FAMILY
ENCYCLOPEDIA
OF WORLD
HISTORY

FAMILY ENCYCLOPEDIA OF WORLD HISTORY
was edited and designed by
The Reader's Digest Association Limited, London.

First edition Copyright © 1996
The Reader's Digest Association Limited, Berkeley Square House,
Berkeley Square, London W1X 6AB.

Copyright © 1996
Reader's Digest Association Far East Limited.
Philippines Copyright © 1996
Reader's Digest Association Far East Limited.

Headword text based on **The Oxford Illustrated Encyclopedia First Edition**
by arrangement with Oxford University Press
© Oxford University Press 1988, 1993

'Timelines in History' on pages 722 to 741 is based on 'Highlights in History'
in *When, Where, Why and How it Happened*, published in 1993 by
Reader's Digest, London.

Printed in France

ISBN 0 276 42287 2

FAMILY
ENCYCLOPEDIA
OF WORLD
HISTORY

Reader's
Digest

PUBLISHED BY THE READER'S DIGEST ASSOCIATION LIMITED
LONDON · NEW YORK · SYDNEY · CAPE TOWN · MONTREAL

CONTENTS

A to Z Encyclopedia

The main 3000 alphabetical entries appear on pages 9 to 721. Use these for quick reference to the essential facts on any subject. Words in SMALL CAPITAL LETTERS within an entry indicate a cross reference to a related entry, or to an associated feature.

Features

These longer articles explore themes and people in greater depth. Each appears close to its appropriate alphabetical position.

A workman perches on a steel frame of the new Empire State Building in 1930.

The British settled on Australia's Norfolk Island in 1778, soon after they claimed it.

A kamikaze pilot prepares to die for his country during the Second World War.

The Battle of Britain fills the skies.

Timelines in History

The time charts on pages 722 to 741 show which events, though widely separated geographically, happened at the same time.

The atom bomb devastates Nagasaki.

At-a-glance reference lists

Look up the dates of key world leaders and major dynasties in this section on pages 742 to 749.

Canada's peoples unite at a 1995 rally.

CONTRIBUTORS

CONSULTANT EDITOR
Asa Briggs

EDITOR • Julian Browne
DEPUTY EDITOR • Mary Devine
ART EDITOR • Sue Mims
EDITORIAL ADVISER • David Kynaston

FEATURE WRITERS

Karen Armstrong
Prof Dudley Baines
Heather D. Baker
Prof T.C. Barker
Frank Barrett
Dr Susan Bayly
Prof Huw Beynon
Prof Vernon Bogdanor
John Booth
Asa Briggs
Prof Peter Burke
Anthony Burton
Dr Paul Cartledge

Prof Martin Carver
Prof David Ceserani
Terry Charman
H.E.J. Cowdrey
Pauline Croft
Prof Nicholas Dent
David Hugh Farmer
Prof Christopher Frayling
Charles D. Gore
Dr Terry Gourvish
Christopher Gravett
Alexander Gray
Roger Griffin

Jonathan P. Grove
Angus Hall
Dr Peter Harvey
Nigel Hawkes
M.J. Inwood
Alan Jackson
Prof Douglas Johnson
Dr H. Kennedy
David Keys
Jeremy Knight
David Kynaston
Brian Lavery
Martin Leighton

Dr Katharine Lerman
John Man
Dr Jan Marsh
P.J. Marshall
Prof G.H. Martin
Kevin McCrae
Dr Charles Melville
Dr Anne Millard
Dr David Miller
Prof G.E. Mingay
Dr David Morgan
Brian Moynahan
Dr Jonathan Phillips

Dr David W. Phillipson
Prof Roy Porter
Eve-Ann Prentice
Prof Keith Robbins
Andrew Robinson
Paddy Scannell
Dr Chris Scarre
Rose Shepherd
Robert Stewart
Rachel Storm
Reay Tannahill
C.C.W. Taylor
Nicholas Timmins

Mark Tully
Prof Irwin Unger
Juliet Vale
Andrew Ward
Andrew Wheatcroft
Michael White
Dr John Whittam
Prof John Wilders
Stephen Williams
Diana Winsor

CONSULTANTS

Prof Keith Branigan • Tony Brett-Young • Colin Bruce • Claire L. Cross • Pam Decho • Mali Edmonds
Lyn Foxhall • John Gillingham • Revd Peter Green • Ailsa Heritage • Dr Carole Hillenbrand • Dr Frank A.J.L. James
Prof Michael Lynch • Sandy Malcolm • John Moore • Prof H.T. Norris • Prof John H. Paterson • Dr Avril Powell
Mark Rowland-Jones • Dr Chris Scarre • Dr G.D. Sheffield • Graham E. Sussum • James Taylor • Dr J.R. Van Diessen

ASSISTANT EDITORS	COORDINATOR	DESIGNERS	Christian Hook
Alison Bravington	Catrina Hey	Emma Gilbert	David Noonan
Charles Clasen	**RESEARCHERS**	Keith Miller	Francis Phillips
Margy Hotson	Deborah Feldman	Tracey Schmidt	Lesli Sternberg
Jane Hutchings	Michael Paterson	Iain Stuart	Malcolm Swanston
Caroline Johnson	**PICTURE**	Jessica Watts	Llewelyn Thomas
Peter Lawson	**RESEARCH**	**ILLUSTRATORS**	Harry Titcombe
David Scott-Macnab	Veneta Bullen	Ian Atkinson	Raymond Turvey
Peter Schirmer	Carina Dvorak	Robert Edwards	Paul Weston
Paul Todd	Jane Lambert	Bob Hersey	

READER'S DIGEST GENERAL BOOKS

EDITORIAL DIRECTOR Robin Hosie • PROJECT ART DIRECTOR Bob Hook • EXECUTIVE EDITOR Michael Davison
EDITORIAL GROUP HEADS Julian Browne • Noel Buchanan • Cortina Butler • PICTURE RESEARCH EDITOR Martin Smith

TRAVEL THROUGH TIME

History is both a useful and a fascinating subject. With its wide sweep it reveals how our world has come into being. Rich in significant detail, it uncovers the motives and explains the actions of the people who have shaped it. As we study it we get behind today's headlines, learning much about how history is made. This encyclopedia, designed both for speedy reference and for absorbing reading, brings history into the home.

The book is arranged alphabetically, the most straightforward means of access to information. It starts with Abbas I, the great shah of Persia, and ends more than 3000 entries later with the Swiss Protestant reformer Zwingli. It includes numerous cross references from one entry to another, and there is a multiple choice of entry points. The alphabetical arrangement makes some odd neighbours – agriculture and Agrippa, explosives and Ezekiel, Hannibal and Hanover, water supply and Waterloo. Browsing through the encyclopedia can be as revealing, therefore, as using it for reference or for reading. History is full of surprises, like the fall of the Berlin Wall or, indeed, the 'discovery' of America: this book springs surprises on almost every page.

Just as no event or idea in history can be understood in isolation, so no single encyclopedia article can be complete in itself. History is concerned with connections. To explore the Industrial Revolution you can start with people, such as Arkwright or Watt, or with resources, such as iron, or with inventions; or you can move out from the British industrial revolution of the 18th century to the sequence of revolutions that followed it in other places.

FROM DETAIL TO THE BROADER VIEW

Some of the entries are concise; others are more exploratory, taking the form of carefully chosen features: the story of Abelard and Héloïse is the first, the origins of writing the last. The features include topics – such as cities or communications or democracy – that link widely separated places and different periods. Other articles challenge you to make your own judgments, such as 'Ten Inventions and Discoveries that Changed the World'. All these features open up debate. A distinctive aspect of history is that historians disagree in their conclusions. Nor are these ever final. The past looks different in the light of the present. The Cold War has stood out in a new perspective since the collapse of the USSR in 1989.

The research, writing and teaching of history now covers all parts of the world, and takes as its subject the lives of all kinds of people, including ordinary men and women as well as long-famous public figures. Women, once left on the sidelines, figure prominently, as do children. In the encyclopedia a feature on childhood follows soon after a short entry on child labour. Play is studied as well as work. Wars cannot be left out, of course, and there are many entries on generals and admirals, battles and treaties.

INSIGHTS THAT BRING HISTORY TO LIFE

History is rich in stories. Every kind of testimony is drawn upon, from eyewitness accounts to statistical tables. Monuments stand like sentinels over time, but ephemera – tickets, forms, posters – bring back a sense of immediacy. Personal records such as diaries can tell more than official documents. The evidence of the arts illuminates both the constant and the transitory in the human condition.

One of the great delights of time travel is to encounter the unfamiliar, for that is what brings history to life, as one of the first historians, the ancient Greek Herodotus, appreciated. This encyclopedia travels back before his age into prehistory, and into every continent. Another dimension of time travel which interests historians is looking into the home – the parlour, the kitchen, even the bedroom – to examine how our ancestors really lived and thought.

Crossing boundaries is one of the attractions of this encyclopedia, which breaks down traditional divisions between constitutional, military, political, diplomatic, economic, social and cultural history. In these pages history is as up-to-date as it can be. The boundary between the present and the past is always moving. Like history itself, this great encyclopedia project has never once stood still.

Asa Briggs

WHO'S WHO ON THE COVER

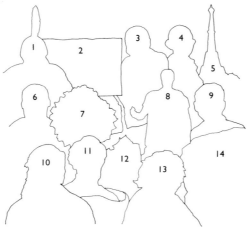

(1) Sitting Bull (2) Bayeux Tapestry (3) Winston Churchill
(4) Mohandas Gandhi (5) Eiffel Tower (6) Martin Luther King
(7) Elizabeth I (8) Julius Caesar (9) John F. Kennedy
(10) Charles Darwin (11) Abraham Lincoln (12) Great Wall
of China (13) Albert Einstein (14) Cleopatra

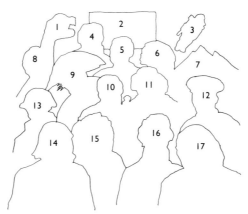

(1) Viking wood carving from the Oseberg ship-burial
(2) Aztec codex depicting Montezuma and Cortés
(3) US space walk (4) Martin Luther (5) Nelson Mandela
(6) Sphinx (7) Pyramids of Giza (8) Mao Ze-dong
(9) Napoleon (10) Louis Pasteur (11) William Shakespeare
(12) Stalin (13) George Washington (14) Rasputin (15) Queen
Victoria (16) Duke of Wellington (17) Mother Teresa

Abbas I (1557-*c*.1628) Shah of Persia from *c*.1588 to *c*.1628, named 'the Great'. His empire stretched from the Tigris to the Indus, and during his reign Persia came to be of prime cultural and commercial importance. In 1590 Abbas ended a war with the OTTOMANS by conceding territory in order to concentrate on driving the Uzbek Turks from north-eastern Persia. By 1618 he had also recovered the lands ceded to the Ottomans. Abbas (who was not a member of the Abbasid dynasty) was renowned for his humanity, mixing with people to learn of their grievances and attempting to redress them.

Abbassids Muslim dynasty which claimed descent from al-Abbas, uncle of the prophet MUHAMMAD, and ruled most of the Middle East for more than 500 years, from 750 to 1258. As caliphs, or successors to Muhammad in the leadership of the Muslim world, the Abbassids developed the idea that the office of caliph could be held only by a descendant of the prophet. Caliph al-Mansur established a new capital at Baghdad, which, under HARUN AL-RASHID, became a centre of culture and prosperity. The Abbassids used an extremist group, known as the Hashimiyya, to exploit

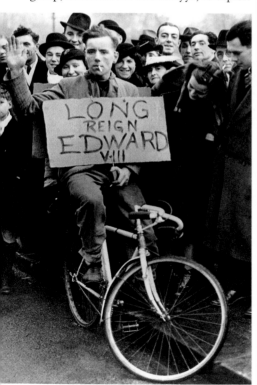

The general public supported Edward VIII, who had to choose between the Crown and the woman he loved during the abdication crisis.

tribal, sectarian and ethnic rivalries and to overthrow the UMAYYAD dynasty which, since it was established in 661, had brought north-west Africa, Spain, western India and portions of central Asia into the Islamic empire. From around 850, central Abbassid power weakened in the face of local dynasties. In 1055, SELJUK Turks took Baghdad and with it, effectively, political control of the caliphate.

abdication crisis Events leading up to the abdication of Britain's King EDWARD VIII in December 1936. Edward announced that he wished to marry Wallis Simpson, a divorcee. This would have required a change in the law and in social attitudes in Britain. The government strongly opposed the king's wish, and Edward, who had been proclaimed king but not yet crowned, chose to abdicate rather than rule 'without the help and support of the woman I love'. His brother, the Duke of York, succeeded him as GEORGE VI.

Ab-dul Hamid II (1842-1918) Last sultan of Turkey in an era of decline, when his country was described by Tsar Nicholas I as 'the sick man of Europe'. Ab-dul Hamid suspended parliament and the constitution, and ruled despotically from 1876 until he was deposed the year after the YOUNG TURKS revolution of 1908. Present-day Armenian hostility to the Turks largely stems from the Armenian massacres of 1895-6, for which Ab-dul Hamid became known as the 'Great Assassin'.

Abelard and Héloïse see feature, page 10

abolitionists Militant opponents of slavery in 19th-century USA, linked to campaigners in Europe. The issue of slavery became a major source of conflict between North and South, involving the right of a state to decide whether to have slavery, and led ultimately to the AMERICAN CIVIL WAR. The first organised effort to oppose slavery was in 1775, when Benjamin Franklin and Dr Benjamin Rush, convinced that slavery went against the ideals of the Declaration of Independence, formed the first colonial antislavery group in Philadelphia. Other founders also included Thomas Paine and Alexander Hamilton.

The spread of cotton-growing in the South gave slavery great economic importance, but by the 1830s abolitionists were demanding an end to slavery in all parts of the country. They had before them the example of the British reformer William WILBERFORCE, who in 1833 was to win his campaign to abolish slavery in the British Empire. They were also able to draw on growing antislavery sentiment in the North which sprang from fear of increasing Southern political power. Other factors included White workers' anxiety over competition from slave labour, growing compassion for the slaves' condition, and the religious

Abolitionist John Brown is led to his execution in 1859 for an attack on a US armoury. His campaigning made him a hero among Blacks.

conviction that slavery was a sin. Boston newspaper-owner William Lloyd Garrison, inspired by the success of the British campaign, in 1833 formed the American Anti-Slavery Society. Prominent campaigners included Harriet Beecher Stowe, whose anti-slavery novel *Uncle Tom's Cabin* sold 1.5 million copies within a year of its publication in 1852. At first the abolitionist cause found little support in Congress or the main political parties, but it played a growing part in the lead-up to the civil war.

During the war, in 1863, convinced that the issue of slavery was the major threat to the preservation of the Union, Abraham LINCOLN issued the Emancipation Proclamation. Two years later, at the close of the war, the 13th Amendment to the Constitution ended slavery in the United States.

Aborigines The original seminomadic inhabitants of Australia, believed to have arrived some 50000 to 60000 years ago, and their descendants. When Europeans arrived, in 1788, there were approximately 300000 Aborigines, who enjoyed sophisticated social organisation, myths and rituals, and spoke more than 200 languages. In a hundred years their numbers declined to around 50000, as a result of loss of land, the effects of European diseases and the introduction of alcohol, falling birthrates and conflict with settlers.

In the mid 1990s Aborigines numbered nearly 257000 and made up 1.5 per cent of the Australian population. Reserves were created in central and northern Australia in the 1930s, and 12 per cent of Australian land is owned by Aborigines. They were made Australian citizens in 1948, and since then there has been a cultural resurgence, and

Star-crossed lovers

The tragic love affair between the great scholar Peter Abelard and his beautiful student Héloïse was immortalised in a rich legacy of poems and letters.

Peter Abelard (*c.* 1079-1142) – philosopher, theologian, teacher and lover – was born near Nantes in Brittany. He studied logic at the cathedral school of Notre Dame in Paris under such leading schoolmen as William of Champeaux, but his brilliant mind and flair for exposition made him more his masters' rival than their pupil. He exerted immense influence over the intellectual life of the day and numbered among his pupils such prominent thinkers as the English humanist John of Salisbury.

Abelard's theology was informed by the Gospels and the Christian tradition of St Augustine, but also by Plato, Aristotle and the classical Greek thinkers. He led the 12th-century movement which emphasised the importance of intention in morality, arguing that sin lay not in the deed but in the knowing consent to wrongdoing.

A PASSIONATE AFFAIR

At the age of 40, while a lecturer at Notre Dame, Abelard fell passionately in love with a private pupil, the 17 year old Héloïse, niece of Canon Fulbert, with whom he lodged. So began a love story that would become celebrated in both

Abelard and Héloïse discuss philosophy, religion and thwarted love, in this miniature from a 14th-century French manuscript.

literature and history. Distracted from his studies, Abelard composed poetry and ballads, which together with the couple's correspondence would later immortalise their story of love against all odds. When the affair was discovered Héloïse was sent to Brittany where she bore him a son, Astrolabe. On her return to Paris the pair

married in secret. Her relatives opposed the match violently. On discovering the truth, they raided Abelard's house and brutally emasculated him. Abelard withdrew in shame to the abbey of St Denis just outside Paris where he became a Benedictine monk, while Héloïse took the veil at Argenteuil.

Abelard's doctrinal reliance upon the testing of truth by discussion, and his rigorous use of reason in analysing the nature of God and the Trinity, laid him open to charges of heresy. In 1121 an ecclesiastical council at Soissons condemned his work *On the Divine Unity and Trinity* as heretical and the book was burnt. Abelard became a hermit at Nogent-sur-Seine, where in 1125 he founded a monastic school which he called the Paraclete. Soon afterwards he left to become abbot of St Gildas de Rhys in Brittany, and entrusted the Paraclete to Héloïse, who became abbess of the convent. Abelard himself continued to teach and write.

In 1141, at a council at Sens, Abelard was again condemned for heresy, by the Christian reformer Bernard of Clairvaux, and banned from lecturing. He retired to Cluny, where he died at the priory of St Marcel-sur-Sâone. His body was sent to the Paraclete, and later moved to the cemetery of Père Lachaise in Paris, to lie alongside that of his beloved Héloïse, who died in 1164. Abelard's life-story is recounted in his autobiography *Historia Calamitatum (The History of My Troubles).*

---

demands for greater equality. Aborigines have a rich spiritual life based on *Tjukurpa* ('Dreamtime'), a golden age when spirits created the world, and 'Dreaming', which restores contact with them. Invisible 'song-lines' guide Aborigines across vast stretches of desert, meeting at sacred sites which often put them in conflict with mining interests. The most famous of these sites is Uluru (Ayers Rock). In 1993 the government overturned the principle that Australia was unoccupied when the Europeans arrived, and recognised that the Aborigines may still hold common law 'native title' to land.

Aboukir Bay see NILE, BATTLE OF THE

Abraham Founding father of the Hebrew nation, from whom the Israelites traced their descent. Around 1800 BC he was divinely

'Guests' from the spirit world take part in the feast after an Australian Aborigine funeral in this symbolic tree-bark painting.

inspired to settle with his family in CANAAN, where God promised them they would become a great nation. The Bible tells how God tested Abraham's faith by asking him to sacrifice his son Isaac. As Abraham raised a knife to kill the boy, an angel appeared and told him to spare Isaac and sacrifice a ram. Abraham's obedience had proved his faith. Muslims regard Abraham as a prophet and an ancestor of the Arabs through his son Ismael.

absentee landlord Landowner who did not normally live on the estate from which he gained income. Such landlords were common in prerevolutionary France and in Ireland, where confiscations led to Irish estates falling into English hands. While some landlords cared for the welfare of their tenants, others would issue short leases in order to raise rents frequently, and evict anyone unable to pay. Their estates were managed by agents such as Charles Boycott, whose tactics in the 1880s so enraged Irish tenants that they refused to harvest crops for him – hence the term 'boycott'.

Absentee landlords, who sometimes lacked personal interest in their lands and tenants, were blamed for evictions such as this on a Fermanagh estate, now in Northern Ireland, in the 1890s.

absolutism Form of government in which all power is concentrated in a monarch. It is especially associated with the 17th-century reign of LOUIS XIV of France, who boasted *'L'état, c'est moi'* ('I am the state'). In the 18th century CATHERINE THE GREAT of Russia and FREDERICK THE GREAT of Prussia used their absolute powers to bring about important administrative and social reforms. From the 19th century absolute monarchy declined with the spread of liberalism, and in the 1990s only the Gulf states of Oman and Qatar remained absolute.

Abyssinia see ETHIOPIA

Acheson, Dean (1893-1971) US politician and major architect of postwar American foreign policy. He served in President Harry S Truman's administration as assistant secretary of state, under-secretary, and secretary of state from 1949 to 1953, and advised succeeding presidents. He urged international control of nuclear power, and supported the formation of NATO. He helped to devise and implement the MARSHALL PLAN for rebuilding Western Europe, and he was also involved in the TRUMAN DOCTRINE which offered US support for nations such as Greece and Turkey, which were threatened by communist expansion in Eastern Europe. His autobiography, *Present at the Creation,* won a Pulitzer prize in 1970.

acropolis The highest part of a fortified Greek city or CITADEL, which includes its principal temples and public buildings. The Acropolis of Athens is the most famous example. (See also feature, page 14.)

Actium, Battle of (31 BC) Decisive naval battle which gave Octavian undisputed supremacy in the Roman world. It took place off the coast of north-west Greece. The town of Actium was the base used by MARK ANTONY and CLEOPATRA in their campaign against Octavian during the last in the series of civil wars which began in 49 BC. After blockading Antony's larger fleet, Octavian scattered it. Antony and Cleopatra escaped to Egypt and committed suicide. In 27 Octavian gained official recognition as Caesar AUGUSTUS.

Acts of Union (1707, 1800) Two Acts of Parliament which established the United Kingdom. The first united the parliaments of Scotland and England; the second abolished the Irish parliament. Union with Scotland became necessary after the Scottish parliament passed an Act of Security in 1704 insisting on guarantees of sovereignty, religion and trade before the successor to the English crown could also inherit the Scottish throne. The 1707 Act maintained a separate Scottish legal system and the Presbyterian Church. It also established one kingdom and one parliament of 'Britain' represented by a Union flag.

After the Irish rebellion of 1798, the British prime minister William Pitt the Younger decided that Ireland should be united with Britain under a single parliament. The Act had to be passed by the British parliament and the Irish parliament, where it was resented. The Act was passed after Pitt promised that the reward would be Catholic emancipation, but he found this impossible to achieve because George III would not go against his coronation oath to defend the Protestant faith.

Adam, Robert (1728-92) British architect and designer. He was the first to design and execute buildings and contents as a unit, from the structure down to the fireplaces, door handles and furniture. A member of a family of architects, Adam worked with his three brothers to create a style of architecture that has become associated with their name. Born in Scotland, Adam was trained by his architect father and began his career in Scotland with his eldest brother, John. From 1754 to 1758 he toured Italy where he studied classical architecture and antiquities. Establishing himself in London on his return, his version of the neoclassical style quickly attracted patrons. The interior of Syon House in Greater London (1762) and Kenwood House, overlooking Hampstead Heath in north London (1767-8), are among the best-known Adam designs; together with the oval staircase in Cluzean Castle in Scotland.

Adams, John (1735-1826) Second US president, from 1797 to 1801. In three separate careers Adams helped to found the United States. First, he campaigned against British oppression and helped to draft the DECLARATION OF INDEPENDENCE. Second, he was an American diplomat in Europe for more than ten years from 1777 and negotiated the treaties which concluded the American War of Independence. Then in 1789 he became America's first vice-president, and in 1797 George Washington's successor as president.

A lawyer from Quincy, Massachusetts, Adams wrote extensively on the right of colonies to self-government, but only reluctantly came to believe in full American independence. For his work in drafting the Declaration of Independence and securing its unanimous adoption in Congress, Thomas JEFFERSON described him as 'The Colossus of Independence'. In Europe, Adams served as a diplomat in France and Holland, finally joining with Benjamin FRANKLIN and John JAY to negotiate the Treaty of Paris which ended the War of Independence in 1783. Adams was the first minister of the independent United

The second United States president John Adams, surrounded by the coats of arms of 16 US states, was derided as a 'vain monarchist'.

States to present his diplomatic credentials to Britain's George III, in 1785. He said he found the vice-presidency 'the most insignificant office the invention of man contrived or his imagination conceived'.

During his presidency, relations with France worsened as the French Revolution progressed, and Adams leaned towards Britain. After an attempt by Adams to conciliate with France had met a rebuff, war fever increased, but he resisted the pressure of his own party leaders to declare war on France in 1799. Faced with the political opposition of his friend Thomas Jefferson, Adams failed to be re-elected and retired to Quincy.

Adams, John Quincy (1767-1848) Sixth president of the USA, from 1825 to 1829, and eldest son of John ADAMS, the second president. At the age of 11, he acted as his father's secretary on a diplomatic mission to France, and went on to pursue a 70-year career of public service as diplomat, statesman, politician and administrator.

Adams served as a Federalist senator for Massachusetts from 1803 to 1808. After five years as minister to Russia, he helped to negotiate the end of the WAR OF 1812 at Ghent in Belgium. He was US minister in London from 1815 to 1817, before becoming secretary of state under John Monroe. In this office he laid the foundations of a century of American foreign policy. In a treaty with Britain, he demarcated the border with Canada as far west as the Rockies; he prevailed upon Spain to cede Florida to the USA; and he was the driving force behind the MONROE DOCTRINE, which declared that the New World was no longer open for colonisation by Europe. Little was achieved during his term as president, partly because of persistent opposition by supporters of Andrew JACKSON to his attempts to extend government powers. He was elected to each congress until his death.

Adams, William (1564-1620) Navigator and first Englishman to enter the service of a Japanese ruler. Adams went to sea at the age of 12 and in 1598 joined five Dutch ships bound for the East Indies, sailing as pilot in the *de Liefde*. The fleet was scattered and his ship arrived off southern Japan with its crew dying. Adams was brought before the shogun Tokugawa Ieyasu in Osaka. Ieyasu was so impressed by Adams's knowledge of ships and shipbuilding techniques that he gave him an estate. Adams mediated between the shogunate and the Dutch and English traders who had come to

Five accidents that changed the world

Not all accidents are undesirable. While some have changed the course of history, or served as dire warnings, others have initiated momentous periods of progress or discovery.

MISTAKEN BEARINGS

On August 3, 1492, the Genoese mariner Christopher Columbus set sail from Spain on his flagship the Santa Maria. Financed by Queen Isabella, he planned to reach the East – with its lucrative trade in silk and spices – by voyaging west across the Atlantic. He reckoned that it was less than 4000 miles to the Indies. By the end of the year he had landed first on one of the Bahamas ('the Indies', he assumed), then on Cuba (just off Japan, or was it China?) and finally on the island of Quisqueya, which he renamed Hispaniola. Columbus returned to Spain as 'Viceroy and Governor of the Islands that he hath discovered in the Indies', and later undertook further westward voyages. He died in 1506, still not understanding that he had by chance discovered a 'new world'.

Christopher Columbus failed to get to India.

THE PLUCKED REED

'I have accidentally made a discovery of the very greatest importance... I have succeeded today in transmitting signals without any battery whatever!' The exultant tone of Alexander Bell, writing to a business associate on June 2, 1875, was understandable. Bell, a young Scottish scientist and professor of vocal physiology, was living in Boston, USA. He had been experimenting for several years with using electricity to transmit sounds. Now, with his assistant Thomas Watson, he had succeeded. The decisive moment occurred that hot afternoon when Bell happened to press against his ear the magnetised steel reed of one of the receivers he

had been developing, at the very moment that Watson in the next room plucked the connecting reed. Bell, to his intense excitement, recognised the note as that of Watson's reed. Eight months later Bell uttered the first intelligible words into his newfangled instrument. The telephone was a reality, and a revolution in personal communications had begun. In 1877 Bell founded the Bell Telephone Company in America, and from there the telecommunications industry burgeoned.

A WRONG TURN

On June 28, 1914, the Archduke Franz Ferdinand, heir to the Austrian throne, was in Sarajevo to inspect the Bosnian army. While out riding with his wife in

The Serbian terrorist Princip is arrested after shooting the Archduke Ferdinand in Sarajevo.

an open carriage a bomb was thrown, and several aides were injured. In haste, the Archduke's driver took a wrong turning, stopped to reverse, and a loitering conspirator, Gavrilo Princip, grasped the opportunity and killed the royal couple with just two shots, shots which initiated the sequence of events that led inexorably to the outbreak of the First World War.

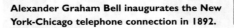

Alexander Graham Bell inaugurates the New York-Chicago telephone connection in 1892.

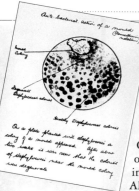

THROUGH THE OPEN WINDOW

On the second floor of a London hospital in September 1928, Alexander Fleming was in his laboratory – with the window open. Just as he was about to throw away a dish containing one of his preparations of bacteria, he noticed that the surrounding bacteria were starting to dissolve. The cause was a strange green mould spreading on the dish – a fungus that had come in through the window. Over the next decade he and others established that the fungus *Penicillium notatum* – 'penicillin' for short – had antibiotic properties, inaugurating a revolution in medicine. Fleming always resisted the claim that he had 'invented' penicillin: 'Nature has been making it for thousands of years. I only discovered it.'

A HARD RAIN

'The odds of a meltdown are one in 10 000 years,' declared a Soviet minister in 1986 about the safety of his country's nuclear power plants. Two months later, on April 26, following a misconceived safety test, the Number Four reactor at the Chernobyl plant near Kiev exploded. A nuclear fallout greater than a thousand Hiroshima bombs sent radioactive clouds across Europe, threatening health and contaminating land. After Chernobyl, it became unlikely that nuclear power would ever again be wholly trusted.

Engineers check levels of radioactivity in the air at Chernobyl after the explosion in 1986.

Japan, and settled permanently. Adams also helped the English East India Company to set up a trading factory in Japan in 1613.

Addington, Henry, 1st Viscount Sidmouth (1757-1844) Unpopular British prime minister and war leader, whose incompetence in office forced him to resign in 1804. He was a firm opponent of Catholic emancipation, and was invited by George III to succeed William PITT the Younger as prime minister in 1801. His peace treaty with France in 1802 won him some acclaim, but when the conflict was resumed the following year it became clear that he lacked the qualities of a war leader and his government was weak and indecisive. He resigned in 1804 and later, as Lord Sidmouth, held other Cabinet posts. As home secretary from 1812 to 1822 he introduced repressive legislation in an attempt to suppress the LUDDITES and other protest groups. He opposed Catholic emancipation in 1829 and the Reform Act in 1832.

Addled Parliament (April 5-June 7, 1614) Nickname given to the second parliament of James I of England. Those opposed to the king's policies were able to divert the House of Commons to discussion of grievances, including Church reform, import duties and court interference at the elections. The king dissolved the short-lived parliament before it had passed any legislation – hence the term 'addled' meaning barren or empty – and ruled without one until 1621.

Aden Port commanding the entrance to the Red Sea. Settled as early as the 3rd century BC, Aden was a Roman trading port. It was captured by the Turks in 1538 and controlled by North Yemen until 1728. In 1839 Aden was captured by a British expedition and annexed. It became a free port in 1850, a trading centre for East Africa and a station on the route from Europe to the East, especially after the opening of the Suez Canal in 1869. Aden was a crown colony from 1937 to 1967 when, after a period of struggle by nationalists, it was combined with the former Aden protectorate to create the Southern Yemen People's Republic, now part of the republic of YEMEN.

Adenauer, Konrad (1876-1967) German statesman and first chancellor, from 1949 to 1963, of the postwar GERMAN FEDERAL REPUBLIC. Adenauer became mayor of Cologne in 1917, but because of his opposition to Nazism he was removed from his post in 1933 and twice arrested. In 1945 he again became mayor and helped to create the Christian Democratic Party, of which he became leader. He adopted a policy of rebuilding a strong West Germany by securing partnerships with Europe and the USA through the Common Market and NATO.

Adrian IV (c.1100-59) The only English pope, from 1154 to 1159. His original name was Nicholas Breakspear. As pope, he reformed the papal administration and reclaimed lands that had been taken over by the Italian nobility. The conflicting claims of the German monarchy and the papacy for political and ecclesiastical control in north and central Italy led to serious rivalry with the Holy Roman Emperor Frederick BARBAROSSA.

Adrianople, Battle of (August 9, AD 378) Defeat of the Roman forces by the VISIGOTHS at the Roman city of Adrianople, 300 miles (480 km) west of Constantinople. Emperor Valens, who had hoped to prevent the Gothic invasion of the Roman Empire, was killed. The outcome shifted the balance of Roman power in favour of the German people.

Adrianople, Treaty of Treaty that ended the Russo-Turkish war of 1828-9. Russia won control of the mouth of the Danube and required the OTTOMAN EMPIRE, centred on present-day Turkey, to pay compensation. The treaty also confirmed self-rule for Serbia and Greece and guaranteed free passage for merchant ships through the Dardanelles.

Aeschylus (c.525–c.456 BC) Greek dramatist who wrote the earliest surviving tragedies. Born at Eleusis in Attica, Aeschylus fought at the battles of Marathon and Salamis during the Greek-Persian Wars. He used drama to explore profound moral conflicts which he expressed in high-flown language, winning the annual prize 13 times at the Athenian drama festival. Although Aeschylus wrote

Konrad Adenauer, West Germany's first chancellor, aimed to produce an economically strong and democratic republic that could ultimately bargain for Germany's reunification.

High point of Greek city life

The best known acropolis, or 'high city', of the ancient world is found in Athens.

Built on a hilltop in the 5th century BC as a temple to the Greek goddess

Athena, it marks the cultural birthplace of Europe.

At the heart of most ancient Greek cities was the acropolis or 'high city'. In the time of the earliest Greek-speaking people, the Mycenaeans, this area of elevated rocky ground was the fortified centre of a city, where the palaces of the king and his retainers stood. After the collapse of the Mycenaean age in about 1100 BC the palaces disappeared, but some 300 years later, with the renewal of Greek civilisation, they began to be replaced by temples for the city's patron deity.

The most famous acropolis is in Athens, centre of the religious life of the greatest of the Greek city-states. Over the ruins of Mycenaean palaces the Athenians built a temple to their patron deities Athena and Poseidon. In the Archaic period (about 800-500 BC) a large temple for Athena was begun, but in 480 BC Athens was sacked by the Persians and the Acropolis was left a ruin.

A Greek confederation led by Athens repelled the Persians the following year. The Athenian statesman Pericles believed the city should look worthy of its status as leader of the confederation. After a 30-year interval, he persuaded the Athenians to embark on a building programme to create a setting for the elaborate ceremonies of the state cults. The overseer of the works, which were to last 40 years, was the sculptor Pheidias.

CROWNING GLORY

Three sides of the Acropolis are steep, but on the more gentle western approach the Athenian architects built the Propylaea (437-432 BC), designed by Mnesicles, an imposing gateway to the sacred enclosure. The northern wing of the Propylaea housed the Pinakotheke, a picture gallery. To its right stands a small temple (427-424 BC), designed by Callicrates in the Ionic style. Dedicated to Athena Nike ('Victory'), its frieze celebrates one of the Greeks' victories over the Persians.

The Acropolis is dominated by the Parthenon, the temple of Athena Parthenos ('The Maiden'), patroness of Athens, built between 447 and 432 BC. Designed by Ictinus and Callicrates, and 65 ft (20 m) high, it is made entirely of marble. Ninety-two panels of sculptured reliefs on the upper part of the temple showed legendary battles. The western pediment depicted the contest between Athena and Poseidon that won Athena her role as protectress of Athens. The frieze around the temple's walls showed the city's religious procession, the Panathenaia.

Inside stood a 40 ft (12 m) statue of Athena, made by Pheidias in gold and ivory. With its perfect proportions, the Parthenon is considered to be the crowning glory of classical architecture.

The Erechtheion (421-406 BC) was built over the spot where Poseidon and Athena gave the Athenians their gifts: a stream of sea water symbolic of the trade that veneration of the god would give the city; and an olive tree, whose fruit and oil were essential to Greek life. Dedicated to Athena, it contained a wooden statue of the goddess, said to have fallen from heaven, and a rock scored with marks made by Poseidon's trident, along which trickled a salt-water stream.

Close to the Erechtheion was the Shrine of Pandrosos, a precinct that protected Athena's sacred olive tree, which had miraculously sprouted anew after being chopped down by the Persians. Around the foot of the Acropolis were other fine buildings: the Odeion, an indoor auditorium where music and poetry could be heard, and the Theatre of Dionysus, which witnessed the first performances of noted playwrights such as Aeschylus, Aristophanes, Euripides and Sophocles. This small hilltop settlement became the birthplace of European civilisation.

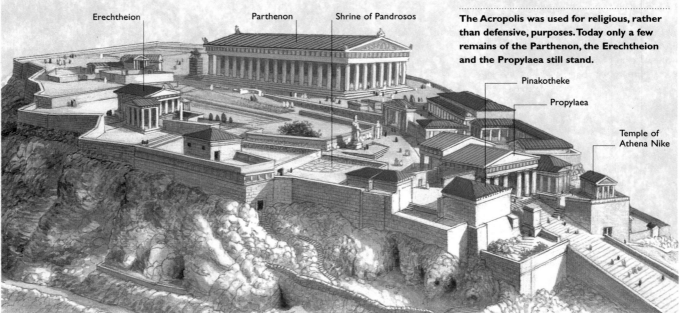

Erechtheion   Parthenon   Shrine of Pandrosos

The Acropolis was used for religious, rather than defensive, purposes. Today only a few remains of the Parthenon, the Erechtheion and the Propylaea still stand.

Pinakotheke

Propylaea

Temple of Athena Nike

more than 80 plays, only seven tragedies survive complete. He left Athens and moved to Sicily around 476 after being defeated in the drama festival by SOPHOCLES. Aeschylus, who appeared in his own plays, introduced costumes and stage decoration and gave new importance to the role of the chorus. In his masterpiece, the *Oresteia* trilogy (*Agamemnon, Choephori, Eumenides*), Aeschylus portrays the killing of Agamemnon by his wife Clytemnestra and the revenge of their son Orestes. Aeschylus's world is dominated by an omnipotent Zeus, the supreme Greek god; wrongdoing and arrogant behaviour bring their own punishment and fearful curses are handed down from generation to generation.

Afghanistan Country between the Indian subcontinent, central Asia and the nations of the Middle East. Despite an inhospitable landscape of rugged mountains and arid deserts, Afghanistan has been almost continuously involved in wars, migrations, trade and power struggles. It was conquered by Alexander the Great, and after his death became part of the state of BACTRIA. A succession of foreign overlords was followed by Arab conquest and conversion to ISLAM in the 7th century. The most important Muslim ruler of all was Mahmud of Ghazna, who made Afghanistan a centre of Islamic power at the beginning of the 11th century. The country was overrun by MONGOLS under Genghis Khan in 1222, only becoming united under an Afghan leader in 1747, when Ahmad Shah founded the Durrani dynasty at Kandahar.

In the 19th and early 20th centuries three wars were caused by British efforts to limit Russian influence in Afghanistan. In the first, fought between 1838 and 1842, a British attempt to replace the Kabul ruler Dost Muhammad was repulsed. The second war, from 1878 to 1880, was fought because the emir favoured the Russians and refused to allow Britain's representative into the city. By the Treaty of Gandamak in 1879, Britain gained control of the Khyber Pass – an important route between present-day Pakistan and central Asia – and with it control of Afghan foreign policy.

Under Abdurrahman Khan, who became emir in 1880, a strong central government was established, and his heirs achieved some modernisation and social reform. The third Anglo-Afghan war began in 1919 when the new emir, Amanullah, attacked British India. Although repulsed, he secured full independence under the Treaty of Rawalpindi in 1919. The monarchy, founded by Amanullah in 1926, lasted until it was overturned by a military coup in 1973. In 1978, after the assassination of General Muhammad Daoud

Khan – who had dominated politics since the early 1950s – the new Democratic Republic of Afghanistan embarked on a series of reforms, but still there was tension and rural unrest.

In December 1979 Soviet troops occupied the country and installed as president Babrak Karmal, leader of Afghanistan's Marxist Party. Guerrilla *mujahidin* (freedom fighters) forces, equipped with US arms, then waged a *jihad* (holy war) against troops armed and supported by Soviet forces. Some 5 million refugees fled to Iran and Pakistan. By 1987 the cost to the Soviet Union had become unacceptable and it began to disengage, all troops being withdrawn by 1989. The Marxist government was ousted in 1992, but the new government was prey to faction fighting and the civil war continued. A UN plan for a transfer of power to an interim council was delayed in 1995 as the *talibaan* (army of students) took control of a third of the country.

> ### DID YOU KNOW?
>
> *According to legend, Aeschylus was killed when an eagle dropped a tortoise on his bald head, mistaking it for a stone on which to smash the shell.*

Africa Second largest continent, after Asia. (For the early history of Africa see also feature, page 16.) The arrival of the Portuguese in the 15th century marked the beginning of European intervention in Africa. Until the 19th century, European interest centred on the trade in slaves, ivory and gold. An estimated 10 million slaves were transported to plantations in the West Indies and the southern USA, mainly by Portuguese, English, French and Dutch slave traders. By 1800 most of the coastline had been explored and in places lightly settled by Europeans, particularly by the Dutch Boers in South Africa.

During the 19th century the interior was gradually opened up by explorers, traders looking for a commercial replacement for the slave trade, and Christian MISSIONARIES such as David LIVINGSTONE, who publicised the mineral and commercial potential of the lands he had discovered. In the years between 1880 and 1914, most of Africa was partitioned by the European powers in the so-called 'Scramble for Africa', with Britain, France,

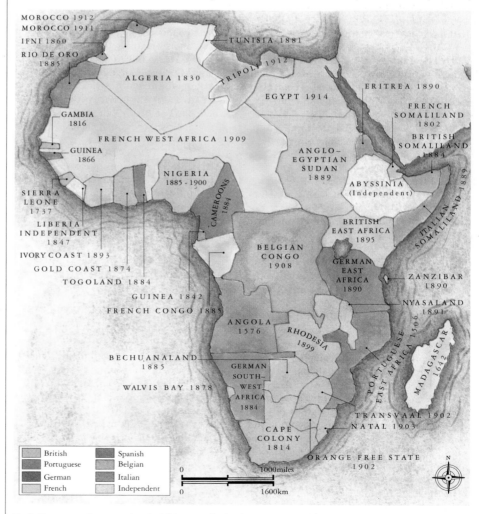

MOROCCO 1912
MOROCCO 1911
IFNI 1860
RIO DE ORO 1885
ALGERIA 1830
TUNISIA 1881
TRIPOLI 1912
EGYPT 1914
ERITREA 1890
FRENCH SOMALILAND 1802
BRITISH SOMALILAND 1884
GAMBIA 1816
FRENCH WEST AFRICA 1909
GUINEA 1866
NIGERIA 1885-1900
ANGLO-EGYPTIAN SUDAN 1889
ABYSSINIA (Independent)
ITALIAN SOMALILAND 1889
SIERRA LEONE 1737
LIBERIA INDEPENDENT 1847
IVORY COAST 1893
GOLD COAST 1874
TOGOLAND 1884
GUINEA 1842
FRENCH CONGO 1885
CAMEROONS 1884
BRITISH EAST AFRICA 1895
BELGIAN CONGO 1908
GERMAN EAST AFRICA 1890
ZANZIBAR 1890
NYASALAND 1891
ANGOLA 1576
RHODESIA 1899
PORTUGUESE EAST AFRICA 1506
MADAGASCAR 1642
BECHUANALAND 1885
WALVIS BAY 1878
GERMAN SOUTH-WEST AFRICA 1884
CAPE COLONY 1814
TRANSVAAL 1902
NATAL 1903
ORANGE FREE STATE 1902

British	Spanish
Portuguese	Belgian
German	Italian
French	Independent

0   1000miles
0   1600km

N

Early European intervention in Africa was limited to coastal regions, where gold, ivory and – most importantly – slaves were traded. But within 20 years of France occupying Tunisia in 1881 the entire continent had been carved up by European colonisers in their 'Scramble for Africa'.

Germany, Italy and Portugal competing for territory. Germany's former colonial empire was divided among the victorious Allies after the First World War and the rise of African nationalism following the Second World War hastened the process of decolonisation. Most of the Black countries became independent between 1957 and 1980, sometimes as a result of peaceful negotiation and sometimes through armed rebellion.

In the south, small, White privileged groups held on to political power, notably in Rhodesia and South Africa, but elsewhere Black Africans assumed responsibility for governing their own countries. But the artificial colonial boundaries on maps that ignored ethnic groupings and nomadic lifestyles, the rapid transition to home rule, and the underdeveloped local economies continued to produce political, social and economic problems.

Many of the new nations remained unstable and prone to single-party rule, while drought in the 1980s and early 1990s caused great suffering in Africa south of the Sahara. New regimes which emerged between 1990 and 1992, including South Africa in 1994, inherited vast burdens of international debt.

African National Congress (ANC)

Largest political party in South Africa, victor in the country's first multiracial general election in 1994. The ANC began in Blomfontein in 1912 as the South African Native National Congress, founded by a Zulu Methodist minister, J.L. Dube. In 1914 Dube led a deputation to Britain protesting against the Native Land Act (1913), which restricted the purchase of land by Black Africans. In 1926 the ANC formed a united front with representatives of the Indian community, with the aim of creating a racially integrated, democratic southern Africa. It sought to achieve racial equality by nonviolent means, as practised by Mohandas (Mahatma) GANDHI in India, and from 1952 until 1967 the party was led by the Zulu chief Albert LUTHULI. The South African government banned the ANC in 1960, together with a more militant breakaway movement, the PAN-AFRICANIST CONGRESS. Faced with Afrikaner rigidity on racial issues, the ANC resorted to a campaign of violence. Maintaining that apartheid should be abolished, and that every South African should have the vote, it formed a liberation army, Umkhonto we Sizwe (Spear of the Nation).

In 1964 its leader, Nelson MANDELA, and some of his colleagues were convicted of sabotage and jailed for life. International support for the group grew throughout the 1970s and the 1980s. The exiled wing of the ANC kept up a campaign of violence during the 1980s, but following the election of President F.W. DE KLERK in 1989 and the release of Mandela in 1990 it entered into cautious constitutional negotiations. The ANC eventually

Africa: birthplace of the human race

The origins of humankind lie in southern and eastern Africa.

By the time our ancestors spread to other continents they stood upright, used fire, cooked food and made tools.

The African continent was almost certainly the birthplace of humanity. Archaeologists are still uncovering the secrets of its remote past, between 4 million and 1.5 million years ago, when the apelike creatures who lived there began to take on the appearance and behaviour of human beings. Humans only colonised Europe and Asia after they had lived in Africa for almost a million years.

Evidence of the earliest human activity has been found in eastern Africa and South Africa, where the environment was best suited to these creatures' way of life, and where conditions helped to preserve their bones and stone tools. The most important sites are Hadar in Ethiopia, Koobi Fora in Kenya, Olduvai Gorge in Tanzania and Sterkfontein in South Africa. The first humans did not necessarily live in only these parts of Africa, but most of their remains have been found there.

The richest and best-preserved fossil finds of the early hominids *Australopithicus* have been made along the Rift Valley of East Africa and in the south.

THE FIRST TOOLMAKERS

Although the skeletons of early Africans are often preserved in a highly fragmented state they show great variation. It is not known what physical differences might have been apparent in even a single population, between males and females, for example, but experts are generally agreed that there were two main divisions: *Australopithecus* ('southern ape') which eventually became extinct, and *Homo* ('man'), to which all living races of humankind belong.

The earliest species, *Homo habilis* ('handy man') probably appeared about 2 million years ago, leaving behind the first traces of human technology – simple stone tools. Yet these artefacts reveal little about their users, and

'Lucy', discovered in Ethiopia in 1976, is 3.6 million years old and the earliest link in the human chain.

archaeologists have looked further for evidence that these creatures were developing humanlike behaviour, such as social cooperation, food-sharing and forward planning.

Homo habilis was eventually superseded by *Home erectus* ('upright man'), the first hominid to spread beyond Africa. Tools gradually became more sophisticated in Africa – as elsewhere in the world before the invention of metallurgy. They also became smaller, resulting eventually in 'microliths' – stone tools so tiny that they must have been fitted to handles. Various cutting and scraping tools were developed, such as arrow points and barbs. The bow and arrow was also probably an African invention. These microliths were widespread in Africa by about 20000 years ago, but they had appeared in the extreme south of the continent some 80000 years earlier.

A CLEAR LINK

African microliths were made by people like ourselves: *Homo sapiens sapiens*. Where and when such people evolved is not known precisely, but the oldest fossils of this type come from South Africa, dating from about 100000 years ago. Genetic evidence confirms that these may be the oldest remains of fully

Footprints fossilised in volcanic ash (Tanzania, 1978) reveal that 3.5 million years ago humans walked upright.

modern people anywhere in the world. As humans became more adaptable and specialised, they were able to respond more readily to environmental changes. Between 10 000 and 6000 BC, the region that is now the southern Sahara underwent a wet period, and lakes and rivers appeared in a region that had previously been too dry to support human habitation. The rich supplies of fish in these waters attracted semipermanent communities where farming developed. Here the foundations of later African cultures were laid.

Fossils from three species found together, all 1.5 million years old, prove that human evolution has not always stemmed from a single species.

agreed to free, multiracial elections in 1994 which resulted in Mandela being elected as the first Black president of South Africa.

Afrikaners White, Afrikaans-speaking people of South Africa, also known as Boers. The name refers to the descendants of the families who emigrated from the Netherlands, Germany and France before 1806, when Britain seized the Cape Colony. The unifying factors of the Afrikaners are the Afrikaans language and the Christian Calvinist tradition, from which arose the controversial concept of APARTHEID.

Aga Khan Imam, or spiritual leader, of the Nizari branch of the Ismaili Muslims, who live mainly in Pakistan, India, Iran and Syria. The Aga Khans – the title comes from the Turkish words *aga*, 'master', and *khan*, 'ruler' – trace their line from Ismail, eldest son of the sixth Shiite imam in succession to the Prophet Muhammad. The first Aga Khan of the present line, Hassan Ali Shah of Kirman (1800-81), fled to Afghanistan and Sind after leading an unsuccessful revolt in Iran in 1838. He won British favour and settled in Bombay. His grandson, Sultan Muhammad Shah (1877-1957), played an active part in Indian politics, attempting to secure Muslim support for British rule, particularly as president of the All-India MUSLIM LEAGUE. Prince Karim Shah, Aga Khan IV (1936-), the 49th imam, is a Harvard graduate and a distant descendant of the chief of the ASSASSINS, the secret order of a fanatical sect which instilled fear in the Crusaders.

Agincourt, Battle of (October 25, 1415) Battle fought near the village of Agincourt in northern France that ended in victory for Henry V's English army over a French force which heavily outnumbered it. By invading Normandy in 1415, Henry re-engaged in the HUNDRED YEARS' WAR, the long-running dispute over English claims to the French throne and lands. After capturing Harfleur, Henry's force attempted to retreat to the safety of Calais but was intercepted by a large French army. The English troops, mainly archers and foot soldiers, dug in behind wooden stakes on a narrow front between thick woods.

The next day the French cavalry advanced across the waterlogged ground, but became bogged down and were picked off by English archers and infantry. A dozen leading French figures, including the Constable of France, died, with up to 1500 French knights and 4500 men-at-arms; these included prisoners massacred after a group of French knights made a surprise attack on a baggage train. English casualties were light, but included the Duke of York and the Earl of Suffolk. Henry's victory paved the way for his recognition as the heir to the French throne.

Selective breeding practised during the agricultural revolution resulted in improbably large but highly profitable farm animals.

agricultural revolution Term used to describe the changes that transformed farming in Britain during the 18th century. The medieval system of open-field cultivation in strips was replaced by farming in large-scale units, which often extended arable farming over heaths and commons. This process was accelerated by private ENCLOSURE Acts in Parliament. Livestock farming became more intensive and the peasants, who had been largely self-sufficient, became agricultural labourers. There were considerable improvements in agriculture through new techniques such as crop rotation. New crops were also introduced, including turnips and potatoes, as well as improved grasses, resulting in a significant increase in year-round food supplies.

Viscount Townshend (1674-1738) and Thomas Coke, Earl of Leicester (1752-1842), were notable for their adoption of crop rotation. Jethro TULL (1674-1741) invented the seed drill – a machine for planting seeds in holes.

agriculture see feature, pages 20-21

Agrippa, Marcus Vipsanius (63-12 BC) Roman general who accompanied the young Octavian to Rome after Julius Caesar's murder. Agrippa later won decisive naval victories over Sextus Pompeius at Mylae and Naulochus in 36 BC, and over MARK ANTONY at Actium in 31. In 27 Octavian (now AUGUSTUS) became the first Roman emperor: he entrusted Agrippa with military and organisational responsibilities – marking him out as his successor in 23 – and allowed his daughter Julia to become his third wife. Agrippa was a prolific builder, and personally financed improvements to public water supplies and roads. His best-known constructions are the Pantheon at Rome and the Pont du Gard and Maison Carré at Nîmes, southern France. He died before he could succeed Augustus.

St Aidan founded churches and monasteries throughout northern England and an ecclesiastical centre on Lindisfarne, or Holy Island, off the Northumberland coast.

Aidan, St (d. AD 651) Irish-born missionary. While still a monk on the Scottish island of Iona, in the inner Hebrides, around 635 Aidan was made a bishop and chosen by King Oswald to act as a missionary in the English kingdom of Northumbria. With Oswald's royal support, Aidan settled on the island of Lindisfarne, establishing a monastery there where missionaries could be trained. His ministers went on to play a key role in converting northern England to Christianity.

AIDS Acquired Immune Deficiency Syndrome is a normally fatal condition in which the body's immune system breaks down. There is no known cure. AIDS was first identified in the United States in 1981, but cases recorded since the 1940s have been retrospectively diagnosed. In 1983, AIDS was discovered to be the result of infection by the Human Immunodeficiency Virus (HIV), which is transmitted when the body fluids of an infected person enter another person's bloodstream. There the virus attacks cells which are part of the immune system. It is possible to carry the virus – that is, to be HIV positive – for ten years or more without developing AIDS. Sufferers usually die of opportunistic infections – those that do not normally affect people with healthy immune systems – such as rare forms of pneumonia and skin cancer.

HIV is believed to have diverged from a virus found in a group of African monkeys as long as 140 years ago, but AIDS went undetected because its symptoms were diagnosed as other infectious diseases such as syphilis and tuberculosis. Not until these diseases had been brought under control in the mid 20th century did it become apparent that AIDS was a separate condition. Those most at risk from infection are homosexual and bisexual men, injecting drug users who share needles, and surgical patients and haemophiliacs treated with contaminated blood. Increasing international trade and tourism made contacts between different countries and continents commonplace. Drugs became used for recreation, and the availability of heroin and disposable plastic syringes led to populations of injecting drug users in large cities.

The growth in prostitution in cities and along trade routes between African countries led to an AIDS epidemic in the early 1980s. In some states as many as 20 per cent of the adult population were said to be infected. Mass immunisation programmes which took place without rigorous sterilisation of needles are also said to have transmitted the disease. By mid 1995, a total of nearly 1.2 million cases of AIDS had been reported to the World Health Organisation, and it has been estimated that more than 4.5 million cases have occurred worldwide since the epidemic began.

air force Aircraft were originally used in the First World War to locate targets for artillery batteries on the WESTERN FRONT. From 1916, aircraft were developed for bombing, while rival fighter planes engaged in gunfights in France and in the MESOPOTAMIA CAMPAIGN, where aircraft were also used for reconnaissance. Germany used Zeppelin airships for bombing attacks against civilian targets. Rapid strides in aircraft design between the wars resulted in both sides possessing formidable bomber and fighter fleets by the start of the Second World War.

During the war, dive-bombing techniques as well as heavily armed bombers for massed high altitude air raids were developed, while the invention of radar helped defenders to locate attacking aircraft, particularly during the Battle of BRITAIN in 1940. Large troop-carrying planes were also built, together with the first helicopters, which later became a key weapon in wars in Korea, Vietnam and Afghanistan. The high costs of the increasingly sophisticated aircraft developed since the Second World War have made it difficult for poorer countries to compete in building and maintaining efficient air forces.

air transport The earliest air transport in 19th-century Europe was by hot-air balloon, glider and airship, first using steam and then petrol engines to drive a propeller. Airships continued to be developed, especially by Germany and Britain in the First World War, and by the USA. The development of airships for transatlantic passenger service was set back when the British *R101* crashed and burned in 1930, and ended with the crash of the German *Hindenburg* at Lakehurst, New Jersey, in 1937, and the loss of 36 lives.

Development of the aeroplane since the first flight of the Wright brothers in 1903 was stimulated by both world wars. Passenger and freight traffic, using land and seaplanes, was developing between the wars. Since 1952, jet airliners have brought huge rises in traffic. In 1970 jumbo jets (Boeing 747s), which can carry up to 490 people, allowed fares to be cut, while in 1976 Concorde cut the trans-Atlantic crossing time to under four hours.

Aix-la-Chapelle, Treaty of (1748) Treaty which ended the War of the Austrian Succession, in which France, Spain and Prussia disputed with Austria and Britain the claim of MARIA THERESA to inherit the Austrian Empire. The treaty restored territory to its former owners, with a few exceptions. The terms were drawn up by the British and French and reluctantly accepted by Empress Maria Theresa, who had to abandon Silesia to Frederick II of Prussia. In Italy Don Philip, the younger son of Philip V of Spain, received Parma. In North America, colonists were forced to hand back the fortress of Louisbourg to the French, so that Britain could secure the return of Madras in India. The treaty left many conflicting interests unresolved, and the SEVEN YEARS' WAR broke out eight years later.

Akbar (1542-1605) Third and greatest of the MUGHAL emperors, who ruled India from 1555 until his death. At 13 Akbar inherited a fragile empire, but military conquests brought Rajasthan, Gujarat, Bengal, Kashmir and the north Deccan under his sway. He introduced a system of civil and military service which ensured personal loyalty and centralised control, and made changes to the land revenue system which reduced pressure on peasant farmers. Although a Muslim, he married RAJPUT princesses, suspended discriminatory taxes and increased the employment of Hindus in the imperial service. Akbar created the basis for Mughal control over much of India until the early 18th century.

Akhenaton (d. 1362 BC) Pharaoh of Egypt from 1379 until his death, husband of NEFERTITI. The pharaoh believed in the existence of only one god, and banned the worship of all but Aton, the sun-god. He built a new city (modern Tell el Amarna) to replace Thebes, the capital, and named it after himself. Akhenaton's religious reforms were unpopular and they were overturned by the priests of Amon at the beginning of TUTANKHAMUN's reign.

The Egyptian pharaoh Akhenaton, here hand-in-hand with his wife, built a great temple without a roof in his new capital city so that devotees could worship Aton the sun-god.

The Mughal emperor Akbar leads his forces in an attack on Ranthambore fort during the conquest of Rajasthan in northern India.

Akkad Area in central Mesopotamia, named after the city of Agade, which was founded by Sargon I around 2350 BC. Sargon conquered the SUMERIANS in southern Mesopotamia after much hard fighting, and in later campaigns penetrated as far as Syria and eastern Asia Minor. He ruled for more than 50 years, crushing a number of revolts in his sprawling empire. His successors maintained Akkadian supremacy for another hundred years.

Alamein, El, Battles of (June–November 1942) Two battles fought in Egypt of decisive importance in the Second World War. In June 1942, the British took up a defensive line, with one flank resting on the Mediterranean at El Alamein and the other on the salt marshes of the Qattara Depression. At the first Battle of Alamein in July, General Claude Auchinleck averted the danger of the Allies losing Egypt by halting the advance towards Cairo of the German Afrika Korps commanded by General Erwin ROMMEL, the 'Desert Fox'. General Bernard MONTGOMERY built up Allied forces at El Alamein to outnumber the enemy nearly three to one before launching an offensive on October 23.

After an artillery barrage, some 1200 tanks advanced, followed by infantry. Rommel was handicapped by a fuel shortage and had only about 500 tanks. The outnumbered Germans never regained the initiative. They were forced to retreat into Libya, and some 10 000 Germans and 20 000 Italians were taken prisoner. The battle was the first major British land victory of the war and marked the beginning of the end for Germany in North Africa.

Alamo, The Mission fort in San Antonio, Texas, and scene of a siege during clashes with Mexico in 1836. A Mexican army of 3000 led by Santa Anna besieged the fort, which was held by fewer than 200 men under the joint command of William B. Travis and James Bowie. The siege lasted from February 24 to March 6, when the Mexicans finally breached the walls. Travis, Bowie, Davy Crockett and all their men were killed. The defence of the Alamo became the symbol of Texan resistance.

Alaric I (c.AD 370-410) King of the Visigoths, who commanded the forces of the Gothic allies of Emperor Theodosius and helped to put down the Western usurper, Emperor Eugenius. On Theodosius's death the Eastern and Western Roman Empires were divided. Alaric revolted against the rule of CONSTANTINOPLE and moved his people in search of a homeland. In 401 he invaded Italy. Twice defeated by Stilicho, the Roman general, he entered into an alliance with him. After Emperor Honorius executed Stilicho, Alaric repudiated the pact and ravaged Italy, laying siege to Rome three times. The city fell in 410. Alaric planned invasions of Sicily and Africa, but his fleet was destroyed by storms.

Alaska purchase Deal of 1867 by which the USA bought Alaska from Russia for $7 200 000. The purchase was arranged by William H. SEWARD, who was convinced of Alaska's strategic importance, while the Russians preferred to sell it to the Americans than risk it falling into British hands. At first known as 'Seward's Folly', Alaska was governed by various US departments until 1884 when a civil government was established. It became the 49th state of the union in 1959.

Alba, Duke of (1507-82) Spanish statesman and general. Born Fernando Alvarez de Toledo, he rose to prominence in the armies of the Holy Roman Emperor Charles V, whose territories extended from the Baltic to the Mediterranean. Alba contributed significantly to the defeat of the German Protestants at the Battle of Mühlberg in 1547. In 1559 he helped to negotiate the treaty of Cateau Cambresis, which ended the war with France, and in 1567 Philip II sent him, in the post of governor-general, to quell uprisings in the Netherlands. A religious fanatic, Alba established a special court at Brussels, the notorious 'Council of Blood', with full civil and military powers. Comprised of seven members, the Council set out ruthlessly to suppress heresy and demands from the Dutch provinces for political self-government, spreading fear as thousands were brought to trial and convicted, and some 18 000 people were executed. Properties were confiscated and taxes raised, fanning resentment even further until eventually the revolts escalated into a war of independence. Alba was recalled to Spain in 1573. Although Philip imprisoned him in 1579 for allowing his son to marry without royal consent, the following year he released Alba to lead the forces that eventually conquered Portugal.

The Visigoth king Alaric I (right) was reputedly buried with his treasure under the Busento river in southern Italy after its waters had been temporarily diverted.

At a sitting of the 'Council of Blood', the Duke of Alba (left) hears pleas from women from the Dutch provinces; meanwhile the 'Council' decides on appropriate punishments for dissenters.

Living off the land

Until modern times land was the basis of life. Most people lived by subsistence farming – and died if harvests failed. This is their story.

From prehistory up until the 19th century, farming was the main support of the population everywhere. The peasant's work varied with the seasons, and the nature of his tasks depended on location and climate. In southern Europe, for example, hot summers and mild winters allowed work to continue throughout the year and determined the crops cultivated, such as olives and vines. Peasants in the northerly parts of Europe were much more restricted in what they could grow.

Every peasant's life included a range of activities. Some worked solely on the land, but others spent time at crafts such as weaving, carpentry, brewing and pottery. In wooded areas they cut timber, made hurdles and burnt charcoal. By the sea many combined fishing with farming.

The peasant's family worked as a unit: when the men were busy elsewhere, wives and daughters kept the farm going, caring for the stock, feeding the chickens, driving the pigs into the woods to forage, gathering fuel and making butter and cheese in the dairy. Women also worked in the fields, even at tasks such as breaking down clods of earth with mallets. They supplemented the family earnings with their own crafts – spinning yarn, making lace or weaving baskets. During busy seasons other tasks had to be set aside, but in the winter extra work, perhaps in a nearby village, was greatly prized. The children also helped on the land, and often left home at an early age to become servants or apprentices in a town.

FROM HOVEL TO HOUSE

Living standards varied widely depending on the nature of the farming, the fertility of the soil and the availability of alternative occupations. The warm climate of southern Europe meant that less clothing and heating were needed, the winter days were longer and the houses could be simpler. Many peasant homes in Spain, Italy and Greece lacked glass in their windows until recent times. The earliest one or two-room homes of wood, dried mud and straw, lath and plaster or other local materials were eventually replaced by more permanent structures of timber, stone or brick. Houses became more elaborate, with a kitchen and dairy, and an upper storey for sleeping or for storing grain, cheese or wool. But in some areas the 'long house', a single-storey dwelling with the family and livestock all under one roof, lingered on.

Celia Fiennes, a gentlewoman journeying in northern England about the end of the 17th century, described a peasant's home: 'I was forced to take up in a poor cottage which was open to the thatch and no partitions but hurdles... the landlady brought me out her best sheets which served to secure my own sheets from her dirty blankets... but no sleep could I get, they burning turf and their chimneys are sort of flues or open tunnels that the smoke does annoy the rooms.'

Bread was often made from inexpensive grains such as barley, oats or rye. The supply of fuel was very important: cheap wood or coal allowed more hot dishes and less sharing of ovens. Housewives exchanged recipes. They were kept in account books which record items such as 'Goodwife Wells, her runnet' or 'Goody Cleaves recipe for Hogs Cheek'. Stilton cheese is said to have derived from such a transfer of recipes. Much use was made

Less than 100 years ago many peasants in Brittany in northern France could not afford teams of horses and had to drag their harrows back and forth by hand before sowing.

Carpenters in all ages used adzes. This one is Roman

Victorian farm workers still used sickles like this one from the Iron Age

The cycle of the seasons marked out the peasant's year. Little ever changed. In this French manuscript from about 1460 labourers are engaged in the main activities of the busiest months.

of what could be gathered from the woods, commons, rivers or sea: offal, eggs, poultry, rabbits and herring featured large in the diet. Seafoods such as sole and oysters were much eaten in places where they were plentiful. The introduction of the potato, which became common in the early 19th century, was a major innovation, offering a nutritious alternative to bread, which could be expensive after a poor harvest.

A PRECARIOUS LIFE

The well-being of the family depended on its good health. A prolonged illness, a serious accident or the early death of a husband or wife was a disaster. Peasants had to rely on folk remedies, and their lives were often short. Marshy areas were infamous for malarial agues. Daniel Defoe, visiting a low-lying part of Essex in south-eastern England, reported that the peasants took their brides from the uplands and the young girls, 'soon getting an ague or two', seldom lasted more than a year. 'It was very frequent to meet with men that had from five or six to 14 or 15 wives.'

In the Middle Ages the majority of European peasants were serfs, holding land in return for services owed to the lord of the manor. These services could be onerous, requiring the peasant to work for two or three days a week on the lord's land and also to help at harvest time, carry produce for him and offer gifts at festivals, such as eggs at Easter and a fat capon at Christmas. The peasant was also obliged to grind his corn at the lord's mill and press his grapes

in the lord's wine-press. The peasant and his family could not appear in the royal courts, and were forbidden to leave the manor without the lord's permission.

In time these obligations broke down under changing economic circumstances or were abolished by statute, though serfdom survived in some countries such as Russia until the late 19th century. In England lords found it more practical to levy a rent in cash rather than in kind. The unfree peasant became a tenant farmer, though in some districts there had always been independent freeholders. Some freeholders prospered and became large-scale farmers.

The status of the agricultural poor was also changed markedly by the 'agricultural revolution', which started in the late 17th century. This was a long-drawn-out process of innovation in crops, livestock, drainage, fertilisers and machinery, accompanied by the cultivation of former waste lands and by changes in the structure of farming. The ancient 'open fields' and commons – the basis of the old system of communal farming – were swallowed up by enclosures, resulting in the modern pattern of farms held by individuals.

The modernisation of farming was a consequence of the rapid

In Asia rice was the staple diet. Workers winnow and store the grain in an illustration from the 13th to 14th century Yuan dynasty.

growth in the population and towns in later 18th and 19th-century Europe. The economic gains were undeniable, but the social consequences were sometimes disastrous. Some peasants lost their few acres of land and became full-time labourers on farms or in industry. Others emigrated, especially to the United States. The potato blight, which in the mid 1840s spread hunger and misery through northern Europe and particularly in Ireland, combined with farming changes and the growth of population to put irresistible pressure on country people to seek cheap land and a new life elsewhere.

Those who remained had to adapt to the sharply declining importance of agriculture in national life. The former peasant, if he was fortunate, joined the ranks of the larger farmers; otherwise he remained a landless farm labourer – though now more respected as a member of a scientific and mechanised occupation and, in time, one who was better rewarded for his labours.

Albania One of the smallest and poorest countries in Europe, bounded on the north and east by Serbia and on the south-east by Greece. Albania was part of the Ottoman Empire for nearly 500 years from the 15th century. Nationalist resistance arose in the 19th century, but was crushed in 1831. Albania finally achieved independence as a result of the BALKAN WARS in 1912.

During the First World War Albania was a battleground for the forces of Austria, Italy and neighbouring Balkan powers. At the Paris Peace Conference in 1919 its independence was secured, and it became a monarchy under King ZOG in 1928. Invaded by Italy in 1939, Albania was established as a communist state in 1944 by Enver Hoxha. It remained a satellite of the Soviet Union until a rift in 1958, when it turned to China for military and economic aid. Albania remained Stalinist in policy and cut off from the rest of the world until the death of Hoxha in 1985.

In 1990 cautious steps were taken to allow opposition political parties to be set up and to restore democracy. Nearly 40000 Albanians took advantage of the easing of restrictions the following year to cross the Adriatic to Italy to ask for refugee status. Most were returned to Albania. The communists held power in the first free elections in 1991, but were defeated in 1992. The following year a democratic parliamentary constitution was adopted, but then the economy collapsed causing widespread poverty and hardship.

Alberoni, Giulio (1664-1752) Italian cardinal and statesman. In 1713 Alberoni arranged the marriage of the Duke of Parma's niece Elizabeth FARNESE to the Spanish king, Philip V. He became effective ruler of Spain in 1715, and increased royal power. His chief aims were to strengthen Spain, recover lost territories and crush Austrian power in Italy. He was doubtful about the wisdom of declaring war on Austria in July 1717. It led to British and French intervention against Spain, and his dismissal by Philip in 1719.

Albert, Prince (1819-61) Husband of Queen VICTORIA, prince consort of Great Britain and Ireland, and father of Edward VII. The younger son of the Duke of Saxe-Coburg-Gotha, Albert married his first cousin Victoria in 1840. At first Albert met with mistrust and prejudice because he was not British. The queen would let him take no part in state affairs, but he became in effect her private secretary and gradually his influence over Victoria increased. Albert took a keen interest in industry, agriculture and the arts, and headed the Royal Commission that raised the money for the Great Exhibition of 1851. He displayed diplomatic skill in softening the government's reactions in disputes with Prussia in 1856 and with the USA in 1861.

Albert's early death from typhoid caused Victoria to go into a lengthy period of seclusion and mourning. She had to be persuaded in the 1870s by Prime Minister Benjamin Disraeli once more to take part in public life.

Alberti, Leon (1404-72) Italian architect, sculptor, painter and writer. He was also a lawyer, papal secretary, playwright, mathematician, grammarian and cryptographer, embodying the Renaissance ideal of the 'universal man'. Alberti was one of the leading architects of his period and the most important writer on the theory of art during the Renaissance, however little survives of his work as a painter and sculptor. His first book about the arts, *On Painting*, written in 1435, contains the earliest description of perspective. Alberti's other books about the arts included *On Sculpture*, probably written in the 1460s, and *Concerning Architecture*, the first printed book on the subject, published in 1485 after Alberti's death. Alberti rejected the medieval notion of art as the expression of religious ideas, emphasising instead its rational and scientific basis. He showed admiration for classical antiquity. As an architect Alberti stressed the intellectual side of the art, such as theories of proportion. His two most important surviving buildings are the churches of San Sebastiano and Santa Andrea, in Mantua.

Albigensians Followers of a form of the CATHAR heresy in the 12th and 13th centuries who took their name from the town of Albi, in Languedoc, southern France. There and in northern Italy the sect was widespread.

The Albigensians rejected priests and, like followers of MANICHAEISM, believed that spirit and matter were opposed to each other. For them, the material world was evil and salvation required freeing the soul from the flesh. This led them in extreme cases to condemn marriage. Eating any form of animal product – even milk or eggs – was forbidden, as was the taking of life and swearing oaths. There was a discinction between a 'pure' initiated elite and the great mass of ordinary believers.

The movement was condemned at the Council of Toulouse in 1119 and by the third and fourth LATERAN councils in 1179 and 1215 as heretical and a threat to family and state. It was also vigorously opposed by St Bernard and St Dominic but, thanks to the protection of Raymond VI, Count of Toulouse, and most of the southern French nobility, the heresy gained wide acceptance in the south. After failing to convert the Albigensians peaceably, Pope INNOCENT III called for a crusade to take place against them. The Albigensian Crusade, in 1209, became a byword for massacre and cruelty and was seen as an onslaught by the nobility of northern France on the civilisation of the south. The French Crown gained most benefit from the defeat of the Albigensians: with the taking of Montsegur in 1244, the Languedoc province could be incorporated into the kingdom. Throughout the remainder of the 13th century the remnants of the Albigensians, together with other Cathar groups and the WALDENSES, were the main targets of the feared INQUISITION, by which the papacy tried to suppress 'deviant' forms of Christianity.

> **DID YOU KNOW?**
>
> Albigensian believers nearing death received baptism by words not water, consolamentum, and then had to embark on the endura, a period of total and suicidal fasting.

Alcibiades (c.450-404 BC) Influential Athenian leader in the PELOPONNESIAN WAR between Athens and Sparta, whose career ended in disaster. The nephew of PERICLES, he took up politics, urging the conquest of Syracuse in Sicily. Alcibiades was appointed one of the commanders of an expedition to Sicily from 415 to 413, but he was charged with the desecration of sacred statues and recalled to Athens. He fled to Sparta, where he changed sides and advised the Spartans on how best to wage war against their long-term enemies, the Athenians.

After breaking with Spartan leaders in 411, Alcibiades went on to win the confidence of the officers of the Athenian fleet based at Samos, leading it with conspicuous success. He again fell under suspicion in 406, when he was blamed for a defeat, incurred by a subordinate officer, of the Athenian navy off Notium. Alcibiades withdrew from public life but was murdered in Phrygia, Anatolia.

Alcuin (c.735-804) English scholar and theologian. He was educated at the cathedral school in York, later becoming its head. Invited by the emperor Charlemagne to set up a palace school at Aachen, German, Alcuin taught there from 782 and established what was to become the core curriculum of the medieval age. It was known as the 'seven liberal arts', and comprised grammar, rhetoric, dialectic, arithmetic, geometry, astronomy and music theory. Alcuin encouraged the large-scale transcription and preservation of ancient texts. He also wrote many letters, school manuals and theological treatises, and revised the liturgy of the Frankish Church. His pupils included leaders of the so-called 'Carolingian Renaissance', in which groups of scholars from England, Spain and Italy joined Franks and Jews at Charlemagne's court. In 796 Alcuin became Abbot of St Martin at Tours, where he worked until his death.

Alexander I (1777-1825) Tsar of Russia from 1801 to 1825. Alexander had been educated by his grandmother, CATHERINE II 'the

Great', whose sudden death frustrated her plan to pass over her unstable son Paul and make Alexander tsar. For five years Alexander's father, Paul I, had tyrannised Russia before his assassination in 1801. Alexander set out to reform Russia and correct many of the injustices of his father's reign. He introduced plans for public education, but he was unable to abolish serfdom because he depended upon the support of the nobility. His adviser, Mikhail Speransky, pressed for a more liberal constitution, but the nobles managed to bring about Speransky's fall in 1812.

In foreign policy, Alexander at first supported the coalition against Napoleon, who defeated him at AUSTERLITZ in 1805 and at Friedland in 1807. These reverses resulted in the Treaties of Tilsit in which Alexander allied himself with Napoleon and supported the CONTINENTAL SYSTEM against trade with the British. His wars with Persia (1804-13) and Turkey (1806-12) brought territorial gains, including Georgia. Napoleon invaded Russia in 1812 to intimidate Alexander, who had failed to join him against Austria in 1809. The invasion roused Alexander to declare: 'Napoleon or I. From now on we cannot reign together.' Alexander refused to make peace even after the loss of Moscow, and his armies helped to defeat Napoleon's *Grande Armée* at Leipzig in October 1813. He pursued him to Paris and secured Napoleon's abdication.

Alexander formed a HOLY ALLIANCE of European monarchs, which was intended to bring a peace based on Christian love. Such idealism gave way to the fear of revolt and Alexander became more hostile to reform at home. He was reported to have died in the Crimea, but rumour persisted that he had disappeared to Siberia and become a hermit.

Alexander I (1888-1934) Serbian monarch who in 1929 renamed his kingdom of Serbs, Croats and Slovenes as Yugoslavia. Alexander came to the throne in 1921 and tried to overcome the ethnic, religious and regional rivalries among the Balkan peoples by dictatorial rule and by uniting his country under a single name. In 1931 his restoration of some civil rights failed to quell rising separatist tension. Alexander was planning to restore parliamentary government when he was assassinated by a Croatian terrorist.

Alexander II (1818-81) Tsar of Russia from 1855 until his death. Known as the 'Tsar Liberator', Alexander was the eldest son of Nicholas I and succeeded to the throne as the CRIMEAN WAR exposed how backward the society of his empire had become. Alexander's Emancipation Act of 1861 freed millions of serfs and he went on to overhaul Russia's antiquated judicial system and inefficient local government.

Conqueror of the ancient world

Alexander the Great became King of Macedon at the age of 20. By the time he died only 13 years later, he had expanded the frontiers of his empire from Greece to India, venturing to the limits of the known world.

When King Philip of Macedon, whose armies had subjugated the Greek city-states, was assassinated in 336BC, his throne passed to his 20-year-old son. The Greek cities saw their opportunity. Believing Alexander to be merely an inexperienced boy, they prepared to fight to regain their independence. This, it turned out, was to be a costly mistake.

Using the new Macedonian tactics of the heavy infantry phalanx with interlocking shields, Alexander broke the Greek armies outside Thebes, close to Athens. He then stormed the city and burned it, selling the survivors into slavery. There were no more revolts, and Alexander was free to turn to his greater design.

EXPEDITION TO THE EAST

By Philip's time Macedon had eagerly adopted Greek culture. As well as having a strict military training, Alexander had been educated by Aristotle, Greece's foremost philosopher. Alexander planned not just military domination of the known world, but a league of Hellenic states under Macedonian leadership. In 334, with an army of 35000 men, he crossed into Persian-dominated Asia.

In a daring cavalry thrust Alexander smashed through the light-armed force of Persian horsemen. He then went on to take the cities of Asia Minor one by one. A far stronger Persian army under King Darius advanced to meet him at Issus on the Syrian border. The Greeks and Macedonians won a crushing victory. Darius fled. Alexander took Syria and Egypt without resistance, and founded the city of Alexandria on the Nile delta.

In 331 Alexander's army crossed the Euphrates into the Persian heartland. Darius had gathered a new, even larger, army, but Alexander defeated it at Gaugemela. Again Darius fled. Darius was killed by his own bodyguard and his empire collapsed. Babylon, Susa and Persepolis fell without a struggle.

How far did Alexander mean to go? At the city of Gordium in Phrygia (Turkey) there was a huge ancient knot; the Fates had decreed that whoever could untie it would be ruler of the world. Alexander hacked it in two with his sword. He told his troops: 'The limits of our empire will be those which the gods have fixed as the limits of the earth.' In the next four years he passed Samarkand into Afghanistan, and crossed the Hindu Kush into the Indus Valley. His last victory, at the river Hydaspes in the Punjab, was against an Indian army with 200 elephants.

Having reached utterly unknown lands, Alexander's exhausted army refused to go on; they believed that the Himalayas marked the end of the world. Alexander began the return journey. At Babylon he became ill, and died in 323, aged 33. His empire was divided between his generals: Antigonus took Greece and Macedonia, Ptolemy Egypt, and Seleucus Syria and the east.

A late 4th-century BC royal sarcophagus at Sidon in the Levant is decorated with a frieze depicting events from Alexander's life. Here Alexander rides to the rescue of a client king, Abdalonymus, whose horse has been attacked by a lion while on a hunting expedition.

Despite his reforms, he still believed in the need to maintain autocratic rule, and his commitment to military strength led him to bring in general military service in 1874. Alexander's reign saw extensive territorial gains in the Caucasus, the Middle East and the Far East to offset the sale of Alaska to the USA in 1867. The growth of a number of secret revolutionary societies such as the Nihilists and Populists, who objected to Alexander's absolute rule, culminated in an assassination attempt in 1866. This caused him to abandon his reforms. After surviving further assassination attempts, he was mortally wounded by a bomb thrown by a member of the People's Will Movement.

Alexander II (1198-1249) King of Scots from 1214 to 1249, successor to William the Lion. After supporting the English barons in the first BARONS' WAR against King John, Alexander had to suppress revolts at home in Moray in 1221, in Argyll and Caithness the following year and in Galloway in 1224. The absence of a fixed border between Scotland and England kept relations between the two countries unstable. To improve them he married Joan, eldest daughter of John and sister of Henry III, in 1221, but she died in 1238 without producing an heir.

In 1244 Alexander led 100 000 Scots into England, but he returned without a fight, agreeing at the Treaty of Newcastle not to ally himself with England's enemies nor to invade England unjustly. He died of fever on an expedition against the Lord of Argyll and the Norse king Haco, whose possession of the islands of the Orkneys and Hebrides threatened the Scottish coast.

Alexander III 'the Great' see feature, page 23

Alexander Nevsky (c.1220-63) Russian soldier, Grand Duke of Vladimir from 1252 to 1263. Born in Vladimir, son of the Grand Duke Yaroslav II of Novgorod, he earned the name 'Nevsky' after defeating the Swedish army on the banks of the River Neva in 1240. Wars against the Germans and Lithuanians reached a climax in his decisive victory two years later over the TEUTONIC KNIGHTS on the frozen Lake Peipus. Nevsky willingly cooperated with the Mongol overlords (suzerains) of Russia and was supported by the Russian Orthodox Church, which enjoyed exemption from taxes under the Mongol emperors, and canonised him in the mid 16th century.

Alexander of Tunis, 1st Earl (1891-1969) British field-marshal whose title reflects his achievements in the North African Campaign in the Second World War. Harold Alexander served in the Irish Guards in the First World War, and later in Latvia and India. In the

Saint Alexander Nevsky was made an official national hero by Soviet leader Joseph Stalin to boost morale during the Second World War.

Second World War he commanded the rearguard at Dunkirk and the withdrawal of British and Indian troops from Burma. As commander in chief of the Middle East, in 1942 he turned the tide against the German General Erwin ROMMEL. As deputy to the American general Dwight EISENHOWER in 1943, he directed the Allied offensive which drove the Germans back to Tunis in North Africa, and subsequently led the invasion of Sicily, afterwards remaining in Italy as commander of Allied forces until the end of the war. In 1946 Alexander was made governor-general of Canada and remained there until his appointment as minister of defence, a post he held from 1952 to 1954.

Alexandria Name given to six cities conquered or founded by ALEXANDER THE GREAT throughout his empire. Their architecture and institutions were Greek in style, contributing greatly to the spread of HELLENISTIC civilisation. The most successful of the six was established at the western edge of the Nile delta in 331 BC. For more than 2000 years Alexandria was the largest city in Egypt. It became the country's main port, took over the trade of Tyre and Carthage, and under Ptolemy I, who reigned from 304 to 284 BC, replaced Memphis as the capital. The harbour's lighthouse, built in 280 BC on the island of Pharos, was famed as one of the SEVEN WONDERS OF THE WORLD. Alexandria

flourished throughout the Ptolemaic dynasty, and when Egypt became a Roman province in 30 BC its location made it a centre of world trade. Enhanced by its library and museum, Alexandria prospered culturally as well as economically. The library, founded by Ptolemy I, was said to contain some 700 000 items. It was burnt down by Arabs who captured the city in AD 641. The city began to decline and in the 14th century this process accelerated when the canal linking Alexandria to the Nile silted up, and in 1324 an earthquake destroyed the lighthouse. The discovery of the Cape of Good Hope at the end of the 15th century opened a new route to the East and reduced the city's standing as a trading centre.

Napoleon occupied Alexandria from 1798 to 1801. In 1882, the city was bombarded and occupied by the British, and it was used as a British naval base during the First and Second World Wars. From the 1950s Alexandria grew more Egyptian in character as the once large foreign community left after the establishment of the republic in 1953.

Alfonso X (1221-84) King of the Spanish kingdom of Castile and León from 1252 to 1284. Known as Alfonso the Wise, he commissioned a law code, the *Siete Partidas,* 'the Seven Divisions of the Law', as well as a history of Spain – the first such works to be written in Spanish (Castilian) – as well as the translation of scientific texts from Arabic to Spanish. Alfonso also wrote poems, mainly in honour of the Virgin Mary. His accomplishment as a scholar was not matched by his political achievements. He spent nearly 20 years trying to become Holy Roman Emperor in opposition to the English claimant, Richard, Earl of Cornwall, until Richard died in 1275 and Pope Gregory X persuaded Alfonso to renounce his claim. He failed to complete his father's crusade against the Moors in southern Spain, and his efforts to impose legal uniformity and increase taxes, together with a dispute over the succession, caused his son Sancho IV to rebel in 1282 and isolate him in Seville, where he died.

Alfred the Great (849-99) Ruler of the English kingdom of Wessex from 871 until his death. Renowned both for his achievements in war and for his love of learning, Alfred is the only English king to be entitled 'the Great'. He ruled south of the Thames (Wessex) and parts of central

The Alfred Jewel – made of gold, rock crystal and enamel – bears the inscription *Aelfred mec heht gewyrcan,* 'Alfred had me made'.

England (English Mercia), so his kingdom included nearly all the English who had not submitted to Danish conquest. The king thus came to be regarded as a symbol of unity.

In 865, the Danes had overwhelmed the English kingdoms of EAST ANGLIA, MERCIA and NORTHUMBRIA, and in 871 began to challenge the defences of Wessex. Alfred was the first English monarch to organise systematically the defence of his realm against the Danes, with whom he fought almost without break from 876 until his death. The most serious attack came in 878 when the Danes, under Guthrum, drove Alfred into hiding in the marshes of Athelney, Somerset. It was during this time, according to a 12th-century account, that Alfred absent-mindedly let burn a batch of barley cakes that he was watching for a herdswoman. Later that year Alfred won a decisive victory at Edington, making peace at the Treaty of Wedmore (present-day Chippenham). Guthrum agreed to withdraw to East Anglia and convert to Christianity. When Alfred captured London in 886, he agreed with Guthrum a clear boundary between Wessex and the DANELAW. The Danes were to remain east of Watling Street, the Roman road from London to Chester.

Alfred improved England's defences by reorganising the army and developing a navy, and by improving the system of fortified towns (known as burghs), many of which are still county towns. He also encouraged learning and was renowned for issuing a law-code. He had translations made of the Latin texts of BOETHIUS, Orosius and GREGORY the Great, adding his own commentaries. Just as his military victories saved the English nation and culture, so his contributions to learning and the legal system were a major civilising influence on his people.

Algeria Country in North Africa whose boundaries, established after French conquest in the 1830s, make it the second largest country of the African continent after Sudan. The earliest inhabitants were Berbers, whose neolithic cave drawings of hunting and herding can be seen at Tasli N'ajjer. Phoenician traders began to colonise the coast in the 9th century BC. In the 2nd century BC the Romans incorporated the region into the province of Africa, and Christianity later took root there. St Augustine (AD 354-430), one of the greatest bishops in the early Christian Church, was born in Algeria and became bishop of Hippo (now Annaba). Invasions by VANDALS in the 5th century brought Roman rule to an end, but by then the Berbers controlled most of the area. In the early 6th century the Byzantine Empire reached as far as present-day Algiers. The Arabs invaded and conquered the region in the 7th century, despite fierce Berber resistance, and it became part of the Ummayyad caliphate, based in

Algerian rebel troops left their mountain bases to take control of villages and cities before the 1962 referendum in favour of independence.

Damascus. Although the Berbers converted to Islam, they continued to resist Arab rule. From the 10th century, Algeria was ruled by a series of local dynasties such as the Fatimids, Almoravids and Almohads, until the area came under nominal Ottoman rule in 1518. This was thanks to the pirate BARBAROSSA (Khayr ad-Din), who conquered the North African principalities, and secured them against the threat from Christian Spain. Relatively independent Barbary pirates – whose name comes from 'Berber' – ranged

> **66 Independence . . . a folly, a monstrosity . . . France must not leave. She has the right to be in Algeria. She will remain there. 99**
>
> *French president Charles de Gaulle during the Algerian war of independence, March 1960*

along the North African coastline and were a menace to European shipping for centuries. Booty and protection money were the chief sources of revenue for the local rulers.

In 1815 the USA, whose ships had been attacked, fought against Algiers, which in 1816 was bombarded by an Anglo-Dutch fleet. Not until the French conquest of Algeria in the 1830s did the piracy end. France formally annexed Algeria in the 1840s and extended its influence south until the current boundaries were drawn in 1902. It was 'attached' to metropolitan France and heavily settled by Europeans, who confiscated lands and refused the Muslim majority the right to political and economic equality. By 1880 there were around 375 000 Europeans living in the country and farming the best land. This provoked increasing instability, until a war of national independence broke out in 1954. In

the face of considerable resistance in both France and among the White Algerians, in 1962 the French president Charles de Gaulle negotiated an end to hostilities in the Evian Agreement, and Algeria was granted independence following a referendum.

Ahmed BEN BELLA became prime minister and a year later was elected as the country's first president. With Algeria devastated by war and weakened by the departure of European capital and skilled labour, Ben Bella nationalised abandoned colonial holdings and supported anticolonial movements in other countries. In 1965 a bloodless coup established a left-wing government under the former defence minister Colonel Houari BOUMÉDIENNE, who nationalised French oil and natural gas concessions in 1971. After Boumédienne's death in 1978, his successor, Benjedid Chadli, relaxed his repressive internal policies and began to re-establish Algeria's foreign relations.

High unemployment, inflation and corruption triggered serious unrest in October 1988; in 1989 Algeria ceased to be a one-party state. The FIS (*Front Islamique du Salut*) made rapid gains, winning almost 65 per cent of the vote in the 1990 municipal elections – the first multiparty elections since 1962. Economic austerity and violence by fundamentalists demanding an Islamic state resulted in Chadli's resignation in 1992. A military regime took control, annulling recent elections and banning the FIS. Mohammed Boudiaf was made head of a new presidential council, but was assassinated in June 1992. FIS supporters continued to wage a campaign of violence and terrorism.

Algonquin Native Peoples inhabiting the Ottawa valley and nearby regions in the 17th century, and southern Ontario in the 18th. They fought the IROQUOIS, their rivals in the fur trade, especially the MOHAWK. They formed an alliance with the Montagnais to the east in 1570, and from 1603 with the French. Although mostly a hunting-fishing culture, some grew corn, beans and squash in cleared areas of the bush. They lived in pointed tepees or dome-shaped wigwams made from birchbark laid over poles, and were known for their light birch-bark canoes and the snowshoes, sledges and toboggans which they used for winter travel. About 2000 Algonquins survive, working as hunters' guides and trappers in modern Canada.

Ali Pasha, Mehmed Emin (1815-71) Turkish Ottoman statesman and reformer. After service in the sultan's foreign ministry he took office as Grand Vizier in 1852. Ali Pasha became one of the leading statesmen of the Tanzimat reform movement, and was responsible for the Hatt-i Humayun reform edict of 1856: this guaranteed Christians security of life and property, opened civil offices to all subjects, abolished torture and allowed foreigners to own property. Ali Pasha believed in autocratic rule and opposed the granting of a parliamentary constitution.

Allenby, Edmund (1861-1936) British field-marshal. Allenby served as a cavalry officer in the South African War between 1899 and 1902. When the First World War broke out he served as a British cavalry commander in France and led the Third Army from 1915 to 1917. He went on to defeat the Ottoman forces in Palestine and Syria, capturing Jerusalem. Allenby routed the Egyptian forces at the Battle of Megiddo in 1918 and ended Turkish resistance. He was appointed special high commissioner for Egypt and the Sudan from 1919 to 1925. Convinced of the case for Egyptian independence he persuaded the British Government to end its protectorate over Egypt in 1922.

Allende, Salvador (1908-73) Chilean statesman who in 1970 became the first Marxist to win the presidency of a Latin American country in a free election. He began his career in radical politics while studying medicine at the University of Chile, but was expelled and briefly imprisoned for his revolutionary activities. In 1933 he helped to found Chile's Socialist Party. He ran unsuccessfully for the presidency in 1952, 1958 and 1964 before a coalition of leftist parties brought him victory in 1970.

During his three years in power he set the country on a socialist path, nationalised many industries in which US businesses had an interest, and speeded up land reform. These measures, coupled with severe economic problems and widespread strikes, provoked the Chilean military establishment to overthrow him in a violent military coup led by General Augusto PINOCHET, with indirect support from the USA, in 1973. Allende died in the fighting, and was finally given a state funeral in 1990.

Almohad Berber dynasty that originated in the Atlas Mountains of North Africa in the early 12th century. The founder, Ibn Tumart, claimed to be the Mahdi ('the divinely guided one'), whose coming was foretold by MUHAMMAD, and he preached a puritanical form of Islam. His successor, Abd al-Mumin, seized North Africa and southern Spain from the ALMORAVIDS in 1145. The Almohad empire became an important Islamic Mediterranean power. A centrally directed administration with a professional civil service collected taxes and maintained a large fleet and army. Clashes in Spain with local princes proved disastrous, and the defeat at Las Navas de Tolosa in 1212 ended the Almohad regime. The dynasty survived in Marrakesh until 1269.

almshouse House where alms – food and money – were distributed. Originally part of medieval monasteries, most medieval almshouses were founded by clergymen such as Bishop Henry of Blois, who established the Hospital of St Cross in Winchester, England, about 1135. The term was also used to describe privately financed dwellings, usually for the elderly and infirm. Merchants, individually and in corporations, became especially active in endowing almshouses as a way of showing their charitable intentions. From the 16th century the relief supplied by almshouses was supplemented by the POOR LAWS which partly filled the gap left by Henry VIII's closure of the monasteries.

Alsace-Lorraine French region west of the Rhine repeatedly disputed by France and Germany. Alsace was part of the Roman province of Upper Germany before it was taken by the Alemanni in the 5th century and the Franks in 496. The region was divided between Charles the Bald and Louis the German in 870, in 911 it passed to the Frankish kingdom, then back to the Germans in 923. France began to dominate the area in the 17th century after confrontations with the Holy Roman Empire. Germany won back Alsace and the eastern part of Lorraine after the FRANCO-PRUSSIAN WAR from 1870 to 1871. Rich in coal and iron ore, Lorraine enabled Germany to expand its naval and military power. The French resented attempts to 'Germanise' the region and took back the province after the First World War under the Treaty of VERSAILLES. In 1940 the Germans occupied the region, until French and US troops recovered it for France at the end of the Second World War.

aluminium The Earth's third most plentiful element, exceeded only by oxygen and silicon. In the 20th century aluminium became valuable because it is light, strong, conducts electricity and resists corrosion. Although it is much less dense than iron, copper or zinc, it can be combined with other metals to form alloys that, for their weight, are stronger than any other metal. Aircraft engines were the first to use aluminium alloy pistons during the First World War, as they had to be of the lightest possible weight. Aluminium alloys were developed in the 1920s and 1930s for aircraft fuselages. Aluminium components are used increasingly in cars as their light weight saves fuel.

Ambedkar, Bhimrao Ramji (1893-1956) Indian leader who led the movement for the constitutional rights of the so-called Untouchables in the 1930s. The Untouchables were beneath the caste (class) system in Hindu society and said to defile members of other castes on touch, or even on sight. After Mahatma GANDHI went on a fast against the British creation of a series of separate electorates for the Untouchables, Ambedkar agreed to the 1932 Poona Pact. The pact retained Hindu joint electorates but provided nearly twice as many reserved seats for Untouchables in the legislative assemblies. After independence in 1947, Ambedkar was the law minister until 1951 and helped to draft the constitution, outlawing discrimination against Untouchables.

Ambrose, St (c.340-97) Bishop of Milan. In 374, Ambrose was Roman governor of the region: within a single week he was baptised a Christian, ordained a priest and made a bishop. Considered one of the 30 Doctors of the Church – exemplary theologians of outstanding merit – he was a renowned preacher and writer who opposed ARIANISM, which held that God the Son was not as divine in all respects as God the Father. He also attacked the pagan revival and the Jews, influenced three Roman emperors, and baptised St Augustine of Hippo and his son in 387. Ambrose opposed the execution of heretics and excommunicated the Roman emperor Theodosius for massacring the people of Thessalonica in 390, and forced him to perform public penance before receiving him back into the Church. Ambrose gave remarkable sermons and composed beautiful hymns. He saw Church and State not as rivals, but as complementary institutions under threat from heretics and barbarians.

American Civil War see feature, page 28

American Revolution see feature, page 31

Bhimrao Ambedkar (left), who was taunted by high-caste boys for being born an Untouchable, waged a campaign against discrimination.

Idi Amin, who was thought to have killed or tortured up to 300 000 people in his eight-year reign, looks on in 1975 as former British army officers swear an oath to serve in Uganda's armed forces.

Amerindians Indigenous peoples of North and South America. They are usually classified as a major branch of the Mongoloid peoples, but are sometimes seen as a distinct racial group. With the Inuits (Eskimos) and Aleuts (inhabitants of the Aleutian Islands) – who are unquestionably Mongoloids – they were inhabitants of the New World when the first European explorers arrived in the late 15th century. Their forebears came from northeastern Asia between 50 000 and 12 000 years ago, when the two continents were joined by a land bridge at what is now called the Bering Strait. The earliest evidence suggests that the American continent was inhabited 15 000 years ago, but finds in Mexico, Chile and Brazil suggest a date as early as 30 000 or more years ago. There may have been several separate colonisations; the Inuits and Aleuts are the descendants of the most recent, which took place by boat within the last 5000 years. The first colonisers brought little more than stone tools and perhaps domesticated dogs for hunting. As hunters and gatherers they spread south, killing the plentiful game with their stone-pointed lances.

Amerindian agriculture developed differently from that in the Old World. Starting 7000 or more years ago, it was based on maize, squash and beans, with cassava being grown in tropical forest regions. With no suitable animals to domesticate apart from the llama and the guinea pig, and no draught animals to pull the plough, the development of more mixed farming was gradual.

Farmers in the Andes developed skills in working metal from 1000 BC. Complex societies arose in South and Central America and grew into highly sophisticated civilisations, for example, those of the AZTECS and INCAS, but most collapsed after the arrival of the CONQUISTADORES and other European explorers during the 16th century.

Amin, Idi (1926-) President of Uganda from 1971 to 1979, notorious for his brutal and oppressive regime. Joining the army after a basic education, Amin rose through the ranks to become commander. In 1971 he overthrew his friend President Milton OBOTE and seized power. He advanced narrow tribal interests, expelled non-Africans and ordered the killing of thousands of his opponents, commenting: 'I ate them before they ate me.' As a Muslim he befriended Palestine and Libya and was personally involved when Palestinians hijacked an Israeli airliner at Entebbe, Uganda's capital. Amin was overthrown by Tanzanian troops and Ugandan nationalists in 1979, and is said to have fled to Saudi Arabia.

Amritsar Massacre (April 13, 1919) Incident in which British-led troops killed unarmed Indian protesters. Discontent with British rule had been mounting as a result of First World War emergency powers against subversion that the administration had extended into peacetime. More than 10 000 demonstrators gathered to protest in the Jallianwala Bagh, a walled park. Fearing a riot, Brigadier Reginald Dyer ordered his Gurkha troops to fire on the demonstrators, killing 379 and wounding more than 1200. The massacre prompted Mohandas GANDHI to form the Non-Cooperation Movement. The holiest shrine of the SIKH religion, the Golden Temple, is also in Amritsar. In 1984 armed Sikh separatists occupied the temple and were killed during a four-day army operation. In retaliation, the Indian prime minister, Indira Gandhi, was shot dead by two of her Sikh guards four months later.

Anabaptism Christian religious doctrine, literally rebaptism, which held that only adult baptism was valid and that people baptised as infants must be rebaptised as adults. Anabaptists are believed to have derived from a sect that originated in Zürich in the 1520s at a time when second baptism was punishable by death. Anabaptists believed that earthly institutions were corrupt and so they denied their authority, claiming the right to disobey the law. For this they were feared and thousands were killed.

anarchism Belief that government and law should be abolished and that equality and justice can only be achieved by getting rid of the State and by substituting free agreements between individuals. Groups of anarchists sought popular support in many European states in the 1860s and 1870s. In 1868 the Russian anarchist Mikhail Bakunin founded the Social Democratic Alliance, which attempted to gain control of the Workers' INTERNATIONAL, an association of socialist organisations. They switched between strategies of mutual association and violence against the State. Anarchists tried to mobilise mass working-class support for general strikes in Russia during the failed 1905 revolution and the 1917 Bolshevik uprising. They were active in the SPANISH CIVIL WAR, and in the latter half of the 20th century anarchism inspired many terrorist groups.

French deputies recoil in fear in 1893 when an anarchist bomb explodes in parliament, in an artist's re-creation of the scene for a magazine.

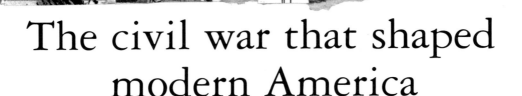

The civil war that shaped modern America

In 1861 war broke out in America that was to determine the future of the USA. This devastating conflict brought an end to slavery and united the states under one federal government, at a cost of 620 000 lives.

The American Civil War (1861-5) was brought about by the inability of the United States to resolve the problem of slavery, and the secession from the Union of the Southern states in February 1861.

Slavery relegated to servitude nearly 4 million Black bondsmen whose heavy labours in the cotton industry made the economy successful for Southern Whites. Majority opinion in the North viewed slavery as an abomination. During the years 1848 to 1861 the nation's party system came to reflect this division, and when in 1860 the Republican candidate, Abraham Lincoln, was elected to the presidency 11 Southern states seceded from the Union rather than accept a government hostile to their interests. They organised themselves into the Confederate States of America with Jefferson Davis as their president, and Richmond, Virginia, as their capital.

The Confederacy demanded that Lincoln evacuate the federal garrison at Fort Sumter in Charleston Harbor. Lincoln refused, and on April 12, 1861, the Confederates attacked the fort, thus marking the opening stage of the American Civil War.

THE BATTLE BEGINS

Patriotic fervour swept both North and South in the weeks following the attack. A London *Times* correspondent travelling through the South noted immense crowds with 'flushed faces, wild eyes, screaming mouths,' shouting the blood-curdling 'rebel yell'. The South's strategy was to make the war so expensive for the Union that it would concede Confederate independence. The North's was to suppress the rebellion and re-establish the authority of the federal government over the seceded states.

The first major battle took place at Bull Run in Northern Virginia in July, 1861. There, inexperienced Confederates under Pierre Beauregard encountered equally untried federals under Irvin McDowell. The 'Yankees' from the North pushed the 'rebels' from the South back until the Confederates rallied and sent the Union forces into flight back to Washington. The

A Northern officer interrogates Confederate prisoners in the painting *Prisoners from the Front*. The war fuelled antipathy between the Northern and Southern states that lasted for many years.

defeat was a sobering experience for the North. Lincoln called for thousands of volunteer soldiers and selected George McClellan to lead the Union offensive.

McClellan turned the flood of blue-clad volunteers into an effective fighting force, the North's new 'Army of the Potomac'. In March 1862 his troops advanced on Richmond, the Confederate capital. Weeks of battling with the Confederate Army of Northern Virginia under Robert E. Lee led to stalemate. McClellan broke off the attack and returned to Washington.

West of the Appalachians, the Union commander Ulysses Grant was showing greater initiative. In mid February, Grant's forces took Fort Donelson in western Tennessee, capturing 15 000 Confederate troops. In April he confronted the rebels under Albert Johnston at Shiloh. The Northerners, or Yankees, won the battle, but both sides paid dearly in lives. That spring and summer Union troops took the South's largest city, New Orleans. By late 1862 both governments had

Confederate general, Robert E. Lee (above) battled against the Union forces of General Grant (right), before surrendering in 1865.

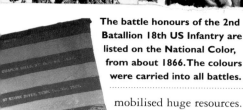

mobilised huge resources. The South was the first to resort to conscription. The Union was also forced to abandon the volunteer system once the early patriotic enthusiasm waned. In some Northern cities the draft provoked vicious riots in which local Republicans were threatened and Blacks were murdered.

At the outset few Northerners considered the abolition of slavery a primary Union war aim. But by mid 1862 Lincoln had concluded that its legal abolition would undermine the Confederacy. On January 1, 1863, Lincoln issued the Emancipation Proclamation, declaring slavery void in those parts of America still in rebellion. After this, where Union troops advanced, many slaves abandoned the plantations to assert their freedom. Before the war's end, almost 200 000 Black men, mostly former slaves, had joined the Union forces.

Financing the war was difficult. The Confederacy resorted to paper money. The Union, too, issued paper money (the first 'greenbacks') to pay its way, but also taxed its citizens and borrowed heavily.

From 1863 to 1865 advantage on the battle fronts shifted back and forth. In 1863 Grant captured Vicksburg on the Mississippi along with 30 000 prisoners. The South was now cut in two along the Mississippi and, as Lincoln said, the 'Father of Waters again goes unvexed to the sea'. Shortly before these victories in the west, George Meade's Army of the Potomac had intercepted Lee and his Army of Northern Virginia at Gettysburg in Pennsylvania, when Lee crossed the North-South border hoping to undermine Union morale with a victory on Northern soil. Lee's forces were savagely beaten back.

Gettysburg has often been considered the turning point of the war, but 20 months of fighting remained. In March 1864 Grant came east to take command of the Army of the Potomac and launched an attack against Lee, while in a coordinated campaign the Union general William Sherman advanced into the heart of the Confederacy. At first the Union forces made little progress while suffering fearsome losses, but in August Sherman captured Atlanta. This victory came in time to help Lincoln to win the Union's presidential campaign against McClellan, who was running as the Democratic candidate on a peace platform.

SOUTHERN SURRENDER

Certain that rebel morale must be broken, Sherman expelled most of Atlanta's civilians. Soon after, fires set to destroy surplus Union supplies consumed a third of the city. In November Sherman's army of 62 000 left Atlanta and set out for the sea across hostile territory to Savannah. Along the route his army cut a swathe of destruction, ripping up railroad tracks, burning crops and livestock and removing slaves. Sherman presented Savannah as a Christmas gift to Lincoln and then turned north up the Carolina coast.

Meanwhile, Grant had brought the depleted Army of Northern Virginia to bay, and on April 2, 1865, the Confederate government evacuated Richmond. Three days later, when Lincoln visited the city that had resisted every assault for four years, one Richmond Black woman shouted: 'I know I am free for I have seen Father Abraham and felt him.'

On April 9, at Appomattox Courthouse, Lee accepted the surrender terms dictated by Grant. The news produced jubilation in the ranks of the Yankees, or Northerners. 'The air is black with hats and boots, coats, knapsacks, shirts, and cartridge boxes,' one soldier wrote. 'They fall on each other's necks and laugh and cry in turns.'

Then, on April 14, while seeking diversion at Ford's Theater in Washington, Lincoln was killed by an assassin, the actor and Southern patriot John Wilkes Booth, who sought revenge for Confederate defeat. Dismay replaced exhilaration and helped to set the stage for a vindictive response towards the ex-rebels during the reconstruction period that followed.

The war exacted a frightful toll. During the four years of battle, around 618 000 men died, either in action or from disease, 360 000 from the Union and 258 000 from the Confederacy. It consumed billions of dollars, and the armies that moved across the landscape wreaked physical havoc. But the war also ended Black slavery and subdued the South, the section that had held in check the modern entrepreneurial energies of the North. The United States, a free society at last, would soon leap to first place among the industrial nations of the world.

Union forces from the North occupy trenches during the long siege of Petersburg, Virginia, July 1864 to April 1865. The photograph was taken by Mathew Brady, a pioneer of war photography.

ancien régime Political and administrative system, French for 'old regime', existing in France in the 17th and 18th centuries under the Bourbon kings before the FRENCH REVOLUTION. The monarch had, in theory, unlimited authority. There was no representative assembly. Privilege was the hallmark of the *ancien régime*: the nobility were privileged in matters of taxation and in the holding of high offices. This was particularly resented by the increasingly prosperous middle class and in practice limited the power of the monarchy. The clergy were equally privileged and the Roman Catholic Church had extensive landholdings. But the *ancien régime* was inefficient: by the mid 18th century reforms in law, taxation and local government were long overdue and government bankruptcy was to be one of the causes of the revolution that destroyed it.

Andrassy, Julius, Count (1823-90) Hungarian statesman. One of the radical nationalist leaders of the unsuccessful Hungarian Revolution of 1848, he rose to prominence in the negotiations leading up to the *Ausgleich* (Compromise) of 1867 which granted Hungary its own parliament and constitution under a dual Austro-Hungarian monarchy. By now a moderate, he served as Hungary's first prime minister from 1867 to 1871. From 1871 to 1879 he served as foreign minister of the AUSTRO-HUNGARIAN EMPIRE.

Angevin Dynasty of the Counts of Anjou in France, founded in the 9th century AD. The English royal line of Plantagenets, of whom Henry II was the first, derived its name from the Angevin emblem, a sprig of the broom plant *Genista*. Henry II

Thousands of complex sculptured scenes from the legends of Vishnu and Krishna cover the walls of the massive Angkor Wat temple in Kampuchea.

was the son of Geoffrey of Anjou, who married Matilda, the daughter of Henry I of England, in 1128. The power of the Angevins under Henry II was formidable. Anjou remained in English hands until 1203, when Philip II of France wrested it from King John. In 1246 Louis IX gave the Angevin title to his brother Charles, who became king of Naples in 1266 and so established a second dynasty. His son, Charles II of Naples, had seven grandchildren. One became Charles I of Hungary in 1308, but the Angevin line in Eastern Europe ended on the death of his son, Louis I, king of Hungary and Poland in 1383. In France, the Angevin line merged with the French crown when Philip IV inherited Anjou and Maine from his mother in 1328.

Angkor Site of several capitals of the KHMER empire in Kampuchea (formerly Cambodia). The city, built on the shores of the vast inland lake of Tonlé Sap, had 8 miles (13 km) of moated walls. It is renowned for the temples which the Khmers built between the 9th and 12th centuries for their god-kings to live in after death. The greatest is the Angkor Wat, 'Angkor Temple', built during the reign of Suryavarman II (1113-50) and surrounded by a moat 590 ft (180 m) wide. It was one of the largest religious structures ever built. To the north in the new capital of Angkor Thom stood the grandiose temple of Jayavarman VII (1181-c.1220); on pinnacle after pinnacle the king's features live on in the faces of the Buddha. The city and its great temples were lost to the jungle for centuries following Angkor's destruction by Thais in 1431. French missionaries rediscovered them in the mid 19th century.

DID YOU KNOW?

The city of Angkor was planned as a symbolic universe based on ancient Indian theories. A pyramid temple was built on the only hill and the city was orientated around it.

Angles Germanic tribe closely linked to the JUTES and SAXONS, thought to have originated in Schleswig-Holstein or Denmark. In the 5th century they settled in eastern Britain, in East Anglia and Northumbria. Later, the land of the ANGLO-SAXONS became known as 'Englaland' and thereby England.

Anglican Church Term used to describe the Church of England, as reformed during the 16th-century Protestant REFORMATION. Although Henry VIII broke with the Roman Catholic Church, and Edward VI made moves to establish Protestant doctrines and practices, the formulation of Anglican principles dates from the reign of Elizabeth I.

The second Book of Common Prayer of Edward VI's reign was revised in 1559 and its use enforced by the 1552 Act of UNIFORMITY. In 1571 the Church of England adopted the THIRTY-NINE ARTICLES as a statement of its beliefs and practices. The aim was to set up a

comprehensive national Church, administered by bishops and having the monarch as supreme governor. Those who refused to attend services were fined. The PURITANS were dissatisfied with the Elizabethan religious settlement, but the queen opposed all their attempts to modify it. Since then, the history of the Anglican Church has reflected the struggle between 'high' and 'low' members to narrow or widen the extent to which it differed from the Catholic Church.

Archbishop William Laud's 'Catholic' policies in the 1630s increased Puritan objections to the power of bishops, and religion was a crucial factor in causing the outbreak of the English Civil War. Anglicanism was banned during the Commonwealth and Protectorate, but returned with Charles II at the Restoration in 1660. The CLARENDON Code and TEST ACTS created a breach between establishment Anglicanism and nonconformists, and James II's pro-Catholic policies played a part in provoking the GLORIOUS REVOLUTION which replaced him on the throne with William and Mary. The Toleration Act of 1689 secured limited toleration for nonconformists, although clergy refusing to swear the oath of allegiance to William III (many of whom were 'high' Churchmen) were deprived of office. Catholics were not allowed to vote or hold office until 1829. During the 18th century Anglicanism formed around three traditions: High Anglicans who broadly followed the Catholic tradition, Low Anglicans, who were closer to the Dissenters, and Latitudinarians, who were less concerned with dogma. The opposition of many influential Anglicans to the evangelism of John WESLEY led to the establishment of an independent METHODIST CHURCH in 1791. From the 1830s there was a religious revival in Britain. John Henry NEWMAN and others led the OXFORD MOVEMENT, which aimed to restore continuity with the Roman Catholic Church and introduce more ceremony into Anglican worship.

This 'High Church' movement was countered by the 'Low Church' or Evangelical movement, which was more Protestant in its views and active in missionary work and social reform. The Anglican Church remains the legally established Church in England, but was disestablished in Scotland in 1690, Ireland in 1871 and Wales in 1920.

Anglican Communion Worldwide family of Christian Churches with the same basic doctrine as the ANGLICAN CHURCH, and all accepting each other's sacraments and ministry. In 1784 the first diocese of the American Episcopalian Church was formed. Most Anglicans live outside Britain, and the Churches

Revolution in the New World

After 1763 the British attempted to tighten their control over their prosperous colonies in North America. By 1776 the colonists' patience was at an end.

For more than a century and a half following their foundation, the English-speaking settlements of North America remained relatively content. Left largely to their own devices, by 1760 the population of the British colonies had risen to 1.6 million, living in 13 separate, self-governing provinces and enjoying one of the world's highest standards of living.

The picture changed following the defeat of France in the Seven Years' War (1763). The cost of the war and the Americans' reluctance to pay their share strengthened British resolve to tighten imperial control. The result was an array of laws, culminating in the Stamp Act of 1765, which taxed legal and business transactions to defray the costs of defence and government in the colonies.

INDEPENDENCE DECLARED

The Stamp Act and subsequent measures threatened colonial autonomy, and the American response was violent. The slogan was heard 'No taxation without representation', and groups of 'patriots' rioted against the imperial tax collectors and imposed a boycott on British imports. In 1774 delegates from 12 colonies gathered in Philadelphia to organise a provisional government for English-speaking America. In July 1776 they adopted the Declaration of Independence, announcing separation from Britain.

In April 1775, even before the Declaration of Independence, British troops and 'minutemen' (colonial militia) had clashed at Lexington and Concord, Massachusetts. Soon after, the United Colonies chose George Washington of Virginia as commander of the Continental forces to wage the war. The Americans solicited and received substantial aid from France.

The war dragged on for eight years. The Americans were divided into Loyalists and Patriots. Many Loyalists enlisted in the king's forces and fought to suppress the rebellion. Patriot officials retaliated by confiscating the property of Loyalists and driving them from their homes.

The early fighting was inconclusive. In June 1775 some 1000 British troops fell when their forces captured Bunker Hill, but by March 1776 the British had evacuated Boston. Farther south, General William Howe defeated Washington at the Battle of Long Island, forcing him out of New York. In 1778 British forces under John Burgoyne surrendered at Saratoga. Now convinced of the Americans' ability to survive, the French sent troop and naval reinforcements.

In the Southern colonies the British swept the Americans out of Georgia, and in 1780 took Charleston. On the western frontier both sides used Native American allies, and fighting was especially fierce.

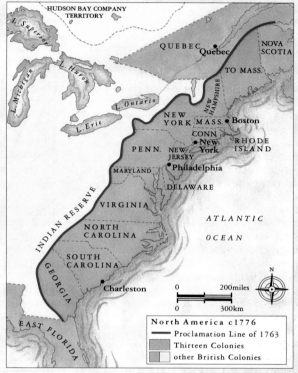

By 1776 the Atlantic seaboard of North America was fully settled and colonists had started moving westwards into the interior.

The French support proved decisive. In 1781 a combined American-French army cornered General Cornwallis' forces on the Yorktown peninsula in Virginia. Cornwallis surrendered on October 19. Yorktown virtually ended the fighting, but the peace negotiations in Paris were not concluded until 1783. Under the terms of the Treaty of Paris, Britain recognised the independence of the United States.

The war not only assured American independence; it also encouraged a liberalisation of American life. Slavery was gradually abolished in the Northern states. Hereditary titles were forbidden, the Anglican Church disestablished, and land ownership laws intended to bolster large family estates repealed. Though not a fully egalitarian society, by 1790, under its new Constitution, the United States had become the most democratic nation in the contemporary world.

Minutemen answer the fire of British infantrymen at Lexington and Concord, the first battle of the War of Independence (left). They later captured British arms and military kettle drums.

The Battle of the Texel was the last great naval confrontation in the Anglo-Dutch wars and ended in a strategic victory for Holland.

of the Anglican Communion vary in practice. Every ten years bishops from all parts of the Anglican communion attend the Lambeth Conference. It has no law-making powers, but its decisions are often influential.

Anglo-Afghan wars see AFGHANISTAN

Anglo-Boer war see BOER WAR

Anglo-Dutch wars Three maritime wars (1652-4, 1665-7, 1672-4) fought between the United Provinces and Britain over issues of commercial and naval rivalry.

The first war began when the English NAVIGATION ACT of 1651 undermined the Dutch freight-carrying trade, and the Dutch refused to salute the English flag in the English Channel. The Dutch admiral Maarten Tromp defeated Admiral Robert Blake off Dungeness in 1652, but the following year the English regained command of the Channel and blockaded the Dutch coast. This reverse brought the leader of the United Provinces Jan de Witt to settle for peace terms from Oliver Cromwell in 1654: the Dutch recognised English sovereignty in the Channel, gave compensation for the massacre of English settlers at Amboina in Indonesia in 1623 and promised not to assist the exiled Charles II.

In March 1665 trade rivalries drove the two countries to war again. Before it was declared, the English had already seized possessions in West Africa and New Amsterdam (renamed New York) in the USA. The English defeated the Dutch off Lowestoft in June. The following year, Cornelius Tromp and Michiel de Ruyter won the Four Days War in the Channel off Broadstairs, but the English recovered command of the sea within a few months. Negotiations for peace began in 1667, but England's attempt to save money by keeping its fleet in dock backfired when de Ruyter made a daring night-time raid on the English dockyards at Chatham on the Thames estuary, burning four ships and carrying off the largest, the *Royal Charles*. By the peace agreed

at Breda in 1667, the Navigation Acts were modified in favour of the Dutch. Under the treaty the Dutch kept Surinam and the British kept Delaware and New England.

The third war was fought in 1672 when Charles II, dependent on French subsidies, supported Louis XIV against the Dutch. The Battle of the Texel in August 1673 ended the threat of an English invasion and the blockade of Dutch ports. The Treaty of Westminster signed in 1674 renewed the terms of Breda.

Anglo-Maori wars see NEW ZEALAND

Anglo-Saxon Chronicle Collection of seven manuscripts written in Anglo-Saxon (Old English) which tell the history of England from the arrival of early Saxon settlers in 495 up to 1154. The major text, known as the 'Parker Chronicle', covers events until 891 and appears to have been written by one clerk. Most of the copies end in the 11th century; after 1079 only the 'Peterborough Chronicle' continues, breaking off abruptly with an unfinished entry for 1154. The 'Chronicle' probably began as notes accompanying the tables used by the Christian Church for calculating the date of Easter.

Anglo-Saxons Name given to the ANGLES, SAXONS and JUTES whose invasions of Britain between 450 and 600 began with the departure of the Romans. They were probably joined by FRISIANS and perhaps a few settlers from southern Sweden and the Rhineland.

The monk BEDE in his *Historia Ecclesiastica Gentis Anglorum (Ecclesiastical History of the English People)* explained how the independent kingdoms emerged. The East Angles (East Anglia), Middle Angles (East Midlands), Mercians (Midlands) and those who lived north of the River Humber were descended from the Angles. The Saxons established the

kingdoms of the East Saxons (Essex), the South Saxons (Sussex) and the West Saxons (Wessex). The Jutes settled in Kent, on the Isle of Wight and in Hampshire.

In the 7th century Northumbria under Edwin, Oswald and Oswy claimed authority over all Anglo-Saxons. By the 8th century dominance had passed to Mercia under Ethelbald and Offa and, in the 9th century, to Wessex, whose kings were able to resist the Vikings. Under ALFRED, Edward the Elder, Athelstan and Edgar, Wessex established undisputed control of England. Renewed Scandinavian raids led to a Danish king, CANUTE (Cnut), becoming king of England in 1016. The West Saxon line returned with EDWARD THE CONFESSOR in 1042, but ended with the Norman Conquest in 1066.

Angola Country in south-western Africa, formerly a Portuguese possession which has been independent since 1975. The Portuguese colonised the Atlantic coast in the 16th century, but did not move inland, where there were vast reserves of diamonds and iron ore, until the 19th century. Angola became an overseas province of Portugal in 1951, and gained its independence in 1975 after a long and bitterly fought guerrilla war.

Some 400 000 Portuguese returned to Portugal, and civil war and economic collapse followed. The ruling Marxist party, the Popular Movement for the Liberation of Angola (MPLA), was supported by Cuba and the Soviet Union. It was opposed by the National Union for the Total Independence of Angola (UNITA), backed by South Africa and the USA. South African raids into Angola took place from time to time, aimed at bases of the South West Africa People's Organisation, a Namibian liberation group operating across the border. A series of cease-fire agreements negotiated in the 1980s collapsed, but a peace

Angolan youngsters, who trained with wooden guns for the day when they could take part in the struggle against Portuguese troops, join the independence day parade on November 11, 1975.

treaty signed in 1991 promised multiparty elections, which took place in September 1992, and were monitored by UN observers. The MPLA won, but the result was disputed by UNITA, which resumed fighting and gained control of half the country by November 1992. UNITA accepted government seats, but sporadic fighting continued.

Anne (1665-1714) Queen of Great Britain and Ireland from 1702 to 1714, the last STUART sovereign. Anne was the younger daughter of James II and, although he was Catholic, she was brought up as a Protestant and supported her brother-in-law William III when he invaded England and forced James into exile. In 1683 Anne married Prince George of Denmark. Her last surviving child died in 1700, and the Act of SETTLEMENT was passed the following year to provide for the throne to pass on her death to her Hanoverian cousins, ending the claim of her Catholic half-brother James, the Old Pretender. The Act of UNION united the English and Scottish parliaments in 1707 to prevent the Old Pretender from ever regaining the Scottish throne.

England engaged France in the War of the SPANISH SUCCESSION two months after Anne succeeded William, and the conflict dominated her reign. Victories were won under the Duke of Marlborough at Blenheim, Oudenarde, Ramillies and Malplaquet. Britain also captured the territory of Gibraltar.

Anne was devoted to the Anglican Church and disliked Catholics and dissenters. Politically, she was easily manipulated by favourites, notably Sarah Churchill, Duchess of Marlborough. At first the WHIGS dominated, through Sarah Churchill's influence, but in 1707 she was ousted by her cousin Abigail Masham, who favoured the Tories. In 1710 the Tories came to power, and remained in office until Anne's death.

Anne was the last English monarch to preside over Cabinets and sessions of the House of Lords, and the last to veto an Act of Parliament, the 1707 Militia Act. She caused controversy in 1712 when she created a dozen peers to give the Tories a majority in the House of Lords. Anne suffered from constant ill health: she was plagued by gout and became so fat that she had to be hoisted into her coach. Her reign was notable for cultural and political achievements. The literary flowering which earned this period the title of 'England's Augustan Age' produced writers such as Alexander Pope. St Paul's Cathedral in London was completed, and 'Queen Anne' houses are among the most graceful examples of British architecture.

Anne of Austria (1601-66) Wife of Louis XIII of France, whom she married in 1615 at the age of 14, and the daughter of Philip III of Spain. Anne was accused of encouraging the advances of the Duke of Buckingham, who in 1625 scandalised the court by revealing his passion for the queen. Her friend Marie de Rohan-Montbazon, Duchesse de Chévreuse, was involved in plots against Louis' chief minister, Cardinal Armand RICHELIEU. Anne failed to persuade Louis to dismiss Richelieu in 1630, and the cardinal exposed her treasonable correspondence with her brother, Philip IV of Spain, while France was at war with Spain in 1637. When her four-year-old son succeeded to the throne as Louis XIV in 1643 Anne became regent and gave her support to Cardinal Jules MAZARIN during the FRONDE, a rebellion by magistrates against a plan to stop their wages for four years to raise money. Her regency ended in 1651, but she influenced her son until her death.

Anne of Cleves (1515-57) German princess and fourth wife of HENRY VIII of England. The king's adviser Thomas Cromwell suggested Henry should take a wife from among the Protestant princesses of Germany: on the strength of a painting Henry chose Anne. He married her in January 1540, even though their first meeting was a disaster and she spoke no English when she arrived. Six months later Henry had the marriage annulled, alleging that it had not been consummated. Anne was given a generous pension on condition that she remained in England.

Anschluss Adolf Hitler's annexation of Austria on March 12, 1938. After several years of Nazi disruption, Hitler summoned Austrian chancellor Kurt von Schuschnigg to Germany in February 1938 and demanded the admission of Nazis into his Cabinet. Schuschnigg tried to hold a referendum on Austrian independence, but he failed and was forced to resign. German troops entered Vienna and the *Anschluss*, German for 'union', was proclaimed. The majority of Austrians welcomed the annexation. Following its liberation in the spring of 1945, Austria was re-established within its prewar boundaries.

Anselm, St (1033-1109) Philosopher, theologian and 36th Archbishop of Canterbury. Anselm was a Benedictine monk at the monastery of Bec in Normandy, where LANFRANC was prior. He succeeded him as prior in 1063, and over the next 30 years turned Bec into a major centre of scholarship. Anslem was known as 'the Father of Scholasticism', and advanced the authority of the early Church fathers and of Aristotle. After making the essential act of faith, Christian truths, he believed, could be understood rationally, so reason could be used in the context of faith.

Anselm succeeded Lanfranc as Archbishop of Canterbury in 1093. His relationship with both William II and Henry I was uneasy, particularly over the issue of INVESTITURE – the

Henry VIII married Anne of Cleves after seeing this flattering portrait by Hans Holbein, but he found the real Anne to be coarse, fat and ugly.

appointment of bishops without interference from the Crown. Twice Anselm went into voluntary exile over this issue between 1097 and 1106. Finally he accepted a compromise under which the king surrendered his claim to invest bishops but kept the right to receive homage for lands held through their office.

Antarctica Ice-covered continent surrounding the South Pole. The first person to sight the continent was probably Fabian von Bellingshausen, a Russian explorer, in 1820. Russian, British, French and American scientific and geographical expeditions were made during the 19th century. The next phase of discovery began when the Norwegian, Carsten Borchgrevink, in command of the British Southern Cross expedition, spent a winter on the continent in 1899. In the next decade, several such expeditions took place, in which international rivalry and the quest for the unknown pushed explorers to the limits of endurance. Otto Nordenskjold, a Swede, explored the east coast of the Antarctic Peninsula from 1901 to 1904.

The Britons Robert Scott and Ernest Shackleton led three separate parties between 1901 and 1913 from bases on Ross Island, just off the Antarctic coast, and proceeded to make important discoveries in geology and meteorology. Shackleton's party sledged to within 97 miles (156 km) of the South Pole in 1909 before turning back mainly because their supplies would not last. Roald Amundsen's Norwegian party was the first to reach the Pole, on December 14, 1911. A month later, Robert Scott's party reached the Pole but all members died on the return journey, the last two just 11 miles (17 km) from their major supply depot and safety. In the following decades much of Antarctica was mapped from the air. A Norwegian-British-Swedish expedition made scientific journeys into the interior between 1949 and 1952, and laid the foundations for the International Geophysical Year, 1957-8, when 12 nations set up more than 50 stations during the Antarctic winter. Since 1957, the Special Committee on Antarctic Research has coordinated all fieldwork. Many countries have made territorial claims in Antarctica, including Britain, New Zealand, Australia, France, Norway, Chile and Argentina. The Antarctic Treaty, signed in 1961 by these countries plus Belgium, Japan, South Africa, the USSR and the USA, and later by Brazil, China, India, Poland, Uruguay, Italy and Germany, preserves Antarctica for peaceful purposes. It pledges scientific cooperation, and prohibits nuclear explosions and the disposal of radioactive waste. A 50-year ban on all mining was agreed in 1991. Antarctica has also been the focus for study of the hole in the ozone layer surrounding the Earth, whose growth is taken to indicate ecological imbalance.

Anthony, Susan B. (1820-1906) American women's rights pioneer. Anthony's campaign for women's suffrage helped to establish the 19th Amendment of the US constitution, which in 1920 gave women the vote. After

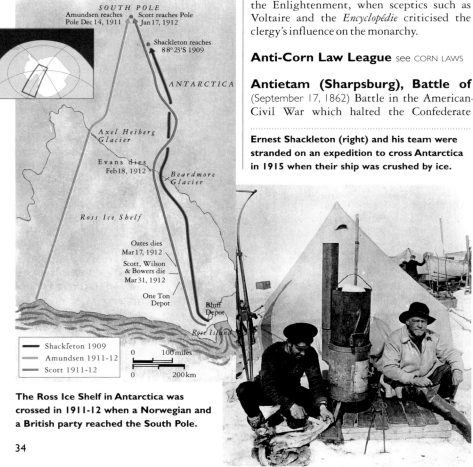

The Ross Ice Shelf in Antarctica was crossed in 1911-12 when a Norwegian and a British party reached the South Pole.

three years as a teacher, she embarked on a crusade for social change. In 1852, she moved from working in the temperance movement to join Elizabeth Cady STANTON in the campaign for women's rights and suffrage, and in the 1850s also became engaged in the fight against slavery. In 1872 Anthony demanded that the political rights granted to Black men by the 14th and 15th Amendments be extended to women, and led a group of women to the polls in Rochester, New York, to test the right of women to vote. She was arrested but refused to pay a fine for violating the voting laws. In the following decades she continued to be chief organiser of the US movement for women's suffrage.

anticlericalism Hostility toward Christian clergy, especially their involvement in political and secular affairs. In medieval Europe prime targets for criticism were the 'absenteeism' of clergy who did not live in their own parishes, and 'pluralism' – the holding of several Church offices at the same time. Those suspected of immoral conduct gave the clergy a bad name, as did the abuse of indulgences, by which remission of the penance imposed on a sinner by his confessor was offered in return for the payment of a fee. Anticlerical feeling prepared the ground for the REFORMATION, and the doctrinal reforms of John WYCLIFFE and Martin LUTHER. Modern political anticlericalism dates from the Enlightenment, when sceptics such as Voltaire and the *Encyclopédie* criticised the clergy's influence on the monarchy.

Anti-Corn Law League see CORN LAWS

Antietam (Sharpsburg), Battle of (September 17, 1862) Battle in the American Civil War which halted the Confederate

Ernest Shackleton (right) and his team were stranded on an expedition to cross Antarctica in 1915 when their ship was crushed by ice.

advance into Maryland and the threat to Washington DC. After his victory at the second Battle of Bull Run, the Confederate General Robert E. LEE invaded the North with 55 000 men. General George McClellan, at the head of the Northern army, attacked Lee on the Antietam Creek at Sharpsburg in Maryland. The Confederates were badly mauled, but they held their positions and were able to make an orderly retreat on the following day. The 26 000 killed or wounded, the worst casualties of any single day of the war, were divided almost equally between the two sides. While the Confederate invasion was driven back, McClellan was blamed for not using his superior forces to pursue and destroy Lee's weakened army and bring the war to an early end. The outcome may have influenced Britain not to recognise the Confederates and provided Abraham Lincoln with the opportunity to issue his Emancipation Proclamation on September 22, 1862, announcing that unless the Confederates laid down their arms by January 1, 1863, he would free their slaves.

Antioch One of the most prosperous cities of antiquity, today called Antakya, near the southern border of Turkey with Syria. Antioch was founded in 300 BC as the capital of the Greek province of Syria by Seleucus I in memory of his father, Antiochus, a Macedonian general, and was the capital city of the Seleucids. In 64 it was annexed by Pompey the Great for Rome and because it stood at a strategic point on the trade routes linking the East with the Mediterranean, it developed into the third largest city in the Roman Empire. It acquired a forum, temples, a theatre, aqueducts and palaces.

Antioch was one of the first centres of Christianity: St Peter preached there, and St Paul came to the city with his first mission to convert the Gentiles. It played an important role in many of the theological arguments which raged in the early Christian Church. The city remained a flourishing commercial and intellectual centre, though it had declined by the time of its capture by the Arabs in AD 637-8. The Crusaders captured the city in 1098, and it remained an important centre of Christianity until in 1268 it fell to the MAMELUKES of Egypt. From 1516 it came under the rule of the OTTOMAN EMPIRE.

antipope One who has claimed to be, or has been elected, pope in opposition to the reigning pope. There have been about 35 antipopes in the history of the Roman Catholic Church, the last being Felix V between 1439 and 1449. They appeared either when electors disagreed over a candidate for the PAPACY, or when a Holy Roman Emperor preferred a pope who would favour his interests and so nominated an alternative pope. During the

The first antipope during the Great Schism was Clement VII, who was elected at Avignon in 1378 and remained in office until 1394.

GREAT SCHISM (1378-1417), and other periods, the existence of two or even three rival popes left the identity of the true pope unclear.

anti-Semitism Prejudice against Jews. The term is imprecise, since Arabs form part of the Semitic race. At many stages of their history Jews have been the object of insult, discrimination, expulsion and, particularly during Adolf Hitler's Nazi HOLOCAUST, mass extermination. The Jews' claim to be a chosen people, their insistence on worshipping their own God, and their adherence to special religious laws often antagonised other peoples. In the Roman Empire, few Jews were allowed to become citizens. Early Christians blamed them for the Crucifixion of Christ, and for centuries this supposed offence was used to justify Church-sanctioned anti-Semitism.

During the Middle Ages persecutions of Jews occurred in England, Spain, France and Germany. From the 12th century, they were often required by law to live apart from other people, sometimes in walled ghettos; outside the ghetto they were obliged to wear an identifying badge. This forced segregation was gradually reduced to restrictions on where they could live in the 19th century. Segregation seems to have been motivated by fear of their influence and by the commercial interests of merchants and craft guilds. They were barred from many professions, so Jews rose to prominence in money lending, banking and trade. Queen Isabella of Castile financed Christopher Columbus's expedition to the New World in 1492 largely with Jewish money, but this did not stop her in the same year expelling the Jews from Spain.

In Eastern Europe Jews first arrived during the CRUSADES after 1096; a second wave of immigration took place following the Black Death in 1348, which it was widely believed Jews had caused by poisoning wells. The communities were allowed to govern themselves at first, but in Poland in 1648 Church-decreed attacks occurred during a power struggle between the Eastern Orthodox Ukrainians and the Polish Roman Catholics. As a result of the three 18th-century partitions of Poland, large Jewish populations were incorporated into Russia. The Russian empress Catherine the Great established the 'Pale of Settlement', an extensive territory for the Jews in the western provinces, and forced Jews to do military service. POGROMS, or mob attacks directed at Jews, began in 1881, and led to large-scale emigration to the United States and the founding of Zionist settlements in Palestine.

In most parts of the Muslim world, Jews dwelt freely until the 18th century, after which they were often required to live in special areas away from mosques and other holy places. Since the establishment of the state of Israel in 1948, tension between the Arab people and Zionist Jews has been both territorial and religious. The Age of Enlightenment in Western Europe in the 18th century and the French Revolution prepared the way for the separation of Church and State that led to the emancipation of Jews, giving them equal legal status and religious freedom. But strong anti-Semitic feeling remained during the late 19th and early 20th centuries in France – illustrated by the DREYFUS case – as well as in Germany and Eastern Europe.

After the First World War, early Nazi propaganda blamed the Jews for Germany's defeat. From the time Hitler came to power in 1933, the Nazis used the claimed superiority of the Aryan German race and the need for 'racial purity' as excuses to persecute Jews throughout the country. By the start of the

Anti-Semitic posters, such as this from Poland in 1939 with caricatures of Jews adulterating food, were used to whip up public hatred.

Second World War, about half the German Jewish population had been driven out. Hitler then put into effect what he called the 'final solution' to the Jewish problem, a programme of mass murder aimed at the extermination of the entire Jewish race. In the holocaust an estimated 6 million Jews were killed in labour and CONCENTRATION CAMPS between 1939 and 1945. Anti-Semitism was also rife within the former Soviet Union, especially after the Second World War. At the time of his death in 1953 Stalin was planning mass Jewish deportations.

In 1961, the World Council of Churches declared anti-Semitism to be against the teachings of Christ, and in 1965 the Second

> **66** For as long as people remain racially pure and conscious of the treasure of their blood they can never be overcome by the Jew. Never ... can the Jew become master of any people except a bastardised people. **99**
>
> *German Nazi dictator Adolf Hitler*
> *(1889-1945)*

Vatican council condemned racism and repudiated the responsibility of Jews for Christ's death. In Europe, the rise of neo-Nazi groups and the sporadic defilement of Jewish monuments in Germany, France and Britain showed that anti-Semitism was still alive.

antitrust laws US laws restricting unfair business practices and monopolies where exclusive control of a product or service allows the provider to sell at unreasonably high prices. In 1890, the Sherman Anti-Trust Act declared illegal 'every contract, combination, or conspiracy in restraint of trade'. In the early 1900s several large corporations, or trusts, were broken up, including American Tobacco, Standard Oil of New Jersey and Du Pont. Further growth in giant multinational corporations after the Second World War led to the Celler-Kefauver Antimerger Act in 1950, which was intended to prevent a monopoly shared between a few large corporations being used to fix prices. In 1982 the 22 local operating companies of the American Telephone and Telegraph Corporation were separated from the parent company. In the 1990s, deregulation of the telecommunications, media and utility industries gave rise to mergers such as the $19 billion Walt Disney Company takeover of ABC in 1995. At the time it was the second largest takeover in American history.

Antonescu, Ion (1882-1946) Romanian military leader, who in 1940 assumed dictatorial powers and forced the abdication of Carol II. Antonescu lent his support to the Axis Powers, Germany, Italy and later Japan, and took part in the Nazi invasion of the Soviet Union. His regime collapsed when the Red Army entered Romania in 1944. He was executed as a war criminal in 1946.

Antony, Mark see MARK ANTONY

Anzac Acronym derived from the initials of the Australian and New Zealand Army Corps which fought in the First World War. Originally the name described members of the Corps who took part in the GALLIPOLI CAMPAIGN, but later it became an informal description for all the Australian and New Zealand forces. Anzac Day, April 25, commemorating the Gallipoli landing, has been observed since 1916.

Anzus Acronym derived from the initials of the members of the 1951 Pacific security treaty between Australia, New Zealand and the USA. The treaty calls on each of the three countries to respond to potential threats in the Pacific area to any one of them. The USA suspended its security obligations to New Zealand in 1986, as a response to an antinuclear policy which banned nuclear-armed ships from its ports.

Apache North American indigenous people. In prehistoric times they were nomads on the central and southern Great Plains, gradually moving southwards into the semideserts between the 9th and 15th centuries. As early as the 13th century, they and the NAVAHO raided towns of the Anasazi people centred in present-day Utah, Colorado, Arizona and New Mexico, and were partly responsible for their downfall. Spanish explorers found the Apache well established in Arizona, New Mexico, Texas and northern Mexico in the late

16th century, and regular contact with Spanish settlements was developed by the early 17th century. As the Apache and other peoples on the eastern edges of the plains acquired horses, competition for buffalo hunting became fierce and the Comanche eventually drove them off the Great Plains into the west by the mid 18th century. Their new homelands brought them into conflict with the expanding USA in the 19th century when it acquired those territories from Mexico. From 1861 they fought alongside the Navaho against US troops but surrendered five years later. However, individual skirmishes continued in the 1870s.

apartheid Racial policy, Afrikaans 'separateness', enforced in South Africa between 1948 and 1991. It involved the strict segregation of Blacks from Whites in land ownership, residence, marriage, work, education, religion and sport. The concept goes back to the segregation practised by the Dutch settlers since the 17th century.

From 1948 onwards apartheid was enforced by laws, by job reservation and trade union separation, and by the denial of parliamentary representation to non-Whites. The creation of BANTUSTANS (homelands) deprived the Bantu-speaking peoples of South African citizenship in return for an illusory independence. From 1984, restrictions began to be softened by creating subordinate parliamentary chambers for Indians and Coloureds (people of mixed descent), by relaxation of rules for sport and leisure, by abolishing the pass laws and by modifying the Group Areas Act. But international pressure demanded the abolition of apartheid, and in July 1991 the government of President F.W. DE KLERK repealed all remaining apartheid legislation.

By the 1880s lands still controlled by Apache leaders such as Geronimo (above) stood in the way of the westward expansion of the USA.

In December 1991 a Convention for a Democratic South Africa (CODESA), comprising the government and 18 political groups, gathered to prepare the necessary changes to a constitution based on segregation.

In March 1992 de Klerk appealed to White voters for a clear mandate to negotiate. The overwhelming support he received, in his words, 'closed the book on apartheid'. Its collapse was confirmed in the multiparty elections of April 1994, after which the African National Congress leader Nelson MANDELA became the first Black president of South Africa and head of a multiracial Cabinet.

appeasement Term used scornfully to describe the efforts by the British prime minister Neville CHAMBERLAIN and his French counterpart Edouard DALADIER to satisfy the demands of the Axis powers of Germany and Italy between 1936 and 1939. Their policy enabled German dictator Adolf Hitler to occupy the Rhineland, to annex Austria, and to acquire the Sudetenland in Czechoslovakia after the MUNICH PACT of 1938. Appeasement ended when Hitler, ignoring assurances given at Munich, invaded the rest of Czechoslovakia in March 1939. Britain and France then promised to protect Romania, Greece and Poland if Germany or Italy attacked them.

Appian Way Ancient Rome's earliest major military road, named after Appius Claudius Caecus, who authorised its construction in 312 BC. It was called the 'Queen of Roads' by the poet Statius. Running from Rome to Brindisi, it was paved with cobblestones. Some of the original paving remains along the first few miles out of Rome.

Appomattox Village in Virginia, USA, scene of the surrender on April 9, 1865, of the Confederate Army of Northern Virginia to the

Members of an Australian and New Zealand Army Corps (Anzac) infantry unit in 1916 relax during a lull in the fighting in France. About 7600 of their colleagues died in the Gallipoli landing.

Union Army at the end of the American Civil War. Forced to evacuate Petersburg and Richmond the week before, General Robert E. LEE was almost completely surrounded by greatly superior forces and decided that further resistance was pointless.

Aquinas, Thomas, St (c.1225-74) Philosopher and theologian. Aquinas was born to a noble Italian family and, despite their opposition, became a DOMINICAN friar, studying under Albertus Magnus of Cologne, one of the great teachers of the day. He then taught in Paris and was for a time attached to the papal court. Aquinas was a powerful force in the movement known as SCHOLASTICISM, which looked to Aristotle as well as to the early Church fathers for authority. It was Aquinas who made the work of Aristotle acceptable in Christian Western Europe; his own explanation of reality, his account of the human mind and his moral philosophy were a development of Aristotle's. Aquinas's main theories were set out in his *Summa Theologica.* His followers are known as Thomists and his work remains as the respected basis for much Roman Catholic philosophy and theology.

Aquitaine A province in south-western France, known by the Romans as Aquitania. Between the 3rd and 7th centuries it suffered from German and Gascon invasions. The Carolingians made it part of their empire in the 8th century. Aquitaine remained semi-independent and, after the collapse of Carolingian power, emerged as a duchy in the 10th century under the counts of Poitiers. It passed briefly to France when Duchess Eleanor married Louis VII, but they divorced in 1152. When her new husband became Henry II of England in 1154 Aquitaine came to the English crown. Control of the territory passed between France and England until France recovered it during the HUNDRED YEARS' WAR in the middle of the 15th century.

Arab League Organisation of Arab states, founded in Cairo in March 1945. The original members were Lebanon, Egypt, Iraq, Syria, Transjordan (present-day Jordan), Saudi Arabia, the Yemen, and representatives of the Palestine Arabs; they were later joined by other Middle East and African states and the Palestine Liberation Organisation. The aim of the league was to protect the independence and integrity of member states. It embodied Syrian and Lebanese hopes of Arab aid in consolidating their freedom from French rule, and confirmed feelings of Arab solidarity over Palestine. Egypt was expelled following the CAMP DAVID ACCORD, and readmitted in 1989. The league survived the GULF WAR, and its headquarters returned to Cairo in 1991.

Arafat, Yasser (1929-) Palestinian politician. Born in Jerusalem, he helped to form the al-FATAH movement, emerging as its leader in 1968. The PALESTINE LIBERATION ORGANISATION (PLO) was founded in 1964; and Arafat became its chairman in 1969 and then commander in chief of the Palestine Revolutionary Forces in 1971. The group aimed to return Palestinians to their own lands, now occupied by Israel. He organised guerrilla raids and terrorist attacks. In 1982 the Israeli army drove the PLO from its headquarters in Lebanon. In 1983 Arafat set up a new base in Tunisia and in 1988 he was invited to address the UN, where he rejected violence, recognised the existence of Israel and called for a political solution to the Palestine problem. Following his support of Iraq during the Gulf War, Arafat was excluded from the Madrid 'peace-process' in 1992, but the following year he signed a peace accord with Israel.

Arafat moved to Gaza in July 1993 to head the new Palestinian National Authority, which controls the Gaza Strip and a number of autonomous Palestinian towns in the West Bank. Since then he has lost support for failing to provide basic facilities and services in the

The Appian Way, which was known as ancient Rome's highway to the East, also had branch roads to Neapolis (Naples) and Barium (Bari).

authority, for allegedly making too many concessions to Israel in the peace talks, and for his autocratic style of leadership. In 1996 he was elected president of the authority.

Aragon Formerly a kingdom, now a province in northern Spain. It became part of the Roman Empire under Augustus, was taken by the Visigoths in the 5th century and by the Moors in the 8th century. It grew with the annexation of Barcelona (Catalonia) in 1137 and Valencia in 1238. During the 14th century Sardinia and Sicily were added and Naples in the 15th century. The marriage of FERDINAND V to Isabella of Castile in 1469 united the kingdoms of Aragon and Castile and led to the unification of Spain in a single kingdom in 1516.

Arcadia Mountainous region in the central Peloponnese, Greece. In ancient times it was an isolated area but rose to political prominence when Megalopolis was founded around 370 by the Theban general Epaminondas. The city led resistance to SPARTA and in 235 joined the confederacy of Peloponnesian states known as the Achaean League after the region of Achaea in north-east Greece. In Roman times Arcadia fell into decay. It was identified during the Renaissance as an earthly paradise, for example in Sir Philip Sidney's *The Arcadia.*

archaeology Study of the past of humanity, through material remains. It can take a variety of forms depending on the nature of the site. Archaeological research can use a number of different techniques. The most obvious are recovery of material by excavation, by chance find, by surface survey, and by observation from the air. Digging remains crucial because it alone can establish the context of finds, without which they lose much of their meaning. The form, composition, date and associations of archaeological finds all bear information. Studying changes in forms

Economic sanctions played a vital part in forcing the South African government in 1991 to abolish its strict apartheid laws, which from 1948 had regulated almost all public aspects of everyday life.

(typology) can link finds from different sites. The results have to be built into a coherent story to give an account of what happened and when. Finally reasons must be sought for the processes of cultural change.

archer Cave paintings show that bows and arrows were used for hunting in prehistoric times, enabling hunters to kill game beyond throwing range. The bow and arrow became a basic military weapon from Egyptian times until the coming of firearms at the end of the Middle Ages in Europe, and even later in China and Japan. Ancient Greek and Roman infantry did not include archers, but both Greeks and Romans employed SCYTHIAN archers often on horseback.

In the Middle Ages the powerful but unwieldy crossbow was widely adopted in continental Europe, despite the pope's ban in 1139 on its use against anyone except unbelievers. The English longbow won a European reputation in Edward III's reign. Nearly 6ft (2 m) long and made of yew, oak or maple, it enabled arrows to be fired accurately up to a range of about 1000 ft (300 m), and helped to give England such victories as CRÉCY in 1346, POITIERS in 1356 and AGINCOURT in 1415. Archery became the English national sport;

> 66 **The air was darkened by an intolerable number of piercing arrows flying across the sky to pour upon the enemy like … rain.** 99
>
> *Thomas de Eltham, account of the Battle of Agincourt, 1415*

the scholar Roger Ascham published a treatise on archery, *Toxophilus*, in 1545. From the later 16th century the musketeer replaced the archer in Europe, but in 19th-century North America the Native Americans proved how devastating the mounted archer could be, even against men armed with rifles.

Archimedes (c.287-212BC) Greek mathematician and inventor. Although best known as a brilliant mathematician and the founder of the sciences of statics and hydrostatics, he was also an ingenious engineer who applied his talents to a wide range of practical problems. When the Romans besieged his native Syracuse in 213 BC, he invented a range of ballistic weapons that delayed the capture of the city. Archimedes also developed the principle of the lever and of the multiple pulley. He claimed that a single man could move any massively heavy object if he were given a long enough lever and a fulcrum was placed near the object to be moved.

Archimedes is said to have run naked through the streets of Syracuse shouting *'Eureka!'* ('I have found it!') when he realised, after getting into his bath, that the volume of an object can be measured by the volume of water it displaces. He used this fact to prove that a supposedly solid gold crown did not have the right density to be pure gold. Archimedes' principle states that a body immersed in a fluid or gas is buoyed up by a force equal to the weight of the fluid displaced. Therefore, a boat floats or a hot-air balloon rises because they are less dense than the water or air they displace.

Arctic Most northerly region of the Earth. The Arctic is centred on the North Pole, and extends to include the frozen Arctic Ocean, the extreme northern parts of North America and Eurasia, and the islands and archipelagoes along their northern coasts.

The search for a north-west and a north-east passage from Europe to the Far East gave rise to Arctic explorations from the 16th century onwards. The British geographer Sir John Barrow promoted explorations in the early 19th century, while an attempt by Sir John Franklin in 1845 to find a north-west passage ended in his disappearance. The 40 or more search parties sent out after him brought back valuable information about the Arctic regions. In 1850 the British Arctic explorer Robert McClure completed a west-east crossing, but the first continuous journey was not achieved until the voyage of the Norwegian Roald Amundsen from 1903 to 1906. The Swedish Baron Nordenskjöld was the first to cross the north-east passage from Norway to the Bering Strait between 1878 and 1879. It was not until 1909 that the North Pole was finally reached – by the American Robert E. Peary, after several unsuccessful attempts, although his success has been disputed.

The concept of countries working together to make systematic meteorological and magnetic observations of the Arctic was put forward at international polar conferences held in 1879 and 1880. By 1882 at least eight major nations had created observation stations.

The Arctic's resources have aroused interest in many nations, and a military presence in the area is maintained by both the USA and Russia. In order to preserve the traditional INUIT way of life, the Inuit (Eskimo) People's Circumpolar Conference was started in 1980 with the aim of formulating an Arctic policy on oil development and the use of the area for military manoeuvres and weapons testing.

Ardennes Campaign The last serious German counteroffensive against Allied armies advancing towards Germany in the Second World War between December 16, 1944, and January 21, 1945. Also known as the Battle of the Bulge, it was the result of Hitler's decision to attack through the hilly, wooded country of the Ardennes in Belgium, and thereby take the US forces by surprise. Last-ditch resistance at several points, notably

German troops advance past burning US vehicles during the Ardennes Campaign before Allied air power finally stopped the attack.

at Bastogne, held the Germans up long enough for the Allies to counterattack and prevent the Germans reaching their objective, which was to retake the port of Antwerp.

Argentina South American country that occupies much of the southern part of the continent. Little is known of the precolonial history of Argentina. The indigenous peoples were nomadic hunters except in the northwest, where the Incas introduced settled agriculture and a road which reached as far south as the present-day city of Mendoza.

The Spanish were the first Europeans to colonise Argentina, but their settlement developed slowly from the early years of the 16th century. Buenos Aires was founded in 1580. Colonists farmed in the areas of Salta, Jujuy and Córdoba and raised stock on the fertile pampas (grass plains). Until 1776 the region was part of the viceroyalty of Peru; in that year the viceroyalty of La Plata was established with its capital in Buenos Aires. It also included Uruguay, Paraguay and Bolivia.

The independence of the 'United Provinces of South America' was declared at the Congress of Tucumán in 1816. Conflict between *unitarios* (centralists) and *federales* (federalists) continued for much of the 19th century. The lack of a political or constitutional legal framework gave rise to an age of Caudillos, or military dictators, until a National Constitution was proclaimed in 1853. In the second half of the 19th century immigrant workers, principally from Spain and Italy, an extensive railway network and the use of refrigerated steamships all contributed to greatly increased cattle and grain exports alongside more intensive use of the pampas lands of the interior. The influx of immigrants between 1870 and 1914 also helped to raise the population from 1.2 million in 1852 to 8 million in 1914.

With a military coup in 1930, the armed forces emerged as the final authority in Argentinian politics. The failure to achieve sustained civilian democratic government and economic growth has led to frequent military intervention. This was true even in the case of Juan Domingo PERÓN, president from 1946 to 1955. Although a former army officer, Perón was elected with the support of the trade unions. His wife Eva, a former actress, also held considerable power and became a popular heroine. Perón was deposed by the army in 1955, but despite military opposition, was re-elected as president in 1973 after an 18 year exile. His death in 1974 was followed by another period of military dictatorship from 1976 to 1983. In a particularly bitter and tragic period of authoritarian rule, an estimated 20000 Argentinians lost their lives in a 'dirty war' when the government arrested, tortured and killed people it suspected of opposing its rule.

In 1982 the armed forces suffered a humiliating defeat in the war with Britain over the FALKLAND (Malvinas) Islands, and in 1983 a civilian administration was elected under President Raul Alfonsín of the Radical Party. The move back towards democracy in Argentina faced severe problems, notably a virtually bankrupt economy. The Perónist Justicialist Party came to power in 1989 with Carlos Menem as president. Diplomatic relations with Britain were restored and the economy was boosted by easing industrial rules. The constitution was amended in 1994, allowing the president to remain in office for two terms. Menem was re-elected in 1995.

Argos Ancient Greek city in the Peloponnese, near present-day Nauplia. It became an important power among the Greek city-states in the 7th century BC under King Pheidon, who defeated SPARTA. After his death it declined as Sparta gained supremacy. Argos remained neutral throughout the Persian Wars (see PERSIA), and over the next century made unsuccessful attempts to reassert itself in the Peloponnese. It supported PHILIP II of Macedonia and finally joined the Achaean League, a confederacy of Peloponnesian states, until defeated by Rome in 146.

Arianism Christian heresy which denies the divinity of Jesus Christ. It was named after Arius (250-336), a priest – probably from Libya – living in Alexandria, who declared that Jesus was simply an exceptional human being. His teachings reached a wide audience, from the imperial household down to humble citizens, but in 325 the Council of NICAEA excommunicated and banished him. After Emperor CONSTANTINE's death the Roman Empire became divided over the controversy, and another condemnation was issued at Constantinople in 381. However, the Arian heresy had already been carried to the Goths then living in what is now Hungary, Croatia and parts of Bosnia and Serbia. As a result the VISIGOTHS became faithful Arians. They also carried Arianism into Spain. The belief persisted in some places until the 8th century.

Aristides (c.530-c.467 BC) Athenian general and statesman. Aristides fought at the Battle of MARATHON in 490, when the Athenians defeated the invading Persians. He was exiled in 482 after a quarrel with rival Athenian politician Themistocles, but was recalled to take part in the naval victory over the Persians at SALAMIS in 480. Aristides led the Athenian contingent at PLATAEA the following year. He assessed the levels of tribute to be paid by members of the DELIAN LEAGUE and played a leading role in the development of the empire. He was famed for being scrupulously fair – hence he was known as 'the Just'.

aristocracy Originally a form of government, from Greek, 'the rule of the best', but now usually a hereditary social class, normally based on landed property. From Plato and Aristotle onwards, it was generally assumed that political power was best placed in the hands of those who through education, occupation or social position had shown their capacity to exercise it. This assumption was challenged by the democratic ideas fostered by the American and French revolutions in 1776 and 1789. Edmund Burke's *Reflections on the Revolution in France* in 1790 and Louis de Bonald's *Theory of Political and Religious Power* in 1796 were among the last explicit defences of aristocracy. Modern political aristocracies have included the British landed gentry who governed Britain until the mid 19th century, the French nobility who lost power after 1789 and the Russian nobility who clung to power until the Bolshevik revolution of 1917.

Aristotle (384-322 BC) Greek philosopher who, with PLATO, has most influenced Western thought. At the age of 17 he joined Plato's Academy where he stayed, first as a student and then as a teacher, until shortly after Plato's death in 348. From 343 to 342 he was tutor to Alexander the Great. In 335 he returned to Athens, where he established his own school, the Lyceum, which pursued a wide range of subjects, with emphasis on a detailed study of nature. When Alexander died in 323 Aristotle was forced to leave Athens, and he died the following year in Chalcis. Aristotle's output was enormous and included dialogues and scientific and philosophical works, such as the *Nicomachaean Ethics*, the *Politics* and the *Metaphysics*. His work was characterised by a love of order, which was shown in his careful classification of the different areas of science.

Aristotle's work was well-known to Roman philosophers, but was nearly lost to the Western world after the fall of the Roman Empire. It was rediscovered by Arab scholars, and brought back to the West when Greek academics fled to Italy with their manuscripts after the fall of Constantinople to the Turks in 1453. Translated into Latin, it shaped the development of medieval thought in the arts and science. St Thomas AQUINAS reconciled Aristotelian ideas with Christian theology, and they remained a key part of higher education in Europe until the 17th century.

Arkwright, Sir Richard see feature, page 40

Armenia Region comprising present-day north-eastern Turkey and the Republic of Armenia in southern Transcaucasia. The Armenians are an Indo-European people with their own language who migrated to eastern Anatolia in the 7th century BC. They were part of the Persian empire, then absorbed into the Syrian Seleucid kingdom after being defeated by Alexander the Great in the late 4th century. In Greek and Roman times Armenia was a self-governing state standing between the Parthian empire to the east and the western Graeco-Roman powers. Under King Tigranes I (c.95-55 BC) the Armenian state was the strongest in the Roman east, stretching from Georgia to Mesopotamia and Syria. Tigranes was eventually defeated by the Roman general Pompey in 66 and Armenia became a Roman tributary.

In AD 300, Armenia became the world's first Christian state when King Tiridates converted to Christianity. This brought about Armenia's permanent break with Persia and the east. Following the Council of CHALCEDON in 451 the Armenian Church broke with Western Christianity, and in 506 the Gregorian Church was established. In 640 Muslim Arabs invaded Armenia but effectively permitted self-rule. In 995 an Armenian dynasty, the Bagratids, gained control until the 11th century when Armenia was conquered by the Byzantines and then by the Seljuk Turks. Most of the Armenian region was ruled by the Ottoman Turks from 1516, though territory was disputed between the Ottoman Empire and Persia until the end of the 18th century, except for a brief period of independence

> **DID YOU KNOW?**
>
> Aristotle formed a collection of manuscripts which was the model for later libraries, and organised research projects such as a comparative study of 158 Greek city-states.

Industrial mastermind

Sir Richard Arkwright harnessed water to power the spinning frame that generated the Industrial Revolution.

Sir Richard Arkwright (1732-92) was a pioneer of the Industrial Revolution. Above all his contribution lay in the commercial exploitation of newly invented machines, particularly in cotton manufacturing, and in his ability to concentrate workers in factories.

Arkwright became one of the richest men in Britain, yet he started with neither financial assets nor social advantages. Born the youngest son of a poor family in Preston, Lancashire, Arkwright was apprenticed to a barber and wigmaker. He set up on his own in Bolton in 1750.

SPINNING SUCCESS

Arkwright had a keen interest in mechanics, but needed capital to develop what was to become his first patent. In 1768 he moved to Nottingham, home of the knitting trade, where he set up a small workshop using machines driven by horses. The rise of cotton manufacturing depended on technical innovation, and Arkwright took out several patents for mechanical inventions. His first was granted in 1769 for a spinning frame powered by water. This was followed in 1775 by an all-embracing spinning frame which included a carding machine. Some of his patents were disputed, and, despite protracted litigation in their defence, they were finally rescinded in 1785.

Arkwright's business breakthrough came in 1771 when he entered into a contract with the hosiers, Samuel Need, Jedediah Strutt and John Smalley. Their joint decision to build an imposing water-driven mill at Cromford, Derbyshire, was a landmark in the industrialisation of Britain. Soon it employed more than 300 people working day and night, accommodated in the first factory village. While other mill owners were building their own factories, Arkwright went on to found new mills in Lancashire and elsewhere, including New Lanark in Scotland, later to be made famous by the socialist Robert Owen. In 1782 Arkwright started to introduce steam engines into his factories.

'We all looked up to him,' said Sir Robert Peel, himself a successful cotton manufacturer and the father of a future prime minister. In Peel's judgment Arkwright was a man who through his innovations and business enterprise 'had done more honour to the country than any man I know'.

Proud of his wealth and his newly acquired social status, Arkwright bought land, built a castle and served as sheriff of Derbyshire in 1787. He understood how important industry had become to Britain's role in the world, and boasted that he could pay off the national debt alone. By the time of his death Lancashire had become the centre of England's cotton textile industry, and ten years later cotton manufacturing accounted for between 4 and 5 per cent of Britain's national income.

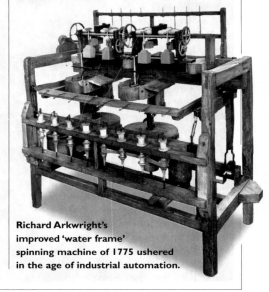

Richard Arkwright's improved 'water frame' spinning machine of 1775 ushered in the age of industrial automation.

---

between 1722 and 1730. In 1828 Russia acquired north-east Armenia. This and the growing influence of European thought led to nationalist agitation in Russian and Turkish Armenia. Calls for independence grew following Turkish atrocities against Armenian Christians. Widespread European diplomatic concern over the 'Armenian Question' did not prevent the massacre of thousands of Armenians between 1894 and 1896.

The YOUNG TURK government, fearing Armenian sympathy for the Russian enemy during the First World War, in 1915 decided to deport the Turkish Armenian population of about 1.75 million. Between 600 000 and a million Armenians are estimated to have died of starvation or been killed while on the way to Syria and Palestine. Some settled in Russian Armenia where an independent republic was founded in 1918. Only two years later the government relinquished power to the communists, and the country became the Soviet Republic of Armenia. Under the terms of the Treaty of Lausanne in 1923, Turkish Armenia

was absorbed into the new republic of Turkey. In 1936, the new Soviet constitution gave Russian Armenia the status of a republic of the USSR. After an earthquake devastated much of the country in 1988, thousands were left homeless and industry was badly affected. In 1989 ethnic violence erupted over the status

> 66 **No fleet in the world can get over the mountains of Taurus to protect the Armenians.** 99
>
> *Marquis of Salisbury, speech against atrocities by Turkey, 1896*

of the Christian Armenian region of Nagornyy-Karabakh within Shi'ite Muslim AZERBAIJAN. Tension continued after the republic declared independence from the Soviet Union in 1991, and erupted into all-out war in May 1992 when Armenian forces entered Nagornyy-Karabakh, taking about 10 per cent of Azerbaijan territory. A cease-fire collapsed in 1994 and Armenia withdrew

from peace talks in 1995. Parliamentary elections were also held in 1995 and a new constitution was approved in a referendum.

Arminius, Jacobus (1560-1609) Dutch theologian, founder of the theological movement known as Arminianism. His Dutch name was Jakob Harmensen, and he studied at Utrecht, Leiden, Basle and Geneva before being ordained in 1588. He became professor of theology at Leiden University, where he opposed the Calvinist doctrine of absolute predestination (see CALVIN, John); this held that God has preordained all things, even the salvation or damnation of souls. Arminius believed that man's free will plays a significant part in his eventual salvation.

Arminianism later gave rise to the Dutch Remonstrant movement, and in England it influenced Archbishop William LAUD.

armistice (November 11, 1918) Agreement which ended hostilities in the First World War, though initially it applied to a period of only 36 hours. The Allied commander Marshal Ferdinand Foch and the British Admiral Rosslyn Wemyss received a German delegation led by Major-General Detlef von Winterfeldt in a railway carriage in the forest of Compiègne, France. The agreement was signed at 5.10 am. The most important conditions required Germany to evacuate the occupied areas of Belgium, Luxembourg, France and Alsace-Lorraine and to surrender 2500 heavy guns, 25 000 machine guns, 1700 warplanes, all its U-boats, 5000 lorries, 5000 locomotives and 150 000 wagons. At 11 am, the armistice took effect. In the United Kingdom a two-minute silence is observed every year at 11am on the Sunday nearest to the anniversary of the Armistice, to commemorate the millions killed in two world wars.

arms control see DISARMAMENT

Armstrong, Louis (c.1900-71) American jazz trumpeter and singer. He first played the cornet at 14, while on remand in the Coloured Waifs Home. For a time he played in and around New Orleans, before joining King Oliver's Creole Jazz Band in Chicago. He played second cornet on Oliver's historic recordings of 1923, the first to feature Black performers. Armstrong then made his own recordings between 1925 and 1928, backed by his 'Hot Five' and 'Hot Seven'. These recordings changed the face of jazz, shifting the focus from ensemble playing to the solo improviser. Armstrong appeared in more than 50 films.

army Armies, people organised and trained for fighting on land, came into existence with the earliest states, and served the great empires of ancient China, Egypt, Babylon and Assyria. The army of Alexander the Great succeeded in conquering the known world between 334 and 323 BC. At this time, siege techniques developed as an important part of military practice.

When Alexander died, the Greek forces were superseded by first the Carthaginian and then the Roman armies, as the most significant armed forces in the Western world. The generals of Carthage, especially Hannibal, hired mercenaries to great effect, but it was the armies of Rome, evolving into professional standing forces, which dominated Europe from the 2nd century BC to the 5th century AD. The Roman army's advantage lay in its flexible but disciplined formations, or legions, and the rapid construction and defence of its fortifications.

Less disciplined but swiftly moving armies which could number up to 100 000 were a feature of the so-called Dark Ages, from those of ATTILA the Hun in the 5th century to the Mongols in the 12th and 13th. Their size gave them a significant advantage over smaller forces. In Europe in the Middle Ages, the heavily armoured mounted KNIGHT dominated warfare. But individual knights combined in small armies lacked organisation and were successfully challenged from the 14th century by Swiss infantry armed with pikes (long spears) and halberds (axes with added spikes), and the English ARCHER armed with the longbow. The use of mercenaries became common at this time. They were led by CONDOTTIERE of various nationalities, who took their name from the Italian *condotta*, 'contract', which they used when hiring their soldiers. From the late 15th century Swiss infantry, which was regarded as the best in Europe, was hired out to other countries.

The major advances of the 15th and 16th centuries were the use of gunpowder and the development of cannon. Organisation, discipline and further advances in weaponry led to the creation of efficient standing armies. The Swedes and the Dutch set up the first 'modern' standing armies in the early 17th century. The Swedes were also the first to use conscript armies in the 17th century, and the system was used in France to build forces to fight the revolutionary and Napoleonic wars. During the 19th century most European countries conscripted young men to train and serve for about two years. Britain only enforced CONSCRIPTION in 1916-18 and between 1939 and 1963. In the 18th century military battles still followed a strict and formal pattern. Infantry were lined into well-drilled rows, firing muskets and advancing with bayonets, backed up by field guns. Cavalry divisions, armed with swords, provided mobility. European armies played an essential role in 19th and early 20th-century imperialism, their superior firepower and military discipline enabling them to dominate the peoples of Africa and Asia.

Since the Industrial Revolution technological development has transformed the way armies operate. The advent of steam power made the transporting of armies much faster and easier. Railways became crucial for the movement of troops in the mid 19th century and were important during the AMERICAN CIVIL WAR (1861-5). At the same time new infantry weapons, such as the breech-loading rifle and the repeating carbine, were developed with improved accuracy, range and rapidity of fire. By the time of the FRANCO-PRUSSIAN WAR (1870-1) artillery was becoming more powerful. Motor transport and armoured vehicles had been used in the RUSSO-JAPANESE WAR in 1905 and were mobilised for the First World War. Advances in tactics meant that by the end of the conflict commanders no longer sent massed waves of infantry against trenches defended with machine guns. By the Second World War most armies were heavily motorised, and tanks played a major part in the North African Campaign and at the Eastern Front. The basic infantry tactics developed in Europe remained essential. They remained so for campaigns in Korea, Vietnam and the Falklands. But the deciding factor was coordination between all the armed forces. During the Cold War balance of power, large armies of NATO troops and the Warsaw Pact continued to face one another in Europe, armed with conventional weapons and nuclear missiles. Allied victory in the GULF WAR in 1991 was achieved through massive tank deployment backed by air power.

Arnhem, Battle of (September 1944) Second World War battle fought in the Netherlands. British, American and Polish parachutists of the 1st Allied Airborne Division were dropped behind German lines in an attempt to capture bridges over the Lower Rhine which would enable the Allied armies to advance into Germany. Only a few troops reached the Arnhem bridge and other key objectives, and German units blocked the path of Allied divisions which were attempting to reach the airborne troops. There were over 7000 casualties, and it was Field-Marshal MONTGOMERY's only major defeat.

Arnold, Benedict (1741-1801) American Revolutionary war leader turned traitor. Arnold was a hero of the early stages of the War of Independence, serving with valour when capturing the frontier fort of Ticonderoga, during the invasion of Canada, and at the victory over the British at Saratoga. From 1778 he began plotting with the British commander in chief, Sir Henry Clinton, to deliver West Point, the key to the Hudson valley, to the British for £20000. When his courier, Major John André, was captured, he escaped on a British ship, leaving André to hang. Because the plot failed, he received only £635 and a brigadiership from the British. He died, neglected, in England.

Artaxerxes II (c.436-358 BC) King of Persia from 405 to 358, the son of Darius II. His long reign over the Achaemenid (Persian) empire was beset by unrest. Egypt revolted in 405 and was lost for the rest of his reign. His younger brother CYRUS hired 10 000 Greek mercenaries in a bid for the throne but was defeated and killed at Cunaxa in 401. By supporting the Greek enemies of Sparta, Artaxerxes recovered the Greek cities of Asia Minor at the peace of Antalcidas. But the king was largely controlled by his wife and mother and relied

> ## DID YOU KNOW?
>
> *Oliver Cromwell's New Model Army during the English Civil War was the first to wear regular uniforms. They were coloured red, which made it easy to distinguish friend from foe and also concealed the blood from wounds, so avoiding damage to morale.*

King Arthur presides over his court at Camelot. Some accounts claim that the king devised the famous Round Table to prevent the knights arguing over which one was the most important.

on his ministers. In 373, various SATRAPS, or provincial governors, formed a coalition to overthrow him. It took him from 366 to 358 to put them down, but Artaxerxes mercifully returned most of the rebels to their governorships. By contrast his son, Artaxerxes III, killed most of his relatives and crushed two rebellious satraps to secure his hold on power.

Arthur Legendary king of the Britons, for whom there might be some historical basis as a Celtic British king or chieftain of the 6th century AD who fought the Saxon invaders of England. Arthur is usually portrayed as a powerful king, attracting to his court at Camelot an elite corps of knights of the 'Round Table', bound by ideals of CHIVALRY and a semimystical form of Christianity. This romantic myth was invented in the 12th and 13th centuries and has little connection with any historical Arthur. The 9th-century writer Nennius claimed that Arthur commanded a British force against the SAXONS, whose raids on Britain increased with the departure of the Roman legions. According to Nennius, Arthur inflicted defeat on the Saxons at Mount Badon in about 516, but was mortally wounded in a later battle at Camlan in 537. The monk and historian Gildas, writing before 547, mentioned Badon but did not connect Arthur with the victory, and neither Mount Badon nor Camlan has been identified.

Aryans People who settled in Iran and northern India in prehistoric times. From their language evolved Sanskrit, the language of classical and sacred Hindu texts, and the Indo-European family of languages. The Aryans moved into India from Persia between 2000 and 1200 BC. Over the following thousand years they expanded eastwards, absorbing the local population. The CASTE, or class, system evolved at this time and India remained divided between warring states.

> **DID YOU KNOW?**
>
> *Legend says Arthur was given the magic sword Excalibur by the Lady of the Lake. After his death the sword was thrown back into the lake and a hand is said to have caught it.*

In the late 4th century BC, northern India was united for the first time by the MAURYAN dynasty which established an administrative system and a regular army. It was overthrown in the 2nd century BC by the Sunga dynasty. The west of India remained the stronghold of the original Aryan culture and the home of HINDUISM. During the 19th century the French diplomat Comte de Gobineau popularised the idea of an 'Aryan race' composed of those who spoke Indo-European languages, who were supposedly responsible for all the progress that mankind had made and who were also morally superior to 'Semites', 'yellows' and 'blacks'. The Nordic, or Germanic, peoples were regarded as the purest 'Aryans'. The NAZIS seized on this idea and made it the basis of the German persecution of 'non-Aryan' peoples.

Ascham, Roger (1515-68) English humanist scholar and influential exponent of the NEW LEARNING, which was based on study of the Bible and of classical literature. From 1540 he was a lecturer in Greek at St John's College, Cambridge, and in 1545 he published a popular treatise on archery, *Toxophilus*, which earned him a royal pension. He was also tutor to the future Elizabeth I.

Ashley Cooper, Anthony see SHAFTESBURY

asiento de negros Contract from the Spanish crown granting a monopoly of the supply of African SLAVES to the Spanish American colonies. The first such contracts were issued in the 16th century to Portuguese, Genoese, French, English and Spanish companies. The last contract, by a provision of the Treaty of Utrecht, went to the British South Sea Company in 1713. The South Sea Company was to supply 4800 slaves a year for 30 years, in return for an annual tax to the Spanish crown of £34000. The profits expected contributed to the speculation

which resulted in the SOUTH SEA BUBBLE. The enterprise was frequently unprofitable, and the illegal trade which accompanied the permitted traffic led to disputes and eventually to the War of JENKINS' EAR between England and Spain which broke out in 1739. This arrangement was ended in the mid 18th century. It was estimated that 450000 Africans were transported to Spanish America under this system between 1600 and 1750.

Asoka (3rd century BC) Last great MAURYAN emperor of India, who ruled from about 269 to about 238 BC. He is remembered for making Buddhism the state religion and for his high ethical standards. Buddhist *dharma* (teaching on religious truth) led him to a concern for the spiritual and material welfare of his subjects, and to toleration of other religions.

Asoka inherited an empire which already extended over the whole subcontinent except the extreme south. After the brutal conquest of the state of Kalinga, he renounced warfare because of the suffering it caused and adopted a policy he called 'conquest by *dharma*'. Asoka had these principles engraved on rocks and pillars throughout India. Inscriptions on these so-called Pillar Edicts record his thoughts and actions and suggest he was an efficient ruler who strengthened and humanised a remarkable administrative system. Asoka erected Buddhist monasteries and sent missionaries to neighbouring nations and as far away as Syria, Egypt and Greece. He also regulated the slaughter of animals and eased harsh laws. Asoka maintained a standing army, a secret service and a large bureaucracy. His empire fell apart after his death, but he is generally regarded as one of the greatest of the country's early rulers.

aspirin Most widely taken drug in the world, used since 1899 to relieve pain and fever, and in the mid 1990s shown to help people with heart disease. Around 400 BC Hippocrates prescribed a brew made from willow leaves to ease the pain of childbirth. Two thousand years later, in 1763, an English clergyman reported that a willow bark brew reduced fevers. A close cousin of its active ingredient, salicylic acid, was later produced from the meadowsweet plant, *Filipendula ulmaria*. But salicylic acid irritates the mouth, throat and stomach. In the 1890s acetyl salicylic acid was found to be less harsh and more effective in relieving pain. By 1899, the Bayer company was marketing it as 'Aspirin'.

Asquith, Herbert (1852-1928) British statesman and Liberal prime minister from 1908 to 1916. He served as home secretary from 1892 to 1895, and in 1905 joined the government of Sir Henry CAMPBELL-BANNERMAN as chancellor of the exchequer. In his third budget he introduced old age pensions, and supported other legislation to ban sweatshops and establish labour exchanges. When Campbell-Bannerman fell ill in 1908, Asquith was appointed prime minister. He supported LLOYD GEORGE in his fight for the People's Budget and for the National Insurance scheme for unemployment and sickness benefits in 1911. Other legislation included the PARLIAMENT ACT of 1911, which took away the power of veto from the House of Lords.

The later years of Asquith's ministry were troubled with industrial unrest and violence in Ireland over his HOME RULE Bill, which proposed an Irish Parliament in Dublin. During the First World War, Asquith formed a coalition with the Conservatives in 1915. But conflict in the Cabinet, military reverses and press attacks caused growing discontent, and in 1916 Lloyd George replaced him.

Assassin Member of a secret sect of the ISMAILI branch of Shiite Islam, known originally for murdering its enemies as a religious duty. The name is derived from the Arabic *hashishiyun*, 'hashish eater'. Hasan ibn al-Sabbah founded the sect in 1094 to support the claim of Nizar to the Fatimid caliphate, and established a headquarters at the hill fortress of Alamut in north-west Persia. The Assassins wielded influence through their reputation for murder, won by suicide squads who were confident of earning a place in paradise if they died carrying out their mission. The Nizari branch of the Ismailis, who revere the Aga Khan, are their spiritual descendants.

assizes Periodic court sessions formerly held in each of the counties of England and Wales for the trial of civil or criminal cases. The first assizes were introduced in the 12th century by HENRY II. They were originally decrees or verdicts made at sessions of the king's council and dealt with criminal trials (Assize of Clarendon, 1166), local defence and public order (Assize of Arms, *c.* 1179), or entitlement to land (the Grand Assize). At first, all writs of assize had to be heard in Westminster, or wait until the judges sat locally every seven years. In order to remedy such delay, MAGNA CARTA provided for writs of assize to be tried every year in every county. The judges who heard these cases came to be called justices of assize, and their sessions were called assizes. The judicial circuits that were established remained in force until a new system of Crown Courts was introduced in 1971.

Assyria Mesopotamian empire based in present-day Turkey and Iraq that flourished from around 2000 until 609 BC. At its height from the 9th to the 7th centuries BC, the Assyrian empire extended over much of the Middle East and was the most powerful the world had seen. The Assyrians were famed as ruthless soldiers, and developed sophisticated forms of administration, architecture and art, though culturally they owed much to their rival in the south, BABYLON. Assyria was named after its first capital, Ashur (or Assur) on the upper Tigris river. The city frequently had to defend itself against warlike neighbours. Defensive sallies into enemy territory brought increasing wealth, and by the 8th century BC the king led his army every year to collect tribute from his territories and to make

> **❝ The Assyrian came down like the wolf on the fold, and his cohorts were gleaming in purple and gold. ❞**
>
> Lord Byron (1788-1824)

new conquests. A city would be besieged then destroyed, and the inhabitants massacred and hung on poles as an inducement for the surrounding region to submit to Assyrian rule without resistance.

The first Assyrian empire was established early in the 2nd millennium BC. Under a series of strong rulers, Assyrian influence spread either side of the middle section of the River Euphrates and into central Anatolia (modern Turkey), where Assyrian traders established commercial colonies. Shamshi-Adad I (1813-1781) brought Mesopotamia under his control, but after he died his empire was attacked by Babylon and then fell to the Mitanni, a people from the west.

Assyria recovered its political and economic dominance under Ashur-uballit I (1362-1327) and his successors. The Mitanni were conquered, northern Mesopotamia was secured, and under Tukulti-Ninurta I, who ruled from 1242 to 1206, Babylon was captured. Under the Babylonian king Nebuchadnezzar I (1150-1110) Assyria was subject to Babylon, but Tiglath-Pileser I (1114-1076) recovered Assyrian independence. The years 911 to 824 saw Assyrian expansion, with the empire extending to the Mediterranean, Arabia and Egypt. Iron, the main source of wealth, was extensively traded. The peak of Assyrian power and civilisation began with the reign of Tiglath-Pileser III who ruled from 744 to 727, reconquered Babylon, but allowed it to retain limited autonomy. This policy did not ensure peace, and Babylon was destroyed in 689 by Sennacherib, who made Nineveh his capital. In 671, his son Esarhaddon even conquered Egypt, which he ruled through native princes. But the Egyptians rebelled against his successor Ashurbanipal, who was weakened by other revolts within his empire. Finally Nabopolassar, a Chaldean, took control of Babylon in 625 BC and, under attack from him and the Medes, Assyrian power collapsed.

Astor, John Jacob (1763-1848) US fur trader, financier and founder of a notable Anglo-American family of capitalists, businessmen and philanthropists. He emigrated from Germany in 1779 and worked in London until 1783, when he set sail for North America. He entered the fur trade and by 1800 had established the beginnings of a commercial empire, with chartered ships plying both the Atlantic and the Pacific. Within ten years his American Fur Company, formed in 1808, dominated the fur trade in the prairies and mountains. In 1834 he sold his interest in the company and spent his remaining years managing his highly profitable property holdings.

astrology Study of the relative positions of the planets and stars in the belief that they influence human affairs. Astrology was practised by the Babylonians, developed by the Greeks and reached Christian Europe via the Arabs. Different systems flourished in China, India and elsewhere. Astrology was considered a practical science linked with medicine and agriculture, and also a philosophical system resting on the belief that movements

Assyrians charge into battle, in a 7th century BC stone frieze. The empire was organised for continuous warfare, which led to a shortage of farmers. Food eventually had to be imported.

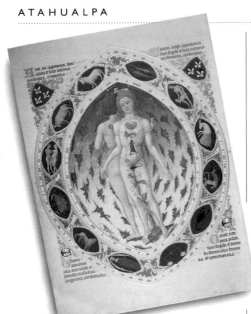

This illustrated zodiac, produced by the Limburg brothers in 1415, was part of the new enthusiasm for astrology that blossomed in the Renaissance.

in the heavens had their counterparts on Earth. By studying eclipses, comets and the movements of the planets in the zodiac, astrologers claimed to predict such effects as wars, plagues and the weather. They found a key to a person's life in the horoscope, which recorded the position at the time of that person's birth of the planets and the zodiac constellations – first named about 2000 years ago.

In the 16th century most Renaissance popes were enthusiastic patrons of astrologers, and many rulers employed court astrologers for political and medical assistance. In England, Elizabeth I appointed John Dee as court astrologer. However, its popularity waned later in the century. In 1586 a papal bull condemned astrological forecasting and, as the Protestant reformers were hostile, astrology met with the disapproval of most Christian Churches. Astrology is today discredited among most scientists, but it still has a large popular following.

Atahualpa (reigned 1525-1533) Last Inca ruler of Peru, executed by Francisco PIZARRO. An illegitimate son of the previous ruler, Huayna Capac, Atahualpa inherited a kingdom divided between himself and the legitimate heir, his half-brother, Huascar. But by 1532, Atahualpa had taken Huascar's capital, Cuzco, and held him prisoner. That year Pizarro and his 180 men ambushed Atahualpa, massacred his bodyguards and captured him. Pizarro then accepted Atahualpa's offer to fill a room with gold in exchange for his freedom. While the ransom was assembled Atahualpa ordered the murder of Huascar to prevent him from conspiring with the Spaniards. For Pizarro, the danger of freeing a potential enemy outweighed the virtue of a kept promise, and Atahualpa was tried on the pretext that he had encouraged an Inca uprising. He was publicly garrotted in the square of his capital, Cajamarca.

Ataturk, Mustafa Kemal (1881-1938) Founder of the Turkish Republic and first president from 1923. Originally named Mustafa Kemal, he was a young military officer when he joined the YOUNG TURKS and played an active part in the coup that in 1908 overthrew the Ottoman sultan Abdul Hamid. Kemal distinguished himself in the First World War when he served in the Dardenelles and played an important part in forcing the Allied forces to withdraw from GALLIPOLI.

Kemal was strongly opposed to the Turkish surrender to the Allies in 1918 and to the foreign occupying powers that remained in Anatolia. He used his wartime reputation and position overseeing the demobilisation of the remaining troops in Anatolia to organise a national army based at Ankara. This army drove out the Allied occupying forces and abolished the sultanate. Sultan Muhammad VI fled to a British warship. In 1922 Kemal proclaimed a republic with its capital in Ankara. In 1923 the peace treaty of Lausanne recognised Turkey's independence.

As president, Kemal began a series of sweeping reforms which modernised the legal and educational systems, adopted the Roman alphabet and encouraged the European and secular way of life. He took the name Ataturk ('Father of the Nation') in 1934, and remained in office until his death.

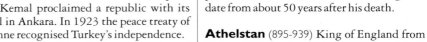

Athanasius, St (c.295-373) Bishop of Alexandria and theologian. Athanasius was a vehement opponent of ARIANISM, the heresy that denied the true divinity of Jesus. In 325, he played a leading part in the Council of Nicaea which met to condemn the heresy, and he refused the Roman Emperor CONSTANTINE's request to receive back into communion the heresy's founder Arius, who had been excommunicated. Arian sympathisers had Athanasius himself exiled five times by Constantine and other emperors. During one exile he completed one of his most important works, *Four Orations Against the Arians*. His theological position was finally confirmed at the first Council of Constantinople in 381 when Arianism was prohibited and the Nicene Creed, a statement of Christian belief largely composed at the Council of Nicaea in 325, was finally approved. Athanasius was believed to be the author of the Athanasian creed, which affirms the doctrine of the Trinity, or three persons in one God, but it is now thought to date from about 50 years after his death.

Athelstan (895-939) King of England from 926 until his death. As king of Wessex, Athelstan established the supremacy of Wessex in England, Wales and southern Scotland. The

Turkish leader Kemal Ataturk is greeted in 1937 by female pilot Sabiha Gökschen. She was able to come to prominence solely because of his radical reforms to the male dominated society.

ANGLO-SAXON CHRONI-
CLE records that in 937 he
defeated a combined force
of Scots and Danes at an
unidentified place called
Brunanburhas. The king
reformed the coinage,
provided sound govern-
ment, granted charters
to towns and, in a century
of legal reforms, issued six
series of laws. These in-
cluded help for the destitute
and reduced penalties for
young offenders, as well as pre-
scribing the punishments for
theft and corruption.

Athens Leading ancient Greek
city-state, and capital of modern
Greece. Athens, named after its
patron goddess Athena, was famous for its
learning, culture and democratic institutions.
Its intellectual and artistic achievements are
symbolised by the Parthenon, which was built
in the 5th century BC – the city's golden age.
SOLON, SOPHOCLES and PERICLES were
among its great figures.

The city-state of Athens was formed when a
number of small villages in Attica united, at
first under hereditary kings, then under an
aristocracy which was successfully challenged
by Solon in 594 BC. A tyranny established by
Pisistratus in 561 lasted until his son Hippias
was driven out in 510. Athenian democracy
was placed on a firm footing by Cleisthenes
who built on the legacy of Solon in the last
decade of the 6th century BC.

At first, the *areopagus,* the council which
had virtually ruled Athens in the 7th century,
retained considerable influence, which lasted
during the Persian Wars from 499 to 449. It
was only after Ephialtes stripped it of its
powers in 462 that a more radical democracy
came into being. Pericles pushed through further reforms, establishing in particular the
important principle of pay for jury service.

A popular assembly was open to all
Athenian male citizens aged over 18. All
members had the right to speak, and it was the
assembly which decided all legislative and
policy matters. The council of 500, elected by
lot for a year from Athenian male citizens over
the age of 30, was an executive body which
prepared business for the assembly and then
saw that its decisions were carried out.
Pericles dominated the democracy until his
death in 429, but none of the 'demagogues'
who followed him achieved the same level of
influence. Radical democracy had its dangers,
however: laws were sometimes overridden by
the assembly, and skilled orators could manipulate listeners' emotions. In 490 and 480-479
the city-state enjoyed success in the Greek-
Persian Wars. The Greek army defeated Persia

**The making of pottery
flourished in and around
the ancient city of
Athens. Artists used a
layer of clay solution,
called slip, which turned
black after firing to
depict scenes like this
of youths collecting
olives from a tree.**

at Marathon in 490 and an
Athenian fleet won a major
victory against Persian forces
off the island of Salamis in
480. The DELIAN LEAGUE,
formed in 478 of Greek states
newly freed from
Persia, was subse-
quently transformed
into the Athenian empire
as Athens, by virtue of its naval superiority,
was able to impose its will on its allies.
Inscriptions and literary sources reveal the
means by which Athens controlled its subjects: the installation of garrisons; the establishment of *clenruchies* (colonies) of citizens in
strategic or rebellious areas; the encouragement of local democracies; the referral of
important judicial cases to Athens; the imposition of Athenian weights and measures
throughout the empire; and the appointment
of officials to keep an eye on its subject cities.

As long as it had a strong navy, Athens
could crush revolts throughout the Aegean,
but the empire died with Athens' final defeat
in 404 at the end of the long PELOPONNESIAN
WAR, when it lost almost all its fleet and the
city walls were destroyed. Nevertheless it
recovered in the 4th century and led the resistance to PHILIP II of Macedon. Athens was prey
to the Macedonian successors
of Alexander the Great, first
falling to Demetrius, the son of
Antigonus I in 307, later
losing its independence in 262
but regaining it in 228. After
backing MITHRIDATES, king of
Pontus (120-63), against
Rome, in 87-86 it was sacked
by its opponent, SULLA. From then on its
importance was as a centre of philosophy, science and the arts, which attracted many young
men from throughout the Mediterranean,
particularly the Romans. It then underwent a
prolonged period of obscurity and economic
decline. It was captured by the Turks in
AD 1456, and suffered during the Venetian
siege of 1687. The modern city came into
being after 1834 when it became the capital of
the newly independent Greece.

Atlantic, Battle of the Name given to a
succession of naval operations in the Second
World War which took place in the Atlantic,

the Caribbean and northern European waters,
when Germany tried to cut the supply line
between the United States and Britain.
German U-boats, sometimes aided by Italian
submarines, were the main weapon of attack,
but aircraft and surface raiders also took part.
The Allies lost about 2800 merchant ships,
mainly British. The critical situation eased
after the summer of 1943, with the use of
better radar, long-distance aircraft and naval
CONVOY escorts, and the breaking of German
codes. Technical innovations later increased
the U-boats' effectiveness, and it was only
when Allied land forces captured their bases
in 1944 that the threat to Atlantic shipping
was finally ended.

Atlantic Charter Joint declaration of
principles to guide a peace settlement after
the Second World War. It resulted from a
meeting at sea between Winston CHURCHILL
and F.D. ROOSEVELT. Issued on August 14,
1941, it called for freely chosen governments,
free trade, freedom of the seas, access to raw
materials for all nations and world economic
cooperation, as well as the disarmament of
aggressors. It condemned territorial changes
and renounced territorial ambitions. The
charter's principles were endorsed by 26 allies
in the United Nations Declaration signed in
Washington, DC on January 1, 1942.

atomic bomb see MANHATTAN PROJECT

Attainder, Act of Law passed in the
English Parliament that pronounced a person
or a group guilty of treason or felony and so
bypassed normal legal procedure. Acts of
Attainder became common in the Wars of the
ROSES as factions used them against their
rival's leaders. In the 16th and 17th centuries,
attainder was used to dispose of
distinguished figures: Henry
VIII rid himself of Thomas
CROMWELL and Charles I dis-
posed of Archbishop William
LAUD after Acts of Attainder
were passed against them.
Charles I's minister Thomas
STRAFFORD went to the scaf-
fold in 1641 after the king signed an Act.
When told of his fate Strafford commented:
'Put not your trust in princes, for in them is no
salvation.' Charles had promised him that no
Parliament should touch a hair of his head.
The MP John Pym commented: 'Has he given
us Strafford? Then he can refuse us nothing!'

But these Acts became unpopular because
those accused did not always have a chance to
defend themselves. The public also knew that
Parliament could declare any conduct it found
offensive to be a crime which could then be
used as the pretext for using the Act. The law
was abolished in 1870 except for 'acts of outlawry', and that provision was ended in 1938.

DID YOU KNOW?

*Lord Edward Fitzgerald was
the last person in Britain to
be condemned to death by
Act of Attainder, for leading
the 1798 Irish rebellion.*

Attila see feature, page 47

Attlee, Clement (1883-1967) British politician, and prime minister from 1945 to 1951 of the first Labour government to have an overall majority in Parliament. Attlee studied at Oxford, then practised law before becoming a social worker in the East End of London. His work there led him to become a Labour Party member in 1908. Entering full-time politics Attlee became mayor of Stepney in 1919, and Member of Parliament for Limehouse in 1922. He served in the Ramsay MacDonald governments of 1924 and 1929-31, resigning in opposition to the formation of a national coalition government in 1931. Attlee succeeded George Lansbury in 1935 as leader of the Labour Party.

During the Second World War he was deputy prime minister between 1942 and 1945 in the coalition government of Winston Churchill. He became prime minister after the landslide Labour victory of 1945, and presided over the difficult postwar transition period as sterling was devalued and rationing and austerity measures had to be continued longer than expected. Under his two Labour administrations, the WELFARE STATE was established, major industries – such as coal, steel, rail and air travel – were nationalised, and independence was granted to India, Pakistan, Ceylon (Sri Lanka) and Burma (Myanmar), marking the beginning of the end of the British Empire. His achievements as prime minister had a profound impact on the economic and social structure of postwar Britain. Attlee retired as leader of the Labour Party in 1955 and accepted an earldom.

Auchinleck, Sir Claude (1884-1981) British field-marshal and one of the ablest commanders in the Second World War. Auchinleck halted the headlong advance of Field-Marshal Erwin Rommel towards Cairo at the first battle of El ALAMEIN in July 1942 and so averted the danger of the Allies losing Egypt and being expelled from North Africa. Nicknamed 'the Auk' by his troops, his skill and courage earned the respect of Rommel, who considered him 'a very great leader'.

Auchinleck had served with distinction in the First World War, and commanded the land forces at Narvik in the Norwegian campaign of April-May 1940. He was promoted to general and appointed commander in chief in India in November before taking up the Middle East Command in mid 1941. When Tobruk surrendered in June 1942, Auchinleck took personal command of the troops, establishing the key defensive line at El Alamein. But he had been in command earlier when Rommel forced Allied troops to retreat and was made a scapegoat by Prime Minister Winston Churchill who replaced him as Middle East chief by General Sir Harold

The citizens of Augsburg show off their finery in a painting of around 1500. The city's success as a commercial centre had also made it a focus for German developments in the sciences and arts.

Alexander, leaving Auchinleck disgraced in many eyes. He returned to India after the war as commander in chief where he founded the modern Indian and Pakistani armies.

Augsburg City in Bavaria, from 1276 one of the free cities of Germany which were subject only to the authority of the Holy Roman Emperor. Augsburg was an important member of the Swabian League of small cities and major landowners, formed to offset the growing strength of the Swiss Confederation and the Bavarian Wittelsbach dynasty. The FUGGERS and the Welsers were the most important of the business families who contributed to the emergence of Augsburg in the 15th and 16th centuries as a major banking, commercial, scientific and cultural centre.

Augsburg was the place chosen by Emperor Charles V for the series of attempts to restore religious unity following Luther's Reformation. In 1530 the Confession of Augsburg was drawn up by Luther's fellow reformer, Philipp Melanchthon. Its 28 articles stated essential Lutheran doctrines in a form that they hoped would be acceptable to Roman Catholics. The Confession was also intended to prevent the misrepresentation of Lutheran ideas. The Lutherans argued for justification by faith, the belief that faith alone was sufficient to win entry to heaven. The Confession was rejected by the Roman Catholics but remains the chief statement of faith in Lutheran churches. In the Interim of Augsburg of 1548, German Catholics attempted to reach provisional doctrinal agreement with Protestants. Concessions to the Lutherans included allowing clerical marriage and communion of bread and wine for the laity. Many Protestant areas refused to

abide by the Interim because they claimed it was biased towards the Catholics. However, in 1555, the Peace of Augsburg was concluded by the emperor Ferdinand and the seven electors – the princes who had the right to elect the Holy Roman Emperor. The agreement led to peaceful coexistence between German Roman Catholics and Lutherans. War on religious grounds was banned within the empire. Both Roman Catholicism and Lutheranism (but not Calvinism) were recognised. The principle of *cuius regio, eius religio*, 'the ruler of a territory chooses its religion', was adopted, so each prince could impose his own faith on territories he controlled. This principle was often not enforced by Protestant princes. Thanks to the Peace of Augsburg serious conflicts in the empire were avoided for more than 50 years.

Augsburg, League of (1686) Defensive alliance formed by Emperor Leopold and some German princes to prevent the French king Louis XIV's advance into the Rhineland. It was joined by the Holy Roman Emperor, the Netherlands, Spain, and Sweden. After the French invaded the PALATINATE in 1688 and William III became king of England, a new Grand Alliance was formed; the ensuing conflict, the War of the Grand Alliance (see NINE YEARS' WAR) is also known as the War of the League of Augsburg or King William's War.

Augustine of Canterbury, St (died c.605) First Archbishop of Canterbury. Sent from Rome by Pope Gregory the Great to convert the English to Christianity, Augustine landed with 40 monks in Kent in 597 and converted King Ethelbert, whose wife was already a Christian. Augustine was consecrated archbishop the same year, and organised the

Warlord of the Huns

Attila the Hun became the scourge of the tottering Roman Empire as he plundered and pillaged his way across Europe.

In AD 440 the armies and fleets of the Eastern Roman Empire were trying to recapture North Africa from the Vandals. The Romans did not consider the possibility of a threat from the Huns, nomadic Asiatic herdsmen who had migrated into Romania and the Ukraine. They thought that the Hunnish kings – Uldin, Rua and now Attila – could be manipulated or, if necessary, defeated. They were to be brutally undeceived.

Early in 441 Attila crossed the Danube frontier and captured the Roman city of Viminacium (Kastolacz). He pillaged it, enslaved its people, then demolished the city stone by stone. The shock struck terror throughout the Balkans.

Attila had welded together his tribes of steppe nomads by imposing centralised kingship and perfecting a military system based on lightning cavalry manoeuvres and the powerful 'Scythian bow'. His object was not territory but plunder with which to reward his warrior horde.

The Huns moved over thousands of miles of plains and, as one Roman observer wrote, seemed to live in the saddle. They dominated an area from the Caspian to Hungary, and north to Poland. To hold this extensive territory, Attila had to travel constantly. His court was a group of richly adorned tents.

Attila was a warlord of considerable presence – he welcomed the ambassador Priscus of Panium with a troupe of dancing maidens. At a banquet at which his entourage wore rich silks and drank from gold goblets, Attila alone sat above them wearing simple leather Hunnish dress and drinking from a wooden cup.

THE HUN MEETS HIS MATCH

Attila was also a tyrant. When the Romans refused his demands for a huge tribute of gold, his hordes destroyed five Roman cities, defeated two Roman armies and were stopped only at the walls of Constantinople itself. Then in 450 the Huns turned west into Europe.

The Roman general Aetius skilfully negotiated a coalition of western European nations, and in 451 met Attila near Chalons, east of Paris. A bloody battle involving 40 000 men ended inconclusively. For Attila, a battle that did not result in plunder amounted to a defeat: his subject nations began to desert.

In desperation he invaded Italy, took Milan, and threatened Rome. Finally, in the spring of 453, after an alcoholic feast

Attila and his son march on Paris (above). On a medallion he appears as the Greek god Pan.

to celebrate his marriage, he was found dead from a haemorrhage following a nosebleed. Within a year the federation of tribes fell apart. Attila had known how to shake the earth, but not how to rule it: he could destroy what others had built, but not create.

St Augustine of Hippo is regarded as one of the founders of Western theology and second only to St Paul in his influence on Christianity.

Church into 12 dioceses. At a meeting with the Celtic bishops in 603 Augustine failed to resolve the differences between the Roman and Celtic Churches of Wales and Scotland, principally over the correct date to celebrate Easter and the ritual to be used in baptism and other sacraments. These differences were eventually resolved at the Synod of WHITBY in 664. Augustine's work was instrumental in re-establishing Christianity in England after its introduction during the Roman occupation had been halted by the Saxon invasions.

Augustine of Hippo, St (AD 354-430)

Christian bishop, the outstanding theologian of the early Christian Church. In his life and his philosophy Augustine combined the classical and Christian worlds into a synthesis which had a profound influence on the development of Western thought and culture.

Born in the Roman province of Numidia (present-day Algeria) of a pagan father and a Christian mother, Augustine received a classical education and studied rhetoric at Carthage, where a treatise by Cicero sparked his interest in philosophy, and where he fathered an illegitimate son. His prayer, 'Lord make me chaste, but not yet' has been echoed by errant Christians ever since. Augustine spent nine years attracted to the heresy of MANICHAEISM, which combined ZOROASTRIAN, Christian and gnostic elements in a dualistic system in which God and Satan reigned as equals.

He taught rhetoric in Rome and Milan, where he found in Neo-Platonism a philosophy which he could reconcile with Christianity. Influenced by Bishop Ambrose of Milan, Augustine was baptised, together with his son, in 387. He resigned his chair in rhetoric and returned to Africa, where he led a monastic life. The popular acclaim he met when visiting Hippo in 391 persuaded him to become a priest, and in 395, Bishop of Hippo (present-day Annaba, in Algeria). Augustine was opposed to heretical Christian sects, including the Pelagians, Manichees and Donatists, as well as pagan philosophies. He affirmed the unity of Christian belief, the nature of original sin and man's dependence on God's grace. In this way he created a theology that has remained basic to Western Christianity, Roman Catholic and Protestant. He was an upholder of order at a time when the Roman Empire was disintegrating, and he died as the VANDALS reached Hippo. Augustine's writings include *The City of God*, a Christian answer to paganism, and the *Confessions*, which contain a vivid account of his early life and conversion. The Rule of St Augustine, which is based on his writings, is followed by AUGUSTINIAN monks and friars.

Augustinian Member of one of the religious orders following the rule or code of conduct laid down by St AUGUSTINE OF HIPPO. Augustine's rule proved practical and adaptable to changing conditions over many centuries, and was used by St Dominic and St Francis as a model constitution for their own orders. It required men to live a communal life apart from the world but allowed them to undertake missionary work and care of the sick. The rule was endorsed by the Fourth Lateran Council of 1215.

Augustus Caesar see feature, right

Augustus II 'the Strong' (1670-1733) King of Poland from 1696. He was Elector of Saxony from 1694 and succeeded John III (John Sobieski) as king of Poland in 1696. Augustus joined Russia and Denmark against Charles XII of Sweden in 1700 in a bid to win land. The Polish Diet (assembly) refused to support him and he was defeated. Charles had him banished and had Stanislaus Leszczynski elected king in his place. Augustus recovered his position after Charles's defeat by Russian forces at Poltava in 1709 and for the rest of his reign brought some economic prosperity to Saxony and Poland, although renewed war with Sweden lasted until 1718. A ruler of considerable extravagance, and said to be the most dissolute monarch in Europe, Augustus was a patron of the arts and gave much support to the Dresden and Meissen china factories.

Aung San (1914-47) Burmese nationalist leader. Head of the prewar Dobama Asiayone (We Burmans' Association), whose members took the title of *Thakin*, 'lord', Aung San was an organiser of a student strike in Rangoon in 1936. After a period of secret military training under the Japanese he returned to Burma in 1942 and became leader of the Japanese-sponsored Burma National Army, which defected to the Allies in the closing weeks of the Pacific War. As head of the Anti-Fascist People's Freedom League, he led the postwar Council of Ministers, and in January 1947 negotiated a promise of full self-government from the British. On July 19, 1947, while

God of the Romans

Augustus Caesar, first emperor of Rome, established an imperial system which transformed the history of Europe and earned him the veneration of his people.

On the ides of March, March 15, in 44 BC the dictator Julius Caesar was assassinated by a group of republican senators led by Brutus and Cassius, who feared that he intended to make himself king. When news of the killing reached Apollonia in Greece, an 18-year-old student made the momentous decision to return immediately to Italy. The young man was Octavius (63 BC-AD 14), Julius Caesar's great-nephew and heir.

Octavius quickly proved to be a shrewd and ruthless politician. Exploiting the reputation of his uncle, whose military conquests had made him a national hero, he hurried to Rome. There he joined forces with Caesar's former ally, the consul Mark Antony, and drove Brutus and Cassius out of the city. Octavius then put to death 300 senators so that he could confiscate their wealth to pay his legions. At the Battle of Philippi in 42 Octavius and Antony destroyed the forces of Brutus and Cassius. The victors went on to divide the empire between them.

Their joint rule lasted only 12 years. Antony had married Queen Cleopatra of Egypt, and with her wealth dominated the East, threatening Octavius' supremacy. Octavius provoked Antony into civil war and crushed him at the Battle of Actium in Greece in 31. Antony and Cleopatra committed suicide. Egypt was annexed as a Roman province, and Octavius became sole ruler of the empire.

Octavius had no wish to share the fate of his uncle. In theory he remained simply the 'princeps' (first magistrate), ruling in equal partnership with the Senate. In practice he acted as a supreme monarch. He manipulated elections for the Roman magistracies, and curtailed the powers of the Popular Assembly. He was careful to retain personal control of the armies.

Octavius was a cold, calculating ruler, supported by his astute wife, Livia. He understood that above all else the people of Rome wanted stability and prosperity. In exchange, they were ready to give up the traditional republican 'liberties', which few had enjoyed. In 27 the Senate voted Octavius the title Augustus and named the eighth month of the new calendar in his honour.

REFORMED STATESMAN

Augustus ruled for 44 years, from 30 BC to his death, and evolved from a revolutionary dictator into a far-sighted, benevolent statesman. He reformed the administration of the Roman provinces, founded cities, and laid the foundations for the Romanisation of Western Europe. His patronage made possible the careers of some of the greatest Roman writers, including Virgil, Livy and Horace, and he initiated so much building that he could boast, 'I found Rome in brick and left her in marble.' After his death at the age of 77 he was succeeded by his

adopted son Tiberius Caesar. Augustus was later declared a god and temples were built in his honour. So secure was the hereditary monarchy he had created that the titles Caesar and Augustus were automatically adopted by every succeeding emperor. The Republic was never to be restored.

A statue portrays Augustus as a warrior (left). After a victory in 15 BC, a scabbard shows Tiberius being received by Augustus (above).

de facto prime minister of a country on the verge of independence, he and six of his colleagues were assassinated at the instigation of a political rival, U Saw.

Aung San Suu Kyi (1945-) Opposition leader in Myanmar, formerly Burma. The daughter of AUNG SAN, Aung San Suu Kyi was two years old when her father was assassinated. She attended schools in Burma until her mother Khin Kyi was appointed ambassador to India. While studying at Oxford University she met her husband, and lived a quiet married life with two children until 1988 when she spoke out against the brutal regime of the military strongman Ne Win.

Aung San Suu Kyi began a nonviolent campaign for human rights and democracy for which the military government placed her under house arrest from 1989 to 1995. In 1991 she was awarded the Nobel peace prize. She was free to leave the country but chose to remain until political prisoners were freed and the country returned to civilian government.

Aurangzeb (1618-1707) Mughal Emperor of India from 1659 to his death. Aurangzeb is considered the last great ruler in his line, despite his despotic tendencies and Muslim fanaticism. After eliminating his brothers, he seized the throne from his father, Shah Jahan, and then imprisoned him in Agra until his death. He proceeded to adopt the title *Alamgir*, 'world-holder'. Until about 1680 Aurangzeb's rule was fairly stable. Then, following a revolt of the Rajputs between 1678 and 1681 which was supported by his third son, Aurangzeb pushed the boundaries of Mughal India to their fullest extent in a series of fierce campaigns against the Hindu kingdoms Bijapur and Golconda, which were finally captured in 1686-7.

Thereafter Aurangzeb fought continuously and ineffectively against the Marathas in the south and west, overextending his resources. In an attempt to reassert Muslim orthodoxy, Aurangzeb reversed the taxation concessions which had won Hindu support, particularly since AKBAR's reign, and destroyed countless Hindu temples and shrines. The result was intensified opposition to Mughal rule among the Marathas and the Sikhs. At the time of his death, the empire was collapsing.

Auschwitz Notorious CONCENTRATION CAMP complex set up by the Nazis at Oswiecim, in Poland. Up to 4 million people, mostly Jews transported from all over Europe, were murdered in the gas chambers or died of starvation, exhaustion and disease there between 1940 and 1945.

Austen, Jane (1775-1817) English novelist, whose treatment of unexceptional people in everyday life gave a distinctively modern

The Mughal leader Aurangzeb, shown on a lion hunt in 1670, extended the empire to its greatest extent, but failed to fight off the Western infiltration that helped to destroy it after his death.

character to the art of the novel. Austen's writings show deep insight into the social life and manners of the country gentry, portraying them vividly and with affectionate irony. Apart from occasional visits to London, Bath, Lyme Regis and her brothers' houses, her life was externally uneventful. She never married. Austen's reputation rests on six major novels: *Sense and Sensibility* (1811); *Pride and Prejudice* (1813); *Mansfield Park* (1815); *Emma* (1815); *Persuasion* (1817); and *Northanger Abbey* (1817). Sir Walter Scott criticised her for her narrow themes but praised her 'exquisite touch which renders ordinary commonplace things and characters interesting'.

Austerlitz, Battle of (December 2, 1805) Decisive Napoleonic victory over Austria and Russia, near the town of Austerlitz in the present-day Czech Republic. Alexander I of Russia persuaded Francis I of Austria to attack before French reinforcements could arrive but their complicated plan to encircle the French allowed Napoleon to split their army and defeat each half. As a result, the Russian army had to withdraw from Austria, which signed the Treaty of Pressburg in 1805, recognising Napoleon as king of Italy and ceding to France Austrian territories in northern Italy, the Alpine regions and on the Adriatic coast.

Australia Island continent in the southwest Pacific. It was first inhabited by ABORIGINES thought to have migrated from South-east Asia more than 50 000 years ago. The first recorded sighting of Australia by Europeans was in 1606 by the Dutch ship *Duyfken*, but there may have been earlier visits by the Portuguese. In 1770 Captain James Cook claimed British possession of the eastern part of the continent, naming it New South Wales. The British penal colony of New South Wales was founded in 1788. It was the first of several similar colonies in which convicts made a considerable contribution to the economic foundation of the country.

For the first half-century of colonisation, Australia was primarily an extensive jail. Government-aided immigration of free settlers from the 1830s helped the colony's development, as did exploration, which opened pastures for the wool industry. Settlement by squatters of much of eastern Australia led to conflict with the Aborigines, resulting in incidents such as the Myall Creek Massacre in 1838, when White station hands killed 28 Aborigines. Separate colonies were formed in Tasmania in 1825, Western Australia in 1829 and South Australia in 1836. The system of convict transportation faded from the 1840s, finally ceasing in 1868.

The GOLD RUSHES of the 1850s and 1860s brought newcomers and furthered exploration of the outback. The WHITE AUSTRALIA POLICY, which restricted non-European immigration to protect the 'white working man' from cheap Asian labour, can be traced to that period: it lasted from 1901 until the 1950s. The colonies federated as self-governing states, becoming the Commonwealth of Australia in 1901. The British monarch is represented by a governor-general; the prime minister and Cabinet are drawn from the federal parliament; and the self-governing states have their own constitutions.

Australia played an important role in both world wars, and after 1945 embarked upon a fresh period of expansion with new mineral finds playing a large part in economic growth. Australia strengthened regional ties with the

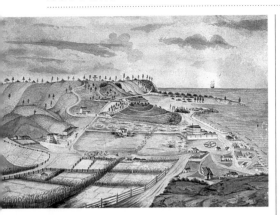

Norfolk Island, discovered in 1774, was used as one of the first Australian prison settlements.

South-east Asian countries, which have provided an increasing proportion of more than 4 million immigrants who have settled in Australia since the Second World War. People born overseas still total 23 per cent of the population. In 1975, the governor-general took the unprecedented step of dismissing the prime minister, Gough Whitlam, after the senate had blocked the government's financial legislation. Since then, Australians have been increasingly in favour of declaring a republic, ending the role of the British monarch as head of state. In 1996 Prime Minister John Howard said a people's convention would be set up to debate the issue.

Austria Country in central Europe. Celtic tribes settled in the area from about 500 to 200 BC and were conquered by the Romans in 14 BC. The region remained part of the Roman Empire. A succession of Germanic invasions, by Vandals, Goths, Huns, Lombards and Avars began in the 5th century AD and ended with a short period of stability under Charlemagne. Magyar invaders then followed, but these were decisively defeated by Otto the Great at the Battle of Lechfeld in 955. Otto invested Leopold of Babenberg with the title of Margrave of Austria, and the Babenberg dynasty lasted until 1246.

In 1282 Rudolf I, Count of Habsburg invested his two sons jointly as Dukes of Austria. The older son Albert, who was Duke of Austria from 1282 to 1308, founded a dynasty which survived into the 20th century. The first Habsburg Holy Roman Emperor was Frederick III (1452-93) and perhaps the greatest was Charles V (1519-56), who was also king of Spain.

Vienna withstood a Muslim siege in 1529 and again in 1683, when a Polish army forced invading Ottoman forces to retreat. The War of the AUSTRIAN SUCCESSION brought to a head the conflict over supremacy in Germany, and the SEVEN YEARS' WAR confirmed Prussia as a power of equal weight. The end of the 18th century saw almost continuous conflict,

with Austrians fighting against the French revolutionary armies in the Netherlands, the Rhineland and northern Italy. By 1806 Francis I, the emperor of Austria, ruled all his lands from the capital city of Vienna.

The GERMAN CONFEDERATION of 38 states formed at the Congress of Vienna in 1815 was dominated by Austria. Prussia, Austria's rival in Germany, in 1866 proposed to exclude Austria from the confederation and achieved this by victory in the AUSTRO-PRUSSIAN WAR. Austria was forced to turn eastwards, and make concessions to the Hungarians to form the AUSTRO-HUNGARIAN EMPIRE. Defeat and revolution destroyed the monarchy in 1918, and the first Austrian republic which followed it was only a rump of the former state. This was destabilised by the Nazis, who wanted to unite Austria and Germany. In 1934, they murdered the chancellor, Englebert Dollfuss, and attempted a coup. They were more successful in 1938, when Hitler's army annexed the country without opposition and declared the ANSCHLUSS. Defeated in the Second World War, Austria was invaded by Soviet troops, and divided into separate occupation

> **❝ A free and independent Austria removed from all rivalries... devoted to the cause of peace, will be an asset for... the world. ❞**
>
> *German poet Karl Theodor Körner speaking in 1951*

zones, each controlled by an Allied power. In 1955 a treaty between the Allies and Austria restored full sovereignty to the country. The treaty prohibited the possession of major offensive weapons and required Austria to pay heavy compensation to the USSR. It remained neutral, democratic and increasingly prosperous under a series of social democratic regimes. It was accepted as a member of the European Union in January 1995.

Austrian Empire (1806-67) When the Holy Roman Empire was dissolved in 1806, Emperor Francis II continued to rule as Francis I, Emperor of Austria. His dominions included the hereditary Habsburg lands of Bohemia, Hungary, Croatia and Transylvania, Galicia (once a province of Poland) and much of northern Italy (Venetia and Lombardy). Nationalist feeling was emerging, and during the reign of his successor Ferdinand I (who ruled from 1835 to 1848) liberal agitation developed for political representation, press freedom and the reform of Chancellor Clemens METTERNICH's police state. In March 1848, at a time of economic depression, riots in the capital led to Metternich's resignation. A new constitution was not sufficiently democratic for radical leaders, who organised a popular protest on May 15, 1848.

The emperor fled to Innsbruck and later abdicated. His 18-year-old nephew Francis Joseph succeeded. There were movements for independence among all the peoples of the empire, including the Hungarians, the Czechs, Slovaks, Serbs, Croats, Romanians and Italians. In June 1848, a Pan-Slav conference met in Prague, but the opposition to the government in Vienna was divided and the prime minister, the Prince of Schwarzenberg, and Francis Joseph were able to regain control. The empire regained some stability, until defeat by France and Piedmont ended Austrian rule in Italy in 1859. In an effort to satisfy nationalist feeling the emperor proposed a new federal constitution, but it came too late and after a further defeat he agreed to the *Ausgleich* (Compromise) of 1867 and the creation of the AUSTRO-HUNGARIAN EMPIRE.

Austrian Succession, War of the (1740-8) A complicated European conflict in which the key issue was the right of Maria Theresa of Austria to succeed to the lands of her father, Emperor Charles VI, and for her husband, Francis of Lorraine, to accede to the imperial title. Francis's claims were disputed by Charles Albert, Elector of Bavaria, supported by Frederick II of Prussia and Louis XV of France. In addition, Philip V of Spain and Maria Theresa were in dispute over who should control Italy, and Britain was challenging domination by France and Spain of the Mediterranean in the War of JENKINS' EAR, and fighting for control of India and America.

The war began badly for Austria. When Charles VI died in 1740, Frederick II of Prussia invaded Silesia, part of the Austrian Habsburg kingdom of Bohemia. The French seized the Bohemian capital Prague, a Spanish army landed in Austrian north Italy, and Charles Albert was elected Holy Roman Emperor. But after Frederick II's seizure of Silesia was confirmed by treaty in 1742, Britain came to Austria's support, and troops under the command of George II defeated the French at Dettingen in 1743. Savoy joined Austria and Britain at the Treaty of Worms in September 1743. In 1744-5 Frederick II re-entered the war, determined to retain Silesia. Meanwhile Charles Albert

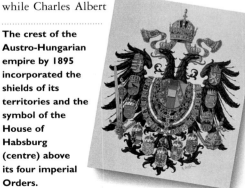

The crest of the Austro-Hungarian empire by 1895 incorporated the shields of its territories and the symbol of the House of Habsburg (centre) above its four imperial Orders.

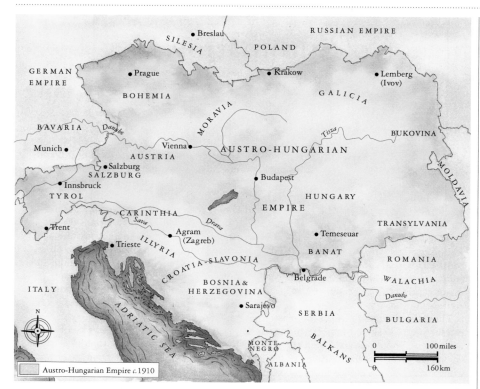

The Austro-Hungarian Empire in 1910 covered a vast area of Europe, including present-day Austria and Hungary, the Czech Republic, Serbia, Bosnia and parts of Poland, Romania and Italy.

died and Francis was elected Holy Roman Emperor in exchange for Austria's return of its Bavarian conquests to the Elector's heir. Frederick II won a series of victories against Austria, and the Treaty of Dresden (1745) confirmed his possession of Silesia. The struggle between France and Britain intensified. The French supported the Jacobite invasion of Britain and in India the French captured British-controlled Madras in 1746. The British won victories at sea: off Cape Finisterre, Spain and Belle-Ile, France, in 1747. By 1748 all participants were ready for peace, which was concluded at Aix la Chapelle.

Austro-Hungarian Empire

Territories and peoples controlled by the dual Habsburg monarchy between 1867 and 1919. After Austria's defeat by Prussia in 1866, Francis Joseph, the Austrian emperor, realised that Austria's future lay along the Danube and into the Balkans. The *Ausgleich* (Compromise) of 1867 made Austria and Hungary self-governing states under a common sovereign. Each had its own parliament to control internal affairs, but foreign policy, war and finance were decided by ministers common to both countries. This system came under increasing pressure from the other subject nations, and the failure to resolve nationalist aspirations in the empire was one of the causes of the First World War. The empire was dissolved by treaties in 1919 and 1920 which were part of the Versailles Peace Settlement after the war.

Austro-Prussian War (June-August 1866)

War fought between Prussia, allied with Italy, and Austria, allied with Bavaria and other German states. War became inevitable after Prussian Chancellor Otto von Bismarck challenged Austria's supremacy in the GERMAN CONFEDERATION. Hostilities finally broke out when Bismarck, having won France's neutrality and the support of Italy, proposed that the German Confederation should be abolished. Prussian troops forced the Austrians out of Schleswig-Holstein, but the Austrians defeated the Italians at Custozza. The Prussians crushed the Austrian army at Sadowa (Königgrätz) in Bohemia. Seven weeks later the Austrians signed the Treaty of Prague, by which the German Confederation was dissolved. Austria ceded Venice to Italy, while Prussia annexed the smaller states into the North German Confederation. The war proved to be the first step towards the establishment of the German Empire in 1871.

autobiography

Autobiographies hardly existed in ancient times, the outstanding exception being St AUGUSTINE's *Confessions*, written around AD 400, a remarkable psychological account of religious crisis and conversion. This pattern of conversion reappears in several 17th-century works such as John BUNYAN's *Grace Abounding to the Chief of Sinners*, 1666, and later in a secular philosophical form in William Wordsworth's poetic masterpiece, *The Prelude,* completed in 1805.

The modern age of autobiography may be dated from the *Confessions* (1781-8) of Jean-Jacques Rousseau, in which the frankness of self-revelation was unprecedented. Benjamin Franklin founded a distinctively American tradition of the success story in his *Autobiography*, published in 1793.

automation see feature, page 52

automobile see feature, page 115

Avars Central Asian nomads who swept into eastern Europe in 568 and formed a large empire centred on the Danube valley. They drove the southern Slavs into the Balkans and the Germanic Lombards into northern Italy, thereby removing Byzantium's Latin-speaking subjects and confirming its Greek character. They unsuccessfully laid siege to Constantinople in 626, but continued to control the Hungarian plain. Their empire was finally destroyed by Charlemagne in 791.

Axis Powers Alliance of fascist states fighting the Allies during the Second World War. In October 1936 the term was used in an agreement between Germany's Adolf Hitler and Italy's Benito Mussolini proclaiming the creation of a Rome-Berlin 'axis round which all European states can also assemble'. Japan joined the coalition in November 1936. A full military and political alliance between Germany and Italy, the 'Pact of Steel', followed in 1939. The Tripartite Pact between the three powers in May 1940 cemented the alliance. Hungary, Romania and Bulgaria, as well as the Nazi-created states of Slovakia and Croatia, later became members.

This US propaganda poster against the Axis Powers carried the message that only military and industrial might could bring final victory.

Into the age of automation

The machine is central to the 20th century. The century began with the start of mass production and the application of science to industry in the USA. It ends with a global revolution associated with technology driven by computers.

Mass production pioneered by the car maker Henry Ford in 1913 put the USA at the forefront of mechanisation. In his factory at Highland Park, Detroit, conveyor belts carried engines along a line of workers who fitted crankshafts and pistons from stationary positions; 'the point is,' Ford noted, 'that no man has anything to do with moving or lifting anything.'

Ford's innovations, known in Europe as 'the American system', established basic production methods for 50 years, making possible the mass production of machines from cars to dishwashers, for sale at a price which transformed people's lives.

However, the Ford system, for all its sophistication, still relied on the human mind, and the work of human operators. The next major step forward came with the introduction of automation, based on machines which think for themselves, acting and correcting themselves without human interference.

In the 1950s, the chemical and nuclear industries developed techniques which made possible the remote operation of physical and chemical reactions within large vessels. These 'process technologies' were important breakthroughs on the path to full automation.

THE SILICON REVOLUTION

The next 'leap forward' came with the application to electronic devices of the properties of silicon – a nonmetallic element which in its impure form acts as a semiconductor of electricity. American involvement in the space race of the 1960s created the need for miniaturised computer systems, and assured generous funds for their development. They were achieved by assembling transistors

Once a moving belt brought the car to the worker for each stage of assembly. Today a technician can direct complex processes in a nuclear power station from a single console.

onto a thin wafer sliced from a crystal of germanium or silicon. The 'silicon revolution' had arrived.

Fairchild Semiconductor developed the first integrated circuit in 1959, and by 1969 the microprocessor firm Intel had invented the microcomputer – the 'computer on a chip'. Intel was based in Santa Clara, California, and its success launched the so-called 'Silicon Valley' as a major centre of the electronics and computing industries.

These developments led to the mass production of desk and laptop computers many times more powerful than their enormous valve-driven predecessors. Computers became a part of daily life. In superstores, for example, they enable check-out and stock control to be automated; in banking, customers withdraw cash through computer-driven machines in the walls.

Some of the earliest industrial applications of computers were to metal working. By the mid 1970s, McDonald Douglas was making aircraft parts using hundreds of these machines integrated into a single computer-aided manufacturing system. The work of designers was transformed by the computer screen and software applications which made computer-aided design possible. Machines once suited only to a single task became more flexible. In car assembly, by 1980, almost all paint spraying and welding had been taken over by robots.

Early in the century the arrival of new technology was greeted with euphoric talk of human liberation. Soon there was concern that machines were displacing people. But technology only offers possibilities: how it is used will be decided by humans.

A robot welder replaces human muscle; the term 'robot' is from the Czech word for servile labour.

Ayodha Town in the Indian state of Uttar Pradesh, scene of militant Hindu violence in 1991. In the 16th century the Mughal emperor Babur built a mosque on the site traditionally identified as the Hindu god Rama's birthplace. In the 1980s Hindu fundamentalist organisations campaigned for a temple to replace the mosque, and in 1990 more than a million Hindus marched on the site. Police stopped the march, and the government fell as a result. Almost two years later, on December 6, 1991, the mosque was attacked and demolished in a few hours, and more than 1500 people died in rioting throughout India.

Ayub Khan, Muhammad (1907-74) Military leader and president of Pakistan from 1958 to 1969. A Pathan from the Hazara district, Muhammad was a professional soldier who, when Pakistan was created in 1947, assumed command of military forces in East Pakistan, now Bangladesh. He was appointed commander in chief of the Pakistan army in 1951, minister of defence from 1954 to 1956, and Chief Martial Law Administrator after the 1958 military coup. For the next ten years he ruled Pakistan as president, pursuing a policy of rapid economic growth, modest land reform, and restricted political life through 'basic democracies', introducing Pakistan's second constitution. He suffered a serious illness in March 1968 and lost political control. He was replaced in March 1969 by General Yahya Khan.

Azerbaijan Area of the Caucasus west and south of the Caspian Sea, home of ancient civilisations such as those of the Urartu and the Media. In the 13th century Azerbaijan became the centre of a Mongol empire which stretched from Syria in the west to the river Oxus, the present-day Amu Darya, in the east.

By 1914 Russian Azerbaijan was the largest oil-producing area in the world, centred on Baku. In 1922 the Azerbaijan Soviet Socialist Republic joined with Armenia and Georgia to form the Transcaucasian Soviet Federated Socialist Republic, but it split up in 1936 and each region became a republic within the Soviet Union. Nagornyy-Karabakh, a self-governing area inhabited by Christian Armenians in the republic, has been the cause of conflict between Azerbaijan and Armenia. In 1989 the Soviet Union imposed direct rule on Nagornyy-Karabakh in a bid to stop the fighting. In 1991 Azerbaijan declared independence as a Shiite Muslim state. A coup took place in June 1993 and a referendum in October confirmed former Communist Party general secretary Geidar Aliyev as president.

Azores Nine volcanic islands in three groups in the Atlantic Ocean about 800 miles (1300 km) west of Portugal, to which they belong. They were discovered, uninhabited, in the 14th century, and the Portuguese crown took control after 1494. The islands were a meeting point for Spanish treasure fleets sailing home from the Americas.

Aztecs People who dominated Central America in the early 16th century. In the 13th century the Aztecs migrated into the valley of Mexico. From the 15th century, they conquered the other cities in the valley. By 1520 the empire stretched from coast to coast, north to the deserts, and south to the Maya kingdoms of Yucatán.

The Aztecs, who worshipped many gods, considered themselves the chosen people of Huitzilopochtli, who required human blood. The Aztecs made war to obtain a supply of captives. Their ruler MONTEZUMA believed that the Spanish conquistador Hernando Cortés was the god-king Quetzalcoatl. But in 1519 Cortés took Montezuma hostage and ruled through him. In the revolt of 1520 Montezuma was killed. The Aztecs continued to fight, but in 1521 Cortés captured the capital of Tenochtitlán and the empire. (See also feature, page 404.)

The Aztec capital of Tenochtitlán was built on an island in the middle of Lake Texcoco, on the site of present-day Mexico City. When the Spanish arrived in 1519, Tenochtitlán had more than 100 000 inhabitants, canals to convey traffic through the city and a central ceremonial temple complex.

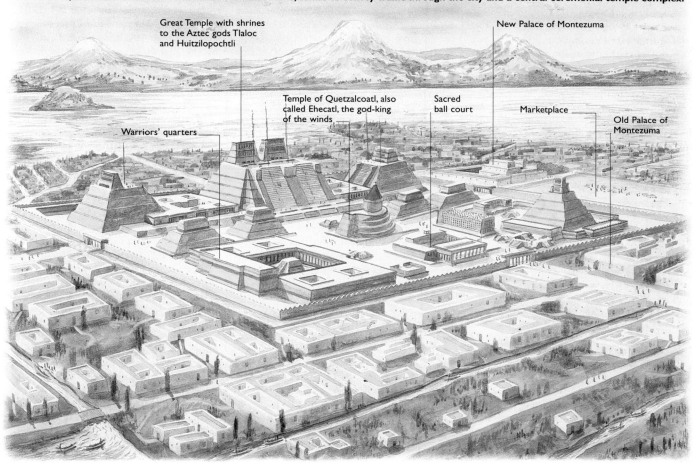

Great Temple with shrines to the Aztec gods Tlaloc and Huitzilopochtli

New Palace of Montezuma

Temple of Quetzalcoatl, also called Ehecatl, the god-king of the winds

Sacred ball court

Marketplace

Old Palace of Montezuma

Warriors' quarters

Baader-Meinhof gang West German terrorist group that carried out a campaign of murders, bombings and kidnappings during the 1970s with the aim of overthrowing capitalism and driving US armed forces out of Germany. Known to its members as the 'Red Army Faction', the group also became identified with the names of two of its leaders, Andreas Baader (1943-77) and Ulrike Meinhof (1934-76). Baader and Meinhof were arrested in 1972 and committed suicide in prison. The group eventually split into a number of cells, some of which carried out several political murders in the 1980s and early 1990s.

Ba'athism Ideology of the Ba'ath Party, founded in SYRIA in 1943 by Michel Aflaq and Salah al-Din al-Bitar. The Ba'ath ('Renaissance') Party promoted Arab nationalism, unity and socialism, and opposed British and French occupation of Arab lands. The Ba'ath took power in Syria in 1963 and in IRAQ in 1968, but became divided between its Syrian and Iraqi wings.

Babbage, Charles (1791-1871) British mathematician and inventor. He worked on the theory of logarithms and designed mechanical calculating machines that could store and manipulate information. His 'analytical engine' was designed to be programmed by punched cards, like a Jacquard loom. The concept was too ambitious to be realised by the

A German 'wanted' poster, issued in 1972, offers a reward for information leading to the arrest of Baader-Meinhof terrorists.

mechanical devices available in Babbage's day, but the analytical engine is now acknowledged as a precursor of the modern computer.

Babe Ruth (1895-1948) Nickname for George Herman Ruth, a US baseball player, also popularly known as the 'Sultan of Swat'; one of the first sporting superstars whose fame spread worldwide. From 1914 to 1919 Ruth established himself as a formidable pitcher with the Boston Red Sox. In 1920 he was sold to the New York Yankees, with whom he proved himself an equally capable batter. Ruth's colourful performances helped to restore baseball's popularity in the 1920s after revelations of a conspiracy to fix the results of the 1919 world series. As a result of the wealth he brought to the Yankees, their stadium became known as 'the house that Ruth built'.

Babeuf, François-Noël (1760-97) Socialist of the French Revolution who campaigned for the equal ownership of property by all. In 1794 he began publishing a small newspaper, the *Journal de la liberté de la presse*, and formed a group called The Equals. Babeuf's plan for an armed uprising on May 11, 1796, was betrayed and he was sent to the guillotine.

Babington Plot Conspiracy by the English Roman Catholics Sir Anthony Babington and John Ballard to assassinate Elizabeth I and replace her with MARY, QUEEN OF SCOTS. Babington acted as go-between in secret negotiations with Spain, but his correspondence was monitored by Sir Francis WALSINGHAM, Elizabeth's secretary of state. Babington and Ballard were executed in 1586, and Mary in 1587.

Babur (1483-1530) Founder of the MUGHAL empire in northern India, and a descendant of the Mongol conquerors GENGHIS KHAN and TAMERLANE. Babur ('Tiger'), whose real name was Zahir ud-Din Muhammad, inherited the central Asian principality of Fergana, north of the Pamir mountains. In 1504 he established a kingdom in Afghanistan after capturing the city of Kabul. From

Lions in glazed brick flanked the Processional Way after Nebuchadnezzar II rebuilt Babylon in the 7th century BC.

1519 Babur began making raids into northern India, and in 1525 he launched a full-scale invasion after receiving a request from Dawlat Khan, the governor of the Punjab, to help him in overthrowing the sultan of Delhi. In April 1526 Babur won a decisive victory against huge odds at Panipat, 52 miles (84km) north of Delhi, and over the next three years secured most of northern India as his empire. Tolerant in matters of religion, Babur was also a gifted poet and diarist, as well as a lover of nature. He was renowned for laying out magnificent gardens.

Babylon Ancient capital of Mesopotamia on the River Euphrates, south of modern Baghdad in Iraq. The city gained huge wealth from its position on important Middle-Eastern trade routes and was twice the centre of major empires. The first great Babylonian empire was established in 1894 BC by the Amorite king Sumuabum and expanded by its most eminent ruler, King HAMMURABI, who came to power in 1792. Following a Hittite attack in about 1595 Babylon fell under the rule of the Kassites, an Indo-European people, for more than 400 years before being looted by the Elamites, also from western Persia, in 1158. They in turn were defeated by Nebuchadnezzar I (ruled 1124-1103), who established a dynasty that lasted for more than a hundred years.

In 625 Nabopolassar, king of the Chaldeans, took control of Babylon. Under his son, NEBUCHADNEZZAR II, the second great Babylonian empire was extended as far as Palestine and Syria. Babylon itself became the largest city in the ancient world. Within its walls stood the Hanging Gardens (one of the SEVEN WONDERS OF THE WORLD), the Temple of Marduk and the Ziggurat, a great pyramidal tower which is popularly identified with the Tower of Babel described in the Bible. During this period Babylon became infamous among the exiled Hebrews for its sensuous lifestyle – giving rise to the opprobrium associated with its name ever since. The Chaldean dynasty continued until the Persian king CYRUS II captured the city in 539. Babylon flourished under the Achaemenid dynasty established by Cyrus, but never again became an independent power in its own right.

Bach, Johann Sebastian (1685-1760) German composer and organist, whose deeply religious compositions include the *Mass in*

B Minor, the *Magnificat*, the *St John Passion* and the *St Matthew Passion*. As a child, Bach was trained first by his father, then his brother. Later he became organist, choirmaster and musical director at several German churches and courts. In 1723 he was appointed director of music at St Thomas's School in Leipzig, where he composed his greatest works. Married twice, he had 20 children, four of whom became outstanding musicians in their own right. Bach's baroque church music, inspired by his own devout Protestant beliefs, expresses in magnificent choral and organ structures the glory of God and human struggle towards salvation. His other works include the six *Brandenburg Concertos* (1720), *The Well-Tempered Clavier* (1722; 1744) and the *Goldberg Variations* (1742). Although he was forgotten for some half century after his death, Bach became fully appreciated in the 19th and 20th centuries.

Bacon, Francis, Viscount St Albans

(1561-1626) English statesman and philosopher. He became a barrister in 1582 and entered Parliament two years later. During the 1590s Bacon prospered at court and in 1597 published his first collection of *Essays* on death, friendship and truth. He was knighted in 1603 and rose to become Lord Chancellor to JAMES I, but in 1621 he was impeached by Parliament for accepting bribes. With his political career destroyed, Bacon retired to devote himself to literary, scientific and philosophical writing. His works *The Advancement of Learning* (1605), *Novum Organum* (1620) and *New Atlantis* (1627) contributed significantly to the European scientific revolution.

Bactria

Ancient country, corresponding approximately to northern Afghanistan, noted for its fertility and for its fierce resistance to Alexander the Great, who conquered it in 329 BC. In the late 1st century BC a nomadic Chinese tribe, the Kushans, occupied the area, making it a centre of Buddhism.

Baden-Powell, Robert, 1st Baron

(1857-1941) British soldier, and founder of the Boy Scout movement in 1907. Baden-Powell's seven-month defence of Mafeking (1899-1900) in the BOER WAR made him a national hero. In developing his Scout movement, he applied his military skills of lone army scouting – exploring enemy territory, escaping detection and surviving in the open – to which he added training in self-reliance and a strict code of moral conduct. With his sister, Agnes, Baden-Powell also founded the Girl Guide movement in 1910.

The 17th-century courtier Francis Bacon was a man of many talents. His writings had a major influence on modern scientific thought.

Badoglio, Pietro

(1871-1956) Italian general who served under Benito MUSSOLINI, but in 1943 helped to depose him and signed an armistice with the Allies. By 1925 Badoglio was Mussolini's chief of staff. He was then appointed governor of Libya, and in 1935 was sent to revive the faltering Italian campaign in Ethiopa. He captured Addis Ababa and became governor of the territory, but resigned in 1940 during Italy's disastrous invasion of Greece. When Mussolini was deposed in 1943, Badoglio was chosen to lead a new non-fascist government, which the Germans promptly overthrew and the Allies subse-·quently restored. He resigned in June 1944 to allow a new Cabinet to be formed.

Bagehot, Walter

(1826-77) British man of letters, economist and journalist best known for his book *The English Constitution,* which he published in 1867. In it he applied a rigorous analysis to his country's political system in order to distinguish between the realities of power, which he considered lay in the Cabinet and the House of Commons, and its formal trappings, which he saw as the Crown and the House of Lords.

Baha'ism

Religion – derived from the earlier Babism – founded by the Persian leader, Baha'ullah, 'Splendour of God' (1817-92). The central idea of Baha'ism is that all religions are essentially one, under a single God. Its goal is world peace and the ultimate unity of mankind. The governing body of the Baha'i faith is in Haifa, Israel. The Baha'is have been persecuted by orthodox SHIITE Muslims, especially in Iran after the Islamic revolution in 1978.

Bahamas

Group of more than 700 islands and cays in the Atlantic Ocean off the east coast of Florida and north coast of Cuba. They are the site of Christopher Columbus's first landing in the Americas in 1492. Britain laid claim to the Bahamas in 1629 and made them a crown colony in 1717. During the 18th and 19th centuries the islands were considered strategically important and were exploited commercially for sugar, produced with the labour of African slaves. By the mid 20th century a civil rights movement had grown up

which led to the Progressive Liberal Party (PLP), representing the Black majority, gaining power in 1967. In 1973 the islands attained independence. The PLP remained in power until 1992, when it was defeated in elections by the Free National Movement (FNM). In August 1995 the Bahamas voted to remain in the British Commonwealth.

Bahrain

Oil-rich sheikdom consisting of a group of more than 30 islands in the Persian Gulf. Iran controlled Bahrain from 1602 to 1783, but was expelled by the al-Khalifah dynasty, which is still in power. Bahrain was a British protected state from 1861 to 1971, when it became fully independent and joined the Arab League. Tension between the country's Shiite and Sunni Muslim communities increased, leading to suspension of the National Assembly in 1975. Together with other members of the Gulf Cooperation Council (Saudi Arabia, Kuwait, Qatar and Oman), Bahrain repeatedly called for an end to the IRAN-IRAQ WAR of 1980-8, while retaining its neutrality both then and later during the GULF WAR of 1991. The country's economy has become increasingly diversified as its oil reserves have dwindled. Increasing opposition to the government led to an outbreak of civil unrest in 1994.

bailiff Estate manager of the lord of the manor in England between the 11th and 14th centuries. In each medieval village there was usually one salaried bailiff whose main

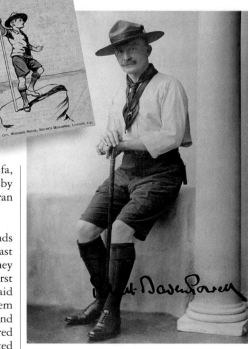

Lord Baden-Powell poses in Scout uniform. Today the movements he founded have more than 20 million members around the world.

Robin Gibb's painting of the 93rd Highlanders' heroic last stand at Balaklava, *The Thin Red Line*, presented Victorians with a romantic image of war. 'The Valley of Death' (left) was more squalid and mundane, littered with spent shot and shells from the Russian guns on the heights of Sevastopol.

task was to ensure that his village had a sufficient supply of labour and reached its annual production target for the lord. He might be sued if it failed to do so, but he gained any surplus produced. The bailiff also played a legal role in the village, prosecuting on its behalf, or acting as the legal representative of individual villagers. From the 14th century, when lords often let out their manors to farmers, the bailiff's role became that of a representative of the SHERIFF, authorised to make arrests, to summon people to court, to seize property and collect rent. (See also REEVE.)

Baird, John Logie (1888-1946) British electrical engineer who gave the first demonstration of a television image in 1926. By 1924 Baird had developed a primitive photo-mechanical television transmission system. In 1928 he demonstrated the first colour television. From 1929 his equipment was used for experimental public broadcasts in the UK, but in 1937 the British Broadcasting Corporation opted instead for a rival system developed by Marconi EMI. Baird also experimented with video recorders, radar, fibre optics and infrared night-vision devices.

Baker, Sir Samuel (1821-93) British explorer who traced many tributaries of the River Nile. Accompanied by his wife Florence, Baker set out in 1861 to reconnoitre the Blue Nile in western Ethiopia. He and his party then travelled down the White Nile, meeting the explorers John SPEKE and James Grant at Gondokoro in 1863. In 1864, with the aid of maps and information supplied by Speke and Grant, Baker located Lake Albert Nyanza (now Lake Mobutu, on the border of

Zaire and Uganda). Speke had heard of the lake but never seen it, and Baker's discovery helped to map the course of the Nile. Five years later Baker was invited by the pasha of Egypt to lead an Egyptian expedition to annex the southern Nile basin in present-day Uganda. He served as Egypt's governor-general of the area from 1869 to 1874, using his position to abolish slavery there.

Bakunin, Mikhail (1814-76) Russian revolutionary, leading exponent of ANARCHISM and founder member of the Russian Populist Movement. He served as an officer in Tsar NICHOLAS I's Imperial Guard, but resigned in

> 66 **The urge for destruction is also a creative urge!** 99
>
> *Mikhail Bakunin*
> *1842*

1835 in protest at the treatment of Polish rebels. After taking part in the REVOLUTIONS OF 1848 he was sentenced to death by both Prussia and Austria and handed over to the Russians, who exiled him to Siberia. In 1861 he escaped to London, then headquarters of militant anarchist and communist groups. The First International (see INTERNATIONALS), an association founded in 1864 to unite socialist and communist groups throughout the world, was split by the conflict between Karl MARX and Bakunin. Marx believed that the existing political and social order would collapse of its own accord, while Bakunin argued that it had to be destroyed by violent means. He died in poverty in Switzerland.

Balaklava, Battle of (October 25, 1854) Inconclusive battle of the CRIMEAN WAR, including the disastrous incident immortalised in Lord Tennyson's poem *The Charge of the Light Brigade*. As Russian forces advanced on the port of Balaklava in order to cut the supply lines of British, French and Turkish troops they met a British cavalry division. The British commander in chief, Lord Raglan, sent orders to the Light Brigade, led by Lord Cardigan, to 'prevent the enemy taking away the guns'. Raglan was almost certainly referring to the Russian guns on the heights above the Balaklava plain, but Cardigan understood him to be ordering a direct assault on Russian guns in the valley. Fired on from both flanks and from the front, he and a few cavalrymen reached the Russian line before retreating, but 247 out of 673 men were killed or wounded.

balance of power Concept of international politics by which one state or group of states increases its power in relation to the power of another state or group of states so that neither can become dominant and threaten the peace. The concept can be traced back to the Greeks and Romans and can be applied to relations between countries anywhere in the world; however, it is usually associated with the nations of Europe between the end of the Napoleonic Wars and the beginning of the First World War. During this period Britain played a crucial role by allying itself with a variety of nations at different times in order to preserve the power balance between them. As a result, Europe remained free from war throughout most of the 19th century. In 1914 the system broke down as the multiplicity of competing nations was replaced by two virtually world-wide power groupings – a situation that became entrenched after the Second World War with the emergence of the Soviet Union and the USA as global superpowers. Some historians argued that the 19th-century balance of power was replaced by a nuclear 'balance of terror', in which neither superpower could afford to allow tensions to deteriorate into open hostility.

Balboa, Vasco Núñez de (c.1475-1517) Spanish explorer and conquistador, the first European to sight the east coast of the Pacific Ocean. He arrived in the New World in 1501 and in 1510 joined an expedition that founded the town of Santa Maria de la Antigua on the Isthmus of Darién (now the Isthmus of Panama) – the first stable settlement on the American continent. After hearing rumours among local Indians about the great wealth of the Incas, Balboa set out in 1513 with 190 conquistadores, including Francisco PIZARRO, and a thousand Indians. Travelling south, he sighted the Pacific Ocean, which he named the 'Great South Sea', and took possession of it in the name of Ferdinand V of Spain. The king made Balboa admiral of the South Sea and governor of the provinces of Panama and Coiba, under the overall authority of an elderly nobleman, Pedro Arias Davila (also called Pedrarias). Pedrarias was jealous of Balboa and eventually had him charged with treason and executed.

Baldwin I (c.1058-1118) Nobleman from Lorraine who joined the First CRUSADE (1096-99) with his elder brother Godfrey of Bouillon. After the capture of Jerusalem in 1099 and the unexpected death of Godfrey in July 1100, Baldwin was invited to become Defender of the Holy Sepulchre. In December 1100 he was crowned first king of Jerusalem.

Baldwin, Stanley, 1st Earl (1867-1947) British statesman who served three terms as Conservative prime minister between 1923 and 1937. Baldwin was elected to Parliament in 1908, and from 1917 to 1921 he served as financial secretary to the treasury in David Lloyd George's coalition government. In 1922 Baldwin persuaded his fellow Conservatives to withdraw from the coalition, thereby forcing an election which they won. He was made chancellor of the exchequer under Andrew Bonar LAW, and was appointed prime minister when Law resigned in 1923.

Baldwin's attempt to introduce tariffs on goods imported from outside the British Empire lost him the 1923 election, but he returned to office in November 1924. His premiership was marked by a return to the GOLD STANDARD, the GENERAL STRIKE of 1926, Neville CHAMBERLAIN's social legislation and the Trades Dispute Act of 1927,

which restricted the rights of trade unions. Baldwin then lost the 1929 election, but served in Ramsay MACDONALD's coalition government, created in response to the 1931 economic crisis, and succeeded him as prime minister in 1935. In that year Baldwin approved the Hoare-Laval Pact, which condoned Italy's annexation of Ethiopia, but he was forced to back down in the face of a public outcry. He then skilfully managed the ABDICATION CRISIS of Edward VIII. Throughout this period Baldwin resisted demands for rearmament, believing that it was not in the best interests of Britain and earning himself considerable criticism for his apparent failure to recognise the threat from Nazi Germany. He retired in 1937.

Balfour, Arthur, 1st Earl of (1848-1930) British statesman and Conservative politician. As chief secretary for Ireland from 1887-91 Balfour opposed Irish HOME RULE and earned from the Irish the nickname 'Bloody Balfour' for his severity in dealing with insurrection. He became prime minister in 1902 and established a national system of secondary education. He created the Committee of Imperial Defence in 1904, and helped to establish the ENTENTE CORDIALE with France. Balfour resigned in December 1905, as a result of a Cabinet split over the issue of abandoning free trade, then saw the Tories lose the general election of 1906. In 1915 he joined Herbert ASQUITH's coalition government as First Lord of the Admiralty, and in 1916 became foreign secretary in a new coalition under David LLOYD GEORGE. In the latter role Balfour is remembered for issuing the so-called BALFOUR DECLARATION supporting the idea of a national home for Jews in Palestine. He helped to negotiate the VERSAILLES PEACE SETTLEMENT and played an important part in the shaping of Europe after the First World War.

Balfour Declaration (November 2, 1917) Declaration by Britain in favour of a Jewish national home in Palestine. It took the form of a letter from the British foreign secretary Arthur BALFOUR to Lord Rothschild, a prominent Zionist, promising British aid for a Jewish homeland provided the civil and religious rights of non-Jews in Palestine were respected. The Arabs of the area saw the Declaration as contradicting many promises that had been made to them, and the British Government formally abandoned the principles of the Declaration in 1939.

Bali Indonesian island off eastern Java with a highly developed agricultural economy and a strong military tradition. Bali's population

was Hindu from the 7th century and it resisted the spread of Islam through the area in the 16th and 17th centuries. At this time Bali was divided into nine warring states which engaged in piracy, slave trading and ship-wrecking. The island suffered three Dutch incursions – in 1846, 1848 and 1849 – which established Dutch control in the north, but rulers in the south and east submitted only after decisive battles in 1906 and 1908; the Hindu rajahs and their retainers allowed themselves to be killed by Dutch forces rather than suffer capture. Bali was occupied by the Japanese during the Second World War, and became part of INDONESIA after 1945.

Balkans see feature, page 58

Ball, John (d.1381) English rebel priest who combined the religious teachings of John WYCLIFFE with an egalitarian social message. He was imprisoned for heresy, but released in June 1381 by the rebels of the PEASANTS' REVOLT. At Blackheath, outside London, Ball incited the crowds to attack anyone who opposed his ideal of social equality. The rebels overran London, and Richard II and his mother had to take refuge in the Tower. But the revolt collapsed when rebels deserted their leaders on the promise of a pardon. Ball was captured, and hanged, drawn and quartered as a traitor.

> **DID YOU KNOW?**
>
> Preaching to the peasants on social equality, John Ball took as his text an early poem: 'When Adam delved and Eve span, who was then the gentleman?'

Balliol, Edward (d.1364) King of Scotland from 1332 to 1356. During a period of internal strife in Scotland, Balliol landed in Fife in 1332 to reclaim the throne that his father John BALLIOL had surrendered in 1296. Balliol defeated an opposing Scottish army at Dupplin Moor and was crowned at Scone. He then acknowledged Edward III of England as his lord and suzerain over Scotland, but in December 1332 was defeated in battle by Sir Archibald Douglas. Edward III subsequently restored Balliol to the throne after defeating Douglas's army at Halidon Hill, but Balliol's position was never secure. In 1356 he resigned his claim to the throne.

Balliol, John (c.1250-1313) King of Scotland from 1292 to 1296. Balliol claimed the Scottish crown through descent from DAVID I and in 1291 this was upheld by EDWARD I of England. Less than a month after his coronation on November 30, 1292, the new king grudgingly paid homage to Edward as his lord. However, in 1295 he attempted to ally Scotland with France, provoking an English invasion. Balliol was forced to give up his kingdom to Edward, and was taken as a captive to England before being allowed to retire to his estates in Normandy.

The long search for peace and independence in the Balkans

Divided between Roman Catholic and Eastern Orthodox Christians, as well as between Christians and Muslims, the Balkan states have for centuries been notorious for their deep and ancient animosities.

The Balkans – the region of south-eastern Europe between the Adriatic, the Aegean and the Black Sea – once formed the greatest part of Turkey's empire in Europe. The name 'Balkans' comes from a Turkish word for 'mountains', while 'to Balkanise' has come to mean 'to divide an area into small, mutually hostile states'. Both the rugged terrain of the Balkans and the bitter divisions between its peoples are reflected in its history. It has been frequently invaded by, among others, Celts, Romans, Thracians, Slavs, Huns, Goths, Hungarians, Bulgars, Turks, Italians and Germans. The ethnic and religious hatreds they have caused have frequently boiled over into violence, often generations later.

The area is a mosaic of disputed borders, once of kingdoms, principalities and provinces, now of republics. It has suffered as a buffer zone between rival religions and empires, marking the divide between the Roman Catholic and Eastern Orthodox Churches, and between Christianity and Islam. There have been periods of apparent stability under the Roman, Byzantine and Ottoman empires, and under postwar Marxist dictatorships, but Great Power involvement has often been destructive.

The area was part of the Roman Empire until 395. Thereafter, the territories of modern Slovenia, Croatia and Herzegovina remained in the Latin Western Empire, while the rest became part of the Byzantine Eastern Empire. In 1054 the Eastern Orthodox Church broke with the Roman Church. The Byzantine region of the Balkans has remained Orthodox, while the Croats and Slovenes are Catholics.

TURKEY IN EUROPE

Ottoman Turks began their conquests in Europe in the 14th century. In the region of the former Yugoslavia, only Montenegro had any success in rebuffing the onslaught. The Serbs were defeated at the Battle of Kosovo in 1389, and the last Bulgarian stronghold was overrun in 1396. In 1453 the Turks captured Constantinople, and within seven years had taken all of Greece. Until 1477 Romanian-speaking Wallachia and Moldavia put up a fierce resistance under leaders such as Vlad Tepes, 'the Impaler', prince of Wallachia, who inspired the legend of Count Dracula.

Albania was overrun in 1479. The Turks defeated Hungary in the Battle of Mohács in 1526, expanding their empire north and west of the Danube. In 1527 Croatia sought the protection of Austria, and remained under Austrian control until 1918. The Turks strengthened their hold on Bosnia-Herzegovina and by the mid 16th century were masters of most of the Balkans. The exceptions were Croatia and the Adriatic coast, where the Turkish fleet was decisively beaten in 1571 at Lepanto by the Christian League of Spanish, Venetian and Genoese ships.

The Turks added a fresh component – Islam – to the existing split between Catholic and Orthodox. Some Christians converted to their conquerors' faith, notably in the regions of modern Albania, Kosovo, Macedonia and Bosnia-Herzegovina. The region was economically and educationally backward, its people reduced to serfdom.

After their defeat at the gates of Vienna in 1683, the Ottomans were in slow retreat. They were driven from Hungary, and many Serbs trekked north into Vojvodina to gain the protection of the Habsburgs and the Austro-Hungarian Empire. European opinion became increasingly unhappy at Muslim domination of Balkan Christians.

Serbia rose against the Turks in 1815, gaining autonomy in 1829, though the last Turkish troops did not leave until 1867. The Greeks began a war of independence against the Turks in 1821. The English poet Lord Byron was among those who sought to help them, but he died of fever in Greece in 1823. The combined British, French and Russian fleets defeated the Turks at Navarino in 1827, and Greece gained its freedom two years later.

A Bulgarian revolt against Turkish rule in 1876 was brutally crushed, but in the same year Romania, helped by France and Russia, declared its independence from the Ottoman Empire. Serbia, Romania and Russia then declared war on Turkey, which

The tragedy of civil war in the Balkans: Croatian guardsmen and an elderly civilian woman take cover from Serbian troops opposed to Croatia's declaration of independence in June 1991.

Balkans mid 16th C
Ottoman Empire c.1572

In the mid 16th century the Ottoman Turks held large areas of south-east Europe

Balkans August 1914

By 1914 several Balkan states were independent nations.

Balkans 1996
boundary of former Yugoslavia

The collapse of communism created many new boundaries.

From the Ottoman Empire to a patchwork of modern republics, the Balkans has been bitterly fought over for most of the past 500 years.

allowed Bulgaria to become autonomous in 1878. Macedonia remained under Ottoman rule, but in the First Balkan War in 1912, Serbia, Greece and Bulgaria formed an alliance to liberate Macedonia and Albania. Turkey in Europe was reduced to a rump. A year later, the Balkan allies turned on each other. Serbia and Greece united against Bulgaria, which had claimed Macedonia for itself. At the same time, Serbia gained control of Kosovo from Albania.

These tensions triggered the First World War. Archduke Franz Ferdinand, heir to the Austro-Hungarian Empire, was assassinated by a Serb nationalist in Sarajevo in June 1914. Austria used the murder as a pretext to overrun Serbia. The Russians felt their position in the Balkans to be threatened and mobilised their armies, involving their British and French allies in war against the Central Powers – the Austro-Hungarian Empire and Germany.

THE RISE OF GERMANY

After the First World War, Vojvodina, Slovenia and Croatia joined with Serbia, Montenegro and Macedonia to form a new country, ruled by the King of Serbia. In 1929 its name was changed to Yugoslavia, meaning 'Land of southern Slavs'. Serbian domination of the government was bitterly resented by the minority peoples, notably the Croats. In 1934 the king was assassinated by Croatian nationalists, but the Serbians held on to power under the profascist regency which followed.

Adolf Hitler invaded Yugoslavia in 1941 and established a fascist puppet regime in Croatia. Armies of the promonarchist Chetniks and communist partisans under Marshal Tito fought the Germans and each other in a savage war of atrocity and counteratrocity in which a tenth of the population was killed.

Greece was overrun by the Germans in 1941. Bulgaria and Romania entered the war with the Germans, but both countries changed sides in 1944. In September 1944, in a truly Balkan twist of diplomacy, Bulgaria was simultaneously at war with Germany, the Soviet Union, Britain and the USA. With the exception of Greece, the Balkans was liberated by the Soviet Red Army, with the help of communist partisans in Yugoslavia and Albania.

Although the Greek monarchy survived a three-year civil war against communist guerrillas after 1946, communist dictatorships were established throughout the rest of the Balkans. The Albanian, Bulgarian, Romanian and Yugoslav monarchies were replaced by republics. With political dissidence crushed in single-party states, an impoverished stability was attained. But ethnic tensions were only partially submerged under the Tito-led regime which controlled Yugoslavia from 1945. Although the federal government was responsible for major policy areas such as defence, foreign policy, economy and human rights, other powers were devolved from 1970 to the six republics and two autonomous regions.

THE FALL OF COMMUNISM

The communist monopoly of power was broken in the aftermath of Mikhail Gorbachev's reforms in the Soviet Union. In November 1989, the day after the Berlin Wall was breached, the 35-year rule of the Bulgarian party leader Tidor Zhivkov ended. After a bloody uprising, the Romanian dictator Nicolae Ceauşescu and his wife Elena were executed in December the same year. In December 1990 the ramshackle communist regime in Albania agreed to allow opposition political parties to be formed.

After Tito's death in 1980, the unwieldy federal structure he had created to unite Yugoslavia proved unable to contain nationalist passions and economic crisis. In 1990, the Serbian nationalist leader Slobodan Miloševic campaigned to bring Kosovo and Vojvodina within Serbia, a move resisted by Kosovo's predominantly Muslim Albanians. In 1991, Croatia and Slovenia declared themselves independent, while fighting broke out between Croatians and Serbs of the Krajina region, who wished to join a 'Greater Serbia'. In Bosnia-Herzegovina, Serbs fought Muslims and Croatians. In December 1991 the federal president, Stipe Mesic, resigned and declared that 'Yugoslavia no longer exists'. Bosnia-Herzegovina and Macedonia declared independence in 1992. Several hundred thousand refugees fled as violence escalated beyond United Nations control.

Serbs under Radovan Karadžić 'ethnically cleansed' Bosnia of Croats and Muslims by forced evacuations and mass killings. UN sanctions were imposed on Serbia, and NATO air strikes were used on Bosnian Serb positions around the besieged city of Sarajevo. After much bloodshed, a peace accord was brokered at Dayton, Ohio, in December 1995, with a NATO-led Peace Implementation Force stationed in Bosnia. However, the patchwork of minorities throughout the region – Hungarians in Romanian Transylvania and Serbian Vojvodina; Turks in Bulgaria; Bulgars in Macedonia; Albanians in Kosovo; Serbs in Bosnia – suggested that the Balkans would remain as volatile as ever.

Balzac, Honoré de (1799-1850) French novelist and one of the world's great fiction writers. As a young lawyer's clerk, Balzac wrote a string of sensational potboilers under a variety of pseudonyms. His first successful book published in his own name was *Les Choans* (1829), an historical novel about Breton peasants. Balzac went on to write more than 90 novels and short stories, presenting a panoramic view of French life, from the peasantry and the provinces to the aristocratic salons of the capital. Among the best known are *Eugénie Grandet* (1833), *Le Père Goriot* (1834) and *Les Illusions Perdues* (1837-43). In 1834 Balzac conceived the notion of collecting his works together under the title *La Comédie Humaine*, creating a vast cycle of events and characters, some of whom appear in more than one book. Balzac's writing is characterised by his power of imagination and detailed observations – the latter quality heralding a new movement in French fiction-writing away from ROMANTICISM towards what came to be called naturalism.

Banda, Hastings (c.1902-) Malawian statesman, and president from 1966 to 1994. Son of a peasant in the British colony of Nyasaland, Banda went to the USA and Britain, where he trained and practised as a doctor. Returning to Nyasaland, he became politically active, was arrested for an alleged plot and imprisoned for a year. On his release, Banda attended the 1953 London conference which set up the Federation of Rhodesia and Nyasaland. When the Federation broke up in 1963, Banda became Nyasaland's first prime minister; a year later, with independence, Nyasaland changed its name to MALAWI.

In 1966 Banda was elected president, becoming president for life in 1971. His timid policies towards South Africa left him an isolated figure, and he was increasingly resented by younger Malawian politicians. Banda's popularity began to wane in the early 1990s as he continued to ignore calls for multiparty politics. In the run-up to the general election of 1992, 40 people were killed in strikes and riots. In May 1994 Banda was defeated in a general election, and was succeeded by Bakili Muluzi. He was put on trial in 1995 for the murder of four politicians in 1983 but acquitted.

Bandaranaike, Solomon (1899-1959) Prime minister of Ceylon (now SRI LANKA) from 1956 until his death. In 1952 he founded the Sri Lanka Freedom Party, and in 1956 formed an alliance with other socialist parties which swept to victory in the election that year. As prime minister, Bandaranaike promoted the Sinhalese language, Buddhism, socialism and neutrality, policies which alienated the Hindu Tamil minority. Assassinated by a Buddhist monk, he was succeeded by his

Rousing words from Robert Bruce rally his troops before the Battle of Bannockburn in 1314, in which the Scottish infantrymen crushed the larger but incompetently led English army.

widow, Sirimavo Bandaranaike, who thus became the world's first woman prime minister (1960-5 and 1970-7). In August 1994, the SLFP won enough seats for their daughter Chandrika Bandaranaike Kumaratunge to become prime minister. Within months she was elected president and her mother again took over the role of prime minister.

Bangladesh Country on the Indian subcontinent, formerly known as East Pakistan. The region is geographically and historically part of Greater BENGAL, which formed part of British India and was partitioned in 1947 to create West Bengal – a province of India – and East Pakistan, a province of PAKISTAN. Physically and culturally remote from western Pakistan, the Bengalis of East Pakistan became increasingly absorbed during the 1960s with the issue of regional autonomy. This reached a peak in 1970 when the Awami League, campaigning for greater autonomy for East Pakistan, won Pakistan's first general

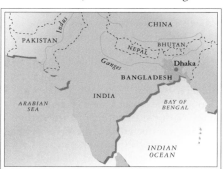

election. However, jubilation turned to frustration when the president of Pakistan's military government suspended the national assembly, and in March 1971 civil war broke out. Indian troops then intervened on the side

of the Bengalis and decisively defeated the Pakistani army in East Pakistan, leading in December to the formation of Bangladesh as a sovereign state with Sheik Mujibur Rahman as its first president. In 1974 famine brought chaos and political instability, resulting in Rahman's assassination the following year in the first of a succession of military coups.

Elections in 1991 restored civilian rule under prime minister Begum Zia, and the presidential system of government was replaced when a parliamentary constitution was adopted. Zia's government was troubled by strikes and mass protests and in a close-run election in 1996, Hasina Wajed, the daughter of Mujibur Rahman and leader of the Awami League, replaced him as prime minister. Bangladesh has suffered disastrous flooding during the annual monsoons, and is one of the world's poorest countries.

Bank of England British central bank, known as the 'Old Lady of Threadneedle Street', after the street in which its London offices stand. It was founded in 1694 as an undertaking by 1268 merchants to lend £1.2 million to William III so that he could finance his wars against France. In return the bank received 8 per cent interest and the right to issue notes against the security of the loan. The founding of the Bank of England, the earlier institution of the National Debt (a debt secured against the national income) and the setting up of the Stock Exchange in 1773 were part of a financial revolution in England. The rewards from financial speculation led investors away from land, the traditional source of wealth, towards the City of London, which became a centre of commercial activity and prosperity. Since the mid 19th century, the Bank of England has been the only English bank authorised to issue banknotes. It was formally nationalised in 1946 and since then has been a central instrument of the British Government's monetary strategies.

Bannockburn, Battle of (June 24, 1314)

Decisive battle between EDWARD II of England and Robert BRUCE of Scotland. The invading army of Edward, about 20000 strong, was overwhelmingly defeated at the Bannock Burn ('River') near Stirling. Edward lost half his army and was himself lucky to escape to safety. The battle ensured that Scotland kept its independence from England, which was formally recognised in 1328.

Bantu see NGUNI

Bantustan

Name for any of the 'Bantu homelands' compulsorily reserved for Black Africans under the former APARTHEID policy of the Republic of South Africa. The Bantu Self-Government Act of 1959 divided South Africa's Black population into separate nations and created ten Bantustans to be their national territories. The Bantu Homelands Constitution Act of 1971 established these territories as Separate Development Self-Governing Areas and envisaged eventual independence for them. Four Bantustans – Transkei in 1976, Bophuthatswana in 1977, Venda in 1979 and Ciskei in 1981 – were eventually granted 'independence', though this was never recognised by the international community. Each of the four began with a democratic constitution, and each suffered military coups and countercoups during the 1980s. The homelands policy began to be dismantled with the ending of apartheid and the democratic reforms which brought Nelson Mandela to power. Most have opted for full integration with South Africa, but a few, notably KwaZulu, are demanding some form of regional autonomy.

Baptist Church

Protestant Christian movement which practises adult baptism in the belief that only those who consciously accept the Christian faith can be accepted into its community. A number of Anabaptist groups arose in Europe in the 16th century (see ANABAPTISM), but the beginnings of the Baptist Church are generally traced to John Smyth, who established a church in Amsterdam in 1609, and Thomas Helwys who founded one in London in 1612. The Baptists insisted on the autonomy of local congregations from any kind of hierarchy of bishops or assemblies of presbyters, and in the 18th century they were recognised as dissenters from the Church of England.

Baptist churches grew rapidly in both Britain and America, and later spread their missions to India, Russia and many other countries. In the USA, Black Baptist churches flourished after the end of the American Civil War in 1865, making an important contribution to emerging Black culture.

Barbados

Easternmost island of the West Indies. It was probably reached by the conquistador Rodrigo de Bastidas in 1501, when it was still inhabited by CARIB and Arawak Indians. By the time the first British colony was established in 1627, Barbados was deserted and slaves had to be imported from Africa to work in the sugar industry that rapidly became the mainstay of the island's economy. In 1966 Barbados became an independent state within the Commonwealth.

Barbarossa (d.1546)

Nickname, meaning 'Redbeard', for the 16th-century Turkish corsair and OTTOMAN admiral Khayr ad-Din. He and his brother Aruj became notorious for their success in attacking Christian vessels in the Mediterranean. When Aruj was killed in 1518, Barbarossa served the sultan of Turkey. He captured Algiers in 1529 and in 1533 became grand admiral of the Ottoman fleet under SULEIMAN I, conquering all of Tunisia in 1534. The following year the Holy Roman Emperor CHARLES V recaptured Tunis, only for his fleet to be defeated by Barbarossa in 1538. Barbarossa died a hero in Istanbul. (See also FREDERICK I 'BARBAROSSA'.)

Barbarossa the corsair sailed the waters of the Mediterranean in the 16th century, terrorising shipping and plundering along its coasts.

Small boys arrive at a Dr Barnardo's home in 1875. Barnardo saw a need for 'orphanages' while working with the poor in the East End.

Bar Cochba, Simeon (d.AD 135)

Leader of the last great Jewish rebellion against Roman rule in AD132, born Simeon Bar Kosba. Emperor HADRIAN had outraged the Jews by prohibiting circumcision and by building a temple to Jupiter on the ruins of the Temple of Jerusalem, destroyed in AD70. The Jews rebelled under the leadership of Simeon Bar Kosba, who was hailed as the Messiah and given the name Bar Cochba (also spelt Kokhba) meaning 'Son of the Star'. For three years Hadrian struggled to reassert control. Bar Cochba was eventually killed in his stronghold at Bether south-west of Jerusalem after severe casualties on both sides.

Barebones Parliament

English assembly summoned by Oliver CROMWELL in July 1653, after he had dissolved the ineffectual RUMP PARLIAMENT. Cromwell believed he could work with a chosen group of honest patriots selected partly by army leaders and partly by congregations of 'godly men'. Known by its supporters as the Parliament of Saints, it was later named after one of its leaders: 'Praise-God' Barbon, or Barebones. The Parliament's attacks on the Court of Chancery and the Church of England alarmed many of the more moderate members, who resigned in December. The Parliament was dissolved and Cromwell became Lord Protector – in effect a dictator, but subject to the rule of law.

Barnardo, Thomas John (1845-1905)

British social reformer. Born in Dublin of a Spanish Protestant family, Barnardo moved to London in 1862. There he became concerned at the plight of deprived children and in 1870 established the first 'Dr Barnardo's Home' for destitute boys in the East End of London. A similar home for girls followed in 1876.

The evolution of banking from medieval to modern times

Banking has oiled the wheels of commerce since ancient times, developing commercially through the centuries to form what is today the financial cornerstone on which the world's economies depend.

Money was minted, exchanged and lent in the ancient world, but it was in medieval Italy, among its merchants and traders, that something akin to modern banking was first introduced. The *bancherius* was a moneychanger in late 12th-century Genoa who received deposits from local businessmen and dispensed credit; the *banchi di scritta* were 13th-century Venetians who not only took deposits but also, through a mechanism known as the bill of exchange, transferred payments from buyers to sellers. This phase culminated in the Medici bank with its headquarters in Florence. It was run as a powerful branch network by the charismatic Lorenzo de Medici until his death in 1492.

During the 18th century the Bank of England issued paper money, such as this £50 note (above). By the 19th century the Bank's Great Hall was a busy centre for the world's financiers and businessmen.

FROM CITY TO NATIONAL BANKS

The Genoese bankers remained important, but gradually the focus moved north to the Fuggers of Augsburg, a German financial dynasty. The key figure, Jacob Fugger 'the Rich' (1459-1525), was instrumental in financing the expansion of the Habsburg Empire under Charles V in the 16th century. He was descended from wool merchants who had also made a fortune from silver mining.

Commercial banking developed significantly in Europe over the next two centuries, led by goldsmith-bankers in London – moneychangers with whom merchants deposited their bullion for safekeeping – but it remained a fragmented, privately capitalised cottage industry, reflecting the preindustrial economy at large.

The breakthrough came with the introduction of state banks, the central banks of the future. The Bank of England led the way. Founded in 1694, its functions became diverse, and included

Moneychangers in medieval Italy give credit to merchants, in a miniature of the Veneto-Bolognese school (left).

acting as the government's day-to-day banker, lending to it during wartime, bringing order to the note issue (1844), and helping to develop the financial system. Today it acts as a banker to the clearing banks, implements monetary and exchange-rate policy and manages the national debt. Other central banks proliferated during the 19th century, and by the 1920s international central banking cooperation had become an indispensable part of the world order.

London in the early 19th century had replaced Amsterdam as the world's leading financial centre, and crucial to its continuing ascendancy until the First World War was the rise of the merchant banks. Barings, Rothschilds, Schroders,

Hambros, Lazards and Kleinworts were all internationally minded, risk-taking dynasties which gravitated towards London and did much to finance the industrialisation of the global economy. Barings was once described as the 'sixth great power' of Europe.

Joint-stock banking heralded a revolution in the 19th century. These banks were owned not privately, as had been the custom, but by a broad range of shareholders, permitting greater capitalisation and scope of operation. The use of cheques for drawing money and settling accounts became widespread.

MODERN BANKING SYSTEMS

By the 1920s banking systems across the developed world had become highly concentrated, hugely capitalised and sensitive to the wishes of the central banks. They offered a wide range of financial services and loan facilities, such as specialised services to private home-buyers. In Britain amalgamations led to the rise of the 'big four' clearing banks: Barclays, Lloyds, Midland and National Westminster. Some smaller banks remained, alongside those offering specialist services, including the savings and investment banks.

Barnado believed that every child deserved the best possible start in life and even went so far as to 'philanthropically abduct' children whose parents were cruel or violent. By the time of Barnardo's death nearly 60000 children had been cared for in more than 90 homes bearing his name throughout England.

baron In the Middle Ages, a tenant who held a barony (estate) direct from the monarch. During the 1290s under Edward I the status of barons changed: hereafter, the summons of barons to the Great Council (Parliament) was by royal writ and was no longer dependent on their tenure of land. The title of 'baron' was introduced by Richard II in 1387. In modern times, baron denotes a title of nobility ranking below a viscount or, in countries without viscounts, a count. The title is now also borne by life peers, first created in 1958.

Barons' Wars (1215-17; 1264-7) Civil wars fought in England between the Crown and most of the BARONS. In June 1215, King JOHN, faced with concerted opposition from the barons and the Church, was forced to concede MAGNA CARTA, the Great Charter of Rights. However, he quickly persuaded the pope to absolve him from this promise, which provoked his barons to offer the crown to Louis, Dauphin of France, who landed in Kent in May 1216. A major civil war was prevented by John's sudden death in October 1216 and the reissue of Magna Carta by the regent acting for John's nine-year-old son, who had become Henry III. In 1217 Louis and the remaining rebel barons were defeated at Lincoln and Sandwich.

Civil war broke out again in 1264 between the barons, led by Simon de MONTFORT, and Henry III after the king repudiated constitutional reforms agreed in 1258. After baronial forces captured the king at the Battle of Lewes in May 1264, de Montfort ruled England until killed by royalist forces under the future Edward I at the Battle of Evesham in August 1265. Hostilities ended in 1267 after a series of new treaties had been concluded.

barrow Large prehistoric burial mound – also called a tumulus if made of earth, or a cairn if made of stone. Barrows were commonly raised from about 3500 BC throughout Europe and parts of Asia. They enclosed burials, cremated ashes, or sometimes elaborate structures of stone or wood built as houses of the dead. Long barrows, such as those at West Kennet in southern England, were used for multiple burials and are typical of the NEOLITHIC age. Round barrows are mainly BRONZE AGE, IRON AGE or even ANGLO-SAXON and were intended as tombs for single highly placed individuals.

Barton, Sir Edmund (1849-1920) First prime minister of Australia. Born in Sydney, Barton was elected to the New South Wales legislature in 1879. Towards the end of the 19th century he emerged as one of the leaders of the Australian Federation Movement, which strove to unite the separate states of Australia. When this was achieved in 1901, with the creation of the Commonwealth of Australia, Barton was elected as the new country's prime minister. He resigned in 1903 to become a High Court judge.

The West Kennet long barrow in Wiltshire, England, contains five distinct burial chambers used by Neolithic settlers. The barrow is 330ft (100m) long, and has a turf-covered dome 6ft (2m) high.

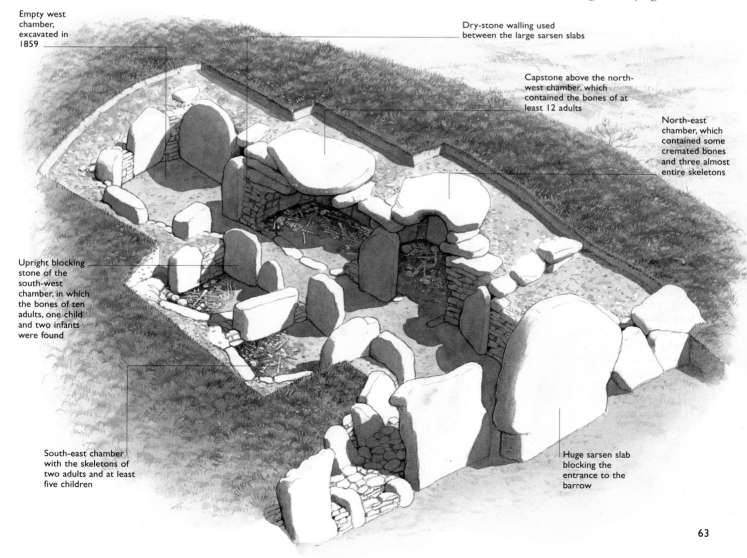

Empty west chamber, excavated in 1859

Dry-stone walling used between the large sarsen slabs

Capstone above the north-west chamber, which contained the bones of at least 12 adults

North-east chamber, which contained some cremated bones and three almost entire skeletons

Upright blocking stone of the south-west chamber, in which the bones of ten adults, one child and two infants were found

South-east chamber with the skeletons of two adults and at least five children

Huge sarsen slab blocking the entrance to the barrow

A contemporary painting shows Parisians storming the Bastille, four centuries after it was built to defend Paris against the English.

Bastille Medieval fortress in eastern Paris which was, in the 17th and 18th centuries, a state prison primarily used for holding political prisoners. The Bastille, a symbol of Bourbon tyranny, was attacked by crowds on July 14, 1789. Its governor and guards were killed, its seven prisoners released and the fortress demolished. The event is celebrated as the beginning of the FRENCH REVOLUTION, and Bastille Day is a French national holiday.

Batista, Fulgencio (1901-73) Cuban president and dictator overthrown in 1958 by Fidel CASTRO. Batista came to power after leading an army revolt against Cuba's provisional government in 1933. He was elected president in 1940 and ruled until 1944, establishing a strong government and overseeing rapid economic growth. After retiring to Florida, Batista saw Cuba descend into corruption and in 1952 returned to power in another military coup. This time, however, Batista's regime was brutally dictatorial, creating popular support for Castro's guerrilla army, which entered Havana in triumph on January 1, 1959.

Battenberg, Prince Louis (1854-1921) British admiral, grandfather of Prince Philip, Duke of Edinburgh. Of Polish-German descent, he became a naturalised British subject in 1868 and married Princess Victoria, granddaughter of Queen Victoria, in 1884. He was appointed First Sea Lord in 1912 but anti-German feeling in the early months of the First World War forced his resignation in

October 1914. He became a marquis in 1917, giving up his German titles and adopting the Anglicised name of Mountbatten.

Baudelaire, Charles (1821-67) French writer and poet. Having squandered his inheritance by the age of 23, Baudelaire started writing art criticism to earn a living. From 1852 he dedicated himself to translating the works of the American author Edgar Allan Poe, and in 1857 he published the only volume of his poetry to appear during his lifetime, *Les Fleurs du Mal* (*The Flowers of Evil*). Major preoccupations of the collection are the inescapable link between beauty and corruption, and the search for meaning in all manifestations of life, whether pure or defiled. The overt eroticism of some of the poems led to Baudelaire, his publisher and the printer being convicted of obscenity and fined in 1864. Baudelaire died disillusioned, but his work was soon acclaimed by poets of the Symbolist movement such as Stéphane Mallarmé, who saw it as paving the way for an entirely new mode of expression.

Bauhaus School of art, architecture and design founded in 1919 by the architect Walter Gropius at the German town of Weimar. Its staff included such eminent artists as Paul Klee, Wasily Kandinsky and Lázló Moholy-Nagy, who taught students to appreciate the relationship between pure artistic design and the requirements of industrial mass production. The characteristic Bauhaus style, in buildings, ornaments and furniture, was functional, geometric and severe, and was based on a close study of the materials being used. These ideas proved too revolutionary for the period, with the result that the Bauhaus was forced to move to Dessau in 1925 and to Berlin in 1932.

The following year Germany's Nazi government closed the school for good, though by then its philosophy had become influential throughout the world. Several Bauhaus teachers and students emigrated to the USA, where they continued to develop the principles of the German school.

Bavaria Largest of the Federal Republic of Germany's states, which from the late 12th century until 1918 was ruled by the Wittelsbach dynasty, first as a duchy and after 1805 as a kingdom. It suffered throughout the 18th century from the wars of the SPANISH SUCCESSION and AUSTRIAN SUCCESSION, and in 1796 and 1800 was occupied by France. In 1806 Bavaria was incorporated into Napoleon's CONFEDERATION OF THE RHINE, but before the Battle of Leipzig (1813) it joined the QUADRUPLE ALLIANCE against him. By the middle of the 19th century Bavaria had become one of the three most powerful states in the GERMAN CONFEDERATION, holding the balance of power between Austria and Prussia. The state was defeated by Prussia after siding

Bauhaus functionalism in the 1920s is exemplified by these staff houses, designed by Walter Gropius at the Bauhaus in Dessau, and the geometric-pattern poster advertising the school's exhibition.

Few remember Johnny and the Moondogs, but with a change of name and image in the early 1960s the same Liverpool pop group rocketed to the top of the charts and a place in history. The Beatles' exuberant new sound, haircuts and suits had enormous worldwide appeal.

with Austria in the Prussian-Austrian War of 1866, but four years later joined Prussia in the FRANCO-PRUSSIAN WAR. In the 1871 constitution of the German Second Empire, Bavaria won a greater degree of independence than any other state.

During the night of November 7-8, 1918, one of Europe's oldest dynasties ended when King Ludwig III was deposed by socialist leader Kurt Eisner, who declared Bavaria a republic. After Eisner was assassinated in 1919, Bavaria became a centre of right-wing politics leading to the first attempted Nazi revolution in 1923 (see MUNICH BEER-HALL PUTSCH). With the end of the Second World War, Bavaria became in 1948 a state in the Federal Republic of Germany.

Bavarian Succession, War of the (1778-9) War between Austria and Prussia resulting from Emperor JOSEPH II of Austria's ambition to add Bavaria to the HABSBURG dominions. When Maximilian Joseph of Bavaria died childless in 1777, the succession passed to Karl Theodor, Elector of the Palatinate, who agreed to sell a third of Bavaria to Joseph II. Prussia's FREDERICK II marched into Bohemia to oppose this plan and there encountered Joseph's army. However, little fighting took place, both armies concentrating on disrupting each other's supply lines. Prussian troops even spent their time digging up potatoes, hence the nickname of 'Potato War'. The Peace of Teschen (1779) ended the conflict by ceding the small but fertile Inn district to Austria.

Baxter, Richard (1615-91) English Puritan minister and author. He was ordained as an Anglican clergyman, becoming chaplain to a Roundhead regiment in 1645. In 1650 he published a devotional work, *The Saints' Everlasting Rest*. At the Restoration he became a royal chaplain but refused a bishopric. The 1662 Act of UNIFORMITY forced his resignation, and in about 1673 he took out a licence as a NONCONFORMIST minister. In 1685 he was imprisoned and fined by Judge George JEFFREYS for 'libelling the Church'.

Bayeux tapestry Large embroidered strip of rough linen showing events leading up to the Norman invasion of England and the Battle of HASTINGS in 1066. The so-called 'tapestry' is about 226 ft (69 m) long and is arranged in a similar way to a modern strip cartoon, with one episode succeeding another in more than 70 scenes.

The tradition that the tapestry was made by William the Conqueror's wife, Queen Matilda, and her handmaidens has been generally discounted. The tapestry is now believed to have been commissioned by Odo, William's half-brother, the bishop of Bayeux in Normandy, and embroidered in an English monastery (perhaps at Canterbury) between about 1067 and 1077 as a triumphant decoration for Bayeux Cathedral.

Bayezid I (c.1360-1403) Ottoman sultan who succeeded his father Murad I and swiftly conquered Bulgaria, parts of Serbia, Macedonia and Thessaly and most of Asia Minor, earning the name Yildirim ('Lightning'). He then blockaded Constantinople from 1394 to 1401 and defeated a Christian army at Nicopolis in 1396. His thrust into eastern Asia Minor, however, brought him to disaster: in 1402 he was defeated by TAMERLANE at Ankara and died in captivity.

Bay of Pigs Bay on the south-west coast of Cuba where a small force of Cuban exiles landed on April 17, 1961, in an attempt to overthrow the Marxist regime of Fidel CASTRO. The exiles had been trained by the US CENTRAL INTELLIGENCE AGENCY but they were swiftly crushed by Castro's troops. The incident was a grave blow to the prestige of the USA and President Kennedy; it also led to Castro strengthening his country's links with the Soviet Union.

Beaker Culture Term for a wide variety of people living in western Europe from about 3000 BC. They are named after the fine, bell-shaped pottery drinking vessels that are found in graves from Spain to northern Germany and from Hungary to Britain. The theory that the wide distribution of these beakers indicated that a single group of people, called 'Beaker Folk', arose in Spain and migrated across Europe in search of metals is no longer accepted by experts. The beakers were probably valuable status symbols since they were buried with their owners along with other items of wealth.

Beatles, The British pop group that achieved worldwide popularity in the 1960s. By this time the group's members were John Lennon, Paul McCartney, George Harrison and Ringo Starr (Richard Starkey). The Beatles' first record, *Love Me Do*, became an instant hit in 1962, and within a year they were followed everywhere by shrieking adolescent fans – a phenomenon that came to be known as 'Beatlemania'. The huge success of most of the Beatles' records allowed them to experiment with unconventional musical forms from 1967. In that year the innovative

Sgt Pepper's Lonely Hearts Club Band marked a new phase in the group's output, winning them admiration from a new serious audience. The Beatles also made several films, including *A Hard Day's Night* (1964), *Help!* (1965) and *Let it Be* (1970). The group disbanded in 1970. Ten years later John Lennon was murdered in New York. In 1995 and 1996 the surviving Beatles brought out two retrospective recordings containing previously unreleased songs by Lennon.

Beatty, David, 1st Earl (1871-1936) British admiral. He earned rapid promotion for his daring leadership in campaigns in North Africa and in the BOXER RISING in China (1900). In 1913 Beatty took command of Britain's battle-cruiser squadrons, achieving minor victories over the German navy at Heligoland (1914) and Dogger Bank (1915). In 1916 he played a major role in the Battle of JUTLAND, and in 1918 as commander-in-chief of the Grand Fleet he received the German naval surrender. After the war Beatty served as First Sea Lord from 1919 to 1927.

Beaufort English noble family descended from three illegitimate sons of John of GAUNT, Duke of Lancaster and fourth son of Edward III. The children were declared legitimate by their half-brother Henry IV, who helped them to become powerful and wealthy. By 1471, however, the entire male line had died or been killed in the Wars of the ROSES. Yet when Henry Tudor

(later Henry VII, and founder of the Tudor dynasty) claimed the English throne, he did so on the basis of his LANCASTRIAN heritage, which he traced through his mother, Margaret Beaufort, who was great-granddaughter of John of Gaunt.

Beauregard, Pierre (1818-93) US Confederate general. Beauregard was appointed superintendent of West Point military academy in 1860, but resigned at the outbreak of the American Civil War to join the Southern Confederacy. As commander at Charleston, he ordered the first shot of the war against FORT SUMTER. He was field commander in the Confederate victory at the first battle of Bull Run in 1861, but suffered a major defeat at Shiloh the following year. For much of the rest of the war Beauregard had limited influence, owing to ill-health and bad relations with President Jefferson DAVIS.

Beaverbrook, Maxwell Aitken, Baron (1879-1964) Financier, statesman and newspaper baron. Born in Canada, Beaverbrook amassed a fortune as a stockbroker and financier before moving to Britain in 1910. There he entered politics as a Conservative and was soon elected to parliament. In 1916 he played a pivotal role in overthrowing Herbert Asquith and manoeuvring war secretary David Lloyd George into the premiership. In 1917 he received a peerage. The following year Beaverbrook was appointed minister of information, and during the Second World War he served in Winston Churchill's Cabinet as minister of aircraft production (1940-1), minister of supply (1941-2) and Lord Privy Seal (1943-5). After the war Beaverbrook devoted himself to the newspaper empire he had been establishing over the previous decades. In 1919 he had taken over the London *Daily Express*, which he made into the most widely read newspaper in the world. He then founded the London *Sunday Express* and bought the London *Evening Standard* and the Glasgow *Evening Citizen*, using these newspapers to campaign for free trade and strong unity within the British Empire.

> **DID YOU KNOW?**
>
> *The newspaper magnate Lord Beaverbrook was caricatured as 'Lord Copper' in Evelyn Waugh's satirical novel Scoop, published in 1938.*

After canonisation Thomas Becket was portrayed throughout all of Western Christendom in religious manuscripts such as this.

Bechuanaland see BOTSWANA

Becket, St Thomas (1118-70) Archbishop of Canterbury, martyr and saint. Born in London and educated in Paris and Bologna, Becket was appointed chancellor of England in 1154. He became a close friend of HENRY II, whom he served ably as statesman and diplomat until 1162, when Henry made him Archbishop of Canterbury. Becket then emerged as a staunch defender of the rights of the Church, coming into conflict with the king at the councils of Westminster, Clarendon and Northampton between 1163 and 1164, particularly over Henry's wish to try in the lay courts clergy who had already been convicted in an ecclesiastical court (see BENEFIT OF CLERGY). Becket then refused to endorse the Constitutions of CLARENDON, which further challenged the authority of the Church, and went into exile in France.

On his return in 1170, Becket excommunicated a number of bishops, including the Archbishop of York, who had participated in a ceremony to crown Henry's eldest son joint king of England. This infuriated the king, who reputedly shouted: 'Will no one rid me of this turbulent priest?' Accordingly four knights took Henry at his word and murdered Becket in Canterbury Cathedral on December 29, 1170. Becket was acclaimed a martyr and canonised in 1173, his tomb becoming one of Europe's most important centres of pilgrimage.

Bede, the Venerable, St (673-735) Early English scholar and author, best remembered for his *Ecclesiastical History of the English People*, written in Latin in 731. Bede received his education from the age of seven at the Northumbrian monasteries of Wearmouth and Jarrow. Here he wrote the lives of five abbots, several biblical commentaries, hymns, verse, books on astronomy, letters and a martyrology of 114 saints. He also popularised a new chronology dating events from the birth of Christ (AD). A synod at Aachen posthumously awarded Bede the title 'Venerable' in 836.

Bedford, John of Lancaster, Duke of (1389-1435) Third son of Henry IV of England. John was made Lieutenant of the Kingdom on several occasions while his brother Henry V campaigned in France during the HUNDRED YEARS' WAR. After Henry's death in 1422, John was appointed Guardian of England and Regent of France. He successfully commanded the English armies in several battles against the French, but in 1429 was forced to raise his siege of Orléans by Joan of Arc. In 1431 he had Joan burnt at the stake and crowned Henry VI king of France.

Beethoven, Ludwig van (1770-1827)

German composer, one of the giant figures of European music and a major influence in the development of musical forms from the Classical period to ROMANTICISM. Born in Bonn, the son and grandson of musicians, Beethoven himself became a professional musician before he was 12. In 1787 he studied briefly under MOZART, and in 1792 he moved to Vienna to become a pupil of Joseph HAYDN. In Vienna Beethoven soon secured generous aristocratic patrons by his virtuoso piano playing, but from 1801 increasing deafness forced him to concentrate on composition.

The first major landmark in Beethoven's development was his Third Symphony (the *Eroica*) of 1803-4, a work of titanic energy which breaks many of the established conventions of classical music and develops simple themes into immense musical structures. This was followed by many of Beethoven's most popular works, among them his Fifth and Sixth symphonies (1808) and his Fifth Piano Concerto (the *Emperor*, 1809). He completed his only opera, *Fidelio*, in 1814.

Many of these compositions demonstrate Beethoven's view of the composer as a Romantic artist expressing his own creative soul or genius, rather than a craftsman fulfilling the requests of patrons. Among his final works, the *Missa Solemnis* (1818-23), the Ninth (*Choral*) Symphony (1817-23) and the late string quartets show Beethoven at his most intense and innovative.

Begin, Menachem (1913-92)

Israeli statesman and prime minister, born in Belorussia. Begin was active in the ZIONIST movement in Poland in the 1930s, and was sent with the Polish army-in-exile to Palestine in 1942. There he eventually commanded the IRGUN, a terrorist group dedicated to establishing a Jewish state in Palestine.

When the state of Israel was created in 1948 the Irgun became the Herut ('Freedom') Party with Menachem Begin as its leader. In 1970 Begin became joint chairman of the Likud ('Unity') coalition, and in 1977 was made prime minister after Likud won the general election. Ending hostilities that had most recently broken out in the YOM KIPPUR WAR of 1973, Begin negotiated a peace treaty with President Anwar SADAT of Egypt, for which they shared the Nobel peace prize in 1978. Begin resigned in 1983 as a result of national and international opposition to Israel's invasion of Lebanon.

Belarus

Country in eastern Europe also known as Byelarus, formerly Belorussia ('White Russia'). During the 14th century the area became part of the duchy of Lithuania, which was itself incorporated with Poland in the 16th century. The three-fold division of Poland in the late 18th century consigned

A proud Menachem Begin, his dream of an Israeli state realised, speaks to a gathering of his fellow Israelis in Jerusalem in 1948.

Belorussia to the Russian empire. It suffered large-scale devastation during Napoleon's invasion of Russia in 1812, the First World War, the Soviet-Polish War of 1919-21 and the Second World War. In 1921 the Treaty of Riga ceded western Belorussia to Poland and in 1922 the eastern territories joined the Soviet Union as the Belorussian Soviet Socialist Republic. A Soviet invasion in 1939 reunited these two regions. In 1991 the Belorussian republic declared its independence from the Soviet Union, becoming the Republic of Belarus. In four referenda in 1995, however, Belarussians voted in favour of establishing closer links with Russia than it had when it was part of the Soviet Union.

Belgae

Large group of Celtic tribes living in the northern Rhineland, the Low Countries, northern France (Gaul) and southern England in the 2nd and 1st centuries BC. The Belgae were a resourceful people who put up fierce resistance to the Romans and whom the Romans soon learned to respect. Within a century of Julius Caesar's conquest of Gaul in 50 BC, Belgic noblemen were admitted to the Roman senate. Present-day Belgium takes its name from the Belgae.

Belgium

Country in north-west Europe, renowned in the Middle Ages for the wealth of its free merchant cities. In the 15th century the region was part of the Duchy of BURGUNDY, before being absorbed by the HABSBURG empire of MAXIMILIAN I in 1477.

Between 1504 and 1713 the territory was ruled by Spain, from 1713 to 1795 by Austria, and then by France. In 1815, it became a province of the kingdom of the Netherlands and in 1830 was declared independent following a national revolution. The following year Prince Leopold of Saxe-Coburg was elected King of the Belgians. An international treaty drawn up in 1839 guaranteed Belgian neutrality, but this was ignored by Germany in 1914 and again in 1940. Constitutional reforms introduced in 1971 divided Belgium into a federation of semiautonomous regions: Flemish-speaking Flanders, French-speaking Wallonia and bilingual Brussels – the headquarters of the North Atlantic Treaty Organisation (NATO) and the European Community (EU). When King Baudouin died in 1993 he was succeeded by his brother, Albert II.

Belisarius (AD 505-65)

East Roman (Byzantine) general, who for a time reversed the ailing fortunes of the Roman Empire. In 530 Belisarius defeated Persian invaders in the east and four years later conquered the VANDALS in North Africa. Between 535 and 540 he recaptured most of Italy from the Ostrogoths, including Naples, Ravenna and Rome, where the Goths surrendered on condition that Belisarius become their emperor. This resulted in his hurried recall by Emperor JUSTINIAN. In 559 Belisarius saved Constantinople from the HUNS, but never again had Justinian's full confidence.

Belize

Formerly British Honduras, a heavily forested country on the Caribbean coast of Central America. The British settled there in the 17th century, proclaiming the area a crown colony in 1862 under the jurisdiction of the governor of Jamaica. In 1964 the colony gained complete internal self-government. It adopted the name Belize in 1973, and in 1981 became an independent state within the British Commonwealth. Guatemala, which borders it on the west and south, had always claimed the territory on the basis of old Spanish treaties, but in 1991 recognised Belize's independence. As a result Britain withdrew most of its troops in 1993.

Bell, Alexander Graham (1847-1922)

Scottish-born US scientist, best known as the inventor of the telephone. In 1872 Bell went to the USA, where he became professor of vocal physiology at Boston University. Together with Thomas Watson, a mechanic, he experimented with ways of transmitting speech electrically, and in 1876 patented the first telephone. The following year Bell founded his own successful telephone company. Later he made improvements to Thomas EDISON's phonograph to develop the graphophone, a practical sound-recording device using wax cylinders and discs. In addition to many other research projects, Bell spent much of his life promoting and developing a system, pioneered by his father, for teaching deaf people to speak.

Belshazzar (6th century BC) Son of Nabonidus, the last Chaldean king of BABYLON. When Nabonidus went campaigning in Arabia in about 550 BC, he left Belshazzar as his regent in Babylon. In 539 BC, however, the city fell to CYRUS II of Persia and Belshazzar was killed.

According to the (historically incorrect) Biblical version (Daniel 5:7-8), Belshazzar was the son of NEBUCHADNEZZAR. At a great feast he committed sacrilege by using sacred vessels looted from the Temple of Jerusalem and was astonished when the mysterious Hebrew words *Mene Mene Tekel Upharsin* appeared on the wall. The prophet Daniel interpreted the supernatural message as a divine judgment announcing the imminent downfall of Babylon and its king.

Benares see VARANASI

Ben Bella, Ahmed (c.1918-) Algerian revolutionary leader and statesman. Ben Bella served in the French army during the Second World War, but in 1947 became a leader of the extremist Algerian nationalist movement, the 'Special Organisation'. He was imprisoned by the French in 1950 for revolutionary activities, but escaped to Cairo where he founded the National Liberation Front (FLN), which began a concerted guerrilla war against France. In 1956 Ben Bella was again interned and released only when Algeria won its independence in 1962. He was then elected his country's first prime minister, becoming president a year later. In 1965 Ben Bella was deposed in a military coup by Colonel Houari Boumedienne and imprisoned until 1979. He returned to Algeria in 1990 after nine years in exile.

Benedictines Monks and nuns belonging to the Roman Catholic Order of St Benedict (OSB), a confederation of autonomous abbeys which adhere to the rule laid down by St BENEDICT OF NURSIA. The order grew rapidly after the founding of the first Benedictine abbey at Monte Cassino in about 525, reaching its peak of prestige and influence in the 10th and 11th centuries. By then there were several thousand Benedictine abbeys throughout Europe, of which the Burgundian Abbey of CLUNY was the most illustrious. Throughout this period the Benedictines played a vital role as scholars, educators and guardians of learning, while at the same time striving to live a life of prayer detached from worldly concerns. From the middle of the 12th century the Benedictine order went

Rembrandt portrays alarm on the faces of Belshazzar and his guests as they read the phantom Hebrew message that presages the fall of Babylon to the Persian army in the 6th century BC.

through several periods of decline and revival, but since the middle of the 19th century the movement has generally flourished.

Benedict of Nursia, St (c.480-c.550) Founder of the BENEDICTINE order of monks, which was later to include nuns. Benedict established a monastery at Monte Cassino in central Italy in about 525, and here drew up his monastic rule, setting out how monasteries should be run and how monks should lead their lives. The qualities and actions expected of a monk were principally humility, prayer, work, obedience, silence and solitude. Benedict's rule was later organised into a system by St Benedict of Aniane (c.750-821), whose code received official approval in 817 as the basis for reforming French monastic houses.

benefit of clergy Privilege of the Church in medieval Europe which allowed clergy, nuns and monks accused of crimes to be dealt with by ecclesiastical courts, which usually treated them with more leniency than secular courts. It was a system open to abuse, and in England it was a major issue in the struggle between Archbishop Thomas BECKET and HENRY II. Benefit of clergy was largely conceded by the Crown in the aftermath of Becket's murder in 1170. Later, its application was limited by various Acts of Parliament. Benefit of clergy was abolished in 1827.

Beneš, Eduard (1884-1948) Czechoslovak statesman. Together with Tomáš MASARYK, Beneš helped to found CZECHOSLOVAKIA in 1918, becoming his country's foreign minister in the same year. In an attempt to keep the BALANCE OF POWER in eastern Europe, he formed the Little Entente with Yugoslavia in

1921 to enforce observance of the VERSAILLES PEACE SETTLEMENT by Hungary and to prevent a restoration of the Habsburg dynasty. In 1935 Beneš succeeded Masaryk as president, a position he held until 1938 when the MUNICH PACT partitioned Czechoslovakia. After spending the Second World War in exile, Beneš returned as president in 1945, but resigned in 1948 when a communist coup backed by Joseph Stalin brought in a new government under Klement GOTTWALD.

Bengal Region of the north-east Indian subcontinent on the deltas of the Ganges and Brahmaputra rivers. From the 8th to the 12th

St Benedict replaced the severity of monastic life with moderation. In this 16th-century fresco he and his monks share a simple meal.

centuries Bengal was governed by Buddhist dynasties, then by Muslim governors of the DELHI sultanate, before becoming part of the MUGHAL empire in 1576. With the decline of the Mughals in the 18th century, the nawabs of Bengal enjoyed a brief period of autonomy, until ousted by the British. In 1757 General Robert CLIVE seized Calcutta and defeated the Nawab of Bengal at the Battle of PLASSEY — the first steps towards British control of Bengal and expansion into the rest of India. With the end of British rule in 1947 Bengal was partitioned into West Bengal, a province of India, and East Pakistan, a province of Pakistan. In 1971 East Pakistan became the independent state of BANGLADESH.

Ben-Gurion, David (1886-1973) Popular first prime minister of Israel, often referred to as the 'Father of the Nation'. Born in Russian Poland, Ben-Gurion migrated to Palestine in 1906, which was then part of the OTTOMAN EMPIRE. He worked as a farmer in Galilee, but was expelled by the Turks at the outbreak of the First World War for political activities, returning in 1917 with the British army's Jewish Legion.

Ben-Gurion then set to work to make the vision of a Jewish homeland, as promised by Britain's BALFOUR DECLARATION, a reality. As part of his campaign for greater Jewish immigration to Palestine Ben-Gurion became secretary of the General Federation of Jewish Labour (Histadrut) in 1921 and, in 1930, leader of the Labour Party (Mapai). In 1939 Ben-Gurion led opposition to Britain's attempts to restrict further Jewish immigration to Palestine, and in 1948 he became first prime minister as well as minister of defence of the new state of ISRAEL. He retired from both positions in 1953, but took them on again from 1955 to 1963. In 1965 he founded Rafi, a small party opposed to Mapai, which he led until retiring from politics in 1970.

Benin Country in West Africa known until 1975 as Dahomey. From the 13th century the area formed part of the powerful trading kingdom of Benin, and had a highly developed artistic tradition (see feature, page 70). In the 1890s Benin was divided between French and British colonial powers. In 1900 its eastern region was incorporated in the protectorate of Southern NIGERIA, while in 1904 the western region became part of French West Africa, under the name Dahomey. After becoming an independent republic in 1960, Dahomey suffered a turbulent period of alternating military and civilian rule. In 1972 the country was declared a Marxist-Leninist state under the presidency of Mathieu Kérékou, and in 1975 it changed its name to Benin.

Benin's first free elections, held in 1991, were won by the former World Bank economist Nicephore Soglo, who moved Benin

Jeremy Bentham's clothed skeleton is preserved at University College, London, and is brought out for council meetings. The head is a wax model. His real head, mummified, lies between his feet.

towards a free market economy. In March 1996, however, Kérékou made a comeback, narrowly winning the presidential vote.

Bentham, Jeremy (1748-1832) British philosopher, best known for proposing the ethical and political system of UTILITARIANISM — the theory that the morality of an action can be measured by its effects on people: the best action is one which results in the greatest happiness and the least pain for the greatest number of people. Bentham argued that all institutions and laws should be judged by the extent to which they fulfil these criteria. He also wrote extensively on economic and legal issues, argued passionately in favour of the French Revolution, campaigned for prison reform and helped to found University College, London. Bentham's most important works are *A Fragment on Government* (1776) and *Introduction to the Principles of Morals and Legislation* (1789).

Bentinck, Lord William (1774-1839) British statesman who served as the first governor-general of all India from 1833 to 1835. Bentinck was a liberal reformer who introduced the use of English, in place of Persian and Sanskrit, in Indian courts, and brought about many educational reforms. He also abolished the Hindu practice of suttee, which required a widow to die on her husband's funeral pyre, and suppressed the THUGS – a Hindu sect of assassins and robbers.

Benz, Karl (1844-1929) German engineer who in 1885 designed and built the first car to be powered by an internal combustion engine. Known as the *Motorwagen*, Benz's first car was a three-wheeled vehicle; it was replaced with a four-wheeled car in 1893. In 1926 Benz's company merged with DAIMLER to form Daimler-Benz, makers of today's Mercedes-Benz vehicles (see feature, page 115).

Berbers People who have lived in northern and north-western Africa since prehistoric times. Renowned for their fierce independence and austere way of life, the Berbers were mentioned by the Greek historian HERODOTUS as early as the 5th century BC. They frequently rebelled against Roman colonial rule, but were conquered in the 7th century by Arab invaders, from whom they adopted the Islamic faith. The Berbers played an important role in the 8th-century invasion of Spain, where they supported the UMAYYAD dynasty. They later set up several dynasties of their own, of whom the Almohads and the Almoravids were the most important. Today the Berbers are scattered across North Africa, but constitute the majority population of Morocco. Most are farmers, but many still follow a nomadic or semi-nomadic way of life.

Beria, Lavrenti (1899-1953) Director of the Soviet secret police who organised large-scale purges of Joseph STALIN's political opponents. Born in Georgia, Beria joined the Communist Party in 1917 and became head of Lenin's secret police, the CHEKA, in Georgia in 1921. From 1936 to 1938 Beria conducted political purges for Stalin in the Transcaucasian republics. He was then appointed head of the People's Commissariat for Internal Affairs, or NKVD – the Soviet secret police. Here he immediately organised a purge of the police bureaucracy and set about expanding the system of prison labour camps (or gulags) throughout the country. In 1941 Beria was appointed a deputy prime minister of the

Lavrenti Beria, a guest at Joseph Stalin's dacha in 1935, holds his host's daughter Svetlana on his lap. Stalin studies documents at the table.

A blossoming civilisation in the West African rain forests

In the tropical rain forests of south-western Nigeria, the Edo kingdom of Benin flourished from the 13th century to the 19th century, developing a unique identity and producing some of the world's great works of art.

At its height, during the European Middle Ages, the Edo kingdom of Benin in the West African rain forests extended from the River Niger in the east to Lagos in the west, and beyond. It produced objects now acknowledged as works of art comparable in quality and sophistication with any in the world. Its political and religious ruler was the Oba of Benin, the kingdom's capital city. (Historical Benin is not the same as the Republic of Benin, a recently renamed nation 250 miles to the west.) The current oba can still trace his descent from the dynasty's founder, who came from the sacred Yoruba city of Ife some time before the 14th century.

ROYAL PATRONAGE OF ART

When the Portuguese first visited Benin City early in the 16th century, they found a powerful nation that was expanding its borders by military prowess and alliance. Benin compared favourably with any European city of the time. Rebuilt by Oba Ewuare in the late 15th century, it had broad streets leading to the oba's palace, itself as large as a European town. The palace and city were surrounded by earthen ramparts covering 2500 sq miles (6476 km²) – the world's largest man-made structure after the Great Wall of China.

Ewuare was the first great warrior king of the Edo. He established a sophisticated hierarchy of chieftains through whom he exercised his power over the kingdom, and developed the court's ceremonial, introducing the coral regalia of kingship supposedly wrested from the sea god Olokun. Under his rule and that of his successors there was a flowering of the arts in ivory, brass, iron, and wood. The work was produced by guilds of artisans who served the palace: ivory and brass were reserved exclusively for the oba and his chiefs, for shrines and ceremonial uses.

The Portuguese had arrived on the coast in search of pepper, ivory, cloth, metals and slaves. They brought with them, among other goods, manillas – bracelets made from brass. The increased supply of the alloy allowed the Edo to expand their output of brass castings using a 'lost wax' method they had developed before contact with Europeans. The castings, whether of memorial heads or plaques, were exceptional in their range and visual power, both as works of art and as religious or ceremonial objects.

The plaque form of brass casting originated in the 16th century to depict ceremonial events. The

A figure of the oba with his symbols of office would be set on an ancestral altar and worshipped. It was removed by its loop for polishing.

plaques were nailed to pillars in the palace. Some 900 survive dating from the 16th and 17th centuries.

At the beginning of the 18th century Oba Akenzua I halted a period of decline by increasing trade with the Dutch, especially in ivory, and by strengthening the religious aspects of kingship. This ritual emphasis resulted in more stylised forms of brass casting.

BENIN'S LIVING TRADITIONS

During the 19th century increasing British influence reduced the power of the Edo kingdom. In 1897 a punitive expedition, sent in retaliation for a massacre of British envoys, occupied the capital and banished the king, Oba Ovoramwen. Several thousand art works in metal, ivory, terracotta and textiles from the palace of the oba were taken to England. It was among the first African art to arrive in the West in quantity, and its skill and artistry astounded the public. Pieces soon found their way onto the international art market, and hold the record at auction as the most valuable to come from Africa.

These disasters did not destroy the kingdom. Seventeen years later the next oba, Eweka II, rebuilt the palace and commissioned new brass castings and other works of art to continue the traditions of the Edo kingdom. Skilled brass casters and ivory carvers are still active, and retain a special relationship with the oba.

Among the works of art produced by Benin's sculptors was a lifelike brass head for the oba's palace (left) and a stylised plaque commemorating a battle victory.

USSR, and in 1945 he became a marshal of the Union. After Stalin's death in March 1953, Beria attempted to manoeuvre himself into power, but was defeated by a coalition led by Georgi Malenkov, Vyacheslav Molotov and Nikita Khrushchev. He was accused of treason, and tried and executed in secret. Beria is thought to be responsible for the deaths of millions of people, including those who died in the infamous gulags.

Berlin airlift (1948-9) Massive British and US airlift of supplies into Berlin after the city had been blockaded by Soviet forces in one of the early crises of the COLD WAR. In June 1948 the USA, Britain and France announced a currency reform in their zones of occupied Germany – including the sectors they administered in Berlin. The Soviet Union, fearing that this was a prelude to the unification of these zones, retaliated by closing all land and water routes to Berlin, which lay behind the East German border within the Soviet zone. The Western Allies responded by organising a round-the-clock airlift of supplies to their sectors of Berlin. In all, they made more than 275 000 flights during the siege, which lasted for nearly a year until May 1949 when the Russians reopened surface routes to the city. The confrontation led to Berlin, and Germany, being divided into two administrative units: East and West.

Berlin, Congress of (1878) Conference held in Berlin by the major European powers to revise the Treaty of San Stefano (1878), which had ended the Russo-Turkish war of 1877-8. Under the chairmanship of the German chancellor Otto von BISMARCK, the congress sought to placate Britain by giving it the right to occupy Cyprus and by limiting Russian naval expansion. It also allowed Austria-Hungary to occupy Bosnia and Herzegovina, reduced Bulgaria to one-third of its former size, and gave Montenegro, Romania and Serbia their independence from Turkey.

The British prime minister Benjamin DISRAELI claimed that the congress had achieved 'peace with honour' but Russia, Serbia, Greece and Bulgaria were all dissatisfied with the results of the congress.

Berlin Wall Barrier built across Berlin by the communist East German government to stem the flood of refugees fleeing to the more prosperous West. Between 1945 and 1961 more than 2.5 million people had defected to the West, seriously threatening the East German economy. In August 1961 the communists closed the 80 crossing points in the city, sealed border buildings and erected a

barbed-wire barrier, which was gradually replaced by a 20 ft (6 m) concrete wall, guarded by troops with instructions to shoot to kill. Ninety-two people were killed trying to cross the wall and many others wounded. Hundreds more died attempting to flee to the West from East Germany. In November 1989 the wall was unexpectedly opened following popular pressure for political reform in East Germany. Soon afterwards the East German government collapsed, and within a few months large sections of the wall had been demolished. During the 28 years that it stood, the wall was the virtual embodiment of the IRON CURTAIN and a stark reminder of the COLD WAR between East and West.

Bermuda Group of about 150 islands in the north-western Atlantic Ocean administered as a self-governing British colony. The islands were discovered in the early 16th century by the Spanish navigator Juan Bermúdez (after whom they were named), but not colonised until a group of English settlers en route to Virginia were shipwrecked there in 1609. The first parliament in the New World was established in Bermuda in 1620, four years after Indian and African slaves began arriving to work on the islands' tobacco plantations. From 1797 Bermuda was an important British naval base, and since 1941 it has housed US air and naval bases as well. A new constitution granted Bermuda a considerable degree of self-government in 1968, but demands for complete independence from Britain continued to grow. In 1973 the governor Sir Richard Sharples was assassinated, and in 1977 political murders and riots led to official efforts to end all racial discrimination. In a referendum held in August 1995 islanders voted for Bermuda to remain a British colony.

DID YOU KNOW?
The shipwreck of colonists in Bermuda in 1609 is thought to have given Shakespeare the inspiration for his play The Tempest two years later.

Bernadotte, Folke, Count (1895-1948) Swedish diplomat and international mediator. The nephew of Gustav V of Sweden, Bernadotte headed the Swedish Red Cross during the Second World War, establishing himself as a skilled and impartial negotiator. In May 1948 he was appointed as UN mediator between Israel and the Arab states that had invaded it at independence. He arranged a ceasefire but outraged some Israelis by suggesting that Arab refugees should be allowed to return to their homes in Israel. In September he and another UN observer were murdered by Jewish extremists.

Bernard of Clairvaux, St (1090-1153) Theologian and reformer who was one of the most influential churchmen of his age. Though he was born into a noble Burgundian

Machine-gunned as he tried to scramble over the Berlin Wall in August 1962, 18-year-old Peter Fechter was left dying for an hour before East German police retrieved his body.

family, Bernard decided on a life of religious study and austerity. In 1112 he entered the CISTERCIAN monastery at Cîteaux and in 1115 founded a new monastery at Clairvaux, which he made into a model for reformed monastic houses. Under Bernard's influence the Cistercian order grew rapidly. He was also a prolific writer and a frequent participant in theological councils and debates. In 1146, at the request of Pope Eugenius III, Bernard preached in support of the Second CRUSADE. A fervent mystical thinker, Bernard clashed with the more intellectual approach of the philosopher Peter ABELARD, whom he helped to convict of heresy.

Berwick, Treaties of Three treaties between England and Scotland named after the border town of Berwick-upon-Tweed where they were signed. The first, on October 3, 1357, arranged for the English to release David II of Scotland in return for a ransom of 100 000 marks. The second treaty, on February 27, 1560, pledged English military aid for Scottish Protestants so that they could overthrow the Catholic regent Mary of Guise. The third treaty, on June 18, 1639, ended the first (bloodless) Bishops' War between Charles I and the Scottish COVENANTERS who opposed Charles's attempts to impose the 1637 prayer book on Scotland.

Bessemer, Sir Henry (1813-98) British inventor and engineer who in 1856 developed a process for mass-producing cheap steel, revolutionising heavy industry in Britain and Europe. Bessemer's process involved blowing air through molten iron to remove carbon and other impurities from the metal. His tilting converter, a large cylindrical furnace for holding the molten iron, was introduced in Sheffield in 1860. In 1875 the process was refined by adding limestone which separated phosphorus from the steel. The converter was widely used throughout Europe. In the USA steel was made in much the same way using a process patented by William Kelly.

Betancourt, Rómulo (1908-81) Venezuelan democratic politician. In 1928, while still at university, Betancourt was briefly jailed for his opposition to the dictator Juan Vicente Gómez. He then spent several years in exile, returning in 1941 to found the left-wing opposition party Acción Democrática. After a military coup in 1945 Betancourt was appointed provisional president, a position he held until 1948 when he resigned to allow a successor to be democratically elected. Soon afterwards Betancourt had to flee Venezuela again after another military coup in which Marcos Pérez Jiménez took power. When Jiménez was himself overthrown in 1958, Betancourt returned to Venezuela and was elected president. He retired in 1964, and made an unsuccessful bid to regain the presidency in 1973.

Bethmann-Hollweg, Theobald von (1856-1921) German statesman who opposed unrestricted submarine warfare during the First World War. Bethmann-Hollweg was appointed Prussian minister of the interior in 1905, secretary of state in 1907 and chancellor in 1909, in which capacity he instituted a number of electoral reforms as well as greatly increasing the size of the German army. Believing that Germany's neighbours would sooner or later force his country into war, Bethmann-Hollweg worked closely with Britain to prevent the First BALKAN War from becoming a major international conflict. In July 1914, however, he gave unconditional support to Austria-Hungary in its dispute with Serbia, and was then powerless to stop Russia from entering the fray. In 1917 Bethmann-Hollweg opposed Admiral TIR-PITZ's proposal to use submarines against all merchant ships supplying Britain, as he feared that this would bring the USA into the war – which it did. He resigned in July 1917, after which generals HINDENBURG and LUD-ENDORFF set up a virtual dictatorship.

Bevan, Aneurin (1897-1960) British politician, best known for creating Britain's National Health Service in 1948. A passionate socialist, Bevan led the Welsh miners in the GENERAL STRIKE of 1926. He was elected to Parliament in 1929 as the Independent Labour representative for Ebbw Vale in South Wales. In 1931 Bevan joined the more moderate Labour Party, though his left-wing views and fiery personality always marked him out as a rebel. He was also a great orator, and one of Winston Churchill's most outspoken critics during the Second World War. Under the Labour government of 1945 Bevan was appointed minister of health with responsibility for establishing the National Health Service, which offered free medical care to all. In 1951 Bevan became minister of labour, but he resigned in protest at government

proposals to impose charges on certain medical services. Soon afterwards a left-wing, socialist group of 'Bevanites' developed within the Labour Party. Despite many conflicts with his colleagues, Bevan was elected deputy leader of the party in 1959.

Beveridge, William, 1st Baron (1879-1963) British academic, economist and social reformer who helped to plan Britain's post-war WELFARE STATE. In 1909, while working for the Board of Trade, Beveridge published *Unemployment: A Problem of Industry* – a report in which he argued that the regulation of society by an interventionist state would strengthen rather than weaken the free market economy. He later became director of the London School of Economics (1919-37) and Master of University College, Oxford (1937-45). As an expert on unemployment Beveridge was commissioned by the government in 1941 to chair an enquiry into the social services. His findings, delivered in 1942 as *Social Insurance and Allied Services*, also known as the Beveridge Report, became the blueprint for Britain's new welfare state.

Bevin, Ernest (1881-1951) British trade union leader and politician. Born into a poor family, Bevin was orphaned at seven and had to leave school only a few years later. His experience of the labour market soon made him an active trade unionist. In 1921 he helped to form the Transport and General Workers' Union, becoming its general secretary until 1940. Bevin played a leading role in the 1926 GENERAL STRIKE and in 1937 he was elected chairman of the Trades Union Congress. Throughout the 1930s Bevin argued strongly in favour of rearmament and a foreign policy that would counter the threat of German and Italian fascism. As a result he was invited in 1940 to become minister of labour in Winston Churchill's wartime coalition government, where he played a vital role in mobilising Britain's workforce. After the war Bevin became foreign secretary in Clement Attlee's Labour government, helping with the economic recovery and defensive reorganisation of Western Europe, especially by incorporating the USA in NATO in 1949.

Bhagavad-Gita Central religious text of the Hindu faith (see HINDUISM). The *Bhagavad-Gita*, Sanskrit for 'Song of the Lord', is a long poem composed some time between the 2nd century BC and the 2nd century AD and forming part of the sixth book of the Indian epic the *Mahabharata*. The poem takes the form of a dialogue between the prince Arjuna and Lord Krishna, an incarnation of the god Vishnu. Krishna explains to Arjuna that, as a member of the warrior caste, he has a duty to fight – even against kinsmen and friends – since virtue consists in the dispassionate and

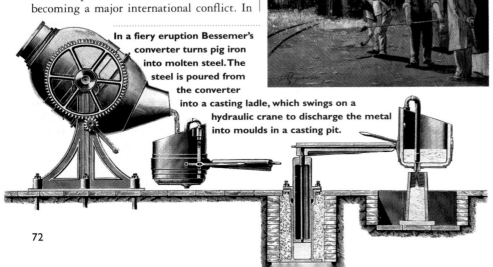

In a fiery eruption Bessemer's converter turns pig iron into molten steel. The steel is poured from the converter into a casting ladle, which swings on a hydraulic crane to discharge the metal into moulds in a casting pit.

President Bhutto inspects the Republican Guard on a visit to France in 1973, amid speculation that his mission was to secure armaments for Pakistan from President Pompidou.

devout acceptance of one's duty. Krishna also tells Arjuna about Brahman, the supreme god, and the different ways in which people can achieve eternal union with him.

Bhutan Isolated kingdom in the eastern Himalayas. The region was probably inhabited by Tibetans migrating southwards from about the 9th century AD. By the 17th century Bhutan had developed its own political identity and system of government. A monarch was spiritual ruler of the country and an appointed joint ruler, called the *deb raja*, exercised control over temporal issues. This system survived until 1907 when, with British support, a hereditary monarchy was established by Sir Ugyen Wangchuk, the country's most powerful provincial governor, and thereafter the first *Druk Gyalpo*, 'Dragon King'. For most of its history Bhutan has been inaccessible to the outside world, partly because of its seclusion and partly because of a deliberate policy of prohibiting foreigners from entering the country. In 1864, however, Britain annexed part of south Bhutan and in 1910 the two countries negotiated a treaty whereby Bhutan agreed to be guided by Britain in its foreign policy in return for a large annual subsidy.

In 1949, as part of its withdrawal from the Indian subcontinent, Britain restored Bhutan's southern territory, and gave India the responsibility of assisting Bhutan in its defence. The 1950 Chinese invasion of Tibet drove Bhutan and India even closer together, while stimulating a programme of modernisation and intensive road-building. In recent years King Jigme Singye Wangchuk has done much to bring the country up to date, but Nepalese immigrants have protested against his measures to preserve Bhutan's culture and language.

DID YOU KNOW?

Until the early 20th century the Bhutanese believed their monarch, the dharma raja, was reincarnated from one generation to the next.

Bhutto, Benazir (1953-) Pakistani politician who became the first woman to lead a Muslim country in modern times. Educated at Harvard and Oxford universities, Bhutto became leader of the Pakistan People's Party (PPP) after the execution of her father, Zulfikar BHUTTO, in 1979. She opposed the military regime of General ZIA ul-Haq, resulting in her exile from 1984 to 1986. She returned after the lifting of martial law and then led the PPP to victory in elections held after Zia's death in a plane crash in 1988. Bhutto became prime minister of a coalition government, which worked to improve the civil rights record of Pakistan, but was unable to do much to alleviate the country's widespread poverty. In 1990 Bhutto's government was dismissed by the president for incompetence and corruption, but she fought her way back to power in the elections of 1993.

Bhutto, Zulfikar Ali (1928-79) Pakistani statesman. A lawyer by training, Bhutto was appointed minister for fuel, power and natural resources in AYUB KHAN's military government in 1958. He became foreign minister in 1963, but left the government in 1967 after opposing a peace treaty with India over Kashmir. Bhutto then formed the Pakistan People's Party (PPP) with a policy of promoting Islam, democracy and socialism. In the elections of 1970 the PPP won a commanding victory in West Pakistan, but refused to cooperate with the overall winner, the Awami League, which had campaigned for independence for East Pakistan. The Pakistani national assembly was then suspended, leading to rioting, civil war and the eventual loss of East Pakistan, which became the state of BANGLADESH. In December 1971 Pakistan's demoralised military leaders handed the government over to Bhutto, who became president and, in 1973, prime minister. He formulated a new constitution, cultivated friendship with China and instituted an ambitious economic programme. In 1977 a military coup led by General ZIA ul-Haq ousted Bhutto, who was later hanged after being found guilty of ordering a political murder.

Biafra Short-lived breakaway state in south-eastern Nigeria. After years of mounting tensions between the Hausa people of northern and western Nigeria and the Ibo people of the south-east, Lieutenant-Colonel Odumegwu Ojukwu declared the oil-rich Ibo territory an independent state in May 1967. In the bitter three-year civil war that followed Biafra was supported by the Ivory Coast, Gabon, Tanzania, Zambia and France, while Britain and the Soviet Union backed Nigeria's federal government. By 1968 Biafra was completely cut off by federal troops and when the war ended in January 1970 more than a million Biafrans had died of starvation and disease.

Bible see feature, page 74

bicycle The first bicycle with pedals (on its front wheel) was made in about 1839 by Kirkpatrick Macmillan, a Scottish blacksmith, but it was not until 1885 that the first recognisably modern bicycle, with a chain-and-sprocket drive to the rear wheel, appeared. This was called the 'safety bicycle' because both wheels were of equal size – unlike the 'penny-farthing', whose rider sat several feet off the ground on top of an enormous front wheel. The safety bicycle created a vogue for cycling in Europe and the USA and provided working people with transport that was cheap and convenient. The arrival of the motor car in the early 20th century gradually diminished the role of the bicycle in developed countries, but it remains a primary form of transport in many other parts of the world.

Bihar State in north-east India comprising the fertile middle Ganges plains and the mineral-rich Chota Nagur plateau. Bihar was a centre for northern Indian civilisation from the 6th century BC. The Magadha kingdom flourished there and gave rise to two of the world's great religious figures: Gautama BUDDHA and the Jain seer Mahavira. The region's capital, Palatiputra (now Patna), was adopted by several empire builders including the Nanda dynasty, the Mauryans and the Guptas, between the 4th century BC and the 5th century AD. In about 1200 Bihar came under the authority of the Muslim sultans of Delhi, until it was absorbed by the MUGHAL empire in the 16th century. The British amalgamated Bihar and BENGAL in 1765, but then separated them in 1936, naming Bihar a province of British India. In 1947 Bihar became a state of the newly independent India.

Holy Writ that reveals the Word of God

The Bible contains the most sacred books of Jews and Christians.
The Hebrew Old Testament includes texts dating back to the 10th century BC.
Later, Christians added their New Testament, inspired by the life of Jesus.

Christians and Jews both revere the collection of ancient texts contained in the Old Testament as inspired scripture and believe that in their pages they encounter the Word of God. But they interpret its divine inspiration differently. Many Orthodox Jews, for example, are convinced that every word of the Pentateuch (the first five books of the Bible) was revealed to Moses on Mount Sinai. Some Protestant Christians insist that all the stories of the Bible are factually true. Other Jews and Christians take a less literal view and regard some biblical material as symbolic or mythical, rather than factual record.

VARIED SOURCES, VARIED TEXTS

History was important to the biblical writers. Jews and Christians both believe that their God has revealed Himself in actual events in the real world. The Hebrew Bible consists of narratives which trace the history of the people of Israel, prophetic oracles which see God at work in the political and social events of their day, and collections of songs and wisdom writings which give practical advice about how to live in the right way in accordance with God's will.

Christians believe that God entered history in the person of Jesus of Nazareth. To the Hebrew Bible they added their own scriptures, written in Greek – the 'New Testament'. These consist of the letters of St Paul and the disciples of Jesus, and accounts of Jesus's life ascribed to the evangelists Matthew, Mark, Luke and John. Christians still

Bibles were often elaborately decorated and embellished. The cover of these Gospels from 1797 is embossed with silver filigree.

The 1611 King James Bible (above) was an English translation. Hebrew Bibles, made by Jews, include this 13th-century French edition.

revere the Jewish scriptures (the Old Testament), which they see as a prelude to Jesus, God's last word to humanity.

Yet the biblical writers were not attempting the kind of objectivity that would satisfy a modern historian. The writers of Genesis – the first book of the Bible – included two different versions of both the Creation and the Flood. Similarly, the Christian writers gave conflicting accounts of such events as the Resurrection. All the writers were mainly concerned with the divine significance of the events they described.

The earliest parts of the Pentateuch were written perhaps as early as the 10th century BC, though some experts place them in the 8th or even the 6th. The prophetic writings date from the 8th to 6th centuries, and the Wisdom books of the Apocrypha, the 'appendix' to the Old Testament, were probably written during the 2nd century BC. The New Testament scriptures were written from about AD 50 to the early 2nd century. The oldest surviving fragments of the Hebrew text are the papyrus of Nash, found in Egypt in 1902, and the Dead Sea Scrolls, discovered in 1947 in caves 15 miles (24 km) east of Jerusalem.

Parts of the Bible have been translated into 1500 languages. The first Latin translation was that of St Jerome in the early 5th century. This forms the basis of the Vulgate, the Roman Catholic authorised version of the Bible. Miles Coverdale, a Protestant priest, carried out the first translation of the entire Bible into English in 1535. Perhaps the most influential translation is William Tyndale's: many of his phrases can be found in the 1611 'Authorised Version' produced under the authority of James I for the Church of England. There are a number of modern translations.

The preoccupation with the literal truth of scripture is a product of Western modernity. In the 16th century, when Europeans embarked on their scientific revolution, they began to expect the same kind of verifiable fact from scripture as they were seeking in the laboratory. The philosophers of the Enlightenment in the 17th century questioned Christianity and the existence of one God. In the 19th century the naturalist Charles Darwin's theory of evolution caused controversy because it contradicted the Book of Genesis. These conflicting views have made the status of scripture problematic for many Jews and Christians today.

Bikini Atoll One of the Marshall Islands in the west Pacific Ocean. From 1946 to 1958 Bikini was the site of 23 US nuclear bomb tests. Despite extensive work to reclaim the land and allow islanders to return in the early 1970s, the atoll remains too contaminated for human habitation.

Biko, Steve (1946-77) South African Black activist and student leader. While at medical school Biko decided that the multiracial National Union of South African Students was dominated by Whites, so in 1968 he co-founded and became president of the all-Black South African Students' Organisation whose

> **I think the central theme about Black society is that it has got elements of a defeated society. People must develop a hope...to look at their problems, and...build up their humanity. This is the point about Black consciousness.**
>
> *Steve Biko,*
> *defence witness 1976*

aim was to raise Black consciousness and increase Black self-esteem. Biko also helped to establish the South African Students' Movement for high-school pupils, and became honorary president of the Black People's Convention. In February 1973 Biko was served with a 'banning order', severely restricting his public statements as well as whom he could see and where he could go. He was arrested several times for defying this ban and in 1977 died in police custody from head injuries after being manacled naked for 24 days. Biko's death made him a martyr of Black nationalism in South Africa.

Bill of Rights (1689) Act of Parliament which formally set out the conditions by which WILLIAM III and Mary II were to become joint sovereigns of England, Scotland and Ireland. The bill's major provisions were that Catholics were barred from the throne; that the Crown could not levy taxes without the consent of Parliament; that the Crown no longer had the power to suspend or dispense with any laws; and that there was to be no peacetime standing army without Parliament's consent. The bill also incorporated the Declaration of Rights, which guaranteed the rights and liberties of British subjects, among them toleration of all Protestants and a general election every three years. The bill was often praised as a worthy result of the GLORIOUS REVOLUTION (1688-9), which began with James II's eviction from the throne.

Bill of Rights (1791) Name given to the first ten amendments to the CONSTITUTION OF THE USA, which were adopted as a single entity. After the constitutional arrangements of 1787 were criticised for being too general in their guarantee of human and civil rights, James MADISON drew up 12 amendments, of which ten were ratified. Based on common law principles and certain features of the English BILL OF RIGHTS of 1689, the amendments guarantee freedom of speech, press, worship and assembly; the right to bear arms; the right to a fair and public trial by jury; the right not to incriminate oneself, nor to suffer unwarranted search and seizure or cruel punishments. The amendments also prohibit the quartering of troops in private houses and specify that powers not reserved for the federal government belong to the states or the people.

Billy the Kid (1859-81) Nickname for William Bonney, US outlaw who was alleged to have killed at least 27 men before he was 22. Born in New York, Billy arrived in New Mexico in 1868 and by the time he was in his early teens was notorious for his lawlessness. In 1878 he took part in a New Mexico cattle war, killing Sheriff Jim Brady. Billy was captured by Sheriff Pat Garrett in 1880, tried and sentenced to hang. He escaped, but was eventually ambushed and shot dead by Garrett near Fort Sumner, New Mexico.

Bismarck, Otto von see feature, page 76

Black and Tans Nickname for emergency police officers drafted in by the British Government to fight the Irish Republican Army in Ireland in 1920-1. After the end of the First World War, Irish nationalists conducted a violent campaign against the Royal Irish Constabulary, with the result that many of the force resigned. The British Government responded by recruiting reinforcements, mostly veteran soldiers, who were given an assortment of military khaki and dark police uniforms to wear – hence the name Black and Tans, after a famous pack of foxhounds. The Black and Tans adopted a policy of harsh reprisals which alienated the Irish and shocked the public in Britain and the USA. They were withdrawn after the Anglo-Irish truce of 1921.

Black Death see feature, pages 78-79

Black Hand Symbol and name of a Serbian terrorist organisation founded by Colonel Dragutin Dimitrijevic in 1911 to liberate Serbs outside Serbia from Habsburg or Turkish rule. The Black Hand wielded a powerful influence in Serbia and was instrumental in the assassination of the Austrian Archduke FERDINAND in 1914. The name was also adopted by several organisations controlled by the MAFIA in New York and other US cities between about 1890 and 1920.

Black Hole of Calcutta Small prison room at Fort William, Calcutta, where many British defenders of the city suffocated during the night of June 20, 1756. The city had been attacked by Siraj ud-Daula, nawab of Bengal, because it was being fortified in violation of earlier agreements. According to the garrison commander, James Holwell, 146 people were imprisoned in the Black Hole and only 23 emerged alive. The incident was widely upheld as an example of the nawab's barbarism, providing justification for Robert CLIVE to seize Calcutta and the whole of Bengal. However, Holwell's account of the number of prisoners and deaths is now thought to have been exaggerated.

Black Muslim Movement see NATION OF ISLAM

Black Panthers Militant Black US movement founded in 1966 by Huey Newton and Bobby Seale. The Panthers were originally dedicated to patrolling Black ghettos to prevent police brutality. They then developed a revolutionary Marxist ideology that called for the arming of all Blacks to fight for civil rights and Black liberation. This led to friction with the police, which culminated in a series of shoot-outs. Panther members were also subject to sustained and widespread police harassment, some of which was itself extremely violent, leading to congressional investigations into police behaviour. By the early 1970s, however, the party had fallen into disfavour with most mainstream Black leaders, provoking Newton and Seale to publicly renounce the Panthers' violent aspirations. By 1974 the Black Panthers had ceased to exist.

Billy the Kid, fair-haired, blue-eyed and 5 ft 3 in (1.6 m) tall, was a feared outlaw with a high price on his head by the time he was only 18 years old.

REWARD ($5,000.00)
Reward for the capture, dead or alive, of one Wm. Wright, better known as
"BILLY THE KID"
Age, 18. Height, 5 feet, 3 inches, Weight, 125 lbs. Light hair, blue eyes and even features. He is the leader of the worst band of desperadoes the Territory has ever had to deal with. The above reward will be paid for his capture or positive proof of his death.
JIM DALTON, Sheriff.
DEAD OR ALIVE!
BILLY THE KID

The Iron Chancellor

Otto von Bismarck, first chancellor of the German Empire, shocked his parliamentarians by embarking on a military 'blood and iron' policy to bring about the unification of Germany.

Otto von Bismarck (1815-98) dominated the history of Germany and Europe from 1862, when he was appointed prime minister of Prussia, until 1890. His formidable reputation as 'The Iron Chancellor' rested on his political successes and his willingness to use war to secure Prussian domination of German-speaking central Europe.

Born into the Prussian nobility, Bismarck was physically impressive and personally courageous. As a young man he excelled at duelling. In 1842 he was commended by King Frederick William IV for rescuing two men from drowning. He was intimidated neither by outbreaks of cholera (which he never believed was infectious) nor by potential assassins, one of whom he seized by the throat in May 1866 after the man had shot at him twice with a revolver.

Bismarck joined the Prussian civil service as a judicial administrator but found himself unable to work within the bureaucratic system and left. Between 1839 and 1847 he lived as a country squire, but soon tired of rural life.

FATHER OF A NATION

In 1847 Bismarck entered the Prussian parliament. The new constitutional government in Prussia offered far-reaching opportunities to a man who was branded a conservative reactionary but had startlingly modern political skills. He defended the monarchy against the liberals, and was rewarded for his loyalty in 1851 when Wilhelm I appointed him Prussian minister to the diet (federal assembly) of the German Confederation at Frankfurt – an unprecedented promotion for a man without diplomatic training. He then served as ambassador to St Petersburg and Paris before being recalled in 1862 as prime minister.

In pursuit of his goal of uniting Germany under Prussian rule, Bismarck embarked on the Austro-Prussian War of 1866 which destroyed the German Confederation dominated by Austria and led to the creation of a North German Confederation dominated by Prussia. Victory over France in the Franco-Prussian War of 1870 made possible

Dropping the Pilot, a cartoon of 1890 from Punch magazine, shows Kaiser Wilhelm II dismissing the aged Otto von Bismarck.

the accession of the south German states. The creation of a German Empire was proclaimed on January 18, 1871.

Now imperial chancellor of a unified Germany under the new Kaiser, Wilhelm I, Bismarck developed an alliance centred on Berlin to counter any coalition of European powers committed to undoing unification. In 1878 he played the role of 'honest broker' at the Congress of Berlin, which met to resolve tensions between the great powers over the Balkans.

In domestic politics Bismarck's style was confrontational. He introduced the first social welfare legislation in Europe in the 1880s, and established a central bank and a common currency. But he resented constitutional constraints. His position depended on the support of the Crown, and when both Wilhelm I and his son Friedrich III died in 1888 Bismarck came into conflict with Wilhelm II, nearly 44 years his junior. Dismissed in 1890, Bismarck retired from public life full of resentment.

Black Power Militant movement among Blacks in the USA during the 1960s to secure civil rights for Black people. Leaders such as Stokeley Carmichael proposed that Black Americans should avoid allying themselves with liberal Whites, and should concentrate instead on achieving political and economic power in their own communities. Several organisations with widely differing creeds were associated with the general aspirations of Black Power, among them the Black Muslims (see NATION OF ISLAM) and the BLACK PANTHERS. They had in common pride in Black culture and a belief that Black people could achieve their own liberation. The riots in the cities in the middle and late 1960s seemed to herald new waves of Black militancy, but the intensity of the Black Power Movement declined in the early 1970s.

Black Prince, Edward the see EDWARD THE BLACK PRINCE

Black September Extreme Palestinian terrorist group, responsible for murdering 11 Israeli athletes at the Munich Olympics in September 1972. Black September emerged after the expulsion of Palestinian guerrillas from Jordan in September 1970, from which event it took its name. The group claimed to be independent but was part of al-Fatah, the dominant faction in the PALESTINE LIBERATION ORGANISATION. The name Black September was eventually dropped by al-Fatah.

Black Shirts Colloquial name for several fascist organisations. The original Black Shirts were the Italian *camicie nere*, militant supporters of Benito MUSSOLINI. They violently attacked socialists, communists and republicans from 1919, and helped Mussolini to take power in 1922. In Germany the Black Shirts were the SS, founded by Adolf HITLER in 1925 as his personal bodyguard, and distinct from the brown-shirted storm troopers of the SA (see BROWN SHIRTS). All three groups inspired other fascist organisations throughout the world, notably the British Union of Fascists led by Sir Oswald MOSLEY.

Blake, Robert (1599-1657) English admiral. Blake lived a quiet life until he was 40. He was then elected to Charles I's Short Parliament and in 1642 joined the Parliamentarians fighting the ENGLISH CIVIL WAR. Blake proved a brilliant commander, leading Oliver Cromwell to appoint him as one of his three navy 'generals' in 1649. The following year Blake destroyed the Royalist fleet under Prince RUPERT off the coast of Spain, and in 1651 he captured the Isles of Scilly. During the first Dutch War between 1652 and 1654 Blake lost only one of four major battles. He proceeded to destroy a fleet of Barbary pirates in the Mediterranean in 1655 and a Spanish

A hooded Black September terrorist is glimpsed outside the Israeli athletes' quarters in the Olympic village, Munich. This sinister image became a symbol of the 1972 Olympic Games.

treasure fleet off the Canary Islands in 1657. Ill health forced Blake to return to England, where he died a few miles from port.

Blake, William (1757-1827) British poet and artist. Born in London, Blake was apprenticed as an engraver in 1772, then studied briefly at the Royal Academy before setting up on his own as a publisher's engraver and illustrator. From an early age Blake also wrote poetry, which is often described as marking the beginning of English ROMANTICISM. Some poems are visionary and deeply mystical, based on Blake's own complex mythology. Other poems such as 'The Lamb' are characterised by childlike simplicity and unstudied directness, which can be combined with a powerful energy (as in 'The Tyger.') that is unique to Blake. Throughout his writings Blake celebrated the power of innocence, love and liberty, while denouncing the hypocrisy and oppression inherent in conventional art, religion and society, especially under the influence of the Industrial Revolution. His best-known works include the *Songs of Innocence* (1789), *Songs of Experience* (1794), *Milton* (1808) and *Jerusalem* (1820).

Blenheim, Battle of (August 13, 1704) Major battle during the War of the SPANISH SUCCESSION, fought at the Bavarian village of Blenheim (now Blindheim). The armies of the French king Louis XIV and his ally the Elector of Bavaria were marching towards Vienna when they were attacked by the combined forces of John Churchill, Duke of Marlborough, and the Austrian commander, Prince EUGENE OF SAVOY. The allies won a decisive victory, thereby saving Vienna, eliminating Bavaria from the war and preserving the Anglo-Austrian alliance. Blenheim Palace at Woodstock, Oxfordshire, was subsequently built for the Duke of Marlborough by a grateful English Parliament. It was later the birthplace of Sir Winston CHURCHILL, a direct descendant of the duke.

Bligh, William (1754-1817) British naval officer. Bligh joined the Royal Navy in 1770 and accompanied Captain James COOK on his second and third voyages. In 1787 he was given command of HMS *Bounty* with instructions to take breadfruit trees from Tahiti to Jamaica. En route to Jamaica the crew of the *Bounty* mutinied under the leadership of Fletcher Christian, allegedly because of Bligh's quick temper and imperious manner. Bligh and 18 loyal crewmen were set adrift in an open boat, which Bligh then guided to Timor in the East Indies some 3600 miles (5800 km) away.

The mutineers returned to Tahiti, where 16 disembarked, while the remainder collected their Tahitian friends and sailed on to Pitcairn Island, 1350 miles (2170 km) to the southeast. There they burned the *Bounty* and lived undiscovered until the arrival of American whalers in 1808. Bligh resumed his career, transporting breadfruit trees and serving with distinction under Admiral NELSON at the Battle of Copenhagen in 1801. In 1805 Bligh was appointed governor of New South Wales, where his attempts to curtail the rum trade led to the RUM REBELLION of 1808. Bligh was appointed vice-admiral in 1814.

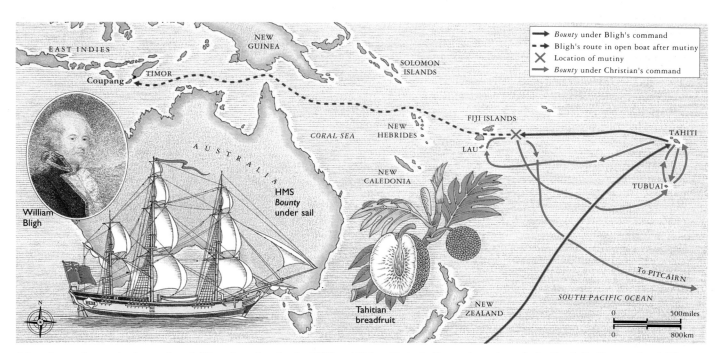

After the mutiny on the *Bounty*, by a brilliant feat of navigation William Bligh guided a frail open boat through the South Pacific to safety in Timor while his second-in-command, Fletcher Christian, and eight other mutineers sailed the hijacked ship in the opposite direction to Pitcairn Island.

The triumph of death:
plague brings horror to Europe

In 1348 the Black Death swept relentlessly across Europe, leaving perhaps 25 million dead. Two years later the ordeal appeared to be over, but outbreaks of plague were to become a recurrent nightmare.

The contemporary French historian Jean de Venette wrote: 'In AD 1348, in addition to Famine and War, Plague appeared in the world'. In fact, rumours had been current in European ports for more than 10 years of something terrible already happening in distant lands, of India depopulated and Syria and Armenia covered with dead bodies.

Then three galleys put into the north Italian port of Genoa, their sailors infected by bites from fleas borne by the ships' rats. Though the sailors were driven back to sea by flaming arrows, 'for no man dared touch them', it was too late. The Black Death had arrived, the most virulent epidemic of bubonic and pneumonic plague ever recorded. In the next two years it was to kill between a third and a half of the population of Europe, perhaps as many as 25 million people.

A QUICK DEATH

Death came quickly. The writer Boccaccio witnessed the plague in Florence. 'It first betrayed itself by the emergence of certain tumours in the groin or the armpits, some of which grew as large as a common apple, others as an egg,' he wrote. He believed that after the tumours, or 'buboes', appeared the infected person would be dead within a day, though others noted that victims usually lingered on for four or five days. The term 'bubonic plague' derives from these tumours; the description 'Black Death' from the colour that they turned. The disease leapt rapidly across countries: it was in France, Spain and England by the end of 1348.

Most unsettling of all was the fact that people at the time did not understand how the infection was spread. The pope's doctor at Avignon, Guy de Chauliac, a remarkable man with more insight into the epidemic than any person then living, declared that you could catch the disease 'simply by looking at the sick people'. A doctor in Paris wrote that 'one sick person could infect the whole world'.

Two plagues made up the Black Death. At the time only de Chauliac noticed that,

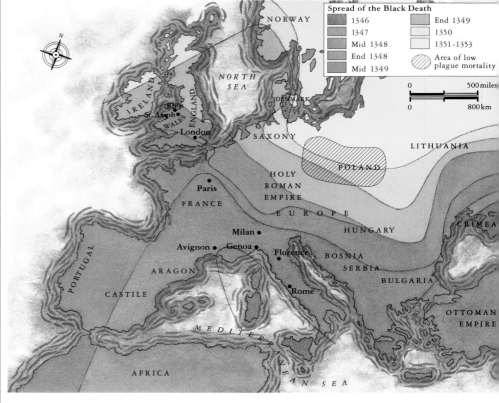

Plague was already advancing overland from the east when it arrived by sea in Genoa in 1348. It rapidly spread throughout Europe, westwards to Portugal and northwards into Scandinavia.

in addition to the buboes, there was another quite distinct set of symptoms: continual fever and coughing of blood. Though he did not realise it, he had identified the far more infectious pneumonic plague, from which, as he noted, a victim died in two days. The bubonic type was spread by the fleas of the black rat; the pneumonic by a person coughing into the air. In an epidemic in Manchuria as recently as 1921, the life expectancy of those who caught pneumonic plague was less than two days.

After two ghastly years during which there seemed no hope, 1348 and 1349, the nightmare seemed to pass as suddenly as it had arrived. In 1350 Pope Clement V announced a jubilee year, and a million pilgrims flocked to Rome to celebrate the survival of humanity. They were all terribly mistaken. Ten years later the pestilence returned, then again in 1369.

Even 1348 was not the beginning, for the plague had come before. Writing in the 8th century, the English historian Bede recorded that in the 5th century, around 450, 'the living could scarce bury the dead'. A great mystery of the British past is how no more than 10 000 immigrant Anglo-Saxons came to conquer a country with a population which may have numbered between 5 and 10 million. The plague might offer an explanation.

Soon after the epidemic struck, the English, who had been held up in their advance for half a century – a check

Citizens of Tournai, Belgium, bury their dead. This Flemish picture of 1352 is one of only a handful to record events as they happened.

In *The Triumph of Death*, a French painting from 1503, the grim reaper inexorably harvests his prey.

The wealthy carried fragrant pomanders to ward off pestilence.

A silver, book-shaped pomander is engraved with a plague rat.

The beak worn by London plague doctors in 1665 was filled with fragrant herbs.

associated with King Arthur – resumed the process which ended with their conquest. It is thought that the English invaders had not been affected by the plague for, unlike the British, they did not trade with Mediterranean Europe. Empty bottles found buried under British hill-forts show that the wine trade was flourishing, and it is possible that with the wine trade came the plague.

No one wrote an eye-witness account, but many did when the disease returned. In AD 543, during the rule of Emperor Justinian, plague swept through the Eastern Roman Empire, and a year later, as a boy, the Frankish historian Gregory of Tours saw it pass through Gaul. In 550 in Ireland the annalists recorded that the 'yellow plague' had come.

There is a glimpse of the terror people must have felt in the accounts of the death of the Welsh king Maelgwn the Tall, who had left his hill-top fortress near modern Llandudno to take refuge in the church at Rhôs, which exists on its slopes to this day. The king is said to have put his eye to the keyhole and seen 'the yellow plague loping towards him'.

In 1382, a generation after the Black Death, the plague returned. The Welsh poet Iolo Goch,

Iolo the Red, wrote an elegy on one of its victims, his patron the archdeacon of St Asaph. Such poems were a stock in trade for any medieval Welsh poet, but this elegy is different, for the writer has been terrified out of all conventional phrases. His imagery is filled with horror. This is no death in old age or in battle; this is a death the poet cannot understand. 'On Thursday the horror began/between the new days and the night…' Out of nowhere the plague had come again, as it was to do every 4 to 12 years until the 16th century.

The last major incidence of the plague in Britain was the Great Plague of London in 1665. Remarkably, for the most part it was confined to the metropolis. In 1910 there was a small outbreak in Suffolk, but in the East it rampaged on, claiming 6 million victims in India as recently as 1896.

A myth about the Black Death is that it was and remains the most infectious disease ever known. The windows in some old houses in East Anglia are bricked up where they face towards London. But the Black Death can now be completely cured by tetracycline, the simplest and cheapest form of antibiotic, discovered in the 1940s. The most extensive use of this drug in the West is for acne.

Not everyone who was infected by bubonic plague died. Well over 60 per cent of those infected did lose their lives, but excavation of a plague cemetery under the Royal Mint in London shows that the epidemic of 1665 may have killed fewer people than was once believed. The population of the city is estimated to have been between 40 000 and 100 000, but bodies found suggest a death toll of no more than 12 400. Moreover, the methodical layout of the cemeteries implies an orderly public health administration.

THE SERFS FIGHT BACK

At the time the Black Death seemed the most terrible event in the history of the world. But for one group in society it provided the chance to realise their power. In this new age when labour was scarce, those who worked for wages demanded more. In 1349, in the middle of the epidemic, the tanners of Amiens called for a rise in pay. Some serfs insisted on paying rent and so freed themselves from their obligations to their masters, while others just slipped away from the land. The Statute of Labourers, enacted by the English Parliament in 1351, attempted to force wages down to pre-plague levels. A poll tax was introduced, riots ensued, and in the Peasants' Revolt of 1381 workers demanded an end to serfdom. Though these rebellions were ruthlessly put down, there could be no going back.

military victories owed more to his dash and courage rather than to any great tactical skill. Blücher served in the Prussian army from 1760 to 1807 with distinction. In 1813, at the age of 71, he came out of retirement to fight Napoleon and achieved several major victories, notably at the Battle of LEIPZIG. Blücher also played a successful role during the invasion of France, entering Paris with other Allied commanders in May 1814. After retiring to his estates in Silesia, Blücher was again recalled when Napoleon returned to the field in 1815. He was defeated at Ligny on June 16, 1815, but withdrew his army and made an invaluable appearance two days later during the closing stages of the Battle of WATERLOO.

Blum, Léon (1872-1950) French socialist politician and writer. After graduating as a lawyer, Blum made a name for himself as a journalist and critic. He was then drawn into politics by the DREYFUS affair, in which he sided with the republicans against the royalists. In 1919 Blum was elected to the National Assembly as a member of the French Socialist Party and soon became one of its leaders. In the early 1930s he formed a coalition of radicals, socialists and communists known as the POPULAR FRONT, which won power in 1936.

As France's first socialist prime minister, Blum presided over sweeping reforms in labour legislation. His government instituted a 40 hour week, paid holidays and collective bargaining, infuriating many industrialists. Blum resigned in 1937 when the Senate refused to give him emergency powers, but returned to lead the government briefly in 1938. Arrested by the VICHY GOVERNMENT soon after the German invasion of 1940, Blum spent the rest of the war behind bars. He formed a brief caretaker government in 1946, and retired once the Fourth Republic was established in January 1947.

Boadicea see BOUDICCA

Boccaccio, Giovanni (1313-75) Italian poet, humanist and scholar. Born in Paris the illegitimate son of a Tuscan merchant, Boccaccio grew up in Florence before going to Naples to study law and commerce. Here he fell in love with a woman whom he was to immortalise in his early poems as Fiammetta. In about 1340 he returned to Florence where he completed his masterpiece, the *Decameron*, between 1349 and 1351. This collection of 100 witty, sometimes licentious, tales is set against the background of the Black Death (see feature, page 78). At this time Boccaccio met his eminent fellow poet Petrarch, whom he joined in the study and imitation of Latin and Greek literature of antiquity, thereby paving the way for later Renaissance humanists. From then on Boccaccio's major writings were all in Latin.

In June 1941 the blitzkrieg stuns Russia and Panzer divisions easily secure Ukraine's fertile plains. Hitler seemed poised to bring the Red Army to its knees but the long Russian winter lay ahead.

blitzkrieg Military tactic employed by the Germans in the Second World War in their campaigns against Poland in 1939; against Belgium, the Netherlands and France in 1940; and against the Soviet Union in 1941. The blitzkrieg, German for 'lightning war', employed fast-moving tanks and motorised infantry, supported by dive bombers, to throw superior but slower enemy forces off balance and thereby win crushing victories rapidly with small expenditure of men and materials. The tactic was copied in 1944 by US general George PATTON in his invasion of France. In 1940 the term 'the Blitz' was coined in Britain to describe the German bombing campaign against British cities.

Blood, Thomas (c.1618-80) Irish adventurer, whose exploits during the English Civil War led Charles II to confiscate his estates at the Restoration. Blood's various attempts to get them back included an assault on Dublin Castle in 1663 and an attempted theft of the crown jewels in 1671. After his arrest Blood was personally interrogated by Charles II, who was so impressed by his audacity and strength of character that he pardoned him and restored his estates.

Blood River, Battle of (1838) Battle fought in South Africa between some 10 000 Zulus and a commando of 468 VOORTREKKERS. After arriving in Natal (now Kwazulu-Natal) in 1837, the Voortrekkers tried to negotiate a land agreement with the Zulu king Dingane. In February 1838 the Voortrekker leader Piet Retief was murdered at Dingane's kraal, and a few days later a Zulu

army swept over the Voortrekker camps, killing some 500 inhabitants. In November a commando set out under the leadership of Andries Pretorius. It located the Zulu army and, on December 16, drew up in a defensive laager on the banks of the Ncome River. In spite of their small numbers the Voortrekkers beat off successive Zulu attacks. By the time the Zulus retreated 3000 of their number lay

> 66 **We swear that if Almighty God on this day brings us through victorious, it shall forever be observed as a day of thanksgiving and we will found a house in memory of His great name.** 99
>
> *Andries Pretorius,*
> *Inscription in a church built on the battle site*

dead, their blood staining the Ncome River red – hence its European name, Blood River. The Voortrekkers suffered three casualties.

Bloody Assizes Trials held in the west of England in 1685 to punish rebels who took part in the abortive MONMOUTH REBELLION against James II. Conducted by Lord Chief Justice George JEFFREYS and four other judges, the assizes became notorious for the severity of the sentences they imposed. More than 300 people were hanged, some 800 transported to Barbados and several hundred flogged or imprisoned.

Blücher, Gebhard Leberecht von (1742-1819) Prussian field-marshal, known affectionately as 'Marshal Forward', whose

During the Boer Wars grandfather, father and son stand shoulder-to-shoulder – simply equipped with rifles and bandoliers – ready to join the guerrilla campaign against the British.

Bodin, Jean (1530-96), French political philosopher, best known for his influential work *Les Six Livres de la République* (known in English as *The Six Books of the Commonwealth*) published in 1576. Bodin was appalled by the chaos suffered in France as a result of a weak monarchy and the conflict between Catholics and Huguenots (see RELIGION, WARS OF). He argued that the ideal state is characterised by religious toleration, a fully sovereign monarch who is kept informed of his citizens' needs, and citizens who respect and obey the decisions of their government. Bodin's ideas were taken up by the English philosopher Thomas HOBBES and contributed to the rise of the modern state.

Boeotia Region in east-central Greece with large, fertile plains well suited to agriculture. In ancient times the Boeotian city of THEBES was an important centre of power. In about 446 BC, the region's city-states formed the Boeotian League – a political and military alliance dominated by Thebes and opposed to Athenian power. The league was at first allied to SPARTA and in 424 won a major victory over the Athenians at Delium. It then opposed Sparta in the Corinthian War (395-387) leading to its defeat and subsequent dissolution. The Boeotians were notorious among the ancient Greeks for their alleged stupidity as well as their good living.

Boer Wars (1880-1; 1899-1902) Two wars (also known as the South African Wars and the Anglo-Boer Wars) fought between Britain and the Boer republics in South Africa. The first arose from the British annexation of the Transvaal (at the time called the South African Republic) in 1877. When the British government under William Gladstone refused the Transvaal its independence in 1880 the Boers, under Paul KRUGER, Petrus Joubert and Andries Pretorius, decided to fight for it. Though vastly outnumbered they won decisive victories in a number of engagements, particularly Majuba Hill in 1881. The resulting Pretoria Convention laid the ground for an uneasy peace, which came under strain when gold was discovered on the Witwatersrand in 1886 and large numbers of British prospectors poured into the area. In 1895 Cecil RHODES, prime minister of the Cape colony, privately financed the abortive JAMESON RAID to overthrow Kruger's government, leading to further Boer suspicion and a defence pact between the Transvaal and the Orange Free State in 1896.

Determined to protect its commercial interests, Britain began reinforcing its garrisons, provoking all-out war in which the Boers achieved several notable successes. British garrisons were besieged at Ladysmith, Kimberley and Mafeking. Only the arrival of huge reinforcements under Lord KITCHENER and Lord Roberts in 1900 turned the tide against the Boers, who resorted to a guerrilla campaign. In response Kitchener adopted a scorched-earth policy, systematically destroying farms and interning the civil population in the world's first CONCENTRATION CAMPS. By 1902 some 450 000 British troops had won the submission of about 50 000 Boer commandos. Peace was at last agreed at the Treaty of Vereeniging.

Boethius, Anicius (c.475-524) Roman senator and Christian philosopher. Boethius was a tireless scholar, writing on mathematics, logic, music, theology and astronomy, as well as translating Aristotle and Plato into Latin. Many of these translations later became the standard texts of medieval scholastic philosophers. In 510 Boethius was appointed consul and in about 520 became chief minister to the Ostrogothic king of Italy, THEODORIC THE GREAT. Shortly afterwards he fell out with Theodoric, who may have suspected him of communicating with his rival, the Byzantine emperor Justin I. He condemned Boethius to death, and while in prison Boethius wrote his masterpiece, *The Consolation of Philosophy*. In this work, which became the most widely read book in the Middle Ages after the Bible, Boethius expresses the Neoplatonic belief that everything on Earth is capricious and unstable – with the exception of virtue; also that the only true wisdom a person can have is knowledge of the existence of God.

Bohemia Historic kingdom in central Europe, now part of the Czech Republic. Bohemia was established as an independent duchy towards the end of the 9th century. Its first notable ruler was Duke (later Saint) WENCESLAS, who was murdered by his brother in 929. In 950 Bohemia came under the control of the German Holy Roman Emperor OTTO I, and early in the 11th century it absorbed the neighbouring territories of Moravia and Silesia. After the crowning of Otakar I in 1198 Bohemia became an independent kingdom in the Holy Roman Empire. The state's boundaries were later expanded by his grandson Otaker II.

Under CHARLES IV, who was crowned Holy Roman Emperor in 1355, Bohemia enjoyed a golden age with Prague as the centre of the empire. This was followed by the religious and nationalistic upheavals of the early 15th century, when the reformer John Huss was burned at the stake and his followers, the HUSSITES, fought a series of wars, from 1420 to 1423, against the Holy Roman Empire and other Catholic armies. In 1526 Bohemia passed into the hands of the Austrian HABSBURG dynasty, which resulted in pressure for the country to revert to Catholicism. Religious discontent eventually exploded in 1618 with the THIRTY YEARS' WAR, which ravaged Bohemia and inaugurated two centuries of Austrian rule.

Czech nationalist aspirations re-emerged in 1848 when a Pan-Slav congress assembled in Prague to demand greater Czech autonomy within a federal Austria. But independence had to wait for the fall of the Austro-Hungarian empire and the founding of Czechoslovakia in 1918. In 1969 Bohemia, Moravia and Czech Silesia were incorporated to form the Czech Socialist Republic, which in 1990 became the Czech Republic – itself an independent country since the breakup of Czechoslovakia in 1993.

This rare portrait of Anne Boleyn is by Hans Holbein, who became court painter in 1536, the year of the queen's execution.

Boleyn, Anne (1507-36) Second wife of HENRY VIII of England and mother of Queen Elizabeth I. By 1527 Anne Boleyn was having an affair with Henry while he was conducting secret negotiations to divorce Catherine of Aragon, who had failed to provide him with a male heir. In January 1533 Henry and Anne were secretly married, and in May Archbishop Thomas CRANMER annulled Henry's marriage to Catherine, allowing Anne to be crowned in June, three months before the birth of Elizabeth. Henry's actions provoked a confrontation with the Roman Catholic Church and led directly to the English REFORMATION. In less than three years Anne had become deeply unpopular at court; she had also failed to produce a son. In May 1536 she was tried on dubious charges of adultery, convicted and beheaded.

Bolingbroke, Henry of see HENRY IV

Bolingbroke, Henry St John, 1st Viscount (1678-1751) English Tory politician and writer. Bolingbroke entered Parliament in 1701, became secretary for war in 1704, secretary of state in 1710 and a peer in 1712. Shortly before the death of Queen ANNE in 1714 he failed to win the leadership of the Tory Party and, because of his JACOBITE sympathies, was later dismissed from office by Anne's successor, George I. Bolingbroke fled to France where he became secretary of state to the Pretender to the English throne, James Edward STUART, but soon became disillusioned with his cause. In 1723 George I allowed Bolingbroke to return to England. Here he conducted a long campaign against Sir Robert WALPOLE, leader of the Whigs.

Bolingbroke's best-known work is *The Idea of a Patriot King* (1749), the theme of which is the importance of monarchy standing above politics and representing the nation.

Bolívar, Simón see feature, page 83

Bolivia Landlocked country in central South America. The region was inhabited from about AD 600 by the Aymara people and after about 1200 became partly absorbed by the INCA empire. In 1538 it was conquered by the Spanish conquistadores, who founded the city of Chuquisaca (modern Sucre) as the capital of Upper Peru. The discovery of tin and silver in the Potosí mountains in 1545 brought great wealth to the area, which fell to the Spanish viceroy of Peru. In 1780 indigenous Indians, led by Túpac Amaru, rebelled against Spanish rule. Túpac Amaru was executed in 1781 and the rebellion crushed the following year. In 1825, local revolutionaries won a long fight for independence from Spain after royalist forces were defeated by Simón BOLÍVAR and his lieutenant Antonio José de Sucre. Bolívar then drew up a constitution for Upper Peru, which was named Bolivia in his honour.

Since independence Bolivia has endured instability. In 1884 it lost the Atacama coastal region to Chile. The CHACO WAR (1932-5) with Paraguay bled the country of resources and territory, paving the way for a series of coups. These ended for a while with the Bolivian National Revolution in 1952, when the Movimiento Nacionalista Revolucionario seized power. In 1964 the country entered another phase of military coups. Since 1982 Bolivia has been governed by elected leaders who have made some progress in dealing with the country's problems: an unstable economy, soaring inflation, an extensive drugs trade and a discontented labour force.

Bolsheviks Hard-line faction of the Russian Social Democratic Workers' Party, formed at the party's second congress in 1903. The Bolsheviks ('Members of the Majority') supported Lenin's proposal that the party should be prepared to achieve their goals by violent means. The opposing faction, whom the Bolsheviks called the Mensheviks ('Members of the Minority'), favoured more moderate, democratic action.

Both factions took part in the RUSSIAN REVOLUTION of 1905, but only the Mensheviks participated in the provisional government formed after the revolution of February 1917. In the following months the Bolsheviks made strong gains in Russian factory committees and workers' councils (see SOVIET), and by

> 66 **You are bankrupts. You have played out your role. Go where you belong – to the dustbin of history.** 99
>
> *Leon Trotsky's speech to the Mensheviks, 1917*

October 1917 they had enough support to overthrow Russia's provisional government. In the subsequent RUSSIAN CIVIL WAR (1918-22) the Bolsheviks succeeded in seizing control of the country. In 1918 they changed their name to the Russian Communist Party, which in 1952 became the Communist Party of the Soviet Union.

Bolshoi Ballet Russian ballet company based at the Bolshoi Theatre in Moscow. The company began as a dancing school for the Moscow Orphanage in the late 18th century. It took its present name when the first Bolshoi ('Great') Theatre was opened in 1825, and developed an individual, spontaneous style

Bolsheviks sweep away the bourgeois ideologies of monarchy, capitalism and imperialism. Such Soviet propaganda cartoons were successfully aimed at Russia's largely illiterate population.

Liberator of Latin America

The courageous exploits of the revolutionary, Simón Bolívar, freed half a continent from Spanish imperial rule.

Standing on the Monte Aventino in Rome, a young Venezuelan aristocrat vowed to free his country from Spanish rule. The man was Simón Bolívar, born to a family of Spanish descent in 1783. He had been educated in Europe at the time of the French Revolution, and would later come to be known by another name – El Libertador, The Liberator.

In 1807 Bolívar returned to Venezuela. Within a year he was plotting the liberation of Latin America. Spanish rule was resented by the Latin American-born Creole elite, who were excluded from positions of authority by the Spanish-born ruling class. In 1811 Venezuela declared itself independent, but was soon overrun again by Spanish forces. Bolívar escaped to New Granada (present-day Colombia). From there he launched an attack on Venezuela, and after a hard-fought campaign he reached the capital, Caracas, in 1813. But the next year he was defeated again, and in 1815 fled to the West Indies. There he wrote *Letter from Jamaica*, in which he set out his belief in the ultimate success of the revolution.

In 1815, with the help of Haiti, Bolívar fitted out seven schooners and raised 250 men to crew them. In his own country he enlisted an army of *llaneros* (cowboys). In 1819 he conceived a plan to catch the Spanish in Bogotá unawares and drive them out of New Granada. He led 2500 men across flooded plains, over mountains and through crocodile-infested rivers. The defenders were taken by surprise, and at the Battle of Boyacá the Spanish army surrendered. Three days later, Bolívar entered Bogotá: New Granada was free.

Cavalry leader Simón Bolívar (left) forced the Spanish back across the bridge at Boyacá to liberate Bogotá.

VICTORY AND INDEPENDENCE

By 1821 the Spanish had been driven from Venezuela; by 1822 they were out of Quito (present-day Ecuador). Bolívar became president and military dictator of the Republic of Great Colombia, made up of the three newly independent countries. Only Peru remained under Spanish control. In 1825, after victories at Junín and Ayacucho, the Spanish were ejected. Upper Peru took the name of Bolivia in honour of the man who had orchestrated its liberation.

South America was now independent, but civil war soon broke out over territorial disputes. Bolívar tried to establish authoritarian constitutions in the countries he had freed, provoking resentment and an assassination attempt. Realising that his belief in strong government had made him an obstacle to peace, Bolívar retired from public life to the estate of an admirer. Here the man who had freed half a continent from Spanish rule died on December 17, 1830, in the house of a Spaniard.

---

distinct from the formal approach of ballet companies in St Petersburg. In the early 20th century, under the directorship of Alexander Gorsky, the Bolshoi began using the strikingly realistic scenes and costumes which have been its hallmark ever since. When it first appeared in the West in 1956 the company caused a sensation with its dramatic, acrobatic performances. After Yuri Grigorovich became artistic director in 1976, the Bolshoi's repertoire has included modern ballets among its more traditional fare of *Swan Lake* and *The Nutcracker*. Since the collapse of communism the Bolshoi has faced serious financial problems caused by cuts in state funding

Bonhoeffer, Dietrich (1906-45) German Protestant theologian. After the Nazis came to power in 1933 Bonhoeffer became a leading spokesman for the Confessing Church, an evangelical movement opposed to the pro-Nazi German Christian Church. During the Second World War Bonhoeffer was active in the German resistance, flying to Sweden in 1942 to offer proposals to the British Government for a negotiated peace. Arrested by the Nazis in 1943, Bonhoeffer was later hanged after the discovery of papers linking him with the failed July Plot (1944) to kill Adolf Hitler.

Boniface VIII (1235-1303) Pope from 1294. Born Benedetto Caetani, Boniface had a long, distinguished career as papal diplomat and lawyer. Soon after his election as pope, he tried to end the hostilities between France and England. Both countries had started to tax the clergy without papal consent in order to finance their war. This led to a disastrous confrontation with the ruthless king of France, PHILIP IV, concerning the limits of royal authority. In 1303 Philip had Boniface kidnapped, and although he was rescued after only two days Boniface never recovered from the shock of his ordeal.

Bonnie Prince Charlie (1720-88) Nickname for Charles Edward Stuart, also known as the Young Pretender, who was the last significant JACOBITE claimant to the British throne. Grandson of the exiled Roman Catholic king JAMES II, Charles sailed to Scotland in July 1745 with fewer than a dozen supporters. After rallying an army he marched into England to claim the throne, but was forced to retreat and was finally defeated at the Battle of Culloden in April 1746. With the help of Flora MACDONALD, the adopted daughter of the clan chief, Charles escaped to France and settled in Rome.

Booth, Charles (1840-1916) British shipowner and pioneering sociologist. From 1866 Booth and his brother ran a successful shipping company. In his spare time, and with the assistance of the sociologist Beatrice Webb, Booth conducted exhaustive research into the causes and distribution of poverty, publishing his findings in a 17-volume study called *Life and Labour of the People in London* (1889-1902). Booth was also involved in promoting old age pensions for all, accelerating the Old Age Pensions Act of 1908.

Real-life drama unfolds as John Booth shoots Abraham Lincoln. Booth's derringer (left) is now housed in the Ford's Theatre Museum.

Booth, John Wilkes (1838-65) US actor who assassinated President Abraham LIN-COLN. Booth was a supporter of slavery and the Confederate cause during the American Civil War. In 1864 he conspired to abduct President Lincoln. The plot failed, but on April 14, 1865, Booth was able to enter the president's unguarded box at Ford's Theatre in Washington and shoot him in the head. Booth then fled to a farm in Virginia where he was discovered and shot 12 days later. Four of his fellow conspirators were later hanged.

Booth, William (1829-1912) British religious leader who founded the SALVATION ARMY. After working as an itinerant Methodist preacher, Booth moved to London in 1864 where, with the help of his wife Catherine (1829-90), he established a Christian association which in 1878 became the Salvation Army. Organised along strict military lines, with Booth as its 'General', the army initially provoked considerable opposition, but by 1890 its caring work was widely admired. Booth's mission was carried on by his children, notably his son William Bramwell (1856-1929) and his daughters Kate (1859- 1955) and Evangeline (1865-1950).

Borgia, Cesare (c.1475-1507) Italian Renaissance general, whose ruthless ambition was admired by Niccolò MACHIAVELLI, and who was probably the inspiration for Machiavelli's book *The Prince*. Born the illegitimate son of the corrupt Pope Alexander VI, Borgia became one of the most powerful men in Italy. His father made him both archbishop and cardinal while he was still in his teens, and then appointed him papal legate to France, where he married the sister of the king of Navarre in 1498. Cesare returned to Italy to become captain-general of the papal armies, leading them in three campaigns to re-establish control over the Papal States, which had fallen into the

Ten books that changed the world

From Plato's Republic *to Chairman Mao's* Little Red Book, *through their novels, treatises on ideal states or exposés of injustice, authors have deeply influenced the way that people think and act.*

The Republic, Plato (c.375BC). The turning point in Plato's life was the trial and execution in 399BC of his friend and mentor Socrates, perhaps the greatest of the Athenian philosophers. These events shocked him profoundly: 'I was forced to the belief that the only hope of finding justice for society or for the individual lay in true philosophy, and that mankind will have no respite from trouble until either real philosophers gain political power or politicians become by some miracle true philosophers.' So was born the notion of the philosopher ruler (or king), developed by Plato in *The Republic*. Plato's depiction of the ideal state – neither aristocratic nor democratic, but based instead on the enlightened virtue of an absolute ruler – was to become a benchmark of Western political thought.

The Confessions of St Augustine (c.397-400). These spiritual memoirs of a North African bishop are not only the first autobiography in the modern sense, but down the centuries they have become a central and inspiring text for Western Christianity. Augustine's conversion, his wrestling with sensual temptation ('Give me chastity and continency, but not yet'), his changing relationship with God – all are related by Augustine in a way that combines dramatic immediacy with authoritative theology.

The Prince, Niccolò Machiavelli (1513). Machiavelli was a moderately successful, personally unattractive Florentine diplomat who came to believe that a strong prince uniting Italy and providing political stability was more important than liberty, traditional civic values or wider ethical considerations. His treatise laid down, with cynical precision and subtlety, the methods needed to achieve an effective tyranny. In an era of strong, centralising governments it soon proved influential across Europe, and left an infamous legacy, based on cruelty and deceit, for future tyrants and would-be tyrants.

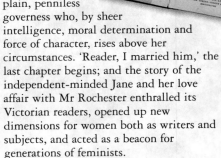

Jane Eyre, Charlotte Brontë (1847). The heroine of this English novel – subsequently adapted and filmed on many occasions – is a plain, penniless governess who, by sheer intelligence, moral determination and force of character, rises above her circumstances. 'Reader, I married him,' the last chapter begins; and the story of the independent-minded Jane and her love affair with Mr Rochester enthralled its Victorian readers, opened up new dimensions for women both as writers and subjects, and acted as a beacon for generations of feminists.

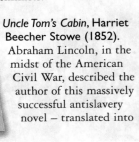

Uncle Tom's Cabin, Harriet Beecher Stowe (1852). Abraham Lincoln, in the midst of the American Civil War, described the author of this massively successful antislavery novel – translated into

23 languages – as 'the little lady who wrote the book that made this great war'. She herself was more modest: 'God wrote the book. I took His dictation.' Either way, the highly sentimental story of a faithful and lovable Black slave proved a powerful catalyst for the momentous events that were shortly to unfold.

All Quiet on the Western Front, Erich Maria Remarque (1929). This most famous of pacifist novels sold half a million copies within four months of its publication in Germany, and by the end of 1930 had been adapted into a classic film. In Germany itself the book and the film became increasingly the object of Nazi attacks, on the grounds that Remarque had stained the honour of the soldiers who had fought in the trenches. Elsewhere, Remarque's work played an important part in the mood of appeasement that, during much of the 1930s, characterised Europe's response to the rise of Adolf Hitler.

Common Sense Book of Baby and Child Care, Benjamin Spock (1946). Dr Spock was a New York psychiatrist whose manual became an all-time best seller. Reacting against interwar behaviourism, which deemed that it was emotionally damaging to bestow undue affection upon an infant, Spock adopted a liberal approach, with 'daily stimulation from loving parents' to foster 'emotional depth and intelligence'. In the 1960s the excesses of the 'permissive society' brought severe criticism down upon Spock's head, a backhanded compliment to the huge influence he had exercised.

Nineteen Eighty-Four, George Orwell (1949). 'Big Brother Is Watching You,' the authorities warn a cowed population in perhaps the best-known work of 20th-century imaginative literature. The English novelist's last book, *Nineteen Eighty-Four* is a terrifying picture of a future totalitarian state, and still retains

its power today. Coining the terms 'newspeak' and 'doublethink', it played a major part in undermining the generally accepted ideas of the postwar world about the automatic benevolence of state control.

One Day in the Life of Ivan Denisovich, Alexander Solzhenitsyn (1962). Published during Russia's brief period of liberalisation after 1956, when the new Soviet leader Nikita Khrushchev criticised the policies of his predecessor Joseph Stalin, Solzhenitsyn's novella – based on personal experience of imprisonment and exile between 1945 and 1956 – described one typical day of squalor and inhumanity in a Stalinist labour camp. Touching on many unmentionables, including the mass deportation of citizens because of their religious or political beliefs or class or ethnic background, it had an enormous and irresistible impact. At home it engendered a torrent of written memoirs by other ex-prisoners; abroad it turned Solzhenitsyn into the leading Soviet dissident. Solzhenitsyn's subsequent accounts of the terrors of Stalinism led ultimately to his exile from the Soviet Union in 1974.

Little Red Book, Mao Ze-dong (1965). In the 1960s the Chinese Communist leader Mao launched the 'Cultural Revolution'. The party bureaucracy was destroyed; the 'bourgeois' intelligentsia dismembered; and the People's Liberation Army utilised as a mass egalitarian force on behalf of 'proletarian' ideals. The bible of this movement was Mao's *Little Red Book* – more properly, *Quotations from Chairman Mao Ze-dong* – a distillation of his thinking described as 'the guiding principle for all the work of the party, the army and the country'. Compulsory reading inside China, it became a cult book in the West, where, with its exaltation of revolution, it did much to mould the radical left-wing student movements of the 1960s.

Better to remove and distract him than to say, 'No, no!'

hands of local rulers. Alexander made Borgia Duke of the Romagna in 1501, but his father's death in 1503 severed Borgia's connection with the papacy. Imprisoned in Spain by Pope JULIUS II, Borgia escaped in 1506 and died the next year fighting for the king of Navarre.

Borgia, Lucrezia (1480-1519) Italian noble-woman, the beautiful, illegitimate daughter of Pope Alexander VI, and sister of Cesare Borgia. To further the ambitions of her father and brother, Lucrezia was married three times. Her first marriage, in 1493, was to Giovanni Sforza, Lord of Pesaro, who later accused her of committing incest with her father. She then married Alfonso of Aragon, who was murdered in 1500 at the instigation of her brother. Lucrezia's third husband (1501) was Alfonso d'Este, who became Duke of Ferrara in 1505. Freed from political intrigue by the deaths of her father in 1503 and brother in 1507, Lucrezia devoted the rest of her life to the patronage of art and literature at Alfonso's court. However, lurid accounts of Lucrezia's life involving murder and incestuous orgies in the Vatican have become her enduring legacy, receiving added impetus through works such as the opera *Lucrezia Borgia* (1833) by the Italian composer Gaetano Donizetti.

Bormann, Martin (1900-45) German Nazi leader who became one of Adolf Hitler's closest advisers. Bormann was jailed briefly in 1924 for his part in a political murder. He then joined the Nazi Party, becoming chief of staff to Hitler's deputy, Rudolf HESS, in 1933. After Hess's flight to Scotland in 1941, Bormann was appointed Reichsminister, or head of the party chancellery – a position from which he wielded great power unobtrusively. He was a leading supporter of Nazi death camps, and was accordingly sentenced to death in his absence at the NUREMBERG TRIALS in 1946. For several decades Bormann was alleged to have escaped to South America. In 1973, however, a skeleton exhumed from a West German building site was identified as Bormann's, and he was subsequently declared to have died from unknown causes soon after Hitler committed suicide in 1945.

Borneo Island lying south-east of the Malay peninsula in South-east Asia. Borneo has four political regions: Kalimantan, the largest, which belongs to Indonesia; Sarawak and Sabah, which are part of Malaysia; and the independent Islamic sultanate of BRUNEI, which in the 16th century ruled most of the island. Borneo's population is mostly made up of coastal Malays and indigenous, inland Dyaks. European traders from Portugal and Spain arrived in the 16th century. The Dutch appeared in the early 1600s and gradually took over the area that is today Kalimantan. The British established themselves in the

The Battle of Borodino opened the way for Napoleon to march on Moscow but at a high price. In 12 hours his once-glorious Grande Armée lost about 30 000 men.

in Sarajevo in June 1914, which precipitated the First World War. In 1918 Bosnia and Herzegovina were annexed to Serbia, and in 1946 the two provinces became a joint republic within the state of Yugoslavia.

Following the collapse of communism in eastern Europe in 1989, and the secession of Croatia and Slovenia in 1991, the people of Bosnia and Herzegovina voted for independence, which was declared in 1992. The new country of Bosnia-Herzegovina was plunged into civil war as Bosnian Serbs, aided by troops from Serbia, began carving out autonomous provinces for themselves and ejecting all Bosnian Muslims and Croats. Intervention by both the United Nations and NATO had little effect until late 1995, when the USA brokered a peace settlement between Serbia, Bosnia and Croatia at Dayton, Ohio.

Boston US city, capital of the state of Massachusetts and a major sea port at the mouth of the Charles River. Founded in 1630 by English Puritans, Boston became the largest colony of New England. In the 18th century it became a centre of opposition to Britain. Bostonians took the lead in protesting against the STAMP ACT of 1765, which imposed direct taxation on Britain's colonies. Increasingly hostile clashes between citizens and British soldiers culminated in the Boston Massacre (March 5, 1770), when troops shot dead five members of a rioting mob. In 1773 the BOSTON TEA PARTY further antagonised the British and led to the start of the AMERICAN REVOLUTION (April 1775). Boston was besieged by American militiamen who were defeated in the Battle of BUNKER HILL but a year later George Washington forced British troops to withdraw from the city.

Today Boston has developed as a leading centre for high-technology research, manufacture, education and culture.

Boston Tea Party (December 16, 1773) Name for an act of defiance taken by American colonists against the British tax on tea imports. Aggrieved colonists threw cargoes of tea from British ships into Boston harbour. Britain retaliated by closing the harbour to commerce, quartering troops in the city and replacing the elected colonial assembly with one appointed by the British governor – punitive measures which helped to provoke the War of Independence in April 1775.

Bosworth Field, Battle of (August 22, 1485) Final battle in England's WARS OF THE ROSES, fought near the town of Market Bosworth in Leicestershire between the armies of RICHARD III and Henry Tudor. Henry had returned from exile with a small contingent of French troops on August 7 and marched from Wales adding to his band of followers. Richard was betrayed by several nobles who failed to give him their promised support. At a critical moment in the battle Sir William Stanley, who had been watching from a distance, joined forces with Henry with decisive effect. Richard's army fled and he was killed; Henry was crowned Henry VII, marking the beginning of the Tudor dynasty.

north in about 1665. In 1841 the British 'white rajah' James BROOKE took control of Sarawak. By the late 19th century North Borneo (modern Sabah), Sarawak and Brunei were under some form of British control, and the rest of the island under the Dutch. Invaded by Japan during the Second World War, Borneo began to shake off colonial rule after liberation in 1945. In 1950 Dutch Borneo (Kalimantan) was made part of the Republic of Indonesia, and in 1963 Sabah and Sarawak joined the Federation of Malaysia. Brunei remained a British protectorate until January 1, 1984, when it gained full independence.

Borodino, Battle of (September 7, 1812) Battle fought between the Russian army under General Mikhail Kutuzov and the French forces of Napoleon some 70 miles (110 km) west of Moscow. After 12 hours of fierce combat and a massive artillery bombardment the Russians withdrew, allowing Napoleon to enter Moscow unopposed on September 14. All told some 80 000 troops were lost, making this the bloodiest one-day battle of the Napoleonic Wars.

Bosnia-Herzegovina Republic in the Balkan peninsula, until 1992 one of the six constituent republics of YUGOSLAVIA. By the 10th century two recognisable territories, Bosnia and Hum (later Herzegovina) had emerged. Turkey occupied Bosnia in 1463 and Herzegovina in 1482. The area stagnated for several centuries until a peasant uprising in 1875 led to the intervention of the Russians, who fought a war with Turkey from 1877 to 1878. At the resulting Congress of BERLIN, Bosnia and Herzegovina were placed under the administration of the Austro-Hungarian empire, which formally annexed the region in 1908. This inflamed Serbian nationalists and led to the assassination of Austria's Archduke FRANZ FERDINAND

Enjoying the Boston Tea Party, enthusiastic bystanders cheer as colonial radicals dressed as Mohawks board three ships of the East India Company and hurl chests of tea into Boston harbour.

Botany Bay Inlet on the east coast of Australia where the English explorer Captain James Cook first landed in 1770. Cook gave the bay its name because of the many new plants discovered there by his botanist Sir Joseph Banks. In 1787 Botany Bay was chosen as the site for a penal colony, but the first arrivals found the bay unsuitable and moved some 5 miles (8 km) north to Port Jackson, now known as Sydney Harbour.

Botha, Louis (1862-1919) South African general and statesman. The son of a VOORTREKKER, Botha emerged as a brilliant commander during the second BOER WAR, from 1899 to 1902, during which he rapidly rose to the rank of general. After the war he worked for reconciliation with the British and was elected prime minister of the Transvaal (1907-10). He then became first prime minister of the newly formed Union of South Africa (1910), a position he held until his death. Supported by his friend and colleague Jan SMUTS, Botha took South Africa into the First World War on the side of the Allies. This resulted in considerable Afrikaaner resentment, which boiled over in 1915 when Botha agreed to a British request to invade German South West Africa. After putting down a revolt led by his former comrade General Christiaan de Wet, Botha personally led the invasion of the German colony. Shortly before his death, Botha attended the Versailles Peace Conference, where he pleaded for moderation in the treatment of Germany.

Bothwell, James, 4th Earl of (c.1535-78) Scottish nobleman, the third husband of MARY, QUEEN OF SCOTS. Though a Protestant, Bothwell was a strong supporter of his Catholic queen. In 1565 he helped to put down a rebellion by the Earl of Moray, Mary's half-brother, and soon became her adviser. When Mary's husband, Lord Darnley, was murdered in February 1567 Bothwell was tried for the crime but acquitted. He then quickly divorced his wife, abducted Mary (or so she later claimed) and married her on May 15. By now Bothwell had been made Duke of Orkney and this, together with his marriage, led to an uprising in June by Scottish nobles, who regarded him as a usurper. Forced to flee, Bothwell was shipwrecked off Norway and died insane in a Danish prison.

Botswana Land-locked country in southern Africa, formerly known as Bechuanaland. Originally inhabited by KHOISAN (Bushman) people, the area was gradually occupied from the late 16th century by Bantu-speaking Tswanas. The first European explorers arrived in 1801, and gold was discovered in 1867. Subsequent encroachment by Boers provoked Britain to declare Bechuanaland a protectorate in 1885. At the same time a large area in

the south was made a crown colony before being annexed to the Cape Colony in 1895. Britain's original intention was to incorporate Bechuanaland into the Union of South Africa. This idea finally faltered with the rise of the National Party in South Africa, with its policies of APARTHEID. Bechuanaland was granted full independence as the Republic of Botswana in 1966, with Sir Seretse KHAMA as the nation's first president. Mineral deposits, including diamonds, copper and nickel, have been discovered, but the benefits that these have brought have been offset by the country's severe droughts and unemployment.

Boudicca (d.AD 61) British warrior-queen, known to the Romans as Boadicea. She was the wife of Prasutagus, king of the ICENI – a tribe of British Celts living in and around Norfolk. The Iceni were semi-independent allies of Rome, and when Prasutagus died in AD 59 or 60 he left his kingdom jointly to his two

> **❝ I am fighting as an ordinary person for my lost freedom, my bruised body and my outraged daughters . . . Let the men live in slavery if they will. ❞**
>
> *Boudicca*
> *AD 61*

daughters and the Roman emperor Nero. The Romans responded by annexing and plundering the Iceni kingdom, driving Boudicca to organise a revolt among the peoples of East Anglia. The rebels sacked Roman settlements at Camulodunum (Colchester), Verulamium (St Albans) and Londinium (London), as well as destroying the entire 9th Legion. According to the Roman historian Tacitus, Boudicca's forces slaughtered some 70 000 Romans before being defeated by the governor Suetonius Paulinus. Rather than submit to Rome, Boudicca committed suicide.

Bounty, mutiny on the see BLIGH, WILLIAM

Bourbon French royal house, and one of Europe's most enduring ruling dynasties. The House of Bourbon arose in 1272 when Robert of Clermont, sixth son of the CAPETIAN king Louis IX, married the heiress of the powerful Bourbon family. In 1327 their son, Louis, became 1st Duke of Bourbon, beginning a line that lasted until 1527, when the 7th duke died without an heir. The title then passed to the La Marche-Vendôme branch of the family, descended from a younger son of the 1st duke. In 1548 Antoine de Bourbon married Jeanne d'Albret and became titular king-consort of Navarre while his brother Louis was made Prince of

CONDÉ. With the death in 1589 of Henry III, the last VALOIS king of France, the crown passed to Antoine de Bourbon's son, who became HENRY IV. His heirs ruled France until 1792, when LOUIS XVI was overthrown by the French Revolution. The Bourbons were restored to the French throne after the defeat of Napoleon in 1814, but in 1830 the crown passed to LOUIS-PHILIPPE, Duke of Orléans and a member of another branch of the family deriving from a younger son of Louis XIII. He ruled until the REVOLUTION OF 1848.

Earlier, in 1700, Louis XIV had proclaimed his second grandson, Philippe d'Anjou, PHILIP V of Spain, thereby sparking the War of the SPANISH SUCCESSION. Philip's descendants ruled Spain (where they were known as Borbóns) until the deposition of Alfonso XIII by Republicans in 1931. In 1975 the throne was restored to Alfonso's grandson JUAN CARLOS. Two further lines of Bourbons ruled in Naples and Sicily (where they were known as Borbone) between 1734 and 1860.

Bourguiba, Habib (1903-) Tunisian politician who led his country to independence from France. In 1934 Bourguiba helped to found the Neo-Destour ('Constitution') Party to campaign for Tunisian sovereignty, and was jailed by the French authorities. He spent ten of the next 20 years in prison, but was released in 1954 to negotiate Tunisian self-rule. In 1956 he became his country's first prime minister, and in 1957 its first president following his abolition of the monarchy. Bourguiba pursued a moderate form of socialism and a neutral foreign policy, but he alienated France in 1961 by using the army to force France to quit its one remaining military base at Bizerte. In 1975 Bourguiba was elected president for life, but in 1987 was deposed by Prime Minister Ben Ali.

Bow Street runners First official British POLICE force, recruited by the magistrate and novelist Henry Fielding in 1748. Their name derived from Fielding's courthouse at Bow Street, London. The Bow Street runners served writs and also acted as detectives. They gained a reputation for efficiency as 'thief-takers' and engendered fear and respect among criminals. The runners were disbanded in 1839, ten years after the formation of the London Metropolitan Police by Sir Robert PEEL.

Model of John Townsend, a Bow Street runner who gained royal favour for saving George IV from an attack by a deranged woman.

Boxer Rising (1899-1900) Anti-Western rebellion in China. During the 19th century China suffered a series of natural and military disasters, which prompted many people to turn to semimystical secret societies as a means of restoring the national spirit. One of these was the 'Righteous and Harmonious Fists', or 'Boxers' as Westerners called them, who practised a form of shadowboxing which they believed endowed them with supernatural powers, including immunity from bullets. The movement was at first opposed to the Manchu rulers of China's QING dynasty, but its hostility was cleverly manipulated by the empress dowager CIXI and redirected against foreigners. In late 1899 the Boxers began attacking Christian missions, and in June 1900 they rampaged through Beijing, murdering Chinese Christians and Westerners, and eventually laying siege to the capital's foreign legations in their walled compound. These were relieved in August by an international expeditionary force, which then looted Peking and the imperial FORBIDDEN CITY. Hostilities were formally ended by the Boxer Protocol (1901), which imposed punitive reparations on China leading to the collapse of the Qing dynasty 11 years later.

boyar Member of the highest nonprincely class of medieval Russian society. Between the 10th and 12th centuries the boyars were the most senior members in the retinues of the princes of Kiev. They also formed an important advisory council, or *duma*, and held the higher posts in the State administration and army. In the 13th and 14th centuries the boyars became powerful landowners, transferring their allegiance between princes as they chose. The boyars retained their influence when political power shifted to Moscow in the 14th and 15th centuries, forming a closed aristocratic class drawn from about 200 families. Thereafter, the boyars became progressively weaker as the grand princes of Muscovy consolidated their own power. Under Ivan IV, who ruled from 1533 to 1584, the boyars lost many of their ancient privileges, and in the early 18th century Peter the Great abolished the rank and title of boyar altogether.

Boycott, Charles (1832-97) Retired British army captain who became the first target of Charles PARNELL's policy of noncooperation with Irish landlords and their agents. After leaving the army, Boycott became agent on Lord Erne's estate in County Mayo. In 1879 he was informed by the Land League that he should reduce his tenants' rents because of a possible famine. Boycott refused and in 1880 began evicting the tenants, who were urged by Parnell, president of the Land League, not to communicate or cooperate with Boycott and his family. Boycott was forced to leave Ireland, and Parnell's tactic became known as 'boycotting'.

Boyle, Robert (1627-91) Physicist and chemist, best known for his detailed study of the nature and behaviour of gases. Born into a wealthy family in Ireland, Boyle was educated at Eton and in Europe before settling in Dorset, England. In 1654 he moved to Oxford, and with the assistance of the inventor Robert Hooke constructed the first vacuum pump, which allowed him to demonstrate, among other things, that air has weight and that its pressure affects the boiling point of water. In 1662 he published his discovery that the volume and pressure of a gas are inversely proportional – a principle now known as Boyle's law. Boyle also helped to establish the modern science of chemistry, separating it from the old discipline of alchemy. His book *The Sceptical Chymist* (1661) rejected contemporary theories of matter and offered the first definitions of chemical elements, mixtures and compounds.

Boyne, Battle of the (July 1, 1690) Battle in Ireland in which the Protestant English king WILLIAM III defeated the deposed Roman Catholic king JAMES II. James had been forced to abdicate in 1688 and had assembled an army of French and Irish troops in an attempt to recapture the throne. His force was heavily outnumbered when it was attacked by William's army on the banks of the River Boyne north of Dublin. Believing he was about to be encircled, James fled the battlefield and returned to exile in France. His army survived to fight again the following year at Aughrim, County Wicklow, where it was decisively defeated. Both battles are commemorated annually in Northern Ireland on

During the savage Boxer uprising against foreign nationals and Christians in China in 1900, bloodthirsty Chinese rebels went on the rampage decapitating their victims and impaling their heads on stakes. In the besieged Beijing compound 231 Europeans, mostly missionaries, lost their lives.

The sounds of war disturb the tranquillity of the Irish hills in July 1690 as the troops of William III engage those of James II. This scene from the Battle of the Boyne was painted by Jan Wyck.

the anniversary of the battle of Aughrim (August 12), their memory kept alive by the Orange Order – a political society founded in 1795 to support a Protestant monarchy.

Bradley, Omar (1893-1981) US general who played a leading role in the later stages of the Second World War. Bradley led the US 2nd Corps to prominent victories in Tunisia in May 1943 and Sicily in August 1943. He was then given command of the US 1st Army and helped to plan the invasion of France. In June 1944 Bradley led his troops in the assault on Normandy, and in August he oversaw the liberation of Paris. He was then promoted to command of the US 12th Army Group, the largest US group in the war, directing it in the battle for Germany. After the war Bradley was instrumental in formulating US global defence strategy and in building up NATO. From 1949 to 1953 he served as the first permanent chairman of the Joint Chiefs of Staff, in which capacity he was promoted in 1950 to the position of General of the Army, which he held until his retirement in 1953.

Bradman, Sir Donald (1908-) Australian cricketer, popularly known as 'the Don', who was the most successful batsman in the history of the game. Between 1928 and 1948 Bradman scored 29 centuries in international Test matches, and in the same period achieved a Test average of 99.94 runs per match. Among his many other records, Bradman achieved a best score of 452 not out. He retired in 1948 and was knighted the following year.

Braganza Royal dynasty which ruled Portugal from 1640 to 1910. The family was descended from Alfonso, an illegitimate son of John I of Portugal, who was made 1st Duke of Braganza in 1442. His descendants gained a claim to the throne when John, the 6th duke, married a niece of John III. From 1580 Portugal was ruled by the kings of Spain, but in 1640 Portuguese independence was restored and the 8th Duke of Braganza was crowned John IV. His descendants ruled Portugal without interruption until 1910 when the country became a republic. When Brazil declared its independence from Portugal in 1822, it was ruled as an empire by two members of the Braganza family until the revolution of 1889.

Brandenburg Eastern German principality which formed the nucleus of the kingdom of PRUSSIA. The area was once populated by Slavic people, who were conquered and Christianised by German kings from the early 12th century. After the THIRTY YEARS' WAR (1618-48), Brandenburg emerged as a significant power under FREDERICK WILLIAM, who secured excellent terms at the Treaty of WESTPHALIA (1648) and subsequently turned Brandenburg-Prussia into a powerful European state with a healthy economy and a highly effective army and bureaucracy. Frederick William's son and successor, Frederick III (1657-1713), persuaded the Holy Roman Emperor to grant him the title King of Prussia, and he was crowned as FREDERICK I in January 1701.

From this date until 1947 the history of Brandenburg is merged with that of Prussia. In 1815 Brandenburg formally became a province of Prussia, a status it kept after the unification of Germany (1871) and the establishment of the WEIMAR REPUBLIC (1919). At the end of the Second World War, Prussia was formally abolished by the victorious Allies (1947), and part of the old territory of Brandenburg re-emerged as a state of East Germany. It was subsequently dissolved in 1952 during the reorganisation of East German states, but reconstituted in 1990, after the reunification of East and West Germany, with Potsdam as its capital.

Brandt, Willy (1913-92) German statesman who was mayor of Berlin, and later chancellor of the former West Germany from 1969 to 1974. Born Herbert Frahm, he adopted the name Willy Brandt after fleeing to Norway in 1933 to escape the Nazis. Brandt returned to Berlin after the war, entered politics and was elected to the federal parliament in 1949. From 1957 to 1966 he served as mayor of West Berlin, earning international renown for resisting Soviet demands in 1958 that Berlin become a demilitarised free city, and then dealing with the crisis of the BERLIN WALL in 1961. Elected chancellor in 1969, Brandt developed a policy of OSTPOLITIK ('East politics'), or détente, towards Eastern Europe,

Willy Brandt kneels at the memorial of the Warsaw ghetto in December 1970. This public acknowledgment of the Holocaust was a historic moment in postwar German-Jewish relations.

A 19th-century lithographer observes the social divide in colonial Brazil. A wealthy Portuguese woman, followed from church by her servants, buys flowers from a Black street vendor.

which led to the signing of non-aggression pacts with the Soviet Union and Poland in 1970, agreement on the status of Berlin in 1971 and a treaty with East Germany in 1972. In recognition of his work, Brandt was awarded the Nobel peace prize in 1971. He was forced to resign in 1974 when it emerged that a senior aide was an East German spy. Between 1977 and 1979 Brandt chaired an international commission (the Brandt Commission) on the state of the world economy, which recommended urgent improvement in trade relations between rich countries in the Northern Hemisphere and poor countries in the developing Southern Hemisphere.

Brazil Largest country in South America and the only one originally established there as a Portuguese rather than Spanish colony. The indigenous inhabitants were mostly nomadic Indians. In April 1500 the explorer Pedro Cabral claimed Brazil for Portugal under the terms of the 1494 Treaty of TORDESILLAS which divided the known world between Spain and Portugal. Over the next century, *bandeirantes* pushed into the southern interior in search of Indian slaves and gold, while in the north-east landowners established great sugar estates, for which they imported large numbers of Black slaves from Africa. The discovery of gold in 1695 created a gold rush to the interior and brought such wealth to the colony that it was soon more prosperous than Portugal. This prompted nationalist agitation and an abortive revolution in 1789 under the leadership of José da Silva Xavier, nicknamed 'Tiradentes', the 'Tooth-puller'.

When Napoleon invaded Portugal in 1807, the heir to the throne, Dom John (later John VI), fled to Brazil and set up court in Rio de Janeiro, which became the centre of the Portuguese empire. In 1821 John returned to Lisbon, leaving behind his son Dom Pedro. The following year Pedro crowned himself emperor (see PEDRO I) of an independent Brazil. The Brazilian empire lasted until 1889 when PEDRO II abdicated and a republic was formed with Deodora da Fonseca as president.

Early in the 20th century the collapse of Brazil's lucrative rubber and coffee markets created a climate of economic instability that allowed Gétulio VARGAS to seize control in 1930. In 1938 he instituted a military-backed dictatorship. His rule brought Brazil many benefits, but failed to curb the country's chronic high inflation and he lost power after the military withdrew their support in 1945. Vargas was elected president again in 1950 but committed suicide four years later. His successor was Juscelino Kubitschek, who was elected president in 1955. Kubitschek's ambitious programme to expand Brazil's economy and construct the futuristic new capital of Brasilia, intended to encourage development of the interior, also produced a severe balance-of-payments deficit accompanied by even worse inflation. These conditions resulted in political instability, marked by widespread terrorism from 1964 to 1979 when the military seized power. The presidency of General João Figueiredo (1979-85) restored order to the country, resulting in a return to civilian rule in 1985 under José Sarney. In 1989 Brazil had its first free election in almost three decades, but in 1992 the winner, President Fernando Collor de Mello, was impeached for corruption. The country faces international concern over the rapid destruction of the Amazon rain forest for timber, mining and cattle-ranching.

Breakspear, Nicholas see ADRIAN IV

Brecht, Bertolt (1898-1956) German dramatist and poet noted for his experimental theatrical writings and productions. Brecht first studied medicine, then turned to writing plays which expressed a deep antipathy to bourgeois values. During the late 1920s Brecht was converted to Marxism, which led him to reject traditional dramatic forms. He began developing a new style, which he called 'epic theatre' – a blend of narrative, commentary, song and loosely related episodes. His intention was to destroy the illusion of the theatre and stimulate the audience into critical reflection on the action, rather than emotional identification with it. From 1924 to 1933 Brecht worked in Berlin, where he produced his first major triumph, *The Threepenny Opera* (1928), an adaptation of John Gay's *The Beggar's Opera*, with music by Kurt Weill. The rise of the Nazis forced Brecht to go into exile, first in Scandinavia from 1933 to 1941, then in the USA to 1947. During this period he wrote many of his finest plays, among them *Mother Courage and her Children*, *The Life of Galileo* and *The Caucasian Chalk Circle* – works which reveal Brecht's characteristic concern for justice, sardonic humour and compassion for humanity. In 1947 Brecht left the USA and in 1949 he returned to (East) Berlin, where he formed the Berliner Ensemble.

Breda City in the province of North Brabant in the south-west Netherlands. In 1566 the city gave its name to a document that marked the first Dutch opposition to Spanish rule in the Netherlands. The so-called Compromise of Breda was signed by a league of Dutch and Flemish nobles and burghers, both Protestant and Roman Catholic, to protest against the infringement of liberties by the Spanish government. The city was captured by the Spanish in 1581 and again in 1625 – the latter event immortalised in Diego Velázquez's

> ### DID YOU KNOW?
>
> *Brazil's name comes from 'brazilin', a red dye extracted from brazilwood, one of the former colony's main products.*

painting *The Surrender of Breda*. In 1660 Breda became home to the exiled Charles II of England. In April of that year he issued his Declaration of Breda, in which he promised an amnesty to his former enemies, religious toleration and payment of salary arrears to the army if he were restored to the throne. Seven years later, Breda saw the signing of the Treaty of Breda, which ended the second ANGLO-DUTCH WAR. The treaty recognised English control of New Netherland (later New York and New Jersey), and Dutch dominion over the East Indies and Dutch Guiana.

Brendan, St (*c*.484-578) Irish abbot and hero of legendary Atlantic voyages, also called Brendan the Navigator and Brendan of Clonfert. Brendan founded several monasteries in Scotland and Ireland, the greatest of them Clonfert (*c*.560) in County Galway, Ireland, where he was abbot. He also gained a reputation as a traveller, visiting holy sites in Brittany, the Hebrides and western Scotland, including St Columba's monastery on the island of Iona. Brendan was later immortalised in a remarkable Irish epic which was translated into Latin prose in about 1050 as *Navigatio Brendani* ('The Voyage of Brendan'). The story tells how Brendan and a group of monks sailed across the Atlantic to the 'Promised Land of the Saints'. Often called St Brendan's Island, this mythical land was sought by sailors for centuries and has popularly been identified as the Canary Islands.

On his legendary Atlantic voyage, St Brendan, at the prow of his boat in this 1911 stained-glass window, meets the penitent Judas.

Brest-Litovsk, Treaty of (March 3, 1918) Peace treaty signed at the Polish city of Brest-Litovsk (now Brest in Belarus) between the Central Powers (Germany, Austria-Hungary, Bulgaria and Turkey) and Soviet Russia towards the end of the First World War. A peace conference, requested by Russia, had opened in December 1917, but had made little headway as Leon Trotsky, head of the Russian delegation, continually stalled the proceedings. In February the Germans renewed hostilities towards Russia, prompting the BOLSHEVIK government to capitulate on Vladimir Lenin's instructions. By the terms of the treaty Russia surrendered nearly half of its European territories: Finland, the Baltic states, Poland, the Ukraine and parts of Belorussia and the Caucasus. The treaty was later annulled by the ARMISTICE of November 1918, which marked the defeat of the Central Powers. Russia's western boundaries were decided by a series of later treaties – among them the VERSAILLES PEACE SETTLEMENT, which resulted in the return of the Ukraine to Russian control.

Brétigny, Treaty of (May 8, 1360) Peace treaty which attempted to end the war (eventually the HUNDRED YEARS' WAR) between England and France. In 1356 the French king John II (1319-64) had been captured at the Battle of POITIERS. The Treaty of Brétigny set John's ransom at 3 million gold écus (crowns), and guaranteed English sovereignty over Aquitaine, Gascony, Calais and other territories in return for an end to English claims to the French throne. In October 1360 John was released to help to raise his own ransom, but in 1363 he surrendered himself back into captivity when his second son, who had been held as a substitute hostage, broke his parole and escaped. John died in London a few months later, and by 1370 hostilities with England had resumed.

Bretton Woods Conference (July 1-22, 1944) Informal name given to the United Nations Monetary and Financial Conference held at Bretton Woods, New Hampshire, USA, to consider global financial arrangements after the end of the Second World War. The conference was attended by 44 nations, including the Soviet Union, and resulted in the formation of two major institutions: the International Bank for Reconstruction and Development (see WORLD BANK) which would make long-term capital available to states urgently needing such aid, and the INTERNATIONAL MONETARY FUND (IMF), with responsibility for financing short-term imbalances in international trade and payments. The conference created an international financial system with stable exchange rates and currency values fixed against US dollars and gold. This lasted until the early 1970s, when the US government ended the convertibility of dollars to gold, and floating exchange rates were introduced.

Brezhnev, Leonid (1906-82) Statesman and leader of the Soviet Communist Party from 1964 to 1982. Brezhnev joined the Communist Party in 1931 and worked his way steadily through its hierarchy, becoming a member of the Central Committee in 1952. In 1960, as a result of his support for Nikita KHRUSHCHEV, he was made chairman of the

> 66 **Peaceful coexistence in no way implies the possibility of relaxing the ideological struggle. On the contrary we must be prepared for this struggle to be intensified...** 99
>
> *Leonid Brezhnev, speaking on East-West détente, June 1972*

presidium of the Supreme Soviet (titular head of state). Four years later Brezhnev resigned this position to become Khrushchev's assistant, but after only three months he helped to oust Khrushchev, and took his position as first secretary (later general secretary) of the Communist Party in October 1964. After initially sharing power with his fellow conspirator Aleksei KOSYGIN, Brezhnev rapidly became the dominant figure in Soviet politics. In 1968 he justified the Soviet invasion of Czechoslovakia by asserting that the Soviet Union had the right to interfere in the affairs of any WARSAW PACT nation if communist rule was threatened or undermined there – a policy that became known as the 'Brezhnev Doctrine'. During the 1970s Brezhnev pursued a policy of détente with the West, and especially the USA. At the same time his administration imposed harsh punishments on Soviet dissidents, and maintained tight control over the Soviet-bloc countries of Eastern Europe. In 1977 Brezhnev was elected chairman of the presidium (thereby becoming both head of state and head of the party), but his failing health resulted in a paralysis in policy-making, which contributed to long stagnation in the Soviet economy.

Brian Boru (*c*.926-1014) Last high king of Ireland – the king to whom all lesser kings paid respect. In 976 Brian acceded to the throne of Munster, which he built into a powerful state, and subdued other kingdoms in southern Ireland. In 997 he defeated the high king Maelsechlainn II and thereby ended the influence of the powerful Uí Néill dynasty which had dominated Ireland for three centuries. In 1002 Brian became high king himself, though his authority was never fully accepted. In 1014 he faced a serious challenge from the king of Leinster, the Norse king of

Dublin and several Scandinavian allies. On April 23, Brian's army decisively defeated his enemies at Clontarf, near Dublin. After the battle, a party of Norsemen found Brian and murdered him. The battle broke the power of the Norse in Ireland, but also resulted in some 150 years of clan warfare.

Briand, Aristide (1862-1932) French statesman who served as foreign minister in 14 successive governments, and as premier 11 times between 1909 and 1929. Briand entered the chamber of deputies in 1902, a dedicated socialist and an impressive orator. In 1905 he played a leading role in obtaining the formal separation of Church and State, and in 1909 he was made premier for the first time. During the First World War Briand headed two coalition governments, but in 1917 he was forced to resign after several failed military campaigns. After the war he devoted himself to supporting international peace and cooperation and the LEAGUE OF NATIONS. Briand returned to power in 1921, only to resign the following year after criticising the VERSAILLES PEACE SETTLEMENT for its harsh treatment of Germany. Returning to the Cabinet in 1925 as foreign minister, Briand worked with Austen CHAMBERLAIN and Gustav STRESEMANN to achieve the LOCARNO PACT (1925), which attempted to normalise relations between Germany and its former enemies. In 1926 he shared the Nobel peace prize with Stresemann and in 1928 he helped to devise the Kellogg-Briand Pact, in which 60 countries declared war an illegal means of achieving foreign policy. In 1930 Briand began championing a federal union of Europe.

Bridgewater, Francis, 3rd Duke of (1736-1803) British landowner who financed Britain's first canal and so inaugurated the great era of English canal building in the 1770s and 1780s. Looking for cheap transport for the coal produced by the mines on his estates, Bridgewater in 1759 commissioned the engineer James Brindley (1716-72) to construct a 10 mile (16 km) canal from Worsley to Manchester. Bridgewater's canal was a marvel of 18th-century engineering, especially where it crossed the Irwell Valley by aqueduct. Later extended to Liverpool, the canal caused a dramatic reduction in the price of coal and brought Brindley commissions for a further 360 miles (580 km) of canals.

Brigantes Celtic tribe (whose name means 'mountain folk') inhabiting northern England in the region of what is now Yorkshire. After the Roman invasion of Britain in AD 43 the emperor Claudius formed an alliance with Cartimandua, queen of the Brigantes, in order to stabilise her territory. Roman troops helped to suppress at least three revolts against her, and in 51 she handed over the rebellious king

CARATACUS after he had fled into her domain as a refugee. In about 68 Cartimandua repudiated her anti-Roman husband, who then led a rebellion which overthrew her. The Roman governor of Britain, Petilius Cerealis, responded in about 71 by conquering the Brigantes and establishing a permanent legionary fortress for the Ninth Legion at Eboracum (York), previously a stronghold of the Britons. In about 155 the Brigantes again rebelled, and this time the Romans subjugated them completely.

Britain, Battle of (August-October 1940) Name given to a series of intensive air raids launched against Britain by the German Luftwaffe in the early stages of the Second World War. After the fall of France in June 1940 Germany prepared for an invasion of Britain by bombing British ports, ships and coastal defences, but suffered heavy losses to fighter planes of the Royal Air Force (RAF). In August the Germans shifted their attention to aircraft factories and RAF airfields, causing considerable destruction – but German losses were still high because of the tenacity of RAF fighter pilots and the accuracy with which they were directed by British RADAR.

With their invasion plans frustrated by failure to cripple the RAF, the Germans turned suddenly, in early September, to bombing British cities – the beginning of the 'Blitz', which caused extensive damage, particularly in London, Coventry and Plymouth. Paradoxically this change in tactics gave the RAF enough breathing space to recover its strength. By the beginning of October the Battle of Britain had reached stalemate and on October 12 Hitler postponed his plan to invade Britain. The barrage of air raids against

British cities continued until April 1941, but Germany had suffered its first major defeat of the war, with more than 2500 aircraft destroyed, against 900 of the RAF.

Britain, Great The countries of ENGLAND, WALES and SCOTLAND, together with neighbouring islands such as the Shetlands, linked together as a political and administrative unit. Often referred to as 'Britain', it does not include the Isle of Man (a crown possession) or the CHANNEL ISLANDS (crown dependencies), all of which have their own systems of government. Neither does it include the province of Northern Ireland, or Ulster, which belongs within the larger political formation known as the United Kingdom.

Great Britain as a political unit has its origins in the 13th century, when the principality of Wales was defeated by Edward I and so became subject to English rule. The two countries were formally joined by Henry VIII's Act of Union in 1536. In 1603 the kingdoms of Scotland and England took a step towards union when James VI of Scotland inherited the throne of England as JAMES I and called himself 'King of Great Britain'. However, the two countries remained separate kingdoms under a single monarch, and each retained its own parliament. From 1653 to 1659 the Scottish and English parliaments were temporarily linked in Oliver Cromwell's PROTECTORATE. Then in 1707 both parliaments voted to merge, and so to unite England, Scotland and Wales as a single Kingdom of Great Britain. By the terms of the resulting Act of Union the Scottish Parliament was abolished, and Scotland gained free access to English trade together with permanent safeguards for its Church and legal system.

Paul Nash's *Battle of Britain* traces aerial warfare above the Thames. In a dance of death over the heads of civilians, RAF Hurricanes and Spitfires fight to halt Hitler's invasion of Britain in 1940.

Top-hatted dignitaries of the British Raj ride high during a *durbar* (imperial public audience) of Akbar II in Delhi, 1815. The splendid ceremonies of the waning Mughal empire were readily adopted by the British later in the 19th century for their own celebrations, especially royal occasions.

Following Wolfe TONE's unsuccessful rebellion against British rule in IRELAND in 1798, the British Parliament passed a second ACT OF UNION in 1801, creating the United Kingdom of Great Britain and Ireland. This lasted until 1921, when Ireland was partitioned into the Irish Free State and Northern Ireland. From then on the Union was restricted to Great Britain and Northern Ireland. Referendums held in Scotland and Wales in 1979 failed to win majority approval for devolution, but in 1995 the Conservative government revealed plans to allow the Scottish Grand Committee of all 72 Scottish MPs to debate uncontroversial legislation which concerned Scotland.

British Empire see feature, page 94

British Expeditionary Force (BEF)
British army contingent formed in 1906 to fight overseas at short notice. Under Richard HALDANE, Britain's secretary for war from 1905 to 1912, the British army was restructured to create a volunteer reserve force called the Territorial Army, and a regular army of professionals that could be sent abroad, as a BEF, in an emergency. Just such an occasion arose with the outbreak of the First World War in August 1914, and a BEF was despatched to France, where it suffered heavy losses. By the end of 1914 on average only one officer and 30 men survived of each BEF battalion of approximately 600 troops. By 1915 the BEF was heavily supported by territorial volunteers, and from 1916 by armies of conscripts. In 1939 another BEF was sent to France, but had to be hastily evacuated from DUNKIRK in 1940. The rest of the war was again largely fought by armies of conscripts.

British Honduras see BELIZE

British North America Act (July 1867)
Act of Parliament uniting the colonies of Nova Scotia, New Brunswick and CANADA (which at the time consisted of the modern provinces of QUEBEC and Ontario) to form the Dominion of Canada. As the American Civil War drew to a close, several British North American colonies began discussing the possibility of forming a federation to prevent US expansionism. In 1867 Canada, Nova Scotia and New Brunswick reached an agreement leading to the British North America Act, which bound them together as 'one Dominion under the name of Canada'. The Act also split the old colony of Canada into the provinces of Quebec and Ontario, defined federal and provincial legislative powers, and made provision for other British territories and colonies in the region to become part of the dominion. By the terms of the Act, the dominion retained the status of a colony, but with a system of parliamentary and Cabinet government similar to that of Britain. The Act functioned as the constitution of Canada until 1982, when it was superseded by the Constitution of Canada Act.

British Raj
Term for Britain's Indian Empire derived from the Hindi word *raj*, 'rule', especially as it existed between 1858 and 1949. From the early 1740s the British EAST INDIA COMPANY (EIC) strove to establish itself as the principal European trading company in INDIA, and also to capture as much territory as possible. Its supremacy was established by Robert CLIVE's defeat of the Nawab of Bengal at PLASSEY in 1757, and later confirmed by the Treaty of Paris in 1763. In the process the EIC became more than a powerful trading organisation; it acquired direct control of certain parts of India, afterwards known as British India. Over the next half century the British Government passed a series of laws giving the EIC formal authority to govern in India, as well as conferring on itself significant power over EIC policies and activities.

By the early 19th century Britain, through the EIC, controlled about half of India. The remainder, the so-called princely states, was ruled by local princes under the guidance of British officials called residents. By the middle of the century British political control of the subcontinent was complete, from the Punjab to Ceylon (now Sri Lanka). Between 1857 and 1859 the colonial establishment in India was thrown into disarray by the bloody Indian Mutiny, which prompted the British Government to assume direct control of all territory administered by the EIC. By the terms of the Government of India Act of 1858, India was to be governed locally by a viceroy answerable to the British Government.

The next 50 years were the heyday of the Raj, the high point in British imperial ambitions, symbolised in 1877 by Queen Victoria's assumption of the title of Empress of India. This period also saw the emergence of Indian nationalism, particularly in the form of the Indian National CONGRESS, founded in 1885 by Indians who wished to see the British sharing political power with local leaders. By 1909 the British Government had introduced a number of political reforms, but its determination to keep control of the reins of power led to some ugly confrontations, among them the AMRITSAR Massacre of 1919. In 1935 the Indian National Congress, led by Mahatma GANDHI and Jawaharlal NEHRU, won an overwhelming election victory and began campaigning for a complete British withdrawal from India. This resulted in the internment of Congress leaders during the Second World War.

Following further elections in 1946, the British Raj officially ended in August 1947 with the partition of the Empire of India into the independent states of India and Pakistan. By this time British rule had brought lasting change to the Indian subcontinent, particularly evident in the widespread use of the English language and in the structure and organisation of the armed forces, civil service and educational systems of several countries in the region.

> **DID YOU KNOW?**
>
> In 1931 Gandhi dominated the first day of London's Conference on India without uttering a word. He had vowed to remain silent on Mondays.

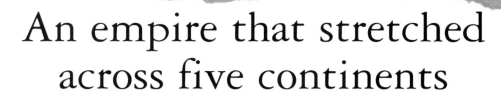

An empire that stretched across five continents

The British Empire was the largest and most enduring of modern times. Its influence is still felt from North America to Australia, from Africa to India, where the language and administration of Britain live on in modern forms.

The first permanent British settlement outside Europe was established on the coast of North America in 1607. From this point on, growth was continuous, and by the end of the 19th century the empire extended from Canada across Africa and South and South-east Asia to Australasia and the Pacific. With additions in the Middle East, it reached its fullest extent in the 1930s, when about a quarter of the world's people lived under British rule.

During the 16th century and the first half of the 17th, England had lagged behind Spain and Portugal in the acquisition of overseas territories. The Spanish had built a powerful empire on the ruins of the Amerindian kingdoms of Central and South America. The English were able to settle only on its fringes, along the North American coast and on the outer islands of the Caribbean. There adventurers tried to carve out estates.

After many failures, two valuable trades were developed: tobacco, centred on the Chesapeake in North America, and sugar on the West Indian islands. The workforce came at first from emigration from the British Isles. Some 400 000 people crossed the Atlantic in the 17th century, mostly as labourers; a small number – such as the Pilgrims in the *Mayflower* of 1620 and the Puritans who colonised Massachusetts in the 1630s – went to create new communities inspired by religious ideals.

EXPANDING TRADE AND POWER

The Portuguese were the first to exploit the route to Asia around the Cape of Good Hope. Until the 19th century, Europeans went to Asia not to conquer, but to trade in the valuable commodities that Asians were already producing, especially spices, silk and cotton cloth. In 1600 the English East India Company was launched to compete with the other European companies in the trade around the Indian Ocean.

By the mid 17th century Asian goods and American tobacco and sugar, now largely cultivated by African slaves imported by English traders, were helping to make England rich. The overseas activities of the English were backed by the armed forces of what was becoming one of Europe's strongest states. London was emerging as a financial centre, and ports such as Bristol and Liverpool prospered on the international trade. During the 18th century Britain's naval and military power won it mastery in North America, the West Indies, along the West African coast and around the Indian Ocean. In a series of wars for imperial dominance, it beat off competition from the Dutch and, above all, Britain's main rival, the French.

The growth of the British Empire was checked by the revolt of the North American colonists against attempts to make imperial rule over them more effective. From 1765 disaffection was apparent; independence was declared in 1776; and by 1783 Britain had to abandon any attempt to rule. The loss of more than 2.5 million people and 13 colonies was a severe but

OUR ALLIES THE COLONIES

As late as the mid 20th century Britain's colonies were still spread across the globe (above). The glamorous imagery of empire appeared everywhere and was used to sell even the most everyday products.

Patriotic fervour reached a peak during Queen Victoria's Diamond Jubilee in 1897. Her procession reaches St Paul's Cathedral (below).

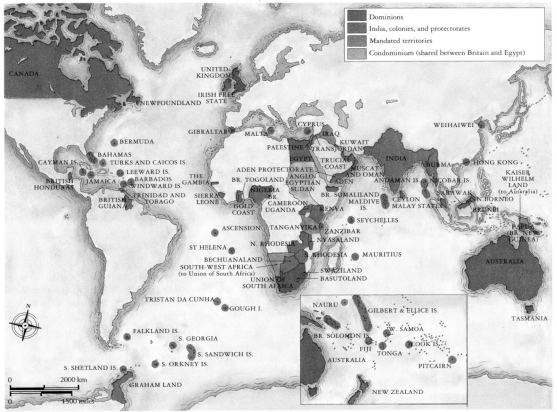

Dominions

India, colonies, and protectorates

Mandated territories

Condominium (shared between Britain and Egypt)

The British Empire reached its greatest extent during the 1930s in the aftermath of the First World War, but by then it was under pressure both from rival powers and from its subjects who were demanding political independence.

only temporary blow. The British remained in North America in Canada, which they had recently conquered from the French.

Spectacular expansion was taking place elsewhere. In India conquests were launched from the East India Company's trading settlements. In Bengal, British forces under Robert Clive intervened in 1757 to depose a ruler and substitute a British ally. From 1765 Bengal was under British rule. Other conquests followed. In 1788 the first European settlement in Australia was established by the shipping of convicts to Sydney. In 1806 the British took possession of the Cape of Good Hope.

For most of the 19th century the empire grew without much competition from other European powers. Armies conquered Indian states and brought the whole subcontinent under British domination by mid century. By 1871 the Indian empire covered some 250 million people. The whole of Australia was claimed by Britain; New Zealand was annexed in 1840; and British Canada was extended westwards to the Pacific. Large

numbers of British migrants moved into all three territories and were increasingly allowed to run their own affairs. During the 19th century the Royal Navy intervened to protect British interests in many parts of the world not directly under British rule, as in the Opium Wars on the China coast from 1839 to 1842 and 1856 to 1860.

FROM EMPIRE TO COMMONWEALTH

British world supremacy was challenged towards the close of the 19th century. France, Germany and Russia developed interests beyond Europe, and the USA and Japan emerged as new powers. Within the empire there were stirrings of nationalism, with people beginning to demand the right to self-government. Britain responded by occupying more territory to protect its interests and head off the claims of others. A large part of tropical Africa, not until then regarded as valuable, was annexed for Britain by such freelance adventurers as Cecil Rhodes, who in the 1890s built up a vast British domain in central Africa extending over what is now Zimbabwe, Zambia and Malawi.

The most overt nationalist challenge, that of the Afrikaner Boers in South Africa, was repressed by the costly Boer War

between 1899 and 1902. Threats to British supremacy also provoked jingoistic assertions of nationalism, glorifying the empire as the source of Britain's greatness – the spirit embodied in Queen Victoria's Diamond Jubilee celebrations in 1897.

The empire survived for much of the 20th century despite threats from Britain's rivals and from those who sought to break free. The most formidable of the independence movements developed in India under the inspiration of Mahatma Gandhi. Increasing self-rule was granted to non-European peoples as well as to the ex-British communities such as Australia. The empire of British rule gradually evolved into a Commonwealth of former British territories voluntarily allied with Britain. Its peoples supported Britain in both world wars: more than 5 million of them served alongside 'the mother country' between 1939 and 1945.

After 1945 Britain's capacity to rule was weakened. Britain had become a second-rate power in relation to the United States and the Soviet Union. Nationalism could no longer be checked, and it no longer seemed in Britain's interests to do so. The focus of its trade had shifted, especially after Britain joined the European Common Market in 1973. By then the Indian empire had been replaced by an independent India and Pakistan, and the African empire was being dismantled. Hong Kong, the last major colony, reverts to China in 1997.

Everywhere they went the British took their language and their institutions with them. English took root and the British liked to think that a respect for law and for human rights, together with sound and honest administration and parliamentary government, were also spread throughout the world. In practice, the advantages these brought were more available to White people than to non-European imperial subjects, who suffered various abuses: especially in southern Africa, many indigenous peoples lost their lands.

The rule of one people by another now seems indefensible, but genuine ideals underlaid the British Empire, even if the British did not always live up to them.

Brittany Region in north-west France with a distinct local culture including a language, unrelated to French, known as Breton. Brittany was conquered in 56 BC by Julius Caesar, who made it part of the Roman province of Lugdunensis. During the 5th and 6th centuries AD many Celts migrated there from Britain, including Christian missionaries who gave their names to towns such as St Malo and St Brieuc. Between the 6th and 9th centuries, petty lords of Brittany maintained independence from the FRANKS. In the 10th century Geoffrey of Rennes assumed the title of Duke of Brittany after his father, Conan of Rennes, had emerged as the region's single, supreme ruler, and for several centuries their successors battled to preserve Breton autonomy against the dukes of Normandy and counts of Anjou.

Control of the duchy eventually passed to the French crown in 1488, after it was inherited by Anne of Brittany, who was successively married to the French kings Charles VIII and Louis XII. The incorporation of Brittany as a province of France was formally confirmed in 1532 by a treaty which also guaranteed some autonomy for the region. At the start of the French Revolution in 1789 the province was a stronghold of republicanism, but by 1792 the antireligious campaign of France's First Republic had made Brittany a centre of anti-revolutionary sentiment. Generally conservative and deeply religious, Bretons have always been wary of centralised government. This led to the steady growth of Breton nationalism during the 19th century, and sporadic acts of violence in the 20th century – such as the bombing of the Palace of Versailles in 1978.

Britten, Benjamin (1913-76) British composer, pianist and conductor. Britten began composing as a young child and rose to international prominence at the 1937 Salzburg Festival with his *Variations on a Theme by Frank Bridge*. In that year he met the tenor Peter Pears, who was to become his companion and artistic associate. After facing a conscientious objector's tribunal in 1942, Britten went on to compose the perennially popular *The Young Person's Guide to the Orchestra* as well as the tragic opera *Peter Grimes* (both performed in 1945), the latter establishing him as the most important opera composer of his generation. In the years that followed Britten wrote some of his best-known works, including the operas *Billy Budd*, *The Turn of the Screw* and *A Midsummer Night's Dream*. He produced his choral *War Requiem* in 1962 for the consecration of the new Coventry Cathedral. In 1976 Britten was made a life peer, as Baron Britten of Aldeburgh – the first musician to receive this honour.

Broken Hill Man Early form of modern human also called Kabwe Man or Rhodesian Man – technically *Homo sapiens rhodesiensis*,

This portrait of Anne, Emily and Charlotte Brontë was painted by their brother, Branwell. The shadowy figure just visible in the centre was Branwell's self-portrait, which he later painted out.

whose fossilised bones were found in 1921 at Broken Hill, Northern Rhodesia (present-day Kabwe, Zambia). The bones represent a population of ancient *Homo sapiens sapiens* who lived in southern Africa between 200 000 and 400 000 years ago. They are in many respects indistinguishable from the bones of modern humans (*Homo sapiens*), yet the skull has certain features typical of NEANDERTHAL Man – who developed in the Northern Hemisphere about 125 000 years ago. Consequently palaeontologists are unsure whether Broken Hill Man was the ancestor of modern humans or of Neanderthals, or perhaps even of both.

Brontë sisters Three British sisters, Charlotte (1816-55), Emily (1818-48) and Anne (1820-49), who were all novelists and poets. The sisters grew up with their only brother, Branwell (1817-48), amid the bleak Yorkshire moors, creating for themselves a rich imaginative life by writing stories. Two other sisters, Maria and Elizabeth, died in childhood. In 1846 the three sisters published a volume of poems under the pseudonyms Currer, Ellis and Acton Bell. The collection shows Emily as the most gifted poet of the three. She also emerged as an inspired novelist with her only work *Wuthering Heights*, a powerful story of passion and hate which is now acknowledged as one of the finest novels in the English language. In 1847 Charlotte published her masterpiece *Jane Eyre* while Anne published *Agnes Grey* and, in 1848, *The Tenant of Wildfell Hall*. As the Brontës were showing their greatest promise they were struck by tragedy – Branwell, Emily and Anne all dying of tuberculosis between September 1848 and May 1849. Charlotte went on to publish the novels *Shirley* in 1849 and *Villette* in 1853. She married in June 1854 but died within a year.

Bronze Age Period in human technological development when the metals copper and then bronze (a mixture of copper and tin) were used as the primary materials for making tools and weapons. The Bronze Age began in China and the Middle East before 3000 BC, in Britain in about 1900 BC and in the Americas in about AD 1100. In all these cases it was preceded by the STONE AGE, and in most cases was followed by the IRON AGE. However, some Bronze Age peoples, such as the Incas, never progressed to iron-working, and some Iron Age peoples, such as the African Nguni, never had a transitional Bronze Age. Among the peoples of the Middle East and also the Mediterranean the early Bronze Age saw the rise of the great civilisations of Mesopotamia, Sumer, Crete and Mycenae. The search for new deposits of copper and tin led to exploration, colonisation and trading across much of Europe, which gradually emerged from the Stone Age as the new technology spread northwards. Before 1000 BC the process for smelting iron – a far more common ore – had been discovered, and a new era was about to dawn under such peoples as the Scythians, Greeks and Etruscans.

Brooke, Sir James (1803-68) British adventurer who established a dynasty of 'white rajahs' that ruled the state of SARAWAK on the island of BORNEO from 1841 to 1946. In 1838, after serving in the army of the EAST INDIA COMPANY, Brooke bought an armed schooner and sailed to Singapore and then Borneo. Here he assisted Muda Hassim, uncle of the Sultan of BRUNEI, in his war against the rebel Dyak tribes of neighbouring Sarawak. As a reward, Brooke was declared Rajah of Sarawak in 1841, a title confirmed in perpetuity by the sultan in 1846. Brooke ruled as a benevolent autocrat, passing laws that respected local customs, but also suppressing head-hunting and piracy. In 1848 he was given a baronetcy by the British Government. Brooke returned to England in 1863 and, with no son to succeed him as rajah, he left Sarawak in the hands of his nephew Charles

Brooke. He in turn was succeeded by his eldest son, also called Charles Brooke. In 1941 Charles, the third White rajah, set up a constitution intended to lead to self-government for Sarawak, but the following year he had to flee from the Japanese invasion of Borneo. In 1946 he ceded Sarawak to Britain as a crown colony.

Brougham, Henry, 1st Baron (1778-1868) British lawyer, politician, outspoken eccentric and reformer. Brougham was born in Scotland and entered Parliament as a WHIG in 1810. With his customary ebullience, he spoke so frequently during his first session in Parliament that he more or less usurped the place of the leader of the Opposition. In 1820 he won popular approval for successfully defending Queen Caroline in the annulment action brought by her husband George IV. As an enthusiast for education Brougham helped to found the Society for the Diffusion of Useful Knowledge in 1825 and the University of London in 1828. Serving as Lord Chancellor from 1830 to 1834, he played an important role in reforming legal procedures and in setting up the Central Criminal Court in London. In 1832 Brougham helped to bring about the Parliamentary REFORM ACT, and achieved a major victory in his campaign against slavery when the 1833 Abolition Act was passed. Among his other achievements, Brougham designed the four-wheeled, one-horse carriage which bears his name.

Brown, John (1800-59) Militant US abolitionist in the years leading up to the American Civil War. In 1855 he moved to Kansas, the scene of opposition between factions for and against slavery, and rapidly became a prominent leader of the abolitionists. In May 1856 a group of slavers sacked the abolitionist town of Lawrence, whereupon Brown led a retaliatory raid on a slavers' camp on the banks of the Pottawatomie River, leaving five men dead.

Brown's most dramatic gesture came on the night of October 16, 1859, when he led 21 armed followers in an assault on the federal arsenal at Harper's Ferry, Virginia, hoping that this would provoke a mass uprising of slaves. The abolitionists captured the arsenal but were overpowered in less than 48 hours by US marines commanded by Colonel Robert E. LEE. Brown was later tried and hanged for treason and murder, but was soon being honoured as a martyr of the abolitionist cause. The song 'John Brown's Body' became a popular marching song for federal troops in the civil war which broke out two years later.

Browne, Robert (c.1550-1633) English Puritan clergyman whose teachings caused an early schism in the Church of England after the Anglican REFORMATION. Browne led his NONCONFORMIST followers, popularly called 'Brownists', in demanding a Free Church, independent of the Anglican hierarchy as well as of the State. In 1581 Browne and his group fled to Holland, where he published several tracts including, in 1582, *Reformation without Tarrying for Any*, which called for immediate doctrinal reform. Returning to England in 1584, Browne was imprisoned and excommunicated. He soon began to show a change of heart and within two years was reconciled with the established Church. He had, however, established a framework of reformist principles which were eventually to become the foundations of the CONGREGATIONALIST Church. At the age of 80 Browne was jailed for assaulting a constable and died in prison.

Brown Shirts Common name for Nazi storm troopers, members of the Sturmabteilung ('Assault Division'), or SA, a paramilitary organisation founded by Adolf Hitler in 1921. The Brown Shirts were recruited from various rough elements of society who were attracted by the emerging Nazi movement. Fitted out in brown uniforms reminiscent of Benito Mussolini's BLACK SHIRTS, they protected the Nazi marches and rallies, and also waged a widespread campaign of violence and intimidation against Jews, left-wing intellectuals, political opponents of Nazism, and even on occasion ordinary voters.

From 1931 the Brown Shirts were led by Ernst Röhm, a radical anticapitalist who hoped to establish the SA as Germany's main military force and use it to bring about a socialist revolution in German society. By 1933 the SA had a membership of approximately 2 million – double the size of the regular army, which was hostile to it. However, Röhm's ambitions threatened Hitler's desire to preserve loyalty to his regime among the German establishment, and especially the military officer corps. Consequently Hitler

The Sultan of Brunei, during his lavish silver jubilee celebrations in 1992, parades in an ornate chariot through the capital city.

had more than 70 senior members of the SA, including Röhm, summarily executed by his personal bodyguard, the SS, during the night of June 29-30, 1934 – thereafter known as the NIGHT OF THE LONG KNIVES. The SA was never again a significant force in Nazi affairs, although it was responsible for training Germany's Home Guard units from 1939.

Bruce, Robert see ROBERT I

Bruegel Family of outstanding Flemish artists, whose name has a number of different spellings: Bruegel, Brueghel or Breughel. Pieter Bruegel the Elder (c.1525-69) was skilled as a draughtsman, etcher and painter. On the customary artist's pilgrimage to Italy Bruegel was deeply affected by his experience of crossing the Alps. His paintings of Alpine landscapes, made in the years after his return to the Low Countries, divulge a deep awe for the grandeur of high mountains. Many of Bruegel's paintings show a parallel interest in expansive landscapes as well as minute details, particularly relating to human figures. His subjects included nightmarish visions in the style of Hiëronymus Bosch, such as *The Fall of the Rebel Angels*; Biblical scenes, including *The Tower of Babel*; satirical and moralising scenes-such as *The Blind Leading the Blind*; landscapes like *Hunters in the Snow*; and cheerful scenes of daily life, for example *Peasant Wedding*. Bruegel enjoyed a considerable reputation during his lifetime and had a profound influence on Flemish painting. He also had two sons to keep up the family's artistic tradition.

Pieter Bruegel the Younger (1564-1638) painted religious and rustic scenes in the manner of his father, as well as copying many of his father's works. He acquired the nickname 'Hell Bruegel' because of his particular predilection for depicting hell and its fires. Pieter the Younger's works include *Census at Bethlehem*, *Attack on a Snow-Covered Village*, and *Aeneas in the Underworld*. His younger brother Jan Bruegel (1568-1625) was nicknamed 'Velvet Bruegel' because of his skill in depicting rich and delicate textures. He specialised in still life and was rated the finest flower painter of his day.

Brunei Country in north-west Borneo, consisting of two separate areas divided and bounded by the Malaysian state of SARAWAK. By the early 16th century Malay settlers had established the independent sultanate of Brunei, an Islamic kingdom which controlled most of Borneo and its neighbouring islands. The arrival of the Dutch and the British in the 17th century gradually drove the sultanate back until, by about 1800, it ruled only the area covered by the present-day states of Brunei, Sarawak and part of Sabah in north and north-west Borneo. During the 1840s the indigenous peoples of Sarawak rebelled, but they were successfully put down with the help of the British adventurer James BROOKE, who was subsequently given control of Sarawak by a grateful Sultan of Brunei. In 1877 the sultan signed away control of Brunei's portion of North Borneo (now known as Sabah) to a consortium of British merchants, and in 1888 his state was made a British protectorate. During the Second World War Brunei was overrun by the Japanese. In 1963 the state resisted pressure to join the Federation of Malaysia, achieving internal self-government in 1971 and full independence in January 1984. By then the Brunei economy was one of the richest in the world, sustained by oil fields discovered in 1929 and gas fields located in 1965.

Brunel, Isambard Kingdom (1806-59) British engineer who designed the Clifton Suspension Bridge across the Avon Gorge at Bristol. The only son of Sir Marc BRUNEL, Isambard Brunel revolutionised Britain's railways by introducing broad-gauge tracks, 7 ft (2.13 m) apart, allowing trains to travel at much higher speeds. As chief engineer of the Great Western Railway, he was responsible for laying more than 1000 miles (1600 km) of track in England, Wales and Ireland, and for designing numerous bridges, tunnels and viaducts. Brunel also made a major contribution in the field of marine engineering, designing and constructing three ships that were wonders of their day. The *Great Western* was the first transatlantic steamship; the *Great Britain* was the first iron-hulled ship with screw propellers; and the *Great Eastern* was the first ship to have a double iron hull and was unrivalled in size for more than 40 years.

DID YOU KNOW?

The work and anxiety of building the Great Eastern proved too much for Isambard Brunel. The day before the huge ship left for sea trials he had a stroke and died ten days later.

Brunel, Sir Marc (1769-1849) French-born British architect, engineer and inventor, who solved the problem of constructing a tunnel through soft or waterlogged earth. While serving in the French navy for six years Brunel built an accurate quadrant. Forced to flee revolutionary France in 1793, he settled in the USA, where he constructed several buildings and was appointed chief engineer of New York, before moving to England in 1799. He invented numerous labour-saving devices in areas as diverse as printing and boot-making. In 1818 he patented his tunnelling shield – a massive iron casing that protected labourers tunnelling in water-bearing strata – and in 1825 he began building a tunnel under the Thames, from Rotherhithe to Wapping in London. The scheme was audacious and without precedent. Work on the tunnel was suspended for seven years for lack of funds, but it was eventually completed in 1842, the year after Brunel was knighted.

Bruno, Giordano (1548-1600) Italian philosopher, astronomer and mathematician who profoundly influenced philosophical and scientific thought throughout the 17th and 18th centuries. Ordained as a priest in 1572, Bruno showed little respect for religious dogma, and was charged with heresy in 1576 for publicly discussing forbidden texts. He then fled Italy to begin a long career as a peripatetic lecturer, teaching as far afield as Geneva, Paris, Oxford and Frankfurt. As a committed free thinker, Bruno outraged many scholars by criticising Aristotle. He also upheld COPERNICUS's theory that the planets in our Solar System revolve around the Sun, and challenged the Bible as a source of astronomical information. Even more threatening to theologians was Bruno's theory that the Universe is infinite, composed of countless worlds and solar systems similar to our own. Having been lured back to Italy in 1591, Bruno was denounced to the Inquisition in 1592. He endured a trial that lasted seven and a half years and was eventually burnt at the stake for heresy.

Bruno of Cologne, St (c.1032-1101) German churchman who in 1084 founded the CARTHUSIAN order of monks. Born and ordained at Cologne, Bruno was summoned in 1057 to teach at the cathedral school at Reims. There he acquired a reputation for the depth of his piety and learning, however in 1076 he was forced to flee after a disagreement with the archbishop of Reims. Bruno and six companions withdrew to the Alps near Grenoble, building a small monastery in the Chartreuse Valley and following a strict regime of self-denial. In 1090 Bruno was summoned to Rome by Pope Urban II, a former pupil, to act as councillor. He turned down the pope's offer to make him Archbishop of Reggio, and went on to establish another hermitage at La Torre in southern Italy.

Brutus, Marcus Junius (c.85-42 BC) Roman soldier and STOIC philosopher, who was one of the leading conspirators against Julius Caesar in 44 BC. As an ardent supporter of the Roman republic, Brutus sided with Gnaeus POMPEY in the civil war against Caesar from 49 to 48. After Pompey's defeat Brutus was pardoned by Caesar, who made him governor of Cisalpine Gaul and, in 44, urban praetor (a form of senior magistrate). Brutus remained sufficiently apprehensive of Caesar's dictatorial rule to join Gaius Cassius Longinus's plot to murder Caesar and restore democracy. Brutus's prestige gave the conspiracy greater respectability, but his idealism cost it dearly. By insisting that the conspirators restrict themselves to the single

act of killing Caesar, Brutus effectively lost them the political initiative, which was seized instead by the consul MARK ANTONY. Forced to flee from Rome, Brutus and Cassius raised an army in Macedonia, and in 42 won an initial engagement. Three weeks later the republican army was soundly beaten at PHILIPPI by a force commanded by both Mark Antony and Octavian, who became emperor as AUGUSTUS CAESAR. Now realising that all was lost, Brutus committed suicide.

buccaneers Sea adventurers, mainly from Britain, France and Holland, who preyed on Spanish settlements and shipping in the Caribbean and South America during the 17th century. Drawing their inspiration from the exploits of men such as Sir Francis DRAKE (c.1540-96), the buccaneers took advantage of the rivalry between the various colonial powers in the New World to plunder Spanish treasure ships and coastal communities. They operated with the tacit approval of their monarchs, or other local authorities, who expected a share of their booty. In this respect the buccaneers are distinct from true pirates, especially of the 18th century, who were outlaws in the eyes of all nations. In many cases they also differed from PRIVATEERS (though this is what they usually claimed to be), who held official commissions from the authorities allowing them to act as a sort of mercenary navy.

The buccaneers made their headquarters on the French island of Tortuga, off Haiti, and on Jamaica, after its capture by the English in 1655. Their most daring commander was Sir Henry MORGAN, whose exploits included the sacking of Puerto Bello in 1668 and the capture of Panama in 1671. When the NINE YEARS' WAR broke out in Europe in 1689 the buccaneers were appointed privateers by their respective nations. During the 18th century the power of the buccaneers declined with the growth of national navies.

Buchanan, James (1791-1868) US politician who was 15th president of the USA from 1857 to 1861. An expert in constitutional law and a brilliant orator, Buchanan played a central diplomatic role in the OREGON QUESTION – a boundary dispute with Britain – and the MEXICAN-AMERICAN WAR of 1846-8. As minister to Britain in 1853-6, he helped to draw up the Ostend Manifesto of 1854, which recommended that the USA should buy Cuba in order to prevent a

A Roman coin bears the profile of Marcus Brutus, who was trusted for his honesty and republican principles.

slave uprising there. This was repudiated by the US government. When Buchanan won the presidency for the Democratic Party in 1856 there was extreme tension over slavery. In attempting to reconcile the opposing factions in the dispute, he ended up being mistrusted by both sides. Buchanan himself believed that slavery was morally wrong, but he tried to safeguard the Southern states' right to the practice for the sake of preserving the Union. This split the Democratic Party and opened the way for the Republican Abraham Lincoln to win the presidency in 1860.

Buckingham, George Villiers, Duke of (1592-1628) English courtier and royal favourite who exercised great power over James I and his son Charles (later Charles I). After meeting James in 1614, Villiers was made an earl in 1617 and Lord High Admiral in 1619 – positions which he used to advance and enrich his own relatives, to the dismay of Parliament and the English nobility. In 1623 Villiers was made Duke of Buckingham, and in the same year he was sent to Madrid in the hope of arranging a marriage between Charles, Prince of Wales, and the daughter of the king of Spain. Negotiations collapsed, largely as a result of Buckingham's arrogance, and he subsequently persuaded James to make war on Spain.

After Charles's accession to the throne in 1625, Buckingham continued to play the part of royal policy-maker, with disastrous consequences. He organised a huge expedition against the Spanish port of Cadiz, but it collapsed in disarray. In 1627 he led a force to assist the French HUGUENOTS in their stronghold of La Rochelle, but after four months of bungling he was forced to withdraw. A year later Buckingham was stabbed to death by a naval officer who was resentful of his mismanagement of the war.

Buddha see feature, page 100

Buddhism One of the world's great religions, derived from the teachings of Gautama Siddhartha, known as the BUDDHA. After the death of Buddha, the 'Enlightened One', in 483 BC, his teachings spread widely through India, receiving considerable impetus from the support of Emperor ASOKA during the 3rd century BC. Asoka sent Buddhist missionaries throughout Asia, so that by AD 1000 the faith was well established as far afield as Afghanistan and Japan, Tibet and Sri Lanka. In India, meanwhile, Buddhism was on the decline as a result of a resurgence of Hinduism. And after the 11th-century Muslim invasion of north India Buddhism progressively disappeared from India.

As it spread to different regions Buddhism developed into two major schools, or traditions, also called 'vehicles'. The *Theravada*

Lavish royal patronage made the Duke of Buckingham wealthy and a power behind the thrones of James I and Charles I of England.

tradition, or 'lesser vehicle', became dominant in south and south-east Asia, including Sri Lanka, Burma, Thailand and Indochina. It maintains that the task of every individual is to become an *arhat*, 'perfect saint', liberated from the cycle of earthly reincarnation and suffering by attaining enlightenment and, through that, blessedness known as nirvana.

The other major tradition, the *Mahayana*, 'great vehicle', spread north, through Sikkim, Bhutan, Nepal, Tibet, Mongolia, China, Korea and Japan. In these countries it taught that the aim of all Buddhists is to become *Bodhisattvas* – beings who have attained purity and enlightenment, but who choose to return to earthly life to help others along the path. There are also several important branches of the *Mahayana* school, notably the *Vajrayana* or Tantric tradition of Tibet, and the Zen and Pure Land traditions of China and Japan. In the last century Buddhism has spread to Europe, North America and other regions across the globe. By the early 1990s there were estimated to be more than 300 million Buddhists throughout the world.

Bukharin, Nikolai (1888-1938) Russian BOLSHEVIK leader and Marxist theoretician. Bukharin played an active part in the Bolshevik RUSSIAN REVOLUTION of 1917, afterwards becoming a leader of COMINTERN, the Communist International, and editor of the Communist Party newspaper *Pravda*, 'Truth'. Bukharin opposed Vladimir Lenin's signing of the Treaty of BREST-LITOVSK, by which Russia withdrew from the First World War, arguing that Russia should use the war to bring about a communist revolution throughout Europe. After Lenin's death in 1924, Bukharin became a full member of the Politburo, where he continued to support Lenin's NEW ECONOMIC POLICY of 1921, designed to bring about gradual economic change, rather than

rapid industrialisation and collectivisation of agriculture. When Joseph Stalin turned against this policy in 1928, Bukharin lost all his party positions. Under extreme pressure he renounced his errors and in 1934 was briefly allowed to edit the government newspaper *Izvestia*, 'News'.

In January 1937 Bukharin was arrested, and in March 1938 he was put on show trial as a spy, a 'Trotskyite' (see TROTSKY) and, for good measure, a counter-revolutionary who was intent on restoring capitalism. He was convicted and executed, but was rehabilitated and posthumously reinstated as a member of the Communist Party in 1988.

Bulganin, Nikolai (1895-1975) Soviet military leader and politician, premier of the Soviet Union from 1955 to 1958. Bulganin joined the Communist Party in 1917. In the 1930s he served as chairman of the Moscow Soviet (in effect, mayor of Moscow), premier of the Russian Republic and deputy premier of the Soviet Union.

During the Second World War Bulganin served on Joseph Stalin's war Cabinet, the State Defence Committee. In 1947 he replaced Stalin as minister for defence, and in 1948 he became a full member of the Politburo. After Stalin's death in 1953, Bulganin served in the government of Georgy Malenkov but he subsequently supported Nikita KHRUSHCHEV in the power struggle between the two men. When Khrushchev won, Bulganin was rewarded in February 1955 with Malenkov's position as Chairman of the Council of Ministers, premier of the

Communist editor Nikolai Bukharin, who was once named 'the darling of the party' by Lenin, met his downfall during Stalin's Great Purge.

Soviet Union. He held this position until 1958, when Khrushchev turned against him because Bulganin had supported an attempt to oust Khrushchev from power in June 1957. Bulganin was also expelled from the Central Committee of the Communist Party.

Bulgaria Country in the Balkans in southeast Europe, bordering on the Black Sea. The region was settled in about 3500 BC by semi-nomadic peoples from Central Asia, who gave rise to the kingdom of THRACE in the 5th century BC. Colonised by the Romans in the mid 1st century AD, the area was invaded by Goths, Huns, Bulgars and Avars from the 3rd century, before being settled by Slavic pastoralists in the 6th century. They were invaded in turn in about 679 by Bulgar tribes, who established the first Bulgarian empire between 681 and 1018, while assimilating the culture of the majority Slavs.

By the 9th century the Bulgarians were a significant power in the Balkans, and in 864 Boris I adopted Orthodox Eastern Christianity as his country's official religion. In 1018 Bulgaria was annexed by the Byzantine Empire, but a second Bulgarian empire rose in 1185 and subsequently dominated most of the Balkans, with the exception of Greece. The mid 14th century brought an invasion by the Ottoman Turks, who finally conquered the Bulgarians in 1396 and ruled over them for the next five centuries.

Bulgarian nationalism increased rapidly during the 19th century, culminating in a major insurrection in 1876, with more than 12 000 Bulgarians massacred. Russia responded by going to war with Turkey, and in 1878 concluded the Treaty of San Stefano, which created a largely independent Bulgaria covering almost three-fifths of the Balkan Peninsula. The powers of Europe responded by calling the Congress of BERLIN, at which Bulgaria was reduced to about a third of its former size. The area south of the Balkan Mountains became a semi-independent Ottoman province called Eastern Roumelia, which was annexed back into Bulgaria in 1885. Bulgaria's rulers still owed nominal allegiance to the Ottoman Empire, but in 1908 Prince Ferdinand of Saxe-Coburg declared Bulgaria an independent kingdom with himself as tsar.

The country lost considerable territory to Greece and Serbia during the Second Balkan War (June-August 1913), and even more as a result of siding with Germany during the First World War. In 1918 Ferdinand abdicated and was succeeded by his son, Boris III. Several years of political instability followed, until Boris established a personal dictatorship in 1934. During the Second World War Bulgaria again sided with Germany, but in 1944 the country was invaded by Soviet forces, enabling a communist-led coalition to take power. Two years later the monarchy was

The enlightened one

Gautama Siddhartha, the founder of Buddhism, rejected his princely lifestyle, found enlightenment, and through his teaching inspired one of the world's great religions.

The Buddha is the title by which Gautama Siddhartha, the founder of Buddhism, was known after experiencing enlightenment at the age of 35.

Gautama lived in north-east India from about 563 to 483 BC. He was the son of a wealthy, elected aristocratic ruler. At 29 he turned his back on his birthright to become a wanderer, living by alms and seeking a way to lasting happiness. He rejected yogic trance as an incomplete solution and harsh asceticism as too extreme. Instead, while sitting under a bo tree at Buddh Gaya in Bihar, he developed his own way to meditate until he reached a state of profound inner stillness that gave him access to three sources of understanding.

The first was through memory of many past rebirths – as a human, animal, ghost, hell-being and mortal god. The second was achieved through an awareness of how people went from rebirth to rebirth according to the quality of their behaviour (karma), selfish

As a young prince, Buddha travels to lessons; with the spread of Buddhism came Nepalese versions (right).

actions leading to unpleasant rebirths, selfless actions to pleasant ones. The third was the most profound. He experienced nirvana, a state beyond all suffering and limitation, which brought release from further reincarnations. Later he formulated his

discoveries as the 'Four Noble Truths', to show others how to attain liberation.

Some of those inspired by the Buddha's teachings became monks, and five years after his enlightenment he ordained the first nuns. When he had gathered 60 enlightened monks, he sent them out to teach others. In time, he had more than 2500 fully enlightened disciples and several thousand lay disciples.

BUDDHA'S TEACHING

After the Buddha's death his monastic disciples convened a council to recollect and arrange his teachings in collections now called the *Vinaya* (monastic discipline), and the five *Nikayas* (the Buddha's discourses). They began as oral compositions passed on by communal chanting. Around 80 BC, in Sri Lanka, they were written down, together with an early version of commentaries on the text of this and other collections.

The Buddha's teaching was precise and compassionately adapted to the state of mind of his hearers. It is said that he once delayed a sermon to a group of well-to-do people until a poor man had eaten a meal and could benefit from his discourse. He did not expect blind belief from his followers, but wanted them to test his teachings so as to discover their power and truth for themselves.

The Buddha's calm and confidence is illustrated in a passage from the *Vinaya* in which he is said to have halted a charging elephant, set loose to kill him by a jealous cousin, by radiating kindness to it. He loved nature. Indeed he was enlightened under a tree, gave his first sermon in an animal park, and died between two trees that were said to be blooming out of season due to his presence. Buddhism quickly spread throughout Asia. As a 'teacher of humans and gods', the Buddha is seen in Buddhist texts as having guided many divine beings towards their liberation.

In the Battle of Bunker Hill, the first pitched battle of the American War of Independence, British ships bombard American positions as redcoat troops cross the river, and Charlestown is torched.

abolished and Bulgaria was declared a people's republic, with Georgi DIMITROV, leader of the Communist Party, as premier. In the ensuing years Bulgaria closely followed the Soviet Union's economic and political policies. As a result it became the most consistently pro-Soviet member of the WARSAW PACT. In 1989 Bulgaria was caught up in the process of reform that was sweeping through Eastern Europe, and in November that year the communist leader Todor Zhivkov, who had been in office since 1954, was forced to resign. Elections held in 1991 brought the country its first noncommunist government in more than 40 years, as well as economic reforms and a new constitution.

Bulge, Battle of the see ARDENNES CAMPAIGN

Bülow, Bernhard, Prince von (1849-1929) German diplomat and statesman, who as imperial chancellor from 1900 to 1909 pursued an aggressive foreign policy that led to Germany's isolation in Europe. Bülow held a string of diplomatic posts before being appointed foreign secretary in 1897. In this position he worked to achieve Emperor Wilhelm II's vision of Germany as a world power, and after three years he was rewarded with the chancellorship.

Following the BOER WARS in South Africa, in which Wilhelm had openly supported the Boers, Bülow attempted to improve relations with Britain. In 1905, however, he antagonised both France and Britain by thwarting French attempts to gain a protectorate in Morocco; and in 1908 he alienated the Russians by supporting Austria-Hungary's annexation of Bosnia and Herzegovina. Bülow was forced to resign in 1909 after the London *Daily Telegraph* published indiscreet remarks by the emperor about German foreign policy towards Britain. Bülow had authorised these remarks without having read them.

Bunker Hill, Battle of (June 17, 1775) Early battle in the American Revolution of 1775-83, which resulted in a costly British victory, and greatly boosted the revolutionary cause. Shortly after the Battle of LEXINGTON AND CONCORD, American troops under General Artemas Ward laid siege to the city of Boston, and in the middle of June began fortifying a hill, called Breed's Hill, overlooking the city. General Thomas GAGE, the British commander besieged in Boston, sent about 2400 troops (a significant proportion of his garrison) to take the heights, which were occupied by some 1200 Americans under Colonel William Prescott.

After two failed uphill charges, the British redcoats managed on their third attempt to dislodge the defenders, who had run out of ammunition. The British won the day, but at a cost of about 1000 casualties, which they could ill afford. The Americans lost some 400 men, but they had put up a stout defence and had badly mauled a formidable enemy who could risk no further sorties to raise the siege of Boston. Although the battle was fought over Breed's Hill, it has come to be called after nearby, and more prominent, Bunker Hill.

Bunyan, John (1628-88) English author and Puritan preacher, best known for his allegorical masterpiece *The Pilgrim's Progress* (1678). Driven by deep religious convictions, Bunyan became a lay preacher for a Baptist church in Bedford in 1653, and soon came into conflict with the QUAKERS, against whom he published his first writings. With the Restoration of the monarchy in 1660 Bunyan was charged with preaching without a licence and imprisoned in Bedford. He remained in jail until 1672, during which time he wrote several books, including *Grace Abounding to the Chief of Sinners*, his impassioned and tormented spiritual autobiography. In 1677 Bunyan was again briefly detained, and the following year he published *The Pilgrim's Progress*, a fervent

and accessible account of Christian salvation. By now Bunyan was a hero to his followers, among whom he continued his ministering work for the rest of his life. He also wrote several other religious books, including *Life and Death of Mr Badman* (1680), *The Holy War* in 1682, and the second part of *The Pilgrim's Progress*, which was published in 1684.

Burghley, Lord see CECIL, WILLIAM

Burgoyne, John (1722-92) British general and playwright, nicknamed 'Gentleman Johnny' and best known for his defeat at Saratoga during the American Revolution. Burgoyne achieved fame by his daring exploits in the SEVEN YEARS' WAR between 1756 and 1763. After the outbreak of the American Revolution he was sent to Canada as a major general with instructions to lead an attack southward towards the Hudson Valley during the summer of 1777. After some initial successes Burgoyne's army was forced to surrender to a much larger force commanded by General Horatio Gates near Saratoga Springs in October that year. Returning to England Burgoyne was severely censured, but in 1782 he was briefly made commander in chief in Ireland. After 1783 Burgoyne lived increasingly as a society gentleman, writing several plays, of which *The Heiress*, published in 1786, is the best known.

Burgundian School Name given to artists and musicians of the duchy of BURGUNDY, especially during its golden age in the late 14th and early 15th centuries. In this period the duchy acquired extensive territories in northern France and the Low Countries by marriage, treaty and conquest. The Burgundian court became renowned for its patronage of the arts, and the capital, Dijon, became one of the leading cultural centres of Europe. Flemish panel painters and miniaturists flourished here, as did sculptors such as Claus Sluter. The duchy's prosperity also allowed its dukes to maintain large chapels of musicians in several major cities, attracting composers such as Guillaume Dufay and Gilles Binchois. Their secular polyphonic songs, or chansons, provided Europe with one of its most important musical styles of the 15th century.

Burgundy Historic region of eastern France that was once a duchy with territories extending over much of the Netherlands and Belgium. With the decline of the Western Roman Empire in the 5th century AD, a Germanic tribe called the Burgundii gradually moved into eastern and southern France, where they established a powerful kingdom. In 534 the Burgundii were conquered by the FRANKS, and their territory was divided between different Merovingian rulers, before being absorbed by the CAROLINGIAN EMPIRE

The dukes of Burgundy gained their vast territories by treaty, conquest and marriage.

Growth of Burgundy
- under Philip the Bold 1363-1404
- under Philip the Good 1419-1467
- under Charles the Bold 1467-1477
- under temporary control
— border of the Holy Roman Empire

in the late 9th century. At this time Burgundian lands extended from the Mediterranean to central France, as well as deep into what is now Switzerland. The majority of these territories passed into German hands, and in 1034 became part of the Holy Roman Empire. Meanwhile the Burgundian heartland, the duchy itself, remained part of the kingdom of France, having been inherited in 921 by the CAPETIAN Rudolph (Raoul), who was elected king of France two years later.

In the centuries that followed the dukes of Burgundy established themselves as the foremost noble family in France. In 1363 the duchy entered its golden age when John II ('the Good') of France, made his son, Philip the Bold (1342-1404), Duke of Burgundy. Through his wife, Margaret of Flanders, Philip inherited several new territories, including Artois, in northern France, and Flanders. Philip's successors – John the Fearless (1371-1419), Philip the Good (1396-1467) and Charles the Bold (1433-77) – acquired further lands, including Lorraine, Alsace, Luxembourg and much of present-day Belgium and the Netherlands. During this period the Burgundian court became one of the finest in Europe, offering patronage to writers, artists and musicians on a grand scale. At the same time the dukes of Burgundy became immensely powerful, posing a considerable threat to the kings of France, especially during the HUNDRED YEARS' WAR when Burgundy allied itself with England. It was during this conflict that the Burgundians captured JOAN OF ARC in 1430 and sold her to the English.

In 1477 Charles the Bold died in battle against Louis XI of France, who immediately annexed the duchy as a province of France. Most peripheral Burgundian lands, including an area called the Franche-Comté, passed to the House of Habsburg when Charles the Bold's daughter, Mary of Burgundy, married the future Holy Roman Emperor Maximilian I in May 1477. In 1668 the Franche-Comté was conquered for France by Louis II of Bourbon, the Great CONDÉ, whose family had been given control of Burgundy in 1631. The province was eventually abolished in the French Revolution of 1789, when it was split into several new *départements*, or regions, including Côte d'Or and Saône-et-Loire.

Burke, Edmund (1729-97) British politician, writer and political theorist. Born in Dublin, Burke moved to London in 1750, and abandoned his law studies to become a writer. In 1758 he founded the *Annual Register*, a survey of world affairs, which he edited for the next 30 years. In 1765 Burke became private secretary to Britain's WHIG prime minister, the Marquis of ROCKINGHAM, and shortly afterwards entered Parliament.

Burke argued for a more tolerant treatment of Britain's American colonies, urging the government to repeal the STAMP ACT, which imposed direct taxation on the Colonies and was a cause of great resentment there. He was critical of Britain's government of Ireland, particularly in so far as it discriminated against Roman Catholics. He also campaigned for many years to reform the administration of British India, which was at that time under the control of the EAST INDIA COMPANY. Burke opposed George III's attempt to increase the political power of the Crown, arguing instead for the formation of political parties that could stand for clear and consistent principles. The outbreak of the French Revolution in 1789 ended Burke's long friendship with the politician Charles FOX. Like many other British libertarians, Fox was delighted by events in France, while Burke saw them as a terrifying manifestation of mob rule. In his *Reflections on the Revolution in France*, published in 1790, Burke set out his beliefs that liberty can exist only under the rule of law and order, and that reform must proceed through evolution, not revolution. Burke's outlook eventually prevailed, convincing most other Whigs to support the Tory government of William PITT the Younger in waging war against France.

Burkina Faso Landlocked country in western Africa, known as Upper Volta (in French, Haute-Volta) until 1984. Originally inhabited by the Bobo, Lobi and Gurunsi peoples, invaders from the south conquered the central and eastern regions in about the 14th century and established the powerful Mossi states. The Yatenga and Ouagadougou states were characterised by complex administrative systems and powerful armies, which included cavalry units. These states were still in existence at the end of the 19th century, when European powers were engaged in their 'scramble for Africa'. In 1895 France negotiated a protectorate over Yatenga, and during the next two years annexed Ouagadougou and Gourma, together with the territories of the Bobo, Lobi and Gurunsi peoples. The entire region was then administered as part of French Sudan (now Mali).

In 1919 Upper Volta was constituted as a separate colony, becoming an overseas territory of the French Union in 1947, and in 1958 an autonomous republic within the French Community. Two years later Upper Volta achieved full independence with Maurice Yaméogo as its first president. A bloodless coup in 1966 brought Lieutenant Colonel Sangoulé Lamizana to power. He suspended the national assembly and introduced two new constitutions, in 1970 and 1977. The latter brought a return to free, multiparty elections, which Lamizana won in 1978. Two years later the country saw the start of a series of military coups, including that of Captain Thomas Sankara in 1983. The following year Upper Volta was renamed Burkina Faso, and by 1986 Sankara had appointed a civilian administration. In 1987 Sankara and other officials were assassinated and Captain Blaise Compaoré seized power in yet another coup. He introduced a new constitution in 1991, leading to elections which his party won.

Burlington, Richard Boyle, 3rd Earl of (1694-1753) English connoisseur, architect and patron of the arts. Burlington was deeply influenced by the buildings of the English architect Inigo Jones (1573-1652), and by the Italian Andrea PALLADIO, from whom Jones had also drawn his inspiration. Burlington designed several buildings in a style which came to be known as Palladianism (or neo-Palladianism), characterised by sober, formal, classical symmetry, contrasting markedly with the exuberant baroque style of the late 17th century. Among his masterpieces are Chiswick House near London, which he built as his country retreat between 1725 and 1729, and the Assembly Rooms at York built shortly afterwards. Burlington also helped to promote the careers of several artists, notably William Kent, another eminent Palladian architect, and was widely regarded as the most distinguished arbiter of taste of his day.

Burma see MYANMAR

Burma Campaigns (1942-5) Series of military offensives launched by British and other Allied armies during the Second World War with the objective of driving the Japanese out of Burma (now MYANMAR). In early 1942 the Japanese overran Burma with the objective of capturing the recently completed 'Burma Road' – a vital supply line between India and Nationalist China. The British withdrew into India, and within a few months were organising offensives against the Japanese. From late 1942 British and Indian troops were fighting to retake the Arakan region of western Burma, and in 1943 Brigadier Orde WINGATE led his Chindit jungle fighters in a highly effective guerrilla campaign deep behind the Japanese lines. After an abortive Japanese invasion of north India in early 1944, culminating in the bloody battles of Imphal and Kohima, the Allies launched a three-pronged offensive in October 1944. They reopened the Burma Road in January 1945, and liberated the capital, Rangoon, on May 1.

Burr, Aaron (1756-1836) US politician who destroyed his career by killing a political opponent in a duel. Burr served with distinction in the early years of the American Revolution, before becoming a lawyer and a politician. From 1791 to 1797 he served as a member of the US Senate, and in 1800 he and Thomas Jefferson, a fellow Democratic Republican (see DEMOCRATIC PARTY), won an equal number of electoral college votes in the presidential election. In the ensuing contest to determine who should be president and who vice-president, Burr lost to Jefferson as a result of strong opposition from the federalist Alexander Hamilton. When Hamilton again thwarted Burr's political hopes in 1804, Burr challenged him to a duel, mortally wounding him. Burr was forced to flee, and by 1806 he had become an adventurer with plans to invade Mexico and perhaps establish an independent republic in south-western America. He was betrayed to the authorities, tried for treason in 1807, and acquitted. He then spent four years vainly trying to convince Napoleon to invade Florida, before settling down in New York to practise law.

Burton, Sir Richard (1821-90) British scholar, writer, diplomat and explorer, who made several pioneering journeys in Africa and the Middle East. Burton was a brilliant linguist, eventually able to speak some 40 languages and dialects. After leaving Oxford in 1842, he joined the EAST INDIA COMPANY and was posted to Sindh in northern India (now part of Pakistan). In Sindh he distinguished himself as an intelligence officer able to pass unnoticed among locals whose languages he had mastered. In 1853 Burton disguised himself as a Pathan – an Afghani Muslim – in order to make a perilous journey through Egypt and Arabia to the holy city of Mecca. The following year he became the first European to enter the forbidden African city of Harar (now in Ethiopia). Between 1855 and 1858 Burton made two journeys with John

In Burma, Brigadier Wingate (centre) and his Chindit guerrillas plan acts of sabotage against the Japanese, such as blowing up a railway bridge.

SPEKE into central Africa to locate the source of the White Nile. On their second expedition Speke discovered Lake Victoria, which he was convinced was the source of the Nile. Burton disagreed, and an acrimonious public dispute flared up between the two men.

From 1861 Burton was British consul at Fernando Po – a Spanish island off the west coast of Africa – at Santos (Brazil), Damascus and Trieste. In addition to his official duties, Burton wrote several studies on the sociology and anthropology of the countries he visited, as well as making a number of translations, including an unexpurgated *Arabian Nights*. Among Burton's many other books are several classics of exploration, including *Pilgrimage to El-Medinah and Mecca*, *First Footsteps in Africa* and *Explorations of the Highlands of Brazil*.

Burundi Landlocked country in east-central Africa. Burundi was originally populated by the pygmy Twa people, but by about AD 1000 they were outnumbered by Hutu migrants. From about the 15th century the Hutu themselves were progressively subjugated by a relatively smaller number of Tutsi.

In 1890 Burundi, together with neighbouring RWANDA, became part of German East Africa. After an Allied invasion in 1916, during the First World War, Belgium was given a mandate from the League of Nations to govern both Rwanda and Burundi – then called Ruanda-Urundi – until the mandate was replaced by a UN trusteeship in 1948. In July 1962 Burundi became an independent kingdom ruled by a Tutsi king. Increasing tensions between the Hutu and Tutsi populations spilled over in 1965, when the Hutu rebelled, only to be bloodily suppressed. The following year a military coup established Burundi as a republic, but tribal rivalries continued. During the early 1970s renewed fighting between the Tutsi and Hutu resulted in the death of up to 150 000 Hutu, and the flight of tens of thousands more to neighbouring countries. A further coup in 1976 made Burundi a one-party state, and another one in 1987 brought Major Pierre Buyoya to power. He introduced reforms intended to reduce ethnic tensions, but a renewed outbreak of violence in 1988 left many thousands more Hutu dead or homeless.

In July 1993 multiparty elections were held and Melchoir Ndadaye was elected president – the first Hutu president in 30 years of independence. After 100 days in office he was brutally murdered. This sparked another wave of civil unrest. Just six months later a plane carrying the new president was shot down. An orgy of violence followed in which more than 1 500 000 Burundians fled to refugee camps in Zaire, where thousands of them died. Civil unrest has continued in Burundi, with massacres perpetrated by both the Hutu militias and the Tutsi-dominated army.

The US policy of busing children to schools in the 1960s stirred up racial tension, and police escorts were needed to safeguard the pupils.

Bush, George (1924-) US statesman, who was vice-president of the USA from 1981 to 1989 and the country's 41st president from 1989 to 1993. Bush served as a US navy pilot during the Second World War, winning the Distinguished Flying Cross. He then studied at Yale University, becoming a successful businessman. In 1966 Bush was elected to the House of Representatives. He held a number of important posts under presidents Nixon and Ford. In 1971 he was appointed the American ambassador to the UN. From 1974 to 1976 he was chief of the US Liaison Office in Beijing, and director of the Central Intelligence Agency from 1976 to 1977. In 1980, and in 1984, Bush was elected vice-president of the USA alongside Ronald Reagan. He then easily won the Republican presidential nomination when Reagan retired, and was duly elected president in November 1988.

Bush's term in office was marked by a series of dramatic world events, notably the Soviet president Mikhail Gorbachev's efforts to reduce global tensions, and the collapse of communism in Eastern Europe. In 1989 Bush ordered an invasion of Panama to arrest General Manuel Noriega on charges of drug trafficking and other offences. The following year he played a leading role in uniting a coalition of Western and Arab countries against Iraq over its invasion of Kuwait. The

subsequent GULF WAR in 1991 was a major triumph for the US military and the Bush administration. In the USA itself Bush had fewer successes. He was unable to stimulate the US economy sufficiently to end a recession that had begun in 1990, with the result that he lost the 1992 presidential election to the Democrat Bill Clinton.

bushranger Australian outlaw who lived in the bush, or OUTBACK, in the 19th century. The first bushrangers were usually escaped convicts who raided White farmers and Aboriginal settlements, either on their own or in organised gangs. From about 1850 most bushrangers were free settlers who had deliberately taken to a life of banditry. They carried out more spectacular crimes, such as hold-ups of stagecoaches and gold convoys. Many bushrangers were hardened killers, but some of them came to be folk heroes through sharing their loot with the poor. The last significant bushranger was Ned Kelly, who was hanged in 1880.

busing Informal name for a practice, introduced in the USA in the 1960s, of taking children by bus from racially distinct neighbourhoods to a variety of schools in order to achieve racially integrated education. After the decision of the US Supreme Court in 1954 that racial segregation in public schools must end, federal courts began ruling in the 1960s that children should be bused to different areas to ensure a 'racial balance' in public schools. The practice met with strong opposition, particularly from White parents in the Southern states, and became an increasingly contentious political issue. In 1971 the Supreme Court ruled that it did not expect a racial balance in every school, and in 1972 the US Congress ordered that further busing schemes should be delayed until all appeals to higher courts had been heard. In the years that followed, busing came to be discredited as a means of achieving racial integration.

Bute, John, 3rd Earl of (1713-92) Scottish courtier and politician who exercised a powerful influence over George III, and served as prime minister from 1762 to 1763. In 1747 Bute joined the household of Frederick Louis, Prince of Wales, becoming tutor to his son George. When Frederick died in 1751 Bute became George's close companion, with the result that he was appointed secretary of state in 1761, after George acceded to the throne. The following year Bute became prime minister, a position he used to assist the king in breaking the WHIG domination of British politics. Bute made himself extremely unpopular when he dismissed the former secretary of state William PITT the Elder from his government, and by signing the Treaty of Paris that ended the SEVEN YEARS' WAR of 1756 to

1763. In April 1763 Bute was forced to resign after imposing a tax on cider, and soon afterwards he lost his influence over the king.

Byng, John (1704-57) British admiral who was executed for failing to save the island of Minorca from besieging French forces during the SEVEN YEARS' WAR between 1756 and 1763. John Byng was the son of George Byng, Viscount Torrington, also an admiral, who achieved fame for his naval victories during the War of the SPANISH SUCCESSION. In 1756 Byng was sent to defend Minorca, but arrived to find it already under siege. After an indecisive naval engagement he decided that his forces were too small for the task and accordingly withdrew to acquire reinforcements.

The British Government responded with fury, hoping to find a scapegoat for its own mismanagement of the war, and after a speedy court-martial Byng was duly found guilty of neglect of duty and executed. This prompted the French writer and philosopher Voltaire to observe in his novel *Candide* that from time to time the English find it necessary to shoot an admiral '*pour encourager les autres*' – in order to encourage the others.

Byron, George Gordon, 6th Baron (1788-1824) British Romantic poet and satirist, who became a hero of the Greek struggle for liberation from the Ottoman Empire. Byron was only ten when he inherited the family title and estates, including Newstead Abbey in Nottinghamshire, from his great-uncle. In 1809 he set off with his friend John Hobhouse for a grand tour of Europe – a journey which included several love affairs, and inspired Byron's semi-autobiographical poem *Childe Harold's Pilgrimage*.

After Byron published the first two cantos in 1812 he was lionised in aristocratic and literary circles, and drawn into liaisons with a number of women, including his half-sister Mrs Augusta Leigh. In January 1815 he married Anne Isabella (Annabella) Milbanke, but separated from her a little over a year later. By early 1816 Byron was a social outcast, and in April he left England for the Continent. After spending some time with the poet Percy Bysshe Shelley and his entourage in Switzerland, Byron settled in Italy, where he wrote the tragic, poetic drama *Manfred* in 1817, and the satire *Beppo* the following year. He also began work on his epic masterpiece, *Don Juan*, in 1818, before meeting the Countess Teresa Guiccioli, who was to be Byron's mistress for the remainder of his life.

In 1823 Byron sailed to Greece, where he worked tirelessly with Prince Alexandros Mavrokordatos to liberate Greece from Turkish rule. Struck down by a fever in February 1824, Byron was further weakened by being frequently bled, which was the standard medical treatment for his condition. He died in April, without seeing any combat, but swiftly became a national hero among the Greeks for his devotion to their cause.

Byzantine Empire Initially, the eastern half of the Roman Empire (also known as the Eastern Roman Empire); later, a great Mediterranean power which survived into the late Middle Ages. In AD 330 the Roman emperor CONSTANTINE I 'the Great' established a new capital for himself on the western shore of the Bosporus. The site he chose was the ancient Greek colony of Byzantium, which he rebuilt and renamed CONSTANTINOPLE.

At the time, the Roman Empire was fragmenting, having already been divided by the Emperor Diocletian in 286 and subsequently reunited by Constantine. In 395 the division between the eastern and western halves of the empire became permanent when the Emperor Theodosius died, leaving his sons, Arcadius and Honorius, as rulers of the East and West respectively. After the sack of Rome by the Visigoths in 410, the Eastern Empire became increasingly powerful, while the Western Empire progressively diminished, finally collapsing to the Vandals and Ostrogoths in 476.

Constantinople then emerged as the 'new Rome', developing its own culture while at the same time safeguarding a notional Roman Empire. Several emperors attempted to drive the 'barbarians' out of Italy and thereby reunite the empire, the most successful being JUSTINIAN I. By now, however, the division between Constantinople and Rome had

> **DID YOU KNOW?**
>
> *Byzantium succeeded in making its own silk after two monks, commissioned by Justinian I, smuggled silkworm eggs out of China in their hollow walking staffs.*

increased, and from the end of the 6th century the popes of Rome asserted greater authority in the West than their Byzantine governors.

Over the next century the Byzantine Empire had to contend with Arab invasions of Persia, the Middle East and North Africa, and threats from Bulgars and Slavs in the Balkans. At the same time the Eastern Orthodox Church grew increasingly distant from the Roman Church, provoking further disunity between rulers of the East and West, and culminating in the EAST-WEST SCHISM of 1054.

By the late 11th century the Seljuk Turks had become a major power in the eastern Mediterranean, leading Emperor Alexius I to request assistance from the West in fighting them. In this way he unwittingly helped to launch the First Crusade, which soon developed into a movement to capture Jerusalem rather than support the Byzantine Empire.

Constantinople was at this time the most magnificent city in Europe, inspiring envy in rival nations. In 1204 the Doge of Venice helped to manipulate the Fourth Crusade into capturing Constantinople, which for a time became the capital of a line of Latin emperors. The city was retaken in 1261 by the exiled emperor Michael VIII, but by now the Byzantine Empire was little larger than Constantinople itself. During the next century the Ottoman Turks emerged as a potent enemy. In 1453 they captured Constantinople, thereby bringing the Byzantine Empire to an end.

Byzantium see CONSTANTINOPLE

Byzantine mosaics line the choir of San Vitale in Ravenna, reflecting the artistic influence of Constantinople in the 6th century. This panel shows the Emperor Justinian and his retinue.

cabal Group of political intriguers. In 17th-century England the term was applied disparagingly to the inner circle of government ministers who were privy to all the nation's secrets. As such it was a precursor of the English CABINET, though today it describes any political group which pursues its aims by underhand methods. From 1667 to 1673, although Charles II's ministers were often at loggerheads, the term was applied to them because the initials of their surnames – Clifford, Ashley, Buckingham, Arlington and Lauderdale – happened to spell 'cabal'.

Cabinet Group of ministers mainly responsible for implementing government policy. England's rulers always had advisers, but not until the restoration of the monarchy in 1660 did a Cabinet (or Cabinet Council) develop. It was made up of the major office-bearers and the king's most trusted privy councillors, who met as a committee in a private room (the 'cabinet') and took decisions without consulting the full Privy Council. During Queen Anne's reign it became the main machinery of executive government, and the role of the Privy Council became formal. From about 1717 the monarch George I ceased to attend and the Cabinet met independently. Insanity and age forced George III to leave the business of government more and more to his ministers, but not until the Reform Act of 1832 was royal control of Cabinets dissolved. Cabinets then began to depend on the support of the majority in Parliament to implement their policies.

Cabot, John (c.1450-98) Venetian navigator who settled in England in 1484. Before he could find sponsors for a voyage seeking a transatlantic route to the Orient he learned that COLUMBUS had already sailed, but in 1496 HENRY VII gave him permission for a voyage of general exploration. Discovering Newfoundland, which he believed was off the Chinese coast, he took possession of it in the king's name. His scond expedition, in 1498, disappeared without trace. In 1526 Cabot's son Sebastian (c.1474-1556) led a Spanish expedition to La Plata in South America, but was turned back by hostile Indians. He returned to Bristol, later organising several expeditions to seek a route to the Orient passing north of Europe and Asia.

Cadbury, George (1839-1922) British businessman and social reformer. A prominent Quaker, with his brother Richard (1835-99) he was part owner of the cocoa and chocolate firm which bears their name. In 1894-5 they built the Bournville garden city

George and Elizabeth Cadbury helped to set new standards of labour welfare with projects such as Bournville, built for their staff.

estate, near Birmingham, for their employees. George Cadbury's concern for adult education and for the welfare of his workers set new management standards in Britain, which were taken up in other parts of the world. With his wife Elizabeth (1858-1935), a noted social worker and philanthropist, he was also influential in various peace movements.

Cade, Jack (d.1450) Irish-born rebel leader. In June 1450 he led a band of Kentishmen protesting against the financial oppression and incompetence of HENRY VI's government. The rebels had more support from the landed classes than had the PEASANTS' REVOLT of 1381, and occupied London for three days, killing the treasurer of England and the sheriff of Kent before the rising was suppressed. Cade was mortally wounded during his arrest.

Cadwallon (d.633) King of Gwynedd, north Wales. When, in 629, his attempted invasion of Northumbria failed he fled to Ireland. There his hatred of the Anglo-Saxon kingdom festered and led to an alliance with the pagan King PENDA of Mercia. Their joint victory over Edwin of Northumbria in 632 devastated Edwin's realm; but Cadwallon was eventually killed in battle by Edwin's nephew Oswald.

Caesar, Gaius Julius (c.100-44 BC) Roman general and dictator. A PATRICIAN by birth, he became *Pontifex Maximus* (High Priest) in 63 BC as part of a deal with POMPEY and CRASSUS, the so-called 'First Triumvirate'; as consul in 59 he obtained the provinces of Illyricum and Cisalpine and Transalpine GAUL. A superb general, inspiring loyalty in his men, he subjugated Gaul, crossed the Rhine and made two expeditions to Britain. Some of Caesar's records of his campaigns,

such as the *Gallic Wars,* have survived and offer insights into both contemporary history and the Roman way of life. He refused to surrender command of his armies until he had secured a second consulship for 48 BC; this would render him immune from prosecution by his enemies, by now including Pompey. When the Senate again demanded his resignation in January 49, Caesar crossed the RUBICON river, took Rome, and in 48 defeated Pompey at Pharsalus in northern Greece. After campaigns in Asia Minor, Egypt, Africa and Spain, he returned to Rome in 45.

Caesar governed Rome as a dictator. His wide-ranging reforms, which included the institution of the Julian calendar, reveal his breadth of vision, but he ignored republican traditions. Conspirators, led by BRUTUS and Cassius, assassinated Caesar on the ides (15th) of March 44. He was later deified and a temple in the forum was dedicated to his worship.

Cairo Conference (November 22-26, 1943) Second World War meeting attended by the US president F.D. Roosevelt, the British prime minister Winston Churchill and the Chinese leader Chiang Kai-shek to chart postwar policy for the Far East. Central to this was Japan's unconditional surrender, while Manchuria was to be returned to China, and Korea to its own people. At a second conference Roosevelt and Churchill met President Ismet Inonu of Turkey to confirm Turkey's future independence.

Caledonia Roman name for Scotland north of the Antonine Wall, an area corresponding roughly to today's Scottish Highlands. In AD 83 the governor of Britain, Agricola, invaded the territory of the Caledonii, ancestors of the PICTS, and defeated them, though they remained a threat to the Roman frontier.

calendar see feature, page 107

Calhoun, John (1782-1850) US statesman who, within a year of his election to Congress in 1811, led the hawks who forced the USA

into war with Britain. Later he served as secretary of war under James MONROE (1817-25), and as vice-president to John Quincy Adams (1825-9) and Andrew JACKSON (1829-32). A proponent of the rights of individual states to self-government, he saw a North-South clash as inevitable.

California US west coast state whose fine climate attracted the early film industry and led to the establishment of Hollywood. The original inhabitants of California were Native Americans. The area was first visited by Spanish explorers in 1542, but was not colonised until the mid 18th century. In 1769 a Franciscan mission was established in San Diego; its members attempted to convert the indigenous peoples, coercing them to work on farms and ranches. Mission properties were given to Mexico on gaining independence from Spain in 1821. The discovery of the 'Mother Lode' in 1848, then the world's biggest potential source of gold, started a gold rush to the state, which Mexico had ceded to the USA a few months earlier. Oil and other mineral finds boosted California's economic development, making it the richest and most populous US state. Its so-called Silicon Valley is the centre of the world's microelectronics and computer industry. Part of the state lies along a major geological fault, and San Francisco, one of its largest cities, has been devastated by earthquakes.

Caligula (AD 12-41) Roman emperor from AD 37 to 41, nicknamed after the tiny army boots (*caligae*) he wore as a child when his father Germanicus was commander in chief on the Rhine. The great-grandson of both AUGUSTUS and MARK ANTONY, and a greatnephew and successor of TIBERIUS, Caligula was crowned as Gaius Julius Caesar Germanicus. His reign was bloody and authoritarian. He outraged the Senate by introducing ritual obeisance to Rome and appointing his horse, Incitatus, as a consul. His mental instability led to personal excesses and eventual delusions of divinity. He was assassinated by a member of his palace guard.

Caligula's name has become a byword for cruel and capricious despotism.

Marking time

Early societies discovered accurate methods of telling the time, but devising a calendar proved more complicated.

Day and night, the medieval monk was alert for the sound of bells. At fixed times, they summoned the brothers to their duties. The dangers of sleeping-in are remembered in the nursery rhyme:

Frère Jacques, Frère Jacques,
Dormez-vous? Dormez-vous?
Sonnez les matines, sonnez les matines,
Ding, ding, dong; ding, ding, dong.

What the monks needed was an alarm clock: an automatic bell to alert them at the appropriate hour. They probably had to make do with *clepsydras*, invented by the Egyptians in about 1450 BC. These were clocks in which time was measured by the flow of water through a hole. They were excellent timekeepers, but needed constant attention.

ACCURATE TIMEPIECES

Sundials were also used for centuries, and, if large enough, could be accurate to within a minute. Indoors, people relied on a burning candle marked in notches to represent the passing of an hour.

The first mechanical clocks appeared at the end of the 13th century. They were made possible by the invention of the 'verge escapement', a device for releasing the driving power of the weights at a steady speed. Genuinely portable clocks and watches driven by springs appeared at the end of the 15th century. Accuracy arrived with the pendulum in the 17th century – inspired, it is said, by Galileo's observations of the lanterns swinging in Milan Cathedral.

The words 'clock' and 'watch' are derived from the duty 'watches' aboard ship. These were recorded by bells, for which the French word is *cloches*. But pendulum clocks were no good at sea, where accurate timekeeping was needed to determine longitude by comparing local time, measured by the Sun and stars, with that at Greenwich – mean time – on the zero line of longitude. The first chronometer precise enough for this task was made by John Harrison in 1762.

To primitive societies the calendar was more important than the time of day. By dividing the year into seasons, the right time for sowing and harvesting could be determined, and the migration of animals predicted. The ancient Egyptians had three seasons: the Nile flood, the sowing season and the harvesting season. But problems arose from the fact that the months, measured by the phases of the Moon, bore no exact relationship to the length of the year – the time the Earth takes to orbit the Sun.

Many different solutions were devised, but the longest-lasting was that of Julius Caesar. To allow for the fact that the year is 365¼ days long, he fitted in an extra day every four years – the leap years. This was not exact: the annual error was 11 minutes. By 1582 this had built up to ten days, and Pope Gregory XIII ordered a revision. Ten days were 'lost' – October 5, 1582, became October 15 – and to avoid future error Gregory decreed that leap years should occur only 97 times in 400 years, so that century years are leap years only if they can be divided by 400. Many countries were reluctant to accept a change dictated by Rome, and the Gregorian calendar was not introduced in Britain until 1752.

Astronomical clocks, such as this 1560 German version, not only told the time, but showed the movements of the planets and the stars.

---

caliphate Originally the central ruling office of Islam. After Muhammad's death in 632, his father-in-law Abu Bakr became the first *khalifa*, or 'successor of the Prophet'. With his successors Umar, Uthman and Ali, he is one of the Rashidun, or 'rightly guided', caliphs. On Ali's death in 661, Islam split: the SHIITES acknowledged the Imams as his successors, while all other Muslims accepted the UMAYYAD dynasty. In 750 the Umayyads were overthrown by the ABBASSIDS, who became puppets of the Turks. Under the Fatimids in North Africa a Shiite caliphate arose (909-1171) which passed to the MAMELUKES in 1258 and, after the OTTOMAN conquest of Egypt in 1517, to the Turkish sultans.

Callaghan, James (1912-) British Labour prime minister from 1976 to 1979. Soon after taking office, he was forced by a sterling crisis to call on the International Monetary Fund to bolster the ailing pound. Relations within the EUROPEAN ECONOMIC COMMUNITY were threatened by Cabinet members opposed to Britain's continued membership. Unable to command a majority in Parliament, Labour was forced to woo the Liberal Party and form the 'Lib-Lab Pact' (1977-8). Weakened during the 'winter of discontent' (1978-9) by strikes opposing proposed wage restraints, the government was defeated and in the ensuing general election the Conservatives won.

Calvin, John (1509-64) French theologian and leading PROTESTANT reformer whose teachings gained a reputation for stern

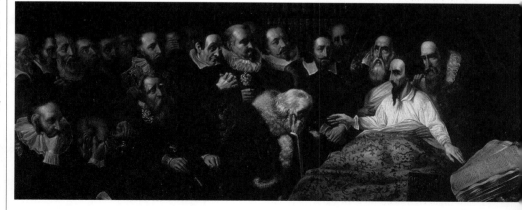

The reformer John Calvin surrounded by the lords and councillors of Geneva, which he had made a bastion of Protestant faith and missionary zeal. Calvin still preached from his deathbed.

morality. Educated in Paris, Orleans and Bourges, in about 1533 Calvin converted to the Reformed faith. He sprang to prominence with the publication in 1536 of his *Institutes of the Christian Religion*, a lucid exposition of Reformed theology, which saw every event as planned by God and minimised the freedom of human will. This was followed in 1541 by *Ecclesiastical Ordinances*, in which he proposed a form of Church government which subsequently became a model for PRESBYTERIANS. For nearly 30 years – from 1536 to 1564, broken only by a three-year enforced exile in Strasbourg – Calvin imposed his version of liturgy, Church organisation, doctrine and moral behaviour on the Swiss city of Geneva, where he had established his own religious community. The city became a Protestant haven and base for missionary activity. His doctrines of predestination and of legitimate resistance to 'ungodly authority' strengthened the faith of many Protestants suffering under oppressive rulers. These beliefs were particularly influential in the Netherlands, France and Scotland, and were also the bedrock, in England and North America, of the PURITAN movement.

Cambodia (Kampuchea)

South-east Asian country which was a flashpoint in the VIETNAM WAR. Part of the Khmer empire until the 16th century, Cambodia was threatened by Thailand to the west and Vietnam to the east until, in 1863, it sought French protection. From 1884 it was treated as part of FRENCH INDOCHINA, though retaining its royal dynasty. Freed from Japanese occupation at the end of the Second World War, it gained semi-independence within the French Union in 1949 and full independence four years later. When, in 1955, Prince Norodom SIHANOUK, who had been elected king in 1941, abdicated to form a broad-based coalition government the USA suspected that he was aiding the Chinese and Vietnamese communists, and Cambodia was drawn into the Vietnam War. Following a US invasion Sihanouk was overthrown by the army under Lon Nol in 1970, but the new regime came under heavy pressure from the communist KHMER ROUGE. When Phnom Penh fell in 1975 the Khmer Rouge under POL POT launched a reign of terror in which as many as 2 million – a third of the Cambodian population – may have died. Border tensions prompted a Vietnamese invasion in 1978. After two weeks, the Pol Pot rule was overthrown and Vietnam installed a client regime under an ex-Khmer Rouge member, Heng Samrin, who proclaimed a new People's Republic of Kampuchea.

A government in exile led by Son Sann, the Coalition Government of Democratic Kampuchea, was recognised by the United Nations in 1983. In Cambodia civil war continued until 1990, when three years of inconclusive peace talks led to an agreement which ended 13 years of strife. Multiparty elections were held in 1993, and a process began of repatriating more than half a million refugees and prisoners.

Cambrai, League of

Alliance of the PAPACY, the HOLY ROMAN EMPIRE, France and Spain against Venice from 1508 to 1510. In 1529 the Habsburg-Valois wars were temporarily halted by the Peace of Cambrai, or Ladies' Peace – so named because it was concluded on behalf of Francis I of France by his mother, Louise of Savoy, while Margaret of Austria signed on behalf of her nephew Charles V.

Cameroon

West African country which is thought to be the original home of the BANTU and was one of the earliest centres of the African slave trade. With more than 150 different ethnic groups, Cameroon has the most diverse population in Africa, and the tribal clashes which this diversity caused created a ready source of slaves which was exploited almost as soon as the first Portuguese explorers reached the coast in 1472. Portuguese, Spanish, Dutch and British slavers all established thriving bases on the Cameroon coast and by the early 19th century British traders and missionaries had established a foothold. In 1884 Germany acquired most of the coastal strip from the powerful Duola tribe, established a protectorate and expanded into the hinterland. Germany gained France's colony in the Cameroons in exchange for its territory in Morocco under the Franco-German Treaty of 1911. The German protectorate was occupied by Anglo-French forces in 1916, and from 1919 was administered under League of Nations (later UN) trusteeship, divided into British and French MANDATES. In 1960 the French Cameroun became an independent republic. It linked in 1961 with part of the British Cameroons – with the remainder joining Nigeria – and in 1972 both merged, eventually becoming the Republic of Cameroon. It was admitted to the UN in 1995.

Campaign for Nuclear Disarmament (CND)

Pressure group formed in 1958 to press for international nuclear disarmament and the scrapping of British nuclear weapons. Frustration at lack of progress led to the creation of a more militant splinter group pledged to civil disobedience, the Committee of 100, led by CND's first president, the philosopher Bertrand Russell. This became involved in protest marches and there were frequent clashes with the police. In the early 1980s CND led protests against the deployment of nuclear-armed US cruise missiles at Greenham Common in southern England. In 1980 European Nuclear Disarmament (END) was formed, working closely with groups in Eastern Europe and similar movements in France, Germany, Australasia and the USA. When the Cold War ended, END turned its attention to nuclear proliferation.

In a 1962 CND protest, 14 000 marchers head for London; by 1980, at Greenham Common (right), the 'bomb' had become a feminist issue.

Campbell-Bannerman, Sir Henry
(1836-1908) British statesman and prime minister of the Liberal government of 1905 to 1908. As secretary of state for war in 1895 he forced the ageing Duke of Cambridge to retire as commander in chief of the army, but during his short tenure failed to introduce any far-reaching reforms. He led the Liberal opposition to British policy during the Anglo-Boer War (1899-1902). During his brief premiership – which ended in his resignation a week before his death – self-government was granted to the TRANSVAAL and ORANGE FREE STATE; the 1906 Trades Disputes Act, which protected trade unions against actions for damages, was passed; and army reforms proposed by Viscount HALDANE were introduced. Campbell-Bannerman also guided the settlement of Anglo-Russian differences, which led to the Anglo-Russian entente in 1907.

Camp David Accord (1978) Middle East peace agreement named after the official country house of the US president in Maryland, where President CARTER met President SADAT of Egypt and Prime Minister BEGIN of Israel to settle disputes which had led to hostilities between the two Middle Eastern countries for 30 years. Under the provisions of the peace, Israel agreed to withdraw from captured Egyptian territory. The accord angered other Arab countries and caused Egypt's isolation from its Arab neighbours.

Camperdown, Battle of (October 11, 1797) Naval engagement off the coast of Holland in which the British destroyed a Dutch fleet. A Dutch strategy to lure the British ships on to the shoals backfired when the British commander accepted the risk, and chased and captured nine Dutch vessels. This victory, coupled with the earlier defeat of the Spanish fleet in February at CAPE ST VINCENT, dashed NAPOLEON's hopes of invading England. It also enabled PITT THE YOUNGER to form another coalition government.

Campion, St Edmund (1540-81) English JESUIT scholar and Catholic martyr. Three years after being ordained in the Church of England in 1568, Campion journeyed to Douai in the Low Countries, where he joined the Roman Catholic Church. In Rome, two years later, he became a Jesuit and in 1580 participated in the first secret Jesuit mission to England, which planned to restore a Catholic monarch to the throne. He claimed he had returned to England only to teach and minister to the Catholic community, but he was tortured, tried and executed for treason.

Canaan Ancient name for PALESTINE, the 'Promised Land' of the Israelites, inhabited by the Canaanites from about 2000 to 1500 BC. Though periodically subjugated by the

In opening up the interior, the Canadian Pacific Railway became a tangible symbol of the ties between the newly federated states. A passenger service, begun within a year, strengthened these links.

Egyptians and Hittites, it was not until the Israelite EXODUS from Egypt in the 13th century that the Canaanites were conquered and confined to the coastal strip of PHOENICIA. Their religion included the worship of local deities called Baals, sacred prostitution, child sacrifice and frenzied prophecy, which were condemned by the Hebrew prophet ELIJAH.

Canada Federation of ten provinces occupying the northern part of America, originally inhabited by Native Peoples and, in the far north, by the Inuit. A Viking settlement established in the 10th century was short-lived; and though the adoptive Englishman John CABOT landed on the island of Newfoundland in 1497, it was the French explorer Jacques CARTIER who in 1534 claimed the mainland for France.

Fur traders established the first French settlement in 1604, and four years later Samuel de Champlain founded QUEBEC on the St Lawrence river. The governor Count Louis de Frontenac defended Quebec against Sir William Phips (1691) and led a successful campaign against the hostile IROQUOIS (1696). Explorers followed the routes of the Great Lakes and the Mississippi Valley – LA SALLE reached the mouth of the Mississippi in 1682. Conflict between Britain and France in Europe was mirrored in Canada in the French and Indian Wars. Under the Peace of UTRECHT (1713) France gave up most of Acadia, Newfoundland and Hudson's Bay. The remainder of New France was conquered by Britain and ceded to it in 1763.

By the end of the American War of Independence, British North America consisted of the former French colony of Quebec – captured during the SEVEN YEARS' WAR in a daring night attack by General James WOLFE, whose troops scaled the Heights of Abraham on which the main town stood – as well as NOVA SCOTIA, St John's Island (renamed Prince Edward Island in 1799), Newfoundland, Cape Breton Island (joined to Nova Scotia in 1820) and the newly created New Brunswick. Areas to the north and west were administered by the Hudson's Bay Company. Fears of US expansion led to the British North America Act (1867), creating the Dominion of Canada with responsibility for its home affairs. In 1870 the Hudson's Bay Company released the first of its lands to federal and provincial control, and three years later the promise of a CANADIAN PACIFIC RAILWAY persuaded Prince Edward Island and British Columbia to join the federation. The railway was completed in 1885. In 1896 the Yukon boomed briefly with the Klondike gold rush. The Hudson's Bay Company gradually ceded all its lands but remains an economic force. As the provinces developed, so did their strength in relation to the federal government, and they enjoy extensive fiscal and legislative autonomy.

Although Canada retains allegiance to the British Crown and membership of the Commonwealth, conflict between its French-speaking and English-speaking citizens has increased in recent years, bedevilling federal politics. French-speaking Quebec, particularly, has pressed for its own distinct 'separatist' status, a move narrowly defeated in a 1995 provincial referendum. In 1993 Canada joined with the USA and Mexico to form a North American economic bloc, so strengthening economic ties with its southern neighbour which had grown in the postwar years.

Canadian Pacific Railway First transcontinental railway in Canada, which was built to transport prairie wheat for export. A plan for the railway was unsuccessfully mooted in the 1840s but revived in 1871, when British Columbia made the construction of the railway a condition of its joining the Confederation of Canada. The planning of the line's development led to a scandal over the award of contracts, which in 1873 forced the prime minister, Sir John Macdonald, to resign. In spite of this, when he was returned to office five years later the railway gained its charter and the line was completed in 1885.

candle Candles probably had their origins in the ancient oil lamps in which floating wicks provided a smoky light. In ancient Egypt bundles of fibre soaked in fat were used to similar effect, and the Romans improved on this technique using harder fats which melted in the heat of the flame and so fed the burning wick. By the 17th century the first moulded candles were manufactured in Europe. These provided an uneven flame from wicks needing frequent attention until, in 1824, the French candle maker Jean-Jacques Cambaraceres developed a plaited wick giving an even, smokeless flame. His invention coincided with the discovery of stearine, a combination of purified fatty acids which gave a harder cylinder as well as a brighter flame. This was replaced in the 1860s with paraffin wax – discovered during the production of lubricating oil in the fledgling petroleum industry.

Cannae, Battle of (216 BC) One of the classic victories in military history in which the Carthaginian general HANNIBAL routed a Roman army numerically many times superior to his own. Defending the southern Italian village of Cannae, densely packed Roman legionaries charged the centre of the shallow crescent which Hannibal's men had formed. As it slowly and deliberately gave ground, and the Romans pushed deeper, Hannibal effected a brilliant double-encirclement. His cavalry, having defeated the opposing right and left wings, closed the trap and fell on the Roman flanks and rear. Of some 50 000 Romans, 35 000 were killed or captured, as against Carthaginian losses of only 5700. Rome's hold on Italy was imperilled, and many of its allies in central and southern Italy defected to Hannibal.

Canning, Charles, 1st Earl (1812-62) British statesman and governor-general of India at the time of the INDIAN MUTINY, who played a notable part in the work of reconciliation which followed. The son of George CANNING, he was subsequently first viceroy of India (1858-62), and known as 'Clemency Canning' for his policy which actively promoted nonretribution.

Canning, George (1770-1827) British statesman, foreign secretary and, briefly, prime minister who from the time he entered

Parliament in 1794 was known as a resolute opponent of revolutionary France. Appointed foreign secretary in 1807 he ordered the destruction of the Danish fleet at the second Battle of COPENHAGEN to prevent it falling into Napoleon's hands, and was responsible for the decision to wage the PENINSULAR WAR. Following a quarrel with Lord CASTLEREAGH, which ended in a duel in 1809, he held no important office until his opponent's suicide in 1822, when he again became foreign secretary. An open supporter of the MONROE DOCTRINE and of the emergent South American republics, Canning also initiated the Anglo-French-Russian agreement which led to Greek independence from Turkey. He was prime minister for a few months before his death in August 1827, but had to rely on Whig support, as his policies, particularly his advocacy of CATHOLIC EMANCIPATION, had antagonised his Tory colleagues.

canon law Law of the Western Christian Church which evolved to deal with discipline, organisation and administration, as well as general morality and liturgy. Guidance was sought from the scriptures, but canon law was also influenced by Roman law, the writings of St PAUL and of the Church Fathers, and from Church councils. Gratian's *Decretum*

(c.1140) introduced order to the profusion of early, often conflicting, canon law established by individual bishops. Significant adjustments were made within the Roman Catholic Church at the Council of TRENT (1545-63), in response to the Protestant REFORMATION, and also at the Vatican Council of 1869.

Canossa Castle in the Apennines where, in the winter of 1077, the German emperor Henry IV (1050-1106) was said to have stood barefoot in the snow while he waited for Pope GREGORY VII to grant him absolution and revoke the excommunication incurred by Henry for his clash with the papacy over ultimate control within the Holy Roman Empire. His penance strengthened his hand against the threat from German princes, who had been allies of the pope but withdrew their support for Gregory when Henry was absolved.

Canton see GUANGZHOU

Canute (c.994-1035) King of England, Denmark and Norway, and one of the most powerful rulers of Europe in his day. When the Danish king SWEYN FORKBEARD invaded England in 1013, his son, Canute (or Cnut), accompanied him and was chosen as king of England on his father's death in 1014. A

Canute was accepted as sole king of England in 1016. He then asserted his hereditary right to the Danish throne, and in 1028 became king of Norway after an uprising had driven out Olaf II.

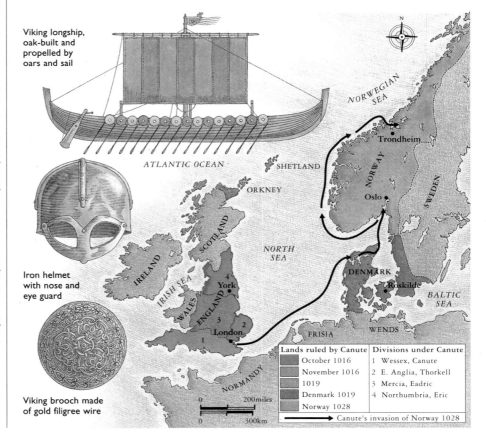

Viking longship, oak-built and propelled by oars and sail

Iron helmet with nose and eye guard

Viking brooch made of gold filigree wire

Lands ruled by Canute	Divisions under Canute
October 1016	1 Wessex, Canute
November 1016	2 E. Anglia, Thorkell
1019	3 Mercia, Eadric
Denmark 1019	4 Northumbria, Eric
Norway 1028	

Canute's invasion of Norway 1028

prolonged struggle with ETHELRED II and his successor Edmund II of Wessex ended with Edmund's death in 1016. The following year Canute married Ethelred's widow, Emma. In a reign marked by displays of piety, legal and military reforms and internal peace, Canute wisely consulted both English and Danish advisers. A later chronicler relates that Canute rebuked his flatterers by showing that even he, as king, could not stop the incoming tide.

Cape Province Originally South Africa's largest province and home of the Khoisan peoples – the Bushmen and the Hottentots – when the Dutch established a settlement on the shores of Table Bay in 1652. Dutch colonisation coincided with the first influx of Bantu-speaking Africans in the east of southern Africa, and in 1779 the first of the Xhosa wars broke out when the white settlers and Bantu peoples clashed in the eastern Cape. From 1795 to 1803 – and again from 1806 onwards – the British held the Cape, taking permanent control of the Cape Colony under the Treaty of Vienna in 1815. The Boers and their new rulers soon fell out over the anglicisation of courts and schools, the official use of English, taxation of farmland and the emancipation of slaves. Many Boers moved north and east in five mass migrations, known as the GREAT TREK, and set up separate republics. In the 1890s, attempts by Cecil RHODES to reassert British rule and unite the Cape with these Dutch-speaking republics led to the Second BOER WAR from 1899 to 1902. The Act of Union of 1910 brought the colony – renamed the Cape Province – into the newly formed Union of South Africa. In 1994 the Cape was split into four semiautonomous administrative regions.

Cape St Vincent, Battle of (1797) Naval battle off the south-west coast of Portugal in which on February 14 the British admirals Horatio NELSON and John Jervis, although outnumbered by almost two to one, defeated a 27-strong French and Spanish fleet. The victory allowed the British fleet to continue its blockade of Cadiz and to pursue Napoleon and his forces, who had invaded Egypt.

Capetian (987-1328) French royal dynasty founded by Hugh Capet in 987. Although successors to the CAROLINGIANS, the Capetians were at first limited to territory around Paris, and did not begin to expand their power until the reign of Louis VI (1108-37). Philip Augustus (1180-1223) seized Normandy and recovered many other areas held by, or under the influence of, the English Crown. He effectively doubled the size of the kingdom and made Paris the centre of government. By the end of the reign of Philip IV (1285-1314) a largely stable France had acquired many of the legal and governmental systems which were

to survive until the Revolution. When Charles IV died in 1328 the throne passed to the House of VALOIS which, with the later BOURBONS, claimed indirect descent from Hugh Capet.

capitalism System of economic organisation developed in Western Europe between the 16th and 19th centuries under which the means of production, distribution and exchange are privately owned and run by individuals or corporations rather than by the State. Initially used in banking and commerce, capitalist methods were applied to industrial production at the time of the Industrial Revolution. At its purest, capitalism minimises the role of the state in economic policy, encouraging FREE TRADE. When, on the other hand, capitalist industry seeks active State intervention against foreign competition it is known as protectionism. International political and economic developments in the 20th century have led to modifications in capitalist societies, which range from the 'welfare capitalism' of Western Europe's WELFARE STATES (see feature, page 695) and the interventionism of President F.D. Roosevelt's NEW DEAL, to the 'mixed economy' concept, in which the production of some goods or services is nationalised, while the rest of the economy is in private hands.

Capone, Al (1899-1947) Flamboyant Italian-American gangster, known as 'Scarface', the most widely publicised criminal of the PROHIBITION era. Capone dealt in bootleg alcohol, extortion, white slavery, prostitution and other rackets. Following his takeover of Chicago's South Side gang from Johnny Torrio in 1925, Capone set out to eliminate all other crime syndicates and thus dominate the city's underworld – aided in this ambition by his control

of the deeply corrupt administration of Mayor Bill Thompson. Capone's campaign, which reached its peak in the slaughter of seven members of 'Bugs' Moran's North Side gang in the St Valentine's Day Massacre of 1929, went unchecked until 1931 when he was jailed for tax evasion. His body and mind broken by syphilis, Capone was freed in 1939.

Caporetto, Battle of (1917) Action, north of Trieste, in which Austro-Hungarian and German forces overwhelmed the Italian army, temporarily forcing Italy out of the First World War. Between October 24 and November 7 some 300000 Italians were taken prisoner before General Luigi Cadorna withdrew his demoralised Italian troops. A new line north of Venice held after being strengthened by British and French reinforcements drawn from the Flanders front. The Italian withdrawal opened the way for Germany's March 1918 offensive on the WESTERN FRONT.

Cappadocia Central area of ancient Asia Minor whose satrap Ariarathes I resisted ALEXANDER THE GREAT's Macedonians until he was killed in 322 BC. Descendants of Ariarathes regained control after 301, though when Ariarathes IV was defeated by the Romans at Magnesia in 190, he and his successors aligned themselves with Rome. When Cappadocia was ravaged by the neighbouring Armenians during the Mithridatic War of 85 BC, Rome granted extensive financial help for the town and its environs to be rebuilt.

Alphonse 'Al' Capone took pride in his snappy dressing, but his bon vivant style and expensive clothes masked a ruthlessness that could order the St Valentine's Day Massacre.

Caratacus (d.AD54) King of the Catuvellauni, a southern British tribe, and son of CUNOBELINUS. Caratacus, also known as Caractacus or Caradoc, succeeded his father about AD40. Continuing resistance after the Roman invasion of Britain in 43 in spite of the fall of his stronghold, Camulodunum, Caratacus was defeated at the Medway and fled to the BRIGANTES, who handed him to CLAUDIUS in 51. Taken to Rome, Caratacus and his family were held as respected hostages.

caravel Small ship favoured by the Spanish and Portuguese and used for early voyages of discovery from the 15th to the 17th centuries. The lightly built caravels were usually single-masted and lateen-rigged, and were also popular as trading ships in the Mediterranean. Christopher Columbus's flagship of 1492, the *Santa Maria*, was a 95 ft (29 m) caravel, and Bartholomew Diaz had rounded the Cape of Good Hope in a similar vessel in 1488. For long ocean voyages they were developed into three or four-masters.

Carbonari Nationalistic secret revolutionary society, formed in Italy but also active in France and the Iberian Peninsula. Founded in the kingdom of Naples during the reign of Joachim Murat, from 1808 to 1815, to free the country from foreign rule, the Carbonari (meaning 'charcoal burners') were influential in fomenting revolts in Naples, Spain and Portugal in 1820, in Piedmont in 1821 and in Romagna and Parma a decade later. After revolts in France failed in 1821 and 1822 the movement there evaporated. All the revolts were suppressed, though that in Naples led to the granting of a constitution to the Kingdom of the Two Sicilies (see SICILY). In Italy, the Carbonari were eventually supplanted by the more broadly based Young Italy movement.

Cárdenas, Lázaro (1895-1970) Mexican revolutionary leader who, during his presidency from 1934 to 1940, gave refuge to Leon TROTSKY. Cárdenas joined the revolutionary army at 18 and within ten years, under the patronage of the former president Plutarco Calles, had become a general. As a military leader in the Mexican Revolution, Cárdenas fought against both Emiliano Zapata and Francisco Villa before becoming governor of his native state, Michoacan, in 1920. Ousting his former mentor, for more than a decade Cárdenas combined a series of political posts with military leadership as civil disturbances continued to plague Mexico. As a committed socialist he was in the forefront of legislation which decreased the number of priests, supported legislation to reduce share-cropping, and broadened the country's educational base. Although conflict with the Church was muted during his presidency, he pushed for a socialist rather than a religious bias in the education programmes of public schools. Although he had given refuge to Stalin's political rival Trotsky, Cárdenas was awarded the Stalin peace prize.

Caribbean Islands and surrounding sea off Central America. By about 5000 BC the Ciboney, a hunter-gatherer-fishing people, had crossed the seas from South America and settled on the two largest islands, HISPANIOLA and CUBA, eventually occupying the other West Indian islands making up the Antilles. Between about 1000 BC and AD 200 they developed agriculture and their own distinctive pottery before being slowly replaced, over the next 800 years, by migrating Arawak Indians. These newcomers from north-eastern South America followed religious, ceremonial and agricultural practices similar to those of Mexico and northern Central America, and some of this 'Taino' Arawak culture survived in the Greater Antilles, though it was destroyed in the Lesser Antilles by the warlike CARIBS who migrated to the islands in about 1000. After COLUMBUS's landfall on the islands and their settlement in the late 15th and 16th centuries, Spain, France, Britain and Holland all fought for various possessions there, and many islands changed hands several times in the 17th and 18th centuries. By then the indigenous peoples were nearly extinct, and African slaves were imported to work in the sugar, tobacco and coffee plantations which dominated the Caribbean economies. From the late 19th century onwards many of the islands gained independence.

Caribs Natives of South America who migrated to the islands of the Lesser Antilles from about AD 1000, replacing the agricultural Arawak culture. The Caribs killed off most of the Arawak men – often eating them in ritual cannibalism – and took their women. The Caribs were the first 'Indians' encountered by Columbus and his men.

Carlist Supporter of claims to the throne of Spain by the Spanish king's brother Don Carlos (1788-1855) and his descendants. His religious orthodoxy and belief in the divine right of kings made Don Carlos the natural leader of traditionalists who – in 1830, after Ferdinand VII preferred his daughter, Isabella, as his successor – formed the Carlist Party. When Ferdinand died three years later, the Carlists proclaimed Don Carlos king, as Charles V, igniting a six-year civil war which ended when the pretender fled to France. His two eldest sons continued the Carlist claims until an unsuccessful rising in 1860; the third son, Juan (1822-87), after briefly advancing his claims, renounced them in favour of his son, Don Carlos VII, in 1868. When in the same year ISABELLA II was overthrown, Carlist support intensified, but was dashed by the new king, Amadeus, in 1872. The establishment of a federal republic in 1873 renewed Carlist hopes, but in 1874-5 Isabella's son was restored as Alfonso XII. The re-establishment of a republic following Alfonso XIII's abdication in 1931 renewed popular Carlist support. In the SPANISH CIVIL WAR the Carlists sided with the nationalists, and for many years obstructed Franco's aim to restore the Bourbon dynasty. But in 1969, overcoming Carlist objections, Franco named Alfonso's grandson, Juan Carlos, as his successor.

Carlyle, Thomas (1795-1881) Historian, essayist and thinker. Born in Scotland, for a time Carlyle taught and contributed to the *Edinburgh Review*. His *Life of Schiller*, first printed in serial form in 1823-4, won critical acclaim, but it was the publication in 1837 of *The French Revolution* which established his literary reputation. In it he expressed the view, to be repeated in his later works, that great men shape the course of history. A severe critic of 19th-century materialism and a keen sympathiser with the sufferings of the poor, he described their plight in *Chartism* (1839) and later in *Past and Present* (1843).

Carmelite Follower of the Order of Our Lady of Mount Carmel who obeys the strict monastic 'rule' of St Berthold of Jerusalem, which isolates both monks and nuns from the secular world. The order has its origins in a group of hermits who lived on Mount Carmel, in Palestine, and were formally structured by Berthold in about 1154. When the Holy Land was conquered by the Muslims the Carmelites moved first to Cyprus and then to western Europe, where the order was approved by Pope Honorius III in 1226. The rule of strict isolation was later relaxed in order to allow some involvement with the care of the laity. Monasteries were established in Oxford, Cambridge and Paris, and the order became active in the academic life of the late 14th century. In 1452 the Carmelite Sisters was formed. Known in Britain as 'Whitefriars', the Carmelites produced such celebrated mystics as St TERESA OF AVILA and St JOHN OF THE CROSS, who reformed the order.

Carnac Town in Brittany, France, noted for its standing stones. More than a thousand stones, or MEGALITHS, arranged in avenues and circles mark the area as having been a major centre of ritual activity between 5000 and 3000 BC. Many tombs dot the area, and at nearby Locmariaquer stands the world's largest known MENHIR, 65 ft (20 m) high.

Multimillionaire Andrew Carnegie was shown as a bricklayer whose library 'blocks' would offer others the chance of self-improvement.

Carnegie, Andrew (1835-1919) Scottish-born US industrialist and philanthropist. A weaver's son, in 1848 Carnegie emigrated to the USA where he swiftly rose to become, at 18, personal assistant to Thomas A. Scott of the Pennsylvania Railroad. Investing in iron and steel production, Carnegie in 1872 launched his own steel company, ultimately gaining control of US steel output through technological and management improvements. When he sold out to the US Steel Corporation for $447 million in 1901 his personal holdings made him a multimillionaire. Carnegie's belief that the rich should act as trustees of their wealth for the public good was set out in his essay *The Gospel of Wealth* (1889), and put into practice in the philanthropic distribution of more than $350 million, a substantial part of which went towards the establishment of some 3000 public libraries in many parts of the world – the first being in his home town of Dunfermline.

Carnot, Lazare (1753-1823) French general and military tactician drawn into political life after the FRENCH REVOLUTION. Two years after joining the army in 1784, Carnot published his influential *Essay on the Use of Machines in Warfare*. Elected to the National Assembly in 1791, his reorganisation of military recruitment and administration was mainly responsible for the successes of the revolutionary armies. Although a staunch republican and member of the Directoire from 1795 to 1797, Carnot accepted the royalist victory in the elections of 1797 rather than the republican coup which followed, fleeing to Germany when this led to false accusations of treason. Returning to France in 1800 to become NAPOLEON's minister of war, Carnot continued the administrative reforms

he had begun in 1791, but resigned a year later. He again served Napoleon during the HUNDRED DAYS of 1815, but chose to go into exile in Germany after Napoleon's defeat.

Carol I (1839-1914) German-born first king of Romania, who ruled from 1881 until his death. As a minor German prince, in 1866 Carol was chosen by the Habsburgs to succeed Alexander John Cuza as Prince of Romania, then part of the Austro-Hungarian empire. While his pro-German leanings during the FRANCO-PRUSSIAN WAR cost him popular support, Carol's skill in manipulating politicians and elections thwarted his opponents' attempts to force his abdication. Experience gained as a Prussian officer proved invaluable to his military leadership in the Russo-Turkish War, which led the Congress of Berlin to grant Romania full independence from the Ottoman Empire as a kingdom in 1881. Carol reformed the constitution, monetary system and army, and also improved communications and encouraged the first exploitation of Romanian oilfields. But he did little to help the peasants, savagely crushing a revolt in 1907. Carol declared Romania neutral at the outset of the First World War, but on his death, his nephew and successor, FERDINAND I, joined the war against Germany.

Carol II (1893-1953) King of Romania and great-nephew of CAROL I. After the birth of his son Michael to his wife Princess Helen of Greece, Carol's scandalous domestic life forced him to renounce the succession in 1925. He went into exile with his mistress in Paris. Though Michael succeeded to the throne two years later, he stepped down in favour of his father and Carol returned as king in 1930 to establish a royal dictatorship. In 1940 his pro-Nazi palace guard forced Carol to abdicate in favour of Michael.

Caroline of Ansbach (1683-1737) German princess who married the future GEORGE II in 1705. Cultured and clever, Queen Caroline also possessed considerable political skill, using her influence in support of Sir Robert WALPOLE. She was a popular queen, and was four times appointed 'Guardian of the Realm' during the king's absences in Hanover. As an amateur botanist and enthusiastic landscape gardener, it was her proposal to enclose 300 acres (121 ha) of Hyde Park in London that led to the establishment of Kensington Gardens.

Carolingian Empire Group of western European territories ruled by, and taking its name from, the family of CHARLEMAGNE (768-814). Charlemagne's Frankish ancestors fought their way to power under the Merovingian kings, the last of whom was deposed by Charlemagne's father PEPIN III in

751. Charlemagne – whose court became a centre of learning – expanded the empire to cover modern-day France, part of Spain, Germany to the River Elbe and much of Italy, and was crowned Emperor of the West by Pope Leo III in 800. When in 843, nearly 30 years after Charlemagne's death, the Treaty of VERDUN divided the empire between three of his grandsons, the empire's power was already under intolerable strain from Viking raids and the rivalries of ambitious families. In spite of this, Carolingians ruled in Germany until 911 and in France until 987, setting a standard of cultural achievement which later kings of the Middle Ages sought to emulate.

carpetbaggers Derogatory US term describing Northern entrepreneurs, educators and missionaries who moved into the American Southern states after the civil war. After the Reconstruction Acts of 1867, numerous northerners moved south to share in the rebuilding of the former states of the Confederacy. They were called 'carpetbaggers' because it was said they could carry all they owned in a single hold-all, known as a carpet-bag. Many of them genuinely wished to help the Black ex-slaves, but others were interested only in making a quick profit. Some were active supporters of the Republican Party and achieved public office, including state governorships. After Rutherford Hayes was elected president in 1876 and self-rule was restored to the Southern states in the following year, carpetbagger influence waned.

Carroll, Lewis (1832-98) English author and mathematician whose two tales about the adventures of Alice in a magical realm have become classics of children's literature. Lewis Carroll was the pen name of Charles Dodgson, who was educated at Oxford and lectured in mathematics there from 1855 to 1881. He became a clergyman in 1861. Four years later, the nursery tales which he had told to the second daughter of his college head were published as *Alice's Adventures*

A much-loved creation of Lewis Carroll, the White Rabbit was always in a hurry.

in Wonderland and proved to be an immediate success. Its sequel, *Through the Looking-Glass and What Alice Found There*, appeared in 1872 and was equally popular. Dodgson also wrote humorous verse and several mathematical works. He was also an enthusiastic and gifted amateur photographer.

Carson, Edward, Baron (1854-1935) Anglo-Irish statesman dedicated to preserving Ireland's constitutional relationship with Britain. Following his election in 1892 to the British Parliament, he became solicitor general in the Conservative government of 1900 to 1905. His opposition to the third Home Rule Bill in 1912 led him to organise a private army of ULSTER VOLUNTEERS, threatening that Ulster would establish its own provisional government if the Bill went ahead. When, two years later, he reluctantly accepted Home Rule for southern Ireland he insisted that the north – including the predominantly Catholic counties of Tyrone and Fermanagh – should remain under the British Crown. His inflammatory battle against Home Rule was resumed after the First World War, and though he grudgingly accepted the Anglo-Irish Treaty of 1921, which gave dominion status to southern Ireland, he continued to campaign for Ulster's interests.

Carter, Jimmy (1924-) President of the United States from 1977 to 1981. Carter's lack of ties with a US political establishment tainted by the Watergate scandal helped him to win the Democratic nomination and election of 1976. His early policy of cutting US aid to regimes which failed to respect basic human rights as agreed at the HELSINKI CONFERENCE was soon abandoned, though measures to pardon Vietnam War draft-dodgers

and to introduce administrative and economic reforms were popular. Despite a Democratic majority in Congress, Carter failed to obtain approval for his plans to reduce oil consumption, while the Senate in 1979 refused to ratify the agreement on STRATEGIC ARMS LIMITATION TALKS (SALT II). But his administration did negotiate the CAMP DAVID ACCORD between Israel and Egypt and the transfer of control of the PANAMA CANAL to Panama. The IRAN HOSTAGE CRISIS may have cost him the 1980 election, in which he was defeated by the Republican Ronald REAGAN. After leaving office he engaged in numerous peace missions in the Middle East and North Africa – where he hosted peace negotiations between Ethiopian and Eritrean separatists in 1989 – before helping to resolve the North Korean deadlock over nuclear arms in 1994 and in the same year brokering democratic changes in Haiti. He also visited Bosnia, laying the groundwork for later peace talks.

Carthage City state founded on the North African coast of what is today Tunisia by Phoenician colonists from TYRE (traditionally by Dido in 814 BC, but probably later). Carthage became one of the major trading cities of the western Mediterranean, with footholds in Spain, Sardinia and Sicily. Between 500 and 300 Carthage was frequently at war with the Greeks of Sicily. On this island, too, Carthage first clashed with Rome, leading to the three PUNIC WARS, so called from the Roman name for the Carthaginians, *Poeni* – hence Phoenicians. In spite of heroic campaigns by the Carthaginian general HANNIBAL, the second Punic War cost Carthage its fleet and all its possessions outside Africa. Although Carthage recovered as a trading power, the city was razed in 146 BC

Carthage made armour such as this fine gilded bronze breastplate as early as 300 BC.

after its third conflict with Rome. Julius Caesar saw it rebuilt as a Roman colony, when it again achieved great prosperity. Later, under St Cyprian, it became a centre of Christianity. Captured in 439 by Genseric, who established it as his capital, it was held by the Vandals until its capture by BELISARIUS in 533-4. It remained part of the Byzantine Empire until it was destroyed by invading Arab hordes in 697.

Carthusian Monk in the austere monastic order founded by St Bruno of Cologne in France in 1084. Though credited with the invention of the liqueur that bears the name of their first community at La Chartreuse, fasting, solitude and silence except for a few hours each week mark the severe discipline of the order. Lay brothers and sisters who attend to the members' non-spiritual needs provide a minimum of contact with the outside world.

Cartier, Sir George Étienne (1814-73) Conservative French-Canadian statesman who was involved in the 1937 PAPINEAU REBELLION but later worked towards Anglo-French accord. From 1857 to 1862 Cartier led the French-Canadian faction in the Canadian government, serving for four years from 1858 as joint prime minister with Sir John Macdonald. In 1867 Cartier became a minister in the first dominion government formed after the establishment of the Canadian Confederation – the unification of the states he had worked so hard to promote.

Cartier, Jacques (1491-1557) French navigator who in 1534 discovered the St Lawrence River while seeking a north-west passage to China. On his next voyage to Newfoundland the following year Cartier followed the river as far as the Île d'Orléans, continuing in longboats to an Indian village which became the site of Montreal. On a third voyage in 1541-2, though he wintered on the river, Cartier made no new geographical discoveries. His work of Canadian exploration was continued more than 60 years later by the French governor, Samuel de Champlain.

cartoon Originally a full-sized drawing made by an artist as a basis for a painting or tapestry, cartoons have come to describe humorous or satirical drawings which are

Following the explorer Jacques Cartier's descriptions, a contemporary artist chose a map of Canada's east coast and the St Lawrence River as his setting for the first French colonists' arrival.

Pioneers of the road

Just over 100 years ago the first petrol engine was patented in Germany. In 1908 mass production of motor cars began in the USA, and by 1995 there were more than 600 million motor vehicles in use across the world.

The invention of the petrol-driven internal combustion engine by Gottlieb Daimler and Karl Benz in Germany in 1885 marked the start of a transport revolution. The first petrol-driven vehicles began to evolve in Europe and the United States in the 1890s. Early examples were a challenge even to the hardy motorists of the time. Drivers sat on – not in – open vehicles, protected against the elements by special clothing. Roads were rough and cars often had to be pulled out of the mud by an obliging farmer and his horse. In the early 20th century cars became status symbols for the well-off, but for ordinary people – especially doctors, who were among the industry's best customers – the growing practicality of the basic models made them a welcome alternative to horses.

FORD SHOWS THE WAY

In 1908 Henry Ford transformed production with the introduction of the assembly line in the USA, and the launch of his Model T Ford. This sturdy open tourer was affordable, and simple to maintain – 15 million had been sold by the time production ceased in 1927.

As purchasing power increased, mass production brought the motor car within reach of more people. In Britain there were 2 million cars in 1940; by 1995

The 1929 Mercedes – named after the daughter of a Daimler concessionaire in Nice – was the first eight-cylinder motor car.

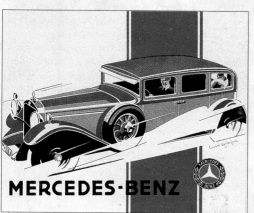

Henry Ford looks nostalgically down at the first Ford motor car, with the 10 millionth Ford behind him. (Inset) Imaginatively designed headgear protected motorists from the elements.

there were more than 20 million. Special roads were built, with German autobahns taking the lead in the 1930s, although most motorway building, even in the USA, dated from the 1950s. By then, motor vehicles were competing with trains for journeys over longer distances.

The assembly of motor vehicles and the manufacturing of components became concentrated in particular areas: around Detroit in the United States, and in the English Midlands. Motor manufacture became a major industry – the second largest in the USA.

By making a range of cars that were smaller and cheaper to run, British manufacturers, led by Austin and Morris, became the world's second largest producers in the 1930s. Just as those of modest means had moved from bicycles to motorcycles before 1930, so they now traded up to small cars.

The most successful model, invented in Germany just before the Second World War and marketed after it, was the Volkswagen 'Beetle', of which 20 million were

sold. From about 1960, the Japanese showed the way by making ever-better and more compact models.

Cars not only changed the face of travel, but influenced how people lived. They no longer had to rely on public transport, but travelled from door-to-door at their own convenience. Families went for day trips or on holiday by car. They travelled farther to shop. Suburbs and out-of-town centres developed.

In 1995 there were more than 600 million motor vehicles worldwide – at least one for every ten people on Earth. Of these, 450 million were cars and the rest buses and commercial vehicles. The increase took place mainly after 1940, when there were a mere 45 million cars and 37 million other vehicles.

While the car has brought unprecedented personal freedom, it has increasingly been blamed for damaging the environment. Manufacturers are under pressure to produce pollution-free models, while the rising cost of fuel has increased demand for smaller, more efficient cars. World car ownership continues to expand by 5 per cent a year.

often pointed commentaries on public figures or current events. Initially part of the process for making stained-glass windows, by the early 15th century cartoons were used by painters in preparing frescoes and other murals. The design was transferred by pressing along the sketched outlines with a stylus or by rubbing powdered charcoal through fine holes pricked along the lines in a process known as 'pouncing'. Early political cartoons were often vulgar and poorly drawn, making their first appearance as a form of social propaganda in 16th-century Germany during the Reformation. Others were skilfully executed caricatures, the work of artists such as Hans Holbein. By the 18th century such caricatures had become an important and effective part of English journalism, attracting artists such as the painter and engraver William Hogarth and the caricaturist Thomas Rowlandson. In France, Honoré Daumier's scathing satirical drawings and etchings awakened and aired public concern about government corruption in the mid 19th century. In the USA the impact of political cartoons on public opinion became evident in the 1870s when the power of New York's Tammany Hall was broken and the corrupt local politician, William ('Boss') Tweed, was imprisoned largely because of the mocking exposures of the *Harper's Weekly* cartoonist Thomas Nast. The term passed into popular English usage after the proposed designs for frescoes in Britain's Houses of Parliament were parodied in the humorous magazine *Punch*.

Carver, John (c.1576-1621) Former deacon of the separatist church in Leiden who led the PILGRIM FATHERS' migration on the *Mayflower* in 1620. Shortly before his death the colonists elected Carver as the first governor of Plymouth Plantation.

Cartoons often rely on puns to make a point. In 1867 this was how Honoré Daumier saw the 'balance of power' between France and Prussia.

EUROPE

By the age of 25 Casanova had been a soldier, secretary to a cardinal, an alchemist and a violinist. But it was his accounts of amorous encounters which gave illustrators ample imaginative scope.

Casablanca Conference (January 14-24, 1943) Meeting in Morocco at which the British prime minister Winston CHURCHILL and the US president Franklin D. ROOSEVELT planned Allied strategy for the next phase of the Second World War, including increased bombing of Germany and the invasion of Sicily. They resolved to continue the war until Germany surrendered unconditionally, and agreed that when this happened British forces should be transferred to the Far East.

Casanova de Seingalt, Giovanni (1725-98) Notorious Venetian womaniser and adventurer who wandered through Europe as a gambler and spy. Casanova's personal charm contributed to the many and varied successful seductions recounted in his voluminous memoirs. Written in French and published posthumously, these provide both a lively account of his adventures and amours, and an entertaining picture of 18th-century society.

Casement, Sir Roger (1864-1916) Irish patriot executed by the British for treason. An Ulster Protestant and respected member of the British consular service, Casement gained a knighthood for his work, as well as widespread respect for exposing ill-treatment of Black labour in Africa, particularly of workers on rubber plantations in the Upper Congo. Freed of official constraints by retirement in 1913, Casement openly supported the cause of Irish independence. In 1914 he visited the USA and Germany, canvassing support for an uprising in Ireland. Efforts to recruit German-held Irish prisoners of war to fight the British in Ireland failed; nor would Germany provide troops. In 1916 Casement landed on the coast of County Kerry from a German submarine, hoping to postpone the EASTER RISING until the rebel forces were strengthened and better armed. But he was arrested and taken to London, where he was tried and hanged for treason. His diaries — leaked by British agents before his trial and the subject of continued controversy — claimed to prove Casement's homosexuality and may have reduced Irish sympathy for him. His request to be buried in Ireland was rejected at the time, but agreed to in 1965.

Castile Former kingdom in northern Spain whose name derives from the extensive castle-building in the region during the 10th century. In the political confusion of the early Middle Ages, alliances with the Spanish MOORS alternated with expansion into their territory, especially under Alfonso VI and Alfonso VII. Castile's cultural life developed under ALFONSO X (1221-84), but his reign was followed by a long period of weak rule and internal turmoil. When ISABELLA I of Castile married FERDINAND II of Aragon in 1469, the two greatest kingdoms of Spain were united.

Castlereagh, Robert, Viscount (1769-1822) British statesman and a leader of the coalition that defeated Napoleonic France and achieved a postwar settlement at the Congress of VIENNA in 1815. Entering the Irish House of Commons in 1790, Castlereagh pushed through the ACT OF UNION in 1800 to unite Britain and Ireland, but later resigned as an MP when George III rejected a plan for CATHOLIC EMANCIPATION which Castlereagh had promoted. He proved a poor secretary for war (1807-9), and George CANNING's attack on his policies led to the two men duelling, forcing Castlereagh to resign his Cabinet post. As foreign secretary from 1812 he threw his energies into defeating Napoleon and maintaining the balance of power in Europe. While his foreign policy was successful, at home Castlereagh became the focus of hostility over his support of repressive legislation introduced in response to the unrest caused by demands for parliamentary reform. Many held him directly responsible for the PETERLOO MASSACRE of peaceful demonstrators in 1819. Blackmailed for his alleged homosexuality, Castlereagh committed suicide.

Castro, Fidel (1927-) Marxist revolutionary who became prime minister and, later, president of Cuba. The son of an immigrant sugar planter, Castro was drawn to Marxism by the poverty he saw around him. After studying law, in 1953 Castro led an unsuccessful uprising against the Cuban dictator General Fulgencio Batista, for which he was imprisoned. He conducted his own defence at the trial and his concluding words, 'history will absolve me', became a rallying-cry and broad statement of philosophy for Castro and his group of revolutionaries. Freed in an amnesty two years later, Castro went into voluntary exile in the USA and Mexico. In 1956, accompanied by the Argentinian revolutionary Ché GUEVARA, Castro invaded Cuba at the head of an 82-strong guerrilla band. They were ambushed as they landed and only 12 of the invaders survived the first assault.

Gaining growing public support, Castro mounted a successful guerrilla campaign from the island's Sierra Maestra mountains, and by December 1958 he had attracted enough followers to march on the capital, Havana. Batista fled and on January 1, 1959, Castro proclaimed the Cuban Revolution and declared himself prime minister. Almost immediately he expropriated foreign industry and soon took farming into public ownership. Unable to gain US diplomatic recognition or arrange commercial agreements with the USA, Castro turned to the Soviet Union to negotiate credit and to obtain arms and food. From 1961 Castro openly aligned Cuba with the Soviet Union and his policies became more strongly Marxist. The abortive US-backed BAY OF PIGS invasion by right-wing exiles in April 1961, and his survival of the CUBAN MISSILE CRISIS the following October, boosted Castro's popularity. His support for revolutionary movements in other South American countries, and of African liberation movements, gained him considerable status in the developing countries and he was chosen to lead the Non-Aligned Movement.

When the Soviet Union and its economic arm COMECON collapsed in 1990, Cuba faced severe economic problems. Austerity measures were followed by a gradual liberalisation of the economy. However, the flight of refugees from the Castro regime to the USA and Cuban attempts to prevent their exodus continued to strain relations between the two countries. Castro has survived several assassination attempts, including one, allegedly planned by the CIA, to blow him up with an explosive device concealed in one of the cigars which he habitually smokes.

catacombs Underground burial galleries of early Christian Rome, named after the tomb of St Sebastian 'in the Hollow' (*ad Catacumbas*) where one of the earliest martyrs was interred. The catacombs became the site of celebrations to mark the anniversaries of martyrs who were among those buried there. Forty chambers are known, tunnelled through soft rock outside the boundaries of the ancient Roman city. The graves, looted during the sack of Rome by Visigoths and Vandals, were almost forgotten until their rediscovery in the 16th century.

Çatal Hüyük Large late Stone Age settlement near Konya in south-central Turkey, spread over about 32 acres (13 ha) and dating from about 6500 BC. First excavated in 1958, the site has yielded evidence of 12 levels of habitation, and it is believed that at the peak of its occupation Çatal Hüyük may have had 10 000 inhabitants. So tightly packed were the small mud-brick houses that their only entrances were through the flat roofs. Bulls' horns mounted in benches and found in many rooms are thought to mark shrines. Richly furnished burials beneath the floors, as well as murals and votive offerings, have been uncovered at the site.

Catalonia Semiautonomous region in north-east Spain centred on Barcelona, with its own distinctive culture and language. Catalonia was a Roman colony until it was overrun by the VISIGOTHS in the 5th century. From 874 it became independent under the counts of Barcelona and later, through marriages, was allied to ARAGON in 1137, and to CASTILE in 1469. Always separatist, the Catalans rebelled in 1462-72 and again in

---

Çatal Hüyük is one of the world's earliest cities and the largest Neolithic site in the Middle East. This early farming community lived in mud-brick houses with a kitchen in one corner of the main room and platforms for working and sleeping lining the walls. Small windows gave the only light.

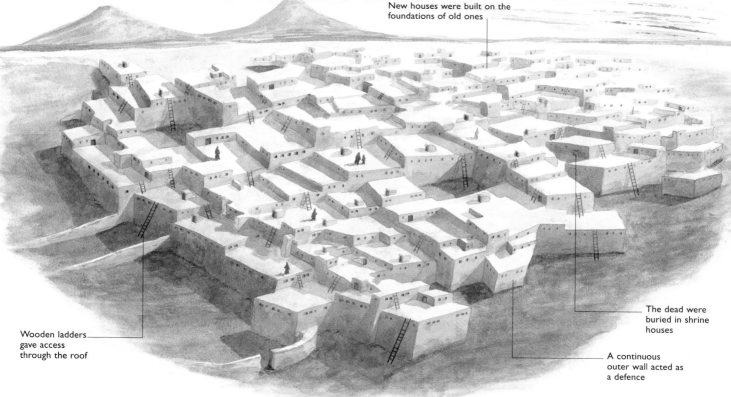

New houses were built on the foundations of old ones

Wooden ladders gave access through the roof

The dead were buried in shrine houses

A continuous outer wall acted as a defence

Castles built for power and prestige

The medieval castle was an awe-inspiring expression of the might of the lord who built it. Once within its formidable walls he knew that only a prolonged siege could threaten him.

A castle was the defended residence of a medieval lord, who might be a king, a nobleman or even a bishop. He did not live there all the time, for an important lord would have several castles and would travel between them with his retinue. When its lord was in residence, the castle had to cater for a large household, as well as house him in the style that his rank demanded. Its architecture could be as much an assertion of the importance of its owner as an expression of military power.

Some features of the medieval castle were present in late Roman forts and town walls, which often had either towers projecting from the curtain wall or twin-towered gatehouses, but many centuries passed before medieval builders copied these. After the fall of Rome, Germanic and Celtic chieftains feasted their war bands in barnlike timber halls, as described in the Anglo-Saxon poem *Beowulf*. By about 1000 similar halls, sometimes defensible, were being built in stone by regional lords in northern Spain and western France. They were surrounded by defences of earth or stone, and many were based upon *mottes*, high circular earth mounds with a timber palisade and tower.

STONE CASTLES FROM NORMANDY

In Britain, the first spate of castle building began with the Norman Conquest of 1066. Chepstow, built by William fitz Osbern from Calvados in Normandy, is the oldest datable stone castle in Britain. It has a defensible stone hall like some in Normandy. Most castles at this date, however, had defences and buildings of timber, often with a motte; the more important acquired stone defences later.

Throughout western Europe, defensible halls developed into square towerlike keeps such as William the Conqueror's Tower of London (now the White Tower); Henry II's keeps at Newcastle (1172-7) and Dover (1181-5); and Domfront or Falaise in France. Such towers were self-contained, with a great hall, accommodation for the king or lord and his household, ample

space for stores, a well and its own chapel. By about 1200 castles such as these were becoming more sophisticated. 'New style' castles, often geometric in shape, had high stone curtain walls. Projecting from them at intervals were rounded towers with batteries of arrow slits so that the space in front could be swept by fire from longbows or crossbows. From about 1220 gate towers and entrance arches were replaced by twin-towered gatehouses. The

entry between a pair of circular towers was defended by gates, portcullises, arrow loops and murder holes – small holes in the roof of the gate passage through which missiles could be dropped. Central keeps were now rarer, but were usually circular, with an all round field of fire. The 'typical' medieval castle had evolved. One influence on this new military architecture may have

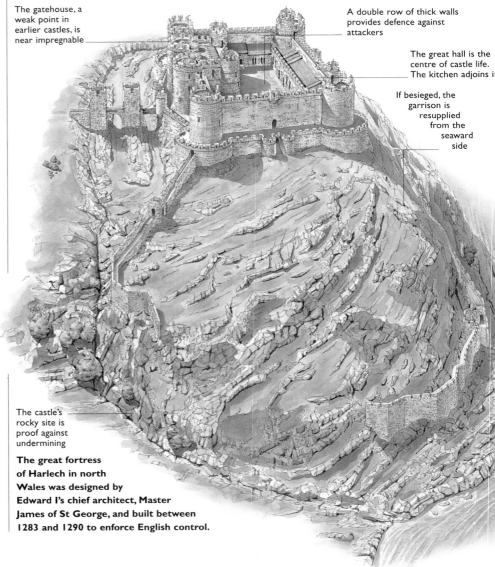

The gatehouse, a weak point in earlier castles, is near impregnable

A double row of thick walls provides defence against attackers

The great hall is the centre of castle life. The kitchen adjoins i

If besieged, the garrison is resupplied from the seaward side

The castle's rocky site is proof against undermining

The great fortress of Harlech in north Wales was designed by Edward I's chief architect, Master James of St George, and built between 1283 and 1290 to enforce English control.

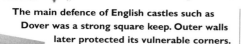

been the Crusades. Many crusading princes were familiar with Byzantine fortifications such as the 5th-century land walls of Constantinople, which anticipated some features of medieval castles. Kings such as Richard I, the builder of Chateau Gaillard near Rouen (1196-8), Philip Augustus of France and Edward I would have cast an eye over such works; however, Crusaders in the East usually preferred to build castles of the type they knew at home.

Whatever its sources, a castle such as Krak des Chevaliers, 'Castle of the Knights', in Syria, built by the Knights Hospitallers and lost to the Saracens in 1271, represents the peak of castle building, along with the Welsh castles of Edward I such as Conwy (1283-7), Harlech (1283-90) and Caernarfon (1281-1330).

The military significance of a castle such as Krak is that in the East the limited forces of the Crusaders faced the more numerous armies of Islam. One solution to this problem was to make stone walls do the work of men. Concentric castles such as these had two lines of defence, set close inside each other. The inner one was higher and stronger so that attackers who scaled the outer line could be picked off by archers on the inner walls. Gateways, particularly those in the north Welsh castles, were monumental in scale. Housing the private apartments of the king, they could be separately defended should the rest of the castle fall.

DEFENCE AGAINST SIEGE

A castle was built to withstand siege, and to resist both direct assault and weapons such as stone-throwing machines and battering rams, and undermining by tunnels. It might be built on a rock like Harlech, Chateau Gaillard or many Rhineland castles, or surrounded by water like Caerphilly. The aim was to commit invaders to a long siege in conditions where the garrison, as long as it had food and water, held a military advantage. In peacetime, a castle also controlled the surrounding land so that its lord could collect taxes and supplies from his peasants.

A castle would be home to a number of people. The garrison would vary in size, but a peacetime complement of between 20 and 40 knights, sergeants (lighter armed cavalry), archers and watchmen would be normal. When the lord was away, a waged constable or steward commanded. There would be many civilians, including priests,

servants and craftsmen such as smiths or masons. There would also be a number of women, from noble ladies to washerwomen.

All needed to be fed and housed. In the hall, the lord, his family and noble guests sat at high table, with lesser folk ranged down its length, while servants were busy in the kitchens and service rooms below. The lord's family would have a great chamber or living room, and, usually on upper floors, a bedchamber equipped with fireplaces, latrines and a private chapel.

Lesser folk would lodge elsewhere, some with their own fireplace. Most made do with a communal latrine. Sanitation was important, for disease was as dangerous as arrows. Latrine shoots emptying into a ditch or river were common. Deep wells were dug to supply fresh water, storage space was necessary for food supplies and wine, and there would be a bake house and brew house for fresh bread and beer.

THE CASTLE BECOMES A HOME

Western European castles were the product of a feudal society with a military, landowning aristocracy. Castles were also built in other countries with similar social systems, such as Japan in the 16th and 17th centuries, but there they were designed to resist earthquakes as well as sieges. Moorish castles in southern Spain were places of refuge in time of war, rather than fortresses with feudal garrisons.

From about 1300 castles tended to be noble residences rather than purely military structures, and a growing taste for privacy sometimes led to the lord's apartments being sited in a separate tower. Not until

the advent of cannon, which could break down a curtain wall, did castles start to become militarily obsolete. Some adapted to the new warfare, and many British castles withstood sieges in the Civil War. In the same period French kings demolished many castles belonging to the nobility, seen as rivals to their own power.

In 19th-century Britain, the castle returned to fashion: landowners built themselves castellated houses with mock arrow slits. The French emperor Napoleon III and Ludwig II of Bavaria built or rebuilt palace-castles for their amusement. The castle was, as it always had been, a symbol of status, power and wealth.

The first Norman castles had a *motte*, or mound, originally topped by a wooden tower, and *bailey*, or enclosure, as at Pleshey in Essex.

The broadly moated Bodiam Castle in Sussex was started in 1385 by Sir Edward Dalyngrigge, who feared that French raiders would come to reclaim the wealth he had looted from them.

119

1640-52, when they sought French help. Their support for the Austrian candidate in the War of the SPANISH SUCCESSION led to political reprisals following the BOURBON victory. Though Catalonia eventually gained independence in 1932, the republic was short-lived: it was abolished in 1939 following the Spanish Civil War, in which parts of Catalonia had supported the royalist cause. Franco also banned all official and educational use of Catalan, the traditional tongue of Catalonia, Andorra and the Balearic Islands. Since the reinstatement of Spain's monarchy, this Romance language, which is similar to Provençal, is regaining its cultural hold.

catapult Device to propel missiles, used by the Romans as part of their siege arsenal. Catapults based on the Roman design were developed in Germany during the early 13th century and used in sieges of castles and walled towns. They consisted of a sling containing a projectile attached to one end of a counterweighted arm which was mounted on a raised triangular pivot. The arm was winched back and when released the abrupt fall of the counterweight launched the projectile towards its target. Decapitated heads of enemies sometimes took the place of the more commonly used rocks, and even corpses were catapulted into besieged towns and castles in the hope of spreading disease among the defenders. In the First World War catapult-like devices were used to throw grenades. A similar principle was used in launching early seaborne aircraft.

Stripped of the worldly goods they claimed to despise, 12th-century Albigensians (Cathars) are driven from the town of Carcassonne.

Cathars Members of a heretical sect which originated in Bulgaria and spread to western Europe in the 1140s. In southern France this Christian heresy was called ALBIGENSIANISM. Seeking a life of moral perfection and taking their name from the Greek *katharos*, 'pure', Cathars believed that if God – being wholly good – was the sole creator, evil could not exist. Thus another, diabolical, force must have taken part in the creation. They saw the material world as irredeemably evil; despised the human body and its appetites; rejected marriage; and admired suicide by starvation. Only a very few, called the 'perfect', could attain a pure life. The rest, known simply as 'believers', could live as they chose, their salvation assured if, just before dying, they took the *consolamentum*, a form of confirmation. The

ceremony was delayed as long as possible to minimise the recipient's chance of again sinning, however unintentionally, before death.

Catherine I (c.1684-1727) Lithuanian servant girl who became the mistress and second wife of PETER I, and empress of Russia (1725-27). When Peter died Catherine was proclaimed ruler with the backing of her husband's close friend and senior adviser, Aleksandr Menshikov, and the royal guards regiments. Menshikov, working through the Privy Council, became the effective head of government, but he fell from power on Catherine's death.

Catherine II 'the Great' (1729-96) Expansionist empress who ruled Russia for 34 years following the death of her husband Peter III in 1762. As the German princess Sophie of Anhalt-Zerbst, in 1745 Catherine married the future emperor. Six months after his accession Peter was murdered – probably by Catherine's lover Alexei Orlov – and with the support of the royal guards regiments of St Petersburg Catherine was proclaimed empress. An intelligent and ambitious woman, she corresponded with VOLTAIRE and considered herself a disciple of the ENLIGHTENMENT. In spite of this, her much-heralded Legislative Commission (1767-74), intended to improve the lot of the peasant masses, achieved little, while her Charter to the Nobility of 1785 not only enshrined the privileges of the nobles but extended serfdom and made it harsher. Her claim to greatness lies

Catalan (later Aragonese) expansion to the mid 15thC

- Aragonese 1380
- under Catalan/Aragonese influence to the mid 13thC
- acquired in the 15thC
- temporary Aragonese fiefs mid 15thC
- 1229 date of acquisition
- — Holy Roman Empire

After Catalonia was united with Aragon in 1137, Catalan traders came to rival those of Genoa and Venice, expanding the House of Aragon's power in the Mediterranean. With the union of Aragon and Castile in 1479, Catalonia began to decline, partly as the result of changes in trade routes.

Catherine the Great was a woman of immense appetites who devoured a string of lovers and also conquered many neighbouring lands.

mainly in her foreign-policy successes. With the help of Aleksandr Suvorov and Grigory POTEMKIN – the only one of her many lovers whom she allowed to influence her decisions – she gained most of Poland in the partitions of 1772, 1793 and 1795, took Azov in the first Turkish War, and annexed the Crimea and the entire northern shore of the Black Sea.

Catherine of Aragon (1485-1536)
Spanish-born first wife of HENRY VIII of England and mother of MARY I. Married to Henry in 1509, Catherine bore him a daughter but no male heir who survived. By 1527 the importance of the Spanish alliance had diminished and Henry – already infatuated with Anne Boleyn – asked Pope Clement VII for an annulment justified by Catherine's earlier marriage, in 1501, to his elder brother Arthur (1486-1502). This, he argued, contravened a common law that siblings could not marry the same spouse. When Henry's claim was rejected by the pope, Thomas CRANMER, Archbishop of Canterbury, was pressed into granting an annulment in 1533, so causing Henry's, and England's, breach with Rome. After the annulment Catherine lived in seclusion in England.

Catherine of Braganza (1638-1705)
Portuguese princess who brought Tangier and Bombay as part of her dowry when she married King CHARLES II of England in 1662. Throughout their empty, childless marriage Catherine had to tolerate not only the king's numerous infidelities but also widespread unpopularity stemming from her Roman Catholicism, although attempts to implicate her in the POPISH PLOT failed. In 1692, widowed and isolated, she returned to Portugal.

Catholic emancipation
The granting in 1829 of full political and civil liberties to British and Irish Roman Catholics. Partial

religious toleration existed in 17th-century Britain, although until 1745 the JACOBITE threat was seen as justifying continued anti-Catholic discrimination, and fears of Catholic emancipation led to the GORDON RIOTS in 1780. During the late 18th century many reformists began to agitate for total religious freedom throughout Britain. Concessions to the Catholic majority in Ireland were made from 1778 onwards and culminated in the Irish parliament's Relief Act of 1793, which provided a wide franchise and freedom of worship, but denied Catholics the right to sit in parliament or hold any public office. By 1798, when Ireland erupted in the rebellion led by Robert Emmet and Wolfe Tone, William Pitt the Younger had accepted the need for full Catholic emancipation and he promised as much when the Irish parliament accepted the Act of Union in 1800. But Protestant landlords and George III resisted emancipation and Pitt resigned. It was not until the election to Parliament of the devout Catholic Daniel O'CONNELL – who had founded the pacifist Catholic Association in 1823 – that the situation changed. As a Roman Catholic he could not take his seat in Parliament, and to avoid civil war the prime minister, the Duke of Wellington, reluctantly introduced the Relief Bill. The ensuing 1829 Act removed most civil restrictions on Roman Catholics.

Catholic League see HOLY LEAGUE

Cato, Marcus Porcius, 'the Elder'
(c.234-149 BC) Roman writer and administrator. Though today remembered for his writings, Cato was a remorseless politician: as consul he suppressed the 195 BC revolt in former Carthaginian Spain and, 11 years later as censor, condemned private extravagance when he drove Publius SCIPIO from public office, prosecuting him for corruption. Although he was active in improving civic amenities, Cato opposed all forms of change. His book on agriculture, *De agricultura*, survives, but only fragments of his history, the *Origines*, remain. *Delenda est Carthago*, 'Carthage must be destroyed', became Cato's slogan, but he did not live to see it fall in 146.

Cato, Marcus Porcius, 'the Younger'
(95-46 BC) Great-grandson of Cato the Elder, and a conservative republican who came to exemplify traditional Roman values. He sided with his long-time opponent Pompey against Julius Caesar. After Caesar's victory at Thapsus, rather than seek a pardon Cato committed suicide at Utica in North Africa, after which he became known as 'Uticensis'.

Cato Street Conspiracy (1820)
A plot to assassinate members of the British Government as a prelude to a general uprising. Led by the revolutionary extremist Arthur

Thistlewood, the conspirators planned to murder Lord CASTLEREAGH and other ministers. When government agents revealed the plan, the plotters were arrested at a house in Cato Street, off Edgware Road in London. Convicted of high treason, Thistlewood and four other ringleaders were hanged, and the rest of the plotters were sentenced to transportation to Australia for life.

Cavalier Parliament (1661-79)
First Parliament in the reign of CHARLES II of England, also known as the Long Parliament of the Restoration. Initially chosen by the king, it was at first made up of 100 Anglican Royalists drawn from the LONG PARLIAMENT of Charles I, and its early years were marked by harsh laws passed against Roman Catholics and Protestant Dissenters. Though it sat for only five of its 18 years in office, its lengthy duration enabled the members of the Commons to claim to play a large part in government. As its membership changed and loyalist numbers diminished, the Commons became increasingly critical of royal policy.

Cavaliers
Royalist party before, during and after the ENGLISH CIVIL WAR. From about 1641 opponents used the word, derived from the French *chevalier*, 'horseman', as a term of abuse, though later it gained a romantic aura in contrast to the puritanical ROUNDHEADS. Defined by loyalty to the Crown and the Anglican Church, the party was drawn from all social classes, but was dominated by country gentry and landowners. The Restoration in 1660 brought the Royalists back to power.

Despite their finery, Royalist Cavaliers, such as these painted by Sir Anthony Van Dyck, proved in battle that steel lay beneath their silks.

At home with her pet dogs, Edith Cavell seems an improbable candidate for martyrdom by a German firing squad.

Cavell, Edith (1865-1915) English nurse and First World War heroine. Eight years after she had helped to establish a training school for nurses at the Berkendael Medical Institute in Brussels, war broke out and Cavell, the daughter of a Norfolk vicar, was left to run the institute as a neutral Red Cross hospital. Though impartial in her nursing of sick or wounded German and Allied soldiers, Cavell believed it her duty to help British, French and Belgian soldiers to escape. She aided 300 men to cross the border into neutral Holland. When her activities were discovered, Cavell was arrested, court-martialled and, in spite of a plea for clemency by US diplomats, executed by the Germans in October 1915.

DID YOU KNOW?

Before her execution, Edith Cavell's last words were: 'I realise that patriotism is not enough. I must have no hatred or bitterness towards anyone.'

Cavour, Camillo, Count (1810-61) Piedmontese politician and leader of the struggle for Italian unification. A financier and industrialist, Cavour set out his reformist views in *Il Risorgimento* (*The Resurgence*), the newspaper he founded in 1847. He believed that unification would come through the action of the strongest of the Italian states, PIEDMONT. Elected to the first parliament of Piedmont, he became prime minister in 1852, and quickly established the state as a model of economic and military progress. The entry of Piedmont into the CRIMEAN WAR gave it a world voice and the chance of alliances essential to end Austrian control in Italy. In secret negotiations in 1858 with Napoleon III, Cavour was promised French support in exchange for the cession of Savoy and Nice to France. This led to victory against the Austrians at MAGENTA and SOLFERINO the following year; but the unexpected Franco-Austrian truce of 1859 led Cavour to resign. He returned to office in 1860, when French support was renewed. After planning

the unification of all northern Italy under Victor Emmanuel II in 1859, Cavour then used GARIBALDI's expedition to Sicily and Naples the following year to bring those states into a united Italy. Appointed Italy's first premier in February 1861, Cavour died four months later, still negotiating for complete Italian unification with the inclusion of Venetia and the Papal States.

Caxton, William (c.1422-91) Father of English printing. After spending most of his life as a cloth merchant in Bruges, in about 1470 Caxton studied printing in Cologne. In 1475 he printed the first book in English, *The Recuyell of the Historyes of Troye*. A year later he set up the first press in England, within the precincts of Westminster Abbey, and in 1477 printed its first book, *Dictes or Sayengis of the Philosophres*. He produced almost 100 books in all, comprising scholarly works, poetry and romances.

Cecil, Robert, 1st Earl of Salisbury (1563-1612) English statesman. Following in the footsteps of his father William Cecil, Lord Burghley, Robert Cecil became chief minister to ELIZABETH I in 1598. Five years later he ensured the succession of her second cousin James I, and in 1608 he was made Lord Treasurer. Faced with crown debts of nearly a million pounds, Cecil introduced additional customs duties and tried to improve the administration of crown lands and revenues. When, in 1610, Parliament rejected his 'Great Contract' – a proposal that it should vote revenues annually to the king – Cecil was forced to continue raising money by selling titles and by such unpopular methods as a forced loan in 1611. After his death the deficit between crown income and expenditure increased dramatically under James's new adviser, the Duke of BUCKINGHAM.

Cecil, William, 1st Baron Burghley (1520-98) English lawyer and statesman, for 40 years principal adviser to ELIZABETH I. Though the politically adept Cecil held office

under both Henry VIII and Edward VI, it was as Elizabeth's secretary of state from 1558 until his death that he exerted great influence on England's domestic and foreign policies, ensuring the stability of the Elizabethan regime. He encouraged new industries, such as glass-making, and introduced financial reforms. More sympathetic than his queen to the Protestant cause, Cecil persuaded her to aid both the French Huguenots in 1567 and the Dutch Calvinists in 1585. As a committed Anglican, he also commissioned Bishop John JEWEL to write his *Apologia pro Ecclesia Anglicana* in 1587, and, because he saw the continued existence of MARY, QUEEN OF SCOTS as a threat to the state, persuaded Elizabeth to sign her death warrant. Cecil was handsomely rewarded by offices – Master of the Courts of Wards and Liveries (1561) and Lord Treasurer (1572) – and wealth. Created Lord Burghley in 1571, he built the mansions of Burghley House, Huntingdonshire, and Theobalds in Hertfordshire.

Cellini, Benvenuto (1500-71) Florentine sculptor, writer and goldsmith whose fame rests as much on his autobiography, published posthumously in 1728, as on the superb quality of his surviving artistic work. Early in his career Cellini worked in Rome, but for five years from 1540 he was employed by Francis I of France, for whom he made a gold saltcellar, regarded as the finest surviving example of the goldsmith's craft from the Italian Renaissance. He spent the rest of his career in Mantua and Florence, where his bronze *Perseus* in the Loggia dei Lanzi is one of the city's landmarks. In his swashbuckling autobiography, Cellini, who was imprisoned several times for duelling, boasted of his amorous conquests and admitted that he had artistic rivals murdered or maimed.

Celtic Church Term applied to the Church in Ireland and other parts of the British Isles inhabited by CELTS from the 5th to the 10th centuries. Ireland probably had early contact with Christianity through Roman Britain, but its widespread conversion to Christianity appears to have occurred under St PATRICK (c.390-460). For the next three centuries Ireland was the most important centre of Christianity in northern Europe, playing a major part in converting Scotland, Gaul and northern Italy, and reconverting England in the 7th century. Largely isolated from the rest of the Church in Europe, Irish missionaries such as St COLUMBA (c.521-97) – who founded a monastery on the island of Iona, off the north-west coast of Scotland – established a form of Christianity with strong individual characteristics. As shown by surviving 'Penitential Codes', the Celtic Church was ascetic and noted for its missionary zeal. It was organised on monastic lines rather than in dioceses or parishes: even bishops were subject to abbots. A rich culture generated works such as the Book of Kells, an 8th-century illuminated manuscript of the gospels. Gradually the Celtic Church lost its distinctive features as it was influenced, and then absorbed, by the mainstream of Western Christendom.

Celts European peoples united by common cultural and linguistic features, and thought to have originated in the Upper Danube region in the 13th century BC. From 800 BC they branched into Galatia in Asia Minor, Gaul (modern France), northern Italy, Galicia, northern Spain and the British Isles. They sacked Rome in 390 and Delphi about a century later. Gifted craftsmen and fierce fighters, the Celts lacked the necessary political cohesion to resist the growing pressures of Rome and migratory Germanic tribes. By the first millennium they had been driven into such remote areas of Europe as Brittany, Wales and Ireland, where their dialects and traces of their culture survive.

Central African Republic Former French colony of Ubangi-Shari and part of French Equatorial Africa, which became a republic within the French Community in 1958 and gained full independence two years later. In 1976 its president, Jean Bédel Bokassa – a former mission school pupil and later chief of the army – declared himself emperor. His regime was marked by violence, torture and intertribal bloodshed. Bokassa was deposed in 1979, and the empire reverted

The intricate ornamentation of the 340 vellum folios of the Book of Kells testifies to the piety of the Celtic monks who illuminated them.

to a republic. Political instability persisted, and in 1981 the military, led by General André Kolingba, seized power. Civilian government was restored in 1986, with Kolingba still president. Demands for multiparty politics led to the emergence of a democratic movement, and a new constitution was adopted in 1992. General elections in 1993 led to a coalition government.

Central America Countries comprising and surrounding the isthmus of Panama, which connects the North and South American continents. When the first Europeans arrived in the early 16th century the region was populated by diverse aboriginal groups, who were enslaved or driven to inaccessible areas as Spain expanded its colonies, drawing manpower from its Caribbean settlements of HISPANIOLA and CUBA. With independence from Spain in 1821, most of Central America was briefly annexed (1821-2) to the Mexican empire. Experiments at confederation between 1823 and 1838 fell victim to political and regional rivalries and – apart from brief intervention by foreign interests in several Central American countries – military strong men dominated the area for the remainder of the 19th century. In 1848 the British gained control of the Mosquito Coast, so thwarting US plans for what was later to become the PANAMA CANAL. The French eventually won canal rights in the region, but the USA continued to see the area as falling within its sphere of influence. In 1951 the Organisation of Central American States was formed to help to solve common problems, but efforts to forge economic links and reduce trade barriers lost impetus in the 1970s. Since then wars – in some of which the USA has been marginally involved – and ideological differences have hampered progress.

Central Intelligence Agency US foreign intelligence agency established by Congress in 1947. Responsible to the president through the National Security Council, the CIA gathers and evaluates foreign intelligence, undertakes counterintelligence operations overseas, and organises secret political intervention and psychological warfare in foreign areas. A series of scandals and widely publicised failures, including the BAY OF PIGS fiasco of 1961, and the later discovery that one of its senior officers was a Soviet agent, steadily eroded the CIA's former immense power and influence. The end of the Cold War forced the CIA to redefine its roles.

Central Pacific Railroad Western part of the first US transcontinental rail route, built eastwards from Sacramento to link, in 1869, with the Union Pacific coming westwards. Promises of a larger federal subsidy for the

While people in the **Central African Republic** starved, Bokassa spared himself no luxuries.

company laying the most track spurred the Central Pacific Railroad (CPR) to build rapidly over extremely difficult terrain. It traversed the sierras and followed the Humboldt River through Nevada and into Utah, where at Promontory Point on May 10, 1869, a golden spike was driven in to mark the two lines' meeting and the completion of the east-west rail link. CPR failed to win the subsidy, but its organisers, Collis P. Huntington and Leland Stanford, sold millions of acres to cover the $90 million construction costs.

centurion Middle-ranking Roman army officer, leader of a combat unit of a hundred men based on citizen lists drawn up for military service. Originally most centurions rose from the ranks, but in the later republic and under the emperors some men enlisted directly as centurions. Their rigorous discipline and experience made centurions vital to the success of the Roman army.

ceorl Free peasant farmer in Anglo-Saxon England, in status above a slave but below a THANE. Ceorls were liable to taxation and to military service. They could own land, but economic pressures and security needs often drove them to accept the control of richer landowners. Their status diminished after the Norman Conquest, the term 'churl' coming to mean an ill-bred serf.

Cervantes, Miguel de (1547-1616) Spanish novelist and playwright who created the bumbling knight-errant Don Quixote and his long-suffering manservant Sancho Panza. Cervantes spent most of his life as a soldier and began writing while still in the army. His military career included a five-year spell as a captive of Barbary pirates. On returning to Spain he fared little better, being imprisoned for the misuse of government funds. During this second prison sentence, in La Mancha, he wrote *The Adventures of Don Quixote*. Published between 1605 and 1615, it won an acclaim that his earlier works had not, and earned him a place in world literature.

Cetshwayo's portrait was commissioned by Queen Victoria after the Zulu king successfully pleaded to her to be restored to his throne.

Cetshwayo (1826-84) Zulu king from 1872 until he was deposed following the British invasion of Zululand in 1879. In the family clashes which followed the death of his father Mpande in 1872, six of Cetshwayo's half-brothers were killed and two exiled before he could claim the throne. Cetshwayo, also spelt Cetewayo, was officially installed by Sir Theophilus Shepstone, Natal's secretary for native affairs, but Shepstone's growing support for the Boers in the Transvaal Republic's long-standing border disputes with Zululand infuriated the king. Cetshwayo, who as a 12-year-old had fought against the settlers in warrior impis – the military divisions based on tribal age groups and developed by SHAKA into effective fighting units – set about enlarging his army. Early in 1878 Shepstone's successor, Sir Bartle Frere, decided to subjugate Cetshwayo, and in January 1897 British forces invaded Zululand, so starting the ZULU WAR. At first Cetshwayo achieved victories against the British – including the Battle of Sandlwana, in which nearly 1200 redcoats were killed – but when Ginginglovu, his capital, fell eight months later Cetshwayo was deposed and exiled to the Cape. He travelled to London to plead his case before Queen Victoria, who reinstated him in 1883. But Cetshwayo's return to power was brief: after a clash with old tribal enemies, he gave up the throne and fled to his birthplace, Eshowe.

Ceylon see SRI LANKA

Chaco War (1932-5) Conflict between Paraguay and Bolivia over control of the Gran Chaco, an extensive lowland plain disputed by the two countries since the early 19th century.

Bolivia's loss of its Pacific coast in 1929 prompted ever-stronger claims to the Chaco, and a series of border clashes eventually erupted into war. Although the Bolivian army was larger and better equipped, its Indian conscripts from the Andean highlands could not acclimatise to the low, humid Chaco. The Paraguayan forces drove the Bolivians back across the Chaco, forcing them to sue for peace in 1935. Paraguay gained most of the disputed territory, but more than 50 000 Bolivians and 35 000 Paraguayans died, creating a climate of economic stagnation that plagued both countries for years.

Chad Mineral-rich former French colony in central Africa, now an independent republic torn by continuing religious and tribal disputes. By the early 1890s, when much of Chad had fallen to Sudanese invaders, French expeditions had begun to penetrate the region. After the FASHODA incident in 1898 led to agreement between Britain and France on the French sphere of influence in Africa, Chad was declared a French protectorate, and ten years later it became part of French Equatorial Africa. In 1920 Chad became a French colony, and its rich mineral deposits were extensively exploited. After gaining full independence as a republic in 1960, under President François Tombalbaye, Chad has since struggled to maintain unity between its Arabic-speaking Muslim north and more economically developed south and west. A Libyan invasion in 1980 sparked seven years of civil war which ended only when French and US intervention led to Libya's withdrawal and the installation of Hissène Habré as president. Habré was deposed in 1990 by his one-time military commander Idriss Déby. A constitutional conference to prepare for a return to democratic rule planned for May 1992 was postponed, and although a transitional legislature was established in 1993, tensions remained, and armed rebels continued to clash with government forces.

Chadwick, Sir Edwin (1800-90) British health reformer whose efforts led to the amendment of the POOR LAWS in 1834. Chadwick's report for the 1833 royal commission into children's work conditions in factories led to the Factory Act of that year, which limited to 12 hours the maximum time that children could work each day. The Ten Hours Act, introduced 14 years later, further reduced children's working hours. In 1840, concerned that cholera was killing so many breadwinners and making paupers of their dependants, Chadwick carried out an *Inquiry into the Sanitary Condition of the Labouring Population*.

Published in 1842, this and later agitation led to an Act of 1848 giving municipalities powers to establish local health boards responsible to Public Health Commissioners. As one of the first of these, during his term of office from 1848 to 1854 Chadwick persuaded urban authorities to undertake major water, drainage and slum clearance schemes.

Chalcedon, Council of (451) Fourth council of the leaders of the early Christian Church, which met in Chalcedon, in Asia Minor. Rejecting the views of an earlier meeting – convened at Ephesus in 449 without papal approval – which declared Christ to have a single nature, the Council of Chalcedon ruled that Christ's nature was both human and divine. The 'Chalcedonian decision' was widely accepted.

Chaldea Area at the head of the Persian Gulf, later to become BABYLON. Conquered by the Assyrians in about 850 BC, Chaldea's first great dynasty of Babylon was established in 626 by Nabopolassar. His son NEBUCHAD-NEZZAR II was responsible for the exile of Jews from Judaea to Babylon – and for the capital's renowned Hanging Gardens. The dynasty was overthrown by Cyrus the Great in 539.

> **DID YOU KNOW?**
>
> *Astronomy and astrology were first studied in Chaldea in the 6th century BC, so that 'Chaldean' came to mean anyone practising these sciences.*

Chamberlain, Joseph (1836-1914) British colonial secretary and advocate of imperial preference, which gave favoured tariffs to trade between countries within the British Empire. Chamberlain first made his mark as a pioneer of municipal reform while Liberal mayor of Birmingham from 1873 to 1876, after which he entered Parliament. The nationwide Liberal Associations that he organised helped to win the election of 1880, when he joined the Cabinet. But six years later he joined the Conservatives as a Liberal Unionist in protest at Gladstone's HOME RULE policy for Ireland. As colonial secretary from 1895 to 1903, Chamberlain supported Alfred MILNER's policies in South Africa which precipitated the second BOER WAR, but distanced himself from the JAMESON RAID. A committed imperialist, he encouraged the formation of the Commonwealth of Australia, and increasingly saw a policy of trade protection as vital to Britain's economy. Chamberlain resigned in 1903 to campaign, without success, for an end to FREE TRADE and the introduction of preferential tariffs which would encourage trade within the British Empire.

Chamberlain, Neville (1869-1940) British statesman noted for his policy of 'appeasement' in the years before the Second World War. Son of Joseph CHAMBERLAIN, he entered Parliament in 1918 and as minister for health was responsible for reforms of the POOR LAW as well as promoting council-house building and streamlining local government. As a skilful chancellor of the exchequer from 1931 to 1937 he guided Britain towards economic prosperity with a policy of low interest rates and easy credit. But his plans for social reform were undermined by Britain's need to rearm, which was already apparent when he became prime minister in 1937. Chamberlain's hopes of averting war by accommodating the European dictators were in vain. In three meetings with Adolf Hitler in 1938 – notably at Munich from which he returned promising 'peace in our time' – Chamberlain made increasing concessions. His policies failed to save Czechoslovakia from German invasion in March 1939, and when Germany attacked Poland later in the year Chamberlain declared war. The debacle of Britain's abortive invasion of Norway in May 1940 forced him to resign in favour of Winston CHURCHILL.

Champagne North-eastern province of France, renowned in the Middle Ages as the site of European merchants' fairs. Champagne was united with France by the marriage in 1284 of Jeanne, daughter of its ruler Henry I of Navarre, to the French king PHILIP IV 'the Fair'. The method of making its celebrated sparkling wine, champagne, is said to be the discovery of a Benedictine monk, Dom Pérignon (1668-1715).

Channel Islands Group of nine rocky islands off the north-west coast of France. The islands are the only part of the former dukedom of Normandy whose allegiance to Britain has survived since the Norman Conquest in 1066. Though the islands, which were occupied by German forces during the Second World War, are a dependent territory of the British crown, they have their own legal system and legislative assemblies. The nine islands are divided between the bailiwicks of Jersey and Guernsey.

Channel Tunnel Submarine rail tunnel between England and France. Its opening in 1994 linked Britain by land with the European continent for the first time since the Ice Age. Although plans for a tunnel were first mooted in 1867, when a company was formed to excavate an undersea link between Dover and Calais, the scheme was abandoned in the face of Francophobe fears and riots which erupted in Dover. The idea was revived in 1880 and drilling started on both sides of the Channel – only to be abandoned when funds ran out two years, and 1¼ miles (2 km), later. During the next century there were several false starts and little practical support from either the British or French governments. Work on the existing 31 mile (50 km) tunnel began in December 1987. Burrowing from

In Chaplin's first full 'talkie' film he satirised Adolf Hitler, but his popularity was based on his role as a bowler-hatted, comic tramp.

both sides of the Channel, engineers linked the first two undersea shafts through a trial bore at the end of October 1990. The first full breakthrough followed in May 1991. By the time the project was completed more than 9 million cubic yards (7 million m³) of spoil had been removed.

Chaplin, Charlie (1889-1977) Film star whose comic genius and talent for mime made him one of the world's best-loved entertainers. The son of two English music-hall performers, Chaplin appeared on stage for the first time before he was eight, but it was in the fledgling silent film industry that he made his mark. During 1914 he made 35 one-reel slapstick films for Mack Sennett and the Keystone Company, establishing the character of the

down-at-heel tramp with a bowler hat, cane and baggy trousers that was to become his trademark. Chaplin's first full-length film, *The Kid* (1921), showed a new dimension in his acting and he brought pathos and a sympathy for the underdog to his role. Chaplin was unhappy with talking pictures and continued to make films without dialogue, such as *Modern Times* (1936), long after the rest of the industry had switched to sound. His satire of Hitler, *The Great Dictator* (1940), was his first film with full sound. Wartime patriotism ensured its success at box offices in both Britain and the USA, but Chaplin's popularity began to decline. When his left-wing sympathies were attacked during Senator Joseph MCCARTHY's 1950s witch hunts, Chaplin settled in Switzerland. He made four more films, which he directed and for which he wrote the music. Only one of these, *Limelight* (1952), was a critical and box-office success.

chariot Fast, two-wheeled vehicle designed for use in war, developed from four-wheeled SUMERIAN battle-wagons of about 2500 BC. The introduction of light horse-drawn chariots to the Near East from the region between the Black Sea and the Caspian in around 2000 BC changed the nature of warfare. Orginally the prized possessions of potentates – as much for prestige as for warfare – their use spread through Greece and Egypt and as far as China throughout the 2nd millennium BC. When, in the 1st millennium, heavier horses led to the development of cavalry, the chariot's importance declined, and

Standing in his chariot with his bow drawn, Tutankhamun leads his troops into battle against an Asian tribe in this 14th-century BC decoration on the side of the pharaoh's tomb at Thebes.

Julius Caesar was surprised to find them still being used in Britain to give warriors mobility on the battlefield. In Rome, they continued to be used for sport in chariot races.

Charlemagne see feature, opposite

Charles I (1600-49) King of Great Britain and Ireland from 1625 to 1649. The second son of JAMES I and Anne of Denmark, Charles was neglected by his father in favour of the Duke of BUCKINGHAM, who later also became a dominant figure in the early years of Charles's reign. The illegal levying of TUNNAGE and poundage which Charles introduced, combined with his tolerant attitude to Roman Catholics and a disastrous foreign policy, enraged Parliament, which in 1628 forced through the PETITION OF RIGHT, intended to curb what his opponents saw as the king's illegal actions. Charles was stubborn and politically naive, and held strong religious convictions.

From 1629 he ruled without a parliament, relying increasingly on the advice of William LAUD, Thomas STRAFFORD and his French Catholic queen, HENRIETTA MARIA. Their influence, coupled with the king's unconstitutional actions, intensified popular antagonism, especially after the SHIP MONEY crisis of 1637 when a Member of Parliament, John Hampden, issued a writ opposing the tax. It had been imposed two years earlier to finance Charles's navy, and was dropped in 1640. Driven to recall Parliament in the same year by the fiasco of the Bishops' Wars with the COVENANTERS, Charles was forced to sacrifice Laud and Strafford, who were impeached and executed. Though Charles accepted new and

Embattled in his wartime capital of Oxford when this £3 gold coin was struck, Charles I might have looked back nostalgically on his royal progress to Hampton Court with his new bride Henrietta Maria.

severe limitations of his powers, an open breach with Parliament came in January 1642 when he tried to arrest five members of the House of Commons, a blunder which united the Lords and Commons against the king and led to the ENGLISH CIVIL WAR. Charles's forces were beaten at MARSTON MOOR (1644) and NASEBY (1645), and in 1646 Charles surren-

> **66 You manifestly wrong even the poorest ploughman, if you demand not his free consent. 99**
>
> *Charles I refutes Parliament's jurisdiction over him, January 21, 1649*

dered to the Scots, who handed him over to Parliament the following year. He escaped from Hampton Court but was recaptured and held at Carisbrooke Castle on the Isle of Wight. Described at his trial as a 'tyrant, traitor and murderer', Charles claimed that the court had no jurisdiction over him. He was found guilty and beheaded in London.

Charles I of Anjou (1226-85) King of Naples and Sicily from 1266 to 1285. The son of Louis VIII of France, Charles of Anjou was given the kingdom of Sicily by Pope Urban IV to curtail the power of the Hohenstaufens, who were threatening the papacy. Charles's victory at Benevento effectively ended the Hohenstaufen influence, but he then went on to take Naples and much of northern Italy – so becoming a new threat to papal interests. His harsh rule led to his assassination and the death or expulsion of his countrymen in the anti-French uprising, the SICILIAN VESPERS.

Charles II (823-77) King of the West Franks from 843 to 877 and emperor of Germany from 875 to 877. After the death of their father Emperor Louis the Pious, Charles, known as 'the Bald', and his brother Louis the German attacked and defeated their elder brother Lothair, who had inherited the West Frankish kingdom. Under the Treaty of VERDUN in 843 Charles took that throne, and in 870 he and Louis divided Lothair's central kingdom between them. Charles gained the

imperial title in 875 and became ruler of the kingdom of Italy a year later. Both titles were contested by a nephew, Carloman, and Charles died while fleeing from him. A noted patron of scholarship and the arts, Charles is credited with reviving the Carolingian renaissance.

Charles II (1630-85) King of Scotland from 1651 and of Great Britain and Ireland from 1660 until his death. As the son of CHARLES I, Charles took refuge in France after the ENGLISH CIVIL WAR. Returning at the invitation of the COVENANTERS and after signing the Solemn League and Covenant – which he later repudiated – Charles was crowned king of Scotland in 1651. Oliver CROMWELL had already defeated the Scots at Dunbar, and Charles's advance into England was halted by his defeat at Worcester. Legend has it that at one stage Charles hid from his pursuers in an oak at Boscobel House in Shropshire, before escaping to nine years' exile on the Continent.

Following his RESTORATION to the English throne in May 1660, Charles adopted conciliatory policies, offering indemnity to all but those responsible for the death of his father and attempting to eliminate religious prejudice in England. However, his marriage to CATHERINE OF BRAGANZA in 1662 increased anti-Catholic feeling and this intensified when their childless union made the Roman Catholic Duke of York – James, the king's brother – heir apparent. Initially a member with Sweden and the United Provinces of the Triple Alliance of 1668 against France, in 1670 Charles signed the Treaty of Dover promising support for the French king Louis XIV against the Dutch. A secret clause in the treaty also committed him to announce his conversion to Catholicism. Charles's moves to undermine anti-Catholic legislation, called the CLARENDON Code, provoked the POPISH PLOT of 1678 and the RYE HOUSE PLOT five years later, as well as the exclusion crisis of 1679-81 in which the Earl of SHAFTESBURY was his chief parliamentary opponent. Defying the law, after March 1684 Charles did not call Parliament. He was, nevertheless, a popular monarch. Although he is remembered for his mistresses – who included Lady Castlemaine, an

Charlemagne: the model of a medieval monarch

As King of the Franks, Charlemagne tried to re-create the glories of the Christian Roman Empire. Crowned emperor by the pope, he united much of Europe under his rule and would influence rulers until the time of Napoleon.

Charlemagne, or Charles the Great, was the most illustrious ruler in the history of medieval Europe. At his death he controlled territory covering modern-day France (excluding Brittany), Belgium, Holland, Switzerland, western Germany, most of Italy, Corsica, the Balearic Islands and north-eastern Spain. Power on such a scale won the admiration of contemporaries and subsequent generations, and perpetuated his fame.

DEFENDING THE FAITH

Charlemagne's personal piety and his conception of the duties of a king caused Church and State to become intimately linked. He saw his task as 'to defend the Holy Church against pagans and infidels, and to fortify it from inside with knowledge of the Catholic faith'. The defence of the faith and the importance of education were the dominant themes of his reign. Later European kings saw Charlemagne as the perfect example of a Christian ruler presiding over a Christian empire.

Charlemagne was born in about 742. On the death of his father, Pepin, in 768, he and his brother Carloman divided the Frankish kingdom between them. With Carloman's death in 771, Charlemagne became sole ruler. He invaded and conquered Italy and Bavaria, but his campaigns in Muslim Spain met with only moderate success. Nevertheless, his efforts against the infidel would make

him a role model for the Crusaders of later centuries. Among his most formidable opponents were the Saxons of north-eastern Germany, who seized the opportunity of his long absences to regain their freedom. Not until a policy of massacre and forcible conversion was implemented were permanent advances achieved.

Charlemagne's rule was a time of cultural revival, and he decreed that 'bishoprics and monasteries should offer earnest instruction in the study of literature to those capable of learning.' He took great interest in reading and enjoyed discussions of the classics, mathematics, astronomy and theology; he assembled a palace school employing many of the most learned men of the day, including the English scholar Alcuin of York. But Charlemagne's court was not solely devoted to intellectual endeavour. He loved hunting and banqueting – although he was said to abhor drunkenness – and he had a magnificent palace constructed at Aachen in 790. This was based on classical models and featured thermal swimming pools and a famous octagonal chapel that can still be seen today.

The high point of Charlemagne's career was Christmas Day 800, when Pope Leo III crowned him Emperor of the Romans. In the decades before this

Charlemagne's empire c814
Border territories controlled by Charlemagne
✕ Site of major battle

Constant warfare carved out Charlemagne's empire. The Saxons were subdued by forced conversion, massacre and transportation.

Charlemagne had acted as the protector of the papacy and had eclipsed its authority, but after 800 his prestige was dramatically enhanced, particularly in relation to his principal rival, the Byzantine Empire, successor to the Roman Empire in the East. In 800 the Greeks of Constantinople were in disarray and Charlemagne clearly saw himself as their superior. He proclaimed that his coronation renewed the glorious days of the Roman Empire.

Acknowledgment of Charlemagne's eminence sometimes took strange forms. In 802 Harun ar-Rashid of Baghdad sent him an elephant: the animal was enrolled in the imperial army and died in service in Denmark in 810.

Charlemagne died in January 814. Despite his success, by the mid 9th century the empire he had created had been fragmented by internal rivalries. Yet his reputation was secure. For centuries to come Charlemagne's reign stood as an ideal for rulers of Western Christendom.

Charles V precedes his archrival Francis I as Europe's two mightiest rulers enter Paris in 1540. A bust (right) of Charles at 20.

Good in 1465, Charles formed the League of the Public Weal, defeating the French king, Louis XI, and forcing the Peace of St Maur to confirm his control of the territory won from France. Within two years Charles also gained much of the Rhineland and Alsace, but failed to persuade the Holy Roman Emperor to grant him the title of king in 1473. Two years later the emperor sided with France, Lorraine and the Swiss to curb Burgundian expansion, and Charles was killed in battle at Nancy.

Charles V 'the Wise' (1337-80) King of France from 1364 to 1380 who earned his nickname from his interest in books, his patronage of the arts and his piety. Becoming regent in 1356 after his father John II was captured at POITIERS, he put down revolts in Paris and by the JACQUERIE in northern France. Charles recovered most of France from invading English forces. His 'scorched-earth' policy contributed to French successes in the HUNDRED YEARS' WAR.

Charles V (1500-58) Holy Roman Emperor from 1519 to 1556, and King Charles I of Spain from 1516 until his death. Coming to the throne of Spain and uniting it with that of the empire which he inherited, Charles was hampered by the differing political and economic needs of his far-flung territories. Surviving an early revolt, he set the foundations of a strong government and overcame papal resistance to the establishment of Spanish rule in Italy. His long, indecisive war with FRANCIS I of France, who had challenged him for the imperial crown, weakened France, and though Charles blunted the OTTOMAN offensive against Christian Europe and maintained control of the Netherlands, he failed to check the spread of Protestantism in Germany or to curb the independence of its princes. Between 1554 and 1556 Charles handed over Naples, the Netherlands and Spain to his son Philip. After abdicating the imperial crown in favour of his brother Ferdinand in 1556, Charles withdrew from public life, retiring to a Spanish monastery.

ancestor of the present Princess of Wales, and NELL GWYN – and his horse-racing, Charles was also a notable patron of arts and science.

Charles III (1716-88) King of Spain from 1759 until his death and, as Charles VII, king of Naples and Sicily from 1734 to 1759. Although his policies were opposed in Spain, Charles tried to improve both agriculture and industry. He reformed the Spanish judicial system and reduced the INQUISITION's powers. His alliance with France involved Spain in the SEVEN YEARS' WAR, during which Florida fell to Britain in 1763, but he regained the territory 20 years later after siding with the colonists in the American Revolution.

Charles III 'the Fat' (839-88) Emperor of Germany from 881 to 887, and King of the Franks from 884 to 887. The youngest son of Louis the German, Charles inherited Swabia, in south-western Germany, and then acquired Italy, Saxony and the east and west Frankish kingdoms, so reuniting all CHARLEMAGNE's old empire except for Provence. However, Charles failed to repel SARACEN invaders and was also forced to pay off VIKINGS to prevent their raids. The resentment this caused led to Charles being deposed, ending the Carolingian monopoly of kingship over the Franks.

DID YOU KNOW?

The spread of the Black Death and wars ravaging Europe in the mid 14th century delayed Charles IV's coronation for six years after his election.

Charles IV (1316-78) King of Bohemia from 1346, and Holy Roman Emperor from 1347 until his death. Charles's promise of concessions to the papacy won the support of Pope Clement VI and ended the long conflict between popes and emperors. Though he was barred from involvement in Italian affairs, he expanded the empire to include Austria and Hungary in 1364. His *Golden Bull* of 1356 set out the imperial constitution, procedures for the election of the emperor and regulated the seven ELECTORS' duties. A scholarly man, he founded the University of Prague in 1348.

Charles Martel (c.688-741) Frankish leader whose defeat of the Muslim forces between Poitiers and Tours in 732 ended their northward expansion and made him an early French national hero. The illegitimate son of Pepin II, Charles took his name from the Old French *martel*, 'hammer'. He extended Merovingian rule to include the two main Frankish kingdoms of Austrasia and Neustria, as well as Burgundy and Aquitaine.

Charles the Bold (1433-77) Duke of BURGUNDY from 1467 to 1477, who almost established a kingdom independent of France. Even before inheriting Burgundy and the Low Countries from his father Duke Philip the

Charles VII (1403-61) King of France from 1422 until his death. His reign was dominated by internal quarrels and war with England. His father, Charles the Mad, had lost considerable French territory to England, and when Charles inherited the throne in 1422 England's Henry VI had already claimed the French crown. It was not until seven years later that Charles was crowned – and then only at the urging of JOAN OF ARC. During his reign Charles regained the French territory captured by England during the HUNDRED YEARS' WAR except for Calais, thus effectively ending the conflict. He made the French Church more independent of the papacy: his Pragmatic Sanction of Bourges, introduced in 1438, upheld the Church's right to administer its own property and nominate clergy to benefices.

Charles X (1757-1836) King of France from 1824 to 1830, whose reactionary rule led to the JULY REVOLUTION and his forced abdication. In 1789 Charles, the dissolute brother of Louis XVI, was exiled to Britain, remaining there until 1814. Throughout the reign of his other brother, LOUIS XVIII, and until he gained the throne, Charles led the ultra-royalist faction. His royal proclamation of his divine right to rule and his choice of ministers, who clashed with parliament's liberal majority, led to civil unrest. In July 1830 Charles reacted to the defeat of his ministers in parliament by issuing ordinances for control of the press, to dissolve the newly elected chamber, and to restrict suffrage. These moves so enraged the bourgeoisie that there was insurrection in Paris and he was forced to abdicate.

Charles XII (1682-1718) King of Sweden from 1697 to 1718, whose reign mirrored the changing fortunes of antagonists in the NORTHERN WAR. Three years after Charles attained the throne Sweden was attacked by a Polish, Danish and Russian coalition. He won a series of victories until in 1709, two years after he invaded Russia, he was defeated at the Battle of Poltava in the Ukraine. He fled to Turkish territory where he spent five years – including a spell in prison – before escaping

and, following a dramatic ride across Europe, remobilising his army. In 1718 Charles was shot during a siege on a fort on the Norwegian border. The financial drain of his wars ended Sweden's role as a European power.

Charles XIV (1763-1844) French commoner who became king of Sweden and Norway in 1818 and ruled until his death. A French lawyer's son, Jean-Baptiste Bernadotte served under Napoleon in the Italian Campaign and supported him when he proclaimed the empire in 1804. He became governor of Hanover in June that year and fought with distinction at Austerlitz a year later and at Wagram in 1809. In 1810 Sweden's parliament invited Bernadotte to succeed the senile, childless Charles XIII. As crown prince, Charles allied Sweden with Britain and Russia and played an important part in Napoleon's defeat at the Battle of Leipzig in 1813. A year later, after invading Denmark, Charles forced the Danes to cede Norway to Sweden. He succeeded Charles XIII in 1818, and though he was autocratic and opposed demands for a more liberal government, he retained popular support throughout his reign. He was the founder of the present Swedish dynasty.

charter Legal document of a ruler or government, conferring rights or laying down a constitution. The best known of these, MAGNA CARTA (1215), sought to define the feudal relationship between the English Crown and its BARONS. Charters in England date from around 600. Initially used to confirm grants of land, they were usually recorded in Latin,

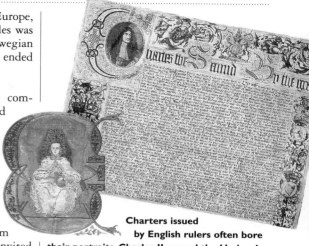

Charters issued by English rulers often bore their portraits. Charles II graced the Hudson's Bay Company's Canadian charter and Elizabeth I (left) illuminated many.

deriving their name from *carta*, the Latin for 'written document'. Between 1066 and 1216 English kings issued charters to more than 300 boroughs, granting them such privileges as self-government and freedom from certain taxes. England's commercial and colonial expansion from the 16th century led to charters authorising trading ventures or forming the first constitutions of the English colonies in America. Such colonial charters were often extensions of trading grants, as was the case in Virginia in 1606, or recognised the self-governing status of colonies such as Connecticut, granted its charter in 1662.

chartered company Form of trading company developed from European medieval trading guilds, and prominent in the voyages of exploration of the late 16th and 17th centuries. The discovery of India and America encouraged groups of merchants to monopolise trade under the safeguard of a royal charter. Exclusive rights were awarded to a few rich merchants whose companies were easy for kings or governments to control and acted as virtual representatives of the Crown, though their restrictive practices often aroused local opposition. Of all these ventures, the English EAST INDIA COMPANY and the Dutch East India Company were probably the most profitable. However, many European chartered companies were costly failures: in the 17th century the French monarchy set up about 30, including the French East India Company in 1664, most of which were unprofitable.

Chartism Popular working-class movement for electoral and social reform in Britain, named after its 1838 manifesto, *The People's Charter*. Widespread discontent after the 1832 REFORM ACT, which had left Britain's masses without a say in government, led to the formation in 1836 of the London Working Men's Association, headed by William Lovett and

Retreating members of his army bear the corpse of Charles XII home to Sweden from his doomed invasion of Norway at Russia's behest. Until this defeat Charles had seemed invincible.

Francis PLACE. The Chartist movement, also strongly influenced by the Irish radical Feargus O'CONNOR, developed from their programme of reforms and was strengthened by the manifesto. This called for universal male suffrage, annual parliaments, vote by ballot, abolition of the property qualification for Members of Parliament – who would also be paid – and fair electoral districts. Meeting in 1839 to prepare a petition to Parliament, the Chartists became so divided on policy that when the petition was rejected the movement's future was uncertain. Following riots in Birmingham and the north of England and the Newport rising in Monmouthshire later that year, several Chartist leaders were imprisoned. In 1842 the Chartists' second petition, with 3 million signatures, was again rejected by Parliament. A mass meeting in London in 1848 to present another petition was abandoned when troops were called in. The movement later collapsed, though many Chartists became active in radical politics.

Chatham, 1st Earl of see PITT, WILLIAM

Chattanooga Campaign Phase in the AMERICAN CIVIL WAR which opened on September 9, 1863 when a Federal army occupied Chattanooga, a strategic Confederacy communication centre. Advancing to the south-east, the army was attacked by Confederate forces and driven back to Chattanooga. There it was besieged for several weeks until General Ulysses GRANT assumed direct command, broke the siege and counterattacked, winning the battles of Chattanooga. The victory opened the way for the advance on Atlanta in 1864 and the subsequent march of General William SHERMAN to the sea.

Chaucer, Geoffrey (c.1342-1400) English poet whose works, particularly *The Canterbury Tales*, are regarded as the starting point of English literature. A London vintner's son, Chaucer became a page in the royal household before serving as a soldier in France. He travelled widely in Europe on diplomatic missions and may have met BOCCACCIO and Petrarch during his travels. In 1387, out of favour with the court and living near to poverty, he started to write *The Canterbury Tales*. These 24 linked stories, told by an assortment of acutely drawn pilgrims travelling from London to St Thomas Becket's shrine in Canterbury, give a vivid insight into medieval life. Chaucer wrote in rhyming couplets, using the iambic pentameter, which came to be the standard English poetic meter.

Cheka Soviet secret police instituted by LENIN in 1917 to enforce the Russian Revolution through terror. Run by Felix Dzerzhinski, a leading revolutionary of Polish extraction, it had its headquarters at the Lubyanka prison in Moscow, which contained torture cells and places of execution. In 1922 the Cheka (Russian initials of the 'All-Russian Extraordinary Commission for the Suppression of Counter-revolution and Sabotage') became the OGPU (State Political Administration) and in 1934 the NKVD (People's Commissariat for Internal Affairs). This eventually became the KGB.

chemical warfare Use of harmful or poisonous chemicals to kill or immobilise enemy forces. Although banned at the 1899 Hague Conference, chlorine gas was used by Germany in 1915 during the First World War – initially with some tactical success in Flanders against the British and French. Cumbersome gas masks were devised as a countermeasure. By 1917 both sides had developed shells containing mustard gas, which was seldom fatal but burned and blistered the skin and caused blindness. Postwar public outcry led to the virtual outlawing of gas warfare, though it was employed in Italy's Abyssinian campaign and by Japan during its invasion of China in 1937. In the Second World War the German discovery of a lethal nerve gas was shelved, as were British and US developments of bacterial agents and gases which interfere with blood functions. Development and stockpiling of potentially devastating chemical weapons have been curtailed in recent decades, particularly since the end of the Cold War. However, both gas and bacteria were deployed in the war between Iraq and Iran from 1980 to 1988, and gas was used in Iraq's attempts to suppress the Kurds during the late 1980s and early 1990s.

Geoffrey Chaucer reads one of his poems in this late-14th-century illustration for the first folio printing of his work *Troilus and Cressida*.

After the Chernobyl disaster Soviet militia prevented inhabitants returning to evacuated zones surrounding towns such as Narodicki.

Chernobyl Soviet nuclear power station near Kiev, in Ukraine, which in 1986 was the site of the world's worst nuclear accident. Operators at the plant deliberately circumvented safety systems so that they could learn more about how it operated. The reactor overheated, causing two major explosions and leading to 250 deaths as well as exposing thousands of people to hazardous doses of radiation. Soviet authorities sealed off the surrounding area, but fallout from the explosions affected much of Europe, and livestock in high-rainfall areas had to be slaughtered. Experts estimate that its effects will be felt for up to 40 years after the disaster, with as many as 30 000 additional cancer victims in Europe and Russia.

Cherokee Native American people who inhabited western Virginia and the Carolinas, eastern Kentucky and Tennessee, and northern Georgia and Alabama. A prehistoric ceremonial centre built in Georgia by the ancestors of the Cherokee was visited by Hernando DE SOTO during explorations from 1540 to 1542. By the 17th century, when French and English traders first encountered them, they had been decimated by smallpox and other 'European' diseases. Although they clashed with settlers moving westwards, after the American War of Independence the Cherokee adapted quickly to their way of life.

Chesterfield, Earl of see STANHOPE

Chiang Kai-shek (1887-1975) Nationalist Chinese leader and general. From his takeover of the GUOMINDANG in 1926, Chiang's ruthless anticommunism stamped China's history for the next half century. Suppressing trade unions and driving the communists out of the Guomindang, between 1928 and 1937 Chiang's nationalist government attempted to unify most of China, introducing major financial reforms and improving communications and education while promoting traditional Confucian values. His government was constantly at war – with provincial warlords, with the communists in their rural bases and with the invading Japanese. In 1936, Chiang, kidnapped at Xian, agreed to cooperate with the communists in resisting the Japanese – a pact that endured through the Second World War. The breakdown of postwar talks with MAO ZE-DONG led to the CHINESE CIVIL WARS, in which the erosion of his armies through casualties and desertions forced his eventual withdrawal from mainland China to the island of Formosa. In 1949 he evacuated his Guomindang survivors to TAIWAN, where the nationalist administration he established, and of which he remained president until his death, still calls itself The Republic of China, though most countries now recognise the Communist People's Republic of China ruled from Beijing.

Chicanos US descendants of Mexicans who lived in the south-west of the present United States when the area was taken by the USA in the MEXICAN-AMERICAN WAR (1846-8), or the descendants of later immigrants from Mexico. Long underprivileged, they were encouraged by the CIVIL RIGHTS movement of the 1950s to launch Chicano organisations to better their conditions. A series of strikes and boycotts in the 1960s led to improved treatment of California grape-pickers, and since the 1970s Chicano children have had access to schooling, many families have moved into better homes, and the Chicanos' choice of jobs has widened and improved. They have also become a growing political force in both local and federal government in the USA.

child labour With the advent of the INDUSTRIAL REVOLUTION, hazardous conditions frequently faced by young children compelled to work in factories and mines began to cause concern. Though Britain's first laws regulating child labour, enacted in 1802, proved ineffective, in 1833 a FACTORY ACT restricted children's working hours and provided for the appointment of inspectors. Later the introduction of compulsory education effectively limited the use of child labour. Other Western European countries followed suit, while some US states also passed laws to restrict child labour, though these were not always enforced. In some developing countries, children are still employed on farms, in factories and in mines, despite international condemnation through the United Nations.

Chile South American country between the Pacific and the Andes which became independent from Spain in 1810. Spanish colonisation began in 1541, five years after Spanish explorers first encountered the dominant indigenous group, the Araucanians. Theoretically subject to the INCA EMPIRE but retaining considerable independence, the Araucanians were gradually driven south. The Spanish colony that developed around the foundation of Santiago in 1541 was overshadowed by

At lines of weaving looms, children squat on cramped benches in a Pakistan carpet factory. As late as 1995 UN efforts had failed to halt exploitation of child labour in developing countries.

wealthier Peru, under whose viceroy it fell. Independence was achieved after Bernardo O'HIGGINS – the son of an Irishman who was viceroy of Peru and governor of Chile – and the South American liberator José de SAN MARTÍN crossed the Andes with 3200 men. They defeated the Spaniards at the battles of Chacabuco in 1817 and of Maipo in the following year. Rich copper deposits discovered in the northern Atacama desert in the late 1840s dramatically improved the new republic's economy, and the boom continued as rich nitrate deposits were annexed following war with Bolivia and Peru from 1879 to 1883. When synthetic nitrates replaced saltpetre during the 1920s, Chile's return to dependence on copper exports placed it at the mercy of the world market. Growing social problems and the failure of a series of political experiments after the Second World War led, in 1970, to the election of Salvador ALLENDE – the first avowed Marxist in history to be chosen as president by popular vote.

Heading a coalition of communists and socialists, Allende confronted both a majority opposition in the Chilean Congress and US hostility, which frustrated his radical plans for nationalisation and land reform. Within three years, inflation, the flight of foreign capital and a balance-of-payments deficit had created an economic crisis during which, in September 1973, the army commander-in-chief General Augusto PINOCHET led a military coup in which Allende and 15 000 other Chileans died. The brutality of the new

regime prompted one in ten of the population to emigrate as the junta suppressed all labour unions and other opposition. Although inflation fell dramatically, so did demand, output and employment, continuing the economy's downward spiral. In 1988 Pinochet accepted a plebiscite decision for the 're-establishment' of 'workable democracy'. Since 1989 democratic elections have been held, and by the mid 1990s the Chilean economy had begun to show strong signs of recovery.

Ch'in see QIN

China Asia's largest country, which is the home of more than 1130 million people. These are predominantly ethnic Chinese (Han) but there are significant minorities, especially in TIBET, Xinjiang and MONGOLIA. China's recorded history goes back nearly 4000 years to the SHANG, who settled in the Yellow River valley and gradually developed a technology which laid the foundations of a civilisation far in advance of any contemporary society in the West. From the 6th century BC, CONFUCIUS and MENCIUS expounded ideas that formed the framework of Chinese society, while TAOISM appeared during the 3rd century BC. As Chinese culture spread, a form of writing was developed which, because its characters represented meanings rather than sounds, could unite people speaking a diversity of dialects and languages. Unification expanded as the QIN (Ch'in) built a territorial and cultural empire that was to survive both fragmentation by barbarian invaders and rule by non-Chinese

Great expectations: the many faces of childhood

Traditionally, the children of the rich have been pampered and protected, while those of the poor have been put to work from an early age. But an adult's view of childhood is not always the same as that of the child.

Childhood wears two different faces: as experienced by the young themselves, and as fantasised through the visions of adults, whether parents, paediatricians or poets. The two may not agree. Victorian painters typically sentimentalised childhood as a time of golden delight, but many autobiographers of that period looked back on their youth as a time of cruelty, neglect or misery.

What childhood was like from early times to the Middle Ages is difficult to gauge because it was little recorded. Greek thinkers, for instance, though greatly concerned with education, wrote little about children – perhaps because infants were largely brought up by women and slaves. Shakespeare's plays tell us little about Tudor childhood. Over the centuries,

children were rarely seen, since wealthy families employed nurses and nannies. This is in striking contrast to more modern outlooks: from the Romantic age at the end of the 18th century, fascination grew with children and the child's view of things.

CHILDREN AT WORK

European societies never gloried in childhood. The fact that up to half of all newborn infants died before the age of five may have discouraged lavish emotional investment in them. Also, societies not enjoying Western affluence have always had to rely heavily on child labour. Most children could neither be pampered nor kept for years at school, but would be sent into the fields or set to spin – or, in the Industrial Revolution, to the factory or

down the mines. Children were made into young adults as fast as possible, as in poorer countries today. In 18th-century Britain, boys were commonly apprenticed and girls sent into service before they reached their teens. In the home and at school they were routinely beaten and brutalised. Such practices were reinforced and even encouraged by preachers and teachers. 'Spare the rod and spoil the child' was the

In a painting of a wealthy German family around 1630, the children are represented as mini-adults in grown-up clothing. A medieval illustration (right) shows boys up to the age-old trick of helping themselves to fruit from the tree.

watchword. Travellers and missionaries to Africa and America complained that the peoples they encountered failed to exercise sufficient discipline over the young.

Christians who believed in original sin had no truck with the innocence of infants. The mother of John Wesley, founder of Methodism, boasted of her babies: 'When turned a year old (and sons before) they were taught to fear the rod, and to cry softly.' Children from the lower orders in particular experienced parents as figures of terrifying power. At the end of the 18th century, Francis Place, born into a working-class family, was often beaten by his father until the stick broke. William Hutton, who became a hardheaded businessman, records that he was never hugged or kissed by his mother; this was probably not untypical. On his mother's death, his nanny upbraided him: 'Don't cry, you will soon go yourself.'

Medieval eyes could see four distinct ages of man: infant, adolescent, man and old man (above). But in the late 19th century the children of the poor had to become old before their time, working in factories to help to support their family (right).

Street Arabs in London's East End in 1888 show a face of childhood far removed from the Victorian ideal.

'I was an economist from my cradle', he wrote. Sentiment was a luxury. In many families youngsters were often expected to stand silently in their parents' presence; obedience was the golden rule.

But change was afoot. The concept of childhood as a special state had early origins. Christianity was an important source, thanks to the glorification of the child Christ, and to the Christian notion that truth could come out of the mouths of babes and sucklings. The children of the rich were always spoilt. Records of the childhood of Louis XIII of France show the infant king being pampered and turned into an object of public attention.

Such ideas were reinforced by certain 18th-century philosophers, notably the French educationalist Jean-Jacques Rousseau, who argued that man was born free, and that evil was not inherent but came through the corruption of society. By

inference, children were naturally good; with a proper upbringing, they would retain their virtue. From then on, two new outlooks developed.

On the one hand, there was a tendency to indulge children and to sentimentalise childhood. The poet Thomas Gray, reflecting upon the child's mind, expressed the sentiment that 'where ignorance is bliss, 'tis folly to be wise'. William Blake, in his *Songs of Innocence and Experience*, saw the child as a visionary and condemned turning boys into chimney sweeps. William Wordsworth's notion that the child is father to the man attributed wisdom to the young, surpassing that of greybeards.

This paved the way for the 19th-century belief that childhood was a magical age, to be looked back on with nostalgia and regret. Charles Dickens put that feeling in a mysterious and sometimes horrifying form, as in *Oliver Twist*. Growing material wealth and a new emphasis on the home and the domestic nuclear family as a nest of emotional warmth and joy also helped to make society more child-centred.

DEVELOPMENTS IN EDUCATION

New attention was devoted to the philosophy of education. From the time of Rousseau, educationalists stressed that children should learn by doing and should be encouraged to find out for themselves – notions incorporated into the educational programmes of Johann Pestalozzi, and Friedrich Froebel, who developed the kindergarten in the 19th century. New playthings combined pleasure with instruction, such as jigsaw puzzles and telescopes.

Child-centredness has been most evident in 20th-century America. In 1946 Dr Benjamin Spock warned, in his *Common Sense Book of Baby and Child Care*, against overrigid disciplining, suggesting that it would create delinquents and neurotics. Ambiguities in our attitudes towards childhood are conveyed by the teachings of psychoanalysis. Sigmund Freud insisted that the early years are the richest of our imaginative lives, stamping themselves on all future development. More attention than ever is now paid to children. But Freud's views on infantile sexuality, and later theories of child development, have torn to shreds the 'innocent child' adored by the Victorians. The 'golden age of childhood' is threatened by commercial exploitation. Once, children were turned prematurely into adults because of the needs of labour; now the same is happening within a consumer culture.

dynasties, such as the YUAN (1279-1368), who were usually won over to Chinese cultural traditions. Under strong dynasties such as the HAN and the TANG (618-907), China's power reached TURKISTAN in the west and Annam in the south, as well as strongly influencing several of its neighbours such as Korea and Japan.

From the 1st century AD BUDDHIST philosophies began to reach China where they were gradually altered and assimilated into Chinese culture. Traditional respect for learning coupled with a remarkable inventiveness kept the Chinese ahead of the West in knowledge and technology until about the end of the SUNG dynasty in 1279. The MONGOL CONQUEST bred widespread change. China drew in upon itself. Learning became a stereotyped study of the Confucian classics, and this, combined with China's new isolationism, stultified intellectual development. The 'Middle Kingdom', as it is called by the Chinese, had always seen itself and its culture as supreme, so that Western attempts to establish trading links with the QING DYNASTY met with little success. It was only when Qing power weakened towards the end of the 18th century that growing external pressures led to direct European involvement in China during the 19th century.

Contact with the West precipitated crisis and decline. After the OPIUM WARS, the so-called TREATY PORTS became the focus for both Western expansion and demands for modernisation. Rebellions devastated the country and undermined imperial rule, and in spite of the abortive HUNDRED DAYS REFORM and more realistic reforms generated by defeat in the SINO-JAPANESE WAR of 1894-5 and the BOXER RISING, the dynasty fell to the CHINESE REVOLUTION of 1911. When the revolutionary leader SUN YAT-SEN resigned his brief presidency in favour of Yuan Shikai, the new republic rapidly degenerated into a patchwork of regimes headed by rival warlords. China's unity was shattered, and it was to remain divided for decades to come.

Although CHIANG KAI-SHEK, the nationalist GUOMINDANG leader, reunited much of the country after the successful Northern Expedition, his Republic of China was weakened by the Japanese invasion of 1937 and could not survive the CHINESE CIVIL WARS with MAO ZE-DONG's communists which followed. In 1949 Chiang was driven from the mainland to the island of Taiwan. Led by Mao, the CHINESE COMMUNIST PARTY established the People's Republic of China on the mainland, introducing land reforms and revolutionising society and the economy. Among the changes of the 1950s, communes were established, urban industry was expanded and nationalised, and the GREAT LEAP FORWARD was initiated. None of the reforms was entirely successful and some failed abysmally. From 1966 to 1976 China's problems were increased by the CULTURAL REVOLUTION, which tore the country apart and ended only with Mao's death. The 1980s saw his successor DENG XIAOPING committed to economic reform, and there has been marked economic growth and progress towards a controlled market economy. But demands for democracy have also grown; a student demonstration in Beijing in June 1989 led to a massacre of some 2000 protesters in Tiananmen Square. Despite continued human rights abuses, in 1994 the USA decided to maintain special trade links with China. Chinese naval manoeuvres off the Taiwanese coast at the time of the island's first democratic elections in 1996 led to a temporary increase in tension between the USA and China.

China-Japan Peace and Friendship Treaty Pact signed by China and Japan in 1978 pledging closer political and economic cooperation between the two nations. Post-war Japanese foreign policy trod a fine line between its economic relations with the USA and popular domestic pressure for closer links with China. The thaw in US-Chinese relations following President Nixon's visit of 1972 and Japan's growing need for Asian markets prompted Chinese-Japanese rapprochement. One of the main aims of the treaty was closer trading links between the two countries.

Chinese Civil Wars (1927-37; 1946-9) Conflicts sparked by ideological differences between Chinese nationalists and communists. During the Northern Expedition of CHIANG KAI-SHEK, anti-leftist purges of the GUOMINDANG led to retaliatory communist urban uprisings in 1927. When these were suppressed, MAO ZE-DONG's communists moved into the countryside, establishing rural strongholds from which their guerrilla tactics could neutralise the nationalists' superior strength. It took Chiang's forces three years to destroy Mao's Jiangxi Soviet, and after the LONG MARCH of 1934-5 the communists re-established themselves in the northern area of Yan'an. From the Japanese invasion of 1937 until the end of the Second World War, the two sides maintained an uneasy truce, fighting separate campaigns against the common enemy. When, in April 1946, the US general George MARSHALL failed to arrange a lasting compromise settlement, fighting resumed. For the first year the numerically superior nationalist troops made large territorial gains, including the communist capital of Yan'an, but as Guomindang morale crumbled in the face of communist victories, confidence in Chiang's administration dwindled. In a successful communist counteroffensive, by November 1948 Lin Biao had taken Manchuria where the nationalists lost half a million men, many through defection. In central China the nationalists suffered further setbacks, and in January 1949 Beijing fell, followed by Nanjing and Shanghai in April. The People's Republic of China was proclaimed on October 1, 1949, and the communist victory was complete when the nationalist government fled from the Chinese mainland to TAIWAN in December.

Chinese Communist Party (CCP) Chinese interest in communism based on Marxist principles was stimulated by the Russian Revolution of 1917 and the May Fourth Movement. The movement evolved from student protest over the Versailles settlement decision to grant Japan former German concessions in Shandong. The CCP was founded by Li Dazhao, librarian of Beijing University, and Chen Duxiu at a congress in Shanghai in July 1921. Instructed by the COMINTERN, CCP members joined the GUOMINDANG, supporting its drive for national liberation while organising trade unions in Shanghai and other large cities. At the same time, under Peng Pai, the CCP developed a peasant movement. It was in China's numerous peasant population that the CCP found a revolutionary base when forced out of the cities by the Guomindang purges of 1927. It set up the Jiangxi Soviet in southern China in 1931 and, when this fell to Chiang's forces, moved north, led by MAO ZE-DONG on the LONG MARCH. An uneasy truce with the Guomindang followed in 1936. It endured throughout the Japanese invasion in 1937 and during the Second World War, but in 1945 civil war resumed. The party's military strength and rural organisation gave it victory, and in 1949 a People's Republic was proclaimed which has ruled China ever since. In the chaos of the CULTURAL REVOLUTION (1966-76) the party seemed bent on self-destruction; after Mao's death and the fall of the GANG OF FOUR, CCP policies stabilised under DENG XIAOPING.

Chinese Revolution of 1911 Overthrow of the Manchu QING DYNASTY, which led to the establishment of a short-lived Chinese republic. A half century of anti-Manchu risings forced the imperial government to give limited authority to provincial assemblies, which then became power bases for constitutional reformers and republicans. Their opposition to the nationalisation of major railways so weakened the government that it could not

> ### DID YOU KNOW?
>
> *Although more than 100 million Chinese speak each of the main dialects, many are so different as to be mutually incomprehensible. Only the written language, containing 30 000 symbols, is understood by all. Knowledge of at least 3000 of these is needed to read a newspaper.*

The 19-year-old Chopin entertains a Berlin salon; and (left) his manuscript score of an 1842 polonaise.

suppress the republican Wuchang uprising of October 10, 1911. By the end of November, 15 provinces had seceded and on December 29 their delegates proclaimed a republic with SUN YAT-SEN as provisional president. By the following February the last Qing emperor, Pu Yi, was forced to abdicate and Sun stepped down to allow Yuan Shikai to become president. A provisional constitution promulgated in March 1912 provided for a democratically elected parliament, but this was ignored and eventually dissolved by Yuan when the abortive Second Revolution of 1913 challenged his authority. By 1915, when Yuan had himself proclaimed emperor, central government had become ineffective and control of much of China had reverted to the warlords.

Ch'ing see QING

chocolate Both chocolate and cocoa are produced from the liquid obtained when the shelled beans of the tropical evergreen cacao tree are finely ground and pressed. Chocolate was drunk by the Aztecs and introduced to the Spanish court by conquistadors returning from the Andean foothills in the 16th century. It rapidly became one of the most fashionable drinks throughout Europe. It was first used in confectionery by the British manufacturers J.S. Fry and Sons in the mid 19th century.

Choiseul, Étienne-François, Duc de
(1719-85) French statesman who as secretary of state for foreign affairs (1758-70) concluded the 1761 alliance between France and CHARLES III of Spain. Given France's weakness, Choiseul's negotiations at the Treaty of PARIS in 1763 were successful, though his later attempts to reform the army and navy failed. He was dismissed in December 1770 when he tried to persuade Louis XV to support Spain against Britain in their conflict over sovereignty of the Falkland Islands.

Chopin, Frédéric (1810-49) Polish composer and pianist whose melodious keyboard works are among the best-loved of the popular classics. Settling in Paris in 1831, Chopin enjoyed seven successful years as a concert pianist before withdrawing from public performance to concentrate on the composition of virtuoso piano music of passionate intensity. Much of Chopin's composition was based on Polish folk-dance forms and rhythms and was said to reflect Chopin's nationalist leanings. He also did much to popularise the nocturne, polonaise and ballade. Chopin's persistent ill-health, widely publicised love affairs – particularly with the French novelist George Sand – and untimely death have made him the archetype of 'romantic' composers.

Christ see JESUS CHRIST

Christian Democrats Members of moderately conservative political groups in various countries sharing a democratic doctrine emphasising a sense of community and moral purpose linked to social reform. Particularly in postwar Italy and Germany, Christian Democracy offered an attractive alternative to previous totalitarian regimes, while in France it offered a focus for political change. In the first decade after the Second World War some of Western Europe's most distinguished statesmen – among them Konrad ADENAUER, Georges Bidault, Alcide DE GASPERI, and Robert SCHUMAN – found their political homes in these parties.

Christian I (1426-81) King of Denmark and Norway from 1448 to 1481, and of Sweden from 1457 to 1464, founder of the Oldenburg dynasty. Chosen as king by the Danish Rigstad, Christian confirmed his new status by marrying his predecessor's widow. After the war of 1451-7 he also took the Swedish throne, but later lost it to the Swedish nobility. He gained Schleswig and Holstein and was at war with England from 1469 to 1474. As a staunch Catholic he founded the Catholic University of Copenhagen in 1479.

Christian Science Religious movement centred on the concept of the power of mind over matter which was founded in the USA by Mary Baker Eddy (1821-1910). A frail and sickly woman deeply interested in medicine and the Bible, Eddy's belief in religious healing was strengthened by her recovery from a severe fall in 1866. Nine years later she published her manual *Science and Health, with Key to the Scriptures*, and in 1879 established the Church of Christ, Scientist. Based on a belief that God is 'divine mind', it teaches that matter, evil, sin, disease and death are all illusory and only the mind is real. In 1908 Eddy founded the international daily newspaper the *Christian Science Monitor*. Although since 1950 Christian Science membership in North America and Europe has fallen, the movement has grown in Africa and South America.

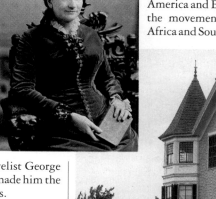

From a balcony of her New Hampshire home Mary Baker Eddy (inset) speaks to followers of Christian Science, the movement she founded.

Defending the honour of Christendom

The strength of the medieval knights as a disciplined fighting force lay in an enduring chivalric code of conduct based on virtue, courage and devotion both to their order and to the defence of their faith.

Chivalry was the code of conduct adopted by the mounted warrior class of medieval Europe. The term originated from the French *chevalier*, 'knight', which meant a man who fought on horseback. By the 9th century, the expensively and heavily armoured cavalryman had mastered the use of stirrups, and by the 12th century he had added the 'couched' lance to his repertoire.

The division of society into knights, clerics and peasants gave the knights the role of keeping the peace. This task sanctified the use of force, and rituals evolved for the blessing of weapons. One 10th-century prayer asked God to 'bless . . . this sword with which your servant desires . . . to defend and protect churches, widows and orphans and all [your] servants against the cruelty of the pagans'.

In the late 11th century, Western Christendom rallied to the call to free the Holy Land from Muslim rule. Companies of knights joined the First Crusade in 1095, and many thousands fought in the Near East in the following centuries. Orders of knights closely modelled on those of monks were formed to fight in Palestine, including the Knights of the Temple of Solomon (Templars) and the Knights Hospitallers of St John of Jerusalem. St Bernard described

A German knight of the 13th century rides into battle wearing a falcon headdress and bearing falcons on his shield and flag.

the Templars as 'valiant men of Israel chosen to guard the tomb of Solomon, each man, sword in hand, superbly trained to conduct war'.

After the fall of Acre in 1291, the last Christian outpost in Syria, crusading energies changed direction, focusing on non-Christian peoples in Spain and Prussia.

Jousting tournaments, such as the one below watched by René of Anjou in the 15th century, were a favourite form of entertainment. The 12th-century ceremonial Seedorf shield (left) was an heirloom for the family of Arnold of Brienz.

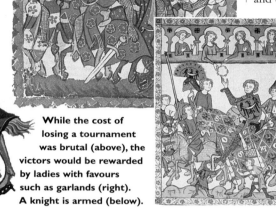

While the cost of losing a tournament was brutal (above), the victors would be rewarded by ladies with favours such as garlands (right). A knight is armed (below).

By the late 13th century, the Knights Templars (left) were feared for their financial strength.

In the late 14th century Geoffrey Chaucer described the knight in the 'Prologue' to his *Canterbury Tales* as campaigning in Lithuania and Russia, as well as Spanish Granada. The Templars became very rich, but were disbanded in 1314, their property confiscated and their last grand master burned at the stake.

Secular rulers also began to found chivalric orders of their own throughout Europe, including the Castilian Order of the Sash in 1332, the Order of the Garter, founded by the English king Edward III in 1347, René of Anjou's 15th-century Order of the Crescent, and the Burgundian Order of the Golden Fleece, established in 1430.

The orders had priests to serve their respective churches. At St George's Chapel in Windsor Castle in southern England, a dean's, canon's and vicar's choral prayed daily for the souls of the knights of the Garter. On an order's feast day, the members gathered for church services and would also review their chivalric deeds and elect new knights.

RICH PAGEANTRY

The building and decoration of the chapel at Windsor provided a splendid setting for the annual ceremony of the Garter. Its richly painted precious relics set with jewels reflected the value King Edward set on the enterprise. For the high altar alone, ten carts drawn by 80 horses brought the carvings of Nottingham alabaster.

The orders were highly structured, often with a limited membership – 25 knights for the Garter. Chivalry proved a highly effective means of bonding together a fighting force and giving it a code of collective loyalty. Both English and French kings were quick to exploit this during the Hundred Years' War from 1337 to 1453.

From the early 12th century, the tournament became a prime form of chivalric ideal, as well as being an important training ground for warfare. By the 14th century, these highly regulated armed encounters between two sides, or between single opponents, could be 'of peace' or 'of war'. Encounters 'of war' were fought with the sharp weapons used on the battlefield; those 'of peace' employed blunted swords and lances. During the Hundred Years' War, Edward III presented a captured French knight whom he considered had fought well with a circlet of pearls from his own head, much as if it were a prize for being the best at jousting in a tournament.

These two chivalric modes, of war and of peace, also determined the knight's choice between two sets of arms, one of war (his family coat of arms), the other of peace (his badge). Edward the Black Prince, who died in 1376, had as his family coat of arms the royal arms of leopards and fleurs-de-lis, as well as a 'peaceful' badge of ostrich feathers on a black background. The colourful shields, banners and pennons illustrated in medieval chronicles served throughout the chivalric world to identify individual knights and to communicate the status and rules of an engagement.

This collective chivalry, in war and in peace, was based on a code of personal honour and devotion, especially to soldier saints such as George, Maurice and Sebastian. The chivalry that took shape in France during the 12th century and which soon spread across Europe was distinguished by the value given to individual qualities of honour, loyalty and courage. Men were not born knights: they had to make a public commitment to this ideal in accepting the sword of knighthood at the hands of their lord. This contrasted with the earlier emphasis on bravery as a member of a group. It was also part of a more general movement in the 12th century towards individualism.

Romances about King Arthur and his knights became hugely popular and embodied a new attitude towards women, who were often the inspiration for the knight's honour. At tournaments, tokens of a lady's love, such as gloves or a handkerchief, for example, were worn openly, and women had a new role as spectators and prize-givers.

The 'courtly love' of a knight for his lady, often had little hope of realisation, since inheritance customs meant that there were large numbers of younger sons who could never hope to marry. Often the knight's 'lady' was remote and inaccessible, although dazzlingly beautiful: 'I intended to live without love/ . . . But my heart . . . drew me back to a madness/Greater than the child's who cries for the beautiful star/He sees shining high and far-off', wrote Guy, the castellan of Coucy in northern France, who was to die on the Fourth Crusade in the early 13th century.

TOWNSPEOPLE ADOPT CHIVALRY

Gradually the chivalric ethos trickled down through society. Rich and ambitious townspeople saw chivalric behaviour as a means of entering the noble classes. In the Low Countries they staged particularly magnificent jousting displays in which the local nobility did not hesitate to participate. One of the most famous emblems of medieval chivalry, a beautifully illuminated manuscript of poems known as the *Manesse Codex*, was produced for a rich burgher family of Zurich.

Throughout society, codes that influenced personal conduct in warfare and duelling, as well as behaviour between the sexes, survived over the centuries as evidence of the enduring power of chivalric ideals long after the Middle Ages had drawn to a close.

Christianity Religion of those who believe in Jesus Christ as the Son of God, and follow his teachings. Its 1300 million adherents are divided into three main groups: the ROMAN CATHOLIC, the ORTHODOX and the Protestant Churches. Christianity had its roots in the faith of a group of Palestinian Jews who saw Jesus as the Messiah, the 'anointed one' – in Latin *Christos* – who would free the Jews from Roman domination. His teachings were spread by his followers, particularly by the converted Pharisee PAUL, who travelled through Asia Minor and visited Greece and Rome preaching that faith in Jesus exempted his followers from obedience to the ritual demands of Jewish Law. This opened Christianity to the many Gentiles (non-Jews) seeking an alternative faith to Roman paganism but unwilling to accept the ritual obligations of Judaism. In spite of intermittent harassment by the Roman authorities, Christianity spread rapidly until the reign of Emperor Decius, whose systematic persecution of them began in 250. Far from eliminating the faith, oppression strengthened it, and throughout the 3rd century Christianity spread across the Roman Empire. In 313 the Emperor CONSTANTINE ended repression, and in 380 Theodosius recognised Christianity as the empire's official religion. By then Christianity had also reached Armenia, Egypt, Persia and, probably, parts of southern India.

Around 200, Church leaders had begun to assemble the most authoritative Christian writings into the New Testament of the BIBLE, though the selection was not finalised until 382. A statement of Christian belief had been agreed at the Council of NICAEA in 325, but as the Church expanded disputes on doctrine and matters of organisation also developed. What had started as a cultural and linguistic gap between the Eastern Church based in Constantinople and the Western Church in Rome became doctrinal and led to the EAST-WEST SCHISM of 1054. The split became permanent following the CRUSADERS' sack of Constantinople in 1204.

In the West, as the Catholic Church, its unity centred on the politically influential papacy in Rome, but this was eroded by the Protestant REFORMATION of the 16th century when autonomous Reformed Churches emerged. By 1800 Rome's political influence was diminishing, but the main moral teachings of the Catholic and Protestant Churches retained their hold both on governments and on individuals. The political, social and scientific revolutions of the 19th century brought new challenges and a weakening of links between Church and State. Growing scientific knowledge challenged biblical beliefs –

in particular the story of the creation, which was questioned by Charles DARWIN's theory of evolution. Nevertheless this was also a time of intense missionary activity, particularly by the Protestant Churches. Their work was inspired by a growing social conscience, and Christian beliefs were often important factors in many of the campaigns to abolish slavery, to introduce legislation protecting workers and to establish education and welfare systems.

> ### DID YOU KNOW?
> *With only 37 members, the Zonda Church of God's True Apostles, in Zambia, is the smallest of the world's 22 189 Christian sects or denominations.*

The 20th century has seen ties between Church and State almost disappear in most countries, and under some regimes Churches have been forcibly suppressed. In Western Europe there has been a steady decline in Church membership, though in many developing countries it continues to rise. A need for greater Church unity was recognised with the establishment of the WORLD COUNCIL OF CHURCHES in 1948.

Christian Socialism Name given to a movement started in Britain in the 1840s by a group of socially conscious Church of England clergy who wanted to improve the conditions of workers. Such efforts were intensified in the face of late-19th-century urban and industrial squalor created by unrestricted capitalism, and led to the establishment of the British Christian Social Union and the US Society of Christian Socialists in 1889. The more radical Social Gospel movement grew from a belief that the sympathies of established Churches lay closer to the interests of employers than to the problems of their workers. The movement's leaders studied Christ's teaching to explore its social and economic implications.

Christina of Sweden remained unmarried after rejecting each suitor proposed by her advisers.

Christina (1626-89) Queen of Sweden from 1632 to her abdication in 1654. Aged six when she succeeded her father GUSTAVUS ADOLPHUS, Christina proved a clever ruler – though restless and headstrong – after she took over the reins from her regent, Chancellor Axel Oxenstierna, in 1644. Christina attracted foreign artists and scholars, including René DESCARTES, to her court. There was a serious constitutional crisis in 1650 and she faced growing social unrest. This, together with her secret conversion to the proscribed Catholic faith, led her in 1654 to abdicate in favour of her cousin, Charles X. Christina spent most of her remaining years in Rome, where she patronised the arts and unsuccessfully intrigued to win the crowns of Naples and Poland.

Chulalongkorn (1853-1910) King of Siam (Thailand) from 1868 to 1910, also known as Rama V. Chulalongkorn was only 15 when his father Rama IV (Mongkut) died, and – represented by a regent – he used the years until he reached his majority in 1873 travelling and studying foreign administrations. On assuming the throne he continued his father's reformist policies, and quickly began to modernise Siam. This, as much as his diplomatic acumen in playing off rival British and French interests against each other, helped to protect Siam from colonisation. However, he was forced to cede some territory to French Indo-China in 1907 and to British Malaya in 1909.

Churchill, Lord Randolph (1849-95) British politician, the younger son of the 7th Duke of Marlborough and father of Winston CHURCHILL. Elected to Parliament as a Conservative in 1874, Churchill swept to prominence as one of the young Tories known as 'the Fourth Party' in the 1880-5 Parliament because of their opposition to the Liberals. A fine orator, Churchill saw himself as the heir to Benjamin DISRAELI, and his comment in 1886 that 'Ulster will fight and Ulster will be right' became a slogan for opponents of HOME RULE for Ireland. Churchill wooed middle and working class voters by emphasising the concept of Tory democracy. He resigned as chancellor of the exchequer when, in 1886, the Cabinet failed to support his proposed cuts in military expenditure. He died mentally disturbed as a result of syphillis.

Churchill, Sir Winston Spencer see feature, page 140

Church of England see ANGLICAN CHURCH

churl see CEORL

Cicero, Marcus Tullius (106-43 BC) Roman statesman whose lasting claim to greatness rests on his writings. Cicero gained a

Posters promoting the Lumière brothers' cinematograph shows appeared on hoardings and walls all over Paris and, as in this 1896 advertisement, often included 'stills' from the film.

reputation as a lawyer in civil and criminal trials, particularly as prosecutor of Verres, a corrupt Roman governor of Sicily, in 70 BC. As his standing grew, the nobility saw him as a contender for the consulship, which he attained in 63. Cicero outmanoeuvred Catiline and his fellow conspirators in their plot to win control of Rome, but his denunciation of the First Triumvirate – comprised of Pompey, Crassus and Julius Caesar – led to his exile, on the trumped-up charge of executing the Cataline plotters without trial. He was

> 66 **I would rather be wrong, by God, with Plato... than be correct with those men.** 99
>
> *Cicero commenting on the Pythagoreans in Tusculanae Disputationes*

recalled in 57 to popular acclaim, returning to Rome on the eve of civil war between Caesar and Pompey, which he tried in vain to avert. In the war his allegiance lay with Pompey and the senatorial cause, but disillusioned by the general's leadership he returned to Italy after Pompey's defeat at Pharsalus in Greece. Although Caesar forgave Cicero's support for Pompey, he quit politics to immerse himself in his philosophical writings. However, after Caesar's assassination it fell to him to rally the Senate. Hoping to revive the republic, Cicero denounced MARK ANTONY in the 'Philippic Orations', and in 43 Antony, Octavian and Lepidus, the new leaders of the empire, ordered his execution. Regarded as the finest Roman orator, Cicero's speeches, correspondence and treatises still have a strong influence on Western thought.

Cid Campeador see EL CID

Cilicia Country in what is today south-eastern Turkey. From early times, the strategic pass through the Taurus mountains in the west of the country was the main gateway for trade between East and West. Known as the Cilician Gates, the pass came under the control of the Hittites, the Assyrians and Alexander the Great, and Cilicia was fought over by the Seleucids and Ptolemies. Pirates whose haven it had been from the 2nd century BC were finally driven out by the Roman general Pompey in 67 BC, and by the end of the century it had become part of the Roman Empire. Occupied by migrating Armenians, Cilicia became a principality in 1080, and an independent kingdom from 1198 until it was conquered by the Egyptian Mamelukes in 1375. Known by then as Lesser Armenia, in 1515 the country was conquered by the Turks and became part of the Ottoman Empire.

Cincinnatus, Lucius Quinctius (c.519-438 BC) Roman hero famed for his devotion to the republic in times of crisis. Appointed dictator in 458 BC when the Aequi had surrounded a Roman army, Cincinnatus's crushing victory rescued the beleaguered force. This mission completed, he immediately resigned his command and returned to his farm. CATO THE ELDER and other later republicans saw in Cincinnatus the epitome of the old Roman values of rustic frugality, duty to fatherland, courage and lack of personal ambition. Their view coloured much of what the historian LIVY wrote about this ideal statesman 'called from the plough' to take supreme command and who, after fulfilling his duty, went 'back to the land'.

cinematography The basic principles of making motion pictures on film have changed very little since the first 'optical toys' were developed in the mid 19th century. These relied on the phenomenon of persistence of vision, in which the eye retains the image of an object for a fraction of a second after the object has been removed. A synchronised, swiftly moving shutter covers the gap between individual images on the film, so creating the impression of continuous movement. Attempts by inventors and scientists to apply this technique to the popular magic lantern were unsuccessful until the 1870s, when the British photographer Eadweard Muybridge and the French physiologist Etienne-Jules Marey developed apparatus to photograph people and animals in motion. In 1889 the US inventor Thomas EDISON produced a working cinecamera which used the recently developed flexible roll film to capture images. His films were viewed in hand-cranked kinetoscopes, similar to peepshow machines. A moving film was shown in public for the first time in Paris in 1895, when the Lumière brothers used a combined camera and projector to throw moving images onto a screen. Similar systems were developed independently in other parts of Europe and in the USA. The first commercial sound films, or 'talkies', were produced in 1926 using a sound-on-disc system, in which the sound was recorded and played to synchronise with the projected images. A range of sound-on-film recording systems were used throughout the 1930s but were superseded by magnetic recording techniques developed during the Second World War.

Cinque Ports Confederation of coastal towns in south-east England which, from the 11th century to the 16th century, provided the Crown with ships and men to patrol the English Channel and convey armies to the Continent. The original five (French, *cinque*) ports – Hastings, Romney, Hythe, Sandwich and Dover, known collectively as the 'head' – were joined by 32 other ports, known as 'limbs'. By the 14th century Winchelsea and Rye were also recognised as 'head' ports. Under a royal charter granted in 1278, ports in the confederation were exempt from taxes, sent representatives to attend the monarch at coronations and, until the 19th century, retained the right to return members to Parliament. The post of Warden of the Cinque Ports, created in 1268, is today only titular; and the establishment of a permanent navy gradually diminished the standing of the Cinque Ports.

Dover's Cinque Port seal bears the date 1305 and is the oldest known example.

His finest hour

Sir Winston Churchill was a wayward genius who, through his leadership of Britain during the Second World War, played a key role in the defeat of fascism in Europe.

When Sir Winston Churchill (1874-1965) became a Member of Parliament at 25, he already had behind him a career as soldier and war correspondent. Churchill was born into politics: his father, Lord Randolph Churchill, had been a Conservative chancellor of the exchequer. Winston's switch in 1904 from the Unionists to the Liberals suggested to some that he was no more than an opportunist. If so, his timing was perfect. Over the next decade he rose rapidly through the Liberal hierarchy to head the Board of Trade, the Home Office and, by 1911, the Admiralty.

The First World War brought Churchill political disaster. He attempted to end the bloody stalemate on the Western Front with an attack on Turkey, but the landing on the Dardanelles proved a failure, and he was made the scapegoat.

'WE SHALL NEVER SURRENDER'
After the war Churchill returned to the Conservatives. He became chancellor of the exchequer from 1924 to 1929, but in the 1930s his romantic attachment to the British Empire and his attacks on the government's policy of appeasing Adolf Hitler kept him out of office. At the outbreak of the Second World War in 1939, no other politician could match his record of steadfast opposition to the rise of fascism. He became prime minister in 1940. Churchill believed he had been born for this hour. His

In a US war poster, Churchill represents the 'bulldog breed'.

speeches roared defiance, and his exuberant confidence in victory inspired the nation. Half-American himself, he cultivated American support and, after the USA joined the war in 1941, promoted the collaboration between the two countries which proved crucial to the war effort. Though an opponent of communism, he also realised that cooperation with Stalin was a necessary evil.

Labour's 1945 election victory curtailed his term of office. Having earlier published biographical and historical works, he turned to writing his own history of the war. His achievements won him the Nobel prize for literature in 1953. He became prime minister again from 1951 to 1955 at the height of the Cold War, when what he had in 1946 described as the 'Iron Curtain' had descended to divide Eastern Europe from the West, but his powers declined after he suffered a stroke in 1953.

Towards the end, Churchill had to accept that Britain's global influence was diminishing. At his state funeral in London, the world's leaders gathered to mark the death of a great British leader and the passing of his country's imperial era.

Churchill visits the Normandy front on June 12, 1944, during the Allied invasion of France. On the left is General Montgomery.

---

circus Place of entertainment in ancient Roman times, featuring CHARIOT races and taking its name from the arena's racing 'circuit'. Rome's largest circus, the Circus Maximus hippodrome, could hold 350000, or one in three of Rome's population. In the races – held on 90 days of the year – four rival teams wearing green, red, blue and white represented the elements, while the four horses that each team drove represented the seasons. On each race day, 24 seven-lap events were contested. Although these days of 'bread and circuses' were meant to defuse the explosive Roman mobs, circuses were often the scene of political assassination and riots.

Cistercian Member of an austere monastic order which follows a strict interpretation of the 'rule' of St BENEDICT. Founded by St Robert of Molesme at Cîteaux in France in 1098, the Cistercian constitution was laid down in the *Carta Caritatis*. A daughter house, founded at Clairvaux by St BERNARD, became equally renowned. As monastic houses expanded in the 11th and 12th centuries, the Cistercians led the reclamation for agriculture of previously unproductive marsh and moorland, pioneering new techniques and prospering as sheep farmers and wool traders. Today's Cistercian monks are divided into two observances: the strict (following the original rule), known as Trappists, and the slightly less austere common observance.

citizenship Membership of a particular country's social structure which usually brings specific legal rights, such as the vote, and civic obligations. In early civilisations citizenship was a privileged status extended only to those who met certain criteria such as owning fixed property; but in modern states citizens' rights are usually regarded as an aspect of nationality, accorded to people born – or permanently resident – in a particular country. In democratic countries citizens are protected by law from arbitrary government decisions which might infringe their rights, and are expected, through the ballot box, to play a part in influencing government policy.

civilisation Stage in a society's development marked by structured social, economic and religious order. In one of the earliest civilisations, that of ancient MESOPOTAMIA, improved irrigation and farming techniques encouraged the change from subsistence farming to specialisation of labour in an ordered society. While farmers still fed the community, their increased output freed others to become builders, craftsmen and priests, each performing a particular task. Gradually, settled communities became towns and cities which were ruled by kings or priests. In this more stable environment written records were kept, and ceremonial and

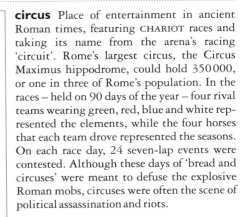

A 17th-century Italian artist's fanciful reconstruction of the Circus Maximus in Rome crammed simultaneous bouts of boxing, gladiatorial combat, athletics and mounted jousts into the arena.

religious buildings were constructed. By 3000 BC urban societies were forming in ancient Egypt and towns had sprung to life independently in the Indus Valley, China, Mexico and Peru. From these centres of civilisation, economic and social organisation spread to areas surrounding them.

Civil Rights Acts Legislation to extend the legal and civil rights of the Black population in the USA. Reversing the Dred Scott decision, which nine years earlier had ruled that slaves were not US citizens, the first Civil Rights Act of 1866 conferred equal citizenship on all people born in the USA, with the exception of Native Americans, who did not gain the right until 1924. Its provisions, which included equal protection in law, were reinforced by the FOURTEENTH AMENDMENT to the Constitution; but both were rendered largely ineffective by later Supreme Court decisions and the apathy of successive administrations. For almost a century little effective federal action was taken to protect Blacks against discrimination, particularly in the South where they were regarded as second-class citizens. A series of legislative Acts, starting with the Civil Rights Act of 1957 and culminating in the Civil Rights Act of 1964 and the Voting Rights Act of 1965, empowered federal agencies to enforce Black rights, opening the way to nondiscrimination.

Cixi (c.1834-1908) Unscrupulous dowager empress of China from 1862 to 1908, who encouraged the BOXER RISING. Manchu-born and a concubine of the emperor Xianfeng, in 1856 Cixi (or Tz'u-hsi) gave birth to a son. Six years later, when the boy inherited the throne as the Tongzhi Emperor, his mother became regent. As such she ruled China for 12 years. After only a year of real power Tongzhi died mysteriously – possibly at his mother's hands – and his four-year-old cousin came to the throne as the Guangxu Emperor, whereupon Cixi resumed the regency. Cixi, no stranger to intrigue and corruption, exercised her power ruthlessly, and when in the 1890s Guangxu tried to reverse her conservative policies through the Hundred Days of Reform, she imprisoned him. As an instigator of the Boxer Rising, Cixi fled Beijing when foreign military forces intervened; and, though conceding some reforms when she returned in 1902, continued until her death to delay the establishment of a constitutional monarchy.

clan Tribal kinship system in which families share a common ancestor and surname. In the British Isles, where clans have always had political as well as social significance, their members are usually fiercely loyal to their chief. Scotland's kings needed clan support, often playing on clan rivalries to maintain power. During the Reformation such rivalries, especially between the Highland and Lowland clans, intensified – often along religious lines. Highland clans clung to Roman Catholicism, siding with the Royalists in the English Civil War, and it was their reluctance to accept William of Orange that led to the GLENCOE MASSACRE in 1692. Their leading role in the JACOBITE rebellions of 1715 and 1745 prompted the British Government to ban the wearing of the kilt and to undermine the system of communal land ownership in an attempt to break the clans. In Ireland, after 16th-century rebellions against English rule,

the clan-based social system was also progressively destroyed by military suppression and a policy of wholesale land confiscation. In other parts of the world, particularly in southern Africa, clan loyalties are often more powerful than tribal allegiances and form the basis of many political alliances.

Clare election (1828) Election in Ireland that led to Roman Catholics being allowed to sit as British parliamentarians. When in 1828 the Irish lawyer Daniel O'CONNELL won the parliamentary constituency of County Clare, he could not take his seat because he was a Roman Catholic. Fears that O'Connell's exclusion would lead to violent disorders in Ireland forced the prime minister, the Duke of Wellington, to push through the Relief Act of 1829, which permitted Catholics to sit in Parliament and hold public office.

Clarence, George, Duke of (1449-78) Younger brother of the English king EDWARD IV. He reputedly drowned in the Tower of London in a butt of malmsey wine. After Clarence intrigued with the Burgundians and fell out with both Edward and his other brother, Richard, Duke of Gloucester – later to become RICHARD III – he was found guilty of high treason and sentenced to death.

Clarence, Lionel, Duke of (1338-68) Second surviving son of EDWARD III and Philippa of Hainault. Known as Lionel of Antwerp, after the town of his birth, in 1361 Clarence was sent to Ireland as governor to reassert English rule. A year later he was

Flanked by princesses Deling and Rongling, the formidable Chinese dowager empress Cixi was photographed in Beijing after the Boxer Rising.

Cities: from mud-brick homes to skyscrapers

Crowded, noisy, dirty, violent — cities are all these things, but they are also glamorous and exciting, centres of power and learning. Civilisation truly began when men and women came together to live in cities.

Large settlements have existed ever since hunting and food gathering gave way to food producing, for crops take time to grow and agriculture led to a more permanent existence. The wealth produced by agricultural surpluses allowed people time to develop specialised skills. City life became enriched by traders and craftsmen, while a ruling class developed and priests began to keep written records. From the beginning, cities have had temples as well as granaries and citadels.

Some of the world's earliest cities developed more than 5000 years ago in Mesopotamia, the broad, fertile valley between the rivers Tigris and Euphrates in present-day Iraq. In cities such as Ur – a great warehousing centre for goods coming by land, river and sea – Uruk and Nippur the Sumerians invented a system of writing, discovered bronze, lived in homes of baked mud-brick and built large pyramid-shaped temples called ziggurats. Mesopotamian pottery workers are probably also the first people to have used wheeled vehicles, around 3500 BC.

Farther east in the Indus Valley of present-day Pakistan small communities of hill farmers colonised the fertile valleys of the river Indus. While Mesopotamia's cities grew up in a more haphazard fashion, those of the Indus were laid out according to set patterns. Although 400 miles (650 km) apart, the cities of Mohenjo-Daro and Harappa had similar layouts – including walls, streets constructed on a grid pattern, a water tank and cloisters – and similar populations, probably around 20000. This was a large figure for the time, and would remain so for centuries to come. As late as AD 1800 there were only an estimated 364 cities in the whole of Europe with a population of 10000 or more.

THE WONDERS OF BABYLON

The Mesopotamian city of Babylon, destroyed and rebuilt, may have reached the same size as the Indus Valley cities when it displayed its hanging gardens. Nearly half a millennium before Christ, it was described by the Greek historian Herodotus as

'an exact square, 120 furlongs each way... surrounded by a deep moat...behind which rises a wall...with a hundred gates, all of brass...The streets all run in straight lines ...[and] the centre of each division of the town is occupied by a fortress.'

In ancient Egypt the hieroglyph for a city was a cross within a circle, the cross perhaps suggesting communication and convergence, and the circle compactness and limits – the wall or the moat. Another suggestion is that the cross was a mason's hammer, a symbol of the craftsmanship on which the construction of cities depended. The city of Memphis was established as the capital of King Menes, who united the rival kingdoms of Upper and Lower Egypt around 3100 BC. Across the Mediterranean,

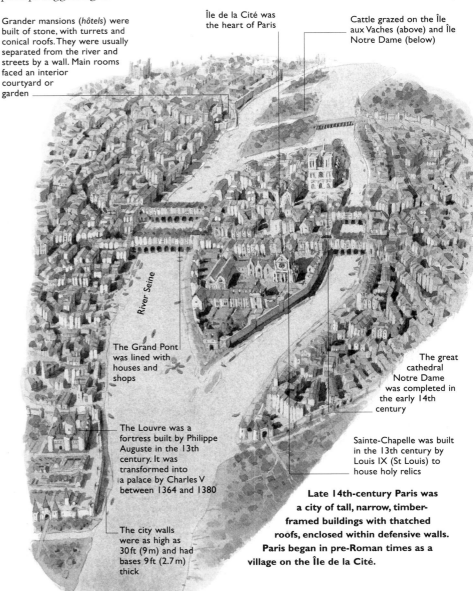

Grander mansions (*hôtels*) were built of stone, with turrets and conical roofs. They were usually separated from the river and streets by a wall. Main rooms faced an interior courtyard or garden

Île de la Cité was the heart of Paris

Cattle grazed on the Île aux Vaches (above) and Île Notre Dame (below)

River Seine

The Grand Pont was lined with houses and shops

The Louvre was a fortress built by Philippe Auguste in the 13th century. It was transformed into a palace by Charles V between 1364 and 1380

The city walls were as high as 30ft (9m) and had bases 9ft (2.7m) thick

The great cathedral Notre Dame was completed in the early 14th century

Sainte-Chapelle was built in the 13th century by Louis IX (St Louis) to house holy relics

Late 14th-century Paris was a city of tall, narrow, timber-framed buildings with thatched roofs, enclosed within defensive walls. Paris began in pre-Roman times as a village on the Île de la Cité.

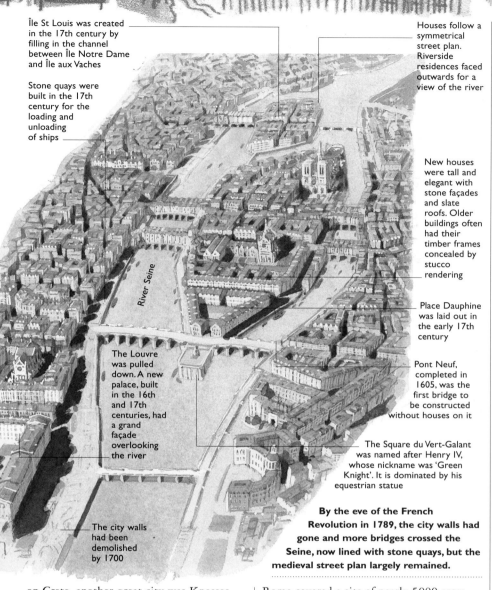

Île St Louis was created in the 17th century by filling in the channel between Île Notre Dame and Île aux Vaches

Stone quays were built in the 17th century for the loading and unloading of ships

River Seine

The Louvre was pulled down. A new palace, built in the 16th and 17th centuries, had a grand façade overlooking the river

The city walls had been demolished by 1700

Houses follow a symmetrical street plan. Riverside residences faced outwards for a view of the river

New houses were tall and elegant with stone façades and slate roofs. Older buildings often had their timber frames concealed by stucco rendering

Place Dauphine was laid out in the early 17th century

Pont Neuf, completed in 1605, was the first bridge to be constructed without houses on it

The Square du Vert-Galant was named after Henry IV, whose nickname was 'Green Knight'. It is dominated by his equestrian statue

By the eve of the French Revolution in 1789, the city walls had gone and more bridges crossed the Seine, now lined with stone quays, but the medieval street plan largely remained.

on Crete, another great city was Knossos, the centre of Minoan culture. It was occupied long before 3000 BC.

In ancient Greece, which flourished after the fall of Crete, there were several hundred politically autonomous city-states, consisting of city and hinterland but varying in size, appearance and importance. It is from the Greek word for city-state, *polis*, that the word 'politics' is derived.

CITIES OF THE ROMAN EMPIRE
Roman cities were designed to a standard pattern, incorporating an enclosing wall, grid-pattern streets, a forum, a temple, public baths and an amphitheatre. The forum served the same function as the Greek *agora*, a meeting place as much as a market. The Romans built towns and cities wherever they extended their empire. In Britain, the provincial town of Verulamium, modern St Albans, was built on a site of 200 acres (80 ha). By contrast,

Rome covered a site of nearly 5000 acres (2000 ha) before the emperor Constantine moved the empire's capital to Byzantium, which he renamed Constantinople (present-day Istanbul), in AD 330. Constantinople fell to the Ottomans in 1453.

It was the marketing function of the city that stimulated the 11th and 12th-century re-emergence of towns and cities in Europe after their eclipse in the years following the fall of Rome. The granting of market charters was a landmark in urban history; another was the formation of guilds of merchants. Market towns and cities also had to be protected with defensive walls and castles; in Britain cities acquired cathedrals, making them the centres of dioceses. The largest urban populations were in Italy; 14th-century Florence had a population of more than 90 000.

In the 16th and 17th centuries, capital cities, with their courts and bureaucracies, increased in number and also gained in

splendour, providing an increasing range of specialised urban services. The population of Paris was 180 000, while London reached 250 000.

It was only with the rise of steam-driven industry that there was a striking growth in the number of provincial cities, which added factories and chimneys to the warehouses and spires, and also created new social classes. At first some of these cities, such as Manchester and Birmingham in Britain, lacked the apparatus of town government, but they were centres of unprecedented productive power, attracting immigrants and provoking new social conflicts. They had their rich and their poor areas, with population densities and rates of mortality varying greatly between city centres and suburbs. Social problems such as public health, which had not been fully identified in the 19th century, generated voluntary movements and, in the case of Birmingham, a new civic gospel to deal with them. Joseph Chamberlain, who was mayor from 1873 to 1876, claimed that municipalities could 'do more for the people than Parliament' by improving the environment and the quality of daily life.

THE AGE OF RAILWAYS
The coming of the railways profoundly affected both the process of urbanisation and the fortunes and layouts of towns and cities. In Britain and most of Europe railways linked existing towns and cities, but in the United States, where there was an unparalleled increase in city populations, railways often placed new cities on the map. Chicago, for instance, attracted a huge immigrant population during the last decades of the 19th century. During the 1880s, the number of cities in the USA with a population of between 40 000 and 70 000 increased from 21 to 35, and the number of still bigger cities from 23 to 39. Where land was scarce, as in Manhattan, developers built upwards, creating the skyscraper-dominated city centres of today.

During the 20th century the number of cities outside the Western world, few of them following the pattern of the 19th-century industrial city, has increased sharply too, creating problems of organisation and scale in Asia, Africa and Latin America that dwarf those of the past. In 1950 there were 75 cities in the world with populations of between 1 and 5 million; by 1970 there were 144; and by 1990, 249. In 1990 there were 12 cities with populations of 10 million or more. Towards the end of the 20th century it is the developing countries that are experiencing the major thrust of urban growth, and the fate of the city is as controversial an issue as it ever was.

created Duke of Clarence, a title derived from his wife's inheritance of the lordship of Clare in Suffolk. He died a few months after his second marriage – to Violante, the daughter of Galeazzo Visconti, Lord of Pavia – arranged after his first wife's death. The title, occasionally conferred on the younger sons or brothers of English monarchs, was last used in 1892.

Clarendon, Constitutions of (1164)

Document issued by HENRY II of England at Clarendon, near Salisbury, in an attempt to define certain relationships between Church and State. The most controversial issue in Henry's 16 proposals concerned his claim to the right to try in his law courts clerics already convicted in ecclesiastical courts. Churchmen, in particular Thomas BECKET, regarded this as Crown interference. After Becket's murder in 1170 Henry conceded the benefit of clergy, which allowed clerics accused of crimes to refuse to be tried by secular courts, but would not agree to any of the other points.

Clarendon, Edward Hyde, 1st Earl of

(1609-74) English statesman, historian and royal adviser. Clarendon's political career began in the Short and LONG PARLIAMENTS as an opponent of royal authority. When, in 1641, he refused to support the Grand Remonstrance, which indicted the king and attempted to change the relationship between Church and State, he changed sides, becoming a trusted adviser of Charles I and, later, of Charles II, with whom he shared exile. After the RESTORATION, as Charles II's lord chancellor he furthered the king's conciliatory policies. His influence reached its peak in the marriage of his daughter Anne to the heir apparent, James, Duke of York. Though Clarendon did not sympathise with the legislation called the Clarendon Code, which was introduced between 1661 and 1665 and aimed to ensure the supremacy of the Church of England over Catholics and dissenters, he went against the king's wishes to enforce the laws. Widely blamed for the naval disasters of the second ANGLO-DUTCH WAR, Clarendon fell from power in 1667, fleeing to France to avoid impeachment. His *History of the Rebellion* (published 1702-4) is a masterly account of the English Civil War, written from a Royalist standpoint but with considerable objectivity.

Clarkson, Thomas (1760-1846) British

philanthropist and a strong opponent of slavery. As a founder member of the Society for Effecting the Abolition of the Slave Trade, Clarkson gathered extensive material about the trade and conditions on slave ships. Published in 1786 and 1787 in pamphlet form, this information was used in William WILBERFORCE's abolitionist campaign which led to the 1807 Act prohibiting British participation in the slave trade. Clarkson became vice-president of the Anti-Slavery Society in 1823, and saw its efforts rewarded ten years later when slavery was abolished throughout the British Empire.

classical architecture Description of the symmetrical structures, often incorporating columns, which characterised major buildings in ancient Greece and Rome, and whose principles continue to influence architecture in many parts of the world. In these classical buildings a fine sense of proportion was allied to an impressive use of space and light. Early classical architecture is classified by the type of column used by the builders. In ancient Greece these became progressively slimmer and more richly decorated – ranging from the simple Doric and voluted Ionian to the elaborate Corinthian decorated with acanthus leaves. They were named after the regions in which they were said to have first been used. The Romans added a further two Grecian influenced forms: the Tuscan, a stark form of the Doric; and the Composite, a rich mixture which includes the more elaborate features of both the Ionic and Corinthian.

As the forms developed they were often combined and the plainer designs were used as a basis for the more exuberant later Grecian styles. During the Renaissance the proportions and details of these forms were classified and illustrated in numerous architectural theses, forming the core of much architectural training in the West until the beginning of the 20th century.

Claudius (10 BC-AD 54) Roman emperor

from 41 to 54. Often mocked for his limp and a speech impediment, the intelligent and scholarly Claudius was the nephew of Tiberius and the uncle of Gaius CALIGULA, with whom he shared consular office. After Caligula's murder, Claudius was found hiding in the imperial palace by the elite Praetorian Guard, who proclaimed him emperor in spite of the senate's reluctance to accept his succession. Taking an active interest in civil and military affairs, he set about repairing the damage of the previous reign. He took part in the invasion of Britain – which, with Mauretania, he incorporated into the empire – adding 'Britannicus' to his son's names to indicate its possession. Claudius's notoriously unfaithful third wife Messalina, the mother of his children Britannicus and Octavia, was eventually put to death after she had gone through a form of public 'marriage' with one of her lovers. Claudius's fourth wife, his niece Agrippina, is thought to have poisoned him to hasten her son NERO's succession to the throne.

Clausewitz, Karl Marie von (1780-1831)

Prussian general and military strategist. Von Clausewitz is remembered for his

A caricature of Georges Clemençeau by André Gill suggests the French leader's ambivalence – armed ruthlessness linked with social concern.

posthumously published, unfinished work, *On War* (1833) which made a significant impact on the shape and direction of strategic studies, and influenced many generals. In it von Clausewitz argues, among other things, that war, as a continuation of politics, must be conducted swiftly and ruthlessly to reach a clear and rapid outcome. After campaigns in the Rhineland, in 1801 von Clausewitz entered the Berlin military academy. Here he was deeply influenced by the military reformer Gerhard von SCHARNHORST, whom he helped to reorganise the Prussian army eight years later. Von Clausewitz served in the Russian army from 1812 to 1814 and

> **❝ War is nothing but the continuation of politics by other means. ❞**
>
> *Karl Marie von Clausewitz*
> *On War, 1833*

was soon involved in the negotiations at Tauroggen, which in 1812 paved the way for Prussia's desertion of France the following year. Von Clausewitz then helped to forge the powerful alliance between Prussia, Russia and Britain against Napoleon.

Clay, Henry (1777-1852) US politician and

orator, known as 'the Great Pacificator'. The son of a Baptist preacher, Clay worked as a mill hand until, aged 15, he obtained an assistant clerical post in the Virginia courts. Five years later he qualified as a lawyer. He was elected to Congress in 1811 and was immediately appointed to be speaker of the House of Representatives. As a leader of the 'War Hawks' in Congress, Clay was a central figure in the events leading to the war against Britain of 1812 – as well as a negotiator of the

Treaty of GHENT which ended it. Clay's nickname stemmed from his roles in drawing up the MISSOURI COMPROMISE and the Compromise of 1850, both of which dealt with the thorny North-South issue of slavery and its spread into the territories, soon to become new states. But Clay also won support for his policy to strengthen national unity through economic legislation introduced while he was secretary of state from 1825 to 1829.

Clemençeau, Georges (1849-1929) French statesman who was chairman of the Versailles Peace Conference. Although he entered the National Assembly in 1871, it was not until his passionate defence of Alfred DREYFUS in 1897 that Clemençeau achieved political prominence. He led the extreme left-wing in the assembly, urging widespread social change and earning the nickname 'The Tiger'. Later as minister of the interior and as premier, from 1906 to 1909, his ruthless suppression of the strikes and demonstrations which beset France during his term of office cost him much of the popular support his earlier stance had won. Towards the end of the First World War in 1917, with French morale at its lowest ebb, Clemençeau again became prime minister and formed his 'victory' Cabinet with himself as minister of war, and persuaded the Allies to accept FOCH as commander in chief. But he was less persuasive at the 1919 conference of Versailles, and although ALSACE-LORRAINE was restored to France, Clemençeau's claim to the SAAR basin and demands that Germany cede all control of the Rhine's left bank as well as pay the total cost of the war were rejected by the other Allies. The failures cost him the presidential election of 1920.

Cleopatra see feature, right

Cleveland, Grover (1837-1908) Twice president of the USA (1885 to 1889 and 1893 to 1897). As governor of New York (1883 to 1884), Cleveland quickly gained a reputation as a reformist independent of the corrupt political machinery of TAMMANY HALL. As the Democratic nominee for president in 1884, Cleveland's support from many reform-minded Republicans – the 'mugwumps', a derisory term coined to describe people who voted against their party – gave him a narrow victory over his Republican rival James Blaine. Cleveland favoured low tariffs and civil service reforms, but these offered no answer to the nationwide economic depression which occurred during his second term of office, when he relied on exorbitant loans from a bankers' consortium led by J.P. MORGAN to balance the federal budget. While opposing the rising tide of imperialist sentiment and resisting US intervention in Hawaii and Cuba, Cleveland's implacable insistence that

Serpent of the old Nile

Cleopatra, Queen of Egypt from 51 BC to her death, was a wise and ambitious ruler whose celebrated affairs with Julius Caesar and Mark Antony enraged the Romans.

Seven queens of Egypt bore the name of Cleopatra, and all were talented and determined women, but the most celebrated is the last of the line, William Shakespeare's 'serpent of the old Nile'.

The seventh Cleopatra (69-30 BC) has been unkindly treated by historians since our information about her comes from her Roman enemies. 'I detest Cleopatra and the insolence of the Queen,' complained the Roman orator Cicero. She proved so dangerous a foe of the Romans that they blackened her name, accusing her of arrogance, debauchery and murder. In fact she was a clever, well-educated, ambitious woman, who ruled her country wisely and tried to regain the provinces Egypt had held in Palestine and Syria. She was the first of her line who bothered to learn Egyptian – Greek was her principal language.

Cleopatra's family came from Macedonia. Its founder, Ptolemy I, had been one of Alexander the Great's generals. When they carved up the empire after Alexander's death, Ptolemy grabbed Egypt, but by Cleopatra's time her father, Ptolemy XII, was just a puppet of Rome. In 51 BC Cleopatra became joint sovereign with her brother-husband Ptolemy XIII, whom she had married when she was 18 and he ten. But Cleopatra soon fell out with Ptolemy's council of regency and left Alexandria.

When Julius Caesar arrived in pursuit of his rival Pompey, Cleopatra returned. According to the historian Plutarch, she slipped into Alexandria harbour in a tiny boat and, wrapped in a carpet, was smuggled into the palace to see him. She persuaded Caesar to act first as an arbiter and then as her champion in her quarrel with her brother. When he died during the ensuing war, Cleopatra married her other brother, Ptolemy XIV. Caesar, however, was the father of her

son Caesarion, born in 47 BC. When Ptolemy XIV conveniently died, she made the baby her co-ruler as Ptolemy XV. Cleopatra joined Caesar in Rome, staying there until his murder in 44 BC. Rome was scandalised when Caesar installed a gold statue of the goddess Venus made in the likeness of Cleopatra in the temple of Venus Genetrix.

CLEOPATRA'S DOWNFALL
A new opportunity for Cleopatra to use Roman might to regain Egypt's lost provinces came in 42 BC. Cleopatra went to Tarsus (now in Turkey) to meet Mark Antony, joint ruler of the Roman Empire with Julius Caesar's great-nephew Octavius, the emperor Augustus. Cleopatra so captivated the general that they became lovers and had three children. Antony's divorce of Augustus's sister, Octavia, to marry Cleopatra caused Augustus to declare war on her in 32 BC.

Defeated at the Battle of Actium (31 BC), she and Antony fled to Egypt, but in 30 BC both committed suicide: Cleopatra by allowing herself to be bitten by an asp, probably an Egyptian cobra.

A bust of Cleopatra made c.30-11 BC contrasts with a more idealised 17th-century image of Caesar and Cleopatra, below.

Britain should go to arbitration over its dispute with Venezuela in 1897 concerning the boundary of Guiana, extended the scope of the MONROE DOCTRINE.

cliff dwellers Name for the Anasazi peoples who inhabited Colorado and Arizona in the 12th century and whose communities built their homes against a protective wall of living rock. These sites were partly defensive against intertribal warfare and against APACHE and NAVAJO raids. Cliff Palace, Mesa Verde, in Colorado, is typical of these dwellings, having several levels of adobe brick structures built against an overhanging cliff face and including stout terrace walls, square and round apartment towers with more than 200 rooms, and 23 large circular ceremonial chambers.

Clinton, Bill (1946-) Democratic politician and 42nd president of the USA, from 1993. Born in Arkansas, Clinton won a Rhodes Scholarship to Oxford, and also studied at Yale University before entering politics and becoming governor of Arkansas. His promises to reduce the federal deficit by cutting military spending and reforming taxation, and to increase investment in education, training, and public health care helped to win him the presidency from the incumbent George BUSH in 1992, but once in office he found them impossible to keep. Clinton's choice of his wife Hillary to head a programme to improve health care was attacked in Congress and by the media.

In 1994 Clinton reached agreement with the Russian president Boris YELTSIN to reduce nuclear armaments, and he made a significant contribution towards the peace process in Northern Ireland, but he was accused of indecision during the early stages of the war in BOSNIA. The Whitewater scandal, concerning alleged financial irregularities during Clinton's term as governor, beset his first years of office, while from mid 1995 a Republican-dominated Congress and Senate created a political climate hostile to his administration.

Like many US presidents, Bill Clinton made much of 'family values' and was often pictured with his wife Hillary and daughter Chelsea.

Lord Clive shows the Nawab of Bengal's son some of the widows and veterans to be aided by a charity partly funded by the nawab.

Clive of Plassey, Robert, Baron (1725-74) British general and administrator, who was governor of BENGAL from 1757 to 1760 and from 1765 to 1767. His achievements in laying the foundations for British rule in the subcontinent led to him being called 'Clive of India'. Sent to south India at 18 as an EAST INDIA COMPANY clerk, Clive was so depressed by his work that he attempted suicide; but when the pistol misfired twice he decided 'I feel that I am reserved for some end or other' and did not try a third time. Given command of a troop of Indian militia, Clive demonstrated such military prowess – notably against the Indian allies of the French in the siege of Arcot in 1751 – that he was appointed to take over the government of Madras, where he quickly imposed Britain's authority. Having secured south-east India for Britain, in 1756 Clive moved his forces into Bengal as the first step in controlling the region. A series of military actions culminated in the defeat of the Nawab of Bengal in 1757, and Clive assumed governorship of the state. He returned home to a peerage, but in 1765 was recalled to Bengal where the Company faced growing economic difficulties. No less honest than other senior officials of his day, Clive's earlier efforts for the East India Company had also gained him a substantial personal fortune – which now hampered his attempts to change the exploitative system from which he had benefited. On his return to Britain he was censured by Parliament, the victim as much of more critical attitudes to overseas ventures as of jealousy of his nabob-like lifestyle. Though Parliament reversed its verdict, Clive committed suicide in 1774.

clocks One of the earliest devices used to measure the passage of time was the shadow clock, known from around 1500 BC, which was the forerunner of the sundial. Other early clocks were the clepsydra, or water clock, which was developed in Greece before 250 BC, and the sand glass – based on the principle still used in an egg timer. Mechanical clocks were first made in China where by the 8th century AD the system of gears – the escapement which is central to all mechanical clocks – had been developed.

In Europe mechanical clocks date from the 14th century; driven by a falling weight, these were only accurate to within an hour in every 24 and so had no minute hand. The first spring-driven clocks appeared about 150 years later, and their smaller mechanisms also led to the manufacture of watches. It was not until the 17th century, when the Dutch mathematician Christiaan Huygens adopted the pendulum and spring balance, that more accurate timekeeping became possible. By the late 18th century accurate chronometers driven by balance springs could be used by navigators to find longitude, but these were not widely available until the 19th century. The development of the quartz crystal clock in 1929 allowed accuracy to within 0.0001 seconds a day. Atomic clocks, the first of which was built at the National Physical Laboratory near London in 1955, allow an even greater accuracy, varying by as little as a second in 3 million years.

Clovis (c.466-511) Founder of the Frankish kingdom and Merovingian dynasty. By leading his small tribe of Salian FRANKS to victory over the last Roman governor in Gaul at Soissons in 486, Clovis extended his control from Tournai, in modern Belgium, to cover the entire area between the rivers Loire and Seine. Ten years later he defeated the Alemanni to gain the upper Rhineland and then conquered the VISIGOTHS near Poitiers, expanding his territory south to the Pyrenees. Clovis also absorbed several small independent kingdoms in northern France into his realm. Strong support from the Catholic Church, which followed Clovis's conversion to Christianity, ensured the continuation of the Merovingian dynasty.

Cluny, Order of see feature, opposite

Cnut see CANUTE

coal Sedimentary rock of organic origin which has been used as fuel for more than 2000 years. As early as the end of the 3rd century BC coal was mined in China where it was used not only for domestic heating but in metalworking, pottery making and other manufacturing for which high temperatures were needed. Around 200 years later alluvial coal was used domestically in Greece and Rome, and it was first mined in Britain during the Roman occupation. Wood, however, remained the main source of heating until the INDUSTRIAL REVOLUTION, when the need for

Heyday of monasticism

The great monastery of Cluny, under a succession of charismatic abbots, won acclaim throughout Europe for its style of worship, while its magnificent buildings inspired the spread of Romanesque architecture.

At the beginning of the 10th century William the Pious, Duke of Aquitaine, founded a monastery at Cluny in Burgundy for the benefit of the souls of his family. William dedicated the new monastery to St Peter and St Paul, apostolic founders of the See of Rome, and thus entrusted it to a papal protection that enhanced its fame and its prestige. For most of the next 250 years it was ruled by powerful abbots, notably Odo (927-42), Maieul (948-84), Odilo (994-c.1048), Hugh (1049-1109), and Peter the Venerable (1122-56). Cluny followed the Rule of St Benedict. It became famous both for its elaborate worship and for its singing.

ABBOT HUGH'S CHURCH

The monastery owed much of its appeal to a belief in the efficacy of its prayers and almsgiving as intercessions for men and women in life and after death. Odilo popularised the observance of All Souls' Day (November 2) 'as a commemoration of all the faithful departed from the beginning of the world until its end'.

Each successive abbot added to its buildings. In 1088 Hugh began to build a third abbey

The new abbey church at Cluny was consecrated by Urban II in November 1095. Opposite the pope stand Abbot Hugh and the monks.

church with a large donation from King Alphonso VI of Leon-Castile. Alphonso believed that the intercessions of Cluniac monks had helped to free him from imprisonment, and he counted on them to help support the reconquest of Spain from the Moors. Henry I of England – like his father, William the Conqueror – was convinced of the value of Cluny's religious and political support and sent further sums. Hugh's church was bigger than St Peter's in Rome and inspired a tradition of Romanesque architecture and sculpture that was to spread throughout Europe.

By Hugh's time, Cluny had numerous dependent abbeys and priories. Its first English priory, Lewes in Sussex, was founded in 1077. By visiting these houses, the abbots were able to keep in close contact with a wide circle of clergy and laity. Pope Urban II, who in 1095 preached the First Crusade, had been a monk at Cluny and later its prior.

Cluny also had its critics. In Odilo's time the monastery was satirised as being over-magnificent. 'Now I'm really a knight,' one of his monks is depicted as boasting, 'for I serve at the command of a king – my lord is King Odilo of Cluny!' Yet under Peter the Venerable, Cluny remained a centre of monasticism. Abbot Peter

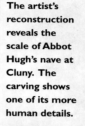

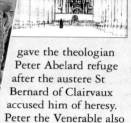

The artist's reconstruction reveals the scale of Abbot Hugh's nave at Cluny. The carving shows one of its more human details.

gave the theologian Peter Abelard refuge after the austere St Bernard of Clairvaux accused him of heresy. Peter the Venerable also sponsored a Latin translation of the Koran, showing that Islam should be understood as well as fought in a Crusading age. After Peter's death, Cluny fell from pre-eminence. Its style did not adapt to the individualism and inward spirituality which emerged with the Cistercians in the 12th century.

WARS OF RELIGION

From 1518 Cluny's abbots were 'commendatory' – absentees chosen by the French king. They included such distinguished names as the 17th-century cardinals Richelieu and Mazarin. Cluny suffered during the French Wars of Religion: in 1563 the Huguenots burnt books from its library and depredations continued until the Edict of Nantes in 1598. Cluny never recovered.

As with most French abbeys, the end came with the French Revolution. Monastic life ceased in 1790, and on October 25, 1793, Mass was celebrated in Hugh's third church for the last time. In 1798 its empty shell was bought by two Mâcon merchants. Parts of the south transept still stand as a reminder of the majesty of Cluniac monasticism in its 11th-century heyday.

more efficient fuel in mills and factories led to growing demand and the extensive development of coal mining. Until the beginning of the 20th century, Britain was the world's largest coal producer, but since then it has been overtaken by North America, which today accounts for almost half of the world's output. Geologists estimate that at the current rate of consumption the world's coal reserves will last for at least 200 years.

Coalbrookdale Bridge World's first all-iron bridge, built across the River Severn in Shropshire in 1779. Designed by the British ironmaster Abraham Darby III, the bridge took only three months to erect. Sections, some weighing as much as 6 tonnes, were cast in the Darby family's Coalbrookdale foundry. Mortise and tenon joints connected the sections to create five semicircular ribs, which formed a 100 ft (30 m) arched span supporting a roadway 24 ft (7 m) wide.

Cobbett, William (1763-1835) British social reformer and journalist. From 1802 when he first published the weekly *Political Register* until his death while a Member of Parliament, Cobbett was involved in political controversy. Using the *Register* as a platform, he denounced the conduct of the Napoleonic War and called for peace. He urged parliamentary reform, condemned the sufferings of the rural poor, and eventually, in 1810, was imprisoned for two years and fined £1000 for denouncing flogging in the army. After his release – and apart from a spell in the USA – Cobbett spent much time travelling in the English countryside, recording his impressions in his *Rural Rides,* published in 1830. He strongly supported the REFORM ACT of 1832 and was elected a Member of Parliament in the same year.

Cobden, Richard (1804-65) British political economist and statesman. Believing that FREE TRADE would help to promote international peace, in 1839 Cobden joined forces with John Bright to found the Anti-Corn-Law League, which played a significant part in forcing the repeal of the CORN LAWS in 1846. His extensive campaigning for free trade in corn led Cobden to neglect his business interests, and he faced financial ruin until a public subscription organised by his supporters raised £80000. Such was his popular support that although Cobden was travelling in Europe throughout the election year of 1848 two constituencies elected him to Parliament. As a Member of Parliament, in 1860 Cobden helped to negotiate an Anglo-French treaty based on tariff reductions and expansion of trade between the two countries. During the

Pot boys are kept on their toes serving cups of coffee to periwigged gentlemen who share market news and the latest gossip of 1668 in a London coffee-house, still then a fashionable novelty.

AMERICAN CIVIL WAR Cobden's open support for the North helped to ease tensions between the US and British governments. His radicalism was tempered by doubts about the extension of the franchise, a belief in minimum state interference and a dislike of trade unions.

Code Napoléon First modern codification of French civil law. Drawn up between 1800 and 1804 by a commission presided over by Napoleon, the *Code Civil* reorganised France's legal system. Its articles were a compromise between revolutionary principles and Roman Law – the old civil law used widely in Europe – and asserted the rights of the individual as opposed to those established by Church and customary law. Revised in 1904, the Code remains the basis of French civil law and has been adopted in many other countries.

Cod War (1972-6) Period of antagonism between Britain and Iceland over fishing rights, sparked by Iceland's unilateral extension of its territorial waters. After Iceland announced plans designed to prevent overfishing, its warships harassed several British trawlers working within the new Icelandic limit – prompting protective action by British naval vessels. A compromise reached in 1976 allowed a maximum of 24 British trawlers to fish inside the 200 mile (320 km) limit, hastening the decline of fishing ports such as Hull and Grimsby.

Cody, William Frederick (Buffalo Bill) see WILD WEST

coffee-house Coffee was introduced into Europe in the 16th century, but its rise to popularity dates from the opening in London in 1652 of the first coffee-houses. These became convenient places to transact business, read newspapers and exchange literary and political opinions. Most of the cities of Europe had coffee-houses by the late 17th century, and Lloyd's coffee-house, which opened in London in the 1680s, became the centre for marine insurance.

Coffee-houses reached the American colonies in 1689, and in New York the Merchants Coffee-house, which opened in 1737, was an important place for the exchange of political ideas in the years leading to the American War of Independence. By the mid 18th century the heyday of coffee-houses was ending. In England gentlemen's clubs took over some of their functions, while specialist exchanges became the venues for commercial activities.

Coke, Sir Edward (1552-1634) English lawyer and politician. As attorney general, Coke prosecuted such defendants as the Earl of ESSEX in 1601, Sir Walter Raleigh in 1603 and the GUNPOWDER PLOT conspirators in 1606. He became lord chief justice of England in 1613. Although he initially supported the royal prerogative, Coke's defence of the common law against Church and Crown led to his dismissal by James I in 1616. As a Member of Parliament he led the opposition to both James I and Charles I, and was largely responsible for drafting the PETITION OF RIGHT, a declaration of civil liberties sent by the English Parliament to Charles I in 1628.

Coke, Thomas William, Earl of Leicester (1752-1842) British landowner and agricultural innovator who established new patterns of land usage by crop rotation. After inheriting Holkham Hall, Norfolk, in 1776, Coke devoted his life to improving its estates. Following the earlier example of his fellow Norfolk agriculturist, the innovator Charles Townshend (1674-1738), Coke planted turnips as a winter fodder crop, replaced rye with wheat, introduced better livestock breeding techniques and improved the quality of the soil by spreading clay. He successfully encouraged his tenants to follow similar practices, granting long leases at fair rents to those who did so. The improved crops and better harvests on these farms encouraged others to introduce crop rotation.

Colbert, Jean Baptiste (1619-83) French statesman and leading adviser to LOUIS XIV of France. Having proved his financial skills by building up Cardinal Jules MAZARIN's private fortune, Colbert was well placed to succeed Nicholas Fouquet when the former superintendent of finance was arrested for embezzlement. The son of a Paris financier, Colbert was loyal, dedicated and hard-working and soon rose to be one of Louis XIV's chief ministers. Becoming controller-general of finance in 1665, Colbert not only halved the expense of tax collection but greatly increased the national revenue.

State documents and robes of high office indicate Jean Baptiste Colbert's power when he sat for his portrait by Claude Lefèbvre.

Although the king's costly wars proved a handicap to Colbert's MERCANTILIST policies, he managed to stimulate industry and improve communications. His aim – to make France great through the prosperity of the people – was hampered by his failure to cure the basic weakness of the French fiscal system, and he tended to burden industry with bureaucratic details. Later, as secretary of state from 1668, Colbert reorganised France's colonies and strengthened its navy. As a patron of industry and the arts, he also supervised the reorganisation of the Gobelins tapestry factory and re-established the Royal Academy of Painting and Sculpture.

Cold War see feature, page 150

Michael Collins solemnly watches the Dublin ceremony marking the birth of the Irish Free State. Five months later he was shot dead.

Coligny, Gaspard de (1519-72) French nobleman and royal adviser, appointed Admiral of France in 1552. His later conversion to Protestantism gave respectability to the HUGUENOT cause in the first phase of the FRENCH WARS OF RELIGION. A Catholic by birth, Coligny became a committed CALVINIST while imprisoned by the Spaniards in 1557. Appointed commander in chief of the Huguenots in 1569, Coligny was among the signatories of the Peace of St Germain a year later. But his influence on the young Charles IX alienated him from Catherine de MEDICI, the king's mother, and he was an early victim of the St Bartholomew's Day Massacre.

collectivisation Replacement of privately owned agricultural holdings in the Soviet Union by collective or communal farms, each covering about 15 000 acres (6000 ha). The policy of collectivisation, introduced by Joseph STALIN, caused the deaths of an estimated 500 000 peasants. Between 1929 and 1933 an acute grain shortage threatened the Soviet Union, much of whose wheat harvest was being exported to pay for industrial development. These export sales of agricultural produce – and the peasants' slaughter of their own livestock in protest – caused the famine of 1932-3. A more moderate approach to state farms followed, allowing families to own small plots for their own use while nine-tenths of the land was cultivated collectively. By the late 1980s private plots made up 3 per cent of the nation's farmland, but accounted for more than a quarter of all Soviet agricultural output. After the collapse of communism they were gradually privatised and supported the 'black' economy. After 1945 a number of socialist countries adopted a similar policy of collectivisation. It formed the basis of mao zedong's first Five Year Plan introduced in China in 1953, though Mao preferred the peasant COMMUNE to Stalin's ruthless subordination of agriculture to meet the needs of industrial development.

Collins, Michael (1890-1922) Irish soldier, patriot and SINN FÉIN leader. As a member of the Irish Republican Brotherhood, Collins fought in the Dublin EASTER RISING of 1916. Elected to the British Parliament two years later, he was one of the rebel MPs who set up their own Irish Parliament, Dáil Éireann, in 1919. He was finance minister in Arthur GRIFFITH's government, at the same time leading the Irish Republican Army. In 1921 Collins was a key player in negotiations leading to the Anglo-Irish truce and the Dáil's approval of the treaty, which in 1922 gave Southern Ireland dominion status. As commander of the government's Irish Free State Army in the Irish civil war, Collins was killed by his former comrades in an ambush at Beal-na-Blath, County Cork.

Colombia Country in the extreme northwest of South America. Home to the Chibcha and other Indians before the Spanish conquest in the early 16th century, Colombia was

initially part of the viceroyalty of Peru, but – with Venezuela, Ecuador and Panama – it became part of the new viceroyalty of New Granada when this was established in the first half of the 18th century. It remained a viceroyalty of Spain until 1819, when it was liberated by Simón BOLÍVAR in the South American wars of independence against Spain. The four Spanish provinces which had made up New Granada were reunited in 1822 as the Republic of Gran Colombia. This collapsed in 1830, and a period of constitutional change followed. In 1863 the country was renamed the United States of Colombia. Constitutional uncertainties continued; member states' sovereignty was abolished in 1886 when the presidential system of the newly named Republic of Colombia was established. Encouraged by the USA, which hoped to cut a canal through its isthmus, Panama broke away from the republic after the War of the

The Iron Curtain falls

*The Cold War between the Western powers and the Soviet bloc between 1945
and 1989 contained many of the elements of war – menace, subversion, high
arms spending, proxy conflicts – but without a direct battle being fought.*

Tension between the Soviet Union and Western powers, including the USA, was evident even when they were allied against Nazi Germany during the Second World War. The Atlantic Charter of 1941 committed Britain and the USA to support free elections and national self-determination in the postwar world. But Joseph Stalin, the Soviet leader, made it clear at the Yalta Conference in 1945 that his country would maintain its influence in the Eastern European states it was liberating from the Nazis. The Cold War, as it came to be called, had begun. Two alliances underpinned the hostilities: the North Atlantic Treaty Organisation (NATO), formed by West European and North American countries in 1949, and the Warsaw Pact, created by the USSR and its East European satellites in 1955.

The Soviets established pro-Soviet communist regimes across Eastern Europe in the three years after the end of the Second World War. This political separation was described by Winston Churchill as the descent of an 'Iron Curtain'. Concerned at the support for communist parties in the West, notably in France and Italy, the USA launched the Marshall Plan to aid economic recovery in Europe. The Soviets refused to allow members of their bloc to participate in the plan and permitted them only to sign trade agreements among themselves. The economic division of Europe was complete.

In 1945 Germany was divided into Soviet, US, British and French occupation zones. Berlin, deep in the Soviet zone, was similarly divided. In June 1948 Soviet forces blocked entry to the city from the west. The blockade was broken by the Berlin airlift, in which for more than a year British and American aircraft operated supply flights into the city. At that time, the US enjoyed a nuclear monopoly, but in 1949 the Soviets successfully tested an atomic bomb. Both NATO and the Warsaw Pact now possessed nuclear strike forces.

'Proxy' wars between the blocs broke out in Korea in 1950, when Soviet-backed communist North Korea invaded the US-backed South; and in Vietnam in 1965 when the US committed troops to back South Vietnam against communist domination. Tension in Europe was reignited by the 1956 Hungarian

A British poster celebrates the tenth anniversary of NATO in 1959 (right). US President Kennedy inspects missiles at Key West in 1962 (below).

uprising, when Soviet forces crushed an attempt by Hungarians to leave the Soviet bloc. In 1961 the communist East German regime erected the Berlin Wall to isolate the Western sector of the city. Seven years later, the Warsaw Pact intervened militarily in Czechoslovakia to re-establish a repressive government.

TOWARDS DETENTE

In 1957 the Soviet launch of the first satellite took the Cold War into space. The USA responded with a programme to develop long-range rockets with nuclear warheads. But the 1962 Cuban Missile Crisis was the only time when global nuclear conflict appeared imminent.

Strategic Arms Limitation Talks (SALT) helped to establish a detente between the blocs with the signing of SALT I in 1972. The thaw in relations was aided by the 1975 Helsinki Conference, but suffered a setback with the Soviet invasion of Afghanistan in 1979. The strain on the weak Soviet economy, and the technical superiority of the US, led the Soviet leader Mikhail Gorbachev to propose steps for nuclear disarmament. In 1989 he withdrew from Afghanistan, and began a period of liberalisation at home. East Europeans took advantage of the change in policy to overthrow their communist regimes. The fall of the Berlin Wall marked the psychological end of the Cold War. Its formal end was declared by the Conference on Security and Co-operation in 1990.

In 1948 the first Allied plane returns after supplying the blockaded sectors of Berlin with vital food and fuel.

Thousand Days from 1899 to 1902. Country-wide violence has erupted spasmodically since, though semirepresentative democracy has been restored and Colombia's economy has benefited from diversification of production and increased foreign investment. An oil field, opened up in 1993, boosted the economy, but Colombia's illegal drugs trade, thought to supply about 80 per cent of the world's cocaine market, dominates internal affairs and its relations with the USA. Extremist guerrilla groups as well as rival drug cartels – whose methods include kidnappings and assassinations – have further complicated domestic and external policies. In 1990 a new constitution led to the surrender of several drug traffickers and an agreement by some guerrillas to demobilise and take part in the political process, but rebel violence continues to be a problem.

colonialism see IMPERIALISM

Colosseum see feature, page 152

Columba, St (c.521-97) Irish-born missionary and first abbot of Iona, a remote island off western Scotland. St Columba was born in Donegal into the family of the Irish High Kings. In 546 he founded the monastery of Derry, in Ireland. In 563, with the help of 12 other monks, he established the monastery of Iona, an establishment which became the centre of Celtic Christianity in the north of Britain. For the next 30 years Columba continued the conversion of the heathen Picts. His consecration of King Aidan in 574 was the first time that a British monarch's investiture was blessed by the Church.

Columbus, Christopher see feature, pages 154-5

Combination Acts British legislation adopted in 1799 and 1800 to prevent two or more people meeting, or 'combining together' to improve their working conditions. The Acts effectively made TRADE UNIONS illegal, and working men who transgressed were sentenced to three months' imprisonment or two months' hard labour. Largely inspired by the fear of radical ideas spreading from France, the Acts were repealed in 1824 following skilful campaigning by Francis PLACE, and were replaced in 1825 by an Act which accepted trade unions but limited their right to strike.

Comecon Organisation established by Joseph Stalin in 1949 – also known as the Council for Mutual Economic Assistance – to encourage the economic interdependence of

DID YOU KNOW?

As well as being revered as a warrior saint whose help was often invoked in battle, Columba is credited with copying nearly 300 books in his own hand and writing three Latin hymns.

Common land at Laxton, Nottinghamshire, is still farmed in the same scattered strips as it was when mapped in 1635.

the Soviet-bloc countries of Eastern Europe. Comecon extended its membership to Cuba, Vietnam and the Mongolian People's Republic, but made little impact on the economies of the Soviet Union or the West. In 1962 Russia enforced agreements limiting its satellites' trade output and tying their economies to the Soviet Union. Discussions on cooperation with the EUROPEAN COMMUNITY began in 1987, but the fall of communism in Eastern Europe led to the council's collapse as its members reverted to free market economies.

Comintern Body dedicated to promoting communist doctrine internationally and so furthering world revolution. It was established by Lenin in 1919 with Grigori ZINOVIEV as chairman. During Comintern's second meeting in Moscow a year later, attended by delegates from 37 countries, Lenin established the Twenty-One Points, which required all parties to expel moderate ideologists and to conform to Soviet patterns of party structure and discipline. In 1943 Stalin dissolved the Comintern, although in 1947 a modified form was revived as the Cominform. This coordinated the activities of European communism until it was dissolved in 1956.

commedia dell'arte Improvised but stylised Italian comic entertainment which was the forerunner of *Punch and Judy* shows, pierrots and the modern pantomime. Developed during the 16th and 17th centuries, the plays relied on stock characters and situations, though plots varied and the professional cast improvised dialogue around a theme devised by the author. Acrobatics, songs and dances formed part of each performance. Punch, Pantaloon, Columbine, Harlequin, the Doctor and the braggart Scaramouche were among the characters, with each member of the troupe specialising in one part. All wore distinctive costumes and masks. Popular throughout Europe, *commedia dell'arte* strongly influenced later playwrights such as Jean MOLIÉRE.

Committee of Public Safety Emergency body established in April 1793 as the first effective government of the French

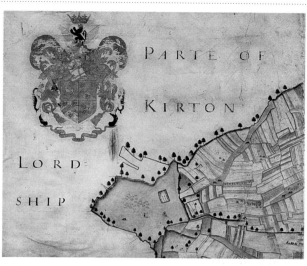

Revolution. During the most critical year of the Revolution, the mainly JACOBIN Committee – its initial nine members later expanded to twelve – contained some of the ablest men in the country. Dominated at first by Georges DANTON and then by Maximilien ROBESPIERRE, the Committee kept France's external enemies at bay, but its ruthless suppression of internal dissent during the Reign of TERROR led to growing opposition. Although in March 1794 an attempt to overthrow it, led by Robespierre's archenemy Jacques Hébert, was quashed, four months later Robespierre's downfall and summary execution removed the Committee's power from every sphere but foreign affairs. By October 1795 its influence had ended.

common Land, usually woodland or rough grazing, set aside for the use of villagers in medieval England. In 1236 the Statute of Merton laid down that the owner of any village – usually the lord of the manor – could only enclose wasteland for his own use if he left adequate pasture for the villagers. By the second half of the 18th century the ENCLOSURE of common land, which had started 600 years earlier, had increased dramatically, often arousing bitter opposition and claims of theft. Many of the village communities in colonial America also shared large areas of surrounding open land, used for defence as well as pasturage. Some of these areas survived and, as public parks, are today used for recreation.

Common Market see EUROPEAN UNION

Commons, House of Lower chamber of the British PARLIAMENT whose members today are elected by universal adult suffrage. The Commons has its roots in the parliament summoned by Simon de MONTFORT in 1265 when for the first time knights of the shire and burgesses of the boroughs joined the body which until then only the barons had been allowed to attend. But it took almost another

Colosseum: a setting for slaughter

The amphitheatre in which the Roman emperors turned human suffering into an entertainment for the masses is a tourist attraction of modern Rome.

The Colosseum in Rome was the largest construction dedicated to gladiatorial combat. Even in ruin it remains one of the most celebrated of all Roman buildings surviving today.

Fights between gladiators may have originated as part of the funeral rites of the Etruscans – who lived between 900 and 200 BC – to provide a human sacrifice in honour of a dead relative. They evolved into public spectacles in Rome in the late 2nd century BC. Early combats were staged in the Forum. An amphitheatre was built in the Campus Martus, but this was destroyed in the great fire of AD 64. When Vespasian, emperor from 69 to 79, emerged victorious from the civil wars following Nero's death, he saw the building of a new amphitheatre as a good way to win popularity.

The site chosen was the basin that had formed an artificial lake in the grounds of Nero's palace, the Golden House. The building was conceived on a grand scale, 620 ft (190 m) across and 165 ft (50 m) in height. Spectators sat or stood on four terraces; the highest-born occupied the front rows, and there was a box for the imperial family and a place of honour for the six Vestal Virgins, Rome's revered priestesses. Behind and beneath the seats were stairways and corridors.

Games were held on as many as 175 days in a year. As well as gladiatorial combats, they included the *venationes* – wild beast hunts involving lions, tigers, bears, hippopotamuses, elephants, boars, panthers, leopards, ostriches, giraffes, wild bulls, crocodiles, hyenas and wolves.

Most gladiators were slaves but some were condemned criminals and prisoners of war, and others were volunteers hoping to win fame and fortune. They were classified by the armour they wore and their style of fighting. The *retiarius* had a net, trident and dagger; the Thracian had a broad-brimmed helmet, a small round shield and a long, curved knife called a sica. The Samnites and *myrmillons* were more heavily armed. Others fought from horses and from chariots.

Although the formal greeting of gladiators was 'Hail Caesar! Those about to die salute you!', not all bouts ended fatally: there were drawn matches, and a gallant loser might be spared. Some survived to retirement and set up training schools for new gladiators. But when prisoners of war and criminals – including Christians – were thrown to the wild beasts it was intended that they should all die. Criminals were killed in other savage ways, including being put in a tunic soaked in pitch and set alight.

A three-day programme would have mixed gladiator fights and hunts for two days. On the third day the arena would be flooded for a *naumachia*, a naval battle with real ships; one staged in the time of Emperor Claudius involved 19 000 men. Like the fights and hunts, the water spectacles were a bloody business.

Ten years in building, the Colosseum opened in 80, during the reign of Vespasian's son Titus; it was originally called the Flavian Amphitheatre after the dynasty of its two builders, and only later dubbed Colosseum meaning 'gigantic'.

The inaugural Games lasted 100 days. Most of the 10 000 men who took part were killed and 5000 animals were massacred. The last recorded Games took place in the Colosseum in 523, a century after they had been officially banned.

Some 50 000 spectators at a time entered the oval Colosseum through 80 arches, then spread left and right along corridors to the terraced seating.

Huge canvas awning, supported on poles, to give spectators shade

Seats on three stone tiers and standing room on uppermost wooden tier

Corridors to eating places and lavatories

Windows and pilasters on top storey, with poles for canopy

Wall arches on two storeys decorated with statues of gods

Entry for spectators by 80 arched gateways

Wooden floor covered with sand: 'arena' is the Latin word for sand

Network of cells, cages for animals and cellars for storage, with ramps and lifts to arena

four centuries before the Commons gained effective authority in the balance of power between it, the hereditary House of LORDS and the monarchy. In the 14th century both Houses gained constitutional rights in relation to the monarchy, and many of the struggles between Richard II and his opponents were waged through the Commons – notably in the Merciless Parliament of 1388. The number of MPs increased in the 16th century from 296 to 462 as the gentry pressed the Crown for extra seats. The Lancastrian monarchs frequently summoned parliaments to authorise taxation, while Henry VIII used Parliament as a constitutional tool to change the Church's status in relation to the Crown during the English Reformation. In the early 17th century, conflicts of interest between the Crown and Parliament became more serious. It was the Commons which, in 1628, ultimately forced Charles I to accept the PETITION OF RIGHT, establishing the principle that taxes could be imposed only with parliamentary assent. During the LONG PARLIAMENT's tenure from 1640 to 1660 the Commons led the moves which curtailed the Crown's authority and abolished the House of Lords, and later established the COMMONWEALTH. Yet it was also the Commons which was instrumental in inviting Charles II to return from exile to take up the throne.

In promoting the BILL OF RIGHTS in 1689 and the Act of SETTLEMENT two years later, the Commons defined the relationship between itself, the Lords and the monarchy, and laid the foundations for Britain's form of government today. But though the Commons had gained constitutional powers, until the end of the 19th century it was no more than an equal partner with the non-representative, hereditary House of Lords. Extension of the franchise, which began in 1832 with the first of seven REFORM ACTS, and the influence of several members such as Robert Peel, Lord Palmerston and William Gladstone increased the Commons' powers until by the end of the century it was effectively regarded as the voice of the people. In the 20th century legislation was passed establishing the Commons as superior to the Lords.

As a rule, politically controversial bills are introduced in the Commons before going to the Lords, and the Commons claims exclusive control over national taxation and expenditure. Members have been paid since 1911.

Commonwealth Period of republican government in England from 1649, when Charles I was executed, until the RESTORATION of King Charles II in 1660. Claiming to be 'the supreme power in this nation', the

RUMP PARLIAMENT's strength was vested in a 40-strong Council of State. It had ordered Charles I's execution and abolished the monarchy, but did not enact further radical reforms. Taxes to finance Oliver CROMWELL's campaigns against Royalist resistance in Ireland and Scotland from 1649 to 1651, and the Navigation Acts which provoked the ANGLO-DUTCH WAR of 1652, fuelled public resentment, and Cromwell expelled the Rump in April 1653. However, his hopes that the BAREBONES PARLIAMENT, which replaced the Rump, would achieve political and religious harmony were shortlived. By December Cromwell accepted that he himself must become the head of State. The period of Cromwell's rule is known as the PROTECTORATE.

Commonwealth of Independent States see RUSSIA

Commonwealth of Nations Inter-

national group made up of the United Kingdom and countries which were formerly part of the BRITISH EMPIRE. Although most of its member states are independent, the Commonwealth accepts the British monarch as its titular head. The term 'British Commonwealth' was first used after the First World War and acknowledged the enhanced status earned by the Dominions' military aid to Britain during the conflict. Their independence was legitimised by the Statute of WESTMINSTER in 1931. By the end of the Second World War, the Commonwealth consisted of countries where the White population was dominant, but with the independence of India, Pakistan and Burma in 1947 and of other former colonies in the next two decades, its racial composition changed and it adopted the title Commonwealth of Nations.

A few countries have left the Commonwealth, including Burma in 1947, the Republic of Ireland in 1949, Pakistan in 1972 and Fiji in 1987. Hostility to its APARTHEID policies forced South Africa to withdraw in 1961, though it was readmitted in 1994 – two years after Namibia's enrolment as what was then the only Commonwealth member never to have been a British colony. Cameroon was admitted in 1995, in spite of criticism by some member states of its human rights record. The same year Mozambique, which has no historical links with Britain, joined as a 'special case'. Conferences and cultural links help Commonwealth members to maintain a semblance of unity.

commune Medieval European town which by purchase or force had acquired specific privileges and often became a bastion of local

power. Initially a commune's privileges ranged from responsibility for local order, justice and trade and the freedom to elect councils, to being empowered to raise taxes and tolls. The enhanced wealth of many individual towns, generated by the boom in trade in the Middle Ages, so increased their power that some – such as Venice, Florence and Milan – became independent city-republics. In Flanders, Germany and Spain the high costs of warfare forced many rulers to surrender direct control of cities in return for financial benefits; these communes often pursued their own diplomatic policies as political alliances shifted. Communes declined as strong national monarchies developed in the 16th and 17th centuries.

Commune of Paris see PARIS, COMMUNE OF

Communism see feature, pages 158-9

Communist Manifesto Primary source of the socioeconomic doctrine propounded by Karl MARX and Friedrich ENGELS in 1848. The manifesto linked SOCIALISM with COMMUNISM in a common political programme for the working-class movement. Arguing that all history reflected the development of class struggles, and asserting that the industrialised proletariat would eventually establish a classless society safeguarded by social ownership, the manifesto set out ways to achieve this. Although Marx suggested that it should be shelved, the work continued to influence worldwide communist movements throughout the 20th century.

Marx's and Engels's *Communist Manifesto* was the blueprint for Russia's revolutionaries.

Columbus sails to the ends of the Earth

On October 12, 1492, lookouts in three ships, the largest just 100 ft (30 m) long, sighted what is now the island of San Salvador in the Bahamas. The collision between the Old World and the New would transform them both.

For two months a tiny flotilla had sailed westwards from Palos in Spain on a voyage no explorer had made before. Often the crews had despaired of sighting land, and once they had mutinied. The ships were named the *Santa Maria*, the *Niña* and the *Pinta*, and their commander was Christopher Columbus.

'Then', says the log of the *Santa Maria*, 'they saw naked people, and the Admiral went ashore in a small armed boat.' He planted the banner of Spain on the land and claimed possession for the Crown. He called the islanders 'Indians' in the belief that he had landed in the East Indies.

Sailing on, he discovered another island, now called Cuba, and then Haiti, which he named Hispaniola because it reminded him of Spain. But on Christmas Eve the *Santa Maria* ran aground on a sand bank and could not be refloated. The two surviving ships had not enough room for the extra men. Believing this to be a sign from God, Columbus put ashore 38 of them to found a colony, and built a small fort that he named Navidad.

On January 18, 1493, Columbus headed for home. His voyage had been the culmination of eight years of frustrating efforts to persuade the courts of Portugal and Spain to support an expedition to find a westward sea route to India and China.

A MASTER MARINER'S AMBITION

Columbus was born in Genoa in 1451 but went to live with his brother Bartolomeo, a chart-maker, in Lisbon. There he took up his brother's trade and became fascinated by the explorations of Portuguese mariners along the West African coast. By his early thirties he was himself a master mariner.

The navigators' ambition was to reach the southern tip of Africa, if there was one, and from there to find a sea route to the Indies, with its rich silk and spices, which would bypass the Genoese, Venetian and Arab middlemen. Columbus had a far more daring plan. Every educated person knew that the Earth was a globe. If so, it should be possible, he thought, to reach India, China and Japan by sailing westwards

Lisbon (above) was the headquarters of Atlantic and African explorers, bustling with nimble caravels such as that used by Christopher Columbus (right).

across the Atlantic. Paolo Toscanelli, a geographer, had calculated the distance as 3500 miles (5600 km). Columbus was not the only person to have had this idea, but he was certainly the most persistent.

He petitioned the Portuguese king John II, who turned him down. In disgust, he turned to King Ferdinand and Queen Isabella of Spain. Here, too, there was doubt, partly because Columbus's arguments were often vague. But supporters at court finally persuaded the king and queen to agree. If Portugal was exploring, why should not Spain do so too?

When Columbus returned in triumph from what he believed was the Indies in March 1493, Ferdinand and Isabella gave him the title 'Admiral of the Ocean Sea, Viceroy and Governor of the islands that he hath discovered in the Indies'. He displayed small gold ornaments as evidence of the fabulous wealth to be had, if only he could make contact with China. Columbus wanted support for a second expedition.

In May 1493 Ferdinand and Isabella obtained from the pope, Alexander VI, ownership of all lands west of a north-south line dividing the Atlantic. Assured that they could legitimately claim any lands he discovered, they gave Columbus what he wanted. In September he left Cadiz with 17 ships and 1500 men, intending to colonise.

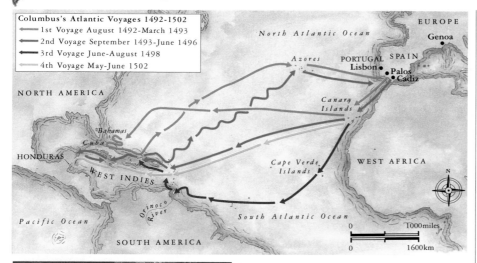

Columbus's Atlantic Voyages 1492-1502
→ 1st Voyage August 1492-March 1493
→ 2nd Voyage September 1493-June 1496
→ 3rd Voyage June-August 1498
→ 4th Voyage May-June 1502

Columbus's voyages revealed the New World to Europe. King Ferdinand and Queen Isabella receive him on his triumphant return (left).

The discovery by Columbus of plants such as the pineapple counted for little after his misrule of Hispaniola had been discovered. He was sent back to Spain in chains (below).

He made landfall on what is now Dominica, and in November reached Puerto Rico. Returning to Hispaniola, he was dismayed to find that the colonists of Navidad had been massacred by the local inhabitants. He resettled the island with a new colony, which he named Fort Isabella, and sent a messenger back to Spain with various proposals. He wrote enthusiastically of the colony's prospects: wax-producing palm trees, cotton-producing kapok trees, and indigenous peoples who would be valuable as slaves. He then sailed on to explore the coasts of Cuba and Jamaica.

Returning to Fort Isabella, he found its occupants quarrelling. Provisions had been allowed to rot, and instead of farming they were obsessed with searching for gold. Despite this setback, Columbus sailed on around the western end of Cuba, where the coast curves south, believing it to be the coast of China. After a brief return to Fort Isabella he made for home, having captured 500 local people as slaves.

This time his reception was cooler. Reports of problems in the colony were filtering back to Spain, and the king and queen were displeased that he had appointed his brother Bartolomeo 'governor' of Hispaniola. Columbus returned with many promises, but little wealth to justify the expedition. He was able to embark on a third voyage in 1498 partly by agreeing to transport convicts as colonists, but this proved even less successful.

He sent three of his ships direct to Hispaniola. While commanding the other three he proceeded south-east to reach Trinidad and the mouth of the Orinoco.

Noticing powerful tributaries flowing into it, he might have realised it was part of a continent. Instead, he had the fantastic idea that these were the four rivers of paradise.

He was brought back sharply to reality on reaching Hispaniola, where a rebellion against Bartolomeo had been crushed and several men hanged. When news of this episode reached Spain, the king and queen sent a new governor to inquire into the troubles and relieve Columbus of his post.

COLUMBUS FACES EXECUTION

The governor arrived in August 1500 with troops, guns and orders to Columbus and his brothers Bartolomeo and Diego to hand over prisoners, stores and forts. They refused, and all three were promptly arrested, put in chains and returned to Spain, expecting to be executed for treason. But the king, shocked at their treatment, ordered their release. Columbus fell at his feet and wept in gratitude.

Columbus was forbidden to sail back to Hispaniola. Yet once more, desperately, he set out with four old ships in 1502. He discovered the island of Martinique, but was refused admission to Dominica on royal orders. He then sailed for Jamaica but had to quell two mutinies before sailing on to Honduras. He was now voyaging in his imagination, writing to the king that he was only ten days' sail from the Ganges.

Storms destroyed two of his ships and badly damaged the others. He was forced into a small cove in Jamaica, which he still believed was off China. Here ill-health, lack of supplies and threats from mutinous men and hostile indigenous peoples obliged him to appeal to the governor of Hispaniola for help. After being stranded for a year, Columbus returned to Spain in late 1504.

Sick, frustrated and mentally unstable, he had a final meeting with Ferdinand in Segovia in 1505, hoping that the king would restore him to the government of the Indies. He finally retired to Valladolid, where he died, worn out, in 1506.

To the end of his life Columbus believed he had discovered the Indies, bordering on China and Japan. Meanwhile, Vasco da Gama had rounded the Cape of Good Hope in 1497 and opened up the sea route to Asia, which was to establish Portugal as the dominant power in the Indian Ocean. The West Indies, and soon Mexico, would be Columbus's unwitting legacy to Spain.

Columbus combined the roles of explorer and exploiter. He made great discoveries, but even by the standards of the time his treatment of the peoples he encountered and of his own men was cruel. His voyages opened up the New World to the Old, but they also began the destruction of Amerindian civilisation.

computers These have been described as 'universal information processing machines' and, in theory, can perform any information processing task that can be specified by an algorithm, or well-defined series of instructions. They are one of the most significant inventions of the 20th century.

While the use of computers became widespread only from about 1970, they are the result of centuries of mathematical and scientific speculation and the culmination of a long history of exploring methods of automatic calculation. As early as the 1st century AD the Greek inventor Hero of Alexandria wrote of the possibility of making mathematical calculations by using a series of gears to represent numbers; but there was little progress until the late 16th century when the first calculators were built, using the principles that had been established by the oriental abacus. In 1679, the German mathematician Gottfried Leibniz speculated on the possibility of building a calculator which would use balls to represent numbers in a binary code.

The breakthrough came in the mid 1830s when the English mathematician and inventor Charles Babbage developed the basic idea of an analytical machine which contains most of the elements of today's general-purpose computer. Babbage began to design an Analytical Engine in 1834 and completed his first specifications two years later, but the development costs were high and the British Government withdrew funding before his machine was completed. His ideas were lost but his instructions and working papers were rediscovered a century later in the 1930s when work on electromechanical computers was started independently in both Germany and the USA. The world's first working stored-program computer was completed in Germany in 1941, while in Britain faster and more reliable computers were developed secretly and used in wartime code-breaking. In the postwar years, faster and smaller computers were rapidly developed using new technology based on microchips.

By the 1990s computers had transformed many aspects of scientific research, not only through their ability to analyse large quantities of numerical data but also by the use of simulation techniques to model complex systems such as the weather. Space travel and advanced aircraft design would probably have been impossible without the processing capacities of computers. As the technology has become more sophisticated and computers have become smaller, manufacturers have applied microtechnology to such fields as television sets, cameras and domestic appliances, and in doing so have changed the pattern of modern living. But the biggest changes have been in communications – which will change even more with the advent of what the experts call the new 'information super-highway'.

A revolution in communication

Gone are the days of carrier pigeons and fleet-footed messengers; today we can communicate instantly with almost anywhere in the world via a network of optical cables and orbiting satellites.

The 19th-century British prime minister Lord Salisbury had no doubt which invention had changed the world most in his lifetime. In 1889 he declared: 'The electric telegraph has achieved this great and paradoxical result. It has, as it were, assembled all mankind upon one great plane, where they can see everything that is done, and hear everything that is said, and judge of every policy that is pursued at the very moment when these events take place.' The Canadian thinker Marshall McLuhan, coining the term 'global village', said much the same thing 80 years later.

SIGNALS IN SEMAPHORE
Throughout human history, distance insulated societies from each other. News spread at the speed of the messenger, horse, carrier pigeon or sailing ship. Empires were controlled at arm's length, with real power lying in the hands of plenipotentiaries on the spot. Kings led their armies on the battlefield because only by being there could they be in command.

The first change came with printing, the second with the semaphore telegraph. On hills across Europe, towers were built with signalling beams mounted on top. They consisted of a horizontal beam with two smaller wings at the ends. By altering the angle of these 'indicators', coded messages could be sent from hill to hill. The system that Napoleon ordered to be built in 1804 could send a signal from Paris to Milan, a distance of 388 miles (625 km), in 30 minutes.

The electric telegraph, developed and patented by Samuel Morse by 1837, used the flow of current along

Claude Chappe's semaphore system used mechanical arms to convey 9999 words, which he recorded in 1794.

In 1984 the Leasat communications satellite was deployed from the space shuttle *Discovery*. Most satellites are stationed 22300 miles (35900 km) above the Equator.

wires to transmit signals instantaneously. It was first successfully applied in Britain in 1837 by Professor Charles Wheatstone of King's College, London, and the entrepreneur William Fothergill Cooke. A line was installed along the track of the Great Western Railway from Paddington station, and in 1844 it enabled *The Times* of London to be first with the news of the birth of Queen Victoria's second son, Alfred Ernest, at Windsor Castle. The following year it helped to catch a murderer. John Tawell killed his mistress at her home near Slough, 20 miles (32 km) west of London, and was later seen boarding the 7.42 pm train to Paddington. Alerted by telegraph, the police were able to arrest Tawell.

The telephone – able to transmit sounds rather than coded messages – was patented by the Scottish inventor Alexander Graham Bell in

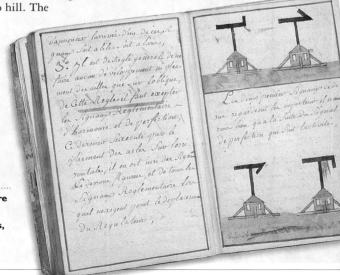

Despite the technological advances made in weaponry during the First World War, carrier pigeons still proved necessary.

1876. Building on the success of the telegraph, its progress was swift. The first long-distance line used 290 miles (467 km) of hard-drawn copper wire to link Boston and Providence, Rhode Island, in 1884.

To begin with, connections were made through telephone operators. The automatic exchange was invented in 1889 by a Kansas undertaker, Almon Brown Strowger, who believed that the switchboard girls were directing callers to his rivals. His 'girl-less, cuss-less, out-of-order-less, wait-less' exchanges operated successfully until fully electronic exchanges appeared during the 1960s.

OPTICAL LINKS

The launch of communications satellites into space in the 1960s, and the development of optical fibres that can carry far more calls at once than copper wires, vastly expanded the range of telephony. Now huge volumes of data can be exchanged between computers over telephone lines, making possible the Internet, a vast and growing network of computers all over the world, linked by cables and able to exchange data and gossip 24 hours a day.

The effect has been to centralise power in the hands of governments, allowing them to gather information and issue instructions instantaneously, while individuals can now communicate more freely than ever before. Business and commerce have multiplied as the telecommunications revolution continues to make the world smaller.

Comte, Auguste (1798-1857) French philosopher whose theories, with those of his compatriot Henri de Saint-Simon, built the foundations of modern sociological study. Comte coined the term 'sociology' in defining his 'Law of Three Stages'. This argued that society was like an organism in which each part had a role to play in contributing to the functioning of the whole. Human knowledge and society evolved through distinct phases, Comte said. In the first of these, the theological phase, man sought explanations in the actions of the gods; in the second, or metaphysical phase, more abstract processes, such as 'nature' were explored for answers; and in the third, positive, stage of man's development he looked for discernible laws, or patterns. Comte's ideas, expounded in his major work *Cours de Philosophie Positive* (1830-42), greatly influenced the social theorist Emile Durkheim, who is widely regarded as the father of sociology.

concentration camps Camps in which civilians regarded as hostile by the authorities were held, or 'concentrated', during periods of war or civil unrest. The first concentration camps were set up by Britain's Lord KITCHENER during the second BOER WAR OF 1900-2 to remove women and children from the effects of his 'scorched earth' policy in the Transvaal and Cape Colony. About 20 000 Boer women and children died in them – mainly from diseases caused by inadequate rations and unhygienic conditions – leading to claims of 'deliberate genocide'. As a result of a campaign in London spearheaded by Emily Hobhouse, conditions were improved and then death rates fell.

It was the similarly named institutions in Nazi Germany of the 1930s which gave the whole concept an obscene notoriety. The early inmates of the Nazis' concentration camps included trade unionists, Roman Catholic and Protestant dissidents, communists, Jews and gypsies. Described by GOEBBELS in August 1934 as 'camps to turn antisocial members of society into useful members by the most humane means possible', before the outbreak of the Second World War they already held as many as 200 000 people described as 'undesirables'. After the outbreak of war the camps were increased in size and number to house armies of slave labourers or as factories of death for the extermination of Europe's Jewish population in what came to be known as the HOLOCAUST. Administered by the Nazi elite SS, the camps became sites of some of the worst acts of torture, horror and mass murder the world has known. In Eastern Europe prisoners were used in labour battalions or helped in killing other inmates, until they were exterminated. In camps such as Auschwitz, gas chambers were used to kill as many as 12 000 people daily. In the west,

Belsen, Dachau and Buchenwald were notorious. An estimated 6 million Jews, some half a million gypsies and other civilians as well as several millions of Polish and Russian prisoners of war died. After the war many camp officials were tried and punished in a series of trials that continued into the 1950s. Others did not face trial until the mid 1990s.

Conciliar Movement (1409-49) Church movement whose original purpose was to heal the rift that had developed from the simultaneous existence of two – and later three – popes in different parts of the Christian world. The movement emerged from ecumenical councils held in Pisa in 1409, in Constance from 1414 to 1418 and in Basle from 1431 to 1449. Though the first council healed the rift by successfully deposing or accepting the resignations of the rivals and establishing a single pope, the movement itself later came into conflict with the papacy. As early as 1415 the ecumenical council's *Haec Sancta*, or *Sacrosancta*, decreed the superiority of a general council of the Church over the papacy and tried to make this concept of religious control a regular feature of the Western Church. The movement also dealt with various heresies, condemning the writings of the dead John WYCLIFFE in 1415 and in the same year ordering that his follower John Huss be burnt at the stake. The papacy eventually defeated the challenge to its authority, but the movement's long-term influence on the hierarchical structures of the Church was considerable.

Concord see LEXINGTON, BATTLE OF

concordat Agreement between the State and the Roman Catholic Church regulating the Church's secular status. Among the most significant, the Concordat of 1801 between Pope Pius VII and Napoleon I re-established the Catholic Church in France and lasted until the separation of Church and State in 1905. It laid down that although property confiscated during the French Revolution was not to be returned to the Church, the government undertook to maintain the clergy. It also gave the government the right to appoint local archbishops and bishops – subject to papal confirmation. Another major concordat, the LATERAN TREATIES of 1929, regulated the status of the papacy in Italy. This had been a source of contention since Italian unification in 1870, when the secular powers of the pope had been abolished. The Lateran Treaties restored the influence of the Catholic Church in Italy as well as giving the pope sovereignty over the VATICAN CITY.

Condé Junior branch of the French royal House of BOURBON. As Prince de Condé, Louis I de Bourbon (1530-69) was the first to bear the title. He was a bitter opponent of the

Communism: the revolt of the working classes

Karl Marx envisaged a communist society in which all would 'work according to their abilities and receive according to their needs'. In 1917 his principles inspired the Russian Bolsheviks and changed history.

Karl Marx wrote that: 'Philosophers have previously tried to explain the world. Our task is to change it.' This urge for action was the key to the transformation of a 19th-century social and economic theory into the mass movement of the 20th century. The ideal of a classless society, in which public ownership replaces private interests, is common in some degree to all forms of socialism. Fundamental to communism is the conviction that the process is historically inevitable, that it must be imposed in its totality, and that the dictatorship of the proletariat is necessary to achieve it.

For Marxists, class struggle is the engine of change, driving society forward from slavery and feudalism to capitalism and, ultimately, to communism. Marx held that existing systems could not be reformed because of the strength of reaction and vested interest; a bourgeois or capitalist revolution was necessary before feudalism could be overthrown. In turn, the working class must advance by destroying capitalism and the bourgeoisie. Only then would the way be prepared for the eventual withering away of the state in a truly communist and classless society. Other socialists based their

campaigns on morality and the ballot box. The ruthlessness of communism flowed from the belief that violent struggle was part of its mission. Such extremism won it the world's largest country, Russia, and the most populous, China.

COMMUNISM'S FIRST SUCCESS

Communism succeeded because, in the highly centralised form devised by Vladimir Lenin, it tolerated no opposition. But its inflexibility and inhumanity came ultimately to undermine it. It collapsed in its Leninist form in the Soviet Union because it lapsed into party and leader worship, and into mass murder.

Russia was communism's first, and until 1945 its only, success. Marx held that communist prospects were best in industrially advanced countries where the bourgeois revolution had already taken place. Russia was backward; four out of five of its people were peasants who desired to own their own land. The Russian triumph tore up the rule book: communism spread most rapidly in poor countries.

Lenin's narrow, disciplined and strictly led Bolshevik Party – which became a template for others – played almost no part

Posters of the 1930s extol Marx, Engels, Lenin and Stalin as the four pillars of communism, while the Soviet proletariat marches towards a new world order.

in Russian affairs until losses at the front in the First World War, food shortages and government corruption produced a spontaneous uprising in 1917. They were a fringe party of interest to few beyond the secret police, who infiltrated them with such ease that the leadership was in prison or exiled when the Petrograd garrison refused to open fire on strikers and mutinied in March 1917.

Within a week, the tsar had abdicated and a moderate provisional government committed to parliamentary democracy was established. The Bolsheviks neither anticipated nor directed this revolution. They were, however, determined to exploit it. For the first time in a decade, Lenin

Flags form the backdrop for a political reading in a house taken from a wealthy peasant in 1930, as part of a campaign against illiteracy (left), and for a guard of honour at Beijing Airport in 1973 (below).

returned to Petrograd from exile in Switzerland. His demand for 'peace, bread and land' was popular, but when the Bolsheviks failed to win a majority in the influential left-wing Soviet, Lenin decided to seize power in a coup d'état. In November 1917, Bolsheviks, on the initiative and under the direction of Leon Trotsky, arrested government members and took control of telephone exchanges, post offices and banks in Petrograd. Lenin declared to the Soviet: 'We will institute workers' control over production. We shall create a proletarian socialist state. Long live the socialist world revolution!'

Lenin had written that the socialist Paris Commune of 1871 failed because of the 'excessive generosity' of the working class. He did not intend to repeat the mistake. The new parliament was dismissed at gunpoint; Soviet Russia became the first one-party state. The Cheka, or secret police, was set up to destroy opponents. The tsar and his family were shot. The Red Army fought against right-wing Whites in a ferocious civil war.

When Lenin died in 1924, his body was mummified and displayed in a mausoleum in Moscow's Red Square. Communism, supposedly scientific, was becoming idolatrous. Lenin's position of pre-eminence in the party was eventually seized and greatly expanded by Joseph Stalin, the party's secretary-general, who forced the Soviet Union through a second, more radical revolution.

From 1930, peasants were stripped of their land and shot, exiled or forced onto new, agriculturally disastrous, collective farms. The terror-famine that accompanied this process probably killed 14 million people. After the farms came the factories.

Five-Year Plans, rigidly controlled from Moscow, were introduced to allow Soviet Russia to overtake American industry. The Soviet economy grew at record rates in the 1930s, but the human cost was immense. Stalin ensured that political rivals, real or imagined, joined the victims of the purges that also swept the country in the 1930s. Show trials, executions and slave labour added millions to the Bolshevik death toll.

In 1941 Hitler turned on Stalin. Russian industrial effort combined with Russian endurance and courage to defeat Nazi Germany in the greatest land conflicts of the Second World War. In 1945 communism was imposed on the swathe of Eastern Europe that was occupied by the Red Army. Elsewhere, a communist revolution was completed in China in 1949 under Mao Ze-dong. Communist-led insurgencies flared in South-east Asia, Africa and Latin America.

CRACKS IN THE SYSTEM

Old failings remained. Party bureaucrats, the 'new class', were pampered. State control failed to ensure that the economy adapted to the demands of the modern world. The brutalities of prewar Soviet Russia were repeated in a new revolutionary ideology in China during the Cultural Revolution. The Soviet invasions of Hungary in 1956 and Czechoslovakia in 1968, the treatment of dissidents, and the Tiananmen Square massacre in Beijing in 1989 all showed the extent to which communism relied on force for survival. 'Personality cults' on Stalinist lines continued with Mao, Kim Il Sung in North Korea, and in Europe with the Romanian dictator Nicolae Ceauşescu.

The Soviet Union, impoverished by the strains of the Cold War arms race, cracked in 1988. The last Soviet leader, Mikhail Gorbachev, believed that his country's communist system could be reformed by perestroika, or economic reconstruction, and by glasnost – political openness. But industry proved resistant to change, and Eastern European satellites, followed by the USSR itself, seized advantage of glasnost to rid themselves of their repressive systems. Yet communism was not dead: in 1995 a revived Russian Communist Party won more than 20 per cent of the vote in a democratic election, while in China the Communist Party remains in political control.

Peasants enrol to join a collective farm in 1931, after Stalin, in the face of poor results and peasant resistance, had ordered a resumption of forcible collectivisation.

The Sforza condottiere Muzio Attendolo leads a Florentine force into battle, in Paolo Uccello's painting *The Rout of San Romano*.

Catholic GUISE family and a military leader of the Protestant Huguenots during the first phase of the French Wars of Religion. Louis was killed at the Battle of Jarnac. His son Henry I de Bourbon (1552-88), who took over as leader of the Huguenots, briefly renounced his faith at the time of the ST BARTHOLOMEW'S DAY MASSACRE in 1572, but subsequently embarrassed his cousin, the future Henry IV, with his Protestant fanaticism.

Henry's grandson Louis II de Bourbon was known as the Great Condé, and excelled as a military commander in the last phase of the THIRTY YEARS' WAR. However, in 1650 disagreements with Cardinal MAZARIN over continuing the war with Spain led to his arrest and brief imprisonment, and when his insurrection of 1651-2 failed, he fled to the Netherlands where he served with the Spanish armies. Allowed to return to France in 1660, the Great Condé conquered Franche-Comté for Louis XIV in 1668 and was a senior commander against the United Provinces of the Netherlands four years later, but Louis never forgave his defection to the Spaniards.

condottiere Medieval leader of a band of mercenary soldiers, whose title derives from the Italian *condotta*, or 'contract'. Motivated by self-interest, condottieri frequently changed sides and loyalties, and the economic prosperity of 14th and 15th-century Italy, which spawned a host of intercity wars, provided rich pickings for their mercenary bands. At first they were recruited from the unemployed mercenary 'free companies' – particularly the so-called Grand Company, a multinational band about 10 000 strong whose knights and followers subcontracted their services to condottieri. The system was refined in the 15th century by the most powerful condottiere, Muzio Attendolo, who assumed the name SFORZA, or 'force', and at one stage controlled three mercenary armies fighting each other. The system died out when the Habsburg-Valois wars of the 16th century led to changes in the financing and organisation of armies.

Confederation of the Rhine (1806-13) Grouping of middle and south German states ordered by Napoleon after his victory at the Battle of Austerlitz in 1805. Members of the Confederation were obliged to leave the Holy Roman Empire, which was thus effectively dissolved. After Prussia's defeat at Jena in 1806, other states joined the Confederation. While Napoleon had annexed all the left bank of the Rhine for France, the new German grouping gradually extended from the Rhine to the Elbe, creating a barrier against Prussian and Austrian power. Initially welcomed by the Germans, who saw the Confederation as a step towards unity, it became less popular as Napoleon's CONTINENTAL SYSTEM and Britain's retaliatory blockade led to growing economic hardship. Although it contributed troops to Napoleon's campaigns of 1813, after his defeat at Leipzig the Confederation broke up and its members gradually made peace with the QUADRUPLE ALLIANCE of Prussia, Britain, Russia and Austria.

Confucius (c.551-479 BC) Chinese philosopher, also known as Kong-zi or Kong-fu-zi, whose teachings, contained in the *Analects* ('Sayings'), probably compiled by his followers after his death, provided the basis for a philosophy of life followed by millions of Orientals. As a minister in the state of Lu (in modern Shandong), and in spite of the political instability which marked the later Zhou period of China's history, Confucius sought to restore what he saw as the earlier 'golden age' of the Zhou dynasty. The ideal society, he taught, could be re-established by harmonising the 'Five Relationships': between husband and wife; ruler and minister; father and son; elder and younger brother; and friend and friend. The inferior must obey; the superior must be righteous but benevolent. When his employers disregarded his advice Confucius resigned and spent years at other courts, unsuccessfully seeking a ruler who would practise his precepts and appoint him to office. Nevertheless, from HAN times (202 BC-AD 220) Chinese administrative conduct and much social behaviour were based on Confucius's ideas, while the Confucian classics and commentaries were central to all Chinese education.

Congo see ZAIRE

Congregationalist Member of a Church organisation – claiming to represent the form of the early Christian church – where each local congregation is independent. In England, Congregationalists believe that Christ is the sole head of the Christian Church and that bishops are unnecessary. Their origins lie in the followers of Robert BROWNE, who broke with the Anglican Church in the 16th century. Driven underground by persecution, Congregationalists resurfaced in Holland in the 17th century, and were among the PILGRIM FATHERS. Later they helped to found the universities of Harvard (1636) and Yale (1701). In England they were prominent in Oliver Cromwell's New Model Army. Their strong traditions of tolerance and freedom of belief led to Congregationalists becoming prominent in the ecumenical movements of the 19th and 20th centuries. In 1972 most Congregational Churches in England and Wales united with the English Presbyterian Church to form the United Reformed Church.

Congress, Indian National India's main political party, which steered India to independence and has held power for much of the time since. The party was founded in 1885 by Indians who wanted more say in the government of their country. By 1907 ideological divisions between moderates and extremists had split the party, but in 1920 its leader Mahatma GANDHI shaped Congress into a powerful nationwide organisation with a mass membership. Campaigning for Indian self-rule and independence, in 1937 Congress easily won elections in a majority of provinces, but two years later withdrew from the government after voting for neutrality at the outbreak of the Second World War. Although many of its leaders were imprisoned during the 1941 'Quit India' campaign, Congress negotiated successfully with Britain for independence after the war ended. After partition in 1947 it continued to dominate India under Jawaharlal NEHRU, but after his death in 1964 the struggle between the old guard and younger, radical elements led by Mrs Indira GANDHI split the party. Although Mrs Gandhi

The Eastern philosopher Confucius failed to restore China's 'golden age', but his teachings shaped Chinese society for more than 2000 years.

Congressmen from the Union states seem involved in their own skirmishes in this contemporary woodcut from December 1861 – eight months after the outbreak of the American Civil War.

quickly rebuilt it, in the 1977 elections Congress was heavily defeated by Morarji Desai's Janata (People's) Alliance Party. In the following year Mrs Gandhi formed a new party, the 'real' Indian National Congress, or Congress (I) Party. In 1979 she led this faction to electoral victory, and resumed the premiership until her assassination in October 1984. Leadership of the party passed to her son Rajiv Gandhi, prime minister from 1984 to 1989; he was assassinated in May 1991 during the run-up to a general election. The Congress (I) Party was re-elected under P.V. Narashima Rao, who became prime minister.

Congress of the USA Legislative arm of the US federal government. It is divided into two houses: the lower, the House of REPRESENTATIVES, membership of which is based on state populations; and the upper, the SENATE, in which each state is represented by two members. Congressmen serve a two-year term and senators a six-year term. Congress was intended to steer the course of federal government, but as the presidency's role grew stronger fluctuations in the balance of power between legislature and executive developed. Today much of Congress's effective work is carried out in standing committees which deal with major areas of policy. Congressional powers include the collection of taxes and duties, provision for common defence – including declaration of war, raising of armies and the maintenance of a navy – the nation's health and general welfare, the regulation of commerce, the control of postal services and the establishment of federal courts.

conquistadores Soldiers and adventurers serving the Spanish crown who were responsible for much of the colonisation of the New World in the 16th century. The term relates to the slow reconquest, or *Reconquista,* of Spain by the Christians after 500 years of Moorish rule, culminating in the fall of Granada to Ferdinand and Isabella in 1492. The conquistadores were driven by two main motives – the search for the legendary wealth of 'El Dorado' and a desire to bring Christianity to the inhabitants of the lands which they explored. Best known among the conquistadores are Hérnan CORTES, conqueror of Aztec Mexico, and Francisco PIZARRO, conqueror of Inca Peru; but there were many others whose explorations and conquests embraced the Caribbean, Latin America, the Philippines and southern and south-western USA. The establishment of formal colonial administrations – and the shrinking of new lands left to conquer – diminished the conquistadores' role, and they could never again find such rich empires as those of the Aztecs or Incas.

conscription Compulsory call-up for military service, usually in times of war though many countries bolster the strength of their armed forces in peacetime by conscripting young men and women for a specific period. China, Israel, Greece and several Middle Eastern countries rely on conscription to provide the bulk of their military manpower, and the Swiss army is comprised almost entirely of conscripts. In Britain and the USA, where conscription was introduced at the start of the Second World War, it was continued in the postwar era as National Service in the UK from 1947, and as Selective Service, or the 'draft', in the USA from 1948. Conscription ended in Britain in 1957. During the 11 years of the Vietnam War an estimated 10 000 young Americans dodged the draft, many of them fleeing the USA rather than undertaking their military obligations. In 1973 the USA abolished conscription.

Conservative parties Political parties – particularly in Britain, Canada and South Africa – whose ideologies tend to be based on the maintenance of traditional values and institutions. In Britain, where the Conservatives remain a major party, the name dates from 1830, when the Tory *Quarterly Review* suggested that a better name for the old Tory Party might be 'Conservative' since it stood for the preservation of existing institutions. Though Sir Robert Peel favoured the name, it was not until the party split over the issue of FREE TRADE and Peel's followers joined the Liberals that the majority, under Lord Derby and Disraeli, gradually adopted the title Conservative. Disraeli outlined the aims of the party as: 'the preservation of our institutions, the maintenance of our Empire and the amelioration of the condition of the people.'

Throughout the first half of the 20th century the British Conservative Party was strongly imperialist. From 1945 until the 1970s its policies tended to be pragmatic, accepting the basic philosophy of the WELFARE STATE and being prepared to adjust in response to a consensus of public opinion. Under the leadership of Margaret THATCHER, however, it seemed to reassert the 19th-century liberal emphasis on individual free enterprise, challenging the need for State support and subsidy, while asserting State power against local authorities. Until the early 1990s Canada's Conservatives retained a traditional approach on national issues, while an extreme right-wing Conservative Party was established in South Africa during the last decade of the Apartheid era, drawing considerable support from traditionalists, particularly among the white Afrikaner minority.

Conservative policies were shown as the sun's rays in this 1929 election poster which drew its inspiration from popular advertising styles.

Constance, Council of (1414-18) Ecclesiastical council – the second of three forming the CONCILIAR MOVEMENT – called at Constance in Switzerland to deal with reform and heresy within the Christian Church. It resolved the schism which had developed in the Church over the rivalry between two popes – one in Avignon and one in Rome. It also presided over the trial and burning of John Huss, the reformist follower of John WYCLIFFE, but the council failed to reform existing abuses in clerical finance and conduct, and to subordinate the powers of the pope to those of the council.

Constantine I 'the Great' (c.274-337) Roman emperor from 324 to 337 under whom Christianity became a permitted faith within the Roman Empire. On the death of Constantius I in 306 the army at York – at that time Rome's strongest army – proclaimed his son Constantine as the new emperor, but there were other powerful contenders for the title and in the ensuing turmoil several claimants competed for the post. It was not until Constantine's defeat of Maxentius at Milvian Bridge north of Rome in 312 that he became emperor of the West, dividing the empire with Licinius, who held the Eastern empire. Eleven years later Constantine defeated and killed Licinius to become sole emperor. He founded a second capital at Byzantium and renamed it CONSTANTINOPLE. Constantine proclaimed tolerance of Christianity in the Edict of Milan, but his own beliefs are uncertain. He was not converted until shortly before he died, and probably supported orthodox Christianity because he thought it would help to unify the empire. In 326 he decreed that Sundays should be holidays. Both Constantine and his mother Helena took great interest in Christian sites, building basilicas over the stable-cave in Bethlehem, on Christ's tomb in Jerusalem and at St Peter's grave on the Vatican Hill in Rome. He also built Constantinople's basilica of St Sophia.

Constantinople Turkish city founded in 657 BC as the Greek colony BYZANTIUM and renamed by CONSTANTINE early in the 4th century AD when he chose the site as capital of the Eastern empire. Constantine designed it as a new Rome, straddling seven hills and divided into 14 districts. Over the centuries its walls withstood siege by Goths, Persians and Arabs. Wealthy and noted for the richness of its culture, Constantinople was looted by Western Crusaders in 1204 after a bloody attack on their fellow Christians, who made up more than half of the city's population. It eventually fell to the Ottoman Turks in 1453 and remained a capital of the OTTOMAN EMPIRE until 1923. Its name was changed in 1930 to become the Turkish city of Istanbul.

DID YOU KNOW?

Although a deathbed convert, Constantine adopted Christian symbols for his battle standards in 312 – after a 'vision' revealed the sign of the cross in the rays of the sun.

Constitution of the USA Fundamental written instrument of American government, and one of the most influential documents in Western history. The US Constitution replaced the Articles of Confederation, which from 1781 to 1787 had served the shared interests of individual states, with a blueprint for an effective centralised national government, which preserved the right of individual states to determine many of their own affairs. Three months of secret debate among the FOUNDING FATHERS at the Federal Constitutional Convention in Philadelphia in 1787 produced a series of modifications to James Madison's original Virginia Plan.

The Great Compromise, between large and small states, gave equal representation in the Senate, but the number of seats in the House of Representatives was allotted in proportion to the size of the population. North and South finally agreed that the slave trade would continue until at least 1808 and that, in terms of representation and taxation, a slave would be counted as three-fifths of a person. The principle of popular sovereignty, with biennial election of congressmen to the House of Representatives, was balanced by indirect election of senators and presidents for renewable six and four-year terms. The federal government comprises the executive (president, vice-president, Cabinet and civil service); the legislature (Senate and House of Representatives, together forming CONGRESS); and the judiciary (Supreme Court and other federal courts). A series of checks and balances shares and divides power between these three components of government. For example, the Supreme Court, appointed by the president with senatorial approval, may declare actions of the executive or legislature unconstitutional, but may not initiate lawsuits or legislation. The 1787 draft had to be considered and then approved by nine state conventions and although there was major opposition in Virginia, Massachusetts and New York the Constitution came into operation in 1789.

Major shortcomings of the Constitution included the failure to foresee the establishment of political parties, the absence of a BILL OF RIGHTS, the complexity of its electoral arrangements and the many obstacles put in the way of central government. The Bill of Rights was introduced in response to antifederalist criticism that the Constitution should define individual rights more clearly, and its amendments – the first to the Constitution – were originally to have been included in the main instrument. However, they were not ratified by all the states until 1791 and thus formed a separate document. All told, the Constitution has been amended 26 times, most notably to abolish slavery and to give the vote to Blacks and women.

containment Basic principle of US foreign policy after the Second World War to curb Soviet expansion with military pacts among countries encircling Russia and its satellites. The policy was initiated in 1949 by President Harry S TRUMAN with the creation of NATO, the major European military grouping. Its forces, armed with conventional and nuclear weapons, stretched from the Arctic Circle to Turkey. Similar pacts in the Far East were the ANZUS PACT (1951) and the South-East Asia Treaty Organisation (1954). In the 1960s the policy was extended to discourage Soviet participation in the affairs of Latin American and African states.

Continental Congress (1774, 1775-89) Assembly of colonists which drafted the American DECLARATION OF INDEPENDENCE. It first met in Philadelphia to prepare a concerted response to the Coercive Acts, the legislation introduced by Britain as a punishment for the BOSTON TEA PARTY. At this session delegates from Massachusetts, Virginia and South Carolina outmanoeuvred the moderates from New York and Pennsylvania to have the Coercive Acts rejected as 'the attempts of a wicked administration to enslave America'. The second congress – called in 1775 after the clash between British troops and colonists at Concord, near Boston and at Lexington – created a Continental Army under George Washington and took control of the American forces during the ensuing War of INDEPENDENCE. Although under the Articles of Confederation drawn up in 1781 the congress became the government of the USA, its delegates were little more than ambassadors from the 13 sovereign states. The congress was superseded with the establishment of the CONSTITUTION OF THE USA in 1789.

Continental System Napoleon's economic strategy of blockading Britain in the hope of crippling its economy. It was based on his Berlin (1806) and Milan (1807) decrees, which forbade France's allies and those countries which were neutral in the Napoleonic War to trade with Britain or her colonies. Britain responded by blockading French ports and only allowing France's allies to trade with each other and neutral countries if they did so through Britain.

The restrictions had serious effects on Britain and her allies, and contributed to war with the USA over the right of neutral ships to trade with Europe. But they also resulted in Napoleon gradually losing support at home

In 1935 France still transported convicts to penal colonies abroad. A batch are herded below decks to begin the long voyage from Marseilles to the notorious prison on Devil's Island.

and being challenged abroad. His unsuccessful invasion of Russia in 1812 was provoked by its refusal to continue the system.

control commissions

Allied administrations established in Germany after both world wars. The first control commission established after the First World War was solely to supervise German demilitarisation, but the administration set up after the Second World War was wider ranging. American, British and Soviet leaders had agreed that after Germany's defeat the country should be divided, and in 1945 four occupation zones were set up. Until 1948 these were administered by the three Allies and France, whose four military commanders acted as a supreme control council with responsibility for all matters relating to the administration of Germany as a whole. In practice each occupying power administered its zone independently, though the commission did carry out some significant work, particularly in screening former Nazis and removing them from important posts. The British and US zones merged at the start of 1947, and were joined a year later by the French zone. Growing tension between the Soviet and Western representatives provoked by the intensification of the COLD WAR led to the collapse of the shared control system in the following year.

convict transportation

Banishment of a criminal to a penal settlement – frequently in a distant colony – as a form of punishment. The French transported convicts to the West Indies and the Russians sent offenders to Siberia, but it was Britain that used this system of punishment most. The first British convicts to be transported were sent to the American colonies, but after the American War of Independence offenders were sent to the Australian mainland and Tasmania. Between 1788 and 1868, when the system was abolished, more than 160 000 men and women were transported to the Australian colonies, many of them for minor offences. Though most Australian transportees had been convicted of theft, some were political prisoners, mostly from Ireland. Initially convicts laboured on public works; later, a system of 'assignment' was introduced and convicts were allotted to colonists as paid servants.

Those who committed further offences after transportation faced a range of punishments which included flogging, solitary confinement, hard labour and lengthy spells in PENAL SETTLEMENTS, where they worked as coal miners or lime burners. The penal settlement at Port Arthur, in Tasmania, became one of the most feared for the harshness of its regime. Founded in 1832, it was widely regarded as one of the most brutal settlements, where floggings were ordered for minor offences and a rule of strict silence was enforced. In its 'model prison' – established in 1852 and intended to reform its inmates, rather than punish them – prisoners spent their time in solitary confinement and many of them, far from being rehabilitated, were driven insane. French convicts were sent to the equally notorious penal colony on Devil's Island, off the South American coast, until 1938.

convoy system

Wartime method of protecting merchant ships by sailing in groups escorted by armed naval vessels. Armed ships had been used to accompany merchantmen since the days of sail, but the convoy system was first introduced on a major scale during the First World War. Merchant ships as well as naval vessels became 'legitimate' targets for German U-boats when, in 1917, Germany adopted a policy of unrestricted submarine warfare. A quarter of all shipping to and from British ports was sunk in the last two years of the war and new construction could replace only a tenth of lost tonnage. Faced by a shortage of imports that soon reached crisis levels, the British prime minister David Lloyd George overruled the Admiralty's refusal to organise convoys. By November 1918, 80 per cent of inward or outward-bound shipping sailed in convoy. At the outset of the Second World War, despite a shortage of destroyers, transatlantic convoys were immediately instituted, later using long-range fighter aircraft for additional protection.

Cook, James

(1728-79) British naval captain and explorer whose Pacific voyages led to the first European settlement of the Australian continent. The son of an agricultural labourer in Yorkshire, Cook was apprenticed to a shipowner plying the Baltic trade before joining the Royal Navy as an able seaman. Here his skills as a navigator earned him promotion to master. While serving in North America from 1759 to 1767 Cook charted the St Lawrence Channel and the coasts of Nova Scotia and Newfoundland. The following year he commanded an expedition to Tahiti in HMS *Endeavour* carrying an expedition to observe the transit of Venus, and mapped the coasts of New Zealand and eastern Australia

> **❝[I wished]...not only to go further than anyone had done before, but as far as possible for man to go. ❞**
>
> *From the journals of Captain James Cook, 1775*

before returning home by way of the East Indies in 1771. On his second voyage, from 1772 to 1775 in the *Resolution*, he became the first navigator to cross the Antarctic Circle. As well as revisiting New Zealand and Tahiti, Cook explored vast areas of the Pacific, discovering New Caledonia and Norfolk Island to the south and charting Easter Island, the Marquesas and Society Islands, the Friendly Isles (Tonga) and the New Hebrides. Rounding Cape Horn on his voyage home, Cook then visited South Georgia and discovered the South Sandwich Islands. Cook sailed for the South Pacific again in 1776 and, seeking a north-west passage from the Pacific to the Atlantic, he reached the islands of Hawaii before mapping part of the Alaska coast. Cook overcame the risk of his crews suffering from scurvy – a disease rife on long sea voyages at

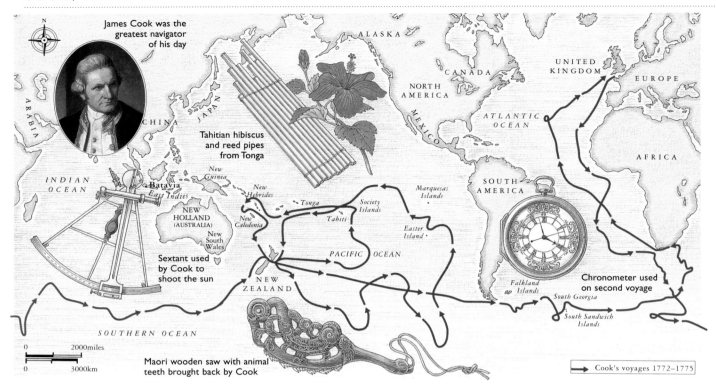

James Cook was the greatest navigator of his day

Tahitian hibiscus and reed pipes from Tonga

Sextant used by Cook to shoot the sun

Chronometer used on second voyage

Maori wooden saw with animal teeth brought back by Cook

Cook's voyages 1772–1775

English navigator James Cook's first voyage of discovery in 1771 was so successful he was made a commander and given control of a second voyage to chart the northern extent of the lands of Antarctica. He completed this task, discovered several islands – and only one member of his crew died.

the time – by including fresh limes in their rations. Largely because of this, he lost only one man during his voyages and the practice was gradually adopted on all ships of the Royal Navy (giving rise to the use of the slang term 'limey' to describe an Englishman). On his way home from his third voyage of discovery Cook was killed by Hawaiians in a skirmish when he revisited the island.

Cook, Thomas (1808-92) British pioneer of popular tourism who introduced the concept of organised guided tours for travellers and whose agency developed into a worldwide organisation. Cook became a Baptist missionary in 1828 and 13 years later organised his first railway excursion – from Leicester to Loughborough – for members of his congregation and their friends to attend a temperance rally. The outing was so successful that he was asked to arrange other, similar trips for church groups. In 1855 Cook organised a more ambitious trip – to Paris – and this proved so popular that others followed and the travel industry was born.

Coolidge, Calvin (1872-1933) President of the USA from 1923 to 1929, known for his thrift, caution and honesty at a time when corruption in public life was common. His firm action as governor of Massachusetts in crushing a Boston police strike in 1919 won Coolidge national fame – and the Republican vice-presidency in the following year. On the

death of President Warren HARDING in 1923 Coolidge succeeded him. He failed to curb easy credit, or the market boom which led to the great Wall Street Crash seven months after he left the White House; and he showed no sympathy for the needs of small farmers, miners or textile workers. Nevertheless Coolidge remained popular throughout his administration. He resisted pressures to stand for office again in 1928.

Cooper, Anthony Ashley see
SHAFTESBURY, EARL OF

Copenhagen, Battles of Engagements in 1801 and 1807 between British and Danish forces during the Napoleonic Wars. In the first clash, the neutral league of Russia, Prussia, Denmark and Sweden opposed Britain's claimed right to search ships at sea. Though war was not declared, a British fleet was sent to destroy its Danish counterpart, anchored in Copenhagen. The British divided their ships, Lord Horatio NELSON attacking the Danes from the more protected south and Admiral Hyde Parker attacking from the north. Fixing the telescope to his blind eye,

British men-of-war were hampered at the Battle of Copenhagen by shallows at the entrance to the port, but Nelson ignored signals to break off the action and went on to win a great victory.

Nelson ignored Parker's signal to discontinue action and sank or captured all but three of the Danish ships, forcing an armistice and the league's disbandment. In 1807 news that Denmark was to join Napoleon's CONTINENTAL SYSTEM and declare war on Britain brought a swift response: Britain landed troops outside Copenhagen and, when the Danes refused to surrender, shelled the city.

Copernicus, Nicolaus (1473-1543) Polish physician, mathematician and astronomer whose revolutionary theories on the nature of the Solar System earned him a place as one of the fathers of modern astronomy. Copernicus's medical studies in Krakow included mathematics and astronomy, a subject which came to obsess him. After graduating, the young physician travelled to Italy where he continued his studies of the stars and planets and experimented with the new science of optics, learning to grind and assemble lenses and building his first simple spyglass, although he did not use it to view the heavens. It was left to GALILEO, nearly a century later, to first use a telescope to explore the night skies. Nevertheless, Copernicus's mastery of the science of astronomy was already such that he was invited to lecture on it in Rome.

Returning to Pomerania in 1505, he was appointed physician to his uncle, the Bishop of Ermland, and – although he was not ordained as a priest – was appointed canon of Frombork, from where he continued to study astronomy. Until Copernicus proved otherwise, Western astronomers believed the theory advanced by Ptolemy in AD150 – and based on even earlier Aristotelian principles – that the Sun, stars and planets revolved around the Earth as centre of the Universe. It was an argument which had been made a significant keystone of early Christian theology.

As observation of the movements of stars and planets expanded, medieval astronomers had formulated an elaborate system to explain the workings of the Universe as intricate cosmic clockwork. Copernicus's studies during his first 25 years in Frombork convinced him that the workings of the Universe were simpler and that the Sun was the centre of the Solar System while the Earth – and all the other known planets – orbited it. His 400-page treatise *De Revolutionibus Orbium Coelestium* (*On the Revolution of the Celestial Spheres*) was completed in 1530, but such was the Roman Catholic Church's hostility to his theory that the book was not published until the year of his death. The Church continued to reject his findings for more than a hundred years. He was threatened with the charge of heresy, though never formally accused. Not until late in the 17th century did the Church shift

from its view, after Galileo's observations and Johannes KEPLER's theory that planets moved in elliptical orbits had confirmed Copernicus's theories.

Copper Age Period of history marking man's discovery of metalworking. The use of copper began in Asia around 6000BC, but emerged at different times in different places. Originally pure copper nuggets or pieces smelted into small ingots were beaten into the required shapes, but archaeological evidence shows that by 3500BC copper ore was mined, smelted and cast into clay moulds in parts of the Middle East. Such metalworking coincided with the growth of permanent settlements and led to the emergence of a class of skilled workers, as well as encouraging the spread of trade in both copper and artefacts made from it. In some parts of the world there was no distinct period before the alloying of tin with copper introduced the BRONZE AGE. In other places, such as the Andes, pure copper was used for many centuries. Initially copper's scarcity confined its use to ornaments and rare daggers or flat axes, often chased with gold and occasionally with silver. Later it displaced the use of stone for tools and weapons, until copper was replaced in turn by the introduction of bronze and iron.

Copts Members of the Coptic Orthodox Church of Egypt and Ethiopia, whose first adherents are said to have been converted by St Mark. Their name derives from the Greek *Aegyptios*, 'Egyptians'. From the 2nd century to the 5th century the Copts' Catechetical School of Alexandria, Egypt, where Christianity and the scriptures were taught in a series of questions and answers, was the most important intellectual institution in Christendom. The Copts split from the rest of the Church in 451 over their insistence that Christ has only a single nature, which is part human, part divine. Christian monasticism originated in the Coptic Church of the 3rd century, spreading through North Africa to Rome, and through Palestine to Asia Minor. The Coptic calendar dates from 284 – the Church's 'Year of the Martyrs' commemorating the severest point of the emperor Diocletian's persecution of the Christians. The Church lost many members to Islam after the Muslim conquest of Egypt in 641, but it survived in Ethiopia, where it is still a strong force.

A Coptic homily, penned in early Greek script, lauds the angel Gabriel.

Corday, Charlotte (1768-93) French noblewoman who murdered the revolutionary leader Jean Paul MARAT. Charlotte Corday d'Armont, who had spent a lonely childhood in Normandy, first heard of Marat at meetings of the GIRONDINS. Persuaded that he was a tyrant, Corday decided to assassinate him. After travelling to Paris, on July 13, 1793, Corday stabbed Marat in his bath. At her trial a plea of insanity was overruled and she died on the guillotine.

Corfu incident Naval bombardment and occupation of the Greek island of Corfu by Italian troops in 1923 in which 16 islanders were killed. Three days before the incident an Italian general and four of his staff had been murdered while surveying a disputed stretch of the Greek-Albanian border on behalf of the LEAGUE OF NATIONS. After the bombardment of Corfu, the Italian leader Benito MUSSOLINI demanded a heavy indemnity from Greece, which was ordered to pay 50 million lire when its appeal to the League's Council of Ambassadors failed. The Italian troops withdrew, but the dispute raised doubts about the efficiency of the League, which was set up after the First World War to maintain peace.

Corinth Port on the Isthmus of Corinth in Greece. By the mid 6th century BC Corinth's strategic situation at the crossroads of major trade routes enabled it to become the most prosperous city-state in Greece. It was a prolific exporter of high-quality pottery, and Corinthians established colonies in northwest Greece and in Sicily. Its power remained unchecked until the rise of the Athenian empire, when Corinth pressed Sparta to embark on the PELOPONNESIAN WAR. Corinth joined the Achaean League in 243BC, becoming involved in wars with its former allies Macedonia and Sparta. Sacked and destroyed by Rome in 146BC, it was rebuilt as a Roman colony a century later. In AD521 an earthquake destroyed the city. Today it is a busy port at the head of the Corinth Canal, which was cut through the isthmus in 1893.

Corn Laws British legislation commonly used in the 18th and early 19th centuries to control the supply and price of grain by regulating its import and export. The best known of the Corn Laws was introduced in 1815. After the Napoleonic Wars, Parliament passed a law permitting duty-free imports of foreign wheat only when the price of local wheat reached 80 shillings a quarter (8 bushels) – leading to an increase in the price of bread. In 1828, to reduce the distress this caused to the poor, a sliding

A contemporary satirist saw Richard Cobden of the Anti-Corn Law League as a fast-stepping father hurrying his small son (a reluctant Sir Robert Peel) towards the chosen goal of free trade.

scale of duties was introduced. But in the late 1830s a slump in trade and a succession of bad harvests worsened the situation, strengthening the hand of the Anti-Corn Law League which, founded in Manchester in 1839 by Richard COBDEN and John Bright, organised mass meetings, circulated pamphlets and sought to influence Members of Parliament. The duties were eventually abolished – except for a nominal shilling a quarter – by the Tory government of Sir Robert PEEL in 1846, a decision which split his party and forced his resignation. The repeal of the Corn Laws came to symbolise the success of FREE TRADE and liberal political economy.

Cornwallis, Charles (1738-1805) General, and 1st Marquis of Cornwallis, who commanded the British forces in the southern campaign of 1780 in the American War of Independence. After defeating the Americans at Camden and Guildford Court House, Cornwallis pursued survivors into the interior, exhausting his troops and severing his contact with the commander-in-chief, Sir Henry Clinton. His choice of Yorktown as a winter base for his troops was ill-advised. Isolated from the main British force by George Washington's army and blockaded by the French fleet, Cornwallis was forced to surrender in 1781. As governor-general of India from 1786 to 1793, he defeated TIPU SULTAN, and reformed land tenure. He was viceroy of Ireland from 1798 to 1801 and a negotiator of the Treaty of Amiens in 1802, before returning to India as governor-general in 1804.

Corsica Mediterranean island which has been part of France since 1769 and was the birthplace of Napoleon Bonaparte. Greeks, Etruscans and Carthaginians set up settlements on Corsica before it was conquered by the Romans in 259 BC. As a Roman province, the fourth largest Mediterranean island became a place of political exile. Corsica was conquered by the Vandals in about AD 469, and for the next 600 years the island was controlled by the dominant Mediterranean power of the time, including Byzantines, Goths, Lombards, Franks and Moors. In 1077 the pope assigned Corsica to the bishop of Pisa, but after Genoa's defeat of Pisa in 1284 the island came under Genoese rule and for 156 years its new masters withstood attempts by Aragon to take possession of Corsica. A similar six-year French campaign begun in 1553 was equally unsuccessful and Genoa retained control throughout the 17th century despite widespread local discontent. A mass revolt failed in 1729, but in 1755 Pasquale Paoli established what was effectively an independent Corsican state. In 1768 France bought all rights to the island from Genoa, defeating Paoli's troops in 1769. Corsica then became a French province.

Cortés, Hernán (1485-1547) Nobleman who conquered Mexico. Six years after sailing to Spain's Caribbean colony of Hispaniola as a 19-year-old, Cortés joined a Cuban expedition with Diego Velázquez and amassed considerable wealth from its spoils. Helped by Velázquez, he equipped an expedition to colonise the Mexican mainland, landing at Veracruz in April 1519. His arrival coincided with the predicted return of the Aztec's mythical god-king Quetzalcoatl and Cortés was welcomed in Tenochtitlán, the Aztec capital, by the emperor MONTEZUMA. When the Aztecs began to doubt that he was a god, Cortés seized Montezuma as a hostage and withdrew to Veracruz. He won over a force sent by Velázquez to seize him and, with his reinforcements, returned to Tenochtitlán, where fighting had broken out following a Spanish massacre of a hundred Aztecs. But Montezuma was mortally wounded and, led by the new emperor Cuauhtémoc, the Aztecs drove the Spaniards from Tenochtitlán. The following year Cortés besieged the city, which fell on August 13, 1521, after 93 days, and the Aztec empire was subdued. Cortés's expedition to Honduras in 1524 failed. He spent the rest of his life fighting in Mexico and Spain.

Cosgrave, William (1880-1965) Politician and Irish patriot who took part in the EASTER RISING in 1916 and two years later was elected to the British Parliament as a SINN FEIN member. Cosgrave, who dedicated his political efforts to the cause of Irish independence, became minister for local government in the provisional government of the Dail in 1919. He was president of the executive council of the (Irish) Free State from 1922 to 1932 and in the following year became leader of the opposition in the Dail. He was the father of Liam Cosgrave, who later became prime minister of the Irish Republic.

Cossacks Groups of south Russians noted for their horsemanship. They are descended from refugees who fled Protestant religious persecution in Poland in the 16th century and were joined by serfs who were escaping feudal taxes and other obligations in Poland, Lithuania and Muscovy. Settling around the rivers Don and Dnieper, the Cossacks helped to shape the history of the Ukraine. Frontier hardships encouraged their horsemanship and military prowess, and they developed their own rough democracy. They were semi-autonomous but gave Russia military service, especially against the Turks, and all men between the ages of 16 and 60 were obliged to bear arms. The Cossacks rose against Russia four times in the 17th and 18th centuries before negotiating their own privileges from

The Spanish adventurer Hernán Cortés, mistaken by the Aztecs for a god they expect to return, is welcomed with gifts by the emperor Montezuma in a contemporary reconstruction.

The free-spirited Cossacks, in defiance of a Turkish invasion of the Ukraine, are said to have hired a scribe to write an insulting letter to the Sultan, captured here by Russian artist Ilya Repin.

the tsar; in exchange they provided Russian royalty with an elite cavalry force in which all Cossack men served for 20 years from the age of 18. By the end of the 19th century, the Russian authorities had divided the Cossacks into 11 distinct regional groups, so weakening their strength. Most of these sided with the tsarist forces against the Bolsheviks in the 1918 revolution, and were later gradually incorporated into the Soviet Union.

Costa Rica Central American country first visited by Europeans during Christopher Columbus's fourth voyage to the New World in 1502. Permanent European settlement did not begin until 1564 when colonisers from Nicaragua led by Juan Vásquez de Coronado established an agricultural community on its upland plateau, the Meseta Central. The small Indian population fell victim to disease, leaving the ethnic make-up of the area mostly European. Until 1821, when it joined the independent Mexican empire, Costa Rica formed part of the captaincy-general of Guatemala. Three years later it became part of the Central American Federation, and in 1838 became an independent republic, attracting British and US investment because of its political stability and agricultural potential.

Apart from the two-year dictatorship of Federico Tinoco Granados from 1917, Costa Rica maintained a democratic tradition until the end of the Second World War when left-wing parties emerged. Between 1948 and 1958 socialist presidents tried to disband the army, nationalise banks and curb US investment. Although a new constitution granting universal suffrage had been introduced in 1949, political dissatisfaction spread and by the 1970s this unrest had been aggravated by

economic problems and by the arrival of political fugitives from neighbouring states. President Luis Alberto Monge (1982-6) had to impose severe economic restraint, and in 1987 his successor, President Oscar Arias Sánchez, proposed a peace plan for Central America which won him a Nobel prize but which ran counter to US policy in the region. The US president Ronald Reagan reacted by reducing American aid. The severe economic problems which continued under President Rafael Calderón Fournier led the International Monetary Fund to insist on a tough

austerity programme. This sparked further industrial troubles, and Costa Rica's economy continued to deteriorate. Attempts by the new president José Mariá Figueres to quell unrest after his election in 1994 proved as ineffective as those of his predecessors.

cotton Fibres derived from the seed pods, or bolls, of the tropical and subtropical cotton shrub have been used since prehistoric times to produce a cloth which remains one of the world's staple fabrics. From the earliest days cotton was used for clothing in China, Egypt and India. In India production of the world's finest cotton cloth coincided with the advent of the British Raj, leading to an unprecedented popularity and descriptive names such

as madras, muslin and calico based on their respective origins. Cotton was a major crop in the southern states of colonial America, and the intensive labour needed for its cultivation and harvesting stimulated the growth of the slave trade. For more than 150 years Britain was the world's leading producer of cotton fabrics, and by 1913 Lancashire was home to the largest spinning and weaving industry the world had seen.

Counter Reformation Roman Catholic revival which stemmed from reform movements within the Church from the mid 16th to the mid 17th century. Although the Counter Reformation was independent of the REFORMATION, it became increasingly identified with efforts to 'counter' Protestant developments. Three factors contributed to the Counter Reformation. First, a succession of popes notably more spiritual than their immediate predecessors initiated reforms in the Church's central government. Secondly, new religious orders such as the Oratorians and Jesuits were established and older orders, including the Franciscans, were reformed. Thirdly, Catholic doctrine on most points in dispute with Protestants was defined and clarified by the Council of TRENT, which met between 1545 and 1563. The Council also instituted important moral and disciplinary reforms and improved clerical education by establishing theological colleges, or seminaries. While this created a climate in which Catholic spirituality flourished at a popular level, it also bred an increasingly anti-Protestant mentality. Links with Catholic rulers, such as PHILIP II of Spain, who sought to re-establish Roman Catholicism by force, gave the Counter Reformation a political edge. The permanent division between Catholics and Protestants was effectively recognised when in 1648 the Treaty of WESTPHALIA ended the Thirty Years' War.

country houses In the 18th and 19th centuries large dwellings built in the grand manner and standing in their own parkland came to symbolise the new riches generated by trade, banking or industry. However, they had been built in England by the wealthy from the 16th century onwards, when the stability of the Tudor period allowed people to plan homes for comfort rather than defence. Although some of the best-known country houses, such as Longleat in Wiltshire and Hardwicke Hall in Derbyshire, date from the 16th century, and Hatfield House in Hertfordshire from the early 17th century, the heyday of country-house building in England was in the 18th century. In this period noble families recovered their estates after the Restoration, increased their income from agricultural land by ENCLOSURES and the development of mineral resources, and built

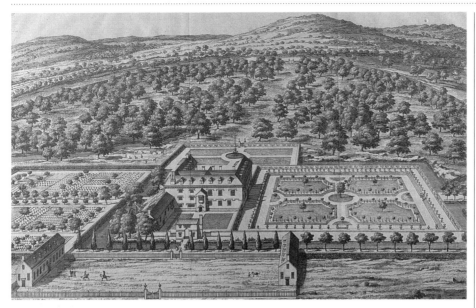

Hardwicke Park Court, in Gloucestershire, surrounded by its formally laid-out gardens, was typical of the gracious country homes built by wealthy landowners in the 17th and 18th centuries.

magnificent residences to display collections of paintings, silver and furniture. Many of these – as well as Greek and Roman statuary which fashionably adorned many country house gardens – were acquired on the GRAND TOURS of Europe (see feature, page 268) by wealthy young men as part of their education.

Courtrai, Battle of Clash between French and Flemish forces on July 11, 1302, sometimes referred to as the 'Battle of the Golden Spurs'. When Philip IV of France invaded Flanders, the burghers of Courtrai defeated his force, including an unusually large number of the French nobility. To celebrate their victory the burghers hung the nobles' spurs in the churches of nearby Bruges. The battle was one of France's most significant 14th-century defeats, but was avenged when Charles VI of France sacked Courtrai in 1382.

Covenanters Scots who opposed the episcopal hierarchy of Charles I of England and instead subscribed to a National Covenant drawn up in 1638. Although the document was also known as the 'Noblemen's Covenant', Covenanters were drawn from almost every part of Scotland and from every level of society. They swore to resist 'episcopal' changes, and when Charles went ahead with them, the Covenanters set up a full PRESBYTERIAN system which they defended in the Bishops' Wars. Hoping to impose the Presbyterian system on England, in 1643 they drew up the Solemn League and Covenant with the LONG PARLIAMENT, but were disappointed. Charles II signed the Covenant in 1650, but abjured it ten years later when, at his RESTORATION, he condemned his oath as unlawful. When the authority of the bishops was re-established in

Scotland in 1661 the Covenanters were discriminated against until the establishment of the Presbyterian Church of Scotland in 1690.

Coverdale, Miles (1488-1568) English priest and scholar said to be the author of the 'Great Bible' commissioned in 1539 by Thomas CROMWELL, who ordered it to be placed in all parish churches. As a priest Coverdale was strongly influenced by William TYNDALE, whose Protestant views he came to share. Coverdale's translation of the psalms is still used in the Book of Common Prayer and his first translation of the Bible was printed in Zurich in 1535 – leading to the commission from Cromwell. Appointed bishop of Exeter in 1551, Coverdale fled abroad during the reign of Mary I and may have contributed to the Geneva Bible of 1560.

cowboy The popular term for a cattle herder on the Great Plains of the USA was originally used to describe a member of the lawless, pro-British gangs that operated in neutral Westchester County in New York state during the American War of Independence. The later cowboys – many of whom were Black or Mexican – became part of the lore of the American West where they rounded up cattle and, dividing them into herds about 2500 strong, drove them hundreds of miles to the nearest railheads. About a dozen cowboys accompanied each herd, serving a cattle industry which spread across the Great Plains from Texas to Canada and westward to the Rocky Mountains. As ranchers' fences encroached on the open ranges, and railway expansion made trail-driving uneconomical, cowboys adapted to a more settled existence.

Cranmer, Thomas (1489-1556) English cleric and a major architect of the reformed Church of England who, as Archbishop of Canterbury, annulled HENRY VIII's marriages to Catherine of Aragon, Anne Boleyn and Anne of Cleves. Cranmer had served Henry as a diplomat, but in 1532 the king made him archbishop to overcome papal rulings on Henry's first marriage. During EDWARD VI's reign, Cranmer was chiefly responsible for liturgical reform, including the first and second Books of Common Prayer, in 1549 and 1552, and the Forty-Two Articles of 1553. His support for Lady Jane GREY's succession in 1553 led to his initial trial for high treason on Mary I's accession and to a second trial for heresy. He was burnt at the stake in Oxford.

Crassus, Marcus Licinius (c.115-53BC) Roman general who sacked Jerusalem. With Gnaeus POMPEY and Julius CAESAR, Crassus was a member of the 'First Triumvirate' that dominated Roman politics from 59 to 53 BC. As a young man he joined Lucius SULLA in his march on Rome, commanding the future consul's troops at the battle of the Colline Gate in November 82. His rewards from Sulla, invested in property speculation, eventually made Crassus one of the richest men in Rome. After he and Pompey defeated SPARTACUS, the leader of a slave revolt, in 71 both men were elected consuls. Rivals for 12 years in office, in 59 the two nevertheless formed an

After roping a calf, cowboys of the Great Plains watch one of their companions check its brand. By the 1880s fences and the advent of railways had ended mass cattle drives across the prairie.

unofficial triumvirate with Caesar. Given the governorship of Syria for a five-year term in 55, Crassus's greed drove him to sack Jerusalem and then to attack the Parthians who defeated his army at Carrhae, where he was captured and executed.

Crazy Horse (c.1842-77) Sioux chief of the Ogala, who opposed White infiltration into the mineral-rich Black Hills and defeated General George CUSTER at Little Bighorn in 1876. Following the first military confrontation between the Sioux and Whites in 1854, Crazy Horse opposed plans to settle Native Americans on reservations and headed the alliance that defeated both General George Crook on the Rosebud River and, later, Custer. Along with his followers, Crazy Horse was starved into surrendering in May 1877. Later he was imprisoned, after rumours that he planned a revolt. He was stabbed to death, allegedly while trying to escape.

Crécy, Battle of (August 26, 1346) English victory in northern France early in the Hundred Years' War. Some historians claim that when the raiding army of England's Edward III was trapped outside Crécy by a larger French force under Philip VI, Edward's archers dug pits to impede advancing cavalry while the English knights, led by Edward the BLACK PRINCE, dismounted and formed three supporting divisions. Those of France's crossbowmen not cut down by English arrows died under the charging French knights, whose horses were shot from under them by English longbowmen. Edward lost only 40 men, while the cream of France's nobility was among its 1500 dead. One of these was the blind Count of Luxembourg, who had ordered his men to lead him into the thick of battle.

Led by Crazy Horse in his protective war paint, victorious Ogala braves race past the corpses of General Custer's defeated cavalrymen in this Sioux illustration of the Battle of the Little Bighorn.

The Battle of Crécy in 1346 as imagined by a French artist in the *Chronique D'Angleterre*, published a century after the English victory.

Creole Native-born White in Spanish colonial America. Although looked down on by the *peninsulares*, or Whites born in Spain, the Creoles soon became a powerful faction in Spain's developing territories, accruing much of the wealth and occupying most of the lower levels of bureaucracy. But few achieved high rank in either the State or the Church and their resentment was a cause of the local wars of independence – in which Creoles formed the bulk of the leadership.

Crete Largest of the Greek islands and legendary birthplace of Zeus and the home of the Minotaur. As the site of the MINOAN civilisation centred on KNOSSOS and Phaestos, which flourished from about 3000 to 1500 BC, Crete contributed significantly to the development of Bronze Age Greek art. Its position on sea routes to Egypt, the Levant and Cyprus gave it an important role in the development of trade and the movement of skills and knowledge in the eastern Mediterranean. By the 3rd century BC, the island was a notorious pirate base protected and encouraged by Philip V of Macedonia. When in 68-67 the pirates supported the Pontian king MITHRIDATES in his war with Rome, Pompey's Roman forces invaded Crete, destroyed Knossos, and established the island as a Roman province.

After Roman and Byzantine rule, Crete spent almost 500 years under Arab control before its recapture by the Byzantines in AD 960-1. Sold to Venice in 1210, it became a major source of grain and wood for the republic until its capture by the Turks in 1669. Crete's long series of unsuccessful revolts against its Turkish overlords culminated in a call for *enosis*, or union with Greece. But when a Greek force landed on the island in 1897, Europe's 'great powers' – Britain, France,

Russia and Germany – gave the island only partial independence. A year later Turkish troops were withdrawn, but unrest continued until, in 1913, Crete finally became part of Greece under a treaty signed in London by Greece and Turkey.

Crimea Peninsula on the northern shore of the Black Sea and main battleground of the CRIMEAN WAR. Colonised by the Greeks in the 6th century BC, the Crimea became a Roman protectorate in the 1st century AD. On the route taken by invaders from the north and the east, the Crimea fell to Ostrogoths, Huns and other tribes until it came under partial Byzantine control from the 6th to the 12th century. The 13th century saw it pillaged by Mongols, while a Tatar khanate was absorbed by the Ottoman Empire in the late 15th century. Russia annexed the Crimea in 1783.

Crimean War (1853-6) War in which Russia fought the combined forces of Turkey, Britain, France and Piedmont and in which Florence NIGHTINGALE established nursing as a profession. War became inevitable when Russia failed to obtain equal rights with France in a dispute over the Palestinian holy places and occupied part of the Ottoman Empire. At a conference to forestall Russian expansion in the Black Sea area and to protect trade routes, Turkey's allies pressed it to placate Russia, but Turkey refused and declared war in October 1853.

In November the Russians destroyed the Turkish fleet at Sinope on the Black Sea, forcing Britain and France to declare war in March 1854. Austria remained neutral, but by mobilising its army forced Russia to evacuate Wallachia and Moldavia. The Allied force led by Lord Raglan, which reached the Crimea in

In the early stages of the Crimean War British troops were poorly fed and inadequately equipped. Later, during a lull in fighting, men from the 8th Hussars draw their rations from a field kitchen.

August 1854, was ill-prepared, but although ravaged by cholera it defeated the Russian army at the battle of the Alma River on September 20, 1854, and laid siege to the armed fort of SEVASTOPOL. Russian attempts to relieve the fort were thwarted by the British defence of the Inkerman ridge, and the tsar's forces retreated after a bloody battle. A winter of siege warfare followed the next Anglo-Russian clash at the Battle of BALAKLAVA, site of the charge of the Light Brigade. The Allied armies were hampered by a lack of fuel, clothing and supplies, and a high death rate among the wounded. Public criticism in Britain was increased by articles in *The Times* written by W.H. Russell, the first war correspondent to use the telegraph to transmit his reports. As a result, Florence Nightingale obtained permission to take nurses to the Crimea, eventually reducing hospital mortality among the Allied wounded from 42 per cent to 2 per cent. When Sevastopol fell, in September 1855, the new Russian tsar, ALEXANDER II, had begun to sue for the peace which was formalised at the Congress of Paris in 1856.

Cripps, Sir Stafford (1889-1952) British politician responsible for the austerity programme introduced after the Second World War. Cripps was called to the Bar in 1913, becoming the youngest barrister in England. He was appointed solicitor general in 1930 and entered Parliament as a Labour member the following year, but refused to serve in Ramsay MACDONALD's coalition government, aligning himself instead with the party's hard left. Cripps was expelled from the Labour Party in 1939 when he advocated the formation of a 'Popular Front' to face the threat of war. During the Second World War Cripps was ambassador to Moscow from 1940 to 1942 and then became minister for aircraft production until the war's end. Between 1945 and 1950 he served successively as president of the Board of Trade and as chancellor of the exchequer in Clement ATTLEE's government, and was responsible for its policy of austerity – continued rationing and new controls intended to adjust Britain to its weakened, postwar economy.

Croatia Balkan state, formerly a region of Yugoslavia, populated mainly by Slavs. Supposedly the Illyria of Shakespeare's *Twelfth Night* – under Roman occupation it was known as the province of Illyricum – Croatia suffered a series of invasions by barbaric tribes from the east and north before being conquered by Charlemagne in the 9th century. When the Carolingian Empire collapsed, the first independent Croatian nation soon fell prey to power struggles between Hungary, Venice and the Byzantine Empire, from which Hungary emerged victorious. Croatia was subject to Hungarian rule until 1301 when the House of Anjou took control for 80 years, after which followed more than a century of civil war. The Battle of Mohács in 1526 brought most of the country into the Ottoman Empire, and the remainder was governed by the Habsburgs. The first stirrings of a renewed Croatian nationalism began between 1809 and 1813 when the country was part of Napoleon's Illyrian province. Resistance to both Habsburg imperialism and Hungarian nationalism boiled over in 1848, and a successful revolution reasserted Croatian independence, ended serfdom and proclaimed all citizens equal. A year later, however, Austria claimed Croatia as Austrian crown land; and in 1868, as part of the newly established Austro-Hungarian empire, it became the autonomous Hungarian Crownland of Croatia-Slovenia – with the exception of the Dalmatian coastline, which remained an Austrian province.

Hungarian attempts to crush Croatian nationalism failed, and after the defeat of Austria-Hungary in the First World War, an independent Croatia was again proclaimed in October 1918. The new state joined the Kingdom of the Serbs, Croats and Slovenes in 1921, which was later renamed Yugoslavia. But the Croats resented what they saw as Serb domination and centralisation. After Germany's Second World War invasion of the Balkans, and with Croatia's leadership predominantly pro-Nazi, in 1941 the country again became independent under the fascist Ante Pavelić, whose brutal government provoked guerrilla resistance. Croatia joined the new Federal Republic of Yugoslavia in 1945, but an underground movement for independence continued, surfacing in the late 1980s.

A noncommunist government was formed in May 1990 and by the end of the year anti-Serbian partisans attacked enclaves of Serbian residents, who were then supported by units of the Serbian-dominated Yugoslav army. A confused military situation deteriorated into civil war and in April 1992 a UN Protection Force was established in the Serb-populated areas, Croatia having been recognised as independent by the European Community. The governments of Croatia, Serbia and Bosnia accepted a US-brokered peace plan for the region in 1995, but tension continues.

Crockett, Davy (1786-1836) US pioneer, adventurer and folk hero. As a hunter and frontiersman, Crockett fought against the Creek Indians in Andrew Jackson's campaign of 1814, going on to serve two terms in the state legislature. When it was jokingly proposed that he should stand in elections for Congress, Crockett took the suggestion seriously and served three terms, initially as a Jacksonian Democrat. He cultivated a backwoods manner and this, combined with his earthy humour and frontier style of dress – which included a 'coonskin' hat and an elaborate beaded waistcoat – won Crockett fame and popularity. Crockett broke with Jackson over the rights of western Tennessee squatters, whom he represented, and defected to the Whigs. The move ended his political career

> **DID YOU KNOW?**
>
> *Though Croats and Serbs speak the same Serbo-Croat language, the Roman Catholic Croats use the Latin alphabet and the Orthodox Serbs use Cyrillic script.*

Davy Crockett won votes by cultivating a 'frontiersman' style, shown by his beaded waistcoat.

and Crockett returned to the frontier. A keen supporter of Texan independence, Crockett was among the defenders who died when, after a long siege, Fort ALAMO fell to a large Mexican army force.

Croesus (died c.546 BC) King of Lydia from 560 BC until his death, whose wealth and power were legendary. His expansion of his kingdom gained him control of all the Greek cities on the coast of Asia Minor. But he was defeated by Cyrus the Great, and Lydia became part of the Persian empire.

Cromer, Evelyn Baring, 1st Earl of (1841-1917) British statesman, colonial administrator and diplomat. Though trained as a soldier, in 1879 Cromer followed a four-year term as secretary to his cousin the viceroy of India with a posting to Egypt where, as commissioner of debt, he rescued the country from near bankruptcy. After another spell in India, in 1883 Cromer became British agent and consul general in Egypt when Britain occupied the country after the battle of Tel-el-Kebir. His ability and imposing personality made Cromer the effective ruler of Egypt until he retired in 1907.

Cromwell, Oliver (1599-1658) English statesman and general who, as Lord Protector of the Commonwealth, was sole ruler of England from 1653 until his death. As an opposition member of the Long Parliament Cromwell rose to prominence during the ENGLISH CIVIL WAR as a Roundhead military leader. His organisational skills and mastery of cavalry tactics led to the foundation in 1644 of the NEW MODEL ARMY. Five years later Cromwell led the group which called for the execution of Charles I, and in the ensuing

Commonwealth became chairman of the Council of State. He brutally suppressed resistance to the regime in Ireland, Scotland and, later, in England. He was also widely blamed for the unpopular policies of the RUMP PARLIAMENT which he expelled in April 1653 to become Lord Protector ruling in its stead. Although his Protectorate – based on an Instrument of Government and upheld by the rule of major-generals in the counties – was unpopular, the new Protectorate Parliament, which had been elected in 1654, offered him the crown in 1657. He refused but spent the rest of his life trying in vain to give constitutional permanence to his military regime.

Cromwell, Richard (1626-1712) Son of Oliver Cromwell, whom he succeeded as Lord Protector of England from 1658 to 1659. More interested in country life than in politics, Cromwell retired after a few months, and 18 months after his father's death a section of the army under General George MONCK called for free elections. When Charles II was recalled from exile Cromwell fled to the Continent, but returned in about 1689 to live quietly in Hampshire.

Cromwell, Thomas (1485-1540) English statesman who organised Henry VIII's break with Rome. As a young man Cromwell appears to have travelled widely, acquiring skills in commerce, law, languages and mercenary warfare before gaining the patronage of Thomas WOLSEY in 1520. By 1529, when Wolsey was discredited, Cromwell had attracted Henry's attention and within two years had joined the inner royal council. From 1533 to 1540 he was the king's chief minister, successively appointed chancellor of the exchequer in 1533, principal secretary of state a year later, vicar-general in 1535 and lord privy seal and Lord Cromwell of Wimbledon in the following year. Cromwell used his administrative abilities to arrange Henry's divorce from Catherine of Aragon, the break with the pope and the Roman Catholic Church, and the subsequent Dissolution of the Monasteries, which earned him the nickname 'Hammer of the Monks'. It was his Protestant sympathies that led to the choice of ANNE OF CLEVES as the king's fourth wife. But this cost him Henry's favour

Oliver Cromwell applied the skilled discipline of his military experience to the iron rule he imposed in government.

and opened a way for the HOWARDS to contrive his execution for treason without a hearing soon after he had been made Earl of Essex.

crop rotation Agricultural system in which different crops are grown in a successive pattern to avoid exhausting the soil in which they are cultivated and to limit the possible spread of disease. Some form of crop rotation was probably practised by the earliest agriculturists. The method of husbandry in which fields were left fallow every three years was widespread in medieval Europe, but systematic crop rotation based on a more scientific approach began only with the agrarian revolution of the 18th century. The British landowner Viscount Townshend, who retired to his family's Norfolk estates in 1730, introduced the turnip as winter fodder for his cattle, so lessening the need for pasturage. He followed this with four-stage rotation – a root crop, followed by barley, clover pasture and oats or wheat. Elsewhere six-stage rotation was practised. Townshend's system was adopted and improved on by Thomas COKE, who also encouraged his tenants to follow it.

crucifixion Early form of capital punishment used by the Persians, Carthaginians and Romans, usually for slaves and others with no civil rights. The victim was nailed or roped to a crossbar and then hoisted onto an upright to form a 'T' or cross. Crucifixion was particularly abhorrent to the Jews as it was a punishment forbidden by the Mosaic law. Though the manner of Christ's death led his followers to adopt the crucifix as a symbol, they did so only after their persecution ended.

Crusades Military expeditions undertaken between the 11th and 13th centuries, initially intended to force Muslims from the holy places of Palestine and reimpose Christian rule, but later becoming the pretext for pillage and plunder. The First Crusade (1095-9) was called by Pope Urban II when the power struggle between the Seljuk Turks and the Byzantines halted all pilgrimages to Palestine. Crusaders were promised forgiveness of their sins. They invaded Jerusalem in 1099, massacred its inhabitants and established a Christian realm ruled by Godfrey of Bouillon. The next Crusade (1147-9) did little more than sour relations between the existing Crusader kingdom, its Byzantine neighbours and nearby

171

The savagery of the Crusades is reflected in a French illustration from 1490. Richard I looks on as an executioner prepares to behead one of hundreds of Saracens captured in the Third Crusade.

Muslim rulers. Prompted by SALADIN's capture of Jerusalem in 1187, the Third Crusade (1189-92) could only regain Acre. Ten years later the Fourth Crusade (1202-4) did not even reach the Holy Land. Enticed by Venetian promises of riches, the fleet diverted first to the Dalmatian coast and then to the Christian city of Constantinople, which the Crusaders sacked and plundered in 1204. The Byzantine territories which they captured were held for 57 years, until Emperor Michael VIII retook the city. Later expeditions to North Africa achieved little, and the fall of Acre in 1291 brought Crusader presence in the Levant to an end.

Throughout the Crusades the papacy was unable to control the forces, and rabble armies slaughtered Jews and Christians as they crossed Europe on the way to the Holy Land. Only the Sixth Crusade (1228-9) was untarnished by greed and brutality. Nevertheless, the Crusades attracted leaders such as England's RICHARD I and France's Louis IX, and influenced European CHIVALRY and literature. They intensified hostility between Christianity and Islam, but they also stimulated contacts which brought aspects of Arab learning and architecture to Europe.

Cuauhtémoc (c.1495-1525) Last Aztec emperor, who succeeded to the throne in 1520 as Hernán CORTÉS prepared for the siege of the empire's capital, Tenochtitlán. Cuauhtémoc defended the city valiantly, but his forces were worn down by illness and hunger as much as by the attacks of Cortés's men. After ten weeks the Spaniards took the last of the city's strongpoints. The emperor was captured and tortured in an attempt to force him to reveal the location of treasure which the Spaniards believed he had hidden. He survived, but four years later was executed, accused of plotting to kill Cortés and others.

Cuba Large Caribbean island which since 1959 has been a socialist regime. Christopher Columbus visited Cuba in 1492, but a further 16 years passed before Spanish navigators sailed round it and realised that it was an island. Settlement began in 1511 with the establishment of Havana and several other towns. The colonists enslaved the indigenous Arawak Indians, who had reached the island from the South American mainland about 2500 years earlier, and exploitation and European-introduced diseases soon drastically reduced their numbers. From 1526 African slaves were imported to cultivate the sugar and tobacco plantations – which remain the island's two major sources of export earnings – and by the end of the century the Arawaks were almost extinct. Although importation of slaves ended in 1865, slavery was not abolished on the island until 1886. Britain captured Cuba in 1762 during its war with Spain, but within a year returned it in exchange for Florida. Spanish rule continued until 1898 when the USA intervened in Cuba's second war of independence. Earlier US attempts to acquire the island – which by then was producing a third of the world's sugar – had failed. But in 1899 Cuba was occupied by US troops, who remained on the island until the proclamation in 1902 of a republic under US 'protection'. Cuba was ruled by a series of corrupt governments supported by the USA, and during the brutal regime of Gerardo Machado, from 1925 to 1933, the first of several abortive revolutions erupted. In 1956 Fidel CASTRO initiated a guerrilla war which led to the overthrow of the US-supported regime of Fulgencio BATISTA.

Castro set up a socialist regime in 1959 which declared itself communist in 1961 after the US placed an embargo on trade with Cuba. Castro seized US land and industries and allied himself with the Soviet Union. The US responded by cutting off diplomatic relations and backing the abortive BAY OF PIGS invasion by Cuban exiles. The following year Castro's regime survived the CUBAN MISSILE CRISIS.

Initial hopes of diversification and industrialisation were not realised, and Cuba had to rely on the export of sugar as well as on substantial financial aid from the Soviet Union. Castro's one-party regime greatly improved Cuba's public health, education and housing, but its human rights record remained poor. Frustrations with the regime led to an exodus of 125 000 Cubans in 1980. When COMECON and the Soviet Union collapsed in 1990 and 1991 the Cuban government survived in spite of an ever-weakening economy. In October 1991 the fourth Congress of the Cuban Communist Party endorsed the policy of centralised control, but an opposition group, the Cuban Democratic Convergence emerged. Attempts to improve US-Cuban relations foundered on the question of the continuing flight of refugees from the island to the US mainland – often in hazardous conditions and in unseaworthy craft. In 1996 relations between the two countries worsened when Cuba shot down two US-based planes which were allegedly being used to spot refugees.

Cuban Missile Crisis International incident which in 1962 brought the USA and the Soviet Union to the brink of nuclear war. The crisis developed when US leaders learned that Soviet nuclear missiles capable of targeting the USA were being secretly installed in bases in Cuba. President J.F. KENNEDY ordered a blockade against Soviet military shipments to

> **DID YOU KNOW?**
>
> *Although opposed to the Cuban regime since 1959, the USA maintains a large naval base on the island at Guantanamo, and used ships from there in 1962 to stop Soviet arms shipments.*

Children of God

In 1212 groups of young people in France and Germany gathered to march to the Holy Land, their aim nothing less than to free Jerusalem from the Muslims.

Few if any of the disorganised rabble of young peasants who set out for the Holy Land in 1212 ever reached it. Yet the idea of an uprising of the poor inspired by religious devotion to capture Jerusalem caught the contemporary imagination. A chronicler described what became known as the Children's Crusade as 'a miraculous affair...nothing of the sort has ever been heard of in the world'.

Wild tales began to circulate about their fate. Some were supposed to have made their way to Marseilles, where unscrupulous merchants offered them free passage to the East. Seven large boats set out; two were wrecked and the other five sailed to Alexandria where the children were sold into slavery – ending their days at the court of the caliph of Baghdad.

THE PURITY OF THE POOR

The background to these events lay in the recent history of the Crusades and the popular piety of the time. In 1187 Saladin had captured Jerusalem and, in spite of the endeavours of Richard the Lionheart, the Third Crusade had made little progress in the recovery of the Holy Land. In 1204 the Fourth Crusade sacked the Christian city of Constantinople rather than fighting the Muslims. The cause of these failures was believed to be the wealth and vanity of the princes who had led the expeditions. By contrast the poor, especially children, were regarded as pure. Support for the concept of the Crusades remained strong: in 1212 the papacy preached campaigns against

the Muslims in Spain and the heretic Cathars of southern France. This combination of crusading enthusiasm and the idea that the poor were God's chosen people provided the inspiration for the Children's Crusade.

The crusade had two elements. In France a young shepherd, Stephen, from Cloyes in the Ile de France, gave bread to a poor pilgrim whom he identified as Christ. In return for his hospitality, the pilgrim gave Stephen letters to present to Philip II of France. Thousands of shepherds gathered around Stephen and they marched to St Denis near Paris, where miracles are said to have taken place. It is possible that in this fevered atmosphere they hoped that the king would lead a new crusade, but instead he instructed the shepherds to return home.

The German part of the children's crusade was led by a young man called Nicholas of Cologne, who felt directed by God to gather people together to recapture Jerusalem. Groups of young people assembled, some no more than six years old. They were poorly equipped and lacked the weapons and horses for a military expedition. Most were no more than simple labourers inspired by faith and the chance of adventure, an escape from humdrum lives on the fields of Europe. Their parents were aghast: who would bring in the crops or care for the animals? Some churchmen were also annoyed: crusades had been authorised by the pope, yet here the masses were acting for themselves.

A romanticised 19th-century view of the crusade recalls a Sunday school outing. The reality was grimmer.

Thousands of children set out on the Children's Crusades, but never achieved their aim of recovering the Holy Land.

Nicholas led his supporters through southern Germany into Italy. The crossing of the Alps in one of the hottest summers of the age proved gruelling: the crusade started to disperse as some realised the impracticality of their aim and others found the going simply too tough. Several thousand followers remained with Nicholas and are known to have reached Genoa on August 25, 1212. It is not clear what happened next. Some may have sailed to the East, but the majority melted away, returning northwards to be ridiculed for their apparent foolishness.

For such an inconclusive event the Children's Crusade left a remarkably strong impression on medieval society. Even today the children's adventure remains a potent symbol of popular, if misguided, religious enthusiasm.

The artist commemorating the English victory at Culloden chose to ignore the bloody and brutal nature of the battle.

Cuba and demanded that Russia withdraw the weapons and close its bases. The forces of both superpowers were placed on full alert, and the danger of war loomed as Soviet merchant ships thought to be carrying missiles approached the island. When they were within 500 miles (800 km), President KHRUSHCHEV recalled the Soviet ships and Russia agreed to dismantle the rocket bases in return for a US pledge not to attack Cuba. The crisis led to the establishment in 1963 of the 'hot line' – a direct, emergency communications link between the president of the USA and the president of the Soviet Union.

Culloden, Battle of Rout by English and lowland Scots troops of the JACOBITE forces of Bonnie Prince Charlie (Charles Edward Stuart) which ended the FORTY-FIVE rebellion and destroyed Jacobite hopes of returning a Stuart to the Scottish throne. On April 16, 1746, on a bleak moor to the east of Inverness, the Young Pretender's enthusiastic amateur army was trounced by professional soldiers led by the Duke of CUMBERLAND. After the battle, fought in a storm, Cumberland's men hunted down and killed Jacobite survivors as well as slaughtering prisoners and the wounded.

Culpeper's Rebellion (1677) Popular uprising by American colonists against the syndicate which owned and administered the new colony of North Carolina. Encouraged by the example a year earlier of a similar uprising in Virginia, local colonists rebelled when the owners of North Carolina attempted to enforce the NAVIGATION ACTS on tobacco and to collect land taxes. An 18-strong 'parliament' proclaimed one of the ringleaders, John Culpeper, governor. He ruled until 1679, when he was replaced by a syndicate nominee. Further rebellions continued in North Carolina until 1714.

Cultural Revolution (1966-76) Chaotic decade of political upheaval in China caused by a factional dispute over the future of Chinese socialism. In the mid 1960s thinly veiled criticisms of MAO ZE-DONG's ideology prompted his sharp retaliation. When he could not counter the threat from pro-Soviet party pragmatists and bureaucratic modernisers by conventional political means, Mao enlisted discontented students and young workers as his RED GUARDS. These attacked local and central party officials – often with army backing – and replaced them with Mao's supporters. Academics and intellectuals were particular targets. They were frequently physically ill-treated and all were forced to undergo humiliating 're-education' programmes which involved abuse, menial labour and public 'confession' of imaginary crimes or doctrinal errors. Liu Shaoqi, who as state chairman since 1959 had been Mao's heir-apparent, lost all his official posts and Lin Biao became the designated successor. In the upheaval much of China's cultural heritage was destroyed. The most violent phase of the Cultural Revolution ended with the Ninth Party Congress in 1969, but its radical policies continued until Mao's death in 1976.

Cumberland, William, Duke of (1721-65) British army commander who defeated the Jacobites at CULLODEN in 1746. The second son of George II, Cumberland was only 24 when he was appointed captain-general of the British army in 1745. A year later, the slaughter at Culloden earned him the nickname of 'Butcher'. In the Seven Years' War against France, Cumberland lost the Battle of Hastenbeck in 1757 and later was forced to withdraw his troops from Hanover and Germany. Cumberland's political influence with his father led to the collapse in 1757 of the wartime coalition dominated by William Pitt, but after his father's death his influence waned. Disgruntled Whig politicians dismissed by his nephew George III looked to Cumberland for support at court, but he died soon after their leader, the Marquis of Rockingham, became prime minister.

Cunard, Sir Samuel (1787-1865) Canadian ship-owner and founder of the Cunard Line. As a successful merchant in Nova Scotia, in 1839 Cunard and his partners George Burns and David MacIver bid successfully for a British Government subsidy to run a steam mail-packet service between North America and the UK. This grew to become the British and North American Royal Mail Steam Packet Company – the shipping line which was later to bear his name.

cuneiform Early form of WRITING developed by the Sumerians in Mesopotamia around 3000 BC. Using split reeds on soft clay, free-hand signs were impressed in groups to represent concepts and words as well as objects. Later this cuneiform, or 'wedge-shaped', script was adapted to more elaborate languages, with signs serving many different purposes. Practice tablets and glossaries that have survived show that long training was needed to master the scripts. In Mesopotamia cuneiform was used for some purposes as late as the 2nd century BC, many centuries after the development of the Phoenician alphabet.

Throughout China's Cultural Revolution the philosophy outlined in Chairman Mao's 'Little Red Book' offered guidance to young soldiers charged with purging bureaucrats and intellectuals.

Cunobelinus King of the Belgic Catuvellauni in England from around AD5 to 40, who is also known as Cymbeline. From his base at Verulamium, the site of modern-day St Albans, Cunobelinus captured Camulodunum (Colchester) and went on to gain control of much of south-east England.

Curie, Marie (1867-1934) Polish-born physicist who, with her husband Pierre, discovered radium and radioactivity. After studying at the 'free university' for Polish women workers in Warsaw, Curie enrolled to study physics at the Sorbonne in Paris in 1891 and married Pierre four years later. Together, in 1898, they discovered polonium – named by Curie for her native land – and radium. For this and the discovery of radiation they shared the Nobel prize for physics in 1903.

After Pierre's death in a road accident three years later, Curie continued her researches. She was appointed to her late husband's chair of physics at the Sorbonne, becoming the first woman to teach there, and won a Nobel prize for chemistry in 1911, becoming the first scientist to win two Nobel prizes. Curie studied the applications of radioactivity in medicine and pioneered mobile X-ray units, heading the French radiological service during the First World War. Afterwards she worked at the newly established Radium Institute, which became the hub of international research into nuclear physics. She died from leukaemia caused by exposure to radiation.

Curragh Incident Demand in March 1914 by the commander of the British military base on the Curragh plain near Dublin that he and his officers should not be used to force Ulster Protestants to accept Home Rule. On the instructions of Colonel John Seely, the secretary of state for war, the officers were told that those with Ulster connections could resign or 'disappear'. Seely's unilateral decision was seen as a threat to army discipline and he was forced to resign.

Curtin, John Joseph (1885-1945) Australia's Labour prime minister throughout most of the Second World War. Elected to the House of Representatives in 1928, Curtin led the Opposition from 1935 until 1941 when he became prime minister. As such he organised Australia's defences in collaboration with US forces and encouraged closer wartime cooperation within the British Commonwealth. Although he opposed conscription during the First World War, he did introduce limited conscription for active service overseas.

Curzon, George (1859-1925) British statesman and viceroy of India from 1899 to 1905. As viceroy Curzon reformed administration, education and currency, but he also

Lord Curzon was still popular as India's viceroy when a Bombay caricaturist portrayed him as Krishna dancing on the serpent Shesha.

provoked Hindu resentment when in 1901 he established the North-West Frontier province and partitioned Bengal – seen by the Hindus as pro-Muslim measures. Curzon, who had been made 1st Marquis Curzon of Kedleston, resigned in 1905 as a result of a bitter dispute with Lord Kitchener, then commanding the Indian army. David Lloyd George included Curzon in his coalition war Cabinet from 1916 to 1918, and made him foreign secretary a year later. In this capacity Curzon gave his name to the frontier line between Poland and Russia proposed by Lloyd George in 1920, which in 1939 became the boundary between the Soviet and German areas of occupied Poland, and in 1945 became the definitive frontier between Poland and Russia. In 1923 he hoped to become prime minister but intrigue robbed him of the job, which went to Stanley Baldwin.

Custer, George Armstrong (1839-76) US soldier who was killed – along with the 212 soldiers in his force – at the Battle of the Little Bighorn, popularly known as 'Custer's Last Stand'. After serving in the American Civil War, in which he gained a reputation for personal courage, in 1874 General Custer led an expedition to look for gold in South Dakota. Although a treaty had established the area as a sacred hunting-ground for the Sioux and Cheyenne, after the discovery of gold these peoples were ordered to move to a reservation. Those who had not left the area by January 1, 1876, were declared hostile. In June, as part of an expedition to round

them up, Custer went ahead of the main force towards Little Bighorn and, encountering a war party led by the Sioux chief Crazy Horse, decided to attack. Underestimating the size of the war party, Custer and his men were forced onto the defensive. They occupied a hill, but were wiped out by some 3500 Plains Indians.

customs and excise Duties charged on goods to raise revenue for governments. Customs charges were levied by the authorities from ancient times, usually for the use of transport facilities for trade, such as ports, roads and bridges and even market stalls. Later these tariffs were imposed on specific commodities. In England, Edward I was the first ruler to add to the royal coffers in this way by imposing duties on wool and leather. His son Edward II introduced TUNNAGE and POUNDAGE, thus setting a precedent for impositions – added levies made by monarchs without Parliament's consent.

In Holland duties on imports were introduced in the late 16th century and similar levies were soon introduced in Britain, where for more than a century royal impositions were a source of friction between Crown and State. Charles I raised money in this way and from monopolies until these were abolished by the LONG PARLIAMENT in 1643. In the same year Parliament introduced excise duty – as a tax on alcoholic drinks – to finance its armies in the English Civil War. In 1799, PITT THE YOUNGER introduced income tax to help to finance the war with France, and gradually direct tax on income became the main source of revenue for most European governments. Colonial powers, particularly France and Britain, used customs duties to protect markets in their overseas possessions. They set high tariffs for imports from noncolonial sources and charged high customs duties for goods imported to their foreign territories.

For many Americans Custer came to epitomise the fearless cavalryman of legend.

customs unions Groups of countries which have agreed to eliminate tariffs on goods imported or exported to each other. The most powerful bloc is the European Customs Union, which provides for duty-free or reduced tariffs on cross-border trade among the member states of the EUROPEAN UNION. Similar unions are planned in other parts of the world – notably in North America, where Canada, the USA and Mexico will reduce and eventually remove customs barriers.

Cuzco City in the Peruvian Andes which was the INCA capital from around AD 1200 and was largely rebuilt in 1438. An inner city which included palaces, administrative buildings and the *Coricancha*, 'Sun Temple', was surrounded by regularly planned wards representing all the provinces of the Inca empire. After the Spanish defeat of the Incas in 1535, Cuzco was replaced by Lima as the viceregal capital of Peru since the victors needed a large port to serve their colonial possessions. Cuzco nevertheless remained an important provincial city sacred to the Incas, who set up a successor state in the hills to the north of Cuzco but failed to recapture their capital in 1538.

Indian hawkers display their wares on a typical Cuzco street where blocks of ancient Inca stone are capped by newer plaster walls.

Cymbeline see CUNOBELINUS

Cynic Member of a sect of philosophers established by Antisthenes of Athens. His pupil DIOGENES became its best-known exponent. Although virtuous self-sufficiency was a common theme, the Cynics were not a formal school and had no fully defined philosophy. Considerable differences emerged among Diogenes' followers, who adopted only those concepts which appealed to them. Diogenes' main disciple, Crates of Thebes, argued that in times of trouble the man who gave up material possessions, had minimal needs and maintained his independence could be happy. In the 3rd century BC the Cynic philosophy flourished in Greece and the itinerant beggar-philosopher was a familiar sight. During the 1st century AD the philosophy enjoyed a brief revival in Rome, where the readiness of its followers to criticise imperial behaviour led to many Cynics being expelled from the city.

Cyprus Island in the eastern Mediterranean divided between Greek and Turkish-speaking Cypriots, and a continuing source of political friction between Greece and Turkey. Colonised by Mycenaeans in the 14th century BC, Cyprus was later ruled successively by the Assyrian, Persian, Roman and Byzantine empires. The English king Richard I conquered it in 1191 and sold it to the French Crusader Guy de Lusignan, who ran the island as a feudal monarchy and made it an important base for the Crusades. Subsequently it was controlled by Venice, falling to the Ottomans in 1571 and remaining part of their empire until 1879, when it came under British administration after the Congress of Berlin. Formally annexed by Britain in 1914, Cyprus was declared a crown colony in 1925, but from the outset the rivalry between the community of Greek-speakers which wanted *enosis,* or union with Greece, and the island's Turkish minority dominated Cypriot politics. After the Second World War this erupted in violence led by the Greek-Cypriot guerrilla organisation EOKA, which was covertly supported by the Greek government. Talks between Britain, Turkey and Greece finally reached a settlement and the island became independent in 1960, under the presidency of Cypriot Orthodox Archbishop Mihail Makarios.

Within five years the government was in chaos and a United Nations peace-keeping force intervened. In 1974, when Greece backed a coup which ousted Makarios, Turkish forces invaded, gaining control of most of Cyprus. Peace talks between Britain, Turkey, Greece and the two Cypriot sides led only to a Turkish withdrawal to the northern part of the island. Although Makarios resumed the presidency in 1975, the Turkish Federated State of Cyprus was formed, comprising about 35 per cent of the island and having its own president. Since then sporadic clashes have erupted between the two Cypriot communities, and though talks between the leaders of the two sides continued into the 1990s they have failed to reach agreement.

Cyril, St (c.827-69) Greek missionary who gave his name to the alphabet still used in Russia. Educated at the Byzantine court, Cyril and his elder brother St Methodius (c.825-85) were sent to central Europe to convert the Slavic tribes. Adopting what became known as the Cyrillic alphabet, the two began a translation of the liturgy and the Bible into Slavic, which Methodius completed after his brother's death. Rival missionaries in Bulgaria, who used Latin, spearheaded opposition to the introduction of a vernacular liturgy, and the ensuing competition for converts increased tension between the Churches in Rome and Constantinople.

Cyrus II 'the Great' (d.530 BC) Founder of the Persian empire and the ruler who freed the Jews from their Babylonian exile. Four years after defeating the Medes, who were the Persians' overlords, in about 550 BC Cyrus gained control of Asia Minor from King CROESUS of Lydia. Victory over the last of the Chaldean kings added Babylonia, Assyria, Syria and Palestine to Cyrus's realm, while further conquests to the north and east created an empire which stretched from Egypt to Turkey and into India. Under Cyrus's enlightened policies conquered peoples were encouraged to retain their customs and religions. He promoted Medians to important posts and allowed the Jews to start to rebuild the Temple, their main religious centre at Jerusalem. Cyrus was probably killed in battle in Afghanistan.

Cyrus the Younger (d.401 BC) Persian prince whose financial support enabled the Spartan general Lysander to defeat Athens in the PELOPONNESIAN WAR. A son of Darius II, Cyrus was given command of Asia Minor in 408 BC. When ARTAXERXES II, his elder brother, became king, Cyrus raised a force – in which the historian XENOPHON served – to depose him, but was killed at Cunaxa.

Czartoryski, Adam Jerzy, Prince (1770-1861) Polish statesman and nationalist leader known as the 'Polish king in exile' who helped to plan unsuccessful rebellions against Russia in 1830 and 1863. As a trusted adviser of Grand Duke Alexander, who became tsar in 1801, Czartoryski – a cousin of Poland's last independent king – was appointed Russian foreign minister. However, when Russia, Prussia and Austria partitioned Poland, he strove to restore his homeland. Czartoryski's nationalist efforts were partly successful when, after the Battle of LEIPZIG in 1813, he sought to re-create Poland from the Grand Duchy of Warsaw which Napoleon had established. As the Polish representative at the Congress of VIENNA he saw Poland restored – but with the Russian tsar as king. Proclaimed president of the provisional government of Poland at the time of the Polish revolt of 1830 to 1831, Czartoryski was condemned to death when the uprising failed, but escaped to Paris.

Czechoslovakia Former central European country carved from part of the old Austro-Hungarian empire at the end of the First World War and today divided into the Czech and Slovak republics. Incorporating part of Bohemia and Silesia, Moravia and the Slovak-speaking part of Hungary, the country was also home to several other national minorities. Its original link to the League of Nations and alliances forged with Yugoslavia and Romania in 1921, with France in 1924 and with the USSR in 1935 ensured a degree of stability; but the national minorities within its borders – especially the Germans and the Hungarians – were a source of tension. In 1938 it was forced to accept Adolf Hitler's terms at Munich, depriving it of the Sudentenland and of nearly 5 million inhabitants. A year later Germany's invasion of Czechoslovakia was a cause of the Second World War. In 1948, after a brief period of independence, Czechoslovakia became a Soviet satellite. Liberal-minded communists tried to gain a degree of independence in what came to be known as the 'Prague spring' of 1968, but their efforts were suppressed by an invasion of WARSAW PACT armies.

Anti-Soviet opposition in the late 1970s and 1980s culminated in a national strike in November 1989, which brought down the communist regime. It was replaced by a federal assembly headed by President Václav HAVEL. The Czech and Slovak National Councils, which were established by the assembly, had equal legislative powers and led a gradual transition to a market economy. However, in June 1992 the people of Slovakia voted to become independent and to develop a more centrally controlled economy. In January 1993 the Czech and Slovak republics formally came into being.

da Gama, Vasco (c.1469-1524) Portuguese navigator who in 1497 became the first European to discover a sea route to India. Da Gama was asked to make the voyage after the discovery by the explorer Bartholomew Diaz of a great ocean east of the Cape of Good Hope. Da Gama rounded the Cape, sailed up the east coast of Africa and across the Indian Ocean to the Malabar coast, and returned to Portugal with a rich cargo of spices.

Da Gama was sent back to India in 1502 with a fleet of 20 ships after Muslim traders attacked a Portuguese settlement at Calicut. He bombarded the town before sailing on to Cochin for another cargo of spices. He also tried to force chiefs on the African coast to acknowledge Portuguese power. In 1524 da Gama was recalled from retirement to restore Portuguese authority in the East as viceroy, but fell ill shortly after his arrival in Goa and died at Cochin two months later. His voyages of discovery and exploration helped to lay the foundation for Portugal's domination as a trading nation in the 16th century.

Daguerre, Louis (1787-1851) Inventor of the first commercially successful photographic process. In 1829 Daguerre, a theatrical scenery painter and joint owner of the Paris Diorama, became the partner of Joseph Niépce, who had taken the world's earliest photograph three years before. In 1839 Daguerre published a development of Niépce's process. Niépce had died in 1833, so it was Daguerre who reaped honours and riches, and his name was attached to the first practical photograph, the daguerreotype, a 'one-off' direct positive with no negative.

Dahomey Kingdom in West Africa which became an important trading partner of Portugal after its foundation as the kingdom of Allada in the 16th century. Dahomey came into existence between 1645 and 1685 when the kingdoms of Abomey and Adjaché (now Porto Novo) were united by the conquest of Abomey. The kingdom was notorious among European travellers for its custom of sacrificing large numbers of captured slaves on the death of a king to provide attendants in the

The photography pioneer Louis Daguerre took this still life picture in 1837, two years before he perfected the process named after him.

spirit world. French trading forts were established in the 18th and 19th centuries, but the rulers of Dahomey succeeded in limiting French influence and restricting the European slave trade. In 1960 the country achieved independence from France, and over the next 12 years there were several switches from military to civilian rule. Dahomey became the People's Republic of Benin in 1975 under the military leader General Mathieu Kerekou. Multiparty politics were introduced after a referendum in 1990, and Nicéphore Soglo became president.

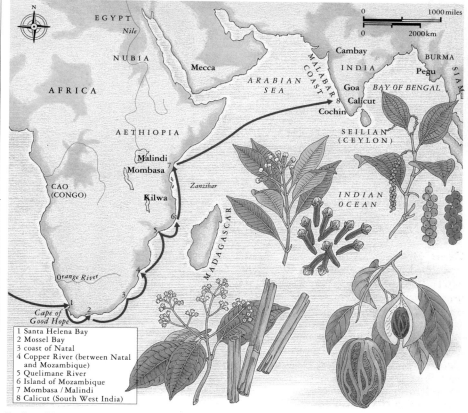

1 Santa Helena Bay
2 Mossel Bay
3 coast of Natal
4 Copper River (between Natal and Mozambique)
5 Quelimane River
6 Island of Mozambique
7 Mombasa / Malindi
8 Calicut (South West India)

Explorer Vasco da Gama discovered a sea route to India by rounding the Cape of Good Hope and returned with a cargo which included (clockwise from top) pepper, nutmeg, cinnamon and cloves.

Gottlieb Daimler, chauffeured by his son Otto, displays in 1886 his first petrol-driven carriage, which had a top speed of 11 mph (18 km/h).

Daimler, Gottlieb (1834-1900) German pioneer of automobile engineering. Daimler developed one of the first high-speed internal-combustion engines in 1885 and perfected a petrol-fuelled carburettor after forming a partnership with Wilhelm Maybach in Stuttgart. They used their first petrol engine to power a bicycle – possibly the first motor cycle. In 1888 they exhibited a two-cylinder motor car in Paris, with an engine provided by the French automotive engineers Rene Panhard and Emile Levassor. Two years later Daimler founded the Daimler Automobile Company at Cannstatt, Germany, and in 1899 he produced the first Mercedes, which was named after the daughter of Emil Jellinek, a major investor in the company. Daimler's successful line of research dated from 1872, when he began working with the German engineer Nikolaus Otto to perfect an oil engine from an earlier gas engine.

Daladier, Edouard (1884-1970) Socialist French premier who joined with the British prime minister Neville Chamberlain in yielding to Hitler's demands at Munich in 1938 to annex to Germany the Sudetenland areas of Czechoslovakia. He was arrested by the pro-Nazi French VICHY government in 1940 and tried with other democratic leaders accused of responsibility for French military disasters. Although acquitted, he remained imprisoned in France and Germany. Daladier was freed at the end of the war and elected to the national assembly in 1945 during the Fourth Republic, in which he served until 1958.

Dalai Lama Title of the religious and political ruler of Tibet (Dalai, 'ocean-wide'; Lama, 'superior one'). Lamaism, a form of Buddhism produced by a merger of Indian Buddhism with ancient shamanism and sorcery, was introduced into Tibet from north-west India in the 8th century. In the 13th century the faith came under the control of a group of monks who allowed corruption to flourish. In the early 14th century monks calling themselves the Yellow Sect seized control, brought in reforms and installed the first Dalai Lama in the capital, Lhasa. He became the temporal leader of the country, while spiritual supremacy was held by the chief abbot of a powerful monastery at Shigatse, who was known as the Panchen Lama. When either lama died, the monks would identify a boy into whom they believed his spirit had passed, and this infant would then become the new ruler.

The 14th Dalai Lama, who was enthroned in 1940, opposed the Chinese occupation of Tibet that took place after the communist Chinese revolution of 1949. Ten years later, after an unsuccessful revolt against the occupying forces, he fled into exile in India. The Chinese, who claimed Tibet had always been part of their country, made the Panchen Lama a puppet ruler. The Dalai Lama then created a government-in-exile in Dharmsala, India, and launched an international diplomatic campaign to expel the Chinese from Tibet. He was awarded the Nobel peace prize in 1989.

Dalhousie, James (1812-60) British statesman and 1st Marquess of Dalhousie who was governor-general of India from 1847 to 1856. Dalhousie oversaw the extension of British rule through the annexation of the Punjab, Lower Burma, Oudh and several smaller Indian states by the use of the so-called doctrine of 'lapse'. This provision allowed Britain to annex any state without an heir it recognised. This policy was one factor which led to the Indian Mutiny, an uprising against British rule in 1857. Dalhousie initiated major developments in public works and in industry and communications, including the railway, the telegraph and postal system and the opening of the Ganges canal. He removed internal trade barriers, promoted social reform through legislation against female infanticide and the suppression of human sacrifice, and fostered the development of an educational system for all Indians.

Dalton, John (1766-1844) British scientist credited with devising the atomic theory of matter. Dalton developed the theory, now known as the Dalton hypothesis, that all matter is composed of small indestructible particles called atoms, which are indivisible by ordinary chemical means.

Dalton received no formal education, but developed an interest in mathematics and the physical sciences while working at a school in northern England. As a young man Dalton studied the weather and recorded his meticulous observations in a journal, and it was his interest in meteorology which led him to investigate the behaviour of gases. This led him to formulate his law of partial pressures: the total pressure of a mixture of gases is equal to the sum of the partial pressures of its components. Dalton was also the first to recognise the existence of colour blindness, a disability from which he suffered and which later became known as daltonism.

Danby, Thomas Osborne (1632-1712) English statesman and 1st Earl of Danby who entered Parliament in 1665 as a supporter of the restored Charles II. Danby received rapid promotion, becoming Treasurer of the Navy in 1671 and Lord Treasurer in 1673. But his reluctant negotiations with Louis XIV of France to supply Charles II with money led to Parliament impeaching him on corruption

Gabriele D'Annunzio (right) who was celebrated as one of the leading writers of his day, became an Italian air force hero during the First World War despite being more than 50 when he enlisted.

Dante's epic poem *The Divine Comedy* was the first major work written in the vernacular rather than Latin, and established the Tuscan dialect spoken in Florence as the literary language of Italy.

charges, and he was imprisoned for five years from 1679. In 1688 he signed the invitation to William of Orange to come to England to take the throne from James II, regained royal favour, and became Duke of Leeds in 1694. Following fresh accusations of corruption and impeachment, he retired from public life the following year.

Danegeld Tribute paid in silver by ETHELRED II 'the Unready' of England to buy peace from the invading Danes. It was raised by a tax levied on land. In 991 the first payment was set at 10 000 lb (4500 kg) of silver. Payments over the next 20 years were greater, rising to 48 000 lb (22 000 kg) in 1012. The tax was no longer levied after this payment, but it was still collected to pay for a navy and the royal bodyguard, when it was known as 'heregeld'. (See also TALLAGE.)

Danelaw Name given to the northern and eastern parts of Anglo-Saxon England settled by the Danes in the late 9th and 10th centuries and where Danish laws and customs applied. The earliest attempt to describe a boundary between these areas and the rest of England was made by King ALFRED and the Danish leader Guthrum around 886. The Danelaw was then defined as being north and east of a line from the Thames estuary through Hertfordshire and Bedfordshire, then along the River Ouse and the Roman Watling Street to Chester. The Danelaw ceased to be recognised after the 12th century.

D'Annunzio, Gabriele (1863-1938) Italian political adventurer, poet, dramatist and novelist who urged Italy to enter the First World War and fought with daring as a soldier, a sailor and in the air force from 1915 to 1918. In 1919 D'Annunzio defied the VERSAILLES PEACE SETTLEMENT and seized the Adriatic port of Fiume, now Rijeka in Croatia. He imposed an authoritarian and fascist government on the town, but it was starved into surrender after 15 months. D'Annunzio retired to Lombardy to write his memoirs.

Dante Alighieri (1265-1321) Italian poet, writer, literary theorist, moral philosopher, and political thinker. His most famous work, *The Divine Comedy*, is a poem in three parts: *Inferno*, *Purgatory* and *Paradise*. It describes Dante's journey to God, accompanied at first by Virgil, symbolising human reason, to the point where only Beatrice, representing divine grace, can guide him. On his journey he stops to talk to all manner of people, both contemporaries and figures from antiquity and mythology. *The Divine Comedy* is a catalogue of medieval lore, underlined by the Christian

The revolutionary leader Georges Danton was fond of boasting that he had been responsible for the overthrow of the French monarchy.

doctrine of fall and redemption. It represents the pinnacle of Italian poetry. Dante spent the first half of his life in Florence until political upheaval forced him into exile in 1302, and he sought refuge in one Italian princely court after another until his death in Ravenna. His Florentine years were marked by his passion for Beatrice Portinari, who died in 1290 in her twenties, but who remained the inspiration of both his poetry and his Christian faith.

Danton, Georges (1759-94) Leading antiroyalist and orator of the French Revolution. He was born at Arcis-sur-Aube and became a lawyer in Paris. At the age of 31 he founded the militant Cordeliers' Club and took part in JACOBIN debates, where he petitioned for the trial of LOUIS XVI and the creation of a republic. He was a favourite of the *sansculottes*, the working classes of the cities, and – though forced to leave France briefly in 1791 for his own safety – he soon returned to become minister of justice. His calm authority during the crises of 1792, when the armies of Austria and Prussia invaded, underlined his growing importance to the revolution. Danton's criti-

> ❝ To conquer the enemies of the fatherland we need boldness, more boldness, boldness now and always, and France is saved. ❞
>
> *Georges Danton reinforcing the morale of the revolutionaries during the crises of 1792*

cism of the harsh judgments of the revolutionary council led to his resignation as a minister. He voted for the king's execution in January 1793, and in April was appointed a member of the Committee of Public Safety, the first effective government of the revolution. For three months he effectively led the government, but his disapproval of the repression of the TERROR, when opponents of the new regime were rounded up and executed, and his growing moderation, soon brought him into conflict with the revolutionary leader Maximilien ROBESPIERRE and led to his own execution in April 1794.

Darby, Abraham (1678-1717) English ironmaster, the first to smelt iron with coke. In the 17th century the growing demand for iron was frustrated because the timber for making charcoal (for use in blast furnaces) was scarce and expensive, and large furnaces were not possible because charcoal was too soft to support a heavy charge of ore. Raw coal was an obvious alternative, but the sulphur and other impurities in it spoilt the quality of the iron. At his Coalbrookdale works in 1709 Darby solved this problem by using coke, which burnt cleanly. Smelting iron with coke became a key process in the development of the English INDUSTRIAL REVOLUTION.

Dardanelles A 38 mile (61 km) strait between Europe and Asiatic Turkey, which joins the Aegean to the Sea of Marmara. In classical times it was called the Hellespont. The strait was of strategic importance for hundreds of years, and in modern times was governed by a series of agreements that restricted its use by warships. The Dardanelles was the scene of an unsuccessful attack on the Ottoman Empire by British and French troops during the First World War in 1915, with Australian and New Zealand contingents (see GALLIPOLI CAMPAIGN). Control of the straits was finally restored to Turkey by the Montreux Convention of 1936.

Darius I 'the Great' (d.486 BC) Ruler of Achaemenid Persia from 521 BC to his death. The first years of Darius's rule were overshadowed by uprisings, but after crushing them he started on major reorganisation. Officials known as SATRAPS were appointed to rule 20 provinces, though Darius allowed considerable local independence. The system was so successful that ALEXANDER THE GREAT adopted it. Darius conducted campaigns to secure his frontiers, but was unable to subdue the Scythians. A revolt by the Ionian Greeks in 499-494 BC was suppressed, but attempts to exact revenge on mainland Greece for assisting the rebels met with disaster. Storms scattered the Persian fleet in 492, and the army was defeated at MARATHON in 490.

Dark Ages Term formerly used to describe the decline of Roman culture and the turmoil in Europe in the 5th and 6th centuries after the collapse of the Roman Empire. Modern historians avoid the term with its implication that only Roman values were civilised values.

Many Germanic peoples travelled through Italy, Germany, France, Spain and North Africa, settling wherever they could. Many groups formed their own kingdoms: Vandals in North Africa; Visigoths in Spain; Franks in France and western Germany; Ostrogoths and Lombards in northern Italy; Anglo-Saxons in England. The Dark Ages saw economic decline, but also the end of high taxation by the Roman Empire and the foundation of monasteries which kept Christian and Roman scholarship alive. The 7th and 8th centuries brought back relative stability, and in the 9th century the encouragement of learning began to emerge at the court of Alfred the Great.

Darnley, Henry, Lord (1545-67) Anglo-Scottish aristocrat who became second husband of Mary, Queen of Scots in 1565 and father of the future James VI of Scotland (James I of England). Mary's reliance on her secretary David Rizzio (who was suspected of being her lover) led Darnley to murder him. Darnley was himself murdered in a conspiracy probably involving the Earl of BOTHWELL.

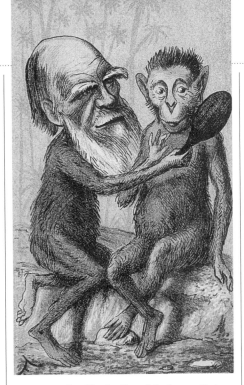

The naturalist Charles Darwin's theory that humans and apes shared a common ancestor was mocked by the cartoonists of his time.

Darwin, Charles (1809-82) British naturalist whose ideas and observations played a decisive role in the science and thought of the 20th century. Darwin's *On The Origin of Species by Means of Natural Selection*, published in 1859, argues that species are not fixed but evolve through selection. Some individuals have characteristics which better fit them for survival, so they are more likely to reproduce and pass their characteristics to offspring. Over a long time distinct species develop. Darwin argued that humanity has evolved in this way. He expanded these theories 12 years later in *The Descent of Man*. His work was based on research in South America and the Galápagos Islands as naturalist on HMS *Beagle* between 1831 and 1836. Darwin's work was soon influential in psychology when his cousin Francis Galton, founder of eugenics (genetic control of human populations by selective breeding), began to study whether intelligence was inherited. Darwin's work gave grounds for belief in the continuity of human and animal evolution. But it caused controversy because it seemed to disagree with a literal reading of the Bible. Debate raged among theological experts, but Darwin did not take part.

> **DID YOU KNOW?**
>
> *During his research in South America, Darwin rode with the Argentinian gauchos, survived an armed political revolt and rescued a boat from a tidal wave.*

dating systems Scientific evidence about the prehistory of the human race and of the Earth depends on the accurate dating of recovered artefacts and rocks. Traditional methods of dating are based on factors such as depth of burial of an artefact and comparison with material from other sites. These methods are now reinforced by several much more reliable scientific techniques. Dendrochronology is based on the measurement of growth rings in timber. Radiocarbon dating uses the decay of the radioisotope carbon-14 to date organic material. A similar technique uses the decay of potassium-40 to argon-40 for dating volcanic rocks, and the decay of rubidium-87 to strontium-87 for dating other rocks.

Dauphiné Former province in south-east France that was conquered by the Romans, Burgundians and Franks. It was once an area controlled by the HOLY ROMAN EMPIRE, but it passed to the kingdom of Arles and, in 1029, to the counts of D'Albon who later took the title of Dauphin of Vienne. After the area was sold to the future Charles V of France in 1349, heirs to the throne began to assume the title of dauphin. It acquired a *parlement* in 1453, but was annexed to the Crown in 1457 and lost its local privileges, especially during the French Wars of Religion.

David (died c.961 BC) Second king of Israel, who appears in the biblical account initially as a harp player at SAUL's court and as the slayer of the Philistine giant Goliath. As a military commander David became a friend of Saul's son Jonathan, and married Saul's daughter Michal, but was exiled by Saul who was jealous of David's talents. After Saul's death, David ruled the tribe of Judah while Saul's son Ishbosheth ruled the rest of Israel.

On Ishbosheth's death, David was chosen as the king of Israel, and his reign marked a change in the fortunes of the Jews from being a confederation of tribes to becoming a settled nation. He moved the capital from Hebron to Jerusalem and made it the religious centre of the Israelites by bringing the Ark of the Covenant, their most sacred object, with him. David expanded the territories over which he ruled and brought prosperity to Israel. His later years were troubled by rebellions led by his sons and by family rivalries at court. His favourite son, Absalom, led a rebellion, but was killed.

David I (c.1084-1153) King of the Scots from 1124 until his death, in succession to his brother Alexander I. David was brought up at the English court of William II and Henry I, whom his sister Matilda later married. His own marriage gave him the earldom of Huntingdon and also a right to intervene in English politics. David's English upbringing prompted him to introduce into Scotland modified English institutions of government and land tenure and to sponsor monasteries and bishoprics. He managed to maintain a

Jacques-Louis David's *The Intervention of the Sabine Women* shows the women, years after their abduction, halting a battle between their Roman husbands and Sabine men on a rescue mission.

balance between old and new, despite four rebellions during his reign. His attempt to consolidate his position in the English north was checked by a heavy defeat at the Battle of the Standard, near Northallerton, in 1138.

David II (1324-71) Only son of ROBERT I (known as Robert Bruce), who became king of the Scots in 1329. At the age of four David was married to Joan, daughter of Edward II of England, and a year later he inherited the throne of Scotland. In 1334 he fled to France after being forced from the throne by Edward BALLIOL, son of the former king John Balliol, who had surrendered the crown in 1296. David returned to Scotland in 1341 and launched an invasion of northern England, but was captured at the Battle of Neville's Cross, County Durham, in 1346. The heavy ransom exacted after his release in 1157 caused problems, but the economy was buoyant and relations with his nobles better than before. His weakness was the lack of an heir.

David, Jacques-Louis (1748-1825) French painter, the outstanding artist of the neo-classical movement. The painting that established David's reputation, *The Oath of The Horatii,* which was finished in 1784, depicts a Roman legend of three brothers who defended Rome against three enemy champions. He was briefly a pupil of the court painter François Boucher and began his career working in the elaborate rococo manner. But during the 1770s, under the influence of the art of ancient Rome, David's work became heroic and severe, and he soon found himself at the head of a movement that rejected the frivolity of rococo in favour of a style more in keeping with the sober social and moral values

that had come to dominate French life. His themes expressed the new cult of the civic virtues of stoical self-sacrifice, devotion to duty, honesty and austerity. David was a supporter of the ideals of the French Revolution and took an active part in it. He was twice jailed and narrowly avoided execution. In 1799 he exhibited his masterpiece *The Intervention of the Sabine Women.* Napoleon appointed him his painter in 1804.

David, St (died c.601) Patron saint of Wales, the son of St Non and of Sant, a local prince, though there is no reliable biography. David is credited with founding 12 monasteries in Wales, the most important at Mynyw (now St David's) where he lived when he became Bishop of Wales. He took a prominent part in the synod of Llandewi-Brevi in about 560 to suppress the Pelagian heresy (which claimed that people can attain salvation by their own efforts), and supposedly persuaded the Synod of Victory at Caerleon around ten years later to adopt the teachings of St AUGUSTINE OF HIPPO. It is said he made the leek a symbol of Wales by telling Welsh warriors to wear the vegetable in battle to distinguish them from their Saxon opponents.

Da Vinci, Leonardo
see feature, page 182

Davis, Jefferson (1808-89) President of the Southern Confederacy during the American Civil War from 1861 to 1865. Davis

was criticised for his aloofness and limited political skill, as well as his interference in military affairs, but it is doubtful whether any other Confederate leader could have been more effective in the wartime conditions.

Davis began his career as a soldier in the Black Hawk War, against Native Americans who resisted attempts to move them from lands west of the Mississippi. He left the army in 1835 to become a Mississippi planter, but ten years later returned to command the Mississippi Rifles in the MEXICAN AMERICAN WAR. Davis served two terms in the Senate and was secretary of war under President Franklin Pierce from 1853 to 1857. He left the Senate when Mississippi seceded from the Union, and in 1861 was named provisional president of the Confederacy. Davis was captured in 1865 and spent two years in jail. The Union dropped plans to try him for treason, and he retired to Mississippi.

Davitt, Michael (1846-1906) Irish patriot who fought against the British-imposed land-holding system in Ireland. Davitt, son of a farmer who had been evicted from his holding, in 1865 joined the Irish Republican Brotherhood, a movement trying to establish an independent republic of Ireland. Five years later he was sentenced to 15 years penal servitude for smuggling weapons to the FENIANS. Davitt was freed in 1877 and two years later helped to found the Irish Land League, an organisation formed to achieve land reform.

With the nationalist leader Charles PARNELL, Davitt sought to protect Irish peasants against evictions and high rents. He was elected an MP in 1882 and again in 1892 and 1895. The agitation which he led helped bring about the 1881 Irish Land Act, guaranteeing the three Fs – fair rents, fixity (security) of tenure, and freedom to sell to tenants.

Davy, Humphry (1778-1829) Inventor of the 'safety lamp', also known as the 'Davy lamp', that provided light for miners without the risk of causing gas explosions. As a 21-year-old laboratory assistant in Bristol, western England, Davy discovered that laughing gas (nitrous oxide) had an anaesthetic effect, and he also isolated elements using electrolysis. It was his research on gases that

Humphry Davy is best remembered for his 'safety lamp', but he also helped to found London Zoo and a gentlemen's club.

Renaissance man

Leonardo da Vinci is regarded as the artistic and scientific genius of the Renaissance. His innovative work in Florence, Milan, and later France, influenced contemporary artists and showed knowledge beyond his time.

Painter, sculptor, engineer and inventor, Leonardo da Vinci exemplifies the creative and versatile 'Renaissance man' inspired by the revival of classical culture in 15th century Italy. He was 'so favoured by nature that to whatever he turned his mind or thoughts, the results were always inspired and perfect,' wrote his first biographer Giorgio Vasari in 1550.

Born in Vinci, after which he was named, in Tuscany in 1452, the illegitimate son of a lawyer, Leonardo's gifts were always exceptional. One early story tells how he decorated a shield for one of his father's tenants with a Medusa's head so impressive that his father kept it for himself. In 1470 Leonardo was apprenticed to the artist Andrea del Verrocchio in Florence. It is said that he took up the humble trade of painting because his illegitimacy barred him from respectable jobs. His first surviving work is a delicate angel in Verrocchio's *Baptism of Christ* and possibly portions of the landscape. Verrocchio, on seeing his own skill eclipsed, vowed never to paint again. Within a few years princes were competing for work by Leonardo.

The beginning of his career coincided with the development of oil-based painting in Italy and a naturalism whose greatest exponent was Leonardo himself. 'It is important to go straight to nature,' he wrote, rather than copy other painters. One of his first dated works was a drawing of the Tuscan landscape (1473). The climax of his art in this period was the unfinished *Adoration of the Magi*, which was commissioned in 1481.

For the following 18 years Leonardo lived in Milan under the ducal patronage of Ludovico Sforza, who presided over one of the most glittering courts in Europe. For Sforza, Leonardo undertook to design a colossal bronze statue of a horse in honour of the duke's father. The project was abandoned when the metal was diverted into armaments, but drawings for the monument exist – Leonardo was himself a fine horseman. He became court artificer, devising elaborate entertainments such as a great 'Masque of the Planets' in 1490.

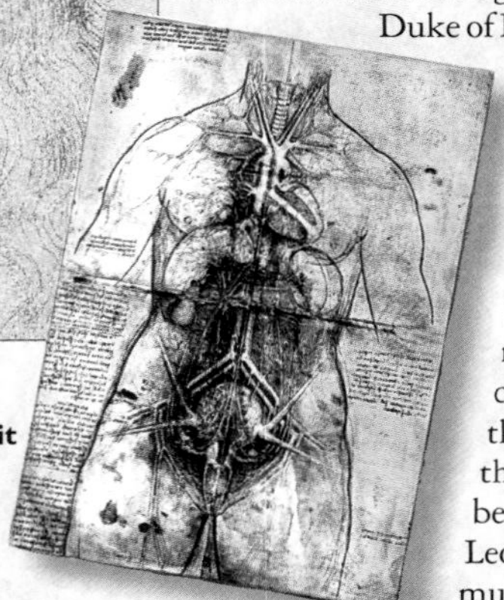

Leonardo's artistic masterpiece in Milan is the fresco the *Last Supper* for the monastery of Santa Maria delle Grazie. Painted on plaster on the wall of the refectory between 1495 and 1498, Leonardo used innovations in perspective with expressive depiction of character in the figures of Christ and his disciples.

SCIENTIFIC STUDIES

He recorded his scientific ideas in a series of remarkable notebooks, which include detailed studies of hydraulics – including an irrigation system for the plains of Lombardy – optics, astronomy and anatomy, military engineering projects, and a water-operated alarm clock. He made repeated attempts to build a flying machine and designed an armoured vehicle like a tank, as well as an astonishingly modern-looking bicycle. Leonardo wrote in mirror-script, so the fertility of his ideas was not fully appreciated until the 19th century, when his annotated diagrams were found to prefigure many discoveries and inventions.

In 1499, after the fall of Sforza, Leonardo returned to Florence and took up a position as architect and designer to Cesare Borgia, Duke of Romagna. From this period in Florence came the *Mona Lisa* (1503). The painting was admired as an unrivalled example of how art can imitate nature. 'On looking closely at the pit of the throat, one could swear that the pulse was beating,' wrote Vasari. Leonardo employed musicians to entertain his sitter while he worked, which perhaps explains her legendary smile – though the same enigmatic look is also seen in his religious figures. In 1503 the city of Florence commissioned both Leonardo and his fellow artist Michelangelo to produce two large wall paintings in commemoration of Florentine battles. Leonardo's was the *Battle of Anghiari*, but like so many of his works it was left unfinished: the original was destroyed and today only copies remain.

Although a large number of drawings have survived, there are few paintings. Of his private life, little is recorded. As he never married and in youth was arraigned on an unproven charge of sodomy, it is inferred that he was homosexual. In mid life he adopted a boy called Giacomo, nicknamed Salai, with angelic features and demonic habits.

Leonardo left Florence in 1516 to work for Louis XII of France. He was given an allowance and a chateau near Amboise where he died in 1519, aged 67.

Leonardo da Vinci, and left, his portrait of Cecilia Gallerani, *Lady with an Ermine*, painted in Milan c.1490. Right, one of Leonardo's finely detailed and annotated drawings which illustrate his profound interest in everything scientific.

The leather and papyrus pages of the Dead Sea Scrolls include poems and an allegorical history of the scrolls' creators.

enabled him in 1815 to construct an enclosed flame that would not set fire to the highly inflammable methane gas often found in coal mines. Davy also worked to popularise science, especially as a professor at the Royal Institution and later as the president of the Royal Society.

Dawes Plan see REPARATIONS

Dayan, Moshe (1915-81) Israeli military leader and politician, minister of defence during the SIX-DAY WAR of 1967. Dayan gained his early military experience in the 1930s with the Haganah, an outlawed armed force that protected early Jewish settlements in what was then Palestine. After losing an eye during the Second World War, he took to wearing a distinctive eye patch.

Dayan was commander of Jerusalem during the 1948 War of Independence and took part in peace talks with Jordan. He became chief of staff of the armed forces in 1953, and won praise for directing the 1956 invasion of the Egyptian Sinai Peninsula. His first government post was as minister of agriculture in 1959. In 1965 Dayan was elected minister of defence and conducted the Six-Day War that ended with Israeli forces occupying parts of Egypt, Jordan, Lebanon and Syria.

Dayan's popularity began to wane after criticism of Israel's lack of preparation for the 1973 October War and he resigned the following year. He came back into government as foreign minister in 1977 and helped to organise the talks that led to the Camp David peace accords with Egypt. He resigned in 1979 in protest at the government's refusal to discuss the future of the Israeli-occupied Jordan West Bank. Dayan founded a party called Telem in 1981 which argued that Israel should withdraw from occupied Arab lands.

Days that changed the world see feature, page 184

Dead Sea Scrolls Collection of ancient Hebrew and Aramaic manuscripts found between 1947 and 1956 by shepherds in caves near the north-western shore of the Dead Sea. They may have belonged to the library of the Essenes, an austere Jewish community sharing some of the beliefs of the early Christians, who lived in a monastery near Qumran, and were probably hidden before the Romans destroyed the group in AD 68. The scrolls include fragments of nearly every book of the Hebrew Bible – the Old Testament, including the oldest known manuscript of the book of Isaiah; a commentary on the book of Habakkuk; a manual of teachings and rules of discipline; and the Temple Scroll, explaining how the ideal temple of Jerusalem should be built. Until the discovery of the scrolls, the earliest surviving Hebrew biblical manuscripts dated from the 9th century AD. The scrolls, which are kept in the Shrine of the Book at the Israeli Museum in Jerusalem, are a key source for scholars on the relationship between Judaism and early Christianity.

Decatur, Stephen (1779-1820) US naval officer who coined the phrase 'our country, right or wrong'. He was promoted to captain following his daring recapture of the frigate *Philadelphia* in the Tripolitan War of 1801 to 1805, which began when the ruling dynasty in what is now Libya demanded an increase in the money America paid to protect its commercial shipping from piracy. As a commodore in 1812 he captured a British frigate during a war with England. Decatur confirmed his heroic reputation by forcing the Dey of Algiers to sign a treaty in 1815 that ended all tributes to the Barbary pirates. He was killed during a duel with a senior naval officer who had been suspended.

Decembrists Members of a number of Russian revolutionary groups, led by the Northern Society, who combined to revolt against the accession of Tsar Nicholas I in December 1825. The group, mostly army officers, were influenced by French liberal ideas. Some of them wanted a republic, while others backed Nicholas's eldest brother Constantine in the hope that he would favour constitutional reform and modernisation. A few guards regiments in St Petersburg refused to take an oath of allegiance and marched to the Senate House, where they were fired on by other troops after a stand-off of several hours. Police spies trapped the conspirators; five were executed, 253 exiled to Siberia and 31 jailed. The Decembrists' revolt led to an increase in police terrorism and to the spread of revolutionary societies among intellectuals.

Declaration of Independence The document which established the United States of America and proclaimed American separation from Britain. It was adopted by the CONTINENTAL CONGRESS on July 4, 1776. Its principal author was Thomas JEFFERSON, who based its arguments on John LOCKE's ideas of contractual government. The famous preamble declared that all men are created equal and have inalienable rights to life, liberty and the pursuit of happiness. There followed a detailed list of acts of tyranny committed by King George III of England and his ministers and Parliament against the American people. The document had 56 signatories.

Defence of the Realm Acts Legislation, known as DORA, passed by the British Parliament during the First World War. Under the Acts Government took powers to commandeer factories and directly control war production, and banned war-workers from moving elsewhere. Left-wing agitators were moved to other parts of the country and strict press censorship was imposed. The Act of May 1915 gave powers over the supply and sale of alcohol, which were widely resented but survived the war as licensing hours. An Emergency Powers Act of 1920 confirmed the government's right to issue regulations in times of emergency, and many such rules were reintroduced in the Second World War.

Defoe, Daniel (1660-1731) English novelist and journalist. Defoe (born Foe) was nearly 60 when he turned to writing fiction. After a career as a journalist, he produced *The Life and Strange Surprising Adventures of Robinson Crusoe* in

THE
LIFE
AND
STRANGE SURPRIZING
ADVENTURES
OF
ROBINSON CRUSOE,
Of YORK, MARINER:
Who lived Eight and Twenty Years, all alone in an un-inhabited Island on the Coast of AMERICA, near the Mouth of the Great River of OROONOQUE;
Having been cast on Shore by Shipwreck, wherein all the Men perished but himself.
WITH
An Account how he was at last as strangely delivered by PYRATES.
Written by Himself.
LONDON,
Printed for W. TAYLOR at the Ship in Pater-Noster-Row. MDCCXIX.

The castaway Robinson Crusoe meets Man Friday in a scene from Daniel Defoe's best-known novel.

Five days that changed the world

History is strewn with events that shaped its course, but five days in particular stand out — struggles for freedom and displays of power that were to have significant and lasting effects.

BATTLE OF SALAMIS

(September 23, 480 BC) For more than 20 years successive Persian emperors had sought to conquer Greece, and in the summer of 480 Xerxes seemed likely to succeed. His huge army of invasion forced its way past stubborn Spartan defenders at Thermopylae to occupy first Attica and then Athens itself, looting the Acropolis. The Greek fleet, led by Themistocles, an Athenian politician, withdrew to the nearby Bay of Salamis. Lured into the bay by this cleverly simulated retreat, the Persian ships were smashed to pieces by the rams of the Greek triremes. Xerxes returned home. The next year his army was defeated by the Greeks at the Battle of Plataea, and over the next 50 years Athenian culture flourished as never before or since.

DEFENESTRATION OF PRAGUE

(May 23, 1618) 'Jesu Maria!' cried Jaroslav of Martinitz, a Catholic governor of Prague, as Protestant rebels pushed him out of a window in Hradčany Castle, the centre of Catholic rule over Protestant Bohemia in the Holy Roman Empire. Martinitz survived his 50 ft (15 m) fall, but this 'defenestration' (from *fenestra*, Latin for 'window') triggered not only an attempt by the Bohemians to achieve independence, but also the Thirty Years' War (1618-48). The rise of France, the emergence of Prussia, and the limitation of Habsburg power were among its consequences. Bohemia itself failed to gain its independence, but the survival of Protestantism was ensured.

FALL OF THE BASTILLE

(July 14, 1789) A 14th-century fortress in Paris, the Bastille had come to symbolise the embodiment of a detested regime. By July 11, rumours had spread that Louis XVI was about to dissolve the newly convened National Assembly, which had sworn not to disperse until it had given France a constitution. The next day a crowd started to attack the Bastille, and on the 14th it fell. Such was the ensuing sense of élan that for the first time revolution, and not simply reform, was on the agenda.

BOMBING OF HIROSHIMA

(August 6, 1945) 'Prompt and utter destruction' or unconditional surrender was the choice that the Allies offered Japan on July 26, 1945. The Japanese rejected surrender and 11 days later an atomic bomb was dropped on Hiroshima. Up to 100 000 people died at once, another 100 000 later. After a second bomb was dropped on Nagasaki Japan surrendered on August 10. The nuclear age that was now dawning magnified the importance of the superpowers, and offered the prospect of world destruction as the ultimate deterrent to all-out war.

The Thirty Years' War begins as Protestants 'defenestrate' members of the Catholic royal council at Hradčany Castle in Prague in 1618 (above). The fall of the Berlin Wall (left) unifies Germany in 1989.

FALL OF THE BERLIN WALL

(November 9, 1989) For 28 years the Berlin Wall had stood as a visible symbol of the Iron Curtain that had cut the Soviet-dominated East off from Western Europe since the end of Second World War. The wall was an object of fear and hatred, and more than 500 East Germans had died attempting to get across it to the West. By 1989, as the communist world began to disintegrate, the East German hardline leader Erich Honecker was succeeded by Egon Krenz, who made unconvincing democratic promises that merely served to intensify the pressure for change. On November 9 the Communist Party announced, as a desperate last throw, that the frontiers would be open from midnight. That night pickaxes were taken to the wall, and East Berliners walked through unhindered amid scenes of joy. Germany was reunified, and an era set in concrete was at an end.

A watch found in the midst of the rubble of Hiroshima stopped at 8.16 am, the very moment the atomic bomb exploded over the city.

1719, based in part on the experiences of Alexander Selkirk, who was marooned on a desert island in the Pacific. It was followed by many works, including *Captain Singleton* in 1720; *Moll Flanders* (1722), the story of a London prostitute and thief; *A Journal of the Plague Year,* and *Colonel Jack. Roxana* was published in 1724. In all, Defoe produced nearly 600 books, pamphlets and journals.

De Forest, Lee (1873-1961) US pioneer of electronics, especially the thermionic valve. In 1906 he improved J.A. Fleming's diode by introducing a third electrode, creating the triode. The triode served only as an improved device for detecting radio waves, but later its ability to act as a high-frequency oscillator and amplifier made it a key component in radio and telecommunications equipment.

De Gasperi, Alcide (1881-1954) Italian statesman who played an important part in creating the Christian Democratic Party as a focus for moderate opinion after the Second World War. He was elected to the Austro-Hungarian Parliament in 1911, and became secretary-general of the Italian People's Party between 1919 and 1925. From 1929 to 1943 he was given refuge from Benito Mussolini's fascist regime by the Vatican. De Gasperi made a strong stand against communism and in favour of European cooperation as prime minister from 1945 to 1953.

de Gaulle, Charles (1890-1970) French statesman who came to international prominence when he fled to Britain in 1940 to lead the Free or Fighting French forces after France had surrendered to the advancing German army. De Gaulle became head of the provisional government in 1944 and provisional president in 1945, but retired a year later following disagreements over the constitution adopted by the Fourth Republic. In 1947 de Gaulle created the *Rassemblement du Peuple Français,* a party calling for strong central government. Its modest success disappointed him, so he dissolved it in 1953 and again retired to his home at Colombey-les-Deux-Églises. He was called back into public life in 1958 because he was generally regarded as the only politician who could deal with the emerging civil war in the colony of ALGERIA over the issue of independence. The Fourth Republic was replaced by the Fifth Republic, with de Gaulle as president, in 1959.

In a surprise move de Gaulle conceded independence to Algeria and the African colonies if they wanted it. He went on to dominate the early years of the European Economic Community. In the 1960s he vetoed two applications from Britain to join the six countries which then formed the Common Market. An approach in 1961 from Prime Minister Harold Macmillan was turned down because de Gaulle believed Britain was too closely linked with America. Six years later Prime Minister Harold Wilson received the famous 'Non' despite the support of the other five members of the EEC. De Gaulle also developed an independent French nuclear deterrent and in 1966 withdrew from NATO.

In 1967 he caused controversy when he lent his support to the movement in Canada which was calling for independence for French-speaking Quebec. During a visit to the city de Gaulle described Quebec as having been 'wrested from its (French) territory 200 years ago'. He ended his speech: *'Vive le Québec libre'* ('Long live free Quebec'). De Gaulle's position was shaken by a serious uprising in Paris in May and June 1968 by students angry over the

> 66 **The French will only be united under the threat of danger. Nobody can simply bring together a country that has 265 kinds of cheese.** 99
>
> *Charles de Gaulle in a speech following the 1951 general election.*

contrast between high spending on defence and the tight budgets for education and the social services. They were supported by industrial workers in what became the most sustained strike in France's history. After riots on the streets of the capital, de Gaulle was forced to liberalise the higher education system and make economic concessions to the workers. The Gaullists won the general election in June, but the following year, after an adverse national referendum on plans for constitutional reform, de Gaulle resigned from office.

De Klerk, Fredrik (1936-) South African president who dismantled the APARTHEID system, giving equal rights to the majority Black population. De Klerk was born in Johannesburg and practised law until entering politics in 1972. In 1982 he became minister of internal affairs under President P.W. Botha and the same year leader of the National Party of Transvaal, advocating the idea of 'limited power-sharing' between races. On becoming president in September 1989 he moved towards the policy of giving Blacks the vote despite opposition from conservative and White extremist groups, many of whom were influencing his police force.

In 1990 De Klerk freed Nelson MANDELA, the AFRICAN NATIONAL CONGRESS (ANC) leader, and his government began to abolish apartheid laws. He established an all-party Convention for a Democratic South Africa and in March 1992 won a referendum to continue negotiations. The following year he was awarded the Nobel peace prize, jointly with Mandela. De Klerk became second deputy to President Mandela after the ANC won the first free all-race elections in April 1994. He resigned in 1996 to form an opposition party.

Delacroix, Eugène (1798-1863) Leading French painter of the Romantic movement. In 1822 he exhibited his first picture, *The Barque of Dante,* at the Paris salon. It was bought by the government, launching him on a highly successful and prolific career. Delacroix favoured dramatic subjects drawn from literature, and he also had a taste for the exotic, stemming partly from a visit to Morocco in 1832. His other subjects included portraits,

Charles de Gaulle is joined by happy crowds as he tours the town of Bayeux in June 1944, after returning to France following four years of leading resistance to the Germans from London.

noted for their spiritual intensity, and from the 1830s he undertook several great mural decorations in public buildings in Paris. His style is characterised by energy, emotional fervour and scintillating colour. His use of colour influenced such diverse figures as Pierre Renoir and Vincent Van Gogh. Delacroix was also a dandy, wit and dashing society figure. His *Journal* is a rich source of information and opinion about his life and times.

Delaware State of the USA situated on the east coast between New Jersey and Maryland. In 1787 it was the first state to ratify the US Constitution. Its name derives from Lord de la Warr, governor of Virginia in 1610, although the English explorer Henry Hudson had visited the region twice on unsuccessful attempts to find a north-east passage to China in 1607 and 1608. Delaware was first settled as New Sweden in 1638, but came under English control in 1664. As the three 'Lower Counties' of Pennsylvania, it enjoyed virtual autonomy under the control of the PENN family, and in 1776 achieved independent statehood.

Delcassé, Théophile (1852-1923) French foreign minister in six successive governments, and the principal architect of a number of key pre-1914 European alliances. Delcassé was the central figure in negotiations which resulted in the ENTENTE CORDIALE with Britain in 1904 and paved the way for the Triple Entente with Britain and Russia in 1907. In 1911, as navy minister, Delcassé arranged for cooperation between the British and French fleets in the event of war. In 1914 he was again foreign minister and helped to negotiate the secret Treaty of London, which persuaded Italy to fight on the side of the Allies in the First World War by guaranteeing that it could keep the Dodecanese islands.

Delhi Capital of India, situated on the banks of the Yamuna (or Jumna) river in the north India plains. According to legend the city has moved many times, and there is archaeological evidence for the existence of at least seven previous strongholds. The earliest finds come from the 6th century BC. In the 1st century BC a certain 'Raja Dhilu' gave his name to the site. Little more is known before the 8th century AD, when the Tomar Rajputs occupied the town and made it their capital. In the 11th century Muslim invaders wrested the city from the Hindu king Prithviraj. From the 12th to the 16th centuries Delhi was the capital of a succession of Muslim dynasties. The first Muslim capital is marked by the Qutb Minar, a carved tower built by the founder of the Mameluke dynasty, Sultan Qutb ud-Din Aibak. Natural and strategic factors caused movements to new sites, but always within a few miles of the original settlement.

In the Mughal era Emperor SHAH JAHAN, who ruled from 1628 to 1658, built the Red Fort, palace and mosque which still dominate walled 'Old Delhi'. Mughal decline led to renewed invasions, notably the sack of Delhi by the Persian king Nadir Shah in 1739. The city was captured by the British in 1803. The capital of British India was moved from Calcutta to New Delhi in 1912.

Delian League Voluntary alliance formed by the Greek city-states in 478-477 BC to seek revenge for losses suffered during the Persian Wars (see PERSIA). All members paid tribute in the form of ships or money, the latter being stored on the sacred island of Delos, the league's nominal base. At first, under the leadership of ATHENS, the league tried to drive Persian garrisons out of Europe and to liberate the Greek cities of Asia Minor. At Eurymedon in about 466 a Persian fleet and army were crushed. Athens, which had the largest navy and dominated the alliance, soon began to make its leadership oppressive. In about 472 the city of Carystus was compelled to join the league, and between 465 and 462 the revolt of Thasos was crushed and its mining and other commercial interests on the mainland taken over by Athens. PERICLES oversaw the conversion of the alliance into the beginnings of the Athenian empire.

Delphi Seat of the most respected ORACLE of ancient times, located in the mountains of central Greece. Individuals and city-states consulted Pythia, the priestess of Apollo, and her ambiguous answers relayed from the oracle were interpreted by a priest. Pythia sat on a golden tripod and went into a frenzied trance before delivering the oracle's messages. One of the most famous answers by the oracle concerns the Greek philosopher Socrates. A disciple of his named Chaerephon journeyed to the mountain and asked whether any man was wiser than Socrates. Pythia replied on behalf of the oracle that no man was wiser, and Socrates based his life and work on this judgment. After his death Socrates was acknowledged as one of the most respected philosophers of ancient times.

Delphi was attacked in 480 BC by Persians and by Gauls in 279 BC but emerged largely unscathed, though the Roman emperor Nero removed 500 statues. The shrine was closed by

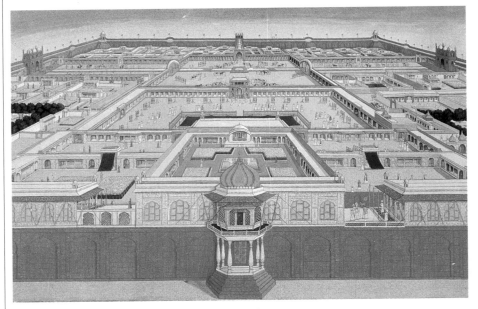

Delhi's huge Red Fort, named after its red sandstone walls and gateways, was built between 1638 and 1658, and includes the imperial Mughal palace, gardens, barracks and other public buildings.

A treasury at Delphi held offerings to the god Apollo, painted here on a cup (right) with his lyre.

the Christian emperor Theodosius in AD390. Remains of a number of buildings survive, including temples to Apollo and Athena, treasuries, a theatre and the *stadion* or running track which was used for the Pythian Games, a sprinting competition and festival held by ancient Athens.

demesne Term used in medieval Europe for the lands retained by a lord under his direct control. The lord, whether a king or VASSAL, needed land to provide food and other necessities for himself and his household. Demesnes were the sites of his homes. They could be manors, palaces or castles. Lords with widespread territories would have demesne lands in several areas, especially where there was any military threat. The day-to-day running of such estates was carried out by servants such as stewards and bailiffs.

democracy see feature, page 188

Democratic Party One of the two major political parties in the USA. The party emerged under Thomas JEFFERSON in the 1790s in opposition to the FEDERALIST PARTY and drew its support from Southern planters and Northern yeoman farmers. In 1828, after a split with the National Republicans under John Quincy ADAMS and Henry Clay, a new Democratic Party was formed led by Andrew JACKSON and John C. Calhoun. Its strong popular appeal kept it in power for all but two presidential terms between then and 1860, when it divided over slavery.

The Democratic Party only returned as a major force in the last decades of the 19th century, retaining the loyalty of the Deep South and gaining support from the expanding west and from the immigrant working classes of the industrialised north-east. In the early 20th century it adopted many of the policies of the PROGRESSIVE MOVEMENT, and its candidate for president, Woodrow WILSON, was elected for two terms from 1913 to 1921. The party was in eclipse in the 1920s, but it re-emerged in the years of the Great DEPRESSION, capturing Congress and the presidency.

The Democrat Franklin D. ROOSEVELT is the only president to have been re-elected for three terms. Since then the party has tended to dominate the House of Representatives, and has generally held the Senate. Following the CIVIL RIGHTS movement and DESEGREGATION in the 1950s and 1960s, the Democrats lost much of their support from the DIXIECRAT southern states, becoming the party associated with the working classes of the big cities and the small farmers as against business and the middle classes. The Democratic presidencies of John F. KENNEDY and Lyndon B. JOHNSON saw working partnerships between Congress and the president, although the VIETNAM WAR caused a major split in the party in 1968.

The Democratic Party won the presidential elections in 1977 for Jimmy CARTER and, in 1992, for Bill CLINTON. It lost control of the Senate in 1980, but regained it six years later. The Democrats lost the 1988 elections when Michael Dukakis stood for president, but the party kept its majorities in both Houses of Congress. However, in mid-term elections in 1994 the Democrats suffered major losses, and the Republicans took control of both Houses for the first time since 1954.

demography Systematic study of human populations, especially their growth, size and structure. The main sources of data are census and registry statistics, which developed in the 19th century. In the 20th century, population studies have developed in two main directions. Formal demography is concerned with the calculation of population trends; it shows how rates of birth, fertility, mortality, marriage and migration combine to produce different population structures, densities and distributions. Social demography relates this abstract study to the economics and culture of particular societies to determine the causes and influences of changing population trends.

Demosthenes (384-322 BC) Greatest orator of ancient ATHENS, who urged the need to resist the encroachments of PHILIP II of Macedonia. He fought at Chaeronea in 338. The high point of his career as a public speaker came when he used his skill to defend himself successfully during his trial for allegedly accepting bribes and for cowardice in battle. He turned the charge against his accusers, the peace party of his life-long enemy Aeschines, by saying: 'Your policies supported our enemy; mine, our country.' After the defeat of Athens by the Macedonians in 322 BC and the death of Alexander the Great, Demosthenes committed suicide to avoid execution on a false charge of stealing money.

Deng Xiaoping (1904-) Veteran Chinese politician. Deng, also known as Teng Hsiaop'ing, was one of the original supporters of Chairman MAO ZE-DONG's Communist Party and took part in the Long March in 1935, when the dwindling Jiangxi Soviet fled its base ahead of government troops and marched 6000 miles (9600 km) to set up a new mountain stronghold. Deng studied in France in the early 1920s and spent some time in the Soviet Union before returning to China and working for the communists in Shanghai and Jiangxi. During the civil wars between 1937 and 1949 he rose to prominence as a political commissar, and afterwards held the senior party position in south-west China. Deng moved to Beijing in 1952 and became general secretary of the Chinese Communist Party in 1956. He was discredited during the CULTURAL

> **❝ The tendency to worship capitalism and advocate bourgeois liberalisation ... must be opposed and repudiated. ❞**
>
> *Deng Xiaoping in a speech supporting a political clampdown in 1980*

REVOLUTION, an attempt by Mao to reassert his pre-eminence over party ideology that spiralled out of his control. After being rehabilitated, Deng suffered again at the hands of the GANG OF FOUR, powerful members of the party leadership – including Mao's wife – who are alleged to have attempted to seize power after the chairman's death in 1976. Deng re-emerged in 1977 as the power behind the administration of Hua Guofeng, who succeeded Mao as chairman of the party's ruling central committee; now Deng became the champion of economic modernisation and set about improving relations with the West.

After 1981 Deng's main policies were to decentralise the running of the economy and to purge corruption. Yet he was not willing to

The Chinese leader Deng Xiaoping reviews the army in 1981. He opened the country to world trade but suppressed political dissent at home.

Votes for all: democracy comes of age

Democracy is a form of government in which the people rule, either directly or by electing representatives. Since its origin in Athens 2500 years ago, it has become the basis for political authority in many countries.

Democracy was introduced in the *polis* or city-state of Athens in the 5th century BC, where the people participated in making decisions at meetings of the assembly. In the democracies of today, the people elect representatives to make decisions for them.

Until the end of the 18th century it was thought that democracy could only work in a small city-state. In the American colonies, following the revolt against Britain after 1775, political thinkers such as James Madison began to develop an idea of representation which would enable democracy to be applied to large states. In the modern world, representation is secured by means of political parties. Almost all democracies today are party democracies.

In France, the outbreak of revolution in 1789 gave rise to an explicit political theory of democracy, embodied in the *Declaration of the Rights of Man and of the Citizen*, issued on August 26, 1789. This document declared that all political power derived not from God or from kings, but from the people.

Today, democracy has become the only lasting and legitimate basis for political authority. Even dictatorships such as the communist regimes which ruled Central and Eastern Europe until 1989 called themselves 'Peoples' Democracies'.

The Athenians, although they invented participatory democracy, limited its scope, excluding both slaves and women. The Americans, when they introduced democratic government in the 18th century, also excluded women and slaves, and the French restricted the vote to

men. It was not until 1893 that a state – New Zealand – was willing to give women the vote. In the United States, women received the vote in 1919, while in Britain women over the age of 21 were enfranchised in 1928. In France, women did not receive the vote until 1945, while in Switzerland women had to wait until 1971 to take part in elections.

MAKING DEMOCRACY WORK

Democracy is not without its problems as a form of government. It works best in homogeneous societies, where there are no deep ethnic, religious or linguistic divisions. In divided societies stability is achieved through forms of power-sharing, as in Switzerland, so that both majority and minority can participate. Democracy can also enable the people to elect to

At the 'Althing' – Iceland's parliament, dating back to around 930 – farmers set up booths, debated public affairs, and made decisions on matters of law by democratic consensus.

government a party which establishes a dictatorship. This happened in Germany in 1933, when Adolf Hitler's Nazi Party was voted into power. Hitler's regime is a prime example of what is sometimes called a totalitarian democracy.

To combat totalitarian democracy, most countries use constitutional checks and balances, so that no government can destroy minority rights. These can include a constitutional court to protect minorities, a second house of parliament to combat the excesses of the first, a strong system of local government, and federalism, to disperse political power away from the centre.

Democracy, the novelist E.M. Forster said, deserved only two cheers. Perhaps the third cheer should be reserved for constitutional democracy, a form of government which combines popular participation in decision-making with respect for the rule of law and the rights of minorities.

These ballot-discs from the 4th century BC, discovered in the Athenian Agora, were dropped into a box to record a verdict. Solid hubs stood for acquittal and hollow for condemnation.

During the Great Depression unemployed American workers desperate for money resorted to selling goods in the street. Wages were reduced and by 1933 around 13 million were out of work.

allow the Communist Party of China to lose its monopoly on power to the growing democracy movement that flourished in the late 1980s. A student demonstration was allowed to occupy Beijing's Tiananmen Square in 1989, but Deng sent in the army when the students' demands for more freedom attracted Western media coverage. Up to 2000 people are estimated to have died as tanks and troops bulldozed tents and makeshift barricades. Deng encouraged economic growth in the 1990s and promoted as his successor Jiang Zemin, who became president in 1993.

Denikin, Anton Ivanovich (1872-1947) Counter-revolutionary general during the Russian OCTOBER REVOLUTION in 1917, who took command of a 'white' army and seized control of a part of southern Russia. The son of a serf, Denikin had served the provisional government as commander on the Western Front in 1917, after the fall of the tsar. In May 1919 he launched an offensive against Moscow which was repulsed by the RED ARMY at Orel. He retreated to the Caucasus, where in 1920 his army disintegrated. Denikin fled to France and later emigrated to the USA.

Denmark Country in northern Europe, which incorporates the Atlantic territories of the Faeroe Islands and Greenland. The Danes took part in the VIKING explorations and conquests after about 800. In the early 11th century the Danish king CANUTE ruled over a great empire which covered Denmark, England, Norway, southern Sweden and parts of Finland. His reign was notable for the spread of Christianity, first introduced in the 9th century. In the 13th century Denmark emerged as the leading Scandinavian nation

after a period of disunity and civil war. But warfare and constitutional troubles continued until Christopher II, who reigned from 1320 to 1332, made concessions to the nobles and clergy at the expense of royal authority. The Protestant Reformation of the 16th century brought in a national Lutheran Church. King Christian IV intervened in the THIRTY YEARS' WAR in 1624 as a champion of Protestantism. A sequence of 17th-century wars with Sweden resulted in Denmark's eclipse as the leading Baltic power.

Denmark supported France during the Napoleonic Wars, and in 1814 was forced to cede Norway to Sweden. In 1863 SCHLESWIG was incorporated into Denmark. This was opposed by Prussia and Austria, whose troops invaded in 1864. Schleswig was absorbed into the GERMAN SECOND EMPIRE. After the First World War north Schleswig voted to return to Denmark.

The Germans occupied Denmark between 1940 and 1945 despite a declaration of neutrality at the start of the Second World War. Denmark joined NATO in 1949, and in 1960 it became part of the new EUROPEAN FREE TRADE ASSOCIATION. It joined the European Community in 1973. A close referendum decision in 1992 rejected the draft Maastricht Treaty, which proposed greater European political and economic unity. The following year another referendum was held and the Danes agreed to ratify the treaty.

Depression, the Great Popular term for the world economic crisis from 1929 to 1933. Panic began on 'Black Thursday', October 24, 1929, when millions of shares were sold on the

New York Stock Exchange. The market collapsed the following Tuesday. As a result, US banks began to call in international loans, including money lent to Germany for industrial development and REPARATIONS after the First World War. In 1931 discussions took place between Germany and Austria for a customs union. The French saw this as a first step towards a full union and in May withdrew their funds from the Kredit-Anstalt bank of Vienna. The bank announced its inability to fulfil its obligations, and soon other Austrian and German banks were forced to close.

President Herbert HOOVER in the USA negotiated a one-year postponement for the payment of reparations, but it was too late. The German collapse was felt in other countries. In the USA and Germany members of the public began withdrawing their savings, and more banks had to close. Farmers were unable to sell their crops; factories, shops and industrial concerns could not borrow and went bankrupt; workers were sacked; and governments could not afford to continue to pay unemployment benefits. In the colonies of the European powers and in Latin America, demand for basic commodities collapsed, increasing unemployment and stimulating nationalist unrest. Unemployment in Germany rose to about 6 million, and in Britain to 3 million. By 1932 about half the banks in the USA had failed. In Europe, where the introduction of greater democracy since the First World War had reduced class tensions, the effect was to foster political extremism.

Renewed fears of a BOLSHEVIK uprising produced right-wing militarist regimes inspired by fascism, not only in Germany but throughout the Balkan countries. In 1932 the Democrat Franklin D. ROOSEVELT was elected president of the USA. Gradually financial confidence was restored, but not before the Nazi THIRD REICH had established itself as the only force that seemed capable of revitalising the depressed German economy.

> **DID YOU KNOW?**
>
> *Popular songs of the Depression such as 'Brother, Can You Spare a Dime?' summed up the feelings of First World War veterans hit hard by unemployment.*

Derby, Edward Stanley, 14th Earl of (1799-1869) British statesman. Derby first entered Parliament in 1820 as a Whig, and as colonial secretary in 1834 he freed 775 000 plantation slaves in the Caribbean. In the next decade he moved over to the Conservatives and joined Sir Robert Peel's government of 1841. He resigned four years later over the repeal of the CORN LAWS. Derby was prime minister in 1852 and for two other terms. His administration from 1866 to 1868 passed the second REFORM ACT, which redistributed parliamentary seats, doubled the electorate and gave the vote to many working men.

Derry see LONDONDERRY

Desai, Morarji (1896-1995) Indian statesman and nationalist leader. Desai made his reputation as revenue minister of Bombay between 1946 and 1952, then as chief minister of the city for four years and as finance minister again in the central government between 1958 and 1963. He oversaw a series of five-year plans for expanding industry which led to a doubling of output in ten years. After the death of Jawaharlal NEHRU in 1964, Desai was a strong contender for the post of prime minister, but his austere and autocratic style made him too many enemies within the Congress Party. In 1977 he was the obvious candidate to head the Janata opposition to Mrs Indira Gandhi and led his party to victory in the election that year. As prime minister for the next two years his inflexible style handicapped him in dealing with economic and factional problems, and he resigned in 1979.

Descartes, René (1596-1650) French mathematician, scientist and philosopher. Descartes based his philosophical reasoning on the principles and methods of mathematics. His quest for certitude started from his aphorism, 'Cogito ergo sum' ('I think, therefore I am'). He advanced mathematics by developing analytical geometry, and optics by his discovery of the law of refraction. Descartes' profound influence can be traced in the works of rationalists, empiricists and materialists who rejected his doctrines but benefited from his intellectual rigour. Educated by the

> The philosopher René Descartes claimed that the nature of his future work was revealed in a dream.

Jesuits, he then went on to take a degree in law. He followed a military career from 1617 to 1619 in the peacetime armies of the Netherlands and Bavaria. After several years travelling, he spent some time in Paris and finally settled in the Netherlands, where he completed his *Regulae ad Directionem Ingenii* (*Rules for the Direction of the Mind*) in 1628. He then produced the works which brought him fame: *Discours de la Méthode* (*Discourse on Method*, 1637), *Meditationes de Prima Philosophia* (*Meditations on First Philosophy*, 1641) and *Principia Philosophiae* (*Principles of Philosophy*, 1644). But Descartes' views exposed him to persecution by theologians, and he finally accepted a royal invitation to take refuge in Sweden, where he died.

desegregation Movement in the USA to end discrimination against its Black citizens. Many segregation laws were passed in the Southern states after the AMERICAN CIVIL WAR, and they were supported by a Supreme Court decision in 1896 which accepted as constitutional a Louisiana law setting up separate but equal facilities for Whites and Blacks in trains. For the next 50 years, many Southern states continued to use this 'separate but equal' rule as an excuse for providing only segregated facilities. Segregation was extended at the beginning of the 20th century to include schools, hospitals, churches and jails.

Black and White Americans alike began making efforts to end segregation with the founding of the National Association for the Advancement of Colored People in 1909, but they met with fierce resistance from state authorities and White organisations, especially in the South. Change was inevitable after the Second World War, during which more than a million Blacks served in the military. In 1948 President Harry S Truman issued a directive calling for an end to segregation in the forces, but it was only with the CIVIL RIGHTS movement of the 1950s and 1960s that significant reforms were made.

The Supreme Court decision in 1954 against segregation in state schools was a landmark. This was followed in the 1960s by the policy of BUSING children from other neighbourhoods to achieve a racial mix of pupils. The efforts of Black minister Martin Luther KING led to the passing of the Civil Rights Act of 1964 and the Voting Rights Act of 1965, which outlawed segregation and ended literacy tests which had been used to keep Black children out of White schools.

Desmoulins, Camille (1760-94) French journalist and revolutionary. Desmoulins became an advocate in the Paris *parlement* in 1785 and four years later, after the dismissal of Jacques Necker as chief minister, he summoned the crowd outside the Palais Royal 'to arms'. On July 14, the mob stormed the Bastille. In November Desmoulins began to publish his famous journal *Les Révolutions de France et de Brabant*, attacking the ANCIEN RÉGIME, and began a close association with revolutionary Georges DANTON. Desmoulins voted for the execution of Louis XVI, but his support of Danton's moderate policies angered Maximilien ROBESPIERRE and led to his arrest and execution on April 5, 1794.

de Soto, Hernando (c. 1496-1542) Spanish conquistadore and explorer who was made governor of Cuba by Emperor Charles V, with the right to conquer the mainland of America. De Soto landed on the Florida coast in 1539 and reached North Carolina before crossing the Appalachian Mountains and returning through Tennessee and Alabama. In 1541 he led a second expedition, crossing the Mississippi (which he was probably the first European to see) and sailing up the Arkansas river into Oklahoma. The expedition was looking for gold and silver, but returned disappointed. De Soto died on reaching the banks of the Mississippi on the return journey.

National Guardsmen enforce desegregation policy at a former Whites-only school in Little Rock, Arkansas in 1957. White parents had threatened to prevent Black children from attending classes.

Despenser, Hugh le (1262-1326) English aristocrat and adviser to Edward I and EDWARD II. Despenser (known as the Elder) and his son, Hugh le Despenser (the Younger), were attacked in Parliament for their allegedly evil counselling of Edward II and were disinherited and exiled from the realm. The sentences were annulled, but after Edward was forced to abdicate in 1326 by his wife and her lover Roger Mortimer, the Despensers were captured and executed.

Dessalines, Jean Jacques (1758-1806) Emperor of Haiti. After escaping from slavery during the slave rebellion of 1791, Dessalines served under TOUSSAINT L'OUVERTURE in the wars that liberated Haiti from France. Although illiterate, Dessalines had a declaration of independence written in his name. In 1803 he led a revolt against French forces which had been severely reduced by yellow fever. With the defeat of France he became governor-general of Haiti, and in late 1804 had himself crowned Emperor Jacques I. He instituted a reign of terror and tried to rebuild

Rebellious slaves led by Jean Dessalines take their revenge on defeated French troops who had tried to reinstall the hated slave masters.

the nation's economy by the use of forced labour. The cruelty of his rule led to a palace revolt in 1805. Dessalines was assassinated while trying to quash the rebellion in 1806.

détente Easing of strained relations, especially between states and particularly between the USA and the Soviet Union. The word, from the French for 'relaxation', is associated with the 'thaw' in the COLD WAR in the early 1970s and the policies of Richard Nixon as US president and Henry Kissinger as national security adviser from 1968 and secretary of state from 1973 to 1977. The more relaxed relations were marked by the European Conference on Security and Co-operation in

Helsinki and Geneva from 1973 to 1975, the arms reduction SALT I treaty in 1972 and the improvement in West Germany's relationships with the Eastern European states.

Dettingen, Battle of (June 27, 1743) Important victory for the British over the French in the War of the AUSTRIAN SUCCESSION. Forty thousand Hanoverian, British, Dutch and Austrian troops, led by Britain's GEORGE II, marched to the banks of the River Main. They were attacked by a French army, but forced it back across the river. George II was the last reigning British sovereign to take personal command of his forces on the battlefield.

> **DID YOU KNOW?**
>
> Sergei Diaghilev's Ballets Russes used some of the finest composers and artists of the time. Debussy, Ravel and Strauss wrote scores, while Picasso often designed spectacular sets.

de Valera, Eamon (1882-1975) Irish statesman who devoted himself to securing Ireland's independence from Britain. De Valera was imprisoned for his part in the EASTER RISING in 1916 and would have been executed but for his American birth. He was freed under an amnesty in 1917 and elected president of SINN FÉIN. De Valera was held again in 1918 for his Sinn Féin activities, but escaped from Lincoln jail the following year and spent two years as a guerrilla fighter in the IRISH REPUBLICAN ARMY. He was elected as a Sinn Féin MP and became president of the independent government (Dáil Éireann), which was set up by Sinn Féin.

De Valera did not attend the negotiations in London leading to the Anglo-Irish Treaty of 1921, and attacked the plan signed by his representatives to set up an Irish Free State from which six Ulster counties were to be excluded. He became the leading opponent of William Cosgrave, president of the executive council of the Free State from 1922 to 1932, and founded the rival FIANNA FÁIL in 1926. De Valera went on to lead his party to victory in the 1932 election. He ended the oath of allegiance to the British crown and in 1937 devised a new constitution, describing his country as a 'sovereign independent democratic state'. During the Second World War he kept Ireland neutral despite an offer from Britain to recognise the principle of a united Ireland in return for an entry into the war. He stopped the payment of annuities to Britain and negotiated the return of naval bases held under the 1921 treaty. De Valera was twice elected president of Ireland, and his last presidency, until 1973, took him into his 90s.

Dewey, George (1837-1917) US admiral. Dewey's victory over the Spanish fleet at Manila Bay on May 1, 1898, was not only decisive for the outcome of the SPANISH AMERICAN WAR but also for the future of American imperialism in the Pacific. He had

served in the Union (Northern) navy during the American Civil War. In 1899 he made a triumphal progress through New York and was created the first US Admiral of the Navy, a rank higher than admiral.

Diaghilev, Sergei (1872-1929) Ballet impresario and founder of the Ballets Russes, which he directed for 20 years. Diaghilev graduated in law in 1896 at the University of St Petersburg but was determined to follow a musical career. In Moscow around the turn of the century Diaghilev made radical suggestions for operas starring the bass singer Fyodor Chaliapin, and founded an international art review, *Mir Iskusstva* (World of Art). He moved to Paris in 1906, where he organised an exhibition of Russian art and produced Modest Mussorgsky's opera *Boris Godunov* at the Paris Opera with Chaliapin in the title role. Diaghilev, with the assistance of three other artists, founded the Ballets Russes (Russian Ballet) in 1909 at the Théâtre du Châtelet, with the dancers Anna Pavlova and Vaslav Nijinsky in the company. His productions were avant garde, using techniques such as mime. Music and scene design were made an integral part of the dance. Diaghilev's experimental method reached a climax in Igor Stravinsky's *The Rite of Spring* in 1913, which caused uproar among the fashionable Parisian audience. The company toured extensively giving performances until Diaghilev's death.

Diane de Poitiers (1499-1566) Mistress of HENRY II of France. Diane de Poitiers came to court during the reign of Francis I, from 1515 to 1547, and Prince Henry, 20 years her junior, fell in love with her. On his accession she became queen in all but name, displacing Henry's wife Catherine de Medici. A beautiful and cultured woman, she enlarged the

The nationalist leader Eamon de Valera (right) inspects a division of the IRA in 1922. It was created to fight for a reunited state of Ireland.

Diane de Poitiers, Henry II's mistress, concentrated on providing for her family rather than taking part in politics.

Château de Chenonceaux and its gardens and became the friend and patron of artists and poets, such as Pierre de Ronsard. On Henry's death in 1559, Catherine forced Diane de Poitiers to surrender the crown jewels and banished her to the grim Château Chaumont.

diaspora Collective term, from the Greek for 'dispersion', for Jewish communities outside Israel or any people dispersed from their native lands. The process of dispersal of the Jews began with Assyrian and Babylonian expulsions in 721 and 586 BC. It was continued by voluntary migration and accelerated by the destruction of the Temple in Jerusalem by the Roman emperor Titus in AD 70. Soon after there were Jewish communities from the Levant to Italy, and in Babylon and Egypt. The diaspora Jews of the Graeco-Roman world were mostly Greek-speaking, but they remained loyal to their faith, visited Jerusalem, and regarded Israel as their homeland. In the early Middle Ages, Spain was the main centre of Jewish scholarship, until the Roman Catholic INQUISITION expelled all Jews in 1492.

Jewish scholars were also found in France and Germany, but from the time of the Crusades anti-Semitism began to develop, with many cities began to confine Jews to particular areas. Poland and Lithuania welcomed Jewish victims of persecution, and by the 17th century Eastern Europe had become the diaspora's centre of gravity, until the pogroms of the 1880s drove many westwards to the USA. Persecution of diaspora Jews continued throughout the 20th century, particularly under the Nazi regime in Germany from 1933 to 1945, which caused the death of more than 6 million Jews as part of Adolf Hitler's 'final solution'.

Díaz, Porfirio (1830-1915) Mexican dictator of part-Indian descent whose harsh rule prompted the MEXICAN REVOLUTION of 1910 and led to civil war from 1911 to 1918. As president Díaz remained in control of his country from 1876 to the civil war. He began his military career by supporting Benito Juárez and the liberals during Mexico's War of Reform from 1858 to 1861 and during the fight against the French intervention in the following year. Díaz was responsible for the economic development and modernisation of his country, but ruled in the interests of a privileged minority. Mineral resources were exploited by foreigners, and much of the rural population was bound to debt slavery.

Dickens, Charles (1812-70) English novelist who highlighted the grim conditions of the working classes and the harshness of life in early-19th-century London. Following his father's imprisonment for debt, the 12-year-old Dickens worked briefly in a blacking factory, an experience which provided him with material for his novel *David Copperfield*. After working as a lawyer's clerk, he began his journalistic career in 1831 reporting Parliament for the *Morning Chronicle*. Five years later Dickens published the first of a monthly series called *The Posthumous Papers of the Pickwick Club*, which were intended as captions to sporting pictures but which became so popular that they were issued as a novel. The success of the *Pickwick Papers* established his reputation and led to a series of books that included *Oliver Twist, Nicholas Nickleby, The Old Curiosity Shop* and *A Christmas Carol*. Dickens campaigned against slavery and for better housing, and travelled to the USA to take part in an exhausting tour of dramatic readings that might have shortened his life. His later novels included *Hard Times, Great Expectations* and *Bleak House*. He died while writing *The Mystery of Edwin Drood*.

Diderot, Denis (1713-84) French novelist, dramatist, critic and philosopher. Diderot was critical of the ANCIEN RÉGIME, and in 1749 was jailed for a few months by royal order. Diderot edited the 35-volume *Encyclopédie,* in which he expressed his belief in science and his scorn for superstition. His accounts of exhibitions of contemporary art inaugurated the genre of art criticism, and he helped to popularise science and philosophy.

Dien Bien Phu (1954) Decisive military engagement in the French Indochinese War. French airborne troops seized and fortified the village of Dien Bien Phu overlooking the strategic route between Hanoi and the Laotian border in November 1953 in an attempt to defeat Vietminh guerrilla forces trying to overthrow French colonial rule in Vietnam.

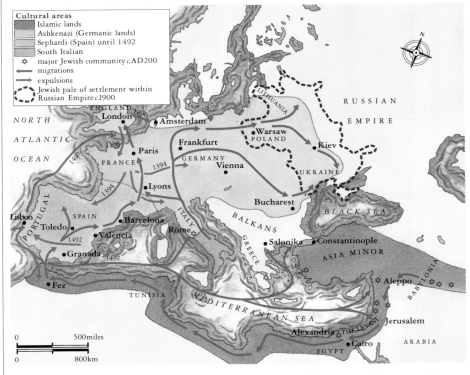

Cultural areas
- Islamic lands
- Ashkenazi (Germanic lands)
- Sephardi (Spain) until 1492
- South Italian
- ✿ major Jewish community c.AD 200
- ← migrations
- → expulsions
- --- Jewish pale of settlement within Russian Empire c.1900

The centuries of expulsions and migrations suffered during the diaspora were interpreted by some Jews as exile, and by others as a positive aspect of the spiritual destiny of Judaism.

Allied troops advance up the beach during the Dieppe raid in this artist's depiction of the failed 1942 attack on the French port. The lessons learnt about seaborne assault were used on D-Day.

But the Vietnamese commander General Vo Nguyen Giap was able to establish an effective siege with Chinese-supplied heavy artillery, preventing the garrison being supplied by air. He subjected it to eight weeks of constant bombardment between March and May 1954, which finally forced its surrender. The guerrillas took about 10000 prisoners. The armistice that followed ended French rule within two months.

Dieppe raid (August 18-19, 1942) Amphibious raid by the Allies on Dieppe, Normandy, in the Second World War. Its aim was to destroy the German-held port, airfield and radar installations, and to gain experience of amphibious operations. Some 1000 British commandos and 5000 Canadian infantry were involved. There was considerable confusion as landing craft approached the two landing beaches, where they met heavy fire. The assault was a failure and the order to withdraw was given. More than two-thirds of the troops were lost, and German shore guns sank one destroyer and 33 landing craft, and 106 aircraft were shot down. Although the raid was a disaster, it taught many lessons for later landings in North Africa, and particularly for the Normandy landings in June 1944.

Diesel, Rudolf (1858-1913) German pioneer of the high-compression diesel engine. Diesel began developing the engine that was to bear his name in 1892 when he obtained a patent on a new type of internal-combustion engine fuelled by oil, in which ignition was produced not by a spark but by the heat generated by compression of the fuel in the cylinder. When the prototype was exhibited in 1897 it attracted worldwide interest, and a factory to manufacture the engine was established in Augsburg. The engine's relatively low power-to-weight ratio at first limited its use to applications where weight was not critical, as in submarines and ships. Refined design and lighter alloys were later used to remedy this drawback.

Diet Word used to describe the estates or representative assemblies of various European countries (from the medieval Latin, 'a meeting for a single day'). The Holy Roman Empire held Diets between emperors and local rulers, or kings and princes, notably at Augsburg in 1500, Constance in 1507 and Frankfurt in 1518. The most famous was that of WORMS in 1521, where the Protestant reformer Martin Luther confronted the Holy Roman Emperor Charles V. As the princes used Lutheranism to challenge Charles V's

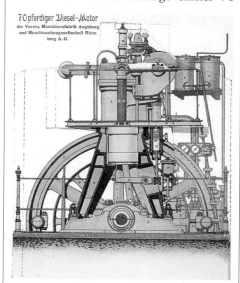

The first engine built by Rudolf Diesel could produce 25 horsepower, but improved versions like this were soon able to triple the output.

authority, further Diets discussed religion. At Speier, a solution offering religious tolerance was submitted in 1526, and a strict Catholic alternative in 1529. The two sides further defined their terms at Augsburg in 1530, and made a last attempt at conciliation at Regensburg in 1541. Meetings at Augsburg in 1547-8 and 1555 brought religious settlement. At another important meeting, held at Regensburg in 1732, the princes agreed to accept the PRAGMATIC SANCTION, which was intended to prevent a struggle for succession to the post of emperor.

The Imperial Diet of the Holy Roman Empire was finally abolished in 1806. The German Confederation established a federal Diet in Frankfurt with Austria holding a casting vote. Other parliamentary bodies, including those of Hungary, Bohemia, Poland, the Scandinavian countries and Japan, have also been called Diets.

Digger Name for a member of a radical Puritan group which flourished briefly in England in the period of political instability between 1649 and 1650. The Diggers earned their name by seizing common land and sharing it out for growing crops as one way to combat soaring food prices. They called themselves the True Levellers, but were denounced by the original LEVELLERS, who disliked their communistic attitude towards property. The Diggers' main settlement at St George's Hill, Surrey, and those in nine other counties were dispersed by the authorities in March 1650.

Dimitrov, Georgi (1882-1949) Bulgarian communist leader. In 1945 Dimitrov was appointed head of the communist government in Bulgaria, which led to the setting up of the People's Republic the following year under his premiership. By 1929 he had been head of the Bulgarian sector of the COMINTERN in Berlin. When the REICHSTAG was burned in 1933 he was accused with other communists of complicity. His defence at his trial was so effective that it forced the Nazis to release him, and he lived in Moscow until the end of the Second World War.

Diocletian (Gaius Aurelius) (245-316) Roman emperor from 284 to 305. Diocletian restored order after a long and chaotic period of short-lived emperors. He had been commander of the imperial household troops when his men made him ruler. Diocletian campaigned vigorously and successfully to protect the empire's collapsing frontiers and to repress internal rebellions, most notably in Britain and Egypt. He introduced far-reaching and lasting administrative, military and financial reforms, and established the 'Tetrarchy', dividing the empire between four rulers. He became senior emperor (titled Augustus) of the eastern half of the empire,

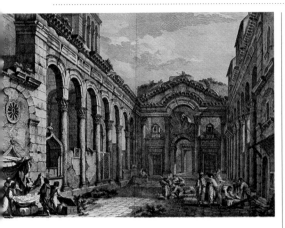

The Roman emperor Diocletian's palace in Salonae was a cross between a sea fortress and a country house of impressive proportions.

with Galerius as his deputy, and Maximian took control of the Western Empire helped by Constantius. From 303 Diocletian ordered the persecution of Christians because he was devoted to the traditional forms of Roman religion. He abdicated in 305, and apart from a brief re-emergence in 308 lived until his death in a palace at Salonae (now Split on the Croatian coast), much of which survives. Diocletian provided the basis upon which CONSTANTINE was to continue to restore the empire's fortunes.

Diogenes (c.400-325 BC) Greek philosopher, popularly credited with being the founder of the CYNICS. He came to Athens, where he lived as a pauper and flouted conventional behaviour. He believed that an individual needed only to satisfy his natural needs in the simplest manner possible to be happy. His apparent shamelessness led to his nickname 'the dog' (Greek *kuon*, hence 'Cynic'). He is said to have lived in a barrel. His debt to Antisthenes of Athens, himself a devoted disciple of SOCRATES, was considerable.

diplomacy see feature, page 195

Directory (1795-9) Government of France in the turbulent years following the JACOBIN dictatorship of the French Revolution. The Directory was composed of two legislative houses, a Council of Five Hundred and a Council of Ancients, and an executive (elected by the councils) of five directors. It was dominated by moderates and sought to stabilise the country by overcoming economic and financial problems at home and ending the war with Spain and Holland.

In 1796 the Directory introduced measures to combat inflation and the monetary crisis, but popular distress increased and opposition grew as the Jacobins reassembled. A conspiracy led by François BABEUF was crushed the same year, but this persuaded the Directory to

seek support from the royalists. In the elections the next year, in which the directors were supported by Napoleon, they annulled some of the results. This second Directory brought in authoritarian policies (often called the 'Directorial Terror'), which for a time established stability as financial and fiscal reforms met with some success. But by 1798, economic difficulties in agriculture and industry led to renewed opposition which, after defeats abroad in 1799, became a crisis. The directors, fearing a foreign invasion and a Jacobin coup, turned to Napoleon, who seized his opportunity to take power in November and then abolished the Directory.

disarmament Attempt to achieve the reduction or abolition of military forces and armaments by international agreement begun before the First World War. It was followed in 1932 by a World Disarmament Conference. In 1952 a permanent United Nations Disarmament Commission was established in Geneva. National pressure groups, for example the Campaign for Nuclear Disarmament, have tended to seek unilateral disarmament. Bilateral agreements are negotiated between two governments for arms reduction and control, while multilateral agreements are sought via conferences or the UN Commission. Since the Second World War most talks have concerned nuclear weapons, leading to the SALT treaties, but chemical and biological arms have also been discussed.

disciple In Jewish society at the time of Jesus Christ many religious teachers attracted disciples who gathered to be taught their master's interpretation of the scriptures. The followers of Jesus differed from these groups in several respects. For example, he actively sought out disciples, and he found many of his followers among people who were judged by society to be social or moral outcasts.

The Apostles, those Jesus chose to preach his gospel, were the 12 chief disciples: PETER (the leader), John, Andrew, James, Philip, Matthew, Bartholomew, Thomas, James (the Less), Thaddeus, Simon and Judas Iscariot. After the suicide of Judas, who betrayed Jesus, his place was taken by Matthias. PAUL and his original companion Barnabas are also considered as Apostles.

Disney, Walt (1901-66) Cartoon animator and film maker. He set up studios in Hollywood in 1923 and created his most famous character,

Walt Disney himself provided Mickey's voice in 1928 when the mouse made his screen debut in *Steamboat Willie*.

Mickey Mouse, in two short films released in 1928. The following year Disney exploited the new film medium of sound in 'Silly Symphonies', cartoons with changing images matched with different soundtracks. The Disney studios grew rapidly and began to produce full length animated movies which included *Snow White and the Seven Dwarfs* in 1937, and *Pinocchio* and *Dumbo* in the 1940s. In the 1950s Disney began to also make films with actors and actresses, such as the popular musical *Mary Poppins*.

The studios also began making programmes for the growing medium of television with the children's series *Davy Crockett*. Disney expanded his empire in 1955 by opening the first Disneyland amusement park in California followed by another in Florida. In 1992 his company opened its first European theme park, EuroDisney, on a 5000 acre (2000 ha) site 20 miles (32 km) east of Paris.

Disraeli, Benjamin (1804-81) British statesman and novelist. Disraeli gave the modern Conservative Party its identity and provided it with a policy of imperialism and social reform. He entered Parliament in 1837 after unsuccessfully fighting four elections and by the early 1840s had become a member of the Young England movement of Tories which favoured an alliance between the old aristocracy and the people, in opposition to the increasingly powerful middle classes.

In 1846 the Tory prime minister, Sir Robert Peel, repealed the CORN LAWS, provoking fierce opposition from Disraeli and a majority of the Tories, who supported a protectionist policy. The controversy split the party. For the next 20 years Disraeli, with the help of the Earl of Derby, led the protectionist Conservatives in the House of Commons and became chancellor of the exchequer in 1852,

Foreign relations

Diplomacy as a method of conducting relations between states is as much in evidence today as it was in the ancient empires of the Middle East, but the role of the ambassador in the 20th century has changed.

The first diplomats are thought to have been the ambassadors sent by the ancient Babylonian and Egyptian empires to neighbouring states or trading partners. Intermittent contact, with envoys authorised to discuss specific matters such as settling a dispute, continued through the Middle Ages. Immense ceremony was usual, particularly if rulers were personally involved. 'The Field of the Cloth of Gold', a meeting outside Calais in 1520 between Henry VIII of England and Francis I of France, was a dazzling extravaganza staged by Cardinal Thomas Wolsey. The two kings feasted and jousted for almost a fortnight – but failed to seal an alliance. One of the earliest Western accounts of imperial China, by a Spanish friar in 1585, described the elaborate receptions given to ambassadors sent by King Manoel of Portugal and the king of Malacca.

In the 15th century, Italian states such as Florence, Venice and the Papacy experimented with keeping full-time envoys at other courts. When King Ferdinand of Aragon sent Rodrigo Gonzalez de la Puebla to London in 1495, he became the first resident ambassador in England. The creation of permanent embassies allowed continuous diplomatic relationships based on a regular flow of news.

In the 17th century France set a new style for diplomacy. Cardinal Richelieu concentrated responsibility in his newly created foreign ministry, and later Louis XIV maintained no fewer than 21 permanent ambassadors. Most capitals acquired a resident diplomatic corps of perhaps half a dozen ambassadors, representing states of particular importance to them. Diplomacy was becoming a salaried professional career. François de Callières, French plenipotentiary at the Treaty of Ryswick in 1697, wrote a classic textbook, *The Art of Negotiating with Sovereign Princes*,

Louis XIV, Europe's most powerful monarch, receives a Spanish embassy at the palace of Versailles. One of his career diplomats, François de Callières, wrote a textbook on his new profession.

outlining the requisite qualities of patience, self-control and attentiveness. More tersely, Sir Henry Wotton, English envoy in Venice, defined an ambassador as 'an honest man sent to lie [live] abroad for the good of his country'.

DIPLOMACY IN ACTION

In Asia diplomatic contacts remained occasional. The Chinese empire had become increasingly introverted, indifferent to both diplomacy and trade expansion. When Lord Macartney, head of the first diplomatic mission, arrived in Peking in 1793 magnificent gifts, known as 'tribute presents', were sent by George III and the East India Company to ease relations with the Chinese government.

The 18th century regarded the 'balance of power' as the central aim of European diplomacy. Each state combined alternately with others to prevent the domination of a single ruler. But after the fall of Napoleon the system became less stable. Complex issues such as the Eastern Question – what to do about Ottoman Turkey, a great power in decay – and the rise of Otto von Bismarck's Germany posed enormous challenges to both France and Britain. Diplomacy failed to solve these tensions, and they led eventually to the outbreak of the First World War. In August 1914, Lord Grey of Falloden, after a lifetime at the British Foreign Office, mourned the end of the old order: 'The lamps are going out all over Europe; we shall not see them lit again in our lifetime.'

In the 20th century the growth of the diplomatic corps has accelerated. Nearly every nation is represented in the major capitals, yet the importance of traditional diplomacy has declined, and instead the emphasis is on trading relations. With electronic communications and air travel, heads of state can directly contact one another on matters of high importance. The 'hot line' between the White House in Washington and the Kremlin in Moscow was established during the Cold War to prevent any misunderstanding from escalating into nuclear disaster. Ambassadors still have cultural and social prestige, but they exercise less power.

Prime Minister Benjamin Disraeli, as Aladdin, offers Queen Victoria the crown of India in a cartoon published in the magazine *Punch*.

1858-9 and 1866-8. As the leader of the Commons he introduced the REFORM Bill of 1867, which gave much of the urban working class the vote, and in the following year he was prime minister for a brief while. In 1874 he again became prime minister. Disraeli bought the largest shareholding in the SUEZ CANAL Company for Britain, obtained the title of Empress of India for Queen Victoria, and averted war with Russia through skilful diplomacy at the Congress of Berlin in 1878.

At home his government passed social legislation which covered slum clearance, public health and trade union reform, and the improvement of conditions in factories. Economic depression and unpopular colonial wars led to a Conservative defeat in the election of 1880 and Disraeli, though in poor health, led his party from the House of Lords until his death, having been created 1st Earl of Beaconsfield in 1876. He began writing novels before his entry into politics and continued after his election as an MP. Books such as *Sybil* and *Coningsby*, written in the 1840s, reflected his concern with social reform.

Dissolution of the Monasteries see
MONASTERIES, DISSOLUTION OF

Divine Right of Kings European doctrine
which held that monarchy was a divinely ordained institution, that hereditary right could not be abolished, that kings were answerable only to God, and that it was therefore sinful for their subjects to resist them actively. The principle evolved during the Middle Ages, in part as a reaction to papal intrusion into secular affairs. The extension of the Divine Right of Kings to justify absolute rule and illegal taxation aroused opposition.

James I of England upheld the doctrine in his speeches and his son Charles I was executed for refusing to accept parliamentary control of his policies. After the GLORIOUS REVOLUTION of 1688 the doctrine became obsolete in England, yielding to antiabsolutist arguments like those of the philosopher John Locke.

In late-17th-century France Louis XIV's monarchy was based on the principle of Divine Right, which was claimed by his successors up to the revolution.

Dixiecrat Popular name once applied in the
USA to a right-wing Democrat in a Southern state opposed to DESEGREGATION. The Southern states were known as Dixieland after the name of a song adopted as the Confederate army anthem during the American Civil War. In 1948 the States Rights Democratic Party was founded by die-hard Southern Democrats (Dixiecrats), opposed to President Harry S Truman's renomination as Democratic candidate for president because of his support for CIVIL RIGHTS. Its members wanted each state to be able to nominate its own presidential candidate without losing the 'Democratic' label. In the 1948 presidential election their vote totalled more than 1 million. After Truman's victory they abandoned their attempts to win presidential candidates from each state, but continued to resist the civil rights programme in Congress. Many Dixiecrats moved to support the Republican Party in the 1960s and 1970s.

Djibouti East African country, formerly part
of French Somaliland. Its importance derives from its strategic position on the Gulf of Aden. The small enclave was created as a port

in the late 1880s by the French, and the town became capital of French Somaliland in 1892. In 1958 French Somaliland was declared by France to be the Territory of the Afars and Issas, but in 1977 the country was granted independence as the Republic of Djibouti under President Hassan Gouled.

The country has since suffered from famine and civil war, and an influx of refugees from Somalia and those fleeing from the Ethiopian civil war. In November 1991 the *Front pour la Restauration de la Unité et la Démocratie* was formed. Fighting in the west and south was ended by French mediation in February 1992, with an assurance of democracy. One party was allowed to oppose Gouled's *Rassemblement Populaire pour le Progrès* (Popular Rally for Progress Party) later in the year, but other parties called for a boycott. Less than half the population voted, and Gouled's party won all the seats. Fighting resumed until a cease-fire was honoured in 1993.

D notice Advisory notice from the British
Defence, Press and Broadcasting Advisory Committee asking newspapers and broadcasters not to publish information which could damage national security. The system allows government departments to tell the media which details of defence and antiterrorist measures could be useful to foreign intelligence services or subversive organisations. Details about nuclear weapons, arms, plans, codes and general military capability are the subjects of notices. The committee was set up in 1912 and consists of media and government department representatives. In 1993 the notices were renamed Defence Advisory (DA) notices to emphasise that they are voluntary.

The leader of Venice sets off on the ancient annual ritual to mark the city's connection with the seas in Antonio Canaletto's painting *The Commemoration of the Wedding of the Doge and the Sea*.

doge Title of the holder of the highest civil office in Venice, Genoa and Amalfi from the 8th century AD to the 18th century. The office originated in the city of Venice as it consolidated its supremacy as an empire in the Adriatic. In 1032 hereditary succession was banned and election was made increasingly complicated to prevent domination by particular factions. But the Participazio and Candiano families still provided most candidates in the 9th and 10th centuries, and the Tiepolo and Dandolo families in the 13th and 14th centuries. The system finally ended with the Napoleonic conquest of 1797.

The Genoese introduced a similar system after 1339; it became an aristocratic office after 1528, and also succumbed to Napoleon. The first doge's palace in Venice was built in 814 and destroyed in 976. Mercantile riches in both the cities later financed lavish residences for civic leaders. In Venice the magnificent 15th-century doge's palace was decorated by the painters Tintoretto and Titian.

dollar diplomacy Term used to describe foreign policies designed to help American business interests. It was first applied to the policy of President William TAFT, who financed the building of railways in China in 1909 with investments and loans. The policy spread to Haiti, Honduras and Nicaragua, where United States loans were backed by US forces and where a US collector of customs was installed in 1911. Dollar diplomacy failed because it was based on a simplistic idea of how economies work, and it often caused social unrest because it was backed by US troops. The policy was abandoned by President Woodrow Wilson after 1913, but intervention in support of business interests, particularly in Latin America, continued.

Dollfuss, Engelbert (1892-1934) Austrian statesman. In February 1934 demonstrations by socialist workers led chancellor Dollfuss to order the bombardment of a housing estate in Vienna. After fierce fighting the socialists were crushed and Dollfuss proclaimed an authoritarian constitution. In 1932 he had managed to negotiate a generous loan from the LEAGUE OF NATIONS, but this had failed to relieve economic depression and social unrest in the country. In March 1933 Dollfuss suspended parliamentary government, which deprived him of any support from the working classes against the Nazi threat. On July 25, 1934 he was assassinated during an abortive Nazi coup.

dolmen see MEGALITH

Domesday Book Survey of property in England conducted in 1086 on the orders of William I, but probably partly based on administrative records. As an assessment of

property and land it was the most comprehensive ever undertaken in medieval Europe. The name came from the general belief that an entry was as final as doomsday. The English shires were visited by royal commissioners and the survey listed the names of landholders, their status, the size of their holding, its use, its tax liability and the number of animals it supported. The information for each shire was then reorganised by 'hundreds' or subdivisions of counties. The final version formed two volumes – Little Domesday (Norfolk, Suffolk and Essex) and Great Domesday (the rest of England except for the four northern shires, which were never surveyed, and London and Winchester – for which no records survive). The survey was carried out by the Normans to assess the resources of the land they had conquered. The information was used to maximise revenue and to bring order into the Norman seizure of English property.

domestic architecture see feature, page 198

Dominic, St (1170-1221) Founder of the DOMINICAN order of friars. St Dominic was born in Spain of a noble family, but as a young man adopted an austere life, becoming a priest and canon of Osma Cathedral. From 1206 he became a missionary to the ALBIGENSIAN heretics of southern France. He embraced

Dominican monks were known as the 'Black Friars' because they wore a black mantle.

poverty to convert by example, and worked with Crusaders who suppressed the heretics by force. In 1215 he founded his own order.

Dominican Member of the Order of Friars Preachers. They were founded by ST DOMINIC in 1215 and in the following year received

papal approval. The Dominicans were a mendicant or begging order, devoted to teaching and preaching and not confined within a monastery. Emphasis on learning was based on a teaching system involving groups of study, the *Studia Generalia*. St Thomas AQUINAS was a member of the order, as were four popes. The popes used the Dominicans for preaching in the Crusades and to search for heretics during the INQUISITION. They were governed by their master-general. The rise of new orders during the COUNTER REFORMATION reduced their influence.

Dominican Republic Country in the Caribbean, the eastern part of the island of Hispaniola which it shares today with HAITI.

It occupies a strategic position on major sea routes leading from Europe and the USA to the Panama Canal. The country was conquered by the Haitians at the end of the 18th century, then briefly controlled by France until Spain took over. Independence was gained in 1821, but Haiti annexed the major seaport of Santo Domingo the following year. In 1843 the Dominicans revolted against Haiti, winning their second independence in 1844 when the republic was founded. Between 1861 and 1865 the Dominican Republic was reannexed to Spain and fought again for independence under Buenaventura Báez. Anarchy, revolutions and dictatorships followed, and by 1905 the country was bankrupt. The USA assumed financial control, but disorder continued and the country was occupied from 1916 to 1924 by US marines.

A constitutional government was then set up, but this was overthrown by Rafael TRUJILLO, whose military dictatorship lasted from 1930 until 1961. On Trujillo's assassination, President Juan Bosch brought in a democratic government which was deposed by a military junta just over a year later. Civil war and fear of a communist takeover brought renewed US intervention, and a new constitution was introduced in 1966. The *Partido Reformista* was returned to power in the 1986 and 1990 elections. An IMF austerity programme in 1991 sharply reduced inflation, and there have been successful efforts to expand the economy. In 1994 the *Partido Reformista* was re-elected, but the opposition claimed there was evidence of corruption and fraud. Fresh elections were scheduled to be held in 1996 to end the political crisis.

House and home

Our homes are the result of the evolution of domestic architecture over thousands of years. Some of their familiar features can be traced back to medieval palaces; others to humble farmhouses.

People must have shelter, but housing has always involved choice and taste as well as necessity. Nomadic peoples use portable shelters, such as the Bedouins' tents, but even seasonal settlements produce semipermanent dwellings. With permanence and security came two key developments: the emergence of the house as the dwelling of individual families, and the separation of people from their animals.

After the family, the most important influence on domestic architecture has come from the definition of a social hierarchy, a process which housing has helped to shape. Architectural display emphasises rank and power, and its details are then copied by those who want to emulate the effect. The palace has influenced the design and use of the humblest of houses.

Sophisticated housing probably spread from Asia. Tomb-houses and models from Han China (200 BC to AD 200) and similar structures of AD 200 to 600 from Sassanid Persia suggest that forms of the multistorey house were established in the east, though clay models from Nayarit (in present-day Mexico) show that there were parallel developments in central America by the last centuries BC.

The Romans owed their domestic architecture, with much else, to Greek examples. The apartment-block, however, like those which survive at Ostia, may have been their own contribution to urban design. The Romans carried an early form of central heating with them when they extended their power into north-western Europe, but their principal architectural legacy to medieval Europe, along with bricks, mortar and masonry vaulting, was the villa-like plan later to be adopted by the Benedictine monastery, with its church and domestic buildings arranged around an arcaded *atrium* or cloister.

The secular equivalent of the monastery was the great hall, probably Germanic in origin, more often built of wood than of stone, providing warmth, accommodation and a place of assembly for a lord and his retainers. During the Scandinavian invasions of the 9th and 10th centuries AD, stone towers known as keeps or donjons were built in Western Europe as refuges, and the castle developed as a complex of defences and subsidiary buildings round the keep. The great hall was then either incorporated into the keep or raised over a stone-vaulted undercroft for greater security. Such first-floor halls were widespread in continental Europe. A hall, built into the keep or free-standing, remained a feature of castles for centuries.

By the time the Norman king of England William Rufus built Westminster Hall in the 1190s, kings and lords expected separate sleeping accommodation, which became known as the chamber. The king might keep state in the hall and dine there with his retainers, but what passed for private life was led in an increasingly elaborate suite of rooms with their own domestic staff of chamberlain, the chief officer, and the esquires and grooms of the chamber. At the opposite end of the hall, their entrances masked by a screen, were the kitchen, pantry or bread cupboard, and the buttery.

Medieval country houses conformed to the same pattern, with a central hall and cross wings, of one or two storeys, at either end. The smallest farmhouses and cottages were simply long rooms with a fireplace at one end, for cooking and smoking meat and fish, and a byre or animal-house at the other. Farmhouses often grew sideways, with the old house becoming a barn or byre, and the new house extending away

Ancient Egyptian model houses found in tombs give a vivid impression of a rural dwelling of about 1900 BC (below) and a tall, narrow town house of the 1st century BC (right), built upwards because of shortage of space.

A water engineer's diagram of the mid 12th century shows the Roman-inspired layout of the Benedictine abbey at Canterbury, Kent.

The Romans pioneered the apartment block. These shops with flats above are in Ostia.

from it. Generally, however, a house of any pretension had a courtyard round it, with a separate kitchen to diminish the risk of fire.

In medieval towns, tightly contained by walls and ramparts for security and with commercial activity focused on the market place, street frontages were expensive: house-plots were narrow and long. In northern Europe, notably in the north German Hanseatic towns whose prosperity depended on long-distance trade, space was gained by building upwards, with gables three or four storeys above the street and a hoist to raise merchandise to the upper floors. At street level everywhere the front was usually occupied by a shop containing a work-room open to the street, with a counter which hinged upwards to make a shutter, and a gateway to the courtyard behind where a hall, kitchen and outhouses were ranged. Larger houses had a garden or orchard beyond.

In both town and country at all levels of society, domestic furniture was sparse and simple. Tables were assembled on trestles, a practice recalled in the expressions 'festive board', and 'sideboard', a table left standing

Easthorpe Hall in Essex is a 15th-century hall house, with a central hall and cross pieces. The windows and door were later enlarged.

to hold cups and dishes. There might be a single chair for the head of the household; the chair is still a symbol of authority in committees. Others sat on benches, stools and chests. Wealth was lavished on bed-furnishings and silver plate, then on hangings, and later on imported carpets used as tablecloths. New luxuries might occur at any time: the English king Edward III had brass taps for hot and cold water over his bath at Westminster in the 1330s.

From 1500 to 1700 the refinement of weapons and artillery helped to strengthen law enforcement and pacify society. Fortification gave place to architectural display; castles were deserted for palaces and large country houses. In Italy, the revival of classical tastes and learning during the Renaissance produced the free-standing villa, which had a profound effect north of the Alps two centuries later. In the greatest households elsewhere, semipublic and private rooms were filled with increasingly elaborate furniture, and the great hall, formerly the heart of domestic life, became a mere entrance, a function which it still performs in modern houses.

Those changes spread rapidly in the 17th and 18th centuries through a growing middle class enriched by the growth of trade and professional services. In Europe long before the Industrial Revolution there was a commercial revolution based on an expanding market for imported food and other commodities, including tobacco. Sugar and potatoes enriched diet, tea and coffee drinking changed social habits and stimulated overseas trade and the use of porcelain and other tableware. Dietary change and increasing wealth promoted a rapid growth of population.

One result was enormous demand for housing built to common standards and, with railway transport available, no longer

Andrea Palladio designed the Villa Capra in Vicenza. His neoclassical style influenced architecture throughout Europe and America.

dependent upon local materials. The back-to-back terrace houses of industrial towns were merely hovels, but villas and semidetached villas multiplied in the suburbs and catered for higher standards of comfort. The increase in numbers imposed more stringent disciplines on society, especially in hygiene. Even medieval towns had public fountains with piped water supplies, but now taps and water-closets in private houses brought new industries into existence. Gas and electric lighting and heating were equally powerful innovations.

The patterns established in the 19th century have largely survived into the 20th. In England the semidetached house in its garden, with its front and back doors, entrance hall, specialised rooms and services all marshalled within four walls, encapsulates 2000 years of experimentation and tradition, while urban apartments everywhere arrange the same amenities on a single floor. Both contain electronic devices which have transformed many domestic rituals, such as family meals. At the same time individual tastes flourish, and the home seems likely to nurture them for centuries to come.

Dutch 17th-century town houses were shaped by commerce. Their ornate gables held hoists for goods.

Gustav Doré's *The Deluge* was one of his many engravings inspired by Biblical accounts.

Don Pacífico Affair International incident between Britain and Greece. In 1847 an angry crowd in Athens ransacked and burnt the house of Don Pacífico, a Portuguese moneylender, and injured his wife and children. Pacífico, who had been born in Gibraltar and could therefore claim British nationality, demanded compensation from the Greek government. Lord Palmerston took up the case in 1850 and decided to enforce Pacífico's entitlement to compensation by blockading Greece with British ships and threatening to bombard the capital, Athens. The move was attacked as 'gunboat diplomacy' by opposition politicians in Britain's Parliament. Greece eventually agreed to pay £4000 compensation, but only £150 was handed over.

Doré, Gustave (1832-83) French artist who produced book illustrations, paintings, etchings and sculptures. He was one of the most prolific and successful illustrators of his time, and once had to employ 40 block-cutters to prepare his illustrations. Doré provided pictures for about 120 books. His drawings, which were often executed in a grotesque style, included scenes from works by Dante, Cervantes and Edgar Allan Poe.

Doria, Andrea (1466-1560) Soldier and admiral who ruled GENOA from 1528 until his death. He fought as a mercenary first for Francis I of France and then Charles V of Italy. He expelled the French from Genoa in 1528 and took power, creating the republic. His descendants contributed six doges and numerous officials to the state.

Dorians Invaders from the north who entered ancient Greece between about 1125 and 1025 BC. They destroyed the MYCENAEAN civilisation and ushered in the Greek 'Dark Age'. The Dorians settled first in the Peloponnese then in the islands of Crete, Melos, Thera and the southern coast of Asia Minor. They spoke a dialect of Greek and seem to have come from southwest Macedonia and EPIRUS. In Sparta and Crete they used the population as HELOTS, or serfs, but elsewhere a gradual merger of conquerors and the conquered took place.

Dostoyevsky, Fyodor (1821-81) Russian author whose realistic fiction has influenced the modern novel. He resigned his commission as a military engineer to concentrate on writing. The subject of his first novel, *Poor Folk*, published in 1846, was suffering amid city squalor. Three years later Dostoyevsky was arrested, charged with being a member of a subversive discussion group and sentenced to death. However, he was reprieved and sent to a penal settlement in Siberia for four years. On his release he wrote *Notes from the House of the Dead* in 1862 and *The Insulted and the Injured*.

After backing two unsuccessful literary magazines Dostoyevsky produced *Crime and Punishment* and *The Gambler* in 1866 to pay his creditors. The books failed to make enough money to cover his gambling debts and the writer fled from the country in 1867. While abroad, he published *The Idiot, The Eternal Husband* and *The Possessed*. He returned to Russia in 1871 and wrote one of his major works, *The Brothers Karamazov*.

Douglas-Home, Sir Alec (1903-95) British Conservative prime minister from 1963 to 1964. Sir Alec was suddenly handed power when Prime Minister Harold MACMILLAN resigned. During his short period in office he made history by renouncing his peerage and fighting a by-election while still premier. His ministry was marked by a dash for economic growth and the acceptance of a controversial report on higher education. Sir Alec became an MP in 1931 and assisted Prime Minister Neville CHAMBERLAIN in negotiations with Adolf Hitler to try to avoid war. He was foreign secretary in Macmillan's government and leader of the opposition after the Conservatives lost the 1964 general election to Harold Wilson's Labour Party. But the following year he lost the leadership of the party to Edward HEATH. He again became foreign secretary after Heath won the 1970 election, and was made a life peer, Baron Home of the Hirsel, in 1974.

Douglass, Frederick (c.1817-95) US opponent of slavery. Douglass was born into slavery in Maryland, but escaped to the free states in 1838. In 1841 he became an agent for the Massachusetts Anti-Slavery Society and a prominent ABOLITIONIST. He also functioned as an adviser to Abraham Lincoln during the American Civil War.

Dowding, Hugh, 1st Baron (1882-1970) British air chief marshal who was commander in chief of Fighter Command during the BATTLE OF BRITAIN from July to October 1940, when the Royal Air Force fought the German Luftwaffe for control of the skies over England. Suffering from both mental and physical exhaustion, Dowding was replaced in November 1940 after Germany had abandoned its daylight attacks. He began his career as a pilot with the Royal Flying Corps and was appointed commander in the First World War. As head of Fighter Command from 1936 he built up a force of fighter aircraft and encouraged the development of radar.

> **DID YOU KNOW?**
>
> *The adjective 'draconian', meaning excessively harsh, derives from the strict laws laid down by the Athenian statesman Draco.*

draconian laws One of the first written codes of law, drawn up in ATHENS, believed to have been introduced in 621 or 620 BC by a statesman named Draco. According to later ancient sources, these laws were strict, even by the standards of the time, and the punishments severe. Even those people found guilty of pilfering received the death penalty. The law also maintained that the State must punish murderers and not leave them to be dealt with in vendettas. A 4th-century BC politician observed that Draco wrote his laws not in ink but in blood. The code was superseded by Solon's laws in 594 BC.

dragoon Mounted infantry soldier, named in 16th-century France after the short musket called the 'dragon'. Dragoons were organised in infantry companies, not cavalry squadrons, but were progressively trained to cavalry standard. By the early 18th century they were known as medium cavalry in the Prussian army, and later as light dragoons in the British army. Their flexibility on horse or foot made them ideal for maintaining public order or for dealing with guerrilla warfare.

Drake, Sir Francis (c.1543-96) English admiral and explorer, the first Englishman to circumnavigate the world. When the SPANISH ARMADA sailed to attack England in 1588 Drake was appointed vice-admiral of the fleet at Plymouth. In command of the *Revenge*, he took a leading part in the defeat of the Armada and its pursuit into the North Sea. The story of his finishing a game of bowls before going into battle is improbable, although it is said he was waiting for the tide to turn.

Drake sailed on a slave-trading voyage with his cousin, John HAWKINS, in 1567 and spent the next few years in privateering raids on the Spanish Main. In 1577 he was employed by a syndicate headed by Elizabeth I to go on a voyage around the world. He passed through the Strait of Magellan in his ship the *Golden Hind*, and raided the Spanish settlements on the west coast of South America. Then he journeyed to present-day California and crossed the Pacific to the Moluccas, returning to Plymouth a rich man. In 1585 Drake commanded an expedition against Spanish possessions in the Indies. He sacked Cartagena, Santo Domingo and St Augustine in Florida. Returning to England he heard news of the preparations for the Spanish Armada, and sailed to Cádiz to destroy some of the Spanish fleet in the operation known as 'singeing the King of Spain's beard'. In 1595 Drake sailed to the Caribbean, where he died of dysentery.

dreadnoughts Class of British battleship which revolutionised naval warfare. They were designed in response to the increasing ranges at which gunnery battles were fought. The first of the new ships was launched in 1906. Their steam turbine engines gave them a top speed of 21 knots, and their fire power enabled them to attack from beyond the range of enemy torpedoes. By the outbreak of the First World War, all the major navies had ships of a similar design.

Dresden raid (February 1945) One of the heaviest Allied air-raids on Germany in the Second World War, and one whose justification and effectiveness have aroused intense controversy. During the main raid on the night of February 13-14, 1945, the Royal Air Force attacked the city with 805 bombers. This was followed by three more raids in daylight by the US 8th Air Force. Dresden was seen as being strategically important as a communications complex, as well as a centre of industry. It was also a cultural centre full of baroque and rococo architecture and famous for German opera. The city was known to be overcrowded with about 200 000 refugees, but it was felt that the high casualties might help to shorten the war. The number of dead and wounded is still in dispute, with estimates varying from 55 000 to 400 000.

Dreyfus, Alfred (1859-1935) French officer involved in a court case that caused a political scandal at the end of the 19th century. Dreyfus, who was Jewish, served in the French war office. In 1894 he was charged with selling military secrets to Germany, found guilty and sentenced to life imprisonment on Devil's

Alfred Dreyfus is unjustly stripped of his rank for spying in this magazine illustration, which captured the anti-Semitic mood of the time.

Island in the West Indies. Doubts arose about the fairness of the trial. In 1896 Colonel Georges Picquart, chief of the intelligence section, satisfied himself that Dreyfus was the innocent victim of a spy, Major Ferdinand Esterhazy. When Esterhazy was pronounced innocent by a military court in 1898 the storm broke. The novelist Émile Zola, in a newspaper article headed '*J'accuse'*, claimed that the

In 1577 Elizabeth I sent Francis Drake to raid and explore the west coast of Spanish America, saying she 'would gladly be revenged on the King of Spain'. Drake sailed round the world and returned home in 1580, his ship laden with Spanish gold. He also brought back a coconut for Elizabeth.

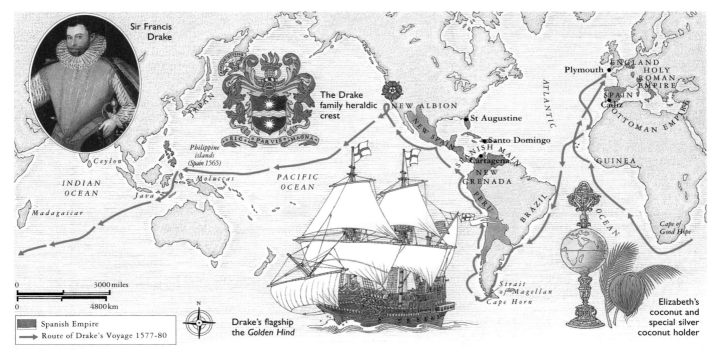

judges had obeyed orders from the war office in deciding their biased verdict. He was tried and jailed for libel, but escaped to England. The case was exploited by nationalist, militarist, anti-Semitic and royalist elements on the one hand, and republican, socialist and anticlerical supporters on the other. The case against Dreyfus collapsed when it was discovered that evidence against him had been forged and Esterhazy confessed. The Supreme Court ordered the military to retry the case against Dreyfus. A military court found him 'guilty with extenuating circumstances', and he was pardoned by the president of the republic. It was not until 1906 that he was fully cleared and reinstated in the army. Anticlericalism increased as a result of the case, and in 1905 Roman Catholicism ceased to be the official religion of France.

Drogheda, Siege of see CROMWELL, OLIVER

Druids Members of the ruling caste of the Gallic CELTS. Knowledge of the Druids comes mostly from the Roman accounts of Julius Caesar and TACITUS. Caesar reports that they exercised legal and priestly functions, worshipped in clearings in forests and cut mistletoe from the sacred oak tree with a golden sickle. The religion was stamped out by the Romans, who feared it might become a force for resistance to Roman rule. Suetonius Paulinus destroyed the Druid centre at Mona (Anglesey, in north Wales) in AD61, after which there is no further mention of Druids living in England and Wales.

The Romans are believed to have started the probably mythical accounts of Druids burning enemies to death in giant 'wicker men'.

Druze Tightly knit religious and political sect who broke away from the Ismaili Shiites in the 11th century. The main communities are in Syria, Lebanon and Israel. In the 18th and 19th centuries the Druze expanded from southern Lebanon into south-western Syria, where they drove out the inhabitants of Jabal

Druze fighters open fire. Their Muslim sect was drawn deeply into the bitter Lebanese civil war of the 1970s and the 1980s.

Hawran and became known as Jabal Druze. Throughout the 19th and 20th centuries the Druze have been involved in clashes with MARONITE CHRISTIANS, but also with the Turks when they were part of the Ottoman Empire. After the French mandate was created in Syria, Druze tribes rebelled in 1925-7 against social and administrative reforms. In 1944 the Druze tribes of Syria became amalgamated under the country's central government, but many chose to leave. After 1945 in Lebanon, the Druze held high political office but became embroiled in the civil war. In the 1970s and 1980s they became involved in the war between the Maronite Christians, Sunni and Shiite Muslims and Palestinians which tore the country apart.

Dual Monarchy see AUSTRO-HUNGARIAN EMPIRE

du Barry, Marie Jeanne, Comtesse (1743-93) Favourite of Louis XV of France, a great beauty who in 1769 became the king's mistress and influenced him until his death in 1774. The powerful Etienne François Choiseul, secretary of state for foreign affairs, criticised her and she may have helped to bring about his dismissal. She was arrested by the Revolutionary Tribunal during the French Revolution, tried on a charge of treason and guillotined.

Dubček, Alexander (1921-92) Czech communist statesman. In what came to be known as the 'Prague Spring' of 1968, Dubček, the government's leader, set about freeing the country from the political and economic controls imposed by Moscow. He promised the introduction of democracy and began to pursue a foreign policy independent of the Soviet Union. In response Moscow sent in a WARSAW PACT invasion force in August which was resisted by mostly unarmed civilians. Dubček, together with other leaders, was taken to Moscow and forced to abandon key reforms. He was removed from office in 1969 and expelled from the party in 1970. He re-emerged in 1989 after popular unrest forced the communist government to resign, and was elected chairman of the new Federal Assembly in 1990. He remained a convinced federalist and was strongly opposed to the successful Slovak bid for independence in 1992.

Dudley, Robert see LEICESTER, IST EARL OF

Dulles, John Foster (1888-1959) US international lawyer and statesman. Dulles served as adviser to the US delegation at the San Francisco Conference which set up the UNITED NATIONS in 1945, and as the chief author of the Japanese peace treaty in 1951. As secretary of state under President Dwight EISENHOWER from 1953 to 1959 he became a supporter of COLD WAR policies. Dulles went beyond the TRUMAN DOCTRINE – the policy of setting up military pacts around the communist countries – and urged a nuclear arms build-up to deter Soviet aggression. He helped to draft the Eisenhower doctrine of economic and military aid to halt aggression in the Middle East, and gave assurances that the United States would defend West Berlin against any communist encroachment.

Duma Elective legislative assembly introduced in Russia by Tsar Nicholas II in 1906 in response to popular unrest. The assembly was boycotted by the socialist parties, and its efforts to introduce taxation and agrarian reforms were blocked by reactionary groups at court which persuaded the tsar to dissolve three successive Dumas. The fourth Duma, from 1912 to 1917, was in constant conflict with the tsar and in February 1917 rejected an imperial decree ordering its dissolution and instead established a provisional government. Three days later it accepted the tsar's abdication, but soon began to disintegrate, causing a power vacuum that finally triggered the Bolshevik RUSSIAN REVOLUTION.

Dumbarton Oaks Conference (1944) International conference at Dumbarton Oaks in Washington, DC, where representatives of the United States, Britain, the Soviet Union and China drew up proposals that served as the basis for the charter of the United Nations. It also discussed the creation of a SECURITY COUNCIL, a permanent peace-keeping organ.

Dunant, Jean-Henri see RED CROSS

Dunbar, Battle of (September 3, 1650) Victory by Oliver Cromwell's force of 14 000 men over 27 000 Scots near the port of Dunbar in Scotland. Large numbers of Scots were

Retreating Allied troops wade out to ships at Dunkirk. They were helped by a pause in the German army advance.

taken prisoner, together with all the Scottish guns. This victory of Cromwell's destroyed the cause of the STUART royal dynasty in Scotland for the best part of a decade.

Duncan I (c.1010-40) King of Scots from 1034 to his death. Duncan I was the ruler of Strathclyde, which was added to the Scottish kingdom he inherited from his grandfather Malcolm II. His accession was unpopular with the northern tribes, and he was killed in battle by the mormaer of Moray, known as MACBETH.

Duncan II (c.1060-94) King of Scots in 1094. Duncan II gained the throne through the support of William II of England, who provided the army with which Duncan defeated his uncle and rival Donald Bane. But Duncan's English alliance was resented, and he was murdered at his uncle's instigation.

Dunkirk evacuation Seaborne rescue of British and French troops in the Second World War between May 26 and June 4, 1940. German forces advancing into northern France cut off large numbers of British and French troops. Allied soldiers withdrew to the beaches of Dunkirk, where warships, aided by many privately-owned boats, carried off some 330 000 men – most, but not all, of the troops. This retreat came to symbolise the fighting spirit of Britain's period of single-handed resistance to the Nazis.

Duns Scotus, John (c.1265-1308) Scholastic philosopher and theologian. In both his writings and lectures Duns stressed the distinction between faith and reason. He argued that the use of reason had to be limited and that the will is superior to the intellect. His ideas were unpopular with 16th-century reformers who regarded his supporters as 'Dunsmen' or 'dunces'. Duns was born in Scotland, and became a Franciscan friar, then a priest, and studied at Oxford and Paris. He returned to both universities as a teacher before moving in 1308 to Cologne University.

Dunstan, St (c.909-88) Archbishop of Canterbury from 959 until his death. Dunstan was a reformer of organised monasticism in England, and a counsellor to its kings. Edmund I of Wessex made Dunstan abbot of the Benedictine house of Glastonbury in Somerset. He was exiled by King Edwy in 956, then recalled by his successor King Edgar the following year and made successively Bishop of Worcester and London. Dunstan founded or re-founded many abbeys with Edgar's support, and helped to draw up a code of monastic observance, the *Regularis Concordis*, at the Synod of Winchester. His formulation of the ceremony for Edgar's coronation became the basis of all coronations. He has been called one of the makers of England.

Dupleix, Joseph-François, Marquis de (1697-1763) Governor-general of the French East India company in India from 1742 to 1754. Dupleix demonstrated able leadership of France's Indian interests, but was outmanoeuvred by Britain's Robert CLIVE during wars in south India. In 1754 he was recalled to Paris where he died in disgrace, aware that Clive's victories in Bengal had destroyed his peronal dreams of extending French influence in India.

French East India company governor Joseph Dupleix claimed to have spent his vast fortune on a failed attempt to found a new French empire in India.

durbar Public audience held by Mughal emperors of India, and used under British rule for ceremonial gatherings, usually connected with some royal event. The word means 'court' in Persian and Urdu. On January 1, 1877, the viceroy, Lord Lytton, held a durbar at Delhi to proclaim the adoption by Queen Victoria of the title Empress of India, and such gatherings became features of the British Raj. The most magnificent was that attended by George V at Delhi in December 1911.

Durham Report (1838) Report on constitutional reform in British North America. In 1837 the liberal reformer John Lambton, Earl of Durham, was appointed governor-general of British North America after the PAPINEAU REBELLION of 1837. His *Report on the Affairs of British North America* recommended that the regions of Upper and Lower Canada should be united and given self government. It also proposed reform of the land laws, extensive railway building to unify the country and an end to French nationalism. The report met with hostility in Britain, but it eventually became the main document for policy in the White dominions for the rest of the 19th century.

Dutch East Indies Islands in South-east Asia now occupied by Indonesia. The archipelago was first influenced by Indian and Chinese culture. Hinduism, Buddhism and later Islam reached the islands and were grafted on to local cultures before the arrival of the Europeans. Empires in the Indies based on sea power were, except for SRIVIJAYA – an important river port in what is now southern Sumatra – relatively short-lived, for example Macassar and Ternate in the MOLUCCAS. The land-based empires lasted longer. Islam spread throughout the Indies after 1300 (Hinduism survived only in BALI), and provided a weapon against the Portuguese and Dutch, who arrived in force in the 16th and 17th centuries. The Netherlands set up the Dutch East India Company in 1602 to control the area. The company was involved in attacks on the Portuguese (then part of the SPANISH EMPIRE), fought with indigenous rulers, and created a virtual monopoly in trade and in fine spices such as cloves, nutmeg and mace. In 1619 the company made Batavia (now Jakarta) its headquarters. It ousted the Portuguese from Ceylon (now Sri Lanka), set up trading bases in India, Persia, and Nagasaki, and made the Cape of Good Hope a base for Dutch ships plying their trade on their way to and from the East. However, low salaries led to corruption among Dutch East India Company officials and in 1799 the company was liquidated and its responsibilities taken over by the Dutch state. In 1949 the islands were granted independence and became known as Indonesia.

Dutch Revolts see NETHERLANDS

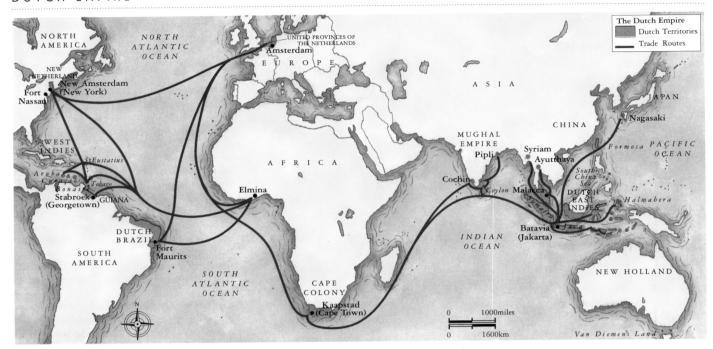

In the 17th century, trading enabled the Dutch to break free from Spanish rule and to challenge the Portuguese monopoly of the spice trade. The new Dutch nation became the greatest maritime power in the world, with a global colonial empire, until the British gained ascendancy after 1678.

Dutch empire Overseas territories of the United Provinces of the NETHERLANDS. Dutch wealth was based on the fishing and shipping industries, assisted by Holland's position on the main European trade routes. In 1602 the Dutch East India Company was created to foster trade in the Indian Ocean and to assist in the revolt against Spanish rule in the Netherlands. From headquarters in Java, the company largely displaced the Portuguese in the East Indies, came to control the spice trade and traded extensively in the China seas.

The Dutch West India Company, a trading and colonising company founded in 1621, struck at Spanish and Portuguese colonies in the West Indies, South America and on the west coast of Africa, where it was involved in the slave trade. In North America it founded the colony of New Netherland, later NEW YORK, in 1609. Trade rivalry with Britain led

The dictator François Duvalier, seen here with his wife Simone, believed himself to be the semidivine embodiment of the Haitian nation.

to the Anglo-Dutch Wars between 1652 and 1678, after which the Dutch lost command of the seas and all Dutch colonies except the DUTCH EAST INDIES, now Indonesia.

Dutch Revolts see NETHERLANDS

Duvalier, François (1907-71) Dictator of Haiti from 1957, known as 'Papa Doc'. After training as a physician he served as director-general of the health service and minister of health. His election as president was the first held under the rule of universal adult suffrage, but within a year he suspended constitutional guarantees and established a reign of terror enforced by his police and spy organisation, the Tontons Macoutes (Haitian Creole for 'bogeymen'). He also exploited voodoo practices and Black nationalism to maintain his power. The Haitian economy declined severely, while 90 per cent of the population remained illiterate. Duvalier ensured the succession of his son, Jean-Claude, but in 1986 'Baby Doc' was forced to flee to France.

earl British nobleman ranked third in the peerage. Anglo-Saxon 'ealdormen' were royal officials, usually noblemen. Originally in charge of single shires, from the 10th century each officer governed several shires. Under the Danish king Canute (*c.*994-1035) they came to be known as earls, from the Scandinavian

jarl, with individual officers controlling the provinces of Mercia, Northumbria, Wessex and East Anglia. After the Norman Conquest in 1066 smaller earldoms were created and shire administration passed to the sheriffs. While the title of 'alderman' was applied to urban dignitaries, earl itself survived as a hereditary title in the British peerage.

East Anglia Region of eastern England made up of the modern counties of Norfolk, Suffolk and parts of Cambridgeshire and Essex. The kingdom of the East Angles was formed around the end of the 5th century AD by Angles, Saxons, Frisians and Swabians from the Baltic coast. The first settlements were made in Norfolk, but those in Suffolk, especially around Ipswich, formed the nucleus of the kingdom. Protection against the Britons to the west was provided by Middle Angles, who settled in the waterlands of the Fens, and by the construction of earth-works such as Devil's Dyke.

Little is known about East Anglian kings. Raedwald, who died around 624, was briefly a Christian and was styled Bretwalda, or overlord, of the south by the scholar and historian St BEDE. The rich ship burial at SUTTON HOO is probably Raedwald's. The kingdom was overrun by Danes in the later 9th century, after which it became part of the DANELAW and eventually one of the English earldoms.

Easter Island South Pacific island 2400 miles (3800km) west of Chile, to which it belongs. The island was originally colonised by Polynesians from the nearest occupied

London's East India Docks were built by the East India Company in 1806 for ships importing indigo, spices and silk. In 1782 a company official's wife (right) superintends tailors in India.

islands 1800 miles (2900 km) to the west. A series of massive stone heads, which ranged from 10 to 40 ft (3-12 m) high and weighed up to 51 tonnes, were probably erected between 1000 and 1500. When the Dutch navigator Jakob Roggeveen landed on the island, on Easter Day 1722, the Polynesians were no longer engaged on voyages of exploration and had developed a complex system of chiefdoms. Following the arrival of foreigners, the island declined. Peruvian slave raiders took about a third of the population in 1862-3; those who returned brought with them diseases such as smallpox and tuberculosis. After the introduction of Christianity in the 1860s the surviving Polynesian traditions died out. The island was annexed by Chile in 1888 and is now administered by a civilian governor. Chile has declared it a historic monument.

Easter Rising Insurrection in Dublin in April 1916 when some 1800 members of the Irish Republican Brotherhood and the Irish Citizen Army took up arms against British rule in Ireland. A few days before the rebellion, the British navy seized a ship carrying a consignment of arms from Germany for the rebels. Roger CASEMENT of the IRB was arrested soon after landing from a German submarine. Nevertheless, the joint military leaders Pádraic Pearse and James Connolly decided to go ahead. Supported by the SINN

FÉIN Party, members of the IRB seized the General Post Office and other strategic buildings in Dublin. On April 24, Easter Sunday, they proclaimed an Irish Republic. A provisional government was set up with Pearse as president. By April 29 British troops had forced the rebels to surrender. The rising had little public support to begin with, but the execution of 15 of the rebellion's leaders provoked popular anger and led to strong backing for the nationalists. In the 1918 general election Sinn Féin won most of the Irish seats.

East Germany see GERMAN DEMOCRATIC REPUBLIC

East India Company, British Company of London merchants whose powerful trading position in India became the basis for British control of the subcontinent. After its foundation in 1600 the company lost the MOLUCCAS to the Dutch, who formed their own company in 1602 to administer the DUTCH EAST INDIES, now Indonesia. By 1700 the British company had secured important Indian trading ports, including Madras, Bombay and Calcutta. During the SEVEN YEARS' WAR of 1756 to 1763 it achieved dominance in India at the expense of the French East India Company, founded in 1664. The English general Robert CLIVE secured south-east India by

outmanoeuvring Joseph-François DUPLEIX, the French governor. With victory over the ruler of Bengal in 1757, the British East India Company emerged as the greatest European trader in India. The French company ceased to exist after 1789, while the British company developed into an instrument of colonial government. It continued to serve as Britain's administrative agent in India even after losing all its commercial monopolies by 1833. The Indian Mutiny in 1857 led to the India Acts, which in 1858 transferred India from the company to British Government control. The company was dissolved in 1873.

East Timor Part of an island in South-east Asia, colonised by the Portuguese in the 16th century. The western part belonged to the Dutch until 1949, when it became part of Indonesia. East Timor remained a province of Portugal, but in 1975 the leftist Fretilin movement declared independence after a brief civil war. Nine days later, Indonesian troops invaded. East Timor was formally integrated into Indonesia in 1976, after which separatist movements were suppressed. Human rights groups claimed that between 1976 and 1991 some 200000 Timorese were killed or died in detention. The United Nations has disputed the legality of Indonesia treating East Timor as its 27th province.

East-West Schism Split between the Eastern ORTHODOX CHURCH and the Western Roman Church, which became final in 1054. Tension between the two Churches dates back at least to the division of the Roman Empire into the Eastern and Western empires, and the transfer of the capital from Rome to CONSTANTINOPLE in the 4th century. While the Eastern Church suffered violent theological disputes, the Western Church remained relatively calm. They moved farther apart when the popes turned to the HOLY ROMAN EMPIRE in the West rather than to the BYZANTINE EMPIRE in the East, especially from the time of Emperor CHARLEMAGNE (c.742-814). There were also disputes over doctrine and over the nature of the pope's

The terraces of stone heads on Easter Island were carved out of rock from the crater of the Rana Raraku volcano. The origin and purpose of these massive carvings remain unclear. In 1958 Easter Islanders re-erected a 32ft (10m) statue weighing almost 30 tonnes using only ropes and two levers (right).

authority. The Churches excommunicated and formally denounced each other in 1054. The breach widened when Constantinople was sacked in 1204 during the Fourth Crusade. There were attempts to heal the schism, but these ended after 1453 when Constantinople was captured by OTTOMAN Turks, who occupied almost all of the former Byzantine Empire. In recent years dialogue between the two Churches has been reopened.

Ebert, Friedrich (1871-1925) German statesman. Ebert was chancellor for one day, November 9, 1918, when Germany collapsed at the end of the First World War. Between 1919 and 1925 he was first president of the WEIMAR REPUBLIC, attempting to steer a course between revolution and counterrevolution to give Germany a liberal, parliamentary constitution. Ebert lost the support of the left for crushing the communists, but was condemned by the right for having signed the Treaty of VERSAILLES in 1919.

Ecuador Country in north-west South America. Coastal Ecuador was the site of the first agricultural villages in the Americas. From about AD 500 diverse Indian peoples developed independent kingdoms. After 1450 the INCAS conquered the central valley, making QUITO their regional capital. Spanish CONQUISTADORES arrived in 1526, and in 1532 used Ecuador as a base from which to invade Inca-controlled Peru. In 1534 they took Quito, and Ecuador fell under the control of the viceroy of Peru. The Spanish then established large estates in central Ecuador, but neglected the coastal plain, which developed its own culture. In 1822 the South American revolutionary Marshal José Antonio de Sucre beat the Spanish at Pichincha. Together with Venezuela and Colombia, Ecuador joined the union of Gran Colombia under Simón BOLÍVAR. After it broke up in 1830 Ecuador became an independent state, its politics reflecting the tension between the conservative landowners of the interior and the more liberal business community of the coast. A near total breakdown in government from 1845 was ended by García Moreno, who during his two presidencies in 1861-5 and 1869-75 re-established order. After the First World War, increasing poverty led to political unrest.

During the Second World War US military bases brought some economic gain, but a disastrous war with Peru in 1941 forced Ecuador to abandon its claims to the Upper Amazon. Between 1944 and 1972 José Maria Velasco Ibarra alternated with the military as ruler. In 1972 the military seized power, holding it until 1979, when a new constitution came

Edgehill was the opening battle of the English Civil War and the first to be fought between Englishmen since the Wars of the Roses nearly 200 years before. Both sides claimed victory.

into force. Despite the discovery of oil in the 1970s most people remained poor and illiterate, although the HACIENDAS, or large estates, survived intact. In the 1980s Ecuador suffered from a major debt crisis and a decline in oil prices. In 1992 a coalition government led by Sixto Duán Ballén introduced public spending cuts and economic reforms, provoking popular unrest. In 1995 a recurrent border dispute with Peru was settled and unpopular economic measures were again introduced.

Eden, Anthony, 1st Earl of Avon (1897-1977) British prime minister from 1955 to 1957, at the time of the SUEZ WAR. Eden served as Conservative foreign secretary from 1935 until 1938, when he resigned because of his opposition to Neville Chamberlain's policy of APPEASEMENT. He again served as foreign secretary from 1940 to 1945 and from 1951 to 1955, when he succeeded Winston Churchill as prime minister. When Egypt nationalised the strategically important Suez Canal in 1956, Eden regarded President NASSER as a threat to world peace and supported an invasion of Egypt by Britain, France and Israel. Domestic opposition to Britain's role in the crisis, together with his own failing health, led to Eden's resignation the following year.

Edgar (c.944-75) King of Northumbria and Mercia from 957 and king of a united England from 959. The younger son of Edmund I, he became king of Northumbria and Mercia after his brother Eadwig was deposed. On Eadwig's death in 959 Edgar also took control of England south of the Thames and in 973 he was recognised as overlord of almost all Britain. During a peaceful reign, Edgar, aided by St DUNSTAN, began to reform the English monasteries. In 973 he introduced a uniform currency based on new silver pennies. He was succeeded by his son Edward the Martyr.

Edgehill, Battle of (October 23, 1642) First battle of the ENGLISH CIVIL WAR. Marching south from Nottingham with the aim of recapturing London, Royalist troops clashed with Parliamentarians led by the 3rd Earl of ESSEX at Edgehill, near Banbury. Prince RUPERT and his Royalist cavalry gained an early advantage, but darkness and the exhaustion of the troops ended the struggle, with no clear victor and heavy losses on both sides.

Edison, Thomas (1847-1931) US scientist and inventor who patented almost 1100 inventions. After only three months' formal schooling, he began his career as a freelance

Thomas Edison, shown here with his perfected phonograph, claimed that genius was 'One per cent inspiration and 99 per cent perspiration'.

A French manuscript illustrates Edward I, who learnt of his succession to the English throne on his return from fighting in the Crusades.

telegrapher in 1862. He developed inventions based on the telegraph and in 1876 moved his laboratory to Menlo Park in New Jersey. In 1877 he invented the phonograph, the first device that could both record and replay sound, and also improved Alexander Graham Bell's telephone transmitter and receiver. Edison produced the first practical electric light bulb in 1879, and in 1882 he built the world's first central electric power station.

Edward I (1239-1307) King of England from 1272 until his death. The eldest son of Henry III, Edward was captured by Simon de MONT-FORT during the BARONS' WAR, but defeated him at the Battle of EVESHAM in 1265. As king, Edward annexed Wales between 1277 and 1284. In 1301 he granted the principality to the future Edward II, his son by ELEANOR OF CASTILE. The statutes covering administrative and legal reforms he initiated between 1275 and 1290 earned Edward the title of the 'English Justinian', after the 5th-century Byzantine emperor and lawgiver. He also did much to establish the House of Commons. Following a request by Scotland's nobility to settle the Scottish line of succession, Edward asserted his overlordship of Scotland before declaring for John de BALLIOL in 1292. Four years later he conquered Scotland, provoking the Scottish wars of independence. At the same time he was forced to defend his lands in GASCONY against the French. Heavily in debt from the wars, Edward died on his way to fight ROBERT I in Scotland.

Edward II (1284-1327) First English Prince of Wales from 1301 and king of England from 1307 to 1327. Edward was notorious for his inordinate affection for his favourite, Piers GAVESTON. By 1308 their relationship had alienated Edward from his barons. In 1311

they drafted ordinances that restricted the king's powers and demanded the expulsion of Gaveston, whom they murdered the following year. The king's prestige fell further when he was defeated by the Scottish king Robert I at BANNOCKBURN in 1314. Edward annulled the ordinances in 1322, but his reliance on Hugh le DESPENSER was resented by his wife, Isabella of France. In 1326 Isabella and her lover Roger MORTIMER deposed Edward in favour of his son, Edward III. Edward II died while imprisoned in Berkeley Castle. He was almost certainly murdered.

Edward III (1312-77) King of England from 1327. Edward succeeded his father, Edward II, at the age of 15, but real power was held by his mother, Isabella of France, and her lover, Roger MORTIMER, until Edward had Mortimer executed in 1330. Edward continued the fight against Scottish independence, which he had reluctantly recognised in 1328, but Anglo-French conflict over Scotland and

> **66** The King of France, hardened in his malice, would assent to no peace or treaty, but called...his strong host to take into his hand the duchy of Aquitaine, declaring against all truth that it was forfeit to him. **99**
>
> *Edward III proclaiming the outbreak of the Hundred Years' War in 1337*

AQUITAINE led to the outbreak of the HUNDRED YEARS' WAR in 1337. In 1340 Edward assumed the title 'King of France'. English victories at SLUYS (1340) and CRÉCY (1346) were followed by a truce. In 1348 Edward founded the chivalric Order of the Garter. At this time the BLACK DEATH reached England.

Fighting resumed in 1355 and the following year Edward's eldest son, EDWARD THE BLACK PRINCE, won a decisive victory at POITIERS, strengthening Edward's position to negotiate the Treaty of BRÉTIGNY in 1360. Edward surrendered his claim to the French crown in return for Aquitaine and other territories, but war broke out again in 1369. After the death of his wife, Philippa of Hainault, in 1369 Edward's health and mind deteriorated and he fell under the influence of his mistress, Alice Perrers. He was succeeded by RICHARD II, son of the Black Prince, who died in 1376.

Edward IV (1442-83) King of England from 1461 to 1470 and from 1471 during the WARS OF THE ROSES between the rival dynasties of York and Lancaster. He became the Yorkist leader in 1460 after the death of his father, Richard, Duke of YORK. Defeat at ST ALBANS was followed by victories at Mortimer's Cross and Towton, and in 1461 Edward and his cousin, Richard Neville, Earl of WARWICK, deposed the Lancastrian king HENRY VI.

In 1464 Edward secretly married Elizabeth Woodville and also promoted her relatives, alienating Warwick. Together with Edward's brother, the Duke of CLARENCE, he captured the king, but they were forced by public opinion to release him after two months. In 1470 Warwick invaded England from France and restored Henry VI, but the following year Edward regained the throne after the Battle of TEWKESBURY and had Henry murdered. Despite a dissolute lifestyle, Edward was a strong ruler who promoted English commerce. His early death left England with the young Edward V.

Edward V (1470-83) King of England in 1483. The eldest son of Edward IV, he succeeded to the throne on April 9, 1483. On May 30, his paternal uncle, Richard, Duke of Gloucester, took Edward into custody, after which he appointed himself Protector and postponed Edward's coronation. On June 26 Edward was deposed and Richard assumed the throne as RICHARD III. Between then and August, Edward and his younger brother, Richard, Duke of York, were murdered in the Tower of London, possibly on the king's orders. Claims that two skeletons discovered in the Tower in 1674 were those of Edward and Richard have never been proved.

Edward VI (1537-53) King of England from 1547. The son of Henry VIII and Jane Seymour, Edward came to the throne aged nine.

In his short life Edward VI was nearly betrothed to the infant Mary, Queen of Scots at six and became king of England at nine.

Effective power was exercised by his uncle, Edward Seymour, Duke of Somerset, until 1549, and then by John Dudley, Duke of NORTHUMBERLAND. A fervent Protestant, Edward endorsed Archbishop Thomas CRANMER's English Prayer Books of 1549 and 1552. Contemporaries noted his studious, unemotional nature and a callous streak reminiscent of his father. Before Edward died of tuberculosis, he attempted to exclude his sister, the Catholic MARY I, from the throne by securing the succession for Northumberland's daughter-in-law, Lady Jane GREY.

Edward VII (1841-1910) King of Great Britain and Ireland and Emperor of India from 1901 until his death. Edward was the eldest son of Queen Victoria, who blamed the stress of Edward's scandalous affair with an actress for Prince Albert succumbing to typhoid in 1861. She excluded Edward from matters of state and he devoted himself instead to high society, horse-racing, gambling and shooting. Although married to Princess Alexandra of Denmark, he continued to have mistresses throughout his life and was cited in two divorce cases. On his succession, Edward embarked on goodwill visits to Germany, Italy and Russia. In 1903 he visited France, where his charm and perfect French helped to promote public acceptance of the ENTENTE CORDIALE in 1904. A popular monarch, he also brought colour and life back to court after Victoria's 40 years of mourning for Albert. He was succeeded by his second son, GEORGE V.

Edward VIII (1894-1972) Uncrowned king of Great Britain and Northern Ireland and Emperor of India from January to December 1936. The eldest son of George V, he became Prince of Wales in 1911. After service in the First World War, his goodwill tours of the British Empire and concern for the unemployed during the Depression made him extremely popular. In 1936 Edward's desire to marry Wallis Simpson, an American divorcee, sparked the ABDICATION CRISIS and he was succeeded by his brother, GEORGE VI. Edward was made Duke of Windsor, but the title 'royal highness' was not extended to the duchess. Following their marriage in 1937, the couple visited Hitler in Germany. Edward was governor of the Bahamas from 1940 to 1945, but thereafter lived in France. He was not invited to any official ceremony with members of the royal family until 1967. After their deaths the duke and duchess were buried side by side in the grounds of Windsor Castle.

Edward the Black Prince (1330-76) Popular name for Edward of Woodstock, eldest son of EDWARD III of England and one of the finest English commanders in the HUNDRED YEARS' WAR. Edward won his spurs by leading part of his father's army at the Battle of CRÉCY in 1346. It was there, legend says, that he wore the black armour that earned him his nickname. In 1356 he captured the French king John II at POITIERS. Edward's victories were a source of pride to the English, who regarded him as a national hero and an embodiment of chivalric ideals. His merciless sack of Limoges in 1370 showed a less attractive side to his character. Edward died before he could accede to the throne, which therefore passed to his son RICHARD II on the death of Edward III.

Edward the Confessor, St (c.1003-66) Anglo-Saxon king of England from 1042 until his death. The eldest son of ETHELRED II, Edward returned from exile in Normandy in 1041 and succeeded to the throne following the death of the Danish king Canute's heirs. He maintained his position against his father-in-law, the powerful Earl GODWIN of Wessex, with the help of his own Norman favourites. In 1051 Edward was said by the Normans to have promised the throne to William, Duke of Normandy. That same year he put down a rebellion by the Godwins, but they regained their ascendancy the following year. Edward remained childless and on his deathbed nominated Harold Godwin his successor as HAROLD II. William's pursuit of his own claim led to the NORMAN CONQUEST in 1066, after which he took the throne as WILLIAM I. Edward founded Westminster Abbey, and had a reputation for piety, although he was too ill to attend its consecration in 1065. After he was canonised in 1161 he was given the title 'the Confessor', which referred to someone who remained loyal to his faith and resisted the temptations of the world.

Edward the Elder (d.924) King of Wessex from 899. Edward continued the policy of his father, King ALFRED, of conquering those areas of England controlled by the Danes and known as the DANELAW. Between 910 and 916 his advance was marked by the building of fortifications known as *burhs*, and in 917 Edward overwhelmed the Danish army of East Anglia. After he gained control of Mercia in 918 following the death of his sister Ethelflaed, Edward's kingdom included all land south of the River Humber. Two years later he conquered Northumbria, and his authority north of the Humber was recognised by all the chief rulers, including the king of the Scots.

Edward the Martyr, St (c.963-78) King of England from 975. He succeeded his father EDGAR, but his accession was disputed by his younger brother, Ethelred. Edward was murdered at Corfe Castle while visiting his brother, who took the throne as ETHELRED II. Miracles were reported at Edward's tomb at Shaftesbury and he was canonised in 1001.

Egbert (d.839) King of WESSEX from 802. Egbert was expelled from England in 789 by the powerful Mercian king OFFA and the West Saxon king Beorhtric. He lived in exile at the court of the emperor CHARLEMAGNE until 802, when he became king. By 829 Egbert had extended his authority over the other southern English kingdoms, but Mercia regained its independence in 830. Egbert styled himself 'King of the English', but his authority was tested towards the end of his reign by Danish raids.

Egypt Country in north-eastern Africa. During the 4th millennium BC two kingdoms, one in the Nile delta (Lower Egypt) and one stretching along the valley (Upper Egypt), came into existence. After the kingdoms were unified around 3100 BC there were 30 dynasties of PHARAOHS or kings. The

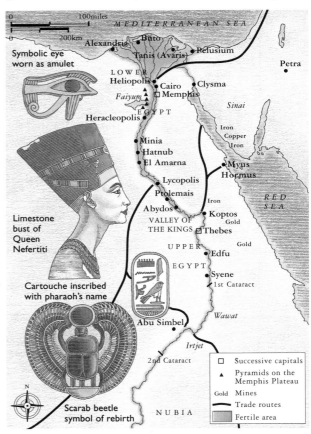

Egypt, whose recorded history goes back 5000 years, is the site of one of the world's most ancient civilisations.

Symbolic eye worn as amulet

Limestone bust of Queen Nefertiti

Cartouche inscribed with pharaoh's name

Scarab beetle symbol of rebirth

MEDITERRANEAN SEA

Alexandria • Buto
Tanis (Avaris) • Pelusium
Petra

LOWER
Heliopolis • Cairo • Clysma
Faiyum □ Memphis
EGYPT
Heracleopolis
Sinai

Iron
Copper
Iron

Minia
Hatnub
El Amarna
Myus
Hormus

Lycopolis
Ptolemais
Iron
RED SEA

Abydos • Koptos Gold
VALLEY OF
THE KINGS □ Thebes

UPPER
Gold
EGYPT
Edfu

Syene
1st Cataract

Wawat

Abu Simbel

Irtjet

2nd Cataract
NUBIA

□ Successive capitals
▲ Pyramids on the Memphis Plateau
Gold Mines
— Trade routes
▭ Fertile area

subsequent history of ancient Egypt is usually divided into three periods. During the Old Kingdom (c. 2700-c. 2200 BC) the pharaohs developed a complex sun-worshipping religion, and the major pyramids, built as tombs of the pharaohs, were constructed at Giza. The Middle Kingdom (c. 2100-1786 BC), when Egypt conquered Nubia and Libya, ended with an invasion by the HYKSOS. During the New Kingdom (c. 1570-1100 BC) Egypt conquered Palestine and Syria, and magnificent temples were built at KARNAK and Luxor. After 1100 Egypt was incorporated into the Assyrian and Persian empires, and in 332 it was conquered by Alexander the Great. In 30 it passed into Roman rule following the suicide of Queen Cleopatra.

As the Roman Empire's power declined, Egypt came under the control of Byzantine governors. Christianity was introduced and until AD 451 Alexandria was the intellectual centre of the Coptic Church (see COPTS). In 642 Arab armies conquered Egypt, but there was little pressure for conversion to Islam. In the 10th century the Fatimid dynasty took control, building the new capital of al-Qahira, present-day Cairo. They were overthrown in 1171 by the Muslim leader SALADIN. From 1250 Egypt was ruled by the MAMELUKES, who also ruled Syria, but in 1517 the country fell to the OTTOMAN EMPIRE.

The French emperor Napoleon invaded Egypt in 1798 in an attempt to restrict British trade with the East, but was driven out by Turkish and British armies in 1801. The opening of the SUEZ CANAL in 1869 made Egypt strategically important and in 1882 it was occupied by the British following a nationalist revolt. Egypt became a British protectorate in 1914 and in 1922 received nominal independence and a constitutional monarchy. Thirty years later, King FAROUK was overthrown in a bloodless coup by army officers led by Colonel Gamal Abdul NASSER, who emerged as president of the new republic.

Nasser's nationalisation of the Suez Canal in 1956 provoked the SUEZ WAR and in the same year he embarked on an unsuccessful war against Israel. Despite Soviet military and economic aid, Nasser suffered a further defeat at Israeli hands in the SIX-DAY WAR of 1967. His successor, Anwar SADAT, continued his aggressive policies but after defeat in the 1973 YOM KIPPUR WAR he turned his back on the Soviet alliance and strengthened contacts with the West. In 1979 Sadat signed an agreement with the Israeli leader Menachem Begin laying down a basis for peace in the Middle East. Egypt was expelled from the ARAB LEAGUE and many Middle Eastern countries severed all ties. After Sadat's assassination in 1981 his successor, Hosni Mubarak, followed a policy of reconciliation and in 1989 Egypt was readmitted to the Arab League. In 1991 Egypt sent troops to support the US-led

In 1961 Adolf Eichmann was put on trial in Jerusalem for overseeing the murder of millions of Jews in the Second World War.

alliance in the GULF WAR and in return had its debts to the US reduced. Poverty remained a major problem, while Islamic fundamentalists grew increasingly violent.

Eichmann, Adolf (1906-62) Austrian Nazi administrator. He joined the Nazi Party in 1932 and three years later took charge of the GESTAPO's Jewish affairs section in Berlin. From 1942 he organised the transportation of Jews to CONCENTRATION CAMPS. After the war Eichmann went into hiding in Argentina. In 1960 he was captured by Israeli agents and smuggled back to Israel, where he was tried for crimes against humanity and executed.

Eiffel, Alexandre (1832-1923) French construction engineer best known for the 985 ft (300 m) Eiffel Tower in Paris. Completed in 1889 to commemorate the centenary of the French Revolution, the tower was the last major structure to be built of wrought iron and the highest building in the world until New York's Chrysler Building in 1930. Eiffel also designed an iron bridge over the River Garonne in Bordeaux and the framework of the Statue of Liberty in New York.

Einstein, Albert see feature, page 210

Eisenhower, Dwight David (1890-1969) American general and 34th president of the USA, from 1953 to 1961. After America entered the Second World War, Eisenhower was swiftly promoted to Allied commander in chief for the invasion of North Africa (1942), Sicily (1943) and Italy (1943). In December 1943 he was appointed supreme commander of the Allied expeditionary force, responsible

for the NORMANDY LANDINGS. At the end of the war, Eisenhower, known as 'Ike', received a hero's welcome home. He was appointed commander of the newly created NATO forces in 1951 but resigned the following year and was nominated as the Republican presidential candidate. Elected president with more popular votes than any previous candidate, he took office in 1953 with Richard Nixon as his vice-president. Six months later the Eisenhower administration ended the KOREAN WAR.

Labelled a 'moderate Republican' during his two terms in office, Eisenhower continued the social welfare programmes of his predecessor, Harry S Truman, sought to reduce taxes, and aided urban renewal. His administration was embarrassed by the anticommunist witch hunts of Senator Joseph MCCARTHY, whom Eisenhower denounced in 1954. In 1957 Eisenhower ordered the use of federal troops to enforce the DESEGREGATION of schools in Little Rock, Arkansas. That same year the Soviet Union launched SPUTNIK, the first artificial satellite to orbit the Earth, and in 1958 Eisenhower formed the National Aeronautics and Space Administration (NASA) to direct the US space programme.

In foreign affairs, Eisenhower together with his secretary of state, John Foster DULLES, tried to contain communism. They developed a strategy of 'massive retaliation' with nuclear weapons in case of attack, and in 1954 created the South-East Asia Treaty Organisation to prevent further communist expansion in that part of the world. After announcing the Eisenhower Doctrine in 1957 to aid Middle East nations threatened by communism, Eisenhower sent US Marines to the Lebanon to forestall a communist takeover there in 1958. He attempted to ease COLD WAR tensions by summit meetings with Soviet leaders in 1955 and 1959, but a planned meeting with the Soviet premier Nikita KHRUSHCHEV collapsed in 1960 after an American U-2 reconnaissance plane was shot down by the Russians over Soviet territory. In 1961 his administration broke off diplomatic relations with Cuba. Eisenhower retired in 1961 and was succeeded by John F. Kennedy.

El Cid (c. 1040-99) Spanish soldier and hero. Born Rodrigo Díaz de Vivar, a Castilian nobleman, El Cid – from the Arabic *al-Said*, 'the lord' – was also known as *el Campeador*, 'the Champion'. He fought against the MOORS for Ferdinand I and Sancho II of Castile, but in 1081 was exiled from Castile by Alfonso VI. He then fought for the Moorish ruler of Saragossa against both Christians and Moors until he returned to favour. In 1094 El Cid became protector and then ruler of Valencia until his death. His exploits have been romanticised in literature, and his reputation as a Christian warrior hero was exploited by the Nationalists during the Spanish Civil War.

How the world works

Albert Einstein's theories of relativity revolutionised contemporary thinking about space, time and motion, and are still considered the best description of the Universe we have.

Understanding of how the physical world works was revolutionised in the 20th century by the Swiss-German physicist Albert Einstein (1879-1955).

Born in the small German town of Ulm, Einstein showed an early interest in machines – his father was an electrical engineer. Einstein studied for his degree at a technical college in Zurich. In 1901 he became a Swiss citizen and took a job with the patent office in Bern, while continuing with his own research. He obtained a doctorate in 1905.

In the following years he began to formulate the ideas which were to transform the conception of physics established by Sir Isaac Newton. In his special theory of relativity (1905) he stated that the speed of light was fixed and that no physical object – such as a spaceship – could travel faster. He also demonstrated that as objects approach the speed of light they shrink, their mass increases and time slows down. In the general theory of relativity (1916) Einstein established a four-dimensional description of the Universe called space-time in which time is considered to be another dimension like length, width and depth. Since their creation, these theories have been repeatedly confirmed.

Albert Einstein broadcasts in the USA. His famous equation (inset) expresses the relationship between mass and energy.

Einstein's paper on the special theory of relativity allowed him to move from the patent office into a series of academic positions around Europe. He settled in Berlin in 1914, where he worked as director of the Kaiser Wilhelm Institute for Physics until 1933.

Einstein achieved world fame when his general theory of relativity was verified by the British astronomer Arthur Eddington. Even though only a handful of people understood his work, he became a symbol of the ultimate achievements of science.

NOBEL PRIZEWINNER

Einstein was awarded the Nobel prize for physics in 1921, not for uncovering the secrets of relativity but for his theory of 1905 explaining the workings of the photoelectric cell.

He was Jewish by birth, and when the Nazis came to power in 1933 he was forced to flee Germany. He lived in France, then moved to his final home in Princeton, USA, to continue his research at the Institute of Advanced Study.

In 1939, Einstein wrote to the US president Franklin D. Roosevelt urging the manufacture of atomic weapons in view of arms developments in Germany. After the war he protested against the Cold War arms race. Although some equations describing the fission of radioactive material come from special relativity, Einstein played no further part in the development of these weapons. In later years he was seen as an eccentric, antiestablishment figure with his greatest work behind him, but respected for his pacifist views. He declined the presidency of Israel in 1952.

Einstein's work is still seen as a central pillar of physics. His theories form the basis of attempts by Professor Stephen Hawking and others to produce a unified theory to explain the entire mechanism of the Universe.

The quest for the legendary wealth of El Dorado was inspired by priceless treasures such as these gold funerary hands from Peru.

El Dorado Legendary kingdom or city in South America, which may have had some foundation in fact. When Spanish CONQUISTADORES defeated the Muisca Indians of Colombia in the 1530s they heard tales of *el dorado*, 'the gilded one', from their captives. According to these tales, when a new ruler was appointed he was taken to a large lake in the Colombian interior, stripped, covered with mud and gold dust, and set on a raft laden with golden objects. He and other chiefs would then offer the gifts to the waters. As the search for treasures by the Spanish and others continued, *el dorado* came to mean an entire kingdom or city. Expeditions seeking El Dorado, especially those by Gonzalo PIZARRO in 1539 and Jiménez de Quesada in 1569-72, hastened the conquest of South America.

Eleanor of Aquitaine (c.1122-1204) Queen consort of Louis VII of France and subsequently of the future HENRY II of England. Married to Louis VII in 1137, she accompanied him on the Second Crusade in 1147, but the marriage was annulled in 1152. She then married Henry, Duke of Normandy and Count of Anjou, who ruled AQUITAINE in her name. When he succeeded to the English throne as Henry II in 1154, their kingdom stretched from Scotland to the Pyrenees. In 1173-4 Eleanor led three of her five sons, Henry, Richard and Geoffrey, into a war against her husband. She was probably fighting for the independence of Aquitaine, but was arrested and imprisoned until Richard's accession as Richard I in 1189. In 1199 Eleanor helped his brother and successor, John, to win Anjou from Arthur of Brittany. She lived out her life in France. After she died, her subjects in Aquitaine transferred their allegiance to the king of France.

Eleanor of Castile (c.1244-90) Queen consort of EDWARD I of England. The daughter of Ferdinand III of Castile, she married Edward I in 1254 and bore him 13 children. During the Crusade of 1270-3 she accompanied Edward and is said to have saved his life by sucking poison from a wound. After her death at Harby in Nottinghamshire, Eleanor's body was embalmed and taken to Westminster Abbey. At each of the 12 overnight stopping places Edward followed her deathbed request and ordered a stone cross to be erected in her memory. The last was Charing Cross in London. Three 'Eleanor crosses' still stand.

Elector One of the princes of the HOLY ROMAN EMPIRE who had the right to elect the emperor. The monarchy was elective by the 12th century, but in 1273 the number of Electors was fixed at seven: the Count Palatine of the Rhine, the Margrave of Brandenburg, the Duke of Saxony, the king of Bohemia and the archbishops of Mainz, Trier and Cologne. Electorates were later created for Bavaria, Hanover and Hesse-Kassel. Because of their independence the Electors exercised considerable power, but after 1452 the imperial crown was secured by the HABSBURG dynasty. The office of Elector disappeared when Napoleon abolished the Holy Roman Empire in 1806.

Electoral College Group of people chosen to elect a candidate to an office, such as the College of Cardinals, which meets in Rome to elect the pope. In 1787 the Founding Fathers adapted the idea as a method of electing the president and vice-president of the USA. Originally the plan was for electors to choose the president, but this was modified with the inception of political parties. Today, each state elects as many electors as it has representatives in both houses of Congress. On a specific day in December after the presidential election, the electors meet in their state capital having pledged to cast their ballot for the presidential candidate who gained the highest popular vote in the state. The votes are counted in Washington on January 6. This winner-takes-all method does not ensure that the electoral vote mirrors the popular vote, as a candidate who loses a state even narrowly loses the state's

Immigrants at New York's Ellis Island look for a better life in the New World. Known as the 'isle of tears' because not all were accepted, the island received 2000 immigrants daily in the early 1900s.

electoral vote. In 1876 Rutherford B. Hayes won a majority of electoral votes although he won fewer popular votes than his opponent. In the event of a tie, the president is chosen by a vote in the House of Representatives.

Elijah (9th century BC) Hebrew prophet at the time of King Ahab. As described in the Old Testament, his mission was to strengthen the worship of the God of the Israelites, to oppose the worship of all other gods, and to promote moral uprightness and social justice. He rebuked Ahab and his queen Jezebel for worshipping the fertility god Baal. Elijah charged his successor, Elisha, with the destruction of the OMRI dynasty. Elisha inspired revolutions in Syria and Israel and caused the downfall of the Omri by anointing Jehu as king of Israel.

Elizabeth I see feature, pages 212-13

Elizabeth II (1926-) Queen of the United Kingdom and head of the Commonwealth of Nations from 1952. The eldest daughter of GEORGE VI, she became heir to the throne in 1936 on the abdication of her uncle Edward VIII. She trained in motor transport driving and maintenance in the Auxiliary Territorial Service during the Second World War, and in 1947 she married her distant cousin Philip Mountbatten, formerly Prince Philip of Greece and Denmark. Their first child and heir to the throne, Prince Charles, was born in 1948. The Queen succeeded to the throne in 1952. Her coronation in 1953 was the first major royal occasion to be televised, and her reign has seen increasing media coverage of the royal family. Although occupying the office in which the nation's supreme power is vested, the Queen generally exercises the royal prerogative only on the advice of ministers. She retains her constitutional role to approve

parliamentary bills and to open sessions of Parliament. The Queen has also shown a strong commitment to the Commonwealth.

Ellis Island Island off Manhattan Island in New York harbour. Originally an arsenal and a fort, from 1892 to 1943 it was a centre for immigration control, dealing with a total of 20 million immigrants. From 1943 to 1954 it was a detention centre for deportees and aliens whose papers were not in order. In 1965 it became part of the Statue of Liberty National Monument and was opened to visitors.

El Salvador Smallest and most densely populated Central American state. Around 1526 the Pipil Indians of El Salvador were conquered by the Spanish and became part of the viceroyalty of NEW SPAIN. After independence in 1821, El Salvador was briefly incorporated into the Mexican empire before becoming a member of the United Provinces of Central

America from 1823 to 1839. In 1841 it became an independent republic. Internal struggles between liberals and conservatives, as well as border clashes with neighbouring countries, impeded El Salvador's development in the 19th century. By the 20th century the conservatives had gained the ascendancy and the presidency was regarded by a few elite families as their birthright. From 1931 El Salvador was dominated by a series of military

Elizabeth II and Prince Philip attend the Order of the Garter ceremony at Windsor Castle, where the chivalric order was founded in 1348.

dictators. Tensions arising from Salvadorians seeking work in Honduras culminated in war in 1965 and in 1969, following a World Cup football match between the two countries. In the 1970s unrest caused by economic instability and repressive military regimes led to an increase in guerrilla activities.

From 1979 El Salvador was torn by civil war between left-wing guerrillas, the Frente Farabundo Martí de Liberación (FMLN), and the US-backed right-wing government. The country was ravaged by right-wing 'death squads' and guerrilla terrorists. In 1980 the murder by the army of Archbishop Oscar Romero caused worldwide outrage. In 1991 UN-sponsored talks led to a peace agreement in 1992. The FMLN took part in the 1994 elections, losing to the right-wing Alianza Republicana Nacionalista (ARENA) Party led by Armando Calderón Sol.

Emin Pasha, Mehmed (1840-92) German explorer and physician who made important contributions to natural history, geography and anthropology. Originally called Eduard Schnitzer, he adopted a Turkish name and lifestyle after joining the Ottoman army as a medical officer in 1865. In 1876 Emin was appointed medical officer under the Sudan's British governor-general, General Charles GORDON, for whom he undertook administrative duties and diplomatic missions. In 1878 Gordon appointed him governor of Equatoria in southern Sudan. Emin surveyed the region and also suppressed slavery there, for which he earned the honorary title of pasha. After the MAHDI gained control of the Sudan he was left isolated and, in 1888, was rescued by the explorer H.M. STANLEY. During an expedition for the German government Emin was murdered by Arab slave-traders.

emir In the Middle East and parts of Africa, the Muslim prince or governor of a province, or a high military official. Under the UMAYYAD dynasty, an emir – from the Arabic *amir*, 'lord' or 'prince' – exercised administrative and financial powers, but the ABBASSIDS introduced a separate financial officer. An emir could be a subordinate of the caliph, the secular and religious head of state, or virtually independent. The second caliph, Umar ibn al-Khattab (*c*.581-644), took the title *amir al-muminin*, 'commander of the faithful', which was borne by his successors. The name could also be applied to a specific office, such as *amir al-umara*, commander in chief of the armies. In 631 the title *amir al-hajj*, leader of the pilgrimage to Mecca, was taken by the prophet Muhammad. '*Amir-al*' is the origin, through medieval Latin, of the English title 'admiral'.

Emmet, Robert (1778-1803) Irish nationalist. In 1798 Emmet joined the UNITED IRISHMEN society and went to live in France,

The glory of the age of Elizabeth

Her mother was executed when Elizabeth was only three, but she survived the perils of the Tudor court to become one of England's greatest monarchs and preside over the flowering of English culture.

When the zealous Roman Catholic queen Mary Tudor died on November 17, 1558, large numbers of her subjects breathed a sigh of relief that the persecution and burning of Protestants would be ended. So did her 25-year-old half-sister Elizabeth, daughter of Anne Boleyn, living in semiretirement at Hatfield. Widely believed to have Protestant sympathies and to be capable of conspiring against the queen, her life had more than once been in danger. While still a child she learned the arts of prudence and deception.

As the new queen, Elizabeth faced huge problems. Her country was weak, poor and surrounded by potential enemies. As a young woman, she was expected to marry. She was the best match in Europe, and by 1559 as many as 12 kings or princes were her suitors. She evaded their offers but gave them continuing grounds for hope in an elaborate charade designed to keep the great Catholic powers of France and Spain disunited.

Building on the achievements of her father Henry VIII, Elizabeth established a national Church of England which avoided the extremes of both Catholics and Calvinist Puritans. But her suppression of a Catholic uprising provoked a total break with Rome: Pope Pius V issued a bull deposing her as a usurper and heretic. This forced Elizabeth into the role of Europe's leading Protestant monarch. She supported the Dutch in their bitter rebellion against Spain, and the Huguenots in

France. Always short of money, she angered Spain by allowing privateers such as Sir Francis Drake and Sir John Hawkins to prey on the Spanish treasure-fleets sailing from the New World.

ELIZABETH'S RIVAL QUEEN

The main threat to her position came from her cousin, the Catholic Mary Stuart, Queen of Scots and widow of the French king Francis II. Mary claimed also to be queen of England. In 1568 she was expelled from Scotland by her Protestant nobles and fled to England, where Elizabeth held her under house arrest. A succession of plots was discovered aimed at placing Mary on the English throne, but only

The Armada Jewel designed by Nicholas Hilliard and the Armada Portrait both commemorate the defeat of the Spanish by the queen, whose hand dominates the globe.

when a full-scale Spanish invasion seemed imminent was Elizabeth persuaded by her ministers that Mary was too dangerous a figure to keep alive. She was executed at Fotheringhay Castle in 1587.

The following year the 'invincible' Armada sailed. It was seen by Spain and the pope as a great and decisive crusade against the Protestant Jezebel. All Europe was watching. It was a huge and complex combined operation. The main Spanish army under the Duke of Parma was to sail from the Spanish Netherlands and land on the coast of England. To escort it across, the Armada of 130 galleons and an additional army would sail up the Channel and link up with Parma.

Elizabeth's position seemed perilous: her available forces could not have withstood the crack Spanish regiments if they had landed in force. At sea the two fleets were roughly equal in numbers, but the English ships were smaller, faster and far more manoeuvrable in the treacherous seas of the Channel.

THE ARMADA IS REPELLED

Elizabeth rallied the troops at Tilbury, mounted on a warhorse, exclaiming: 'I know I have the body of a weak and feeble woman, but I have the heart and stomach of a king, and the King of England too.' The English fleet was commanded by Lord Howard, John Hawkins and Francis Drake, and harassed the Armada so that it was forced to put into Calais to regroup. In a daring attack, Howard's fleet scattered them with fireships, and completely disrupted the junction with Parma. The weather did the rest. The remainder had to return to Spain via the North Sea and the Scottish coasts, where at least half were wrecked.

The Armada's failure was a catastrophic blow to Philip II of Spain, who shut himself away and gave himself up to prayer. England's prestige, and with it Protestant morale, rose everywhere in Europe. Even the new pope, Sixtus V, did not withhold his admiration for her.

Throughout her reign Elizabeth shrewdly cultivated her public image and remained hugely popular. Her refusal to marry has sometimes been seen as a sacrifice of her personal happiness, but to remain the 'Virgin Queen' was a political choice. Like her father, she was utterly determined to be sole and absolute ruler. She died on March 24, 1603, after 45 years on the throne, honoured at home and abroad as no queen of England, and few kings, had ever been before.

A team of surveyors mark out the boundaries of the land in preparation for its enclosure by Act of Parliament in 1798.

from where he travelled the Continent for the Irish cause. He returned in 1802 together with a small band of followers and planned an insurrection in Dublin. This proved to be little more than a riot and it collapsed within an afternoon. Emmet was captured and executed, but during his trial his speech from the dock caused him to become a powerful symbol in the cause of Irish nationalism.

Ems telegram (July 13, 1870) Dispatch from the Prussian king WILHELM I to his chancellor, Otto von BISMARCK, which precipitated the FRANCO-PRUSSIAN WAR of 1870-1. In June 1870 Leopold of Hohenzollern-Sigmaringen, a member of Prussia's ruling family, was persuaded by Bismarck to accept an offer of the Spanish throne. The French, fearing Prussian influence south of the Pyrenees, declared they could not tolerate such a move and Leopold, under pressure from Wilhelm, withdrew. The French ambassador then approached Wilhelm at the German spa town of Ems asking for an assurance that Leopold's candidacy would never be renewed. The king refused, politely but firmly, and sent his chancellor a telegram describing the meeting. Bismarck, intent on provoking war with France in the belief that victory would lead to German unification, published a shortened version that made it appear as though the parties had insulted each other. On July 19, Napoleon III declared war. The ensuing Prussian victory led to the creation of the GERMAN SECOND EMPIRE.

enclosure Conversion of open pasture or COMMON land into closed fields by fencing or hedging it. From the 12th century enclosures began to transform English farming from the medieval system of communally controlled open fields, farmed in strips by the villagers, into a system of individually owned fields. From 1450 to 1640 the process progressed rapidly as sheep farming grew more profitable and lords sought to increase the amount of land available for pasture. Villagers lost both employment and grazing rights. In the 16th century enclosures were denounced by the Church and penalised by statutes and royal proclamations. Between 1750 and 1860 enclosures were undertaken to improve agricultural efficiency. Most were obtained by Acts of Parliament, and in 1801 the General Enclosure Act standardised the procedure. Although they received compensation, the loss of rights for rural people already close to poverty made many dependent on charity and the Poor Law. The process of enclosure was virtually completed by the late 19th century.

Encyclopédie French encyclopedia published in 35 volumes between 1751 and 1780. Edited by Denis DIDEROT and Jean le Rond d'Alembert, the *Encyclopédie* was a complete review of the arts and sciences of the day. It was notable for its innovative coverage of the industrial arts as well as for its scepticism, liberalism and criticism of legal, judicial and clerical abuses. Its contributors, known as the *Encyclopédistes*, included such leading figures of the French ENLIGHTENMENT as VOLTAIRE, ROUSSEAU and MONTESQUIEU. The rational, secular emphasis of the first volume alienated the Jesuits in particular and in 1759 it was placed on the index of books forbidden to Catholics. Nevertheless, the *Encyclopédie* continued to circulate and the critical attitudes it promoted had a widespread influence in the years leading up to the French Revolution.

Engels, Friedrich (1820-95) German socialist philosopher and, with Karl MARX, one of the founders of modern COMMUNISM. The son of a Rhineland textile manufacturer, Engels became his father's Manchester agent in 1842, attracted by the growth of radical thought in England. He became interested in

Friedrich Engels, seen here in 1891, left school at the age of 16 to work in his father's business. The family's factories later made Engels a wealthy man.

CHARTISM, and came to believe that England's advanced industry and growing working class would lead the world in social upheaval. In 1844 he met Marx in Cologne and in 1845 published *The Condition of the Working Class in England in 1844*, based on his own observations and on parliamentary reports. Two years later he and Marx joined the socialist League of the Just. They transformed it into the Communist League and in 1848 published the COMMUNIST MANIFESTO. That same year Engels took part in a revolutionary movement in Baden and later published a penetrating work on the failure of the REVOLUTIONS OF 1848 in Germany. He returned to England, working in the family's Manchester cotton mill and supporting Marx financially. After Marx's death in 1883 he continued to work on *Das Kapital* from Marx's drafts, publishing the second and third volumes in 1885 and 1894. In 1889 he played a major part in forming the Second INTERNATIONAL, a merger of revolutionary and reformist socialist parties.

Enghien, Louis de Bourbon-Condé, duc d'

(1772-1804) Last member of the house of CONDÉ, the junior branch of the French royal house of BOURBON. From 1792 to 1801 he was commander of a force of exiled royalists known as the *armée des émigrés* who left France after the Revolution and fought against French Republican armies in Europe. After the force was dissolved in 1801 Enghien retired to Baden. In 1804 he was wrongly accused by the French emperor Napoleon of being involved in a plot to assassinate him. Enghien was kidnapped by the emperor's agents, tried by a military court and shot.

England

Largest political division within the United Kingdom. There were settlements in England from early Stone Age times, and considerable remains exist of Neolithic and Bronze Age cultures. These were followed by the CELTS, whose civilisation spread over the whole country. The Romans under Julius CAESAR raided the south of England in 55 and 54 BC, but full-scale invasion only took place a century later. The country was then ruled as a Roman province until the withdrawal of the last Roman garrison in the 5th century AD. From the 3rd to the 7th centuries Germanic ANGLES, SAXONS and JUTES raided England, establishing independent kingdoms. WESSEX became dominant in the 9th century and England emerged as a distinct political entity. Following the NORMAN CONQUEST in 1066, England, under its Norman and PLANTAGENET kings, was closely linked to France.

The principality of WALES was conquered by EDWARD I between 1277 and 1284 and incorporated politically in the 16th century. During the period of TUDOR rule from 1485 to 1603 England emerged as a naval power and a Protestant state with a strong monarchy. The

upheavals of the ENGLISH CIVIL WAR of 1642 to 1651, followed by the period of republican government under Oliver CROMWELL, gave way to the RESTORATION of CHARLES II in 1660. In 1688 those opposed to the Roman Catholic king JAMES II invited the Dutch Protestant WILLIAM III and his wife MARY, both grandchildren of CHARLES I, to invade England. Scotland, ruled from England since 1603, was united with England in 1707 under the Act of UNION, and it was then that Great BRITAIN was created.

English Civil War

(1642-51) Conflict in which Parliamentary forces, or ROUNDHEADS, led by Oliver CROMWELL defeated the CAVALIERS of King CHARLES I. The war arose from constitutional, religious and economic differences between the king and Parliament, particularly the LONG PARLIAMENT. Religion became a decisive factor after the Archbishop of Canterbury, William LAUD, attempted to impose one system of worship on Roman Catholics and Puritans, alienating large numbers of clergy, gentry and craftsmen.

In the first Civil War (1642-6) Charles's main objective was to capture London, which was controlled by Parliament. After an indecisive battle at EDGEHILL, he was forced to take refuge in Oxford, which became his wartime capital. In 1643 his plan to bring together Cavalier armies from Oxford, Newcastle and

By 1645, Royalists fighting the English Civil War had lost control of the country.

the south-west, followed by a march on London, failed to be realised. The Roundheads acquired help from the Scots by the SOLEMN LEAGUE AND COVENANT and in 1644 they won the Battle of MARSTON MOOR. Charles's attempt to march on London that year was frustrated by the Battle of Newbury. Cromwell, meanwhile, had formed the NEW MODEL ARMY and in 1645 he was able to inflict a crushing defeat at NASEBY. Charles, who had rejected terms previously offered to him, surrendered near Newark in 1646 after Oxford had fallen.

Charles's attempts to profit from divisions between the Parliamentary factions prevented a settlement from being reached in 1647. He escaped to the Isle of Wight and in 1648 the second Civil War began. This consisted of unsuccessful Cavalier risings in Wales, Essex and Kent and an invasion by the Scots, now fighting on the Royalist side, which came to grief at the Battle of PRESTON. PRIDE'S PURGE, in which MPs who wanted to reach a deal with Charles were expelled from Parliament, cleared the way for the trial and execution of the king in 1649 and the establishment of the English COMMONWEALTH. Cromwell then recaptured most of Ireland, and defeated an alliance of Charles II and the Scots in 1650-1. It has been estimated that 100 000 people died in the Civil War.

Enigma

Device used by German military intelligence to encode strategic messages in the Second World War. The Enigma machine was acquired from its Dutch inventor by the German armed services in 1926. The Poles began to decipher Enigma from 1932 and in July 1939 passed on their information to the British and French. The Enigma ciphers were cracked by cryptographers and mathematicians at the top-secret Government Code and Cypher School based at Bletchley Park, northwest of London. In 1939 British secret services set up the Ultra project at Bletchley Park to intercept Enigma signals and to distribute their information. Messages from the highest levels, including Hitler himself, gave an accurate picture of German plans. Information from Enigma played a major part in the Allies winning the Battle of the ATLANTIC. Ultra's existence was an official secret until 1974.

Thinkers of a new era

In the 17th and 18th centuries the radical ideas of the philosophers of the Age of Enlightenment overturned established beliefs and influenced reform.

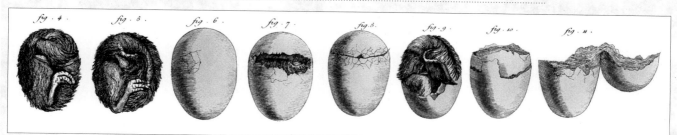

The Enlightenment was an intellectual movement inspired by the resurgence of the sciences in 17th-century Europe. It tried to apply the methods of the natural sciences to social and political affairs. The English poet Alexander Pope spoke for the Enlightenment when he said: 'Presume not then the ways of God to scan/The proper study of mankind is man.'

No European nation and no sphere of culture escaped its influence. Its main doctrines were that man is by nature rational and can attain to perfection by the use and education of his reason; that men (and, in the view of some thinkers, women) are equal, and should be given equality before the law and individual liberty; and that beliefs are to be accepted not on the basis of authority or tradition, but only if they pass the test of reason. This emphasis on reason favoured atheism or deism, the belief that God's existence can be established by reason.

The 'Age of Enlightenment' or 'Age of Reason' began in Britain in the 17th century with the lawyer, politician and thinker Francis Bacon, and the political philosophers Thomas Hobbes, John Locke, David Hume and Adam Smith. In 18th-century France it became an organised, self-conscious movement, which influenced the French Revolution in 1789. The

New ideas circulated at Madame Geoffrin's salon where gifted women presided over these 'men's debates' under the marble gaze of the French writer and thinker Voltaire.

publication between 1751 and 1780 of the *Encyclopédie* edited by Jean le Rond d'Alembert and Denis Diderot, with contributions by Voltaire, Jean-Jacques Rousseau and others, provided a focal point for proponents of Enlightenment. It was advertised as a 'systematic dictionary of the sciences, arts and trades', and was marked by anticlericalism and political radicalism.

THE USE OF REASON

In Germany the Enlightenment achieved its most significant philosophical expression in the writings of Moses Mendelssohn, Gotthold Lessing, Immanuel Kant and Johann Fichte. Kant described Enlightenment as the 'emergence of man from his self-imposed infancy': its watchword was: 'Have the courage to use one's own reason!'

The most typical, if

Diderot's *Encyclopédie* contained detailed studies of nature such as this hatching chick.

not the most distinguished, representative of Enlightenment was François Marie Arouet (1694-1778), better known by his pen name, Voltaire. He was a playwright, historian and novelist, and a gifted populariser of scientific and philosophical ideas. His sometimes spiteful but invariably witty assaults on authority were rewarded with lawsuits, imprisonment and exile. Voltaire was a deist rather than an atheist, but he believed that the world contains much pointless evil, and in his novel *Candide* attacked, in the person of 'Dr Pangloss', the doctrine of Gottfried von Leibniz that God has created the best of all possible worlds.

Voltaire was a relentless critic of established religion, and waged a lifelong war in defence of justice, humanity, tolerance and liberty. He was a true spokesman of the Enlightenment.

Enlightenment see feature, page 215

enosis (Greek, 'union') Campaign by Greek Cypriots for the union of CYPRUS with Greece. It began in the 1930s, but became a sustained guerrilla campaign from 1955, when Colonel Georgios Grivas, supported by Archbishop MAKARIOS III, founded EOKA, the National Organisation of Cypriot Fighters. In 1958 Makarios's acceptance of independence without union led to renewed demands for *enosis*. Makarios proscribed EOKA in 1974, three months before Turkey invaded and partitioned Cyprus to protect its Turkish minority.

Entente Cordiale Name given to the agreement signed between Britain and France in 1904. The Entente Cordiale – French for 'cordial understanding' – aimed to end Anglo-French colonial competition by allocating spheres of influence. Britain was to be given a free hand in Egypt while recognising French interests in Morocco. It also led to greater cooperation between the countries against perceived German ambitions. In 1907 the Entente was extended to Russia, leading to the formal alliance of Britain, France and Russia in the First World War.

Enver Pasha (1881-1922) Turkish general and statesman. He played a prominent part in the YOUNG TURK revolution, which in 1908 restored the liberal constitution of 1876 and the following year deposed the Ottoman emperor Abdülhamid II. From 1913 to 1918 Enver was one of the three real rulers of the OTTOMAN EMPIRE. As minister of war from 1914 he helped to bring the empire into the First World War on Germany's side. Enver's aim was to unite Ottoman Turks with the Turks of Russian central Asia. After the war he fled to Germany, and was later killed in Bukhara in a rebellion against Soviet rule.

Ephesus Ancient Greek city on the west coast of Asia Minor, in present-day Turkey. Founded by the Ionians, the city became wealthy as the region's leading seaport. In the middle of the 6th century BC it was captured by the Lydian king CROESUS, who contributed to the rebuilding of the Temple of Artemis, founded in about 600 BC and one of the SEVEN WONDERS OF THE WORLD. The city then passed to Cyrus II of Persia (d. 530 BC). Ephesus was a member of the DELIAN LEAGUE, an alliance formed by Greek city-states in 478. In 334 Alexander the Great took the city, which thrived under his successors, the SELEUCID dynasty. After it became Roman territory in 133 BC, Ephesus became the administrative capital of the Roman province of Asia and one of the wealthiest cities of the eastern Mediterranean. In AD 262 it was sacked by the Goths and its temple destroyed. Ephesus fell into decline in the Middle Ages

Ephesus is one of the world's largest archaeological sites. Hadrian's Temple, with its Corinthian pillars, was built in AD 118 as a tribute to the Roman emperor, to Artemis and to the city itself.

and by the 14th century had been abandoned. The site was excavated from 1863. The remains of streets, shops, temples and a magnificent theatre have since been uncovered.

Epictetus (c. AD 50-135) Phrygian philosopher of the STOIC school. His philosophy, together with his belief in one God, has many superficial similarities with the teachings of Jesus Christ. He insisted that trust in God was the only answer to the mysteries of pain, loss and death. Epictetus, a freed slave, was banished from Rome in about AD 90 when the emperor Domitian proscribed philosophers.

Epicurus (341-270 BC) Founder of the philosophical school of Epicureans, who believed that pleasure was the only worthwhile aim in life. This did not mean that life should be an endless search for pleasure, but that pleasure was a state of being in which natural and necessary desires were satisfied. Epicureans chose to avoid any deep emotional attachments and the stresses associated with politics and public life. Epicurus was educated at the Academy in Athens and in 307 established his own school there. His followers, who included women and slaves, lived modestly, but his desire for privacy and his hedonistic doctrine led to accusations from rival philosophers that he was advocating the selfish pursuit of pleasure.

Epidaurus Ancient Greek city-state in the north-east Peloponnese. In the early 4th century BC a sanctuary was built to Asclepius, the god of healing. The city's Greek theatre, marvellously well preserved and renowned for its acoustics, seats 14 000 people and is still used.

Epirus Coastal region in north-western Greece, well known in ancient times for the ORACLE of Zeus at Dodona. From 303 to 272 BC PYRRHUS expanded and strengthened its territory by invading neighbouring lands. Rome attacked the region in 197 BC after it gave its support to Macedonia, and 150 000 of its people were taken as slaves. When the Roman Empire split in two in AD 395, Epirus became a province of the Eastern Empire. After Crusaders occupied the empire's capital, Constantinople, in 1204 it became the independent Despotate of Epirus until it was reunited with the Byzantine Empire in 1337. Epirus became part of the Ottoman Empire from 1430 to 1913, when it was divided between Greece and Albania.

Erasmus, Desiderius (1469-1536) Dutch priest and Renaissance scholar, the leading exponent of Christian HUMANISM. The illegitimate son of a priest, Erasmus entered the Augustinian order in 1485 and was ordained a priest in 1492. He came into contact with humanist groups while studying in Paris from 1495. During one of his several visits to England he was professor of divinity and Greek at Cambridge University between 1509 and 1514. In 1516 he published his edition of the Greek text of the New Testament, followed by a Latin translation. This was to have enormous significance to European disciples of humanism, which made classical antiquity the basis of Western Europe's educational system. Editions of early Christian authors followed; his reputation was also enhanced by works such as *In Praise of Folly* (1509), a witty satire on monasticism and the Church dedicated to his friend Thomas MORE.

Until 1521 Erasmus moved throughout Europe, lecturing and debating. He wished for peaceful, rational reform of the Church, but ultimately repudiated the Protestant Reformation. In 1521 Erasmus retired to Basle, disillusioned by the religious conflict.

He died the most renowned scholar of his age, but after his death his works were held suspect and in 1558 were forbidden by Pope Paul IV.

Erhard, Ludwig (1897-1977) German economist and statesman. As Christian Democrat finance minister from 1949 to 1963, Erhard was the main architect of West Germany's 'economic miracle', which trebled the country's gross national product following the devastation of the Second World War. In 1963 he succeeded Konrad ADENAUER as chancellor, but three years later economic difficulties and Cabinet defections forced him to resign.

Eric the Red Tenth-century Norwegian explorer who founded the first European settlement on GREENLAND. After moving to Iceland as a child, in about 982 he and his household left in search of new land to the west. They reached Greenland, where they remained for three years, but in 986 Eric returned to Iceland. After persuading others to join him, he established the settlement of Brattahlid in southern Greenland.

Eric's son Leif Ericsson (c. 970-c. 1030) was one of the first Europeans to reach North America. According to the Norse *Eirik's Saga*, in about 1000 he sailed off course on his way from Greenland to Norway, landing at a place he named VINLAND, probably Nova Scotia. Other Icelandic sagas cite Bjarni Herjulfsson as the first European to reach North America.

Eritrea Province of ETHIOPIA, on the Red Sea. It was part of an ancient Ethiopian kingdom until the 7th century AD, remaining under Ethiopian influence until the Turks took control in the 16th century. Italy invaded Eritrea and declared it a colony in 1889, and from there launched a disastrous campaign against Ethiopia in 1896. From 1941 the region was administered by Britain, but in 1952 the United Nations voted to make it a federal area subject to Ethiopia. Ten years later Emperor HAILE SELASSIE declared the region a province of Ethiopia, provoking a battle for independence led by the Eritrean People's Liberation Front (EPLF). Fighting between the EPLF and the Ethiopian regime continued throughout the 1980s, despite drought and famine. In 1991 the EPLF, together with its allies, defeated government forces and set up a transitional Eritrean government. Two years later a referendum led to independence.

Essex, Robert Devereux, 2nd Earl of (1567-1601) English courtier, a favourite of Elizabeth I. He distinguished himself as a soldier during the Dutch Revolt in 1586, but four years later earned Elizabeth's displeasure by marrying the widow of Sir Philip Sidney. The love-hate relationship between queen and courtier continued throughout the 1590s. In 1591-2 Essex commanded an English contingent sent to help the French king Henry IV during the French Wars of Religion, and in 1596 he was one of the commanders responsible for sacking the Spanish seaport of Cadiz. Appointed Lord Lieutenant of Ireland in 1599, Essex concluded an unsatisfactory truce with the Irish rebels. He returned to England in 1600 to justify himself to Elizabeth, but was stripped of his offices. In 1601 his attempt to raise the people of London in a revolt led to his trial and execution for treason.

Estonia Country on the east coast of the Baltic. Independent states occupied the area from the 1st century AD. They came under the control of German Christian invaders in the 13th century. By the 16th century the land was mostly owned by German nobles, but thereafter the Swedes took control of the north while Poland governed the south. The country was annexed by the Russian empire in 1709, but regained its independence in 1918 after the Bolsheviks took power in the Russian Revolution. In the early 1920s the great estates of the mostly German Baltic barons were broken up, and a more prosperous peasantry was created. The economy was badly affected by the Great Depression and from 1934 until 1939 Estonia experienced a neofascist regime led by Konstantin Paets. His attempt to make a pact with Hitler was invalidated by the 1939 Nazi-Soviet Pact, by which Estonia was incorporated into the Soviet Union. On the outbreak of the Second World War, Soviet troops occupied key ports and in 1940 seized the whole country. In 1941 Estonians welcomed the invading German troops, but anti-Bolshevik resistance forces were unable to prevent the Red Army from reoccupying it in 1944, after which it became a constituent republic of the Soviet Union. In 1990 there were mass rallies in the capital, Tallinn, to demand independence. Talks began

with the Soviet Union, which recognised the republic's independence in 1991, when it was admitted to the UN General Assembly. In 1992 a new constitution was adopted. The last Russian troops withdrew two years later.

Etaples, Treaty of (November 9, 1492) Truce between Charles VIII of France and Henry VII of England after Charles attempted to annex the duchy of BRITTANY. Following a token invasion, Henry was bought off for a sum to be paid in annual instalments. Charles was left free to proceed with his plans to invade Italy, while Henry had gained international recognition of the new Tudor dynasty.

Ethelred I (d.871) King of Wessex from 866. His rule coincided with the beginning of the Danish invasion of England. Short-lived success against Danes advancing into Mercia in 868 and into Wessex in 870 was followed by defeat at Reading in 871. Later that year Ethelred won a notable victory at Ashdown, but he failed to gain any real advantage against the Danes. He died, perhaps of wounds received in battle, leaving his brother ALFRED THE GREAT to continue the fight.

Ethelred II 'the Unready' (c.968-1016) King of England from 978 to 1013 and from 1014 until his death. Ethelred succeeded his stepbrother, EDWARD THE MARTYR, in whose murder he was implicated. His authority was further undermined by blunders that earned him the title 'Unrede', meaning 'devoid of counsel'. Within two years of his accession, the Danes resumed their invasions. Five times between 991 and 1012 Ethelred was forced to buy peace with DANEGELD, a tribute paid in silver. After his 991 treaty with Richard, Duke of Normandy, by which each promised not to aid the other's enemies, Ethelred married Richard's daughter, Emma, in 1002. Later that year his order to massacre all Danes who had settled in his kingdom provoked further Viking invasions. In 1013 the Danish king SWEYN FORKBEARD was accepted as king of England by all the people living north of the

The Renaissance scholar Erasmus was the first major European figure whose fame and influence were based on the printed page.

An Ethiopian manuscript dating from the 10th century illustrates Jesus Christ sitting between Heaven, the World and Hell.

Thames. Sweyn then took the cities of Oxford, Winchester and London. Ethelred fled to Normandy, but was restored after Sweyn's death in 1014. By the time of Ethelred's own death two years later, England was under attack from Sweyn's son, CANUTE.

ether Ether's effect as an anaesthetic was known by the 19th century, but it was not tried on people until 1846. In 1844 William Morton, an American dentist, was working with Horace Wells, who had been attempting to relieve pain with nitrous oxide. After discussing the problem with Charles Jackson, a Boston chemist, Morton decided that ether would be more effective and in 1846 used it to anaesthetise a patient during the removal of a neck tumour. He spent the rest of his life in costly battles with Jackson and Wells over who first used an anaesthetic during surgery. In Britain, the obstetrician Sir James Young Simpson used ether in 1847 before discovering that chloroform was more effective at relieving the pain of childbirth. The technique was opposed by colleagues and clergy until it was made respectable by Queen Victoria, who in 1853 accepted chloroform as an anaesthetic for the birth of Prince Leopold.

Ethiopia Country in north-east Africa, formerly called Abyssinia. By the 2nd century AD Axum in northern Ethiopia had a brisk trade with Egypt, Syria, Arabia and India in gold, ivory and incense. In the 4th century the court became Christian. The Zagwe dynasty emerged after the collapse of Axum around 1150, but it was replaced in 1270 by the Solomonic dynasty, which claimed descent from the Hebrew king Solomon and the queen of Sheba. In the mid 15th century European Christians believed the region to be the kingdom of the legendary Christian monarch PRESTER JOHN. In 1543 Muslims from the lowlands attacked the Christian highlands, but were repulsed with Portuguese help. Emperor Fasilidas (1632-67) made Gondar his capital but the empire foundered because it was surrounded by Islam and divided by warring factions. The only unifying force was the Ethiopian Coptic Church. The empire was eventually reunited in 1855 under Tewodros II. Menelik II defeated an Italian invasion at Adowa in 1896, but in 1935-6 the country fell to Benito MUSSOLINI. Emperor HAILE SELASSIE was restored with British aid in 1941, and during the 1950s and 1960s Ethiopia emerged as a leading African neutralist state. Haile Selassie's failure to deal with social and economic problems, however, led to an army coup in 1974.

In 1977 a coup brought to power Colonel Mengistu Haile Mariam, whose centralised Marxist state faced a guerrilla uprising in ERITREA. After severe droughts in the 1980s, famine on a massive scale broke out between 1984 and 1987. Despite Soviet and Cuban military assistance and an international relief effort, neither peace nor plenty returned. In 1991 Mengistu was forced to flee the country by the Ethiopian People's Revolutionary Democratic Front (EPRDF) and its allies. Peace talks in London led to the recognition of an EPRDF government, which largely succeeded in restoring order. In 1991 the country was divided into nine regions, although Eritrea became independent in 1993. The following year a new constitution was adopted, giving the regions considerable autonomy, and in 1995 the first multiparty elections were won by the EPRDF under Meles Zenawi.

Etruscans Inhabitants of the ancient kingdom of Etruria in present-day Tuscany and Umbria. In the 7th and 6th centuries BC 12 independent cities, including Vulci, Clusium and Cortona, formed a league that came to dominate central Italy. Tradition held that the Etruscans came from Asia Minor in the 10th century BC, although it is now believed that they were native to Italy and culturally influenced by the Greek colonies of the south. In the 6th century BC they were driven out of southern central Italy by the Greeks, Latins and Samnites. Traditionally, TARQUIN, the last Etruscan king of Rome, was expelled in 510 BC. In the 4th century the Etruscans were driven out of Elba and Corsica, and in 390 they were defeated by the Gauls. After allying themselves with Rome in 283, they began to lose their cultural identity.

The Etruscans' art is known from tombs discovered north of Rome. These reveal an aristocratic society in which women had an emancipated style of life. The technical skill of the Etruscans' bronze and metal work and terracotta statuary is impressive. Their language, which was still spoken and written in the 1st century AD, has so far proved untranslatable.

Eugène of Savoy (1663-1736) Prince of the House of SAVOY and one of Austria's greatest generals. Born in Paris, he was refused a commission by the French king Louis XIV and joined the Austrian army when Vienna was besieged by the Turks in 1683. In 1697 he was given command of the Danube army and annihilated the Turks at Zenta, thereby freeing Hungary from Turkish domination. As president of the council of war during the War of the SPANISH SUCCESSION (1701-14) he successfully cooperated with the British general John Churchill, Duke of MARLBOROUGH at BLENHEIM, Malplaquet and OUDENAARDE, and won control of north Italy at the Battle of Turin in 1706. In 1716-18 he led a campaign against the Turks and recovered Belgrade.

Eugénie (1826-1920) Empress of France and wife of NAPOLEON III, whom she married in 1853. A Spanish-born countess, she was christened Eugénia María de Montijo de Guzman. During Napoleon's reign from 1852 to 1870 Eugénie contributed much to the brilliance of his court and on three occasions acted as regent while he was away fighting. She also encouraged French intervention in Mexico. Following the collapse of the French Second Empire in 1870, Eugénie fled to England.

eunuch Castrated man or boy, from the Greek *eunoukhos*, 'one in charge of a bed'. Eunuchs were used as guardians of harems in ancient China, in the Persian empire of the Achaemenids, and at the courts of the

An Etruscan funerary urn shows a young boy being punished after having been caught spying on Diana, goddess of the moon.

Li Lien-Ying (right) was chief eunuch to the Chinese empress Tze-Hsi (1834-1908). Eunuchs were used as servants in women's quarters.

Byzantine emperors and the Ottoman sultans. They often became the friends and advisers of rulers. Castration was also imposed as a form of punishment and was practised voluntarily by some Christian sects. In Italy castration was used to produce male sopranos – *castrati* – until Pope Leo XIII banned it in 1878.

Eureka Stockade (1854) Armed conflict between diggers and authorities in the gold fields of Ballarat in Australia. Gold was discovered there in 1851, and by 1853 more than 20 000 diggers had arrived. The rebellion was the result of long-standing grievances over the licence system, corrupt officials, lack of political representation and limited access to land. Following clashes with troops, the diggers built a stockade, where, in December, 150 of them were surrounded by soldiers. A short battle followed in which about 25 diggers and five soldiers died. The battle hastened reforms in the administration of the gold fields.

Euripides (c.485-c.406BC) Greek dramatist. From about 455 Euripedes produced 80 or 90 plays, of which 19 survive, including the tragedies *Electra, Medea, The Trojan Women* and *The Bacchae*. He was accused by his contemporaries of distorting traditional Greek myths and also of being a misogynist. Euripedes' plays are parodied in the works of the comic poet Aristophanes.

Europe Continent of the Northern Hemisphere that throughout history has exerted an influence out of proportion to its size. Its most important ancient civilisations developed in the Mediterranean region. Greek civilisation reached its zenith between 500 and 300 BC, succeeded by that of ROME. Christianity became the official religion of the Roman Empire in the late 4th century, shortly before the western part of the empire was overrun by Germanic invaders. The eastern part lived on as the BYZANTINE EMPIRE.

During the MIDDLE AGES a politically fragmented Europe was invaded and colonised by MOORS, VIKINGS, MAGYARS and others. In Western Europe the CAROLINGIAN EMPIRE gave way to the HOLY ROMAN EMPIRE. The Roman Catholic Church became a unifying force throughout the continent. In the 14th century the RENAISSANCE of classical art, literature and learning spread from Italy to the rest of Europe. Attempts to reform the Church in the 16th century led to the REFORMATION and an era of political and religious warfare.

Postmedieval Europe was marked by the rise of nation-states such as France, England, the Netherlands, Spain and eventually Russia, all of which built vast empires outside Europe. Imperial expansion continued during the age of European revolutions, of which the FRENCH REVOLUTION, beginning in 1789, was the most momentous. The revolution was followed by the NAPOLEONIC WARS until the Congress of VIENNA in 1815 heralded almost a century of relative peace.

The INDUSTRIAL REVOLUTION began in England during the late 18th century and soon spread throughout most of Europe. The unification of the German states into a powerful nation in 1870 alarmed some European nations. By 1914 an alliance of Britain, France and Russia faced Germany and the Austro-Hungarian empire. The assassination of the Austrian archduke Franz Ferdinand on June 28, 1914, was the immediate cause of the First World War, which led to the end of monarchies in Germany, Austria-Hungary and Russia, and to the creation of several small nations. In Russia the communists took power in the RUSSIAN REVOLUTION of 1917 and created the Union of Soviet Socialist Republics. In Germany, NAZIS gained a grip on a nation crippled by war reparations and rampant inflation. In 1939 the Second World War broke out after the German chancellor Adolf Hitler invaded neighbouring countries. The Axis powers of Germany, Italy and Japan were defeated by the nations of Western Europe allied with the USA and the USSR. Western Europe experienced postwar growth and eventually set up the European Economic Community, later the EUROPEAN UNION, while Eastern Europe stagnated under communist rule. The eastern nations gained their freedom in 1989-90 in a wave of mostly bloodless revolutions. The Soviet Union collapsed, with each republic setting up its own government. In the former Yugoslavia a bloody ethnic war between the new republics raged from the early 1990s until 1995.

European Economic Community (EEC) see EUROPEAN UNION

European Free Trade Association (EFTA) Customs union of European states. EFTA was brought into existence by the Stockholm Convention in 1959, and has at times included Austria, Britain, Denmark, Norway, Portugal, Sweden, Switzerland, Liechtenstein, Finland and Iceland. It was created as an alternative trade grouping to the European Economic Community (EUROPEAN UNION) on a basis suggested by Britain. In 1973 Britain and Denmark left EFTA and entered the European Community; Portugal made the same move in 1985. In 1977 EFTA signed an agreement with the EEC to set up free trade between the two organisations. This was followed in 1984 by the Luxembourg Declaration to form a European Economic Area, which came into force in January 1993.

European Parliament Legislative assembly of the EUROPEAN UNION, which meets alternately in Strasbourg and Luxembourg. From 1958 it was composed of representatives

The battle of the Eureka Stockade in Australia lasted only 15 minutes. The British Government offered rewards for the capture of rebels, but none was convicted.

Growth of the European Union
- Treaty of Rome 1957
- admitted 1973
- admitted 1981
- admitted 1986
- admitted 1995
- admitted to Customs Union Jan 1996 but not full membership
- non E.U. Countries

After 40 years the European Union has mushroomed into the world's largest trading bloc, but the prospect of federation leads some members, notably Britain, to fear loss of national sovereignty.

drawn from the assemblies of the member states, but since 1979 direct elections have taken place every five years. Treaties signed in 1970, 1975 and 1986 gave the parliament important powers over budgets and constitutions, but the Single European Act of 1986 ensures that national parliaments retain a degree of sovereignty. The 1992 Treaty of MAASTRICHT envisaged a further extension of the European Parliament's powers.

European Union (EU) Association of European states whose goal is to promote closer economic and political cooperation between its members and to achieve monetary union by 1999. It has its origins in the desire for reconciliation that followed the Second World War. In 1951 France, the Federal Republic of Germany (West Germany), Italy, Belgium, Luxembourg and the Netherlands formed the European Coal and Steel Community (ECSC) to pool their resources. Six years later they signed the Treaty of Rome, which founded the European Economic Community (EEC) and the European Atomic Energy Community (Euratom). Within ten years the EEC had abolished customs duties between member states and set up grants to help poorer countries to improve their farming and industries. In 1967 the EEC, Euratom and the ECSC were merged to create the European Community (EC). The principle of economic and monetary union was advanced from the late 1960s and in 1979 the Economic Monetary System (EMS) was established with

a view to eventual currency union. The EC was joined by Britain, Ireland and Denmark in 1973, Greece in 1981, and Portugal and Spain in 1986. In 1992, EC members signed the Treaty of MAASTRICHT, which led to the creation of the European Union. The member countries added a shared foreign policy and commitment to cooperation on security matters, including justice and policing, to their economic and political links. By the mid 1990s the EU was the world's biggest trading power. The main institutions are the European Commission, the Union's administrative body; the Council of Ministers, responsible for political decision-making; the EUROPEAN PARLIAMENT; and the European Court of Justice, whose decisions overrule any national Act of Parliament on the same issue.

In 1994 dissent over many issues and doubt over the future led to Norway voting in a referendum to reject the offer of a place in the Union. Austria, Sweden and Finland joined in 1995, bringing the total number of members to 15. The EU also has agreements of association with many countries. Turkey, Malta and Cyprus have been promised eventual admittance to the Union after they have fulfilled certain conditions. Applications from Poland and Hungary are under consideration. The EU has also agreed to cooperate and negotiate with many countries of the former Soviet

Union, as well as Bulgaria and Romania. In 1994 more limited cooperation agreements were made with both Russia and the Ukraine.

Evesham, Battle of (August 4, 1265) Decisive engagement fought in the second BARONS' WAR. Prince Edward, the future EDWARD I, defeated Simon de MONTFORT and rescued his father, HENRY III, who had been captured by de Montfort's forces the previous year. De Montfort's headless corpse was buried in the abbey at Evesham, which later became a place of pilgrimage.

evolution, human Process of development in which modern human beings, *Homo sapiens sapiens*, emerged from ape-like ancestors to take on their present form. The process took at least 5 million years by way of the HOMINIDS: Australopithecines, *Homo habilis*, *Homo erectus* and *Homo sapiens*. Many details are unknown, including the link between the Australopithecines and the *Homo* lines. The discovery of BROKEN HILL MAN suggests there was another stage in human development. The modern theory of evolution derives from Charles DARWIN's theory of natural selection. (See also features, pages 16-17 and 444-5)

Exchequer English government department in charge of the collection and dispersal of national revenue. It was named after the chequered cloth on which revenues were reckoned and became the government's main financial agency under Henry I. The lower Exchequer received money and was connected to the Treasury; the upper Exchequer regulated accounts but it was gradually superseded by the Treasury from the 16th century and abolished in 1833.

Exclusion Crisis (1679-81) Attempt to exclude Charles II's Catholic brother James, Duke of York, later JAMES II, from the English throne. After the discovery in 1678 of the Catholic POPISH PLOT, the WHIGS tried three times to pass Bills excluding James. Charles survived the crisis by dissolving Parliament so that the Bills were lost. The Whigs eventually triumphed when the Protestant William of Orange became WILLIAM III in 1688.

excommunication Deprivation of the right to receive Holy Communion. In the Roman Catholic Church it was first used against those with heretical religious beliefs, but it later became a disciplinary and political weapon against rulers who opposed the Church and the papacy. Subjects would then be released from their duty to obey their lord, which could threaten a weak monarch. The English king JOHN was excommunicated, as was the Holy Roman Emperor Henry IV, who submitted to Pope Gregory VII at CANOSSA in 1077 after standing in the snow for three days.

Exile Captivity of the Jews in BABYLON, also known as the Babylonian Exile. There were two mass deportations: in 598 BC, when King Jehoiachin was deposed, and in 586 BC, when the Babylonian king NEBUCHADNEZZAR II destroyed Jerusalem, forcing thousands of Jews into exile in Babylon. Many settled in communities, enabling Jewish teaching, religion and life to continue. During this period institutions such as the synagogue developed. In 539 BC Babylon fell to Persia, and in 538 CYRUS II allowed Jews to return home. The number who returned was probably small.

Exodus Liberation of the Israelites under MOSES from their captivity in Egypt around 1300 BC, recorded in the Old Testament book of Exodus. According to the biblical account, the Israelites were pursued by the pharaoh's army, but were saved when the Red Sea parted to allow them across and then closed, drowning the pharaoh's troops. The Israelites then spent more than 40 years in the wilderness of the Sinai desert. During this time they received the Ten Commandments through Moses. Moses was succeeded by Joshua, whose capture of Jericho led to the occupation of CANAAN, the promised land of Palestine. The variety of sources make it impossible to regard this narrative as a reliable historical account, but it is central to Jewish history as evidence of God's favour to his chosen people.

exploration For the first explorers, travel was easier by sea than by land. PHOENICIAN traders were sailing to Galicia in Spain, to Brittany and Cornwall by around 900 BC. In the early Middle Ages the VIKINGS sailed as far as Greenland and North America, while curiosity about the 'marvels of the East' led the Venetian MARCO POLO overland to China between 1271 and 1295, although some people believe that in his writings he exaggerated the extent of his travels. The Chinese Ming emperors supported seven voyages by ZHENG HE between 1405 and 1433.

Under the patronage of HENRY THE NAVIGATOR, the Portuguese sailed to the Indian Ocean in the 15th century, and in 1498 Vasco DA GAMA crossed the South Atlantic. In 1492 Christopher COLUMBUS left Spain aiming to reach the East, but landed on San Salvador in what is now the Bahamas. The North American landmass was such an obstacle that searches were long made for a navigable passage to the north. The search for a north-west passage led the Venetian Sebastian CABOT to what was probably Hudson Bay in 1509, and the Frenchman Jacques CARTIER along the St Lawrence River in 1534-41. Exploration of the North American interior began in the

17th century, and the continent was first crossed in 1792-3 when the Scottish-born Alexander Mackenzie traversed Canada. The United States was crossed in 1804-5 by the American LEWIS AND CLARK EXPEDITION. Scientific research enabled Captain James COOK to secure backing for his voyages to New Zealand and Australia in 1768-79.

The Portuguese charted the coasts of part of Africa in the 15th century; exploration of the interior was carried out by the Britons David Livingstone, Henry Stanley, John Speke and Sir Richard Burton during the 19th century. The Russians began exploration of the Arctic in the 1730s and by the end of the 19th century much of it had been covered. In 1909

Robert Peary reached the North Pole. In the 19th century, American, French and British explorers mapped parts of Antarctica. Sledge journeys to the interior were made by the Briton Robert Scott in 1901-4, and in 1907-9 by his fellow countryman Ernest Shackleton. But in the race to the South Pole the Norwegian Roald Amundsen arrived first, on December 14, 1911, a month before Scott. Scott's party died on the return journey. The aeroplane made possible further exploration of the globe. In the second half of the 20th century, explorers faced the new challenges of SPACE EXPLORATION (see feature, page 610).

explosives see feature, page 222

A 15th-century Italian manuscript illustrates Moses guiding the Israelites across the Red Sea during their Exodus from Egypt. The Exodus is commemorated annually in the Passover feast.

From fireworks to fission

Gunpowder was introduced into Europe from the East in the 13th century. As explosives and firearms developed, the nature of warfare changed from muscle-powered combat into a struggle for technological superiority.

The origins of gunpowder are unknown. The Chinese used saltpetre in fireworks, and their first formula for gunpowder – a mixture of saltpetre, charcoal and sulphur – to make bombs appears in 1044. Soon they were using gunpowder to fire projectiles from tubes of bamboo, bronze or iron. This 'black powder' was to form the charge for guns for the next 800 years.

From the mid 13th century the Moors used gunpowder in projectiles launched from catapults. It was from the Muslims that the West received knowledge of explosives. The first surviving recipe for gunpowder is mentioned in 1267 by the English Franciscan friar Roger Bacon.

CANNON POWER

Illustrations of cannons appear in two English manuscripts of 1326. Each is shaped like a vase and fires a large dart rather than a ball. Primitive cannons are mentioned at the Battle of Crécy in 1346. Huge bombards were employed in siege warfare: Mons Meg, built in 1449 and still in existence at Edinburgh Castle,

Greek fire was an early form of napalm. The Byzantine navy struck fear into its enemies by showering them with burning liquid.

could hurl a stone ball weighing 5 cwt (250 kg). These early guns could be as great a danger to the user as to the enemy – in 1460 James II of Scotland was killed by an exploding cannon at Roxburgh.

The word 'barrel' derives from the method of constructing bombard barrels from wrought-iron strips bound by hoops. Lighter guns were often of cast bronze or brass and mounted on wheeled carriages. Handguns were no more than small tubes fitted with stocks. The charge was lit by hand with a hot wire or slow taper – a cord of hemp or flax impregnated with saltpetre and applied to a touch-hole. Then came the matchlock, in which a slow match attached to an arm was lowered onto a pan of priming charge when the trigger was pulled.

By the 18th century the flintlock musket had become the soldier's principal armament. It used a flint to strike a steel to produce the spark. In the mid 19th century it was superseded by a percussion cap of explosive which was struck by a hammer to set off the main charge, and enclosed with the bullet in a paper cartridge. Soon fixed ammunition, a metallic cartridge case with primer in the base and a bullet or shot at the other end, became standard.

THE TECHNOLOGY OF WAR

Artillery had become increasingly important by the mid 18th century. Cannons fired solid shot or grape and canister (clusters of smaller balls). Shells were designed to explode in the air or on hitting the ground. Ships were adapted to become floating gun platforms.

From the 1880s 'smokeless' propellants based on nitrocellulose began to take over from black powder, and 'high explosive' shells were developed, like those used in the First World War. Machine guns rendered cavalry useless on the battlefield. In the Second World War explosives were turned on civilians, who suffered bombing from the air. A more recent development is plastic explosives such as Semtex.

In 1867 the Swedish chemist Alfred Nobel invented dynamite, a powerful explosive used largely for nonmilitary purposes. Gunpowder is still used for fuses, fireworks and quarry blasting.

Today the most awesome power can be unleashed by splitting and fusing the atom, but conventional explosives are still an essential part of the modern arsenal.

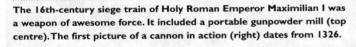

The 16th-century siege train of Holy Roman Emperor Maximilian I was a weapon of awesome force. It included a portable gunpowder mill (top centre). The first picture of a cannon in action (right) dates from 1326.

Ezekiel (6th century BC) Hebrew prophet. According to tradition a priest who was taken into EXILE in Babylon in 597 BC, Ezekiel denounced religious apostasy and idolatry and prophesied the forthcoming destruction of Jerusalem and the Jewish nation. As soon as Jerusalem fell, in 586, he began to prophesy that God would restore the nation, all exiles would return and that the Israelites would begin life back in their land in a new relationship with their God.

Ezra (5th and 4th century BC) Jewish priest instrumental in reforming Judaism after the EXILE in Babylon. It is thought that Ezra arrived in Jerusalem in 397 BC with authority from the Persian king Artaxerxes I or his successor Artaxerxes II. He reformed the system of worship at the Jerusalem Temple and established a written code of laws and the priestly leadership of Judaism. He is sometimes regarded as the second Moses and the father of Judaism because of his extensive reforms.

Fabian Society British socialist movement seeking gradual social reforms, such as better municipal facilities, improved factory conditions and a fairer tax system, through non-confrontational means. It took its name from the Roman general Maximus Quintus FABIUS, who was regarded as an archetype of gradualism. The society, founded in 1884 by a group of left-wing intellectuals including George Bernard SHAW and Beatrice and Sydney WEBB, believed in 'the inevitability of gradualism'. In 1900 its members helped to found the Labour Representation Committee, which became the Labour Party. At its peak in 1946 the Fabian Society had 8400 members. It still carries out research and holds meetings.

Fabius, Maximus Quintus (d.203 BC) Roman general who served as consul to the republic five times between 233 and 209. Fabius was nicknamed *Cunctator*, 'Delayer', because of his hesitation in entering into battle against Hannibal and his superior Carthaginian army during the second PUNIC WAR. The wisdom of his strategy of slow harassment was recognised too late; in 216, when he was no longer in command, the Roman army hurried to annihilate the Carthaginian forces and was defeated at Cannae.

Factory Acts Laws introduced to regulate conditions of employment of 19th-century textile factory employees, mainly women and children who often worked between 12 and 16 hours a day, sometimes in dangerous conditions. Britain's Factory Act of 1833 banned

The Factory Act of 1833 banned the use of young children in Britain's coal mines. Pit owners had employed children because some of the coal seams were too narrow for adult miners to work.

the employment of children under the age of nine, restricted the working hours of older children and appointed factory inspectors. Further acts between 1844 and 1920 legislated for the protection of workers in mines and other industries, reduced the working day to ten hours and raised the minimum age of workers to 14 years. By the 1890s most European countries had adopted a complicated structure of industrial law, and in 1938 the Fair Labor Standards Act was passed in the USA. With CHILD LABOUR, excessive hours and poor conditions for women still rife in many countries, especially the Far East, in 1919 the League of Nations formed the International Labour Organisation to protect the rights of workers throughout the world.

fair Named after the Latin *feriae*, 'holiday', the fair as a temporary market was a feature of religious festivals in China as early as the 12th

Rural fairs, such as this in 16th-century Italy, sold mainly local livestock and food. Town fairs also traded in exotic imports such as spices.

century BC. Fairs were also held during the early Olympic Games of Greece and were a common fixture of the Roman Empire. A fair held in St Denis, near Paris, in AD629 was probably the first in Western Europe, though by the 10th century fairs were common across the whole of Europe. Typical goods traded included cloth and furs. The fairs of Champagne and Brie in France attracted merchants from as far as the Middle East and Africa and lasted up to six weeks. By the 14th century international fairs had declined, with merchants leaving long-distance trading to their overseas agents. The 20th century saw the emergence of trade fairs, such as the annual Frankfurt Book Fair.

Fairfax, Thomas (1612-71) English general who in 1645 became commander-in-chief of Parliament's NEW MODEL ARMY and played a prominent part in the defeat of the Royalists during the ENGLISH CIVIL WAR. Fairfax won a string of victories, including the Battles of Marston Moor in 1644 and Naseby in 1645, but he refused to carry the campaign against the Royalists into Scotland. He disapproved of the purge of Parliament by his soldiers and disassociated himself from the decision to execute Charles I. He resigned in 1650.

Faisal I (1885-1933) King of Iraq from 1921 until his death. The son of Hussein ibn Ali, ruler of Mecca, Faisal I commanded the northern Arab army in Jordan, Palestine and Syria in alliance with Britain's T.E. LAWRENCE, 'Lawrence of Arabia', in the Arab Revolt of 1916. He was elected king of Syria in 1920 by the Syrian National Congress, then expelled by France, the governing power. The British achieved some influence over the territory and made the cooperative Faisal king of Iraq to ease resistance to British rule. In return, they agreed to the country's eventual independence, which was finally achieved in 1932.

Falange Fascist political party founded in Spain in 1933 by José Antonio Primo de Rivera, the son of General Miguel Primo de RIVERA. The movement, which was equally opposed to the reactionary Right and the revolutionary Left, sought to run Spain along the lines of Italian fascism. During the Spanish Civil War, General Francisco FRANCO realised the value of the Falange if it could be made more acceptable to traditionalists and monarchists. He adopted the movement in April 1937, after Antonio was executed by the Republicans, and used it alongside his military attempt to take power. The Falange was abolished in 1977 after Franco's death.

Falkirk, Battles of Two battles that took place at the Scottish town of Falkirk. The first, in July 1298, resulted in victory for Edward I of England over Sir William WALLACE, leader of the Scottish resistance to English sovereignty. In the second battle, in January 1746, Royalist forces were defeated by the Jacobite army of Bonnie Prince Charlie in the FORTY-FIVE rebellion.

Falkland Islands Group of 202 islands in the South Atlantic, ruled by Britain. Since the 16th century the islands have been occupied by the French, British and Spanish. In 1820 they were claimed by Argentina, where they are known as 'Las Malvinas'. The British, objecting on the grounds that their sovereignty had never been renounced, reclaimed the islands as a crown colony in 1833. Argentina continued to dispute their possession and invaded the islands in 1982, leading to the FALKLANDS WAR.

Falklands War Confrontation between Argentina and Britain over possession of the FALKLAND ISLANDS. The Argentinian military junta headed by General Leopoldo Galtieri sparked the war in March 1982 by invading the outlying island of South Georgia after years of negotiations for a transfer of sovereignty became deadlocked. On April 2, General Galtieri said he was reclaiming the Falklands and landed an invasion force which took control of all the inhabited islands. The United Nations, the United States and Peru tried to negotiate a peaceful solution, but failed. Britain launched a task force of aircraft,

A helicopter plucks survivors from a raft after Argentinian planes bombed the British landing ship *Sir Galahad* in the Falklands War. Fifty-one personnel died as the ship caught fire and sank.

30 warships and troops to retake the islands. The war lasted ten weeks, claimed the lives of nearly 1000 British and Argentinian troops and civilians and ended with the surrender of the Argentinians on June 14. It was believed that General Galtieri had launched the invasion to boost the popularity of his junta, and in 1983 his government collapsed. The islands were declared part of the new province of Tierra del Fuego by the Argentinian Congress in 1990, but remained British.

Faraday, Michael (1791-1867) British physicist whose discovery of electromagnetism made possible the continuous generation of electric current. Faraday trained as a bookseller and bookbinder, but became laboratory assistant to Humphry DAVY at the Royal Institution, eventually succeeding him as director in 1827. Faraday was fascinated by electrical phenomena and conducted many experiments with electricity and magnets, leading to the discovery that a current could be produced by a change in magnetic intensity – the basis of electromagnetism. In 1831 he published his 'laws of electromagnetic induction'. Among Faraday's many achievements were constructing the first electric transformer, isolating the compound benzene and discovering diamagnetism – a weak magnetic effect present in all materials. He turned down a knighthood and the presidency of the Royal Society, fearing that the honours would compromise his integrity.

Farnese Italian noble family which ruled the duchy of Parma from 1545 to 1731. The first prominent member of the family, which originated in the 11th century, was Alessandro (1468-1549), who became Pope Paul III in 1534 and created the duchy of Parma and Piacenza by detaching lands from the papal dominions. The most distinguished descendant was another Alessandro (1545-92), who became Duke of Parma in 1586. A brilliant military tactician, he successfully served in many battles, including the crushing victory over the Ottomans at the Battle of LEPANTO in 1571. When the last Farnese male descendant Antonio died in 1731 Parma and Piacenza passed via Elizabeth Farnese – queen of Spanish king Philip V – to her son Don Carlos, the future Charles III of Spain, and then to his brother Philip, who founded the line of Bourbon-Parma.

Alessandro Farnese, who was Pope Paul III for 15 years in the 16th century, holds an audience in Venice with former Barbary pirate Barbarossa, who had become admiral of the Ottoman fleet.

Farouk (1920-65) King of Egypt, who ruled from 1936 to 1952. Farouk's sympathies with the fascist alliance during the Second World War resulted in a clash with the British, who appointed as premier the Wafd leader Mustapha an-Nahas Pasha, a supporter of the Allies. Farouk's defeat in the Arab-Israeli conflict of 1948, together with his extravagant lifestyle, led to a military coup in 1952 headed by Gamul Abdul NASSER. He was forced to abdicate in favour of his infant son, Fuad II, who was deposed a year later.

fascism see feature, page 226

Fashoda Incident Climax on September 18, 1898, of a long series of territorial disputes between Britain and France over Africa. In 1896 French forces under Jean Baptiste Marchand set out from Gabon to claim the Sudan. At the same time Britain's Herbert KITCHENER was heading towards the Nile to recover the city of Khartoum. The two sides met at a fort in Fashoda, in south-east Sudan, and a potentially disastrous conflict was delayed while talks took place in London and Paris. The French ordered Marchand to withdraw and an agreement was reached allowing each side to retain its colonial possessions as far as the Nile and Congo watersheds.

Fawkes, Guy see GUNPOWDER PLOT

Federal Bureau of Investigation Branch of the US Department of Justice which investigates violations of federal law, especially those involving espionage, racketeering and security of the nation. It now has jurisdiction over 185 crimes ranging from subversion and spying to bank robbery and gambling violations. Originally set up as the Bureau of Investigation in 1908 by attorney general Charles J. Bonaparte, the organisation was restructured by J. Edgar HOOVER, who was made director in 1924 and led the FBI until his death in 1972.

In the 1930s the organisation became renowned for its successful campaign against gangsters such as John Dillinger, though its reputation has not always been untarnished. In 1964 it was criticised by the Warren Commission over its investigations into the assassination of President John F. KENNEDY. In 1973 its acting director Patrick Gray resigned when it was discovered that he had destroyed documents about the Watergate investigation, which eventually led to the resignation of President Richard NIXON in 1974.

federalism System of government in which individual regional governments recognise the control of a national government while retaining some local powers. The USA, whose federal constitution was drawn up in 1787-8, became a model for federations, including Canada and Australia. Examples of federal governments include Mexico, South Africa, India, Germany and the former USSR.

Federalist Party American political party that evolved after the signing of the US constitution in 1788. George Washington and John Adams were both members of the party, which was named after *The Federalist Papers*, a collection of essays written by James Madison, Alexander Hamilton and John Jay, to persuade New York state voters to approve the constitution. The party saw itself as helping 'the wise, the good, and the rich', and its belief in a strong central government and firm domestic laws appealed to the commercial sector and wealthy landowners in New England and the north-east. The party disappeared in 1825 after it was undermined by changes in political opinion and disagreements over commercial and foreign policy. It laid the foundations of national government and a policy of neutrality in foreign affairs which allowed the newly formed nation to develop in peace.

Fenian Member of an Irish-American secret society formed in 1857-8 and named after the Fianna – Irish warriors of the 3rd century AD. The Fenian movement was established to achieve Irish independence from England by force. John O'Mahony, who along with many other disaffected Irish people had emigrated to the USA after the IRISH FAMINE, founded the US branch, known as the Fenian Brotherhood, in 1857. In 1858 James Stephens established the Irish branch, known as the Irish Republican Brotherhood (IRB). The British Government took steps to suppress the movement, imprisoning many of its members. In the late 1860s the Fenian Brotherhood split into three separate factions, and while they all claimed allegiance to the IRB they were bitterly divided over policies. The Fenian movement died out in the 1870s. One of its members, Arthur GRIFFITH, went on to found the political party SINN FÉIN, which continues the Fenian aim of achieving a unified Ireland.

Ferdinand II (1578-1637) Holy Roman Emperor from 1619, and king of Bohemia and Hungary. Ferdinand was a forceful opponent of Protestantism and became a leader in the Roman Catholic Counter Reformation, which aimed to reform the Church and to secure its traditions against Protestant influence. In 1619 Ferdinand was temporarily deposed as king by Bohemia's largely Protestant parliament, in favour of Frederick V of the Palatinate. Ferdinand formed an alliance with Maximilian I of Bavaria which

The Holy Roman Emperor Ferdinand II spent his reign trying to end the Thirty Years' War but failed to gain a military or diplomatic victory.

won him back sovereignty, but provoked the THIRTY YEARS' WAR. With the help of Spain and the Catholic princes of Germany at the beginning of the war, Ferdinand gained significant victories over his German opponents and the king of Denmark.

Ferdinand issued the Edict of Restitution in 1629, ordering the return of all Roman Catholic property seized since 1552. His fortunes changed when he removed the religious rights of German Protestants, and the Protestant princes began to see him as a threat to German liberty. The Swedes and the French joined the opposition and a compromise was finally achieved through the Peace of Prague in 1635, which greatly modified the Edict of Restitution. This appeased both the Catholics and the Protestants for a while, though the war resumed and continued into the reign of Ferdinand's son and successor Ferdinand III, who became emperor in 1637.

Ferdinand V (1452-1516) Spanish ruler from 1474, also known as Ferdinand II, king of Aragon, and Ferdinand III, king of Naples. The son of John II of Aragon, in 1469 he married Princess ISABELLA of Castile, and in 1481 they ruled the kingdoms of Aragon and

> **DID YOU KNOW?**
>
> In 1866 the US Fenian group decided to strike a blow against Britain by invading its colony, Canada. About 800 men captured Fort Erie but they were cut off and 700 were arrested.

The dictator-states

Fascism was used to describe the regime of the right-wing dictator Benito Mussolini in Italy in the 1920s. Dedicated to the cause of national rejuvenation, it was later adopted in a more radical form by Hitler's Germany.

The term 'fascist' conjures up the image of someone intolerant, fanatical and violent. Yet those in Italy in 1919 who called themselves fascists were idealists, convinced they had a mission to rid Italy of the evils which they believed were undermining its greatness, and to transform it into a land of productivity, justice, joy and heroism.

Fascism took its name from the Latin *fasces*, symbols of authority in ancient Rome. In Italy in 1919 it described the struggle of the *Fasci di combattimento*, 'fighting leagues', to create a new political and social order out of the chaos following the First World War. They were set up by the former socialist leader Benito Mussolini to spread the heroic spirit of the trenches throughout society.

Italian fascist officials are toughened up by gymnastics at Rome's Foro Mussolini, and (below) 'legions' of youth gather in Milan.

FULFILLING A DREAM

As leader between 1925 and 1943 Mussolini created a single-party state which introduced radical institutional reforms. But the dream of the 'Fascistisation' of society proved impossible to realise. It was relatively easy to suppress opposition parties, but the attempt to turn everyone into worshippers of the state and its leader had little impact. Equally, the claim to have built a powerful economy and armed forces was more rhetorical than real.

In the 1930s Mussolini embarked on foreign expansion. He turned Ethiopia into a colony and entered an alliance with the German Third Reich. This 'Axis' with Adolf Hitler was to prove fatal to his regime: when the Second World War turned against the Axis powers, Italy's armed forces proved inadequate. In April 1945 Mussolini was shot by partisans.

The term 'fascist' came to refer to other right-wing nationalist movements. The most destructive to seize power was Nazism in Germany, which attempted to destroy Marxist socialism so as to inaugurate a 'new order' based on a strong national community. Hitler's aims included the reversal of the humiliating peace settlement imposed on Germany after the First World War; the integration of ethnic Germans within new national frontiers; the seizure of a colonial empire in Poland and western Russia; and the creation of a Germany populated only by the culturally and biologically 'pure'.

The Nazi reconstruction of Germany involved fighting a war against 'inner enemies'. These included Jews, gypsies, communists, homosexuals, the handicapped and anyone with the courage to resist. In 1939 Germany's foreign policy led to war against external enemies as well. To wage these two wars, the Third Reich was ruthlessly determined to use the force of arms, social engineering, propaganda, state terror, persecution and murder, causing suffering on an inconceivable scale. The slaughter was halted only by Allied victory in 1945.

Adolf Hitler prepares to address a rally of brown-shirted *Sturmabteilung*, 'storm troopers', in Dortmund in 1938. The picture appeared in a propaganda book entitled *Germany Awakens*.

Ferdinand V (left) married Isabella of Castile to help her to gain succession to her throne and strengthen his aim to control the kingdoms that would later form the basis of modern Spain.

Castile, uniting the two most powerful Spanish monarchies. In 1492 they completed the 'Reconquest' of Spain from the Moors by expelling them from Granada. Ferdinand and Isabella banned all religions except Roman Catholicism, and in 1478 introduced the Spanish INQUISITION to suppress heresy. After Isabella's death in 1504 Ferdinand controlled Castile as regent for his daughter JOANNA THE MAD, and later for his grandson CHARLES V. In the same year Ferdinand married Germaine de Foix, a niece of Louis XII of France. Ferdinand's ruthless foreign policies enabled him to create a strong realm with a network of allies, and by 1515 his kingdom stretched from the Pyrenees to Gibraltar. He left his grandson a unified Spain together with control of Naples, Sicily and Sardinia.

Ferdinand VII (1784-1833) King of Spain

from 1808 until his death. Having succeeded to the throne after his father Charles IV was forced to abdicate by Napoleon, Ferdinand was deposed in favour of Joseph Bonaparte, Napoleon's brother. He was held captive while the PENINSULAR WAR between France and Spain raged, and it was left to the Spanish populace to defy the French in the name of Ferdinand – their 'desired one'. When he was eventually released and restored to the throne in 1814, he abolished the administration achieved through the Constitution of Cadiz of 1812 and began a rule of repression, supported by the Church and the military. Liberal uprisings forced him to reinstate the constitution. When Spain lost its American colonies during the Spanish-American wars of independence the military mutinied and held him prisoner. He was restored to the throne after a liberal uprising in 1820 set up a new radical government, which he accepted until French troops arrived in 1823 to help him overthrow the revolutionaries. Those behind the uprising were arrested or hounded into exile.

Ferry, Jules François (1832-93) French

statesman, notable for his opposition to clerical education and his success in extending French colonialism. Ferry served as mayor of Paris during the siege of 1870 to 1871 and became known as 'Ferry-la-Famine'. In 1879 Ferry rose to prominence as minister of education in the French government, and became prime minister the following year until 1881 and again from 1883 to 1885. He established the modern French education system, reducing the influence of the Roman Catholic Church and making primary schools free and compulsory. Ferry presided over wide French colonial development in Tunisia, the Congo and Madagascar. The conquest of Tonkin in Indochina in 1885 was a costly affair that led to Ferry's dismissal from office. He was assassinated by a religious fanatic in 1893.

Fertile Crescent Agricultural area in the Middle East stretching from the Nile Valley to the Euphrates. It is regarded by the Western world as the cradle of CIVILISATION, home of the ancient peoples of Babylon, Assyria, Egypt and Phoenicia. Carbon dating has confirmed the existence of agricultural communities there as far back as 8000 BC.

feudalism see feature, page 228

Fianna Fáil Irish political party seeking to remove all British influence and create an independent, unified Ireland. The group, whose Gaelic name means 'warriors of Ireland' but members interpret as 'soldiers of destiny', was founded in 1926 by Eamon DE VALERA, an opponent of the Anglo-Irish Treaty of 1921. The party came to power in 1932, gaining 47 per cent of seats in the Dáil – the Irish assembly. Fianna Fáil was successful throughout the 1930s and 1940s and remained the dominant political party until 1973, when it lost to an alliance of Fine Gael and the Labour Party. Charles Haughey led a Fianna Fáil government from 1987 to 1994.

Field of the Cloth of Gold Site near Calais of a meeting in June 1520 between Henry VIII of England and Francis I of France to discuss an alliance. The name refers to the sumptuous tents and the lavish displays made by both kings. For two and a half weeks Henry and Francis paraded their riches amid scenes of great pageantry. But the political result of the meeting was negligible because the two kings could not overcome their mutual reservations and parted without agreement.

Henry VIII built a temporary palace outside Calais in northern France for his meeting with Francis I at the Field of the Cloth of Gold. Entertainment included jousting and mummers' plays.

field systems The layout and management of fields by man. The most obvious example is terracing, the creation of narrow shelves on the side of a hill, as seen on Andean slopes, European vineyards and Asian rice paddies. The earliest field lines can be found in ancient drained and cultivated plots in the Amazonian and Central American forests. The effects of the plough from as long ago as the 4th century BC are evident in man-made terraces and fields in north-west Europe.

Fifth-Monarchy Men Extreme Puritan sect in England in the mid 17th century. They believed that Jesus Christ and his saints would soon become the 'fifth monarchy' to rule the world, after those of Assyria, Persia, Greece and Rome. The sect supported Oliver CROMWELL in the hope that their prophecy would be fulfilled through his Barebones Parliament, chosen from nominees of the independent churches in July 1653. But their hopes were dashed when in December Cromwell replaced the Barebones Parliament with the Protectorate. The sect turned against him, but their two rebellions were easily suppressed and the movement gradually died out.

Fiji Group of about 840 islands in the southwest Pacific. They were first settled by Melanesian and Polynesian peoples between 2000 and 1000 BC. Before the islands became a British colony in 1874, Fiji was notorious for intertribal wars and cannibalism, and the unrest was made worse by deserting seamen, traders and whalers. The British set up the

> 66 **The men of Fiji are formidable on account of the dexterity with which they use their bow and slings; but much more so on account...of eating their enemies whom they kill in battle.** 99
>
> *Captain James Cook on his third voyage to the Fiji islands, 1774*

Western Pacific High Commission to establish calm and to control the labour trade, importing Indians to work on the sugar estates. Fiji became independent in 1970 within the British Commonwealth, and as Indians were now outnumbering Fijians, an Indian government was voted into power.

In 1987 ethnic tension resulted in two military coups to restore control to the indigenous people. Fiji declared itself a republic and left the Commonwealth. Civilian rule with guaranteed Melanesian control was restored in 1990. The new constitution was seen as racist by the Indians, who emigrated in large numbers the following year. A military coup was suppressed when the Fijian Political Party headed by Major-General Sitiveni Rabuka, the leader of the coups of 1987, won the

Vassals, villeins and serfs: a hierarchy of power

Feudalism, the right to land and privileges in return for allegiance to one's lord and the provision of military services, took root in Europe in the Middle Ages.

Harold of England swears allegiance to Duke William in a scene from the Bayeux tapestry.

Late in the 9th century the Frankish Emperor Charlemagne's system of government, loosely based on that of the Roman Empire, disintegrated under pressure from Viking raids in the west and Hungarians to the east. The vacuum was filled by a new social order based on land-holding, a system which came to be known as feudalism.

The term 'feudalism' was invented by the Victorians in the 19th century. It comes from the Latin word 'feudum', meaning a fief – a piece of land held in return for certain services, often military. The man who held the fief was usually a noble or a knight, but feudalism was more than just a system of land-holding.

HOMAGE AND REWARD
The personal allegiance of the holder of the fief (or 'vassal') was just as important. This obligation of loyalty was expressed by the oath of homage. In early instances, a clod of earth was exchanged as a symbol of the grant of land by the feudal lord.

Later, in 1127, when Count William Clito of Flanders first received his vassals, the ceremony had three parts. He asked each vassal to confirm that he wished unreservedly to become his man; and, after the reply 'I wish it', with the vassal's hands clasped between his own, they kissed. The vassal then pledged his

allegiance with the words, 'I promise [that]...I will be faithful to Count William and steadfast in my allegiance to him against every other person, in good faith and without deception.' Finally, he swore this oath on holy relics. A scene in the Bayeux tapestry shows Earl Harold Godwinson (the future King Harold of England), standing between two chests of relics placed on top of altars, one hand on each, and swearing just such a solemn oath to Duke William of Normandy.

The fief was not only a grant of land: with it came the peasants who lived on it and the right to hold courts and pass judgment on them. This gave feudal lords huge social control, with command over the personal lives of those living on their estates in both town and country. They controlled the marriage and movement of serfs, and could levy fines on new tenants. An English law of the early 12th century states: 'Every lord may summon his man in order to do justice upon him in his court; and if the man is resident in the most remote manor...he shall nevertheless go...if his lord shall summon him.'

Each vassal could then grant parts of his fief to other men (or subvassals) and they in turn could make grants to their subvassals or villeins. Feudal Europe can be pictured as a pyramid, with layers of subvassals, with other vassals above them, and the king at the top.

DIVIDED LOYALTIES

In practice things were not so simple: perhaps a spider's web gives a better idea, for Western Europe was covered by a complex network of allegiances, with one man owing allegiance to several lords. Sometimes this led to divided loyalties: in 1101 the Count of Flanders became the vassal of Henry I of England and promised to serve him in all conflicts except those in which the king of France, his other lord, was involved.

In England feudalism died out at the end of the Middle Ages, but it survived elsewhere. In France and Austria it was finally abolished in the 18th century and in Russia in 1861. The Japanese feudal system with its samurai, the equivalent of Western knights, survived until 1868, when it was eradicated by the new Meiji emperor. Since then the term has been applied to other non-European societies which have been thought of as passing through a 'feudal stage' in their history.

Jean de Sainte-Maure makes a vow of fealty to the French king René (left) and a lord's castle (below) looms over his toiling serfs.

Most Fijians are Methodists today, but in the past these towering temples were built in homage to the spirits.

general election in 1992. The government collapsed in 1994, but was re-elected with Rabuka's party increasing its majority.

filibusters Term used to describe political speakers who deliberately set out to delay legislation by using obstructionist tactics, such as making prolonged speeches. Originally it was used to describe pirates or buccaneers who pillaged the Spanish colonies in America in the 17th century. Filibustering came to mean the attempts made by the USA in the 19th century to take over countries with whom it was at peace through privately-financed expeditions. The practice came to an end in 1861 and the term was then applied to those interfering in parliamentary attempts to set laws.

fin de siècle Phrase from the French for 'end of century' often used to refer to the world-weary mood of the arts in Europe during the 1880s and 1890s. The movement originated in France where there was a general feeling of despondency and cynicism after defeat in the Franco-Prussian War and the bad planning and bankruptcy associated with the building of the Panama Canal. Among those involved in the movement were the poets Paul Verlaine and Jules Laforgue, whose works were permeated with a feeling of disenchantment and the sense that the world was decaying – so-called 'decadence'. They adopted the slogan *l'art pour l'art*, 'art for art's sake', believing that art existed for its own beauty alone. In Britain the influences of the movement are apparent in the works of Oscar Wilde – particularly his novel *The Picture of Dorian Gray* – the illustrator Aubrey Beardsley and the artist James McNeill Whistler.

Fine Gael Irish political party, whose name means 'Gaelic Nation' and which seeks to unite Ireland through peaceful, conciliatory methods. It was founded in 1933 as an amalgamation of Cumann na nGaedheal – 'Society

> ### DID YOU KNOW?
>
> The first book to be published in Finnish was prompted by the Protestant reformer Martin Luther's ruling that Latin should not be used in church. The Bishop of Turku, Michael Agricola, translated the New Testament in 1548 and became known as 'the father of Finnish literature'.

of Gaels' – and two other lesser parties. They were all supporters of the Anglo-Irish Treaty, which led to Northern Ireland remaining part of the United Kingdom while the rest of Ireland became the Irish Free State. Cumann na nGaedheal won 41 per cent of the seats in the Free State's first elections in 1923 and formed a minority government under William COSGRAVE. Its fortunes waned in 1932 when its main rival, FIANNA FÁIL, came to power after fresh elections. As Fine Gael, the party entered government again in 1948 as the principal partner in a coalition led by John Costello, and declared Ireland a republic. Fine Gael governed from 1973 to 1977 and from 1981 to 1987, with coalition support.

Finland Northern European country bordering the Baltic Sea. Human habitation dates back to at least 7200 BC when melting ice allowed hunters to travel farther north. Between the 1st and 8th centuries AD the indigenous population of Lapps were driven into the far north of the country by the first Finnish-speaking people, who migrated to Finland from the south. During the Middle Ages Finland was the subject of constant Swedish-Russian rivalry until 1558 when Gustavus Vasa of Sweden proclaimed it a separate Swedish duchy with its own legislative Diet. In 1807 the Treaty of TILSIT between Tsar Alexander I and Napoleon led to the annexation of Finland as a grand duchy of Russia. The Russian Revolution of 1917 gave the Finns the chance to assert their independence. This was achieved in 1919 under Marshal Carl MANNERHEIM, and a democratic, republican constitution was introduced. When new Russian claims on Finnish lands were rejected Russia invaded, starting the Finnish-Russian War in 1939. Finland put up resistance but the Soviets broke through the Mannerheim Line in 1940 and the country was forced to cede its eastern territories and the port of Viipuri (Viborg). The Finns' attempt to regain these by fighting on the side of the Axis Powers in the Second World War was foiled in 1944. Since the war Finland has remained neutral and in 1992, after the break up of the Soviet Union, a treaty was signed with Russia. Finland became a member of the EUROPEAN UNION in 1995.

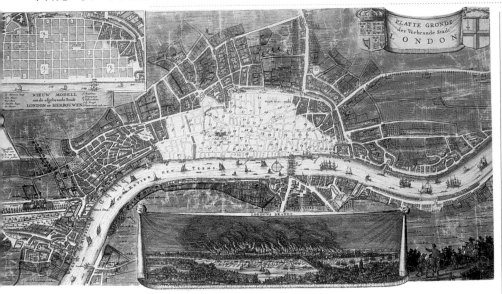

The Fire of London devastated 395 acres of the city centre. It destroyed the Royal Exchange, badly damaged the Guildhall and the Custom House and made nearly 250000 people homeless.

Fire of London Major fire which destroyed much of London in September 1666. The fire, which made the diarist Samuel Pepys 'weep to see it', swept through the city for four days. It consumed more than 13000 houses and 87 churches, including St Paul's Cathedral, and was only stopped by blowing up buildings in its path. The fire was so devastating that the city had to be reconstructed. Sir Christopher Wren rebuilt St Paul's and many other churches and public buildings. He also designed the Monument which commemorates the fire, and which was built in 1671-7 near the site of the baker's shop where it started. The fire was not a complete disaster for it cleared most of the tumble-down slums in which the Great Plague of 1665 still lingered.

First World War see feature, page 232

Fisher, John, 1st Baron (1841-1920) British naval officer and First Sea Lord from 1904 to 1910 and 1914 to 1915, whose reforms helped the Royal Navy to achieve dominance in the First World War. Fisher joined the navy in 1854 at the age of 13, serving as a midshipman in the Crimean War and in China. He went on to specialise in gunnery and in 1872 helped to introduce the torpedo. As First Sea Lord, Fisher's recommendation to modernise the navy resulted in the building of a fleet of major warships, in time to play a key role in the First World War. He helped to plan the GALLIPOLI expedition of 1915, in which the Allies tried to force a passage through the Dardanelles strait, but its failure led to his resignation later the same year.

fishing industry As one of the primary forms of food production, fishing probably predates farming. The hunter-gatherers of prehistory took fish from waters by hand, and prehistoric remains show that shellfish formed a large part of the diet of early humans living near lakes and shores. Many civilisations were using traps, hooks and nets to catch fish as early as 6000 BC. Boats also came into general use about this time, leading to the operation of small fishing fleets.

By the Middle Ages large fisheries had developed around the coasts of Europe, the principal catch being herring. Cod fishing started off the Newfoundland coast at the end of the 15th century, and in the 17th century whaling, using spears and harpoons, became a huge industry in the Atlantic and the South Pacific. By the end of the 19th century the fishing industry had become mechanised: steam and diesel powered boats replaced sail, and power winches took over from traditional hand-worked tackle. Today commercial fishing has become even more sophisticated with the use of radar, underwater sonar, on-board refrigeration holds and computers which operate massive fishing vessels.

The increasingly advanced technology used to catch fish has led to overfishing and the depletion of fish stocks. Pollution has also contributed to the decline. Concern about fish stocks has caused governments across the world to implement measures to protect and conserve the resource. Limitations on catches have been introduced, the size of boats and nets have been regulated and some waters have been closed to commercial fishing. The restrictions have created hostility among the international fishing communities, leading to disputes over fishing rights. The COD WAR

> **DID YOU KNOW?**
>
> *Accounts of fishing go back to the 4th century BC when the Chinese used a silk line, a hook made from a needle and a bamboo rod with congealed cooked rice as the bait.*

between Britain and Iceland from 1972 to 1976 was an early indicator of unrest. In 1995 Brittany's parliament in France was burned down by fishermen protesting against cheap fish imports, and conflict broke out between Spain and Canada over the division of catch quotas off the coast of Newfoundland.

flagellant Religious fanatic who whipped his or her own body in public processions, usually to the accompaniment of psalms. Often a reaction to disaster and disorder, the practice originated in ancient Sparta and Rome in the 4th century BC and subsequently spread to the Christian world. The most notable demonstrations of flagellation took place during political unrest in Perugia in Italy in 1260, and at the height of the Black Death throughout Europe in the mid 14th century. Religious flagellation subsided after Pope Clement VI condemned the practice in 1349, but it was temporarily revived by the Jesuits in the 16th century. It is still practised by some Shiite Muslims.

Flanders Region of Belgium that in medieval times was a principality of the Low Countries. In the 5th century AD the area was won from the Franks by Celtic tribes, and in the Middle Ages it became extremely prosperous under the Counts of Flanders, especially through its cloth trade with England, with which it allied itself during the HUNDRED YEARS' WAR. Flanders has been the scene of many battles throughout its history, especially during the two world wars. During the First World War thousands died in major battles at Passchendaele in 1917 and Ypres in 1915 when the German forces used poison gas for the first time. The Battle of Flanders in the Second World War began when the Germans invaded neutral Belgium in May 1940 and ended with the surrender of Belgian troops and the mass evacuation of the British Expeditionary Force and Allied troops at Dunkirk as the Germans advanced into France in June.

Fleming, Sir Alexander (1881-1955) Scottish bacteriologist whose discovery of penicillin was a major advance in antibiotic therapy. Having studied medicine at St Mary's Hospital Medical School in London, Fleming went on to become its professor of bacteriology in 1928. In the same year, while conducting research on antibacterial substances that would be nontoxic to humans, he noticed that a culture was being contaminated by a mould which was producing an antibiotic. He discovered that while the antibiotic, which he later called penicillin, killed organisms that caused certain infectious diseases, it had no ill

Sir Alexander Fleming discovered penicillin by accident in 1928 but had to wait 12 years for Howard Florey and Ernst Chain to isolate the mould and then perfect a way of producing it.

effects on animals or humans. Later researchers also found the drug was effective against diseases such as pneumonia. In 1945 Fleming shared the Nobel prize for medicine.

Fleming, Sir John (1849-1945) British electrical engineer. His most notable invention was the thermionic valve, a diode which allowed electric current to flow in one direction only, which he patented in 1904. The device was later improved by Lee DE FOREST, who added a third electrode to create a triode. For half a century thermionic valves were an essential part of most radio transmitters, radio receivers and other electronic devices, until the development of the transistor.

Fleury, André Hercule de (1653-1743) Cardinal and French statesman who controlled the government of Louis XV. Fleury began his association with the king when he became his tutor in 1715. In 1726 he became chief minister in Louis's government, distinguishing himself by his skill in handling foreign policy. Fleury forged close links with the British prime minister, Sir Robert Walpole, and strove to reduce tensions between Britain and Spain. This enabled him to avert the spread of conflict into Europe and France when hostilities between Britain and Spain broke out in 1727.

flight see feature, page 236

Flodden, Battle of (September 9, 1513) Conflict in which English forces halted a Scottish invasion of England. To honour his alliance with France, James IV of Scotland crossed the English border with a 30000-strong army supported by artillery. He was met by a much smaller, but much better equipped, English army led by Thomas Howard, Earl of Surrey, representing Henry VIII. The English also had a superior troop of archers. By nightfall the Scots were annihilated, and James IV had been killed with about 10000 of his subjects.

Florence Northern Italian city, first founded as a military colony for Roman army veterans in the 1st century BC. It flourished as a banking city and cloth trade centre during the 12th century, and in the 13th century it witnessed the rivalry between the GUELPHS, who supported papal control, and the Ghibellines, supporters of imperial power. During the 14th and 15th century Florence became one of the principal centres of the Italian RENAISSANCE under the patronage of the powerful Medici family which ruled the city from 1434 until 1737. Successive members of the family acted as patrons to the astronomer and philosopher Galileo Galilei, the painter Sandro Botticelli and the sculptor, painter and poet Michelangelo.

In the mid 18th century control of Florence passed to the Habsburg rulers of Austro-Hungary. In 1860 the city was annexed to the new kingdom of Italy, and served as the provisional capital from 1865 until 1870.

Florey, Howard Walter, Baron (1898-1968) Australian pathologist who played a major part in developing penicillin as a medicine. In 1940 Florey and Sir Ernst Chain, after managing to purify penicillin, developed a way to produce it. Florey successfully tested it on wounded British troops in North Africa in 1943, then it was mass produced in the USA to treat casualties of the D-Day battles in 1944. The following year Florey shared the Nobel prize for physiology and medicine with Chain and Alexander FLEMING – the scientist who had first discovered penicillin in 1928.

Florida Southernmost state of the US east coast. Native Americans first settled the area 10000 years ago. The first European to visit was the Spanish explorer Juan Ponce de Léon in 1513. He named the area Florida after the season in which he found it – Pascua Florida, 'the feast of flowers', or Easter time. Other Spanish explorers claimed the land for Spain. From 1763 the British ruled Florida, after their victories in the SEVEN YEARS' WAR, before the Spanish regained control 20 years later. In 1819 the Adams-Onis Treaty led to Spain ceding Florida to the United States in return for the recognition of Spanish sovereignty over Texas. Florida became an American state in 1845.

The Santa Maria del Fiore cathedral dominates the Florentine skyline. It was built during the 14th century and the impressive dome was added by Filippo Brunelleschi in the 15th century.

The killing fields of Europe

The First World War brought onto the battlefield the power of the modern mechanised state. After four years of slaughter few political issues had been resolved, but 10 million people lay dead.

The shots fired by Gavrilo Princip, a Serbian nationalist, that killed Archduke Franz Ferdinand, heir to the Austro-Hungarian throne, in Sarajevo on June 28, 1914, provoked the First World War. But the underlying causes were more complex. The rise of a united Germany after the Franco-Prussian War of 1870-1 upset the European balance of power. Tensions were heightened by conflicting national ambitions, economic competition and colonial rivalries. By 1914 a system of alliances divided Europe into two camps: the Triple Alliance of Austria-Hungary, Germany and Italy; and the Triple Entente between Britain, France and Russia. Any incident involving one country threatened to drag them all into conflict. The assassination was that incident. A month later Europe was mobilising for war.

Britain declared war on Germany on August 4, 1914, after Wilhelm II's forces had invaded Belgium, whose independence Britain had guaranteed. While the Royal Navy was the world's largest, Britain alone in Europe possessed no conscript army. Britain's secretary of state for war, Lord Kitchener, set about creating a volunteer army which by the end of 1915 numbered 2.5 million men. But in January 1916, as recruiting figures slumped and casualties rose, Britain was forced for the first time to introduce compulsory military service.

THE COST OF TRENCH WARFARE

The German attempt to inflict a knockout blow against France before the Russian mobilisation was completed was checked at the Battle of the Marne in September 1914. By then it had become clear that the range, accuracy and firepower of modern weapons, especially the machine gun, were such that soldiers could survive on the battlefield only by taking shelter in trenches. All attempts by both sides to outflank the other failed. By the end of the First Battle of Ypres in November 1914 the British Expeditionary Force under Sir John French was almost wiped out, and by December 1914 opposing lines of trenches extended from the English Channel to Switzerland.

For the next four years the Allies and the Germans tried to find a means of ending the stalemate of trench warfare. This resulted in successive attempts to breach the enemy lines by the use of artillery bombardments, poison gas and the development of the tank. Casualty rates were enormous. In 1916 Allied losses in the Battles of Verdun and the Somme were more than 1.1 million, with the Germans losing almost as many. In that year the British Army under Sir Douglas Haig was suffering an average monthly casualty rate of 44000 men, a figure which by 1918 had increased to 75000.

The most important theatre of war after France was the Eastern Front, where Austria-Hungary and Germany confronted Russia. The Russians had achieved initial successes, invading East Prussia and even, it was thought, threatening Berlin itself. But with the rushing of reinforcements from the Western Front, Generals Paul von Hindenburg and Erich Ludendorff were able to secure a stunning victory over the Russians at the Battle of Tannenberg, where more than 100000 prisoners were taken.

By 1917 the Russian army had suffered enormous losses and, despite winning a great victory over the Austrians during General Alexei Brusilov's offensive in the summer of 1916, was exhausted. After the success of the February 1917 Revolution, the Provisional Government under Alexander Kerensky

A lightly armed raiding party of the 10th Scottish Rifles moves out from the trenches into no-man's-land on the Western Front in the spring of 1917.

War is declared (left). Among its heroes would be air 'aces' such as Albert Ball, the top-scoring British pilot before his death in a crash at 21.

mounted another offensive in the summer of 1917. This failed, due in part to mass disaffection of the troops. The Bolshevik-led October 1917 Revolution ended Russia's war effort and in March 1918 Lenin concluded a humiliating peace with the signing of the Treaty of Brest Litovsk.

In addition to the Eastern Front, there were a number of 'sideshows'. More than a million British and Empire troops took part in campaigns against Germany's ally Turkey – on the Gallipoli peninsula, where Australian and New Zealand forces distinguished themselves – and in Egypt, Palestine and Mesopotamia. In the Balkans the Serbs threw back the Austrians, but were defeated by a force of Austrians, Germans and Bulgarians in the winter of 1915-16. To assist the Serbs an Allied force which eventually totalled 600 000 men was landed at Salonika. In May 1915 Italy joined the Allies after having been given lavish promises of enemy territory. The Italian front was stabilised along the River Isonzo for two and a half years before the Italians were forced back from Caporetto to the River Piave in October 1917 by an Austro-German force. An Anglo-French force was sent to aid the Italians, who avenged Caporetto a year later at the Battle of Vittorio Veneto. Farther afield there were campaigns in Africa to mop up German colonies. Most fell quickly, but in German East Africa defending forces were still fighting at the time of the Armistice.

The First World War had a profound effect on civilian life in all the warring nations. In Britain the government introduced the Defence of the Realm Act, which gave it sweeping powers. News was censored, the coal mines were nationalised, property was requisitioned, the sale of alcohol was restricted and Summer Time was introduced. Food rationing was imposed in 1918. Germany suffered greatly from the Allied blockade, and turnips became Germans' staple diet during the winter of 1917. In all countries the influx of men into the armed forces caused labour shortages which resulted in women doing jobs in industry, transport, agriculture and commerce that had until then been done by men. In Britain more than 100 000 women joined the auxiliary services of the forces.

CIVILIANS IN THE FRONT LINE

Aircraft were used for the first time in large numbers during the war: the Germans raided British and French cities both with aircraft and Zeppelin airships, while Paris was also bombarded by long-range guns. These raids put the civilian in the front line for the first time, and some 1500 British civilians died as a result of this new form of warfare. Above the trenches airmen engaged in combat, and 'aces' such as Manfred von Richthofen (the 'Red Baron'), Albert Ball, Georges Guynemer and Eddie Rickenbacker became national heroes.

At sea Britain looked to the Royal Navy for protection and to keep the sea lanes open for supplies of food and raw materials. There were engagements between British warships and German commerce raiders, of which the *Emden* was the most successful, in the Indian Ocean, South Atlantic and the Pacific. The long-awaited clash between the British Grand Fleet and the German High Seas Fleet took place at the Battle of Jutland on May 31, 1916. Although the battle was indecisive and the Royal Navy lost more ships, the High Seas Fleet, apart from one or two abortive sorties, remained in port for the rest of the war.

The Allied blockade made the Germans retaliate with a campaign of unrestricted submarine warfare against merchant shipping. In the spring of 1917 this campaign brought Britain close to defeat, but it also precipitated the USA's entry into the war on April 6, 1917. The adoption of the convoy system and a huge increase in British and American shipbuilding enabled the Allies to overcome the U-boat threat.

After the collapse of Russia, the Germans attempted a knockout blow to defeat the British and French before American aid could become effective. Their offensive, which began on March 21, 1918, was initially successful and the Allies' situation appeared desperate. But the tide turned during the summer of 1918 and the Allies, joined by General John Pershing's American 'doughboys', went onto the offensive. The British won a spectacular series of battles and the Germans were forced to ask for an armistice. This came into effect at 11am on Monday, November 11, 1918.

A final settlement, determined at the Paris Peace Conference dominated by the US president Woodrow Wilson and the British and French premiers David Lloyd George and Georges Clemenceau, was embodied in the Treaty of Versailles signed in June 1919. Germany lost territory and her army was restricted to 100 000 men. She had to pay massive compensation – $5 billion in gold marks to be paid between 1919 and 1921, with reparations to be fixed later – for war damage and to admit her guilt for starting the conflict. These terms created great bitterness in Germany, where a fervent desire to upset the Treaty was soon apparent. As Marshal Ferdinand Foch, the Allied commander, observed: 'This isn't peace, but an armistice for 20 years.'

German guards officer's helmet. The spike diverted sword strokes

British trench club

German gas mask

Weapons of war: the best of their time, but primitive by today's standards.

Vickers Mark I machine gun, deadly against attacking infantry

French commander and strategist Ferdinand Foch (right) with George V on a visit to the Western Front during the First World War.

Foch, Ferdinand (1851-1929) Marshal of France during the First World War, and as commander of the Allied forces in 1918 regarded as the leader most responsible for the Allied victory. Foch began his military career in 1870 and attended several training schools, including the Ecole Supérieure de Guerre where he spent 25 years learning and then teaching the art of warfare .

In 1913 Foch was put in command of an army corps responsible for defending the Lorraine frontier when the First World War began. He proved his talent for strategy in the Battle of the Marne in 1914 and in 1916 he led the French forces on the Somme, where he tried to break through the German line at Artois. In 1918 the British prime minister David Lloyd George and the French premier Georges Clemenceau agreed that there was only one man with the spirit and determination to secure victory for the Allies, and Foch was appointed commander in chief. His tactics of relentless attack resulted in the German surrender at Compiègne on November 11.

Fontenoy, Battle of (1745) Conflict of the War of the AUSTRIAN SUCCESSION. The battle took place in Fontenoy, a village in the Hainaut region of south-west Belgium on May 11, and was fought between the French led by Marshal Maurice de Saxe, and an allied army of British, Austrian and Dutch troops led by the the Duke of Cumberland. De Saxe had already overrun the Austrian Netherlands, but he was threatened by the duke's army, which was advancing to relieve the besieged town of Tournai. The duke found a gap in the French line of fortifications, but he was eventually driven back to Brussels. The victory was de Saxe's greatest triumph, and in the following four months he overran Tournai and most of Flanders.

Forbidden City Private domain of China's emperors within the inner city of Peking, now Beijing, from 1421 to 1911. It gained its name because no commoners or foreigners were allowed to enter without permission. The city housed the Imperial Palace, containing 9999 rooms, and was surrounded by a high wall. When the communists won power in 1949, the palace became a museum.

Ford, Henry (1863-1947) American industrialist and car manufacturing pioneer, who revolutionised factory production. In 1903 Ford set up the Ford Motor Company in Detroit, producing his first car – the Model T – in 1908. In 1913 he brought in assembly-line production, which not only enabled him to mass produce cars at the rate of one every three minutes, but also allowed him to sell them at a price which was within the means of a large proportion of the middle class. He told potential customers the car was available in 'any colour – so long as it's black'. During both wars, Ford's factory produced military transport, including aeroplanes and tanks. After Ford retired in 1919 his son, Edsel, took over the company.

Fort Sumter Military fort in Charleston Harbor, South Carolina, the site of the first military engagement of the American Civil War. On April 12, 1861, the fort was bombarded by Confederates led by General Pierre Beauregard, after Major Robert Anderson and his Union troops refused to evacuate it. His refusal was backed by President James Buchanan. Two days later the intensive bombardment forced Anderson to surrender the fort. This shelling of US property by the Confederates provoked and united the North.

Forty-Five, the Jacobite rebellion of 1745, which aimed to remove the Hanoverian George II from the English throne and replace him with James Edward STUART, the 'Old Pretender'. James sent his son Charles Edward – Bonnie Prince Charlie – to represent him and the rebellion achieved some success. A Jacobite victory at Prestonpans, east of Edinburgh, was followed by the invasion of England as far south as Derby. The advance was checked by the approach of the English armies of Field-Marshal George Wade and the Duke of Cumberland, forcing Charles to retreat. The rebellion evaporated and all serious challenges to the Hanoverians ended with the defeat of the depleted Jacobite army at CULLODEN on April 16, 1746. The defeat also ended the CLAN system in Scotland.

forum Open assembly place in a town or city of the Roman Empire. Forums were used from the 6th century BC for civic meetings and religious and military ceremonies. They comprised the Curia – Senate House – and civic buildings, along with markets, libraries and courts. Later forums were built in Rome by emperors including Augustus and Trajan. A forum was built in almost every empire town.

Fosse Way Major Roman road which crossed Britain from Seaton, 25 miles east of Exeter, in the west to Lincoln in the east. Named after the fossa, or drainage channel, that ran beside it, the road was probably laid as a military route along the frontier established

Fort Sumter in South Carolina was bombarded by more than 4000 Confederate shells in 1861 at the start of the American Civil War – but nobody was killed. The Union regained the fort in 1865.

The main forum in Rome, originally smaller than five acres, was expanded under the dictator Sulla in 78 BC and later by Julius Caesar to include many of the empire's administrative buildings.

after the Roman invasion of Britain in AD 43. The road passed through Bath and Leicester, and as it left Lincoln to turn north towards York, it joined Ermine Street.

Foucault, Michel (1926-84) French historian and philosopher, noted for his examination of the concepts and codes by which humans operate. Influenced by Friedrich NIETZSCHE, Foucault was interested in the 'sciences' of man, including psychology and social administration, and his earlier work concerned the study of mental illness. His various books, including *Madness and Civilisation* and *Discipline and Punish: The Birth of the Prison*, reveal the sometimes sinister power relations that exist in society, as seen in institutions such as asylums and prisons which use systems of discipline to encourage 'normal' behaviour. He argued that those in power decide what constitutes crime or insanity and then apply these labels to anybody they want to oppress as 'deviant'.

Fouché, Joseph, duc d'Otrante (c.1759-1820) French statesman. Fouché became politically active in the French Revolution as a principal member of the JACOBIN Club, which opposed the monarchy. An advocate of the club's violent policies, he joined in the demands for the execution of the king. Fouché clashed with the club's founder, the revolutionary Maximilien ROBESPIERRE, and was expelled in 1794. But he went on to play a role in the coups that led to the downfall of

Robespierre. After Napoleon's accession to power in 1799 Fouché became minister of police, and in 1809 he was appointed interior minister. He went into exile in 1816 after France banished those who killed the king.

Founding Fathers Popular name given to the 55 delegates who drafted the Constitution of the USA in 1787. The group was led by

> ❝...to form a more perfect Union, establish Justice...promote the general welfare and secure the Blessings of Liberty. ❞
>
> *Founding Fathers of the USA, excerpt from the Constitution, 1787*

James MADISON, George Mason, Gouverneur Morris, James Wilson, Roger Sherman and Elbridge Gerry, and included George WASHINGTON and Benjamin FRANKLIN. The Constitution, written to amend the original Articles of Confederation of 1781, established the system of Federal government in the USA.

foundling hospital Institutions set up to care for abandoned children. Until the founding of the first hospital in Milan in the 8th century, unwanted children were generally left to die in places built for that purpose. Of the many foundling hospitals that emerged in Europe, the Paris Foundling Hospital, set up in 1670, was probably the most famous. Britain's best-known foundling hospital was

founded in Holborn, London, in 1739 by Thomas Coram. Foundling hospitals have been replaced for the most part in Britain and the USA by foster care programmes.

Fourteen Points Peace programme for the settlement of the First World War drawn up by the American president Woodrow WILSON and addressed to the US Congress on January 8, 1918. Its 14 clauses included reduction of arms, the evacuation of Russian and of Belgian territory, independence for Poland, and the establishment of a 'general association of nations', which later became the League of Nations. The programme, reluctantly accepted by the Allies, formed the foundation of the VERSAILLES peace settlement

Fourteenth Amendment Most significant of the three amendments made to the US Constitution following the AMERICAN CIVIL WAR. The amendment was set out in 1866 by the Joint Committee of Fifteen – nine members of the House of Representatives and six members of the Senate. The amendment, which was ratified in 1868, aimed to extend civil liberties and included among its clauses the right to citizenship for all people, including ex-slaves, and the right of all people to equal protection under the law. In the 20th century the Fourteenth Amendment has been a tool of civil rights groups.

Fox, Charles James (1749-1806) British statesman and renowned champion of liberal reform. He entered Parliament in 1768 as a member of the Whigs in opposition to Frederick, Lord North, and soon developed a reputation as an eloquent and persuasive debator. Fox was a bitter critic of George III and was therefore almost always in political opposition. When North's government was brought down in 1782 a Whig ministry under Lord Rockingham took over and Fox became Britain's first foreign secretary. After Rockingham's death in July the king chose William Shelburne as his successor and Fox, who considered the king's interference as unconstitutional, resigned.

In 1783 a coalition with his old adversary Lord North ejected the Shelburne government, but was itself dismissed by the king after the House of Lords rejected Fox's bill to reform the government of India. William PITT became prime minister and so ensued a long period of antagonism between the two, though Fox did support Pitt's struggle for Catholic emancipation. Fox alienated himself from his supporters by supporting the French Revolution, causing the 'Old Whigs' to move over to the government. When Pitt died in 1806, Fox became a member of the new 'Ministry of all the Talents' under William GRENVILLE, which succeeded in persuading Parliament to agree to an antislavery bill.

How flying machines shrank the globe

From the time of Columbus, the North Atlantic crossing has been one of the most commercially important. Every advance in transport has speeded the journey — none more so than the advent of flight.

For the first man to fly solo across the Atlantic, one of the greatest dangers was colliding with the masts of ships. Charles Lindbergh, skimming the wave tops, took 33½ hours to fly from New York to Paris in his monoplane *Spirit of St Louis* in 1927. Concorde now makes the journey in less than a tenth of the time, flying at 60 000 ft (18 300 m) with more than a hundred passengers cosseted in comfort.

The conquest of flight began in Kitty Hawk, North Carolina, in 1903, when Orville Wright covered about 120 ft (36 m) in the first controlled powered flight in a heavier-than-air machine. By 1905 his brother Wilbur had made a flight of 25 miles in a new aircraft, the *Flyer III*. The Wrights' claims to have flown were doubted, but they conclusively answered their critics by public demonstrations. By the First World War the aircraft was a practical device, used for reconnaissance, bombing and aerial combat.

It was a converted Vickers Vimy bomber that made the first transatlantic crossing in 1919, piloted by the British aviator Captain John Alcock and his navigator Lt Arthur Whitten Brown. They carried 870 gallons (3960 litres) of fuel and a toy black cat called Twinkletoes, and made the 2000 mile (3218 km) crossing from Newfoundland to Ireland in just under 16½ hours, landing in a bog near Clifden, County Galway.

The Atlantic had long been the arena for competition in transport. The first man known to have crossed it, Christopher Columbus, took more than two months to complete the voyage from Spain to the New World in 1492. In 1838 the paddle-steamers *Sirius* and *Great Western* raced from Britain to New York, *Sirius* winning by a bare three hours after starting four days earlier and taking 18 days for the crossing. By the 1930s, the heyday of the great ocean liners, the journey could be completed in less than five days. The fastest was the SS *United States*, whose maiden voyage in 1952 set a record not beaten by a passenger ship until 1990, when the catamaran *Hoverspeed Great Britain* crossed in 3 days, 7 hours and 54 minutes.

In the late 1920s, the first rivals to ocean liners appeared in the form of airships. The biggest of these, the *Hindenburg*, carried 50 passengers and a crew of 60, and made 10 round trips in 1935. But the brief airship era came to a tragic close in the disastrous fire that consumed the *Hindenburg* at Lakehurst, New Jersey two years later.

Captain Alcock and Lt Brown pose in front of their Vickers Vimy a few weeks after their epic Atlantic crossing in 1919. Their log (right) records the moment they crossed the Irish coastline.

Enthusiasts at Reims in 1909 shelter under a Wright biplane. The pilot sat in front and propellers mounted at the rear 'pushed' the machine along. The same summer, Louis Blériot made the first flight across the English Channel in a more advanced monoplane.

The German airship *Hindenburg*, filled with inflammable hydrogen, explodes after clipping its mooring mast at Lakehurst, New Jersey, in May 1937, with the loss of 36 lives.

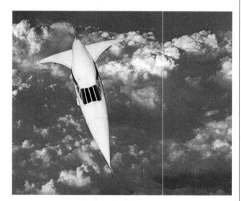

Charles Lindbergh in his plane *Spirit of St Louis* gets a hero's welcome at Boston two months after his solo flight across the Atlantic to Paris.

Concorde first flew in 1969 and remains the world's only supersonic airliner, getting New Yorkers to London in less than three hours.

IN 2 TAGEN NACH NORD-AMERIKA!
DEUTSCHE ZEPPELIN-REEDEREI

Airships carried more than 10 000 passengers on scheduled services.

The first airlines used aircraft left over from the 1914-18 war. The combatants had produced more than 200 000 between them, and many planes had survived undamaged. They were cheap to buy, and pilots were also plentiful. On February 5, 1919, Germany's Deutsche Luft Reederei was the first European airline to launch services, using five-seater AEG biplanes for a daily run between Berlin and Weimar. The French were not far behind, opening the first international route between Paris and Brussels, and in August a converted de Havilland 4a bomber of Air Transport and Travel inaugurated flights between Hounslow in London and Paris. Only the wealthy or the adventurous considered it worth paying the single fare of £21, for the same journey could be made by train and boat for less than £4.

Airlines proliferated but struggled to make a profit. Long journeys could take several days or even a week, with overnight stops. The lack of airports made flying boats the most practical aircraft for such

trips, and by the late 1930s the well-heeled could take a leisurely trip to the Far East on board Imperial Airways Empire flying boats, the Short S-23 'C' class. With a range of 700 miles (1130 km) and a maximum speed of 200 mph (320 km/h), the Empire flying boats landed on lakes and harbours to refuel.

Although the USA can boast the first airline – the St Petersburg-Tampa Airboat Line which for a few months in 1914 carried one passenger at a time across Tampa Bay in Florida in a flying boat – it was slower to establish services after the war. Mail planes operated by the US Post Office led the way, finding their way at night by following a chain of beacons. When the mail planes were privatised by Congress in 1925, they provided a basis for passenger services. By the end of 1929 the USA had 11 airlines and was carrying more passengers than any other nation. Mergers followed, establishing four big airlines by 1931: TWA, United, Eastern and American.

By the end of the 1930s, aircraft were reliable enough to use on a service on the Blue Riband route – the North Atlantic. The Empire class did not have the range, but Boeing's Type 314 flying boat did. With this aircraft Pan American launched the first scheduled North Atlantic service on June 27-28, 1939, completing the flight between Botwood, Newfoundland and Southampton in 18 hours 42 minutes, carrying 19 passengers. The Pan Am 'Clippers' continued the flights during the Second World War, carrying high-priority passengers and mail. But by 1947 there were adequate runways for conventional aircraft; the era of the flying boat was over.

The development of the jet engine during and after the war greatly increased speed, and the first scheduled jet service, launched by the British Overseas Aircraft Corporation in 1958 with the Comet 4, took seven hours for the crossing. That remains roughly the time taken for the flight today by wide-bodied jets such as the Boeing 747, which inaugurated mass travel across the Atlantic. When time is vital, passengers can take the world's only supersonic jet transport, Concorde.

Jets have made journeys to anywhere in the world into everyday experiences. Today, hundreds of thousands of people – the population of a good-sized city – are aloft at any one time, flying hundreds of routes in thousands of different aircraft. The 747 can cover 60 miles (96 km) per gallon of fuel per passenger – excellent mileage for a car, and at a speed ten times faster.

Fox, George (1624-91) English founder of the QUAKERS, or the Society of Friends. The son of a Puritan weaver, Fox left home in 1643 to wander the country, preaching a simple way of life and worship. Three years later he had a divine revelation telling him to set up the society. He stressed the importance of being guided by the inner voice of the spirit. Fox's sincere oratory together with his captivating personality attracted thousands of converts; by 1660 there were more than 20 000 followers. The restoration of the monarchy in the same year led to legislation and action against the Quakers. To counteract the hostility Fox encouraged local Quaker groups to organise regular meetings and occasional national meetings – a practice that became a permanent feature of the organisation.

Fox's missionary journeys took him as far afield as the West Indies, North America and Holland, though he was imprisoned eight times for his beliefs – between 1649 and 1673. His *Journal*, which describes the founding of the Quakers and reveals details of his life's work, was published posthumously in 1694.

Foxe, John (1516-87) English Puritan and clergyman, best known as the author of *The Book of Martyrs*. The book was a history of the persecution of Christians, especially Protestants, from the radical reformer John WYCLIFFE's time in the 14th century to Foxe's own time. The first part of the book was published in Latin in 1554. The English edition of 1563, *Acts and Monuments of Matters Happening in the Church*, was popular with the government and the clerical establishment, and became the most widely read book among the Puritans, after the Bible.

France Western European country with coastlines on the North Sea, the Atlantic Ocean and the Mediterranean Sea. Human settlement dates back to prehistoric times; remains have been discovered from 100 000 years ago. The GAULS – a mainly Celtic people – migrated to France from the Rhine valley around 1200 BC. They were conquered by the Romans by about 50 BC. After the fall of Rome in AD 476 the area was invaded by tribes from throughout Europe, and fought over by many rival rulers. One of the most powerful was the Emperor CHARLEMAGNE, who between the 7th and 8th centuries expanded the empire to encompass most of Western Europe.

Charlemagne's dynasty, the Carolingians, were succeeded by the Capetians until 1328 when the throne passed to Philip I. He embarked on the HUNDRED YEARS' WAR, which led to England losing all the French territories it had acquired by conquest and royal marriage, except Calais. France finally emerged as a unified state after the defeat of the English and the Burgundians at the end of

St Francis of Assisi, who became the patron saint of animals, preaches to birds in a painting by Ambrogio Giotto.

the 15th century. After conflict with the growing might of Spain, France became by 1650 the leading power in Europe. The French Revolution of 1789 brought the demise of the monarchy and the establishment of the first French Republic in 1792. The First Empire of Napoleon I replaced the Republic in 1804. Napoleon's forced abdication in 1814 saw the restoration of the Bourbon monarchy with Louis XVIII. In 1830 Charles X's attempts to reintroduce an absolute monarchy led to a revolution which overthrew him and placed Louis Philippe on the throne. When he abdicated in 1848 the Second Republic was created, which survived until the Second Empire of Napoleon III in 1852. By this time France's empire had expanded into North Africa, South-east Asia and the Pacific.

The Third Republic was established in 1870 after the exile of Napoleon III and French defeat in the FRANCO-PRUSSIAN WAR. This republic fell in 1940 to Nazi Germany. The FREE FRENCH resistance movement, established by Charles de Gaulle, assisted the Allied forces in liberating France in 1944, paving the way for the Fourth Republic in 1946. The Indochina war and growing nationalism among the French colonies brought about the downfall of this republic in 1958. It was replaced by the Fifth Republic under the presidency of Charles de Gaulle, who helped to re-establish France's prominence in Europe and granted most of the colonies independence. In 1957 the country became a founder member of the EUROPEAN ECONOMIC COMMUNITY. François Mitterrand became France's first socialist president in 1981. He called a referendum in 1992 that narrowly endorsed the Maastricht Treaty, which aimed to unify Europe. In 1995 Jacques Chirac took over the presidency.

Francis I (1494-1547) King of France from 1515. Francis spent most of his reign engaged in an inconclusive struggle with the Habsburgs. In his bid to become Holy Roman Emperor he tried but failed to enlist the support of England's Henry VIII at the FIELD OF THE CLOTH OF GOLD in 1520. In 1521 he launched a war against the elected emperor Charles V, king of Spain, but was captured at the Battle of Pavia in 1525. Francis was released after renouncing his claims in Italy,

but hostilities continued until the Peace of Crespy was agreed in 1544. He did achieve success in some other areas: he secured a concordat with the papacy and an alliance with Switzerland, and during his reign the French Renaissance saw its fullest development.

Francis of Assisi, St (1182-1226) Italian monk and founder of the Franciscan order of friars. Born in northern Italy, Francis abandoned his family trade as a merchant in favour of a religious life of extreme poverty. His work with the poor and sick, and his deep respect for the natural world and all its creatures, gained him many supporters.

In 1209 he founded the Franciscans, who adopted a vow of strict poverty. The order eventually split into two factions – the 'spirituals', who believed in the original interpretation of the rule, and the 'moderates' whose views triumphed and allowed the order to own property. After reforms in the 16th century three branches survived, including the Capuchins and the nuns known as the 'Poor Clares'. The Third Order consists of lay people who try to follow Franciscan ideals. Pope Innocent III made Francis a deacon, but his humility prevented him from accepting a full priesthood. Francis made many missionary journeys to southern Europe and a number of miracles and visions were later attributed to him. He was canonised in 1228.

Francis Xavier, St (1506-52) Spanish missionary priest. In 1534 Francis and six others, including St Ignatius LOYOLA, took vows at Montmartre, then on the outskirts of Paris, and formed the nucleus of the Society of Jesus, or JESUITS. Francis became the first Jesuit missionary in the East and was later called the 'Apostle of the Indies'. He travelled for 11 years, establishing missions in the Indies,

Japan and Ceylon and making thousands of converts. Francis died on an island near Hong Kong while waiting to enter China.

Franco, Francisco (1892-1975) Spanish general and head of state, who led the Nationalist forces to victory in the SPANISH CIVIL WAR. At the age of 14 Franco enlisted in the Infantry Academy of Toledo, graduating three years later. In 1915 he became the youngest captain in the Spanish army, and quickly gained a reputation for professionalism and dedication. His career was halted in 1931 when a republic replaced the king, Alfonso XIII, and adopted an antimilitary policy. Elections in 1936 returned a more left-wing government, prompting Franco to lead the army into revolt and sparking the Spanish Civil War. He then became commander in chief of the rebel forces.

From 1937 the Nationalists were supported by the FALANGE, a movement adopted and expanded by Franco into a fascist party. Franco emerged victorious two years later, after military aid from Adolf Hitler and Benito Mussolini, and became dictator of Spain. During the Second World War he remained neutral, despite his sympathies with the AXIS POWERS. His regime became less oppressive in the 1950s and 1960s as he reduced the powers of the Falange and tried to negotiate good relations with the USA, where

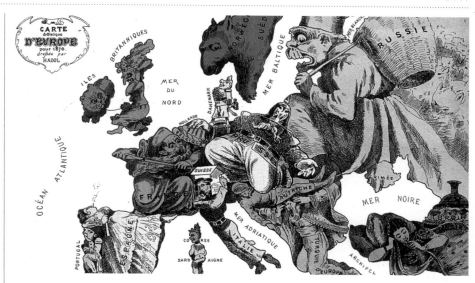

Napoleon III's France tries to fight off the aggressive Prussian leader Otto von Bismarck while the Russian giant looks on in this comic map produced in 1871 during the Franco-Prussian War.

he had been labelled 'the last surviving fascist dictator'. After Franco's death in 1975 a democratic system of government was reinstated and Prince Juan Carlos, grandson of Alfonso XIII, became king.

Franco-Prussian War Conflict between France, under Napoleon III, and Prussia from 1870 to 1871. It was provoked by the attempt by the Prussian leader, Otto von BISMARCK, to install a German prince on the Spanish throne. Before he made his move Bismarck had checked that Russia, Italy and Britain would remain neutral in any war. When Napoleon declared war on July 19 Prussian armies advanced into France, causing French forces under Marshal Marie Macmahon and Marshal François Bazaine to retreat. Napoleon's subsequent capture on September 1, seen by the French as a national humiliation, led to his fall as emperor. On September 19 the Prussian army besieged Paris, but attempts by Bismarck to impose peace were repelled by Parisian radicals, who established the COMMUNE OF PARIS – a council dedicated to preventing a surrender. The French government was eventually persuaded to sign the Treaty of Frankfurt on May 10, 1871, resulting in the proclamation of the German Second Empire at Versailles, the royal palace outside Paris, where William I of Prussia was crowned emperor. Bismarck's troops remained until an indemnity of 5 billion gold francs had been paid. The Prussian victory signalled the end of French predominance in Europe and the emergence of Germany as its leading power.

Frank, Anne (1929-45) German Jewish girl whose diary, published in 1947, provides a moving account of suffering under Nazism. Anne and her family moved to the Netherlands at the beginning of Adolf Hitler's

Nazi regime. When the country was occupied by the Germans the Franks spent two years, from July 1942 to August 1944, hiding from them in a secret apartment in Amsterdam. The family was betrayed, and Anne was eventually taken to the concentration camp at Belsen where she died of typhus. The detailed diary she kept while in hiding has gained worldwide recognition.

Anne Frank, who hid from the Nazis for two years in Amsterdam, died in Belsen but the vivid testament of her diary lives on.

franklin English freeholder in the 13th and 14th centuries. Franklins were not nobles and did not owe military service to their lord, but they owned extensive property for which they paid rent. The end of the Black Death in 1349 saw a more favourable economic climate from which many franklins benefited. The newly rich and social-climbing franklin was satirised by the medieval poet Geoffrey CHAUCER in his *Canterbury Tales*.

Francisco Franco gives a fascist salute in 1938 after a Mass in memory of the Nationalist movement founder General Antonio de Rivera.

Franklin, Benjamin see feature, page 241

frankpledge System of maintaining law and order in English communities between the 10th and 14th centuries, also known as the 'peace pledge'. Each community was made up of a tithing, an association of ten households overseen by a headman, a 'chief pledge' or 'tithing man'. Members of the community were all responsible for one another's conduct. The system developed from laws passed by King Canute which required communities to put up sureties to guarantee members' behaviour. It was gradually replaced by other means of ensuring law and order, such as justices of the peace.

Franks Germanic people who from the 6th century established the most powerful Christian kingdom in Western Europe after the collapse of the Roman Empire. The Franks were made up of three groups: the Salians, the Ripuarians and the Chatti, or Hessians. The Franks' first conquest was Gaul, roughly modern France, after the Salians under CLOVIS defeated the Romans at Soissons. Most of their conquests were achieved under two dynasties – the Merovingians, who ruled until 751, and the Carolingians who replaced them. The most influential leader of the Carolingians was CHARLEMAGNE, who expanded his empire to create a territory that stretched from France in the west to Hungary in the east. The empire disintegrated at the end of the 9th century, the western Franks merging with the Gallo-Roman population to form France, and the eastern Franks occupying the lands that became Germany.

Franz Ferdinand (1863-1914) Archduke of Austria and heir to the throne of Austria-Hungary, whose assassination led directly to the outbreak of the First World War.

Ferdinand's quest to make the Austro-Hungarian empire a triple monarchy with the inclusion of a Slavic kingdom under Croatian leadership was opposed by the Hungarians and by Slav nationalists, including Serbs, who saw no future with the empire. On June 28, 1914, while on a visit to Sarajevo, Ferdinand and his wife Sophie were shot dead by the Serbian nationalist Gavrilo Princip.

Franz Joseph (1830-1916) Emperor of Austria from 1848 and emperor of Austro-Hungary from 1867. Franz Joseph succeeded to the throne during the Revolutions of 1848, a period of economic unrest and rising nationalist fervour in Europe. Although he managed to hold the empire together, he spent most of his reign struggling against the forces of nationalism. In the Italian War of 1859 he lost

> **DID YOU KNOW?**
>
> *Emperor Franz Joseph faced a string of tragedies. His son killed himself, his brother was executed, his wife was stabbed to death and his nephew shot dead.*

Lombardy and Sardinia to Napoleon III, then Venetia in the Austro-Prussian War of 1866. The growing dominance of Prussia combined with Hungarian unease at their loss of influence over German affairs caused Franz Joseph to form in 1867 the 'Dual Monarchy', which gave both the Habsburg kingdoms of Austria and Hungary equal power within the empire. As well as Austria and Hungary, the empire embraced Moravia, Bohemia, Slovenia, Austrian Poland, Transylvania, Croatia, Austrian Silesia and parts of the Dalmatian coast. The association, though it brought material prosperity, failed to appease the minority nations, especially the Balkan states, which became disturbed by Hungary's growing influence in the empire. These states eventually became the Dual Monarchy's bitter enemy. Franz Joseph's declaration of war on Serbia, after the assassination of his nephew and heir Austrian Archduke FRANZ FERDINAND by a Serbian nationalist in 1914, was the spark that ignited the First World War.

Frederick I (c.1123-90) Nicknamed 'Barbarossa', meaning 'red beard', Frederick was king of Germany and Italy from 1152, and emperor from 1155. Lack of crown resources in Germany led Frederick to spend 16 years in Italy, often at war with the northern city states. His quarrel with Pope ADRIAN IV over the control of papal lands led to him setting up an 'imperial pope'. After his defeat by Milan in the Battle of Legnano in 1176 Frederick made peace with the Lombard cities and the pope. This enabled him to concentrate on Germany, where he defeated HENRY THE LION and strengthened the position of his own family, the Hohenstaufen. In 1189 Frederick led the Third Crusade, but was drowned crossing a river in Asia Minor.

Frederick I (1657-1713) Elector of Brandenburg from 1688, and first king of Prussia from 1701 until his death. After succeeding to the electorate – an association of princes which had the right to elect the Holy Roman emperors – Frederick was determined to make himself king of Prussia. He allied himself with Austria and the Holy Roman Emperor, Leopold I, in the War of the SPANISH SUCCESSION against France, and in return the emperor allowed him to crown himself king in January 1701. Frederick created new industries, acquired new provinces and stimulated culture. He also established the Academy of the Sciences, the Academy of Arts and the University of Halle at Berlin.

Frederick II (1194-1250) Holy Roman Emperor from 1220. He was the grandson of Frederick 'Barbarossa', and was known as *Stupor Mundi*, 'Wonder of the World', because of the breadth of his power and his administrative, military and intellectual abilities. His reign as emperor was dominated by a long and unsuccessful conflict with the papacy. While on a Crusade during 1229 he gained Jerusalem,

Frederick the Great's many victories had made Prussia the foremost military power in Europe by 1763. His tactics of anticipating attack and then striking first earned the admiration of Napoleon.

Franklin's formula

Benjamin Franklin, the US politician and scientist, negotiated the treaty by which Britain accepted American independence.

Printer, publisher, author, diplomat, statesman, eminent scientist and inventor, Benjamin Franklin (1706-90) had the versatility of a Renaissance man. That he was born into a community barely past the pioneer stage – early 18th-century Boston, Massachusetts – and left school at the age of ten makes his achievements all the more remarkable.

When he was 12, Franklin was apprenticed to his brother, James, a printer and publisher. He found the work of the print shop congenial and used his free time to read the ancient classics and the best English authors of the day. In 1723 he departed for Philadelphia, Pennsylvania.

INTERNATIONAL FAME
In Philadelphia Franklin married, established himself as a printer, publisher and bookseller, and became a force in Pennsylvania's political affairs. As the creator of 'Poor Richard', a fictional farmer whose wise maxims were featured in his popular almanac, Franklin's reputation soon spread.

It was as a part-time inventor and scientist that Franklin achieved international fame. In 1752 he sent a kite aloft in a thunderstorm with a key

Franklin, shown drawing electricity from lightning in Benjamin West's painting, characteristically wore simple, sober black.

attached. By showing that the key became electrified he proved the electrical nature of lightning. Soon after he devised the lightning conductor to provide the first effective protection for houses during storms. Later he invented bifocal spectacles. Franklin was awarded honorary degrees by European universities for his work, and became known as 'Dr Franklin'.

During the 1760s and 1770s he was sent to England to lobby Parliament about Pennsylvania's tax grievances. He defended the American position in the growing dispute after 1763 with Britain over colonial autonomy. In 1775 he returned to Philadelphia in time to help to draft the Declaration of Independence proclaiming freedom from Britain.

FOREIGN DIPLOMAT
During the War of Independence Franklin was American minister to France. Lionised by the liberal French elite, who saw him as the beau ideal of the 'natural man' beloved of the philosophers of the Enlightenment, he helped to draw France into the war as America's ally. In 1783 he and his colleagues negotiated the Treaty of Paris by which Britain accepted American independence.

Franklin returned to America in 1785 and joined the debate over a new form of government for the United States. He was a Pennsylvania delegate to the Constitutional Convention of 1787 and supported the adoption of a stronger federal union. One of his last public acts, at the age of 84, was to sponsor a petition to end slavery in the USA. To the end, Benjamin Franklin remained a soldier in the army of progress and enlightenment.

Nazareth and Bethlehem for Christendom, and crowned himself 'King of Jerusalem'. Despite his clashes with the papacy Frederick achieved some support from the lay and clerical princes of Germany by transferring a substantial amount of power to them. But continued papal opposition and subsequent military defeats gradually wore him down. All Frederick's heirs became victims of the conflict he had produced with the papacy and were dead within 22 years of his own death.

Frederick II 'the Great' (1712-86) King of Prussia from 1740. Frederick significantly expanded Prussia's territory and created the strongest military power in Europe. He was cultured, diligent and a brilliant soldier, and though he ruled as a despot he believed that absolute power should be exercised only for the good of his subjects. He applied this principle by abolishing torture and establishing full religious tolerance. Frederick's understanding of the art of warfare won him many new territories. In 1740 in the War of the AUS-TRIAN SUCCESSION he attacked the Habsburg ruler Maria Theresa and gained Silesia, and in 1757, during the SEVEN YEARS' WAR, he won notable victories over the French and Austrians. He was routed by Austro-Russian forces at Kunersdorf in 1759, but when his ally Peter III became tsar of Russia, Peter withdrew Russian troops, allowing Frederick to retain Silesia and to establish Prussia as a leading power in Europe.

Frederick III (1415-93) King of Germany from 1440, and Holy Roman Emperor from 1452 until his death in 1493. As Archduke of Austria, Frederick inherited the Habsburg domains, and by 1439 had become the dynasty's most senior member. His reign was beset with conflicts with relatives and the nobility, though he did achieve better relations with the Church. His most notable achievement was the marrying of his son, Maximilian I, to Mary, daughter of Charles the Bold, Duke of Burgundy, which greatly extended the kingdom.

Frederick William I (1688-1740) King of Prussia from 1713. The son of Frederick I, he developed his country into a prosperous state. His nickname was 'the Royal Drill-Sergeant', as he was obsessed with maintaining a well-disciplined and efficient army. By the time he died almost 40 per cent of the population were enlisted in the army and Prussia was the third largest military power in Europe, after Russia and France. Frederick made the Prussian state financially independent by scaling down his court and introducing taxes. When he died, his heir, Frederick II (Frederick 'the Great'), inherited an efficient, centralised state with a strong army.

Frederick William III (1770-1840) King of Prussia from 1797. The victim of repeated bullying by his father, Frederick William II, he developed a reticent, pedestrian nature which made him an ineffectual ruler. After his defeat at the Battle of Jena he was forced by the Treaty of TILSIT (1807) to surrender half his dominions, and his decision to remain neutral

An apprentice, left breast bared, prepares to be initiated into an English Freemasons' lodge in the early 19th century. Many of the ritual symbols on the floor, including compasses, are in use today.

in the Wars of the Second and Third Coalitions between France and Austria diminished Prussia's prestige and lost him all of his provinces west of the River Elbe. To try to reverse his empire's decline Frederick supported the efforts for reform made by his statesmen Karl Stein and Karl von Hardenberg, and at the Congress of VIENNA he won back Westphalia and much of the Rhineland and Saxony for Prussia.

Free French Organisation of French men and women which sought to continue the war against Germany after the military collapse of France in 1940. Its leader was General Charles DE GAULLE, and from its base in London it organised forces to participate in military campaigns. Initially the movement consisted of French troops in England and units of the French navy, but eventually de Gaulle was able to mobilise most of France's resistance forces. The Free French joined the Allies in a number of significant victories against the Axis powers, and 300 000 of them were involved in the Allied invasion of Normandy in 1944. On August 24 the same year de Gaulle returned to Paris in triumph and helped to rebuild the state of France.

free trade Economic doctrine advocating the free movement of goods between countries. Free trade is based on the theory that each country produces what it can most cheaply and efficiently in exchange for what it cannot. The doctrine was first championed in Britain by the Scottish economist Adam SMITH, who in his 1776 work *An Enquiry into the Nature and Causes of the Wealth of Nations* stated that the division of labour between countries leads to specialisation, greater production and wealth. The British prime minister Robert PEEL took up the cause of free trade between 1841 and 1846 by reducing import duties and repealing the CORN LAWS, which had restricted the import and export of grain to protect the interests of landowners. After the Second World War increased efforts were made to reduce tariff barriers and currency restrictions and, at a conference in Geneva in 1947, a first schedule to free world trade was drawn up – the General Agreement on Tariffs and Trade, known as GATT. In 1959 Britain helped to found another trading group, the European Free Trade Association, EFTA.

The European Economic Community, EEC or Common Market, was set up in 1958 by six central European nations to encourage free trade among its members. COMECON, communist Eastern Europe's equivalent community, was established in 1949. In 1993 the EEC, which had become the EUROPEAN UNION, removed all barriers to the free movement of trade between member countries.

Freemason Member of the world's largest secret society. The fraternity, which accepts men only, exists for the mutual support and fellowship of its members and has a complex system of secret signs. The first 'free masons' were probably skilled itinerant stonemasons and cathedral builders of the 14th century, who recognised their fellow craftsmen by these signs. By the 17th century cathedral building had declined and the masons began to accept honorary members. In 1717 a 'grand lodge' of Freemasons in London established a new constitution and system of rituals and went on to become the parent of other 'lodges' in Britain and around the world. By the 1990s there were about 6 million members worldwide. Notable freemasons were Wolfgang Mozart, Franz Josef Haydn and Johann von Goethe.

> **DID YOU KNOW?**
>
> The first American Freemasons' lodge was founded in 1750, with Benjamin Franklin as one of its members. Since then 13 American presidents have been Freemasons.

Frelimo War Conflict between Frelimo – the Mozambique Liberation Front – and Portuguese troops from 1964 to 1975. Rising nationalist feeling against Portuguese rule resulted in military operations, headed by Eduardo Mondlane, to achieve independence. Frelimo was supplied with arms by China, Czechoslovakia and the Soviet Union, and the Portuguese were unable to quell the conflict. By 1968 Samora Machel, who commanded the army after Mondlane's assassination, claimed one-fifth of the country. Portugal was forced to cede independence in 1975, and Frelimo became the principal political force in Mozambique's new People's Republic.

Frémont, John (1813-90) US explorer, soldier and political leader. Known as 'the Pathfinder', Frémont was largely responsible for mapping the area between the upper waters of the Mississippi and Missouri rivers. Between 1842 and 1846 he led three major expeditions to the far west, and he was also involved in the controversial American conquest and development of California during the MEXICAN-AMERICAN WAR. He became a multimillionaire in the gold bonanza of 1848. Frémont was the first presidential candidate of the new Republican Party in 1856, but was defeated by James Buchanan.

French, John, 1st Earl of Ypres (1852-1925) British field-marshal. In 1914, after his successes in the Sudan and the Second Boer War, French was made the commander in chief of the British Expeditionary Force in France. Although he halted the German advance through Belgium and Flanders, French proved unable to coordinate the movements of his forces, and in December 1915 he resigned in favour of General Sir Douglas HAIG after he was criticised for indecision. In 1916, as commander in chief of the Home Forces in the UK, he sent two divisions to put down the Easter Rising in Ireland. Two years later he was made Lord Lieutenant of Ireland – a position he held until 1921.

French empire Territories controlled by France after rivalry with England in the 18th century over lands in North America, India and Africa. France was left with French Guiana, SENEGAL, GABON and some West Indian islands. French Guiana, secured by France in 1817, was developed as a penal colony, to which more than 70 000 convicts were sent between 1852 and 1939. It became an overseas *département* in 1946 and in 1968 the launch site for the European Space Agency's Ariane rockets. The French empire expanded rapidly in the 19th century under Napoleon I and

Napoleon III. Algeria was claimed in 1830, followed by Cochin China, Cambodia and New Caledonia. The South-east Asian empire became known as French Indochina. By 1912 the 'Scramble for Africa' had given France many other territories, including Tunisia, Morocco, French Somaliland and Madagascar. After the First World War, the German colonies of Togoland and the Cameroons were added, together with Syria and Lebanon from the former Ottoman Empire. But the empire began to crumble following German occupation in the Second World War.

In 1946 the empire was replaced by the French Union, which reclassified the former colonies as territories and *départements*, and allowed autonomy, with a voice in decision-making in Paris. A guerrilla war between France and Indochina from 1946 to 1954 ended in French withdrawal from the union of Laos, Cambodia and Vietnam, while in 1962 Algeria was lost after six years of bitter civil war. Morocco and Tunisia achieved independence more peacefully. By 1958 all the protectorates had gained independence and the union was replaced by the French Community, which soon began to disintegrate after

the former possessions developed their own political and economic structures. Within three years the system had virtually collapsed.

French Foreign Legion Armed force based in France, formed mainly of foreign volunteers. Louis-Philippe established the *régiment étranger* – 'foreign regiment' – in Algeria in 1831 to control colonial possessions in Africa. The legion fought in many wars during the 19th century and in both world wars. When Algeria gained independence in 1962 the legion was transferred to France. No questions are asked about the origin or past of the recruits, who bind themselves completely to the legion and its unofficial motto, *legio patria nostra* – 'the legion is our fatherland'.

French Revolution see feature, page 244

French Wars of Religion Series of civil conflicts between 1562 and 1598 that brought the French state close to disintegration. Key factors were the spread of French Protestantism, a weak monarchy and the dynastic ambitions of the principal noble houses of Bourbon and Guise. The wars were

aggravated by support for the opposing sides from Catholic and Protestant powers abroad. Efforts at religious compromise by Catherine de Medici, mother of the last three Valois kings, Francis II, Charles IX and Henry III, failed with the outbreak of the first war in 1562. Subsequent attempts by the Crown, aided by the Catholic Guise faction, to repress the Protestant Huguenots led to two further outbreaks of fighting during the following eight years. The slaughter of Huguenots in the ST BARTHOLOMEW'S DAY MASSACRE of 1572 sparked the fifth war, which ended in 1576 with the promise by the Crown of freedom of worship for Protestants.

Catholics responded by forming the extremist Holy League, headed by Henri duc de Guise and his brother Cardinal Lorraine, supported by Spanish money. Wars of 1577 and 1580 proved inconclusive, but recognition of the Protestant Henry of Navarre as heir presumptive in 1584 prompted the War of the THREE HENRIES (1584-9). Isolated by the conflict and forced to submit to the power of the league, Henry III used desperate measures to preserve his monarchy. De Guise was lured to an audience with the king in 1588 and stabbed to death, but the following year Henry III was himself assassinated by an insane monk. From 1589 to 1594 Henry of Navarre fought his way to the throne, becoming the first Bourbon king of France as Henry IV. He converted to Catholicism and restored calm through a policy of religious toleration and royal absolutism.

Freud, Sigmund see feature, page 246

friar Named after the French *frère*, 'brother', friars first emerged in the Middle Ages as members of Roman Catholic religious orders forbidden to hold property. They follow a written rule which stipulates poverty, celibacy and obedience, and they preach and heal among the community. As mendicants they rely on the support and aid of the people. There are ten orders, the principal four being the AUGUSTINIANS or Austin Friars, the Franciscans (Grey Friars), the DOMINICANS (Black Friars) and the Carmelites (White Friars). The Black and White Friars are so-called because of the colour of their robes; the Grey Friars originally wore grey habits, though today they wear brown.

friendly society Mutual-aid organisation to protect members against debt through old age, illness or death. Friendly societies first emerged in the 17th century and had their origins in the burial societies of ancient Greek and Roman artisans. In the Middle Ages their idea of mutual assistance was extended to cover illness and old age. When friendly societies were established they expanded this principle by trying to calculate how much

Foreign Legionnaires go into action in Algeria in 1903. In 1962 one regiment was disbanded after it attempted a coup against President Charles de Gaulle for negotiating with the Algerian rebels.

Revolution in France that changed the face of Europe

From 1789 to 1799 France experienced events which brought down the monarchy, created the Republic, ended feudalism and instigated a charter of human rights. It was a time of turmoil, mob rule, and the guillotine.

In 1789 a political upheaval began in France that changed the face of Europe. Some contemporaries regarded it with admiration: 'How much the greatest event it is that ever happened in the world: and how much the best,' declared the English politician Charles James Fox. Others looked upon it with horror, for although it swept away entrenched privilege and injustice, it ushered onto the political stage the unpredictable: the mob, the psychology of intimidation, the carrying of ideological struggles across international borders.

The sequence of events leading to the French Revolution began with Louis XVI's announcement that the States-General, the French 'parliament', would meet on May 5, 1789, for the first time in 175 years. The king summoned the assembly because his treasury was bankrupt and he hoped to persuade the delegates to grant him funds. The peasantry could no longer raise enough revenue to support the government, especially in the wars against England, and rising prices coupled with France's lack of an adequate banking system had served to make the situation even worse.

A STATE IN CRISIS

Attempts were made during 1787 to reform state finances and the tax system, but the privileged classes demanded constitutional reform against the government's attempts to break their immunity from taxation. With the calling of the States-General, these attempts were abandoned and the Swiss banker Jacques Necker, who until 1781 had handled finance by raising loans, was recalled.

The turmoil was all the greater because the harvest in 1788 had been disastrous. Peasants were required to hand over money or produce to the owner of the land, to the Church and to the State, while speculators in the towns sold food at high prices. At the same time, the economy was in recession. This far-reaching crisis brought rich and poor alike, in town and country, into unprecedented conflict.

Although well-intentioned, the king had neither the experience nor the ability to lead the State out of crisis. He had assumed that when the States-General met it would sit, as before, separately in three sections: clergy, nobility and 'Third Estate' – commoners. But the Third Estate was inspired by thinkers of the Enlightenment, who believed that the State should be run on modern, rational principles rather than by a privileged hereditary elite. Its spokesman insisted on its members' rights as fellow citizens to meet as equals of the nobles and clergy. On June 17, after much procedural wrangling, it declared itself to be a National Assembly.

It was hardly the best moment for a rational debate. Rioters demanded that the price of bread be fixed, workers seized grain, others protested because they had not been paid. On April 28, 1789 the factory of a wallpaper manufacturer named Réveillon was attacked by the Paris mob, who had heard that he was proposing a reduction in his workers' wages. Troops opened fire on the rioters, killing some 300 of them.

Rumours of conspiracies appeared to be confirmed when the king dismissed Necker on July 11. Would the army be used to re-establish royal power? Orators in Paris urged the mob to take action. On the night of July 12-13 some 50 customs posts were attacked. Buildings were ransacked for food. The National Assembly appeared to encourage these demonstrations. The critical moment occurred on July 14, 1789, when bands of malcontents broke into the armouries and stormed the hated royal fortress of the Bastille in Paris. After the attack the Duc de Liancourt is said to have broken the news to the king. 'This is a riot,' said the king. 'No, Sire, it is a revolution,' de Liancourt replied.

The king recalled Necker; he expressed his sympathy with the crowds of Paris by wearing a tricolour cockade of red and blue for the city and white for the Bourbons; and he made the Marquis de Lafayette, a

On June 20, 1789, the Third Estate defy the king, vowing in the tennis court at Versailles not to disband until France had a constitution.

The Paris mob surges towards the Hotel de Ville, the town hall, after seizing the Bastille on July 14, 1789. The French Revolution has begun.

popular aristocrat, the commander of a militia called the National Guard. In August the National Assembly abolished the feudal structure of France and adopted the Declaration of the Rights of Man, which set out the principles of fundamental human rights.

Rumours grew that the king was plotting to restore privileges to the aristocracy. In October, inflamed also by a bread shortage, the women of Paris marched to Versailles and forced the king to return to the city. For the next two years Louis remained a prisoner of the mob.

Fanning the revolution was this fashion accessory decorated with La Fayette's portrait set in a tricolour cockade and flanked by songs.

Louis XVI appears on a balcony before the rabble bring him back to Paris on October 6, 1789. Thereafter he was effectively a prisoner.

'The Marseillaise', sung by volunteer troops, became the national anthem in 1795, the year Centigrade replaced Fahrenheit.

A new, more democratic constitution was devised. Deputies and officials were to be elected by those citizens who paid the equivalent of three days' labour in taxes. The country was divided into 83 departments. It was, for the time being, a rational, middle-class revolution.

The constitution required skill and goodwill on the part of the king. He possessed neither. Two key developments compelled the revolution forward again. One came from the need to solve the financial crisis. It was decided to sell Church land, on the grounds that it belonged to the nation. Government bonds, based on the value of land and known as assignats, were issued. Religious orders were suppressed. As a result, the Catholic Church turned against the revolution, creating ideological division, and the assignats became a form of currency that eventually hampered trade and raised prices.

The other development was the outbreak of war. Some politicians hoped that war would allow the revolution to go forward by spreading its principles across Europe. In August 1792 the French declared war against Austria, whose forces invaded France and threatened to destroy Paris if the royal family were harmed. The ensuing conflict, in which Britain, Holland and Spain joined Austria and Prussia in a coalition against France, threw the people behind the revolution in a struggle for national survival.

The tempo quickened. The constitution was abolished and a new National Convention was elected. The enemy was now seen not only to be foreign powers; it was also the enemy within. Rooting out internal opponents was the job of the Terror and its weapon, the guillotine. The king was executed on January 21, 1793.

NEW REPUBLIC

France was ruled by the Committee of Public Safety. Maximilien Robespierre was the dominant figure from the spring of 1793 to the summer of 1794. A new calendar was introduced; a new religion was organised, the Cult of the Supreme Being. The Republic made war on the peasantry of Brittany and the Vendée because they would not accept the rule of Paris. When this conflict was won, it was seen that the Republic was no longer in danger and the need for the Terror had passed. All men feared Robespierre, and he was guillotined in 1794.

The revolution began to stabilise. From 1795 to 1799 France was ruled by five directors, 'The Directory', to ensure that there would not be another Robespierre, and by a two-chamber parliament based on wealth. It was a time of corruption, and although the assignats were abolished the economy remained weak. Royalist plots continued. French armies fought on in Europe. As dissension grew, politicians turned to the army to maintain control. And in November 1799 the most famous of the generals was Napoleon Bonaparte.

Louis XVI was guillotined for treason on January 21, 1793, an event which shook the thrones of Europe.

Freud on the mind

Sigmund Freud's pioneering work in psychoanalysis overturned established thinking on human behaviour.

Sigmund Freud's study of the unconscious mind had a powerful impact on 20th-century thought and literature. Born in Austria to Jewish parents, Freud (1856–1939) trained as a doctor in Vienna before specialising in the study of the brain and its disorders. He pioneered psychoanalysis, in which the patient's 'free association' of ideas in conversation and the interpretation of his or her dreams replaced drugs and electric shocks as a treatment for mental illness.

Freud believed human behaviour to be rooted in sexual desire, present from infancy. He argued in *The Interpretation of Dreams* (1900) that the dream, like the neurosis, was a disguised manifestation of repressed desire and provided the 'hidden meaning' to behaviour.

CONTROVERSIAL THEORIES

Freud divided the mind into the id, the unconscious and primitive mass from which emerges instincts for food and sex, the ego, or rational self, and the superego, the ethical element which inhibits the ego with feelings of guilt.

His excellence as a writer won him the Goethe prize in 1930. He was an inspired phrase-maker, coining the terms 'Oedipus complex', 'guilt complex', 'sublimation' and 'depth psychology', and he used his own patients' case histories to great effect. His work *Beyond the Pleasure Principle* (1920) offered the idea of the 'death instinct' – man's urge to destroy himself – as an explanation for the trench slaughter of the First World War. He shocked his readers when, in *The Future of an Illusion* (1927), he declared that religions 'must be classed among the mass-delusions' of mankind. He added: 'No one, needless to say, who shares a delusion ever recognises it as such.'

The same point was made of Freud's own followers, artists and intellectuals hungry for fresh explanations of human conduct and eager to discuss sexuality openly. There was no experimental evidence to support his theories, and his own patients fared no better than those of his rivals.

Freud's fall from fashion has been dramatic. His conviction that his opponents were mentally disturbed – 'My inclination is to treat those colleagues who offer resistance exactly as we treat patients in the same situation,' he wrote to his colleague Carl Jung before breaking with him – is seen by some as a precursor to the detention of Soviet

After escaping from the Nazis in 1938 Freud went straight back to work at his desk in Hampstead, London.

dissidents in psychiatric wards. Feminists are outraged by his belief that sexual abuse suffered by his female patients as children was imagined and not real. But if his insights are no longer seen as the key to the human mind, many therapists still follow his method of listening to patients with care and respect.

His sense of humour has also survived. Before leaving Vienna for England in 1938 to escape Nazi persecution, he was asked by Adolf Hitler's Gestapo to sign a form confirming its proper behaviour: 'I can recommend the Gestapo to anyone,' he wrote. Freud died in London the following year.

---

members should pay, based on the size of each risk. In Britain friendly societies have taken the form of building societies, though they can also be trade unions or fraternal orders.

Frisians Germanic seafaring people. In Roman times they occupied northern Holland and north-west Germany – an area known as Frisia. Between 12 BC and AD 69 the Frisians rebelled on several occasions against Rome. After the 5th century they were conquered by the Franks, who tried to convert them to Christianity. During the Middle Ages the Frisians maintained some autonomy, but in 1524 they came under the domination of the Habsburgs.

After their alliance with the Dutch in the revolt against Spanish rule, the Frisian colony was made part of a Dutch republic in 1579. In 1815 Frisia was divided into Friesland, a province of the Netherlands, and the Ostfriesland and Nordfriesland areas of north-western Germany. Their language is now spoken in only three small areas of the region.

Froissart, Jean (c.1337–c.1410) Flemish poet and court historian, whose *Chroniques* provide one of the most significant accounts of medieval Europe. The earliest books were based on the work of chronicler Jean le Bel (c.1290–c.1370), while the others were drawn from Froissart's own travels abroad, particularly the time he spent at the English court. Froissart used his privileged position to interview notable figures and follow closely events such as weddings, funerals and the battles and campaigns of the HUNDRED YEARS' WAR. His observations of courtly extravagance, chivalrous ideals and the behaviour of the aristocracy are vividly related, while the victims of the time are usually ignored.

Fronde Series of revolts against the growing power of the Crown in France while LOUIS XIV was a child and power was in the hands of his mother Anne of Austria and her chief minister Jules MAZARIN. The word in French means a sling used in a children's game and was first used by Cardinal de Retz to describe street fighting in Paris. The first Fronde was started by court magistrates of the judicial PAR-LEMENT in 1648 in reaction to the decision made by Anne of Austria and Mazarin to raise money by stopping magistrates' wages for four years. The magistrates were joined by the

This page from Jean Froissart's *Chroniques* portrays the Battle of Sluys (1340), when the English king Edward III's navy destroyed a French fleet in a harbour on the Flemish coast.

The prison reformer Elizabeth Fry reads the Bible to inmates at London's Newgate prison. She travelled to Europe to spread her ideas and later set up soup kitchens for the poor in London.

nobility, whose influence was also being undermined by Mazarin. The main instigators were arrested in 1649. The second Fronde began in 1650 after the arrest of the military leader the Prince de CONDÉ. The nobles rebelled and Mazarin was forced to flee France. But Condé was not supported by the *Parlement* and his popularity waned, compelling him to leave Paris. Mazarin was able to return to France after the army had taken control of Paris on behalf of the king. The Fronde was suppressed in October 1652, allowing Louis to strengthen the position of the monarchy.

Fry, Elizabeth (1780-1845) British philanthropist and advocate of prison reform. Married to Joseph Fry, a QUAKER, she became a preacher in the Society of Friends. Her determination to improve conditions for women prisoners was inspired by a visit to Newgate prison in London in 1813, where she witnessed their brutal treatment. Fry's campaigning for improvements such as separation of the sexes, female supervision for women and useful prison jobs led to reforms stressing rehabilitation rather than punishment.

Fuchs, Klaus (1911-88) German-born British physicist and spy, and a member of the team that developed the atomic bomb at Los Alamos in the USA in 1943. Fuchs returned to Britain to work for the Atomic Energy Research Establishment at Harwell. He was arrested in 1950 and charged with passing information about the atomic bomb to Soviet agents. Fuchs pleaded guilty and was imprisoned. After his release in 1959 he went to East Germany, where he became director of the Institute for Nuclear Physics near Dresden.

Fugger Family of bankers and merchants from south Germany who were the creditors of many rulers in the Middle Ages and who were deeply involved in the finances of the papacy. The family established its position in the 14th century through Hans Fugger, who twice married daughters of wealthy masters of the weavers' guild in Augsburg. His fortune began to accumulate through trade and banking. His descendant Jacob I became head of the guild, marking the family's first step to prominence. The family's most distinguished member was Jacob II, who brought the Fuggers to their peak of prosperity in the early 16th century.

Jacob II lent vast sums to the Holy Roman Emperor Maximilian I, but his most notable achievement was the financing of Charles V's candidacy for the same title in 1519. In return Charles ennobled the family and allowed them to coin their own money. The Fuggers' downturn in fortunes was brought about by the bankruptcies of the HABSBURG dynasty, whose wars they had helped to finance, and the ravages of the THIRTY YEARS' WAR. Only astute management of their remaining assets saved the Fuggers from complete ruin. A few descendants were prominent after the 17th century, but little was left of their wealth.

Fulbright, James (1905-95) US politician. In 1943 Fulbright, as a member of the House of Representatives, introduced a resolution calling for the creation of the UNITED NATIONS. He sponsored the Fulbright Act to provide funding for the exchange of students between the USA and other countries. He became chairman of the Senate Foreign Relations Committee in 1959, a position he held for 15 years. An outspoken critic of foreign policy, Fulbright was opposed to the Bay of Pigs invasion of Cuba in 1961 and his country's involvement in the Vietnam War.

fundamentalism Religious movements which seek to promote and defend a literal interpretation of the doctrines of a faith. Christian fundamentalists emerged in the USA in the late 19th century in opposition to the influence of the evolutionary theories of Charles DARWIN and growing scepticism about the Bible as an historical source. The movement grew in the early 20th century and its followers emphasised among other things, the importance of a literal interpretation of scripture along with the orthodox Christian teachings of the divinity of Jesus Christ and the reality of the virgin conception. In 1919 they formed the much larger World Christian Fundamentals Association. A partial religious revival in the 1950s brought more converts, and today it is thought there are as many as 60 million Christian fundamentalists in the USA, with a growing worldwide following.

The term fundamentalism is also applied to ultraconservative or militant movements in other faiths. Shiite fundamentalists in Iran followed the Ayatollah KHOMEINI in violent opposition to Western influences in the country in the 1980s, while in 1981 Muslim fundamentalists in Egypt, outraged by a peace initiative with Israel, assassinated President Anwar SADAT. The 1990s saw continued Islamic fundamentalist uprisings in the Middle East, Africa and Asia.

Jacob Fugger (right) known as 'the Rich', became wealthy because he held a monopoly in the mining and trading of precious metals.

Fur trappers review their catch in the wilds of North America. They formed part of a major industry: between 1853 and 1877 the Hudson's Bay Company sold more than 3 million skins.

fur trade Animals have been killed for their fur since prehistoric times, but as civilisation developed, furs for clothing became more of a luxury than a necessity. Trading in furs was a significant part of the economy of the Roman Empire and by the Middle Ages the trade had spread across most of Europe. Early fur trappers were responsible for opening up many of the wilderness areas of Siberia and North America. Their main sources of fur were beavers, muskrats, racoons, skunks and sea otters. The fur trade reached its peak between the 17th and early 19th centuries, by which time the USA and Canada were the biggest producers, and huge agents such as the British-owned Hudson's Bay and American Fur companies flourished. The chief producers today are the USA, southern Canada and the Scandinavian countries. Many of the hunted species have become endangered, and countries such as the USA and Britain have banned the import and sale of pelts from such animals as tigers, polar bears and jaguars. In the 1980s the protests of animal rights groups led to a decrease in the popularity of furs and an increase in the demand for synthetic furs. There has also been growing condemnation of the methods used to kill fur-bearing animals.

fusilier Historically a soldier armed with a 'fusil' – a flintlock musket – in the French army of the 17th century. The name was subsequently given to a member of other infantry regiments, including machine-gunners.

fyrd Military force of freemen in Anglo-Saxon times. From the 7th century, freemen were obliged to perform three duties – the *trinoda necessitas* – for their kings: maintain strongholds, repair roads and provide military service. Anyone who failed to comply with a summons to join the fyrd incurred a fine known as *fyrdwite*. The system was modified by ALFRED THE GREAT in the 9th century and was further restructured by Henry II's Assize of Arms in 1181, which required all freemen to possess arms suitable to their rank. In 1285 Edward I's Statute of Winchester allowed the fyrd more control over maintaining public order. It was superseded by the MILITIA.

Gabon Country in equatorial West Africa. The Portuguese visited Gabon in the 15th century and began to trade in slaves. In 1839 the French made Gabon a naval base to suppress slavery, and a French colony developed, exploiting the country's rare woods, gold, diamonds and other minerals. Gabon became an overseas territory of France in 1946, gained its autonomy in 1958 and its full independence in 1960. After early years of political instability, there was considerable support for the presidency of Omar Bongo, who was first elected in 1967. In the November of 1990 his Gabonese Democratic Party won a general election, following a decision to restore multi-party politics, and in 1993 Bongo was again re-elected. By making good use of its natural resources Gabon has achieved one of the fastest economic growth rates in Africa.

Gaddafi, Moammar al- see QADDAFI, MUAMMAR AL-

Gage, Thomas (1721-87) British general whose incompetence contributed to the loss of the American colonies. In 1763, after he had served in Flanders, at CULLODEN and in France and India, Gage was appointed commander of all British forces in America, where he seriously misjudged the colonies' mood in favour of independence. As military governor of Massachusetts in 1774, he tried to quell rising unrest. It was Gage who sent troops into LEXINGTON AND CONCORD where skirmishes touched off the AMERICAN REVOLUTION. Gage resigned in 1775.

Gaitskell, Hugh (1906-63) British politician, leader of the Labour Party in opposition from 1955 to his death. Gaitskell represented the moderate right-wing of the Labour Party and fought for a balance between private and state industry. He opposed the Conservative government over the 1956 SUEZ WAR and resisted those within his own party who supported unilateral nuclear disarmament. Gaitskell entered Parliament in 1945, and held several posts in the Labour government of Clement ATTLEE, including that of chancellor of the exchequer from 1950 to 1951.

Galen (c. AD 130-c.200) Greek physician whose teachings dominated medicine for nearly 1500 years. When Galen was a boy he regularly visited the medical school in his home town of Pergamum (the present-day Bergama) in Turkey. There he examined gladiators' wounds to see how they responded to treatment. As a young man he studied medicine and visited schools in Greece and Egypt to learn different medical techniques. Galen returned home in 157 and became chief doctor at the school for gladiators, enabling him

Gaitskell's fortunes soar as the government is embarrassed when accusations of spying erupt during the Summit of Nuclear Powers, 1960.

to increase his extensive knowledge of anatomy and wounds. Four years later he moved to Rome where success in treating important citizens gained him a place at the court of Marcus Aurelius, who was then joint emperor with Lucius Verus. After the death of Verus, Galen was appointed personal physician to Commodus, the son of Aurelius. His many writings on blood, the heart, the kidneys and the bladder were translated by Arabs during the 9th century. Further translations of his Greek notebooks into Latin in the 11th century made his work available to 16th and 17th century physicians who repeated his experiments and corrected some of his findings.

Galicia Region in north-western Spain. In the 6th century AD it was a kingdom of the GOTHS. It became a centre of resistance against the Moors in the 8th century and in the 13th century passed to Castile.

Galileo see feature, page 250

galleon Sailing warship of the late 16th century. Galleons eventually replaced the less manoeuvrable carracks as the principal type of European fighting ship. They were masted and square-rigged, with two decks and two main batteries of cannons. Lighter, swifter galleons developed by the English seaman Sir John HAWKINS played a large part in defeating the more cumbersome old-fashioned galleons used by the Spanish Armada in its attack on England. This improved design was later incorporated in the great Portuguese and Spanish galleons which opened up the New World to trade with Europe.

galley Warship equipped with oars and sail, which was propelled mainly by oars in battle. The Phoenicians are thought to have invented the bireme, with two banks of oars, around 700 BC. Athens used the TRIREME, with three banks, as its principal warship. One of the greatest trireme battles was at SALAMIS in 480. In Hellenistic times the quinquereme became standard; this was equipped with five banks of oars. The Viking longship was a small but durable type of galley, simpler than the larger designs used by the major Mediterranean powers such as Byzantium and Venice. The longship, with its high bow, could negotiate heavy seas, and carried the Vikings to Greenland and America in the 10th century. But Mediterranean galleys had severe limitations: they were slow because much of the oarsmen's effort was wasted, and they could not be used in storms because they had a low freeboard.

Gallicanism The tradition of resistance to papal authority in French Roman Catholicism dating back to Philip IV's struggle with Pope Boniface VIII from 1294 to 1303. It was founded on the principles that the papacy had

At Gallipoli, the bravery and spirit of Anzac troops won them recognition as 'worthy sons of the Empire', and fame for being 'jokers in the midst of death'.

no secular power over the French monarchy, that the clergy and secular powers would cooperate to limit papal power in France, and that an ecumenical council was superior to the papacy. These principles were set out in the four *Gallican Articles* of 1682 and approved by the assembly of the French clergy. Eighteenth-century rationalism and the French Revolution weakened concern about Gallican issues.

Gallic Wars Campaigns fought by Julius CAESAR from 58 to 51 BC which established Roman rule over central and northern Europe west of the River Rhine. Caesar crossed into Transalpine GAUL, now southern France, and stopped German tribes from advancing in the south and east, the Belgae in the north and the Veneti in the west. He even crossed the Rhine

Galleys such as this, drawn by Raphael, last played a crucial role at the Battle of Lepanto in 1571 when Christian allies defeated the Turks.

to demonstrate Roman control of that crucial natural frontier. A combination of Caesar's speed and ruthlessness and a lack of unity among his opponents enabled him to subdue the northern and western coasts of what is now France. Caesar invaded Britain, which was regarded as a Belgic refuge and a threat to Rome, in 55 and 54 BC. Then, in the winter of 53-52 BC, VERCINGETORIX rallied the central Gauls in an unusual display of unity. In a long and bitter campaign, Caesar defeated him and his successors, and the tribal leader was executed. Caesar's account of the campaign was published as the *Gallic Wars*.

Gallipoli Campaign (1915-16) Allied attempt to force a passage through the DARDANELLES during the First World War. Its main aims were to make Turkey abandon the war, and to open a safe sea route to Russia. After the failure of a naval expedition in February 1915, a military expedition was attempted, relying mainly upon British, Australian and New Zealand troops, with some naval support. The first landings, on the Gallipoli peninsula and on the Asian mainland opposite, were made in April 1915. Turkish resistance was strong and, despite Allied reinforcements, fighting on the peninsula reached a stalemate. After nine months the Allied troops were withdrawn. About 36 000 Commonwealth troops died. Winston CHURCHILL, who as First Lord of the Admiralty was largely responsible for the campaign, was blamed for its failure. ANZAC Day, April 25, commemorates the part played by Australian and New Zealand servicemen during the landings and later campaigns.

Galton, Francis (1822-1911) British psychologist, explorer, meteorologist, founder of eugenics and pioneer of the study of Human

Exploring a secret Universe

Despite opposition from the Church, the Italian astronomer, mathematician and physicist Galileo laid the foundations of modern science.

Galileo Galilei was born at Pisa in 1564, 20 years after the publication of Nicholas Copernicus's treatise stating that the Earth was a planet that revolved around the Sun, not the centre of God's universe. Galileo accepted the theory, and his career, which together with that of Johannes Kepler laid the foundations for Isaac Newton's laws of motion, was spent in fear of ridicule and denunciation.

Galileo was born into an impoverished household of the lesser Italian nobility. His father wanted him be a merchant, but recognising his gifts sent him to study medicine at Pisa. Unable to get a scholarship – despite showing that a pendulum of a given length swings at a constant frequency, regardless of amplitude – he left without a degree.

He continued his experiments at home, inventing a hydrostatic balance and writing a treatise on it which gained him a lectureship in mathematics at Pisa. Three years later, in 1592, he was given the chair of mathematics at Padua. There, for the next 18 years, he laid the foundations of the science of moving bodies – dynamics – though the story of his dropping weights from the leaning tower of Pisa is mere legend. Galileo's work depended on the telescope, invented in 1608 by a Dutch spectacles-maker and improved by Galileo the following year.

One of Galileo's first discoveries was of four moons of Jupiter, which helped to undermine belief in an earth-centred Universe. He published his findings in 1610, the year he left Padua to become philosopher and mathematician to Cosimo II de'Medici, Duke of Tuscany. Three years later he issued a tract on Sun spots. He also observed the oval shape of Saturn and the phases of Venus, proof that it revolved around the Sun.

AND YET IT MOVES

Galileo had supported Copernican theory all his life, fearing that, like his forerunner, he would be 'laughed at and hissed off the stage'. In 1613, provoked by a dinner-table dispute, he wrote an open letter upholding Copernicus and the Church entered the fray. In 1616 the papacy denounced Copernicanism. Galileo, summoned to Rome, was told not to teach the new science. He published nothing more until in 1632 he issued the *Dialogue on the Two Great Systems of the World*, which irrefutably overthrew the Aristotelian Universe.

In 1633 Galileo recanted before the Inquisition in Rome, though he probably did not whisper the defiant words '*e pur si muove*', 'and yet it moves', of the Earth at the end of the trial. He was sentenced to house arrest; his health failed and, after becoming blind, he died in 1642.

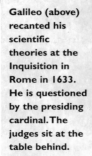

Galileo (above) recanted his scientific theories at the Inquisition in Rome in 1633. He is questioned by the presiding cardinal. The judges sit at the table behind.

intelligence and of the differences between individuals. Galton was inspired by his cousin Charles DARWIN's *On The Origin of Species,* published in 1859, to produce his own *Hereditary Genius* ten years later. He relied on biographical information to show that particular talents often run in families. He carried out the first study of twins in 1876. Identical twins have identical genes, so twin studies remain the principal method of distinguishing between the effects of heredity and those of experience or the environment. Galton's development of methods in psychology was as important as his ideas: his main contribution was to show how to apply statistics to psychological data.

Gambia, Republic of The Small West African country, which was originally part of the Mali empire, a Muslim dominion based on gold trading that flourished in West Africa between the 7th and 15th centuries. The Portuguese arrived at the end of this period, and monopolised trade with Europeans for a century until the English took over by setting up trading posts which they controlled from Sierra Leone. A fort was built by the British at Banjul in 1816, as a base for operations against the slave trade. The new town, renamed Bathurst, became the capital in 1821, and The Gambia became a British colony in 1843. A British Protectorate over the interior was proclaimed in 1893.

The Gambia became an independent member of the Commonwealth in 1965, and a republic in 1970, with Sir Dawda Kairaba Jawara as the first president. Tourism has been developed and is now an important source of foreign revenue. In 1982 The Gambia and its neighbour, Senegal, formed a limited confederation called Senegambia for defence, economic, and foreign policy purposes, but this collapsed in 1989. In April 1992 Jawara was re-elected president for his fifth term of office, but in July 1994 was ousted in a military coup led by Lieutenant Yahya Jammeh.

Gamelin, Maurice (1872-1958) French general. As a staff officer in the First World War he helped to plan the battle of the MARNE in 1914, which successfully prevented the Germans from invading Paris. In the Second World War, as commander-in-chief of the French forces, he was unprepared for the German thrust through the Ardennes in 1940 which resulted in the fall of France. In mid May 1940 Gamelin was replaced by General Maxime WEYGAND. He refused to defend himself when tried for 'war guilt' by the German-backed Vichy government in 1942, and was held in Germany until he was freed in 1945.

Gandhi, Indira (1917-84) Indian stateswoman, prime minister from 1966 to 1977 and again from 1979 to 1984. Gandhi, the daughter of Jawaharlal NEHRU, joined the

Indian National CONGRESS Party in 1939, and spent more than a year in prison for resisting British rule. Her first years in politics were spent as an aide to her father when he was prime minister, and she was president of the Congress Party in 1959 and 1960. She became minister for broadcasting and information in Lal Bahadur Shastri's Cabinet, and on Shastri's sudden death in 1966 was chosen by the party to succeed him as prime minister.

In her early years as prime minister she faced a protracted struggle with the older leadership of the party, which she overcame with the aid of the left wing in 1970. After the successful INDO-PAKISTAN WAR of 1971 her popularity stood high, but it waned during the 1970s. In 1975 she was threatened with being ousted as prime minister after a court declared that electoral rules had been broken in the 1971 general election.

Gandhi declared a state of emergency and ruled India as a virtual dictator. After two years of autocratic rule, she called elections in 1977 but lost to Morarji DESAI. Gandhi's career seemed finished, but in 1979 her faction of the Congress Party was re-elected and she ruled until she was assassinated by a Sikh extremist member of her bodyguard. Her elder son, Rajiv GANDHI, succeeded her as prime minister.

Gandhi, Mohandas see feature, page 252

Gandhi, Rajiv (1944-91) Indian statesman and prime minister from 1984 to 1989. As a young man Gandhi was an airline pilot and showed no interest in politics. But he came from an Indian political dynasty: he was the elder son of Indira GANDHI, who had been prime minister twice, and grandson of India's first premier, Jawaharlal NEHRU. When his brother Sanjay was killed in a plane crash, Gandhi stood in the 1981 by-election and was elected to his brother's parliamentary seat. He was so popular that his Congress Party won the 1984 election with a record majority, but he failed to gain re-election in 1989 after government officials were accused of accepting bribes to award a major arms contract to the Swedish Bofors company. Gandhi was assassinated during the 1991 election by a young Tamil woman with a bomb strapped to her.

Gang of Four Radical Chinese leaders who rose to prominence during the CULTURAL REVOLUTION of the mid 1960s. The four — Wang Hong-wen, Yao Wen-yuan, Zhang Chun-zhao and Jiang Qing, who was MAO ZE-DONG's fourth wife — had a power base in Shanghai and occupied important positions in the Politburo after the Tenth Party Congress of 1973. Following Mao Ze-dong's death in 1976 their enemies alleged that they plotted

Jiang Qing, Mao's widow, sits in the dock with others of the accused during the Gang of Four trial in Peking in 1980. After Mao died, the Gang was publicly denounced on wall posters.

to seize power, and in 1980 they were found guilty of conspiring against the state and were blamed for the revolution's excesses. Jiang and Zang received suspended death sentences, Wang was jailed for life and Yao received a jail term of 20 years.

Garbo, Greta (1905-90) Swedish film star whose alluring screen presence made her a Hollywood legend during the 1920s and 1930s. Garbo worked in a number of menial jobs in her native Stockholm before appearing as a bathing beauty in 1922 in a film called *Peter the Tramp*. In the same year she enrolled for two years at the Royal Dramatic Theatre, Stockholm, where she met the director Mauritz Stiller. He taught her how to play to the camera and gave her a role in his 1924 film *The Story of Gösta Berlings*. Stiller went to Hollywood the following year and took Garbo with him. She appeared in 27 films, including *The Torrent* in 1926 and *Love* in 1927. In 1930 she made her first 'talkie', *Anna Christie,* and appeared in *Queen Christina* in 1933, *Anna Karenina* in 1935 and *Camille* in 1936. Savage criticism of her role in *Two-faced Woman* in 1941 made Garbo retire at the age of 36. She thereafter became a recluse and fended off all requests for interviews.

Garrick, David (1717-79) Actor, dramatist and joint manager of the Drury Lane Theatre in London. Garrick was the greatest English actor of the 18th century, and restored the popularity of William SHAKESPEARE's plays.

In April 1740 the Drury Lane theatre staged Garrick's first comedy, *Lethe*. The following year he replaced a sick actor to play

> **DID YOU KNOW?**
>
> At 16, Garbo turned down her first offer of a part in a feature film. She could not get time off work selling hats in a department store.

Harlequin at a small, unlicensed London theatre. Soon after, he was offered the role of Richard III and was an instant success, with nobles flocking to the tiny theatre to see the new actor who dared to portray a tragic Shakespearean character. A string of successful roles followed and he was offered a large salary to appear at Drury Lane.

In 1747, with the help of friends, he raised £8000 to buy the theatre in partnership with James Lacy, a failed actor. Lacy dealt with business while Garrick concentrated on radical reforms, such as the introduction of sidelights and footlights. He staged Shakespeare's plays purged of Restoration rewrites and alterations, and rewrote existing plays for specific actors. He continued to appear on stage himself, playing the parts of King Lear, Macbeth, and Richard III, and touring in Europe. He also wrote and published about 20 plays, but his works were not popular. Towards the end of his life he sold his share in the theatre and retired.

Gardiner, Stephen (c.1490-1555) Bishop, diplomat and secretary to HENRY VIII. As a protégé of Thomas WOLSEY, Gardiner assisted in the negotiations to secure Henry's divorce from Catherine of Aragon, and was made Bishop of Winchester in 1531. Though he defended royal supremacy over the Church, notably in his treatise *On True Obedience*, he opposed Protestant doctrines. For this he was deprived of office and imprisoned in 1548 under EDWARD VI. In 1553 the Roman Catholic MARY I restored him to his bishopric and made him Lord Chancellor; in these offices he persecuted Protestants until his death.

Spirit of India

Mohandas Gandhi, the outstanding figure in India's struggle for independence from Britain, dedicated his life to the cause of peace, reform and self-rule for his country.

The teacher and reformer Mohandas Karamchand Gandhi (1869-1948) is still known by the title 'Mahatma', or great spirit. Gandhi was born in Porbandar in western India. In 1888 he went to London as a law student and began studying religion. His attention focused on the Bhagavad-Gita, the Hindu text which was to inspire him throughout his life. Gandhi then settled in South Africa, where he worked as a lawyer. He mobilised mass support to fight laws that discriminated against the Asian community and gained some concessions from the government.

Gandhi returned to India in 1915, having written a booklet advocating Indian self-rule. He adopted a simple style of life and dress. For Gandhi personal conduct and social reform mattered as much as politics. He worked for the elimination of untouchability – the isolation of India's lowest caste – and for women's rights, and believed in good Hindu-Muslim relations.

CIVIL DISOBEDIENCE

In 1920 Gandhi persuaded the Indian National Congress, the organisation leading the drive for freedom, to launch a noncooperation movement against the British. The movement evoked a huge response. Gandhi called for a boycott of British cloth made with cheap Indian cotton, and adopted the spinning wheel as a symbol of self-reliance. He was arrested and imprisoned for six years.

In 1930 Gandhi began a second civil disobedience movement. He led a march through western India to the coast to make salt with his own hands, defying a government monopoly. Again he was arrested. In 1931 he attended the Round Table Conference on India's future in London, but the negotiations failed.

As a young lawyer, Gandhi – flanked here by his practice staff – used his legal skills to fight against racial injustice in South Africa.

During the Second World War, Gandhi launched the Quit India movement. The British responded by arresting the leaders of the Congress, but in their absence the movement turned violent, with the government losing control of large areas of the country.

After 1944 Gandhi increasingly devoted himself to bringing calm to areas stricken by Hindu-Muslim riots, leaving negotiations with the British to Congress. He was opposed to partition – the political division of India between its Hindu and Muslim-dominated regions which led to the creation of Pakistan. On independence day, August 15, 1947, Gandhi fasted and prayed for peace. The transfer of Hindus and Muslims at partition left hundreds of thousands dead.

On January 30, 1948, Gandhi was shot dead at his regular evening prayer meeting in Delhi by a Hindu extremist.

At 77 Gandhi was widely respected for his peaceful campaigns of civil disobedience.

Garfield, James (1831-81) President of the USA, who held office briefly in 1881. Garfield was a lay preacher who entered politics in 1859 by winning a place in the Ohio state senate. He served in the AMERICAN CIVIL WAR, retired as a major-general and then entered national politics as a Republican Congressman in 1863. He emerged as the compromise candidate to fight and win the presidential election of 1880 after the Republican Party had split into two factions. A feud had developed between the self-styled 'Half-Breeds' – members who favoured a conciliatory policy towards the South after the American Civil War and advocated civil service reforms – and 'Stalwarts', the more conservative faction that resisted reform. Within four months of becoming president he was assassinated by a disappointed 'Stalwart' office-seeker.

Garibaldi, Giuseppe (1807-82) Italian leader and military commander of the RISORGIMENTO movement, a campaign from 1831 to 1861 that led to the creation of the united kingdom of Italy. In 1834 Garibaldi led an unsuccessful republican plot in Genoa in support of Giuseppe MAZZINI, the leader of the Risorgimento movement. He fled, and spent the next 12 years in exile in South America, where he became a master of guerrilla warfare. He returned to Italy and took part in the REVOLUTIONS OF 1848. He became a popular hero when he formed a volunteer army of 'Redshirts' to defend the short-lived Roman Republic against French forces fighting for Pope Pius IX in June 1849. His resistance and gallant retreat were hailed by the people.

After another period of exile, in 1858 he was invited by Count Camillo CAVOUR to help to defeat the Austrians in northern Italy. This was achieved in 1859. Sicily was captured the following year, and then Naples, capital of the kingdom of the two Sicilies. The whole of southern Italy was then handed to VICTOR EMMANUEL II four months later. In 1862, in an attempt to secure the Papal States, Garibaldi led his forces unsuccessfully against Rome. In 1867 he was defeated by French and papal forces at Mentana while attempting once more to capture Rome. He spent his last years as a recluse on the island of Caprera.

Garvey, Marcus (1887-1940) Jamaican Black leader who inspired the first important Black nationalist movement in the USA. He organised the Universal Negro Improvement and Conservation Association (UNICA) in Jamaica in 1914 to encourage racial pride and Black unity with the slogan 'Africa for the Africans at home and abroad'. Two years later Garvey went to the USA, where he promoted an independent Black economy, set up a range of businesses and promised repatriation of American Blacks to a new African republic, to

'Here, we either make Italy or we die!' Garibaldi rallies his troops as battle hangs in the balance at Calatafimi, Sicily, in May 1860. His red-shirted 'Thousand' defeated twice as many regular troops.

be created out of former German colonies. Garvey's followers clashed with more moderate Blacks in the 1920s. Although personally honest, he mismanaged his movement's finances and was convicted in 1923 of attempted fraud. The Rastafarian religious cult in Jamaica draws on many of his ideas.

Gascony Former duchy in south-western France. Named after the Vascones, or Basques, who took it in the 6th century AD, it enjoyed a great measure of independence until 819 when it came under the control of King Louis the Pious of France. Henry II of England took possession of the region on his marriage to ELEANOR OF AQUITAINE. Rebel nobles were subdued by Simon de MONTFORT, but the duchy was lost to the French in the HUNDRED YEARS' WAR. Edward III regained it, and Gascony was recognised as an English possession by a treaty in 1360. The English were finally driven out by the army of Charles VII of France. Royal authority was only fully realised when the House of Armagnac was defeated and Gascony was formally joined to the crown of France by Henry IV in 1607.

Gates, Bill (1955-) Chairman and co-founder of the American computer software giant Microsoft and one of the richest men in the world, with his estimated stake in the company alone worth $13.4 billion in 1995. At the age of 13, Gates became obsessed with computers at school and learned all he could about them in his spare time. He soon graduated to helping a company in his home town of Seattle to find errors in their computer programs. In 1971, while still at school, he enlisted the help of his friend Paul Allen to set up a company called Traf-O-Data to write a program that analysed volumes of traffic. The success of this enterprise encouraged Gates and Allen in 1975 to move to Albuquerque

and form Microsoft. The company grew by providing programs to companies entering the personal computer (PC) market in the late 1970s. In 1980 Gates, who had moved his growing company to Seattle, secured a deal with the computer giant IBM that began Microsoft's domination of the PC industry. Microsoft started to produce applications programs for the growing number of computer users. Convinced that there would be a computer in every home within a decade, Gates placed his company in a strong position to play a major role in the multimedia revolution that began in the early 1990s. Gates has tangled with the US government over his near monopoly of parts of the PC industry.

GATT see GENERAL AGREEMENT ON TARIFFS AND TRADE

gaucho Horseman of the South American pampas, or grasslands, in Argentina, Uruguay and Paraguay. Gauchos, often Indian or of mixed European and American or Black ancestry, hunted the herds of escaped horses and cattle that roamed the pampas. Early in the 19th century they took part in the Spanish South American wars of independence, supporting rival *caudillos*, leaders, in regional power struggles. Gauchos lost much of their free-spirited independence by the late 19th century as landowners fenced off the pampas into huge estates, and many were forced to become farmhands or *peones*, landless peasants.

Gaul Roman name for the lands of the CELTS in Western Europe, approximately the area covered by present-day France and Belgium.

The Gauls invaded northern Italy in the 4th and 3rd centuries BC. In 390 they invaded and plundered the city of Rome, but as Rome's power grew, it began to extend into Gaul. In 222 land south of the Alps was declared the Roman province of Cisalpine Gaul. The RUBICON (believed to be the Fiumicino river) formed part of the frontier with Rome proper. Beyond the Alps the southern coast of modern France and its hinterland was known as Transalpine Gaul, or often 'Provincia' (hence modern PROVENCE), after its annexation in 121.

Julius CAESAR was given command of the Gallic provinces in 59. His successful military campaigns in the GALLIC WARS had extended Transalpine Gaul to the Atlantic, the English Channel and the Rhine. In 52 the tribal leader VERCINGETORIX amassed an army to challenge Roman rule, but by 46 Caesar had successfully suppressed the revolt and captured Vercingetorix. In general, however, there was little in the way of Gallic resistance to Roman

Gauchos wearing traditional *bombachas*, loose trousers gathered at the ankles, leave a calf little room for manoeuvre. Gaucho folklore inspired 19th-century South American writers and poets.

conquest. Augustus divided Gaul north of the Alps into Narbonensian Gaul (centred on Narbonne) – under the authority of the Senate – and Lugdunensian Gaul (Lyons), Aquitania and Belgic Gaul – under his own legates or provincial governors. In the later 3rd century usurper emperors created a semi-independent Gallic empire which served as a buffer against Germanic invasions, but Gaul was increasingly devastated by GOTHS, HUNS and VANDALS until it was finally ceded to the FRANKS in the 5th century. The colonies in the east became independent kingdoms; those in the west evolved into the kingdom of France.

Gallic noblemen wore intricately decorated gold and bronze parade helmets during the 4th century BC.

Gaunt, John of (1340-99)

Duke of Lancaster from 1362. The fourth son of EDWARD III of England, he was born in Ghent, of which his name is a corruption. His father provided him with the vast inheritance of Lancaster by marrying him to the heiress Blanche of Lancaster in 1359. This made him the greatest landowner in England. A second marriage, to Constance, elder daughter of King Pedro the Cruel of Castile, gave him a claim to the throne of Castile and León, which in 1388 he renounced in return for £100000 and an annual pension. From 1390 he was Duke of Aquitaine. Katharine Swynford, his third wife, brought to prominence her family, the BEAUFORTS. Although Gaunt proved loyal to his nephew RICHARD II, his ancestry, power and wealth made Richard wary of him. When John of Gaunt died, Richard II prevented Gaunt's son Henry of Bolingbroke, later HENRY IV, from taking up his inheritance.

Gautama, Siddhartha see BUDDHA

Gaveston, Piers (c.1284-1312)

French-born English noble. He was a Gascon who was brought up in the English royal household as the foster-brother of the future EDWARD II, and Gaveston exploited Edward's infatuation with him. In 1307 Edward made Gaveston Earl of Cornwall and appointed him regent of England. The English barons, indignant at Edward's favouritism towards Gaveston, called for his banishment. Edward was forced to exile him in 1308 and again in 1311, but Gaveston returned and in 1312 was killed by the Earl of Warwick.

General Agreement on Tariffs and Trade (GATT)

International trade agreement established by the United Nations in 1948. By the end of 1994 there were 125 participating countries. GATT aimed to promote trade by removing obstacles and barriers, to set low tariff rates and to agree trading policies. It promoted the postwar expansion of world trade, but the poorer countries felt that it favoured the developed world. This criticism led to the founding of the United Nations Conference on Trade and Development (UNCTAD) in 1964, and to an agreement in 1965 for developing countries to be able to negotatiate more favourable terms with developed countries than they would have to give in return. By the 1980s there were demands for modification of the GATT agreements. In 1986 the 'Uruguay round of talks' attempted to deal with outstanding agricultural issues. The discussions, frequently deadlocked, continued into 1993, as a compromise was sought over EUROPEAN COMMUNITY farm subsidies which the USA opposed. In April 1994, the Final Act of the Uruguay round was signed in Geneva. It established cuts in tariffs and export subsidies and created GATT's successor, the World Trade Organisation (WTO).

General Strike (1926)

National strike by British trade unions, whose failure weakened the power of organised labour for decades. The action was taken in support of the National Union of Mineworkers, whose members were being pressed to accept longer hours and lower wages because of trading difficulties. Owners had locked the miners out of the pits to try to force them to accept the reduced terms. The miners fought back and called for

Volunteers in the General Strike are in the hot seat as they keep London buses on the road, protected by both bobby and barbed wire.

solidarity from the rest of the union movement. The Trades Union Congress responded by calling upon some 2 million workers to strike in key sectors such as the docks, transport, printing, building and electricity and gas supply. The action began on May 4, 1926, and collapsed nine days later because of poor trade union leadership, skilful government propaganda and the use of troops and volunteers to do the strikers' jobs. The miners fought on alone until November, when they returned to work, accepting lower wages. In 1927 a Trade Union Act restricted union privileges.

genetics

Study of heredity and genes. The science of genetics began in 1866 when the Austrian monk Gregor Mendel formulated the basic laws of heredity after experimenting with garden peas. In 1910 the American scientist Thomas Hunt Morgan was able to prove that genes were located on chromosomes and both were inherited together. Oswald T. Avery discovered in 1944 that DNA (deoxyribonucleic acid) was the part of the chromosome that carried the genetic information. Francis Crick, James Watson and Maurice Wilkins discovered the molecular structure of DNA, for which they shared the Nobel prize for medicine and physiology in 1962. Later Crick discovered the 'code' that DNA uses to tell cells how to grow and what forms to take. Genetics is used to prevent and treat hereditary diseases, for breeding plants and animals, and has the potential to create new organisms.

Geneva

Swiss city situated at the southwestern corner of Lake Geneva. First mentioned in the 1st century BC as a settlement of the Celtic Allobroges, it fell to the Romans and later became a bishopric. From the mid 12th century to 1401 the bishops ruled the city and region, then the dukes of Savoy took effective control. In 1535 the citizens, under the leadership of the Protestant theologian John CALVIN, rejected the authority of bishop and duke and accepted the Protestant religion. Geneva became self-governing and a key centre of the REFORMATION. This 'Protestant Rome' became a haven for religious refugees who added to its economic prosperity, and a training ground for HUGUENOT ministers. Annexed by France in 1798, the city joined the Swiss Confederation in 1814.

Geneva Conventions

Series of international agreements on humane treatment for victims of war. The first in 1864 was the direct result of the work of the Swiss Henri Dunant, who also founded the RED CROSS. It laid down rules for the proper treatment of prisoners of war and wounded enemy soldiers, as well as for the protection of medical workers. It was amended and extended in the second convention of 1906, which required that all modern facilities for treating the sick and wounded must be available. The First World War led to a third convention in 1929, in which the USA and 46 other nations banned the military use of poison gas and agreed on rules about the treatment and rights of prisoners of war. A fourth convention in 1949 extended protection for the sick and wounded, for shipwrecked sailors, for prisoners of war and for civilians in areas occupied by an enemy. Protocols were added in 1977 to cover guerrillas captured while fighting wars of liberation.

Genghis Khan see feature, page 256

Genoa

Port on the coast of north-west Italy, for four centuries an independent republic and major seafaring and trading power. It was captured by the Romans in the 3rd century BC. Genoa fell to the Lombards in AD634, and was repeatedly sacked by the SARACENS. It recovered its fortunes by the 10th century and entered its heyday as an independent republic. Its influence and colonisation spread to Sicily, Spain, North Africa and the Crimea. Unpopular rulers were ousted in a coup in 1257 and the office of DOGE, or ducal ruler, was created in 1339. Rivalry gave rise to intermittent warfare with neighbouring city states. Pisa was defeated in 1284, and in 1380 the Genoese nearly captured Venice. The city also contributed many mercenaries, particularly crossbowmen, to foreign armies. The advance of the Venetian and OTTOMAN empires weakened Genoa, and after the 15th century its importance diminished.

Genscher, Hans-Dietrich (1927-)

German politician, who was vice-chancellor of the Federal Republic and foreign minister from 1974 to 1992. In 1982, as leader of the Free Democratic Party, Genscher brought down the Social Democratic government of Helmut SCHMIDT by switching his party's support to the Christian Democratic Union. Genscher remained foreign minister in the new coalition with the Christian Democrats, and championed *ostpolitik*, the policy of improving links with the communist East German Democratic Republic. This culminated in German reunification in 1990. After retiring from office in 1992 Genscher continued as a member of the German parliament.

George I (1660-1727)

King of Great Britain and Ireland from 1714 to 1727, and Elector of Hanover from 1692. His mother Sophia was a granddaughter of JAMES I, and her children were recognised as heirs to the throne of England by the Act of SETTLEMENT of 1701, which excluded the Roman Catholic Stuarts. In 1714, George succeeded Queen Anne and a year later the JACOBITE rebellion, an attempt to restore the Stuart dynasty, helped to unite the country behind him. He disliked the way the British political system required the king to share power with Parliament and his ministers, and spent all the time he could in Hanover. But his unswerving support for Sir Robert WALPOLE from 1721 helped to establish the Whig Party's supremacy. Cruel to his wife Sophia Dorothea, he divorced her in 1694 for alleged adultery and imprisoned her in a castle near Hanover until she died 32 years later.

George II (1683-1760)

King of Great Britain and Ireland, and Elector of Hanover from 1727. He resented his father, GEORGE I, for treating his mother Sophia Dorothea cruelly.

George II was the last English king to lead his troops in battle, at Dettingen in 1743, during the War of the Austrian Succession.

George's own marriage to Princess CAROLINE OF ANSBACH was happy, and through her influence he learned to accept Sir Robert WALPOLE as his prime minister. He had a fiery temper and was intolerant in his dealings with others – he insisted on the execution of Admiral BYNG in 1757 – and he was always on bad terms with his son, Prince Frederick Louis. He disliked William PITT the Elder but eventually accepted him as prime minister in 1757. This paved the way for Pitt to mastermind many British successes in the SEVEN YEARS' WAR against France.

George III (1738-1820)

King of Great Britain and Ireland, and Elector of Hanover from 1760. He is believed to have suffered from porphyria, a disease which causes mental disturbances. This flared up briefly in 1765, and plans were made for a regency council. For several months in 1788-9 his illness was so severe as to raise again the prospect of a regency. George III was the first Hanoverian ruler to be born in Britain. The son of Frederick Louis, he succeeded the throne on the death of his grandfather George II. He was a devoted family man and a keen patron of the arts. George was against making major concessions to the demands of the American colonists and was deeply affronted when they won their independence. He came to rely increasingly on William PITT the Younger, but in 1801 the king refused to contemplate

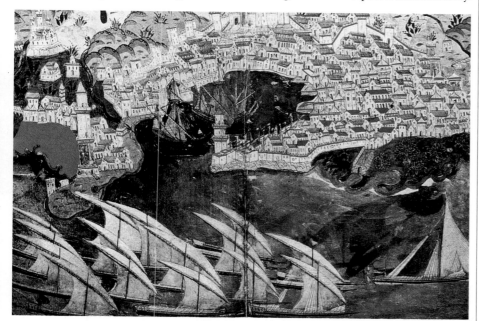

The Ottoman fleet sails past Genoa in this Turkish miniature, illustrating how the city's role in the Mediterranean had been eclipsed by the rise of Ottoman naval power by the mid 16th century.

Conqueror of Asia

Genghis Khan, creator of the vast Mongol empire, was a far-sighted administrator who instituted a stable political system.

The largest continuous land empire in the history of the world was the 13th-century Mongol empire founded by Genghis Khan (1167-1227). Originally named Temujin, Genghis was a member of a princely family of a nomadic Mongol tribe which lived by hunting and herding in the present-day Republic of Mongolia. His father was killed when he was young, and the child grew up to be a bandit with a reputation for ruthlessness.

Building up his position by allying with powerful tribal leaders, and then betraying them, Genghis came to dominate the steppe grasslands of Mongolia. In 1206 an assembly of princes and nobles acknowledged his supremacy and he took the title Genghis Khan, 'universal ruler'.

CHINA SUBMITS TO KHAN

After decades of internal strife, the Mongols, finally united, turned their attention to external enemies. Their first target was China, the nearest and richest source of plunder. The country was divided into three states: Hsi-Hsia, Chin, and Sung. Hsi-Hsia was the weakest and quickly submitted (1207-10), but Chin resisted until seven years after Genghis Khan's death, finally falling under Kublai

Genghis Khan sits enthroned, with his sons close by. While still a boy, Genghis had murdered his half-brother, a potential rival.

Khan, Genghis's grandson, in 1234.

In 1218 Jebei, one of Genghis's finest generals, seized control of the central Asian kingdom of Qara-Khitai, which extended from Lake Balkhash in Kazakhstan to Tibet. The shah of the neighbouring Islamic kingdom of Khwarazm deliberately provoked war by

plundering a Mongol trading caravan and murdering the merchants and an ambassador. Genghis retaliated by invading Khwarazmian territory in 1219. An appallingly destructive four-year campaign followed in which many hundreds of thousands were massacred, and the great Islamic cities of Bukhara, Balkh, Samarkand and Herat destroyed. Citizens who surrendered were spared, but those who resisted were exterminated. Genghis turned home in 1223 to fight his last campaign against Hsi-Hsia, at the end of which he died.

ELITE MILITARY FORCE

Though not a great innovator, Genghis Khan achieved astonishing military successes. His formidably large Mongol army, mainly mounted cavalry, was organised in multiples of ten, the trusted commanders hand-picked by Genghis himself. Military service, for which all adult males were liable, was a normal part of the nomadic Mongol way of life, so a large proportion of the population could be mobilised at any time with ease. This, coupled with the Mongols' remarkable manoeuvrability, probably account for what appeared to be the vast size of the Mongol army. But Genghis Khan was not merely a soldier notorious for destruction and massacre. He was also a constructive statesman who laid the institutional foundations for a lasting empire that continued to expand for half a century after his death. He was buried in the mountains of northern Mongolia.

CATHOLIC EMANCIPATION, and Pitt resigned. From 1811 the king's insanity brought about the regency of the profligate Prince of Wales, which lasted until he succeeded as George IV.

George IV (1762-1830) King of Great Britain and Ireland and Hanover from 1820 to 1830. His dissolute life as prince regent from 1811 to 1820, and later as king, caused a decline in the prestige of the monarchy. In 1785 he secretly married a Roman Catholic widow, Maria Fitzherbert. The marriage was declared invalid, and ten years later he reluctantly married Caroline of Brunswick, separating from her after the birth of their only child, Princess Charlotte. As regent he gave his support to the Tories, but soon quarrelled with them, leaving himself without a significant following in Parliament. His reign saw the passage of the CATHOLIC EMANCIPATION ACT in 1829. His attempt to divorce Caroline for adultery in 1820 only increased his unpopularity. His time as prince regent came to be known as the REGENCY period.

George V (1865-1936) King of Great Britain and Ireland (from 1920, Northern Ireland) and Emperor of India, from 1910 to 1936. The major event of his reign, the First World War, caused George to change the family name from the German Saxe-Coburg-Gotha to Windsor. He convened the Buckingham Palace Conference in 1914 to discuss Irish HOME RULE. He was active in politics, and chose Stanley BALDWIN to be prime minister in 1923 and then Ramsay MACDONALD to lead a coalition government in 1931.

George VI (1895-1952) King of Great Britain and Northern Ireland from 1936 to 1952, Emperor of India until 1947. He and Queen Elizabeth played an important role in sustaining public morale during the wartime German bombing of British cities. George succeeded his brother, EDWARD VIII, after the ABDICATION CRISIS. He strongly supported Churchill during the Second World War, as he did Clement ATTLEE's Labour government over the granting of independence to India.

After the battle for the Georgian parliament house in January 1992, President Gamsakhurdia fled the capital, but civil disorder remained rife.

Georgia Caucasian republic on the east coast of the Black Sea. Between the 14th and 19th centuries the region suffered from repeated onslaughts – by the Mongol leader TAMERLANE, the Ottoman Turks, and Persians. From 1821 to 1829 Russian invasions brought the different kingdoms in the area firmly under tsarist control. A strong Social Democrat Party of MENSHEVIKS briefly formed a republic in 1918. In 1921 Georgia was part of the Transcaucasian Soviet Federal Socialist Republic together with Azerbaijan and Armenia, but in 1936 it became a full member of the Soviet Union in its own right. Large-scale anticommunist uprisings were suppressed in 1924 and 1956, as were anti-government riots in 1989.

In April 1991 Georgia gained independence under Zviad Gamsakhurdia, but he was deposed in January 1992 for 'dictatorial methods'. The former Soviet foreign minister Eduard Shevardnadze became president the following September, but forces loyal to Gamsakhurdia attempted to recover control until they were routed in November 1993. Other armed conflicts beset the country, notably in South Ossetia, and the frontier region of Abkhazia. In December 1993 the republic joined the Commonwealth of Independent States, and in February 1994 Georgia signed a ten-year treaty of friendship and cooperation with Russia. Shevardnadze was re-elected president in 1995.

Georgia

State of the USA on the southern Atlantic coast, founded as a colony in 1732 with English parliamentary support as a bulwark against the Spanish in Florida and as a place for English debtors to start a new life. The trustees under James OGLETHORPE, who founded the colony, established tightly controlled settlements at Savannah in 1733 and elsewhere. At the outset, slavery and rum were prohibited, and silk and wine production encouraged. But from the 1750s this regime was relaxed and, with immigration from Europe and other colonies, Georgia slowly began to prosper. After the invention in 1793 of the cotton gin, a machine that separates the fibre from cotton seeds, Georgia began to profit from its large crop of cotton, mostly picked by Black slaves. By the 1840s a major textile industry had been established.

In 1861 Georgia joined the Confederate side in the AMERICAN CIVIL WAR. Three years later General William Sherman decided to take the war to the heart of the Confederacy, set fire to Atlanta and marched through Georgia to the sea causing heavy destruction. The state remained under military rule until 1870 when it was readmitted to the Union. Following the First World War Georgia was badly hit when the cotton crop failed. After the DEPRESSION there was an upsurge in racial conflict. In 1946 Black Georgians were allowed to vote in a Democratic primary election only after a ruling by the US Supreme Court.

German Confederation

(1815-66) The alliance of German sovereign states whose constitution formed the model for the united GERMAN SECOND EMPIRE forged by Otto von

BISMARCK in 1871. At the Congress of VIENNA in 1815 the 38 German states formed a loose grouping to protect themselves against French ambitions. Austria and Prussia lay partly within and partly outside the confederation. The Austrian chancellor Prince Lothar METTERNICH devised the confederation and exercised a dominant influence in it through the Federal Diet at Frankfurt, whose members were delegates of state governments. As the rival power to Austria in Germany, Prussia attempted to increase its influence

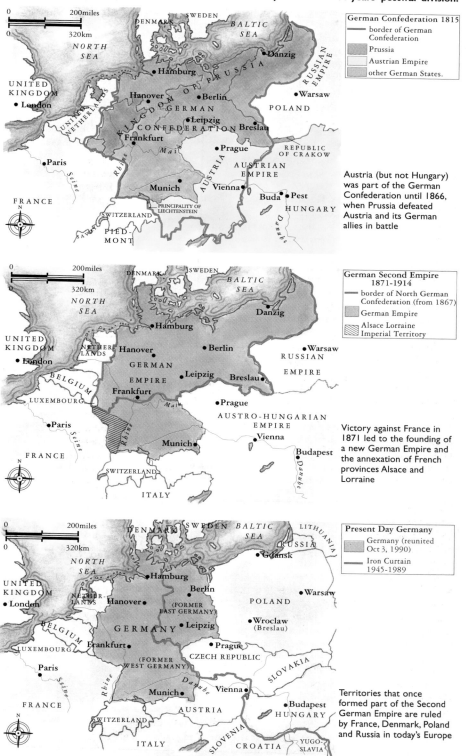

Modern Germany takes shape: in 1815, the German Confederation allies smaller states; Otto von Bismarck's Second Empire forms in 1871; in 1995 Germany unites after 50 years' postwar division.

German Confederation 1815
— border of German Confederation
Prussia
Austrian Empire
other German States.

Austria (but not Hungary) was part of the German Confederation until 1866, when Prussia defeated Austria and its German allies in battle

German Second Empire 1871-1914
— border of North German Confederation (from 1867)
German Empire
Alsace Lorraine Imperial Territory

Victory against France in 1871 led to the founding of a new German Empire and the annexation of French provinces Alsace and Lorraine

Present Day Germany
Germany (reunited Oct 3, 1990)
— Iron Curtain 1945-1989

Territories that once formed part of the Second German Empire are ruled by France, Denmark, Poland and Russia in today's Europe

over other states by founding a ZOLLVEREIN, or federal customs union. In the REVOLUTIONS OF 1848 a new constituent assembly was elected at Frankfurt, and tried to establish a constitutional German monarchy. But the Austrian emperor refused the crown for fear it would weaken his authority in Hungary, while the Prussian king, Frederick William IV, refused it because the constitution was too liberal. The pre-1848 confederation was restored, with Bismarck as one of Prussia's delegates. In 1866 Bismarck proposed to reorganise the German Confederation and exclude Austria. When Austria opposed this measure Bismarck dissolved the confederation and opened hostilities against Austria in the AUSTRO-PRUSSIAN WAR. After Prussia's victory, in 1867 the 21 governments above the River Main combined together into the North German Confederation (Norddeutscher Bund), with its capital in Berlin. In 1871 the GERMAN SECOND EMPIRE was established.

German Democratic Republic (East Germany)

Former Eastern European country which emerged in 1949 from the Soviet occupied zone in postwar Germany. Its capital was East Berlin, but the existence of West Berlin, part of the German Federal Republic (West Germany) although deep inside GDR territory, caused serious problems (see BERLIN AIRLIFT and BERLIN WALL).

In the first five years the republic had to pay heavy reparations for war damage to the Soviet Union, and Soviet troops were used to put down disorder. In 1954 the republic proclaimed itself a sovereign state, and the following year it became a founder-member of the WARSAW PACT, a military alliance of the Soviet-controlled Eastern European countries. In 1972 the German Federal Republic, as part of its policy of OSTPOLITIK, established diplomatic relations with the republic. Admission to the United Nations followed in 1973, after which the republic won diplomatic recognition worldwide.

Economic recovery from the Second World War was slower than in West Germany, but East Germany succeeded in establishing a strong industrial base. This began to weaken when its highly bureaucratic, centralised system of control steadily decayed, corruption spread from the top, and its secret police, the Stasi, became ever more ruthless.

During 1989 a series of huge demonstrations took place, mostly in Berlin and Leipzig, with a reform group, New Forum, demanding political democracy. In November 1989 the authorities opened the Berlin Wall and the Socialist Unity Party (communist) surrendered its monopoly of power. The first free elections were held in March 1990, and on October 3, 1990, the republic was absorbed into the Federal Republic of Germany. The united country was placed under the heavy

financial strain of bringing the eastern economy up to date. A number of trials opened in 1992 involving East German politicians, including Erich HONECKER, the former head of state. Extra measures were taken in 1993 to fund the restructuring of the eastern German economy, notably the imposition of a 7.5 per cent 'solidarity surcharge' on income tax and cuts in social welfare spending and unemployment benefits.

German Federal Republic

Country in north-west Europe created in 1949 from the British, French and US zones of occupation after the Second World War, and since 1990 embracing the former Soviet-dominated GERMAN DEMOCRATIC REPUBLIC in eastern Germany. The federal republic became a sovereign state in 1955, when ambassadors were exchanged with world powers. As chancellor between 1949 and 1963, Konrad ADENAUER was determined to see eventual reunification of Germany and refused to recognise the legal existence of East Germany. As the COLD WAR intensified the Soviet Union demanded the withdrawal of Western troops from the Allied areas of the city and in 1961 authorised the building of the BERLIN WALL to separate the East from the rest.

Tensions over Berlin began to ease in 1971, during the chancellorship of the socialist Willy BRANDT with his policy of OSTPOLITIK, the opening of relations with the Eastern Bloc. This led to treaties with the Soviet Union, Poland and Czechoslovakia and one of mutual recognition and cooperation with the German Democratic Republic. Membership of the United Nations was obtained in 1973.

Economic recovery was assisted after the Second World War by the Marshall Plan. Shattered cities were rebuilt, many millions of refugees from Eastern Europe were absorbed and systems of social welfare and health provision were re-created. The Federal Republic joined NATO in 1955, and in 1957 it signed the Treaty of Rome, becoming one of the founder-members of the European Economic Community. The pace of economic growth slackened, but the economy remained one of the strongest in the world, under a stable democratic regime.

Following economic and monetary union with the German Democratic Republic in June 1990, a Treaty of Unification was signed in August and unification took place in October. Chancellor Helmut Kohl's Christian Democratic Union won control of four out of the five new *Länder* (states) in former East Germany; but their economic problems were so serious that unemployment rose to 17 per cent and disillusionment with the political achievement of reunification set in. Germany's liberal policies on asylum resulted in a large influx of immigrants, both legal and illegal, with accompanying social problems

including a degree of neo-Nazi resurgence. In May 1994 Roman Herzog was elected president and in October Kohl's federal coalition, in office since 1982, was re-elected with a greatly reduced majority. By early 1996 unemployment had risen to a postwar high of more than 4 million, 10.8 per cent of united Germany's workforce.

German Second Empire (1871–1918)

Period between the end of the GERMAN CONFEDERATION and the WEIMAR REPUBLIC when Germany rose to become a first-rate industrial and colonial power. The Second German Empire, or Reich (the first was the Holy Roman Empire) was the union of 25 German states created by Chancellor Otto von BISMARCK. The Prussian king became the first emperor, or kaiser, WILHELM I. The growth of German industry between 1870 and 1910 made Germany the greatest industrial power in Europe, and the search for new markets led to tension with other powers, but at first Bismarck's authoritarian ministry gained him fewer friends at home than abroad. He won important allies for Germany in the TRIPLE ALLIANCE between Germany, Austria and

> 66 **Place in the hands of the king of Prussia the strongest possible military power; then he will be able to carry out the policy you wish; this policy ... can only be carried out through blood and iron.** 99
>
> *Otto von Bismarck to the Prussian House of Deputies, January 1886*

Italy, and in the THREE EMPERORS' LEAGUE between Germany, Austria and Russia. After Kaiser WILHELM II forced Bismarck to retire in 1890 he let the alliance with Russia lapse in favour of Austria, and turned to Admiral Alfred von TIRPITZ to launch a naval arms race with Britain. He also plunged into colonial adventures which antagonised both Britain and France and led to the ENTENTE CORDIALE between the two countries. In 1914, Germany declared war on Russia and France in support of its Austrian ally's dispute with Russia over Serbia. By 1918, Germany had lost its overseas colonies, and the German people, long deprived of democratic reforms and starved of food during wartime shortages, rose in revolt against their leaders. William went into exile, and the weimar REPUBLIC was proclaimed by the Social Democrats.

Germany

Country in central Europe. It was occupied by Teutonic tribes who were driven back across the Rhine by Julius Caesar in 58 BC during the GALLIC WARS. When the Roman Empire collapsed, eight Germanic kingdoms were created, and in the 8th century CHARLEMAGNE consolidated these under

In 1933, their first year of operation, the Gestapo began arresting Jews. Two Gestapo agents, here supervised by an SS officer, inspect the papers of Jews about to be taken into custody in Berlin.

the FRANKS and imposed Christianity. The region became part of the HOLY ROMAN EMPIRE in 962, and Emperor Otto I began colonising the lands east of the Elbe. The Germanic princes gradually regained their power in the 11th and 12th centuries. Imperial power was replaced in 1438 when the long rule of the HABSBURGS began.

In 1521 the Emperor Charles V confronted the Protestant leader Martin Luther at the Diet of Worms: as the REFORMATION spread, it increased the fragmentation of Germany. The region, now made up of hundreds of states, was finally torn apart during the THIRTY YEARS' WAR. When the war ended in 1648, Brandenburg-Prussia emerged as a force ready to challenge Austrian supremacy.

By the end of the NAPOLEONIC WARS the states had been reduced to 39. At the Congress of Vienna in 1815 these states were formed into a loose grouping, with new lands, in the GERMAN CONFEDERATION, under Austrian leadership. Demands for national unity led to demonstrations and uprisings and calls for a national parliament as part of the REVOLUTIONS OF 1848 which swept through Europe. The Confederation was dissolved as a result of the AUSTRO-PRUSSIAN WAR, and in 1867 all northern Germany formed a new North German Confederation under the leadership of Prussia. This in turn was dissolved in 1871 after victory in wars with Austria and France, and the new GERMAN SECOND EMPIRE was proclaimed with William I of Prussia as emperor.

After Germany's defeat in the First World War, a revolution overthrew the monarchy and the WEIMAR REPUBLIC was set up. But the crippling effects of war reparations and the world economic DEPRESSION helped Adolf HITLER to become chancellor and found the THIRD REICH in 1933. Germany followed a policy of rearmament and Hitler triggered the Second World War in 1939 by invading Poland. Upon defeat in 1945, the country was divided into the GERMAN FEDERAL REPUBLIC (West Germany) and the GERMAN DEMOCRATIC REPUBLIC (East Germany), which were reunited in 1990 after the collapse of communism in the east.

Gestapo Nazi secret police, an abbreviation of Geheime Staatspolizei (German: 'secret state police'). In 1933 Hermann GOERING reconstituted the Prussian plain-clothes political police as the Gestapo. In 1936 control of the force passed to Heinrich HIMMLER, who had restructured police forces in other German states and headed the SS (Schutzstaffel: 'protective squads'), the elite police corps of the Nazi Party. The Gestapo was effectively absorbed into the SS and in 1939 was merged with the SD (Sicherheitsdienst: 'Security Service'), the intelligence branch of the SS, in a Reich Security Central Office under Reinhard HEYDRICH.

The turning point in the Battle of Gettysburg, and in Southern fortunes, came on the third day when a Confederate charge failed to break Union lines on Cemetery Ridge.

The SS and the Gestapo controlled Nazi CONCENTRATION CAMPS and instituted a reign of terror in every occupied country, killing suspected troublemakers and 'undesirables,' as well as large numbers of civilians in retaliation for partisan attacks on occupying forces.

Gettysburg, Battle of (July 1-3, 1863) Turning point in the AMERICAN CIVIL WAR, and the bloodiest battle fought on American soil. On July 1, elements of the Confederate Army of Northern Virginia under General Robert E. LEE and the Union Army of the Potomac under General George Meade came into contact west of Gettysburg, Pennsylvania. Early Confederate attacks were fought off, but the arrival of reinforcements forced the Union troops to retreat through the town. The following day fresh Union soldiers in strong defensive positions on Cemetery Ridge repelled Confederate attacks. On the third day, a charge against the centre of the Union line was repulsed, with heavy losses, and Lee was forced to abandon his invasion of the North. The Southern forces suffered 28 000 casualties from a force of 75 000, while the Northern casualties totalled 23 000 from among 83 000 troops. On November 19, 1863, at the dedication of the Gettysburg National Cemetery, President Abraham Lincoln reaffirmed the principles of freedom, equality and democracy in his 'Gettysburg Address,' considered a masterpiece of oratory.

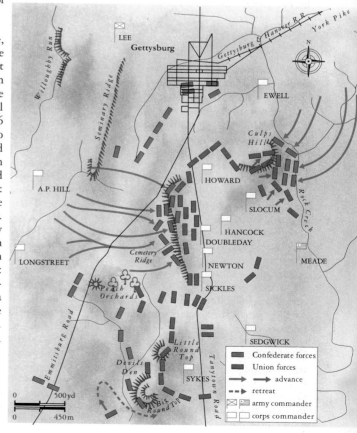

Ghana The ancient kingdom of Ghana included the area now known as east Senegal, south-west Mali and southern Mauritania, as well as present-day Ghana. As early as AD 800 Ghana was called 'the Land of Gold'.

In 990 the king of Ghana took the BERBER kingdom of Audaghost, and so gained control of the gold and salt caravan trade. The country fell to the Algerian Almoravids in 1054, to another tribe in 1203 and to the Mali empire in 1240.

In 1800 there were British and Danish trading forts along the so-called Gold Coast and the British Colonial Office bought out the Danes in 1850. After wars with the Ashanti in 1824 and 1874, the British established the colony of the Gold Coast to exploit deposits of gold inland. Further wars against the Ashanti followed in 1896 and 1900. After 1920 economic growth based on mining and the cocoa industry, combined with high standards of mission schooling, produced a sophisticated people who demanded home rule.

The west African territories of the Gold Coast and British Togoland were combined in 1957 to form the independent Republic of

Ghana, led by Kwame NKRUMAH. He transformed the country into a one-party state. Economic problems and resentment over political repression and mismanagement led to his overthrow by the army in 1966. After a succession of coups, a group of junior officers under Flight-Lieutenant Jerry Rawlings took power in 1979, executed three former heads of state and installed a civilian government.

When this government failed, Rawlings again seized power in December 1981. Some economic and political stability was regained with the help of the International Monetary Fund, but Western aid donors added to pressure from internal groups to restore democracy. A new constitution legalised political parties in April 1992, and in November that year Rawlings was victorious in multiparty presidential elections, but opposition parties contested the result.

Ghent, Pacification of (1576) Alliance forged during the revolt of the NETHERLANDS, the struggle by the Low Countries for independence from Spain. Revolt had broken out in 1567 against a Spanish reign of terror and high taxation. Spanish countermeasures

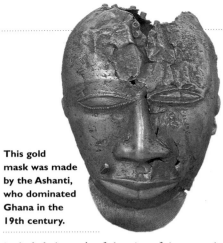

This gold mask was made by the Ashanti, who dominated Ghana in the 19th century.

included the sack of the city of Antwerp in 1576. This precipitated an alliance between the Catholics and the Protestants (Calvinists) against the common enemy. They called for the removal of imperial troops and an end to religious persecution. The pact lasted three years until Calvinist excesses provoked the Catholic southern provinces into making a separate peace with the Spanish.

Ghent, Treaty of (1814) Treaty negotiated in the city of Ghent, in Flanders, which ended the WAR OF 1812 between Britain and the USA. The treaty failed to tackle differences over British trade restrictions and opposition to US westward expansion which had caused the war, but it did free all prisoners, restore all conquered territory and appoint a commission to settle boundary disputes between the US and Canada. Other issues, such as fishing rights, were left for future settlement.

Gibbon, Edward (1737-94) British historian, author of *The History of the Decline and Fall of the Roman Empire*, which was published in six volumes between 1776 and 1788. Gibbon travelled widely, and was inspired to write his history after a visit to Rome in 1764. The book was attacked for suggesting that Christianity played a significant role in the decline of Rome. Gibbon's work, although its conclusions have been modified by later research, is still regarded as a masterpiece of historical writing.

Gibraltar Coastal town and rocky headland of southern Spain, which dominates the sea passage from the Mediterranean Sea to the Atlantic Ocean. It was captured by the Moors in 711 and their leader, who fortified it, gave it its name, Jabal al-Tariq (Mount of Tariq). It became Spanish in 1462 but in 1704, during the War of the SPANISH SUCCESSION, the fortress surrendered to Britain, which kept it at the Treaty of UTRECHT.

Spain repeatedly attempted to recapture it, notably in 1779 during a long siege by powerful Franco-Spanish forces. Gibraltar was an important naval base during the two world wars and remains a British dependency with

the support of its inhabitants. From 1969 to 1985 the border with Spain was closed by the Spanish in order to support their claim to Gibraltar, a claim which they maintain to the present day.

Gilbert, Sir Humphrey (c.1539-83) English navigator and daring early pioneer of English overseas colonies. In 1566 Gilbert wrote a *Discourse* proposing a voyage to discover a north-west passage to China, but the idea was turned down. In 1583, with the help of his half-brother Sir Walter RALEIGH, he set off with five ships for NEWFOUNDLAND where he established the first English colony in North America. On the return voyage, Gilbert's ship went down with all hands in a fierce storm off the Azores.

Giolitti, Giovanni (1842-1928) Italian statesman who was elected prime minister five times. Giolitti was a skilled conciliator and liberal, who introduced the vote for all men over 30 years old and did not oppose the growth of trade unionism. He agreed to the conquest of Libya but argued against Italy's entry into the First World War. In 1914 he was ousted from his post by a general strike. Giolitti was re-elected as prime minister in 1920 but resigned a year later as Benito MUSSOLINI's fascists prepared to seize power.

Girondins Moderate political grouping in the French Revolution, closely associated with, but less radical than, the JACOBINS. It took its name from the Gironde region, home of its leading figures. Jacques Brissot, Étienne Clavière and Jean-Marie Roland quickly gained key positions in the Convention, the republican assembly that governed France from September 1792. They were responsible for provoking a series of wars with France's enemies. The eventual failure of these wars led

Moderately republican, the Girondins failed to meet the economic demands of Parisian workers and were ousted by the mob. Here, 21 deputies await the guillotine in October 1793.

William Gladstone's Irish Home Rule bill of 1886 gave him a bumpy ride: it was kicked out of the Commons and he resigned office soon after.

to the downfall of the party. A mob expelled them from the Convention in June 1793 and the Reign of TERROR ensued. Later, more than 20 of their ministers were guillotined.

gladiator In ancient Rome, a prisoner or slave trained to fight other gladiators, wild beasts or condemned criminals for the entertainment of the people. The word 'gladiator' means, literally, a swordsman. Categories of gladiator included the Samnite, heavily armed with oblong shield, visored helmet and short sword; the Retiarus, fighting with net and trident; and the Thracian, bearing a round shield and curved scimitar. Thumbs up or down from the crowd spelt life or death for the loser. Women and even the physically handicapped fought at times. The Christian emperors CONSTANTINE and THEODOSIUS banned the combats, despite public opposition.

Gladstone, William Ewart (1809-98) British political figure in the Victorian era who was four times prime minister. Gladstone entered Parliament as a Tory in 1832. He was a firm supporter of FREE TRADE and had to resign, together with the prime minister Sir Robert PEEL, after the repeal of the CORN LAWS in 1846. Gladstone's views were much shaped by his admiration for Peel's economic liberalism. He served as chancellor of the exchequer from 1852 to 1855 and again from 1859 to 1866, and introduced a series of budgets which cut tariffs and restricted government spending. Gladstone was chosen as leader of the Liberal Party in 1867 and took

office as prime minister in 1868. His first administration passed notable measures, including the disestablishment of the Church of Ireland, a secret ballot at elections, reforms in the legal position of trade unions, in the legal system and in education. Gladstone claimed to have liberated the people from unjust laws and paved the way for their personal advancement. He also arranged the settlement of disputes with the USA through international arbitration.

He was defeated by Benjamin DISRAELI in 1874, but became prime minister once more in 1880 after the MIDLOTHIAN CAMPAIGN, and secured the passage of the third REFORM ACT in 1884. However, he incurred much unpopularity, and in June 1885 resigned after the fall of Khartoum (see GORDON, CHARLES).

Back in office the following year, Gladstone introduced a bill to give Ireland HOME RULE. This policy split the Liberal Party and his government was defeated. However, he became prime minister again in 1892, and made a further attempt with a new Home Rule bill in 1893, but it was rejected by the House of Lords. In 1894 Gladstone resigned for the last time. His liberalism included measures to reform laws, to curb public spending and to help to promote trade.

glass Prehistoric peoples made small objects from rock crystal, a colourless quartz, or from volcanic obsidian. Glass-making was well established in Egypt before 2000 BC, and many different types of glass were produced by the Romans, including drinking goblets, mirrors, prisms and window panes. Little is known of glass-making between the fall of the Rome Empire in the 6th century and the invention of stained glass in the 10th century. France became supreme in the production of plate glass after a casting process was invented around 1680. England specialised in flint glass which was suitable to be made into fine

cut glass. Mass-produced glass was first made by the American Boston and Sandwich Glass Company after the invention of a glass pressing machine in 1827. Modern glass includes glass fibre, which is pulled into continuous strands and used for insulation; and safety glass which does not shatter into dangerous fragments when broken.

glebe Land belonging to a parish church in medieval England and used to support its priest. The size of glebes varied enormously from 2½ acres (1 ha) to several hundred acres. Some priests were wealthy enough to hire labourers but others had to work the land themselves. Many parishes had to levy additional taxes to support their priests.

Glencoe massacre Cold-blooded murder of members of the MacDonald CLAN, named after the Scottish glen in which the incident took place in February 1692. The clan was technically guilty of treason for failing to swear allegiance to WILLIAM III by January 1, 1692. Bad weather added to the clan chief's deliberate delay and he took the oath six days late. The Campbells, hereditary enemies of the MacDonalds, led troops to the glen where, after enjoying MacDonald hospitality for 12 days, they butchered the chief and 38 of his clan; about 300 escaped. William did little to punish the killers.

Glendower, Owen see GLYNDWR, OWAIN

Glorious Revolution Bloodless English revolution of 1688-9 which replaced JAMES II with WILLIAM III and Mary, and established a constitutional form of government.

After his accession in 1685 James II defied the law and appointed Roman Catholics to important positions in the army, the Church, the universities and government. Claiming the royal right to suspend laws as he pleased,

Survivors of the Glencoe massacre escaped death because troops under Archibald Campbell disobeyed orders and used guns instead of swords. Their shots awoke clansmen in time to flee.

Goa's daily market in the main square was a magnet for both Portuguese and Indians, according to this 17th-century print. Water vendors shoulder a large urn slung from a pole, a nursemaid holds a child and talks to a slave girl and, near the centre, an auctioneer takes bids for a cloak.

James cancelled the effects of penal laws against Roman Catholics and dissenters in two Declarations of Indulgence. Seven bishops were tried for stating that the second declaration was illegal, but they were found not guilty of seditious libel. The birth of a son to James in 1688 appeared to ensure the Roman Catholic succession and provoked leading politicians to invite the king's Protestant son-in-law William of Orange to England. William landed with a Dutch army at Torbay, Devon, in November. James's army refused to obey its Catholic officers, his daughters deserted him and he was allowed to escape abroad. Parliament invited William and Mary to take over the vacant throne.

A revival of arbitrary government was made impossible by the BILL OF RIGHTS of 1689, which offered the crown to the new monarchs but limited their powers. James II landed in Ireland with French troops in March 1690 and besieged LONDONDERRY. He was defeated at the Battle of the BOYNE in July and returned to exile in France. The Act of SETTLEMENT of 1701 was passed in order to ensure that future British monarchs were Protestant.

Gloucester, Humphrey, Duke of (1391-1447)
Youngest son of HENRY IV. From 1422 he was guardian of his infant nephew HENRY VI, but his claim to be Regent of England was rejected by the House of Lords. He was popular with the House of Commons and the people of London, and came eventually to be seen by Henry VI as a threat. In 1441 his wife, Eleanor of Cobham, was imprisoned on a charge of treason and heresy. His own death six years later, after he himself had been arrested for treason, was believed to have been murder.

Glyndwr, Owain (c.1354-c.1416)
Welsh national hero who led the last revolt against English rule. In September 1400 Glyndwr

was proclaimed Prince of Wales by a band of rebels who wanted to free the country, most of which had been annexed by England in the 13th century. Glyndwr set up an independent Welsh parliament and led a revolt against the LANCASTRIAN English rulers of north Wales. Harlech and Aberystwyth were captured in 1404, and Welsh parliaments were held that year and in 1405. But the English under HENRY IV recaptured the towns and the rebellion was over by 1408. Glyndwr spent the rest of his life as a fugitive.

Goa
District on the west coast of India. The Portuguese captured the settlement in 1510, and expanded it to form a base for South-east Asian trade until it became the administrative centre of Portugal's Asian empire. When Portuguese power declined elsewhere in Asia, Goa remained an enclave of European influence. The region was taken from the Portuguese by India in 1961 and, together with two other former Portuguese west-coast territories, Daman and the island of Diu, it was absorbed into India in 1962. It became an Indian state in May 1987 with three elected members of parliament.

Gobineau, Joseph, Comte de (1816-82)
French diplomat and scholar, the intellectual founder of 'racism'. His most famous book, *Essay on the Inequality of Human Races*, written between 1853 and 1855, argued that races are unequal and that the White Aryan race is the purest and superior to all others. The NAZIS used Gobineau to justify ANTISEMITISM.

Godolphin, Sidney, 1st Earl of (1645-1712)
English statesman who gave loyal service to Charles II, James II and Queen Anne. Godolphin was Queen Anne's Lord Treasurer for most of her reign and secured the Act of UNION with Scotland in 1707. He maintained

close links with the Jacobites when he served William III, until he quarrelled with his colleagues in 1696. Godolphin's fortunes were linked with the Duke of MARLBOROUGH's – he financed the duke's campaigns in the War of the SPANISH SUCCESSION – so when Marlborough lost favour and the Tories regained influence in 1710 his career ended.

Godunov, Boris (c.1551-1605)
Russian tsar. Born into a noble family, Godunov began his career of court service under IVAN IV 'the Terrible'. Appointed guardian of Ivan's feeble-minded son Fyodor, Godunov gradually took control of Russia after Fyodor ascended the throne in 1584. On the tsar's death in 1598, Godunov was elected to succeed him, but never secured the support of all the BOYARS, or nobles, many of whom regarded him as a usurper.

Godunov reformed the judicial system but also pursued his opponents ruthlessly and thereby increased the hostility of the boyars. In 1604 a pretender, claiming to be Fyodor's half-brother, gathered a large army against Godunov, whose own forces held out until his sudden death the following year. There ensued years of chaos known as the 'Time of Troubles', which ended with the crowning of the first ROMANOV tsar in 1613.

Godwin (d.1053)
Earl of the English kingdom of Wessex, who used his influence to help to secure the accession of HAROLD I in 1035 and EDWARD THE CONFESSOR in 1042. When his daughter Edith married Edward in 1045, Godwin's dominance in English politics seemed assured. But Edward preferred to rely on Norman advisers, and when Godwin rebelled in 1051 he exiled him with his son Harold. They invaded England in 1052 and Edward was forced to reinstate Godwin and his family. Harold later became HAROLD II.

Goebbels was a brilliant showman who had studied at eight universities before becoming master of the Nazi Party propaganda machine.

Goebbels, Joseph (1897-1945) German Nazi propagandist. He joined the Nazi Party after being rejected by the army because of his club foot, and founded a new paper for party propaganda, *Der Angriff (The Attack)*.

His theatrical parades and mass meetings helped Adolf HITLER to attain power. In 1933 Goebbels became Hitler's Enlightenment and Propaganda minister, with control over the press, radio and all aspects of culture. His mastery of these media made him one of the first modern mass-manipulators. After Germany's defeat at STALINGRAD he was put in charge of the policy of 'total war' within the country. After the Soviet army entered Berlin in 1945, Goebbels and his wife killed their six children and then committed suicide.

Goering, Hermann (1893-1946) German Nazi leader and commander of the Luftwaffe. An air ace during the First World War, Goering joined the NAZIS in 1922, commanded their BROWN SHIRT paramilitary organisation, and fled the country after being wounded in Adolf HITLER's unsuccessful MUNICH 'beer-hall' putsch the following year. After Hitler came to power in 1933, Goering was made commander of the German air force, the Luftwaffe, and was responsible for the re-armament programme.

Until 1936 Goering headed the GESTAPO, which he had founded. The same year Hitler put him in charge of a four-year economic plan to prepare the country for war, and he directed the German economy until 1943. In 1937 he became minister for foreign affairs and in 1938 Hitler's first deputy. Goering was ordered by Hitler to prepare for the invasion of

Britain in 1940 with the campaign of bombing and aerial fighter attacks that became known as the BATTLE OF BRITAIN. Goering was stripped of all authority in 1943 after he became increasingly dependent on drugs, and was sacked in 1945 for secretly trying to negotiate peace with the Allies. Sentenced to death at the Nuremberg trials, he died in his cell after swallowing poison.

Goethe, Johann (1749-1832) German poet, novelist, dramatist and philosopher. Goethe was one of the greatest figures of the German Romantic period and one of the most prolific. Goethe studied law before turning to writing. He became part of the Sturm und Drang (Storm and Stress) Romantic movement, which used literature and music to depict violent passions. His drama *Götz von Berlichingen* (named after the historical figure of that name), 1773, and the novel *Die Leiden des jungen Werthers (The Sorrows of Young Werther)*, 1774, were typical examples. In 1775 Goethe moved to Weimar where he fell in love with Charlotte von Stein, who inspired many of his lyrics and other works. Nine years later he produced two plays and a volume of poetry which were heavily influenced by his contact with classical culture during a stay in Italy. In the last years of his life Goethe wrote *Wilhelm Meisters Wanderjahre (Wilhelm Meister's Travels)*, 1821-9, and his most famous work, *Faust*.

Golden Horde Name given to the TATARS who lived in a Muslim state set up by the Mongol conquerors of a large part of Russia between 1242 and 1480. In 1238 Batu Khan, a grandson of GENGHIS KHAN, invaded Russia with a Mongol force. He burned Moscow and in 1240 took Kiev. After sweeping through Eastern Europe he established his camp at Sarai on the Lower Volga. He ruled a region extending from central Asia to the River Dnieper, demanding tribute in money and military contingents, but interfering little with the Russian princes, who in general avoided trouble by cooperating. The Horde's destruction of Kiev led to the rise of a more northerly, forest-based Russian civilisation, and it was from Moscow that resistance to the Horde developed. Independent khanates emerged in the Crimea and Kazan, but in 1480 their power was broken by Ivan 'the Great' in his campaign as self-proclaimed 'Ruler of all Russia'. The word 'horde' is from the Mongol *orda*, a camp. 'Golden' recalls the magnificence of Batu Khan's tent.

gold rush see feature, page 264

gold standard System which linked the value of a country's currency to a specific weight of gold. Paper money was convertible into gold on demand, the metal could be freely imported and exported, and exchange rates

between countries were based on their relative values in gold. Britain was the first country to introduce a gold standard, in 1821. It was followed some 50 years later by France, Germany and the USA, and by 1900 the world's leading countries had adopted the standard. Most countries were unable to maintain the gold standard during the First World War because gold could no longer be moved about easily and inflation devalued paper money. Britain returned to the gold standard in 1925 but abandoned it in 1931 because of the Great DEPRESSION. Other countries were soon forced to do the same.

Gomulka, Wladyslaw (1905-82) Polish politician and leader of the Polish Workers' Party from 1943 to 1948. He was jailed in 1951 when he defied the Soviet dictator Joseph Stalin. He was restored to power five years later by Nikita Khrushchev in an attempt to restore calm after Polish and Soviet frontier troops exchanged fire, following riots in Poznan and a workers' trial. Gomulka helped to produce a degree of post-Stalin liberalism, but resigned in 1970 following popular protests caused by rises in food prices.

Gorbachev, Mikhail (1931-) Russian statesman, president of the Soviet Union from 1988 and executive president from 1990 to 1991. His efforts to carry out perestroika, the economic and social reform of Soviet society, led to a gradual process of liberalisation. He encouraged a greater degree of glasnost, or openness and accountability, in the face of

Gorbachev won the 1990 Nobel peace prize but lost popularity in his own country as his reforms brought confusion and rising prices.

Gold fever!

The discovery of gold in northern California in 1848 attracted a sudden influx of prospectors, but the living was tough and not all made their fortunes. 'Forty-Niners' came from as far afield as China and Australia.

On a cold morning in January 1848 James Marshall noticed a shiny pebble in the tailrace of a new sawmill he was building in the foothills of the Sierra Nevada mountains of northern California. Marshall rushed off to show his fellow workers. 'Boys, by God, I believe I have found a gold mine,' he shouted. He then told his employer, John Sutter. Sutter tried to keep the find a secret, but by mid April most of his employees had decamped for the gold streams, leaving his grand ranchero of New Helvetia a ghost community.

Within a few months the news of the Californian gold finds had spread. By the end of 1848 some 6000 men were working at the diggings along the rivers and streams running from the Sierras. The following year brought the great rush of 'Forty-Niners'. By the end of 1849 more than 100000 'argonauts' had reached California by land or sea in search of sudden wealth.

Life was hard. The miners lived in canvas tents or log shacks. Working in groups of three or four, they cleared loose stones and surface earth from sandbanks at stream edges or from bars in midstream. Then they shovelled the soil into the hopper of a 'rocker' or 'cradle'. One member of the team poured buckets of water into the apparatus, another rocked it back and forth. The gold flakes, if any, were trapped by ridges or cleats.

THE DIGGER'S LOT

Few enjoyed the grind of the diggings. One Forty-Niner wrote to his family from the banks of the Feather river: 'You can scarcely form any conception of what a dirty business this gold digging is and of the mode of life which a miner is compelled to lead. We live more like brutes than humans.'

The mining camps were crude, but not chaotic. At first men could leave their possessions unguarded while they worked their claim. As competition grew, crimes proliferated, and the miners soon turned to vigilantism for protection.

The earliest contingent of miners was the luckiest. Some made as much as $500 a day at a time when the typical skilled worker back east earned about $2. Those who arrived towards the end of 1849 seldom did as well, and neither Sutter or Marshall had any benefit at all from their discovery. William Swain, a New York farmer who reached the diggings in November 1849, returned east in the autumn of 1850 carrying a disappointing $500 in gold dust and an IOU for $280.

If materially Swain had little to show for his hard work, he never forgot his participation in one of his country's great epics. Above all, the Californian gold rush helped to open up the Pacific coast of America to successive groups of settlers.

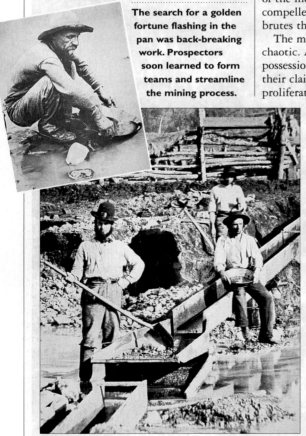

The search for a golden fortune flashing in the pan was back-breaking work. Prospectors soon learned to form teams and streamline the mining process.

inefficiency and corruption, especially after the nuclear disaster at CHERNOBYL in 1986. Gorbachev released many political dissidents, including the physicist Andrei Sakharov, and for the first time the Russian people were told the extent of the crimes against humanity perpetrated by Stalin's regime. A directly elected parliament, called the Congress of People's Deputies, was introduced in 1988.

Together with his foreign minister, Eduard Shevardnadze, Gorbachev negotiated an ARMS CONTROL treaty in 1987 to reduce nuclear forces in Europe. He withdrew Soviet forces from Afghanistan after ten years of military intervention, and it was his refusal to use significant force against the breakaway movements in Soviet satellite states that opened the way to their eventual independence.

In August 1990 he negotiated a deal with the German chancellor Helmut KOHL that allowed a united Germany to join NATO. Gorbachev also supported United Nations demands that Iraq should end its occupation of neighbouring Kuwait, and was active in last-minute attempts to avoid the GULF WAR.

At home Gorbachev faced increasing hostility to his radical changes from a conservative, bureaucratic hierarchy. Tensions during 1991 led to an attempted coup in August, which he survived with the support of his rival Boris YELTSIN. He had by then accepted that the Communist Party's political monopoly of the Soviet Union had ended, but he still believed that the Union could be reformed along evolutionary lines.

As the Soviet economy fell apart, his power base collapsed, along with the Soviet Union itself. He resigned in December 1991 as the last leader of the Soviet Union. Despite his considerable reputation abroad, Gorbachev was discredited at home, and in the 1996 Russian presidential elections he captured only 1 per cent of the vote.

Gordon, Charles (1833-85) British general and administrator. His diplomatic career began in 1860, after he had served with distinction in the CRIMEAN WAR, when the Chinese government appointed him to turn a small army of 3500 peasants into a fighting unit able to defend Shanghai against TAIPING REBELS. This achievement earned him the nickname 'Chinese Gordon'. In 1873 the governor of Egypt, Khedive Ismail, appointed him governor of Equatoria, an area of southern SUDAN, where he brought peace and order and helped to stamp out the slave trade.

Gordon returned to the Sudan in 1884 at the request of the British Government to evacuate British and Egyptian forces from Khartoum. The town was threatened by an army of the rebellious Muhammad Ahmed, calling himself the MAHDI, who in March besieged the city and finally captured it after ten months. Gordon and his staff were killed

Gordon stands outside his office at Khartoum as a dervish prepares to spear him. His corpse was then beheaded. Britain was outraged.

two days before a relief expedition, which had belatedly been sent from Britain, reached the garrison. In Britain, indignation at his death brought down the GLADSTONE government.

Gordon Riots

Gordon Riots Anti-Catholic riots in London in 1780, led by Lord George Gordon, leader of the Protestant Association. This was formed to force the government to repeal the 1778 Catholic Relief Act, which had lifted some of the repressive laws used against Catholics. On June 2, Gordon led a mob to present Parliament with a petition against the Act. The riots that followed lasted for more than a week, prisons were broken open, property destroyed and 235 people killed. Gordon was acquitted of high treason, but later convicted of libelling the queen of France, the French ambassador in London and English justice. He died in Newgate prison.

Gorky, Maxim (1868-1936) Russian short-story writer and novelist. He is considered to be the 'father' of Soviet literature and helped to consolidate the literary doctrine of socialist realism which was to turn Soviet writers into political propagandists.

As a youth he wandered over Russia, working at many trades. In the 1890s he began writing short stories based on his experiences, and achieved international fame. *Twenty-Six Men and a Girl* (1899) contains the central idea of all his work – that the strong, self-aware individual can overcome moral and physical misery. The heroine of *Mother* (1906) is Gorky's most poignant embodiment of the struggle between the heroic human spirit and its degrading environment. He lived in Italy from 1906, but returned to Russia during the

First World War. Although his articles incurred LENIN's censorship, Gorky did much to defend writers and scholars in the postrevolutionary years. In 1928 he became the first chairman of the Union of Writers and the figurehead of Stalin's control of literary life.

Goths Germanic peoples who overran the Western Roman Empire. By the 3rd century AD peoples from the Baltic area had migrated to the northern Black Sea and the Lower Danube. The eastern group around the Black Sea were known as OSTROGOTHS and the western settlers, on the Danube in Dacia, as VISIGOTHS. In the 4th century the Visigoths settled within the Roman Empire under treaty. They expanded over the Western Empire, finally bringing about its fall. The Ostrogoths allied themselves with the HUNS, then in the 5th century they were converted to Christianity and under THEODORIC established their kingdom in Italy.

In Spain the Visigothic kingdom survived until it was overrun by the Muslims in 711. The architectural style of the 13th century onwards was called 'Gothic' or 'barbarous' by Renaissance artists, who preferred Roman and Romanesque simplicity.

Gotland Baltic island which was a major trading centre during the Viking period. Its capital, Visby, was a town of the HANSEATIC LEAGUE from the 11th to the 14th centuries.

When a young man, Gorky was a close friend of Leo Tolstoy and Anton Chekhov. In later life he was the undisputed leader of Soviet writers.

Gotland's 8th-century Viking picture-stone shows souls on their way to Valhalla, the great hall of immortality. An armed rider and a woman are above a sailing ship with two on board.

Under the Treaty of Stettin in 1570, Denmark gained control of the strategically important island, but it has been part of Sweden since the Treaty of Brömsbro in 1645.

Gottwald, Klement (1896-1953) Founder member in 1921 of the Czechoslovak Communist Party, and its general secretary from 1927. In 1938 Gottwald went to the Soviet Union, remaining there until 1945.

He became prime minister in a postwar coalition government from 1946 and in 1948 became president after engineering a communist coup. For five years he dominated the country through purges, forced labour camps and show trials. He agreed with Stalin's plan to reduce Czechoslovakia to satellite status within COMECON, an economic grouping of the Eastern bloc countries.

Gowon, Yakubu (1934-) Nigerian soldier and national leader from 1966 to 1985. Gowon was a colonel in the Nigerian army when he played a leading part in a military coup of July 1966 and was invited to lead a new government. He rewrote the constitution to replace the federal republic of four regions with a federation of 12 states. The eastern Ibo region rejected the constitution and declared itself the state of Biafra. The Biafran War that followed ended in 1970, and Gowon provided aid for the defeated Ibo people. He was largely responsible for the creation of the Economic Community of West African States. By the mid 1970s Gowon was emerging as an international figure, but corruption was rife within Nigeria and he was deposed by the army in July 1975.

Gracchus, Gaius Sempronius (c.158-121 BC) Roman TRIBUNE in 123 and 122 BC and brother of Tiberius Sempronius GRACCHUS. Gracchus was determined to solve the problem of falling army recruitment caused by an increase in the number of peasants who were disqualified from serving because they owned no land. He introduced extensive reforms to reduce poverty and to curb senatorial corruption and abuse of power. His innovations included the introduction of a corn subsidy and the foundation of an overseas colony in Carthage. In 121 riots in protest at plans to dissolve the colony at Carthage gave the Senate the excuse it needed to move

Granada's Moorish rulers took refuge from the summer heat amid the watercourses and fountains in the Generalife gardens of the Alhambra.

parliament, but was arrested in 1926 and imprisoned by fascist ruler Benito MUSSOLINI until he died 11 years later. His *Prison Notebooks* influenced the left wing in Europe during the 1970s and 1980s.

Granada City, probably of Roman origin, and capital of a province of the same name in south-eastern Spain. Granada was conquered by Moorish invaders in the 7th century and was the last of the Muslim kingdoms to be taken in the Christian reconquest of Spain that spanned seven centuries. The Alhambra, Granada's citadel and royal palace, is the finest surviving monument to the splendour of Moorish civilisation in Spain. Granada's surrender in 1492 to the 'Catholic Kings' FERDINAND and ISABELLA made them the first sovereigns of a united Spain. Both Jews and Muslims were expelled and the Spanish INQUISITION hunted down heretics. Granada never recovered the glory of its period under Muslim rule.

Grand Alliance, War of the see NINE YEARS' WAR

Grand Remonstrance (1641) Document condemning the rule of the English king CHARLES I since 1625 and containing drastic proposals for reform of Church and State. Many MPs saw the document as a vote of no confidence in the king. The Remonstrance was passed in the House of Commons by just 11 votes, and swords were drawn in the House for the first time in a row over how it was to be printed. It drove Charles into a disastrous attempt to arrest its five main supporters, including John PYM, an act which further angered MPs. The crisis between the king and LONG PARLIAMENT deepened and led to the outbreak of the ENGLISH CIVIL WAR in 1642.

grand siècle Name given to the 'great age' of LOUIS XIV, king of France from 1643 to 1715, the period of France's greatest magnificence, when it established its cultural leadership and replaced Spain as the dominant power in Europe. Its strength stemmed from strong political control, fertile land and a population which, at almost 20 million, was far greater than that of any other European state. Cardinal Armand RICHELIEU, as chief minister from 1624 to 1642, had established the authority of the monarchy and achieved for France a far greater degree of internal unity than its rivals possessed. Europe was impressed by the splendours of the Court of VERSAILLES.

French military predominance, achieved partly through the creation of the first modern standing army, led to brilliant victories. The frontiers of France were strengthened by the acquisition of Artois, Alsace and the province of Franche-Comté. French fashions in dress were copied widely, as were the elegant products of French craftsmanship. The works of the writers Racine, Molière and La Fontaine were accepted as models, and French became the polite language of Europe. The splendour of the *grand siècle* depended on heavy taxation of the poor and expensive military campaigns.

Grand Tour see feature, page 268

Grant, Ulysses (1822-85) US general, and 18th president of the USA from 1869 to 1877. After a distinguished military career in the early years of the AMERICAN CIVIL WAR, in

against him. Gracchus was forced to commit suicide, but most of his laws survived and formed a solid legal base for the next generation of Romans.

Gracchus, Tiberius Sempronius (168-133BC) Roman TRIBUNE in 133BC, brother of Gaius Sempronius GRACCHUS. He introduced a bill to repossess common land seized by unscrupulous landlords and to redistribute it among the needy. When Tiberius stood for re-election, extremists in the Senate, claiming to uphold law and order, attacked and killed him and many of his supporters.

Graf Spee see PLATE, BATTLE OF THE RIVER

Grafton, Augustus Henry, 3rd Duke of (1735-1811) British prime minister from 1768 to 1770. Grafton favoured conciliating the Americans who were moving towards the War of Independence but he was overruled in Cabinet. As prime minister he was ineffective, and the ferocious anonymous personal attacks he suffered in the press, particularly over his handling of the radical MP John WILKES's return from exile, contributed to his resignation in 1770. He held the office of Lord Privy Seal under Lord Frederick NORTH in 1771 but resigned in 1775 over British policy towards the North American colonies.

Gramsci, Antonio (1891-1937) Founder of the Italian Communist Party in 1921. During the Turin general strike of 1920 he advocated that workers should take over and run factories, as the starting point for a new communist society. He led the communists in

Grant (fifth from right) stands among his staff at City Point, Virginia. His civil war fame led him to office as president in 1868, but Grant proved politically inept and the dupe of corrupt officials.

The Great Exhibition attracted more than 6 million visitors, many on excursions from the provinces, to see England's award-winning industrial products in Britain's most futuristic building.

Great Exhibition International exhibition held in Hyde Park, London, from May to October in 1851. It was promoted by Henry Cole, a civil servant and designer, and strongly backed by Albert, the Prince Consort. Its aim was to demonstrate to the world the industrial supremacy and prosperity of Britain. The exhibition was housed in the Crystal Palace, a vast glass and iron structure with more than 300 000 panes of glass, designed by Joseph Paxton and covering 22 acres (9 ha). It was erected, using prefabricated parts, in only 22 weeks. Britain's leadership as 'workshop of the world' was confirmed when an international jury awarded it 17 medals out of 24 in the class of manufacturing machines and tools. Profits from the exhibition were used to buy land in South Kensington on which the Albert Hall, the Royal Colleges of Art and Music and London's main museums were built. Later, the Crystal Palace was re-erected in Sydenham, south London, and burned down in 1936.

Great Leap Forward (1958) Chinese drive for industrial and agricultural expansion through the establishment of 'backyard' industries in the countryside and increased production quotas. The policy of switching resources from agriculture to industry led to great human suffering. Ambitious increases in production were announced, but quality and distribution posed serious problems.

In agriculture, COMMUNES became almost universal. The Leap fell apart after two years, undermined by poor products and disastrous harvests which caused a famine in which at least 30 million died. Its most important advocate, Chairman Mao ZE-DONG, stayed in the background. The CULTURAL REVOLUTION of the 1960s can be seen partly as his attempt to reintroduce radical policies.

February 1864 Grant was promoted to the supreme command of all Union (Northern states) forces. He maintained relentless pressure on General Robert E. LEE in a bloody year-long campaign, and finally forced him to abandon Richmond and surrender at APPO-MATTOX in 1865, bringing the war to an end.

Grant had entered the war as a colonel of volunteers in support of the Union, and success brought him rapid promotion. He was active in most of the early battles in the western theatre, winning for himself the nickname 'Unconditional Surrender' for his capture of Fort Donelson in February 1862. As a major-general, he captured Vicksburg in 1863 and was again successful at CHATTANOOGA.

Grant was twice elected Republican president of the USA, but although one of the greatest of all American soldiers, he was one of the least successful American presidents. His governments were politically corrupt, poorly run and marred by financial scandals.

Granville, John Carteret, 1st Earl of (1690-1763) English statesman. Granville was employed as a diplomat by the soldier and statesman James, Earl of STANHOPE before becoming secretary of state in 1722. Sir Robert Walpole, chief minister to George I, saw Granville as a potential rival and, to get rid of him, in 1724 sent him to Ireland as Lord Lieutenant. He returned in 1730 to lead the opposition to Walpole in the House of Lords. After Walpole fell in 1742, Granville dominated the government but he relied too much on royal support, and in 1744 George II was persuaded by Henry PELHAM and the Duke of NEWCASTLE to accept Granville's resignation.

Grattan, Henry (1746-1820) Irish statesman and a champion of Irish independence. A member of the Anglo-Irish ruling class, he was a brilliant orator. Grattan led the movement to repeal POYNING'S LAW, which made all Irish legislation subject to the approval of the British Parliament. Giving way to considerable pressure, the British government repealed the Act in 1782. Grattan strongly opposed the merging of the British and Irish parliaments in the 1801 ACT OF UNION. In 1805 he sat as MP for Dublin in the British House of Commons and devoted himself to furthering the cause of Catholic emancipation.

The Great Leap Forward turned out to be a muddy slide backwards. In spring 1958, 60 million Chinese peasants were put to work on water conservation projects, but the result was famine.

Broadening the mind

The education of a young British aristocrat of the 18th and 19th centuries was not considered complete without an expensive, and often perilous, Grand Tour to experience the cultural and linguistic delights of Italy.

During the late 18th century, some 40 000 Britons, most of them aristocrats aged between 15 and 21, set out on 'The Grand Tour' from London to Rome. Before taking up their duties as the heads of their estates, these eldest sons of the nation's grandest families were sent abroad to increase their knowledge of the world and to learn foreign languages. 'A man who has not seen Italy,' said Dr Johnson, the English writer, 'is always conscious of an inferiority. The grand object of travelling is to see the shores of the Mediterranean.' The Grand Tourists' fathers spent as much as £10 000 a year, for three to five years, to round off their heirs' education.

THE LONG ROAD SOUTH

The idea of such journeys came from the father of Thomas Coke, the future Earl of Leicester, who began his Grand Tour at the age of 18. Until then it was thought that attending an English public school, or being tutored at home, was enough to prepare young men for their future responsibilities. What was lacking was an opportunity to view art treasures such as the paintings of Titian and Raphael on their native ground. 'As the great works of art cannot come to us,' said Coke's father, 'then we must go to them!'

From the moment the tourists set foot in France they were the prey of highwaymen, prostitutes, and tricksters. To protect their money, the young men concealed gold coins in their buckled shoes; to protect their health they took well-stocked medicine chests and supplies of sheep-gut contraceptives.

At Marseilles the voyagers faced a choice of routes to Italy: by sea, at the risk of

As a souvenir of his visit to Italy, the tourist was expected to bring home a portrait of himself painted in front of a famous antiquity. This group scene in Rome dates from around 1750.

capture by Barbary Coast pirates, or by land through the Alpine passes. Usually they chose the way across the Maritime Alps. Muffled in furs, they were borne in wicker chairs by porters. Their coach, split into sections, followed on the backs of mules. At the St Gotthard Pass the travellers had to crawl along a bridge above a sheer drop to the river below.

On reaching Italy, the tourists made for Venice, which they arranged to reach during the annual carnival. There they attended masked balls, exhibitions of bull-baiting and gondola races, as well as surveying the Palace of the Doge and the Accademia di Belle Arte, and admiring the works of Canaletto. But it was Rome that proved to be the greatest magnet. Although many Britons returned from Rome with fakes, others

brought back genuine masterpieces, including landscapes by Claude and Poussin, works which inspired gardeners such as Lancelot 'Capability' Brown. The more conscientious tourists went south to visit the ruined towns of Pompeii and Herculaneum under Mount Vesuvius, a coach ride away on the Bay of Naples. Their sketches of the classical architecture found on these sites formed the basis of the new design for the English country house, remodelled on Italianate lines by the brothers Robert and James Adam.

The Grand Tourists returned to Britain more sophisticated beings. Even so, their ornate clothes, extravagant wigs and foppish attitudes were much castigated. The Scottish philosopher and economist Adam Smith, who accompanied the Duke of Buccleuch on his tour, wrote that the average traveller came back 'more conceited, more unprincipled, more dissipated' and more incapable of study or business than 'had he lived at home'.

Many Grand Tourists kept travel diaries. This one from 1839 describes and depicts Florence.

Great Schism Term used to describe two splits in the Christian Church. The Great or EAST-WEST SCHISM in 1054 marked the separation of the Eastern (Orthodox) and Western Christian Churches. The Great Schism of 1378 to 1417 was caused when the papacy was moved back to Rome after nearly 70 years of being based at Avignon in France. The new pope, Urban VI, elected as a result of pressure by the Roman mob, was so hostile to the French cardinals that they elected their own pope in Avignon, Clement VII. The period of popes and rival ANTIPOPES lasted until the Council of CONSTANCE in 1417 elected pope Martin V of the Roman party and deposed his French rival.

Great Trek see feature, page 270

Great Wall of China Fortification built across northern China as a protection against incursions by the nomadic tribes of Mongolia and Manchuria. In the early 3rd century BC the first Qin emperor Shi Huangdi ordered that defensive walls already built by some frontier states should be joined together and extended, using the forced labour of vast gangs of troops and civilian men and women. The wall ran from the Gulf of Liaodong 1400 miles (2250 km) across mountain, steppe and desert to southern Mongolia. It was extended by the Han emperors in the 1st century BC to Yumen (Jade Gate) in Gansu province to aid their expansion into central Asia, and 25 000 turrets were added.

Later much of the wall was rebuilt on different routes, notably by the Northern Wei kingdom, the Sui dynasty, and lastly by the Ming between the 14th and 17th centuries. The wall today is largely of Ming construction. It is about 25 ft (8 m) high and 12 ft (4 m) wide at its top and is built of earth, with stone facings on the eastern sections. The wall acted as a dividing line between the steppe and cultivated land. Properly defended it could delay raiding parties; otherwise the steppe-dweller could ride through its undefended gates.

Greece Mountainous country in south-east Europe. Archaeological evidence suggests that Greek speakers arrived in the mainland from the north around 2000-1700 BC. But the first writing in Greece, dating from around 1650-1600 BC, is of a language known to have been used in Crete in the Bronze Age MINOAN CIVILISATION. Called Linear A, it has never been deciphered. The MYCENAEAN CIVILISATION – whose script, Linear B, dates back to 1450 BC – flourished until it collapsed from unknown causes during the 13th and 12th centuries BC. After an obscure period of history (the Greek 'Dark Ages') the city-state, or POLIS, emerged, and with it the Greek 'Golden Age'.

The new civilisation produced democracy, art, philosophy, politics and literature that laid the basis for much of modern Western culture. In the early 5th century the Greeks repulsed Persian attempts to annex their land. ATHENS and SPARTA were now the major sea and land powers. By the end of the prolonged PELOPONNESIAN WAR in 404 Sparta had crushed Athens and destroyed its empire. In the 4th century THEBES toppled Sparta, but Greece as a whole soon bowed before an outside conqueror – PHILIP II of Macedonia. His son, ALEXANDER THE GREAT, spread Greek thought and culture throughout the Middle East; and after his death in 323 the Greek world was dominated by the Hellenistic kingdoms established by his successors, the cities of Greece itself playing comparatively minor parts in the power struggle.

But then Rome defeated Carthage, became the major power in the Mediterranean, and turned its attention to the Greeks. In the MACEDONIAN WARS Rome secured mainland Greece. In 146 BC Rome sacked Corinth and incorporated Alexander's empire into the Roman Empire. Later Greece became part of the BYZANTINE EMPIRE, to fall like Byzantium itself under the control of the Ottoman Turks in AD 1460.

The GREEK WAR OF INDEPENDENCE from 1821 to 1832 led to an independent Greece, with Duke Otto of Bavaria as king. Otto was deposed in 1862 and a Danish prince, William, was installed, taking the title George I of the Hellenes. In 1924 a military coup established a republic. George II was restored in 1935 but fled into exile in 1941.

Greece was occupied by the Germans in the Second World War, and suffered bitter fighting between rival factions of communists and royalists. In 1946 the British restored the Greek monarchy, and a civil war broke out which lasted three years and ended with the defeat of the communist forces. Recovery and reconstruction began in 1949, with the help of the Marshall Aid programme, and in 1952 Field-Marshal Alexandros Papagos became civilian prime minister.

In 1967 Constantine II was ousted by a military coup, and Greece was governed by a junta (the 'Colonels') for seven years. The king fled to Rome and the monarchy was abolished in 1973. A civilian republic was established the following year and in the 1981 general election Andreas Papandreou became the first socialist prime minister, remaining in office for eight years. Greece joined the European Community, whose agricultural policies boosted its economy, but as tariff barriers were reduced a balance-of-payments crisis developed. In June 1993 the government of Constantine Mitsotakis fell and Andreas Papandreou was returned to power. His government officially opposed the recognition by other European Union countries of the republic of Macedonia in former Yugoslavia, since Greece regards its own northern province of Macedonia as having the right to the name. Papandreou resigned in January 1996 (died June) and was succeeded by Costas Simitis.

Greek drama see feature, page 272

Greek religion The religion of the ancient Greek world was polytheistic, involving the worship of many gods and goddesses. The

> ### DID YOU KNOW?
>
> *Only free-born males — about one in ten of the population — could vote in ancient Greece. Women, slaves, freed slaves and immigrants were excluded.*

The Great Wall of China did not prevent the conquest in 1644 of the Ming dynasty. A traitor let invading Manchus pass through a gate in the wall.

most important deities were the sky-god Zeus (ruler of Olympus), his wife Hera (goddess of marriage), Poseidon (god of sea and earthquakes), the virgin goddess Athena (learning and the arts), Apollo and his sister Artemis (Sun and Moon, the one patron of music and poetry, the other of chastity and hunting), Hephaestus (fire and metalwork), Aphrodite (love and beauty), Ares (war), Demeter (crops), Hestia (hearth and home), and Hermes (the gods' messenger). Although all were revered, different cities had different individual gods as their special patrons. Apollo's shrine at DELPHI was recognised throughout the Greek world.

The Greek gods never lost their essentially human character, and Greek religion largely lacked the emphasis on high standards of personal morality which characterises Christianity, Judaism and Islam. It had no developed concept of an afterlife. Religious beliefs were modified by some of the more mystical aspects of Near-Eastern religion, especially in the period after Alexander's conquest of Asia Minor and Egypt. It finally gave way to Christianity during the 5th century.

Greek War of Independence (1821-32)

Revolt by Greek subjects of the OTTOMAN EMPIRE against Turkish domination. It had its origins in the nationalistic ideas of the *Hetairia Philike* (Society of Friends), who chose Alexander Ypsilanti, a Russian general and son of the ruler of Wallachia, to lead the revolt. He established links with Romanian peasants, Serb rebels and Ali Pasha, the warlord of western Greece. Ypsilanti crossed into Turkish territory with his supporters in March 1821, but only after his defeat in June did the mass of Greeks rebel. Atrocities took place on both sides, but the revolt gained the popular support of the Christian world, and there were many foreign volunteers, including the English poet Lord Byron, who joined in support of the Greek forces.

By the end of 1821 the Greeks had achieved striking successes on land and sea, and in January 1822 an assembly met to declare Greece independent. Four years later, however, MEHEMET ALI, pasha (viceroy) of Egypt reconquered the Peloponnese and threatened to restore Turkish control. At the Treaty of London in 1827, Britain and Russia offered to mediate and secure an autonomous Greek state. When the Turks refused, Britain, France and Russia sent a combined fleet which destroyed the Egyptian-Turkish fleet at Navarino. In 1829 the Russian army seized Adrianople and threatened Constantinople. The Turks agreed to make peace, and the Conference of London in 1832 confirmed Greek independence. The following year a Bavarian prince, Otto I, was crowned king of Greece in Athens, and reigned until he was deposed in 1862.

The Great Trek

The Afrikaners of South Africa regard the Great Trek as the central event of their history and the origin of their identity as a people.

Between 1835 and 1840, some 14000 Afrikaners packed their belongings into ox wagons and left their farms in the Cape Colony to find a land of their own. Grievances had been building up among the Afrikaners – many of them descendants of the original Dutch settlers of 1652 – ever since the British seized control of the colony in 1805. The abolition of slavery, laws giving Blacks equal legal status with Whites and the introduction of English as the principal language in schools and churches all caused discontent. Land in the Eastern Cape had become scarce. Many Afrikaners began to think of moving, and plans for a large-scale exodus were laid.

The Great Trek was not one journey. *Voortrekkers* (forward journeyers) came from all over the eastern Cape and used a variety of routes. The first two parties to leave were led by Louis Trichardt and Hans van Rensburg. Together they set off northwards across the Orange river in 1835, splitting just south of the Limpopo river after a quarrel. Van Rensburg took his party north along the river, where they were wiped out by the Tsonga. Nearly three years later Trichardt found his way to the port of Delagoa Bay, where he and nearly half of his party died of malaria. The survivors took a ship to Port Natal.

Meanwhile, trekkers had been leaving the Cape in droves on the 300 mile journey to the mountain of Thaba Nchu, north of the Orange river. Light and mobile enough to cross vast stretches of dusty veldt and treacherous mountains, their ox wagons were loaded with clothes, food, tools, weapons and even furniture. At night they were drawn into a *laager* (ring) for defence against attack.

ADVANCING TOWARDS A HOME

From Thaba Nchu the trekkers headed eastwards over the Drakensberg Mountains. Even on relatively flat terrain they averaged only around 6 miles (10 km) a day. On the mountains' steep slopes every yard became a struggle. To prevent their wagons running out of control down the mountainside, the trekkers had to remove their rear wheels and tie branches under the axles.

Having crossed the Drakensberg and broken the power of the Zulus at the Battle of Blood River in December 1838, the Boers (farmers) set up the Republic of Natal. They were forced to move again in 1843 when the British annexed Natal, and finally settled in the Highveld to the west and north. In the 1850s the British recognised the two Boer republics of Transvaal and the Orange Free State. The Voortrekkers had found a home.

After 1835, waves of Afrikaner trekkers left their farms in the Cape and moved inland. When the British annexed their new settlement in Natal, the Boers retreated into the Highveld.

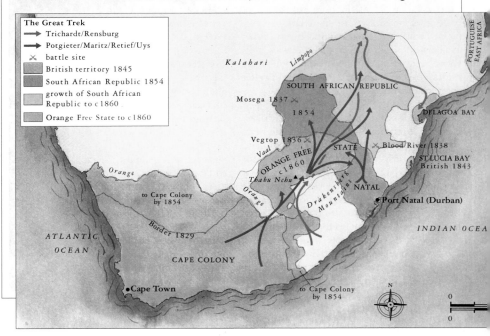

The Great Trek
→ Trichardt/Rensburg
→ Potgieter/Maritz/Retief/Uys
✕ battle site
British territory 1845
South African Republic 1854
growth of South African Republic to c1860
Orange Free State to c1860

Petra Kelly, the 'mother' of the German Green Party, campaigned on streets and in parliament before her death at the age of 44 in 1992.

Greenland Large island, lying mainly within the Arctic Circle. It was sighted in the early 10th century by the Icelander Gunnbjörn Ulf-Krakuson, but it was not settled until 985, by ERIC THE RED. The climate was warmer than today and the south-western region habitable; farming was difficult but was supplemented by fishing and the export of furs and walrus ivory. Christianity came with Eric's son Leif Ericsson around 1000. At its height the population reached approximately 3000, but the Black Death reduced it in the 14th century. The settlement died out around 1400 because of increasingly severe winters and trade problems. European explorers charted the coast of Greenland during the 16th century, and the island was settled in 1721 by the Norwegian missionary Hans Egede under the aegis of the Danish crown. In 1729 the Danish crown assumed control of the colony and, from 1774, established a state monopoly on all trade with Greenland, which stayed in force until 1951.

During the Second World War when Denmark was under German occupation, the US government took over Greenland as a protectorate and offered to buy it in 1946, but the Danish government refused. Self-government was granted in 1981 after a referendum. Greenland retains two seats in the Danish national assembly, and the Danish government handles some of Greenland's external affairs. In 1985 Greenland withdrew from full membership of the European Community.

Green movement Organisations and pressure groups, formed in many countries to protect the environment against pollution and exploitation. Among the first was Greenpeace, founded in 1971 in British Columbia to oppose US nuclear testing. The US Green Party was founded in 1973. In politics, the 'Greens' have had most impact in the Federal Republic of Germany, where the Green Party was formed in 1979. A high point was reached when it won 42 seats in the 1987 federal elections, but it lost them all in 1990, though the party remained in a number of state coalition governments. In the 1989 elections to the European parliament, the UK Green Party won 15 per cent of the vote. Throughout the 1980s Green parties developed in Belgium, France, Italy, Switzerland, Finland and the Netherlands as well as in countries such as Australia, Canada, New Zealand, Argentina and Chile. In 1992 the UN Conference on Environmental Development was held in Rio, attended by 103 heads of state or government. Known as the 'Earth Summit', it made a Declaration of 27 principles intended to promote environmentally sustainable development on the planet.

Gregory I, 'the Great', St (540-604) Pope from AD 590 to 604 who sent St AUGUSTINE OF CANTERBURY on his mission to convert England to Christianity. When Gregory became pope Italy was in a state of crisis, devastated by floods, famine and Lombard invasions. The position of the Roman Catholic Church was threatened by the imperial Roman power at CONSTANTINOPLE. Gregory made peace with the Lombards in 592, and appointed governors to the Italian cities, thus establishing the temporal power of the papacy. Throughout his time in office he effectively opposed the double assault on the Church from paganism and the ARIAN heresy. His interest in music led to developments in the liturgical singing known as plainsong, or Gregorian chant.

Gregory of Tours, St (538-94) Churchman and historian at the court of the Frankish king Childebert II. He was educated by his uncle, St Gall, and resisted attacks on the Church during the reign of King Chilperic. Of his many works the best known is his ten-volume *Historia Francorum* (*History of the Franks*), a source of early MEROVINGIAN history. His canonisation soon after his death was greatly aided by his reputation as a chronicler.

Gregory VII, St (c.1021-85), Pope from 1073 to 1085. Gregory argued for the moral reform of the Church and sought to unite the Christian West under the leadership of the papacy. He was one of the first popes to urge celibacy of the clergy and opposed simony, or the buying of offices within the Church. Many secular rulers objected to the pope's attempt to lead the West, but he stubbornly defended the Church's liberty against the encroachments of secular power. Gregory's most formidable opponent was Henry IV, the Holy Roman Emperor. In 1076 Gregory excommunicated Henry because the emperor would not give up his right to dismiss bishops and formally confer, or invest new candidates in their office. The following year Henry began to lose support abroad because of the pope's action, so he travelled to the Italian mountain castle of CANOSSA to plead for absolution. The pope granted the emperor's plea, but Henry's submission was merely tactical. In 1080 he attacked Rome, appointed an antipope, Clement III, and forced Gregory to retreat to Salerno in southern Italy, where he died.

Grenada West Indian island, the southernmost of the Windward Islands, which Columbus sighted in 1498. It was colonised by the French governor of Martinique in 1650, and passed to the control of the French crown in 1674. The island was conquered by the British during the SEVEN YEARS' WAR and ceded to them by the Treaty of Paris in 1763. An uprising in 1795 against British rule, supported by many slaves, was put down the following year. After the end of slavery in 1838, the island survived by exporting cocoa,

bananas and spices. The vote was granted to all adults in 1950 when the United Labour Party, led by Eric Gairy, emerged. He was deposed in a nearly bloodless coup in 1979 by Maurice Bishop, leader of a left-wing group, the New Jewel Movement. Bishop encouraged closer relations with Cuba and the Soviet Union, but following a quarrel within his party he was overthrown and killed by army troops in 1983. The USA invaded to prevent a Marxist revolutionary council from taking power, and to protect US interests. In June 1995 a general election brought the New National Party (NNP) to power under Keith Mitchell.

Grenville, George (1712-70) British prime minister from 1763 to 1765. Grenville entered Parliament in 1741, and became treasurer of the navy three years later, but was dismissed in 1755 for criticising the ministry's foreign policy. He returned under the administration of his brother-in-law, William Pitt the Elder, in 1757 and became First Lord of the Treasury. As prime minister, Grenville devised the Stamp Act of 1765 which caused so much anger in the American colonies that it helped to provoke the American Revolution. George III disliked Grenville and used his policy failures as a pretext for dismissing him.

Theatrical highlights

The ancient Greeks were enthusiastic theatregoers who would sit for hours in the open air watching the tragedies of playwrights such as Euripides, or the comedies of Aristophanes. Today their drama lives on in modern theatre.

English drama draws much of its vocabulary of the theatre from ancient Greece. The word theatre itself is Greek: so, too, are drama, ode, tragedy, comedy, scene, poetry, music, orchestra and chorus. Like so much in Western cultural life, the idea of the theatre was born in Greece, specifically in Athens during the 6th century BC, where Thespis (hence 'thespians') is credited with inventing the Greek tragedy. From Athens the new art form spread throughout the cities of the Greek world to southern Italy, Rome and, through the Renaissance, Britain. Modern texts of ancient Greek dramas descend from official versions prepared in the 4th century for the public archives in Athens.

PRESERVED FOR POSTERITY

With the rise of Christianity, the plays ceased to be part of general education and culture, but throughout the Middle Ages texts were preserved and copied on papyrus and vellum in Western monasteries as well as in Constantinople, the faithful custodian of pagan Greek heritage. The few that survived to the age of printing had a pronounced influence on modern European theatre, but it was not until the 19th century that the plays themselves began to be restaged, in the original Greek or in vernacular translations.

Greek drama was created and staged under the sign of Dionysus, god of wine and exuberance, of transformation and illusion, but also of paradox – since he engendered in his worshippers murderous violence as well as ecstatic bliss. Although staged as part of a religious ritual, Greek tragedy and, later, comedy was also concerned with the deepest human matters in an almost secular way: such as relations within the family (Aeschylus' *Oresteia* trilogy), political power and civil disobedience

Admission tokens (right) entitled the citizens of ancient Athens to watch open-air performances in the theatre of Dionysus.

The playwright Menander inspects a mask. On the table are actors' masks for a young woman and an older man, similar to the terracotta mask (inset).

(Sophocles' *Antigone*), and war and slavery (Euripides' *Trojan Women*).

The three 'classical' tragedians, Aeschylus, Sophocles and Euripides, were all probably alive at the same time, in the mid 5th century BC. Later Greeks canonised them, but original if less accomplished tragedies continued to be written and performed long after the deaths of Euripides and Sophocles. Although the tragedians normally took their plots from traditional myths and legends set in the distant past, they gave them new and sometimes shocking twists. Their presentation of moral, political and theological issues must have struck home to their contemporary audiences – mainly men, as many as 15 000, who sat in the open air during daylight for hours on end.

Modern Western comic tradition stems not from Aristophanes, whose career stretched from 420 to 380 BC, but from Menander, an Athenian who flourished in the decades around 300 BC. Little of Menander survives in the original, but the Roman playwrights Plautus and Terence lifted plots from his lost work, so present-day audiences have a fairly good idea of Menander's style of comedy.

MODERN INTERPRETATION

Greek tragic playwrights also wrote satyr-dramas, humorous companion pieces in which the chorus consisted of satyrs – mythical half-men, half-beasts – who formed Dionysus' intimate entourage and habitually behaved disgracefully. In Egypt in the 19th century a papyrus text was found preserving part of *The Trackers*, one of Sophocles' satyr-dramas. This fragmentary Greek original was incorporated and updated by the modern playwright Tony Harrison in his verse drama *The Trackers of Oxyrhynchus*, which included a chorus of clog-dancing satyrs: a perfect example of the continuing ability of Greek drama to relate meaningfully to modern theatre and its audiences.

Sir Thomas Gresham, portrayed in his wedding finery in 1544, was more than just a shrewd financier. He smuggled cargoes of arms and gunpowder to England from Antwerp.

Grenville, Sir Richard (1542-91) English naval commander, renowned for his epic battle aboard the *Revenge* against the Spanish which led to his death. He became MP for Cornwall in 1571, and in 1585 led the unsuccessful expedition, planned by his cousin Sir Walter RALEIGH, to colonise ROANOAKE, an island which later became England's first North American colony. He supplied three ships to the force assembled in May 1588 against the Spanish Armada. In 1591 his ship *Revenge* held out for 15 hours against a powerful Spanish fleet in a battle off the Azores after it was cut off from other English raiding vessels. Fatally wounded in hand-to-hand fighting, Grenville died aboard a Spanish ship.

Grenville, William, Baron (1759-1834) British statesman who formed the coalition 'Ministry of all the Talents', between February 1806 and March 1807, during which he championed successfully the abolition of the British overseas slave trade. His attempts to end the Napoleonic War failed, however, and he left politics when a bill to emancipate Roman Catholics was rejected by George III. Grenville's career in the House of Commons began in 1782, and nine years later he served as secretary of state for foreign affairs under William Pitt the Younger. After Pitt's death he passed the law abolishing slavery but failed to agree on other initiatives.

Gresham, Sir Thomas (c.1519-79) English cloth merchant, financier, diplomat and founder of the Royal Exchange. Gresham negotiated loans for the English Government, in Antwerp, provided William CECIL with valuable information from the Continent, and influenced Elizabethan economic policy. He

founded Gresham College in 1579 as a venue for public lectures. He also formulated the financial rule that 'bad money drives out good', which became known as Gresham's Law. He said this was illustrated by people passing on clipped money (gold or silver coins that had had their edges illegally sheared off to be melted down and sold separately) and keeping 'good' or unclipped coins.

Grey, Charles, 2nd Earl (1764-1845) British statesman. From the beginning of his political career in the House of Commons in 1786, Grey was an advocate of electoral reform. As leader of the Whigs, he was prime minister from 1830 to 1834 in the government which passed the first great parliamentary REFORM ACT in 1832. Factory laws were passed in 1833 along with an act abolishing slavery throughout the British Empire.

Grey, Edward, Viscount Grey of Fallodon (1862-1933) British politician who as foreign secretary from 1905 to 1916, negotiated the Triple Entente, which brought Britain, France and Russia together. In 1914 he persuaded a reluctant British Cabinet to go to war because Germany had violated Belgian neutrality. He summed up the fears of his generation at the start of the First World War: 'The lamps are going out all over Europe; we shall not see them lit again in our lifetime.'

Grey, Lady Jane (1537-54) 'Nine Days' Queen' of England in July 1553. She had some claim to the English throne as a descendant of

Henry VII's younger daughter Mary, and her father-in-law, John DUDLEY, persuaded Edward VI to name Jane as his successor. MARY I ousted her, and she was beheaded at the age of 17 after her father had incriminated her by taking part in WYATT'S REBELLION, when 3000 men marched on London in protest at Mary's planned marriage to Philip II of Spain.

Griffith, Arthur (1872-1922) Irish statesman. He helped to found the Republican Sinn Féin Party, which became a radical political force in favour of Irish independence from Britain. In 1906 Griffith founded the newspaper *Sinn Féin* (*We Ourselves*), which he edited until 1914. He took part in gun-running for the Irish Volunteers in 1914 and opposed Irish participation in the First World War, but did not take part in the Easter Rising of 1916 against British rule. Griffith was elected to the Westminster Parliament in 1918, and was a major figure in the formation of the Dáil Éireann in 1919. When the Irish Republic was declared he became vice-president and later president. In 1921 he led the Irish delegation that signed the Anglo-Irish Treaty, establishing the IRISH FREE STATE.

Grotius, Hugo (1583-1645) Dutch jurist and scholar. His work, *De Jure Belli et Pacis*, (*Concerning the Law of War and Peace*), published in 1625, is considered to be the first definitive book on international law. In 1613 he supported his patron Johan van OLDEN-BARNEVELDT in a bitter dispute between two factions of Calvinism, for which he was

About to meet her death, Lady Jane Grey, the hapless victim in a political power struggle, declares that she 'never desired the Crown' and that she dies 'a true Christian woman'.

arrested by Maurice of Nassau, and sentenced to life imprisonment. In 1621 his wife helped him to escape and he fled to Paris, entered Sweden's diplomatic service, and was Swedish ambassador to France from 1634 to 1644, just before his death in a shipwreck off Pomerania.

Group of Seven Seven major industrial countries whose heads of government have met annually since 1976 to try to agree global economic policies and exchange rates. They are the USA, Japan, Germany, Canada, Britain, France and Italy.

Guadalupe, Virgin of Apparition of the Virgin Mary, said to have appeared twice to Juan Diego, a Christian convert, on a hill near Mexico City in December 1531. When he requested proof that she was the Virgin, the image materialised on the inside of his cloak. A basilica was built to display the cloak in the town of Guadalupe, near the hill. News of the apparitions and cloak itself helped to attract many Mexicans to Christianity, even though, or perhaps because, the spot where the Virgin appeared had also been sacred to one of their pagan goddesses. In the 18th century the Virgin became the symbol of the nation and was carried on banners during the War of Independence. The feast of the Virgin of Guadalupe is still celebrated on December 12, the day the image appeared.

Guam Pacific island east of the Philippines. It is a US naval and air base, one of the most important centres for US strategic intelligence. The island was first visited by the Portuguese explorer Ferdinand Magellan in 1521, and ruled by Spain from 1688 until it was ceded together with the Philippines to the USA after the Spanish-American War in 1898. Between 1941 and 1944 it was occupied by Japanese forces. Its people voted in a referendum in 1982 to accept the status of a commonwealth nation with the USA.

Guangzhou Capital, formerly known as Canton, of the Chinese province of Guangdong. After 1757 it was the only port in China open to Europeans, who were restricted to 13 'factories' or trading posts outside its walls. There they bought tea and silk, and after about 1800 sold increasing amounts of opium.

Guatemala Country in Central America. In pre-Columbian history Guatemala formed part of pre-Mayan and Mayan civilisations (see feature, page 404). In 1523 Spanish conquistadores led by Pedro de Alvarado arrived and the country became a colony under the viceroyalty of NEW SPAIN. In 1821 it declared itself independent. However, Mexico invaded and held Guatemala until 1823, when the United Provinces of Central America formed. In 1839 the country declared independence as

a republic, with Rafael Carrera as its first president. Carrera's successors became increasingly despotic. Ten years of social reform began with the election of Juan José Arévalo to the presidency in 1944. In 1954 the US Central Intelligence Agency backed a coup.

Ten years of disorder followed, and during the 1970s and early 1980s the army, trained and funded by the USA, controlled the country. In 1985 democracy was restored and Vinico Cerezo was elected president. In 1991 his successor, Jorge Serrano Elias, opened talks with the left-wing guerrilla movement URNG, and began a purge against the military for its corruption. In June 1993 Ramiro de Léon Carpio was elected president. Talks with the URNG guerrillas to end the 32-year civil war were resumed, but they broke down and there were subsequent heavy clashes. In 1995 Alvaro Arzu became president.

Guelph Member of a faction originating in the German Welf family, dukes of Saxony and Bavaria. The Welfs were traditional opponents of the HOHENSTAUFENS in Germany and Italy. In the 12th century the Guelph leader was HENRY THE LION, who supported the papacy against the aspirations of the Holy Roman Emperors. Guelph support was in the major Italian towns and cities. Their rivals the Ghibellines, named after the Hohenstaufen castle of Waiblingen, were the imperial party whose strength came mainly from the great aristocratic families. In local feuds, no matter what the cause, the antagonists came to associate themselves with one or other of the opposing factions whose names continued to be used for many years after the original disputes were forgotten.

guerrilla The term, Spanish for 'little war', for a member of an irregular military unit. It was coined during the PENINSULAR WAR (1808-14) to describe the Spanish partisans fighting the armies of Napoleon. During the American Civil War the Confederate ranger John Mosby used guerrilla warfare tactics to attack the federal army, and in the Arabian desert Arab cavalry under the British commander T.E. Lawrence (Lawrence of Arabia) harassed superior Turkish forces between 1916 and 1918. The Chinese revolutionary leader Mao Ze-dong conducted a large-scale guerrilla campaign during the 1920s and 1930s against the government and Japanese

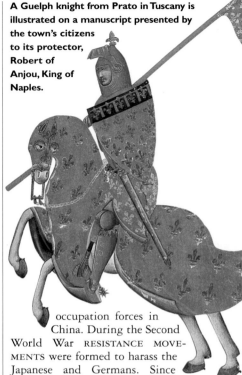

A Guelph knight from Prato in Tuscany is illustrated on a manuscript presented by the town's citizens to its protector, Robert of Anjou, King of Naples.

occupation forces in China. During the Second World War RESISTANCE MOVEMENTS were formed to harass the Japanese and Germans. Since 1945 guerrillas have become associated with revolutionary movements in South America, Asia, the Middle East and Africa.

Guevara, Che (1928-67) Argentine-born revolutionary and political leader. A doctor by training, Ernesto 'Che' Guevara met the insurgent Fidel CASTRO in Mexico in 1954 after fleeing from Guatemala when its procommunist regime was overthrown. He helped to prepare the guerrilla force which landed in Cuba in 1956 and fought its way to power. Shortly after Castro's victory Guevara was given a Cabinet position in charge of economic policy, and played a major role in the transfer of Cuba's traditional economic ties

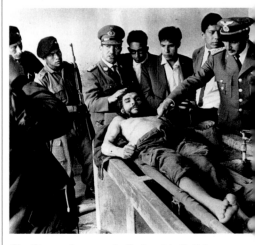

Che Guevara's corpse is displayed in Bolivia before being buried in an unmarked grave. In Cuba the official wake included a 21-gun salute.

from the USA to the communist bloc. He moved to Bolivia in 1967 in order to persuade the peasants and tin-miners to take up arms against the military government, but was captured and killed. He became a role model for radical students in the West in the 1960s.

Guiana see FRENCH GUIANA, GUYANA, SURINAM

Guicciardini, Francesco (1483-1540) Italian statesman and historian. For four years he worked on his monumental *Storia d'Italia* (*History of Italy*), which covered the years from 1494 to 1534. He died before completing the final revision, but it stands as the most objective contemporary history of the country during the period of Italy's wars with France. Guicciardini was Florence's ambassador to Aragon from 1511 to 1514, and served the papacy from 1515 to 1534.

guild Association of townspeople formed to protect trading practices. Guilds may have developed in Syria and Egypt or in Roman and Byzantine trade associations, but probably arose in Western Europe in the 7th century. In Anglo-Saxon England they took the form of *frithguilds*, family associations which protected members' interests, including those of trade. These early benevolent associations were usually based in towns, and engaged in charity and local administration. They were often religious in character, and throughout the Middle Ages religious guilds performed social and charitable work in towns and parishes. From the early 11th century merchants and traders combined to regulate trade. These merchant guilds controlled markets, weights and measures and tolls, and negotiated the CHARTERS that granted their towns borough status. Before the end of the 12th century small crafts and trades formed their own guilds, each setting quality standards within a hierarchy of master, journeymen and apprentices. From the 16th century guilds were unable to adapt to the new international markets that were developing. They survived in a largely ceremonial role in the City of London, and continued to control some apprenticeships. Guilds built residences, called guildhalls, to hold banquets and conduct business. They were often major features of European cities and towns and many of these fine buildings still exist.

In 1517 Venetian carpenters hung this guild sign at the Venice Arsenal, where they built a large part of the state's merchant fleet. By the 17th century the power of the fleet, like that of guilds throughout Europe, was in decline.

Queen Marie Antoinette's head, displayed to the crowd in October 1793, was one of 2639 that 'Madame La Guillotine' claimed in Paris between March 1793 and August 1794.

guillotine An instrument for beheading, in which a weighted blade is dropped between grooved vertical posts. Execution by this method was recorded in Ireland as early as 1307 and was used in Europe in the Middle Ages. It had generally fallen into disuse by the time of the French Revolution when the revolutionary and doctor Joseph Guillotin suggested the introduction of a 'mechanical decapitator'. 'La Guillotine' was erected in 1792 on the Place de Grève in Paris. During the TERROR, when some 16 000 were executed in France, the Paris guillotine was used to behead 1376 victims in only seven weeks between June 10 and July 27, 1794. The guillotine's use continued in France until 1981.

Guinea Country on the west coast of Africa, formerly a French colony. The area was part of the Muslim Mali empire between the 7th and 15th centuries. From about 1879 most of eastern Guinea became a part of the empire of the military leader Samori Ture, who fought against the French. In 1904 Guinea was made part of French West Africa, and it remained a French colony until 1958, when a popular vote called for independence. Ahmed Sekou Touré became the first president, and there was severe unrest, repression and almost complete isolation from the outside world, although before Touré's death in 1984 more freedom was allowed. This trend continued under the military regime of President Lansana Conté. In 1990 he established a committee for national recovery, following a referendum on a new constitution. After a general strike in 1991, a multiparty system was introduced, but opposition parties refused to recognise Conté's re-election in 1993.

Guinea-Bissau Country in West Africa, formerly Portuguese Guinea. The Portuguese used the country as a slave-trading centre after their arrival in 1446. After being part of the Portuguese Cape Verde Islands, a group of islands to the west, it became a separate colony in 1879. Opposition against colonial rule intensified in the 1960s, led by Amilcar Cabral, and in 1974 Portugal recognised its independence. In 1977 an unsuccessful attempt was made to unite with Cape Verde, a newly formed republic. In 1980 a military coup established João Vieira as president with a national assembly elected from the ruling Marxist Party, the PAIGC. In 1989 Vieira was re-elected, and again in 1994, when the first multiparty elections also returned a PAIGC majority in the assembly.

Gujarati culture draws on Hindu, Buddhist, Muslim and Jain influences. This 14th or 15th-century miniature shows the Jain hero Halaka.

Guise Branch of the ducal house of Lorraine that rose to prominence in 16th-century France. The Catholic Guise family was the most influential in France by the 1550s. Its conflicts with the Protestant HUGUENOTS and the BOURBONS led directly to the outbreak of the FRENCH WARS OF RELIGION. Claude de Lorraine was created Duke of Guise in 1527 after distinguishing himself in a number of French victories. He was succeeded by his son, François, who became the most effective commander serving under Henry II. François was responsible for the capture of Calais from the English in 1558 and their subsequent withdrawal from France. His brother Charles became Cardinal of Lorraine in 1550, and his sister Mary, who married James V of Scotland, was the mother of MARY, Queen of Scots.

A Huguenot assassinated François in 1563. His son and successor, Henry, fought in the third and fourth Wars of Religion and planned the murder of the man he believed responsible for his father's death – Gaspard de COLIGNY – an act which initiated the ST BARTHOLOMEW'S DAY MASSACRE of 1572. In 1576 he organised the Holy League, an alliance between Venice, Spain and the Papacy against Turkish encroachment in the eastern Mediterranean. When he was put forward as a possible heir to the throne in 1588, Henry III, the last Valois king of France, had him assassinated. His brother, Charles, kept the Guise and extremist Catholic causes alive until 1595, when he submitted to HENRY IV. The power of the Guise family then waned, and the ducal line died out in 1675.

Gujarat Region of India, including the Kathiawar peninsula on the north-western coast and a narrow hinterland. Remains of INDUS CIVILISATION sites indicate early urban settlements, after which the area became part of numerous Hindu and Buddhist empires from as early as the MAURYAS in the 3rd century BC. The Jainist religion was also introduced. The name of the region comes from a Hun tribal dynasty, the Gurjaras, who ruled in the 8th and 9th centuries. Muslim rule began in 1298 with the invasion of the KHALJI Delhi sultan, Ala ud-Din. An independent Muslim sultanate, based on the new capital city of Ahmadabad, ruled from 1411 until 1573, when Mughal invasion reduced the region to a province. In the mid 18th century the area came under the control of the expanding MARATHAS, until it was taken over by the EAST INDIA COMPANY based in Bombay. Many Gujaratis emigrated abroad, particularly to East Africa and Britain. Gujarat is now one of the states of India.

Gulf War (1991) International conflict in the Gulf region of Kuwait and Iraq. On August 2, 1990, Iraqi troops invaded Kuwait after President Saddam HUSSEIN declared it the 19th province of Iraq, intending to take control of its large and valuable oilfields. The UN Security Council imposed economic sanctions, and a US-led coalition of 29 countries mobilised a joint military task force of some 725 000 troops. Intense diplomatic activity failed, and on January 17, 1991, a large-scale air attack known as 'Operation Desert Storm' was launched. Strategic targets, some in densely populated areas, were destroyed by electronically guided bombs. Within seven days, Allied forces established air supremacy and Iraqi forces were bombed in the open desert spaces of southern Iraq. The land war, named 'Operation Desert Sabre' by the UN forces under Commander in Chief General Norman Schwarzkopf, began on February 24, and in four days the Iraqi forces, demoralised by the bombardment, were routed. The Allied forces used such high-technology weapons as laser-guided bombs and antiballistic missiles. Iraq's defences included chemical and biological weapons and Soviet Scud ballistic missiles. Saddam set fire to several hundred Kuwaiti oil wells before he withdrew from Kuwait and accepted the UN cease-fire terms at the end of February.

gunboat diplomacy Negotiations which are supported by the threatened use of force by one country in order to impose its will on another. The term was used originally in the 19th century when the great maritime nations, notably Britain, used their naval power to exercise their will on the rulers of small or weak countries. In 1882 a British fleet bombarded Alexandria in Egypt to crush a nationalist movement. During the BOXER uprising in China in 1900, the European powers combined their forces to protect their interests and punish the rebels. Gunboat diplomacy has also been used by the US to quell revolutionaries in the Philippines and to enforce its policies in Latin America.

Gunpowder Plot Roman Catholic conspiracy to murder JAMES I of England and the members of his Parliament at the state opening on November 5, 1605, to be followed by a national Catholic uprising and seizure of power. On the eve of the opening, Guy Fawkes was discovered in a rented cellar beneath the House of Lords. He was standing guard over 20 barrels of gunpowder, which the plotters, led by Robert Catesby, intended to use to blow up the Lords and the House of Commons.

Kuwait burns in the aftermath of the Gulf War. Many Iraqi troops fled, despite the determination of Saddam Hussein that the war would be 'the great showdown, the mother of all battles'.

Robert Winter, Christopher Wright, John Wright, Thomas Percy, Guido Fawkes, Robert Catesby, Thomas Winter

Guy Fawkes joined the Gunpowder Plot believing that 'a desperate disease requires a dangerous remedy', but death came for the conspirators, not for Parliament, after his discovery and arrest.

The other conspirators were overcome in the Midlands after brief resistance. Fawkes and seven others were tried and executed in January 1606. The plotters saw violent action as the only way to gain toleration for English Catholics. They were later disowned by the majority of Catholics, who had little sympathy for their methods. It has been suggested that the statesman Robert CECIL manufactured the plot in order to discredit the Catholic cause. Immediately afterwards, the laws against Catholics were stiffened and an Oath of Allegiance imposed, but use of the new laws soon became sporadic. Bonfires, fireworks, and the burning of 'guys', or effigies of Guy Fawkes, still mark November 5 in Britain.

Guomindang Chinese political party, now the official ruling party in TAIWAN. In 1912, following the overthrow of the QING dynasty, the political leader SUN YAT SEN replaced his revolutionary Alliance Party with the republican Guomindang (Kuomintang), or National People's Party. With Soviet help, Sun reorganised the Guomindang along the lines of a Bolshevik Party in 1923-4, and in 1924 the party allied itself with the Chinese Communist Party (CCP). At the party congress that year the Guomindang adopted Sun's 'Three Principles of the People': nationalism, democracy and 'people's livelihood'. After his death in 1925 the party was led by CHIANG KAI-SHEK, who in 1926 undertook the Northern Expedition to extend the Guomindang's power from its base in southern China. In 1927 a break between the Guomindang and the CCP led to civil war, but in 1928 Beijing fell to the Guomindang, who established a government in Nanjing until 1937. The Japanese invasion of northern China in the same year led to a period of co-operation between the Guomindang and the CCP, but fighting resumed at the end of the Second World War. In 1949 the Guomindang was defeated by the CCP under Mao Ze-dong and forced to retreat to Taiwan.

Gustav I (Gustavus Vasa) (1496-1560) King of Sweden from 1523 and founder of the Vasa dynasty. His election as king ended the 126-year-old Union of KALMAR which had subordinated Sweden to Denmark. He had fought against the Danes in 1517, but was successful only after 1520, thanks to financial and naval backing from the Baltic city of Lübeck. He created a national army of volunteers and built an efficient navy. He also modernised the economy, and in 1527 broke with the Roman Catholic Church for mainly political reasons. In 1544 the Swedish crown became hereditary in the Vasa family.

Gustav II (Gustavus Adolfus) (1594-1632) King of Sweden from 1611 to his death, generally recognised as the country's greatest ruler. Gustavus inherited three Baltic struggles. His father and predecessor, Charles IX, usurped the Swedish throne from the Catholic Sigismund III, who was also king of Poland; struggles with Poland were endemic. The country was also at war with Russia and Denmark. Gustavus paid an indemnity to the Danes and cut off Russia from the Baltic by annexing territory connecting Finland with Estonia, a Swedish province west of Russia. At home, his partnership with the chancellor, Count Axel OXENSTIERNA, bore fruit in reforms in the government, the armed forces, the economy and education.

Gustavus crossed to Germany in 1630 to take part in the THIRTY YEARS' WAR, and proceeded to turn the tide against the Imperial forces of the Holy Roman Emperor FERDINAND II. Originally he intended to prevent the Catholic Habsburgs from dominating the Baltic, but by 1632 his successful campaigns had ensured that Protestantism survived in Germany, and his opposition to the Habsburgs helped to delay the creation of a united Germany for another 200 years. Sweden defeated the Imperial forces at the Battle of Lützen, where Gustavus was mortally wounded.

Gutenberg, Johann (c.1400-68) German craftsman and printer, credited with the introduction to Europe of movable type – separate letters moulded in metal, which could be put together in any combination and used again and again. In the late 1430s, Gutenberg persuaded three partners to help him to develop new printing techniques. In 1450 he raised money from a Mainz goldsmith, Johann Fust, and about five years later produced the first book printed with movable type, the Mazarin Bible, or 42-line Bible, after the number of lines in each column. But Fust wanted a faster return on his investment than Gutenberg could give and sued him for debt, then seized his printing equipment as payment for the loan. Gutenberg's later career is obscure, although he seems to have continued printing in Mainz. In January 1465 the Archbishop of Mainz gave him a pension.

Guyana Country on the north-east coast of South America. The area was inhabited by Carib, Warrau and Arawak Indians when Europeans arrived in the 1500s. The Dutch created the first settlement in the 1620s, and colonies were later established by Britain and France. By the Treaty of Breda, which brought an end to the second Anglo-Dutch war of 1664-7, the Dutch gained the English colonies in Guyana. Britain gained the territory at the Congress of Vienna in 1815, and secured control in 1831, merging three settlements at Essequibo, Demerara and Berbice to form the crown colony of British Guiana. Disputes with neighbours over borders dominated the 19th century. In 1953 Britain

Gustavus Adolfus made his uniformed and well-drilled Swedish forces models for European armies of the future.

Nell Gwyn, actress and mistress of Charles II, created many original comic roles for 17th-century playwrights such as John Dryden.

suspended the constitution because it feared a possible communist takeover after the elections were won by the left-wing People's Progressive Party. The PPP won elections under a revised constitution in 1957, and in 1961 the country gained internal self-government under the party leader, Cheddi Jagan. In 1963, a small PPP majority in a new election forced them to form a coalition with the People's National Congress, and in 1964, further elections excluded the PPP from the coalition.

Britain granted independence in 1966, and Guyana became a republic in 1970. The economy, based on agriculture and mining, began to suffer from the fall in price of its main exports: rice, sugar and minerals. In December 1991, prime minister Desmond Hoyte declared a state of emergency, and the return of Cheddi Jagan in the election of October 1992 brought 28 years of rule by the PNC to an end. The new government pledged to follow the free market policies of the previous administration, while economic crisis continued.

Gwyn, Nell (1650-87) English comic actress, mistress of CHARLES II of England. Nell Gwyn sold oranges at Drury Lane Theatre in London before taking up acting. Charles made her his mistress in 1669, and she bore him two sons. Nell Gwyn was popular with the people, proclaiming 'I'm the Protestant whore' when a mob attacked her coach during the anti-Catholic fervour which followed the POPISH PLOT of 1678. She had been mistaken for another of the king's mistresses, the French-born Roman Catholic Louise de Kéroualle, Duchess of Portsmouth. Charles's deathbed instruction – 'Let not poor Nelly starve' – was carried out by his brother James II, who gave her a pension of £1500 a year.

Haakon VII (1872-1957) King of Norway from 1905 until his death. In April 1940 Haakon was driven out by the German invasion, but he refused demands by the pro-Nazi government of Vidkun QUISLING to abdicate and vowed to continue the resistance struggle from London. Haakon returned to Norway after it was liberated in 1945. He dispensed with much of the regal pomp and ceremony traditionally attached to the monarchy, and became known as the 'people's king'.

Habsburg Royal dynasty which dominated Europe from the 15th to the 20th century. The dynasty, sometimes spelt Hapsburg, was named after Habichtsburg (Hawk's Castle), Switzerland, where the family originally held lands. The founder of the Habsburg family's power was Rudolf I, king of the Romans from 1273 to 1291 and conqueror of Austria and its province of Styria, which he passed on to two of his sons in 1282. Habsburg domination of Europe resulted from the shrewd marriage policy of MAXIMILIAN I in the late 15th century. His marriage gained the Netherlands, Luxembourg and Burgundy, while that of his son, Philip, brought Castile, Aragon and the Spanish New World possessions.

From 1493 the family controlled the HOLY ROMAN EMPIRE. The zenith of its power came in the 16th century under the Holy Roman Emperor CHARLES V, who was also Charles I, king of Spain. Hungary and Bohemia were added to the empire in 1526, and Habsburg control extended over Naples, Sicily and Sardinia. After Charles' death, his brother Ferdinand ruled Germany and Austria, while his son, PHILIP II, ruled over the Spanish

inheritance. The Habsburgs' grip on Europe was weakened by the THIRTY YEARS' WAR, which broke out in 1618, despite the addition of Portugal to their territory. In the 18th century the Austrian Habsburgs flourished again under MARIA THERESA and her son JOSEPH II, but by the end of the Napoleonic wars the dynasty had lost the Austrian Netherlands and the title of Holy Roman Emperor.

The family survived the REVOLUTIONS OF 1848, but after the Austro-Prussian war of 1866 they were forced to make concessions to Hungarian nationalism and formed the dual monarchy of Austria-Hungary. The Habsburg emperor, Francis Joseph, clashed with Russia over control of the Balkans, and formed an alliance with Germany in 1879. Nationalist aspirations led to the breakup of his empire during the First World War. The last Habsburg monarch, Charles I of Austria, renounced his title in November 1918.

hacienda Large working estate, including the landowner's house, mainly in Latin America. The growth of these estates, known as *estancias* in Argentina and *fazendas* in Brazil, began in the late 17th century to supply produce for local markets. By the end of the 18th century, prominent families owned several such estates. In the 19th century, laws favouring the landowning classes and a rise in population created resentment in rural areas. The MEXICAN REVOLUTION called for the breakup of the haciendas in 1910 and 1911. Most Latin American countries have faced similar demands, and haciendas remain a political issue to this day.

Hadrian (c.AD 76-138) Roman emperor from 117 to his death. After the death of his parents while he was still a boy, Hadrian, Publius Aelius Hadrianus, was adopted by the Emperor TRAJAN, becoming his heir when he

The court of the Habsburg Emperor Francis Joseph and Queen Elisabeth receives Hungarian magnates in 1896 at celebrations commemorating 1000 years of the Hungarian monarchy.

The 4500 Jewish refugees aboard the Haganah ship *Exodus* found themselves in German camps after interception by the Royal Navy.

married Trajan's niece. Hadrian travelled to most parts of his empire during his reign, visiting the western empire from 121 to 126 – including Britain, where he ordered the building of the defensive HADRIAN'S WALL – and the eastern parts between 128 and 134. A Jewish rebellion led by Simeon BAR COCHBA broke out after Hadrian visited Palestine and announced his plan to rebuild a Romanised JERUSALEM. The Jews were also angered by the emperor's ban on the traditional practice of male circumcision. Hadrian expelled them from the Holy City and destroyed it. The remains of the ruined Temple became a place of pilgrimage known as the Wailing Wall. Hadrian enjoyed the arts, and supported a building renaissance in the empire. He designed his own villa at Tibur, now Tivoli, in Italy, the ruins of which can still be seen.

Hadrian's Wall
Defensive fortification in northern Britain, built between AD 122 and 126 during the reign of the Roman Emperor HADRIAN. It was 73 miles (117 km) long and about 15 ft (4.5 m) high, and was a stone barricade in the east and a turf barricade in the west. Large forts, milecastles and signal towers marked its length, and there were defensive ditches on both sides. Substantial remains of forts can still be seen in Northumberland at Housesteads, Great Chesters and Vindolanda. The Picts damaged the wall several times, and the Romans finally left it to decay in 383. Several long stretches still stand, and are protected as heritage sites.

Haganah
Jewish defence force in Palestine, established in 1920 as an independent, armed organisation, and then transformed into a semiofficial group to defend Jewish settlements. During the Arab rebellion of 1936 to 1939 the force was considerably expanded, gaining a general staff; it organised illegal Jewish immigration and prepared for the fight against Britain, which held the mandate over Palestine. In 1941 the organisation formed the Palmach (assault platoons). The Haganah took 4500 Jews to Palestine on board a single immigration ship, *Exodus*, chartered in the hope of forcing the British authorities to provide for them. They turned to violence after British foreign secretary Ernest Bevin refused to allow the passengers to disembark; instead they were sent back to Germany. In 1948 Haganah provided the core of the Israeli Defence Force, formed to protect the newly created state of Israel; the force later became the Israeli army.

Haig, Douglas, 1st Earl (1861-1928)
British field-marshal, army commander in chief in the First World War. Haig was criticised for his strategy of attrition, described by commentators as 'kill more Germans', while being prepared to accept heavy casualties on the SOMME in 1916 and at PASSCHENDAELE the following year. His conduct of the final campaign ended the war in 1918 more quickly than the French marshal Ferdinand FOCH expected. He then devoted himself to working for ex-servicemen, and instituted the 'Poppy Day' appeal in Britain.

Haile Selassie (1892-1975)
Emperor of Ethiopia from 1930 to 1974, though from 1935 until 1941 his rule was interrupted by the ABYSSINIAN WAR and occupation by invading Italian troops. He became Prince Ras Tafari Makonnen and heir to the throne in 1916 after leading a revolution against ruler Lij Eysu. He was crowned king in 1928 and emperor in 1930, and put a constitution into effect which limited the powers of parliament. The constitution failed, and Selassie sought exile in Britain. He regained power in 1941, with British aid, but lost touch with the social problems of his country and was deposed in 1974 by a committee of left-wing army officers. The belief that Selassie was the Messiah is the basis of the Rastafarian religion, followed by many descendants of Black Africans and Jamaicans in Britain and the USA.

Haiti
Caribbean country occupying the western third of the island of HISPANIOLA in the West Indies. Hispaniola, reached by Christopher Columbus on his first voyage to the New World in 1492, became a Spanish colony in the 16th century. The crews of French pirate ships settled in the west in the 17th century, and in 1697 Spain recognised French claims in the Treaty of Ryswick. The area was known as Saint Domingue in the 18th century, and became a profitable source of sugar and coffee for the European market. African slaves replaced a decimated Indian population, and by the end of the 18th century the population was predominantly Black.

French rule was challenged in 1791 by a successful slave rebellion led by Toussaint L'Ouverture. Under the control of former slaves, the country declared its independence in 1804, and an escaped slave, Jean DESSALINES, was proclaimed emperor. After his assassination in 1806 a separate kingdom was set up in the north, while the south and west became republican. These kingdoms were

Haile Selassie, whose name means 'Might of the Trinity', arrives at Addis Ababa in triumph in 1941. The Ethiopian capital was recaptured with British help after Italy's six-year occupation.

reunited in 1820 as an independent republic. Haiti and the eastern part of the island (later the DOMINICAN REPUBLIC) were united from 1822 to 1844.

In 1859 Haiti faced increasing unrest because of hostility between the mulatto population and the Black majority. The USA, fearing that its investments were in danger and that Germany might seize Haiti during the First World War, landed marines in 1915; they stayed until 1934. The country was then dominated for several decades by President

François DUVALIER, known as 'Papa Doc', and by his son and successor Jean Claude, 'Baby Doc'. Their secret police force, the Tonton Macoutes, terrorised the population. 'Baby Doc' was exiled to France in 1986, and a National Council of Government was formed under army commander Henri Namphy. In 1988 Namphy was overthrown and replaced by General Prosper Avril. Avril's regime ended in violence, and the Roman Catholic priest Jean-Bertrand Aristide was elected, only to resign seven months later in response to popular discontent. He was replaced by Haiti's first female president, Ertha Pascal-Trouillot, who was seized by rebel troops in September 1991. Civil violence flared up

against a new military regime. Aristide fled to Venezuela and appealed to the Organisation of American States (OAS) for help, but trade sanctions and talks failed. Violence sponsored by the army and the police prevented Aristide's return to the country, and increased sanctions held the economy in a state of crisis. In September 1994 US troops landed on Haiti to oversee the transfer of power to Aristide. Presidential elections in 1995 were won by René Préval, an associate of Aristide.

Haldane, Richard, 1st Viscount (1856-1928)
British politician who recognised the growing danger from German militarism while serving as secretary for war from 1905 to 1912, and used his knowledge of the German army to redevelop Britain's services in the face of modern war. He created an Imperial General Staff to organise military planning, and a Territorial Army as a reserve. He also formed the highly trained Expeditionary Force, mobilised later in 1914. Haldane was sent on a mission to Berlin in 1912, but failed to persuade Germany to reduce its naval arms. He subsequently served as chancellor, first under the Liberal Herbert Henry Asquith, and after the war, for Ramsay Macdonald's Labour government.

Halifax, Edward, 1st Earl of (1881-1959)
British politician, an advocate of APPEASEMENT – Neville CHAMBERLAIN's efforts to satisfy the demands of the Axis Powers. Halifax served as foreign secretary in Chamberlain's Conservative government in 1938 after Anthony EDEN resigned in protest over attempts to negotiate with the European

dictators. He accepted the absorption of Austria by Nazi Germany in 1938, and the occupation of parts of Czechoslovakia after the MUNICH PACT. He refused an invitation to Moscow, losing the chance of a possible agreement with the Soviet Union, and leaving the door open for Hitler and Stalin to draw up the NAZI-SOVIET PACT in 1939.

From 1925 to 1931 Halifax, as Lord Irwin, was governor-general and viceroy of India. He wanted the country to become a dominion and opposed the campaign for independence. In 1930 he jailed the nationalist leader Mahatma Gandhi for organising a 200 mile salt march in protest at the British monopoly of the mineral. During the Second World War Halifax was British ambassador to the USA.

Hallstatt
Prehistoric burial place in Austria which has given its name to the culture of the early IRON AGE, from about 750 to 450 BC. Many of the burials were near ancient salt mines, and as a result their contents were well preserved. At first cremation was practised, followed by burials in flat or low graves. Later the tumulus or raised BARROW became standard. Hallstatt was superseded by the Celtic La Tène culture.

Hamilcar Barca (died c.229 BC)
General, father of HANNIBAL and HASDRUBAL. Hamilcar commanded the forces of his native Carthage in the later part of the first PUNIC WAR against Rome and negotiated the peace of 241 BC. With his rival Hanno, Hamilcar defeated rebellious mercenaries. In 237 he brought southern and eastern Spain under Carthaginian control before dying in battle.

Hamilton, Alexander (1755-1804)
Shot dead by Republican Aaron BURR in a duel, Hamilton was an American Federalist statesman and financial expert. He fought in campaigns in New York, during the American Revolutionary War, before becoming George Washington's private secretary and aide-de-camp in 1777. He served in the CONTINENTAL CONGRESS from 1782 to 1783, and in 1787 he was a delegate at the Constitutional Convention in Philadelphia, PENNSYLVANIA, where he called for a strong central government. In the same year, Hamilton instigated *The Federalist*, a series of 85 essays, of which he wrote 51, which did much to persuade people to ratify the new US Constitution.

As secretary of the treasury from 1789 to 1795, Hamilton devised a financial programme which recommended setting up a Bank of the United States and advised the government to take over the debts accumulated by the Continental Congress. This 'Hamiltonian System' was supported by the FEDERALISTS and opposed by James MADISON and Thomas JEFFERSON, so helping to create the Democratic Republican Party. Hamilton

Terrified plantation owners plead for their lives during an 18th-century slaves' revolt in northern Haiti. Plantations were burned to the ground and many Whites and mulattos were slaughtered.

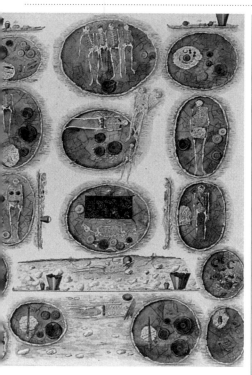

Excavations of the Hallstatt cemeteries in Austria in the 19th century uncovered more than 2000 graves showing many types of burial.

resigned from the Cabinet in 1795 and returned to New York to practise law. He constantly frustrated Aaron Burr's political ambitions, which led to their duel.

Hamilton, James, 1st Duke of (1606-49) Scottish nobleman, a supporter of the king during the ENGLISH CIVIL WAR. Charles I appointed Hamilton his commissioner in Scotland in 1638. Despite negotiations with the Scottish Presbyterian COVENANTERS he was unable to prevent their conflict with Charles, known as the Bishops' Wars. Hamilton attempted to keep Scotland neutral in the Civil War, and was made a duke in 1643, only to be forced out of Scotland a few months later by the Covenanters. He was suspected of treachery, expelled from the king's supporters and imprisoned for more than two years. In 1646 he led an army against Oliver Cromwell's Parliamentary forces at PRESTON, but was defeated and later executed.

Hammarskjöld, Dag (1905-61) Swedish diplomat, secretary-general of the UNITED NATIONS from 1953, who once described himself as 'the curator of the secrets of 82 nations'. Dag Hammarskjöld set up an emergency force to help to maintain order in the Middle East after the SUEZ CRISIS, and UN observation forces were sent to Laos and Lebanon. Hammarskjöld initiated and directed the UN role in the CONGO CRISIS by using Article 99 of the UN Charter, which he believed allowed the secretary-general to use his initiative independently of the Security Council or the General Assembly. While on his way to visit the Congo, Hammarskjöld was killed in a plane crash which some speculated was caused by sabotage.

Hammurabi (d.1750BC) Amorite king of BABYLON who greatly extended his inherited lands until they stretched from the Persian Gulf to parts of Assyria. He also encouraged agriculture and literature. In 1901 a code of laws bearing his name was found inscribed on a column at Susa, near Dizful in Iran. This code, although based on traditional law, has given him a personal reputation for justice.

Hampden, John (1594-1643) English politician and Parliamentarian. He became a national figure when he was prosecuted in 1637 for refusing to pay SHIP MONEY, a tax revived by Charles I to pay for the Royal Navy. Ship money was even levied on inland towns and their residents. Hampden's stand gave many the courage not to pay the tax. Ten years earlier he had been jailed for refusing to pay a 'forced loan' to finance unpopular foreign campaigns. A member of the LONG PARLIAMENT, Hampden survived the king's attempt to arrest him and four other MPs in 1642, and was appointed to the Committee of Safety to organise the Parliamentary forces in the ENGLISH CIVIL WAR. He died of wounds received at a Civil War battle in Oxfordshire.

Hampton Court Conference (1604) Meeting in which JAMES I, the new king of England, presided over an assembly of bishops and Puritans to discuss a 'Millenary Petition' presented to him by the Puritans in April 1603, listing Church practices offensive to them. The king refused most of the Puritans' demands, although agreement was reached on the production of a new translation of the Bible known as the Authorised Version of 1611, now called the King James Bible.

Han Chinese dynasty established in 206BC at the overthrow of the QIN, the first imperial dynasty, by the rebel peasant Liu Pang. The dynasty lasted for more than 400 years, with only a short interruption from AD9 to 25. The Chinese distinguish themselves from other Mongoloid peoples by calling themselves the 'men of Han'. After 'the Martial Emperor' Wudi – ruler from 141 to 87BC – halted onslaughts by nomad horsemen, the Xiongnu, Chinese armies were able to penetrate deep into central Asia. Some marched more than 2000 miles (3200km) west of the Western Han capital Chang'an, now Xi'an. Envoys seeking alliances against the Xiongnu also travelled far west, returning with news of the Roman Empire. Camel trains taking out silks, bringing back jade and horses larger than those known in China, travelled the SILK ROAD. Much of south China and Annam was conquered, and Han rule extended over part of Korea. The teachings of CONFUCIUS were gradually accepted as the state philosophy.

By AD9, the court was oppressed by economic problems and torn by strife. Wang Mang, chief minister of a boy-emperor he had placed on the throne, seized power and established the Xin dynasty, which lasted until a Taoist-inspired rebellion and renewed invasions by the Xiongnu caused his downfall. In 25, the Han dynasty was restored when Prince Liu Xiu set up a court in Luoyang. Soon, Chinese armies again penetrated central Asia.

The Han period was notable for its artistic achievements and its technological advances, and for the arrival of the first Buddhist missionaries. But by the end of the 2nd century, Taoist rebellion and the ambitions of empresses and eunuchs led to the near collapse of the dynasty and the growth of regional armies. The last Han emperor abdicated, and China split into three warring states, the THREE KINGDOMS.

Hancock, John (1737-93) American merchant and Revolutionary leader, the first to sign the American DECLARATION OF INDEPENDENCE in 1776. Hancock inherited his uncle's mercantile business in Boston and supplemented his fortune by smuggling. This brought him into open conflict with British customs officers with the seizure of his sloop *Liberty* in 1768. He helped to organise the BOSTON TEA PARTY, and signed the Declaration of Independence while president of the Second CONTINENTAL CONGRESS. Hancock became the first governor of independent Massachusetts, a position which he held for 11 years.

Handel, George (1685-1759) German-born composer of the *Messiah* oratorio who spent most of his working life in Britain. Handel became an organist at Halle Cathedral in 1702, while studying law. He gave up his studies in 1703 to become a violinist at the composer Reinhard Keiser's Opera House in Hamburg. In 1705 his first operas, *Almira* and *Nero*, were successful and led to an invitation to work in Italy. Handel became a leading composer of Italian opera, but went to Germany in 1710 to take up the post of Kapellmeister (director of music) to the Elector of Hanover – later GEORGE I of England. After he took up residence in England in 1712, his operas dominated the London stage. Pressure of work damaged his health, and financial difficulties in 1736 forced him to work in the less costly field of oratorio. His fortunes were restored after the successes of *Israel in Egypt* (1739), *Saul* (1739), and the *Messiah* (1742), and Handel died a wealthy man.

Hanna, Marcus Alonzo (1837-1904) US
businessman and politician, one of the most powerful political organisers of modern times. Hanna joined his father's wholesale grocery business in Cleveland, and started a successful partnership with him in 1862 dealing in coal, iron and shipping. By 1890, he was the most powerful man in the Ohio Republican Party, and supported the election of Republican William MCKINLEY to the governorship of the state. Hanna used campaign contributions from big business to back McKinley for the presidency in 1896. In an expensive and well-organised campaign paid for by the deft use of patronage, he undermined the support for Democrat William Bryan in the presidential election of 1896. McKinley won, and Hanna was elected to the Senate in 1897.

Hannibal (247-c.182BC) Carthaginian general, an outstanding tactician and leader. As a young man Hannibal accompanied his father HAMILCAR BARCA to Spain. Hamilcar established a province there. Hannibal was given supreme command in Spain in 221BC and adopted an aggressive policy towards the Romans. During the second PUNIC WAR in 218 he marched over the Alps in 15 days with about 40000 troops and a procession of elephants, intending to march into northern Italy and take the Romans by surprise. Many elephants and troops died during the arduous journey, but Hannibal inflicted three crushing defeats on the Romans, at Trebia in 218, at Lake Trasimene in 217 and at CANNAE in 216.

Despite winning over many southern Italian communities, central and northern Italy remained largely loyal to Rome. Hannibal was unable to break Rome's resistance and the tide of war gradually turned against him, until in 203 he was recalled with his army to Africa. The next year, he was defeated at Zama by the Roman general SCIPIO AFRICANUS. Hannibal pursued a programme of political reforms in Carthage around 196 which provoked his enemies to complain to Rome, and he fled abroad. He spent time at the courts of Antiochus III of Syria and Prusias of Bithynia, both enemies of Rome, before committing suicide in 183 or 182 to avoid capture by the Romans.

A Carthaginian
coin commemorates
the epic journey of
Hannibal across the Alps.

Hanover Former north German kingdom.
The city of Hanover was a member of the HANSEATIC LEAGUE, a north German trading alliance, from 1386, and became capital of the kingdom in 1692. The name also continued through the German dynasty who ruled Britain and Ireland from GEORGE I in 1714 to the death of VICTORIA in 1901.

In 1658 Sophia, the daughter of Elizabeth of Bohemia and granddaughter of James I of England, married Ernest Augustus, Duke of Brunswick-Lüneburg. In 1692 Ernest became an Elector of Germany and took Hanover as his title. Sophia and Ernest's son became George I, the first Hanoverian king of Great Britain, in 1714. The Hanoverian territories included the strategic towns of Göttingen and Hildesheim in the north-west, and their defence was an important factor in British foreign policy during the 18th century. In the NAPOLEONIC WARS of 1796 to 1815, most of Hanover became part of the Kingdom of Westphalia, created by Napoleon in 1807. In 1810 the rest of the territory was divided between Westphalia and France, but in 1815 the British crown regained it at the Congress of Vienna. Hanover became a kingdom in its own right as a part of the new GERMAN CONFEDERATION in the same year.

Succession in Hanover – unlike in Britain – was governed by Salic Law, which barred a woman from succession to the throne. When Victoria became queen of England in 1837 her uncle Ernest Augustus became king of Hanover. He revoked the liberal constitution of 1815, but was forced to restore it after unrest during the Revolutions of 1848, a series of revolts across Europe against autocratic government. In 1866 Hanover was annexed by Prussia, whom it had opposed in the AUSTRO-PRUSSIAN WAR. The kingdom was dissolved and it became a province of Prussia within the North German Confederation. After the Second World War Hanover was incorporated into adjoining territories to form the state of Lower Saxony.

Hanseatic League Trading alliance of
north German cities, named after the German word *hanse*, meaning 'group' or 'society'. The alliance originated from a league formed by Hamburg and Lübeck in 1241 to guarantee security and special trading rights to one another. By the 1280s, many other German cities had joined the association, which was led by Lübeck. League members dealt mainly in wool, cloth, linen and silver. They also joined together to combat pirates, and took other measures to keep ships safe, building lighthouses and training helmsmen. In the later Middle Ages the Hanseatic League had between about 100 and 160 member towns, and became an independent political power with its own army and navy. It also fought a number of successful wars between

Hamburg's key role in the Hanseatic League as a major centre of maritime trade is shown in this illustration from its 1497 City Charter.

1350 and 1450. In the early 17th century the League began to disintegrate, until only Hamburg, Bremen and Lübeck remained.

Hapsburg see HABSBURG

Hardie, Keir (1856-1915) British politician,
leader from 1906 of the first Parliamentary Labour Party. Hardie worked as a miner in Scotland from the age of ten, and entered journalism and politics after he was barred by the coal-owners for militant union activities. Originally a Liberal, he broke away in 1888 to form the Scottish Labour Party, but his first attempts to become an MP ended in defeat. He succeeded in 1892, becoming chairman of the INDEPENDENT LABOUR PARTY the following year. Hardie lost his seat in the Commons in 1895, and afterwards worked towards linking the party with other socialist organisations to form the Labour Representation Committee in 1900. Hardie was also an outspoken pacifist, and in 1903 he became chief adviser to the SUFFRAGETTE movement.

Harding, Warren (1865-1923) President of
the USA from 1921 until his death. Warren Harding was used by an ambitious lawyer, Harry Daugherty, who helped him to win the office of lieutenant-governor of Ohio in 1904 and to become a senator in 1915. Five years later, Daugherty successfully promoted him as a compromise Republican candidate for the presidency. Harding brought many of his self-seeking friends, the 'Ohio Gang', into office, which resulted in a series of political scandals such as the TEAPOT DOME scandal, in which US navy oil reserves stored at Teapot Dome, Wyoming, were illegally leased to an oil company. Albert Fall, the secretary of the interior and a member of the 'Ohio Gang', was jailed for three years for accepting a $100 000 bribe

in the case. The scandals obscured Harding's achievements, such as the 1922 Washington National Conference, aimed at reducing naval strength among the world powers. He died suddenly, and it was only after his death that the corruption behind his administration was fully revealed.

Harley, Robert, 1st Earl of Oxford

(1661-1724) English statesman, head of the Tory government from 1710 to 1714. Harley entered Parliament as a Whig, but before the accession of Queen Anne, he became a Tory, serving as speaker of the House of Commons and secretary of state. His greatest achievement was the Peace of UTRECHT, which ended the Spanish War of Succession in 1713. In the power struggle among the Tories just before the death of Queen Anne in 1714, Harley lost to Viscount Henry BOLINGBROKE. The Whig administration of GEORGE I imprisoned him on suspicion of treason as a Jacobite, and prepared a case against him. Harley was acquitted and released two years later, but he took no further part in public affairs.

harness

In the Middle East, oxen were harnessed as draught animals as early as 4000 BC. A bar was tied to the horns of a pair of oxen to take the strain of hauling a plough or a cart. By 2500 BC in Mesopotamia asses were being harnessed for farm work and for pulling vehicles. The neck collars they wore could choke an animal pulling too heavy a weight. Loads remained small until the European Dark Ages, when the addition of a chest strap to a well-padded collar distributed the strain. This allowed heavier loads to be drawn, and its design has survived to the present day.

Harold I

(c.850-933) First king of all Norway, from 872 until his death. A series of battles with minor kings ended with Harold's victory at Hafrsfjord in about 890, giving him control of the western coastal districts. His taxation system and conquests forced many to emigrate to Britain and Iceland. Harold followed the emigrants to Britain, and brought the Orkney and Shetland islands, together with much of northern Scotland, into his kingdom. Harold is mostly known through poems in 13th-century Icelandic manuscripts.

Harold II

(c.1020-66) King of England in 1066, the second son of the powerful Earl GODWIN of Wessex, whom he succeeded in 1053. Harold's sister Edith was married to King EDWARD THE CONFESSOR, and his brother Tostig was Earl of Northumbria. Harold, Godwin and Tostig were exiled for defying royal authority, but in 1052 they returned to political life in England. In 1065 the Northumbrians revolted against Tostig. Harold supported their choice of Morcar, the brother of the Earl of Mercia, as the new earl, a

On the Bayeux Tapestry, Harold II is offered the crown and axe (left), symbols of authority, by members of the witan, or council. He is then crowned in Westminster by Archbishop Stigand.

choice which split the family. He succeeded Edward the Confessor as king in 1066, despite the Norman claim that Edward had made the French Duke William of Normandy his heir. Tostig raided the south-east coast, then joined the invasion of northern England by Harald Hardrada, the Norwegian king. Harold defeated them at STAMFORD BRIDGE, killing Tostig and Hardrada, and marched 250 miles (400 km) south to face Duke William at the Battle of HASTINGS, where he was killed.

Harrington, James

(1611-77) English philosopher and political theorist. Harrington is said to have influenced the framing of the US Constitution with his insistence on a written constitution and a two-chamber legislative system. His work *The Commonwealth of Oceana* (1656) showed his Republican sympathies, but he was a friend of Charles I and was briefly imprisoned with him. Even so, Charles II arrested him for treason in 1661. He was freed, but his health had been destroyed.

Harrison, Benjamin

(1833-1901) President of the USA from 1889 to 1893, grandson of former president William Henry Harrison. During Harrison's Republican administration, the US desire for more markets helped to stimulate the Pan-American movement of co-operation between South, Central and North America, while Pacific imperialist interests were pursued in Hawaii and Samoa. His domestic policies included the ANTI-TRUST LAWS, which limited company monopolies; the McKinley Tariff Act, which raised import duties in the interests of domestic manufacturers; and the Sherman Silver Purchase Act, giving a federal subsidy to silver producers in the west. Harrison also created extra benefits for Civil War veterans unable to work. He retired to Indianapolis to practise law after his defeat by Grover CLEVELAND in 1893.

Harun ar-Rashid

(c.766-809) From 786 he was the fifth ABBASSID caliph (from the Arabic *khalifa*, 'deputy of God'), whose name means 'Aaron the rightly guided'. Harun's court and capital provided the setting for many stories in the *Thousand and One Nights*. He was a competent commander and a patron of the arts. Under his rule, Baghdad reached its greatest brilliance, partly through the ability of his court officials, the Persian VIZIERS. The Persian Barmakid family controlled the empire at the time Harun came to power, but court intrigues turned Harun against them in 803, and many of them were imprisoned. Hostilities between civil servants and religious scholars within the empire accelerated, and Harun's division of his inheritance led to nine years of further conflict after his death.

Harvey, William

(1578-1657) English scientist, physician to James I and Charles I, who discovered how blood circulated in the body. Harvey advanced the theory, which was later proved, that blood was pumped by the heart through the arteries and back through the veins. The theory was first made public in 1616 and was greeted with disbelief. Harvey's reputation suffered as a consequence, and only later was his theory accepted.

The original notebooks in which William Harvey recorded his discoveries still survive.

A cartoonist showed Warren Hastings (centre), accused by Edmund Burke (left) and protected by Edward Thurlow and the Devil (right). He holds a pie representing Elijah Impey, (imp-pie), chief justice in India, with whom Hastings was accused of arranging the murder of a moneylender.

Hastings, Battle of (October 14, 1066) Battle fought at Senlac Hill, 6 miles (10 km) inland from Hastings in south-east England, between the English under HAROLD II and an invading army of about 8000 men under Duke William of Normandy, later to become WILLIAM I. Harold heard of the Norman invasion after his defeat of the Norwegian invader Harald Hardrada in September at the Battle of STAMFORD BRIDGE. He immediately marched south to confront William. The English troops resisted Norman attack for many hours and William was nearly killed, but the Norman crossbowmen and cavalry eventually proved superior. Harold was killed during the battle, and William marched on London to be crowned king on December 25.

Hastings, Warren (1732-1818) British administrator and the first governor-general of BENGAL from 1774 to 1785. Hastings worked his way up from being a clerk in the EAST INDIA COMPANY to the management of a trading post in Bengal and appointment to the administrative councils of Calcutta and Madras. While serving as governor-general, he faced difficulties when enemies on his council continually attempted to obstruct his policies. Hastings consolidated the conquests of the British general Robert CLIVE in north-eastern India, but was afterwards accused of dishonest practices, a charge instigated by the British statesman Edmund BURKE. A quarrel with a council member, Philip Francis, ended in a duel; both survived and Francis spread tales of Hastings's alleged malpractices. The impeachment charges he faced in 1787 included the waging of unjustified wars, extortion from Indian rulers and collaborating with the chief justice of Bengal to bring about the judicial murder of an Indian moneylender who had threatened him. Hastings had the support of the British Lord Chancellor, Edward Thurlow. After a seven-year trial, beginning in 1788, he was acquitted, and lived to see his policies vindicated by the company's success in India.

Hatshepsut (c.1540-c.1481 BC) Ruler of ancient Egypt, the daughter of THUTMOSE I. After the death of Thutmose II, her half-brother and husband, Hatshepsut's young nephew THUTMOSE III succeeded, but he was too young to fight for his position and Hatshepsut took over as effective ruler. She was crowned as pharaoh, even donning a false beard to persuade officials to accept her authority as if she were a man. Hatshepsut extended her father's buildings at KARNAK, the religious centre of Thebes. Her rule came to an end after 20 years; she may have been forced out by Thutmose III, or may have died. When her nephew took power, many of Hatshepsut's monuments were defaced to erase signs of her reign.

The idealised face of Queen Hatshepsut was carved on her magnificent funerary temple at Deir el-Bahri in western Thebes.

Hausa Inhabitants of northern Nigeria. The original Hausa states, including the cities of Kano and Zaria, were the vassals of the neighbouring state of Bornu to the north-east in the 14th and 15th centuries. Muslim missionaries arrived in the 14th century, and in the late 15th century the *shariah*, the Muslim code of law, was introduced, along with the mystic practices of the Sufis and a code of constitutional theory. The Hausa were conquered in 1513 by the Songhay, rulers of a powerful trading empire centred on the middle reaches of the Niger river.

In the early years of the 19th century the Fulani, who ruled an Islamic empire in western Africa, launched a series of holy wars to 'purify Islam' and took control of the country. They settled in the area and adopted the Hausa culture and language.

Havel, Václav (1936-) Czech statesman, president of Czechoslovakia from 1989 to 1992 and president of the Czech Republic from 1993. Havel was born in Prague. As the son of a family of bourgeois descent living under a communist regime he was excluded from university. He worked as a laboratory assistant and taxi driver until he obtained a job as a stagehand at a theatrical academy. He wrote and published a number of plays before 1968, when his work was declared subversive and banned, but he continued to write and to publish abroad. His plays include *The Garden Party* (1963) and *Largo Desolato* (1985).

In 1977 Havel formed a Committee for the Defence of the Unjustly Persecuted. Twelve years later, after years of imprisonment by the government for supporting Charter 77, a manifesto demanding human rights, he helped to form the Civic Forum, a coalition of noncommunist opposition groups.

In December 1989 the Forum led a popular uprising, the Velvet Revolution, which forced the government to resign, and was followed by the downfall of communism in the country. Havel was elected president at the end of the year, but resigned when the country split into the Slovak and Czech nations in 1993. He was elected president of the new Czech Republic in the same year.

Hawaii State of the USA comprising a chain of islands in the North Pacific. The populated islands, inhabited by Polynesians and ruled by kings, were named the Sandwich Islands by the English explorer Captain James Cook in 1778, after his patron the Earl of Sandwich. American missionaries went to the islands in the 1820s and helped to evolve a written language: the first constitution was written in 1839. The main crops of Hawaii are pineapple and sugar cane. The sugar industry was introduced in the 1830s, and by 1893 a number of the new settlers, backed by American sugar interests, wanted the USA to take over the

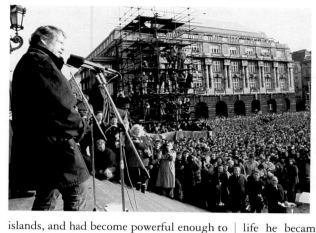

Václav Havel addresses a rally in Wenceslas Square, Prague. Havel consistently campaigned for the recognition of human rights in Czechoslovakia.

islands, and had become powerful enough to overthrow the Hawaiian monarchy under Queen Liliuokalani. Five years later, the USA was persuaded to annex the region. It declared Hawaii a territory of the USA in 1900, and installed its chief Pacific naval base in PEARL HARBOR on the island of Oahu. Hawaii became the 50th US state in 1959.

Hawkins, Sir John (1532-95) English admiral, largely responsible for creating the fleet which defeated the SPANISH ARMADA in 1588. Hawkins made the first English slave-trading voyage from Africa to the West Indies in 1562. His third voyage in 1567 ended in disaster when Spaniards attacked his ships at San Juan de Ulua, Mexico. Only two ships, commanded by Hawkins and Sir Francis DRAKE, were able to escape.

Hawkins became a Member of Parliament in 1572, and succeeded his father-in-law as treasurer of the navy in 1577. He was third in command of the Armada fleet in 1588, after Lord Howard of Effingham and Sir Francis Drake, and was knighted at sea during the battle. Hawkins died during a raiding expedition in the Spanish West Indies.

Hawkins, Sir Richard (c.1560-1622) Commander in the Elizabethan navy, son of Sir John HAWKINS. He served under Sir Francis DRAKE in an expedition to the West Indies in 1585 and during the battle against the SPANISH ARMADA in 1588. In 1593 he left

England with the intention of surveying eastern Asia, where he was hoping to establish an English trading empire. On the way there, he plundered Valparaíso, a port in Spanish America, and was held by the Spaniards until 1602, when a ransom of £3000 was paid. In the final years of Hawkins' life he became vice-admiral of Devon in south-west England and mounted a campaign to combat coastal pirates.

Haydn, Joseph (1732-1809) Austrian composer, one of the most skilled musical craftsmen of all time. As a boy, Haydn was a chorister, and in 1740 he was chosen for the choir of St Stephen's Cathedral, Vienna, where he remained for 20 years. In 1761 he entered the service of the aristocratic Magyar family of Esterházy, directing all the musical activities which took place at their palace at Eisenstadt. He composed church, opera, chamber and orchestral music, including 104 symphonies. His employer, Nikolaus Esterházy, died in 1790, and Haydn moved to Vienna, though he continued to work for Esterházy's grandson. Two successful visits to London over the next five years led to his last 12 'London' symphonies, and increased his interest in choral music. In collaboration with the amateur musician Baron von Swieten, Haydn composed two oratorios in the English instead of the Italian manner, giving an important role to the choir rather than using just the aria for a solo singer. *The Creation* was completed in 1798 and *The Seasons* in 1801.

health services Ancient civilisations cared for their sick in religious communities. In the first millennium BC, temples dedicated to gods of healing appeared; these were the earliest type of HOSPITAL. Disease was rife in

Europe in the Middle Ages, where sufferers were looked after in monastic communities. After the Dissolution of the Monasteries by Henry VIII from 1535 to 1541, civil authorities made provision for the sick in England.

The Industrial Revolution led to an increase in ill health among late 18th century workers. By the early 19th century, a population explosion and progress in medical science in Europe led to an increased awareness of health hazards and ways of improving public health. Voluntary hospitals were founded to care for the sick and better SANITATION systems were built. Towards the end of the century Russia established state health services, and the first system of health insurance was set up in 1883 by Otto von Bismarck in Germany.

In the early 20th century, the development of state hospitals and health insurance became one of the main concerns of nations which had developed a WELFARE STATE – a society which

> 66 **I would rather be kept alive in the efficient if cold altruism of a large hospital than expire in a gush of warm sympathy in a small one.** 99
>
> *Aneurin Bevan, British Labour politician, on creating the National Health Service, April 30, 1946*

attempted to look after the basic requirements of all of its citizens. In Britain, the National Health Service was set up in 1946. Two years later, the United Nations established the World Health Organisation to look after the needs of both industrialised and developing countries. Longer life-expectancy and rising costs in industrialised countries are imposing greater strains on public health services, and developing countries are still disadvantaged by a lack of skilled physicians and funding.

Hearst, William Randolph (1863-1951) US newspaper publisher and journalist. From newspapers Hearst branched out into magazines and films, and he amassed a colossal fortune. His exaggerated accounts of Cuba's struggle for independence from Spain were popularly believed to have helped to provoke

Joseph Haydn conducts from the piano as a smartly uniformed orchestra rehearses. He is dressed in gentleman's attire, showing his rise in social status and reputation since his early days in the service of his patron, Nikolaus Esterházy, when he would have dressed as a liveried servant.

William Hearst (right) entertained the stars on a grand scale at San Simeon, his Californian castle, complete with opulent swimming pool.

the SPANISH-AMERICAN WAR in 1898. He opposed US entry into the First World War, and he was always hostile to the League of Nations. His own incursions into politics, for example as candidate for the post of mayor of New York, were unsuccessful. Hearst was the model on which the megalomaniac newspaper magnate played by Orson Welles in his 1941 film *Citizen Kane* was based.

Heath, Edward (1916-) British politician, leader of the Conservative Party from 1965 to 1975 and prime minister from 1970 to 1974. Heath entered Parliament in 1950 and became minister of labour in 1959. In July 1961 he began negotiations to make Britain part of the European Economic Community, now the EUROPEAN UNION. His achievement of this ambition just over a decade later in 1973 stands as his principal legacy. Heath took over the leadership of the party from Alec Douglas Home in 1965; he was defeated in the 1966 general election but won a surprise victory in 1970.

As prime minister, Heath froze workers' wages in 1973 in an attempt to solve Britain's growing economic crisis. In protest, the coal miners led a wave of strikes, which forced him to introduce a three-day working week to conserve dwindling reserves of coal at the electricity generating stations. He called an election to try to strengthen his position, but was defeated. Labour's Harold WILSON returned to office as prime minister. Heath lost the leadership of the Conservative Party to Margaret Thatcher in 1975.

Hebrides Group of islands off the west coast of Scotland. They comprise two archipelagos lying parallel to the mainland: the Outer Hebrides, consisting of Lewis, Harris, the Uists and Barra; and the Inner Hebrides of Skye, Mull, Islay and Jura. The largest few dozen islands have been inhabited since around 3800 BC, first by PICTS and then, from the 3rd century AD, by Scots. St Columba converted the islands to Christianity in the 6th century. Scandinavians settled there from about 800, and the area was controlled by Norway from 890 to 1266. The islanders' way of life, which was based on subsistence farming and fishing, changed little until the 19th century, when sheep farming on a large scale and the clearance of crofters gave rise to depopulation and widespread deprivation.

Hegel, George (1770-1831) German philosopher who was influenced by Romanticism and the work of Immanuel KANT. Hegel began by arguing that Kant's division of reality into knowable and unknowable areas was wrong. In *The Phenomenology of Mind* (1807) he viewed the world as a *Geist*, 'spirit', which evolved to become more rational as *Geist* moved on to higher levels of self-consciousness. This process was to be described by the dialectic, a method of argument different from deduction, in which every stage of history is composed of a thesis, or form of idea, contradicted by an antithesis, or its opposite. This conflict would produce a higher thesis, which is contradicted by a new antithesis, and so on. Hegel's vision, in which history is governed by laws and the world forms an organic whole, proved that 'the rational is the real'.

His concept of dialectics was adopted by Karl MARX to prove that revolutionary social changes were inevitable. Hegel's work also inspired the theories of the French philosopher Jean-Paul Sartre and the German socialist Ferdinand Lassalle. His theory of the state was adopted by a group known as the Young Hegelians, who argued for the unification of the German states.

hegira Name for the secret departure of MUHAMMAD from Mecca in AD 622 to live among the people of Yathrib, later Medina, so founding the first Muslim community. The word comes from the Arabic *hjira*, meaning 'exodus' or 'migration'. Muhammad believed in the existence of only one god and preached against the practice followed in Mecca of worshipping many gods. He left because of the hostility of merchants who earned their living from the pilgrims who visited Mecca. Under the second caliph, Umar, this key event in the history of Islam was chosen as the starting-point for the Muslim calendar.

Heisenberg, Werner (1901-76) German physicist who expanded on Albert EINSTEIN's quantum theory using matrices. Heisenberg studied theoretical physics in Munich before lecturing at Göttingen in 1924, where he began to formulate his radical reinterpretation of how atomic particles behave. In 1927 Heisenberg published a revolutionary theory, the uncertainty principle, based on the limited precision of simultaneous measurements of position and velocity. Three years later he published his work on the matrix theory in *The Physical Principles of the Quantum Theory*, which influenced the development of atomic and nuclear physics. Heisenberg taught at Leipzig from 1927 to 1941, and subsequently at physics institutes in Berlin and Göttingen.

Helena, St (c.250-c.330) Wife of Emperor Constantius Chlorus and mother of the first Christian emperor, CONSTANTINE. Constantine made Helena empress dowager, and influenced her conversion to Christianity when she was already over 60. She became known for her piety and acts of charity, and for building churches on the sites of the Nativity and the Ascension. She died while on pilgrimage to Palestine and was buried in Rome.

Heligoland Small island in the North Sea. Originally the home of FRISIAN fishermen, Heligoland was Danish from 1714 until it was seized by the British navy in 1807. It was ceded to Britain eight years later, then exchanged with Germany in 1890 in return for ZANZIBAR and Pemba in the Indian Ocean. Germany developed the island into a naval base of great importance. Its naval installations were demolished after the First World War under the terms of the VERSAILLES PEACE SETTLEMENT. Rebuilt by the Nazis, they were demolished a second time after the Second World War. The island was returned to the Federal Republic of Germany in 1952.

Heliopolis Greek name, meaning 'Sun City', for the ancient Egyptian city of Iunu or Onu, now a suburb of Cairo. Heliopolis was a centre for the worship of the Egyptian sun-god, Ra.

St Helena uncovers wooden crucifixes while building a church for her son, Constantine, at Golgotha in Jerusalem. Legend tells how she discovered the cross on which Jesus was crucified.

Its temple was the largest in Egypt after that of Amun at KARNAK. The city has few remains; its buildings were broken up between the 3rd and the 1st centuries BC. 'Cleopatra's Needle', now in London, and a similar obelisk in New York were both originally erected in Heliopolis by THUTMOSE III.

Hellenistic civilisation Art and culture of Greece which spread widely in the Middle East and beyond after the conquests of Alexander the Great in Assyria, Asia Minor, Egypt and the Punjab between 336 BC and his death in 323. The cities founded by Alexander and his successors were centres for a fusion of Greek and local ways of life. ALEXANDRIA in Egypt became a cultural focus of the Mediterranean world. Greek became the dominant language, and an important element in the spread of the new culture was the development of a common Greek dialect, *Koine*. The Hellenic world had fallen to Rome by 146 BC, but its culture had a profound influence on subsequent Roman civilisation.

Hellespont Strait now known as the Dardanelles that joins the Aegean Sea with the Sea of Marmara and separates Europe from Asia. It has long been a key strategic point. Ancient Troy stood near the western end. King Xerxes I crossed the strait with his Persian army using a bridge of boats around 481 BC, and it was crossed by Alexander the Great in 334 BC. Control of the Hellespont allowed the Spartans to cut

'Cleopatra's Needle', a red granite obelisk from Heliopolis, was erected on the Embankment of the Thames in London in the 19th century.

off corn supplies to Athens from the Black Sea area, an act which brought an end to the PELOPONNESIAN WAR in 404 BC.

Hell Fire Club English secret society founded by Sir Francis Dashwood in 1745. The club met in Medmenham Abbey and West Wycombe Park in Buckinghamshire. Its members were reputed to indulge in debauchery and mock religion with blasphemous 'black masses'. Many politicians were members, among them John WILKES, John BUTE and the Earl of Sandwich.

Helot Bondsman or SERF in ancient Spartan society. Helots were used as agricultural labourers, and to a lesser extent in domestic service. The inhabitants of Laconia in the southern Peloponnese became Helots when they were conquered by the Dorians around 1000 BC. The Spartans emerged as the dominant faction among the Dorians, and during the 8th and 7th centuries BC they conquered Messenia, a large fertile region in the south-western Peloponnese. The Spartans were greatly outnumbered by the Messinians, and kept them as Helots under tight military control to guard against rebellion.

Helsinki Conference (1973-5) Meetings at Helsinki, and later Geneva, attended by leaders of 35 nations who represented the membership of NATO, the WARSAW PACT and the non-aligned countries, at which the Conference on Security and Cooperation in Europe was launched in 1975. The conference was proposed by the Soviet Union to confirm post-1945 frontiers and to arrange further economic and technical cooperation. It produced the Helsinki Final Act, a list of agreements on technical cooperation and human rights. All signatories agreed to

respect 'freedom of thought, conscience, religion and belief'. These provisions were not always honoured but the meetings did help to reduce East-West tension.

Helvetii Celts who migrated from southern Germany to the areas south and west of the Rhine in the 2nd century BC. In 102 BC they joined the Cimbri and Teutones invading Italy, and were defeated by the Roman general Gaius Marius. Their quest for land led them to attempt a mass migration into Roman GAUL in 58 BC, but Julius Caesar drove them back. The Roman emperor Augustus then incorporated their territory into Belgic Gaul. The Helvetii were finally overrun in the 5th century by a succession of Alemanni, Franks, Swabians and Burgundians.

Helvétius, Claude Adrien (1715-71) French philosopher and wealthy financier. Originally a tax collector, he retired to become a writer. His book *De l'Esprit* (*On the Mind*), published in 1758, was condemned by the French court and Church as immoral and publicly burned. Its theme was that self-interest is

> 66 **What makes men happy is liking what they have to do. This is a principle on which society is not founded.** 99
>
> *Claude Adrien Helvétius*
> *De l'Esprit, 1758*

the basis of all human action and should be used by government in the public interest: the well-being of the human race could be ensured by enlightened government, without changing human nature. Helvétius also contributed to the *Encyclopédie*, a key publication of the age of ENLIGHTENMENT.

Hengist and Horsa Brothers from the Germanic tribe of JUTES, leaders of the first Anglo-Saxon invasion of England. According to legend, Hengist and Horsa were invited by the 5th-century Romano-British king, VORTIGERN, to help to reinforce British resistance to the raiding Picts and Scots around AD 449. The ANGLO-SAXON CHRONICLE describes how they turned against Vortigern and seized land in Kent, and it recounts the death of Horsa in battle and the succession of Aesc, the son of Hengist.

Henrietta Maria (1609-69) French princess, queen consort of CHARLES I of England from 1625 until his death. Henrietta Maria's Catholicism made her unpopular and increased public fears about the religious sympathies of the court. As the Puritan opposition to the Crown strengthened, Henrietta began to take an active part in politics. Her efforts to win support for Charles from the pope, the

Henrietta Maria of France married Charles I at 16. A devout Catholic, she refused to attend her husband's Protestant coronation service.

Dutch and the French angered the English. The rumour that Parliament was to impeach the queen drove Charles to attempt the arrest of five Members of Parliament – one of the incidents that led to the ENGLISH CIVIL WAR. From 1644 Henrietta lived mainly in France, visiting England again only briefly in October 1660, after the Restoration.

Henry I (c.876-936) Duke of Saxony from 912 and king of Germany from 919 until his death. A successful warrior, Henry brought many new territories under his control. He was elected king by the Franks and Saxons in 919. He laid a strong foundation for his son, OTTO I, despite challenges from his nobility. Henry's system of fortified defences foiled Hungarian invaders, whom he defeated in 933 at the Battle of the Riade. The following year he invaded Denmark in one of his last campaigns, and took over the region of Schleswig. He was also known as Henry the Fowler; it is not known why, though one legend tells that he was laying bird snares when he was told he had been elected king.

Henry I (1068-1135) King of England from 1100 until his death, son of William the Conqueror. When his brother WILLIAM II died in a hunting accident, Henry seized the treasury – and control of royal funds – at Winchester, and was crowned three days later in London while his eldest brother Robert was out of the country on a Crusade. In compensation Robert received the Duchy of Normandy and an annual pension of £2000. In 1106 Henry invaded Normandy, and defeated his brother at Tinchebrai. Robert was imprisoned in Cardiff Castle, where he died in 1134. Henry was a determined ruler, and he clashed with the Archbishop of Canterbury, St ANSELM, over the king's traditional right to appoint bishops, a practice which was known as lay INVESTITURE. After two years of debate, Henry retained control of appointments, but he agreed not to carry out the traditional rituals. He needed money to defend the Duchy of Normandy, and this spurred him to make improvements to royal administration, particularly at the EXCHEQUER, by making the collection of taxes more efficient. He also reformed the courts: his law code combined the old laws of the country with Norman ideas of justice. A political crisis was triggered when in November 1120 his only legitimate son, William, drowned on a journey to England from Normandy, supposedly because the crew was drunk. After Henry's death the crown was seized by his nephew STEPHEN instead of going to his designated heir, his daughter MATILDA, leading to a long civil war.

Henry II (1133-89) King of England from 1154 until his death, and the founder of the Plantagenet dynasty. Henry was the son of MATILDA, queen of England, and Geoffrey IV, count of Anjou. His reign saw rebellions led by his sons and the murder of the Archbishop of Canterbury, Thomas BECKET, who had opposed the king over his attempts to restrict the rights of the Church. Pope Alexander III received Henry's penance for provoking this crime.

Henry's first task on becoming king was to bring to an end the anarchy of King STEPHEN's reign. He dealt firmly with barons who had built castles without permission, and brought in important legal reforms. Local administrations were given authority to deal with routine matters of justice and finance, leading to the development of a system of common law which has survived until the present day. As the son of Geoffrey of Anjou, Henry II also controlled Normandy, Maine, Touraine, Brittany and Anjou. His marriage in 1152 to ELEANOR OF AQUITAINE, the former wife of Louis VII of France, brought him even greater estates in France, so that his kingdom stretched from northern England to the Pyrenees. These territorial gains were reinforced by the homage of Malcolm III of Scotland and by the recognition of Henry as overlord of Ireland in 1171.

Between 1173 and 1174 Henry II crushed a rebellion led by his wife and sons Henry, Geoffrey and Richard. His oldest son, Henry, had been crowned king in 1170 while his father still ruled. He resented his lack of power and was in revolt against his father once more when he died in 1183. Henry II was succeeded by his third son, RICHARD I.

DID YOU KNOW?

According to legend, Henry I decreed that the standard measurement of a 'foot' should be one-third of the length of his arm, which happened to be 36 inches long.

Henry III (1207-72) King of England from 1216. Henry came to the throne at the age of nine after the death of his father, JOHN, and England was managed until he came of age by William Marshal, 1st Earl of Pembroke, Peter des Roches, Bishop of Winchester, and Hubert de Burgh, Earl of Kent. The king declared himself of age in 1227, but did not take control until he was 29. He made ambitious policy plans, but lacked the drive and determination to see them through. Throughout his reign, Henry was preoccupied with cultural activities, including the rebuilding of Westminster Abbey, and he showed a preference for foreign advisers and favourites. In 1258 the barons, dissatisfied by Henry's lack of control, called for government by ministers rather than the king. The king clashed with them in 1264, and civil war broke out. After apparently accepting a number of reforms from the nobles under the Provisions of Oxford, he then sought to recover his independence. The war led to the temporary control of England by the Earl of Leicester, Simon de MONTFORT – the French husband of Henry's sister, Eleanor – who no longer had confidence in Henry's ability to rule. De Montfort defeated the king at the Battle of Lewes, but Henry recovered control after the forces of his son and successor, Edward, killed de Montfort and many of his supporters at the Battle of Evesham in 1265.

Henry IV (1553-1610) King of Navarre as Henry III from 1572 to 1589, and the first BOURBON king of France from 1589 until his death. Henry was a Protestant nobleman and the head of the HUGUENOTS, a position that nearly cost him his life. Between 1562 and 1598 there were nine conflicts over the throne between Catholic and Protestant factions. Henry claimed to be a Catholic during the ST BARTHOLOMEW'S DAY MASSACRE in August 1572, when Huguenot leaders were murdered by Catholic mobs in Paris and thousands died in violence across France. He was kept a virtual prisoner at court until 1576, when he escaped and returned to his Protestant beliefs.

Henry won the War of the THREE HENRYS, the eighth of the FRENCH WARS OF RELIGION, started by Duke Henry of GUISE and Henry III of France to prevent him succeeding to the throne. The duke and Henry III were murdered, and Henry became king of France in 1589. He professed himself a Catholic again in 1593, an occasion which led to his famous declaration: 'Paris is well worth a Mass.' He faced conflict with Spain over its claims to the throne through the Valois line, but negotiated a successful peace three years later. His Edict of NANTES in 1598 granted political rights and some religious freedom to the

Huguenots. Henry is sometimes regarded as the founder of the centralised regime of late 17th-century France, but the breakdown of royal authority after his assassination by a Catholic fanatic showed that his power had depended on his personal popularity.

Henry IV (Bolingbroke) (1366-1413)

King of England from 1399 until his death, first ruler of the House of Lancaster. In 1398 RICHARD II exiled Bolingbroke, known by the name of the Lincolnshire town in which he was born, after charges and countercharges of treason. The following year Richard confiscated the vast estates which John of GAUNT, Bolingbroke's father, had left to his son. While Richard was in Ireland, Bolingbroke returned to England with a small army and seized the crown. Richard surrendered after losing two armies in two weeks and was imprisoned. The following year Henry had Richard killed after a failed escape attempt.

Henry's position as king was not a strong one. He needed the support of the Church, the nobles and the House of Commons, and they resented his frequent requests for money. Cash shortages also crippled his attempts to deal with the rebellions of Owain GLYNDWR in Wales and the PERCY family in Scotland. After 1405 he was in poor health, but in 1411 he fought off an attempt to make him abdicate in favour of his eldest son, the future HENRY V.

Henry V (1387-1422)

King of England from 1413 until he died, the eldest son of HENRY IV (BOLINGBROKE). Henry came to the throne at the age of 26, immediately crushed two plots against him and laid claim to the French crown. He invaded France in 1415, captured Harfleur and marched through Normandy to AGINCOURT where he won a decisive victory. In 1417 he invaded France again, and after a successful campaign he negotiated the Treaty of Troyes. Its terms stated that Henry would succeed to the French crown at Charles VI's death and would marry Charles's daughter, Katherine of Valois. The marriage took place in 1420, but Henry died of a fever in 1422, a few weeks before he would have become king of France on the death of his father-in-law. Henry's military successes made him a popular hero. He built a strong navy, cleared the English Channel of enemy ships and used profits from increased trade to pay for the fleet. He was succeeded by his son, Henry VI.

Henry VI (1421-71)

King of England from 1422 to 1461, and again from 1470 until his death. Henry inherited the throne from his father HENRY V when he was nine months old, leading to a power struggle at court. After Henry was declared of age in 1437, tension increased between the Plantagenet Houses of York and Lancaster, who were in competition for the throne. The LANCASTRIANS supported the king, and the YORKISTS supported his heir, Richard of YORK. Henry was a pious and withdrawn monarch. He became unpopular after a series of defeats between 1449 and 1453 in the HUNDRED YEARS' WAR with France, and the loss of Normandy and Aquitaine. His marriage to MARGARET OF ANJOU in 1453 brought him a son, Prince Edward, who displaced Richard of York as his heir.

Two years later Richard started the Wars of the ROSES against the House of Lancaster by winning the first Battle of St Albans. In 1460 Richard claimed the crown for himself. When he was killed at the Battle of Wakefield, his son seized it and became Edward IV. Henry, who had earlier suffered a temporary breakdown and fled to Scotland, was captured and spent the rest of his life in the Tower of London, apart from a brief period when the Earl of WARWICK restored him to the throne. Edward IV defeated Warwick, reimprisoned Henry and won back the throne. Prince Edward was killed at the Battle of TEWKESBURY in 1471, and Warwick died soon afterwards. Edward IV decided that Henry, as the last representative of the Lancastrians, could not be allowed to live; he was murdered in the Tower in April 1471.

Henry VII (1457-1509)

King of England from 1485, and founder of the Tudor dynasty. The deaths of his rivals in the Wars of the ROSES strengthened his tenuous claim to the throne through his mother Margaret BEAUFORT. He was taken to France for safety, but in 1485 gathered his Lancastrian supporters and landed at Milford Haven in Wales. His forces defeated and killed King Richard III at the Battle of BOSWORTH FIELD. Henry honoured his promise to marry Elizabeth of York, Edward IV's daughter, the following year, but refused to rule jointly with her. His son Arthur married CATHERINE OF ARAGON, but died in 1502, and his daughter Margaret wed JAMES IV of Scotland. Henry quashed repeated dynastic rebellions, and manipulated the law to control discontented aristocrats. He left his son, HENRY VIII, a peaceful country with its finances and administration in good order.

Henry VIII (1491-1547)

King of England from 1509. Henry passed laws to sever the connection between the English Church and Rome when the pope, despite the efforts of Cardinal WOLSEY, refused him permission to divorce his wife, CATHERINE OF ARAGON. Catherine's children, except for a daughter who later became Mary I, had died as babies. Henry made himself head of the English Church in 1534 and divorced her. The king's advisers, led by Thomas CROMWELL, created the theory of royal supremacy, and Henry used this new power to sanction the Dissolution of the MONASTERIES and nunneries. But he remained conservative in doctrine, believing

Henry IV prepares to confront the Spanish at the Siege of Amiens. The Spanish took the town in March 1597, and did not surrender until September, when their only remaining leader was killed.

Henry VIII, the perfect Renaissance prince, was nicknamed 'Bluff King Hal', but turned into a feared, ill-tempered tyrant in later years.

in Catholicism without the pope and retaining the title 'Defender of the Faith', granted in 1521 for his treatise against the Protestant reformer Martin LUTHER. Meanwhile Henry married in succession Anne BOLEYN, Jane SEYMOUR, ANNE OF CLEVES, Catherine HOWARD and Catherine PARR in an attempt to father male heirs. Anne Boleyn was accused of adultery and beheaded in 1536; the king divorced Anne of Cleves, beheaded Catherine Howard, and was survived by Catherine Parr. Only Jane Seymour bore him a son, the future EDWARD VI, but she died soon afterwards.

Little was achieved by Henry's expensive wars with France and Scotland, but a powerful English navy was created. His attempts to take advantage of the struggles between FRANCIS I of France and CHARLES V of Spain severely undermined the English economy.

Towards the end of his life Henry became ill and overweight. He had begun his reign as a young monarch with a genuine interest in the flowering of Renaissance learning, and ended it as a paranoid tyrant who blamed his mistakes on his advisers. However, his reign was important, not only for the reformation in religion, but also for the centralisation of national government.

Henry the Lion (1129-95) Duke of Saxony and Bavaria, and a member of the Guelph family. Henry obtained his duchies with the help of the Holy Roman Emperor Frederick BARBAROSSA, expanding his territories to the Baltic. As he became more ambitious he lost the emperor's favour, and was banished for three years in 1182. His second wife – Matilda, daughter of Henry II – secured him a welcome in England. Ten years later, after Barbarossa's death, he regained some of his former territory. His son, Otto IV, challenged Barbarossa's descendants for the German throne.

Henry the Navigator (1394-1460) Portuguese prince, the third son of John I of Portugal and the grandson of the English duke John of GAUNT. Henry was the patron of a succession of Portuguese seamen. He sponsored voyages of exploration to the Atlantic islands and down the west coast of Africa, leading to the discovery of the Cape of Good Hope and the sea route to India. He founded a school of navigation, astronomy and cartography, and built Portugal's first observatory.

heraldry Coats of arms worn for individual identification, and their accessories of crests, badges, mottoes and flags. Its origins are military: medieval knights in armour could not easily be identified in battle, so the practice evolved of displaying a sign or device on the shield and on the linen coat worn over the armour, hence the term 'coat of arms'. The first heraldic designs may have been worn in the Crusades, but their use became widespread in Europe in the 12th century. In Japan a similar system emerged. By the 13th century, heraldry had developed its own terminology based on Old French. Its colours are called 'tinctures', of which there are two metals, gold (*or*) and silver (*argent*), and five colours, blue (*azure*), black (*sable*), green (*vert*), purple (*purpure*) and red (*gules*). In England in 1484 the College of Arms was formed to administrate heraldic regulations.

Herculaneum Small coastal town near Naples in Italy. Herculaneum was the first town to be buried when the volcano Vesuvius erupted in AD79; the lava also overwhelmed neighbouring POMPEII. More than 8in (20cm) of ash fell on August 24, followed by blast clouds and avalanches of lava early the following day. Many of the population are thought to have been killed as they fled across the beach, and were buried, like the town, under 60ft (20m) of volcanic mud. The site was discovered accidentally by a well-digger in 1709.

heresy Belief or doctrine considered by Church authorities to be a distortion of the Christian faith. During the Middle Ages it was believed that the one 'true' religion provided the only guarantee of salvation and afterlife. Those who argued against orthodox teaching risked being declared heretics. The Church maintained the unique validity of its doctrine, so conflict was inevitable. The early Church condemned the Gnostics in the 2nd century, who claimed to possess a secret and mystical knowledge separately revealed to their sect, and the doctrines of ARIANISM and the beliefs of the NESTORIANS in the 4th century. Iconoclasts, who objected to the worship of religious images, were condemned at the Council of NICAEA in 787. The condemnation of the CATHARS in southern Europe led to the ALBIGENSIAN Crusade. Later dissatisfaction with orthodox Catholic teaching led ultimately to the emergence of PROTESTANTISM.

A 15th-century King of Arms presents new coats to a duke. The King of Arms oversaw the administration of heraldic regulations, and granted coats of arms to those whom the College of Arms deemed eligible.

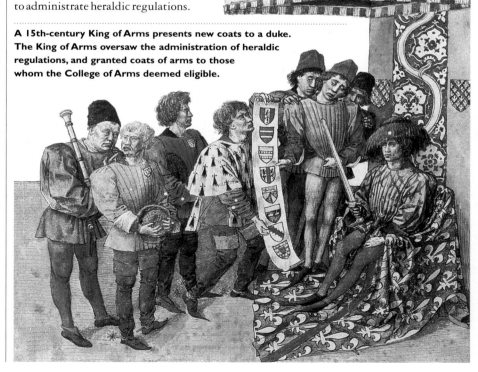

The Roman Catholic Church set up a tribunal in 1232, the INQUISITION, to search for unorthodoxy. The medieval Church revived the pagan punishment of burning alive for heretics. In England a law was passed in the early 15th century allowing secular authorities to carry out this punishment. The practice was abandoned several times in the 16th century and finally banned after James I burnt a group of ANABAPTISTS in 1612.

Hereward the Wake (11th century) Anglo-Saxon outlaw, best known for his resistance to the Norman conquerors of England. He supported a Danish raid on the monastery of Peterborough in revenge for the appointment of a Norman abbot. He then set up camp on the Isle of Ely in eastern England, where he was joined by Morcar, the English Earl of Northumbria. Morcar later surrendered, but Hereward escaped capture. His exploits inspired many legends.

hermit Person who, for religious reasons, takes up a solitary life. The word comes from the Greek *eremites*, meaning 'living in the desert'. The first Christian hermits of the late 3rd century were numerous in and around Egypt. Some were venerated and were visited by pilgrims. The hermit's way of life influenced strict European monastic orders such as the CARTHUSIANS and the CARMELITES.

Herod Dynasty which ruled Palestine with the support of Rome. It was founded by Antipater, who was appointed governor of Judaea in 47 BC by Julius Caesar, and was

A 15th-century Italian painting shows the solitary life of a hermit, whose prayer is rewarded with a vision of the infant Christ.

Herod Antipas (left) promised any reward to Salome, the daughter of his new wife Herodias, after she danced for him at a feast. Herodias persuaded Salome to ask for the head of John the Baptist.

murdered in 44 BC. Herod the Great was appointed 'King of the Jews' in 40 BC; he ruled Judaea ruthlessly and maintained an unaccustomed peace. His encouragement of Greek culture was resented by Jewish nationalists and the end of his reign was marked by violent palace feuds. After his death, the kingdom was divided between three of his sons: Archelaus, Herod Antipas and Philip.

Archelaus ruled Judaea, Idumaea and Samaria from 4 BC to AD 6, until he was deposed and his territory put under a Roman governor. Herod Antipas ruled Galilee and Peraea from 4 BC to AD 39, during the lifetime of Jesus Christ. According to the Bible, he imprisoned John the Baptist for criticising his marriage to his half-brother's former wife, Herodias, and eventually had John beheaded. Religious riots led to his exile by the Roman emperor Gaius Caligula. Philip ruled the territory east of Galilee from 4 BC to AD 34. Herod Agrippa I, a grandson of Herod the Great educated at the imperial court in Rome, reunited the territories, helped by the Roman emperor Tiberius CLAUDIUS, and ruled from 41 to 44. He ordered the execution of the apostle James, and imprisoned the apostle Peter. His son, Herod Agrippa II, the last of the dynasty, ruled only in northern Palestine until about 93. He helped the Romans to crush the JEWISH REVOLT between 66 and 70.

Herodotus (c.484-c.425 BC) Greek historian, who was often called the 'Father of History'. Herodotus wrote a comprehensive nine-book account of the Greek-Persian Wars of 500 to 449 BC. His work included the history of the Persian empire and a digression on Egypt. He visited places as far apart as Athens, Babylon, Egypt and the Black Sea, gathering information from people he met and making his own observations. His *History* contains information about the contemporary Persian and Greek worlds, and is an outstanding achievement. It is the earliest prose work preserved from ancient Greece.

Hertz, Heinrich (1857-94) German physicist and pioneer of radio communication, the first to broadcast and receive radio waves. Hertz began studying electromagnetic waves in 1883. The British physicist James Clerk MAXWELL had predicted the existence of these waves with his electromagnetic theory, but Hertz demonstrated it experimentally. He discovered that the waves behaved like light and radiant heat, proving that they were electromagnetic. His work was used by Guglielmo MARCONI to develop a system of radio telegraphy in 1896, followed by short-wave radio experiments establishing the basic principles for all long-distance radio.

Hertzog, James (1866-1942) South African statesman, prime minister from 1924 to 1939. In 1914 he formed the National Party, aiming to achieve South African independence and to oppose support for Britain in the First World War. As prime minister, he made Afrikaans an official language, instituted the first Union flag and followed a policy of protecting domestic industry from foreign competition. He also supported strict segregation of the races in South Africa. In 1933 he formed a coalition with Jan Christian SMUTS, and they united the Nationalist and South African Parties as the United Party. Hertzog won the 1938 election, but his opposition to joining Britain in the Second World War brought about his downfall in 1939.

Herzl, Theodor (1860-1904) Hungarian Jewish writer, founder of modern ZIONISM. Herzl decided that a Jewish national state was the only solution to ANTI-SEMITISM, which he witnessed in 1894 while covering the trial of the Jewish officer Alfred DREYFUS in Paris for a Vienna newspaper. His 1896 pamphlet *Der Judenstaat* (*The Jewish State*) set out his aims, and he convened the first Zionist Congress at Basel in 1897. His arguments were underlined by a series of POGROMS – attacks by mobs often backed by the authorities – against Jews in Russia. His objective was 'to lay the foundation stone for the house which will become the refuge of the Jewish nation' in PALESTINE, but he died before achieving his aim.

Hess, Rudolf (1894-1987) German Nazi leader who was imprisoned with Adolf Hitler after the Munich 'beer-hall *putsch*', a failed attempt by the Nazis to take control of the country in 1923, and was his deputy as party

> 66 **The reasons why I simulated loss of memory were tactical ... my capacity to follow the trial is not being affected.** 99
>
> *Rudolf Hess*
> *Nuremberg trials, 1945-6*

leader and minister of state. In 1941 Hess parachuted into Scotland, apparently without Hitler's knowledge, in an attempt to negotiate peace between Britain and Germany. He was jailed by the British for the rest of the war, then jailed for life by the Allies following the postwar NUREMBERG TRIALS. He initially affected amnesia to appear unfit for trial, but later admitted the deception. From 1966 he was the only prisoner at Spandau prison in Berlin, where he remained until his death.

Heuss, Theodor (1884-1963) Politician and first president of the Federal Republic of Germany. Before the Second World War, Heuss belonged to the German Democratic Party, and was a member of parliament from 1924 to 1928 and from 1930 to 1933. He helped to found the Free Democratic Party in 1946, becoming its leader in 1949, and he served on the committee that wrote the new republic's constitution. Heuss was elected president of the new state in the same year, and served until his retirement ten years later. Many books and newspaper articles written by Heuss were burned as 'un-German' after Adolf Hitler came to power.

Hexham, Battle of (May 15, 1464) Battle during the Wars of the ROSES in which a YORKIST force led by John Neville, Lord Montagu, captured the Lancastrian leader Henry BEAUFORT, Duke of Somerset, three miles from the town of Hexham in Northumberland. Beaufort was beheaded on the field of battle and many of his followers were executed afterwards. Neville was rewarded with the estates of the PERCY family, and received the earldom of Northumberland.

Heydrich, Reinhard (1904-42) German Nazi police official. Heydrich joined the SS, the elite corps of the Nazi Party, in 1931, and in 1934 became deputy head of the GESTAPO. From 1941 he controlled the Czechoslovak territory of Bohemia-Moravia, where his inhumanity and executions earned him the nicknames 'Hangman of Europe' and 'the Beast'. He was assassinated by Czech nationalists in 1942. Germany retaliated with one of the most extreme reigns of terror in the Second World War, systematically executing civilians, including the entire male population of the villages of Lidice and Lezáky.

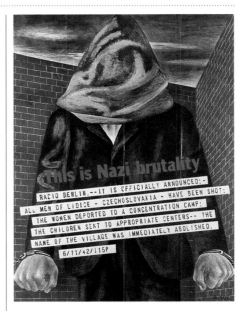

Following the death of Reinhard Heydrich, Lidice was destroyed to 'teach the Czechs a final lesson of subservience and humility'.

Hezekiah (d.687 BC) King of Judah in southern Palestine from 715 to 687 BC. When Hezekiah came to power, Judah was a vassal state of the Mesopotamian empire of ASSYRIA; with the leaders of neighbouring states he was involved in a number of rebellions, and suffered defeat in 701 when the Assyrian king SENNACHERIB invaded; only Jerusalem escaped destruction. The Bible describes Hezekiah's work of religious reform, destroying local shrines and cult objects and trying to prevent the worship of local gods. The reform was short-lived, and after his death pagan practices were reintroduced by his son and successor Manasseh.

hieroglyphs Pictorial signs used for formal inscriptions in ancient Egypt. Hieroglyphs stand for whole words, syllables or alphabetic sounds. They were devised mainly for religious and monumental purposes around 3000 BC, and were used until the late 3rd century AD. Their structure was too clumsy for practical use, and cursive or 'long-hand' versions required long professional training. Hieroglyphs have played an important part in archaeological research, extending written history to 2000 years before classical times. The term has been applied more loosely to other ornamental scripts used by the MINOAN CIVILISATION, the HITTITES and the MAYA.

Highland Clearances Removal of Scottish 'crofter' peasant farmers by landlords to clear the land for leasing to sheep-farmers. In the late 18th and early 19th centuries, Scottish society in the Highlands and the Isles suffered severely from the collapse of its system of chiefs and fighting clans. As the

Theodor Herzl (centre) sits among Zionist missionaries in 1898. He approached rulers, statesmen and financiers in many countries, seeking their support for a Jewish national home.

population increased, overcrowding occurred and subsistence, or 'hand-to-mouth', farming did not meet food needs. Major landowners cleared their land, evicting crofters and sometimes burning their cottages.

highwayman Travellers had fallen victim to thieves since Anglo-Saxon times, but during the 17th and 18th centuries better roads, more frequent travelling and the growth of coaching inns made rich pickings for thieves on horseback. Their cry of 'stand and deliver!' was, in reality, much less romantic than is suggested in fiction, and they often murdered their victims to avoid being identified. Some robbers, such as Swift Nick Levison (hanged at York in 1684), Dick Turpin and Jack Sheppard became notorious. Eventually, their appearance in daylight in central London in the mid 18th century provoked vigorous efforts to stamp them out, and by the early 19th century the menace of highwaymen had been largely overcome.

Hill, Sir Rowland (1795-1879) British administrator and inventor, originator of the penny postage stamp system, subsequently adopted throughout the world. In 1837 he published a pamphlet, *Post Office Reform*, in which he proposed a uniform, low rate of postage, prepaid by the sender. He described the postage stamp as 'a bit of paper just large enough to bear the stamp, and covered at the back with a glutinous wash'. He adopted the idea from a proposal in 1834 that the postage on newspapers should be collected by using wrappers that were uniformly stamped. Despite bureaucratic opposition, his proposals were put into effect in 1840.

Himmler, Heinrich (1900-45) German Nazi police chief, the second most powerful man in the Third Reich, who terrorised his own party and all German-occupied Europe. Himmler began his working life as a poultry farmer in Bavaria. As an early member of the Nazi Party he took part in the Munich 'beerhall *putsch*', a right-wing attempt to take control of the state in 1923. Six years later Hitler appointed him chief of the SS, the elite corps of the party. He shared the racist views of Adolf Hitler and organised the persecution and murder of more than 6 million Jews, incarcerating many in wartime CONCENTRATION CAMPS. He constructed the Third Reich's first concentration camp at Dachau in 1933. He became the chief of all police services, including the GESTAPO, three years later. As head of the Reich administration from 1939, his repression extended to occupied countries. Himmler put down a conspiracy to kill Hitler, the JULY PLOT of 1944, but within a few months he undertook secret negotiations to bring about Germany's surrender to the Allies in a bid to save himself. He was expelled from the party by Hitler and attempted to escape from Germany in disguise, but he was caught in 1945 by British troops and committed suicide by swallowing poison.

Hindenburg, Paul von (1847-1934) German general and statesman who began his career as a soldier. He fought at the Battle of SADOWA and in the AUSTRO-PRUSSIAN WAR of

1866 and the FRANCO-PRUSSIAN WAR of 1870-1, and retired in 1911. At the outbreak of the First World War, Hindenburg was recalled, and his reputation benefited from victories against Russian forces. He became chief of the general staff in 1916, and his record as a war hero led to his election as president in 1925. After his re-election in 1932, his advisers compelled him to appoint Adolf Hitler as chancellor, who took control of the country as Führer the following year.

Hinduism Name given to religious beliefs and social customs originating in India. Hinduism is based upon a complex mixture of elements drawn from Indo-European culture, brought by the ARYAN invasions of 1500 BC onwards and from the native pre-Aryan and Dravidian societies. The religion of the early period is called Vedic, from the texts and rituals of the VEDAS, which retain an important place in Hinduism. Many other texts and sources have also become significant, for example the *Bhagavad-Gita* (*The Song of the Lord*), believed to have been revealed to mankind by the deity Vishnu. Vishnu is one of a trinity of supreme Hindu gods, also including Siva, the god of destruction and reproduction, and Brahma, the creator. Hindus have diverse beliefs, but most maintain that people are trapped in a cycle of death and rebirth, and seek to escape from this into union with God, the principle and entity behind existence. This release is sought by a variety of ascetic and devotional paths, as well as by actions appropriate to an individual's caste or hereditary class (see feature, pages 312-13).

Many reform movements appeared in the 19th century as the religion came under the influence of European ideas. In the first half of the 20th century, religious discord arose between Hindus, who comprised more than 80 per cent of India's population, and Muslims, who made up just over 10 per cent, eventually leading to the establishment of the separate Muslim state of Pakistan. In the 20th century, Hindu leader Mohandas Gandhi (see feature, page 252) became the champion of the Untouchables – people of the lowliest social category. Gandhi called for noncooperation, nonviolence, *satyagraha* (truth-force) and self-rule for the Indian people. Since India's independence in 1947, religion has remained one of the main reasons for ethnic and separatist violence. The Hindus clashed with the Sikhs in 1984, after hundreds of separatist Punjabi Sikhs were killed by troops during an invasion of the sacred Golden Temple in Amritsar. In the same year, Prime

> **DID YOU KNOW?**
>
> The ancient Hindus were among the first to use wedding rings, and the tradition was exported to the West by the Greeks and Romans. The ring remained a 'property sold' sign until the 9th century, when the Christian Church adopted it as a symbol of fidelity.

Evictions during the Highland Clearances forced many families of crofters to emigrate. Many others, betrayed by their clan chiefs, were left behind to suffer overcrowding, poverty and famine.

The Hindu deity Vishnu has many avatars, or incarnations. He assumes the form of a fish in this 17th-century illustration from Kashmir.

Minister Indira GANDHI was assassinated by her Sikh bodyguards in a revenge attack, prompting riots in Delhi in which Hindu mobs killed more than a thousand Sikhs.

hippodrome Stadium in which the ancient Greeks and Romans held chariot and horse races. Competitors raced on U-shaped courses with a barrier along the centre; spectators watched from tiered stands. The Greek sanctuary of OLYMPIA had an early example, and hippodromes were a typical feature of major Greek cities and temple sites of classical and Hellenistic times. The Roman hippodrome at Constantinople held about 100 000 spectators, and was the scene of fierce rivalry among partisan supporters. The CIRCUS Maximus at Rome was modelled on Greek hippodromes.

Hirohito (1901-89) Emperor of Japan from 1926 until his death. In the 1930s Hirohito had little opportunity to exercise his technical sovereignty against the aggressive policies of the general and statesman TOJO HIDEKI. Throughout the Japanese invasion of China and during the Second World War, he followed his counsellors' advice not to weaken the throne by becoming involved in politics. But in 1945, realising that after the nuclear destruction of HIROSHIMA and NAGASAKI the war must end, he forced the armed services to accept unconditional surrender. Hirohito was saved from trial as a war criminal by making a deal with the American general Douglas MACARTHUR, commander of the Allied occupation forces, requiring him to renounce his divine status. He remained a symbolic monarch, without governing power.

Hiroshima Japanese city in southern Honshu, the largest of Japan's four islands and an industrial heartland. It became the target of the first atomic bomb attack on August 6, 1945, launched by the USA, which destroyed the city centre and killed about a third of the 300 000 inhabitants. This attack, together with an attack on NAGASAKI three days later, led directly to the unconditional surrender of Japan and the end of the Second World War.

Hispaniola Second largest island of the West Indies. Ciboney Indians from South America had settled there by 5000 BC. Agriculture reached the island around 1000 BC with the arrival of Arawak Indians from South America. By about AD 200 a Taino Arawak culture from Mexico began to develop. The Arawaks grew maize, built ceremonial centres and worshipped human and animal spirits. In 1492 Christopher Columbus landed on the island, and four years later the town of Santo Domingo was established – the first European settlement in the Americas. Spaniards developed plantations at the eastern end of the island but lost control of western Hispaniola to France, which established the colony of Santo Domingue, later known as HAITI. The eastern half of the island became the DOMINICAN REPUBLIC. Exploitation and European diseases virtually eradicated the Arawak culture by the 18th century.

Hiss Case (1949-50) Controversial legal case in the USA. Alger Hiss, a State Department official, was found guilty of perjury for his denial, on oath, that he had passed secret documents to a self-confessed Communist Party courier, Whittaker Chambers. Hiss pleaded innocence and government officials testified for him, but he was imprisoned for five years. His trial was a symptom of the fears aroused by the COLD WAR, when the USA and the former Soviet Union spied on each other's military and industrial secrets. The FEDERAL BUREAU OF INVESTIGATION was believed to have tampered with evidence to convict Hiss.

historiography The writing and interpretation of history. Historiography developed from oral history – the retelling of legends handed down through the spoken word, such as the epic tales of the Greek poet HOMER. In the classical age of ancient Greece, Herodotus and Thucydides wrote narrative histories of their own times. In China, Sima Qian, who lived from around 145 to 85 BC, is known as the 'Father of Chinese History'. The works of Roman historians such as Tacitus, Livy and

> ❝ **History is indeed little more than the register of the crimes, follies and misfortunes of mankind.** ❞
>
> *Edward Gibbon, historian*
> *(1737–94)*

Suetonius served as models for medieval and Renaissance historians. In the Arab world al-Tabaric, who lived from AD 838 to 923, wrote the *Annals*, a history of the world from its creation to 915, and Ibn Khaldun, who lived from 1332 to 1406, wrote the *Kitab a'ibar* (*Book of Examples*), a history of Islam.

In medieval Europe, history was written by the literate clergy, and mostly confined to works such as the *Anglo-Saxon Chronicle*. During the Renaissance, ancient historical texts were studied and reinterpreted by the HUMANISTS, but it was not until the 18th century that the ENLIGHTENMENT brought a measure of rationalism and scepticism into historical writing, encouraging such masterpieces as Edward Gibbon's *The History of the Decline and Fall of the Roman Empire*. Napoleon's campaigns in Europe during the French Revolution engendered feelings of national pride in occupied territories which led to the study of history in schools. The teaching of history began in Germany and spread to other European countries, providing a basis for the expansion of historical scholarship over the past 200 years.

Hitler, Adolf see feature, page 296

Hitler Youth Organisation for training young Germans in Nazi principles. In 1936, Adolf HITLER outlawed other youth groups and announced that all young Germans

Emperor Hirohito enjoyed the longest reign in Japan's history – his rule became known as the time of Showa, or 'enlightened peace'.

Festivals for young people, promoted in propaganda posters (right) and on badges, recruited new members for training in the Hitler Youth movement.

should join the Jungvolk ('Young Folk') at the age of ten. They were instructed in activities such as sports and camping, and received Nazi training. At 14 the boys entered the Hitler Youth, which exposed them to semimilitary discipline and Nazi propaganda. Girls joined the League of German Maidens to learn about motherhood and domestic duties. In March 1939, membership was made compulsory.

Hittites

Ancient people of Asia Minor, who flourished from 1700 to 1200 BC. The Hittites were Indo-Europeans, probably from north of the Black Sea, and entered Anatolia towards the end of the 3rd millennium. They established Hattusas – near modern Bogazköy in Turkey – as their capital, and gradually extended their power into much of Anatolia and Syria. Hattusas has yielded an invaluable collection of Hittite records in the form of cuneiform inscriptions. Mursilis I penetrated as far as Babylon by about 1595 BC, but his death was followed by internal discord. The high-point of Hittite rule was under the leadership of Suppiluliumas, ruler from about 1375 to 1335. Nearly 200 years later, invasions by the migrating Sea Peoples – probably Greeks, Sardinians and Tyrrhenians who were specialists in seaborne attacks – led to the empire's collapse. Migrants then took newly developed Hittite iron-working techniques to southern Europe, Asia and Africa, and the IRON AGE began.

Hobbes, Thomas

(1588-1679) English philosopher and political theorist. In the political turmoil preceding the English Civil War, Hobbes' manuscript of *The Elements of Law, Natural and Politic*, circulated in 1640, was condemned by Parliament for its support

DID YOU KNOW?

Each Hittite king enjoyed supreme rule as a monarch, military leader and chief judge. When a Hittite king died, he became a god.

of the concept of royal power, and Hobbes left England for Paris. In his best-known work, *Leviathan*, published in 1651, Hobbes argued that people are motivated by selfish concerns. Fear of death and anarchy lead to the surrender of individual rights and the acceptance of the rule of an absolute monarch – the Leviathan – a monster to whom all submit in the interests of security. He believed that the alternative, popular government, leads to civil war. These ideas were regarded by Royalists as an inducement to Oliver CROMWELL to set himself up as an absolute ruler. Despite his views, Hobbes returned from Paris in 1651 and regained his reputation at the court of Charles II.

Ho Chi Minh

(1890-1969) Vietnamese statesman, the central figure in his country's struggle for independence. Ho Chi Minh was born Nguyen Tat Thanh, and was also known as Nguyen Ai Quoc. As a young man in 1917, he moved to Paris and became a socialist, and in 1920 he helped to create the French Communist Party. He went to Moscow in 1923, where he took part in the fifth Congress of the Communist International, and left for Guangzhou (Canton) in China in 1924 to form a Vietnamese nationalist movement. Chiang Kai Shek expelled the communists from Guangzhou in 1927 and Ho left once again for the Soviet Union. He returned in 1930 to found the Indochinese Communist Party, and established the Vietminh guerrilla movement in North VIETNAM in 1943 to fight the Japanese occupying forces, adopting the name Ho Chi Minh ('he who enlightens'). In 1945, leading the

resistance after the Japanese surrender, he proclaimed the Democratic Republic of Vietnam, but was forced back into guerrilla war after the return of French colonial forces, who were defeated in 1953. The Geneva Conference of 1954 accepted the Vietminh triumph and left Ho Chi Minh in control of North Vietnam. From 1963 in the Vietnam War, he committed his communist forces to the struggle to take over American-dominated South Vietnam. The actions of North Vietnamese troops helped to reunify the country in 1976.

Hogarth, William

(1697-1764) Painter and engraver, the most important English artist of his generation. Hogarth was apprenticed as a silversmith, and he later joined a drawing school run by James Thornhill, an artist who he admired. His first dated painting is a scene from John Gay's *Beggar's Opera*, painted in 1728. In the early 1730s Hogarth invented the use of sequences of anecdotal theatrical pictures to satirise social abuses. The best known is *A Rake's Progress*, eight scenes portraying the punishment of vice which he began painting in 1732. Engravings of each series were extremely popular, and were so much pirated that Hogarth succeeded in having copyright legislation passed in 1735, known as the Hogarth Act, as a defence against imitators and profiteers. His satire was directed as much at pedantry and affectation as at immorality, and he saw himself as a

Ho Chi Minh gave his name to the former capital of South Vietnam, Saigon, after Vietnam was reunited through his efforts in 1976.

Scourge of Europe

Adolf Hitler, the German dictator, set out with extraordinary determination to impose his ideal of 'One Empire, One People, One Leader' on his country at the expense of millions of lives.

Adolf Hitler (1889-1945) took fascism to its extreme with his creation of the Nazi Party in 1921. He achieved absolute power in Germany, provoked the Second World War by invading Poland in 1939, and conquered much of Europe before committing suicide in the ruins of Berlin in April 1945. Hitler shared with the Soviet leader, Vladimir Lenin, a craving for power, attention to detail, dislike of luxury, and an inhumanity stemming from utter conviction in his historic mission. Unlike Lenin, his revolutionary principle was based on race, not class, and the objects of his hatred were Jews, Slavs, and gypsies.

Hitler was born in Austria, the son of a customs official who wanted him to become a civil servant. He saw himself as an artist, whose spirit was repelled by his father's office. A performance of Wagner's opera *Rienzi* convinced him that it was his destiny to rescue the German people as Wagner's hero had rescued the Romans. 'In that hour it began,' he said.

As a failed art student taking odd jobs in Vienna, Hitler sympathised with the anti-Semitism prevalent in the city. He served in a Bavarian regiment in the First World War, and won the Iron Cross for bravery. In 1919, while working as an army informer spying on political parties, Hitler became a member of one, the National Socialist German Workers' Party (later known as the Nazi Party); by 1921 he was its leader.

HITLER'S VISION

Hitler failed to overthrow the Bavarian government in a coup in 1923, and took advantage of his brief imprisonment to write *Mein Kampf (My Struggle)*. This political manifesto laid the basis of his appeal for '*Ein Reich, Ein Volk, Ein Führer*' ('One Empire, One People, One Leader') which would crush the Jews, tear up the Versailles peace settlement imposed on his country at the end of the First World War, and lead a greater Germany to eastern conquests.

German democracy was undermined by weak government. By 1933 the Nazis had become the largest party, and Hitler was appointed chancellor. He achieved totalitarian powers after the burning of the Reichstag (parliament) the same year. A secret police, the Gestapo, was formed on Soviet lines. Dissenters and Jews began to be murdered, or to disappear into concentration camps.

A shrewd political opportunist, Hitler incorporated Austria and Czechoslovakia into the Third Reich before turning on Poland in September 1939. He overran France and the Low Countries in 1940, and invaded the Soviet Union in 1941. His recklessness and savagery brought him a multiplicity of enemies that no army could withstand. Proof that absolute power corrupts absolutely, he railed that the German people were 'not worthy' of him.

Nazi leaders (below, left to right) Hermann Goering, Wilhelm Keitel, Karl Dönitz and Heinrich Himmler support Hitler, who saw himself as a hero (right) destined to rescue the German people.

William Hogarth trained himself to visualise the subjects of his paintings in his mind's eye. In this self-portrait, he depicts the comic muse without recourse to any preliminary drawings.

defender of native virtues against a fashion for French and Italian mannerisms. In his treatise, *The Analysis of Beauty* (1753), Hogarth argues that the views of the practising artist should carry more weight than the theories of learned connoisseurs.

Hohenzollern Part of the state of Baden-Württemberg in the Federal Republic of Germany, formerly a province of Prussia. The province gave its name to a dynasty which steadily gained power in Germany from the 11th century. From 1415 the dynasty ruled the electorate of Brandenburg. The following century saw great expansion, with Margrave Albert, 1st Duke of Prussia, becoming Grand Master of the TEUTONIC KNIGHTS in 1511. In 1614 the Duchy of Cleves was acquired, and in 1701 the Elector Frederick III of Brandenburg became Frederick I of Prussia. In 1871 William I of Prussia became Emperor William I of the German Empire. Prince Charles Hohenzollern-Sigmaringen of the second branch of the dynasty, was elected Prince of ROMANIA in 1866, becoming King Carol I in 1881. His brother Leopold was offered the throne of Spain in 1870, but turned it down. His candidature angered France, and provoked the FRANCO-PRUSSIAN war. The last important Hohenzollern, the German emperor William II, was overthrown at the end of the First World War.

Hokusai, Katsushika (1760-1849) Japanese artist and leading printmaker born in Edo, now Tokyo, who studied wood engraving and book illustration. Hokusai adopted his name in about 1797, and used as many as 50 others during his lifetime. He was a versatile artist who produced pictures of many different subjects, but was best-known for illustrating scenes from everyday life. In 1814 he began a 13-volume book of sketches called *Manga*, and from 1823 to 1829 worked on the outstanding *36 Views of Mount Fuji*.

Holland see NETHERLANDS, THE

Hollywood

Area of Los Angeles, California, which became a base for the US film industry in the 20th century. The streets were originally laid out in 1887 by Horace Wilcox, a prohibitionist interested in real-estate, but its mild climate – the Los Angeles Chamber of Commerce 'guaranteed' 350 days of sunshine a year – attracted film makers. In 1911 the first studio was set up on Sunset Boulevard, and soon more than 20 companies were filming in Hollywood. The Motion Picture Patents Company, established in 1909, enforced a rule that all actors should remain anonymous. This was revoked the following year, and film companies began to promote their leading actors, creating the celebrity status enjoyed by Hollywood film stars ever since. In 1913, director and producer Cecil B. De Mille created what is generally regarded as Hollywood's first feature film, *The Squaw Man*, using a converted barn as a studio.

By 1920, Hollywood was producing more than 800 films a year. Many of the new celebrities had moved to the area, and Hollywood became a byword for glamour. The next two decades saw a series of revolutions within the industry. The 'talkies' arrived with Al Jolson in *The Jazz Singer* (1927), and the use of colour tints on film was superseded in 1935 by the first feature film in three-colour Technicolor, *Becky Sharp*, by Robert Mamoulian.

Hollywood entered its golden years with a surge of creativity which produced musicals, westerns, cartoons, romances, comedies, and gangster and horror films. After the Second World War, many companies began filming abroad, attracted by the benefits of lower taxation. The emergence of television also led to a decline in film-making; many Hollywood studios began to be used for television production. Since the 1960s the motion picture industry has moved more towards independent productions filmed on location, but the legacy of Hollywood, the 'dream factory', remains.

Holocaust, the see feature, page 298

Holy Alliance

(1815) Loose alliance of European powers pledging to uphold the principles of the Christian religion. It was proclaimed at the Congress of VIENNA by the emperors of Austria and Russia and the King of Prussia, and signed by all European leaders except the Prince Regent of Britain, for constitutional reasons, and the pope and the Ottoman sultan, for religious reasons. The restored French king Louis XVIII was among the signatories. As a diplomatic instrument the Alliance was short-lived and ineffective, and became associated with autocratic and repressive regimes.

Holy Roman Empire (962-1806)

European empire in the West, conceived as a replacement for the CAROLINGIAN EMPIRE, in the Christian imperial tradition of the Roman emperor Constantine. It has been called the greatest mistake of the medieval popes, for rather than establishing a powerful secular

> 66 **The Holy Roman Empire was neither holy, nor Roman, nor an empire in any way.** 99
>
> *Voltaire, French writer and philosopher (1694-1778)*

deputy to rule Christendom as they intended, they created a rival. From OTTO I's coronation in 962, the empire became associated with the German crown, even after it passed to the Austrian branch of the HABSBURGS in the 15th century. The empire consisted of duchies, counties and bishoprics owing formal allegiance to the emperor. But clashes occurred between the emperor and the nobility, especially over the emperor's claims to sovereignty in Italy, leading to his frequent absences from Germany. Emperor Henry IV struggled with the Church over the right

Hollywood triumphs of 1927 (below) and 1939 (right), broke new ground in the history of film-making.

to appoint bishops and senior clergy in the 11th century. Frederick I made a sustained attempt to bring Italy and the papacy under his military control but was finally defeated at the Battle of Legnano in 1176. Open warfare broke out between the GUELPHS (allies of the pope) and the Ghibellines, the imperial party. After the death of Emperor FREDERICK II in 1250, German imperial power waned in Italy and at home. The empire became virtually hereditary, ruled by successive members of the same princely family. The first Habsburg emperor was Rudolph I, from 1274, and the empire remained in the family's hands until its dissolution in 1806.

In 1530 King Charles I of Spain was crowned as Holy Roman Emperor Charles V. His empire included Spain, Germany, the Netherlands, Sardinia and Sicily, together with newly conquered territory in the Americas. But the Reformation and the Thirty Years' War were upheavals which challenged the power of the Catholic Habsburgs, and the emperors suffered a loss of prestige and power during a series of wars against Louis XIV. In the 18th century Prussia under Frederick II emerged as the leading German power, and the imperial crown was surrendered to Napoleon in 1806. The empire was not revived after his downfall.

In the splendour of wide screen, 70mm. and full stereophonic sound!

DAVID O. SELZNICK'S PRODUCTION OF MARGARET MITCHELL'S "GONE WITH THE WIND"

Winner of Ten Academy Awards

STARRING
CLARK GABLE
VIVIEN LEIGH
LESLIE HOWARD OLIVIA de HAVILLAND

...NICK INTERNATIONAL PICTURE · VICTOR FLEMING · SIDNEY HOWARD · METRO-GOLDWYN-MAYER INC · MAX STEINER METROCOLOR

WARNER BROS. SUPREME TRIUMPH
AL JOLSON IN "The JAZZ SINGER"

Slaughter of the innocents

In his quest for the ideal master-race, Adolf Hitler set about systematically exterminating the Jewish population, first in Germany and then across Europe. Six million Jews lost their lives in what became known as the Holocaust.

The Holocaust is the term used to describe the attempted genocide of the Jews of Europe by the German leader Adolf Hitler between 1939 and 1945. In January 1933 Hitler's National Socialist (Nazi) Party took power with the aim of creating a 'racially pure' nation populated by a 'master-race'. Anyone who did not fit his vision would be eliminated: the disabled, homosexuals, and 'racial aliens' – Blacks, Gypsies and, especially, Jews. Concentration camps brutally run by the Schutzstaffel (SS), the elite Nazi paramilitary force, were set up to imprison political opponents and 'asocials'. Jewish businesses were boycotted. Jews were purged from government employment.

DEPRIVED OF CITIZENSHIP

The 1935 Nuremberg 'race laws' deprived Jews of citizenship and forbade them to marry Aryans. In 1938, during *Kristallnacht* ('The Night of Broken Glass'), more than 90 Jews were murdered, 20000 were put into camps and 7000 businesses were destroyed.

The German conquest of Poland in 1939 brought 1.5 million Polish Jews under Nazi control, and the Germans overran most of western Europe the following year. Polish Jews were sealed inside ghettos. Between 1940 and 1942, hunger and disease claimed 300000 lives.

When Germany invaded the Soviet Union in June 1941, killing squads

The Holocaust
✝ Death Camps
1,000 Total number of Jews murdered from each country (1937 borders)

operated behind the advancing troops; about a million Russian Jews were murdered. In July 1941 Hitler authorised the 'Final Solution' of the 'Jewish Question'. Death camps equipped with gas chambers were built in Poland, concentration camps such as at Auschwitz were brought into use. From spring 1942, Jews were transported by train to the death camps. The 'Final Solution' relied on secrecy and the connivance of Germany's allies. In December 1942, after proof of the genocide reached the west, the Allies condemned Nazi war crimes but did little to impede the slaughter. Those Jews who could fled; those trapped concealed their identity or hid. Armed resistance was almost impossible, yet in April

Thousands of prisoners died at the Buchenwald concentration camp, Germany, through forced labour, disease, and starvation.

The map shows the number of Jews killed in the Holocaust, and the Nazi death camps to which many were taken by train, right.

1943 several hundred young Jews in the Warsaw Ghetto fought back in an inspiring gesture of defiance.

In 1944, 437000 Hungarian Jews were deported to Auschwitz-Birkenau, where the majority died. For the first time, the Red Cross, the Vatican and neutral countries intervened and the remaining ghettos were 'liquidated'. During the last winter of the war, Jews were forced on 'death marches' from camps in the path of the invading Red Army.

Of the millions of Jews killed by the Nazis, their fate is unique because they were victims of the only attempt by a modern state, using all its resources, to annihilate a special group of people.

Home Guard Second World War military force formed in Britain from volunteers. The Home Guard, known as the Local Defence Volunteers (LDV) until it was renamed by the prime minister Winston Churchill, existed from 1940 to 1944. In 1942 enrolment became compulsory for sections of the civilian population. About a million men served in their spare time; in its first year the Home Guard possessed more men than firearms, and its members occasionally resorted to using broom handles for drill. The unit was never put to the test, but it helped to boost British morale in the early years of the war.

Homer Traditionally the author of the *Iliad* and the *Odyssey*, the greatest of the early Greek epic poems. Many scholars dispute Homer's authorship of the poems, which were put together from a variety of sources and probably not written down until the 8th century BC. The *Iliad* describes the Greek siege of Troy after a Trojan prince abducted Helen, the wife of the king of Sparta. The *Odyssey* tells the story of Odysseus, one of the Greek leaders at Troy, on his protracted and adventurous return to his kingdom of Ithaca ten years after the siege. The poems stand as the final flowering of a long oral bardic tradition which told legends of the 'heroic age' of Greece. Homer was studied by ancient Greek scholars, who considered him their most outstanding poet, and the reputation of the *Iliad* and the *Odyssey* as prominent works of literature still survives.

Home Rule Nationalist movement to reestablish self-government in Ireland. The Home Rule movement grew from resentment against English domination which began at the end of the 12th century when Norman barons seized land after defeating the Vikings. Henry II of England became king of Ireland in 1172, and successive English monarchs attempted to tame the rebellious island. The extortionate policies of CHARLES I led to the Irish Rebellion of 1641, brutally crushed by Oliver Cromwell and the Parliamentary army. The rising of the UNITED IRISHMEN in 1798 had the reverse of its intended effect, bringing about the ACT OF UNION in 1800 which stripped Ireland of its own parliament. Serious lobbying to repeal the Act began in 1870, when the nationalist leader Isaac Butt set up a Home Rule association. The first Home Rule Bill of 1886, submitted by the Liberal Party under William Gladstone after much work by the Irish MP Charles PARNELL, was defeated, as was a subsequent bill in 1893. A third was passed in 1912, causing an outcry among Protestants, who feared Roman Catholic domination. The bill was to establish a separate legislative body in Ireland, but was postponed when war broke out in Europe in 1914. It left unresolved the question of how many of the northern counties of the mainly Protestant, pro-British ULSTER were to be excluded from the new Irish state. The EASTER RISING in 1916 and the sweeping majority for SINN FÉIN in the 1918 general election were followed by unrest and guerrilla warfare. The Dáil Eireann, a republican Irish assembly, was elected by Southern Ireland in 1918. The Home Rule Bill of 1920 proposed parliaments in Dublin and Belfast linked by a Federal Council of Ireland, and the Northern Ireland Parliament was set up in 1920. By the Anglo-Irish Treaty the following year, the 26 southern counties became the IRISH FREE STATE. The new state was still in allegiance to the British crown, and though the situation contradicted claims for independence, the Dáil Eireann approved the treaty. The oath of loyalty to the British crown was abolished in 1937 by a new constitution set up by Eamon DE VALERA, leader of the FIANNA FÁIL, a political party supporting separation from Britain. Ireland demanded total independence in 1948, and the following year the Republic of Ireland was proclaimed, severing the connection with the British Commonwealth.

hominids Members of the family *Hominidae*, including modern humans, *Homo sapiens*, their presumed forebears *Homo erectus* and *Homo habilis*, and forms believed to be closely related, collectively called the *Australopithecines*. Remains of *homo habilis*, 'handy man', were first found at Olduvai Gorge in Tanzania in the early 1960s and then at other sites in Africa, and date from about 4 million to 1.5 million years ago. Simple pebble and flake artefacts found at Olduvai Gorge indicate that *Homo habilis* may have made stone tools. Their faces were more humanlike than the earlier *Australopithecines*. They are believed to have evolved into *Homo erectus*, 'upright man', in Africa, about 1.5 million years ago.

Upright man was a larger creature with a brain almost the size of a modern human's, but with relatively large facial bones and a longer skull. These hominids developed sophisticated tools with axelike heads, discovered how to control and use fire, and made basic clothing. Around a million years ago, *Homo erectus* is thought to have begun travels to places such as China and Indonesia. Their last representatives disappeared 400 000 to 200 000 years ago, as they evolved into *Homo sapiens*, 'wise man'. By this stage the brain had enlarged, and the now rounded skull was lighter. The *Homo sapiens* line is believed to have split into two branches, one leading to NEANDERTHALS, *Homo sapiens neanderthalensis*, the other to modern people, *Homo sapiens sapiens*. The development of this branch into *Homo sapiens sapiens* happened gradually in the past 130 000 years. Anatomical and genetic evidence supports the theory that this happened in Africa, but it is possible that there was one parallel development in the Far East. In the Middle East, anatomically modern humans appeared around 50 000 years ago, and arrived later in Europe, around 45 000 years ago. The earliest modern Europeans are called Cromagnons. Neanderthals may also have interbred with modern people entering Europe from Africa via the Middle East.

The evolution of modern people led to increases in population, social activities, the first appearance of art and advances in tool technology. By this period, the UPPER PALAEOLITHIC, spoken languages had probably evolved. Humans reached New Guinea and Australia from Indonesia by 40 000 years ago, and developed different characteristics in isolation there. The timing of the first settlement of the New World is more controversial. There is little firm archaeological evidence for colonisation earlier than 15 000 years ago, but genetic, linguistic and anatomical evidence of modern Native Americans suggests that hominids may have appeared in North America as early as 40 000 years ago.

Honduras Central American country. A lieutenant in the service of the Spanish conquistador Hernán Cortés, Francisco de las Casas, founded the first settlement – the port of Trujillo – in 1523. Honduras was attached administratively to the captaincy-general of Guatemala throughout the Spanish colonial period. When independence came in 1821 it briefly became part of the Mexican empire of Agustin de Iturbide, then joined the United Provinces of Central America in 1825. The

union broke up in 1838, and a succession of *caudillos*, or military dictators, dominated the country for the rest of the 19th century.

Military dictators continued to be more prominent than civilian presidents until the election in 1957 of Ramón Villeda Morales. The army overthrew his liberal regime before the reform programme he had pushed through Congress in 1963 could come into effect. In 1969 Honduras fought a border war with El Salvador, a conflict which led to a humiliating defeat for the military, and led to the establishment in 1971 of a short-lived civilian government under Ramón

Ernesto Cruz. Cruz was ousted by the army the following year, and the country was once more controlled by military juntas until in 1982 a new US-backed constitution was established with the aim of increasing democratic activity. As a condition for support from the USA, Honduras allowed antigovernment guerrillas or 'Contras' from neighbouring NICARAGUA into the country.

In 1985 a new president, José Azcona del Hoyo, took control. He was faced with popular unrest towards the Contra presence in 1988, and he threatened to stop Contra activity and reduce the power of the military. But Honduras remained economically dependent upon the USA, and in 1989 Rafael Callejas of the National Party was elected president with US support. He faced economic turbulence, left-wing guerrilla activity, and security forces which were responsible for 40 assassinations and more than 4000 known violations of human rights in one year. The Contras withdrew from Honduras in 1990. The government launched an economic investment plan the same year. Despite loans from the IMF and the World Bank, the plan provoked hostility from unions, peasant groups and private business, causing unrest in 1992. Presidential elections at the end of 1993 were won by liberal Carlos Roberto Reina, who took office the following year, but political and economic difficulties continued.

Honecker, Erich (1912-94) East German politician. As a young man Honecker was jailed for ten years in 1935 for underground resistance to Adolf Hitler's dictatorship. Released by Soviet forces at the end of the Second World War, he became chairman of the Free German Youth in the newly formed German Democratic Republic. In 1958 Honecker joined the ruling Communist Politburo, and supervised the construction of the Berlin Wall in 1961, built to prevent escape to the West. His loyalty to the party and reputation as a Cold War warrior helped him to become party chief in 1971 and head of state in 1976. Honecker was deposed by the anticommunist revolution which swept through the East European communist countries in 1989. After the fall of the Berlin Wall the same year, he was ousted and entered a Soviet military hospital in Berlin. He was transferred to Moscow and the Soviets refused to extradite him for trial on charges of manslaughter for ordering border guards at the Berlin Wall to shoot to kill. When the USSR collapsed in 1991 he took refuge in the Chilean embassy, but the following year he was returned to Germany. The charges were dropped in 1993 when it was revealed that he was suffering from a terminal illness. Honecker was allowed to leave for Chile, where he died.

In the 1980s, Honduras provided a base for Contra rebels fighting the revolutionary Sandinistas in neighbouring Nicaragua.

Hong Kong British crown colony southeast of Guangzhou (Canton) on the coast of China, consisting of Hong Kong Island, Kowloon and the New Territories. In the 19th century, Hong Kong became a centre for commerce. A large quantity of opium was confiscated from British merchants and destroyed between 1839 and 1841, and Britain's frustration with Chinese restrictions on foreign trade led to their occupation of the island in the first of the Opium Wars. Hong Kong was ceded to the British at the end of the war by the Treaty of Nanking in 1842. In 1898, part of Hong Kong north of Kowloon Peninsula was leased to Britain by China for a period of 99 years, and became known as the New Territories. During the Second World War, after two weeks of fighting, the colony surrendered to the Japanese on December 25,

1941, but Britain reoccupied it in 1945. The communist victory in China led to an influx of refugees and wealth after the war, especially from Shanghai. The United Nations embargo on trade with China during the Korean War in the 1950s stimulated the development of its industry and financial institutions, and in the 1970s and 1980s it became an important international economic and business centre.

In 1984 Britain agreed to transfer sovereignty of the entire colony to China in 1997 when the treaty on the New Territories was due to expire. China agreed not to alter Hong Kong's economic and social structure for 50 years, but unease in the colony led to

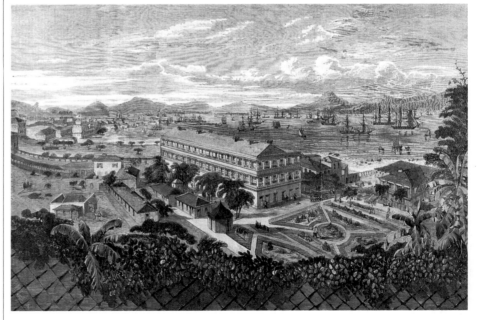

Hong Kong harbour, shown here in 1856, was well positioned on the trade routes of the Far East. The colony grew as a trading centre in the 19th century, attracting both Europeans and Chinese.

increasing pressure for more democratic government before the handover. A dispute with China arose over reform of the colony's political system proposed by Chris Patten, appointed governor of Hong Kong in July 1992. China argued that the reforms contravened the 1984 Sino-British Declaration. Talks between the two countries over the proposals failed in November 1993. By June 1994, the whole reform package had been passed by the Hong Kong Legislative Council (Legco), despite objections from the Chinese government, who announced that the Legco would be disbanded following Hong Kong's reversion to Chinese sovereignty. Talks in April 1995 failed to alleviate Sino-British tensions. In June, an agreement was finally reached on the creation of a Court of Final Appeal as a replacement for Britain's Privy Council, to ensure the continuation of law in Hong Kong after the handover.

Hood, Samuel, 1st Viscount (1724-1816)
British admiral who served in the Seven Years' War, the American War of Independence and the French Revolutionary Wars. Hood entered the navy in 1741 and was promoted to post-captain in 1756. In 1780, he went to the West Indies as rear-admiral, second-in-command to Lord George RODNEY, and played a prominent part in the defeat of the French fleet near Dominica in the Battle of Les Saintes two years later. During the French Revolutionary Wars, Hood commanded the British fleet in the Mediterranean.

Hoover, Herbert (1874-1964)
Thirty-first president of the USA, from 1929 to 1933. Hoover was an engineer and businessman who earned a reputation as a humanitarian by organising the production and distribution of food in the USA and Europe during the First World War. He became secretary of commerce in 1921 and served for seven years under Republican presidents Warren Harding and Calvin Coolidge. Hoover received the Republican nomination for president in 1928 and used his reputation as a moderate liberal to defeat Alfred E. Smith, his Democratic rival. His presidency was marked by failure to prevent the Great DEPRESSION following the STOCK MARKET CRASH of 1929. The shanty towns of the homeless that soon sprang up around cities were seen as evidence of this, and became known as Hoovervilles. He ran for re-election in 1932, but was heavily defeated by the Democrat Franklin D. ROOSEVELT.

Hoover, J. Edgar (1895-1972)
Director of the US Bureau of Investigation, now the FEDERAL BUREAU OF INVESTIGATION (FBI) from 1924 until his death. Hoover was given the task of raising its standards after the disrepute it had earned during the corruption scandals

FBI director J. Edgar Hoover (centre) kept extensive files on John F. Kennedy (left) and his brother Robert (right).

connected with the presidency of Warren HARDING. He achieved this by rigorous selection and training of personnel, and by creating a scientific crime detection laboratory and an FBI National Academy. In the 1930s, the FBI earned a reputation for integrity with Hoover's campaigns against prominent criminals, although the wide publicity they were given for this tended to mask the growth of syndicate crime. In his later years Hoover's persistent interest in the private lives of various public figures, possibly with a view to blackmail, clouded his supposed political impartiality. His opposition to CIVIL RIGHTS activities also earned widespread criticism.

Hopkins, Harry (1890-1946)
US administrator and public servant who played a number of key roles behind the scenes during important national and international events in the first half of the 20th century. Hopkins began his career as social and welfare policies adviser to Franklin D. ROOSEVELT when he was governor of New York state. During the years of the NEW DEAL, he was in charge of many projects set up to salvage the economy and create jobs after the Great Depression. He was Roosevelt's manager when he ran for a third term as president in 1940. Before and after US entry into the Second World War, he served as Roosevelt's untitled second-in-command. He played a pivotal role in the San Francisco conference of 1945, which launched the charter of the UNITED NATIONS, and in the last of the Second World War summit conferences at POTSDAM.

horse
Archaeological evidence shows that horses were kept in the Neolithic period, towards the end of the Stone Age, in about 9000 BC. They were not used as work animals, but as a source of food, milk and hides. Later, horses were used to drag loads, but they were mostly too small to ride. Selective breeding eventually produced horses big enough to be used as transport. The Hittites of Asia Minor harnessed horses to chariots in around 2000 BC, and in 590 BC the Assyrian army included 12 000 archers on horseback. In ancient Athens in around 1700 BC wealthy men bought mounts and simple weapons and became fighters in the service of the state. The Roman Empire became more dependent on horses to cover large distances as it conquered new territories and expanded. As cavalry soldiers became more heavily armoured,

stronger animals were needed to carry them. The German tribes bred the first of the 'Great Horses' which helped them to resist the Roman Legions in the 5th century AD. Arab cavalry conquered the Middle East and North Africa in the 7th century, and the Mongols used cavalry to extend their 13th-century empire from China to eastern Europe.

The horse also existed on the American continent but died out in prehistoric times. It was reintroduced to North America by the early settlers, and in the 18th century enabled Plains Indian tribes to become more efficient hunters. The Portuguese took horses to South America in the 16th century; many escaped, developing into large, wild herds on the plains of Argentina. In Asia, horses were also vital to the Cossacks of the Russian steppes.

Cavalry evolved through the ages: the heavy armour of medieval knights was abandoned with the development of guns, and lighter horses came into use. During the mechanised battles of the First World War the military use of horses decreased. They are used today more for ceremonial and recreational activities than for practical purposes.

Horthy de Nagybánya, Nikolaus (1868-1957)
Hungarian admiral who became regent of his country. In 1919, during the chaos following the First World War, the communist regime of Béla KUN seized power in Hungary. Counter-revolutionary forces invited Horthy to lead them, and Kun was overthrown. In 1920, the Hungarian parliament voted to restore the monarchy, and elected Horthy regent. He ruled virtually as dictator, and agreed to join Germany in the Second World War. In 1944 he unsuccessfully sought a separate peace with the Allies. He was imprisoned by the Germans at the end of the war, and was later released by the Allies.

hospital
The first 'hospitals' were probably temples dedicated to gods who were believed to possess powers of healing. They existed in the Middle East and south Asia in the 1st millennium BC. Hospitals for wounded legionaries were established by the Roman Empire in the first century AD, and contained

as many as 40 wards supervised by an army surgeon. In the 4th century, temples associated with healing were closed down after the Emperor Constantine made Christianity the religion of the Roman Empire. Private civilian hospitals were established, mostly by Christians, in Rome and other major cities, and more appeared in Europe, sponsored by the Church. In the Middle Ages, monasteries in Europe set aside areas for treating the sick. The huge increase in urban populations in the 16th century led to the establishment of hospitals by governments. Many developed in England after the Great Plague of 1665 and an epidemic of typhus in 1710. Government and wealthy citizens began to consider it their social duty to provide funding for hospitals.

Towards the end of the 19th century hospital treatment was revolutionised by the introduction of anaesthesia, better sanitation, antiseptics and training for nurses. Before these innovations, about one in four of all hospital patients died. In addition to caring for patients and training staff, many hospitals are now centres for research into the treatment and cure of disease.

Hospitaller see KNIGHT

Hotspur see PERCY

Howard, Catherine (c.1521-42) Queen consort of HENRY VIII from 1540. She was the king's fifth wife, as a result of the ambitious lobbying of her Catholic relatives, the dukes of Norfolk. After the king's marriage to ANNE OF CLEVES failed, they removed the principal opponent to the new marriage – Henry's Protestant chief adviser Thomas Cromwell, Earl of Essex – by executing him for alleged treason. Henry appeared to be deeply in love with his new wife, but Protestant enemies of the Howards accused Catherine of being unfaithful and having affairs with courtiers. The king was incredulous at first, but eventually he became convinced, and Catherine was beheaded.

Howe, Richard, 4th Viscount (1726-99) British naval officer, commander of the British fleet off North America in 1776. He attempted to negotiate a peace settlement with the rebellious American colonists, and when his efforts failed his fleet helped the British army to capture New York and Philadelphia. In 1782 Howe raised the siege of Gibraltar after defeating a combined Franco-Spanish force. He brought his career to a triumphant conclusion with a victory over the French fleet off Ushant in 1794 in the Battle of the 'Glorious First of June'.

Howe, William, 5th Viscount (1729-1814) British general, the younger brother of Richard HOWE. He joined the British army in 1746, won rapid promotion, and took part in the successful assault on Quebec in 1759. He led the march to the PLAINS OF ABRAHAM above the city, and took a major part in the battle there which ended French hopes of ruling Canada. He sympathised with the rebellious American colonists, but as supreme commander of the British forces in North America in 1776 he inflicted a series of defeats on US forces under George WASHINGTON. In 1778 he resigned in protest at the lack of support from the British Government.

Hudson's Bay Company Firm chartered in 1670 to govern and trade in a huge area of Canada called Rupert's Land, which borders Hudson Bay. The Company granted land to Scottish emigrants in 1803, which brought them into murderous conflict with the North West Company – founded by French and Scots traders who had settled in Montreal – over control of the highly profitable fur trade. Resolving this crisis led to the amalgamation of the two companies in 1821. The company still exists, based in Toronto; it has oil and gas interests, and trades general merchandise through department stores.

hue and cry Term given to the practice in medieval England of calling out loudly for help in pursuing a suspected criminal. All who heard the call were obliged by law to join in the chase; failure to do so would incur a heavy fine. Any misuse of the hue and cry was also punishable. The system was set out by Edward I in the Statute of Winchester of 1285, which detailed how communities should be policed. Members of the public are still, in principle, obliged to help the police to arrest a suspect.

Hugo, Victor (1802-85) French poet, novelist and dramatist, regarded by many as one of the greatest French poets of the 19th century. Hugo's poetry until the mid 1840s is predominantly lyrical. Later collections are more philosophical, and contain some of his finest poems. *Les Châtiments* (*Punishments*), published in 1853, is a satire against the loss of political liberty in France. *Les Contemplations*, published three years later, is a review of his life. The success of his verse drama *Hernani* (1830) signalled the triumph of romanticism over the classical dramatic conventions that governed French theatre. His novels, notably *The Hunchback of Notre-Dame* (1831) and *Les Misérables* (1862) demonstrated his concern for social and political issues. He was

banished in 1851 to Brussels for opposing NAPOLEON III's coup. He settled in Guernsey in 1855, and returned to France after the fall of the empire in 1870.

Huguenots French Protestants of the 16th and 17th centuries who followed the beliefs of the religious reformer John CALVIN. By 1561 there were more than 2000 Calvinist churches in France, and the Huguenots had become a political faction that seemed to threaten the state. Persecution followed, and they fought eight civil wars against the Catholic establishment during the FRENCH WARS OF RELIGION between 1562 and 1598. In August 1572, hatred of the Huguenots culminated in the deaths of 3000 at the hands of Catholic Parisian mobs in the ST BARTHOLOMEW'S DAY MASSACRE. Thousands more died in further disturbances outside the city. Henry IV finally gave them liberty of worship and a 'state within a state' in the Edict of NANTES in 1598. Their numbers grew, particularly among merchants and artisans, until further persecution when the Edict was revoked in 1685; many thousands of Huguenots fled to England, the Netherlands and Switzerland. In France, they had no civil rights until the revolutionary National Assembly restored them in 1789.

humanism Philosophical and cultural movement of the 15th-century European RENAISSANCE. Humanists were originally scholars who studied and taught humanities – grammar, rhetoric, history, poetry and moral philosophy – using classical Latin, Greek and Hebrew texts. They based their educational system and cultural outlook on classical antiquity. They included the theologians Desiderius ERASMUS and Marsilio Ficino, the

On his return to Paris after exile, Victor Hugo was elected to the national assembly and became a senator in the Third Republic.

DID YOU KNOW?

In 15th to 17th century England, the colour red was thought to bring down fever. Hospital patients were dressed in red nightgowns to aid their recovery.

Artisans among the Huguenot refugees who fled to Britain set up a flourishing business creating textiles in Spitalfields, London.

statesman and historian Francesco GUIC-CIARDINI and the political theorist Niccolò MACHIAVELLI. Humanists rejected abstract reasoning and narrow-minded approaches to religion in favour of basic human values, believing in well-being in this life rather than in the next. The invention of printing helped to spread the movement's ideas from its birth-place in Italy to western Europe. Humanism's spirit of sceptical enquiry prepared the way for the Reformation and some aspects of the Counter Reformation.

Humayun (1508-56)
Second MOGUL emperor of India, from 1530 to 1540, and ruler again from 1555 until his death. After his first ten years of precarious rule he was exiled in Persia, and recovered his empire only shortly before dying. His reign is significant because he returned from exile accompanied by Persian scholars and artists, and introduced Persian influences to India. Persian became the court language, and the Islamic SHIITE religion spread through parts of India.

Humboldt, Alexander, Baron von
(1769-1859) German explorer and scientist who travelled in Central and South America from 1799 to 1804, investigating natural history, meteorology and physical geography. Humboldt proved that the Amazon and Orinoco river systems are connected, and his measurements of the Peru, or Humboldt, Current off South America showed that the flow was colder than the surrounding sea. Humboldt climbed peaks in the Andean Highlands, and was the first to suggest that mountain sickness was caused by lack of oxygen. He pioneered the use of isotherms – lines on weather maps connecting

points with the same mean temperature – and examined the relationship between geography and plant distribution. Humboldt published his findings between 1804 and 1827, and settled in Paris. When his financial means were exhausted, he returned to Berlin, where he served at the Prussian court. In his last 25 years, he wrote *Kosmos*, a work describing the mid-19th-century understanding of the structure of the Universe.

Alexander von Humboldt developed many interests and friendships. More than 8000 letters survive from his correspondence.

Hume, David
(1711-76) Scottish philosopher and historian. In his *Treatise of Human Nature* (1739-40) he claimed it was impossible to establish certain knowledge through reason. He believed that man could only rely on his experiences, and that there is no overall scheme of things. He was accused of atheism, which lost him a hoped-for professorship at Edinburgh University. Hume was sent on diplomatic missions between 1746 and 1748, but returned to Edinburgh where he wrote his *History of Great Britain* between 1754 and 1762. He became friends with fellow philosopher Jean Jacques ROUSSEAU while serving at the British Embassy in Paris from 1763 to 1765. In his work, Hume attempted to rationalise moral issues and to undermine the idea of a religion based on the need for the Universe to have a creator. He also contributed ideas to economic theory, and his political views influenced the American Constitution.

hundred
Administrative subdivision of an English shire – a division of land managed by an alderman – between the 10th century and the setting up of district councils in 1894. Hundreds were probably based upon units of 100 hides; a hide was a measure of land calculated to be enough to support a family, and ranged from 60 to 120 acres (24 to 48 hectares). A hundred court of freeholders met each month to deal with military defence, private pleas and tax, and to prepare court cases.

'Hundred Days' (March 20-June 28, 1815)
The period between the French emperor NAPOLEON I's return from exile on the island of Elba and the second restoration of LOUIS XVIII. Napoleon landed at Cannes on March 1, while the European powers were meeting at the Congress of Vienna to discuss the affairs of Europe after his defeat. He won great popular acclaim as he moved north through Grenoble and Lyons. He arrived in Paris on March 20, a week after Louis had fled, and prepared to defend his empire against a hastily revived coalition of the European states. By the end of April he had raised an army of 105 000 troops to face an allied European force of almost 130 000. Nevertheless, Napoleon took the offensive and forced the Prussians to retreat at Ligny. Two days later, on June 18, he was decisively defeated at WATERLOO by British and Prussian forces. He returned to Paris and on June 22 abdicated for the second time. Six days later Louis XVIII was restored to the throne.

Hundred Flowers Movement (1956-7)
Political and intellectual campaign launched by the Chinese communist government under MAO ZE-DONG, based on the idea that self-criticism by officials and the people would benefit China's development. The campaign

was named after a slogan from Chinese classical history: 'Let a hundred flowers bloom, and a hundred schools of thought contend.' In February 1956, Soviet Union leader Nikita KHRUSHCHEV denounced the former Soviet dictator, Joseph Stalin. This encouraged free speech, and led Mao to invite criticisms of party policy. Denunciations of the Communist Party and its institutions began to appear in the press. Social unrest followed, and the party reacted by attacking critics and sending many into exile in an antirightist campaign. It has been claimed that Mao initiated the Hundred Flowers Movement to flush out his enemies and destroy them.

Hundred Years' War Conflict surrounding a series of attempts by English kings to dominate France between the 1340s and 1450s. The key issues were the sovereignty of AQUITAINE and EDWARD III's claim to the French throne through his mother Isabel, daughter of Charles IV of France, after the death of the last CAPETIAN king. Rivalry over

the profitable Flanders wool trade and French support for the Scots against England also contributed. Philip of Valois was crowned king of France in 1328 and confiscated Aquitaine – under English control since the marriage of Henry II to ELEANOR OF AQUITAINE in 1152. Edward III retaliated by invading France in 1338, winning a naval battle at Sluys in 1340 and victories at CRÉCY and Calais in 1346 and 1347. At the Battle of POITIERS in 1356, Edward's son, EDWARD THE BLACK PRINCE, captured Philip's successor, John II. John was ransomed for £50 000 in the Treaty of BRETIGNY of 1360, which gave Edward territories in France in return for abandoning his claims to the French throne.

The French gradually strengthened their position, and most of the hostilities ended during the reign of Edward's successor, Richard II. But England retained control of Calais and Bordeaux, preventing a permanent peace. HENRY V revived English claims to France by capturing Harfleur and winning a crushing victory at AGINCOURT in 1415. Four

years later, he occupied Normandy and then much of northern France. The Treaty of Troyes in 1420 forced Charles VI of France to disinherit his son in favour of Henry V, who married Charles's daughter, Katherine. After Henry's death in 1422 at the age of 35, the regents of his ineffectual son, HENRY VI, kept the initiative until the recovery of French morale under the leadership of JOAN OF ARC. The English were defeated at Orléans in 1429, and by 1450 France had conquered Normandy and much of Gascony. The last English stronghold, Bordeaux, was captured in 1453. This ended the war, although Calais was not recovered by the French until 1558.

Hungarian Uprising (1956) Revolution in Soviet-controlled Hungary after the Second World War, which led to famine and low standards of living. At the Twentieth Congress of the Communist Party of the Soviet Union in February 1956, the new Soviet leader Nikita Khrushchev criticised the former dictator, Joseph Stalin. Khrushchev's speech and anticommunist riots in Poland later in the year sparked demonstrations calling for 'de-Stalinisation' in Budapest on October 23. Soviet tanks arrived in response, but when Hungarian soldiers joined the uprising, Soviet forces withdrew. Imre NAGY became prime minister, appointed noncommunists to his coalition, and then withdrew Hungary from the WARSAW PACT, seeking neutral status for the country. This was unacceptable to the Soviet Union, who attacked Budapest on November 4 and brought the resistance to an end. Nagy was replaced by the communist leader János KADAR. The Soviet Union broke a pledge of safe conduct, and handed Nagy and other prominent figures over to the new Hungarian regime. They were executed in secret.

Hungary Country in central Europe. The Roman provinces of Pannonia and Dacia once existed where Hungary is today, but were overrun by Germanic tribes between the 5th and 6th centuries and then conquered by the Holy Roman Emperor, CHARLEMAGNE. By 896, the Arpád family had been appointed rulers of the region by the Holy Roman Emperor, Arnulf. The family was part of the MAGYAR tribe which had emigrated from Russia, and Hungary emerged as the centre of a strong Magyar kingdom in the late Middle Ages. A Mongol invasion devastated the population in 1241, and when the Arpád line died out in the 14th century the crown passed to a succession of foreigners. The advance of the OTTOMAN EMPIRE threatened the country, especially after the Battle of Nicopolis in 1396, when Sigismund, King of Hungary, was defeated by the Turks. A period of peace followed the defeat of the Turks at Belgrade in 1456, but the death of the Hungarian king

In the Hundred Years' War France fought against English domination. Joan of Arc's victory at Orléans in 1429 was a turning point, but it took until 1453 for the French to regain control.

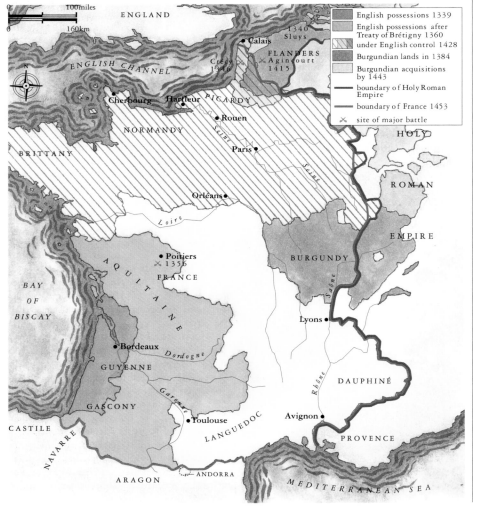

English possessions 1339
English possessions after Treaty of Brétigny 1360
under English control 1428
Burgundian lands in 1384
Burgundian acquisitions by 1443
boundary of Holy Roman Empire
boundary of France 1453
✕ **site of major battle**

Hungarians burn Russian propaganda material during the uprising of 1956. The revolution was crushed, and when János Kadar came to power more than 190 000 Hungarians fled into exile.

Louis II in battle in 1526 led to the partition of the country between the Habsburgs and the Ottomans. By 1711 all Hungary had come under Habsburg rule, and was to remain so until 1919. Revolutionaries led by the political reformer Lajos Kossuth set up a Hungarian republic in 1848, but it was suppressed by the Austrians. The AUSTRO-HUNGARIAN EMPIRE or Dual Monarchy, an alliance of Magyars and Austrian Germans against the Slav peoples, was established in 1867. Defeat in the First

World War led to revolution and independence, first as a democratic republic, then briefly under Béla KUN's communist regime. Dictatorship followed from 1920 to 1944 under Nikolaus HORTHY.

In the Second World War Hungary was allied to the defeated Axis powers of Germany, Italy and Japan; it was brought under the control of the Soviet Union in 1946, and a communist one-party system was installed in 1949. The HUNGARIAN UPRISING in 1956 was an unsuccessful attempt to end domination by the Soviet Union, but demonstrations in Budapest in 1988 led to the restoration of multiparty politics. Elections in 1990 brought the MDP, or Hungarian Democratic Forum, to power. Freedom from the disintegrating Soviet bloc also led to a fall in trade and a rise in unemployment. Refugees from Romanian Transylvania and from civil war in

the Balkans caused more problems. Reforms to revive the economy and introduce a free-market system were instigated in 1990. The privatisation of many companies in 1991 and an increase in foreign investment could not prevent continued economic recession. In the election of May 1994, the MDP lost to a new coalition led by Gyula Horn of the Hungarian Socialist Party. Despite a sense of economic crisis in the country, slight economic growth was recorded in 1995.

Hungry Forties Period in the early 1840s in Britain when economic depression caused widespread misery among the poor. A serious slump in trade led to high unemployment in 1839, and three years of poor harvests followed. The CORN LAWS kept the price of bread artificially high and increased the suffering. In 1845, potato blight struck England and Scotland, spreading to Ireland later in the year and ruining most of the crop. The blight returned the following year, causing the IRISH FAMINE, in which a million people starved to death and another million were forced to emigrate.

Huns Pastoral nomads famed for their horsemanship. The Huns entered recorded history when they invaded south-eastern Europe in around AD 370. They drove the Germanic VISIGOTHS into Roman territory in 376 and advanced west, pushing the Alans, VANDALS and other tribes into Gaul, Italy and finally Spain. Under ATTILA in the mid 5th century they ravaged the Balkans and Greece, but were beaten in 451 by the Romans and Visigoths. They plundered Italy before retreating after the death of Attila in 453. The White Huns, believed to be the remainder of the Hunnish people, went on to establish an empire in northern India.

hunting Early man hunted for food and clothing, and later, as agriculture developed, to protect crops. Hunting for sport began among the rulers of ancient societies. Huntsmen of ancient Egypt formed a social class, and scenes depicting hunts have been found on the walls of Assyrian and Babylonian buildings from the second and third millennia BC. Coursing – using fast dogs to run down prey – and hunting on horseback occurred in the second millennium BC, and falconry first appeared in early India and China. Hunting was a popular pastime in medieval Europe, reserved for the privileged classes by game laws protecting the king's quarry. It gradually became more widespread, and guns were introduced in the 16th century. Codes of fair play have emerged, stating that prey should be given a chance to escape, and that wounded game should be tracked down and killed to prevent further suffering. Concerns of conservationists have led to restrictions protecting certain species of animal.

hussar Soldier of a light cavalry regiment. The name comes from the mounted troops raised in 1485 by Matthias Corvinus, king of Hungary, to fight the Turks. In the 18th century most European armies used hussar regiments for scouting. Britain sent hussars hired from several German states to America, where they were hated by the colonists. Regiments of hussars were formed in the British army in the 19th century by converting regiments of light dragoons, or mounted infantry. They wore distinctive uniforms with a dolman or braided jacket worn loosely over the left shoulder. British hussar regiments have seen action throughout the 20th century, most recently in the Gulf War.

Hussein (ibn Talal) (1935-) King of Jordan from 1953, the grandson of Abdullah ibn Hussayn, who was installed in 1920 as emir, or princely ruler, of the country known as Transjordan under the British mandate. Jordan achieved independence in 1927. When Hussein became king, he tried to revive the economy, but was forced to rely on aid from the West. In the Arab-Israeli War of 1967 he lost territory on the West Bank of the River Jordan to Israel. Palestine Liberation Organisation (PLO) guerrillas moved into the country, but Hussein expelled them in 1971. He reasserted his authority, surviving accusations by Arab neighbours that he had undermined Palestinian resistance to Israel. From 1979 his policies became more flexible. He was reconciled with PLO leader Yasser Arafat, and became central to a peace initiative in the Middle East. In 1988 he renounced Jordanian claims to the West Bank, and in 1992 relaxed a 34-year ban on political parties. He signed a peace treaty with Itzhak Rabin, then prime minister of Israel, in 1994.

Saddam Hussein presents a young British hostage on Iraqi television. Expatriate families were kidnapped in August 1990 when an Allied attack loomed.

Hussein, Saddam (1937-) President of Iraq from 1979. Hussein began his climb to power by joining the Ba'ath Socialist Party in 1957, and in the early 1960s he was involved in several coups and plots. He was imprisoned in 1964 for attempting to overthrow the regime, and after his release two years later he took a leading part in the revolution of July 1968 which brought General Ahmed Bakr to power. The following year he became deputy-chairman of the Revolutionary Command Council, following the execution of 51 prominent Iraqis on spying charges. In 1979 Hussein succeeded Bakr as chairman of the council and president of Iraq.

At home Hussein concentrated on expanding the Iraqi oil industry, and in 1980 he launched the IRAN-IRAQ WAR with technical support from the West, which saw revolutionary Iran as a threat to supplies of Middle East oil. In 1988 the inconclusive war of attrition ended. The same year Hussein carried out a campaign of repression against the Kurds of northern Iraq, attacking their mountain homes with chemical weapons and poison gas. In August 1990 he ordered an Iraqi invasion of KUWAIT, and in 1991 he was defeated in the Gulf War by an international coalition of United Nations troops.

Hussites Followers of John Huss (c. 1372-1415), a Bohemian religious reformer who was excommunicated for heresy and put to death by the Catholic Church. His execution at the stake provoked a nationwide protest in Bohemia for religious freedom and against German rule. The Hussite movement then split into two main parties: the moderate Utraquists and the Taborites – named after Mount Tabor, their fortified stronghold – who held more radical theological and social views. The Taborites were eventually defeated by an alliance of Utraquists and Catholic forces at the Battle of Lipany in 1434.

Most of the moderate demands made by the Utraquists were granted in 1436 by the Church at the Compactata of Prague. Some Hussite congregations survived into the 20th century, but the movement was largely overtaken by the 16th-century Reformation.

Hyde, Edward see
CLARENDON, EDWARD HYDE

Hyderabad One of the largest and most powerful of the former princely states in south-central India. It rose to dominance under the Mughal viceroy Asaf Jah Nizam ul-Mulk, who in 1724 established largely independent rule. His successors ruled as nizams, or governors, of Hyderabad. Since they lacked the forces to combat European armies, they arranged in 1798 for Hyderabad to become a British protectorate in return for the upkeep of EAST INDIA COMPANY troops. On British withdrawal from India in 1947, the nizam accepted the Indian Union. In 1956 the territories of Hyderabad were divided among new language-based states.

Hyksos Invaders, probably desert nomads from Palestine, who conquered the pharaohs of the Middle Kingdom (c. 2100-1786 BC) in Lower Egypt and part of Upper Egypt. The name means 'rulers of foreign lands'. The Hyksos' power lasted until about 1550, when

Soldiers in the Hussite army of the Taborites used a mobile battle wagon to convey arms and supplies, and to outflank their enemies.

they were overthrown by a rebellion started by the Egyptians of Thebes. The Hyksos probably introduced the horse and chariot to Egypt.

Iberians Early inhabitants of eastern and southern Spain, who migrated from Africa between the 8th and the 6th centuries BC. From the 4th century the northern peoples intermingled with the Celts and became the Celtiberians. In the 3rd and 2nd centuries both peoples became increasingly allied with Carthage, and formed a vital part of the Carthaginian armies that fought the Romans and the Sicilians. Today the word Iberia refers to the peninsula of Spain and Portugal.

Ibn Battutah (c. 1304-68) Moroccan explorer. A Berber Muslim, he travelled widely across the entire Muslim world and a large part of the Far East, including China. His motto was 'never to travel any road a second time'. After some 25 years of continuous travelling, in which he covered 70000 miles (112000 km), he returned to Morocco in 1349, where he dictated his adventures to a writer, Ibn Juzayy. *Rihlah* (*Travels*) survives as a vivid account of the Muslim world of Battutah's day.

Ibsen, Henrik (1828-1906) Norwegian dramatist and poet. Generally considered the founder of modern realistic theatre, he achieved international renown for his often disturbing plays exploring social, political and psychological themes. *Pillars of Society*, written in 1877, established Ibsen's reputation, but his best-known works are *A Doll's House* (1879), *Ghosts* (1881) and *Hedda Gabler* (1890), all of which powerfully exemplify his deep mistrust of the social rules by which individuals are supposed to abide.

ice ages Periods during which the Earth experienced repeated expansion, movement and retreat of ice sheets. Average temperatures during these ages were about 6°C (11°F) lower than at present. The most notable ice age – often referred to as 'the Ice Age' – occurred about 10 million years ago. The most recent, lesser ice age began in the 16th century and advanced and retreated until 1880. The cause of ice ages is not fully understood, but it is thought that they are chiefly brought about by a change in the tilt of the Earth in relation to the Sun.

Iceland North Atlantic island near the Arctic Circle. After its conquest by VIKING invaders between 874 and 930, Iceland was governed by 36 chieftains. They assembled at one of the world's oldest surviving parliaments – the Althing. The islanders were converted to Christianity in about 1000. Icelandic sagas from around this time, such as *Egils Saga* and *Njals Saga*, are among the earliest examples of European literature.

In 1262 Iceland passed to Norway, before coming under the rule of the Danish crown in 1380. The Althing was restored in 1845, and in 1918 the country became a sovereign state in union with Denmark. Iceland was an Allied base during the Second World War, and in 1944 became an independent republic. In

1946 it joined the United Nations and NATO. The country was entangled with Britain over fishing quotas in the COD WAR disputes of the 1970s, and in 1985 national opposition to the presence of US naval bases led Iceland to declare itself a nuclear-free zone. In 1991 it secured restrictions on fishing in its waters, and in 1993 it began negotiations for membership of the European Union.

Iceni Eastern English tribe of the 1st century AD. From 43 the Iceni were controlled by the Romans through an allied English ruler, Prasutagus. After his death in 60 the Romans broke the alliance. Prasutagus's widow, BOUDICCA, led the tribe into revolt with some success, but she was eventually defeated. The much diminished tribe lived on with a small capital in Caister, Norfolk.

ideology Since Karl MARX used the term in the 19th century, 'ideology' has meant a system of ideas representing the beliefs and values of a particular group or class. However, when the word was coined in 1796 by the French writer Destutt de Tracy he used it to mean simply the 'science of ideas'. De Tracy's ideal of a democratic, rational and scientific society was adopted by the Directory – the revolutionary government of France between 1795 and 1799. In the 19th century Karl Marx argued that the conflicting interests of social classes, particularly those of the working class and the bourgeoisie, produced conflicting ideologies expressive of their class interests. His ideas stemmed from the belief that the narrow interests of the bourgeoisie were forced on society as a whole to maintain its social and economic superiority. Marxism expanded on the earlier ideologies of SOCIALISM and COMMUNISM. In the first half of the 20th century the collection of beliefs that have

Ife produced naturalistic bronze sculptures, such as this head of a Yoruba king, from around the 14th century. It may have been cast for a burial ceremony.

subsequently been grouped under the name of FASCISM emerged in Germany, Italy and Spain. Its common features include a violent opposition to Marxism together with the insistence that the individual should be subjugated to the needs of the state and that the state should be governed by a strong, authoritarian leader.

Ife Holy city in Oyo Province, south-west Nigeria. By the 11th century Ife was the capital of a kingdom considered by its Yoruba population to be the birthplace of all mankind. In the following century the city's craftsmen began to produce superb terracotta sculptures and bronze heads. During the 16th century Ife progressively lost influence among the Yoruba as Old Oyo – capital of the province – became a seat of more powerful political kingdoms.

Ile-de-France Area of the Paris basin where the rivers Marne and Oise join the River Seine. In the 10th century it was part of the original duchy of France and, as such, was the birthplace of the French monarchy. In 987 its first ruler was Duke Hugh Capet. The early French kings exerted their authority over the entire country from this region, and by the time Louis XI had acceded to the throne in 1483 the realm covered most of present-day France. In the French Revolution Ile-de-France was partitioned and became a province. Today it is an agricultural region that supplies the capital with dairy produce and vegetables.

Illyria Area on the eastern coast of the Adriatic, now Albania and the former Yugoslavia. From around 1000 BC it was inhabited by several related Indo-European peoples, who antagonised their neighbours in Epirus and Macedonia. When King PYRRHUS of Epirus annexed their southern territory around 290, the Illyrians reasserted their power southwards. In 168 the Romans conquered them after the surrender of the last Illyrian king. The people became a military asset to the Romans, and some of the Roman army's greatest military leaders were Illyrians, including Aurelian and Constantine the Great. In AD 395 the kingdom was divided and fell subsequently to the Huns and the Slavs who, by the 7th century, had intermarried with the population of all the Illyrian-speaking territories. The only direct descendants of the Illyrians are the Albanians.

IMF see INTERNATIONAL MONETARY FUND

Imhotep Egyptian architect and astrologer, who was chief adviser to King Zoser, the ruler around 2700 BC. Imhotep is thought to have designed the first temple at Edfu and the first PYRAMID – the so-called Step Pyramid at Saqqara. In about 525 BC, he was elevated to become the Egyptian god of Memphis. The Greeks associated Imhotep with their god of healing, Asclepius. His temples subsequently attracted many worshippers.

impeachment Process of removing an official such as a president, judge or viceroy from office for wrongdoing. First invoked in England in the 14th century, the prosecution was frequently used in the 17th century against Charles I's supporters and ministers, including the Duke of BUCKINGHAM, Archbishop William LAUD and the Earl of STRAFFORD. It was last used in Britain in 1806 against Viscount Melville for his financial abuses when treasurer of the navy. In the United States the procedure requires the House of Representatives to submit articles of impeachment – effectively a list of complaints – for examination by the Senate. In 1974 the House voted to impeach President Richard Nixon over the WATERGATE affair, but he resigned before the case could be heard.

imperialism System of rule whereby one country exerts its influence over others, either by force or political control. One of the earliest empires was created by Alexander the Great in the 4th century BC; it covered an area from Greece to India. The two main periods of empire building in the modern era occurred between the 15th and 18th centuries and then between the mid 19th century and the First World War. France, England, Spain, Portugal

Imhotep designed the world's first pyramid, the Step Pyramid at Saqqara, around 2700 BC. Its shape may symbolise a staircase by which the dead pharaoh could ascend to the Sun.

Ten images that changed the world

Visual records can reveal as much about the past as written sources – and sometimes more. These ten paintings and photographs, in addition to being striking images in themselves, inspired or reflected new approaches to life and art.

LASCAUX CAVE PAINTINGS

The prehistoric paintings on the limestone walls of the Lascaux Caves in south-western France – dating from some 16 000 years ago and accidentally discovered as recently as 1940 – are among the earliest known works of art. In what seems today like incredibly difficult circumstances, a group of human beings thought it worth their while to find the means to give visual form to their thoughts and experiences. Did they intend to record their world, celebrate it, exorcise it, or reassure themselves that the wild beasts were not so wild after all? We cannot know. But image making starts here.

BOOK OF KELLS

This brilliantly illuminated manuscript of the four Gospel stories, dating from the late 8th century, was produced by an anonymous team of monks in remote parts of Scotland and Ireland. It consists of 340 folios of thick vellum, most of them decorated with miniature, jewel-like images – a rich anthology of early medieval symbolism. The page which opens the Gospel according to St Matthew shows four winged figures: Matthew the Man, Mark the Lion, Luke the Calf and John the Eagle.

THE CREATION OF ADAM

Between 1508 and 1512, Michelangelo Buonarroti – then in his mid thirties – decorated the ceiling of the Sistine Chapel in the Vatican, Rome, with a gigantic fresco which told stories based on the Bible's Old Testament. He worked virtually alone, on scaffolding, never able to stand back from what he was painting. The central image of the Creation shows God stretching out to give life and energy to the earthbound Adam – energy which is passed through his outstretched finger. Adam lies on the ground, the model of Renaissance beauty. Part of his body is energised, the rest inert. This is still the greatest image of the act of creation.

THE ALHAMBRA

The Alhambra Palace, overlooking Granada, was mainly built in the 14th century under the supervision of two rulers of the last Spanish Moorish kingdom: Yusuf I and Mohammed V. It is a fabulous monument to Moorish culture, a meeting-point of Eastern and Western visual languages and a reminder that both the medieval and Renaissance eras in Europe depended on the learning and creativity of the Islamic world.

LAS MENINAS

Las Meninas, 'The Maids of Honour', was painted in 1656 by Diego Velázquez. It is set in his huge, gloomy studio in Madrid's royal palace, and shows the five-year-old Princess Margareta attended by two companions. Velázquez himself is painting a double portrait of the king and queen, who are reflected in a mirror on the back wall. The artist is looking out at his subjects and the viewer, so the focus of the composition lies in front of the painting.

This has been called 'the most daring pictorial experiment ever made', a celebration and analysis of the process of image-making.

THE DEATH OF MARAT

The Death of Marat by Jacques-Louis David, painted in Paris between July and October 1793 during the French Revolution's 'Reign of Terror', shows the revolutionary Jean-Paul Marat lying in a medicinal bathtub lined with patched sheets (he had a serious skin disease) with a fatal stab wound in his left lung. He has a quill pen in his hand, and an upended packing case doubles as his desk. The composition and lighting are those associated with a late Renaissance Christ taken down from the Cross; the figure resembles a classical sculpture. These effects are used, though, to create an image of a down-to-earth modern hero and martyr.

MUYBRIDGE'S HORSES

Before photography revealed that the legs of galloping horses move independently of each other, artists had drawn and painted 'rocking horse' images. The Englishman Eadweard Muybridge took the first successive still photographs of 'limb displacement in motion' in the USA in 1878 – they were published in Paris – and provided a rich source for late 19th-century image-makers. One commentator had observed, on seeing a photograph for the first time, 'from today, painting is dead'. In fact, the photograph became just one more distinctive way of seeing.

THE SCREAM

The Scream, painted by the Norwegian artist Edvard Munch in 1893, shows an anguished figure in the foreground beneath a red and yellow sunset made up of rhythmic, streaky lines. The 29-year-old Munch described the experience which inspired it: 'I was tired and ill…I felt as though a scream went through nature'. His painting has been called 'the most painful expression of the anxieties of modern life': the skeletal face, the desperation of the colours, the wavy lines of the sky, seem outward signs of inner turmoil. Sigmund Freud started his researches into psychoanalysis at about the same time.

THE BATTLESHIP POTEMKIN

This renowned still from the Soviet film-maker Sergei Eisenstein's *The Battleship Potemkin* (1925) shows the face of a woman as she is struck by a Cossack's sword. She stands on steps at the Black Sea port of Odessa in 1905, watching a mutiny aboard the *Potemkin*. The film, and especially the Odessa Steps sequence, was a model of cinematic montage – the ferocious mounted Cossacks are crosscut with their fleeing victims and events on the battleship – and became a cornerstone of modern narrative film technique. The film also produced stills, often based on the director's drawings, which themselves were to influence 20th-century image-making.

MAN ON THE MOON

Pictures of American astronauts taking a 'giant leap for mankind' on the surface of the Moon were relayed back to Earth on July 21, 1969. Together with images of Earth itself – looking very small and insignificant – they had a huge impact on the way we see ourselves, and became key icons of scientific and technological achievement for that time. Science fiction would never look the same again, and the astronaut took over from the cowboy as the great American hero. These images were created by 'remote control', showing that the effect of a mass-produced picture of the 20th century could be as powerful as the work of an individual artist.

The 19th-century imperialist powers of Britain, Germany, Russia, France and Japan divide the cake of China, as its anxious emperor looks on.

and the Netherlands built the most significant empires. Indigenous populations gained some benefits from imperial rule, but often they lost their traditional identity and were forced to accept new religions and social doctrines. In the 1920s condemnation of imperialism increased, and several anti-imperialist movements sprang up. Since the Second World War most of the countries under Western control have achieved independence. France's remaining territories became the French Community. Many of the states within the BRITISH EMPIRE formed the COMMONWEALTH OF NATIONS. In postwar years the concept of neoimperialism emerged, which held that the highly industrialised countries controlled developing countries through restrictive trading practices, multinational companies and monopolies.

Impressionism Major art movement which developed in France in the 1860s. The central figures were Claude Monet, Edouard Manet, Camille Pisarro, Pierre August Renoir, Edgar Degas and Alfred Sisley. They reacted against academic teaching and conventions and rejected the idea of Romanticism, which required art to convey personal emotions. Instead they favoured a more objective recording, or 'impression', of what they saw at a particular moment. The Impressionists' aim was to capture the effects of light on different surfaces. Abandoning the landscape paints of greens, browns and greys they used bright colours to convey sunlight and reflection, with dabs and specks of colour that seemed shocking to traditionalists. Landscapes are the theme most typical of Impressionist paintings, though many other subjects,

including people and animals, were also painted. In 1874 the Impressionists held their first exhibition, independent of the official Salon of the French Academy, which had consistently rejected most of their works. After the exhibition the term 'Impressionism' was coined for the first time by Louis Leroy, a writer for the satirical magazine *Le Charivari*. He took the term from the title of one of Monet's paintings, *Impression: Sunrise*, and used it derisively. Impressionism did not win critical acclaim until the 1880s, by which time the Impressionist group had begun to disintegrate as each member pursued individual aesthetic interests and principles. But in its short existence Impressionism had a revolutionary effect, influencing painters of the same era such as Paul Cézanne, Vincent van Gogh and Paul Gauguin, and liberating subsequent painters from traditional techniques.

Incas People of South America, predating the Colombian Indians, who built a huge empire spanning present-day Ecuador, Peru, Bolivia and parts of Argentina and Chile.

The ruling dynasty was founded by Manco Capac around AD 1200, though the civilisation did not expand until the 15th and 16th centuries. The Inca empire grew through the conquests of three rulers – Pachacuti (1438-71), Topa Inca (1471-93) and Huayna Capac (1493-1525). It began to break up in civil wars during the reign of ATAHUALPA, and was further fragmented by the arrival in 1532 of Spanish troops led by Francisco PIZARRO. By 1537 most of the empire had been subdued by Spain. Each Inca ruler, or Sapa Inca, was

believed to be descended from the sun-god. The Sapa Inca oversaw an efficient army and a vast administrative bureaucracy in charge of regional agriculture, food distribution, road building and commerce. The Incas were skilled engineers, builders and farmers; they produced intricate ceramics and textiles, grew a variety of crops on terraced hillsides, and herded llamas and alpacas for wool. Many of their buildings were made of stone blocks fitted together with precision. Writing was unknown, but records were kept on *quipus* – sets of cords of different colours and thicknesses tied with a system of coded knots. (See also feature, pages 404-5.)

income tax Direct tax levied on annual income. It was first introduced in December 1798 in Britain by William PITT THE YOUNGER, to help to finance the wars with France. The property-owning classes were made to pay 10 per cent tax on incomes over £200, amounting to two shillings (10p) in the pound. Temporarily abolished by Parliament in 1816, income tax was revived in 1842 by Sir Robert Peel and thereafter remained in force. In the 20th century 'progressive' income tax, imposing different levels of tax on higher and lower income earners, was introduced in Britain. Other European countries adopted the income tax system in the second half of the 19th century, as did the United States, which introduced it in 1864 to help to finance the American Civil War. When federal income tax was reintroduced in the USA in 1913, most individual states were already levying their own income tax.

Impression: Sunrise (1872) by Claude Monet gave its name to the Impressionist movement, which flourished in France in the late 19th century. Monet advised his followers to paint a view 'just as it looks to you, the exact colour and shape, until it gives your own naïve impression of the scene'.

Independence, American War of see feature, page 31

India Greater part of the south Asian subcontinent. It was first inhabited by aboriginal Adivás peoples, and from around 2500 BC to 1700 the Dravidian-speaking peoples built up the INDUS CIVILISATION. Over the next 1000 years there were several migrations to India of peoples from the north-west, and they became dominant in the Indo-Ganges plain.

The first empire unifying all of India, was established by the MAURYANS between 325 and 185, after Alexander the Great left India. When their empire disintegrated, power struggles occurred between competing kingdoms, including those of the SCYTHIANS and the Parthians (see PARTHIA). In the 8th century AD Arab traders brought Islam to India, and between the 11th and 16th centuries India was invaded by Muslim Turks who gained control of the north and the Deccan plateau. Only in a few areas, such as the RAJPUT states, was Hindu power maintained.

The power of the Islamic MUGHAL empire was at its strongest from 1526 to 1707, and then declined as religious conflict with Hindus and European colonial intervention undermined it. The EAST INDIA COMPANY, formed by the English in 1600 as a trading group, gradually gained control of coastal enclaves. From these, the company grew to become the main power in the subcontinent for more than 200 years until the 1857 Indian Mutiny, led by soldiers of the company. The immediate cause of the mutiny was the soldiers' refusal to use cartridges greased with pig and cow fat – an outrage to Muslims and Hindus respectively. It was reinforced by a civil rebellion against the rapid imposition of European civilisation and harsh land policies.

Although the rebellion gained several military successes, including the massacre of the British garrison at Kanpur, it was crushed by the British in 1858. In the same year the East India Company's rule was replaced by direct British rule under the Act for the Better Government of India, one of a series of India Acts aimed at improving the country's administration. Central government remained under the viceroy, but the council was represented by Indian and European members. Under the Acts further improvements were made to the systems of land ownership, communication and education.

British rule was initially embraced, but the Indians gradually became more critical of it, and social reform movements such as the Brahmo Samas and the Arya Samaj attracted support. Substantial progress towards independence was made through the Indian National CONGRESS. Founded in 1885, the Congress provided an all-Indian forum for political activity, and under Mahatma GANDHI, who became its leader in 1920,

Native Americans gather at Standing Rock Indian Reservation in 1919 to hear President Woodrow Wilson. European style hats and suits have replaced the men's traditional dress.

conducted a political campaign for Swaraj, or self-rule, and independence. Although many Indians were killed during the PASSIVE RESISTANCE campaign, such as during the massacre at AMRITSAR in 1937, the Congress easily won the elections held under the 1935 Government of India Act, which provided for provincial autonomy in British India. Support for the Congress grew after the arrest of Gandhi and other leaders in 1942, and the subsequent founding of the 'Quit India' movement.

In 1947 independence was granted, Jawaharlal NEHRU became prime minister, and the Muslims were granted PAKISTAN as a separate homeland. In 1966 Nehru's daughter Indira GANDHI was made prime minister of India. After the army stormed the Sikh temple at Amritsar in 1984, she was assassinated by a militant Sikh. Her son Rajiv GANDHI succeeded her. Following Indian intervention in SRI LANKA between 1987 and 1990 to quell rebel TAMILS, he was assassinated in 1991 by a militant Tamil. Ethnic conflict between Hindus and Muslims and violent separatist movements in KASHMIR and the PUNJAB intensified under Rajiv's successor, P.V. Narasimha Rao. Following elections in May 1996 a United Party coalition led by H.D. Deve Gowda came to power.

Indian caste system see feature, pages 312-13

Indian reservations Land designated by the USA for Native Americans. The reservations were first established by Congress in 1786. President Andrew JACKSON introduced the Indian Removal Act in 1830, which led to Creek, Seminole, Chickasaw, Choctaw and CHEROKEE peoples being sent to reservations in the so-called Indian Territory, in modern Oklahoma. Around 200 reservations were set aside in more than 40 states, most on poor land which exacerbated the Indians' poverty. The status of Native Americans continued to deteriorate until the 1960s and 1970s, when their rights began to be recognised.

Indo-Chinese War Dispute on the border of India and China between October 20 and November 21, 1962. The conflict began over claims made by China that the region had been wrongly given to India by the British in 1914 in the McMAHON decision. The Chinese launched an offensive which made substantial gains in Assam, but they declared a cease-fire and retreated to the Tibetan side of the McMahon Line, retaining parts of Ladakh in Kashmir. Some border areas are still disputed.

Indonesia Archipelago of some 13700 islands in the South-east Asian Pacific. The population consists of around 300 ethnic

groups who speak 250 different languages. The majority of the population follow Islam. In 1816 the islands became the Netherlands Indies, and by the early 20th century independence was being demanded by indigenous political movements, the most prominent of which was the Indonesian Nationalist Party – *Partai Nasionalis Indonesia*. The party, led by Ahmed SUKARNO, was banned by the Dutch in the 1930s, but after Indonesia's defeat by the Japanese in 1945 Sukarno declared the country independent. Although the Dutch tried to regain control, fighting an open war with the independence movement from 1947 to 1949, they were finally forced to transfer power and left the islands.

Sukarno's popularity began to fade when his political democracy gave way to a semi-dictatorship or 'guided democracy', with a strong executive and special powers reserved for the army. In 1965 inflation, peasant unrest and the concern of right-wing Muslims about the influence of communism within the party led to a military coup under General Thojib SUHARTO. Sukarno remained a figurehead president until 1967 when he was deposed. Under Suharto, Indonesia's economy grew and a degree of stability was achieved. But his regime remained authoritarian and his political opponents, including fundamentalist Islamic groups, were brutally repressed.

In 1975 EAST TIMOR declared its independence from Portugal, and in the following year it was annexed by Indonesia. Throughout the 1980s conflict continued between government forces and the independence movement. In 1995 talks took place about East Timor between Portugal and Indonesia, under United Nations sponsorship.

Indo-Pakistan War Border conflict in September 1965 between India and Pakistan. It broke out when Pakistan attempted to assist Muslim opponents of Indian rule in KASHMIR, and spread when fighting reached the PUNJAB. A UN cease-fire was accepted, and complete troop withdrawal was achieved on January 11, 1966, by the Tashkent Declaration. War broke out again in December 1971 in Kashmir and East Pakistan, leading to the creation of the state of BANGLADESH to replace the former East Pakistan.

indulgence Partial or total annulment by the Christian Church of the temporal punishment still owed for sins after they have been forgiven. Though the practice was found in the early Church, it did not become widespread until the 11th century. Indulgences could be granted by saying specific prayers, carrying out good deeds and by going on Crusades. Corruption often occurred when money was offered in return for indulgences, an abuse vociferously criticised by Martin LUTHER during the Protestant Reformation.

Indus civilisation Highly developed civilisation which flourished in the lower valley of the River Indus in south Asia between 2500 and 1500 BC. Archaeological excavation of

Sacred castes: the hierarchy of India

The hereditary caste system in India developed from religious scriptures written 3500 years ago, and still forms the basis on which society is structured and marriages are arranged.

Even in present-day India it is common for parents to use the classified columns of newspapers to find a marriage partner for their children. The advertisements specify to which of India's thousands of castes a prospective bride or groom belongs. Castes are the social units into which most of those who follow the majority religious faith of the subcontinent believe themselves to have been placed at birth.

India's oldest religious scripture, the Rig Veda, written between 1500 and 900 BC, says that at the time of creation humans were divided into four orders, each with a particular skill or occupation, all mutually supportive and interdependent. This idealised model of society is known as the four-fold scheme of varnas. It holds that the most gifted and upright people are those who were created to serve the gods as priests. Members of this priestly varna are known as Brahmans. Below them, in descending order of rank, are the varnas of kings or warriors (Kshatriyas), merchants (Vaisyas), and the toiling people (Sudras), who serve the others.

The word caste was probably applied by the Portuguese who were greatly struck by the elaborate ways in which Indians classified one another.

LOWLIEST OF THE LOW
The system is based on the idea of unequal hierarchies: members of the same caste are said to share an intangible corporate essence, or blood bond, and to be of either higher or lower rank than members of other castes. Most castes are associated with a particular livelihood. Some occupations are held to be inherently degrading: a sweeper or hereditary remover of ordure belongs to the lowliest of all social categories, once called the Untouchables and now known as Dalits or the 'downtrodden'.

According to ancient teaching, it is sinful for Hindus to marry outside their caste or share food with those whose caste background is unlike their own. The statesman B.R. Ambedkar (1891-1956),

The political power of Indian Kshatriyas (right), or warriors, was subject to the Brahmans (above), or priests, who often acted as their advisers or ministers.

the first Indian Untouchable to gain a university degree, wrote of the humiliation of growing up as a child of unclean caste, aware that high-caste mothers would make their children bathe and change their clothes if touched by his 'impure' hands or even his shadow.

The Indian caste system may have developed to cope with wide extremes of social inequality, as has been the case with similar systems elsewhere. The livelihoods of most Indians were so precarious that caste helped both the weak and the strong to relate themselves and their colonisers to a fixed social structure. Although caste helped rulers and landowners to dominate those whom they defined as their inferiors,

The merchant selling grain, above, is a Vaisya, belonging to an Indian caste of higher status than the accountant, left, who is a Sudra – a member of the traditionally lower caste of peasants and labourers.

it also offered security to the poor through the bonds of mutual obligation. Lowly people could hope to find patrons of their own 'blood'.

By the time the first European travellers arrived, most parts of India were developing increasingly refined versions of these ideas. New Hindu rulers confirmed their royal standing by showering their favoured Brahman dependants with gold. One 18th-century prince from south India, the Maharajah of Travancore, had his Brahman priests proclaim a more prestigious caste origin for him by having himself reborn from a golden statue of a sacred cow.

The 20th-century Indian leader Mohandas Gandhi campaigned against what he saw as the evils of caste, coining the term Harijan or 'children of God' for the Untouchables. The constitution which came into effect when India gained independence in 1947 made it illegal for people born into the high castes to discriminate against those ranked below them, and since the 1970s the government has tried to correct inherited social disadvantage. However, the richest and most powerful people in India are still likely to come from the upper levels of the regional caste hierarchies, and the poorest from the lowest.

the area has been in progress since the 1920s. The most significant sites of more than 70 excavated are those at MOHENJO-DARO, Harappa, Kalibangan and Lothal, which reveal evidence of an advanced society with bronze and copper tools, baths, drains and straight streets. The civilisation died out suddenly, possibly due to flooding, overpopulation or an invasion by ARYANS.

industrialisation Transition from an essentially land-based economy to an industrialised one with high levels of manufacturing and service industries. In the late 18th century Britain became industrialised during the INDUSTRIAL REVOLUTION. After 1800 the continent of Europe followed, and in the USA the process spread across the country after the American Civil War of 1861 to 1865. By the 1870s industrialisation had reached Belgium, France, Germany and Japan.

Within the next 30 years industrial growth was rapid in most countries, especially in Germany and the USA where output had by 1900 surpassed that of Britain. The world's major industries at this time were iron and steel, chemicals, engineering and shipbuilding. In the final decade of the 19th century Russia rapidly industrialised, and in the 20th century industrialisation spread to most other countries, including India, China, Mexico and Brazil.

Industrial Revolution see feature, pages 314-15

Inkerman, Battle of see CRIMEAN WAR

Innocent III (1160-1216) Pope from 1198, and a Church reformer who increased control over the PAPAL STATES. Innocent excommunicated England's King John for refusing to recognise Stephen Langton as the archbishop of Canterbury, and declared Magna Carta void; he also attempted to curb the independence of Philip II of France. He instigated a Crusade against the ALBIGENSIANS in southern France, and in 1204 supported the Fourth Crusade. In the Fourth LATERAN COUNCIL – a meeting of Church leaders – summoned by Innocent in 1215, 70 reforms were decreed, and a new Crusade was subsequently launched in 1217 to convey them.

The Inquisition attempted to exterminate all heresy. Pedro Berruguete's 16th-century painting shows Dominican friars burning heretical Albigensian books.

Inns of Court The four legal societies of England and Wales, comprising Inner Temple, Middle Temple, Lincoln's Inn and Gray's Inn in London. They were set up in the 14th century, probably as hostels for students of common law. All barristers must be admitted to one of them before they are 'called to the bar' – the partition, real or imaginary, that separates the judge, jury and certain lawyers from the public.

Inquisition Court established by the Roman Catholic Church around 1232 to try cases of heresy. Concern about the activities of heretics such as the ALBIGENSIANS led to Pope Gregory IX's appointment of monks, mostly from the Franciscan and Dominican orders, as inquisitors. Those found guilty of heresy endured a range of punishments, including confiscation of goods, torture and death by burning at the stake. In 1557 a list of books condemned by the Church was published as 'The Index'. The Spanish Inquisition was a similar, but separate, organisation established in 1479 by the Spanish monarchy.

insurance The oldest known forms of insurance date back to around 4000 BC when Babylonian traders assumed the risks of the caravan trade through loans which were repaid, with interest, only after safe delivery of the insured goods. The Phoenicians and Greeks applied a similar

The three industrial revolutions that made the modern world

The changes that turn a country from reliance on basic agriculture and commerce into a modern industrial society using powered machinery are known as an industrial revolution. There have been three kinds.

French visitors investigating Britain's innovations at the end of the 18th century coined the phrase 'industrial revolution' as a counterpoint to the recent political revolution in their own country. The term describes a decisive advance in the way technology is used. With each such revolution economic growth rates have greatly increased – unless war or political disturbance has intervened.

FIRST INDUSTRIAL REVOLUTION

Preindustrial economies were not unchanging, but spurts of growth were followed by periods of decline. The main constraint was shortage of energy. In 17th-century England, for example, two-thirds of the land area was needed to provide basic subsistence. The remaining third had to produce the principal source of energy, wood, all animal feed and most raw materials (for example, for housing, shoes and clothes). The land could produce little more than 44 lb (20 kg) of wood per person per week, which is equivalent in energy to just half that amount in coal. The only abundant energy sources were wind and water; everything else had to be accomplished by muscle power. It was the introduction of fossil fuels, initially coal, that enabled economies to escape these limitations.

The first industrial revolution, in the late 18th and early 19th centuries, occurred in the most prosperous continent. Western Europe was then the richest part of the world and Britain, which had the most productive agriculture, was its wealthiest country. As an island, Britain had been protected from the worst

W. Bell Scott's painting *The Industry of the Tyne* shows the intensity of labour needed by early factories.

ravages of Continental wars and it had cheap coastal trade, a major reason why London was the biggest city in Europe. The process of industrialisation started in the richest country because it was there that demand was putting the greatest pressure on resources. Britain also had ample supplies of coal. By 1850, preindustrial energy levels had been augmented by 110 lb (50 kg) of coal per person per week, making the extra energy available to get industry started.

In general, technical change is not caused by the 'inventions' of inspired individuals. The steam engine was introduced not because James Watt observed the boiling of a kettle but because a number of people were then trying to solve a 'bottleneck' in the production of energy. The wealth of 18th-century Britain had created a demand for new technology: it would be profitable if it could be developed. Similarly, textile production was mechanised because cotton entrepreneurs such as Sir Richard Arkwright and James Hargreaves could not satisfy the market with existing technology. Most 'inventors' were really entrepreneurs.

Once one industrial country came into being the world was transformed, for it was not necessary to invent the steam engine twice. Businessmen could copy or adapt British technology. Governments also became important agents of industrial change as pressure grew to emulate Britain.

But industrialisation spread most quickly through trade and investment. It became possible for a country to export raw materials and food in return for industrial products. The 19th-century development of the United States was a classic example of industrialisation spreading to a 'follower' country. The USA exported cotton, timber and later wheat and beef to Britain in exchange for manufactures. This allowed the USA to develop faster than if she had had to rely on domestic industry. Once industrialisation was under way the United States erected tariffs to 'capture its own market' – to force its people to buy American goods. Russia, Germany and Japan all followed suit.

Industry created a new sort of urbanisation. Large cities had existed for

Affordable mass-produced Model T Fords await shipment by river to their expectant owners. For most of them it would be their first car.

thousands of years but, in the main, preindustrial cities were where the government was, where the rich people lived and where the people who lived off the rich people lived. By the late 19th century, industry in most countries had become highly concentrated, often on coalfields, creating dirty, overcrowded cities housing large populations of impoverished factory workers. It was a long time before the poor benefited from industrialisation to the same extent as the rich.

SECOND INDUSTRIAL REVOLUTION
Most of the classic products of the first industrial revolution – steam engines, locomotives, machinery, ships, reapers – were 'capital goods', items which are used to make other goods rather than consumed by their purchasers. Technical change in consumer goods was often difficult to achieve and in most countries consumers remained relatively poor.

As long as only a small number of wealthy people formed the main market for sophisticated consumer goods, such as early motor cars, it was not profitable to mass-produce them. The 'second industrial

Before computer control, an American circular knitting machine makes low-priced goods, but still needs many workers to tend it.

revolution' came about because of the rise of a mass consumer market.

This happened first in the USA where, in the late 19th century, the consumers were the world's richest. The essential advance was the development of new production processes. On the production line, each operative carried out only one task. The system required great coordination to perfect – it took three years in the case of the Model T Ford. This explains a second important change: the growth in the size of firms and the revolution in management techniques associated with the rise of the business corporation and eventually the multinational company.

The production line revolutionised the world of work, reducing the importance of many skills and replacing the partial independence enjoyed by artisans with the drudgery of repetitive tasks. But it also rewarded unskilled workers with a significant increase in wages and political power, especially through trade unions, and made good products at low prices affordable for far more people than before.

THIRD INDUSTRIAL REVOLUTION
The later 20th century saw a 'third industrial revolution'. New, science-based industries such as pharmaceuticals and petrochemicals and materials such as plastics were developed. But the most important change was the introduction of computers, which allowed the close control of production. The cost of modifying the

Robots replace workers on a production line in Japan (below). Filipinos hand-finish footwear (inset), providing cheap, high-quality labour.

output of a production line, for example, fell sharply. It was no longer necessary to make large numbers of identical products such as the Model T Ford for them to be inexpensive, and the quality of cheap goods rose sharply.

Computer technology also caused communications to become faster and cheaper. The result was that markets became global, making it easier for 'follower' countries to acquire technology and allowing investment to flow to the most dynamic economies. In combination with state planning in some countries, these two factors explained the late 20th-century success of the countries of the Pacific Rim.

Japan developed into one of the world's major economic powers within 30 years of a disastrous defeat in the Second World War. South Korea was able to develop a huge export trade in heavy engineering products, notably ships. Taiwan concentrated on exporting consumer goods. The success of countries such as Singapore, Malaysia, Hong Kong, South Korea and Taiwan was based on the combination of quality technology with low-cost labour, undercutting and destroying some industries in the older industrial countries.

In the developed world at the end of the 20th century, people took economic growth for granted. They expected their incomes to rise each year and would vote only for governments offering the prospect of greater prosperity. Yet continuous growth began in Europe just 200 years ago. It was the crude technical breakthroughs of the first industrial revolution that made the silicon chip possible.

An International Brigades recruitment poster of the 1930s proclaims that all the peoples of the world are supporting Spanish republicans.

system of insurance to seaborne commerce, using a 'bottomry' contract in which a shipowner borrowed money for a voyage and pledged his ship as security. In the Middle Ages bottomry contracts became more specialised, in the form of marine and land insurance. After the Great Fire of 1666, fire insurance emerged in London. Life insurance spread in the 17th century, and in the 18th century LLOYD'S OF LONDON – established as Lloyd's Coffee House in 1688 – became an important mercantile insurance company. By the 20th century people could protect themselves financially against many risks, including accidents at work, ill health, disability, house theft and car accidents.

intendant Royal administrator during France's ANCIEN RÉGIME. The office originated in the 1630s as an emergency measure to counter disobedience to the Crown. Intendants would carry out tours of inspection in the provinces and report any trouble to the provincial governor. During the 18th century they became a vital link between the provinces and central government, supervising the tax system and keeping the Crown informed of political developments. Their local power made intendants unpopular and in 1789 the office was abolished during the French Revolution.

International One of several associations established to unite socialist and COMMUNIST organisations throughout the world. The First International was set up in 1864 in London, and its most prominent figure was Karl MARX. It was disbanded in 1876 because

of irreconcilable differences between Marxists and anarchists. The Second, or Socialist, International was formed in 1889 to bring together the numerous new socialist parties in Europe. It was made up of representatives from Europe, the USA, Canada and Japan. It disintegrated at the start of the First World War, when its plan to prevent war by general strike and revolution was sunk by a surge of nationalism in all countries.

The Third International, known as the Communist International or COMINTERN, was founded in 1919 by LENIN and the Russian Bolshevik Party. Its doctrine of Twenty-One Points, through which it sought to promote world revolution, was accepted by communists but not socialists. In 1943 Stalin disbanded the organisation.

The Fourth International was founded in 1937 by Leon TROTSKY. After Trotsky's assassination in 1940 it was controlled by two Belgian communists, Michel Pablo and Ernest Germain. In 1953 their disagreements led to the group's collapse.

International Brigades International groups of left-wing volunteers supporting the republicans against General Franco in the SPANISH CIVIL WAR. Organised by the COMINTERN, they fought mainly in 1936 in the defence of Madrid and in 1938 in the Battle of the River Ebro. The French formed the largest foreign group of volunteeers. The men, and the few women, of the Brigades were finally withdrawn from Spain in 1938.

International Monetary Fund (IMF) Organisation set up in 1945 by the UNITED NATIONS to help to expand world trade after the Second World War by encouraging international financial cooperation and stabilising exchange rates. It was originally planned at the BRETTON WOODS CONFERENCE. Today member countries subscribe funds depending

on their wealth, and in times of economic difficulties may draw on the reserve fund created to meet foreign obligations.

international organisations see feature, page 317

Inuit Indigenous inhabitants of northern Canada and Greenland. The Inuit are closely related to the Aleut peoples of Alaska and similar groups in north-east Siberia, all of whom are commonly known as Eskimos. While the

> 66 **Nothing is more gorgeously clean than a new snow house. It is like a fairy grotto of an unearthly whiteness. The walls sparkle with a myriad diamond pinpoints.** 99
>
> *Lord Tweedsmuir*
> *January 1939*

Aleut and others have no objection to the term 'Eskimo', their counterparts in Canada and Greenland insist on being called Inuit – meaning 'people' in their language.

Like the Aleut, the Inuit migrated from Asia between 2500 and 1000 BC. Traditional Inuit culture was based on a seminomadic lifestyle, fishing and hunting whales, seals and caribou. In the 20th century most Inuit have taken to living in permanent settlements.

inventions see feature, pages 320-1

Invergordon Mutiny Rebellion by sailors on 15 ships of the British Atlantic Fleet in September 1931 at the naval port on the Cromarty Firth, Scotland. They refused to go on duty after Ramsay MACDONALD's National Government imposed severe pay cuts. The mutiny ended after the cuts were slightly revised, but more than 20 ringleaders were discharged from the navy.

A 19th-century Inuit mask (left) worn for fishing expeditions, and representing the soul of a salmon. Fish and animals such as the polar bear remain vital to modern Inuit existence.

Peace at all costs

The dream of an organisation dedicated to freeing the world from conflict was born in the suffering of the trenches during the First World War. In 1920 the League of Nations was formed, followed 25 years later by the United Nations.

The flags fluttering outside the United Nations building in New York and its sister palace near Lake Geneva in Switzerland symbolise global harmony, although it has proved a hard dream to realise. The League of Nations, forerunner of the United Nations, evolved after devastating losses in the First World War to prevent armed conflicts and to help countries to assist each other in times of natural disaster.

This marked a radical change in international relations. Europe had for centuries been a cauldron of shifting alliances. The British prime minister Benjamin Disraeli summed up this attitude when, after the Congress of Berlin in 1878, he told Queen Victoria of his dealings with the German leader, Count Otto von Bismarck: 'His idea of progress is evidently seizing something.'

In the League of Nations, rivalries would be set aside: governments would provide collective security for all countries through a system of economic and military sanctions against any aggressor. The League would also protect national minorities, and improve health and working conditions.

The League was largely the idea of the American president Woodrow Wilson, but the American Congress refused to join because it did not want the USA to be dragged again into European squabbles. It was also weakened by the omission of Germany and Russia.

In the 1920s it had some success in solving disputes in Europe, preventing an invasion of Albania by Yugoslavia, and resolving a dispute between Germany and Poland over Upper Silesia. But increasingly it came to be ignored.

Pressure for a new organisation to preserve world peace emerged at the end of the Second World War. The founding conference of the United Nations in June 1945 declared that the UN's aim was to 'save succeeding generations from the scourge of war which twice in our lifetime has brought untold sorrow to mankind; and to reaffirm faith in fundamental human rights, the dignity of the human person, the equal rights of men and women and of nations large and small'. Its charter was signed by 51 nations, and headquarters were established in New York.

AGENCIES WITH A MISSION

A number of autonomous specialist agencies were set up under the auspices of the UN, including UNESCO, which promotes collaboration through education, science and culture; the World Bank, to provide financial aid to developing member countries; and the World Health Organisation. The Security Council is responsible for maintaining world peace: 13 peace-keeping operations were established between 1946 and 1988 in countries from the Middle East to Korea; 21 between 1988 and 1995. Yet, regardless of the ideals of the UN's founders, national interests tend to hold sway when disputes arise.

In the 1990s the organisation was criticised for not doing enough to halt the civil war in the former Yugoslavia, but it did supply aid, thereby saving thousands of Bosnians from starvation.

Since its founding the UN has helped countless millions of people afflicted by war, famine and natural disaster.

UN peacekeepers – at risk as they escort food relief convoys in the former Yugoslavia.

The League of Nations Council consider the future as they listen to Hitler's foreign minister, Joachim von Ribbentrop, at St James's Palace, London, in 1936. A stamp (left) records NATO, an international defence organisation.

UNITED FOR FREEDOM
NATO
1949-1959
4c
UNITED STATES POSTAGE

At the investiture of the bishop and soldier Martin of Tours, spurs are fitted to his ankles, in a 14th-century painting by Simone Martini.

investiture Formal act of conferring office upon senior clergy. In the early Middle Ages kings 'invested' bishops with their bishoprics, but the practice was denounced by 11th-century churchmen, who were opposed to lay authorisation of the bishops' spiritual powers. The dispute over rival claims of Church and State for authority over Church appointments erupted into an investiture conflict, part of a wider movement for Church reform. The struggle between Pope Gregory VII and Emperor Henry IV over the reforms led in Germany to civil war, which was ended in 1122 by the Concordat of Worms – an agreement between Pope Calixtus II and Emperor Henry V. This abolished the king's right to invest, but allowed him to retain much practical control over the appointment of bishops.

Iqbal, Sir Muhammad (1876-1938) Indian philosopher, poet and political leader. Born in Sialkot (now in Pakistan), he taught philosophy at Lahore, studied law in England and was knighted in 1923. Active in politics in the Punjab, he became president of the Muslim League in 1930 and he advanced the idea of a Muslim state in north-west India.

Iran Islamic republic in south-west Asia, known until 1935 as Persia. In the 19th century Russia and Britain competed for influence in Persia. Britain's importance in the southern sector increased in 1909 with the founding of the Anglo-Persian Oil Company, later renamed BP (British Petroleum). In 1921 Reza Khan, a Persian officer, seized power from the Qajar ruler and declared himself the new ruler as REZA SHAH PAHLAVI. Throughout the Second World War Iran was occupied by British and Soviet forces. In September 1941 the shah abdicated in favour of his son Muhammad Reza Shah Pahlavi, who sought better relations with the West. He was opposed by the political leader Mohammad Mossadeq, who resented foreign interference in Iran's affairs and, in 1951, forced parliament to nationalise Iran's oil industry. The shah ousted him from office in 1953 and allowed foreign oil companies to operate, provided Iran was awarded a share of their profits.

In the 1960s the shah began a programme of economic reform and social modernisation which alienated religious leaders such as Ayatollah Ruhollah KHOMEINI. In 1978 riots against the shah led to the imposition of martial law. The following year Khomeini headed a rebellion which overthrew the shah. He established an Islamic republic hostile to the West and to its neighbour Iraq. Khomeini instigated the IRAN HOSTAGE CRISIS, which involved the seizure of the American embassy in Tehran, and entered the IRAN-IRAQ WAR. After Khomeini's death in 1989, the moderate Hashemi Rafsanjani became the country's leader. Iran remained neutral in the GULF WAR of 1991 and, after the break-up of the Soviet Union in that year, spread its influence in the newly independent central Asian states.

Sanctions were announced by the United States in 1995, after evidence emerged that Iran was sponsoring international terrorism and pursuing a nuclear weapons programme.

Irangate see REAGAN, RONALD

Iran Hostage Crisis Prolonged crisis between IRAN and the USA that lasted from November 4, 1979, to January 20, 1981. The American embassy in Iran's capital, Tehran, was seized by followers of the Ayatollah KHOMEINI, who believed the USA was involved in a plan to reinstate the shah, Muhammad Reza Pahlavi. Sixty-six American citizens were taken hostage, and efforts by President Jimmy CARTER to free them, including an abortive helicopter rescue in April 1980, were foiled. The crisis was ended through Algeria's mediation. The incident undermined Carter's re-election campaign, and he lost to Ronald Reagan.

Iran-Iraq War Border dispute between IRAN and IRAQ which escalated into a major conflict. It began in 1980 after President Saddam HUSSEIN of Iraq, retaliating against Iran's assistance to Kurds fighting for independence from Iraq, repudiated a 1975 border agreement which gave Iran an area north of the Shatt-al-Arab waterway. A border skirmish started by the Iraqi army was followed by an armoured assault into Iran's oil-producing region. Despite a shortage of arms and equipment, after 1982 the Iranians recaptured territory from the Iraqis, who were receiving arms from the West and the former Soviet Union. Iran relied on repeated, and often ineffective, infantry attacks by an army of poorly trained conscripts. The war entered a new phase in 1987 when Iran increased attacks against commercial shipping in and around the Gulf. The USA and other nations responded by sending naval escorts to protect Kuwaiti and Gulf state tankers. UN secretary-general PEREZ DE CUÉLLAR achieved a peace settlement in August 1988, by which time 1.5 million lives had been lost.

Iraq Middle Eastern country. Much of Iraq formed ancient MESOPOTAMIA, where the SUMERIANS established one of the world's

At the height of the Iran Hostage Crisis a bound and blindfolded American hostage is held by an Iranian soldier outside the US embassy in Tehran. In the background hangs a poster of Khomeini.

earliest civilisations. They lived in the fertile valleys of the Tigris and Euphrates rivers, possibly as early as 3500 BC. The Babylonian empire (see BABYLON) arose in 1894 BC and fell around 550 BC to the Persians, who were in turn conquered by Alexander the Great in 330 BC. Iraq was subsequently fought over by Parthian, Roman, Sassanid and Byzantine armies, until it became Muslim in the 7th century AD. The OTTOMAN EMPIRE took control of Iraq in the 16th century and ruled until 1917. The British occupied Iraq after the First World War under a League of Nations mandate. In 1921 Britain agreed to recognise Abd Allah FAISAL, the sharif (prince) of Mecca, as king, and in 1932 Iraq became independent.

British influence weakened in 1958 after an army coup d'état toppled the monarchy. In 1968 political rivalry ended with a coup by the Ba'ath Socialist Party. From the 1970s the party was led by Saddam HUSSEIN, who used oil revenues from some 3 million barrels produced a day to industrialise the country and implement social improvements. He has since ruled oppressively, appointing himself both president and prime minister and suppressing opposition with a secret police force.

In 1990 Hussein's invasion of Kuwait led to the GULF WAR. The conflict was ended in February 1991 by a US-led coalition of 29 countries acting on behalf of the United Nations. In 1992 Iraqi Kurds, who controlled an area of northern Iraq, elected a national assembly and defied a government blockade. In the following year attacks by government forces on the SHIA communities in southern Iraq led the Western victors of the Gulf War to declare the area an exclusion zone. Violations of the zone by Iraqi forces in 1993 resulted in air attacks by Western forces.

Ireland Island of the British Isles, west of Britain. It was inhabited successively from the 6th century BC by CELTS and PICTS. Celtic kings and chiefs ruled until the Middle Ages. Viking occupation of Ireland's shores from the late 8th century was ended in 1014 when BRIAN BORU defeated the Scandinavians at Clontarf. The Anglo-Norman conquest began in 1171 and was largely completed by 1172. But resistance to English rule persisted for 400 years, becoming particularly bitter when Henry VIII imposed Protestantism and when Elizabeth I encouraged 'plantations' of English and Scottish settlers in NORTHERN IRELAND, or Ulster. The religious and settlement disputes led to an Irish rebellion, suppressed in 1649 by Oliver Cromwell. His extension of Protestant settlement was confirmed by the GLORIOUS REVOLUTION of 1688, when the Roman Catholic James II was forced from the throne by William of Orange.

In 1782 Henry GRATTAN's party in the Irish Parliament achieved a degree of independence. This lasted until the defeat of the rising

A round tower in Ardmore, County Waterford, is one of many still standing in Ireland. Built as a secure place of retreat in the 12th century, it is almost 100 ft (30 m) high and tapers to a point.

led by the UNITED IRISHMEN in 1798 and the subsequent Act of Union, under which Ireland became part of Britain. Growing resentment against direct British rule, exacerbated by the IRISH FAMINE from 1845 to 1851, led to the establishment in 1858 of the Irish Republican Brotherhood (IRB) to agitate for an Irish republic. Its members were known as FENIANS, after the Fenian Brotherhood of the USA, which supported the group with funds and men. The partial independence offered by the HOME RULE bill

> **❝ I believe this treaty will lay the foundations of peace and friendship between the two nations. What I have signed I shall stand by in the belief that the end of the conflict of centuries is at hand. ❞**
>
> *Arthur Griffith, President of the Irish Free State, speaking of the Anglo-Irish Treaty, 1921*

failed to satisfy the Brotherhood, and in 1916, led by Padraic Perse, they mounted a rebellion in the abortive EASTER RISING.

The 1920 Government of Ireland Act allowed for two Irish parliaments: one which presided over the six counties of Ulster, and another parliament for the remaining 26 counties. But in 1921 the Anglo-Irish Treaty resulted in Northern Ireland remaining part of the UK and the 26 counties becoming the Irish Free State. Republicans led by Eamon DE VALERA rejected the treaty and fought a civil war against the Irish Free State forces, but in 1923 they were defeated. De Valera's party, FÍANNA FÁIL, won the 1932 elections and began to sever the Irish Free State's

connections with Britain. A new constitution renamed the Irish Free State as Ireland – or, in Irish, Eire. In 1949 it became a republic and De Valera was elected president. Subsequent governments have been controlled alternately by the Fíanna Fáil and a coalition between FINE GAEL and Labour. In 1991 Ireland elected its first female president, Mary Robinson.

The 20th century has seen a continuing struggle for a unified Ireland. The principal organisation advocating unity has been the Irish Republican Army (IRA), founded in 1919 by SINN FÉIN. Its first commander was Michael COLLINS. From 1969 the IRA and various Protestant paramilitary groups have been responsible for a campaign of bombings and assassinations in Northern Ireland in which more than 3400 people have died and another 35 000 have been injured. In December 1993 talks about peace began between the Irish and British prime ministers, John Bruton and John Major, and in August, 1994, the IRA declared a cease-fire. During 1995 a deadlock developed in the peace talks, and in February 1996 the IRA resumed its bombing campaign in Britain.

Ireland, Republic of see IRELAND

Irene (c.752-803) Ruler of Byzantium from 780 to 802. After the death of her husband Leo IV in 780 she became joint ruler with her 10-year-old son, Constantine VI. The adult Constantine resented his mother's controlling influence in the empire, and in 790 he banished her and became sole ruler. Allowed to return in 792, Irene had Constantine blinded and imprisoned, and ruled as emperor – not as empress – until deposed by a conspiracy of

Ten inventions and discoveries that changed the world

From the first appearance of early humans on Earth, the advance of civilisation has been marked by innovations that have transformed the way people lived. Here are a few of them.

FIRE

The control of combustion – 'the furnace of all human invention' – provided warmth and protection from wild animals and transformed the efficiency of tools and weapons. Fire was first mastered by *Homo erectus* – the ancestor of *Homo sapiens*, our own species – who lived 1.6 million to 200 000 years ago. More recently, *Homo sapiens* learned how to apply heat to create pottery and smelt metals. Fire was soon perceived as having spiritual power: it could create and destroy.

AGRICULTURE

After the last great ice age, which ended around 10 000 BC, hunting and gathering began to be supplemented by farming as people learned to cultivate plants and to domesticate animals. The growing of plants from seeds encouraged observation and experimentation, qualities that led to the development of buildings. Cities came into existence by 3500 BC. In one of the first, Sumer in Mesopotamia, two skills were developed that made possible all later progress: counting and writing.

COUNTING

The Sumerians of the 4th millennium BC developed a system of counting using units and tens – concepts that clearly derived from counting using the ten fingers of a person's hands. (Even in modern English the word *digit* derives from the Latin for 'finger'.) In Babylon, 60 was the base of a measuring system that still survives in divisions of time: hours, minutes, seconds. Early advances in counting derived from the practical needs of farmers and merchants; later, ancient Greece introduced into mathematics abstractions such as infinity. The subsequent development of mathematics, and with it science, depended most on India, where the system of what later came to be called Arabic numerals was devised. It was through the Muslim world that they made their way into the West.

WRITING

Sumer also developed a means of recording ideas and words. Using the wedge-shaped end of a reed, they made patterns of marks called cuneiform on wet clay tablets. In ancient Egypt, messages and records were stored by means of hieroglyphs – stylised pictures representing objects and sounds. The ancient Chinese used graphic symbols, or characters, which became increasingly abstract. The first alphabet to use letters to stand for sounds was devised in Asia Minor around 1300 BC. From the start the uses of writing were multiple and diverse, yet for centuries literacy was confined to an elite class of priestly scribes, who jealously guarded the secret of their skill.

PRINTING

The advance that threw open public access to words of every kind was devised in China and Korea. Printing made its way to the West, and then to the rest of the world after the invention of the printing press using movable type by Johann Gutenberg in the 1430s. Printed materials – from the ephemeral advertisement to the bound book, from the ballad sheet to the novel – met a huge variety of different needs, material, spiritual, economic, social and cultural. By speeding up the flow of information and ideas through the pamphlet, newspaper and periodical, and by affording entertainment, printing influenced all aspects of life.

STEAM POWER

In early 18th-century England, Thomas Newcomen devised a steam engine for pumping water from coal mines; in the late 18th century James Watt developed an

Putting fire to good use: a baker prepares to take a freshly baked loaf out of his oven in this Roman mosaic.

Egyptian agriculturists at work (above). Early farmers used flint-edged sickles such as this.

This Mesopotamian clay tablet with its intricate cuneiform script (above) dates from around 3200 BC.

These tokens from ancient Mesopotamia were used for counting items of merchandise, such as jars of oil or specific quantities of honey, metal, grain and livestock.

Thomas Newcomen's steam engine, connected to a pump designed to remove water from flooded mines.

engine capable of moving machines. The age-old dependence on water and wind power was eliminated. For Karl Marx the steam engine ushered in modern times, vastly increasing the world's wealth but generating social conflicts that he believed would lead to revolution. In fact, steam was supplanted by other technologies based on electricity, oil, and, in the 20th century, nuclear power. The climax of the steam age was the steam locomotive, the most important invention in the history of transport since the discovery of the wheel.

INTERNAL COMBUSTION
The possibility of private locomotion revolutionised transport. In the 1880s Karl Benz and Gottlieb Daimler built the first vehicles powered by petrol engines. Cars remained a luxury until Henry Ford so reduced their cost that cars could be afforded by millions. Increased individual mobility affected both work and leisure; with the increase of traffic, landscapes and townscapes were transformed. The first aeroplane, produced by the Wright brothers in 1903, also used a petrol-driven motor, and the 'conquest of the skies' followed.

With this printing press (above) – the first to use movable type – Johann Gutenberg revolutionised book production.

PHOTOGRAPHY
The process of capturing images on light-sensitive materials, as demonstrated in the 1830s by Louis Jacques Daguerre in France and William Fox Talbot in England, made possible the recording of persons, scenes and events. The camera became the 'eye of history'. By the end of the 19th century, after the invention of the Kodak camera and roll film in the 1880s, photography had become a popular pastime. With the development of moving pictures the way was prepared for the age of the cinema, which began in 1895 with film demonstrations by the Lumière brothers.

RADIO AND TELEVISION
Radio, exploited by Guglielmo Marconi after he had transmitted radio messages in 1895, used Morse code, not words, until the invention of the thermionic valve in the first decade of the 20th century. It was not until the 1920s that radio broadcasting systems were introduced, building up huge

audiences. Television, which had been forecast a generation earlier, began on an experimental basis in the 1930s, but not until the 1960s did it become the dominant medium of information and entertainment. In 1969 the first global satellite communications system enabled viewers in their own homes to watch Neil Armstrong stepping on to the Moon.

COMPUTERS
There would have been no journey into space without computers. The first of them were huge: ENIAC (Electronic Numerical Integrator and Calculator), installed at the University of Pennsylvania in 1946, was almost 100 ft (30 m) long. The invention of the silicon microchip made it possible to reduce size and multiply capacity. As the price of computers fell, they entered the home: in 1996 there were more than 1000 million in use worldwide. They now direct not only the way we calculate, but the way we are educated and entertained. Digital technology carries more information – as words, images, documents and music – to more people than any previous medium.

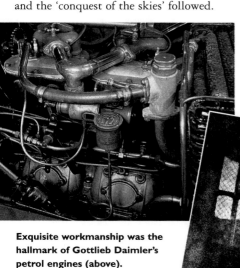

William Fox Talbot took this photograph of his own home, Lacock Abbey, in 1835 (below).

Exquisite workmanship was the hallmark of Gottlieb Daimler's petrol engines (above).

Guglielmo Marconi (above) waits beside his radio apparatus to receive the first transatlantic broadcast in 1901.

The massive ENIAC computer, built in 1946, looks more like a primitive telephone exchange with its many external wires.

The Byzantine ruler Irene is depicted in resplendent regalia in this 11th-century mosaic which graces Hagia Sophia church in Istanbul.

officials and generals and exiled to Lesbos in 802. Irene's vehement opposition to the icon-oclasts – opponents of the use and veneration of icons, or religious images – led to her canonisation by the Greek Orthodox Church.

Ireton, Henry (1611-51) Parliamentarian commander and politician, who fought in the ENGLISH CIVIL WAR battles of Edgehill in 1642 and Marston Moor in 1644. He helped to pass the SELF-DENYING ORDINANCE of 1645 and assisted in bringing Charles I to trial. In 1646 he married Oliver Cromwell's daughter Bridget. Ireton was Cromwell's second-in-command during the Irish campaign between 1649 and 1650, and was made Lord Deputy of Ireland. He died of plague.

Irgun Zionist terrorist group, whose full Hebrew name is Irgun Zvai Leumi (National Military Organisation). The group was active in Palestine between 1937 and 1948 against Arabs and Britons, whom it saw as occupiers. In July 1946 Irgun blew up the King David Hotel in Jerusalem, killing 91 people, 29 of whom were British. In the war of 1947 Menachem BEGIN led the group.

Irish Famine Period of famine in Ireland between 1845 and 1851. In 1845 potato blight deprived the Irish peasantry of adequate supplies of their staple food, resulting in the starvation of around a million people. An epidemic of typhus killed another 350000 people between 1846 and 1847. Farmers who could not pay their rents were often evicted and their cottages destroyed. During this period 2 million Irish people emigrated, principally to the United States and Australia.

Irish Republican Army (IRA) see NORTHERN IRELAND

Iron Age see feature, page 323

ironclads Wooden battleships whose hulls were protected by armour plating. France built the first ironclad, the *Gloire*, in 1859, and the design was quickly adopted by most nations. The first ironclad battle took place in 1862 during the AMERICAN CIVIL WAR between the *Monitor* and the *Virginia* (formerly *Merrimack*). Ironclads were superseded by steel-hulled battleships in the 1890s.

Iron Curtain Frontier between the Soviet Union and its East European dependants, and Western non-communist countries. The term originated in an article written in 1945 by the Nazi propaganda minister Joseph GOEBBELS and was first used in English by Winston Churchill when he said at Fulton, USA, in 1946: 'An iron curtain has descended across the Continent'. After the disintegration of the Soviet bloc in 1989, the term fell out of use.

Iron Mask, Man in the see MATTHIOLI, ERCOLE

Ironsides see NEW MODEL ARMY

Iroquois Confederacy of Native American peoples – the MOHAWK, Oneida, Onondoga, Cayuga and Seneca, and after 1723 the Tuscarora – who inhabited New York State and formed the Six Nations. As a reward for their support of the English fur trade in the 17th century, the Iroquois received a land grant which they used to found homelands in Ontario. Today a confederation of Iroquoian-speaking peoples, including the Huron, live by Lake Huron and in the St Lawrence Valley.

In a contemporary etching of the Irish Famine a starving rural family carefully combs through an infertile field for potatoes without blight.

A victorious Iroquois warrior forces a bound French prisoner to his knees and proceeds to scalp him, in an 18th-century print.

Isabella I (1451-1504) Queen of Castile from 1474 until her death. The daughter of John II of Castile and Isabella of Portugal, she united her kingdom with that of Aragon in 1469 through her marriage with its king, FERDINAND V. Known as 'the Catholic' because of her piety, in 1492 Isabella expelled the Jews from Castile. She also urged the conquest of Granada and the conversion of the Moors, and supported the Spanish Inquisition. Isabella helped to finance Christopher Columbus's first voyage to the New World and, with her husband, was a patron of Spanish artists.

Isabella II (1830-1904) Queen of Spain from 1833 to 1870. The daughter of FERDINAND VII, her accession was disputed by her uncle, Don Carlos, giving rise to the CARLIST Wars which raged for six years until 1839. Isabella fled to France in 1868 after a rebellion against her unstable rule, during which she was involved in a succession of personal scandals. A new constitution was accepted by the Duke of Aosta, who ruled as Amadeus I. When he abdicated in 1873 Spain became a republic.

Isaiah (8th century BC) Hebrew prophet. His preachings were centred on the message that the safety of the kingdom of JUDAH was assured if the king put his trust in God, instead of relying on foreign allies. Despite repeated invasions by the Israelites, the Syrians and the Assyrians, Isaiah promised that faith in God would ensure the people's deliverance. He prophesied the coming of a future king and redeemer of Israel, whom later Christian writers took to mean Jesus Christ.

Islam see feature, pages 326-7

Ismail I Safavi (c.1486-1524) First ruler of the Safavid dynasty in PERSIA, from 1501 until his death. Ismail's main achievement was the conversion of his realm from the Sunni to the SHIITE form of Islam. In 1514 the

Iron, the world's wonder-metal

As early as 2000 BC iron was used to make weapons, tools and other functional items, but it was not until the 18th century that innovative smelting techniques heralded a new 'Iron Age' and a vastly increased range of products.

The story of metalworking stretches back more than 6000 years. It was so important in antiquity that two periods of history, the Bronze Age and the Iron Age, are named after metals. The Iron Age started around 700 BC in Europe and 100 years later in China. Its final years in Europe overlapped with the beginnings of the Roman Empire. But iron was first used long before the Iron Age, and many centuries afterwards it became the key material of the early Industrial Revolution.

The people of Anatolia made iron weapons between 2000 and 1500 BC. Its use spread from them to Europe, Asia and Africa. Iron was brought to Britain by the Celts, who had created an Iron Age culture at Hallstatt in the Austrian Alps before their dispersal westwards.

Iron had three advantages over bronze: it gave a sharper, harder-wearing edge, it did not need to be combined with another metal, and supplies were widely scattered. It was used for nails, tools, weapons, horse equipment, cooking

A sword of the 3rd century BC shows the skills of early peoples in working with iron. But the furnaces glowing in the night sky near Coalbrookdale introduced better quality iron.

utensils, jewellery and also for religious articles.

But in prehistory it was impossible to create a high enough furnace temperature to melt iron ore for casting in a mould. After smelting, pieces of iron were picked from the slag, reheated and hammered out. Furnaces were fuelled with charcoal, and for centuries ample supplies of trees and deposits of ore were needed to make iron. Many important mines were in Germany.

A NEW IRON AGE

Sweden was exporting iron by 1300 and remained a major producer until the 18th century. In 1709 Abraham Darby of Coalbrookdale in England ended the dependence on finite supplies of wood for charcoal when he discovered how to produce quality iron smelted with coke, but the impact of his invention was not felt until the 1750s and 1760s.

In peace and war, demand for cast iron and wrought-iron products increased, and the production of iron and coal rose in an unprecedented fashion. By the end of the 18th century more than three-quarters of

iron production in Britain was located in the coalfields. The world's first iron barge, built by John Wilkinson, was launched in 1787 on the River Severn, where the first iron bridge had been constructed at Coalbrookdale in 1779. With the rise of steam power, iron was in ever greater demand for machines, railways and ships. The early Industrial Revolution depended on it.

Britain was the leader in this new 'age of iron', but lost ground in the 19th century when other countries followed their own paths to industrialisation. With the development of technology, iron gave way to steel – formed from iron, carbon and other elements – a more flexible and adaptable metal that had been made for centuries in small quantities. By 1914 the USA was producing almost four times as much steel as Britain.

In the late 20th century the low-cost, high-grade ores of Latin America and Australia played a major role in the international market. But iron, shaped by humans for nearly 4000 years, remains the most important metal in use today.

James Nasmyth's steam-powered hammer, invented in 1839, could forge heavy pieces such as the steel drive shaft of a steamship.

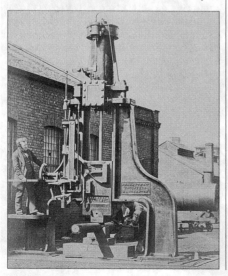

Ottoman Sunni sultan Selim I, who opposed Shiite Islam, invaded north-west Persia. Ismail was defeated, but a long series of border skirmishes continued.

isolationism American policy that opposes any active involvement in the affairs of other nations. Popular feeling prevented Woodrow Wilson from taking the USA into the League of Nations in 1919 and 1920, and delayed US participation in the Second World War. After 1945 America's economic power led it to take on a world role, though isolationists favoured withdrawal from overseas military bases and the establishment of a 'fortress America' protected by nuclear missiles. When the COLD WAR ended in 1991, the USA was left as the world's most powerful nation and continued to be active in foreign affairs.

Israel Middle Eastern country. First inhabited around 100 000 years ago, it was originally known as Palestine. Occupation by the Israelites, or Hebrews, was completed in the 13th century BC. The Hebrews who lived in the northern kingdom of Israel in the 12th and 11th centuries called themselves 'the children of Israel'. Israel was also the name of the kingdom over which Saul, David and Solomon ruled in Palestine during the 10th and 9th centuries. Palestine was overrun by the Assyrians in 722 and was subsequently conquered by the Babylonians. Independence was achieved in 141 under the Hasmoneans, but rivalries within the dynasty led to civil war and Roman intervention in 65 BC. The

During the Italian Campaign US troops are applauded by civilians as they drive towards Palermo, Sicily, in July 1943. Later that year, Italy switched allegiance and declared war on Nazi Germany.

Romans put down Jewish revolts, and emigration from the 4th century AD when the emperor Constantine converted to Christianity reduced the Jewish population to a fraction of its former size.

Muslim Arabs conquered Palestine in the 7th century and ruled for some 900 years, except for a period from 1099 to 1187 when Christian Crusaders ruled the Latin Kingdom of Jerusalem. The OTTOMAN Turks conquered Palestine in 1516 and remained for more than three centuries.

In the late 19th and early 20th centuries Zionists campaigned to secure a Jewish state in Palestine. In 1917 the British foreign secretary wrote the BALFOUR DECLARATION, a pledge of British support for a Jewish national home in Palestine. At the imposition of the British mandate in 1923 there were around 90 000 Jews in Palestine. By 1939 there were 445 477, about 30 per cent of the total. Calls for the partition of Palestine and the formation of separate Jewish and Arab states by the Peel Commission – an enquiry led by Lord Peel from 1936 to 1937 to determine the causes of unrest among the Arabs and Jews – were rejected by Britain. After the end of the British mandate in May 1948, the independent State of Israel was established.

The modern State of Israel was founded in 1948. It occupies a long, narrow belt of land in the south-eastern corner of the Mediterranean.

The ensuing Arab-Israeli conflict led to five wars, including the 1967 SIX-DAY WAR, the 1973 YOM KIPPUR WAR and a war in Lebanon in 1982. Jews from Europe and Arab countries continued to emigrate to Israel, swelling the population to 4.2 million by 1985. Israel became the most advanced country in the region, with an economy based on services and manufacturing. In September 1993 a peace accord, signed by the Israeli prime minister, Yitzak RABIN, and the Palestinian leader, Yasser ARAFAT, gave the Palestinians limited self-rule in Gaza and the West Bank town of Jericho. JORDAN also made peace with Israel. In November 1995 Rabin was assassinated by a Jewish extremist, Yigal Amir, who was opposed to peace.

In January 1996 elections were held in Gaza and on the West Bank, and Arafat became the Palestinian president. In March the extremist Islamic organisation Hamas sent a series of four suicide bombers into Israel to try to sabotage the peace process, killing more than 60 people. Israel launched a two-week offensive in Lebanon in April after rocket attacks by Islamic Hezbollah guerrillas in the north of the country. Israeli elections held in May were won by the right-wing Binyamin Netanyahu.

Italian Campaign Second World War military campaign from July 1943 to May 1945. It began with the invasion of Sicily by British and US troops under the command of General Montgomery and General Patton. Allied troops captured the cities of Palermo and Catania and forced German soldiers allied to Italy to withdraw. Subsequent invasions of southern Italy in September 1943 led to an armistice which ended hostilities between Anglo-American forces and those of the new government of PIETRO BADOGLIO. When the ports of Taranto and Brindisi were captured in October, Italy declared war on Germany. The

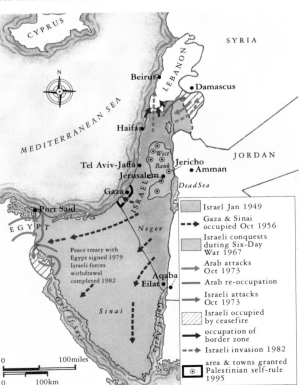

CYPRUS

SYRIA

LEBANON

MEDITERRANEAN SEA

Beirut

Damascus

Haifa

Tel Aviv-Jaffa
West Bank
Jericho
JORDAN
Jerusalem
Amman
Gaza
Dead Sea
ISRAEL

Port Said

EGYPT

Negev

Peace treaty with Egypt signed 1979 Israeli forces withdrawal completed 1982

Aqaba
Eilat

Sinai

Gulf of Suez
Gulf of Aqaba

	Israel Jan 1949
▪▪▪	Gaza & Sinai occupied Oct 1956
	Israeli conquests during Six-Day War 1967
→	Arab attacks Oct 1973
—	Arab re-occupation
→	Israeli attacks Oct 1973
▨	Israeli occupied by ceasefire
→	occupation of border zone
▪▪▪	Israeli invasion 1982
⊙	area & towns granted Palestinian self-rule 1995

0   100 miles

0   100 km

Allied campaign continued with the capture of Rome in June 1944 and Florence in August. In May 1945 the German army in northern Italy and southern Austria surrendered.

Italian Wars (1494-1559) Series of conflicts between European powers for control of the independent states of Italy. When most of these states sought foreign alliances to increase their power, they fell prey to emerging national states, particularly France and Spain. The wars began when Charles VIII of France invaded Italy and seized Naples. He was forced to retreat by the armies of Spain, Venice, Milan, the Holy Roman Emperor and the Papal States. His successor, Louis XII of France, occupied Milan and Genoa, and agreed to partition the kingdom of Naples between himself and Ferdinand V of Spain. However, in 1502 a disagreement over its division resulted in war. The fight for control of Naples continued in a further six phases of war under a number of different monarchs and states. The major conflict of the long wars was the Battle of PAVIA in 1525, in which France under Francis I suffered defeat by Spain under Charles V. The 1526 Treaty of Madrid forced Francis to renounce his Italian claims. Spanish supremacy in Italy was achieved through the Treaty of Cateau-Cambrésis in 1559, which gave Sicily and Milan to PHILIP II.

Italy Country in southern Europe. People have lived in the region since early Stone Age times, and its later development was influenced by the ETRUSCANS, Greeks and Celts. The Romans united Italy around 262 BC. When the Roman emperor Constantine converted to Christianity in the early 4th century the ROMAN CATHOLIC CHURCH and the PAPACY became established there. In the 5th century AD the Western ROMAN EMPIRE was destroyed by invading peoples, including the Visigoths and the Huns. The Byzantines later claimed part of Italy, while the rest succumbed successively to the Lombards, Franks and Germans. The Normans established a kingdom in southern Italy in the 11th century, and city-states emerged in the north.

The country remained fragmented during the next two centuries but developed as a cultural centre of Western Europe, experiencing the revival of classical arts and literature in the RENAISSANCE period. In the 15th century the country was divided between five major rival states – Milan, Florence, Venice, the central Papal States and the kingdom of Naples. These came under Spanish rule between 1559 and 1700 and then, after the Treaty of UTRECHT in 1713, largely under Austrian domination. When NAPOLEON invaded Italy

in 1796-7, hopes for unification grew. Partial unity was achieved but short-lived, and after 1815 Italy was again ruled by both the Austrians and the French.

The 19th-century RISORGIMENTO unification movement created renewed hopes for a unified Italy. Assisted by the French, the Austrians were removed from Lombardy, which proceeded to unite with the Italian kingdom; while the Neapolitan monarchy was overthrown by an army led by Giuseppe GARIBALDI. In 1861 VICTOR EMMANUEL II was crowned king of Italy, and complete unification was attained in 1870 when Venice and Papal Rome were annexed.

After the First World War FASCISM developed under Benito MUSSOLINI. His invasion of Ethiopia was followed in 1936 by the formation of an alliance between Italy and Germany – the Rome-Berlin Axis. In the Second World War Mussolini sided with Adolf Hitler, but when the Allies invaded Italy he was arrested by Victor Emmanuel III and the country joined the war against Germany. After the war the country experienced rapid economic growth, but political instability led to frequent changes of government. Italy was mainly governed by complicated coalitions dominated by the Christian Democrats. Dissatisfaction with corruption in politics grew to the point where calls were made in 1991 by President Francesco Cossiga for constitutional reform. In 1994 a new electoral system brought victory to a right-wing coalition led by Forza Italia, a party owned by a media magnate, Silvio Berusconi. In 1995 Berusconi was forced to resign when a minority coalition partner withdrew its support. In April 1996 a centre-left coalition formed a government with the support of the Communist Refoundation under Romano Prodi.

Ithaca Island off the north-west coast of Greece, kingdom of Homer's legendary hero Odysseus. Remains dating from MYCENAEAN times, around 1400 to 1150 BC, indicate the importance of Ithaca as a staging post for trade between the island of Sicily and southern Italy. By classical times its significance had declined, and by the 16th century AD the island was virtually uninhabited. After an earthquake in 1953, Ithaca was rebuilt.

Ivan IV 'the Terrible' (1530-84) Grand Prince of Muscovy (now Moscow) from 1533, and the first ruler to assume, in 1547, the title 'Tsar (Emperor) of Russia'. His nickname refers to his violent temper, though 'the Terrible' is more accurately translated as 'awe-inspiring'. A precocious child, Ivan took part in affairs of state from the age of five. His early

reign was spent reducing the powers of the BOYARS – the Russian aristocracy who had governed the country since the 10th century. He reorganised the army and embarked on a campaign of territorial expansion into Kazan, Astrakhan and Siberia. In 1547 Ivan married the first of seven wives, Anastasya Zakharina-Yureva. His subsequent marriages were short-lived: Ivan rid himself of unwanted wives by arranging their murder or forcing them into convents. In 1564 Ivan began a reign of terror, partly due to his mistrust of the boyars, and introduced a secret police force – the *oprichniki* – to break their power. Shortly before his death he killed his son, Ivan, in a fit of rage, after which he reputedly repented for some 3000 murders. His favourite adviser, BORIS

Tsar Ivan IV 'the Terrible' gazes sternly from a contemporary engraving. He was responsible for ruthless executions of boyars across Russia.

GODUNOV, eventually succeeded him after the reign of Fyodor I (1584-8). Ivan was not without positive qualities: well-read and erudite, he introduced printing into Russia and opened up relations with the rest of Europe.

Ivory Coast Former French colony in West Africa which became independent in 1960. Although France obtained rights on the coast in 1842, it was not until 1893 that a colony was established, which in 1904 became a territory of French West Africa. In 1933 most of Upper Volta was added to the Ivory Coast, but in 1948 this area was returned to the reconstituted Upper Volta (now BURKINA FASO). In 1958 the Ivory Coast became an autonomous republic within the French Community, gaining full independence two years later, with Félix Houphouet Boigny as its president. In its first multiparty elections in November 1990, the president's Democratic Party won almost all the seats in the National Assembly.

By the word of Allah a new religion is born

When the Angel Gabriel is said to have appeared to Muhammad in AD610 and revealed the first verses of the Koran, the seeds were sown of a new faith, Islam, whose followers were to conquer an extensive empire.

The essence of Islam is contained in an early verse of the Koran, or Qu'ran, revealed to Muhammad in the barren hills near Mecca in about AD610: 'In the name of God, the Merciful, the Compassionate: Say: God is One, the Eternal God. He begat none, nor was He begotten. None is equal to Him.'

Muhammad was born around 570. He was an Arab, and came from the town of Mecca in western Arabia. Mecca was a trading city and the meeting place of many caravan routes. It was also the site of an ancient shrine, dedicated to a number of gods and looked after by the tribe of Quraysh. The fairs where merchants met were held under the protection of this shrine. Muhammad himself came from a family of Quraysh, the sons of Hashim, who had been wealthy but seem to have fallen on hard times. When he was a young man he married an older woman, Khadijah, and acted as her business manager, joining trading caravans to Syria, where he is said to have met Christian monks with whom he discussed religious issues.

MUHAMMAD'S CONVERSION

Around the year 610, Muhammad believed that he was visited by the Angel Gabriel, who instructed him to preach in Mecca and dictated to him the first verses of what was to become the Koran. His sense of being chosen by Allah set him apart from his fellows and was a passionately held conviction that never left him.

The message was simple: there was only one God, Allah, and all people should worship him alone. Rich men should be generous to the poor. After death, all souls would be judged and those who had obeyed Allah in their lives would go to heaven, which was described as a beautiful garden. Those who had not were destined for the eternal fires. The followers of the new faith were called Muslims, that is those who practise Islam, or submission to Allah.

The Koran, which was revealed gradually throughout Muhammad's life, is believed by Muslims to be the exact and unalterable word of Allah. It was the directness and simplicity of Islam, compared with the complexities of Christian doctrines such as the Trinity and the virgin birth, that made it so attractive.

Muhammad abandoned his career as a merchant, and his preaching attracted a number of followers, including his wife, his cousin Ali, and Abu Bakr and Umar, two members of the tribe of Quraysh who later became the first Caliphs, as Muhammad's successors were known. He also became the object of violent hostility from adherents of the old religion, who feared that he wished to destroy the shrine on which the prosperity of Mecca depended.

Muhammad's position in the city became precarious, but he was saved by an invitation from the oasis settlement of Medina, 200 miles (320 km) to the north. The people of Medina were divided by tribal conflicts. They appealed to Muhammad, as both a famous preacher and member of the elite tribe of Quraysh, to act as their arbiter.

In 622 Muhammad, Abu Bakr and 20 of Muhammad's followers left Mecca to settle in Medina. This migration, known to the Muslims as the *Hijra*, or Hegira, marked the beginning of the Islamic state. It is the date from which the Muslim era is counted.

Muhammad soon established himself not just as arbiter but as ruler. His authority and administration were confirmed by the revelation of further suras, or chapters, of the Koran. He and his followers soon began a struggle with their religious enemies in Mecca. The Muslims won a famous victory at Badr in 624 when they captured a Meccan caravan, but the Meccans fought back.

It was not until 630 that Muhammad was accepted by the Meccans as their ruler. Mecca became the centre of worship and pilgrimage for the new religion. By the time of his death in 632 Muhammad was accepted as both Prophet of Allah and ruler over wide areas of Arabia.

Muhammad never claimed to be more than an ordinary mortal, chosen by Allah to deliver his message. When he died, Muslims debated anxiously about his successor. It was Abu Bakr (632-4) and the shrewd Umar (634-44) who laid the foundations of the Muslim expansion.

After Muhammad's death, many of the Bedouin tribesmen of Arabia, who had accepted his authority tried to break away

Many Islamic artefacts, whether an illuminated 16th-century Bukharan Koran (left), or a spiral minaret in Iraq (below), move the soul to union with Allah.

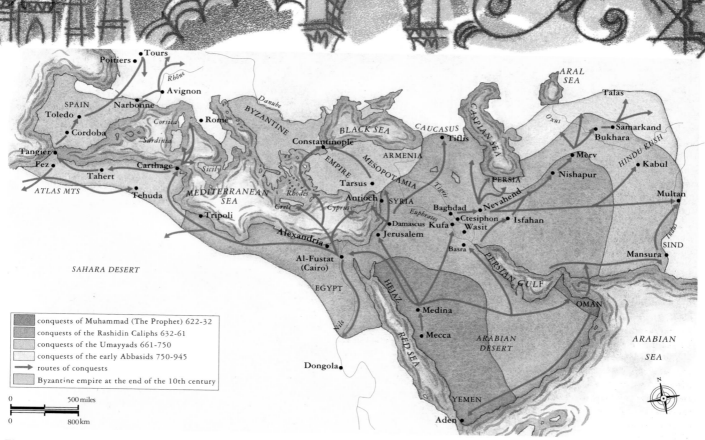

The spread of Islam between the 7th and 10th centuries was fuelled by religious zeal and Arab expansionism, and made easier by the relative weakness of the Byzantine and Persian empires.

conquests of Muhammad (The Prophet) 622-32
conquests of the Rashidin Caliphs 632-61
conquests of the Umayyads 661-750
conquests of the early Abbasids 750-945
→ routes of conquests
Byzantine empire at the end of the 10th century

0   500 miles
0   800km

Above, the Kaaba, the shrine at the geographic centre of the Islamic world, adorns a 16th-century manuscript. This Uzbeki plate is 1000 years old (right).

from the control of the Caliphs. Abu Bakr dispatched military expeditions that soon reduced them to obedience. The tribesmen then had to be given an outlet for their military energies, so he sent them against the neighbouring countries, Iraq, Syria and Palestine. These were all settled agricultural areas with substantial cities. Iraq was part of the Sassanian Persian Empire, while Syria and Palestine belonged to the Byzantines. However, the Muslims were able to take these areas with ease and by 638 both Iraq and Syria were in Muslim hands; in 641 they took Egypt.

Before long Muslim armies were pressing east from Iraq to conquer Iran. By 651 the last of the Sassanian kings, Yazdgard III, had been killed and almost the whole of present-day Iran was under Arab rule. More conquests followed in Uzbekistan, including the ancient trading cities of Bukhara and Samarkand, which was taken by 714, and Sind (in present-day southern Pakistan).

In the north of Syria, the Arab advance was halted by the Byzantines at the Taurus Mountains, but Arab expansion continued in the west. The conquest of North Africa began after the fall of Egypt, but there was bitter and prolonged resistance from the indigenous

Berber peoples. It was not until 700 that the entire area was subdued. In 711 a joint force of Arab and Berber Muslims invaded Spain. Expansion continued into France, but was finally halted by Charles Martel at the Battle of Poitiers in 732.

CONQUERED LANDS

In the century following Muhammad's death, the Muslims conquered the most extensive empire the world had seen, stretching from the Atlantic in the west to the borders of India and China in the east. Not all the peoples of these areas immediately became Muslim. There was no conversion by force, and Christians, Jews and Zoroastrians – Zoroastrianism was the religion of the old Persian Empire – were given the status of protected people. As such they were free to practise their beliefs, but were not allowed to bear arms and they had to pay a poll tax. Meanwhile, the Muslims tended to keep separate from the conquered peoples, living in special garrison cities such as Kufa and Basra in Iraq, Fustat (Old Cairo) in Egypt, and Qayrawan in Tunisia.

It was not until after 750 that large numbers of these conquered peoples began to convert to Islam. Thereafter, slowly and peacefully, Islam extended throughout the area. At the end of the 20th century, Islam predominates in the Arab world, parts of Africa, central Asia, Pakistan, Malaysia as well as in Indonesia. It is also the second largest religion of Britain today.

Jackson, Andrew (1767-1845) Seventh president of the United States, from 1829 to 1837. Jackson became a national hero in 1815 when, as an army major, he defeated the British at the Battle of NEW ORLEANS. He increased his popularity by invading Florida in 1818, forcing Spain to relinquish that territory to the USA. Jackson was a frontiersman who trained as a lawyer and helped to draft the constitution of his home state of Tennessee. He spent two years in the Senate (1797-8), but was forced out of public life as a result of financial problems.

Entering national politics again as a senator in 1822, Jackson became a leading figure in the Democratic Party. In 1828 he won the presidential election. Relying on his reputation as a hard-headed frontiersman, he greatly increased the independence of the presidency while promoting a new style of popular democratic politics. He was freer in the use of the presidential veto than his predecessors. In 1832 he opposed the renewal of the charter of the Bank of the United States in his belief that the centralised control of money was working against him, and he distributed federal deposits to state banks. This policy won him re-election in the same year. He retired in 1837.

Jacobin Member of the most radical political club of the FRENCH REVOLUTION. It met from 1790 to 1794 in a former Jacobin (Dominican) convent in Paris, from which it derived its name. Membership grew steadily throughout the country and its carefully prepared policies had a great influence in the National Assembly. In 1792, however, ROBESPIERRE, the revolutionary leader, seized control and the moderates were expelled. The club became the focus of the Reign of TERROR and overthrew the moderate GIRONDIN group. It was closed after the fall of Robespierre in 1794, and the name is now most commonly used to describe a left-wing extremist.

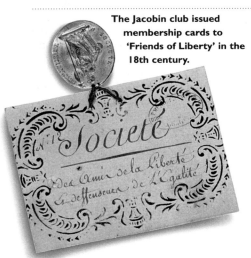

The Jacobin club issued membership cards to 'Friends of Liberty' in the 18th century.

A defeated Jacobite rebel is reunited with his wife and young child in *The Order of Release* (1853) by Sir John Everett Millais.

Jacobite Scottish or English supporter of the exiled royal house of STUART after the GLORIOUS REVOLUTION. When JAMES II was deposed in 1688-9 the Jacobites took their name from the Latin for James (Jacobus). Their principal strength lay among the Highland CLAN fraternity of Scotland. The Fifteen and the FORTY-FIVE (1715 and 1745 respectively) were their major rebellions, but neither succeeded in restoring the Stuarts to the throne. The Jacobites were defeated at the Battle of CULLODEN in 1746, the government suppressed the clans, and Jacobitism ceased to be a serious force.

Jacquerie Rebellion of peasants in northern France from May to June 1358. Its name comes from 'Jacques Bonhomme', an aristocratic nickname for a French peasant. Under the leadership of Guillaume Carle (or Cale), and with the help of a rebel group in Paris, peasants looted and demolished castles. Their grievances were the result of increased feudal burdens, the ravages of the BLACK DEATH and the devastation of the countryside by English soldiers during the HUNDRED YEARS' WAR. The rebellion collapsed after the execution of Carle by Charles II of Navarre.

Jahangir (1569-1627) Emperor of India from 1605 to 1627. The huge MUGHAL empire that he inherited from his father, AKBAR, expanded under Jahangir. However, he left politics and court intrigue to his strong-willed Persian wife, Nur Jahan, who quashed frequent rebellions by his son, Prince Khurram (later SHAH JAHAN, who built the Taj Mahal). As the fame of the Mughal empire spread, Portugal and the British East India Company sent ambassadors to Jahangir's court. He was a patron of the arts, particularly miniature paintings.

Jainism Ancient Indian religion based on the avoidance of injury to any living creature (*ahimsa*) and spiritual training through austerity, leading to nirvana (absorption into the supreme spirit). The concepts of karma (destiny) and nirvana are shared with HINDUISM. Jainism follows the teachings of Vardhamana Mahavira, the 24th tirthankara, or prophet, (*c.*599-527 BC). It has no deity, is monastic and, like BUDDHISM, follows the doctrine of reincarnation. In the 1st century AD Jainism divided into two main sects over the question of nudity: the Digambaras ('sky-clad') who went naked, and the Swetambaras ('white-robed'), for whom nakedness was not necessary. Today there are about 4 million Jains, the majority of whom live in India.

Jaipur Capital city of Rajasthan, north-west India. In the 12th century a RAJPUT tribe made it the capital of the state of Jaipur. Around 1550 it was forced to pay feudal dues to the Mughal empire. The city was rebuilt in 1727 by Maharajah Jai Singh II, who ordered it to be painted pink, the colour that his astrologers declared auspicious for him. In the 18th century the city fell to the MARATHA, a Hindu warrior people, and in 1818 its rajah signed a treaty which acknowledged British supremacy. In 1949 the state of Jaipur merged with neighbouring Rajasthan.

Jamaica Third largest island in the West Indies and a former British Crown colony which gained independence in 1962. Jamaica was originally settled by Arawak Indians. It was sighted by Christopher Columbus in 1494 and settled by the Spanish 15 years later.

The Jain god Sakra, on the right, orders the transference of an embryo from the goddess Devananda to the womb of the goddess Trisala.

The original pink stone of the harem in the 18th-century Chandra Mahal, the city palace of Jaipur, has faded to a dusky red beneath its tarnished domes. Jaipur is often described as the 'Pink City'.

In 1655 the island was captured by the British and became a prosperous base for BUCCANEERS who preyed on Spanish ships. Slaves were imported to work on the sugar-cane plantations, and by the 18th century Jamaica had become both a leading sugar producer and one of the world's largest slave markets (see feature, page 598). After the abolition of slavery in 1833 its economy suffered considerably.

In 1865 a rebellion at Morant Bay was ruthlessly suppressed by the governor General John Eyre, and the following year Jamaica became a crown colony. Representative government gradually evolved, but racial tension, economic depression and dissatisfaction with the crown colony system in the 1930s led to widespread rioting. Adult Jamaicans won the right to vote in 1944 and the economy finally began to recover after the Second World War.

In the late 1950s Jamaica took a lead among the Caribbean islands of the Commonwealth by founding the Federation of the West Indies. This was dissolved in 1962 when Jamaica became an independent dominion within the COMMONWEALTH OF NATIONS. Subsequent administrations have alternated between the Jamaican Labour Party (JLP) and People's National Party (PNP), whose leader Michael Manley became a driving force in Jamaican politics during the 1970s and 1980s and introduced a number of economic and social reforms. Ill-health obliged Manley to retire in March 1992, and he was succeeded by Percival J. Patterson. In 1993 the PNP won a landslide election victory, but the JLP charged it with fraud and boycotted the new parliament. The following year both parties agreed to suspend elections until constitutional reforms had been arranged.

James I (1394-1437) King of Scots from 1406, though assuming power only in 1424. Following the murder of his elder brother by the Duke of Albany, his uncle, James was sent to France for safety. On the way, he was shipwrecked and captured by the English; his invalid father, ROBERT III, died on hearing the news. James, the successor to the Scottish throne, was held in England from 1406 until a ransom of £33 000 was agreed for his release. During his detention, he received a good education and exposure to the courts of Henry IV and Henry V. Meanwhile Scotland was governed by the Duke of Albany, followed by his son Murdoch under whom disorder prevailed.

On assuming power in Scotland in 1424, James's rule was firm and often brutally effective. His policy of reducing the powers of the nobility and making more use of the Scottish Parliament, in addition to raising taxes to pay off his ransom, ultimately led to a reaction. In February 1437 he was murdered in Perth by a group of dissidents. James was a cultured king and a patron of the arts. In 1423 he wrote a collection of poems, *Kingis Quair* (*King's Book*).

James II (1430-60) King of Scots from 1437 until his death. James was six years old when his father, JAMES I, was murdered. He was brought up in Edinburgh Castle under the charge of his mother and Sir Alexander Livingston. There was much unrest during his minority; when he began to reign in his own right he regarded the Douglas clan as a serious threat to his authority, and he stabbed the 8th Earl of Douglas to death in an argument at Stirling Castle. But James also improved the courts of justice and regulated the coinage. He was killed by an accidental cannon blast while leading a siege against Roxburgh Castle, held by the English.

James III (1452-88) King of Scots from 1460, the son and successor of JAMES II. He came to the throne aged eight, following the death of his father, although he did not take control until 1469. Inspired by his tutor, the humanist Archibald Whitelaw, James had a great love of culture. He married Margaret, daughter of the king of Denmark, who brought with her the islands of Orkney and Shetland as part of her dowry. His rule was the subject of many challenges by members of his family and their supporters, and in 1479 he imprisoned his brother, Alexander Stewart, Duke of Albany, who later led a rebellion against him. He was defeated and killed in battle at Sauchieburn by his own nobility, supported by his 15-year-old son, who succeeded him as JAMES IV.

James IV (1473-1513) King of Scots from 1488 until his death. James was an able and popular king, and the last to speak Gaelic. He restored order to Scotland, quelling an uprising of nobles and enriching the kingdom. He spent lavishly on his castles, which became the setting for an embryonic Renaissance court filled with musicians and poets. James' marriage to Margaret TUDOR, the daughter of Henry VII of England, was to bring the Stewart line to the English throne – as the STUART dynasty – in 1603 with the accession of his great-grandson, James VI of Scotland. His alliance with France against England led to a disastrous border raid in 1513. In the ensuing battle at FLODDEN FIELD against Henry VIII's army, James was killed alongside 10 000 fellow Scots. He was succeeded by his son, JAMES V.

James V (1512-42) King of Scots from 1513 until his death. He succeeded his father JAMES IV at the age of only 18 months and grew up to preside over a glittering court. His mother Margaret Tudor, her second husband, the Earl of Angus, and the Duke of Albany struggled for control of the kingdom during his minority. When James came to power in 1528 he implemented judicious policies, replenished crown revenues, and established a college of justice. His alliance with France, strengthened by his marriages to Madeleine, daughter of FRANCIS I of France, and on her death to Mary of GUISE, enraged his uncle, Henry VIII of England. The English invaded in 1542 and defeated James's army at Solway Moss. He died the same year, leaving his only child, a one-week-old daughter, to succeed him as MARY, QUEEN OF SCOTS.

James VI (1566-1625) King of Scots from 1567 and also King James I of England from 1603. The son of MARY, QUEEN OF SCOTS and Henry, Lord Darnley, James was one year old when he acceded to the Scottish throne on his mother's abdication. As King of Scots he fostered good relations with England, and strengthened the power of the Crown over the Scottish Parliament.

James ascended to the throne of England as the great-grandson of James IV of Scotland's English wife, Margaret TUDOR. He was a popular king at first, but his reign was marked by several errors of judgment. He angered the Puritans by refusing to accept their demands for reform of the Anglican Church, including the abolition of bishops; and he insisted on the maxim 'no bishop, no king'. However, he did agree to a new translation of the Bible, the Authorised Version of 1611. His court was tainted by sexual and financial scandal, and while his chief minister Robert CECIL attempted reform, the king's promotion of his favourite, the Duke of BUCKINGHAM, alienated Parliament. He married Princess Anne of Denmark in 1589 and was succeeded by his second son, CHARLES I.

James VII (1633-1701) King of Scots, and King James II of England from 1685 to 1688. The second son of CHARLES I, he was the last Stuart king to rule in either country. As Duke of York, he was Lord High Admiral in the ANGLO-DUTCH WARS, during which the Dutch settlement of New Amsterdam was captured and in 1664 renamed New York in his honour. Following the death of his first wife, Anne Hyde, the mother of Mary and Anne (the future Queen ANNE), he converted to Catholicism and married Mary of Modena. Parliament reacted in 1673 by passing the TEST ACT, which declared that anyone holding public office must be a communicant of the Church of England. However, on the death of his brother CHARLES II in 1685 James acceded to the throne without opposition from Parliament. His rival, the Protestant James, Duke of MONMOUTH, illegitimate son of Charles II, subsequently led an unsuccessful rebellion to assert his claim to the throne. Monmouth was beheaded and his followers persecuted in the BLOODY ASSIZES, causing deep resentment among Protestants.

Within three years of his accession James had suspended the Test Act, promoted Roman Catholics to positions of power within the Church, and provoked widespread opposition resulting in the GLORIOUS REVOLUTION and his replacement on the throne by WILLIAM III and MARY II. He fled to France with his wife and son, James Stewart (the future 'Old Pretender') and, following an abortive attempt to regain his throne at the Battle of the BOYNE in 1690, he died in exile.

Jameson Raid (December 1895-January 1896) Disastrous revolt against the Boers in the Transvaal Republic in southern Africa, led by Leander Starr Jameson, a British pioneer. Many Britons had been attracted to the region following the discovery of gold and diamonds. These UITLANDERS (foreigners) were detested by the Boers. Jameson, under orders from Cecil RHODES, prime minister of the Cape Colony and founder of the De Beers Mining Company, led an armed raid to support the uitlanders and try to overthrow the government of Paul KRUGER. His forces were overpowered by the Boers, and Jameson himself

was captured and handed over to the British for punishment, his hopes for a united South Africa dashed. He was tried in London and sentenced to imprisonment, but soon released. Rhodes, who had financed the raid, was forced to resign as premier of Cape Colony. The defeat of Jameson's raid prompted WILHELM II, emperor of Germany and king of Prussia, to congratulate the Boers on suppressing the British, in a famous telegram to President Kruger.

Jamestown First permanent English settlement in North America. It was founded by an expedition dispatched by the Virginia Company from London in 1607, and named in honour of James I. The site, 40 miles (64 km) up the James River in Virginia, was chosen mainly for strategic reasons, but the surrounding malarial swamp and typhoid-infected river water caused endemic illness. Only the determination and military skills of John Smith, a colonist and member of the governing council, saved the new outpost from being captured by Native Americans. Jamestown was the seat of the colonial assembly from 1619 and the capital of Virginia; in 1676 it was burnt down in a rebellion led by Nathaniel Bacon, and in 1699 Williamsburg became the new capital.

Janata Party Indian political organisation, composed mainly of right-wing Hindu political parties, which in 1977 ousted Indira GANDHI from power. It was a broad coalition based upon the Jana Sangh – the People's Party, which was founded in 1951 – and was formed to oppose Gandhi after she had been found guilty of breaking electoral rules. The Janata Party successfully wrested control from Gandhi's Congress Party in the 1977 elections

> **DID YOU KNOW?**
>
> James VII's favourite pastime was riding to hounds. He is said to have introduced fox-hunting to Britain as a court pursuit.

and formed a government under the prime ministership of Morarji Desai. Its rule was short-lived; Gandhi was re-elected in 1980 at the head of the new Congress I Party, an offshoot of the Congress Party. In the late 1980s Janata joined a centre-left coalition as part of an anti-Congress national front known as Janata Dal, formed by V.P. Singh, who was prime minister briefly from 1989 to 1990. The party split over the issue of political representation for the untouchable castes, and the Congress I Party returned to power. Following elections in April 1996 the Janata Party briefly formed a government under Atal Vajpayee, but it lost a vote of confidence in May and was replaced by a United Party coalition.

janissaries Soldiers in an elite guard of Turkish troops formed in the 14th century. The name comes from the Turkish *yeni çeri*, 'new troops'. The janissaries served the OTTOMAN sultans until their abolition in 1826 when, following a mutiny, they were massacred by Sultan Mahmud II. They were originally recruited from prisoners of war, but from the time of BAYEZID I (1389-1403) they were largely raised by means of the *devshirme* ('gathering'), a levy of the fittest youths among the sultan's non-Muslim subjects. After converting to Islam, most served as foot soldiers, while the ablest moved into civil administration and exercised a powerful role in political life. Decimation in the great wars against Persia and Austria (1578-1606) lowered the traditionally high quality of the intake, and also opened the corps to Muslims.

Jansen, Cornelius (1585-1638) Dutch bishop and founder of the Catholic school of theology known as Jansenism. He studied in Paris and Louvain before becoming the director of a newly founded college at Louvain in 1617, and in 1636 he was made Bishop of Ypres. His ideal was the reform of Christian

Before the Jameson Raid of 1895-6, volunteers in the Transvaal line up for kit inspection. Their raid proved unsuccessful, and further soured relations between British uitlanders and the Boers.

Three people dressed in traditional kimonos face the moon from behind characteristically Japanese wooden balconies. Japan evolved its own artistic themes and styles over the centuries. This series of prints, entitled *The Moon*, was made with woodblocks in 1857 by Utagawa Kunisada (1786-1864).

life outlined in his major work, the *Augustinus*, which was published posthumously in 1640. In it he attempted to prove that the teachings of St Augustine on a number of subjects, including free will and predestination, were in opposition to the teachings of the JESUITS. This work inflamed the Jesuits and caused a deep rift in the Roman Catholic Church. In 1653 it was condemned by Pope Innocent X. Jansen called himself a Catholic, but a number of his tenets resembled those of John CALVIN. His supporters included the French philosopher Blaise PASCAL. The controversy over his theories lasted well into the 18th century, during which time Jansenists suffered persecution in France and excommunication. They were tolerated in the Netherlands, and in 1723 the Dutch Jansenists nominated their own bishop of Utrecht.

Japan Country set between the mainland of east Asia and the Pacific Ocean, chiefly made up of the four islands of Hokkaido, Honshu, Kyushu and Shikoku, with Tokyo as its capital. Evidence of human life goes back 3000 years; Japan was originally inhabited by native Ainu, but the Japanese themselves are thought to be descendants of people who migrated from mainland Asia. The reign of the first emperor, Jimmu, was recorded in 600 BC. By the 5th century AD the Yamato clan controlled much of Japan. The state was greatly influenced by China, from which it derived the art of writing and the skills of administration and farming. BUDDHISM was introduced in the 6th century and, after a brief conflict, coexisted with the Japanese religion, SHINTO. By the 9th century the Fujiwara family controlled the imperial court.

The growing strength of feudal lords and of Buddhist monasteries led to civil war for most of the 12th century, the ultimate victor being Minamoto Yoritomo, who in 1192 became the first shogun and established a military administration, a SHOGUNATE, that ruled until 1868 when the emperor was restored.

Europeans had begun to trade with Japan in 1542, as Portuguese, then Spanish and Dutch traders arrived. Christianity was introduced and missionaries made numerous converts. The shogunate responded in 1639 by excluding all foreigners and banning Christianity.

During the 18th and 19th centuries the wealth and power of merchants increased and Japan extended its influence over the northern island of Hokkaido. In the first half of the 19th century the power of the shogunate was gradually undermined by economic problems, insurrection and the arrival of Western trading and naval expeditions. The shogunate's failure to resist this foreign penetration served as the catalyst for armed opposition, which in 1868 replaced the shogunate with a new regime led by the emperor Meiji (see MEIJI RESTORATION). He proceeded to create a centralised state, introduced the Western calendar and, in 1889, established a constitution. Rapid industrialisation followed.

Japan's new strength brought victory in the SINO-JAPANESE WAR (1894-5) and the RUSSO-JAPANESE WAR (1904-5), and established it as the dominant power in north-east Asia. Japan fought on the Allied side in the First World War. Its occupation of MANCHURIA from 1931 to 1945 provoked full-scale war with China in 1937. In December 1941 Japan, having already allied itself with Germany and Italy, entered the Second World War with a surprise attack on the US fleet at PEARL HARBOR. Initially overrunning the colonial empires of south-east Asia at great speed, Japanese forces were gradually driven back in the PACIFIC CAMPAIGNS. In August 1945, after the dropping of two atomic bombs,

Japan was forced to surrender, accepting occupation by the Allied forces led by General Douglas MACARTHUR. The military occupation was dominated by the USA, its two main objectives being the demilitarisation of Japan and the establishment of democracy. In 1952 a new constitution was introduced, and full independence was restored. Japan embarked on another period of rapid industrial development, to become a major economic power (see feature, page 332). American influence did not go unquestioned and in the late 1960s the country was shaken by the guerrilla attacks of the anarchic Red Army. Internationally, Japan's relations with China and south-east Asian countries improved, but a trade imbalance, in its favour, with Western nations – particularly the USA – resulted in economic instability.

The Liberal Democratic Party held office from 1955 to 1993, despite several political and financial scandals. A series of short-lived coalitions followed. Emperor Hirohito, who died in 1989, was succeeded by his son, Akihito. In 1995 an earthquake shook the city of Kobe, killing more than 5000 people; and a gas attack in the Tokyo underground railway system by Aum Shinrikyo, a religious sect, claimed 18 lives. In the same year, the 50th anniversary of the end of the Second World War, Japan formally apologised for its treatment of Allied prisoners of war.

Java Island situated between the Indian Ocean and the Java Sea. One of the Sunda Islands, now the heartland of Indonesia, Java includes the three largest cities of Indonesia – Jakarta (the capital), Surabaya and Bandung. Indian traders began arriving in Java in the 1st century AD, bringing Hinduism with them. From the 8th to the 16th centuries Hindu dynasties reigned, the last of which was the Majapahit (1298-1520). In the 8th century

Japan's economic miracle

*Only 30 years after its catastrophic defeat in war, and occupation by
a foreign power, Japan had adapted its social traditions to create a unique
business culture. The prize was world economic leadership.*

Within five years of its defeat in the Second World War, Japan was experiencing phenomenal growth. Economic output increased by more than 9 per cent a year between 1950 and 1973, and by 3.5 per cent annually between 1973 and 1994.

Until the Meiji Restoration of 1868, Japan was a relatively undeveloped country. In the late 19th century its economy did not keep step with its emerging military power, though by 1939 an industrial structure had been created based on cotton and silk textiles, food processing and iron and steel. The first steelworks had opened in 1902. Conglomerates called *zaibatsu* had also emerged, led by families such as Mitsui, Mitsubishi and Yasuda.

The country's competitiveness was transformed after the US occupation ended in 1952, stimulated by the import of American technology – for example in engineering and shipbuilding – and by exploiting American ideas better than Americans did. Japan made a smooth transition from the industries of the first industrial revolution (textiles, iron and steel, shipbuilding) to those of the second (cars, machinery, engineering) and finally to the high-tech industries of the third (computers, semiconductors, electronics).

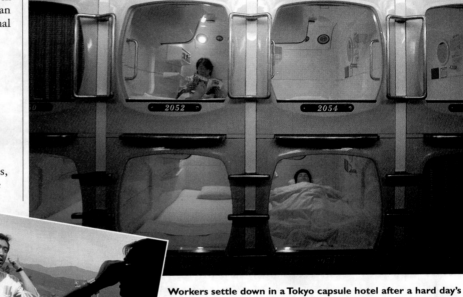

Workers settle down in a Tokyo capsule hotel after a hard day's labour. At management training school (left), elite students cast aside traditional reserve to develop a forceful telephone manner.

The stability of government institutions was one factor in Japan's success. Another was the nature of government-industry relations, especially the role of the Ministry of International Trade and Industry as a development agency. The relationship evolved to the benefit of both sides: governments moved from a dictatorial role in the 1950s to one of 'administrative guidance' in the 1960s, especially under Hayato Ikeda between 1960 and 1964. Assistance included tax concessions and import controls.

Entrepreneurial zeal was also crucial, as was Japanese industrial management. The US occupation force had disbanded the *zaibatsu* but they were reborn as the *keiretsu*, groups of closely knit

After the surrender in 1945, many returning soldiers found their homes wrecked by air raids, and their families living in makeshift shelters.

businesses led by a cadre of well-trained professional managers. Entrepreneurs such as Akio Morita and Masaru Ikuba of Sony and Soichiro Honda and Takeo Fujisawa of Honda characterised the dynamism of postwar business leaders who saw international competition as a battle to be won.

THE SECRET OF SUCCESS

But the secret of Japan's success in manufacturing owed most to its *kaisha*, or business corporations, where close attention was paid to engineering, research and, above all, the management of people. Leading companies established networks to share market intelligence and technology, and to make joint approaches to government, mixing cooperation and competitiveness. Workers were offered employment for life, promotion by seniority, job rotation and training.

Although Japan later struggled to maintain its momentum, it remains a leading economic power. Eight of the world's largest enterprises, including Toyota, Hitachi and Nissan, are Japanese.

Jazz from America was 'hot' in Paris in the 1920s (right), and later the epitome of 'cool', relaxing music in the 1960s.

Buddhism briefly displaced Hinduism in central Java. At this time Borobudur, one of the largest Buddhist temples in the world, was constructed by the Sailendra dynasty. During the 16th century the island was converted to Islam. In 1619 the Dutch captured Jakarta, on Java's north coast. They renamed it Batavia after the Batavii, the Germanic tribe who lived in the Netherlands in Roman times, and made it the headquarters of the Dutch East India Company. The Javanese put up a fight in 1628-9 when Sultan Agung (1613-46), the ruler of the kingdom of Mataram, unsuccessfully besieged the city. The Dutch proceeded to consolidate their position, and by the mid 18th century the whole island was under direct or indirect Dutch rule. The British took over for a brief period between 1811 and 1816, and the Japanese occupied the island from 1942 to 1945 until the founding of the Republic of Indonesia.

Jay, John (1745-1829) American statesman and jurist who, as a member of the CONTINENTAL CONGRESS in 1777, drafted the constitution of New York state. From 1789 to 1795 he was first chief justice of the Supreme Court. Jay was sent as a special envoy to England to conclude a treaty following the War of Independence. The treaty enforced the terms of the Peace of Paris (1783) which recognised American independence, and ordered the British to leave their trading posts in the American Northwest Territory. As a result, the British lost control of the lucrative FUR TRADE and ceded a share in the trade with the West Indies to the Americans.

jazz Musical style created by Black Americans in New Orleans at the start of the 20th century. Jazz has its roots in the blues songs of Black slaves; in 19th-century 'Negro spirituals' and hymns; in the black-face minstrel shows of the 1830s; and in the rhythms of ragtime popularised in the 1890s by composers such as Scott Joplin. It evolved via the big band jazz of the 'swing' era in the 1930s with band leaders such as Duke Ellington and Count Basie, through the experimental 'bebop' of the 1940s developed by musicians such as Dizzy Gillespie and Charlie Parker, to the lighter 'cool jazz' movement of the late 1940s launched by Miles Davis. In the 1950s 'free', improvised jazz emerged. Since the 1960s there has been a fusion of jazz and rock music with an increasing use of elecronic instrumentation. Today many jazz groups draw on musical influences worldwide, while others play jazz styles from earlier periods.

Jefferson, Thomas (1743-1826) Third president of the United States, from 1801 to 1809, chiefly responsible for drafting the DECLARATION OF INDEPENDENCE (July 4, 1776) during his term as a delegate to the federal legislature, the CONTINENTAL CONGRESS.

Jefferson was a wealthy Virginia planter, and in 1769 he was admitted to the Bar. A slave owner who favoured gradual emancipation, he felt unable to implement such a policy, although the Northern states did abolish slavery during his presidency. Jefferson served as governor of Virginia (1779-81), US minister to France (1785-9), and as President George WASHINGTON's secretary of state (1789-93). In 1791 he formed a political alliance against the FEDERALIST government, which grew into the Democratic Republican Party (the forerunner of the modern Democratic Party). His opposition to Alexander HAMILTON's economic policies led to his resignation, but in 1796 he was called to the vice-presidency under John ADAMS and in 1801 he was chosen as president by the House of Representatives.

Jefferson's two terms in office witnessed a war against Tripoli (1800-15), which ended tribute payments to Barbary pirates along the North African coast; the LOUISIANA Purchase from the French in 1803; and the LEWIS AND CLARK EXPEDITION (1803-6) overland to the Pacific coast of America. Although seen as head of the Democratic Republican Party, he presided over a Cabinet of federalists. In 1809 Jefferson retired to his estate in Monticello, Virginia, and ten years later he founded the University of Virginia.

Jeffreys, Judge George (c.1645-89) Welsh judge and Lord Chief Justice of the King's Bench from 1683, known as the 'Hanging Judge' for his harshness. He presided over the trials of the RYE HOUSE conspirators in 1668 and Titus Oates after the POPISH PLOT.

Following the failure of the Duke of MONMOUTH's rebellion against the Roman Catholic king James II in 1685, Jeffreys tried the rebels at the BLOODY ASSIZES. In the same year the king made him a peer and appointed him Lord Chancellor. At the accession of William III, Jeffreys was imprisoned while attempting to flee the country disguised as a sailor. He died in the Tower of London before proceedings were taken against him.

Jellicoe, John Rushworth, 1st Earl (1859-1935) British admiral who commanded the Grand Fleet in 1916 at the Battle of JUTLAND, a crucial sea battle between the British and German fleets during the First World War. Jellicoe was widely criticised for his tactics, but his strategy confined the German fleet to the Baltic for the rest of the war.

In 1916 he was promoted to First Sea Lord, and implemented the CONVOY SYSTEM. He was subsequently dismissed from office in December 1917 following a disagreement with Sir Eric Geddes, a member of the War Cabinet. In 1919 he became an admiral of the fleet and served as governor-general of New Zealand from 1920 to 1924.

Jefferson rises after drafting the American Declaration of Independence while Benjamin Franklin examines it, and John Adams looks on.

The walls of Jericho fall to the victorious Israelite army of Joshua, in this 16th-century illustration from a Nuremberg Bible. The martial event is related in the Book of Joshua in the Old Testament.

Jena, Battle of (October 14, 1806) Decisive victory of Napoleon's French forces over the Prussian army near the German town of Jena, in Saxony. The Prussians, led by Prince Hohenlohe, had grossly underestimated the size of the French army. On the same day Napoleon's marshal Louis Davout defeated the Duke of Brunswick's principal Prussian army at Auerstädt, leaving the road to Berlin unprotected. Within six weeks Napoleon had completed his conquest of Prussia.

Jenkins' Ear, War of (1739-42) War fought between Britain and Spain in defence of Britain's trade with South America. A merchant captain named Robert Jenkins was brought before a committee of the House of Commons to tell a story of torture and the loss of an ear in 1731 at the hands of Spanish coastguards in the West Indies. British merchants had been protesting at a tightening-up of Spanish control, despite the British South Sea Company's limited trade monopoly with the Spanish American colonies, granted by the Peace of UTRECHT (1713). Sir Robert WALPOLE, England's first prime minister, was keen to preserve peace with Spain, but popular clamour was such that he reluctantly declared war. In 1740 the war merged into that of the AUSTRIAN SUCCESSION.

Jenner, Edward (1749-1823) English physician and naturalist who pioneered the use of vaccination against the deadly SMALLPOX virus. Jenner was born in Gloucestershire and trained as an apprentice to a surgeon near Bristol. In 1770 he went to London to study under the surgeon John Hunter, before returning to Gloucestershire to set up his practice. Jenner observed that infection with the mild disease called cowpox made people immune to smallpox. In 1796 he inserted cowpox matter into two scratches made on the arm of a healthy eight-year-old boy. A few months later the boy was inoculated with smallpox; the disease refused to take. The exercise met with some opposition, but before Jenner's death, smallpox vaccination was being practised throughout the world.

Jeremiah (c.640-570 BC) Old Testament Hebrew prophet during the reign of King JOSIAH who predicted the fall of Jerusalem and the coming of a messiah. Jeremiah was the son of Hilkiah, a priest. As Babylonian power increased, he maintained that resistance was useless as the fall of the city was inevitable – a view popular with neither the king nor the people. When Jerusalem finally fell in 586 BC to NEBUCHADNEZZAR, king of Babylon, Jeremiah remained until he was taken to Egypt by Jewish dissidents. His messages, always intensely personal, were preserved and edited by his scribe-secretary Baruch.

Jericho Ancient city in the Jordan valley, north of the Dead Sea. It is one of the oldest continuously inhabited cities in the world, having been occupied from around 9000 BC. According to the Old Testament, Jericho was the first Canaanite stronghold to be captured and destroyed by the Israelites.

Archaeologists have unearthed a succession of towns and cities on and around the site. By 7000 BC Jericho was a walled settlement of some 10 acres (4 hectares). In the course of its subsequent history the principal mound, or tell, accumulated more than 50 ft (15 m) of deposit, even though the later occupation levels, from 2000 to 500 BC, have been swept off the summit by erosion. Traces of the magnificent winter residence of Herod the Great (4 BC) have been discovered to the south on the site of the Roman Jericho mentioned in the New Testament. In the 20th century the city has been the subject of dispute between Palestinians, ISRAEL and JORDAN. In 1994 Palestinian self-rule began in Jericho under the PALESTINE LIBERATION ORGANISATION.

Jeroboam I (d.901 BC) First monarch of the northern kingdom of ISRAEL, from 922 until his death. He first held office during the reign of SOLOMON, but was forced to flee to Egypt after an unsuccessful revolt. On Solomon's death, he returned and led a successful revolt of the northern tribes against the new king, REHOBOAM. Jeroboam took advantage of Syrian and Assyrian weakness to extend and strengthen the kingdom. The prophet Amos criticised him for oppression, and for encouraging idolatry at Dan and Bethel, in rivalry to Judaism at the temple in Jerusalem.

Jerome, St (c.342-420) Christian leader, priest and scholar who made the first Latin translation of the Bible from Hebrew. Known as the Vulgate ('popular tongue'), it was the authorised Latin version of the Bible for the Roman Catholic Church in the 16th century.

Jerome, born Eusebius Sophronius Hieronymus in Stridon, Dalmatia, studied in Rome and learnt Hebrew while living as a hermit. Following his ordination in Antioch, he returned to Rome in 382 and it was there, while employed as secretary to Pope Damascus, that he began his work on the Bible. When the pope died Jerome settled in Bethlehem where he completed his translation. He was a vigorous disputer, attacking, among others, the heretical British theologian, Pelagius. Jerome advocated asceticism and believed priests should be celibate. His annual feast day is September 30.

Jerusalem see feature, page 335

Jesuit Member of the Society of Jesus (SJ), a Roman Catholic religious order founded in 1534 by St Ignatius LOYOLA. Its original aim was to convert non-Christians, but it also fostered reform within the Roman Catholic Church, which was facing the challenge of the Protestant Reformation. In 1540 it received the approval of Pope Paul III, but some religious orders, including the Dominicans and Jansenists, accused the Jesuits of immorality. By the early 17th century Jesuits had made an important contribution to the COUNTER-REFORMATION, establishing many schools and colleges and setting up missions in India, China, Japan, Africa and South America. The Jesuits' involvement in nonreligious matters led to their expulsion from France in 1764 and from Spain in 1767; and in 1773 they were suppressed by Pope Clement XIV. Jesuits continued to teach in Germany and Austria, and also survived in England. In 1814 the order was restored by Pope Pius VII.

Stronghold of faith

Destroyed by the Romans, pillaged by the Persians, invaded by Islam, and a centre of continuing conflict in the 20th century, yet the holy city of Jerusalem remains a place of worship and pilgrimage.

The city of Jerusalem is revered as holy by Jews, Christians and Muslims, who all worship the same God. Yet it was originally dedicated to the Syrian deity Shalem, god of the setting sun. The city is first mentioned in the 19th century BC: its name probably meant 'Shalem has founded'. Later, the Jebusites established themselves in Jerusalem's citadel of Zion around 1200 BC and may have brought the cult of Baal, chief god of the Phoenicians and the Canaanites.

Jerusalem had already had a long pagan history when David, king of Israel and Judah, conquered it in 1000 BC and made it his capital. His son Solomon built a temple to Yahweh, the god of Israel, on Mount Zion. The temple enjoyed a special status because it contained the Ark of the Covenant, the portable shrine that the Israelites had carried during their 40 years wandering in the desert, but it was not the only shrine in Israel. Later, King Josiah (c. 649-609 BC) tried to institute reform by declaring Jerusalem to be the only place where sacrifice could be offered to Israel's God.

DEPORTED TO BABYLON

In 586 BC, King Nebuchadnezzar of Babylon destroyed Jerusalem and its temple and deported most of the population, but some 50 years later the Jews were permitted to return and rebuild the temple. After the Babylonian exile, Jerusalem truly became the centre of the Jewish world. It was thought that the temple occupied the site of the Garden of Eden and was the place where Abraham had bound Isaac for sacrifice. During his reign from 37 to 4 BC, King Herod built a magnificent new temple, after which thousands of pilgrims flocked to Jerusalem from all over the world.

In AD 70, however, during the great Jewish revolt against Rome, the Roman emperor Titus destroyed both the city

A 13th-century map places Jerusalem at the centre of the world (above). The Dome of the Rock mosque in Jerusalem (right) is the world's earliest surviving example of Islamic architecture.

and its temple. Yet Jerusalem remained central to the Jewish imagination, even though in 135 Jews were banished for more than 500 years when Emperor Hadrian built the Roman city of Aelia Capitolina on its site. Meanwhile the city had also become sacred to the new religion of Christianity.

In 327 the Christians discovered the tomb of Jesus, which had been buried under a Roman temple, and the Emperor Constantine built a beautiful basilica on the site. Thousands of Christian pilgrims began to flock to Jerusalem in order to visit the places associated with Jesus's passion, death and resurrection.

The Christians lost their holy city to the new religion of Islam in 638; Jerusalem became the third holiest city in the Muslim world after Mecca and Medina. Muslims honoured Jerusalem because it had been the city of Abraham, David, Solomon and Jesus, whom they revered as great prophets.

CAPTURED BY THE CRUSADERS

In 691 Muslims built the splendid Dome of the Rock to commemorate Abraham's sacrifice of his son, rededicated the Temple Mount (which the Christians had left in ruins), and came to believe that their prophet Muhammad had ascended to heaven from the Temple Mount during his greatest spiritual experience.

The Muslims did not exclude Christians and Jews from Jerusalem: they were allowed to live there and cultivate their own holy places in the city. But by the 11th century Christians were finding their pilgrim trail to Jerusalem increasingly barred by Seljuk Turks who had conquered large areas of Asia Minor. The first Crusader armies, with the support of Pope Urban II, succeeded in capturing the city in 1099. They were ousted by Saladin, sultan of Egypt, in 1187, and the city reverted to Muslim domination. In 1516 Jerusalem became part of the Ottoman Empire, where it remained until the British conquered it in 1917. In 1948 it was divided between Jordan and the new Jewish state of Israel. Jordanian Jerusalem was annexed by Israel in 1967 and today its future remains fiercely contested by both Jews and Arabs.

Muhammad Ali Jinnah (right), president of the Muslim League, strolls in 1946 with Pandit Nehru, leader of the Indian National Congress.

Jews see JUDAISM

jihad Muslim 'holy war' against non-believers, which does not necessarily involve military force. One of the basic duties of a Muslim, prescribed as a religious duty by the KORAN, is to struggle against external threats to the Islamic community and also against personal resistance within oneself to the rules of divine law. Jihad is controlled by the strict laws of war in Islam, which lay down conditions under which war may be declared (either by heart, tongue, hand or sword), usually against a particular enemy who inhibits the observance of the faith.

jingoism British term for a mood of inflated, uncritical patriotism. It originated in 1878, when the prime minister Benjamin DISRAELI nearly involved Britain in a war. Russian successes against the OTTOMAN EMPIRE had created, at the Treaty of San Stefano, a Bulgaria which Britain considered a threat to its Eastern interests. Anti-Russian feeling grew, as shown in the music-hall refrain: *'We don't want to fight, yet by Jingo! if we do, / We've got the ships, we've got the men, and got the money too.'*

Jinnah, Muhammad Ali (1876-1948) Founder and first governor-general of PAKISTAN from 1947 until his death. Jinnah was born in Karachi. He studied law in London, and in 1897 became a barrister. He moved to Bombay and in 1913 joined the Indian MUSLIM LEAGUE. As president of the League, in 1916 he helped to bring about the Congress League Lucknow Pact in which the Congress accepted the principle of separate electoral representation for Muslims. He

The coming of the Messiah

Jesus was a Hebrew teacher upon whose ministry Christianity was founded. He attracted a large following in Palestine before antagonising the Jewish authorities and being put to death.

The focus and inspiration of the Christian religion was a Jew called Jesus, born in Roman-controlled Palestine in about 4BC and brought up in the Galilean village of Nazareth. He seems to have been at first a disciple of the preacher John the Baptist, but later he attracted a following of his own.

Jesus travelled around the small towns of Galilee, preaching the imminent arrival of the Kingdom of God foretold by the prophets – an era of universal peace when Israel would vanquish its enemies and God would rule the world from his temple in Jerusalem. The four Gospels of the New Testament tell how Jesus performed miracles of healing and exorcism, which suggested that the powers of God were already at work in the world in an entirely new way. He spoke in parables, telling a simple story to illustrate a moral principle in a way that would appeal to his listeners.

We do not know whether Jesus claimed to be the Messiah, the leader whom Jews expected to usher in the Kingdom of God. Nor can we be certain of the reasons for his agonising death. In about AD30, Jesus and his disciples arrived in Jerusalem for the festival of Passover. He was, it appears, aware of his impending death and had taken time to train 12 chosen disciples.

CHRIST IS CRUCIFIED

In Jerusalem Jesus seems to have fallen foul of the authorities. The Jewish priests may have feared that he would provoke a riot during Passover, always a sensitive time in Jerusalem; in the past Romans had savagely put down such riots. The priests handed Jesus over to the Roman prefect Pontius Pilate who reluctantly sentenced him to death. On the evening before his crucifixion, Jesus held what has become known as the Last Supper, a feast with his disciples still celebrated by Christian communities in remembrance of him.

Jesus died nailed to a cross outside the city and was buried in a nearby rock tomb. Three days later some of his followers claimed that the tomb was empty. Others said they saw Jesus in startling visions and

Jesus offers bread and wine, his 'body' and his 'blood', to his 12 disciples to eat and drink in his memory in Fra Angelico's *The Last Supper*.

believed that he had risen from the dead. They became convinced that Jesus had indeed been the Messiah (in Greek, Christos); he had died for the sins of the people, and God had rewarded his sacrifice by raising him to an exalted position. He was the Son of God – an ambiguous term, but broadly indicating a relationship of unique intimacy with God.

Soon, the first Christians believed, Jesus would return to Earth in glory to inaugurate the Kingdom. The writings of the New Testament show the gradual refinement and definition of this belief. The first Christian teachings committed to paper are those contained in the letters of St Paul, which were written in the 50s and 60s. Paul believed that the significance of Jesus, as Messiah, was not limited to the Jews. His death had cancelled the old Law of Moses and now Gentiles, or non-Jews, could become members of the New Israel. The precise influence of Paul's theology on the four evangelists, who wrote accounts of Jesus's birth, teaching and ministry, is

Jesus is crowned with thorns before his crucifixion, in a painting by the 17th-century Flemish artist Sir Anthony van Dyck.

uncertain, for they used sources now lost to us. It is believed that Mark wrote his Gospel in 70, some 40 years after Jesus's crucifixion; Matthew and Luke wrote during the 80s, using Mark as their main source, and John wrote in about 100, with a structure wholly different from that of the other three Gospels.

In developing their beliefs still further, Christians during the 4th, 5th and 6th centuries became involved in a series of bitter disputes that the earliest Church could not have anticipated. Gradually they evolved the complex doctrines of the Trinity and the Incarnation to define – with an accuracy not demanded by Jesus's first followers – how Jesus could have been divine without being a second God. Today these doctrines are accepted in some form by most Christians.

A 16th-century Italian earthenware panel shows Christ on the Cross. At his feet stand his mother, St John and Mary Magdalene.

led the Muslim League in the 1937 elections. In 1946 the League won an overwhelming victory in Muslim seats, confirming Jinnah's claim to speak on their behalf. After the partition of India and the establishment of the independent Muslim state of Pakistan in 1947, he had to contend with communal riots in the Punjab, fighting in Kashmir and a severe refugee problem.

Joanna the Mad (1479-1555) Nominal queen of Castile from 1504 and of Aragon from 1516, and the mother of the future Holy Roman emperors CHARLES V and his successor Ferdinand I. She was the daughter of FERDINAND and ISABELLA of Spain and the wife of PHILIP IV, Duke of Burgundy, Archduke of Austria and son of the emperor Maximilian I. On the death of Isabella in 1504 she became, by right, queen of Castile; however, since she was mentally unstable, Ferdinand declared himself regent. After Philip's death in 1506 Joanna became totally insane and from 1509 was imprisoned by Charles in Tordesillas with her husband's embalmed corpse.

Joan of Arc see feature, page 338

Jodhpur City and former state in Rajasthan, north-west India. From 1459 to 1947 it was the capital of the largest RAJPUT princely state. The city occupies a magnificent site, commanded from a rocky outcrop by its red sandstone fortress. Formerly known as Marwar, the state had existed since the early 13th century but reached its peak after the construction in 1459 of the new capital named after its founder, Rajah Rao Jodha. Despite Mughal invasions in the 16th and 17th centuries, its rajahs maintained their independence, but fell under MARATHA control in the 18th century. In 1818 the British brought it under their control, and in 1949 Jodhpur merged with the state of Rajasthan.

John (1167-1216) King of England from 1199 until his death. John was nicknamed 'Lackland' because, unlike his elder brothers, he did not receive lands from his father, Henry II.

When his brother Richard I, the Lionheart, acceded to the throne in 1189, John received the earldom of Gloucester, but during Richard's absences on Crusades he secretly intrigued against him with PHILIP II of France. On Richard's deathbed, John was pardoned. From 1206 to 1214 King John lost royal and baronial lands in Normandy, Anjou, Maine and Brittany.

A further crisis arose from his refusal to recognise Stephen LANGTON as Archbishop of Canterbury, which led to John's excommunication and England being placed under papal interdict from 1208 to 1214. His ruthless policies brought him into conflict with his barons who in 1215 forced him to seal MAGNA

CARTA, a statement of his obligations. His repudiation of it caused the first of the BARONS' WARS, which only ended with his death.

John Birch Society US ultraconservative private political organisation. It was formed in 1958 by Robert Welch, a Boston confectioner, in order to expose the 'communist conspiracy' which was allegedly infiltrating the highest federal offices. The group took its name from John Birch, a Baptist missionary who was killed by Chinese communists in 1945 while working as a US army intelligence officer. It gained most support in California and the South. The society bitterly attacked Chief Justice Warren for his part in forcing the Southern states into desegregation of Blacks and Whites. It operates from Belmont, Massachusetts, and its supporters are known as Birchites or Birchists.

John Bull Character created by John Arbuthnot in 1712 in his satire, *The History of John Bull*, which soon came to be regarded as representative of the typical patriotic Englishman. He was depicted as a prosperous Tory farmer and was the subject of many, not always flattering, caricatures in the late 18th century. He was later popularised by the cartoonists of *Punch* magazine and is, to this day, often used as a label for anything British.

John Bull strides confidently across the world in an advertisement of 1905. His purposeful smile symbolises Britain's imperial confidence.

John I (1357-1433) King of Portugal from 1385 until his death, known as John the Great. His reign marked the start of Portugal's colonial expansion. He encouraged African and westward exploration; and his sons, including HENRY the Navigator, later consolidated his achievements. John fostered an Anglo-Portuguese alliance with a treaty in 1386 and his marriage in 1387 to Philippa, daughter of John of Gaunt of England.

John II (1455-95) King of Portugal from 1481 until his death, known as John the Perfect. He continued to sponsor Portuguese exploration, particularly in Africa, and in 1494 negotiated the Treaty of TORDESIL-LAS, which divided the lands of the New World between Spain and Portugal.

John III (1502-57) King of Portugal from 1521 until his death, known as John the Pious. He was a fervent Catholic who sponsored the Portuguese Inquisition and the Jesuit missionaries in Brazil. During his reign Portugal became a major sea power. John encouraged Portuguese settlement in Brazil, claimed the Spice Islands (Moluccas islands), traded with Siam (Thailand) and in 1535 conquered the Indian island and city of Diu.

John IV (1604-56) King of Portugal from 1640 until his death, known as John the Fortunate. As the Duke of BRAGANZA, he founded the dynasty of that name, expelling a Spanish usurper and proclaiming himself king. He defeated the Spanish at Montijo in 1644, drove the Dutch out of Brazil in 1654, and restored Portugal's world position. In 1622 his daughter, Catherine, married Charles II of England.

John of Austria, Don (1545-78) Spanish general and admiral. Born in Ratisbon, Germany, John was the illegitimate son of Emperor Charles V (Charles I of Spain) and was educated in secret in Spain. He was recognised by Philip II of Spain as his half-brother and in 1559 he was given the name Don John of Austria. In 1571 he commanded the fleet of the Holy League, formed by Pope Pius V, Spain and Venice, and defeated the Turks at LEPANTO; and in 1573 he conquered Tunis. His career began to founder in 1576 after his posting to the Spanish Netherlands as governor-general, during the DUTCH REVOLTS against the return of Catholicism. Meanwhile, he entertained grandiose schemes of marrying Mary, Queen of Scots and supplanting Elizabeth I on the English throne. He died of typhus before he could effect these plans.

John of Salisbury (c.1115-80) English philosopher and theologian who was with Thomas BECKET, Archbishop of Canterbury, in 1170 when Becket was murdered in Canterbury Cathedral. John studied under Peter ABELARD in Paris and, after a short period at the papal court, in about 1148 was appointed secretary to Archbishop Theobald of Canterbury. He continued as secretary to Becket, Theobald's successor, but antagonised HENRY II of England, who thought him too keen a champion of ecclesiastical independence. He went into exile in France from 1163 to 1170 and was soon joined by Becket, who was also in dispute with Henry II. A reconciliation with the king led to the two men returning to Canterbury in 1170, and to Becket's murder. In 1176 John became Bishop of Chartres. He was the author of a number of works, including *Metalogicon*, on logic and

The Maid of Orléans

The peasant girl Joan of Arc was executed at 19, but her courage helped to inspire the French to eject the English from their country.

The fame of Joan of Arc owes everything to the romance of her short life and the pathos of her death. She remains a heroine of the French for her spectacular intervention in the Hundred Years' War with England, but for all her courage and devotion to the cause of Charles VII she was not what popular mythology has made her, the saviour of her country.

She was born the daughter of a farmer in the Champagne region of eastern France in about 1412. She grew into an intelligent and frank young woman who, despite hearing 'voices' of saints from an early age, had little of the fanaticism of a religious mystic. When she was about 16, in 1428, those voices exhorted her to come to the aid of Charles, who had been proclaimed king six years earlier but had been kept from his throne by an English occupation force. Joan prevailed upon Robert de Baudricourt, a French commander, to give her letters of introduction to the king.

She arrived at Charles's castle at Chinon on the Loire dressed as a man and with six companions. After correctly identifying the king from among a crowd of courtiers and passing a theological examination of her authenticity, she was granted an audience. It took only a few minutes for her to convince the demoralised king that she had been sent by God to save France: with her help he could successfully assert his title to the throne.

Joan witnesses Charles VII's coronation, as imagined by Ingres. The only image made during her life (inset) dates from 1429.

THE RELIEF OF ORLEANS

Charles supplied her with troops and she went into battle with them. Though she probably played no part in deciding military strategy, she inspired the relief of the besieged town of Orléans in May 1429 by her resolution and bravery, despite being seriously wounded by an arrow. She then persuaded Charles to go to Reims, the traditional place for the coronation of French kings, which lay deep inside English territory.

In July Charles was at last crowned: Joan stood by his side throughout the ceremony. Her mission accomplished, she did not return to her humble life as a shepherdess. She remained on the field of battle as a freelance captain, and was captured by the Burgundian allies of England at Compiègne in May 1430. By then the Maid of Orléans was becoming a symbol of national revival, and the English paid a ransom of 10 000 golden crowns to have her delivered into their hands. Her fate was sealed.

To escape responsibility for her death, the English delivered Joan to an ecclesiastical court at Rouen, where she was convicted of heresy for claiming direct inspiration from God without the intercession of the Church. Charles, to his shame, did not come to her aid. Joan, having courageously resisted her inquisitors throughout a lengthy trial, recanted and was sentenced to life imprisonment. Shortly afterwards, however, she renounced her recantation, was brought before a secular court and condemned to death. She was burnt at the stake at Rouen in May 1431.

Her tragedy played on Charles's mind: 25 years later he had Joan absolved of her crime at a rehabilitation trial. She was beatified in 1909 and canonised by the Roman Catholic Church in 1920.

philosophy, and *Policraticus* on Church and State diplomacy (both written in 1159). He also wrote about the life of Becket.

John of the Cross, St (1542-91) Spanish

Roman Catholic friar, mystic and poet. His rigorously intellectual verse has been called the finest poetic expression of Spanish Christian mysticism. He helped St TERESA of Ávila to found the Order of the Discalced Carmelites. A CARMELITE monk himself, in 1567 he was ordained priest. His collaboration with St Teresa, who wanted to restore the Carmelite philosophy of austerity, led to friction within the order of the Calced Carmelites. In 1577 he was imprisoned at Toledo, but escaped to a monastery at Úbeda the following year. He was canonised in 1726.

John Paul II (1920-) Pope from 1978. Born

Karol Wojtyla near Kraków, Poland, John Paul became the first non-Italian pope since 1522, earning renown for his energy and analytical ability, and travelling more widely on papal missions than any other pope. On his visit to Britain in 1982 he took part in a service in Canterbury Cathedral, the first pope to enter the building since the Reformation.

During the Second World War Wojtyla was conscripted by the Germans to work in quarries and a chemical factory, but in 1942 he started studying illegally for the priesthood. In 1946 he was ordained. He became professor of moral theology at the universities of Lublin and Kraków, then in 1964 Archbishop of Kraków. In 1967 he was made a cardinal, and in 1978 he succeeded Pope John Paul I.

John Paul II's term of office, burdened by financial deficits, has seen a slowing down of reforms advocated since the Second Vatican Council (1962-5) on the devolution of responsibility to the priesthood and laity. It has also been marked by opposition to the ordination of women, to artificial birth control and to practising homosexuals. While engaged in the revival of Roman Catholicism in Russia and Eastern Europe, he has shown less support for left-wing worker-priests in Latin America. He has also remained cautious about ecumenism – unity among Christian Churches. In 1981 he survived an assassination attempt in St Peter's Square, Rome.

John the Baptist, St (c. 12 BC-c. AD 27)

Jewish preacher and prophet who baptised Christ. John was born in Nazareth, Galilee, the son of Zacharias, a priest, and Elizabeth, cousin of Mary, the mother of Jesus. He proclaimed the coming of the Messiah, and baptised his followers. Around AD 27 he began preaching against social injustice and religious hypocrisy, mainly as practised by the PHARISEES and SADDUCEES, urging baptism to prepare for the imminent coming of the kingdom of God. John's denunciation of

HEROD Antipas for marrying his niece and brother's wife Herodias led to his imprisonment. He was executed at the request of Herod's stepdaughter Salome, who asked that his head be brought to her on a platter.

John XXIII (1881-1963) Pope from 1958

until his death. During his pontificate he made energetic efforts to liberalise Roman Catholic policy, especially on social questions. He also summoned the Second Vatican Council (1962-5) to revitalise the life of the Church by bringing up to date its teaching, discipline and organisation, with the unity of all Christians as its ultimate goal.

Born Angelo Giuseppe Roncalli, he was the son of a peasant from near Bergamo in northern Italy. Following his ordination in 1904 he served as a chaplain in the First World War. As an apostolic delegate John worked in Bulgaria, Turkey and Greece, and in 1944 became the first Papal Nuncio to France after its liberation. Particularly notable was his encyclical in 1961, *Mater et Magistra*, on the need to help the poor, and another in 1963, *Pacem in Terris*, on the need for peace between East and West. He was succeeded as pope by PAUL VI.

Johnson, Andrew (1808-75) Seventeenth

president of the USA, from 1865 to 1869. Johnson was thrust into the presidency on the assassination of Abraham Lincoln in April 1865, shortly before the end of the American Civil War (1861-5). He was born in Raleigh, North Carolina, and worked as a journeyman tailor before moving to Greenville, Tennessee. There he rapidly climbed the political ranks, serving as governor of Tennessee from 1853 to 1857 and becoming a US senator in 1857. A pro-Union

Southern Democrat, in 1864 he was elected vice-president. After becoming president, he pursued a policy of conciliation towards the defeated, Southern confederate states, which failed to insist on political reforms or to protect the interests of the ex-slaves. This brought him into conflict with the Republican majority in Congress, and his vetoes of several reconstruction measures were overridden by large majorities. His dismissal of his secretary of war, Edwin Stanton, in defiance of the Tenure of Office Act, led in 1868 to his impeachment – the US legal procedure for removing officers of state before their term of office expires – and Johnson survived only by a single vote in the Senate. He retired in 1869.

Johnson, Lyndon Baines (1908-73)

Thirty-sixth president of the USA, from 1963 to 1969. As vice-president to John F. Kennedy, Johnson was in the motorcade in Dallas, Texas, when Kennedy was assassinated, and he was immediately sworn in as the next president. He went on to win a sweeping victory in the presidential election of 1964, with Hubert Humphrey as vice-president.

Johnson was born in Stonewall, Texas. He became a teacher and secretary to a congressman before being elected as a Democrat to Congress (1937-49). In the Second World War he was decorated for his service in the US navy. In 1948 he was elected senator, and in 1960 became vice-president.

As president, Johnson acted decisively to restore confidence and pressed Congress to pass the former president's welfare legislation, especially the CIVIL RIGHTS proposals. The administration introduced an ambitious programme of social and economic reform, including Medicare (medical aid for the aged),

John Paul II slumps down in his popemobile after an assassination attempt on May 13, 1981, in St Peter's Square, Rome. Four bullets fired by a Muslim Turk, Mehmet Ali Agca, failed to kill him.

housing and urban development, increased spending on education, and federal projects for conservation. Urban tension, however, increased. The Black civil rights campaigners Martin Luther KING and MALCOLM X were assassinated and there were race riots. As the USA became increasingly involved in the VIETNAM WAR, with conscription and high casualties, Johnson's popularity waned. In 1968 he chose not to seek re-election.

Johnson, Samuel (1709-84) English writer, poet, lexicographer and critic who won widespread acclaim in 1755 for his *Dictionary of the English Language* and his ten-volume *Lives of the Most Eminent English Poets* (1779-81).

Johnson was born in Lichfield, Staffordshire, the son of a bookseller. He left Oxford without a degree and turned to teaching. In 1737 he moved to London where he wrote articles and poems for *The Gentleman's Magazine*, and in 1750 started his own journal, *The Rambler*. His poems include 'London' (1738) and 'The Vanity of Human Wishes' (1749).

His work was recognised in 1762 by GEORGE III, who awarded him a pension. In 1764 Johnson founded the Literary Club with a group of friends, including Edmund BURKE and the artist Joshua Reynolds. Johnson's friend and biographer James BOSWELL portrayed his brilliant conversation in his *Life of Samuel Johnson* (1791).

In a stained-glass window at his home in Gough Square, London, Samuel Johnson is depicted before the cathedral of his birthplace, Lichfield.

joint-stock company see CHARTERED COMPANY

Jordan Semi-arid Middle Eastern Arab state, to the east of the Jordan river, bordered by Syria, Iraq, Saudi Arabia and Israel. Its capital is Amman. Territory to the west of the river, known as the West Bank, was administered by Jordan from 1949 until 1967 when it was occupied by Israel in the SIX-DAY WAR. The first states of the kingdom of Jordan are

Josephine kneels before Napoleon Bonaparte to receive her imperial crown. Jacques-Louis David's enormous canvas, *The Coronation of the Emperor Napoleon*, is set in Notre Dame Cathedral, Paris.

known to have existed in the 13th century BC. Around 1000 BC Jordan was incorporated into the ancient kingdom of Israel under David and Solomon. The region then passed through the hands of the Assyrians, Babylonians, Persians and Seleucids, before being occupied around the 4th century BC by the Nabataeans. It was conquered by the Romans in 63 BC and the Arabs in the 7th century AD. After the fall of Jerusalem to the Crusaders in 1099, it became part of the Latin Kingdom of Jerusalem. In the 16th century it came under Turkish rule as part of the OTTOMAN EMPIRE.

In 1920, following the Arab Revolt and the dissolution of the Ottoman Empire, the League of Nations placed the territories of Transjordan, on the east of the Jordan river, and Palestine, on the west, under British control in the form of a MANDATE. Abdullah ibn Hussein was recognised as ruler and given British advisers, a subsidy and assistance to create a security force. Separating from Palestine in 1923, Transjordan achieved full independence from Britain in 1946 as the Hashemite Kingdom of Jordan, with Abdullah ibn Hussein as king. Two years later the mandate in Palestine came to an end and Arabs and Israelis fought for control of the region. A ceasefire was called in 1949, by which time Jordanian forces had occupied what was to become known as the West Bank, as well as the Old City of Jerusalem; this territory was annexed to Jordan.

King Abdullah ibn Hussein was assassinated in 1951, his son Talal was deposed in 1952, and in 1953 Talal's son, Talal ibn HUSSEIN, became Jordan's ruler. Under Hussein's leadership Jordan's economy improved until the Six-Day War with Israel in 1967 and the resultant loss of the West Bank and Old City of Jerusalem, including prime agricultural land and half the country's industrial base. The early 1970s witnessed conflict between Palestinian groups and the government. Relations with other Arab countries began to improve when Jordan accepted in 1974 that

the PALESTINE LIBERATION ORGANISATION was the 'sole legitimate representative of the Palestinian people'.

From 1980 to 1988 Jordan supported Iraq in the IRAN-IRAQ WAR. It criticised the West's attack on Iraq during the GULF WAR in 1991, and its economy subsequently suffered from United Nations trade sanctions imposed on its main trading partner. In the same year the government's ban on political parties, in place since the Six-Day War, came to an end. A pact with the PLO and a peace treaty with Israel were signed in 1994. In an agreement between Israel and the PLO, self-rule of the West Bank was granted, and in 1995 Israeli forces began their withdrawal.

Joseph II (1741-90) Holy Roman Emperor from 1765 until his death. The son of Francis I and MARIA THERESA, he was co-regent of Austria with his mother from 1765 and sole ruler from 1780. Dedicated to the ENLIGHTENMENT, he used autocratic means to implement liberal reforms. Joseph enacted the Edict of Toleration, granting religious equality to Protestants and Greek Orthodox Christians, removing restrictions on Jews and guaranteeing the freedom of the press. In 1781 he abolished serfdom and curtailed the feudal privileges of nobles. His alliance with CATHERINE II of Russia led to a disastrous war from 1787 to 1792 against the Turks.

Josephine (1763-1814) Empress of the French and wife of NAPOLEON Bonaparte. Born Marie Josèphe Rose Tascher de la Pagerie in Martinique, in 1779 she married the Vicomte de Beauharnais, who was subsequently executed by order of the JACOBIN club for his part in the French Revolution. Two years later, in 1796, Josephine married Napoleon in a civil ceremony. She accompanied him on his Italian campaign (1796-7), but preferred to remain in France where she attracted around her the most brilliant of French society and used her position to promote Napoleon's career. In 1804 Napoleon became emperor and she insisted on a second wedding with religious rites. Five years later Napoleon, seeing a political match in Marie Louise, daughter of the Austrian emperor FRANCIS I, had his childless marriage to Josephine annulled. She retained the title of empress and died at Malmaison, near Paris.

Josephus, Flavius (c.AD 37-c.100) Jewish historian, priest and soldier, and one of the main sources of written information on the Jewish background to early Christianity. His most notable works were his histories of the Jewish people from the Creation to AD 66 (*Antiquitates Judaicae, The Antiquities of the Jews*) and of the Jewish revolt and its antecedents (*Bellum Judaicum, The History of the Jewish War*).

Josephus was born Joseph ben Matthias in Jerusalem, the son of a priest. Accomplished in his knowledge of Hebrew and Greek literature, he stood out as a remarkable PHARISEE – a deeply religious Jew who was willing to submit to Roman rule provided he could maintain his faith – and at the age of 26 he was chosen as a delegate to Emperor Nero in Rome to secure the release of Jewish priests imprisoned there. His visit left him with a lasting impression of Rome's power and culture. He was a commander in Galilee in the Jewish revolt against Nero, but after his capture in 67 went over to the Romans. He settled in Rome, and having found favour with Emperor Vespasian he became a Roman citizen, was given a pension and devoted himself to his writing.

Josiah (c.649-609 BC) King of JUDAH from 640 until his death. The son of Amon, he succeeded to the throne at the age of eight. Renovations to the temple in Jerusalem in 621 BC led to the discovery of the *Book of the Law*, thought to be chapters 12-26 of the Old Testament Book of Deuteronomy. This revelation encouraged Josiah to undertake major reforms, re-establishing the worship of Yahweh (Jehovah) and suppressing that of local gods. He closed shrines and made the temple in Jerusalem the sole centre of worship. In the Bible he is described as a model king, because of his concern for the Jewish faith. He died at the Battle of Megiddo, defeated by the Egyptians.

journeyman Qualified late-medieval artisan who had successfully served his apprenticeship. He was one of three grades of workers (apprentices, journeymen and masters) who were recognised by a craft GUILD.

The name derives from the French *journée* (a day), as journeymen were paid daily. A journeyman could become a master of his own business, but most were prevented from doing so by the guilds, which restricted the number of masters without limiting the number of

apprentices. In the 16th century the English Parliament passed legislation compelling masters with apprentices to employ journeymen. The Industrial Revolution in the 18th century, with its developing factory system and use of unskilled labour, spelled doom for the journeyman. Associations of journeymen were the earliest trade unions in both Britain and the USA, one of the longest-lived being the Federal Society of Journeymen Cordwainers in Philadelphia.

Joyce, James (1882-1941) Irish writer who influenced the 'stream of consciousness' style in novels. Educated at a Jesuit boarding school and then at University College, Dublin, Joyce became disillusioned with the power imposed by Roman Catholicism on his country and in 1904 he left Ireland. Thereafter he lived mainly in Trieste, Zurich and Paris with Nora Barnacle, whom he married in 1931.

Joyce began by writing poetry, and in 1907 *Chamber Music* was published. His first collection of short stories, *Dubliners* (1914), was greeted with enthusiasm by Ezra Pound, the American poet and critic, who encouraged Joyce's writing. His next important work, the autobiographical novel *A Portrait of the Artist as a Young Man* (1914-15), introduces Stephen Dedalus, who reappears in Joyce's masterpiece, *Ulysses* (1922). This work follows one day – June 16, 1904 – in the life of an 'everyman' figure in Dublin, a Jewish character named Leopold Bloom. Together with *Finnegan's Wake* (1939), it pushed linguistic experiment in the 20th-century novel to the limits of communication and continues to attract a mass of critical commentary.

Two journeymen, a mason and a carpenter, are tested by a ceremonially robed guild warden before being admitted as master craftsmen.

Joyce sits with Sylvia Beach, the publisher of *Ulysses*, in her Paris shop. Held to be obscene, the novel was banned in Britain and the USA.

Juan Carlos (1938-) King of Spain from 1975. Juan Carlos has presided over Spain's peaceful transition to democracy. Born in Rome, he was the grandson of Alfonso XIII. He was educated in Switzerland, and from 1948 in Spain following an agreement between his father, Don Juan de Borbón, and General FRANCO that Juan Carlos could be a possible successor on Franco's death. He graduated from military academy and received commissions in the army, navy and air force. He also served in several government departments. In 1962 he married Princess Sophia of Greece and they have three children. In 1969 Juan Carlos was named by Franco as the future monarch, and on the general's death in 1975 was proclaimed king. In 1981 he successfully opposed an attempted military coup.

Juárez, Benito (1806-72) First Indian president of Mexico, from 1861 to 1864 and then from 1867 until his death, and regarded as the embodiment of the republic. A Zapotec Indian, Juárez was born in the state of Oaxaca. He qualified as a lawyer and in 1848 was elected governor of Oaxaca. He was concerned with the low status of the Indians and implemented a programme of public works and schooling. Exiled with fellow liberals to New Orleans during the presidency of the reactionary Antonio López de Santa Anna, Juárez returned after Santa Anna was overthrown in 1855 to serve as minister of justice, and head of the supreme court.

In 1858 conservatives forced the resignation of President Comonfort, leaving Juárez to declare himself president. He fled with his supporters to Veracruz where he established his government. Victorious in the elections of 1861, Juárez returned to Mexico City. In 1863 France invaded the country, supported by conservative Mexicans, and installed Archduke Maximilian of Austria as emperor (1864-7). Juárez moved to the north of the country from where he led the war effort until the French were defeated and he was re-elected president.

Judah Southern part of ancient Palestine – also known as Judaea – settled by Judah, one of the 12 tribes of Israel. After King SOLOMON's death in about 937 BC, the kingdom of Judah supported his son, REHOBOAM, and the line of David, while the northern kingdom of Israel elected JEROBOAM. Judah resisted repeated invasions before falling to NEBUCHADNEZZAR of Babylon, who destroyed its capital, JERUSALEM, in 586. When the Jews returned from exile in Babylon, the land they occupied was named Judaea. Desecration of the Temple in 167 by the SELEUCID army prompted the revolt of the Jewish Maccabee dynasty. Independence lasted until the Roman conquest of 63. In AD 135 the area was absorbed into Roman Syria. Today it forms the southern region of the West Bank.

Judaism Religion of the Jews. Practised by 14 million people worldwide, centred in the 3.6 million population of ISRAEL. According to Hebrew scriptures, the Jews owe their foundation to ABRAHAM, who was promised the land of Israel for himself and his descendants by God. In pursuit of this promise Abraham took his people in 2000 BC from Mesopotamia to Egypt. Moses, 550 years later, led an EXODUS from Egypt, and under Joshua the Jews conquered Palestine.

The kingdom was divided into Israel and JUDAH, both of which were invaded by the Babylonians, who deported many of the inhabitants. It was during the Babylonian EXILE (597-538 BC) that many of the characteristics of Judaism emerged, including the idea of one all-powerful God and the emphasis on teaching and prayer. The teachings of MOSES, recorded in the Torah (the first five books of the BIBLE), provided instruction in religious belief and moral matters.

Jewish communities became widely scattered in the DIASPORA after the destruction of the Temple at Jerusalem in AD 70 by the Romans. Leaders, or rabbis, of these communities encouraged a greater loyalty to the Torah and its daily demands. During the following centuries various interpretations of scriptures were written down in the TALMUD, and Judaism revolved around the study of the Torah and the Talmud. Jewish communities were centred on the synagogue and they lived by their own religious laws.

Jews who moved to Mediterranean countries were known as Sephardim, and those who went to north-western and eastern Europe were called Ashkenazim. They lived in ghettos or legally enforced residence areas, worshipping in their homes and synagogues, and guided by rabbis.

By the 18th century pressures were growing within the Jewish community for the granting of equal rights. In Berlin the philosopher Moses Mendelssohn (1729-86) campaigned for Jewish emancipation. From his work there grew the Haskalah, or Jewish Enlightenment. New religious reforms which emphasised ethical content rather than traditional adherence to Jewish law, as well as racial ANTI-SEMITISM and POGROM attacks, led to large-scale emigration, especially to the USA.

Three strands of Judaism emerged in the 19th century: Reform, Orthodox and Conservative. Mendelssohn's followers tried to reconcile Judaism with contemporary Europe by means of a reform movement, which among other things allowed modern languages to be used in the synagogue. Orthodox Jews reacted by seeking to preserve ancient practices, and supporters of the mystical Hasidism movement stressed the development of an inner spiritual life and rejected modernity. Between these grew Conservative Judaism.

When ZIONISM – the movement to establish a Jewish homeland – emerged in the late 19th century, Reform and Conservative Jews supported it. However, most Orthodox Jews were hostile to the establishment of a Jewish state and believed that only the long-awaited Jewish Messiah could re-establish Israel.

In the 20th century some 6 million Jews were murdered in the HOLOCAUST. In 1948 the state of Israel was established. Most Jews outside Israel have assimilated into the population of their country while preserving their distinctive traditions.

Julian (c.331-363) Roman emperor from 360. During his short reign he restored paganism as the state cult in place of Christianity. Born

Judaism's holiest shrine, the Wailing Wall in Jerusalem, unites Orthodox Jews and Israeli soldiers in prayer.

This 4th-century statue of the Roman emperor Julian 'the Apostate' portrays a noble man modestly dressed in a plain toga.

Flavius Claudius Julianus, he was the youngest son of Julius Constantius and the half-brother of CONSTANTINE the Great. Following the death of Emperor Constantine, there was a brutal massacre of males in Julian's family to ensure that only the emperor's sons would reign. Julian was spared because of his youth, but the murders precipitated his loss of belief in Christianity and his subsequent conversion to paganism, earning himself posthumously the title 'Apostate'. He went on to receive a classical Greek education and devoted himself to NEO-PLATONISM. He was a soldier and governor of Gaul in 355, winning the respect of his troops for his courage and the simplicity of his life. On the death of Constantius II, his troops proclaimed him emperor. He was killed in a campaign against the Persians.

Julius II (1443-1513) Born Guiliano della Rovere, he was pope from 1503 and patron of numerous artists, including MICHELANGELO. He strove to restore and extend the PAPAL STATES and to establish a strong independent papacy. He joined the League of CAMBRAI (1508-10), an alliance between Louis XII, Emperor Maximilian I and Ferdinand of Spain, which regained the papal provinces on the Adriatic from Venice. In 1510 he entered into a Holy League with Spain and England which forced the French out of Italy. Politics and war dominated Julius's reign and he devoted little time to Church reform. He did, however, send missionaries to India, Africa and America. Julius was a generous patron of the arts, commissioning Bramante to design St Peter's in Rome in 1503, RAPHAEL to decorate his private apartments and Michelangelo to paint the ceiling of the Sistine Chapel.

Julius Caesar see CAESAR, GAIUS JULIUS

July Plot (July 20, 1944) Unsuccessful attempt by German military leaders to assassinate the Nazi dictator Adolf HITLER and overthrow the regime. Disenchanted with Hitler's leadership and policies, a number of senior army officers believed that he had to be assassinated and an alternative government established which would negotiate peace with the Allies. Count Claus von Stauffenberg left a bomb in a

conference room at Hitler's headquarters at Rastenburg. The bomb exploded, slightly injuring Hitler and killing four of his staff. Stauffenberg, believing that he had been successful, flew to Berlin where the plotters aimed to seize the Supreme Command headquarters. An immediate countermove led to the arrest of some 200 plotters, including Stauffenberg, and generals Beck, Olbricht, von Tresckow and, later, Fromm. They were shot, hanged, or in some cases strangled. Field-Marshal Erwin ROMMEL was implicated and subsequently committed suicide.

July Revolution

(1830) Insurrection in France that overthrew the Bourbon monarch CHARLES X in favour of LOUIS-PHILIPPE. The revolt began when Charles issued his ordinances of July 26, which suspended the liberty of the press, dissolved the new Chamber of Deputies, reduced the electorate and allowed him to rule by decree. Opponents erected barricades in Paris, and after five days of bitter street fighting Charles was forced to abdicate. The duc d'Orléans, Louis-Philippe, was invited to become 'King of the French' (1830-48), a title which replaced the more traditional 'King of France'. His accession marked the victory of constitutional liberal forces over arbitrary and absolutist rule.

Jung, Carl Gustav

(1875-1961) Swiss psychiatrist and a pioneer of analytical psychology. Jung was born in Kesswil, Switzerland, and studied medicine in Basel. His early research while working at the Burghölzli mental clinic in Zurich brought him to the attention of Sigmund FREUD and led to their first meeting in 1907 in Vienna. Jung became a collaborator with Freud in the early development of psychoanalysis, but his dissatisfaction with Freud's emphasis on the sexual basis of

Shells explode into the North Sea during the Battle of Jutland on May 31, 1916, while burning British and German battle cruisers billow smoke, in a contemporary picture by Norman Howard.

neurosis led in 1913 to the breakup of their partnership. Jung developed the theory of 'archetypes', naturally inherited ideas in the individual unconscious that derive from the collective experience of humanity as a whole. Although his belief in the power of the occult and the significance of dreams has prejudiced some against his ideas, his theories of symbolism and pioneering work on personality types – he coined the terms 'introvert' and 'extrovert' – have been hugely influential. Jung's best-known works are *Psychology of the Unconscious* (1912) and his autobiography, *Memories, Dreams, Reflections* (1962).

jury

The system of conducting criminal and civil cases in a court of law, whereby 12 sworn lay people determine the truth from the evidence submitted and reach a verdict, may have originated in England; in the Anglo-Saxon 'compurgation' an accused person could be cleared on the sworn word of 12 neighbours to his or her good character.

In 1166 the Assize of Clarendon instructed jurors to present their evidence and suspects before the king's justices. Trial by jury was adopted in civil cases in 1215 when the Lateran Council forbade trial by ORDEAL, and it was made compulsory in 1275 for some criminal cases by the Statute of Westminster. In England jurors are chosen at random from the electoral roll. The jury system has been adopted by most English-speaking and some European countries.

Justinian I

(483-565) Byzantine emperor from 527. His codification of Roman law in the *Corpus Juris Civilis* has had a major influence on the law of most European countries.

Justinian was born in Illyria, the nephew of Emperor Justin I, and educated in Constantinople. On Justin's death he was proclaimed emperor. He successfully restored the Roman Empire to its former extent; his general, BELISARIUS, crushed the Vandals in

Africa (533-48) and the Ostrogoths in Italy (535-54). His reforms of provincial administration were strongly influenced by his powerful wife, THEODORA. A lasting contribution to the development of jurisprudence was provided by Justinian's codification of the 4652 imperial ordinances (*Codex*), his summary of the views of the best legal writers (*Digest*), a student handbook (*Institutiones*), and a collection of laws (*Novellae*) which made up the *Corpus Juris Civilis*. Justinian remained an orthodox Christian throughout his life; he built the original Church of St Sophia, in Constantinople, to be his great memorial, but in 532 it was burnt down in a riot.

Jutes

Germanic people said to have invaded Britain in the 5th century AD under HENGIST and Horsa. According to BEDE, the Anglo-Saxon historian (who is supported by archaeological evidence), they occupied the Isle of Wight, the Hampshire coast and Kent – the former land of the Belgic Cantii people, with its capital at Canterbury. Here they permitted St AUGUSTINE to pursue his religious mission of re-Christianising Britain. The name of the Jutes survives today in Jutland, Denmark.

Jutland, Battle of

(May 31, 1916) Indecisive battle fought off the coast of Jutland in the North Sea between Britain and Germany. It was the only major sea conflict of the First World War and began between two forces of battle cruisers, the British under David BEATTY and the Germans under Franz von Hipper. Suffering heavy losses during the day, Beatty joined the main British Grand Fleet under John JELLICOE, which engaged the German High Seas Fleet.

The battle resumed at 6pm at long range, but as the Germans headed for home they met the British fleet. Both sides claimed victory. The British lost 14 ships, including three battle cruisers; the Germans lost 11 ships; but the British retained control of the North Sea.

Jung considers a psychoanalytical work in 1952 at Basel University, Switzerland, where from 1944 to 1961 he was professor of psychology.

Women Kabuki actors were forbidden in 1629 because competition for their favours led to violence. The young male actors who replaced them were in turn banned in 1652 because, dressed as women, they caused even more scandal. Thereafter all parts were played by adult men.

Kabuki Form of popular Japanese drama. Kabuki – Japanese for 'art of singing and dancing' – evolved in the 17th century from classical NOH DRAMA to provide entertainment for the expanding merchant class. A Kabuki programme is accompanied by music and consists of domestic and historical dramas separated by dance episodes. Actors, always male, are trained from childhood, and their art lies in their ability to express emotions through stylised movements of the whole body. Scenery, costumes and make-up are elaborate and lavish.

Kádár, János (1912-89) Hungarian leader. After training as a mechanic, Kádár joined the outlawed Communist Party in 1931 and helped to organise underground resistance to German occupation during the Second World War. A communist regime was established in Hungary at the end of the war, and in 1949 Kádár was admitted to the Politburo and appointed minister of the interior. A year later he was expelled from the party after coming into conflict with the Stalinists, and was imprisoned between 1951 and 1953.

In 1954 Kádár was rehabilitated and joined the government of Imre NAGY, who had promised to liberalise the Soviet-backed regime. In October 1956 the HUNGARIAN REVOLUTION broke out, and on November 1 Kádár declared the Communist Party dissolved. However, when Soviet troops suppressed the uprising, Kádár deserted Nagy, whom he later had executed, and formed a new government under Soviet auspices. Kádár served as premier until 1958 and again from 1961 to 1965. From 1958 he was also general secretary of the Hungarian Communist Party. Kádár remained loyal to Moscow in foreign affairs, but his policies at home allowed for an increasingly diversified economy and a higher standard of living. During the 1960s, Hungary became the most prosperous nation in Eastern Europe, but by the 1980s reform had stopped and the economy had entered a period of stagnation. Kádár was ousted as general secretary in May 1988 and replaced by the prime minister Karoly Grosz.

Kafka, Franz (1883-1924) Czech novelist and short-story writer. Born in Prague to prosperous German Jewish parents, Kafka studied law and worked in an insurance company before tuberculosis forced him to leave. Kafka's writing depicts the terrors and frustrations of modern life. The individual is portrayed as lonely, tormented or victimised, living in an incomprehensible and sinister environment and afflicted by surreal, nightmarish events. One of his best-known short stories, *The Metamorphosis* (1915), pursues with relentless logic the effect on a family of the hero's metamorphosis into a giant insect. Kafka's three novels, *The Trial* (1925), *The Castle* (1926) and *Amerika* (1927), were published posthumously against his wishes by his friend Max Brod. In *The Trial*, the hero's unexplained arrest and trial provide a picture of the workings of inscrutable authority and of an individual's desperate attempt to deny the guilt of his own existence.

Kamakura City south-west of Tokyo and seat of Japan's first SHOGUNATE. In 1180, the Japanese general Minamoto Yoritomo made the small fishing village his clan's headquarters. After he became military leader, or shogun, in 1192, he established his administration, or *bakufu*, in Kamakura. This became Japan's second capital for the next 300 years. The Kamakura shogunate (1192-1333) established the rule of the SAMURAI class. During this period *seppuku*, ritual suicide by disembowelment, emerged as an honourable way of avoiding shame following defeat or betrayal. The shogunate also officially sponsored ZEN BUDDHISM, and Kamakura remains famous for its *daibutsu*, or 'great Buddha', a 42 ft (13 m) high bronze figure of Buddha, which was cast in 1252.

kamikaze Japanese air force pilot trained to make a suicidal crash attack on an enemy target in an aircraft laden with explosives. The name means 'divine wind' in Japanese and refers to typhoons that dispersed Mongol invasion fleets threatening Japan in 1274 and 1281. The Japanese adopted these desperate tactics during the Philippines campaign in 1944 to try to stop the advance of Allied naval forces. There was no lack of volunteers inspired by the honour of dying for their emperor and country. At OKINAWA in 1945, more than 300

A kamikaze pilot ties Japan's flag around his head before take-off. Suicide attacks sank 34 American ships and damaged hundreds more.

kamikaze pilots inflicted the greatest losses ever suffered by the US navy in a single battle, killing nearly 5000 men. Kamikaze missions continued to the end of the war.

Kampuchea see CAMBODIA

Kant, Immanuel (1724-1804) German philosopher. He was born in Königsberg, East Prussia, where he attended university and in 1770 was appointed professor of logic and metaphysics. In his works, including the *Critique of Pure Reason*, published in 1781, Kant attempted to bridge the gap between empiricism, which stresses experience, and rationalism, which stresses reason. Kant was concerned that conventional metaphysics had failed to resolve issues such as the existence of God, the immortality of the soul and the operation of free will. The first step to answering such questions was to investigate the limits of human understanding and reasoning – a type of investigation he called a 'critique'. Kant concluded that we cannot ever know a 'thing-in-itself', but only as it appears to the human mind. He also argued that 'right action' could not be based on intuition or desire but must conform to a law of reason, the 'categorical imperative', which urges people to behave as they would wish everyone else to. Kant led a regular life: the people of Königsberg set their clocks by his punctual afternoon walks.

Karageorge (1762-1817) Serbian revolutionary leader, founder of the Karageorgević dynasty. Born George Petrović, the son of a peasant, he was known as Karageorge ('Black George') because of his dark complexion. An effective guerrilla fighter, he led the Serbian revolt against the Turkish army in 1804 and played a major part in forcing the Turks out of SERBIA. Four years later he was proclaimed 'first and supreme Serbian hereditary leader'. From 1809 he fought with Russia against the Turks, but the peace of 1812, concluded by Russia as it prepared for Napoleon's invasion, left Serbia vulnerable to attack. In 1813, the Turks invaded and crushed all opposition. Karageorge fled to Austria and on his return in 1817 was murdered, probably on the orders of a rival Serbian leader, Miloš OBRENOVIĆ. The Karageorgević dynasty competed with the Obrenović dynasty for control of Serbia in the 19th century, ruling from 1842 to 1858 and again from 1903 to 1945.

Karnak Village on the eastern bank of the Nile in Egypt, the religious centre of ancient THEBES. Karnak was the seat of worship of Amon, the Thebans' chief god and the god of life and reproduction. The great temple of Amon at Karnak was built between 1320 and 1237 BC, mainly by the pharaohs Seti I and RAMESES II. It includes a vast hypostyle hall with 134 columns, each 78 ft (24 m) high, and

is Egypt's largest temple. Other temples are dedicated to Mont, the god of war, and to Mut, the wife of Amon. A statue-lined avenue once linked Karnak to Luxor 2 miles (3.2 km) away.

Károlyi, Mihály, Count (1875-1955) Hungarian statesman. A member of one of the country's wealthiest aristocratic families, Károlyi entered the Hungarian parliament in 1910 as a conservative, but soon moved to the left. He advocated a less pro-German policy for the AUSTRO-HUNGARIAN EMPIRE, equal rights for all the nations within it and universal suffrage. These policies were too radical for wide acceptance in Hungary. Károlyi emerged as an influential figure only towards the end of the First World War. He became prime minister of the new republic of Hungary in 1918 and president in January 1919, but resigned in March on learning that Hungary had to cede territory to Romania, Czechoslovakia and Yugoslavia. His government was replaced by the communist regime of Béla KUN.

Kashmir Former principality on the northwestern border of India. In the late 14th century, Muslims conquered the region and converted many of the population; in 1586 it became part of the MUGHAL empire. In 1846 the British installed a Hindu maharajah. At Indian independence in 1947, the maharajah acceded to the state of India, and Kashmir, with its predominantly Muslim population, became a source of conflict between India and Pakistan. In 1949 it was divided into Jammu and Kashmir, an Indian state, and Azad ('free') Kashmir, under Pakistani control. The Indian Ladakh region in the east is culturally Tibetan.

Conflicts flared up again in 1965 and 1971, since when there have been demands for a UN-supervised referendum. In 1990 India imposed direct rule on Jammu and Kashmir following Muslim separatist violence. Border fighting and civil unrest have continued.

Katyn massacre Mass execution of Polish military officers in Katyn forest near Smolensk, western Russia, during the Second World War. In 1941, after Germany had invaded Russia, the Soviet government agreed to cooperate with the Polish government-in-exile in London, who requested the return of 15 000 Polish prisoners taken in 1939, when the Soviet Union had occupied the eastern half of Poland during the period of Nazi-Soviet collaboration. The Soviet government claimed the prisoners had escaped to Manchuria and could not be found, but on April 13, 1943, the German army discovered the mass graves of 4443 Polish officers. The victims had been shot from behind. Soviet claims that the invading German army had killed the prisoners in 1941 were disproved, but the Soviet government denied responsibility until 1990. The fate of the other missing prisoners has never been established.

Kaunda, Kenneth (1924-) Zambian politician, president from 1964 to 1991. Kaunda trained as a teacher and in 1949 joined the African National Congress (ANC). In 1959 he became president of the new Zambian ANC and led the opposition to British plans for a Central African Federation to be composed of Northern Rhodesia, Southern Rhodesia (present-day Zimbabwe)

German officers stand at a mass grave uncovered at Katyn, 1943. Not until 1990 did the Soviets finally admit that Stalin, fearing a national revival in Poland, had Polish officers killed by his secret police.

and Nyasaland (Malawi). After instituting a campaign of 'positive nonviolent action' he was imprisoned by the British.

On his release in 1960 Kaunda was soon elected president of the United National Independence Party (UNIP), which took Northern Rhodesia to independence in 1964, with Kaunda becoming president of the new republic of Zambia. Ethnic differences, the Rhodesian and Angolan conflicts and the collapse of copper prices caused unrest and political violence, which led Kaunda to institute a one-party state in 1972. In 1976 he took emergency powers. He demanded sanctions against South Africa because of its policy of apartheid , and joined in the economic blockade of Rhodesia, formerly Southern Rhodesia, albeit at great cost to Zambia's own economy. Kaunda was re-elected in 1978 and in 1983. In 1990, faced with antigovernment demonstrations, he legalised opposition parties, but lost the 1991 elections to Frederick Chiluba.

Kaunitz, Wenzel Anton, Count von

(1711-94) Austrian statesman. He served as state chancellor from 1753 to 1792, controlling Habsburg foreign policy under Empress Maria Theresa and Emperor Joseph II. A lifelong enemy of Prussia, his main diplomatic achievement came in 1756-7 when he allied France and Russia with Austria at the outbreak of the Seven Years' War against Prussia, reversing traditional European alliances. The allies were unable to subdue Frederick the Great, but Kaunitz was a leading negotiator of the Treaty of Paris (see PARIS, TREATY OF), which ended the war in 1763. The French Revolution destroyed his system of alliances and in 1792 he resigned.

Kazakhstan Republic in north-western Asia, formerly part of the Soviet Union. Conquered by the Mongols during the 13th century, by 1848 the region had come under Russian rule and large numbers of ethnic Russians were encouraged to settle on lands used by the nomadic Kazakhs.

In the early 20th century a Kazakhstan nationalist movement developed and led to a bloody anti-tsarist revolt in 1916. Two years later, Kazakh nationalists established an autonomous republic, which in 1936 became a constituent republic of the Soviet Union. Russian settlement increased during the 1930s, while the Kazakhs were forced to settle on collective and state farms. From 1954 to 1960 Soviet premier Nikita Khrushchev's policy of ploughing 'virgin lands' for grain was followed vigorously in the region. Large mineral deposits, including uranium, were also discovered and exploited. Semipalatinsk in eastern Kazakhstan was used as a testing ground for nuclear weapons, and in 1990 the Soviet government declared that eastern Kazakhstan was an ecological disaster zone after an explosion at a nuclear fuel plant. Kazakhstan proclaimed its sovereignty in October 1990. The Communist Party was replaced by the Independent Socialist Party the following year. The Kazakhstan Republic joined the new Commonwealth of Independent States in December 1991, and the UN within 1992. Since then Western companies have invested heavily in huge oil and gas reserves.

Keitel, Wilhelm (1882-1946) German field-marshal during the Second World War. As chief-of-staff of the high command of the German armed forces from 1938 to 1945, Keitel helped to direct most of the Third Reich's campaigns. He was Hitler's chief military adviser and bore some responsibility for repressive measures the army adopted in occupied territory. On May 8, 1945, he signed Germany's surrender. He was tried for war crimes at Nuremberg and hanged.

Kelly, Ned (1855-80) Australia's most notorious bushranger and folk hero. After serving time in prison for receiving a stolen mare and for resisting arrest, Kelly was later hunted for killing three policemen in Victoria. The Kelly gang – Ned, his brother Dan, and two friends – took to the bush, seizing a sheep station, robbing two banks, and capturing a hotel, where they eventually fought it out with the police. Kelly emerged from the hotel encased in roughly made armour, but was captured and hanged in Melbourne. The others died in the hotel.

Kempis, Thomas à (c.1380-1471) German Augustinian monk and probable author of *Imitatio Christi* (*Imitation of Christ*), a devotional treatise that follows the soul's progress to Christian perfection. With its emphasis on the spiritual life, and on the importance of asceticism and moderate austerity, it was a reaction to the worldliness of the 15th-century Roman Catholic Church. Its sincerity and simplicity brought it wide popularity, and it has since proved to be one of the most influential works in Christian literature.

Kennedy, John Fitzgerald (1917-63) Thirty-fifth president of the United States and the fourth to be assassinated in office. After service in the US navy during the Second World War, Kennedy became a Democratic member of the House of Representatives and subsequently a senator. In 1953 he married Jacqueline Lee Bouvier. After winning the 1960 Democratic nomination he defeated Vice-President Nixon in the closest presidential election since 1884, becoming the youngest-ever president – and the first Roman Catholic – to win office.

At his inauguration Kennedy declared, 'Ask not what your country can do for you – ask what you can do for your country.' He brought a new spirit of hope and enthusiasm to the office and became an immensely popular figure both at home and abroad. In 1961 he established the Alliance for Progress to provide economic assistance to Latin America. Congress supported his foreign-aid proposals and also his goal of landing a man on the Moon within the decade, which was achieved in 1969. But Congress was reluctant to accept his programme for civil rights and social reform, known as the 'New Frontier' proposals.

In foreign affairs Kennedy recovered from the BAY OF PIGS fiasco in 1961, and resisted Khrushchev over the CUBAN MISSILE CRISIS, which in 1962 brought the world to the brink of nuclear war. The following year he helped to secure a NUCLEAR TEST-BAN TREATY with the USSR and Britain. Kennedy became involved in Vietnam, dispatching increasing numbers of US 'military advisers' there.

On November 22, 1963, Kennedy was assassinated while visiting Dallas, Texas. The Warren Commission, appointed by his successor, Lyndon B. Johnson, concluded that he had been shot by Lee Harvey OSWALD, acting alone, but unanswered questions and inconsistent evidence have led to speculation that Oswald was framed, or not the sole killer.

John F. Kennedy was a member of a noted political family. His brother Robert F. Kennedy (1925-68) was a key member of the Kennedy administration as attorney general from 1961 to 1964 and ran for the Democratic

Kennedy electioneers with his wife Jackie in Wall Street, 1960. During their tenure the White House was called 'Camelot' because of the mythic quality surrounding them.

nomination for president in 1968. While campaigning in California, he was shot dead by a Jordanian immigrant, Sirhan Sirhan. Edward M. Kennedy (1932-), brother of John and Robert, is a senator and an influential figure in the Democratic Party.

Kenneth I (died c.858) First king of a united kingdom of Scotland from about 843until his death. Also known as Kenneth MacAlpin, in 834 he succeeded his father, Alpin, as king of the Scots of Dalriada in Argyll, and in about 843 became king of the Picts, who occupied the area north of the Forth. Kenneth combined the territories of both peoples to form the united kingdom of Alba (Gaelic for Scotland), north of a line between the Forth and Clyde rivers. He moved St COLUMBA's relics from Iona to Dunkeld, which became the seat of the Scottish Columban Church.

Kenneth II (d.995) King of Scotland from 971, son of Malcolm I. In 973, in return for recognising the lordship of King EDGAR of England, Kenneth was given the area known as Lothian between the Tyne and the Forth rivers. This was the first time the River Tweed was recognised as the effective border between England and Scotland.

Kenya Country in East Africa. The Portuguese first visited Kenya's coast in 1498, gaining control of much of it by the end of the 16th century. In 1698 they were driven out by Arabs from Oman who conquered nearby Zanzibar. Little is known about inland Kenya until the 18th century, when the Masai – a pastoral people – came into the region from the north. During the 19th century the Masai were largely displaced by the Kikuyu, farmers who advanced steadily from the south.

European missionaries first reached the interior in the 1840s, but other Europeans did not explore the region until the 1880s. In 1886 the British, French and German governments established spheres of influence in East Africa, with most of present-day Kenya going to Britain. The British East African Association was given a royal charter in 1888 to develop and administer the British sphere in East Africa. After it suffered financial problems, its territory was taken over by the British Government, which in 1895 established the East Africa Protectorate.

European immigration increased after the railway from the coast to Lake Victoria in the far west was completed in 1903. Settlers took over the highlands region and established themselves as large-scale farmers. In 1920 the East Africa Protectorate became the British crown colony of Kenya, while a coastal strip leased from the Sultan of Zanzibar became the Kenya Protectorate. By then a great area of the 'White Highlands' had been reserved for White settlement, with 'Native Reserves'

Kenyatta returns home in 1961, following his release from prison. Despite completing his sentence in 1960, he had been kept in detention.

established to separate the two communities.

During the 1920s considerable immigration from Britain was accompanied by the development of African political movements demanding a greater share in the government of the country. In 1944 Kenya became the first East African country to include an African in its Legislative Council; by 1951 there were eight African seats in the legislature. Kikuyu nationalism developed steadily, culminating in the MAU MAU rebellion of 1952-7 against the British colonial government. A number of nationalist leaders, including Jomo KENYATTA, were imprisoned. After the rebellion, political progress resumed. By 1960 there was an African majority in the legislative council and the Kenya African National Union (KANU) and the Kenya African Democratic Union (KADU), formed a coalition government in 1962.

In May 1963 Kenya became self-governing with Kenyatta as prime minister. Full independence was declared in December when Zanzibar also surrendered its sovereignty over the Kenya Protectorate. The following year Kenya became a republic with Kenyatta as president. Under his leadership Kenya remained generally stable, but after his death in 1978 growing opposition to his successor, Daniel arap Moi, culminated in a bloody attempted coup in 1982. Elections in 1983 saw the return of comparative stability, with Moi still president of an increasingly corrupt and autocratic regime. In December 1991 Moi reluctantly ended single-party politics following pressure from the Forum for the Restoration of Democracy (FORD), supported by Western aid-donor nations. He was

> **DID YOU KNOW?**
>
> It was Kepler's attempt to confirm his teacher Tycho Brahe's theory that the Sun revolved around the Earth that led him to prove exactly the opposite.

re-elected in 1992 in a result condemned by opposition parties. Despite the controversy, donors committed more than $800 million in aid for 1994, but in July 1995 they declared that further assistance depended on political and economic progress.

Kenyatta, Jomo (c.1892-1978) President of KENYA from 1964 until his death. The son of a Kikuyu farmer, Kenyatta was brought up in a Church of Scotland mission. Later he joined the Kikuyu Central Association, which aimed to recover Kikuyu lands from White settlers. In 1928 he visited England as Secretary of the Kenya Central Association, campaigning for land reforms and political rights for Africans. He lived in Britain from 1932 to 1946, when he returned to Kenya and became president of the Kenya African Union. In 1953 he was convicted and imprisoned for directing the MAU MAU rebellion to remove British rule, a charge he steadfastly denied. While in jail he was elected leader of the Kenya African National Union (KANU). Soon after his release in 1961 he entered parliament, winning a decisive victory for his party at the 1963 elections. He led his country to independence in 1963 and was its first president. He reconciled Asians and Europeans with liberal policies and a sound economic strategy but, intolerant of dissent, in 1969 he outlawed opposition parties.

Kepler, Johannes (1571-1630) German astronomer and mathematician. He studied in Prague under the Danish astronomer Tycho Brahe, and on Brahe's death in 1601 succeeded him as imperial mathematician of the Holy Roman Empire. He also inherited Brahe's astronomical data which he used to deduce that the Earth and the planets travel around the Sun in elliptical orbits. This was the first of Kepler's three laws of planetary motion, published between 1609 and 1619. His observations gave Isaac NEWTON the basis on which to develop his theory of universal gravitation.

Kerala India's most densely populated state, in the narrow Malabar coastal plain between the Western Ghats and the Arabian Sea. The region was known as Keralaputra during the reign of the emperor Asoka in the 3rd century BC, but from the 5th century AD it fragmented into separate kingdoms and was never again united, although the Malayalam language maintained some cultural unity. The arrival of the Portuguese explorer Vasco da Gama at Calicut in 1498 began an era of European intervention in the spice trade. By the late 18th century British influence predominated, and in 1795 the southern principalities of Travancore and Cochin accepted

British protection. When India gained independence in 1947 the area was known as Travancore-Cochin state. Kerala received its present name in 1956.

Kerensky, Aleksandr Feodorovich
(1881-1970) Moderate socialist revolutionary and prime minister of the Russian provisional government from July to October 1917. After graduating, Kerensky became a prominent lawyer and around 1905 joined the Socialist Revolutionary Party. In 1912, he was elected to the fourth DUMA as a delegate of the Labour group. After the outbreak of the Russian Revolution in February 1917, he was made minister of justice and then minister of war in the provisional government of Prince Lvov, succeeding him as prime minister in July. His determination to continue the war against Germany and his failure to implement agrarian and economic reforms alienated both moderates and the left. When the Bolsheviks seized power in the October Revolution, he escaped and went into hiding. In May 1918 Kerensky fled to Paris and in 1940 moved to the USA.

Kesselring, Albrecht (1885-1960)
German field-marshal and one of Hitler's leading military strategists during the Second World War. Kesselring commanded air offensives over Poland in 1939 and France in 1940. His assault on Britain's airfields (see BRITAIN, BATTLE OF), intended to destroy the Royal Air Force in advance of a German invasion, was on the brink of succeeding when, in September 1940, Hermann GOERING decided to redirect the attack to British cities instead. This gave the RAF time to recover and defeat the German offensive. Kesselring was made commander in chief of German forces in Italy from 1943 to 1945 and on the Western Front in 1945. In 1947 he was condemned to death for war crimes which had occurred in Italy, but had his sentence commuted to life imprisonment and was released in 1952.

Kett's Rebellion
English peasant protest from July to August 1549 against the profiteering and ENCLOSURES of Norfolk landlords. Led by Robert Kett, a small landowner, 16000 small farmers encamped on Mousehold Heath outside Norwich and blockaded the city. The rebels aimed to impress the authorities and shame the local magnates with their disciplined self-government. Kett refused a royal amnesty, saying that innocent men did not need to be pardoned, and on August 1 attacked and took control of Norwich. On August 24 Norwich was retaken by forces under John Dudley, Earl of Warwick and later Duke of NORTHUMBERLAND, who easily routed the main body of rebels at Dussindale on August 27. Kett and his brother William were among those later executed.

Keynes, John Maynard, Baron (1883-1946)
British economist whose ideas dominated economic policy from the 1930s to the 1960s. During the First World War he was employed in the Treasury and was economic adviser to Lloyd George at the Versailles Peace Conference in 1919. Resigning in protest at the harsh war REPARATIONS imposed on Germany, he won an international reputation for his book, *The Economic Consequences of the Peace*, which predicted that Europe would be economically ruined as a result of them. Keynes wrote his most influential work, *General Theory of Employment, Interest and Money* (1936), in response to the failure of conventional LAISSEZ-FAIRE economic policies to deal with the Depression and chronic unemployment. Keynes revolutionised economic thought by proposing deficit financing – using money raised by government borrowing for public spending projects that would increase employment, even though this policy would result in a budget deficit.

During the Second World War, Keynes served in the Treasury as an adviser and played a major role in the BRETTON WOODS CONFERENCE of 1944, which resulted in the setting up of the INTERNATIONAL MONETARY FUND and the WORLD BANK. His support of a policy of full employment influenced governments

> 66 **Practical men, who believe themselves to be quite exempt from any intellectual influences, are usually the slaves of some defunct economist.** 99
>
> *John Maynard Keynes*, General Theory of Employment, Interest and Money

in the immediate postwar years and also the 1942 BEVERIDGE Report, which had set out the principles of the British WELFARE STATE.

In more recent years, the validity of 'Keynesian economics', which seeks to establish a mix of capitalism and interventionism, has been questioned, particularly by monetarists who favour controlling the economy by regulating the money supply.

KGB
Secret police of the Soviet Union from 1954 to 1991. Its title is an abbreviation of the Russian for 'Committee of State Security'. The KGB's responsibilities were both domestic and international and included overt and covert intelligence and counterintelligence, the protection of state and military secrets, surveillance of key members of the Communist Party, the monitoring of dissidents and the supervision of censorship. Unlike predecessors such as the Cheka and the NKVD, it was firmly under Communist Party control. The KGB successfully infiltrated every intelligence service in the world, and at home subjected dissidents such as Andrei Sakharov and Alexandr Solzhenitsyn to internal exile. Its importance was reflected in 1982 when Yuri Andropov, chairman of the KGB from 1967, was appointed Soviet leader. In August 1991, the head of the KGB, Vladimir Kryuchkov, took part in the attempted coup against Mikhail GORBACHEV, and as a result the KGB was stripped of many of its military units and internal security functions. In 1992 it was abolished and replaced by the External Intelligence Office and the Federal Security Service of the Russian Republic. At the end of the Soviet period the KGB was estimated to employ between 400000 and 700000 people.

Khama, Sir Seretse (1921-80)
First president of BOTSWANA from 1966 to 1980 after the former protectorate of Bechuanaland gained independence. Khama's marriage to Ruth Williams, an Englishwoman, in 1948 created controversy both at home and in Britain. In 1950 the British Government exiled him to Britain until he agreed to give up the chieftainship he had inherited from his father at the age of four. He returned as a private citizen in 1956 and in 1962 established the Democratic Party. Three years later, the party won the elections and Khama became his country's leader, taking it to independence in 1966, when he was made president. A strong believer in multiracial democracy, Khama strengthened the economy of Botswana and achieved universal free education.

Khmer Rouge
Communist movement that ruled Cambodia from 1975 to 1979. It was set up in 1967 as the armed wing of the Communist Party of Cambodia and in 1970 formed a coalition with Prince SIHANOUK after he had been overthrown by the right-wing, US-backed regime of Lon Nol. In the early 1970s the Khmer Rouge received aid from North Vietnam and won increased support in the countryside, helped by the US bombing of Cambodia during this period. After five years of civil war, the Khmer Rouge captured the capital, Phnom Penh, in 1975. Under POL POT's leadership, a bloody purge liquidated almost the entire professional elite, as well as most of the government officials and Buddhist monks. The majority of the urban population was relocated to work in the countryside, where large numbers perished. The regime was responsible for up to 2 million deaths in Cambodia and for the serious disruption of the country. In 1979 Pol Pot was overthrown by a coup backed by Vietnam, but continued to wage a guerrilla war against the new regime from bases in Thailand.

In October 1991, the Khmer Rouge, as the Party of Democratic Kampuchea, and with Pol Pot still influential, agreed to join the UN-backed Supreme National Council following a peace agreement.

Khomeini, Ayatollah Ruholla (c.1900-89)

Religious and political leader of IRAN from 1979 to 1989. In 1950 he was acclaimed ayatollah (Persian for 'miraculous sign of God'), the highest rank of religious leader in the SHIITE branch of Islam. During antigovernment demonstrations in 1963 he spoke out against the land reforms and Westernisation of Iran by MUHAMMAD REZA SHAH PAHLAVI, and was briefly imprisoned.

After being forcibly exiled from Iran in 1964 he went to live in Iraq, but was made to leave by Saddam HUSSEIN and in 1978 settled near Paris, from where he agitated for the overthrow of the Shah. On February 1, 1979, two weeks after the Shah had left Iran, Khomeini returned amid wild celebrations. He was acclaimed as the religious leader of Iran's revolution and four days later he appointed a government. A referendum in December 1979 established a new constitution that named him political and religious leader for life. Islamic law was once more strictly imposed, and he enforced a return to fundamentalist Islamic tradition. All opposition was suppressed and the Shah's pro-Western foreign policy abandoned.

In November 1979, Khomeini sanctioned the seizure by Iranian militants of the US embassy in the capital Tehran, which began the IRAN HOSTAGE CRISIS. He prolonged the IRAN-IRAQ WAR in the hope of overthrowing Saddam Hussein; only with deep bitterness did he accept the UN armistice of 1988. Khomeini supported Islamic revolution and terrorist groups throughout the Middle East.

Khomeini is welcomed back to the holy city of Qum in 1979. He had studied and taught there until his arrest in 1963.

Khrushchev, Nikita (1894-1971)

Leader of the Soviet Union from 1958 to 1964. The son of a miner, Khrushchev joined the Bolshevik Party in 1918 and enlisted in the Red Army a year later. After training at a technical institute, his technical and organisational abilities allowed him to rise in the Communist Party hierarchy and escape Joseph STALIN's purges in the late 1930s. From 1938 to 1949 he was political head of the Ukraine, organising resistance there during the Second World War and subsequently creating and enlarging state farms. In the power struggle following the death of Stalin in 1953 Khrushchev emerged as first secretary of the Communist Party.

In 1956 Khrushchev caused a sensation by denouncing Stalin and the 'cult of personality'. In the subsequent process of 'destalinisation', thousands of political prisoners were released, and many prison camps closed. Security controls were relaxed and concessions made to a consumer economy. Khrushchev introduced widespread changes in regional economic administration and raised agricultural output dramatically. Abroad, in 1956 Khrushchev agreed to allow the Poles more freedom under Wladyslaw GOMULKA, but he subdued the HUNGARIAN REVOLUTION by sending in Soviet troops. In March 1958, he assumed the additional role of premier of the Soviet Union. Although Khrushchev followed a policy of 'peaceful coexistence' with the West, in 1962 he brought the Soviet Union close to war with the USA in the CUBAN MISSILE CRISIS. The following year he signed the NUCLEAR TEST-BAN TREATY with the USA and Britain. Khrushchev's ideological feud with MAO ZE-DONG threatened war with China. In 1964 members of the Politburo led by his successor, Leonid BREZHNEV, unseated him, largely as a result of failures in agricultural production.

Khyber Pass

Strategically important mountain pass on the Afghan-Pakistan frontier that has been a major trading and invasion route. In the 5th century BC DARIUS I of Persia marched through the pass to reach as far as the Indus river. Among other invaders who used it were ALEXANDER THE GREAT, Mahmud of Ghazni, the 11th-century emperor of Afghanistan, TAMERLANE and BABUR. The Khyber area was

The jovial ebullience with which Khrushchev brandishes an ear of corn during a 1959 US tour alternated with menacing belligerence.

the scene of many skirmishes with fierce Pashtun tribes during the Afghan Wars (see AFGHANISTAN), and the British won control of it under the Treaty of Gandamak (1879). A railway through the pass required 34 tunnels and 94 bridges, and was opened in 1925. The Khyber is now controlled by Pakistan.

kibbutz

Collective farm or settlement in Israel. Decisions about the running of a kibbutz are taken collectively, and responsibilities such as laundry, cooking and child care are shared by all the residents, who work for the benefit of the community rather than for personal gain. The first kibbutz (Hebrew for 'gathering') was founded in 1909 at Deganya in Palestine by Zionist settlers, partly as an experiment in socialist living. By the 1950s, kibbutzim played an important role in the Israeli economy, supplying more than a third of Israel's agricultural output, often with crops grown in poor soil and reclaimed desert. Today most kibbutzim run factories as well as farms, and some 270 of them house around 130 000 Israelis.

Kiel Canal

Artificial waterway connecting the Baltic with the North Sea. Conceived by Bismarck in 1873 to give German ships quick access to the North Sea, the canal was built between 1887 and 1895 and widened in 1907. Until the end of the First World War it was owned by the German government, but was internationalised in 1919 because of its strategic importance. In 1936 Adolf Hitler repudiated its international status, which was restored after the Second World War.

Kiev Capital of Ukraine. Probably founded in the 6th or 7th century, Kiev is known as 'the mother of Russian cities'. From the 9th to the 13th centuries it was a leading European cultural and commercial centre as the capital of Kievan Rus, the forerunner of both Russia and Ukraine. In 1240 Kiev was destroyed by Tatars and passed into the control of Lithuania, Poland and the Cossacks before Russian rule was established in the 17th century. It is also the original centre of Orthodox Christian faith in Russia, for which it is known as 'the Jerusalem of Russia'.

Killiecrankie, Battle of Defeat of the troops of the English king William III by JACOBITE forces on July 27, 1689. John Graham, Viscount Dundee, led this first Jacobite attempt to restore James II and VII to the English and Scottish thrones, in a narrow, densely wooded pass near Pitlochry in Scotland. The Jacobites overwhelmed the inexperienced forces of General Mackay, who lost 2000 dead and 500 taken prisoner, but Dundee was killed at the moment of victory. The Highlanders were unable to follow up their success, although the rising was not finally put down until May 1690.

King, Martin Luther, Jr (1929-68) Black minister who led the CIVIL RIGHTS movement in the United States. As the pastor of a Black Baptist church in Montgomery, Alabama, King won national fame in 1955-6 by leading the Black boycott which ended racial segregation on Montgomery's buses. King then organised the Southern Christian Leadership Conference, and through this launched a nationwide civil rights campaign. A powerful orator, King looked to Mohandas GANDHI's example and urged reform through nonviolent means. He was arrested and imprisoned several times. In 1963 he organised a peaceful march to the Lincoln Memorial in Washington, in which some 200 000 people took part. It ended in a rally at which he delivered, in his celebrated 'I have a dream' speech, his vision of an America free of racial prejudice. In 1964 King was awarded the Nobel peace prize. His campaign broadened from civil rights for the Black population to criticism of the Vietnam War and of society's neglect of the poor. King was planning a Poor People's March on Washington when, on April 4, 1968, he was assassinated in Memphis, Tennessee, by James Earl Ray.

King, William Mackenzie (1874-1950) Liberal politician and Canada's longest serving prime minister. Mackenzie King entered the Canadian parliament in 1908 and was minister of labour from 1909 to 1911 under

Kipling's own illustration from the *Just So Stories* shows 'the Elephant's Child' crying as the Crocodile lengthens his nose by pulling on it. The writer was painted by his cousin Philip Burne-Jones convalescing in 1899.

Sir Wilfrid Laurier. In 1919 he became leader of the Liberal Party. Between 1921 and 1948 he was prime minister for all but six years. King combined support from French-Canadian Liberals with endorsements from the Progressives, the farmers' party of western Canada. He helped to preserve the unity of the country's French and English-speaking population, and in 1926 was instrumental in establishing equal status for Canada with Britain in the Commonwealth.

During the Second World War King led the Canadian war effort, surviving two political crises over conscription, and at the same time prepared Canada for economic development and advances in social welfare after the war. From 1945 he promoted the Canadian role in postwar reconstruction, the United Nations and NATO.

Kinnock, Neil (1942-) Leader of the British Labour Party from 1983 to 1992. Kinnock was elected to Parliament in 1970, and became a member of the party's national executive committee in 1978. He never held ministerial office, but after Labour lost office in 1979, Kinnock was an effective opposition education spokesman. He was elected leader of the Labour Party in 1983 and led the Opposition to Margaret THATCHER's second administration. As leader, Kinnock reduced the influence of Labour's left wing and persuaded the party to drop its unpopular commitment to unilateral nuclear disarmament. He also made major reforms in policy and presentation, and began modernising the party structure to make it less dependent on trade union backing.

Although Labour's standing in the opinion polls had increased from just over 25 per cent to 45 per cent by 1992, Labour lost the general elections of 1987 and 1992. Kinnock resigned as party leader and was replaced by John Smith. Kinnock became a Commissioner of the European Union in 1995.

Kipling, Rudyard (1865-1936) British author of poems, short stories and novels, many of which are set in India, where he was born. His father was an artist and curator of the museum in Lahore. At the age of six Kipling was sent back to England for schooling. He was unhappy and missed his home and family terribly. His adult masterpiece, the novel *Kim* (1901), about an orphan English boy growing up in Lahore, is full of Kipling's love for India. He returned there in 1882 to work as a journalist, and left again seven years later. In 1892 Kipling married the American Caroline Balastier and moved to Vermont for ten years. He finally settled in England in 1902. In Kipling's own time his poems, such as 'Mandalay', 'Gunga Din' and 'The Ballad of East and West' were highly valued. He is now generally regarded as the 'poet of empire', but he was a man of complex views. He was a political conservative, a liberal in social matters, a fervent supporter of war and empire though not a racist. In many ways he was both an English and an Indian writer. Kipling's books for children included *The Jungle Book* (1894), about Mowgli, a child brought up by wolves, and *Just So Stories* (1902). In 1907 he was the first British writer to receive the Nobel prize for literature.

Kirov, Sergei (1886-1934) Russian communist leader. He began his revolutionary activities in 1917 as a Bolshevik agitator in the Caucasus. In 1926 Joseph Stalin transferred him to Leningrad, where he became a member of the politburo in 1930 after loyally supporting Stalin against his opponents. Kirov's power increased during the early 1930s, but in 1934 he was assassinated by a young party member, Leonid Nikolayev. Stalin then claimed that he had discovered an anti-Stalinist conspiracy, and used Kirov's murder to launch the show trials and party purges of the late 1930s. In February 1956 Khrushchev implied that Stalin himself had instigated Kirov's assassination.

Kissinger, Henry (1923-) US adviser on foreign policy. Kissinger acted as government consultant on defence from 1955 to 1968 before serving as President Richard NIXON's head of the National Security Council from 1969 to 1975 and secretary of state from 1973 to 1977. Kissinger was largely responsible for improved relations with the Soviet Union, resulting in the Strategic Arms Limitation Treaty (SALT) of 1969. He helped to achieve a resolution of the Indo-Pakistan War in 1971 and a rapprochement with Communist China in 1972, which the USA recognised for the first time. Kissinger at first supported the Vietnam War, but changed his views and after prolonged negotiation reached an agreement for the withdrawal of US troops in 1973. For this he was awarded the Nobel peace prize jointly with North Vietnamese negotiator, Le Duc Tho, who refused the prize. That year Kissinger also helped to resolve the Arab-Israeli War and restored US diplomatic relations with Egypt. After Nixon's resignation following the Watergate scandal, he remained in office to advise President Gerald Ford.

kitchen cabinet Popular term for unofficial advisers to a president or prime minister. The term was coined in the United States after Andrew JACKSON was elected president in 1829. During the early years of his presidency, Jackson's official Cabinet contained many strong but opposed personalities, including his first vice-president, John Calhoun, and his secretary for war, John Eaton. Official Cabinet meetings were therefore held as seldom as possible, and Jackson took most of his advice from Martin Van Buren (his second vice-president and successor), John Eaton, the newspaper editors Amos Kendall and Francis Blair, and personal friends appointed as minor government officials. After a Cabinet reorganisation in 1831 Jackson relied rather more on members of his official Cabinet.

Kitchener of Khartoum, Lord (1850-1916) British field-marshal and statesman. Between 1896 and 1898 Kitchener commanded an Anglo-Egyptian army in the SUDAN. His organisation of supplies and his troops' use of the recently invented machine gun helped him conquer the Sudan and earned him a knighthood. From 1900 he was chief of staff and then commander in chief during the second BOER WAR, which the British won in 1902. Afterwards he was much criticised by Liberal politicians for his 'scorched earth' policy and use of CONCENTRATION CAMPS for

noncombatants. Kitchener was serving in Egypt when the First World War broke out in 1914. As secretary of state for war he campaigned successfully to secure volunteers and it was largely due to his determination that Britain survived the disasters of 1914-16. His advice to abandon the DARDANELLES CAMPAIGN, which ended in a bloody defeat, provoked considerable criticism from colleagues but he refused to resign. In 1916 Kitchener was on his way to Russia when his ship was sunk by a German mine off Orkney.

knight The first knights were armed and mounted professional soldiers of the Middle Ages in Europe. In the 9th and 10th centuries knights were raised above the peasantry by their expensive military equipment, particularly their body armour and well-trained horses. Knights formed an essential part of a society in which land was granted in return for military service. From the late 10th century the Church sought to impose a religious discipline on them. The ceremony of knighthood, which came to be known as dubbing, was sanctified. The Christian ideal of knightly behaviour demanded religious devotion, loyalty to one's social and military superiors and the maintenance of personal honour. This ideal developed into the code of conduct known as CHIVALRY. Knights rose to become the lowest rank of the nobility during the 11th century, but knighthood came to be an honour prized by all ranks. The ideal of the knight as the 'soldier of Christ' was most nearly achieved during the CRUSADES, when

A kneeling knight in an Austrian armoury embodies the mingling of 14th-century Christian and military values.

the Church established military religious orders such as the Knights of the Holy Sepulchre in 1113 and the Knights Templar in 1118. The Knights of the Hospital of St John of Jerusalem, founded around 1070 to care for sick and wounded Crusaders, came to be known as the Knights Hospitaler, and began to take part in fighting during the Second Crusade of 1146-9. The orders were bound by monastic vows to defend Christendom, but as their numbers and wealth grew some were drawn into other pursuits. The Knights Templar, for example, became bankers to most of Europe's nobility, attracting much hostility. In 1307 they were charged with heresy and immorality and their order was suppressed.

From the late Middle Ages, secular orders of knights were instituted. One of the first was the Order of the Garter, founded in 1348 by the English king Edward III to honour nobles who fought alongside him in France. In the 16th century new firearms, and the development of musket balls that pierced armour, made the knight in armour obsolete on the battlefield. But the title of knight survived as a rank of the nobility and as an honour given in recognition of civil or military service.

Knossos Principal city of Crete's MINOAN civilisation and capital of the legendary King Minos. The heyday of Knossos was from around 2000 BC, when its original palace was built, to 1400 BC. This palace was severely damaged about 1700 BC, probably by an earthquake. During the 15th century BC,

This poster of Kitchener's stern face and pointing finger encouraged 887000 men to enlist in four months after September 1914.

In the New Palace at Knossos, built around 1450 BC, a dolphin fresco lines the walls of the Queen's Room situated at the top of the royal staircase (right).

Knossos came under the control of the Mycenaeans from mainland Greece, and some time around 1370 the last palace was destroyed. Although the city was no longer a palatial centre, it continued to be inhabited in classical times until it was sacked by the Romans in 68-67 BC. From 1900, the site was excavated by the British archaeologist Sir Arthur Evans, who reconstructed the palace throne room and the labyrinth. Lively and stylish frescoes showing processions, bull sports and dolphins were also revealed. The Greek myth of the maze that housed the half-man, half-bull Minotaur may have arisen from the complex floor plan of the palace.

Knox, Henry (1750-1806) American general who commanded the Continental Army artillery during the War of Independence. In the winter of 1775 Knox was sent from Boston to Ticonderoga, New York, to bring back captured British artillery. He used oxen, horses and men to haul the weapons, which weighed a total of 120000lb (55000kg), across 300 miles (480km) of snow and ice. In March 1776 this artillery was used to force the British evacuation of Boston. Knox was one of General George Washington's most trusted advisers, and succeeded him as commander of the army after the war ended in 1783. In 1785 Knox became secretary of war to the Confederation and four years later joined Washington's first Cabinet.

Knox, John (c.1513-72) Scottish Protestant reformer and one of the founders of the Church of Scotland. During the early 1540s Knox converted to Protestantism under the influence of the preacher George WISHART. In 1546 Wishart was burnt for heresy on the orders of Cardinal David Beaton, and the following year Knox joined a group of conspirators who, after assassinating Beaton, fortified themselves in St Andrew's Castle. Although a scholar and teacher by inclination, Knox now became a passionate preacher for the Scottish

Protestant cause. After the castle was stormed by the French, he was imprisoned as a galley slave. On his release in 1549, still staunchly Protestant, he went to England and became chaplain to EDWARD VI in 1551. On the accession of the Roman Catholic MARY I in 1553, Knox fled to Frankfurt and then Geneva, where he ministered to Protestant refugees and met John CALVIN. Knox returned to Scotland in 1559 to lead the fight against Catholicism. Although his *First Blast of the Trumpet Against the Monstrous Regiment* [or Rule] *of Women* in 1558 had alienated him from ELIZABETH I, in 1560 she sent troops to help the Scottish Protestants defeat French plans to unite the three kingdoms of Scotland, England and France under MARY, Queen of Scots and her French husband, Francis II. Protestantism became the established religion in Scotland in August 1560, and the Scottish Parliament adopted Knox's *Confession of Faith*. In 1561 he was one of the key authors of the *First Book of Discipline*, outlining a reformed Church of Scotland. After her return to Scotland in 1561, Mary, Queen of Scots and Knox were fierce opponents, but she failed to have him convicted of treason and in 1567 the Protestant nobles forced her abdication. Knox died in 1572 after giving his last sermon as minister of St Giles', Edinburgh, a protest against the St Bartholomew's Day Massacre of French Huguenots.

Kohl, Helmut (1930-) Chancellor of the Federal Republic of Germany from 1982 to 1990, and of a united Germany from 1990. After studying in Frankfurt and Heidelberg, Kohl became a lawyer. In 1959 he was elected to the Rhineland-Palatinate state parliament, and in 1969 became the state premier. He was elected chairman of the Christian Democratic Union (CDU) in 1973, and three years later was the joint candidate of the CDU and Christian Social Union for the chancellorship. After losing to Helmut SCHMIDT, chairman of the Social Democratic Party, he led his party in opposition. When Schmidt's government collapsed in 1982, Kohl became interim

chancellor, and the following year his coalition government won the national elections. He was re-elected in 1987 after being cleared of involvement in a scandal over the funding of political parties. In 1989-90, as the Soviet Union abandoned its control over Eastern Europe, Kohl's government gave asylum to an ever-increasing number of refugees from the German Democratic Republic. Two months after East and West Germany were reunited in October 1990, Kohl was elected the first chancellor of a unified Germany since 1945. He adopted a positive stance towards the eastern part of his country, but the cost of unification and of modernising East Germany was far higher than he had calculated. By 1992 rapidly rising unemployment in the east, increased taxation, high interest rates and the presence in Germany of an estimated 1.5 million migrants and asylum seekers had led to a

> **66 To attain German unification without obtaining European unification would mean that I have not accomplished my goal. 99**
>
> *Helmut Kohl, Time magazine June 25, 1990*

loss of public support for Kohl. That same year, Germany experienced a wave of neo-Nazi rioting. Kohl remained committed to European political and monetary union.

Koniev, Ivan (1897-1973) Soviet field-marshal. Koniev was conscripted into the tsarist army in 1916, and joined the Red Army and the Communist Party in 1918. During the Second World War he led the offensive against the Germans, commanding several different fronts. Koniev was made a marshal of the Soviet Union in 1944. In 1945 his 1st Ukrainian Army advanced through Poland and Silesia to play a major part in the capture of Berlin. Koniev was commander in chief of Warsaw Pact forces from 1955 to 1960.

Königgratz, Battle of see SADOWA, BATTLE OF

Konoe Fumimaro, Prince (1891-1945) Japanese prime minister three times between 1937 and 1941. Konoe entered politics after the First World War, becoming a member of the upper house of the Diet by virtue of his rank. During the 1920s he advocated a popularly based parliamentary democracy and opposed the military domination of government. In 1937 Konoe became prime minister, but his Cabinet fell in 1939 after he failed to end the conflict with China, which had become a full-scale war in July 1937. During his second Cabinet from 1940 to 1941, he concluded an alliance with Germany and Italy and began negotiations with the US in the belief that American mediation would resolve the Sino-Japanese war. Konoe formed a third Cabinet in July 1941, but in October was forced out of office by his war minister, Tojo Hideki. In 1944 Konoe helped to engineer the collapse of the Tojo government. He committed suicide in December 1945 after being charged with war crimes.

Koran Islamic sacred book held by believers to be the word of Allah (God) as revealed to the Prophet MUHAMMAD by the archangel Gabriel over a period of 20 years. The revelations were memorised by Muhammad's followers but not compiled until the reign of Uthman (644-56), the third caliph, or successor to the Prophet, who in 651-2 established a committee to reconcile various versions. The Koran, or Qu'ran (Arabic, 'reading' or 'recitation') is divided into 114 *surahs*, or chapters, which are generally arranged according to length, the longer ones first. Its central message is belief in one God and absolute submission (*islam*) to Him as creator and sustainer of the universe. The Koran contains many parallels with the Old Testament. It venerates Jesus as a prophet, or messenger of God, but maintains that God saved him from dying on the Cross. The Koran also lays down the religious principles that form the basis of Islamic law, although details of the law's requirements are not given. Because it is the verbatim word of God, translation of the Koran has traditionally been forbidden.

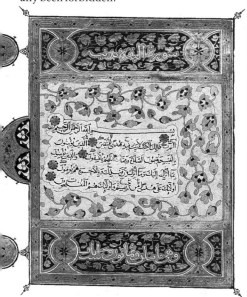

The ornate decoration of the Koran honours the revealed words of God that it contains. This manuscript dates from 1389.

Korea Country in north-eastern Asia. Buddhism reached Korea in the 4th century. The Silla kingdom in the south became a tributary state of China from 658 and ruled a unified Korea for 200 years. A period of civil war ended with the supremacy of the Koryo kingdom (918-1392). Under the Yi dynasty (1392-1910) Korea was greatly influenced by Ming China. Confucianism largely replaced Buddhism, and a new capital was built at Seoul. Korea became a battleground during the RUSSO-JAPANESE WAR (1904-5), and a Japanese colony in 1910. After the Second World War Korea was divided along the 38th parallel into US and Soviet zones of occupation. In 1948 the US zone became the Republic of Korea (SOUTH KOREA) and the Soviet zone became the Democratic People's Republic of Korea (NORTH KOREA).

Korean War War between SOUTH KOREA and Communist NORTH KOREA from 1950 to 1953. In 1945, at the end of the Second World War, the Allies divided KOREA into a Soviet occupied zone north of the 38th parallel and a US zone south of it. Plans to reunify the country failed, and in 1948 the communist Democratic People's Republic was set up in the north and the pro-Western Republic of Korea in the south.

In 1949 the US withdrew its troops. On June 25, 1950, fighting began with a surprise attack by North Korean troops, who soon held most of the south. The conflict became part of the larger COLD WAR when the invasion was condemned by the United Nations, which, in the temporary absence of the Soviet delegate, voted to send assistance to the south. A 16-nation UN force under the supreme command of General Douglas MACARTHUR arrived in September 1950, and by the end of October had pushed the North Koreans back to the border with Communist China. China retaliated by sending troops to support the North Koreans.

In January 1951, the Communist armies reached the South Korean capital of Seoul, but in the spring were driven back across the 38th parallel. After months of fighting, the conflict reached a deadlock close to the original boundary. In July General Mathew Ridgway,

Koreans flee south as US troops advance to face the North Korean forces led by Kim Il Sung (below).

MacArthur's replacement, started peace negotiations. But it was not until 1953, after around 4 million people had been killed or wounded, that an armistice was signed at Panmunjom. A ceasefire was agreed and a demilitarised buffer zone was established between north and south at approximately the 38th parallel.

Kosovo, Battle of Decisive battle fought at Kosovo Polje (the 'Field of Blackbirds') in SERBIA in June 1389 between the Serbian army of Prince Lazar and the Turkish forces of the Ottoman Sultan Murad I. The Serbs enjoyed an early success when the sultan was killed by a Serbian noble, but Murad's son BAYEZID quickly took command, surrounding and then crushing the Serbs. Victory opened the way for a Turkish invasion of central Europe. At a second Battle of Kosovo from October 17 to 20, 1448, Sultan MURAD II defeated the Hungarians and thereby consolidated Ottoman control of the Balkans.

Kosygin, Alexei (1904-80) Soviet politician, premier from 1964 to 1980. Kosygin joined the Communist Party in 1927. He held posts in the Leningrad city government and industry before becoming a member of the party's central committee in 1939 and the politburo in 1948. Following Joseph Stalin's death in 1953 he lost his position in the party, only regaining his authority in 1957 under Nikita KHRUSHCHEV, with whom he worked closely on economic matters. While his role in Khrushchev's downfall is obscure, Kosygin succeeded Khrushchev as premier in 1964, sharing power with Leonid BREZHNEV, general secretary of the Communist Party. Kosygin achieved a notable diplomatic success in bringing to an end the 1965-6 INDO-PAKISTAN WAR, but from the late 1960s his authority declined as Brezhnev's increased. Kosygin retired because of ill health in 1980 and died soon afterwards.

Kronshtadt Mutiny Rebellion against the Bolshevik government by the Russian Baltic fleet at its headquarters in Kronshtadt in the Gulf of Finland. In 1917, the Kronshtadt naval garrison had supported the Bolsheviks, but in March 1921, as urban workers demonstrated against the hardships of the civil war, the sailors rose against what they now regarded as the communist dictatorship. They formed a Provisional Revolutionary Committee to demand economic reform and political freedom, but on March 17-18 were brutally suppressed by Red Army troops led by Leon Trotsky. The revolt forced the Communist Party to adopt Lenin's more liberal New Economic Policy in 1921.

Kruger, Paul (1825-1904) Afrikaner statesman, president of the TRANSVAAL from 1883 to 1900. As a child Kruger took part in the Boers' GREAT TREK, which in 1852 resulted in the establishment of the Dutch-speaking republic of the Transvaal. After the republic was annexed by Britain in 1877, Kruger led the Transvaal's fight for independence in the first BOER WAR of 1880-1, and in 1881 helped to negotiate the Pretoria Agreement granting the Boers limited independence. Elected president of the Transvaal in 1883, Kruger followed a policy of resistance to the British.

In 1886 the discovery of gold in the Witwatersrand led to large numbers of mostly British immigrants settling in the Transvaal, but despite pressure from the British and the prime minister of the Cape Colony, Cecil RHODES, Kruger refused to grant these 'Uitlanders' (foreigners) political equality. Relations between Britain and the Transvaal and ORANGE FREE STATE continued to deteriorate and in 1899 the second Boer War broke out. Despite early Boer successes, Kruger was forced to retreat in 1900 and moved to Europe, where he vainly sought allies against the British. He died in exile in Switzerland.

Krupp German steelmaking and armaments firm that armed Germany from 1857 to 1945. The Krupp family business was founded in 1811 by Friedrich Krupp (1787-1826). Under his son Alfred (1812-87) the company pioneered the first cheap method of making steel, invented by Henry BESSEMER in 1856, and soon diversified into arms manufacture. In 1870-1 Krupp heavy guns helped the Prussians to win the Franco-Prussian War. Alfred's son-in-law, Gustav Krupp von Bohlen und Halbach (1870-1950), developed Germany's long-range artillery in the First World War. Big Bertha, the gun used in 1918 to shell Paris from a distance of 82 miles (131 km), was named after Gustav's wife.

Gustav helped the Nazis to rearm Germany in the 1930s, but during the Second World War Krupp was run by his son Alfried (1907-67), who used concentration-camp prisoners as slave labour in Krupp factories. Alfried was tried at Nuremberg and was imprisoned from 1948 to 1951. Krupp became a public company after Alfried's death in 1967.

Kublai Khan (1214-94) Fifth of the Mongol Great Khans, and first Mongol emperor of China, from 1279 until his death. The grandson of GENGHIS KHAN, Kublai was elected Great Khan in 1260. In 1267 Kublai made Cambaluc (present-day Beijing) the Mongol capital and in 1271 founded the Yuan dynasty, with himself as emperor. In 1279 he finally conquered south China and became ruler of an empire stretching from the East China Sea to the River Danube. He established Buddhism as the state religion, and was a patron of learning and the arts. He followed Chinese forms of government, although civil service examinations were abandoned. Privileged status was given to Mongols, while other foreigners, mostly from central Asia, were appointed to important civil and military posts. The Venetian traveller MARCO POLO wrote that he served as Kublai's agent from 1275 to 1292.

Kublai's rule was a period of prosperity for China. The Grand Canal linking north and central China was extended, post roads were built, and food was stored for periods of shortage. But while the foreign merchant class benefited, ordinary Chinese people grew poorer. Obedience was enforced by a curfew and much spying. Determined to establish China as the centre of the world, Kublai also undertook

Golden tents surround Kublai Khan's capital, Cambaluc, at the centre of this 15th-century map based on Marco Polo's information. The map is typical of the period in being drawn with North at the bottom and East on the left hand side – the opposite of modern map-making practice.

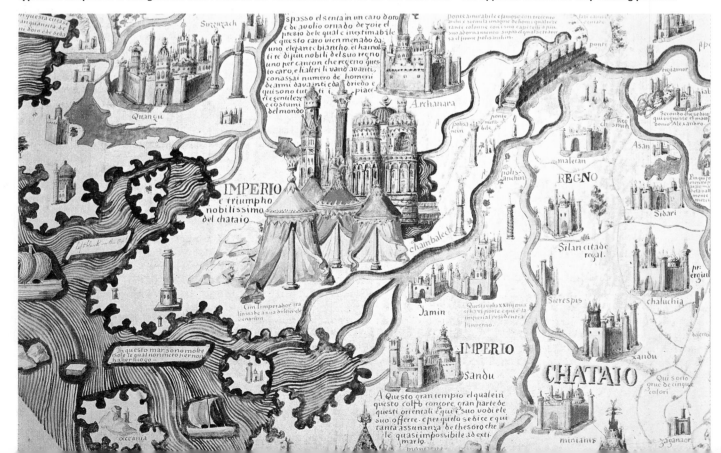

Klan members celebrate a Supreme Court ruling in June 1992, stating that the US constitution's First Amendment protects 'reprehensible' manifestations of free speech such as cross burnings.

costly foreign campaigns which had limited success. His attempts to annex Japan failed disastrously when his invasion fleets were destroyed by typhoons in 1274 and 1281.

Ku Klux Klan American secret organisation dedicated to White supremacy. The first Ku Klux Klan was founded by Confederate soldiers in Tennessee in 1866, immediately after the American Civil War. The name came from *kyklos*, the ancient Greek word for a circle. Members, who soon numbered half a million, opposed the federal government's policy of Reconstruction, which had allowed Black men to vote and hold positions of power. Wearing hooded white robes and carrying burning crosses, Klansmen intimidated and killed Blacks and destroyed their property. In 1869, General Nathan B. Forrest, the Klan's 'Grand Wizard', disbanded the organisation, partly because of its use of violence, after which laws suppressing the Klan were passed.

In 1915 a second Klan was founded in Georgia by William Simmons, a former minister, to promote White supremacist, anti-Semitic, anti-Catholic and anti-Communist views. At its peak in the mid 1920s the Klan elected high federal and state officials, but by 1930 its membership had dropped from 4 million to fewer than 10 000 after revelations of the Klan's corruption of state politics. The civil rights movement of the 1960s led to a revival, and the Klan was denounced by President Lyndon B. Johnson following the murder of civil rights demonstrators in Alabama in 1965. The Klan survives at a local level in the Southern states.

kulak In Russia, a rich peasant or village usurer. In late 19th century Russia a class of wealthy peasants developed, who owned large farms and could afford to hire labour or act as moneylenders. The other peasants called such a man a kulak – a 'fist'. The kulaks became significant after the emancipation of the serfs and the agrarian reforms of the Russian premier Peter STOLYPIN from 1906. Kulaks gained land in the revolution of 1917, but during the civil war from 1918 to 1921 the communists organised committees of poor peasants to help the Red Army requisition grain from the kulaks. This stopped with Lenin's New Economic Policy in 1921. But in 1927 Stalin increased their taxes, and in 1929 he called for the 'liquidation' of the kulaks. During the 1930s their animals were seized and their land was taken for collective farms. Many kulaks were killed – estimates put the death toll at 3 million, with up to 10 million kulaks deported to Siberia and other remote parts of the Soviet Union.

Kulturkampf 'Cultural struggle' by the German chancellor, Otto von BISMARCK, between 1881 and 1887 to bring the German Roman Catholic Church under state control. The conflict began in 1871 when Bismarck, suspicious of the loyalty of German Catholics to the newly created German empire, abolished the Roman Catholic bureau in the ministry for education and ecclesiastical affairs. In 1872, Bismarck extended state control over religious schools and diplomatic relations with the Vatican were broken off. The May Laws of 1873 further restricted the powers of the Catholic Church, and in 1875 civil marriage was made obligatory. Clergy who failed to comply could be exiled. Strong Catholic opposition in the German parliament caused Bismarck to repeal many of his anti-Catholic laws, although education remained under state control. In 1887 Pope Leo XIII declared the conflict finished.

Kun, Béla (1886-c.1939) Hungarian communist leader. During the First World War Kun fought in the Austro-Hungarian army, but was captured on the Russian front and joined the Bolsheviks. He returned to Hungary in November 1918 and founded the Hungarian Communist Party. After the government of Mihaly KAROLYI fell in March 1919, Kun persuaded the Communists and Social Democrats to form a coalition government and set up a Soviet republic under his leadership. After an unsuccessful military campaign against Rumania the regime collapsed on August 1. Kun fled to Vienna and then to the USSR, where he was executed in one of Stalin's purges.

Kuomintang see GUOMINDANG

Kurdistan Mountainous area in western Asia, divided between Turkey, Iran, Iraq, Syria and Armenia and inhabited by Islamic Kurds. Kurdistan has never known political unity. In the 7th century it was conquered by Arabs, who converted its people to Islam, and it became successively part of the Seljuk, Mongol and Ottoman empires.

On the dissolution of the Ottoman Empire at the end of the First World War, the region was split between Turkey, Syria, Iraq, Iran and the USSR. The Kurds in all these countries have been fighting for an independent state ever since. The Treaty of Sèvres in 1920 promised an independent Kurdistan, but it never materialised.

Kurds in Iraq began an armed struggle for autonomy in 1958. In 1970 the Iraqi government promised Iraqi Kurds limited autonomy in the Kurdish-controlled region of northern Iraq. The Kurds refused to accept the terms of the agreement and after the government tried to impose its plans in 1974 heavy fighting resumed, with Iran giving the Kurds

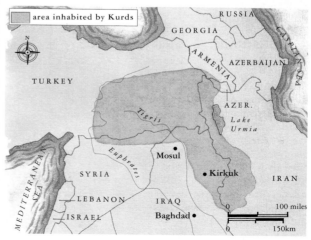

area inhabited by Kurds

Kurds have never had their own country. Their homeland covers parts of Syria, Iraq, Iran, Turkey and Armenia.

military assistance. Four years later, Iran granted its Kurds limited autonomy, but political persecution continued. Kurdish unrest in Iraq grew throughout the 1980s, and brought retaliation from the Iraqi leader Saddam Hussein in 1987-8, in the form of chemical warfare. Thousands of Kurds were killed and approximately 1.5 million more were forcibly removed from their mountain villages to townships.

The Gulf War of 1991 precipitated another Kurdish revolt in Iraq that was ruthlessly suppressed until Kurdish 'safe havens' protected

> **❝** We don't want to be like the Palestinians and ask for the impossible. If there were a democratic government in Iraq, we would be happy to be Iraqis. **❞**
>
> *Jalal Talabani, Kurd Democratic Party*
> *New York Times, March 27, 1991*

by French, British and US troops were established in northern Iraq. After failing to negotiate a new autonomy agreement with the government, leaders of the two main Iraqi Kurdish parties – the Patriotic Union of Kurdistan (PUK) and the Kurdistan Democratic Party (KDP) – called for elections for an Iraqi Kurdistan National Assembly. These were held in May 1992 and in July a government was formed, although its authority was not recognised by Baghdad. In October the PUK and KDP approved a motion calling for an independent Kurdish state within a democratic Iraq. Since May 1994 the PUK and KDP have been at war with each other, but in August 1995 talks began in Ireland between the two factions to try to end the civil war.

In Turkey the Kurdistan Workers' Party (PKK) began an armed struggle for an independent Kurdistan in 1984. In 1994-5 the Turkish government launched offensives against PKK rebels in south-eastern Turkey and northern Iraq, bringing the number of deaths since the PKK started its campaign in 1984 to more than 15 000.

Kursk, Battle of Largest tank battle of the Second World War, fought between the armies of the Soviet Union and Germany. In an attempt to regain the offensive on the Eastern Front, Adolf Hitler ordered a surprise attack to eliminate the key railway junction of Kursk in the western Soviet Union. Almost 900 000 German troops and 2700 tanks and mounted assault guns were supported by more than 1000 aircraft. The Soviets anticipated the attack and when the Germans struck on July 5, 1943, they were confronted by even larger numbers of Soviet guns, tanks and aircraft. Forced to retreat, the Germans lost 120 000 men killed, wounded or missing.

By August 23, the Soviets had regained the nearby cities of Orel and Kharkov. The battle ensured that the German army never recovered the initiative on the Eastern Front.

Kut-al-Amara, Siege of British defeat by the Turkish army during the First World War. In December 1915, British troops defeated by the Turks at Ctesiphon in southern Iraq were forced to retreat to Kut-al-Amara on the River Tigris, where they were besieged by the Turks from December 1915. After badly organised relief forces had failed to break through, the British finally capitulated in April 1916. Ten thousand British and Indian prisoners were marched across the desert. Two-thirds died on the way; and some 23 000 troops of the relieving force were also lost. Kut-al-Amara was recaptured in February 1917, but the defeat severely weakened Britain's prestige as an imperial power.

Kutuzov, Mikhail (1745-1813) Russian army commander, and prince of Smolensk who drove back Napoleon Bonaparte's invasion of Russia in 1812. In 1805 Kutuzov was given command of the joint Russian-Austrian army against Napoleon, but was removed from command after the defeat at the Battle of Austerlitz in 1805. From 1806 he fought in the Russo-Turkish War, and in May 1812 he concluded the Treaty of Bucharest on terms favourable to Russia. In August he was appointed commander in chief of all the Russian forces against Napoleon. After losing almost half his troops at the Battle of BORODINO on September 7, Kutuzov withdrew beyond Moscow, abandoning it to the French, who entered on September 14. In October, faced with Tsar Alexander I's refusal to surrender and the grim prospect of a Russian winter, the French turned back. Kutuzov forced them to retreat along the same devastated route they had used to enter the country. He harried and almost annihilated the French, and pursued them into Poland and Prussia, where he died of disease.

Kuwait Independent state on the north-west coast of the Persian Gulf. Kuwait was settled in the early 18th century by Arab tribes, and has been ruled since 1756 by the al-Sabah family. In 1899 the sheik of Kuwait gave control of his country's foreign affairs to the British, and in 1914 Kuwait became a British protectorate. The discovery of oil in 1938 transformed the economy, and after the Second World War Kuwait became one of the world's largest oil producers.

The country gained independence in June 1961, but in July Britain provided troops to defend it against annexation by Iraq. After its defensive pact with Britain lapsed in 1971 Kuwait tried to pursue a policy of neutrality. However, when the Iran-Iraq War broke out

in 1980 it posed a threat to Kuwait's own security and oil shipments. Kuwait sided with Iraq, to which it made large loans throughout the 1980s. In 1990 talks with Iraq on the repayment of these war loans and other issues broke down, and on August 2 Iraq invaded Kuwait on the basis of a long-held claim to sovereignty. The country was stripped of its economic assets and an estimated 7000 Kuwaitis were killed, and 17 000 held in camps in Kuwait and Iraq, before a US-led military coalition defeated Iraqi forces in the GULF WAR of January-February 1991.

Oilfield fires set by the retreating Iraqis, and perhaps accidentally by US bombing, were put out by the end of 1991. Oil production was quickly restored to help to meet reconstruction costs estimated at up to $100 billion. Most Kuwaitis returned, but the government decided that in future non-Kuwaitis would make up no more than half the country's population – out of a prewar population of 2 million, only 800 000 had been Kuwaitis. In 1992 demands for the restoration of parliamentary democracy, suspended since 1976, led to elections. Although only 13 per cent of the population was eligible to vote, many candidates opposed to the royal family won seats in the National Assembly.

Labor Party Australia's oldest surviving political party. Labor groups were formed in individual states in the 1880s and 1890s and merged to become the Australian Labor Party in 1918. Labor had provided state governments briefly in 1904 and again in 1908, but it was not until the federal election of 1910 that it gained control of both houses of parliament. During its administration of 1915-17 Labor introduced some social reforms, but split over the issue of conscription in 1916 and was replaced by a National-Country coalition until 1929, when it returned to power for two years. It split a second time in 1931 over policy differences. Labor regained power in 1941 and continued in office until 1949, when the party split again. Labor was in opposition for the next 17 years until the defeat, in 1966, of Robert MENZIES' Liberal Party. The crisis of 1974-5, in which the governor-general tried to force the resignation of the premier, Gough Whitlam, brought down the next Labor government. In 1983, for only the second time in 33 years, Labor won power and dominated Australian politics until 1996.

Labour Party British political party. In 1982, three years after the Scottish Labour Party was formed by trade unionists and socialists, the party gained three parliamen-

TO-MORROW – WHEN LABOUR RULES

The Labour Party issued three election posters in 1923. The first two attacked unemployment and war. The third, shown above, promised working class happiness under a Labour government.

tary seats. One of these was won by Keir HARDIE, who the following year helped to form the Independent Labour Party, advocating pacifism and SOCIALISM, and representing the interests of workers. In 1900 a Labour Representation Committee was formed which in 1906, still under Hardie, won 29 seats in the general election. The name was changed to the Labour Party, and in 1918 its members adopted a constitution drawn up by Sidney WEBB and Arthur Henderson.

Party membership was over 4 million by 1920, and Labour had replaced the Liberals as the main opposition party to the Conservatives by 1922. It shared office with the Liberals in national elections in 1923 and 1929, but its first overall majority was gained in 1945 under Clement ATTLEE. Attlee's government created the WELFARE STATE and nationalised British industries, such as the railways. Labour lost the 1951 general election, but held power again from 1964 to 1970 under Prime Minister Harold WILSON, and from 1974 to 1979 under Wilson and then James CALLAGHAN. By 1979 increasingly left-wing policies alienated many of the party's leaders, four of whom left to form the Social Democratic Party in 1981.

In 1983 Neil KINNOCK took over the leadership and set about eliminating many of the party's more radical policies in an attempt to win back the support of the electorate. He resigned in 1992 after Labour failed to win the general election. John Smith took over as leader, but died of a heart attack two years later and was replaced by Tony Blair. Blair antagonised Labour's left-wing by forcing changes to the party's constitution, particularly the 'block vote' which had weighted internal decision making in favour of the trade unions – and by moving Labour's policies towards the centre. With these moves the party was dubbed 'New Labour'.

Labourers, Statute of English legislation introduced in 1351 to counter the scarcity of labour caused by the Black Death. It forbade landless men to seek new masters or higher wages, provoking hostility which contributed to the PEASANTS' REVOLT of 1381.

Lafayette, Marie Joseph, Marquis de (1757-1834) French soldier and aristocrat. An advocate of liberty and humanism, Lafayette joined the American War of Independence in 1777 as a volunteer in the American forces, and fought at Brandywine and Monmouth Court House. He was given command of an army in Virginia and was present at the surrender of British troops at Yorktown in 1781, a victory that ensured American independence. Returning to France in 1782 Lafayette became an early supporter of the French Revolution, and perhaps its most important leader among the nobility. But when the revolution turned against the king, he had to flee the country because the Jacobins suspected him of supporting the king and the enemies of France. In exile he was imprisoned by the Prussians and the Austrians, returning to France only when Napoleon gained power in 1799. Lafayette remained active as a liberal spokesman until his death. Already a citizen of several states in the USA, his popularity was reaffirmed when he returned there on a visit in 1824. He was subsequently hailed as the hero of 'Two Worlds', France and America.

laissez-faire Phrase used to refer to a government's policy of limited interference with the actions of the individual or society. It was based on the belief that society as a whole

would benefit most if individuals were allowed to pursue their own personal goals. From the French meaning 'allow to do', it was first used as the doctrine of the physiocrats – 18th-century French economists – and was adopted in Britain by the Scottish economist Adam Smith.

Lake Erie, Battle of Naval engagement during the WAR OF 1812. Both the USA and Britain built warships to use on the strategically important Lake Erie. On September 10, 1813, the two squadrons clashed and ten US ships engaged and captured six British vessels, paving the way for a renewed US attack on Canada.

Lambert, John (1619-83) English Roundhead major-general. He loyally supported Oliver Cromwell both in battle during the 1650 invasion of Scotland and in his subsequent government, but when his own political ambitions seemed thwarted he resigned his commissions. He was tried for treason in 1662 after the Restoration of Charles II and spent the rest of his days in prison.

Lancastrian Descendant or supporter of John of GAUNT, Duke of Lancaster. The Lancastrians, whose emblem was a red rose, held the throne of England under HENRY IV, HENRY V and HENRY VI. But their rule was overturned in the Wars of the ROSES, a series of battles against their bitter rivals, the YORKISTS, which began in 1455. When Henry VI was deposed by EDWARD IV in 1461, the Lancastrian die-hards took refuge in France. Their subsequent invasion of England under MARGARET OF ANJOU restored Henry VI briefly to the throne in October 1470 until the Yorkist victories at Barnet and TEWKES-BURY a few months later. The Lancastrians' persistence was rewarded when their support of Henry Tudor at the Battle of BOSWORTH FIELD in 1485 led to his enthronement as HENRY VII.

Land League Irish organisation set up in 1879 to seek reforms in land tenure. Founded by Michael Davitt and with Charles PARNELL as president, it refused to deal with anyone who replaced a tenant evicted because of non-payment of rent. The British Government declared the League illegal and Davitt and Parnell were imprisoned. Branches of the League were formed in Australia, the USA and elsewhere. The worst aspects of the Irish tenure system were eventually eliminated through a series of Land Acts passed by British governments between 1881 and 1903.

> ### DID YOU KNOW?
> When Lafayette first offered his services to the American Revolution, Congress informed him that he was a troublesome adventurer and that Philadelphia contained too many of his sort already ... before realising its mistake and appointing him major general.

This miniature of Lanfranc as Archbishop of Canterbury, from a manuscript of around 1100, typifies the style of English pre-Conquest art.

Lanfranc (c.1010-89) Scholar and teacher, and Archbishop of Canterbury from 1070. Born in Italy, in 1042 Lanfranc joined the abbey of Bec in Normandy, becoming its prior four years later and developing it into one of Europe's finest schools. Lanfranc became a close adviser to William I, and after William's conquest of England was made Archbishop of Canterbury. During his archbishopric he sought to reform the English Church and helped to maintain its independence, while continuing to acknowledge the king's authority to intervene in Church affairs.

Langton, Stephen (c.1150-1228) Archbishop of Canterbury from 1207, and a major figure in the drafting of MAGNA CARTA in 1215. Although King JOHN strongly opposed Langton's appointment as archbishop, he was forced to accept it in 1213, when England was placed under papal authority. In 1215, after Langton had tried to mediate between John and his barons, he was suspended by Pope Innocent III and summoned to Rome to explain his actions. He was allowed to return to Canterbury in 1218, where he began a significant revision of the relations between Church and Crown. In 1222 he declared a set of constitutions, still considered binding in English ecclesiastical courts.

Languedoc Historical and cultural region of southern France. Colonised by the Romans, overrun by the Visigoths in the 5th century and later settled by the Carolingians, the province eventually passed to the French crown in 1271. Although part of France, it retained its independence, traditional culture and language called *langue d'oc*, *oc* meaning 'yes' in southern French – as distinct from the *langue d'oïl* (modern *oui*) of northern France. Its ruling body, or *parlement*, became the second most important in France after that of Paris. A 16th-century Protestant stronghold, Languedoc's towns supported the 'Camisard' peasants in their rebellion against Louis XIV between 1702 and 1710. Today Languedoc is a renowned wine-producing region, and the traditional language is still widely spoken in many districts.

Laos South-east Asian country. The Lao people, a branch of the Thais, emigrated to Laos from southern China after the 8th century AD, but were driven south by the Mongols. They established the Buddhist kingdom of Lan Xang – 'A Million Elephants' – in 1354, which in 1701 was split into three separate kingdoms: Vientiane, Champassak and Luang Prabang. The kingdoms gradually fell under Siamese (Thai) domination before Siam was forced to cede its claim to France in 1893. After the Second World War, during which the country was occupied by the Japanese, Laos experienced a brief period as an independent monarchy until 1953. But guerrilla warfare instigated by the communist political faction PATHET LAO undermined the monarchy. Relative stability was restored by Prince Souvanna Phouma in 1962, but fighting soon resumed and lasted until the 1970s, with Laos suffering badly from its involvement in the VIETNAM WAR. Following a cease-fire in 1973, the prince

agreed to share power with the Pathet Lao leader, who was also his half-brother. By 1975 the Pathet Lao had gained almost complete control and the monarchy was abolished, paving the way for the establishment of a new party – the People's Democratic Republic – led by Kaysone Phomvihane, a close ally of Vietnam. His tyrannical rule eased in 1989 and steps were taken to rebuild the economy. Under a new constitution, Kaysone was elected president in 1992 but died within months of taking office. He was succeeded by Nouhak Phoumsavan, who soon afterwards negotiated a development loan from the IMF. The USA restored diplomatic relations in 1992, and lifted its aid embargo in 1995.

Largo Caballero, Francisco (1869-1946) Spanish statesman and prime minister from 1936 to 1937. As Secretary-General of the socialist General Workers Union, Largo Caballero was imprisoned in 1917 for taking part in a general strike. Although he received a life sentence, he was released when he was elected to parliament the following year. After the fall of Primo de Rivera, Largo Caballero joined the Second Republic government as minister for labour. When the republic collapsed in 1934 he was again imprisoned, but was acquitted and freed in 1935. He led the Popular Front to victory in the election of February 1936, and became prime minister in September, two months after the outbreak of the Civil War. He resigned after the communist takeover in Barcelona in May 1937.

La Rochelle Port in south-west France which was a focus of power struggles between Roman Catholics and Protestants in the 16th

The determination of Languedoc's people to preserve their independence in turbulent times is reflected in the turreted bastions and crenellated walls of the medieval town of Carcassonne.

and 17th centuries. As a HUGUENOT stronghold during the French Wars of Religion, La Rochelle was besieged by Catholic forces in 1573. The siege ended when a treaty was signed allowing the Huguenots freedom of worship. Cardinal RICHELIEU finally wrested the town from Huguenot control after a 14 month siege in 1627-8 in which many of the inhabitants starved. La Rochelle later played a significant part in trade with French colonies in North America, until the Revocation of the Edict of Nantes deprived its mainly Protestant inhabitants of their religious and civil liberties. Its role diminished further when France lost Canada in 1763.

La Salle, René Robert Cavalier, Sieur de (1643-87) French explorer of Canada and North America. In 1682 La Salle discovered Louisiana, which he named after King Louis XIV. He returned to France in 1683, where he was given authority to govern the entire region between Lake Michigan and the Gulf of Mexico. But when he set out the following year, he was unable to find the mouth of the Mississippi. His men mutinied and murdered him, and it was another 12 years before Louisiana was finally settled by the French.

Las Casas, Bartolomé de (1474-1566) Spanish missionary, known as the 'Apostle of the Indies'. In 1502 he settled as a planter in the Spanish colony of Hispaniola in the West Indies. Horrified at the treatment of the indigenous Indians, he became an outspoken critic of colonial rule and in 1510 joined the priesthood. In 1514 he began travelling between the colonies, and for the next 50 years fought for the abolition of slavery. Las Casas wrote several books promoting Indian equality, including his *History of the Indies*. His tireless campaigning resulted in the imposition of the New Laws, giving the Indians some protection, though their effectiveness was limited by the CONQUISTADORES' opposition.

Lascaux caves Site in the south-west of France where a system of caves contain some of the most important prehistoric art in the world. First discovered in 1940 by four boys following their dog, the caves' walls are covered in Stone Age paintings dating from between 15 000 and 13 000 BC. In vivid colours, these paintings show animals such as reindeer, bears, horses, aurochs – extinct cowlike animals – and a creature which looks similar to the legendary unicorn. Near many of the animals are pictures of arrows and traps, suggesting that Lascaux was used over a long period as a centre for hunting magic. The tableaux are executed in at least 13 different styles, probably from different eras. Their natural pigments and charcoal were applied by finger painting, daubing with moss or fur and spraying through hollow bones.

Lateran Councils Five meetings of senior churchmen at the Lateran Palace in Rome. The first, in 1123, confirmed the Concordat of Worms of 1122, which had ended the king's right to confer office on senior clergy, and clarified which aspects of life should be governed by the Church and which by the secular authorities. The second council was convened in 1139 to simplify doctrine and to heal divisions resulting from the activities of the antipope Anacletus II. The third, in 1179, condemned SIMONY (the buying or selling of ecclesiastical offices) and set out a procedure for papal elections. The fourth, or 'Great Council' was called by Pope INNOCENT III in 1215. It denounced the ALBIGENSIAN heretics of southern France, clarified doctrine on transubstantiation and reaffirmed orthodoxy. The fifth council, begun in 1512, condemned heresy and revoked the claim by Charles VI of France to authority over the Church. It also restored peace among Christian rulers.

Lateran Treaty Agreement, signed in February 1929 in the Lateran Palace, Rome, between Benito Mussolini and Pope Pius XI to improve relations between the Vatican and the Italian government. Although the treaty laid down financial compensation for papal lands lost during the unification of Italy, it was hailed as a propaganda victory for the Fascist regime. The Lateran Treaty also led to the acceptance of the VATICAN CITY as a fully independent state under papal sovereignty and the recognition of Roman Catholicism as the sole religion of the Italian state.

A chance discovery brought archaeologists in 1940 to an entrance to caves at Lascaux in France. Inside they found an amazing gallery of prehistoric animal paintings, regarded as the beginnings of human art.

Latimer, Hugh (c.1485-1555) English Bishop of Worcester. Appointed in 1535, Latimer resigned over the Act of the Six Articles of 1539, which restricted his power to introduce Church reforms. Latimer was a vigorous Protestant preacher and condemned social injustice during Edward VI's reign. On Mary I's accession in 1558 he was arrested for heresy along with Thomas CRANMER, Archbishop of Canterbury, and Nicholas Ridley, Bishop of London, and eventually burned at the stake with Ridley in Oxford.

Latvia Country on the east coast of the Baltic Sea. Originally settled by Lettish peoples, it was overrun by the Russians and Swedes during the 10th and 11th centuries, and converted to Christianity by German-speaking neighbours in the 13th century. By 1230 the Teutonic Knights had conquered Latvia and imposed a feudal system, with German landowners ruling over Latvian peasants. Between the 17th and 18th centuries the country was partitioned between Sweden and Poland, before being annexed by Russia at the end of the 18th century. Independence in 1918 was followed by recognition as a republic two years later. Soviet occupation in 1940 was interrupted by German troops in 1941, but the USSR regained control just three years

later and made Latvia a constituent republic of the Soviet Union. Although Latvia prospered and became industrialised under the Soviets, its fight for independence continued and was won in 1991.

Laud, William (1573-1645) Archbishop of Canterbury from 1633. The son of a draper, Laud rose to prominence when he was made president of St John's College, Oxford, in 1611. Ten years later he was appointed Bishop of St David's in Wales, and in 1628 Bishop of London – becoming one of Charles I's closest advisers. Appointed Archbishop of Canterbury, he continued to support the king. The two worked together to bolster the Church of England, thus provoking Puritan opposition. Laud's religious beliefs were constantly questioned as his policies seemed to tend towards the Roman Catholicism of Charles's queen, Henrietta Maria. He provoked further controversy by trying to 'Anglicanise' the Church of Scotland, a policy which led to the Bishops' Wars of 1639 to 1640. Laud was arrested by the Long Parliament in 1644. The Lords found him innocent of treason, but he was summarily executed on January 10, 1645.

Laval, Pierre (1883-1945) French politician, who began his political career as a socialist but gradually drifted to the right. Laval was prime minister from 1931 to 1932 and from 1935 to 1936. He made his mark as foreign minister when, in 1935, he helped to draw up the Hoare-Laval pact with the British foreign secretary Samuel Hoare, conceding part of Ethiopia to Italy. He fell temporarily from power but was reinstated in 1940 as chief minister in the collaborationist VICHY regime – the right-wing government of the unoccupied part of France. He was tried and executed in 1945 for his support of Adolf Hitler and fascism during the Second World War.

Law, Andrew Bonar (1858-1923) British politician, born in Canada. Law became leader of the Conservative Party in 1911 and supported Ulster's resistance to Irish Home Rule. In 1915 he joined a coalition with Herbert ASQUITH, serving as chancellor of the exchequer from 1916 to 1919, when he shrewdly managed war loans and war bonds. Law then served as Lord Privy Seal until 1921. The following year the Conservatives rejected the coalition with the Liberals under David LLOYD GEORGE, and Law was appointed prime minister. He was forced to resign in May 1923 because of ill health.

Law, John (1671-1729) Scottish financier. After failing to convince the Scottish Parliament of the merit of his proposals for revolutionary banking reforms based on increasing the circulation of paper money, Law tested his ideas in France in 1716. The

Dubbed 'France's last chance' in 1942, Pierre Laval, the French Nazi collaborator, was extradited from Spain and executed in 1945.

French government was heavily in debt and the regent, Philippe, Duc d'Orléans, authorised Law to set up a state bank and a trading company with exclusive rights to develop overseas trade. In January 1720 Law became the French controller-general of finance, but in December the same year he was forced to flee the country, hounded by political intrigue and blamed for a wave of financial speculation which had ruined many people.

Lawrence, T(homas) E(dward) (1888-1935) British soldier and author. He worked as an archaeologist in the Near East and became known as 'Lawrence of Arabia' for the prominent part he played in organising the Arab revolt against the Turks during the First World War. The events and Lawrence's adventures during the revolt are recalled in his book *The Seven Pillars of Wisdom*, published in 1926. His wartime exploits had established Lawrence – essentially a shy man – as a popular public figure, but after a postwar spell as Winston Churchill's adviser in the newly established Middle Eastern Department he withdrew from public life. He enlisted as a mechanic in the Royal Air Force under the assumed name of John Hume Ross, and later joined the Tank Corps in 1923 as T.E. Shaw, before returning to the RAF in 1925. He was killed in a motorcycle accident.

League of Nations Organisation for international cooperation established by the VERSAILLES PEACE SETTLEMENT of 1919. Initiated by the victorious Allied Powers, the aim of the League of Nations was to solve international disputes and to achieve collective security. It succeeded in bringing about cooperation on a range of issues, including health, labour problems and a reduction of armaments. But the League proved powerless

in the face of Italian, German and Japanese expansionism, and it failed to prevent the outbreak of the Second World War. It was replaced by the UNITED NATIONS in 1946.

Lebanon Country on the east coast of the Mediterranean. Much of Lebanon formed part of the empire of the Phoenicians, who arrived around 3000 BC. It was invaded by, among others, the Amorites, Hyksos, Egyptians and Achaemenians. In the 7th century AD a Christian tribe from Syria – the Maronites – established a community on Mount Lebanon, which became a refuge for religious minorities. Around the same time Arabs settled in southern Lebanon, and 400 years later these Arab groups merged their beliefs into the Druze faith. Late in the 18th century the Maronites began to expand their mountain community, threatening the peace with the Druze. In 1842 the Ottoman Turks crushed the power of the Druze princes, and in 1860 the Druze initiated a massacre of Maronites. France intervened on behalf of the Maronites and forced the Ottoman sultan to establish an autonomous Christian province for them.

After the Second World War a National Pact led to equal representation of all religious communities in Lebanon. This mutual tolerance created a climate in which Lebanon prospered and its capital, Beirut, became the financial hub of the Middle East. However, the influx of thousands of Palestinian refugees from the Arab-Israeli Wars sparked off new fighting between the Arabs and Maronites, and in 1975 a protracted civil war broke out, leading to military intervention by Syria.

In 1978 Israel, provoked by the activities of the PALESTINE LIBERATION ORGANISATION (PLO), invaded Lebanon and occupied an area

Augustus John's portrait shows T.E. Lawrence in the Bedouin robes that he used to hide his true identity when he was fighting the Turks.

in the south of the country. A full-scale Israeli invasion followed in 1982 and Israeli troops did not withdraw until 1985. By this time the country was in ruins, thousands of lives had been lost and the conflict remained unresolved. The Syrians intervened again in 1987, sending troops into Beirut and taking over much of the country. Peace attempts failed, and in March 1989, with Israeli support, the Maronite Christian General Aoun launched an all-out war against Syria. Six months later an accord, negotiated by the ARAB LEAGUE, reduced Maronite political dominance and brought a fragile peace to the country. A formal treaty, accepted in 1991, did little to ease Lebanon's instability. In 1992 the first general elections for 20 years were boycotted by the Maronites, allowing Muslim parties to gain political control; but attacks and bombings did not end until 1995 when Israel agreed to establish an autonomous Palestine.

Lebensraum Political doctrine of the Nazi Party in Germany in the 1930s. *Lebensraum*, literally 'living space', sought to justify German claims to former Austrian and Prussian territories in Eastern Europe. It was the basis of Adolf Hitler's *Drang nach Osten* – the 'drive east' – which prompted the German invasions of Czechoslovakia and Poland and led to the outbreak of the Second World War.

Le Corbusier (1887-1965) Swiss-born French architect and interior designer, who greatly influenced 20th-century architecture. His real name was Charles-Edouard Jeanneret – his pseudonym, from the French, *corbeau*, was a pun on his facial resemblance to a raven. His designs are best known for their strong sense of Expressionism – many of his buildings took their forms from such unlikely models as steamships – combined with functionalism. He believed that a house should be 'a machine for living in'. Le Corbusier was the first person to advocate the use of reinforced concrete. Largely self-taught, he formed most of his ideas while travelling through central Europe and the Mediterranean between 1907 and 1911. In the 1920s and 1930s he was one of the leaders of the 'New Spirit' movement, designing a series of highly influential white cubic houses which were often raised on stilt-like pillars. After the Second World War his style became more imposing and sculptural. Among his best-known works are a huge housing estate complete with shops in Marseilles and the pilgrimage chapel Notre-Dame-du-Haut, at Ronchamp. His largest project was the layout of the new city of Chandigarh in India, begun in 1951.

Lee, Robert E. (1807-70) Leading Confederate general in the AMERICAN CIVIL WAR. Raised in a prominent military family, Lee graduated from West Point with a commission in the engineers. He was wounded in the Mexican-American War of 1846-8, and then commanded the Military Academy for three years. Lee was offered the field command of the Union Army at the start of the American Civil War in 1861. Instead he became military adviser to the president of the Southern Confederacy, Jefferson DAVIS, and his tactical and strategic mastery proved a powerful weapon against the North. In June 1862 he took command of the Confederate Army of Northern Virginia, leading it to victories at Fredericksburg in December 1862 and Chancellorsville the following May. Though defeated at GETTYSBURG, Lee withstood General Ulysses GRANT at Richmond for almost a year before being forced to surrender at APPOMATTOX on April 9, 1865.

Lee Kuan Yew (1923-) Singaporean statesman, and prime minister from 1959 to 1990. Lee's democratic socialist People's Action Party dominated Singapore's politics from the late 1950s. When Singapore gained full independence from the Federation of Malaysia (see MALAYA) in 1955, Lee set about strengthening national identity and embarked on a shrewd and determined programme of economic development and social improvement. When he resigned in 1990, Singapore was Asia's second most affluent country after Japan, with one of the world's most successful economies.

> **DID YOU KNOW?**
>
> *The Druze, who worship the 11th-century Fatimid caliph Al Hakim, draw on the Gospels and the Jewish Torah as well as the Koran for spiritual guidance.*

Leibniz, Gottfried Wilhelm (1646-1716) German philosopher and mathematician. A scholar of almost encyclopedic knowledge, in 1684 Leibniz invented a form of mathematics known as infinitesimal calculus. When, three years later, Isaac NEWTON published his own discovery of calculus the two men were caught up in a controversy that lasted until 1711, when the Royal Society declared for Newton, on the basis of work the English scientist had published before 1684. But Leibniz was also absorbed by other branches of science and philosophy and employed rational thought to explain natural phenomena. He believed that the Universe was composed of a series of units – monads – which were placed in harmony with one another by God, who existed at the top of the monad framework.

Leicester, Robert Dudley, 1st Earl of (c.1532-88) Favourite courtier of ELIZABETH I. Dudley and his father were sentenced to death for their support of Lady Jane GREY. His father was executed but Dudley was freed in 1554 and quickly won Elizabeth's favour. She showered him with offices and lands and, in 1564, made him Earl of Leicester. He apparently hoped to marry Elizabeth. But the suspicious circumstances surrounding the death of his wife, Amy Robsart, foiled this plan. In 1563 Elizabeth's suggestion that he marry Mary, Queen of Scots came to nothing, and in 1573 he secretly married Dowager Lady Sheffield and in 1578 bigamously married again. Sent to command 6000 troops against Spain in the Netherlands, Leicester proved incompetent and was recalled in 1588 to organise forces at Tilbury to fight the Spanish Armada. He died suddenly of poisoning later that year.

Elizabeth's favourite, the Earl of Leicester, whirls the queen off her feet in a contemporary court scene. She dismissed rumours that he had poisoned his first wife and forgave his later bigamy.

From a hill overlooking the cannon smoke and carnage of the Battle of Leipzig, Napoleon and his staff watch the brave but vain efforts of the French cuirassiers to halt Blücher's attacking forces.

Leipzig, Battle of (1813) Turning point in the NAPOLEONIC WARS, also known as the 'Battle of the Nations'. In the engagement outside Leipzig in Saxony, Napoleon's army of about 185 000 French, Saxon and other German allies was defeated by a force of some 320 000 Austrian, Prussian, Russian and Swedish troops led by Field-Marshal Karl Schwarzenberg. At first, Napoleon's men beat off attacks from the north by Schwarzenberg and General BLÜCHER, but when Russian and Swedish reinforcements arrived and his Saxon troops deserted Napoleon, he was forced to withdraw. In the retreat 30 000 French troops were captured when a bridge was accidentally blown up, stranding them. The defeat and the retreat of Napoleon's forces effectively ended French power east of the Rhine.

Lend-Lease Act Second World War agreement under which the USA supplied equipment to Britain and its allies. The Lend-Lease Act was introduced by President Franklin D. ROOSEVELT and enabled him to lend or lease arms and supplies to any state whose defence was considered vital to US security. Most of the supplies went to Britain.

Lenin, Vladimir see feature, opposite

Leningrad, Siege of Second World War siege of Russia's second largest city, which lasted for almost 900 days and cost nearly a million lives. German forces reached the outskirts of Leningrad (now St Petersburg) in September 1941 and swiftly surrounded it. Although the city was ill-prepared to withstand a siege, the civilian population was forbidden to evacuate and soon faced starvation and disease as well as relentless bombing and shelling. Soviet counterattacks began early in 1943 but the siege was not fully lifted until January the following year. In 1965 the Soviet government awarded St Petersburg the title 'Hero City of the Soviet Union'.

Leo I, St 'the Great' (c.390-461) Pope from 440 until his death. Leo extended papal authority to Spain, Gaul, North Africa and the Middle East. At CHALCEDON in Greece in 451 he established a basic Christian liturgy by clarifying the relationship of God the Father to God the Son in a way that both the Eastern and Western Churches could accept. The following year Leo prevented Rome's destruction by the Huns by buying off their king, ATTILA. In 455 Leo again saved the city when he persuaded the VANDALS not to sack Rome.

Leo III (c.750-816) Pope from 795 to his death, who surrendered supreme papal authority to CHARLEMAGNE. Leo's predecessor, Hadrian I, had used the Eastern Empire's opposition to Charlemagne to maintain papal independence, but in 799, when Leo was accused of perjury and adultery, he fled to the emperor's court for protection. In 800, Leo returned to Rome where, at Charlemagne's insistence, the complaints against Leo were dropped and his detractors were arrested and deported. The emperor acquitted Leo of all charges and, in return – in St Peter's on Christmas Day 800 – the pope crowned his apparently unsuspecting protector as Emperor of the West, establishing the precedent that only a pope could crown an emperor.

Leo IX, St (1002-54) Pope from 1048 until his death. An able reformer, Leo tried to end what were regarded as the main ecclesiastical evils of the day. He opposed clerical marriages, the investiture of the clergy by lay authorities, and SIMONY (the buying and selling of religious offices), and succeeded in having these practices condemned at the Easter synod of 1049. Leo was imprisoned by the Normans in 1053 when he tried to establish papal control in southern Italy, where his interference in areas claimed by the BYZANTINE EMPIRE led to Rome's break with the Eastern Church in 1054. Leo was released after nine months but died soon afterwards. He was posthumously canonised for restoring papal prestige.

Leonidas (d.480BC) King of Sparta and a hero of the PERSIAN WARS. Leonidas led a small Greek force which for two days resisted Xerxes' vast Persian army at THERMOPYLAE. Leonidas ordered the bulk of the Greek troops to withdraw, remaining with a force of 1000 Spartans who fought to the last man, allowing their allies to escape to safety.

Leopold I (1640-1705) King of Hungary from 1655, and of Bohemia from 1656, and Holy Roman Emperor from 1658 until his death. Having spent his formative years preparing for the Church, Leopold was ill-equipped to rule and relied heavily on the counsel of his ministers and generals. He was at war for much of his reign, repulsing Ottoman attacks in the east, and the French under Louis XIV in the west. Early military success against the Ottomans expanded his realm, but Leopold could not end the Ottoman threat while he was still at war with France. In 1686 he enlisted English and Dutch support to resist French expansion, and in 1701 this culminated in the war of the SPANISH SUCCESSION. Leopold ended the Ottoman threat with the Treaty of Karlowitz in 1699. In the ensuing years of peace on his eastern borders, Leopold developed Vienna into a centre of European culture.

> **DID YOU KNOW?**
>
> *Leopold I was a talented composer and a patron of the theatre. He sometimes took part in the costly theatricals at his court and wrote music for them.*

Leopold II (1835-1909) King of the Belgians from 1865 until his death. Leopold's main interest was in expanding Belgium's colonial interests but, becoming king of the newly created independent state of the Congo in 1885, he treated the African territory as his personal fief, exploiting its rubber and ivory trades for personal gain as well as using its resources to develop Belgium's economy and expand its military forces. In 1908, an Englishman, Edmund Morel, drew world attention to Leopold's mishandling of the Congo, and he was forced to relinquish control of the territory to the Belgian government.

Founder of a dictatorship

*The state that Lenin set up lasted for almost 80 years,
bringing tyranny and suffering across a large swathe
of Europe and Asia before its collapse in 1991.*

The world's first communist state, the Soviet Union, was the creation of one man, Vladimir Ilyich Ulyanov, alias Lenin. His establishment of a one-party state, underpinned by secret police and labour camps, profoundly influenced the course of the 20th century.

Unswervingly ruthless – he complained that 'the Russian…is incapable of applying the harsh measures of revolutionary terror' – Lenin was a mixture of brilliance and incompetence, insight and blindness. To one contemporary he was 'crazy with vanity', but to another he seemed 'more of a provincial grocer than a superman'. He suppressed an early love of music because it led to sentimentality. His marriage was childless.

'Lenin will live for ever' declares a propaganda poster from 1967.

MARXISM AND REVOLUTION
The champion of the working class was born into a middle-class family at Simbirsk on the Volga in 1870. He qualified as a lawyer, and spent most of his adult life with emigré intellectuals outside Russia. His elder brother was hanged for plotting to assassinate the tsar in 1887, and Lenin became convinced that 'any correctly thinking and truly honest person must be a revolutionary'. His study of Karl Marx led to his belief in 'class war' as the engine of progress: the proletariat must destroy the bourgeoisie. The state would then seize all property and mature into an ideal communism in which all would receive according to their needs.

Exiled for his views, his insistence on a party dominated by an elite split the Russian Social Democrats at a 1903

congress in which the Leninists emerged as the 'Bolsheviki', or majority. The Bolsheviks played little part in the failed 1905 rising, and none in the February 1917 revolution that swept away the tsar: Lenin was in Zurich, complaining that there would be no revolution in his lifetime. He returned in April, but after a failed Bolshevik coup fled to Finland in July. A second coup in October brought Lenin to power as head of the new Soviet government. His success in the subsequent civil war was partly due to Leon Trotsky's Red Army.

At gunpoint Lenin dissolved Russia's first freely elected Constituent Assembly. He elevated the party to a godhead, and extended the righteous atrocity that was once the preserve of the religious to party politics. His prescription for nonbelievers was 'Despatch to the front, compulsory labour, confiscation, arrests, execution by shooting'. When he died in 1924, after a series of strokes, his embalmed body was displayed in a mausoleum in Moscow's Red Square, a holy relic of dictatorship.

Lenin inspects troops in Red Square in 1919 as civil war rages between the new Soviet regime and the anti-Bolshevik White Army.

Of 200 Turkish galleys which put to sea, only 40 escaped the crushing defeat at Lepanto, where more than 10000 Christian slaves were freed.

Lepanto, Battle of (1571) Major naval battle in the Gulf of Corinth, and the last fought by galleys manned by oarsmen. On October 7, the Ottoman fleet and ships of the Holy League – Venice, Spain, Genoa and the Papacy – clashed off the northern entrance to the Gulf. Led by Don JOHN OF AUSTRIA, the League administered the first significant naval defeat of the Turks by Christian forces. Although 117 Turkish galleys and thousands of men were captured, the victory did little to reduce Ottoman power in the long-term.

Lesotho Mountainous southern African state founded, as Basutoland, by King Moshoeshoe I in 1832. Although Boers from the Orange Free State had helped to defend Basutoland against Zulu invasions, in 1868 tensions developed between the former allies and Moshoeshoe asked for British protection.

Basutoland was administered from the Cape Colony until 1884, when it came under direct British control. In 1910 control passed to the British high commissioner in the newly formed Union of South Africa. The territory was renamed Lesotho in 1966, when it became independent under King Moshoeshoe II. Its prime minister, Chief Leabua Jonathan slowly eroded royal power, and in 1974 set up a national assembly to govern in conjunction with hereditary chiefs instead of the king.

Jonathan frequently clashed with South Africa, to which Lesotho's economy was closely linked, and his government was overthrown in 1986 by a South African backed military coup led by Colonel Elias Ramaena. The coup replaced the Jonathan regime with a military council acting in consultation with the king, but in 1990, when Moshoeshoe tried

Members of the Lewis and Clark expedition encounter a party of Plains Indians on an upper reach of the Missouri. The records of their journey helped to open up the American West.

to overrule him, Ramaena deposed him and replaced him with the crown prince Letsie III. The next year Ramaena was ousted in a bloodless coup and his successor, Major General Justin Lekhany, established a democratic constitution. Multiparty elections held in 1993 led to a political crisis and the following year Letsie suspended the government and constitution. Civil unrest led to negotiations between Letsie and the former government and he was forced to abdicate in favour of his father, who returned to the throne in 1995. In 1996 Moshoeshoe died in a road accident and Letsie resumed the throne.

Lesseps, Ferdinand, Vicomte de (1805-94) French civil engineer and architect of the SUEZ CANAL. Lesseps' 20 year dream of building a canal across the Suez isthmus became possible when his friend Sa'id Pasha was appointed khedive (viceroy) of Egypt in 1854. The engineer personally raised more than half the funds needed for the project and work began in 1860. Almost 10 years later the canal was completed. In 1881 Lesseps started work on ambitious plans for a Panama Canal, but work was abandoned in 1888 and Lesseps and his fellow directors were charged in France with breach of trust. Their five-year prison sentences were later reversed.

Levellers English radical republican group active in the 1640s, led by John LILBURNE, John Wildman and William Walwyn. The Levellers agitated for religious freedom, wider voting powers, freedom of expression and the abolition of the monarchy and aristocracy. Their early support was among London's poor, but by 1647 they had won over many of the rank and file of Oliver Cromwell's NEW MODEL ARMY. Representatives from each regiment, known as 'Agitators', met Cromwell and the army grandees but failed to resolve disagreements and the Levellers mutinied. When they mutinied again in 1649 Cromwell crushed the movement.

Lewis, John Llewellyn (1880-1969) US labour leader. Lewis worked as a miner and rose to become in 1920 president of the United Mine Workers of America, which he built into one of the most powerful labour unions. His bulldog appearance was matched by a tenacity that enabled him to negotiate major improvements in miners' wages and working conditions, but also led to many acrimonious strikes during the the Second World War. Though Lewis had always been a Republican, at the 1947 MCCARTHY hearings he refused to swear that he was not a communist. He retired in 1960 but remained as adviser to the union's welfare body.

Lewis, Sir Samuel (1843-1903) African jurist and statesman, who in 1896 became the first African to be knighted. The son of freed slaves, Lewis trained in England as a barrister before practising in Nigeria, the Gold Coast and Sierra Leone, where he was also chief justice. He was a member of its legislative council from 1882 to 1902.

Lewis and Clark expedition (1804-6) Transcontinental journey which blazed the way for the settlement of the American West. The 40-strong expedition – commissioned by President Thomas JEFFERSON and commanded by his secretary Meriwether Lewis (1774-1809) and William Clark (1770-1838) – included botanists and zoologists as well as experts in Indian lore. The men left St Louis in 1804, sailing up the Missouri to North Dakota, where they wintered, before crossing Montana in spring to reach the Rocky Mountains and Lemhi Pass in Idaho. In 1805 the expedition reached the Pacific after canoeing down the Clearwater, Snake and Columbia rivers. They spent a bleak winter on the coast before recrossing the Rockies the following year. The expedition split into two groups to widen its exploration before returning to St Louis. It brought back detailed maps as well as valuable scientific data. In spite of several clashes with hostile Native Americans only one member of the expedition died during the long journey.

> **DID YOU KNOW?**
>
> A Shoshone Indian named Sacagawea, 'Bird Woman', acted as interpreter to Lewis and Clark and guided them on their search for a route across the Rockies.

Lexington and Concord, Battle of (1775) Opening battle of the American War of Independence. When, on April 19, the English general Thomas Gage learnt that patriots were gathering arms and munitions at Concord, 20 miles (32 km) north of Boston, he sent about 700 men to confiscate them. Alerted to the move the settlers sent 77 of their MINUTEMEN militia to face the English force at Lexington. Who fired the first shot is uncertain, but in the ensuing skirmish eight minutemen were killed. The British did not fare so well upon reaching Concord, where a force of about 300 patriots drove them back. During the English retreat to Boston the red-coats came under constant musket fire and lost more than 250 men.

Liaqat Ali Khan (1895-1951) Pakistani politician, and prime minister from 1948 until his assassination in 1951. Liaqat was a Muslim leader in the United Provinces of British India when in 1933 he became the right-hand man of Pakistan's founder, Mohammed Ali JINNAH, in the Muslim League. On Jinnah's death in 1948, Liaqat Ali Khan became prime minister, distinguishing himself as the architect of Pakistan's domestic and foreign policy, and as the driving force in efforts to achieve reconciliation with India through the 1950 Delhi Pact.

Liberal Party British political party, which succeeded the Whig Party in the mid 19th century. Lord Palmerston's administration of 1855 is regarded as the first Liberal government, advocating FREE TRADE and civil and political liberty. William GLADSTONE's Liberal government of 1868 to 1874 instituted the secret ballot and reformed the army, the judicial system and education. The party split in 1886 over Irish Home Rule, when a breakaway group formed the Unionist Party. A lesser party split in 1900 over the Second Boer War allowed the Conservative Party to form a government from 1902 to 1905, but when this fell the Liberals returned to office at the end of 1905. An overwhelming victory the following year gave the Liberal Party a mandate to resume its social reforms. After the outbreak of the First World War it formed a coalition with the Conservatives and went on to form another five coalition governments between 1916 and 1945. In the postwar years the party's fortunes declined and it was supplanted by the Labour Party as the main opposition party. In 1988 the Liberals merged with the Social Democratic Party to form the Liberal Democrats.

Liberal Party (Australian) Political party formed in opposition to the Labor Party in 1909. Originally the Fusion Party, it adopted the name Liberal on winning the federal election in 1913. From 1916 to 1929 and 1932 to 1941 'Liberals' governed in coalitions under various names. The new Liberal Party was founded by Robert MENZIES in 1944, and from 1949 a Liberal-Country coalition governed Australia continuously for 23 years, and again from 1975 to 1983. The Labor Party was then in power for the following 13 years until the Liberals were re-elected.

Liberal Party (Canadian) Prominent political party formed in 1867 by a group of radical reformers seeking social change. Following the establishment of the Dominion of Canada in the same year, the Liberal Party developed into a powerful political force and governed, under Alexander Mackenzie, from 1873 to 1878. In the early 1900s the party sought Canadian autonomy and in 1931 Mackenzie KING, its longest serving leader, helped to negotiate the Statute of Westminster, recognising the right of British dominion parliaments to control their own domestic and foreign affairs. With its power base in Quebec, the party suffered from the demands of the Québécois secessionists and failed to win federal office from 1984 until 1993, when it was returned to power.

Liberia West African country, established in 1822 by the American Colonisation Society as a home for freed slaves from the USA. Liberia is the oldest independent republic in Africa. The name was adopted in 1824, and the country's first non-White governor, Joseph Jenkins Robert, declared independence in 1847. From the 1920s the Firestone Rubber Company developed Liberia's natural rubber resources, giving the country its first taste of prosperity. But when world rubber prices fell in the 1970s the economy suffered, and in 1980 a bloody revolution brought a military government under Master-Sergeant Samuel Doe to power. Doe's corrupt and autocratic 10 year rule as president and commander in chief ended in 1990 when he was killed by peacekeeping forces from the Economic Community of Western Africa. These had been sent to Liberia to intervene in the civil war between two rebel groups which had wracked the country for two years. An uneasy truce, negotiated between the forces of Charles Taylor and those of Prince Yormie Johnson was agreed later that year, but did not last long. Civil war continued even after 1992 when Taylor accepted Amos Sawyer as interim president and himself became vice-president. By 1996 the carnage had become so widespread that US forces evacuated some 150 aid workers and other foreign nationals.

libraries The practice of keeping records began as long ago as the 3rd millennium BC, when the Babylonians inscribed and stored information on clay tablets. From early in the 4th century BC collections of writings were kept in Greek temples, and by 340 BC great libraries, such as that of Aristotle, were widely known and visited by scholars. The library at ALEXANDRIA in Egypt, established at around the same time, came to be regarded as one of the Seven Wonders of the World. In Europe, the monasteries became the main repositories of knowledge until the advent of printing – and the Renaissance – encouraged the spread of literacy, and libraries expanded in response to the new desire for knowledge.

Libraries became accessible to a wider public in the 19th century, when public lending libraries were established – supported by philanthropists such as Andrew CARNEGIE (1835-1919) – to encourage self-improvement among the working classes. Better education, the accompanying explosion of literacy and increased leisure time created a demand for fiction, which today makes up two-thirds of the bookstock of most public libraries. The world's largest library is the United States Library of Congress in Washington DC. It contains around 110 million items, including more than 16 million books.

Children choose books in the New York Free Circulating Library in 1900. Though many of their parents were illiterate, the new generation was turning to books for entertainment and learning.

Libya North African country, most of which lies in the Sahara desert. Although its coast was colonised by Greek communities in the 7th century BC, and from the 1st century BC Libya became part of the Roman Empire, for much of its history the interior has been the sole province of Arab and Berber nomads. Even the Turks, who gained control of the coastal region in 1561, were unable to assert their rule over the desert tribesmen led by the Sanusi brotherhood. Italy met the same obstacle when it wrested control of the area from the Turks in a brief war from 1911 to 1912.

In the Second World War the Allies placed Libya under military government, and it gained independence as a monarchy under Emir Sayyid Idris al-Sanusi in 1951. When the emir was overthrown in a military coup 18 years later, Libya emerged as a radical Islamic socialist state under the leadership of Colonel QADDAFI. Using the wealth from its oil resources, Qaddafi turned Libya into a military state, and in 1978 set up the Revolutionary Committee Movement, which he used as a vehicle for international political intrigue. Qaddafi's links with terrorist groups alienated Libya from the international community and provoked armed confrontation with US forces in the Mediterranean. In April 1986 US aircraft struck Tripoli and Benghazi. By the early 1990s Qaddafi appeared to have adopted a more conciliatory stance, condemning the Iraqi occupation of Kuwait in 1990 and attempting to restore relations with Egypt and other Middle Eastern countries. But Libya again clashed with the USA during 1992 over its refusal to extradite terrorists, leading to the imposition of increasingly tough United Nations sanctions.

Lie, Trygve (1896-1968) Norwegian politician and first secretary-general of the United Nations, from 1946 to 1952. As a leading Labour politician, Lie was forced to flee the country in 1940 when it was occupied by Germany. In Britain he served as foreign minister in the exiled Norwegian government until 1945. A year later Lie became secretary-general of the United Nations, and in 1950 he authorised the use of UN forces in South Korea after its invasion by Soviet-backed troops from North Korea. This decision alienated the USSR, which ceased to recognise him as secretary-general. He was forced to resign in 1952 amid US accusations that he had employed communists and disloyal American citizens on the UN staff.

Liebig, Justus, Baron von (1803-73) German chemist and one of the fathers of modern agricultural chemistry. Liebig's

In his laboratory at Giessen, north of Frankfurt, the chemist Justus Liebig established the cycle in which plants obtained their nourishment, leading to the development of early artificial fertilisers.

DID YOU KNOW?

In 1801 the USA went to war with Libya in a dispute over the amount of tribute US ships should pay to the Bey of Tripoli to protect them from the fleets of pirates he controlled.

laboratory, which he had established at Giessen in 1825, gained international renown and drew students from all over Europe. Some of these – such as August Wilhelm von Hoffman whose researches helped to found the synthetic dye industry, and Sir Edward Frankland, who studied the structure of elements and their atoms – went on to win fame as chemists in their own right. Liebig came to be regarded as the ultimate authority on his subject. In the sphere of pure chemistry he established new techniques of organic synthesis and analysis, while his studies of the volatile oil benzaldehyde – carried out in conjunction with Friedrich Wöhler – led to its widespread use in perfumery and as a solvent. Liebig's research into plant physiology and nourishment progressed to experiments with artificial fertilisers. In later life he concentrated on the broader effects of chemistry on human life.

Liebknecht, Wilhelm (1826-1900) Co-founder of the German Social Democratic Party. Liebknecht's socialism led to his expulsion from Berlin in 1846, when he was 20. In 1849 he went to England and became a close associate of Karl Marx in the Communist League. Returning to Germany in 1863 he founded the League of German Workers' Clubs and in 1867 joined the Reichstag, the legislative body of the German Empire, as a leading opposition spokesman. A pacifist, Liebknecht's outspoken opposition to the FRANCO-PRUSSIAN WAR of 1870 led to two years' imprisonment. In 1874 he returned to the Reichstag, helping to form the German Social Democratic Labour Party a year later. Otto von Bismarck, the creator of a unified Germany, tried to suppress the party and forbade the publication of socialist literature. Despite this, the party continued to grow and in 1891 became the German Social Democratic Party (SPD).

Light Brigade, Charge of the see BALAKLAVA, BATTLE OF

Lilburne, John (c.1614-57) English republican agitator who became leader of the radical LEVELLERS. Lilburne, nicknamed 'Freeborn John', came from a well-to-do family but developed an early interest in workers' rights. He was imprisoned in 1638 for smuggling Puritan pamphlets into England, the first of many stays in prison for his outspoken opinions. A master propagandist, Lilburne was renowned for his attacks on the monarchy and Parliament until, in 1649, Oliver Cromwell suppressed the Leveller movement. Shortly before Lilburne died he became a Quaker.

Lin Biao (1908-71) Chinese military leader and a key figure in the communists' 22 year struggle for power. Graduating from the Whampoa military academy in 1926, Lin quickly established himself as one of the best commanders in Mao Ze-dong's RED ARMY. In 1945, after the Second World War, he became commander of the North-West People's Liberation Army, which conquered nationalist controlled Manchuria in 1948. Lin never lost a battle, and rose to become minister of defence in 1959. He popularised the idea of a 'people's war', with the army relying upon support from the peasants. After his close collaboration with Mao Ze-dong during the CULTURAL REVOLUTION it was widely assumed that he would succeed Mao as China's leader. Mystery surrounds his death, but he is thought to have died in an plane crash while trying to flee the country following involvement in an abortive coup attempt.

Lincoln, Abraham (1809-65) President of the USA from 1861 until his death. Born into a poor Kentucky frontier family, Lincoln taught himself law, earning the nickname 'Honest Abe' through his fairness and candour. After serving as a WHIG in the Illinois state legislature, he was elected to Congress for one term in 1846. He joined the newly formed REPUBLICAN PARTY in 1856, and in 1858 he ran for the senate against the Democratic incumbent, Stephen Douglas. Lincoln lost, but a series of debates with Douglas attracted national attention and established him as an advocate for a strong federal union and opponent of any extension of slavery.

In 1861 Lincoln was elected president as a Republican. This precipitated the secession of eleven Southern slave holding states, and led to the AMERICAN CIVIL WAR. In 1863, in the middle of the war, Lincoln proclaimed the slaves in rebel territory free. This measure freed only 200 000 people, but it marked the death knell of American slavery, and in 1865 Lincoln secured the Thirteenth Amendment to the Constitution freeing all slaves. Lincoln said the war was fought to determine 'that the government of the people, by the people, for the people, shall not perish from the earth'. After the South surrendered in April 1865 Lincoln argued for peaceful reconciliation 'with malice towards none, and charity towards all.' Lincoln was fatally wounded by a fanatical Confederate sympathiser, John Wilkes BOOTH, while attending *Our American Cousin* at Ford's Theater, Washington.

Lindbergh, Charles (1902-74) American aviator who made the first nonstop flight across the Atlantic. Lindbergh joined the US Army Air Corps reserve in 1925 and a year later became an airmail pilot. On May 21, 1927, he landed in Paris after a 33 hour solo flight from New York in the monoplane *Spirit of St Louis*. He became an overnight hero.

In 1932, after the kidnapping and murder of his two-year-old son, Lindbergh moved to England temporarily. In the years leading up to the Second World War he warned of German air superiority and called for US neutrality. But once the USA entered the war Lindbergh flew on 50 combat missions.

Lister, Joseph (1827-1912) English founder of antiseptic surgery and pioneer of preventative medicine. After Louis PASTEUR's researches established that microorganisms caused disease and infection, Lister sought a way of destroying the bacteria in the environment in which he carried out surgery. His antiseptic of diluted carbolic acid was first used in an operation on August 12, 1865, and his reports showed that over the next four years the mortality rate of patients undergoing surgery fell from 45 per cent to 15 per cent. In spite of success and honours, Lister remained unassuming, believing his work was directed by God.

Lithuania Country on the east coast of the Baltic, whose original Lith inhabitants settled along the Nemen river as early as 1500 BC. By the 13th century AD, threatened by invading Teutonic Knights and the Livonian Brothers of the Sword, the Liths merged with other neighbours to form a vast grand duchy, incorporating Lithuania, parts of the Ukraine and Belorussia. This became one of the major states of medieval Europe and at its peak stretched to the Black Sea. In 1386 the marriage of the Lithuanian grand duke Jagello and the 12-year-old Polish queen Jadwiga forged a loose alliance with Poland. The two countries united in 1569. This commonwealth, formed by the Union of Lublin, was absorbed into Russia in 1795. In the 1880s strong nationalist and cultural movements developed in opposition to Russia. German troops occupied the country in 1915

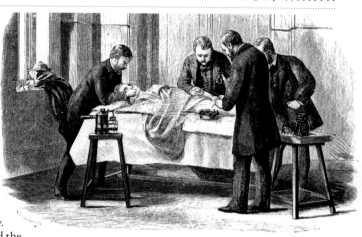

Lincoln towers above General George McClellan, third from left, the commander whom he dismissed after five months.

and three years later a German king was installed, only to be deposed in November the same year. Russian and Lithuanian communists then fought Polish and Lithuanian nationalists until 1920, when Russia signed a peace treaty giving Lithuania independence. Germany occupied the country again at the start of the Second World War. In 1940 the Red Army wrested it from Germany, and Lithuania once more became a republic of the Soviet Union. A unilateral declaration of independence in March 1990 was recognised by Russia in September 1991. During 1992 Lithuania negotiated a treaty of friendship with Poland, and adopted a new constitution.

Little Rock Capital of Arkansas, USA. In 1957 Little Rock achieved notoriety when the state governor, Orval Faubus, called out the National Guard to prevent nine Black children from entering local segregated schools. A test of power between federal and state governments ensued, compelling President Eisenhower to send federal troops to secure the entry of the children to the schools. By the end of the next decade segregation in American schools was abolished.

Litvinov, Maxim (1876-1951) Soviet revolutionary politician and advocate of world disarmament. A Bolshevik from 1903, Litvinov was the Soviet commissar for foreign affairs when he attended the League of Nations' disarmament conference and in 1928 signed the Kellogg-Briand Pact. Under this the USA, France and other powers renounced war and agreed to settle all future disputes by peaceful means. Litvinov's cooperation led to US recognition of the USSR and establishment of diplomatic relations between the two in 1933. Litvinov fell out of favour with the Soviet leader Joseph Stalin and was dismissed in 1939 when he opposed the Soviet pact with Germany and instead urged action against Germany, Italy and Japan. After the German invasion of the Soviet Union in 1941, Litvinov was reinstated and was appointed ambassador to the USA later that year.

Liverpool, Robert, 2nd Earl of (1770-1828) British statesman and Tory prime minister from 1812 to 1827. Elected to Parliament in 1790 he became prime minister reluctantly after the assassination of Spencer PERCEVAL. Liverpool hoped to find someone he considered more suitable for the position, but he went on to serve for 15 years. Although a FREE TRADER and opposed to tariffs, he bowed to Cabinet pressure and agreed to the introduction of the CORN LAWS. He also initiated the tough 'Gagging Acts' after the PETERLOO MASSACRE in 1819. Liverpool was strongly opposed to slavery and in 1815 at the Congress of Vienna urged its abolition. He resigned after a stroke.

livery company One of the companies of traders and craftsmen in the City of London which replaced the medieval craft GUILDS. Liverymen, so called because of their distinctive 'livery', or dress, of fur-trimmed gowns, were indirectly responsible for electing the mayor as well as the aldermen. Many livery companies, including Goldsmiths, Cutlers and Carpenters, formed regulatory bodies for their individual trades, and many of the original companies still function.

Livingstone, David (1813-73) British missionary and explorer who did more than any other individual to change Western attitudes towards Africa. Sent in 1841 to Bechuanaland – present-day BOTSWANA – by the London Missionary Society, he made it his goal to 'open up the interior, or perish'. For the next 15 years he travelled across Africa, preaching Christianity and mapping the territory through which he travelled. By 1842 he had already gone farther north into the continent than any other European. In 1855 he reported the existence of the Victoria Falls, and his last journey in search of the sources of the Nile took him deeper into the interior.

Livingstone's disappearance in 1865 caused widespread concern until Henry STANLEY, sent to Africa by the *New York Herald*, tracked down the ailing explorer at Ujiji near Lake Tanganyika six years later, greeting him with the famous words: 'Doctor Livingstone, I presume?' Though he survived attacks by lions and local people, Livingstone finally succumbed to fever, his guides finding his body kneeling by his bed as if in prayer in his camp at Chitambo, in what is today Zambia.

Livy (Titus Livius) (59 BC-AD 17) Roman historian whose account of the city from 753 BC to 9 BC became a classic in his own lifetime. Livy began to write his *History of Rome* around 29 BC, adopting a style unique among his fellow historians in that it was free of political views. His work broadened to include contemporary observation after he arrived in Rome from Patavium (Padua) to

Accounts of the missionary-explorer David Livingstone's adventurous African treks kindled worldwide interest in the 'Dark Continent'.

tutor the future emperor Claudius. Livy's personal touch enlivened his writings, and his individual way of relating events influenced historians up to the 17th century – from Tacitus to Lord Clarendon. Of the 142 books of his *History of Rome* 35 survive in full, the rest in summary and fragments. They provide a fascinating record of Rome from the foundation to the early days of the empire.

Lloyd George, David (1863-1945) Liberal statesman who dominated British politics in the later stages of the First World War. He began his career in 1890 as Liberal Member of Parliament for Caernarfon Boroughs, a seat he retained for 55 years. He quickly established himself as a powerful and eloquent orator, earning the nickname 'the Welsh Wizard'. As chancellor of the exchequer in Herbert ASQUITH's government he introduced health and employment insurance and caused a constitutional crisis in 1909 when his 'People's Budget', intended to pay for welfare measures, was rejected by the House of Lords. This led to the Parliament Act in 1911 to limit the Lords' powers. During the First World War growing discontent with Asquith as a war leader forced him to step down in 1916, and Lloyd George assumed the premiership, creating a new coalition with the Conservatives. He masterminded the establishment of a unified Allied command which went on to secure victory in the war, and he was a leading figure in the VERSAILLES PEACE SETTLEMENT. But his handling of Irish demands for independence and scandals surrounding Liberal campaign funds cost him the support of many Conservatives in the coalition. In 1922 a group of Conservatives led by Stanley Baldwin forced an end to the coalition and Lloyd George resigned as prime minister. He continued to lead a weakened Liberal Party until 1931. He completed his *War Memoirs* in 1936, and in 1940 he declined Winston Churchill's invitation to join the War Cabinet.

Lloyd's of London One of the world's most important insurance markets. It dates from 1688, when Edward Lloyd opened a coffee house where merchants, seafarers, bankers and underwriters drank coffee and conducted their business. The underwriters accepted insurance on ships for the payment of a premium, and in 1774 they formed an association and moved to the Royal Exchange; the company has since moved to its own building. In 1871 the Lloyd's Act gave the company self-regulating powers, with responsibility for the control and supervision of its members and

David Lloyd George's fiery oratory held Welsh voters in his spell for more than 50 years; but allegations that he 'sold' peerages and honours to swell Liberal coffers cost him the premiership.

of the market itself. Although marine insurance remains Lloyd's principal business, it also underwrites other branches of insurance. In the late 1980s and early 1990s a series of disasters in various parts of the world wiped out the profits of many of its member syndicates and bankrupted hundreds of 'names' who had invested in them.

Lloyd's marine links are symbolised by the bell from the wreck of HMS *Lutine* in 1799. Until the 1970s it was rung when a ship was lost.

Llywelyn ap Gruffydd (c.1225-1282) The only Welsh ruler officially recognised by the English as Prince of Wales. By signing a treaty recognising Henry III of England's overlordship, Llywelyn, the grandson of Llywelyn the Great, was authorised to receive homage from other Welsh princes. In 1277 Wales was invaded by Henry's son EDWARD I, who was determined to reduce Llywelyn's authority and reinforce English sovereignty. Llywelyn struggled unsuccessfully to drive out the English and in 1282 was killed by Edward's forces near Builth, after which Wales came permanently under English rule.

Llywelyn the Great (1173-1240) Prince of Gwynedd, north Wales. Llywelyn drove the English out of the north of the country in 1212 to become the most powerful ruler in medieval Wales. His rule was recognised by King JOHN of England in Magna Carta, and his authority over other Welsh leaders was confirmed by the Treaty of Worcester in 1218. In 1205 he married King John's illegitimate daughter and, assisted by barons opposed to the king, extended his influence over south Wales. Before he died he passed the government of the country to his son David.

Locarno, Treaties of A series of international agreements made on December 1, 1925, aimed at maintaining peace in Europe. The treaties sought to achieve this by guaranteeing the common boundaries of Germany, Belgium and France as specified in the VERSAILLES PEACE SETTLEMENT of 1919. The German foreign minister Gustav STRESEMANN refused to accept Germany's borders with Poland and Czechoslovakia as permanent, but agreed his challenge would be peaceful. However, in 1936, claiming that the Franco-Soviet Alliance of the previous year had negated the Locarno pact, Adolf Hitler sent German troops first into the demilitarised Rhineland and then in 1939 into Czechoslovakia to annex SUDETENLAND before invading Poland – so precipitating the Second World War.

Locke, John (1632-1704) English philosopher whose ideas still influence Western thinking. Locke rebelled against academic tradition while a student at Oxford, becoming involved in experimental medicine and science with such thinkers as Robert BOYLE and John Wilkins. He was appointed personal physician to the future Earl of SHAFTESBURY, and later became his scientific and political adviser. When Shaftesbury gained the post of chancellor, Locke became secretary to the council of trade and plantations. But when Shaftesbury fell from favour his friendship with the earl led to Locke being suspected as a Whig supporter of liberty. Locke fled to Holland, and only returned to England after James II was deposed in 1688.

His *Essay Concerning Human Understanding* (1690) expounded the view that human experience was the only source of knowledge. Locke helped to shape contemporary ideas on liberal democracy, spending his later years writing such philosophical works as *Letters on Toleration*, which called for sympathetic treatment of dissenters other than atheists and Roman Catholics, and *Two Treatises on Government*, published anonymously in 1690,

> 66 **It is one thing to show a man that he is in error, and another to put him in possession of the truth.** 99
>
> *John Locke*
> Essay Concerning Human Understanding *(1690)*

which explained the Whig doctrine and refuted the absolutism of Thomas HOBBES. Locke's ideas on a mixed form of constitution with a balance of power greatly influenced the authors of the American constitution.

Lodge, Henry Cabot (1850-1924) US politician. A conservative Republican, he led the successful fight against US membership of the LEAGUE OF NATIONS. He bitterly opposed Woodrow WILSON's peace policy, arguing that US sovereignty would be threatened and that linking America's interests with international politics would be fatal. Lodge became one of the leading exponents of US isolationism.

Lollard A derisory term for a follower of the 14th-century English reforming theologian John WYCLIFFE. The name was derived from the Dutch word *lollaerd*, meaning a mumbler of prayers. The Lollards opposed such Roman Catholic practices as clerical celibacy, indulgences and pilgrimages. Although the movement was initiated by Oxford-trained clerks, it soon attracted a broad range of educated people, including some lower clergy. It was driven underground when HENRY IV came to the throne and instigated a wave of repression against heresy. In 1414 an uprising led by Sir John Oldcastle failed and Lollardism lost support, though it was a precursor to the 16th-century REFORMATION.

Lombardy Region of central northern Italy named after the Lombards, a Germanic people from the Danube region who arrived there in the 6th century. In the late 8th century it became part of Charlemagne's empire. By the mid 12th century the cities of the area, including Milan, Pavia and Brescia, had become economically and politically powerful and formed the Lombard League to resist interference by Holy Roman emperors, including FREDERICK I. Later the region was ruled by Spain, France and Austria before becoming part of Italy in the 19th century. Today it is a densely populated, heavily industrialised region which also contains some of Italy's most fertile farming areas.

London Corresponding Society An organisation founded in London in 1792 by the shoe maker Thomas Hardy to agitate for universal male suffrage. The first working-class political movement in Britain, the society circulated literature and initiated debates on the reform of Parliament. It established contacts with similar bodies in other towns, such as the Sheffield Society of Constitutional Information. The political writer Thomas PAINE encouraged the growth of the society and a national convention was suggested; but Britain was at war with Revolutionary France, and in 1794 the government, alarmed by the society's activities, imprisoned its committee, but they were acquitted. The society was suppressed in 1799.

London dockers' strike Dockers strike in 1889 at the Port of London, demanding better pay and conditions of employment. The dockers' action succeeded in securing them the 'dockers' tanner' – a pay rate of sixpence an hour, instead of the five pence they

London's striking dockers in 1889 were backed by parading coalmen, and by Cardinal Manning, later honoured in a union banner.

had been paid previously – and a reduction in working hours. The incident strengthened the effectiveness of other strikes throughout industry and acted as a spur to the growth of the trade union movement in Britain.

Londonderry City on the River Foyle in Northern Ireland. Originally known as Derry, it grew from a monastery founded by St Columba in 546. Though relatively unaffected by Viking and Norman invaders it was frequently attacked by Norsemen. Before the 17th century the city had little contact with England. But in 1613 it was granted to the city of London for colonisation, took the name of Londonderry and became staunchly Protestant. It withstood a 105 day siege by the deposed Catholic king James II of England in the Irish rising of 1688 to 1689, becoming renowned for its defenders' cry of 'No surrender!'

Londonderry was at the centre of many disturbances in Ulster in recent times. In 1969 violent demonstrations against British rule led to British troops being stationed there to keep the peace for the first time in the history of the Province. During a banned civil rights march on January 30, 1972, 13 people were shot dead by British troops in clashes which became known as 'Bloody Sunday'.

Long, Huey (1893-1935) US politician and governor of Louisiana. Long rose through various elected public offices in Louisiana to become state governor from 1928 to 1931. Nicknamed 'The Kingfish', he gained popular support through an expensive programme of road building, new state-owned hospitals and improved schooling in remote rural areas, financing these measures and an extravagant personal life style through increased taxation of big business. When Long was elected to the US Senate in 1930, he declined to take his seat until he had ensured that his choice of a successor as state governor had gained office. Through his successor, Long extended his

grip on Louisiana. Although he initially supported President F.D. Roosevelt's NEW DEAL he soon became one of the president's most outspoken critics. Long's decision to run against Roosevelt for the presidential nomination almost split the Democratic Party, but he was assassinated before he could run for the nomination.

Long March Epic trek made by retreating Chinese communists between 1934 and 1935, from which MAO ZE-DONG emerged as the undisputed leader of the Communist Party. Weakened by repeated nationalist GUOMINDANG attacks, 100 000 troops from the Jiangxi SOVIET in south-eastern China evacuated their rural base. In January 1935 Mao took over the leadership of the march as it headed towards the Soviet base in Yan'an in the north-western province of Shensi. In nine months the troops crossed 24 rivers and 18 mountain ranges, travelling 6000 miles (9600 km), while fighting off further attacks

Peasant soldiers trudge through some of China's harshest mountains on their nine-month Long March to a communist 'utopia'.

by the Guomindang. Their bravery inspired many young men to join the communist cause. In October Mao finally reached Yan'an. Only 10 000 of the original 100 000 survived – the others had died in the fighting or from starvation and disease. Safe from Nationalist attacks Mao began to establish a powerful base from which the communists eventually won the struggle to control mainland China.

Long Parliament A session of the English Parliament which lasted 20 years. It was called by CHARLES I in 1640 after the Bishops' Wars had bankrupted him. Historians called it the Long Parliament to distinguish it from the earlier Short Parliament of April to May 1640. Led by John PYM, it attempted to curb many of the royal powers that had aroused opposition following Charles's accession. Tension between king and Parliament – which could only be dissolved by its own consent – was exacerbated when the king's attempt to arrest five of its members failed, and the crisis developed into the ENGLISH CIVIL WAR. After Charles was defeated the army exercised political power, with Colonel Thomas Pride expelling all but 60 members of the Long Parliament – PRIDE'S PURGE – in 1648. The remnant, or Rump Parliament, arranged the trial and execution of Charles, and the establishment of the COMMONWEALTH in 1649. It was forcibly ejected by Oliver Cromwell in 1653, only to be reinstated in 1659 after the failure of Cromwell's son Richard as Lord Protector. The Long Parliament dissolved itself in March 1660, having brought back the members forced out in Pride's Purge and paved the way for the succeeding Convention Parliament which restored the monarchy.

Lord Lieutenant English representative of the Crown, originally commissioned to muster, administer and command the militia of a specified district in times of emergency. Henry VIII was the first to appoint them, and during Edward VI's reign there were attempts to establish them on a permanent basis. From 1585 most shires had their own lieutenant and deputy lieutenant, and by the end of the 16th century they assumed additional roles, including the appointment of magistrates. Though the military responsibilities of lord lieutenants have fallen away, they still represent the Crown in a mainly ceremonial role.

Lords, House of Upper chamber of the British PARLIAMENT whose members include senior bishops of the Church of England, hereditary and life peers and peeresses, and Law Lords. The Lords grew from the body of nobles who advised Anglo-Saxon kings and became the 'Great Councils' of the 13th and

14th centuries, where the king met barons and bishops to discuss policy. By the 15th century a council of prelates and hereditary peers met regularly. For centuries the House of Lords had similar powers to the lower House of Commons, proposing its own legislative measures, but its influence diminished after the 1832 REFORM Bill, which changed parliamentary representation. The Lords' powers were further reduced by the Parliament Act of 1911, which provided for all finance bills to become law, with or without the Lords' approval, one month after being sent to the upper house. Today its main function is to review legislation sent to it by the House of Commons and to suggest amendments. Proposals to abolish the legislative functions of hereditary peers have been mooted from time to time. The Lords remains the supreme appeal court.

Lorenzo the Magnificent see MEDICI, LORENZO DE

Louis I (1326-82) King of Hungary from 1342 to 1382, and of Poland from 1370 to 1382. Known as Louis the Great, he succeeded his father, Charles I, in Hungary. For much of his reign he attempted to strengthen the Hungarian state in wars against Venice and Naples. Louis achieved two significant victories over Venice and won control of virtually all Venice's Dalmatian towns. He became king of Poland after the death of Casimir III, who had proclaimed Louis his successor. When Louis died his daughter Mary succeeded him in Hungary while his other daughter, Jadwiga, became queen of Poland.

Louis I (778-840) King of the Franks, and German emperor from 813 to 840. He was known as 'the Pious' for his deep religious belief and Christian charity. A son of CHARLEMAGNE, Louis was determined to keep intact the huge empire his father had created by dividing it among his sons Lothair, Pepin I and Louis the German. But they protested when he tried to establish a kingdom for Charles, his son by another marriage. Louis spent the rest of his reign fighting off claims to the throne by all four sons. These conflicts continued after his death, leaving the empire in disarray and jeopardising the unity of the Frankish kingdom.

Louis IX, St (1214-70) King of France from 1226 and 1270, and leader of the Seventh Crusade. The son of Louis VIII, his effective administration and personal charm made him the most popular of the Capetian monarchs. Louis's most notable achievement was the securing of a lasting peace with the English Plantagenets, who maintained territorial claims in France. He used his prestige in Western Christendom to negotiate successfully with Henry III of England, and on May 28, 1258, Henry recognised Louis's rule over Aquitaine. In return he was allowed to keep some neighbouring territories. Louis was profoundly religious and after his recovery from a severe form of malaria raised the Seventh Crusade against Egypt in 1248. He was captured by Sultan Turanshah and only released upon payment of a ransom in 1250. Obsessed by the Holy Land, he mounted another Crusade to Tunis where he died. He was canonised by Pope Boniface VIII in 1297.

Louis XI (1423-83) King of France from 1461 until his death. He continued the work of his father, CHARLES VII, of strengthening and unifying France. A fat and ugly child, Louis was raised in seclusion where he developed a furtive and creeping character that earned him the nickname 'the universal spider'. In 1445 he was banished from the kingdom after he was suspected of plotting to kill one of his father's advisers. He became a guest at the court of Philip the Good of Burgundy in the Netherlands, where he waited patiently for his father's death.

Louis returned to take the throne in 1461 and one of his first actions was to dismiss his father's ministers. He also attempted to curb the powers of the nobility, who retaliated by forming a coalition against him which waged the 'War of Common Weal'. Louis's greatest enemy was CHARLES THE BOLD of Burgundy, to whom he had to cede much territory after the Battle of Montlhéry in 1465. In 1475 he subsidised the Swiss confederates and René II of Lorraine in their war against Charles the Bold, and after Charles was defeated by them in 1477 Louis set about breaking up the Burgundian state. He achieved full sovereignty over the duchy in 1482 and continued to acquire other territories, including Picardy and Boulannaise. By the time of his death only the duchy of Brittany remained independent.

Louis XIV (1638-1715) King of France from 1643 to 1715. Known as the 'Sun King' for his might and splendour, he took France to the zenith of its power. Louis was five when he succeeded his father, Louis XIII, in 1643. His mother ANNE OF AUSTRIA became regent and Jules MAZARIN chief minister. Louis married the Infanta Maria Theresa in 1660 and a year later, after Mazarin's death, he took over the government and embarked on a long period of personal rule. He believed that as king he had a divine right to exercise absolute power over his subjects, and tried to extend his control to every aspect of national life, including court behaviour, public works, the military and industry. He saw no necessity to call the States-General – a body to advise the king on matters of policy – and largely ignored the *Parlement*, choosing instead to rely on a close circle of expert ministers and councils. He also created a larger and more efficient army and defeated various European alliances in wars between 1667 and 1697. The success of the army led to an expansion of the French empire.

A 13th-century manuscript (far left) and a stained glass window from St Chapelle (left) both show St Louis, revered in his own time as a mild, just, gentle and holy king.

Louis XIV enjoyed flamboyance and dressing up. Here the Sun King poses as the Greek sun god Apollo, surrounded by his family. Queen Maria Theresa, right, appears as Diana, the moon goddess.

But the NINE YEARS' WAR and the War of the SPANISH SUCCESSION saw France hardpressed as Europe united to curb Louis' aggression. After 1700 France suffered a series of crushing defeats and in 1713 the Treaty of Utrecht ended France's supremacy in Europe. Louis left a heritage of political, economic and religious problems which were to grow during the reigns of his heirs and would ultimately destroy the monarchy.

Louis' reign became known as the *grand siècle* (great age) due to his support and development of literature and arts based on the court, which he moved out of Paris to a magnificent new palace at VERSAILLES. He also initiated a programme of improvements which included redesigning towns, altering the landscape, authorising the building of monuments and establishing new royal residences, though his extravagance increasingly incurred the disapproval of his subjects.

Louis XV (1710-74) King of France from 1715 until his death. Though he was a greatgrandson of Louis XIV, he did not inherit his predecessor's strong will and powers of command. He decided to rule without a chief minister, but lacked the confidence to give firm direction to his secretaries of state in their attempts to initiate social reform. Louis' faltering foreign policy did little to strengthen France's power in wars against Prussia and Britain, and, under the provisions of the Treaty of PARIS in 1763, at the conclusion of the SEVEN YEARS' WAR, most of France's overseas territories were lost to the British. Though married at the age of 15 to Marie

Leszczynska, daughter of the King of POLAND, Louis kept a string of mistresses, including Madame de POMPADOUR and Madame DU BARRY, on whom he lavished enormous amounts of money. The extravagance of the court and the high cost of war absorbed all France's resources, and by the time Louis XVI succeeded to the throne the country was insolvent and the government in disarray.

Louis XVI (1754-93) Last king of France before the FRENCH REVOLUTION. Lacking any authority or strength of character, Louis was dominated by his Austrian wife, MARIE ANTOINETTE. He was sympathetic towards his subjects, but his failure to consolidate the economic and social reforms proposed by his ministers Anne-Robert-Jacques Turgot and Jacques NECKER caused widespread hostility. France's involvement in the AMERICAN REVOLUTION had drained the exchequer, and in 1787 Louis attempted to remedy this by gaining the approval of the largely aristocratic Assembly of Notables to tax the nobility. They refused, and in 1789 he recalled the STATES-GENERAL, a body of political advisers representing the clergy and commoners as well as the nobility, which had not met for 175 years. This precipitated the revolution.

Louis' dismissal of the popular Necker helped to provoke the storming of the BASTILLE on July 14, 1789. Louis and his family tried to flee Paris in June 1791, but they were caught at Varennes and returned to the Tuileries palace. He hoped for foreign intervention to restore him to power, but in August 1792 the Parisians overran the Tuileries

palace and took the royal family prisoner. In September 1793 France's first republic was declared and the monarchy was abolished. Louis was tried for treason and executed in January, and Marie Antoinette followed him to the guillotine in October. Their eight-year-old son, Louis XVII, became titular king of France but died in prison two years later.

Louis XVIII (1755-1824) King of France from 1795 to 1824. The brother of Louis XVI, during the French Revolution he fled to England to promote the royalist cause. His exile ended in 1814 with the fall of NAPOLEON and he returned to the throne of France with the help of Charles Maurice de TALLEYRAND, a shrewd diplomat. Louis issued a constitutional charter which promised to recognise the citizens' rights and religious tolerance established by the revolution, and retained many of Napoleon's reforms to the law, administration, Church and education.

Louis' liberal policies changed when in 1820 his nephew the Duc de Berry was assassinated by an antiroyalist intent on destroying the Bourbon line. He deposed his moderate ministers and replaced them with ultraroyalists led by the duc's father – Louis' brother, the Comte d'Artois. Civil liberties were subsequently curbed and Louis' earlier attempts to heal the wounds of the revolution were set aside. After Louis' death the comte assumed the throne as Charles X.

Louisiana US state in the Mississippi valley. It was discovered by the French explorer Robert de LA SALLE in 1682, who named it after his king, Louis XIV. French settlers began arriving there in 1699. Its largest town, New Orleans, was founded in 1718 as part of a chain of French forts and trading posts surrounding British settlements in North America. France sold Louisiana to the USA in 1803 for $11.25 million – the so-called Louisiana Purchase. In 1812 it became the 18th state of the union. The state's economy boomed in the early 19th century as huge sugar and cotton plantations were developed in the fertile lowlands. The large Black population – mainly descendants of former slaves – were exploited to work on the plantations after the American Civil War, and were often victimised by the White supremacist group the KU KLUX KLAN. A state constitution, introduced in 1898, denied Blacks the right to vote and enforced a policy of racial segregation which remained in force until the 1960s.

Louis Philippe (1773-1850) King of the French between 1830 and 1848. Louis Philippe was a descendant of Philippe I, Duc d'Orléans, brother of Louis XIV. During the French Revolution he joined a group of progressive nobles who supported the Revolutionary government. In 1809 Louis

Louisiana's flat-bottomed steamboats plied the Mississippi and helped to turn the river into a major commercial waterway and New Orleans into the USA's second largest port.

Philippe went to Sicily, where he married Marie-Amélie of Naples. On the restoration of LOUIS XVIII to the French throne he returned to France and recovered the Orléans estates. After the JULY REVOLUTION in 1830, which forced Charles X to abdicate, the legislature elected Louis Philippe King of the French – the 'citizen king'. His accession to the throne was a victory for the new class of upper bourgeoisie – his chief supporters – over the aristocracy. During his reign Louis strengthened France's position in Europe and improved Anglo-French relations. He instituted reforms to combat political corruption and judicial malpractices, appeasing both the liberals and extremists by appointing moderate ministers. However, his refusal to enfranchise the lower bourgeoisie caused frequent rebellions and several attempts on his life. He responded with repressive measures which alienated his former supporters, and he was compelled to abdicate in February 1848. He retired quietly to Surrey, England, where he used the name 'Mr Smith'.

Low Countries see BELGIUM and NETHERLANDS

Loyola, St Ignatius (1491-1556) Spanish ecclesiastical reformer who founded the JESUITS, or Society of Jesus. Loyola began his career as a soldier attached to the court of Ferdinand II of Aragon, but developed a deep interest in religion when he underwent a spiritual transformation during his convalescence from a leg wound. In 1522 the formerly vainglorious soldier abandoned the comforts of his home to make a pilgrimage to north-eastern Spain where he began a life of poverty and penance, spending seven hours a day in prayer. In 1523 he went on a pilgrimage to Jerusalem, and from 1528 to 1535 he attended the University of Paris, where with six others, including St FRANCIS XAVIER, he took vows of poverty, chastity and obedience to the pope. Their 'Society of Jesus' was recognised as an order of the Church by Pope Paul III in 1540.

Luce, Henry (1898-1967) American media magnate whose publishing empire included *Time, Life* and *Fortune* magazines. In 1923 Luce and Briton Hadden launched *Time*, a weekly news magazine to educate what Luce considered to be a poorly informed American public and to provide international news coverage, which he felt was neglected by American newspapers. The style of the magazine was lively and its stories reflected Luce's personal opinions – he believed that objective reporting was impossible. After Hadden's death in 1929, Luce became *Time*'s editor-in-chief. He went on to found the business magazine *Fortune* in 1930 and the pictorial news magazine *Life* in 1936. *Life*, which pioneered the creative combination of photography and text to tell a story, became one of the most popular magazines ever published.

Lucknow, Siege of Key event during the Indian Mutiny of 1857-8 when, facing a force of mutineers that outnumbered it by almost seven to one, the British garrison at Lucknow held out for over five months. Lucknow had been the capital of the Kingdom of Oudh, and the mutiny was partly the result of the British ending the kingdom's existence in 1856. Some 3000 British and Indian troops, including women and children, were besieged in the residency. They suffered heavy casualties as they held out against more than 20 000 Indian mutineers. Lucknow was relieved in November 1857 by troops led by General Sir Colin

Relief comes at last to Lucknow garrison, under siege since May 1857. On November 17 Sir James Havelock and Sir James Outram greet Sir Colin Campbell, called 'Sir Crawling Camel' for his slow advance. Havelock died of dysentery within days, and Lucknow was not retaken until March 1858.

Campbell, but the city was not recaptured until the following March. Lucknow is now the capital of the state of Uttar Pradesh.

Luddite Member of an early 19th-century group of British craftsmen who destroyed textile machinery which they believed was displacing them. The movement began in the knitting factories of Nottinghamshire in 1811 and quickly spread to other textile industries in Yorkshire, Lancashire, Derbyshire and Leicestershire. The men involved – claiming to be acting under the leadership of a certain, probably mythical, 'Ned Ludd' or 'King Ludd' – stormed the cotton and woollen mills to attack the power looms. The government's response was to make machine-breaking an offence punishable by death, and though there were further sporadic outbreaks in 1816, the movement died out.

Ludendorff, Erich (1865-1937) Prussian general and chief architect of Germany's military strategy in the later stages of the First World War. Ludendorff had planned Germany's successful strategy in the Battle of Tannenberg which in 1914 prevented a Russian invasion. In 1916 he assumed overall military control alongside the iron-willed General Paul von Hindenburg. They proved a formidable pairing and directed the war effort until the final offensive failed in spring 1918. Ludendorff fled to Sweden after his dismissal by the German emperor. In 1919 he returned, sitting in the Reichstag as a pro-Nazi National Socialist between 1924 and 1928. As a propagandist of 'total war', Ludendorff argued that politics should further the conduct of war, with peace merely an interval between conflicts. He wrote extensively, blaming the Roman Catholic Church, the Jews and Freemasons for contributing to Germany's downfall.

Lumumba, Patrice (1925-61) Congolese nationalist and politician, and first prime minister of the Democratic Republic of the Congo – present-day Zaire. In 1958 he founded the Belgian Congo's first national political party – the influential Mouvement National Congolais (MNC). In January 1960 at the Brussels conference on the Congo, Lumumba emerged as a leading negotiator, and when the Congo gained independence in June, he was appointed prime minister and minister of defence. Later that year the province of Katanga declared its independence, and Lumumba called unsuccessfully for United Nations intervention to help to suppress the Katangese revolt. President Joseph Kasavubu, his rival for power, dismissed him in September 1960 and soon afterwards he was arrested. He escaped, but was recaptured and killed. His death caused riots in many parts of Africa where he had been regarded as a hero.

Lusitania British transatlantic liner torpedoed and sunk by a German submarine in May, 1915. The unarmed liner, returning from New York, was attacked without warning off the Irish coast, after the Germans had discovered that it was carrying 173 tonnes of munitions. In all 1198 people drowned, including 124 Americans. The incident created intense indignation in the USA, which until then had accepted President Woodrow Wilson's policy of neutrality. The sinking was cited in 1917 as one of the reasons that led the USA to join the war on the side of the Allies.

Luther, Martin see feature, opposite page

Luthuli, Albert (1898-1967) South African political leader and president of the AFRICAN NATIONAL CONGRESS (ANC) from 1952 to 1960. As a Zulu tribal chief, Luthuli served on the Native Representative Council – an elected body which advised the South African government on matters affecting the country's Black population – until it was abolished in 1946. He became president of the ANC soon after the Afrikaner Nationalist Party came to power and began to impose a policy of apartheid. Luthuli, who subscribed to Mohandas GANDHI's pacifist views, became an international symbol of nonviolent opposition to oppression of the Blacks. His political rallies attracted White support, and there was a multiracial response to his appeal for a 'stay at home' strike in 1957. The South African government constantly harassed him, banishing him to his village in 1959 and outlawing the ANC a year later. In 1961 Luthuli became the first African to receive the Nobel peace prize.

Luxembourg Small country in Europe. Occupied by the Romans, and then by the FRANKS in the 5th century, Luxembourg became independent in 963 under Siegfried, Count of Ardennes. In 1060 Conrad, one of his descendants, became the first Count of Luxembourg. The duchy of Luxembourg was created in 1354, after which it passed between the House of Burgundy, the Habsburgs and Spain. It was created a grand duchy and awarded to William I of the Netherlands by the Congress of Vienna in 1815. In 1867 the grand duchy was made an independent state and its perpetual neutrality was guaranteed by the major European powers, though Germany twice violated the guarantee, occupying the country in both World Wars. After liberation by the Allies in 1944, Luxembourg abandoned its neutral status and became a founder member of the United Nations (UN) and the North Atlantic Treaty Organisation (NATO). It joined the European Economic Community (EEC) in 1957, and is host to the European Court of Justice and the European Investment Bank. In the 1970s and 1980s Luxembourg became an important financial centre.

Luxemburg, Rosa (1871-1919) Polish revolutionary, a founder of the Polish Social Democratic Party and leader of the German Social Democratic Party (SPD). Gaining German citizenship by her marriage to Gustav

After the *Lusitania*'s fate caused huge outrage at 'Germany's murderous piracy', U-boat commanders had secret orders not to sink passenger ships without warning.

Luther defies the pope

In 1517, the German friar Martin Luther nailed 95 theses to the door of Wittenberg Castle church. These points for debate about the Roman Catholic Church led to the upheaval of the Reformation.

When he spoke out, nothing could have been further from the Augustinian friar Martin Luther's mind than to divide the Church between Roman Catholics and Protestants. Born in 1483 of peasant stock and conservative outlook, he was not part of the movement among humanist Renaissance scholars to liberalise the mind of Europe.

In 1505, at the age of 22, he had abandoned his study of law at Erfurt University to enter a monastery. He was transferred to Wittenberg in central Germany in 1511. Two years later, while preparing lectures, he was struck by a passage in Paul's Epistle to the Romans: 'the just shall live by faith alone'. The more he considered this, the more determined he became to restore purity of faith to religious life. The Church's emphasis on 'good works' as a path to salvation – especially the debt-ridden papacy's sale of 'indulgences' in return for a reduction in the time a purchaser's soul would spend in purgatory – seemed mere worldly vanity. 'Justification by faith alone' was a revolutionary slogan, for it made the hierarchy of the clergy and the teachings of Church Fathers superfluous.

THE CHALLENGE TO ROME

Luther meant only to start a debate but, borne on a tide of nationalistic fervour and piety, he found himself leading a fundamental challenge to Rome. 'The song', he said, 'was pitched in too high a key for my voice.' In June 1519 he was drawn into debate at Leipzig by the Dominican friar John Eck, who got him to admit that scripture was the ultimate religious authority. The destiny of individuals, armed with the Bible, was in their own hands: 'the priesthood of all believers'.

Luther's position was becoming more radical. In 1520 he challenged the doctrine of transubstantiation – that at the Eucharist the wine and bread are turned into the blood and body of Christ – and was branded a heretic by Pope Leo X. In 1521 he was excommunicated. Meanwhile he published three influential pamphlets: *The Address to the Christian Nobility of the German Nation*, calling upon secular rulers to take up the Protestant cause; *The Babylonian Captivity of the Church*; and *The Freedom of a Christian Man*. The Emperor Charles V, alarmed at Luther's support, invited him to explain his views at a diet, or parliament, called at Worms in 1522. Asked to recant, Luther replied: 'I cannot and will not recant anything, for it is neither safe nor honest to act against one's conscience. God help me.'

After then Luther's decisive influence on the Reformation waned. In 1525 he married a former nun, Katharina von Bora, and the couple had six children. He lived the rest of his life quietly spreading the new faith, translating the Bible into the German language and composing hymns. He died at Eisleben, the Saxon village of his birth, in 1546, after several years of infirmity.

In protest at the sale of indulgences, Luther posts his theses, provoking a rift between Christians that would convulse Europe.

Rosa Luxemburg and Karl Liebknecht agitated for revolution and proletarian government, and in 1918 founded Germany's Communist Party.

Lübeck, she settled in Berlin in 1898. A persuasive writer and orator, Luxemburg argued the cause of revolution in the SPD. In 1905 she took part in the Polish revolution against Russian rule, advocating mass action to achieve international socialism. She became active in the second International, and collaborated with Karl Liebknecht to establish the SPARTAKIST MOVEMENT, which in 1918 fiercely opposed Germany's role in the First World War. During the Spartakist rebellion against military suppression of radical uprisings in 1919, both she and Liebknecht were shot after being captured by right-wing soldiers in Berlin.

Lydia Territory in western Asia Minor. Believed to have made the world's first coins, of a gold and silver alloy, in the 7th century BC, the Lydians grew wealthy on trade. Lydia's position astride the two main routes linking the Aegean coast to the interior increased its prosperity. The kingdom reached its pinnacle of power under CROESUS, who was deposed by the Persians around 540 BC. In 133 BC it became part of Roman Asia, attaining provincial status under Diocletian.

Lysander (d. 395 BC) Admiral and statesman of the Greek city of Sparta. His victory at Aegospotami in 405 BC secured triumph for

Sparta over Athens in the Peloponnesian War, which had begun in 431. With the financial support of CYRUS, son of the king of Persia, he expanded and improved the Peloponnesian fleet, and in 404 sealed Athens's fate by blockading the HELLESPONT, which cut off corn supplies and starved Athens into surrender. Lysander was killed while leading a campaign against the Boetians.

Maastricht, Treaty of (1992) Agreement by the leaders of the European Community member states – then 12 in number – to progress towards greater European unity. The treaty, which was to be ratified at national level, envisaged political union, with shared citizenship for the populations of all member states; eventual monetary union under a European Central Bank; and common policies on foreign affairs and security. Under the treaty, the Western European Union would provide a joint military defence for the Community, there would be greater cooperation on domestic and environmental matters, and the European Parliament would be strengthened. The treaty also laid down rules for 'subsidiarity', demarcating powers and responsibilities between EC institutions and individual member states. Britain and Denmark were quick to distance themselves from aspects of the Maastricht agreement, which continues to cause political friction both at national and inter-European levels.

MacArthur, Douglas (1880-1964) US army chief of staff from 1930 to 1935 who was recalled to service by President Franklin Roosevelt when the USA entered the Second World War in 1941 to build up a defence force in the Philippines. Soon after his appointment, Japanese troops invaded the islands, forcing General MacArthur to evacuate his operational headquarters to Australia, vowing 'I shall return'. He commanded the victorious Allied counterattack in the Papuan campaign in New Guinea from July 1942 to January 1943, and from this base his troops advanced on the Philippines, which were recaptured in the first months of 1945. As commander of all US army forces in the Pacific, MacArthur received the Japanese surrender on board the USS *Missouri* on September 2, 1945, and later commanded the Allied occupation forces in Japan, where he introduced reforms and helped to draft the new Japanese constitution. As head of UN forces in the KOREAN WAR MacArthur led his troops into North Korea in October 1950, but was forced to retreat by an invading Chinese army. He resumed the offensive early in 1951, but was dismissed in

Macau, the oldest permanent European settlement in the Far East, was developed as a trading base by the Portuguese. Its name derives from the Ma Kwok temple built in the 14th century.

April by President Harry S TRUMAN who feared that MacArthur might lead the USA into a nuclear war.

Macau Small Portuguese territory (also spelt Macao) on the coast of mainland China, across the Pearl River estuary (now Zhu Jiang) from Hong Kong. Macau was established by Portuguese traders and missionaries in 1557. The settlement had a flourishing trade with Japan until the late 17th century. In the 19th century Macau lost its trading pre-eminence to Hong Kong and became dependent on gambling, tourism and transit trade, but in recent years it has developed manufacturing industries. It is due to be returned to China in 1999.

Macaulay, Thomas, 1st Baron (1800-59) British historian, essayist and politician. During a long parliamentary career which began in 1830, Macaulay was a prominent advocate of reform, religious toleration and the abolition of slavery. From 1834 to 1838, as a member of the supreme council in India, he played a significant part in drafting the penal code which was to become the foundation of India's criminal law. Returning to England, Macaulay wrote his partially completed *History of England*, published in 1849 and 1855. Lauded as a major work of art, it stressed the importance of the 'Glorious Revolution' of 1688 in forming British institutions and liberal values. Macaulay's view of British history, known as the 'Whig interpretation' was strongly influential for nearly a century.

Macbeth (c.1005-57) King of the Scots from 1040. His attainment of the throne and death 17 years later form the basis of William Shakespeare's tragedy, *Macbeth*. A grandson of Malcolm II, the historical Macbeth challenged his cousin DUNCAN I for the throne, defeating and killing him in battle near Elgin in 1040. In 1050 Macbeth made a pilgrimage to Rome. He was killed by Duncan's son at the battle of Lumphanan, in Aberdeenshire.

Macdonald, Flora (1722-90) Scottish Jacobite who helped Prince Charles Edward Stuart, 'Bonnie Prince Charlie', to escape his pursuers after the collapse of the FORTY-FIVE REBELLION. The Young Pretender, disguised as Flora's maidservant, accompanied her to the safety of the isle of Skye, and in June 1746 to France. She was arrested, but released in 1747.

MacDonald, James Ramsay (1866-1937) British statesman and first Labour prime minister, briefly in 1924 and again from 1929 to 1931. Elected as a Labour Member of Parliament in 1906, five years later MacDonald became leader of the small but growing parliamentary Labour Party. His pacifist attitude at the outbreak of the First World War cost him popular support and he resigned, but he

For helping Bonnie Prince Charlie to escape, Flora Macdonald was imprisoned in the Tower of London until pardoned in 1747.

returned to lead the opposition from 1922 and became prime minister two years later, the first time Labour had formed a government. But this lasted only nine months and it was not until 1931 that MacDonald could form a second Labour government. When nine ministers quit the Cabinet over proposals to reduce unemployment benefits, he continued as prime minister of the coalition National government until 1935. MacDonald was closely involved in the international disarmament schemes of the early 1930s when, like many others, he did not grasp the Nazi threat to world peace. Failing health led to his leaving office in 1935.

Macedonian wars

Series of armed conflicts between Rome and Macedonia in the 3rd and 2nd centuries BC. In the first of three wars – from 211 to 205 – Philip V of Macedonia clashed with Rome and her allies Aetolia and Pergamum. But the alliance was weakened by Rome's military commitment on a second front – the second PUNIC WAR – so that Philip could force Aetolia to accept terms and then negotiate a similarly favourable settlement with Rome. Three years after the resumption of hostilities in 200, Philip was decisively defeated. His son Perseus came to the throne in 179, but Rome was wary of the Macedonian king's attempts to woo the Greeks and declared a third war, which it eventually won with a crushing victory at Pydna in 168. Nearly 20 years later, in 149, Andriscus, who claimed to be Perseus' son, attempted to regain the throne but was defeated in 148 and Macedonia became a Roman province.

Machel, Samora

(1933-86) Mozambique freedom fighter who led his country's struggle for independence and became its first president. After training as a guerrilla in Algeria, from 1966 Machel commanded the Mozambique Liberation Front, FRELIMO (Frente de Libertaçao de Moçambique). For almost ten years he led the war against the Portuguese, gaining independence in 1975. As president of the Peoples' Republic of Mozambique until his death in a plane crash, Machel nationalised multinational companies and allowed his country to be used as a base for forces fighting for independence in Rhodesia and South Africa. Although a Marxist, Machel's politics became increasingly pragmatic; he accepted Portuguese aid and developed contacts with South Africa.

Machiavelli, Niccolò

(1469-1527) Italian statesman and political theorist whose name has come to be a byword for deception and manipulation. One of the outstanding figures of the RENAISSANCE, by 1498 Machiavelli had been appointed secretary and second chancellor to the republic of Florence. On diplomatic missions between 1499 and 1508 he dealt with some of the most powerful political figures of the age, but after the MEDICIS regained control of Florence in 1512 Machiavelli was forced to quit public life. In retirement he wrote extensively on the art of war and on political philosophy. In *The Prince* (1513), he offered advice intended to keep a ruler in power. Modern interpretations of the term 'Machiavellian' tend to ignore the subtleties of his observations on the relationship between ethics and politics. In *Discourses on the First Ten Books of Titus Livius,* written between 1513 and 1517, Machiavelli advocated a republic with a mixed constitution modelled on that of ancient Rome, but he also stressed the need for an incorruptible and strongly moral political culture very different from the climate of the Italy of his day. Though he again found favour with the Medicis and was appointed chief historian of Florence in 1520, when the Medici family lost control of the city seven years later Machiavelli failed to obtain an official position in the new republic and died within a month of its establishment.

Machiavelli was not only a theorist: he helped to create Florence's militia and in 1509 was put in command of it against Pisa.

> **DID YOU KNOW?**
>
> Arguing that mercenaries had contributed to Italy's instability, in 1506 Machiavelli replaced those in Florence with Europe's first citizens' militia.

Mackenzie, Alexander

(1822-92) Canadian statesman who became the country's first Liberal prime minister. As leader of the Liberal opposition in the first House of Commons when the Dominion of Canada was formed in 1867, Mackenzie was a dominant figure in his country's early nationhood. During his term as premier – from 1873 to 1878 – voting by ballot was introduced, the Canadian supreme court was formed and the territorial government of the North-west Territories was reorganised.

MacMahon, Marie, Comte de

(1808-93) French statesman who despite his Irish descent became president of France from 1873 to 1879. Although MacMahon fought successfully in the Crimea and at the battles of Magenta and Solferino in 1859, as a general in the Franco-Prussian War he was defeated at Worth in 1870 and, with NAPOLEON III, capitulated at SEDAN. A year later MacMahon commanded the army that crushed the Paris Commune; but though he had little sympathy with the Third Republic, he was opposed to a royalist restoration and agreed to succeed Louis Thiers when he was ousted as president by right-wing deputies. MacMahon considered the Chamber of Deputies to be too republican and dissolved it in 1877. But the electorate returned an even more republican chamber – so effectively establishing the principle that governments were accountable to the chamber rather than to the president.

Macmillan, Harold

(1894-1987) British statesman, and Conservative prime minister from 1957 to 1963. A critic of APPEASEMENT throughout the 1930s, in 1940 Macmillan joined Winston Churchill's coalition government. When the Conservatives returned to power in 1951 Macmillan, as minister for housing and local government, was responsible for Britain's largest-ever local authority building programme. In 1954 he became minister of defence and in Anthony Eden's government he served as foreign secretary and, later, chancellor of the exchequer.

After the SUEZ crisis Macmillan succeeded Eden as prime minister, going on to win the general election of 1959 with a comfortable majority. A year later, addressing a joint sitting of South Africa's Houses of Parliament, he spoke of a 'wind of change' blowing through Africa, in a speech that was seen as an encouragement to African nationalism and a criticism of APARTHEID. Overseas, Macmillan enjoyed friendly relations with President John F. Kennedy, supporting him throughout the CUBA crisis and reaching an agreement that the USA should provide nuclear missiles for British submarines.

During Macmillan's premiership – in which Britain tasted an affluence which inspired Macmillan to claim that 'our people have never had it so good' – legislation was passed to limit entry of Commonwealth citizens into the UK. His government was weakened by President Charles de Gaulle's veto of Britain's application to join the EUROPEAN ECONOMIC COMMUNITY in 1963, and by scandal involving his secretary of state for war, John Profumo, who was forced to resign. Nevertheless in July 1963 Macmillan's government succeeded in negotiating a nuclear-test ban treaty between the USA, the Soviet Union and Britain. Macmillan became Earl of Stockton in 1984.

Macquarie, Lachlan (1762-1824) Aust-

ralian governor, the last to have virtually autocratic power. Appointed governor of New South Wales after the RUM REBELLION of 1808, Macquarie saw the colony as a convict settlement where prisoners should be treated fairly and humanely, and free settlers had little place. But Australia was developing beyond its role as a penal colony, and conflict arose between ex-convicts who wanted to make a new life there and those who wanted to deny them civil rights. Both sides clashed with Macquarie, who returned to Britain in 1821.

Madagascar Island off the south-east

African coast, once a pirate stronghold and today an independent republic. The island's people are of Indo-Melanesian and Malay

descent, but among some 18 ethnic groups there are also Bantu, Arab, Indian and Chinese minorities which together reflect Madagascar's chequered history.

Arab traders probably visited Madagascar before the 10th century, but not until 1500 when a Portuguese sea captain, Diego Dias, discovered the island – already named by Marco Polo from hearsay knowledge – was it added to seamen's charts. In the following centuries Dutch, English and Portuguese vessels called there frequently, while trading centres set up by the French were often used as lucrative pirate bases.

Concessions were granted to a French trading company in 1860 and 30 years later the island became a French protectorate, but resistance to France continued until 1895. Madagascar became an Overseas Territory of the French Republic in 1945 and a republic in 1958. It gained independence as the Malagasy Republic in 1960; it changed its name back to Madagascar in 1975.

Social and economic problems led to recurrent unrest and frequent changes of government. Although one-party rule ended in 1990, there were antigovernment riots in April 1991. Six months later the revolutionary council and national assembly were both dissolved, pending agreement on a new constitution. In 1992 a new multiparty constitution was adopted, and in elections held the following year Albert Zafy, leader of the opposition coalition Committee of Living Forces, became president.

Madeira Island in the Atlantic Ocean,

belonging to Portugal. Uninhabited when it was discovered by Portuguese colonists in the 14th century, Madeira was cultivated for sugar and vines. Later Dutch, Spanish and Italian immigrants, as well as Jews and Moors expelled from Spain in the 15th century and slaves from Africa, settled on the island.

Madison, James (1751-1836) Fourth presi-

dent of the USA, from 1809 to 1817, and one of the most influential figures in the Constitutional Convention of 1787, which four years later proposed the Bill of Rights. Madison helped to draft the Virginia State Constitution, served in the Continental Congress from 1780 to 1783 as a Republican and ensured the passage of President Thomas JEFFERSON's Bill, which guaranteed religious freedom in the USA. As Jefferson's secretary of state from 1801 to 1809, Madison was involved in disputes with France and Britain over the USA's rights to neutrality and, on becoming president, took his country to war with Britain. In 1816 he introduced the first protective tariff in US history.

Mafia International secret society with

Sicilian roots which has become a major force in modern crime. Today's Mafia dates from 1806 when, during the Napoleonic Wars and for almost a decade afterwards, Britain encouraged the breaking up of the feudal estates of the Sicilian aristocracy.

Former members of the aristocrats' private armies often formed bands of brigands who, although operating outside the law, developed their own system of rule and justice. By

The Mafia mobster Dutch Schultz slumps over a restaurant table in Newark, New Jersey, after being gunned down in 1935 by rival gangsters.

1860 they controlled many police and government officials in Sicily, and efforts by the new government of King Victor Emanuel II to crush them proved unsuccessful.

Two decades later, when many Sicilians emigrated to the USA, the Mafia became established in New York and Chicago, and membership increased in the 1920s when leaders escaped from attempts by the Italian fascist government to prosecute them. The Mafia – organised in 'families' and with a

> **What is organised crime? If the rich didn't try to use the poor for their selfish interest, organised crime could never exist. What have I done that's worse than all those fixers on Wall Street?**
>
> *Meyer Lansky, gangster*

command structure similar to that of a feudal army – was active during the US PROHIBITION era. After the Second World War Mafia activities became international and increasingly focused on drug trafficking. In the USA and Italy, where businessmen and politicians have been linked to the Mafia, periodic high-profile trials have failed to erase its influence.

Magellan, Ferdinand (c.1480-1521) Portu-

guese explorer who was killed during the first round-the-world voyage. Posted by the Portuguese crown to the East Indies, between 1509 and 1512 Magellan explored the Spice Islands, today's Moluccas. Five years later he offered his services to Spain to sail to the same islands by a westward route. Magellan left Spain with five ships in 1519, sailing down the coast of South America and through the strait north of Tierra del Fuego that now bears his name. Although Magellan named the peaceful ocean into which he emerged the 'Pacific', it was more than three fraught months before he reached the Philippines. Here Magellan was killed in a skirmish with the islanders, but under the command of his lieutenant Juan del Cano the *Victoria* rounded the Cape of Good Hope and reached Spain to become the first vessel to sail round the world.

Magenta, Battle of (June 4, 1859) Clash in

Lombardy in which French and Sardinian forces routed their Austrian opponents. Earlier in 1859, at a meeting between the French emperor Napoleon III and the Piedmontese statesman Count Camillo CAVOUR, France offered military support for an expanded kingdom of Piedmont. The Battle of Magenta was fought soon after the outbreak of war and the Franco-Sardinian victory opened the way to the occupation of Lombardy and Milan, part of the RISORGIMENTO. Three weeks later the allies were again victorious at the Battle of SOLFERINO.

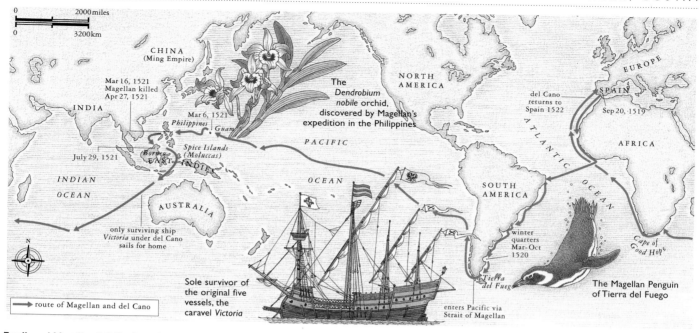

Ferdinand Magellan left Spain to lead an expedition which sailed around the world. In 1520 after a rough passage, he sailed into a calm ocean that he named the Pacific. He was killed in the Philippines, and after mutiny, desertion, starvation and scurvy only the *Victoria* returned home in 1522.

Maginot Line Fortifications along France's eastern frontier, stretching from Switzerland to Luxembourg. Begun in 1929, the construction of the Maginot Line stemmed from the French military theory that defence would be paramount in any future war in Europe. It also reduced the need for a large army. Belgian objections, based on the fear that their country would be left exposed, prevented the defences from being extended along the Franco-Belgian frontier to the coast. This meant that the Maginot Line could be outflanked – as it was in the spring of 1940 by invading German armies. However, the defences did prove impregnable to frontal assault.

Magna Carta (June 15, 1215) List of rights and privileges – also known as the Great Charter of Liberties – sealed by King JOHN of England under pressure from his barons at Runnymede, west of London. Magna Carta set certain bounds to the king's powers, but though its 63 clauses covered a wide spectrum of subjects it mainly represented landowners' interests. The charter dealt with matters ranging from the right to trial of all freemen and justice for everyone, to weights and measures, fish weirs and foreign merchants.

Magna Carta also restricted the powers of sheriffs, preserved the liberties and privileges of boroughs and confirmed the Crown's agreement not to interfere with the rights of the Church, nor to levy SCUTAGE or any special tax without the consent of the king's council.

The charter was safeguarded by its final clauses, which empowered a group of 25 barons to take up arms against the king if he failed to keep its conditions. Three days after

sealing Magna Carta, John sought – and later obtained – papal condemnation of it, leading four months later to the first BARONS' WAR. Although the charter was largely ignored by medieval and Tudor monarchs, it has come to be regarded as an important influence on principles of English constitutional liberty, and as a model for the constitutions of newly independent countries across the world.

Magyars Hungarian people whose ancestors came from the steppes of Eastern Europe, and who by AD 830 had settled near the River Don in Russia. In the 9th century, led by Prince Arpád, the Magyars entered what became Hungary and from there attacked the German territories to the west and north. They were defeated and repulsed in 955 by the Holy Roman Emperor Otto I at the Battle of Lechfeld, near Augsburg. Their first king, Stephen (about 975 to 1038), who unified the Magyars and converted many of them to Christianity, was crowned with regalia sent by Pope Sylvester II in 1000. Stephen was canonised in 1083.

Mahabharata Epic Sanskrit poem about the Bharata dynasty which contains the *Bhagavad-Gita,* one of the most sacred texts of HINDUISM. Written between the 2nd century BC and the 2nd century AD, the *Bhagavad-Gita* – which is a central part of the *Mahabharata* – takes the form of a dialogue between the Pandava prince Arjuna and his charioteer Krishna, who is an incarnation of

the god Vishnu. It relates in 18 books the victory of the Pandava dynasty over the Kaurava usurpers of their throne.

In the *Bhagavad-Gita,* Krishna discusses the nature of God and the paths which can be taken to reach eternal union with Brahman, emphasising the need to follow the dharma, the ultimate code and pattern of all things.

Mahdi Spiritual and temporal saviour who, according to Islamic belief, is a divine teacher sent to prepare humanity for the end of earthly time. Best known of the many who have claimed to be the Mahdi is Muhammad Ahmad bin Abdallah (1844-85). A Nubian by birth, he claimed descent from Muhammad. He proclaimed himself Mahdi in 1881, gathered followers in Sudan, and eluded or defeated all Egyptian government armies. By 1884 he had gained control of all Sudan except Khartoum, which he besieged. The English general Charles GORDON was recalled from retirement to relieve the Egyptian garrisons in rebel-held territory. Gordon was killed in Khartoum on January 26, 1885. Five months later the Mahdi also died, probably of typhus, but the Mahdist struggle continued until the rebel forces were defeated in 1898 by General Horatio KITCHENER at the Battle of Karari, near Omdurman.

> **DID YOU KNOW?**
>
> *When Kitchener asked to exhibit the Mahdi's skull at the Royal College of Surgeons, Queen Victoria objected on the grounds that the Mahdi was 'a man of a certain importance'.*

Mahler, Gustav (1860-1911) Austrian-Jewish composer of songs and symphonies including *Das Lied von der Erde (The Song of the*

Mahler was composing his *Songs on the Death of Children* – the *Kindertotenlieder* – when this etching was completed in 1902 by Emil Orlik.

Earth). Born in Bohemia, Mahler studied in Vienna and for 12 years was conductor and artistic director of the Vienna Court Opera before resigning to spend his time composing. He created a vast repertoire of songs and wrote nine major symphonies. He was working on his tenth symphony when he died.

Maimonides, Moses (1135-1204) Jewish physician and philosopher whose writings influenced Judaic and medieval Christian scholars. Born in Córdoba in Spain, Maimonides – sometimes referred to as Rambam from the initials of his Hebrew name Rabbi Mosheh ben Maymun – was driven out by the persecution of the Muslim conquest, and in 1165 he moved to Egypt. There he wrote the *Mishnah Torah*, a huge codification of rabbinical law and ritual, and a *Guide for the Perplexed,* which attempts to reconcile faith and reason.

Maine North-easternmost state of the USA, occupying an area where Sebastian Cabot landed in 1496. Settled by Sir Ferdinando Gorges and his heirs in the early 17th century, Maine was infiltrated by colonists from neighbouring Massachusetts who in 1677 purchased it. From 1687 to 1699 Abnaki Native Americans and their French allies devastated the territory, but its fortunes improved after the American War of Independence, and in 1820 it became an independent state.

Major, John (1943-) British Conservative politician, and prime minister since 1990. The son of a circus performer, Major left school at 16 and, after cutting his political teeth as a Conservative member of Lambeth Borough

Council in London from 1968 to 1971, was elected to Parliament in 1979. As a protégé of Margaret THATCHER, Major held several Cabinet posts, including that of foreign secretary. In October 1990, as chancellor of the exchequer, he took Britain into the European Monetary System (EMS). In November Thatcher was ousted in a party leadership struggle and Major was chosen as the next prime minister. In the following general election of April 1992 Major emerged victorious. But his government soon faced an unfavourable foreign exchange rate and a currency crisis which forced Britain in September to withdraw from a system for regulating the relations of currencies, the Exchange Rate Mechanism (ERM).

There was also growing internal criticism of his continued acceptance of the MAASTRICHT TREATY among those Conservatives who were against closer European integration. This led to conflict within the Conservative Party and the temporary withdrawal of the whip – party recognition – from a group of 11 Tory rebels in 1995. Major pre-empted a possible challenge to his position by resigning as party leader and forcing a leadership election, which he won.

Prolonged negotiations with the Irish government and covert talks with SINN FÉIN finally brought a cease-fire and an uneasy peace to Northern Ireland in 1995. The following year the IRA ended its cease-fire and, after losses in by-elections and defections of Conservative MPs to other parties, Major's parliamentary majority was reduced to one.

Makarios III (1913-77) Greek Cypriot archbishop, president of CYPRUS from 1960 to 1976. As primate and archbishop of the Greek Orthodox Church in Cyprus for 27 years from 1950, Makarios reorganised the movement for *enosis*, the union of Cyprus with Greece. Deported to the Seychelles by the British in 1956 for his alleged support of Colonel George Grivas' EOKA terrorist campaign against the British and Turks, Makarios was allowed to return in 1959, and in 1960 was elected president of an independent Cyprus.

A coup by Greek officers in 1974 forced his brief exile to London, but he was reinstated in 1975 and held office until his death.

Daniel Malan stands among White political supporters in 1948 in Pretoria, South Africa. His racist campaign won him the year's election.

Malacca Malayan port which commands the strait connecting the Indian and Pacific oceans. Founded in 1402 by a refugee Hindu prince who converted to Islam and took the title Iskandar Shah, Malacca, or Melaka, soon became a Chinese vassal state. Thus secured against Thai and Javanese attacks, by 1500 it had become an entrepôt for trade. Spices from the Moluccas, Chinese silk, camphor from Borneo, Burmese teak, Indian cloths and woollens from Europe all passed through the port, and its merchants helped to spread Islam through south-east Asia.

In 1511 Malacca was captured by the Portuguese governor of the East Indies, Alfonso de Albuquerque, as part of his campaign to monopolise trade throughout Asia; and in spite of attacks from local and European rivals, Portugal continued to control the port for more than a century. In 1641 it was captured by the Dutch, but as the Dutch East India Company's main base was in Java, Malacca's commercial importance soon diminished and it became a fortress city protecting the strait.

Malan, Daniel (1874-1959) South African prime minister (1948-54) whose regime initiated laws which came to be known as APARTHEID. In 1905 he became a minister of the Dutch Reformed Church, preaching White supremacy as the Afrikaners' divine destiny. When General James HERTZOG split with Prime Minister Louis BOTHA to found the National Party in 1914, Malan became an early recruit. In 1915 he was appointed first editor of the party's mouthpiece, *Die Burger*,

and in 1918 he was elected to parliament. In 1924 Hertzog came to power, and Malan was appointed minister of the interior. In 1933, when his leader formed a coalition with General Jan SMUTS, Malan led a breakaway group of Nationalists seeking independence from Britain. From 1948 to 1954 he was prime minister, until ill health forced him to retire. Malan's administration enacted the early racial separation laws which were to be tightened and harshened by his successors J.G. Strijdom and Hendrik VERWOERD.

Malawi Central African country, formerly known as Nyasaland. A major source of 'black ivory', or slaves, for Arab traders and raiders from Zanzibar, Malawi's resultant desolation was described by David LIVINGSTONE, who reached it in 1859. Spurred by his account, Scottish missionaries settled there in 1875, and for more than a decade governed parts of the country. In 1889 the Shire Highlands were proclaimed a British protectorate, and two years later became British Central Africa. Renamed Nyasaland in 1907, the country gained independence in 1964 as Malawi.

In 1966 Dr Hastings BANDA, the country's first prime minister, declared Malawi a republic. Banda became president and in 1971 he was proclaimed president for life. Although a façade of democracy was maintained and regular elections to the National Assembly were held, all candidates had to be members of the Malawi Congress Party and Banda adopted almost dictatorial powers. He enjoyed economic aid from the White regimes of South Africa and Rhodesia, but faced growing internal opposition to the one-party system. By 1992, when the opposition leader Chakufwa Chilana was arrested, political protest exploded in riots and all nonhumanitarian aid from the West was suspended. Although the one-party system remained in place for the general election of June 1992, a referendum in October led to the adoption of a multiparty political system. In 1993 a new constitution was approved and elections in 1994 were won by the United Democratic Front, with Bakili Muluzi becoming the new president.

Malaya Country in south-east Asia which since 1963 has been part of the Federation of Malaysia. Over a period of several thousand years Malaya's original Negrito inhabitants were gradually replaced by settlers from Yunnan, in China. By AD 400 north-western Malaya had come under Indian influence, and later the powerful Sumatran empire of Srivijaya, the Javanese Hindu state of Majapahit and Siam all exerted some control over Malaya. In 1402 the port of MALACCA was founded and Islam introduced. The strong Dutch influence in Malaya after the capture of Malacca in 1641 diminished when Britain occupied Penang in 1786 and in 1819 leased

the island of SINGAPORE. Following the Dutch withdrawal in 1824, Penang, Malacca and Singapore were combined in 1826 as the STRAITS SETTLEMENTS and were ruled from India by Britain.

In all the states other than Johore, by 1888 Britain had established a system whereby local sultans had to accept the advice of British

officials on everything except religion and customs. Linked as the Federated Malay States in 1896, their economies progressed with the introduction of rubber and Western tin-mining technology. But the arrival of Chinese and Tamil labourers for the plantations and mines turned Malaya into a multiracial society and created some resentment among the indigenous Malays.

During the Second World War, after securing a free passage through Thailand, Japanese troops invaded northern Malaya in December 1941 and marched south to attack Singapore. As British, Indian and Australian troops retreated, a small guerrilla resistance force, the Malayan People's Anti-Japanese Army (MPAJA), was organised to conduct sabotage behind the Japanese lines.

The Malayan Communist Party was an influential part of the MPAJA, and after the defeat of Japan they tried briefly – and failed – to take power before the return of the British. Britain then experimented briefly with a centralised Union of Malaya, and in 1948 set up a Federation of Malaya.

But soon afterwards the 'Malayan Emergency' began. Building on resentment of Malay dominance in the federation the mainly Chinese communist guerrillas initiated a series of attacks on planters and other estate owners, which between 1950 and 1953 flared up into a full-scale guerrilla war.

Led by Chin Peng and supported by their own supply network, the guerrillas of the Malayan Races Liberation Army caused severe disruption in the early years of the campaign. But the insurgents were gradually contained, and the loyalty to the British of Malays and Indians, combined with Britain's skilful use of local leaders in the administration, allowed a peaceful transition to independence. In 1957

the Malay Peninsula became the self-governing Malayan Federation. By then the insurrection was all but beaten, although the emergency did not end officially until 1960.

In 1963 Tungku Abdul RAHMAN became the first prime minister of the Federation of Malaysia – which included Singapore, Sarawak and Sabah – and held office until 1970. Singapore was forced to secede in 1965 because of fears that its largely Chinese population would challenge Malay political dominance. BRUNEI refused to join the federation, and Indonesia waged an intermittent guerrilla war against it. The Indonesian president Achmad SUKARNO sent forces to Malaysia's Borneo territories, which were defeated with Commonwealth military assistance.

In 1969, inequalities between the politically dominant Malays and economically dominant Chinese resulted in riots in the capital Kuala Lumpur, and parliamentary government was suspended. A major restructuring of political and social institutions followed to ensure Malay predominance, the New Economic Policy being launched to increase the Malay (*bumiputra*) stake in the economy. In 1971 elections were won inconclusively by the largest political party, the United Malays National Organisation, which ruled in a coalition – the National Front – with the Malaysian Chinese Association and some ten other parties.

In 1994 Malaysia's relationship with Britain was strained when it was revealed that a British Government loan of £234 million to build the Pergau dam was linked with local agreements to purchase British armaments.

Malcolm III (c.1031-93) King of the Scots known as Canmore, who defeated MACBETH and reigned from 1058 until his death. After his father Duncan I was murdered by Macbeth, Malcolm was brought up in England at the court of Edward the Confessor. With English assistance, he returned to Scotland in 1054 to defeat Macbeth and claim the throne. In 1069 he married the future Saint MARGARET. Malcolm's support for Saxon exiles from the Normans led the English king William I to invade Scotland in 1072. Malcolm accepted William as king, but when William died in 1087 Malcolm attacked England. He was killed at Alnwick, Northumberland, while invading England for the fifth time in 32 years.

Malcolm X (1925-65) US Black leader who rejected the cooperation with White liberals that was a mark of the CIVIL RIGHTS movement. Born Malcolm Little, he was a spokesman for the BLACK MUSLIM movement during the 1950s, until he was suspended in 1963 by

DID YOU KNOW?

Modern Malaysia's largest state, Sarawak, was ruled by the British Brooke family from 1841 until the end of the Second World War. The 'white rajahs' had their own currency, stamps and flag.

MALDIVES

Malcolm **X** wears a striking ring decorated with symbols of Islam following a visit to Mecca in 1964.

its leader Elijah Muhammad for stating that President John F. KENNEDY's assassination was a case of 'the chickens coming home to roost'. After his conversion to Orthodox Islam in 1964, he preached Black and White brotherhood, without abandoning Black nationalism, and formed the Organisation of Afro-American Unity. He was assassinated by Black Muslim opponents while speaking at a rally in Harlem, New York.

Maldives Chain of coral islands in the Indian Ocean. The Maldives came under Portuguese influence in the 16th century, and in the 17th century the islands were a sultanate under the protection of the Dutch rulers of Ceylon. When Britain captured Ceylon in 1796, the Maldives came under British protection; a status which was formalised in 1887. In 1932 the country proclaimed a democratic constitution, though it remained a sultanate. Full independence was gained in 1965, and three years later the sultanate was abolished and a republic declared.

In 1985 the Maldives became a full member of the Commonwealth. In 1988 India helped to suppress an attempted coup against President Maumoun Abdul Gayoom, who had been elected ten years earlier. He was re-elected that year, but faced continuing criticism from young Maldivians.

Maldon, Battle of (August 991) Clash in Essex, England, which is the subject of an epic, near contemporary poem. During the battle a party of Viking raiders defeated an English force led by Ealdorman Byrhtnoth. The verse, celebrating the loyalty and heroism of the defenders, is one of the few surviving accounts of an Anglo-Saxon battle.

Mali West African country which, as a 13th and early 14th-century empire, controlled trade across the Sahara and became a major supplier of gold. By the 1330s large cities, including TIMBUKTU, had been built.

In the 15th century Mali fell to Moroccan rule which lasted until the end of the 18th century, when the country was divided among the Tuareg and two other African peoples, the Macina and Ségou. Colonised by France in the late 19th century, in 1946 Mali became an Overseas Territory of France and, as the Sudanese Republic, was made an autonomous state within the French Community 12 years later. In 1959 it united with Senegal as the Federation of Mali in 1959, but in 1960 Senegal withdrew and Mali became independent. In 1963 it joined the Organisation of African Unity. A military government which took over in 1968 under Lieutenant Moussa Traoré gradually reintroduced civilian participation and Traoré was elected president in 1974 and again in 1985. Reform, however, proved slow and in 1990 prodemocracy riots erupted. The following year Traoré was arrested and replaced by a National Reconciliation Council. More than 40 political parties emerged, of which the Alliance for Democracy in Mali won a majority in the general election of 1992, its leader Alpha Oumar Konare being elected president. In the same year he concluded a peace agreement with rebellious Tuareg nomads and granted them limited autonomy in the north of the country.

Malplaquet, Battle of (September 11, 1709) Last victory of the Duke of MARLBOROUGH over the French in the War of the SPANISH SUCCESSION (1701-14). Attempting to make LOUIS XIV agree to harsh peace terms, the allied forces of England, the Netherlands and the Holy Roman Empire fought the French army near Malplaquet, a village in north-east France close to the Belgian frontier. Although the allies were victorious and forced a French retreat, their losses were so great that a planned advance on Paris was abandoned.

Malta Island in the Mediterranean which was awarded the George Cross by George VI of Britain in recognition of the islanders' bravery during the Second World War.

Settled possibly as long as 6000 years ago, Malta later became a Carthaginian outpost and in 218 BC fell to Rome. As part of the Byzantine Empire, in 870 it was conquered by Muslim Arabs. In the next 650 years it was captured by the Normans, recovered by Muslim forces, and finally fell to Spain. In 1530 the Holy Roman Emperor and Spanish king Charles V gave the island to the religious and military order of the Knights Hospitallers who defended it against Turkish attacks. The knights were expelled by Napoleon in 1798, and a year later the island was captured by the British. It became a base for the Royal Navy's Mediterranean Fleet, and during the Second World War withstood prolonged bombing raids by the German Luftwaffe.

In 1964 Malta gained independence within the British Commonwealth and ten years later became a republic. In 1979 Britain closed its military base on the island. Malta applied to join the European Community in 1990, but negotiations for admittance were postponed until economic reforms had been achieved.

Malthus, Thomas (1766-1834) British political economist and demographer whose theory that a nation's population growth always outstripped its capacity to produce food greatly influenced 19th-century political thought. In his *Essay on the Principle of Population*, published in 1798, Malthus argued that, because of this imbalance between people and food, the general standard of living could never rise above subsistence level. Population numbers were kept down by natural disasters such as famine and war as well as contraception and 'moral restraint'.

Malvinas see FALKLAND ISLANDS

Mameluke Name of two successive Egyptian dynasties established by Turkish and then Circassian slave soldiers. Mamelukes – from the Arabic *mamluk*, 'possessed' or 'slave' – were a feature of Islamic armies from the 9th century. Captured as children, Mameluke slave soldiers were trained in all aspects of warfare and converted to Islam.

On the death of Sultan Al-Salih in 1249, after a power struggle between his Turkish and Mongol bodyguards, the Turkish Mamelukes emerged victorious and elected one of their generals as sultan. After internal struggles the Turkish succession became hereditary. The new dynasty recruited Burji – mainly Circassian – slaves as bodyguards, and in 1390 they, in turn, usurped the sultanate and ruled continuously until 1517.

Mameluke control stretched from Egypt and Syria to western Arabia. Both dynasties had a highly organised civil service and judiciary. They encouraged commerce and traded across Africa as far as Mali and Guinea as well as throughout the Indian Ocean. The Mamelukes were overthrown in 1517 when the Ottoman Turks captured Cairo, but as

Mameluke warriors ride towards one another with swords raised in this 13th-century illustration from a cavalry manual. The Mamelukes fought Christian and Mongol invaders in the Middle East.

Turkish power waned they re-established themselves as rulers. They were defeated by Napoleon in 1798 and their rule was finally ended in 1811 by the PASHA Muhammad Ali.

Mameluke sultanate Muslim dynasty based in Delhi which ruled a north Indian empire from 1206 to 1290. The founder, Qutb ud-Din Aibak, who ruled until 1211, had risen in the service of Muhammad of Ghor, the previous ruler of Delhi. Qutb's son-in-law and former slave Iltutmish (1211-36) consolidated his hold on the Punjab, Bengal and Rajputana, and conquered Sind. The Mameluke sultanate survived Mongol threats in the mid 13th century and reached its peak under Ghiyas ud-Din Balban (1266-87), but soon after his death fell to the Khaljis.

Manchester School Group of British economists, businessmen and politicians, identified in the 1840s through their opposition to any interference by the State in commerce. Based in Manchester, the centre of the Victorian cotton industry, the group – whose leaders included the Members of Parliament John Bright and Richard COBDEN – followed the laissez-faire philosophy of Adam Smith, and supported FREE TRADE and economic freedom. Their influence faded when, in the 1880s, State intervention in economic affairs became more widely accepted.

Manchuria Region of China, now called Dongbei, north-east of the GREAT WALL. Between 200 BC and AD 900 there was little central control of China's various nomadic peoples, and Manchuria was ruled by a succession of dynasties established by different peoples. Some of these – such as the Liao, the Jin and the Manchu – later extended their empires into China and by 1644 the Manchu had become dominant and ruled China. Their homeland became part of the QING empire.

Japan used the MUKDEN INCIDENT in September 1931 as a pretext to establish Manchuria as a puppet state, Manchukuo, from 1932 to 1945. Though notionally ruled by the last Chinese emperor Pu Yi, effective control of Manchuria was in the hands of the Japanese army until the Chinese communists, supported by the Soviet Union, took over at the end of the Second World War.

Manchus Descendants of nomads who settled in northern China and established a powerful Chinese dynasty in the 17th century.

The Manchus first established a kingdom in the north of the Liaodong Peninsula of Manchuria, and imported Chinese technicians and advisers while maintaining military control.

In 1616 the Manchu leader Nurhachi claimed the title of emperor; his son, Abahai, proceeded to campaign extensively in Korea, Mongolia and northern China; and by 1680 his grandson had become the first QING emperor of China. While the Manchus adopted many aspects of Chinese life, they remained racially segregated, forbade intermarriage with the Chinese and kept separate quarters in all Chinese cities. Segregation began to break down during the 19th century, and the process accelerated in 1912 after the Qing dynasty was overthrown. In the 20th century Manchus have merged into the mass of the Chinese people.

mandarin Senior official in imperial China, named from the Portuguese term *mandarim*, 'governor'. Charged with the efficient running of China's empire, the mandarins were scholars and bureaucrats whose disdain of physical work was manifested by the great length of their fingernails. There were nine grades of mandarin, recruited after examinations in the Confucian classics.

mandate International trusteeship devised by the LEAGUE OF NATIONS after the First World War to administer former German and Ottoman colonies in Africa and Asia, including PALESTINE and CAMEROON.

In 1919 the League assigned each of these possessions to one of the Allied nations. The mandate powers were to be responsible for the administration, welfare and development of local populations until they were considered ready for self-government. Mandated territories were to be supervised by the League's Permanent Mandates Commission, but since this had no way of enforcing its decisions the mandate powers were in effect free to govern as they wished. In 1946 the mandates were replaced by the UNITED NATIONS' trusteeship system, which had a similar purpose.

Mandela, Nelson see feature, page 384

Manfred (c.1232-66) King of SICILY from 1258 until his death. The illegitimate son of the Holy Roman Emperor FREDERICK II, Manfred ruled in Italy for his legitimate half-brother Conrad IV until 1257 when, with Saracen support, he captured the Sicilian Kingdom. He was crowned king in the following year, which led to his excommunication by Pope Alexander VI. He proceeded to invade papal territories in Tuscany. Again excommunicated by Pope Urban IV, who gave the crown to Charles I of Anjou, Manfred was defeated and killed at the Battle of Benevento.

Manhattan Project Code name for the secret Second World War project to develop the atomic bomb in the United States. In the late 1930s scientists established that it was possible to build a bomb by harnessing the power generated by splitting the atom.

When it was learnt that German scientists were working on the same technology, the project received high priority and a team was assembled at Los Alamos, New Mexico, to design and make an atomic bomb.

Led by the US physicists J. Robert OPPENHEIMER and Enrico Fermi, who had built the first atomic pile at the University of Chicago, the project led to the detonation of the first atomic bomb at Alamogordo, New Mexico, on July 16, 1945.

A mandarin strolls with his servants, in this 18th-century painting by Tiepolo. His lordly air reflects his role as an imperial Chinese official.

Manichaeism Religious philosophy based on a belief in the warring forces of good and evil. Manichaeism sprang from the teachings of the Persian mystic Manes (or Mani), whose beliefs combined elements of Christianity, Buddhism, Zoroastrianism and Gnosticism. He argued that good and evil were in perpetual conflict – an idea that influenced several heresies of medieval Christianity. In AD 276, aged 60, Manes was driven into exile in India by followers of the ZOROASTRIAN faith who eventually flayed him alive before crucifying him. Although the Roman emperor Diocletian persecuted Manes' followers, Manichaeism spread to Rome and Africa in the 4th century and survived in Chinese Turkistan until the 10th century.

manifest destiny US political doctrine, popular in the 19th century, advocating territorial expansion. Originally referring to the desire of expansionists in the 1840s to extend US boundaries from the Atlantic to the Pacific, it became a tenet of Democratic Party policy. The doctrine then gained support from the WHIG, and later the Republican, Party and was important in justifying the annexation of Texas in 1845 and, a year later, the MEXICAN-AMERICAN WAR. It was again invoked by William SEWARD who arranged the purchase of Alaska from Russia in 1867, and re-emerged in the 1890s when Hawaii was annexed and when Spanish territories were acquired after the SPANISH-AMERICAN WAR.

Man in the Iron Mask see MATTHIOLI, ERCOLE

Mannerheim, Carl Gustav, Baron von (1867-1951) Finnish statesman who as president from 1944 to 1946 brought his country into the Second World War against Germany.

As an officer in the tsarist army, Mannerheim rose to the rank of general and in 1918 led a successful war against the Finnish Bolsheviks and expelled Soviet forces from FINLAND. He was appointed chief of Finland's National Defence Council in 1930 and planned the Mannerheim Line – a fortified defence across the Karelian Isthmus to block any potential aggression by the Soviet Union. When Soviet forces attacked Finland in 1939, Mannerheim led the resistance, later forming an alliance with Germany. In 1944 he signed an armistice with the Soviet Union and in March 1945 brought Finland into the war.

Manning, Henry (1808-92) Anglican priest, who, after conversion to Roman Catholicism, became a cardinal actively supporting HOME RULE for Ireland. As a Church of England priest, Manning was strongly influenced by the OXFORD MOVEMENT and by its interest in the Church Fathers and the pre-Reformation Catholic Church. Becoming a

Father of a Nation

After 27 years as a political prisoner and branded a terrorist, Nelson Mandela emerged unbowed and without animosity to become president of his country.

On May 10, 1994, watched by tens of thousands of spectators in Pretoria, South African air force jets trailed ribbons of smoke in the colours of the new national flag. Once potent weapons of the regime that had enforced White supremacy for nearly 50 years, now the planes were saluting a Black man, the newly inaugurated president, Nelson Mandela.

Rolihlahla Mandela – he gained his English first name at school – was born in 1918 in the town of Umtata on South Africa's east coast, the son of a chief of the Xhosa-speaking Tembu tribe. At a time when few Black people were gaining any form of higher education, he studied law at the universities of Fort Hare and the Witwatersrand.

In 1944 Mandela joined the African National Congress (ANC), a political organisation that called for full citizenship for Black South Africans, the right for them to own land and the repeal of discriminatory legislation. His activities soon attracted the attention of the police. He was briefly imprisoned in 1952, and in 1956 was arrested for high treason. After policemen killed nearly 70

unarmed Black protesters in Sharpeville in 1960, Mandela came to believe that only armed resistance would have any effect.

When he began to advocate acts of sabotage against the apartheid regime he was forced to go underground, abandoning his wife, Winnie, and their children. He travelled in disguise throughout South Africa, giving interviews, trying to reorganise the ANC as a clandestine movement and helping to set up its military wing, Umkhonto we Sizwe (Spear of the Nation). He was named 'the Black Pimpernel' for his elusiveness.

When Mandela was caught in August 1962, he was sentenced to five years' imprisonment for inciting workers to strike and leaving the country without travel documents. The following year, after police uncovered piles of weapons at the Umkhonto we Sizwe headquarters, his sentence was increased to life.

FROM PRISONER TO PRESIDENT

From 1964 to 1982 Mandela was held on Robben Island, off the coast of Cape Town. Life there was one of mind-numbing routine, 'each day like the one before; each week like the one before it'. But he was far from forgotten, for he became the focus of a campaign against apartheid that during the 1980s spread far beyond South Africa.

Finally, on February 10, 1990, President F.W. de Klerk, recognising the end of apartheid, announced that the world's most famous political prisoner would be released. The next day, in front of a barrage of television cameras, Mandela walked free.

In 1991 he became president of the ANC. His stature was such that no one opposed him. For three years he led the party in negotiations with the government as they sought to develop a new constitution. In April 1994 the first elections for the whole population took place. In May, the man so long the government's enemy became its leader.

A jubilant Mandela leaves court in 1961 with Moses Kotane after being acquitted of treason in a trial that lasted five years.

Roman Catholic in 1851, he was made Archbishop of Westminster in 1865 and a cardinal ten years later. Although theologically conservative, Manning was an early supporter of trade union rights, and in 1889 his mediation helped to secure a just settlement in a London dockers' strike.

manor house Originally the home of the lord of an estate in medieval Europe. The word 'manor' comes from the Old French *maneir*, a term introduced into England after the Norman Conquest in 1066. As well as accommodating the lord and his family, the manor was the administrative hub of the manorial estate. Manor houses varied widely in size and design, depending not only on available local materials but also on the need for fortification – some were enclosed within walls or moats. Many houses had a manorial court in which the lord exercised periodic jurisdiction over his tenants. At the centre of all manor houses was the great hall, reflecting the wealth and power of the lord who entertained his guests there. Until the 17th century in France, Spain and other parts of battle-scarred Europe, defensive considerations were paramount and fortified tower-houses were commonplace.

In England the move towards more comfortable homes began earlier, and by the 14th century the traditional great halls were being divided into private living apartments and service rooms. By the 17th century the English manor house had developed into the COUNTRY HOUSE set in landscaped parkland.

manorial system Social, economic and administrative system which emerged in the 5th century from the chaos following the collapse of the Roman Empire. In return for the protection of powerful lords, farmers surrendered certain rights and control of their lands, and a system of obligations and service gradually emerged. These were set down in records called custumals. The manor consisted of a DEMESNE, or the lord's private land, and the holdings of tenants, each of whom was free or a tied VILLEIN. Rank depended on personal status or the size of the tenant's land enclosure. Meadows known as common land on which livestock could graze were open to the entire community; sometimes access to woodland for timber and to graze pigs was also shared. Tenants paid the lord in cash or by contributing regular labour, known as week work or seasonal boon work. In the 12th century cash rents began to replace labour, but this was reversed after about 1200 when inflation encouraged landlords again to exact services in kind. Rebellions such as the PEASANTS' REVOLT of 1381, enclosures, tenant unrest and labour shortages caused by Europe's death toll of 25 million during the BLACK DEATH, effectively ended the manorial system.

Maori Eastern Polynesian peoples thought to have migrated to NEW ZEALAND from the central Pacific in several waves from about AD 800. By the time the English navigator Captain James COOK explored New Zealand in 1776 more than 100 000 Maoris had settled on the islands. Until the arrival of European settlers, shared language and customs, intermarriage and trade links had not prevented local feuds; but the arrival of the newcomers was seen as a threat which united the people as Maori – a word meaning 'normal' or 'ordinary'. Though they welcomed traders, there was growing resistance to shore-based settlement. Under the Treaty of WAITANGI, signed by the chiefs and British representatives in 1840, the British crown gained the right to govern and to settle in New Zealand. The Maoris kept authority over their lands and all their affairs and gained the rights of British citizens.

By 1896 disease had reduced the Maori population to 42 000. After the Second World War their numbers increased and many Maoris migrated to towns seeking improved opportunities; but in the 1980s, threatened by rising unemployment and loss of identity, the Maoris demanded national recognition of their language and culture and the preservation of remaining Maori land. During a royal visit to New Zealand in November 1995, Elizabeth II signed legislation providing for compensation worth about £70 million, and including 39 000 acres (15 800 ha) of land, to the Tainui federation of peoples, much of whose land was confiscated by colonists. The Queen also made a personal apology to the Maori people.

Mao Ze-dong see feature, page 386

Maquis Resistance movement, formed from young people hiding in the hills and forests to avoid forced labour in Germany, which went underground to fight the Nazi occupation

Marat clutches a note from his killer, Charlotte Corday, as he lies dead in his bath in Jacques-Louis David's painting of the same year, 1793.

forces after the fall of France in 1940. The name 'maquis' means shrubland – a reference to undergrowth as a hiding place. The various groups of the Maquis, supported by the French Communist Party, operated independently but in 1944 they were coordinated into the Forces Françaises de l'Intérieur.

Marat, Jean Paul (1743-93) French revolutionary leader and extremist whose opposition to the moderate GIRONDIN group led to his murder by Charlotte CORDAY.

After studying medicine in Scotland, Marat practised as a doctor in London, where in 1773 his *Philosophical Essay on Man* attacked the view of HELVETIUS that science was unnecessary for a philosopher. In 1777 he returned to Paris. From 1789, he was editor of a radical journal, *L'ami du peuple*. A leader of the extremist Cordelier Club, he became a key figure in the French Revolution. Although Marat's attacks on those in power led to his brief exile in 1790, two years later he was elected to the National Assembly. He was murdered on July 13, 1793, soon after masterminding the Girondist defeat.

Maratha Wars (1779-82, 1803-5, 1817-18) Conflicts in India between troops of the English EAST INDIA COMPANY and the Maratha peoples. By the late 18th century more than 90 clans of Maratha Hindus had formed a confederacy, and though the British

In 1769, Sidney Parkinson, Cook's artist, portrayed a tattooed Maori chief wearing an ornamental *heitiki* round his neck and greenstone ear-pendants.

China's Great Helmsman

The dominant figure in late 20th-century China, Mao Ze-dong mobilised the peasants to throw off centuries of repression. Yet his policies led to 30 million deaths from starvation and the destruction of his country's rich culture.

The Chinese Communist Party (CCP), over which Mao Ze-dong (Mao Tse-t'ung) maintained almost total control, came to power in 1949 after two decades of struggle against nationalists, warlords and Japanese occupation forces. The party's successful guerrilla campaign, for which Mao supplied both strategy and ideology, became a template for liberation movements everywhere. He continued to lead China until his death in 1976. His long period in power was marked by totalitarianism, the economic failures of the 'Great Leap Forward' and the bizarre cruelties of the 'Cultural Revolution'.

Mao was born in Hunan province in 1893, the son of a successful peasant farmer. During his youth, China was weak, anarchic and preyed on by its own warlords and the gunboat diplomacy of foreign powers. He learned that force fills a political vacuum, later coining the dictum that 'Power grows from the barrel of a gun'. Working in the library of Beijing (Peking) University, he studied the works of Marx and helped to found the CCP in 1921. He was close to Chiang Kai-shek's nationalist Guomindang movement, which also sought to revive and reunify China. In 1927, however, Stalin ordered the CCP to break with Chiang, whose troops began to hunt down communists. Mao realised that China was too backward for the CCP to rely on the small urban proletariat, and he established a peasant-based soviet in south-central China. His reliance on the peasantry brought a new strand into Marxist-Leninist theory.

In 1934 the soviet was overrun by Chiang's forces. Mao and his followers set off on the dangerous and epic 'Long March'. Manoeuvring with great skill to avoid pursuing nationalists, they reached Shaanxi province in the north-west in 1936. Mao was elected CCP chairman during the march. From their remote base in Yan'an, moving swiftly in small, lightly armed groups and living off the countryside, the communists successfully resisted the Japanese forces in China. After the Japanese surrender in 1945, Mao turned against and defeated Chiang's regime. The People's Republic of China was proclaimed in Beijing in 1949.

THE GREAT LEAP FORWARD

Mao's impatience, allied to a belief in the power of slogans, led to a misconceived effort to achieve rapid advances in farming and industry. The communes set up by the 'Great Leap Forward' in 1958 proved to be a large step backwards, causing widespread starvation. Its failure caused Mao to assume a lower profile, but he continued as party chairman. Always xenophobic, in 1962 he split with the Soviet Union. In 1966, feeling his position weakened, he launched a 'Cultural Revolution' to destroy liberal opponents. He called for a 'permanent revolution' to crush the emergence of new elites, ignoring

In 1970 a portrait of Mao, named supreme commander of China and its army that year, reminds the citizens of Beijing of his status.

his own status as 'the Great Helmsman' whose thoughts, published in the 'Little Red Book', were required reading. Young Red Guards, spurred on by Mao, carried out a brutal campaign of intimidation against their elders. In 1968, at last admitting the revolution's excesses, Mao brought the Red Guards under control with the help of his deputy Zhou En-lai.

The atrocities he unleashed, and his failure to modernise industry, undermined Mao's reputation after his death. The survival of communist rule in China, however, meant that Mao's influence continued to be a crucial factor in the world's most populous country.

People 'from the rivers and mountains' unite as Mao proclaims the Republic in 1949 (above). The Long March (right) was a 6000 mile (9600 km) trek for survival.

exploited rivalries between chiefs their alliance became a significant threat to the company's control of northern and central India. In the second of the wars, Sir Arthur Wellesley, later Duke of WELLINGTON, won the battles of Assaye and Argaon. No further British acquisitions of Indian territories were envisaged when the company's charter was renewed in 1813, but in 1817 troops invaded Maratha territory to put down Pindari robber bands supported by local princes. With the final defeat of the Maratha princes in the following year, Britain's domination of the subcontinent was almost complete.

Marathon Narrow coastal plain to the east of Athens where in 490 BC some 9000 Athenians and their Plataean allies defeated an army of 25 000 invading Persians, marking a turning point in the Persian Wars. Cleverly using the terrain to protect their flanks, the Greeks killed more than 6400 invaders and marched quickly back to Athens to prevent a seaborne attack on the city. The Athenian herald Pheidippides, sent to summon help, ran the 150 miles (240 km) to Sparta in two days. The modern marathon race commemorates the tradition that a messenger ran the 26 miles (42 km) from the battlefield to Athens with news of victory and fell dead from exhaustion as he delivered the news.

Marconi, Guglielmo (1874-1937) Italian-born pioneer of radio communication. Marconi began experimenting with wireless communication in 1894, after reading about Heinrich HERTZ's research into electric waves. In less than a year he had sent and received signals over a distance of more than 1¼ miles (2 km). Failing to gain Italian support for his research, Marconi went to London, took out a UK patent and in 1896 demonstrated his

invention to the British Post Office. By 1899 he had sent messages from England to France, and in 1901 his signals crossed the Atlantic in MORSE code.

In 1902 he patented a magnetic detector of electrical signals, and in 1905 added a horizontal directional antenna to his string of lucrative inventions. In 1909 Marconi shared the Nobel prize for physics with the German physicist Karl Braun who had invented a coupled wireless transmitter and receiver.

Marco Polo (c.1254-1324) Venetian traveller whose tales of China and the Mongol court stimulated European interest in the East. Between 1271 and 1275 Polo accompanied his father and uncle on a journey from Acre, Palestine, into central Asia along the Silk Road. He reached China and the court of the Mongol emperor KUBLAI KHAN whose service he entered, travelling widely in the MONGOL EMPIRE for 17 years. In 1295 Marco Polo returned to Venice and three years later was captured by the Genoese. While in prison, he dictated an account of his travels which was widely read. Although it is thought that many of his adventures and observations were based on hearsay, scholars agree that the descriptions of the places he visited and the customs of the inhabitants are an informative geographical and social commentary of the time.

Marcos, Ferdinand (1917-89) President of the PHILIPPINES from 1965 to 1986, whose regime ended when he was forced to flee after a military-led popular revolt. Marcos, who entered Congress in 1949 and became senate leader in 1963, initially achieved some success as a reformer. His anticommunist stance as president gained him US support and financial aid, but his ruthless suppression of nationalist and communist guerrilla groups led to

Ferdinand Marcos and his wife Imelda wave to supporters after parliament had declared him president following the election in 1986.

widespread dissent and in 1972 he declared martial law. Although this was lifted in 1981, US support for his regime waned in the face of his misuse of foreign aid for personal gain and the murder of political opponents, including in 1983 the opposition leader Benigno Aquino. In February 1986 his attempts to retain power after an election which was disputed by Benigno's widow, Corazon Aquino, led to strikes and mass demonstrations. Marcos fled to Hawaii where, until his death, he fought attempts to extradite him on corruption charges. His widow Imelda faced similar accusations after 1989 as she battled in the courts to unfreeze her husband's assets.

Marco Polo and companions travel in a camel caravan along the Silk Road in this detail from a 14th-century Catalan map. They journeyed through Baghdad, Yarkand and the Gobi desert before arriving in 1275 at the court of the Mongol emperor Kublai Khan in Beijing, China.

Mapping the world

More than 8000 years ago, people began to try to record the details of their surroundings. As knowledge increased, scholars found inventive ways of representing the world, producing by AD 150 the precursor of the modern map.

Long before the first true maps, the people of prehistoric societies were aware of the landscape around them and wanted to record it. A wall painting excavated at Çatal Hüyük, a Neolithic settlement in central Anatolia dating from about 6500 BC, shows its buildings in plan view, with a nearby volcano in the background.

The earliest recorded attempts to make maps were in Mesopotamia and Egypt. Mesopotamian surveyors in 2300 BC produced plans of properties for legal and practical purposes. Fragments of city maps also survive. There are a few examples of Egyptian maps, including the Turin Papyrus of about 1300 BC, which identifies gold and other mines, with routes leading from them to the Red Sea. The 'Babylonian World Map', inscribed on a clay tablet in about 600 BC, shows a flat world, with Babylon and other cities labelled. Beyond them, seven or eight remote regions project like the points of a star. The map is a scholarly attempt to illustrate ideas about cosmology. The ancient Greeks were the first to write about the theory and practice of map-making. They applied their skills in science, mathematics and philosophy to the problems of how to measure the world and represent it accurately.

The idea of a spherical Earth was probably first proposed by Pythagoras in the 6th century BC. Parmenides divided the globe into the five zones we use today: one hot, two temperate and two cold. The problem of representing a sphere on a flat surface was tackled by various scholars. Most arrived at a rectangular shape, with Greece at the centre.

Anaximander of Miletus (*c*.611-546 BC) was acknowledged as the first map-maker. Eratosthenes (*c*.275-194 BC) measured the Earth's circumference: he calculated it to be 250 000 stadia (about

The Babylonian World Map shows Babylon, with other cities and the Euphrates river, circled by the ocean. Legendary lands lie beyond.

25 000 miles, 40 230 km), an overestimate of less than 200 miles (322 km). The efforts of these scholars, and knowledge provided by Greek military expeditions and voyages, established the basis of scientific cartography.

The *Geography* of Claudius Ptolemaeus (*c*.AD 90-168) represented the peak of ancient cartography. Ptolemy discussed the principles of cartography and introduced the use of latitude and longitude. His map of the world, as it survives in later reproductions, is a clear forerunner of modern maps.

After Ptolemy, progress in scientific map-making slowed. Arab geographers of the 7th to the 12th centuries used translations of Ptolemy's work and filled in details of previously unexplored regions. Cartography also developed in China in the Middle Ages: maps were used for military and administrative purposes. Plans drawn on silk have recently been found in a general's tomb of 168 BC. A map of the whole country, which had been drawn in AD 1193, was copied on stone and set up in a temple in 1247. But European world maps, known as *mappae mundi*, of the 8th to the 15th centuries were usually symbolic or religious rather than practical.

The Age of Exploration awakened a new interest in technical map-making. Many editions of Ptolemy's work were published in 15th-century Germany and Italy. From the 14th century sailors from the Mediterranean began to make detailed sea charts, known as 'portolans', using improved instruments such as the magnetic compass. The advances of this period culminated in the production of sophisticated maps such as those of Gerard Mercator (1512-94) of Flanders, whose methods are still used in many modern maps.

Ptolemy, the Egyptian astronomer and geographer, produced a map in AD 150 which remained the most accurate representation of the world until the Middle Ages.

The Holy Roman Empress Maria Theresa sits opposite her husband Francis I, with some of their children, in a painting by Martin van Meytens (1695-1770). Maria bore 16 children in 19 years.

Marcus Aurelius (AD 121-80) Spanish-born thinker and STOIC philosopher who was Roman emperor from 161 until his death 19 years later. Although Marcus Aurelius preferred literature, philosophy and law, his efforts to defend the empire against Parthian, German and British insurrection forced him to campaign as a fighter in Asia and Europe. His *Meditations*, written while he was on campaign and which record his thoughts on philosophy, survive, together with some letters.

Margaret, Maid of Norway (c. 1283-90) Queen of Scotland at the age of three who drowned when she was seven, ending the 200-year-old Canmore dynasty. The daughter of Erik II of Norway and granddaughter of Alexander III of Scotland, Margaret inherited the Scottish throne in 1286 and six guardians were appointed as regents. EDWARD I of England proposed a marriage between Margaret and his son Edward, the first English Prince of Wales.

Her death, while crossing the North Sea from Norway to the Orkneys, led to a year-long dispute over the succession involving 13 claimants. Edward I eventually judged in favour of John BALLIOL.

Margaret of Anjou (1430-82) Queen of England who led the briefly successful Lancastrian attempt to restore her husband HENRY VI to the throne. Margaret's marriage in 1445 ensured a truce in the war between England and France, and in the face of Henry's weakness the Lancastrians rallied to his indomitable wife. In February 1461 she defeated the Yorkists at the second Battle of St Albans, but her hesitation in pressing forward her advantage cost Henry the throne, and she had to flee to Scotland and then to France. From there she led the invasion which for a few months in 1470-1 regained the throne for Henry. When he was again ousted after EDWARD IV's victory at the Battle of TEWKESBURY in 1471, Margaret was taken prisoner. In 1476 the French king Louis XI paid a ransom for Margaret, who returned to her native Anjou for the rest of her life.

Margaret, St (c. 1046-93) Queen consort of MALCOLM III of Scotland from 1069, whose piety led in 1250 to her canonisation.

Descended from the House of Wessex, Margaret was the daughter of Edward the Atheling and the granddaughter of Edmund Ironside. She encouraged the Church of Scotland to replace its Celtic practices with the Roman form of Christianity, refounded the abbey of Iona and brought the Benedictine monastic order to Scotland. She was also responsible for building Dunfermline Abbey, a burial place for the Scottish royal family.

margrave Governor appointed to protect vulnerable borders, or 'marks', of the Holy Roman Empire which were the equivalent of English marches. Charlemagne introduced the office, which in the 12th century became hereditary, and the medieval German title *Markgraf*, 'count of the mark', came to rank equally with a prince of the empire.

Maria Theresa (1717-80) Ruler of the Habsburg dominions from 1740 until her death. The daughter of Charles VI, Maria succeeded to the Habsburg lands in Austria, Bohemia, Hungary, the southern Netherlands and north Italy in 1740 under her father's PRAGMATIC SANCTION – which he had promulgated in April 1713 to ensure that his territories would not be divided between future Habsburg heirs. She was only 23 when she inherited, and her claim to the various thrones led to the War of the AUSTRIAN SUCCESSION (1740-8). But Maria courageously rallied her peoples in both this war and the SEVEN YEARS' WAR (1756-63). In the first war Maria lost Silesia, but she gained Galicia in 1772 in the first partitioning of Poland.

Francis, Duke of Lorraine, whom she had married four years before coming to the throne, became Holy Roman Emperor in 1745. When he died in 1765, their son Joseph II became co-regent with his mother. Maria chose able ministers, and under her rule control of Austria and Bohemia became more centralised. She reorganised local government, introduced military and educational reforms and was a patron of the arts.

Marie Antoinette (1755-93) Queen of France, wife of LOUIS XVI. The daughter of MARIA THERESA and Francis I of Austria, Marie Antoinette was married at 14 to the French Dauphin. Surrounding herself with frivolous court favourites, she indulged in extravagant and unconventional behaviour which made her unpopular with the people. Opposed to new ideas, she encouraged Louis to ignore the advice of his more liberal ministers and continued to intrigue with Austria against the Revolutionary forces. While attempting to escape from France the royal couple were arrested at Varennes and taken back to Paris. During their incarceration and the events leading up to the king's trial and execution, and her own nine months later, Marie Antoinette behaved with great courage and dignity.

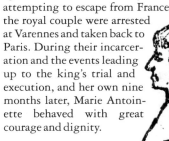

In 1793 Marie Antoinette was sketched by the artist David on her journey to the guillotine.

The Duke of Marlborough, seated on a white horse, surveys his troops at the Battle of Oudenarde in the Netherlands on June 30, 1708. The allied forces won a resounding victory over the French.

Mark Antony (83-30 BC) Roman general who delivered the oration at Julius CAESAR's funeral and later became CLEOPATRA's lover. In 49, after serving with Caesar in the GALLIC WARS, Antony defended his comrade in the Senate and fought at his side when Pompey was defeated in the following year at the Battle of Pharsalus. He represented Caesar in Italy during Caesar's African campaign, and in 44 led the faction which offered the crown to Caesar in vain.

After Caesar's murder in the same year Antony took the political initiative against the assassins, and when they fled Rome he

> **His captain's heart, / Which in the scuffles of great fights hath burst / The buckles on his breast, reneges all temper, / And is become the bellows and the fan / To cool a gypsy's lust.**
>
> *Description of Mark Antony in Shakespeare's Antony and Cleopatra, 1607*

assumed virtually dictatorial powers in the city. Defeated at Mutina in 43 by the forces of the consuls and OCTAVIAN, Caesar's designated heir, Antony escaped to Gaul. He was reconciled with Octavian when he returned at the head of a strong army, and joined Lepidus and Octavian to form the Second Triumvirate. The trio disposed of their political enemies, including CICERO, and defeated Brutus and Cassius in 42 at the Battle of PHILIPPI.

Within months of being given control of Rome's eastern Mediterranean territories, Antony began his liaison with Cleopatra. Although a powerful ally, she cost Antony much support in Rome where their marriage was considered to be illegal. When in 34 Antony declared Caesarion – Cleopatra's son, allegedly by Caesar – rather than Octavian as Caesar's heir, war became inevitable. Defeated by Octavian's forces at the sea battle of ACTIUM, off the Greek coast, Antony fled to Egypt where he committed suicide.

Marlborough, John Churchill, 1st Duke of (1650-1722) English military campaigner whose victories were rewarded by the nation's gift to him of Blenheim Palace.

After his marriage to Sarah Jennings, a favourite of James II's daughter Princess Anne, the king appointed him second-in-command in 1685 against MONMOUTH's REBELLION. But three years later Marlborough, opposed to James's Roman Catholicism, switched his allegiance to William of Orange. By 1701 war over the SPANISH SUCCESSION seemed inevitable, and William III chose Marlborough as his commander in chief. When Anne became queen a year later Marlborough was given a dukedom and also became commander in chief of the allied armies. His European campaigns led to spectacular victories at BLENHEIM in 1704, Ramillies in 1706, Oudenarde in 1708 and MALPLAQUET a year later; but the increasingly heavy casualties among his forces led to growing parliamentary criticism.

The influence which Marlborough's wife Sarah (1660-1744) had exercised over the queen had also been steadily eroded and in 1710, when the Whig ministry was replaced by Tories, the duke was charged with embezzlement of public money and dismissed. He left England in the following year to live on the Continent until the accession of George I in 1714, when Marlborough was restored to his old offices. Two years later ill-health ended his career. After his death Sarah devoted herself to supervising the completion of Blenheim Palace at Woodstock, Oxfordshire.

Marne, Battles of Two First World War battles (September 5-12, 1914 and July 15-August 7, 1918) fought along the River Marne in eastern France. The first clash was the climax of a successful French counter-offensive at the start of the war, driving back the invading German forces from within 15 miles (24 km) of Paris and dashing their hopes of destroying the French forces before Russia could fully mobilise. Setting the pattern for trench warfare on the WESTERN FRONT, the retreating Germans dug themselves in north of the River Aisne. The second battle ended the German General Erich von LUDENDORFF's final offensive.

Maronite Member of a Christian sect, which claims to have been founded in Syria by St Maron in the 4th century, and which dominated politics in LEBANON in the 20th century.

Condemned in the 7th century for its monotheistic belief that Christ was divine but not human, the Maronite Church has been in full communion with the Roman Catholic Church since the 11th century. Its 1.5 million adherents live mainly in Lebanon, but are also represented in Cyprus, the Palestinian autonomous areas adjacent to Israel, and Egypt.

A DRUZE massacre of Maronites in Lebanon and Syria in 1860 led to French intervention and eventual French control of both countries. With the collapse of the Ottoman Empire in 1920 Lebanese Maronites became self-ruling under French protection, and when Lebanon became independent in 1945 they formed the dominant group. It was agreed that every future Lebanese president would be a Maronite, the prime minister a Sunni Muslim, and the speaker of parliament a Shiah Muslim. There would also be six Maronites for every five Muslims in the chamber of deputies.

In the 1930s the Maronites became divided by interclan rivalry into several groupings, among which was a right-wing Phalange ('Phalanx') faction, and in 1958 the National Liberal Party led by a former president of Lebanon, Camille Chamoun, and known as 'Chamounists'. When civil war began in 1975 the Phalangists attempted to gain control of Lebanon, but the war weakened the Maronite hold on the country. In October 1989 the Taif Accord negotiated by the ARAB LEAGUE ended the Maronites' built-in political majority over the Muslim population, bringing a fragile peace to the country under Syrian protection.

Marprelate Tracts Satirical pamphlets published in England in 1587-9, featuring scurrilous attacks on Anglican bishops.

The Puritan authors, who shared the pseudonym 'Martin Marprelate', mocked the Elizabethan Church, angering Elizabeth I and leading to prosecutions for sedition. One of the alleged authors, John Penry, was executed in 1592 and another died in prison. Appearing when Puritan fortunes were already at a low ebb, the tracts led to several statutes against dissenting sects.

From barter to Big Bang

All the familar features of capitalism — the New York stock exchange, the City of London — have their origins in the first market places, where peasants came to sell agricultural goods and swap the local gossip.

In primitive societies goods were bartered — exchanged directly one for another. But the system had limitations: a man with a pig who wanted a sheep would have to find a partner interested in the reverse transaction, and bartering took no account of differences in the value of goods being exchanged. This problem was solved by the introduction of a common currency; both grain and silver were being used as money in Mesopotamia before 2000 BC. The development of coinage in ancient Greece and Rome allowed complex chains of buyers and sellers to trade goods of different value for money. As soon as the process of exchange in an economy developed beyond bartering, markets emerged. The arrival of the market place, often in a town square where traders could meet conveniently, marks a turning point in the evolution of society.

Market places developed in all parts of the world. Cheapside in London and several English towns such as Chipping

Campden derive their names from *ceap*, Anglo-Saxon for market. German towns such as Frankfurt held annual fairs that attracted traders from throughout Europe. But any European market place of the medieval period would probably have been dwarfed by Tenochtitlán, the Aztec city in Mexico discovered by the Spanish conquistador Hernando Cortés in 1519, where 60 000 traders were said to assemble daily.

BUYING AND SELLING

In preindustrial Europe, market places were the focus for the commercial activities of rural societies. Towns grew up around them. On market day peasants would flock to town to trade livestock and set up stalls to sell food. They were also attracted by the sellers of cloth, shoes, pots and pans and other items which they could not produce at home. The weekly market was an important social occasion, bringing a dash of colour into lives dominated by agricultural labour. It was an eagerly anticipated event, not least for the opportunity to drink with friends in the market tavern.

From earliest days, market places were subject to regulation. Town corporations

recognised that markets were a useful source of revenue and levied a charge, or toll, on all traders. The *Institutae Lundoniae* of about 1000 lists details of tolls charged in London. In return the trader gained the advantage of operating in a regulated market place, sometimes a covered hall, with a system of weights and measures and rules to ensure that competition was fair and prices were just.

As industrialisation developed, communications improved and sellers sought higher profits in distant markets, local price regulation broke down. Market places often became the scene of food riots as protesters called upon the authorities to enforce controls. During Nottingham's Great Cheese Riot of 1764, crowds rolled cheeses through the streets.

Retail trading in market places continues to be a feature of urban life. But modern economists think of the market place not as a particular location but as the whole area in which goods might be traded — the 'global market place'. All capitalist economies, though they differ in the degree to which they follow 'free market' principles, are based on the idea of the market, where goods are traded in open competition.

This medieval market scene, bustling with prosperous burghers, was painted in the 16th century by the German Pieter Aertsen.

Marshall, George (1880-1959) US general and diplomat who, from 1947 to 1949, fostered the Marshall Plan to promote postwar European economic recovery. As army chief of staff from 1939 to 1945, Marshall enlarged the US army when his country entered the Second World War and was responsible for overall strategic military planning. After the war, as secretary of state Marshall first organised aid to Greece and Turkey, and then to the rest of Europe.

The Marshall Plan was a US programme approved by President TRUMAN and Congress in 1948 to aid European recovery after the war,

> ❝ It has not fallen to your lot to command the great armies. You have had to create them, organise them, and inspire them. ❞
>
> *Winston Churchill, letter to George Marshall, 1945*

and between 1948 and 1951 $13.5 billion of material and financial aid was distributed. The Organisation for European Economic Co-operation was set up to administer the plan. When growing Soviet hostility undermined his aid plan for Eastern Europe, Marshall helped to create a Western defence alliance, NATO. He was US secretary of defence from 1950 to 1951, and in 1953 he was awarded the Nobel peace prize for the Marshall Plan.

Marshall Islands Country consisting of a cluster of atolls and islands in the central Pacific, and the site of the first postwar atomic bomb tests. Named after a British captain who visited them in 1788, the Marshall Islands became a German protectorate in 1886 and after the First World War were administered by Japan. The islands became a UN Trust Territory under US administration after the Second World War, and from 1946 the United States used BIKINI and other atolls in the group for atomic bomb tests. Forty years later the Marshall Islands were given semi-independence in a 'compact of free association' in which the USA maintained control over military activities. In 1990 the country became independent, and the following year it joined the United Nations.

In 1992 the United States began making payments in compensation for injuries relating to the atomic tests.

Marshall, John (1755-1835) US lawyer who as chief justice from 1801 until his death moulded the constitution through his interpretations, despite his frequent opposition to the views of incumbent presidents. Elected to Congress as a supporter of FEDERALISM in 1799, Marshall established the Supreme Court's power to review state and federal

laws and to pronounce on their constitutional validity. Between 1810 and 1830 the Supreme Court, guided by Marshall in a series of major decisions, proved the US constitution to be both a precise document that established specific powers and a living instrument to be interpreted. Marshall's rulings gave the federal government power to act effectively, and limited the powers of individual states.

Marston Moor, Battle of (July 2, 1644) First major Royalist defeat of the ENGLISH CIVIL WAR. After relieving the besieged city of York, the Royalist general Prince RUPERT pursued the Roundhead troops to Marston Moor, where he was unexpectedly attacked. Oliver Cromwell's disciplined cavalry routed the Royalist forces, capturing 4500 Cavaliers and killing some 3000 men. As a result, Charles I lost control of the north of England and Cromwell emerged as the leading Parliamentary general.

Martí, José (1853-95) Cuban revolutionary, poet and national hero. As a young man, Martí was a student of Rafael de Mendive, an outspoken critic of Spain's administration in CUBA, who encouraged the young man's revolutionary leanings. Martí became a journalist, and a year after the 1868 anti-Spanish rising which developed into the Cuban Ten Years' War he was charged with treason as a result of his writings. He was sentenced to six months' imprisonment, and in 1870 was deported to Spain. There, though technically still a convict, he was allowed complete freedom and enrolled as a law student in the University of Madrid. Spells in Mexico and

While living in London Karl Marx wrote a three-volume critique of political economy, *Das Kapital.*

Guatemala followed his graduation, but he returned to Cuba in 1878 under the amnesty which marked the end of the war. In 1879 he was detained for conspiracy against the administration and was again deported to Spain. Martí remained in exile – mainly in the USA – for most of the rest of his life, founding the exiled Cuban Revolutionary Party, writing in support of independence and plotting an armed invasion and rebellion, which in 1895 was finally launched. Martí returned to Cuba with the invaders and was killed in May 1895 by Spanish forces at the Battle of Dos Ríos. Cuban independence from Spain was achieved, with US aid, seven years later.

martyr Person dying for his or her spiritual or, later, political beliefs. After Stephen, the first Christian martyr, was stoned to death in Jerusalem around AD 35, the term came to denote anyone put to death or tortured because of their Christian beliefs. Martyrs' graves became shrines, and after the last persecution in the early 4th century were often marked by new churches where services were celebrated over a martyr's remains.

In later centuries the persecution of Protestants, Catholics and nonconformists created countless martyrs, as did the deaths of missionaries sent abroad during the years of European imperial expansion. More recently, the term has also been applied to non-Christians killed for upholding their faith and people persecuted for political reasons.

Marx, Karl (1818-83) Radical German philosopher and economist whose works inspired COMMUNISM in the 20th century. Marx studied law at Bonn and Berlin, and took a doctorate in philosophy at the University of Jena. After an antigovernment newspaper, which he helped to run at Cologne, was suppressed by the censor in 1842, Marx moved to Paris. There he met Friedrich ENGELS with whom he collaborated in works of political philosophy.

In 1847 he joined the Socialist League of the Just – later renamed the *Communist League* – and with Engels wrote its *Communist Manifesto* the following year. Expelled from most European countries, Marx settled in London where, supported by Engels, he lived for the rest of his life. Marx saw constant conflict between the working class and the capitalists who controlled the state, and hoped this conflict would lead to a world-wide political and social revolution. Uniting all workers, Marx argued, would give them political power.

A key figure in founding the First INTERNATIONAL, formed in London in 1864 to unite

Mary I married Philip of Castile by proxy. It was months before they met, and they lived together for only 14 months.

socialist and communist organisations throughout the world, Marx later became its leader. But clashes in IDEOLOGY between Marx and followers of the anarchist leader Mikhail BAKUNIN led to its disintegration eight years later. Marx developed his theories at length in the three volumes of *Das Kapital*, which were edited by Engels after his death.

Mary I (1516-58) Queen of England and Ireland, whose persecution of Protestants during her brief reign from 1553 until her death earned her the nickname 'Bloody Mary'. The only surviving child of Henry VIII and Catherine of Aragon, Mary Tudor was separated from her mother during her parents' divorce proceedings in 1531 and was never reunited with her. Banished from court, Mary was declared illegitimate, losing her rights to succeed to the throne, though these were restored in 1544 by a Succession Act.

Throughout the reign of her half-brother Edward VI, and in spite of his pro-Protestant legislation, Mary remained staunchly Roman Catholic, which stood her in good stead when she outmanoeuvred the Protestant Lady Jane GREY to gain the throne. Many English people had remained loyal to Catholicism, and Mary enjoyed broad public support both as ruler and for her reversal of Edward's Protestant legislation. Even though her projected marriage to the future Philip II of Spain provoked WYATT'S REBELLION, the Kentish landowner and his 3000 supporters found to their cost that England's affection for Mary was stronger than its fear of Spain. The rebellion was swiftly quelled, and in 1554 the Anglo-Spanish marriage took place. Unhappy and childless,

Mary turned increasingly for guidance to the Roman Catholic Archbishop of Canterbury, Cardinal Reginald POLE. In the four years preceding her death Mary approved the execution of nearly 300 Protestants including the Archbishop of Canterbury Thomas CRANMER, and the bishops Nicholas Ridley and Hugh LATIMER. In 1557 Philip dragged England into Spain's war with France, which cost England Calais, its last territorial outpost on the European continent.

Mary II (1662-94) Joint monarch of England, Scotland and Ireland with WILLIAM III from 1689 until her death. She was the daughter of James II by his first wife Anne Hyde. In 1677 Mary married William of Orange, and 11 years later she supported William against her father when James was removed from the throne in the GLORIOUS REVOLUTION. Mary shared the throne with her husband, who became William III. She administered England during William's frequent absences and was popular in both the Netherlands and England. Her inability to bear children and her quarrel with her sister Anne, the successor to the throne, clouded her last years.

Mary, Queen of Scots (1542-87) Queen of Scotland from 1542 to 1567 who, forced to abdicate, fled to England where she was held prisoner by Elizabeth I and eventually executed for treason.

The daughter of JAMES V of Scotland and his second wife Mary of GUISE, Mary inherited the throne when she was a week old and was betrothed to the future Edward VI of England when she was one. The Scottish Parliament's subsequent veto of the royal engagement led to war with England in which the Scots were defeated in 1547 at the Battle of Pinkie, near Edinburgh.

Sent to the French court, Mary received a Roman Catholic upbringing and in 1558, at the age of 16, married the Dauphin who acceded to the French throne as Francis II a year later. He died in 1560 and within a year Mary had returned to Scotland. The anti-Catholic and anti-French atmosphere of Reformation Scotland was ill-suited to Mary, whose marriage to her cousin the dissolute Lord DARNLEY in 1565 further alienated her Scots subjects. Although she bore Darnley a son – the future JAMES VI of Scotland and James I of England – her husband's involvement in the murder of

her Savoy-born private secretary David Rizzio widened the gap between Mary and her nobles. Darnley was killed in a mysterious explosion and only three months later, in May 1567, the Scottish queen married the divorced Earl of BOTHWELL, who had been implicated in his death. A coalition of Scottish lords then rose against Mary, and she was forced to abdicate after the Battle of Carberry in June. After almost a year's imprisonment in Loch Leven Castle she escaped, but the army raised to fight for her was defeated at the Battle of Langside in May 1568, and she fled to England, where she threw herself on the mercy of Elizabeth I. Confined in various strongholds until her death, Mary was accused of complicity in several Roman Catholic conspiracies against Elizabeth. The pro-Catholic Northern Rising of 1569, while protesting loyalty to Elizabeth, sought to have Mary declared heir to the English throne. Then the Ridolfi and Throckmorton plots, of 1571 and 1583 respectively, attempted to place Mary on the English throne. And finally in 1586 the BABINGTON PLOT provided enough evidence for a commission to find Mary guilty of treason. Even then Elizabeth, who for years had refused Protestant pleas to execute her fellow monarch, delayed signing the death warrant. And when Mary was executed at Fotheringhay in February 1587, Elizabeth disclaimed responsibility.

Mary the Virgin Mother of Jesus and the pre-eminent saint in Roman Catholic and Orthodox Christianity. Her name comes from the Hebrew, Miriam. She is also revered by Muslims, as Maryam. Episodes in Mary's life, described in the gospels, range from the Annunciation by the angel Gabriel of Jesus' birth and the birth itself, to her presence at his Crucifixion. Mary was originally given the title 'God Bearer' ('Mother of God') at the Council of Ephesus in 431 and is also referred to variously as Our Lady, the Madonna and the Blessed Virgin. Protestants,

Mary, Queen of Scots, depicted in a cameo pendant, was brought up in France and signed her name in French.

The serious business of arranging a match

The purpose of marriage has not only been to raise and protect children. In all societies it has been a vital means of creating family alliances and of specifying who should inherit rights, possessions and authority.

The view that love and marriage go together 'like a horse and carriage' has never been universal. In most societies marrying for love would have seemed a giddy choice, and partners would have been stopped from committing such an irresponsible act. Before the 18th century most Europeans thought that love should arise from marriage, rather than marriage follow love. Since the implications of wedlock went far beyond the parties betrothed, it required social and legal sanction. Medieval Europe was certainly acquainted with the idea of romantic love: it appeared in the songs of the troubadours, tales of King Arthur's court and in poems such as Jean de Meun's *Roman de la Rose*, written in about 1220. But it had nothing to do with marriage; it was an aristocratic display of sophisticated adultery.

FROM CUSTOM TO TRUE ROMANCE

In most communities, unions have been arranged as settlements between families or clans, sometimes brokered, as in traditional Jewish society, by matchmakers. Especially in upper-class families, the aim has been to further economic interests or political alliances. Parents have had the right to dispose of their offspring as they please, daughters in particular, in pursuit of family strategies and to perpetuate the line. Arranged marriages have usually involved legally binding transfers of money, especially the dowry provided by the bride's father, to facilitate the match and to set the couple on a sound footing.

While writers such as William Shakespeare in *Romeo and Juliet* have shown the tragic results of families obstructing the course of true love, there is little evidence worldwide that arranged marriages have been opposed by bride and groom or have led to unsuccessful matches. All depends on customs and expectations. In the preindustrial West, practical considerations came first: a man would seek a wife known to be virtuous and skilled at housewifery; a woman would hope to find a reliable breadwinner. An old saying taught: 'Never marry for money, but marry where money

is.' Men would not wed until they had achieved financial security; historically, European males have delayed marriage until their late twenties and teenage marriages have been unusual.

Similar patterns can be seen elsewhere. The development of the silk industry in Japan from the 16th century changed marriage customs. It made economic sense for families to keep their daughters at home to help with spinning and weaving. The result was that the average age of female marriage went up from 21 to 24.

With the rise of individualism in Europe during the past 300 years, marrying for love has triumphed. Even in aristocratic families, where property transfer and family lineage were most significant, parents gradually ceased to exercise the privilege of matchmaking, retaining only a veto. In England, Restoration plays and 18th-century novels such as Henry Fielding's *Tom Jones* exposed mercenary matches and celebrated the victory of romance. The climax of Charlotte Brontë's 19th-century novel *Jane Eyre* comes with the heroine declaring: 'Reader, I married him'. When ladies could not earn their own living, and the spinster was regarded as a sad case, securing a husband was crucially important. As the right of the young to choose their partner gained acceptance, elaborate courtship rituals had to be developed to give them opportunities to meet – hence the balls and tea parties in Jane Austen's fiction of the 18th century.

REMAINING 'ON THE SHELF'

Yet, as Austen's own case shows, things did not always work out: she remained unmarried, as did her sister Cassandra. The move from arranged marriage to personal choice meant that increasing numbers of people from the middle class and the gentry never married at all. The 'spinster problem' was one of the forces behind the Victorian women's movement.

Though Roman Catholicism has prized celibacy over matrimony, all the Christian churches have accepted St Paul's dictum that it is 'better to marry than to burn'

A girl prepares her wedding trousseau in this 5th-century BC terracotta tablet from a sanctuary of Persephone in southern Italy.

(with unquenched sexual desire). With Catholics, the aim of marriage was the procreation of children; the Protestant churches, which allowed their clergy to wed, have placed more stress upon companionship. Within Christianity, premarital and extramarital sex was sinful and bastardy carried a stigma. But from the 18th century, it became normal among the labouring classes for a couple to embark upon sexual relations once they had started 'going steady'. If pregnancy occurred, they would then normally marry.

Those eager to marry, perhaps against parental wishes, had things made easier for them by chaotic nuptial procedures. Before the 18th century in Europe it was possible to ask a priest to marry you on the spot: the ceremony did not have to be performed in church. A union was also considered valid if the partners declared themselves man and wife in the company of witnesses, or performed in public some ritualised act such as jumping backwards over a broomstick. The Church also accepted a union as binding in the eyes of God

A French couple (left) plight their troth in this miniature from the end of the 13th century, when even quite young children might become engaged. This elegant wedding ceremony (right) in 18th-century Japan was painted by Kiyonaga, an artist acclaimed for his images of beautiful women.

The wedding day of 'Ludwig and Thea', married in a suburb of Berlin in September 1919, appears to have been a solemn occasion.

Not every woman was allowed to marry for love in the 19th century. This arranged Russian marriage was painted by Vasili Pukirev.

A Hindu wedding in Willesden, London, shows how different marriage customs have spread across the world from their place of origin.

if a couple had made solemn vows to each other, even in private. Elopements were common and confusion reigned. To put a stop to clandestine marriages, from the 18th century the laws governing marriage procedures were made stricter – for example, requiring banns to be read in church – so as to 'protect' heiresses (or their family acres) from adventurers.

TILL DEATH US DO PART

In the 19th century, civil marriage became available in many countries. In modern England, marriages can be performed according to the ceremonies of the Church of England or those of other faiths, or in a register office. In most European countries and in the USA, civil registration of marriage, as well as (or instead of) a religious ceremony, is mandatory. Common law marriages – cohabitation as man and wife without a legal ceremony – has some legal recognition in many states.

By the 18th century in Europe and North America, marrying for money was less universally accepted: the new ideal of

romantic love spoke of marriages made in heaven. This squared with the Christian ideal of marriage as an indissoluble tie, a binding contract 'till death us do part'. In case of marital breakdown, judicial separations were possible but full divorce with remarriage was hardly sanctioned. In pre-19th-century England, divorce required a private Act of Parliament and was extremely expensive and very rare. Legal divorce was introduced slowly and inconsistently. In Victorian times, a man could petition for divorce on account of his wife's adultery; a wife needed to prove additional offences against her husband, such as cruelty. In 18th-century England it was not cruel in the eyes of the law for a man to beat his wife, so long as the stick he used was not thicker than his thumb.

The most spectacular change in the West during the last century has been the growth

of divorce. Obtaining a court divorce has been made far easier. As romantic ideas have inflated expectations, there has been a corresponding increase in disappointment. Contraception, a reduction in the stigma of 'living in sin' and of illegitimacy, and the greater economic independence of women have combined to reduce the pressure on unhappy couples to stay together.

There is no doubt that married women were for long legally disadvantaged: in England wives were not allowed to hold property in their own name until Victorian times. The social 'double standard' allowed husbands to seek sexual gratification outside marriage – though in Mediterranean societies, as the English poet Lord Byron found, it was accepted that married ladies might take a lover once they had given their husband an heir. In the last 25 years some women in the West have rejected marriage altogether, adopting the view of the pioneer 18th-century feminist Mary Wollstonecraft that marriage, inevitably exploitative, is no more than 'licensed prostitution'.

Roman Catholics and Muslims believe that she was born without original sin and remained a virgin – despite giving birth to Jesus, known as 'Isa to Muslims.

Mary is the subject of much Christian doctrine, while according to the Koran she is said as a child to have been miraculously fed while praying in a temple niche.

It is claimed that Mary has appeared miraculously in several places, which have since become centres of pilgrimage, including Guadeloupe in Mexico, Lourdes in France and Fatima in Portugal. Among the many Marian shrines are those at Loreto in Italy, Walsingham in England and Ephesus in Turkey.

Maryland State on the central east coast of the USA, named after the English queen HENRIETTA MARIA. Situated around the northern end of Chesapeake Bay, Maryland was founded as a privately owned colony in 1632 when Charles I of England granted a charter of the area to the Roman Catholic Lord Baltimore. Although in 1648 it passed a Toleration Act which guaranteed freedom of worship, Puritan settlers in the 1650s launched a series of anti-Catholic religious uprisings and repealed the Act.

Since the 1730s tobacco has been Maryland's staple product. In 1776 the state adopted its constitution and a declaration of independence. Despite its population of some 87 000 slaves in the 1860s, it elected to fight alongside the northern ABOLITIONISTS in the American Civil War, as its wealthy industrialists sought to stay in the Union. By the end of the 19th century railways from the north and south of the country were meeting in Maryland, and contributing to its growth. Its capital is Washington DC, home of the United States government.

Masada see feature, page 396

Masaryk, Jan (1886-1948) Czech diplomat and statesman who helped to establish the Czech Republic and died in mysterious circumstances soon after the communist takeover of his country. The son of Tomás MASARYK, Jan was ambassador to Britain from 1925 to 1938, when he resigned in protest at the British prime minister Neville Chamberlain's deal with Adolf Hitler over the future of Czechoslovakia at a meeting in MUNICH. After the Second World War, when Czechoslovakia was liberated from Nazi occupation by the Allies, Masaryk became foreign minister. He opposed the Soviet veto of Czechoslovak acceptance of US aid under the MARSHALL PLAN but, at the request of the Czech president Eduard BENEŠ, remained in his post after the communist coup of February 1948. Three weeks later Masaryk either committed suicide or was murdered when he fell from a window of the foreign ministry in Prague.

Masaryk, Tomás (1850-1937) First president of Czechoslovakia. Masaryk was a member of the Austrian parliament in the early 1890s, and sat as a representative of the Czech People's Party from 1907 to the outbreak of the First World War. He was a keen supporter of Slav and Jewish minority rights within the Austro-Hungarian empire.

As a refugee in London during the war, he worked alongside Eduard BENEŠ to establish the Czechoslovak national council, which in 1918 was officially recognised by the Allies as the *de facto* government. That year Czech independence was proclaimed in Prague, and Masaryk was elected president. A strong supporter of the League of Nations, he also favoured friendly relations with France, Germany and Austria. He resigned in 1935 in favour of Beneš, arguing that Czechoslovakia needed a younger president to face the rising Nazi menace in Europe.

> **DID YOU KNOW?**
>
> *Tomás Masaryk visited the novelist Leo Tolstoy on his estate and was appalled at the poverty he found there. He complained to Tolstoy that ideals must be matched by actions.*

Mason-Dixon line Former political boundary between Pennsylvania and Maryland, USA, later seen as the division between the Northern and Southern states.

Between 1765 and 1768 British astronomer Charles Mason and surveyor Jeremiah Dixon charted the Pennsylvania border with Maryland along longitude 36° 43´N. In 1799 the line was extended as the boundary between Pennsylvania and Virginia. In the years before the American Civil War the phrase 'Mason-Dixon line' was used to refer to the border between all Southern slave states, like Virginia, and all Northern free states, like Pennsylvania. It may be the origin of the term 'Dixie', applied to the Southern states.

mass production System of industrial production which breaks down manufacturing processes into a range of specialised operations. While mass production involves the division of labour advocated by Adam Smith in his book *The Wealth of Nations* (1776), its principles were probably first applied by the Scottish inventor James Watt, who in the 1780s designed standard, interchangeable parts for his steam engine.

In the United States, Eli Whitney began the mass production of muskets in 1798, making machine tools to turn out the weapon's parts. Criticism arose during the 19th century from thinkers such as John Ruskin and William Morris in England who witnessed the rapid replacement of traditional skilled crafts by the mechanised factory operations of mass production.

But it was in the United States in 1903 that mass production came of age. The Ford Company's factories assembled standard parts on a conveyor belt to turn out cheap cars, and profits soared. Other manufacturers adopted similar methods, and increasingly sophisticated automation accelerated production.

Tomás Masaryk, wearing a white peaked cap and a goatee beard, addresses a peasant gathering in 1926. A coachman's son, the Czechoslovakian president's down-to-earth style won him support.

The Zealots' last stand

In AD 73, in one of the grimmest acts of defiance, the Jewish defenders of Masada, a mountain fortress in the Judaean desert, chose mass suicide rather than surrendering to the besieging Romans encamped below.

On the south-western shore of the Dead Sea in present-day Israel, a mountain rises 1500 ft (457 m) from the desert floor. This natural bastion, known as Masada, is the site of a mass suicide by Jewish Zealots in the first century AD.

Its flat-topped pinnacle had been fortified by Herod the Great in about 37 BC. His palaces, aqueducts and cisterns were among the marvels of the ancient world. In 4 BC Masada became the focus of a rebellion against Rome led by Judas of Galilee, founder of the Zealots, a sect whose members believed themselves chosen by God to initiate a violent apocalypse. The Romans crushed this rebellion, and occupied Masada.

SIEGE OF MASADA

When the Zealots rose again in AD 66, the Roman garrison of Masada was a prime target. The fortress was taken by Menahem, a descendant of Judas of Galilee, and its defenders exterminated. After the rebellion had failed in the rest of Judaea, Masada became a symbol of resistance to Roman rule. Its 1000 inhabitants withstood several assaults from a besieging army of 15 000.

In 73, the Roman 10th Legion prepared for a decisive strike, building a ramp up the mountainside and moving siege machines within range of the walls.

The Zealot leader, Eleazar ben Jair, knew that the Jews' situation was hopeless: the men faced certain death, the women and children imprisonment or worse.

He addressed the garrison. 'Life is the calamity for man, not death,' he said. 'Death gives freedom to our souls and lets them depart to their own pure home where they will know nothing of any calamity.' Basing his message on Zealot law, in which separation and defilement were regarded as worse than death, he said: 'Let us die unenslaved by our enemies, and leave this world as free men in company with our wives and children.'

The ruins of Herod the Great's palace stand on the mountain of Masada in Israel, where determined Jews fought the Roman army.

The garrison agreed. On April 15, the men killed their wives and children, then divided into groups to organise their own deaths; a lone survivor set fire to the town and committed suicide. Altogether 960 inhabitants perished, leaving the Romans a city of ash and corpses.

The story was revealed by two women who had hidden with their children in the water conduits beneath the fortress. The testimony of one of them was quoted by the Jewish historian Josephus. The Zealots' decision conforms with the concept of resurrection they took from Old Testament prophecies such as Ezekiel's: 'You will know that I am Yahweh, when I open your graves and raise you from your graves…and I shall put my spirit in you, and you will live.'

These words were quoted in scrolls found beneath the synagogue when Masada was excavated in 1963. Other finds, including Roman camps, provided further evidence of the accuracy of Josephus' account. Israelis today see Masada as a symbol of national heroism.

Erected in AD 81, the Arch of Titus in Rome displays a procession carrying the menorah, a candelabrum from the Temple of Solomon in Jerusalem. On a Roman coin, 'Judaea Capta' (inset), two Jewish captives, one bound and the other grieving, symbolise the defeat of the Jews.

Massachusetts New England colony, whose capital was the scene of the BOSTON TEA PARTY in 1773. Founded in 1620 by the Puritan Massachusetts Bay Company, in the following decade the colony became a magnet for some 20 000 immigrants fleeing religious persecution in England. Their numbers included leading Puritan ministers and gentry who were granted a royal charter to trade and colonise. BOSTON was chosen as the capital and seat of the general court and the legislature, and the state's first governor, John WINTHROP, established a regime based on strict CONGREGATIONALIST rules. After a political struggle against royal interference, in 1684 Massachusetts' charter was revoked and direct government imposed. Five years later it became a royal colony which incorporated the older Plymouth Colony to the south. In 1773 Bostonians led the resistance to British attempts to increase taxes in the American colonies, and Massachusetts was in the forefront of the American War of Independence. After Shays' Rebellion in 1786, when state troops had to defend a federal arsenal from destitute farmers who had marched on the seaboard towns from the west of Massachusetts, a new constitution strengthening the powers of the federal government was introduced. This later became a pattern for other American states.

mass media see feature, pages 400-1

Massey, William Ferguson (1856-1925) New Zealand premier from July 1912 until his death. As founder of the Reform Party, which campaigned for freehold tenure and free enterprise, Massey made extensive purchases of remaining MAORI lands within months of his election as prime minister. Challenged by militant members of the farming unions in 1912 to 1913, he enrolled some farmers as special constables – nicknamed 'Massey's Cossacks' – to break strikes. From 1915 to 1919 Massey headed a wartime coalition. After the First World War he continued to favour strong ties with Britain, with New Zealand as a dominion within the empire.

Matabeleland see ZIMBABWE

Match Girls' Strike (1888) Industrial dispute which advanced the cause of women's rights and of the nascent TRADE UNION movement in England. The strike involved young women working in the London factory of Bryant & May, who suffered low pay and gangrene of the jawbone – nicknamed 'phossy jaw' – caused by the phosphorus used in match-making. Organised by the journalist Annie Besant, the strike and its associated demonstrations – which highlighted the girl's disfigurement – won the sympathy of the public and gained them increased pay.

matches Though prehistoric people may have used portable quartzite 'firestones', the first easily carried means of making fire was a flint and steel gadget, used to produce a spark which could be blown to a flame. Tinderboxes combined both flint and steel and dry kindling, or tinder, to make the process simpler. Combustion was sometimes aided by the use of sulphur-tipped wooden splints, and from these developed the modern match. Matches of various types were first made in Paris in 1805 and by the late 1820s were being produced in England. Many early matches were unpredictable in quality, and the use of poisonous white phosphorus to improve their ignition added a further hazard. These early matches were popularly known as 'lucifers'. In 1845 a nontoxic form of phosphorus was discovered, and in 1855 safety matches were invented which ignited only when struck on a combustible material attached to a matchbox.

Mather, Cotton (1663-1728) American Puritan clergyman, one of the founders of Yale University and the first American-born member of Britain's Royal Society. The son of the clergyman Increase MATHER, Cotton wrote nearly 500 works on theology, history, politics, science, medicine, social policy and education. His *Memorable Providences relating to Witchcraft and Possessions* (1689) probably helped to stir the superstitions which led to the SALEM WITCH TRIALS, though he did not support them. When the learned Mather was passed over for the presidency of Harvard, which his father had previously held, he became a driving force in establishing its rival university, Yale, in 1702. He was an advocate of Church involvement in social welfare, and an early champion of smallpox inoculation.

Mather, Increase (1639-1723) Boston minister, who as colonial agent in London for four years from 1688 negotiated a liberal royal charter for the state of Massachusetts. The son of Richard Mather, who had helped to define the beliefs of the new Congregational Church, Increase was a prolific author and was regarded as the foremost American preacher of his generation. On his return from London Mather helped to end the SALEM WITCH TRIALS which his son Cotton may have inadvertently helped to spark. From 1685 to 1701 he was a president of Harvard college.

Matilda (c.1102-67) Only legitimate daughter of Henry I, who challenged King STEPHEN's right to the throne of England. She is also known as Maud. In 1114 Matilda married the Holy Roman Emperor, Henry V. On her husband's death in 1125 she returned to England, now bearing the nickname the 'Empress'. Two years later – as the king's only remaining legitimate child – she was

Match girls at a factory in Victorian London cut and pack wooden splints, in this etching from *The Illustrated London News.* **Harsh conditions at Bryant & May led to a successful strike in July 1888.**

acknowledged by the Anglo-Norman barons as Henry's successor. In 1128 she married Geoffrey, Count of Anjou. Despite their oaths of allegiance to Matilda, however, when Henry died in 1135 most of the barons accepted his nephew STEPHEN as king. Four years later Matilda invaded England from Normandy, plunging the country into civil war. Plans to have her crowned at Lincoln in 1141 after the defeat and capture of Stephen were abandoned. The civil war continued, and in 1148 Matilda was forced to return to Normandy. Nevertheless, she lived to see her son succeed Stephen in 1154 as HENRY II.

Matthias I (1443-90) King of Hungary from 1458, also known as Matthias Corvinus, whose military successes won an empire that dominated south-central Europe. The son of the Hungarian king and national hero John Hunyadi, Matthias was 18 when his father died. Almost immediately he was embroiled in conflict, and he remained at war for most of his reign. He had to repulse the threats of the Holy Roman Emperor Frederick III and resist Turkish aggression even before his coronation in 1464.

Four years later Pope Pius II persuaded him to lead a crusade against the HUSSITES in Bohemia, although he was still at war with the Turks, who remained a threat throughout his reign. Fighting continued until 1478 when Matthias concluded a treaty with the Bohemian king Ladislaus II at the Peace of Olomuc. This gained him extensive territories and the shared title of King of Bohemia. By then he had also been waging war against Austria for a year, and in 1485 he beseiged and captured Vienna. Matthias introduced military, fiscal and administrative reforms, codified the law, founded the University of Buda, and encouraged the arts and learning.

Matthioli, Ercole Probable identity of the Man in the Iron Mask, one of history's most mysterious figures. Alexander Dumas wove his story of *The Man in the Iron Mask* (1847) around an unknown prisoner held for 40 years in the Bastille for alleged treason on the orders of the French king LOUIS XIV. The prisoner's identity was kept secret even from his jailers, but he is thought by some to have been Count Matthioli, an agent of the Duke of Mantua, who had tricked Louis over a secret treaty to gain the strategic fortress of Casale. The prisoner, who died in the Bastille in 1703, wore a velvet mask, not the iron mask of Dumas's tale. Other theories claim that he may have been a brother or illegitimate son of the king.

Maud see MATILDA

Mau Mau Nationalist movement in Kenya headed by Jomo KENYATTA, who was to become the country's first president in 1964.

Mau Mau's origins can be traced to the Kikuyu Central Association, which Kenyatta formed in 1920 and whose members argued that Kenya's White Highlands belonged to the Kikuyu people. Using an oathing ceremony designed to overcome local religious taboos on murder and disfigurement, Mau Mau committed its members to a campaign of violence in which some 11 000 Africans and 30 White settlers died. Kenyatta was jailed as an alleged Mau Mau leader in 1953, and then exiled to his native village. British colonialists launched a counterinsurgency campaign and placed more than 20 000 Kikuyu in detention camps. Widespread political and social reforms followed the campaign and led in 1963 to Kenyan independence.

Mauritania West African country whose interior forms part of the Sahara desert. French penetration of the hinterland began in 1858, and Mauritania was variously a French protectorate and a territory of French West Africa, before becoming autonomous a century later. It gained full independence in 1960, with Moktar Ould Daddah as its first president. After Spain withdrew from the western Sahara in 1976, war broke out between Mauritania and Morocco over rights to the southern part of the former Spanish territory, known as Tiris-el-Gherbia. In 1978 Daddah's government was overthrown in a military coup, and a year later Mauritania relinquished its territorial claims. Following ethnic violence in 1989, some 40 000 Black Mauritanians were expelled to SENEGAL, sparking a border war which lasted until April 1992. A referendum

A Parisian song-sheet portrayed the Bastille's mysterious prisoner – perhaps Ercole Matthioli – as 'Always Alone !!!' in his 'Mask of Iron'.

in 1991 showed majority support for a new constitution in a multiparty 'Islamic, African and Arab republic', and the following year Maaouiya Taya was elected president.

Mauritius Island in the Indian Ocean east of Madagascar and an independent state since 1968. Discovered by the Portuguese in 1511, Mauritius was controlled successively by the Dutch (1598-1710) and the French, before being captured by the British in 1810.

Under British rule there was a large influx of Indian labour to work the island's sugar plantations. In the 1980s the fall in world sugar prices led to a successful programme of agricultural diversification. The country remains politically stable, with a multiethnic population. The Mauritian Socialist Party, led by Aneerood Jugnauth, has held power since 1982. Mauritius became a republic in 1992, but remains a member of the Commonwealth.

Mauryan empire (c.325-185 BC) First empire to extend over most of the Indian subcontinent. The founder of the dynasty, Chandragupta Maurya, overthrew the Magadha kingdom in north-eastern India and then expanded westwards across the River Indus, annexing some provinces deep in Afghanistan from the Greek successors of Alexander the Great. On Maurya's death in around 297 BC, his son Bindusara expanded the empire southwards into the Deccan as far as Mysore.

Although the third emperor, ASOKA – who ruled from 265 to 238 – renounced military expansion, he developed a centralised bureaucracy through which he consolidated the huge empire, which he divided into four princely provinces. Revenue came from both agriculture and trade, and surviving sculptures point to a flourishing of the arts during Asoka's reign. After his death in 238 the dynasty declined. It ended in 185 BC when Emperor Birhadratha was assassinated by the founder of the new Sunga dynasty.

Maximilian I (1459-1519) Archduke of Austria, who in 1486 was elected King of the Romans and in 1493 inherited the Habsburg Holy Roman Empire. In 1477 Maximilian married Mary, the daughter and heiress of Charles the Bold, thereby adding the duchy of Burgundy, including the Netherlands, to the Habsburg lands. This angered France, and though two years later Maximilian defeated the French at the Battle of Guinegate, Habsburg-Valois rivalry continued in both the Netherlands and Italy.

After driving the Hungarians out of the Austrian territory they had seized under MATTHIAS I, Maximilian was recognised as the future king of Bohemia and Hungary by the Treaty of Pressburg in 1491. Two years later he repulsed the Turks, but the war in Italy

The making of the mass media

In 1865, it took 12 days for news of the assassination of President Abraham Lincoln in Washington to reach Britain. Now, for the first time in history, world events are shared and shaped through communications.

Newspapers, radio and television – the media – are so much part of daily life that it is hard to imagine a world without them. Yet all are recent innovations. Although daily newspapers began publication in the 18th century, the popular press in its modern form goes back only to the 1920s. Radio, which began at the same time, reached large national audiences in Britain and America by the end of the 1930s. Mass audiences for television were established in America in the early 1950s, and throughout Europe by the end of the 1960s.

The impact of the media has been vigorously debated. Newspapers have been accused of betraying their responsibility to report facts accurately and of vulgar sensationalism. Television has been blamed for the death of conversation, for increasing violence, decreasing sexual morality and destroying family values. None of these effects has been conclusively demonstrated. What is certain is the media's profound effect on public life and politics throughout the 20th century.

A WEDDING FOR THE MASSES

Before the development of mass media, public persons and events were remote. In early-19th-century Britain royal ceremonies were inaccessible rites performed for the privileged few, but in 1953 the coronation of Elizabeth II was seen by millions of television viewers in Britain, and the wedding in 1981 of Prince Charles and Lady Diana Spencer drew a global audience of 750 million watching in 74 countries. The world's media have created not only shared national cultures – a Brazilian soap opera, for instance, is just as likely to be enjoyed in Russia as in its country of origin – but a common global culture of news, sport and entertainment.

Celebrity O.J. Simpson evades arrest for alleged murder. Fans applauded his acquittal.

In the 1920s, John Reith, first Director General of the British Broadcasting Corporation, became keenly aware of the importance of new media to the health of another 20th-century innovation – mass democracy. In 1918 the Representation of

Children run from a misplaced napalm strike on Trang Bang, South Vietnam, in June 1972. Images such as this strengthened domestic opposition to American involvement in the Vietnam war.

Pravda ('truth') was the Soviet Communist Party newspaper. Its circulation exceeded 11 million, but its content was propaganda.

A televised debate between Kennedy and Nixon helped the better-looking candidate to win the 1960 presidential election.

the People Act had given the vote to most British adults. Lord Reith thought radio could help them to exercise their voting rights by broadcasting news and political debate. But the government refused to let the BBC develop its own news service and banned the discussion of controversial political issues.

In 1924 Reith complained: 'To disregard the spread of knowledge, with the consequent enlargement of opinion, and to be unable to supplement it with reasoned arguments, or to supply satisfactory answers to legitimate and intelligent questions, is not only dangerous but stupid.' It was not until the late 1950s in Britain that current affairs programmes included probing political interviews; until then, politicians continued to be treated with deference.

There has been a continuing struggle, in all countries, over the control of information. In totalitarian regimes such as Soviet Russia or Nazi Germany, the media were the propaganda arm of the state. A free press did not exist and public criticism was ruthlessly suppressed. Even in democratic countries the media have had to fight to open up politics to public scrutiny.

The media have made politicians more accountable – not just for their policies but their appearance. It is said that Richard Nixon lost the American presidential election in 1960 because he looked less trustworthy than John F. Kennedy in a televised debate. Many who heard the debate on radio thought Nixon had won the argument. Nixon always had an uneasy relationship with the media, and 14 years later a newspaper caused his downfall: as a result of the *Washington Post*'s investigations into the

Watergate scandal, he was forced to resign the presidency. The British prime minister Margaret Thatcher understood the importance of public presentation: after opinion surveys indicated that she sounded shrill and bossy she took voice coaching.

The conduct of war has been deeply influenced by modern media. Even as early as the Crimean War of 1854-6, the reports of military incompetence sent back to *The Times* of London by William Howard Russell contributed to the fall of the British Government. Almost a century later, the Second World War was the first to be followed on film, radio and in newspapers on every continent, so the enemy powers fought not just with weapons but with competing versions of events. Television coverage of the Vietnam War was influential in turning American public opinion against further involvement and helped force America's withdrawal. One lesson of Vietnam learnt by governments was to keep the media under control. It was not lost on the British during the Falklands War of 1982, and the Gulf War ten years later was carefully stage-managed by the military so that their version of events would be the one to appear on the world's television screens.

INSIDE THE ELECTRONIC VILLAGE

Today we live in what the Canadian sociologist Marshall McLuhan called the 'electronic village'. Everyone knows the faces of global celebrities, even those who are famous only for being famous. In a way which would have been inconceivable at any earlier time, the instantaneous transmission of information by electronic media has created a shared world in which we are all involved and for which we all feel responsible. The arrival of the internet may have the effect of drawing every person with a computer into a global web of personal communication in which national boundaries and restrictions become increasingly irrelevant.

Princess Diana, a nursery assistant in 1980, flees the cameras (right) after 14 years' exposure to the press.

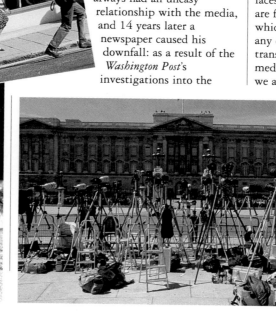

The world's media gather outside Buckingham Palace to cover the Trooping the Colour ceremony.

between French and Habsburg forces dragged on until 1516. Here Maximilian was hampered by the German princes' refusal to finance his campaigns. Despite an alliance with England against France, at the end of the war the emperor had to cede Verona to the Venetians and Milan to France. He also failed in his attempts to impose centralised rule on the self-governing German princedoms.

As a dynast, Maximilian had more success. He secured Spain for the Habsburgs through his son Philip's marriage to the infanta Joanna (the daughter of FERDINAND II and Isabella), while Hungary and Bohemia were added to their empire by the double marriage of a grandson and granddaughter to the daughter and son of Ladislaus II of Hungary in 1521.

Maximilian (1832-67) Austrian archduke who ruled Mexico as emperor from 1864 until his death. A brother of the Austrian emperor FRANZ JOSEF, Maximilian accepted the imperial crown reluctantly and only after pressure from NAPOLEON III of France and conservative Mexican landowners with royalist leanings.

Although the Mexican empire had been established following independence from Spain in 1821, the new country had suffered

Maximilian (inset), Emperor of Mexico, faces a firing squad at Querétaro. The soldiers in this painting by Edouard Manet support the liberal Benito Juárez.

civil wars and indigenous Indian rebellions until 1861, when President Santa Anna's repressive regime was replaced by a liberal republican government led by Benito Juárez. Maximilian was, effectively, imposed on a reluctant nation by the French after their invasion of Mexico in 1863. However, he immediately antagonised the wealthy landowners who had originally backed him by instituting a series of liberal reforms, and he further alienated Juárez's supporters in 1865 when he ordered the execution of several of their leaders. Maximilian's only protection was a French military force, and this was withdrawn in 1867 after pressure from the United States. He was left with a small army and was captured by Juárez's forces at Querétaro, where he was executed by firing squad.

Maxwell, James (1831-79) Scottish physicist who developed the theory of electromagnetism. Appointed the first director of the Cavendish Laboratory in Cambridge in 1871, Maxwell proved the existence of electro-magnetic radiation – the physical waves which include light, X-rays, gamma rays and microwaves. His theory was based on four mathematical equations covering the laws of magnetic and electric attraction and the links between magnetic fields and electric currents. In 1871 Maxwell devised an imaginary creature, 'Maxwell's demon', as part of a paradox on the second law of thermodynamics, which states that heat from a cool body cannot of its own accord flow into a hotter body. The 'demon' – and the paradox – remain a matter of contention among scientists.

This classical 6th-century Maya mask, made mainly of jade mosaic, was found by archaeologists in a Guatemalan tomb.

Maya Central American people whose culture dominated southern Mexico, Guatemala, Belize and the Yucatán peninsula from about 2600 BC to the 15th century AD. Archaeologists divide Maya influence into four areas: the Guatemalan highlands; the Petén, or central Guatemala; the Yucatán peninsula; and the lands to the east and west of Guatemala called the Southern Lowlands. All the regions had political and trade links with the cities of southern and central Mexico. From about 300 to AD 900 the southern lowlands were dominant, with cities such as Tikal, Uaxactún and Palenque. After 900, TOLTEC influence led to a mixed Toltec-Maya culture. Around 1200 power shifted to the Yucatán peninsula and particularly Mayapán, which became the leading Maya city after its ruler, Hunac Ceel, conquered its principal rival, Chichén Itzá. The city contained nearly 4000 buildings, enclosed within an outer wall more than 5½ miles (9km) long. Mayapán dominated politics and trade until 1441, when it was defeated and sacked by a coalition led by the city of Uxmal. (See also feature, pages 404-5.)

Mayflower see PILGRIM FATHERS

Mazarin, Jules (1602-61) French statesman and cardinal, who as France's chief minister during LOUIS XIV's minority built the kingdom into the most powerful in Europe. An Italian by birth, Mazarin acted as France's unofficial papal representative from 1631 to 1639, before becoming a cardinal two years later. After the death of Cardinal RICHELIEU in 1642 and of Louis XIII in the following year, Mazarin became virtual ruler of France, continuing Richelieu's policies and deriving his authority mainly from his close relationship with Louis XIV's mother, Anne of Austria. Mazarin used his diplomatic skills to negotiate good terms for France when, in

1648, the Treaty of Westphalia ended the Thirty Years' War, but his decision to raise taxes to continue the war against Spain led to the antiroyalist FRONDE uprisings in Paris in 1648 and 1653. Surviving these crises, Mazarin successfully ended the Spanish War in 1659 at the Treaty of the Pyrenees.

Mazzini, Giuseppe (1805-72) Italian revolutionary and a leader of the RISORGIMENTO. Mazzini's membership of the CARBONARI, a secret society dedicated to Italian self-rule, led in 1830 to his arrest and exile by the region's Austrian rulers. A year later he formed the Young Italy Society in Marseilles and in 1834 led a fruitless invasion of the Piedmontese province of Savoy from Switzerland. He returned across the Swiss border and was sentenced to death *in absentia* by the Piedmontese authorities. From 1837 he spent a period of exile in London, returning to Italy in 1848 during Europe's REVOLUTIONS. Pope Pius IX's flight from Rome the following year led to Mazzini's proclamation of a short-lived republic (February-June 1849).

Abortive anti-Austrian risings in Mantua and Milan weakened his influence and in 1858 he returned to London. As a confirmed republican, he never accepted the monarchy of VICTOR EMMANUEL II, and refused to return openly to Italy. In 1868 he settled in Switzerland, secretly crossing the border in 1872 to die at Pisa in his homeland.

McAdam, John (1756-1836) Scottish road engineer who developed the system of macadamised roads. After amassing a fortune as a financier in the USA, McAdam returned to Scotland in 1783 to experiment with designs to improve road-building. In 1815 he was appointed surveyor to the Bristol Turnpike Trust, for whom he devised a durable road surface composed of stones and gravel laid down to form a dense, firm base and raised to improve drainage. Later, engineers added tar to bind the stones together, calling the surface 'tarmacadam' or 'tarmac' after him.

McCarthy, Joseph (1908-57) American politician who persecuted alleged communist sympathisers. A Republican senator for Wisconsin from 1947 until his death, McCarthy claimed in 1950 that he had a list of 205 communists in the highest levels of government. Feeding on fears of infiltration by the Soviet Union, he gained national publicity for his campaign against subversive influences within the US government. Although a senate investigating committee concluded that there was no substance to his charges, McCarthy continued his attacks on the government, the military and public figures.

> **DID YOU KNOW?**
>
> McCarthy boasted that he had been wounded in action in the Marine Corps. In fact, he fractured his foot when he fell off a ladder.

The term 'McCarthyism' became synonymous with the anticommunist hysteria that gripped the United States from 1950 to 1954 at the height of the COLD WAR. In 1953, as chairman of the senate permanent subcommittee on investigations, McCarthy's merciless questioning and unsubstantiated accusations on television destroyed numerous reputations, including those of diplomats, academics and Hollywood film stars. In 1954 McCarthy was finally censured by the senate.

Joseph McCarthy points to alleged communist power bases in the USA (below), and stars of the film world confer before confronting him.

McKinley, William (1843-1901) Twenty-fifth president of the United States, from 1897 to 1901. He served in the Union army during the American Civil War and entered Congress as a Republican in 1876, giving his name to the tariff of 1890 which steeply raised import duties on foreign goods. Aided by the wealthy industrialist Marcus HANNA, he was elected governor of Ohio in 1892. His victory in the presidential election of 1897 was due largely to his conservative support of the GOLD STANDARD. The following year McKinley embarked on an expansionist foreign policy, taking the USA into the SPANISH-AMERICAN WAR and acquiring Puerto Rico, Guam and the Philippines, as well as annexing Hawaii. He was re-elected in 1900, but the following year was assassinated in Buffalo by an anarchist, Leon Czolgosz. He was succeeded by his vice-president, Theodore ROOSEVELT.

McMahon Line Boundary drawn between Tibet and India in 1914. The line was marked out by British representatives led by Sir Henry McMahon at the Simla Conference in India between Britain, Tibet and China – whose government refused to ratify the agreement. After China regained control of Tibet in 1951, boundary disputes eventually led to war in 1962 between India and China.

Mecca Birthplace in around AD570 of the Prophet MUHAMMAD, and Islam's holiest city. Forced in 622 to flee from Mecca to Medina, Muhammad returned to capture the city a few years later. Although he criticised Mecca and the pre-Islamic cult associated with its central shrine, the Kaaba, he taught that life was fulfilled by making a pilgrimage to the shrine. The city remained a prosperous trading centre until it was sacked in 930 by the Qarmations, a heretical Islamic sect. In 1517 it was captured by the Ottoman Turks, and in 1924 it fell to Ibn Saud, the future king of independent Saudi Arabia. The KORAN decrees that all Muslims should make a pilgrimage, or *hadj*, to Mecca once in their lifetime, after which they can take the title *Hadji*. (See also feature, pages 326-7.)

Medes Indo-European people who occupied Media, an area south-west of the Caspian Sea, in the 7th century BC. The Median empire was probably established around 675 by Phraortes. It was extended in 612 by his son Cyaxares (625-585), who, in alliance with Babylon, conquered the Assyrians and captured NINEVEH. He was succeeded by Astyages, who added various Babylonian territories to the empire before his overthrow around 550 BC by CYRUS II 'the Great', the founder of the Persian Achaemenid empire.

Three empires of Sun, gold and sacrifice

About 15000 years ago the first people walked into America across a land bridge between Siberia and Alaska. In Central and South America their descendants would build the civilisations we know as Maya, Aztec and Inca.

In 1492 Christopher Columbus made his first voyage to the Americas. Two of history's most dramatic events followed: the destruction of the resplendent Aztec and Inca empires at the hands of the Spanish conquistadores.

Spanish soldiers entered the Aztec capital of Tenochtitlán (on the site of present-day Mexico City) in the early 16th century. Set on an island in Lake Texcoco, it had some 200000 inhabitants and was laid out on a grid of canals and streets, with elaborate temples and palaces. It was said to resemble an 'enchanted city'.

The Aztecs established the centre of their empire at Tenochtitlán in 1325. They had forged a society bountiful in gold and rich in culture, yet also demanding religious rituals of notorious savagery. The Spanish invaders referred to the Aztecs as barbarians – a description used, at least in part, to justify their conquest and looting.

Yet Aztecs and Spanish had much in common. Both saw themselves as chosen people destined to prevail. Such was the Aztecs' commitment to warfare that at their baptisms baby boys would be dedicated to the battlefield. For Aztecs, conquest was not just a means of gaining riches through tribute; it was essential to cosmic survival. Huitzilopochtli, their sun god, was said to need constant nourishment with blood: the life of the Universe could only be extended by the sacrifice of prisoners. At a ceremony during the reign of the last emperor, Montezuma II, 12000 enemy soldiers were put to death. Sometimes, Aztecs would eat the limbs of victims, and priests would wear human skins as ceremonial dress. If a brave warrior was sacrificed, they believed that his strength would pass into their soldiers.

Despite such practices, the Aztecs respected humility, compassion, obedience

The Aztec and Mayan empires flourished in present-day Central America, and the Inca people dominated South America.

and hard work. They enforced a strict legal system and imposed harsh penalties for crime. Upper class boys were sent to boarding schools where they were prepared for war and taught law, politics, history and music. Other boys were trained in the trades as well as warfare; girls were taught to be housewives and mothers. Life was regulated by rituals which were governed by two calendars: one for the civil year and one for the sacred year.

Just as the Aztecs built their empire on conflict so, according to their mythology, the act of creation was one of adversity: four times the gods created an era and four times they destroyed it before bringing our current era into

being. The Aztecs recorded their myths in books as well as on vases and in carvings on wood, bone and stone. They spoke Nahuatl and wrote in pictographs.

It was a myth concerning the god Quetzalcoatl which helped to cause the collapse of the Aztec empire. The Spanish conqueror Hernando Cortés exploited the prophecy that Quetzalcoatl would one day return from the east to claim his throne. Emperor Montezuma was so unsettled by the tale that he believed Cortés to be the fabulous god himself, come home across the seas to take possession of his kingdom. So it was that, on August 13, 1521, the glorious city of Tenochtitlán fell to the Spaniards.

Four years earlier, in 1517, the Spaniard Francisco de Cordoba had sailed to the coast of Yucatán. There he uncovered the remnants of an elaborate and artistic culture – that of the Maya people. At their height from about AD300 to 900, the Maya controlled present-day Guatemala,

A jade bead (below, left) showing the Mayan sun god and a colossal stele put up in 771 bear witness to the complexity of Mayan civilisation.

Map labels:

NORTH AMERICA

ATLANTIC OCEAN

AZTEC EMPIRE

Gulf of Mexico

Tenochtitlán

Chichen Itza

MAYA

A Maya noble of about AD800

SOUTH AMERICA

Montezuma's quetzal-feather headdress

PACIFIC OCEAN

INCA EMPIRE

Cuzco

N

0   800miles

0   1000km

Gold Inca pouch to store coca leaves

Aztec empire in 1519
Maya territory 600-800
Inca empire in 1525

Belize and part of Mexico. Although they were ignorant of iron or bronze, their culture features finely detailed carved stone pottery, monoliths and arches. They are renowned for their elaborate hieroglyphic writing, their accurate calendars and their advanced knowledge of astronomy and mathematics. The calendars were used to regulate ceremonies, the most important of which took place at sacred centres such as Chichén Itzá in North Yucatán, where large pyramids were built. Many of the Maya's myths concerned humanity's creation and their belief that a succession of previous worlds existed before their own.

By the time the Spanish arrived, civil war had brought about the decline of Maya civilisation; in many regions it had more or less disappeared. Chichén Itzá had been overgrown by forest. The Spaniards encountered the remains of this fabulous civilisation when they found a fortified town with stone buildings, market places and temples still standing.

Maya society was highly structured. A gulf lay between the nobility who possessed the wealth, accumulated

The Aztecs mistook Cortés for their god Quetzalcoatl (right). The codex below shows great captains of the Aztec army.

through trade and commerce, and the peasants who worked the land. The aristocracy admired elongated, flattened foreheads and tied boards to their children's heads to deform their skulls. The Maya produced finely worked gold objects, jade carvings and pottery, and exported salt and cotton as far south as the Gulf of Honduras.

THE RISE OF THE INCAS
In the early 16th century, while the Aztec capital of Tenochtitlán was the most important city in Central America, Cuzco, the Inca capital, dominated South America. The Incas settled there around AD 1200 under the leadership of their founder, Manco Capac, a shadowy figure supposedly descended from the sun god. But it was not until the mid 15th century, under the emperor Pachacuti, that the Incas began to expand beyond their capital, seizing booty, exacting tribute and accumulating riches.

At its height, their realm stretched for 3500 miles, from northern Ecuador to central Chile. It was the Incas' engineering skills more than their weapons which enabled them to pursue their conquests. Their roads were far more advanced than those of the Romans: one stretched more than 1500 miles. But it was not only their political and organisational skills which enabled them to build such an immense empire; they believed, as did the Aztecs, that they had a divine mission to spread the light of the sun god.

Because the Incas regarded their ancestors as direct descendants of this god, their leader ruled by divine right and wielded absolute power. The emperor's directives were administered by governors, who organised the agricultural communities and instilled Inca ideas. Laziness was regarded as a serious crime: even children as young as five were supposed to work. An advanced system of state care provided orphanages and storehouses.

Some rituals were carried out by Sacred Virgins of the Sun, who lived in convents where they guarded the sacred fire for the festival of the sun and prepared food and clothing for state occasions. Myths were perpetuated by word of mouth. In 1471 Topa Inca, Pachacuti's son, made Quechua the official language. It is still spoken.

The last emperors claimed not only to be descended from the sun god, but to be the god himself. The centre of Cuzco was redesigned around the sun temple, the walls of which were lined with gold.

Despite the splendour of the Inca empire, it was overcome by a handful of Spanish soldiers led by Francisco Pizarro. This feat was accomplished partly because of the Incas' belief in Emperor Atahualpa's invulnerability. The power of the Incas was concentrated in the emperor; when he was taken captive, his subjects had no one left to obey. Also the Incas, like the Aztecs, had no weapons that could withstand guns and men on horseback. Within 50 years, the Spanish conquistadores succeeded in marking out the boundaries of an empire twice as large as Europe.

Machu Picchu (below) was the Incas' ceremonial centre. The bulging cheeks of the silver female figure (right) show that she is chewing the narcotic coca leaf.

Lorenzo de Medici leads a procession as one of the Magi, or three Biblical kings, in a painting by Gozzoli. Behind him ride his father Piero, on a white horse, and his grandfather Cosimo, in blue.

Medici, Catherine de

Medici, Catherine de (1519-89) Queen of France from 1547 to 1559, whose support for the Roman Catholics against the Huguenots (French Protestants) led to the ST BARTHOLOMEW'S DAY MASSACRE of 1572. Born the daughter of Lorenzo de Medici, Duke of Urbino, in 1533 Catherine married the Duc d'Orléans, who in 1547 became Henry II of France. When her second son Charles IX (1550-74) became king in 1560, Catherine acted first as regent during his minority and then as his adviser until his death.

As queen, Catherine encouraged tolerance between Catholics and Huguenots. But she abandoned this policy in 1562 when the first of the FRENCH WARS OF RELIGION broke out. She allied herself with the Catholic GUISE faction, so sparking the brutal massacre of hundreds of Protestants. She continued to rule the court when her third son became Henry III in 1574. Though she tried to reconcile Catholics and Protestants, her earlier policy change cost her the trust of both factions.

Medici, Cosimo de (1389-1464) Banker and patron of the arts who established the power of the Medici dynasty, the dominant family of Renaissance Florence. During the intense power struggle between rival Florentine factions in the early 15th century Cosimo was banished from the city by the Albizzi family, but a year later, in 1434, he returned with the popular support of the citizens. For the next 60 years he and his descendants were the virtual, though un-elected, rulers of the city. Cosimo's wealth and power stemmed from the Medici bank, which he managed prudently while expanding the family's interests into other areas. By around 1455 he owned a company for the manufacture of silk and two wool-making companies, and had opened further branches of the bank in Geneva, Bruges, London, Avignon, Rome, Milan, Pisa and Venice. He was also a patron of several sculptors, including Lorenzo Ghiberti and Donatello.

Medici, Lorenzo de (1449-92) Joint ruler of Florence with his brother Giuliano, and the sculptor MICHELANGELO's first patron – known as 'Lorenzo the Magnificent'. In 1478 he survived an assassination attempt (in which his brother was killed) made by the rival Pazzi family backed by Pope SIXTUS IV. Hoping to seize power, the plotters struck during high mass in Florence Cathedral, but Lorenzo's escape served to rally the citizens in support of the Medicis. Politically, Lorenzo worked to preserve peace among the various Italian states by establishing a balance of power. He was a poet and a lavish patron of the arts and sciences. His second son became Pope Leo X.

Medina Sidonia, Duke of (1550-1619) Spanish nobleman (Alonso Pérez de Guzmán), who in 1588 commanded the SPANISH ARMADA against England. When PHILIP II gave Medina Sidonia responsibility for the Armada, the duke – who knew little of naval warfare – asked to be excused the task, but his appeal was rejected. In fact, Medina Sidonia organised the expedition efficiently, and its eventual failure was due mainly to a vigilant English navy and adverse weather conditions. He himself survived and returned to Spain, where he continued in royal service.

Medway, Battle on the (AD 43) Two-day battle for control of the River Medway in Kent, England, between the British under CARATACUS and the invading Roman armies, commanded by Aulus Plautius. The Roman victory allowed the imperial forces to advance to the River Thames and, later, to consolidate their conquest of ROMAN BRITAIN.

megaliths Huge stone blocks used to build monuments in Europe between around 4000 and 1500 BC. Similar stones are known from Inca Peru, ancient Egypt and the Orient. The European monuments belong to a number of different periods and cultures. During the later NEOLITHIC and early BRONZE AGE, megaliths were used singly as 'standing stones' or MENHIRS, or arranged in rings as 'stone circles' or in rows as 'avenues'. All these structures are thought to be places of ritual. Megaliths were also used to construct tomb chambers with side-slabs and capping stones, which were then covered with earth mounds (called barrows) or stone cairns. Examples which have lost their covering mound are commonly known as DOLMENS. One of the largest megaliths recorded is the capstone of a tomb at Browneshill, County Carlow, Ireland, estimated to weigh 100 tonnes.

Mehemet Ali (c.1769-1849) Albanian-born Egyptian pasha (viceroy) from 1805 to 1849. Mehemet unsuccessfully led the Ottoman army in Egypt against Napoleon in 1799, and

Mehemet Ali, the independent and reforming pasha of Egypt, reclines in splendour in Cairo, in a watercolour by John Frederick Lewis.

returned in 1801 at the head of the sultan's Albanian troops to subdue the anarchy which had erupted when Napoleon's forces withdrew. Helped by the British, he overthrew the MAMELUKE dynasty within a decade. Although officially viceroy of the Ottoman sultan Mahmud II, Mehemet was effectively independent and, with the aid of French advisers, reorganised Egypt's entire economic and administrative structure.

From 1811 to 1818 Mehemet campaigned against the Wahhabis in Arabia and he occupied the Sudan from 1821 to 1823. However, his six-year campaign against Greece, begun in 1822, angered Britain, France and Russia, whose navies destroyed his fleet in 1827 at the Battle of Navarino. From 1831 to 1833 Mehemet took control of Syria, and in 1839 defeated the Ottoman forces at the Battle of Nizip. Threatened by the continuing opposition of the major European powers, he accepted Ottoman suzerainty in 1841, and was granted a request that his family become hereditary pashas of Egypt.

Meiji Restoration Return to imperial rule in Japan in 1868 following the overthrow of the Tokugawa SHOGUNATE. The restoration period stretched from the fall of the shogunate to the institution of a constitution in 1889.

The failure of the shogunate to exclude foreigners from Japan after the arrival of the US admiral Matthew PERRY in 1853, combined with internal economic problems, united its opponents in demands that the emperor should be restored to full power. Faced by an alliance of regional forces, the last shogun formally surrendered his powers to the Meiji emperor Mutsuhito, who in January 1868 resumed imperial rule. Mutsuhito dismantled the feudal Daimyo and SAMURAI system of overlords who each maintained a private army of warriors, and replaced it with a European-style peerage. This formed part of a two-chamber parliament shared with an elected lower house. A Cabinet system was introduced as part of the new Meiji constitution in 1885, and a privy council three years later. A policy of government-sponsored industrial development initiated by the emperor gradually transformed Japan into a modern state.

Meir, Golda (1898-1978) Israeli prime minister from 1969 to 1974. Born in Kiev, Ukraine, Meir emigrated with her parents to the USA when she was eight. As a student she was inspired by the growing movement to establish a Jewish state in Palestine, moving there when she was 23. As head of the political department of the Jewish Agency from 1946 to 1948, Meir was closely involved in the negotiations that led to the foundation of Israel. She served from 1949 to 1956 as Israel's first minister of labour, and for the next decade as foreign minister. In 1966 Meir

Golda Meir, the first woman prime minister of Israel and leader of the Labour Party, robustly states her beliefs. Behind her is the Israeli flag.

became secretary general of the Mapai Party, which the following year was renamed the Labour Party. Elected prime minister of a coalition government in 1969, she gained Israel many friends through her international stature, but she faced strong domestic criticism in 1973 over Israel's lack of military readiness for the YOM KIPPUR WAR. She resigned in 1974 and was replaced as prime minister by Yitzhak RABIN.

Melanchthon, Philip (1497-1560) German religious reformer and the main draughtsman of the AUGSBURG Confession of 1530, which laid down the principal Lutheran doctrines. Appointed professor of Greek at Wittenberg in 1518, Melanchthon soon came under the influence of the priest Martin LUTHER. His *Loci Communes* (1521) was the first ordered presentation of Reformation beliefs, and won many converts. More conciliatory than his mentor, when Melanchthon signed the Schmalkaldic Articles – a statement on doctrine drawn up by Luther in 1537 – he did so with the reservation that he would accept the papacy in a modified form. Deeply influenced by Christian HUMANISM, Melanchthon was particularly active in reforming Germany's educational system.

Melanesians Peoples of New Guinea, New Caledonia, Fiji and neighbouring groups of Pacific islands. The Melanesians arrived from South-east Asia in several waves of migration starting about 10000 years ago. As early as 7000BC they had successfully developed methods of subsistence farming. The people are related ethnically to the Australoids and Mongoloids of East Asia. Traditional society is based on village units, generally without hereditary kings or chiefs. Today the most important part of their economy is fishing.

Melbourne, William Lamb, Viscount (1779-1848) British prime minister in 1834 and between 1835 and 1841, and one of Queen Victoria's closest advisers during the early years of her reign. The 2nd Viscount Melbourne was elected to Parliament as a Whig in 1806 and acted as chief secretary for Ireland from 1827 to 1828. Two years later, as home secretary, he dealt harshly with agrarian riots in southern England, and during his brief tenure as prime minister in 1834 he upheld the sentences of transportation passed on the TOLPUDDLE MARTYRS. He was prime minister in 1837 at the time of Queen Victoria's accession to the throne.

His wife, Lady Caroline Lamb, wrote novels. For nine months in 1812 to 1813 she had a notorious love affair with the poet Lord BYRON, whom she described as 'mad, bad and dangerous to know'.

Memphis Capital of Egypt's Old Kingdom from around 2700 to 2200BC, at the head of the Nile delta. According to tradition, Memphis was founded by King Menes, the first ruler to unite the Upper and Lower Kingdoms, on whose boundary the city stood. The city was sacred to the god Ptah. Among the most impressive remains are an alabaster sphinx and two colossal statues of the pharaoh Rameses II. At nearby Sakkara there is a necropolis which was a favoured burial place among the kings of the Old Kingdom. From Sakkara, a line of PYRAMIDS stretches some 20 miles (32km) to Giza. Memphis retained its importance during the long dominance of THEBES and remained Egypt's second city, after ALEXANDRIA, until Roman times.

This alabaster sphinx stands guard near the temple of Ptah at Memphis. Ptah was the god of craftsmen and the city's special protector.

Mencius (c.372-289 BC) Chinese philosopher whose influence was second only to that of his predecessor CONFUCIUS. A consistent champion of Confucius, Mencius believed in the innate goodness of every individual and that the right environment would reveal it. He argued that rebellion against oppressive rule was justified and that, conversely, a ruler who attended to the welfare of his state would attract all people to his sway; 'all under Heaven' would obey him.

Mendès-France, Pierre (1907-82) French prime minister from 1954 to 1955. Elected as a radical socialist to the Chamber of Deputies in 1932 and first gaining office as economics minister six years later, Mendès-France was imprisoned by the Vichy government in the Second World War. In 1941 he escaped to London where he joined General Charles DE GAULLE's exiled Free French government.

A critic of French postwar policy in Indo-China, Mendès-France's promise that France would withdraw from its former colony helped to gain him the premiership in 1954, soon after the defeat of French forces at DIEN BIEN PHU. Mendès-France honoured this pledge and also supported Algerian claims for independence. An austere economic policy led to his downfall in 1955. Though Mendès-France served in Guy Mollett's government the following year, he was unhappy with de Gaulle's Fifth Republic and resigned from the Radical Socialist Party in 1959. Lacking an effective power-base, his opposition to de Gaulle foundered and in 1973 he retired from political life.

menhir Monumental upright stone erected in prehistoric times. Its name derives from the Breton language and means 'long stone'. Between 3000 and 2000 BC the practice of

A towering menhir casts its long shadow past a solitary farmhouse in Brittany, France. It may mark the site of an ancient ceremonial burial.

Five meetings that changed the world

From curtailing the powers of an English king to wiping out the entire Aztec civilisation, five meetings over the centuries have radically altered the course of world history.

THE ENGLISH KING AND THE BARONS

The position of King John of England was parlous by 1215. He was hated by his nobles because of his arbitrary rule and heavy taxation, and widely despised for his cruelty and loose living. London fell to rebel barons on May 17, and on June 15 they met the king at Runnymede, on the banks of the River Thames, where John reluctantly placed the royal seal on Magna Carta, or the Great Charter. He would not have done so without the skilful mediation of Stephen Langton, Archbishop of Canterbury. The charter pledged that no free man was to be imprisoned, outlawed or exiled, or dispossessed of his goods 'except by the lawful judgment of his equals or by the law of the land', and set out a range of rights and liberties. Although John tried to retract on it, Magna Carta survived as not only the foundation stone of the English constitution, but an inspirational symbol of freedom everywhere.

A gathering of nobles persuade King John to give Magna Carta his seal of approval.

THE AZTEC AND THE CONQUISTADOR

The Aztec civilisation of Central America, centred on Tenochtitlán, Mexico, was one of the glories of the world during the 15th and early 16th centuries. An empire of 15 million people was run with great efficiency, while the beauty of its craftsmanship in gold and silver was matched by the splendour of its architecture. Then came the Europeans, hungry for conquest. Hernán Cortés, a Spanish adventurer accompanied by 400

other conquistadores, reached Tenochtitlán on November 8, 1519. 'With such wonderful sights to gaze on we did not know what to say, or if this was real that we saw before our eyes,' a companion of Cortés would recall. One of those sights was the Aztec emperor, Montezuma II, carried on a litter beneath a canopy of green feathers, decorated with gold, silver and pearls. Gifts were exchanged and the Spaniards were warmly welcomed, a hospitality that Cortés soon repaid by taking Montezuma hostage. Cortés, helped by the Aztecs' belief that he was the bearded white god Quetzalcoatl who had returned in accordance with legend, used Montezuma as his spokesman. The unfortunate emperor was eventually stoned to death by some of his subjects as he pleaded for calm, and Tenochtitlán fell to the forces of Cortés in 1521. The Aztec era was over, that of 'New Spain' just beginning.

THE AMERICAN COMMODORE AND THE SAMURAI

For more than two centuries, Japan was a wholly closed society. On July 8, 1853, that era was brought to an end when Commodore Matthew Perry of the US Navy arrived in Edo Bay near Tokyo with

The Aztec emperor Montezuma II welcomes the Spanish conquistador Hernán Cortés at Tenochtitlán.

a fleet of six steam-powered ships and presidential instructions to open up the country to American trade. 'Like wild birds at a sudden intruder,' was how one of his party described the panic-stricken reaction of the fleeing local fishermen. Eventually Perry handed over a casket containing his demands and promised to return the next year – which he did, in February 1854, but this time with nine ships. Over the following weeks a stately diplomatic dance was performed. The Americans proffered gifts: five gallons of whisky for each official, and for the rulers a miniature steam engine as well as drink. The Japanese laid on a display of sumo wrestling, which Perry matched with an exhibition by his men of arms drill on the beach and finally, reluctantly, the hosts signed a Treaty of Amity and Friendship opening up two Japanese ports. Two civilisations had collided, and the one with the big black ships was the winner.

THE BIG THREE

In January 1919, following the end of the First World War, the victorious allies met at Versailles, outside Paris, to forge a peace settlement that, it was hoped, would end war for ever. But from the start the three key figures were at odds: David Lloyd George of Britain sought conciliation and, for the general good, Germany's return to full economic strength; Georges Clemenceau of France never forgot his country's sacrifices and was unyielding in his determination to keep Germany a permanently vanquished power; while Woodrow Wilson of the United States, a former professor of political science, was guided more by abstract considerations of justice than practical realities. The resulting treaty, signed in June, was deeply flawed. Germany lost much of her territory; a demilitarised Rhineland was to be occupied by the allied powers; and a notorious 'war guilt' clause committed Germany to the payment of huge reparations.

Germany faces the guillotine in a cartoon of the Versailles Treaty, and (left) Commodore Perry seeks friendship with Japan.

Germany's sense of grievance never abated. Versailles had sown the seeds for the rise of Adolf Hitler and the Nazis.

THE STUDENTS AND THE TANKS

In April 1989, following the death of the Chinese reformist politician Hu Yaobang, hundreds of students met in Beijing's Tiananmen Square. Their declared purpose was to mourn Hu, but they were also protesting against government corruption, and demanding greater democracy. Over the weeks the number of students grew, and by mid May 200 000 troops circled Beijing. Finally, the ruling Communist Party lost patience. On June 3 and 4 tanks entered Tiananmen Square, massacring about 2000 protesters. World opinion was outraged. In China it was clear that economic liberalism without political reform was untenable. The waiting began for the elderly leadership to pass away.

In the aftermath of the Tiananmen Square massacre in Beijing in 1989, a tank patrols the area where protesters had gathered.

raising MEGALITHS on end became widespread in western Europe, particularly Brittany. The stones stood in avenues, as at CARNAC, France, or in circles such as those found at STONEHENGE and Avebury in Britain. Whether menhirs commemorated the dead, served as places of worship or were used as route-markers or astronomical observation points remains a subject of conjecture.

Mennonite Member of a Protestant sect that evolved in Friesland in the Netherlands in the 16th century. Mennonites have their roots in ANABAPTISM, a movement whose members emphasise that only adult believers should be baptised and deny the validity of infant baptism. In 1536 a Dutch ex-priest, Menno Simons (1496-1561), became an anabaptist and shepherded fellow members of the sect in northern Europe into congregations which were soon named after him. Support for the sect was particularly strong in the Netherlands and Switzerland, where the Mennonites became the target of Catholic persecution. Many were driven from their homes in the 17th century and fled to the United States, where they settled mainly in Pennsylvania, Ohio and the Middle West.

Menon, Krishna (1896-1974) Indian politician and preindependence nationalist leader. Prominent in Britain as a promoter of Indian nationalism in the years before 1947, Menon subsequently served as India's high commissioner in London and in 1952 as representative to the United Nations. Returning to India to become minister of defence in 1957, he was blamed for India's defeat in the war with China over the Tibetan border demarcation and in 1962 he was forced to resign.

Menshevik see BOLSHEVIK

Menzies, Sir Robert (1894-1978) Australian prime minister from 1939 to 1941 and from 1949 to 1966. Menzies practised as a barrister before he began his political career in 1928 in the Victoria parliament. In 1934 he moved to the federal parliament as a member of the United Australia Party, and from 1935 to 1939 served as commonwealth attorney general – the country's most senior law officer.

He was prime minister of a coalition government from 1939 to 1941, and in 1944 he founded the Liberal Party, which replaced the United Australia Party. Menzies was again prime minister from 1949 until his retirement in 1966, making him the longest continuously serving Australian premier. A staunch conservative, in 1951 he tried unsuccessfully to ban Australia's Communist Party.

mercantilism Economic practices based on the theory that the volume of trade is fixed, and that one party's increase in a share of the market must be at another's cost. The theory, widely held from the 16th to the 18th centuries, stated that natural resources could best be fully exploited by promoting exports while limiting imports. Mercantilists, such as the French finance minister Jean Baptiste COLBERT, believed that the possession of gold or 'bullion' was all-important and that countries without a source of precious metal must obtain it by commerce. Government-backed companies controlled trade, tariffs were imposed and maritime rivalry provoked conflicts such as the ANGLO-DUTCH WARS (1652-74) – though prolonged warfare led to higher taxation which weakened industrial prosperity. In the 18th century supporters of LAISSEZ-FAIRE free trade, such as Adam SMITH, opposed the mercantilist theory.

Mercator, Gerardus (1512-94) Flemish cartographer who developed the world's first maps on which longitude and latitude were

A merchant sells cloth at a Dutch market in a painting of 1530. Merchant Adventurers had a monopoly on cloth exports to Holland by 1560.

represented by straight lines (see feature, page 388). The system he developed is known as Mercator's projection and allows navigators to plot their courses as simple, uncurved lines. After gaining a master's degree in philosophy in Belgium in 1532, Mercator studied and worked with the mathematician Gemma Frisius and the engraver and goldsmith Gaspar a Myrica. The three collaborated to prepare maps and to build globes and astronomical instruments. In 1537 Mercator published the first of a series of maps that over the next 32 years, culminating with his map of the world, established him as the finest 16th-century cartographer.

Merchant Adventurers English exporters who dominated the European cloth trade for most of the 15th and 16th centuries. A trading company of Merchant Adventurers was incorporated in 1407 and flourished for almost 300 years. Like its counterparts, it originated from loosely grouped merchants in the major English ports who sold cloth to continental Europe, especially the Netherlands. In cities such as Bristol and London these groups acquired royal charters and forged numerous links with guilds in European towns to strengthen their control of the trade, soon ousting their rival merchants of the HANSEATIC LEAGUE.

By around 1550 the Merchant Adventurers accounted for three-quarters of England's foreign trade. Until 1564 and the outbreak of the Anglo-Spanish War the merchants used Antwerp – then the commercial capital of north-western Europe – as their principal continental base, switching to Hamburg from 1567 to 1579 and then from 1611 onwards. The Merchant Adventurers' royal charter was withdrawn in 1689 when its traders were accused of furthering their own interests at the cost of England's economy. The importance of Merchant Adventurers declined with the rise of the great CHARTERED COMPANIES.

Mercia Central English kingdom formed in the 7th century mainly from 6th century settlements established by the ANGLES. The original communities in the Trent Valley were set up by peoples from the Fenland in the east and from the Humber estuary to the north. In the 7th century this loose tribal confederation was welded into a realm by the military and political skills of PENDA, who became its first king, and his son Wulfhere. They extended Mercia's borders to Wales, Wessex, the east coast and as far north as Northumbria, with whom they were almost constantly at war. By the 8th century and the reigns of Ethelbald and OFFA, whom the Emperor Charlemagne treated as his equal, Mercia was the supreme power in England south of the Humber. But the kingdom was shaken by defeat at the hands of King EGBERT of Wessex at the Battle

of Ellendun in 825 and then foundered under Scandinavian attack in the 870s. In 877 it was finally partitioned between the DANELAW and Wessex.

Mesolithic Transitional period in social evolution, about 10 000 years ago, between the PALAEOLITHIC and NEOLITHIC Ages. Mesolithic – literally 'middle stone age' – people were the hunter-gatherers of western Europe whose culture developed as the climate became warmer at the end of the last Ice Age. Their societies, which lasted until about 3000 BC in the north-west, continued to exist with Neolithic farming groups farther east.

Mesopotamia campaign British campaign against the Turks during the First World War in which T.E. LAWRENCE – known as Lawrence of Arabia – played a key role. When Turkey joined the war in October 1914 Britain was concerned to protect both the oilfields of Abadan in present-day Iran, which it had acquired the previous year, and to safeguard the route to India. British and Indian troops occupied Basra in what is now Iraq and advanced on Baghdad, but were halted and defeated at Kutalamara. A bitter campaign raged for more than two years before March 1917 when General Sir Frederick Maude took Baghdad.

Earlier in the campaign Arab partisans, organised and led by Lawrence, had harassed the Turkish lines and aided the northward drive from Egypt of General Sir Edmund Allenby. His troops occupied Jerusalem in December 1917 and moved on to take Damascus the following October. After the armistice of Mudros on October 1918, British troops briefly reoccupied Baku as a base against the Bolsheviks in the Russian Civil War and to deprive them of its oil. By now Britain occupied all Mesopotamia and – until forced by international opinion to abandon the plan – considered making it one British dominion comprising Palestine, Jordan, Iraq and Iran, so providing a bulwark against Bolshevik plans for expansion.

metals Mineral elements used to make artefacts played a central part in the development of early civilisations. Stages in human progress are commonly measured against the mastery of the skills needed to work different types of metals, giving rise to the BRONZE and Iron ages (see feature, page 323). The earliest metal-working was of pure lumps of mineral found in their natural state – particularly copper and gold, which are soft and easily shaped. Greater skills were needed to extract copper or gold ores from rocks, but by the 5th millennium BC this technique had been mastered in western Asia, and by around 4000 BC the skill had reached Mesopotamia. It was almost another thousand years before it

The founder of the Methodist movement, John Wesley, preaches to an open-air congregation at Epworth, denied entry to the village church.

was discovered that tin and copper could be alloyed to produce bronze, a stronger and more durable metal than copper alone. By 1500 BC copper ores were being mined at depth and extracted by smelting in various parts of Europe and the Middle East, leading to an abundance of the metals and increasing use of bronze.

The production of iron involves more sophisticated techniques than working copper or bronze, but the ore is more widespread than tin or copper. In Egypt, Mesopotamia and Asia Minor iron artefacts were made at about the same time as bronze alloy was produced, but their use was limited to working pieces of the mineral or rare nuggets of pure iron. Crude extraction of iron from ores was first achieved by the Hittites around 1400 BC but, except in China, where iron was cast as early as 700 BC, all iron was wrought by blacksmiths until the 16th century AD, when the first blast furnaces were built in Europe. The production of steel from crude iron was not achieved until 1865, when Henry BESSE-MER developed an industrial process to remove impurities from the metal.

Methodist Follower of the non-Anglican Protestant religious movement that had its origins in the 18th-century evangelical revival, mainly started by the English preacher John WESLEY. Wesley's followers were formed into 'societies' and their regular attendance at classes for religious instruction was a precondition of church membership. Wesley's views on predestination led to friction with followers of John CALVIN, while his evangelical meetings and the difficulty of keeping his societies under ecclesiastical control caused conflict with the Church of England. He was forbidden to use the pulpit in many parishes. In spite of these disagreements, Wesley

managed to keep his followers within the Anglican community until his death in 1791 – when Methodism became a separate Church, or 'connexion'. In Wales a religious revival inspired by Howel Harris and Daniel Rowlands led to the establishment in 1811 of a dominant, Calvinist form of Methodism, while in the United States the Church split into several groups divided over attitudes towards slavery. The World Methodist Council, which was founded in 1881, spearheaded moves towards unity and today links the world's 40 million Methodists.

Metternich, Prince Clemens von (1773-1859) Austrian statesman who for more than 30 years was the most powerful conservative politician in Europe. As Austrian ambassador in Paris in 1806, Metternich attracted Napoleon's favour and was involved in all the major negotiations with him, concluding a treaty at Fontainebleau in the following year. In 1809 Metternich returned to Vienna to become Austrian foreign minister, and negotiated Napoleon's marriage to the Austrian Princess Marie-Louise. Metternich dominated the Congress of VIENNA in 1814-5, called after Napoleon's defeat at the Battle of Leipzig, where he promoted the concept of a GERMAN CONFEDERATION – though not a union, which he feared might come to be dominated by Prussia.

From 1815 Metternich was the strongest voice of reaction in Europe. From 1821 to 1848 as Austria's court chancellor and chancellor of state, he master-minded a political 'system' for Europe based on diplomacy and cooperation between the great powers and the suppression of revolutionary movements, and gained strong support for his views from fellow conservatives in other governments. He put his policies into practice in Austria, where he did not hesitate to use force against liberal political elements, and encouraged other leaders to follow suit. His system created stability in Europe – but led to tensions which found expression in the liberal REVOLUTIONS OF 1848.

Mexico Central American country. Before the arrival of the Spanish conquistadores in the early 16th century, several civilisations flourished in Mexico, including those of the MAYA (from around 300 to 900), the TOLTECS (900 to 1200) and the AZTEC people (1200-1519) (see feature, pages 404-5). Hernán CORTÉS began the conquest in

1519, overthrowing the Aztec ruler MONTEZUMA II, and in 1535 the territory was made the viceroyalty of New Spain under Antonio de Mendoza. Spain imposed MERCANTILISM from the 16th to the 18th centuries, forbidding manufacture and leaving the colony poor. Discontent increased, and when the French emperor NAPOLEON I conquered Spain in 1808 revolution soon broke out in New Spain between 1810 to 1815. The revolution was crushed, but Mexico gained independence in 1821 following the rise to power of a liberal government in Spain in the previous year. In 1823 Mexico became a republic, and the following year Guadalupe Victoria became its first president.

In 1845 America's annexation of TEXAS led to the Mexican-American War. By the Treaty of Guadalupe Hidalgo in 1848, the US claim to Texas was confirmed and for a payment of US$15 million, Mexico relinquished its rights to two-fifths of its territory, an area which included New Mexico, Arizona and California. After the war President Santa Anna established a dictatorship which lasted until 1855, when it was overthrown in a liberal revolution. Conservative opposition to a new constitution in 1857 led to civil war, the War of Reform, from 1858 to 1861. Three years later the French emperor Napoleon III installed Ferdinand-Joseph MAXIMILIAN, a Habsburg prince, as Mexican emperor. The empire collapsed when France withdrew its support in 1867, and the liberals resumed power under President Benito JUÁREZ.

In 1876 Porfirio DÍAZ led an armed rebellion against Juárez's successor Lerdo de Tejada and then held power almost continuously as president until 1911. Díaz's authoritarian regime favoured Mexico's élite and failed to bring the middle class or labour groups into national politics. The 30 year Mexican revolution began in 1910 when Francisco Madero, leader of the Anti-Re-electionist Movement, threatened an armed rebellion against the dictator. Díaz resigned in May

Leading his armed faction in the Mexican revolution, Pancho Villa, third from right, pauses in 1915 from the fighting in the civil war.

1911 and Madero was elected president. Madero was assassinated in 1913 in a coup led by General Victoriano Huerta. Huerta's tenure was brief. Within two years a coalition of revolutionary factions led by Emiliano ZAPATA, Francisco VILLA, Venustiano Carranza and Alvaro Obregón had overthrown his government. Political differences soon split the revolutionaries into constitutionalists who sought to reform the 1857 constitution, and a faction led by Zapata and Villa who wanted to implement radical proposals drawn up in the 1914 convention of Aguascalientes.

In the ensuing civil war of the revolution, Carranza's constitutionalist forces gained the upper hand and in February 1917 he proclaimed a reformed constitution. However, this was largely ignored and in 1920 Carranza was assassinated. In 1928 in the War of the Cristeros Christian peasants rose against the 'godless' state, and were only defeated in 1930. Clashes continued for a further ten years until the election of President Manuel Avila Camacho led to a period of reconciliation.

During the Second World War Mexico fought alongside the Allies from 1942. Industrialisation advanced rapidly in the post-war years until the 1980s when Mexico's – and the world's – oil reserves fell in value. Unemployment and inflation followed. In 1993 Mexico joined Canada and the United States in the North Atlantic Free Trade Agreement (Nafta). In 1994 the Zapatista National Liberation Army led an uprising in the state of Chiapas, reaching a peace agreement with the government of President Ernesto Zedillo in September 1995.

MI5 and MI6 British government agencies charged with gathering intelligence and the protection of state security in Britain and abroad. The sphere of MI5, founded in 1909 as Division 5 of the British Directorate of Military Intelligence, covers both internal security and counterintelligence on British territory while MI6, formed three years later, covers all areas outside the United Kingdom.

MI6 cooperated with RESISTANCE MOVEMENTS in the Second World War, and during the COLD WAR infiltrated Soviet intelligence – Colonel Oleg Penkovsky, a senior KGB officer, spied for MI6 until he was executed in Russia in 1963. Some MI5 and MI6 staff spied for the Soviet Union during and after the Second World War, including Kim Philby, Guy Burgess and Anthony Blunt who were double agents, recruited in the 1930s at Cambridge University. In the 1990s both MI5 and MI6 have combated terrorism, particularly of the Irish Republican Army (IRA).

Michelangelo Buonarroti (1475-1564) Italian painter, sculptor, architect and poet acknowledged to be one of the greatest artists of the RENAISSANCE. Born of an impoverished

Double-agents (clockwise from top left) Anthony Blunt, Guy Burgess, Kim Philby and Donald Maclean were recruited by Soviet intelligence to report back on British Government secrets.

Tuscan family, Michelangelo was raised by a stonemason who apprenticed him to the Florentine painter Domenico Ghirlandaio. In Florence, his work caught the eye of the local prince, Lorenzo de MEDICI, who became his patron. After Lorenzo's death Michelangelo spent three years in Bologna where his sculpture *Cupid* was bought by Cardinal San Giorgio. The cardinal summoned him to Rome and he produced the *Pietà* in St Peter's. Returning to Florence in 1501, Michelangelo began his huge statue of *David*, completed three years later. Again summoned to Rome in 1505, he undertook two major commissions – a tomb for Pope Julius II, of which only the figure of *Moses* was finished, and the decoration of the ceiling of the Sistine Chapel, in the Vatican. Later, from 1536 to 1541, he painted *The Last Judgement* in the Sistine Chapel. It was this work – as much as any of his sculptures – which established Michelangelo as one of the most influential artists of his age.

Mickiewicz, Adam (1798-1855) Polish poet whose verse, based on his country's folklore, started a wave of national romanticism.

In 1823 Mickiewicz was arrested for nationalist activities and deported to Russia where he wrote a verse drama, *Forefather's Eve*, and an epic poem of patriotic revenge, *Konrad Wallenrod* (1828). When the latter was banned by Russia's censors, Mickiewicz fled to France and travelled widely in Europe. In 1834 he published *Pan Tadeusz*, which depicted Poland's aristocracy. During the revolutions of 1848 he organised legions for Polish emancipation. He died in Constantinople in 1852 while raising a force to fight against Russia.

Micronesia Comprising some 600 Pacific islands, the name Micronesia means 'world of little islands'. The forebears of today's population arrived there from Asia around 3000 BC. In 1529 Spain colonised the islands, and sold them in 1899 to Germany. They were occupied in 1914 by Japan, and captured in the Second World War by US forces. In 1947 they were made part of the US Trust Territory of the Pacific Islands, and in 1979 became the self-governing Federated States of Micronesia. Trust status ended in 1990, and the following year Micronesia joined the United Nations.

Mesopotamia: civilisation is born

Mesopotamia is the ancient Greek name for the land between the rivers Tigris and Euphrates. Its fertile soil made possible the start of agriculture, and soon many features of the modern world began to take shape.

Mesopotamia, which covers a large part of modern Iraq, northern Syria and south-east Turkey, saw the earliest innovations in agriculture, literacy, urban communities and complex bureaucracy.

Between 10000 and 6000 BC in the 'Fertile Crescent' – the mountain fringes to the north and north-east of Mesopotamia – sheep, goats, cattle and pigs were domesticated, and staple cereal crops of wheat and barley were developed. Communities which had survived by hunting and collecting edible plants now adopted a more settled existence, as the discovery of early villages in northern Mesopotamia demonstrates.

RISE OF THE FIRST CITIES

When the benefits of agriculture were introduced into southern Mesopotamia, the effects were spectacular. In this arid region an extensive network of canals and ditches is needed to water the fertile soils deposited by the annual flooding of the rivers. Once irrigation agriculture was developed between 6000 and 5000 BC, the surplus food produced could support the expanding populations of the first cities, including their new breed of specialist bureaucrats and craftsmen.

Boosted also by trade, Mesopotamia became the home of three major civilisations: Sumerian and Babylonian in the south, and Assyrian in the north. At many cities, such as Babylon, Ur, Ashur, Nineveh and Nimrud, archaeologists have uncovered monumental palaces, temples, ziggurats (temple-towers) and defensive walls. Spectacular works of art include the carved stone slabs which decorated the royal palaces of the Neo-Assyrian kings, vividly depicting scenes of foreign conquest, hunting and magnificent banquets.

Mesopotamia is credited with the earliest invention of writing. As urban bureaucracy became more complex, simple accounting measures

A bronze and gold figure at prayer, from about 1750 BC, may be King Hammurabi.

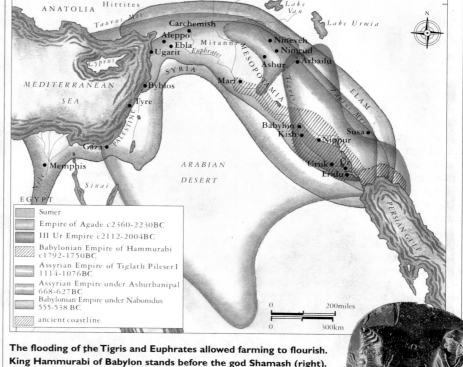

The flooding of the Tigris and Euphrates allowed farming to flourish. King Hammurabi of Babylon stands before the god Shamash (right).

Map legend:
- Sumer
- Empire of Agade c2360-2230 BC
- III Ur Empire c2112-2004 BC
- Babylonian Empire of Hammurabi c1792-1750 BC
- Assyrian Empire of Tiglath Pileser I 1114-1076 BC
- Assyrian Empire under Ashurbanipal 668-627 BC
- Babylonian Empire under Nabonidus 555-538 BC
- ancient coastline

such as clay tokens became inadequate. The first written tablets, dating from just before 3000 BC, consisted of pictographs in which each sign was a simple drawing of an object, such as a sheep or jar. Before long the signs were impressed more schematically using the wedge-shaped end of a reed stylus, forming cuneiform script. Soon these signs came to represent language as well as objects. Sumerian, the oldest surviving written language, was replaced by Akkadian as the spoken language around 2000 BC, though both continued to be written for another two millennia.

Mesopotamian scribes wrote on clay tablets, which are very durable when baked. Many thousands of cuneiform tablets have been preserved. They vary from accounts, contracts, letters and school exercises, to lists of kings and treaties, as well as literary works, such as the *Epic of Gilgamesh*, incorporating a version of the flood story familiar from the Bible. The school curriculum included many compositions which trainee scribes had to copy out. Important texts were also inscribed on stone, such as the Law Code of King Hammurabi of Babylon (1792-1750 BC), who claimed to have established justice so 'that the strong might not oppress the weak'.

Some of the greatest achievements of Mesopotamian culture, such as its advances in astronomy and mathematics, were transmitted to the western world through the ancient Greeks, who ruled over the region in the later part of the 1st millennium BC.

413

Middle Ages Period of European history from about 700 to 1500 marked by the development of forms of centralised government and an expansion of education and the arts. After the decline of Roman power in the West, Europe was plunged into the so-called DARK AGES of the 5th and 6th centuries as invading hordes swept across the continent. In their wake separate kingdoms gradually emerged, bringing to much of Europe more orderly rule and ending more than two centuries of comparative anarchy. The coronation of CHARLEMAGNE as Holy Roman Emperor in 800 not only ended much of this unrest but marked a revival of civilisation and learning across continental Europe.

In England the reign of ALFRED (871-99) saw a similar blossoming of learning. Even the violent territorial incursions of the VIKING hordes in the 9th and 10th centuries and the scattered conflicts of the 11th century did not stem the spread of civilising influences, since descendants of invaders were gradually assimilated into local populations.

The rise of papal power in the 12th and 13th centuries challenged secular rulers, who increasingly came into conflict with a succession of popes over their respective spheres of jurisdiction. But while war dominated this period, the creation of new monastic orders encouraged scholarship, and GOTHIC art and architecture found its finest expression in the cathedrals built from the 12th century onwards. Although wars meant that societies were ruled by aristocracies which held land in return for military service – a system later known as FEUDALISM – trade expanded, universities were founded and philosophy flourished as it had not done since the days of classical Rome. The ferment of ideas led to the emergence of heresies; it led also to the religious enthusiasm shown by the popularity of pilgrimages to holy shrines, and of the CRUSADES in which thousands of Christian knights went to Palestine to try to recapture Jerusalem and to kill or convert Muslims and Jews. The latter half of the Middle Ages was also marked by social and economic unrest as the effects of the BLACK DEATH and the HUNDRED YEARS' WAR (1337-1453) between France and England substantially reduced populations. The coming of the RENAISSANCE, with its conscious revival of the values and styles of antiquity, ended the medieval period.

Midlothian campaigns (1879-80) Series of electioneering speeches to mass audiences made by the British statesman William GLADSTONE, which helped the Liberal Party to win a large majority in the general election of 1880. The campaigns recognised the importance of the new mass electorate created by the 1867 Reform Act, and the growing influence of newspaper reports of political speeches. Before setting out by train from London to his Edinburgh constituency Midlothian, Gladstone addressed the crowds, repeating his speech at each station. The climax of the campaigns came in speeches in Edinburgh and other Scottish cities in which he criticised the government. Gladstone won the Midlothian seat from the Conservative, Lord Dalkeith.

> **DID YOU KNOW?**
> Merchants flourished in the walled towns of the Middle Ages. Before pockets were invented, purses dangling from the belts of the rich were easy prey for stealthy 'cutpurses' with knives.

Mihailovich, Draza (1893-1946) Serbian army officer who led the Yugoslav royalist partisans against Nazi forces in the Second World War. After the fall of YUGOSLAVIA in 1941, Mihailovich organised his forces into guerrilla bands, or *chetniks*. The royalists' relations with the communist partisans led by Josip TITO were often riven by mutual antagonism. When Tito gained power after the war, Mihailovich was accused of war crimes and collaboration with the Nazis. Found guilty after a show trial, he was shot.

Milan Northern Italian city which was originally a settlement of the ETRUSCANS and is today capital of Italy's industrial heartland in LOMBARDY. From 222 BC Milan prospered as the second city of the Roman republic – Mediolanum. It gave its name to the Roman emperor Constantine's edict of AD 313, which recognised Christianity and provided for religious toleration. In 374, its governor – later canonised as St AMBROSE – was chosen by its citizens as bishop, despite not being baptised as a Christian. Within a week he was consecrated in his new position.

Four centuries later, after Charlemagne defeated the Lombards in 773, the city – which had briefly functioned as capital of the old Western Roman Empire – was placed under the rule of patriarchs, or prince-bishops. Throughout the Renaissance Milan was an important cultural centre where from 1450 to 1535 the ruling SFORZA family extended its patronage to artists, including Leonardo DA VINCI, in its ducal court.

Milan during the Renaissance witnessed a flourishing of the arts. In the 15th century, Piero della Francesca painted Battista Sforza and her husband Federigo da Montefeltro, Duke of Urbino.

Miletus Ionian city and port in Asia Minor which in 499 BC led a revolt against Persia. In the 7th and 6th centuries BC Miletus traded widely and established a number of colonies on the Hellespont and Black Sea coasts. Even towards the end of the 6th century, when it became subject to the Lydian king Croesus, Miletus continued to thrive.

During the Persian Wars in 494 Miletus was razed by Persia. Though rebuilt, it never regained its former power, but remained an important port and trading city. In 479 it joined the DELIAN LEAGUE, led by Athens. It broke away from the Athenian empire in 412, but in 334 fell to ALEXANDER THE GREAT. Later, as part of the Roman Empire, Miletus's decline was hastened when its port silted up.

militia Conscripted military force drawn from citizens enlisted for local defence in times of emergency. In medieval England, where the concept of raising militia developed from the Anglo-Saxon FYRD, men were usually recruited forcibly under the local sheriff's supervision. By the late 16th century this responsibility passed to lord lieutenants who continued to exercise these powers for the next 300 years. When control of the militia was disputed between Charles I and Parliament in 1642, Parliament prevailed, but at the RESTORATION the militia was again placed under royal command; it survived until 1907, when it was renamed the Special Reserve.

In both Britain and Europe the militia's importance fluctuated with the conflicts of the times. However, in colonial America the militia were the only form of defence and, as MINUTEMAN forces, played a significant part in the Revolution. The US Militia Act of 1792 required every free, able-bodied, White male between 18 and 45 to enrol in the militia, but the fighters proved unreliable and in the WAR OF 1812 the law was not enforced. During the next century voluntary militias developed into the National Guard — supervised, armed and paid by the federal government.

Mill, John Stuart (1806-73) English philosopher and economist who championed individual liberties and women's rights. From an early age Mill was subjected to a rigorous system of education by his father James, a Scottish philosopher and advocate of UTILITARIANISM. In 1859 he wrote *On Liberty*, which argued that individual liberty should be protected against state interference. He further refined Jeremy BENTHAM's philosophy of utilitarianism, and in 1863 published a book called *Utilitarianism*. Mill proposed that Bentham's doctrine of the greatest happiness of the greatest number should be pursued through legislation. His progressive *On the Subjection of Women* (1869) became an influential exposition of the case for female emancipation and the equal treatment of women.

Milner, Alfred, Viscount (1854-1925) British colonial administrator during the second of the BOER WARS. In the post of private secretary to the chancellor of the exchequer, G.J. Goschen, Milner developed a grasp of government finance which served him well as an administrator in Egypt from 1889 to 1892, and also when he returned to Britain to become chairman of the board of inland revenue for the next five years.

In South Africa, where he served as high commissioner from 1897 until 1905, Milner's inability to comprehend Boer aspirations and his policies, which were widely perceived as jingoistic, contributed to the outbreak of war between Britain and the Boer Republics. However, his innovative schemes for reform following the Boer Wars and his careful choice of talented young administrators — popularly known as 'Milner's kindergarten' — gave stability to the emergent Union of South Africa. In 1916 Milner joined Lloyd George's War Cabinet, and from 1919 to 1921 he served as secretary of state for the colonies.

John Stuart Mill, who learned Greek at three, earned an affectionate caricature in *Vanity Fair*.

Milton, John (1608-74) English poet, scholar and pamphleteer who dictated the epic poem, *Paradise Lost*, when he was blind. One of the supreme masters of the rhythm and sounds of the English language, Milton nevertheless spent some 20 years of his creative life writing political pamphlets and polemics in support of the English republican Commonwealth. From 1641 to 1660 Milton produced little poetry to justify the promise of such earlier

> 66 As good almost kill a man as kill a good book: who kills a man kills a reasonable creature, God's image; but he who destroys a good book, kills reason itself. 99
>
> John Milton, in his pamphlet Areopagitica, 1644

works as *Lycidas* (1637). His sight had begun to fail while he was a young man and by the age of 43 he was blind, dictating his work — including a celebrated sonnet on his own blindness — to his daughters, nephews and such admirers as the poet Andrew Marvell.

At the Restoration Milton went into hiding, but he was arrested and fined for his Puritan activities. He completed *Paradise Lost* — an epic in blank verse on the Biblical version of man's fall from grace — in 1667, and its sequel, *Paradise Regained*, appeared some four years later. Also in 1671 he published *Samson*

Agonistes, a powerful drama in blank verse modelled on classical Greek tragedies. After his death Milton's reputation continued to grow, and his influence on poets of the 18th century was enormous.

Minden, Battle of (August 1, 1759) Decisive action in Germany during the SEVEN YEARS' WAR and one of the few battles of the conflict in Europe in which British troops were involved. When a French army seized Minden, the town guarding access to Hanover, the French were surrounded and defeated by a large force of British, Hanoverian and Hessian troops under Prince Ferdinand of Brunswick.

Mindszenty, Jozsef (1892-1975) Outspoken anticommunist Roman Catholic cardinal and prelate of Hungary who was charged with treason in 1948 by the Communist government. Born Jozsef Pehm, Cardinal Mindszenty took his ecclesiastical name from that of the village in Vas where he was born. Found guilty of treason after a show trial staged by the Budapest government in 1949, he was sentenced to life imprisonment. Six years later this was commuted to house detention, and following a national uprising in 1956 he was granted asylum in the US legation in Budapest. In 1971 he went to Rome, but left to spend the last years of his life in a religious community in Vienna.

Ming (1368-1644) Last dynasty of native-born Chinese rulers, founded by Zhu Yuanz-hang after his armies had driven the Mongol YUAN dynasty from Beijing (Peking). Orphaned when his parents died in a famine, Zhu became a Buddhist novice. He was living as a beggar when he joined an uprising against the Yuan emperor and led the rebels against Beijing. Crowned as the Emperor Hong Wu in 1368, he abolished the post of prime minister to strengthen his own autocratic powers. He developed a strong central administration before leading his forces to invade Mongolia and bring YUNNAN under Ming rule. Before his death in 1398 Zhu had united most of central China and forced Korea to pay tribute.

In the reign of Yung-lo (1403-24) the Great Wall of China was extensively rebuilt, and after this 150 years of peace were marred only by brief Mongol incursions and the activities of Chinese and Japanese pirates. The appointment of provincial governors improved administration, and major public works — such as Beijing's Temple of Heaven and the Forbidden City — were undertaken.

European traders and missionaries began to appear on the coast from 1517 onwards. The Portuguese were permitted to settle in Macao and Jesuits were allowed into Beijing. Although the Ming emperors successfully resisted a Japanese invasion of Korea in 1592 and prevented an incursion into China, these

A Ming bowl from the 15th-century Chenghua period is decorated with blue plant patterns on a fine, white porcelain background.

clashes destabilised the country. In the 17th century the MANCHUS attacked Beijing, banditry in the provinces became rife and the government's bureaucracy fell into disorder. A growing population strained the agricultural resources of the country, and famine and discontent spread, creating a climate ripe for rebellion. An uprising, started in Shaanxi Province and led by the bandit Li Zicheng, cost around a million lives. In 1644 Li occupied Beijing and the last Ming emperor hanged himself. The Manchu QING dynasty followed.

Minoan civilisation Bronze Age culture, named after the legendary King Minos, which developed in central CRETE from 3000 BC. Its major city was KNOSSOS; other centres included Phaestos, Malia and Gournia. Though it is not clear whether the Minoans were immigrants from Asia Minor or the successors of an indigenous Neolithic people, archaeological evidence points to early trade contacts with Egypt and, after 2200, trade throughout the Mediterranean as Minoan longships gained control of the Aegean. Sea power combined with the Minoans' island situation to make land defences scarcely necessary, and their chain of palaces and cities remained unfortified.

Several cities besides Knossos, including Phaistos and Malia, possessed luxurious palaces. These were of complex design, usually centred on a large courtyard, with many staircases, smaller courtyards and temples. Magnificent frescoes adorned the walls, and most major buildings were decorated with 'horns of consecration' which related to a popular cult of bull-worship. Minoan civilisation reached its peak between 2200 and 1450 BC, a period in which artistic achievements in pottery, metal-working, gem-engraving and mural painting reached their height. The early Minoans developed a form of pictorial writing on clay tablets; neither this nor the script known as Linear A – which superseded pictograms around 1800 and was probably used by a sophisticated palace bureaucracy – have been deciphered.

Around 1700 both Knossos and Phaestos were destroyed – probably by earthquakes – but were later rebuilt. Within a century Knossos suffered a further, and final destruction when Crete appears to have been invaded, probably by a MYCENAEAN army from the Greek mainland.

minuteman Member of an 18th-century militia in the AMERICAN REVOLUTION who was ready at a minute's notice to take up arms to defend his property or country. In skirmishes and short-term guerrilla actions such as Lexington and Concord, minutemen distinguished themselves. But their tendency to leave the conflict and return to their farms to sow or reap crops made the volunteers so unreliable in long campaigns and pitched battles that George Washington instituted longterm recruitment. The US constitution's guarantee of a citizen's right to bear arms is said to reflect the 'minuteman philosophy'.

Mirabeau, Honoré Riqueti, Comte de (1749-91) French revolutionary who attempted to impose a constitutional monarchy in France, based on the English model. Mirabeau joined a cavalry regiment in 1767 and his early life was marked by drunken bouts and hedonistic excesses. During the 1780s he wrote several political pamphlets which led to spells in jail as well as a brief period of exile in England in 1784. When the French States General was summoned in

> **❝ I came back ... and I found to comfort me all the horrors of opprobrium and dementia conspiring to swallow up my country. ❞**
>
> *Mirabeau, in a letter to Major Mauvillon, September 1789*

1789 Mirabeau was elected not as a noble, but as a delegate for the Third Estate, or commoners. He led the protest when, at the royal session in June, Louis XVI disregarded the delegates' TENNIS COURT OATH, in which they had established a National Assembly and claimed to be the only true representatives of the people. When the French king

A Minoan wall painting from Knossos shows two girls and a somersaulting boy involved in what appears to be a bull-leaping ritual. The bull was an object of worship in ancient Crete, and may have given rise to the legend in which Theseus slays the Minotaur – a creature half-man and half-bull.

A thousand-year rule by the saints

*Since the earliest days of the Christian Church people have speculated about
a sacred millennium associated with the end of the world
and the Second Coming of Jesus Christ.*

Millenarianism is the belief in a future period of a thousand years – the holy millennium – during which saints will rule on earth, either in preparation for the Second Coming of Christ, or immediately following the Last Judgment. It has Biblical origins in the Book of Daniel (Chapter 7) and in the Apocalypse described in the Book of Revelation (Chapter 20), as well as in Jewish apocalyptic literature, such as the Book of Enoch. However, the doctrine has never been officially sanctioned by any mainstream Christian Church.

Millenarianism arose in the century after Christ's death, when many Christians believed that the end of the world was imminent; it became widespread in the years leading up to AD 1000, which was prophesied to be the year in which the world's last millennium would begin. When no signs of anything untoward appeared, other events were suggested as turning points for the dawn of the world's final age: the capture of Jerusalem, for example, as was preached in 1095 by Peter the Hermit, and Walter the Penniless, with the result that tens of thousands of peasants set out on the First Crusade to 'liberate' Jerusalem from the Turks. The city was taken by Crusaders in 1099, but not by the peasants, whose expeditions all met with complete disaster.

The involvement of the peasants in the First Crusade was no accident, as many millenarian doctrines explicitly associated the coming of the sacred era with the toppling of established rulers, the rise of the peasantry and the

founding of a new, egalitarian social order. Ideas such as these have contributed to the popularity of millenarianism among disadvantaged groups through the ages.

A new impetus was given to millenarian beliefs by the writings of the Italian mystic Joachim of Fiore (*c.*1132-1202). Joachim believed that he had discovered a hidden key to the meaning of the Bible. He wrote that the time of the Law was the age of the Father and the time of the Gospel the age of the Son, while the third age would be that of the Holy Spirit – the imminent culmination of human history. In it there would be no property or wealth, because all would live in voluntary poverty. People would need neither food nor institutional authority: all would live in freedom and joy with no clergy, sacraments or Bible.

TOWARDS AD 2000

Through the later Middle Ages, especially in Germany, millenarianism continued to flourish, sometimes as an underground movement. It helped to fuel the Reformation's virulent opposition to the pope, and occasionally inspired

violent social upheaval. The radical Protestant reformer Thomas Müntzer, for example, encouraged the overthrow of both Church and State in order to establish equality between all people. Believing that the poor were the chosen instruments of God's will, Müntzer actively supported the German peasants in their uprising of 1524, and was duly executed by the authorities in 1525.

In 17th-century England an extremist Puritan sect called the Ranters held many similar ideas. But they also claimed that sin is an illusion and that believers are free to do as they choose. As a result, they were suppressed by Parliament for allegedly encouraging immorality.

Two modern Christian groups have millenarian beliefs at the heart of their teachings. The Seventh-Day Adventists and the Jehovah's Witnesses, both founded in the USA in the 19th century, regard the end of the world and the beginning of the sacred millennium as imminent. In the decades leading up to the year 2000, numerous other sects started claiming that a turning point in world history was about to occur, and a new age about to begin.

According to the Book of Revelation the end of the world, here depicted by Charles Mottram (1807-76), will follow a sacred millennium of peace ruled over by saints.

Mirabeau, at the front of a platform, looks down on Dreux-Brézé, whose red coat marks him as an envoy of King Louis XVI. Mirabeau is refusing to dissolve the revolutionary National Assembly.

ordered the delegates to debate apart from the nobles and clergy, Mirabeau declared: 'We are here by the will of the people and will not leave our seats unless forced by bayonets.' Though he dominated French politics almost until his death, Mirabeau failed to persuade the king to

A missionary nun holds up a gourd and cup in play while Nigerian Yoruba children reach for her hands, in a wooden sculpture of 1881.

establish a constitutional monarchy. As the revolution grew more radical, Mirabeau lost the support of former allies.

missionaries Attempts by members of particular groups to spread their faith among peoples of other religions or cultures go back to the spreading of Christianity throughout Europe by missionaries such as St Paul and St Augustine. Europeans reaching the Far East in the 16th century were followed by missionaries, and by 1601 Matteo Ricci had founded a Jesuit mission in Beijing (Peking).

The growing evangelical movements within the Protestant Church in the early 19th century sparked a new missionary spirit in Europe and the USA. Indigenous peoples of the British, German and French colonial territories were the initial targets of the missionary thrust, while mission societies established in the USA took their faith to Native Americans, African-Americans and the INUIT people.

In India, Africa, China and the South Seas missionaries provided medical services and schooling, often exploring new territories in order to persuade people of other cultures to accept their faith, and often becoming the victims of persecution. Followers of faiths other than Christianity, including Islam and Buddhism, have also sought to spread their beliefs through missionary activities.

Mississippi cultures Interrelated cultures of the Mississippi valley of North America from around AD 700 to 1700. They made huge, flat-topped earthen PYRAMID-shaped temple mounds which were probably inspired by Maya and Aztec buildings of Mexico (see feature, pages 404-5). They were used for religious ceremonies in the Southern cult – a local

variant of Mexican faiths. Spectacular sites include those at Cahokia in Illinois, Aztalan in Wisconsin and Macon in Georgia.

Missouri Compromise (1820-1) Laws passed by the US Congress to ensure a balance between slave states and free states in the Senate. Senator Henry Clay proposed the compromise, admitting Maine as a free state and Missouri as a slave state; the remainder of the LOUISIANA Purchase north of latitude 36° 30´ (the southern boundary of Missouri) was to be free territory.

The issue of slavery was temporarily laid to rest by the compromise, but the drawing of geographical lines between slave and non-slave areas led to deep national divisions, the seeds of the AMERICAN CIVIL WAR. The compromise was repealed in 1854 when the Kansas-Nebraska Act allowed new states to decide their constitution, slave or free, by popular vote.

Mithras Persian god of light and wisdom, and central figure of a religion which emphasised courage and strength and had a large following in the Roman Empire, particularly among soldiers on the empire's frontiers. In the 2nd century the cult flourished in Britain and along the rivers Rhine and Danube. The Roman cult involved rituals in cave sanctuaries devoted to sculptures of Mithras killing a sacred bull, where initiates underwent tests to prove their manliness. In the late 3rd century it succumbed to Christianity.

Mithridates VI (Eupator) (c.132-63 BC) King who led Pontus in Asia Minor to become Rome's main rival for power in the east,

In a 2nd-century Roman marble relief, the god Mithras clutches a dagger and pulls back a holy bull's head to sacrifice it in a secret ritual.

bringing the northern coast of the Black Sea under his control and expanding his realm through much of Asia Minor. In 88 BC Mithridates – who had acceded to the throne in about 120, while still a boy – invaded Roman Asia and advanced into Greece. But his armies were crushed at Chaeronea in 85 and he made peace with the Roman general Lucius SULLA. Two more Mithridatic wars followed before he was finally defeated in 66 by Gnaeus POMPEY. When after three years of minor clashes he failed to re-establish himself in the Crimea, he ordered one of his guards to kill him.

Mitterrand, François (1916-96) Socialist president of France from 1981 to 1995. Though in later years Mitterrand's political enemies suggested that he had collaborated with the Vichy government during the Second World War, his role as a leader of the French resistance movement ensured his election to the French National Assembly as a deputy in 1946. He served in all the governments of the Fourth Republic (1946-58), and in 1965 – seeking to build a left-wing coalition between the Radical, Socialist and Communist parties – he founded the Federation of the Democratic and Socialist Left.

Despite attracting 7 million votes in that year's presidential elections, Mitterand failed to oust General de Gaulle and was again defeated in 1974 by Giscard d'Estaing. Finally elected president of France in 1981, his moves to raise basic wages, increase social benefits and nationalise key industries led to a series of economic crises. Nevertheless, in 1988 he was re-elected.

Mitterrand was a staunch supporter of closer political and monetary ties within the European Community and took France with him along this path in a 1992 referendum over the Treaty of MAASTRICHT. The final years of his presidency, in which he had to work with a right-wing government, were marked by ill-health and in 1995 he did not stand for re-election. He was succeeded by Jacques Chirac.

Mixtec People of the mountainous regions of Oaxaca, Mexico, forerunners of the AZTECS. The dynastic history of the Mixtecs can be traced back to AD 692 and the reign of King Eight-Dear-Tiger-Claw. Around 1000 they formed a confederation of city-states, and by the 14th century they had occupied the valley of Oaxaca where they defeated the rival Zapotec people.

Mobutu, Sese Seko (1930-) African soldier and politician who seized office as president of ZAIRE in 1965 and retained power for the next three decades.

As a representative of the Force Publique, the colonial Belgian Congo army that he had joined in 1949, Mobutu attended a conference in Brussels on Congolese independence in 1960. Appointed commander in chief of the new Congolese army when the country became independent the following year, Mobutu attempted to end the five years of chaos and civil war that followed independence by snatching the presidency. Although under his control the military used harsh tactics to maintain order, Mobutu appointed civilian ministers and encouraged foreign mineral exploitation in his efforts to attain economic stability. In 1971, as part of a policy of Africanisation, he changed the country's name to the Republic of Zaire.

Mobutu survived rebel invasions from Angola in 1977 and 1978; however, his popularity waned and there was growing criticism of his corrupt regime. In May 1990 he announced political reforms to end one-party rule, but against a background of unrest, strikes and shootings in December 1991 Mobutu postponed new presidential elections. In 1994 he agreed to a transitional constitution to reduce the president's powers and implement democratic reforms.

Mochica Pre-Inca people who flourished in the northern coastal regions of PERU from about 400 BC to AD 600. Archaeologists have uncovered the remains of a densely populated site, possibly a city and ceremonial centre. It is dominated by two PYRAMID-shaped structures of adobe bricks, known as the Temple of the Sun and the Temple of the Moon. While the Temple of the Sun, 135 ft (41 m) high, was probably used as a temple, that of the Moon is thought to have been a palace. Some of the finest sculpture in pre-Columbian Peru has been found there, as well as gold jewellery and vases in the shapes of realistically figured human and animal heads, and fine ceramics. The Mochica were also skilled in irrigation and built canals up to 75 miles (120 km) long.

A partly painted golden mask made by the Mochica people gains its hypnotic stare from two mussel shells inserted into its eye sockets.

Model Parliament Parliament called by EDWARD I of England in November 1295 to enlist countrywide support in his wars with Wales, France and Scotland. As well as his nobles, the senior hierarchy of the Church and heads of religious houses, Edward summoned two knights from each shire, two representatives from every city or borough and representatives of the lower clergy – one from each cathedral chapter and two from each diocese.

The Model Parliament, which Edward hoped would raise money to finance his forces, passed no legislation. Although its composition was later idealised as the 'model' for future democratic assemblies, many of its members, particularly the knights and burgesses – freemen of a borough – did not attend regularly until the mid 14th century. By this time the lower clergy had withdrawn to their own convocations, and during the 16th-century Reformation representatives of religious houses were removed.

modernism Experimental trends in the arts – particularly in literature – which were pioneered in the early 20th century. Seen by both its originators and critics as a rebellion against the formal structures of the 19th century, modernism embraced several movements, including Cubism (see PICASSO) in the visual arts, the music of such composers as Igor Stravinsky and Béla Bartók and the BAUHAUS architecture of Walter Gropius.

It is with literature, however, that the term 'modernism' has become most closely associated. Many writers rejected what they saw as traditional bourgeois values and adopted an avant-garde style whose obscure and complex forms shocked and disturbed their readers. Such writers as Marcel Proust led a movement away from the accepted continuity of chronological development; other authors, such as James JOYCE, John Dos Passos and Virginia Woolf, adopted a 'stream of consciousness' approach which traced the random flow of their characters' thoughts. Ezra Pound, T.S. Eliot and William Carlos Williams used free verse instead of traditional rhymes and metres, and in the theatre Berthold BRECHT, Luigi Pirandello and Eugene Ionesco created new abstract forms.

Mogadishu East African city which from the 10th to the 16th centuries was a trading port for gold and slaves. In the 10th century Persian and Arabian merchants founded a settlement in Mogadishu. It grew into a major commercial port and was visited around 1432 by the Chinese admiral Zheng He. In the 16th century it was conquered by the Portuguese.

The town was seized by the Sultan of Zanzibar in 1871, sold to the Italians in 1905, and taken by the British in 1941 during the Second World War. In 1960 it became the capital of the newly independent SOMALIA.

Mohács Hungarian port on the River Danube, which was the site of two important battles between European powers and the OTTOMAN Turks. In 1526 Louis II of Hungary and Bohemia led 28 000 men into battle against the 200 000-strong force of Sultan Suleiman II, and was decisively defeated. As a result, the Ottomans were able to overrun most of Hungary and control the country for the next 150 years. In a second battle at Mohács in 1687, an army led by Charles of Lorraine routed the Ottomans and ended their attempts to conquer more European territory.

Mohawk Native American people belonging to the large IROQUOIS-speaking group of nations. Based in what is now eastern New York state, the Mohawk played an important role in the late 16th century in establishing the Iroquois League – a confederation of five Iroquois nations (six, after 1722) dedicated to abandoning cannibalism and advancing peace, prosperity and civil authority among its members. According to tradition, the Mohawk leader Hiawatha was the first to embrace the idea of the league when it was proposed by the prophet Dekanawida.

During the 17th century the league helped to keep its members ahead of other Native Americans as trade rivalry developed between them. Guns obtained from Dutch and English traders enabled them to defeat neighbouring ALGONQUIN peoples, and many Mohawk sided with the British during their wars with the French. The Mohawk also supported the British during the AMERICAN REVOLUTION, and in consequence they were all driven out of New York to Canada in 1777.

Mohenjo-Daro Ancient city of the INDUS CIVILISATION, which flourished from around 2500 to 1500 BC. Situated near the west bank of the Indus river in modern Pakistan's Sind province, Mohenjo-Daro is about 3 miles (5 km) in circumference and comprises a hill citadel with a larger city laid out on a grid pattern to the east. Its buildings are made entirely of brick and include a large granary and an oblong hall which may have been a temple.

Molière (1622-73) Pen name of the French playwright, actor and director Jean-Baptiste Poquelin, whose comedies and social satires were a major influence on the development of theatre. Molière began his career at the age of 21, forming an acting troupe called *L'Illustre Théâtre*, which was first based in Paris and then toured the provinces from 1645 to 1658. He returned to Paris to set up his own theatrical company and won acclaim as an actor-manager as well as a dramatist, staging simple farces and, later, elaborate ballets. However, Molière is best remembered for his comedies of manners and characters satirising vices or extreme forms of behaviour. *Le Misanthrope*

(1666) and *Le Malade Imaginaire* (1673), which dramatise the miser and the hypochondriac respectively, won immediate acclaim. But Molière also scandalised many people with plays such as *Tartuffe* (1664), which deals with religious hypocrisy. This was initially banned, even though Molière maintained that it attacked neither true faith nor morality.

Molotov, Vyacheslav (1890-1986) Soviet leader who was an adviser to both Vladimir Lenin and Joseph Stalin. He served as foreign minister under Stalin from 1939 to 1949, and under Nikita Khrushchev from 1953 to 1956.

A committed communist from 1906, he changed his name from Skriabin to Molotov ('the hammer') to escape the imperial police, but was arrested and exiled in 1909. Molotov returned to Moscow in 1911 to help to establish the official communist paper *Pravda*, becoming editor the following year.

> ❝ **In such an enormous country as the Soviet Union you cannot make an omelette without breaking eggs. There are no revolutions without victims... All the rest are bagatelles.** ❞
>
> *Vyacheslav Molotov, 1986*

When the BOLSHEVIKS seized power in the RUSSIAN REVOLUTION of 1917, Molotov supervised their programme of compulsory nationalisation. Later he took a leading part in the liquidation of the Mensheviks, and in 1926 put down the ZINOVIEV opposition. As foreign minister in 1939, he signed a non-aggression pact with Nazi Germany (see NAZI-SOVIET PACT), and two years later, after Adolf Hitler ignored the pact and invaded the Soviet Union, he signed a treaty with Britain.

Molotov was Stalin's closest adviser at both the Yalta and Potsdam conferences of 1945, which established the Soviet sphere of influence in postwar Europe. On Stalin's death in 1953, Molotov was reappointed foreign minister, emerging as a major antagonist in the COLD WAR. In 1957 he attempted to oust Nikita Khrushchev and was consequently expelled from all his party posts. He was subsequently given a number of minor positions, including that of ambassador to the Mongolian People's Republic from 1957 to 1960. Molotov was rehabilitated by the Communist Party two years before he died.

Moltke, Helmuth, Count von (1800-91) Prussian field-marshal, one of the first European military leaders to grasp the potential of railways in warfare. As chief of the Prussian general staff from 1858 to 1888, von Moltke argued that men and equipment could be

more rapidly deployed and maintained over wider areas by rail. He proved this argument in victorious wars against Denmark (1864), Austria (1866) and France (1870).

Moluccas Group of islands in eastern INDONESIA, also known as the Spice Islands, and nowadays called Maluku. As the original source of cloves and nutmeg, the Moluccas were coveted by the Portuguese, who landed there in 1512, and established a settlement at Ternate. In 1603 the Dutch East India Company created trading posts on the islands, and by 1666 it had acquired a monopoly over the islands' spice trade. Britain twice occupied the Moluccas during the French Revolutionary and NAPOLEONIC WARS, but in the 19th century the Dutch reasserted complete control over the islands. Following occupation by the Japanese in the Second World War, the Moluccas became part of independent Indonesia in 1949. The South Moluccas have since tried to secede, so far without success.

Mombasa East African seaport settled by Arabs in the 8th century, and a major trading centre for ivory and slaves. The Portuguese explorer and navigator Vasco DA GAMA reached Mombasa in 1498 and it was sacked seven years later in Portugal's campaign to dominate Africa's eastern coastline. After beating off a Turkish assault on Mombasa in 1589, the Portuguese fortified the settlement and made it their main trading centre on the coast; but after several battles they lost it – and the rest of the coast – to the sultanate of Oman in 1698. Control passed to the sultan of Zanzibar in 1837, and in 1886 the port came under British control following a treaty with Germany over imperial spheres of influence. Subsequently, Mombasa was the starting point for Britain's colonisation of East Africa.

monastery Community of celibate monks dedicated to a life of meditation and prayer. BUDDHA was probably the first religious leader to found a monastic order in the 6th century BC. The code of discipline he laid down is still followed by Buddhist monks. In the 2nd century BC, the Essenes, a Jewish messianic sect, founded a community on the shores of the Dead Sea. Christian monasticism has its origins in 4th-century Egypt, where St Pachomius founded the first community at Tabennisi. From around 330 Christian monasticism spread rapidly in Eastern Europe through the rule of St Basil, while St BENEDICT's rule gained momentum from the 6th century in Western Europe. Islam did not develop a monastic organisation until the 12th century, when the SUFI sect formed the Rifaite and Mawlawite brotherhoods.

The great orders of European monasteries flourished from the 10th century. The house of CLUNY, founded in France in 909, built a

The world's religions have produced many different monastic traditions: Buddhist monks at Sera Monastery in Tibet (above), and the ruins of Rievaulx Abbey, Yorkshire (left).

chain of 'daughter houses' through most of Europe, all under the direct control of the powerful Abbot of Cluny. The CISTERCIAN order, which was founded in 1098, also built monasteries in Europe and England, as did the Carthusians and the Gilbertines. As centres of pilgrimage, medical care and learning, monasteries were an integral part of medieval life. Many monks were artists and chroniclers, and monastery libraries housed classical texts and Biblical manuscripts.

From 1536 to 1540, during the English REFORMATION, the English monasteries were abolished and monastic property was seized by the Crown. By 1540, some 800 monasteries had been closed and 11000 monks, nuns and their dependants had been ejected from their communities. As well as destroying many monastic buildings and distributing former monastic lands among England's nobility, the Dissolution of the Monasteries increased the role played by the aristocracy in the appointment of some of the parish clergy, which continues to exist in a small way down to the present day.

In Continental Europe, between the 13th and 15th centuries, monasteries were weakened by wars, plagues and religious schisms, but their fortunes revived with the establishment of orders such as the Society of Jesus, or JESUITS, in the 16th century. These were a powerful force in the COUNTER REFORMATION and continued to exercise lay and ecclesiastical influence in Roman Catholic Western Europe until the ENLIGHTENMENT in the 18th century.

Monck, George, 1st Duke of Albemarle (1608-70) English politician and soldier. During the ENGLISH CIVIL WAR, Monck initially fought for the Royalists, before being captured by Parliamentarians in 1644. Released in 1646, he changed sides and in 1652 he completed the suppression of the Royalists in Scotland. After the death of Oliver CROMWELL in 1658, Monck again emerged as a Royalist, playing a leading role in the RESTORATION of Charles II. The king placed Monck in charge of London during the Great PLAGUE of 1665 and the Great Fire (see FIRE OF LONDON) of 1666.

money Before tokens, coins or notes were used in buying and selling goods and services, most early communities relied on barter – a system that depends on the parties concerned having commodities that each wants to exchange. As industries developed and trade grew, goods began to be exchanged for tokens representing units of fixed value, such as cowrie shells or small discs of precious metal.

The first coins with fixed values to be issued by a state appeared in both Lydia, in Asia Minor, and in China during the 8th century BC. Early Lydian coins were made of a mixture of gold and silver, but during the reign of Croesus in the 6th century they were minted from gold of a standard weight and a guaranteed value. From the 4th century coins with a head or figure on one side and a government symbol on the other became widespread.

Copper, silver and gold coins were widely used as currency throughout Rome's territories in Europe, Africa and Asia Minor. These were imitated in neighbouring regions from about the 1st century AD, so that by the early Middle Ages coins were the standard means of effecting a transaction. Milled edges were introduced in Europe in the 18th century to prevent the practice of clipping – that is, cutting small pieces from coins made out of valuable metal. In the USA gold remained in use as legal tender until the 1934 Gold Reserve Act.

Notes accompanied the development of BANKING and were first issued by banks which undertook to pay the sum of money that appeared on the note from their deposits of gold. The BANK OF ENGLAND has issued notes since its foundation in 1694.

Advocates of MERCANTILISM from the 16th to the 18th centuries equated wealth with the possession of gold or 'bullion' from commerce. In 1821 Britain was the first country to introduce the GOLD STANDARD, a currency system in which the value of money is fixed in terms of a specific weight of gold. In the second half of the 20th century money has been increasingly supplemented by cheques, credit cards and charge cards, leading many economists to speculate that a world without coins or notes – a so-called 'cashless society' – may be a possibility for the 21st century.

Mongol empire Empire founded early in the 13th century by GENGHIS KHAN, whose armies conquered much of Asia and Eastern Europe. Under Genghis Khan's leadership, the loosely confederated Mongol nomads were united into a formidable fighting force and swept westwards across central Asia into Europe and southwards into China.

The Mongol empire was founded by Genghis Khan's armies of mounted warriors, capable of astonishing feats of horsemanship.

After Genghis's death in 1227, his four sons vied for the succession, which passed in 1229 to Ogodei. He continued his father's programme of conquest, defeating the Poles, the Russians and the Hungarians. In 1241 the Mongol armies had reached the outskirts of Vienna, when Ogodei suddenly died. His commanders immediately withdrew to their capital at Karakorum to elect a new overlord from among Genghis's descendants.

Under Mongke, a grandson of Ghengis, Mongol armies advanced into Mesopotamia, sacking Baghdad in 1258. Two years later Mongke was succeeded by his brother, KUBLAI KHAN, who expanded the Mongol empire to its greatest extent by completing the conquest of China begun by Genghis 65 years earlier.

Kublai moved the Mongol capital from Karakorum to Khanbaligh – now known as Beijing. From here, however, it became increasingly difficult to control remote parts of the empire, and after 1300 the provinces, or khanates, became fully independent. By 1368 the Mongols had been completely driven out of China by the native MING dynasty, and in 1372 a Chinese army razed Karakorum.

Mongolia Region on the immense, sparsely populated central Asian steppe, divided between the independent Mongolian People's Republic – or Outer Mongolia – and the Inner Mongolian Autonomous Region of China.

Originally inhabited by scattered nomadic tribes, Mongolia became the heartland of one of the world's greatest empires (see MONGOL EMPIRE). During the 17th century China's Manchu rulers gradually wrested control of both Inner and Outer Mongolia, and the region remained part of the Chinese empire until the fall of the QING dynasty in 1911.

When this occurred, Outer Mongolia declared its independence with the support of Russia. It was reoccupied by China between 1919 and 1921 but attained full independence in 1924 as the communist Mongolian People's Republic, strongly allied to the Soviet Union. Inner Mongolia meanwhile remained part of China.

Although the Mongolian People's Republic became a full multiparty democracy in 1990, the communists have continued to hold power in that country in their new guise as the Mongolian People's Revolutionary Party.

> **DID YOU KNOW?**
>
> *Mongolia has a tradition of ūligers – epic verse stories which are recited from memory. Highly stylised, they relate adventures of Mongol heroes, including the emperor Genghis Khan.*

Monitor and Merrimack, Battle of (1862) First naval battle in the AMERICAN CIVIL WAR between warships known as IRONCLADS. Troops of the Confederate South raised the scuttled Union frigate *Merrimack* at the start of the war and converted it into an ironclad. In March 1862, the *Merrimack* (renamed *Virginia* by the Confederacy) easily defeated a Union squadron at Hampton Roads. It was then confronted by the Union's *Monitor*, a warship with a revolving armoured turret. In the resulting 5-hour battle neither vessel was able to secure victory over the other, and both withdrew. The battle marked the beginning of the end of wooden warships.

Monmouth's Rebellion (June-July 1685) Attempt by the Duke of Monmouth to win the crown of his uncle, the English king JAMES II. An illegitimate son of Charles II, Monmouth openly opposed the succession of James II, and was forced to flee to Holland in 1683 after the RYE HOUSE PLOT had been exposed. Supported by the Earl of Argyll, a Scottish Protestant, Monmouth returned to England in June 1685. Landing at Lyme Regis in Dorset, he assembled a small army and was proclaimed king at Taunton. The following month his force of about 4000 men was routed at the Battle of SEDGEMOOR, after which Monmouth was executed and his followers severely punished by the BLOODY ASSIZES.

Monnet, Jean (1888-1979) French economist, one of the leading proposers of the EUROPEAN UNION. In 1947 he drew up the so-called Monnet Plan for revitalising France's ailing postwar economy through strong government planning and assistance. Monnet went on to draft the SCHUMAN PLAN, and in 1952 became the first president of the resultant European Coal and Steel Community (ECSC), a post he held until 1955. An internationalist with a strong belief in European unification, Monnet envisaged the ECSC as the first step towards full European union, and in 1956 he became president of the Action Committee for a United States of Europe. Many of his ideas were adopted in 1958 when the Treaty of Rome established the Common Market.

Monroe, James (1758-1831) Fifth president of the USA, from 1817 to 1825. His insistence that the European powers refrain from interfering in US affairs, in return for US non-intervention in Europe, became known as the Monroe Doctrine – a cornerstone of US foreign policy for the rest of the 19th century.

Screen idol Marilyn Monroe manages to look alluring even when applying her make-up.

After fighting in the American Revolution, Monroe began a political career which saw him serving in the Senate from 1790 to 1794. He enjoyed moderate successes as ambassador to France and governor of Virginia, but his political fortunes were transformed when Thomas JEFFERSON's Democratic Republicans came to power in 1801.

In 1802 Jefferson sent Monroe to France where he helped to negotiate the purchase of LOUISIANA. From 1814 to 1815 he was secretary of war under President James MADISON, before being elected president himself in 1816, and again in 1820. In 1820 he prompted the MISSOURI COMPROMISE – an early step towards ending slavery. However, it was Monroe's opposition to European colonisation of the Americas and his refusal to take part in the political affairs of Europe which marked his presidency. This approach, spelt out to Congress in 1823, was Monroe's response to Spain's threat to restore its South American colonies and Russian claims to the north-west coast of America. Though repudiated by Britain, the Monroe Doctrine was often invoked by the USA in the 19th century, and continued to influence US foreign policy until well into the 20th century.

Monroe, Marilyn (1926-62) US film actress and sex symbol. Born Norma Jean Baker, Monroe spent much of her childhood in foster homes before becoming a photographer's model in 1946. She was married three times: her second husband was the US baseball star Joe Di Maggio and her third the playwright Arthur Miller. Monroe sparkled in films such as *Gentlemen Prefer Blondes* (1953), *The Seven*

Year Itch (1955) and *Some Like It Hot* (1959). Seeking more serious dramatic roles, she studied at Lee Strasberg's Actors Studio and went on to win acclaim in *The Misfits* (1961), written by Arthur Miller. In 1962 she enjoyed a friendship with President John F. KENNEDY, and died in the same year from a drug overdose in unexplained circumstances.

Mons Early inhabitants of eastern Burma, now MYANMAR, who were first conquered by southward migrating Burmese in the 11th century. By 825 the Mon people had founded the powerful cities of Pegu and Thaton. They were converted to Theravada BUDDHISM and adopted the Indian script known as Pali, spreading both the religion and the script throughout Burma. In 1057 they were overrun by the Burmese of PAGAN, but retained partial control of the south until overthrown by the Toungoo from northern Burma in 1539. In the early 1750s, the Mons cast off Toungoo rule, but in 1757 they lost their independence finally to the Burmese leader Alaungpaya, founder of the dynasty which ruled Burma until 1885.

Montcalm, Louis-Joseph, Marquis de (1712-59) French general killed defending Quebec from British forces under General James WOLFE. Before 1756, when he was made military commander in Canada, Montcalm had fought in the Rhineland, Bohemia and Italy. Under his leadership, the French defeated British forces at Fort Oswego in 1756, at Fort William Henry in 1757 and at Ticonderoga in 1758. They also withstood Wolfe's siege of Quebec, which involved a number of direct assaults, but a daring night climb up Quebec's steep cliffs on the night of September 12, 1759, took Montcalm by surprise, and the French were decisively defeated on the PLAINS OF ABRAHAM the following day.

Montenegro One of the six constituent republics of the former YUGOSLAVIA. From the 14th century, Montenegro was the only region in the BALKANS not to fall under the domination of the OTTOMAN EMPIRE. During the Balkan Wars of 1912-13, Montenegro greatly extended its territory when it sided with Greece, Serbia and Bulgaria to drive out the Turks. It was absorbed into Serbia in 1919 and united with the new kingdom of Yugoslavia a decade later. In 1946 Montenegrans voted to accept the federal constitution of the Yugoslav leader Marshal Tito. Following Tito's death in 1980, the region saw a rapid growth of an independence movement, leading to riots in 1989. However, in multiparty elections held the following year, the communists were returned to power, and in 1991 they allied Montenegro with Serbia. The following year both republics declared themselves sole partners in a new Federal Republic of Yugoslavia.

Montespan, Françoise Athénaïs, Marquise de (1641-1707) Mistress of the French king LOUIS XIV, by whom she had seven children. In 1663 Françoise married the Marquis de Montespan and became a lady-in-waiting to Queen Maria Theresa. By 1668 she had ousted the king's mistress, Louise de la Vallière, from his affections. After her marriage was annulled in 1676, Françoise's status as Louis' mistress was formally acknowleged, their children were legitimised and for the next 20 years – until ousted from the king's affections by Françoise de Maintenon – she exercised considerable political power. Her influence was destroyed when she was accused by court intriguers of involvement in black magic. She left the court in 1691, retiring to a convent where she became mother superior.

Montesquieu, Charles (1689-1755) French lawyer and writer, and a major figure of the ENLIGHTENMENT. Montesquieu made his mark with the publication in 1721 of *Lettres Persanes*, in which two imaginary travellers from Persia criticise current political and religious institutions. In *De l'Esprit des Lois* (1748), he argued that while different forms of government should relate to the nature of each society, all should establish the rule of law. He admired the British parliamentary system, and his analysis of the separation of powers into executive, judicial and legislative branches strongly influenced European liberals, as well as the drafters of the United States constitution.

Monteverdi, Claudio (1567-1643) Italian composer and musician whose operas revolutionised the form. Monteverdi's first works were published in 1587, and in 1590 he was appointed court musician to the Duke of Mantua. In 1602 he became director of music at the duke's court. Monteverdi's first opera, *Orfeo*, written for the duke in 1607, established him as a leading composer of his day. In it he showed how the diverse elements of solo songs, recitatives, chorus and orchestral interlude could be woven into a harmonious whole using music to portray emotions and bring characters convincingly to life. Monteverdi composed at least six major operas, of which only three survive. His church music – which includes the *Vespers of 1610*, several masses, at least 30 motets and two magnificats – was equally successful. In 1613 he was appointed director of music at St Mark's, Venice, a post he held until his death 30 years later.

Montezuma (c.1480-1520) Ninth king of the AZTECS, also called Montezuma II. His empire stretched from Mexico to present-day Honduras and Nicaragua, but was unstable owing to increasing resentment among many of his subject peoples. In 1519 the Spanish explorer Hernán CORTÉS arrived in the area,

apparently fulfilling an Aztec prophecy that the legendary god-king QUETZALCÓATL would return as a white, bearded stranger. As a result, Cortés was widely feared and made easy alliances with peoples who resented Aztec rule. Montezuma offered the Spaniards gifts if they would leave, and in November 1519 he invited them into his palace at Tenochtitlán (the site of present-day Mexico City), where Cortés promptly took him prisoner. The Spaniards attempted to rule the Aztec empire through Montezuma, but in June 1520 the Aztecs rose in rebellion. According to Cortés, Montezuma died while trying to address his people, but the Aztecs claimed that the Spaniards had already murdered their emperor.

Montezuma, king of the Aztecs, in his regalia, as imagined by an anonymous European artist.

Montfort, Simon de, Earl of Leicester (c.1208-65) Leader of the English rebels in the second of the BARONS' WARS. In 1238 Montfort married Henry III's sister Eleanor. After distinguishing himself on a Crusade in Syria, he was made Lieutenant of Gascony in 1248, with orders to crush resistance to English rule there. Four years later Montfort was recalled to England to answer charges of misrule in Gascony. He was allowed to return, but was shortly afterwards again recalled.

Angered by the king's behaviour, Montfort joined the English barons in 1258 to demand constitutional reforms to the way the country was governed. Henry's repudiation of these in 1264 led to the Battle of Lewes, in which he was captured. In 1265 Montfort summoned knights and burgesses to Parliament for the first time in an attempt to broaden his support base. He ruled England until his death at the Battle of EVESHAM in August 1265.

Montgomery, Bernard, 1st Viscount Montgomery of Alamein (1887-1976)

Outstanding British general of the Second World War. A professional soldier, Montgomery served with distinction in the First World War. But it was as commander of the 8th Army in the Second World War's NORTH AFRICAN and ITALIAN campaigns that he inspired deep loyalty and affection in his men, who referred to him simply as 'Monty'. His tactics at the Battle of EL ALAMEIN in 1942 led to a decisive victory and began an Allied advance that drove the Germans out of North Africa by May 1943. In 1944 Montgomery commanded the British Commonwealth armies in the NORMANDY CAMPAIGN with considerable success, though his support for an ambitious airborne attack on ARNHEM led to his only defeat. He played a major role in beating back the German counteroffensive in the ARDENNES before accepting the surrender of Germany's northern forces at Luneberg Heath in 1945. Appointed a field-marshal in 1944, and a viscount in 1946, Montgomery held several senior postwar military posts.

Montrose, James, 5th Earl of (1612-50)

Scottish Royalist general who supported CHARLES I during the ENGLISH CIVIL WAR. In 1637 he joined the Scottish Presbyterian COVENANTERS in opposing Charles's proposed introduction of Anglican reforms in Scotland, and in 1640 he took part in the Covenanters' invasion of northern England.

Montrose subsequently fell out with the strongly anti-Royalist Earl of Argyll, by whom he was imprisoned in 1641. On his release Montrose decided to support the king instead, and was made lieutenant-general of Scotland in 1644. Montrose's army of Highlanders and Irishmen achieved six successive brilliant victories against Argyll, but disaster struck when Charles was defeated at NASEBY in June 1645. Most of Montrose's men slipped away, and the remainder were routed at Philiphaugh. Montrose himself escaped to Europe, from where he set out in March 1650 with about 1200 men to raise another Royalist army in Scotland. He was defeated the following month and was captured by the Covenanters, who hanged him in Edinburgh.

> **DID YOU KNOW?**
>
> The Marquis of Montrose's knowledge of weaponry when he led the Royalist forces in 1644 was limited to bows and arrows. In his youth he had won three archery competitions.

Moor Medieval European name for a Muslim of North Africa or Spain, and later extended to all Muslims. The word became a synonym for SARACEN, referring particularly to those Arabs and Berbers that conquered Spain.

Field-Marshal Montgomery said that his black beret bearing the Royal Tank Regiment badge and his general's badge was 'worth two divisions', as it made him instantly recognisable to his men.

The Moors first landed in Spain in 710, and the following year the Visigoth kingdom collapsed as an army of BERBERS under Tariq ibn Ziyad swept through the country. Reaching the Pyrenees, the invaders crossed into France, where they were defeated by the Franks under Charles Martel near Poitiers in 732.

By 756 the Moors had consolidated a new Arab state in Spain, calling it al-Andalus, or Andalusia, with its capital at Córdoba. In 912 the state became a CALIPHATE, which broke up in 1031 as disagreement grew between local leaders – the *reyes de taifas*, 'party kings'. The Moors' grip on Spain loosened somewhat under pressure from Christian kingdoms to the north, but in 1090 new Berber warrior invaders, the Almoravids, gained control of the country. They gave way in 1145 to another Berber group, the ALMOHAD dynasty, and it was not until the 13th century that European Christians began to reassert control over the region. By 1235 only the Moorish kingdom of GRANADA remained. Torn by rival factions, it could not withstand the united monarchy of FERDINAND II of Aragón and ISABELLA I of Castile, and in 1492 it fell to their armies.

Moorish culture left Spain a rich heritage of science, poetry, art and architecture, including the Great Mosque of Córdoba and the Alhambra palace at Granada. During the 16th century those Moors who remained in Spain either secretly kept their faith as *Mudejares* or converted to Christianity as *Moriscos*. The former were often tortured and killed by the Spanish INQUISITION, and the latter were expelled in 1609.

Moore, Henry (1898-1986) British sculptor. The son of a Yorkshire coal miner, Moore studied art in Leeds and London. Although his

technique varied, he worked mainly in bronze and stone and looked to organic forms in the natural landscape for the inspiration of many of his works. These forms reflected his fascination with the spatial possibilities of sculpture and are seen at their best in the *Madonna and Child*, created during the Second World War for St Matthew's Church, Northampton, and the huge reclining figures made in 1965 for the Lincoln Centre in New York.

Moore, Sir John (1761-1809) British general whose death at Coruña, Spain, during the PENINSULAR WAR was immortalised by the poet Charles Wolfe. Moore, who joined the army in 1776 and served with distinction

This doorway in Córdoba bears testimony to centuries of Moorish settlement in Spain.

Sir John Moore, who lost his life holding off French forces (far right) so that his troops could embark from the Spanish port of Coruña.

during the war with Revolutionary France, was appointed commander of the British army in Portugal in 1808 and ordered to drive the French from the Iberian Peninsula. Finding himself confronted by an overwhelming French force, he retreated some 250 miles (400 km) to the port of Coruña. There he launched a rearguard action in which he was mortally wounded, but which drove off the French so that his troops could be successfully evacuated.

Moravia Region of the Czech Republic. In the 4th century AD the Romans conquered the Celtic and Germanic tribes occupying Moravia, but as the Roman Empire declined Moravia came under the control of the nomadic AVARS and then the MAGYARS. Like most of BOHEMIA, which controlled the area from 1029, Moravia was strongly influenced by the 15th-century religious teachings of the HUSSITES. A moderate form of Hussitism survived persecution and, under the influence of 16th-century ANABAPTISM, evolved as the Moravian Brethren; in the 18th century the Brethren were active as missionaries in southern Africa and formed exiled communities, particularly in North America.

In 1526 Moravia passed under Austrian HABSBURG control after Louis II of Hungary and Bohemia was killed at the Battle of MOHÁCS. After a failed attempt by the Czechs of Bohemia and Moravia to unite their territories in 1848, Moravia was made an Austrian crown land. At the end of the First World War, Moravia became a province of the newly formed state of CZECHOSLOVAKIA.

More, Sir Thomas see feature, page 426

Morgan, Sir Henry (c.1635-88) Welsh buccaneer who caused havoc with Spanish ships and settlements in the Caribbean in the 17th century. Morgan's early career is obscure, but he emerged in the 1650s as one of the BUCCANEERS raiding Dutch and Spanish settlements in Central America and the West Indies. In 1668 he became commander of the buccaneers and thereafter received semi-official licences from British authorities in the Caribbean to act as a PRIVATEER. His exploits included the capture and ransom of Portobelo in 1668, the sacking of towns around

Lake Maracaibo in 1669 and the destruction of the city of Panama in 1671. The last of these raids coincided with a temporary improvement in Anglo-Spanish relations. To placate the Spanish, Morgan was arrested and taken to London in 1673. However, hostilities were renewed before he was brought to trial, and in 1674 he was knighted by Charles II and appointed lieutenant-governor of Jamaica, where he spent the remainder of his life.

Morgan, John Pierpont (1837-1913) US banker, industrialist and philanthropist. Born into a family of financiers from Connecticut, Morgan became the New York agent of his father's firm, J.S. Morgan & Company, in London in 1860, and manager of the entire company after his father died in 1890. Morgan proceeded to develop interests in steel, shipping and railways, and by 1895 he

Sir Henry Morgan, the ruthless buccaneer, became a popular English hero, as this depiction of him reveals.

owned sufficient wealth to lend the US government gold to stabilise falling financial markets. In 1901 he formed the US Steel Corporation, the world's first billion-dollar company, and in 1907 he again came to the aid of panicking US financial markets. Morgan bequeathed his massive private art collection to New York's Metropolitan Museum of Art.

Morínigo, Higinio (1897-1985) Paraguayan dictator. Morínigo was an army officer from 1932 to 1935 during the CHACO WAR against Bolivia, and subsequently became minister of war. When President José Félix Estigarribia was killed in an air crash in 1940, Morínigo succeeded him, immediately suspending the constitution and establishing a military dictatorship. As the country recovered from the Chaco War, there were many improvements in housing and public health, but Morínigo became increasingly unpopular owing to the severity of his rule. He crushed the civil war that broke out in 1942, but was deposed in 1946 by a coup which drove him into permanent exile in Argentina.

Morley, John (1838-1923) British journalist, biographer and politician. An editor of the literary *Fortnightly Review* from 1867 to 1872, and of the liberal *Pall Mall Gazette* from 1880 to 1883, Morley entered Parliament in 1883 as a supporter of William Gladstone. He was chief secretary for Ireland in 1886 and from 1892 to 1895, helping to draft two HOME RULE bills. As secretary of state for India from 1905 to 1910, he worked with the viceroy Lord Minto to increase Indian participation in government through the India Councils Act of 1909 – popularly known as the Morley-Minto reforms. He resigned from the Indian council in 1914. Among Morley's biographies are lives of the free trade economist Richard Cobden (1881) and Gladstone (1903).

A man for all seasons

Sir Thomas More was Henry VIII's unwilling chancellor, whose disapproval of the king's behaviour cost him his head.

In 1529 Henry VIII of England abruptly dismissed his Lord Chancellor, Thomas Wolsey. Wolsey's offence was that he had failed to persuade the pope, Clement VII, to allow the king to divorce his queen, Catherine of Aragon. The man chosen to replace Wolsey was a successful London lawyer whose scholarship was respected throughout Europe, Sir Thomas More (1478-1535).

More knew only too well the poisonous intrigues of Henry's court, but an invitation from the king amounted to a command and he accepted the position reluctantly.

More was firmly of the Roman Catholic faith: he wanted to reform the Church, not to destroy it. He was inspired by the new humanist thinking which looked to the ideals of the Greek and Roman world. In his satire *Utopia* (Greek, 'No place'), written in 1516, More describes a just, rationally governed republic under God, and by implication strongly criticises English Tudor society. Described by a contemporary, Robert Whittington, as 'a man for all seasons', More was no dry jurist: his sense of humour and gaiety

Sir Thomas More (left); and with his family and members of his household (above), by Rowland Lockey, 1593.

would always break out, sometimes shocking the morals of his day. Suitors to his daughters were invited to view them naked, so they would have no surprises about what they were getting.

Henry had appointed More because of his stature as a scholar and a judge. The king had promised that he would never 'molest his conscience' on the delicate issue of his divorce. More took him at his word, respectfully refusing to consent to

its lawfulness. Henry continued to defy the pope, and in 1532 More resigned his chancellorship. In 1533 Henry divorced Catherine and married Anne Boleyn.

The Act of Supremacy of 1534 declared the king head of the English Church in place of the pope. Henry then abolished the Church's privileges and confiscated the lands and treasures of the monasteries. The response of the bishops was confused: some accepted the king's new status, some rejected it. A further Act passed in 1534 stated that anyone openly disagreeing with the king's actions was guilty of treason.

Bishop John Fisher of Rochester refused to accept the Act of Supremacy, and was tried and beheaded. Henry intended Fisher's execution to be a warning to More to conform. It had the opposite effect: More steadfastly refused to accept Henry as head of the Church, and was charged with high treason. He was imprisoned in the Tower of London for a year, and went to the block on July 6, 1535. More joked with the executioner, saying, 'Let me put my beard aside, for it has committed no treason.'

The executions of Fisher and More shocked Catholic Europe, and made permanent the breach between England and Rome. Four centuries later both men were canonised by the Catholic Church.

Mormons Members of the 5 million-strong Church of Jesus Christ of Latter-Day Saints, founded in 1830 by the American visionary Joseph SMITH (1805-44). Smith, who heard his first call to prophecy when he was 15, said that in 1827 an angel revealed to him the whereabouts of gold tablets containing a secret religious book written by a Native American prophet called Mormon. Smith memorised the prophesies and dictated his translation of them to a number of followers. The resulting Book of Mormon was published in 1829, and the following year Smith established his Church in New York state.

In 1831 Smith relocated his headquarters to Ohio, but increasing hostility among other Christians drove him to move to Nauvoo in Illinois in 1838-9. By 1844 opposition to Smith had grown among the Mormons themselves, and in that year he used the Mormon militia to quell a dissident uprising. The state authorities responded by arresting Smith, and three days later he was murdered by an angry mob. Led by Brigham YOUNG, the Mormons

then undertook an epic journey to a remote location in what is now the state of Utah, establishing a community which rapidly grew to become Salt Lake City. Their practice of polygamy continued to provoke hostility among many Americans, but in 1890 the Church abolished the custom. As a result, Utah was able to join the USA in 1896.

Moro, Aldo (1916-78) Italian politician kidnapped and murdered by the RED BRIGADES. A lawyer by training, Moro entered parliament as a Christian Democrat in 1946. As minister of justice from 1955 to 1957, he comprehensively reformed the Italian prison system. From December 1963 he served as prime minister on several occasions until 1968, returning to the position again between 1974 and 1976. Abducted by Red Brigades terrorists in 1978, Moro was shot when the government refused to accede to the terrorists' demands for the release of a number of their colleagues. At the time, Moro was expected to become Italy's next president.

Morocco North African country and the original home of the BERBERS, which became a target of French and Spanish imperial ambitions in the 19th century.

By the 5th century BC the Phoenicians had passed through the Strait of Gibraltar and established trading posts on the Moroccan coast. In the following century a kingdom of

The body of assassinated Italian politician Aldo Moro is discovered lying in the back of a car.

MAURITANIA was formed in northern Morocco and this eventually became a Roman province. Although first Vandals from Spain and then Byzantines occupied the coastal areas during the decline of the Roman Empire in the 5th century, Berbers controlled the interior – eventually forming ruling dynasties in the 8th century. The last of these, the Sharifian dynasty founded in 1524, still reigns today.

From the 16th century Morocco remained independent until increasing European imperialist rivalries during the 19th century led to the country becoming a French protectorate in 1912 under the Treaty of Fez. Spain was given possession of a small protectorate in the north, while the main port of Tangier became an international zone.

In the 1920s Berber rebels began armed struggles with both occupying powers, and in 1956 Morocco became an independent monarchy under Muhammad V. Following violent protests against the monarchy, parliamentary government was suspended from 1965 until 1970. Since then, royal authority has been precariously maintained in the face of several attempted coups.

In 1979 Morocco took possession of part of the Western Sahara, previously known as the Spanish Sahara. Its occupation of this territory has been vigorously opposed by the Polisario Front, leading to the posting of UN peacekeeping troops there in 1991.

Morris, William see NUFFIELD, VISCOUNT

Morrison, Herbert, 1st Baron of Lambeth (1888-1965) British politician who devised the concept of an urban 'green belt', and drafted Labour's programme of NATIONALISATION and the development of a national health service for the 1945 election.

Morrison, who began his political career as one of the founders of the London Labour Party in 1914, went on to unify the capital's transport system under public ownership in the 1930s. He was minister of supply and then home secretary in Winston Churchill's Second World War coalition government, before becoming deputy prime minister in 1945. Ten years later he was defeated by Hugh GAITSKELL in the contest for the Labour leadership.

Morse, Samuel (1791-1872) US inventor and portrait painter who, with his assistant Alexander Bain, developed the signalling code which bears his name. In 1835 Morse made the first electric telegraph which could operate over a long distance, and developed a code using short and long signals to represent the alphabet. Eight years later the US Congress granted him $30 000 to develop an experimental line between Baltimore and Washington, and in 1844 his first message – 'What hath God wrought' – was sent. Subsequently Morse code was widely adopted.

Mortimer, Roger de, 1st Earl of March (c.1287-1330) Prominent member of a powerful English family in the march (border) lands between England and Wales. Mortimer opposed EDWARD II and in 1323 was forced to flee to France, where he became the lover of Edward's wife, Queen Isabella. In September 1326 Mortimer and his royal mistress invaded England and forced Edward to abdicate in favour of Edward's 14-year-old son, who became EDWARD III. For almost four years Mortimer and Isabella ruled in the young king's name, but in October 1330 Edward had Mortimer seized and executed for treason.

Mortimer's Cross, Battle of (February 2, 1461) Yorkist victory in the English Wars of the ROSES. Led by Edward, Earl of March, the Yorkist forces defeated the Earl of Wiltshire's Lancastrian army near Wigmore in Herefordshire. Although this was avenged by Queen Margaret of Anjou's Lancastrian army at St Albans less than a fortnight later, Margaret failed to win the support of the citizens of London, who the following month acclaimed the Earl of March as EDWARD IV.

Morton, John (c.1420-1500) English prelate whose argument that the obviously rich could afford to pay tax and that the apparently poor must have hidden savings supported HENRY VII's attempts to gather revenue. Trained as an academic lawyer, Morton was a protégé of Archbishop Thomas Bourchier, under whose patronage he became a master in the chancery court and a member of Henry VI's council. As a Lancastrian, Morton was forced to flee to France in 1461 during the Wars of the ROSES. Ten years later he joined the Yorkists after the Battle of TEWKESBURY, thereby gaining Edward IV's favour and winning appointment as bishop of Ely in 1479. Morton next supported Henry Tudor, who made him archbishop of Canterbury shortly after gaining the throne as Henry VII. In 1487 Morton was appointed chancellor of England, in which capacity he introduced his ruthless tax assessment principle, dubbed 'Morton's Fork' by its opponents. In 1493 he became a cardinal.

Moses (c.13th century BC) Central character of JUDAISM who, according to the biblical Book of Exodus, led the 12 Hebrew tribes – or Israelites – out of slavery in Egypt.

According to the Old Testament, Moses was born in Egypt and escaped a massacre of Hebrew male children when his mother hid him in a basket which floated down the Nile. He was found by one of the pharaoh's daughters, who raised him herself. As a young man Moses received divine inspiration when he

Moses listens as God speaks to him from a burning bush (top); much later he receives the Ten Commandments from God's own hand.

heard the voice of God speaking from a burning bush. He became leader of the Israelites, and guided his people across the Red Sea and into the desert in search of a Promised Land. During the journey Moses is said to have written the first five books of the Old Testament, which are known in Judaism as the Torah, or the Books of Moses. He also received the Ten Commandments from God on Mount Sinai, but broke the stone tablets on which they were inscribed in rage when he found the Israelites worshipping a golden calf. The Israelites were condemned to wander the desert for 40 years, and Moses never reached the Promised Land of Canaan. However, he was granted a glimpse of it from Mount Pisgah before he died and was buried in the land of Moab.

Mosley, Oswald, Sir (1896-1980) British politician who promoted FASCISM. A Member of Parliament from 1918 to 1931, Mosley sat successively as a Conservative, Independent and Labour supporter before forming his own New Party in 1931. Advocating state intervention, Mosley's brand of socialism called for a dictatorial system of government. After visiting Benito MUSSOLINI in Italy in 1932, Mosley founded the National Union of Fascists, whose black-shirted supporters staged violent marches and rallies in the East End of London. Mosley's views led to his internment during the Second World War, and on his release he briefly attempted to re-establish his party.

mosque Building which provides the focal point of Islamic religious life, from the Arabic word *masjid*, meaning 'place of prostration'.

427

Lord Louis Mountbatten (foreground) and his wife Edwina at the official ceremony to grant India its independence in 1947. Edwina is chatting to Pandit Nehru, India's first prime minister.

The first mosque was established at the house of the prophet MUHAMMAD at Medina after his journey there in AD 622, and all subsequent mosques have been based on the design of that building. Small mosques may be little more than a square or rectangular building with a simple veranda, while larger ones usually have a colonnaded courtyard containing a fountain or other washing facility. A minaret, or tower, normally stands at the front of any large mosque, providing a platform for the *muezzin* to call the faithful to prayer five times every day, or to chant the KORAN on special occasions. Other minarets may stand at each corner of the building.

Prayers are said inside a covered prayer hall, where the Friday sermon is preached. Shoes are removed on entry and women must cover their heads. A *mihrab*, niche, is set into one of the walls of the prayer hall, indicating the *qibla*, direction of Mecca (the prophet's birthplace), which all Muslims face when saying their prayers. There is usually a partitioned area for female worshippers, whose attendance at mosque prayers is not compulsory.

Professional chanters may be heard reciting the Koran according to strict conventions, but no singing or music are allowed in a mosque. Also forbidden are any sculptures or pictures of humans or animals, as these are thought to be blasphemous imitations of God's work. Instead, mosques are often richly decorated with intricate geometric designs and ornate calligraphic extracts from the Koran.

Mother Teresa see feature, page 429

Mountbatten, Louis, 1st Earl Mountbatten of Burma

(1900-79) British admiral and administrator who in 1947 became the last viceroy of India. The younger son of Prince Louis of Battenberg, Mountbatten served as a midshipman in Admiral David Beatty's flagships in the First World War and later accompanied the then Prince of Wales – later Edward VIII – on two empire tours. A professional sailor, Mountbatten commanded a destroyer flotilla at the start of the Second World War, taking part in the 1941 Battle of Crete before becoming chief of combined operations in 1942. The following year he was appointed supreme Allied commander, South-east Asia, and worked to restore the morale and capacity of the Commonwealth forces fighting the Japanese in· Burma. Throughout 1943 and 1944 he was also involved in planning the Italian campaigns and the D-Day landings in Normandy.

Appointed viceroy of India after the war, Mountbatten took responsibility for the country's transition to independence in 1947. Although the transfer of sovereignty was marked by riots and massacres, the new Indian government invited Mountbatten to remain until 1948 as the first governor-general.

Returning to his naval career in 1952, Mountbatten became chief of the defence staff from 1959 to 1965, supervising the merger of the service ministries into a unified ministry of defence. In retirement he was an outspoken critic of reliance on nuclear weapons. He was murdered by the Irish Republican Army while sailing near his holiday home in Ireland.

Mousterian Prehistoric culture of the Middle PALAEOLITHIC period in and around Europe, named after the NEANDERTHAL cave site of Le Moustier in the Dordogne, France. Artefacts from this culture are more sophisticated and cover many more uses than the Acheulian tools of earlier STONE AGES. They consist of small, neat axes and scrapers made from delicately flaked stone, as well as spearheads and arrowheads manufactured from bone as well as stone. Mousterian artefacts, produced throughout Europe from about 130 000 to 30 000 years ago, are also found in North Africa and the Middle East. The Mousterian culture came to an end at about the start of the Upper Palaeolithic period.

Mozambique South-east African country. In 1498 the Portuguese explorer Vasco DA GAMA visited the territory, and in 1505 the Portuguese established themselves at the Arab port of Sofala, near present-day Beira. Further settlements and trading stations were created throughout the 16th and 17th centuries, and in 1752 the Portuguese gave Mozambique its own administration, separate from that in GOA, from where it had previously been governed. From the 1750s to the 1850s many Africans were exported as slaves, mainly to Brazil and the Mascarene Islands.

In the 1890s anticolonial resistance was suppressed, and it was not until 1964 – when a Marxist guerrilla group began the FRELIMO WAR – that Portugal's control of the country was seriously challenged. After a military coup in Portugal in 1974, a ceasefire was negotiated with the rebel leader Samora MACHEL, and in 1975 Mozambique became an independent Marxist People's Republic.

Machel's support for guerrillas fighting the white minority governments of Rhodesia (see ZIMBABWE) and South Africa led to a Rhodesian invasion in 1979, as well as South African support for anti-Frelimo forces – the Mozambique National Resistance Movement (Renamo). In 1984 Mozambique and South Africa signed a non-aggression pact, and in 1986 Machel's successor, Joaquim Chissano,

These typical Mousterian tools – a scraper (right) and a spearhead (bottom right) – have been made from rough pieces of flint, such as that below.

Sister of charity

Mother Teresa, a Roman Catholic nun, has dedicated her life to alleviating the suffering of the slum-dwellers of Calcutta.

For millions of people, Mother Teresa of Calcutta embodies the spirit of Christian goodness in a late 20th century often afflicted by materialism and greed. Some even hail her as a living saint. She was born Agnes Gonxha Bojaxhiu, on August 26, 1910, in Skopje, Yugoslavia, the youngest child of an Albanian grocer. At 18 she studied English in Dublin with the Irish Sisters of Loreto before sailing for India, arriving in Calcutta in January 1929. She spent a year as a novice in Darjeeling, then returned to Calcutta to teach geography at a convent school, where she later became principal.

CALL FROM GOD

Mother Teresa was aboard a train in 1946 when, she said, she received a call from God: she was to work among the sick and needy. In 1948 she left the convent and went among the people of the slums. In Paris she received some medical training before opening a home in Calcutta for the destitute and dying, which she named Nirmal Hriday, 'Sacred Heart', in a wing of a Hindu temple. Later projects included a home for abandoned children, a home for the elderly, a colony for lepers and a workshop for the unemployed. In 1950 she founded her sisterhood, the Order of the Missionaries of Charity.

Mother Teresa continues to work tirelessly among the destitute and dying of Calcutta, as she has done for the last half-century.

In 1971 Mother Teresa visited Britain for the foundation of a house for novices, one of the Mission's first outside India, although her missionaries – nuns, of whom there are now some 2000, and coworkers – would spread throughout the world. Returning to India via Rome, she received the first Pope John Paul XXIII peace prize. In 1979 Mother Teresa was awarded the Nobel peace prize. Characteristically, she called off the celebratory banquet, decreeing that the money allocated to it should be used instead to feed the poor.

This tiny, frail woman cuts a highly distinctive figure in her rough cotton habit and headdress, and her influence is both powerful and international. The Indian prime minister Indira Gandhi was a supporter. The Calcutta Mission has had many distinguished visitors: in 1986 it was visited by both the pope and the archbishop of Canterbury. In 1983, in Delhi, Queen Elizabeth II made Mother Teresa an honorary member of the Order of Merit. The US president Ronald Reagan presented her with the Presidential Medal of Freedom.

But while she is an inspiration to millions, her outspoken opposition to contraception and abortion has proved abhorrent to some feminists and others. In India one group protested at the award of the Nobel prize to someone whose 'sole objective is to influence people in favour of Christianity. Missionaries are instruments of Western imperialist countries – and not innocent voices of God.' Even her fiercest critics, though, could not question Mother Teresa's hard work, her faith or her commitment.

---

agreed to negotiate with Renamo. In 1992 a peace treaty brought an end to the civil war which, together with severe drought, had left Mozambique one of the world's poorest countries. In multiparty elections held for the first time in 1994, Frelimo was returned to power with President Chissano as head of state.

Mozart, Wolfgang Amadeus (1756-91) Austrian composer whose music includes some of the world's greatest classical works. Mozart first toured Europe when he was six, dazzling kings and courtiers with his virtuoso keyboard playing. By the age of 13 he had composed symphonies, sonatas, concertos and two operas. In 1781, after an unhappy ten years as concert master to the archbishop of Salzburg, Mozart moved to Vienna, where he became a rival of the Italian composer Antonio Salieri. Mozart claimed that Salieri tried to poison him, but there is no evidence to support the allegation. Mozart's success with the operas *The Marriage of Figaro* in 1786 and *Don Giovanni* in the following year led to his appointment as court composer to Emperor Joseph II in 1787. Mozart wrote more than 600 compositions, including 41 symphonies. He died while working on a requiem mass.

Mugabe, Robert (1924-) First prime minister of ZIMBABWE. Mugabe campaigned for Black majority rule in Rhodesia from the 1940s, and in 1963 he helped to found the Zimbabwe African National Union (ZANU), a rival party to Joshua NKOMO's Zimbabwe African People's Union (ZAPU). The following year Mugabe was imprisoned for making a 'subversive speech'. He was freed in 1975, and spent the next five years in Mozambique preparing for independence and commanding the guerrillas of the Zimbabwe Patriotic Front, ZANU's military wing.

After winning a landslide victory in the country's first full elections in 1980, Mugabe headed Zimbabwe's first majority-rule government, including Whites as well as his rival, Joshua Nkomo, in his Cabinet. In 1987 Mugabe proclaimed himself president, and the following year he merged his party with Nkomo's ZAPU, making Zimbabwe a single-party Marxist state. Officially abandoning Marxism in 1991, Mugabe announced multi-party elections, which he again won. He played an active role in organising sanctions against the apartheid regime in South Africa.

Mughal Muslim dynasty of mixed MONGOL and Turkic descent, which invaded India in 1526, gained control over the subcontinent and ruled it until the early 19th century. The first Mughal (or Mogul) emperor, BABUR (1483-1530), was succeeded by a line which included HUMAYUN, AKBAR, JAHANGIR and SHAH JAHAN whose TAJ MAHAL – a tomb for himself and his favourite wife – is a masterpiece of Mughal architecture.

The original Persian-speaking Mughals not only established a strong administration in India, but encouraged religious harmony through an attitude of conciliation towards their more numerous Hindu subjects. Their introduction of Persian artistic styles led to

The US boxer Muhammad Ali – articulate, proud and successful – was a role model for young Black Americans in the 1960s and 1970s.

distinctive Indo-Muslim architecture and miniature paintings which can still be seen in the tombs and palaces of DELHI and Agra.

During the 18th century Hindus rebelled against their Muslim rulers, and British and French armies fought for power in India. Mughal court rivalries further undermined central government, allowing provincial governors to seize local power. By 1803, when Delhi fell to the EAST INDIA COMPANY, the Mughals had lost most of their power. Though they enjoyed a twilight era as nominal kings of Delhi for another half-century, they depended on British goodwill. In 1857 the last Mughal king was exiled and his title abolished.

Muhammad see feature, page 431

Muhammad Ali (1942-) American boxer who proclaimed himself 'the Greatest' and proved it by dominating heavyweight boxing between 1964 and 1979. Born Cassius Clay in Louisville, Kentucky, he was known as the 'Louisville Lip' for his repartee and boasts of being able to 'float like a butterfly and sting like a bee'. In 1960 he won a gold medal at the Olympic Games, and in 1964 he became world heavyweight boxing champion by defeating Sonny Liston. Shortly afterwards he joined the NATION OF ISLAM and changed his name to Muhammad Ali. In 1967 Ali became a figurehead for those opposing the Vietnam War when he refused to serve in the US army – for which he was stripped of his world title. He returned to the ring in 1971 and regained the title three years later by defeating George Foreman in an epic battle. Ali retired in 1981.

Muhammad Reza Shah Pahlavi (1919-80) Shah of IRAN from 1941 until 1979. The son of REZA SHAH, Muhammad succeeded to the throne after his father was forced to abdicate by the British. He took supreme power in 1953 after dismissing his prime minister, and staged a lavish coronation ceremony for himself and his third wife in 1967. While suppressing his political opponents, the shah used Iran's growing oil revenues to fund social reforms and economic development. However, his pro-Western regime was bitterly opposed by Iran's Shiite clergy, who for years fomented a popular revolt which eventually drove him into exile in January 1979.

Mukden incident (September 18, 1931) Seizure by the Japanese army of the Chinese city of Mukden (now Shenyang), marking the beginning of the Japanese occupation of all MANCHURIA. A Japanese army detachment sent to guard the South Manchurian Railway alleged that the Chinese had caused an explosion on the line, and used this as a pretext for occupying Mukden and a large part of south Manchuria. Despite protests from the League of Nations and the Japanese Cabinet, the army occupied the rest of Manchuria by February 1932. The crisis led to the collapse of the Japanese government in May of that year, and to Japan's entry into the Second World War in 1941.

Muldoon, Sir Robert (1921-92) Prime minister of New Zealand from 1975 to 1984. Muldoon became leader of the National Party in 1974 and won the general election the following year. He immediately faced economic difficulties caused by a sharp rise in world oil prices in 1973 and Britain's entry into the Common Market, which threatened New Zealand's traditional market for farm produce. Muldoon's freeze on prices and wages led to a conflict with the trade unions, and when the National Party lost power to Labour in 1984, Muldoon was ousted from the party leadership.

mummy Human or animal body preserved by natural processes – such as immersion in a peat bog or exposure to dry air – or by embalming, as was perfected by the ancient Egyptians.

In Egypt, embalming was originally reserved for royalty. Its purpose was apparently to keep the body of the deceased intact so that it could be re-animated in the afterlife. By the time of the New Kingdom, which started in 1570 BC, embalming had reached its highest standards. It involved removing the corpse's brain and intestines,

This mummified Egyptian cat has a head made from painted plaster.

The shah of Iran, Muhammad Reza Shah Pahlavi, takes the hand of his third wife during their belated coronation ceremony in 1967.

replacing them with herbs and then wrapping the body in layers of specially prepared bandages. By this period, sacred animals such as cows, hawks and cats were often embalmed, as were courtiers and servants so that they could provide a royal retinue in the afterlife.

Munich Beer Hall putsch (November 8-9, 1923) First attempt by Adolf HITLER to seize power in Germany. Hitler and his small Nazi Party joined a right-wing political meeting being held in a Munich beer hall on the night of November 8 and forced its leaders to agree to join them in a march on Berlin. The following day the German police dispersed the Nazi marchers with gunfire, killing 16 of them. Hitler was sentenced to five years' imprisonment for treason, but was released after only eight months in Landsberg fortress.

Munich Pact (September 29, 1938) Treaty signed by Britain, France, Germany and Italy which allowed German troops to occupy the Sudetenland region of Czechoslovakia, and which thereby became a symbol of Western APPEASEMENT towards Nazi Germany. The British prime minister Neville CHAMBERLAIN claimed to have won 'peace in our time', but the Czechoslovakian president Edvard BENES felt compelled to resign. On October 1, German troops entered the Sudetenland, and in the same month Poland and Hungary were permitted to occupy regions of Czechoslovakia in which they had minority populations. In March 1939 the Germans proved that the Munich Pact was only a ploy by taking possession of the whole of Czechoslovakia.

Murat, Joachim (1767-1815) Brilliant French cavalry officer who became one of NAPOLEON I's most successful marshals. Murat fought with distinction in Napoleon's campaigns in Italy in 1796-7, and in Egypt in 1799. Later that year he supported Napoleon's coup which overthrew the Directory, and in 1800 he married Napoleon's sister, Caroline. Eight years later Murat was chosen by Napoleon to succeed Joseph

Prophet of Islam

Muhammad founded the religion of Islam around AD 600 after receiving word from Allah in a series of visions.

Muhammad was born about AD 570 in the city of Mecca, in western Arabia. Mecca was both a centre of the caravan trade through Arabia and the site of a pagan shrine which had developed around a black meteoritic stone. Muhammad was born into the tribe of Quraysh, which controlled the shrine and organised much of the city's trade. Although part of this elite group, he was not rich. He became a trader working on behalf of a wealthy Meccan woman, Khadijah, whom he married. Acting for her, he is said to have visited Syria and met Christian monks who aroused his interest in religion.

In about 600, Muhammad began to devote himself to spiritual matters. He roamed the hills around the city, and received visions in which Allah spoke to him through the angel Gabriel, commanding him to be his messenger. The angel revealed that there was only one God, Allah, whom all people should worship – in contrast with the numerous gods worshipped in Mecca – and that the rich should be generous to the poor, for after death all souls would be judged, the virtuous going to heaven

The name of the prophet Muhammad (left) in calligraphy, and the great mosque housing his tomb at Medina (above).

and the wicked to hell. Muhammad was to be the prophet of this new religion.

His message attracted a number of converts, including his wife, his cousin Ali, and Abu Bakr and Umar, who were to become the first caliphs – rulers of Islam – after Muhammad's death. His attack on the traditional religion made him enemies, and in 622 he was forced to leave Mecca with his followers for the agricultural settlement of Medina. This migration, or *hijra*, marks the beginning of the era from which all Muslim dates are calculated.

Medina had long been troubled by tribal feuds. Muhammad was invited to be an arbiter, but he soon took over leadership of the community, and for the next eight years the Muslims of Medina waged war against the Meccans. In 630 an agreement was reached: the Meccans accepted that Allah was the only God and that Muhammad was his prophet; Muhammad acknowledged that Mecca's shrine should become the focus of Muslim devotion and pilgrimage.

In ten years Muhammad had founded a new religion and a new state. The revelations from Allah continued and were collected in the form of the Qur'an (Koran). His house became the first mosque, and he established the fundamentals of Muslim worship and law. Muhammad received the allegiance of most of the Bedouin tribes of Arabia.

Muhammad died in 632, leaving a daughter, Fatima, but no generally accepted successor. It was his followers, led by Abu Bakr and Umar, who consolidated the new religion and launched the Arab conquests which were to spread the new faith as far as Spain in the west and India in the east.

Bonaparte as king of Naples. Murat fought with Napoleon at the battles of BORODINO and LEIPZIG, and in 1814 he made peace with Austria in an attempt to safeguard his own

'Peace in our time', proclaimed British prime minister Neville Chamberlain after signing the Munich Pact with Adolf Hitler in 1938.

throne. When Napoleon returned from exile in 1815 Murat abandoned his Austrian allies to support the emperor during his HUNDRED DAYS in power, and was subsequently defeated by them at the Battle of Tolentino. Murat fled to Corsica, and in October 1815 he made a last attempt to recapture Naples, which had been restored to Ferdinand IV by the Congress of VIENNA. Murat was captured and shot, and his democratic reforms in Naples were annulled.

Murdoch, Rupert (1931–) Australian-born media proprietor. Educated at Oxford, Murdoch inherited an Adelaide newspaper business which he built into an Australian newspaper and radio empire. Moving to Britain, he bought the struggling title *The Sun* for £250 000 in 1969 and, pioneering mass-circulation popular journalism, transformed it into the nation's best-selling tabloid. Profits from *The Sun* funded further acquisitions in Britain, including *The Times* and *The Sunday Times*, and launched Murdoch into the American media, where he bought

magazines, newspapers and the 20th-Century Fox Film Corporation. Further additions to his empire in the form of pay-TV and interests in emerging media markets in Asia have made Murdoch a central figure in the late-20th century global communications revolution.

Muscovy State in west-central RUSSIA, also called the duchy of Moscow, which emerged in the late 14th century as the dominant power in the region, and which came to rule all of Russia. Until the 13th century western Russia was dominated by the duchy of KIEV, before this was overrun by the Mongols or TATARS in 1237-40. In the 1330s, Ivan I consolidated his power at Moscow, though at this stage with the sanction of the Tatar GOLDEN HORDE. After the Tatars were defeated in 1380, Muscovy grew rapidly in importance, especially under Ivan III (1440-1505) and Vasily III (1479-1533). Under IVAN IV 'the Terrible', the grand duke of Moscow became Tsar of all Russia in 1547, and from then on Moscow lay at the heart of the Russian empire.

The Night Watch, painted by Rembrandt van Rijn in 1642, depicts musketeers in Amsterdam. The painting was commissioned for the headquarters of the city's six musketeer militias.

music hall Popular form of mass entertainment which flourished in Britain from the mid 19th century, and was finally eclipsed by the cinema in the 1930s. Music halls had their origins in the special saloons of London taverns set aside as 'music rooms' for convivial singsongs, which were interspersed with solo performances rewarded by a cash collection among the patrons. Enthusiasm for such entertainment became so great that in 1849 the London publican Charles Morton built a 'hall' next door to his tavern specifically to meet the demand. Three years later, London's first purpose-built music hall, the Canterbury, was opened.

The early musical halls comprised a simple stage, a bar and chairs and tables, while the proceedings were controlled by a chairman, who selected the evening's programme. This often contained as many as 25 varied 'turns', including singers, tap and clog dancers, acrobats, comedians and jugglers. Even dramatic sketches were sometimes added. As the simple halls gave way to two and three-tier auditoriums with elaborate stages, programmes expanded to include abridged extracts from popular ballets and tableaux-vivants based on classical myths or patriotic themes. In America, where they were known as vaudeville theatres, the first music halls opened in the 1880s and were as successful as their British counterparts. On both sides of the Atlantic, leading music hall artists such as Marie Lloyd, Vesta Tilley, George Robey and Dan Leno became prominent public figures.

musketeer Soldier whose cumbersome and relatively short-range weapon, the musket, transformed warfare in the late 16th century. Aimed from the user's shoulder, the musket was a large-calibre, smooth-bore firearm that replaced the inefficient hand cannons of 15th-century Europe and the similarly clumsy matchlock harquebuses – in which powder was lit by a match – which were difficult to load and aim. Spanish troops pioneered the use of the more powerful *mosquete* (musket) in the 16th century, and evolved new battle tactics, since the weapons needed forked stands as props for firing. Moreover, since muskets were slow to load, pikemen had to protect musketeers from enemy cavalry charges. The development of the bayonet in the late 17th century removed the need for supportive pikemen.

Muslim League Political party which forced the partition of INDIA in 1947 and the creation of the independent Muslim state of PAKISTAN. Ten years after it was founded by the AGA KHAN Sultan Muhammad Shah in 1905 to protect the interests of India's Muslims against a Hindu majority in any future independent democracy, radical nationalist elements in the Muslim League forged a pact with the mainly Hindu Congress Party. The League was promised separate electoral representation and reserved seats in Muslim minority provinces, tempting some of its members to join the Congress. Although the League gained few seats in the provincial elections of 1937, it went on to convince most

Muslims that the Congress ministries were oppressing them and in 1940 demanded an autonomous Muslim homeland – Pakistan. In negotiations preceding India's independence, the League's leader, Muhammad JINNAH, repeated this demand. The League won nearly all of the Muslim vote in the 1946 elections and, following Muslim rioting, both Britain and the Congress agreed to partition.

Mussolini, Benito (1883-1945) Fascist ruler of Italy from 1922 to 1943. He became dictator in 1928 and, as an AXIS partner of Adolf HITLER's Germany, led Italy into the Second World War in 1940.

After a brief spell as a teacher, Mussolini turned to journalism as editor of the socialist newspaper *Avanti!* (*Forward!*) in 1913. Soon after the First World War, in which he reached the rank of corporal, Mussolini turned his back on socialism and organised his followers into the Fasci di Combattimento, which was the nucleus of his Fascist Party. Its right-wing nationalistic policies struck a chord with Italy's conservative clergy, landowners and industrialists. They turned a blind eye to the thuggery of Mussolini's BLACK SHIRTS, the uniformed arm of the fascists.

In 1921 Mussolini was elected to parliament and the National Fascist Party was recognised officially. Playing on King Victor Emmanuel III's fears of a communist revolution, in October 1922 Mussolini organised tens of thousands of fascist supporters in a 'march on Rome' and was subsequently made prime minister. Within six years his 'corporate state' had unlimited control over Italian

> **66 Fascism is a religion; the 20th century will be known in history as the century of fascism. 99**
>
> *Benito Mussolini, 1933*

economic life and had replaced parliament with totalitarianism. In spite of this, Mussolini won popular support. In 1929 the dictator ended a 60-year-old land dispute between Church and State through the LATERAN Treaty which established the Vatican State.

Mussolini's dream of reshaping Italy along the lines of the Roman Empire led to the annexation of Ethiopia in 1936 and Albania three years later. In spite of these successes, Italy was ill-prepared for a major conflict and Mussolini's alliance with Hitler, one of the dictator's early admirers and imitators, exposed the country's military weakness almost as soon as Italy entered the Second World War in June 1940. A series of military defeats in the Balkans and North Africa swiftly demoted Mussolini to a junior partnership in the Axis. They also weakened his

Mussolini postures in 1938, and Pope Pius XI is caricatured as looking on (right) as the fascist dictator prepares for war.

grip at home, and in July 1943 he was deposed and imprisoned by his former fascist supporters. Rescued in September in a daring raid by German paratroopers, Mussolini established a puppet government in the small town of Salo in north Italy, but in April 1945 he was captured and executed by Italian partisans.

Mutesa I (d.1884) Autocratic monarch of Buganda during whose reign – from 1857 until his death – the first missionaries arrived in what is today UGANDA. As kabaka, or dynastic ruler, Mutesa enriched his country by opening it to Arab traders. He also strengthened the army which he used to acquire the slaves that were Buganda's main merchandise. He captured more slaves when he subdued Bunyoro, the leading state in what is now south Uganda. Although a Muslim, Mutesa welcomed the first Christian missionaries, until the arrival in his kingdom of the British East Africa Company caused social tensions that had not been resolved by the time he died.

Mutesa II, Sir Edward (1924-69) Last regional kabaka, or dynastic ruler, of Buganda, who reigned from 1939 until 1962, when he became first president of UGANDA. Mutesa was 18 years old when he assumed the throne of what had become, in 1900, a British protectorate linked administratively to a larger neighbouring territory, Uganda. Fearing that Buganda's independence was threatened by its neighbour's growing autonomy, in 1953 Mutesa claimed the right of his kingdom to secede. When the Ugandan High Court rejected his claim he was deported by the British, but was allowed to return as a constitutional monarch in 1955. When Uganda

became a republic in 1962, Mutesa was elected its first president by an overwhelming majority. In 1966 he was deposed by the prime minister Dr Milton OBOTE, with whose left-wing policies he disagreed.

Mutiny Act (1689) Legislation passed by the English Parliament with the aim of weakening traditional links between the monarchy and the army. The Declaration of Rights, passed earlier in 1689, had established that no full-time army could be maintained without parliamentary consent, even if it was being paid for by the king. Parliament intended the Mutiny Act – which took its title from its provisions for enforcing army discipline – to strengthen its control over the army. The Act was passed for one year only, which gave Parliament the right to an annual review, and from 1697 to 1701 the Act was not in force. In spite of the Act, the Crown's links with both the army and the navy were not greatly affected.

Myanmar (Burma) Country in Southeast Asia on the eastern side of the Bay of Bengal. The first Burmese arrived from their original homeland in south-west China in the 7th century AD. By 850 they had established the powerful city-state of PAGAN, and in 1057 they conquered their main rivals, the MONS. Following a Mongol invasion in 1287 the Burmese endured centuries of anarchy that lasted until 1758, when Alaungpaya reunited the country and established its last dynasty.

Tension along the Indian-Burmese border prompted a British invasion of Burma in 1842, resulting in the loss of some territory in the north of the country. A second Anglo-Burmese war broke out in 1852 and a third in 1885. Both led to further losses of territory and the third resulted in the deposition of King Thibaw and the establishment of Upper Burma as a province of British India. In 1931, during a two-year peasant uprising, the nationalist Dobama Asi-ayone (Thakin) Party demanded independence. Although six years later Burma became a crown colony, with a Burmese premier and an elected assembly, Japan's invasion in 1942 was initially welcomed by a Burma National Army which was promised independence by the Japanese. Later, during the Allied campaign to regain the area, this force changed sides. Burma

gained full independence in 1948 and elected not to join the Commonwealth. Almost immediately the Karens of the Irrawaddy Delta as well as the Chin, Kayah and Kachin hill peoples challenged the central government in a civil war which lasted until an army coup in 1962. Its leader, Ne Win, established an authoritarian state based on quasi-socialist and Buddhist principles, maintaining a policy of neutrality; however, civil conflict involving insurgent ethnic groups continued.

General Saw Maung seized power in September 1988 and imposed martial law – changing the country's name to the Union of Myanmar – but social, economic and political problems worsened as private armies financed by illegal traffic in drugs took control of many remote areas. During 1989 AUNG SAN SUU KYI emerged as a leader who could unite the opposition, but she was placed under house arrest. Her National League for Democracy (NLD) nevertheless won a two-thirds majority in the 1990 elections for a constituent assembly. Saw Maung responded by refusing to allow the assembly to meet and by arresting other NLD leaders, prompting widespread international condemnation. In 1991 Aung San was awarded the Nobel peace prize for her efforts to establish democracy. A slight shift towards political liberalisation followed Saw Maung's replacement by his deputy, General Than Shwe, in April 1992, and in 1995 the house arrest of Aung San was lifted. However, many emergency powers remained in force.

Mycenaean civilisation Culture which dominated mainland Greece from around 1580 BC until about 1100, when it inexplicably declined and was overrun by invading DORIANS. More than a century before the Mycenaeans conquered MINOAN Knossos in about 1400, their culture had been greatly influenced by the Minoans, whom they replaced as the dominant power in the eastern Mediterranean. Centred on the cities of Mycenae and Tiryns and the port of Pylos, Mycenaean culture spread throughout the Peloponnese and as far north as southern Thessaly. Unlike Minoan cities which were totally unfortified, Mycenaean cities had heavy, complex fortifications. These rich cities had extensive trade links with Egypt, Asia Minor, Cyprus and Syria, and archaeological evidence discovered by Heinrich Schliemann in the 19th century suggests it may have been the Mycenaeans who sacked the city of TROY in about 1200, though this is still the subject of much debate. Other archaeological finds from the early Mycenaean period reveal accomplished artistic skill in creating frescoes, bronze weapons and highly decorative earthenware pots. Ivory

> ### DID YOU KNOW?
>
> Mycenaean kings were buried in great dome-shaped 'beehive tombs'. One tomb – the so-called Treasury of Atreus – has a chamber measuring over 43ft (13m) in height.

from Egypt was a popular medium for ornaments, and the Mycenaeans also produced gold jewellery, utensils and death masks.

Mysore Former Princely State in south-west India which for more than 30 years withstood invasions by the British East India Company. As one of many small Hindu kingdoms, Mysore became the hub of the great Hindu empire of Vijayanagar which emerged in the 14th century to halt Muslim expansion from the north. When Vijayanagar declined, the local Wadiya family attempted to establish an independent kingdom, but strong neighbours prevented its consolidation, and in 1761 the Wadiya raja surrendered power to the Muslim forces of Hyder Ali. He and his son Tipu Sultan were successful in repelling East India Company forces in the four Mysore Wars fought from 1767 until 1799, when their capital, Seringapatam, finally fell. The British annexed almost half of Mysore, but restored the core of the kingdom to the Wadiya rajas. In 1947 Mysore became part of the Indian Union.

mystery plays Medieval performances of scenes from the Bible, also called miracle plays. They were usually enacted on feast days from the 13th to the 16th century, and each episode was presented by a different trade GUILD. Mystery plays probably developed from parts of the Latin Easter Mass celebrated on Corpus Christi, a Roman Catholic holy day, from 1311 onwards. They became popular entertainments through being presented in local languages – rather than Biblical Latin – and scenes were added which were not from the Bible. In several English towns the plays were performed in cycles: wagons in the churchyard or the marketplace were used as stages on which different Biblical episodes were acted out at predetermined stops on a route through town. A full cycle, such as the 48 scenes performed in York, covered the story of Christian redemption from the Creation to the Day of Judgment. Other cycles survive from Chester and Wakefield. The anonymous 'Wakefield Master' created some of the most celebrated mystery plays.

This delicate funeral mask made from solid, beaten gold was the product of Mycenaean civilisation in about the 16th century BC.

mysticism Any system of religious belief which attempts to experience God, or a higher absolute reality ('transcendence'), directly in this present life. Mysticism is central to all religions which conceive of transcendence as an essential part of the material world – such as Hinduism, Buddhism and Taoism. It plays a lesser role in religious systems which present transcendence as radically different from the material world – such as Christianity, Judaism and Islam – though even these religions have their own strong mystical traditions.

Some mystics have had a profound effect on the development of Christianity, among them St BERNARD OF CLAIRVAUX, St FRANCIS OF ASSISI and St TERESA OF ÁVILA. It has also been argued that Christ and Mohammad themselves had mystical experiences which shaped the faiths that were built on their teachings.

A mystic can often not describe his or her experiences in everyday terms and resorts to metaphors; and because these may share common themes, regardless of the faith involved, some experts argue that all mystical experiences are fundamentally similar.

myths Traditional tales often containing elements of fantasy or religion which are found in most societies. Some of the more ancient myths are seen as explanations of the origins of humans, animals and the Universe, as in Egyptian, Greek and Roman myths; others relate to local taboos or social structures. Often they describe the deeds of gods, heroes or ordinary people endowed with supernatural powers. Some myths, such as Homer's account of the Trojan wars, clearly have their origins in historical fact. Others may have been

Tipu's tiger – a life-sized wooden model of a tiger mauling a European – was made for Sultan Tipu of Mysore in about 1795. It contains a miniature organ, which allows it to make fearsome roaring noises.

early forms of religious or quasi-scientific thought. Scholars of anthropology and folklore interpret a society's myths as reflecting how it sees its position in the world. Psychologists such as Carl JUNG thought myths revealed that all people shared some of the same universal mythic symbols.

Mzilikazi (c.1796-1868) First ruler of the Ndebele people of southern Africa, who were united from a loose grouping of clans into a single nation under his leadership. A war leader under the Zulu King SHAKA, Mzilikazi rebelled in 1822 and led his people from Zululand into the western Transvaal. In 1837, as the Zulu empire expanded, the Ndebele were forced to flee north where, subduing the Shona, Mzilikazi and his subjects settled in the area of Bulawayo in modern Zimbabwe.

nabob Term of derision applied in the 18th century to EAST INDIA COMPANY officials who had amassed fortunes in India, which they used to better their positions in England. The term is corrupted from the Persian title *nawab*, a governor administering an Indian province for the MUGHAL emperors. Rulers of some Muslim Princely States continued to use the title during the British Raj period.

Nagasaki Japanese city that was largely destroyed by an American atomic bomb in the Second World War. The bomb was dropped on August 9, 1945, three days after the first A-bomb attack on HIROSHIMA had failed to force the Japanese to surrender. The hilly terrain of Nagasaki protected the population of 230 000 from the full effects of the explosion, but 40 000 people were killed and widespread destruction was caused. The following day Japan offered to surrender, and the ceasefire began on August 15. The city was rapidly rebuilt and is now a centre for shipbuilding.

Nagy, Imre (1896-1958) Hungarian prime minister from 1953 to 1955 and briefly in 1956. Nagy was a popular premier because of his policy of liberalisation, ending collectivisation and loosening police control. He was denounced by the Soviet Union for being too liberal and in 1955 he was removed from power by the Soviet-backed Matyas Rakosi. Anti-Soviet Hungarians rioted and looked to Nagy for leadership, and in 1956 he was reappointed prime minister. Nagy brought non-communists into his coalition and announced in October that Hungary was leaving the WARSAW PACT, the military alliance of Eastern European states allied to the Soviet Union. The latter reacted by invading Hungary in

November and crushing the revolution. Nagy was seized by the Soviet authorities and eventually handed over to the new prime minister, János KADAR, who had him executed. In 1989 a successful revolution led to his rehabilitation and reburial with full honours.

Namibia Republic in southern Africa, originally inhabited by the Hottentot, Bushman and Herero peoples. The Portuguese charted the coasts in the late 15th century, and English and Dutch navigators followed in the 17th and 18th centuries. German missionaries landed in the 19th century, and in 1884 the German protectorate of South West Africa was set up. During the First World War the territory was captured by South African forces, and in 1920 South Africa was granted a League of Nations mandate over it. In 1946 the United Nations refused to allow it to be incorporated into South Africa and ended the mandate. In 1964 it was renamed Namibia but South Africa ignored the move and continued to occupy the country. In 1971 the International Court of Justice ruled that the occupation was illegal, and the UN recognised the Black nationalist group the South West Africa People's Organisation (SWAPO) as the representative of the people. A national assembly was set up by South Africa in 1979 but SWAPO guerrillas continued to operate from neighbouring Angola, which South African troops invaded on several occasions. In 1985 South Africa set up a puppet regime, but it failed to gain control of the country. Three years later South Africa was persuaded by the UN to negotiate with the SWAPO leader Samuel Nujoma. An agreement was signed in August, followed by elections in November 1989, independence and a multiparty democracy in 1990. SWAPO won the elections, and Nujoma became Namibia's first president. He was re-elected in 1994.

Nanak (1469-c.1539) Founder of SIKHISM. He was born in a village in the Punjab, northwestern India, in the mercantile Khatri caste, but abandoned his family and job to travel in search of religious inspiration. On his return he preached a new path to the orthodox Hindu goal of release from the cycle of rebirth and attainment of union with God. He practised a form of meditation on the name of God, the hallmark of the new Sikh faith which soon spread in the Punjab. Many details of his life and travels remain uncertain, although biographical collections of anecdotes, called *Fanam-sakhis*, are in circulation among the Sikhs (disciples) who worship him as the first of their ten gurus (religious teachers).

Nanjing, Treaty of (August 29, 1842) Treaty between Britain and China that ended the first of the OPIUM WARS, which arose in 1839 after the Chinese government confiscated 20 000 chests of illegally imported opium from British warehouses in Guangzhou (Canton). The treaty ceded Hong Kong to Britain, broke Chinese restrictions on trade, and opened five TREATY PORTS to British trade.

Nantes, Edict of (1598) Decree declared by the French king Henry IV which ended the FRENCH WARS OF RELIGION – eight religious and political conflicts. The edict, which was signed at Nantes, a port on the Loire estuary in western France, defined the religious and civic rights of the HUGUENOT (Calvinist Protestant) community, giving them freedom of worship and a state subsidy to support their troops and pastors. It virtually created a state within a state, and in the 1620s clashed with the policies of Cardinal Armand Richelieu, his ally the papal envoy Cardinal Jules Mazarin and the French king Louis XIV. The fall of the Huguenot stronghold of La Rochelle to Richelieu's army in 1628 marked the end of these political privileges. After 1665 Louis XIV embarked on a policy of persecuting Protestants, and in 1685 he revoked the edict.

Naoroji, Dadabhai (1825-1917) Indian nationalist leader and the first Indian to be elected to the British House of Commons, serving as Liberal MP for Central Finsbury in London from 1892 to 1895. His campaign against the drain of wealth from India to Britain, defined in his study *Poverty and Un-British Rule in India* (1901), stimulated economic nationalism in the subcontinent. He was a founder of the Indian National Congress, and served as its president in 1886, 1893 and 1906. In his later years Naoroji was known as the Grand Old Man of India.

Napier, Robert, 1st Baron of Magdala (1810-90) British field-marshal and civil engineer. He served with distinction in the SIKH WARS and during the Indian Mutiny (see INDIA), and was the engineer chiefly responsible for the programme of public works in the Punjab from 1849 to 1856. He took his title from an incident during service in Africa when he led an expedition of 32 000 troops to Ethiopia in 1867-8 and captured the town of Magdala, releasing the British consul who was being held because King Tewodros II mistakenly believed that Queen Victoria had ignored a letter from him. In 1870 Napier became commander in chief in India, and later served as governor of Gibraltar.

Naples City on the Bay of Naples in southwest Italy, overshadowed by the smouldering volcano Vesuvius. It was settled by Greeks from Chalcis and Athens in the 6th century BC, and overrun by the Romans in 328. When Roman rule weakened, Naples was invaded by the Goths, but revived under Byzantine influence in the 6th century AD and survived as an independent duchy until 1139, when it was conquered by the Normans. It became part of the Kingdom of the Two Sicilies in the 12th century and passed successively to the Angevins, the Aragonese, and from 1504 to Spain, becoming a key base for Spanish and Habsburg power in their Italian disputes with the Valois kings of France. It passed to the Austrians in the War of the SPANISH SUCCESSION, but was conquered for the Bourbons in 1734. Napoleon conquered it in 1799, and

The mushroom cloud (above) from an atomic explosion over the Japanese city of Nagasaki. About 40 per cent of the city was flattened; the buildings (left) were more than a mile from the blast centre.

Napoleon III welcomed any opportunity to assert French power and glory. This painting records an embassy from Siam arriving at court, even though the event was without historic significance.

in 1815 the Neapolitan king was restored as Ferdinand I. Naples fell to the forces of Giuseppe GARIBALDI in 1860.

Napoleon I see feature, page 438

Napoleon III

(1808-73) Emperor of the French from 1852 to 1870. After the final fall of his uncle NAPOLEON I in 1815, Louis Napoleon Bonaparte began a period of exile in Switzerland, where he was associated with the CARBONARI, a nationalistic secret revolutionary society which sparked revolts in France, Spain, Italy and Portugal. On the death of Napoleon I's only son, the King of Rome, in 1832, Louis Napoleon became Bonapartist pretender to the French throne, and twice attempted to overthrow King Louis Philippe. After the first attempt in 1836 he was deported to the USA. Four years later he embarked upon the disastrous 'Boulogne conspiracy', when he landed in the French northern coastal town with 56 supporters and tried to persuade the garrison to support him. He was captured and jailed in the fortress of Ham, near Amiens, but escaped to London in 1846 disguised as a mason by the name of Badinguet, which became his nickname.

During the REVOLUTIONS OF 1848 Louis Napoleon returned to France, and was elected president of the French Republic under the new constitution. Three years later his half-brother, the Duke of Morny, launched a coup against the national assembly, and in 1852 Louis Napoleon was installed as Napoleon III, Emperor of the French. His empire became more liberal in the last ten years of his reign as Napoleon widened the powers of the legislative assembly and lifted restrictions on civil liberties. He underestimated the power of the German leader Otto von BISMARCK, and allowed the belligerent EMS TELEGRAM of the 'Iron Chancellor' to provoke him into going to war with Prussia. He was captured by the Prussians and deposed, spending the last three years of his life in exile in England.

Napoleonic Wars

Campaigns fought by NAPOLEON I against the European powers from 1803 to 1815. In the closing stages of the Revolutionary Wars, Napoleon had achieved a series of decisive victories over the Austrians in northern Italy in 1796-7. In 1798 he led an expedition to Egypt, but his ambitions there were thwarted by a British naval victory at the Battle of the NILE.

Napoleon returned to France and in 1802 signed an uneasy truce with Britain. However, his continued aggression led to a resumption of hostilities in 1803 – the start of the so-called Napoleonic Wars proper. In 1805, the combined French and Spanish fleets were destroyed at the Battle of TRAFALGAR, though in the same year Napoleon defeated the Austrians at Ulm and a combined Austrian-Russian army at AUSTERLITZ. In 1806 he went on to break the Prussian armies at JENA and Auerstadt, and in June 1807 he again defeated the Russians, prompting both the Prussian king and the Russian emperor to sign the Treaties of TILSIT in July that year.

After a victorious campaign against Sweden in 1808, the French armies were dominant on the Continent, but from August that year they suffered a number of defeats in Spain and Portugal during the so-called PENINSULAR WAR. Encouraged by these signs of weakness, the Austrians challenged Napoleon in 1809, and after an initial victory at Aspern they were defeated at Wagram in July. In spite of the fact that both these battles had cost France dearly, Napoleon assembled the largest army ever seen in Europe, and in 1812 invaded Russia.

After an initial success at the Battle of BORODINO, Napoleon occupied Moscow, but his *Grand Armée* was then forced to retreat in severe winter conditions which cost the lives of nearly half a million men. In October 1813 an alliance of Russia, Prussia and Austrian forces inflicted a crushing defeat on the French at the Battle of LEIPZIG, driving Napoleon to abdicate and apparently bringing the Napoleonic Wars to an end. However,

Napoleon's return from exile on the island of Elba in March 1815 led to a resumption of hostilities, which culminated in the Battle of WATERLOO in June that year. The defeat of the French armies there finally brought the Napoleonic Wars to a close.

Narva, Battle of

(November 30, 1700) Crushing defeat for Russia under PETER I 'the Great' at the Estonian port of Narva at the outset of the NORTHERN WAR with Sweden. Russia regained Narva in 1704.

NASA

Civilian agency founded in 1958 to coordinate and direct aeronautical and space research in the USA. In June 1969, NASA (National Aeronautics and Space Administration) succeeded in winning the 'space race' with the Soviet Union by landing the astronauts Neil Armstrong and Edwin Aldrin on the Moon. The agency was also responsible for launching communications

By 1810 Napoleon had brought most of Europe under his control. But his triumph was not to endure: in 1813 an allied coalition defeated him at Leipzig on his way back from his disastrous Russian campaign; and less than two years later he was crushed for good on the fields of Waterloo.

ATLANTIC

OCEAN

La Coruña

Oporto

Burgos

Sarago

Torres Vedras
Lisbon

Madrid

SPAIN

PORTUGAL

Ciudad Real

Vale

Córdoba

Bailén

Trafalgar ✕

AFRICA

and weather satellites, and for developing the space shuttle – a spacecraft able to make repeated journeys into space. The agency's funding was drastically reduced in the 1980s. In the early 1990s NASA concentrated its efforts on building an orbiting space station.

Naseby, Battle of (June 14, 1645) Decisive victory for Parliamentary forces during the ENGLISH CIVIL WAR. The battle took place near Naseby in Northamptonshire. The Cavalier force led by King Charles I and Prince RUPERT was outnumbered about three to one by Cromwell's New Model Army, and almost half its troops were killed or captured.

Nash, Richard (1674-1762) English dandy, known as 'Beau' Nash. In 1705 he moved to the resort of Bath, attracted by its gambling. He became the town's Master of Ceremonies, organising lavish balls as well as numerous improvements, such as street lighting and the

suppression of duelling, all of which helped to turn Bath into a fashionable SPA. Nash was also known for defining and insisting upon correct dress. In the 1740s new antigambling laws caused difficulties for Nash, but in 1758 the city corporation granted him an annual pension out of gratitude for his public works.

Nash, Sir Walter (1882-1968) Prime minister of New Zealand from 1957 to 1960. From 1919 Nash was on the executive of New Zealand's Labour Party, formulating policies that in 1935 led to the election of the country's first Labour government. While minister of finance from 1935 to 1949, he played a major role in establishing a system of child allowances and free medicine, creating the most extensive social security system in the world. From 1942 to 1944 he was a member of the Pacific War Council. In 1957 Nash led Labour to a narrow election victory, serving as prime minister until the party's defeat in 1960.

Nasser, Gamal Abdel (1918-70) Egyptian president from 1954 to 1970. In 1942 Nasser founded an antiroyalist, anti-British movement, known from 1948 as the Free Officers' Movement. In 1952 he and 89 followers staged a coup, forcing the abdication of King FAROUK. A republic was declared and a revolutionary council set up, with Major-General Muhammad Neguib as president. Nasser deposed Neguib in 1954, becoming head of state. After failing to receive British and US support for a project to extend the Aswan Dam, in 1956 Nasser nationalised the Suez Canal Company, whose shares were owned mainly by French and British investors. Britain, France and Israel invaded Egypt, but the SUEZ WAR was halted by international disapproval and diplomatic intervention from the USA. In 1967 Egypt's defeat by Israel in the SIX-DAY WAR led Nasser to resign, but he changed his decision after demonstrations of support throughout Egypt. He died in office.

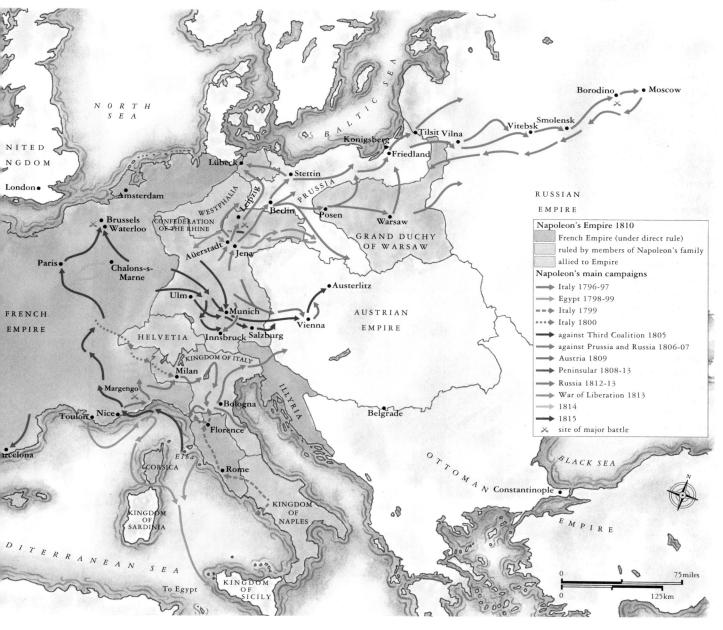

A man of destiny

Napoleon Bonaparte was France's greatest national hero, a conqueror who briefly united much of Europe under his rule and developed political and legal institutions that still influence present-day governments.

Born on the island of Corsica in 1769, Napoleon Bonaparte was sent to France at the age of nine for a military education. Graduating in 1785, he became a lieutenant of artillery. Four years later France was plunged into revolution. By 1793 he had risen to adjutant general in the revolutionary army and made his name in Paris by scattering a royalist mob with a 'whiff of grapeshot' – firing cannon at them.

His fame gained him entrance to the salons of Paris, where he met Joséphine de Beauharnais, a beautiful Creole widow. The couple were married in March 1796. Two days later he took command of the French army in Italy to counter the threat of Austrian invasion.

The young general had won his promotion by boldness and unorthodoxy. He fought by new rules: marching at night; concentrating his forces on the enemy's weakest point; attacking in the rain and on Sundays. Within a year he had driven the Austrians out of Italy. He then tried to repeat these victories in Egypt to damage Britain's Mediterranean interests. Though he was at first successful, a British fleet under Admiral Nelson destroyed the French at the Battle of the Nile.

NAPOLEON SEIZES THE CROWN

In November 1799 Napoleon helped to instigate a coup which installed him as virtual ruler of France. 'I acted not from love of power,' he said, 'but because I felt I was better educated, more perceptive and better qualified than anyone else.' He reformed the government and education system, introducing legal reforms under the Code Napoléon which still form the basis of French law. In 1804 he organised his own coronation in the cathedral of Notre Dame. The climax of the ceremony was to be the crowning of the emperor by the pope. But Napoleon himself took the gold laurel crown and placed it on

A distribution of eagle standards in Napoleon's army in 1810 recalls the military glories of the Roman Empire. Napoleon demands the return of Malta from the British in 1803 (left).

his own head. Although he was popular in France, Napoleon was distrusted by the courts of Europe. Already at war with England, France was soon threatened by Russia, Austria and Prussia. Napoleon reacted swiftly: within two years he had defeated his three continental enemies, and most of Europe was his. He divorced Joséphine – who had failed to bear him an heir – and married Marie Louise, daughter of the Austrian emperor Francis I.

Now Napoleon's luck began to turn. He attacked Portugal to enforce a blockade against British trade. The Spanish government's decision to let the French pass through Spain provoked political instability, allowing British troops to land on the Iberian Peninsula. Under Arthur Wellesley, later Duke of Wellington, Anglo-Spanish-Portuguese forces achieved decisive victories. In 1812 Napoleon invaded Russia. He reached

Moscow only to find the city deserted and the Russians refusing to negotiate. Reports of insurrection at home caused him to turn back. The winter retreat in temperatures as low as -30°C (-22°F) took a horrific toll: fewer than a quarter of his 450000 men returned.

In 1814, Austria, Russia, Prussia and Britain attacked France. After they reached Paris, Napoleon was exiled to the island of Elba. He escaped the following year and landed at Cannes. Moving at speed, he crossed the Alps, gathering the support of soldiers sent to arrest him, and 20 days later arrived in Paris. The king, Louis XVIII, fled. But three months later, on June 18, 1815, Napoleon was defeated by the British and Prussians under the Duke of Wellington at the Battle of Waterloo. He spent the rest of his life exiled on St Helena, a remote Atlantic island. The man who had ruled most of Europe and created the institutions upon which the modern French state was built died of a stomach ailment in 1821.

Natal Eastern coastal province of the Republic of South Africa. Natal was settled by Black farmers probably from the 1st century AD. Between 1819 and 1838 the region was devastated by wars between the related NGUNI and Difagane peoples. During this period, European settlers also arrived. In 1840 the Boers set up an independent Republic of Natal, but after this was annexed by Britain in 1843 many Boers migrated to the ORANGE FREE STATE. Natal became a self-governing colony in 1856, annexing Zululand in 1897. It was invaded by Afrikaner troops in the second BOER WAR, but these were checked at Ladysmith in 1900. Natal joined the South African Union in 1910. In 1994 it became part of the new region of Kwazulu-Natal.

Natchez North American Indian people of the middle Mississippi River region. The Natchez way of life survived long enough for it to be documented, giving a unique insight into the prehistoric MISSISSIPPI CULTURES. Natchez society was organised into a complex hierarchy of nobility, comprising 'suns', 'nobles' and 'honoureds', and commoners, called 'stinkards'. Nobility were required to marry commoners and descent was through the female line. Children of stinkard fathers took their mother's rank, while those of commoner mothers were one rank below their fathers. An attack on Fort Rosalie in 1729 led to a French counterattack and the destruction of many Natchez villages. In 1731 more than 450 Natchez captives were sold as slaves and most of the remainder joined the CHICKASAW.

nationalisation Policy of taking land, firms or industries into public ownership and running them under government-appointed management. From the early 20th century, nationalisation was a declared aim of Labour and socialist parties in developed countries such as the UK and France. In Russia, land, industry and other enterprises were taken into state ownership after the 1917 revolution. Nationalisation has since been carried out by many Western European governments.

The typical nationalised industry is a public utility such as water, gas, post, electricity or telecommunications. This is partly because these industries may be natural monopolies and seen as part of a country's basic services, therefore appropriately kept in the public sector. Nationalisation has been used as a means of increasing efficiency and breaking up concentrations of private wealth, but critics claim that nationalised industries suffer from inefficiency and poor performance due to lack of competition and incentives for workers. In the UK, the Conservative government of the 1980s privatised public utilities and industries that had been nationalised by the Labour government following the end of the Second World War.

In 1995 the Nation of Islam organised a 'Million Man March' in which 400 000 of its members marched on the White House in Washington.

nationalism see feature, pages 440-1

Nation of Islam Islamic Black separatist organisation in the USA, also known as the Black Muslim Movement. The Nation of Islam was founded in Detroit in 1930 by Wallace Fard Muhammad, who encouraged his followers to believe that he was an incarnation of Allah. He taught that Black people are descended from an ancient Muslim tribe and that Islam offers the only escape from racial oppression. The movement grew under his successor, Elijah Muhammad (1934-75), especially in the late 1950s when the charismatic MALCOLM X became Muhammad's spokesman. In 1975 control passed to Elijah Muhammad's son, Warith Deen Muhammad, who repudiated the divinity of the movement's founder and renamed it the American Muslim Mission. In 1985 he disbanded the movement so that its members could follow a more orthodox form of Islam. A New York splinter group under Louis Farrakhan continues to uphold both the name and the original principles of the Nation of Islam. In October 1995 it organised a rally in Washington DC to protest against continuing racial discrimination in the United States.

nation-state Territorial and social entity formed when state and nation coincide. The people of such a state, united by a common sense of culture, history, race, religion or language, feel themselves to be a 'nation'. The state forms a single political community whose institutions are accepted as legitimate by a majority of the population. Nation-states are regarded as the international norm, based on mutual recognition and membership of organisations such as the United Nations.

NATO Military defence alliance of Western powers. NATO (North Atlantic Treaty Organisation) was set up in 1949 during the early years of the COLD WAR, primarily to counter the perceived military threat from the Soviet Union and its allies. The collapse of communism after 1989, followed by the dissolution of the WARSAW PACT in 1991, led to a reassessment of NATO's role as a provider of economic aid to emerging Eastern European democracies. In 1994 the former communist republics were invited to join a 'partnership for peace' in preparation for membership of NATO. In 1994 and 1995 NATO attempted to end the civil war in Bosnia.

Navaho Indigenous North Americans who, like the related APACHES, originated in western Canada. Originally a nomadic people, the Navaho moved to north-eastern Arizona in the 17th century and adopted sheep raising from the Spanish. From 1846 attacks on American settlements in New Mexico led to reprisals until Kit CARSON subdued the Navaho in 1863-4 by destroying their sheep. The majority were then imprisoned in Fort Sumner, New Mexico. In 1868 they were released and given a reservation on the borders of Arizona and New Mexico that now measures more than 16 million acres (6.5 million hectares). The discovery of oil, gas and other minerals has increased Navaho annual income to about £10 million.

Navigation Acts Laws passed by England to prevent foreign merchant vessels from competing on equal terms with English ships. The earliest law dates from the reign of Richard II, but the most important was passed under Oliver Cromwell in 1651. It stated that goods entering the country must be carried in English ships or ships of the country where the goods originated. Its aim was to destroy the Dutch carrying trade and it provoked the

The Navaho originally learned metalworking from the Mexicans and weaving from the Pueblo of New Mexico in the 17th century.

The ties and tribulations of nationhood

Nationalism is the desire of members of a nation to govern themselves and to protect their interests – even at the expense of outsiders. It has been an explosively powerful political force.

Nations are communities of people who have a common history and share an attachment to a particular place or to cultural features such as language and religion. Poland, for instance, is a nation because Poles speak their own language; because they are mainly Roman Catholics; because they consider an area of land bounded by the river Oder to the west and the Carpathian Mountains to the south to be their homeland; and because their history is one of struggle to protect that homeland from their neighbours.

Although people have not always thought of themselves as belonging to distinct nations, the vast majority now do, and this has given rise to nationalism. It can take different forms. Sometimes members of a minority within an existing state, such as Scots or French Canadians, try to form a state of their own. Or, as with the 19th-century movements to unify Germany and Italy, nationalists may try to unite in a single large state fellow-nationals who are divided among several communities. There is also the nationalism of established states whose governments try to increase their power over neighbours, or to resist incorporation into larger entities such as the European Union. The common thread is

the wish to be politically self-determining, usually by creating a state whose borders coincide with the physical boundaries of the nation and by fending off interference by other states.

Nationalistic rhetoric encourages the idea that nations have existed from time immemorial and emphasises the glorious deeds of national heroes. But in reality fully-fledged nationalism is a recent phenomenon. In the past, most political societies were formed on the basis of personal ties between subjects and their rulers. Authority descended through families; provided that the current ruler kept the peace and observed customary law his subjects did not insist that he should belong to their cultural group.

THE RISE OF NATIONS

Outside rule would sometimes give rise to patriotic feelings, as among the Scottish nobles who in 1320 signed the Declaration of Arbroath, pledging that 'so long as . . . one hundred of us remain alive, we will never consent to subject ourselves to the dominion of the English'. But such cases were rare before the modern period.

Nationalism first appeared alongside the modern state, with its formal authority structure and unitary legal system. Britain

Germania, symbol of her nation, holds aloft the new imperial crown.

developed such a state during the 16th and 17th centuries, followed by several of its neighbours. The governments of these states, although not granting democratic rights to all their people, claimed to act on their behalf. The ties of nationhood bound the people into a body which gave governments the authority to act on its behalf.

Historians, philosophers and poets began to describe, and sometimes invent, national identities for their societies. Such identities were invoked above all at moments of political crisis – sometimes in conflicting ways. During the French Revolution, for instance, monarchists claimed that the king was the embodiment of national unity; at the same time revolutionary pamphleteers such as Abbé Sieyès defined the French nation in a way that deliberately excluded the king and the nobility. In the

Revolutions promoting nationalist ideals swept Europe in 1848. In Vienna, the people celebrate as the Austro-Hungarian Empire's liberal new constitution is read out.

In an 1880 allegorical picture, France is offered the talents and patriotism of her great men.

19th century the established nation-states tried to strengthen themselves by promoting the national culture among their citizens, while peoples still under alien rule struggled for liberation. This was the age of European nationalism. Philosophers and poets were once more called upon to demonstrate that, for example, all Germans, whether they lived in Prussia, Bavaria or Saxony, formed part of a single people with its own language, traditions and culture, and ought to be united. In Eastern Europe,

The romantic poet de Lamartine headed the government during France's 1848 revolution.

Czechs, Hungarians and Romanians sought to break free from Habsburg rule. The poet Sandor Petofi, statues of whom can still be seen around Budapest, declaimed his 'National Song' in the city and helped to inspire the popular uprising of 1848.

Not all welcomed these developments. Although many liberals and socialists supported the desire for self-determination, they also hoped that national loyalties would eventually take second place to a cosmopolitan sympathy with humanity as a whole. Such hopes were shattered by the First World War, when young men in their millions chose to fight and die for their countries. After the war, national self-determination seemed less important than efforts to establish peace through binding nation-states together in bodies such as the League of Nations and, after the Second World War, the United Nations.

COLONIES FIGHT FOR FREEDOM

Among the advanced democracies, nationalism tended to become less of a preoccupation during the second half of the 20th century. But elsewhere new nations were being formed during the struggle against colonial rule, and the same methods were used to bind together people who often fell by chance within boundaries set by colonial administrations. These states spawned a new wave of secessionist movements: Pakistan from India, Biafra from Nigeria, Eritrea from Ethiopia. People whose language, culture or religion differed from that of the national majority were prepared to fight, often at great cost, for the right to form their own state.

The most recent wave of nationalist movements has sprung from the collapse of communist regimes in the Soviet Union and Eastern Europe after 1989. These movements illustrate both the strengths and weaknesses of nationalism. They show that it is now virtually impossible, except by military force, to hold together peoples who do not wish to be united. Given the chance of political freedom, Slovenes, Serbs

Bangladeshis invoke Indian allies in their struggle for independence, gained in 1971.

and Croats demonstrated that they wanted to exercise it independently of one another. And historical precedent supports them.

The nation-state has proved to be a successful invention. A shared culture makes it easier to build a flourishing economy and also helps to create the mutual trust needed to make democracy work. As Lord Balfour said of Britain, 'our whole political machinery presupposes a people so fundamentally at one that they can safely afford to bicker'. But conflicts such as the civil war of the early 1990s in Bosnia reveal nationalism's darker side.

Nations are not well-defined entities geographically adjacent to one another. Sometimes, as in Bosnia, populations with conflicting national loyalties are intermingled; sometimes, as in the case of the border between Serbia and Croatia, there is disputed territory which both sides are willing to fight for. Here the idea that the borders of the state should coincide with the boundaries of the nation creates the problem rather than the solution. Fervent nationalism makes people willing to suffer terrible harm to achieve objectives, such as re-establishing what they take to be historic borders, which are of little practical benefit to them.

Ana Ipatescu led a Romanian national uprising in 1848. It was put down by the Russians.

The British navy defeated the larger French and Spanish fleet at the Battle of Cape St Vincent in 1797. British commanders adopted the tactic of the close-quarter melee with great success.

ANGLO-DUTCH WARS in 1652. The Acts applied to the colonies and included measures against the manufacture of goods competing with English products. Despite boosting New England shipping, the Acts were widely resented and helped to cause the American Revolution. They were withdrawn in 1849.

navy In the 5th and 4th centuries BC Athens and Corinth relied on triremes (galleys with three banks of oars), while the Macedonians developed fast and manoeuvrable quinqueremes (five-banked galleys). During the First Punic War of 264-241 BC, the Roman Empire fought Carthage at sea, gaining control of the Mediterranean. Navies also had a role in protecting trading vessels against pirates, and in the 9th century AD King Alfred developed a fleet to defend England against Viking invasions. The Italian city-states had squadrons of galleys and adapted merchant ships to defend their ports against Ottoman Turks. The English navy was reorganised in the 17th century under Samuel PEPYS, while the Dutch and French expanded their fleets in the 18th century as trade and colonial expansion accelerated.

By 1800 many countries had developed fleets of warships. Officers were professionals, but they relied on press-gangs to kidnap or to use threats to force men to join up. During the Napoleonic Wars, naval vessels were wooden sailing ships armed with cannons that fired broadsides. After Nelson's victory at the Battle of Trafalgar in 1805, the British navy dominated the oceans for a century. Steam power gradually replaced sail, and in 1859 the French navy pioneered a technique of protecting the wooden hull of a ship with iron plates. With the development of the iron and steel

industry from the late 19th century, rapid advances were made in designing both ships and their armaments. The submarine also emerged as a fighting vessel.

Early in the 20th century, as a response to advances abroad, the British navy developed the huge steel battleships known as DREAD-NOUGHTS. In the First World War, warships and merchant ships sailed in convoy to prevent attacks by German submarines. Between the wars aircraft were developed further, and in the Second World War naval warfare was increasingly fought by aircraft from aircraft carriers, particularly in the Pacific campaigns. The postwar development of submarines armed with long-range nuclear missiles has reduced the number of surface ships. Most countries retain fleets of small, fast vessels for coastal patrol. In 1982, the Falklands War between Argentina and Britain revealed the extent to which there remained a place for a conventional navy, but also showed how exposed surface ships are to missile attack. During the 1991 Gulf War, the Allied navies played an important strategic role, with six aircraft carriers providing launch sites from which air strikes against Iraqi ground targets were made. The threat of an Allied invasion of Kuwait from the sea meant that many Iraqi troops were tied down defending Kuwait's coastline.

Naxalite Movement Indian revolutionary movement named after the village of Naxalbari in the Himalayan foothills of West

Bengal where it began. The founder of the movement and veteran communist, Charu Majumdar, broke away from the Marxist Communist Party of India and established the Marxist-Leninist Communist Party of India. His group organised armed risings of landless agricultural labourers, particularly in eastern India, and developed into an urban guerrilla movement. Its programme of terror was suppressed with considerable violence. The party eventually split into several factions, one of which adopted a policy of participating in constitutional politics, but Naxalite atrocities continued into the early 1990s.

Nazi Member of the Nationalsozialistische Deutsche Arbeiterpartei (National Socialist German Workers' Party). Founded in 1919 as the German Workers' Party by Anton Drexler, a Munich locksmith, it adopted its new name in 1920 and was taken over by Adolf HITLER in 1921. The Nazi Party, which dominated Germany from 1933 to 1945, based its policies on an opposition to democracy. Theories of the purity of the Aryan race, which led to the persecution of the Jews, were allied to the Prussian military tradition and an extreme sense of nationalism. Nazi ideology drew on the racist theories of Joseph GOBINEAU, the national fervour of Heinrich von Treitschke and the superman theories of Friedrich NIETZSCHE. The success of the National Socialists is explained by the desperation of the German people, who had suffered the humiliation of the VERSAILLES Peace Settlement ending the First World War, as well as years of economic depression and inflation, and by their fear of the communists' power and influence in the Soviet Union. After Hitler gained power by constitutional means, Nazi policies became the foundation of the THIRD REICH. Rival parties were banned, terrorised or duped, and institutions of state and the army were won over.

> ### DID YOU KNOW?
> The layout of the Nazi newspaper Das Reich, founded by the minister of propaganda Joseph Goebbels, was modelled on the British Observer. Goebbels wrote the leaders, and prominent contributors included Theodor Heuss, who later became West Germany's first president.

Before the Second World War broke out, aspects of Nazi ideology found some supporters in countries throughout the Western world. Nazi systems were imposed on occupied Europe from 1938 to 1945, and millions of Jews, Russians, Poles, homosexuals, gypsies, political subversives and others were held in concentration camps and murdered. The German Nazi Party was disbanded in 1945 and its revival officially forbidden by West Germany. Resentment against immigrants at a time of high unemployment in the former East Germany led to neo-Nazi demonstrations in 1992. During the early 1990s there was an increase in racist attacks by neo-Nazis in both Western and Eastern Europe.

The Egyptian queen Nefertiti makes an offering, as shown in a wall painting from the 14th century BC in the Valley of the Queens in Thebes.

Nazi-Soviet Pact Agreement between Germany and the Soviet Union, signed on August 23, 1939, by the German and Soviet foreign ministers Joachim von Ribbentrop and Vyacheslav Moltov. It renounced warfare between the two countries and pledged neutrality if either country was attacked by a third party. Both signatories promised not to join any grouping of powers 'directly or indirectly aimed at the other party'. The pact contained secret plans to divide Poland, and the Soviet Union was to be given a free hand to deal with the Baltic states. Germany ignored the pact when it attacked the Soviet Union in 1941.

Neanderthals see feature, pages 444-5

Nebuchadnezzar II (d.562 BC) King of Babylon from 605 BC, shortly after leading his father's army to victory over the Egyptians. Nebuchadnezzar campaigned vigorously in the west, capturing Jerusalem for a second time in 587 and sending many of the Judaeans into EXILE in Babylon. He carried out a major building programme in his capital, including massive city walls and the Hanging Gardens, one of the SEVEN WONDERS OF THE WORLD.

Necker, Jacques (1732-1804) French financier and statesman during the French Revolution. He restored the French economy after being appointed director general of finances in 1777. In 1781 his demands for reforms were opposed and he resigned, but he was recalled by Louis XVI in 1788, when France was bankrupt. Necker then recommended calling a meeting of the States-General, which represented clergy, nobles and the people, and the introduction of reforms, but he was dismissed in 1789. This angered the people, and after the attack on the BASTILLE in July 1789, Necker was reinstated, but resigned in 1790.

Nefertiti (14th century BC) Wife and queen of AKHENATEN, pharaoh of Egypt. She was often depicted as a devoted worshipper of the sun-god Aten, whose cult was the only one permitted by her husband. After falling from favour, she was supplanted by one of her six daughters. Nefertiti is known through inscriptions, reliefs and a limestone bust found at ancient Akhetaton (Tell el-Amarna).

Negroids One of the major ethnic divisions of mankind, encompassing the indigenous peoples of Africa south of the Sahara and their descendants in other parts of the world. Traditionally, Bantu-speaking Negroid pastoralists and crop-growers are thought to have moved from western to eastern and southern Africa during the past few thousand years, but more recent evidence suggests that Negroids speaking other languages were elsewhere in sub-Saharan Africa much earlier. They may have originated in southern rather than in western Africa. In the east there has been intermixing with Hamitic-speaking Caucasoids – fair-skinned people such as Ethiopians and Egyptians – and in the south with the related cattle-raising Khoikhoi and the hunting and gathering San. Also of Negroid stock are the pygmies of central Africa. There are large Negroid populations in the USA, Brazil and the West Indies, brought from Africa by slave traders in the 16th to 19th centuries.

Nehemiah (5th century BC) Jewish leader, cupbearer to the Persian king Artaxerxes I. In 444 BC Nehemiah was given permission to return to Jerusalem, where he supervised the restoration and rebuilding of the city walls, while facing opposition from officials. In 432 he visited Jerusalem again and introduced moral and religious reforms. Nehemiah's firm action at a time of crisis probably saved the new state of Judaea from collapse. It also enabled the Jewish priest EZRA to undertake his reforms of Judaism.

Nehru, Jawaharlal (1889-1964) Indian statesman also known as Pandit ('teacher'), first prime minister of the Republic of India from 1947 until his death. He was elected president of the Indian National CONGRESS in 1929, following the party's campaign for self-rule instigated by Mahatma GANDHI. Nehru was convinced that India's future lay as an industrialised society, in contrast to Gandhi's ideal of a social structure centred on self-sufficient villages. In order to maintain a united front against British rule, Nehru conducted campaigns of civil disobedience and was frequently imprisoned. On his release in 1945 he took part in the negotiations that created the independent states of India and Pakistan.

As both prime minister and minister of foreign affairs, Nehru implemented a series of five-year economic plans. His successes included the partition of KASHMIR following the first Indo-Pakistan War of 1947-9, the integration of the princely states into central government and the annexation of the Portuguese colony of Goa in 1961. His foreign policies did not rely upon seeking alliances with other powers, but Nehru did seek Western aid when China invaded India in 1962. On his death two years later he was succeeded by his daughter, Indira GANDHI.

Nelson, Horatio, Viscount (1758-1805) British admiral who twice broke the naval power of France. The son of a Norfolk rector, Nelson entered the navy at 12 and became a captain at 20. On the outbreak of war with

> **❝ I have only one eye – I have a right to be blind sometimes...I really do not see the signal! ❞**
>
> *Horatio, Lord Nelson, ignoring orders at the Battle of Copenhagen, 1801*

France in 1793 he was given command of the man of war *Agamemnon*, serving under Admiral Samuel HOOD. He lost the sight of his right eye during a successful attack on Corsica in 1794. Nelson played a notable part in defeating the French and Spanish fleets at CAPE ST VINCENT in 1797, and was promoted to rear-admiral. Later that year he lost his right arm during an unsuccessful attempt to capture Santa Cruz. After victory against the French at the Battle of the NILE in 1798, Nelson sailed to Naples. There he began an

When we shared the Earth with a different kind of human

The Neanderthals looked after their elderly and buried their dead. They may even have been capable of some form of speech. But they were not able to survive competition from our ancestors.

Neanderthal man is probably the best known prehistoric human being, but also the least relevant to the origins of present-day humankind. Although Neanderthals were widespread in Europe, the Middle East and western Asia, they suddenly died out about 25 000 years ago. The precise reasons for this are not known for certain, but the best explanation seems to be that they were unable to cope with the arrival of more intelligent and innovative competitors: the ancestors of modern humans.

Well over half a million years ago our distant hominid ancestor *Homo erectus* ('upright man') began evolving into *Homo sapiens* ('wise man') – a line which then split into two branches or subspecies: *Homo sapiens neanderthalensis* (Neanderthal man), named after the Neander Valley in Germany where its remains were first found; and *Homo sapiens sapiens* (*Homo sap. sap.* for short) – the branch to which all people in the world today belong.

STRANDED IN EUROPE

The Neanderthals were anatomically essentially the same as us, though with certain marked differences. These led some early archaeologists to think that Neanderthal bones belonged to ordinary *Homo sap. sap.* individuals, but had been distorted by disease. We now know that this is not the case, and that Neanderthals had short, stocky bodies with large, chinless heads. They had big teeth, their brows jutted out as massive ridges, their foreheads sloped back at around 45 degrees, their wide noses emerged from a mid-face area, which itself bulged slightly outwards, and the backs of their heads protruded massively. Their brains were long and flat, with the bulk at the back and sides of their heads – indicating a high degree of brain activity relating to action and perception, and rather less involving reasoning.

Whether Neanderthals were capable of speech is a long-debated question. Many scholars believe that the evidence suggests a poorly developed, 'infantile' voice box, incapable of rapid speech but able to produce a range of sounds suited to limited vocal communication.

The story of Neanderthal man is a classic tale of evolutionary isolation. Europe was, during the early Stone Age, a remote and backward region. The Neanderthals' forebears became disconnected from the rest of humanity and evolved into a separate subspecies simply because they ventured into Europe and got stranded there.

The story began over half a million years ago, when the ancestors of the Neanderthals first reached Europe, possibly by crossing the Dardanelles and Bosporus during a period when the sea level was low. Then, when the seas rose again, they were cut off and forced to evolve to adapt to a colder climate. When the Ice Age was at its most severe, the populations were driven into the southern half of the continent.

Among the earliest European ancestors of the Neanderthals were groups of Stone Age hunters whose activities have been deduced by archaeologists in Britain, Germany and Spain. The most important British site – Boxgrove in West Sussex – has yielded spectacular finds, such as bones bearing butchering marks, which indicate that horses, deer and rhino were hunted by humans in England 500 000 years ago. These early Britons used flint, bone, chalk and wood to make implements, and one of the clues they left behind – the shoulder blade of a horse with a spear hole in it– is the world's oldest example of the use of a weapon by a human.

At another location, Bilzinggleben in Germany, archaeologists have found what appears to be a 500 000-year-old campsite complete with stone anvils and hammers, possible tent sites and a series of graffiti-covered stones – the world's oldest 'art'.

But the most spectacular early site was discovered in Spain as recently as the 1980s. Dating back 300 000 years, it has revealed what appears to be the world's oldest evidence of religious feeling. Excavations at Atapueroa in northern Spain

Neanderthals made flint tools, such as these axes (above and below) and scraper (bottom left) from France, but lacked the imagination to develop them further

This skull of a Neanderthal woman was found in Israel. She lived 90 000 years ago

The bones of an arthritic Neanderthal man were found in a French cave

suggest that 3000 centuries ago generation after generation of proto-Neanderthal humans used a pit deep inside a cave in the heart of a mountain as a burial place for their community. So far 32 dismembered skeletons have been found in the pit. The eventual total could rise to as many as 70.

It took hundreds of thousands of years for these early Europeans to adapt to the severe European climate, the major adaptation transforming them into true *neanderthalensis* probably occurring in the intensely cold period which lasted from around 190 000 to 120 000 years ago. Classic Neanderthal man dominated Europe between 125 000 and around 30 000 years ago, but as only a tiny proportion of Neanderthal sites have been found it is likely that isolated communities survived in marginal areas of Europe until much later, perhaps until as recently as 25 000 or perhaps even 20 000 years ago.

Discoveries of remains so far suggest that classic Neanderthals flourished in France, southern England, Italy, Germany and central Europe. At some stage they also appear to have broken out of their European heartland and colonised the northern Black Sea coastal region and parts of the Middle East – the last being the only place in which they coexisted over a long period with our own subspecies.

FALL OF THE NEANDERTHALS

In their European heartland, the Neanderthals survived contact with *Homo sap. sap.* for only about 15 000 years before disappearing for ever. Around 45 000 years ago the first *Homo sap. sap.* hunters migrated into Europe, probably from the Middle East. Like the Neanderthals, they had originated in Africa (evolving from around 130 000 years ago) and had already colonised much of Asia and Australia before expanding into Ice Age Europe. When they did so they drove the Neanderthals to extinction fairly rapidly. Precisely how this happened is not known, but the Neanderthals probably suffered fierce competition from *Homo sap. sap.* for hunted prey. Our ancestors probably also fought and killed large numbers of Neanderthals to eliminate competition, and may have introduced new diseases that also reduced the Neanderthal population.

More than anything else, our ancestors probably eliminated the Neanderthals simply by being brighter. Compared with *Homo sap. sap.*, Neanderthal man seems to have lacked imagination, technological ability and the capacity for innovative thought. Although he was able to imitate some specifically *Homo sap. sap.* toolmaking traditions when he came into contact with them, Neanderthal man stuck to the same limited techniques and range of flint tool manufacture. Although he had plenty of animal bone, he rarely used it to make tools. He did not produce true art and seems to have been constantly on the move.

By contrast *Homo sap. sap.* developed sophisticated art, a wide range of stone and bone tools and a habit of setting up long-term campsites. But both *Homo sap. sap.* and Neanderthal man were equally human. Their shared custom of burying their dead suggests that they had rituals concerning death, and that they almost certainly pondered on what lay beyond the grave. Both were capable of love and care. At several sites, archaeologists have found evidence that Neanderthals looked after their elderly and infirm.

But in the end the common humanity of two subspecies did not prevent our ancestors from driving their less advanced competitors into extinction. It was the last time we were to share our planet with another species of human.

Neanderthals may not have been as innovative as modern humans, but by burying their dead they showed that they possessed a high level of self-awareness.

445

Nelson portrayed after his victory at the Battle of the Nile. The hole left by the bullet that fatally wounded him can be seen in the left shoulder of the coat he wore at Trafalgar.

affair with Lady Emma Hamilton, wife of the British ambassador, that was to last the rest of his life. In 1799 Naples was seized by the French and Nelson helped to recapture the city. Later that year, the British commander in chief Lord Keith, expecting a French attack, ordered Nelson to Minorca. Nelson refused, claiming that his presence in Naples was necessary, but the Admiralty, which knew of his affair, suspected his motives. Commanded to return home, Nelson travelled with the Hamiltons and received a hero's welcome.

In 1801 Nelson was sent to the Baltic with Admiral Sir Hyde Parker to attack the Danish fleet. When Parker gave a command to stop offensive action, Nelson claimed not to see the signal, holding the telescope to his blind eye. His actions led to the defeat of the Danish fleet at Copenhagen. He was created viscount, and when war with France broke out again in 1803 he was given command of the Mediterranean. For two years Nelson blockaded the French fleet at Toulon. When it escaped he gave chase across the Atlantic and back again, finally engaging the French and Spanish fleets at the Battle of TRAFALGAR in 1805. The victory saved Britain from the threat of invasion by Napoleon, but left Nelson mortally wounded.

Neoclassicism Dominant artistic movement in European art and architecture in the late 18th and early 19th centuries, characterised by a desire to re-create the spirit and forms of the art of ancient Greece and Rome.

In literature, neoclassicism emerged earlier. It flourished in 17th-century France in the plays of Jean Racine, and in a moderated form during the English 'Augustan Age' in the works of John Dryden and Alexander Pope. Interest in ancient Rome and Greece was further stimulated in the 18th century by the discovery and excavation of remains at Herculaneum and Pompeii. Early influences on the development of the movement were the German archaeologist and art historian J.J. Winckelmann, and the Italian etcher and archaeologist Giambattista Piranesi, who unlike Winckelmann championed Roman over Greek architecture.

Neoclassicism was perhaps most influential in architecture, in the works of Robert and James ADAM and John Nash in Britain; Claude-Nicolas Ledoux and Jean-François Chalgrin in France; and Andreyan Zakharov in Russia. Among the pioneers in architecture were Ange-Jacques Gabriel, who built the Place de la Concorde in 1755 and the Petit Trianon at Versailles in 1768, and Jacques-Germain Soufflot, who was instrumental in introducing neoclassical ideas into plans to reconstruct Paris. Post-revolutionary architecture displayed clear lines, strict symmetry and Greek and Roman motifs in a reaction against the flamboyance of rococo. The greatest exponent of neoclassical art was Jacques-Louis David in France. The movement spread to the USA through the sculptors Hiram Powers and Horatio Greenough and the artist John Vanderlyn. Among the most successful furniture designers were Thomas Sheraton and George Hepplewhite in Britain. In music, the term is used of 20th-century composers such as Igor Stravinsky, François Poulenc and Aaron Copland, who rejected the ROMANTICISM of composers such as Richard Wagner for a new clarity of form and structure.

Neolithic Later part of the STONE AGES, characterised by the discovery of farming around 10000 BC, also known as the New Stone Age. Neolithic populations learned to cultivate wheat and barley, which they cooked in pottery vessels. They domesticated animals, developed new tools such as axes to clear forests and hoes for tilling, and established permanent villages. As a result, much of Asia, Europe and extensive parts of Central America and Africa were opened up by farmers. The first farmers at sites such as Jericho had not discovered pottery, and are called prepottery Neolithic. The discovery of farming created food surpluses, a growth in the population and permanent settlements. It thereby ended the slow development of the hunting societies of the PALAEOLITHIC and MESOLITHIC periods

and initiated a time of rapid change that soon produced metalworking and led to the establishment of cities (see feature, pages 142-3), states and, eventually, empires.

Neo-Platonism Doctrine of the followers of PLOTINUS (205-70) and other Greek thinkers of the school of PLATO in the 3rd century AD who searched for an intellectual basis for religious belief. God, described as the 'One' or 'Absolute', was the unifying factor making sense of Plato's two worlds of the mental or 'ideal' and the physical. Mystical experience, known as 'ecstasy', brought each person closer to the 'One'. Both the Roman emperor JULIAN and AUGUSTINE of Hippo were influenced by Neo-Platonic beliefs.

Nepal Kingdom running along the southern Himalayas, between China and India. The Buddhist-influenced Licchavi dynasty established the first era of centralised control from around the 4th to the 10th centuries. Under the Malla dynasty, which ruled from the 10th to the 18th centuries, Hinduism became the dominant religion. The Gurkhas invaded in 1769, wielding absolute power over the indigenous Nepalese tribes from their capital at Kathmandu. Their incursion into northwest India led to a border war in 1814-16 and to territorial concessions to the British. Effective rule passed to a family of hereditary prime ministers, the Ranas, who cooperated closely with the British. Gurkhas were recruited into the British and Indian armies.

A coup in 1950 reaffirmed royal powers under King Tribhuvan, who ruled from 1951 until 1955. His successor, Mahendra, experimented with a more democratic form of government until 1960, when this was replaced with monarchic rule, continuing from 1972 under Mahendra's son, Birendra Bir Bikram. Following prodemocracy demonstrations and mass arrests in 1989, Bikram agreed to legalise political parties and in 1990 granted a new constitution. In 1991 the first democratic election was won by the Nepali Congress Party led by Girija Prasad Koirala. Three years later a vote of no confidence in the government led to its resignation. New elections were won by the United Communist Party of Nepal led by Man Mohan Adhikar, but government disputes led to its collapse in 1995.

Neri, Philip, St (1515-95) Italian mystic, known as 'the Apostle of Rome'. After moving to Rome in 1533, Neri established the Confraternity of the Most Holy Trinity in 1548 for the care of pilgrims and convalescents. Ordained a priest in 1551, he joined the ecclesiastical community at San Girolamo, where his popular religious conferences took place in a large room known as the Oratory. Those who took part in the devotional activities and teaching there became known as the

This lid from a Chinese Neolithic pottery vessel dates from about 2500 BC, making it one of the earliest intact prehistoric images. It may illustrate a shaman, or medicine man.

Congregation of the Oratory, or Oratorians. In 1595 Neri helped Henry IV of France to secure papal absolution from excommunication. Neri was canonised in 1622.

Nero, Claudius Caesar (c.AD 37-68) The Roman emperor notorious for his vanity and abuse of power. He was adopted by CLAUDIUS, who had married Nero's mother, Agrippina. On Claudius' death in 54, Nero became emperor and poisoned Britannicus, Claudius' son by Messalina. To rid himself of two constraining influences in his life, he arranged the murder of his mother, and compelled SENECA, his boyhood tutor and counsellor, to commit suicide. He also had his wife Octavia murdered, so that he could marry Poppaea Sabina.

Nero's tyranny extended beyond his family. He was the first emperor to put Christians to death: according to the historian Tacitus, persecuted victims were covered in wild-animal skins and torn apart by dogs. Nero blamed the Christians for a fire that swept through Rome in 64, but many suspected Nero himself after he announced plans to build a 'Golden Palace' over one-third of the area of the original city. The palace was to feature a huge statue of himself depicted as the sun-god. Nero's power waned when a revolt against Roman rule broke out in Palestine in 66. Following an army rebellion in Gaul and the mutiny of his palace staff, Nero committed suicide.

Nestorian Member of a sect largely found in the Middle East, a follower of Nestorius, who was appointed bishop of Constantinople in 428. Orthodox Christianity has considered Nestorianism heretical since Nestorius' lifetime. He taught that Jesus was a conjunction of two distinct persons, one divine and one human, in whom the divine and human were indivisible. He disliked describing Mary as the 'Godbearer', believing that she could only have given birth to Jesus' humanity. His teaching was thought to undermine seriously the belief that Jesus was a single person. His followers established a breakaway Church in northern Greece, and missionaries founded groups in Sri Lanka and China. Expelled from Greece in 489, they moved to Persia but were crushed by Mongols in the 14th century.

Netherlands, the Country in northwestern Europe, also called Holland after one of its regions. The area was conquered by the Romans as far north as the River Rhine, and by Saxons and Franks in the early 5th century. The collapse of the Frankish empire in the mid 9th century led to political fragmentation, but consolidation began under the 14th and 15th-century dukes of Burgundy. After the marriage of Maximilian I to Mary of Burgundy, the region, known as the Low Countries, passed to the HABSBURGS in 1477. The Low Countries became part of the Spanish empire in the 16th century, when the Spanish crown passed to Maximilian's grandson, CHARLES V. Under PHILIP II, high taxation, unemployment and the exclusion of local nobles from government aroused opposition, and in 1568 WILHELM I began the Dutch Revolts against the Duke of ALBA's Spanish forces. The sack of Antwerp by the Spanish in 1576 led to a union of the Netherlands, but Calvinist excesses caused the southern provinces to form the Union of Arras in 1579 and to make peace with Spain, which reintroduced Catholicism. In response, Wilhelm gathered the northern provinces into the Union of Utrecht. The war then became a religious struggle for Dutch independence until the UNITED PROVINCES OF THE NETHERLANDS were acknowledged by the Treaty of WESTPHALIA in 1648.

During the 17th century the Netherlands was a formidable commercial power, acquiring a sizable DUTCH EMPIRE. It began to decline following the ANGLO-DUTCH WARS of 1652-74 and protracted wars against Louis XIV's France. Britain took over the colonies of Ceylon (now Sri Lanka) and Cape Colony in South Africa, important trading posts of the Dutch East India Company. At the Congress of VIENNA in 1815 the entire Low Countries formed the independent kingdom of the Netherlands. Despite Belgium's secession in 1830, the Netherlands flourished under the House of ORANGE. It adopted a constitution based on the British system in 1848 and became the third largest colonial power, controlling the DUTCH EAST INDIES, various West Indian islands and Guiana in South America. During the First World War the country remained neutral, but was occupied by the Germans in the Second World War. The Japanese invaded the East Indian islands in 1942, installing Achmad SUKARNO in a puppet government. Sukarno declared independence in 1945, and after four years of war the Netherlands transferred sovereignty. The Netherlands was a founder member of both the European Union and NATO. In the early 1990s its export-led economy suffered a recession and an increase in unemployment.

During the revolt of the Netherlands, the Spanish artist Velázquez commemorated the Dutch surrender of the besieged city of Breda to the Spanish commander Ambrogio Spinola in 1625.

New Amsterdam see NEW YORK

New Australians Immigrants to Australia immediately after the Second World War. Before 1939 the population of the continent consisted of ABORIGINES and the descendants of predominantly British settlers. The war greatly stimulated industrial production, and a labour shortage was met by a programme of assisted immigration: a passage from London to Sydney cost only £10. Between 1947 and 1952 more than half the 575 000 new arrivals were Polish, Dutch, Austrian, Italian, Greek, Maltese and Yugoslav, which accounts for Australia's cultural diversity.

New Brunswick Province on the east coast of Canada, south of the St Lawrence estuary. The Bay of Fundy separates New Brunswick's southern coastline from Nova Scotia; its western frontier adjoins Maine. First settled in 1604 by the French, it formed part of the French colony of Acadia until ceded to Britain in 1713 by the Peace of UTRECHT. The forests of New Brunswick, dissected by numerous rivers, were good hunting grounds for French fur traders and trappers, who were joined in the 1760s by small settlements of Scottish farmers. The population of New Brunswick expanded with the arrival of large numbers of loyalists during the American Revolution.

New Caledonia Group of islands in the south-west Pacific Ocean. New Caledonia's main island was inhabited for at least 3000

THIS IS ONE RABBIT THAT NEVER FAILED ME!

SPENDING

OLD RELIABLE!

President Roosevelt's New Deal aimed to prevent further economic disasters during the Depression by an avalanche of legislation, but the heavy spending required was criticised.

years before Captain James COOK reached it in 1774. The French annexed the island in 1853 and 11 years later began to use it as a penal colony. With the discovery of nickel in 1863, New Caledonia became economically important to France. The islands were occupied by US troops from 1942 to 1945, but became a French Overseas Territory in 1946. From the mid 1980s outbreaks of violence occurred as the indigenous Melanesian population began a struggle for independence. Although a referendum in 1987 favoured the continuation of French sovereignty, the issue of independence remains unresolved.

Newcastle, Thomas Pelham-Holles, 1st Duke of (1693-1768) English statesman, Whig prime minister from 1754 to 1756 and from 1757 to 1762. Born Thomas Pelham, Newcastle inherited substantial estates from his uncle, whose name he added to his own in 1711. As secretary of state from 1724, he supported Robert WALPOLE and then his own brother, Henry PELHAM. On succeeding Pelham, Newcastle's management of the early stages of the SEVEN YEARS' WAR proved disastrous and he resigned in 1756. After returning as prime minister in a coalition ministry with William PITT THE ELDER from 1757 to 1761, he coordinated financial and political support and British fortunes improved. George III, when he acceded to the throne in 1760, was antagonistic to the domination of government by a few powerful Whig families, believing that it sapped power from the monarchy. Newcastle was forced to resign in 1762 and never again enjoyed high office.

New Deal Programme of relief measures instigated between 1933 and 1940 by US president Franklin D. ROOSEVELT to salvage the economy and end the Great DEPRESSION. Coined by Judge Samuel Rosenman, the term was used by Roosevelt in 1932 in his speech accepting the Democratic presidential nomination. Legislation proposed by progressive politicians and administrators was passed by overwhelming majorities in Congress. The first New Deal of 1933 to 1935 established the TENNESSEE VALLEY AUTHORITY and the WORKS PROJECT ADMINISTRATION to stimulate productivity and reduce unemployment. Emergency legislation granted government insurance for deposits in banks affiliated to the Federal Reserve System or the US Central Bank, and protected investors from stockmarket fraud. This ended the bank crisis and restored public confidence.

Attacks from left and right, and a series of Supreme Court decisions that struck down key New Deal acts, led Roosevelt to launch the second New Deal of 1935-40. Measures such as the Social Security Act provided old-age retirement benefits, while the Wagner Act guaranteed labour's right to organise.

Although the New Deal did not pull the USA out of the Depression entirely, it revitalised morale. It extended federal authority in all fields, supporting small businessmen, labour-

> 66 **The country demands bold, persistent experimentation. It is common sense to take a method and try it. If it fails . . . try another.** 99
>
> *Franklin D. Roosevelt*
> *1933*

ers and farmers, and introduced legislation to equalise opportunities and establish standards for wages, hours, relief and security.

New Economic Policy Policy introduced in the Soviet Union by LENIN in 1921. It permitted private enterprise in agriculture, trade and industry, encouraged foreign capitalists, and informally recognised the right to own private property, which had been abolished after the Russian Revolution. It represented a shift from the policy of 'War Communism' adopted during the Russian Civil War, which had alienated the peasants with its forced requisition of food to supply the cities and the Red Army. Under the New Economic Policy, peasants controlling their own property used their land profitably, and domestic trade improved. Light industry flourished, but heavy industry needed more government investment and when Joseph STALIN came to power he looked to the peasant landholders for funds, forcing them to join collective farms and sell much of their produce cheaply to the state. Rapid industrialisation under Stalin's Five-Year Plans ended the policy in 1928.

New England North-eastern region of the USA comprising the states of Connecticut, Massachusetts, Rhode Island, Maine, New Hampshire and Vermont. Named by Captain John Smith in 1614, the area was granted to the Council for New England, a company of English nobles founded in 1620. The council gave land patents to the PILGRIM FATHERS in 1620 and to the Puritan Massachusetts Bay Company in 1628. From 1643 to 1686 New Haven, Connecticut and Massachusetts Bay formed the New England Confederation to coordinate their mutual defence.

In 1675 conflict between King Philip, a Native American chief, and the confederation led to colonial New England's bloodiest war, in which most Native Americans were killed, driven away or sold into slavery. In 1686 James II established the Dominion of New England to combine the northern colonies under royal control, but it collapsed after he was deposed in 1688-9 and separate colonial governments were revived. During the fight for independence New England was a leading revolutionary centre.

Newfoundland Atlantic offshore island in the Gulf of St Lawrence, forming part of Canada. Claimed for England by John CABOT in 1497, the island's rich cod shoals quickly attracted European fishermen. Colonisation was attempted by Humphrey Gilbert in 1583 and Lord Baltimore in 1621, but by 1650 the settlers numbered only 2000. France contested Britain's claims and Newfoundland changed hands several times until 1713, when British sovereignty was accepted in the Peace of UTRECHT. In 1728 Newfoundland became a chartered colony. French claims ended with the Treaty of PARIS in 1763, although France retained some fishing rights.

New France French territorial possessions in North America, discovered and settled from the 16th to the 18th centuries. The centres of New France were Quebec, founded in 1608, and Montreal, founded in 1642. It became a royal province in 1663, and by 1712 stretched from the Gulf of St Lawrence to beyond Lake Superior and included NEW-FOUNDLAND, Acadia – comprising NOVA SCOTIA, NEW BRUNSWICK and Prince Edward Island – and the Mississippi valley as far south as the Gulf of Mexico. Although France lost Acadia, Newfoundland and Hudson Bay in the Peace of UTRECHT in 1713, New France remained a major competitor for the fur trade and expansion into western territories, and a threat to British colonies to the south. Britain attacked during the French and Indian War of 1755-63, which formed the first phase of the SEVEN YEARS' WAR. The British general James Wolfe took Quebec in 1759 and Montreal in 1760. The French government surrendered Canada to Britain, but secretly gave all of Louisiana west of the Mississippi to Spain. In 1763 the Treaty of PARIS stripped France of almost all its American claims and holdings. Napoleon forced the Spanish to return Louisiana in 1800, but sold it to the United States in the Louisiana Purchase of 1803.

New Guinea see PAPUA NEW GUINEA

New Hampshire NEW ENGLAND state of the USA, one of the original 13 states. First settled in 1623, it was named by Captain John Mason, who, with Sir Ferdinando Gorges of the Council for New England, obtained rights to the region in 1629. The area was mainly settled from Connecticut and Massachusetts, which annexed southern New Hampshire in 1641-3. In 1679 it became a royal colony, although Massachusetts laid claim to parts of the colony until its eastern and southern boundaries were agreed on in 1739-41. New Hampshire was prized by the British crown for its shipbuilding timber, and was attractive to land speculators. Its territorial claims west of the Connecticut River were relinquished in 1782 and became Vermont in 1791.

Ne Win, U (1911-) Burmese general and statesman, the last to hold power before the country's name changed to MYANMAR. From 1936 Ne Win was a member of the extreme nationalist Dobama Asiayone ('We Burmans' Association'). In 1943 he became chief of staff in AUNG SAN's Burma National Army, defecting with it to the Allies in 1945.

After Burmese independence in 1948, Ne Win became home and defence minister, and led campaigns against communist guerrillas. From 1958 he served as prime minister in a caretaker government until the election of U Nu in 1960. Following a coup in 1962, Ne Win abolished the parliamentary system and proclaimed the Socialist Republic of the Union of Burma, expelling 300 000 foreigners in an attempt to regain Burmese control of the economy. He became president in 1974, and although the country was constantly harassed by guerrilla disturbances, he maintained power as a military dictator until he stepped down in 1981. Ne Win's influence remained considerable until 1988, when government corruption and inefficiency led to riots and he resigned as party chairman.

New Jersey State of the USA situated on the east coast between the Hudson and Delaware estuaries. Originally claimed by the Dutch, New Jersey was taken by the British in 1664, split into two colonies with English governors, and became a united crown colony in 1702. Its western part was closely linked with Quaker Pennsylvania and tended to pro-British loyalism and union, but the eastern part was settled by New Englanders and Scottish Presbyterians, who supported independence. The new state, one of the original 13 states of the USA, was a battleground in the early stages of the American Revolution, with actions at Trenton, Princeton and Monmouth between 1776 and 1778. In 1787 delegates from New Jersey led the smaller states in ratifying the Constitution.

New Learning Approach to education pioneered in the 15th and early 16th centuries by the European followers of HUMANISM. The advocates of New Learning applied new critical techniques to a close scrutiny of the Bible and ancient Christian texts with the aim of reaching a deeper understanding of Catholic

New France reached its zenith in 1672-98 under the dynamic Comte de Frontenac, who as governor briefly broke the power of the Iroquois. French holdings expanded to include the Great Lakes and the Mississippi River valley, and a chain of forts was established as far as New Orleans.

Christianity. In England, humanist thinking also influenced advocates of Protestantism during the REFORMATION. This was partly due to the work of exponents of New Learning such as Sir John Cheke (1514-57), the first professor of Greek at Cambridge University and tutor to Edward VI, and Nicholas Udall, headmaster of Eton and Westminster schools. They helped to establish a new educational ideal in which formal training produced valuable servants of the state through rigorous study of the Bible and classical literature.

New Left Movement in Western Europe during the 1960s and 1970s that rejected CAPITALISM and took its inspiration from socialism, revering such figures as Che GUEVARA and HO CHI MINH. Arising out of the Soviet invasion of Hungary in 1956, the New Left was more libertarian in practice than orthodox COMMUNISM in Eastern Europe, and was critical of existing socialist and communist parties in the West. During the 1960s, increasing consumption and technological advances created a division between the skilled and the unskilled: machines took over unskilled jobs, causing unemployment, and the gap between the affluent and those living on the poverty line became greater.

The New Left believed that workers should have a controlling interest in industry. It rejected party politics and believed in direct action, such as strikes and demonstrations. Opposition to the Vietnam War at the end of the 1960s acted as a catalyst for the New Left, which gained prominence with its antiwar demonstrations. In 1968 students in France, Britain, West Germany and the USA agitated for the right to influence the running of the universities. In Paris, the student demonstrations broadened to involve factory workers and led to educational and administrative reforms. Once US troops were withdrawn from Vietnam in 1973, the movement lost momentum and the radicalism it had created declined.

Newman, John Henry (1801-90) British theologian. Newman was a leading figure in the Oxford Movement, which in the 1830s attempted to reform the Church of England by emphasising the Catholic aspects of its tradition. The movement was originally known as Tractarianism, after the tracts written by Newman and other theologians. The tracts opposed Protestant and rationalist tendencies in the Church, promoting it as an inheritor of the faith that predated the REFORMATION and the EAST-WEST SCHISM. This inspired some to reintroduce Roman Catholic patterns of ritual and worship, initiating Anglo-Catholicism. In 1841 Newman's *Tract 90*, which argued

that the 39 Articles of the Church of England could be reconciled with Roman Catholic doctrine, caused a scandal and was the last to be issued. Newman became a prominent convert to Roman Catholicism in 1845, and the following year was ordained a priest in Rome. In 1864 he published *Apologia pro Vita Sua* (*In Defence of My Life*). Newman was created a cardinal in 1879, and his cause for beatification is being examined in Rome.

New Model Army English ROUNDHEAD army of the ENGLISH CIVIL WAR. Established in February 1645, it became the most powerful force in the country and the instrument of Oliver CROMWELL's rise to power. A single army of 22 000 men, it was organised on a national scale and was formed largely from the uncoordinated Roundhead forces of the first phase of the Civil War. Its first commander in chief was Thomas FAIRFAX, with Philip Skippon commanding the infantry, and, after the SELF-DENYING ORDINANCE of 1645, Cromwell in charge of the cavalry. Derided at first by the Cavaliers as the 'New Noddle Army', its men, who were regularly paid, well disciplined and properly trained, became known as the Ironsides. Promotion was achieved through merit. The army's engagements at NASEBY in 1645 and PRESTON in 1648 were resounding victories and won the war for the Roundheads.

After Pride's Purge in 1648, when Colonel Thomas Pride was sent to remove from the House of Commons those who wished to reinstate the king, the New Model Army became involved in national politics. The army formed the basis of government in the following years. Between 1647 and 1649 radicalism permeated its ranks through the influence of the LEVELLERS, agitators for religious freedom and the abolition of the monarchy. The Levellers almost destroyed the discipline of the army, inciting the lower ranks to mutiny, but Cromwell crushed their influence, confronting insubordinate troops, who rallied to his leadership. The New Model Army's power remained considerable until the PROTECTORATE was brought to an end in 1659.

New Orleans, Battle of (January 8, 1815) Battle in the WAR OF 1812 between the USA and Britain. A numerically superior British force led by General Edward Pakenham tried to seize the city of New Orleans but was repelled by US forces under Andrew JACKSON. British losses in dead and wounded topped 2000; only seven Americans were

An instruction manual shows a pike drill exercise performed by New Model Army soldiers. The lobster-tail helmet was part of the equipment for the light cavalry.

killed. The Treaty of GHENT had ended the war two weeks earlier, but the news did not arrive in time to prevent the battle. Jackson's triumph significantly raised US morale and made him a national hero.

New Right Intellectual movement of the 1970s and 1980s that supported conservative values and opposed socialism. Most influential in the USA and Britain, it emphasised a commitment to law and order and a belief in strengthening the family. The libertarian view that, wherever possible, the state should not encroach on individual freedom could be seen in the New Right's defence of FREE TRADE and in its belief in reducing the role of government. New Right ideas marked a radical break from the postwar consensus about the role of the state in society, and challenged the thinking of the NEW LEFT. Its influence could be seen in the governments of Margaret THATCHER in Britain and Ronald REAGAN in the USA in the 1980s.

New South Wales State in the eastern part of Australia, originally the name given to all of known Australia by Captain James COOK, who took possession for Britain in 1770. The first White settlement was a penal colony established in 1788 at Sydney Cove in Port Jackson. The colony was generally peaceful, with officers of the New South Wales Corps, who had been sent to supervise the convicts, using their time to trade goods arriving at Sydney, but disagreements with Governor William BLIGH over trading led to the RUM REBELLION of 1808, and in 1809 the Corps was recalled to Britain.

The colony became peaceful under the governorship of Lachlan Macquarie from 1810 to 1821. Settlement had been confined to an area around Sydney, but Macquarie encouraged exploration and in 1813 adventurers crossed the Blue Mountains. Increasing numbers of free settlers and emancipists, or ex-convicts, led to changes in the colony's nature, as did the Bigge Inquiry, which was carried out by the British Government in 1819-21. This recommended liberal land grants to settlers and extensive use of convict labour to open up the country. Convict transportation to New South Wales ended in 1840. Partial representative government was granted in 1842, and responsible government in 1855. The Port Phillip District, now VICTORIA, separated from New South Wales in 1851; the Moreton Bay district, now QUEENSLAND, separated in 1859. New South Wales became a state of the Commonwealth of Australia in 1901. In 1911, the Australian Capital Territory to the south-west of Sydney was transferred to the Australian Commonwealth to provide a site for the national capital of Canberra.

New Spain

Spain's colonial empire in North and Central America. The formation of New Spain began in 1518 with an attack by Hernán CORTÉS on the AZTEC empire in central Mexico. Following his destruction of Aztec power, Cortés founded a new capital at Mexico City and in 1522 was named governor and captain-general of New Spain. He and his lieutenants extended Spanish authority south into Salvador, Guatemala and Honduras, as well as north into remoter areas of Mexico. The Spanish colonies were divided into viceroyalties in 1535. New Spain grew to encompass California, the American southwest and Florida, although in many areas Spanish settlement was very limited. Spanish America proved to be a rich source of gold and silver from its mines, and paid Spain well for goods sent to the colonies. As a result, the price of Spanish produce rose dramatically during the second half of the 16th century. Riches from America were used to pay creditors, and also to pay for goods sent from Spain to Spanish forces abroad. Consequently, Spain remained a poor country.

In the 18th century, European wars affected Spain's colonial possessions. In 1763 it ceded Florida to Britain and received Louisiana from France; it regained Florida in 1783 but was forced to return Louisiana to France in 1800. In an agreement with Spain in 1821, the lands of New Spain became part of the independent Mexican empire briefly established by the Mexican general Augustín de Iturbide. Iturbide was overthrown in 1823, and Mexico became a republic, free of Spanish control.

newspapers

Around 59 BC the Roman *Acta Diurna* was put up daily in public places, but the circulation of news began in the 16th century with pamphlets and sheets on items of public interest passed from person to person. Newspapers were established in the 17th century in Holland, Germany, Denmark, France, Sweden, Italy and England. The Dutch were pioneers of international newsgathering, with *corantos*, 'current news', translated into French and English. Social news appeared in the form of broadsheets in Japan at the same time. The first British newspaper, the *Weekly News*, appeared in 1622; the first American paper, *Publick Occurrences Both Forreign and Domestick*, in 1690. Newspapers with large circulations spread as printing techniques improved.

Once matters of Parliament began to come into the public domain, government censorship became an issue. The freedom of the press was often curbed, but a radical underground

A newspaper boy announces the Relief of Mafeking in 1900. During the Boer War the *Daily Mail* was selling a million copies a day.

press soon began to voice anti-Establishment views. One of the earliest crusaders for press freedom was John WILKES, accused of libel in 1763 when he attacked George III's ministers in his paper, the *North Briton*. In the mid 19th century, competition for circulation led to the emergence of the popular press in the USA and Britain. Popular papers were geared more towards entertainment than political debate, and maintained low cover prices by earning revenue from advertisers. Newsgathering became faster following the invention of the telegraph, first used by W.H. Russell of *The Times* in 1854 when reporting from the Crimean War. With new printing technology at the end of the century a larger volume of newspapers could be produced. Together with the growth in literacy, these factors led to the emergence in the late 19th century of newspaper empires through which their owners exercised considerable power. The first British press baron, Alfred Harmsworth, Viscount Northcliffe, founded the first tabloid newspaper, the *Daily Mirror*, in 1903 and introduced to England the sensational journalism pioneered by the newspaper proprietor William Randolph HEARST in the USA.

In the 1970s and 1980s a major change in production technology led to writing and editing directly on to computers. In 1983 the American *Wall Street Journal* used electronic and satellite transmission to publish the same newspaper simultaneously over large territories. After News Corporation, the world's largest publisher of English-language newspapers, introduced 'cold type' technology to its London newspaper titles in 1986, all British newspapers followed, with the result that many print workers lost their jobs. Circulation wars between newspapers have

Port Jackson in New South Wales was the first Australian colony established by the British, here shown founding the settlement in 1788. The harbour is now spanned by Sydney Harbour Bridge.

provoked complaints about journalistic techniques. The invasion of privacy and paying perpetrators of illegal activities for their stories – so-called 'chequebook journalism' – are areas of contention. In Britain the Press Complaints Commission was set up in 1991 to maintain standards. The increasing concentration of ownership in the MASS MEDIA, have also become causes for concern.

New Sweden Swedish colony in America, founded on the Delaware River in 1633 by the New Sweden Company with the support of the Swedish statesman Axel OXENSTIERNA, the Finnish admiral Klas Fleming and the Dutchman Peter Minuit. After reaching the Delaware in 1638, Minuit bought land from the Native Americans and established Fort Christina, named after the Swedish queen. Between 1643 and 1655 Sweden established more settlements, to the chagrin of the Dutch, who, led by Peter STUYVESANT, besieged Fort Christina in 1655, took control of the colony and absorbed it into New Amsterdam, which was renamed NEW YORK in 1664.

Newton, Sir Isaac (1642-1727) English mathematician and physicist who discovered the law of gravitation and who is regarded as the founder of modern physics. Newton was at his most productive between 1666 and 1667 – which he called his *annus mirabilis*, 'wondrous year' – when he laid the foundations of his successes in mathematics, optics, dynamics and astronomy. Newton's contributions to mathematics include his theory of differential calculus – the problem of calculating how objects or quantities change, using measurements of their values at fractionally different intervals – which was written in 1671. The German philosopher Gottfried

LEIBNIZ discovered the same theory independently, and a bitter quarrel then ensued as to who had discovered it first. Experiments on the nature of light, which he began in 1666, revealed to Newton that white light is made up of a mixture of coloured rays.

Newton is most famous for the ideas he developed in his major treatise, *Philosophiae naturalis principia mathematica* (*Mathematical principles of natural philosophy*), of 1686-7, which gives a mathematical description of the laws of mechanics and gravitation and applies this theory to explain planetary and lunar motion. Newtonian mechanics has for most purposes survived even the 20th-century introduction of relativity theory and quantum mechanics. Newton's interests were not confined to scientific pursuits. He was appointed Warden of the Mint in 1696 and was responsible for an urgently needed reform of the coinage. He greatly increased the reputation of the Royal Society after his election as president in 1703. Newton also interested himself in alchemy, astrology and theology, and even attempted a Biblical chronology. The newton, a unit of force, is named in his honour.

New York State bordering Canada in the north-eastern USA. Before colonisation it was inhabited by Algonquian and Iroquoian-speaking native peoples. European exploration began in 1609 when the French first sailed down Lake Champlain and Englishmen in Dutch service sailed up the River Hudson. The Dutch then established Albany on the Hudson as a fur-trading post and in 1626 they founded their capital at the mouth of the river on Manhattan Island. The capital was named New Amsterdam, while the colony itself became New Netherland.

In 1664 the Dutch administrator Peter STUYVESANT surrendered the colony to the British before the outbreak of the second ANGLO-DUTCH WAR. The Dutch had already set up a system of proprietary and manorial rights that created a landholding aristocracy, and this system survived when British colonists joined the Dutch settlers. In 1664 the colony and its capital were both renamed New York after the Duke of York, later

James II of England. During the French and Indian War of 1755-63, a confederacy of IROQUOIS allied themselves with the British to prevent French interference. After the war, landowners, merchants and pirates all prospered for a hundred years.

During the American Revolution the state was a major battleground, with the British occupying New York City for most of the war. George WASHINGTON's entry into the city in 1783 was welcomed tumultuously. New York City was the new national capital from 1785 to 1790, and Washington's presidential inauguration took place there in 1789. By 1800 it had become the country's most important commercial and financial centre. During the American Civil War, New York contributed more men, money and supplies to the Union than any other state. As the city's population escalated during the 19th century due to a flood of immigration, power in New York shifted to the popularly based TAMMANY society, which until the 1930s was notorious for its corruption. In the 1990s New York was the most populous city in the USA.

New Zealand Country comprising a group of islands in the southern Pacific Ocean. The islands were first peopled by the Polynesian MAORI from about AD 800. European contact began in 1642 with a sighting by the Dutch navigator Abel Tasman. Captain James COOK charted the islands for the British in explorations from 1769. Commercial colonisation began with whaling companies from New South Wales in 1792, followed by British settlers through the NEW ZEALAND COMPANY founded by E.G. WAKEFIELD in 1837. To regulate Maori-settler relations, the islands were annexed by the British in 1840 in the Treaty of WAITANGI, which guaranteed Maori chiefs ownership of their land. An attempt by the New Zealand Company to assert authority over the powerful Maori chief Te Rauparaha led to the deaths of 22 settlers.

In 1846 the British Government conferred a limited constitution on New Zealand. It was rescinded in 1848 and in 1852 the islands were divided into six provinces and granted representative government. Responsible self-government came in 1856. Settlement of the South Island prospered, assisted by the gold rushes of the 1860s. At the same time, insurrection broke out over the settlers' disregard of the Treaty of Waitangi. In 1858 a number of Maori tribes united to form a kingdom. They soon came into conflict with land-hungry colonists. The fighting escalated into the disastrous Anglo-Maori Wars, which continued until 1872, when the Maoris were defeated and as a result lost much of their land.

In 1881 regulations restricted the influx of Asians, who were resented as a threat to the ethnic purity of the New Zealand people. The terms, confirmed by the 1920 Immigration

One of Isaac Newton's many achievements was the first reflecting telescope, which has been preserved by the Royal Society.

A New York workman helps to build the Empire State Building in 1930. Introduced in the 1880s, skyscrapers became the solution to the problem of a rising population living on a small island.

the Maori chief Te Rauparaha resulted in the deaths of 22 settlers. By 1841 the company had received a British Government charter of incorporation, a loan and a settlement of its land claims. It was responsible for the European settlement of Wellington, Nelson and New Plymouth, but it became commercially unviable and was dissolved in 1858.

Ney, Michel, duc d'Elchingen (1769-1815) Marshal of France, the most celebrated of Napoleon Bonaparte's generals during the NAPOLEONIC WARS, particularly for his victory at Friedland in 1807, which led to the Treaty of TILSIT. During the retreat from Moscow in 1812 Ney commanded the defence of the Grande Armée against the Russians. After the battles of Smolensk and Borodino in 1813 he was created Prince of Moscow by Napoleon, who praised him as 'the bravest of the brave'. On Napoleon's abdication in 1814, which Ney had urged, Ney himself took an oath of allegiance to the restored monarchy, but when sent to check Napoleon's advance in 1815 during the HUNDRED DAYS, he joined the advance, fighting for Napoleon at WATERLOO. After Louis XVIII's second restoration, Ney was tried for treason and shot.

Ngo Dinh Diem (1901-63) South Vietnamese statesman during the VIETNAM War, prime minister in 1954 and president from 1955 to 1963. During the French occupation of Vietnam following the Second World War, Diem formed the anti-French and anticommunist National Union Front. His sympathies alienated him from the communist Vietminh and led to his exile in 1947, but in 1954, with American and French support, he returned to Vietnam just before it was partitioned and was appointed prime minister. The following year he abolished the monarchy and became president.

In his struggle against the communist Vietcong, Diem sought US aid and adopted increasingly authoritarian practices, uprooting peasants and regrouping them in compounds to isolate them from the guerrillas. A Roman Catholic, he was unsympathetic to the Buddhist majority, and also installed members of his family in positions of power. His brother, Ngo Dinh Nhu, earned notoriety as head of the political police. Both brothers were killed in a coup in 1963.

Nguni Related ethnic groups in southern Africa, including the ZULU and Xhosa, who between 1779 and 1879 fought the XHOSA WARS against Dutch and British colonists. In the 1820s the Zulu in the Natal area developed a superior military force under King SHAKA, attacking neighbouring peoples in the Difagane Wars. During the apartheid era, the BANTUSTANS created in South Africa had little connection with original Nguni culture.

Restriction Act, were gradually liberalised. The property qualification for voting was abolished and women were enfranchised in 1893. In 1931 the country became an independent dominion, although it did not choose to ratify the Statute of WESTMINSTER until 1947. Between 1891 and 1947 the country won a world reputation for state socialist experiment, providing comprehensive welfare and education services.

New Zealand actively supported the Allies in both world wars, at the same time enjoying political stability and a high standard of living. After the Second World War, its defence policy concentrated on the Pacific and the Far East. In 1951 it joined the ANZUS security alliance with Australia and the USA, later sending a military force to the Vietnam War. After 1973, when Britain joined the European Community, New Zealand strengthened its trading links with Australia and its Pacific Asian neighbours. When the Labour Party returned to power in 1984 it adopted a nonnuclear policy, which led to New Zealand withdrawing from Anzus in 1986. The National Party under Jim Bolger won the 1990 election at a time of economic recession. It confirmed Labour's non-nuclear stance, but introduced social-welfare cuts. Bolger was narrowly re-elected in 1993, but after losing his majority in 1996 he formed a coalition government. Maori activists continued to demand compensation for land seized illegally by European settlers, and in 1994 the government agreed to pay compensation to the Waikato people.

New Zealand Company Organisation formed in 1837 by E.G. WAKEFIELD to colonise New Zealand. Originally called the New Zealand Association, it was denied a charter by the British Government, largely because of fears that it would come into conflict with the MAORI. Nevertheless, in May 1834 the company began sending out agents and settlers to buy land from the Maori. The establishment of a crown colony in 1840 led to a review of the company's grandiose land claims. This, and Maori resistance, prevented the settlements from developing as planned and in 1843 a rash attempt at Wairau, near Nelson, to assert authority over

Nguyen Van Thieu (1923-) South Vietnamese statesman, president from 1967 to 1975 during the Vietnam War. Originally a member of HO CHI MINH's Vietminh, Thieu took part in Vietnam's struggle against the French after the Second World War. He left the movement because of its communist policies and became a general in the South Vietnamese army. In 1963 he helped to overthrow NGO DINH DIEM's government and, with another military strongman, Nguyen Cao Ky, dominated the politics of his country.

Elected president in 1967 and again in 1971, Thieu pressed hard against the communist Vietcong and their North Vietnamese allies, despite growing opposition to his dictatorial methods. With the promise of US aid, Thieu reluctantly signed the 1973 Paris Agreement providing for the end of hostilities and the withdrawal of US and allied troops, but fighting between South Vietnam and the communists continued, leading to a North Vietnamese offensive in 1975. When the USA rejected his requests for aid, Thieu abandoned the northern half of his country to the advancing communists. With his army in disarray and enemy forces closing on the capital Saigon, Thieu fled to Taiwan and then to Britain days before the communist victory.

Nicaea, Councils of Two councils of the Christian Church that took place in Nicaea (present-day Iznik in Turkey) to combat threats to Orthodox Christian belief. The first council, held in 325, was summoned by the Roman emperor CONSTANTINE and issued a statement against ARIANISM. The statement's contents form the greater part of what later became known as the Nicene Creed. The second council, in 787, was called by the Byzantine empress IRENE to end the controversy that surrounded the iconoclasts, who objected that the veneration of religious images could too easily become a form of idol worship. The council permitted the veneration of icons and condemned iconoclasm.

Nicaragua Largest Central American country, first colonised by the Spanish, who in 1524 founded the towns of Granada on Lake Nicaragua and León on Lake Managua. Part of the viceroyalty of NEW SPAIN and the captaincy-general of Guatemala, the area grew slowly. It depended on agriculture, which developed substantially in the 18th century. Following independence from Spain in 1821 and brief annexation into the Mexican empire, Nicaragua formed part of the Central American Federation until its independence in 1838. Early in the 17th century, the British had established control over the Miskito Indians inhabiting the swampy Caribbean littoral of Nicaragua and Honduras – the so-called Mosquito Coast. In 1848, the British took the port of San Juan del Norte, holding it

until 1860. William Walker, an American adventurer, seized control of Nicaragua in 1855, making himself president in 1856, but the hostility of the Central American states led to his being ousted in 1857. At the same time, peace was made with Britain and a separate Mosquito kingdom was recognised.

The country remained under conservative control until 1893, when José Santos Zelaya took over and extended Nicaraguan authority over the Mosquito kingdom. The USA, suspicious of Zelaya's financial dealings with Britain, supported a rebellion that overthrew him in 1909. In 1912 a civil war brought about Nicaragua's occupation by US marines, who dominated the country until their withdrawal on the election of Juan Bautista Sacasa as president in 1933. Having instigated the assassination of Augusto César Sandino, the remaining liberal rebel leader of the anti-American forces, in 1934, General Anastasio Somoza, commander of the US-trained National Guard, took control of Nicaragua and ruled as president from 1937 until his own assassination in 1956. He was succeeded by his sons Luís (1957-63) and Anastasio (1967-72; 1974-9) Somoza Debayle. The rule of the Somoza family and their associates was characterised by brutal repression and financial mismanagement.

In 1961, the left-wing Sandinista guerrilla movement, Frente Sandinista de Liberación Nacional (named after Sandino), was formed to oppose Luís Somoza Debayle's dictatorial regime. It gained increasing support from the landless peasantry and became one of the most broadly based and popular insurrections in Latin American history. After many clashes with the National Guard, leading to civil war from 1977 to 1979, the Sandinistas established themselves as the ruling party and

expropriated large estates, or HACIENDAS, for landless peasants. The exiled owners of the estates then organised opposition, recruiting a 'Contra' rebel army funded by the American CENTRAL INTELLIGENCE AGENCY. Mines and forests were nationalised and relations with the USA deteriorated. In 1981 US aid ended and the regime was accused of receiving help from Cuba and the Soviet Union. President Ronald REAGAN sought more support from Congress to give aid to the exiled Contra forces in Honduras and Miami but was seriously embarrassed by the exposure in 1986-7 of the illegal diversion of money to the Contras from the US sale of arms to Iran. Military funding to the Contras ended in 1989 under President George Bush.

In the 1990 elections, opposition groups were funded by the USA, and the Sandinistas lost to a coalition group led by Violeta Barrios de Chamorro, widow of Pedro Joaquín Chamorro, a liberal newspaper publisher assassinated in 1978. Despite a US loan of $300 million, a severe economic recession set in and Chamorro only just managed to resist right-wing pressure for the return of the confiscated haciendas to their former owners. In 1992 there were clashes between left-wingers, renamed *recompas*, and rightist *recontras*, which led to talks and constitutional reform in 1993. A cease-fire agreement was reached in 1994.

Sandinista soldiers take part in the campaign leading up to the Nicaraguan elections held in February 1990. They sport red bandanas bearing President Daniel Ortega's name in yellow.

Nicholas II was devoted to his wife Alexandra and their children Olga, Maria, Tatiana, Anastasia and Alexei. His son's haemophilia led his wife to seek help from the mystical healer Rasputin.

Nicholas I (1796-1855)

Tsar of Russia from 1825 until his death. Third son of Paul I, Nicholas succeeded his brother ALEXANDER I as tsar after crushing a revolt by the DECEMBRISTS, who had conspired to dethrone him to gain Western-style reforms. The motto of his reign was 'Orthodoxy, Autocracy, Nationality', and his dictatorial and paternalistic rule allowed for little social reform. Russia was run by a military-style bureaucracy and the secret police were given a bigger role. Nicholas attempted to suppress liberal ideas by controlling the universities and increasing censorship. Religious minorities came under greater persecution. His wars with Persia from 1826 to 1828 and with the Ottoman Empire in 1828-9 extended Russia's empire. In 1830 he brutally suppressed a Polish nationalist uprising. In the REVOLUTIONS OF 1848, he helped Austria to crush the nationalists in Hungary. Attempts to dominate Turkey led to the CRIMEAN WAR of 1853-6, in which Russia was defeated by France and Britain. Nicholas was succeeded by his son ALEXANDER II.

Nicholas II (1868-1918)

Last tsar of Russia from 1894 to 1917. The first two years of his rule saw rivalry between Japan and China over Korea; Nicholas sided with China, as had Germany and France. Relations with Japan became increasingly strained, resulting in the RUSSO-JAPANESE WAR of 1904-5. Russia's defeat and the tsar's autocratic approach to domestic affairs provoked the 1905 RUSSIAN REVOLUTION. Nicholas was forced to issue the October Manifesto, which promised a representative government and basic civil liberties; an elected Duma and an Upper Chamber were also set up. Russia was prosperous under Premier Piotr STOLYPIN (1906-11), and Nicholas won support for the war against Germany in 1914. Unwisely he took personal command of the armed forces, leaving the government in the hands of his wife, Alexandra, who fell under the influence of the notorious mystic RASPUTIN. Mismanagement of the war and government chaos followed and in March 1917 Nicholas abdicated. He and his family were imprisoned by the BOLSHEVIKS, who, fearing the advance of the counterrevolutionary White Army, murdered the entire family in July 1918 at Ekaterinburg in the Urals. After years of speculation about their fate, scientific analysis of the nine skeletons found in a pit in eastern Russia in 1991 confirmed that they belonged to Nicholas and his family. Depending upon official acceptance of the scientific findings, the tsar will be given an official burial in the Cathedral of St Peter and St Paul in St Petersburg.

Nicopolis, Battle of (September 23, 1396)

Siege of the Ottoman Turkish stronghold of Nicopolis on the River Danube by a force of Crusaders under SIGISMUND of Hungary and John, son of Philip the Bold of Burgundy. The combined force of Hungarians and European knights had answered an appeal to relieve Constantinople from Turkish attack. After initial success, they were heavily defeated by the Turks under Sultan Beyazid I. Thousands were killed, with some 10 000 more taken prisoner, but Sigismund escaped. The Turks tightened their control over the Balkans and became a yet greater threat to central Europe.

Niemöller, Martin (1892-1984)

German Lutheran churchman and Protestant leader in Nazi Germany. A U-boat commander during the First World War, Niemöller was ordained in 1924. In 1933 he founded the Pastors' Emergency League to help to combat rising discrimination against Christians of Jewish background. He opposed the nazification of Germany's Christian Church and was imprisoned in a concentration camp from 1938 to 1945. He later became president of the World Council of Churches from 1961 to 1968.

Nietzsche, Friedrich (1844-1900)

German philosopher who developed a concept of *Übermensch*, 'superman', as the only hope for mankind. Trained as a classical philologist, he regarded the literary quality of his writings as inseparable from their philosophical content. At the university of Basel, he was made professor of classics at 24 and became a friend of Richard WAGNER. Nietzsche's first book, *The Birth of Tragedy* (1872), associated Wagner's operas with Greek tragedy, maintaining that man was motivated by his unconscious and was inherently and tragically self-destructive. In subsequent works such as *Beyond Good and Evil* (1886), Nietzsche rejected Christian moral concepts and argued for a more heroic, positive morality: an affirmation of life manifested in a 'will to power'. In *Thus Spake Zarathustra* (1883-92) he describes

Friedrich Nietzsche, portrayed on his sickbed in 1899, had become insane in 1889 and was cared for by his sister for the rest of his life.

a free and powerful will that turns man into superman. The Nazis subverted this idea into a philosophical basis for their belief in the superiority of the Aryan race, ignoring Nietzsche's condemnation of nationalism and praise for the Jews.

Niger

Country in West Africa. In the 14th century, the HAUSA peoples founded several city-states in the south. The Songhai empire of the Niger river ruled much of the country in the 16th century. North Nigerian Fulani tribes waged a holy war against the Hausa in the early 19th century and took control of the south. In 1884 and 1885, at conferences held in Berlin to resolve disputes over possession of central Africa, Niger was assigned to the French, who arrived in 1891 but colonised it fully only in 1914. Part of French West Africa from 1922, Niger became an autonomous republic within the French Community in 1958 and independent in 1960, after agreements with France on finance, defence, technical assistance and cultural affairs. From 1974, a Supreme Military Council governed and political associations were banned until 1988. In 1989, under President Ali Saibou, a referendum approved a new constitution and a new ruling council was set up. Saibou still opposed multiparty democracy, but after strikes and demonstrations in 1990 he agreed to reforms. A year later Amadou Cheiffou was appointed prime minister of a transitional government pending elections. A multiparty constitution was approved by a referendum in 1992, and in 1993 open elections led to a coalition government, with Mahamane Ousmane as president. Catastrophic floods in eastern and central Niger ended years of drought in 1994. The following year, peace was made with nomadic Tuareg rebels who had been fighting government forces for a greater share of uranium earnings since 1991.

Nigeria West African country consisting of a federation of 21 states. Lagos and other coastal trading stations were major centres for the 18th-century slave trade. Explorers made their way inland, but malaria was rife and earned the region the title 'white man's grave' until the discovery of quinine in 1854 alleviated the problem. Having bought Lagos from King Dosunmu in 1861, the British made it a separate protectorate in 1886. In the same year, the British Royal Niger Company was given a charter to administer the Niger River and northern Nigeria, but its monopoly was resented by both Europeans and Africans and in 1900 its charter was revoked. By 1903 forces under Frederick Lugard had occupied the north, which became the protectorate of Northern Nigeria; by 1906 the British had also conquered the kingdom of BENIN, establishing the protectorate of Southern Nigeria, into which Lagos was absorbed in 1906, and in 1914 the two were merged to form the largest British colony in Africa. Lugard governed the colony indirectly through his authority over the chiefs and emirs of its 150 or more tribes. The Muslim chiefs of the Fulani people maintained a conservative rule over the majority of the country's HAUSA population. The YORUBA dominated the west, and the Ibo the east.

Under the 1954 constitution, these regions were formed into a federation of Nigeria together with the trust territory of Cameroons and the federal territory of Lagos. In 1960, the federation became an independent nation within the Commonwealth of Nations, and in 1963 it became a republic. An Ibo independence movement began in 1966, when Ibo army majors murdered the federal prime minister, the premiers of the northern and western regions and leading politicians. In retaliation, a group of northern officers installed General Yakubu GOWON as head of state. Thousands of Ibo living in the north were killed, and later that year the regions were made into 12 states. Attempts at constitutional remedies failed and many Ibo returned to their homeland in the eastern region. There they declared its secession and in 1967 established the republic of BIAFRA. Civil war broke out between the Hausa and Ibo and in 1970 Biafra collapsed. Gowon was deposed in 1975 and the country was further divided into 19 states the following year.

In 1979 the government organised multiparty elections. Unrest and corruption led to military takeovers in 1983 and 1985, and General Ibrahim Babangida became head of state. Violence between Christians and Islamic fundamentalists threatened the restoration of full civilian rule. In 1989, the ban on political parties was lifted, but only two were allowed to register for elections, both with manifestos devised by the government. In 1993, open presidential elections unofficially reported to have been won by Moshood Abiola were annulled by Babangida, prompting civil unrest. Babangida resigned and handed power to the military, promising an elected civilian government for 1994. Abiola fled the country and sought international aid, protesting that the elections had been free and fair. In 1993, Sunni Abacha became head of state, dismantled many existing political institutions and replaced the 1979 military constitution. Abiola returned to Nigeria to campaign for democracy and was arrested in 1994. In 1995, the government postponed civilian rule until 1998, but ended the ban on political activity. There was international outrage when the famous writer Ken Saro-Wiwa and eight other prodemocracy activists were tried on murder charges which they claimed were false and executed in November 1995.

Nightingale, Florence (1820-1910) British hospital reformer, called 'The Lady with the Lamp' for her care of sick and wounded soldiers during the CRIMEAN WAR. In the early 1850s, despite strong opposition

Hitler used the press to announce the Night of the Long Knives and justify the arrest and dismissal of Ernst Röhm (above centre) for treason.

from her family, she trained as a nurse at Kaiserswerth in Prussia and in Paris. As superintendent of the Institution for Sick Gentlewomen in London in 1853, she earned recognition for her achievements. In 1854, she took a team of nurses to Scutari in Turkey to care for British soldiers fighting in the Crimean War. In the face of official hostility, she succeeded in improving beyond recognition the state of British military hospitals, whose insanitary conditions had largely been responsible for the high mortality rates among the wounded. After returning home a national heroine in 1855, she used a gift of money raised by the public to found a training school for nurses at St Thomas's Hospital in London in 1860. For the rest of her life she took an active interest in nursing and hospital matters. In 1907 Florence Nightingale became the first woman to receive the Order of Merit.

> ### DID YOU KNOW?
>
> *Florence Nightingale was named after her birthplace, the Italian city of Florence. Once given to men and women, the name was rare until she made it popular.*

Night of the Long Knives (June 29-30, 1934) Phrase used by Adolf HITLER in referring to a weekend during which political opponents throughout Germany were murdered. After Hitler became chancellor in 1933, the SA (*Sturmabteilung,* 'Storm Division'), the Nazi private militia also known as the BROWN SHIRTS, was given the freedom to persecute Hitler's enemies, but earned the opposition of the army generals, whose support Hitler needed if he was to become head of state after President Paul von HINDENBURG's death. Within the Nazi Party, the founder of the Gestapo, Herman Goering, and the SS leader Heinrich Himmler also regarded the SA leader, Ernst Röhm, as a rival and persuaded Hitler that Röhm was plotting against him. On June 30, Hitler had Röhm arrested and shot. Several other prominent leaders were murdered, and subsequently the SS arrested hundreds of people all over Germany, including some nonparty figures as well as the former chancellor Kurt von Schleicher. Hitler announced that 77 people had been executed that weekend for alleged conspiracy. The Night of the Long Knives ended any hopes for democratic reform in Germany, and its violent methods set the style of political operation until Hitler's death in 1945.

nihilism Total rejection of traditional values, involving the denial of authority as exercised by Church, State and family, and complete belief in scientific truth to the exclusion of any other values. Nihilism was the doctrine of a group of Russian extremist revolutionaries active from the mid 19th to the early 20th century. In their struggle against the conservative elements in Russian society, the nihilists justified violence, believing that the forcible elimination of existing institutions was the only way to secure the freedom to move forwards. They were severely repressed by the government of ALEXANDER II, who was assassinated in 1881 by the People's Will Movement, a terrorist group influenced by their ideas. After the Russian Revolution of 1917, nihilist groups became small and diffuse and were overtaken by better coordinated revolutionaries with other philosophies.

Nijmegen, Treaty of (1678) Treaty signed at Nijmegen in the Netherlands ending the Franco-Dutch War of 1672-8. The treaty was signed by the United Provinces of the Netherlands, France, Spain and the Holy Roman Empire. Louis XIV had invaded the Netherlands in a campaign to expand his empire. France gained substantially from the terms, which extended its eastern frontier.

Nile, Battle of the (August 1, 1798) Decisive naval battle fought between the British and French at Aboukir Bay on the Mediterranean coast of Egypt after the French fleet had escaped Admiral Horatio NELSON's blockade of Toulon. The French admiral François de Brueys had anchored his fleet of 13 vessels in the bay, believing that they were safe from attack, but Nelson was able partially to encircle the French fleet and destroy nine ships, including the flagship *L'Orient*. This conclusive victory towards the end of the French Revolution established Nelson's reputation, destroyed Napoleon's plans to conquer Egypt and curb British colonial power, and also resulted in a second coalition against France.

Nimeiri, Gaafar Muhammad al- (1930-) Sudanese statesman, president from 1971 to 1985. Nimeiri became politically active in the 1950s as his country approached independence. An army colonel, he led campaigns against rebels in the south, who feared that their interests would be subordinate to those of the north when independence came, and joined leftist attempts to overthrow the

civilian government. Following a coup, he became prime minister in 1969 and chairman of the Revolutionary Command Council. Nimeiri was elected president in 1971 and the following year he ended the civil war in southern Sudan, granting it local autonomy. In an effort to make the Sudan a major food producer, Nimeiri switched from socialist economic policies to capitalism, but government corruption and lack of effective organisation hindered his plans. A devout Muslim, he further damaged his popularity by proposing a new constitution in 1984 that would make all Sudanese subject to Islamic law. This was opposed in southern Sudan, where the majority are non-Muslim, and he was overthrown by a military coup in 1985.

Nimitz, Chester William (1885-1966) US admiral who with General Douglas MAC ARTHUR directed the PACIFIC CAMPAIGNS against Japan in the Second World War. Nimitz took command of the Pacific Fleet in 1941, after the Japanese had destroyed much of it at PEARL HARBOR. In June 1942 he used aircraft carriers to win the decisive Battle of Midway. His strategy of closing in on Japan by amphibious attacks on enemy-held islands led to successful assaults on Guadalcanal in the Solomon Islands in 1942 and Iwo Jima and OKINAWA in 1945, after his victory at Leyte Gulf had destroyed the Japanese navy in 1944. On September 2, 1945, Nimitz signed for the USA the document that formalised Japan's surrender. After the war he was chief of naval operations from 1945 to 1947.

William Anderson's painting of 1801 shows the start of the Battle of the Nile as the British fleet is led into action against the French anchored parallel to the shore (left). In the middle distance, *Goliath* attacks *Guerrier*, while, on the right, *Culloden* opens fire on an Egyptian dhow.

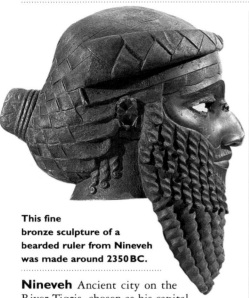

This fine bronze sculpture of a bearded ruler from Nineveh was made around 2350 BC.

Nineveh Ancient city on the River Tigris, chosen as his capital by SENNACHERIB of Assyria, who ruled from 704 to 681 BC. Sennacherib instituted a major building programme at Nineveh, but the city was sacked by the MEDES in 612 BC and never regained its former prestige. Extensive excavations have revealed much of Nineveh's former magnificence, including five of the 15 gateways in the city's 7 mile (12 km) wall, royal palaces with fine sculptured reliefs, and a remarkable store of cuneiform tablets that have proved a valuable source of historical information.

Nine Years' War (1688-97) Also known as the War of the Grand Alliance or the War of the League of Augsburg, a conflict in Europe that resulted from French aggression in the Rhineland and which subsequently became a power struggle between Louis XIV of France and William III of England. In 1688, French armies invaded Cologne and the PALATINATES with the promise of support from the English king James II. Members of the League of AUGSBURG, formed to restrain Louis' expansionist policies, took up arms. Meanwhile, William drove James II from the English throne, and a Grand Alliance of England, the United Provinces of the Netherlands, Spain, Austria and Savoy was formed against France in 1689. The French withdrew from the Palatinates, and in 1690 the deposed James II, while attempting to regain the throne with French support, was defeated in Ireland at the Battle of the BOYNE. That same year, the French navy won a victory in the English Channel off Beachy Head, but in 1692 it was defeated at La Hogue (now Barfleur), near Cherbourg. French campaigns in northern Italy and Catalonia were successful, but the war in the Spanish Netherlands reached a stalemate as one lengthy siege succeeded another. William's only gain was the retaking of Namur in 1695, which had

fallen to the French three years earlier. In spite of its military successes, France suffered an overall defeat because it lacked the financial resources of both Britain and the United Provinces. Peace was eventually concluded by the Treaty of RYSWICK.

Nixon, Richard Milhous (1913-94) Thirty-seventh president of the USA, the first to resign from office. Elected to the House of Representatives in 1947 and 1949, Nixon was prominent in the investigations that led to the indictment of the alleged Soviet spy Alger HISS in the MCCARTHY era. In 1953 he was elected vice-president under Dwight D. Eisenhower and earned a reputation for skilful diplomacy. In the 1960 presidential election, Nixon was narrowly defeated by John F. Kennedy. Two years later he failed to win the governorship of California, blaming a hostile media for his loss. His political career seemed to be over until in 1968 he was chosen as the Republican presidential candidate and defeated the Democrat Hubert Humphrey. In 1971 the Nixon administration initiated a New Economic Policy to counteract inflation, control prices and wages and also reverse many of President Lyndon JOHNSON's social policies. To achieve a balance of trade, the dollar was twice devalued, in 1971 and 1973.

In foreign affairs, secretary of state Henry KISSINGER was partly responsible for the achievements of the administration. Nixon at first extended the Vietnam War, invading Cambodia in 1970 and Laos in 1971, and initiating saturation bombing. From 1971, during negotiations, a policy of gradual withdrawal of US troops began, ending with the cease-fire accord of 1973. Nixon's government supported OSTPOLITIK, and his visit to the Soviet Union in 1972 brought about agreements on trade, joint scientific and space

programmes and nuclear arms limitation. The communist regime of the People's Republic of China was recognised, and in February 1972 Nixon made a state visit there. That year, Nixon was re-elected president with 61 per cent of the popular vote, but revelations about his involvement in the WATERGATE SCANDAL soon followed and he resigned on August 9, 1974. His successor, President Gerald Ford, granted him a pardon in September 1974, and in 1981 Nixon took on the role of a Republican elder statesman.

Nkomo, Joshua (1917-) Zimbabwe politician. A passionate nationalist, Nkomo fought for the independence of Southern Rhodesia as secretary-general of the Rhodesian Railways African Employees Association, and as president of the African National Congress from 1957 until it was banned in Rhodesia in 1959. He founded the National Democratic Party in 1960 followed by the Zimbabwe African People's Union (ZAPU), both of which were banned. Nkomo's involvement with ZAPU led to antagonism with the police. He was sentenced to imprisonment in 1963, and released in 1974. After ZAPU split into two factions, a breakaway group led by Robert MUGABE named itself the Zimbabwe African National Union (ZANU). Following constitutional reform in 1979, ZAPU and ZANU formed the Patriotic Front Alliance, and in 1980 both leaders stood for election in the independent republic of Zimbabwe. Mugabe won and gave Nkomo a position in his government, but his sympathies changed in 1982 on the discovery in Matabeleland of arms caches, which Nkomo was accused of preparing to use in a military coup against ZANU. Unity talks and the release of ZAPU detainees in 1986 led to a reconciliation, and Nkomo became vice-president on Mugabe's re-election in 1990.

Richard Nixon says goodbye to White House staff in August 1974 after resigning as president over his involvement in the Watergate scandal. With him is his son-in-law, David Eisenhower.

Kwame Nkrumah accompanies Elizabeth II and Prince Philip on a tour of Ghana, the first British African colony to gain independence.

Nkrumah, Kwame (1909-72) African statesman, prime minister of the Gold Coast from 1952 to 1960 and Ghana's first president from 1960 to 1966. He was an outstanding African nationalist and a firm believer in PAN-AFRICANISM. After studying in the USA and Britain, Nkrumah returned to the Gold Coast in 1947 as general secretary of the nationalist United Gold Coast Convention. In 1949, he founded the Convention People's Party to secure self-government and led a series of strikes and boycotts. After a short term of imprisonment by the British for sedition, he became prime minister and in 1957 led the Gold Coast to independence as Ghana. Despite his autocratic style of government, Nkrumah's policy of Africanisation made him immensely popular during his first years in power. In 1964, he was declared president for life, but his dictatorial methods together with economic pressures led to civil unrest and two years later, while on a visit to China, he was deposed by a military coup. He took refuge in Guinea, where President Sékou TOURÉ made him 'copresident'. Nkrumah died in exile.

NKVD Soviet secret police agency responsible for internal security and the labour prison camps from 1934 to 1953. The NKVD (People's Commissariat for Internal Affairs) absorbed the functions of the former OGPU. Mainly concerned with political offenders, it implemented Stalin's Great Purges of the Communist Party from 1936 to 1938. Under Lavrenti BERIA (1938-46), the agency split into two parts: one looked after state security; and the other was responsible for internal security and later become the MVD (Ministry of the Interior). After Beria's fall in 1953, the Soviet secret police was placed under the control of the KGB (Committee of State Security).

Nobel, Alfred (1833-96) Swedish industrialist and philanthropist, founder of the NOBEL PRIZE. He was brought up and educated in St Petersburg. Nobel travelled widely throughout Europe and the USA, becoming fluent in five languages and acquiring a knowledge of chemistry, engineering and foreign business methods. In 1866, he invented dynamite, and his experiments with explosives also led to the invention of gelignite and smokeless gunpowder. As a pacifist, Nobel hoped that the destructive power of his inventions would deter warfare. His financial interests in his inventions together with his investments in Russia's Baku oil fields earned him a vast fortune. When he died, he left the greater part of his money to support the international Nobel prizes.

Nobel prize International award made annually for exceptional contributions in the areas of physics, chemistry, medicine or physiology, literature and peace. In 1968 a sixth prize for economics was set up by the Swedish National Bank. The prize of a gold medal and a sum of money is given from a trust fund set up by the will of Alfred NOBEL. In 1995 the prize money was 7.2 million Swedish kronor, just over $1 million (£664000), the first year in which the value of the prize was greater in real terms than it had been when the first prizes were given in 1901.

Noh drama Classical Japanese theatre that relies upon gesture and metaphor rather than on the direct representation of events. The performance is stylised, involving dance, mime and the wearing of masks. It was developed in the 14th and 15th centuries and is based on set themes, including religious worship; supernatural beings or devils; warriors and battle; and contemporary life. Schools of acting grew around the main types of character: the *shite* (old man), the *waki* (subordinate actor) and *kyogen* (more general actors, one often being involved as a narrator). Noh

Alfred Nobel wished to reward those who have 'conferred the greatest benefit on mankind'. Peace prize winners receive this medal (left).

drama declined towards the end of the 19th century, but its popularity revived following the Second World War.

Nomads see feature, page 460

Nonconformist Usually a Protestant who does not conform to the disciplines or rites of the ANGLICAN CHURCH, also known as a dissenter. The term covered many religious groups, including PURITANS, PRESBYTERIANS and RECUSANTS. After the Reformation, a group of Nonconformists known as the Separatists and led by Robert BROWNE left the Anglican Church. Nonconformists were subject to penalties such as fines for their refusal to attend Anglican services. In 1620 the PILGRIM FATHERS emigrated to escape persecution. During the ENGLISH CIVIL WAR, Nonconformists, especially CONGREGATIONALISTS and members of the BAPTIST Church, fought on the side of the Parliamentarians. The Restoration of Charles II in 1660 proved disastrous for dissenting subjects. The king's promise of religious amnesty was anulled by the Anglican Cavalier Parliament of 1661-79. A series of crushing statutes known as the Clarendon Code restored and emphasised the authority of the Church of England. The 1662 Act of Uniformity deprived Nonconformists of freedom of worship and broadened the term to include dissenting groups such as QUAKERS. Persecution led to a further exodus to North America, and in 1681 Pennsylvania was founded as a refuge for Quakers. The 1689 Toleration Act brought greater liberalisation in England, but until 1828 Nonconformists were debarred from holding political office. By 1900 the term 'Free Church' had replaced 'Nonconformist'.

Nore mutiny (May-June 1797) Mutiny by sailors of the British navy stationed at the Nore anchorage in the Thames estuary during the French Revolutionary Wars. Encouraged by the SPITHEAD MUTINY of the previous month, the sailors demanded improvements in their conditions, the removal of unpopular officers and a greater share of the prize money for sinking and capturing enemy vessels. At Nore, the Admiralty refused to repeat the concessions they had made at Spithead. The mutineers blockaded London and threatened to sail to France but eventually surrendered. Their leader, Richard Parker, was tried and executed with at least 36 others.

Norman Conquest Period that began in 1066 when William of Normandy defeated the English at the Battle of HASTINGS and seized the English crown. As WILLIAM I, he quickly established military superiority over the English, crushing rebellions between 1067 and 1071 and building about 5000 castles before his death in 1087. English

Nomads: the last of the desert travellers

Nomad civilisation is thousands of years older than that of Greece or Rome.
In the form of Islam it conquered much of the world, but it could not
withstand the pressures of life in the 20th century.

The first nomads were pastoral people whose way of life around 3000 BC was herding animals. They were often on the move in search of pasture and possessed little but weapons, tents and cooking utensils. Their wealth lay in camels, horses, sheep or goats. About 2000 BC, perhaps because of a period of dry climatic conditions, fully nomadic societies evolved in eastern Europe and inner Asia.

CARAVAN FOR HIRE

Nomads then and later tended to live in deserts and steppes that could not support agriculture. There they traded goods such as meat, leather and wool with townspeople and the farmers who lived in the oases and lands round the edge of the desert. They also provided camels for transporting goods and guided merchants along caravan routes, such as the gold route across the Sahara and the silk route across central Asia to China.

Nomads formed themselves into tribes and did not acknowledge any other ruler. Pride in their traditions set them apart from 'civilised' societies, while their endurance and riding skills gave them

formidable fighting qualities, which they developed by raiding the animals of other groups, by hunting and by competing for scarce resources, including water. Settled communities often suffered from raids and from attacks on caravan routes. In the 3rd century BC the Great Wall was constructed across northern China by the emperor Shih Huang Ti to repel the steppe nomads.

Throughout history, confederations of nomadic tribes have joined together under military leaders to conquer huge expanses of territory. The invasions of the Germanic Goths and Vandals into the Roman Empire helped to cause its collapse. Having inherited territories stretching from the Baltic to the Caspian Sea, Attila the Hun suffered only one defeat, outside Orléans in France in 451, during a long career of conquest in central Europe. The Mongols Genghis Khan and Tamerlane had similar careers as nomadic conquerors in Asia and the Middle East in the 13th and 14th

A palanquin, or covered litter, carries a harem belonging to a wealthy North African nomad through the desert in 1870.

centuries. When the power of the tribes was harnessed by such leaders, the nomads proved to be irresistible.

The most enduring of nomadic achievements were the Islamic conquests of the 7th century AD. The nomads of Arabia, called Bedouin, were inspired by the teachings of Muhammad and by the prospect of plunder. Within a century of Muhammad's death they had subdued an area from southern Spain in the west to China in the east. But there was no great increase in nomadism in the conquered territories, as the nomads themselves became settled.

Later, various minor Bedouin dynasties flourished, while the tribes of the Syrian desert remained important as auxiliaries in the armies of Saladin and his successors, and as suppliers of horses for the rulers of Egypt and Syria. They also controlled routes from the Levant to the East, and the pilgrim routes across north Arabia to the Holy City of Mecca.

The deserts now yield oil, and many Bedouin are employed in the industry. Modern communications combined with a severe drought in the 1960s and government efforts to extend agriculture have reduced nomadic populations. Centralising states have tried to break the tribes' independence by forced settlement. Their customs are preserved now largely for the benefit of tourists.

These Kazakh horsemen of 1899 (left) maintained the nomadic life of their ancestor Genghis Khan. In a timeless scene, Bedouin nomads say their evening prayers in the Sahara.

institutions, such as the Treasury and the King's Council, and the shire system were retained and developed, and the Church was reorganised under Archbishop LANFRANC. The English language was no longer used for government, and the language of the court became Norman French. English towns and population continued to grow, while the English lost heavily in terms of status, public office and land holdings. Taxation was also heavier, and harsh forest laws were maintained: good hunting areas, royal preserves for the king's enjoyment, were subject to special legislation. Norman bureaucratic skills produced a unique survey of England's wealth, recorded in DOMESDAY BOOK in 1086.

Normandy

Region and former province in north-western France named after the Norsemen, or NORMANS, who settled it in the 10th century. Originally part of ancient Gaul, the region was conquered by Julius Caesar and subsequently taken over by the Frankish king CLOVIS. Viking invasions began in the 9th century AD and in 912 the area was ceded to the Viking leader ROLLO. The power of the Normans, who converted to Christianity and adopted the French language, soon came to rival that of the French kings. In 1066 Duke William of Normandy conquered England, taking the throne as WILLIAM I. France recovered the duchy in 1204, but it fell to England during the HUNDRED YEARS' WAR. Normandy was permanently reunited with France after the Battle of Formigny in 1450.

Normandy Campaign

(June-August 1944) Allied invasion of France during the Second World War. Five beaches codenamed Utah, Omaha, Gold, Juno and Sword were designated for the Allied invasion, known as Operation Overlord, with General Dwight D. EISENHOWER as supreme commander. After months of preparation, the greatest amphibious landing in history began on June 6, 1944 – 'D-Day' – when 2727 ships sailed to the Normandy coast and landed 156000 troops. Having expected the invasion to come in the Pas de Calais, the Germans were unprepared. Four beaches were taken easily, but on Omaha the Allies met with fierce resistance. At the same time Allied assault troops landed in France by parachute and by glider. Allied air forces destroyed most of the bridges over the Seine and the Loire, preventing the Germans from reinforcing forward units. By June 9 the bridgeheads had been secured.

Two vast artificial harbours built of iron and steel and codenamed 'Mulberries', were towed across the Channel. One was sunk by a storm, but the second, at Arromanches, provided the campaign's main harbour. Meanwhile, a series of 20 oil pipelines laid across the Channel supplied the thousands of vehicles being landed. Under General Omar BRADLEY, US forces cut

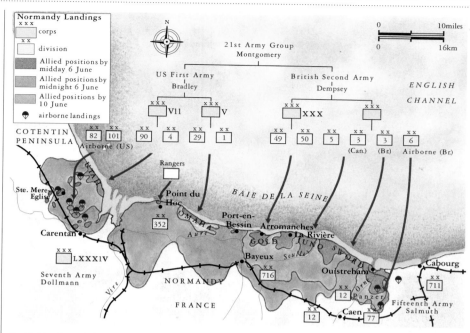

On D-Day, June 6, 1944, an Allied armada landed forces on five Normandy beaches, opening up the Second Front in Europe. The first wave of US troops land at Omaha (right).

off the Cotentin Peninsula and on June 26 accepted the surrender of Cherbourg. After vicious fighting that left the town a waste of rubble, British troops secured Caen on July 9 before advancing on Falaise. US troops captured the vital communications centre of Saint-Lô. The Germans launched a counterattack, but were caught between the US and British armies in the 'Falaise Gap' and lost 60000 men in fierce fighting. A US advance swept across France to Paris, while the British army moved along the north coast. Paris was liberated on August 25, and Brussels on September 3. More than 2 million troops, 4 million tonnes of supplies and 450000 vehicles had been landed at a cost of 224000 Allied dead or wounded and half a million German casualties.

Normans

VIKING people, known as Northmen or Norsemen, who conquered NORMANDY in the 10th century; also the inhabitants of Normandy who invaded England in 1066. After securing Normandy in 912, the Viking invaders established it as a duchy and adopted French as their language. Norman control expanded rapidly, and in 1066 William, Duke of Normandy invaded England to become WILLIAM I. The Normans were to go on to conquer or annex parts of Wales, Ireland and Scotland. Other Normans had already moved into the Mediterranean, under the leadership of Robert Guiscard. By the 12th century they controlled Sicily as well as southern Italy. In both England and Sicily the Normans took over and developed sophisticated systems of

justice and administration. The Normans also left a legacy of imposing castles and inspiring church architecture, notably the cathedrals of Monreale and Cefalu in Sicily and those of Durham and Ely in England.

Norseman see VIKING

North, Frederick, Lord

(1732-92) British WHIG statesman, prime minister from 1770 to 1782. North was given a ministerial post by NEWCASTLE in 1759, was an able chancellor of the exchequer under GRAFTON, and became prime minister in 1770, restoring stability after a decade of frequent changes. He kept taxes low, avoided expensive foreign ventures, and tried to deal with the rebellious American colonists by withdrawing all but one of the Townshend Acts, which imposed import duties on them. While North refused to be provoked by incidents such as the 1770 Boston Massacre, when a mob threatened troops and five people were killed, in 1773 his divided Cabinet would not allow the BOSTON TEA PARTY to go unpunished. As a result he was led into a position that made the AMERICAN REVOLUTION inevitable.

Although North was popular as a peacetime prime minister and in the early years of the American War, frustration with the failures in

the American colonies, as well as opposition propaganda from supporters of Charles ROCK-INGHAM, led to suggestions that the power of his ministry was sustained by excessive crown patronage. North resigned in 1782. He held office again in a coalition with Charles FOX in 1783, but after 1786 failing eyesight caused him to withdraw from politics.

North African Campaigns (June 1940-May 1943)
Series of military campaigns in Africa fought between Allied and AXIS troops during the Second World War. When Italy declared war on the Allies in June 1940, it had 300 000 troops in North Africa. In July it occupied parts of British Somaliland and the Sudan, and by September had reached Sidi Barrani in Egypt. Under General Archibald WAVELL the British counterattacked in 1941, forcing the Italians out of Sidi Barrani, TOBRUK and Benghazi. In February, Germany sent the Afrika Korps under General Erwin ROMMEL to help the Italians. The exhausted British forces withdrew, leaving a garrison to defend Tobruk against Rommel's assaults.

Operation Crusader under General Claude AUCHINLECK relieved Tobruk, but the town fell to another attack by Rommel in June 1942, and the British then took up a defensive position at El ALAMEIN. From there the reinforced 8th Army launched an attack in October led by General Bernard MONT-GOMERY and Rommel fell back to Tunisia.

On November 9, 1942, US and British troops under General Dwight D. EISENHOWER landed in Algeria and Morocco. The German army was squeezed between the 8th Army advancing from the east and the Allied forces advancing from the west until Tunis surrendered on May 7, 1943. Some 250 000 prisoners were taken, and although Rommel withdrew the best of his Afrika Korps to Sicily, the activities of the Axis powers in North Africa had ended.

North American Indians
Original AMERINDIAN inhabitants of North America who migrated from Asia between 60 000 and 20 000 years ago. The main groups are usually divided geographically into the North-west Coast (for example Nootka and Kwakiutl); Plateau and Basin (Paiute, Nez Percé); South-east (CHEROKEE); North-east (ALGONQUIN and IROQUOIS); Plains (APACHE); South-west (NAVAHO and PUEBLO); California (Pomo); Subarctic (Chipewyan); and Arctic (INUIT).

By the time of European colonisation, the Native American population probably numbered fewer than 900 000, mostly living along the coasts rather than in the barren interior. Except from in the south-west, their small villages were organised around hunting, with

At a rally in 1985, Loyalists oppose Northern Ireland's independence from the UK.

agriculture a secondary activity. Conflict with Spanish settlers in the south-west in the 16th century, and with British and French settlers in the north-east in the 17th century, provoked wars between Native Americans and settlers and forced the former inland. After Europeans introduced horses to North America in the late 18th century, mounted hunters and warriors roamed the Great Plains, while trade between groups led to the sharing of customs.

From early colonial times European policy was to gain official surrender of tribal lands through formal treaties. Some 370 treaties were signed between 1778 and 1871, but most were broken, altered or ignored as land was increasingly opened up to settlers. Native Americans were pushed farther west, and from 1830 the Indian Removal Act enabled the president to remove them to INDIAN RESERVATIONS. The disruption of tribal lands by settlers, gold prospectors and railways continued to provoke conflicts. In 1876 the Sioux and Cheyenne united under CRAZY HORSE and SITTING BULL, killing Lieutenant-Colonel CUSTER at the Battle of the Little Big Horn. The last of the hostilities took place at WOUNDED KNEE in 1890. In 1887 the Dawes Act awarded Native Americans who renounced tribal allegiance US citizenship and 160 acres (41 440 ha) of reservation lands. The Native American population of the USA now stands at about 1.5 million.

> ### DID YOU KNOW?
> In November 1942 Hitler sent a message to Rommel in Tunisia stating that the German troops had one choice: victory or death.

North Atlantic Treaty Organisation
see NATO

North Carolina
Colony and state of the USA, on the east coast between Virginia and South Carolina. After Sir Walter RALEIGH's ill-fated attempt in 1585 to colonise Roanoke Island off the north coast, official colonisation of the Carolinas only began in 1663, when the English king Charles II issued a grant to eight proprietors. The colony's northern and southern halves developed separately, and in 1713 it was divided. North Carolina endured unrest against its administrators, including CULPEPER'S REBELLION, until it became a royal colony in 1729.

Finding themselves under the growing control of plantation owners and also subject to heavy taxation, angry frontiersmen formed the Regulators of North Carolina in 1768 in order to fight for self-government, but they were routed in 1771. After a failed British

campaign to assert control during the American Revolution, North Carolina settled to a planter-dominated regime.

Northern Ireland
Province of the United Kingdom made up of six north-eastern counties of the ancient Irish province of ULSTER. The British Government proposed the division of IRELAND after SINN FÉIN proclaimed an Irish republic in 1918, leading to near civil war. The 1920 Government of Ireland Act founded separate parliaments for the mainly Protestant north-east and the Catholic south-west, but Republican resistance led to the 1921 Anglo-Irish Treaty, which gave dominion status to Ireland except for the north-east, which maintained its union with Britain.

In the 1960s Catholic dissatisfaction over discrimination and the Protestant-dominated political system erupted into violence. Civil rights marches led to riots in 1968, with clashes between Republican paramilitary groupings such as the Irish Republican Army (IRA) and militant Loyalist organisations such as the Ulster Defence Association (UDA) and the Ulster Defence Force (UDF). British military forces were sent to the province in 1969 at the request of its government, based in STORMONT, but the bombings and sectarian killings escalated. The IRA split into Provisional and Official wings, with the Provisionals launching a terrorist campaign in Northern Ireland and Britain. In 1972 the British Government suspended the Stormont Parliament and imposed direct rule from Westminster. The Sunningdale Agreement of 1973 led to the establishment in 1974 of a power-sharing Northern Ireland Executive, but it was brought down by a strike organised by the Protestant Ulster Workers' Council and was replaced with rule by a secretary of state for Northern Ireland. In 1980 two IRA prisoners died on hunger strike in an attempt to gain political, not criminal, status.

Closer cooperation between Britain and the Republic of Ireland led to the 1985 Anglo-Irish Accord, or Hillsborough Agreement, which gave the Republic a consultative role in the government of Northern Ireland. It also provoked strikes and protests from Ulster Unionists. By 1992 more than 3000 lives had been lost since the Troubles began. In 1993 the Downing Street Declaration between the British and Irish governments promised political talks and aimed to include Sinn Féin in the peace initiative if they renounced IRA violence. In 1994 the IRA declared a 'complete cessation' of military activities, followed by similar declarations by Loyalist paramilitary groups. By late 1994 the number of British troops in Northern Ireland had almost halved since 1969. During 1995 the British Government refused to negotiate with Sinn Féin until a permanent cease-fire had been established by the IRA decommissioning its weapons. The cease-fire ended in February 1996 when the IRA set off a bomb at Canary Wharf in London.

Northern Territory State in north central Australia bordered by the Arafura Sea in the north and reaching beyond Uluru (Ayers Rock) in the south. The Dutch ship *Arnhem* brought the first Europeans in 1623. Scientific explorations were carried out by the Britons Matthew Flinders in 1803 and Phillip Parker King in 1818. Settlers from New South Wales arrived at Port Essington in 1824. They took formal possession of the area in order to forestall French colonisation, but were forced to leave before relief supplies could reach them.

In 1860 the South Australian government offered a cash reward for the first to cross the continent from south to north. Two years later John McDouall Stuart, a Scottish explorer, crossed Australia from Adelaide to the northern coast. In 1863 the Northern Territory was annexed to South Australia. The discovery of gold at Pine Creek in the 1870s attracted more settlers, while a labour shortage led to an influx of Chinese from Singapore. In 1911 the Australian government took over the administration of the area. A Legislative Assembly was created in 1974, and four years later the Northern Territory was granted internal self-government. The state capital is Darwin.

Northern War (1700-21) Conflict in which Russia, Denmark and Poland sought to curb Sweden's power in the Baltic. At the time of CHARLES XII's accession to the Swedish throne in 1697, his empire included Finland, Estonia and Livonia on the eastern coast of the Baltic Sea, and territory in northern Germany. An attack on Swedish Livonia was launched in 1700 by Augustus the Strong of Saxony and Poland, Frederick IV of Denmark and PETER I of Russia. In the same year the Danes invaded Schleswig. Charles landed in Copenhagen, forced Denmark to make peace, and defeated Peter at NARVA. He then invaded Poland and placed Stanislaus Leszczynski on the throne.

Charles pursued Augustus into Saxony in 1706, forcing him to recognise Stanislaus, and by 1708 he was deep into Russia. After victory at Holowczyn Charles turned south, but his COSSACK ally Mazeppa was defeated by Peter's general Aleksandr Menshikov in the Ukraine.

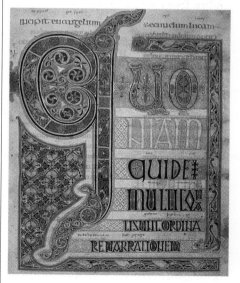

The Swedes' capture of Narva during the Northern War is celebrated in a bronze bas-relief of around 1720.

In 1709, cut off from reinforcements, Charles was defeated at the Battle of POLTAVA. He took refuge in Turkish territory, drawing the sultan into the war against Russia while his subjects fought desperate rearguard actions. Expelled by the Turks, Charles returned to Sweden in 1714, but was killed during an offensive against Norway in 1718. His sister, Ulrica Leonora, then initiated the peace negotiations Charles had refused to consider. By the treaties of Stockholm in 1719 and Frederiksborg in 1720, Bremen and Verden were ceded to Hanover and most of Pomerania to Prussia. After further Russian naval successes, the Treaty of Nystadt ended the war. Sweden recognised Peter I's title to Estonia, Livonia, Ingria, Kexholm and part of Finland.

North Korea North-east Asian country in the northern half of the Korean peninsula. The Democratic People's Republic of Korea was proclaimed on May 1, 1948, formed from the zone occupied by the Soviet Union at the end of the Second World War. Intent on reuniting Korea, North Korea launched a suprise attack on South Korea in June 1950, suffering considerable damage and loss of life in the three years of the indecisive KOREAN WAR. After the war, the ruling Communist Party of Kim Il Sung (1912-94) undertook a programme of reconstruction. From the 1980s, the economy stagnated and then declined, but after North and South Korea held a series of economic talks in 1985 there was a marked upturn in trade between the two countries. Kim Il Sung was re-elected in 1990, supporting a policy of 'normalising' relations with South Korea, but not one of reunification. Talks began in 1990, and in 1992 an economic agreement was signed. Tensions flared again in 1994 when North Korea refused to allow international inspectors to examine its nuclear reactors, amid allegations that it was building nuclear weapons. After US intervention North Korea agreed to inspections, but disputes between the two Koreas continued. In 1995 Kim Jong Il (1942-) succeeded his father as president.

Northumberland, John Dudley, Earl of Warwick, Duke of (c.1502-53) Ruler of England on behalf of EDWARD VI from 1549. Dudley began his career as governor of Calais in 1538. On Edward's accession in 1547 he

backed Edward Seymour, Duke of SOMERSET, as Lord Protector. As Earl of Warwick and a member of the Privy Council, he defeated KETT'S REBELLION in August 1549. After Somerset's downfall in October, he became Lord President of the Privy Council in 1550. The following year he created himself Duke of Northumberland before ordering Somerset's imprisonment and execution. The new government was committed to Protestantism and produced Archbishop Thomas CRANMER's second *Book of Common Prayer* in 1552.

Although condemned by tradition as an evil schemer, Northumberland's regime promoted stability. He ended the wars against France and Scotland initiated by Somerset, and introduced important financial reforms. Northumberland brought about his downfall by persuading the dying Edward VI to agree to the succession of his own daughter-in-law, Lady Jane GREY. She was ousted by MARY I and Northumberland was executed for treason.

Northumbria Kingdom in northern Britain founded by the Angles, who arrived from Denmark and northern Germany in the 5th century AD. Northumbria was formed in 604 when King Ethelfrith merged the kingdoms of Bernicia and Deira. At its height, it extended from Yorkshire to the Firth of Forth. Its greatest period was the 7th century, when powerful kings such as Edwin, OSWALD and OSWY dominated the politics of the Anglo-Saxon kingdoms. Northumbrian learning flourished in the 7th and 8th centuries, developed by scholars and monks such as BEDE and Benedict Biscop at Jarrow. Northumbria attracted Danish raiders – the monastery of Lindisfarne was plundered in 793 and 875 – and its southern part, known as the kingdom of York, was settled by Danes from 876. It was

Northumbria's 'golden age' produced the *Lindisfarne Gospels*, a superbly illuminated manuscript made on Holy Island about 698.

conquered by WESSEX in the 10th century, and was reduced to an earldom in the newly created kingdom of England.

North Vietnam see VIETNAM

North-West Frontier Province

Mountainous province in Pakistan bordered by Afghanistan and India and inhabited by Pathan and Baluchi peoples. Features such as the KHYBER PASS leading into India made the region strategically important. Alexander the Great conquered the area around 326 BC, but was unable to hold it. The Pathans came in the 7th century AD. After it was annexed by the emperor BABUR the region payed allegiance to the MUGHAL empire during the 16th and 17th centuries before passing to the Sikhs and then, in 1849, to Britain.

The British policy of extending control into the tribal territories began with the acquisition of Quetta in 1876, followed by the nearby towns of Pishin, Sibi and Kurram in 1879. This led to wars with a number of the Pathan and Baluchi peoples living along the frontier territory from 1891 to 1898. To control the frontier, the British employed several forces, including the Punjab Irregular Force and the Frontier Constabulary. In 1893 Mortimer Durand, the Indian government's foreign secretary, and the Afghan emir agreed the border with Afghanistan. In 1901 the North-West Frontier was constituted a province with a number of tribal agencies. On the partition of India in 1947 the province joined Pakistan and the new government withdrew military forces from tribal territory.

Norway

Country comprising the western part of Scandinavia. In prehistoric times it was inhabited by primitive hunting communities. In the 9th century AD rivalry between chiefs and the desire for land provoked excursions by VIKINGS to Greenland, Iceland and England. Political organisation strengthened in the 10th century under Harald Fairhair, and under OLAF I and OLAF II. In 1028 the Danish king CANUTE asserted his rights to overlordship and Olaf II fled to Russia. Helped by Norwegian nobles, Canute took control until his death in 1035, after which the throne returned to Norway. Following Harald Hardrada's failed attempt to assert his claim to the English throne in 1066, civil war ensued. The Norwegian throne was finally taken by Sverrir, who claimed to be the illegitimate son of the Norwegian king Sigurd. Under Haakon IV (1204-63) Greenland and Iceland were added to the Norwegian crown, and from 1254 its trade with the HANSEATIC LEAGUE initiated a period of prosperity.

In 1397, Norway, Sweden and Denmark were united under one monarch, the Danish Margaret I, wife of Haakon VI. The union was dissolved in 1523, but Norway continued to be ruled by Danish governors until, having established its own parliament in 1807, it was ceded to Sweden in 1814. A literary revival and a new national consciousness emerged, leading to demands for complete independence. Responsible government was granted in 1884. The union with Sweden was finally dissolved in 1905, and Prince Charles of Denmark was elected as HAAKON VII.

Norway maintained neutrality during both world wars, but in 1940 Germany invaded and imposed a puppet government under the Norwegian fascist Vidkun QUISLING. After Quisling gave himself up in 1945, the monarchy and a Labour government returned. The exploitation of North Sea oil during the 1970s boosted the country's economy, and oil production continued to expand in the 1990s. Norway's first woman prime minister, Gro Harlem Brundtland, led three minority Labour governments between 1981 and 1993, and was re-elected a fourth time in 1993. In 1991 King Olav V was succeeded by his son, Harald V. Although a founding member of the EUROPEAN FREE TRADE ASSOCIATION (EFTA), by 1990 the majority of Norway's export revenue was coming from trade within the European Community and only 15 per cent from EFTA. As a result, in 1992 Norway led the negotiations for the establishment of the European Economic Area – the EC plus Norway, Iceland and Lichtenstein – which came into force in 1993. In a referendum in 1994 Norwegians voted against joining the European Union.

Nostradamus (1503-66) French astrologer and physician. Nostradamus first won fame for his innovative use of medicines and pioneer treatments during plague outbreaks at Aix and Lyons in 1546-7. In 1555 his *Centuries*

Nostradamus, the Latinised name of Michel de Nôtredam, has been credited with prophesying events such as the Second World War.

of rhyming prophecies, decidedly apocalyptic in tone, caught the contemporary imagination. His reputation won him royal favour and an enlarged second edition was dedicated to Henry II of France in 1558. Nostradamus was appointed physician-in-ordinary to the king on the accession of Charles IX in 1560. The prophecies continued to excite speculation and controversy, despite their condemnation in 1781 by the Roman Catholic Church.

Nova Scotia Mainland Canada's easternmost province, a peninsula adjacent to New Brunswick. In 1603 the area was claimed by the French, whose settlement at Port Royal became the centre of France's American empire, Acadia. Britain contested the French claim, naming the peninsula Nova Scotia in 1621 and launching several invasions before capturing it in 1710 and accepting its surrender in 1713. The French retained the nearby Cape Breton Island and built a fortress at Louisburg, which was captured in 1745 but returned to France in 1748. In continued colonial conflicts between France and Britain, some 6000 Acadians were forcibly deported to British colonies to the south in order to prevent insurrection. The second capture of Louisburg in 1757, and the Treaty of PARIS in 1763, placed Nova Scotia in British hands. Settlement was vigorously encouraged, and during the American Revolution large numbers of loyalists emigrated there.

Novgorod Province and capital in northwest European Russia. One of Russia's oldest cities, Novgorod is said to have been the site of the founding in 862 of the first Russian state under the Scandinavian warrior Rurik. It was forcibly converted to Christianity in 989 and became self-governing in 1019. Novgorod survived an invasion by the Mongol GOLDEN HORDE, but submitted to their control in 1238. That same year it resisted an attack launched by Swedish Vikings. In 1242 the city also held fast against the land-hungry TEUTONIC KNIGHTS, a military and religious order from Palestine. Trade flourished in the 14th century, but a struggle with MUSCOVY resulted in submission to Ivan III in 1478. In 1570 a massacre at the hands of IVAN IV suppressed further resistance, and the city was occupied by the Swedes from 1611 to 1619. Novgorod retained its political and commercial importance until the building of St Petersburg under Peter I in 1703.

Nubians Inhabitants of the area between the First and Fourth Cataracts of the River Nile, chiefly in Egypt and the Sudan. Around 2613 BC their country, then known as Kush, was raided by Egyptians. Egyptian troops occupied the region up to the Second Cataract in about 2000 BC, and reached the Fourth Cataract 500 years later. From about 920 BC

A wall painting at Thebes shows Nubian chiefs in Egyptian dress bowing before the pharaoh Tutankhamun.

a Nubian dynasty ruling at Napata between the Third and Fourth Cataracts conquered all Egypt. The Nubian Shabaka ruled as king of Kush and Egypt, with Thebes as his capital, but Assyrians forced his successor, Taharka, to withdraw between 680 and 669 BC. After several further struggles the Nubians drew back to Napata, and from about 530 BC their capital moved south to Meroë. The dynasty lasted until AD 350, when it was destroyed by Aezanas of Axum, a kingdom occupying the area of modern Ethiopia.

After Nubia was converted to Christianity in about 540, three Christian kingdoms emerged. In 652 an Egyptian army conquered the kingdom at Dongola between the Third and Fourth Cataracts, granting it peace in return for an annual tribute of slaves. In the late 13th century Turkish MAMELUKES took the north. The southern kingdom remained until the 16th century, when it was absorbed by the Sudanese Funj kingdom based at Sennar on the Blue Nile.

nuclear age see feature, pages 466-7

Nuclear Test-Ban Treaty (August 5, 1963) International agreement not to test nuclear weapons in the atmosphere, outer space or under water, signed by the USA, the Soviet Union and Britain. The issue of DISARMAMENT was raised at the Geneva Conference of 1955 and discussions on banning nuclear testing began in Geneva in 1958. The treaty was the result of an agreement between US president John F. Kennedy, Soviet premier Nikita Khrushchev and the British prime minister Harold Macmillan. There was no agreement on banning underground nuclear testing, but the treaty stated an intention to resolve this issue and was a step towards ending the COLD WAR. Between 1963 and 1965 the treaty was signed by more than 90 other governments, but not by China or France, who continued to test nuclear weapons in the atmosphere.

Nuffield, William Morris, Viscount (1877-1963) British car manufacturer and philanthropist. Nuffield set up a bicycle business at Cowley in Oxford when he was 16. By 1912 he was repairing cars and the following year he bought a factory at Cowley, where he began production of the Morris Oxford, the first British car planned for family use. Mass production kept Morris cars cheap, while Nuffield's business acumen earned him a vast fortune, much of which he gave away. He established Nuffield College, Oxford, for postgraduate research, and the Nuffield Foundation, a trust to encourage educational developments. Nuffield was created a viscount in 1934.

nunnery Building that houses a community of religious women living under strict vows of poverty, obedience and chastity. Christian religious orders for women date from the 4th century, when monastic communities for men and women were established in the deserts of Egypt, and the first community for women was established by Macrina, sister of St Basil the Great, on her family estate in Cappadocia in Italy. In the 6th century, St Benedict at the abbey of Montecassino in Italy created the vows of poverty, obedience and chastity taken by those entering what became known as the Benedictine monastic communities. In the 11th century the lives of those in the communities were devoted to prayer, reading and work such as spinning and weaving. From the 16th century sisterhoods were founded for more active work, including teaching and nursing. In England, monasticism was abolished during the Reformation, but some groups were refounded in the 19th century after a general revival of interest in the establishment of religious communities.

Nuremberg Trials (1945-6) International tribunal hearing charges of war crimes against Nazi leaders following the Second World War. The trials were complex and controversial: there were few precedents for using international laws that related to the conduct of states in order to judge the activities of individuals. Charges were brought for conspiracy against peace, crimes against peace, violation of the laws and customs of war, and crimes against humanity. As a result of the trials, several Nazi organisations, such as the GESTAPO and the SS, were declared to be criminal bodies. Individual judgments were made on 24 Nazi leaders, punishment being death or imprisonment. Robert Ley committed suicide in prison before his trial, while the industrialist Gustav KRUPP was declared physically and mentally unfit to be tried. Twelve of the remaining 22 were sentenced to hanging, but Hermann GOERING, founder of the Gestapo, committed suicide in prison after being sentenced. Three, including Hitler's deputy, Rudolf HESS, were sentenced to life imprisonment; four were sentenced to imprisonment for between 10 and 20 years; and three were acquitted.

Nyasaland see MALAWI

Nyerere, Julius (1922-) African statesman, first prime minister of Tanganyika in 1961, and first president of TANZANIA from 1964 to 1985. In 1954 he founded the Tanganyika African National Union (TANU), working with the British Government to achieve independence for Tanganyika in 1961. He became prime minister, but resigned the premiership the following month. Nyerere was elected president of the Tanganyika Republic in 1962 and two years later, after a revolution in ZANZIBAR, he effected its union with Tanganyika as the Republic of Tanzania. Nyerere was deeply committed to the concept of *ujamaa*, a belief that the country's land and resources should belong to the people within their village communities. In the Arusha Declaration of 1967 he outlined the socialist policies that were to be adopted in Tanzania. Banks and large companies were nationalised, and the country's major means of production placed under the collective ownership of farmers and workers. After 1987 the policy was largely abandoned. Nyerere was a major force in the ORGANISATION OF AFRICAN UNITY, as well as a strong supporter of the Commonwealth. He retired from the presidency in 1985 and as chairman of TANU five years later.

Nystad, Treaty of see NORTHERN WAR

Goering, Hess, Ribbentrop (front row) and their fellow Nazi defendants listen to the Nuremberg trial proceedings.

Learning to live with the Bomb

The last nuclear device to be used against an enemy exploded over Nagasaki in August 1945. The rest of the 20th century saw an uneasy stand-off between superpowers wielding the threat of annihilation.

The atomic bomb 'Little Boy' killed 70 000 people in Hiroshima in 1945, and exposed thousands more to radiation sickness.

The nuclear age dawned with the first detonation of an atomic device by the United States at 5.30 am on July 16, 1945. It appeared, the watching physicist Sir James Chadwick wrote in his diary, as 'a great blinding light that lit up the sky and the earth as if God himself had appeared among us'.

The exploitation of the immense energy created by reactions in atomic nuclei resulted from weapons research during the Second World War. Despite civilian developments, notably in the nuclear power generation industry, it remains an essentially military concept involving weapons of mass destruction and the efforts to prevent their use and proliferation. Although only five nations have formal status as nuclear powers – the USA, Russia, Britain, France and China – several others, including Israel, India, Pakistan and South Africa, are also believed to have their own nuclear capabilities.

A TERRIBLE NEW WEAPON

In 1942 the Manhattan Project, an intense Anglo-US research programme under Robert Oppenheimer, director of the Los Alamos laboratory, was charged with translating theoretical physics into usable atomic weapons as part of the war effort. Germany had surrendered before the first test device was prepared, but Japan remained in the war and high casualties were expected during its imminent invasion. The atom bomb tested in the deserts of New Mexico used nuclear fission – the splitting of the nucleus of an atom – to produce a massive release of energy in a chain reaction. On August 6, 1945, a US aircraft dropped a bomb on the Japanese industrial city of Hiroshima. Three days later, another was dropped on the port of Nagasaki. Each had the nominal force of 200 000 tonnes of high explosive. The immense destruction they wrought forced the Japanese to surrender and brought the Second World War to an end.

The USA expected to enjoy a nuclear monopoly for at least a decade after the war, but to force through its own nuclear project the Soviet Union launched Operation Borodino, which used espionage and slave labour. On August 29, 1949, an atomic weapon was exploded in Soviet Kazakhstan. No announcement was made, but a US aircraft over the Pacific sucked in a radioactive air sample a few days later.

The USA now pressed ahead with thermonuclear weapons, in which hydrogen nuclei are fused at extremely high temperatures to release energy in the same reaction as that found in the Sun. The first thermonuclear device was detonated by the USA in 1952. The first transportable hydrogen bomb detonated with a force equivalent to 15 million tonnes, or 15 'megatons', of TNT at Bikini Atoll in the Pacific in 1954. The Soviets responded with a less powerful but still devastating hydrogen bomb the following year. The two superpowers now both possessed superbombs.

Brute strength having been achieved, the emphasis switched to delivery systems. The main effort went into rockets. The Soviets launched the world's first satellite – *Sputnik* – in October 1957, the Americans replying two months later with the launch of their first intercontinental ballistic missile (ICBM), the Atlas.

The dangers of a holocaust intensified dramatically with the developments in missiles. The Soviet Union lacked the ships, aircraft, logistical support and industrial base necessary to carry out a conventional invasion of the USA. With rockets, however, nuclear warheads ceased to be weapons of last resort but were seen as first-strike weapons. 'A deep rocket strike will replace land invasion as the first act in war,' the Soviet leader Nikita Khrushchev said. 'Not a single capital, no large industrial or administrative centre and no strategic area will remain unattacked in the first minutes, let alone days, of war.'

The Cuban missile crisis of 1962 marked the most extreme point of danger. The Soviets installed on the Caribbean island rockets with the range to destroy New York and Washington. Unprotected by silos, or hardened shelters, they were first-strike weapons. The Americans, who had clear superiority in ICBMs, submarine-launched missiles and long-range bombers, declared a blockade of Cuba and put their forces at Defcon-2, a Red Alert one step below war itself. Lack of sea power together with his

The Polaris missile (left), developed by the US and used by the Royal Navy, was a target for British antinuclear protesters (below).

A 15-megaton hydrogen blast rises above Bikini Atoll on March 1, 1954, seen here from 50 miles (80 km) away. The spectators at a 1951 atomic test (left) were a little over 12 miles (20 km) away.

underestimation of Western resolve, persuaded Khrushchev to withdraw the missiles after seven tense days.

The crisis inspired nuclear protest movements. In Britain, the Campaign for Nuclear Disarmament (CND) had been created by the philosopher Bertrand Russell and the churchman Canon John Collins in 1958. It called for the global abolition of nuclear weapons while urging a unilateral first step by Britain. Annual marches were held from London to Aldermaston in Berkshire, the centre for nuclear research.

The movement gathered much support; in the early 1980s large demonstrations in Britain and West Germany were mounted against the deployment of a new generation of American cruise and Pershing missiles in Europe. Protesters also campaigned against the neutron bomb, a small hydrogen bomb with a low blast and enhanced radiation, which leaves buildings largely intact but kills through radiation. The two superpowers, however, controlled the overwhelming majority of nuclear weapons, and no similar mass movement developed in the USA or the USSR.

Arms control became a matter of painstaking diplomacy, underpinned by the concept of Mutually Assured Destruction (MAD). This was based from 1968 on the development of multiple independently targetable re-entry vehicles (MIRVs), or

clusters of warheads on top of each missile. A single submarine, carrying 288 warheads on 24 missiles, had sufficient destructive power to make the concept of a first strike irrelevant since both sides would be devastated. Negotiations between the USA and the USSR in the Strategic Arms Limitation Talks (SALT) limited the expansion of nuclear forces. In the 1980s, presidents Ronald Reagan and Mikhail Gorbachev agreed significant reductions.

THE BIRTH OF STAR WARS
The Strategic Defence Initiative ('Star Wars') undertaken by the Reagan administration during the 1980s was an attempt to use laser and particle-beam technology to destroy incoming missiles during their trajectory. Space exploration, guidance systems, telemetry, computer miniaturisation and lasers are among the many technologies to have benefited from nuclear-age research spending. The Soviet economy was increasingly unable to compete with American technical advances.

A long-feared disaster in the Soviet nuclear-power industry took place at Chernobyl in the Ukraine in April 1986. Clouds of radioactive material were blown as far as Sweden after an explosion caused by overheating. The accident emphasised the decay of Soviet industry, caused in large part by the distortions of arms spending.

It was a chilling reminder of Bertrand Russell's comment on the nuclear age. 'You may reasonably expect a man to walk a tightrope safely for ten minutes,' he said. 'It would be unreasonable to do so without accident for 200 years.'

The end of the Cold War in 1990, and the collapse of the Soviet system, led the nuclear age into a new phase. Tension between the superpowers was replaced as the main source of anxiety by nuclear proliferation, particularly in politically unstable parts of the world. Israel was believed to have a stockpile of nuclear weapons, while Iraq and Iran had civil nuclear programmes which it was feared were being adapted to military ends. In the event, the rockets fired by Iraq at neighbouring states after its invasion of Kuwait in 1990 had conventional warheads. Neither did Israel retaliate against Iraqi rocket attacks with nuclear weapons. Iraqi nuclear facilities were inspected after Iraq was defeated in the Gulf War, but nuclear potential continued to raise tension in the region.

The collapse of the Soviet Union also heightened fears of nuclear terrorism. Although agreements covering the control of major missiles were reached by the newly independent Soviet republics, the fate of thousands of less sophisticated nuclear shells and land mines was less certain.

OAS see ORGANISATION DE L'ARMÉE SECRÈTE; ORGANISATION OF AMERICAN STATES

Oastler, Richard (1789-1861) British social reformer known as 'the Factory King' for his efforts to improve conditions of employment. Oastler was working as an estate manager when in 1830 he learned of the abuses of child labour and began a journalistic attack on the employment of young children in factories. In

> 66 **I had been on terms of intimacy and friendship with many factory masters, and I had all the while fancied that factories were a blessing to the poor.** 99
>
> *Richard Oastler, 1830, on his earlier ignorance of working conditions in factories*

1831 he began a campaign for a ten-hour working day, which was achieved in the 1847 Ten Hours Act. After he condemned the Poor Law Amendment Act of 1834, which forced those in need of help to enter a workhouse, Oastler was dismissed by his employer, who had him jailed for debt from 1840 to 1844.

Oates, Titus see POPISH PLOT

OAU see ORGANISATION OF AFRICAN UNITY

Obote, Milton (1924-) First prime minister of Uganda and twice president. In 1950 Obote moved to Kenya, where he joined the independence movement. On his return to Uganda in 1957 Obote became a member of the Uganda National Congress, and in 1960 formed the Uganda People's Congress (UPC). Despite the opposition of the UPC to the existence within Uganda of the powerful kingdom of Buganda ruled by MUTESA II, in 1961 Obote concluded an alliance with Buganda's Kabaka Yekka ('King Only') Party. Obote was elected prime minister in 1962 on Uganda's independence, and the following year Mutesa II became the country's first president. After three years of conflict between prime minister and president, together with increasing tension within the government between ethnic groups, Obote deposed Mutesa with the help of Lieutenant-

Colonel Idi AMIN and declared himself president. The following year he proclaimed a new constitution, but in 1971 was ousted by Amin in a military coup. Obote fled to Tanzania, returning only after Amin was overthrown in 1979 in a Tanzanian-led invasion. In highly controversial elections in 1980, Obote was re-elected, but was unable to control Uganda's inflation or the divided and vengeful army. In 1985 he was ousted by General Titus Okello and exiled to Zambia.

Obrenović Ruling dynasty of SERBIA, founded by Miloš I in 1817. Originally a cattle drover, Miloš rose to power as a national leader after directing Serbia's second uprising against the Turks in 1815. In 1817 he had his rival, the Serbian leader KARAGEORGE, murdered. He presented Karageorge's head to the sultan, and persuaded the Turks to accept his election as Prince of Serbia under the sultan's suzerainty, but in 1839 he abdicated in favour of his son Milan III, who died 25 days later. In 1839 Milan was succeeded by Michael III, who was forced into exile when the Karageorgević dynasty returned to power three years later.

In 1858 the Obrenović dynasty was reinstated, first under Miloš, now in his dotage, and then, in 1860, under Michael, who was an effective leader until his assassination in 1868. There followed 30 years of unpopular rule by his cousin, Milan IV, who declared himself king in 1882 but was forced to abdicate in favour of his son Alexander in 1889. After Alexander's murder, the Karageorgević dynasty again returned to power.

obsidian Acid-resistant, lustrous volcanic glass. Obsidian is usually black or banded, and when fractured displays curved, shiny surfaces. It was used in preindustrial societies to make weapons and tools, and then became a trading currency. After about 10 000 BC obsidian from central and eastern Turkey was traded as far as south-west Iran and Jordan. It was also used extensively in the Americas, the Mediterranean, South-east Asia and the Pacific. In the 4th century BC the obsidian used in cutting tools was superseded by copper alloy, but it may have been the foundation for the wealth of the Mexican city of Teotihuacán from the 2nd to the 7th centuries AD.

Obsidian was used for ornaments as well as for weapons and tools. Its volcanic lustre creates striking eyes on this Egyptian coffin mask.

Daniel O'Connell's campaign for an independent Ireland earned him the nickname 'the Liberator'.

O'Connell, Daniel (1775-1847) Irish nationalist leader and social reformer. It was his condemnation of the 1800 ACT OF UNION abolishing the Irish Parliament that first brought O'Connell to prominence. In 1823 he founded the pacifist Catholic Association in order to campaign against anti-Catholic discrimination, and in the 1820s he raised support for the right of Catholics to sit in the British Parliament. After O'Connell was elected a Member of Parliament in the 1828 CLARE ELECTION, the British Government, threatened with civil disorder, passed the Roman Catholic Relief Act of 1829. This granted CATHOLIC EMANCIPATION, thereby allowing O'Connell to take his seat in the House of Commons.

In the 1840s O'Connell campaigned for an independent Ireland, but lost the support of many nationalists, including the radicals in the Young Ireland movement, who supported revolutionary action rather than constitutional methods. He was imprisoned for sedition for several weeks in 1844, and in 1847 he left Ireland for Italy, where he died.

O'Connor, Feargus (c.1796-1855) Irish radical politician and Chartist leader. In 1832 O'Connor was elected Member of Parliament for County Cork. After losing his seat in 1835, he moved to England and became involved with CHARTISM, a radical working-class movement campaigning for universal male suffrage and other parliamentary reforms. In 1837 he founded the Leeds *Northern Star*, the most influential Chartist newspaper. O'Connor's energy, humour and skill as an orator helped to make Chartism a mass movement, and in 1841, after a year in prison for seditious libel, he became undisputed leader of its cause. In 1847 he was elected Member of Parliament for Nottingham, but he failed to lead the movement to victory. He was declared insane in 1852.

Octavian see AUGUSTUS CAESAR

October Revolution see RUSSIAN REVOLUTION (1917)

Oda Nobunaga (1534-82) Japanese military leader who fought to restore unity to a divided Japan. As a young *daimyo*, 'feudal lord', Nobunaga took control of his own province of Owari, and in 1560 he began to conquer the country. In 1562 he allied with the warlord TOKUGAWA IEYASU and in a series of battles defeated rival daimyo. Nobunaga marched on Kyoto, the centre of Japanese power, in 1568, on the pretext of establishing Ashikaga Yoshiaki – a priest and member of the hereditary Ashikaga shogunate – as shogun in place of Yoshiaki's cousin. In 1573 he ousted Yoshiaki, ending the shogunate, and assumed control of central Japan.

Taking the title of regent, Nobunaga destroyed the daimyo, using new technology such as muskets, and also suppressed powerful Buddhist monastic armies. He worked for a uniform system of currency, allowed missionaries to spread Catholicism, and built castles on a grand scale. In 1582, while preparing to extend his rule farther west, Nobunaga was assassinated by one of his generals. The task of reunifying Japan was then completed by TOYOTOMI HIDEYOSHI and Tokugawa Ieyasu.

Oder-Neisse Line Border between Poland and Germany formed by the Oder and Neisse rivers, set by the Allies after the Second World War. At the Yalta Conference in February 1945 the Allied powers agreed to extend Poland's western frontier into Germany to compensate for large losses in eastern Poland – almost a third of its prewar territory – to the Soviet Union. No agreement on the exact location of the border was reached until the end of the POTSDAM CONFERENCE in August, when Britain and the USA agreed to the Soviet proposal for a line following the Oder and West Neisse rivers from the Baltic to the Czechoslovak border. Poland would administer Pomerania, Silesia and most of East Prussia, and was authorised to expel almost 3.5 million Germans.

A treaty recognising the Oder-Neisse Line as a permanent frontier was signed by East Germany and Poland in 1950. West Germany regarded it as a temporary administrative border, but in 1970 recognised it as part of its OSTPOLITIK to normalise relations between the two Germanys. The Oder-Neisse Line was confirmed on reunification in 1990.

Odoacer (*c*.433-93) German king of Italy from 476 until his death. A member of the Rugian or Sciri tribe, Odoacer joined the Roman army as a mercenary in about 470. In 475 he led his tribesmen in a revolt against the Roman general Orestes, who had reneged on a promise to give the tribal leaders land in Italy. In August 476 Odoacer was declared king of Italy by his troops. Four days later he deposed Orestes' son, the emperor Romulus Augustus, and brought the Western Roman Empire to an end. Odoacer's rule was recognised by the Eastern emperor Zeno until he attacked Zeno's western provinces in 484. In 488 Zeno appointed the Ostrogoth THEODORIC THE GREAT king of Italy, and in 489 Theodoric invaded Italy. After Ravenna, Odoacer's capital, surrendered in 493, Theodoric assassinated Odoacer at a banquet.

Odysseus In Greek mythology, king of Ithaca and a leader in the Trojan War. He is known as Ulysses in Roman history. Odysseus was said to have helped to bring about the fall of TROY with the Trojan horse, a hollow wooden model masquerading as a gift to the gods, inside which Greek soldiers hid to enter the city. On their way home, Odysseus and his men were captured by savage, one-eyed giants, the Cyclopes. They escaped by blinding the Cyclopes' leader, Polyphemus, the son of Poseidon, god of the sea. Poseidon then frustrated their journey for ten years, burdening it with difficulties. Odysseus's adventures included resisting the sirens – sea nymphs who lured sailors to destruction with sweet singing – and Circe, a sorceress who transformed his followers into swine. His troublesome journey and return to Ithaca, where he killed the suitors of his faithful wife, Penelope, are recounted in the *Odyssey*, the epic poem by HOMER.

Offa (d.796) King of MERCIA from 757 until his death. After the murder of a distant cousin, King Aethelbald, in 757, Offa seized control of the kingdom of Mercia, which incorporated most of England south of the River Humber between East Anglia and Wales. The kingdom became a formidable power under Offa, who gradually, although not permanently, unified most of southern England by becoming overlord of the kingdoms of Kent, Sussex, East Anglia and Wessex. Offa was the first ruler whose charters refer to the 'King of the English', and he considered himself the equal of CHARLEMAGNE.

During his reign Offa introduced a uniform silver penny that remained the basis of English currency until the 13th century, stimulated the economy and accepted greater papal control of the English Church. In 796 Offa and Charlemagne negotiated the first recorded English commercial treaty. The earthwork rampart known as Offa's Dyke, which originally stretched some 170 miles (270 km), was built between 784 and 796 to define and defend the boundary between Offa's kingdom and Wales. It formed the first border between England and Wales.

> **DID YOU KNOW?**
>
> *Offa's slaying of the East Anglian king Ethelbert merited just one phrase in the Anglo-Saxon Chronicle: 'In this year Offa ordered the head of Ethelbert to be struck off.' But tradition has it that Offa's remorse for his actions led him to become the first to pay Peter's pence to Rome.*

Oglethorpe, James Edward (1696-1785) English army general, philanthropist and founder of the North American colony of GEORGIA. Oglethorpe entered Parliament in 1722. In 1729 he headed a committee for prison reform, which led to his idea of establishing a colony in the New World to provide asylum for debtors, who might otherwise be imprisoned for years. In 1732 he and his associates received a royal charter and a subsidy from Parliament. The following year Oglethorpe led some 120 to 130 settlers to Georgia, founding a settlement at Savannah. He governed the colony on paternalistic lines, banning alcohol and slavery. He also launched a short-lived silk industry, offered sanctuary to persecuted Protestants from Europe, and from 1739 to 1742 defended Georgia against Spanish invaders. Returning to England in 1743, Oglethorpe fought against the Jacobite rebellion of 1745.

OGPU Soviet secret police, an acronym for the Russian Unified Government Political Administration. In 1922 the GPU replaced Lenin's secret police unit, the Cheka, but it was renamed the OGPU after the formation of the USSR in 1923. The OGPU existed to suppress counterrevolution, to uncover political dissidents and, after 1928, to enforce the collectivisation policy of Joseph STALIN. It had its own army and a vast network of spies. In 1934 the OGPU was replaced by the NKVD.

O'Higgins, Bernardo (1778-1842) Chilean national hero. O'Higgins was the illegitimate son of Ambrosio O'Higgins, an Irish-born soldier who later became governor of Chile and viceroy of Peru. Educated in Peru and England, he returned to Chile after his father's death in 1801, and after 1810 he led Chile's fight for independence from Spain. In 1814 he became commander in chief of the forces fighting a Peruvian-sponsored invasion to re-establish Spanish rule in Chile.

After his defeat at Rancagua, O'Higgins fled to Argentina, where he joined the independence leader José de SAN MARTÍN. They prepared their combined army for an invasion of Chile, and in 1817 defeated Spanish troops at Chacabuco. After declaring Chile's independence in 1818, O'Higgins was appointed supreme director, but his reforms met with much opposition and he was forced to resign in 1823. He died in exile in Peru.

oil see feature, page 471

Okinawa Japanese island between Taiwan and Japan, the largest of the Ryukyuan chain. During the Second World War,

Tracer fire lights up the sky as US warships shell Okinawa in 1945. As the fighting intensified, Japanese kamikaze, or suicide, attacks sank 36 US ships and damaged at least another 370.

Okinawa was captured from the Japanese by US forces in an assault that lasted from April to June 1945. The island was a key objective because its harbour and airfields were needed for the invasion of Japan. The Japanese lost 110000 of their 120000 garrison defending Okinawa, while the USA suffered its heaviest casualties of the war in the Pacific: 36600 Americans were wounded in the battle and a further 12500 were killed.

Okinawa remained under the military control of the US until May 1972, when it was returned to Japan. In the 1990s pressure grew for the closure of American bases on the island. The island's governor, Masahide Ota, refused to sign renewal leases for the bases in 1995, but the government in Tokyo gained a court ruling that enabled Japan's prime minister, Ryutaro Hashimoto, to sign on Ota's behalf.

Olaf I Tryggvassön (969-c.1000) King of Norway from 995 until his death. After his chieftain father was killed by the sons of the Norwegian king Erik Bloodaxe, Olaf fled to the court of Prince Vladimir I in Novgorod, Russia, and became a Viking mercenary. In 991 and 994 he led Viking attacks on England, where he was converted to Christianity. The English king ETHELRED II, forced to sue for peace, paid Olaf with the proceeds of a tax known as DANEGELD, but later in 994 he became Olaf's godfather at his confirmation. Olaf returned to Norway and became king on the death of Haakon the Great in 995. He imposed Christianity on Norway's coast and western islands, the Shetland, Faroe and Orkney islands, Greenland and Iceland, but had little influence elsewhere. Olaf was killed at the Battle of Svolder, fighting the Danish and Swedish fleets.

Olaf II Haraldsson (c.995-1030) King of Norway from 1016 until his death, also the country's patron saint. As a young Viking warrior, Olaf fought the English from 1009 to 1011, but in 1013 he sided with the English king ETHELRED II against the Danes. Later that year he was baptised in France. After his return home in 1015, Olaf conquered territory held by Sweden and Denmark. By 1016 he had taken control of all Norway and made himself king. Using English missionaries, force and bribery, Olaf continued the conversion of his country to Christianity, and established the Church of Norway in 1024. In 1028 he was overthrown by the Anglo-Danish king Canute, and forced to flee to Russia. Olaf returned to Norway in 1030 in an attempt to regain his throne, but was killed by rebel and Danish forces at the Battle of Stiklestad. His zealous Christianity, patriotism and martyr's death led to his canonisation in 1031.

Oldenbarneveldt, Johan van (1547-1619) Dutch statesman. Oldenbarneveldt was a lawyer in The Hague when, in 1572, he joined the Dutch revolt against Spanish rule, becoming a supporter of its leader, WILLIAM I 'THE SILENT'. Between 1578 and 1579 he helped to negotiate the Union of Utrecht, in which the newly united seven northern provinces of the Netherlands declared their independence from Spain. After his appointment in 1586 as head of the States of Holland, the pre-eminent province in the union, Oldenbarneveldt became the country's leading statesman alongside Maurice of Nassau, William the Silent's son and successor.

Oldenbarneveldt oversaw the expansion of Dutch trade, helped to found the Dutch East India Company in 1602, and in 1609 he negotiated the Twelve Years' Truce with Spain. But his attempts to safeguard the individuality of the provinces against a centralised government brought him into conflict with Maurice, and became part of a bitter quarrel between rival schools of Calvinism in which he and Maurice took opposing sides. Maurice took Oldenbarneveldt prisoner and in 1619 had him beheaded for subversion, although no evidence against him has ever been found.

Olympia Ancient Greek religious centre and site of the first Olympic Games (see feature, page 473), situated in the western Peloponnese. From around 1000 BC, Olympia was the location of the sanctuary of Zeus, whom the Greeks believed to be chief of the gods, and the father and ruler of the human race. Between the 8th century BC and the 4th century AD, the Olympic Games were held at the sanctuary every four years as part of a religious festival. At the centre of the sanctuary was the Altis, or Sacred Grove of Zeus. This contained the largest and most important building in Olympia, the Temple of Zeus, which was completed around 456 BC.

Made of stuccoed limestone and marble, the Temple of Zeus measured 210 ft by 90 ft (64 m by 27 m), with six columns across the front and 13 along the sides. Inside was one of the Seven Wonders of the World (see feature, pages 584-5): a gold and ivory statue of Zeus by the Athenian sculptor Phidias. Also outside the walls of the Altis were a stadium, a hippodrome, a gymnasium, a wrestling area, hostels, baths and guesthouses for officials and competitors who were taking part in the Games. The Christian emperor THEODOSIUS

Oil: driving force of the global economy

To call oil 'black gold' undervalues its importance to the global economy. For half a century producer countries and consumer countries have fought and wrangled over the world's dwindling reserves.

As the Iraqis retreated from Kuwait during the 1991 Gulf War, pillars of flame leapt into the sky from oil wells they had set alight on the orders of their leader, Saddam Hussein. The pyres were symbolic of the central issue at stake in the war: control of more than half the world's oil reserves.

Until the 19th century oil had been used only for primitive lighting and cooking. Though the first well was drilled by the Chinese a few centuries before Christ, using percussion bits and bamboo piping, oil was extracted there and in the Middle East mainly by the crushing and heating of shale. It was not until 1859 that an American entrepreneur, Edwin L. Drake, used a steam engine and punching device to drill the world's first modern oil well 69½ ft (21 m) into the rock under Titusville, Pennsylvania.

A quarter of a century later in Germany, Gottfried Daimler developed the liquid-fuel internal-combustion engine and invented the carburettor. After this the petroleum industry grew with spectacular speed.

A GLOBAL INDUSTRY

Today oil is crucial to transport, heating and petrochemicals – for agriculture and the manufacture of plastics, synthetic fibres, glues, paints, dyes, pharmaceuticals and detergents. Oil supplies about 40 per cent of all the energy consumed in the world today.

Oil has been the basis of private and national fortunes. John Paul Getty, the American eccentric, dug his first well in Oklahoma in 1913, was a millionaire by 1916, and, after purchasing a concession in Saudi Arabia in 1949, entered the multibillionaire league in the 1950s. At his death in 1976 he was believed to be the world's richest man. Other dynasties whose wealth was built on oil include the Rockefellers and, east of the Atlantic, the Gulbenkians.

Until about 1945 the United States produced nearly two-thirds of the world's supply of crude oil. Its closest competitors were Mexico, the Soviet Union and Venezuela, the largest exporter. But the discovery of vast reserves in the Middle East between the

After running aground off the Shetland Islands in 1993, the MV *Braer* lost almost 80000 tonnes of light crude oil (left).

two world wars and, more recently, in China and the North Sea, altered the balance of economic and political power. Today the United States is a net importer of oil and has been overtaken as largest producer by Saudi Arabia; other major producers include the countries of the former Soviet Union, Iran, the Gulf States, Libya, Venezuela and Mexico.

OIL, WAR AND ECONOMIC CRISIS

Oil revenue is crucial to producer countries: in Saudi Arabia the state – effectively the royal line of Saud – owns all oil production and controls refining and marketing, which generates two-thirds of the national revenue.

Oil has often caused tension between producer countries, few of which have established democratic regimes, and the industrial giants of the West. An early example was the Suez War of 1956, which resulted in part from the desire of Britain and France to maintain control of oil supplies from the Gulf.

In 1960 the major producers, led by the Middle Eastern states, established the Organisation of Petroleum Exporting Countries (OPEC) to protect their interests. In 1973 OPEC raised oil prices, first by 70 per cent and then by 130 per cent, at a time when Western Europe depended on the Middle East for 80 per cent of its supply. The result was a world economic crisis that damaged industrial production and led to serious unemployment. But since 1986 prices have fallen or remained relatively stable.

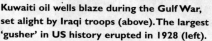

Kuwaiti oil wells blaze during the Gulf War, set alight by Iraqi troops (above). The largest 'gusher' in US history erupted in 1928 (left).

The Sacred Grove of Zeus – the Altis – at Olympia contained the temples, main altars, treasuries and the administrative buildings.

closed the sanctuary in AD 390, and three years later he banned the Games. The first excavations of the site began in 1829.

Olympic Games see feature, page 473

Oman Middle Eastern sultanate on the south-eastern Arabian peninsula, until 1970 known as Muscat and Oman. Arab migration to Oman began in the 9th century BC, but Arab dominance dates from Oman's conversion to Islam in the 7th century AD. In 1507 the Portuguese gained control of most of its coast, but were expelled in 1650 by the Yarubid dynasty, who also took over Portuguese settlements along the Persian and East African coasts. Civil war in Oman enabled the Persians to invade in 1737, but they were driven out in 1741 by Ahmad ibn Said of Yemen, who in 1744 founded the Al Bu Said dynasty that still rules Oman. Under his grandson, Said ibn Sultan, in the early 19th century Oman became the most powerful state in Arabia, controlling the coastal regions of Persia and Baluchistan, as well as ZANZIBAR. Following Said ibn Sultan's death the Al Bu Said empire was split between two sons, one of whom received Zanzibar and the other Oman.

From 1932 Oman was ruled by Sultan Said ibn Taimur, who crushed two major revolts with British assistance, but in 1970 he was overthrown by his son Qaboos bin Said, who began a programme of liberalisation and modernisation using revenues from oil, which had been discovered in 1964. With Britain's support, Jordan and Iran, Sultan Qaboos crushed a long-running rebellion in Dhofar in the south-west by 1975. In 1976 Oman joined the Arab League and the United Nations. It remained neutral during the Iran-Iraq War, but Omani troops fought in the 1991 Gulf War against the Iraqi occupation of Kuwait. Oman has no political parties, but in 1992 Sultan Qaboos moved towards limited political reform when he appointed a Consultative Council. In 1993 oil production in the sultanate reached record levels.

opera The idea of conveying a dramatic story in words set to music originated in the 1570s in Florence with the Camerata, a society of poets and musicians who were inspired by the ancient Greeks' use of music in drama. The earliest surviving opera, *Eurydice*, was composed in 1600 by Giulio Caccini and Jacopo Peri. Originally performed in private theatres, the opera soon gained in popularity and in 1637 the first public opera house opened in Venice. Early works were little more than dramas retold in recitative, or melodic speech, interspersed with ballet.

Opera became a more cohesive art form with the works of Claudio Monteverdi (1567-1643), who supplemented recitative with choruses, arias and duets. In the 17th century and early 18th century the dominant form was opera seria, developed by composers such as Alessandro Scarlatti and George HANDEL. Comic opera forms also developed, including the more sophisticated Italian opera buffa. Change in opera seria came in 1762 with Christoph Gluck's *Orpheus and Eurydice*, which had a stronger role for the orchestra and a plot based on human relationships. Wolfgang Amadeus MOZART (1756-91) reformed opera through his musical and dramatic genius in works such as *The Marriage of Figaro* (1786), *Don Giovanni* (1787) and *The Magic Flute* (1791).

In the 19th century, opera showed stronger national characteristics. After the French Revolution, composers such as Giacomo Meyerbeer developed the arias, choruses and spectacular scenic effects of grand opera, which became popular with a wealthy French middle class. German opera veered towards folklore and fantasy, culminating in the 'music dramas' of Richard WAGNER. In Italy Giuseppe Verdi extended the dramatic range of the Italian tradition of bel canto with operas such as *Aida* (1870).

In the late 19th century overt nationalism came to the fore in Russia with Alexander Borodin and Nikolai Rimsky-Korsakov, and in Czechoslovakia with Antonin Dvořák and, later, Leoš Janáček. A taste for realistic, low-life subjects was first shown in Georges Bizet's *Carmen* in 1875 and developed by Giacomo Puccini. By the 19th century the term operetta had come to describe a play with an overture, songs, interludes, spoken dialogue and dances. Notable composers include Johann Strauss (1825-99) and Sir Arthur Sullivan (1842-1900). Opera in the 20th century has embraced many styles with composers such as Benjamin Britten, Alban Berg and George Gershwin.

Opium Wars Two wars between China and Britain over trading rights in China. The first Opium War began in 1839 after the Chinese government tried to enforce its ban on the opium trade, which was causing social and economic disruption. Officials confiscated some 20000 chests of opium held in British warehouses in Guangzhou (Canton), smuggled there by British merchants as payment from India for exports of tea, porcelain and silk. Looking for a way to end Chinese trade restrictions, Britain responded in 1840 by sending 16 gunboats to besiege Chinese coastal cities. In 1842 the Chinese were forced to sign the Treaty of Nanjing, followed by the British Supplementary Treaty of the Bogue in 1843. Hong Kong was ceded to Britain and the treaty ports of Guangzhou, Jinmen, Fuzhou, Ningho and Shanghai were opened up to British trade and residence.

In 1856 the second Opium War began after Britain renewed hostilities following a search by Chinese officials of a British-registered ship, the *Arrow*. British and French troops took Guangzhou and Tianjin in 1857, and in 1858 the Chinese were obliged to agree to the treaties of Tianjin with Britain, France, Russia and the USA. These opened up a further ten ports and provided freedom of travel to the Chinese interior for European merchants and Christian missionaries. In 1860 Chinese opposition to the agreement led to the allies occupying Beijing and burning down the imperial summer palace. The Chinese then signed the Peking Convention, in which they agreed to observe the treaties of Tianjin and legalise the opium trade.

The huge influx of Indian opium into China led to the Opium Wars. Money flowed out of the country as millions became addicted.

The world celebrates the Olympic spirit

Although the aim of the Olympic Games is to bring nations together in peace, they have sometimes achieved the opposite effect. Even in ancient Greece, the Games did not always live up to the ideals that inspired them.

According to Baron Pierre de Coubertin, the French educationist who led the revival of the Olympic Games in 1896: 'The important thing in life is not the victory but the contest.' Sport may have abandoned his ideals, but every four years the Games still unite the world.

The original Games, held in Olympia, Greece, lasted from 776 BC to AD 394, when they were stopped by the Christian Emperor Theodosius. The first winners were rewarded with olive wreaths, but soon athletes trained full-time to compete for cash, leading to cases of corruption. Events included the pentathlon (running, javelin and discus-throwing, wrestling and long jump) and chariot races.

One story tells how a leading chariot racer challenged a succession of men who sought his beautiful daughter and raced them to their deaths – until a suitor tampered with the father's chariot, causing his death, and won the girl.

THE FATAL MARATHON

The marathon supposedly derives its name from the story of Pheidippides, a professional runner and soldier sent from the battlefield of Marathon to Athens, 22 miles (35 km) away, to convey news of victory over the Persians in 490 BC. Arriving in Athens, he called out, 'Be joyful, we win,' then dropped dead of exhaustion. The modern distance of 26 miles (42 km) was established in 1908, with 385 yards (352 m) added to allow runners to finish near the Royal Box at the London Games.

The origins of the first Olympics are lost in mythology. It is likely that they were held to celebrate victories, and they were always associated with a religious event. The entrants,

Boxers and wrestlers fight on an amphora painted by Nikosthenes, who lived from about 550 to 525 BC.

all male, mostly competed in the nude. They had to swear that they were law-abiding citizens of pure Hellenic birth and paraded in the stadium so members of the public could veto outsiders or lawbreakers. The earliest known hero was Coroebus of Elis, a cook who won a sprint in 776 BC.

The modern Games arose out of a French concern in the 1890s that their countrymen were lagging behind Germans and Czechs in physical well-being: young men, moving from agriculture into industry, might not be fit for war. De Coubertin was asked to find a solution, and he proposed a revival of the Olympic Games.

In 1894 de Coubertin's plan was accepted. The International Olympic Committee was formed, and the congress resolved that 'sports competitions should be held every fourth year on the lines of the Greek Olympic Games and every nation should be invited to participate'. Twelve nations were represented at the 1896 Olympics, held in Greece.

The 1900 Games in Paris lasted five months. The 1904 Games in St Louis, USA, were just as chaotic. The marathon winner was disqualified for riding 10 miles (16 km) in a car. But successes in London (1908) and Stockholm (1912) established the event.

Wars caused the cancellation of the 1916, 1940 and 1944 Olympics. Nazi propaganda dominated the 1936 Berlin Olympics; the 1956 Games, held only a month after the Soviet Union's invasion of Hungary, featured a water-polo match between the two that degenerated into a brawl; and in 1968 two

The Nazis hoped the 1936 Games (left) would prove White superiority, but Jesse Owens (above) won four gold medals. The Greeks used weights (inset) for jumping.

Americans gave 'Black power' salutes during the 200 metres awards ceremony.

In 1972 Palestinian terrorists murdered two of the Israeli team in the Olympic village. A further nine members, taken as hostages, were killed in crossfire. As politicians saw how the Olympics had captured the world's attention, they organised boycotts. African nations, incensed at the New Zealand rugby tour of apartheid South Africa, withdrew from the 1976 Games; the USA led boycotts of the 1980 Moscow Olympics to protest against the Soviet invasion of Afghanistan, and in revenge Eastern European countries boycotted the 1984 Los Angeles Games. Recent Olympics have been dogged by drug-taking.

The 1996 Games in Atlanta in the USA marked a centenary of the global celebration of physical prowess.

Oppenheimer, Sir Ernest (1880-1957)

South African mining magnate and politician. Backed by the bank of the US financier J.P. MORGAN, Oppenheimer founded the Anglo-American Corporation of South Africa in 1917 to exploit the gold reserves of east Witwatersrand in the Transvaal. After forming the Consolidated Diamond Mines of South West Africa in 1919, he gained control of De Beers Consolidated Diamond Mines. By the time of his death, Oppenheimer's interests controlled more than 95 per cent of the world's diamond supply. He was knighted in 1921 and served as MP for Kimberley in Cape Province from 1924 to 1938.

Oppenheimer, J. Robert (1904-67)

American nuclear physicist. Oppenheimer was teaching at the California Institute of Technology when in 1943 he was made director of the MANHATTAN PROJECT, created to develop an atom bomb for Allied use in the Second World War. In October 1945, two months after atomic bombs were dropped on the Japanese cities of Hiroshima and Nagasaki, Oppenheimer resigned and became a leading advocate of civilian and international control of atomic energy. From 1946 to 1952 he served as chairman of the general advisory committee of the Atomic Energy Commission, but in 1953 he was labelled a security risk because of his opposition – on both moral and practical grounds – to the hydrogen bomb. In a highly controversial move Oppenheimer was suspended from secret nuclear research, but he continued as

A priestess of the Delphic oracle, seated on a golden tripod, enters a trance to relay the oracle's message to Aegeus, king of Athens.

director of the Institute for Advanced Study at Princeton University, a post he had held since 1947. He was formally reinstated in 1963.

oracle In ancient Greece, a sacred place at which a deity was consulted about the future. By association, the priest or priestess through whom the prophecy was given was also known as the oracle, as was the prophecy itself. Of the many oracles in ancient Greece, the best known were the oracles of Apollo at DELPHI and of Zeus at Dodona in north-western Greece. There were also oracular shrines in Egypt, Syria and Italy. Individuals underwent rites of purification and sacrifice before consulting an oracle on religious, moral, political, commercial or military matters.

One of the most common methods of divining the god's reply was for the inquirer to sleep in a holy precinct and receive the answer in a dream. At Dodona, the oldest oracle, priests interpreted the rustling of leaves on the sacred oak. The pronouncements of the Delphic oracle, made by the Pythia, or priestess, in a frenzy and then interpreted in verse by priests, could be particularly enigmatic. King Croesus of Lydia, told by the oracle that he would 'destroy a great empire' if he went to war, promptly attacked his neighbour Persia in 546 BC – only to be decisively beaten, and to realise that the empire referred to by the oracle was his own.

Oracles were also known in China from the 16th century to the 11th century BC: Shang monarchs, members of the earliest known Chinese dynasty, used 'oracle bones'. The shoulder blades of pigs, oxen and sheep were heated and the resulting cracks were interpreted as guidance from royal ancestors. The information was recorded on the bones, using the earliest known form of Chinese writing.

Orange, House of Princely dynasty and the ruling house of the Netherlands since 1815. The dynasty derives its name from the medieval principality of Orange in south-eastern France. During the 16th century the princes of Orange married into the German house of Nassau. In 1544 the principality was inherited by WILLIAM I 'THE SILENT', Count of Nassau and, from 1568, leader of the Dutch revolt against Spanish rule. In 1579 William was appointed first stadholder, or chief magistrate, of the recently formed United Provinces of the Netherlands, an office held by members of the House of Orange-Nassau until the republic fell in 1795. William's descendants include WILLIAM III, stadholder from 1672 to 1702 and king of England after the overthrow of his father-in-law, James II, in 1689. In 1815 the Netherlands was established as a kingdom, and the House of Orange-Nassau was restored as the ruling family. Queen Beatrix, born in 1938, is a direct descendant of the Netherlands' first king, William I, who ruled from 1815 to 1840. While the title remained with the Dutch family, the principality of Orange itself was seized by Louis XIV in 1672 and incorporated into France by the Peace of UTRECHT in 1713.

Orange Free State Former province of the Republic of South Africa. In the early 19th century the region was inhabited by the Bantu-speaking Sotho people, until the Great Trek of 1835-43 (see feature, page 270) brought in large numbers of Dutch settlers, or Boers. In 1848 the British annexed the region as the Orange River Sovereignty, but in 1854 they granted it independence as the Orange Free State. From the late 1880s conflicts over the rights of British immigrants prospecting for gold in the TRANSVAAL caused British-Boer relations to deteriorate, and in 1896 the two Boer republics formed a military alliance.

When British troops were sent to protect the goldfields, the Boer states responded by declaring war on Great Britain on October 12, 1899. Despite early successes, the Boers lost the second BOER WAR and in 1902 accepted British sovereignty. Self-government was restored to the Orange Free State in 1907 and in 1910 it became a founding province of the Union of South Africa. In local government reorganisations of 1994 the Orange Free State became a region.

Orange Order Secret society formed in 1795 to maintain Protestant rule in Ireland. It was named after William of ORANGE, who in 1688 replaced the Roman Catholic James II to become WILLIAM III. The order was established to fight the growing agitation for Catholic Emancipation in Ireland, particularly by Wolfe Tone's Society of United

J.R. Oppenheimer, on the left, views the melted remains of the steel tower that contained the first atomic bomb, tested in New Mexico.

Irishmen, which was formed in 1791 to campaign for religious equality, parliamentary reform and, from 1793, an Irish republic. From the 1880s the order formed the backbone of resistance to the call of the HOME RULE movement for Irish self-government. Since the partition of Ireland in 1921, Orangemen have been staunch defenders of Northern Ireland's union with the United Kingdom. The Orange Order's main holiday is July 12, the anniversary of William III's victories over James II in Ireland at the battles of the BOYNE in 1690 and of Aughrim in 1691.

ordeal Form of trial in which the accused was subjected to a painful or dangerous test in order to determine guilt or innocence. The outcome was regarded as a divine judgment. During the early Middle Ages, trial by ordeal was widely practised in Western Europe. It is still practised in parts of the East and in traditional societies. Ordeal by fire required suspects to carry hot irons or to walk barefoot over red-hot ploughshares or heated coals. If they emerged unhurt, or if their wounds were clean when inspected three days later, they were innocent. Women suspected of witchcraft could be subjected to trial by water. The accused would be bound and thrown into water that had been blessed. If she floated, the water had rejected her and she was guilty. If she sank, she was adjudged innocent and pulled out. Trial by ordeal was repudiated by the pope in 1215.

Oregon Question Dispute from 1843 to 1846 between the USA and Britain over the ownership of Oregon territory in the northwest USA. In 1818, Britain and the USA agreed on joint occupation of 'Oregon country' – the vast region west of the Rockies, north of California and south of Alaska. The question of who owned the territory only became an issue in the early 1840s when 'Oregon fever' struck and hundreds of pioneers travelled the OREGON TRAIL to the region each year. As the immigrants poured in, pressure mounted for all of Oregon up to the southern tip of Alaska to become part of the USA. In 1844 James K. POLK won the presidency with the campaign slogan 'Fifty-four forty or fight', a reference to the settlers' wish for their northern boundary with the British to be north of Vancouver Island on the 54° 40′ parallel. The British refused to cede any territory and the two countries came close to war until a compromise was reached in 1846, setting the US-Canadian boundary at the 49th parallel.

Oregon Trail Route from the Missouri to the Columbia rivers, the main path of pioneer travel to the American West from 1843 to 1860. The trail was first used by explorers and fur traders, but in the early 1840s reports of the pleasant climate and rich soil of Oregon country began to attract settlers from the east. The first wagon train of emigrants reached Oregon in 1842, and in the 'great emigration' of 1843 more than 900 people made the 2000 mile (3200km) journey. Covered wagons in convoys of 100 set out from Independence or Westport on the Missouri river, crossed the Rockies, and drove alongside the Snake river, Blue Mountains and Columbia river to reach Oregon. With the coming of the railroads the trail fell into disuse, and by the 1870s it had been abandoned.

Organisation de l'Armée Secrète French terrorist 'Secret Army Organisation' that opposed ALGERIA's campaign for independence from France. The OAS was formed in Algeria in 1961 by a group of French army officers led by General Raoul Salan. Their attempted coup in Algiers in 1961 led to a campaign of terrorism and sabotage in Algeria and France, including a failed attempt to assassinate the French president Charles de Gaulle. The OAS collapsed in 1962 after the Franco-Algerian cease-fire in March, the capture of Salan, and Algerian independence in July. Salan was sentenced to life imprisonment, but was released in 1968.

Organisation for Economic Co-operation and Development Body of representatives of the world's advanced industrialised countries, based in Paris. The OECD was established in 1961 to promote economic growth and stability for its members and to help less developed countries to expand. It replaced the Organisation for European Economic Cooperation, formed in 1948 to administer the US-funded Marshall Plan (see MARSHALL, GEORGE) for the rebuilding of postwar Europe. Membership of the OECD has risen from 20 to 24. Each member receives an annual evaluation of its economy in terms of achievements and projections.

Organisation of African Unity African association to promote unity and solidarity, to coordinate political, economic, defence and social policies, and to eliminate colonialism in Africa. The organisation was established in 1963 at Addis Ababa in Ethiopia. It began with 32 members, but 51 African states belonged to the OAU by 1992.

Organisation of American States Association providing mutual defence and assistance for the countries of North, Central and South America. The OAS was established in April 1948 in Bogotá, Colombia, by the USA and 20 Latin American republics. In August 1961 it established the Alliance for Progress, a ten-year programme for economic development in Latin America initiated by President John F. KENNEDY. During the Cuban Missile Crisis of 1962 the OAS suspended Cuba's membership and supported the US blockade of the island. It also supported US intervention in the Dominican Republic in 1965, but not in the 1979 Nicaraguan revolution. The OAS functions as a regional agency of the United Nations, and in 1994 it had 35 members.

Organisation of Petroleum Exporting Countries Group of oil-rich countries, mainly in the Middle East, operating a cartel to control oil production and secure favourable prices for member nations.

The pioneers of the Oregon Trail journeyed in wagons across prairies, deserts, mountains and rivers, fending off disease and starvation to reach the fertile Willamette Valley six months later.

The neolithic inhabitants of the Orkney Islands left a legacy of standing stones such as the Ring of Brodgar (above) and the Unstan burial chambers (left) at Stenness.

OPEC's activities extend through all aspects of oil negotiations, including prices, royalty rates, production quotas and government profits. The first moves to create closer links between oil-producing countries were made in 1949 by Venezuela, Iran, Iraq, Kuwait and Saudi Arabia. The permanent organisation was set up in Venezuela in 1960. Other countries joined later.

In 1973 OPEC increased oil prices by 70 per cent during September and October, and by 130 per cent in December, partly for commercial reasons, but also to retaliate against the USA and other Western countries for supporting Israel in the Yom Kippur War against Egypt. The increases made some Arab states extremely rich and caused international shortages and inflation in oil-importing countries. Further increases between 1973 and 1980 caused the price of a barrel of crude oil to rise from US$3 to $30, with the result that oil-importing nations began to pursue other energy sources such as coal and nuclear power. Alternative oil suppliers also emerged, and conservation concerns encouraged a decrease in the demand for energy, making OPEC less effective. In 1994 total OPEC oil production was frozen at 24 520 000 barrels per day.

Orkney Islands Group of about 90 islands off the north coast of Scotland, about 20 of which are inhabited. The Orkney Islands were occupied during prehistoric times: the underground village of Skara Brae, which dates from about 2000 BC, is one of the most complete relics of the late Stone Age in Europe. Celtic missionaries arrived in the 7th century AD, and from about 800 the islands were settled by Norwegian Vikings.

In 875 the Orkneys were conquered by Harald I Fairhair of Norway and became a semiautonomous Norwegian earldom. After the death of the last Viking earl in 1231, the islands were ruled by a series of Scottish earls. In 1472 the Orkneys were annexed by the Scottish crown following the marriage of JAMES III and Margaret of Denmark. SCAPA FLOW, lying between the islands of Hoy and Mainland, was a major British naval base during the First and the Second World Wars.

Orlando, Vittorio Emanuele (1860-1952) Italian statesman, prime minister from 1917 to 1919. As minister of justice in 1915, Orlando supported Italy's entry into the First World War. He became prime minister in the crisis that followed Italy's humiliating defeat by Austro-German forces at the Battle of CAPORETTO. Two years later he clashed with the US president Woodrow Wilson at the Versailles Peace Conference. Wilson opposed Orlando's demands for the Allies to fulfil the 1915 Treaty of London, which had promised Italy territory in Dalmatia as compensation for entering the war. Orlando failed to gain British and French support, and resigned.

Initially a supporter of the Fascist leader Benito Mussolini, Orlando resigned from parliament in 1925 after the Fascists murdered Giacomo Matteotti, the leader of the Socialist Party. In 1943 Orlando came out of retirement, serving as first president of the Constituent Assembly from 1946 to 1947 before making an unsuccessful bid for the presidency in 1948, at the age of 88.

Orléans, Duc d' Title of the younger princes of the French royal houses of VALOIS and BOURBON. There were four lines of dukes. The title was first given in 1344 by PHILIP VI of France to his son Philippe de Valois (1336-75), who died without an heir. In 1392 Charles VI bestowed the duchy on his brother Louis I of Orléans (1372-1407), whose power struggle with his uncle Philip the Bold led to his assassination in 1407 by Philip's son, John the Fearless. Louis' grandson succeeded to the French throne as Louis XII in 1498, but died without issue. The throne then passed to his cousin Francis I, while the dukedom passed to Francis's descendants.

In 1626 the Bourbon king Louis XIII revived the title for his brother Jean-Baptiste-Gaston (1608-60). Gaston was involved in a series of conspiracies against the government, but was pardoned and became lord lieutenant of France under Louis XIV, his nephew. He was exiled for four years in 1652 for his part in the aristocratic rebellion known as the FRONDE.

The fourth dynasty was established in 1661 when Louis XIV gave the title to his younger brother Philippe I of Orléans (1640-1701), a notorious libertine who was excluded from state affairs. He was succeeded by his son Philippe II of Orléans (1674-1723), regent of France for the young king Louis XV from 1715 to 1723. His great-grandson, Louis Philippe Joseph, inherited the dukedom in 1785. A supporter of popular democracy, he was one of the liberal nobles who joined the Third Estate of the States General at the start of the French Revolution in 1789. In 1792 he took the name Philippe Egalité (Philip Equality) and voted for the execution of his cousin Louis XVI, but was suspected of wanting to become a constitutional monarch and was guillotined in 1793. In the JULY REVOLUTION of 1830 Philippe Egalité's eldest son was elected LOUIS-PHILIPPE I, King of the French, by the Chamber of Deputies. After he was deposed in 1848 his descendants became the Orléanist pretenders to the French throne. The line died out in 1926 when Louis-Philippe's great-grandson died without heirs.

Ormonde, James Butler, 1st Duke of (1610-88) Anglo-Irish nobleman and leading representative of royal authority in Ireland from 1641 to 1685. Ormonde was appointed a lieutenant general in the English army on the outbreak of the Irish Rebellion in 1641. Under the command of Charles I he fought for the Royalist cause in Ireland during the English Civil War. In 1644 he was appointed lord lieutenant of Ireland and given full discretionary powers to conclude a peace. Two weeks after he achieved this in January 1649, Charles I was executed and Ormonde proclaimed Charles II king of Ireland.

Defeated during Oliver Cromwell's brutal subjugation of the island from August 1649, Ormonde fled to the court-in-exile in Paris in December 1650 and was one of Charles II's closest advisers until the Restoration in 1660. As lord lieutenant of Ireland from 1662 to 1669 and from 1677 to 1684, Ormonde encouraged Irish trade. In 1685 he proclaimed James II king, but his loyalty was tested by James's pro-Catholic policies.

Ormonde, James Butler, 2nd Duke of (1665-1745) Irish general who acceded to his title in 1688 on the death of his grandfather, the 1st Duke of Ormonde. He supported William III in the GLORIOUS REVOLUTION of

1688, which deposed the Catholic James II, and during Queen Anne's reign he became one of the most powerful men in England, serving as lord lieutenant of Ireland from 1703 to 1707 and from 1710 to 1713. In 1711 he was appointed commander in chief of British forces in the War of the SPANISH SUCCESSION. Ormonde opposed the Hanoverian succession to the English throne and was removed from his command by George I. Impeached for treason in 1715, Ormonde fled to France and joined the unsuccessful Jacobite rising of that year. He spent the rest of his life in exile.

Orsini, Felice (1819-58) Italian revolutionary guillotined for his attempt to assassinate the French emperor Napoleon III. During the Italian REVOLUTIONS OF 1848 Orsini was a follower of Giuseppe MAZZINI, leader of the RISORGIMENTO movement to unify Italy and free it from its French and Austrian rulers. When a republic was briefly established in Rome in 1848, Orsini was elected to the Constituent Assembly. The following year he took part in defending the city, but after the republic was crushed by French troops he became an agent for Mazzini in Switzerland, Hungary and England.

Orsini was imprisoned in Mantua in 1855 for his revolutionary activities, but a year later he escaped to England, where he wrote two accounts of his experiences. In 1858 he went to Paris where, on January 14, he threw a bomb underneath the carriage of Napoleon III in revenge for the emperor's betrayal of the Italian cause. Napoleon was unhurt, but ten people died and many others were wounded. Orsini was sentenced to death. While in prison, he appealed to the emperor to help free Italy. Napoleon, who had been pro-Italian

during his youth, was influenced by the plea, and subsequently helped to expel Austria from Lombardy from 1859 to 1860.

Orthodox Church Group of Churches, also known as the Eastern Orthodox Church, which together with Roman Catholicism and Protestantism forms one of the main branches of Christianity. It includes the Greek and Russian Orthodox Churches, as well as Churches in Eastern Europe and the Middle East, all of whom are self-governing, although they recognise the honorary primacy of the patriarch of Constantinople.

The division of the Christian Church began when the Roman Empire was split into Eastern and Western empires in AD 276. In 330 CONSTANTINE I moved his capital from Rome to Constantinople, which became the centre of Christianity in the East. The fall of the Western Roman Empire in 476 increased the division between Constantinople and Rome. The Western Church developed along Latin lines, while the Eastern Church retained its Greek heritage. The word orthodox, from the Greek *orthodoxos*, 'of the right opinion' and 'giving the right glory', was current from 753.

During the 9th century, missionaries and emigrants began to spread the Orthodox Church to Eastern Europe. In 988 the Russian Orthodox Church originated in KIEV and now contains the majority of the estimated 150 million members of the Orthodox Church worldwide. From the 9th century, conflict between the two Churches increased. The final rift, known as the EAST-WEST SCHISM, occurred in 1054 with the mutual excommunications of Pope Leo IX and Michael Cerularius, the patriarch of Constantinople. The immediate reason for the break was a change by the Western Church to the statement of faith known as the Nicene Creed, issued by the Council of NICAEA in 325. This added the word *filioque*, meaning 'And the Son', to read 'the Holy Ghost... who proceedeth from the Father and the Son', rather than from the Father alone. The Eastern Church also refused to accept that the pope had the power to

make unilateral decisions about the doctrine and government of the Church. The rift increased during the Crusades, when the Crusaders occupied Constantinople from 1204 to 1261. Attempts at forging a reunion in 1274 and 1439 both failed. In 1965 the excommunications were lifted, and there has since been some rapprochement between the Churches.

Orthodox rituals, known as the Greek rite, differ from rituals in other branches of the Christian Church. There is no instrumental music, and rites are commonly celebrated in archaic forms of the local language, such as Old Slavonic. Clergy below the rank of bishop are allowed to marry.

Osborne judgment (1909) British ruling outlawing the trade-union political levy. In 1909 the Liberal trade unionist W. V. Osborne brought an action against the trade-union practice of using part of its subscriptions to pay salaries to Labour Members of Parliament. At that time MPs received no parliamentary salary, although this was remedied in 1911. Judges in the House of Lords found in favour of Osborne, a decision that threatened to undermine the political activities of the unions and the Labour Party.

The 1913 Trade Union Act authorised unions to have a political fund, but subscriptions to it were optional, members being able to 'contract out'. In 1984 a further Trade Union Act ruled that any trade union with a political fund should ballot its members every ten years in order to decide whether the fund should be maintained.

Osman I (1259-1326) Founder of the OTTOMAN EMPIRE in about 1299. Born in Bythnia, Osman was the son of a border chief. He turned his band of Turkish nomads from raiding to permanent conquest. In 1290 he declared his independence from his Seljuk Turk overlords and in about 1299 declared himself emir of a small state in north-west Anatolia. As the power of the Seljuk dynasty declined, Osman and his Muslim warriors appropriated territory from the BYZANTINE EMPIRE. In 1326 he captured the Bythnian city of Bursa, which became the empire's first capital. The Osmanli, or Ottoman, dynasty continued with Osman's son Orkhan, who took the title of sultan.

Ostpolitik German term meaning 'policy towards the East', used in West Germany in the early 1970s to describe the opening of relations with the Eastern bloc. The policy was a reversal of the 1955 Hallstein Doctrine, which asserted that West Germany would

An essential part of worship in the Orthodox Church is the veneration of icons, such as this one of God the Father.

sever diplomatic relations with any country, except the Soviet Union, that recognised East Germany's independence. Ostpolitik was vigorously pursued by the West German politician Willy BRANDT, both as foreign minister and as chancellor. In 1970 West Germany recognised the ODER-NEISSE LINE marking East Germany's frontier with Poland. Two years later the General Relations Treaty normalised relations between the two Germanys.

ostracism Method of banishing unpopular citizens in ATHENS during the 5th century BC. The aim of ostracism was to curb tyranny. Each year the Athenian assembly voted on whether or not it wanted an ostracism, which would be held two months later. Every citizen who wished to take part wrote a name on a shard of pottery known as an *ostrakon*. Provided that at least 6000 valid *ostraka* were counted, the man with the most votes against him had to leave the state of Attica for ten years, although he did not lose his citizenship or his property. Ostracism often functioned as a vote of confidence for the policies of the most powerful rival of the man ostracised. Such trials of political strength were most notable in the ostracisms of the statesman and naval commander Themistocles in around 471, and of Pericles' rival, the politician Thucydides, in 443. The practice of ostracism ceased around 416.

Ostrogoths see GOTHS

Oswald, St (c.605-42) Ruler of the English kingdom of NORTHUMBRIA from 633. In 616 Oswald fled to the Hebridean island of Iona after his father, Ethelfrith, first ruler of a united Northumbria, was killed in battle and replaced by Edwin, the son of King Aelle of the Northumbrian kingdom of Deira. After Edwin's defeat by CADWALLON of Gwynedd and PENDA of Mercia in 632, Oswald returned and in 633 he gained control of Northumbria by killing Cadwallon in battle near Hexham in present-day Northumberland.

Oswald, who had become a Christian during his exile, then invited St AIDAN and his missionaries from Iona in order to convert Northumbria to Christianity. For a few years Oswald's military successes made him overlord of other kingdoms; he was one of the seven 'overkings' said by the historian Bede to have exercised power over many of the kingdoms south of the River Humber. Killed at the Battle of Maserfelth – possibly present-day Oswestry – by the pagan king Penda, Oswald was venerated as a Christian martyr soon after his death.

Oswald, Lee Harvey (1939-63) Supposed assassin of US president John F. KENNEDY at Dallas, Texas, on November 22, 1963. An ex-marine and a communist sympathiser,

Jack Ruby shoots Lee Harvey Oswald (centre). Was Oswald silenced to stop him from revealing details of a conspiracy to kill Kennedy?

Oswald lived in the Soviet Union from 1959 to 1962. Two hours after the assassination of President Kennedy while driving in a motorcade through Dallas, Oswald was arrested for the murder of a police officer. On November 23 he was also charged with shooting the president from the sixth floor of the Texas State School Book Depository, Oswald's own workplace. Oswald protested his innocence, claiming that he was a scapegoat, but the following day he was killed by nightclub owner Jack Ruby in Dallas police headquarters. The Warren Commission of 1964 concluded that Oswald had acted on his own. In 1979 the House Assassination Committee confirmed that Kennedy was killed by a shot fired from Oswald's rifle. The evidence has been repeatedly re-examined amid rumours linking Oswald and Ruby to Cuban exiles, the Mafia and the American secret services.

Oswy (c.612-70) Ruler of the English kingdom of NORTHUMBRIA from 651 until his death, also known as Oswiu. After the death of Oswy's brother OSWALD in 642, Northumbria was divided into its two original kingdoms of Bernicia and Deira. Only after he had killed the king of Deira did Oswy of Bernicia reunite the two. In 655, at the Battle of the Winwaed near Leeds, Oswy defeated the Mercian king PENDA to become overlord of many of the kingdoms south of the Humber. Two years later he lost Mercia to Penda's son Wulfhere. Oswy spread Christianity to Mercia and Essex and in 664 summoned the Synod of WHITBY to decide between Roman and Celtic Church usage. He accepted St Wilfrid's arguments in favour of Rome.

Otis, James (1725-83) American lawyer who led the radical opposition to British colonial rule in Massachusetts. Otis achieved fame in 1760 by resigning his position as advocate general of the Vice Admiralty Court in protest against writs of assistance – general search warrants allowing royal customs officials to search houses for smuggled goods without having to show cause. Despite an impassioned argument that such writs violated the colonials' natural rights, Otis lost the case, but in 1761 he became leader of the radical forces in the Massachusetts provincial assembly. He led the colonial protest against the 1765 STAMP ACT, which taxed items such as newspapers and legal documents, but he did not advocate

a complete break with Britain. A fight with a British officer in 1769 brought an end to Otis's career: he suffered head injuries that brought on fits of madness for the rest of his life. He died after being struck by lightning.

Ottawa Agreements Series of agreements on tariffs and trade between Britain and its Dominions, concluded at the 1932 Imperial Economic Conference in Ottawa, Canada, at the height of the Great Depression. In 1931 Britain began to tax food imports from outside the empire, but allowed quotas of meat, wheat, dairy goods and fruit from the dominions to enter the country free of duty. In the Ottawa Agreements the UK promised continued free entry for most empire goods and tariffs on certain food and metal imports. In return, the Dominions granted tariff benefits to imported British produce unless it was to the detriment of their own goods.

The agreement was not officially renewed after its initial five-year period, but continued after 1937. The economic gains of this 'imperial preference' policy were helpful but not huge. In 1947 the GENERAL AGREEMENT ON TARIFFS AND TRADE prohibited any extension of the preferences. Parts of the policy were in force until Britain joined the European Economic Community in 1973.

Otterburn, Battle of (August 5, 1388) Scottish victory over the English at the village of Otterburn in Northumberland. A Scottish raiding force led by the earls of Douglas, Moray and March was attacked by Sir Henry PERCY, known as Hotspur. The Scots captured Percy and his brother, but Douglas was killed. English control of the north was jeopardised for years afterwards. The battle was immortalised in the English ballad 'Chevy Chase'. The Scottish version is 'The Ballad of Otterburn'. These later ballads present the battle as the climax of a private feud between the Percy and Douglas families.

Otto I 'the Great' (912-73) King of Germany from 936 until his death, crowned emperor at Rome (see HOLY ROMAN EMPIRE) in 962. After his election as king of Germany on the death in 936 of his father, HENRY I, known as 'the Fowler', Otto defeated the independent dukes of southern Germany in a three-year war. Afterwards he used members of his own family and churchmen to govern the realm. At the same time he extended Germany's frontiers, bringing Bohemia and Burgundy under German control by 950.

In 951 Otto marched on Italy to defeat the Italian king Berengar II, and crowned himself king of the Lombards. His Italian campaign ended in 954 when he was forced to contend with a revolt in Germany led by his son Liudolf. The rebellion was suppressed in 955, thereby freeing Otto to defend Germany from MAGYAR invaders, whom he defeated decisively at Lechfeld, near Augsburg, in August.

Otto again invaded Italy in 961, following a request from Pope John XII for his help against Berengar II. Arriving in Rome on February 2, 962, Otto was crowned emperor – a title that had lapsed since 924 – by the grateful pope. On February 13 they concluded the *Privilegium Ottonianum* to regulate relations between pope and emperor. In 963, afraid that the emperor had become too powerful, John XII turned against Otto, who replaced him with Leo VIII.

Two years later Leo's death led to a Roman revolt, and in 966 Otto was forced to invade Italy again. By 972 he had subdued Rome and advanced as far as the Byzantine-controlled south of Italy, where he arranged for his son, the future Otto II, to marry Theophanu, a Byzantine princess. Otto's reign was noted for the flowering of culture and learning in the 'Ottonian Renaissance', which was fostered by the imperial court.

Otto III (980-1002) King of Germany from 983 and emperor from 996 until his death. Otto's mother, Theophanu, and then his grandmother ruled as regent until he came of age in 996. Otto had ambitions of re-creating the glory and power of the old Roman Empire with himself as leader of world Christianity. To control the papacy he installed his cousin as Gregory V, and then his tutor as Sylvester II. His short life was torn between periods of intense religious devotion – he lived in a monastery for a year – and dreams of secular power wielded from Rome, where he lived in Byzantine splendour. His attempt to make Rome his capital failed, however, and he was forced out by the Romans in 1001. Otto was preparing to retake the city when he died.

Ottoman Empire Turkish Muslim empire that ruled large parts of the Middle East and Europe from the 14th century to the 20th century. The Ottoman Empire was founded in north-west Anatolia by OSMAN I around 1299 from territories ruled by the Seljuk Turks. The early expansion of the empire in the 14th century during the reigns of Osman I, Orkhan, Murad I and Beyazid I was achieved chiefly at the expense of the BYZANTINE EMPIRE, but Ottoman victories at KOSOVO in 1389 and NICOPOLIS in 1396 also placed large parts of the Balkans under Ottoman rule. Under Mehmed II, who ruled from 1451 to 1481, the Byzantine Empire was brought to an end after its capital, Constantinople (present-day Istanbul), fell to the Ottomans in 1453 and became the Ottoman capital. Ottoman rule was also extended over Serbia, Trebizond in Greece, Albania and the Crimea. The basis of Ottoman success was its military organisation. In a system known as the *devşirme*, 'collecting', the army's senior ranks were recruited from subject Christian families of the Balkans. Conscripts were converted to the Muslim faith, and received strict training before they entered the sipahis (cavalry) or the elite JANISSARIES (infantry).

Ottoman expansion reached its peak during the 16th century under SELIM I from 1512 to 1520, and SULEIMAN I from 1520 to 1566. Selim annexed parts of Persia in 1515, and between 1516 and 1518 conquered Syria, Palestine, Egypt and Algeria. Most of ARMENIA also came under Ottoman control. After the conquest of Egypt, Selim assumed the title of caliph – spiritual and secular head of Islam – a title held by Ottoman sultans until 1924. During the golden age of Suleiman the Magnificent the empire expanded as far as Hungary, Iraq and Libya, while the Ottoman navy dominated the eastern Mediterranean.

Decline set in after Suleiman's death. The first blow came in 1571 when the Ottoman navy was defeated by Christian forces at the Battle of LEPANTO. With no accepted line of succession, the rule of each new sultan was marked by rivalry and bloodshed, while the powerful clergy and janissaries became corrupt. Rule was usually exercised by ministers known as grand VIZIERS.

The empire's decline continued in the 17th century and accelerated in the 18th century due to the breakdown of central authority, increased internal unrest and widespread famine. Despite his policy of reform, Selim III (1761-1808) was unable to stop the decline. New European technology rarely reached the empire, and by the 19th century it was known as 'the Sick Man of Europe'. Greece was lost in 1832 as a result of the GREEK WAR OF INDEPENDENCE, while the Russo-Turkish War of 1877 to 1878 led to the Congress of Berlin, in which the empire abandoned all claims over Romania, Serbia, Montenegro, Bulgaria and Cyprus. In 1876 Abdülhamid II agreed to a Western-style constitution, the first in any Islamic country. Elections to the new parliament were held in 1877, but the following year both parliament and the constitution were suspended indefinitely.

The reformist and nationalist YOUNG TURKS movement began in the late 19th century, and in 1908 led a rebellion to restore the 1876 constitution. The following year, the restored parliament deposed the sultan and put Mehmed V on the throne. In 1913 the Young Turk leader ENVER PASHA seized control of the government. During the Balkan Wars of 1912 to 1913 the empire lost almost all its territory in Europe, and by the end of the First World War, which it joined on Germany's side, the empire had collapsed. It was formally ended in 1920 with the Treaty of Sèvres. In 1922 the last sultan, Mehmed VI, was overthrown, and the Republic of TURKEY proclaimed under Mustafa Kemal ATATÜRK.

Oudenaarde, Battle of (July 11, 1708) Victory for allied British, Dutch and Austrian troops during the War of the SPANISH SUCCESSION. At the Flemish town of Oudenaarde, now in Belgium, the allied commanders EUGÈNE OF SAVOY and John Churchill, Duke of MARLBOROUGH, joined armies, forcing the French under the Duke of Vendôme to fight. It was Marlborough's third great victory after Blenheim in 1704 and Ramillies in 1706, and led to the capture of Lille.

The Ottoman sultan Selim III, guarded by a janissary and an attendant, was a poet and composer. He was murdered by his nephew, Mustapha IV.

outback Colloquial Australian term for the vast inland country well away from the centres of population. The Bigge inquiry of 1819-21 recommended that poor settlers and emancipists – those arguing in favour of rights for former convicts – should be excluded from taking up land. In 1829 a vain effort was made to forbid land settlement beyond the original 'Nineteen Counties' around Sydney. Anybody going beyond this boundary would be an illegal SQUATTER. But as the demand for wool grew, so did the number of squatters pressing farther inland. In 1836 a £10 annual licence fee gave them rights over any tract of land on which they were already grazing sheep, and sheep farming became the major industry of the outback. Its other commercial enterprises are cattle and minerals.

Outremer Old French name for the Crusader states, 'the land overseas'. The Latin Kingdom of JERUSALEM was established in Palestine after Jerusalem was captured by the Crusaders in 1099. Godfrey of Bouillon was appointed 'Protector of the Holy Sepulchre', but after his sudden death in 1100 his brother and successor, BALDWIN I, took the title of king. Baldwin and his successors also became nominal overlords of the counties of Edessa (1098-1144) and Tripoli (1109-1289) and of the principality of Antioch (1098-1268).

Western customs and forms of government were imposed on the Jewish and Muslim populations. Latin clergy were installed, followed by monastic orders. Fighting brotherhoods of KNIGHTS were established, including the Knights Templars – 'soldiers of Christ' who were devoted to the defence of the Holy Land. Until the mid 12th century the king of Jerusalem had considerable power, but this was later weakened by noble revolts and rivalry over the succession. Muslim armies under the generals Nur al-Din and SALADIN united against the invaders, and in 1187 Jerusalem fell following the Christian defeat at the Battle of Hattin.

Overbury, Sir Thomas (1581-1613) English poet and victim of court intrigue. In 1606 Overbury became secretary and adviser to James I's favourite, Robert Carr. In 1611 Overbury opposed Carr's plans to marry Frances Howard, the divorced wife of the 3rd Earl of Essex. This earned the king's displeasure, and the powerful Howards imprisoned him in the Tower of London. He died there after being slowly poisoned, probably on the orders of Frances Howard. Three months later, Carr, now Earl of Somerset, married Frances. In 1615 suspicions arose over Overbury's death. The Somersets were tried and sentenced to death for the crime, but were pardoned by James. The episode damaged the reputation of both king and court, especially in the eyes of the Puritans.

In the outback, the demand for wool led to the development of vast sheep stations covering many thousands of acres, and rich pastoralists became a powerful force in Australian society.

Owen, Robert (1771-1858) British social reformer and industrialist, one of the founders of English socialism. In 1800 Owen took over the New Lanark textile mills in Scotland and proceeded to create a model community for his employees. He reduced working hours and provided better housing, and in 1816 established the first infant school in Britain. From 1817 Owen advocated 'villages of unity and cooperation' in which the unemployed would be mutually self-supporting instead of relying on poor relief. Between 1825 and 1839 he established such villages in Scotland, Ireland, England and the United States.

Although the communities lived harmoniously, they were unsuccessful, as differences arose over methods of administration and religious beliefs. In 1834 Owen helped to found the Grand National Consolidated Trades Union, which aimed to break the capitalist system with a general strike. After the government retaliated by prosecuting the TOLPUDDLE MARTYRS for forming a trade union, Owen withdrew and the union collapsed in October. He spent the rest of his life campaigning and writing.

Oxenstierna, Axel, Count (1583-1654) Swedish statesman. Oxenstierna joined the council of state in 1609. In 1611 he persuaded the young king GUSTAV II to agree to the Accession Charter, which limited royal power. The following year Gustavus appointed him chancellor, beginning 20 years of close collaboration that temporarily ended the rivalry between the Crown and the nobility, and allowed them to reform all aspects of Swedish life. Oxenstierna was also a skilful diplomat, negotiating favourable peace treaties with Denmark in 1613 and Poland in 1629. Despite his opposition to Sweden's entry into the THIRTY YEARS' WAR in 1630, he joined the king in Germany the following year. After Gustavus's death at the Battle of Lützen in 1632, Oxenstierna assumed supreme command of the Swedish forces, continuing the fighting until favourable terms were obtained in the Treaty of WESTPHALIA in 1648. During Queen CHRISTINA's minority, Oxenstierna led the council of regency and became virtual ruler. Their relations were not always harmonious, especially after Christina came of age in 1644, but Oxenstierna remained in control until his death.

Oxford Movement see NEWMAN, JOHN HENRY

Pacific, War of the (1879-84) Conflict pitting Chile against Bolivia and Peru for control of Bolivia's nitrate-rich north Atacama Desert. In 1879 Bolivia revoked an agreement with Chile not to raise taxes on Chilean mining interests in the Atacama Desert. Chile retaliated by occupying Antofagasta, Bolivia's Pacific port. Bolivia declared war on Chile, calling on Peru for help, but with its superior land and sea forces Chile quickly won control of Atacama, Bolivia's only coastal province. Chile also captured Peru's capital, Lima, in 1881. In 1883 a humiliated Peru signed over its southernmost provinces to its invader. After ceding its coastal territory to Chile in a truce in 1884, Bolivia was left landlocked.

Pacific campaigns (1941-5) Series of naval and land battles between the Allies and Japan fought in the Far East and the Pacific during the Second World War. In December 1941 Japanese aircraft bombed the US naval base at PEARL HARBOR, bringing the USA into the Second World War. The American colonies of Guam and Wake Island fell soon after, closely followed by the British colonies of Hong Kong, Malaya and Singapore. The Japanese won the Battle of the Java Sea in February 1942, moving on into the Dutch East Indies (Indonesia) to threaten Australia. By May, Japan had forced the British out of Burma (Myanmar) and the Americans from the Philippines. By cracking Japanese naval codes the US learned of plans to take Port Moresby in Papua New Guinea. In June, the Battle of Midway ended Japanese naval supremacy.

US Admiral Chester Nimitz and General Douglas MACARTHUR, commander of Allied forces in the south-west Pacific, devised a plan to retake the smaller islands and bypass the heavily occupied ones, moving closer to Japan and cutting off its supply routes. In August 1942 US marines landed on Guadalcanal and Tulagi in the Solomon Islands for the first major Allied land offensive in the Pacific. After six months the Japanese evacuated Guadalcanal, having lost more than 24000 men. The Allies lost only 1600, with 4250 wounded, and made Guadalcanal their base.

The Japanese suffered a heavy defeat in the Battle of the Philippine Sea in June 1944, and in July the USA captured the Mariana Islands. The Battle of Leyte Gulf in October effectively ended Japanese naval power. On the mainland, the BURMA CAMPAIGNS succeeded in reopening land communication with China in January 1945. US forces had reoccupied the islands of OKINAWA by June, and Iwo Jima in the face of fierce KAMIKAZE attacks. Japan surrendered after the US dropped an atomic bomb on HIROSHIMA on August 6, 1945, and one on NAGASAKI three days later.

Pagan Ancient city and place of pilgrimage on the Irrawaddy River in central Burma (present-day MYANMAR). Founded around AD 849, Pagan was originally populated by people from the north. By the 11th century they had conquered the rest of Burma, and Pagan was made the capital. Theravada BUDDHISM spread to the city and magnificent shrines and monasteries were built over the next 200 years. In 1287 Pagan was captured by Mongol hordes of the Chinese emperor KUBLAI KHAN. After looters from the east ransacked the city in 1299 it never recovered its importance. In 1975 an earthquake destroyed or damaged many historic buildings.

Paine, Thomas (1737-1809) Revolutionary British writer and political theorist. After losing his job as an excise officer in 1772 over demands for higher wages, Paine went to the American colonies in 1774. In 1776 he wrote the radical pamphlet *Common Sense* which justified American demands for independence. A best seller, it played an important part in boosting American morale during the War of Independence. In 1787 Paine returned to England and in 1791 published the first part of his masterpiece, *The Rights of Man*, a reply to the British politician Edmund Burke's *Reflections on the Revolution in France*, which denounced the changes happening there. The following year the second part of *The Rights of Man* suggested practical policies to help governments to achieve democracy, and it called for the overthrow of the monarchy. It also recommended free education, old age pensions and income and wealth taxes. Paine's theories stimulated the development of the LONDON CORRESPONDING SOCIETY, the first working-class political movement.

In 1792 Paine fled to France to escape arrest for treason. He was elected to the revolutionary National Convention, which campaigned for the abolition of the monarchy. Paine opposed the execution of Louis XVI and suggested that he should be banished instead. In 1793 he opposed the Reign of Terror and was

The free-thinker Thomas Paine's book *The Rights of Man* is commemorated by this inscribed medal.

imprisoned by the revolutionary leader Robespierre for a year under threat of the guillotine. While in prison Paine wrote the second part of *The Age of Reason*, an attack on organised religion. After his return to the USA in 1802 he was shunned as an atheist and died a social outcast.

Pakistan Muslim country in southern Asia, formerly West Pakistan. From 1906 the Muslims of British India, led by Muhammad Ali JINNAH of the Muslim League, demanded a separate state because they feared increasing Hindu domination. Pakistan was created in 1947 when Britain decided to end its control of the Indian subcontinent. The new nation comprised two regions on either side of India. West Pakistan included the provinces of the North-west Frontier, while East Bengal became East Pakistan. India kept Muslim-dominated KASHMIR.

Widespread rioting followed partition. About a million people died as 7 to 8 million Hindus and Sikhs left Pakistan for India, and a similar number of Muslims moved to Pakistan. Prime Minister LIAQAT ALI KHAN's plans for a liberal constitution were opposed by orthodox Muslims, and he was assassinated in 1951. The Muslim League lost the 1952 general election in East Pakistan to the Awami League, which sought autonomy for the East. In 1956 a new constitution declared Pakistan an Islamic republic, with a parliament representing East and West. With the failure of the multiparty system in 1958, President Iskander Mirza imposed martial law under General AYUB KHAN, who quickly took the presidency for himself. His decade of autocracy led to economic growth but also

Observed from a US aircraft carrier during the Pacific campaigns in 1944, a Japanese plane plunges towards the sea.

resentment between the two regions. Bengalis in the East, believing that the West was taking an unfair share of the state's assets, increasingly supported the Awami League. Discontent and rioting forced Ayub to resign in 1969. In the 1970 general election the Islamic socialist Pakistan People's Party (PPP), led by Zulfikar Ali BHUTTO, took the majority of votes in West Pakistan, while the Awami League won overall. Civil war broke out over the future of East Pakistan. With Indian help, Bengali dissidents defeated a Pakistani army in 1971 and established the new state of BANGLADESH.

After becoming prime minister in 1973, Bhutto became increasingly autocratic and in 1977 a military coup placed General ZIA UL-HAQ in power. Zia committed Pakistan to an Islamic code. Martial law was officially lifted in 1985, with Zia promising a return to democracy, but he held on to power until his death in 1988. The general election held in November of that year was won by the PPP, led by Benazir BHUTTO. Her government collapsed in 1990 following charges of corruption, but she regained power in 1993. Against a background of ethnic and sectarian violence in major cities, Benazir faced opposition from her estranged brother, Murtaza, when he formed a breakaway faction in 1995.

Palaeolithic era Earliest period of the STONE AGES, characterised by flaked stone tools. The term often includes all human existence as scavenger, hunter-gatherer and maker of tools before and during the last Ice Age. The longest stage of human cultural development, from 2.5 million to 10 000 years ago, the era is divided into three phases, Lower, Middle and Upper. Flaked stone fragments have been discovered at Olduvai Gorge in Tanzania, where some of the earliest stone tools of the Lower Palaeolithic era were unearthed. Called Oldowan tools after the location of their discovery, they were found alongside fossils of *Homo habilis*, an apelike creature dating from about 2 million years ago and believed to be the earliest ancestor of the human race. More advanced hand axes and cleavers were used from 1.5 million years ago for more than a million years by *Homo erectus*, the first human-like creature to stand upright. In the Middle Palaeolithic era, beginning around 150 000 to 125 000 years ago, a greater variety of stone tools were made by Neanderthal people and their contemporaries (see feature, page 444).

Palatinate Major principality of the HOLY ROMAN EMPIRE in Germany, divided into the Lower and Upper Palatinates. In 1156 the Holy Roman Emperor FREDERICK I bestowed the title of count palatine on his brother Conrad, who held lands east and west of the River Rhine. In 1214 this region passed to the Wittelsbach family, whose lands in Bavaria

became the Upper Palatinate. The count palatine of the Rhine was the empire's most important prince and from 1356 was one of the electors who chose the emperor. During the 16th and 17th centuries the REFORMATION centred on the Palatinates. The election of Count Palatine Frederick V as king of Bohemia in 1619 intensified the THIRTY YEARS' WAR, with the Palatinates becoming a major battleground. Frederick lost the Upper Palatinate to Bavaria, and in 1648 the Treaty of Westphalia gave the Lower Palatinate to Frederick's son, Charles Louis. Forty years later Louis XIV invaded and devastated the Lower Palatinate in the War of the Grand Alliance. More divisions followed, including France taking land west of the Rhine in 1797. The 1815 Congress of Vienna split the Palatinate between Prussia, Bavaria, Hesse-Darmstadt and Hesse-Nassau. After the Second World War the state of Rhineland-Palatinate was created.

pale Fourteenth-century term for a distinct area of jurisdiction. In Latin *palus* means 'stake' and the original medieval pales were usually enclosed by a wooden palisade, fence or ditch. The most important pale controlled by England was in eastern Ireland and was a large area conquered by Henry II in 1171-2. It remained in force until the conquest of Ireland under Elizabeth I. England also established pales around Calais from 1347 to 1558 and in Scotland in Tudor times. Catherine the Great created a Jewish pale in 1792 in lands annexed from Poland. Until the 1860s Jews were forbidden to live or travel outside the area, which included much of the Ukraine, Belarus, Lithuania and Russian Poland.

Palestine Country on the east coast of the Mediterranean, occupied in Biblical times by the kingdoms of Judah and Israel. Also known as the Holy Land, Palestine is sacred to Jews, Christians and Muslims. The name derives from Palaistina or Philistia, the land of the PHILISTINES, who arrived in the 12th century BC, joining the Canaanites who had lived there since 2000 BC. The Hebrews, who believed that the region had been promised to them by God and that they had been led into the land by Moses, came partly under the control of the Philistines until around 1000 BC, when they set up an independent kingdom. After the death of their king Solomon in 922 BC they split into two kingdoms, Israel and Judah. Israel was defeated by the Assyrians in 722, and Judah in 586 by NEBUCHADNEZZAR II, who destroyed Jerusalem and exiled its inhabitants to Babylon. In 536 the Persian emperor CYRUS II overthrew the Babylonians, freeing the Jews from their exile.

The Jews became independent again in 168 BC, when the Jewish Maccabee dynasty rebelled against the Seleucids, ruling until the Romans invaded in 63 BC. The HEROD dynasty controlled parts of Palestine until the Jewish Revolt broke out in AD 66. During Roman rule Palestine became Christian after the empire was converted under the emperor Theodosius in 380. In 641 the country was conquered by Arabs. In 1095 a conflict between the Seljuk Turks and the Byzantines halted pilgrimages to the

State of Israel under UN partition plan 1947
State of Israel after War of Independence 1948
Israeli conquests during Six-Day War 1967
Israeli front line 1973 (Yom Kippur War)
area returned to Egypt 1981
area and town granted Palestinian self-rule 1995

The territory which formed Palestine has been partitioned in many ways since 1947 following the series of wars between the Jewish state of Israel and its Arab neighbours.

In July 1994 the PLO leader Yasser Arafat arrives in the Gaza Strip to a hero's welcome after negotiating Palestinian self-rule.

Holy Land. Pope Urban II reacted by calling the First Crusade. In 1099 the Crusaders captured Jerusalem, massacring its inhabitants and establishing the Latin Kingdom of Jerusalem, or OUTREMER. It was later controlled by the Mamelukes and, from 1516, by the Ottoman Turks.

Palestine remained part of the OTTOMAN EMPIRE until 1918, when Turkish and German forces were defeated by the British. Land west of the River Jordan became officially known as Palestine and was made a British mandate in 1920. This was officially accepted by the League of Nations in 1922 in order to help to implement the 1917 BALFOUR DECLARATION which promised support for a Jewish homeland in Palestine. Jewish immigration intensified, leading to a war between Arabs and Jews in 1936. The flood of incoming Jews at the end of the Second World War led to increased tension. In 1948 Britain ended the mandate and Israel was established. The Arab-Israeli War that followed from 1948 to 1949 led to Palestine losing its political identity and being divided between Israel, Egypt, which occupied the Gaza Strip, and Jordan, which took over the West Bank of the Jordan.

After the 1967 Six-Day War with Egypt, Syria and Jordan, Israel dominated the West Bank, the Gaza Strip, Sinai and the strategic Golan Heights on the border with Syria. Attempts to achieve a settlement between the Arabs and Israelis failed as the PALESTINE LIBERATION ORGANISATION and most Arab countries refused to recognise Israel's right to exist, and Israel would not negotiate with what it considered to be a terrorist group. In 1978 however, under the terms of the CAMP DAVID ACCORD, Israel withdrew from captured Egyptian territory but anti-Israeli violence continued in the remaining occupied

territories, culminating in an *intifada*, 'uprising', by Palestinians in January 1988. That year Jordan withdrew its claim to the West Bank and the PLO declared an independent Palestinian authority there, while recognising Israel's right to exist.

Peace negotiations began to progress in 1992 when a Labour-led coalition came to power in Israel. A year later the Washington Accords were signed, agreeing to PLO recognition of Israel in return for Palestinian self-rule in the Gaza Strip and Jericho. The Accords were implemented in 1995. In 1996 Yasser ARAFAT became the first elected president of the Palestinian National Authority.

Palestine Liberation Organisation

Organisation, also known as the PLO, formed in 1964 to unite Palestinian Arab groups opposed to the Israeli occupation of PALESTINE. From 1967 the PLO was dominated by al-Fatah, the largest and richest faction of the group, and its leader Yasser ARAFAT became chairman in 1969. The PLO was based in Jordan, but its aim of establishing a state of Palestine conflicted with Jordan's desire to regain control of the West Bank. Civil war between the guerrillas and the army broke out in 1970, ending with the PLO moving to Lebanon and Syria. Splinter groups of activists such as the BLACK SEPTEMBER terrorists were responsible for kidnappings, hijackings and political murders.

In 1974 the PLO was recognised by the Arab nations and the UN General Assembly as the representative of all Palestinians. Two years later it became a full member of the Arab League. Driven from its Beirut headquarters by the Israelis in 1982, the PLO was dispersed throughout the Arab world. In 1988 Arafat persuaded the movement to renounce violence. After Jordan severed its links with the West Bank, the PLO declared the area a Palestinian state and recognised the state of Israel. Arafat was made president in 1989 and the PLO gained international acceptance as a government-in-exile. In 1992 it took part in the US-sponsored Middle East peace talks. After Arafat secretly met the Israeli prime minister Yitzhak Rabin in Oslo, the two leaders signed the Washington Accords in 1993. Palestinian self-rule in the West Bank and Gaza Strip was implemented in 1995, with Arafat elected chairman of the Palestinian National Authority the following year.

Palladio, Andrea (1508-80) The Italian

Renaissance architect whose style, inspired by the temples of ancient Rome, has been a major influence on Western architecture. Born Andrea di Pietro in Padua, he started out as a stonemason but in the 1530s became the protégé of Count Gian Giorgio Trissino. Trissino gave him the name of Palladio and took him to study in Rome. In 1554 Palladio

wrote *The Antiquities of Rome*, which was used as a standard guide for two centuries. His career coincided with the desire of great families around Vicenza to build palaces in the city and villas in the countryside. His most famous, begun in 1566, is the Villa Rotonda near Vicenza, a square, domed building with a portico in the shape of a Roman temple front on each of its sides. His fame spread to the rest of Europe with the publication in 1570 of his *Four Books of Architecture*. His style, which became known as Palladian, influenced architects for centuries to come.

Palmerston, Henry, 3rd Viscount

(1784-1865) British statesman whose career included serving as secretary of war, foreign secretary and prime minister. He entered the House of Commons as a Tory at the age of 23 and was appointed secretary of war. He clung to this relatively minor post for 20 years because it allowed him to stay in London. In the 1820s Palmerston was known as Lord Cupid and is said to have had three mistresses, one of whom he married, after she was widowed, in 1839. Politically, he moved towards the WHIGS and in 1830 joined the new Whig government as foreign secretary. Over the next 11 years he fought for Belgian independence from the Netherlands, formed an alliance with France, Spain and Portugal to put down Iberian rebellions; and helped to prevent the disintegration of the Ottoman Empire following a revolt in Egypt.

After five years in opposition to Sir Robert Peel's government, Palmerston returned to the foreign office in 1846. His brusque temperament and actions often upset other governments. He encouraged the revolutionaries

Lord Palmerston, returned as prime minister with a clean sweep in the April 1857 elections, courts a sceptical John Bull in a *Punch* cartoon.

during the European REVOLUTIONS OF 1848, and blockaded Greece to secure compensation for a merchant in the DON PACIFICO affair. He was dismissed in 1851 after unofficially supporting Louis Napoleon's coup d'état in France, but used his popularity to secure the post of home secretary in 1852. In 1855 he succeeded Lord Aberdeen as prime minister. The following year he also helped to bring the CRIMEAN WAR to an end and in 1857 he suppressed the Indian Mutiny. In 1858 Palmerston lost the office of prime minister, but was re-elected in 1859.

Palmyra Syrian oasis settlement that grew rich in the 1st century BC by organising and protecting caravans crossing the desert on a trade route between Babylonia and Syria. Probably incorporated within the Roman Empire after AD 17, Palmyra reached its peak of prosperity under Odaenathus (d. 267) and his wife, Zenobia, who for two or three years governed Syria, Egypt and most of Asia Minor. In 273 the Roman emperor Aurelian destroyed Palmyra, which never recovered.

Pan-Africanism Movement seeking unity between African countries, which became a powerful force after the first London Pan-African Conference in 1900. An international convention called in the USA in 1920 to build support for a republic of Africa was inspired by the Jamaican leader Marcus GARVEY, who campaigned for Blacks to return to Africa. When Italy invaded Abyssinia (now Ethiopia) in 1935, a wave of anticolonial sentiment swept the continent.

Africans called for national unity at the 1945 Pan-African Congress in Manchester, which was dominated by the nationalist leaders Jomo KENYATTA and Kwame NKRUMAH and by the 'father of Pan-Africanism', the American William Du Bois. The ORGANISATION OF AFRICAN UNITY was founded in 1963 to bring the ideals of Pan-Africanism into practical politics.

Pan-Africanist Congress South African political movement, also known as the PAC, which believed the use of violence was legitimate in the fight for racial equality. It broke with the AFRICAN NATIONAL CONGRESS over this issue. Formed by Robert Sobukwe in 1959, the group launched a campaign against the Pass Laws, organising a demonstration at SHARPEVILLE in which 69 Black Africans were killed and 180 wounded by police.

As a result the South African government banned both the PAC and the ANC, imprisoning Sobukwe and other leaders. In 1990, after agreeing to change its policy and stop the violence, the PAC was legalised. Four years later it participated in the first South African multiracial elections, and won five seats in the National Assembly.

For more than a thousand years the ruins of Palmyra lay forgotten in the desert. In the 2nd century AD this arch stood at the end of a colonnade.

Panama Central American republic on the narrowest part of the isthmus linking North and South America. Home to the Cuna, Guaymi and Chocó peoples, Panama was sighted by the Spaniard Rodrigo de Bastidas in 1501 and visited by Christopher COLUMBUS in 1502. The Spanish explorer Vasco Núñez de BALBOA established a successful colony in 1510 and in 1513 became the first Spaniard to see the Pacific Ocean. Portobelo became the main port for trade between the New World and Spain. In 1717 Panama became part of the viceroyalty of New Granada.

In 1821 Panama broke away from Spain to join the South American liberator Simón BOLÍVAR's Gran Colombia. Regular nationalist uprisings continued, but Panama did not become an independent republic until 1903. The United States was instrumental in the coup that established independence and in return received the right to build the PANAMA CANAL across the isthmus and to have an indefinite lease of the zone along either side of it. Panamanian attempts to gain control of the Canal Zone led to its occupation by US forces in 1908, 1912, 1918 and 1989.

In 1987 anti-American demonstrations organised by the government led to US economic sanctions on Panama. The following year, General Manuel Noriega seized power. The US increased sanctions after he was charged with drug trafficking and after he invalidated the elections of May 1989. That December, US forces invaded Panama and deposed Noriega. He was put on trial in the USA and convicted of drug trafficking in 1992. Frequent strikes took place against the government of Guillermo Endaras, which was

itself accused of being illegally involved in drugs. In 1991 constitutional reforms included the abolition of the army. Ernesto Balladares was elected president in 1994.

Panama Canal Manmade waterway across the isthmus of PANAMA. The canal, which is about 51 miles (82 km) long, connects the Atlantic and Pacific oceans and is one of two key strategic artificial waterways in the world – the other is the Suez Canal. The idea for the canal was conceived by the Spanish in the 16th century. Work started in the 1880s under the French engineer Ferdinand-Marie de LESSEPS, builder of the Suez Canal, but was abandoned in 1889 due to bad planning, disease and bankruptcy. After Panama became independent in 1903, President Theodore ROOSEVELT negotiated perpetual control of a 10 mile (16km) wide Canal Zone for the United States in return for $10 million and an annual rent of $250 000. The Americans completed the canal in 1914 at a cost of nearly $400 million. After years of negotiations, in 1977 US president Jimmy CARTER agreed to the Panama Canal Treaties, which gave control of the canal to Panama by January 1, 2000, with the guarantee that it remains neutral. Since 1979 the canal area has been jointly controlled by Panama and the United States.

Pankhurst, Emmeline (1858-1928) Feminist and leader of the militant SUFFRAGETTE campaign that fought for British women to have the right to vote. After founding the Women's Social and Political Union in Manchester in 1903, Mrs Pankhurst and her daughters Christabel (1880-1958) and Sylvia (1882-1960) moved to London to lobby the Liberal government. At first they limited tactics to attention-seeking stunts at processions and meetings and to heckling leading politicians, but in 1912 they became more militant. The actions were mainly directed by Christabel from Paris, where she had gone to avoid arrest.

During her own periods of imprisonment Mrs Pankhurst went on hunger strike and was force-fed, but during the First World War she called off the campaign and concentrated the energies of the organisation on national service. At the end of the war, British married women over the age of 30 were given the vote. Mrs Pankhurst joined the Conservatives with Christabel, while Sylvia remained a socialist. In 1928, weeks before Mrs Pankhurst died, women were given the right to vote at 21.

Pan-Slavism Political and cultural movement in Eastern Europe during the 19th century that aimed to unite all Slavs as one nation. Originally conceived in Prague by Slav intellectuals searching for a national identity through literature, folklore and language, Pan-Slavism became political in 1848 when the movement tried to improve the treatment of Slavs in Austria. It changed direction in the 1860s as more Slavs looked to Russia for protection against the Austrian and Ottoman empires. The Russian Pan-Slavs claimed that the culture of Western Europe was morally bankrupt and the spread of its cultural reforms would damage the soul of Russia. Pressure from the powerful Pan-Slav groups probably helped to provoke the Russo-Turkish War of 1877-8. Russia's support of Serbia against Austria-Hungary in the Balkan Wars was a major factor leading to the crisis that precipitated the First World War. After the war the influence of Pan-Slavism waned due to nationalistic differences and rivalries.

papacy Office of the pope, head of the Roman Catholic Church. The name comes from the Greek *papas* and Latin *papa*, 'father'. There have been 265 recognised popes from St PETER to John Paul II. In the early Church many bishops and even priests were called *papas,* but in the West the term gradually evolved into the title pope for the bishop of Rome. In 1073 Gregory VII forbade its use by anyone else. The institution grew from the belief, supported by the New Testament, that Jesus Christ appointed St Peter to be leader of his Church, with jurisdiction to be passed to his successors. St Peter is believed to have been martyred in Rome, as was St Paul, and by the 3rd century the bishops of Rome were claiming to be Peter's successors.

As Christianity, bolstered by inheriting the remnants of the Roman Empire's power, spread across the known world, the papacy gradually extended its control over the Church. The early popes gained authority from their ability to repel attacks by barbarians as well as from their doctrinal strengths. In the 8th century the papacy acquired temporal and political power when it received a donation of land for supporting the Frankish king Pepin the Short (see PAPAL STATES). This was reinforced in 800 when Pope Leo III crowned Charlemagne Holy Roman emperor. The early medieval popes were frequently caught up in rows over secular issues with rulers. Pope Innocent III (1198-1216) made his bid for secular power against the opposition of emperors Otto IV and Frederick II. During the so-called Babylonian captivity from 1309 to 1378 all the popes were French, were crowned at Avignon in southern France and were controlled by the French monarchy. There followed the GREAT SCHISM, when

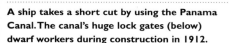
A ship takes a short cut by using the Panama Canal. The canal's huge lock gates (below) dwarf workers during construction in 1912.

popes and antipopes were elected simultaneously at Avignon and Rome and vied with each other for power.

During the Renaissance the popes became as wordly as secular princes. The decadence of some led to the challenge of the Protestant REFORMATION led by Martin Luther. By 1530 most of northern Europe had adopted the new religion. The COUNTER-REFORMATION began following the election in 1534 of Paul III and the setting up of orders for reform and missions such as the Jesuits. However, the papacy was used as a pawn in the personal power struggles of Catholic princes. In the 18th century Clement XIV was forced to suppress the loyal Jesuits and after the fall of Napoleon in 1815 anticlericalism grew in many countries, including France and Mexico.

In 1870 Pius IX put forward the doctrine of papal infallibility at the First Vatican Council, and laid the ground for the growth of Catholicism outside Europe in the 20th century. Social encyclicals concerning how Catholics should live were issued by Pius XI in 1931 and John XXIII in 1961, and restated by Paul VI in 1967. The Second Vatican Council (1962-5) was followed by a growing tendency for churchmen to question papal authority and a drive to increase the power of local churches. JOHN PAUL II – the first non-Italian pope for more than 450 years – elected in 1978, laid emphasis on the international responsibility of the papacy and worked to implement the mandates of the Second Vatican Council.

Papal States Lands in central Italy ruled by the pope from 756 to 1870. In 321 the first Christian Roman emperor, CONSTANTINE, passed a law allowing the Church to own land. In 754 the Franks gave the pope lands they had conquered from the Lombards in central Italy and guaranteed to protect them, thereby increasing the papacy's secular power. During the early Middle Ages, the pope's control over the Papal States weakened, with successive rulers taking land from them until Innocent III (1198-1216) tightened papal control over central Italy and increased the Church's territory. During the reign of Julius II (1503-13) the Papal States included Romagna, Ferrara, Ravenna, much of Tuscany, Umbria and land covered by the Patrimony of St Peter, dividing Italy in two. The papal lands were split when the papacy was based in Avignon in the early 14th century, and during the GREAT SCHISM of 1378 to 1417, when an attempt to move the papacy back to Rome resulted in popes being elected in both Avignon and Rome. The Papal States were taken by the French during the Napoleonic Wars, but were returned in 1815 and then incorporated into the new kingdom of Italy in 1870. In 1929 the state granted papal sovereignty to the lands around the Vatican known as VATICAN CITY.

Papen, Franz von (1879-1969) German politician who helped Adolf Hitler to become chancellor. Papen entered politics in 1921 after being accused of spying and sabotage as military attaché to Washington during the First World War. He belonged to the right wing of the Catholic Centre Party. In 1932 he was appointed chancellor by President Paul von HINDENBURG. Papen tried to appease the Nazis, who formed the second largest party, by lifting a ban on their paramilitary SA organisation; and he won the cancellation of most of Germany's crippling war reparations. But his attempt to impose authoritarian rule failed and his lack of popular support forced his resignation after six months.

In January 1933 he persuaded Hindenburg to appoint Hitler as chancellor and the grateful Nazi leader made Papen vice-chancellor. Papen thought he could restrain the worst excesses of the Nazis, but he realised his mistake in 1934 after narrowly surviving the NIGHT OF THE LONG KNIVES, in which many of his political friends were murdered. He resigned the vice-chancellorship three days after the massacre and was sent to Austria as ambassador. At the outbreak of the Second World War Papen was sent as ambassador to Turkey charged with the task of preventing the country entering the war on the side of the Allies, and remained there until 1944. After the war he was cleared of war crimes by the Nuremburg tribunal but sentenced to eight years in jail by another court for his part in the Nazi government. He was released after two years and fined.

Papineau's Rebellion (1837-8) Uprising by the French-Canadian minority against the British rulers in Lower Canada (now QUEBEC) after their demand for self-government had been rejected. The speaker of the Lower Canada Assembly, Louis-Joseph Papineau (1786-1871), who inspired the French Canadian reformist movement with a series of eloquent speeches, called on the French Canadians to fight against the British. When rebellion broke out he was forced to flee to the United States where he argued the Canadian colonial cause. Hundreds of his supporters were involved in clashes with regular troops in November 1837, and another revolt was suppressed the following year, when 12 supporters were executed. After receiving an amnesty in 1844 Papineau, who had been living in Paris, returned to Canada, by which time Lower and Upper Canada (now Ontario) had been united. He sat in the Canadian parliament but never regained support.

Papua New Guinea Eastern half of the island of New Guinea, together with a number of islands in the south-west Pacific, separated from Australia by the Torres Strait. The western half of the island is called Irian Jaya and forms part of Indonesia. When the Portuguese Jorge de Meneses explored the island in the 16th century, he named it Ilhas dos Papuas, meaning 'frizzy-haired' in Malay. Later the Spaniard Ortiz Retes christened it New Guinea, because it reminded him of the Guinea coast of Africa. The Dutch arrived in 1828, occupying the western half of the island, and in 1884 the Germans and British divided the eastern half between them.

In 1906 the British gave their share, now called Papua, to Australia which, at the start of the First World War, seized Germany's New Guinea territory. After the Second World War, in which Allied troops fought off a determined Japanese invasion, Australia combined the two territories, administering the country until it became self-governing in 1973. Two years later Papua New Guinea was granted independence within the British Commonwealth. Relations with Indonesia were strained during the 1980s over the conflict in Irian Jaya and troops were sent to Bougainville in 1992 to quell the uprising by the Bougainville Revolutionary Army, which demanded secession. A new provincial administration was set up in 1995 to negotiate the island's future status.

Paraguay Land-locked country in South America, bordered by Brazil, Argentina and Bolivia. Part of the Spanish Empire, Paraguay was only sparsely settled by Spaniards. In the 17th and 18th centuries it was known for the self-governing Jesuit missionary villages established among the Guaraní Indians.

Paraguay became independent in 1811 after local military leaders led a bloodless revolt against the Spanish governor. The first to rule the new republic was José Gaspar Rodríguez de Francia who controlled the country as supreme dictator from 1814 to 1840. After his death the government was dogged by bankruptcy, coups and corruption.

Francisco Solano López led the country to disaster in the destructive War of the Triple Alliance against the combined forces of Brazil, Argentina and Uruguay between 1864 and 1870. Political turmoil continued into the 20th century, relieved for a while by the Liberal Eduard Schaerer (1912-17), who encouraged foreign investment and economic progress. These were brought to a standstill with the CHACO WAR (1932-5) when Paraguay won from Bolivia, at great cost, a large part of the long-contested border territory of Gran Chaco. In 1954 General Alfredo STROESSNER seized power and set up a repressive, militarist regime. A massive hydroelectricity project was started and some progress made in settling landless peasants; but cattle exports to Europe fell, the economy declined and the regime became even more brutal. In 1989 Stroessner was deposed in a coup led by General Andrés Rodríguez, who was immediately elected president. With military backing, Rodríguez's Colorado Party retained power when Juan Carlos Wasmosy was elected president four years later.

pardoner Official of the medieval Roman Catholic Church licensed to receive money in return for INDULGENCES – the remission of punishment imposed on sinners who had confessed their wrongs. Money received in this way was meant to be used for charity and good works. It also frequently enriched corrupt Church officials, who misled gullible people into believing that their payments bought them forgiveness, or pardon, for their sins. In 1517 Martin LUTHER condemned the selling of indulgences as an abuse of Church doctrine, and in the 1560s the practice was ended by the Council of Trent and Pope Pius V.

Paris, Commune of (1871) Revolutionary council, set up in Paris after France's defeat in the Franco-Prussian War. During Prussia's siege of Paris from September 1870 to January 1871, the people suffered bitter hardship and starvation, yet became hardened in their opposition to peace. However, in the national elections of February 1871 the rural south and

Papua New Guinea's remote terrain led isolated highlanders to develop some of the country's 700 languages.

In 1871 women of the Paris Commune make their last stand at Montmartre against the royalist Versailles troops.

west of France voted for a royalist National Assembly and peace with Prussia. Parisians remained isolated in their support of radical socialists and a continuation of the war. When in March 1871 the head of the National Assembly, Adolphe THIERS, attempted to disarm the National Guard in Paris and to remove all cannon from the city, Parisians responded by electing a radical socialist municipal council, or Commune – a reference to the JACOBIN Commune of 1793. It proceeded to confiscate the property of people who had fled Paris, establish workers' cooperatives and erect barricades.

Thiers sent in government troops to suppress the revolt and for six weeks Paris was besieged, and its centre destroyed. On 21 May its defences were breached and a week of bitter street fighting, called Bloody Week, followed. Before surrendering, the Communards murdered their hostages, including the Archbishop of Paris. After the collapse of the Commune, more than 18000 people were massacred by government forces, leaving France deeply divided between Parisian radicals and rural monarchists.

Paris, Treaty of (1763) Treaty signed by Britain, France and Spain which brought the SEVEN YEARS' WAR to an end and left Britain as the world's supreme colonial and naval power. Under its terms, France lost Canada and all its North American territories east of the Mississippi to Britain. France also ceded the Louisiana Territory and New Orleans to its ally, Spain, in compensation for Florida, which Spain gave to Britain. France lost some West Indian islands, including Dominica and Tobago, but recovered Guadeloupe and Martinique from Britain, in return for which Britain gained Grenada and the Grenadines. In India, France kept its trading stations but was forbidden to maintain troops, leaving India under British control. In Africa, France ceded Senegal to Britain; and in Europe, Britain recovered Minorca in exchange for Belle Isle, Newfoundland. Cuba and the Philippines were returned to Spain.

parish Smallest unit of ecclesiastical and administrative government in England. The parish developed in the 7th and 8th centuries as the district served by a priest or religious community under the jurisdiction of a bishop. Parish churches, originally found only in important centres, or minsters, became widespread during the 10th century. When the Church of England became independent of Rome at the REFORMATION, it retained the parish as the basic church unit. The parish council, England's smallest unit of local government, dates from the 16th century.

Park, Mungo (1771-1806) British explorer. In 1795 the African Association employed Park to chart the course of the Niger river. Travelling north-east from the Gambia river, he crossed to the Senegal river basin and the Upper Niger. On his return to Britain he wrote *Travels in the Interior Districts of Africa* (1799), which established the direction of the Niger's flow. Park's second expedition to the Niger in 1805 reached as far as Bamako and Ségou (both now in Mali), before Park and his companions were attacked in their canoes by local people at Bussa, and Park was drowned.

Parkes, Sir Henry (1815-96) Australian politician who became prominent as a campaigner against convict transportation before entering the colonial parliament in 1854 as a federalist. He was premier of NEW SOUTH WALES five times between 1872 and 1891, campaigning for free trade, civil-service reform and the federation of the Australian colonies. Often called 'the father of federation', Parkes helped to draft a constitution in 1891, but died before FEDERALISM was achieved in 1901.

Parlement Chief judicial authority in France during the ANCIEN RÉGIME, a social and political system which existed from the 16th century until the FRENCH REVOLUTION. First established in Paris in the 12th century, the Parlement functioned as a court of appeal, and as a source of final legal rulings. From the 15th century there were also provincial Parlements, such as those in Toulouse, Bordeaux and Rennes. Their political importance derived from their power to examine royal decrees and to accept or reject them as they saw fit. The king, however, could always override this power, either by written order or by personally attending the Parlement.

From the 16th century until the French Revolution, Parlements systematically opposed royal reform measures, joining the aristocratic rebellion known as the FRONDE from 1648 to 1653. Their strength continued to grow throughout the 18th century, and in 1771 Louis XV reduced their administrative and political powers. But in 1774 Louis XVI restored them in order to gain support from the aristocracy. Parlements proceeded to lead the opposition to the monarchy, posing as defenders of liberty but chiefly representing aristocratic privilege, and blocking attempts at the financial reforms required to save France from bankruptcy. Their resistance led eventually to the king calling a meeting of the national assembly, or STATES-GENERAL, in 1789 – a decision which sparked the French Revolution. As bastions of privilege and reaction, Parlements were abolished in 1792.

Louis XV attends the Paris Parlement in 1723. By then places in France's 13 Parlements were sold or hereditary. Parlements blocked attempts at reform until Louis reduced their powers in 1771.

Parliament Supreme law-making body in Britain, comprising the sovereign, as head of state, the House of Lords and the House of Commons. Its origins go back to the 13th century when the king summoned barons and prelates to his feudal council – which developed into the House of Lords – and assembled occasional meetings of knights and burgesses, borough representatives. The Parliament of Simon de MONTFORT in 1265 and the MODEL PARLIAMENT of Edward III in 1295 were early attempts at representation determined by status and locality.

In the 14th century the two-chamber system developed as lords debated in one chamber, and knights and burgesses in the other. Petitions, or bills, appeared at this time. Such bills became Acts of Parliament if the king assented; but by the 15th century, the assent of a majority of the members of the Lords and Commons had also become necessary. Henry VIII used the long Reformation Parliament, which sat from 1529 to 1536, to establish the Church of England. Both chambers grew in importance during the 16th century, as the monarch became less able to impose taxation without their approval.

After 11 years of ruling without Parliament, from 1629 to 1640, Charles I was forced by shortage of funds to call one. It accused him of despotism, and the conflict developed into the ENGLISH CIVIL WAR, which the Parliamentary side won. During the COMMONWEALTH period Britain was first ruled, between 1649 and 1653, by a republican Parliament after which Oliver CROMWELL became a dictator, or Lord Protector of the Commonwealth. Parliamentary power resumed in 1659, a year after Cromwell's death.

In 1660 the House of Commons negotiated the restoration of Charles II and in 1688 the accession of William III and Mary II. Acts passed in the GLORIOUS REVOLUTION of 1688 and the Act of Settlement in 1701 established the relationship between Crown, Lords and Commons which continues today. However, British membership of the EUROPEAN UNION now means that Parliamentary Acts can in some instances be overruled by the European Court of Justice.

Parnell, Charles (1846-91) Irish nationalist leader. The son of a Protestant Anglo-Irish landowner, Parnell was elected to Parliament in 1875, where he used the delaying tactic of the filibuster to make speeches about Irish nationalist grievances. Joining the republican FENIANS in their fight against Irish land laws, he became president of the LAND LEAGUE in 1879, successfully organising boycotts of English settler landlords who were setting high rents and evicting tenants. These activities led to his imprisonment in 1881. He was released in 1882, the year of the PHOENIX PARK MURDERS of two British politicians. These

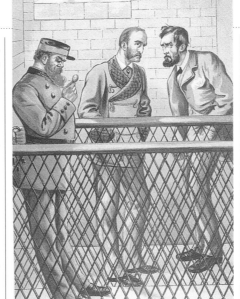

Charles Parnell and his fellow Land League member John Dillon were imprisoned in 1881 for defending the rights of Irish tenants.

murders damaged his reputation, although a letter allegedly implicating him was later shown to be a forgery. Parnell's support for the Liberals enabled William GLADSTONE to form a government in 1886 and to introduce the first Irish HOME RULE bill; but the bill split the Liberals who lost the next election.

Parnell's career came to an end in 1890 when his long-standing relationship with Mrs Katharine O'Shea, the wife of a political supporter, resulted in a divorce case. The scandal lost him the support of Gladstone and English Liberals, and split Irish nationalists into Parnellites and anti-Parnellites.

Parr, Catherine (1512-48) Sixth wife of HENRY VIII. Already twice widowed, she married the king in 1543, and dedicated herself to the education of his children Mary, Elizabeth and the future Edward VI. A devout Protestant, she wrote *A Lamentacion or Complaynt of a Sinner*. Soon after Henry's death in 1547 she married Thomas, Baron Seymour of Sudeley, but died a year later after bearing his daughter.

Parsi see ZOROASTRIAN

parson From the 11th to the 17th centuries a parson was the holder of a church living, and was supported by its revenues. The word comes from the Latin for person, *persona*, and may have indicated that a parson was the person who held the property of God in his parish. Since the 17th century, the term has referred to all clergymen, particularly in the Anglican Church.

Parthia Ancient country of Asia, originally a satrapy – or province – of the Persian Achaemenid empire, which later passed into the

control of the SELEUCIDS. A Parthian empire lasting 400 years was established in 247 BC when Arsaces I led a rebellion against the Seleucids. At the end of the 2nd century BC Parthian territory stretched from the River Euphrates in the west to Afghanistan in the east, and north as far as the River Oxus. When Roman forces under CRASSUS attempted to invade Parthia, they were defeated at the Battle of Carrhae in 53 BC. Although the Parthian empire did not develop beyond a feudal aristocracy, its geographical position enabled it to profit from trade between East and West. In AD 224 the empire fell when Ardashir I of Persia defeated Artabanus V in battle, founding the Sassanian empire.

Pascal, Blaise (1623-62) French mathematician, physicist, religious philosopher and author of the *Pensées* (*Thoughts*). Pascal was a child prodigy who had worked out 23 of Euclid's propositions in geometry by the age of 11. Between the ages of 19 and 21 he designed the world's first calculating machine to help his father with his accounts. By turning dials, which engaged with other dials through cogs, he fed numbers into the machine which could add and subtract. In physics, his study of hydrostatics led to the invention of the barometer, syringe and hydraulic press. In mathematics, he laid the foundations for the theory of probability, developed from a problem sent to him by a notorious gambler. Suffering from overwork, he had a religious revelation in 1654 that led him to join the Jansenist (see JANSEN) monastery at Port-Royal. Here he joined battle with the Jansenists against the JESUITS of the Sorbonne in *Les provinciales* (1656-7), which significantly undermined Jesuit prestige. His *Pensées*, published posthumously in 1669,

Catherine Parr, admired for piety and learning, persuaded Henry VIII to restore the succession to his daughters, later Mary I and Elizabeth I.

established his principle of intuitionism, which held that God is only experienced through the heart, not through reason.

pasha Highest official title of honour in the OTTOMAN EMPIRE. It was personal rather than hereditary, and was used after the proper name. Soldiers, VIZIERs and provincial governors were eligible for the title. First used in the 13th century among the SELJUKs, the title is still used colloquially in Turkey.

Pašić, Nikola (1845-1926) Serbian statesman and a founder of the former Yugoslavia. Five times prime minister of Serbia between 1891 and 1918, his ideal was a Greater Serbia, including much of Croatia and Dalmatia, with Serbs dominating the South Slavs. Pašić signed a pact with his Slav neighbours in 1917, creating the Kingdom of Serbs, Croats, and Slovenes which he represented at the Versailles Peace Settlement in 1919. He was premier from 1921 to 1926 of the new kingdom, which in 1929 became Yugoslavia.

Passchendaele, Battle of (1917) Third battle of Ypres, fought between July 31 and November 6, 1917, on the Western Front in the First World War. Although heavy bombardment and rains reduced Flanders to mud, the British commander in chief Douglas HAIG was convinced, despite huge British losses at the Battle of the SOMME, that frontal assaults v in superior numbers would succeed. When

Knee-deep in a porridge of mud, British soldiers at Passchendaele struggle to carry a wounded comrade.

the British reached the ruined village of Passchendaele after three months of fighting, they had advanced just 5 miles (8 km) and suffered 300 000 casualties. Even this small gain was surrendered in the retreat before General Erich LUDENDORFF's final offensive in April 1918.

passive resistance Nonviolent opposition to a ruling authority or government. It frequently involves refusal to cooperate with the authorities, or a defiant breach of laws. One of the most successful campaigns was waged by Mohandas GANDHI against British rule in India. It influenced the British to grant India independence in 1947. Gandhi's example inspired the civil rights movement in the USA from the 1950s, where demonstrations and the breaking of segregation laws brought considerable gains for the Black population. The failure of passive resistance against harsh regimes was evident in 1989 when Chinese prodemocracy demonstrations in Tiananmen Square, Beijing, were suppressed by the army.

Pasteur, Louis see feature page 490

Patagonia Region set on a plateau in Argentina and Chile, forming the southernmost tip of South America. Originally occupied by South American Indians called the Tehuelches, the territory was settled by Argentine and Chilean rangers in the late 19th century. Europeans, particularly of Basque, Welsh and Scottish origin, migrated to Patagonia in the early 20th century. Since the 1940s, the exploitation of iron ore, petroleum, uranium and natural gas deposits has altered the region's agricultural character.

Patel, Sardar Vallabhbhai (1875-1950) President of the Indian National Congress, who was instrumental in creating the two states of India and Pakistan. Influenced by the PASSIVE RESISTANCE strategy of Mohandas GANDHI, Patel joined the struggle against British rule in India and organised civil disobedience campaigns from 1918 until independence in 1947. In 1931 he was elected president of the Indian National Congress and played a key role in the negotiations that led to the partition of the subcontinent into India and Pakistan. As deputy prime minister of India from 1947 to 1950, he peacefully integrated the country's many princely states into the new political structure.

Pathet Lao Communist movement that fought for the independence of LAOS from France. It was formed in 1951 by the nationalist leader Prince Souphanouvong, who in 1953 led its forces alongside the North Vietnam communist Vietminh army into Laos and established a government in the north of the country. That same year Laos became independent and civil war broke out between the royalist government and the Pathet Lao. A conference held in Geneva in 1954 made the Pathet Lao a partner in a coalition ruling Laos, and the war ceased. But in 1959 the coalition broke down, and the Pathet Lao fought for power against noncommunist government forces. Aided by North Vietnamese troops, the Pathet Lao took control of Laos in 1975, and renamed it the People's Democratic Republic of Laos.

patrician Hereditary aristocrat of the Roman republic. In 510 BC the last king of Rome, TARQUIN, was deposed and sent into exile by the patricians, leaders of Rome's wealthier families who were hereditary members of the senate. They proceeded to consolidate their power by gaining control of all magistracies and priesthoods. However, during the 4th century BC the less wealthy plebeian class struggled for political equality and in 367 the senate was opened to them. The influence of the patricians continued to wane during the ROMAN EMPIRE.

Patrick, St (c.390-c.460) Christian missionary and patron saint of Ireland. Born in Britain, Patrick was captured by Irish pirates when he was 16 and taken as a slave and herdsman to their country. After six years, he escaped and went to Gaul where he probably became a monk at Tours and Lérins. He returned to Ireland as a missionary bishop in about 435, challenging the influence of the DRUIDS and converting the Irish royal family to Christianity.

Patrick chose to site his episcopal see at Armagh and founded the cathedral there. According to tradition, he also performed

Patagonia's windswept plateau stretching from the Andes to the Atlantic proved ideal for the sheep ranching which provided a livelihood for most of the region's settlers.

The founder of health sciences

Louis Pasteur pioneered the application of science to medicine, discovering the unseen causes behind devastating diseases.

Though not a physician, the French chemist and microbiologist Louis Pasteur (1822-95) is indisputably a giant of modern medicine. Feted in his lifetime, since his death he has assumed an almost saintly status as a hero of science for pioneering the new field of bacteriology. His apparent simplicity, devotion to family values and fervent patriotism helped to hide a burning ambition. He went on to become a prominent public figure, with streets and squares throughout France named after him.

Of quite humble background, Pasteur won himself a place at the famous Ecole normale supérieure in Paris, where he studied chemistry. Early in his career he explored the practical problems of why wine and beer went bad and milk soured: to prevent this happening Pasteur developed a new process of heat treatment, now called pasteurisation. Investigation of fermentation led him, through a series of elegant experiments, to refute the ancient theory of spontaneous generation, and he became persuaded of the universal

Pasteur looks on as Joseph Meister is inoculated with fluid from a rabid animal. Two weeks later the boy had recovered.

presence of microorganisms – microbes and germs – which affected living beings.

The next development was the application of these biological ideas to medicine. Convinced that many diseases resulted from infection by invisible bacteria, Pasteur showed that immunity could be conferred by inoculation with a weakened variety of the agent which caused the disease. First he worked on animal diseases: in a celebrated anthrax trial held on a farm south of Paris in 1881, a control group of untreated sheep died while all those he had vaccinated with his new anthrax vaccine survived.

THE CONQUEST OF DISEASE

But Pasteur's most spectacular success was with rabies, then still a common and lethal disease. On July 6, 1885, Joseph Meister, a boy who had been bitten by a rabid dog, was brought to him. Pasteur tried out the new vaccine he was developing, and the boy did not contract the disease. The vaccine was then widely adopted; it proved successful and its use quickly spread throughout the world. The microbiologist became a national hero, and funds flooded in to found a superb new research laboratory in Paris, the Pasteur Institute.

Pasteur was the founder of bacteriology as a practical science, rivalled on the theoretical side by the German, Robert Koch (1843-1910). After centuries of confused speculation, it was finally established that infectious and contagious diseases were caused by living microorganisms. Effective vaccines followed shortly for dangerous disorders such as diphtheria and cholera. However, the production of drugs that would destroy bacteria – the antibiotics revolution – had to wait until the 1940s with the introduction of penicillin.

---

miracles, the most famous being the expulsion of snakes from Ireland. His *Confessio* is the main source of information about his life.

Patton, George (1885-1945) US Second World War general, whose stern and occasionally bullying leadership won him the nickname of 'old blood and guts'. After taking part in the NORTH AFRICAN CAMPAIGNS, Patton commanded the 7th Army in Sicily, capturing the capital, Palermo, in 1943 with a decisive tank attack. He lost his command after striking a soldier suffering from shell shock, but in August 1944 was promoted to lead the 3rd Army in the Normandy Campaign. After the war, his outspoken criticism of the Allied denazification programme in Germany led to his dismissal. He died from injuries sustained in a car crash, and his memoirs, *War As I Knew It*, were published posthumously in 1947.

Paul I (1754-1801) Tsar of Russia from 1796 until his death. Paul was the son of Peter III and CATHERINE II, the empress who seized power from her mentally unstable husband in 1762. On acceding to the throne, he introduced a law of succession based on PRIMOGENITURE and placed limits on the nobility's exploitation of the labourer SERFS attached to their estates. He also outlawed foreign travel and the import of Western music and books. Driven by fear of revolution, he joined a coalition against France in 1798, but his erratic foreign policy led to poor relations with Britain and an abortive raid on British-held India. He was murdered in a conspiracy of army officers and nobles, with the support of his son, ALEXANDER I.

Paul VI (1897-1978), Pope from 1963. Born Giovanni Battista Montini, he continued the work of his reforming predecessor JOHN XXIII, and reconvened the Second Vatican Council after being elected pope. A conservative, he aimed to change Church practices only where they were clearly inappropriate in the modern world. Following the recommendations of the Council in 1965, Paul supervised many reforms, such as translating the Latin liturgy into vernacular languages. However, he condemned artificial methods of birth control in his public letter *Humanae Vitae* (*Of Human Life*) in 1968. He also remained unyielding on the issues of priestly celibacy, divorce and women priests.

Paul, St (1st century AD) Early Christian missionary, said to have been converted to Christianity by a vision of Christ while on a journey to Damascus. Originally named Saul, he was a Jew from Tarsus in Asia Minor (now Turkey). As a PHARISEE, he was strongly opposed to Christianity, but while on a journey to Damascus to suppress the new religion in AD 33 he was dramatically converted after seeing a vision of Christ. Paul then began to preach, and travelled as a missionary in Asia Minor and the Aegean. He stressed that Gentiles – non-Jews – who became Christians needed only faith in Christ, and did not need to follow Jewish laws. This message provoked hostility on a visit to Jerusalem in 57, and a

A tapestry of the Battle of Pavia shows Francis I in arms against his arch rival Charles V.

riot against him led to his arrest by the Roman authorities. He was taken to Rome around 60, where he is thought to have died a martyr's death by decapitation (perhaps after a further period of freedom) in about 64. The sources for his life are the Acts of the Apostles and the Epistles of St Paul to the Galatians, the Romans and the Ephesians which make up about a third of the Bible's New Testament. Paul's ideas exerted a powerful influence on the development of Christianity through commentators such as St AUGUSTINE, St Thomas AQUINAS and Martin LUTHER.

Paulus, Friedrich von (1890-1957) German field-marshal in the Second World War whose army was defeated at the Battle of STALIN-GRAD. As Adolf Hitler's deputy chief of staff, Paulus planned the German attack on Russia, which was code-named Operation BARBAROSSA. In one of the bloodiest battles of the war, some 300 000 Germans were killed trying to capture Stalingrad before Paulus surrendered in February 1943, contrary to Hitler's orders. Held prisoner in the USSR, he joined a Soviet-sponsored German organisa-tion, the National Committee for a Free Germany, and urged the overthrow of Hitler's dictatorship. Following his release in 1953 he lived in East Germany, where he lectured on military strategy.

Pavia, Battle of (February 24, 1525) Decisive battle in the ITALIAN WARS of 1494 to 1559. In October 1524 the French under FRANCIS I invaded Italy. Their army of 28 000 laid siege to the city of Pavia, in Lombardy, until CHARLES V's Habsburg army of 23 000 relieved the city and took Francis prisoner. In 1526, Francis was released and concluded a peace in which he surrendered all French claims to Italy to the Habsburgs.

Paxton, Sir Joseph (1801-65) Designer of the Crystal Palace for Britain's GREAT EXHIBI-TION of 1851 in London. As superintendent of gardens to the Duke of Devonshire at Chatsworth from 1826, Paxton designed two glass and metal greenhouses. He based his design of the world's first major prefabricated

building of sheet glass and iron, the Crystal Palace, on the greenhouse structure. It took just six months to construct in Hyde Park, and Paxton's achievement was recognised with a knighthood. Paxton became MP for Coventry from 1854 until he died. The Crystal Palace was dismantled and re-erected in Sydenham, in south London, where fire destroyed it in 1936.

Peabody, George (1795-1869) US financier and philanthropist. Peabody set up a thriving trading business in the eastern USA before settling in London in 1837, where he turned to banking. There he used his vast fortune for such philanthropic purposes as slum clearance in London, building tenements for working men which survive as Peabody Buildings. In 1867 he established the first educational foundation in the USA, the Peabody Education Fund, to promote education in the American South.

Pearl Harbor United States naval base in Hawaii that was attacked without warning by the Japanese air force on Sunday, December 7, 1941. A surprise attack by 180 Japanese carrierborne bomber aircraft and torpedo planes on the US Pacific Fleet brought America into the Second World War. In less than two hours a total of 188 US aircraft were destroyed, and 18 naval vessels including eight battleships were sunk or damaged. Some 2400 Americans were killed, and more than 1100 were wounded. But the bombs had missed important fuel depots, and US aircraft carriers had been safely at sea during the attack. The next day the USA and Britain declared war on Japan, whose allies, Germany and Italy, in turn declared war on the USA.

Pearson, Lester (1897-1972) Canadian politician, diplomat and international states-man. Pearson was chairman of NATO in 1951

and president of the General Assembly of the United Nations from 1952 to 1953. During the SUEZ WAR of 1956 he played a key role in resolving Arab-Israeli disputes, and received the Nobel peace prize the following year. He was leader of the Canadian Liberal Party in 1958, and prime minister from 1963 to 1968. Pearson's administration, which had no over-all majority, attempted to conciliate QUEBEC's separatists by setting up a commission on French-English equality.

Peasants' Revolt (1381) Uprising in England led by Wat TYLER and John BALL. During the Black Death, the plague which swept through England in 1348, around one in three of the population died. The result was a shortage of labour and a rise in peasants' wages. In 1351 Parliament passed the Statute of Labourers to peg wages at their exisiting level, causing widespread anger. Resentment increased when landlords tried to stop peas-ants leaving for new work by claiming ancient manorial rights which bound the peasants to their lands. Discontent became rebellion when a POLL TAX was increased in 1380, and the following year peasants from Essex and Kent marched to London. The 14-year-old RICHARD II met some of the men at Mile End, and persuaded the rebels to disperse by agree-ing to fair rents, to the abolition of serfdom and to the punishment of traitors. Meanwhile other rebels captured the Tower of London, and beheaded the treasurer and the chancellor, the Archbishop of Sudbury, who were respon-sible for the poll tax. The following day Tyler met the king at Smithfield and demanded an end to Church ownership of property. After an exchange of blows with the mayor of London Tyler was wounded and later beheaded. The king persuaded the rebels to disperse, and the revolt was put down. His advisers immedi-ately revoked the promises made at Mile End.

Pedro I (1798-1835) First Emperor of Brazil, from 1822 to 1831. John VI, king of Portugal, fled with his son Pedro to Brazil in 1807, when Napoleon invaded his country. When he returned to Portugal in 1821, he left Pedro as regent of Brazil. In 1822 John VI attempted to tighten colonial restrictions on Brazil, leading to widespread unrest. Pedro I responded by defying his father and declaring the independence of Brazil. But Pedro's rule was weakened by republican uprisings and nationalist resentment over his Portuguese connections, and in 1831 he abdicated in favour of his son PEDRO II.

After Japan's strike on Pearl Harbor a boat tries to rescue survivors from a US battleship.

Pedro II (1825-91) Emperor of Brazil from 1831 to 1889. He succeeded to the throne, under a regency, at the age of five when his father PEDRO I abdicated. In 1840, Brazil's general assembly declared the 14-year-old Pedro of age and confirmed his emperorship. His long and popular reign was marked by economic progress, the abolition of slavery and wars with Uruguay from 1851 to 1852 and with Paraguay from 1865 to 1870. As Brazil's economy grew, a coalition of industrialists, coffee planters and the military turned against the monarchy, and Pedro was ousted in favour of a republic in 1889. He spent his remaining years in exile in Europe.

Peel, Sir Robert (1788-1850) British prime minister and founder of the Metropolitan Police. Entering Parliament as a Tory in 1809, Peel introduced sweeping reforms as home secretary from 1822 to 1827, and from 1828 to 1830. He removed about a hundred offences from the list of crimes punishable by death, founded the Metropolitan Police, London's police force, in 1829, and supported CATHOLIC EMANCIPATION. Although Peel opposed the Whig government's REFORM ACT of 1832, in his 1834 election speech, known as the TAMWORTH MANIFESTO, he agreed to moderate reform 'without infringing on established rights' – a position which was later to characterise Benjamin Disraeli's new Conservative Party. Peel was briefly prime minister from 1834 to 1835. During his second term from 1841 to 1846 he supported free trade by reducing import duties and introduced the Bank Charter Act of 1844, which made the Bank of England solely responsible for issuing paper money. Faced with the miseries of the IRISH FAMINE, he repealed the CORN LAWS, splitting his party in the process and ending his political career.

Peking man Common name for early human fossils, first found near Beijing (Peking) in China in 1927. Peking man was at first called *Homo erectus*, but some scientists now feel it was closer to modern humans and should be called *Homo Sapiens Pithecanthropus*. Dates of remains vary from 250 000 years old to up to 800 000 years old.

Pelham, Henry (1696-1754) British prime minister from 1743 to 1754. Pelham, a supporter of Robert WALPOLE, became secretary for war in 1724 and prime minister in 1743. Ushering in a period of peace and prosperity, he signed the treaty of AIX-LA-CHAPELLE in 1748, ending the War of the AUSTRIAN SUCCESSION, and then set about reducing the national debt. In 1752 Pelham changed the calendar from the Julian solar measurement to the more accurate Gregorian system in line with continental Europe, which entailed a loss of eleven days from the earlier calendar.

Peloponnesian War Conflict between Athens and Sparta for control of ancient Greece, between 431 and 404 BC, in which Sparta was victorious. Athens and Sparta had long been rivals. Athens was a democracy where all adult free male citizens had the vote. Sparta was an undemocratic state in which a small number of Spartan citizens ruled over a large number of helots, or serfs. Athens led a Greek empire of democratic island states. Sparta led a federation of undemocratic city states, the Peloponnesian League.

According to the historian THUCYDIDES, the war was caused by Spartan fear of Athenian power. In 431 Sparta invaded Attica, the countryside surrounding Athens. PERICLES, the Athenian leader, persuaded his fellow citizens to rely on sea power. They sheltered the whole population of Attica within the walls of Athens, and launched a successful series of coastal raids against Sparta's allies. Pericles died in 429, after overcrowding in Athens led to a plague which killed a substantial proportion of the city's population. The war ground on, for Athens could not defeat Sparta on land and Sparta could not win at sea.

In 422 both the Spartan leader Brasidas and Pericles' successor Cleon were killed, and the following year peace was finally negotiated. The statesman and general ALCIBIADES persuaded the Athenian leader Nicias to attack Sparta's ally Syracuse in 415. He then deserted to Sparta, leaving Athens to fight a disastrous war, in which by 413 it had lost much of its fleet. The fortunes of Athens revived briefly with victories at Cynossema in 411 and Cyzicus the following year, but the tactical skills of the Spartan leader LYSANDER tipped the balance. Sparta destroyed what was left of the Athenian navy at Aegospotami in 405, and its control of the Hellespont starved Athens into surrender in 404. Lysander proceeded to install an oligarchic government – the Thirty Tyrants – in Athens, which never regained its former power.

penal settlements Colonies established to punish criminals by forced labour, principally developed by Britain, France and the former Soviet Union. The British established penal settlements in 18th-century America, in Virginia and Georgia. Later British convicts who were shipped to Australia between 1788 and 1868 and committed further crimes were sent to penal settlements, such as Norfolk Island and Port Arthur, and subjected to harsh punishment. The French empire established penal settlements in Africa, New Caledonia and at Devil's Island in French Guiana. Under the Soviet leader Stalin, hard labour settlements were built in Siberia. During the 1930s the mortality rate in these camps was about 90 per cent, the average lifespan was two years and some 10 million people died.

Penda (d. 655) King of Anglo-Saxon MERCIA, an area roughly corresponding to today's English Midlands. Penda was a noble of the Mercian royal house. In alliance with the king of Gwynedd, CADWALLON, he defeated the king of Northumbria, Edwin, in 633, and declared himself king of Mercia. Penda killed Edwin's successor Oswald in battle in 642 and waged successful war against Wessex and East Anglia. Although a pagan, Penda allowed Christian missionaries into his kingdom. He was killed in battle by OSWY, king of Northumbria, in 655.

penicillin First antibiotic used to treat bacterial infection in humans. Investigations into penicillin began in 1928 when the Scottish biologist Sir Alexander FLEMING identified a fungal mould, *Penicillium notatum*, on a bacteria culture in his laboratory. He noticed that the bacteria died wherever the fungus grew. But it was not until 1940 that the pathologist Howard FLOREY and the biochemist Ernst Chain stabilised and purified penicillin, and confirmed that it was effective against infections and not toxic to humans. It was first used to treat casualties of the Second World War in 1941. Since then it has saved millions of lives.

Peninsular War (1808-14) One of the NAPOLEONIC WARS, fought in Spain and Portugal, in which Britain, allied with Spain and Portugal, defeated France and helped to force Napoleon's abdication. When the French invaded Portugal in 1807 to compel it

> **❝ I don't know what effect these men will have upon the enemy, but, by God, they terrify me. ❞**
>
> *The Duke of Wellington, writing in a letter of the soldiers sent to him from England during the Peninsular War in 1809*

to cease trading with Britain and to conform to the CONTINENTAL SYSTEM, the Portuguese king John VI fled to Brazil without resisting. The following year French troops invaded Spain, and Napoleon placed his brother Joseph Bonaparte on the Spanish throne. The Spanish revolted, and Joseph Bonaparte fled from Madrid in August 1808. In the same month Arthur Wellesley (made Duke of WELLINGTON in 1809) landed in Portugal, where revolt had spread from Spain. Within weeks he had routed the French forces at Vimeiro and expelled them from Portugal. The British forces then turned their attention to Spain, where Napoleon had taken personal command of the army. Despite the efforts of Sir John MOORE, the British commander, Napoleon's army recaptured Madrid in December 1808. In January 1809 Moore was

William Penn meets chiefs of the Delaware tribes in 1682 to sign a treaty intended to promote lasting friendship between Native Americans and Quaker settlers in Pennsylvania.

defeated and killed at the Battle of Corunna, and the British were driven out of Spain. Wellington's forces returned to fight alongside the Spanish army in April 1809, and defeated the French forces at Talavera in July 1809. However, a French attack led by André Masséna forced Wellington back into Portugal, and from October 1810 to March 1811 the French army laid siege to Torres Vedras, Portugal. But Wellington had built a system of defensive lines, and eventually the starved and demoralised French forces retreated. In 1812 Wellington was able to invade Spain again, defeat the French at Salamanca and capture Madrid. The following year he routed the French forces under Joseph Bonaparte at the battle of Vitoria, pushing them back into France. The long attrition of the Peninsular War and the French army's disastrous Russian campaign had weakened Napoleon's forces. Wellington's troops pushed on into France, and had already reached Toulouse when the news came that the allied European armies had captured Paris and Napoleon had abdicated.

Penn, William (1644-1718) QUAKER and founder of PENNSYLVANIA, USA, who drafted

a state constitution based on political and religious tolerance. Expelled from Oxford University for refusing to follow the teachings of the Anglican Church, Penn joined the Quakers in 1664. His tract refuting the doctrine of the Trinity, *The Sandy Foundation Shaken*, led to his imprisonment in the Tower of London in 1668. After his release in 1669 he preached in England, the Netherlands and Germany and continued writing pamphlets on religious toleration. In 1675 Penn became involved in the American colonies when he was appointed a trustee for a Quaker owner of West Jersey.

He subsequently purchased East Jersey with 11 other Quakers in 1681. In the same year Charles II granted him a charter for the colony of Pennsylvania, in payment of debts owed to his father. Penn visited his 'holy experiment' in 1682, and drew up a liberal constitution which he named the 'Frame of Government'. He also established friendly relations between the Pennsylvania colonists and Native Americans. From 1684 to 1699 Penn stayed in England, only returning to Pennsylvania to answer settler discontents by granting more political power to the provincial assembly. He left the American colony in 1701 and spent his last years in England, harassed by debt and, following a stroke in 1712, removed from public life.

Pennsylvania State in the eastern USA,

named after its founder William PENN. From 1681, when the Quaker William Penn was given Pennsylvania by the English king Charles II, until the AMERICAN REVOLUTION in 1776, the state grew rapidly under Quaker control. German farmers, known as Pennsylvania Dutch, worked the rich farmlands of the coastal plain, and from around 1718 Scots-Irish immigrants settled the western frontier.

By the 1770s Philadelphia was the state's finest city, and the largest in the American colonies. During the American Revolution Philadelphia became the national capital. The assembly of the thirteen colonies, the CONTINENTAL CONGRESS, began meeting there in 1774. In 1776 the city was host to the signing of the Declaration of Independence from Britain. British troops captured Philadelphia in 1777, but the Americans retook the city within the year and the Continental Congress returned. The Constitutional Convention which drafted the US Constitution took place in

Philadelphia in 1787, and the federal government was based there from 1790 to 1800, when it moved to Washington.

Pennsylvania was the site of several battles during the American Civil War, including GETTYSBURG in 1863. As the steel industry grew there during the 19th and early 20th centuries, the fortunes of such industrialists as Andrew CARNEGIE, Henry Frick and John Pierpont MORGAN were made.

In 1979 an accident occurred at the nuclear power station on Three Mile Island, 10 miles (16km) south of the capital, Harrisburg, resulting in a partial meltdown of its uranium core, and raising concerns about safety standards. During the 1980s thousands of manufacturing jobs were lost, and such service industries as pharmaceuticals and computers began to grow.

penny post see HILL, SIR ROWLAND

Pentagon Papers Official study of

American defence policy, commissioned in 1967 to examine US involvement in Southeast Asia from the Second World War to May 1968. Leaked to the *New York Times* by Daniel Ellsberg, a former government employee, they revealed miscalculations, deceptions and military actions pursued without the public's knowledge. Their publication provoked demands for more open government.

Pepin Name of three Frankish, or Germanic,

rulers in Europe under the Merovingian and CAROLINGIAN dynasties in the 7th and 8th centuries. Pepin I ruled Austrasia, a region comprising present-day eastern France, western Germany and Holland, from 623 to 629. He was succeeded by his grandson Pepin II who also ruled Neustria, a region in the west of modern France, under the Merovingian kingdom. Pepin II's grandson Pepin III, also known as Pepin the Short, persuaded the last Merovingian, Childeric III, to abdicate in 751, and was crowned the first Carolingian King of the FRANKS.

The pope, who was a close ally, sent a bishop from Rome to consecrate Pepin III and the new dynasty. In return, Pepin III defended Rome from northern Lombard attacks and presented conquered cities, such as Ravenna, to the papacy. These formed the basis for the independent territory known as the PAPAL STATES, which survived until 1870. Pepin III also added Aquitaine, in south-west France, to his kingdom. On his death in 768 he was succeeded jointly by his brother Carloman and his son CHARLEMAGNE.

Pepys, Samuel (1633-1703) English diarist

and naval administrator. Pepys began public life as a clerk for the navy in 1660, the year he started his diary. In 1673 he was promoted to the post of secretary to the admiralty, and sat

Samuel Pepys
was a talented
adminstrator but is best
remembered for his 1.3 million-
word coded diary.

as a Member of Parliament. In 1697 Pepys was charged with betraying naval secrets to the French and briefly imprisoned in the Tower of London, but he was declared innocent and released the following year. He became president of the Royal Society and was reappointed as secretary to the admiralty in 1684. Pepys kept a diary from 1660 to 1669, which vividly documented Restoration London and his private life. It includes descriptions of the FIRE OF LONDON and the Great Plague. It was written in a private code which was not deciphered until 1825.

Perceval, Spencer (1762-1812) British prime minister, the only holder of the office to be assassinated. Perceval entered Parliament in 1796 as a Tory, and supported William PITT the Younger in the wars against revolutionary France. In 1801 he was appointed solicitor-general and held the post of attorney-general from 1802 to 1806. In the Duke of Portland's government he became chancellor of the exchequer, succeeding him as prime minister in 1809. Despite disagreements with the Duke of Wellington over costs, he steadfastly pursued the PENINSULAR WAR against Napoleon. In 1812 Perceval was shot dead in the lobby of the House of Commons by a bankrupt broker, John Bellingham, who was hanged for the murder.

Percy Family of Northumberland lords who supported Henry BOLINGBROKE's bid for the English throne, but rebelled against him after

he was crowned Henry IV in 1399. The Percy family arrived in England with William I in the 11th century. Sir Henry Percy (1364-1403), whose bravery won him the popular name of Hotspur, first won renown at the battle of OTTERBURN against the Scots in 1388. Both Hotspur and his father, the Earl of Northumberland, supported Henry Bolingbroke when he landed in the north of England in 1399 to capture the crown; and, as Henry IV, he rewarded them. However, within four years their desire for greater rewards led the Percys into open rebellion. Hotspur was killed at the Battle of Shrewsbury in 1403 and his uncle Thomas, Earl of Worcester, was captured and executed. Five years later Hotspur's father invaded England from Scotland, but he too was killed, and the Percy estates were forfeited to the king. Subsequently restored to their estates, later generations of the family resumed their role as guardians of England's northern frontier.

Pérez de Cuéllar, Javier (1920-) Peruvian diplomat, and secretary-general of the United Nations from 1982 to 1991. Pérez de Cuéllar entered the Peruvian foreign service in 1940, becoming his country's first ambassador to the USSR from 1969 to 1971 and envoy to the United Nations from 1971 to 1975. As secretary-general of the UN, his patient commitment to peacekeeping efforts led to such successes as the ceasefire that ended the IRAN-IRAQ WAR in 1988 and independence for Namibia in 1990.

Pergamum Ancient city in Mysia (now part of Turkey), where parchment was first used in the 2nd century BC; it takes its name from the city. Under the Attalid dynasty in the 3rd to 2nd centuries BC it developed into a major power, allying itself with Rome against the SELEUCID empire. Attalus I, who ruled from 241 to 197 BC, wrested most of Asia Minor from the Seleucids; and his successor Eumenes II achieved further victories, such as the defeat of the king of Syria, Antiochus III, at Magnesia. The kingdom's pro-Roman policy culminated in Attalus III's will, which bequeathed the kingdom to Rome in 133. It was made a part of the Roman province of Asia in 129, and Pergamum was soon eclipsed by Ephesus as the chief city of the region.

Attilid Pergamum flourished as a centre of HELLENISTIC CIVILISATION. It produced much sculpture, painting and decoration, and its library was second only to Alexandria's.

Pericles (c.495-429 BC) Statesman, orator and champion of democracy in ancient ATHENS. Praised by the historians THUCYDIDES and PLUTARCH as an incorruptible leader, Pericles dominated the cultural and political life of Athens during its golden age in the later part of the 5th century BC. He rose

to prominence in 462 BC as a critic of the privileges of the Areopagus, a powerful council of aristocrats, and became a leader of the movement for greater democracy. Around 454, he extended Athenian democracy by opening every government post to most free male citizens, making all decisions in the courts and the city's ruling assembly subject to a majority vote and paying officials state salaries.

Pericles expanded the Athenian empire through domination of the DELIAN LEAGUE, a confederation of Greek states; he quashed the island rebellion at Samos in 440; and he personally led an expedition into the Black Sea to secure the passage of grain from its shores to Athens. In 447 Pericles started a major programme of monument building, which included a temple to Athena – the Parthenon – on the ACROPOLIS. When the PELOPONNESIAN WAR with Sparta broke out in 431, he persuaded the Athenians to abandon the countryside and retreat behind the city walls, relying on Athens' naval power for protection. However, this strategy led to a plague in 430, and Pericles was removed from office. Re-elected the following year, he died of the disease soon afterwards.

Perón, Eva (1919-52) Argentinian political leader, popularly known as Evita. A minor actress before she met Juan PERÓN, she became active in politics and helped to organise the mass demonstration of workers that secured his release from prison in 1945. As Perón's wife during his presidency from

Eva Perón sits with her husband in 1951. Her stirring speeches and democratic policies won them both huge popularity in Argentina.

1946 to 1951, she unofficially ran the ministries of labour and of health, and set up the Eva Perón Social Aid Foundation to help those in need. She was also an outspoken champion of women's rights. Evita was revered as a saint by the poor and dispossessed, but the army opposed her in 1951 and blocked her bid for the vice-presidency. Perón's regime lost considerable popular support after her death from cancer at the age of 33.

Perón, Juan (1895-1974) Argentinian president. Perón was the leader of a group of Argentinian colonels which admired the Nazi dictator Adolf Hitler and the Italian fascist leader Benito Mussolini, and which in 1943 overthrew the government of President Ramón Castillo. He became minister of war and secretary for labour in the military government. His support for labour reforms and unionisation made him popular with workers. Following his imprisonment after a coup in 1945, Perón was released and elected president of Argentina with mass worker support in 1946. Working with his wife Eva PERÓN, he tried to implement a populist programme of rapid industrialisation, economic self-sufficiency and nationalisation of foreign firms which he called *peronismo*. But the price of Argentinian beef and wheat fell, and the economy faltered. In 1955 Peron was deposed by the armed forces and went into exile in Spain. In 1973 President Alejandro Lanusse permitted free elections in Argentina. Although Perón was not allowed to take part in the elections, his followers were. The Perónist Hector Campora was elected president, and then resigned so Perón could return home and take his place. Re-elected in the same year, Perón died in office in 1974, to be succeeded by his third wife Isabel Perón.

Perry, Matthew (1794-1858) US naval officer, and the first American to make official contact with 19th-century Japan. Assigned to the New York naval yard, Perry commanded America's first steamship, the *Fulton*, in 1837. He was promoted to commander in 1841. After helping to suppress the slave trade on the African coast in 1843, he fought in the MEXICAN AMERICAN WAR from 1846 to 1848. In 1852 Perry was ordered to enter Japan, at a time when the country had just one port, Nagasaki, open to foreigners. He entered Edo Bay (now part of Tokyo) in 1853, returning with a larger fleet the following year. Perry's display of pomp and military force convinced Japan's military government, the shogunate, to open two ports to US trade, as agreed in the Treaty of Kanagawa.

Persepolis Ceremonial capital of the Achaemenid empire in Persia (modern Iran). It was built in the reign of DARIUS I, from 522 to 486 BC, and a spring festival was held there

Ancient Persepolis was set high on a mountain terrace. Stonemasons carved this limestone bas-relief of guards on the base of the city's Tripylon, or council chamber, 2500 years ago.

each year at which tributes were made to the king. Persepolis was looted and burnt by ALEXANDER THE GREAT's troops in 331 BC. Excavations of the palaces of Darius I, Xerxes I and later kings have revealed fine examples of Achaemenid architecture, and bas-reliefs of officials from distant parts of the empire bringing gifts to the king at the festival.

Pershing, John (1860-1948) US general and commander of the American Expeditionary Forces in the First World War. Having served in the Spanish-American War of 1898, Pershing went on to fight in the Philippines and, from 1916, in Mexico. Following America's entry into the First World War, he was appointed commander of the US forces in France in May 1917. Here he successfully organised hastily trained troops into combat units. The Battle of St Mihiel in September 1917 was the first of Pershing's several victories on the WESTERN FRONT. In 1919 he was promoted to general, and was army chief of staff from 1921 to 1924.

Persia Country in south-west Asia, now called IRAN. Several dynasties ruled Persia, from the Achaemenids in the 6th century BC to the Pahlavis in the 20th century. In 546 BC CYRUS II (Cyrus the Great) established the Persian Empire under the Achaemenid dynasty, and defeated the Lydian king CROESUS. The empire was vast, stretching across what is now called the Middle East, and existed for some 200 years. Under DARIUS I, who reigned from 522 to 486, it was united under an

efficient centralised government, and palaces were built in the magnificent capitals of Susa and PERSEPOLIS.

In 500 the Persian Wars broke out when Greek city states on the coast of Asia Minor, aided by Athens and Eretria, revolted against Darius' rule. He put down the rebellions and destroyed Eretria in 490, but his attack on Athens failed when he was defeated at the Battle of MARATHON in the same year. Darius' son XERXES I attacked Athens again, defeated Greek troops at THERMOPYLAE in 480 and captured Athens. But in the same year the Persian fleet was crushed in the naval battle of SALAMIS, ensuring a Greek victory in the war. Artaxerxes I succeeded Xerxes in 464. During his reign there were several rebellions within the empire, as satraps (governors) attempted to seize control of their provinces, and Egypt began a 60 year struggle for independence. Signs of domestic dissent appeared in 425 when Xerxes II, the son of Artaxerxes, was murdered after a reign of only 45 days by his brother, who was in turn overthrown by another brother, Darius II, in about 423. CYRUS THE YOUNGER, the second son of Darius II, then led a revolt against his brother ARTAXERXES II and was defeated at the Battle of Cunaxa in 401.

Following Persia's support for the Greek states fighting Sparta in the Corinthian War from 395 to 386, Persia signed a peace treaty with Sparta, agreeing not to support Sparta's enemies in return for Persian control of the Greek city states in Asia Minor (now part of Turkey). But dynastic instability continued

> **DID YOU KNOW?**
>
> To keep in touch with his empire Darius I of Persia built a Royal Road 1677 miles (2699 km) long, with 111 post stations to provide fresh horses for royal messengers.

to weaken the empire. In 358 the son of Artaxerxes II, Artaxerxes III, murdered his brother's family for the throne and was himself killed in 338. His successor Darius III was the last of the Achaemenids, defeated by the Macedonian ALEXANDER THE GREAT in 331.

But Alexander died in 323 and his generals divided the empire. Subsequently Persia came under the control of Seleucus I and his successors the SELEUCID kings. In 247 PARTHIA, a country in northern Persia, broke from Seleucid rule and established itself as an independent Persian empire, becoming an important rival to Rome. The Parthians defeated a Roman force of 44 000 at the Battle of Carrhae in 53 BC.

In AD 224 Parthia fell to the Sassanid dynasty, and its king Ardashir I built a new empire which replaced Parthian and Seleucid rule. Persia thrived again as a strong state united by the ZOROASTRIAN religion. Magnificent cities were built, such as Ctesiphon and Firuzabad. In 642 invading Arabs toppled the Sassanids, and made Islam Persia's state religion. After invading Turkish armies defeated the Arabs in the 10th century, the Persians were governed by the SELJUK Turk dynasty until the 13th century, and the MONGOL EMPIRE from the 13th to the 15th centuries. In the 16th century Persia won its independence under ISMAIL I, the first king of the Safavi dynasty, who converted the population to the SHIITE sect of Islam.

> 66 **I was not hostile, I was not a follower of the Lie, I was not a doer of wrong – neither I nor any of my family.** 99
>
> *Inscription on the monument of Darius I, 486 BC*

During the 18th century the Afshar and Zand dynasties proved to be shortlived, unpopular regimes, and were succeeded by the Qajar dynasty in 1794. Ruling from Tehran, the Qajars remained in power until 1925. In 1935, following a coup d'état which established the Pahlavi dynasty, Persia's name was changed by royal decree to Iran.

Peru Country in the northwest of South America, former centre of INCA civilisation. Several highly developed cultures have flourished there since around 1000 BC, including the CHAVIN in the central Highlands, the MOCHICA on the northern coast and the Nazca on the southern coast. Between AD 600 and 1000 the Huari people dominated the central Andes, and around 1000 the Chimú became powerful on the northern coast. The Incas founded a capital at CUZCO, and began to conquer surrounding territory around 1200, acquiring a vast empire which during the 15th century stretched from Chile to Ecuador.

Around 1530 the empire was weakened by civil war between ATAHUALPA and Huáscar, brothers and equal rulers who each wanted to control the whole empire. Atahualpa was victorious in 1532, but he was in turn defeated by the Spanish adventurer Francisco PIZARRO, who captured Cuzco in 1533. Pizarro also founded Lima, Peru's capital, which in 1542 became the administrative centre of the Spanish viceroyalty of Peru. Francisco de Toledo was Spain's viceroy in Peru from 1561 to 1589. He expanded the viceroyalty to include all of Spanish South America except Venezuela.

During the 18th century national discontent spread among Indians and creoles – born in Peru, but of Spanish descent – as they remained poor and without political power. Led by a man of Inca ancestry, Tupac Amarú II, they revolted in 1780, but were defeated by the Spanish colonial government three years later. Following Napoleon's conquest of Spain in 1808, independence movements grew throughout Latin America. The revolutionary José de SAN MARTÍN captured Lima in 1821, and proclaimed Peru an independent republic. His fellow revolutionary, the Venezuelan Simón BOLÍVAR, took command of a liberation army to rid Peru of the Spanish troops which remained in the rest of the country. In 1824 Bolívar won the battles of Junín and Ayacucho, forcing the Spanish army to withdraw. Peru was briefly united with Bolivia from 1836 to 1839, but the confederation ended after a military defeat by Chile.

In 1844 General Ramón Castilla became president. He abolished slavery, established a public education system and subsidised Peru's guano fertiliser and nitrates industries. From 1872 to 1876 the country's first civilian president, Manuel Pardo, continued reforms, but he was hampered by the decline in value of nitrate and the cost of the WAR OF THE PACIFIC against Chile (1879-83), which led to the loss of the nitrate rich province of Tarapacá and to national bankruptcy in 1889.

At the end of the 19th century two political parties, the Democrats and the Civilians, were formed. The Civilians were an elected government from 1908 to 1912, and then part of a military dictatorship from 1919 to 1930. Peru's economy grew, benefiting from the opening of the PANAMA CANAL in 1914 and an increase in nitrates exports during the First World War. In 1924 a new party, the Alianza Popular Revolucionaria Americana (APRA), led by Haya de la Torre, called for greater Indian participation in politics. It was banned until the end of the Second World War when Peru, having sided with the Allies, emerged

victorious. In the 1945 elections APRA backed the winning candidate, José Luís Bustamante, but split with him in 1947. The resulting instability ended in a military coup led by Manuel Odría in 1948. Odría remained president until 1956, to be succeeded by Manuel Prado y Ugarteche. In 1962 the military seized power, and conducted elections which were won by Fernando Belaúnde Terry. In 1968 Belaúnde Terry was ousted by a military junta, or council of army officers, which set out a programme to nationalise US-controlled industries. The junta successfully exploited Peru's petroleum resources with foreign aid, but without foreign ownership.

In 1975 another military coup replaced the ruling junta, and in 1980 a new constitution was created and civilian rule was restored. Belaúnde Terry was re-elected president, but there was much unrest led by a Maoist guerrilla group, Sendero Luminoso ('Shining Path') and the Tupac Amarú Revolutionary Movement (MRTA). Elected in 1985, President Alan García Pérez fought a costly war against the guerrillas. In 1990 the son of Japanese immigrants, Alberto Fujimori of the Cambio 90 Party, was elected president. Riots, continuing strikes and guerrilla attacks led him to suspend the constitution in 1992. In September of that year Abimael Guzmán Reynoso, who had founded and led Sendero Luminoso since 1970, was captured and imprisoned, an important government victory against terrorism.

Pétain, Henri-Philippe (1856-1951) French army officer and head of state during the VICHY GOVERNMENT. Pétain became a national hero during the First World War when he stopped the advance of German troops at Verdun. In 1917 he was appointed commander in chief, and was made a marshal in the following year. Under his command, French armies took part in the final victorious offensive led by Marshal Ferdinand Foch in 1918. Pétain fought in Morocco in 1926, and became war minister in 1934.

When German armies attacked France in May 1940 during the Second World War, he was named vice-premier by the premier Paul Reynaud. Pétain urged an armistice, and in June he succeeded Reynaud as premier. The armistice he concluded with the Nazis left two-thirds of France occupied by Germany, with Pétain formally in charge of unoccupied France. Its capital was the spa town of Vichy in central France. His government was heavily authoritarian, backed by French fascists, and passed anti-Jewish laws. Following the allied invasion of France in 1944, Pétain was taken

St Peter pictured in a mosaic in the ceiling of Santa Constanza, Rome, receives from Christ the keys to the kingdom of heaven.

by the Nazis to Germany. He voluntarily returned to France in 1945 to face trial for treason, and he was condemned to death. President Charles de Gaulle commuted the sentence to solitary confinement for life, and Pétain was sent to a fortress on the Île d'Yeu, off the west coast of France, where he passed his final years.

Peter I 'the Great' see feature, page 498

Peter, St (died c.AD 64) One of the 12 apostles, originally named Simon. Peter was a married fisherman in Bethsaida (now in Israel) when Jesus called him, with his brother St Andrew, to be a disciple. Peter appears throughout the Gospels as leader of the disciples. According to the Gospel of St Matthew Jesus renamed Simon as 'Peter' – which means 'the Rock' – and said 'upon this rock I will build my church.' Matthew also says that Jesus entrusted Peter with 'the keys of the kingdom of heaven.' The New Testament also refers to Peter as 'Cephas' which is merely the Aramaic for 'the rock'. Following the arrest of Jesus by the Romans, Peter three times denied knowing him, as Jesus had predicted he would do. Peter probably left Antioch for Rome in 55, where he became the city's first bishop and died a martyr under the Emperor Nero. St Peter's Basilica, seat of the pope and the principal shrine of Roman Catholicism, stands on the supposed site of Peter's crucifixion.

Peterloo Massacre (August 16, 1819) Confrontation in Manchester, England, between parliamentary reformers and government troops. A crowd of some 60 000 people had gathered in St Peter's Fields to hear the radical politician Henry Hunt urge parliamentary reform and the repeal of the CORN LAWS, which had inflated bread prices. Local magistrates ordered the meeting to disband and sent in a body of cavalry to help the untrained constables to arrest Hunt. In the ensuing riot 11 civilians were killed and some 500 injured. The government's endorsement of the magistrates' actions caused national outrage, lending moral force to the reform movement. The name Peterloo was a pun used in the newspapers to compare the massacre unfavourably to the British victory over Napoleon at the Battle of Waterloo four years earlier.

Peter's pence Tax paid annually by lay persons in medieval Europe towards the support of the pope. Peter's pence was levied in England from the 9th century at the rate of one penny per householder. After some interruptions in payment, the tax was revived in the 11th century by William I who paid a single lump sum of £200 for the whole nation. In 1534, during the REFORMATION, the tax was abolished in England.

Petition of Right (1628) Declaration of civil liberties sent by the English Parliament to Charles I. The Petition of Right was drafted by Sir Edward COKE as a result of the expense of wars against France and Spain. It asserted four principles: no taxation without Parliament's consent; no forced billeting of troops on private citizens; no imposition of martial law in times of peace; and no imprisonment without just cause. Although Charles assented to the petition, he continued to exact customs duties on imports – known as tonnage and poundage taxes – and to imprison citizens arbitrarily during the period from 1629 to 1640 when he governed without Parliament.

Petra Ancient city in Jordan. The Nabataeans, a nomadic tribe who settled along the caravan routes from Arabia to the Mediterranean, made Petra their capital from the 4th century BC. After its occupation by the Romans in AD 106, the city's prosperity declined, like that of PALMYRA a century later. Muslims captured Petra in the 7th century, and Crusaders subsequently built a citadel there in the 12th century. The ruins of ancient Petra remained unknown in the modern world until 1812, when the Swiss explorer Johann Burckhardt discovered the city. Accessible only by a narrow gorge cut through steep rock walls, the ruins are extensive, with spectacular tombs carved in the pink rock of the surrounding hills. The Biblical name for the city is Sela.

phalanx Ancient Greek formation of infantry, consisting of a block of soldiers 8 or 16 rows deep. Originally deployed by Sparta in the 6th century BC, the phalanx reached its peak in the armies of the Macedonian kings PHILIP II and his son ALEXANDER THE GREAT in the 4th century BC. Armed with spears some 13 ft (4 m) long and sweeping over their enemies' ranks in a heavy wall of tightly packed men, Macedonian soldiers conquered Greece and the Middle East. By the 2nd century BC the spears used by the phalanx had grown to 21 ft (6.5 m) in response to the improved strength of defensive armour and swords. The now unwieldy phalanx could not match the more flexible Roman legions, and after the Romans conquered the Macedonians at Pydna in 168 BC it fell into disuse.

pharaoh Name given to the kings of ancient Egypt after 1500 BC, from the Egyptian word for palace. Ancient Egyptians considered the pharaoh to be a deity, identifying him with the sky god Horus and with the sun gods Re, Amon and Aton. After a pharaoh's death, he was said to change into the god of the underworld, Osiris, and to pass his powers to the new pharaoh. He was held to be all-powerful, controlling nature and human fertility. A succession of pharaohs expanded Egypt's territory. THUTMOSE I, pharaoh from around 1525 BC, conquered much of Nubia and subdued lands as far east as the Euphrates. From 1468 THUTMOSE III conquered nearly all of Syria, and strengthened Egyptian rule in Africa. Under RAMESES II, who reigned from 1292 to 1225, peace was made with the kingdom of the HITTITES, and the magnificent temples at KARNAK, THEBES and Luxor were built.

The remarkable sight of Petra's tomb-temple Khazneh Firaun greets the visitor after a long approach through the Siq, a shadowy gorge.

Architect of modern Russia

Tsar Peter the Great inherited a backward, eastern-looking country. Through titanic energy and ambition, he turned it into a modern power.

In the spring of 1703 Peter I, the young Tsar of Russia, was inspecting a marshy island at the mouth of the River Neva, where it opened into the Gulf of Finland. Suddenly he snatched a bayonet, carved a square in the turf and said: 'There shall be my city!'

This unpromising site offered Peter a key strategic advantage: an outlet to the Baltic giving direct contact with Europe. Work began first on a defensive fortress against the Swedes and then on a magnificent modern capital, St Petersburg, to replace Moscow. Peter was the first tsar to have travelled in Europe, admiring its technology and learning its trades. He was now determined to transform a backward, eastward-looking country into a modern power.

Typically for Russia, the policy had to be imposed from the top. Thousands of conscript workers died from exposure, undernourishment and even attacks by wolves. The imperial family and other

Peterhof (above) was the most lavish of the tsar's summer palaces. Peter took a personal interest in architecture and produced his own sketches (left).

nobles were compelled to build houses in the city. Within 50 years St Petersburg was a dazzling metropolis rivalling Venice for beauty and Versailles for opulence.

Peter wanted to underpin his reforms with modern armed forces and industries to support them. Experts from Europe were hired to establish ironworks, cannon foundries, powder mills and shipyards, and to train and lead his army. The new army faced its first test in 1709, when Charles XII of Sweden invaded from the north. The Swedes were routed at Poltava, near the River Dnieper, and Charles fled to Turkey. Then in 1714 a Russian-built fleet defeated the Swedes at Hangö and gained control of Finland.

REFORM THROUGH FEAR

Peter's energy matched his ambitions. He reformed the nobility, compelling them to choose a career and creating a more efficient bureaucracy based on ability as well as birth. He encouraged trade, reformed the calendar and the alphabet, founded the Academy of Sciences, started newspapers and even tried to launch a scheme of elementary education for all. By the time of his death in 1725, Russia was the largest iron producer in Europe.

Like Ivan IV 'the Terrible' before him and later Catherine the Great and Stalin, Peter forced through his modernisation by fear. A middle class barely existed and there was no democracy, only the absolute monarchy of the tsar. The Soviet regime used the same centralised power to industrialise the USSR.

If Peter's reforms did not turn Russia into a western nation, they did make her a leading European power. A historian later wrote: 'Peter the Great found at home in Russia only a blank sheet of paper. With his powerful hand he wrote on it: Europe and the West.'

Pharisee Member of a Jewish religious party in ancient Israel which stressed the importance of interpreting the first five books of the Old Testament, or Torah, according to changing social conditions. The Pharisees emerged around 165 BC as a distinct group in opposition to the party of the high priests, the SADDUCEES. When interpreting the Torah, they gave equal importance to the oral law and traditions of the Jewish people, and challenged the reliance of the Sadducees on just the written text. The Pharisees fostered the development of Jewish places of worship, or synagogues, away from the temple in Jerusalem. After the fall of Jerusalem to the Romans in AD 70, and the failed Jewish revolt of 135, Judaism survived in the Diaspora (the dispersal of the Jews) through the synagogues and schools of the Pharisees. Their influence on Christianity was also substantial.

Philip I 'the Handsome' (1478-1506) Spanish king of Castile whose marriage to JOANNA THE MAD, daughter of FERDINAND V and ISABELLA I of Spain, in 1496 united the Habsburg and Spanish dynasties. The son of the Habsburg Holy Roman Emperor MAXIMILIAN I and Duchess Mary of Burgundy, he inherited BURGUNDY and the Low Countries of Holland, Belgium and Luxembourg after his mother's death in 1482. Philip became joint ruler of Castile in 1504, after Queen Isabella's death, and sole ruler in 1506, when Joanna's mental condition worsened. He died of fever the same year.

Philip II (382-336 BC) King of Macedonia from 359 to 336 BC who organised his army in the PHALANX formation, conquered surrounding Greek states and bequeathed a powerful federation, the League of Corinth, to his son ALEXANDER THE GREAT. He created an army based around blocks of pike-armed infantrymen, the phalanx, and pursued a policy of expansion by war and diplomacy. After defeating Athens and Thebes at the battle of Chaeronea in 338, he established the League of Corinth, a federation that stretched

Philip II's gold coinage shows him driving all before him as he turns Macedonia into a major power.

from the Black Sea to the southern Peloponnese. During preparations for an invasion of Persia he was assassinated, possibly at the instigation of his wife OLYMPIA.

Philip II (1527-98) Habsburg king of Naples and Sicily from 1554, of the Low Countries (Holland, Belgium and Luxembourg) from 1555, of Spain from 1556 and, as Philip I, of Portugal from 1580. Philip acceded to the Spanish throne when his father, Holy Roman Emperor Charles V, abdicated in 1556. His first wife, Mary of Portugal, died in 1546, and he was subsequently married three times: to Mary I of England from 1554 to 1558, to Elizabeth of Valois from 1559 to 1568, and

The troubled Philip II of Spain failed to solve the many religious, military and financial problems that beset his reign.

from 1570 to 1598 to Anne of Austria, by whom he had a son and successor, Philip III of Spain. He stayed in the Iberian peninsula from 1559 until his death, and from there he laboured to preserve the far-flung lands owned by the Habsburgs, which included the SPANISH EMPIRE in Italy and the Americas. As a devout Roman Catholic, Philip was concerned to combat heresy and strongly supported the Spanish INQUISITION, which he also saw as a means of extending control over his dominions. His Catholic religious policies provoked the Protestant Dutch revolts in 1568 and the Revolt of the Moriscos – Spanish Moors who had converted to Christianity – from 1568 to 1570.

English support for the Dutch rebels led Philip to launch the SPANISH ARMADA against England in 1588; it was soundly beaten. His support for Catholics in the FRENCH WARS OF RELIGION from 1590 bankrupted Spain by 1596, despite moneys from the Americas and heavy domestic taxation. Philip's major military success in the later years of his reign was the conquest of Portugal in 1580. He left an empire in severe economic straits and fiercely divided between Protestants and Catholics.

Philip III 'the Good' (1396-1467) Duke of Burgundy from 1419. Philip was the founder of a Burgundian state which in the 15th century rivalled France. His first act as duke was to forge an alliance with Henry V of England, the Treaty of Troyes, in 1420 and to recognise Henry as heir to the French throne. His power increased substantially when he conquered the surrounding lands of Namur in 1421, Holland and Zeeland in 1428 and Brabant in 1430. In 1435 Philip recognised Charles VII as the king of France, and was permitted in turn to pursue a foreign policy independent of royal control.

Philip's territorial expansion continued with the conquest of Luxembourg in 1443, but prolonged war taxes provoked an uprising in the city of Ghent, which was ended by the bloody battle of Gavere in 1453. Under Philip the Burgundian court was one of the most refined and prosperous in Europe. In 1430 he founded a chivalric order, the Order of the Golden Fleece, and patronised a number of outstanding Flemish painters, including Rogier van der Weyden and Jan van Eyck.

Philip IV 'the Fair' (1268-1314) King of France from 1285. Philip's quarrels with the pope led him to call the first STATES-GENERAL and move the papacy from Rome to Avignon, France. Popes had generally supported 13th-century kings by calling their campaigns crusades and so letting them tax the clergy. In 1296 Pope Boniface VII explicitly forbade such taxation without papal consent. Philip reacted by forbidding the export of coin to Rome. The pope backed down in 1297, saying kings could tax 'in cases of necessity', even without specific papal approval. A second quarrel broke out when Philip arrested Bernard Saisset, the Bishop of Pamiers, calling the first states-general in 1302 in order to justify his action. Threatened by Boniface with excommunication, Philip had the pope seized and imprisoned in 1303. Boniface died soon afterwards, and Philip secured the election of his successor, Clement V, who in 1309 moved the papacy from Rome to Avignon. At Philip's insistence the pope suppressed the Knights Templar in 1313 and allowed him to confiscate their property. Seeking more wealth, Philip also persecuted the Jews and the Lombards, who were Italian bankers.

Philip V (1683-1746) Duke of Anjou and first Bourbon king of Spain from 1700. A grandson of Louis XIV of France, Philip was bequeathed the Spanish throne by the last Habsburg king of Spain, Charles II. When Louis XIV accepted the throne on behalf of his grandson, the prospect of a French prince ruling Spain plunged Europe into the War of the SPANISH SUCCESSION from 1701 to 1713. Philip's claim was confirmed at a peace conference held in UTRECHT in 1713, but Spain lost Gibralta and Minorca to the British, the Spanish Netherlands and Naples to Austria, and Sicily to the duchy of Savoy. Within Spain, Catalonia had been in open revolt since 1705, and its capital, Barcelona, was recaptured by Philip in 1714. For the rest of his reign Philip's government was dominated by his second wife, Elizabeth Farnese. A war with Austria from 1733 to 1736 enabled Philip to regain Naples and Sicily. At his death, Spain was embroiled in the War of the AUSTRIAN SUCCESSION which lasted from 1740 to 1748.

Philip VI (1293-1350) First French king of the VALOIS dynasty. Philip's reign began in 1328 and saw the start of both the HUNDRED YEARS' WAR with England and the plague, or BLACK DEATH. Invoking the SALIC LAW, which ruled that those descended in the female line could not inherit the crown, Philip denied the rival claim of Edward III of England to the French throne, and in 1337 the Hundred Years' War began. The English destroyed the entire French fleet at Sluis in 1340. In 1346 Edward III invaded Normandy and defeated Philip at the battle of CRÉCY. The following year the English captured Calais, which they held for two centuries. A truce was concluded in 1347, just as the Black Death was beginning its ravages of France.

Philippi, Battle of (42 BC) Octavian Caesar and Mark Antony defeated the armies of Gaius Cassius Longinus and Marcus Brutus at Philippi in Macedonia, Greece, and so avenged the death of the Roman dictator Julius Caesar. Cassius and Brutus had conspired to assassinate Caesar in 44 BC and then raised an army to fight in the name of the republic. In the aftermath of their defeat, both Cassius and Brutus committed suicide. In 29 Octavian, Julius' grandnephew, became Rome's first emperor, and in 27 the senate gave him the title of AUGUSTUS, or imperial majesty.

> ### DID YOU KNOW?
>
> *Philip IV grew up with his future queen, Joan of Navarre. They married when he was 16, she 12, and he wanted to abdicate when she died in 1305.*

Philippines South-east Asian country of over 7000 islands. The Philippines were a Spanish colony from the 16th century but at the end of the Spanish-American War in 1898 control passed to the United States. The islands achieved internal self-government in 1935 and full independence in 1946. Waves of Malay peoples displaced the indigenous Negrito inhabitants around 2000 BC. By AD 1000 the islands were prosperously trading within South-east Asia. In 1521 Spaniards under the Portuguese explorer Ferdinand MAGELLAN visited the islands for the first time. The following year an expedition from the Spanish colony of Mexico named the islands after Prince Philip, later Philip II of Spain. In 1564 the Spanish navigator Miguel de Legaspi set out from Mexico to conquer the islands, convert the Filipinos to Christianity, open up commerce with the Far East, and secure a share of trade in the MOLUCCAS, or Spice Islands. By 1571 the Spanish had established the future capital of Manila, from where a flourishing trade with China, India and the East Indies was developing towards the end of the 16th century.

As Spanish control spread through the islands, the colonial governor was made a viceroy in 1589. During the 17th and 18th centuries the harsh treatment of groups such as the Chinese and the local Muslims, or Moros, led to several revolts. Spanish Jesuit power also contributed to nationalist resentment. In 1896 a popular revolutionary writer, José Rizal, was executed in Manila. His death inspired a full-scale rebellion against Spanish rule. In 1898 the revolution was interrupted by the Spanish-American War. The Filipino leader General Emilio Aguinaldo, given arms by the United States, declared the country independent. In the same year the USA concluded a treaty with Spain in Paris, transferring the Philippines to America. Aguinaldo led an insurrection against the United States from 1899 to 1901 but was defeated, and the islands passed to the USA.

In May 1935 the United States offered the Philippines self-government, and in November 1935 the Commonwealth of the Philippines was established under President Manuel QUEZON. During the Second World War, Japan occupied the islands. In February 1945 they were liberated by the US forces, and the Philippines were granted independence the following year. The Philippines president, Manuel Roxas, agreed that the USA should continue to keep military bases there for 99 years. Between 1946 and 1972 the country faced severe social and economic problems, as communist-led guerrillas fought for power, Moros rebelled against Christian settlement, and inflation soared.

In 1972 President Ferdinand MARCOS declared martial law, claiming that a communist rebellion was imminent. Throughout the 1970s poverty and government corruption grew, and in August 1983 the opposition leader Benigno Aquino was assassinated at Manila airport. Anti-Marcos dissent rallied behind Aquino's widow, Corazon, and her United Nationalist Democratic Organisation. In the 1986 elections both Marcos and Aquino claimed the victory. Strikes and

protests in support of Aquino followed. In February 1986 Marcos fled to America, and Corazon Aquino became president, restoring the country to a fragile democracy. No fewer than six attempted military coups were made against President Aquino in the six years of her government. She was succeeded in 1992 by her first choice as successor, the former defence secretary Fidel Ramos.

Following talks with the rebel Moros, Ramos agreed in February 1995 to allow a Moro National Liberation Front government to be formed on the island of Mindanao. In May that year, Ramos was re-elected president, and Imelda Marcos, widow of Ferdinand Marcos, won a seat in the House of Representatives.

Philippines Campaign
(1944-5) US naval and air campaign that recaptured the Philippines from the Japanese in the Second World War. In the Battle of the Philippine Sea, fought in June 1944 by Japanese and US aircraft carriers, American aircraft destroyed some 400 Japanese planes and three carriers. In October American ships destroyed the Japanese navy at the Battle of Leyte Gulf, five days after US forces had captured the island. American troops under General Douglas MACARTHUR landed on the island of Luzon in January 1945, and in July he announced that 'all the Philippines are now liberated'. The Luzon campaign alone was greater in scale and cost than the entire US involvement in either Italy or North Africa. More than 425 000 Japanese lost their lives in the course of the Philippines campaign.

Philistines
Non-Semitic people who settled in CANAAN in the 12th century BC and gave the region the name Philistia, or PALESTINE. Originally a sea people who may have come from the Aegean, they settled in Canaan (present-day Israel and the Autonomous Palestinian Territories). Their five coastal cities – Ashdod, Askelon, Ekron, Gath and Gaza – formed a prosperous confederacy in an area that was known as Philistia.

The Philistines were enemies of the Israelites and inflicted a defeat on the first Israelite king, SAUL, but were defeated in turn by Saul's successor, King DAVID. In the 10th century the Hebrew kingdom was divided into JUDAH and ISRAEL, and the Philistines regained their independence. They frequently fought battles with both Jewish kingdoms until the 7th century, when they fell under the successive rule of the Assyrians, the Egyptians and the Babylonians. After these defeats the Philistines were never able to recover their political and military power. The

use of the name Philistine to mean an uncultured, crudely materialistic person dates from Hebrew records of the wars between the Philistines and the Israelites.

Phoenicians
Mediterranean traders who around 1500 BC, used a phonetic alphabet which forms the basis of the modern Roman alphabet. Phoenicians lived in an area which roughly corresponds to modern Lebanon and Israel in about 3000 BC. They were Canaanites who originally spoke one of the Semitic group of languages. Canaanite merchants established cities such as Byblos, Sidon and Tyre on the Levant coast, and traded with Egypt from about 2800.

By 1250 the Phoenicians were a successful sea power, with markets stretching as far as Spain. As they expanded their trade, they established several important colonies between the 9th and 7th centuries, including CARTHAGE. Phoenicia was dominated by ASSYRIA at this time, then in the 6th century fell to PERSIA's empire. ALEXANDER THE GREAT conquered the country in the 4th century, and in AD 64 it became a part of the

The Phoenicians, lords of the sea for 1000 years, treasured their trading vessels. This one is carved on the side of a sarcophagus.

Roman Empire. Phoenician exports included cedar and pine wood, glass and cloth dyed purple – the name Phoenicia is derived from the Greek word for the colour purple.

Phoenix Park murders
(1882) Assassination in Dublin of high-ranking British officials by Irish terrorists. On May 6, 1882, the Invincibles, a splinter group of the Irish nationalist FENIANS, murdered the British chief secretary for Ireland, Lord Frederick Cavendish, and his under-secretary, Thomas Burke, while they were strolling in Dublin's Phoenix Park. Widespread disgust against extremist violence enabled the moderate Irish member of Britain's Parliament, Charles PARNELL, to strengthen the position of the nonviolent Irish HOME RULE movement. He was

accused in 1887 by *The Times* of being involved in the murder plot, but was cleared of guilt by a parliamentary commission in 1890.

Photius (c.810-c.893) Bishop, or Patriarch, of Constantinople whose condemnation of the Roman Catholic Church marked the first stage in the separation of the Eastern ORTHODOX CHURCH from Rome. When Ignatius, Patriarch of Constantinople, was deposed in 858 Photius succeeded him, but Pope Nicholas I refused to recognise the new patriarch since he was a layman who had been rushed through holy orders expressly to take office. Photius responded by excommunicating the pope at a synod in 867 and condemning many points of doctrine of the Roman Catholic Church. In the same year the Byzantine emperor Basil I banished Photius and reinstated Ignatius. On Ignatius' death in 877, Photius regained his position and was recognised by the new pope, John VIII. In emphasising the differences between the Eastern and Western Churches, Photius created what was known as the Photian schism and sowed the seeds of final separation, the EAST-WEST SCHISM, which occurred in 1054.

photography Aristotle wrote about the principles of photography in his *Physics* in the 4th century BC. However, the *camera obscura*, or dark chamber, was not developed until the 16th century; this filmless apparatus consisted of a small box with a pinhole at one end and a screen on the opposite side. Inverted images from the pinhole appeared on the screen, which were used by artists to sketch outlines of views.

In 1727 a German professor of anatomy, Johann Schulze, discovered that the darkening of silver nitrate was caused by light, rather than heat. Thomas Wedgwood and Sir Humphry DAVY exploited this discovery early in the 19th century to create photograms, which used paper soaked in silver nitrate to record the shapes of objects placed on it. However, these images faded rapidly as they could not be permanently fixed. In 1816 a French physicist, Joseph Niépce, made the world's first negative, on paper, and in 1827 the first photograph, on metal. From 1827 to his death in 1833 Niépce collaborated with a French painter, Louis DAGUERRE, who developed the daguerreotype in 1839. Daguerre's invention fixed a positive image on a silver plate for the first time. In England in the following year, Henry Fox TALBOT invented a paper negative from which paper positives could be made, and called his photographic method the calotype process. In 1846 Talbot published *The Pencil of Nature*, which was the world's first book with photographs. A further technical advance was made in 1851 by Frederick Archer, with the collodian process. This combined the focus and definition of the daguerreotype with the reproductive method of the calotype, and soon replaced both its predecessors. The collodian process for the first time enabled images of a high quality to be reproduced and distributed in large numbers.

In the 1870s, in the United States, the Englishman Eadweard Muybridge devised a mechanical camera shutter to take a series of photographs of a horse in motion. When these were mounted on a zoetrope, a cylinder which was spun, the horse appeared to be in continuous motion. This demonstrated the phenomenon of 'persistence of vision', whereby a series

> 66 **God created man in His own image, and no man-made machine may fix the image of God.** 99
>
> *Religious objections to photography in the Prussian newspaper,* Leipziger Stadtanzeiger, *1839*

of images passing before the human eye in rapid succession appears to move without interruption. Muybridge's invention for projecting these images, the zoopraxiscope, was a significant step in the evolution of CINEMATOGRAPHY. In 1881 the introduction of the halftone process, which reduced a photographic image to a dotted pattern and allowed for greater precision of reproduction, resulted in the spread of photographic images in books and newspapers. In 1888 photography became a popular pursuit after George Eastman invented the relatively inexpensive Kodak box camera. In the 20th century developments have included the introduction of colour film for transparencies in 1935 and for prints in 1942. The Polaroid camera, which could produce prints seconds after the film was exposed to light, was created by Edward Land and appeared in 1947. In 1963 the Kodak company produced a compact 'instamatic' camera, which made photography even more popular. In the 1990s computer technology has led to the development of the digital camera which records visual images electronically without using a film, but uses a 'card' which can be inserted into a computer to produce images on screen.

Phrygia Territory in Anatolia, Turkey, which dominated Asia Minor from the 12th century to the 7th century BC and whose kings Midas and Gordius passed into Greek mythology. When the empire of the HITTITES collapsed in about 1200 BC, Phrygian speakers, perhaps from the Balkans, settled in a former Hittite territory which became known as Phrygia. Between the 12th and 9th centuries Phrygia formed part of a loose confederation of peoples in Anatolia. In the 8th century the Assyrians seized the eastern half of the confederation, and a Phrygian kingdom under Midas flourished in the west. The kingdom was defeated by the Russian Cimmerians in the 6th century and soon became dominated by the empire of LYDIA. Subsequently it fell under the sway of PERSIA, the SELEUCIDS and the kingdom of PERGAMUM. In 133 Pergamum was bequeathed to the Roman Empire, which later divided Phrygia between the Roman provinces of Asia and Galatia.

Picasso (1881-1973) Spanish painter, sculptor, graphic artist and designer, who became one of the 20th century's most celebrated artists. Picasso was a child prodigy, producing exquisite classical drawings by the age of ten. He lived in Barcelona where from 1901 to 1904 he developed the early style known as his 'Blue period', named after the predominant colour in paintings that depicted the poor and down-and-outs in attitudes of despair. In 1904 he moved to Paris where he embarked on his life-affirming 'Rose period', warmer but more enigmatic than the Blue. In 1907, influenced by the work of Paul Cézanne, the French

Photography races towards the silver screen. In 1878, using a mechanical shutter operating 25 times a second, Eadweard Muybridge took a series of photographs of a galloping horse. When the photographs were viewed through slits in a spinning drum the horse appeared to be moving.

The masterly hand of Picasso could turn a lump of clay into a priceless collector's ceramic.

artist, and by primitive African and ancient Iberian art, Picasso produced the *Demoiselles d'Avignon* (1907) – a work that pioneered the movement known as Cubism. Developed by Picasso and the painter Georges Braque over the next seven years, Cubism analysed the geometry and structure of subjects to combine different viewpoints into one image, rather than simply depict their normal appearance.

Picasso's output was prolific and he experimented with different ideas – from using more decorative elements to producing works of almost classical poise and weight. He also produced collage and sculpture. One of his best-known works, *Guernica* (1937), was painted in response to the Spanish Civil War and was a powerful attack on fascism and war. Picasso's creativity and playful approach gave a freedom to 20th-century art which is still exercised by artists today.

Picts Ancient inhabitants of a Pictish kingdom who united with the southern kingdom of Dalriada to form Scotland. The Romans called them *picti*, 'painted people', because they painted or tattooed their bodies. They lived north of HADRIAN'S WALL, making frequent attacks on Roman Britain. In AD 367 they were joined in a major assault on Britain by the SAXONS on the North Sea coast and the Irish on the western seaboard, but were defeated. In the 5th century Scottish invaders from Ireland established the kingdom of Dalriada to the south of the Picts. By the 7th century there was a unified Pictland north of the river Forth with its own language and culture, in which family titles and land were

inherited through the female line. Viking attacks in the 9th century led the Picts to unite with the Scots under Kenneth MacAlpin, king of Dalriada. This union in 843 marked the birth of the kingdom of Scotland, with distinct Highland and Lowland cultures reflecting the former divide between the Pictish kingdom and Dalriada.

Piedmont Region of northwest Italy, centred on Turin, which was the centre of the RISORGIMENTO, the movement for Italian unification, from 1831 to 1861. It was ruled from the 11th century by the dukes of SAVOY, who became kings of Sicily in 1713. Spain conquered Sicily in 1718, and by the Treaty of The Hague in 1720 Spain ceded Sardinia to the kings of Savoy. France annexed Piedmont in 1794, but it was restored to the kingdom of Sardinia after the defeat of Napoleon I in 1815, and the Sardinian King Victor Emmanuel I returned to its capital, Turin. From 1831, when the liberal King Charles Albert acceded to the throne, Piedmont became the centre of the movement for Italian unification. Camillo Cavour (1810-61), the statesman who prepared Italy for unification, came from Piedmont. Following a treaty with Napoleon III in 1860, Savoy and Nice were forfeited to France in return for France's recognition of votes in Tuscany, Parma and Modena for union with Piedmont-Sardinia. In 1861, after Giuseppe GARIBALDI had taken Sicily and Naples, VICTOR EMMANUEL II was proclaimed king of a united Italy with Turin as the capital, which it remained until 1864.

Pilate, Pontius (1st century AD) Roman governor of the province of Judaea, who condemned Jesus Christ to death by crucifixion. Pilate's part in the trial of Christ is described in the New Testament of the Bible. The ancient Jewish historian Josephus accused him of

corruption and abuse of Jewish customs. Pilate was summoned to Rome by the emperor Tiberius in 36 to answer charges of cruelty. He is said to have committed suicide.

pilgrimage see feature, page 504

Pilgrimage of Grace (1536-7) Rebellions in the north of England which challenged the religious and economic changes introduced by Henry VIII during the REFORMATION. In October 1536 rebels marched to Lincoln after hearing rumours that the king was about to seize Church jewels. The rebels were badly organised and easily dispersed, but their cause was embraced in the county of Yorkshire. A lawyer, Robert Aske, rallied some 30 000 men, and rebel leaders met the king's representative, the Duke of Norfolk, at Doncaster. The rebels pledged their loyalty to Henry VIII, but asked that Thomas CROMWELL, the king's chief minister who had been sending out agents to suppress the MONASTERIES, be removed from office. They also complained of high rents, taxes and the enclosure of land that had previously been in common use. Norfolk assured the rebels that the monasteries would be restored, and promised them a full pardon. However, after Aske and other leaders of the Pilgrimage of Grace had ordered the protesters to disperse, another uprising began in Beverley in January 1537. Although Aske and his confederates helped to put down this new uprising, they were arrested and executed in June 1537. Henry VIII proceeded to impose martial law in the north of England to stamp out further religious opposition.

Pilgrim Fathers The 102 founders of Plymouth, Massachusetts, the first European settlement in New England, who sailed there from Plymouth, England, in 1620 on board the *Mayflower*. Puritan Separatists, who rejected the Anglican Church, fled their village of Scrooby, Nottinghamshire, in 1608 and settled in Holland. In 1617 they sent

A tapestry commemorates the Pilgrim Fathers' thankful landing at Plymouth Rock, but the Puritans were ill-prepared for the hard winter ahead.

Robert Cushman and John CARVER as representatives to London to negotiate with the Virginia Company for permission to settle in the colony of Virginia. By 1619 the permission had been granted and a syndicate of London merchants, the Merchant Adventurers, had agreed to finance a profit-sharing company. In August 1620, 36 Separatists embarked at Plymouth. There were also 66 non-Puritan emigrants on board the *Mayflower*, whom the Separatists called 'Strangers'.

On the voyage to America the emigrants agreed on a document for self-government in their colony, the Mayflower Compact, which the sixth president of the United States, John Quincy Adams, later hailed as 'the first example in modern times of a social compact... instituted by voluntary agreement... by men of equal rights and about to establish their community in a new country'. In December 1690 they dropped anchor off Cape Cod, Massachusetts, and disembarked at a site they named Plymouth Plantation. Conditions were harsh and only half the settlers survived the first winter.

After governor John Carver's death in 1621, William Bradford was elected the Pilgrims' leader, and he was subsequently re-elected 30 times. His *History of Plimoth Plantation* provides a vivid account of how the colony survived with the help of an English-speaking Native American named Squanto who, with other Native Americans, taught the settlers how to plant corn, trap animals and even use herring as fertiliser. In 1643 Plymouth joined the New England confederation. Fur trading provided a lucrative export, enabling the colonists to repay their debts to the Merchant Adventurers by 1648. By the mid 17th century more than 80000 colonists had followed the Pilgrim Fathers. In 1691 Plymouth was incorporated into Massachusetts.

pillory and stocks Medieval wooden frames with holes for holding the head and hands of an offender and exposing him to public ridicule. Pillory and stocks were a means by which local communities in the Middle Ages could punish minor offenders convicted in the court of a manor or a town. They were abolished in 1832 in France, and 1837 in England.

Pilsudski, Joseph (1867-1935) Polish general and the first president of independent Poland from 1918 to 1922. Pilsudski was exiled to Siberia from 1887 to 1892 for an alleged attempt on the life of the Russian tsar Alexander III, who ruled a large area of Poland. On his return, Pilsudski joined the Polish Socialist Party, and in 1894 he started a secret party newspaper called *Robotnik*, 'The Worker'. After the failed revolution in Russia in 1905, Pilsudski resolved to put national

Scientists scrutinise the 'Piltdown Man' in 1912. They took the fake so seriously that the supposed hominid was reconstructed (right).

independence before socialist revolution in Poland. When the First World War broke out, he commanded three Polish Legions which fought with Austrian arms against Russia.

In 1917 he refused to fight for Germany on the Eastern Front unless he received Germany's guarantee of Polish independence. When Germany refused, Pilsudski withdrew his support from their war effort and was imprisoned in Madgeburg. After the war he was released, and returned to Poland to declare national independence. A national committee agreed that Pilsudski should be chief of state and chief of the army staff. From 1920 to 1921 he successfully fought against the Russian Bolshevik army which had invaded Poland to spread revolution. In 1922 Poland adopted a democratic constitution and Pilsudski stepped down as chief of state. Disillusioned with Poland's democracy, he led a coup d'état in 1926 and became Minister of Defence. In this office, he established a virtual dictatorship until his death. In his continuous quest to guarantee Poland's independence, he signed nonaggression pacts with Hitler's Germany and Stalin's Soviet Union in 1934. He died in office the following year.

Piltdown Man Skull found at Piltdown, Sussex, in 1912, and hailed by many scholars as the 'missing link' which proved that humans and apes share a common ancestor, as suggested in Charles DARWIN's theory of evolution. It was not until 1953 that scientific tests showed that the remains of *Eoanthropus Dawsoni*, named after Charles Dawson, the amateur geologist who found them, were in fact the jaw of a orang-utan and a human

cranium. Its bones had been stained to simulate age. In May 1996 the fake was revealed to be the work of Martin Hinton, a disgruntled curator at London's Natural History Museum.

Pinochet, Augusto (1915-) Chilean president and dictator from 1973 to 1990. Pinochet began his military career in 1933 at the age of 18. In 1973 he became commander of the Chilean army and led a military coup against the left-wing government of President Salvador ALLENDE in September of that year. As head of a four-man military junta, the Council of Chile, he declared himself president in June 1974.

During his first three years of military rule, about 130000 opponents were arrested, some of whom were tortured, and there were some 2000 political assassinations. A plebiscite held in 1978 confirmed his presidency. In 1980 he promised a return to democracy after nine years. Despite an economic depression from 1980 to 1983, his free market policies created steady economic growth. Persecution of political opponents continued, and in October 1988 Chile voted in a plebiscite for open elections and against Pinochet continuing as president.

He remained in office until free elections installed a new president, the Christian Democrat Patricio Aylwin, in March 1990. Pinochet continued to hold the post of army commander in chief.

Punishing journeys to sacred places

From earliest times in all cultures, people have seen certain places as sacred. In medieval Europe, pilgrims journeyed to Jerusalem and other shrines, undergoing hardships to gain the benefit of contact with the saints.

One of the oldest and most universal symbols of the divine is the sacred place. When people enter it they feel that they have walked into another dimension, different from but compatible with their ordinary lives. Before the development of scientific ways of looking at the world, people developed a sacred geography. Certain places were thought to be essentially different from others. The sacred dimension of life was believed to have broken into the mundane world at that spot. Perhaps a god had appeared there and so forged a link between heaven and earth. Other places were regarded as sacred because they stood out from their surroundings. Mountains – Mount Fuji in Japan or Mount Olympus in Greece, for example – could be symbols of the transcendence of the divine. When people ascended them, suspended midway between heaven and earth, they felt that they could meet their gods.

EDIFICES OF GOD

The religious experience did not happen automatically at these holy places. Often people were helped by means of liturgy; often they built shrines and temples at these sacred sites. Their architecture was profoundly inspiring: sometimes the plan of the temple symbolised the inner path that men and women had to take to reach the divine. The cathedrals of medieval Europe were such extraordinary architectural and engineering feats that they filled worshippers with awe: people felt that they had entered a wholly different realm of experience.

People felt the sacred as a powerful force. They wanted to share the richer, fuller lives of the gods and to reach beyond the limitations and perils of their own fragile existence. Consequently they wanted to dwell as near as possible to the sacred. The temple or the cathedral was at the heart of a city or settlement and by clustering around these holy places people believed that they could pass their lives close to the divine.

But people were also prepared to make long journeys in order to visit a particularly sacred spot. The pilgrimage, a holy journey to the source of power, has been an important devotion in almost all the major religions. The journey itself acquired spiritual significance. In medieval Europe, a pilgrim would wear special clothes and badges – the scallop shell of St James, the fisherman saint, for example – and begin his journey by making a solemn vow to reach his destination, whatever hardships he might have to endure on the way. The pilgrimage was a powerful symbol of the religious quest. It demonstrated the readiness of the pilgrims to turn their backs upon their ordinary lives and make a new start. Pilgrims were compared with Abraham, who left his family and home in order to obey his God, and with the Israelites who made the Exodus from slavery in Egypt: they too were liberating

At journey's end, pilgrims reach the walls of Canterbury. On sale were badges, such as the one above showing St Thomas Becket riding in triumph, and flasks (left) said to contain the diluted blood of the saint, capable of curing illness.

Pilgrims, like these 14th-century travellers equipped with staffs for their journey, would often cross great distances to visit shrines.

themselves from their ordinary concerns in order to find God.

In Europe the pilgrimage played a crucial role in educating the laity in Christian values. After the fall of the Roman Empire in the late 5th century, much of Europe had become a pagan backwater. In the 11th century, the Benedictine monks of the Abbey of Cluny in Burgundy initiated reforms designed to reintroduce Christianity to Europe. In particular, they promoted the pilgrimage to such special places as Conques in southern France, where the relics of the martyr St Faith were enshrined, or Compostela in north-western Spain, the most important place of pilgrimage in Europe after Rome, where visitors could find what purported to be the tomb of St James the Apostle.

For the monks of Cluny it was the journey, not the arrival, that counted. They hoped that the pilgrims, during their long trek to the sacred place, would live in some respects like monks or nuns. They would be celibate; they were not allowed to fight or carry a sword; because of the hardships of the journey, they would have to live austerely. Because it was not safe to travel alone, pilgrims would travel together, just as they do in Geoffrey Chaucer's poem *The Canterbury Tales*. Only an armed escort was allowed.

They would thus learn how to live in community; rich and poor, men and women would live together, sharing the same trials, and so transcend the normal divisions of society. As a result, the lessons of the road really did teach the pilgrims far more effectively than any sermon what it meant to live a true Christian life.

THE POWER OF PRAYER

But for many of the pilgrims, it was their arrival at the holy place which had most significance. When they came into contact with the bones of a saint who was now in heaven, they felt that they had bridged the gap between the divine world and the mundane. Holiness was experienced as a tangible power emanating from the relics: pilgrims would sometimes be healed of illness and it was said that the sacred bones had the power to kill an evil man. To help the pilgrims along their way, smaller shrines containing the relics of lesser saints sprang up all along the pilgrim routes to such places as Compostela.

The more illustrious the saint, the greater the power. The tomb of St Peter in Rome became one of the most important holy places in Europe. Peter had been the chief of the Apostles and was thought to open the gates of heaven. Pilgrims could also visit what they were told were the burial sites of the other Apostles. But no holy place could rival Jerusalem, where Jesus had died and

Every Muslim should make the *hajj*, or journey to Mecca, once in his lifetime. A cheerful caravan of pilgrims sets off in this 13th-century Persian illustration.

risen from the dead. Some time before AD 330 Helena, mother of the Roman Emperor Constantine, is said to have discovered the True Cross of Christ there. From the 4th century, pilgrims from Europe made the arduous journey to the Middle East simply to pray at Christ's tomb. While they were in Jerusalem, they took part in long, exhausting processions, marching all around the city to visit the places associated with Jesus. They felt that they were literally following in their saviour's footsteps and making contact with him in a new way.

Often the pilgrimage powerfully reinforced the values of society. The most important shrine in England was the tomb of St Thomas Becket in Canterbury Cathedral, Kent. Becket had been killed by the knights of Henry II in 1170 because he had defied the king to protect the rights of the Church. Henry had been scourged at Becket's tomb to prove that he had repented of his crime. It was a powerful symbol of the authority of the Church, which lay at the heart of Europe's political system. When pilgrims processed around Becket's shrine, these lessons were impressed upon them by the spectacular stained-glass windows, completed in the 13th century, depicting Becket's martyrdom and Henry's humiliation. It is not surprising that in 1538 Henry VIII destroyed the shrine to ensure that the Becket cult did not inspire resistance to the monarchy, which was emerging as the chief power of the new Europe.

Pilgrimage seems to answer a fundamental human need that goes deeper than any specific ideology. A striking example of this is the history of the *hajj* to Mecca in Arabia, which was originally a pagan pilgrimage. For centuries before the coming of Islam, pilgrims had gathered at the Kaaba, the ancient cube-shaped shrine, and performed elaborate rituals there. These old pagan rites were so deeply loved that when the Prophet Muhammad conquered Mecca in 630 he gave them a new monotheistic interpretation. Today they are devoutly performed by Muslim pilgrims. For many of them, the *hajj* marks the climax of their experience of Islam.

Even though the scientific tenor of the modern world has little time for the myths of sacred geography, pilgrims continue to make the journey to Lourdes in France or Knock in Ireland because they believe that the Virgin Mary appeared there and created a new link between heaven and earth. The sick who seek a cure in the miraculous waters of Lourdes are still convinced that the sacred has a healing power in our world whose effects can be felt tangibly, in defiance of the laws of nature.

Piraeus Ancient port of Athens, destroyed in 86 BC and redeveloped in the 19th century after Greek independence. In the 7th and 6th centuries BC Athens' principal port was Phaleron. Around 483 the Athenian statesman THEMISTOCLES arranged for the fortification of another port, Piraeus, to protect the large fleet of TRIREMES which he had just built. From 461 to 456 a pair of parallel Long Walls were built to link Piraeus to Athens. The walls were about 600 ft (183 m) apart and enabled Athens to receive supplies from the port during the Peloponnesian War. From that time, Piraeus became the trading centre of the Athenian empire. In 404 the Spartans knocked down the Long Walls but they were rebuilt in 393. The city and fortifications of Piraeus were destroyed by the Roman general Lucius Cornelius SULLA. Subsequently, Piraeus remained insignificant as a port until it was redeveloped after 1832.

pirate Sea robber who attacks unprotected merchant, or commercial, shipping for personal gain. From around 1250 BC pirates preyed upon Phoenician and then Greek vessels, and in the 1st century BC they threatened Rome with starvation by intercepting the city's grain convoys. The Roman general POMPEY cleared pirates from the Mediterranean at this time, but with the decline of the Roman Empire in the 5th century AD piracy revived. From the 8th to the 12th centuries VIKINGS from Scandinavia harassed the commerce of the Baltic Sea, and Muslims from southern Arab countries operated in the western Mediterranean. In the 15th century Venetians, who dominated the eastern Mediterranean, also plundered the maritime trade of rival city-states. From the 16th to the 18th centuries the north African Barbary states derived most of their revenue from piracy, robbing merchant ships from the Spanish and Portuguese imperial fleets.

From the 16th century buccaneers, or sea adventurers, also operated. Drawing their inspiration from the exploits of English seamen such as Sir Francis DRAKE and his cousin Sir John HAWKINS, who had plundered the Spanish Main, the buccaneers, mainly British, French and Dutch, preyed on Spanish settlements and shipping in the Caribbean and South America. The buccaneers robbed with the tacit approval of their governments, who expected a share of the booty, and differed in this respect from pirates who were outlaws in the eyes of all nations.

As England's international trade grew in the 18th century, its merchantmen became prey to pirates around the world. Piracy flourished as naval crews were disbanded following wars, and unemployed men were recruited for outlawry. In 1815 and 1816 the United States, Britain and Holland defeated the Barbary pirates. Following the Opium Wars in 1858, the last stronghold of piracy in the China Seas was broken. The increased size of merchant ships, improved naval patrols and the international outlawing of piracy led to its virtual eradication in the 20th century. However, small boats are still vulnerable to pirates in certain parts of the world, and the nonpolitical hijacking of ships and aeroplanes follows the criminal tradition of piracy.

Pitt the Elder, William, 1st Earl of Chatham (1708-78) Prime minister who oversaw the emergence of Britain's world empire. Pitt entered Parliament in 1735 and became a WHIG opponent of the first British

Pitt the Younger's pockets bulge with taxes and war bills as he bestrides Parliament and toys with world politics in James Gillray's cartoon.

prime minister Robert WALPOLE. After the fall of Walpole's ministry in 1742, he was supported by the leader of the new Whig ministry Henry PELHAM, and became a minister in 1746. In 1755 he became paymaster general of the forces. The following year, after the resignation of Pelham's brother and successor, the Duke of NEWCASTLE, secretary of state Pitt was left effectively as prime minister. The following year he resigned but was recalled to form a coalition ministry with Newcastle.

During the SEVEN YEARS' WAR against an alliance of countries that included France, Pitt conducted a victorious war strategy. He expanded Britain's navy, defeated the French in India and captured French Quebec in Canada. When the Cabinet refused to declare war on Spain in 1761, Pitt resigned. By the end of the war in 1763 Britain was the world's leading colonial power. Hailed as a national hero, he refused offers by George III to form a ministry in 1764 and 1765. He opposed the STAMP ACT in 1765, which required all American legal documents and newspapers to bear a revenue stamp, and favoured conciliation of the American colonies.

In 1766 he accepted the title of Viscount Pitt and Earl of Chatham and agreed to form a new ministry. Troubled by gout and mental illness, he was in virtual retirement from 1767 and resigned in 1768. When the AMERICAN REVOLUTION broke out in 1775, Pitt favoured a peace settlement which would not grant independence to the colonies. His final speech in the House of Lords in April 1778 was a plea for the importance of retaining all Britain's colonies. After the speech, he collapsed and died soon afterwards. His second son was William PITT the Younger.

For three centuries Barbary pirates were notorious for robbing Portuguese merchant ships. This 16th-century Portuguese drawing shows a lively bout of pirate infighting in the Indian Ocean.

Pitt the Younger, William (1759-1806)

British prime minister from 1783 to 1801 and from 1804 to 1806. He was the second son of William PITT, 1ST EARL OF CHATHAM. At the age of 23, he became chancellor of the exchequer. On the fall of the coalition government of Lord North and Charles FOX in 1783, Pitt, then 24, was made prime minister by George III. He secured Britain's steady economic recovery from the American War of Independence by increasing taxation and curbing government expenditure.

In 1793 France, which was in the throes of revolution, declared war on Britain. In response Pitt raised two European coalitions in 1793 and 1798 to fight France. His subsidies to Britain's allies created a national financial crisis, and in 1799 Pitt introduced the first income tax, with a top rate of 10 per cent, to pay for the war. Rebellion in Ireland hampered the war effort and convinced Pitt that the union of Ireland and England was necessary. He achieved the union in 1800 but the

> **England has saved herself by her exertions, and will, as I trust, save Europe by her example.**
>
> *William Pitt the Younger, after the Battle of Trafalgar, 1805*

following year, when George III refused to consider CATHOLIC EMANCIPATION, or restoring full political and civil rights to English and Irish Roman Catholics, he resigned.

He was recalled in 1804 to repel an expected invasion by Napoleon I and organised a third European coalition against France. Pitt died soon after Napoleon's victory at the Battle of AUSTERLITZ in December 1805. Although he called himself an independent WHIG politician, his followers went on to form the nucleus of the emerging TORY PARTY.

Pius II (Aeneas Silvius Piccolomini) (1405-64)

Pope from 1458. Piccolomini, a poet and humanist scholar, became secretary to the Bishop of Fermo in 1432 and to antipope Felix V, in 1439. In 1442 he was appointed secretary and court poet to the Holy Roman Emperor FREDERICK III. Three years later, Piccolomini resolved to reform his dissolute personal life and in 1446 became a priest. He was made Bishop of Trieste in 1447 and a cardinal in 1456. By October 1458 he had become Pope Pius II. He proclaimed a crusade against the Ottoman Turks, but the enterprise came to nothing due to antipapal movements in France and Germany.

Pius V, St (Antonio Ghislieri) (1504-72)

Pope from 1566, during the COUNTER REFORMATION. Revered as an austere Dominican, he was made a cardinal in 1557 and became grand inquisitor in the following year. He directed the Roman Inquisition against heretics with zeal, and in 1566 he was elected pope. During his papacy he worked to further the aims of the Counter Reformation, opposing Protestant innovations, and strove to enact the decrees of the Council of TRENT on Catholic doctrine. He was active politically, excommunicating Elizabeth I of England in 1570 and organising the Holy League forces of Venice, Spain, Genoa and the papacy. The League achieved a momentous victory under Don JOHN OF AUSTRIA in 1571 when its forces defeated the Ottoman Turks at the Battle of LEPANTO. Pius was canonised in 1712.

Pius VII (Luigi Chiaramonti) (1740-1823)

Pope from 1800, who restored papal fortunes after being freed from imprisonment under Napoleon I. Following the occupation of the Papal States by French troops in 1797 and the death of Pope Pius VI as a French prisoner in 1799, Pius signed a CONCORDAT with Napoleon I in 1801 and French troops withdrew from the papal territory. In 1804 Napoleon forced Pius to come to Paris, supposedly to consecrate him as emperor, and then humiliated him by seizing the crown and crowning himself. When Pius refused to support Napoleon's CONTINENTAL SYSTEM of economic blockade against Britain, France annexed Rome in 1808 and the Papal States in the following year. Pius excommunicated the French forces in 1809, and Napoleon responded by imprisoning him at Fontainebleau, France. After Napoleon's downfall in 1814, Pius returned to Rome in triumph. He condemned secret revolutionary societies and re-established the Society of Jesus, the JESUIT organisation. A congress at VIENNA in 1815 restored the Papal States to the Holy See.

Pius IX (Giovanni Mastai-Ferretti) (1792-1878)

Pope from 1846 during the period of Italian unification. Elected as a progressive pope, he initially relaxed press censorship, freed political prisoners and opened negotiations for an Italian customs union. After nationalist revolts in 1848, Pius fled from Rome. On the establishment of a secular Roman republic under Giuseppe MAZZINI in 1850, Pius asked Louis Napoleon, president of the French republic, to help him to regain the city, and French forces ousted the republican army of Giuseppe GARIBALDI.

In 1854 Pius declared that the Immaculate Conception of the Virgin Mary was an article of faith, and in 1869 he convened the First Vatican Council which proclaimed the infallibility of the pope. French emperor Napoleon III fell from power in 1870, and in the following year Rome was incorporated into the new Italian kingdom. Pius refused to recognise the united Italy and never again set foot outside the Vatican.

Pius XII (Eugenio Giuseppe Giovanni Pacelli) (1876-1958)

Pope from 1939, during a period of fascist and communist totalitarianism. From 1917 to 1929 he was a papal nuncio, or ambassador, in Germany. As secretary of state for Pope Pius XI he negotiated a concordat with Nazi Germany in 1933, repeated violations of which led the pope to brand Nazism as anti-Christian in 1937. In his first encyclical, or papal letter, in 1939 Pius XII made a general attack on totalitarianism. He remained politically impartial between the Allies and the fascist AXIS powers in the Second World War, supervising a programme for the relief of war victims through the Pontifical Aid Commission and making the Vatican City an asylum for refugees. He was much criticised for not condemning Nazi persecution of the Jews and was accused of doing little for them in Italy. After the war he spoke out against communism, and in 1949 he excommunicated Italian Catholics who joined the Communist Party. His concern about the persecution of the Church in Eastern Europe led him to excommunicate the communist leaders of Yugoslavia, Hungary, Romania, Poland and Czechoslovakia.

Pizarro, Francisco (c.1475-1541)

Spanish explorer and conquistador, or conqueror, of Peru. He accompanied Vasco Núñez de BALBOA on his expedition across Panama in 1513, when Balboa discovered the Pacific Ocean. Hearing of the fabled wealth of the INCAS, a people who by the 16th century had built a huge empire in present-day Peru, he joined with Diego de Almagro on two expeditions from 1524 to 1525 and from 1526 to 1528. Together they explored the Colombian, Ecuadorian and Peruvian coasts, collecting information about the Incas. In 1532 Pizarro met the Inca emperor ATAHUALPA at Cajamarca, Peru. He imprisoned Atahualpa, extorted a vast ransom and in 1533 had him murdered. His conquest of Peru was virtually completed in the same year by the capture of CUZCO, the Inca capital. Here he established Atahualpa's brother, Manco Capac, as nominal monarch under Spanish rule and was created a marquis by the Holy Roman Emperor Charles V. Pizarro consolidated his position by founding new settlements, including the future capital Lima in 1535, and dividing the spoils of conquest

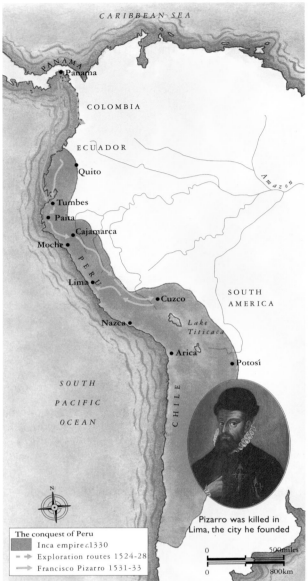

The conquest of Peru
- Inca empire c.1330
- Exploration routes 1524-28
- Francisco Pizarro 1531-33

Pizarro was killed in Lima, the city he founded

Peru was conquered by Francisco Pizarro who set up new settlements during his search for the Incas' treasure.

unsuccessful. In 1542 Charles V of Spain ordered Peru's first viceroy, Blasco Núñez Vela, to implement the New Laws, drafted by the Spanish missionary Bartolomé de LAS CASAS, to protect Indian rights and limit the powers of the conquistadores. Gonzalo became leader of conquistadores opposed to the New Laws, and in the ensuing civil war defeated Vela at the Battle of Anoquito in 1546. Having executed Vela in the same year, he was himself executed in 1548 by the new viceroy, Pedro de la Gasca.

Place, Francis (1771-1854) British radical reformer. A self-educated tailor, he organised an unsuccessful tailors' strike in 1793. For three years from 1794 he was a member of the London Corresponding Society, one of the earliest working-class movements. In 1799 he opened a tailor's shop in London which soon became a meeting place for radicals, and earned him the title of 'the radical tailor of Charing Cross'. From 1814 to 1824 he campaigned successfully for the repeal of the COMBINATION ACTS which banned trade unions. Place was a political activist in the period leading up to the 1832 REFORM Act and, as an early leader of CHARTISM, the popular movement for electoral and social reform he helped to draft the People's Charter of 1838.

plague Epidemic disease, particularly the contagious bubonic plague and the BLACK DEATH, transmitted by fleas from infected rats. The first reported instance of the plague in Europe was in Athens in 430 BC. The ancient historian THUCYDIDES recounted in his *History of the Peloponnesian War* how the plague caused the death of the great statesman PERICLES and about a third of the city's population. In the 3rd century AD plague devastated the Roman Empire, at its height killing some 5000 people daily. In the 14th century the form of plague known as the Black Death swept through Europe from Constantinople, killing about three-quarters of Europe's population from 1334 to 1354. The Great Plague of London from 1664 to 1665 caused 12400 deaths. In 1894 an epidemic of plague occurred in Canton and Hong Kong, and the disease continues to appear in parts of Asia. (See also feature, page 78.)

Plaid Cymru Nationalist political party seeking self-government for Wales and the preservation of Welsh language and culture. Founded in 1925 as Plaid Genedlaethol Cymru, the Welsh Nationalist Party, it became active in the 1960s and won its first parliamentary seat in 1966. In a referendum in Wales in 1979 the party's platform for a separate representative assembly was supported by just 20 per cent of voters, a figure corresponding to the number of native Welsh speakers. By 1996 the party held four seats in the British Parliament.

Plains of Abraham, Battle of (September 13, 1759) Decisive battle in the French and Indian War, part of the SEVEN YEARS' WAR which ended French rule in Canada. On a plateau above the city of Quebec, General James WOLFE ferried British troops up the St Lawrence River past a French fort. Having tricked the sentries into believing them to be French, the British climbed the Heights of Abraham to the fort. In the ensuing battle on the plains, the French garrison under General Louis Montcalm was routed and Quebec surrendered. Both commanders were killed in the fighting, and the subsequent Treaty of PARIS in 1763 gave control of New France (henceforth Quebec) to Britain.

Plantagenet English dynasty descended from the counts of Anjou in France, providing 14 kings of England from 1154 to 1485. The name may derive from the Latin word *genista*, meaning broom, a sprig of which plant Geoffrey (1113-51), Count of Anjou, wore on his cap. Geoffrey's son Henry became Henry II of England who reigned from 1154 to 1189 and established the dynasty. As descendants of the House of Anjou, Henry II, Richard I and John were known as Angevins.

The dynastic line was unbroken until 1399 when Richard II was deposed by Henry of Bolingbroke, who became Henry IV. He established the LANCASTRIAN branch of the dynasty which was descended from Edward III's son John of Gaunt, and was continued by Henry V (reigned 1413-22) and Henry VI (reigned 1422-61 and 1470-1). Between 1455 and 1483 the House of Lancaster contended with the House of York for the throne in the Wars of the ROSES.

The House of York claimed the throne through Edward III's son Edmund of Langley, the first Duke of York. Edward IV (reigned 1461-1470, 1471-1483), Edward V (reigned 1483) and Richard III (reigned 1483-5) were all Yorkists. When the Lancastrian Henry

among his supporters. He pledged the territory of Chile to his old partner Diego de Almagro, but when Pizarro reneged on his promise Almagro seized Cuzco in 1537. Pizarro sent his half-brother Hernando to recapture Cuzco, and in 1538 Hernando executed Almagro on Pizarro's orders. A band of Almagro's followers took revenge three years later by assassinating Pizarro in Lima.

Pizarro, Gonzalo (c.1506-48) Spanish conquistador, or conqueror, who led a revolt against the viceroy of Peru. He was a half-brother of Francisco PIZARRO and between 1531 and 1533 he assisted Francisco in the Spanish conquest of the INCAS. He defended CUZCO against the attacks of the Inca leader Manco Capac from 1536 to 1537, and in 1538 he was appointed governor of Quito (now in Ecuador). His expedition from 1540 to 1541 down the Amazon in search of EL DORADO was

Tudor defeated Richard III at the Battle of BOSWORTH FIELD in 1485 he married Elizabeth of York, ended the Plantagenet line and then, after he became Henry VII, founded the House of TUDOR.

Plassey, Battle of (June 23, 1757) Victory of General Robert CLIVE over the Nawab Siraj-ud-Dawlah of Bengal, leading to British control of north-eastern India. After Calcutta had fallen to the nawab in 1756 Clive, commander of the EAST INDIA COMPANY's army, was sent to Bengal to retake it. He recaptured the city in January 1757. The victory, however, was not sufficient to satisfy Clive, who sought a decisive battle with the nawab. Although his troops were outnumbered by 15 to 1, Clive had prepared for the Battle of Plassey by buying support from the nawab's enemies, and promising the nawabship to Siraj-ud-Dawlah's rival Mir Jafar. Mir Jafar's defection from Siraj helped Clive to a decisive victory. The nawab fled to his palace where he was murdered. The following day his body was paraded through the streets of Murshidabad on the back of an elephant. Mir Jafar was subsequently appointed nawab, and Clive assumed the governorship of Bengal.

plastics Versatile synthetic products generally made from petrochemicals by a process called polymerisation. This involves joining small molecules, or monomers, to make large molecules, or polymers. The first commercial plastic was celluloid, invented by John H. Wyatt in 1869. It was used as a substitute for more expensive substances such as ivory and tortoiseshell. Bakelite was invented in 1909 by Leo Baekeland, a Belgian-born chemist working in the USA. Since it could be moulded into almost any shape, was heat resistant and a good electrical insulator, it was widely used in the manufacture of objects such as light switches and kitchenware. More plastics were developed during the next 40 years, but it was not until the 1950s that they started to flood the market.

The vast potential for plastics was still to be realised when this Bakelite bracelet and wireless were produced in the 1930s.

After the Battle of the River Plate the battleship *Graf Spee* belches flame and smoke as its commander scuttles the pride of the German war fleet to prevent it falling into British hands.

Plataea Ancient Greek city in BOEOTIA, and the site of a Greek victory against the Persians in 479 BC. Before the Persian Wars began in 500, Plataea voluntarily placed itself under Athenian protection. In 490 about a thousand Plataean men fought alongside the Athenian army against Persia at the Battle of MARATHON. In 479 Persian troops were defeated by the Greek army at Plataea, effectively ending PERSIA's attempts to conquer the mainland. At the start of the PELOPONNESIAN WAR in 431, forces from the other main Boeotian city of THEBES attacked Plataea, and a prolonged siege by the Spartans from 429 to 427 led to its capture and destruction. It was rebuilt and occupied by Thebes until 387, then destroyed again in 373. Alexander the Great reconstructed Plataea in 338 in honour of Greek resistance to Persia.

Plate, Battle of the River (December 13-17, 1939) First major naval engagement of the Second World War. The German battleship *Graf Spee* had sunk many cargo ships in the South Atlantic when it was attacked by three British cruisers and forced into the harbour of Montevideo, Uruguay, for repairs. Faced with several British ships which had converged on the Plate estuary, the German captain Hans Langsdorff decided to scuttle the ship rather than renew the battle. In the first, relatively uneventful winter of the war, the British hailed this as a major victory.

Plato (c.428-c.348 BC) Ancient Greek philosopher, and one of the most important figures in Western philosophy. Plato was a pupil of the philosopher SOCRATES, and after the latter's forced suicide in 399 BC he and other disciples of Socrates went into hiding. He then travelled widely in Greece, Egypt, southern Italy and Sicily before returning to Athens where he founded a college, the Academy, in about 387. Here he taught mathematics and philosophy until his death.

Plato's surviving works consist mainly of dialogues. In the earliest group of dialogues, the *Apology*, the *Meno* and the *Gorgias*, he portrays Socrates in argument with someone

> **❝Our object in the construction of the state is the greatest happiness of the whole, and not that of any one class. ❞**
>
> *Plato*
> The Republic (Book IV)

whose philosophical statement is shown to be untrue by a logical series of questions and answers, a process known as dialectic. In his middle years Plato wrote several masterpieces, including the *Republic*, the *Symposium* and the *Phaedo*. In these dialogues he developed the theory that abstractions such as truth or the good – which he calls 'forms' or 'ideas' – exist in a realm beyond the physical world. Unlike objects which are perceived with the senses, forms can be grasped only through reason – which is why philosophy is so important. In the *Republic* – the first Utopia, or an idealistic vision of a social system – Plato argued that the ideal state would not be a democracy, instead it would be ruled by a 'philosopher-king'. The poetic *Symposium* describes the path to the highest good as the ascent by lovers to true beauty; and the *Phaedo* argues that the soul is immortal and finds eternal truth after death. Plato's longest work

Plato's philosophical ideas have survived for more than 2000 years, and have profoundly influenced the history of Western civilisation.

from his middle and late period is the *Laws*, which rejects Athenian democracy and argues that extremes of government are to be avoided. Plato was teacher to the philosopher ARISTOTLE. His works were translated into Latin in the late 15th century and became central to RENAISSANCE scholarship and ideas.

plebs Common people of ancient Rome. When the Roman Republic was established around 500 BC, the plebs were excluded from public office and from intermarriage with the hereditary aristocrats, or patricians. To protect their rights against abuses by the senate the plebs in the 5th century BC created the post of TRIBUNE of the people. The plebeian class struggled for political equality until 367 when the senate became open to them. The word plebiscite, meaning a vote of the people, comes from plebs.

Plekhanov, Georgi (1856-1918) Russian revolutionary and Marxist philosopher. In 1876 Plekhanov led a massive student popular demonstration in St Petersburg and a year later became leader of a secret society, Land and Liberty, which promoted revolution, but he left when it turned to terrorism. As a refugee in Geneva in 1883 he helped to found the first Russian Marxist organisation, the League for the Liberation of Labour, which merged in 1898 with the Russian Social Democratic Workers' Party. When the party split in 1903 into the BOLSHEVIKS, and the Mensheviks ('Members of the Minority') who believed that Russia was not ready for revolution and needed to be reformed, he supported the latter. He

returned to Russia in February 1917, but failed to prevent the Bolsheviks from seizing power in the October Revolution.

Pliny the Elder (Gaius Plinius Secundus) (AD 23-79) Roman author of the *Natural History*, a 37 volume encyclopedia which remained a major source of scientific knowledge until the 17th century. By 52 Pliny was a cavalry commander, serving in Germany. He returned to Rome, studied law and then went to Como, where he devoted himself to study. He wrote seven works, of which only the *Natural History* survives.

Upon the accession of the Emperor VESPASIAN in 69 Pliny re-entered public life, holding various official positions. In 71, following the death of his brother-in-law, he adopted his nephew PLINY THE YOUNGER. As commander of a fleet in the Bay of Naples in 79, he went ashore to observe an eruption of Vesuvius, and was choked to death.

Pliny the Younger (Gaius Plinius Caecilius Secundus) (61-i12) Roman author and administrator, the nephew of PLINY THE ELDER. Born into a wealthy family and adopted by his uncle, Pliny began to practise law at the age of 18. In AD 100 his legal and political success enabled him to reach the highest Roman administrative post of consul.

A close friend of the Emperor TRAJAN and the historian Publius Cornelius TACITUS, he wrote letters to them and other contemporaries which he published in ten volumes. These give a detailed picture of the upperclass Roman lifestyle and a first-hand account of the eruption in 79 of Mount Vesuvius, near POMPEII. In 110 Pliny became governor of the province of Bithynia (now in Turkey) where he died two years later.

PLO see PALESTINE LIBERATION ORGANISATION

Plotinus (205-270) Philosopher, and founder of NEO-PLATONISM. Born in Egypt, possibly of Roman descent, his first language was Greek. From 232 to 242 he studied philosophy in Alexandria under Ammonius Saccas, a follower of PLATO. To learn about the philosophies of India and Persia, Plotinus joined an expedition of the Roman Emperor Gordian III from 242 to 243. In 245 he went to Rome where he established himself as a teacher. In 254 he began writing his six *Enneads*, or groups of nine treatises. These set out his rigorous intellectual search for a basis to religious belief, and had considerable influence on the early Christian Church.

plough The wooden plough superseded the digging stick in the BRONZE AGE as the growth of large settlements brought about an increasing demand for food. The iron ploughshare was first used in south-west Asia in the 12th century BC, and in Roman times played a major role in colonisation. An innovation in the 11th century was a mouldboard, or curved plate which could turn over the furrow. The plough remained largely unchanged until the 18th century when population expansion demanded greater food production. In 1760 the Rotherham plough, which had a triangular frame, was designed. Lighter and stronger than its antecedents, it determined the basic form of the modern plough. During the 19th century steel ploughs were manufactured and experiments with steam power began. Horsedrawn ploughs, however, were not superseded until after the tractor had been perfected.

Plutarch (c. AD 46-126) Greek essayist, biographer and philosopher. He lived mainly in Boeotia, in northern Greece, but travelled in Egypt and Italy and lectured on philosophy in Rome. His surviving works include a collection of essays, the *Morals,* and *The Parallel Lives*, 46 paired biographies of famous Greeks and Romans which concentrate on the moral character of their subjects, touching only briefly on associated events. Through the translations of Sir Thomas North in 1579 the *Lives* have had a lasting influence on English literature, notably in the Roman plays of Shakespeare, including *Antony and Cleopatra, Julius Caesar* and *Coriolanus*.

poaching In medieval Europe lands owned by kings and feudal landowners were protected by laws against poaching, which was punishable by imprisonment. Game for the sport of the king and his nobles in royal forests

Poaching was commonplace in Victorian England but poachers needed to keep a wary lookout for mantraps (left) laid by keepers to protect the landowners' game.

Victims of a Russian pogrom are laid out in a Jewish cemetery. After the failed revolution of 1905 the government channelled national discontent into anti-Semitism and the pogroms escalated.

was similarly protected. During the 17th century poaching in the English royal forests became a common pursuit of impoverished peasants. In the 18th and 19th centuries gamekeepers were hired to protect private estates, and iron mantraps and spring guns were used to catch intruders. Today poaching for sport or commercial profit is threatening some species with extinction.

Pocahontas see feature, page 512

pocket borough British parliamentary borough, or constituency, that was 'in the pocket' of a single wealthy individual or family. The term was first used by 19th-century British parliamentary reformers to describe the many boroughs in which voters were bribed or coerced by powerful local patrons to elect their choice of representatives. Throughout the 18th century more and more boroughs had come under the influence of patrons. In the election of 1806-7 more than 300 of the 658 Members of Parliament were elected by pocket boroughs. As a result Parliament was firmly under the control of the landed gentry. The REFORM ACTS of 1832 and 1867 put an end to most pocket boroughs by increasing the numbers of people who could vote, and redistributing seats to reflect the movement from country to the towns. In 1872 the secret ballot finally removed pressure on voters. (See ROTTEN BOROUGH.)

> ### DID YOU KNOW?
> In 1686 Lady Rochester requested a pocket borough for her 13-year-old great-grandson because she thought Parliament was 'a good school for youth to be improved in'.

pogrom Mob attack condoned by a government authority against religious, racial or national minorities, most often against Jews. The word means 'riot' or 'devastation' in Russian, and is usually applied to attacks on Russian Jews between 1881 and 1917. The first pogroms occurred in the Ukraine in 1881 following the assassination of Tsar ALEXANDER II. Although the assassin was not a Jew, false rumours incited mobs in more than 200 cities to attack Jews and destroy their property. In 1903 a three-day pogrom took place in Kishinev, Moldavia, in which 45 Jews were killed, 600 wounded and 1500 Jewish homes ransacked. After a failed Russian revolution in 1905, there was an increase in violent demonstrations of ANTI-SEMITISM, spurring many Jews to emigrate to the USA and western Europe and to support a political movement advocating the return of Jews to Palestine (ZIONISM). The Bolshevik Revolution in 1917 ended the Russian monarchy and the government's anti-Semitic policies. After 1917 widespread pogroms ceased in Russia. In 1933 the anti-Semitic dictator Adolf Hitler came to power in Germany and encouraged pogroms. Nazi-organised attacks against Jews increased during the Second World War throughout most of Europe, and led to the extermination of the Jewish people in the HOLOCAUST.

Poincaré, Raymond (1860-1934) The president of France from 1913 to 1920, who favoured the payment of heavy REPARATIONS by Germany following the VERSAILLES PEACE SETTLEMENT. As prime minister from 1911 to 1913, Poincaré increased security in anticipation of the First World War by raising military service from two to three years and strengthening alliances with Britain and Russia. After the Allied victory against Germany in 1918, he insisted that the terms for German reparation payment, drawn up in the Versailles Peace Settlement, were too lenient. In 1922 he was again prime minister, and in the following year he sent French troops to occupy the German steel and mining area of the Ruhr when Germany defaulted on their payments. Nationalist feelings were fuelled in Germany by soaring inflation caused by the occupation and Germany refused to continue paying the reparations. In 1924 Poincaré resigned.

In his last period as prime minister from 1926 to 1928 he led a government of national unity and stabilised the economy. He retired in 1929, but continued to press for reparation payments and to urge France to prepare for further German aggression.

Poitiers, Battle of (September 19, 1356) One of the worst French defeats in the HUNDRED YEARS' WAR between England and France. While leading an English and Gascon force of about 7000 men on a raid into central France, EDWARD THE BLACK PRINCE, heir of Edward III, was met by a French army of more than 16000 soldiers near Poitiers on September 17. A temporary truce was concluded for the following day, a Sunday. This enabled Edward's forces to position themselves alongside marshland, and in the battle on Monday French knights became bogged down, dismounted and became easy targets for the English archers. The French king John II was captured, and was held prisoner until he agreed in May 1360 to the Treaty of BRETIGNY, which marked the end of the first phase of the Hundred Years' War.

At the Battle of Poitiers, vividly recorded in Froissart's medieval chronicle, standards are unfurled as English and French armies meet.

Pocahontas: the 'playful' princess

*Within her short life, the Native American princess Pocahontas became
a celebrity of the new Virginia colony, and of English society.*

Although her story may have been to some extent mythologised, Pocahontas (*c.*1595-1617) was a real person who played a key role in the lives of the first British colonists in North America. By birth she was a Native American princess, the daughter of Powhatan, chief of the Powhatan confederacy of tribes in Virginia. Her name meant 'playful one' – she refused to let the English settlers know her real name, Matoaka, for fear that it would enable them to put the 'evil eye' on her.

It is unlikely that the British in the new settlement of Jamestown, founded in 1606, would have survived their first winter if the Powhatan tribes had not given them food and introduced them to crops such as yams and corn. Yet what the indigenous people did not give, the English took, and there often ensued ferocious fighting.

SAVED FROM EXECUTION

A former soldier, Captain John Smith, was among those who urged the colonists to grow food crops and abandon the search for gold. (Virginia's own 'gold' would prove to be tobacco.) In 1607, while Smith was exploring the colony, he fell into Powhatan's hands and would have perished but for the intervention of

Pocahontas appears as 'Lady Rebecca' in court dress on her visit to England, during which she was presented to the king.

Pocahontas. The young girl had already been a force for peace between the colonists and the indigenous population: she played among the English children and mediated between the two peoples. Smith was to have been clubbed to death, but Pocahontas, aged just 12 or 13, laid her head upon his to prevent the execution. Nor was this the only time she came to his rescue. 'Blessed Pocahontas,' he wrote in his *Generall Historie of Virginia* (1624), 'the great King's daughter of Virginia, oft saved my life.' He also said of her, 'She, under God, was the instrument to preserve this colony from death, famine and utter confusion.'

After Smith returned home, Pocahontas married a native warrior named Kocoum. Knowledge of her life at that time is sketchy, and of his fate there is no record.

But she was taken into 'honoured captivity' by Captain Sir Samuel Argall and held as security against the slaughter of English prisoners. In 1613 she was in the care of the acting governor of Jamestown, Sir Thomas Dale, and was baptised with the English name Rebecca. John Rolfe, first secretary and recorder-general of Jamestown, fell in love with Pocahontas, and secured not only the governor's consent to marry her but also Powhatan's blessing. They were married in April 1614, helping to secure eight years of peace for the colonists.

In 1616, Pocahontas sailed for England. To the citizens of London she must have seemed an exotic creature. She was feted as a princess and presented at the court of James I. She so impressed people with her gracious manner that the English were forced to review their prejudices about Native Americans. Ben Jonson even wrote Pocahontas into one of his plays.

The following year she prepared to return to Virginia with her husband, but died of smallpox before sailing. She was buried in St George's Church, Gravesend, leaving a son, Thomas, who later settled in Virginia. Through him she has many descendants living there today.

Pol Pot (1928-96) Cambodian leader of the KHMER ROUGE guerrilla movement under whose totalitarian regime, from 1975 to 1979, at least a million people were murdered or starved to death – one in eight of the population. Pol Pot, whose real name was Saloth

Sar, was schooled under the French education system but failed to reach baccalaureate standard. In 1948 he enrolled as a carpentry student. From 1949 to 1953 he lived in France, studying radio electronics in Paris, where he became a member of the French Communist Party.

On returning to the Cambodian capital Phnom Penh he joined the communists fighting against the French colonial presence in CAMBODIA. He spent the next 12 years organising the Communist Party, supported by the People's Republic of China. Civil war broke

out in 1970, and after five years the Khmer Rouge toppled the military government of General Lon Nol. In 1975 Prince Norodom SIHANOUK returned from exile in China to become nominal head of state. In the following year Pol Pot was elected prime minister and proceeded to set up a dictatorship which perpetrated one of the worst campaigns of mass murder in history.

Overthrown by invading Vietnamese forces in 1979, he retreated with the Khmer Rouge to the borders of Thailand, from where he directed guerrilla activity against the new government. In 1985 he resigned as leader of the Khmer Rouge but remained influential within the movement. Cambodian elections were held in May 1993 under a United Nations peace plan, but the Khmer Rouge refused to participate and in the following year resumed its guerrilla activities.

Poland Country in central Europe. The first king was the Piast monarch Mieszko I who reigned from about 963 to 992 and adopted

Pol Pot sits in his hideout in 1980, and (above) a charnel house where bones of some 8500 of his victims were amassed.

Christianity as the state religion. The Piast line continued to rule Poland until 1386 when it was succeeded by the Jagiellon dynasty from Lithuania. In 1569 a Polish-Lithuanian state was created by a treaty in Lublin. After the death of Sigismund II in 1572, the Jagiellon dynasty ended. In 1655 Poland was invaded by Sweden, and in a treaty of 1660 gave up a large swathe of territory. In 1667 the eastern Ukraine was ceded to Russia. John III, John SOBIESKI, drove the Ottoman Turks out of southern Poland, but after his death in 1696 Russia, Prussia and Austria took control of Poland. In 1697 Tsar Peter I arranged for the Elector Frederick Augustus I of SAXONY to become king of Poland as AUGUSTUS II.

In 1772, 1793 and 1795 Poland was successively partitioned between its three powerful neighbours. Following the treaties of TILSIT in 1807, Napoleon I created a French puppet state, the Grand Duchy of Warsaw. After Napoleon's defeat at the Battle of LEIPZIG in Saxony in 1814, the duchy collapsed. At a Congress in Vienna in the following year, most of the duchy became the kingdom of Poland. In 1830 a failed national revolution resulted in the kingdom being incorporated into Russia. Revolts in 1846 and 1863 were crushed by Russia and Prussia.

Following the Allied victory in the First World War in 1918, Poland became a republic led by Marshal Joseph PILSUDSKI. By the VERSAILLES PEACE SETTLEMENT in 1919 the country was granted access to the Baltic Sea through German territory via a POLISH CORRIDOR. The existence of this corridor caused friction with Nazi Germany, and in September 1939 Germany invaded Poland, starting the Second World War. As a result of the NAZI-SOVIET PACT, an agreement between the Soviet Union and Nazi Germany, Poland was divided between the two dictatorships. When Germany invaded the Soviet Union in 1941 all of Poland fell under Nazi rule. In 1943 the discovery of a mass grave of Polish officers murdered by the Soviet army in the KATYN MASSACRE led to a rift between the Polish government in exile in London and the Soviet Union. When an uprising in Warsaw in 1944 was organised by the government in exile, it was crushed by German troops while Soviet forces remained passively outside the capital.

In the winter of 1944-5 the Soviet army drove the Germans from Poland, and a provisional government was established under Soviet protection. In 1945 its boundaries were redrawn at conferences in YALTA and POTSDAM The Polish communist leader Boleslaw Bierut worked with the Soviet leader Joseph Stalin to give the country a Soviet style of dictatorial government, and in 1952 Poland became a communist republic. In 1956 Polish workers went on general strike to protest against Soviet control of Poland and chronic food shortages. In 1970 there were further strikes and Wladyslaw Gomulka was replaced as party leader by Edward Gierek.

In 1980 strikes were held at the Lenin shipyards in Gdańsk and SOLIDARITY, an illegal trade union, was formed under the leadership of Lech WALESA. Strikes spread to other cities, and in December 1981 the Polish prime minister General Wojciech Jaruzelski imposed martial law and arrested the union's leaders. In January 1983 martial law officially ended, but the government maintained its ban on Solidarity. Renewed strikes in 1988 led to government talks with Solidarity and the drafting of a new constitution. Multiparty elections in the following year led to an overwhelming victory for Solidarity, and in December 1990 Lech Walesa became president. In the 1990s his radical programme for transforming Poland into a noncommunist market economy led to hardship and a series of unstable governments. In 1995 Poles elected a communist prime minister Wlodzimerz Cimoszewicz, and Walesa lost the presidency to Aleksander Kwasniewski.

Pole, Reginald (1500-58) English cardinal and Archbishop of Canterbury who attempted to restore Catholicism in England. He held a YORKIST claim to the throne of England through his mother, the Countess of Salisbury. As a devoted Catholic, he objected to the English Protestant Reformation and in 1532 he left the court of Henry VIII and travelled to Italy. In 1536 he was made a cardinal by Pope Paul III. He repeatedly urged France and Spain to invade England to reinstate Catholicism; Henry VIII took vengeance by beheading Pole's mother and brother. In 1553 Pope Julius III made Pole a papal representative, or legate, to England, and in the following year he returned home. Pole assisted the English queen Mary I in her COUNTER-REFORMATION programme against Protestants, and declared England Catholic. In 1556 Pole became Archbishop of Canterbury. Nearly 300 Protestants were executed by Mary while Pole was her religious adviser. Ironically, in 1557 Pole was denounced by Pope Paul IV as a heretic and his papal authority was ended. He died a demoralised man on November 17, 1558 – the same day as Mary I.

police The first body of civilian officers responsible for maintaining public order and safety and enforcing the law was instituted in Britain in the 1740s, when the BOW STREET RUNNERS were established in London as a voluntary force to catch thieves. The French ministry of police was founded in 1796 and centralised in 1800. The first professional British force was created in 1814 by Sir Robert PEEL, after whom its members were dubbed 'peelers' or 'bobbies'. In 1829 Peel founded London's Metropolitan Police Force, which was soon copied in other British cities. Most other European countries followed the French pattern of a national police force, and this has been adopted by the majority of developing countries in Africa and Asia.

Several countries, including Australia, the USA and Canada, have followed the British model of local forces. In 1842 the Criminal Investigation Department (CID), a division of London's Metropolitan Police, was formed, the first non-uniformed detective unit. In 1908 the FEDERAL BUREAU OF INVESTIGATION was created in the USA as a detective

By 1850 English police were uniformed and paid regular salaries. As well as preventing crime by patrolling, 'bobbies' were expected to light street lamps, call the time and watch for fires.

agency under national control. The Nazi GESTAPO was formed in Germany in 1933 as a secret police force which operated independently of the civil police for political purposes. Such organisations are typical of police states, totalitarian countries which use the police to repress social and political opposition.

poliomyelitis Acute viral infection which can cause inflammation of the central nervous system. Polio may be mild, with symptoms no worse than a fever and headache, or severe, leading to paralysis or death. The first vaccine against polio was prepared by a Pittsburgh physician, Jonas E. Salk, in the early 1950s and used in 1954. It contained a polio virus that had been killed with formalin. Three years later a Cincinnati virologist, Albert Bruce Sabin, began immunisation with a weakened live polio virus. Vaccination has reduced the incidence of polio in Britain from 6000 in 1956 to fewer than ten a year today, and in the same period in the USA from more than 57 000 to fewer than ten.

polis City-state in ancient Greece. The polis probably emerged in Greece around the 8th century BC. There were several hundred such communities, each consisting of a walled town with villages in the surrounding countryside. A polis contained an ACROPOLIS, or citadel on raised ground, and an agora, or marketplace. Local civic institutions might include an assembly of citizens, a council and magistrates, and various priesthoods. Slaves and foreigners were not citizens of the polis and, like women, took no part in its political life even though they lived there permanently. Politics, philosophy, literature and art flourished in the polis, particularly in Athens. In 338 Greece fell to Philip II of Macedonia following the Battle of Chaeronea. After the death of his son Alexander the Great in 323, Greece was dominated by the Hellenistic kingdoms and the authority of the polis was limited to local matters.

Polish Corridor Belt of Polish territory that separated former East Prussia from Germany, the invasion of which by Adolf Hitler started the Second World War. It was granted to POLAND in 1919 as part of the VERSAILLES PEACE SETTLEMENT and provided the country with access to the Baltic Sea. In September 1939 Hitler's forces annexed the Polish Corridor, which had a large German-speaking minority. Since Britain and France were bound by treaties with Poland, they declared war on Germany and the Second World War began. After the war, the territory was restored to Poland.

Polish Succession, **War of the** (1733-5) War between the allied armies of Russia and Austria against France, for control of Poland.

From 1955 mobile vaccination clinics starting touring the cities of the United States in a mass immunisation programme to conquer poliomyelitis. A similar policy was adopted in Britain.

After the death of the Polish king AUGUSTUS II in 1733, Austria and Russia supported his son, Frederick Augustus of Saxony, as Poland's future king. The French, however, promoted the father-in-law of Louis XV, Stanislaus Leszczynski, who was duly enthroned as Stanislaus I by a majority of Polish nobles.

In 1733 Russian troops invaded Poland and ensured that Augustus III acceded to the throne. Stanislaus fled to Danzig where he was pursued by the Russian army. Fighting between Russia and France spread along the Rhine to Italy, with Spain and Sardinia joining France, and Austria joining Russia. Peace negotiations began in 1735, but the final treaty was not signed until 1738. Stanislaus I renounced the Polish throne, but inherited the duchies of Lorraine and Bar, which reverted to France on his death; Spain gained Naples and Sicily from Austria; and France guaranteed the PRAGMATIC SANCTION by which Charles VI's daughter Maria Theresa was to inherit the Austrian throne.

Politburo The chief political and executive committee of the Communist Party of the USSR. In 1917 the BOLSHEVIKS formed the Soviet Politburo to provide leadership during the RUSSIAN REVOLUTION. After 1952 it was replaced by a larger committee called the Presidium, which operated until 1966 when the name Politburo was reintroduced. Although it was nominally elected by the party's central committee, the Politburo was

The Politburo in 1977 was at the apex of the Communist Party hierarchy in the USSR and wielded absolute power.

a self-regulating body that ruled the country as it saw fit. Its chairman was the general secretary of the Communist Party and leader of the USSR. Following the break-up of the USSR and the banning of the Communist Party in Russia in 1991, the Politburo ceased to exist. There was a similar Politburo in each eastern European satellite country of the USSR, and one still functions in China.

political parties Groups vying for power to form a government, originating in their modern form in Europe and the United States in the 19th century. In Europe, parties were allied to the aristocracy if they were CONSERVATIVE and to the mercantile classes if they were LIBERAL. In Catholic countries, such as France and Italy, conservative parties were supported by the Church. In the USA, which was a republic without an established aristocracy, both the REPUBLICAN PARTY and the DEMOCRATIC PARTY were generally liberal. (In the American Civil War, from 1861 to 1865, the aristocratic plantation holders in the South were defeated by the liberal North.)

In 1900 the British LABOUR PARTY was formed from an association of trade unions and organisations supporting SOCIALISM.

ПОЛИТБЮРО ЦК КПСС

Similar socialist parties developed within continental Europe, including Germany, where in 1913 the Social Democratic Party had more than a million members. Following the Russian Revolution in 1917, revolutionary socialist parties promoting COMMUNISM were formed in other European countries. In 1919 an authoritarian party with a military style of organisation emerged in Italy, supporting FASCISM. In Italy in 1922 and in Germany in 1933 fascist political parties achieved power.

Democracies such as Britain and the USA have a two-party electoral system, although smaller parties may also exist. In continental Europe there is a multiparty system, in which small parties often share power. Communist states such as China have a single party system of government, as do many developing countries in Africa and Asia.

Polk, James (1795-1849) Eleventh president of the USA, from 1845 to 1849. In 1844 Polk won the presidential election as a Democrat, advocating territorial expansion as the United States' MANIFEST DESTINY. The annexation of Texas by the United States in 1845 provoked the Mexican-American war of 1846-8, in which the USA conquered an area comprising New Mexico, Arizona and California. In 1846 Polk reached a settlement with Britain over the sovereignty of Oregon (the OREGON QUESTION), thereby establishing the US-Canadian boundary at the 49th parallel.

poll tax A tax levied on every 'poll', or head, of a population. A poll tax introduced by the English government in 1380 sparked off the PEASANTS' REVOLT of 1381. A similar tax introduced by the British Prime Minister Margaret THATCHER in 1989-90 – officially called the community charge but known as the 'poll tax' – led ultimately to her fall from power. The tax provoked widespread riots and a non-payment campaign and was replaced in 1993 because of its unpopularity. In the USA, between 1889 and 1910, poll taxes were tied to voting rights in Southern states, with the result that many poor people, particularly Blacks, lost their vote. By the 1940s some of these taxes had been abolished, and in 1964 poll taxes tied to voting rights in federal elections were banned. In 1966 this ban was extended to all American elections.

Poltava, Battle of (1709) Decisive Russian victory against Sweden in the NORTHERN WAR. Although CHARLES XII of Sweden had the support of the Cossack military leader, or hetman, Ivan Mazeppa, his army was defeated by the troops of the Russian tsar PETER THE GREAT at the city of Poltava in the Ukraine. When the Northern War ended in 1721, Sweden had lost its Baltic empire and Russia had become a major Baltic power.

Polynesians practised magical rituals to bring success, or misfortune, to rivals. This wooden figure from Tahiti was possibly used for sorcery.

Polybius (c.204-122 BC) Greek historian of the rise of the Roman Empire. Polybius was born into a wealthy Arcadian family, and was captured and taken to Rome after the Roman conquest of Macedonia in 168 BC. He became a protégé of the consul Aemilius Paullus, and later of the SCIPIO family. Under their patronage he wrote a 40-volume *History* of the rise of the empire from 220 to 146. Only five books survive intact, but there are large fragments of other volumes. He attributed Rome's success to the army's fair administrators and a balance of regal, aristocratic and democratic elements in the ROMAN REPUBLIC.

Polynesians Inhabitants of Pacific islands within the triangular area formed by Hawaii, EASTER ISLAND and New Zealand. They probably came from India and Indonesia more than 3500 years ago, settling in Tonga around 1140 BC and Samoa by 1000-500. They later spread to other parts of French Polynesia, and by AD 500 had settled as far east as Easter Island and north to Hawaii. Within the next 500 years they reached the Cook Islands and New Zealand. The principal MAORI immigration, from the Marquesas Islands, to New Zealand took place around 1350, but it was not the first.

Pombal, Sebastião, Marquês de (1699-1782) Portuguese prime minister. On the accession of José I in 1750, Pombal became chief minister for foreign affairs and war. When an earthquake devastated Lisbon in 1755, he organised relief work and the rebuilding of the city. In 1756 he was made prime minister. He believed that the Church

held too much power, and in 1759 he expelled the JESUITS from Portugal and its colonies in South America. He also brought the INQUISITION under the control of the king. In 1770 he was made Marquês of Pombal. After the death of José in 1777, the pro-clerical Maria I banished Pombal from Lisbon.

Pomerania Region of north-east Europe on the Baltic Sea between the rivers Oder and Vistula. In the 10th century it was inhabited by Slavic tribes. Poland conquered it in the 10th century and introduced Christianity. In 1227 eastern Pomerania became independent and was known as Pomeralia. When the Treaty of WESTPHALIA ended the THIRTY YEARS' WAR in 1648, western Pomerania was divided between Sweden and Brandenburg (now in Germany). In 1721, after the NORTHERN WAR, Sweden lost most of western Pomerania to Prussia. In 1772 eastern Pomerania was annexed by Prussia.

Following the NAPOLEONIC WARS in 1815 both western and eastern Pomerania were given to Prussia at the Congress of VIENNA. After the VERSAILLES PEACE SETTLEMENT in 1919 part of eastern Pomerania became the POLISH CORRIDOR. Following the Second World War in 1945 most of Pomerania was given to Poland, while the remainder was incorporated into the former East Germany.

Pompadour, Jeanne, Marquise de (1721-1764) Mistress of LOUIS XV of France, who exercised enormous influence over his policies. A middle-class woman of beauty and intelligence, she became the king's mistress in 1745. Pompadour admired and patronised VOLTAIRE and other philosophers of the ENLIGHTENMENT. She was also a generous patron of the arts, and founded a porcelain factory at Sèvres. She encouraged the French alliance with Austria which embroiled France in the disasters of the SEVEN YEARS' WAR.

The pampered Madame de Pompadour attracted the eye of Louis XV at a ball in 1745. For 20 years she influenced the French king.

Pompeii Settlement on the Bay of Naples destroyed by an eruption of Mount Vesuvius in August AD 79. Pompeii was a fashionable and prosperous colony of Rome, dedicated to the Roman goddess of love, Venus, with a population of some 20 000, including Greeks, Jews and Christians. In AD 62 an earthquake severely damaged both Pompeii and neighbouring HERCULANEUM. Only 17 years later, avalanches of molten lava erupted from Mount Vesuvius and engulfed both towns within three days. PLINY THE YOUNGER witnessed the eruption and described it in letters to the historian Tacitus. PLINY THE ELDER choked on the fumes, and later died. In the 16th century the ruins of Pompeii were rediscovered by the architect Domenico Fontana. Excavation work began in 1748, contributing to the revival of classical art and architecture known as NEOCLASSICISM.

Pompey, Gnaeus Pompeius Magnus (106-48 BC) Roman general and rival of Julius CAESAR, known as Pompey the Great. He fought for General Lucius SULLA and in 81 BC was granted the title of Magnus, meaning great, by the senate. In 72 he helped to quell the slave revolt led by SPARTACUS. He was elected consul in 70 and proceeded to restore the power of the TRIBUNE. In only three months in 67 he cleared the Mediterranean of pirates and in the following year defeated MITHRIDATES VI of Pontus.

When the senate refused to support him in 60 BC, Pompey entered into a pact to rule Rome with Julius Caesar and Marcus Crassus – the First Triumvirate – and married Caesar's daughter Julia. Following Julia's death in 54 and the death of Crassus in the following year, the rivalries between Pompey and Caesar became more pronounced. In 52 Pompey was appointed sole consul with the aim of restoring order after gang warfare had terrorised Rome. Caesar reacted by resigning from the senate, and in 49 crossed the RUBICON, a small river, from Gaul to fight Pompey's army. In 48 Caesar defeated Pompey at the Battle of Pharsalus. Pompey escaped to Egypt, where he was murdered by Pothinus, a eunuch in the court of Ptolemy XII.

Pompidou, Georges (1911-74) French president from 1969 to 1974. He served in the RESISTANCE movement in the Second World War and in 1944 became an adviser to Charles de Gaulle, the president of the provisional government of France. From 1946 Pompidou held a variety of government posts until he became prime minister in 1962. In that year at Evian-les-Bains he agreed with the provisional government of ALGERIA to end French colonial rule there. Following strikes and riots in May 1968, de Gaulle dismissed Pompidou. When de Gaulle resigned in 1969, Pompidou was elected president. He immediately devalued the franc, introduced a price freeze and lifted France's veto on Britain's membership of the European Economic Community. The French national cultural centre in Paris, commissioned under Pompidou's administration, was named in his honour.

Pondicherry Former French colony in south-east India from 1674 to 1954. It was founded by the French East India Company, and was the capital of French India. During the 17th and 18th centuries colonial rivalries led to its capture by the Dutch and the British on several occasions. From 1816 to 1954 it was secured as the administrative centre for French interests in India. In 1954 the Indian government took over its administration, and in 1962 a formal transfer from France to India was concluded.

Pontiac (c. 1720-69) Chief of the Ottawa tribe and leader of a Native American uprising against British colonists in North America. After defeating the French in 1759 at the Battle of the PLAINS OF ABRAHAM near Quebec, the British built forts and permitted White settlement on tribal lands. Pontiac formed an alliance of several ALGONQUIN tribes to repulse the settlers. In May 1763 Ojibwa, Potawatomi and Wyandot tribesmen attacked the forts at Detroit and Fort Pitt but failed to destroy them. The Delaware, Seneca and Shawnee tribes, however, destroyed many forts. The British responded with punitive expeditions between 1764 and 1766 until Pontiac was forced to agree to a peace treaty.

Pontus Kingdom in Asia Minor (now northeastern Turkey) established in the 4th century BC. In the 3rd and 2nd centuries Pontus grew in power and in 183 Pharnaces I annexed the Black Sea port of Sinope as his capital. Pontus reached its zenith under MITHRIDATES VI who conquered Asia Minor and gained control of the Crimea, challenging Roman rule in these places. In 66 he was defeated by the Roman general Gnaeus Pompey, and in 62 Pontus was incorporated into the Roman Empire.

Poor Laws System of social welfare in England, culminating in statutes in 1597 and 1601, which made each PARISH responsible for looking after its own poor and needy. The parish organised work for the able-bodied poor, but sent vagrants and vagabonds to houses of correction to be punished. In 1795 the Speenhamland system (named after Speen in Berkshire where it was devised), which supplemented the wages of poorly paid workers, was adopted by many parishes. In 1834 a Poor Law Amendment Act restricted the allowance to WORKHOUSE residents in order to cut the rising cost of parish subsidies, or poor relief. During the 19th and early 20th centuries

A legacy of Georges Pompidou's presidency, the innovatively designed Pompidou Centre was a bold attempt to bring art to the people.

The Poor Laws produced an austere workhouse system. Mealtimes in 1900 were bleak and regimented occasions.

harsh conditions in the workhouse, where families were often separated by sex and age, provoked widespread social criticism. The Poor Laws were gradually dismantled by social legislation in the 20th century, and replaced by the WELFARE STATE.

Popish Plot (1678) Alleged conspiracy by Catholics to murder CHARLES II of England and replace him with his Catholic brother James, Duke of York (later JAMES II). The plot was hatched by a defrocked Anglican parson Titus OATES, who asserted that a massacre of Protestants and the burning of London were imminent. The discovery that Edward Coleman, secretary to the Duchess of York, had been in treasonable correspondence with France, and the murder of a magistrate to whom Oates had sworn his statement, sparked off a frenzy of anti-Catholic violence. Thirty-five Catholics were executed and Parliament attempted to exclude James from the succession before Oates was eventually discredited. In 1685 he was punished for perjury, but survived to receive a pension from the Protestant king, William III.

Popular Front Coalition of left-wing and centre parties in the 1930s united in opposition to FASCISM. The French Popular Front was in power from June 1936 to October 1938, led successively by the prime ministers Leon BLUM, Camille Chautemps and Edouard DALADIER. It implemented a programme of social reforms and suppressed fascist groups. In Spain the Popular Front governments of the prime ministers Manuel Azaña, Fernán Caballero and Juan Negrín were in office from February 1936 to March 1939, and fought the SPANISH CIVIL WAR against the fascist general Francisco FRANCO. A Popular Front government ruled in Chile from 1938 to 1947.

population By around 8000 BC the world was inhabited by between 5 and 10 million people. At the beginning of the Christian era the number had increased to some 300 million. Despite setbacks such as the BLACK DEATH, world population grew gradually over the following centuries until the industrial revolution around 1750, by which time there were about 800 million people. Improved public health care in 19th-century Europe and the United States then led to an unprecedented rise in the human population. In 1800 it stood at around 1 billion, and the British economist Thomas MALTHUS predicted that it would soon increase beyond the capacity of the world to feed it. By 1930 world population had reached 2 billion. Over the next 30 years another billion was added – and just 14 years later another billion. Since 1950 there has been a population explosion in Asia, Africa and Latin America, raising the world's population to 5.3 billion in 1990. By the year 2025 it is expected to reach 8.3 billion.

Major migrations of population have also taken place through the ages as a result of nomadism, exploration, war and slave trading. Amongst the mass migrations of the 19th and 20th centuries some 37 million people crossed the Atlantic from all parts of Europe to North America. Immigration to Australia and New Zealand came mainly from Britain until the arrival of the NEW AUSTRALIANS from continental Europe after the Second World War.

porcelain White, translucent, fine-grained pottery which originated in China around AD 900. During the Chinese Tang dynasty, from 618 to 906, porcelain was exported to the Middle East, where it was highly prized. The process was refined during the Song period from 960 to 1279. During the Yuan dynasty, from 1280 to 1368, blue and white porcelain was produced using cobalt from the Middle East. The Ming period from 1368 to 1644 produced exquisite coloured porcelain.

In Europe, porcelain was first made around 1575 in Florence in Italy. From 1710 it was being produced commercially in Germany at Meissen. Around 1800 the Englishman Josiah Spode developed bone china, a fine type of translucent porcelain, by adding bone ash to the ingredients of Chinese porcelain.

This porcelain jug was made in 1760 at Meissen – famed for the Meissen ware it produces from local kaolin.

Portsmouth, Treaty of (1905) Treaty signed in Portsmouth, New Hampshire, marking the end of the RUSSO-JAPANESE WAR. Russia had suffered several defeats in 1904 and 1905 when the US president Theodore Roosevelt intervened to end the war. By the treaty both sides agreed to evacuate Manchuria, restoring it to Chinese rule. Russia acknowledged Japanese supremacy in Korea, transferred its lease of Port Arthur (now Lüshun) to Japan and gave up the southern half of the island of Sakhalin. The treaty ended Russian expansion in the Far East, established Japan as the region's strongest country and confirmed the USA as a diplomatic power.

Portugal European country on the western coast of the Iberian peninsula. Around 500 BC Portugal was settled by Celtic tribes and some 350 years later Roman troops made it the Roman province of Lusitania. The Germanic Suebi people conquered the peninsula in the 5th century AD, and in 469 they were in turn subdued by the Germanic GOTHS. In 711 Arab Moors conquered most of Portugal, but an area in the north remained in Christian hands. In 1179 the Christian area was recognised by the papacy as the kingdom of Portugal under Alfonso I. By 1249 the Christian army had conquered all of Portugal.

Under the Aviz monarchs from 1385 to 1580 a vast PORTUGUESE EMPIRE took shape. In 1580 PHILIP II of Spain conquered the country, and union with Spain lasted until 1640, when a nationalist revolt brought the native BRAGANZA monarchy to power. During the PENINSULAR WAR (1808-14) the Braganza royal family fled to the Portuguese colony of BRAZIL. In 1821 John VI returned after a revolution against the Crown at the head of a new liberal constitution.

Conflict during the 19th century between supporters of ABSOLUTISM and DEMOCRACY led in 1910 to a revolution which overthrew the monarchy and established a republic. In 1926 there was a military coup, and from 1932 to 1968 the prime minister Antonio SALAZAR ruled the country as a virtual dictator. In 1974 there was a coup led by Marxist military leaders disillusioned with Portugal's costly colonial wars, particularly in ANGOLA and MOZAMBIQUE. In the following year these colonies were granted independence. In 1986 Mario Soares was elected president, with Anibal Silva leading a centrist government, and Portugal became a member of the European Community. In 1991 Soares was re-elected as president of Portugal, which was now both prosperous and stable. He was succeeded in January 1996 by Jorge Sampaio, former leader of the Socialist Party.

Portuguese empire The foundations of Portugal's overseas empire were laid by voyages of exploration in the 15th century under the patronage of Prince HENRY THE NAVIGATOR (1394-1460). By 1530 the Portuguese empire included the Atlantic islands of Cape Verde, Madeira and the Azores; a large area of Brazil; settlements in East and West Africa; coastline stretches of Angola and Mozambique; Indian Ocean bases including Ormuz, Goa and Colombo; and Far Eastern posts in the Moluccas, Macao, Java and Malacca.

The empire brought increasing wealth, particularly from the Far Eastern spice trade. During the 17th century much of the Portuguese territory in the Far East was lost to the Dutch, and Portugal was never again a great power. In the 20th century all the remaining Portuguese colonies were either regained by revolutionaries or given independence, with the exception of Macao which reverts to Chinese sovereignty in 1999.

Potatau Te Wherowhero (d.1860) First MAORI king. In 1858 he was elected by New Zealand Maoris on North Island as King Potatau I. He supported the Kingitanga ('all things kingly') Maori movement in its resistance to selling land to British settlers. When the Anglo-Maori TARANAKI WAR broke out in 1860, he spoke out against involving the Kingitanga. Descendants of Potatau still lead the Kingitanga.

Potemkin, Grigori Aleksandrovich (1739-91) Russian field-marshal and favourite of Empress CATHERINE II. Potemkin entered the Russian Horse Guards in 1755. Having distinguished himself in Russia's first war

> **❝...my love for you dazzles me. I forget everything my reason tells me and I feel I become quite stupid when I am in your presence. ❞**
>
> *Catherine II, writing to Grigori Potemkin, 1774*

with the Ottoman Empire he was created count in 1774. About the same time he became Catherine's lover. Potemkin played an important part in the annexation in 1783 of the Crimea, for which he was created prince. Although licentious and unscrupulous, he was an able administrator, and he did much to develop the Crimea.

Potosí Bolivian city established in the 16th century. In 1546 the Spaniards Juan de Villarroel and Diego Centeno founded the city, and began to mine its immense deposits of silver. By 1650 Potosí had grown into the largest and wealthiest city in the Americas. Many fine colonial buildings were erected

At the Potsdam Conference the broad smiles of Winston Churchill, Harry Truman and Joseph Stalin belie the growing tension between Britain and the USA on one side, and the USSR on the other.

during the 17th and 18th centuries, and the city is now a world heritage site. Although the silver deposits are exhausted, the mines still yield tin, zinc, copper and lead.

Potsdam Conference (July 17-August 2, 1945) Final conference of the Allied war leaders, held in Potsdam, outside Berlin, near the end of the Second World War. It was attended by the president of the United States Harry S TRUMAN, the dictator of the USSR Joseph STALIN and the British prime minister Winston CHURCHILL (who was replaced on July 27 by his successor Clement ATTLEE). As a result of the conference control of Germany was transferred to American, British, French and Russian zones of occupation. German territory east of the Oder and Neisse rivers was allotted to Poland, creating a new German-Polish border, the ODER-NEISSE LINE. War REPARATIONS were imposed on Germany, the Nazi Party was outlawed and the way opened for democratic government. Orders were made for the NUREMBERG TRIALS to take place. Japan was offered the choice between unconditional surrender or total destruction, but the atomic bomb was not mentioned.

Poynings' Law (1494) Irish parliamentary Act which made all legislation subject to the prior approval of the English Parliament. It was named after Sir Edward Poynings, Lord Deputy of Ireland, who summoned the Irish Parliament to announce it at Drogheda. It also specified that laws passed in England should apply in Ireland. The Statutes of Drogheda, as the Act was officially called, were a major grievance to Irish parliamentarians. In 1782 an Irish politician, Henry GRATTAN, successfully campaigned to have them repealed .

Praemunire, Statutes of (1353, 1365 and 1393) English antipapal laws designed to prevent judgments made in the king's courts

being referred to foreign courts. Although papal courts were not specifically mentioned until the second statute of 1365, the intention of all three statutes was to exploit feelings of English nationalism and antipapalism. The statute of 1393 imposed further restraints on communication between England and the papal court. The Statutes of Praemunire were revived in the 16th century by Henry VIII to aid him in his legal battle with the papacy.

Praetorian Guard Member of the emperor's personal corps of bodyguards in ancient Rome. In 27 BC AUGUSTUS CAESAR established nine cohorts, divisions of between 300 and 600 Praetorians, in Rome. A tenth cohort was added at the end of the 1st century AD. A Praetorian belonged to an influential

Praetorian Guards, here in marble relief, were concentrated in fortified barracks near Rome in AD23, and wielded great political power.

elite which accompanied the emperor wherever he went. Two prefects, who were military officers but sometimes took on civil duties, usually commanded the Praetorian Guard and frequently intervened in imperial politics. In 312 Emperor CONSTANTINE abolished the Praetorian Guard and replaced it with a new corps of guards, the Scholae.

pragmatic sanction Edict issued by a sovereign that becomes part of the fundamental law of the land, particularly in matters of royal succession. The term, which originated in Roman law, usually refers to the pragmatic sanction of April 1713 by which the Holy Roman Emperor Charles VI (reigned 1711-40) altered the succession of the Habsburg monarchy. Charles aimed to ensure that in the event of his having no male heir, his eldest daughter would inherit all the Habsburg lands, thereby disinheriting the daughters of his deceased brother, the previous emperor Joseph I. In 1717 his daughter MARIA THERESA was born and the law took on great importance. Despite the pledges of support that Charles obtained from European monarchs, Maria Theresa had to fight for her crown from 1740 to 1748 in the War of the AUSTRIAN SUCCESSION.

Prague, Defenestration of (1618) Act of rebellion by Bohemian Protestant nobles against Catholic Habsburg rule. On May 23, 1618, two Habsburg counts, Martinic and Slavata, were tried by an angry assembly of Protestants in Prague and found guilty of violating Protestant rights. They were then thrown with their secretary, Fabricius, through a 50 ft (15 m) high window of the Hradčany Castle. The men landed on a pile of rubbish below and escaped with their lives.

This unorthodox punishment was a method of disposing of opponents which had been used by the Bohemian religious reformers for more than a century. On this occasion it sparked the Catholic-Protestant THIRTY YEARS' WAR, which was to change the political face of Europe.

Prasad, Rajendra (1884-1963) First president of India. Prasad was a lawyer who in 1917 began working with the political and spiritual leader Mohandas GANDHI. In 1920 he joined the Indian National CONGRESS, and was its president in 1934 and 1939. During the Second World War the British imprisoned him from 1942 to 1945. In 1947 he was again elected president of Congress, and in 1950 he became the first president of an independent Indian republic, serving until 1962.

> **DID YOU KNOW?**
>
> *Scotland is perhaps the world's most strongly Presbyterian country, with a traditional dislike of the theatre. In 1784, however, the Church of Scotland cut short the annual meeting of its general assembly so that members could see the much-acclaimed actress Mrs Siddons.*

Press gangs were ruthless in their pursuit of recruits. Even a bridegroom on his wedding day could be hauled off for service on the high seas.

Prempeh I (d.1931) Last king of the Ashanti people of West Africa. In 1888 he was elected king of the Ashanti, but the British deposed him in 1896 after an Anglo-Ashanti war. In 1902 the Ashanti state was declared a British colony. In 1924 Prempeh was invited to return to the Ashanti capital Kumasi (in present-day Ghana), and in 1926 he was made a Kumasihene, a territorial chief. When he died his nephew, Prempeh II, was elected Kumasihene in 1931. In 1935 the Golden Stool, the traditional throne of Ashanti kings, was returned by the British and Prempeh II became a figurehead monarch, the Asantehene. The British established an Ashanti Confederacy Council during the 1930s, but political power remained in British hands.

Presbyterians Members of a Protestant Reformed Church which is governed by presbyters (elders) rather than by bishops, and in which Church courts oversee the conduct of the congregation. Their form of government follows the model laid down by the French Protestant reformer John CALVIN in 1541. In 1559 the French Protestants, the HUGUENOTS, established the first national Presbyterian Church. The only Presbyterian state Church to be established by law was founded in Scotland in 1560 under the leadership of John KNOX. Catholic persecution of Presbyterians in France was a major factor in the FRENCH WARS OF RELIGION between 1562 and 1598. A Reformed Church was established in the NETHERLANDS following the Eighty Years' War against Catholic Habsburg rule. The Presbyterian Church of England was formed in 1876, and it became part of the United Reformed Church in 1972. In the USA the first Presbyterian Church was founded in 1706 in Philadelphia, and by the 1990s the largest Presbyterian organisation in the USA had some 4 million members.

Presley, Elvis see feature, page 520

press gang Detachment of sailors employed by the British navy to impress, or force, men into naval service. From the Middle Ages until the early 19th century a press gang was legally entitled to recruit merchant seamen for the navy. It generally limited its activities to seaport towns where it could find recruits with suitable experience, but it was empowered to recruit able-bodied men throughout the realm. In British wars between 1688 and 1815 press gangs were especially active. In the port cities popular feeling against the 'press' was often strong, and the press gang did not dare go ashore in Cornwall or parts of Devon and Dorset. Fishermen and gentlemen were exempted from the press. Naval officers disliked the system but argued that there was no alternative. US resentment over impressment of American citizens was one cause of the War of 1812 with Britain. The army used the press gang less than the navy and ended the practice after the NAPOLEONIC WARS. The navy continued to rely on press gangs until the 1830s, when improvements in pay provided enough volunteers. In 1853 the Continuous Service Act gave seamen permanent positions and made the press gang redundant.

Prester John Legendary Christian monarch of the Middle Ages, at first believed to rule a kingdom in Asia, and later in Africa. His name means 'Priest John', from the Greek word *presbuteros* (priest). Prester John was first mentioned in a 12th-century German chronicle where he was identified as a descendant of the Magi. In the time of the CRUSADES many journeys were made to find his country in the

The king of rock'n'roll

The rise of the mass media in the 20th century created the new phenomenon of global celebrity. No one was to become more famous than Elvis Presley.

The career of Elvis Aaron Presley showed that 20th-century technology could give pop stars a fame possibly surpassing even that of military or political giants in earlier eras. He lived and died before the eye of the world's media and, hence, a fascinated public.

A pioneer of rock'n'roll and its outstanding performer, Presley was born on January 8, 1935, in Tupelo, Mississippi. His earliest musical influences came from the Pentecostal Church and the country and blues played on local radio stations, styles which he blended to form something uniquely his own. His potential was spotted by Sam Phillips, owner of Sun Studios in Memphis, Tennessee. Recordings made there attracted the attention of the flamboyant promoter Colonel Tom Parker, who decided to 'sell' the 21-year-old singer to the emerging teenage market of the USA.

Under Parker's management, Presley signed up with RCA Records. His first session for them produced 'Heartbreak Hotel', and triggered a period of intense creativity that included the recording of worldwide hits such as 'Hound Dog' and 'Don't Be Cruel' and the launch of a parallel film career with *Love Me Tender*.

On stage with the *Blue Moon Boys* in Miami in August 1956, the raw vitality of the young Elvis Presley electrified American teenagers.

The combination of interpretative ability and magnetic personal style was new in popular music, and a postwar generation hungry for excitement readily embraced him as an antihero.

In 1958 Presley was conscripted into the US army, and the singer whose sometimes suggestive stage act had once caused him to be condemned as a danger to morals found himself cited as a model for the nation's youth. He served as a soldier for two years, mainly in Germany, and some fans claim that it was a lesser Elvis who re-emerged into civilian life: his stage act was toned down and the material was pitched at a broader audience. But by widening his appeal he entered his period of greatest commercial success, with hits such as 'It's Now or Never' and 'Wooden Heart' and several undemanding films-with-music.

PILGRIMAGE TO MEMPHIS

But things soon changed. The mid 1960s saw the rise of British groups such as 'The Beatles', and this, with the dilution of Presley's rebellious image, now made him seem old-fashioned. An appearance on *Elvis*, a television special in 1968, reminded viewers how electrifying he could still be, but by the early 1970s he had sunk into self-parody. The icon of youth ended his career as a cat-suited crooner, bloated by drugs, alcohol and excess, performing for middle-aged tourists in Las Vegas. He died of a heart attack on August 16, 1977.

Pilgrims from all over the world still journey to Gracelands, his preserved home in Memphis, to pay homage to his achievements and to the drama of a life made and broken by the 20th-century phenomenon of global celebrity.

---

hope that he would help Christendom in its fight against Islam. From the mid 14th century the search focused on Ethiopia.

Preston, Battle of (August 17-19, 1648) Battle in Lancashire between Royalists and Parliamentarians which effectively ended the ENGLISH CIVIL WAR. In July 1648 a Scottish aristocrat, James HAMILTON, led one of the last attempts by the Royalists to regain power, and invaded England. The highly disciplined NEW MODEL ARMY of Oliver CROMWELL caught up with Hamilton's raw recruits at Preston, and pursued them in a series of running battles. On August 25 Hamilton surrendered at Uttoxeter.

Prestonpans, Battle of (September 21, 1745) Victory of Charles Stuart (BONNIE PRINCE CHARLIE), the JACOBITE claimant

The search for the legendary kingdom of Prester John led to Ethiopia, depicted here in a 16th-century Portuguese atlas.

to the British throne, in the FORTY-FIVE rebellion. In July 1745 Charles rallied an army of Highland supporters. They marched across Scotland, seized Edinburgh and at nearby Prestonpans they surprised and routed government forces led by Sir John Cope. The victory persuaded Charles and a narrow majority of his Highland chiefs to launch an invasion of England.

pretender One who puts forward a claim to the throne of a monarch. In the 15th century two impostors, Lambert SIMNEL and Perkin WARBECK, claimed the crown of Henry VII of England. After the GLORIOUS REVOLUTION of 1688-9, the Catholic king James II was removed from the English throne. His descendants, the Stuart Pretenders, were banned from power because they were Catholics. When James died in 1701 his son James Edward Stuart (1688-1766), 'The Old Pretender', claimed the throne. In 1715 and again ten years later unsuccessful JACOBITE rebellions were organised by his supporters.

The FORTY-FIVE rebellion to dethrone the Hanoverian king George II was led by his son BONNIE PRINCE CHARLIE, 'The Young Pretender' (1720-88).

Pride's Purge (December 6, 1648) Expulsion of about 140 Members of Parliament from the House of Commons by an army officer after the ENGLISH CIVIL WAR. Following orders from Oliver CROMWELL's army council, Colonel Thomas Pride assembled troops to arrest or expel PRESBYTERIAN Members of Parliament who sought a compromise agreement with CHARLES I. The remaining Members formed the RUMP PARLIAMENT and voted to put the king on trial for treason. In January 1649 Pride was a member of the court that condemned the king and was one of the signatories of his death warrant.

primary election Preliminary election in the United States in which the registered voters of a political party nominate candidates for office, including the presidency, and choose delegates for their party's national convention. During the 19th century state delegates for the national party convention were selected and instructed how to vote by a caucus of senior party members who operated an undemocratic system of party control. In 1903 Wisconsin became the first state to hold a democratic primary election for the nomination of candidates. In 1917 all except four US states held primary elections. Today all states hold primary elections, or 'primaries', for some or all offices.

Primo de Rivera, Miguel (1870-1930) Spanish general and dictator of Spain from 1923 to 1930. In the SPANISH-AMERICAN WAR of 1898 Rivera fought in Cuba and the Philippines, and from 1909 to 1913 he served in Morocco. In 1922 he became governor of Barcelona, and in the following year he led a military coup. Rivera was supported by the Spanish king Alfonso XIII, and in 1925 he changed his government from a military to a civil dictatorship. However, his support for

feudal landlords aroused the opposition of nationalists in Catalonia and Spanish liberals. In 1930 the economic and political failures of his regime led to the withdrawal of army support and forced his resignation. Rivera escaped to Paris where he died in exile.

primogeniture Legal system under which the estate of the father descends to the oldest son. It means 'the condition of being the first born'. In the Middle Ages it was widely practised in western Europe. In the 11th century the NORMANS introduced it to England as a means of preserving intact the landed wealth of a BARON, a warlord who held land directly from the king in return for military service. Exceptions to the practice of primogeniture included burghs in Scotland, and the county of Kent in England where *gavelkind*, a system of equal division of estate among all sons, persisted to 1925. In 1540 the Statute of Wills permitted the disinheritance of an oldest son, and in the 17th century the practice of holding land in return for military service was ended. In 1926 primogeniture was abolished in most cases in England and Wales, and in 1964 in Scotland, though it still applies to royal inheritance and to most peerages.

Primrose League Political organisation founded in 1883 by the TORY Party politicians Sir Drummond Wolf and Lord Randolph CHURCHILL. The emblem of the League was the favourite flower of the Tory Party leader Benjamin DISRAELI. Its aim was to broaden support for the party by demonstrating its capacity to improve living conditions for the whole nation. It developed into a mass organisation which was particularly successful in recruiting women to campaign for the Tories.

printing see feature, page 522

privateer Privately owned armed ship, its captain or crew member, authorised by a government at war to attack enemy vessels. From the 13th century such ships were issued with government licences in order to distinguish them from PIRATE vessels. Successful English privateers in the late 16th century included John HAWKINS and Francis DRAKE. In the following century English BUCCANEERS, including Henry MORGAN, claimed to be privateers and operated with the tacit approval of the

monarch, but without official government commissions. In the AMERICAN REVOLUTION and the WAR OF 1812 the United States relied on privateers in the absence of a national navy. Privateers frequently ignored naval discipline and violated the rules of war, and most European nations signed a declaration in Paris in 1856 making them illegal.

Progressive Movement (1890-1914) Campaign in the USA by members of the Republican and Democratic parties to effect social, political and economic reforms. Progressives were committed to FREE TRADE, internal party democracy, and government control of trusts – that is, commerrcial cartels and monopolies. They proposed PRIMARY ELECTIONS to nominate candidates, legislation to improve conditions of employment, ANTITRUST laws, and PROHIBITION. Progressive policies were adopted by the Republican president Theodore ROOSEVELT from 1901 to 1909 and by the Democratic president Woodrow WILSON from 1913 to 1921.

Progressive Party (1912, 1924 and 1948) Name of three separate political parties which grew from the PROGRESSIVE MOVEMENT in the USA and challenged the dominant Democratic and Republican parties. In 1912 some Republicans, disillusioned with their right-wing president William TAFT, formed a Progressive Party, and in the same year their candidate Theodore ROOSEVELT won more than 4 million votes in the presidential elections, overtaking Taft but losing to the Democrat Woodrow WILSON. In 1924 a new Progressive Party was formed. Although its presidential candidate Robert La Follette won more than 5 million votes nationwide, only Wisconsin nominated him. In 1948 former Vice-president Henry A. WALLACE founded another Progressive Party, supported by the communists and the New York Labor Party. Wallace campaigned for an end to the COLD WAR with the Soviet Union, winning about a million votes but not the presidency.

Prohibition (1920-33) Period in the USA when alcohol was prohibited. In the 19th century the US TEMPERANCE MOVEMENT, which included the Prohibition Party and the Anti-Saloon League, campaigned for a government ban on alcohol. During the First World War US alcohol output was limited, and in 1919 the Volstead Act brought into effect the Eighteenth Amendment, which banned alcohol. Drinking continued between 1920 and 1933 in illegal bars called 'speakeasies', and bootlegging – the smuggling and illegal production of alcohol – flourished. Gangsters, including Al CAPONE, controlled the supply of alcohol, and corruption spread through police forces and city governments. In 1931 a government commission reported that

At a primary election rally in Philadelphia in 1980 Senator Edward Kennedy waves to his supporters. He later withdrew from the presidential race.

From manuscript to information technology

Up to the 15th century, manuscripts were copied out laboriously by hand and circulated among the few who could read – mostly churchmen. The introduction of printing opened the human mind to a vast range of new possibilities.

The invention of printing made possible two key developments: the spread of literacy beyond the educated elite, and the storage of large quantities of information. It created the book, the pamphlet, the newspaper and the periodical. Its uses extended to commerce, religion, politics, literature and art. Its influence over religion and politics became so powerful that the authorities resorted to censorship, regulation and taxation to control it.

Printing was invented in China in the 7th or 8th century AD, at first using wooden blocks rather than metal type. The first known book produced in this way was *The Diamond Sutra*, a translation from Sanskrit dated 868. The first movable type was made in China in the 11th century from a mixture of clay and glue. Movable type made from metal moulds was used for a wide range of publications in Korea and China in the 15th century, before Johann Gutenberg developed his own similar printing system, using a hand press, at Mainz in Germany.

EXCHANGING IDEAS

The first printed document from Mainz was a papal indulgence of 1454. A Bible followed in 1455. Both in Asia and Europe religion was the first subject for printers. But while Chinese printing conserved traditional values, in Europe its growth in Germany and beyond transformed the evolution of ideas during the Reformation. Readers could now study the text of the Bible in the vernacular and ideas could spread rapidly from one country to another.

In England William Caxton, who had learned printing in Germany, published the first dated book in English at Westminster in 1477. He saw the value of books for instruction and entertainment as well as devotion. Two years before, in Bruges, Belgium, he had published

Caxton's press brought reading to a much wider English public (right), though movable type cast in bronze had already been in use in Korea since 1403.

his first book in English, *The Recuyell of the Historyes of Troye*.

Hand presses remained in use for printing until the 19th century. It was the newest medium of communication, a newspaper – *The Times* of London – which first acquired a steam-powered press in 1814 in response to the need for a quicker way to circulate news to a growing readership. A high-speed rotary press, with the printing surface wrapped round a cylinder, was invented in the United States in 1847. Along with later inventions in telegraphy, in paper folding (and later in paper production) and in typesetting by machine, it made possible the advance of large-circulation newspapers. The freedom of the press, proclaimed by the poet John Milton during the English Civil War of the 17th century, was among the great liberal causes of the 19th century. As literacy rates rose, the century also became the great age of the book. Reading was deemed essential for industrial societies advancing towards political democracy.

During the 20th century the speed of technological and commercial innovation in printing and publishing accelerated. Old patterns of industrial relations were broken as multimedia mergers linked print and electronic communications to form a new 'information society'. Yet books survived despite predictions of their demise, and newspapers gained in power. There was universal recognition that the story of the 'communications revolution' that had started with Gutenberg's little printing press in Mainz was far from finished.

Some of the earliest rotary printing presses were installed at *The Times* in 1848. As a result, production was quickly tripled.

During the Prohibition years, from 1920 to 1933, US federal agents poured gallons of whiskey down city drains. Widespread illicit stills meant law enforcers could do little to stop bootleggers.

the Prohibition laws were unenforceable, and in 1933 the Eighteenth Amendment was repealed by the Twenty First Amendment. By 1966 every state had abandoned prohibition.

Protectorate Government of England under Oliver CROMWELL from 1653 to 1658, and Richard CROMWELL from 1658 to 1659. After the ENGLISH CIVIL WAR and the execution of Charles I in 1649 England became a republic, the COMMONWEALTH. A RUMP PARLIAMENT ruled through a Council of State, chaired by Oliver Cromwell. In April 1653 Cromwell accused the Rump Parliament of corruption and replaced it with the BAREBONES PARLIAMENT. In December a council of army officers drafted an Instrument of Government which made Cromwell the Lord Protector of England, Scotland and Ireland, ruling with a single House of Parliament.

In 1655 Cromwell divided England into 11 military districts ruled by major generals. In 1657 Parliament offered Cromwell the crown and the right to name a successor. He refused to be king, but chose his son Richard to succeed him. When Cromwell died in 1658, Richard became Lord Protector but he failed to control the army and Parliament. Richard resigned the following year, bringing the Protectorate to an end. General MONCK then recalled the LONG PARLIAMENT, and in May 1660 Charles II was restored to the throne.

Protestantism One of the three main branches of Christianity, with the Roman Catholic Church and the Orthodox Church. Protestantism arose from the REFORMATION in the 16th century. The word comes from the *Protestatio* of the Lutheran minority at the DIET, or meeting, of Speyer in 1529. These reformers were protesting against the decision by the Catholic majority to outlaw the reforms of the German priest Martin LUTHER. Protestantism emphasises the Bible as the main source of doctrinal authority, rather than the pope or general councils. In the 16th century, it reacted against the corruption and worldliness of some of the institutions of the Roman Catholic Church. It also condemned certain Catholic practices as superstitious.

Some Protestant Churches were based on the teachings of Luther. Others followed the French theologian John CALVIN or the Swiss Ulrich ZWINGLI. In England Henry VIII broke with the Roman Catholic Church in 1534 and became the head of a national Church. Under Elizabeth I the Church of England was reformed as a compromise between Catholicism and Calvinism. It became the foundation of ANGLICANISM. In 1689 the BILL OF RIGHTS declared that the monarch must be Protestant and a member of the Church of England. Several Protestant denominations have evolved since the 17th century, including QUAKER, BAPTIST CONGREGATIONALIST and METHODIST Churches.

Proudhon, Pierre Joseph (1809-65) French journalist and socialist. In 1840 he published the pamphlet *What is Property?* This began with the bold paradox 'Property is theft', and maintained that the owners of private property robbed tenants of their wages by taking rent. Proudhon was elected to the National Assembly after the REVOLUTIONS OF 1848 and tried unsuccessfully to establish a national bank to give workers interest-free credit. He was imprisoned from 1849 to 1852 for publishing an attack on the president, Louis Napoleon. His writings influenced later supporters of ANARCHISM and FEDERALISM, as well as the philosopher Karl Marx.

Provence Region of south-east France. In the 6th century BC colonies were established there by Greece. In the 2nd century BC the Romans made it their first *provincia* beyond the Alps, from which it derives its name.

In the 5th century AD the Germanic Goths conquered the region, followed in the 6th century by the Germanic Franks and in the 8th century by Arabs from the Levant. In 933 it became part of the Kingdom of Arles, and at the end of the 10th century a local dynasty, the counts of Provence, came to power. By the 12th century Provence was thriving through trade with the Levant; its cultural achievements included TROUBADOUR music, poetry in the local Provençal language and superb Romanesque churches. In 1246 it passed to the ANGEVIN dynasty, and in 1481 its last king, Charles of Maine, bequeathed it to France. It retained administrative independence until 1790 when the French Revolution brought it under French rule.

Prussia Former north German kingdom, comprising parts of present-day Germany, Poland and countries of the former USSR. It was established in the 13th century by the TEUTONIC KNIGHTS who defeated the pagan Prussian tribes. In 1525 it became a hereditary duchy ruled by the HOHENZOLLERN dynasty, with Poland controlling its foreign policy. In 1618 the duchy of Prussia was inherited by German princes, the Electors of BRANDENBURG, and in 1701 the Elector Frederick III had himself crowned 'king in Prussia', FREDERICK I.

During the 18th century the kings FREDERICK WILLIAM I, FREDERICK II and Frederick William II made Prussia the greatest military power on the European continent. It was defeated in the NAPOLEONIC WARS, but the Congress of VIENNA in 1815 granted it further territories and created a GERMAN CONFEDERATION. Following victory in 1870 in the FRANCO-PRUSSIAN WAR, the Prussian king William I became emperor in 1871 of a united Germany. After the First World War Prussia became a *Land*, a German province, in the German WEIMAR REPUBLIC. After the Second World War Prussia was occupied by the allied victors from 1945 to 1947. It was then abolished and divided between Poland, the USSR and the German Democratic Republic.

Ptolemy Macedonian dynasty ruling Egypt from 323 to 31 BC. Ptolemy I was one of ALEXANDER the Great's generals who, after Alexander's death, seized the governorship of Egypt. In 304 he proclaimed himself king and proceeded to conquer Cyprus, Palestine, many of the Greek islands and parts of Asia Minor (now Turkey). Under his rule a huge library was built in ALEXANDRIA, and the city became a centre of art and learning.

The reigns of the Ptolemys who succeeded him were characterised by wars with the Seleucids, a dynasty founded by Alexander the Great's general Seleucus I (*c.*356-280 BC) and based in Mesopotamia, and by rebellions in Egypt. In 48 the Roman army of Julius Caesar supported CLEOPATRA VII in a successful revolt against her brother Ptolemy XII. In 31 the Roman general Octavian, later the Emperor Augustus, defeated Cleopatra and Mark Antony at ACTIUM, bringing Egypt under the rule of Rome and ending Ptolemaic power.

Pueblos Name given to the Native Americans who lived in stone or adobe houses in the south-west of the present-day USA; from the Spanish *pueblo,* (people). Around the 1st century AD Pueblo villages were built with pits for houses. By 1000 these pits had been replaced by adobe and stone houses up to five storeys high. Each storey was usually set back from the floor below, so that the building looked like a stepped pyramid. At Mesa Verde in the 13th and 14th centuries the Pueblos lived in multi-storey cliff houses.

In the 16th century Spanish conquistadores entered the region of the Rio Grande occupied by the Pueblo dwellers. By 1630 they had converted 60 000 Pueblos to Christianity. The Pueblos successfully revolted against Spanish rule in 1680, but they were reconquered in 1692. Some Pueblos in western settlements stayed independent; they include the Hopi, whose towns have remained continuously occupied for some 700 years.

Puerto Rico Self-governing island in the Caribbean. In 1493 Christopher Columbus arrived in Puerto Rico. In 1508 the Spaniard Juan Ponce de Léon began colonising the island. Since the indigenous Arawak peoples had been massacred or killed by European diseases, African slaves were brought in to work on the sugar and tobacco plantations. Trade flourished during the 17th century, and coffee plantations were established in the 18th

century. In 1873 slavery in Puerto Rico was abolished. The island came under US military rule in 1898 during the SPANISH-AMERICAN WAR, and was ceded to the United States at the end of the war. Puerto Ricans were granted US citizenship in 1917, and in 1952 they voted to become a self-governing commonwealth in

association with the United States. In a referendum held in 1993 Puerto Ricans voted to maintain their commonwealth status, rather than claim full independence or become the 51st state of the USA.

Pugachev, Emelian (c.1742-75) Cossack Pretender and leader of a revolt against the Russian Empress CATHERINE II. In 1773 he declared himself to be Tsar Peter III, the assassinated husband of Catherine II. He harnessed the support of the lower classes, including factory and mine workers, Cossacks, serfs and Tatars, and led a rebellion in the south of the country. In 1774 he captured Kazan, where he established a court and announced the abolition of serfdom. Catherine sent an army against Pugachev, which easily defeated his forces. He was brought in an iron cage to Moscow, where he was executed.

Pullman strike (1894) US labour dispute with the Pullman Palace Car Company of Chicago. In May 1894 the company cut wages and sacked union representatives without consulting employees. The workers' cause was taken up by the American Railway Union. About 50 000 workers supported the strike, bringing Chicago's railways to a standstill. The dispute ended in bloodshed when the federal court declared the strike illegal and in July President CLEVELAND sent in troops.

Punic Wars Three wars fought in the 3rd and 2nd centuries BC between ROME and CARTHAGE. The first (264-241) was fought for control of the Strait of Messina, dividing

Sicily from mainland Italy. Rome's navy was victorious and conquered Sicily. After the first war, tensions between Rome and Carthage grew when Rome seized Corsica and Sardinia, and in 237 the Carthaginian general HAMILCAR BARCA captured southern and eastern Spain. The second war (218-201) arose from the capture of Saguntum (now Sagunto) in Spain by Hamilcar Barca's son HANNIBAL. He invaded Italy by crossing the Alps with a huge force. Rome suffered several defeats, notably in 217 at Lake Trasimene and in 216 at CANNAE. In 207 Hannibal's brother Hasdrubal was defeated in north Italy, and in 203 Hannibal was forced to return to Africa to defend Carthage against the Roman general SCIPIO Africanus Major. In the following year Hannibal was conclusively defeated at Zama, and in 201 Carthage made peace and surrendered its province of Spain to Rome.

The third Punic War began in 149 when Rome, spurred by the writer CATO (the Elder), declared war on Carthage. In 146 Scipio Africanus Minor destroyed Carthage and declared Africa a Roman province.

Punjab North-western region of the Indian subcontinent, divided between Pakistan and India. In the 8th century Muslims conquered western Punjab and converted the population to Islam. In the 12th century they conquered eastern Punjab, but failed to convert the mainly Hindu people. From the 16th to the late 18th century the region prospered under the Muslim Mughal empire. In 1799 Sikhism, a religion with roots in Hinduism, became dominant and Sikhs established a

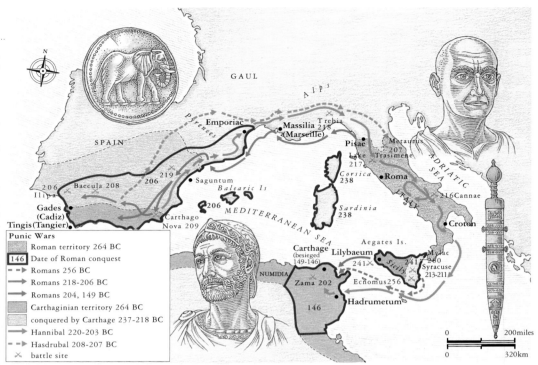

The First Punic War ended in Roman victory when Carthage abandoned Sicily in 241 BC. In the second, Hannibal (above) and his elephants took the war into Italy – but in 202 Scipio (top right) defeated Hannibal at Zama, and in 146 the legions returned to burn Carthage to the ground.

Punic Wars
- Roman territory 264 BC
- 146 Date of Roman conquest
- Romans 256 BC
- Romans 218-206 BC
- Romans 204, 149 BC
- Carthaginian territory 264 BC
- conquered by Carthage 237-218 BC
- Hannibal 220-203 BC
- Hasdrubal 208-207 BC
- × battle site

kingdom under the maharajah RANJIT SINGH. In 1849 they were defeated by the British in the SIKH WARS. When the British withdrew from occupation of India in 1947, the Punjab was divided into Muslim West Punjab in the newly created country of Pakistan, and Punjab in India for Hindus and Sikhs. In 1949 West Punjab was renamed the province of Punjab. In 1966 the Indian state of Punjab was divided into the states of Haryana, with a Hindu majority, and Punjab, with a Sikh majority. In the 1980s militant Sikhs violently campaigned for an independent Sikh nation, and in 1987 the Indian government declared a state of emergency. Elections were held in 1992 and separatist violence declined.

Puritanism Extreme form of PROTESTANTISM, originating in England in the 16th century. Its followers believed that the ANGLICAN CHURCH had not gone far enough in rejecting Roman Catholic dogma and rituals. Since most Puritans followed the teachings of John CALVIN, they welcomed Calvinist PRESBYTERIANS and other NONCONFORMIST Church members into the movement. In 1604 a Puritan petition for changes in the practices of the Anglican Church was rejected by James I at the HAMPTON COURT CONFERENCE. Subsequent persecution, organised by William LAUD, drove many Puritans to emigrate to the Netherlands and the New World. In 1620 the PILGRIM FATHERS, Puritans who rejected the Church of England, travelled to New England on board the *Mayflower,* and founded the Puritan Commonwealth of Massachusetts. From 1642 to 1660 Puritanism became a powerful political force and helped to bring about the ENGLISH CIVIL WAR. After the restoration of Charles II, Puritans were repressed under the CLARENDON code. They disbanded and were absorbed into various Nonconformist Churches.

Pushkin, Aleksandr (1799-1837) Russian poet, novelist and playwright, regarded as the founding father of Russian literature. He was born into an aristocratic family in Moscow. In 1817 he entered government service but in 1820 he was exiled by Tsar Alexander I to southern Russia for writing political verse, including an *Ode to Liberty*. He returned six years later, but remained subject to censorship. His works include the tragic historical drama *Boris Godunov* (1824-5), which was made into an opera by Mussorgsky. *Eugene Onegin* (1833), a novel in verse, was also turned into an opera in 1879, by Tchaikovsky. In 1837 Pushkin was fatally wounded in a duel with a French aristocrat, Baron Georges D'Anthès, whom Pushkin had been told in anonymous letters was his wife's lover.

Pym, John (1584-1643) English Puritan leader of the House of Commons during the LONG PARLIAMENT. Pym entered Parliament in 1614 and attached himself to the Country Party. In 1626 he organised the impeachment of George Villiers, 1st Duke of BUCKINGHAM, on charges of corruption and financial mismanagement. In 1628 he was a leading advocate of the PETITION OF RIGHT, a declaration of civil liberties by Parliament. In 1641 he persuaded Parliament to pass the Acts of ATTAINDER, pronouncing his friend Thomas Strafford and William Laud guilty of treason.

He published the GRAND REMONSTRANCE, a document condemning the rule of Charles I. When Charles attempted to arrest Pym and four other MPs, the crisis between the king and Parliament deepened and in 1642 led to the outbreak of the ENGLISH CIVIL WAR. In 1643 Pym arranged the SOLEMN LEAGUE AND COVENANT with Scotland, promising Scottish Presbyterians cash and religious reforms in exchange for military aid to Parliamentarians.

pyramid Large monument built to house a tomb or temple, especially in ancient Egypt. Most Egyptian pyramids were constructed around 2700 to 2200 BC, during the Old Kingdom. The architect IMHOTEP designed the first pyramid, the Step Pyramid at Saqqara, for King Zoser. Three pyramids at Giza, near Cairo, include the Great Pyramid of Cheops, which rises 450ft (137m) above the desert and is the only one of the SEVEN WONDERS OF THE WORLD to survive.

The ZIGGURAT, a temple in the shape of a stepped pyramid, appeared in ancient Babylonia and Assyria from the 3rd millennium BC to the 6th century BC. The Romans built pyramidal tombs, including the pyramid of Cestius (62-12) in Rome. Similar structures were erected by pre-Columbian Native American civilisations in Central America between AD 250 and 1520, including the magnificent Temple of the Sun in Tenochtitlán, Mexico. In 1989 Ieoh Pei, the Chinese-American architect, built a controversial glass pyramid in the courtyard of the Louvre art museum in Paris.

Pyrrhus (319-272 BC) King of EPIRUS, a country in Greece, from 307 to 303 BC and from 297 until his death. In 280 Pyrrhus sent troops with elephants to Tarentum, a Greek colony in southern Italy, to do battle with Rome. He was victorious at Heraclea and in 279 at Asculum. The phrase 'a Pyrrhic victory' is based on the king's supposed remark after his victory at Heraclea, achieved with severe losses to his own army: 'We cannot afford another victory like that'. In 278 he went to Sicily where he unsuccessfully attempted to expel the Carthaginians. In 275 Pyrrhus was defeated on the Italian mainland by the Romans at Beneventum. In 273 he failed to conquer Macedonia, and then the Peloponnese. The following year he fled to the city of Argos where he was killed by a mob.

Pythagoras (c.582-c.507 BC) Greek philosopher and mathematician. Around 530 BC Pythagoras settled in Crotona, a Greek colony in southern Italy, where he established a religious community, perhaps based on a mystical Orphic cult. He and his followers preached the transmigration of souls, the passing of a soul on the death of a person to another body. He led an ascetic life of moral purification in order to raise his soul to a higher level for the next life. He believed that the world could only be understood through numbers and worshipped the equilateral triangle as 'the fount and root of ever-flowing nature'. Pythagoras evolved the theorem that the square on the hypotenuse of a right-angled triangle is equal to the sum of the squares on the other two sides. He influenced the Greek philosopher PLATO (c.428-c.348 BC) and the 3rd century AD followers of NEOPLATONISM.

Mayan and Toltec architecture blend together in the Castillo Pyramid at Chichén Itzá in Yucatán, Mexico. On each of the four sides of the pyramid 91 steps lead up to the temple at its summit.

Qaddafi, Moammar al-

Qaddafi, Moammar al- (1942-) Libyan leader who seized power in 1969 by overthrowing his country's monarchy. Born to a family of Bedouin farmers, Qaddafi joined the Libyan army and rose to the rank of captain. In September 1969 he led an officers' coup that deposed Idris I (1890-1983), and installed himself as commander in chief of the armed forces and chairman of the country's new governing body, the Revolutionary Command Council. Qaddafi soon became renowned for his anti-Western rhetoric. Within four years he had closed British and American military bases, nationalised foreign petroleum assets and confiscated the property of all Jews and Italians before expelling them from Libya.

As a devout Muslim, Qaddafi restored traditional Islamic laws, while as a vociferous Arab nationalist he strongly opposed any concessions to Israel. He also used his nation's oil wealth to support a number of revolutionary

Qaddafi in full regalia at the 1981 passing-out parade of Libya's women's military academy. He opened Libyan military training to women.

organisations across the world, including the Black Panthers, the PLO and the IRA. Under Qaddafi, Libya has been implicated in several attempted coups in the Middle East, and numerous acts of terrorism in Europe. In an attempt to end Libyan sponsorship for such activities US warplanes in 1986 bombed several sites in Libya, including Qaddafi's palace. He escaped unhurt, though several of his children were killed or injured. Since then Qaddafi's politics have been less provocative towards the West, though he refused British and US requests for the extradition of two Libyan intelligence agents believed to be responsible for the bombing in 1988 of an American airliner over Lockerbie, Scotland. During the Gulf crisis in 1990 Qaddafi first supported Iraq's invasion of Kuwait, but also condemned the taking of civilian hostages and offered to join the UN naval blockade of Iraq.

In 1995 Qaddafi expelled 30 000 Palestinian refugees, claiming that this exposed the 'lie' of an Israeli-PLO accord that failed to find a place for them in Palestine.

Qatar Country occupying the Qatar peninsula on the west coast of the Persian Gulf. For most of its history Qatar, like its neighbours, has been inhabited by nomadic Arab herders. Towards the end of the 18th century it fell under the control of the powerful al-Khalifah dynasty of Bahrain, but in 1868 the country broke free with British help and established its own monarchy. Three years later the Ottoman Empire claimed authority over Qatar, only to be defeated by the forces of the sheikh. The First World War brought an end to Turkish power in the area, and in 1916 Qatar agreed to become a British protected state. The discovery of oil in 1939 led to the rapid development of the Qatari economy after the Second World War, bringing with it wealth that is among the highest in the world per head of population. In the 1960s Qatar seemed set to become part of the United Arab Emirates, but chose instead to become fully independent in 1971. During the GULF WAR of 1991, Qatar permitted UN coalition forces to be stationed on its soil, and expelled many Palestinians because of the PLO's pro-Iraqi stance. Since the war Qatar has strengthened its links with Iran, owing to the perceived threat from Iraq.

Qin dynasty (221-206 BC) China's first imperial dynasty, from which the name China is derived. During the 4th century BC, the small but warlike state of Qin began conquering its neighbours, and by the middle of the 3rd century it had expanded over most of China. The process was completed by King Cheng, who in 221 proclaimed himself Qin Shi Huang Di – 'First Qin Emperor' – of all China. In order to govern his huge territory, he abolished feudalism, standardised systems of writing and measurement, and created a strong, centralised government. He also set about building China's Great Wall by strengthening and linking a number of ancient defensive walls along the country's northern frontier. Qin Shi Huang Di's grandiose projects, harsh laws and heavy taxation resulted in a series of rebellions which broke out soon after his death in 210. In 206 his son was overthrown. A period of civil strife ensued, until the HAN emerged as China's next ruling dynasty in 202.

Qing dynasty (AD 1644-1912) China's last imperial dynasty, sometimes called the Manchu dynasty. By 1644 the MING dynasty was fatally weakened by several years of rebellion and civil war. A rebel leader called Li Zicheng had captured part of Beijing, and pronounced himself emperor. The Ming general Wu Sangui then made the error of inviting Manchu troops to assist him in fighting Li Zicheng, and in the resulting turmoil the Manchus seized Beijing and pronounced their own ruler emperor of China. The Qing emperors made themselves acceptable to the Chinese by adopting many aspects of Ming government, and emphasised their continuity with the past by fostering ancient traditions and classical Confucian values (see CONFUCIUS). Under the emperor Kangxi, who reigned from 1661 to 1722, China expanded to include Mongolia, Turkistan, Tibet and Taiwan, while the emperor Qianlong, ruling from 1736 to 1796, made further conquests that expanded the empire to its greatest extent. During the 19th century the Qing dynasty suffered a number of setbacks, most notably from the First OPIUM WAR with Britain (1839-42), the TAIPING REBELLION (1850-64) and the First SINO-JAPANESE WAR of 1894-5. The situation was exacerbated by the actions of the dowager empress CIXI, who dominated the Chinese court from 1895, stifling all attempts at modernisation and manipulating the BOXER REBELLION in an attempt to drive foreigners out of China. Three years after her death in 1908 China was declared a republic under SUN YAT-SEN, resulting in the abdication of the six-year-old emperor Pu Yi in February 1912.

Qin Shi Huang Di see QIN DYNASTY, and feature, page 527

Quadruple Alliance Name given to several alliances formed by four European powers. The Quadruple Alliance of 1718 arose when Austria, France, Britain and the Netherlands joined forces to prevent Spain from seizing Sicily and Sardinia, contrary to the Peace of UTRECHT which had been concluded in 1713. The allies forced Spain to withdraw its claims to Italy under the terms of the Treaty of the Hague (1720).

Another Quadruple Alliance was formed in 1813 by Britain, Prussia, Austria and Russia to ensure the defeat of Napoleon Bonaparte. The resulting Battle of Leipzig (1813) helped to bring about Napoleon's abdication, but the allies had to go to war against him again in 1815 after he returned from exile on Elba. After Napoleon's final defeat at the Battle of Waterloo (1815), the allies renewed their alliance at the Congress of Vienna, to ensure that France could not again threaten peace in Europe. In 1818, however, France joined the

> ### DID YOU KNOW?
>
> The long pigtail worn by Chinese men from the 17th century was not a traditional Chinese hairstyle. It was imposed on them by their Qing, or Manchu, rulers.

China's eternal army

Qin Shi Huang Di was the first emperor to unite China. To guard his tomb in his afterlife, he had his fearsome army of conquest reproduced in terracotta.

One of the most spectacular archaeological finds of this or any century was made by Chinese labourers excavating wells near Xi'an in the northern province of Shaanxi in March 1974. Buried in the reddish soil of the Huang He (Yellow River) valley they uncovered the first of a vast army of 7000 life-size terracotta figures. These were part of the 20 sq mile (50 km²) funerary compound of King Zheng of Qin (259–210 BC), who in 221 united the Chinese states into an empire, assuming the name of Shi Huang Di, or 'First Emperor'.

According to the historian Sima Qian, writing a century after Zheng's death, work began on his tomb soon after he became King of Qin in 246. More than 700 000 labourers were conscripted. They dug through three underground streams, lining the burial chamber with copper to prevent flooding. Inside the chamber they created a miniature version of China, building models of pavilions, palaces and temples. The Huang He and Chang Jiang (Yangtze) rivers were reproduced in mercury, and mechanically made to flow into a miniature ocean. Birds of gold and silver and pine trees of carved jade were set beneath a sky sparkling with constellations of pearls.

To guard these riches from robbers, Shi Huang Di ordered the setting of traps, including crossbows ready to shoot at anyone entering the tomb. Whether this proved a successful deterrent is not yet known, as the huge mound covering the emperor's burial chamber has never been excavated. The glorious treasures described by Sima Qian may still be in place, awaiting discovery.

BODYGUARDS FOR A TYRANT

The purpose of the terracotta army, which stands about a mile (1.6 km) away from the burial chamber, was to protect the emperor in the afterlife. Each figure was probably modelled from life, as no two are exactly the same. Originally brightly painted, they have hollow heads and torsos, though their legs are solid to bear

Qin Shi Huang Di's reign was one of terror and harshness. To crush opposition, he had many books burned and scholars executed.

the weight. The figures are deployed in the corridors of underground chambers, arrayed as the Qin army would have been as it prepared to charge into battle.

In front stand 200 bowmen and crossbowmen. These were the Qin army's equivalent of modern artillery. Moving swiftly, clad only in cotton, they fired continuous streams of arrows from long range, avoiding hand-to-hand combat. The heavy bolts of the crossbows would have ripped straight through the shields of the Greek and Macedonian soldiers of the time.

Behind the bowmen stand six chariots, each drawn by four horses. Two of the chariots were command vehicles, equipped with drums and bells, which in battle would have been struck to issue orders. Ranked behind the chariots are the foot soldiers. Though they would have been expected to engage in close combat with the enemy, they carry no shields,

and their armour covers only the upper part of their bodies. The vigilance, bravery and fierce discipline of the Qin soldier were considered sufficient protection, as the armies of Qin never defended: they always attacked.

The swords and spears of the terracotta soldiers – most of which had long since been looted by grave robbers – were made of an unusual alloy. Thirteen elements, including copper, tin, nickel, magnesium and cobalt, went into its composition. The metal was treated with a preservative so effective that the weapons have not corroded, even after 22 centuries. The blades of some were still sharp enough to cut a hair when they were dug up.

A second chamber, separate from the one containing the infantry, holds 1400 cavalry and 90 chariots. A third may have held the commander in chief – for his chariot and guard are certainly there. But none of the chambers has been fully excavated: the terracotta army still has many secrets to yield.

The underground army faces east – the direction from which Qin's enemies would have come. Yet, despite Shi Huang Di's grandiose preparations – his terracotta army and the Great Wall of China – his dynasty fell within five years of his death, a victim of its own tyranny.

The terracotta army represents the full range of Chinese warfare, and each figure is different.

alliance to make it a Quintuple Alliance, and in 1834 France joined Britain, Portugal and Spain to form another Quadruple Alliance to support the liberal monarchies of Spain and Portugal against rival, conservative claimants (see CARLIST).

Quakers Members of the Religious Society of Friends, a Christian movement founded by the English Puritan George FOX in the mid 17th century. Early Quakers worshipped without preachers or liturgy, as they believed God would inspire a member of the congregation to speak as required.

The name 'Quaker' was originally a term of derision, used by opponents of the Friends, in reference to their frequent shaking or other signs of religious emotion at their gatherings. Over the years, however, 'Quakers' has become an acceptable semi-official name for the Friends. Before the Toleration Act of 1689 the Quakers suffered frequent violent persecution for their beliefs which, in addition to the rejection of an established Church and ordained ministers, included a refusal to take oaths and bear arms, and a belief in the equality of all men and women.

By 1670 there were Quaker converts throughout the British Isles, continental Europe, the West Indies and Britain's North American colonies. In 1681 William PENN obtained a royal charter to found the Quaker colony of Pennsylvania, with guarantees of political and religious freedom, and the colony became a haven for Quakers fleeing persecution. During the 19th century two branches of Quakerism emerged – the evangelical Orthodox followers of Elias Hicks (1748-1830) and the Conservative followers of John Wilbur (1774-1856). In recent years the division has diminished. Quakers are respected worldwide for their efforts to promote peace and international understanding.

The fleur de lys and maple leaf, symbols of Quebec separatism and federal Canada, are happily reconciled on smiling faces at a rally for national unity, 1995.

Quebec Canada's largest province, situated in the east of the country, as well as the capital of that province, often called Quebec City to distinguish the two. Originally populated by the Algonquin, Montagnai and Cree Native Peoples, the region was claimed for France in 1534 by Jacques CARTIER. In 1608 Samuel de Champlain established a trading post on the St Lawrence River, which would eventually grow into the city of Quebec. The territory of NEW FRANCE was much larger than present-day Quebec, and was subject to constant incursions by British forces and their Iroquois allies. Anglo-French rivalry came to a head during the SEVEN YEARS' WAR, and resulted in a major British victory on the PLAINS OF ABRAHAM outside Quebec City in September 1759. The subsequent Treaty of PARIS (1763) gave control of New France (thenceforth Quebec) to Britain, which attempted to conciliate the colony's French inhabitants by passing the Quebec Act of 1774, guaranteeing them a number of special privileges regarding language, religion and customs.

In 1791 the colony was divided into two provinces: Upper Canada (now the province of Ontario), with a predominantly English-speaking, Protestant population, and Lower Canada (present-day Quebec), with a French, Roman Catholic population. By 1837 both of the provinces had become economically stagnant and rose in rebellion (see PAPINEAU'S REBELLION), with the result that the British Government decided to reunite them. This was achieved in 1841 with the creation of the new United Province of Canada, in which Quebec became known as Canada East, and Ontario as Canada West.

The separate provinces of Quebec and Ontario finally emerged in 1867, when the BRITISH NORTH AMERICA ACT created the Dominion of Canada. Since that time Quebec has become increasingly concerned with asserting and protecting its French character within the Canadian federation.

During the 1960s a number of separatist groups rose to prominence, among them the Front de Libération du Québec, which launched a bombing campaign and in 1970 kidnapped Pierre LaPorte, the provincial minister of labour, who was later found dead. In 1976 the separatist Parti Québécois, led by René Lévesque, won power in the province, and four years later it held a referendum to determine whether Quebec should secede from the rest of Canada. The party lost the referendum and in 1985 it lost the provincial elections too. After a separatist alliance won a majority of the province's seats in the 1994 federal elections, the Parti Québecois organised another referendum in October 1995, which it again lost, though by the narrowest of margins. Jacques Parizeau, leader of the Parti Québécois, subsequently announced his retirement from public life.

Queen's shilling Coin which, when accepted from a military officer, obliged the recipient to serve in the British army. Also called the King's shilling when appropriate, the coin was deemed to be the first instalment of army pay, and was used by recruiting officers in the 18th century to effect a binding agreement. The shilling became notorious through the actions of unscrupulous recruiting officers, who would ply likely young men with drink and then persuade them to accept a coin. As soon as they did so, they would be marched off to the nearest barracks.

Queensland Australia's second-largest state, after Western Australia, situated in the north-east of the country. The Queensland coast, much of which shelters behind the Great Barrier Reef, was first charted in 1770 by Captain James Cook. From 1824 a number of penal settlements were established in the region known at the time as Moreton Bay and administered as part of New South Wales. In

Early attacks on the Quakers included ridiculing meetings 'when wemen doe hold forth' and 'talke of light within'.

1859 Queensland was given its present name and declared a separate British colony with its own government. The discovery of gold in the 1860s and 1870s led to a rapid increase in the population of the colony, which in 1901 became a constituent state in the Commonwealth of Australia. In 1922 the upper house of the Queensland parliament voted itself out of existence, making this the only Australian state with a single-chamber legislature.

Quesnay, François (1694-1774) French economist who led a group of fellow thinkers called the Physiocrats in defining the first systematic theory of political economy. Quesnay originally trained as a doctor and served as physician to the French king, Louis XV. At the age of 62 Quesnay turned his attention to economics, publishing a number of influential articles in Denis Diderot's *Encyclopédie*, and a major study called *Tableau économique* (1758). Together with his Physiocrat colleagues, Quesnay argued that land was the only source of wealth, and agriculture the only productive sector in the economy. He opposed MERCANTILISM, which sought to maximise exports and minimise imports through the imposition of tariffs, arguing instead for LAISSEZ FAIRE, or free trade. Much of Quesnay's analysis anticipates the work of Adam SMITH and J.M. KEYNES.

Quetzalcóatl Ancient Central American deity, often represented as a feathered snake. Quetzalcóatl was the principal god of the TOLTECS, who inhabited Mexico from the 9th to the 12th century AD, and of the AZTECS who succeeded them. Two of the

---

It is unclear which Quetzalcóatl came first, the feathered god of wind, light and good, or the Toltec ruler who introduced the calendar.

most impressive temples dedicated to the god are those at Cholula and Teotihuacán. Among the MAYA, who preceded the Toltecs, Quetzalcóatl was known as Kukulkán. According to one myth, Quetzalcóatl was a priest-king who was driven out of Tula, the Toltec capital, and then sailed away, having promised to return. The arrival of the Spanish under the conquistador Hernán CORTÉS in 1519 corresponded with aspects of the myth, and led the Aztecs to believe at first that Quetzalcóatl's promise had been fulfilled. This proved to be their downfall.

Quezon, Manuel (1878-1944) Political leader who became first president of the Commonwealth of the PHILIPPINES – the political structure created by the USA as a forerunner to a fully independent republic. A champion of Filipino independence, Quezon fought against the USA in Emilio Aguinaldo's insurrection of 1899-1901. In 1907 he was elected to the Philippine Assembly, and from 1909 to 1916 he served as resident commissioner in Washington. Returning to the Philippines, Quezon became president of his country's Senate, and in 1935 he defeated Emilio Aguinaldo to become president of the newly constituted Philippine Commonwealth. Re-elected in 1941, Quezon led a government in exile in the USA after the Japanese invasion of the Philippines in 1942. He died before his country was liberated and granted independence in 1946.

Quiberon Bay, Battle of (1759) Naval battle fought between Britain and France at Quiberon Bay, on the north-west coast of France, during the SEVEN YEARS' WAR.

After a six-month British blockade of Brest harbour, a French fleet of 21 ships managed to slip away to embark troops for a planned invasion of Britain. They were pursued by the British fleet, under the command of Admiral Edward HAWKE, driven into Quiberon Bay and decisively defeated. The battle put paid to French ambitions to invade Britain at that time.

quilombo Fortified settlement of fugitive Brazilian slaves in the 17th and 18th centuries. For much of its colonial history Brazil depended heavily on imported African slaves, thousands of whom fled into the forests. There they set up their own communities, called *quilombos*, which were distinctly African in culture. In north-eastern Brazil the *quilombo* of Palmares declared itself an independent republic, and survived repeated Portuguese attacks for almost a hundred years. When it was finally conquered in 1694, Palmares had some 20 000 inhabitants.

Quisling, Vidkun (1887-1945) Norwegian fascist leader who in 1940 helped Nazi Germany to prepare for its invasion of Norway. As an army officer, Quisling served as Norwegian military attaché in Russia and Finland from 1918 to 1921. He returned to Russia as a diplomat in the 1920s before becoming minister of defence in 1931. Two years later Quisling resigned from the government to found the fascist Nasjonal Samling (National Unity) party, which never won a seat in the Norwegian parliament. In 1939 he met Adolf Hitler, and in the following months helped the Nazis to plan their conquest of Norway. After this took place in April 1940, Quisling served in the occupation government and was declared president by the Germans in 1942. Though fervently opposed by the great majority of Norwegians, Quisling remained in power until the liberation of Norway in 1945, when he was convicted of high treason and executed. 'Quisling' has became a synonym for 'traitor'.

Quito Capital city of the South American country of Ecuador, and once the most northerly city of the Inca empire. Situated beneath the volcano Pichincha, which last erupted in 1666, Quito was the ancient royal capital of the Quito kingdom, which flourished before the 11th century. In the late 15th century this kingdom was conquered by the Incas, who made Quito their northern provincial capital. Only a few decades later, in December 1534, the conquistador Sebastián de Belalcázar captured the city for Spain. The following year the Franciscans established the church and monastery of San Francisco – one of the finest examples of Spanish colonial architecture. Quito is now the oldest capital city in South America.

Qur'an see KORAN

Rabelais, François (c.1494-1553) French satirist and physician. His most popular books are *Pantagruel* (1532) and *Gargantua* (1534) in which he satirised medieval scholasticism and superstition. His work is noted for its wit and wisdom, containing much high-spirited vulgarity which belies the author's piety – Rabelais was first a Franciscan then a Benedictine monk. Having access to a large library in the monastery of Fontenay le Comte, he learned Greek, Hebrew and Arabic, and read extensively. He studied medicine in Montpellier, and practised it throughout his life. While accompanying Jean du Bellay, the bishop of Paris, on a visit to Rome, Rabelais, a keen plant collector, came across melons, artichokes and carnations, all of which he introduced to France.

Rabin, Yitzhak (1922-95) Israeli general and prime minister. As chief of staff of the armed forces between 1964 and 1968 he planned the Israeli victory in the SIX-DAY WAR (1967). Between 1968 and 1973 Rabin served as Israel's ambassador to Washington. Returning to Israel in 1973, Rabin entered politics and in June 1974 became Israel's first native-born premier. He secured a ceasefire with Syria in the Golan Heights and ordered the raid on Entebbe airport in July 1976 to rescue hostages seized by Palestinian terror-

> **66** There are enemies of the peace process, and they try to hurt us. But violence undermines democracy and must be denounced and isolated. **99**
>
> *Yitzhak Rabin, at the peace rally the night he was killed, November 4, 1995*

ists. Rabin resigned as prime minister in 1977 after falling foul of technical currency regulations, but regained prominence as defence minister from 1984 to 1990, directing Israel's tough response to the Palestinian uprising, the *intifada*, which began in December 1987. In 1992, Rabin recaptured the leadership of the Labour Party from his rival Shimon Peres, and succeeded Yitzhak Shamir as prime minister in June. He halted the building of Israeli settlements in the occupied territories. Secret talks on Palestinian self-rule led to the peace accord with the Palestine Liberation Organisation in September 1993, for which Rabin, foreign minister Shimon Peres and Yasser ARAFAT were jointly awarded the Nobel peace prize. Arab and Jewish ultra-nationalists remained opposed to the accord. After addressing a peace rally in Tel Aviv on

November 4, 1995, Rabin was assassinated by Yigal Amir, a Jewish extremist who considered he had a religious duty to act as he did.

Racine, Jean (1639-99) French dramatist and poet, most noted for his tragedies based on classical Roman and Greek themes, including *Andromaque* (1667), *Britannicus* (1669) and *Phèdre* (1677). Racine was born in northern France and received a strict Roman Catholic Jansenist upbringing. He soon discovered an aptitude for verse, writing an ode, *La Nymphe de la Seine* (1660), on the marriage of Louis XIV. He gradually gained recognition for his work, becoming friends with the poets Nicolas Boileau and Jean de la Fontaine and the playwright Molière, whose company performed Racine's first play in 1664. In the same year he received a gratuity from the king for a congratulatory ode, and during the next 13 years he produced his most acclaimed work.

racism Belief that human abilities are determined by race or ethnic group, often expressed in the form of the assertion of superiority by one race or group over another. It can appear as discrimination, violence and verbal abuse. Racism has often been a factor in wars. The NAZIS expressed extreme racism in their conviction that fair-haired Germanic 'ARYAN' peoples were superior to others. Nazism led to the genocide of millions of Jews, Slavs and gypsies in Europe between 1933 and 1945. Racism was also the basis of South Africa's APARTHEID system, which forcibly separated the country's different races.

radar Method of locating objects or determining one's own position by transmitting and measuring the reflections of high frequency radio waves. The radio waves travel at the speed of light, and distance can be calculated by timing their progress to

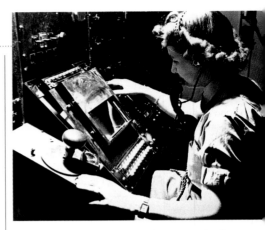

The first British radar system began service in September 1938 and operated round the clock until 1945. Believing the war was nearly over, the Germans stopped radar research in 1940.

and from the object concerned. Radar (Radio Detection And Ranging) is a valuable aid in navigation, particularly for ships and aeroplanes and especially in darkness or bad weather. It is used in warfare to detect enemy aircraft, vessels or missiles.

During the Battle of Britain in 1940 radar played an important role in helping to prevent a German invasion. Radar stations positioned along the English south coast determined the number and position of attacking aircraft, allowing the Royal Air Force to plan its response. Radar is also used in meteorology, in underground surveys of pipe-work or archaeological remains, and by the police in speed traps for motorists.

Radek, Karl (1885-c.1939) International communist leader and writer born in Galicia, Austria-Hungary. He joined the Polish Social Democratic Party, and became involved in the Russian Revolution of 1905, for which he was imprisoned. On his release he wrote for Polish and German newspapers, gaining a reputation as a witty political commentator. In 1917 Radek accompanied Vladimir Ilich Lenin on his return to Russia after the outbreak of the revolution. He remained to become a leading member of COMINTERN, the international organisation of communist parties, and one of the editors of *Izvestia*, the Russian state newspaper. In 1927 he was expelled from the party for allegedly supporting Joseph Stalin's opponent, Leon Trotsky. Radek was re-admitted after recanting, and helped to draft Stalin's constitution in 1936, but was accused of treason in the same year. In 1937 he was sentenced to imprisonment, during which he is believed to have died in a Siberian labour camp.

Radetzky, Josef, Count of Radetz (1766-1858) Austrian field-marshal and hero. Radetzky fought in the Revolutionary Wars against France between 1792 and 1802. After Austria's defeat by French imperial and Italian forces at Wagram, near Vienna (1809), he was

Rabin's handshake at the White House in 1993 led eventually to the shot that killed him as he left a peace rally in 1995.

appointed to assist Field Marshal Prince Johann of Liechtenstein with the reorganisation of the army. In 1813 his strategy at the Battle of Leipzig proved decisive in Austria's defeat of Napoleon. Radetzky was placed in command of the Austrian forces in Lombardy between 1831 and 1857 to protect Habsburg interests during the Risorgimento, Italy's campaign for national unity and independence. He won a number of victories over the Italians and French, and held the Lombardo-Venetian territories for the Austrians, a region which he continued to rule until the age of 91.

Radhakrishnan, Sir Sarvepalli (1888-1975) President of India from 1962 to 1967. A professor of philosophy at the universities of Mysore and Calcutta, and professor of Eastern religions and ethics at Oxford University, Radhakrishnan wrote widely on Hinduism and philosophy. Committed to establishing a classless and casteless society, he became a member of the Indian Assembly in 1947, chairman of UNESCO in 1949, and served as the first Indian ambassador to the Soviet Union from 1949 to 1952. In 1952 Radhakrishnan was appointed vice-president of India, becoming president ten years later. Radhakrishnan was knighted in 1931.

Raeder, Erich (1876-1960) German naval commander who was convicted as a war criminal for his activities in the Second World War. He was Admiral von Hipper's chief of staff in the First World War, and in 1928 became commander in chief of the German navy, secretly rebuilding it in violation of the Versailles Peace Settlement and developing the submarine (U-boat) fleet. The German leader Adolf Hitler promoted him to grand admiral. In 1943 he resigned after Hitler became outraged by the apparently poor performance of the surface fleet against Allied convoys. Raeder was tried before the International Military Tribunal at Nuremberg for contributing to a war of aggression, and sentenced to life imprisonment.

Raffles, Sir Thomas Stamford (1781-1826) British colonial administrator, founder of SINGAPORE, and also a founder of London Zoo. Raffles was born in Jamaica, the son of a merchant seaman. He joined the British East India Company in 1795, and in 1805 was appointed to Penang. After participating in the capture of Java in 1811 he served as its lieutenant-governor (1811-16), instituting costly administrative and social reforms which led to his recall to London. At his next posting, to the lesser position of lieutenant-governor of the Sumatran port of Bengkulu

(1818-24), Raffles recognised the commercial potential of Singapore at the tip of the Malay Peninsula and acquired it from the Sultan of Johore for the East India Company in 1819. Ill-health forced him to return to Britain in 1824, but Singapore rapidly developed into an important trading port. Public interest in his Malayan natural history collections led to him helping to found the Zoological Society of London. He was knighted in 1817.

Raglan, FitzRoy Somerset, 1st Baron (1788-1855) British general who gave the ambiguous order at the Battle of BALAKLAVA, during the Crimean War, which led to the disastrous charge of the Light Brigade. After joining the army in 1804, Raglan (at the time known as Somerset) served as aide-de-camp to Sir Arthur Wellesley (later the Duke of Wellington) during the PENINSULAR WAR in Spain and Portugal (1808-14), and was seriously wounded during the Battle of Waterloo in 1815.

Raglan served as secretary to the Horse Guards from 1827 to 1852 – the year in which he was made a peer. After Britain declared war on Russia in 1854, Raglan was appointed commander of British forces in the Crimea. He won victories at Inkerman and Alma, but was criticised in England for his conduct of the campaign. In fact much of the hardship endured by his troops was the fault of the Treasury, which at the time was responsible for supplies and transport. Raglan died while on campaign in the Crimea.

> **DID YOU KNOW?**
>
> Raglan's right arm was amputated at the Battle of Waterloo. He bore the operation without a word. Then, as an orderly carried off the arm, he called for a ring that his wife had given him to be returned.

Rahman, Tungku (Prince) Abdul (1903-73) First prime minister of Malaya from 1957 to 1963 and of Malaysia from 1963 to 1970. Rahman studied law in Britain. He entered the civil service in his home state, and in 1952 founded the Alliance Party, which brought together the factional Malay, Indian and Chinese populations. He became leader of the United Malay National Organisation, and played a central role in organising its alliance with the Malayan Chinese Association, which provided the political base for gaining independence from Britain. Rahman was elected prime minister after Malaya became independent in 1957, and in 1961 he proposed the formation of the Federation of Malaysia, which came into existence in 1963. Political unrest and riots between Malays and Chinese forced him to stand down in 1970.

Raikes, Robert (1735-1811) British printer, newspaper proprietor and philanthropist, who in 1780 opened the first Sunday school in Gloucester. Raikes's school taught reading and the catechism, primarily to poor children who worked in factories during the week, so

that they could read the Bible. This led to a national Sunday school movement, founded in 1785. By 1831 more than 1.25 million children were attending SUNDAY SCHOOLS.

Railways see feature, page 532

Rajagopalachari, Chakravarti (1879-1972) Indian politician and the only governor-general of independent India. He was a prominent member of the National Congress and a close friend of Mohandas GANDHI. While Gandhi was in prison in the 1920s, Rajagopalachari edited the newspaper *Young India* in his place. He became chief minister of his home state Madras (now Tamil Nadu) from 1937 to 1939. He served as governor-general of India from 1948 to 1950 during the country's transition to independence from Britain, and again as chief minister of the Madras government from 1952 to 1954. His opposition to the socialist policies adopted by Congress led him to found the Swatantra (Independent) Party in 1959 to act as a non-communist alternative to Congress. After its heyday in the 1960s, the party merged with the right-wing Janata Party.

Rajput Hindu warrior caste, descended from central Asian warlike tribes of Scythians and Huns, who established territories across northern India from the 4th to the 7th centuries. From the 8th century the Rajputs lived in kingdoms throughout Rajputana, the 'country of the kings' (today's Rajasthan). The Rajputs – their name comes from the Sanskrit for 'sons of kings' – held out against Muslim invaders for nearly a thousand years until they finally submitted to MUGHAL control in the 16th century. Rajput princes continued to rule their conquered territories until the collapse of the Mughal empire in the 18th century. The area fell to Hindu MARATHAS from western India and, in the early 19th century, to the British. Under British rule, the largest princely states of JODHPUR, JAIPUR and Udaipur were allowed considerable autonomy. When India gained independence in 1947, the territories were merged to form a single state of Rajasthan, and were deprived of power. Some Rajput titles still survive.

Rákosi, Mátyás (1892-1971) Hungarian ruler who played a key role shaping Hungary as a communist state after the Second World War. As first secretary of the Hungarian Communist Party, Rákosi imposed a ruthless Stalinist regime from 1949 to 1953, while his secret police instituted a reign of terror. On Joseph Stalin's death he was replaced by the reforming Imre NAGY. Rákosi returned to power in 1955 only to face opposition culminating in the HUNGARIAN UPRISING of 1956. The Russians removed him from power and he died in exile in the Soviet Union.

The train arrives

No one invented the railway. Track, signals and locomotives were devised over three centuries for different purposes. But when they were put together in the 19th century, they opened up the world.

The first transport on railed tracks was horse-drawn. In 18th-century Britain, mine owners used horses to pull coal trucks along wooden, and later iron, rails from the pithead to barges or ships. It was in 1804, on just such a line linking the Merthyr Tydfil ironworks with the Glamorgan Canal, that a tiny steam locomotive built by the Cornish engineer Richard Trevithick first hauled a train of wagons. The age of the steam railway had begun.

The many technical problems still to be overcome were worked out on the lines serving the collieries of north-east England. This first stage of development ended with the opening of the Stockton and Darlington Railway in 1825. Now passengers, too, were invited to use the railway, in what was still, in effect, a

When the Liverpool and Manchester Railway was opened in 1831, public interest was so great that sets of fine prints were issued illustrating the different types of train using the line.

stagecoach pulled by a horse. The difference was that this one had flanged wheels running on iron rails instead of flat-rimmed wheels rolling along the open road. But the main objective of the system remained clear: to carry goods, not people.

The next advance came with the construction of the Liverpool and Manchester Railway under the direction of the engineer George Stephenson. Yet many still doubted whether steam locomotives would ever be strong or fast enough to work a line on their own. Doubts were dispelled in 1829 when Stephenson's son Robert introduced his *Rocket*, a locomotive which could haul heavy loads and dash along at an undreamt-of 30 mph (50 km/h).

Passenger trains were soon to become the wonders of the age. But it was the plodding freight train, linking the port of Liverpool with the textile heartland of Lancashire, that kept the profits rolling in. Coal for the steam engines of the factories, and raw materials such as iron and cotton – these were the goods that helped the railway network to spread. By the mid 19th century, Britain had become the greatest industrial nation on Earth, with an appetite for materials that only the railways could feed.

RAILWAYS UNITE THE WORLD

The rest of the world began to demand railways of their own, and turned to British engineers for their expertise. The Liverpool and Manchester Railway had been built to carry cotton to the mills, and part of the cotton came from the fields of India. But most transport in India consisted of heavy bullock carts. A railway was the answer, but between the port of Bombay and the plantations there lay the cliffs of the Western Ghats. The engineers conquered them by building a line that zigzagged up the hills.

As the engineers moved round the world, they left behind more than railways. In Kenya, what began as a camp for the Uganda Railway developed into the city of Nairobi. Wherever rail networks were built, change followed. Land was developed, towns grew, once isolated areas could look to a wider world in which to sell their goods. Railways were no longer serving purely local interests: they were uniting global markets and industries.

But the greatest impact was less tangible: people who had never even considered travelling more than a few miles from home could now cheerfully contemplate crossing whole continents.

The paymaster's train brings the wages during the building of the Union Pacific Railroad across the USA. 'Puffing Billy' (right), built in 1813, is the oldest locomotive in existence.

The expedition Sir Walter Raleigh sent to the New World in 1584 made landfall on Roanoake island and returned with enthusiastic reports.

Raleigh, Sir Walter (c.1552-1618) English explorer, courtier and poet, and a favourite of ELIZABETH I. Born in Devon, Raleigh joined a privateering expedition against the Spanish in the West Indies in 1578. Two years later he was sent to suppress a rebellion in Ireland, which he did successfully. On his return to England in 1581 he became a favourite of Elizabeth, who indulged him with honours and large estates in Ireland, where he is reputed to have introduced the potato crop.

From 1585 to 1589 Raleigh successfully organised several colonising expeditions to VIRGINIA, all of which ended in failure.

His position as the queen's royal favourite was taken by the Earl of Essex in 1587, and when in 1592 Raleigh's secret affair with Elizabeth Throckmorton, one of the queen's maids of honour, was discovered, the couple were imprisoned in the Tower of London. Raleigh bought their release, but was exiled from court; he later married Throckmorton.

In 1595 he sailed for the Orinoco River in Guiana, South America, where the gold mines of EL DORADO were thought to lie. His account of the voyage, *The Discoverie of Guiana*, is one of the finest narratives of Elizabethan adventure.

James I, on his accession, saw Raleigh as an enemy, and the explorer was convicted of treason and sentenced to death. Winning a reprieve, he was again incarcerated in the Tower, where between 1603 and 1616 he wrote poetry, and embarked on his unfinished *History of the World*.

In 1616, in return for his freedom, he promised to discover gold for the king in Guiana. The expedition failed, and Raleigh was executed on his return.

Ramayana One of two epic Sanskrit poems of ancient India, written in about 500 BC; the other is the *Mahabharata*. The *Ramayana* is reputed to have been written by the poet Valmiki, and recounts the legendary adventures of Rama, an incarnation of the god Vishnu, and his attempts to recover his wife, Sita, from the hands of her abductor, Ravana, king of Lanka. The stories from both poems, representing family life and intrigue, have inspired dance, drama and painting over the centuries. Numerous translations have been made. Even today the events of the *Ramayana* are enacted in an annual pageant in northern India, and signs of their influence can be seen in present-day Indian comics and films, as well as statues and temples throughout South-east Asia.

Rambouillet, Marquise de (1588-1665) French aristocrat who presided over the first of the salons which dominated the intellectual life of 17th-century Paris. Born Catherine de Vivonne in Rome, she was married at the age of 12 to the son of the Marquis de Rambouillet. She had a low opinion of the manners and morals of the French court, and at her home, the Hôtel de Rambouillet, she gathered together leading nobles and writers. Emphasis was placed on refinement and good taste as expressed by the term *précieuse*, which was later mocked by Jean-Baptiste Molière in his comedy *Les Précieuses Ridicules*. Among the visitors were the dramatist Pierre Corneille, the letter-writer Madame de Sévigné and the orator and writer Jacques Bossuet. The French word *salon* (drawing room) was used thereafter to describe a literary circle of this type.

Rameses II, shown as a child in this carving found in the Valley of the Kings. At ten, he held the honorary rank of an army captain.

Rameses II 'the Great' Pharaoh of Egypt between about 1279 and 1213 BC, regarded by his subjects and posterity as the most successful of all rulers of Egypt. After years of skirmishes with the HITTITES, he concluded a peace treaty with them around 1258 BC and strengthened ties by marrying the daughter of the Hittite king in 1245. His reign brought prosperity to Egypt, allowing him to embark on an ambitious building programme which included the temple to his father Seti I at Luxor, the colonnaded hall at KARNAK, the two temples carved out of rock at Abu Simbel and the temple at Abydos.

Rameses III (d.1166 BC) Pharaoh of Egypt from about 1198 BC. Rameses successfully repelled three major invasions, two by the Libyans and one by the SEA PEOPLES. He won a victory over the PHILISTINES at a time when Egypt held much territory in Palestine.

Ramillies, Battle of (May 23, 1706) Victory by British, Dutch and Danish forces under the Duke of MARLBOROUGH, over the French during the War of the SPANISH SUCCESSION. The battle took place north of Namur, at the village of Ramillies, in Belgium. Marlborough duped the French commander, the Duc de Villeroi, into believing his main attack was coming from the right, and broke through the French line from the left. French losses were 8000 dead and wounded; the allies lost 1066 men, with 3633 wounded. Marlborough went on to overrun much of Flanders and Brabant.

Ranjit Singh (1780-1839) Ruler from 1799 of the Sikh kingdom of the Punjab in India. At the age of 12 Ranjit Singh succeeded his father to become leader of a minor Sikh group, inheriting a town and surrounding villages. He developed a powerful army trained by European officers, and worked to establish a kingdom to unite the Sikh provinces.

In 1799 he captured Lahore, taking the title 'Maharajah of the Punjab' in 1801. In 1802 he extended his rule over the Sikh holy city of Amritsar. Expanding farther afield, Ranjit Singh took control of Kashmir and Peshawar to become the most powerful ruler in India, earning the nickname 'Lion of the Punjab'.

He became a strong ally of the British, with whom he reached an agreement over his borders. By the end of the SIKH WARS, ten years after Ranjit Singh's death, most of his territory had been taken by Britain.

ransom The demanding and payment of money for the release of a prisoner or for the return of property formed an accepted part of medieval warfare and diplomacy. Knights who were vassals of a lord, as well as his family

and friends, felt obliged to help to pay for his release if he was captured in war. In 1193 RICHARD I of England was recognised while trying to cross Austria in secret and was handed over to the emperor, Henry VI. Henry demanded 150 000 marks in ransom, most of which was paid.

Rapallo, Treaties of Two international treaties named after the north Italian port in which they were signed. In the first treaty (1920) frontiers were settled between Italy and Yugoslavia. Italy obtained the Istrian peninsula; Dalmatia went to Yugoslavia; and Fiume (Rijeka) became a free city.

In the second treaty (1922) Germany and the Soviet Union agreed to abandon any financial claims which each might bring against the other following the First World War, and resumed diplomatic relations.

Raphael (Raffaello Sanzio) (1483-1520) Italian painter, one of the leading figures of the High RENAISSANCE. Raphael was born in Urbino, the son of Giovanni Santi, a court painter. In Perugia he studied under the artist known as Perugino and in 1500 received his first recorded commission. His early work, which included the *Marriage of the Virgin* (1504), reflected his mentor's style. In 1504

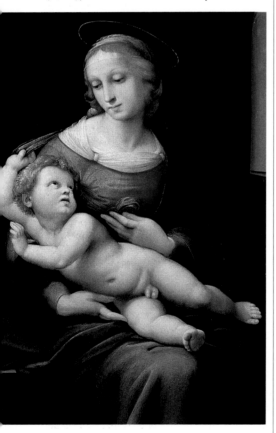

Raphael painted this Madonna shortly after he arrived in Rome in 1508. There his abilities and charm won him fame as 'the Prince of Painters'.

Raphael moved to Florence where he learned from LEONARDO DA VINCI, MICHELANGELO and Fra Bartolomeo. His *Ansidei Madonna*, among other work from this period, shows the influence of Leonardo. In 1508 Pope Julius II gave Raphael his first major commission: to decorate a new papal apartment in the Vatican in Rome. The resulting masterpiece, which includes the frescoes *School of Athens* and *Disputà*, established Raphael's reputation as one of the greatest artists of his time.

He was appointed architect of St Peter's, working alongside Donato Bramante on the building of the Basilica, and took over the direction of the work after Bramante's death.

Rashid Ali al-Ghailani (1892-1965) Iraqi prime minister between 1940 and 1941. Rashid Ali was hostile to the British presence in Iraq. He believed that an alliance with Germany during the Second World War would force the British to leave Iraq. Rashid Ali was overthrown in January 1941, but three months later he seized power in a military coup which also deposed Abdul Illah, the pro-British regent for the child-king Faisal II. Britain sent forces to support those already present, and at the end of a 30-day war, in May 1941, Iraqi forces surrendered. The Germans had failed to come to Rashid Ali's aid as promised, and he and his supporters fled to Iran. A pro-British government was installed.

Rasputin (c.1865-1916) Russian faith healer and wandering 'holy man'. Rasputin won the devotion of Tsarina Alexandra by his treatment of the haemophiliac crown prince, Alexis, and soon became an influential member of the Imperial court. Born Grigori Efimovich Novykh, he was a Siberian peasant who arrived in St Petersburg in 1903 at a time when royal circles were interested in mysticism and the occult. He came to the attention of the royal family, and in 1908 first attended Alexis. Tsar NICHOLAS II and his wife were quickly taken in by Rasputin's striking appearance and magnetic personality, by his apparent loyalty, and by his ability to ease their child's suffering. Yet outside court he was notorious for his immoral behaviour; his nickname, Rasputin, meant 'debauched one'.

When Tsar Nicholas left the court to command his army during the First World War, Alexandra took over the country's internal affairs. Influenced by Rasputin, she replaced reputable ministers with incompetent politicians favoured by Rasputin, causing discontent and discrediting the monarchy. Nicholas ignored the protestations of his advisers.

A number of unsuccessful attempts were made to assassinate Rasputin before a group of nobles, led by Prince Yusupov, first poisoned him and then, when this had no effect, shot him five times. They finally threw him into the ice-cold River Neva.

Ratana, Tuhupotiki Wiremu (1870-1939) Maori religious and political leader in New Zealand. 'Bill' Ratana, a farmer and faith healer, gave the Maori people a strong identity both spiritually, through the founding of the Ratana Church, and politically, through a Ratana-Labour Party alliance which emphasised Maori land rights. Ratana began having visions in 1919 and after some success as a healer, became the centre of a new religion based on Christianity but with its own rituals and character. People flocked to hear him, calling him *Te Mangai* (God's mouthpiece) and by 1936 almost one in five Maoris was an adherent. Both the religious and political aspects of this movement survived his death. Ratana candidates held all four Maori seats in parliament between 1943 and 1963 and the Church gained many non-Maori members.

Rathenau, Walther (1867-1922) German industrialist and politician. Rathenau, who was born in Berlin of Jewish parents, was responsible for directing the economy of Germany during the First World War. In 1921 he became minister of reconstruction, with responsibility for reparations, and he was foreign minister a year later. Convinced of Germany's ability to gain ascendancy in Europe he negotiated the Treaty of RAPALLO with the Soviet Union in 1922. The treaty, which normalised relations between the two countries after the First World War, was a diplomatic success and a demonstration of German independence which affronted the Western allies. Rathenau was assassinated by anti-Semitic nationalists in 1922.

Reagan, Ronald (1911-) Fortieth president of the USA, from 1981 to 1989. A former film star, Reagan won a landslide victory in the 1980 presidential election on a programme of reduced taxation and increased defence expenditure to combat world communism. He was a popular Republican president and an effective communicator.

Reagan was born in Tampico, Illinois, the great-grandson of an Irish immigrant. In 1937 he joined the film company Warner Brothers and appeared in 50 films, mainly B productions, in which he played romantic leading roles. In 1952 he married the actress Nancy Davis, his second wife.

His political interests lay initially with the Democrats, but as president of the Screen Actors' Guild (1947-52) his views grew steadily more conservative. He campaigned for the Republican Dwight D. EISENHOWER in 1952 and 1956, and joined the Republican Party in 1962. Encouraged by colleagues in business, he was elected governor of California in 1966 and remained in office for eight years. He stood unsuccessfully for the Republican presidential nomination in 1968 and 1976, losing to Richard Nixon and Gerald Ford respectively, but won on his third attempt in 1980 and defeated President Jimmy Carter. Shortly after taking office in 1981, Reagan survived an assassination attempt.

As president, Reagan cut federal social and welfare programmes, reduced income taxes by 25 per cent, and presided over America's largest increase in peacetime defence spending. He adopted a hard-line policy against communism and the Soviet Union, and campaigned against alleged Soviet involvement in Latin America, especially Nicaragua. In 1983 he proposed the controversial Strategic Defense Initiative ('Star Wars') to protect the USA against nuclear missile attack, and committed large sums to research. In the same year he sent a battalion of marines to support a cease-fire in the Lebanon, but a terrorist bomb killed 260 marines, resulting in a US withdrawal. His successful invasion of the island of Grenada, following a left-wing military coup, was condemned abroad but helped to revive American self-confidence.

Economic recovery and the promise of further tax cuts helped Reagan to win re-election in 1984. Talks on ARMS CONTROL were a prominent feature of this period. Responding to the new era of openness in Soviet foreign relations, Reagan met the Russian leader Mikhail GORBACHEV four times. Their meetings, held between 1985 and 1988, culminated in the Intermediate Nuclear Forces Treaty with the Soviet Union (1988), which eliminated intermediate-range nuclear missiles.

President Reagan's position came under threat at the end of 1986 with the 'Irangate' scandal.

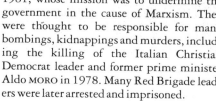

Reagan's best film performance was in *King's Row*, in which the future US president starred with Ann Sheridan.

This revealed that the administration had begun illegal negotiations for arms sales to Iran in return for American hostages being held by Islamic groups in the Middle East, with profits being channelled to anti-Marxist Contra forces in Nicaragua. Members of Reagan's staff were forced to resign; the president emerged weakened but still in office. Though Reagan had solved the short-term problems of inflation, he did so on borrowed money, and he passed on record budget and trade deficits to his successor, George BUSH.

Rebecca riots (1839, 1842-4) Protests by tenant farmers in south-west Wales, named after the Old Testament figure of Rebecca, who was told: 'Let thy seed possess the gate of those which hate them'. Each band of men was led by a 'Rebecca', often a man dressed as a woman. They resented the tollgates set up by the turnpike trusts (licensed roadbuilders), and objected to their low wages, high rents and unfair landholding system. Troops were called in to restore order and a commission took evidence and investigated their grievances. In 1844 the turnpike laws were amended and the causes of the riots were removed.

recusant Roman Catholic who refused to attend Church of England (ANGLICAN) services between the 16th and 18th centuries. Fines were imposed on recusants by Acts of Uniformity (1552, 1559) at the rate of one shilling a Sunday, which increased to £20 a month in 1581. The term was an abbreviation of 'Catholic Recusants', distinguishing them from 'Church Papists', who were Catholics who attended Anglican services rather than pay the fines. Nonconformists could also be penalised for recusancy. The laws against Catholics were repealed in the late 18th and early 19th centuries (CATHOLIC EMANCIPATION).

Red Army Army raised in Russia by Leon TROTSKY as commissar for war in the aftermath of the Russian Revolution (1917). The

Watched by a number of compatriots, a soldier of the Red Army fixes the Soviet flag to the top of the German Reichstag in 1945.

Workers' and Peasants' Red Army was composed mainly of recruits and former officers of the Imperial Army. This army of the communist Bolshevik Party fought and overcame counterrevolutionary forces ('Whites') in the bitter RUSSIAN CIVIL WAR between 1918 and 1920. Trotsky maintained conformity by appointing political commissars to every unit to disseminate propaganda and report on malcontents. After Trotsky's downfall, Joseph Stalin conducted a purge of army officers in 1937 to remove possible opposition. More than 40 000 officers were arrested, including senior generals, and most of them were killed. Consequently the efficiency of the army was greatly reduced during the early months of the German invasion in 1941, but younger officers emerged to lead their country to victory. By 1945 the Red Army had become the largest in the world, numbering 11 million. It was renamed the Soviet Army in 1946. Since the break-up of the Soviet Union in 1991, each republic has had its own army.

Red Brigades Extreme left-wing terrorist groups, active in Italy between 1977 and 1981, whose mission was to undermine the government in the cause of Marxism. They were thought to be responsible for many bombings, kidnappings and murders, including the killing of the Italian Christian Democrat leader and former prime minister Aldo MORO in 1978. Many Red Brigade leaders were later arrested and imprisoned.

Red Cross International agency concerned with the alleviation of human suffering. Its founder, the Swiss philanthropist Jean-Henri Dunant (1828-1910), was horrified by the plight of the wounded at the Battle of SOLFERINO between France and Austria in 1859. He proposed the formation of voluntary aid societies for the relief of war victims. The Red Cross was established at his instigation under the first GENEVA CONVENTION in 1864. This drew up terms for the care of soldiers and was extended to include victims of naval warfare (1906), prisoners of war (1929) and, 20 years later, civilians. The Red Cross also helps refugees and victims of natural disasters. Its conventions have been ratified by almost 150 nations.

The agency's flag in Christian countries is a red cross on a white background; the symbol used in Muslim countries gives the agency its alternative name of Red Crescent.

Red Guards Militant young supporters, mainly students, of MAO ZE-DONG in China during the CULTURAL REVOLUTION (1966-9). Taking their name from the army units organised by Mao in 1927, the Red Guards, who numbered several million and wore red armbands, provided the paramilitary vanguard of the revolution. They attacked reactionaries, the Communist Party establishment, China's cultural heritage and all vestiges of Western

A Red Cross worker gives rice to a refugee in Zaire, one of half a million people who fled Rwanda on July 15, 1994. The Red Cross was already caring for 600 000 refugees in two makeshift camps.

influence, maintaining the momentum of the movement through mass demonstrations, a poster war, and attacks on people and property leading to thousands of deaths. Mao brought the Cultural Revolution to an end in 1969, and many Red Guards were sent to the country for enforced 're-education'.

Redl, Alfred (1864-1913) Austrian-born spy. A colonel from a modest background in the Austro-Hungarian army, Redl employed modern criminological methods in the gathering of intelligence, and became chief of espionage and counter-espionage in the Vienna Secret Service from 1907 to 1912. At the same time he earned ten times his officer's salary acting as chief spy for Russia in Austria. Redl would pass Austrian strategic plans to Russia, and in turn withhold information about Russia from Austria. When detected in 1913, he confessed, asked to be left alone with a revolver, and shot himself. His treason contributed to the Austrian defeats in Serbia in 1914.

Redmond, John (1856-1918) Irish politician and leader of Ireland's Nationalist Party. Like his predecessor Charles PARNELL, Redmond

Red Guards brandish copies of Chairman Mao's 'Little Red Book'. In 1971 they spearheaded what has been called 'the most ruthless cretinisation of the most sophisticated nation on earth'.

sought the repeal of the Act of Union (1801) that joined Ireland to Britain, and the establishment of an Irish parliament. After the 1910 elections to the British House of Commons, Redmond's party held the balance of power. In return for his support the Liberal prime minister, Herbert ASQUITH, introduced the third Home Rule Bill in 1912. It was passed, but its enactment was postponed until after the First World War, by which time Redmond had died.

His hopes for a peaceful transition to Home Rule in Ireland were dashed by the EASTER RISING in Dublin in 1916, and the rise of the nationalist party, SINN FEIN.

reeve Local official in Anglo-Saxon and medieval England. The most important category of reeve was the shire reeve (later known as sheriff), who was appointed by the king to administer justice and collect royal revenues. Manorial reeves were appointed as general overseers to organise the peasant labour force on estates, and in return received a wage, grazing land and remission of rent. Even if he were of VILLEIN status, a reeve was an important figure in village society The poet Geoffrey Chaucer (1340-1400) first characterised such an official in 'The Reeve's Tale'.

Reform Acts (1832, 1867, 1884) Series of laws which extended the right to vote for males in 19th-century Britain, and prepared the way for universal suffrage in the 20th century. The first Reform Act of 1832, under Prime Minister Charles GREY, eliminated ROTTEN BOROUGHS – largely uninhabited rural constituencies controlled by the nobility and gentry – created new boroughs and redistributed seats. It enfranchised inhabitants of the new and rapidly expanding industrial towns – hitherto unrepresented – but still left effective power in the hands of the landed aristocracy. The second Reform Act of 1867, largely the work of Benjamin DISRAELI, doubled the size of the electorate by giving many urban working-class men the vote. The third Reform Act of 1884 extended the vote to male agricultural and domestic workers.

The right to vote for all men over the age of 21 was achieved in 1918, and for women in 1928 (peers, criminals and the insane were excluded). In 1969, the minimum voting age was reduced to 18.

Reformation see feature, page 538

refrigeration Techniques for preserving food by chilling it existed as much as 4000 years ago. The ancient Greeks and Romans took ice from the mountains and buried it in 'snow cellars' to use later to store food. Even in tropical countries ice was collected by placing water in trays on cool nights. Its rapid evaporation would cause ice to form, even though the air temperature remained above freezing.

In 1806 a young American, Henry Tudor, shipped ice from Boston, Massachusetts, to Martinique in the West Indies and so began the business of transporting ice around the world. It was used to reduce fevers and cool drinks, in addition to chilling food. In Britain in the 1830s ice was collected in rural areas in winter and taken by carts to London, where it was stored in underground icehouses and used to keep fish fresh on city stalls in summer.

In America and Australia ways were sought to ensure that meat and dairy exports arrived fresh and edible at their destination several weeks later. In 1857 James Harrison patented a process which produced the first synthetic ice in Australia. He then developed a refrigeration chamber that would keep meat cool on board ship for the long voyage to Britain. After several failures, the first cargo of frozen meat and butter from Australia reached London in 1880. By this time, Louis Pasteur had established scientifically the role played by bacteria in food decay, and how chilling inhibits this and freezing stops it.

These advances opened up world markets, especially to the food producers of the USA, Australia and New Zealand. Refrigerated railway wagons and trucks were introduced, families began to buy iceboxes for their homes. The development of refrigerated cabinets and deep freezers cooled by chemical refrigerants has continued during the 20th century. In the 1920s Clarence Birdseye worked out how to fast-freeze food so that it retained its original condition on thawing, and he distributed the first packages of frozen food. Refrigeration has helped to increase living standards worldwide and brought prosperity to producers in many countries.

refugee Individuals and sometimes whole populations who have been forced to leave their homelands for as long as war has existed. The word refugee was first applied to the HUGUENOTS who fled from France after religious persecution in the 17th century. The largest movements of refugees in Europe in the 20th century included Jews fleeing from the POGROMS in Russia at the turn of the century and from Germany in the 1930s and 1940s; White Russians fleeing from the Soviet Union after the RUSSIAN REVOLUTION in 1917; Spanish Loyalists escaping from the regime of General FRANCO in 1939; and those who were displaced in the Second World War. In the early 1990s some 3 million people were displaced during the conflict between the republics of the former Yugoslavia. Troubles in Afghanistan, Rwanda, Liberia and Bosnia generated more than 5.3 million refugees, and in 1995, $225 million was used to fund aid for the 1.6 million people taking refuge in Zaire.

> ### DID YOU KNOW?
> One person in every 115 has been forced to flee. In 1995, there were nearly 50 million refugees around the world, including displaced persons still living in their own countries.

The Office of the UNITED NATIONS High Commission for Refugees (UNHCR) was established in 1951 to extend international protection to refugees. Under the terms of the 1951 UN convention relating to the status of refugees, its aims include ensuring that refugees are given political asylum and are not forcibly returned to a territory where they fear persecution; providing emergency relief such as food, shelter and medical assistance; and, in the long term, assisting in their voluntary repatriation, or resettlement and integration into a new community. Despite UNHCR efforts, governments have been known to close their borders to refugees, or treat them as illegal immigrants and harass or imprison them. Many refugees find themselves trapped in ill-equipped long-term refugee camps.

Since the fall of the Berlin Wall in 1989, the increasing number of refugees in Europe has forced traditionally hospitable countries such as Germany and Britain to tighten the criteria used for admitting asylum seekers.

Regency Period in Britain from 1811 to 1820 when the Prince of Wales, who later reigned as GEORGE IV, acted as regent for his father, GEORGE III, during the king's periods of insanity. The Prince Regent reacted against his strict upbringing, leading a flamboyant and extravagant lifestyle with his high-living friends, who included 'Beau' Brummel, the arbiter of fashion. During the period, fashions, architecture and domestic furniture combined classical elegance with exotic detail and exuberant ornamentation.

The Prince Regent was an enthusiastic patron of the arts and recognised the talents of the architect John Nash, who designed many of the magnificent buildings in the area of London between Pall Mall and Regent's Park. He also redesigned the Royal Pavilion at Brighton, adding domes, minarets and pierced stonework, to create an architectural icon.

Regulus, Marcus Atilius (died c.251 BC) Roman consul and statesman and a hero of his time. Regulus defeated the Carthaginian fleet in 256 BC and invaded Africa during the First PUNIC WAR. He took Tunis but was defeated and captured by the Carthaginians. Five years later his captors sent him on parole to Rome to negotiate peace terms involving the exchange of prisoners. He advised the Senate to refuse the terms and then returned to captivity in Carthage, where he was tortured and executed.

Rehoboam (10th century BC) King of Judah from around 932-915 BC. He succeeded his father, SOLOMON, as King of ISRAEL, but the northern tribes, restive from the constraints of Solomon's rule, broke away and set up a new kingdom under JEROBOAM. Rehoboam continued as the first ruler of the southern kingdom of JUDAH. His military efforts to regain control of the north failed.

This mahogany sideboard displays the quintessential characteristics of the Regency style: slim, elegant lines, enriched with finely carved detail and brass inlays and handles.

'Faith alone' challenges authority for the soul of the Church

Europe was torn asunder in the 16th century by the ideas of a German friar who sought a more direct relationship with God. The political and religious conflicts that ensued shattered the certainties of the medieval world.

At the start of the 16th century, all European Christians were Roman Catholics and accepted the spiritual rule of the pope. Within 50 years, the continent was bitterly divided between Catholics and those who protested against the authority of Rome, or Protestants. Historians use the term Reformation to describe this split and the religious and civil conflicts it provoked.

At its heart, the Reformation was an ecclesiastical and spiritual revolution, but there were also economic and political elements. Its roots can be traced to the late 14th century, when the Englishman John Wycliffe and the Bohemian John Huss attacked the corruption of the papacy. Simmering discontent came to the boil in 1517 when a German Augustinian friar, Martin Luther, challenged the Church to respond to his 95 'theses', or propositions, about its condition.

Luther (left) and others of the Wittenberg reformers stand protected by their champion, John Frederick I, Elector of Saxony.

Luther was outraged by the sale of 'indulgences', or pardons for sin, which had increased to help to pay off the debts of Pope Leo X. Luther nailed his theses to the door of the chapel of Wittenberg Castle, so lighting the fuse that led to the explosion of the Reformation.

Germany was then in the grip of an agricultural recession. The peasantry and lesser nobility were ready to vent their anger on the great landlords, especially ecclesiastical landlords who controlled the wealth of the Church. The temporal authorities of many European states, such as England with its increasingly powerful central monarchy under the Tudors, also saw in Luther's challenge an opportunity to press their claims for independence from papal interference, and for an end to the payment of various dues and taxes to the Vatican. Their political ambitions found justification in Luther's assault on the worldliness of the Church.

Luther's message was purely spiritual. He proclaimed a doctrine of 'justification by faith alone' and 'the priesthood of all believers'. Formal religious observance would not bring eternal salvation; a man was justified by his belief in the redemptive power of Jesus Christ alone. And every man was his own 'priest', with direct access to God and the truth of the Gospels. It followed that the rigid hierarchy of the Church was an irrelevance to spiritual health.

CATHOLICISM FIGHTS BACK

Luther was excommunicated by the Diet of Worms in 1521 after refusing to recant his opinions, declaring *Ich kann nicht anders* – 'I can do no other'. By siding against the German peasants in their revolt of 1525, he helped to stifle the democratic implications of his teachings, but nothing could stop the spread of 'Protestant' ideas. The invention of movable type by Johann Gutenberg in the mid 15th century had made the Bible accessible to readers who spoke no Latin. Only the extremities of Europe – Russia and Ireland, for instance – remained almost untouched by the new ideas.

The Counter Reformation, a renewal of the Catholic Church through reform, kept Spain, Portugal, Italy and France loyal to the papacy. But in northern Europe Protestantism gained sway – often in the extreme form preached by John Calvin, who established a Puritan theocracy in Switzerland in 1541. National churches, such as the Church of England established by Henry VIII in the 1530s, asserted their independence, and for the next century Europe was thrown into turmoil by a series of bitter religious wars.

Protestants celebrate aspects of their creed, in a tableau dated 1601 from Windsheim. On the left, John Frederick I of Saxony disputes with the Catholic Emperor Charles V.

The destruction caused by the Reichstag blaze took two generations to restore. In 1991 it was decided to rebuild the Reichstag to house the parliament of a reunited Germany.

Reichstag Legislative and representative assembly of the GERMAN SECOND EMPIRE from 1871 to 1919 and of the WEIMAR REPUBLIC from 1919 to 1933, when fire destroyed the building. Its origins date back to the DIET of the Holy Roman Empire in the 16th century. Revived by Otto von BISMARCK in 1867, the Reichstag's role was confined to legislation. It was forbidden to interfere in federal government affairs and had limited control over public spending. Under the Weimar Republic it enjoyed greater power. In July 1932 the Nazis became the largest party in the Reichstag, and in January 1933 Adolf HITLER formed a government.

On February 27, 1933, fire swept through the Reichstag. The Nazis blamed the communists, and on the day after the fire Hitler issued a decree suspending all civil liberties and installing a state of emergency. Many communist and some socialist deputies to the Reichstag were arrested and sent to the newly established concentration camps. The Nazis executed a Dutch communist, Marius van der Lubbe, for starting the fire. At the time, and since, many have argued that the Reichstag fire was in fact organised by the Nazi leader Hermann GOERING. The Enabling Act of March 23, 1933, effectively voted the Reichstag out of existence.

Reith, John, 1st Baron (1889-1971) Director-general of the British Broadcasting Corporation from 1927 to 1938. From 1922, as general manager of the BBC, Reith developed radio services within Britain and around the empire, and inaugurated the world's first

television service in 1936. His strongly Calvinistic temperament moulded the early years of broadcasting, with an emphasis on programmes which were educational in the widest sense: classical music, book reviews, news and drama. Reith's aim was that the BBC should earn respect for its impartiality and sense of responsibility. During the Second World War, Reith held ministerial positions in Winston Churchill's government. In honour of his contribution to broadcasting, the annual BBC Reith Lectures were instituted in 1948.

relic Part of the mortal remains of a saint, or an object closely associated with one. The relics of early Christian martyrs were said to produce miracles, but the most prized were fragments of the cross on which Christ died. Pilgrims returned from distant shrines with relics for their home churches or monasteries, and these in turn became places of pilgrimage as their prestige grew because of the relics they contained. During the Middle Ages the expectation of miracles from relics increased, fuelled by the flood of relics into Europe during the Crusades. LOUIS IX of France built Sainte-Chapelle in Paris in the 13th century to house relics from Constantinople. Abuses led the LATERAN COUNCIL in 1215 to forbid their sale and decree that only relics authenticated by the papacy might be venerated. Their use was attacked by the Protestants, and in 1563 the Council of Trent ruled that the veneration of holy relics was permitted as an aid to devotion. Similar devotions are officially sanctioned in Buddhism, but not in Islam.

Religion, Origins of see feature, page 540

Religion, Wars of see FRENCH WARS OF RELIGION

Renaissance see feature, page 544

reparations Compensation or remuneration required of a defeated nation for damage inflicted during a war. The VERSAILLES PEACE SETTLEMENT between the Allied Powers and Germany at the end of the First World War required Germany to pay £6.5 billion in reparations. When Germany was unable to keep up the payments in 1923, France and Belgium occupied the RUHR, provoking an outcry in Germany. The occupation ended in 1924, after an Allied commission devised the Dawes Plan, which reduced the amounts required of Germany. Inability to meet even these payments led to the YOUNG PLAN in 1929 which lowered the debt to a third of the original sum. The Lausanne Pact in 1932 converted it into a bond issue; repayments never resumed.

After the Second World War the Allies occupied Germany and Japan and collected reparations. Britain, France and the USA ended the collection of reparations in 1952. The Soviet Union removed assets and industrial equipment from East Germany and seized Japanese assets in Manchuria. Victims of Nazi persecution, including the state of Israel, received about $2 billion from West Germany, but other payments were modest.

Representatives, House of Lower house of the Congress of the USA. When the House first met in 1789 there were 59 members. Membership grew steadily until it was stabilised in 1912 at 435 representatives, who are elected for a two-year term. The seats are reapportioned among the states every ten years to reflect population changes shown in a census. The presiding officer, the Speaker of the House, is elected by members. The Constitution states that if the president and vice-president were both to die, the Speaker of the House would then become president. The House and the SENATE have an equal voice in legislation, though all revenue bills must originate in the House. Since 1900 Democrats have held the majority in the House for a total of 68 years, but in 1995 a Republican majority was returned for the first time since 1954.

Republican Party One of the two major political parties in the USA, founded in 1854. The Republican Party brought together groups opposed to slavery, and supported protective trade tariffs. It won its first presidential election with Abraham LINCOLN in 1860 and from then until 1932, apart from a few brief periods, dominated the US Congress.

The party's early success was based on the support of the farmers and industrial workers of the north and west, and on its conservative

The elephant was a cartoonist's symbol for the Republicans – 'sure to win if kept pure and clean and has not too heavy a load to carry.'

What the first humans believed about their world and the next

How did religion begin? The mysterious caves of Lascaux, the burial sites of Neanderthals or the Great Mother figurines of the Mediterranean tell an extraordinary story of human imagination.

We know little about the origins of religion. Archaeological evidence of spiritual activity in the prehistoric era is scanty and literary evidence non-existent, so it is impossible to be certain about the religious experience of the first human beings. Some scholars have studied the beliefs and practices of such peoples as the Australian Aborigines or the Native Americans in the hope that they can supplement our knowledge. But these more traditional societies have themselves developed and changed; their genesis is now lost beyond recall.

We do know that the Neanderthals, who lived from about 100 000 to 50 000 years ago, buried their dead. Some remains have been discovered with flint tools and implements beside their hands. Skulls have also been found, either surrounded by a ring of stones or dyed in red ochre. These practices probably indicate some belief in the soul or an afterlife, but it is impossible to reconstruct the mythology or theology that might underlie this concern for the relics of the dead. Many more burial sites have been discovered in the late Palaeolithic age, also splashed with ochre, which shows some continuing preoccupation with mortality.

We know that the practice of leaving personal objects in the grave of the deceased is still common in traditional societies. Often it is thought that these objects will help the dead during the next phase of their existence. It is also felt that a person's life-force informs his or her possessions. Among pre-literate peoples, there is a strong sense of the continued presence of the dead, expressed in a veneration of the ancestors of the clan.

DIALOGUE WITH THE DEAD

These legendary personages help to unite the group by providing it with a common origin. It is also assumed that the ancestors are still concerned about the survival of the group, so their cult is often connected with fertility rituals. The spirits of the dead are felt as a strong accompanying presence, regarded with affection and awe but also

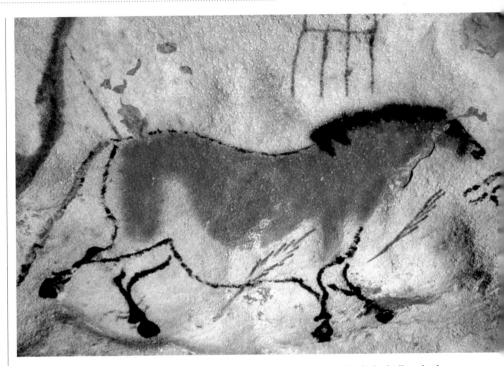

Prehistoric paintings found in the caves of Lascaux in France depict animals, including the horse, above, being attacked with arrows, and indicate a connection with magical hunting rituals.

with dread if they met a violent death. Ancestor cults demonstrate the conviction that the spirit of individuals has a dimension that transcends this mundane existence. It is possible that prehistoric human beings, who were clearly concerned for their dead, shared this belief.

Burial rites could provide the earliest evidence of a religious response to the world, but it is probably mistaken to imagine that our earliest ancestors saw religion as a separate human activity, as we do today. In more traditional societies, religion still permeates the whole of life. Hunting, for example, is not regarded merely as a means of getting food. An Australian Aborigine will meditate, pray and purify himself before a hunt. During an expedition he feels that he is one with the First Hunter, an archetypal hero, and that this identification with a larger world keeps him in existence.

Anthropologists have noted that in pre-literate societies from Siberia to Tierra del Fuego, men and women are continuously aware of a sacred dimension that informs the entire world. Sometimes this is felt as an impersonal force, sometimes as spirits or gods – even a High God who created the world. This power, which scholars often call *mana*, pervades all things and is indestructible. It is present in human beings, animals, rocks, plants, rivers, the sun and the moon. Sometimes it fills people with awe and dread, sometimes it makes them ecstatic, exuberant or contemplative. In this way the whole of existence shares the same divine nature.

Mana is unseen but regarded as a tangible fact of life. The Shaman, a universal figure in traditional societies, is trained in ecstatic techniques to make spiritual journeys and make contact with the spirit world. But the sacred element is

The painting of a half-man, half-stag creature in the cave at Les Trois Frères, France, represents a spiritual figure, c. 15 000 BC.

felt by everybody to some degree. It is almost certain that prehistoric men and women were equally conscious of this powerful and holy dimension.

Today, even though *mana* is omnipresent and all-pervasive, it is felt to imbue certain people, objects and actions with particular intensity. These are regarded as *tabu* and can only be approached by trained personnel. The common folk must keep their distance from their chief, who is specially endowed with

mana. In much the same way, members of the lower Hindu castes must make no contact with the Brahmins. Certain states connected with the great changes of life are also *tabu*. In many traditional societies, people avoid contact with blood, a dying person, a warrior on the eve of battle or a corpse.

This embracing vision of religion is also shown in the reverence for a totem, a non-human creature which is felt to have a special relationship with the tribe. An animal, plant, stone or river can be a totem and is often thought to be the great ancestor of the group. Members of a tribe are forbidden to hunt or eat their totem, except on special ritual occasions that constitute a form of communion, which unites the clan with its essential spirit. This practice had practical ecological and economic reasons; it prevented the over-hunting of certain species. But at a deeper level it also expresses the kinship that is felt to exist between humanity, the sacred and the non-human world.

It is likely that some such feeling inspired the extraordinary cave paintings, executed between 20 000 and 8 000 years ago, which have been discovered at such sites as Lascaux in France and Altamira in Spain. These depictions of deer, bison and horses – animals which were an important source of food – were possibly connected with hunting rituals. Frequently they are presented with spears in their sides. Perhaps the ability to capture an animal in paint was thought to influence its later capture in the field. The inaccessibility of these caves suggests that they had a cultic significance. Some show a man disguised as

an animal: perhaps he was a priest, whose dress emphasised the bond between the hunter and his prey. Or perhaps he was a dancing god, the lord of the beasts, or the totem of the tribe.

If so, prehistoric human beings had begun to imagine gods who, perhaps, personified the sacred *mana* of life. Figurines unearthed throughout the Mediterranean world and the Near East depicting a woman with large belly and breasts and, often, pronounced genitals, may show evidence of this. At a time when agriculture was developing, this cult of the Great Mother expressed a sense that the fertility which was wondrously transforming human life was itself sacred and connected with human fecundity.

WHERE RELIGION MEETS MORALS

Some scholars argue that religion originally sprang from magic, a primitive attempt to control the environment by rituals. But this interpretation leaves out the sense of the sacred and the desire to celebrate it which appears crucial to primal religion. In many societies magic has been a precursor of science rather than religion and may represent a quite different sphere of activity.

We cannot generalise about the ethics or beliefs of prehistoric humanity. Today in traditional societies we find myths that point to an afterlife which can be attained by good deeds and which imply a divine judgment of some kind. But we have no idea whether this was an element of early faith. Certainly in later pagan religion, immortality was thought to be the privilege of the gods alone.

As men and women gained a greater mastery over their world, their religions inevitably changed. They may have felt a new alienation from their environment. The sacred was now becoming less ubiquitous and more concentrated in special holy places and in divine personages who occupied a separate world. Yet the paganism of the cities and early civilisations retained aspects of the old vision. The Great Mother appeared in new guises: Aphrodite, Isis, Venus, Inana, Astarte. The old kinship of human and non-human was preserved in myths of the gods who had human traits and were also identified with such natural forces as the sun or the wind. The gods, human beings and the natural world were still thought to share the same essentially divine nature.

The Great Mother has taken on forms such as, from left to right, Venus of Willendorf, c. 20 000 BC, the Maltese Lady in Limestone, c. 3400 BC, and the Greek Venus de Milo, 2nd century, right.

541

financial policies and trade tariffs. The party split in the early 20th century when Theodore ROOSEVELT launched the liberal Progressive Party (see PROGRESSIVE PARTIES). The Republicans lost office to the DEMOCRATIC PARTY during the 1930s and 1940s, returning to power in 1952 through the popularity of President Dwight EISENHOWER. Under more recent Republican presidents since 1968– Richard NIXON, Gerald FORD, and Ronald REAGAN – the party became associated with military spending and a forceful assertion of US presence worldwide. It is strongly backed by corporate business.

Requerimiento Document prepared on the orders of FERDINAND II of Spain in 1513 by which the Indians of South America were required to acknowledge the supremacy of the pope and the king of Spain over their lands. They were also made to receive Christian preachers. The penalty for refusal was enslavement to the Spanish. By law the document had to be read to all Indians, but few understood enough Spanish to comprehend its terms. The Spanish used it to justify their continued conquests, until it was superseded by a new law in 1573.

resistance movements Underground resistance movements fought against German and Japanese occupations of France, Italy, Malaya, Vietnam, and many other countries during the Second World War (1939-45). Their activities involved helping Jews and

prisoners of war to escape, publishing underground newspapers, conveying intelligence by secret radios, and committing acts of espionage and sabotage. In Eastern Europe the long German lines of communication were continually harassed by partisans, and the Polish resistance was the largest and most elaborate in Europe. There were often deep divisions between the communist and the noncommunist resistance. In Yugoslavia, for instance, the communist partisans and the Serb nationalist Chetniks hated, and occasionally attacked, each other.

Restoration (1660) Re-establishment in England, Scotland and Wales of the Stuart monarchy by placing CHARLES II, the exiled son of Charles I, on the throne after the English Civil War. As Lord Protector, Oliver Cromwell never succeeded in reconciling the Royalists to his republican regime. His death in 1658 undermined the PROTECTORATE, and his son and successor Richard Cromwell was brushed aside by the army. The negotiations of General George MONCK in Scotland and England, and the Earl of CLARENDON in exile with Charles II, brought about the peaceful Restoration in May 1660. The Restoration was accompanied by the revival of the Church of England and a flourishing cultural and social life.

Retz, Paul de Gondi (1613-79) French statesman and cardinal. The designated successor to his uncle, the Archbishop of Paris,

Retz plotted to replace Jules MAZARIN as chief minister of France. He was active in the first years of the FRONDE revolts (1648-53) against Mazarin's government and was afterwards imprisoned. He escaped and fled to Rome. In 1662 he resigned his claim to the archbishopric in order to be allowed to return to France. He became abbot of St Denis. Retz's *Mémoires*, published after his death, give a spirited account of the personalities and intrigues of mid-17th-century France.

Reunification of Germany (October 3, 1990) Restoration of West Germany and East Germany as one united state. It followed a growing tide of reform during the 1980s, initiated by the Soviet leader Mikhail Gorbachev, which led to the fall of communist regimes throughout the Eastern Bloc.

In 1989 the East German government, led by the communist Erich HONECKER, was under pressure from the example of reforms instituted in the Soviet Union. Threatened by mass demonstrations, East Germany opened its borders with Hungary and precipitated a vast exodus of people through Hungary into Austria and West Germany, severely disrupting the East German economy. The pro-democracy movement gathered momentum, Honecker was replaced by Egon Krenz in October 1989, and borders with the West were opened. The dismantling of the BERLIN WALL that divided the city began.

In December 1989 the West German chancellor, Helmut KOHL, drew up a ten-point plan for the reunification of the two countries. Revelations about the corruption of Honecker's regime led to Krenz's resignation and Honecker's arrest. The communists suffered a crushing defeat in multi-party elections in East Germany in March, 1990. As the Eastern economy deteriorated further and the emigration continued, negotiations began for the unification of the two Germanies. A treaty ratifying monetary and economic union was signed in July. Official reunification came in October, with Berlin as the capital of a Federal Republic of Germany and Bonn as the seat of government. In December the first unified elections in 58 years resulted in victory for Kohl and a coalition government.

Reuter, Paul, Baron (1816-99) Founder of one of the first news agencies. Born in Germany and originally named Israel Josaphat, he established a pigeon-post service between Aachen and Brussels in 1850 to relay commercial information. In 1851 he settled in London, where he opened a telegraph office near the Stock Exchange. Linked by telegraph with correspondents in other countries, Reuter supplied the daily newspapers with information about share prices, eye-witness reports of foreign conflicts such as the CRIMEAN WAR,

In a photograph probably posed for propaganda purposes, French soldiers and civilians listen to BBC broadcasts. A German drawing pin tin, right, concealed a secret radio.

Revolution sweeps into St Mark's Square, Venice, on March 23, 1848, as Daniel Manin proclaims a Venetian republic. Manin became its president and led a heroic defence against an Austrian siege.

and other international news. By the 1870s his agency had become a worldwide organisation which still operates today. In 1871 the German Duke of Saxe-Coburg-Gotha made him Baron Julius von Reuter, a title later recognised in England, where he took British nationality in 1857.

Reuther, Walter (1907-70) US trade union leader. Originally a socialist, Reuther spent two years in the 1930s working for a car factory in the Soviet Union, where he developed a strong dislike of communism. Returning to Detroit, he became a foreman in a car plant and one of the leaders of the factory sit-ins of 1937 that made General Motors recognise the new United Automobile Workers (UAW). Ford recognised the UAW in 1941, and it became one of the largest unions in the world. Reuther was president of the UAW from 1946 to 1970. He negotiated guaranteed employment, wage increases, holidays, medical insurance and welfare provisions for his members, and fought against communist influence within the union. Reuther was president of the Congress of Industrial Organisations (CIO) from 1952 to 1955.

Revere, Paul (1735-1818) American patriot. Revere was a silversmith, engraver and printer in Boston. He published anti-British cartoons and joined the Sons of Liberty, a group which resisted British colonial oppression in the American colonies, particularly taxation. Revere was involved in numerous patriot activities including the BOSTON TEA PARTY of 1773. He rode from Boston to Lexington to warn of the approach of British troops before the Battle of LEXINGTON AND CONCORD in

1775, a feat immortalised in Henry Wadsworth Longfellow's *Midnight Ride of Paul Revere* (1863). Revere served in the War of Independence, and died a wealthy merchant and manufacturer. He designed and printed the first US currency.

revisionism Term used primarily within the communist movement to describe the revision of Marxist theory, usually in the direction of greater moderation. A noted 'revisionist' was Eduard Bernstein (1850-1932), a German socialist who challenged the central tenets of Marxism and argued for a gradual, nonrevolutionary transition to socialism. Recently the term has been applied to those who believe that the basic aims of Marxism can be achieved without extensive public ownership of industry. The term is often used derogatorily.

revivalism Protestant movement, mainly in the USA, in which travelling preachers encourage repentance, prayer, forgiveness of sin through Jesus Christ, and emphasise direct personal experience. The first 'Great Awakening' or intense religious revival lasted from about 1720 to 1770. Jonathan Edwards and George Whitefield were notable preachers. A 'Second Awakening' between 1797 and 1820 began with 'camp meetings' in tents along the frontier for prayer and exhortation. In the early 19th century revivalism was an accepted method of worship among Presbyterians, Congregationalists, Baptists and Methodists. The tradition was renewed in the 1950s by preachers such as Billy Graham, who attracted mass audiences to their meetings in football stadiums. Radio and television

extended their audience: on a single day in 1996, an estimated 1.5 billion viewers around the world tuned into Graham's television crusade to reach younger people.

Revolutions of 1848 Series of revolts across Europe against autocratic government. These revolutions challenged the rule of the monarchy and the feudal rights of the landowning aristocracy. The first major revolution was in France, where supporters of universal suffrage under the socialist Louis Blanc caused the overthrow of LOUIS-PHILIPPE and established the Second Republic. In German states there were uprisings and a movement for an elected national parliament and a united Germany. Rioting in Austria resulted in the flight of both Prince METTERNICH and the emperor, the formation of a constituent assembly and the emancipation of peasants. The Hungarian independence movement led by Lajos Kossuth formed a short-lived republican government. Revolutions in the Italian states caused the temporary expulsion of the Austrians and the flight of Pope PIUS IX from Rome. The revolutions failed to achieve lasting success. By the end of 1849 counterrevolutionary forces had restored order.

Reynaud, Paul (1878-1966) French politician. Reynaud was prime minister at the time of the fall of France in 1940 when he unsuccessfully tried to prevent German occupation. He was arrested and imprisoned throughout the Second World War. After liberation Reynaud served as finance minister and deputy prime minister. He assisted in the formation of the Fifth Republic, but later quarrelled with Charles DE GAULLE's insistence on a presidential regime. He published a number of works, including his *Mémoires* (1960-3).

Reza Shah Pahlavi (1878-1944) Shah of Iran from 1925 to 1941. Reza Khan was an officer of the Persian Cossack Brigade when he seized power through an army coup in 1921, established a military dictatorship and founded the Pahlavi dynasty. He followed a policy of rapid modernisation and economic development in a country that had suffered from centuries of misrule and the ravages of war. He crushed tribal and other opposition to his policies. In the Second World War his refusal to expel German nationals led to the invasion and occupation of Iran by Soviet and British forces. In 1941 Reza Khan abdicated in favour of his son, MUHAMMAD REZA SHAH. He died in exile in South Africa.

Rhee, Syngman (1875-1965) President of South Korea from 1948 to 1960. Rhee was an early supporter of Korean independence from Japan. He was educated at a Methodist school learned English, and in 1896 joined the campaign for Korean independence. After serving

Art and culture are reborn, as a new age dawns in Italy

Renaissance means 'rebirth'. From its roots in late medieval Italy, this rediscovery of ancient Greek and Roman culture flowered across Europe, profoundly affecting its intellectual outlook.

The Renaissance was a cultural revival, a wave of enthusiasm for the ancient world, especially Rome, that might be called a 'craze' had it not lasted for more than two centuries. The essential idea, expressed frequently by men of letters in Italy and elsewhere in the 14th, 15th and 16th centuries, was that of rebirth. Literature, sculpture and architecture were viewed as having flourished in ancient Rome, then to have declined in the age of the barbarians or Goths – hence the term 'Gothic' to describe medieval architecture – and finally to have been reborn in Italy in the time of the poet Petrarch (1304-74).

'Not only has no one spoken Latin correctly for many centuries,' lamented the Italian scholar Lorenzo Valla (1405-57), 'but no one has even understood it properly when reading it ... as if, after the fall of the Roman Empire, it was not fitting for the Roman language to be spoken or to be understood.' But now, thought Valla, at last things were changing.

EMERGING FROM THE 'DARK AGES'
Writers and artists developed an increasingly acute sense of the past. They began to see it as divided into distinct periods – a glorious antiquity, followed by a barbarous epoch which they were the first to call the 'Dark Ages' or 'Middle Ages'.

One sign of this enthusiasm for antiquity was the desire to discover, collect and preserve what remained of it. Petrarch was delighted to discover manuscript copies of works by the Roman writer Cicero. The Florentine architect Filippo Brunelleschi (1377-1446) and his friend the sculptor Donatello (*c*.1386-1466) studied, measured and sketched the ruins of ancient Rome.

Another sign was the attempt to imitate classical masterpieces, in the belief that culture would flourish again if people returned to the style of the age when it had flourished before. Petrarch

Antonio da Sangallo's classically inspired plan for the completion of St Peter's in Rome was never carried out. Andrea Palladio produced several influential designs for neoclassical villas (top).

wrote a long epic poem called *Africa* in the style of Virgil. Architects followed the models of Roman buildings such as the Colosseum and the Pantheon. Sculptors, including Michelangelo (1475-1564), were inspired by classical statues discovered in Rome and elsewhere. Of one of these, the so-called Belvedere Torso, Michelangelo remarked that 'this is the work of a man who knew more than nature'. Painters such as Raphael (1483-1520) also studied ancient statues, since no

Raphael's fresco *The School of Athens* (1509-11) depicts a group of philosophers, with Aristotle and Plato in the centre, and symbolises the rational pursuit of truth.

In Botticelli's *Birth of Venus*, painted about 1485, Venus represents a beauty that can inspire nobility of thought. Her pose – known as 'Venus pudica' (modest Venus) – uses a prototype found in ancient Greek statues (left).

This sculpture by Michelangelo is a 'Pietà', or study of the Virgin Mary holding the body of Jesus. It was made between 1497 and 1500 for a French cardinal.

Greek or Roman paintings had survived. And composers tried to reconstruct the forms of ancient Greek music.

Teachers in schools and universities encouraged their students to perform Latin dramas. They also revived the Roman system of education, based on the study of grammar, rhetoric, poetry, history and ethics. These subjects, they thought, made students more fully human – hence the description of these teachers as 'humanists'.

Despite their veneration for antiquity, these artists and writers also had great confidence in their own abilities. The Florentine sculptor and goldsmith Benvenuto Cellini (1500-71) told the Duke of Florence that although 'the great Donatello and the marvellous Michelangelo' were 'the greatest artists since the time of the ancients', yet 'I have it in me to produce a work which will be three times better'.

Men such as Cellini were not going to imitate the ancients slavishly: they tried to adapt ancient models to the conditions of their own times. The Florentine philosopher Marsilio Ficino (1433-99) wrote what he called a 'Platonic Theology' – an attempt to combine the ideas of the Greek Plato with Christian tradition. Niccolò Machiavelli (1469-1527) argued that rulers should imitate the example of the ancients, and wrote a commentary on the early history of Rome in order to guide them. 'Considering in what honour antiquity is held, and how … a bit of an old statue has fetched a high price', he declared himself to be full of 'astonishment and grief' at the lack of interest in the political practices of the Romans. All the same, his *Prince*, which gives advice to rulers on how to keep themselves in power, was a new kind of book, not grounded on classical models.

FROM LATIN TO VERNACULAR

Poets such as Petrarch wrote not only in Classical Latin but in the vernacular as well – in Petrarch's case, in the dialect of Tuscany, which was being adopted in other parts of Italy and later developed into modern Italian. In a similar way, architects adapted the plans of pagan temples in order to build churches. They not only revived something old, they also strove to create something new.

Intellectuals and artists in other countries learned with excitement about the Italian cultural revival. Some came to Italy to see things for themselves. The German artist Albrecht Dürer (1471-1528) visited Venice to learn about new developments in painting, while the Englishman John Colet, a friend of Thomas More, went to Florence to discuss Plato with Ficino. Another friend of More's, the Dutchman Erasmus (1469-1536), liked Italy less; all the same, he saw a golden age at hand, since literature and learning 'which were almost extinct' were reviving throughout Europe.

Many learned books were translated from Italian and Latin into French, Spanish, English and other European languages, and became more widely available after 1450 with the invention of the printing press. Some Italian artists were invited to work abroad. Leonardo da Vinci (1452-1519) went to France at the invitation of Francis I, while Pietro Torrigiano, a Florentine sculptor who had broken Michelangelo's nose in a fight, decided to emigrate and moved to England, where he worked on the tomb of Henry VII in Westminster Abbey.

THE EXCITEMENT OF A NEW AGE

Poets all over Europe imitated Italian as well as ancient models. The use of the vernacular rather than Latin for works of literature was encouraged particularly by the examples of Petrarch and Lodovico Ariosto (1474-1533), whose poem *Orlando Furioso* (*The Madness of Roland*) was read and imitated from Portugal to Poland.

Picture-books with designs for houses in the new style circulated so that people intending to build could select doorways or fireplaces. Statues of rulers on horseback erected in public squares imitated Roman models, and even the symmetrical public squares constructed in European cities were inspired by the ancient Roman Forum.

As the Renaissance spread, the idea of a 'new age' was extended to other areas of discovery, such as exploration, science and medicine. In the words of a 16th-century physician, Jean Fernel (1497-1558): 'The world circumnavigated, the largest of Earth's continents discovered, the compass invented, the printing press sowing knowledge, gunpowder revolutionising the art of war, ancient manuscripts rescued and the restoration of scholarship all witness to the triumph of our New Age.'

a prison sentence from 1897 to 1904 for his nationalist activities, he went to the USA, becoming president of a government-in-exile in 1919. On the surrender of Japan in 1945 Rhee returned to the US-controlled area of Korea. In 1948 he became the first president of the Republic of SOUTH KOREA, advocating the unification of Korea both before and after the KOREAN WAR (1950-3). Rhee was re-elected in 1952 and 1956, but opposition to his corrupt and autocratic government grew, and a third re-election in 1960 brought accusations of vote-rigging and serious rioting. Rhee was forced into exile.

Rhineland Region in western Germany adjoining the River Rhine. A former province of Prussia, the Rhineland has been much fought over. In 1794 the success of the French revolutionary armies brought the left bank of the Rhine to France, but it was ceded by the Congress of VIENNA to Prussia in 1815 as a bulwark against French expansion. With the formation of the GERMAN SECOND EMPIRE in 1871 the nearby French provinces of ALSACE and Lorraine, both rich in iron and coal, were annexed to the Rhineland. In 1918 these were restored to France and the Rhineland was demilitarised but allowed to remain within the WEIMAR REPUBLIC. Adolf HITLER's troops marched into the region in 1936 with only token protests from Britain and France. The Rhineland was the scene of heavy fighting in 1944 when it was recaptured by US troops. After the Second World War it became a state within West Germany.

Rhode Island Smallest state in the USA, located on the southern coast of New England around Narragansett Bay. Rhode Island was settled in 1636 by Roger Williams, a religious dissident from Massachusetts, and was chartered as a colony by Parliament in 1644, becoming a Quaker and Baptist refuge. Both Providence, the capital, and Newport thrived on slave-trading and rum-distilling in the 17th and 18th centuries, while the eastern part of the region became prosperous through agriculture and horse-breeding. Rhode Island was occupied by the British during the War of Independence (1776-9). After the American Revolution (1775-83), it remained independent in its views and had to be greatly pressured to ratify the constitution.

Rhodes Largest of the islands in the Greek Dodecanese located off the south-west coast of Turkey. Rhodes, the capital, was founded in 408 BC, and was the site of the Colossus of Rhodes, one of the ancient SEVEN WONDERS OF THE WORLD. The Colossus was a huge statue of the sun-god Helios, over 100 ft (30 m) high. It was destroyed by an earthquake in 244 BC. Rhodes was inhabited by speakers of Doric Greek, who established

---

Painting Africa red

In 1888 Cecil Rhodes bought South Africa's Kimberley diamond mines. Soon his company, De Beers, controlled most of the world's diamond production. He then went on to change the face of Africa.

Cecil Rhodes was not simply an entrepreneur: he had an almost mystical belief in British imperialism. While other European countries were seeking colonies in Africa, Rhodes had even more grandiose imperial dreams for Britain which included building a railway from the Cape to Cairo.

Born in England in 1853, Rhodes left for Africa at the age of 17. By 1881 he had been elected to the parliament of Cape Colony, and in 1890 he became its prime minister. A domineering man, he had little but contempt for missionaries, humanitarians and the cautious policies of the Colonial Office in London. Rhodes wanted northward expansion into the interior, and he wanted it quickly, before the Belgians or Portuguese beat him to it.

There were two main obstacles. One was King Lobengula of Matabeleland to the north; the other was Paul Kruger, president of the Afrikaner Republic of the Transvaal to the north-east, the site of Africa's great gold fields.

A reluctant Lobengula was persuaded to sign a treaty of 'friendship' which gave Rhodes mineral rights. He and his agents promptly moved in. The result was a royal charter from London which allowed him to extend his company's control to the Zambezi and beyond – far more than Lobengula had conceded. In 1890 Rhodes sent an expedition as far north as Mashonaland (Zimbabwe), where a fort was established named Salisbury, after the prime minister. Railways soon followed. In 1893 a revolt by Lobengula was crushed, the king was killed and his kingdom snuffed out. The vast new territory, nearly half the area of Europe, was named Rhodesia.

RHODES IN DISGRACE

Kruger's Boer Republic was a bigger obstacle. He needed British workers in the gold fields, but as foreigners they were denied political rights. Kruger had already defeated the British at Majuba Hill in 1881; now he sealed off the frontier of the Vaal river. Rhodes concocted a desperate adventure to overthrow the republic.

In December 1895 a force of nearly 50 cavalry led by Leander Starr Jameson invaded the Transvaal, making for Johannesburg, where they were to join an uprising. The expedition – the 'Jameson raid' – was a fiasco. There was no uprising; Jameson's forces were defeated easily; and Rhodes was sacked as premier.

In 1899 Kruger, hoping for German backing, began a disastrous war against the British. Rhodes died in 1902, the year the British finally defeated the Boers and won domination of all southern Africa. By now he was a national hero. As one historian put it: 'Rhodes was an Elizabethan – the endless rolling plains of Africa his sea.'

Cecil Rhodes in his later years relaxes on safari with a book. Throughout his life he maintained a deep interest in all aspects of the continent he helped to open up.

Richardus.I.

Richard I – the Lionheart – himself a poet, became the hero of many romantic poems and legends. Here he is shown wrestling with a lion.

three city-states – Ialysus, Lindos, and Camirus. The mountainous island was well placed to benefit from trade, and the opening up of the Persian Empire by Alexander the Great made Rhodes exceptionally prosperous. The island later formed part of the Byzantine Empire, and from 1309 to 1522 it was occupied by the Knights Hospitallers of St John of Jerusalem. They were ejected by SULEIMAN I and Rhodes became part of the OTTOMAN EMPIRE. Italy occupied the island in 1912 and ceded it to Greece in 1947.

Rhodes, Cecil see feature, page 546

Rhodesia see ZIMBABWE

Ribbentrop, Joachim von (1893-1946) German NAZI politician and close associate of Adolf HITLER. Ribbentrop joined the Nazi Party in 1932. From 1936 to 1838 he was ambassador to Britain. As foreign minister from 1938 to 1945, Ribbentrop conducted negotiations with states destined to become Hitler's victims. The 1939 NAZI-SOVIET PACT on non-aggression between Germany and the Soviet Union was regarded as his major achievement, opening the way for the attack on Poland and the Baltic States. Ribbentrop was also responsible for the Tripartite Pact in 1940 between Germany, Italy and Japan. After trial at NUREMBERG as a war criminal he was executed.

Ricardo, David (1772-1823) British economist. Ricardo, a wealthy stockjobber, wrote *Principles of Political Economy and Taxation* (1817), supported the law of supply and demand in a free market, and proposed that the value of a commodity rests on the amount of labour required for its production – a theory later adopted by Karl MARX. In 1819 he entered Parliament as a Radical, where he supported FREE TRADE, a return to the GOLD STANDARD and the repeal of the CORN LAWS.

Richard I (1157-99) King of England, Duke of Normandy and Count of Anjou from 1189. Richard's military exploits earned him the nickname Lionheart, or *Coeur de Lion*. Richard was the third son of HENRY II – against whom he rebelled – and ELEANOR OF AQUITAINE. He was made Duke of Aquitaine at the age of 12. Having taken the Crusader's vow, Richard left England in 1190 with the Third CRUSADE. In Palestine he captured Acre and defeated the sultan SALADIN at Arsuf. In 1192, after concluding a truce with Saladin, he set out for England, but was imprisoned while crossing Austria by Emperor Henry VI. A large ransom was raised in England for Richard's release, and he returned home in 1194. Almost immediately he crossed the Channel to defend his family's dominions in Aquitaine, Anjou and Normandy. Richard spent the rest of his life in France trying to protect his lands, and died while attacking the castle at Châlus.

Richard II (1367-1400) King of England from 1377 to 1399. Richard was the only son of EDWARD THE BLACK PRINCE, and grandson of Edward III, whom he succeeded at the age of ten. Until he came of age, the country was governed by a council controlled by his uncle, John of Gaunt. Richard faced his first crisis in 1381, the PEAS-ANTS' REVOLT, provoked by the imposition of a poll tax. Courageously, he rode among the rioters in London making empty promises to persuade them to disperse. The Lords Appellant, a group led by another of Richard's uncles, Thomas of Woodstock, Duke of Gloucester, opposed John of Gaunt's rule. In 1388 the Lords Appellant executed or imprisoned Richard's chief supporters and created a commission to oversee the king. Richard repudiated it, gained control of the country and took revenge on his enemies. But then in 1399 Gaunt's son

Richard III was characterised as a wicked, scheming hunchback by Tudor historians, but this may have been political propaganda.

Henry Bolingbroke deposed Richard and assumed power as HENRY IV. Richard died in prison at Pontefract Castle.

Richard III (1452-85) Duke of Gloucester from 1461 and king of England from 1483 until his death. Richard was a younger brother of EDWARD IV and son of Richard Plantagenet, Duke of YORK. As Duke of Gloucester he served Edward faithfully and was an able soldier, helping to win victories over the Lancastrians in 1471. On the accession of his 12-year-old nephew EDWARD V in 1483, Richard became Protector of England. In the same year he alleged that his brother's children were illegitimate and took the crown for himself. Edward V and his younger brother disappeared, many said murdered by Richard's men at the Tower of London. To this day controversy continues as to his guilt. But several powerful lords believed him guilty and in 1485 they went over to support the rebellion led by Henry Tudor, the future HENRY VII. Henry and Richard fought at the battle of BOSWORTH FIELD. Richard was defeated, but refused to flee and was killed.

Richard, Duke of York see YORK, RICHARD PLANTAGENET, 3RD DUKE OF

Richelieu, Armand Jean du Plessis, Duc de

Richelieu, Armand Jean du Plessis, Duc de (1585-1642) French cardinal and statesman. As chief minister to Louis XIII from 1629, Richelieu greatly strengthened the power of the monarchy, crushing conspiracies by the nobles. He was also responsible for his country's dominant role in Europe. Richelieu was born near Chinon. He was consecrated Bishop of Luçon in 1607, became an adviser to the regent, Marie de Médici, in 1616, and later gained the king's confidence. On the domestic front he destroyed the political strength and military might of the HUGUENOTS. Richelieu's excessive taxation led to revolt, but he needed money to finance France's anti-HABSBURG foreign policy. He took France into the THIRTY YEARS' WAR in 1635 and subsidised the Protestant Dutch, Danes and Swedes to fight against Austria. His successor was Jules MAZARIN, whom he had trained to continue his policies.

From 1629, Richelieu effectively ruled France, and was at the centre of constant intrigue both at home and abroad. Under Richelieu, France overtook Spain as Europe's leading power.

Ridolfi Plot (1571) Abortive Roman Catholic conspiracy to overthrow ELIZABETH I of England and put MARY, Queen of Scots on the throne. It was organised by Roberto Ridolfi (1531-1612), a Florentine banker who had settled in England. With papal finance and Spanish military aid the English Catholics were to rise up under Thomas Howard, 4th Duke of Norfolk, whom Mary would marry, deposing Elizabeth. A messenger was seized, leading to the arrest of the plot's leaders except for Ridolfi, who was abroad at the time.

Rights of Man, Declaration of the

Rights of Man, Declaration of the Document which contained the guiding principles of the FRENCH REVOLUTION, which was approved by the National Assembly in 1789. Its full title was 'The Declaration of the Rights of Man and of the Citizen'. Its 17 articles set forth the individual's rights to equality and liberty on the grounds that 'men are born free and equal in rights'. They affirmed equality before the law, equality of opportunity, freedom from arbitrary imprisonment, freedom of speech and religion, rights of private property and taxation in proportion to ability to pay. The declaration was influenced by the constitutions of the newly independent North American states.

Riot Act (1715) British Act of Parliament to curtail civil disorder, passed in the wake of JACOBITE disturbances which followed the accession of George I. If 12 or more people assembled and disturbed the public peace a magistrate could 'read the Riot Act' ordering them to disperse. To disobey was regarded as a serious offence. Frequent use was made of the Act in the 18th century. Its use declined in the 19th century and it was superseded by the Public Order Act of 1986.

Ripon, George, 1st Marquess of

Ripon, George, 1st Marquess of (1827-1909) British statesman, viceroy of India from 1880 to 1884. Ripon entered Parliament as a Liberal in 1853 and served as secretary for war (1863-6) and secretary for India (1866-8). As Lord President of the Council (1868-73) in William GLADSTONE's government he was responsible for the 1870 Education Bill which his deputy, William Forster, took through the House of Commons. This established compulsory, government-financed elementary education. In 1873 Ripon became a Roman Catholic and resigned both from public office and as grand master of the Freemasons. Gladstone appointed him viceroy of India in 1880, where he introduced a system of local self-government and ended restrictions on the freedom of the press. His Ilbert Bill (1883) gave qualified Indians jurisdiction over Europeans and established trial by a jury, of which half were to be Europeans. On his return to Britain he again held office in Liberal governments.

Risorgimento see feature, page 549

river navigation Since early times, people have widened and deepened rivers to allow easy passage by boats. Weirs were often

The Declaration of the Rights of Man was intended to correct the ills of the old regime in France and to state fundamental principles, but it served as a charter for real democracy.

built across rivers to raise the water level. The oldest weir in Britain, dating from around AD 1100, can still be seen on the River Dee at Chester. Manmade channels, such as canals with locks, enabled boats to pass the weirs and to travel upstream. Canals were also used to avoid bends in rivers and to bypass treacherous stretches of water. One of the oldest ship canals still in operation is the Grand Canal in China, linking the Yellow River and Chang Jiang. The building of the Grand Canal, which is 1085 miles (1747 km) long, began in the 4th century BC and continued over hundreds of years. In north-east America the St Lawrence river connects, with the use of canals and deepened channels, the Great Lakes with the Atlantic Ocean, creating 9500 miles (more than 15 000 km) of waterways.

road First among road-builders were the Persians, and the earliest long-distance route was probably the 1677 mile (2698 km) Royal Road from the imperial city of Susa to Sardis in Lydia, which is thought to have been in use as early as 500 BC. The first important European road-makers were the Romans. They developed a network joining Rome to its expanding empire, principally to speed troop movements. The APPIAN WAY was the first major stretch, leading south to Brindisi. Streets were made of large polygonal blocks of stone, and minor roads of gravel. By AD 200 the road networks of the Roman, Mauryan

Italy becomes an independent nation

The vision and bravery of three remarkable men turned Italy from a divided collection of principalities suffering under foreign domination into a unified modern state.

After 20 years of war and French domination, Italy was as divided in 1815 as it had been since the fall of the Roman Empire. Instead of Napoleon, Prince von Metternich, chancellor of the Austrian Empire, controlled the destiny of the peninsula. Lombardy-Venetia was incorporated into the empire, the duchies of central Italy were all client states, the pope was under Austrian protection. Only the north-western state of Piedmont possessed limited autonomy. A growing number of Italians, inspired by the French Revolution, conspired to expel the hated foreigners. They called for the 'Risorgimento' or 'revival' of Italy. After 1830 Giuseppe Mazzini assumed leadership of this liberation movement.

Always dressed in black as a sign of mourning for his oppressed country, Mazzini advocated an uprising against the Austrians to create a united republic, with Rome as its capital. Although his attempts failed, his role as prophet and propagandist was crucial.

Garibaldi receives a hero's welcome on landing at Marsala with his 'Red Shirts' in 1860 (right).

Metternich regarded Mazzini as 'the most dangerous man in Europe', and Italian moderates too deplored his aims. They planned a federal Italy in which the princes could retain their thrones and the pope would be president. Piedmontese liberals such as Camillo Cavour believed in creating an independent Italy with their own kingdom as its nucleus.

The revolutions which swept through most of Europe in 1848 provided an ideal opportunity for the Mazzinians, the federalists and the Piedmontese to pursue their aims. The Austrians appeared unable to maintain control in Italy, but political differences prevented a united effort while the peasant masses wanted no part in the unrest. Pope Pius IX, believed to be liberal and nationalist, proved to be neither and turned against the Risorgimento. His decision virtually ruined the federalist cause.

The Piedmontese army advanced against the Austrians but was twice defeated. Mazzini returned from exile and was joined by Giuseppe Garibaldi, already a legendary guerrilla fighter who had fought for an independent Uruguay. Together, Mazzini and Garibaldi defended the Roman Republic established after the pope's flight. Although eventually defeated by the French, Garibaldi's heroic exploits captured the world's imagination.

THE YEAR OF MIRACLES
During the remainder of 1849 the Austrians restored the old rulers. But Piedmont retained its constitution, and prime minister Cavour transformed his country into a modern, liberal state, well equipped to lead a second war of independence. Cavour's diplomatic skill secured an alliance with Napoleon III, leading to a successful war in 1859 which forced the Austrians out of Lombardy and secured the liberation of central Italy.

The 'year of miracles' was 1860. Against all odds, Garibaldi and 1000 volunteers, the 'Red Shirts', conquered Sicily and Naples and presented them to Cavour's master, Victor Emmanuel III of Piedmont. In 1861 he was proclaimed king of a united Italy. Rome became the capital in 1870. 'We have made Italy,' it was said. 'Now we must make Italians.'

A small minority of Italians had created a united state which could claim to be both liberal and national. Regionalism, Church-State conflict and class war remained constant threats to its unity, and they persisted throughout the next century. But the memory of the Risorgimento and the respect felt for its three leading personalities has helped successive generations of Italians to preserve their national unity.

Italians head for Piedmont, celebrating their success after voting for unification in 1860.

(Indian), and Chinese empires provided trade routes from most of Europe to India and the Far East.

In Roman Britain major highways, comprising several thick layers of stone and drained by side ditches, fanned out from London. These included Watling Street, built in the mid 1st century AD to link Dover with London, St Albans and Chester. Roman methods of construction, and poor maintenance prevailed until the arrival of the Scottish engineers Thomas TELFORD and John Loudon MCADAM in the 18th century. They developed a more refined form of construction, dispensing with large and expensive foundation blocks and introducing a thinner surface with improved drainage. Tarmacadam dates from the 1830s, when tar was first used in Nottinghamshire to bind the surface stones.

By the 1920s highways designed specifically for heavy and fast traffic were being built in the USA, Germany and Italy. In Britain at this time some dual carriageways were constructed, but it was not until the late 1950s that work began on a motorway network. Concrete and other hard-wearing compounds have been introduced, and machinery developed to speed up construction.

robber baron Ruthlessly aggressive businessman. The term was first applied to a feudal lord who robbed travellers passing through his domain. In the USA, financiers who made fortunes during the American Civil War and thereafter exploited the stock market, railways and public utilities became known as 'robber barons'. A notable example was Jay Gould (1836-92), who made $25 million out of railway and bullion speculation. Cornelius VANDERBILT made an even larger fortune of some $100 million out of railways.

Robert I (Robert the Bruce) (1274-1329) King of the Scots from 1306, who won a decisive victory over England at the Battle of BANNOCKBURN in 1314. Robert seized the crown and gradually extended his control over Scotland, which was partly occupied by the English. His victory over EDWARD II at Bannockburn secured his position on the throne but hostilities with England did not end until the Treaty of Northampton in 1328, when EDWARD III recognised Robert as king and confirmed Scotland's independence. Robert was succeeded by his son, DAVID II. Legend

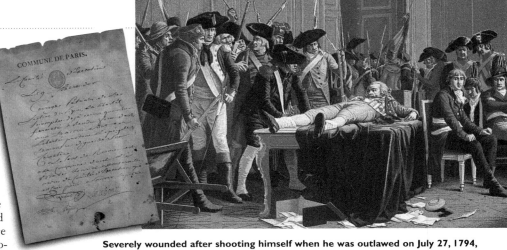

Severely wounded after shooting himself when he was outlawed on July 27, 1794, Robespierre wrote a bloodstained appeal. But he was arrested and guillotined the next day.

has it that Robert was a fugitive, his fortunes low, when he was inspired to fight on by the persistence of a spider building a web.

Robert II (1316-90) First Stewart king of the Scots, from 1371, who inherited the throne from his uncle, DAVID II. Robert was the son of Walter, Steward of Scotland, and Marjory, daughter of ROBERT I. As regent while David was in exile in France and imprisoned in England, he spent many years leading the Scottish nationalists against the invading armies of Edward III. Shortly after his accession Robert concluded a treaty with CHARLES V of France which reaffirmed the Franco-Scottish alliance.

Robert III (c.1337-1406) King of the Scots from 1390. Robert, christened John, was the eldest son of ROBERT II. As a result of a kick from a horse, Robert was an invalid, and his reign was marked by a struggle for power between his brother, Robert, Duke of Albany, and his eldest son, David, Duke of Rothesay. Rothesay became lieutenant of Scotland in 1398; his fall and death in 1402 brought Albany to power. Robert, fearing for the safety of his younger son James (later JAMES I of Scotland), sent him to France, only to die on hearing news of James's capture by the English.

Robertson, Sir William Robert (1860-1933) British field-marshal, the first officer from the ranks to pass through the Staff College, Camberley (1897), of which he later became commandant (1910). He served in intelligence in the Boer War in South Africa and as quartermaster-general of the

Robert I proudly rides at Bannockburn, site of his triumphant victory over the English in 1314.

British expeditionary force in France at the start of the First World War. Robertson became chief of the Imperial General Staff from 1915 until criticisms of British strategy by the prime minister, David LLOYD GEORGE, led to his resignation in 1918. He published his autobiography *From Private to Field-Marshal* in 1921.

Robespierre, Maximilien de (1758-94) French politician, a principal figure in the FRENCH REVOLUTION and leader of the JACOBIN Club. He supported the execution of LOUIS XVI in 1793, but was later overthrown and sent to the guillotine himself.

Robespierre trained as a lawyer and practised in Arras, championing the rights of the poor. At the age of 30 he was elected a deputy, and became influential in the National Assembly. Two years later he joined the Jacobin Club and began a bitter struggle with the powerful republican GIRONDINS. Noted for his honesty – Thomas Carlyle later called him 'the Seagreen Incorruptible' – Robespierre fought for social reform. He welcomed the Declaration of the RIGHTS OF MAN and became popular in Paris. He was instrumental in the overthrow of the Girondins in 1793 and was elected to the COMMITTEE OF PUBLIC SAFETY, the governing body of the Revolution.

Although Robespierre did not instigate the Reign of TERROR, he did support moves to rid the revolution of its enemies, denouncing the radicals and ordering executions. As Robespierre's power grew so did the ranks of his enemies, who disliked his dictatorial style and his so-called moderate policies. In July 1794 he was seized and beheaded.

Rob Roy (Robert MacGregor) (1671-1734) Scottish outlaw and cattle dealer. Rob Roy maintained a band of armed followers to protect his herds from frequent cattle raids. However, he and his men were not above plundering for themselves in the JACOBITE cause. He borrowed money from the Duke of

Montrose to engage in unsuccessful cattle speculation, and in 1712 he suffered financial ruin. His lands were seized by the duke, and Rob Roy declared war. In 1727 he was arrested and escaped transportation by the timely arrival of a pardon. His exploits are the subject of many stories, and Sir Walter Scott's novel *Rob Roy* (1818) was based on his life.

Rochdale Pioneers Lancashire weavers who founded the first consumers' Cooperative society in Toad Lane, Rochdale, in 1844. The Rochdale Society of Equitable Pioneers was based on the theories of the social reformer Robert OWEN (1771-1858). The 28 weavers opened a grocery store, each contributing £1 towards buying supplies and dividing the profits. The store was followed by a cooperative factory and textile mill, establishing the British cooperative movement.

Rockefeller, John D. (1839-1937) US industrialist and philanthropist and founder of the Standard Oil Company, one of the USA's first monopolies. Rockefeller was born in Richford, New York. He entered business in 1858 as a partner in a firm dealing in hay and grains. Five years later, seeing the potential of the expanding oil industry, he built a refinery in Ohio which became the nucleus of Standard Oil. By 1879 the company controlled 90 per cent of the nation's refining capacity, and in 1881 it became one of the first trusts in the USA, setting a precedent for other monopolies. The public's growing dislike of these monopolies led to the Sherman ANTI-TRUST Act of 1892 and the eventual division of Standard Oil in 1911 into 34 separate companies. A pious Baptist,

A German V-2 rocket stands in the abandoned underground assembly plant at Nordhausen in 1945. Both the Americans and Russians benefited from captured German rocket technology.

Rockefeller had turned to philanthropy by the 1890s, and established various organisations for the promotion of medical research and education such as the Rockefeller University in 1901, and the Rockefeller Foundation for 'the well-being of mankind' in 1913. He gave away $600 million in his lifetime. His work was continued by his son, John D. Rockefeller Jr (1874-1960), who bought for the United Nations the site for its headquarters in New York.

rocketry Rockets propelled by gunpowder were first used in China around AD 1300 as incendiary bombs; today, propelled by liquid fuel, they launch craft into space. Their use, both as fireworks and weapons, spread to Europe in the 14th century. The British artillery expert William Congreve (1772-1828) developed a rocket with a range of 9030 ft (2750 m), which was employed against France in 1806. At the end of the 19th century the possibility of using a rocket to thrust a capsule into space was mooted, and experiments led to the US physicist Robert H. Goddard launching the first liquid-fuelled rocket in 1926.

Rocket research made great advances during the Second World War, particularly in Germany where it was funded by the military authorities. Wernher von Braun developed the V-2 missile in 1942, and it was this technology that formed the basis of the Soviet Union's Earth satellites, *Sputnik 1* and *2*, launched in 1957. Advances in the USA produced the Saturn V booster rocket to launch the Apollo Moon missions in the 1960s and 1970s. In the 1980s in the USA the emphasis shifted towards a reusable launch vehicle, the space shuttle. The most powerful rocket of the 1990s is the Russian Energia

which can send 100 tonnes into orbit. Rockets have also been used over the centuries to fire lifelines and distress signals.

Rockingham, Charles Watson-Wentworth, 2nd Marquis of (1730-82) British prime minister from 1765 to 1766 and in 1782. Rockingham led a political group known as the Rockingham WHIGS which supported the American colonists' claim to independence from Britain. During his first term as prime minister Parliament repealed the STAMP ACT, which had imposed a much criticised tax on the colonists. Internal dissent within Rockingham's administration caused GEORGE III to replace him with William PITT. Rockingham led a vociferous opposition, and during his second short term of office he started peace negotiations with the colonists. On his death in office the Rockingham Whigs split into further factions, one of which developed into the new Whig Party.

Rodney, George Rodney, 1st Baron (1718-92) British admiral. Rodney gained his early naval expertise with the well-respected British admiral Edward Hawke, in Hawke's victory against the French off Cape Finisterre in 1747. As a rear-admiral in 1759 at Le Havre, Rodney destroyed the French flotilla poised to invade England in the SEVEN YEARS' WAR. His most notable victory was over the French in 1782 at the Battle of Les Saintes in the Caribbean, where he restored British supremacy at sea in the closing stages of the American War of Independence.

Rollo (c.860-932) Leader of a band of VIKINGS which invaded north-western France and an ancestor of William the Conqueror, who became a figure of legend in France as well as

Philanthropist John D. Rockefeller gives part of his fortune away as he takes his daily dose of oil. His oil company monopolised the industry.

in Scandinavia and Iceland. Rollo was the son of a Norse earl. He sailed south from Norway, landing marauding parties in Scotland, England, Ireland and France. In a peace settlement with Charles III of France in 911 he was offered the duchy of Normandy on the lower Seine. Rollo was baptised, gave land in Normandy to his followers, and began the chapter of NORMAN influence on Europe.

Roman Britain (AD43-410)

The Romans first raided Britain under Julius CAESAR in 55 and 54 BC, but their occupation did not begin until CLAUDIUS I invaded in AD43, attracted by the island's reputation for wealth. Some inhabitants were quick to absorb Roman ways. With their failure to conquer Scotland the Romans established barriers to contain them, HADRIAN'S WALL (122-126) and the Antonine Wall (142). Army veterans settled in Britain, as did traders, scholars, craftsmen and soldiers from all parts of the Roman Empire (see feature, pages 554-5). Eventually Christian bishoprics were established. Roman villas and ROADS abounded, but little Latin was spoken and the people remained essentially Celtic. In 406 and 409 the Britons rebelled against Roman rule. The Romans withdrew around 410, leaving a legacy of towns, including London, York, Chester and Bath, and a network of roads.

Roman Catholic Church

Largest branch of the Christian Church (see CHRISTIANITY) in the world, with about 960 million members. The Roman Catholic Church is under the jurisdiction of the pope, who as Bishop of Rome claims direct apostolic descent from St Peter as chief apostle, and his hierarchy of cardinals and bishops. One of the main differences between the Roman Catholic Church and other Christian denominations is that it claims the right to settle disputes over vital points of doctrine without consulting other bishops and Churches, a claim commonly known as 'papal infallibility'. In the vast majority of cases, the Roman Catholic Church insists that its priests remain unmarried.

In the early Christian centuries, the role of the Bishop of Rome grew in importance, especially in Western Europe. Disagreements about the proper extent of the pope's authority in the Church led to its final separation with the Eastern ORTHODOX CHURCH in 1054, and with the PROTESTANT Churches in the REFORMATION of the 16th century. It was at the time of the Reformation that the term Roman Catholic Church came into use, initially by Protestants as a way of implying that the Roman Catholic Church was only one branch of the Christian Church. The term was, in fact, acceptable to many Catholics, in that it asserted the primacy of the pope over Christians. Attempts to modernise the Church were resisted by Pope Pius X at the beginning of the 20th century, but the second Vatican Council (1962-5) introduced the use of everyday languages instead of Latin in the liturgy and set out to modernise the Church's teachings and organisation. Under JOHN PAUL II (1978-), friendly contacts between the Catholic Church and the Eastern Orthodox and Protestant Churches, and with other faiths, continue to be developed.

Roman Empire see feature, pages 554-5

Romania

Country in south-east Europe bordering the Black Sea, formed by the union of Wallachia and Moldavia in 1861, and bounded by Ukraine, Moldova, Bulgaria, Yugoslavia and Hungary. Romania is dominated by the Carpathian Mountains in the north-west which level out to the plains of the River Danube in the south-east. The capital is Bucharest. The area of present-day Romania was first populated by Illyrians, Thracians and Scythians. Greek colonies appeared on the Black Sea coast in the 7th century BC. Dacians, Romans and Goths followed.

The states of Wallachia and Moldavia were founded in the 14th century and absorbed into the OTTOMAN EMPIRE in the 15th century. Moldavia (Bessarabia) fell to Russia in 1812. The Congress of BERLIN in 1878 recognised Romania's independence, and CAROL I (1881-1914) became king. Romania joined the Allies in the First World War and was rewarded by the doubling of its territories. Ferdinand I (1914-27) succeeded Carol I, and CAROL II (1930-40) imposed a fascist regime. He was forced to cede much territory to the AXIS POWERS in 1940.

Romanian forces cooperated with the German armies in the Second World War, but with the advance of the Red Army lost land to the USSR and Bulgaria. After the war Romania became a Soviet satellite; a republic was proclaimed, dominated by the Communist Party. The country retained a degree of independence, which increased when Nicolae Ceauşescu became president (1967-89). He imposed a ruthless regime. During 1989 a movement towards democracy culminated in the execution of Ceauşescu and his wife on December 25. A National Salvation Front (NSF) was formed, led by Ion Iliescu, who was elected president. Romania moved towards a market economy, a new constitution was adopted in 1991 and the Eastern Orthodox Church was legalised. Demonstrations against steeply rising prices were crushed by a government composed mainly of former communists. In spite of opposition, Iliescu

retained power in the 1992 presidential election, having secured a $748 million loan from the International Monetary Fund.

Romanov

Ruling house of Russia from 1613 until the revolution of 1917. The dynasty began with the accession of Tsar Michael Romanov who ruled until 1645, followed by Alexis (1645-76) and Fyodor III (1676-82). Under these tsars Russia emerged as the major Slavic power. PETER THE GREAT, sole ruler from 1689 to 1725, and CATHERINE THE GREAT, who ruled from 1762 to 1796, established Russia as a great power in Europe. The last tsar, Nicholas II, was forced to abdicate in 1917. Nicholas and his family were murdered in 1918, and the other Romanovs fled or faced execution.

The orator Cicero saves the Roman republic by alerting the senate to a conspiracy planned by the demagogue Catiline, who intended to seize power. Cicero's rhetoric forced Catiline to flee.

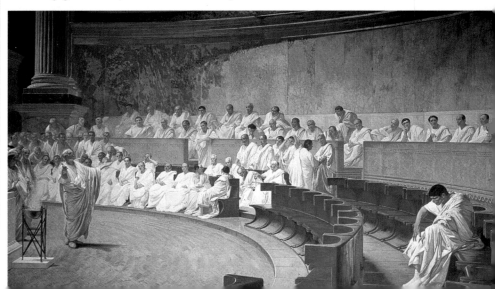

Lord Byron, Leigh Hunt and John Trelawny mourn at the funeral pyre of their fellow Romantic, the poet Percy Bysshe Shelley, who was drowned in a sudden squall off the Italian coast in 1822.

Roman republic Roman state which existed for 400 years after the expulsion of Lucius TARQUIN, the last Etruscan king of Rome, in 510 BC. Lucius BRUTUS, who had led the rising against Tarquin, established a republican government centred on Rome, and the power previously held by the monarchy gave way to that of the landed aristocracy, the PATRICIANS, who ruled through two chief magistrates or consuls, appointed for brief periods in rotation, and a senate. The lower classes, plebeians, had their own representatives. The reputed modesty of the rulers was exemplified by Lucius CINCINNATUS who, when a messenger arrived in 460 BC to tell him he had been chosen as consul, was found ploughing on his farm.

Marcus CATO (234-149 BC), known as 'Censor' because of his devotion to duty, attempted to retain the simple lifestyle in the face of Greek refinement and luxury. This system of rule did not suit the autocratic generals who, in a time of overseas expansion – including the Punic Wars for control of the Mediterranean which led to Rome's victory over its great rival, CARTHAGE – were used to wielding great power abroad. The last of these commanders, Octavius (see AUGUSTUS CAESAR), became the sole ruler by appearing to combine republican ideas with military power, and so the Roman Empire (see feature, pages 554-5) succeeded the republic.

Romanticism Literary and artistic movement which originated in Europe in the late 18th century. Romanticism emphasised individual emotions and imagination against the claims of reason and intellect that had characterised the preceding period. The movement developed at the time of the French Revolution as a reaction to the strict rules of classicism, and reached its peak in Britain, France and Germany in the early 19th century. In painting Romanticism exuded passion, imagination and a love of the exotic, with an emphasis on natural beauty and the supernatural, as represented in the work of the French artist Eugène DELACROIX (1798-1863). In literature and music, emotional expression was seen as more important than formal structure; such writers as Lord BYRON, Percy Bysshe Shelley, Sir Walter Scott, William Wordsworth, Johann GOETHE and Honoré de BALZAC, among others, were at the centre of the movement, which influenced composers such as Hector Berlioz, Franz Liszt, Robert Schumann, Frédéric CHOPIN and Richard WAGNER.

Rome Capital of Italy on the River Tiber and bishopric of the pope. Rome was once the heart of the Roman Empire (see feature, pages 554-5), and evidence of the ancient city still exists, including the Colosseum and the Forum. According to tradition, the twins Romulus (after whom the city was named) and Remus began the first settlement on the Palatine Hill, one of the seven hills on which the city was built, in 753 BC. Etruscans dominated in the 6th century BC, introducing art and culture, a coinage and the Greek alphabet, all of which were refined by the Romans. Overseas expansion under the ROMAN REPUBLIC and early empire brought great wealth to Rome. According to the Roman historian Suetonius, the Emperor AUGUSTUS claimed to have 'found the city brick and left it marble.'

As the empire declined, the seat of power moved to Constantinople. Rome remained a centre of Christianity from the 6th century AD, and as such was ruled by the PAPACY. Its influence on art, culture and law spread throughout Europe, and in the 16th century it became a focal point of the RENAISSANCE. It was occupied by the French from 1789 to 1867. In 1870 Rome was declared capital of a newly unified Italy; the pope moved into the VATICAN CITY, which became an independent ecclesiastical state in its own right in 1929.

Rome, Treaties of (1957) Two international agreements which established the European Economic Community, later the EUROPEAN UNION, and Euratom (European Atomic Energy Commission). They were signed in Rome by Belgium, France, Italy, Luxembourg, the Netherlands and the Federal Republic of Germany. The treaties included provisions for the free movement of labour and capital between member countries, the abolition of customs barriers and the fostering of common agricultural and trading policies. New members of the European Community would be required to adhere to the terms of these treaties. Euratom's function was to establish cooperation in nuclear research. The treaties remain the basis for all moves towards closer political and economic union among European states.

Rommel, Erwin (1891-1944) German field-marshal. Rommel distinguished himself in the Second World War by leading a German Panzer division in a militarily acclaimed assault on France in 1940. The following year he was promoted to command the Afrika Korps, a tank formation sent to aid Italian campaigns in Libya. In 1942 he advanced to El-ALAMEIN, but was defeated by the British and forced to retreat. Adolf HITLER appointed him to take charge of coastal defences in northern France in 1944 in anticipation of an Allied invasion. He was subsequently wounded in the NORMANDY CAMPAIGN and recalled to Germany. The Gestapo, suspecting Rommel of being involved in the JULY PLOT against Hitler, offered him the choice of death by firing squad or suicide. Rommel committed suicide by taking poison.

Rommel's tactical skills earned him his opponents' admiration in France and North Africa, where he was nicknamed 'Desert Fox'.

The power and the glory of Rome

A modest settlement on the banks of the River Tiber in Italy grew 2000 years ago into a mighty empire centred on the Mediterranean. Its impact on the culture, language and politics of Europe is still felt today.

The Roman Empire was the greatest of the ancient world. At its height it stretched from the Atlantic Ocean in the west to the Syrian desert in the east, and from the Sahara in the south to the Rhine estuary and Scottish lowlands in the north. It has left us an enduring legacy of monuments, literature and institutions; vivid characters such as Augustus and Nero; and a mass of historical evidence.

The Romans did not set out to create an empire, but their reserves of manpower, rigid military discipline and determination in adversity gave them the upper hand in conflict after conflict. They soon learned that conquests brought security and wealth.

THE CARTHAGINIANS DEFEATED

The first phase of Roman expansion was the conquest of the Italian peninsula. It was largely complete by 264 BC, when the Romans took up arms against the Carthaginians over control of the island of Sicily. Victory over the Carthaginians in the First Punic War (264-241) was won only by Rome becoming a naval as well as a land-based power. The Romans' first important overseas acquisitions after the Second Punic War (218-201) were southern Spain and a foothold on the shore of the Adriatic. During the 2nd century BC they took Greece, Macedonia and Tunisia (146) and western Asia Minor (133).

These possessions turned Rome from an Italian into a Mediterranean power. Although Rome was now the centre of an empire, it was not ruled by an emperor: it remained a republic until the late 1st century BC. Power rested in the hands of the senate (an assembly of leading citizens) and of annually elected magistrates who performed a variety of government functions. The

Trajan built the city of Timgad in conquered territory in North Africa for veteran legionnaires who had served in the area.

most important of the magistrates were the consuls, who presided over senate meetings and were also supreme commanders in wartime. The overseas territories were organised into provinces ruled by a governor (often an ex-consul) appointed by the senate.

Changes came in the 1st century BC, when a series of powerful generals used their military followings to undermine the republic. Among these was Sulla, a supporter of aristocratic privilege, who ruled as uncrowned king of Rome from 82 to 79. He was followed by Pompey and then Julius Caesar. Caesar conquered Gaul during the Gallic Wars from 58 to 51, and defeated Pompey at the Battle of Pharsalus in 48 to become 'dictator' and undisputed ruler of Rome. Opposition to Caesar's government resulted in his murder in 44 by conspirators led by Brutus and Cassius.

A centurion such as Marcus Facilis (right) would be promoted on merit to command 100 men.

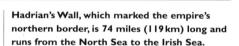

Hadrian's Wall, which marked the empire's northern border, is 74 miles (119 km) long and runs from the North Sea to the Irish Sea.

The assassins may have thought they had 'saved' or 'restored' the republic, but the rule of one man had by now become inevitable. After Caesar's death, two rivals jockeyed for power: Octavian, Caesar's adopted son, and Mark Antony. For a while they co-existed in peace, dividing the empire between them. Antony took control of the eastern provinces, where he became romantically involved with Cleopatra, queen of Egypt, while Octavian ruled the west. In 31 Octavian felt strong enough to force the issue, and defeated Antony and Cleopatra at the sea battle of Actium. Four years later, Octavian was accepted by the senate as the constitutional first citizen of Rome, with control of the army and all the key provinces. Taking the title Augustus, he became the first in a line of Roman emperors which was to last in the west until AD 476, and in the east until the fall of Byzantium (Constantinople) to the Ottoman Turks in 1453.

The empire governed by Augustus had grown considerably during the 1st century BC. It now included most of Asia Minor and Syria (added by Pompey), Gaul (added by Julius Caesar) and Egypt (conquered by Augustus himself). Roman rule

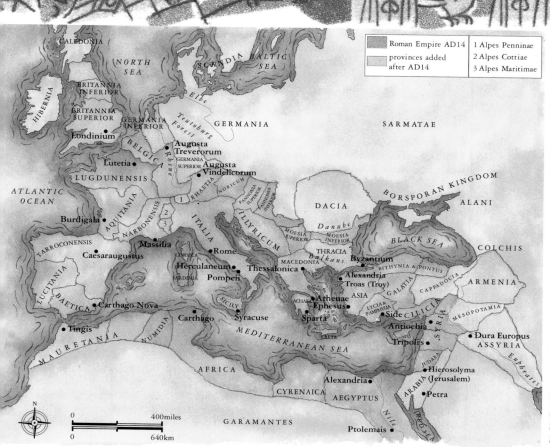

At its greatest extent under the Emperor Trajan (98-117), the empire stretched from northern Britain to southern Egypt and from the Iberian peninsula to the shores of the Caspian Sea.

stretched to every corner of the Mediterranean. Augustus embarked on a programme to establish strong natural frontiers – campaigning in the Balkans, for example, to conquer all the lands up to the Danube. In Germany, he attempted to extend the frontier to the Elbe, but withdrew to the Rhine again when three of his legions were annihilated by the Germans at the Teutoburg Forest in AD 9. When Augustus died five years later, he warned his successor not to expand the empire beyond the frontiers he had set, though further territories were gradually added, especially during the reigns of Claudius (54-68), Trajan (98-117) and Septimius Severus (193-211).

The reign of Augustus was a golden age for the arts. He considered patronage to be one of his duties as first citizen, and gave support and encouragement to Horace, Virgil and Livy. Other wealthy Romans added their patronage of the poets and historians of the day. The greatest literary product was Virgil's *Aeneid*, an epic poem which retold the origins of Rome in the legend of Aeneas fleeing the sacking of Troy to make a new beginning in Italy. Augustus also took pains to make the city of Rome a capital worthy of a great

empire. Rome by this time had outstripped Alexandria to become the largest city of the western world, with a population of about a million. Alongside dynastic monuments such as his new Forum, Augustus built aqueducts and reorganised the grain supply, the regular shipment of grain at state expense on which the urban poor depended.

THE EMPIRE AT ITS HEIGHT

Roman culture continued to flourish under Augustus' successors: the dour Tiberius, the autocratic Caligula, the eccentric Claudius and the art-loving Nero. The wealth of Italy during this period is reflected in the remains of cities and villas such as those of Pompeii and Herculaneum, and in luxury metalwork and jewellery. Italian merchants and entrepreneurs, stimulated by home demand and sheltered by Roman prestige, travelled far afield in search of new commercial opportunities, establishing small colonies as distant as Arikamedu in southern India.

At the same time, provincials began to take on an increasingly prominent role in the government of the empire. During the 2nd century AD provinces such as Spain and North Africa (modern Tunisia) became the wealthiest regions of the empire,

outstripping Italy itself. It was a time of relative stability, though frontier wars were a recurrent problem. Emperor Trajan made vast conquests in the east, taking Roman control briefly as far as the Persian Gulf. Most of these territories were abandoned by Hadrian (117-138), who adopted a policy of consolidation, exemplified by the wall he built across northern Britain to shield the Roman province from 'barbarian' invaders from the north. The army became increasingly a frontier garrison, with the redoubtable legions each based in a permanent stone-built fort. This meant that units had to be withdrawn from other sectors to raise a field army for any campaign. The problem was only solved with the creation of a permanent field army, separate from the frontier forces, in the 3rd century.

By the middle of the 3rd century the empire was in crisis. Internal unrest and external invasion brought it to its knees. In the east, a powerful new neighbour, the Sassanian empire of Persia, invaded Syria. In north and west, Germanic peoples including Goths and Alamanni crossed the Rhine and Danube to raid deep into Roman territory. Faced by these threats, the imperial government became increasingly militarised and autocratic, and the empire less prosperous. Italy and the provinces were now on an equal footing: since 212, full Roman citizenship had been extended to all provincials save women and slaves.

The empire weathered the 3rd century crisis and was strengthened and reorganised by powerful rulers such as Diocletian (284-305) and Constantine (306-337), who rejected the traditional Roman gods in favour of Christianity as the state religion. Constantine also founded a new imperial capital at Byzantium in the east. The empire survived broadly intact until 395, when it was officially divided. The eastern half lived on as the Byzantine empire until 1453, but the western provinces fell to Germanic invaders during the 5th century. The last western emperor, Romulus Augustulus, abdicated in 476, and Italy itself became a Germanic kingdom. So too did Britain, France, Spain and (for a while) North Africa. Yet key elements of Roman culture lived on. Latin, for example, was not only the language of the church but the origin of most west European languages, and Roman law has remained the basis of most western legal systems up to the present day.

Eleanor Roosevelt believed passionately that the lack of human rights the world over was a major cause of friction between nations.

Roosevelt, Eleanor (1884-1962) US humanitarian and United Nations diplomat, wife of President Franklin D. ROOSEVELT. Eleanor Roosevelt was actively involved in human rights projects, and advised her husband on social policy. Following the president's death in 1945, his successor, Harry S TRUMAN, appointed her as a delegate to the UNITED NATIONS, where as chairman of the UN Commission on Human Rights in 1947 she played a major role in the drafting and adoption of the UN's Universal Declaration of Human Rights (1948). When Eleanor Roosevelt died, US statesman Adlai Stevenson said of her: 'She would rather light candles than curse the darkness, and her glow has warmed the world.'

Roosevelt, Franklin Delano see feature, page 557

Roosevelt, Theodore (1858-1919) Republican president of the USA from 1901 to 1909. Roosevelt was born in New York and educated at Harvard College. He was elected to the New York State Assembly in 1881, and became assistant secretary of the US Navy in 1897. Roosevelt raised and commanded the volunteer ROUGH RIDERS cavalry to fight in the SPANISH-AMERICAN WAR in Cuba in 1898, and became a hero for his exploits. On his return home he was elected governor of New York. Roosevelt was nominated vice-president in 1900, and the assassination of William MCKINLEY the following year brought him the presidency. Roosevelt introduced the Square Deal (1902) to regulate business monopolies, secured US control of the construction of the PANAMA CANAL in 1903 and won the Nobel peace prize for his role in negotiations to end the Russo-Japanese War (1904-5). In 1904 he was overwhelmingly elected president in his own right. His introduction of the Pure Food and Drug Act in 1906 was one of the first moves towards modern consumer protection. In reaction to the conservative policies of his successor, William TAFT, he formed a splinter group of Republicans, the PROGRESSIVE or 'Bull Moose' Party, but failed to regain the presidency in 1912.

Root, Elihu (1845-1937) US statesman and diplomat, and Nobel peace prize winner in 1912 for his promotion of international arbitration. A Republican, Root was secretary of war from 1899 to 1904. He reorganised the army and formulated the Platt Amendment of 1902 which gave the USA greater control over Cuba. As secretary of state under Theodore ROOSEVELT from 1905 to 1909 he negotiated the Root-Takahira Agreement of 1908 in which Japan agreed to uphold the Open Door Policy which furthered US commercial interests in China. Root opposed US neutrality at the outbreak of the First World War in 1914 and supported the Allied cause.

Root-and-Branch Petition (1640) Document drawn up by a London alderman, Isaac Pennington, calling for the abolition, 'with all its dependencies, roots and branches', of the government of the Church by bishops. The 15 000 signatures testified to the Puritan radicalism of some London citizens. A Root-and-Branch Bill was introduced into the LONG PARLIAMENT in May 1641, supported by John PYM. It was dropped in favour of more urgent measures such as the GRAND REMONSTRANCE, a catalogue of grievances against CHARLES I.

Rosebery, Archibald, 5th Earl of (1847-1929) British Liberal prime minister from 1894 to 1895. Rosebery served in William GLADSTONE's Cabinet as foreign secretary in 1886 and from 1892 to 1894. He briefly became prime minister on Gladstone's retirement, until the defeat of his government in the 1895 general election. His support for British imperialism alienated many Liberal supporters. Rosebery published biographies on the Earl of CHATHAM, Chatham's son William PITT, NAPOLEON and Sir Robert PEEL. He was also a successful racehorse owner; his horses won the Derby three times.

Roses, Wars of the (1455-85) Sporadic fighting for possession of the throne of England between the House of York, whose badge was a white rose, and the House of Lancaster, symbolised by a red rose. Both houses claimed the crown through their descent from EDWARD III, and armed conflict was sparked by bitter rivalry between the Lancastrian Edmund BEAUFORT (1406-55), Duke of Somerset, and Richard, 3rd Duke of YORK. Beaufort was a close supporter of the simple-minded HENRY VI and his ambitious queen MARGARET OF ANJOU. Richard, protector of the realm during Henry's illness (1453-5) and eager to protect his power, backed by the Earl of Warwick, became their opponent.

In 1455 Richard won the first Battle of ST ALBANS. An uneasy truce lasted until 1459 when further fighting erupted. YORKIST successes were followed by the death of Richard in a surprise attack by the LANCASTRIANS at the Battle of Wakefield in 1460. Henry VI's supporters won a further victory at the second Battle of St Albans in February 1461. In the

> **❝ England is the best place to conduct your affairs. Neither the countryside nor the people are destroyed. Disaster and misfortune fall only on those who make war – the soldiers and the nobles. ❞**
>
> *Philippe de Commynes (c.1447-1511), French political commentator, on the Wars of the Roses*

same month, Richard's son, Edward, defeated the Lancastrians at Mortimer's Cross in Herefordshire, marched to London and was proclaimed king as EDWARD IV, the first Yorkist king. He defeated Margaret's forces at Towton on March 29, and Margaret fled to Scotland with her husband and son.

In 1470 a Lancastrian invasion led by the disaffected Earl of Warwick restored Henry VI to the throne, but in 1471 Edward regained it at the Battle of Barnet. Margaret was captured and most of the Lancastrian leaders were killed at TEWKESBURY in May 1471, but the struggle ended only in 1485 when Henry Tudor defeated RICHARD III at BOSWORTH FIELD. The following year, as HENRY VII, he married Edward IV's daughter, Elizabeth of York, to unite the two houses.

The Wars of the Roses turned in the Yorkists' favour at the Battle of Tewkesbury in 1471. The Lancastrian heir, the Prince of Wales, was slain.

A New Deal for the USA

Franklin D. Roosevelt was the only US president to be elected to four terms of office. He led his country out of the Depression and to victory in war.

In 1933 the Democrat Franklin D. Roosevelt swept into the White House ready to solve the daunting problems of the Great Depression. Born in 1882 into a political family, Roosevelt's career had almost been wrecked in 1921 by polio. For the rest of his life he could not walk unaided. But what followed his election was the most innovative reform wave ever to roll over the USA.

This was his New Deal, a series of measures to provide a federal dole and launch public works projects to sustain the millions of jobless. The government borrowed to fund investment and devised ways to stabilise industry, agriculture and banking. Reaching beyond the immediate crisis, it sought to end business abuses and create opportunities for organised labour. Its crowning achievement was the 1935 Social Security Act, which provided old age pensions, unemployment insurance and aid to the disabled and to poor families.

Despised by most business leaders and by upper middle class conservatives, Roosevelt became a hero to poorer Americans, including many Blacks

Roosevelt joins Uncle Sam on a wartime poster (left). The extent of his disability was kept from the public.

who had traditionally voted Republican. In 1936 he was re-elected by a landslide.

Despite the support of millions, it had become clear by 1938 that the New Deal would not restore full employment. But by this time he was becoming absorbed by the emerging crisis that followed the rise of

Adolf Hitler. Americans wanted no part of Europe's problems, but Roosevelt struggled to induce Congress and voters into supporting an active role for the USA in checking fascism. After the fall of France in 1940, he manoeuvred a reluctant nation into an alliance with Britain as a provider of arms and naval support on the vital North Atlantic sea lanes.

On December 7, 1941, angry at America's efforts to block their expansion in Asia, the Japanese attacked the American Pacific fleet at Pearl Harbor in Hawaii. Three days later the USA was at war with Germany and Italy as well. For the next four years, in collaboration with Britain's Winston Churchill and Russia's Joseph Stalin, Roosevelt led the Grand Alliance against the Axis powers. As war president, he converted the USA into the 'arsenal of democracy'. Despite Japan's early gains in the Pacific, he accepted a Europe-first approach that led to Germany's defeat in early 1945. He believed that the Allied powers could continue to cooperate after the war and accommodated Soviet demands at the Yalta Conference in 1945.

He did not live to see the peace. On April 12, 1945, just as the Allied armies converged on Germany's heart, Roosevelt died of a stroke. The nation mourned the man who had restored hope to millions and helped to defeat the greatest threat that liberal democracy had ever known.

Rosetta Stone Slab of black basalt bearing an inscription in three languages of a decree of Ptolemy V written in 197 BC. The Rosetta Stone provided the key to deciphering Egyptian HIEROGLYPHS. It was found in 1799 near the town of Rosetta in Egypt by a French soldier. Its three inscriptions are in Greek, Egyptian demotic and Egyptian hieroglyphs. By comparing the three texts Thomas Young and Jean-François Champollion finally unlocked the secrets of hieroglyphs in 1821, giving access for the first time to the written history of ancient Egyptian civilisation.

Rosicrucian Member of a secret religious society active in the 17th and 18th centuries. Rosicrucians claimed to have discovered a secret and ancient form of esoteric and anti-Catholic Christianity. They venerated the emblems of the rose and the cross as symbols of Jesus Christ's resurrection. Two anonymous texts published in Germany between 1604 and 1614, now generally attributed to the

Lutheran Pastor J.V. Andreae (1586-1654), are thought to have launched the movement. The works were intended to be satirical, but were taken seriously. The most notable text, the *Account of the Brotherhood*, told of a mythical German knight of the 15th century, Christian Rosenkreutz – possibly the author – who travelled extensively to learn the wisdom of the East before he founded the order. The English physician and mystic Robert Fludd later helped to spread Rosicrucian ideas with his treatise *Apologia Compendiaria Fraternitatem de Rosea Croce* in 1616. The modern Rosicrucian Order is devoted to the application of esoteric religious doctrine to everday life.

Roskilde, Treaty of (1658) Settlement which obliged Denmark to surrender to Sweden land it had held for many centuries in southern Scandinavia. The treaty gave

> **DID YOU KNOW?**
>
> *Queen Elizabeth I's favourite scientist and astrologer, Dr John Dee, was influenced by the Rosicrucians. Elizabeth fixed the day of her coronation on Dee's astrological advice.*

Halland, Scania, Blekinge, the island of Bornholm and the Norwegian territories of Trondheim and Bohuslän to Sweden, thus evicting Denmark from the Swedish mainland for the last time. It ended the war between Sweden and Denmark (1657-8), during which Charles X of Sweden had marched his army across the ice to attack Denmark.

Rothschild Banking family which exerted considerable influence on both the economic and political affairs of Europe during the 19th and early 20th centuries. The Rothschild banking house was founded in the 18th century by Mayer Amschel Rothschild (1744-1812), a Frankfurt moneylender. He and his five sons set up prosperous business houses in London, Paris, Vienna and Naples, and negotiated some of the most notable European government loans of the 19th century. Mayer's son

Waddesdon Manor, Bucks, was built with the Rothschild fortune. The shadow of Nathan Rothschild (right), missed by his London colleagues, remains in the City after his death.

Nathan (1777-1836) established the London branch in 1804; his son, Lionel (1808-79), became the first Jew to sit in the British House of Commons in 1858.

Lionel lent the British Government £4 million in 1875 to buy the SUEZ CANAL shares. His son, Nathan (1840-1915), the first Jewish British peer, was regarded as the unofficial head of French and British Jews. It was to his son Lionel Walter (1868-1937), the second baron, a scientist, scholar and the chairman of the British Zionist Federation, that the BALFOUR DECLARATION was addressed in 1917 concerning a national home for Jews in Palestine.

His daughter, Miriam (1908-), is a distinguished entomologist. Lionel's nephew, Nathaniel (1910-90) was also a scientist and head of the British Government's central policy review staff from 1971 to 1974. In the 1990s, the 50 or so living descendants of Mayer Rothschild have maintained the family tradition of banking, and also support charities and the arts.

rotten borough

British constituencies whose population had virtually disappeared by 1832, generally through migration to cities, but which were still entitled to elect Members of Parliament. There were some 148 such boroughs at that time, 50 of which had fewer then 50 voters. This made it easy for landowners to secure the election of MPs favourable to their interests, making the boroughs 'rotten' with bribery and coercion. The constituency of Old Sarum had two seats in Parliament, though it had just seven voters. Rotten boroughs were abolished by the REFORM ACT of 1832.

Rough Riders

Popular name for the 1st Volunteer Cavalry Regiment that fought for the USA in the SPANISH-AMERICAN WAR of 1898. This band of cowboys, miners and college students, among others, was largely recruited by Theodore ROOSEVELT, who left his position as assistant secretary of the navy to become lieutenant-colonel under the leadership of Colonel Leonard Wood. Their most notable exploit was a successful uphill charge on foot during the Battle of Santiago in Cuba in July 1898.

Roundheads

Term applied to Puritans and Parliamentarians during and after the ENGLISH CIVIL WAR (1642-51). The Puritans showed their disapproval of the fashion for long hair among CHARLES I's Cavaliers by adopting a close-cropped style. It is thought that the term originated as a form of abuse during parliamentary debates in 1641.

Round Table Conferences

Meetings held in London from 1930 to 1932 between British and Indian representatives to discuss the constitution of India. The conferences formed the basis of the 1935 Government of India Act, which planned a federal organisation involving the Princely States, and autonomy for the provinces. The first session (November 1930-January 1931) agreed on the federal principle. It was attended by 73 representatives from India, but was boycotted by the Indian National CONGRESS which was conducting a Non-Cooperation Campaign against the British Government. Following the Gandhi-Irwin Pact of March 1931, Mohandas GANDHI attended the second session (September-December 1931). With the renewal of non-cooperation, Gandhi was imprisoned and Congress took no part in the final session (November-December 1932).

Rousseau, Jean-Jacques
see feature, page 559

Rowntree, Joseph

(1801-59) British businessman and philanthropist. At the age of 21 Rowntree founded a grocery shop in York, which later developed into a family cocoa and chocolate manufacturing firm. He was a Quaker, and showed a keen interest in civic affairs and education. Rowntree's son, also Joseph (1836-1925), became a partner in the firm with his brother, Henry Isaac. Joseph consulted his employees about conditions and provided housing, unemployment insurance and pensions. In 1904 he founded the Joseph Rowntree Village Trust, which still supports research into social policy and housing. Seebohm Rowntree (1871-1954) continued in

Reformers hack at the tree of rotten boroughs in this cartoon by George Cruikshank, while its corrupt defenders crowd the other side to prop it up, fearful of losing their livelihoods.

Confessions of a radical

Jean-Jacques Rousseau argued that civilisation had corrupted man – 'the noble savage'. All institutions were flawed: the sovereignty of a nation rested with its people alone. Few thinkers have been more influential.

The philosopher Jean-Jacques Rousseau (1712-78) is best known for his ideas about political theory. He said that all people are born free and equal, and that a just state must protect the dignity of all its citizens without distinction of birth or rank. 'Man is born free; and everywhere he is in chains,' he wrote in his most famous work, *Du contrat social* (*The Social Contract*), published in 1762. Rousseau's defence of the rights of common people against entrenched privilege made him, along with Voltaire, a principal figure of the Enlightenment, the movement committed to clearing away the mysteries of religion and superstition and replacing them with rational inquiry.

Rousseau's criticism of the Roman Catholic Church in his book *Émile* (also of 1762) resulted in his persecution, and he suffered prolonged mental illness after fleeing Paris to avoid imprisonment. He spent 17 months in England from January 1766, but returned to France still convinced he was being victimised. His personality was marked by paranoid suspicion.

Émile is principally a treatise on education, describing the upbringing of an imaginary pupil, stating that people are by nature good, but are corrupted by social contact. To prevent this, children should as far as possible be left free to develop at their own pace and on their own terms. Only when self-reliant should they take their place in society, for then they will not be sucked into envious and competitive relationships.

ROUSSEAU'S DARK SECRET

When he was 56 Rousseau married his long-time mistress Thérèse Levasseur. He almost certainly sent their children to the foundling hospital to be brought up. This allegation created scandal in his lifetime, and causes many to question his status as an expert in child-rearing.

An illustration from his *Confessions* shows Rousseau releasing rabbits on an island, back into the nature he loved.

His autobiography, *Confessions*, remains one of the most candid and self-revealing books ever written. Among lesser-known aspects of his work are his achievements as a composer (including an opera performed at Versailles in 1745); his writings on botany, a study he loved; and his novel of torrid and illicit passion, *La Nouvelle Héloïse* (1761).

Although born in Geneva, Rousseau is considered to be one of France's greatest men and a major influence on the French Revolution of 1789. The themes of his political philosophy – the need for liberty, fraternity and equality – became the rallying cry of the revolutionaries in their efforts to overturn aristocratic privilege and domination. In 1794 his remains were transferred to the Panthéon in Paris, which contains the remains of many of France's heroes. To this day he has impassioned admirers and vociferous detractors. It is impossible to be indifferent to him.

---

the family tradition as a progressive employer. He became chairman of his father's chocolate firm in York (1925-41), where he had instituted a number of social reforms, including a pension plan (1906), a five-day week (1919) and a profit-sharing scheme for his employees (1923). Rowntree achieved national prominence for his life-long study of social conditions and welfare and published many books, including *Poverty: a Study of Town Life* (1901), the findings of his research into working-class homes in York.

Roy, Ram Mohan (1772-1833) Indian religious leader and reformer. Roy devoted his life to modernising Indian society. He attacked idolatry, suttee (burning of widows), polygamy, discrimination against women and the Indian caste system (see feature, pages 312-13). Roy founded the Atmiya Sabha (Friendly Association) to serve as a platform for his liberal ideas. He also helped to establish the Hindu College in Calcutta in 1816 and several secondary schools in which English educational methods were employed. In 1828, in an attempt to purify Hinduism, he set up the Brahmo Samaj (Society of God) in Calcutta, which has had a profound influence on intellectual, social and religious life.

Royal Academy of Arts Society founded by GEORGE III in London in 1768 to foster fine arts, including painting, engraving, sculpture and architecture. The academy's first president was the painter Sir Joshua Reynolds. The number of academicians is limited to 40, all of whom contribute to its fine collection of art. Members have included the painters Thomas Gainsborough, J.M.W. Turner, John Constable and Augustus John; the sculptor John Flaxman; and the architects Sir William Chambers, Sir John Soane and Sir Edwin Lutyens.

Royal African Company English trading company which dealt mainly in slaves and gold. Charles II granted the company a monopoly charter in 1672. Its trading posts along the Gold Coast (present-day Ghana) were built as forts for defence against European aggressors, local Fante chiefdoms and pirates. It lost its monopoly of trade with England by an Act of 1698; in 1750 it was succeeded by the African Company of Merchants.

Royal Society Oldest scientific society in Britain, founded in 1660, and granted a royal charter by CHARLES II in 1662. The Royal Society become world famous for its stimulation of scientific thought and development. Political and religious topics were excluded from its debates, and only those who had made a distinguished contribution to the sciences were eligible for election as fellows. Among its earliest members were the diarist

Essen foundries helped to make the Ruhr Europe's largest steel producer and the powerhouse of Germany's military machine. Krupp arms factories and Thyssen steelworks were located there.

Samuel PEPYS, the architect Sir Christopher WREN and the scientists Robert Boyle, Robert Hooke and Sir Isaac NEWTON. Newton's theory of gravitation, *Principia Mathematica,* was published in 1687 with the encouragement of the society. The organisation's *Philosophical Transactions,* begun in 1665 to publish scientific papers, was the first journal of its kind in the West.

Rozvi Aristocratic ruling clan in the Karanga empire which extended across present-day Zimbabwe, parts of Botswana and the Transvaal. Hereditary priests, they exercised political and military authority over the Karanga from the late 17th century. Though cut off from outside influences for more than a century, they attained the highest level of stone architecture in southern Africa, particularly in Great ZIMBABWE. Their empire collapsed in 1831 when the Angoni tribe invaded.

rubber The elastic material produced mainly from the milky liquid of the tree *Hevea brasiliensis* is today supplemented by a synthetic form of rubber derived from petroleum and other chemicals. Both forms of rubber are used to make products such as tyres, latex foam, soles for shoes and industrial components. The substance was first called 'rubber' in 1770 by an English chemist, Joseph Priestley, who found it useful for rubbing out pencil marks. The tree originated in Brazil, where it was 'tapped' by cutting the bark diagonally with a sharp knife to allow the latex to be drawn off. This liquid was then coagulated over a fire. Its tendency to soften in hot weather was overcome by the American inventor Charles Goodyear, who

devised the process of vulcanisation in the 1840s. He discovered that the combination of rubber with sulphur and white lead, and exposure to heat, improved the product's strength. Its commercial potential then began to be realised. Trees were transplanted to Southeast Asia, and Indonesia, Ceylon (Sri Lanka) and Malaya became major rubber-producing countries. The Second World War encouraged the production of synthetic rubber, while further developments have increased the durability of natural rubber. Rubber components form important parts of most machinery.

Rubicon River in north-east Italy which flows into the Adriatic, now called the Rubicone. In Roman times the Rubicon formed part of the border between the province of Cisalpine Gaul and Italy. By leading his troops across it in 49BC, Julius CAESAR declared war on the Roman Republic, giving rise to the expression to 'cross the Rubicon', meaning to take a step after which there can be no turning back.

Ruhr Industrial and coal-mining region in the valley of the river Ruhr in western Germany. The region has been mined for coal since the Middle Ages, but it was the Ruhr valley's restoration to Prussia in 1815 that marked the beginning of its development as a major industrial centre producing coal and steel. From 1923 to 1925 its economy suffered when the Ruhr was occupied by French and Belgian troops following Germany's default on REPARATIONS payments to France. In the 1930s war industries were established in the Ruhr as Germany rearmed. Allied bombing during the Second World War caused extensive destruction, and

after the war the recovery of the Ruhr was monitored by an international commission. Control passed to the European Coal and Steel Community in 1952 and to the Federal Republic of Germany in 1954.

Rump Parliament Puritan remnant of the English LONG PARLIAMENT, which continued to sit in the House of Commons after PRIDE'S PURGE of 121 royalist Parliamentarians in 1648. In January 1649 the Rump ordered CHARLES I's execution, abolished the monarchy and established the COMMONWEALTH. Oliver CROMWELL dissolved the Rump in 1653 and called a short-lived 'Barebones' Parliament of army officers, before becoming Protector of England and ruling without Parliament. Six years later, after Cromwell's death, the Rump was recalled to mark the end of the PROTECTORATE. In 1660 members excluded by Pride were readmitted, and the Long Parliament was restored. It soon dissolved itself in preparation for the restoration of the monarchy.

Rum Rebellion (1808) Insurrection in Australia in which officers of the New South Wales Corps overthrew the governor, William BLIGH, and appointed their commander, George Johnston, in his place. The rebellion was provoked by Bligh's determination to limit the increasing power of the corps, which was known as the 'Rum Corps' for its involvement in the liquor trade. Bligh, whose irascible temper had helped to provoke a mutiny on his ship the *Bounty* earlier in his career, further inflamed the corps by accusing it of corruption and arresting its chief supporter, the entrepreneur John Macarthur. On becoming governor Johnston released Macarthur and imprisoned Bligh. When Governor Lachlan MACQUARIE took office in 1810, the corps was recalled to England, along with Johnston and Macarthur. Johnston was court-martialled and dismissed in 1811. Macarthur returned to Australia to make his fortune in the wool business. Bligh was exonerated, and promoted to the rank of admiral.

Rundstedt, Karl Rudolf Gerd von (1875-1953) German field-marshal who commanded the German forces in the Battle of the Bulge (1944) during the ARDENNES CAMPAIGN of the Second World War. His army mounted a surprise attack on the Allies but failed to reach their goal of Antwerp. Rundstedt served during the First World War. In the 1930s he was dismissed for criticising Adolf HITLER. He was recalled in 1939 and commanded in the invasion of France in 1940 and in Russia in 1941, but was dismissed for withdrawing from Rostov in the Ukraine against Hitler's orders. From 1942 to 1945 he commanded the Western Front from Holland to the Italian border. Relieved of his command in March 1945, Rundstedt was later captured by US troops and imprisoned in Britain. He was not tried for war crimes because of his ill-health, and was released in 1949.

Rupert of the Rhine, Prince (1619-82)
English cavalry officer and admiral. Rupert was the son of Frederick V, the Elector Palatine of the Holy Roman Empire, and Elizabeth, daughter of JAMES VI of Scotland (James I of England). He grew up in the Low Countries, and fought in the THIRTY YEARS' WAR. In 1642 Rupert, a nephew of Charles I of England, joined the CAVALIERS, and became commander of the royal army during the ENGLISH CIVIL WAR. He was a daring, skilful cavalryman; though his forces were initially successful, they were eventually defeated by the Parliamentarians. After Rupert surrendered Bristol in 1645, Charles dismissed him. Later, in the West Indies, he commanded privateers against English shipping. Under Charles II he was given naval commands in the ANGLO-DUTCH wars. Rupert helped to found the Hudson's Bay Company. He was also interested in chemical research and developed a technique to improve the method of engraving prints known as mezzotint.

Ruskin, John (1819-1900)
Influential British art critic. The son of wealthy parents, Ruskin studied at Oxford and travelled throughout Europe. His meeting with the artist J.M.W. Turner in 1840 inspired him to publish the first of his five-volume *Modern Painters* (1843-60), in order to win recognition for Turner. Ruskin's literary output was prolific and he had a hold over public opinion, raising the appreciation of artists' work and defending the Pre-Raphaelites in 1851. He believed that art, in particular as expressed in the GOTHIC style, could be a means of solving social problems, and in the second half of his life, using his inherited fortune, he devoted himself to philanthropic work and to writing on economic, social and political questions. He was a watercolourist, and the first Slade professor of art at Oxford, from 1869 to 1879.

Russell, Bertrand, 3rd Earl (1872-1970)
British philosopher, mathematician and author. Russell introduced English-speaking philosophers to the advances made in mathematical logic by the German philosopher Friedrich Frege. In 1913 he published *Introduction to Mathematical Philosophy*, in which he argued that mathematics was an extension of logic. The grandson of the Liberal prime minister Lord John Russell, he studied mathematics and philosophy at Trinity College, Cambridge, becoming a fellow in 1895. Although his work mainly concentrated upon philosophy, he also wrote on social, educational and religious issues. Russell was a controversial figure. He was

imprisoned for his pacifist activities during the First World War, and later ostracised for his views on sexual morality expressed in *Marriage and Morals* (1929). He travelled widely, visiting the USSR and lecturing in China and the USA. Russell was married four times. After the Second World War he became a leading spokesman for the Campaign for Nuclear Disarmament (CND). In 1950 he was awarded the Nobel prize for literature.

Russell, John, 1st Earl (1792-1878)
British prime minister from 1846 to 1852 and 1865 to 1866. Russell entered the House of Commons in 1813. A firm advocate of CATHOLIC EMANCIPATION, he urged the repeal of the Corporation Act and the Test Act (1828) under which no Catholic or Protestant nonconformist could hold public office. Russell was largely responsible for drafting the first REFORM Bill (1831). As home secretary from 1835 to 1839, he reduced the number of crimes punishable by death. He became prime minister after the fall of Sir Robert PEEL. Russell's government was overshadowed by the dominant personality of his foreign secretary, Lord Henry PALMERSTON, whom he dismissed in 1851. He later served as foreign secretary in Palmerston's government from 1859, succeeding him as prime minister in 1865. Russell resigned the same year when his proposal for a new Reform Bill split his party.

Russia
Country in eastern Europe and northern Asia. The Russian Federation extends from the Baltic Sea to the Pacific Ocean, and from the Arctic Ocean to the Black Sea. It includes 16 autonomous regions. The capital is Moscow. Russia, once the Russian empire, was known from 1922 until 1991 as the Russian Soviet Federated Socialist Republic, the largest republic of the UNION OF SOVIET SOCIALIST REPUBLICS (USSR).

The northern part of the country was originally inhabited by Slavs, the south by nomads. In the 9th century the Vikings began to dominate, establishing the first Russian state with its capital at KIEV. The Mongols established control from the 13th to the late 14th century. The principality of MUSCOVY developed in the 15th century. IVAN the Terrible was the first Muscovite ruler to assume the title of tsar (emperor) of Russia in 1547. He put an end to Mongol domination, and expanded the state to the south and east into Siberia. He was followed by the ROMANOV dynasty (1613-1917). PETER THE GREAT (1672-1725) partially Westernised the old Muscovite state, and transformed it into an empire stretching from the Baltic to the Pacific. In the 18th century

Russia played a major role in European affairs. Under the empress CATHERINE II (1729-96), it dominated Poland, and won a series of victories against the Ottoman Turks. Between 1798 and 1814 Russia took a leading part in the NAPOLEONIC WARS and the overthrow of Napoleon. Conflicting interests in the Balkans led to the CRIMEAN WAR (1853-6), between Russia and the Western powers.

At home, SERFDOM among the peasants was abolished in 1861, and industry grew. Attempts to reform local government, the judicial system and education were only partially successful, and a revolutionary undercurrent developed. Russia's defeat in the RUSSO-JAPANESE WAR (1904-5), led to the RUSSIAN REVOLUTION (1905), and the tsar, NICHOLAS II, conceded to demands to establish the first DUMA (parliament).

Russia's involvement in the First World War created great hardship at home. A series of revolts culminated in the RUSSIAN REVOLUTION of 1917, the abdication of the tsar and the RUSSIAN CIVIL WAR. The Russian republic was the largest of the 15 members of the USSR, which was established in 1922 under Vladimir Ilyich LENIN and the Communist Party. It was drawn into the Second World War in 1939 to combat a German invasion.

The postwar years were dominated by the COLD WAR and deteriorating relations with the West. In the WARSAW PACT of 1955 the USSR agreed a military alliance with other East European communist states which lasted until 1991. The Communist Party kept firm control until the mid 1980s when pressure began to develop among the republics, including Russia, for independence from the USSR. Mikhail GORBACHEV came to power in 1985. His policies of glasnost (openness) and perestroika (restructuring) set Russia on the path to reform, democratisation and a market economy, but not without opposition from conservatives at home. Abroad, he initiated a period of détente and built on previous discussions with Western leaders on arms reductions.

In 1989 the first Soviet parliament since 1918 was held. Gorbachev, the newly elected president, faced economic problems as well as nationalist unrest in the republics. In 1991, following an attempted coup and the demise of the USSR, Boris YELTSIN was elected president, and a new body, the Commonwealth of Independent States (CIS), was formed. State subsidies were withdrawn and private enterprise was encouraged. Prices soared, fuelling discontent and support for the right-wing nationalist parties. A new constitution was adopted in 1993 setting up a 450-seat lower house, or Duma, and a 178-seat Federation

> **DID YOU KNOW?**
>
> In 1985, when Mikhail Gorbachev came to power, the US dollar was officially worth 1.7 Russian roubles; in 1991, when he left power, it was worth 222; and in June 1996, 5000.

mounting distress to the poor, and Russia's defeat in the RUSSO-JAPANESE WAR had highlighted the weakness of the tsarist government. On January 22, 1905, thousands of unarmed workers demanding reform marched on the Winter Palace in St Petersburg. Imperial troops opened fire on the crowd, killing many on what was to become known as Bloody Sunday. The country was gripped by a general strike. In October, following the formation of a SOVIET (council) of workers' delegates in St Petersburg, the tsar yielded to demands for reform, including the establishment of a legislative duma. Social democrats continued to fight for a total overthrow of the system, and were met with harsh reprisals.

Russian Revolution (1917)
Overthrow of the tsar, NICHOLAS II, and the imperial government, by the BOLSHEVIKS under the leadership of Vladimir Ilyich LENIN. The revolution of 1917 marked the end of 300 years of ROMANOV rule and led to the foundation of the UNION OF SOVIET SOCIALIST REPUBLICS (USSR) in 1922. There were two stages: the first, in February 1917 (March in the Western calendar), was led by the liberal intelligentsia, the Mensheviks, who sought the establishment of a democratic, Western-style republic. The second, in October (November, Western calendar), was a Bolshevik revolution led by communists who were prepared to use violence to establish a MARXIST proletarian state. Years of government repression and the extreme hardships of the First World War prompted the February revolution, when strikes and riots in Petrograd, formerly St Petersburg, led to the tsar's abdication. A provisional government was appointed under Prince Lvov, who was replaced by the socialist Alexander KERENSKY. Opposition mounted within the Petrograd Soviet of Workers' and Soldiers' Deputies, and in October the Bolsheviks, led by Lenin, seized the tsar's Winter Palace, arrested the members of the provisional government and took control of the cities. A new government, the Council of People's Commissars, was created, land was distributed to the peasants and banks were nationalised. A Soviet constitution was proclaimed in July 1918 and Lenin transferred the government from Petrograd to Moscow. Counterrevolutionaries fought back in the RUSSIAN CIVIL WAR, which ended three years later in victory for the Bolsheviks.

Russo-Japanese War
(1904-5) Conflict between Russia and Japan over Manchuria and Korea. The Japanese launched a surprise attack on Russian warships at anchor in Port Arthur (now Lüshun), Manchuria, after Russia had reneged on its agreement to withdraw its troops from Manchuria. Port Arthur fell to the Japanese, as did Mukden, the capital of Manchuria. At sea, the Japanese soundly defeated the Russian Baltic fleet in the Tsushima Straits. The war was ended by the Treaty of PORTSMOUTH under which Russia surrendered its claims to Korea and Port Arthur. This was Japan's first victory over a Western power on both land and sea. For Russia, the humiliating defeat contributed to the RUSSIAN REVOLUTION (1905).

Rutherford, Ernest Rutherford, 1st Baron
(1871-1937) New Zealand physicist and pioneer of atomic science. Rutherford was one of 12 children born to a wheelwright and a

Council. The growth of regionalism in territories rich in resources became a political issue. Yeltsin was in failing health by 1996, but a threat from the communist leader Gennady Zuganov failed to materialise and he was re-elected with the support of his security overlord, Alexander Lebed, whose intentions to boost Russia's military power made him a controversial figure in the eyes of the West.

Russian Civil War
(1918-21) Bitter conflict in Russia between the counter-revolutionary White Army and the Bolshevik RED ARMY in the aftermath of the RUSSIAN REVOLUTION (1917). The Whites began organised resistance against the BOLSHEVIKS in December 1917, clashing with a Red Army hastily assembled by Leon TROTSKY. Fighting broke out in northern and southern Russia, in the Ukraine, the Baltic States and Caucasus.

In northern Russia a force of French and British units landed at Murmansk in 1918, occupied Archangel and set up a puppet government which survived until 1920. In Siberia, where US and Japanese forces landed, the Russian naval commander Alexander Kolchak acted as minister of war in a White government at Omsk until the city fell to the Bolsheviks and he was executed in 1920. The Red Army, under the firm control of Trotsky, was a more effective fighting force than the fragmented Whites. It put down peasant risings caused by famine, and suppressed a mutiny of sailors at KRONSTADT. Lack of co-operation between different elements of the counterrevolutionary White forces contributed to their collapse and to the establishment of the UNION OF SOVIET SOCIALIST REPUBLICS (USSR).

Russian Revolution (1905)
Rebellion that overthrew the government of Tsar NICHOLAS II and led to the formation of a parliament (DUMA). Heavy taxation had brought

The head of Tsar Nicholas II, toppled in Moscow during the Russian Revolution, mirrors the fate of the tsar himself. After abdicating in March 1917, Nicholas was shot in July 1918.

flax miller near Nelson. He won a research scholarship in experimental physics at the Cavendish Laboratory, Cambridge, in 1895 where he made the first radio transmissions over a distance greater than 2 miles (3 km). Working in the field of radiation, he became professor of physics at McGill University in Canada, and then at Manchester. With his assistant, Niels Bohr, he developed the concept of the Rutherford-Bohr atom. While researching into radioactivity Rutherford discovered alpha, beta and gamma rays. He observed that alpha radiation consists of positively charged helium atoms, and discovered the atomic nucleus in 1906. Rutherford published many papers and books, and won the Nobel prize for chemistry in 1908.

Ruyter, Michiel de (1607-76) Admiral who commanded the Dutch fleet in the ANGLO-DUTCH WARS. Ruyter went to sea at the age of nine, and became a merchant captain at 18. In the First Anglo-Dutch War (1652-4) he served under Maarten TROMP and won promotion to vice-admiral. In the Second War (1665-7) he won the Four Days' Battle off Dunkirk, and sailed up the Medway to destroy much of the English fleet in a daring raid. His victories over English and French forces off Solebay, Ostend and Kijkduin in the Third War (1672-4), prevented an invasion of the Dutch Republic.

Rwanda Republic in central Africa which is bounded by Uganda, Tanzania, Burundi and Zaire. The capital is Kigali. Rwanda is a densely populated, mountainous country, and is mainly inhabited by two ethnic groups, the majority Hutus and the minority Tutsis. The country's economy relies on exports of coffee and tea, although its considerable mineral resources are being developed. From the 16th century it was linked to Burundi, and administered by Belgium as Ruanda-Urundi from 1919 until independence in 1962. Violence between Hutus and Tutsis resulted in the overthrow of the Tutsi hierarchy and monarchy in 1959. A republic was proclaimed in 1961 and self-government granted in 1962. The warring groups agreed to make peace, but fighting began again in the 1970s. A new constitution was adopted in 1978 and civilian rule restored.

In 1990, Tutsi forces of the Rwandan Patriotic Front (FPR) invaded from Uganda. Fighting continued in spite of a peace accord in 1993. In April 1994 the presidents of Rwanda and Burundi were killed in an air crash. Fighting escalated, and in the ensuing violence hundreds of thousands of Rwandans – mainly Tutsis – were killed. Others fled across the borders, while Hutu bands carried out genocide attacks on remaining Tutsis. A cease-fire was called in June 1994 and a government of national unity was formed. In the following year, attempts by the United Nations and the new government to repatriate refugees were thwarted by the threat of reprisal killings. An International Criminal Tribunal for Rwanda opened in 1995 to investigate the killings.

Rye House Plot (1683) Conspiracy of Whig extremists who planned to murder CHARLES II of England and his brother James, Duke of York (later James II), after the failure of an attempt to exclude James, a Roman Catholic, from the succession. The plot takes its name from the house in Hertfordshire where the assassination was to have taken place. The Duke of MONMOUTH, an illegitimate son of Charles II and a claimant to the throne, was among those involved. When the plot was discovered, Monmouth fled to the Low Countries while his fellow conspirators, Lord Russell and Algernon Sidney, were condemned to death and the Earl of Essex committed suicide.

ryotwari system Form of land taxation in India whereby cultivators paid their dues to the government direct, without the intervention of a landlord. The ryotwari system was devised by Governor Thomas Munro in Madras in 1820. Previously tax was collected by the landlord, which often worked against the interests of the *ryot*, 'peasant'.

Ryswick, Treaty of (1697) Agreement which ended the NINE YEARS' WAR (1688-97) between the Grand Alliance (England, the United Provinces, Austria, Spain and Savoy) and France. The treaty was drawn up in Ryswick in the Netherlands. LOUIS XIV agreed to recognise WILLIAM III as king of England, give up his attempts to control Cologne and the Palatinate, to end French occupation of Lorraine and to restore Luxembourg, Mons, Courtrai, and Barcelona to Spain. The Dutch were allowed to garrison a series of fortresses in the Spanish Netherlands as a barrier against France.

Saarland Coal-producing state in southwest Germany bordered by France and Luxembourg. By the Middle Ages the Saar consisted of several small German-speaking territories. Twice occupied by France in the 17th and 18th centuries, it was divided between Bavaria and Prussia following the French emperor Napoleon's final defeat in 1815. It became a major industrial area after German unification in 1871, when Germany also acquired Alsace-Lorraine and its coal and iron deposits. Following Germany's defeat in the First World War, the Saar Territory was placed under the administration of the League of Nations and its coal fields were awarded to France. It was restored to Germany in 1935, but became part of the French zone of occupied Germany at the end of the Second World War. The Saarland became the tenth state of the Federal Republic of Germany in 1957.

Sabines Ancient tribe who inhabited the foothills of the Apennines north-east of Rome. The Romans are said to have based many of their religious practices on the customs of the Sabines. According to legend, the Romans abducted the Sabine women during a festival to provide wives for themselves. An army was raised to take revenge, but the women appeared on the battlefield with new-born babies and the two sides were reconciled. The Sabines were conquered by the Romans in 290 BC and became Roman citizens in 268.

Sacco-Vanzetti case Controversial American criminal trial. In 1920 two Italian immigrants, Nicola Sacco and Bartolomeo Vanzetti, were arrested for the murder of a paymaster and his guard in Massachusetts. Despite conflicting evidence, both men were found guilty in 1921. It was widely believed that they had been convicted for being anarchists and immigrants, and worldwide anti-USA demonstrations followed, including one protest in Paris in which a bomb killed 20 people. Attempts to secure a retrial were made, but both men were executed by electrocution in 1927.

Sacheverell, Henry (1674-1724) English divine and political preacher who brought about the fall of the Whig government in 1710. In 1709 Sacheverell, a Tory and a High Church Anglican, preached sermons in Derby and London attacking the government's policy of religious toleration towards Protestant dissenters. The Whig Lord Treasurer Sidney GODOLPHIN, also a victim of the preacher's attacks, condemned the sermons as seditious, and in March 1710 Sacheverell was impeached before the House of Lords.

The trial was accompanied by riots in favour of Sacheverell, who became a popular hero for a nation tired of the Whig-directed WAR OF THE SPANISH SUCCESSION of 1701 to 1713. Although he was convicted and suspended from preaching for three years, the light sentence was seen as a moral victory for Sacheverell. The impeachment contributed to Queen Anne's dismissal of Godolphin in August, and a general election held in the autumn was won decisively by the Tories under Robert HARLEY.

Sadat, Anwar (1918-81) President of EGYPT from 1970 to his assassination, who in 1979 secured the first Arab peace treaty with Israel. Sadat met many Egyptian nationalists, including Gamal Abdul NASSER, during his military training from 1936 to 1938. During the Second World War he was imprisoned by the British for being a German agent. He escaped, but was jailed again from 1946 to 1949 for terrorist acts. A member of Nasser's revolutionary Free Officers movement, Sadat took part in the 1952 coup that deposed King Farouk and brought Nasser to power. During Nasser's rule he twice served as vice-president, from 1964 to 1966 and from 1969 to 1970,

In his quest for peace in the Middle East, Anwar Sadat (left) talks to Prime Minister Menachem Begin during a visit to Israel.

and on Nasser's death in 1970 he became president. Sadat moved Egypt away from Soviet influence, and in 1972 expelled thousands of Soviet technicians and advisers. The following year he launched the YOM KIPPUR WAR against Israel and became a popular hero in the Arab world when Egyptian troops recaptured part of the Sinai Peninsula that had been taken by the Israelis in 1967.

Under US influence, Sadat then worked towards peace in the Middle East. His visit to Israel in 1977 marked the first recognition of Israel by an Arab state and brought strong condemnation from most of the Arab world. In September 1978, at the invitation of US president Jimmy CARTER, Sadat met the Israeli prime minister Menachem BEGIN at Camp David in Maryland. The resulting CAMP DAVID ACCORD provided a framework for the settlement of the Middle East conflict, and led to the Egyptian-Israeli peace treaty of March 1979. Sadat and Begin were jointly awarded the Nobel peace prize in 1978. The treaty increased opposition to Sadat inside Egypt, and he was assassinated by Muslim fundamentalists on October 6, 1981.

Sadducees Jewish political-religious faction in ancient Israel. Formed around 200 BC, the Sadducees probably took their name from Zadok the Priest, whose descendants held priestly office from the time of Solomon. Most Sadducees were rich landowners, and their conservative religious beliefs brought them into conflict with the PHARISEES. Unlike the Pharisees, they accepted only the written Torah (the first five books of the Old Testament) and denied the legal force of oral traditions. As a result, they refused to believe in bodily resurrection after death and in the existence of angels. The Sadducees were influential in the Temple of Jerusalem at the time of Christ and may have played a role in his trial and crucifixion. They ceased to exist after the destruction of the Temple by the Romans in AD 70.

Sadowa, Battle of (July 3, 1866) Battle that ended the AUSTRO-PRUSSIAN WAR, fought near the village of Sadowa near Königgratz, east of Prague. With superior mobility and new breech-loading rifles, the Prussians, led by Helmuth von MOLTKE, were able to overcome Ludwig von Benedek's Austrian troops. Benedek took responsibility for the defeat and retired. The Prussians lost fewer than 15 000 men, but Austrian casualties reached 40 000. The battle marked the end of Austrian influence in Germany and confirmed Prussian domination of the North German Confederation, established after the war.

saga Medieval Icelandic or Scandinavian heroic prose tale, from the Old Norse for 'saw' or 'saying'. Originally sagas were recited, but from the 12th century, scribes began to write them down. There are three main categories: legendary sagas such as *Völsunga saga* (*c.* 1270) which retell pagan Norse legends; kings' sagas, which are fictionalised accounts of early Danish or Norwegian kings, for example Snorri Sturluson's *Heimskringla* (*Orb of the World*), written between 1223 and 1235; and family or Icelandic sagas, tales of the heroic settlers of Iceland in the 9th and 10th centuries such as the anonymous *Njáls saga*. Many of the stories are brutal, painting a picture of a fierce warrior society dominated by superstition, long and bitter feuds, and acts of heroism and loyalty.

St Albans, Battles of (1455; 1461) Two major battles in the English Wars of the ROSES, fought in the Hertfordshire town of St Albans. The first Battle of St Albans was the opening action of the wars. In 1455 the Lancastrian king Henry VI recovered from a spell of insanity during which his rival for the throne, Richard, Duke of YORK, had been appointed protector of the realm over Henry's queen, MARGARET OF ANJOU. Richard took up arms and marched on London, believing that the queen and Edmund Beaufort, Duke of Somerset, were plotting to destroy him. On May 22 the two factions met at St Albans. After Somerset was killed and Henry captured, Richard continued his advance on the capital, where he had himself proclaimed Constable of England.

The second Battle of St Albans took place on February 17, 1461. Lancastrian forces attacked the Yorkist army under Richard Neville, Earl of WARWICK, who was holding Henry VI prisoner. The Lancastrians recaptured Henry, but were slow to exploit their victory. Warwick and Edward, Duke of York, reached London first, where Edward was proclaimed king as EDWARD IV.

St Bartholomew's Day Massacre (August 24-25, 1572) Murder of French Huguenots, or Protestants, by Roman Catholics during the FRENCH WARS OF RELIGION. The massacre followed Catherine de MEDICI's approval of a plot by the Catholic GUISE faction to assassinate Admiral de COLIGNY, the Huguenot leader influencing her son, the young king Charles IX. After the failure of the assassination attempt on August 18, 1572, Catherine persuaded Charles to approve the murder of the Huguenot leaders who were in Paris for the marriage of her daughter Marguerite de Valois to the future HENRY IV, a Huguenot, on August 22. The massacre

> ### DID YOU KNOW?
>
> Anwar Sadat had an English mother-in-law who objected to her daughter's choice of husband, until Sadat discovered their mutual passion for the novels of Dickens.

The body of Gaspard de Coligny is pushed out of a window (right) during the St Bartholomew's Day Massacre, as the corpses of other Huguenots are piled up and pushed into the Seine.

began before dawn on August 24; Coligny was one of the first victims. A royal order on August 25 failed to stop the bloodshed, which spread to Rouen, Lyon, Bourges, Orléans and Bordeaux and lasted until October. As many as 70 000 Huguenots were killed, including 3000 in Paris. The massacre revived hatred between Huguenots and Catholics, and led to a resumption of the Wars of Religion.

Saint-Just, Louis de (1767-94) French revolutionary, who became a leader of the extreme left with Maximilien ROBESPIERRE. An administrator during the early French Revolution, Saint-Just attracted attention in 1791 with his essay *Esprit de la Révolution et de la Constitution de France* (*Spirit of the French Revolution and Constitution*). A loyal supporter of Robespierre, he was elected to the National Convention in 1792 and in his first speech attacked Louis XVI, who was tried and executed by the Convention in 1793. In the same year Saint-Just joined the COMMITTEE OF PUBLIC SAFETY, supervising military affairs, and became a zealous advocate of the Committee's Reign of TERROR. The following year he was instrumental in the overthrow of Georges DANTON; he passed the Ventôse Decrees, which redistributed property to the poor; and in June he led the victorious attack against the Austrians at Fleurus in Belgium. On July 27, 1794, Saint-Just was arrested in the coup that overthrew Robespierre, and was guillotined the next day.

Saint-Simon, Henri de (1760-1825) French social philosopher and founder of French socialism. Having entered military service at the age of 17, Saint-Simon fought in the American War of Independence in one of the regiments sent by France to aid the colonists. During the French Revolution he was briefly imprisoned in Paris and then made a fortune by buying nationalised land, but after coming close to bankruptcy he turned to the study of science. He envisaged a government run by industrialists, scientists and poets, representing action, thought and feeling. His major work, *Nouveau Christianisme* (*The New Christianity*), 1825, developed his belief that religion should guide a community towards improving the conditions of its poorest members. After Saint-Simon's death his disciples spread his ideas, which influenced the English historian Thomas Carlyle and the German socialist Friedrich Engels.

Saladin (c.1137-93) Kurdish general and leader of Muslim forces against the Crusaders. His Arabic name, Salah ad-Din ibn-Aiyub, means 'the Welfare of the Faith'. In 1152 Saladin entered the service of Nur al-Din, sultan of Syria, taking part in campaigns against the Fatimid rulers of Egypt. In 1169 he succeeded his uncle, Shirkuh, as vizier of Egypt, and abolished the Fatimid caliphs in 1171. On Nur al-Din's death in 1174 Saladin proclaimed himself sultan of Egypt and took control of Syria. Over the next ten years he also gained control of Mesopotamia and received homage from the Seljuk princes of Asia Minor.

Saladin then mounted a campaign against the Latin Kingdom of Jerusalem, also known as OUTREMER. In 1187 he routed Christian forces at Hattin near Tiberias to capture Jerusalem and Acre, thus provoking the Third CRUSADE in 1189. The Crusaders recovered Acre in 1191 when the English king RICHARD I also defeated Saladin at Arsuf, but they were unable to regain Jerusalem and agreed to a three-year truce. After Saladin's death, his fame as a shrewd and chivalrous commander became part of European legend. His dynasty fell to the Mongols in 1250.

Saladin did not become famous in the Muslim world until Crusader songs about him were translated into Arabic in the 19th century.

Salamis, Battle of (480 BC) First great naval battle in recorded history, which occurred during the Persian wars of 500 to 449 BC (see PERSIA). The Persian king XERXES had gained control of most of Greece when, in 480, the Athenian commander Themistocles lured the Persian navy into the narrow straits between the island of Salamis and the mainland. The Persians found it difficult to manoeuvre their 800 galleys in such a confined space. The Greeks destroyed almost half of the Persian vessels and lost only 40 of their own 370 nimbler, more expertly handled triremes. The rest of the Persian fleet was scattered, forcing Xerxes to withdraw to Asia Minor. This gave the Greeks time to regroup and repel the remaining Persian invaders from northern Greece.

Salazar, António (1889-1970) Prime minister and virtual dictator of Portugal from 1932 to 1968. Salazar was elected to parliament in 1921, but after one session returned to his post as professor of political economy. He served as finance minister after a military coup in 1926, and again from 1928 to 1932. In July 1932 Salazar was named prime minister by President António Carmona. In 1933 he introduced a new constitution, giving himself dictatorial powers and naming the new regime the Estado Novo (New State). Salazar also served as minister of war from 1936 to 1944 and as minister of foreign affairs from 1936 to 1947.

A supporter of General Francisco Franco in the Spanish Civil War, Salazar kept his country neutral during the Second World War, although he allowed Britain to use the Azores as a base. Poverty and illiteracy were not substantially reduced under Salazar's rule, and he faced numerous wars of independence in Portugal's African colonies. In 1968 he suffered a stroke and Marcello Caetano succeeded

A Salem woman accused of witchcraft is examined at her trial for the 'Devil's Mark'. It was believed that Satan sucked blood through a wart-like protuberance on the body of a witch.

him as prime minister. In 1974 an army coup ushered in democracy and ended the dictatorship Salazar had founded.

Salem witch trials Series of witch trials which took place from May to October 1692 in Salem, Massachusetts. The hunt for witches began after three girls living near Salem began to act as if possessed by the devil and accused a slave of being responsible. After the slave was beaten, she confessed and also accused two local women of being witches. Hysteria about devil worship and further accusations of witchcraft (see feature, page 706) spread through the surrounding towns. A special court was set up in Salem to try the accused, who by October numbered 150. A clergyman, Increase MATHER, called for trials, but as the investigations continued the initial public hysteria gradually turned into scepticism. Mather persuaded Governor William Phips to end the proceedings in October; 14 women and six men had been executed. In 1696, the jurors apologised publicly for their wrongs. The girls who made the first accusations are thought to have read *Memorable Providences Relating to Witchcraft and Possessions* (1689) – a book by Mather's son Cotton MATHER – with its lurid account of the alleged symptoms of possession.

Salic Law Legal code of the Salian FRANKS, who conquered Gaul in the 5th century. Salic Law, *Lex Salica* in Latin, was issued around 507-11 in the reign of Clovis. It was reissued under his descendants, and under the Carolingian dynasty was altered and translated from Latin into Old High German. Concerned with both civil and criminal law, the code contained a list of fines for various offences and crimes, and also declared that

daughters could not inherit land. In 14th-century France, Salic Law was invoked in order to justify excluding women from inheriting the throne, although it only became a law of the kingdom in the 16th century. In 1328 it was used against Edward III of England, who claimed the French throne through his mother. Salic Law was established as a principle in Spain in 1713.

Sallust (86-c.34 BC) Roman politician and historian Caius Sallustius Crispus. Sallust was appointed to political office in 52 BC, but was expelled from the senate two years later on charges of immorality. A supporter of Julius Caesar, he was given command of one of Caesar's legions when civil war broke out in 49. For his part in Caesar's African campaign in 46, Sallust was made governor of Numidia (present-day Algeria), but he resigned in about 44 after allegations of extortion. In his retirement, Sallust turned to historical writing. *Bellum Catalinae* is an account of the Catiline conspiracy to overthrow the Roman government in 62-63, while *Bellum Iugurthinum* describes the war against the Numidian king Jugurtha in the 2nd century. Fragments of his history of Rome between 78 and 67 also survive. Despite their errors and bias, Sallust's narratives influenced historians such as TACITUS.

SALT see STRATEGIC ARMS LIMITATION TALKS

Salvation Army International Christian evangelical and charitable organisation. In 1865 the Methodist revivalist preacher William BOOTH founded the Christian Revival Association in London's East End, where he established mission stations to feed and house the poor. After renaming his

association the Salvation Army in 1878, he organised it on military lines, with brass bands and military uniforms and ranks. Booth himself became general for life. The Army's open-air meetings, informal services and public conversions attracted a large following, and the Army expanded rapidly both in Britain and overseas. In 1896 General Booth's son Ballington Booth set up a splinter group, the Volunteers of America. Today the Salvation Army is well known for its social work helping the poor and homeless. It also operates a missing persons investigation service.

Samaria Hill city in ancient Palestine, now a village in Jordan. Samaria was founded by King Omri around 875 BC as the new capital of the Northern Kingdom of Israel. The kingdom had been established by northern tribes – including those of the central Palestinian region also known as Samaria – when they separated from the Southern Kingdom of Judah in the 10th century. In 722 the Northern Kingdom was crushed and the city of Samaria captured by the Assyrians. The Assyrians deported most of its inhabitants and replaced them with non-Jewish settlers, mainly from Syria and Mesopotamia. Descendants of the settlers, who were known as Samaritans, were disliked by the Jews of Judah for their mixed ancestry, for building a rival temple, and for splitting away from true Judaism. In the New Testament Jesus tells the parable of a man from Samaria – the Good Samaritan – who finds a Jew attacked and left to die at the roadside, and helps him despite the hostility between Jews and Samaritans. Samaria was destroyed in 120 BC, but it was rebuilt and enlarged between 37 and 34 by Herod the Great, who renamed it Sebaste.

Since establishing its first mission stations in 1865, the Salvation Army has created over 3000 welfare institutions across the world.

Samoa Chain of volcanic islands in the southern Pacific. The islands were first settled around 1000 BC by Polynesians, probably from Tonga. The first European to discover Samoa was the Dutch navigator Jacob Roggeveen in 1722, but the islands were visited mainly by convicts and runaway sailors until the arrival of English missionaries in the 1830s. Thereafter Britain, the USA and Germany were rivals for control of Samoa. In 1878 the three powers each signed treaties promising to protect the islanders against foreign seizure in exchange for naval rights. They agreed to a tripartite protectorate in 1889, but after the outbreak of tribal warfare in 1899 the two largest islands, known as Western Samoa, were annexed by Germany, while the seven eastern islands were given to the USA. In 1914 New Zealand occupied Western Samoa, governing it through serious nationalist disturbances in the 1920s to independence in 1962. American Samoa remains an unincorporated territory of the USA.

Samuel Israelite leader and prophet who lived in the 11th century BC. In the Old Testament, Samuel, which in Hebrew probably means 'name of God', was the last judge, or leader, of the tribes of Israel before the establishment of hereditary kingship. After the defeat of Israel and the loss of the Ark of the Covenant to the Philistines, Samuel rallied his people in opposition to them. He was instrumental in creating the Hebrew monarchy, anointing SAUL as the first king of Israel and providing him with prophetic advice until they had a disagreement over Saul's priestly duties, after which Samuel anointed DAVID as Saul's successor.

samurai Member of the warrior class that dominated Japanese society from the 12th to the 19th century. Samurai emerged in the 10th century as warriors in the service of

Samurai warriors were expected to display skill in battle and to be fearless in the face of their enemies.

provincial officials, and they became a dominant force during the 12th century when warrior clans such as the Minamoto took power out of the hands of the court and the aristocracy.

In 1192 the emperor secured the military leadership – the SHOGUNATE – for Minamoto Yoritomo, marking the beginning of almost 700 years of military rule in Japan. Samurai became military vassals of the shogun and the aristocracy, and they were granted land in return for military service. Their distinctive martial culture developed, influenced by the self-discipline of ZEN Buddhism.

The ideal warrior followed a strict code of conduct, formalised as *bushido*, the 'Way of the Warrior', which held bravery, family honour and loyalty above life itself. During the TOKUGAWA shogunate of 1603 to 1867, samurai became a hereditary closed caste with superior status, but during the long peace of the period many turned to administration. In 1868 samurai from Choshu and Satsuma brought about the MEIJI RESTORATION of imperial rule. With the abolition of feudalism in 1871, samurai lost their privileged position. A national army was established in 1872, and four years later samurai lost their income and their right to carry swords. Some rose in rebellion, others moved into government, the armed forces or business. The influence of the samurai continued long after they ceased to exist as a privileged class.

DID YOU KNOW?

For a Samurai warrior, honour was more important than life. Samurai who suffered dishonour or defeat were expected to kill themselves in hara-kiri, a ritual that lasted several hours, even days, a practice which continued until the end of the Second World War.

sanctuary Sacred place, such as a church or temple, recognised as a refuge for fugitives. The right of sanctuary existed in ancient Egypt, Greece and Rome, and was extended to Christian churches at the end of the 4th century. In medieval England all churches could provide a temporary refuge for criminals accused of a felony. The accused could choose to be tried for his crime, or to confess and leave the realm by a specified port within 40 days. If he failed to choose, he was starved into submission. There were also about 22 places in England that were exempt from the Crown's authority and offered permanent sanctuary. In

1540 Henry VIII restricted the number of towns with sanctuary privileges to seven, but these were abolished in 1603. In England the right of sanctuary for crime was abolished in 1623 and for civil processes in 1723. The right of sanctuary is the basis for the custom of claiming diplomatic asylum in embassies.

Sandinista Liberation Front see NICARAGUA

San Francisco Treaty of Peace Peace treaty between Japan and the nations it had fought against in the Second World War, signed on September 8, 1951. When the treaty came into force in April 1952, the post-war Allied occupation of Japan was formally ended and Japanese sovereignty restored. Japan recognised the independence of Korea and renounced its rights to Taiwan and other islands mandated to it before the war by the League of Nations. Japan was allowed the right of self-defence, but the USA would maintain forces in the country until the Japanese could maintain their own defences. The Soviet Union did not sign the treaty, but diplomatic relations were restored in 1956.

Sanhedrin Ancient Jewish council of elders, from the Greek word for 'council', *synedrion*. The name is usually applied to the supreme Jewish council known as the Great Sanhedrin, which met in Jerusalem before and during the time of Christ. The composition and function of the Sanhedrin remain unclear. In the Gospels it is described as a political and judicial council headed by a high priest, whereas in the Talmud, the compilation of Jewish traditions, law and commentary, the Sanhedrin is a religious, legislative body headed by sages, and has some political and judicial functions. After the fall of Jerusalem in AD 70 it was replaced by the Beth Din (Court of Judgment).

sanitation The world's first known drainage system was built around 2500 BC in the town of MOHENJO-DARO in the Indus Valley of present-day Pakistan. Bathrooms and toilets were connected to the city's drains by earthenware pipes and the waste disposed of in surrounding fields. Ancient Rome had a small network of sewers, the largest of which, the Cloaca Maxima, was built in about the 6th century BC. Rome had an efficient plumbing system, in which water entered the city on aqueducts and was distributed through lead pipes. After the fall of the Roman Empire, plumbing and drainage systems were neglected. In medieval Europe, monasteries provided relatively good sanitation, but generally people threw their rubbish and the contents of their chamber pots out of windows, and public latrines were often built on platforms over rivers. In South America, the Incas of the city of Cuzco built a system of stone channels into the streets through which mountain water could course.

During the 19th century, overcrowded cities in Britain and the USA suffered from grim housing conditions, inadequate water supplies and few sewers. Major epidemics of typhoid led to improvements in sanitation. Public Health Acts made towns appoint medical officers and improve the water supply and drainage facilities. In Western Europe the steadily improving health of the population and the rise in life expectancy achieved by 1939 were largely due to safer and more abundant water supplies and efficient sewerage.

In the mid 19th century links between bad sanitation and disease led to the construction of more effective drainage systems such as the Abbey Mills pumping station in London, built in 1862.

San Martín, José de

San Martín, José de (1778-1850) Argentinian leader of the fight against Spanish rule in South America. As a child San Martín moved from Argentina to Spain, where he later trained as a military officer. He fought against Napoleon from 1808 until 1811. In 1812 he returned to Buenos Aires and joined the revolution against Spain. In January 1817, with Argentine independence threatened by Spanish troops in Chile and Peru, San Martín led an army across the Andes into Chile. Together with Bernardo O'HIGGINS, he defeated the Spanish at Chacabuco in 1817, and after his victory at Maipú the following year he declared Chilean independence. Two years later he reached Peru by sea and took Lima.

After declaring independence in Peru in 1821 San Martín was made protector of the country, but his position remained insecure. In 1822 he met Simón Bolívar (see feature, page 83), the liberator of Venezuela and Quito – present-day Ecuador. In 1822, after differences with Bolívar, he resigned as protector of Peru, and after staying for a while in Chile he returned to Argentina. Refusing to become involved in the internal quarrels of Argentina, San Martín left for Europe in 1824 and died in exile in France.

sans-culottes

sans-culottes French term meaning 'without breeches' applied to the poorer classes during the Revolution, referring in particular to small shopkeepers, workers and city poor. It was also a political label for militant revolutionaries between 1792 and 1795, so named because they wore long trousers rather than the kneebreeches of the upper classes.

The original sans-culottes were the Paris workers who stormed the Bastille and led the food riots in 1789. They became an important political force with the outbreak of the French Revolutionary Wars in April 1792, after which they dominated the National Guard. In August, sans-culottes and other radicals stormed the Tuileries palace and overthrew the monarchy. Thereafter they dominated the city government and the local revolutionary committees. In June 1793 they helped to bring the JACOBINS to power, and the following September they forced the National Convention to institute the Reign of TERROR. During the Terror, public functionaries also wore the sans-culotte costume of trousers, short-skirted coat, red cap of liberty and clogs. In March 1794 Robespierre ordered the arrest of their Jacobin leader Jacques René Hébert, who was executed together with leaders of the Commune. In despair over a poor harvest and soaring inflation, the sans-culottes rebelled in May 1795, but were crushed.

Sappho

Sappho (c.612-c.580BC) Greek lyric poet born on the island of Lesbos. Sappho is said to have married Cercolas, a wealthy man from the island of Andros. She was probably exiled to Sicily with other aristocrats, but returned to Mitylene on Lesbos, where she was the centre of a circle of female friends and admirers who composed poetry.

Seven or nine books of Sappho's poetry are known to have existed, but only fragments survive. The poems, probably all meant to be sung as songs, are written in the local dialect and are mainly concerned with her friendships and enmities with other women. The longest is an invocation to Aphrodite over Sappho's love for a young girl. Her passionate poetry was greatly revered in the ancient world and influenced later poets such as Catullus and Ovid. Sappho's supposed homosexuality gave rise to the term 'lesbian', after the island of her birth.

Saracen

Saracen Originally a nomad belonging to tribes of the Syrian and Arabian deserts, but by the time of the CRUSADES a name used by Christians for all Muslims. The word comes from the Arabic *sharqiyun*, 'Easterners'. In the Middle Ages, writers often used the term MOOR as a synonym.

Saragossa

Saragossa Capital city of a province bearing the same name in north-eastern Spain. The city was built on the site of the Roman colony of Caesaraugusta, from which its Arabic name Saraqusta and Spanish name Zaragoza are derived. One of the first towns in Spain to be Christianised, it fell to the Visigoths in the 5th century and to the Moors around 714. In 1118 Saragossa was conquered by Alfonso of ARAGON, and subsequently prospered as the capital of his kingdom. The city declined in importance after the unification of Spain in 1492, but became famous during the Peninsular Wars for its citizens' heroic resistance to the long French siege of 1808 to 1809, in which about 50 000 of the defenders died.

Sarawak

Sarawak State of Malaysia on the north-west coast of the island of BORNEO. In the 15th century, Sarawak became the southern province of the sultanate of BRUNEI. In 1841 the sultan ceded it to the English adventurer James BROOKE after he helped to put down a

James Brooke negotiates with the sultan of Brunei in 1841 over the new state of Sarawak, the first British dominion in Borneo.

revolt by indigenous tribes. Sarawak became an independent state with Brooke as rajah. Although it became a British protectorate in 1888, it remained under the control of the Brooke family until its occupation by the Japanese during the Second World War. In 1946 the Brooke family ceded the territory to Britain and it became a crown colony. Sarawak gained independence in 1963 after a guerrilla war, and joined the Federation of Malaysia.

Sarnoff, David (1891-1971) Russian-born American pioneer of radio and television broadcasting. Sarnoff began his career in 1906 as a messenger boy for a telegraph company. Six years later he became famous when, as a radio operator, he picked up the distress signals of the sinking *Titanic* and reported the disaster for 72 hours without a break. In 1915 Sarnoff proposed to the company management the idea of marketing a 'simple radio music box' for use in the home. This revolutionary idea developed into the American radio industry and the Radio Corporation of America (RCA), of which Sarnoff became president in 1930. In 1926 he founded the National Broadcasting Company (NBC), the first national radio network. Two years later he launched an experimental NBC television station, and in 1939 held a successful demonstration. Sarnoff served as a communications consultant to General Dwight D. Eisenhower in the Second World War.

satrap Provincial governor in ancient Persia. Satraps were appointed by the king and were usually members of the royal family or the nobility. As well as being responsible for collecting taxes and for raising and maintaining the army, they were the highest judicial authority. DARIUS I, who ruled from 522 to 486 BC, divided his empire into 20 satrapies, each of which paid him an annual tribute. Although the satraps nominally owed allegiance to their king, the autonomy vested in them fostered disloyalty and there were frequent uprisings, notably the rebellion of 366 BC against ARTAXERXES II. Alexander the Great retained the system after his conquest, as did the Parthians, but during the Sassanian empire of AD 224 to 651 the term designated a less important figure.

satyagraha Policy of nonviolent resistance, including fasting and economic boycotts, developed by Mohandas Gandhi (see feature, page 252) as a means of pressing for political reform. The word 'satyagraha' comes from Sanskrit, and means 'force of truth'. Gandhi conceived the idea in South Africa in 1906 to combat laws discriminating against Asians. The first satyagraha campaign in India began in 1917. It was the basis of Gandhi's Non-Cooperation Movement of 1920 to 1922, which boycotted British institutions and

goods in protest against the AMRITSAR MASSACRE of 1919. The movement ended after violence broke out, but Gandhi continued to use hunger strikes, nonviolent protests and civil disobedience, such as refusing to pay taxes, to achieve Indian independence in 1947.

Saudi Arabia Country in south-west Asia occupying four-fifths of the Arabian peninsula. The religion of ISLAM was founded in Medina in the west by the prophet Muhammad in 622, and by the mid 8th century the Islamic empire stretched from India to Spain. Rivalry among different sects led to its decline and by the mid 13th century it had split into small sheikhdoms. In 1517 it was taken over by the Ottoman Empire.

From 1745 the Wahhabi movement, a puritanical Islamic group, tried to unite Arabia, but was crushed by Egypt between 1811 and 1818 and again in 1891. In 1902 a descendant of the Wahhabi rulers, Abd al-Aziz Ibn Saud, began a struggle to rid Arabia of the Turks. After Turkey entered the First World War against Britain, the British gave arms and aid to the Arabs and from 1915 held Saudi lands as a protectorate. Colonel T.E. LAWRENCE, known as 'Lawrence of Arabia', helped the tribes to fight Turkish forces. After the war Ibn Saud defeated his rivals and in 1926 unified the kingdoms of the Hejaz on the north-west coast and Nejd in central Arabia, west of Riyadh. The independence of the new state was recognised by Britain in 1927 and in 1932 was renamed Saudi Arabia by Ibn Saud, who ruled until 1953. In 1936 oil was discovered. By 1944 the kingdom controlled the world's largest known oil reserves, and it became one of the founding members of the ORGANISATION OF PETROLEUM EXPORTING COUNTRIES (OPEC) in 1960.

Ibn Saud was succeeded by his son Saud, who ruled from 1953 until 1964, when he was deposed by his family and replaced by his half-brother Faisal. Faisal's use of Saudi oil power helped the country's rise to prominence. In 1973 he helped to organise the OPEC oil embargo against the USA and other nations supporting Israel in the YOM KIPPUR WAR against Egypt. Two years later Faisal was assassinated and succeeded by Ibn Saud's fourth son, Khalid, who ruled until 1982. In 1979 Saudi Arabia broke off diplomatic relations with Egypt following an Egyptian-Israeli peace treaty. Saudi Arabia supported Iraq in the IRAN-IRAQ WAR, but in August 1990 Khalid's successor, King Fahd, agreed to station UN troops to protect Saudi oil fields from Iraqi invasion. Thousands of Saudi troops took part in the 1991 GULF WAR against Iraq, while Saudi Arabia also took in

Kuwait's royal family. The Gulf War led to increased criticism of Fahd's regime by pro-democracy liberals, and by the increasingly influential Islamic fundamentalists. In 1992 Fahd created a Consultative Council, comprising 60 members chosen by the king. The council could give advice but could not make laws. Fahd also denounced the spread of Islamic fundamentalism, and international concern arose over the abuse of human rights and public executions in Saudi Arabia. In January 1996 the ailing King Fahd transferred power to his half-brother, Crown Prince Abdullah, and remained monarch in name only.

Saul (11th century BC) First king of ancient Israel, from about 1021 to 1000 BC, whose story is told in the Old Testament. Initially anointed by the prophet SAMUEL, Saul earned his anger by usurping some of Samuel's priestly duties. In his later years the king witnessed the rise to power of his son-in-law, DAVID. Saul was jealous of David's military successes and of his friendship with Jonathan, Saul's son. Samuel secretly anointed David as Saul's successor. On the eve of a battle against the neighbouring PHILISTINES at Mount Gilboa, Saul visited a witch at Endor who foretold his defeat and death. The following day, vanquished and wounded, he committed suicide to evade capture.

Saul became deranged as he grew older and threatened to kill his son-in-law David, who fled to escape Saul's unprovoked attacks.

Savage, Michael (1872-1940) First Labour prime minister of New Zealand. Savage was born in Australia, where he worked as a gold miner, but settled in New Zealand in 1907. In 1916 he joined the newly formed Labour Party, becoming its deputy leader in 1923. Ten years later he took over as leader and in 1935 became prime minister following Labour's landslide victory. He was re-elected in 1938 but died in office, and was succeeded by Peter Fraser. Savage's advocacy of social security legislation and anti-Depression economic measures helped to make him one of the most popular of New Zealand's political leaders.

Savonarola, Girolamo (1452-98) Italian religious reformer. Savonarola entered the Dominican order in 1475. As lecturer in the convent of San Marco in Florence, his sermons attacking Church corruption and state tyranny attracted large attendances, and in 1491 he was made prior. In 1494 Charles VIII of France invaded Italy – an event Savonarola had predicted in 1492 – and the Medici rulers of Florence were overthrown. Savonarola became the spiritual leader of a new democratic republic of Florence. He introduced laws against vice and frivolity and attacked the notoriously corrupt pope, Alexander VI.

In 1497 Savonarola's followers burnt personal ornaments, gambling equipment and pictures in a public 'bonfire of the vanities'. In the same year, Savonarola ignored an order from the pope to stop preaching, and was excommunicated. In 1498, one of his disciples accepted an ordeal by fire to prove the invalidity of the excommunication. The event did not take place, but disputes between his supporters and opponents became rife. He was brought to trial, tortured and found guilty of heresy, and was executed on May 23.

Girolamo Savonarola was stripped of his vestments, hung and burnt in the Piazza della Signoria, Florence, with two of his most devoted followers.

Savoy Region on the French-Italian border in the western Alps. The area was first inhabited by Celtic tribes who were conquered by the Romans in 121 BC. It became known as Savoy after 534, when it came under the control of the kingdom of Burgundy. From the mid 11th century Savoy was ruled by the House of Savoy, which during the Middle Ages extended its territory into Switzerland, Nice and PIEDMONT. In 1416 Savoy became a duchy. It was occupied by the French in 1536, but in 1559 Duke Emmanuel Philibert regained most of his territories and in 1563 moved the ducal residence to Turin, after which Savoy became an Italian state.

By the Treaty of Utrecht, which ended the War of the SPANISH SUCCESSION in 1713, the duke of Savoy was made king of Sicily. In 1720 he exchanged this for control of Sardinia, and Savoy and Piedmont became part of the kingdom of Sardinia. Savoy was annexed by France during the French Revolutionary Wars, but was returned in 1815. On Italian reunification in 1860-1, French Savoy was ceded to France in return for Napoleon III's help against the Austrians. The House of Savoy became the ruling house of Italy until the Italian Republic was established in 1946.

Saxe, Maurice, Comte de (1696-1750) Marshal of France and military theorist, the illegitimate son of AUGUSTUS II 'THE STRONG', king of Poland. At the age of 12 Saxe was sent by his father to join the army of John Churchill, Duke of Marlborough, in Flanders. In 1720 he went into service for the French, and he fought in the War of the POLISH SUCCESSION of 1733 to 1738. In the War of the AUSTRIAN SUCCESSION, Saxe took Prague in 1741 and in 1744 was appointed marshal of France by Louis XV.

After his victory at FONTENOY in 1745, Saxe gained control of most of the Austrian Netherlands, which strengthened France's position at the Treaty of AIX-LA-CHAPELLE in 1748. Saxe's treatise on warfare, *Mes Rêveries*, was published in 1756-7.

Saxons Germanic people who in ancient times lived in the area of modern Schleswig in Germany and along the Baltic coast, from where they ravaged the coasts bordering the North Sea in the 3rd and 4th centuries. Saxons appear to have arrived in Britain, together with ANGLES and JUTES, as mercenaries in the late period of the Roman occupation. After the Romans withdrew from Britain in 409, Saxons and other Germanic tribes again raided the British coast, and from the 430s they began to arrive in large numbers. According to tradition, the tide of settlement was halted in the early 6th century by British resistance led by chieftains such as ARTHUR, but began again around 550. By the 7th century Britain was organised into seven ANGLO-SAXON kingdoms, including Wessex (the West Saxons), Essex (the East Saxons) and Sussex (the South Saxons). After the migration to Britain, Saxons on the Continent occupied SAXONY in northwest Germany and in 566 were subjugated by the Franks.

Saxony Area of north Germany, the original home of the SAXONS. Between about AD 200 and 700 an area between the Elbe and Ems rivers, including south Jutland, was conquered by the Germanic Saxons. Saxons migrated to Britain from the 5th century, but in the late 8th century the Continental Saxons were conquered by CHARLEMAGNE. On the division of Charlemagne's empire in 843, Saxony became part of the German kingdom and by the early 10th century was a hereditary duchy. In 919 HENRY I, duke of Saxony, was elected king of Germany, and in 962 his son OTTO I founded the Holy Roman Empire.

In 1356 the duke of Saxony became one of the seven permanent imperial Electors with the right to elect the Holy Roman Emperor. Saxony was the leading state of Protestant Germany from the 16th century until the Thirty Years' War of 1618 to 1648. In 1806 Napoleon conquered Saxony and made it a kingdom. After his defeat, Saxony lost much of its territory to Prussia at the Congress of VIENNA of 1814 to 1815, and became a member of the GERMAN CONFEDERATION. In 1871 it became part of the German Second Empire. At the end of the Second World War Saxony became a part of the German Democratic Republic, but was abolished as a formal territory in 1952. The state of Saxony was re-created on German reunification in 1990.

scalawag White supporter of the Republican reconstruction programme in the American South in the early years following the AMERICAN CIVIL WAR. Scalawags were a diverse group, including some profiteers, but also businessmen, reformers, former Southern Whigs and yeoman farmers who supported the Republican regime. A Republican from the North was known as a CARPETBAGGER.

Scandinavia Northernmost part of Europe, traditionally Denmark, Norway and Sweden; a broader definition includes Finland, Iceland and the North Atlantic islands that have come within Scandinavia's influence. In the VIKING age (c.800-1050) Scandinavia was an important centre of civilisation. It sent colonists to Iceland, the North Atlantic islands and Greenland, while Scandinavian rulers dominated much of England, Ireland, Normandy, Finland and western Russia. This primarily seaborne civilisation also made contact with the shores of North America, which the Vikings called VINLAND.

By the early 11th century, Norway, Denmark and Sweden had become kingdoms. Overseas conquests led them to join together in the Union of Kalmar of 1397. In 1523 Sweden under GUSTAV I VASA broke away, but Norway and Denmark remained united until 1814. Sweden rose to prominence in Europe in the 17th century under GUSTAV II ADOLPH and his chancellor OXENSTIERNA, eclipsing Denmark-Norway as a Baltic power, and until the NORTHERN WAR of 1700 to 1721 held the balance of power in Europe.

Scapa Flow Sheltered stretch of sea in the ORKNEY Islands, Scotland, the main base of the British Grand Fleet during the First World War. On June 21, 1919, the German High Seas Fleet, then interned at Scapa Flow, was scuttled by German crews as an act of defiance against the terms of the Versailles Peace Settlement. In October 1939 the defences of Scapa Flow were penetrated when a German U-boat sank HMS *Royal Oak*, and its eastern entrances were sealed up as a result.

The SMS *Konig Albert*, a dreadnought belonging to the surrendered German fleet scuttled at Scapa Flow, is towed away for destruction.

Schacht, Hjalmar (1877-1970) German banker and finance minister between the two world wars. Schacht was appointed Germany's special currency commissioner in 1923. His policy halted the Weimar Republic's rampant inflation and in December he was appointed president of Germany's leading financial institution, the Reichsbank. In 1929 he took part in the Paris conference on Germany's reparations payments, but rejected the resulting YOUNG PLAN and resigned his position. Schacht admired Hitler, and brought him to the attention of wealthy industrialists who were in a position to offer financial support. He was reappointed as Reichsbank president by the Nazis in 1933, and became minister of economics in 1934. Rivalry with Hermann Goering over the economy caused his resignation in 1937, and two years later he was dismissed from the Reichsbank for disagreeing with Hitler over rearmament expenditure, and was imprisoned in a concentration camp in 1944. He was acquitted of war crimes in the NUREMBERG TRIALS, and set up his own bank in 1953.

Scharnhorst, Gerhard von (1755-1813) Prussian general and military reformer during the NAPOLEONIC WARS. A Hanoverian, he entered the service of the Prussians in 1801. After Prussia's defeat by Napoleon at the Battle of JENA in 1806, Scharnhorst reorganised the Prussian army. He abolished capital punishment, promoted non-aristocrats to the officer corps and introduced the *Krümpersystem* – 'shrinkage system' – in which citizens were trained and sent into reserve forces. This increased the number of trained soldiers while maintaining the size of the standing army within the limit of 42 000 men imposed by Napoleon. Scharnhorst was appointed chief of staff to Field Marshal Gebhard Leberecht von BLÜCHER in 1813, but he died of wounds received at the Battle of Lützen. His reforms enabled the Prussian army to defeat Napoleon at the Battle of LEIPZIG in the same year.

Schiller, Friedrich von (1759-1805) German Romantic poet, dramatist and historian. Forced into studying law by his father's employer, Schiller was later allowed to transfer to medicine, and in 1780 he became an army surgeon in Stuttgart. His anonymously published first play, *Die Raüber* (*The Robbers*, 1781), attacked political tyranny and was an instant success. Schiller fled his post and in 1785 moved to Leipzig. He wrote *Don Carlos* (1785), a verse-drama about Philip II of Spain, followed by a history of the Dutch Revolts in the NETHERLANDS. This gained Schiller the professorship of history at Jena University, where he produced his *History of the Thirty Years' War* (1791-3). From 1793 he lived in Weimar, plagued by ill health. There he wrote his final great dramas: *Wallenstein*

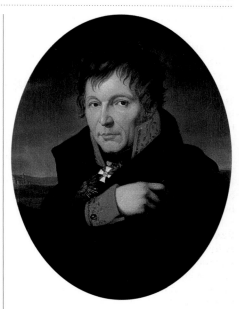

Gerhard von Scharnhorst wrote directly to the king of Prussia asking permission to become a lieutenant colonel and reorganise the army.

(1798-9), about the commander in chief of the armies of the Holy Roman Empire during the Thirty Years' War; *Maria Stuart* (1800) about Mary, Queen of Scots; *Die Jungfrau von Orleans* (*The Maid of Orleans*, 1801), about Joan of Arc; and *Wilhelm Tell* (1804), the story of the Swiss revolt against Habsburg rule.

Schlegel Family name of two German scholars, August Wilhelm von (1767-1845) and Friedrich von (1772-1829), pioneers of the study of art history, literature and comparative philology. In 1798 August Wilhelm became professor of literature and fine art at Jena University. There he founded *Das Athanäum*, the principal organ of German ROMANTICISM. He translated 17 of Shakespeare's plays between 1797 and 1810 which are still used on the German stage. In 1808 he gave a series of lectures in Vienna on dramatic art and literature, helping to spread Romantic ideas throughout the Continent. He served as press secretary to Bernadotte, later Charles XIV of Sweden, in 1813 and 1814, and from 1818 to 1845 was professor of art and literary history at Bonn.

Friedrich developed many of the philosophical ideas of the early German Romantic movement. He studied oriental languages in Paris from 1802 to 1804, and in 1808 published a pioneering work on Sanskrit and Indo-Germanic linguistics. While living in Paris, Friedrich was also a spokesman for the anti-Napoleonic movement for German liberation. Between 1810 and 1812 he lectured on history. His *History of Ancient and Modern Literature* (1815) reflected his notion of the inseparability of a nation's intellectual, spiritual, political and economic development.

Schleswig-Holstein Province of Germany, bordered by Denmark. In the Middle Ages the duchies of Schleswig and Holstein owed allegiance to the Danish crown, but were not part of Denmark. By the Congress of VIENNA of 1814 to 1815, Holstein, with its German-speaking majority, was incorporated into the GERMAN CONFEDERATION, but the mainly Danish-speaking Schleswig remained outside it.

In 1848 war broke out in both duchies after Denmark's annexation of Schleswig. Prussian troops drove out the Danish army, but Britain, Russia and France intervened, forcing Prussia's withdrawal in 1850. The Schleswig-Holstein question became a burning issue in Europe. A compromise peace agreement was reached: by the 1852 London Protocol, Denmark undertook not to attempt to incorporate Schleswig, but in 1863 the Danish king Christian IX signed a common constitution for Denmark and Schleswig.

In 1864 Prussia and Austria declared war on Denmark, which was easily defeated and surrendered the duchies to its adversaries. In 1866, Prussia used a dispute over the administration of the duchies to start the AUSTRO-PRUSSIAN WAR. Following Austria's defeat, Prussia annexed both duchies, which in 1871 became part of the unified German Empire. In 1920 plebiscites were held in North Schleswig. The northern part passed to Denmark as the province of South Jutland, the rest of Schleswig-Holstein remaining in Germany.

Schlieffen Plan Basis for Germany's strategy at the outbreak of the First World War. The plan was devised by General Alfred Schlieffen, German chief of staff from 1891 to 1905. After the Franco-Russian alliance of 1894, he developed a strategy that would enable Germany to avoid fighting on two fronts. Initially the Russians, who took several weeks to mobilise, would be held by defensive operations, while French fortifications facing Germany were outflanked by a scythelike attack through Holland, Belgium and Luxembourg. France could be defeated within six weeks, after which Germany's forces could be transferred east. A modified version of the plan formed the basis for Germany's strategy on the outbreak of the First World War, but failed due to the French counteroffensive at the Battle of the MARNE in September 1914. It was abandoned when Germany withdrew forces from the Western Front to stem Russian advances into East Prussia. In 1940 Adolf Hitler employed the principles of the Schlieffen Plan in his BLITZKRIEG, or 'lightning war', in the West.

Schmidt, Helmut (1918-) Chancellor of West Germany from 1974 to 1982. Born in Hamburg, Schmidt served in the German

A portrait of Kaiser Wilhelm II looks over a class of Berlin schoolchildren, who benefited from the earliest state school system, as they are taught history at the outset of the First World War.

armed forces during the Second World War and won the Iron Cross. A member of the Social Democratic Party, in 1953 he was elected to the Bundestag, the West German parliament. In 1969 Schmidt became minister of defence in the government of Willy BRANDT, and in 1972 was appointed minister of finance. Following Brandt's resignation in 1974, Schmidt was elected federal chancellor. He was re-elected in 1976 and 1980.

Schmidt continued Brandt's OSTPOLITIK, or dialogue with the German Democratic Republic (East Germany) and the Soviet Union, while maintaining close ties with the USA. His refusal to cut social-welfare programmes in October 1982 lost him the support of his partners in the alliance government. He resigned after a vote of no confidence and was succeeded as chancellor by Helmut KOHL.

Schoenberg, Arnold (1874-1951) Austro-Hungarian composer and teacher. Schoenberg was brought up in Vienna, where he learned the violin and began composing before the age of nine. Almost entirely self-taught, his early works were in a late Romantic style, but in 1907 he began to abandon tonality – music written in a specific key and centred on a specific tone. Early 'atonal' works – a term coined by a disapproving critic – such as his second *String Quartet* (1907-8) caused an uproar when first performed because of their harsh, dissonant style. In 1923, with his *Five Piano Pieces*, Opus 23, Schoenberg introduced a method of composition known as the 12-note method, or 'serialism'. The lack of melody provoked public hostility, but thereafter Schoenberg only occasionally returned to traditional tonality. Dismissed from his Berlin teaching post by the Nazis in 1933, Schoenberg moved to the USA and taught at the University of California from 1936 to 1944.

Scholasticism Method of philosophical and theological enquiry that aimed at a better understanding of Christian doctrine by a process of definition and systematic argument. The educational tradition of Scholasticism arose in medieval universities, or 'schools', in the 11th century, and flourished in the 12th and 13th centuries. The writings of Aristotle and St AUGUSTINE played a crucial part in the development of Scholastic thought. One of the earliest Scholastics was St ANSELM, who lived from 1033 to 1109. In his writings, St Anselm sought to understand and defend religious belief by intellectual reasoning rather than by arguments based on the Scripture and other authorities.

The crowning achievement of Scholastic thought was St Thomas AQUINAS' *Summa Theologica*, written between about 1265 and 1273, in which he attempted to establish a complete theological system which reconciled reason with faith. His main rival was the Franciscan philosopher John DUNS SCOTUS, whose writings and lectures stressed the distinction between faith and reason. Scholasticism declined in the later Middle Ages. In the 14th century the writings of WILLIAM OF OCCAM challenged the scholastic position by claiming that faith has no rational basis.

school systems In medieval western Europe, education was usually provided by religious orders. After the Reformation both Protestant and Roman Catholic groups offered formal education to more people, and there was an increase in the number of private and public schools. Nevertheless, before 1800 the concept of education for all emerged only in a few Calvinist countries such as Scotland and the Netherlands, and in the New England colonies of America. State systems developed from the late 18th century. Prussia was the first country to establish compulsory attendance in the 18th century, and in 1794 recognised the state's responsibility to provide education. In 1810 the Prussian ministry of the interior introduced state examinations for teachers to regulate teaching standards. In the USA, officials in Massachusetts established a state board of education in 1837, and the provision of a secular school system spread to other states throughout the 19th century. France laid early foundations for the centralised control of education when in 1854 the country was divided into *académies*, educational administrative districts, each run by a rector, and secular state schools were established by the end of the 19th century.

In England and Wales, church schools and Sunday schools provided voluntary primary education before the Education Act of 1870 introduced free, secular primary education. The Education Act of 1880 introduced compulsory education, while the Act of 1902 laid the basis for a state system of primary and secondary education. The 1944 Education Act of England and Wales established a system of universal secondary education provided by grant-assisted independent schools and local-authority schools. Similar acts came into force in Scotland in 1945 and in Northern Ireland in 1947. After 1988, primary and secondary schools in England and Wales could elect to become grant-maintained, receiving direct funding from central government.

School systems divide broadly between the centralised Prussian and French systems, and the more decentralised US and British systems, although the introduction of a national curriculum in the late 1980s in Britain marked a shift towards centralisation. Four systems have acted as models: the Prussian in the mid 19th century in Russia, Turkey and Japan; the French in most of western Europe, Egypt, the Middle East, French-speaking Africa and much of South-east Asia; the US system throughout much of South America, China and present-day Japan, where a national system of universal education was established in 1871; and the British system in India and the Commonwealth. In the late 20th century primary education became almost universal, while secondary and technical education for all are priorities for developing countries.

Schopenhauer, Arthur (1788-1860)
German philosopher who believed that human will is an irrational, impelling force. Schopenhauer reacted against the German idealist tradition represented by George HEGEL. In his main work, *Die Welt als Wille und Vorstellung* (*The World as Will and Idea*, 1819), he emphasised the role of the will in human nature. Intellect and consciousness are instruments in the service of will, while conflict between individual wills is the cause of the world's strife; pleasure is the absence of pain. In Schopenhauer's profoundly pessimistic view of human life, art and aesthetic contemplation provide a temporary antidote. In 1820 Schopenhauer began teaching in Berlin, but failed to attract students. With his book almost ignored, he moved to Frankfurt, where he lived an unhappy, reclusive life and reworked his ideas. Schopenhauer's work began to attract attention from the 1850s, greatly influencing Friedrich NIETZSCHE, Richard WAGNER and Sigmund FREUD.

Schuman Plan
Proposal made in May, 1950, to pool the coal and steel industries of France and the Federal Republic of Germany under a common authority that other European nations might join. The plan was drafted by the French economist Jean MONNET and put forward by the French foreign minister Robert Schuman. It became effective in July 1952 with the formation of the European Coal and Steel Community, to which Italy, Belgium, Holland and Luxembourg as well as France and West Germany belonged. Britain declined to join. Its success ultimately led to the formation of the EUROPEAN UNION.

Schumpeter, Joseph (1883-1950)
Moravian-born economist and sociologist. Schumpeter served as Austria's finance minister from 1919 to 1920 and as professor of economics at Bonn from 1925 to 1932, when he moved to the USA and became professor of economics at Harvard University. Schumpeter's theory of the entrepreneur as the dynamic factor in fostering the business cycle had a powerful influence, as did his theory of capitalist development. In *Capitalism, Socialism and Democracy* (1942), he predicted that the success of capitalism would lead to its demise. Economic enterprises would grow, leaving less scope for the individual entrepreneur. The result would be a form of socialism where economic decisions were made centrally by bureaucratic means.

Schuschnigg, Kurt von (1897-1977)
Chancellor of Austria during the Nazis' rise to power. Elected a Christian Socialist deputy in 1927, Schuschnigg served as minister of justice from 1932 to 1933, and of education from 1933 to 1934, before becoming chancellor after the assassination of Engelbert DOLLFUSS. In July 1936, with Austria isolated from the Western powers, Schuschnigg signed a compromise agreement with Adolf Hitler. Germany agreed to respect the sovereignty of Austria if it acknowledged itself a German state. In February 1938 Schuschnigg attempted to defeat a conspiracy by Austrian Nazis by meeting Hitler, but was humiliated. On March 9 he announced a plebiscite to decide in favour of Austrian independence. On March 11, two days before the plebiscite, Germany annexed Austria in the ANSCHLUSS. Schuschnigg was forced to resign and was imprisoned by the Germans throughout the Second World War. After the war he became a professor of political science in the USA.

Schwarzenberg, Felix, Prince of
(1800-52) Austrian statesman, nephew of Karl Philipp SCHWARZENBERG. Schwarzenberg was a diplomat before becoming political adviser to Field-Marshal Joseph RADETZKY on the outbreak of the REVOLUTIONS OF 1848 in Prague and Vienna. Appointed chief minister in November 1848, Schwarzenberg persuaded Emperor Ferdinand I to abdicate in favour of his nephew, FRANZ JOSEF. The Hungarian nationalist uprising of 1848-9 was crushed with the aid of Russia, and Habsburg supremacy was restored in northern Italy. Schwarzenberg opposed autonomy for the states of Austria and in 1849 he drew up a constitution that transformed the Habsburg Empire into a centralised and absolutist state with strengthened imperial powers. In 1850, Schwarzenberg secured formal recognition by the Prussians of Austrian leadership in the GERMAN CONFEDERATION. Two years later he died suddenly in office.

Schwarzenberg, Karl Philipp, Prince of
(1771-1820) Austrian field-marshal and diplomat. Schwarzenberg entered the imperial cavalry in 1787. In 1809 he was general of cavalry at the Battle of WAGRAM, after which Austria was forced to concede defeat to the French emperor Napoleon. The following year Schwarzenberg negotiated the marriage between Napoleon and Maria Louisa of Austria. Austria assisted Napoleon in his Russian campaign of 1812, but in 1813 joined the allies against the French. In October 1813 Schwarzenberg was commander of the victorious allied armies at the decisive Battle of LEIPZIG, which shattered the French army and led to Napoleon's defeat in 1814. Schwarzenberg retired in 1815.

science, rise of see feature, pages 576-7

Scipio
Ancient Roman patrician family which produced outstanding Roman leaders in the 2nd and 3rd centuries BC. Scipio Africanus Major (236-184) was one of the greatest soldiers of the ancient world. During the Second PUNIC WAR of 218 to 201 between Rome and CARTHAGE, Scipio forced the Carthaginians out of Spain in 206, and in 202

DID YOU KNOW?

The ancient Greeks had a highly developed system of elementary education, but it emphasised physical training more than reading, writing and arithmetic. Fitness was important because the country's highest priority was to produce good athletes and capable soldiers.

Scipio Africanus (centre) listens as the captive Numidian prince Syphax explains his reasons for reneging on an agreed alliance with the Romans during the Second Punic War. Syphax claims to have been led astray by his wife, Sophonisba (left), who was a Carthaginian and an enemy of Scipio.

his defeat of HANNIBAL at the Battle of Zama in Africa broke the power of Carthage. For this he was honoured with the title 'Africanus'. Scipio's pro-Greek policies contributed to the rivalries that led to his downfall in 184, when CATO accused him of corruption.

Scipio's son was the adoptive father of Scipio Africanus Minor (185-129), who became a national hero during the Third Punic War of 149 to 146, and was given the title 'Africanus' for his destruction of Carthage in 146. He also won the title 'Numantinus' after capturing Numantia and subjugating Spain in 133. Scipio was at the centre of an intellectual group, the 'Scipionic Circle', which included the historian POLYBIUS. In 129 Scipio lost support after showing his disapproval of the reforms of his brother-in-law, the tribune Tiberius GRACCHUS, and implying that Gracchus' murder was deserved. He died in the upheaval that followed.

Scotland Country occupying the northern part of Great Britain, part of the United Kingdom since 1707. By the early 2nd millennium BC there were settlements on the west coast, SHETLANDS and ORKNEY Islands. The region was known as CALEDONIA to the Romans, who invaded it unsuccessfully several times between AD 82 and 208. From the 5th century Scotland was divided between Picts, Britons, Gaelic Scots from Dalriada in northern Ireland, and ANGLES. Christianity, introduced in late Roman times and established by Celtic clergy from Ireland, helped to unify the diverse peoples. KENNETH I united the kingdoms of the Scots and the Picts in about 483 to form one kingdom, Alba, where Scots culture and language became dominant.

The kingdom expanded to include Lothian and Strathclyde in the reigns of Malcolm II, from 1005-34, and Duncan I, from 1034-40. Attempts by the English king EDWARD I to

impose direct rule over Scotland in 1296 led to war, but in 1328 ROBERT I 'the Bruce' secured Scottish independence. From 1371 the Stewart dynasty maintained Scotland's alliance with France, but this came under attack during the Scottish Reformation, led by John KNOX. Protestantism was established as Scotland's national religion in 1560, and in 1567 MARY, QUEEN OF SCOTS was forced to abdicate by Protestant nobles. In 1603 the English and Scottish crowns were united when James VI of Scotland became JAMES I of England, but political union was not established until 1707. After the Hanoverians succeeded to the throne in 1714, JACOBITE supporters of the STUART dynasty staged unsuccessful rebellions in 1715 and 1745.

In the mid 18th century, Scotland experienced a cultural Enlightenment. At the same time, the failure of the Jacobite rebellions led

In 18th-century Scotland, the river Clyde was deepened to allow access to Glasgow. The city became famous for its shipbuilding industry.

to the suppression of the CLAN system. Landowners needed to clear space for the introduction of sheep farming, leading to the evictions of crofters and tenants, known as the HIGHLAND CLEARANCES, during the 19th century. Scotland's industrial revolution began in the late 18th century, but during the 20th century heavy industries declined. New industries such as microelectronics and North Sea oil slowed the decline but did not halt it. In the 1970s a tide of support for Scottish nationalism provoked a referendum on the issue of limited self-rule. Scotland faced high unemployment in the recession of the early 1990s, partly alleviated by regional and social funding by the EC (see EUROPEAN UNION) and UK regional enterprise grants.

Scottish National Party Scottish political party dedicated to the achievement of Scottish independence. It was formed in 1934 from a merger of the National Party of Scotland and the Scottish Party. The party gained its first parliamentary seat in 1945 at a by-election in Motherwell. In the October 1974 general election, 11 of its candidates won parliamentary seats. In 1979 a referendum in Scotland on a Scottish representative assembly failed to gain the required majority, and in the 1979 general election all but two of the candidates were defeated. Three were elected in 1987, and four in 1992.

Scottsboro Case (1931) Notorious American civil rights case in which two White girls accused nine Black youths of rape on an Alabama freight train. A lynching was averted and the youths were put on trial in Scottsboro, Alabama, defended by two lawyers who volunteered on the day.

An all-White jury convicted the youths. Eight of them were sentenced to death, but the jury could not decide whether the ninth

Protesters marched to the White House in 1933 to demand freedom for those convicted in the Scottsboro Case. They were joined by one of the alleged victims, who repudiated her testimony.

defendant, a boy of 12, should be executed or imprisoned for life. In 1932 the US Supreme Court overturned the convictions on the grounds that the defendants had been denied adequate counsel, but one of the boys, Clarence Norris, was retried in 1933. Despite one of the alleged victims admitting the rape had not taken place, Norris was convicted again. In 1935 the conviction was overturned by the Supreme Court because Blacks had been deliberately excluded from the grand jury that indicted Norris.

Haywood Patterson, another of the defendants, was retried and sentenced to 75 years in jail; the others were also retried and convicted again. Patterson escaped in 1948, only to die in prison three years later after a conviction for manslaughter. Following appeals from pressure groups, the four youngest defendants were eventually freed because of their age and probable innocence, and the others were paroled. Clarence Norris, the only known surviving defendant, received a full pardon in 1976.

scutage In medieval English law, payment made by a knight to the Crown in lieu of military service. The term comes from the Latin *scutum*, meaning shield. Scutage was accepted in England by 1100. It was demanded by the Crown from those liable for knight service as a means of raising money for military campaigns. The need for more permanent and flexible forces meant that the wars fought by RICHARD I and JOHN in France led to the hire of an increasingly large number of mercenaries. The barons' opposition to the frequent and heavy scutages exacted by King John to finance campaigns was a factor in their revolt in 1215 and was reflected in clause 12 of the MAGNA CARTA, which stated that the king was

not to levy scutage without the consent of a great council. Changes in land law meant that scutage began to bring in less and less money for the king. By the late 13th century it was being replaced by taxes voted in Parliament, and it became obsolete, as did the feudal army.

Scythians Ancient Indo-European nomadic people. The Scythians briefly occupied part of Asia Minor in the 7th century BC. After they were driven out by the MEDES, they established a kingdom in southern Russia in the 6th century and traded with the Greek cities of the Black Sea. The Scythians were famed for their horsemanship and skill as archers. They resisted the attempts of the Persian ruler DARIUS I to subdue them in about 512 BC. Around 325 BC they crushed a large detachment of Macedonian troops before making peace with Alexander the Great, but were driven out of the Balkans by the Celts after 300. In the 2nd century BC they were displaced by the related Sarmatian tribe. Gold and bronze objects found in graves of Scythian kings and nobles, many of which were made for them by the Greeks, show outstanding artistic skills.

A Scythian, sculpted in stone from the fortress city of Ahicchattra in the 3rd century BC, would have provoked fear with his skill on horseback.

Seacole, Mary (1805-81) Jamaican nurse during the CRIMEAN WAR. Seacole gained her medical experience in Kingston, Jamaica, a garrison town where British soldiers preferred local healers to their own, often incompetent, regimental surgeons. In 1853 she volunteered to serve alongside Florence NIGHTINGALE, but despite her experience in treating illnesses affecting troops in the Crimea, her offer was rejected because of her colour. Nevertheless, she left for the Crimea the following year at her own expense. Based outside Balaklava, she sold goods to the soldiers, using the profits to care for the sick, dispense medicine and provide healthy meals. Seacole's work set a new standard for army suppliers. After the war she returned to Britain bankrupt. Her debts were cleared by war veterans and well-wishers.

Second Front Invasion of German-occupied France by the Allies in the Second World War. The Soviet leader Joseph Stalin pressed for an early opening of the Second Front from August 1941 to relieve pressure on the Red Army in the east. The British argued for a delay, as combined operations on a large scale needed long planning and specialised equipment. This was confirmed by the disaster of the DIEPPE RAID in August 1942. In 1943 at the CASABLANCA CONFERENCE, the British prime minister Winston Churchill persuaded the US president Franklin D. Roosevelt that the invasion of Italy should come first, but the Soviet government criticised British hesitancy throughout 1943. The NORMANDY CAMPAIGN eventually opened the Second Front in June 1944.

Second Reich see GERMAN SECOND EMPIRE

Security Council Principal council of the UNITED NATIONS responsible for maintaining world peace. It is composed of five permanent members – Britain, the United States, Russia, the People's Republic of China and France – and ten non-permanent members elected to two-year terms by the General Assembly. The Security Council may investigate any international dispute; its recommendations, which might involve a peaceful settlement, the imposition of trade sanctions, or a request to UN members to provide military forces, are to be accepted by all member countries. In deciding upon a course of action, the Security Council requires the votes of nine members, but each of the five permanent members can veto a resolution. By 1992 it was felt by many, including the secretary-general Dr Boutros Boutros-Ghali, that its membership needed revising to recognise the current world power structure. In 1994 the proposal was advanced that permanent Security Council membership be doubled.

How humans learnt to observe their world

Medieval Europe was founded on faith in God and the received wisdom of the ancients. When humans began to explore the natural world through observation and experiment, modern science was born.

Science is regarded today as the systematic attempt to understand the natural world through the use of observation, experiment and reason. In that form it originated among ancient Greek thinkers from the 6th century BC onwards, though they built upon a knowledge of the heavens and skill in the handling of numbers earlier developed by the Mesopotamians and Egyptians.

Greek philosophers took the view that the cosmos was governed according to the orderly operations of nature. It was not the result of blind chance, nor was it subject to the arbitrary interventions of the gods. Aristotle and his disciples believed that the natural world, despite all its diversity, was composed of four basic elements – earth, fire, water and air – and that health and disease could be explained by the activities of four humours or body fluids. Following Pythagoras and Plato, most Greeks believed that the orbits of the planets and other aspects of the order of nature could be understood through the sciences of numbers and geometry: astronomy was systematised by Ptolemy. So from astronomy to biology, antiquity created a coherent and comprehensive scientific outlook which held sway for some 2000 years, becoming harmonised with the Christian world-view of the Middle Ages.

EXPLORING THE COSMOS

Though the Greeks pioneered the concept of science, the 16th and 17th centuries produced the theories and methods which form the core of science today. Change came first in astronomy. In 1543 Nicolaus Copernicus, a Polish canon, argued in his *On the Revolutions of the Heavenly Spheres* that the cosmos was not, as most Greeks had believed, Earth-centred, but was heliocentric, with all the planets, the Earth included, orbiting the Sun. The implications of this view were staggering, for it suggested that mankind might not, after all, be at the centre of creation.

By the early 17th century the work of the German mathematician Johannes Kepler and the Italian Galileo Galilei (the first astronomer to look through a telescope) had finally convinced the scientific world of the correctness of the Copernican hypothesis – though the Roman Catholic Church put Galileo on trial for his supposedly heretical view that the Earth moved. When Galileo finally submitted to the Church and stated that the Earth did not move round the Sun, some accounts say that he muttered under his breath *'e pur si muove'* ('and yet it moves'). Seventeenth-century astronomers went on to deny that the Sun was at the centre of the system, arguing instead for an infinite Universe in which it was just one of an infinite number of stars.

The same year as Copernicus published his treatise on astronomy, Andreas Vesalius, professor of medicine at the University of Padua, equally broke with the authority of the Greeks by showing, through the findings of dissections, that the human body was not formed as described in the long-revered writings of the Roman physician Galen.

Vesalius's work inaugurated a period of intense and dramatic anatomical investigations which led, within a couple of generations, to the epochal discovery of the circulation of the blood, announced by the English physician William Harvey in his 1628 book, *On the Motion of the Heart*.

Harvey viewed the heart as a pump, encouraging a mechanical view of the workings of the bodily parts. Sadly, he

Andreas Vesalius (above) laid bare the secrets of the human body. Nicolaus Copernicus charted the Earth's orbit (left).

believed that his discovery had done him little good. The antiquarian John Aubrey reported, 'I have heard him say that, when his book on blood circulation came out, his practice suffered and people called him mad'.

Many of the great thinkers of the 17th century deplored what they condemned as the over-confident rationalism of Aristotle and other Greek philosophers. They maintained that science could progress only through meticulous observation and recording of facts, on the basis of sensory experience. This outlook was memorably expressed by Francis Bacon, a courtier and Lord Chancellor of England as well as an influential scientific thinker. Bacon denounced idle speculation and insisted that facts must always precede theory.

Because of the crucial role of fact-gathering, Bacon and others argued that science could thrive only by becoming a collective endeavour. His vision of a flourishing fact-based science was boosted in England in 1660 by the founding of the Royal Society, shortly to be followed by the

and strange man who devoted much of his time to alchemy and theology. Following Bacon, Newton stressed the key role of facts: *'Hypotheses non fingo'* was his claim – 'I do not make hypotheses'. Nevertheless his great achievement lay not in discovering new facts but in unifying astronomy, physics and mathematics.

In his *Mathematical Principles of Natural Philosophy*, published in 1687, Newton formulated the basic laws of mechanics and developed his conception of the law of gravity, a force operating throughout the Universe and explaining the motions of the planets no less than the falling of apples from trees. Newton was to become the outstanding hero of the 18th-century intellectual movement known as the Enlightenment on account of his seemingly godlike capacity to penetrate the inner workings of nature. According to the English poet Alexander Pope, 'Nature and Nature's laws lay hid in night; God said, *Let Newton be!* and all was light'.

Perhaps the greatest transformation in 17th-century science lay in its view of the basic composition of things. Greek science had regarded nature as a kind of organism – a living whole interacting and combining to bring about certain ends. Thus rain fell to make the grass grow, and heavy bodies fell because they 'wished' to return to the solid ground where they belonged. Later scientists rejected this notion, insisting that nature was essentially mechanical and atomistic; matter was composed of various invisible particles and corpuscles, driven by short-range forces and governed by mathematical laws. This 'mechanical philosophy' was encouraged by contemporary technological developments, above all by advances in clock-making.

THE CONQUEST OF NATURE
The idea of a clockwork Universe, subject to laws, opened new possibilities for science. No longer a living being but rather a machine, nature was an object which could be studied, taken apart, dissected, put together again, improved and transformed. All of nature – the animal kingdom included – was opened to human experimentation. No longer mysterious, sacred or alive, nature was now viewed as raw material for scientists to work upon. The thinkers of the Enlightenment proclaimed the domination of human beings over nature, and stressed their right to control it for their own good.

This breathtaking vision underpinned the technological changes of the Industrial Revolution, although each individual advance depended less on pure science than on improvements in processes. It also led to the antiscientific revolt of the Romantics. The artist and poet William Blake had attacked Newton even before the Industrial Revolution got underway, and the novel *Frankenstein* by the English writer Mary Shelley, published in 1818, warned against man overreaching himself. The promise and the perils of the vision of science created by the 17th century are with us still. The possibility of manipulating life through genetic engineering, the forces unleashed by nuclear energy, the opportunity to prolong human life despite old age and the ability to alter the environment, all show that the dilemmas created by science are far from resolved.

Vesalius's *De Humani Corporis Fabrica* (above left) revolutionised anatomy when it appeared in 1543. Galileo's defence of Copernicus (above right) led to a charge of heresy.

setting up of the Academie des Sciences in France. The Royal Society staged pioneering experiments devised by the chemist Robert Boyle, the physicist Robert Hooke and others (commemorated in Boyle's Law and Hooke's Law), and published its findings in the *Philosophical Transactions*, the world's first enduring scientific journal. The modern cosmopolitan scientific community began to emerge, though as yet there were few professional scientists – the word 'scientist' did not enter the English language until the 1830s.

What historians now call the 'scientific revolution' culminated in the work of another Englishman, Sir Isaac Newton, a towering genius if a solitary, difficult

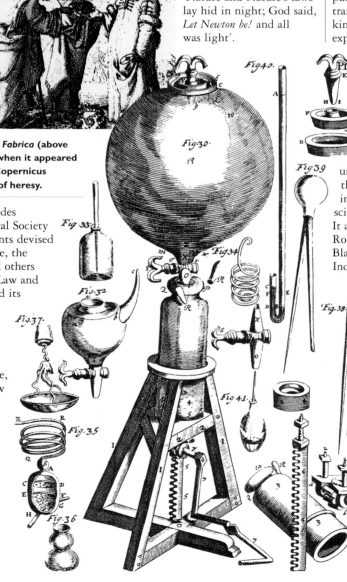

Robert Boyle's vacuum pump revealed the relationship between the pressure and volume of a gas.

The Prussian forces, on the right, wreak havoc at the Battle of Sedan in 1870, proving that their new steel, breech-loading field guns were far superior to the muzzle-loading guns of the French.

Sedan, Battle of (September 1-2, 1870)

Decisive battle during the FRANCO-PRUSSIAN WAR. On discovering that the French army under Marshal MACMAHON had set out to relieve Metz, the Prussians diverted two armies marching on Paris and encircled the army of NAPOLEON III at Sedan on the River Meuse, near the Belgian frontier. The Prussians were equipped with new guns from the KRUPP factory that were far superior to the French guns. The French surrendered unconditionally and Napoleon III was taken prisoner, together with 100000 troops. The battle marked the downfall of the French Second Empire. Germany replaced France as the dominant military power in Europe.

Seddon, Richard John (1845-1906)

Prime minister of New Zealand from 1893 until his death. Born in England, Seddon worked in the Australian gold fields before moving to New Zealand in 1866. He became the miners' spokesman and in 1881 was elected parliamentary member for Kumara. He was minister of public works in the first Liberal government in 1891 and two years later became premier. Seddon oversaw the introduction of a range of radical legislation, including low-interest credit for farmers, women's suffrage, William Pember REEVES' industrial conciliation and arbitration Act, old-age pensions, and free places in secondary schools. Seddon sent troops to support Britain during the second Boer War (1899-1902).

Sedgemoor, Battle of (July 6, 1685)

Battle that ended MONMOUTH'S REBELLION against the English king James II. Retreating from Bristol, James Scott, Duke of Monmouth, was trapped in Somerset by James II's army under Lord Feversham and John Churchill, later Duke of MARLBOROUGH. Monmouth attempted a night attack to give his raw recruits some advantage over the professionals of the Royalist army, but his plans miscarried and he was captured and later executed.

Seeckt, Hans von (1866-1936)

German general who began the work of restoring his country's military power between the two world wars. Seeckt was a chief of staff during the First World War, fighting in eastern Europe and the Balkans. Appointed commander in chief of the German army in 1919, he evaded the terms of the Versailles Peace Settlement, which limited the German army to 100000 men, by training his soldiers as an efficient nucleus for a much larger army. Short-term enlistment created a large reserve, and Seeckt made a deal with Gustav KRUPP and other industrialists to produce weapons in factories abroad. In 1922 he concluded a secret agreement allowing German troops to train in the Soviet Union. In 1926 Seeckt was forced to resign because of President Hindenburg's jealous hostility, but his work enabled Adolf Hitler to transform a small army into a formidable fighting force by 1940.

Seleucids

Hellenistic dynasty founded by ALEXANDER THE GREAT's Macedonian general Seleucus I (c. 356-280 BC). After the death of Alexander, Seleucus became governor and then ruler of Babylonia in 312. He extended his kingdom to the frontiers of India and Syria, where he founded the city of ANTIOCH in 301. He secured control of Asia Minor in 281, but the following year he was murdered. Antiochus III the Great, who ruled from 223 to 187, recovered Syria and Palestine, lost by his predecessors, but when he conquered Thrace and then invaded Greece he came into conflict with Rome. He was defeated at THERMOPYLAE and Magnesia, and in 188 made peace on terms that excluded him from Asia Minor. Seleucid power subsequently declined. Tyre regained its independence in 126, as did other cities and chiefdoms, until in 64 BC Pompey annexed what was left of the empire to form the Roman province of Syria.

Self-Denying Ordinance

English parliamentary regulation passed on April 3, 1645, during the ENGLISH CIVIL WAR. Proposed by Zouch Tate, who had been prompted by Oliver CROMWELL, the ordinance forced Members of Parliament to resign military and naval offices and commands granted since November 1640. It was intended to remove inadequate generals and was the result of Cromwell's determination to create an efficient national army controlled and paid from Westminster rather than by the counties. The House of Lords amended the ordinance so that it was possible for certain Members of Parliament to be reappointed to Cromwell's NEW MODEL ARMY, enabling Cromwell to continue his military career as lieutenant-general.

Selim I (c.1470-1520)

Sultan of the OTTOMAN EMPIRE from 1512 until his death, nicknamed 'Yavuz' and known in English as 'the Grim' or 'the Relentless'. Recalled from Crimean exile after an aborted attempt to ensure his own succession, Selim succeeded to the Ottoman throne after forcing his father Bayezid II to abdicate and causing him, his brothers and his nephew to be put to death. In 1514 Selim crushed the Persian army at Chaldiran and took Diyarbakir and Kurdistan. Turning against the Egyptian MAMELUKE dynasty, Selim conquered Egypt, Syria and the Hejaz in 1517. He took the titles of caliph and protector of the holy cities of Mecca and Medina, thereby becoming spiritual and secular head of the Islamic world. Selim was succeeded by his son, SULEIMAN I.

Selim I, in a 16th-century miniature, receives the severed head of Sultan Kansu Gavri Mameluke to mark his conquest of Egypt.

Seljuk Turkish dynasty that conquered much of western Asia and Asia Minor in the 11th and 12th centuries. The dynasty was founded by Seljuk, chief of the nomadic Oguz tribes, which in the 10th century converted to the Sunniye form of Islam. Seljuk's grandson, Toghril Beg, conquered Persia and in 1055 entered Baghdad and was proclaimed sultan. Toghril's son Alp Arslan (ruled 1063-72) conquered Syria and Palestine and in 1071 defeated and captured the Byzantine emperor Romanus IV at the Battle of Manzikert, opening the way for Turks to settle in Asia Minor. The empire reached its height under Toghril's son Malik-Shah (ruled 1072-92).

In 1095 the CRUSADES to recapture the Holy Land from the Seljuks began, and by the early 12th century the empire was beginning to fragment. Seljuk kingdoms were eventually conquered by GENGHIS KHAN and his successors in the 13th century. The former Seljuk sultanate of Rum in Anatolia fell to the Mongols in 1243, but in the 14th century became the nucleus of the OTTOMAN EMPIRE.

Semites Group of Middle Eastern peoples said in the Old Testament to be descended from Shem, the eldest son of Noah. The Semites were nomadic farmers in the Arabian peninsula who from 3000 BC spread to Mesopotamia, Syria, the eastern shores of the Mediterranean and the Nile delta. The inhabitants of Akkad in ancient Babylonia were Semites, as were the Assyrians, the Egyptians, the Aramaeans, the Canaanites, the Phoenicians, the Carthaginians and the Hebrews. Over the centuries, distinctions between Semitic tribes broke down through intermarriage and trading contacts, only the Hebrews keeping themselves apart because of their distinct religion.

The Semites are grouped together mainly because their languages were found to be related, deriving from a common origin in Mesopotamia around 3000 BC. An alphabet that developed among the Semites in about 1700 BC is believed to be the forerunner of all the world's alphabets. (See feature, pages 712-13.)

Senanayake Family name of two politicians from Ceylon (now Sri Lanka). Don Stephen Senanayake (1884-1952) was born in Colombo and worked on his father's rubber plantation before entering politics in 1915. He was elected to the State Council in 1931 and served as minister of agriculture until 1946. Senanayake led the movement for constitutional reform, and as head of the United National Party became the country's first prime minister after independence, and also served as minister of defence and external

affairs. In 1952 he was succeeded by his son, Dudley Senanayake (1911-73), who also became leader of the United National Party. Dudley Senanayake resigned in 1953 as pressure mounted from the socialist Sri Lanka Freedom Party associated with Solomon BAN-DARANAIKE, but he was prime minister again in 1960 and from 1965 to 1970, when he pursued a policy of communal reconciliation between the country's Sinhalese and Tamil communities.

> **DID YOU KNOW?**
>
> *Seljuk soldiers had to play polo at least once a week to keep themselves fit and alert, and had regular training in archery.*

Senate Upper house of the CONGRESS of the USA, established at the Constitutional Convention of 1787 and inaugurated in 1789. Senators, two from each state, have six-year terms. They must be at least 30 years old, have been a US citizen for nine years, and be a resident of the state they represent. The Senate was originally intended as a check upon possible excess by the President or the House of REPRESENTATIVES, and senators were chosen by the state legislatures rather than by direct popular vote, until the 17th Amendment in 1913 provided for their direct election. A third of senators are subject to re-election every two years. The Senate must ratify all treaties with foreign governments by a two-thirds vote, confirm presidential appointments by a majority vote, and take an equal part in legislation with the House of Representatives. Much of its work is done through committees rather than by a meeting of the full house. The vice-president serves as president of the Senate, but may vote only to break a tie.

Seneca, Lucius Annaeus, also known as Seneca the Younger (*c.*4 BC-AD 65), STOIC philosopher and politician. Seneca was banished to Corsica in AD 41 by Emperor Claudius on a charge of adultery, but was recalled by Claudius's wife Agrippina in 49 to act as tutor to their 12-year-old son, NERO. After Nero became emperor in 54, Seneca was made his political adviser. In 59 he found himself a reluctant accessory to the murder of Agrippina and composed the emperor's explanation for the Senate. No longer influential, Seneca retired in 62 but three years later Nero accused him of treason and he was compelled to commit suicide. His surviving works include essays, letters, plays and dialogues.

Senegal Country in West Africa (see map on page 582). In the 14th and 15th centuries the region was part of the empire of Mali. In 1659 the French established their first African colony at Fort St Louis, which became a slave-trading centre. Senegal became part of French West Africa in 1895, and in 1946 all inhabitants were made French citizens. In 1958 Senegal was made an autonomous republic within the French Community. The following year it joined with French Sudan to form the Federation of Mali, but in 1960 Senegal withdrew to become an independent republic with Léopold SENGHOR as its first president. He was succeeded in 1980 by Abdou Diouf.

From 1982 to 1989, Senegal joined The GAMBIA to form the Senegambia Confederation. Senegal and Mauritania engaged in a violent frontier war between 1989 and 1992. At the same time, a separatist movement began to develop in the southern part of

The US Senate hears Senator Henry Clay outlining plans that became the Compromise of 1850, which by keeping a balance between slave and free states delayed the Civil War by a decade.

The whole world goes to war

The Second World War began as a local European conflict. After nearly six years of increasingly widespread fighting, it ended with the dropping of atom bombs made in the United States on Japan.

St Paul's Cathedral survived the Blitz on London almost unscathed to become a potent symbol of British resistance to the Nazis.

Hopes for lasting peace after the end of the First World War in 1918 were short-lived. The next 20 years witnessed a series of diplomatic crises that foreshadowed a new world war. Fascist dictatorships bent on territorial expansion and cultural domination were established in Italy under Benito Mussolini and in Germany, where Adolf Hitler became Reich Chancellor in January 1933, while Japanese militarism threatened the peace of Asia.

Under Hitler, Germany embarked on a rearmament campaign. In March 1936, in defiance of the Treaty of Versailles, he reoccupied the Rhineland, and two years later annexed Austria. In September 1938 at Munich, Hitler persuaded Britain and France to make the Czechs give up the German-speaking Sudetenland region. In March 1939 Hitler occupied the rest of Czechoslovakia, prompting Britain and France to give a guarantee to Poland. This failed to deter Hitler from invading on September 1, 1939, and Britain and France declared war two days later. Poland was overwhelmed in a *blitzkrieg* campaign, Warsaw capitulating on September 27.

In April 1940 Hitler invaded Denmark and Norway. A month later on May 10, the day Winston Churchill became British premier, the Germans launched their offensive in the West. The main attack was directed through the Belgian Ardennes. Tanks and assault troops with air support broke through the French line and drove northward towards the Channel, splitting the Allied armies. The British and the French 1st Army were cornered at Dunkirk, but 338 000 men escaped to Britain. The Germans continued their advance until the French government concluded an armistice on June 22, 1940.

Britain then stood alone against Germany and Italy, which had entered the war on June 10. In July Hitler gave orders to draw up an invasion plan, but first he had to win mastery of the skies over southern England. The Luftwaffe under Reichmarschall Hermann Goering began its main offensive on August 13, and Air Chief Marshal Hugh Dowding's RAF Fighter Command was down to its last reserves when the Germans switched their attack from airfields to targets in London on September 7. Ten days later Hitler postponed his invasion.

Hitler next attempted to bomb Britain into submission. The campaign, which Britons called the Blitz, lasted from September 1940 until May 1941, but it failed in its objective. As in the First World War, command of the seas was vital to Britain. Again Germany's U-boats presented the biggest threat and by 1942 they were sinking 92 ships a month. But within a year Admiral Karl Dönitz's U-boats were taking heavy losses. Of his 40 000 men, only 10 000 survived.

THE DESERT WAR

Conflict came to the Mediterranean and Middle East after Italy's entry into the war. Mussolini invaded Greece in October 1940, but was badly beaten. Hitler had to come to his assistance in April 1941, also attacking Yugoslavia and sending aid to the Italians in North Africa, where in June 1942 Erwin Rommel's Afrika Korps captured Tobruk and threatened the Suez Canal. In October 1942 German and Italian forces were decisively beaten by General Bernard Montgomery's British 8th Army at El Alamein, and surrendered in May 1943 after a campaign in Tunisia. The invasion of Sicily on July 10, 1943, and the

Fighter pilots of the County of London Squadron scramble to engage the enemy in January 1941. The engines of their Hurricanes have already been started by mechanics to save vital seconds.

1943, and at Kursk in July 1943. By the summer of 1944 the Red Army had driven the Germans from Soviet soil, but at a staggering cost. The exact number of Russian casualties will never be known, but certainly more than 20 million died.

In the occupied territories of Europe the Nazis set about a policy of ruthless economic exploitation, repression and genocide. Six million Jews were murdered in the gas chambers or shot as a result of Hitler's 'Final Solution'. More than 3 million Poles were slaughtered, while some 3.5 million Russian prisoners of war also perished. Resistance to the Nazis intensified. In Yugoslavia Josip Tito's partisans tied down whole German divisions, while in Warsaw and other ghettos Jews took up arms.

The US aircraft carrier *Franklin* lists after being hit by a Japanese kamikaze bomber in March 1945. A German submarine commander (left) peers through his periscope at a British convoy.

landings on the Italian mainland in September, gave the Allies, now including the USA, their first foothold in Europe since 1941, but their advance in the face of stiff German resistance was painfully slow. The Germans finally surrendered on May 2, 1945. Four days earlier, Mussolini had been executed by Italian partisans.

Strategic, economic and ideological motives lay behind Hitler's invasion of Russia in June 1941. Initially successful, the Germans came to a halt outside Moscow and Leningrad, and the Russians under General Georgi Zhukov successfully counterattacked in December 1941. Hitler then turned to the south to gain oil fields and other economic plunder, attacking the Caucasus in the spring of 1942. His armies were decisively beaten at Stalingrad, where 91000 prisoners including Field-Marshal Friedrich Paulus were captured in February

BOMBED INTO SUBMISSION

The Allies' strategic bomber offensive played a major part in Hitler's defeat. From February 1942 RAF Bomber Command under Air Marshal Arthur Harris adopted 'area bombing' of German cities to wreck industry and break morale. On May 30/31, 1942, the first thousand-bomber raid took place on Cologne. In August 1942 the US Army Air Force joined the offensive with precision daylight attacks. In 1943 the RAF and USAAF attacked Hamburg, the Ruhr and Berlin, but the Luftwaffe's fighters took a heavy toll and under the armaments minister Albert Speer German production actually increased. Long-range escort fighters transformed the last phase of the bomber offensive, culminating in the destruction of Dresden in February 1945, in which perhaps 50000 died. Allied losses were also heavy; nearly 100000 British and US aircrew were killed.

On June 6, 1944, the Allied liberation of Western Europe began with the D-Day landings. Under the command of the American General Dwight Eisenhower, more than 156000 Allied troops were transported across the Channel and landed in Normandy on the first day. After a month of heavy fighting Caen fell to the

Three days after invading Poland in September 1939, German troops pause by the roadside.

British and Canadians. At the end of July US troops broke through and advanced to the east and south. Paris was liberated on August 25 and Brussels on September 3. Montgomery's plan to open a back door to Germany through Holland ended in failure on September 26 when the British 1st Airborne Division was forced to withdraw at Arnhem. Hitler's last offensive was made in December through the Ardennes but was repulsed, and in March 1945 the Allies crossed the Rhine.

The Western Allies halted on the Elbe, as agreed at the Yalta Conference, allowing the Russians to take Berlin on May 2, 1945. Hitler had committed suicide two days before. On May 4 German forces in north-west Europe surrendered to Montgomery, while Germany's surrender took place on May 7 at Eisenhower's headquarters in Reims in Northern France.

In the Far East, Japan's territorial ambitions had led by 1941 to a serious deterioration in relations with the United States. On December 7, 1941, without a declaration of war, the Japanese bombed the US Pacific Fleet at Pearl Harbor in Hawaii, while at the same time attacking British colonial possessions. The Allies were ill-prepared and by the summer of 1942 the Japanese had overrun the Philippines, Malaya, Burma and the Dutch East Indies, resulting in·the capture of about 250000 Allied personnel and civilians. They had to endure appalling conditions of imprisonment, with more than a quarter of British prisoners dying as a result.

At Midway in June 1942, which like most Pacific naval battles was dominated by the aircraft carrier, the Japanese suffered their first decisive defeat. Soon they were being pushed back throughout their Pacific conquests. General Douglas MacArthur's American forces fought their way through New Guinea to the Philippines, while the Solomon Islands were recaptured after bitter fighting on Guadalcanal. In the Central Pacific Admiral Chester Nimitz carried out a series of operations which brought US forces within bombing range of Tokyo. In Burma, the British 14th Army under General William Slim won a decisive victory at Imphal-Kohima before retaking Rangoon and Mandalay. By spring 1945 an invasion of Japan was being prepared.

The Japanese rejected Allied calls for surrender and put up fanatical resistance on Iwo Jima and Okinawa. In order to swiftly end the war, the US president Harry S Truman gave the order to use the newly developed atomic bomb. The first was dropped on Hiroshima on August 6, 1945, followed three days later by a second on Nagasaki. On August 14, 1945, the Japanese surrendered unconditionally.

Senegal. In 1993 violence by the separatists marred the presidential election, won by Diouf, but later in the year a cease-fire agreement was concluded. In spite of aid from France and the International Monetary Fund, by 1994 the Senegalese economy was on the verge of bankruptcy.

Senghor, Léopold (1906-)

African statesman and poet, first president of Senegal from 1960 to 1980. The son of a rich landowner, Senghor was educated in Paris, where he helped to formulate the concept of Negritude, which he defined as 'the sum total of cultural values of the Negro-African world'. Captured during the Second World War, Senghor was in a Nazi concentration camp from 1940 to 1942, after which he joined the French Resistance. After the war he was elected to the French National Assembly as a socialist deputy.

In 1958 Senghor formed the Senegalese Progressive Union – known as the Socialist Party from 1976 – which took Senegal to independence in 1960. Elected president, Senghor sought unsuccessfully to achieve unity among the former French West African colonies. Re-elected in 1963, 1968 and 1973, he was succeeded in 1980 by Abdou Diouf.

Sennacherib (d.681 BC)

King of ASSYRIA from 704 BC until his death. For much of his reign Sennacherib was fighting rebels. In 701 he crushed a revolt in Palestine led by HEZEKIAH, king of Judah. Tyre and Jerusalem both defied capture, but the latter was compelled to pay a large indemnity. Babylonia was a source of more persistent discontent, and Babylon itself was destroyed and looted in 689. Sennacherib restored the Assyrian capital, NINEVEH. He was murdered by two of his sons and succeeded by a third, Esarhaddon.

Serbia

Independent republic, largest of the republics of the former YUGOSLAVIA. Slavic tribes from the Danube region won the area from Greeks and Romanised peoples in the 7th century. In the 14th century STEPHAN DUSHAN established a short-lived Serbo-Greek empire, but in 1389 Serbia came under the control of the OTTOMAN EMPIRE. Serbian nationalism re-emerged in 1804 with a rebellion led by KARAGEORGE, who was murdered in 1817 by his rival, Milos OBRENOVIC. In 1830 the Turks recognised Serbian autonomy, followed by full independence in 1878. In the 20th century Serbia sought to liberate Serb peoples within Turkey and Austria-Hungary. Fearing a Serb expansion, Austria annexed the neighbouring region of BOSNIA and Herzegovina in 1908 and also tried to control Serbia. This policy led to the assassination in 1914 of the Austrian archduke Franz Ferdinand by a Serbian nationalist, precipitating the First World War.

In 1918 Serbia absorbed Bosnia and Herzegovina and joined Croatia and Slovenia to form a kingdom that in 1929 was renamed Yugoslavia. Croatia was a reluctant partner, and during the Second World War tensions arose between Croats and Serbian partisans. In 1946 Bosnia and Herzegovina became an autonomous republic within Yugoslavia. By playing off ethnic groups against each other Marshal TITO kept tensions in check, but they increased after his death in 1980.

In 1989 the ardent Serbian nationalist Slobodan Milosovic became president of Serbia, reviving a vision of a 'Greater Serbia' comprising Serbia, Vojvodina, Kosovo, the Serbian-populated parts of Croatia, large parts of Bosnia and Herzegovina and possibly Macedonia. Serbia also made moves to annex the autonomous province of Kosovo, sending troops to suppress the protests of its 90 per cent Albanian population. Following the collapse of communism in Europe (1989-90), Slovenia and Croatia declared their independence in 1991, after which Milosovic authorised military action against the breakaway republics. By July the Serb-led Yugoslav army had pulled out of Slovenia, and in January 1992 there was a UN-sponsored cease-fire in Croatia that left 30 per cent of the land in Serbian hands. Slovenian and Croatian independence was recognised by the EC on January 15. After Bosnian independence was recognised by the EC and the US in April, Serbian troops from Serbia and the local Serb population seized about 65 per cent of the new state's territory and declared the Serbian Republic of Bosnia and Herzegovina.

Following a policy of 'ethnic cleansing', Serbs, backed by the Belgrade government, evicted the mostly Muslim communities in eastern Bosnia. UN sanctions were imposed in the summer of 1992, and in 1994-5 there were NATO air strikes against Bosnian Serb positions and advances by Bosnian government forces. A settlement between Croatia and Serbia saw the return of eastern Slavonia, including the town of Vukovar, to Croatia. In late 1995 the governments of Serbia, Croatia, and Bosnia and Herzegovina accepted a US-brokered peace settlement. (See also feature, pages 58-59.)

serf

Peasant bound to the land and under the control of a lord. From the Middle Ages serfs represented the bottom tier of society, after the decline of slavery. Unlike slaves, serf families could not be split up and sold; nor could their lords kill or mutilate serfs, as masters could do to slaves. But serfs had no personal freedom, and unlike free tenants they had to submit to the justice administered by their lord in his manorial court. In Western Europe the BLACK DEATH and war undermined serfdom in the 14th century; they led to labour shortages, enabling some serfs to escape from their lords' estates, while many who stayed became free tenants. Most remaining serfs bought their freedom in the 15th and 16th centuries. In Eastern Europe, however, the increased power of the nobility and the development of absolutism led to

Serfs in medieval England held their smallholdings in return for the hard agricultural labour they were forced to perform on the estates of their manorial lords.

the consolidation of serfdom. Formally ended in France in 1789, it lingered in Austria and Hungary until 1848, and was abandoned in Russia only in 1861. Serfdom has never been formally abolished in Britain.

Settlement, Act of

(1701) British statute that determined the succession to the throne after the death of Queen ANNE. Intended to prevent the Roman Catholic STUARTS from regaining the throne, the Act stipulated that the crown should pass to James I's grand-daughter, the Electress Sophia of Hanover, or to her Protestant heirs. The Act also placed further limitations on royal power, and made the judiciary independent of crown and Parliament. On Anne's death in 1714, Sophia's son became Britain's first Hanoverian monarch as GEORGE I.

Sevastopol

Russian port and naval base on the south-west coast of the Crimean penin-sula. Founded in 1783, Sevastopol became the main base of the Russian Black Sea fleet in 1804 and was strongly fortified during the 1840s. It was a prime military target in the CRIMEAN WAR (1853-6). From September 1854 the British and French laid siege to Sevastopol until the Russians finally with-drew on September 8, 1855, after which it was almost completely destroyed. At the end of the war, Sevastopol was demilitarised under the terms of the 1856 Congress of Paris, but it regained its importance during the 1870s. During the Second World War it fell to the Germans after a 250-day siege in 1941-2.

Seven Weeks' War see AUSTRO-PRUSSIAN WAR

Seven Wonders of the World see feature, pages 584-5

Seven Years' War

(1756-63) Conflict in which Prussia, Britain and Hanover fought against Austria, France, Russia, Saxony, Sweden and Spain. Britain and France were fighting for control of North America and India, while FREDERICK II of Prussia wanted to enlarge his kingdom at Austria's expense. Following the War of the AUSTRIAN SUCCES-SION (1740-8) each side was dissatisfied with its former allies. In 1756 Frederick II con-cluded the Treaty of Westminster with Britain, while MARIA THERESA of Austria and her minister Count von KAUNITZ made alliances with France and Russia.

War began with Prussia's invasion of Saxony in 1756. Despite victories at Rossbach and Leuthen in late 1757, Frederick II was in a desperate situation by 1758, but the follow-ing year saw a series of British victories: General James WOLFE captured Quebec, Ferdinand of Brunswick defeated the French army at MINDEN, and Admiral Edward Hawke destroyed the French fleet at QUIBERON BAY. In India, General Robert CLIVE won control of Bengal at PLASSEY. In 1760 Montreal was taken. In 1762 Elizabeth of Russia was succeeded by Frederick II's ally, Peter III, who made peace with Prussia and then with Sweden. The following year Prussia, Austria and Saxony signed the Treaty

of Hubertusburg, while Britain, France and Spain concluded the Treaty of PARIS. Prussia emerged as a leading European power, and Britain as the world's chief colonial power.

Severus, Septimius

(c.145-211) Roman emperor from 193 until his death. Born in North Africa, Severus became a professional soldier and was governor of Upper Pannonia, south of the Danube, when Emperor Pertinax was murdered in 193. Severus was proclaimed emperor by his troops and entered Rome unopposed. His first act was to disband the PRAETORIAN guard, replacing it with his own men. After defeating his rivals between 195 and 197 Severus restored order to the empire and consolidated the eastern frontier. In 208 he embarked on a campaign to restore order in Britain, but severe Roman losses following the invasion of CALEDONIA (present-day Scotland) led to a temporary peace in 210. The following year Severus died at York.

Sèvres, Treaty of

Final treaty of the VER-SAILLES PEACE SETTLEMENT at the close of the First World War. Its effect was to end more than six centuries of Ottoman power in the Middle East and Balkans. Negotiated between the Allies and the OTTOMAN EMPIRE and completed in August 1920, the treaty ended Turkish rule of the Arabian peninsula; made territorial concessions to Greece, the Kurds and the Armenians; gave Britain the

A triumphal arch (left) in Rome commemorated the glory of Emperor Septimius Severus, an autocrat who headed a military regime and also founded a personal dynasty. In a mosaic (above) Severus appears with his Syrian wife, Julia Domna, and his son Caracalla. Severus named Caracalla co-emperor in 197 to ensure that he became his successor.

The seven wonders of the ancient world

Among the remarkable architectural and artistic achievements of the ancient civilisations described by contemporary writers and detailed by archaeologists, seven were recognised as the most outstanding.

The ancient Greeks were great travellers. They visited the lands around the Mediterranean where other civilisations flourished, some much older than their own. They noted the splendid buildings and works of art, and compiled lists of those they considered the most magnificent. In the 2nd century BC they thought the edifices depicted here were the seven greatest wonders.

THE PYRAMIDS OF GIZA

The oldest of the seven wonders – seven was regarded as a magic number by the Greeks – and the only one still standing, the pyramids were built in Egypt's fourth dynasty (about 2584-2465 BC) for the kings Khufu, Khafre and Menkaure and their queens, and by the time of the ancient Greeks had already stood for 2000 years. The pyramids were tombs, intended to protect the royal mummies and their treasures for eternity. They were also the sites from which the god-king's spirit was launched to join his divine relatives in heaven, and where daily offerings were made to him. The Great Pyramid of King Khufu is the largest, 480 ft (147 m) tall and 750 ft (230 m) along each side of the base. The sides are orientated to the four points of the compass. About 2 300 000 blocks were used to build it; most weigh about 2.4 tonnes, but those over the burial chamber are heavier. The blocks were so perfectly cut that it is impossible to get a knife blade between them. The outer casing was made of fine white limestone from the quarry at Turah. A labour force of about 5000 skilled masons worked on it, and as many as 100 000 peasants joined them for three or four months each year to haul stones during the annual flood of the Nile, when they could not cultivate their fields. The Great Pyramid and its surrounding complex took about 23 years to build.

THE HANGING GARDENS OF BABYLON

After King Nebuchadnezzar II of Babylon (605-562 BC) married Amyitis, a princess of the Medes, tradition says that life on the flat plains of Mesopotamia caused the queen to pine for the mountains of her homeland. To please her the king ordered the building of an artificial mountain. It may have resembled a Babylonian ziggurat or temple platform – a series of platforms one on top of the other, decreasing in size as they rose. The whole structure may have reached a height of about 130 ft (40 m) and its terraces were covered with plants, trees and shrubs brought from all over the empire and beyond. Each terrace would have needed artificial irrigation to keep the vegetation alive. This could have been supplied by slaves working a treadmill that raised up buckets of water. Such a system could have maintained pools and even small waterfalls. The Babylonian empire fell prey to the Persians in 538 BC. The city itself eventually declined and by the end of the 2nd century BC, during the later stages of Greek civilisation, was already a desolate ruin. Modern archaeology has revealed the massive foundations of a great four-sided building situated near the Southern Palace, which may be all that is left of the fabulous hanging gardens.

THE TEMPLE OF ARTEMIS AT EPHESUS

A temple dedicated to the moon goddess Artemis was built in the mid 6th century BC with the help of Croesus, the Lydian king of legendary wealth. Artemis, daughter of Zeus and twin sister of Apollo, also protected young girls and animals. She was known to the Romans as Diana. The temple was built of limestone and marble on a stepped platform 430 ft by 260 ft (131 m by 79 m), it had 117 marble columns, each 65 ft (20 m) in height, and was decorated with superb sculptures. It was one of the biggest temples in the Greek world, considerably larger and more magnificent than the Parthenon though possibly not as perfect in its proportions. It housed a strange multi-breasted marble statue of the goddess and attracted many pilgrims. The temple was destroyed by fire in 356 BC and later rebuilt on the orders of Alexander the Great, who was born on the day of the fire. In the 3rd century AD it was plundered by the Goths, and today only a few blocks survive.

THE STATUE OF ZEUS AT OLYMPIA

Olympia was the main cult centre of Zeus, king of the gods. As part of their festivals honouring the gods, the Greeks held athletic contests and Olympia hosted the most famous of them all, the Olympic Games. An impressive temple to Zeus was built at Olympia between 466 and 456 BC, but it was several years before an appropriately awe-inspiring statue was commissioned. The artist chosen for this important task was Pheidias, the most celebrated of all ancient sculptors. In about 435 BC he completed a seated figure of Zeus holding his eagle-topped staff in his left hand and the figure of Nike (Victory) in his right. The colossal statue, some 43 ft (13 m) tall, had gold clothing and ivory skin attached by plates to a wooden 'skeleton'. The Olympic Games were banned after the Roman Empire became officially Christian in AD 394 and the statue was later shipped to Constantinople. It was destroyed in 462 when the palace in which it was housed burned to the ground.

THE MAUSOLEUM AT HALICARNASSUS

King Mausolus of Caria (377-353 BC) and his sister-wife Artemisia planned a spectacular tomb for themselves at their capital, Halicarnassus, on the west coast of Asia Minor – present-day Bodrum, Turkey. Mausolus died before the monument was finished, but Artemisia carried on the work which was completed in about 350 BC. The solid base of the monument rose in three tiers, each smaller than the one below. Magnificent statues decorated each tier. Greek sculptors were employed to decorate the building which was adorned on its four sides by more than 300 images of people and animals. The central part of the building, above the tiered base, was surrounded by columns and more statues. On top rose a pyramid surmounted by a flat platform on which stood a horse-drawn chariot, probably containing a statue of Mausolus. The monument was about 140 ft (43 m) high. The royal couple's ashes were buried in golden caskets below this splendid pile. The building was called the Mausoleum after the king, and its magnificence gave the word mausoleum, meaning a tomb, to posterity. It was destroyed by an earthquake in the Middle Ages and in 1489 the Knights of St John reused the stones when they began building a nearby castle.

THE COLOSSUS OF RHODES

After successfully withstanding a desperate siege by Demetrius Poliocretes from 305 to 304 BC, the people of Rhodes decided to erect a huge statue of their sun god Helios as a thank-offering for the victory. It took 12 years to build, being completed about 280 BC, and was the work of the architect Chares of Lindos (a town on the island). It probably had an iron frame to which the bronze plates of the figure were attached, and was filled with stones to help to keep it

An artist's impression of the white marble Mausoleum at Halicarnassus. Contemporaries wondered at the magnificence of this tomb for King Mausolus and his wife Artemisia.

stable. The colossus stood over 98 ft (30 m) in height. Popular imagination sees it straddling the entrance to the harbour, but in fact it stood in the town, overlooking the sea – but not for long. In 226 BC there was an earthquake and the colossus snapped off at the knees. A convenient oracle said it should not be rebuilt, so it lay

where it had fallen until AD 654, when the bronze was salvaged and carried off by a Syrian invader to turn into coins.

THE LIGHTHOUSE OF ALEXANDRIA

A lighthouse completed in about 280 BC in the reign of Ptolemy II stood on the island of Pharos, which lay at the hazardous mouth of Alexandria's harbour. The marble structure was of unusual design. On the base, made of huge stone blocks, stood a rectangular tower with a ramp spiralling up to a third, cylindrical tower with a statue of Zeus on the top. The fire was in the third tower and its light was reflected out to sea by sheets of bronze. The whole edifice was about 380 ft (117 m) tall. At night its light could be seen 30 miles (50 km) out to sea; during the day a column of smoke guided shipping. The lighthouse was destroyed by an earthquake in the 14th century AD and a fortress was built over the ruins. Recently, marine archaeologists have brought to the surface statues from the lighthouse and from ancient Alexandria, then Egypt's capital and one of the great centres of Greek learning.

The pyramid is topped by a marble statue of King Mausolus driving a chariot drawn by four fine horses

Lions associated with sun worship emphasise Mausolus's connection with Helios, the sun god

Between Ionic columns larger than life-size statues of men and women in mourning surround the Mausoleum

At the base of the third tier of the Mausoleum a frieze depicts battle scenes between Greek and Amazon warriors

mandate for Palestine, Iraq and Transjordan; and made Syria a French mandate. However, Turkey failed to ratify the treaty and it was rejected by the newly elected Turkish leader Mustafa Kemal Ataturk who secured a redefinition of his country's borders under the 1923 Treaty of Lausanne.

sewage treatment see SANITATION

Seward, William Henry (1801-72) US politician who as secretary of state in 1867 arranged for Alaska to be bought from Russia for $7 200 000. After serving as governor of New York State, Seward was elected to the US Senate in 1849 as a Whig; but as a convinced opponent of slavery he left them to join the newly formed Republican Party in 1855. He failed to gain the US presidency five years later, but instead served as secretary of state under President LINCOLN.

Although wounded in a separate attack at the time of Lincoln's assassination, Seward remained in office during the presidency of Andrew JOHNSON, supporting him against his radical fellow Republicans. Seward believed that the USA should expand its influence in the Pacific; he advocated friendly relations with China, and pressed for the annexation of Hawaii and other islands as coaling stations for a US Pacific fleet.

Seychelles Group of 92 Indian Ocean islands, only the largest of which, Mahe, has any major urban development. First visited by Vasco da Gama in 1502, the Seychelles were claimed by France in 1756 and settled by colonists and their Mauritian slaves 12 years later. Captured by Britain during the Napoleonic Wars, the islands were administered from Mauritius before becoming a British crown colony in 1903.

The Seychelles gained independence in 1973, and two years later a coup established a one-party republic with the former prime minister, France-Albert René, as president. The coup marked the start of two decades punctuated by unrest, failed countercoups and demands for multiparty rule.

Seymour, Jane (c.1509-37) Third wife of HENRY VIII of England. Jane supplanted the executed Anne BOLEYN as queen in 1536. The following year she gave birth to a son, the future EDWARD VI, but died 12 days later.

Seyss-Inquart, Arthur (1892-1946) Austrian pro-Nazi interior minister, organiser of the ANSCHLUSS with Germany in 1938. After the German takeover, Adolf HITLER appointed Seyss-Inquart governor of Austria. Later, while Nazi commissioner in the occupied Netherlands, he was responsible for thousands of executions and deportations to concentration camps. In 1946 Seyss-Inquart

was sentenced to death at the postwar NUREMBERG TRIALS of war criminals, and was executed on October 16.

Sforza Family which controlled Milan for much of the 15th and 16th centuries. The family became prominent patrons of the arts, and its court was a centre of RENAISSANCE culture. Although Muzio Attendolo (1369-1424), one of the most powerful CONDOTTIERI of the period, assumed the name Sforza, or 'force', it was his illegitimate son Francesco (1401-66) who established the powerful Sforza dynasty. In 1450, after his armies triumphed in a three-way war with the Milanese republic and Venice, Francesco married the daughter of Duke Filippo Maria Visconti and entered Milan as duke. His eldest son Galeazzo, who succeeded him, was assassinated in 1476. His younger son Ludovico, nicknamed 'the Moor' because of his swarthy complexion, then usurped the regency from Galeazzo's widow and ruled Milan from 1480.

Five years after aiding the invasion of Naples by Charles VIII of France in 1494, he was driven out of his own duchy by Louis XII. Ludovico, who died in 1508, had been an early patron of Leonardo da Vinci. Aided by the Swiss, in 1512 Ludovico's 17-year-old son Massimiliano regained Milan – only to be defeated at Marignano three years later by Francis I of France who forced him to cede his territory, but granted him a pension of 30 000 ducats. Holy Roman Emperor Charles V restored Massimiliano's younger brother to the duchy as Francesco II in 1522, but Francesco's death in 1535 ended the male ducal line, and Milan fell to Spain.

The Mughal emperor Shah Jahan, builder of the Taj Mahal, wrote on this painting by Bichitr: 'A good portrait of me in my 40th year'.

Shaftesbury, Anthony Ashley Cooper, 1st Earl of (1621-83) English opportunist politician who lent credibility to the POPISH PLOT, so sparking the EXCLUSION CRISIS. Entering Parliament as a Royalist in 1640, he changed sides three years later and rose to become a member of Oliver Cromwell's Council of State. In 1660, he helped to bring about the Restoration of Charles II, and was rewarded by being made Baron Ashley in 1661 and Earl of Shaftesbury in 1672. After Lord CLARENDON's flight from England in 1667, Shaftesbury became one of Charles' CABAL, but was dismissed in 1673 when he supported the TEST ACT. As a relentless opponent of Roman Catholicism, Shaftesbury attempted to exclude Charles II's brother, the Roman Catholic James, Duke of York, from the succession. When this failed, Shaftesbury fled to exile in Holland in 1682.

Shaftesbury, Anthony Ashley Cooper, 7th Earl of (1801-85) British Tory politician and reformer. Shaftesbury entered Parliament in 1826 and almost immediately initiated an unsuccessful campaign to abolish the Indian practice of *suttee*, in which Hindu widows commit suicide on their husbands' funeral pyres. He was more successful in persuading Parliament to pass an Act reforming the treatment of lunatics, and was largely responsible for the Ten Hours Factory Act of 1847, shortening the working day in textile mills. Shaftesbury supported the establishment of the 'Ragged Schools' – charity schools for children in slums – and championed the abolition of boy chimney sweeps. Although he campaigned for better urban housing for the poor as well as shorter working hours, he

Members of the Sforza dynasty, depicted with the Madonna in an idealised family portrait, were the rulers of Milan from 1450 to 1535.

opposed the development of trade unionism and also the reform bills of 1832 and 1867, fearing that they could provoke class warfare.

Shah Jahan (1592-1666) Builder of the TAJ MAHAL and Mughal emperor of India from 1628 until 1658, when he was imprisoned by AURANGZEB, his son and successor. Jahan extended Mughal power and rebuilt the capital at Delhi where his buildings, with those in Agra, mark the peak of Indo-Muslim architecture. In a war of succession between his four sons, which erupted in 1657 while Jahan was severely ill, Aurangzeb killed two of his three brothers, imprisoned his father in the Agra palace and seized the throne. Shah Jahan was buried with his favourite wife in the Taj Mahal, which he had built as her mausoleum.

Shaka (1788-1828) African military leader also known as Tshaha or Chaka, who united the Zulus and became their first paramount chief from 1818 until his death. The son of a minor chief, after his father's death in a clash with a rival clan Shaka fled with his mother to Dingiswayo's Mthethwa tribe where his military skills quickly became apparent. As Dingiswayo's military commander, when the Mthethwa chief was murdered by a rival, Zwide, Shaka assumed command of the tribe and wiped out Zwide's forces.

With the aid of his ruthlessly disciplined impis – regiments organised by age group and armed with long shields and the short stabbing spears he had developed – Shaka subjugated the surrounding tribes to become ruler of all the territory from the huge Drakensberg mountain range to the coast. Fear of his forces spread beyond the Zambezi river and caused mass tribal migrations. His relations with the white settlers were cordial, but his cruel and tyrannical reign was increasingly resented by the nation he had forged. Shaka was assassinated by his half-brother Dingane, who succeeded him as paramount chief.

Shaker Member of a QUAKER sect. Called 'Shakers' because of their uncontrolled jerkings in moments of religious ecstasy, the revivalist group left the Quaker movement in 1747. Ann Lee, a visionary who joined the sect in 1758, declared herself the female Christ and in 1774 established a prosperous community near Albany, New York, which gained a reputation for its skilled craftsmen. The sect reached a peak of about 6000 members in the 1820s, but a decline set in after 1860.

Shakespeare, William see feature, page 588

Sharpeville massacre (March 21, 1960) Clash between rioters and police in the South African township of Sharpeville, near Johannesburg, in which 69 Africans were shot and

Crowds flee the violence at Sharpeville, which focused world criticism against South Africa's apartheid policy.

another 180 were wounded. When the African National Congress and Pan African Congress jointly organised an illegal, but peaceful, demonstration against the apartheid regime's pass laws the police opened fire. The slaughter was internationally condemned. Two days later, when an armed mob attacked the police station in Langa, near Cape Town, killing six innocent bystanders, the South African government declared a state of emergency, arrested nearly 1700 people and soon afterwards banned the two political organisations responsible for the demonstrations. The deaths led to increased Commonwealth criticism of apartheid and South Africa withdrew from the body, becoming an independent republic in 1961.

Shaw, George Bernard (1856-1950) Irish dramatist, essayist and critic, whose 'drama of ideas' had an electrifying impact on 20th-century theatre. Aged 20, Shaw was already an enthusiastic writer of letters to newspapers when he left Dublin to join his mother, a singing teacher in London. There Shaw first read Karl Marx, becoming drawn to socialism while struggling as an impoverished and unsuccessful novelist for several years. Then he obtained work as a theatre and music critic and began to make his intellectual mark.

George Bernard Shaw was alert, irascible and still typing his own manuscripts at the age of 90 in the wooden hut he called his 'retreat'.

Shaw also joined the FABIAN SOCIETY, of which he was to become a leading figure. He wrote his first play, *Widowers' Houses* (1892), in response to his own call for a change of theatrical attitudes and the development of a new drama of ideas. It was followed by *Arms and the Man* (1894) and *Mrs Warren's Profession* (1898), which was banned for its frank treatment of prostitution. Though the dramatist did not use his plays as a platform for socialist propaganda, themes of social concern run through many of them, and in their published versions many are prefaced with introductory essays in which Shaw explores and argues his views.

Discussion of social and political ideas is at the heart of many of Shaw's plays, and his 'Shavian' wit, his unorthodox views and love of paradox convinced his audiences that mental and moral passion could produce absorbing drama. Shaw's most popular play, *Pygmalion* (1913), a human comedy about love and class, was later adapted as the musical and film *My Fair Lady*. His 50 plays include *Man and Superman* (1903), *Major Barbara* (1905), *The Doctor's Dilemma* (1906) and *Saint Joan* (1923). Other significant works include *The Quintessence of Ibsenism* (1891) and *The Intelligent Woman's Guide to Socialism and Capitalism* (1928). Shaw campaigned for many causes, including women's rights, vegetarianism, electoral reform and reform of the English alphabet. He was awarded the Nobel prize for literature in 1925.

Sheba, Queen of Legendary wise ruler of the wealthy realm of Sheba, a part of southwest Arabia first occupied by Semitic tribes in the 10th century BC. According to the Bible, the queen visited King SOLOMON to test for herself his legendary wisdom, while the KORAN also mentions – and greatly embellishes – her visit. In the Koran's account, she is called Bilqis and is tricked into revealing her hairy legs, which have to be shaved before Solomon will marry her. In Ethiopia, where the queen is known as Makeda, the son of her union with Solomon, Menelek I, is said to have founded the royal Ethiopian dynasty.

All the world his stage

Little is known about the life of William Shakespeare, but in his plays the whole of human experience is explored.

The son of a prosperous leather trader, William Shakespeare was christened in Stratford-upon-Avon, Warwickshire on April 26, 1564. He probably attended the town's grammar school and received an education based on Latin language and literature. The first performances he saw were likely to have been put on by travelling actors. In 1582 he married Anne Hathaway, a local farmer's daughter eight years his senior.

Shakespeare is next mentioned, in 1592, as a dramatist in London where his play *Henry VI*, Part II moved 'ten thousand spectators' to tears. He was also an actor with the Lord Chamberlain's Men. As well as appearing in public, the company gave performances for Elizabeth I and her court. By 1598 he had written a number of successful plays, including *Richard III*, *Romeo and Juliet*, *A Midsummer Night's Dream* and *The Merchant of Venice*. The company performed in Shoreditch, but later ferried the theatre's timbers over the Thames to build a new playhouse,

Mr. WILLIAM SHAKESPEARES COMEDIES, HISTORIES, & TRAGEDIES. Published according to the True Originall Copies. LONDON Printed by Isaac Iaggard, and Ed. Blount. 1623

Shakespeare converses with his friends, as seen by a 19th-century artist. The First Folio of his plays, dating from 1623, may show a better likeness.

The Globe, on the south bank. There *Henry V* and *Julius Caesar* were first performed. Shakespeare was now a shareholder in the theatre and was able to buy a fine house in Stratford.

With the accession of James I in 1603 the company became the King's Men. During the early years of James's reign he wrote his tragedies *Hamlet*, *Othello*, *King Lear* and *Macbeth*. In 1608 the company acquired an indoor theatre, The Blackfriars, in the city centre near St Paul's Cathedral. For this playhouse Shakespeare wrote *The Winter's Tale* and *The Tempest*. He retired to Stratford, where he died in 1616. He had written 37 plays, a collection of sonnets and two long narrative poems. He was buried at the church where he had been christened.

Shakespeare was recognised in his lifetime as exceptionally gifted and is now considered to be the finest of all dramatists. How the son of a provincial tradesman achieved this cannot be explained, but the culture of Elizabethan and Jacobean England gave him certain crucial advantages. His education had introduced him to Latin authors such as Virgil, Cicero and Ovid. Some of his early works were modelled on the plays of the Latin dramatists Plautus and Seneca. He could also have gained an appreciation of the riches of medieval drama by seeing the cycles of religious plays regularly performed at Coventry. He was fortunate to write when English - the language of the King James Bible - was exceptionally expressive, and he lived in London when playgoing was becoming popular. All this helped to make his achievement possible, but it would have made no difference had he not also been a genius.

Sheridan, Philip Henry (1831-88) US general. He emerged as the outstanding cavalry leader on the Union (Northern) side in the American Civil War, distinguishing himself in Tennessee and in the Chattanooga campaign (November 1863) before being appointed in April 1864 to command the cavalry of the Army of the Potomac. His campaign in the Shenandoah Valley (September-October 1864) laid waste one of the South's most important supply regions, while his victory at Five Forks on April 1, 1865, effectively forced Robert E. LEE to abandon Petersburg and Richmond. After the war Sheridan commanded the 5th military district in the South, and in 1884 he succeeded Sherman as commander in chief of the US army.

sheriff Chief representative of the Crown in the shires (counties) of England from the early 11th century, taking over many of the duties earlier performed by ealdormen. The word comes from 'shire reeve'. Sheriffs assumed responsibility for the fyrd (militia), royal taxes, royal estates and shire courts, and presided over their own court, the Tourn. They abused these powers, as an inquest of 1170 showed, when many were dismissed. However, by around 1550 the office had become purely civil, as a result of the proliferation of specialist royal officials such as coroners (1194), justices of the peace (1361) and lords lieutenant (1547).

Shetlands Group of around 100 islands some 100 miles (160 km) off the north coast of Scotland. They were settled by the Norse people from the end of the 8th century; a Norse language remained in use up to the 19th century. Controlled by the earls of Orkney, the Shetlands became part of the kingdom of Scotland in the marriage contract of James III and Margaret of Norway in 1472.

Shiite Adherent of the second-largest branch of ISLAM, distinguished from the Sunni majority. The name is taken from the Shiat Ali, the 'party of Ali', the cousin and son-in-law of Muhammad. Ali and his descendants are regarded by Shiites as the only true heirs to Muhammad as leader of Islam. Important differences of doctrine, ritual and spiritual organisation have developed between Shiism (also known as Shia Islam) and Sunnism, notably with reference to the status of imams, the religious leaders. Shiite tradition, which emphasises sacrifice, martyrdom and belief in an inner hidden meaning of the Koran, has generated many different subgroups, such as the Ismailis. Most, however, revere the sites associated with the deaths of Ali and his sons, Hasan and Husain, and the tenth day of the month of Muharram, the first in the Islamic calendar, which marks their martyrdom.

Shimonoseki, Treaty of (April 17, 1895) Treaty between China and Japan ending the Sino-Japanese war of 1894-5. With its navy destroyed and Beijing in danger, China was forced to grant independence to Korea, pay a large indemnity, give favourable trade terms, and cede Taiwan, the Pescadores Islands and the Liaodong peninsula, including the naval base at Port Arthur (present-day Lüshun). International pressure forced the return of Port Arthur and the abandonment of the claim to the Liaodong peninsula shortly afterwards, but Japanese domination over north China had been established.

Shinto Japanese religion that reveres ancestors and nature spirits. The name means 'Spirits' Way'. Things which inspire awe – twisted trees, contorted rocks, dead warriors – are believed to enshrine *kami* ('spirits'). In early times each clan had its *kami*. With the supremacy of one clan in the Yamato region, its sun goddess, Amatesaru, enshrined at the temple at Ise, became paramount. The name Shinto was adopted in the 6th century AD to distinguish it from Buddhist and Confucian cults, though most Japanese practised both Shinto and Buddhism. Shinto offers no code of conduct and no philosophy. It stresses ritual purity – early Western visitors were amazed at the Japanese custom of frequent bathing. At simple shrines worshippers rinse hands and mouth, bow, and offer food and drink.

In the 18th century scholars began stressing the emperor's descent from the sun goddess. After the Meiji restoration in 1868, the government encouraged State Shinto, classed not as a religion but as a code requiring loyalty and obedience to a divine emperor, and clearly distinguished from Sect Shinto with its simple rites and local festivals.

ship money Originally, an occasional sum of money paid by English seaports to the Crown to meet the cost of supplying ships to the Royal Navy. Charles I revived the tax in 1634 while he was ruling without Parliament, and in 1635 extended it to inland towns, raising up to £200 000 as a result. In 1637 John Hampden was taken to court for refusing to pay and claimed that Charles needed Parliament's approval to levy such a regular tax. The judges decided by seven to five in Charles's favour, but the narrowness of

the king's victory encouraged a widespread refusal to pay the tax. The LONG PARLIAMENT abolished ship money in 1641.

shipping, evolution of see feature, page 590

shogunate System of government under which the military effectively ruled Japan and the emperors became mere figureheads. Generals had been appointed as shoguns since the 8th century, but only for limited terms and with specific objectives. In 1192 Minamoto Yoritomo set a new pattern which was to last until 1867 when he was granted unlimited authority as the first *Sei-i dai-shogun* ('barbarian-conquering great general').

After Yoritomo died there was a succession of Hojo regents subject to both emperors and shoguns. From 1339 to 1573 the shogunate was held by the Ashikaga family, who ruled ineffectively but with absolute authority.

Under their TOKUGAWA successors the power of the shogunate became supreme. But from the 1840s Japan's growing exposure to foreign influences began to undermine the system, and resistance to its conservative policies led to demands for a return to full imperial rule. Between 1866 and 1869 the Tokugawa armies were gradually defeated by an alliance of provincial forces from Choshu, Satsuma and Tosa acting for the MEIJI emperor, who formally resumed imperial rule in January 1868.

shops Shops developed gradually from the stalls of produce and simple crafted goods that were bartered or sold in the world's earliest towns and cities – a system of retail trading that is still found in less developed countries

Shinto priests (above) attend a festival. At the Himenomiya Shrine, women may pray for good marriages and safe births.

Paris was a centre of fashionable shopping in the early 1900s. Ladies flocked to department stores such as the elegant Au Printemps.

and which is echoed in the traditional weekly markets held in Europe's towns. In the cities of ancient Greece and Rome a covered area was often set aside for merchants and craftsmen to display their wares, and these developed in time into walled spaces.

As crafts developed and towns became the focus for trade, a merchant class developed across much of medieval Europe who sold or produced goods in their dwellings. Similar developments occurred in Asia and the Middle East. There was little change in this pattern until the industrial revolution and the subsequent explosion in manufactured goods. This led to the growth of more specialist shops and the establishment of set prices for goods. This pattern remained throughout the early 19th century; Au Bon Marché in Paris, the first 'department store' offering a wide range of items, opened in 1852. The French experiment was followed in the USA by Macy's in 1858 and in England when Whiteleys opened five years later. Japan did not get its first department store until 1904, though it soon established 14 branches.

The self-service and supermarket concept developed in the USA in response to staff shortages caused by the demand for factory workers during the Second World War, and spread quickly in the postwar years. Although the first shopping centre was built in Kansas City in 1922, the growth of these giant complexes often housing hundreds of shops was also a postwar phenomenon. Claimed to be the biggest in the world, the West Edmonton

Merchant ships ply the oceans

The power and success of the world's great maritime nations have never depended only on their warships. Humble merchant vessels have played a crucial role as well.

For thousands of years, merchant ships have carried goods and people across the oceans. Their cargoes have included necessities, luxuries and countless emigrants, setting out to live in the most far-flung regions of the Earth.

The great traders and empire-builders of the Mediterranean – the Phoenicians, Egyptians, Greeks and Romans – had little need for ocean-going vessels. As a result, their merchant ships were relatively light, employing a single mast with a large, square sail.

By the Middle Ages, the Vikings had built ships capable of withstanding the rigours of the open Atlantic Ocean. Their longships inspired the development of the cog, the main cargo vessel of medieval northern Europe. Cogs carried a stern rudder instead of a steering oar, and their sides were built up to provide defence as well as enclosed cabins.

A great revolution in shipping occurred in the 15th century, when ships were fitted with two and then three masts. These vessels were used by explorers such as Christopher Columbus, Vasco da Gama and Ferdinand Magellan in their great voyages of discovery.

In the 17th century the Dutch developed the *fluyt* as a small but efficient cargo carrier, able to carry the maximum cargo with the minimum crew.

Sailing ships such as the medieval cog (inset) and the 19th-century clipper *Flying Cloud* (above) played an invaluable role in the development of trade across the world's oceans.

These vessels helped to make Holland a great maritime power, prompting rivalry and then war with England.

BRITANNIA RULES THE WAVES

After the defeat of Holland in the Anglo-Dutch wars, England quickly established itself as the world's leading merchant marine power. By the middle of the 18th century, Britain dominated the trade routes to India and the Far East. Its largest East Indiamen – the biggest merchantmen of their day – could carry over 1000 tonnes of freight.

By about 1850 the East India companies had lost their monopoly of trade with India, so competition was much more intense. Designers concentrated on speed, with the result that the *Cutty Sark*, launched in 1869 to carry tea from India, was able to reach Britain in three months – half the time taken by an old East Indiaman.

By this time the next revolution in ship design was already well under way: steamships, which had first appeared in about 1800, were about to take over from wind-driven vessels. From 1838, when Isambard Kingdom Brunel's *Great Western* was launched, steam-powered passenger liners began to make regular crossings of the Atlantic. The opening of the Suez Canal in 1869 hastened the decline of sailing ships, as their need for space to tack made them unable to use this shorter, but narrow, route from the East.

The final revolution in shipping began in the late 1950s, as oil tankers expanded from 30000 to over 500000 tonnes, and container ships were developed to carry cargoes in self-contained units, easily transferred from ship to road or rail. The latest container ships, operating with a crew of only 14, can carry up to 6000 containers, each of which would need a vehicle to itself when carried by road.

Isambard Kingdom Brunel's steam-powered *Great Western* took only 15 days to reach New York on its maiden voyage in April 1838.

Mall in Canada has 128 acres (52 hectares) of floor space and contains more than 800 shops, 11 department stores, 110 restaurants, 13 nightclubs and 19 cinemas – as well as a full-size replica of Christopher Columbus's ship *Santa Maria*.

Shostakovich, Dmitri (1906-75) Russian composer, born in St Petersburg, where he later studied at the city's Conservatory. Shostakovich composed his first symphony when he was 19. His tonal and often dramatic music met with initial success in Russia but was slow to gain international acclaim. As his overseas popularity grew, his operas and ballets were condemned by the Soviet authorities and critics for their lack of 'Soviet realism'. However, in 1937 his fifth symphony led to his reinstatement and he went on to compose prolifically, writing chamber music, violin, piano and cello concertos, choral works and a total of 15 symphonies.

Siam see THAILAND

Sicilian Vespers Massacre of French inhabitants of Sicily on Easter Tuesday, 1282, marking the start of an uprising which ended ANGEVIN rule of the island and scotched the French dynasty's ambitions in Italy. In 1266 Pope Urban IV granted the Kingdom of the Two Sicilies to Charles of Anjou, who, in pursuit of his claim, had defeated Manfred, son of the Holy Roman Emperor Frederick II. Heavy taxation and Charles' severe rule created intense hatred of the French; within a month of the massacre all the French had been killed or forced to flee.

Sicily Mediterranean island near the southwest coast of Italy. For 300 years – from the 8th century BC when Greeks colonised its eastern and southern coasts and Phoenicians

established trading posts in the west – the two powers coexisted harmoniously. But early in the 5th century conflict between Phoenicia's North African port of Carthage and the Greek port of Syracuse on Sicily turned the island into an intermittent battleground. War between the two Mediterranean powers continued through the eclipse of Greece and until the first of the PUNIC WARS between Carthage and Rome in 264 BC.

By 210 BC Sicily had fallen under Roman control. Later it was occupied by the Vandals and then the Ostrogoths. Belisarius added the island to the Byzantine Empire in AD 535, a rule which lasted until the 9th century. Then, after prolonged and ferocious fighting, the Arabs won control. Sicily flourished under two centuries of Arab rule which was ended by Norman colonisation. In 1139 Roger II formed the Kingdom of the Two Sicilies by linking the island to the Kingdom of Naples. Norman rule was followed by Surabian and then ANGEVIN rule, which ended in the infamous SICILIAN VESPERS of 1282.

The island was ruled by princes of Aragon and Spanish kings until 1799, when the Spanish Bourbon Ferdinand, king of Sicily and Naples, was defeated by the French Revolutionary army, which had already taken Naples. Sicily was proclaimed the Parthenopean Republic. Ferdinand sought British protection in the island's capital, Palermo. In June, escorted by Admiral Horatio NELSON, Ferdinand returned to Naples where he ordered the mass execution of 100 Italian patriots accused of collaborating with the French. He again sought British protection for his position in Sicily in 1806,

when Napoleon established first his brother Joseph and then General Joachim MURAT as kings of Naples. Pressed by Britain, in 1812 Ferdinand promulgated a British-style constitution and parliament, but could not break the power of the feudal lords. Three years later he was restored to the throne of Naples as Ferdinand I, King of the Two Sicilies. But his regime and that of his son Ferdinand II were unpopular, and Sicily became a hotbed of nationalists seeking Italian unification.

The first revolution in Italy took place in Palermo in 1848. In 1860 Giuseppe GARIBALDI and his 'Thousand' landed in Sicily and defeated Ferdinand at a battle near his palace of Caserta. Sicily was united with the kingdom of Italy by a plebiscite in October 1861, but retained much of its old feudal tradition; this gave rise to the MAFIA. The island gained regional autonomy in 1947.

Siegfried Line Fortified defensive system built by the Germans in the First World War after their failure to capture Verdun, stretching across France from Lens to Rheims. It was also known as the Hindenburg Line. In 1917 the line allowed the German army to maintain a defensive front even after their forces had been severely depleted. In the Second World War Adolf HITLER referred to the fortifications along Germany's western frontier as the Siegfried Line, some of which was defended by the German army – the Wehrmacht – during its retreat in 1944.

Siemens German industrial empire founded by (Ernst) Werner von Siemens (1816-92). He and his younger brother Sir (Charles) William (Karl Wilhelm) Siemens (1823-83) were pioneers in electrical engineering and key figures in the development of telegraphy. As a Prussian army officer in charge of the artillery workshops in Berlin, Werner set up Prussia's telegraph system, gaining knowledge and experience which later led to the establishment of the Siemens communications company. Werner also carried out chemical experiments that resulted in the invention of an electroplating process which, with William and his third brother, Frederick, he developed commercially after leaving the army.

William Siemens studied engineering. In 1843 he moved to Britain where he sold Werner's electroplating process while developing inventions of his own, including an open-hearth furnace for use in glass-making – and later used in steel production – patented in partnership with Frederick. Meanwhile, in 1847, Werner and a partner founded a firm of electrical manufacturers which laid telegraph cables across the Mediterranean and from Europe to India. William managed the London office, promoting electric lighting, electric tramways, telegraph cables, and

Early Sicily's mixed heritage includes Greco-Roman temples. The mosaic (left) with vivid mythical themes decorated the 3rd-century BC Roman villa at Casale Piazza Armerina.

The first telegraph cables made in Britain were produced at William Siemens' factory by the Thames at Woolwich.

designing the steamship *Faraday*, the first undersea cable-laying vessel. William was naturalised in 1859 and knighted in 1883.

Sierra Leone West African coastal state, which was a centre for the slave trade and piracy during the 16th and 17th centuries. The country's main Mende and Temne tribes moved from the African interior to Sierra Leone about the same time as the Portuguese navigator Pedro de Cintra arrived there in 1462. The slave trade dominated the coastal area and the interior from the 16th century until 1787, when the British-based Anti-Slavery Society bought the coastal territory from the local ruler and established Freetown as a private refuge for freed slaves. The purchase followed a British legal ruling 15 years earlier that any escaped slave who came to Britain would become automatically free. Though the initial venture failed, in 1791

Alexander Falconbridge formed the Sierra Leone Company for the same purpose, landing the first colonists at Freetown in 1792. In 1808 Freetown became the first British crown colony in Africa, and after 1815 British warships which had captured slave ships landed their freed captives there. During the 19th century the hinterland was gradually explored and in 1896 Sierra Leone became a British protectorate, remaining separate from the colony of Freetown until 1951. The country became independent in 1961. Food shortages, corruption and tribal tensions produced serious violence in the early 1980s, and though Sierra Leone became a one-party state in 1985

the rule of its All People's Congress remained corrupt. In April 1992 an army coup formed a National Provisional Defence Council, committed to eliminating corruption and rebuilding the economy.

Sieyès, Emmanuel (1748-1836) French churchman and politician, and one of the chief theorists of the Revolutionary era; usually known as Abbé Sieyès. In 1788, while vicar-general of the diocese of Chartres, Sieyès wrote a pamphlet entitled *What is the Third Estate?*, stimulating bourgeois awareness and gaining widespread popular acclaim for its author. A year later, as a member of the States General, he led the attack on the aristocracy and helped to write the new French constitution. When asked what he did in the Revolution, he replied 'I survived'. But his popularity waned and he withdrew from politics until 1799 when, appointed to the Directory, Sieyès conspired with NAPOLEON and organised the coup which brought him to power. Sieyès set about producing the 'perfect' constitution but when Napoleon modified it, he retired from public life. Exiled at the restoration of Louis XVIII in 1815, Sieyès did not return to France until after the July Revolution of 1830.

Sigismund (1368-1437) Bellicose Holy Roman Emperor whose broken promises to the reformer John Huss sparked a war in Bohemia that continued for a decade after Sigismund's death. The son of Emperor Charles IV, Sigismund became king of Hungary in 1387. Despite defeat by the Turks at Nicopolis in 1396, he went on to acquire and secure a large number of territories and titles in a long and violent reign. In 1411 he inherited the German throne. Almost at once he was again at war — with the HUSSITES, Venetians and rivals for the thrones of Hungary and Germany. An orthodox Catholic, Sigismund was particularly savage in his treatment of the Hussites. After pressurising Pope John XIII into calling a council at Constance to put an end to the

Hussite Schism, Sigismund disregarded his promise of safe conduct for Huss to attend it. He imprisoned the reformist leader and in 1415 acquiesced in Huss's execution by burning at the stake. These actions not only sparked the Hussite War but provoked intense opposition when Sigismund ascended the throne of Bohemia — the Hussite heartland — four years later. The Czechs refused to accept him as their king in spite of a series of bloody campaigns to quell their opposition. Sigismund became king of Lombardy in 1431 and two years later was crowned Holy Roman Emperor — the last of the House of Luxembourg to hold that office.

Sihanouk, Prince Norodom (1922-) Cambodian politician who won independence for his country; he ruled first as king and then as prime minister and head of state. Soon after his election as king of the French-ruled territory in 1941, the Paris-educated prince threw in his lot with Cambodia's budding nationalist movement. He rapidly became a master of political subtlety and manoeuvring. He used his skills to exploit the complicated political situation that had developed at the end of the French Indochinese war to gain full independence for Cambodia (now Kampuchea) in 1953. Two years later he abdicated in favour of his father and formed a political union in which he acted as prime minister. He became head of state in 1960.

Initially Sihanouk remained neutral in the VIETNAM War, but when he became convinced that the communist forces would win he began to lend them covert assistance. This earned him the enmity of the USA, which contributed to his overthrow in Lon Nol's military coup of 1970. From exile in China, Sihanouk continued to support the KHMER ROUGE, and following their victory in 1975 he returned as nominal head of state. The next year he was removed from office and again went into exile to collaborate with the nationalists who sought to overthrow the Vietnamese-backed regime of Heng Semrin. In 1982 he again allied himself with the

Prince Norodom Sihanouk returns to Phnom Penh in 1991 as president of Cambodia's Supreme National Council.

Khmer Rouge, and in 1987 entered discussions which led to a peace agreement and the establishment in 1991 of the frail, UN-backed Supreme National Council of Cambodia, with himself as head of state. He reascended the throne in 1993.

Sikhism Religion based on the teachings of the 15th-century Indian mystic Guru NANAK and the nine gurus who succeeded him. Though it has its roots in HINDUISM, Sikhism stresses meditation on the name of the one God. Hymns compiled by the first five gurus and collected as the *Adi Granth* by Guru Arjun in 1604 reflect the core of the faith and provide guidance to its followers, the Sikhs. Orthodox Sikhs wear 'the five Ks': the *kesh* (uncut hair and beard), the *kangha* (a comb), the *kaccha* (shorts), the *kara* (an iron or steel bangle), and the *kirpan* (a sword or dagger). Clashes with the Mughals in the 17th century resulted in the execution of the fifth and ninth gurus. In 1699 the tenth and last guru, Gobind Singh, established the *khalsa* (military brotherhood) whose members are called *akalis*. A century later Ranjit Singh (1780-1839) set up a powerful Sikh kingdom in the Punjab, but its short-lived dominance was ended by British annexation in 1849.

Sikh Wars (1845-9) Conflicts between the Sikhs of Lahore and the British EAST INDIA COMPANY. In 1845, in the first of two wars, Sikh troops crossed the Sutlej River into British India where they fought inconclusive battles at Mudki and Firozshah. The battles were the toughest fought by the British in India, against determined forces which Ranjit Singh had trained in European methods of warfare before his death in 1839. The following year the Sikhs were defeated at Aliwal and Sobraon, and by the Treaty of Lahore ceded the area of Jullundar Doab to Britain. Britain also took Kashmir and established control of the Lahore government through a Resident.

Sikh resentment of the treaty's terms led to a second war in 1848, when the bloody but inconclusive battle of Chilianwallah was followed, in 1849, by a decisive British victory at Gujerat over 60000 Sikhs. The governor-general, Lord Dalhousie, annexed the Punjab later the same year.

Sikkim Small mountainous state on the borders of Nepal in the eastern Himalayas, absorbed by India in 1975. From the 14th century until it joined India Sikkim was ruled by *chogyals*, or kings, of the Namgyal dynasty, which survived continual invasions by Himalayan neighbours, especially Bhutan and Nepal. Sikkim's strategic interest to Britain, which feared Russian imperial expansion in the region, resulted in the Anglo-Sikkimese Treaty of 1861, making the country a protectorate within British India.

A Sikh stands before the Golden Temple, the holiest shrine of Sikhism, in the Indian city of Amritsar. In 1984 Indian troops stormed the temple to end an occupation by Sikh extremists.

Despite internal criticism of his feudal rule, the *chogyal* had hoped to retain autonomy when Britain left India, but a referendum in 1975 came down in favour of transfer into the Indian Union.

Sikorski, Vladislav (1881-1943) Polish general and politician who organised a Polish army in exile on the Allied side in the Second World War. From 1919 to 1920 Sikorski commanded Polish army divisions against the Bolsheviks, and in 1922 he headed a non-parliamentary coalition which governed

Sikorski, pictured the year after Poland's defeat by Germany in 1939, headed the Polish government in exile in the Second World War.

Poland until the following year. Sikorski fled to France in 1939 and from there to London to become head of the Polish government in exile. After the Soviet Union joined the Allies, Sikorski encouraged Polish prisoners of war in Russia to join a 'Polish Army in Russia'. The moderately harmonious relations he had maintained with the Soviet Union ended when news broke of the KATYN MASSACRE. Sikorski was killed in an air crash.

Silesia Industrial and mining region in central Europe, mostly in modern Poland, with the remainder in the Czech Republic. Long peopled by a mix of nationalities, Silesia has been the subject of frequent disputes since the 17th century. Its seizure by Frederick the Great in 1740 triggered the War of the AUSTRIAN SUCCESSION. Austria finally ceded its Silesian lands to Prussia at the end of the SEVEN YEARS' WAR, though Poland did not relinquish Upper Silesia until 1800. After the defeat of Germany and her allies in the First World War, and following a series of plebiscites, the coal and steel-producing area of Silesia was returned to Poland in 1919. Most of what had been Austrian Silesia was given to Czechoslovakia, while Germany retained Lower Silesia. Territorial disputes over their interests in Silesia soon emerged among the three countries and developed into ethnic clashes and civil unrest. In 1939 Upper Silesia was occupied by Germany, and by the end of 1940 the whole region was under Nazi control. After the Second World War the POTSDAM CONFERENCE of 1945 decreed that all non-Czech Silesia should pass to Poland and the German nationals were repatriated, mainly to the Federal Republic of Germany.

California's Silicon Valley – the centre of the world's computer industry – stretches 25 miles (40 km) from San Jose to Palo Alto.

Silicon Valley Nickname given to Santa Clara County in California, the heartland of US microelectronics, COMPUTER and database technology since the late 1950s. The name derives from the tiny silicon chips – each can contain a complete electronic circuit – which transformed the industry and paved the way for the widespread use of computers. The moderate climate, clean air, good communications and relatively low price of land in the area made it an attractive site for the fledgling industry; after the first companies had established themselves there, others followed suit.

silk trade see feature, page 595

Simnel, Lambert (c.1475-1534) English impostor and royal pretender. Born the son of a carpenter, Simnel was trained as a child by an Oxford priest to impersonate Edward IV's younger son Richard, Duke of York, who is thought to have been murdered in the Tower of London. In spite of obvious discrepancies, many Yorkists acknowledged him as heir to the throne. In 1486 the Yorkists changed their plan and forged a new identity for Simnel – this time as Edward of Warwick, son of the murdered Duke of Clarence, another claimant to the throne. Crowned 'Edward VI' in Dublin in 1487, Simnel crossed to England where the Yorkists, supported by 2000 German mercenaries, challenged and were defeated by Henry VII at the Battle of Stoke. Showing mercy to the young impostor, Henry later employed Simnel as a scullion, or dish washer, in the royal kitchens.

simony The buying or selling of any ecclesiastical living or source of income, such as the sale of pardons for sins. Simony was one of the main criticisms levelled at the Roman Catholic Church during the REFORMATION. The name comes from the account in the New Testament of Simon Magus' bid to buy spiritual powers from St Peter. Simony became a means for secular landholders – and venal clergy – to circumvent the Church's policy of not selling its assets, particularly parish lands. The richer of these lands often generated large incomes, and many medieval nobles claimed the estates as their own to exploit or sell as they pleased. Where the Church thought its ownership of such holdings was in jeopardy it sold offices – the administration of parishes, monastic lands, or even entire dioceses – to members of wealthy families. The Church lost the income from the benefice, but it retained legal ownership of the land, and payments of simony swelled its coffers. Simony later came to embrace the buying or selling of any form of Church preferment.

Singapore South-east Asian island state. It was acquired from the sultan of Johore in 1819 for the British EAST INDIA COMPANY by Sir Stamford RAFFLES, and rapidly developed into an important trading port on the tip of the Malay Peninsula. In 1867 it was removed from British Indian administration and incorporated within the new colony of the STRAITS SETTLEMENTS; its commercial development, dependent on Chinese immigrants, proceeded alongside its growth as a major naval base. Its fall in 1942 marked one of Japan's greatest victories in the SECOND WORLD WAR.

Singapore had strong coastal defences, but no preparations had been made against a land attack from the Malay Peninsula other than mining the 1 mile (1.6 km) causeway across the Strait of Johor. Having swiftly overrun MALAYA, early in February 1942 Japanese forces under General Yamashita massed opposite the island, surprised the garrison and pursued a relentless eight-day attack. On February 15 the 80 000-strong garrison of British, Indian and Australian troops surrendered and Singapore remained in Japanese hands until the end of the war. The island became a separate colony in 1946 and enjoyed internal self-rule from 1959 under the leadership of LEE KUAN YEW. It joined the Federation of Malaysia in 1963 but was expelled in 1965 because of fears that its predominantly Chinese population would discriminate in favour of non-Malays. A member of the COMMONWEALTH OF NATIONS and the Association of South-east Asian Nations, Singapore has maintained close ties with Malaysia and Brunei. It has been governed by the People's Action Party since 1965.

Sinn Féin Irish political party dedicated to the creation of a united Irish republic. Founded in 1902 by Arthur GRIFFITH as a

> **DID YOU KNOW?**
>
> The Japanese spent ten years preparing their invasion of Malaya and Singapore in 1942, infiltrating the region in many disguises such as photographers, merchants and brothel keepers, photographing and mapping the landscape for strategic purposes.

As Singapore faces imminent attack from Japanese forces in 1942, women and children, clutching their belongings, gather on the quayside for an evacuation that would take them to safety.

The camels' precious burden

The ancient civilisations of Rome and China were linked by trade in luxury goods, transported at great risk across desert and sea.

Of all the commodities brought into the ancient world from the east, the most highly valued was Chinese silk. It began to appear in the Eastern Mediterranean around 500 BC, the first time East and West had been linked by trade. The routes across the arid expanses of central Asia along which it was carried – in caravans of camels, horses, mules and even bullocks – became known collectively as the Silk Road.

The routes crossed the Chinese frontier at the western end of the Great Wall, then continued through central Asia and northern Persia to Mesopotamia and the Mediterranean ports. Individual merchants did not travel the whole way; most worked only one stage, selling their wares to other traders at the oasis markets which dotted the route. Merchants were continually menaced by bandits and also had to contend with the central Asian climate, especially in the remote regions north of Tibet and the Hindu Kush. Here the Silk Road forked to pass either side of the Takla Makan Desert, reputedly the most terrible in the world. Its name warned travellers of their likely fate: it means 'Go in and you will not come out'.

SILK FOR SALE

Silk cloth had been made in China since at least the 3rd millennium BC, but until the 6th century AD, when silkworm moths were smuggled to the West, the Romans believed that silk grew on trees. It became a badge of wealth in the Roman Empire from the 1st century AD.

The Silk Road was not the only connection between East and West at this time. More important were the sea routes bringing spices from India and beyond, through the Gulf of Aden to the Red Sea ports. This trade was given an enormous boost around 100 BC when western sailors discovered the monsoon wind system, making it possible to sail directly across the Indian Ocean; with steady winds the

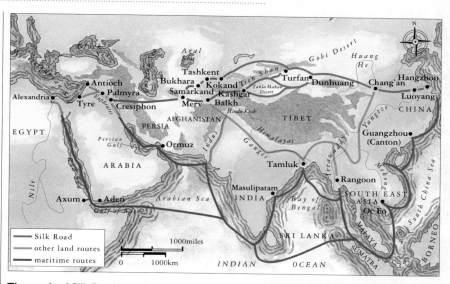

The overland Silk Road was pioneered by Chinese merchants in the 2nd century BC, and remained one of the main links between Europe and the Far East until the Renaissance.

2000 mile (3218 km) voyage from the mouth of the Red Sea to the west coast of India could be made in only 20 days.

Apart from silks, the Romans required spices and gems, which could be sold for enormous prices in Eastern Mediterranean markets such as Antioch and Alexandria. The Roman merchants had nothing to trade in return which could equal the value of these products, so they paid in gold and silver. The flow of precious metal to India was causing concern to the Roman government as early as the reign of Tiberius (AD 14-37). The historian Tacitus relates how in AD 22 Tiberius contemplated measures to curb luxurious living among the rich, and wrote to the senate complaining of 'the specially female extravagance by which, for the sake of jewels, our wealth is transported to alien or hostile countries'.

Roman trade with India and the East flourished throughout the 1st and 2nd centuries. Soon Greek and Roman traders were not only exploring coastal areas but penetrating inland, occasionally visiting the courts of central Asian rulers. These rulers sent ambassadors who were received by emperors such as Hadrian and Antoninus Pius. Merchants born in the Roman Empire must have found India a strange and mysterious land of jungles and deserts, of Hindus Buddhists, and Jains, with tales of still more fabulous countries beyond such as Chryse (Malaysia) – 'the farthest extremity at the east of the inhabited world, lying under the rising sun itself'.

Chinese women of the 12th century prepare newly woven silk by ironing it. Working silk was a vital female task.

Graffiti and wall paintings express support for Irish Republicanism in the Bogside district of Londonderry – known to Nationalists as Derry – a power base of Sinn Féin in Northern Ireland.

movement purporting to encourage an Irish cultural revival, Sinn Féin – in Gaelic, 'We Ourselves'– soon showed its political colours. Militantly nationalist, Sinn Féin actively supported the EASTER RISING of 1916 and three years later was a driving force behind the creation of the Irish Republican Army (IRA). The party gained a large majority of Irish seats in the 1918 British general election, but its MPs refused to take their seats in London and met instead in Dublin, where they proclaimed Irish independence in 1919. Though many of the MPs were in prison or on the run from the British authorities, they set up an independent parliament called Dáil Éireann.

Guerrilla warfare against the police and British troops followed, and violence continued even after the partition of Ireland and the establishment of the Irish Free State in December 1921. Sinn Féin's bitter resentment of these moves kept it out of both the Dáil and the Northern Ireland Parliament for many years. For much of the 25 years of civil strife in Ulster that preceded the 1994 ceasefire and subsequent 'peace process', Sinn Féin was prohibited in Northern Ireland. In 1993 the British Government offered Sinn Féin, which had evolved into the 'political arm' of the IRA, a role in discussions on Northern Ireland. But its credibility as a party to the peace negotiations was severely damaged when, in February 1996, the IRA renounced an 18 month truce and resumed its campaign of bombing in mainland Britain.

Sino-Japanese Wars (1894-5; 1937-45) Two armed conflicts between China and Japan which helped to shape much of Asia's later history. Sparked by Japanese expansionist policies, both wars erupted without formal declaration of hostilities by either side.

Although Korea had been a vassal state of its neighbour China since the 17th century, it was opened to Japanese trade in 1876. Soon it became an arena for rivalry between China and the expanding Japanese state, and a rebellion in 1894 gave both sides a pretext to send in troops. The Chinese forces were swiftly overwhelmed by the superior and better-equipped Japanese troops. The conflict spread to China, where the main Chinese fleet was defeated at the battle of the Yellow Sea; Port Arthur (now Lüshun) was captured and the Chinese capital Beijing was threatened by the advancing Japanese. China was forced to grant Korea independence and to make commercial and territorial concessions, which opened the way for a Japanese confrontation with Russia in north-east Asia.

China remained a target of Japanese expansionism, and after the MUKDEN INCIDENT of 1931, in which Japanese troops overran a Chinese garrison in a surprise attack, tension increased and a second war became inevitable.

Hostilities broke out after a clash near the Marco Polo bridge west of Beijing in 1937. Within a year the Japanese had overrun northern China and moved along the Chang Jiang (Yangtze) river and the railways to capture Shanghai, Guangzhou, Hankou and Nanjing, where they massacred more than 100 000 of the civilian population. The GUOMINDANG army of the nationalist leader Chiang Kaishek and the Communist 8th Route Army made common cause against the invaders. Faced with their tenacious resistance and the problems of massive distances and poor communications, the Japanese halted their thrust and a virtual stalemate ensued by the time the fighting was absorbed into the global pattern of the Second World War. Supplied with British and US arms, the Chinese kept more than a million Japanese troops tied down throughout the war, defeating them heavily at Jiangxi in 1942 and successfully repelling a final series of offensives in 1944 and 1945.

On September 9, 1945, the Japanese surrendered to Chiang Kai-shek, and the contest for the control of China was resumed between Chiang's nationalist forces and MAO ZEDONG's Red Army.

Sino-Soviet border dispute (1969) Six-month conflict, which twice erupted into armed clashes, between China and the Soviet Union over the ownership of a small island in the Wusul Jiang river (also known as Ussuri). As part of the disputed border between northeast China and the Soviet Union, possession of parts of the river had long been contentious. Efforts to resolve the dispute had been hampered since 1960 by the widening ideological rift between the two countries. The problem was intensified by the militant nationalism which surfaced as part of China's CULTURAL REVOLUTION. In March 1969 two battles were fought for possession of the island of Zhen Bao (also known as Damansky) and it seemed that the conflict between the two major communist powers might escalate into war. However, talks in September ended the crisis with China retaining control of the island.

Sioux see DAKOTA INDIANS

Sitting Bull (c.1834-90) Native American chief of the Dakota Sioux, whose resistance to the resettlement of his people on reservations led to the Battle of the Little Big

Japanese troops enter Guangzhou in 1939. Defeat in the Second World War ended Japan's bid to expand into China.

Horn in 1876, in which US General George CUSTER died. Sitting Bull's reputation as a warrior was established in wars against the Crow Indians and was enhanced by his armed opposition to White incursions on to the Great Plains in the 1860s and 1870s. His belligerent resistance to the enforced resettlement of the Dakota tribes provoked Custer's ill-fated expedition against the Sioux; but, though he defeated Custer's force, Sitting Bull had to flee to Canada, where he remained until 1881, when a US government amnesty tempted him back. Four years later he joined Buffalo Bill's 'Wild West' Show but continued to lead Indian resistance to the sale of their lands to White settlers. This resistance centred on the Ghost Dance religion, whose promise of a Native American 'messiah' to restore the country to its indigenous people sparked off new uprisings, during which Sitting Bull was killed while resisting arrest.

Sivaji (c.1630-80) Indian hero, who as founder of the Maratha kingdom in 1674 withstood MUGHAL expansion into the west of the subcontinent. From an early age Sivaji planned the downfall of the Muslim sultanates which surrounded his home in the Deccan. He gained a reputation for remarkable daring after unexpected victories in battle against the numerically superior forces of both the Sultan of Bijapur and AURANGZEB, the last great Mughal emperor. After one of his few defeats by the Mughals, Sivaji escaped in disguise and returned to regain and expand his domain, creating a nucleus for subsequent Maratha expansion. In spite of his earlier battles with the Muslims, Sivaji's fair but firm reign was marked by religious tolerance.

Six Acts (1819) Contentious British laws introduced to curb the public protests that followed the PETERLOO MASSACRE of 1819, and to halt what was regarded as dangerous radicalism. Passed in swift response to public anger aroused by the massacre, in which 11 protesters seeking electoral reforms had died, the Acts gave the Tory government wide-ranging prohibitive powers. These included a

ban of meetings 'for military exercises', the regulation and control of all public meetings, and the wider application of stamp duty on newspapers and periodicals. Regarded as a threat to freedom, these three measures were strongly resented. The Acts also contained procedures for bringing cases to trial and for the issue of warrants to search for arms, and provided powers for the seizure of seditious or blasphemous literature. The Acts provoked so much opposition that three years later the government of Lord LIVERPOOL swung towards more liberal policies.

Six-Day War (June 5-10, 1967) Arab-Israeli conflict (known to the Arabs as the 'June War') provoked by Egypt's closure of the Gulf of Aqaba to Israeli shipping and its build-up of troops in Sinai. The suddenness of the pre-emptive strike ordered by Israel's defence minister, Moshe Dayan, took the newly formed military alliance between Egypt, Jordan and Syria by surprise. An Israeli air strike destroyed most of Egypt's air force and Israeli troops occupied Sinai, from which United Nations troops had withdrawn a few days earlier in response to Egyptian demands. Israel's successes were swiftly followed by the occupation of the Arab-held old city of Jerusalem, the West Bank and the strategic Golan Heights. Israel's spectacular and easy victories severely damaged Egypt's claim to leadership of the Arab world. Since the war Israel has been slow to relinquish its territorial gains, other than parts of the West Bank.

Sixtus IV (1414-84) Franciscan priest, born Francesco della Rovere, who as pope from 1471 authorised the Spanish INQUISITION and commissioned the magnificent Sistine Chapel in the Vatican, which is named after him. Originally a monk and teacher, Pope Sixtus lavished funds both on the arts and on the military campaigns which made him a powerful secular ruler. His two expeditions against the Turks between 1472 and 1476 strengthened the political and territorial power of the papacy. He was less successful in his war against Venice in 1483, and in his support of the Pazzi family's failed conspiracy to overthrow their powerful MEDICI rivals in Florence. Sixtus' bid to re-unify the Russian Orthodox and Catholic Churches also failed. In 1478 he authorised the establishment of the Spanish Inquisition, appointing Tomás de TORQUEMADA as its Grand Inquisitor in 1483.

Victorious Israeli troops enter Arab East Jerusalem during the Six-Day War of June 1967 to reunite their ancient capital.

This pious portrait of Pope Sixtus IV belies the political schemer whose dynastic ambitions involved him in numerous political scandals.

In the last years of his papal reign Sixtus concentrated on furthering the ambitions of his family: of the 34 cardinals he created, six were his own nephews.

Sixtus V (1521-90) Pope, who in the five years following his election in 1585 as a compromise candidate, transformed Rome from a medieval into a baroque city. Born Felice Peretti, Sixtus was a noted Franciscan preacher who had been directly involved in the INQUISITION in Venice for three years before his elevation to the papacy. His reforms of central Church administration – including reducing the number of cardinals to 70 – contributed to the success of the COUNTER-REFORMATION, while the order he brought to the administration of the Papal States generated an increase in revenues that funded an extensive building programme in Rome.

slavery see feature, page 598

Slavs Peoples of eastern and central Europe who today form the continent's largest group sharing a common ethnic and linguistic heritage. Worldwide, they are estimated to number around 230 million. Though their origins are obscure, the Slavs are probably descended from Neolithic tribes who occupied the area of the Polesie marshes in Galicia. Some were absorbed by the Scythians and

Taken into servitude

Though slavery has been common in history, only in the 18th century did the means arrive to transport millions of Africans across the oceans to alien lands.

One of the earliest records of slavery comes from the Bible, which tells how Joseph was sold in Egypt. In the ancient world, slavery was thought normal. The Greek philosopher Aristotle wrote that slaves should be of an 'inferior' race, and as their master's property had no rights. The civilisations of the ancient world were often supported by slave labour, but the slaves were not always prepared to accept their lot. The most famous slave rebellion in the Roman Empire, in 73 BC, was led by Spartacus. Other forms of forced labour obliged men such as the peasants who built the Great Wall of China or the serfs of medieval Europe to work for their overlords, often without pay.

In ancient times most slaves were prisoners of war, taken into captivity to toil for their conquerors. A different form of slavery began to emerge in the 15th century, after Portuguese explorers travelled to Africa then to the Americas. In 1482 Diogo d'Azambuja built Elmina Castle in what is now Ghana, the first of the fortresses built to hold Africans before they were packed into ships for the voyage to New World plantations. Other nations wanted a part in this trade. A British slaving company, later called The Royal African Company, was set up in 1660 and Britain soon dominated the slave trade.

TRADING HUMANITY FOR SUGAR

Ships sailed from Bristol and Liverpool loaded with trade goods for West Africa: the standard currency was the iron bar. On arrival, the goods were traded for slaves. It was rare for the British to capture slaves themselves: they were bought from other Africans who had acquired them through wars or raids. The orders of George Merrick of the *Africa* were typical: he was instructed 'not to buy any old slaves or children but goo d healthy young men and women'.

An 1823 broadsheet from Richmond, Virginia, advertises Negroes for sale. On Antigua in the same year (below) slaves plant sugar cane. Copper tags (right) from Charleston, South Carolina, identified slaves who had been rented out by their owners.

Family ties were ignored, elderly parents abandoned, children effectively orphaned.

Once the ships were full, they set off on the Middle Passage to America and the West Indies. The captives were packed in tightly. Disease was rampant and many died, their bodies thrown out to the sharks. Many slaves tried to kill themselves by jumping overboard or fasting. One, Equiano, described how men were whipped hourly until they ate and wrote: 'I have never seen among my own people such instances of brutal cruelty.' The survivors were sold for work in the plantations, sugar in the West Indies and tobacco and later cotton in the USA. These goods formed the main cargo for the return journey to England. It was a lucrative trade, for profit was made on each leg of the voyage.

The African trade was unique. Never had so many people been taken not just to a different land but to another continent. From 1795 to 1804 some 400 000 slaves were taken from Africa by ships operating out of British ports. The total for the 18th century may be as high as 4 million.

The conditions under which they worked were not necessarily worse than those of paid workers in other countries, for owners had no wish to damage their valuable 'property'. But the hopelessness of their condition made their lives especially bitter. There were attempts at uprisings, of which Nat Turner's in 1830 was the most famous, but they could never hope to succeed.

Denunciations of slavery began as early as 1688 with a pamphlet by Francis Daniel Pastorius of Pennsylvania, and in Britain Granville Sharp raised the issue in the courts in 1772. The philanthropist William Wilberforce led the opposition to the slave trade, and saw it outlawed in the British Empire in 1807, a lead soon followed by other European countries. But it was 1833 before slavery itself was abolished in Britain's colonies, and in the USA it took a Civil War to bring emancipation to the Southern states.

10 LIKELY and VALUABLE

SLAVES
AT AUCTION.

On THURSDAY the 24th inst.
WE WILL SELL,
In front of our Office, without any kind of suit or reserve for cash,
AT 11 O'CLOCK,

10 AS LIKELY NEGROES

As any ever offered in this market; among them is a man who is a superior Cook and House Servant, and a girl about 17 years old, a first rate House Servant, and an excellent seamstress,

BROOKE & HUBBARD, *Auctioneers.*

Wednesday, July 22, 1823.

Sarmatians, and others by the GOTHS, the HUNS and the AVARS, whose westward invasions they shared, often as slaves. By the end of the 6th century AD Slavs had settled in Germany east of the river Elbe and others had challenged Byzantium's grip on the Balkan Peninsula, where a second invasion in 746 led to their settlement of parts of Greece. In Germany, where they were known as Wends, the Slavs were subdued by the Emperor CHARLEMAGNE and eventually driven back beyond the river Oder. In the 9th century the Byzantine missionaries CYRIL and Methodius evangelised the southern Slavs, or Slovenes, so beginning the division into the Eastern and Western Churches in which Slavs are still loosely grouped – by their faith and by their use of either the Cyrillic or Roman alphabets.

Slim, William Joseph, 1st Viscount

(1891-1970) British field-marshal who commanded the Allied forces in the BURMA CAMPAIGNS. As a professional soldier, Slim fought at Gallipoli and in France and Mesopotamia during the First World War, before transferring to the Gurkha Rifles. He led an Indian division against the VICHY forces in the conquest of Syria in 1941, and early the following year joined the Burma Campaigns, taking command of the 14th Army in 1943. After victory at Kohima, he led his 'forgotten army' down the Irrawaddy river to recapture Rangoon and most of Burma. After the war, Slim served as chief of the imperial general staff from 1948 to 1952, and as governor-general of Australia from 1953 to 1960.

Slovenia

Small north-Balkan country whose centuries-long struggle for independent nationhood finally bore fruit in 1990. As part of the western Slavonic migration, the Slovenes were dominated by the Franks and their descendants until the 14th century, when the Habsburgs gained control of the country, establishing a reign which survived intermittent independence movements until 1918. After the First World War most of the land peopled by Slovenes was incorporated

into the new Kingdom of Serbs, Croats and Slovenes, which later became YUGOSLAVIA. In 1941 their lands were again divided, this time between Italy, Hungary and the Third Reich. Although in the immediate postwar years

parts of the Istrian peninsula were added to what was nominally the Republic of Slovenia, the country was effectively a client state of the Federal Republic of Yugoslavia. Being predominantly Roman Catholic and sharing a strong Western heritage, Slovenia's people remained the most economically and educationally advanced of any group in the Slav republics. Pressure for independence mounted in 1989, when a coalition of six parties formed the Democratic Opposition of Slovenia (DEMOS). In May the following year it established a noncommunist government, which almost immediately declared independence. Intermittent fighting erupted between Slovene partisans and units of the mainly Serbian Yugoslav army before Serbia tacitly accepted the situation. In April 1992 DEMOS split and a Liberal Democrat government was formed under Janez Drnovsek.

Sluys, Battle of

(June 24, 1340) Naval clash in the Zwyn estuary in Flanders which gave England its first significant victory of the HUNDRED YEARS' WAR. A fleet of 200 French, Genoese, and Castilian ships intercepted a smaller English force commanded by Edward III, but the fighting was dominated by massed archers on Edward's vessels. Only 24 enemy ships survived the encounter, the two French commanders were killed, and the victory gave England control of the English Channel.

smallpox see feature, page 600

Smiles, Samuel

(1812-1904) British author and social reformer. Born in Scotland, Smiles abandoned a successful medical career in Leeds to become a journalist. A course of lectures given to a group of young working-class men who had set up their own evening school proved so popular that he had them published as *Self-help* (1859). The book consisted of a series of short biographies of successful men, accompanied by the injunction 'Do thou likewise', and was an immediate success. Its basic message — that poor people who wanted to improve themselves held the remedy in their own hands — appealed to the underprivileged; while its celebration of such Victorian 'virtues' as the Protestant work ethic and its promise of material and spiritual progress reinforced comfortable middle-class beliefs.

Smith, Adam see feature, page 602

Smith, Joseph

(1805-44) US founder of the MORMON Church. As a young man Smith claimed that an angel, Moroni, had visited him and revealed mystical religious writings on sheets of gold, buried a thousand years earlier on a hill near New York. Published as the *Book of Mormon* in 1829, the revelations formed the basis of the Church of Jesus Christ of the Latter-Day Saints and of the first

Joseph Smith receives the golden tablets containing the *Book of Mormon* from the angel Moroni in this late 19th-century lithograph.

Mormon community, organised by Smith at Fayette, New York. Persecuted by the locals and already split by internal bickering, the community moved west to Ohio, then to Missouri, and finally in 1840 to Illinois, where Smith founded Nauvoo, proclaiming himself its mayor. Despite the mistrust that followed the Mormons, within three years Smith had attracted 20 000 followers. He had also accumulated a harem of 'spiritual wives' – in effect sanctioning polygamy. In June 1844 Smith and his brother Hyrum were arrested and imprisoned in Carthage, Illinois. A mob of about 150 masked men broke into the jail and lynched both men. Leadership of the Church passed to Brigham YOUNG, who led the Mormons on to Utah.

Smithsonian Institution

US museum which houses one of the world's finest and widest-ranging collections of scientific and technological exhibits. Founded with a $100 000 bequest by the English chemist and mineralogist James Smithson, the Institution was established in Washington DC 'for the increase and diffusion of knowledge among men'. Smithson had prescribed three aims: to promote research, to maintain a library and to serve as a museum. Although he died in 1829, legal wrangles over his legacy delayed the Institution's establishment for 17 years. The original library was transferred to the Library of Congress 20 years later and, as other private and government-funded research bodies developed, the Smithsonian's activities in this field diminished. But the museum went from strength to strength and today the Institution also embraces an art gallery, a zoological park and an astrophysical observatory.

The life and death of smallpox

*After wiping out millions of people in successive deadly onslaughts
through the ages, smallpox was finally conquered by human intervention – the
first major disease to have been successfully overcome in this way.*

A highly infectious viral disease, smallpox (*variola major*) for centuries killed millions throughout the world. Its symptoms included high fever, but above all a severe rash: pustules could cover the body. Even those it did not kill it left blind, or disfigured with pitting and scarring.

Smallpox probably evolved from the cattle disease cowpox, which subsequently transferred to humans. It was common in the Egypt of the Pharaohs and in other early civilisations of the Near East, and also through the Roman Empire. The first great plague that spread through the Mediterranean – the Antonine plague of the 2nd century AD – was probably smallpox.

DEVASTATING IMPACT

Smallpox became particularly severe in 17th and 18th-century Europe – Queen Mary II of England and King Louis XV of France died of it. Smallpox accompanied Hernán Cortés to Mexico and Francisco Pizarro to Peru, slaughtering countless Amerindians. The Spanish had acquired some immunity; the Aztecs and Incas had none. Between 1518 and 1531 perhaps a third of the indigenous population died of smallpox, while the Spanish suffered only lightly. The disease did not merely exterminate millions; it utterly destroyed the Amerindians' capacity to resist. The psychological impact was as devastating as the physiological.

The first breakthrough against the disease came not from a physician but from Lady Mary Wortley Montagu (1689-1762), wife of the British consul in Constantinople, once a great beauty who herself had been scarred by smallpox. She reported how Turkish peasant women performed inoculations by breaking the skin and introducing minute quantities of infective material. The aim was to induce a mild dose which would confer lifelong protection without permanent pock-marking. Lady Mary had her three-year-old daughter Mary inoculated when an epidemic struck in England in 1721; the idea caught on, and the era of mass

The pioneering English doctor Edward Jenner (above) vaccinates his son in the late 18th century, in a painting by Monro S. Orr. French children are vaccinated in the 19th century (right).

inoculation came to the country after 1750 thanks to travelling inoculators who treated entire villages. The practice spread slowly through Europe. Catherine the Great of Russia had her family inoculated by Thomas Dimsdale, an English surgeon who was given £10000 and a title for his services.

Inoculation was not completely safe: one of George III's sons died after treatment. Therein lies the significance of the introduction of vaccination by the English doctor Edward Jenner. He discovered that it was common knowledge in his native Gloucestershire that dairymaids who contracted the benign cattle disease cowpox were subsequently immune to smallpox. Building on this knowledge, on May 14, 1796, Jenner inoculated an eight-year-old boy, James Phipps, with some matter taken from a cowpox pustule of a dairymaid, Sarah Nelmes. The boy developed a slight rash and fever, but recovered in a few days. Sometime later Jenner inoculated him with a potentially deadly dose of smallpox virus: it did not take, proving that he had been successfully immunised. What came to be called 'vaccination' was a huge success. By 1799, Jenner could report that 5000 people had been vaccinated. Parliament granted him £30000 as a reward. Smallpox vaccination was made compulsory in many European countries in the 19th century, though in England protesters claimed that the state had no right to impose such medical interventions. By 1900 the disease was almost eradicated in most of western Europe. After a coordinated vaccination programme conducted under the auspices of the World Health Organisation, the worldwide elimination of smallpox was achieved. In 1975, the world's last known case of ordinarily transmitted smallpox was reported: a three-year-old Bangladeshi girl.

Smallpox lives on only in research laboratories in Atlanta, USA, and Koltsovo, Novosibirsk, in Russia. The WHO has scheduled its final extinction for June 1999.

smuggler The smuggler's trade has existed since the beginning of civilisation: in ancient Egypt those caught taking cats out of the realm were subject to the death penalty; those attempting to smuggle silkworms out of China met a similar fate. The rapid development of organised smuggling came in the late 17th century with higher customs duties. In Britain, smugglers were popular because they made brandy, tea, silks and perfumes available at reasonable prices. In colonial America they were regarded as patriotic heroes defying the hated NAVIGATION ACTS enforced by Britain. In the 18th and early 19th centuries smuggling was used as a weapon of economic warfare. Britain encouraged smugglers to run British goods into France and Spain; Western powers used similar methods to overcome imperial China's trade barriers. The reduction of duties in the late 18th century, the spread of free trade and the development of the coastguard system all led to a decline in the smuggling of traditional contraband goods; today's smugglers trade in commodities such as arms, drugs and ivory.

> ### DID YOU KNOW?
>
> *Smugglers in England used boats with false bottoms, plaited tobacco into the rigging, and greased their horses to make them hard for excisemen to catch.*

Smuts, Jan Christian (1870-1950) South African statesman. Of Afrikaner stock, Smuts was educated at Cambridge but returned to practise law in the Transvaal. In 1898 he was appointed state attorney in Johannesburg and a member of Paul KRUGER's government. Smuts contributed to the Boer propaganda pamphlet *A Century of Wrong*, and rose to power in the second BOER WAR as a guerrilla leader. His skills as an orator and lawyer made him a leading Boer negotiator at the 1902 Treaty of VEREENIGING, where he believed that the future lay in cooperation with Britain.

Elected to parliament in 1907, Smuts held a succession of Cabinet posts under Louis BOTHA. At the outbreak of the First World War he was minister of defence, but resigned to lead the South African campaign against German East Africa. In 1917 Smuts joined the Imperial War Cabinet in London, playing a part in establishing the Royal Air Force. He attended the Versailles Peace Conference in 1919, when he helped to set up the LEAGUE OF NATIONS. That year he returned to South Africa and was elected prime minister, but his use of troops against striking White miners in the 1922 Rand revolt cost him public support and he lost the general election of 1924. Smuts led the opposition until 1933, when he became deputy prime minister in a coalition government led by General J.B.M. HERTZOG.

In 1934 Hertzog's National Party and the South African Party joined to form the United Party, supporting a policy of segregation. At the outbreak of the Second World War the coalition foundered when Hertzog wanted South Africa to remain neutral. Smuts became prime minister and leader of South Africa's armed forces, and in 1941 was appointed field-marshal. In 1945 Smuts wrote the preamble to the Charter of the United Nations. Three years later, Smuts's preoccupation with international rather than domestic issues cost him the general election. He was succeeded by an alliance of the Afrikaner Party and the Nationalist Party under D.F. MALAN, with its programme of apartheid.

Snowden, Philip, 1st Viscount (1864-1937) British Labour politician. After he was crippled in a bicycle accident, Snowden left the civil service and started his political career as a journalist working for the Independent Labour Party. In 1906 he was elected to Parliament. Snowden was opposed to British intervention in the First World War and throughout his career also advocated self-government for India. He was chancellor of the exchequer in 1924, from 1929 to 1931, and again in 1931-2 under Ramsay MacDonald. Snowden did not support the general strike of 1926, and his cautious approach to welfare spending alienated many Labour supporters. His 1931 budget further antagonised them by reducing unemployment benefits because of the crisis of the Great DEPRESSION. The following year he resigned when the OTTAWA AGREEMENTS led Britain to abandon its policy of free trade.

Sobieski, John (1624-96) Polish noble who, after defeating the Turks at Khotin in 1673, was elected King John III, reigning from 1674 until his death. As king, John not only drove the Turks out of southern Poland but in 1683 was largely responsible for expelling them from Vienna. John channelled all his abilities into his crusade against the Ottoman Empire, which he regarded as a mission to be pursued at all costs. As a result he neglected to strengthen the Polish monarchy.

socage Term applied in Anglo-Saxon and Norman England to a free tenure of land that did not require the tenant to perform military service; instead he paid rent in cash or in kind and performed some agricultural duties on his lord's estates. However, tenants were liable for three feudal dues: 20 shillings when their lord's daughter married and also when his son came of age, and a year's rent should his lord need to be redeemed from captivity. In contrast to military tenure, there were no restrictions attached to the inheritance of the tenure, nor to the marriage of the heir.

social contract Voluntary agreement among members of a society to behave in ways that are mutually beneficial. The concept, which explores the relationship between the state and the individual, was developed by Thomas HOBBES and later expanded upon by John LOCKE and Jean-Jacques ROUSSEAU, whose book *The Social Contract* (1762) greatly influenced the shaping of the CONSTITUTION OF THE USA.

All three thinkers examined the condition of humanity in a state of nature – that is, without law or government – and the transition by means of a 'contract' to ordered society. The theory of the social contract argues for the existence of an unwritten agreement that those ruled accept the authority of their ruler in exchange for a just and ordered society. To some degree these thinkers shared Hobbes's

John Sobieski relieves Vienna by capturing the Turkish leader Kara Mustapha's tent at the Battle of Kahlenberg on September 12, 1683, during the Great Turkish War of 1683 to 1699.

Enlightened economist

Adam Smith, the 18th-century Scottish thinker, laid the foundations
for capitalism with his theories about the market economy.

In 1776 a book appeared in London which argued that competition for wealth between individuals leads to prosperity for society as a whole. The process works through supply and demand, the 'invisible hand' which is the mechanism of the marketplace. The book was called *An Inquiry into the Nature and Causes of the Wealth of Nations*, and its author was a Scottish professor, Adam Smith (1723-90). It revolutionised economic thinking, and remains one of the foundations of economic theory.

Smith came from Kirkcaldy, near Edinburgh; his father was a customs controller. At the age of 14 he was sent to the University of Glasgow, where he was influenced by the new Enlightenment views of moral and political philosophy. In 1752 he became professor of moral philosophy at Glasgow. All over Europe intellectuals were keenly discussing the nature of government, the state, morality and civil society. Thinkers such as the French political theorist Charles Montesquieu, the Scottish philosopher David Hume and the English historian Edward Gibbon saw people as selfish yet able to create harmonious institutions by use of their reason. Ordered systems of property ownership, law and government all demanded that people voluntarily curb their natural self-interest for the common good. In his first book, *The Theory of the Moral Sentiments* (1759), Smith argued that selfishness is tempered by sympathy, and by the ability of our reason to act as an 'impartial spectator', weighing our own interests with those of others. But, he believed, these sentiments by themselves are too weak to guarantee social harmony, and have to be buttressed by laws.

During travels in France, Smith was influenced by economists such as François Quesnay, who argued that commerce should be freed from government monopolies, duties and taxes, which were stifling the economy. These views contributed to Smith's *Wealth of Nations*.

SUPPLY AND DEMAND

In his book Smith charted the evolution of societies from primitive hunting to complex commercial production and exchange. In this last stage the stability of prices results from supply and demand, a self-correcting mechanism which tends to restore prices and wages to 'natural' levels. Mankind's drive to acquire wealth, says Smith, 'comes with us from the womb and does not leave us until we go into the grave'. This, combined with the market, and the growing division of labour through commercial exchange, provides a social machine for continual economic growth.

Wealth of Nations made a deep impression in Smith's own time. Businessmen, industrialists and thinkers absorbed his ideas, and in the 1830s a reforming British Government dismantled the old restrictions on trade and enterprise. Capitalism was poised for its great leap, which would make Britain the first industrial nation.

Adam Smith's masterpiece, *Wealth of Nations* (1776), had a major influence on succeeding generations of economic policy-makers.

---

view that if no government existed people would turn to any absolute authority that offered security. Locke believed human nature was such that it is guided by reason and conscience even while accepting government. Rousseau believed that we are 'noble savages' in our natural state and only acquire a moral and civic sense when we become part of a larger democratic community. Thomas JEFFERSON later argued that 'to preserve natural rights was essential to the social contract'.

social credit Monetary theory advanced by the British engineer and economist Major Clifford Douglas as a way of eliminating the concentration of economic power. According to the theory, in every productive establishment the total cash issued in wages, salaries and dividends is less than the collective price of the product. To remedy deficiencies of purchasing power, either subsidies should be paid to producers or additional money should go to consumers. The concept gained currency in Britain in 1921-2 and in Canada and New Zealand in the Great DEPRESSION. In Canada, a Social Credit Party led by William Aberhart won an overwhelming victory in Alberta in 1935. The party remained in power until 1971 without, however, implementing many of Douglas's ideas. It also won an election in British Columbia in 1952, but never gained more than a handful of federal seats in Ottawa and largely disappeared after 1980. A New Zealand Social Credit Party formed in 1953 has held between one and three seats in the New Zealand parliament.

social Darwinism Theory of social and cultural evolution adapted from Charles DARWIN's theory of biological evolution. Even before Darwin published *On The Origin of Species* in 1859, the writer Herbert SPENCER was inspired by current ideas of evolution to write *Principles of Psychology* (1855), in which he applied the concept of evolution to the development of society. The theory, based on the belief that natural selection favours the most competitive or aggressive individual, was often used to support political conservatism. It was exploited to justify inequality among individuals and races, and to discourage attempts to reform society because they interfered with the natural process of selection of the fittest. In the 20th century it has been used to justify racist ideologies, and to explain the operations of the 'free economy'.

social democracy Socialist theory that advocates change through reform rather than revolution. The term was first adopted by Wilhelm Liebknecht and August Bebel when they founded the German Social Democratic Workers Party in 1869. The party's aims were based on Karl MARX's political theories, but it advocated evolutionary reform by democratic and constitutional means. In 1875 the party merged with the German Workers' Union to form the Social Democratic Party, which became the target of antisocialist legislation from the chancellor Otto von Bismarck. In the last quarter of the 19th century similar parties emerged in Europe, the USA and Russia, where in 1903 the grouping split into the revolutionary BOLSHEVIKS and the more moderate Mensheviks. Elsewhere many social democratic parties were absorbed by growing labour movements, while in France, Italy and Spain the term 'Socialist Party' was adopted from the beginning.

After the First World War the German Social Democratic Party formed a government in 1919 and was the largest party in the Weimar Republic until it was banned by Adolf Hitler in 1933. After the Second World War it reformed in West Germany and ended all Marxist connections. Swedish politics has been dominated by the SDP since the 1930s. In Britain the Labour Party has been allied with the European Social Democrats since the party's foundation in 1906, but in 1981 a more moderate Social Democratic Party was formed by four prominent Labour Party members. In 1988 it merged with the Liberal Party to form the Social and Liberal Democrats, changing to Liberal Democrats in 1989.

socialism

Political and economic theory advocating communal ownership and control of all production, distribution and exchange as an equitable way to share a nation's wealth. The term was first applied to the concept during the early 19th century in the writings of the Frenchmen François Fourier and Count Claude de SAINT-SIMON, although Robert OWEN's experiments in the cooperative control of industry at his works at New Lanark in Scotland from 1800 predated them.

Almost 50 years later Karl MARX revolutionised socialist political ideals with his claim that capitalist profit was derived from the exploitation of the worker, and his argument that only the working masses could achieve a socialist society. Both the way this society would be established and the manner in which it would be run provoked disagreement, leading to a wide variety of socialist parties. These ranged from moderate reformers to extreme left-wing communists who saw violent revolution as the only means for change. In most developed countries, aspects of socialism such as SOCIAL SECURITY are accepted, but by the 1990s much of its pure ideology was no longer viable and it has become a political and social philosophy interdependent with market forces.

social sciences

The study of societies and social relationships, usually including such topics as anthropology, economics, demography, sociology, psychology and political science. When 18th-century scholars first attempted to investigate man and society, they set about their inquiries using the methods that had been applied to the natural sciences, postulating laws for which they then sought evidence. In some disciplines this approach – termed naturalism or positivism –

Socialism rises victorious from the constricting toils of the capitalist serpent in a May Day poster dedicated to the 'workers of the world'.

worked and is still used, particularly among economists and psychologists who use experiments and statistics to test hypotheses and explain or predict phenomena. As studies of social sciences developed, however, a growing body of opinion argued for a more flexible approach in which the social scientist, rather than seeking 'laws' or gathering statistics, should be more interpretative and intuitive. This approach, often favoured by anthropologists and sociologists, stresses observing and

interpreting actual occurrences, rather than experiments, and canvassing the views of those being studied instead of propounding formulae. Although quantitative and qualitative approaches serve different purposes, the topics social scientists deal with often require a combination of both approaches. Today, governments and public and private bodies use the work of social scientists in their attempts not only to understand the world, but also to regulate it.

social security

Assistance provided by the state to those lacking adequate means. The first comprehensive social security scheme was introduced in Germany between 1881 and 1889 by Otto von BISMARCK; it provided for insurance benefits that were paid by the state in the event of accident, sickness or old age. Similar schemes were begun in New Zealand in 1898 and in France in 1905. Britain did not follow suit until the government of H.H. ASQUITH introduced old age pensions in 1908 and compulsory health and unemployment insurance in 1911. In 1941 Winston Churchill appointed a government committee headed by William BEVERIDGE to review social insurance schemes. Its recommendations, known as the Beveridge Report (1942), proposed a comprehensive national insurance scheme that formed the basis of the postwar WELFARE STATE.

In the USA the vast increase in unemployment and hardship during the years of the Great DEPRESSION prompted Franklin D. Roosevelt's NEW DEAL, in particular the Social Security Act of 1935. Based on a payroll tax, this provided for old age, the death of a spouse and disability. US social security was extended in the 1960s but reduced in the 1980s, and

The social security system pioneered by Otto von Bismarck gave unemployed Germans a degree of support in the years of poverty and rampant inflation that followed the First World War.

became a contentious political issue in the 1990s. With people living longer, and a certain level of unemployment becoming a permanent feature of many societies, the governments of many developed countries face escalating social security costs.

social work Occupation directed towards the alleviation of social and personal problems. Beginning in the 19th century as an unpaid activity associated with voluntary organisations and churches, in the USA and many welfare states social work has emerged in the 20th century as a professionally trained occupation. Social workers play a major role in social care services by assisting children and families, old people and those incapacitated by illness or handicap, and by counselling people with personal problems such as alcohol addiction or marriage breakdown.

In many countries, social workers are being asked to play a bigger role in controlling deviant, delinquent and criminal behaviour, but are required not to intrude on family privacy or abrogate the civil rights of those with whom they work. In some countries, notably in the developing world, they are involved in assessments for financial assistance, in relief work and in community development.

Society of Friends see QUAKER

Socinus, Laelius (1525-62) Latinised name of Lelio Sozzini, an Italian theologian whose monotheistic views contributed to the growth of UNITARIANISM. After studying law in Bologna, Socinus travelled extensively in Europe before settling in Zurich in 1548 to study Greek and Hebrew. There he corresponded with leading Protestant reformers and conducted his own theological enquiries, but his *Confession of Faith* (1555) shows that he had reached few clear conclusions of his own. His nephew Faustus Socinus (1539-1604) developed Laelius' views into a well-defined system, which led to the founding of the Socinian sect, an early form of Unitarianism.

Socrates see feature, page 605

Solemn League and Covenant (1643) Agreement between the English Parliament and Scottish COVENANTERS during the ENGLISH CIVIL WAR. By the terms of the pact, Parliament promised the Scots payment of £30000 a month in return for their military help against the army of Charles I. Parliament also agreed to preserve the Presbyterian Church of Scotland and to introduce Presbyterianism into England. Covenanter forces contributed to the defeat of the Royalists, but realised that the Westminster Assembly of Divines would not impose Presbyterianism on England, which put considerable strain on Anglo-Scottish relations.

Solidarity supporters proclaim their allegiance to the Polish trade union movement, which began in the shipyards of Gdánsk. By the middle of 1981, Solidarity had some 9 million followers.

Solferino, Battle of (June 24, 1859) Battle fought in Lombardy during the RISORGIMENTO to unify Italy. Under the leadership of Count Camillo CAVOUR, Piedmont, which was the centre of the movement for Italian unification, persuaded the French to provide military support against Austria. Having defeated the Austrians at MAGENTA on June 4, the French and Piedmont-Sardinian armies, commanded by Napoleon III, captured the elevated position at Solferino near Verona in northern Italy. They successfully defended it after a fierce counterattack by the Austrians, who began to retreat. A meeting between the Austrian emperor Franz Josef I and Napoleon took place shortly afterwards at Villafranca, where the Austrians agreed to an armistice. Austria handed Lombardy over to France, who later passed it to Sardinia, but retained Venetia as an Austrian province. The rulers of the central Italian duchies were restored. Piedmont acquiesced and Cavour resigned.

Solidarity Independent Polish trade union movement. It emerged in 1980 out of a wave of strikes at Gdánsk organised by the Free Union of the Baltic Coast. Demands included the right to a trade union independent of Communist Party control. Under the leadership of Lech WALESA membership rose rapidly as Poles began to demand political as well as economic concessions. In 1981, following further unrest aggravated by bad harvests and poor distribution of food, General Jaruzelski was appointed prime minister. He proclaimed martial law and arrested Solidarity leaders. The movement was outlawed in 1982, but continued to grow as an underground force.

Under pressure from both left and right, in 1989 the government agreed to round-table talks, from which Solidarity emerged as Poland's dominant political organisation. In the freer political climate that followed the collapse of communism in Eastern Europe, Walesa was elected president of the republic in 1990. But ideological differences within Solidarity together with popular disappointment with Poland's slow economic recovery weakened both the movement and the position of its charismatic leader. Solidarity split into a number of separate political parties, with only one, a minority party, retaining the name *Solidarnosc*. In 1995 Walesa failed in his bid for re-election.

Solomon (died c.922BC) Third and last king of a united Israel from about 961BC until his death. The second son of David and Bathsheba, Solomon succeeded his father at a time

> 66 **Wisdom is the principal thing; therefore get wisdom: and with all thy getting get understanding.** 99
>
> *Proverbs, chapter 4, verse 7, traditionally attributed to Solomon*

when Israel was expanding as a political and economic force. His riches and wisdom became legendary, and under his rule the nation grew wealthier. He forged alliances with Egypt and Phoenicia to maintain peace in the region, but they provoked discontent by leading to the official establishment of foreign religious cults in Jerusalem.

Solomon organised the land into administrative districts to facilitate government, and also introduced a system of forced labour to sustain an unprecedented programme of building works. These included cities, palaces and in about 970BC the first Temple at Jerusalem, which became the central sanctuary of the Jewish religion. Partly because of the high taxes imposed to support court luxury, the northern tribes seceded under JEROBOAM after Solomon's death. Solomon's reputation for wisdom has caused various

A question of philosophy

Socrates is said to have been described by the oracle at Delphi as the wisest man in Greece. Through his conversations he attracted a circle of young followers who recorded his dialogues for posterity.

A philosopher who lived in Athens from 470 to 399 BC, Socrates wrote nothing, and was never a professional teacher. His philosophical activity consisted of informal conversations, chiefly on questions of ethics, with small groups of friends and acquaintances. In these conversations his aim was not so much to propound his own views as to challenge his hearers to examine their own beliefs, and to abandon those which could not stand up to critical examination. A few writers who knew him personally have left vivid portrayals of Socrates' argumentative method and of his extraordinary personality. Despite his remarkable physical ugliness – he had a snub nose and protruding eyes – the keenness of his intellect and his personal integrity, together with his physical toughness and outstanding courage, made him magnetically attractive to a wide range of people.

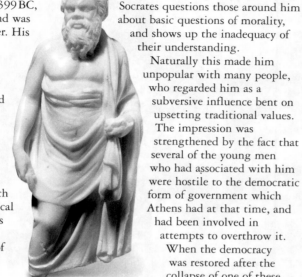

Socrates, above, was noted for his intellectual integrity.

the form of dialogues in which Socrates questions those around him about basic questions of morality, and shows up the inadequacy of their understanding.

Naturally this made him unpopular with many people, who regarded him as a subversive influence bent on upsetting traditional values. The impression was strengthened by the fact that several of the young men who had associated with him were hostile to the democratic form of government which Athens had at that time, and had been involved in attempts to overthrow it. When the democracy was restored after the collapse of one of these antidemocratic regimes, which had briefly seized power, Socrates was brought to trial on vague charges of hostility to the state religion and of corruption of the young. He was condemned to death and executed by the administration of poison.

IMMORTALISED BY PLATO

Socrates' circle included a number of intellectually and politically ambitious young men, the most famous of whom was Plato, who in his own writings immortalised Socrates as the ideal philosopher. Most of these writings are in

The treatment meted out to Socrates had the effect of converting Plato from his earlier political ambitions to a life dedicated to philosophy. One of Plato's aims was to show how his mentor had been unjustly condemned by an ungrateful people, corrupted by the false beliefs from which Socrates had tried in vain to free them. Largely as a result of Plato's portrayal, Socrates became for later ages a representative not merely of the philosophic life, but also of the wider ideals of moral and intellectual integrity.

Condemned to death by drinking a potion of poisonous hemlock, Socrates converses with his friends to the end.

Solomon proposes to divide a baby between two women, so that he can tell by their reactions which of them is the true mother.

Old Testament and apocryphal writings to be attributed to his authorship, including Proverbs, the Song of Solomon, Ecclesiastes and the Wisdom of Solomon.

Solomon Islands Chain of six large and many smaller south-western Pacific islands. They were occupied by Melanesians for some 3000 years before a Spanish explorer Alvaro de Mendeña de Neira arrived in 1568 and named the islands. European settlers and missionaries came in the 18th and 19th centuries. The German New Guinea Company established control of the north Solomons in 1885, while the southern islands became a British protectorate in 1893. In the PACIFIC CAMPAIGNS of the Second World War the Solomon Islands were the scene of fierce battles between Japanese and Allied forces. In 1978 the islands became independent. Solomon Mamaloni was elected prime minister in 1989, but two years later faced criticism for ignoring the constitution. The independent Francis Hilly was premier from May to November 1993, when Mamaloni regained power.

Solon (c.640-560 BC) Statesman whose code of laws introduced major reforms in Athens in the 6th century BC. His code divided Athenian citizens into four classes, based on wealth, each with its own political responsibilities and prerogatives. This moderated aristocratic power, which was based solely on birth. It also included the bringing home of Athenians who had been sold into slavery abroad. Solon may have created a new council to prepare business for the citizen-assembly, thereby challenging the position of the traditional council, or Areopagus. He replaced the DRACONIAN LAWS with a less harsh legal code that remained the basis of later classical laws.

Somali children wait for food at a Red Cross kitchen. In the West, shocking reports of the famine helped to fund relief for the starving.

Somalia Country in East Africa. Originally populated by Somali nomads who converted to Islam in the 7th to 10th centuries, the area known as the Horn of Africa, or Somaliland, was divided between France, Italy and Britain in the late 19th century. Modern Somalia was created in 1960 from former Italian and British possessions in Somaliland. The new republic was soon involved in border disputes

with Kenya and Ethiopia, which has a large Somali population. In 1969 the Marxist Somali Revolutionary Socialist Party seized power in a military coup. Under General Muhammad Siyad Barre, the renamed Somali Democratic Republic entered 21 years of dictatorship, with a sharply deteriorating economy and civil war between government forces and rebel groups such as the Somali National Movement (SNM). In 1977-8 war with Ethiopia ended in defeat and the loss of support from the Soviet Union.

By 1988 Somalia had descended into one of the world's worst man-made disasters as warfare, internal strife and drought brought widespread suffering and famine. When Siyad

Barre fled office in 1991, the SNM proclaimed the Somaliland Republic in the north. By mid 1992 control of the country was in the hands of rival warlords, and millions of Somalis faced starvation. After a UN-sponsored truce in 1992, UN peace-keeping forces were sent to secure food and aid distribution, but they were unable to maintain the cease-fire and had been withdrawn by March 1995.

Somerset, Edward Seymour, Duke of (c.1506-52) Protector of England and effective ruler on behalf of his nephew EDWARD VI from 1547 to 1549. As the brother of Henry VIII's third wife, Jane SEYMOUR, he rose rapidly in the king's favour and was created Earl of Hertford in 1537. In 1543-4 he commanded the English forces that invaded Scotland and sacked Edinburgh, and in 1545 he defeated the French at Boulogne.

On Henry's death, Seymour assumed the titles of Lord Protector and Duke of Somerset, and immediately defeated Scotland at the Battle of Pinkie after the Scots refused to join a voluntary union with England. In 1549 the introduction of a Protestant English Prayer Book, enforced by an Act of Uniformity, led to uprisings in western England. These coincided with KETT'S REBELLION in Norfolk, as well as increasing discontent among magnates grouped around his rival, John Dudley, Earl of Warwick. They overthrew and imprisoned him in 1549, and in 1551 Somerset was executed for treason on the orders of Warwick, now Duke of NORTHUMBERLAND.

Somme, Battle of the (1916) Allied offensive against German troops along the river Somme in northern France during the First World War. It was planned by France's General Joffre and Britain's Field-Marshal HAIG as a joint offensive, but before the campaign could be launched the French army was almost destroyed defending Verdun, leaving Lord KITCHENER's new volunteer armies to bear the brunt of the fighting. The battle began on July 1. British troops advanced from their trenches, but proved an easy target for enemy machine gunners. More than 19000 died on the first day of the offensive alone.

The Germans fell back to the concrete pill-box emplacements of the Hindenburg Line, from which they repulsed wave after wave of poorly supported infantry. In September Haig launched a major assault preceded by 32 tanks. It was the first time tanks had been used in battle, but there were

The appalling conditions and heavy losses suffered during the Battle of the Somme destroyed the morale of Kitchener's army of volunteers.

not enough to make a difference. By the time the conflict ended on November 15, the Allies had advanced just 5 miles (8 km) at the cost of 615 000 lives. German losses numbered at least 420 000.

Sonderbund Alliance of Swiss Catholic cantons. In 1845 seven cantons formed the Sonderbund – German for 'Separate League' – to preserve their Roman Catholicism and to retain their autonomy against the Protestant Radical Party's attempts to establish a more centralised government. In 1847 the Radical majority in the federal Diet sent an army against the Sonderbund. After a month of civil war the Sonderbund capitulated, and the following year a new federal constitution ended the virtual sovereignty of the cantons.

Sophia (1630-1714) Electress of HANOVER, the daughter of Elizabeth of Bohemia and granddaughter of James I of England. In 1658 Sophia married Ernest Augustus, duke of Brunswick-Lüneberg, who became Elector of Hanover in 1692. As the only surviving Protestant descendant of the STUARTS, Sophia was named Anne's heir to the British throne by the terms of the 1701 Act of Settlement. However, she died a few weeks before the queen, and her son succeeded as GEORGE I.

Sophist Itinerant professional teacher who taught a wide range of subjects in much of Greece during the 5th century BC. Gorgias of Leontini (c.483-376) specialised in teaching rhetoric, and his visit to Athens in 427 spurred the development of oratory among young Athenian democrats. The alleged ability of Sophists – from the Greek *sophistes*, 'wise man' – to train men to 'make the weaker argument the stronger' led to popular distrust. Opposition to their teaching methods was strengthened by the fact that they questioned not only conventions and morals, but also the nature of the gods. By the time of the Roman Empire, Sophists taught only rhetoric and were still viewed with some suspicion.

Sophocles (496-406 BC) Greek dramatist, who, with AESCHYLUS and EURIPIDES, was one of the three greatest classical tragedians. Sophocles' impact on the development of the

theatre was immense. He introduced scene painting, and was the first to expand a play's cast beyond the traditional two actors and chorus. Where Aeschylus looked to the gods

> **❝ I depict men as they ought to be, but Euripides portrays them as they are. ❞**
>
> *Sophocles,*
> *Antigone*

for his themes and Euripides wrote of human foibles, Sophocles depicted the deeds of heroes and the impact upon them of the Fates. He wrote some 123 plays, but only seven remain, including *Antigone*, *Electra* and *Oedipus Rex*. A general and a priest, Sophocles was also a friend of the Athenian statesman PERICLES and held important civil and military posts. After his death he was worshipped as a hero.

South Africa Heavily industrialised country on the southern tip of Africa. Originally populated by San peoples, the region was settled by the Khoikhoi about 2000 years ago. In 1488 the Portuguese navigator Bartolomeu Dias was the first European to sight the Cape of Good Hope, but European settlement only began in 1652, when the Cape became a base for Dutch ships en route to and from the East. Conflict between Xhosa peoples and White farmers, known as AFRIKANERS or Boers, led to the XHOSA WARS of 1779 to 1877.

The British first arrived in 1795, and in 1815 the Cape was assigned to Britain by the Congress of VIENNA. After the British introduced restrictions on the acquisition of land, some 12 000 Boers joined the GREAT TREK inland between 1835 and 1843. In 1838 they defeated the Zulus at BLOOD RIVER, and the following year founded the first Boer republic in NATAL. In the 1850s the ORANGE FREE STATE and TRANSVAAL were both recognised by the British, but from 1886 the discovery of diamonds and gold increased Anglo-Boer rivalry, leading to the BOER WARS. In 1910 Natal, Orange Free State, Cape Province and Transvaal formed the Union of South Africa.

Following the First World War, J.B.M. HERTZOG's republican National Party vied with General Jan Christian SMUTS' South African Party before they formed an uneasy coalition in 1933. In 1939 Hertzog and D.F. MALAN created a reunited Nationalist Party opposing South Africa's entry into the Second World War. Following victory in the 1948 general election, Malan became prime minister and was responsible for initiating a strict system of APARTHEID. After the SHARPEVILLE MASSACRE of 1960, Black nationalism grew increasingly radical. The AFRICAN NATIONAL CONGRESS (ANC) and Pan-African Congress (PAC) were outlawed, and during the 1960s

their leaders, including Nelson MANDELA, were imprisoned. In 1961 South Africa left the Commonwealth and became a republic.

While its economic strength allowed it to dominate southern Africa, the rise of Black nationalism both at home and in surrounding countries such as NAMIBIA led to increasing violence, emphasising South Africa's isolation in the diplomatic world. In 1985 attempts by P.W. Botha to interpret apartheid more liberally failed to satisfy either the increasingly militant non-White population or extremist White right-wing groups. The domestic and international sides of the problem remained inseparable, with South African troops fighting SWAPO guerrillas in Namibia and Angola. International sanctions were introduced in 1988, and in 1989 Botha's successor, F.W. de Klerk, began the quest for racial conciliation.

In February 1990 the ANC ban was lifted and Mandela was released from prison. After the last apartheid legislation was repealed in July, sanctions were eased. In 1991 multiparty delegations representing all races and political parties in South Africa formed the Convention for a Democratic South Africa (CODESA), but during 1992 its deliberations were interrupted by violent racial incidents and armed clashes between the ANC and the Zulu Inkatha Movement. In April 1994 the country's first multiparty elections were won by the ANC and its allies. Mandela became president and de Klerk one of two vice-presidents. South Africa rejoined the Organisation of African Unity (OAU) and the Commonwealth. In 1996 de Klerk and the other Nationalist ministers resigned to join the opposition.

South America Southern half of the American landmass. The indigenous AMERINDIAN inhabitants developed several sophisticated cultures, most notably that of the INCAS. After Christopher COLUMBUS sailed along the coast of Venezuela in 1498, and the Portuguese reached Bahia in Brazil in 1500, most of South America was colonised by Spanish CONQUISTADORES and Portuguese explorers. In the 17th century, the Netherlands, England and France founded small colonies on the continent's north-eastern coast.

Between 1816 and 1825 Simón de BOLÍVAR and José de SAN MARTÍN led most of Spanish South America to independence. The continent remained politically independent in the 19th century, but attracted some 15 million European immigrants. European investment in agriculture and mining was considerable, but the poverty of the peasant masses created

economic and political instability. The Roman Catholic Church still occupies a central position as a conservative force, although in the 20th century it has been challenged by industrialisation. Development projects and rapidly increasing oil prices in the 1970s have burdened many South American countries with debts their economies find almost impossible to service.

South Carolina State of the USA on the southern Atlantic coast. Yamasee Indians inhabited the area when failed attempts to settle were made by the Spanish in 1526 and by the French in 1562. In 1663 Charles II granted a charter to eight of his favourites, and in 1670 the first English colonists arrived. In 1713 the colony was divided into North and South Carolina. A prosperous plantation culture based on rice and indigo grew up around Charleston and was greatly dependent on slavery: by 1724 slaves outnumbered Whites two to one. With slave labour essential to the prosperous cotton and tobacco plantations, South Carolina led the battle of the Southern states against the abolitionists. In 1860 it seceded from the Union, the first state to do so, and the following year the opening shots of the American Civil War were fired on Fort Sumter in Charleston harbour. For a decade after the war CARPETBAGGERS ruled South Carolina with the support of Black votes. The state was readmitted to the Union in 1868.

A stately South Carolina plantation house in the 1880s still shows signs of a previous era of elegance and affluence when the planter aristocracy ruled the American South.

South Korea North-east Asian country covering the Korean peninsula south of the 38th parallel. Formed from the zone occupied by US forces after the Second World War, South Korea was proclaimed an independent republic in 1948. Hopes of postwar recovery were dashed by the KOREAN WAR of 1950-3. Lack of industrial and power resources, and a severe refugee problem, were also handicaps. The reputation of President Syngman Rhee's regime was damaged by high unemployment and inflation, and its increasing brutality and corruption led to its overthrow and Rhee's exile in 1960. When a second civilian government failed to improve matters, the army seized power in 1961. As president, General Park Chung Hee organised a successful reconstruction campaign that saw South Korea emerge as a strong industrial power, but his repressive policies caused serious unrest and in 1979 he was assassinated by the head of South Korea's Central Intelligence Agency.

Park's successor, General Chun Doo Hwan, continued his policies until student unrest in 1987 forced him to concede a national referendum and a new constitution. Roh Tae Woo was elected president, and in 1990 his Democratic Justice Party merged with others to form the Democratic Liberal Party (DLP), which advocated reunion with the North. After widespread student demonstrations in 1991 and internal feuding, the DLP lost the general election of 1992. In 1994 tension between North and South Korea grew when the North Korean regime refused to submit its nuclear research programme to international scrutiny. In 1995 allegations of corruption against government leaders in South Korea continued to stir unrest.

South Sea Bubble (1720) English financial crisis that had political repercussions. The South Sea Company was founded in 1711 to trade with Spanish America. George I became its governor in 1718, and in 1720 Parliament allowed it to assume 60 per cent of England's national debt from the Bank of England. In order to raise funds from the sale of shares, the company forced up their value by encouraging rumours of future profits. Bribes of cheap or free shares persuaded politicians to promote the company, increasing the value of shares tenfold. Expectations of high dividends rose accordingly. Bogus companies secured investment by exploiting the speculative fever, but confidence in them soon collapsed and South Sea shares fell to less than 10 per cent of their original price, ruining thousands. Sir Robert WALPOLE began his period in office by saving the company, restoring financial stability and limiting the political damage so that only two ministers were implicated in the scandal.

South Vietnam see VIETNAM

soviet Russian elected governing body, from the Russian *sovet*, 'council'. Soviets first gained revolutionary connotations in 1905, when the St Petersburg Soviet of Workers' Deputies was established to coordinate strikes and other antigovernment activities in factories. Each factory sent its delegates, and for a time other Russian cities were dominated by soviets. Both BOLSHEVIKS and Mensheviks appreciated the potential importance of soviets and appointed delegates. In 1917 a new soviet was established in St Petersburg, now renamed Petrograd, and was strong enough to dictate industrial action and to control the use of armed force. It did not try to overthrow the Provisional Government, but grew increasingly powerful representing opposition to Russian participation in the First World War. Other soviets were established in provinces, and in 1917 the first All Russian Congress of Soviets met. The Bolsheviks gradually dominated policy, and later that year seized power in the Russian Revolution. During the ensuing civil war, village soviets commonly controlled local affairs and agriculture. In 1922 the Supreme Soviet, comprising delegates from all the Soviet republics, became the legislative power of the new Union of Soviet Socialist Republics (USSR).

Soweto Mostly Black South African township south-west of Johannesburg. In June 1976 Black schoolchildren demonstrated against legislation that proposed to make Afrikaans the compulsory language of instruction. Police broke up the demonstration using guns and tear gas, triggering a wave of violence. By the end of the year some 500 Blacks and Coloureds, many of them children, had been killed by the police. Plans for teaching in Afrikaans were dropped, but the anniversary of the demonstration continued to be marked by unrest until the multiracial elections of 1994.

spa Resort noted for its thermal or mineral springs. The name derives from the Belgian town of Spa, celebrated since the Middle Ages

Sulphur and alum springs in the French spa town of Aix-les-Bains, at its peak in 1905, have been frequented since Roman times.

for the restorative quality of its water. In 18th-century England spas such as those at Buxton, Harrogate and Bath were fashionable resorts offering cures and amusements for the upper and middle classes. Sea bathing also became popular, and in the 1790s the patronage of the future George IV ensured Brighton's social success. Spas flourished in Europe in the 19th century, particularly the German resort of Baden-Baden and the French town of Vichy.

space exploration see feature, page 610

Spain Country occupying the greater part of the Iberian Peninsula in south-west Europe. Originally controlled by CARTHAGE, it came under Roman rule after 201 BC

During the apartheid era in South Africa, riots in Soweto were frequent occurrences. In 1990 supporters of the African National Congress were attacked by the Inkatha Party.

and remained part of its empire until the Visigoth invasion of 415. The defeat of the Visigoths by Muslim invaders between 711 and 718 heralded three centuries during which Moorish art and architecture reached its zenith under the UMAYYAD dynasty. After the fall of the Umayyads in 1031, Moorish Spain became fragmented. Christian reconquest consolidated small kingdoms such as ARAGON and CASTILE, and by 1248 only Granada remained in Muslim hands. In 1479 the marriage of FERDINAND II of Aragon and ISABELLA of Castile united their realms. They reconquered Granada in 1492, establishing a powerful and unified Spain. A vast overseas SPANISH EMPIRE took shape, which entered its 'golden age' under CHARLES V and PHILIP II.

The decline in Spain's fortunes began in the 17th century, culminating in the War of the SPANISH SUCCESSION (1701-14), which saw the transition from HABSBURG to BOURBON rule. Spain's power was finally destroyed when the Napoleonic Wars severed Spain's contact with its South American empire, leading to a spate of wars of independence. In a Europe fast becoming industrialised, Spain remained undeveloped and torn by struggles between its absolutist monarchy and the forces of liberalism. In 1898 the SPANISH-AMERICAN WAR led to the loss of Spain's last New World possessions. The virtual dictatorship established by General Miguel Primo de Rivera in 1923 was followed in 1931 by republican rule and the SPANISH CIVIL WAR. Nationalist victory in 1939 led to the harsh dictatorship of General FRANCO, which only eased in the late 1960s.

Franco's death in 1975 was followed by the accession of King JUAN CARLOS, who established a democratic constitutional monarchy and accelerated the liberalisation of Spain. In 1978 and 1981 he survived attempted military coups. The left-of-centre regime elected in 1981 governed Spain until 1996, when it was replaced by a right-wing coalition. The often violent agitation by Basque separatists, which surfaced during the Franco regime, continues to pose problems.

Spanish-American War (1898) Conflict between the USA and Spain that had its roots in Cuba's struggle for independence from Spain, and in US economic and imperialist ambitions. In 1895 a major rebellion against the Spanish broke out in Cuba. Lurid accounts of Spanish treatment of the rebels circulated in the US press, provoking American outrage. Cuban agents in the USA were allowed to agitate for US intervention in Cuba. The pressure for war grew, particularly among expansionists such as the future president Theodore ROOSEVELT, who saw it as a chance to establish the USA as a world power.

In January 1898 loyalist Cubans rioted in Havana against the USA. President William MCKINLEY sent the battleship *Maine* to

A contemporary cartoon caricatures the Spanish–American War, with Uncle Sam rescuing the 'Lady of the Sea', representing Cuba. For Spain, defeat meant the loss of its New World empire.

protect American lives and property, but in February it was mysteriously blown up in Havana harbour. US public opinion blamed Spain. Congress authorised the use of force to expel the Spanish from Cuba, and on April 25 formally declared war. By June 1, US forces had destroyed the Spanish navy in both the Philippines and Cuba. In July, a US expeditionary force including Theodore Roosevelt and his ROUGH RIDERS swept through Cuba. Santiago surrendered on July 17, and on July 28 a third US force took Spanish-held Puerto Rico. On August 12 a cease-fire was declared. By the Peace of Paris in December, Cuba became a US protectorate. Spain ceded Puerto Rico and the Pacific island of Guam to the USA, which also bought the Philippines for $20 million. In 1899 the USA was forced to suppress a rising of Filipino nationalists.

Spanish Armada Large naval and military force sent by PHILIP II of Spain to invade England. The Armada – from the medieval Latin *armata*, meaning fleet or army – set sail from Lisbon in May 1588. Commanded by the Duke of MEDINA SIDONIA, its 130 ships, carrying 19000 infantry, were manned by 8000 sailors. After being delayed by a storm off Corunna, the Armada was sighted by the smaller English fleet led by Lord Howard of Effingham and Francis DRAKE on July 19. The lighter, more manoeuvrable English ships were armed with accurate cannon and harassed the Spanish fleet in a running battle up the Channel until it anchored off Calais.

Unable to link up with an additional force from the Low Countries, the Spanish fleet was further damaged by English fireships during the night of July 28-29. The surviving ships suffered another pounding from the English cannons before a strong wind drove the vessels

into the North Sea. Many of them were wrecked as they made their way to Spain round northern Scotland and western Ireland. Barely half the Armada returned to port.

Spanish Civil War Conflict that engulfed Spain from 1936 to 1939. Following the establishment of the Spanish Republic in 1931, Spain was split between the republic's supporters – moderates, socialists, communists, Catalan and Basque separatists, and anarchists – and its nationalist opponents, including monarchists, CARLISTS, conservative Catholics and the fascist Falange Party. In February 1936 the general-election victory of

> 66 **Whoever wins now, these have lost. / These have seen faces of bad dreams / Look at them down a levelled gun.** 99
>
> *Margot Heinemann,*
> *'On a Lost Battle in the Spanish War'*

a left-wing Popular Front government led to strikes, riots and military plots. In July, generals José Sanjurjo and Francisco FRANCO led an unsuccessful coup against the republic, and civil war exploded. Both sides attracted international support: 50000 Italian soldiers and 10000 Germans fought with Franco, while the Soviet Union sent advisers and supplies to the Republicans. Left-wing and communist volunteers from many countries fought for the Republican cause as part of the INTERNATIONAL BRIGADES.

Despite an international outcry following the indiscriminate bombing in April 1937 of the Basque town of Guernica by German planes, the nonfascist European governments remained aloof from the war. Franco's forces

Superpowers race to reach the Moon

Less than 25 years after V-2 rockets had struck terror into Londoners, Americans built on German technology to put a man on the Moon. Though a 'giant leap for mankind', it proved a false dawn for space exploration.

During the 1950s the motive and means to propel people into space coincided. The motive was the Cold War rivalry between the USA and the Soviet Union; the means, rockets developed by their mutual enemy, Nazi Germany, during the Second World War. The Soviet Union won the race, putting Yuri Gagarin into space on April 12, 1961. But the USA gained revenge by being the first to land men on the Moon.

The roots of space travel lay in pre-Revolutionary Russia. Konstantin Tsiolkowsky, a teacher born in 1857, was the first to realise that the only form of propulsion possible in airless space was the rocket, and that to escape the Earth's gravity several stages would be needed, each falling away to reduce deadweight as its fuel was exhausted. Tsiolkowsky proposed a rocket driven by mixing and igniting two liquid fuels. This was first achieved by the American Robert Goddard in the 1920s; but it was the German V-2, fuelled by oxygen and alcohol and launched against London and Antwerp in the last months of the Second World War, that proved that orbital flight was possible. The V-2, designed by Wernher von Braun, reached a height of 50 miles (80 km), the very edge of space.

After the war, the USA and the Soviet Union drew on German expertise to design their own derivates of the V-2. By 1953 the Soviet rocket engineer Sergei Korolyev had designed the SS-6, as powerful as 20 V-2s and the first intercontinental ballistic missile (ICBM). It flew in August 1957, four months before Atlas, the first American ICBM.

Seeing the chance for a propaganda coup, the Soviet leader Nikita Khrushchev ordered Korolyev to launch an unmanned satellite, Sputnik. Its success, on October 4, 1957, galvanised the USA into a race to put the first man into space. Thanks to Korolyev's powerful launchers, the Soviets triumphed. Yuri Gagarin made a single orbit in Vostok 1 and landed a world hero. In fact, he had been given virtually nothing to do: engineers had controlled the entire flight from the ground.

CLOSING THE MISSILE GAP

John F. Kennedy – who had won the US presidency partly by claiming that a 'missile gap' existed between the Soviet Union and the USA – responded in May 1961 by setting the target of landing an American on the Moon 'before the decade is out'. To do so, one of the most complex programmes ever attempted in peacetime was initiated. At first nobody even knew how it could be done. But eight years later the Apollo 11 mission went flawlessly and on July 20, 1969, Neil Armstrong became the first man to set foot on the Moon.

Nothing since has matched the drama of the lunar missions. The Soviet Union concentrated on permanently manned space stations such as *Salyut* and *Mir*, while the USA developed the space shuttle, a reusable craft intended to make space travel cheaper. But the huge success of unmanned missions – both space probes for the exploration of deeper space and Earth satellites for communications, navigation and observation – has made it clear that for most purposes manned missions are an unnecessary luxury. The end of the Cold War removed much of the political motivation. Manned space flight, though a technical triumph, remains a costly enterprise with no immediate prospect of economic returns.

The reusable American space shuttle (left) made its maiden flight in 1982. A Soviet stamp shows a 'walk in space', first performed by a cosmonaut in March 1965.

Neil Armstrong (left), the commander of Apollo 11, sits with fellow crew members Michael Collins and Edwin 'Buzz' Aldrin.

During the Spanish Civil War, Republicans unsuccessfully besieged the city of Toledo for two months. Nationalists fought back behind barricades.

soon took control of the pro-Republican Basque region as well as the strategic town of Teruel. They then conquered territory between Barcelona and Valencia in 1938, driving a wedge between Republican forces weakened by internal rivalries and the withdrawal of Soviet support. After a desperate Republican counterattack failed, Barcelona fell to Franco in January 1939, followed by Madrid in April. Franco became head of the Spanish state and the Falange was made the sole legal party. The war cost 700 000 lives in battle, 30 000 executed or assassinated, and 15 000 killed in air raids.

Spanish empire Overseas territories controlled by Spain from the late 15th century. At the peak of Spanish power these included Central America, much of South America, the Canary Islands, most of the West Indies and the Philippines. The foundations of the empire were laid between 1492 and 1504 during Christopher COLUMBUS's four voyages seeking a western route to the East. Initially small groups of CONQUIS-TADORES colonised Mexico and Peru as almost personal fiefs. But the New World soon attracted more direct Spanish rule. The colonies were a rich source of gold and silver, and made Spain the wealthiest country in Europe. From 1524 until the final stages of the colonial period the empire was run by the Council of the Indies. All the colonies were eventually divided

The Spanish empire grew rapidly during the 16th century in Mexico, South America and the Philippines. It continued its expansion and consolidation until the late 18th century.

into viceroyalties: New Spain in 1535, Peru in 1569, New Granada in 1717 and Rio de la Plata in 1776. In the Treaty of Paris after the American War of Independence (1776-83), Spain achieved its last imperial success when it regained Florida which it had lost to Britain 20 years earlier.

During Spain's years of empire, despite government regulations after 1542, the authorities failed to prevent exploitation of indigenous peoples. As Spain's power waned under pressure from England, the Netherlands and France, its empire was eroded.

Spanish missions Attempts by Spain to reconcile a desire to convert the indigenous inhabitants of its empire to Christianity with the need of the CONQUISTADORES and settlers for cheap labour. In 1540 St Francis Xavier, co-founder of the JESUITS, responded to an appeal by John III of Portugal for missionaries to his colonies in the East. They set the pattern for Jesuit activity in Spain's colonies. The missionaries claimed that the indigenous peoples were enslaved by a system that obliged them to work in the mines and on the plantations for a specific period each year. In 1542 CHARLES V promulgated laws to protect the rights of Amerindians, but when the settlers revolted, the laws were modified and the system was reinstated. In order to escape it, large numbers of Amerindians converted to Christianity.

This new drain on a source of labour already halved by European diseases led to the introduction of African slaves not protected by Spanish laws.

Spanish Succession, War of the (1701-14) Western European conflict to determine the succession to the Spanish throne after the death of Charles II without heirs. The French king LOUIS XIV, who had married one of Charles's sisters, supported the claim of his grandson Philip of Anjou, but was opposed by the English king WILLIAM III and Leopold of Austria, who had married another of Charles's sisters and supported the claim of his own son, the Archduke Charles. William and Louis tried to pre-empt a crisis with two partition treaties. In the first, in 1698, they agreed to divide Spain and its possessions between France, Austria and the Elector of Bavaria, Leopold's grandson. After the Elector died, a treaty in 1700 made the Archduke Charles the principal heir. But the Spanish king had left his empire to Philip of Anjou, who, supported by Louis, succeeded as Philip V.

Faced with growing French power, in 1701 England, Austria and the Netherlands formed a grand alliance against France. On the outbreak of formal hostilities in 1702 they were joined by most of the German princes, and in 1703 by Portugal and Savoy. Forces under John Churchill, Duke of MARLBOROUGH and EUGÈNE OF SAVOY won a series of victories, including BLENHEIM, RAMILLIES and OUDENAARDE. In 1711 Leopold died and was succeeded by his son Charles. England, faced with war weariness at home and the new possibility of an allied victory uniting Austria and Spain, pressed for peace in 1712. The Treaty of UTRECHT confirmed Philip V's succession and ended French expansionism under Louis.

Spanish Empire c1790

main trade routes

Spartan soldiers developed their military prowess in athletic events, one of which involved running in full armour, as depicted on a Greek amphora of the 6th century BC.

Sparta Common name for the ancient Greek state of Laconia, whose capital was the town of Sparta. By about 700 BC Sparta had emerged as the dominant state in the Peloponnese, rivalled only by Argos. Within a century of taking control of Laconia, the Spartans defeated and annexed their western neighbour, Messenia. Agricultural work and other menial tasks were done by a large slave class, the Helots, leaving the Spartans free to perfect their military skills.

From the age of seven, boys underwent a rigorous communal physical and military training that produced Greece's finest soldiers. The austerity, militarism and discipline of Spartan society, much admired by later Greeks such as Plato, were traditionally ascribed to the great legislator Lycurgus, who lived some time between 900 and 700. The fully developed Spartan system probably took shape between 700 and 600. By then the state was headed by two 'kings', the hereditary commanders of the army. An assembly of all adult male Spartans had ultimate sovereignty, but usually took its lead from a senate comprising the kings and 28 'elders'.

From the 6th century Sparta became the hub of the Peloponnesian League, an alliance of states dominated by Sparta that excluded its traditional rival, Argos. The league led Greece's successful resistance in the Persian Wars (see PERSIA) and then turned on Athens in the PELOPONNESIAN WAR. From 404 Sparta dominated Greece and the Aegean, but hostility to new ideas, the threat of Helot revolts and a steep decline in the numbers of the ruling group of citizens all undermined Sparta's bid for lasting domination of the Greek world. Crushing defeats by Thebes at Leuctra in 371 and at Mantinea in 362 finally broke Sparta's power.

Six speeches that changed the world

Whether in the cause of justice, or to galvanise troops to victory, certain speeches have had a remarkable impact both at the time and on succeeding generations.

'BLESSED ARE THE POOR IN SPIRIT' Jesus Christ's Sermon on the Mount, *c*.33. Jesus spent the last three years of his earthly life preaching in Galilee, but his address from a mountain, the traditional place of divine revelation, was for his disciples only. In it he distilled his ethical as well as spiritual message for mankind: a repudiation of riches for their own sake; a blessing upon the meek, the merciful and the peacemakers; and an insistence on looking at one's own faults before those of others. Christ's sermon includes the Lord's Prayer and, almost 2000 years later, remains a central pillar of Western morality.

Jesus Christ instructs his disciples in the Sermon on the Mount, c.33, by Fra Angelico.

'I SHALL YET PROVE VICTOR' William of Normandy, 1066. At the Battle of Hastings in 1066, 8500 English troops led by King Harold faced 8000 Norman invaders. Although the numbers were almost even, the English held the superior position at the top of a hill. By mid morning the battle seemed about to end as ferocious English housecarls wielding axes charged down, causing panic in the Norman ranks. At this crucial moment the Norman leader, William, calmly

King Harold is struck in the eye by an arrow at the Battle of Hastings, 1066.

pushed up his helmet and, his face visible, exhorted his troops: 'Look at me well. I am still alive and by the Grace of God I shall yet prove victor.' So it proved as the Normans found the courage to fight back and, over a long day, vanquished their opponents. Harold was fatally wounded, possibly by an arrow in his eye, and William took the English throne, becoming the 'Conqueror'. Norman rule replaced Anglo-Saxon rule, setting England on the road towards a more feudal, centralised and European future.

'HERE I STAND' Martin Luther at the Diet of Worms, 1521. As an obscure professor of theology at the University of Wittenberg, Germany, Martin Luther had in 1517 nailed 95 theses – condemning the abuses of the Catholic Church, especially its sale of

Martin Luther defends his views on the Church before the Diet of Worms, 1521, by Anton Van Werner.

indulgences – on the local church door and initiated what would become the Protestant Reformation. Now, summoned by the Holy Roman Emperor, Charles V, to a formal imperial assembly, the heretic gave no ground. Steadfastly, he refused to retract his teachings and his condemnation of the pope. Eyeball to eyeball with the pious emperor, Luther continued his fierce attack on the corruption of the Church. He concluded his defence by saying: 'Here I stand! I can do no other. God help me!' By the time Luther had finished, a schism in Western Christianity was certain.

'GOVERNMENT OF THE PEOPLE, BY THE PEOPLE, FOR THE PEOPLE'
Abraham Lincoln's Gettysburg address, 1863. Dedicating a cemetery for the fallen at the Battle of Gettysburg during the American Civil War – the battle that virtually ensured the defeat of the proslavery Confederate forces of the South – President Lincoln invoked the principles of liberty and democracy to justify the sacrifices that had been made. His language had a religious solemnity and was deliberately unflowery; and his speech, only three minutes long, made such an impact that it would become one of the most-quoted in history, and would be learnt by generations of American schoolchildren.

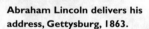

Abraham Lincoln delivers his address, Gettysburg, 1863.

'I HAVE NOTHING TO OFFER BUT BLOOD, TOIL, TEARS AND SWEAT'
Winston Churchill, 1940. Three days after becoming prime minister, as the Second World War moved out of its 'phoney' phase and Britain prepared to meet the German challenge, Churchill made a short speech to the House of Commons that set the defiant note for the next critical two years. Partly personal, Churchill also ruled out the possibility of a compromise peace with Hitler. 'What is our policy? It is to wage war, by sea, land and air.... What is our aim? I can answer in one word: victory – victory at all costs....' The speech instantly cemented Churchill's position as British leader, and during the dark hours of the fall of France and the Blitz that followed later in

Winston Churchill roused the nation with his broadcasts during the Second World War.

1940 his commitment to an ultimate victory never faltered.

'I HAVE A DREAM'
Martin Luther King, 1963. The centenary of Abraham Lincoln's proclamation freeing American slaves culminated in a mass gathering in Washington that called for greater justice for America's Blacks. It was addressed by Martin Luther King, the foremost civil rights leader. To the many thousands who had marched to the Lincoln Memorial, he set forth his message of nonviolence, his dream of 'a beautiful symphony of brotherhood' between Black and White, his call to 'let freedom ring'. Probably the most celebrated speech of the 20th century, it not only hastened civil rights legislation in the United States but acted as a beacon of hope elsewhere in the world, anticipating the eventual abolition of apartheid in South Africa.

Martin Luther King's speech in 1963 inspired civil rights reforms in the US and elsewhere.

Spartacus (d.71 BC) Thracian gladiator who in 73 BC led a slave revolt that defeated several Roman armies before it was suppressed. A shepherd, then a Roman military auxiliary, Spartacus deserted and on recapture trained as a GLADIATOR in Capua, near Naples. In 73 he escaped to the dormant crater of Mount Vesuvius, where he was joined by other fugitives. His followers, who swelled to 90000, devastated southern Italy before they were defeated by CRASSUS and POMPEY in 71. Spartacus was killed in battle and 6000 slaves were captured and crucified. After his death some 3000 Roman prisoners were found unharmed in the rebels' camp. Spartacus later became a hero to revolutionaries. The early German Marxists called themselves the SPARTACUS PARTY.

Spartacus Party Group of German radical socialists. Led by Karl Liebknecht and Rosa LUXEMBURG, it was formed in 1915 with the aim of overthrowing the imperial government and replacing it with a communist regime. The party took its name from the pseudonym

> **66 Freedom is always and exclusively freedom for the one who thinks differently. 99**
>
> *Rosa Luxemburg, leader of the Spartacus Party, 1918*

used by Liebknecht in his publications denouncing international warfare as a capitalist conspiracy and calling on the modern 'wage slave' to revolt like the Roman gladiator SPARTACUS. Following the overthrow of the German emperor Wilhelm II in November 1918, the Spartacists opposed the government of Friedrich EBERT. In December 1918 they became the German Communist Party and in January they attempted to seize power in Berlin. Gustav Noske, as leader of the armed forces, ordered the suppression of all radical uprisings in Germany. Within days the rebellion in Berlin was brutally crushed and the two leaders were arrested and murdered without trial. In 1920 a Spartacist rising in the Ruhr was equally unsuccessful.

spectacles In the 1st century AD the Roman emperor Nero held a faceted jewel to his eye to make out the details of gladiatorial games. In 1268 the English scientist and scholar Roger Bacon suggested using pieces of curved glass to correct faulty vision, but did not develop the idea. At about this time many people in both Italy and China were using magnifying lenses to improve their sight. The first Italian spectacles were probably those

A detail from a German altarpiece of 1404 shows an early pair of spectacles, which were little used until printing spread from the 1450s.

made by the Florentine monk Alessandro di Spina in 1280. He produced spectacles which corrected long sight only. Glasses to correct short sight first appeared in the mid 15th century, again in Italy. In 1785 the US statesman and scientist Benjamin FRANKLIN invented bifocal spectacles.

Speer, Albert (1905-81) German Nazi leader. After becoming the official architect for the Nazi Party, in 1934 Speer designed the grandiose stadium at Nuremberg. An efficient organiser, in 1942 he became minister of armaments and was mainly responsible for the planning of Germany's war economy, marshalling conscripted and slave labour to work in factories and to build strategic roads and defence lines. After the war Speer was imprisoned from 1946 to 1966 for war crimes.

Albert Speer explains his model for Berlin's technical high school, opened in 1939.

Speke, John Hanning (1827-64) British explorer. Speke saw service in the Punjab with the Indian army before he joined Richard BURTON's expedition to Somaliland in 1854. In 1857 the two men were sent back to Africa by the Royal Geographical Society to search for the great equatorial lakes and discovered Lake Tanganyika. Speke quarrelled with Burton and was travelling on his own when, in 1858, he found Africa's largest lake and named it after Queen Victoria. In 1860 he returned to confirm the discovery, identifying the lake as the source of the White Nile. Speke was about to attend a meeting of the Royal Society to defend his discoveries against Burton's doubts when he accidentally shot himself.

Spence, Thomas (1750-1814) English radical social reformer who advocated the nationalisation of all land. Spence's 1775 pamphlet *The Real Rights of Man* argued that all land should be taken over by local corporations who should lease it out fairly and distribute the money earned among the community. A London-based printer of radical tracts, Spence was imprisoned twice, on the second occasion for publishing Thomas PAINE's *Rights of Man*.

Spencer, Herbert (1820-1903) British philosopher and sociologist. Spencer received little formal education and was a railway engineer before turning to writing and the study of philosophy. He published his first book, *Social Statics*, in 1851. His interest in current theories of evolution led to *Principles of Psychology* (1855), in which he explored the idea of SOCIAL DARWINISM. He welcomed Charles DARWIN's *Origin of Species* (1859) and coined the phrase 'survival of the fittest'. Spencer sought to trace the principles of evolution in all branches of knowledge in a projected ten-volume work, *A System of Synthetic Philosophy*, of which the third volume, *The Principles of Sociology* (1896), was the most influential. He attacked all forms of state interference, which he believed would lead to the loss of individual freedom. His optimistic belief in human progress through evolution won him a large following.

Speransky, Mikhail, Count (1772-1839) Russian statesman and chief adviser to ALEXANDER I. After the defeat of Russia by Napoleon and the subsequent Treaty of TILSIT, Speransky drew up a new constitution at the tsar's request. It proposed popular participation in legislation, but was only partially implemented.

He also increased taxation of the nobility, sought to educate the bureaucracy and established promotion on merit. This aroused the enmity of both the aristocracy and the bureaucrats, and in 1812 Speransky was exiled after being charged with treason and secret dealings with the French. Reinstated in 1816, he rejoined the council of state in 1821 and spent his final years codifying Russian law.

Spice Islands see MOLUCCAS

Spinoza, Baruch (1632-77) Dutch-born Jewish philosopher and theologian. After he was expelled from the Amsterdam synagogue in 1656 for his unorthodox views, Spinoza made a living by grinding and polishing lenses. He rejected the concept of personal immortality, and argued that God and the Universe were one and that God was in everything. His critical questioning of the Bible was regarded as blasphemous and most of his writings, of which the most important were the *Ethics*, were published posthumously. Politically Spinoza argued for a SOCIAL CONTRACT in which people surrendered some of their natural rights to the state in exchange for guaranteed security.

Spithead mutiny Mutiny by British sailors that led to improved conditions in the Royal Navy. In April 1797 the fleet anchored at Spithead, outside Portsmouth harbour, and refused to put to sea, demanding higher pay, better food, improved medical services and shore leave. The Admiralty, acknowledging that the sailors' grievances were justified and fearing that the mutiny would spread – by May the NORE MUTINY had already begun in the Thames fleet – agreed to their demands and issued a royal pardon to the mutineers.

spoils system Term used in US politics to describe the practice whereby a victorious political party rewards its supporters with public appointments. The spoils system also refers to the awarding of contracts, especially defence contracts, to a region in return for its representative's support for presidential policies in Congress, and to the granting of public contracts to party contributors on favourable terms. The term was coined in 1832 by Senator William Marcy of New York in connection with President Andrew Jackson, who during his two terms of office replaced 20 per cent of federal office-holders with his political supporters. After the American Civil War, attempts were made to reduce patronage in the civil service – for example with the Pendleton Act of 1883, which created the Civil Service Commission.

Sputnik Series of Soviet satellites, the first of which orbited the Earth in 1957, inaugurating the conquest of space. At the end of the

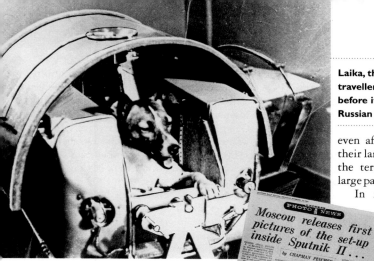

Laika, the world's first space traveller, settles in her cabin before it is installed in the Russian satellite *Sputnik 2*.

19th century, Konstantin Tsiolkovsky, a Russian schoolteacher, proposed that liquid-fuelled rockets could be used to power spacecraft. Significant progress in space exploration (see feature, page 610) was not made until the national rivalry of the Cold War (see feature, page 150) intensified. Soviet and US scientists directed their attention to rocket-powered missiles that could carry nuclear warheads, and modified versions of these were used to launch the first artificial satellite, *Sputnik 1*, on October 4, 1957. This spurred the so-called 'space race', and on January 31, 1958, the USA launched its first satellite, *Explorer 1*.

The first *Sputnik* – Russian for 'fellow traveller' – orbited Earth for 92 days before burning out in the atmosphere. It was only 23 in (58 cm) in diameter and weighed a mere 184 lb (84 kg), but immediately captured the public's imagination. Less than a month after the first launch, *Sputnik 2* carried a dog, Laika, but there was no way to return her to Earth and she died in space. The main purpose of the first ten *Sputniks* was to prepare for a manned space flight. Subsequent *Sputniks* (*11-24*) were also designated by the name *Cosmos*.

squatter Illegal occupant of land or housing belonging to others. In the USA in the 18th century, the term was applied to any settler without legal title to the land he farmed.

In Australia, squatters were often former convicts who occupied land beyond the official limits of settlement established in 1829. They mainly raised sheep, often starting their flocks with stolen stock, and made an important contribution to Australia's growing wool industry. In 1836 squatters were granted grazing rights to their land in return for an annual licence fee. They also demanded the right to buy any land they improved, and were granted this in 1847. Securing the land most suitable for agricultural and pastoral purposes, they became a powerful group, socially, economically and politically. During the second half of the 19th century squatters and small farmers struggled bitterly over land. Squatters continued to be known by this name even after they had acquired their land freehold. Eventually the term was applied to all large pastoralists in Australia.

In many underdeveloped parts of the world, particularly Africa and South America, squatting is a social and political problem. There the poor often occupy public land, particularly unwanted land such as marshy areas or rubbish dumps, and then build shanty towns, for example the *favellas* outside Rio de Janeiro in Brazil and the shacks of the Alexandra township on the outskirts of Johannesburg in South Africa. Some of these have developed on such a scale that the authorities have granted the squatters legal title to the patches they have claimed.

squire Originally an apprentice knight in medieval Europe. Squires, or esquires, were usually young men and served as the personal attendants of fully fledged knights. The title was then one of function rather than birth and derived from the Latin *scutarius*, 'shield', which referred to the squire's duty of carrying his master's shield to and from jousts. In later medieval England the term came to be applied to all gentlemen who were entitled to bear arms. By the 17th century 'squire' had become synonymous with a district's leading landowner, sometimes even the lord of the manor. The considerable local influence, both political and ecclesiastical, of the 'squirearchy' has since diminished.

Sri Lanka Island republic in the Indian Ocean, lying off south-eastern India and formerly known as Ceylon. The origins of the dominant Sinhalese racial group go back to Indo-Aryan invaders from north India, who in the successive kingdoms of Anuradhapura and Polonnaruwa dominated the north central plain from the 5th century BC until about AD 1200. Buddhism gained ground among the Sinhalese from the 3rd century AD, but it's spread spawned rival religious factions. Parakramabahu I of Polonnaruwa reformed the quarrelling sects during his reign from 1153 to 1186. By then, repeated invasions from south India had begun to create a strong Tamil Hindu enclave in the north of the island. Continuing Tamil expansion from the 14th to the early 16th centuries gradually forced the Sinhalese into the south-west of the island, fragmenting Polonnaruwa into several smaller kingdoms, of which Kandy became the most powerful.

Profiting from the divisions, in 1505 Portuguese merchants established a foothold on the island's west coast, from which they expanded their economic and political influence for more than a century. Their grip weakened after 1638 as the Dutch East India Company gained control of the spice trade, but in 1796 the company was ousted by British forces. By 1815 the British had conquered the island, which they called Ceylon. From 1860 coffee gave way to tea as the island's main commodity. A plantation-based economy – to which rubber was later added – also developed.

The island's growing wealth gave rise to an expanding middle class which began to press for self-government. A new constitution was established in 1931, giving the island a degree of self-rule, but it was not fully implemented because of tensions between Sinhalese and Tamils. Ceylon remained a crown colony until 1948, when it was granted independence as a dominion within the Commonwealth. The United National Party established a government led by Don SENANAYAKE, who was succeeded in 1952 by his son Dudley. In elections four years later Solomon BANDARANAIKE led the Socialist Sri Lanka Freedom Party to power. He was the country's dominant political force until his assassination by a Buddhist monk in 1959. His widow Sirimavo Bandaranaike succeeded him. The world's first woman prime minister, she led the government until 1965 and again from 1970 to 1977. In 1972 a new constitution established the island as the Republic of Sri Lanka.

> **DID YOU KNOW?**
>
> *Muslim traders called Sri Lanka the island of Serendib, from which came the word serendipity – 'the faculty of making happy discoveries by accident'.*

In the late 1970s tensions between the Sinhalese majority and the Tamils erupted in violence, which escalated into a full-scale civil war in 1983. Tamil guerrilla groups established control of the Jaffna peninsula and much of northern Sri Lanka. A cease-fire arranged by the Indian government in 1987 did little to defuse the situation, and in the following year government forces faced a second front – an uprising led by the Marxist and mainly Sinhalese People's Liberation Front (JVP), in which 30 000 civilians died. All-party peace talks initiated by President Ranasinghe Premadasa in 1989 failed, and though the JVP rebellion was suppressed in 1990, army and police brutality during the campaign drew international condemnation of the Sri Lankan government and led to the suspension of some Western aid. Premadasa was assassinated in a Tamil suicide attack during the 1993 Labour Day parade in the island's capital, Colombo.

Chandrika Kumaranatunge, the daughter of Solomon and Sirimavo Bandaranaike, was elected prime minister in 1994. Later that year she became president and was succeeded as prime minister by her mother. In 1994 a cease-fire between the government and Tamil guerrillas was abandoned and fighting resumed the following year. Government forces launched a successful assault on the Tamil guerrilla stronghold in the Jaffna peninsula. By the end of 1995 the civil war had cost up to 100 000 lives, and left a once successful economy in decline.

Srivijaya River port near Palembang in southern Sumatra. Once the greatest port in South-east Asia, it was described by a Chinese Buddhist pilgrim of the 7th century as 'a great fortified city'. Srivijaya's position 50 miles (80 km) upstream from the mouth of the Musi River enabled it to trade easily with the mountain peoples of the interior while also protecting it from seaborne attack. There

After the British introduced tea to Sri Lanka, brands such as Lipton's helped to establish it as a major producer, and tea as Britain's national drink.

were probably two separate states known as Srivijaya, the first flourishing from the 7th to the 9th centuries, the second from the 10th to the 13th centuries. The latter developed into a commercial empire extending from Java to Kedah on the Malay Peninsula and had trading contacts with China. But Tamil raids from India weakened its power and in the 14th century it fell to the Javanese Majapahit empire. Its port declined and became a base for Chinese pirates.

SS Elite German Nazi corps, also known as the BLACK SHIRTS. The SS – Schutzstaffel, 'protection squad' – was founded in 1925 by Adolf HITLER as his personal bodyguard. Members of the SS were schooled in absolute loyalty and obedience, and in total ruthlessness towards opponents. From 1929 until the dissolution of the Third Reich, the SS was headed by Heinrich HIMMLER, who divided it into the Allgemeine SS (General SS) and the Waffen SS (Armed SS), which was an elite combat group independent of the armed forces. The SS was subordinate to the SA, or BROWN SHIRTS, until the NIGHT OF THE LONG KNIVES in 1934, when it helped Hitler to murder Ernst Röhm and other SA leaders. By 1936 Himmler, with the help of Reinhard HEYDRICH, had gained control of the national police force. Subdivisions of the SS included the GESTAPO, or political police, and the Sicherheitsdienst (the SD), which dealt with foreign and domestic intelligence. The SS also administered the Nazi CONCENTRATION CAMPS. The activities of the SS were condemned at the Nuremberg Trials in 1946.

Staël, Madame de (1766-1817) French-Swiss literary critic and political propagandist who was an influential figure in early French ROMANTICISM. She was born Anne Louise Germaine Necker, the daughter of a prominent banker in Paris, and in 1786 she married the Swedish diplomat Baron Staël-Holstein. Her ardent advocacy of personal political freedoms earned the displeasure of Napoleon, and in 1803 she was banished from Paris. Fame in Europe came with the publication of her semi-autobiographical novel *Corinne* in 1807. Three years later de Staël established herself as a significant literary figure with *De l'Allemagne*, 'Germany', a literary critical work imbued with her enthusiasm for German Romanticism. In 1811 Napoleon ordered the destruction of the first edition for being 'un-French' and de Staël fled to Russia and then to England before returning to Switzerland.

Stalin, Joseph (1879-1953) Soviet revolutionary who ruled the USSR with an iron fist from the mid 1920s until his death. Born Joseph Dzhugashvili, his father was a Georgian shoemaker and his mother a washerwoman. He joined the Social Democrats in 1900, and became a member of Vladamir LENIN's left wing BOLSHEVIK faction. He was twice exiled to Siberia, in 1902 and 1913. Around 1913 he adopted the name Stalin, 'man of steel'. At the start of the Russian Revolution in 1917, Stalin escaped from Siberia to St Petersburg, where he became the editor of the Bolshevik newspaper *Pravda*. In 1922 he became general secretary of the Communist Party, and used his position to

build a power base by appointing party functionaries and provincial leaders. On Lenin's death in 1924, Stalin, committed to 'creating socialism in one country', began a three-year leadership struggle with Leon TROTSKY, who argued that a European revolution must precede the establishment of a communist state in the USSR. As the victor, Stalin became sole dictator of the Soviet Union. He forced Trotsky into exile and then had him murdered in Mexico. In the 1930s he used show trials and executions to purge both those party colleagues who disagreed with him and those who fawned on him. In this reign of terror as many as 10 million people were executed and twice that number sent to remote prison camps.

The rapid drive towards industrialisation instituted by Stalin in a series of Five-Year Plans built the Soviet Union into the world's second industrial and military power after the USA, but his enforced COLLECTIVISATION of agriculture into large, state-owned farms led to famine; more than 7 million peasants starved to death. In 1939 Stalin signed the NAZI-SOVIET PACT with Adolf Hitler, but in 1941 Germany invaded the Soviet Union. Stalin, surprised and appalled, entered the Second World War on Britain's side. At meetings with the US president Franklin Roosevelt and the British prime minister Winston Churchill in Tehran in 1943, and at YALTA and POTSDAM in 1945, Stalin's skilful diplomacy laid the foundations for a new Soviet sphere of influence in Eastern Europe. After Stalin's death his successor, Nikita KHRUSHCHEV, attacked many of Stalin's policies and methods, and at the 20th All-Party Congress in 1956 he accused the former dictator of terror and tyranny.

Stalingrad, Battle of (1942-3) Long and bitter battle in the Second World War that reversed the German advance into the Soviet Union. During 1942 the German 6th Army under General Friedrich von Paulus occupied

During the Battle of Stalingrad, a long line of German soldiers are marched to prison camps from their last emplacements near the city. Stone blocks mark fortifications blasted by the Russians.

Kursk, Kharkov, the Crimea and the Maikop oil fields before reaching the river Volga and its key city of Stalingrad (now Volgograd). Here, an ill-equipped and relatively small Russian force brought the invaders to a halt, preventing them from crossing the Volga in a campaign of grim and prolonged house-to-house fighting. By November, with the city and its defenders reduced to starvation, Stalin had assembled sufficient reserves to launch an offensive of six Soviet armies led by marshals ZHUKOV, KONIEV, Petrov and Malinovsky. By January 1943 the Germans were surrounded and Von Paulus surrendered, losing 330 000 troops killed or captured. The Russians then advanced to recapture Kursk, marking the end of German success on the Eastern Front.

Stamford Bridge, Battle of (September 25, 1066) Clash in which HAROLD II of England defeated a large army of Norwegian invaders at Stamford Bridge on the River Derwent near York. The invaders, who five days earlier at Fulford had defeated the Saxon forces of Earl Edwin of Mercia and Earl Morcar of Northumbria, were almost annihilated. Their leaders – Harold's exiled brother Tostig and the Norwegian king Harald Hardrada – were both killed. After the battle, Harold's army marched south to face the Norman invasion and fight the Battle of HASTINGS.

Stamp Act (1765) British taxation measure, introduced by George GRENVILLE, to cover the costs Britain had incurred defending its North American colonies during the SEVEN YEARS' WAR of 1756-63. The Stamp Act required all legal documents, newspapers, pamphlets and advertisements issued in the colonies to bear a revenue stamp, as in Britain. Many Americans saw the Act as an attempt to impose 'taxation without representation', and it met with widespread resistance. In October 1765, nine colonial delegations met at the Stamp Act Congress in New York to petition for the repeal of the Act. American boycotts of British goods and civil disobedience persuaded the newly appointed prime minister, the Marquis of ROCKINGHAM, to accede in 1766, but the Declaratory Act revoking the tax reasserted the British Parliament's power over the colonies. The Act helped to initiate the campaign for American independence.

Stanhope, James, 1st Earl of (1673-1721) English soldier and statesman. He entered Parliament as a Whig in 1701, but spent most of the next ten years as a soldier in the War of the SPANISH SUCCESSION, commanding the British forces in Spain from 1708 until his capture in 1710. On his return, Stanhope re-entered politics to play a major part in securing the succession of George I, whose chief minister he became. He organised the government's swift response to the Stuart rebellion of 1715, but Stanhope's genius lay in foreign diplomacy. He ended Britain's isolation, securing a treaty of alliance with France, its recent enemy; put forward a feasible solution to Austro-Spanish rivalry over Italy; and worked for a settlement in the NORTHERN WAR. Accused, probably unjustly, of involvement in ministerial corruption arising from the SOUTH SEA BUBBLE, Stanhope died of a stroke while defending himself against his accusers in the House of Lords.

Stanislaus II (1732-98) Last king of Poland from 1764 to 1795. Originally Count Stanislaus-Augustus Poniatowski, he was the lover of CATHERINE II of Russia and her candidate for the throne of Poland, which had fallen under Russian control in the 17th century. In the first partition of 1772, Russia, Austria and Prussia took slices of Polish territory. From 1773 to 1792 there was a period of national revival encouraged by Stanislaus, but in 1793 he was forced to accept a second partition that left him a virtual vassal of Russia with a truncated kingdom. In 1795 a nationalist rising was crushed and a third partition completed Poland's destruction. In November Stanislaus was forced to abdicate.

Stanley, Sir Henry Morton (1841-1904) British-American journalist and explorer. Born John Rowlands, an illegitimate orphan, he was raised in a Welsh workhouse before he ran away to the USA in 1859. There he was adopted by a New Orleans merchant, Henry Stanley, whose name he took. He served as a Confederate soldier during the American Civil War and as a seaman on US ships before becoming a journalist on the *New York Herald*, which sent him to Africa to find the missing missionary David LIVINGSTONE. The two met at Ujiji on November 10, 1871, and explored Lake Tanganyika. Fêted on his return to England, Stanley resumed his British citizenship. He made three more trips to Africa, exploring Uganda and the Congo, where, under the auspices of the King of the Belgians, he helped to found the International Association of the Congo, later the Congo Free State. Stanley was knighted in 1899.

Stanton, Elizabeth Cady (1815-1902) American social reformer, known as the mother of the women's rights movement. Cady studied law in the office of her father, US congressman Daniel Cady, and learned about the laws discriminating against women. In 1840 she married the lawyer and abolitionist

> **❝Woman's degradation is in man's idea of his sexual rights. Our religion, laws, customs, are all founded on the belief that woman was made for man. ❞**
>
> *Elizabeth Cady Stanton*
> *June 14, 1860*

Henry Brewster Stanton. As the result of her speeches and petitions, a bill was passed in 1848 granting property rights to married women in New York State. Also in 1848 Cady Stanton introduced her Declaration of Sentiments calling for extensive reforms, and insisted that a suffrage clause be included in the bill of rights drawn up at the convention. From 1852 she and Susan B. ANTHONY led the US women's movement; they also compiled three volumes of the *History of Woman Suffrage* (1881-6).

staple see WOOL STAPLE

Star Chamber, Court of English civil and criminal court noted for its summary and arbitrary procedures. It was named after the decorative ceiling of the room in the palace of Westminster where it sat. The court was thought to have originated in a statute of 1487, but in fact had its roots in the reign of Edward IV, when the King's Council began to act in a judicial capacity. From the 1540s it consisted of the Privy Council and the chief justices. Mainly concerned with offences affecting Crown interests, it dealt with cases concerning public order, the judicial system and the enforcement of proclamations. It fell into disrepute when Charles I used it against his opponents in the 1630s, and was abolished by the LONG PARLIAMENT in 1641.

States-General Gathering of representatives of a realm's three estates – the clergy, the nobility and the commons (corporations of the towns) – called to advise French or Dutch sovereigns on matters of policy. In France it began as an occasional advisory body, usually summoned to register support for controversial royal policy. It was developed by Philip IV, who held a meeting in 1302 to enlist support in a quarrel with the pope, but the first proper States-General was in 1484 in the reign of Louis XI. Thereafter it was used by the House of GUISE during the French Wars of Religion as a device against the Huguenots. With the rise of absolutism in the 17th century, the States-General was neglected, but in 1789 it was urgently summoned by Louis XVI and his minister Jacques NECKER in an effort to free much-needed revenue and to break a deadlock caused by the nobles' resistance to administrative reforms. Its summoning and procedure were based on the precedent of 1614, when it was called against Marie de Medici, and its members were encouraged to draw up *cahiers*, representative lists of grievances. Voting was carried out by head rather than by order, giving the radicals a majority. No longer controlled by the nobles, the States-General formed itself into a National Assembly, helping to precipitate the FRENCH REVOLUTION (see feature, pages 244-5).

In the Netherlands the term was applied to the representative body of the United Provinces in their struggle for independence from Spain in the 16th century. As an elected assembly of the various provinces of the Dutch Republic it wielded considerable power, although in times of emergency it delegated its authority to the House of ORANGE. It was replaced in 1795 by a national assembly, but was restored as a legislative body for the kingdom of the Netherlands in 1814.

states' rights US political doctrine that upholds the rights of individual states against the power of the federal government. The framers of the US Constitution created a federal system in which the delineation of power between the federal government and the states was open to interpretation, and from the outset divergent views on this issue have influenced US politics. In the early years Alexander Hamilton and his Federalist Party saw the Constitution as a sanction for a strong central government, while Thomas JEFFERSON and his followers believed that the states should retain all powers not specifically granted to the federal government. The controversy led to the Nullification Crisis of 1828-33, when South Carolina invoked its right to refuse to levy a specific federal tax within its borders. It also formed the constitutional basis of the Southern case in the dispute before the Civil War. In recent years the doctrine of states' rights has been central to controversies over civil rights and welfare expenditure.

The composition of the French and Dutch States-Generals mirrored the hierarchical nature of the medieval world – first the Church, then the king and nobles, and finally the common people.

statistics Branch of mathematics involved in compiling and interpreting numerical data. Simple records, ranging from details of crops and taxes to censuses of slaves, were kept by early civilisations, and often help archaeologists to piece together the lifestyles of those times. But it was the German mathematician Johann Gauss and his French contemporary Siméon-Denis Poisson, who in the early 19th century first used statistics as a mathematical tool to assess past trends and predict probabilities – the main function of the modern statistician. In Britain the Central Statistical Office was established in 1940 to provide comprehensive national data on economic and financial topics, and most governments now operate similar organisations. Their findings – and those of the many international bodies that gather statistics – are regarded as vital tools in economic planning and in forecasting the needs and trends of the population.

Statue of Liberty One of the world's best-known landmarks, the colossal statue of a woman bearing a tablet in one hand and a torch in the other stands on Bedloe's Island

> 66 **Give me your tired, your poor, / Your huddled masses yearning to breathe free, / The wretched refuse of your teeming shore...** 99
>
> *Emma Lazarus*
> 'The New Colossus'

(renamed Liberty Island) in New York harbour. On the tablet is inscribed the date July 4, 1776 – American Independence Day. In the late 19th and early 20th centuries the statue symbolised the opportunities of the USA to the hundreds of thousands of European immigrants entering New York City by ship.

A towering 152 ft (46 m) high, the statue was executed by the French sculptor Frédéric-Auguste Bartholdi, as a gift from France to commemorate the first century of American independence and the role that the French had played in attaining it. The statue was created in France, where it was first exhibited before being taken apart for its voyage to New York. Bartholdi supervised its assembly on American soil in 1886. It has been an official national monument since 1924.

The statue is made of copper sheets hammered into shape and assembled over a steel framework. It is set on top of a 150 ft (45 m) tall concrete pedestal faced with granite. A lift runs to the top of the pedestal, and stairs within the statue lead to the crown. 'The New Colossus', a poem written by Emma Lazarus in 1883 as a tribute to the statue, appears on a plaque over the entrance into the pedestal.

Stauffenberg, Claus Graf von see JULY PLOT

steam power Steam was first harnessed to drive machinery when Thomas Newcomen made a steam-powered pump to drain water from Cornish tin mines in 1712. But it was not until 1781, when James WATT adapted his improved steam engine to drive factory machinery, that steam power's potential to change manufacturing methods was grasped. With its promise of a reliable source of industrial power, Watt's development lay at the heart of the INDUSTRIAL REVOLUTION (see feature, pages 314-15). Until then most factories relied on water power and were sited near streams, usually in the countryside where transport was difficult, and their production depended on the weather. However, the first steam engines were expensive and only large businesses could afford to install them.

As steam power became more widely used, the textile industry and other manufacturing processes were transformed. Larger factories had to be built near coal mines, and towns grew to house factory workers. Steam power applied to railways and steamships led to faster and cheaper travel and transportation of goods. The steam hammer introduced in 1808 made working large pieces of metal possible, while the steam-driven threshing machine accelerated the harvesting cycle and reduced farmers' reliance on water and windmills. The direct use of steam engines began to decline in the early 20th century with the development of petrol and diesel engines and the use of steam-driven turbines to generate electricity – an energy source that could be applied more cleanly and easily in industry.

Stein, Karl, Baron von (1757-1831) Prussian statesman and reformer. Stein undertook various diplomatic and administrative duties before becoming minister of commerce in 1804. He was dismissed by FREDERICK WILLIAM III for attempting to increase the responsibilities of the ministers of state. After Prussia's defeat by Napoleon at JENA and Auerstadt, Stein was recalled to begin his enlightened reforms, which transformed Prussian society. He persuaded Frederick William to abolish the serf system, to end restrictions preventing the sale of land owned by nobles to commoners, and to open the Prussian officers corps to non-nobles.

Stein failed to induce the king to promise a 'free constitution' as an encouragement to a Prussian insurrection against the French, but so alarmed Napoleon that the French emperor persuaded the king to dismiss Stein in 1808. In self-imposed exile in St Petersburg, Stein established a coalition between Russia, Prussia and Sweden against Napoleon and served as an adviser to Tsar Alexander I. His pleas for a united Germany were ignored at the Congress of VIENNA in 1815.

Stephan Dushan (1308-55) King of Serbia from 1331 until his death. The greatest ruler of medieval Serbia, Stephan deposed his father in 1331 and soon gained control of Bulgaria through a marriage alliance. After seizing Macedonia, Albania and much of Greece from the Byzantine Empire, he assumed the title of emperor of the Serbs and Greeks in 1345. He introduced a new code of laws throughout his territories, but his achievements were short-lived, as his son could not hold the new empire together against Ottoman invasion and regional challenges.

Stephen (c.1096-1154) King of England from 1135 to 1154. Stephen joined the other barons of England and Normandy in acceding to the request of his uncle, Henry I, that Henry's daughter MATILDA should be recognised as his heir, but on Henry's death Stephen seized the crown. Stephen was supported by his brother, the Bishop of Winchester, and most of the barons of both England and Normandy. Stephen's reign was marked by rebellion and intermittent civil war. In 1138 Matilda's half-brother Robert rebelled, and the Scots invaded northern England. The following year Matilda landed in England. Stephen was captured at Lincoln in 1141, but his wife (also called Matilda) continued the fight. Matilda's forces were defeated at Winchester later that year and Stephen was released, but meanwhile Matilda's husband, Geoffrey of Anjou, took control of Normandy. In the end Stephen became discouraged by the deaths of his wife and their eldest son; a year before his own death he recognised Matilda's son as his successor, Henry II.

The torch and flame of the Statue of Liberty, made from hand-beaten copper, is assembled by workers at the Gauthier et Cie workshop in Paris in 1876, before being shipped to New York City.

Stephen I, St (975-1038) First king of Hungary from 997 until his death. Stephen was crowned by the authority of Pope Sylvester II in 1000, and the crown Sylvester sent him remains a symbol of Hungarian nationalism. Stephen was chiefly concerned with thoroughly establishing Christianity within his realm, and setting up a durable code of laws. His reign was troubled by persistent warfare, particularly with the Bulgars but later with the German emperor, Conrad II, whom he defeated. Stephen was canonised in 1083. He is the patron saint of Hungary.

Stephenson, George (1781-1848) and **Robert** (1803-1859) British railway engineers. The son of a colliery fireman, George was familiar with the steam engines used in mines for pumping and hauling. He began to manufacture stationary steam engines, then turned to steam traction. In 1814 George built his first colliery steam locomotive, and seven years later he took charge of the building of the world's first public railway, between Stockton and Darlington. This opened in 1825, followed by the Manchester-Liverpool line in 1830. At his Newcastle upon Tyne works, in 1829 he and his son Robert built the *Rocket*, which pulled passenger coaches at a record speed of 29 mph (46 km/h), and many of the next generation of railway locomotives.

Robert Stephenson worked as a mechanical engineer in his father's locomotive works at Newcastle until 1824, when he spent three years superintending mines in Colombia. He then returned to collaborate with George in many railway ventures. He also won fame as a bridge-builder, constructing among others the Menai Bridge in Wales and the Victoria Bridge over the St Lawrence River in Canada.

Sterkfontein Archaeological site west of Johannesburg, South Africa, where fossilised remains of an ape-like hominid found in 1936 were hailed as the evolutionary 'missing link' between man and primates. Before the discovery of the Sterkfontein fossils by the Scots-born palaeontologist Robert Broom, theories that early man had evolved in Africa were based on a fossil fragment found at Taung, in South Africa, 11 years earlier. The fragment was identified by Professor Raymond Dart, an anatomist, as part of the skull of a million-year-old ancestor of man, which he named *Australopithecus africanus*. It was 900 000 years older than NEANDERTHAL man, and Dart argued that the Taung find pointed to man's African origins. His theory was controversial, but many archaeologists accepted that the Sterkfontein find supported it and supplied a 'missing link' 2.5 to 3 million years old. Other finds at Sterkfontein, including the skull of a young female adult, dubbed 'Mrs Ples', confirmed the site's importance in the study of human evolution.

Stern Gang British name for a Zionist guerrilla group operating in Palestine during the British mandate and dedicated to the creation of an independent Jewish state. Founded in 1940 by Abraham Stern, Lohamei Herut Israel Lehi (Fighters for the Freedom of Israel) conducted a campaign of terror until 1948, when it was outlawed by the new Israeli state. Seldom numbering more than a few hundred, members of the Stern Gang operated in small groups and concentrated on the assassination of government officials. Among their victims were Lord Moyne, the British minister for the Middle East who was assassinated in 1944, and Count Folke BERNADOTTE, the United Nations mediator in Palestine killed in 1948. Stern was killed by British forces in 1942.

Stevens, Thaddeus (1792-1868) US statesman. As a member of the Anti-Masonic Party, whose attacks on Freemasonry won popular support in the 1820s and 1830s, Stevens served in the Pennsylvania state legislature before being elected to Congress as a Whig in 1849. He left Congress in 1853 as a result of his strong abolitionist views and helped to organise the Republican Party before returning in 1859 as one of its most formidable representatives. He was one of the chief architects of the Fourteenth Amendment giving former slaves full rights as US citizens, adopted in 1868. That same year, Stevens chaired the committee that brought charges of impeachment against President Andrew JOHNSON.

Stevenson, Adlai (1900-65) US statesman who, despite his brilliance as an orator, twice failed to win the presidency for the Democratic Party. In 1948, after serving in various government posts, Stevenson was elected governor of Illinois with the largest majority in the state's history. A liberal reformer and internationalist, he was chosen as the Democratic candidate in the presidential elections of 1952 and 1956, but both times was beaten by Dwight D. EISENHOWER. In 1961 President John F. Kennedy appointed Stevenson ambassador to the United Nations, a post he held until his death.

Stilwell, Joseph (1883-1946) US general. A West Point graduate and veteran of the First World War, Stilwell gained a reputation as an expert on China during his service as US military attaché in Peking from 1932 to 1939. When the USA entered the Second World War after Pearl Harbor, Stilwell commanded US and Chinese forces in south China and Burma (Myanmar), cooperating with the British in the BURMA CAMPAIGNS. Stilwell technically held authority by virtue of his appointment as chief of staff in this region by CHIANG KAI-SHEK, but differences of opinion with the Chinese leader led to his recall, and he later commanded the US 10th Army at OKINAWA. Stilwell was popularly known as 'Vinegar Joe' on account of his tactlessness.

Stimson, Henry (1867-1950) US statesman. A Republican, Stimson was President William Taft's secretary of war from 1911 to 1913. He later went to France as a soldier in the First World War. Stimson was governor-general of the Philippines from 1927 to 1929, and then President Herbert Hoover's secretary of state until 1933, taking a tough line against the Japanese invasion of Manchuria in 1931, when the Stimson Doctrine refused to grant diplomatic recognition to actions that threatened China's territorial integrity. He served as secretary of war under Democratic Presidents Franklin D. Roosevelt and Harry S

The Stern Gang blew up the Cairo-Haifa troop express in southern Palestine in April 1947, killing 11 and injuring 40, at the height of the Zionist campaign against the British presence in Palestine.

The New York Stock Market Crash of autumn 1929 reduced many investors to selling treasured possessions at rock-bottom prices to raise cash. This car sold on Wall Street for a mere $100.

Truman from 1940 to 1945, and he made the recommendation to drop the atomic bomb on Hiroshima in 1945.

stirrups The stirrup was first used by the nomadic Scythians, who lived in the Ukraine in the 4th century BC. It took the form of a leather loop to help riders vault into their saddles. By AD 300 the Chinese had adapted it to take the width of a foot, but only in the 6th century was the stirrup first used as a riding aid. Avars from central Asia brought the stirrup to Western Europe during clashes with the Franks in the 8th century, thereby revolutionising the nature of warfare. Along with the saddle, it gave horsemen far greater stability, allowing them to use long, heavy lances, and to hold their spears under their arm.

Stock Market Crash Sudden, massive fall in the value of shares on Wall Street, home of the New York Stock Exchange, which began in September 1929, precipitating the worldwide Great DEPRESSION of the 1930s. During the first half of 1929 an unprecedented boom took place on the New York Stock Exchange. In late September 1929, however, prices started to fall and panic selling began. In less than a month there was a 40 per cent drop in stock value, and this fall continued over the next three years. The causes of the 'Wall Street Crash' or 'Great Panic', as it was known, were numerous. Although the postwar US economy seemed to be booming, it was on a narrow base and there were fundamental flaws. The older basic industries, such as mining and textiles, were weak; agriculture was depressed; unemployment at 4 million was unacceptably high; and international loans were often poorly secured. Speculators across the USA tried to emulate the flamboyant lifestyles of

the new postwar rich by means of credit and stock-market speculation. Once the business cycle faltered, panic set in and accelerated a downward economic spiral. Property values collapsed, factories closed, and as banks began to call in loans, more and more investors and businesses went under. The effects of the crash reached across the Atlantic to erode the economies of the other industrialised nations, and the Great Depression had begun.

Fears that history would repeat itself in a similar worldwide crisis surfaced during the boom years of the late 1980s. On October 19,

> 66 **Fear struck . . . Thousands threw their holdings into the whirling Stock Exchange pit for what they could bring.** 99
> New York Times
> October 25, 1929

1987 – known as 'Black Monday' – unexpectedly poor US trade figures plunged the world's stock markets into a spate of panic selling. A week of trading saw the values of US shares drop by a third, with a domino effect on stock markets across the globe. On the London Stock Exchange alone the total loss on paper was estimated at £94 billion. However, the expected world slump did not develop, although several years' slowdown in economic growth occurred.

stocks see PILLORY

Stoic Member of the philosophical school founded by Zeno of Citium around 300 BC. The name derives from the *Stoa poikile*, 'Painted Colonnade', where Zeno taught in Athens. At the core of his philosophy were the

beliefs that virtue is based on knowledge, that reason is the governing principle of nature, and that individuals should live in harmony with nature. The vicissitudes of life were viewed with equanimity: pleasure, pain and even death were irrelevant to true happiness. In time, the idea that only the consummately wise man – the philosopher – could attain virtue was challenged, and Stoicism became more relevant to the reality of politics and statesmen. The Stoic belief in the brotherhood of man helped the philosophy to make a real impact in later republican Rome, upon such men as CATO the Younger, whose suicide brought him a martyr's fame, BRUTUS and CICERO. Later it underlay much aristocratic opposition to the emperors, but even so its disciples included SENECA, tutor and adviser to Nero, and the emperor MARCUS AURELIUS.

Stolypin, Piotr Arkadevich (1862-1911) Russian premier from 1906 until his death, the last effective statesman of the Russian empire. While governor of Saratov province, Stolypin ruthlessly suppressed local peasant uprisings and was hated for his severe punishment of activists in the RUSSIAN REVOLUTION of 1905. Appointed prime minister by Nicholas II, Stolypin dismissed the Duma, or parliament, in spite of the tsar's promises to end autocratic rule and to invest it with legislative powers, and also introduced harsh measures against Russia's Jews. His constructive work lay in his agricultural reforms. Believing that a contented peasantry would check revolution, he allowed KULAKS, or peasants, to have their land in one holding instead of strips that were periodically reallocated within the community. Those taking advantage of this prospered, but they were not powerful enough to stem the revolutionary tide. Stolypin was assassinated in a Kiev theatre.

Stone Age Period of prehistory characterised by the use by early humans of stone to manufacture tools and weapons. In Europe the Stone Age is usually divided into three stages: the Old, or PALAEOLITHIC; the Middle, or MESOLITHIC; and the Late, or NEOLITHIC. In other parts of the world, where human development occurred over a different time span and there was often overlapping of techniques, the Stone Age has other subdivisions.

Stone Age peoples used suitably shaped stones as hammers or hand-axes, gradually learning to flake these into more effective tools or to work sharp slivers of stone into heads for arrows and spears. In Europe about 500 000 years ago, flaked stone tools were being made from flints; in Africa, quartz, chert and basalt were worked more than 2 million years ago. In much of the Middle East OBSIDIAN, a natural form of glass, was favoured, often being carried over long distances. The people of the Old Stone Age led a

Stonehenge has aroused the awe of visitors for centuries – the Normans, for instance, called the ruins one of the wonders of Britain.

hunter-gatherer existence, but by the middle of the Neolithic period, in Europe at least, man had begun to cultivate a few primitive crops. As man progressed from stone to metal artefacts there was often a cultural overlap of the two stages of development.

Stonehenge Prehistoric monument on Salisbury Plain in southern England. Built in several stages, Stonehenge is a unique monument to the Stone Age and Bronze Age peoples who colonised the region during their transition from nomadic hunter-gatherers to settled cultivators. Experts disagree as to the function of Stonehenge – whether it was a temple, a secular ceremonial centre or an astronomical observatory.

The earliest part of the structure, built between 3100 and 2100 BC, consists of a circular bank and external ditch surrounding a ring of narrow pits, known as the Aubrey holes after the 17th-century English antiquary John Aubrey, who was the first scholar to provide a detailed description of Stonehenge. The earthworks housed a wooden structure and a single MEGALITH, known as the 'Slaughter Stone'. Later, a double stone circle was erected inside the bank, and this was replaced around 1500 BC by the stone structure seen today. A horseshoe of seven trilithons – each comprising a lintel supported on two uprights – stood inside 30 giant stone uprights whose lintels formed a continuous circle. Some of these blocks of sarsen, a local sandstone, weigh as much as 54 tonnes. Within the trilithons stood a horseshoe of smaller blocks of bluestone, weighing up to 4 tonnes each. These bluestones came from the Preseli Mountains in Wales, 140 miles (220 km) away.

The construction of Stonehenge called for advanced technical and engineering skills. Symbols which apparently represent Minoan daggers and double-headed axes have been discovered on some of the sarsens. This has led to theories that Minoan seafarers, who are known to have ventured as far as Britain, may have advised the local builders. Although one of the Stonehenge megaliths, the outlying Heel Stone, aligns on the midsummer sunrise, Druid association with Stonehenge began only in 1905 and has no historical roots. Another example of a megalithic monument is at CARNAC in Brittany.

Stopes, Marie (1880-1958) Controversial British pioneer of birth control. Stopes obtained degrees in botany, geology and geography from University College London and was the first woman scientist to be appointed a lecturer at Manchester University. Concerned by what she perceived as the ill-informed and 'unscientific' way in which men and women approached married life, in 1918 Stopes published *Married Love*, which stressed that both partners in a marriage could and should enjoy sex, and followed it the same year with *Wise Parenthood*, in which she advocated birth control and described methods of contraception. Both books created an immediate furore. In 1921 Stopes founded the first birth-control clinic in Britain, in London. Though her books and activities provoked vigorous opposition, her views on contraception attracted steadily increasing support among the medical profession and the general public.

Stormont Belfast suburb and seat of the Northern Ireland Parliament until its suspension in 1972. Created in 1920 as a subordinate body to Westminster, the Stormont Parliament was dominated by the Unionist Party. With the breakdown of law and order in Northern Ireland in the late 1960s, direct rule from Westminster was imposed, to be administered by civil servants of the Northern Ireland Office based in Stormont Castle.

Stowe, Harriet Beecher (1811-96) American author of *Uncle Tom's Cabin*, a novel that helped to turn the tide of public sentiment in favour of the antislavery movement. 'I did not write it. God wrote it. I merely did his dictation,' Stowe said of her novel, published in 1852. Its depiction of slave life had a huge impact in the USA and England, and has been cited as one cause of the American Civil War. It sold 300 000 copies within a year, and was translated into 23 languages. The daughter of Lyman Beecher, a prominent Congregationalist minister, Stowe remained a devout Christian and student of theology throughout her life. In 1836 she married Calvin Stowe, a clergyman and seminary professor. The year

after the book's publication she compiled *The Key to Uncle Tom's Cabin*, which contained many documents and testimonies against slavery. Stowe toured Europe three times in connection with *Uncle Tom's Cabin*, winning tremendous popularity. She campaigned for social change throughout the rest of her life.

Strachey, (Giles) Lytton (1880-1932) English critic and biographer whose *Eminent Victorians* (1918) proved to be an influential landmark in biographical writing. Strachey was a member of the Bloomsbury group of writers and artists, among whom he gained acclaim as a critic. His witty, mordant and iconoclastic biographical essays on such eminent Victorians as Florence Nightingale, Thomas Arnold and General Gordon won him a wider audience; his work was described as 'a breath of fresh air blowing dust off the turgid tomes of earlier biographers'. In 1921 Strachey published the equally irreverent *Life of Queen Victoria*. In *Elizabeth and Essex* (1928), Strachey explored the queen's relationship with her favourite courtier in a work that shows a clear debt to the teachings of Freud.

Strafford, Thomas Wentworth, 1st Earl of (1593-1641) English politician who was beheaded for treason on the eve of the English Civil War. Despite entering Parliament in 1614 as an opponent of royal policies, Wentworth believed that England needed strong government and in 1632 he was appointed lord deputy of Ireland by CHARLES I. His extreme and autocratic methods of effecting the royal will made Wentworth extremely unpopular in both England and Ireland, and most of his achievements proved temporary. Charles recalled him to England in 1639 on the outbreak of the war against the Scottish COVENANTERS. In 1640 he was created Earl of Strafford, but was impeached for treason by opposition members of the LONG PARLIAMENT who thought that he intended to impose a Catholic dictatorship on England. Deserted by the king, Strafford was found guilty and sentenced to death by Parliament.

Straits Settlements Former British crown colony bordering the Malacca Strait in South-east Asia. The English EAST INDIA COMPANY combined the colonies of Penang, Malacca and Singapore to create the Straits Settlements in 1826. After 1858 they passed to British Indian control and became a crown colony in 1867. Labuan was added in 1912. The Straits Settlements were dismantled in 1946, with Singapore becoming a separate colony, and Penang, Malacca and Labuan joining the Malayan Union.

> **DID YOU KNOW?**
>
> *Marie Stopes advocated selective breeding for the 'improvement' of the human race, and held ideas about racial superiority which many condemned as racist.*

Strategic Arms Limitation Talks

Agreements between the USA and the Soviet Union aimed at limiting the production and deployment of nuclear weapons. A first round of meetings between 1969 and 1972 produced the SALT I Agreement. This prevented the construction of comprehensive antiballistic missile (ABM) systems and also placed limits on the construction of intercontinental ballistic missiles (ICBMs) for an initial period of five years. In 1979 the SALT II Treaty sought to set limits on the numbers and testing of new types of intercontinental missiles, but it was not ratified by the US Senate. In 1982 new STRATEGIC ARMS REDUCTION TALKS began.

Strategic Arms Reduction Talks

Discussions aimed at nuclear arms control between the USA and the Soviet Union, and after 1991 between the USA and the four republics of the former Soviet Union that inherited nuclear weapons: Belarus, Ukraine, Russia and Kazakhstan. START negotiations began in 1982, but were suspended in 1983 in protest at US deployment of intermediate nuclear missiles in Western Europe. They resumed in 1985 and the subsequent START I Treaty of 1991 committed the USA and the Soviet Union to a 30 per cent reduction in their nuclear weapons stockpiles. The four republics of the former Soviet Union acceded to START I in November 1993. In January 1993 Russia and the USA signed START II, which provided for the dismantling of two-thirds of their strategic nuclear warheads.

Strathclyde

Romano-British kingdom embracing parts of north-west England and south-west Scotland. Established in the 2nd century, it was the last kingdom of the Britons to disappear, having survived invasions by Eadbert of Northumbria in 750 and 756, raids by Danes in 870, and a brief loss of independence to Edward the Elder of England in 920. Strathclyde was eventually subdued by King Edmund of Wessex, who gave it to Malcolm II in 945, but it retained a measure of autonomy until 1018 when Duncan I united Strathclyde with three other territories. These became the kingdom of Scotland in 1034. The name has been revived for a region of Scotland.

Streicher, Julius (1885-1946)

German Nazi leader and propagandist. Originally a school-teacher, Streicher expounded his anti-Semitic views in his periodical, *Der Stürmer*. As Gauleiter, or district leader of the Nazi Party, in Franconia in southern Germany from 1933 to 1940, Streicher continued to edit the magazine, becoming increasingly virulent in his attacks on Jews. He was sentenced to death as a war criminal at the NUREMBERG TRIALS.

Stresa Conference (April 1935)

Meeting between Britain, France and Italy on Lake Maggiore in Italy. It proposed measures to counter Adolf Hitler's open rearmament of Germany in defiance of the 1919 VERSAILLES PEACE SETTLEMENT. Together these countries formed the 'Stresa Front' against German aggression, but their decisions were never implemented. In June Britain negotiated unilaterally a naval agreement with Germany, and in November 1936 the Italian leader Benito Mussolini proclaimed his alliance with Hitler in the Rome-Berlin AXIS.

Stresemann, Gustav (1878-1929)

German statesman of the WEIMAR REPUBLIC. During the First World War Stresemann's views were strongly nationalistic, but they mellowed during his spell as chancellor in 1923 and as foreign minister from 1923 to 1929. He ended passive resistance to the Franco-Belgian occupation of the Ruhr, and accepted the Allies' plans for postwar reparations. Stresemann negotiated terms for Germany in the LOCARNO treaties of 1925, as well as Germany's admission to the League of Nations in 1926. Stresemann advocated that Poland should return Danzig, the Polish Corridor and Upper Silesia to Germany.

Stroessner, Alfredo (1912-94)

Military leader and president of Paraguay from 1954 to 1989. The son of a German immigrant and Paraguayan mother, Stroessner's military career began with the CHACO WAR of 1932-5. He rose to become commander in chief of Paraguay's armed forces in 1951, and in 1954 led the coup that overthrew Federico Chavez to give Stroessner the presidency. His army-backed regime was essentially totalitarian, using harsh, repressive methods to quash all but token political dissent. It also gave sanctuary to former Nazis.

Stroessner's administration favoured Paraguay's large landowners and international commercial interests at the cost of the peasantry. Although he used some foreign aid to improve schooling and build hospitals, the bulk of development funds went to Paraguay's armed services, highways and hydro-electric power stations. In 1989 Stroessner was overthrown in a military coup.

Stuart

Family name of the Scottish monarchs from 1371 to 1714 and of the English monarchs from 1603 to 1714. The name – spelled 'Stewart' until about 1567 – came from the occupation of the first Stewart, Walter Fitzalan (d.1177), who was steward to the king of Scotland. But it was not until 1371 that ROBERT II became the first Stewart king of Scotland. The marriage of Henry VII's daughter Margaret Tudor to James IV of Scotland in 1502 linked the two royal houses, and a century later, on the death of the childless Elizabeth I in 1603, James VI of Scotland succeeded to the English throne as James I.

With the execution of Charles I in 1649, the Stuarts lost the throne until the Restoration of his son Charles II in 1660. When, in 1688, the GLORIOUS REVOLUTION sent James II, brother of Charles II, into exile, the crown passed first to James's daughter Mary, who ruled jointly with her husband William, and then to his second daughter Anne.

When Anne died without leaving a living son or daughter in 1714, the Protestant Hanoverians, headed by George I, replaced the Stuarts, although JACOBITE supporters of the son and grandson of James II from his second marriage – James Edward Stuart and Charles Stuart – rebelled unsuccessfully in 1715 and 1745. Thereafter the Stuart cause faded, and George III felt able to grant a pension to the last direct Stuart claimant, Henry, the younger brother of BONNIE PRINCE CHARLIE, who died in 1807.

Alfredo Stroessner (left), president of Paraguay, rides in a motor cavalcade with General Francisco Franco, dictator of Spain. Both men were leaders of repressive, right-wing regimes.

student revolts Protests by student groups which began in the West in the early 19th century have since become a worldwide phenomenon. Students are responsive to new ideas and radical teachers, and the expression of their views has played a significant part in almost every major revolution of the past 200 years. In the early 19th century German university students fanned the flames of nationalism and attacked the anti-democratic and pan-European policies of Prince METTERNICH. In tsarist Russia students agitating for liberal reforms were put in prison, exiled or executed. German and Japanese universities spawned both right-wing and left-wing revolutionary movements between the two world wars. In the developing countries, schools and colleges became the seedbeds in which anti-imperialist, nationalist and Marxist movements flourished.

By the 1960s left-wing movements drew strong support from the student bodies of many universities and colleges in Europe, the USA and Japan. In the USA, protests began on the Berkeley campus of the University of California in 1964 and culminated six years later in strikes at some 200 campuses across the country against US policy in Vietnam. In Paris in 1968 student riots were supported by workers who staged a general strike against the government of Charles DE GAULLE.

Demonstrations by South Korean students in 1987 won constitutional amendments, free elections and the release of political prisoners. Students were also an important element in the demonstrations in Prague in 1989 which led to the fall of the communist regime in Czechoslovakia. But prodemocracy rallies and hunger strikes in Beijing were brutally suppressed in the Tiananmen Square massacre in June 1989, in which some 2000 students were killed and hundreds more arrested.

sturdy beggars Able-bodied people classed as workshy by the English Poor Law of 1531, and regarded by Tudor governments as a threat to public order. Tudor arguments against the sturdy beggars were based on the presumption that there was ample work for everyone. But there was not, and soldiers returning from wars to a seemingly jobless future frequently banded together to prey on travellers. Law-abiding folk who took to the roads in search of jobs or charity were seen by the authorities as being no different from the lawless bands, and were frequently severely punished. By the end of the century new poor laws forced parishes to provide work for the genuinely unemployed and made provision for 'incorrigible rogues' to be whipped, returned to their own parishes, or banished overseas in the case of persistent offenders.

In May 1968 students fought riot police on the streets of Paris. Their poster (left) mocks President de Gaulle with the words 'Havoc, that's him!'

Stuyvesant, Peter (c.1592–1672) Dutch colonial administrator in the New World. Soon after becoming governor of Curaçao in the Dutch West Indies, Stuyvesant lost a leg at the battle of St Martin in 1644. In 1646 he became Director of the Dutch colony of New Netherland, centred on Nieuw Amsterdam (now New York City). A man of authoritarian temperament and a strict sabbatarian and opponent of religious freedom, Stuyvesant soon upset the Dutch colonists in north America, indirectly making it easier for English settlers to infiltrate the territory. He expanded Dutch influence and in 1655 gained control of the rival colony of New Sweden. But by now so many English were settling in his own colony that he was unable to offer resistance when the Duke of York's invasion gained it for England in 1664.

submarine For centuries the idea of submerged navigation attracted inventors, and as early as 1620 the Dutch scientist Cornelius van Drebbel constructed an underwater boat for James I of England. Propelled by oars, it was kept watertight with animal hides. Other scientists and inventors modified and improved on van Drebbel's design, but the first successful submarines were the *Turtle*, built in the USA by David Bushnell around 1760, and Robert Fulton's *Nautilus*, built for Napoleon in 1800. Fulton's 'submersible', fitted initially with an air tube and later with a tank of compressed air, could remain under water for six hours. Neither of these vessels was used in naval engagements. However, several submarines were developed by the Confederates during the American Civil War; one succeeded in blowing up a Union ship, but was itself destroyed by the explosion.

French and US engineers, particularly, continued to experiment with submersible craft. But true submarines did not become possible until the 1890s, with the development of the internal combustion engine, sufficiently powerful electric motors and effective batteries. The earliest workable designs shared basic features: ballast tanks, which were flooded when diving and emptied when surfacing; electric motors for underwater propulsion, with steam or petrol engines to recharge the batteries and for surface travel; periscopes; and an internal circular hull to withstand high pressures.

These early submarines spent more than 80 per cent of the time on the surface. They were soon armed with torpedoes and played major roles in both world wars, notably the German

In 1989 a leak in the cooling system forced this Soviet nuclear-powered Echo-2 submarine to shut down and surface off the coast of Norway.

U-boats. Nuclear submarines, introduced in 1954, are today's most effective warships. They can operate at great depth and remain submerged almost indefinitely at speeds of up to 30 knots, and are armed with intercontinental ballistic missiles which can be fired from the surface or from under water.

Sudan Country in north-eastern Africa. The north of the country is largely desert or semidesert, except where the Nile permits intensive irrigation. The people of the north are Muslim and mostly Arab. The south is more fertile, with good pasture for cattle. The different peoples of the south – the Nuer, Dinka, Anuak and others – once each had their own religion, but are now mostly Christian.

In 1800 an Islamic revival shook the Muslim empire of the Funji in northern Sudan and led to local conflicts. The expansionist Egyptian pasha Mehemet Ali took advantage of the situation to conquer the Sudan in 1820. Egypt's rule was uneasy, and in 1874 Khedive Ismail, the viceroy of Egypt, appointed the British general Charles GORDON as governor. Gordon's unpopular attempts to stamp out the slave trade intensified local opposition to Egyptian rule, and he resigned in 1880. The next year Muhammad Ahmad declared himself Mahdi – in Islam the 'mahdi' is a messiah who comes to prepare a just world. His increasingly successful Islamic rebellion threatened to spread through North Africa. In 1882 Britain intervened, occupying Egypt and invading the Sudan. Gordon was recalled in 1884, and held Khartoum against the Mahdi's besieging army for ten months until the city fell and he was killed. Resistance continued even after Lord Kitchener led an Anglo-Egyptian force which defeated the Sudanese Muslims at Omdurman in 1898. After the FASHODA incident in the same year the Sudan was placed under joint Anglo-Egyptian rule, headed by a British governor.

The Sudan had to wait 50 years before being granted a measure of autonomy under the constitution of 1948. Then in 1951 Egypt's King FAROUK proclaimed himself King of Sudan. After his abdication in 1952 Egypt agreed to Sudan's right to independence, granting it self-government in 1953 and full independence in 1956. Even then the political and religious tension between northerners and southerners undermined stability. In 1969 General Gaafar Numeiri became prime minister and negotiated an end to the civil war by granting local autonomy to the south in 1972. In practice this autonomy was limited, and in the early 1980s the collapse of the economy and widespread starvation led to renewed fighting in the south, where the Sudan People's Liberation Army (SPLA) gained effective control. A military coup in 1989 was followed by a ban on all political parties, but the civil war continued.

'We thank our Führer' says this postcard, issued to celebrate the Nazi seizure of Sudetenland.

Sudetenland North-western frontier region of Czechoslovakia, formerly with a substantial German population. At the end of the First World War Sudetenland was declared part of Czechoslovakia, despite the fact that Germans had been settled over much of the area for several centuries. The Nazi leader Konrad Henlein fomented local resentment against the Czech government and demanded incorporation into Germany. This gave Hitler the excuse to annex Sudetenland into the Third Reich in 1938 and expel its Czech inhabitants. Under the POTSDAM agreement of 1945 the region was returned to Czechoslovakia and authorisation was given for the expulsion of most of its German-speaking inhabitants.

Suetonius, Gaius (c.AD 69-140) Roman lawyer, Emperor Hadrian's private secretary, and biographer of the first 12 Caesars, from Julius Caesar to Domitian. Partly grounded in fact and partly drawn from informed anecdote and court gossip, Suetonius' *Lives of the Caesars* preserved much valuable information, though some of his raw material is inaccurate. He was one of the first non-Christian historians to record the early following of Jesus Christ.

Suez Canal see feature, page 626

Suez War (1956) Invasion of Egypt by British, French, and Israeli forces, following Egypt's nationalisation of the Suez Canal Company. In 1956 Israel was poised to retaliate against the increasing number of raids by *fedayeen* guerrillas based in Egypt. With tacit British and French approval, Israel used the nationalisation of the canal as the pretext for a pre-emptive strike into Sinai on October 29. A Franco-British ultimatum demanded that both Israel and Egypt should withdraw from the canal; this would have placed the canal again under international control, and the ultimatum was rejected by Egypt's President Gamal NASSER. British and French troops landed at Port Said and their planes attacked Egyptian bases. But in the face of US pressure and growing international criticism, the Anglo-French forces withdrew and a United Nations peace-keeping force was sent to the region. Israeli forces were withdrawn in March 1957 after a UN Emergency Force was established in Sinai, and Egypt agreed to reopen the Straits of Tiran to Israeli shipping.

suffragette Member of a militant British feminist movement fighting for votes for women. The suffragettes were part of an international movement which started in the USA in 1848 and won voting rights for women in New Zealand in 1893, Australia in 1902 and the USA in 1920.

The movement in Britain began in the 1870s, when women organised a petition to Parliament with almost 3 million signatures demanding the vote. After 1903 Emmeline PANKHURST's Women's Social and Political Union (WSPU) spearheaded the movement, which quickly gained wide public support.

The bullet-riddled windows of the Port Said lighthouse look out over a Norwegian tanker trapped for two months during the Suez War.

Gateway to the East

*The Suez Canal opened a new route from Europe to the East,
cutting out the long journey around Africa. Its strategic importance
also made it the focus of international conflict.*

The history of canals stretches back 3000 years. The Nahawan Canal, built in the valley of the River Tigris during the Babylonian period, was more than 330 ft (100 m) wide and 185 miles (300 km) long, and its waters fed an extensive network of smaller irrigation canals. Babylonian canals were also used by boats, but many centuries passed before waterways were built intended only for transport. The great age of the ship canal came in the 19th century and reached its climax with the construction of the Suez Canal, the first to be designed specifically for steam-powered ships. The scale was immense: 100 miles (160 km) long, 72 ft (22 m) wide and, originally, 26 ft (8 m) deep.

The need for a canal was clear. Trade between Europe and the Far East involved a long journey round the tip of Africa, and the cost of fuel and lack of coaling stations meant that steamers could not compete with the swift clippers in such lucrative trades as China tea.

Ferdinand de Lesseps was a French consul in Egypt and a passionate believer in the value of a canal. When he left the diplomatic service he formed a French company whose plans were approved by an international commission. It took him several years to persuade the Viceroy of Egypt to give his permission; finally, in 1854, it was granted.

A MIGHTY UNDERTAKING

The effort involved in the canal's construction was colossal. There was at first a work force of around 20 000 fellahin (local forced labourers), but they were gradually replaced by machinery. By 1867, 60 specially designed dredgers were at work. Even so, 1500 experienced navvies had to be brought in from Piedmont in Italy to clear a vast rock shelf at Shaluf. A harbour was built at Port Said. By the time the canal opened in 1869 the labourers had shifted 2650 million cu feet (75 million m³) of earth. It was one of the greatest engineering feats of the 19th century.

The canal carried 3 million tonnes of shipping in its first ten years. Sailing ships were driven from their routes by

**The British troopship *Malabar* passes
through the canal shortly after its opening.
In the foreground are bucket-dredgers.**

the steamers. The clipper *Cutty Sark*, for example, launched in 1869 for the tea trade, was redeployed to carry wool from Australia. De Lesseps went on to promote an equally promising short cut through the isthmus of Panama, but this scheme collapsed in a financial scandal which ruined him. When the Panama Canal was finally built, it was with American finance and American engineering skills; it opened in 1914.

The Suez Canal continued to prosper, but after the Second World War it became a source of contention between Egypt and both Britain and France, which regarded it as essential for securing their Middle East oil supplies. In July 1956 the Egyptian president Colonel Gamal Abdel Nasser nationalised the canal, and by November the countries were at war. It was a short-lived campaign, from which the Anglo-French forces were persuaded to withdraw under pressure from the United Nations.

If their aim was to keep the canal open, then the war failed. Sunken ships blocked the waterway, and by the time it was permanently reopened in 1975 the world had moved on to another era. Airliners had replaced passenger ships and the new oil tankers were too large for the canal. Its great days had ended.

**The need to connect the Mediterranean with the Red Sea had long been obvious. The route
was so important that free passage through the canal was guaranteed even in wartime.**

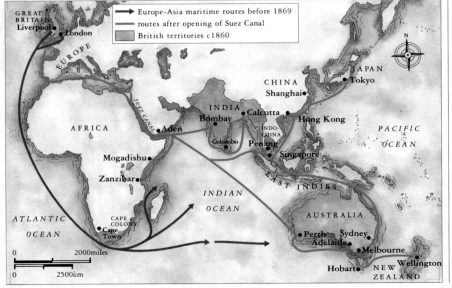

GREAT
BRITAIN
Liverpool
London

Europe-Asia maritime routes before 1869
routes after opening of Suez Canal
British territories c1860

EUROPE

SUEZ CANAL

JAPAN
Tokyo

CHINA
Shanghai

INDIA
Bombay Calcutta
Hong Kong

AFRICA Aden

INDO-
CHINA
Colombo Penang

PACIFIC
OCEAN

Mogadishu

Zanzibar

Singapore

EAST INDIES

INDIAN
OCEAN

ATLANTIC
OCEAN

CAPE
COLONY
Cape
Town

AUSTRALIA

Perth Sydney
Adelaide
Melbourne

Hobart NEW
ZEALAND
Wellington

0   2000miles

0   2500km

Suffragettes picket Parliament in London in 1928. Their propaganda (right) stressed that, electorally, women were treated like the dregs of society.

But Parliament refused all pleas, and the suffragettes became more militant. Attacks on property and disruption of parliamentary debates were added to their earlier armoury of demonstrations and refusal to pay taxes. Imprisoned suffragettes went on hunger strike, and the suffragette Emily Davison was fatally injured when she flung herself in front of the king's horse in the 1913 Derby.

When Britain declared war on Germany in 1914 the WSPU abandoned these tactics and directed its efforts to supporting the war effort, though Emmeline's daughter Sylvia Pankhurst left the WSPU and continued to campaign for the vote. In 1918 British women over 30 who met certain criteria related to education and property were given the vote. In 1928 these restrictions were removed and women voters were placed on a par with men.

Sufi Muslim mystic who seeks union with God through ascetic and other devotional practices, including the ecstatic dancing of dervishes, rather than through the formal rituals and orthodox teachings of Islam. Sufis take their name from the *suf,* a simple woollen garment worn by early ascetics, and follow the teachings of sheikhs whose personal powers are thought to set initiates on the path to communion with God. Often at odds with Muslim orthodoxy, Sufis have nevertheless helped to spread Islam through Africa and southern Asia. They have included outstanding poets and scholars in their number, as well as forming religious orders such as the Qadiriyya and Tijaniyya.

sugar Though widely known in parts of the East, where it originated, in Europe sugar remained an expensive luxury until the early 19th century, when locally cultivated beet sugar began to replace honey as a sweetener. Sugar was first introduced to western Europe in the 8th century. Later, Crusaders brought it back to Britain from the Near East. From 1319 small quantities were imported regularly from Arab traders. Portugal began to grow sugar cane in its tropical possessions in the 15th century. Cultivation soon spread to the Spanish, British and Dutch colonies in the Caribbean, and soon a massive trade grew up in African slaves to work these sugar plantations.

Suharto, Thojib (1921-) Indonesian president since 1968. Suharto played a leading role in the postwar Indonesian Revolution and in 1965 became army chief of staff. Having crushed an attempted communist coup, he accused President Ahmed SUKARNO of involvement in the coup, forcing the Sukarno government to give him wide powers. He used these powers to unite student and military opponents of Sukarno in toppling the regime and ending the three-year conflict with Malaysia. Suharto became acting president in 1967 and the following year assumed full presidential powers. His policies generated an economic recovery and brought Indonesia back into the Western capitalist fold. But his increasingly dictatorial style of government met considerable opposition from Islamic fundamentalists and trade unionists.

Sukarno, Ahmed (1901-70) Leader of the Indonesian independence movement and his country's first president, from 1945 to 1967. He formed his radical Indonesian Nationalist Party in 1927 and soon attracted wide support for his fiery brand of nationalism. The Dutch

> **DID YOU KNOW?**
>
> Suharto became a hero in 1949 when his troops captured Yogyakarta from the Dutch — even though he held it for only six hours.

authorities jailed him for two years in 1929, and then exiled him from Java. During the Second World War he cooperated with the Japanese occupation forces and consolidated his position as a nationalist leader.

After the defeat of Japan in 1945, Sukarno was proclaimed president by a preparatory council set up by the Japanese. He led the war of independence against the Dutch, who finally recognised Indonesian independence and withdrew in 1949. He acted as a spokesman for Asia's nonaligned movement and hosted its Bandung Conference in 1955. But by the mid 1960s his autocratic rule, Indonesia's growing economic problems, and its confrontation with Malaysia all combined to undermine his position. Seeking support from the communists, Sukarno encouraged a coup by left-wing officers in 1965, but lost power to the army when the coup failed. He was officially stripped of his presidency in 1967.

Suleiman I see feature, page 628

Sulla, Lucius Cornelius (c.138-78 BC) Roman soldier and statesman, whose bitter feud with Gaius Marius twice plunged the republic into civil war. This clash of two ruthless personalities began in 107 BC, when Sulla served as quaestor (magistrate and paymaster) under Marius during the Jugurthine Wars in Africa. It continued to fester, and in 88, while favourite consul of the aristocratic faction in the senate, Sulla chose to turn his army on Rome rather than surrender command in the war against the Mithridates of Asia Minor to his rival. Returning victorious from this eastern campaign, Sulla again marched on Rome where, after defeating Marius' forces in 82, he was appointed dictator and assumed the name Felix ('Lucky'). Sulla reformed the state and imposed strict controls on the tribunes and other magistrates, thus strengthening the senate's power. He retired abruptly in 79.

Sully, Maximilien de Béthune, Duc de (1560-1641) French statesman, who as HENRY IV's chief minister rebuilt France's economy after 30 years of civil war. Béthune was raised as a Huguenot (French Protestant) and narrowly escaped death during the ST BARTHOLOMEW'S DAY MASSACRE of Huguenots in 1572. Four years later he distinguished himself in Henry of Navarre's army, contributing significantly to his commander's successful bid for the throne. As the new king's trusted councillor, Béthune negotiated Henry's marriage to Marie de Medici in 1600. But it was his financial and economic skills which served Henry best. Béthune's stringent economies,

Ottomans at the gates of Vienna

Suleiman the Magnificent, the greatest ruler of the Ottoman Empire, added swathes of Europe to his vast imperial domains.

Suleiman confers with his generals during the siege of Buda in 1541. The drawing below is by the German artist Albrecht Dürer.

During his 46-year reign as sultan of the Ottoman Empire, Suleiman I, nicknamed 'the Magnificent', became the most feared general of his age, expanding the empire to its greatest territorial extent. He might have been called 'the Conqueror' if his great grandfather Mehmed had not already earned that title. But Suleiman was an untried young man of 27 when he first marched his armies north from Constantinople in the spring of 1521. Belgrade, the capital of Serbia and the strongest fortress in the Balkans, had resisted the Ottoman expansion into Europe for decades. Now Suleiman besieged the city, and within three weeks had taken it.

The following year his forces attacked the Christian stronghold of Rhodes in the Aegean. The island's garrison was reduced to eating rats before they surrendered in December 1522. In 1526, Suleiman again turned his attention to conquest by land, joining his troops at Belgrade to invade Hungary. There, at the Battle of Mohács in August 1526, he won the most devastating of all his victories. Some 15 000 Christian knights were slaughtered and the young king, Louis II, was found drowned in a ditch. Most of the Balkans were incorporated into the Ottoman Empire, and the Christian West feared that the Turkish armies would march straight on into the heart of Europe.

The high-water mark of Ottoman advance came in 1529. Suleiman camped with his armies outside the walls of Vienna. The few defenders fought desperately against the vast besieging army, but an early winter saved the city after only 19 days. Suleiman turned back from the ice and snow to winter quarters in Belgrade.

CONQUEROR, LAWGIVER, POET

For the next 30 years Suleiman was busy elsewhere in his empire. He made three campaigns against the Safavids of Persia, gaining control of eastern Asia Minor and Mesopotamia. He reformed the laws and system of government – the Ottomans knew him as *Qanuni*, 'the Lawgiver' – and with his architect Sinan he built the ornate mosque in Constantinople that bears his name. Western visitors came to marvel at the splendours of the sultan's city. But Suleiman was more than a warrior and statesman: he was a patron of the arts and literature, and celebrated his love for a Circassian woman called Roxelana, later his wife, in lyric verses published under an adopted nom de plume.

In 1566 the frail and elderly sultan launched a final attempt to crown his career with the capture of Vienna. But the campaign proved too much for him and he died only a few days' march from the city. He had told his generals to keep his death a secret until they were well on the way home. His sorrowing soldiers carried him back to his capital, where he was buried in his mosque. Warrior, statesman, poet and lover, Suleiman possessed all the accomplishments of a 'Renaissance prince', like his contemporaries Henry VIII of England, Francis I of France and the Holy Roman Emperor Charles V.

---

his agricultural reforms and his tight rein on administrative abuses put France's finances back on a healthy footing. He was created Duc de Sully in 1606, but was forced out of office soon after Henry IV's assassination in 1610.

sultanate Sovereign independent Muslim state or trading empire. The term derives from 'sultan', used in the Koran and Islamic tradition to denote authority and applied initially to the Muslim ruler Mahmud of Ghazni. Later 'sultan' became a general title for any Muslim who held secular power, and, under the Ottomans, was used as a mark of respect for princes and princesses of the imperial house. A number of independent centres of Muslim power – such as Delhi prior to India's Mughal empire, and the Sulu trading empire in the southern Philippines between the 16th and 19th centuries – were also called sultanates.

Sumatra Westernmost part of Indonesia and the world's fifth largest island. Indian traders introduced Hinduism and Buddhism to the several small indigenous kingdoms of Sumatra. From the 7th century to the 13th century Sumatra was the core of the Buddhist kingdom of Sri Vijaya, which MARCO POLO claimed to have visited. By the time Sri Vijaya's long dominance ended, Islam had gained a footing in the north of the island and soon spread across Sumatra and on through Malaya and the East Indies. The Portuguese arrived in 1509 and the Dutch in 1596. In 1613 the English set up a trading station. The Dutch later secured a base at Padang on the west coast and began to incorporate Sumatra into the Dutch East Indies.

Sumerians Inhabitants of southern Mesopotamia in the 4th and 3rd millennia BC. The Sumerians developed cuneiform, probably the world's oldest system of writing; it takes its name from the Latin *cuneus* (wedge), after the shape of the symbols made with a cut off reed. By 3000 BC the fertility of the plains and valleys between the Tigris and Euphrates rivers had given birth to city states such as Uruk, Eridu and Ur. The need for administration and an accompanying form of records led the Sumerians to develop pictographs, which gradually became stylised as cuneiform. Many simple inscriptions survive as evidence of this.

The early city states were first united as the empire of Sumer under Sargon, whose Semitic Akkadians conquered their weaker neighbours in about 2350. But his dynasty lasted little more than 150 years, and by 2150 the kings of Ur had not only re-established themselves in Sumer but had also conquered Akkad. The new empire was equally short-lived. Around 2000 Ur was sacked by the Elamites and Amorites and in the devastation which followed Sumer was destroyed as a political power, though its influence on the culture of subsequent Mesopotamian civilisations was far-reaching.

summoner Minor lay Church official who summoned people before the ecclesiastical courts of the later Middle Ages. Also known as apparitors, summoners gradually gained

A mosaic from the early dynastic period, around 2750 BC, depicts the 'peace side' of the royal standard of the Sumerian city of Ur. The other side presents images of war and bloodshed.

inquisitorial powers in cases leading to excommunication. Their extortion and other abuses of these new powers became notorious and were condemned not only by Geoffrey Chaucer in *The Canterbury Tales,* but by the Council of London in 1342 and by Parliament in 1378. More than 10 000 excommunication writs served by summoners survive from late medieval England and Scotland and cover such sins against the Church as witchcraft, nonpayment of tithes, and heresy – including incidents of LOLLARDRY – as well as the civil offences of usury and slander.

Sumner, Charles (1811-74) Abolitionist US statesman and political reformer. After lecturing at Harvard law school, Sumner was elected to the Senate by Massachusetts' Free-Soilers and Democrats in 1851 and served in the Senate until his death. A powerful orator, he soon emerged as a leading member of the antislavery campaign and thus became a target of Southern opposition. In 1856, in a swingeing attack on slavery entitled 'The Crime Against Kansas', Sumner singled out South Carolina senator Andrew Pickens Butler for bitter personal attack.

Two days later Butler's nephew, Congressman Preston S. Brooks, stormed into the Senate Chamber intent on avenging his elderly uncle's honour. He thrashed Sumner with a cane so severely that it took the abolitionist more than three years to recover and return to the Senate. Young Brooks immediately resigned from Congress, but so bitter was the North-South rift that he was immediately re-elected – with an increased majority. Sumner went on to help to organise the new Republican Party, serve as chairman of its Foreign Relations Committee, and maintain the pressure for the emancipation of the slaves. In the years after the American Civil War Sumner supported the radical reconstruction programme and was relentless in his attacks on the corruption and inefficiency of President Ulysses S. Grant's administration .

sumptuary laws Laws and regulations introduced at various times and by various regimes, intended to limit overindulgence, luxury or personal excesses. Though officially justified on religious, moral or social grounds, such laws frequently acted as a tangible way of marking and emphasising class distinctions. Sumptuary laws go back at least to early Greek and Roman societies. The Roman *lex Orchia* – 'law of the orgy' – introduced in 182 BC, was typical in limiting the number of courses that could be served at private banquets. Other early sumptuary laws dealt with dress and even the degree of ostentation permitted on the facades of homes and other dwellings.

In England both Edward III and Henry IV introduced sumptuary laws dealing with dress and diet. But where the laws of the classical age were intended to prevent the wealthy from exercising too much influence, the English laws were designed to maintain class distinctions. Both kings limited not only the sumptuousness of feasts according to a defined order of precedence among the nobility and gentry, but laid down the materials that might be used in clothing and the amount of ornamentation worn. The nobility and the peasantry each had its own set of rules; this made rankings within each group immediately apparent, thus preventing what today might be termed 'social climbing'.

Sunday schools The first Sunday school was probably that established in Gloucester in 1780 by the journalist Robert RAIKES to teach reading, writing and the scriptures to poor children, who often worked during the rest of the week. Organisations such as the Sunday School Society, founded in 1785, and the London Sunday School Union, founded in 1803, soon enrolled several hundred thousand children. In the USA the movement rapidly

developed in the 1790s, and the American Sunday School Union, formed in 1817, set up classes throughout the country.

Sunderland, Robert Spencer, 2nd Earl of (1641-1702) English politician with a knack of ending up on the winning side. After successful diplomatic missions in Europe for Charles II, Sunderland was appointed secretary of state in 1679. He was dismissed two years later when he misjudged the mood at court and supported efforts to bar the Duke of York, later to become James II, from the succession on the grounds of his Catholicism. Sunderland was eventually restored to favour through the wiles of the king's mistress, the Duchess of Portsmouth. James admired Sunderland's 'finesse' but distrusted him. The new king was won over by the earl's apparent support for the Catholics and his arguments urging the suppression of MONMOUTH – who had proof of Sunderland's duplicity and earlier negotiations with the Prince of Orange.

In 1685 James appointed Sunderland Lord President of Council. The earl then embarked on a new round of intrigue: he discredited the Earl of Rochester and replaced him in the lucrative post of First Lord of the Treasury in January 1687. While continuing secret negotiations with the Prince of Orange, Sunderland curried favour with James and in 1688 renounced Protestantism in favour of Roman Catholicism. But with the growing threat of revolution against James, Sunderland fled to Holland, joined William of Orange and turned Protestant again. When William became king of England Sunderland was already his trusted adviser. His power and fortune grew, and he made enemies of both Whigs and Tories. William appointed him Lord Chamberlain in 1697, but an antagonistic Parliament forced his resignation.

Sung dynasty (960-1279) Chinese dynasty, also called Song. The first emperor, Zhao Guangyin (Chao K'uang Yin) was a general who came to power in a coup. But under the Sung civilian officials became more powerful than the generals, and the bureaucracy's Neo-Confucian philosophy partly replaced Buddhism and Taoism. Large tracts of new land were claimed for agriculture, cotton became an important crop, the compass and paper money were invented, examinations came to dominate education, and landscape painting flourished. In the 12th century the invention of movable type produced a flood of books, particularly encyclopedias, science, histories, poetry and short stories.

Sunni see ISLAM

Sun Yat-sen (1866-1925) Revolutionary regarded by both communist and nationalist Chinese as the founder of modern China. The son of a farming family, Sun was educated at an Anglican school before studying medicine in Hong Kong. He practised as a doctor in several Chinese cities but fled in 1895 after organising an unsuccessful revolt against the ruling QING dynasty. A world tour to drum up support for the Chinese nationalist cause, interrupted by a brief spell of imprisonment in the Chinese legation in London, sharpened the appeal to Sun of the theories of Karl Marx and the US economist Henry George. Both Marx and George influenced the manifesto of the Tongmenghui (United League) which Sun formed after settling in Tokyo in 1905. This revolutionary society and Sun's Three Principles of nationalism, democracy and people's livelihood became the nucleus of the future GUOMINDANG.

In 1911, at the start of the Chinese Revolution, Sun returned home from Japan and became provisional president of the fledgling republic, but soon resigned in favour of Yuan Shikai. When Yuan suppressed the GUOMINDANG in 1913 Sun accepted warlord support to set up a separate government in Canton. A decade later Sun accepted Soviet help to reorganise the GUOMINDANG. The move inaugurated an uneasy cooperation with the Chinese Communist Party, but Sun was still attempting to negotiate a unified government when he died.

Supremacy, Acts of (1534 and 1559) Laws confirming the supremacy of the English monarch over the Anglican Church. Henry VIII was styled 'Supreme Head' of the Church in the act of 1534, but after Elizabeth I came to the throne this title was changed to 'Supreme Governor' in an attempt to reduce opposition. The acts required all public officials and clergy to swear an oath of obedience to the monarch in all things, civil and ecclesiastical.

Supreme Court Highest judicial body of the USA, established by the constitution and independent of both the president and Congress. The judges of the Supreme Court are appointed by the president with the approval of the Senate. For the first 80 years the number of Supreme Court justices varied between five and ten, but since 1869 it has remained nine. During the court's early years it established its right to decide whether congressional or state laws conform to the provisions of the constitution, but the court can exercise jurisdiction only when specific cases

A German surgeon of 1540 amputates a leg (left). Many modern instruments resemble the 18th-century Italian surgeon's tools (above).

arising from the laws are referred to it. The court's decisions have had an important bearing on the development of the US political system, often shaping the social, economic and legal policies of different administrations.

surgery Holes found bored into skulls of Stone Age people may well be evidence of a form of prehistoric surgery. Such treatment was still being used in medieval times to draw blood and ease pressure on the brain. Ancient Egyptian and Chinese scrolls describe surgical instruments and the use of splints to set broken bones. Greek and Roman surgeons were often skilful, grasped the need to prevent infection and knew how to use soporifics to deaden pain. These skills were inherited by the Arabs but lost in Europe, where barber-surgeons cut hair, extracted teeth, let blood and set bones. Their patients were as likely to die of shock or infection as from the operation.

Some early European surgeons did achieve good results. The mid-18th-century French monk Jean de Saint Come, who performed operations to remove more than a thousand bladder stones, reported that nine out of ten of his patients recovered. However, in general the high mortality rate discouraged surgery. It was not until the mid 19th century that the American dentist William Morton's use of ether as an anaesthetic and the British surgeon Joseph Lister's techniques to avoid sepsis opened the doors to successful modern surgery. Today's techniques rely heavily on new tools and devices, for both diagnoses

and operations, while modern materials are used to create artificial organs and limbs. Transplant surgery to replace failing organs with donor organs or man-made devices has become almost commonplace.

Surinam Small republic on the north-east coast of South America. Settled by Britain in 1651 and taken by the Dutch 14 years later, control of Surinam alternated between the two colonial powers until it was ceded to Holland as Dutch Guiana in 1815. At first African slaves worked the country's tropical plantations, but in the late 19th century labour was recruited from Holland's colonies in the East Indies and Java. The descendants of this last wave of workers now comprise nearly half the population of Surinam. In 1975 the

country became fully independent, but political and racial conflicts developed almost immediately, and in 1980 the military took power. Civilian rule was restored in 1986, but was disrupted by the guerrillas of the Surinamese Liberation Army (SLA) operating from the jungle of neighbouring French Guiana. A second military coup in 1990 was followed by a negotiated peace with the SLA and the formation of a coalition, the New Front for Democracy and Development, whose leader Ronald Venetiaan was elected president.

Sutton Hoo see feature, page 631

Swabia Region of south-western Germany. Named after the Suevi people of Roman times, the medieval duchy of Swabia was ruled by the Hohenstaufen dynasty from 1079 until

A royal cemetery revealed

Sutton Hoo, now a sheep pasture by the banks of the River Deben in Suffolk, south-east England, is thought to be the last resting place of some of the earliest English kings.

In 1939, excavation at a group of mounds near the River Deben revealed the richest burial artefacts ever to have been found in Britain. The body had lain in a wooden chamber in the centre of a ship (90 ft) 27 m long, the largest found until those dating from the Viking era. The ship was buried in a trench, and on top of it had been piled a mound of earth several feet high. This seagoing ship must have required a huge effort from men and oxen to drag it uphill more than a mile from the river.

THE KING'S TREASURE

Although all trace of the body had disappeared, the finds suggested the interment of a man. He had been dressed in parade gear, with an iron helmet, a jewelled sword and a shield ornamented with a dragon and a hawk. He wore a belt decorated with a solid gold buckle and shoulder clasps of gold inset with red garnets, all ornamented with writhing animals. A fine yellow cloak was thrown over the coffin; on it were placed a board game, drinking horns and a large silver dish. In the chamber were spears, silver bowls, cauldrons and buckets, and two special emblems of power: a 'sceptre' made from a whetstone which carried a stag, and a 'standard' made of iron. Since the date of the objects is mainly 7th century and the site is in East Anglia, the burial is probably that of one of the kings of East Anglia mentioned by the historian Bede, perhaps Raedwald, who died about 625, or his brother Sigebert, who died in 635.

The investigation was halted by the Second World War. When it resumed, ten other mounds were explored. The earliest held cremations which had been placed in bronze bowls. Another covered the grave of a young man in a coffin

The king's ornate belt buckle is made of solid gold. His body lay in a clinker-built ship which was dragged up from the nearby river.

The ceremonial helmet, (reconstructed, left) lay by the king's sword, shield and sceptre. These trappings would have identified him as a figure of awesome power.

with a sword and knife; his grave also contained a cauldron and iron-bound bucket, a spear, a shield and the harness of a horse, with decorated gilt or silvered bronze traces. The horse had been buried in an adjacent pit.

About 40 other graves found at Sutton Hoo contained no objects; the remains in them were often distorted by hanging or beheading. They were in two groups, one round a mound and the other near a wooden structure, probably the remains of a gibbet. The radiocarbon dates of these remains range from the 7th to the 10th centuries, so executions began at the time of the ship burials and went on after the cemetery was abandoned. The killings may have started as sacrifices and continued as capital punishment. A gibbet remained until the 17th century.

Sutton Hoo is now thought to be the burial ground of the first kings of East Anglia. They were pagans, and their funeral rites imitated those of Scandinavia; cremation and ship burial is also found in 7th-century Sweden. This suggests that some of the English, at least, wanted to form kingdoms and obtain trade without joining the new Christian confederation led by the Franks.

The site ceased to be used as a cemetery in the late 7th century, when the East Angles gave their allegiance to Christian Europe. Although it remained a place of execution, it became a remote sheepwalk, its significance lost until the 19th century, when a passion for digging ancient mounds swept England. Most of those at Sutton Hoo were pillaged and ploughed. Nothing is known to have survived from these amateur forays, but the king's resting place was spared.

1268, when it was divided among other rulers. In 1488 a group of cities and magnates in the region formed the Swabian League to counter the threatened expansion of the Swiss Confederation and Bavaria's Wittelsbach dynasty. The league recruited most small states in the area, but religious issues divided them and the league broke up in the 1530s.

Swanscombe man One of the earliest-known human inhabitants of Britain, who lived in southern England around 250 000 years ago. The name derives from a village in Kent, where three humanoid bones were discovered in river gravels in 1935, 1936 and 1955. The bones are from the skull of an adult, probably a young female. The skull is closely related to one found near Steinheim in Germany. Both skulls probably represent a transitional stage between *Homo erectus* and *Homo sapiens*, and seem to have features which link them to Neanderthal man.

SWAPO Acronym for the South West Africa People's Organisation which after 30 years of war gained independence for Namibia and became its first ruling political party. The earliest steps toward independence by the indigenous peoples of South West Africa were brutally suppressed by the area's German colonists. After the First World War the colony was taken from Germany and given to South Africa, first under a League of Nations mandate and then under a UN mandate. The tribal differences which had weakened earlier revolts made it difficult to resist South African domination. But in 1960 the apartheid regime was forced to quit the British Commonwealth: nationalist groups took heart and began to bridge the tribal divisions. As the South African government toughened its authority and began to extend apartheid legislation to South West Africa, these groups gradually combined to form SWAPO between 1964 and 1966. Banned from open activity, they went underground. Led by Sam Nujoma, SWAPO launched a terrorist campaign with their Soviet-trained guerrillas who operated largely from neighbouring Angola. The war ended in 1988 when South Africa allowed open political activity and free elections. SWAPO won the first general election in

The swastika on a Tibetan Buddha symbolises good luck, a different meaning from its later Nazi associations.

1989 and Nujoma became prime minister. In 1994 SWAPO won a two-thirds majority of the national assembly in the first elections in an independent Namibia.

swastika The square cross whose arms bend at right angles, either clockwise or anticlockwise, became notorious as the symbol of the German Nazi Party. In many early cultures, however, the swastika symbolised prosperity and good fortune. Deriving its name from the Sanskrit *svastika* (conducive to well-being), it was a decorative motif in ancient Mesopotamia and may have formed the basis of the 'key pattern' used in classical Greece and Rome. It occurs in early Christian and Byzantine art, in South and Central America and among the Hindus and Buddhists of India. In 1910 the German poet Guido von List, who wrongly believed that the swastika's origins were Teutonic, proposed that all anti-Semitic organisations take it as their symbol. The Nazi Party adopted it in 1920 and in 1935 incorporated it into Germany's national flag.

Swaziland Small mineral-rich kingdom in southern Africa. In the mid 18th century Swazis from the north drove out or enslaved the indigenous Bushmen. A century later their king formed a series of protective alliances with the independent Boer republics. Swaziland came under British rule in 1902, after the Second Anglo-Boer War. Although Swaziland retained its paramount chief – later king – his role was largely ceremonial until independence was gained under Sobhuza II in 1968. Sobhuza suspended the constitution in 1973 and assumed absolute power. Under revised constitutions in 1974 and again in 1978, the monarchy retained wide powers. Sobhuza's successor, Mswati III, has faced growing demands for broader democracy. Parliamentary elections in 1993, held on a non-party basis, were widely criticised as undemocratic.

Sweden North European country comprising the eastern part of the Scandinavian peninsula and the Baltic islands of Gotland and Öland. The Roman historian Tacitus refers to Suiones tribesmen – who probably founded the first Swedish state. Vikings from Sweden raided in the Baltic, into Russia and as

far as the Arab caliphate of Baghdad. In 1397 Sweden joined Norway and Denmark in the Union of Kalmar. Denmark dominated the union until 1523 when GUSTAVUS VASA led a successful revolt, reasserted Swedish independence, established his own royal dynasty and introduced Lutheranism as the state religion. Swedish power and territory expanded during the 16th and 17th centuries, especially in the reign of the great military commander GUSTAVUS ADOLFUS (1611-32). However, the strains of maintaining a scattered empire began to tell during the reign of Charles XII (1682-1718). When the NORTHERN WAR ended in 1721 the empire broke up and a parliamentary government replaced the monarchy until the coup of Gustavus III in 1772. During the Napoleonic Wars Sweden was part of the Third Coalition against the French. In 1818 Charles XIV became king and by his death in 1844 had established the present Swedish monarchy.

Sweden pursued a policy of non-alignment in both world wars, which allowed it to develop into one of the world's wealthiest and also most socially progressive states. After a long period of Social Democratic power, proposals to fund welfare spending by raising taxation cost the Social Democrat prime minister Olaf Palme the general election in 1976. His party regained power in 1982, and although Palme himself was assassinated four years later, the Social Democrats held office until 1991. The Moderate Unity Party then took power and paved the way for membership of the European Community and reduced public expenditure on welfare provisions, particularly health and education. Sweden was admitted to the European Union in 1995.

Sweyn Forkbeard (d.1014) King of Denmark from 986, and briefly King of England. Sweyn deposed his father Harald Bluetooth as Denmark's ruler and spent the early years of his reign in Viking raids before conquering Norway in 1000. Sweyn attacked England from 1002 onwards in spite of payments by Ethelred the Unready. By 1013 he had subdued enough of the country to march on London, force Ethelred into exile and proclaim himself king. Sweyn died before he could consolidate his rule, but he had shattered English resistance, and when Ethelred returned to reclaim his throne he was easily defeated by Sweyn's son Canute.

'Swing, Captain' Name widely used as a signature on threatening letters to landowners and farmers during riots by agricultural workers which swept south and east England in 1830 and 1831. Farm workers faced low wages, high unemployment and the threat

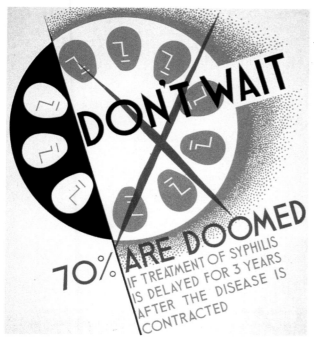

DON'T WAIT

70% ARE DOOMED

IF TREATMENT OF SYPHILIS IS DELAYED FOR 3 YEARS AFTER THE DISEASE IS CONTRACTED

In 1940 the New York prison system warned inmates that syphilis killed. Penicillin was not used as a cure until 1943.

of mechanisation. In a series of spontaneous risings, quickly and ruthlessly suppressed, they threatened employers, burnt hay ricks and destroyed the new threshing machines.

Switzerland Small mountainous central European country which straddles the Alps. Occupied by the Celtic Helvitii from the 2nd century BC, Switzerland's strategic position across Europe's north-south routes invited a succession of invaders and temporary conquerors. Roman, Alemanni, Burgundian, Goth and Frankish armies all conquered or traversed the landlocked territory before it came under the control of the Holy Roman Empire in the 11th century. Declaring independence of their Habsburg overlords in 1291, the cantons of Uri, Schwyz and Unterwalden established the Alliance for Mutual Defence and were later joined by Lucerne, Zürich and Bern. Other cantons joined the alliance throughout the 15th century. After Swiss successes against Burgundy, France and the Holy Roman Empire the soldiers of the new confederation were much in demand as mercenaries. The Reformation and Counter Reformation led to religious warfare, and there were continued clashes with the Habsburgs until they were eventually forced to acknowledge Swiss independence in 1648 in the Treaty of Westphalia.

French Revolutionary armies invaded the country in 1798 and established the Helvetic Republic, but Swiss control was restored and the country's neutrality guaranteed by the Congress of Vienna in 1815. However, religious differences continued to create political problems. Seven predominantly Catholic cantons formed the breakaway SONDERBUND in 1845 to counter the power of the liberal central government. Their move sparked a brief civil war which was resolved by a new, democratic federal constitution adopted in 1848.

Switzerland remained neutral during both world wars. A national referendum in 1992 rejected Swiss membership of the European Economic Area and dashed its government's hopes of eventually joining the European Community.

syndicalism Early 20th-century industrial workers' movement seeking to replace capitalism with workers' control. The syndicalists were influenced by the French anarchist Pierre Proudhon and the writings of George SOREL, who advocated nationwide general strikes as tools of change. They were mainly active in France, Italy, Spain, Russia and the USA, but the growth of communism and the spread of complex labour organisation after the First World War reduced their influence.

syphilis Contagious venereal disease whose origins remain obscure. In 1493 an epidemic of syphilis cut a swathe of death across Europe. It was believed to have come from South America, because symptoms of what later proved to be syphilis had been noted among sailors returning from the New World. However, recent archaeological studies have pointed to the existence of syphilis in ancient Greece and Rome, and some sources suggest that both Caligula and Tiberius may have suffered from the disease. In the Middle Ages it may have been wrongly diagnosed as leprosy, for early writings on leprosy describe symptoms akin to those of syphilis.

The disease was specifically identified and named by the Venetian physician Girolamo Frascatoro, who described it in verse and dubbed it the 'French Disease' early in the 16th century. In 1530 Paracelsus enraged the civic dignitaries of Nuremberg by publishing a clinical description of syphilis and recommending its treatment with careful oral doses of mercury compounds – a cure adopted by England's Henry VIII and widely used until the discovery of penicillin.

Syria Middle Eastern country, originally settled by Akkadians, who were succeeded by Arameans and then by Canaanites. Syria later became a province of successive empires, from the Phoenicians to the Byzantines. The Arabs conquered Syria in the 630s, and the city of Damascus became the brilliant capital of the Umayyad Arab caliphate from 661 until the fall of the dynasty in 750. It reverted to

provincial status under the Fatimids and the Egyptian Mamelukes before coming under Ottoman control in 1516.

After the Ottoman Empire disintegrated in the First World War Syria became a French mandate. Following the fall of France in the Second World War Syria was occupied by the Allies, who encouraged it to become independent in 1941. Different army factions staged coups in 1949, 1951 and 1954. Syria briefly joined Egypt in the United Arab Republic, but the alliance was ended by another coup. The Ba'ath, the dominant party, was split by personal and ideological rivalries. In 1970 a new regime under General Hafiz al-Assad crushed internal opposition and asserted Syrian influence over neighbouring Lebanon. Syria suffered major defeats by Israel in both the 1967 SIX-DAY WAR and the YOM KIPPUR

WAR of 1973. Deeply involved in the Lebanese civil war, Syria remained hostile to Israel. But the country joined the GULF WAR allies, making possible an economic opening to the West and the Arab Gulf states after the war. Syria cautiously supported the Middle East peace process after 1992.

Tacitus (c. AD 55-120) Roman historian and public official who lived through the tyrannical rule of Emperor Domitian and the golden age of Emperor Trajan. Publius Cornelius Tacitus became governor of Asia in 112, and his best known work, the *Annals*, displays a keen knowledge of Roman power politics. About two-thirds of the *Annals*, a history of Rome from AD 14 to 68, survives but most of his *History*, covering the period from 69 to 96, is lost. His book on the German tribes is still the main source on ancient Germany, and his biography of his father-in-law AGRICOLA, governor of Britain, tells us much about Roman Britain. Tacitus was one of the earliest non-Christian writers to record the Crucifixion of Jesus Christ, which he mentions in connection with the persecution of Christians in AD 64. As a historian Tacitus has always been admired for his scrupulous accuracy and also for his succinct style.

Taff Vale case (1901) British court action that established that trade unions could be sued for damages. After a strike by railwaymen employed by the Taff Vale Railway Company, the company sued the Amalgamated Society of Railway Servants for loss of income. On appeal to the House of Lords the company won damages and costs. The judgment significantly increased support for the LABOUR PARTY. The Trade Disputes Act of 1906 effectively reversed the decision by exempting trade unions from this type of action; the Act was amended in 1984.

Taft, William Howard (1857-1930) Judge and 27th president of the USA from 1909 to 1913. Son and grandson of judges, Taft's first love was the law and he came reluctantly to politics. He served as President Theodore ROOSEVELT's secretary of war from 1904 to 1908. Taft was Roosevelt's chosen successor as president in 1908. But Taft, a Republican, lacked the political skills to avoid conflict with the PROGRESSIVE faction in his party, and it split on the issue of tariff reform. He had been elected on a pledge to reduce tariffs on imports, but the 1909 Payne Aldrich Act failed to satisfy many who believed that large corporations could continue to set high prices and make excessive profits because cheap imports were not allowed to compete.

When Taft ran for re-election in 1912 Roosevelt had become his bitter opponent and came out of retirement to run against him as a Progressive. The Republican vote was split and the Democrat, Woodrow WILSON, was elected. Taft served as Chief Justice of the Supreme Court from 1921 until his death, and though considered an arch-conservative was responsible for many progressive judgments. He was the only man to serve as both chief justice and president.

Tahiti Island in the southern Pacific, part of the overseas territory of French Polynesia. The first European to visit Tahiti, the English navigator Samuel Wallis in 1767, was followed a year later by Louis Antoine de Bougainville who claimed the island for France. At the beginning of the 19th century English missionaries converted the majority of Tahitians to Protestant Christianity. The French government established a protectorate in 1842 and annexed Tahiti as a colony in 1880. In 1940 the Tahitians backed the FREE FRENCH government of Charles de Gaulle. In 1946 French Polynesia became an overseas territory of France. At that time many Polynesians, led by the First World War veteran Pouvanaa a Oopa, demanded independence from France. In 1958 Pouvanaa was sentenced to imprisonment in France. Since 1977 French Polynesia has had limited local autonomy, but in 1995 Tahitians rioted against French nuclear tests in the neighbouring Tuamotu islands.

In 1860 the Taiping rebels advanced north on Shanghai but were defeated by the emperor's 'Ever-Victorious Army' with its Western arms and American commander, Frederick Ward.

Taiping Rebellion (1850-64) Radical revolt in China which cost 20 million lives and left the QING dynasty permanently weakened. It was inspired and led by Hong Xiuquan (1813-64), whose visions had convinced him he was the younger brother of Jesus Christ and had a mission to overthrow the Qing. The rebellion began in Guangxi province and gained control of most of the central and lower Chang Jiang (Yangtze) region. The rebels, a million strong, captured Nanjing in 1853 and made it the capital of their Taiping ('Great Peace') kingdom. This kingdom was founded upon idealistic moral precepts, full equality for women, economic modernisation and equal distribution of land, but it was weakened by rivalries among its leadership. In 1864 the Qing armies, partly commanded by such foreigners as the British general Charles GORDON, retook Nanjing. Hong killed himself and over 100000 rebels died. Later revolutionaries, including the communists, drew on the egalitarian Taiping ideology.

Taiwan Island about 100 miles (160 km) off the coast of China. Sparsely settled by Malayo-Polynesian people, Taiwan was a Chinese and Japanese pirate base for many years. Spanish and Dutch trading posts were established in the 1620s, and the Dutch drove out the Spaniards in 1664. In 1661 the Dutch were driven out in their turn by the pirate Koxinga (Zheng Chenggong), who since 1644 had made Taiwan a refuge for supporters of China's deposed Ming dynasty. In 1683 Taiwan surrendered to the Qing dynasty and became part of China's Fujian province. Outbreaks of fighting between its original inhabitants and the Chinese settlers continued into the 19th century. In 1895 Taiwan was ceded to Japan in the Treaty of SHIMONOSEKI at the end of the first Sino-Japanese War and was developed as a Japanese colony.

Taiwan reverted to China in 1945. In 1949 the island became a refuge for the Republic of China's ousted Nationalist government, following the communist takeover of the Chinese mainland at the end of the CHINESE CIVIL WAR. By 1950 almost 2 million refugees from the mainland had arrived on the island. From their base on Taiwan, the Nationalists led by CHIANG KAI-SHEK continued to claim sovereignty over all China and to seek recovery of the mainland. The United States supported Nationalist claims and in 1954 signed a mutual defence pact. Chiang Kai-shek remained Taiwan's unelected president until his death in 1975, and was succeeded by his son, Chiang Ching-kuo. In 1971 Taiwan lost its seat in the United Nations to the People's Republic of China. It lost additional international support when in 1978 the USA ended the United States-Taiwan security pact and recognised the People's Republic of China the following year. However, American military aid continued and the USA and Taiwan maintained unofficial ties.

Taiwan's economic success, especially in the manufacture and export of electronic goods, contributed to demands for political liberalisation. Chiang Ching-kuo, who had been elected president in 1978 and was re-elected in 1984, launched a policy of gradual democratic reform before his death in 1988. Martial law, in effect since 1949, was lifted in 1987 and bans on travel to and trade with the

Chinese mainland were eased. Chiang Ching-kuo's successor Lee Teng-hui was Taiwan's first native-born president. From 1991, as Taiwanese nationalism developed, China became concerned over the prospect of a democratic and permanently independent Taiwan.

Taj Mahal This masterpiece of Indian Mughal architecture, completed in 1648, stands beside the Jumna river in the city of Agra. Designed as a representation of the throne of God in paradise, the Taj Mahal was commissioned as a mausoleum for the Mughal emperor SHAH JAHAN's beloved consort Arjunand Banu Begum. She had died in childbirth in 1631 and had been known by the title Taj Mahal ('Crown of the Palace'). Plans were prepared by a council of the best architects from India, Persia and central Asia, and work began in 1632. The ethereal domed building rises 187 ft (57 m), and is laid out in perfect symmetry along four axes.

Talbot, William (1800-1877) British photographic pioneer who discovered how to produce negative images on light-sensitive paper which could be developed so that any number of positive copies could be made. He called them calotypes or Talbotypes. His method proved to be the forerunner of modern photography, as only single prints could be made from the earlier daguerrotypes.

tallage Medieval tax generally imposed by a lord upon his tenants. The amount and frequency of tallage varied. In England it was a royal tax levied on boroughs and royal lands from the 12th century. Condemned by the barons in MAGNA CARTA (1215), tallage had become less important with the rise of parliamentary taxation, and was abolished in 1340. In France the 'taille' was extended in the 14th century to meet the expenses of the HUNDRED YEARS' WAR. The nobility and clergy were exempted from payment and the burden of the taille lay upon the peasants. By the 18th century it was the main form of direct taxation, caused great resentment and was abolished during the FRENCH REVOLUTION.

Talleyrand-Périgord, Charles de (1754-1838) French diplomat and statesman who held high office during the French Revolution, under Napoleon and under the restored French monarchy. Born to a noble family, Talleyrand's club foot prevented him joining the army. He entered the Church instead, and by 1780 had become agent-general of the French clergy – the representative of the Church to the French government – and an energetic defender of the Church's privileges. But when the French Revolution began he supported the nationalisation of Church property and the pope excommunicated him for consecrating bishops loyal to the new regime.

In 1791 Talleyrand left the Church and began a diplomatic career in London, where he tried to prevent war between Britain and France. Expelled from Britain in 1794, he spent two years in the United States amassing a fortune through financial speculation before returning to France in 1796. In barely a year he succeeded in becoming foreign minister. Involved in the coup that brought NAPOLEON to power, Talleyrand became his trusted adviser and foreign minister from 1799 to 1807, and his formidable skills were applied to most of the peace negotiations during the NAPOLEONIC WARS. In 1807 he resigned from the foreign ministry and secretly plotted with

Talleyrand, a servant of three kings, two revolutions and one emperor, scorned those who 'forgot nothing and learned nothing'.

the Allies against Napoleon. When the allied armies entered Paris in 1814, he persuaded the senate to depose Napoleon, and as head of a provisional government Talleyrand himself recalled LOUIS XVIII to the throne. As the king's foreign minister, he represented France at the Congress of VIENNA. Towards 1830, aware of the growing unpopularity of the government of CHARLES X, he entered into relations with LOUIS PHILIPPE and helped to make him king during the JULY REVOLUTION of 1830. Talleyrand was reconciled with the Church on his deathbed.

Talmud Compilation of Jewish oral tradition, law and commentary. The destruction of the Temple in Jerusalem in AD 70 and the dispersal of Jewish communities, or DIASPORA, prompted a vigorous effort to preserve traditional teachings. Around 100, Judah ha-Nasi compiled the *Mishnah*, an organised summary of the oral tradition. This, together with a subsequent commentary, the *Gemara*, constitutes the Talmud; the word means study. Two versions of the work survive: the Palestinian Talmud dating from about 450 and the Babylonian from around 500. The later version is more complete and for traditional Jews it remains the final authority on the law. Summaries of Talmudic teachings were subsequently prepared by scholars such as MAIMONIDES in the 12th century and Joseph Caro in the 16th century. Caro's *Shulhan Arukh* (*Prepared Table*) found wide favour as a work of ready reference. Study of the Talmud has been central to Jewish intellectual and religious life and its rules are strictly followed by Orthodox Jews.

From 1658 until his death Shah Jahan was imprisoned in the Agra fort by his son Aurangzeb. But he was allowed a window to gaze on the Taj Mahal, the tomb he had built for his beloved wife.

Tamerlane see feature, opposite

Tammany Political society founded in New York city in 1789 and named after Tamanend, a friendly Delaware chief who reputedly signed a treaty with the Quaker William PENN. The society, which was also known as Tammany Hall after its Manhattan headquarters, based its ceremonies on mock American Indian rites, and was originally formed to promote the interests of middle-class Americans against the powerful Federalist Party. In 1800 Tammany's support for the Democratic-Republican Aaron BURR helped him to become vice-president of the USA. From then on, the society became increasingly influential until it dominated New York state and city politics. By the 1870s, however, Tammany had become notorious for its unscrupulous political methods and for the corruption of its leaders. Following a succession of scandals and investigations, Tammany lost an important municipal election in 1932, after which its influence gradually declined.

John Kelly, an influential Tammany politician, helps himself to funds from the New York city treasury, in a political cartoon from 1884.

Tamworth Manifesto (1834) Election address given by the future English prime minister Sir Robert PEEL to his constituents at Tamworth, Staffordshire, in which he accepted the notion of changing existing institutions from within where necessary. In the speech Peel pledged himself to accept the Whig government's Reform Act of 1832 (see REFORM ACTS) and declared his support for a policy of moderate reform, while stressing the need to preserve what was best and most valuable from Britain's past. The speech came to be accepted as a manifesto – hence its name – for the new, enlightened Conservative Party which was developing under Peel's leadership out of the old, repressive Tory Party.

Tanaka, Kakuei (1918-93) Japanese Liberal-Democratic politician, elected in 1972 as his country's youngest postwar prime minister. Soon after taking power, Tanaka signed an agreement to establish diplomatic relations with the People's Republic of China. He was forced to resign in December 1974 under suspicion of corruption, and two years later he was formally accused of accepting bribes from the American aircraft company Lockheed. Though sentenced to four years' imprisonment in 1983, Tanaka remained an influential figure in the Liberal-Democratic Party.

Tanganyika see TANZANIA

Tang dynasty (618-906) Chinese dynasty which forged an empire stretching from Korea to Turkistan, and established one of the most artistically creative periods in Chinese history. The first Tang emperor, Li Yuan, was an official of the Sui dynasty and came to power by defeating a number of rivals and rebels. He adopted and improved the highly effective administrative system of the Sui, recodified China's laws and established a copper coinage that was to last as long as the dynasty. In 626 Li Yuan was forced to abdicate by his ambitious son, Li Shih-min (Taizong), who expanded China's western boundaries to their farthest extent.

During the reign of the third Tang emperor, Gaozong, who ruled from 649 to 683, a formidable woman rose to power. In 655, the concubine Wu Hou (Wu Zetian) became empress after having the previous empress deposed, and over the following 50 years took an increasingly firm hold on the reins of power. After Gaozong died in 683, Wu governed China through two puppet emperors, before seizing the throne for herself in 690. Her rule was ruthless, but also competent and enlightened: above all, she appointed advisers and administrators on the basis of ability rather than social status. This policy helped to pave the way for a great flowering of Chinese civilisation in the 8th century.

The Tang dynasty achieved its high point during the reign of Emperor Xuanzong, which lasted from 712 to 756. During this period there was a flourishing of the arts of painting, music and poetry, largely as a result of strong royal patronage. Foreigners were welcomed, leading to a growth in trade, the expansion of towns, and the introduction of fresh artistic ideas and new religions, such as Christianity and ZOROASTRIANISM.

In 751 the imperial armies were defeated by the Arabs in Turkistan and the Tang dynasty started to fall into decay. A major rebellion between 755 and 763 caused serious disruption, and over the succeeding decades the machinery of government gradually fell apart. Riven by the intrigues of court officials, and under almost constant threat from the

Mongolians and the Tibetans, the country began fragmenting into a patchwork of states controlled by local warlords. The collapse of the dynasty became inevitable, and when it occurred in 906 China entered a period of intense civil strife that was to last for 53 years.

tank Heavily armoured fighting vehicles moving on linked metal belts called tracks were developed by both Britain and France during the First World War, with the aim of crossing German trenches. They first saw action in September 1916, but achieved no significant victory until November 1917, when more than 450 British tanks spearheaded an attack that overwhelmed German defences at Cambrai in northern France.

By the late 1930s the tank had become a major offensive weapon, and it played a decisive role in a number of campaigns during the Second World War. Using the tactic known as *blitzkrieg,* 'lightning war' , German armoured divisions swept rapidly across Poland in 1939, through western Europe in 1940, and deep into the Soviet Union in 1941. Soon a new type of warfare had emerged involving battles between massed battalions of tanks with relatively few infantry.

In spite of the development of sophisticated antitank weapons, such as guided missiles, tanks remain the offensive mainstay of most modern armies. They were used with devastating effectiveness by Allied forces during the 1991 Gulf War.

The British Mark V (male) tank first saw service in 1916. 'Male' tanks were equipped with cannons; 'female' with machine guns only.

Tanzania Country in East Africa created in 1964 by the union of the former republic of Tanganyika and the offshore islands of Pemba and ZANZIBAR. When the Portuguese mariner Vasco da Gama arrived in the region in 1498 it was populated largely by Bantu-speaking people, while Arab trade settlements dotted the coast. The Portuguese made no attempt to explore the interior, but gradually supplanted the Arabs along the coast before being driven out in 1698 with the help of Arabs from

A cruel conqueror

Timur, or Tamerlane, modelled himself on Genghis Khan. During a 35-year reign of terror he laid waste many of the great cities of central Asia.

Europeans speak of Tamerlane or Tamburlaine the Great, as in Christopher Marlowe's play of that name. The historical figure was the 14th-century central Asian conqueror Timur, nicknamed Timur-i-Leng ('Timur the Lame') by his Persian enemies because he walked with a limp. He was born around 1336 near Shahr-i Sabz, not far from Samarkand in present-day Uzbekistan. He was Turkish in language and culture, but of Mongol descent. He claimed to be related to Genghis Khan by a common ancestor, and enhanced his prestige by marrying two princesses of Genghis's family.

THE LURE OF PLUNDER

Like Genghis, Timur rose to supreme power in his homeland by attracting followers through military successes, and then exploiting alliances with those stronger than himself. By 1370 he had become the dominant figure in the western half of the Chaghatai khanate – one of the states into which the Mongol empire had dissolved. He then spent the remaining 35 years of his life in a series of military campaigns of conquest and plunder. The loot was used to adorn his capital Samarkand. Many of the buildings put up there by Timur survive, especially mosques, religious colleges and shrines. They are particularly treasured for their beautiful tilework.

Persia was repeatedly invaded from 1383, before being absorbed into Timur's empire. The other areas attacked and looted were not incorporated: as well as conquering the Golden Horde, Timur's expeditions took him to India, where he destroyed Dehli in 1398; to Syria, where he sacked Damascus, and Iraq, where he razed Baghdad, in 1401; and to Asia Minor, where in 1402 he defeated and captured the Ottoman sultan Bayezid I at the Battle of Ankara.

Timur's final expedition was to be against China, but he died in 1405 as he was about to set off with his army. He was buried in a magnificent tomb, the Guri Mir, in Samarkand. When his body was exhumed in 1941, it was found to show evidence of the disability that had earned Timur his nickname. Parts of

This 16th-century miniature shows Timur's troops building a tower from the rubble of a fortress and the heads of its dead defenders.

Timur's empire were retained by his descendants – one of whom, Babur, founded the Mughal empire in India in the 16th century.

Despite his military talents Timur did not have Genghis Khan's constructive qualities, and his cruelty far exceeded Genghis's. Both massacred hundreds of thousands, but Timur is said to have enjoyed inflicting suffering. One of his particular pleasures was allegedly to erect towers using the heads of his victims.

Oman. Over the next 250 years Arab traders in search of slaves and ivory penetrated into the interior, establishing trading posts as far west as Lake Tanganyika.

During the 1880s much of the country fell under the control of the German East Africa Company, and in 1891 it was made a German

protectorate. After the First World War Tanganyika came under British rule as a League of Nations MANDATE, and in 1961 it became an independent state within the British Commonwealth. In 1962 Tanganyika was declared a republic with Julius NYERERE as its first president, and in 1964 it joined with Zanzibar and Pemba to form the United Republic of Tanzania.

In 1967 the country embarked on a programme of socialist redevelopment set out by Nyerere in his Arusha Declaration. Banks and industries were nationalised and millions of peasants were resettled in agricultural cooperatives. The policy collapsed in 1977 as a result of inefficiency, corruption and huge price rises. Tanzania became a one-party state. In 1979 its army invaded Uganda and drove the dictator Idi Amin from power. Nyerere resigned in 1985 and was succeeded by Ali Hassan Mwinyi, under whose leadership the economy has undergone a marked revival.

Taoism Chinese philosophy and religion, along with Confucianism one of the two main systems of traditional Chinese thought. The central concept and goal of Taoism is *tao*, 'the way' – an elusive idea denoting the force inherent in nature and, by extension, behaviour that is in harmony with the natural order.

Such behaviour cannot be defined since it has to be instinctively and spontaneously recognised, but it is invariably achieved by following a path of least resistance, amounting even to inaction. The central principles of Taoism are set out in the *Tao te Ching* ('The Way of Power', also written *Dao de Jing*), a

Lao-tzu, the founder of Taoism, is often depicted riding comfortably on a buffalo.

text ascribed to Lao-tzu (or Laozi, 'Master Lao'), a mysterious sage who is said to have lived in the 6th century BC and is regarded by Taoists as the founder of their movement. The *Tao te Ching*, however, dates from the 3rd century BC, and many modern scholars doubt that Lao-tzu ever existed.

By the 2nd century AD, the austere philosophy of the *Tao te Ching* had developed into a popular cult with many gods, including Lao-tzu himself. The religious form of Taoism became associated with mysticism, alchemy, superstition and magic – beliefs and practices essentially at odds with the original principles of the *Tao te Ching*. It acquired priests, rituals and numerous sacred writings; it also took from Buddhism the concept of reincarnation, and developed sets of practical instructions on how to achieve immortality. Over the centuries the cult has at times been favoured by China's rulers, and at others persecuted by them. It now survives mainly in Taiwan, having been suppressed on the mainland during the Cultural Revolution of 1966-8.

Tara Ancient seat and coronation place of the high kings of Ireland, situated on a hill in County Meath 20 miles (32km) north of Dublin. The site consists of six earthwork enclosures, the largest some 850ft (259m) in diameter. According to legend, St Patrick preached at Tara in AD432; a statue of him is said to mark the location of the coronation stone on which the high kings were crowned. The site was abandoned in the 6th century, but was used in 1843 for a mass rally of Irish nationalists addressed by Daniel O'CONNELL.

Taranaki Wars (1860-1, 1863-4) Series of conflicts between Maoris and colonial forces in New Zealand's North Island. The first Taranaki War began after Te Teira, a Maori of the Taranaki region, sold land to the colonial government without the permission of his tribal chief. Fighting broke out when supporters of the chief resisted surveyors sent to inspect the newly purchased land. The war was inconclusive and ended in April 1861 with a truce that left the colonists dissatisfied. Fighting flared up again in April 1863, ending a year later with the loss of large tracts of Maori land. Further hostilities continued throughout the North Island until 1872, but they are not usually considered to be part of the Taranaki Wars.

tariff reform Protectionist fiscal policy proposed by the British colonial secretary Joseph Chamberlain in 1897, aimed at ending Britain's practice of FREE TRADE which had been adopted in 1860, 14 years after the repeal of the CORN LAWS. Chamberlain campaigned to introduce duties on imported goods, believing that this would improve Britain's tax revenue as well as its international trading

Having struck terror into the populations of Russia and eastern Europe, the Tatars settled in western Russia where their warlike skills were diverted into violent equestrian sports.

position. He also hoped to strengthen links within the British Empire through a policy of 'imperial preference', by which lower rates of duty would apply between member countries. Tariff reform was repeatedly rejected up until the international financial crisis of 1929-31, but was finally adopted by the coalition government of Ramsay MacDonald in 1931.

Tarquin Family name of the semilegendary fifth and seventh kings of Rome, Lucius Tarquinius Priscus and Lucius Tarquinius Superbus ('the Proud'), who ruled from about 616 to 578BC, and 534 to 510 respectively. According to tradition, Tarquinius Priscus usurped the throne after the death of King Ancus Marcius, and was eventually killed in a plot orchestrated by Marcius' sons. Priscius's widow, the prophetess Tanaquil, managed to secure the throne for her son-in-law, Servius Tullius; he was later murdered, however, by Priscius's son (or perhaps grandson) Superbus.

Rome then endured 24 years of tyranny, in which many senators were put to death. This period came to an end with a rebellion led by the senator Lucius Junius Brutus, and closed with the expulsion of the Tarquins and the abolition of the monarchy. The immediate cause of the rebellion was alleged to be the rape of a noblewoman named Lucretia by Superbus's son Sextus. During the republican era which ensued, the title 'king' became a term of abuse, while the reigns of the Tarquins were often cited as evidence of the inherent dangers of monarchy.

Tasman, Abel (c.1603-59) Dutch navigator who became the first European to discover Tasmania, New Zealand, Fiji and Tonga. In 1642 Tasman sailed around the west and south coasts of Australia, thereby demonstrating that the continent did not extend over the

whole of the Southern Hemisphere, as some people believed. He landed in TASMANIA, and then explored the west coast of New Zealand. Sailing into the Pacific, he discovered the islands of Tonga and Fiji. His next voyage, in 1644, resulted in a survey of the north coast of Australia including the Gulf of Carpentaria.

Tasmania Mountainous island lying off the south-east coast of Australia. The first inhabitants probably arrived some 40000 years ago, when Tasmania was still connected to the Australian mainland. The first European to sight the island was the Dutch navigator Abel TASMAN, who named it Van Diemen's Land after the governor of the Dutch East Indies. In 1803 the island was claimed by Britain, which established a penal colony at Port Arthur. Until 1825 Van Diemen's Land was governed as part of New South Wales; it was then constituted as a separate colony, before being granted self-government in 1855-6, when it was renamed Tasmania. The colony became a state within the newly federated Commonwealth of Australia in 1901.

By this time there were no Aborigines left on the island. They had come into conflict with free settlers and BUSHRANGERS from the earliest years and been all but exterminated. By 1831, only 200 Tasmanian Aborigines survived, prompting the authorities to relocate them as a group on Flinders Island off the Tasmanian coast. But they failed to flourish, and the last full-blood indigenous Tasmanian died in 1876.

Tatars Predominantly Muslim people living in and around the Tatar Republic in western Russia. They are descended from Turkic-speaking nomadic tribes, originally resident in north-eastern Mongolia, who joined forces with the Mongol conqueror Genghis Khan in the 13th century. Europeans and Russians who suffered the onslaught of these armies identified their attackers indiscriminately as 'Tartars', probably through association with Tartarus, the place of punishment in ancient Greek mythology. Many Tatars settled in the khanate of the GOLDEN HORDE – the huge state set up by Genghis and his successors in western Russia. When this started breaking up during the 14th century four major Tatar khanates emerged: Kazan, Astrakhan, Sibir and Crimea. By 1783 these states had all been conquered or annexed by Russia.

taxation The first taxes arose from the ability of the powerful to demand payment from the weak in return for protection. Their subsequent development was largely driven by the need of rulers to finance wars and conquests. In the ancient world, most tax revenue came from tribute paid by conquered peoples, which spared the home economy the need to provide revenue. Tribute was essentially a form of protection money, paid to buy off aggression; it also enabled rulers to maintain large armies which could be used to conquer further territories – from which more tribute would flow. This pattern served as an engine of empire throughout the world.

Until modern times taxes were paid in kind, with grain, livestock and other produce as well as money. Two of the oldest forms of taxation are poll tax – levied directly on people rather than on their property or earnings – and excise duty, which is charged on imported goods. Both are among the easiest taxes to calculate and, in theory, to collect. But there have been unusual taxes in the past, such as those levied on wigs, beards and windows.

Taxes have played a part in at least four major revolutions. A new poll tax contributed to the PEASANTS' REVOLT in England in 1381, while the ENGLISH CIVIL WAR of 1642-9 arose partly over the question of who controlled taxation – the king or Parliament. The taxation policy of the British Government was a major issue in the AMERICAN REVOLUTION of 1776,

Ancient Egyptian officials used tally boards to assess wealth and calculate taxes, as illustrated in this wall painting from around 1400 BC.

while one of the main grievances underlying the FRENCH REVOLUTION of 1789 was the fact that the nobility and the clergy were largely exempt from taxation.

Taylor, Zachary (1784-1850) US army general who served as twelfth president of the USA from 1849 until his death. Taylor grew up in Kentucky, where he received little formal education, before joining the army in 1808. He enjoyed a distinguished military career, fighting in a number of campaigns, such as the WAR OF 1812 between the USA and Britain, and the Black Hawk War of 1832. He became a national hero following his victories in the Mexican-American War of 1846-8, particularly in the decisive battle against the Mexican general Antonio de Santa Anna at Buena Vista in 1847. At the end of the war Taylor was elected to the White House, where he took a firm stand against slavery. He died of cholera after only 16 months in office.

Teamsters US trade union, also known as the International Brotherhood of Teamsters. The union was formed in 1903 for workers in the transport industry, and by the 1940s it had become the largest single union in the USA. The Teamsters was successfully led by Daniel Tobin from 1907 to 1952, but later suffered a series of corruption scandals. In 1958 its president, David Beck, was imprisoned for tax offences, and in 1967 his successor James Hoffa was found guilty of attempting to influence a federal jury while on trial for misusing union funds. Hoffa was released from prison in 1971 after the Teamsters had made substantial contributions to President Richard Nixon's re-election campaign. Hoffa disappeared in 1975, presumably murdered by gangsters with whom he was known to have had strong links. The Teamsters remains one of the most influential trade unions in the United States.

Teapot Dome scandal (1922-4) US fraud scandal perpetrated by Albert Fall, secretary of the interior in the government of President Warren Harding. In 1921 Harding transferred responsibility for oil fields earmarked for the navy to the department of the interior. The following year Fall secretly leased the oil fields – at Teapot Dome, Wyoming, and at Elk Hills, California – to two private oil companies without inviting competitive bids. A Senate investigation found that Fall had received substantial gifts of cash from the oil companies concerned. He was convicted of accepting bribes and jailed for a year.

Tehran Conference (November 28-December 1, 1943) Meeting held by the three Allied leaders, Winston Churchill, Franklin D. Roosevelt and Joseph Stalin, in the Iranian capital Tehran to coordinate the opening of a

James Hoffa was a powerful and effective president of the Teamsters union, retaining control even while serving a prison sentence.

SECOND FRONT in Europe by means of a Soviet offensive against Germany. The three men also discussed the establishment of the United Nations after the war, and Stalin pressed for a future Soviet sphere of influence in the Baltic States and Eastern Europe, while agreeing to the independence of Iran.

Te Kooti Rikirangi Te Turuki (c.1830-93) Maori guerrilla and spiritual leader who founded the Ringatu Church in New Zealand. Te Kooti rose to prominence during the Anglo-Maori wars of the early 1860s. He led resistance on the east coast of the North Island but was captured in 1865 and deported to the Chatham Islands, 500 miles (800 km) east of Christchurch in the Pacific Ocean. While in exile, Te Kooti evolved Ringatu – a new form

A political cartoon from 1922 shows US government officials desperately trying to escape the runaway Teapot Dome scandal.

Time for tea

The introduction of tea in the 1600s had a sobering effect on the West. Before then, forced to choose between often tainted water and milk, or the safer ale and wine, many people drifted through life in a mild state of intoxication.

Tea – 'cups that cheer but not inebriate...' as the 19th-century temperance movement called it – is made from the dried leaf of the tree *Camellia sinensis*, a native of south-west China. The Chinese had been drinking *t'e* (which in English became 'tay', then 'tea') for more than 3000 years before it reached the West. When tea was first imported into Holland in 1610, customers scoffed at it as 'hay water'. It was not until the merchants decided to publicise it as a cure for all ills, from paralysis to gallstones, that sales picked up. By 1660 it had reached England, and the diarist Samuel Pepys recorded trying his first 'cup of tee (a China drink) of which I never had drank before'.

Spreading across Europe a few years after coffee, tea encountered stiff resistance from the opinion-forming classes, who had turned the new coffee-houses into centres of social and political influence. This, and the fact that in England 1 lb (450 g) of tea cost ten times an ordinary weekly wage, meant it was to be more than a century before the market for it became established.

DEMAND SOARS

It was a century during which national drinking preferences also became fixed. Tradition has it that the Swedes abandoned tea for coffee after Gustav III, who ruled from 1771 to 1792, carried out a test by reprieving twin brothers who were due to be executed on condition that one drank nothing but tea and the other nothing but coffee. The tea drinker died first, at the age of 83.

Britain soon became one of the greatest tea drinkers of the Western world. The East India Company had the monopoly in trade with Asia and good reason to promote a crop that would pay its shareholders' dividends. Ironically, the effectiveness of the company's campaign became most apparent when Parliament ended its monopoly in 1833. Prices dropped and demand soared.

Green tea from China being best drunk fresh, the competitive London market was ready to pay a premium on the first

Afternoon tea brings a genteel etiquette to a New England home in 1900. An advertisement (right) attempts to cultivate brand loyalty.

consignment of the new season's crop. An annual race soon developed between specially designed ships known as 'tea clippers'. So close-run were the contests that in 1866, 98 days and 16 000 miles (25 750 km) out from Foochow, the *Ariel* and *Taiping* were still neck and neck as they raced up the English Channel.

The Suez Canal helped to put an end to the China tea trade. Cutting the voyage time from India by more than half, the canal opened in 1869, just when tea planting in India was ripe for expansion. In 1851, production had been 22 000 lb (9980 kg), but by the 1880s most of the 160 million lb (72.5 million kg) imported annually to meet British demand was Indian – a tea that was strong, fermented and long-keeping.

Tea has had a profound influence not only on the economies of Britain, China, India, Sri Lanka (formerly Ceylon) and East Africa, but on the course of history. In the 18th century, American colonists came to resent British taxation of tea. On December 16, 1773, demonstrators emptied 342 tea chests from East India Company ships into Boston harbour. The 'Boston Tea Party' set in train the sequence of events leading to the American War of Independence. In Asia more than 60 years later, Western traders became frustrated by China's insistence on selling tea in exchange not for Western manufactures but for silver. The traders acquired the silver by smuggling Indian opium into China, and the First Opium War of 1839 to 1842 was the result. China lost and was forced to cede Hong Kong to Britain, and to open her ports to Western trade.

Tea has made its mark elsewhere. The 19th-century labouring classes in Britain abandoned the nourishing ale and brown bread for tea and white bread. Their physique deteriorated until, by 1901, the army had to turn down half of all volunteers for service in the Second Boer War because they were too unhealthy to fight. But at least they were sober.

John Logie Baird (left) supervises an early experiment in colour television during rehearsals at the BBC in London in 1943. But his system proved impracticable and was never adopted.

of Christianity that included aspects of traditional Maori belief. He escaped with several followers in 1868, captured a government ship and sailed back to New Zealand.

Te Kooti survived several skirmishes with the authorities, and in 1872 retreated to the area known as the 'King Country' in the centre of the North Island, where he devoted himself to spreading the new faith. As a result of his peaceful activities, Te Kooti was pardoned in 1883. The Ringatu Church, whose followers regard Te Kooti as a prophet and martyr, survives to the present day.

telegraphy Transmission of encoded information over a distance – from Greek words meaning 'far writing'. Fires and drums were used for thousands of years to send simple messages, and by 300 BC the Greeks used a method of spelling out words with rows of vases big enough to be seen from a distance. A more sophisticated form of such signalling was developed in France and England in the late 18th century. Known as semaphore, it used flags, lights or mechanical devices with movable arms, mounted on towers that could be viewed by telescope from another tower.

The first practical electric telegraph was patented in 1837 by the British scientists Sir William Cooke and Sir Charles WHEATSTONE. Their system employed five dials with moving needles and was widely used in Britain, particularly by the railways. In 1844 the American Samuel MORSE introduced his new electromagnetic telegraph, sending a message encoded as dots and dashes from Washington to Baltimore, about 50 miles (80 km) away. Morse's invention, first demonstrated seven years earlier, and the code it used revolutionised communications; by the end of the 19th century telegraph cables had been laid throughout most of Europe and North America, as well as across the Atlantic Ocean.

The invention of the wireless transmitter by Guglielmo MARCONI in the 1890s made long-distance communications possible between parties that could not be connected by cable,

such as ships. In 1901 colleagues in Cornwall, England, transmitted the first wireless message – in Morse code – to Marconi across the North Atlantic in Newfoundland, Canada. Although the telephone soon eclipsed the telegraph, the older system continued to develop, eventually resulting in devices such as the teletypewriter, telex and teletex.

Tel-el-Kebir, Battle of (September 12-13, 1882) Battle between British and Egyptian forces 52 miles (83 km) east of Cairo; also called al-Tal al-Kabir. British troops under Sir Garnet WOLSELEY defeated an army led by the Egyptian nationalist commander in chief Arabi Pasha. Cairo fell three days later, completing the British conquest of Egypt. Egypt did not recover its independence until 1936.

telephone Within a decade of the patenting of the telephone by Alexander Graham BELL in 1876, there were almost 200 000 units in use worldwide. At this time telephones were not powerful enough to be used over long distances, becoming unacceptably faint after only a few hundred miles. This problem was largely overcome by the installation of a series of repeaters, or amplifiers, which made transcontinental conversations possible. From the 1940s such long-distance transmissions relied on microwave, or high-frequency radio, links, rather than on cables. Since the 1960s, these microwaves have been transmitted between continents by way of orbiting satellites. On the ground, optical fibres transmitting digitised pulses of light have largely replaced electric cables.

The Menai Bridge, designed by Thomas Telford, has a main span 579 ft (176 m) long suspended from iron chains.

television The first true television, capable of transmitting a picture from one point to another, was developed in the 1920s by the British engineer John Logie BAIRD. His system was experimented with briefly by the British Broadcasting Corporation (BBC) when it began television transmissions in 1932, but was dropped in favour of a rival system developed by the company Marconi EMI. Three years later the BBC introduced the world's first regular high-definition television service, and in 1951 Columbia Broadcasting System (CBS) began colour transmissions in the USA. In 1962 the *Telstar* satellite made the first live link between the European and American networks, and seven years later a network of satellites made it possible for some 100 million viewers to watch a live broadcast of Neil Armstrong stepping on to the Moon.

Subsequent technological developments that have made television an increasingly successful entertainment medium include cable television (which can provide subscribers with more than 100 channels) and NICAM digital stereo sound. High-definition digital pictures are promised for the near future.

Telford, Thomas (1757-1834) Scottish engineer, renowned for his innovative roads, bridges and canals. The son of a shepherd, Telford worked as a stonemason while teaching himself architecture. In the 1790s he achieved instant fame by building two huge aqueducts for the Ellesmere canal in Wales. Telford went on to construct and improve a number of roads and bridges in Scotland, Wales and England, and he also rebuilt the docks at Aberdeen and Dundee. His crowning achievements were the design and construction of two suspension bridges, over the River Conwy and the Menai Strait, in Wales; the latter, completed in 1826, was on a scale never previously attempted and served as a spur to the future development of bridge-building.

Tell, William Legendary Swiss hero of the struggle against Austrian oppression. Tell was said to be a peasant in the canton of Uri, who defied the authority of an Austrian bailiff, and was then forced to shoot a crossbow bolt through an apple placed on top of his son's head. This he did, and later went on to kill the bailiff in an ambush. The legend of Tell is thought to be a garbled account of historical events that led to the formation of a defensive league between three Swiss cantons in 1291.

Teller, Edward (1908-) Hungarian-born physicist who played a major role in developing the hydrogen bomb. Teller emigrated to the USA in 1935 and took up a post at George Washington University. Six years later he joined the atomic bomb project under Robert OPPENHEIMER at Los Alamos, but became increasingly convinced that he should be working towards creating a far more powerful device than the fission bomb that Oppenheimer's team had in mind. After the atomic detonations over Japan in 1945, many scientists, including Oppenheimer, were reluctant to pursue atomic weapons research, while Teller felt compelled to develop a thermonuclear, or hydrogen-fusion, bomb. Teller's proposals were initially vetoed by Oppenheimer, but after the British atomic scientist Klaus Fuchs admitted to passing vital secrets to the Soviet Union, the US government gave Teller the go-ahead. As a result, the USA detonated the first hydrogen bomb on November 1, 1952, and Teller became known as 'the father of the H-bomb'. Over the next three decades he was a government adviser on nuclear-weapons policy, and in the early 1980s he strongly supported US president Ronald Reagan's idea of a Strategic Defense Initiative, otherwise known as 'Star Wars'.

> **DID YOU KNOW?**
>
> Edward Teller is said to have been the inspiration for the nuclear scientist Dr Strangelove, in Stanley Kubrick's film of that name.

temperance movements Campaigns to restrict the consumption of alcohol first appeared in New England, USA, where meetings were held to encourage people to 'take the pledge' to renounce alcohol. By 1833 some 6000 local temperance societies had been formed in the USA, and the movement had spread to Britain, Norway and Sweden. In 1851 the state of Maine became the first to pass laws prohibiting alcohol, and in 1869 a national PROHIBITION Party was formed. Together with the Women's Christian Temperance Union (founded in 1874) and the Anti-Saloon League (founded in 1895), the Prohibition Party campaigned for a total ban on alcohol across the USA. The movement received an unexpected boost from the need to conserve grain during the First World War, and the pressure led in 1917 to the 18th Amendment to the US constitution, banning the manufacture, sale and transport of alcohol in the USA. The law introducing the period of prohibition came into force in January 1920, but it proved unenforceable, and was repealed in 1933 by the 21st Amendment.

Temple, Sir William (1628-99) English diplomat and author. As English ambassador to The Hague, he negotiated the anti-French TRIPLE ALLIANCE of 1668 between England, Sweden and the United Provinces of the Netherlands. He also helped to arrange the marriage between William of Orange and Princess Mary, daughter of James II, in 1677. In 1679, at a time of anti-Catholic hysteria and political crisis between king and Parliament, Temple proposed that a 30-member council should replace the large and unwieldy Privy Council to transact the business of government, but the experiment was not a success. Temple refused political honours from William III, and devoted his retirement to writing books on history and politics and essays on literature and antiquity.

Temple, William (1881-1944) Anglican churchman and educationalist. Temple served as Archbishop of York from 1929 to 1942, and Archbishop of Canterbury from 1942 to 1944. He assisted in drawing up the 1944 Education Act, which established compulsory secondary education throughout the United Kingdom. His work in forging a greater common purpose between different Christian denominations led to the formation of the World Council of Churches in 1948.

Templer, Sir Gerald (1898-1979) British field-marshal. During the Second World War Templer commanded the 6th Armoured Division. After the war he served as vice-chief of the Imperial General Staff before becoming high commissioner and commander in chief in Malaya from 1952 to 1954, during the communist guerrilla insurgency known as the Malayan Emergency. Templer turned the tide of war decisively against the guerrillas through a combination of military efficiency, adaptability to local circumstance and the fostering of good relations with villagers.

Tennessee Valley Authority (TVA) Independent US federal government agency created in 1933 as part of President Franklin D. Roosevelt's NEW DEAL proposals to reduce unemployment through a programme of public works. The TVA set out to develop the whole Tennessee river basin, which extends over large areas in seven states. The agency was authorised to construct dams to control floods and generate cheap hydroelectric power, to check erosion, to plant forests and to establish recreational facilities. Its dams now form an integrated flood-control system on the Ohio, Tennessee and Mississippi rivers, and its many power plants are a major source of energy for the region. The TVA remains the only agency of its kind, largely as a result of opposition to the formation of similar agencies by state and federal departments fearful of the loss of some of their authority and functions.

Tennis Court Oath (June 20, 1789) Act of defiance by representatives of the Third Estate, or commons, at the beginning of the FRENCH REVOLUTION. In 1788, Louis XVI was forced to summon the STATES-GENERAL, an assembly composed of the three 'estates': nobility, clergy and commons. The States-General had not met since 1614, and it was soon overwhelmed by grievances and demands for large-scale reform. Representatives of the Third Estate feared that moves were afoot to ensure that they would be constantly outvoted, and countered this threat by declaring a National Assembly on June 17, 1789. Three days later they found their usual meeting place at Versailles locked, and concluded that the king was trying to force them to disband. They then adjourned to a nearby indoor tennis court, where they swore never to separate until France had a written constitution. On June 27 Louis capitulated, ordering the clergy and the nobility to join with the Third Estate in the National Assembly.

Teresa of Ávila, St (1515-82) Spanish nun and mystic who undertook a major reform of the CARMELITE religious order. Teresa entered a Carmelite convent at Ávila in about 1535, and 20 years later she underwent a profound religious experience. This convinced her of the need to return to the strict observance of the austere Carmelite rule, which had been

In Giovanni Bernini's portrayal of the mystical ecstasy of St Teresa of Ávila, the saint's heart is about to be pierced by the arrow of God's love.

somewhat relaxed during the 14th and 15th centuries. In the face of strong opposition, but with the blessing of Pope Pius IV, she opened the first reformed convent in 1562, and from 1567 she worked tirelessly with another great mystic, St John of the Cross, in spreading the work of Carmelite reform among both nuns and friars. St Teresa received strong support from Philip II of Spain, and her ideals led to a resurgence of religious fervour in Spain and much of the rest of Europe, being a major force behind the COUNTER-REFORMATION. She was canonised in 1622, and her writings – notably *The Way of Perfection, The Interior Castle* and *Life of the Mother Teresa of Jesus* – have come to be regarded as classics of mystical literature.

Terror, Reign of (September 1793-July 1794) Period of the FRENCH REVOLUTION which began when the revolutionary government, known as the Convention, having executed Louis XVI, set about attacking opponents and anyone else considered to be a threat to the regime. A Revolutionary Tribunal was set up in March 1793 to bring 'enemies of the state' to trial, and in April the COMMITTEE OF PUBLIC SAFETY was created to preserve the reforms of the Revolution.

Following the defeat of the moderate GIRONDIN faction in the Convention in May, the Committee began to exercise virtual dictatorial control. Under its guidance, in September, the Convention proclaimed a 'Terror' against the enemies of the Revolution; it also passed the Law of Suspects, setting out in the broadest possible terms who such enemies might be. In the months that followed at least 200 000 citizens were arrested, of whom 10 000 are thought to have died in prison and some 12 000 on the guillotine.

By June 1794 Maximilien ROBESPIERRE emerged as the most prominent member of the Committee, having eliminated his two most influential rivals – the radical republican Jacques Hébert and the moderate Georges DANTON. By now, however, the Terror was seen as oppressive even by revolutionaries and those who had demanded the measures, and Robespierre had become feared. His enemies joined forces, and he was arrested and executed in July 1794. Robespierre's death ended the Terror, though it was briefly followed by the so-called White Terror, in which many former agents of the Terror were executed.

terrorism The use or threat of violence for political purposes have been practised throughout history, although the term derives specifically from the period known as the Reign of TERROR during the French Revolution. Since the 19th century, terrorism has come to refer to actions such as bombing, kidnapping, hijacking, and assassination carried out by groups of political dissenters, often called guerrillas or freedom fighters by their

Smoke billows from three passenger aircraft blown up in the Jordanian desert in September 1970 after being hijacked by a Palestinian terrorist group. Passengers held as hostages were later freed.

sympathisers. Such groups include the anarchists and nihilists who fought against the tsarist government of Russia during the 19th and early 20th centuries, and numerous organisations guilty of more recent outrages, such as Germany's BAADER-MEINHOF gang, Italy's RED BRIGADES, Peru's Shining Path, the IRISH REPUBLICAN ARMY, and a multitude of Middle-Eastern groups, among them IRGUN, Hamas and BLACK SEPTEMBER.

Occasionally a lone activist with a personal political agenda will wage a one-person terror campaign. Whatever their motivation, terrorists attempt to achieve their goals by producing fear among their opponents and the public at large, often by the use of indiscriminate violence.

Tertullian, Quintus (c.160-c.230) Early Christian theologian whose prolific writings contributed to the developing terminology and doctrine of the Western Church. Tertullian was born in Carthage, and practised as a lawyer in Rome before converting to Christianity in about 193. He then devoted himself to writing on theological matters, using a forceful and imaginative literary style which was widely copied. In about 207, Tertullian broke away from mainstream Christianity, which he considered too lax, and joined the austere Montanists, who preached the need for strong moral discipline. Within a few years, however, Tertullian had founded his sect of even more severe Tertullianists, which existed in North Africa until the 5th century.

Tesla, Nikola (1856-1943) Croatian-born US electrical engineer who discovered the principle behind alternating-current (AC), dynamos and motors. After emigrating to the

USA in 1884, Tesla worked briefly with Thomas EDISON on direct-current (DC) electric generators, but in 1885 he sold patent rights to his own AC system to the Westinghouse Electric company. This provoked a struggle between the DC and AC systems for recognition as the industry standard – a contest won by AC. Tesla went on to found his own laboratory, where in 1891 he invented the Tesla coil, which is still widely used in radio and television sets. Among his many research interests, Tesla worked on wireless electric power transmission, remote control and wireless communications systems.

Test Acts Laws passed in post-Reformation Scotland, England and Ireland to bar anyone who was not a member of the established Church from holding public office. The first such Act was passed in Scotland in 1567, at a time when England had a range of harsh laws that effectively deterred any possible RECUSANT from seeking office. After the restoration of Charles II in 1660, there were widespread fears that Roman Catholicism might return as the national religion – fears fostered by Charles's alliance with France and his Declaration of Indulgence (1672), suspending England's punitive laws against Roman Catholics. Legislation passed in 1661 had required all members of town corporations to receive Holy Communion according to the rites of the English Anglican Church – a requirement extended to all holders of civil and military office by the Test Act of 1673. A further Act of 1678 barred all Roman Catholics, except the future James II, from Parliament. England's Test Acts were formally repealed in the 1860s and 1870s; Scotland's in 1889.

The Grand Master of the Teutonic Knights, Hermann von Salza, pays homage to the Holy Roman Emperor Frederick II in 1226.

Teutonic Knights

Religious and military order of German knights, founded in 1190 at Acre during the Third Crusade. The order was made up of noblemen who took the monastic vows of poverty, chastity and obedience, and it initially flourished in Syria and Palestine. In the early 13th century the Teutonic Knights moved to eastern Europe, where they waged a crusade against the pagan Prussians, and carved out an independent territory for themselves in the process.

In 1237, the Teutonic Knights merged with the similar order of Livonian Knights, which had acquired territories around the Baltic. Together, they were frequently at war with Poland, and in 1410 they were decisively defeated by the Poles and Lithuanians at Tannenberg. The two orders separated in 1525, when the grand master of the Teutonic Knights, Albert of Brandenburg, accepted the Reformation and was invested as duke of a secular Prussia. The Teutonic Knights soon declined, though the order survives in Austria, where it is dedicated to health care and Catholic pastoral work.

Tewkesbury, Battle of

(May 4, 1471) Battle in the English Wars of the ROSES, in which the Yorkists under EDWARD IV decisively defeated the Lancastrians, led by Margaret of Anjou, wife of the deposed king HENRY VI. Margaret had been seeking Lancastrian support in Wales when her army was intercepted by Edward near Tewkesbury in Gloucestershire. In the rout that ensued, several Lancastrian leaders were killed, including Margaret's son, Prince Edward. Margaret was captured and ransomed back to France. Henry VI died, or was probably murdered, in the Tower of London less than three weeks later, leaving the throne securely in Edward's hands.

Texas, Republic of

(1836-45) Short-lived independent republic in the south-western USA. In 1821 the government of Mexico gave permission for Stephen Austin to enter Texas with a number of US settlers. A decade later the Mexicans attempted to stem what had become a steady influx of Americans, but in 1835 the Texans rebelled and on March 2, 1836, they declared their independence from Mexico. A huge Mexican army, under the dictator and general Antonio de Santa Anna, invaded Texas and achieved several victories – the best known being the defeat of a tiny force at the ALAMO, which soon became a byword for Texan heroism. On April 21, Santa Anna was himself defeated by the Texan commander Samuel Houston, who became president of the now secure Republic of Texas. Some nine years later, in July 1845, Texas joined the USA – an event which helped to precipitate the Mexican-American war of 1846-8.

textiles

The earliest textile fibres were coarse materials such as grasses, reeds and rushes. They were used in prehistoric times to make screens, basket-work, fishing nets and ropes. Later, techniques for using finer natural materials such as flax, jute and animal hair were developed. Surviving examples of linen from

Wool was used to produce this Peruvian burial cloth, below, at least 2500 years ago, and cotton for this 9th century European priest's vestment.

ancient Egypt date back more than 7000 years. From the 3rd millennium BC other fibres were developed, notably cotton in India and silk in China. Wool was probably in use earlier than this in the Near East. These textiles all became important trade items for the countries producing them.

John Kay's flying shuttle, invented in 1733, and Sir Richard Arkwright and Samuel Crompton's spinners mechanised cotton production and helped to stimulate Britain's Industrial Revolution. Since the end of the 19th century, artificial fibres have become widely used, among the best known being rayon, nylon, Terylene and Lycra.

Thailand

South-east Asian country, which was known until 1939 as Siam. The Thai people originate mainly from the southern Chinese province of Yunnan. They migrated into Siam in large numbers when their homeland was devastated by Mongols in the 13th century. In about 1238, the first Thai state was founded at the town of Sukhothai, and was succeeded in about 1350 by the kingdom of Ayutthaya. During the 16th century, relations with neighbouring Burma (Myanmar) soured, and in 1569 the Burmese occupied Siam, ruling the country for 15 years.

The arrival of Portuguese traders in 1511 marked the beginning of Siam's relations with the West. The British, Dutch and French followed during the 17th century, but a French bid for dominance in the country in 1688 provoked a reaction which closed Siam to most foreigners for more than 100 years. In 1767 the Burmese again invaded Siam, but they were driven out within a decade.

Shortly after the present Chakkri dynasty of kings came to power in 1782, the capital was moved to Bangkok. In the 19th century Siam's rulers succeeded in maintaining Thai independence, despite the imperial aspirations of Britain and France. The country was modernised in the early 20th century, but remained an absolute monarchy until a bloodless coup in 1932 established a constitutional monarchy with an elected system of government. The first general elections were held in 1934, and in 1939 Siam's first premier, Pibul Songgram, renamed the country Thailand.

During the Second World War, Thailand sided with Japan, but it has subsequently become a strong ally of the USA, largely as a result of the strong anticommunist stance of its military rulers. Since the end of the war, Thailand has been highly politically unstable, with numerous military coups and several periods of martial law. In spite of this, the country has one of the most vigorous economies in South-east Asia.

thane Anglo-Saxon nobleman, also known as thegn, who held land from a lord in return for service, usually of a military nature. The earliest thanes owed their allegiance directly to the Crown, but by the 10th century there was a complex hierarchy of thanes, ranging from king's thanes to bishop's thanes, and even thane's thanes. The most important of these were the king's thanes, who were required to attend the WITAN, or king's council, and to perform administrative duties of state. They answered to no one but the king. Certain thanes possessed their status by hereditary right, while others were given the rank by promotion. The title disappeared after the Norman conquest of England in 1066.

Thatcher, Margaret (1925-) British prime minister from 1979 to 1990, the first woman to hold that office and the longest serving British premier of the 20th century. Born in Grantham, Lincolnshire, where her father was mayor, she studied chemistry at Oxford University and worked as a research chemist before becoming a barrister in 1954. Elected a Conservative MP in 1959, Thatcher served under Edward HEATH as education minister from 1970 to 1974. In 1975 she successfully challenged Heath for the party leadership; she then led the Conservatives to victory in the general election of 1979.

Proud of her middle-class, small-town background, Thatcher believed in the virtues of freedom, hard work, thrift and personal responsibility, and heartily disliked socialism. As prime minister, she promoted lower taxes, a free-enterprise economy, tight monetary policies to control inflation, reduced government spending, privatisation of nationalised industries and restrictions on trade unions. The strict monetary policy and reduction of government subsidies to industry led to many bankruptcies and brought unemployment to levels not seen since the 1930s. Thatcher's popularity declined markedly, but revived equally promptly after Britain's victory in the FALKLANDS WAR of 1982. As a result, she was

About 3400 years ago these sphinxes formed part of a row lining the road which linked the temple at Luxor in the ancient Egyptian city of Thebes to the vast temple complex at Karnak.

again able to secure a landslide victory for the Conservatives in the 1983 general election. From 1984 to 1985 Thatcher successfully resisted a prolonged strike by the National Union of Mineworkers over her decision to shut down uneconomic collieries. The confrontation came to be seen as a decisive test of union power, and the government's ability to resist it. In October 1984, Thatcher narrowly escaped being killed by an IRA bomb planted in her hotel at the Conservative Party Conference in Brighton.

Following a third general election victory for the Conservatives in 1987, Thatcher introduced free-market reforms to the education system and the National Health Service. These met strong opposition, while the introduction of the community charge, known as the poll tax, provoked widespread protest and riots in March 1990. By then, divisions were appearing in the Conservative Party, especially in relation to monetary and political union with the European Community. In November 1990, Thatcher was challenged as party leader, and resigned after an inconclusive first ballot.

Firmly committed to the Western Alliance, Thatcher had close ties with US presidents Ronald Reagan and

Margaret Thatcher, at her constituency of Finchley, north London, celebrates her third general election win in 1987.

George Bush. She was the first Western leader to give public backing to the reforming Soviet leader Mikhail Gorbachev, and stoutly defended the interests of Britain within the European Community. At home, her government ended the moderate political consensus which had dominated British politics since the end of the Second World War, and exposed every area of British society to the rigours and uncertainties of the free-market economy.

Theatre see feature, pages 646-7

Thebes A capital city of ancient Egypt, and one of the great cities of antiquity, situated in and around modern Luxor, some 420 miles (675 km) south of Cairo. The main city area was located on the east bank of the Nile, and included the temple of Luxor, built by Amenhotep III, who reigned from around 1411 to 1372 BC. North of Luxor lies the massive temple complex of Karnak, which was dedicated to Amon, the supreme deity of the ancient Egyptians. On the west bank of the Nile there are a number of magnificent mortuary temples built for the worship of pharaohs after their deaths. Behind these lie the secret burial grounds of the pharaohs and other nobles in the Valley of the Kings and the Valley of the Queens.

Themistocles (c.525-c.460 BC) Athenian statesman and naval commander who crushed the Persians at the Battle of SALAMIS in 480 BC. After the Greek victory over the Persians at the Battle of Marathon in 490, most Greek leaders ignored the Persian threat. Themistocles said that Athens should

Inside the Globe Theatre at a Shakespearean premiere

Join the audience in the wooden theatre beside the river Thames for all the excitement of Hamlet, a new play by William Shakespeare, with the famous author himself playing the ghost.

A new play by Will Shakespeare was always sure of a packed house, especially when the playwright himself was to appear. Queues started forming at the Globe Theatre for *Hamlet, Prince of Denmark*, with Shakespeare as the ghost, as soon as the flag went up on the turret of the theatre on that morning in June, 1601, to announce the performance. It would start at two in the afternoon, 'the idlest time of the day', wrote Thomas Nashe; or, as Sir Thomas Overbury said, 'betweene meals, the most unfit time either for study or bodily exercise'. Besides, winter and summer, plays at the Globe had to be performed under the open sky.

Public theatres were relatively new: James Burbage had built the first in London in 1576, basing its design on the inn yards in which plays had previously been performed. At a time when there was little other entertainment people flocked to them, even if the City of London authorities disapproved. The actors were said to attract undesirables, to encourage the poor to waste their money, and to corrupt young people with shameless posturings. An Act of Parliament in 1572 had classified freelance strolling players as 'Rogues, Vagabonds and Sturdy Beggars', but many wealthy aristocrats, like the Earl of Leicester, who 'loved a play and players', formed their own companies of actors and provided them with protection and patronage. By the time of the first night of Shakespeare's *Hamlet* at the Globe, London's most successful commercial theatre, actors were almost respectable.

IN WITH THE GROUNDLINGS

The audience had to queue for a popular play, because although the Globe could accommodate 2000 people they all had to go through the same single-file entrances and drop a penny in a box. Some then paid as much as sixpence for a cushioned seat in one of the three high tiered galleries that looked down upon the central canopied stage. Even if a penny was all you could afford and you had to take your own stool as one of the 'groundlings', crowding into the open space that surrounded the stage on three sides, you still had a good view. And you were as entitled to clap or boo as much as the aristocrats, who sometimes paid 12 times as much for a box.

The theatre, wrote the playwright Thomas Dekker, 'was so free in entertainment, allowing a stool as well to the farmer's son as to your Templar, that your stinkard has the selfsame liberty to be there in his tobacco fumes, which your sweet courtier hath; and sit to give judgment on the play's life and death, as well as the proudest carper among the tribe of Critic'.

The Globe was set amid the bustle of Bankside, south of the Thames in Southwark, full of taverns and bear pits and pleasure gardens. Above the tumult of carts and coaches, shouting tradesmen, church bells ringing and boatmen calling on the busy river, you might just hear the three blasts of a trumpet from the theatre's high turret signalling that the performance was due to begin.

Not that you might be there just for the play. A writer called Stephen Gosson observed: 'In our assemblies at plays in London you shall see such heaving and shoving, such itching and shouldering to sit by women; such care for their garments that they be not trod on, such eyes to their laps, that no chips light in them; such pillows to their backs, that they take no hurt; such masking in their ears, I know not what, such giving them pippins to pass the time...such tickling, such toying, such smiling, such winking and such manning them home when the sports are ended, that it is a right comedy to mark their behaviour – every wanton and his paramour, every man and his mistress, every John and his Joan, every knave and his queen, are there first acquainted.'

There was plenty of food and drink, of course, and much cracking of nuts in the audience. Certainly many people smoked, although it was less than 40 years since Sir Walter Raleigh had brought tobacco back from the New World. But in the end the play was the thing. Once inside that shadowy, noisy pit, despite the crush and the wealthy layabouts who tried to sit on the edge of the stage and obstruct your view, despite the lack of scenery – only a black curtain at the back of the stage showed that this was to be a tragedy – despite all that, you knew that these rogues and vagabonds could transport you from

It is shortly after 2pm and the play has begun. The king's ghost, played by Shakespeare, takes form in front of Hamlet, who is attended by Horatio and Marcellus.

A fire in the thatched roof destroyed the Globe in 1613

your world of poverty and plague into one of magical make-believe. There might not have been scenery, but the costumes were magnificent. So were the special effects. The stage at the Globe was typical in being thrust out into the centre, about waist-high, with room underneath for all manner of things to arise from trapdoors: above it, supported on two pillars, was a wooden canopy bearing the 'hut', which concealed ropes, pulleys and other devices required for the play. It was a cannon, fired on stage during a performance of Shakespeare's *Henry VIII*, which caused the Globe to be burned down in 1613. A lump of wadding ignited the thatched roof. The only casualty was a man whose breeches caught fire: he doused the flames with a bottle of beer.

Plays were not considered serious literature, and were certainly not historically authentic in costume or direction. Sir Philip Sidney, writing in 1580, said 'Now you shall have three ladies walk to gather flowers, and then

we must believe the stage to be a garden. By and by we hear news of shipwrecks in the same place, and then we are to blame if we accept it not for a rock. Upon the back of that comes out a hideous monster, with fire and smoke, and then the miserable beholders are bound to take it for a cave...'

SEX AND VIOLENCE

But Shakespeare knew what his public wanted: adventure, comedy, romance, a touch of pathos and a lot of sex and violence. Not only was he resident dramatist with the most celebrated theatrical company of the time, the Lord Chamberlain's Men, whose permanent home was the Globe, but one of the seven 'Actor-Sharers' who owned the theatre and profited from its success.

He sold his plays to the company, not to the public: unlike poetry and prose, plays were not published. A dramatist would sell a play to an actors' company for a fee. It then became the property of the company

and, if successful, was jealously guarded by 'the Book-keeper'. Only a few written copies were made by a scrivener, one of which went to the Court for official licence to perform it. Texts of their individual parts were copied for the actors. Although two printed copies of *Hamlet* were in circulation in 1603 and 1604, they were probably pirated; the full texts of all Shakespeare's 36 plays (save *Pericles*) were not printed until after his death, when two of his surviving colleagues at the Globe published them in 1623 in what is known as the First Folio.

Shakespeare's portion of the Globe's profits enabled him to buy New Place, one of the finest houses in Stratford-upon-Avon. He had retired there when his beloved 'Wooden O' burned down. He was still a regular visitor to his old friends in London and the accident must have been more than a financial blow to him. He died three years later in 1616, when he was still only 52. A reconstructed Globe Theatre officially opens near the original site in June 1997.

The stage was raised and projected well into the auditorium

A canopy contained stage machinery and also protected actors from rain and sunshine

Wealthier members of the audience watched the play from boxes

The 'groundlings' filled the central space, eating and sometimes jeering the players

The Athenian naval strategist Themistocles argued for a strong navy to face the threat of a Persian sea invasion, which came in 480 BC.

greatly increase the size of its navy, so it would be able to meet any new Persian invasion at sea.

In 483 he succeeded in obtaining funds for his programme, with the result that a greatly strengthened Athenian navy sailed to confront the Persians when they did arrive in 480. After an indecisive battle, Themistocles managed to lure the Persians into the narrow straits at Salamis, where they were ambushed and convincingly defeated. After the battle, Themistocles was fêted by Sparta, but became increasingly unpopular in Athens. He was banished in 472, and later accused of treason. Escaping to Persia, he was accepted into the service of King Ataxerxes I.

Theodora (c.500-548) Byzantine empress, wife of JUSTINIAN I and probably the most powerful woman in Byzantine history. She is said to have been an actress and a prostitute before marrying Justinian in 525. From 527, when Justinian inherited the throne, Theodora exercised considerable influence over the Byzantine Empire. Although she was never officially appointed co-ruler, her intelligence and political wisdom led Justinian to grant her remarkable freedom in conducting affairs of state. Among Theodora's finest achievements were laws aimed at improving the rights of women – among them a prohibition on the trade in young girls and reform of the divorce laws.

Theodoric I (d.AD 451) First king of the VISIGOTHS. Theodoric became ruler soon after the Visigoths settled in the Aquitaine region of France in 418. His attempts to expand his territory brought him into conflict with Rome, and in 439 he was defeated at Toulouse by the Roman general Flavius Aetius. In 451, however, Theodoric joined forces with Aetius to combat their common enemy, ATTILA. The combined Roman-Visigoth forces defeated Attila at the Battle of the Catalaunian Fields, but Theodoric was killed in the conflict.

Theodoric the Great (c.455-526) King of the Ostrogoths, who became king of Italy in 493. Theodoric spent much of his boyhood in the Eastern Roman capital of Constantinople as a hostage and a pledge for the good behaviour of his people, who had recently

been allowed to settle in Roman territory. In 471 he succeeded his father as king of the Ostrogoths, and in 488 he was asked by the Eastern Roman emperor Zeno to invade Italy and to oust the German chieftain Odoacer, who had deposed the legitimate Western emperor 20 years earlier.

In 493 Theodoric completed his conquest of Italy, and proceeded to rule as king. He carried out a sytem of public works repairing buildings and roads and enlarging harbours. His reign, which saw the beginning of a synthesis of Roman and Germanic cultures, was largely benign, though it was marred by the execution of the philosopher BOETHIUS on dubious suspicion of treason in 525.

Theodosius I 'the Great' (c.349-95) Roman emperor who ruled the eastern half of the empire from 379 to 395, and both the eastern and western halves from 394 until his death. After serving as a provincial military governor under Emperor Gratian, Theodosius was appointed co-ruler – emperor of the Eastern Empire – in 379. He made peace with the Visigoths and the Ostrogoths, who were threatening the stability of the Eastern Empire, and then used them to bolster his armies. After Gratian was murdered in 383, Theodosius defeated a series of usurpers in the West, eventually taking control there in 394. He appointed his sons Arcadius and Honorius as co-rulers in the East and West respectively, with the result that the empire remained divided after his death. Theodosius is remembered for his religious orthodoxy, which drove him to crush the doctrine of ARIANISM.

Thermopylae Narrow, strategic pass in east-central Greece, about 85 miles (137 km) north-east of Athens. The pass was the site of three notable battles in antiquity. The first and most celebrated took place in 480 BC between the Spartan king LEONIDAS and a numerically superior army of Persians. When Leonidas realised that he was about to be outflanked, through treachery, he ordered most of his men to retreat, while he stayed behind with a small contingent to delay the Persians. The Greeks were all killed, but Leonidas' heroic stand cost the Persians dearly.

In 279 BC, the Greeks held back an invading army of Gauls at Thermopylae for several months before again being outflanked; and in 191 BC the Romans defeated the SELEUCID forces of Antiochus III at the pass.

Thiers, Adolphe (1797-1877) French republican statesman, writer, founder and first president of France's Third Republic. After studying law, Thiers became a journalist in Paris, where he wrote a ten-volume history of the French Revolution. In 1830 he helped to found *Le National*, a liberal daily which stirred up opposition to the reactionary king, CHARLES X. Following the July Revolution which overthrew Charles and brought LOUIS-PHILIPPE to the French throne, Thiers held a variety of ministerial posts. He was banished in 1851, when NAPOLEON III took power, but was permitted to return two years later. From 1863 Thiers led the parliamentary opposition to Napoleon III, and after France's disastrous defeat in the FRANCO-PRUSSIAN WAR of 1870-71 he was chosen to head the new provisional

King Leonidas of Sparta prepares to fight to the death to hold back a massive invading Persian army in the pass of Thermopylae, in a painting of 1814 by the French artist Jacques-Louis David.

government. In 1871 Thiers negotiated peace with the Prussians, crushed the uprising of the radical COMMUNE OF PARIS, and became president of the Third Republic. His efficient economic management led to early repayment of war reparations to Prussia, and the evacuation of German troops from France in 1873. In spite of these achievements, Thiers' conservative republicanism alienated the monarchist majority in the National Assembly, and in 1873 he was forced to resign.

Third Reich (1933-45) Period of NAZI rule in Germany, following the end of the WEIMAR REPUBLIC. The Reich, or 'empire', was said to be third in succession to the medieval Holy Roman Empire and the German Empire of 1871-1918. Adolf HITLER promised that the Reich would last a thousand years, but it ended with Germany's ignominious defeat in the SECOND WORLD WAR.

After Hitler was appointed chancellor of Germany in January 1933, he used the fire which damaged the parliament building – the REICHSTAG – as a pretext to seize dictatorial power. Germany became a national rather than a federal state; all political parties other than the National Socialists were outlawed; and opponents of Hitler within the party were eliminated during the NIGHT OF THE LONG KNIVES. In addition, the Nuremberg Laws of 1935 deprived Jews of German citizenship and placed restrictions on whom they could marry and where they could work. Many Jews and other opponents of the regime were sent to CONCENTRATION CAMPS, while a propaganda machine, masterminded by Joseph GOEBBELS, assured Germans of their innate superiority over other nations and races.

In March 1936 Hitler dismayed the nations of Europe by remilitarising the Rhineland in violation of the Treaties of LOCARNO. His subsequent annexation of Austria and the SUDETENLAND in Czechoslovakia deepened the crisis, and his invasion of Poland on September 1, 1939, precipitated the Second World War. In its early years the war brought rapid gains for Germany, so that by the end of 1941 the Third Reich controlled territory from the Arctic Circle to the Sahara, and from the English Channel to the outskirts of Moscow. By then, however, German forces were severely overstretched, and when the United States entered the war in December 1941 the turning point was not far off. In 1942 the Allies won victories in North Africa and began a bombing campaign against German cities and factories. By mid1943 German armies were on the defensive, and by May 1945 Hitler's Third Reich lay in ruins.

Thirteen Colonies, the Name given to the 13 colonies of British North America which in 1776 ratified the DECLARATION OF INDEPENDENCE to form the USA. They were

The combined armies of Ferdinand II and his allies crush the forces of the rebellious Bohemian nobles in 1620 at the Battle of White Mountain, near Prague, during the Thirty Years' War.

Connecticut, Delaware, Georgia, Maryland, Massachusetts, New Hampshire, New Jersey, New York, North Carolina, Pennsylvania, Rhode Island, South Carolina and Virginia.

Thirty-Nine Articles Statement of belief of the Church of England, as drawn up in 1563 on the basis of the Forty-Two Articles largely composed by Thomas CRANMER and issued in 1553. The Articles are not a creed as such, and many are open to a range of interpretations. They do, however, set out to define the position of the Church of England in relation to the Roman Catholics and Anabaptists. By an Act of Parliament of 1571, Church of England clergy were required to accept the Articles; they now need only promise to accept them as an inspiration and guide.

Thirty Years' War (1618-48) Name given to a series of wars, fought mainly in Germany, in which Protestant-Catholic rivalries and German constitutional disputes gradually developed into a major European conflict.

The wars began in 1618, when Protestant noblemen in Bohemia rebelled against the Roman Catholic Habsburg king and future Holy Roman Emperor, FERDINAND II. They deposed Ferdinand and offered the Bohemian throne to the Protestant Frederick V, Elector of the Palatinate. Aided by several Catholic rulers, Ferdinand crushed the rebellion in Bohemia in 1620, before going on to conquer the Palatinate in 1623.

A new phase began two years later, when Christian IV of Denmark, aided by England and the United Provinces of the Netherlands, invaded northern Germany. His avowed aim was to protect Protestant interests against

Habsburg domination, but he clearly hoped to enlarge Danish territory as well. After suffering a series of defeats, the Danes withdrew from the conflict in 1629 after negotiating the Treaty of Lübeck. The following year, however, the Swedish king, GUSTAV II, entered the fray, fearful that the Habsburgs might threaten Swedish domination of the Baltic. The Swedes joined forces with the Protestant Saxons to win a number of battles, including that at Lützen (1632), in which Gustav himself was killed. By 1635 the northern Germans had negotiated the Treaty of Prague. This united Protestants and Roman Catholics in the common aim of driving the Swedes and other foreigners off German soil.

At this point France, under the guidance of Cardinal RICHELIEU, formed an alliance with Sweden and the United Provinces in a final attempt to limit Habsburg power. Fighting spread through most of Europe, including the Low Countries, Italy, France, Spain, the Baltic and Germany. This stage of the war was generally disastrous for the Holy Roman Empire, which suffered numerous major defeats. Peace negotiations began in 1640, but the issues had become so complicated that progress was painfully slow. In 1648 peace terms were finally secured by the Treaty of WESTPHALIA, although a Franco-Spanish war continued in the Pyrenees until 1659.

At the end of the Thirty Years' War the balance of power in Europe had been radically altered: Spain had lost the Netherlands, France had become the dominant power in Western Europe, and the Holy Roman Empire existed in little more than name. Germany was devastated; its industry, commerce and agriculture lay in ruins.

Thrace Area in the Balkans corresponding roughly to north-eastern Greece, European Turkey and southern Bulgaria. In the ancient world, Thrace was renowned for its soldiers, who were often recruited as mercenaries. By the 7th century BC the Greeks had set up a number of colonies along the Thracian coast, among them Byzantium. Between about 516 and 479 BC much of Thrace was conquered by Persia; it was then briefly independent, before being assimilated into Macedonia by PHILIP II – a process completed by 342 BC. During the 2nd century BC the region fell gradually to the Romans, who divided it among several of their provinces. In AD 46, the emperor Claudius I created a new Roman province of Thrace, much smaller than the area known by that name to the Greeks.

After the 3rd century AD, Thrace was repeatedly invaded by Gothic and Slavic peoples, and by the 7th century a large part of it had been incorporated into the emerging Bulgarian state. The whole region then fell to the OTTOMAN Empire in 1453. From 1878, Thrace was at the heart of numerous territorial disputes in the Balkans as the Ottoman Empire began to fall apart. The region was finally divided between Bulgaria, Greece and Turkey by the Treaty of Lausanne in 1923.

Three Emperors' League (1872-5, 1881-7) Alliance between the emperors of Germany, Austria-Hungary and Russia. It was set up largely by the German chancellor Otto von BISMARCK with the aim of keeping the peace between Austria-Hungary and Russia in the Balkans; a further aim of the alliance was to isolate France, Germany's defeated enemy in the FRANCO-PRUSSIAN war of 1870-1. The League was shaken by the Russo-Turkish war of 1877-8, but it was secretly renewed in 1881. Further tension in the Balkans ended the alliance in 1887. It was replaced by a Reinsurance Treaty between Germany and Russia, which lasted until 1890.

Three Henrys, War of the (March 1585-August 1589) Name given to the eighth and last of the FRENCH WARS OF RELIGION. It was provoked by the efforts of the Roman Catholic Duke Henry of GUISE to exclude the Huguenot King Henry of Navarre from succeeding Henry III as king of France. In 1585 Henry of Guise, supported by the Catholic Holy League, confronted Henry III and forced him to renounce Henry of Navarre as his successor. Henry of Navarre promptly took up arms against the Holy League, which was nominally headed by the king but actually dominated by Guise. By 1588, the League had emerged triumphant, enabling Guise to force further concessions from Henry III. Unable to endure this humiliation, the king had both Guise and his brother, the scheming Cardinal de Guise, murdered later that year. In 1589

Henry III joined forces with Navarre and had all but defeated the League when he was himself struck down by an assassin. As he lay dying, the king renamed Henry of Navarre as his heir, urging him to convert to Roman Catholicism. This he did in 1593, allegedly saying, 'Paris vaut bien une messe', 'Paris is well worth a Mass'.

Three Kingdoms (AD 220-80) Bloody period in Chinese history, characterised by constant warfare between the three kingdoms that emerged after the collapse of the HAN dynasty: the Wei in the north, the Wu in the south-east, and the Shu Han in the south-west. During this time China also suffered invasions from the Huns living in Mongolia. In 265 the throne of Wei was seized by the general Sima Yen, who proceeded to conquer both the Wu and the Shu Han. From 280, China was united under the Western Jin dynasty founded by Sima Yen, but it again fell apart after his death in 290.

Throckmorton Plot (1583) International Catholic conspiracy to replace ELIZABETH I of England with MARY, QUEEN OF SCOTS. The plot is named after Francis Throckmorton (1554-84), a devout English Roman Catholic, who was its chief agent in England. The conspiracy intended that Henry of GUISE would invade England with a French Catholic force and free Mary from prison; English Catholics would then depose Elizabeth in favour of Mary, who would restore papal authority. In late 1583, agents of Elizabeth's principal secretary, Sir Francis WALSINGHAM, uncovered the plans. Throckmorton confessed under torture and was executed.

Thucydides (c.460-c.400 BC) Ancient Greek historian, whose *History of the Peloponnesian War* is regarded as the first attempt to record historical events in a scholarly manner. In 424 BC, seven years after the outbreak of the PELOPONNESIAN WAR between Sparta and Athens, Thucydides received an important command as an Athenian general. He failed, however, to prevent the city of Amphipolis from falling to the Spartans and was therefore exiled from Athens. He devoted the next 20 years to writing an account of the conflict, more or less as it unfolded, and making every effort to verify his sources, even when they claimed to be eyewitnesses.

thug Member of a Hindu sect dedicated to Kali, the goddess of destruction. From about the 13th century, bands of thugs roamed central India, murdering and robbing travellers. Their practices included strangling their victims with a scarf, and then burying them, after consecrating a ritual pickaxe – the entire ceremony being known as 'thugee'. The thugs

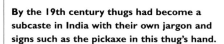

By the 19th century thugs had become a subcaste in India with their own jargon and signs such as the pickaxe in this thug's hand.

were protected by a strict code of secrecy and their own arcane language. During the 1830s, William BENTINCK, the British governor-general of India, successfully eliminated the sect by means of mass arrests and executions.

Thutmose I Pharaoh of Egypt from about 1525 to 1512 BC. Thutmose made extensive improvements to the temple of Amun at KARNAK and was the first pharaoh to be buried in the VALLEY OF THE KINGS.

Thutmose III Pharaoh of Egypt from about 1504 to 1450 BC, considered one of the greatest of ancient Egypt's rulers. During the first 22 years of his reign he was overshadowed by his aunt and stepmother HATSHEPSUT, widow

Pharaoh Thutmose III (left) makes a ceremonial presentation of wine to Amon, the highest of the ancient Egyptian gods.

of Thutmose II, who had declared herself regent in 1503. After Hatshepsut died in 1482, Thutmose distinguished himself as a formidable warrior. He mobilised the army and defeated a strong coalition of enemies at Megiddo, near Haifa in present-day Israel. He proceeded to conquer nearly all of Syria, together with the kingdom of Mitanni on the eastern side of the river Euphrates. Thutmose's exploits are recorded on the many temples and monuments he built throughout Egypt, but especially at the Temple of Amon at KARNAK, which he greatly expanded.

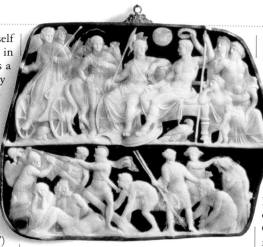

Tiberius Claudius Nero (42 BC–AD 37) Second emperor of Rome, from AD 14 to his death, whose reputation as a military leader and capable ruler was ruined by his final years as a tyrannical recluse. Tiberius was the eldest stepson of Emperor AUGUSTUS, who had no sons of his own. He received his first military command at the age of 22, and rapidly proved himself an exceptional leader; he achieved several notable victories and was revered by his troops. In 12 BC, Augustus forced Tiberius to divorce the wife he loved in order to marry Julia, Augustus's recently widowed daughter. Tiberius soon learned that Julia was being unfaithful to him. He therefore requested to be sent on campaign, and in 6 BC he withdrew to self-imposed exile on the island of Rhodes. Seven years later Augustus recalled Tiberius to Rome, and in AD 4 adopted him as his son and successor.

On becoming emperor in AD 14, Tiberius began a programme of reform. He strengthened the navy, but attempted no new large-scale conquests; he abandoned the practice of providing gladiatorial games and refused to have a month named in his honour. After the death of his son Drusus in 23, Tiberius increasingly delegated the responsibilities of state to Sejanus, Prefect of the PRAETORIAN GUARD. In 27, Tiberius withdrew to the island of Capri, where he was said to devote himself to strange perversions and cruelties. By 31, he realised that Sejanus was becoming too powerful, so he denounced him to the senate. In the final years of his life, Tiberius carried out a spate of wanton political murders, which all but obliterated his earlier achievements. He was succeeded by CALIGULA Gaius Caesar.

Tibet Country in central Asia, since 1951 an autonomous region of China. Tibet was first unified in the early 7th century AD, when it emerged as an independent kingdom with its capital at Lhasa. By the 8th century, a Tibetan empire stretched from Lanzhou in China to Kashgar in central Asia, as well as south into northern India. For a time it was a serious rival to the Chinese TANG empire. During this period a distinctive religious culture emerged in Tibet, based on a blend of Theravada and

Tiberius sits in triumph in a cameo recording his success as a brilliant military commander. As emperor he achieved important reforms.

Tantric BUDDHISM combined with ancient shamanistic beliefs. The result was Tibetan Buddhism, or Lamaism, which encourages an unusually large proportion of the population to devote itself to a monastic life. Thousands of religious communities sprang up throughout Tibet, some of them the size of small cities.

In the 13th century, Tibet was conquered by KUBLAI KHAN, Mongol emperor of China. He was subsequently converted to Buddhism by the abbot of Sakya monastery, who returned to Tibet to become the country's first priest-king under the patronage of the Khan. The defeat of the Mongols by the MING in 1368 allowed Tibet to regain its independence, but the country voluntarily accepted Mongol patronage again some two centuries later. In 1642 a Mongol prince granted full spiritual and political control of Tibet to the DALAI LAMA – or 'Oceanwide Lama' – leader of the reformed Gelukpa Buddhist sect. Two years later the Manchus took control of China (see QING),

and in 1720 they invaded Tibet in order to end two decades of unrest there. This intervention was generally welcomed by the Tibetans as the start of a new era of patronage.

From 1792, Tibet rejected contact with the outside world, especially the West. By the late 19th century the country had become virtually independent, and its self-imposed isolation was frustrating the British who saw it as controlling valuable trade routes into

central Asia. In 1904 Britain invaded Tibet to secure its interests in the region, and in 1906 it formally recognised Chinese sovereignty over the country. This infuriated Tibetans, who responded by evicting the Chinese after the fall of the Qing dynasty in 1912. Tibet remained independent until it was invaded by China in October 1950. The following year the Tibetan government had no option but to capitulate to China, but in March 1959 the populace rose in rebellion. China's violent supresssion of this revolt forced the Dalai Lama to flee into exile. During China's CULTURAL REVOLUTION of 1966-8, Red Guards set about systematically destroying monasteries and other centres of Tibetan culture. Religious practices were banned until 1976. Further protests against Chinese occupation during the 1980s and 1990s were violently suppressed.

ticket-of-leave Certificate which could be granted to a convict in Australia during the period of CONVICT TRANSPORTATION (1788-1868). The ticket was usually granted for good conduct, and allowed a convict to be excused from compulsory labour, to choose his or her own employer and to work for wages. There were some restrictions and the ticket could be withdrawn.

Tilak, Bel Gangadhar (1856-1920) Indian scholar and militant nationalist who helped to lay the foundations for Indian independence. Popularly known as Lokamanya, 'Revered by the People', he owned and edited the weekly nationalist paper *Kesari,* 'The Lion', in which he was strongly critical of British rule. Tilak was imprisoned in 1897 for sedition, but on his release in 1899 he continued his campaign, advocating a boycott of British goods and passive resistance towards the authorities. He was sent to prison again in 1908, on this occasion being deported to Mandalay in Burma (Myanmar). Released in 1914, Tilak formed the Indian Home Rule League, which adopted the slogan, '*Swaraj* [independence] is my birthright and I will have it.' Through the Lucknow Pact he signed with Muhammad Ali JINNAH in 1916 Tilak helped to establish vital Hindu-Muslim unity in the struggle for Indian independence.

Tillett, Benjamin (1860-1943) British trade unionist and politician. Tillett was a leading force behind the LONDON DOCKERS' STRIKE of 1889, which succeeded in gaining assurances for a minimum wage of sixpence an hour and eightpence for overtime. He played an important part in the London Transport Workers' strike of 1911, and was expelled from both Hamburg and Antwerp for supporting dock strikes in those cities. Tillett served as a Labour Member of Parliament from 1917 to 1924, and from 1929 to 1931.

Tilsit, Treaties of Agreements signed in 1807 between France and Russia (July 7) and between France and Prussia (July 9) at the Prussian town of Tilsit – now called Sovetsk in western Russia. The treaties followed Napoleon's defeat of Russia at the Battle of Friedland in June 1807, and his earlier defeat

> 66 **All nations rejoice to see England's malign influence on the Continent destroyed for ever.** 99
>
> *Napoleon Bonaparte*
> *August 1807*

of Prussia at the Battle of JENA in October 1806. Under the first treaty, France and Russia became allies, effectively dividing Europe between themselves; France would assist Russia in its conflict with Turkey, and Russia would join the CONTINENTAL SYSTEM to boycott British trade if Britain remained hostile to France. Under the second treaty, Prussia lost almost half its territory, agreed to pay a huge war indemnity and was obliged to join the Continental System against Britain.

The treaties were so effective in blockading British trade that Napoleon sought to widen their scope as well as to ensure their enforcement. This placed great strains on his allies, who were finding themselves suffering from the boycott. At the end of December 1810 the Russians opened their ports to neutral ships, and in June 1812 Napoleon launched his invasion of Russia. The following year Prussia revoked its treaty to join the Russians in fighting Napoleon.

Timbuktu City in the West African state of Mali, which flourished as a major trading post and as a centre for Islamic culture. Founded as a seasonal camp by Tuareg nomads in about AD 1100, Timbuktu rapidly grew to become one of the most important commercial sites in West Africa – a focal point for North African merchants trading salt, cloth and horses for gold, ivory and slaves.

In the 13th century the city was included in the Mali empire, and in 1468 it became part of the Songhay empire, which at that time dominated West Africa. By then Timbuktu was also renowned for its population of Muslim scholars, many of whom had studied in Mecca. The city reached a high point in the 16th century, but declined after being captured by Moroccan invaders in 1591. It was repeatedly attacked over the following centuries, before falling under French control in 1893.

Timur see TAMERLANE

Tipu Sultan (c.1753-99) Sultan of MYSORE in south-west India from 1782 until his death, nicknamed 'the Tiger of Mysore'. He inherited the kingdom created by his father, Haidar Ali,

and was a formidable enemy to both the British and neighbouring Indian states. He provoked a British invasion of Mysore in 1799 by attempting to negotiate with Revolutionary France, but his failure to secure active French support left him without allies. He was finally besieged in his own capital, Seringapatam, where he died leading his troops against allied British and Indian forces.

Tirpitz, Alfred von (1849-1930) German admiral, chief architect of the German High Seas Fleet and one of the most powerful figures in the imperial government of WILHELM II. Entering the Prussian navy in 1865, Tirpitz took charge of the ministry's torpedo division in 1871. Promoted to secretary of state for the navy in 1897, he immediately embarked on an ambitious programme to build a powerful battle fleet. This included DREADNOUGHTS to rival those of Britain.

In spite of receiving strong initial support, Tirpitz found his plans being scaled down by the German government, which had decided to use its resources to maintain the army. As a result, the German fleet was not a match for the British navy when the First World War broke out, and after the Battle of JUTLAND in May 1916 it was largely confined to port. Realising that his policy had failed, Tirpitz resigned from the navy to re-enter politics. He served as a deputy of the right-wing German National People's Party from 1924 to 1928.

tithe One-tenth of a person's annual income paid to support the Church and clergy. The payment of tithes, in the form of produce, was decreed by Mosaic law for Hebrews, and was encouraged by the early Christian Church in the 6th century. By the 8th century, the paying of tithes was required by law in much of Europe, and it became compulsory in England during the 10th century. Many of the great cathedrals built during the Middle Ages depended on tithes, both for their construction and their maintenance. Tithes were abolished by the French revolutionary government in 1789, and fell into disuse in Italy, England, Scotland and Ireland during the 19th century.

Titian (c.1490-1576) Venetian painter – his full name was Tiziano Vecellio – who was one of the leading artists of the Italian Renaissance. Titian was born in the town of Pieve di Cadore in northern Italy and received his early training from the Venetian masters Giovanni Bellini and Giorgione. By 1516 Titian was recognised as the finest painter in Italy. He received commissions and honours from the Venetian Republic, Italian nobles, Pope Paul III and the Holy Roman Emperor Charles V. Titian was particularly renowned among artists for his innovative use of colour, and for the dramatic scale of his mature works. These include *Bacchus and*

Ariadne (1523), *The Venus of Urbino* (1537), *Christ Crowned with Thorns* (c.1542) and *Charles V at the Battle of Mühlberg* (1548).

Tito (1892-1980) Yugoslav statesman, commonly referred to as Marshal Tito. He was born Josip Broz in Kumrovec, Croatia, in what was then Austria-Hungary. In 1913 Tito was drafted into the Austro-Hungarian army, and was decorated in 1915 for bravery. Later that year he was gravely wounded and taken prisoner by the Russians. By the time Tito returned to Croatia in 1920 it had become part of Yugoslavia. He joined the Communist Party and rose rapidly through its ranks, in spite of being arrested as a subversive on three occasions, the last of which resulted in a five-year prison sentence. After his release in 1934, he became a member of the party politburo. About this time, to avoid government surveillance, he started using the name 'Tito'. It meant 'this that' and was derived from the way he ordered people to 'do this … do that'. In 1937 he was appointed secretary-general of the Communist Party of Yugoslavia.

Following the German and Italian invasion of Yugoslavia in April 1941, Tito emerged as leader of the partisan guerrilla resistance. His enemies included not only the occupying Axis forces, but also the Ustase – Croatian separatists who supported the invaders – and the Serbian nationalist Chetniks. Aided by the Allies, Tito's partisans withstood seven major German offensives, pinning down 30 German divisions, and liberated the country without needing an Allied invasion. In 1943 he was chosen to head a provisional revolutionary

Yugoslav communist leader Tito poses in 1942, at the height of the liberation struggle against occupying Axis forces and their Croatian allies.

government, and was given the title Marshal of Yugoslavia. After the end of the war, Tito rejected Joseph STALIN's attempts to control the communist states of Eastern Europe. Instead, he guided Yugoslavia into adopting a decentralised form of socialism and an independent foreign policy of non-alignment with either the Soviet Union or the United States. Under Tito, Yugoslavia became the most liberal communist country in Europe. What may yet count as Tito's greatest achievement was his ability to hold Yugoslavia together: little more than a decade after his death the country was torn apart by bitter factionalism, which soon erupted into full-scale civil war.

Titus Vespasianus Augustus (AD39-81)

Roman emperor from AD79 until his death. Titus was the son of Emperor VESPASIAN, who was originally a general of Emperor NERO. Titus served in the Roman army in Britain and Germany before joining his father in putting down the Jewish rebellion in Judaea in 67. When his father became emperor in 69, Titus was left in command of the Judaean campaign, which culminated the following year in the capture and destruction of Jerusalem, including its great temple.

On his triumphant return to Rome in 71, Titus was made commander of the PRAETO-RIAN GUARD, and in the years that followed he exercised considerable power over Roman military affairs. Succeeding Vespasian as emperor in 79, Titus proved a capable and popular ruler. He granted generous assistance to inhabitants of Campania who had survived the eruption of the volcano Vesuvius in 79, and he financed the rebuilding of Rome after it was swept by fire in 80. Titus's sudden death was rumoured to have been caused by his brother Domitian, his successor as emperor.

tobacco

The practice of smoking tobacco originated among the indigenous peoples of the Americas, many of whom believed the plant had medicinal properties. Others used it in specific rituals, such as sealing a peace accord. Early European explorers found the Aztecs smoking hollow reeds stuffed with tobacco, while other tribes simply rolled the leaves into a thick tube – the prototype of the cigar. It was in this form that tobacco was first introduced to Europe in the early 1500s, both as a luxury and as a mild panacea.

Within 150 years, tobacco was known throughout Europe, and had spread to Asia and Africa. By 1600, the commercial cultivation of tobacco plants was well established among Spanish colonies in the Americas. In 1612 John Rolfe harvested the first tobacco crop of the English colony at JAMESTOWN, Virginia. Less than a decade later tobacco was a major export commodity for the colony, where it was even used as a form of currency. The habit of inhaling snuff – tobacco that has been

By the 19th century tobacco was an accepted stimulant for virtually every order of society. Here a gang of chained labourers queue to buy supplies from a Brazilian tobacconist.

fermented and then finely ground – became popular in England during the 17th century. In the USA tobacco users took increasingly to chewing their leaf, especially during the 19th century. Improved growing techniques in the early 1900s lowered tobacco's acid content, making it easier to inhale, and contributed to a large increase in cigarette smoking.

Tobruk

Mediterranean port city on the north-east coast of Libya, and scene of some of the most prolonged fighting in North Africa during the Second World War. In January 1941 British forces under the command of General Archibald WAVELL captured Tobruk from the Italians, taking some 25000 of them prisoner. By April, the British had been forced to withdraw several hundred miles to the east by the arrival of General Irwin ROMMEL's Afrika Korps. They had, however, left an Australian garrison at Tobruk, which endured an eight-month siege by the Germans. In December 1941, the British 8th Army, led by Field-Marshal Claude AUCHINLECK, relieved the siege, only to have to retreat again in the face of a German counterattack in May 1942. On this occasion Tobruk was left in the hands of some 35000 South African and Australian troops, whose commander soon realised that he was faced with an impossible task. The garrison accordingly surrendered to Rommel on June 21, after a one-day siege. Less than five months later, on November 13, Tobruk was recaptured by the British 8th Army, now commanded by General Bernard MONTGOMERY.

> ### DID YOU KNOW?
>
> When Tobruk was finally recaptured by the Allies in November 1942, the Australians celebrated their return by running a digger's hat up the flagpole.

Tocqueville, Alexis de

(1805-59) French politician and historian, best known for his analysis of democracy in the USA in the early 19th century. Tocqueville spent nine months touring the USA between 1831 and 1832, ostensibly studying that country's penal reforms for the French government. His real interest was in American democratic institutions, and how they might work in Europe. On his return to France, Tocqueville began the writing of his four-volume masterpiece, *Democracy in America* (1835-40), which was recognised as a classic of political theory as soon as it was published.

Tocqueville was particularly impressed by the political freedom that existed in the USA, and the degree of equality that existed between people living there. He contrasted this with Europe, and especially France, which were still governed by an aristocratic elite; even France, he pointed out, had failed to live up to the promise of its revolution.

In 1839 Tocqueville was elected to the Chamber of Deputies, and in 1848 he was nominated to help in drawing up the constitution of France's Second Republic. He served briefly as foreign minister in 1849, but was forced to leave politics after refusing to pledge his allegiance to NAPOLEON III, following the latter's coup d'état in 1851.

Togliatti, Palmiro

(1893-1964) Italian politician and leader of the Italian Communist Party for almost 40 years. Togliatti helped to form the Italian Communist Party when it broke away from the Socialist Party in 1921.

In 1926, while Togliatti was attending a meeting of the Communist International (see COMINTERN) in Moscow, Benito MUSSOLINI banned the Italian Communist Party and arrested nearly all its leaders. Togliatti was forced to live in exile, mainly in Moscow, from where he arranged secret meetings of the Italian communists. He returned to Italy in 1944, serving in the government of Pietro BADOGLIO and becoming vice-premier under Alcide DEGASPERI in 1945.

Like Marshal TITO of Yugoslavia, Togliatti rejected Stalin's notion of an internationally coordinated communist movement, preferring to develop his own 'Italian road to socialism'. This included forging links with the Roman Catholic Church, rather than promoting atheism, as in the Soviet Union. Unlike Tito, Togliatti never openly defied Stalin, and managed to remain on good terms with him.

Togo Country in West Africa, independent since 1960. Togo was originally part of a far larger region called Togoland, situated between the powerful kingdoms of Ashanti to the west and DAHOMEY to the east. The Ashanti kingdom, in particular, traditionally raided Togoland for its slaves. German missionaries arrived in the area in the mid 19th century, and in 1884 several coastal rulers accepted a German protectorate over southern Togoland. During the 1890s the Germans forcibly annexed northern Togoland.

In 1914 British and French troops achieved their first victory of the First World War by capturing Togoland from the Germans. In 1922 the League of Nations divided it into two unequal parts: a smaller, eastern region, which was given to France to administer, and a western region, which was placed under British control. In 1956 British Togoland became part of the British Gold Coast protectorate, which a year later received its independence as the Republic of GHANA. In 1960, French Togoland followed suit, becoming the independent Republic of Togo.

Togo's first president, Sylvanus Olympio, was killed in an unsuccessful coup in 1963; he was succeeded by his brother-in-law, Nicolas Grunitzky, who was himself toppled in 1967 in a bloodless coup led by Lieutenant-Colonel Gnassingbe Eyadema. In early 1991 Eyadema agreed to reinstate multiparty democracy, but then used the army to win back powers he had surrendered. Continuing prodemocracy agitation and civil unrest forced Eyadema to agree to elections, which in 1994 resulted in a coalition government composed of Eyadema's party and a minor opposition party.

Tojo Hideki (1884-1948) Japanese general and politician who was prime minister of Japan through most of the Second World War. During his long career with the Japanese army, Tojo earned a reputation as both a harsh disciplinarian and a talented commander. In 1937 he was appointed chief of staff of the Japanese army in Manchuria. The following year he became vice-minister of war and one of the leading proponents of the Tripartite Pact, signed in 1940, between Japan, Germany and Italy. After being promoted to minister of war in 1940, Tojo persuaded France's VICHY GOVERNMENT to allow Japan to occupy strategic bases in French Indochina — a move that led to splits within the Japanese government, and dramatically heightened tension with the USA. In October 1941 Tojo succeeded in forcing the resignation of the prime minister KONOE FUMIMARO and immediately took his place.

With Tojo heading the government, Japan entered its most militaristic phase. Less than two months after taking office, Tojo gave the order for the Japanese air force to attack the American Pacific fleet at PEARL HARBOR. He then led Japan through a series of successful campaigns in South-east Asia and the Pacific, riding high on the popularity that followed. However, when the tide of war began to turn against Japan in 1943, Tojo became increasingly dictatorial. He was forced to resign in July 1944, after the loss of the Mariana Islands to the USA. Tojo nevertheless remained defiant, urging that Japan should fight to the end and never surrender. After the end of the war, he was tried and executed as a war criminal.

Tojo Hideki, Japan's wartime prime minister, listens as he is sentenced to death by the International Military Tribunal in 1948.

> **DID YOU KNOW?**
>
> Japan under Tokugawa rule was noted for the pleasure-seeking life of its townsfolk. Wood-block artists captured the colour and display of what came to be called 'the floating world'.

Tokugawa Name of the family that ruled Japan during its last SHOGUNATE, from 1603 to 1867 — a period known variously as the Tokugawa shogunate, or the Edo period.

In the late 16th century, Tokugawa Ieyasu emerged as a dominant figure in feudal Japan. By 1603 he had overcome all his main rivals, and was accordingly awarded the title of shogun, 'overlord', by the emperor. Ieyasu established his capital at Edo — present-day Tokyo — which under his successors became the hub of a highly centralised feudal system. The Tokugawa insisted that their *daimyo*, 'lords', should maintain their residences at Edo, and leave hostages there whenever they left the city. One consequence of this was that Japan enjoyed more than 250 years of peace and stability.

Less favourably, the Tokugawa imposed rigorous constraints on Japanese society. Travel was closely monitored, and peasants were forbidden to undertake nonagricultural labour. From the 1630s, the Tokugawa effectively closed Japan to foreign influence, both economic and cultural. Christianity was banned, and overseas commerce restricted to a single Dutch trading post at the port of Nagasaki.

By the early 19th century, the shogunate was politically and technologically stagnant. In 1867, combined pressure from two powerful rivals forced the last shogun, Tokugawa Keiki (1827-1913), to resign. Less than a year later the MEIJI RESTORATION returned the emperor to supreme power in Japan.

Toleration Act (1689) Law passed by the English Parliament granting freedom of worship to Baptists, Methodists and other dissenting Protestants — that is, those who would not accept the authority and teaching of the ANGLICAN CHURCH. Dissenters were allowed their own ministers, teachers and places of worship, subject to taking oaths of allegiance. The TEST ACTS, which barred dissenters from public office, remained in force, but from 1727 annual indemnity Acts allowed them to hold certain local offices. The Act did not apply to Roman Catholics and Unitarians, who remained subject to civil and religious constraints until the 19th century.

Tolpuddle Martyrs Name given to six English farm workers from the village of Tolpuddle in Dorset, who were transported to Australia for trade union activity. The six were arrested after they had formed a local branch of the Friendly Society of Agricultural Labourers to press for higher wages. In March 1834 they were convicted of the exaggerated charge of administering unlawful oaths and sentenced to seven years' transportation. The severity of the sentence provoked a storm of protest that included large demonstrations in London. The government stood firm for two years, before remitting the sentences in 1836. The 'martyrs' became heroes of early British trade unionism, but only one returned to England; five preferred to emigrate to Canada.

Tolstoy, Count Leo see feature, right

Toltecs Native American people who flourished in central Mexico between the 10th and 12th centuries AD. Their name is taken from their capital, Tollan, near present-day Tula, about 50 miles (80 km) north of Mexico City. In about 900 the Toltecs sacked the great city of Teotihuacán and went on to build an empire from among its surrounding states, including that of the MAYA.

Toltec religion centred on the cult of the feathered serpent, QUETZALCOATL – which was also the name of the second Toltec king and founder of the cult. Their ceremonies included human sacrifice and sun worship, for which they built a number of imposing temples. The Toltecs were overrun in the middle of the 12th century by a variety of nomadic people, collectively called the Chichimec, from whom the great AZTEC empire arose some two centuries later.

Tone, Wolfe (1763-98) Irish revolutionary who led a French invasion of Ireland in 1798. Inspired by the French Revolution, Tone helped to found the Society of UNITED IRISH-MEN – an organisation dedicated to achieving equal political rights for Protestants and Roman Catholics. By 1795 he was negotiating with French ministers for military aid from France, and in 1796 he accompanied an abortive French invasion of the west coast of Ireland. Following the outbreak of widespread insurrection in Ireland in 1798, Tone sailed with another invasion force, which was defeated by the British in County Donegal. Tone was sentenced to death, but committed suicide on the morning of his execution.

Tonga Independent island kingdom in the southern Pacific Ocean, comprising an archipelago of 170 small islands, of which between 36 and 40 are inhabited. The archipelago was first located by the Dutch in 1616, and was named the Friendly Islands by Captain James Cook, who landed there in 1773 and 1777.

Tonga became a unified nation under King George Tupou I, who ruled from 1845 to 1893. In 1900 George Tupou II negotiated a treaty of friendship with Britain, in which Tonga became a British protectorate. During the Second World War, Queen Salote Tupu III placed the islands' resources at the disposal of the Allies. In 1958 and 1968 British controls were reduced, and in 1970 Tonga became an independent nation within the British Commonwealth.

Master of the moral tale

Count Leo Tolstoy, the Russian writer, philosopher and moralist, had a prolific literary career, producing such masterpieces as War and Peace *and* Anna Karenina. *In later years he became obsessed by religion.*

Leo Tolstoy (1828-1910) has been claimed as the world's greatest prose writer. His three panoramic novels brilliantly combine art, realism and moralism; he also wrote many stories and novellas, powerful memoirs of his emotional and spiritual turmoil, and influential tracts on personal and political behaviour.

Born into the Russian aristocracy, Tolstoy spent his early adulthood in the army, took part in the Crimean War and was nearly killed by a grenade. Abandoning a soldier's life, he travelled widely in Europe, set up his own school, and spent most of the 1860s writing *War and Peace* (1865-9), a long, multicharacter historical novel set during the Napoleonic Wars. Resonating with Russian patriotism, *War and Peace* sought to demonstrate that a so-called 'great man' such as Napoleon exercises only a limited control over the course of events, and began Tolstoy's dogged exploration of life's ultimate mysteries.

His second masterpiece, *Anna Karenina* (1875-7), combined two novels in one: the tragic story of the book's heroine, with her wretched marriage, her doomed affair, her suicide under the wheels of a train; and the quest for fulfilment on the part of Levin, clearly modelled on the author himself. *Anna Karenina* brought Tolstoy international renown and marked the summit of his literary achievement. Then, in mid life, came his spiritual crisis. A supreme egotist, and unhappily married, he wrote *Confession* (1878-9), in which he examined the meaning of life, contemplated suicide, and in erratic but inspiring fashion pursued the search for God. His creative writing took on a religious hue, including a fierce repudiation of the temptations of the flesh, a phase that culminated in his final great novel, *Resurrection* (1899).

FOLLOWERS WORLDWIDE

By this time Tolstoy had become a world-famous prophet, writing letters, essays and pamphlets on a wide range of subjects. Money and property as the root of all evil, the abolition of governments and the nation-state, denunciation of war, nonresistance to evil – all were themes that inflamed his followers, including Mohandas Gandhi, who adopted his doctrine of nonresistance.

The tsarist regime looked on Tolstoy and his predictions of an inevitable revolution with deep unease, but because of his reputation it was almost powerless to act.

Tolstoy died in a stationmaster's cottage, having fled by train from his wife. His last words were: 'I do not understand what it is I have to do.'

Leo Tolstoy playing chess, 1908, surrounded by Sofia, his wife, centre, and their family. He adopted a simple lifestyle and denounced his great works as worthless.

Tonypandy Mining town in Wales, which was the scene of a violent dispute over pay rates for miners in 1910. Miners interfered with pit machinery, and there was looting and disorder in the town. After the local police requested government help the home secretary, Winston Churchill, sent 300 extra police from London and placed military detachments on standby. During a later incident in Llanelli the following year, troops mobilised by Churchill opened fire on strikers, killing four of them. As a result of these incidents, trade union hostility to Churchill was intense.

Tooke, John Horne (1736-1812) British radical politician and philologist. Born John Horne, he assumed the additional name Tooke in honour of a rich friend who made him his heir. In 1769 Tooke founded the Society of Supporters of the BILL OF RIGHTS, largely to support the journalist John WILKES, who had been imprisoned for libelling George III. In 1771 Tooke set up the Constitutional Society to agitate for British parliamentary reform and lend support to the American colonists' demand for self-government. He was imprisoned in 1778 for his outspoken criticism of the British Government over its handling of the American Revolution, and was tried for treason, but acquitted, in 1794.

Tordesillas, Treaty of (7 June 1494) Treaty signed between Spain and Portugal, dividing between them the territories that had been discovered by their voyagers in the Americas and elsewhere. In 1493, Pope Alexander VI had approved a line of demarcation stretching between the poles 100 leagues, or 300 miles (483 km), west of the Cape Verde islands. Spain was to control everything to the west of the line (the Americas), and Portugal everything to the east (Africa and India).

At a meeting held at Tordesillas, Spain, the following year, the Portuguese managed to get the line moved another 270 leagues, or 810 miles (1300 km), to the west, ostensibly to give them room to catch the best winds for rounding Africa. As a result, they were able to lay claim to much of Brazil, which is cut by the line near the mouth of the river Amazon. The treaty was sanctioned by Pope Julius II in 1506, but was never recognised by any other European power.

Torquemada, Tomás de (1420-98) Spanish Dominican friar who was made first Grand Inquisitor of the Spanish INQUISITION. Torquemada was confessor and adviser to Ferdinand II and Isabella I, and succeeded in convincing them that Jews and Muslims posed a serious threat to Spanish Catholicism and culture. In 1478 an inquisition was appointed to enquire into this issue, and in 1483 Torquemada was appointed Grand Inquisitor, head of the Spanish Inquisition.

He drew up guidelines detailing offences that the inquisition should investigate, and authorised the use of torture to extract confessions. Torquemada became notorious for the harsh methods he devised, and for his rigour in enforcing them. During his tenure, some 2000 people were burnt at the stake, and many more tortured. Under his influence, Ferdinand and Isabella expelled more than 160 000 Jews from Spain in 1492 for refusing to convert to Christianity.

torture Deliberate infliction of pain in order to intimidate, obtain information or break the will of the victim was commonplace in ancient civilisations. Both Greece and Rome legalised the torture of slaves, though freemen could only be tortured in cases of treason. The right to torture slaves was abolished by the Romans in AD 240.

Torture became increasingly common in Europe from the beginning of the 12th century, as confessions became a standard means of determining guilt. Through the INQUISITION, which sought to find and punish apostates, heretics and witches, the Roman Catholic Church gave official sanction to the use of torture. Legal proceedings in most European countries made use of torture almost as a standard procedure until the end of the 18th century. England was an exception: most of the more barbarous forms of torture used on the Continent were unknown.

From about 1750 opposition to torture grew in Europe, both for humanitarian reasons, and because torture was increasingly perceived as an unreliable means of obtaining true evidence. By the early 19th century most European countries had abolished torture, while the 8th amendment of the US Constitution – banning cruel and unusual punishment – effectively ended it in the USA.

During the 20th century, torture has re-emerged as a common practice, particularly among totalitarian regimes. Dictators such as Adolf Hitler, Benito Mussolini and Joseph Stalin have all made systematic use of torture, leading the United Nations to issue its Universal Declaration of Human Rights in 1948, explicitly denouncing torture. In 1984 the UN adopted the Convention against Torture, which obliges states to make torture an offence punishable under law. By 1995 only 90 countries had ratified the convention, and some of these are known to be states in which torture is still used regularly.

Tory Party (c.1769-c.1832) British political party traditionally opposed to the WHIG party. The name 'Tory' originally referred to Irish Catholic outlaws, and it was adopted as a term of abuse for those royalists who supported the succession of JAMES II, in spite of his Roman Catholic background. The word was first used in this sense during the political crisis of 1679, when the Earl of SHAFTESBURY tried to get Parliament recalled in order to pass a bill excluding James from the throne. The Tories opposed this because of their belief in the divine right of hereditary royal succession.

Following the GLORIOUS REVOLUTION of 1688, which many Tory leaders supported, the division between Tories and Whigs was somewhat reduced on the issue of royal rights. The two parties remained opposed, however, in their attitudes towards religious tolerance and English involvement in foreign wars. The Tories stood for staunch Anglicanism and limited military activity abroad – in most respects representing the interests of the country gentry. By contrast, the Whigs were identified with the aristocratic landowners and the wealthy middle classes.

The Tories were particularly influential under the leadership of Robert HARLEY, during the later years of Queen ANNE's reign (1702-14). They were discredited by the association of Henry BOLINGBROKE, another leading Tory, with the JACOBITE rebellion of 1715, and remained out of favour for the following 60 years.

In 1784 William PITT THE YOUNGER won a long-delayed general election, and over the next 22 years a revitalised Tory faction formed around his policies. This group succeeded in controlling the government until 1830, and then saw their power in the House of Commons destroyed by the REFORM ACT of 1832. The party was thoroughly demoralised, but soon gave birth to a new group calling itself the CONSERVATIVE PARTY.

totalitarianism Political system in which all individual activities and social relationships are subject to surveillance and control by the State. The term gained currency in the 1930s and 1940s, when observers noted points of similarity between NAZI Germany and the Soviet Union under Joseph STALIN. Both had one-party governments headed by a single, powerful individual; both promoted a single official ideology through all media of communication; and both made use of terror tactics by the secret police. Together, these features indicated a society in which power was highly centralised and in which no individual could escape the attention of the state. A totalitarian regime is a specifically modern form of authoritarian state, requiring as it does an advanced technology of social control.

Touré, Sékou (1922-84) African statesman who was president of GUINEA from 1958 to 1984. As a postal worker in his early twenties,

---

DID YOU KNOW?

The ancient Chinese were probably the first to use water torture. Water was slowly dripped onto victims' heads until the repetition sent them insane.

Touré organised the first successful strike in French West Africa and thereafter became closely involved in the labour movement. In 1948 he became secretary-general of the *Confédération Générale de Travail* (General Confederation of Labour) for Africa, and in 1958 he was elected president of Guinea after leading that country's campaign for independence from France. In 1982 he led an Islamic delegation to mediate in the Iran-Iraq war.

tourism see feature, page 658

tournament Medieval sport (also called a tourney) in which knights engage in armed combat to demonstrate their skills and valour. Tournaments originated in the early 12th century in France, from where they spread to England, Germany and southern Europe. The earliest versions consisted of large-scale mock battles, called *mêlées*, fought between groups of knights using real weapons of war. By the late 13th century blunted weapons were adopted, though even these could cause serious injury and even death. Alongside the *mêlée*, more controlled forms of tournament developed involving smaller groups of knights. These culminated in the joust, or tilt, in which two knights armed with lances charged at each other on horseback along a dividing, cloth-covered barrier. Combat on foot was equally popular, and some of the more elaborate tournaments staged mock sieges on specially constructed 'castles'.

Toussaint l'Ouverture, François (c.1743-1803) Haitian patriot who helped his country to become independent from France. Toussaint was born a slave, but received his freedom in 1777. In 1791 he joined a rebellion of slaves, and rapidly emerged as an outstanding leader, forming his own army, which he trained in guerrilla tactics. In 1793 he briefly allied himself with the Spanish of Santo Domingo (the present-day Dominican Republic) in order to secure victories over the French. At about this time he adopted the name l'Ouverture ('The Opening'). Later that year British troops occupied the Haitian coast, helping to inflict further defeats on the French.

In a surprise move in May 1794 Toussaint turned against his Anglo-Spanish allies. Assisted by his generals Jean-Jacques DESSALINES and Henri Christophe, he

François Toussaint l'Overture never saw Haiti become a fully independent nation, but he laid the foundations that made its independence possible.

won a series of battles that resulted in the expulsion of both the Spanish and the British. In return, the French governor of Saint-Domingue, as Haiti was then called, made Toussaint his lieutenant. By 1796 Toussaint was ruling the colony as governor general, and in 1801 he conquered neighbouring Santo Domingo, where slavery still persisted.

Although Toussaint constantly professed his loyalty to France, Napoleon Bonaparte decided to reassert French control over the territory. A French invasion began in January 1802, and after furious fighting Toussaint agreed to surrender if the French promised not to restore slavery. Within a few weeks he was arrested and deported to France, where he died in prison. The following year Haiti became the second country in the New World, after the USA, to win its independence.

Toyotomi Hideyoshi (c.1537-98) Japanese warlord who completed the unification of Japan begun by ODA NOBUNAGA. The son of a peasant, Hideyoshi rose from being a foot soldier in Nobunaga's army to one of his leading generals. After Nobunaga was assassinated in 1582, Hideyoshi continued his work of unifying Japan, which had been riven by over two centuries of civil war. In 1584 he formed a pact with another great warlord, Togukawa Ieyasu, after they had fought an inconclusive battle, and the following year he was appointed chief minister by the emperor. In 1590, with Ieyasu's help, Hideyoshi completed the overthrow of rebellious clans. He then commissioned land surveys, disarmed the peasants, and banned Christian missionaries. In 1592 and 1597 Hideyoshi led invasions of Korea, both of which were unsuccessful.

His vision of a unified Japan was carried forward after his death by Ieyasu.

tractor The earliest prototypes of tractors were steam engines for performing agricultural tasks such as winnowing. These machines appeared in the early 19th century, and had to be hauled into position by teams of horses. The earliest self-propelled steam engines, or traction engines, were built in the UK in 1855, and were in widespread use by the end of the century. The first true modern tractor was built in 1892 by John Froehlich, an blacksmith from Iowa. Powered by a petrol engine, this machine was much lighter, and therefore far more mobile, than a comparable steam engine. By the beginning of

Members of a Soviet collective farm prepare their tractor for a day's work in the 1930s.

the First World War, the tractor had established itself as a vital piece of farm equipment. The war inspired the development of new types of tractor and all-terrain traction systems, one of which was adapted by the British and French to build the first tanks.

Until 1932-3, when oversize rubber tyres were first successfully made, tractors were fitted with ridged or spiked steel wheels. They have subsequently been built with Caterpillar tracks, such as tanks and bulldozers use.

trade and commerce see feature, page 660

Trades Union Congress (TUC) Organisation of British TRADE UNIONS founded in 1868 to hold national conferences on trade union activities. In 1871 the TUC set up a Parliamentary Committee to lobby MPs on the unions' behalf. From 1889 it began to be more politically militant, and in 1900 it helped to found the Labour Representation Committee, known from 1906 as the LABOUR PARTY, with which it has had close links ever since. The General Council, elected by trade union members, replaced the Parliamentary Committee in 1920. After the GENERAL STRIKE of 1926, relations between the TUC and successive British governments were cautiously conciliatory.

During the Second World War the TUC was closely involved in British industrial planning and management – to a greater or

Travel becomes tourism

Until the 19th century only the rich travelled; few country dwellers would see the sea even once. But growing affluence and new forms of transport soon turned everyone into tourists.

The word travel derives from the Latin *trepalium*, the Roman three-pronged instrument of torture, for until the arrival of the train any journey was seen as something of a penance. From the 15th century Europeans began to explore the world, but still most journeys had a practical purpose: to wage war, to conquer new lands, to conduct trade, to gain spiritual salvation through pilgrimage. Holidays were 'holy days' set aside for religious observance.

Only a privileged minority could afford to travel for pleasure. Among them were the young gentlemen of the 18th century who completed their education by seeing the art treasures of Venice and Rome on the Grand Tour. A journey of any distance was likely to be slow, expensive and uncomfortable. In the 1830s the stagecoach from London to Edinburgh could take two weeks to cover the 400 miles: atrocious roads could tip a coach over, with fatal results.

Even so, in the 18th century spas such as Bath in England and Baden-Baden in Germany started to attract affluent visitors who came to take the waters. Early in the 19th century, following a fashion set by the English Prince Regent with his pseudo-oriental Pavilion in Brighton, seaside resorts became the places to go, and the trend was followed in France. But for the vast majority there was still little opportunity to travel beyond their homes.

The train, developed in England, ushered in the age of cheap, convenient travel. A Leicestershire printer, Thomas Cook, was the first to realise its leisure potential. In July 1841 Cook organised a train from Leicester to Loughborough, taking a party of 500 on a day trip to a Temperance Festival. The expedition

Families enjoy the Normandy resort of Etretat in 1900, and a poster of 1937 promotes the healing waters that Baden-Baden had offered since the 1700s.

By 1918 world travel could be booked through Thomas Cook.

proved such a success that Cook began offering other excursions, notably to the London to see the Great Exhibition of 1851. He soon began to sell tours abroad, extending the experience of the Grand Tour to the middle classes. 'Tourism' – a word first used in 1811 – was becoming a reality.

The railway companies also started offering trips to the seaside, and in the 19th century resorts connected by rail to the big cities developed rapidly. Londoners travelled to Brighton; Parisians headed for Normandy, where small fishing ports such as Deauville and Trouville grew into major holiday destinations. As workers became better paid and gained holiday rights, a new generation acquired leisure. The first holiday camp was opened by Billy Butlin in Skegness, England, in

1937. Workers' associations promoted travel, and cheaper cars brought motoring holidays within the reach of millions.

SMART TO SUNBATHE

'Sun and sand' holidays began in southern France. Tans had been associated with manual labour, so smart society avoided the sun, but in the 1920s fashionable travellers began to visit the Riviera during the summer. For those who lived in a cold climate, a tan became desirable.

After the Second World War, war-surplus aircraft and pilots to fly them stimulated the package holiday business, but it was not until the end of rationing and postwar austerity in the late Fifties that Europeans began to travel abroad in large numbers. Spanish fishing villages such as Torremolinos and small resorts such as Benidorm were transformed into Europe's busiest holiday destinations.

Tourism is now the world's biggest industry, employing 212 million people – or one in nine of the entire workforce.

Clouds of smoke from repeated cannonades surround the men-of-war engaged in the Battle of Trafalgar. Admiral Nelson's crew aboard his flagship *Victory* included a boy of ten.

lesser extent it continued to play this role under both Conservative and Labour governments until 1979. Since then it has tended to be on the defensive, particularly against a wave of legislation designed to weaken trade union power in industrial disputes.

trade union Organised association of workers in a particular trade or profession (see also feature, page 662). In the USA trade unions are known as labor unions. During the late 18th century in Britain, groups and clubs of working men in skilled trades developed in order to regulate admission of apprentices, and sometimes to bargain for better working conditions. By 1861 a number of trade unions of skilled workers existed in Britain, forming the TRADES UNION CONGRESS in 1868, and gaining the right to picket peacefully in 1875.

A parallel development had proceeded in the USA. Small local unions appeared in the 1820s and a national organisation called the Knights of Labor flourished from 1869 to 1886, having as its main aim the abolition of child labour. In 1886 the Knights of Labor was succeeded by the American Federation of Labor, an organisation of skilled workers.

The development of MASS PRODUCTION in Europe and the USA brought the recruitment of large numbers of semiskilled and unskilled workers, and from the 1880s they began organising themselves into unions. As industrialisation spread to Australia and other British dominions in the 19th century, it was followed by the development of trade unions, although in South Africa trade union activity among Black workers was illegal until 1980.

In the Soviet Union and communist Eastern Europe, 90 per cent of industrial workers belonged to government-controlled unions which concerned themselves with training, economic planning and social insurance.

Trafalgar, Battle of (October 21, 1805) British naval victory secured by Admiral Horatio NELSON against a combined Franco-Spanish fleet, commanded by Admiral Pierre de Villeneuve, off Cape Trafalgar, near the Spanish port of Cadiz. The Franco-Spanish fleet left Cadiz on the night of October 19-20, hoping to slip into the Mediterranean without engaging the British in battle. It was attacked at midday on October 21, after Nelson had signalled to his ships, 'England expects that every man will do his duty'. Nelson himself was mortally wounded by a sniper firing from the French ship *Redoubtable*, but by the time he died – at 4.30 pm, about half an hour before the end of the battle – he was confident of a complete British victory. Some 1500 British seamen were killed or wounded, but no British ships were lost. In contrast, Villeneuve lost 20 ships and was himself captured. The engagement put an end to Napoleon's plans to invade Britain, and guaranteed British control of the seas for the rest of the 19th century.

Trajan (c.AD53-117) Roman emperor from AD 98, who expanded the empire eastwards, notably in Romania, Armenia, Arabia and Mesopotamia. Trajan was born in Spain and served in the Roman army before being granted a consulship by Emperor Domitian in 91. The elderly Emperor Nerva adopted Trajan as his successor in 97, and within three months Trajan had himself become emperor.

Trajan immediately embarked on a series of campaigns, carving out a new province of Dacia, centred on present-day Romania, and conquering a large part of the Parthian empire in Armenia and Upper Mesopotamia. He also undertook an ambitious building programme of roads, aqueducts and bridges throughout the empire. In Rome, Trajan's constructions include public baths, a theatre and an enormous new forum, at the entrance to which he erected a triumphal column – still standing – depicting scenes from his Dacian campaigns. Trajan was also remembered for his generosity towards the poor of Rome. He died in Asia Minor and was succeeded by Hadrian, who abandoned Trajan's Parthian conquests while keeping the province of Dacia.

Trans-Siberian Railway World's longest continuous railway which opened up vast areas of Siberia, advanced Russian interests in the Far East and provided a link 5786 miles (9311 km) long between Moscow in the west and Vladivostok in the east.

The railway was begun in 1891 with the aid of French loans and was virtually completed by 1904. Its original route passed through Manchuria, and the suspicion that this aroused in Japan was one factor leading to the RUSSO-JAPANESE WAR of 1904-5. By 1916 a longer route had been completed passing wholly through Russian territory. Since then several branch lines have been added, and between 1974 and 1989 an alternative route passing north of Lake Baikal was built. This has opened up new areas for mineral exploitation, but has proved difficult to maintain as it passes over swampy areas. The journey from Moscow to Vladivostok takes about six days.

The Trans-Siberian Railway, linking the Ural mountains to the Pacific Ocean by way of the great steppes of Asia, was one of the most ambitious engineering undertakings of the 19th century.

Trade on the high seas

*The maritime explorations of Spanish and Portuguese sailors in the
15th century heralded the beginning of trade and commerce on a global scale.*

A quicker and safer route to the Orient than the overland haul across Asia had been the dream of Europeans since the 13th century, when merchants such as Marco Polo regaled Venetians with tales of the wealth and power of Emperor Kublai Khan's China. By the 15th century they had developed the marine technology which made long-distance travel possible, and in 1492 Christopher Columbus, unaware of the existence of the Americas, sailed westwards across the Atlantic, bound for the Orient. Though he never reached China, he pioneered a decade of European exploration that changed the course of history. Six years later the Portuguese navigator Vasco da Gama rounded the Cape of Africa into the Indian Ocean.

China was then the world's largest manufacturing country. Chinese porcelain and silk were traded throughout the Indian Ocean in exchange for African gold and exotic animals. Muslim merchants controlled China's business with Europe as well as the trade in textiles, tea and jewellery from India, and spices from the East Indies. These goods reached Europe through Egypt and the Ottoman Empire, and enriched the merchant banks of

Venice, Genoa and Florence. The Portuguese, once in the Indian Ocean, lost no time in seizing Arab trading posts along the east coast of Africa. By 1542 they were trading directly with Japan and China, and although the voyage around the Cape took several months, the investment was justified by profits of around 400 per cent for each cargo.

NATIONS VIE FOR SUPREMACY

Gold plundered by the Spanish during their conquest of the Aztec and Inca empires, and South American silver mining financed this trade. It also caused crippling inflation, especially in Spain.

First the Dutch, who won their long war of independence from Spain in 1648, and then the English, who had defeated the Spanish Armada in 1588, became the

Saffron and spices arrive in Nuremberg, Bavaria, in 1640, products of the burgeoning trade between Europe and the East Indies.

ascendant commercial nations in Europe. Using their naval power, they seized control of European trade with the Orient. As the supply of bullion from the New World declined in the 17th century, economies based on plantation crops expanded. Sugar was produced in Brazil and the Caribbean; tobacco and cotton in American colonies. The growth of these plantations depended on the import of slave labour from Africa, which reached a peak in the 18th century. Britain was one of the main beneficiaries of a profitable 'triangular trade': slaves were shipped from Africa to America, raw commodities were transported from the New World to Britain, and manufactured goods were exported overseas from England.

After their victory over the Indians at the Battle of Plassey in 1757, the British, who came as traders, found themselves with an Indian empire. From then on, Chinese economic dominance was challenged by increasing volumes of manufactured goods from Britain. In the 1830s and 1840s, the richest man in the world was not the German-born British merchant banker Nathan Rothschild, but a Cantonese trader called Howqua who spoke pidgin English. He was rich enough to subscribe more than a million silver dollars towards reparations to England after the Opium War (1839-1842). China's favourable trade balance finally vanished in the 1870s, a decade which saw the development of the United States as a major industrial power.

A catalogue (left) advertises the sale of imported porcelain from the Orient in 1764. Portuguese merchant ships (below) took up to eight months to sail from Lisbon to the East Indies in the 1540s.

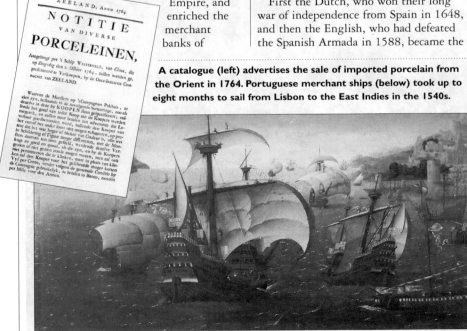

An American passenger ship towers above Chinese vessels in the port of Guangzhou (Canton) – one of the first five treaty ports opened to Westerners by the Treaty of Nanjing in 1842.

Transvaal Former province in the Republic of South Africa, named after its situation across – that is, north of – the Vaal river. The area was inhabited by early hominids up to 3 million years ago, but was populated by Ndebele peoples migrating south from about the 2nd century AD. The first Europeans to reach the Transvaal were Boer trekkers from the Cape, who arrived in the mid 1830s (see feature, page 270). Their numbers increased significantly after Britain annexed the ORANGE FREE STATE in 1848; and four years later, at the Sand River Convention, Britain recognised the right of the Transvaal Boers to govern themselves.

The discovery of diamonds at Kimberley in the 1860s led to further immigration and the chance for some individuals, such as Cecil Rhodes (see feature, page 546), to amass huge fortunes. In 1877 Britain decided to annex the Transvaal, prompting the first BOER WAR of 1880-1. The 1881 Treaty of Pretoria granted the Transvaal (then calling itself the South African Republic) self-government, but the discovery of huge deposits of gold in 1886 prompted further British attempts to gain control of the region. These culminated in the second Boer War of 1899-1902, during which the Transvaal was again annexed by Britain. The Treaty of VEREENIGING of 1902 made the Transvaal a crown colony, but five years later the region gained self-government, and in 1910 it became a founding province of the Union of South Africa. Following South Africa's first multiracial elections of 1994, the Transvaal ceased to exist, being broken into four new regions.

Transylvania Historic area in present-day Romania. Transylvania formed the nucleus of the Roman province of Dacia from AD 106 to around 270. The region was then overrun by Goths, Huns and Slavs, prior to the arrival of the Magyars, or Hungarians, in about 900. In 1003 Transylvania was incorporated into the Hungarian state by STEPHEN I, although it continued to enjoy a large measure of autonomy. It was allowed to develop its own constitution, which safeguarded a 'brotherly union' between its three dominant ethnic groups: Magyars, Szeklers and Saxons. Excluded from this union were the Romanians, who were established in the region in the early 13th century, but were treated as little more than serfs.

In 1526 Hungary was defeated by the Turks, allowing Transylvania to emerge as an independent principality, albeit (after 1566) under OTTOMAN overlordship. During the 17th century Transylvania established itself as an international power with a reputation for religious tolerance. However, the defeat of the Turks at Vienna in 1683 allowed Austrian HABSBURG power to spread eastwards, and in 1711 Transylvania was officially incorporated into Austrian-controlled Hungary.

A Romanian national revival coincided with the defeat of Austria-Hungary in the First World War, and in 1920 Transylvania was incorporated into Romania as a reward to that country for having sided with the Allies. Large areas of Transylvania were annexed by Hungary in 1940, but these were restored to Romania in 1947.

Travancore see KERALA

treaty ports Name given to Asian ports, especially in China and Japan, that were opened in the 19th century to foreign trade as a result of a series of treaties. These treaties ended long periods when both countries had been closed to Westerners.

In China, the first five treaty ports were opened following the Treaty of NANJING in 1842. Eleven more opened as a result of the Treaty of Tianjin (1858) and the Conventions of Beijing (1860), and approximately 35 more before the CHINESE REVOLUTION of 1911. The treaties allowed foreigners to live in their own areas, where they were protected by their home governments. They did not have to pay Chinese taxes and were not subject to Chinese laws – privileges that were strongly resented by Chinese nationalists, and were consequently withdrawn by 1943.

In Japan, the Treaty of Kanagawa in 1858 established five treaty ports, but the foreign powers were obliged to surrender all their privileges in these ports in 1899.

trench warfare The digging of trenches as a means of protecting troops was well-known as early as the Middle Ages. Trenches were used extensively during the AMERICAN CIVIL WAR (1861-5), but they became an especially important feature of the FIRST WORLD WAR.

At the start of the First World War in 1914, army commanders still believed that victory would come from mass infantry charges – in spite of the widespread use of machine guns and artillery capable of inflicting unprecedented casualties. After the first battle of the MARNE in September 1914, both sides dug thousands of miles of parallel trenches along the Western Front. The trenches were linked by intricate networks of communication trenches and were protected by acres of barbed wire. Very soon the warring sides found themselves in a position of stalemate that called for the use of new weapons, such as hand grenades, poison gas, trench mortars and tanks. Mass artillery bombardments were used to weaken the enemy defences, usually with little effect. As the war wore on the trench systems became ever more elaborate to prevent an enemy breakthrough, and they proved virtually impregnable until late 1917, when Allied tanks achieved their first major victory.

During the First World War enemy trenches were at times only yards away from each other, within easy reach of a hand grenade.

Workers of the world unite

From the early 19th century workers combined to fight for better working conditions in their trade or industry; the strike was their ultimate weapon. For employers trade unions became a force to be reckoned with.

Between 1780 and 1820 cotton mill owners, among the key entrepreneurs of the early Industrial Revolution in England, saw their profits rise 20 times faster than the wages they paid their millhands. Workers, including women and children, were forced to toil for 12 hours a day or more in factories and mines. In Manchester a doctor described mill workers as 'a degenerate race of human beings, stunted, enfeebled and depraved – men and women that were not to be aged – children that were never to be adults'.

Since the days of the French Revolution of 1789, which had caused the governing classes of Europe to fear for their privileges, combinations of workers to fight for better conditions, shorter working hours and higher wages had been outlawed.

In 1825 trade unions were legalised in Britain and began to spring to life in industry after industry. Among the first to make use of their freedom – and almost immediately to strike – were shipbuilders and spinners. The ambitious effort made by the socialist reformer, Robert Owen, to amalgamate all workers in the Grand

This ornate certificate from the National Union of Railwaymen, 1912, is a sign of rising confidence within the trade union movement.

National Consolidated Trades Union (1833) foundered, but throughout Europe workers followed the English example. By the end of the 19th century unions were legal in almost every western European country.

In the United States, the Knights of Labor campaigned actively during the late 19th century for equal pay for equal work, an eight-hour day, and the abolition of child labour. The National Labor Union had been formed as early as 1866, and the National Labor Relations Act of 1935 acknowledged the legal right of workers to organise themselves into trade unions.

The strike has always been the ultimate weapon of trade unionists. Two of the most disruptive this century were the

The American trade unionist, Jimmy Hoffa, led a successful campaign to become president of the Teamsters' Union in 1957.

General Strike of 1926 in Britain and the mass strike in Paris in 1968. The first was called by the Trades Union Congress to support the miners' action against a proposal to reduce their wages and increase their hours. Their slogan was: 'Not a penny off the pay, not a minute on the day.' Two million workers downed tools, but the strike lasted for only nine days. It was defeated by a combination of middle and upper-class volunteers, who kept essential services going, and the loyalty of the armed forces to the government.

STRIKING POWERS

The Paris strike of 1968, which saw a rare alliance between workers and students, was as much a general protest against the government of Charles de Gaulle as an industrial action. The streets of the Latin Quarter of Paris were barricaded; Molotov cocktails and ripped-up cobblestones were hurled at riot police. The strike nearly became a national uprising, and was a significant factor in de Gaulle's departure from office the following year.

In the USA, despite the positive achievements of trade unions, the most prominent union leader of modern times was remembered mainly for his corruption. Jimmy Hoffa, head of the Teamsters' (transport workers') Union, was convicted of fraud, embezzlement and jury-tampering, and served four years in prison from 1967 to 1971. Later he disappeared, presumed murdered.

Since the 1980s trade unionism has declined throughout the Western world. Its weakened position is partly a result of legislation to increase the competitiveness of industry. There is greater flexibility within the labour market. Employers, in an age of rapid communications, are able to hire labour from all regions of the world. Together with high levels of unemployment caused by economic recession, these new patterns of work have robbed collective bargaining of much of its strength.

Trenchard, Hugh, 1st Viscount (1873-1956) Creator of the British Royal Air Force. In 1913 Trenchard joined the Royal Flying Corps (RFC), then a branch of the army. Two years later he was appointed commander of the RFC in France, and in April 1918 he succeeded in having the RFC separated from the army as the Royal Air Force. Trenchard became Britain's first Chief of Air Staff, and in 1927 first Marshal of the Royal Air Force. From 1932 to 1935 he served as Commissioner of Police, establishing a police college and a forensic laboratory at Hendon, London.

Trent, Council of (1545-63) Ecumenical council in which the Roman Catholic Church attempted to deal with the crisis brought about by the Protestant REFORMATION. The council met in the city of Trento in northern Italy in three sessions, each presided over by a different pope. The first, from 1545 to 1547, was held under Paul III; the second, from 1551 to 1552, was under Julius III; and the third session, from 1562 to 1563, was convened and chaired by Pius IV.

The intention of the council was to bring about reform of the Roman Catholic Church in answer to the criticisms of the Protestants, and also to set out a clear statement of Roman Catholic doctrines. It achieved these aims, and at the same time produced explicit rejections of certain central Protestant ideas, including Martin LUTHER's doctrine of justification by faith alone. In doing so, the council effectively made reconciliation with the Protestants impossible, and provided firm guidelines for its agents of the COUNTER-REFORMATION.

Trent affair (November-December 1861) Diplomatic furore between the USA and Britain during the AMERICAN CIVIL WAR. In November 1861 the US warship *San Jacinto* stopped the British mail ship *Trent* in the Bahama Channel and forcibly removed two Confederate diplomats bound for Europe. The British Government demanded their release, setting a seven-day deadline and implying that it might enter the civil war on the Confederate side. By late December the incident had fallen sufficiently from public view in the USA for the Cabinet to agree to release the diplomats, officially because the captain of the *San Jacinto* had not brought the *Trent* into port as international maritime law required.

Triads Name given by Western observers to a number of Chinese secret societies, many of them dedicated to overthrowing the Manchu QING dynasty in the 17th century in order to restore the indigenous Chinese MING emperors. The Triads had names such as the White Lotus Society and the Heaven and Earth Society, and they shared a number of rituals and beliefs. These included a common belief in the mystical significance of the number three – hence the name 'Triad'. In peacetime most Triads operated as cooperative brotherhoods, but many were also involved in crime.

The Triads grew in strength during the time of the TAIPING REBELLION, which lasted from 1851 to 1864. In 1900 the BOXER RISING marked an attempt by one powerful secret society to rid China of Western and Christian influence; and in the years that followed other secret societies assisted the nationalist leader SUN YAT-SEN in his efforts to overthrow the old imperial order and found a republic.

Soon after the communists came to power in 1949, they set about eliminating the Triads: membership of a secret society remains punishable by death in mainland China. In the rest of the world, Triads have followed wherever Chinese immigrants have settled. They are now best known as criminal organisations akin to the Mafia, specialising in the trade in drugs from South-east Asia.

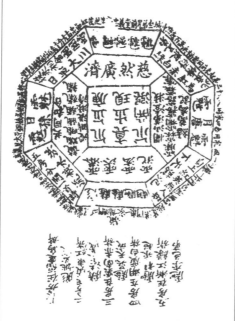

This secret emblem of a Triad society, made up of standard and invented Chinese characters, expounds the society's benevolent nature. Below the octagon are listed family branches.

tribune Either of two types of official in ancient Rome – one military, the other civilian. Military tribunes were originally infantry officers appointed or elected to help to command a legion: every legion had six tribunes among its senior officers. During the empire, the position of military tribune became an important early posting for a young man embarking on a political career.

Civilian tribunes, known as tribunes of the people, were elected officials charged with safeguarding the rights of the PLEBS, or common people. From the mid 5th century BC there were ten tribunes presiding over the plebian assembly in Rome. Their duties included introducing legislation to the assembly and ensuring that the interests of the plebs were suitably represented. They had the authority to veto the decisions of magistrates, the legislation of consuls and even decrees by the senate. Because they were immune from prosecution, the tribunes became some of the most powerful officials in Rome. During the empire, the tribunes lost their power to the emperors, who presented themselves as champions of the people.

Trieste Italian port city at the northern end of the Adriatic Sea. From the 12th century Trieste was a free commune under constant threat from its powerful neighbour Venice. In 1382 the city placed itself and its surrounding territory under the protection of Duke Leopold III of Austria, and consequently flourished as the only port of the Habsburg Empire. From the 1860s, Trieste became a centre for Italian nationalists and in 1919 the city and its coastal lands were annexed by Italy. After the end of the Second World War the entire area was claimed by Yugoslavia, but in 1947 it was declared a UN free territory. Following continuing tension between Italy and Yugoslavia, the area was partitioned between the two in 1954, the city of Trieste going to Italy. The coastal region of Istria is now part of the Republic of Slovenia.

Trinidad Island in the West Indies which, together with its smaller neighbour to the north, comprises the Republic of Trinidad and Tobago. Originally inhabited by Arawak and Carib Indians, the islands were sighted by Christopher Columbus during his third voyage in 1498. The Spanish established a token settlement on Trinidad in 1532, but at first largely ignored the island. Trinidad was raided by Sir Walter RALEIGH in 1595, followed by the Dutch and the French in the 17th century. During this period the Spanish established sugar and tobacco plantations, worked by slaves imported from Africa.

In 1797 a British fleet captured Trinidad from Spain, and in 1802 the island was formally ceded to Britain in terms of the Treaty of Amiens. Britain had already taken possession of Tobago, in 1762, and in 1809 the two islands were united politically.

From 1958 to 1962 Trinidad and Tobago formed part of the short-lived Federation of the West Indies, which collapsed after Jamaica pulled out of it in 1961. As a result, Trinidad and Tobago became an independent nation within the British Commonwealth in 1962, and a republic in 1976. The country's first prime minister was Eric Williams, founder of the People's National Movement, which has dominated the islands' politics for over three decades. In 1987, Tobago was granted full self government. Three years later, in 1990, the prime minister was briefly seized by militant Black Muslims protesting against economic hardship.

Triple Alliance (May 1882) Secret alliance created between Germany, Austria-Hungary and Italy, largely under the influence of the German chancellor, Otto von BISMARCK. The three powers agreed to support each other, either militarily or by remaining neutral, in the event of war with France or Russia.

The alliance had its origins in the Dual Alliance signed three years earlier between Germany and Austria-Hungary – a defence pact joined by Italy in 1882. Each country had its own reason for entering the alliance: Germany wanted protection against France, which it feared was plotting to avenge its defeat in the FRANCO-PRUSSIAN WAR of 1870-1; Austria-Hungary sought support against Russia, its rival in the Balkans; and Italy, although fearful of Austro-Hungarian

expansion, wanted help in pursuing its territorial ambitions in North Africa. The alliance created a major central European power bloc, especially after it was joined by Romania in 1883. Partly as a response to this, Britain and France concluded their own informal alliance, known as the ENTENTE CORDIALE, in 1904, which became the Triple Entente when they were joined by Russia in 1907. The Triple Alliance was broken in May 1915, when Italy declared war on Austria-Hungary.

trireme Principal Mediterranean war galley from the 6th to the 4th century BC. The trireme derived its name from having three banks of oars (a smaller version with two banks of oars was called a bireme). Lightly built for speed and manoeuvrability and unable to venture far from land, each trireme carried a crew of some 200 men, the majority being rowers. They were probably seated on three tiers of benches, so that each rower could pull a separate oar. Triremes were about 120 ft (37 m) long, and were fitted with a bronze ram at the bow for splintering enemy ships. In 480 BC a Greek fleet of triremes scored a decisive victory over a much larger Persian fleet

at the Battle of SALAMIS. In the decades that followed, triremes played an important part in helping Athens to emerge as the most powerful city-state in Greece.

Tromp, Maarten (1597-1653) Dutch admiral who made decisive contributions to Dutch naval success in the 17th century. In 1639, with only 18 vessels at his disposal, Tromp defeated a Spanish fleet of 45 warships in the English Channel, at the Battle of the Downs – a victory which marked the passing of Spanish sea power. During the First ANGLO-DUTCH War, Tromp defeated the English admiral Robert BLAKE off Dungeness in December 1652, fought magnificently to protect Dutch convoys in the English Channel and was killed in 1653 trying to break George MONCK's blockade of the Dutch coast.

His son Cornelis (1629-91) also achieved renown as an admiral, although his career was obstructed by Admiral Michiel de RUYTER. An impulsive commander, Cornelis Tromp won victories against Mediterranean pirates and against the English and French in the second and third Anglo-Dutch wars. In 1676 he defeated a Swedish fleet at Gotland.

The trireme was the fastest oar-driven ship ever built. In good weather it could keep up a steady speed of 8 to 9 miles per hour (13 to 15 km per hour) for an entire day.

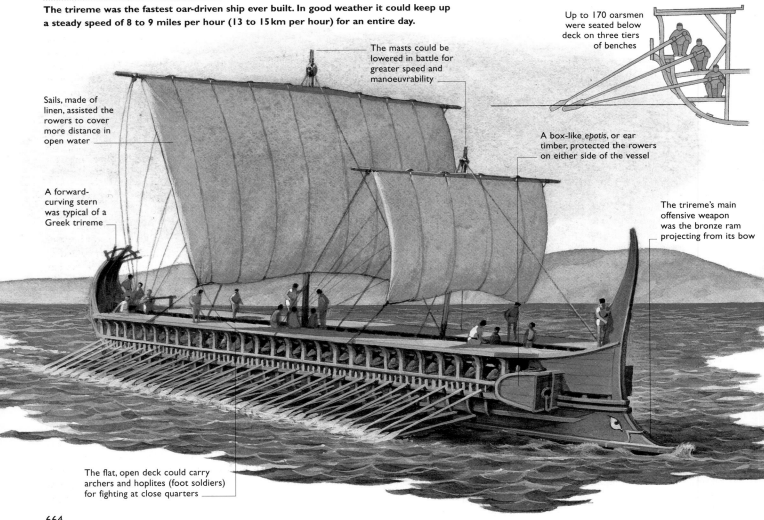

Up to 170 oarsmen were seated below deck on three tiers of benches

The masts could be lowered in battle for greater speed and manoeuvrability

Sails, made of linen, assisted the rowers to cover more distance in open water

A box-like *epotis*, or ear timber, protected the rowers on either side of the vessel

A forward-curving stern was typical of a Greek trireme

The trireme's main offensive weapon was the bronze ram projecting from its bow

The flat, open deck could carry archers and hoplites (foot soldiers) for fighting at close quarters

Trotsky, Leon (1879-1940) Russian communist revolutionary and military leader. Born Lev Bronstein, the son of prosperous Jewish farmers in the Ukraine, he became a Marxist in 1896. By 1900 he had been jailed several times as punishment for revolutionary activities. In 1902 he fled from Russia under the name of Trotsky – adopted from one of his jailers – and settled in London, where he met the exiled Social Democrat Vladimir LENIN.

Trotsky admired Lenin, but feared that his methods would lead to dictatorship. He therefore sided with the Menshevik faction against the BOLSHEVIKS when the Social Democratic Party split in 1903. Two years later, Trotsky returned to Russia to take part in the first RUSSIAN REVOLUTION. He was arrested, exiled to Siberia and in 1907 again managed to escape. In 1917 he was back in Russia, where he played a leading role in the second Russian Revolution which brought the Bolsheviks to power.

As Commissar for Foreign Affairs in the first Soviet government, Trotsky negotiated the Treaty of BREST-LITOVSK by which Russia withdrew from the First World War in 1918; however, its terms were so humiliating that Trotsky felt compelled to resign. Between 1918 and 1924 he was Commissar for War, in which capacity he built up the RED ARMY and directed it during the RUSSIAN CIVIL WAR of 1918-21. When Lenin died in 1924, Trotsky was his obvious successor, but he lacked the prestige of Joseph STALIN, who had become general secretary of the Communist Party in 1922. As an internationalist, Trotsky was dedicated to world revolution, and strongly

Trotsky, probably the most formidable thinker among the early Russian communists, continues to study during his exile in Mexico.

opposed Stalin's cautious approach of 'Socialism in one country'. Steadily losing influence, Trotsky was expelled from the party in 1927, and in 1929 he was forced to leave the Soviet Union. He settled in Mexico in 1936, only to be murdered four years later by Ramón Mercader, a Spanish communist strongly suspected of acting on Stalin's orders.

Troubadours make merry with cymbals, zither and lute in this manuscript preserved at Monte Cassino, Italy.

troubadour Poet-musician of southern France and northern Spain and Italy from the 11th to the 13th century. One of the most distinctive features of troubadour verse is that it is written in *langue d'oc*, the dialect of Provence, whatever the nationality of the poet. Many troubadours were men of noble or aristocratic birth, and some were kings, among them Richard I of England and Alfonso X of Castile and Léon. Minstrels from the lower classes who set the troubadours' poetry to music and helped them to perform it were usually known as *jongleurs*.

The troubadours' verse dealt with courtly love, chivalry, religion and politics, but often the matter was heavily disguised in formal, decorative language. Some of it was heretical, and in the 13th century many troubadours were persecuted. Their poetry was nevertheless among the most important to be written during the Middle Ages, exercising a strong influence on later poetic developments.

Troy Ancient city in north-west Asia Minor, also known as Ilion (Latin Ilium). According to Greek legend, Troy was subjected to a ten-year siege by the Greek king Agamemnon. The city fell to the Greeks after its citizens opened their gates to receive a wooden horse, without realising that it was filled with Greek warriors. Part of the story of the Trojan War is recounted in HOMER's epic poem the *Iliad*.

Convinced that Homer's account contained more than mere myth, the German archaeologist Heinrich Schliemann set about proving that the Roman ruins of Ilion, contained in the mound of Hissarlik in Turkey, were the site of Homeric Troy. His excavations of the mound, conducted between 1870 and 1890, revealed a city with ten distinct periods of occupation. This city is now referred to as Troy.

The first five periods of Troy (Troy I-V) belong to the Early Bronze Age, ending soon after 2000 BC. Troy II, in particular, was a flourishing community, with impressive fortifications and domestic buildings. Troy VI and VII saw an influx of new settlers, who introduced horses, but an earthquake shattered their city in about 1300 BC. The next period, Troy VIIa, did not last long before the city was destroyed by fire. The date of this conflagration, *c.*1250 BC, coincided with a flourishing of Mycenaean civilisation in mainland Greece, suggesting that this event may lie behind the Homeric story, and that

the conquerors of Troy VIIa were Greeks. The site remained unoccupied for perhaps 400 years before Troy VIII was established there. Troy IX consists of the Hellenistic city of Ilion, which lasted well into Roman times.

Trucial States (1820-1971) Former name for the seven states comprising the UNITED ARAB EMIRATES. In the early 19th century the region was notorious for its pirate attacks on British and Indian ships. British naval action induced the area's sheikhs to sign a general peace truce in 1820, followed by a perpetual maritime truce in 1853 – hence the names Trucial States and Trucial Coast. Further treaties with Britain banned trading in arms and slaves, and in 1892 the sheikhs granted Britain control of their foreign affairs. In December 1971 Britain withdrew its armed forces from the Persian Gulf, enabling the Trucial States to form themselves into the United Arab Emirates.

Truck Acts Measures passed by the British Parliament in the 19th century regulating the payment of wages. Certain employers paid their workmen in goods or tokens which could be exchanged only at shops owned by the employers – the so-called truck system, from a now obscure sense of *truck*, meaning 'to barter'. The Truck Act of 1831 listed many trades in which payment of wages had to be made in coins. It was amended by an Act of 1887, which extended its provisions to cover virtually all manual workers. In 1896 a further Act regulated the amounts that could be deducted from wages for bad workmanship.

Trudeau, Pierre (1919-) Canadian statesman who was prime minister of Canada from 1968 to 1979 and from 1980 to 1984. Born to French and Scottish parents, Trudeau was elected to the Canadian parliament in 1965. Three years later he succeeded Lester PEARSON as both leader of the Liberal Party and prime minister of Canada. His Bilingual Languages

Act of 1968 gave French and English equal status throughout Canada, and helped to improve relations between French and English-speaking Canadians. However, he opposed the separation of QUEBEC from the rest of Canada, and in 1969 and 1970 he took firm measures against separatist terrorists.

Throughout the 1970s Trudeau tried to secure economic growth while combatting ever-increasing inflation and unemployment. He improved relations with France, but made little real progress in his efforts to make Canada more independent of the USA. By 1979 Canada was experiencing serious economic problems, and Trudeau's Liberal Party lost the election of that year. The Progressive Conservative Party briefly took power as a minority government, before a new election returned the Liberals to government in 1980.

During his second period in office, Trudeau set in motion a number of major political reforms. Following a referendum in May 1980 in which the partition of Canada was overwhelmingly rejected, he proposed that the power to amend the Canadian constitution should be surrendered by the British Parliament. This was accepted in both Canada and Britain, and on April 4, 1982 Canada's parliament became independent from its British counterpart. Trudeau then devoted himself to improving the Canadian economy before announcing his retirement in early 1984.

Trujillo, Rafael (1891-1961) Dictator of the Dominican Republic from 1930 to 1961. Trujillo received military training from United States Marines during the US occupation of his country between 1916 and 1924. Rising to become chief of the army, he seized power in a coup in 1930, and spent the next 31 years ruthlessly holding on to it. In 1937 Trujillo ordered his troops to halt illegal migration from Haiti; the result was a bloodbath in which up to 15 000 people were killed. In spite of achieving many improvements to the Dominican Republic, Trujillo's repressive methods aroused strong opposition and he was assassinated by conspirators in May 1961.

Truman, Harry S (1884-1972) Thirty-third president of the USA, from 1945 to 1953. Truman served as a Democratic senator from 1935 to 1944, representing Missouri. He became vice-president only 82 days before the death of President Franklin D. ROOSEVELT. Truman automatically succeeded Roosevelt, and immediately took a leading role on the world stage. In July he attended the POTSDAM CONFERENCE to plan for the future of Europe, and in September he authorised the dropping of two atomic bombs on Japan. In 1947 Truman announced a policy of helping countries that were under threat from armed minorities or foreign interference – the so-called TRUMAN DOCTRINE. At home,

Harry S Truman, the 'sure loser', beams as he holds aloft a premature *Chicago Tribune* headline after winning the 1948 US presidential election.

Truman largely continued Roosevelt's NEW DEAL policies, but he fell out with Congress through his efforts to introduce social reforms in areas such as public health and housing, social security and employment.

In 1948 Truman unexpectedly defeated the Republican Thomas Dewey in that year's presidential elections. He went on to take the USA into NATO, and in 1949 initiated the Point Four scheme for giving technical aid to less-developed nations. After the outbreak of the Korean War in 1950, Truman ensured that Western forces entered the conflict under UN, rather than US, authority. The following year he was forced to dismiss General Douglas MACARTHUR for publicly advocating a war with communist China.

Truman did not run for re-election in 1953, but remained active in politics long after his retirement. Although he was poorly regarded during his term in office, he is now thought of as one of the strongest US presidents.

Truman Doctrine (1947) Former guiding principle of US foreign policy designed to contain communism. It was announced by President Harry S TRUMAN in March 1947, when Greece and Turkey were in danger of a communist take over. Truman pledged that the USA would 'support free peoples who are resisting attempted subjugation by armed minorities or by outside pressures'. Congress voted large sums to provide military and economic aid to countries whose stability was threatened by communism. The policy played a important role in launching the Cold War (see feature, page 150).

Tshombe, Moise (1920-69) Leader of the short-lived African state of Katanga – now Shaba province in ZAÏRE – which broke away from the Republic of the Congo two weeks after that country became independent from Belgium in 1960. As president of the Conakat Party, Tshombe proposed that the Congo should consist of a loose federation of states, but his ideas were rejected in favour of

Patrice LUMUMBA's vision of a strongly centralised republic. A fortnight after Lumumba took office as the Congo's first premier, the army mutinied, allowing Tshombe to seize the opportunity and declare his home province of Katanga an independent republic.

Supported by White mercenaries and the Belgian mining company Union Minière, Tshombe held on to power until January 1963, when United Nations troops intervened and he was forced to flee to Spain. The following year he was recalled to the Congo to act as prime minister, but he was dismissed in 1965 and charged with treason. Tshombe again fled to Spain, but in 1967 he was kidnapped and taken to Algeria, where he died after being placed under house arrest.

Tubman, Harriet (c.1820-1913) American antislavery leader. In 1849 Tubman escaped from slavery in Maryland, making her way to freedom in the northern United States by the UNDERGROUND RAILROAD – a network of safe houses established for this purpose. She returned to Maryland the following year to help her family to escape, and over the next 12

Harriet Tubman stands beside a group of slaves whom she had helped to liberate. Her modest appearance helped her to avoid detection.

years she became one of the foremost 'conductors' on the 'railroad', leading some 300 slaves to freedom. She was said to have forced weary or fainthearted escapees onwards by threatening them with a revolver. During the American Civil War Tubman served as a nurse for the Federal forces, and even operated as a spy behind Confederate lines. After the war she devoted herself to Black education.

Tudor English royal house which ruled the country from 1485 to 1603. The Tudors were originally a family of Welsh aristocrats, whose fortunes improved dramatically when Owen Tudor married Catherine of Valois, HENRY V's widow, in the late 1420s. Their eldest son, Edmund (c.1430-56), was made Earl of Richmond by Henry VI, and married Margaret BEAUFORT, great-granddaughter of John of GAUNT – an ancestry that gave her a distant Lancastrian claim to the English throne.

Edmund was executed after the Yorkist victory at the Battle of Mortimer's Cross in 1461, but his only son, Henry Tudor, became HENRY VII after defeating RICHARD III in 1485 at the Battle of BOSWORTH FIELD. This victory ended the Wars of the ROSES and gained Henry the throne as the first Tudor king.

Henry safeguarded his claim to the throne by marrying Elizabeth of York and thereby uniting the previously warring houses of York and Lancaster. He was succeeded by HENRY VIII, whose only surviving legitimate son, EDWARD VI, died in his youth in 1553. Edward was succeeded by his elder half-sister MARY I, who died in 1558 after a childless marriage to Philip II of Spain; and she was succeeded in turn by her younger half-sister, ELIZABETH I, who never married. With Elizabeth's death in 1603 the House of Tudor came to an end, and the throne passed to JAMES VI of Scotland. James was a member of the House of STUART, which derived its claim to the English throne from Margaret Tudor, elder sister of Henry VIII, who had married James IV of Scotland.

Tuileries Former royal palace situated next to the Louvre in Paris, which was commissioned by Catherine de Medici in 1564 and destroyed by fire in 1871. During the French Revolution, the French royal family were forcibly moved from Versailles in October 1789 and placed under virtual house arrest in the Tuileries. In June 1792 the palace was attacked by a crowd of revolutionaries, and again on August 10, when the mob massacred Louis XVI's Swiss guards and forced the royal family to take refuge in the National Assembly. In 1793 the Tuileries was headquarters for the COMMITTEE OF PUBLIC SAFETY; it was later the principal residence of Napoleon I and all subsequent French rulers. The palace was burned down by arsonists during the Commune of PARIS, but its gardens remain part of the Louvre.

Tull, Jethro (1674-1741) British engineer who made an important contribution to the AGRICULTURAL REVOLUTION. Tull studied law, but he abandoned his legal career in 1699 in favour of farming. In 1701 he constructed a horse-drawn mechanical seed drill, which planted seeds in neat rows rather than scattering them wastefully, as was currently the practice. Tull's drill also covered the seeds with soil, protecting them from birds. He also recommended aerating the soil and invented a horse-drawn hoe for the purpose. Tull's ideas and inventions created the basis of modern, efficient farming practice.

Tunisia North African country, the strategic centre of the Mediterranean. The Tunisian coast was settled by the PHOENICIANS from about 1200 BC. By the 6th century the coastal city of CARTHAGE, situated near present-day Tunis, lay at the heart of a powerful kingdom, which was destroyed by the Romans at the end of the PUNIC WARS in 146 BC. The region then became part of Rome's Africa province, providing the Romans with large quantities of corn, olives and wine. In 44 BC the Romans began rebuilding Carthage, which soon became one of their administrative centres in the region.

In AD 439 VANDALS from Spain invaded Carthage and its surrounding territory. They remained there until they were driven out by the Byzantine general BELISARIUS in 533. During this time, most of the region's interior was held by BERBERS, who gave way only in the face of the overwhelming Arab invasions of the mid 7th century. The Arabs destroyed Carthage and built their own capital of Kairouan, or Al Qayrawan, as an inland base from which to control north-central Africa. The city soon became one of the holiest places of pilgrimage in Islam.

Successive Arab dynasties ruled Tunisia, among them the Aghlabids, the Fatimids and the Zirids. In 1159 the region was conquered by the ALMOHAD caliph of Morocco, and in 1228 it fell under the control of a local Berber dynasty – the Hafsids – who ruled until they were defeated by the OTTOMAN Turks in 1574. From the 17th century Tunisia became increasingly independent under its Ottoman governor, the bey of Tunis. By the mid 19th century, however, Ottoman power was weakening, enabling the French to invade Tunisia and establish a protectorate over it in 1881.

After the end of the First World War, demands for Tunisian independence grew rapidly within the country. Fighting erupted between nationalists and the colonial government in the early 1950s, leading the French to negotiate with the imprisoned nationalist leader Habib BOURGUIBA. In 1956 the country became fully independent with Bourguiba as its first prime minister. The following year Bourguiba forced the last bey of Tunis to abdicate so that Tunisia could become a republic, and in 1961 he challenged the French over their continuing use of a naval base at Bizerte. This resulted in a French withdrawal in 1963.

Bourguiba led Tunisia until 1987, when he was deposed by General Zine el-Abidine Ben Ali as being mentally unfit to govern. Since then the country has seen a rise in Islamic fundamentalism, which was partially suppressed in 1990. Tunisia remained neutral during the

For centuries, Barbary pirates based in Tunisia raided European shipping. This 19th-century French print shows them on a raid.

GULF WAR, as a result of which both Kuwait and Saudi Arabia withdrew investments and the USA cut back its aid to the country.

tunnage and poundage Duties levied in England on each tun (a large cask) of imported wine and on every pound of most imported or exported merchandise. From the 15th century Parliament had granted the revenue from these duties to the king for life, but in 1625 CHARLES I's first Parliament granted him the duties for one year only in an attempt to reassert parliamentary control over customs revenue. When Charles continued to collect the duties, Parliament issued its PETITION OF RIGHT in 1628, which Charles also ignored, further enraging the Commons. The duties were eventually abolished in 1787.

Turenne, Henri, Vicomte de (1611-75) Marshal of France and one of Louis XIV's greatest commanders. Turenne forged his reputation on the battlefields of the THIRTY YEARS' WAR. His victories in 1652 helped to conclude the civil wars of the FRONDE in favour of the young king Louis XIV, and his capture of Dunkirk in 1658 placed France in a strong position for negotiating the Treaty of the Pyrenees the following year. In 1674, when France was threatened on all sides, Turenne showed his supreme ability in deploying troops against superior forces. He was killed in battle, near Strasbourg.

Turin Shroud Cloth preserved since 1578 in Turin Cathedral in Italy, which was long venerated by some as the shroud in which JESUS CHRIST was buried. The cloth bears the

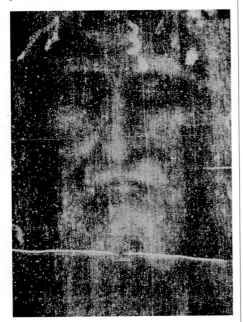

For centuries people believed that this face on the Turin Shroud was the image of Jesus, imprinted on the cloth after his crucifixion.

image of a man who had suffered scourging and had received a puncture wound in his midriff and in each of his wrists and feet. Recent carbon-dating has shown that the cloth dates from between 1260 and 1390, and the Roman Catholic Church now accepts that it can no longer be regarded as authentic.

Turing, Alan (1912-54) British mathematician who pioneered computer theory. In 1937 he published a ground-breaking paper, entitled 'On Computable Numbers', which was in effect a mathematical analysis of how a computer should work. During the Second World War, Turing worked for British Intelligence, playing an important role in building a device that could break the ciphers of the German coding machine known as Enigma. After the war he helped to design the earliest British electronic computers, and in 1948 he joined the University of Manchester to direct the building of a computer with a larger memory than any previous machine. His work laid the foundations of the emerging sciences of computer programming and artificial intelligence.

DID YOU KNOW?

Alan Turing argued that for computers to be able to 'think' like human beings they would need to contain a device which introduces totally random information to their processes.

Turkey Country in south-west Asia occupied since antiquity by numerous peoples, including the Hittites, the Persians, the Greeks and the Romans. The BYZANTINE EMPIRE, based at Constantinople, lasted until 1453, when it fell to the OTTOMAN sultan Mehmed II. The Ottomans then dominated the region, and extensive neighbouring territories, until their empire collapsed at the end of the First World War.

Under the terms of the Treaty of SÈVRES (1920), the defeated Ottoman state was reduced to a fraction of its former size. This triggered off fierce nationalist resistance led by Mustafa Kemal, later known as ATATURK – 'Father of the Turks'. A Greek army invaded Turkey, but was defeated, and Ataturk was able to negotiate more generous terms for Turkey at the Conference of Lausanne in 1923. This established the country's boundaries largely as they exist today, and required the repatriation of some 1.5 million Greeks and half a million Armenians.

In October 1923 the Republic of Turkey was proclaimed, with Ataturk as its first president. Earlier, in November 1922, Ataturk had declared the end of the Ottoman sultanate, and in 1924 he abolished the country's ancient CALIPHATE. Governing as a virtual dictator, Ataturk instituted radical social and economic reforms, modernising, secularising and Westernising the country. He was succeeded by Ismel Inonu, who kept Turkey neutral for most of the Second World War, and instituted multiparty elections in 1950. These were won

by the opposition Democratic Party, which maintained Turkey's alignment with the West. In 1952 the country joined NATO, in spite of tension with Greece over the island of CYPRUS. This boiled over in 1974, when Turkish troops invaded Cyprus following a Greek-led coup d'état there.

Political instability and violence led to a bloodless coup and the imposition of martial law in Turkey itself in 1980. Elections were again held in 1983, and by 1987 martial law had been lifted in most areas. The exceptions were provinces dominated by the country's Kurdish minority, whose nationalistic aspirations have increasingly been expressed by armed confrontation with Turkish troops as well as terrorist acts.

In 1989, Turkey applied for membership of the European Community, but consideration of this has been regularly postponed owing to the country's poor reputation for respecting human rights.

Turkistan Area of central Asia north of the Himalayas, stretching from the Caspian Sea to the western provinces of China. It includes both deserts and highlands and the fertile Ferghana valley, and among its historic centres are Bukhara, Samarkand and Tashkent, all on the ancient caravan trail known as the Silk Road. The western part of the region was under Persian rule from the 6th century BC, Muslim control from the 7th century AD, and Russian overlordship from the 18th century. The eastern portion was contested between the Chinese empire and various nomadic peoples, such as the Mongols and the Khojas.

During the 19th century, Russia, China and Afghanistan began to impose centralised governments on the region. In 1884 East Turkistan became the Chinese province of Sinkiang – now known as the Xinjiang Uygur Autonomous Region. West Turkistan likewise came under Russian control, resulting in the creation of five central Asian Soviet republics after the end of the Russian Civil War in 1921: their names were Turkmenistan, Uzbekistan, Tajikistan, Kyrgyzstan and Kazakhstan. These republics all gained their independence following the collapse of the Soviet Union in 1991.

Turner, Nat (1800-31) Black American leader of the Virginia slave revolt – the only sustained slave uprising in US history. A gifted preacher, Turner believed himself to be divinely appointed to guide his people out of bondage. In August 1831 he led about 60 slaves in a rebellion in Southampton County, Virginia. Some 55 Whites were killed before the state militia arrived and dispersed his followers. Several slaves were hanged at once, including a number who had taken no part in the uprising. Turner himself remained at large for six weeks before being captured and hanged. His rebellion led to a tightening of laws against slaves in the Southern states, and increased hostility towards abolitionists. He has been popularised by William Styron's novel *The Confessions of Nat Turner* (1967).

Tuscany Region in west-central Italy that was one of the great centres of the RENAISSANCE, particularly in the city of Florence. From 1569 to 1737 Tuscany was ruled by the powerful Medici family. It then passed to the Austrian Habsburgs, before being annexed to France by Napoleon I in 1808. Six years later Habsburg rule was restored, and in 1848 Grand Duke Leopold II granted the duchy a liberal constitution. When Tuscan rebels declared a republic in early 1849 Leopold fled, but he was soon restored by the Austrian army. He was driven out again in 1859, and in 1861 Tuscany joined the new kingdom of Italy.

Tutankhamun Pharaoh of Egypt from around 1361 to 1352 BC. Little is known about Tutankhamun's reign and early death at the age of about 18, apart from the fact that he restored polytheistic religion to Egypt after his father AKHEN-ATEN had replaced it with monotheistic worship of the sun god, Aton.

Tutankhamun would have been little more than an obscure minor pharaoh were it not for the fact that his tomb in the VALLEY OF THE KINGS near Luxor was the only one to escape looting in antiquity.

The pharaoh's tomb was hidden by rubble excavated during the construction of a later tomb, and it was not discovered until 1922 when the British Egypt-ologist Howard Carter and his patron, Lord Carnarvon, found it with the burial chamber intact. Tutankhamun's mummi-fied body was inside three coffins, of which the inner was made of solid gold, and

Tutankhamun's exquisite inner coffin, made from gold inlaid with coloured glass and chalcedony, shows the high level of sophistication of ancient Egyptian culture.

the outer ones of gold-covered wood. Over his face was a magnificent gold funerary mask, and the burial chamber and other rooms housed a unique collection of jewellery, weapons and other items. These provided scholars with a wealth of new information about life in ancient Egypt. Asked by Lord Carnarvon what he could see when he first looked inside the tomb, Carter could only reply: 'Wonderful things.'

Twain, Mark (1835-1910) Pen name of the American writer Samuel Langhorne Clemens. He spent his boyhood near the Mississippi river, and in the late 1850s he trained as a river pilot on Mississippi steamboats. When the American Civil War ended river traffic in 1861, Clemens tried his hand at a variety of occupations before emerging as a journalist and humorous writer under the name Mark Twain – derived from a boatman's call indicat-ing that the river is two fathoms deep.

Twain won acclaim in 1869 with the satir-ical novel *The Innocents Abroad*, but his best known works are his two accounts of boy-hood escapades, *The Adventures of Tom Sawyer* (1876) and *The Adventures of Huckleberry Finn* (1884). Another of Twain's works to remain popular is *A Connecticut Yankee in King Arthur's Court*, published in 1889.

Tyler, Wat (d.1381) Leader of the English PEASANTS' REVOLT against the imposition of a heavy poll tax and other government policies during the reign of RICHARD II. Tyler was a former soldier who was chosen by the rebels of Kent to be their captain and spokesman in June 1381. On June 10, Tyler led the rebels in an assault on Canterbury, followed swiftly by a two-day march on London, where they cap-tured the Savoy palace of John of GAUNT, London Bridge and the Tower of London.

On June 15 Richard met the rebels, promised concessions and ordered them to go home. In response, Tyler made a series of ever more radical demands, prompting an angry exchange of words with the mayor of London, William Walworth. In the fighting that en-sued Tyler was wounded and he was taken to St Bartholomew's Hospital. The 14-year-old king kept the mob at bay until reinforcements arrived. The rebellion was then swiftly put down and order restored. Tyler was beheaded.

Tyndale, William (c.1494-1536) English humanist scholar who believed that people should be free to read the Bible in their own languages. Prevented by the Church authori-ties from translating the Bible into English in England, he set to work in Germany with funding from wealthy London merchants. By 1525 he had completed his translation of the New Testament, which found a ready, if illicit, market in England. Tyndale proceeded to the Old Testament, to the great rage of Church

William Tyndale angered both Protestant and Roman Catholic authorities by daring to translate the Bible from Latin into English.

officials. He compounded his unpopularity in England by writing a tract denouncing the divorce of Henry VIII. Tyndale was captured in Antwerp and executed as a heretic. By then 50 000 copies of his New Testament had been printed, inspiring numerous later translators.

Tyre Ancient city of the PHOENICIANS, and the site of modern Sur in Lebanon. The city was famous for its manufactured goods, and especially for its rich dye, known as Tyrian purple. In 587 BC Tyre fell to the Babylonian king Nebuchadnezzar II, and in 332 BC it was razed by Alexander the Great. In spite of such setbacks, the city always recovered its status as a major commercial centre – until 1291, when it was destroyed by the Mameluke Turks.

Tyrone, Hugh O'Neill, 2nd Earl of (c.1540-1616) Irish chieftain who rebelled unsuccessfully against the English from 1595 to 1603. Tyrone grew up in London and helped the English to suppress an Irish revolt in 1580. He then settled in Ulster, where he established himself as the most powerful chief in the area. Dissatisfaction with English rule led him to form an alliance with other chiefs and to rebel against Elizabeth I. In 1598 Tyrone achieved a spectacular victory at the Battle of Yellow Ford, but in 1601 he was defeated at Kinsale. He fought on until 1603, surrendering on March 30 – six days after the death of Elizabeth. Pardoned by James I, Tyrone stayed on in Ulster until September 1607, when he and some 100 northern chiefs secretly fled to the Continent. This so-called 'flight of the earls' ended tribal Gaelic rule in Ulster, enabling the English to take control of the whole island of Ireland.

United Arab Emirates Federation of Arab states bordering the Persian Gulf whose great wealth is derived from large reserves of oil and natural gas. It was founded in 1971 by the former TRUCIAL STATES of Abu Dhabi, Dubai, Sharjah, Ajman, Umm al-Qaiwain and Fujairah. Ras al-Khaimah joined in 1972. Britain had maintained a presence in the area from the 17th century, gaining control over foreign policy on the Trucial Coast in 1892 through treaties with individual rulers. The British withdrew from the Persian Gulf in 1971. In the same year the emirates came together as an independent state and signed a Treaty of Friendship with Britain. The federation is governed by the Supreme Council of Rulers under President Sheikh Zayed bin Sultan al-Nahayan of Abu Dhabi.

United Arab Republic Political union of Syria and Egypt from 1958 to 1961. It was dissolved when, following a military coup, Syria declared itself independent. Yemen withdrew from the loose federation it had joined with the Republic in 1966. Egypt used the name United Arab Republic until 1971, when it became the Arab Republic of Egypt.

United Empire Loyalist Title adopted by 40 000 Americans who were loyal to the British king GEORGE III and who emigrated to Canada during and after the American Revolution (see feature, page 31). By 1784 about 30 000 were settled in Nova Scotia and 10 000 in Quebec and around Lake Ontario. They included townspeople from the eastern seaboard, farmers and artisans, who played an important role in Canada's development. In 1789 the governor-general ordained that all those who had arrived by 1783 could put 'UE' for United Empire Loyalist after their own and their descendants' names.

United Irishmen Society established in Belfast in 1791 by Wolfe TONE and others to bring about parliamentary reform in Ireland and to unite Catholics and Protestants in one nation. By 1796 the society had become secret with the aim of establishing an Irish republic by violent means. Inspired by the French Revolution, the Irishmen sought military assistance from France, and in December 1796 a French fleet of 35 ships carrying thousands of troops arrived in Bantry Bay. Scattered by violent storms, the ships returned without landing their troops. Wolfe Tone, who was with them, remarked that England had not had such an escape since the scattering of the Spanish Armada. In 1798 sporadic uprisings occurred, especially in Wexford and Carlow, but the conspiracy was broken by the swift and ruthless tactics of the British military. Another French force was intercepted and Tone was captured. He was tried and condemned, but committed suicide.

United Kingdom see BRITAIN, GREAT; UNION, ACTS OF

United Nations International organisation established in 1945 as the successor to the LEAGUE OF NATIONS with the aim of promoting world peace and security. The UN has played an important role in bringing peace to areas of conflict, help to refugees and relief to areas of disaster, as well as in the promotion of international trade, scientific and cultural collaboration, and the support of child welfare and education.

The founding of the United Nations was discussed by the UK, the USA and the USSR at the YALTA CONFERENCE in February 1945. Its charter was signed in San Francisco in June, and it came into being in October 1945 with 51 members. The UN headquarters are in New York. Membership stands at 185 states. The annual budget of the UN is currently $1250 million, with members contributing according to their means.

The UN comprises six principal bodies: the General Assembly, the Security Council, the Economic and Social Council, the Trusteeship Council, the Secretariat and the International Court of Justice. Representatives of all the member states sit in the General Assembly, which is responsible for the UN's budget and makes recommendations on any question concerning the work of the organisation. The Security Council is the UN's most powerful body. It is concerned with the maintenance of international security, and has five permanent members – the UK, the USA, the Russian Federation, China and France – and ten elected members. It has sent peace-keeping forces to many trouble spots, including Cyprus (1964), Lebanon (1978), Kuwait (1991) and Bosnia (1992). The Economic and Social Council deals with cultural and humanitarian improvements. The Trusteeship Council looks after territories that are preparing for self-government. The Secretariat handles the UN's administrative affairs under the secretary-general. The first secretary-general was Trygve Lie of Norway (1946-53); since 1992 the post has been held by Boutros Boutros-Ghali of Egypt.

The International Court of Justice is the judicial body of the UN. It consists of 15 elected judges, each from a different country, and it sits in The Hague in the Netherlands. The UN oversees a number of specialised agencies, including the United Nations Children's Fund (UNICEF), the United Nations Educational, Scientific and Cultural Organisation (UNESCO), the United Nations Conference on Trade and Development (UNCTAD) and the Office of the United Nations High Commissioner for Refugees (UNHCR). Other organisations supervised by the United Nations include the World Bank, the International Monetary Fund and the World Health Organisation.

DID YOU KNOW?

The USA is so vast that dawn comes to western Alaska eight hours later than it does to eastern Maine. Even California is three hours behind the east coast.

United States of America Country in North America. The USA is bounded by the Atlantic Ocean to the east and the Pacific Ocean to the west, Canada to the north and Mexico to the south. It is a federal republic consisting of 50 states, including Alaska and Hawaii. The country was originally inhabited by AMERINDIANS, descendants of Asian aboriginals who crossed from Siberia to Alaska during the Ice Age around 50 000 BC or even earlier. They did what they could to resist European settlers, but colonisation gathered momentum after the arrival of the Spanish in Florida in 1565, and the English in Virginia in 1607. The Dutch and French followed. In the struggle for supremacy in the region, the SEVEN YEARS' WAR between Britain and France ended in 1763 with the Treaty of PARIS, which marked the final triumph of Britain.

However, British attempts to reassert central authority over the colonies were resisted. The First CONTINENTAL CONGRESS met in 1774 to consider action to regain lost rights, and the first armed encounters at LEXINGTON AND CONCORD in 1775 led directly to full-scale revolt, and to the formal proclamation of the separation of the THIRTEEN COLONIES from Britain in the DECLARATION OF INDEPENDENCE on July 4, 1776. In the American Revolution (see feature, page 31) the American cause was assisted by France and Spain. In 1783 the second Treaty of PARIS recognised American independence, and the new state was given legislative form by the CONSTITUTION OF THE USA in 1787. A federal system was established that divided power between central government and the constituent states, with an executive president. George WASHINGTON was elected the first president in 1789.

The new legislature was made up of two houses, the SENATE and the House of REPRESENTATIVES, and there was an independent judiciary headed by the SUPREME COURT. Territorial expansion followed with the LOUISIANA Purchase of 1803, the acquisition of Florida in 1819 and of TEXAS, California and the south-west following the Mexican-American War from 1846 to 1848 (see MEXICO). Success in the war, together with the California GOLD RUSH in 1848, helped to open up the WILD WEST and the Pacific coast, while the spread of the railway network and the ever-increasing immigration from Europe began to fill the Great Plains. Between 1812 and 1861 the Mississippi Valley and the Great Lakes region were settled. The mid 19th

Seats of higher learning

Universities broke the monopoly on learning enjoyed by monasteries.
Eventually the laity would be allowed to study, and to build a secular world.

Institutions of higher education existed in ancient China and the Muslim world – colleges for the study of Islamic theology and law were attached to mosques – but the Western 'university' was an invention of the 11th and 12th centuries. It took higher education out of the monasteries for the first time and combined the teaching of different subjects in one place, in what was known as a *studium generale*.

Students began with the arts course, which covered the seven 'liberal arts': the three basic subjects of grammar, logic and rhetoric (the *trivium*) followed by arithmetic, geometry, astronomy and music (the *quadrivium*). Graduate courses were available in law, medicine and theology.

These universities were international institutions, which often attracted students from afar. Masters of Arts were given the right of teaching 'everywhere'. Two of the oldest and most renowned universities were Bologna and Paris, and their different modes of organisation became models for the many universities founded in the later Middle Ages, including Prague in 1347 and Cracow in 1364. In Paris the dons dominated; in Bologna candidates for professorships gave lectures that had to be approved by the students. Oxford and Cambridge both followed the Paris pattern.

Teaching in medieval universities was mainly oral. Lectures consisted of readings from textbooks, such as works by Aristotle with a commentary by the lecturer. Instead of writing essays and examination papers, the students engaged in 'disputations', formal debates for and against a particular proposition or 'thesis'. The debates took place in the 'schools' or lecture rooms, which led to the label 'scholastic' for the philosophy and theology taught there. The students, apart from those studying medicine, were mainly clergy. It was only after 1500 that laymen began to attend universities.

The revival of classical learning in the Renaissance sometimes met with resistance from European universities. The Renaissance humanists wanted to reform the arts course, placing more emphasis on rhetoric and less on logic, and introducing the teaching of Greek. The Protestant reformer and professor Martin Luther was supported by his university of Wittenberg, and certain German universities, such as that at Marburg, were founded on the wealth of suppressed monasteries, but other universities, including Paris and Ingolstadt, opposed the new heresy.

ACADEMIC REACTIONARIES

Although Galileo taught at Padua and Sir Isaac Newton at Cambridge, the 17th-century scientific revolution mostly took place outside the universities, led by discussion groups such as the Royal Society of London. The ideas of the Enlightenment gained supporters in some of the universities, but once again the movement's centre of gravity was outside the academic system, which was increasingly viewed as old-fashioned, notably for continuing to teach in Latin.

The 19th century was the 'age of reform' in the universities and saw the introduction of new subjects, from chemistry and engineering to modern history and vernacular literature. The model was now Berlin, which emphasised research rather than undergraduate teaching, and seminars rather than lectures. It was imitated across the world from Tokyo to Chicago.

In the 20th century, the multiplication of disciplines has continued; the German model has generally been replaced by an American one; and the universities have opened their doors to women – the biggest change in their social history since the admission of the laity towards the end of the Middle Ages.

A **Cambridge seal of about 1261 (above) shows the chancellor seated between the proctors. A class pays close attention (below) at Bologna, Italy, and (inset) a professor teaches in Paris.**

century was dominated by a political crisis over slavery (abolished in 1865) and STATES' RIGHTS. This led to the secession of the Southern states, which were reconquered in the American Civil War of 1861 to 1865 (see feature, pages 28-29). The final decades of the century saw the 1867 purchase of Alaska and the acquisition of Spanish overseas territories after the SPANISH-AMERICAN WAR of 1898.

In the 20th century the USA has become a world power. Reluctantly it was drawn into the First and Second World Wars, contributing to the end of the Second World War by dropping atom bombs on the Japanese cities of Hiroshima and Nagasaki. Since then it has played an active role in 'world policing' and diplomacy, with the UNITED NATIONS' headquarters based in New York. In its determination to prevent the spread of communism it fought in the KOREAN WAR (1950-3) and the VIETNAM War (1964-75), and has supported anticommunist regimes, particularly in Latin America. In the 1970s and 1980s, with the easing of the COLD WAR with Eastern Bloc countries, the USA conducted arms reduction negotiations with the Soviet Union. The USA also fought in the GULF WAR of 1991.

At home, the 20th century in the USA was marked by a severe depression following the STOCK MARKET CRASH in 1929; a campaign of civil unrest that led to the Civil Rights Act of 1964; the assassination of President John F. KENNEDY in 1963; the programme that landed the first men on the Moon in 1969; and the WATERGATE scandal that led to President Richard Nixon's resignation in 1974.

universities see feature, page 673

Upanishads Collection of more than 100 philosophical treatises composed in Sanskrit, probably after 600 BC, which contributed to the theology of HINDUISM. The word is Sanskrit for 'sitting near to', that is, at the feet of a master. The Upanishads contain extracts from the VEDAS (the most sacred of the Hindu scriptures dating from 2000 BC) and the Brahamanas (commentaries on the Vedas), and are known as the Vedanta, 'conclusion of knowledge'. The Upanishadic era marks the emergence of the concept within Hinduism of a single supreme God, Brahman, who is knowable by the human self, the *atman*.

Upper Palaeolithic era Final division of the PALAEOLITHIC ERA or Old Stone Age, associated with the appearance of *Homo sapiens sapiens* about 40 000 years ago, and with the first examples of cave art in south-west France and Spain. The Upper Palaeolithic era occupies the second half of the last glaciation, ending 10 000 years ago. Compared with the Middle Palaeolithic era it was a time of increasing population and larger communities. The most developed cultures lived on the

Carved on the back of an Upper Palaeolithic limestone lamp, some 15 000 years old, is an ibex. The lamp is from La Mouthe in France.

steppe and tundra belts south of the ice sheets, with their plentiful herds of horses, reindeer and mammoths. Several styles of toolmaking can be distinguished in Europe: the earliest is Aurignacian, named after Aurignac in southern France where the first blade tools were used. These cultures disappeared with the end of the Ice Age.

Ur City of the SUMERIANS in southern Mesopotamia (see feature, page 413). In the Old Testament Ur was the home of Abraham, and it is often mentioned in the Bible. During the 19th century remains of the city were discovered, including a great ziggurat, or pyramidal temple tower, that was built by King Ur-Nammu around 2060 BC. Ur was occupied from around 5000 BC and became a commercial and cultural centre. It survived several empires and thrived under the Chaldean kings of Babylon during the 6th and 7th centuries BC. A change in the course of the River Euphrates, upon which it depended, led to the final abandonment of Ur during the 4th century BC.

Urban II (c.1035-99) Pope from 1088. Urban was born in France and belonged to the Cluniac order of Benedictine monks. He became Bishop of Ostia in 1079 and a cardinal under Pope Gregory VII. At the Council of Clermont in 1095, he preached in favour of sending the First Crusade to regain Palestine after its fall to the Muslims. Urban II continued Gregory's Church reform and his councils condemned clerical marriage, SIMONY and lay INVESTITURE.

Urban VIII (1568-1644) Pope from 1623. Urban, who was born in Florence, became a

A 17th-century statue of Pope Urban VIII by Giovanni Lorenzo Bernini sits on a marble pedestal in the Vatican.

cardinal in 1606 and Bishop of Spoleto in 1608. As pope, he canonised both the mystic Philip NERI and the founder of the Jesuits, Ignatius LOYOLA. Urban also condemned the astronomer Galileo and the Roman Catholic Jansenist sect (see Cornelius JANSEN). Urban VIII was a poet, scholar and patron of the arts. In diplomacy his fears of Habsburg domination in Italy led him to favour France during the THIRTY YEARS' WAR (1618-48). He fortified the PAPAL STATES, and suffered a humiliating defeat in the War of Castro (1642-4) against the Duke of Parma, which crippled papal finances and made him unpopular with the Roman people.

Uruguay Country on the east coast of South America. Its capital is Montevideo. Uruguay has emerged as one of the most prosperous nations in the continent due to the wealth created by its livestock industry. It lies between Brazil and Argentina, whose colonists, the Portuguese and Spanish respectively, vied for control. By the 17th century Spain controlled the entire country. Brazil ousted the Spanish rulers in 1814 and the dispute over who should control the country continued until 1828, when Uruguay declared its independence. European immigrants began to arrive in the 1830s.

Throughout the 19th century the liberals, known as Colorados, 'reds', and the conservatives, or Blancos, 'whites', struggled violently for political control. In 1872 the Colorados began a period of 86 years in office, during

which Uruguay was moulded into South America's first welfare state. The Blancos' victory in the 1958 elections was followed by a period of economic and political unrest that saw the emergence of the Tupamaro urban guerrillas. A repressive military regime took over in 1973. Civilian rule was reinstated with a return to democracy in 1985, when Julio Maria Sanguinetti, leader of the Colorados, became president. He was succeeded in 1989 by Lacalle Herrera of the Blanco Party, but in 1995 Sanguinetti was re-elected.

Uruk Ancient Mesopotamian city of the SUMERIANS. A community occupied the site as early as 5000 BC and by about 3000 BC the city was surrounded by a 6 mile (9.5 km) wall attributed to the mythical hero Gilgamesh. Excavations since 1928 have revealed successive cities within the walls. The cities were inhabited until Parthian times (126 BC–AD 224). Ziggurats, or pyramidal temple towers, dedicated to the two gods Anu and Inanna have been uncovered, the latter bearing witness to the reign of King Ur-Nammu, who came to the throne around 2060 BC.

Ussher, James (1581–1656) Irish Calvinist theologian, Archbishop of Armagh from 1625. On the outbreak of the Irish Rebellion in 1640 Ussher escaped to England, where he settled. Among his many writings was a chronology of scripture, *Annales Veteris et Novi Testamenti* (1650–4), which set the date of the Creation as October 23, 4004 BC.

USSR see UNION OF SOVIET SOCIALIST REPUBLICS

U Thant (1909–74) Burmese statesman, and secretary-general of the UNITED NATIONS from 1961 to 1971. He entered the Burmese diplomatic service in 1948 and served at the United Nations from 1957 until he succeeded Dag HAMMARSKJÖLD as secretary-general. U Thant's achievements included the resolution of the CUBAN MISSILE CRISIS in 1962, the formation of a UN peace-keeping force in CYPRUS in 1964, and the admission of China to full UN membership in 1971.

utilitarianism Ethical theory dating from the late 18th century. The idea that all human activity should be directed in order to bring about 'the greatest happiness of the greatest number' was outlined by the English philosopher Jeremy BENTHAM in his *Introduction to the Principles of Morals and Legislation*, published in 1789, and was later clarified by John Stuart MILL in *Utilitarianism* (1863). Utilitarianism applied to organisations, principles and actions the question: What is the use of it? Bentham and his followers had a profound

influence on political and social reform in Britain in the 19th century. In the 20th century, utilitarianism has continued to develop, particularly in the study of economics.

utopianism Visionary thinking in which ideal worlds are depicted, often in order to highlight the defects of existing societies. The original *Utopia* (Greek, 'no place'), which was published in 1516 by Sir Thomas MORE, Lord Chancellor to Henry VIII, featured a society whose members lived communally, sharing property and working under the direction of spiritual leaders. This idealistic state contrasted with the greed and self-interest that More saw in the world around him. Other utopian writings include the Greek philosopher PLATO's *Republic* from the 4th century BC, the English writer Samuel Butler's *Erewhon* (1872) and the English socialist and craftsman William Morris's *News from Nowhere* (1891).

Utopian communities have been established by religious groups, notably by the Shakers in the USA, but few have outlived the lifetime of their founder. In the 20th century utopianism has been challenged by 'dystopia' (Greek, 'bad place'), in which a pessimistic vision of the future is presented, such as Aldous Huxley's *Brave New World* (1932).

Utrecht, Peace of (1713–14) Series of treaties signed in the Dutch city of Utrecht between France and other European nations to end the War of the SPANISH SUCCESSION, which had begun in 1701. Under the terms of the peace PHILIP V remained king of Spain but renounced his claim to the French throne and lost Spain's European empire. The southern Netherlands, Milan, Naples and Sardinia went to Austria. Britain's significant commercial and colonial gains enabled it to increase its role in world affairs. Britain kept Gibraltar and Minorca, obtained the ASIENTO DE NEGROS – the right to supply the Spanish American colonies with African slaves – and gained Newfoundland, Novia Scotia, Hudson Bay and St Kitts from France, as well as recognition of Queen Anne and the Hanoverian succession. The Duke of Savoy gained Sicily. The Austrian emperor Charles VI accepted the terms of the peace at two treaties signed at Rastatt and Baden in 1714.

Uzbekistan Landlocked country in central Asia that borders Kazakhstan, Kyrgyzstan, Tajikistan, Afghanistan and Turkmenistan. Its capital is Tashkent. Uzbekistan lay on the great Silk Road (see feature, page 595) from China to Europe, and for 2000 years from around 1000 BC the cities of Samarkand and Tashkent flourished as trading centres. The

country was overrun by Mongols under GENGHIS KHAN in 1220, and in the late 14th century it was the home of TAMERLANE the Great. From the 14th to the 16th centuries the Uzbeks, a Sunni Muslim people, moved into Transoxania (present-day Uzbekistan). Three khanates (states) emerged based around Bukhara, Khiva and Kokand.

Uzbekistan came under frequent attack from RUSSIA, which annexed the state in 1876. The people rebelled in 1918, were suppressed by the Bolshevik Red Army, and in 1929 the country became a Soviet Socialist Republic. Under Joseph Stalin, cotton was planted on a grand scale; today Uzbekistan is the world's fourth largest producer. In the first general election on gaining independence in 1991, the People's Democratic Party (the former Communist Party) was victorious, and Islam Karimov was elected president. The country then joined the Commonwealth of Independent States. In 1992 a new constitution made Uzbekistan a multiparty democracy, but Karimov used war in neighbouring Tajikistan as a pretext to ban opposition. In 1994 Uzbekistan formed an economic union with Kazakhstan and Kyrgyzstan.

Until well into the 19th century, Uzbekistan fought off tsarist Russia. This dashing Uzbek, in traditional costume, was portrayed in 1840.

vaccination Process of producing active immunity against a disease by inoculation with live, weakened or killed microorganisms. The name, derived from the Latin *vacca*, 'cow', was coined by the British physician Edward JENNER who, in 1796, pioneered the process of providing immunity to smallpox through inoculation with cowpox. His breakthrough came after he had noticed that patients who had suffered from the milder disease of cowpox did not catch smallpox.

The principle of inoculation was not new to medical science. As early as AD590, the Chinese had tried inserting smallpox scabs into patients' noses to give them immunity. As the smallpox spread to Europe in the 14th century, this form of inoculation followed, but patients were always in danger of developing a severe form of the disease as a result. In the late 19th century, the French bacteriologist Louis PASTEUR introduced the first vaccines against cholera, anthrax and rabies, and in the 20th century further vaccines against tuberculosis, POLIOMYELITIS and measles were developed.

vagabonds see STURDY BEGGARS

Valley Forge (1777-8) American Revolutionary winter camp 20 miles (32km) northwest of Philadelphia which marked the lowest point in the revolutionary struggle. The American army, led by George WASHINGTON, suffered defeat at the hands of the British in Philadelphia in September 1777 at the Battle of the Brandywine, and in October at the Battle of Germantown. British occupation of Philadelphia followed and Washington's men spent a bitter winter at Valley Forge, where the lack of supplies and consequent hardships caused many to desert. The 11 000 men of the Continental Army who remained loyal to Washington and the revolutionary cause were hardened by the harsh winter, and Valley Forge became a symbol of endurance.

Valley of the Kings Narrow gorge in western Thebes containing the tombs of at least 60 Egyptian pharaohs of the 18th to 20th dynasties, who ruled between 1550 and 1050 BC. The first pharaoh to be buried there was Thutmose I, who died in 1512 BC. Although supposedly secret, the Valley of the Kings was a rich hunting-ground for grave robbers. Of the tombs discovered, only that of TUTANKHAMUN, hidden by rubble from the construction of the tomb of Rameses VI above it, had not been plundered.

Valmy, Battle of (September 20, 1792) First engagement of the French Revolutionary wars in which the French defeated Austrian and Prussian troops advancing on Paris. The Austrian and Prussian force led by the Duke of Brunswick were engaged at Valmy, a village east of Paris, by the French Revolutionary Army. Commander in chief Charles Dumouriez and Marshal François Kellermann led the French, who forced Brunswick to retreat to Germany. French spirits soared after the battle, and its outcome was a motivating force for continued revolution.

Valois Royal family of France, a branch of the CAPETIANS, who ruled from 1328 to 1589. The last king of the Capetian dynasty was Charles IV, and when he died in 1328 an assembly of nobles used SALIC LAW to prevent his daughter's accession. Instead Philip, Count of Valois and grandson of the French king Philip III, succeeded. The direct Valois line ended with the death of Charles VIII in 1498, but the dynasty continued with Louis XII of Valois-Orléans and FRANCIS I of Valois-Angoulême.

The power of the House of Valois was weakened by struggles with the HABSBURG dynasty and by the regency of Catherine de MEDICI.

The Valois king Charles VIII rides triumphantly into Naples after his conquest in May 1495, but within weeks he and his army were driven out.

Under Catherine's rule from 1560 to 1574, conflicts between the HUGUENOT nobles, who were Protestants, and the Roman Catholic dukes of GUISE erupted into the FRENCH WARS OF RELIGION from 1562 to 1598. Catherine's third son, Henry III, provoked the Catholics by having Henry, the 3rd Duke of Guise, assassinated. The Valois line ended when Henry III was stabbed to death while leading a siege of Paris in 1589. The throne passed to the Bourbons, headed by the Huguenot leader Henry of Navarre, who became HENRY IV.

Van Buren, Martin (1782-1862) Eighth president of the USA, from 1837 to 1841. Van Buren was elected to the state senate as a Democratic Republican in 1813. He served in the US Senate from 1821 to 1828 and then as governor of New York, resigning his post in 1829 to become secretary of state during the presidency of Andrew JACKSON. He resigned in 1831 to give Jackson the opportunity to reorganise the Cabinet and remove supporters of vice-president John Calhoun.

Van Buren ran successfully as Jackson's vice-president in the election of 1832, and was elected president in 1837. The economic crisis of that year and the hard times that followed lost Van Buren a great deal of his support. His unpopularity was increased by his decision not to annex Texas, which was struggling to remain independent of Mexican rule, as he feared war with Mexico and the extension of slavery. He lost the election of 1840 to William Harrison and failed to secure the nomination in 1844.

Vancouver, George (1757-98) English naval captain and explorer of North America's Pacific coast, who gave his name to Vancouver Island, British Columbia. Vancouver began his expedition in 1791, sailing by way of Australia and New Zealand to Hawaii, and then on to the Californian coast. Travelling northwards, he sailed around the island which now bears his name to establish that

At Valley Forge, George Washington watches pensively as the tattered remnants of his American Continental Army stumble through snow into their bleak camp during the winter of 1777-8.

it was separate from the mainland. He returned to spend the winter in Hawaii in preparation for surveying the coast the following year. Sailing north to Alaska in 1794, Vancouver examined Cook's Inlet on the south shore, last visited by Captain James Cook in 1778. The expedition then steered south, rounded Cape Horn and reached England after an absence of four and a half years.

Vandals Germanic tribe that migrated from the Baltic coast in the 1st century BC. The Vandals settled in the ancient Roman province of Pannonia in the valley of the Danube in the 4th century, but were driven farther west by the invading Asiatic HUNS between AD 376 and 406. They crossed the Rhine into Gaul and Spain where the name Andalusia, from the Arabic *al-Andalus,* 'the island of the Vandals', survives from their settlement on the Iberian Peninsula. Moving southwards through Spain, they laid waste to the country. The Visigoths, a division of the GOTHS, moved into Spain in the 5th century, and the Vandals took ship to North Africa under King Genseric in 429. They captured Carthage in 439 and set up an independent kingdom under the leadership of Genseric three years later. There they gathered their resources to return to Italy in 455 and sack Rome. The Byzantine general BELISARIUS, sent by the emperor Justinian to recapture Roman territory, finally conquered the Vandals in 534.

Vanderbilt, Cornelius (1794-1877) US businessman who amassed a fortune from his shipping and railway interests. Vanderbilt started a business ferrying passengers and freight around New York City, and later gained a virtual monopoly over the ferry lines along the coast. The Californian gold rush of

At the age of 16 Vanderbilt began to build his transport empire, ferrying passengers and freight from Staten Island to Manhattan.

On the banks of the Ganges, at the Holy City of Varanasi, Hindus tend funeral pyres, believing that cremation there releases the dead from the endless cycle of birth and death.

1849 created a demand for transport, and Vanderbilt seized the opportunity to connect New York with California. He ran a shipping line south from New York to Nicaragua, and constructed roads for overland travel to Lake Nicaragua and so to the east coast. During the AMERICAN CIVIL WAR, Vanderbilt created a railway business and quickly came to dominate the network in and out of New York and as far west as Chicago. Amassing a vast fortune, he made an endowment of $1 million to found Vanderbilt University at Nashville, Tennessee.

Van Diemen's Land see TASMANIA

Vane, Sir Henry (1613-62) Leading Parliamentarian, civil leader of the Parliamentary cause during the ENGLISH CIVIL WAR while Oliver CROMWELL directed the army. Vane served briefly as governor of Massachusetts from 1636 to 1637, then took the leading role in the English LONG PARLIAMENT, originally convened to curb the powers of CHARLES I, until 1660. He was a promoter of the SOLEMN LEAGUE AND COVENANT of 1643, which recruited the support of the Scottish Covenanters for the Parliamentary cause.

Vane opposed the trial and execution of Charles I, and believed that Cromwell was wrong to make himself head of state and leave government in the hands of the army rather than the people. He disagreed with Cromwell's expulsion of the remains of the Rump Parliament in 1653, and was briefly imprisoned for publishing a pamphlet expressing his views in 1656. Vane then withdrew from politics, until he helped to bring about the recall of the Rump in 1659. After the Restoration he was arrested, accused of treason for his past political activities and executed.

Varanasi Holy city in north India, formerly known as Benares. Thought to be one of the world's oldest cities, it is a centre of pilgrimage for Hindus from all over the country. Varanasi is on the north bank of the Ganges and Hindus descend the flights of steps, or *ghats*, which line the river there, to seek ritual purification in its sacred waters, and cremate their dead on cremation grounds along its banks. The city contains hundreds of temples, most of them built since the 17th century as Muslim invaders in earlier times destroyed many Hindu shrines.

Varennes, flight to (June 20, 1791) Unsuccessful attempt by LOUIS XVI to escape from France during the revolution and join the exiled royalists. On the night of June 20 the royal party, disguised and carrying forged passports, left Paris. They were pursued and stopped at Varennes, after having been recognised at Sainte-Menehould by Jean-Baptiste Drouet. The fugitives were returned to Paris and confined in the Tuileries Palace until it was overrun by the Parisians, when they were imprisoned in the Temple. The king and queen were tried and executed in 1793.

Vargas, Getúlio (1883-1954) Brazilian statesman. He was successively head of a provisional government (1930-4), constitutional president elected by Congress (1934-7), dictator (1937-45) and finally constitutional president elected by universal suffrage (1950-4). The country's first or Old Republic, established in 1889, was brought to an end by political corruption and fraud during the 1930 elections, and by the growing impact of the Great DEPRESSION on Brazil's vulnerable agricultural economy. Vargas assumed absolute power, and in 1937 he announced a state of emergency, a ban on all political organisations, the dissolution of Congress and the organisation of a new constitution. The new constitution would create a nationalist *Estado Novo*, 'New State', backed by the military.

Vargas's economic strategy concentrated on diversifying agricultural production and expanding industry. Growing commercial and diplomatic cooperation with the USA led Brazil to join the Second World War on the side of the Allies in 1942. After the defeat of the Axis powers, Vargas came under renewed pressure to relax the authoritarianism of the *Estado Novo*. His reluctance prompted a military coup in 1945, but his popularity and courting of the left resulted in his return to power by popular vote in 1950. However, thwarted by a growing economic crisis after 1952 and then falsely accused by the army of political corruption, Vargas resigned and committed suicide.

vassal In the Middle Ages a holder of land by contract from a lord. This tenure was an essential component of FEUDALISM. The land received was known as a fief and the contract was confirmed when the recipient paid homage by kneeling and placing his hands between those of his lord. Noblemen received their lands from kings in the same way. A vassal received protection in return for allegiance to his lord, and the contract could legally be broken only by a formal act of defiance. In some cases, vassals acquired more territory and consequently greater power than their nominal masters. Norman kings of England paid homage to kings of France to receive the duchy of NORMANDY as a fief.

Vatican City Independent Papal State in Rome, the seat of the Roman Catholic Church. The other Papal States – the modern Italian provinces of Lazio, Umbria, Marche and parts of Emilia-Romagna – became incorporated into the kingdom of Italy in 1870 by the movement for Italian national unity, the RISORGIMENTO. By the Law of

Guarantees, passed in 1871 to administer relations between the first government of Italy and the papacy, the Vatican was granted extraterritoriality. This made it exempt from local legal jurisdiction, though the temporal power of the pope was suspended until the Lateran Treaty of 1929, signed between Pope Pius XI and Benito Mussolini, which recognised the full and independent sovereignty of the Holy See in the City of the Vatican. The pope has absolute executive and legislative power inside the city, which covers 109 acres (44ha) and has its own police force, diplomatic service, postal service, coinage and radio station

Vauban, Sébastien le Prestre de (1633-1707) Marshal of France and an innovative military engineer. He controlled siege operations and designed fortications for LOUIS XIV, earning prestige for sieges conducted during wars against European alliances between 1667 and 1697. He designed a fortress for Strasbourg, defences for the city of Luxembourg and the fortification of Landau in Bavaria. In addition to his treatises on siege warfare, *De l'attaque et de la défense des places* (*On Siege and Fortification*) (1705-6), Vauban wrote on many other subjects. Of these, his most significant work was *Projet d'une dîme royale* (*Project for a Royal Tythe*) (1707), which advocated a single tax in preference to the existing tax system. It was suppressed by the government and within a few weeks the disappointed Vauban was dead.

Vedas Earliest corpus of Hindu sacred literature, composed in Sanskrit around 1500 to 1200 BC during and following the ARYAN invasions of India. Fire sacrifices were central to Vedic rituals, and the hymns and spells chanted by priests during these ceremonies were incorporated into the Vedas (from the Sanskrit *veda*, 'knowledge'). They comprise four collections of writings: the Samhitas, which contain prose and verse used in ceremonies; the Brahmanas, which explain the purpose of sacrifice; the Aranyakas, giving instructions for meditation during sacrifice; and the Upanishads, containing mysticism and speculation.

Vendée Large area on the Bay of Biscay in western France officially formed in 1790, the centre of a series of counter-revolutionary insurrections from 1793 to 1796. Its inhabitants

were devoutly religious, and objected to the government's introduction of the Civil Constitution of the Clergy in 1790, which tightened controls over the Roman Catholic Church. The introduction of conscription Acts in 1793 provoked widespread rioting. In March, exiled royalists from Lyon, Marseille, Bordeaux and Normandy joined the rebels by forming the 'Catholic and Royal Army'. The Vendéans' superior knowledge of the area led to several victories against the revolutionaries, but republican armies finally crushed the revolts at Le Mans and Savenay in December 1793.

Venezuela Country in South America with its coast on the Caribbean Sea. First sighted by Columbus in 1498 during his third voyage, it was visited by Amerigo Vespucci in 1499 who is said to have named it Venezuela (Spanish for 'Little Venice') because of the Amerindian villages built on stilts in Lake Maracaibo. It was colonised by the Spanish in the 16th century, and by the end of the 18th century its people were fighting for independence from Spanish control.

In its capital, Caracas, a movement for independence began in 1810. One of its leaders, Simón BOLÍVAR, a member of a rich planter family, created Gran Colombia, a union of Venezuela, New Granada, Panama and Ecuador, in 1821. While Bolívar continued his struggle against Spanish forces farther south, rivalries developed in Gran Colombia. José Antonio Páez, Bolívar's chief commander, took control of the separatist movement that had emerged and in 1829 Venezuela broke away from Gran Colombia. Páez was elected first president of the new republic from 1831 to 1835. He maintained his power even when not officially president until 1848 and was the first of the *caudillos* (Spanish, 'chieftains') or dictators who were to rule Venezuela until 1935. He provided a strong administration, allowed a free press and kept the army under control and out of politics.

The period following his second presidency of 1839 to 1843 degenerated into political violence as Páez conducted revolts against his own choice for president, José Tadeo Monagas. Control passed to Monagas's brother and then to his son, who was finally overthrown by Antonio Guzmán Blanco, president from 1870 to 1888. Moves were made towards democracy with the first election in 1881, and economic activity grew, but authoritarian government returned under the *caudillos* Cipriano Castro (1899-1908) and Juan Vicente Gómez (1908-35).

During the 19th century, Venezuela was the world's third largest coffee producer. Oil was discovered before the First World War, and by 1928 Venezuela was the world's leading oil exporter. After 1935, military juntas continued to dominate with some attempts at

The dome of St Peter's overlooks Vatican City. Piazza San Pietro is on the right. In the foreground is the papal audience hall, built in 1971, with its undulating roof.

A 17th-century town plan of Venice focuses on the Piazza San Marco. The Rialto bridge spans the Grand Canal above.

introducing more democratic rule until the military regime of Marcos Peréz Jiménez (1948-58). Rómulo Betancourt completed a full term as a civilian president from 1959 to 1964, and was peacefully succeeded by Dr Raúl Leoni from 1963 to 1969. Democratic politics have continued to operate, with two parties, *Acción Democrática* ('Democratic Action'), founded by Betancourt, and *Partido Social-Cristiano* ('Social Christian Party') alternating in power, although terrorists of both left and right have been active. A post-war oil boom brought considerable prosperity, but an increasing population and rising inflation caused problems for President Dr Jaime Lusinchi (1984-8). After the end of the oil boom in 1983, falling oil prices and an increase in drug trafficking were additional problems for his successor Carlos Andrés Pérez (1974-8, 1989-93), who faced riots over austerity measures in 1989 and two attempted military coups in 1992.

Charged with embezzlement and the misuse of public funds, Pérez was suspended from office in May 1993. Senator Rámon José Velásquez led a government of national unity until Rafael Caldera Rodríguez, head of National Convergence, a 17-party coalition, was elected president in December. Further discontent in 1995 led to demonstrations against official corruption, economic policies, police repression and military control.

Venice City built on the islands of a lagoon on the Adriatic coast of north-east Italy, enclosed by a promontory to the north-east and the islands of Malamocco and Pellestrina to the east and south. Mainland people first fled to the islands to escape from invading GOTHS and HUNS in the 5th century, finally settling there after the Lombard invasion of AD 568. In the 8th century, large buildings began to be built in Venice on wooden piles driven into the clay beneath the muddy surface of the islands. From 727, rulers known as doges were elected, and the islands' defences were strengthened. Venice became a republic independent of the Byzantine Empire in the 9th century, and gained control of the Adriatic by securing Dalmatia in the Balkan Peninsula in the 10th century. Maritime trade grew, and the city became rich trading with the ports of the eastern Mediterranean. Its prominence in the Crusades, with the sack of Constantinople in 1204 under doge Enrico Dandolo, brought great benefits to Venice, and its control extended into the Ionian and Aegean seas. By the 15th century, Venice also ruled the large adjoining province on the mainland of Italy known as Venetia, and many of the Greek islands. The republic was at the height of its powers and dominated the Mediterranean, gaining Cyprus in 1489 and ruling the towns of Bergamo, Brescia, Padua, Verona and Vicenza in north-east Italy, comprising 'the Veneto'. Government was in the hands of a few great families. Although Venice was successful in alliance with Spain and Genoa at the naval battle of LEPANTO against the Turks in 1571, it lost Cyprus the same year and its power began to decline. Venice succumbed easily to invasion by Napoleon in 1797 and was given to Austria in the early stages of the French Revolution, but became part of the kingdom of Italy in 1866.

Venizélos, Eleuthérios (1864-1936) Greek statesman, premier on five occasions between 1910 and 1933 while Greece alternated between monarchy and republic. When he first became premier, Venizélos modernised Greek political institutions and expelled the Turks from their European territory in the Balkan Wars of 1912 to 1913. When the First World War broke out, his intention to join the Allies was resisted by the country's pro-German king, Constantine. Constantine forced him to resign over this issue twice during 1915, but Venizélos was re-elected and in 1917 the king was compelled to abdicate. Constantine's son Alexander became king, and Greece entered the war on the side of the Allies. At the VERSAILLES PEACE SETTLEMENT at the end of the war, Venizélos negotiated promises of considerable territorial gains: Western and Eastern Thrace, several Aegean islands and Smyrna in Asia Minor. Turkey resisted the cession of Eastern Thrace and the Aegean islands. Turkish hostility and the death of King Alexander contributed to the election of a monarchist coalition in Greece in 1920. King Constantine returned and Venizélos exiled himself in Paris. He briefly returned as premier after the dethronement of Constantine by republicans, but exiled himself again in 1924 after disagreements with republican leaders. Becoming premier again in 1928, he lost the elections of 1932 following the Great DEPRESSION, and died in exile.

Vercingetorix (d. 46 BC) King of the Averni, a tribe living in Gaul. Towards the end of the GALLIC WARS in 52 BC, he revolted against Roman occupation and was acclaimed king of the united Gauls. Caesar triumphed against the revolt in 46, paraded Vercingetorix through Rome as a trophy, and then executed him.

Verdi, Giuseppe (1813-1901) Italian operatic composer whose early operas gained popularity as symbols of Italian nationalism. Verdi was the son of peasants from a small village in the state of Parma. His musical aptitude was noticed by a local merchant and amateur musician, Antonio Barezzi, whose daughter Verdi later married. Barezzi paid for Verdi to study in Milan. His first opera,

IL MAESTRO VERDI, PAR GÉDÉON

The patriot Verdi is caricatured playing *Don Carlos* on a barrel organ and holding laurels labelled *Rigoletto* and *Il Trovatore*.

Oberto (1839), met with considerable success, winning him an influential publisher and commissions for further operas.

During 1839 and 1840, while Verdi was completing *Un Giorno di Regno*, his wife and two children died. The opera was a failure, and it was some time before he could be persuaded to compose again. His third opera, *Nabucco* (1842), was a Biblical drama on the theme of Jewish exile. The Italians, fighting to unify their country and throw off the yoke of the Austrian Empire, identified with the exiled Jews, and the opera was a triumph. Worldwide success followed with *Rigoletto* (1851), *Il Trovatore* and *La Traviata* (both 1853), though Verdi's patriotic story lines were sometimes compromised by the disapproval of the Austrian censors. In 1859, he married the soprano Giuseppina Strepponi.

Italy achieved unification in 1860, and themes with political implications were no longer subject to foreign censorship. Verdi's next two masterpieces, *La Forza del Destino* (1862) and *Don Carlos* (1867), were followed by *Aida*, commissioned for the opera house in Cairo, which was built in celebration of the opening of the Suez Canal in 1871, and by his great *Requiem* of 1874.

During his later years, Verdi surprised the world with the creation of two further masterpieces based on Shakespearean plays: the tragedy *Otello* (1887) and a comedy, *Falstaff* (1893), based on *The Merry Wives of Windsor*, written in his 80th year.

Verdun, Treaty of (AD 843)
Division of the territories of the CAROLINGIAN Empire, forming the basic structure of modern Europe, between the Frankish kings Lothar, Louis and Charles, the grandsons of Charlemagne. Their father, Louis the Pious, partitioned his empire between Lothar and Charles before his death in 840, causing conflict with the younger Louis and civil war, which lasted until 842. Long negotiations culminated in a meeting at Verdun where the empire was divided into three kingdoms. Charles and Louis received West and East Francia, roughly present-day France and Germany, while Lothar retained the imperial title of Emperor of the West, and held the middle kingdom, a long strip of territory stretching from the North Sea over the Alps to Rome and bordered in the west by the rivers Scheldt, Meuse and Saône, and in the east by the Rhine. This territory, known as Lotharingia, soon lost its own identity and became a battleground for the embryonic kingdoms of France and Germany.

Vereeniging, Treaty of (May 31, 1902)
Peace treaty that ended the Second BOER WAR. The Boers acknowledged British sovereignty, while on their part the British accepted a civil administration leading to self-government, the use of Afrikaans in schools and law courts,

a repatriation commission and compensation of £3 million for the destruction inflicted on Boer farms during the war.

Versailles
see feature, page 681

Versailles Peace Settlement (1919-23)
Series of four peace treaties between the Allied and Central Powers ending the First World War, also known as the Paris Peace Settlement and the Treaty of Versailles. The Allies and Germany concluded an armistice in 1918 based on a peace programme, the FOURTEEN POINTS, set out by US president Woodrow WILSON. The main treaty was based in part on the Fourteen Points, which included establishing a LEAGUE OF NATIONS to ensure international cooperation. It was signed at Versailles in June 1919 by the Allied powers and Germany. Germany was required to sign without negotiation, and accept responsibility for provoking the war by a 'war-guilt' clause. German-speaking territories were surrendered, including ALSACE-LORRAINE, which returned to France. In the east, parts of Upper Silesia and the Polish corridor to the Baltic Sea were ceded to Poland. Gdánsk (Danzig), formerly the capital of west Prussia, became a free city. Parts of East Silesia went to Czechoslovakia; Moresnet, Eupen and Malmedy, west of Germany, went to Belgium; and the SAAR Valley was placed under international control for 15 years, as was the newly demilitarised Rhineland. Overseas colonies in Africa and the Far East were to be mandated to Britain, France, Belgium, South Africa, Japan and Australia. The German army was restricted to 100 000 men, and the manufacture of submarines, military aircraft and armoured vehicles was to stop. Compensation for damage caused during the war was fixed in 1921 at £6500 million, a sum which proved impossible for Germany to pay. Many aspects of the treaty were criticised as excessive, and its unpopularity in

Germany created a political and economic climate that enabled Adolf Hitler to come to power. The Allied powers signed the second treaty with the new republic of Austria at St Germain-en-Laye, near Paris, in September 1919, the third with Bulgaria at Neuilly in November 1919, and the fourth treaty with the new republic of HUNGARY at the Palace of the Trianon, Versailles, in June 1920.

The treaties were ratified in Paris during 1920. A fifth treaty – that of Sèvres in August 1920 between the Allies and the Ottoman sultanate of Turkey – was never implemented, as it was followed by the final disintegration of the Ottoman Empire and the creation by Mustafa Kemal ATATÜRK of the new republic of Turkey. It was replaced by the Treaty of Lausanne in July 1923.

Verwoerd, Hendrik Frensch (1901-66)
South African statesman who as minister of native affairs from 1950 to 1958 instigated policies of APARTHEID, or racial segregation. Verwoerd edited the nationalist newspaper *Die Transvaler* from 1938 to 1948. After entering politics he became Nationalist Party leader and prime minister from 1958 to 1966. During his government, the enforcement of racial separation provoked unrest, including a demonstration in 1960 which led to the deaths of 69 Africans in the SHARPEVILLE MASSACRE. The government took harsh measures to silence opposition, banning two organisations seeking racial equality: the AFRICAN NATIONAL CONGRESS and the PAN-AFRICANIST CONGRESS. Verwoerd broke away from the British Commonwealth when South Africa became a republic in 1961. An unsuccessful attempt on his life was made by a White farmer in 1960. Six years later he was assassinated in the House of Assembly by Demetrio Tsafendfas, a parliamentary messenger of Greek origin from Mozambique.

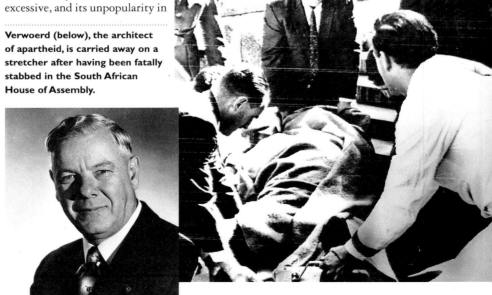

Verwoerd (below), the architect of apartheid, is carried away on a stretcher after having been fatally stabbed in the South African House of Assembly.

The palace of France's 'Sun King'

Louis XIV intended Versailles to be the most splendid royal residence in Europe,
reflecting his own magnificence as well as that of France.

King Louis XIV was nine years old when he developed an implacable aversion to Paris and its citizens. In 1648 the young king was taken hostage by a mob that had broken into his home in the Louvre palace, and he suffered many deprivations before peace was restored the following year.

Louis never forgot the experience, nor forgave what he called the 'Parisian rabble'. In the early 1660s he decided to leave Paris for good and to turn a modest royal hunting lodge at Versailles, 11 miles (18 km) south-west of the capital, into a magnificent palace. He had fond boyhood memories of the place, and he dismissed his courtiers' objections that it had no 'proper view'. He was determined to

The king's bedchamber (right) and the Hall of Mirrors (below) reveal the sumptuous grandeur that was created at Versailles.

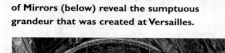

make it the centre of his world and the powerhouse of his ambitions to extend France's influence and territory.

Louis' motto was *L'Etat, c'est moi*, 'I am the state', and his orders, however odd, had to be obeyed. Accordingly, he hired three of France's outstanding talents: the architect Louis Le Vau (and, later, Jules Mansart), the landscape gardener André Le Nôtre, and the decorator and historical painter Charles Le Brun. Under the supervision of Le Vau, they began in 1662 to create a huge palace with a 1361 ft (415 m) façade around the lodge's

original 20 rooms. An army of 30000 workmen set about levelling the hillock on which the palace was to stand, damming a nearby stream and pumping water uphill from the River Seine over 5 miles (8 km) away, to create a reservoir for the new Versailles.

Known as the 'Sun King' from the role he had danced in the ballet *Le Nuit*, 'The Night', when he was 15, Louis resolved that everything at Versailles should reflect his glory. The roof of the palace was covered with gold leaf which, according to onlookers, 'caught fire' as it was lit by the morning

sun. The immaculately landscaped gardens contained over 1400 fountains with their own pools and waterfalls, though there was never sufficient water to keep them all operational for more than three hours at a time.

ARMIES OF ATTENDANTS

More than 7000 officials were squeezed into the palace's public reception rooms and private apartments. Visitors sometimes got lost in the maze of corridors, and some servants in the outermost areas lived in idleness for years, with no one knowing what their duties were supposed to be. There were another 7000 Household Troops and a floating population of painters, dramatists, musicians, philosophers, poets, priests, craftsmen and doctors, whose purpose was to entertain, enlighten and care for the king.

The court followed a strict routine. Twice a day the king held *levées*, or 'risings', at which he was attended by the Gentlemen of the Bedchamber, the Royal Barber, the First Physician and First Surgeon, and the Royal Clockmaker, who wound his watch. During these *levées* Louis was washed, dressed, fed and given the latest news by a flock of valets, cronies and hangers-on. Afterwards he received ambassadors in an ornate reception room-cum-Turkish bath, and fitted in amorous appointments with his wife or current favourite mistress.

In 1682, with building work continuing, Louis decided that the whole country should be run from Versailles. From there he personally supervised every aspect of government, from court etiquette to the building of roads and the movement of troops. By the time the king died in 1715 at the age of 77, a town of some 30000 people had grown up around the still-unfinished palace.

Louis XIV inspects the reservoirs specially built to ensure a water supply for his palace at Versailles.

Vespasian (AD 9-79) Roman emperor from AD 69 until his death, the first of the Flavian emperors. First known as Titus Flavius Vespasianus, he became consul in 51 and a governor in North Africa in 63. On the outbreak, in 66, of the Jewish Revolt – a nationalist uprising against Roman rule – NERO sent him to quell Palestine, but on Nero's death Vespasian suspended operations, leaving his son Titus in command. Civil war broke out over who should succeed Nero, and two imperial commanders, Marcus Otho and then Aulus Vitellius, in turn became emperor. Vespasian was proclaimed emperor by his legions in 69, entered Rome and defeated Vitellius' troops. He restored discipline in the army after the civil war, pacified the frontiers and restored the exhausted economy, largely by taxation. He kept the administration under tight control so that, after a peaceful rule, he died leaving Rome solvent.

Vespucci, Amerigo (1454-1512) Merchant and adventurer from Florence, whose explorations became known through two sets of documents describing his voyages to the New World – thought to have been named America after him. There is some controversy over whether a voyage between 1497 and 1498 around the Gulf of Mexico and the Atlantic coast – in some documents but not others – took place, but all the documents describe two voyages in South America. Vespucci acted as navigator for the Spanish conquistador Alonso de Ojeda, setting out from Spain in 1499 to sail around the north eastern coast. He is believed to have split from Ojeda and sailed on to discover the mouth of the Amazon. On his next voyage, in the service of Portugal, he was the first European, in 1502, to reach the Río de la Plata on the southern coast. Vespucci was not only an explorer: he evolved a system for computing nearly exact longitude, and calculated the circumference of the Earth to within 50 miles (80 km) of the accurate figure.

Vestal virgin Priestess of Vesta, Roman goddess of fire, hearth and home. Six Vestal virgins were chosen by lot from a select group of girls of wealthy freeborn parents, and were taken to live in the House of the Vestals in the forum at Rome. They carried out their duties dressed as brides, and remained chaste throughout their 30 years of service: Vestals who broke their vow of chastity were buried alive. Their duties included officiating at the Vestalia – the public festival of Vesta – each June, cleaning the goddess's shrine, tending its constant fire and preparing ritual food.

Vichy government (1940-5) French government established in areas of the country not occupied by the Germans after the Franco-German armistice in the Second World War. The French vice-premier Marshal PETAIN concluded the armistice with Germany following its military victory over France in 1940. Two-thirds of France remained under German occupation, but the unoccupied areas, including the colonies, were administered by a government set up in the spa town of Vichy by the French National Assembly. France's Third Republic was dissolved, and the Vichy government headed by Pétain issued a new constitution establishing an autocratic state. In 1941 it granted Japan right of access to air bases in Indochina, from which the Japanese launched campaigns in Malaya and Burma. It was dominated first by Pierre LAVAL as Pétain's vice-premier in 1940, then by French admiral François Darlan in collaboration with Hitler from 1941 to 1942, and again by Laval from 1942 to 1944 after German forces moved into the unoccupied areas of France. The Vichy government was never recognised by the Allies, and after the Allied liberation of France in 1944 the Vichy government established itself under Pétain at Sigmaringen in Germany, where it collapsed when Germany surrendered in 1945.

Victor Emmanuel II (1820-78) First king of a united Italy from 1861 until his death, and previously king of the Italian kingdom of Sardinia, which included the island of Sardinia and the state of Piedmont in northwest Italy, from 1849 to 1861. Victor Emmanuel succeeded to the throne of Sardinia after the abdication of his father, Charles Albert. He fought in the REVOLUTIONS OF 1848 against Austrian control, and was a central figure of the RISORGIMENTO, the fight for Italian unification and independence. He appointed Camillo CAVOUR, the leader of the struggle for Italian unification, as prime minister of Piedmont in 1852, and sought the support of Britain and France by entering the Crimean War as their ally. After becoming king of Italy, he supported Prussia in the AUSTRO-PRUSSIAN WAR of 1866, during which Italy annexed Venice. His troops seized the Papal States in 1870, and complete unification was attained.

Victor Emmanuel III (1869-1947) King of Italy from 1900 to 1946. Succeeding Umberto I, he retained good relations with France and Britain, although Italy belonged to the secret TRIPLE ALLIANCE with Germany and Austria, and he maintained neutrality in the First World War until he joined the Allies in 1915. With the breakdown of parliamentary government after the First World War, Victor Emmanuel declined to suppress a fascist uprising and asked Benito MUSSOLINI to form a government in 1922, fearing the alternative to be civil war and communism. He was created Emperor of Ethiopia in 1936 and King of Albania in 1939, following successful occupations led by Mussolini. In 1943, however, Victor Emmanuel dismissed Mussolini because of his alliance with Hitler. Soon afterwards, the new premier, his former chief of staff Pietro BADOGLIO, helped to conclude an armistice with the Allies. German troops occupied Rome following the armistice, and the king fled. In 1946 he abdicated and died in exile in Egypt a year later.

Victoria (1819-1901) Queen of Great Britain and Ireland and of dependencies overseas from 1837, and Empress of India from 1876. The last monarch of the House of Hanover,

Amerigo Vespucci, exploring the South American coastline and islands, is watched by curious Amerindians. This woodcut illustration was published in *Mundus Novus* (*New World*) in 1505.

Victoria, flanked by her son Edward, Prince of Wales, observes Olga, the firstborn of her granddaughter Alexandra and Tsar Nicholas.

Victoria was the only child of George III's fourth son, Edward, Duke of Kent. She came to the throne in 1837 on the death of her uncle, WILLIAM IV, during whose reign the political influence of the Crown declined. By the time she died, Victoria had restored the popularity of the monarchy. As queen, she was at first guided by the prime minister, Lord MELBOURNE. Her reign saw the benefits of the Industrial Revolution: the GREAT EXHIBITION of 1851 was a testament to its success. The family life of the monarchy became the foundation of the 'Victorian Era', along with the moral virtues of thrift, hard work and respectability, which sprang from the era of prosperity between the 1850s and the 1870s. Victoria's marriage in 1840 to Prince ALBERT of Saxe-Coburg-Gotha was happy, and his early death in 1861 was a blow from which she never fully recovered. Her withdrawal from public life during the early years of her widowhood damaged her popularity, but Benjamin DISRAELI persuaded her to take her place once more in public life. Largely at her own instigation, she was declared Empress of India by the Royal Titles Act of 1876. By the 1880s she had won respect and admiration from her subjects; her Golden and Diamond Jubilees were great imperial occasions. Her death ended an era in which Britain had become the world's leading industrial power at the centre of the BRITISH EMPIRE.

Victoria State situated on the most south-easterly point of mainland AUSTRALIA, facing Tasmania. In the 1830s and 1840s Victoria, then part of the NEW SOUTH WALES colony, was settled by Europeans in search of pasture-lands. The Aboriginal population in the area was decimated by disease and slaughter.

Victoria became a separate colony from New South Wales in 1851. GOLD RUSHES, notably to Ballarat and Bendigo in central Victoria, increased the number of settlers that year. Disputes over the administration of the gold fields led to the EUREKA STOCKADE of 1854, a conflict between gold diggers and the authorities in Ballarat. Restrictions on Chinese immigration to the area imposed in 1855 marked the beginning of the WHITE AUSTRALIA POLICY, instigated to preserve ethnic purity. Attempts were made between 1860 and 1890 to make more land available for small farmers. Victoria became a state of the newly created Commonwealth of Australia in 1901. NEW AUSTRALIAN immigration immediately after the Second World War increased its population.

Vienna, Congress of (1814-15) International peace conference that settled the affairs of Europe after the defeat of Napoleon. The Congress continued to meet through the HUNDRED DAYS of March to June, 1815, when Napoleon returned to France from exile only to be defeated at the Battle of Waterloo. The dominant powers – Austria, Britain, Prussia and Russia – were represented by Clemens METTERNICH, Robert CASTLEREAGH, FREDERICK WILLIAM III and ALEXANDER I. Charles de TALLEYRAND-PÉRIGORD represented Louis XVIII of France.

The Congress agreed that the new kingdom of the Netherlands would absorb what had been the Austrian Netherlands – and is today Belgium – but otherwise the Habsburgs regained control of all their domains, including Lombardy, Venetia, Tuscany, Parma and TYROL. Prussia gained parts of Saxony, and regained the Rhineland and much of Westphalia. Denmark, which had allied itself with France, lost Norway to Sweden. In Italy the pope regained the Vatican and the Papal States, and the Bourbons were re-established in the south Italian kingdom of the Two Sicilies. The GERMAN CONFEDERATION, an alliance of German sovereign states, was established, replacing the Holy Roman Empire. Napoleon's Grand Duchy of Warsaw was replaced by a restored kingdom of Poland as part of the Russian empire, with the Russian emperor also becoming king of Poland. The Congress restored Europe's political stability but often at the cost of nationalist sentiments channelled into the REVOLUTIONS OF 1848 in west and central Europe.

Vietnam Country on the eastern coastline of the South-east Asian peninsula. The area used to be made up of three regions: Tonkin in the north, Annam in the centre and south, and Cochin China at its southernmost point. The Chinese conquered the area in 111 BC and ruled until 939, when the inhabitants of Tonkin and Annam drove them out, and by the 16th century separate dynasties ruled the two regions. Annam took over Cochin China in the 18th century. In 1802 the two states of Annam and Tonkin were reunited by the Annamese general Nguyen Anh, who became Emperor Gia-Long, with military assistance from French overseas territories. The influence of France increased in the 19th century, and by 1883 Vietnam was part of French Indochina, France's South-east Asian empire.

In the Second World War the Japanese occupied the region but allowed VICHY France to administer it until March 1945. The Vietminh, a communist guerrilla movement formed in Vietnam in 1941, opposed French and Japanese intervention. In September 1945 the movement's founder, HO CHI MINH, established a republic with its capital at Hanoi. In the postwar years, the Vietminh resisted the returning French and brought their rule to an end, defeating them at DIEN-BIEN PHU in 1954. The GENEVA CONVENTION of that year, trying to solve the conflict, partitioned Vietnam into two military areas, leaving a communist Democratic Republic with its capital at Hanoi in the north and – after the deposition of the former emperor Bao Dai in 1955 – a noncommunist republic with its capital at Saigon in the south. Ho Chi Minh, the North Vietnamese leader, remained committed to a united communist country.

In South Vietnam, opposition to the president NGO DINH DIEM was growing in the form of the Vietcong, also known as the National Front for the Liberation of South Vietnam, founded in 1960. In 1961 the USA signed a military and economic aid treaty with South Vietnam. Vietcong communist insurgence that year led to the declaration of a state of emergency by Diem, and his overthrow by the military in 1963. Communist attempts to take advantage of the political confusion in the south increased in opposition to massive US military intervention the following year. The USA perceived Vietnam as a bastion against the spread of communism in Southeast Asia. After a supposed Vietnamese attack on US warships in the Gulf of Tonkin in 1964, President Lyndon Johnson was given congressional approval to take military action. Throughout the late 1960s and early 1970s the Vietnam War raged throughout the area, even the heavy use of US airpower failing to crush growing communist strength. By 1967, 400 000 US troops were serving in Vietnam. The war provoked growing domestic opposition in the USA which helped to accelerate a US withdrawal. After abortive peace negotiations, the North Vietnamese and their Vietcong allies finally took the port of Saigon in South Vietnam in April 1975, and a united

Socialist Republic of Vietnam was proclaimed the following year. Although the war had severely damaged its economy, the Republic, adopting an aggressively pro-Soviet foreign policy, dominated Laos and invaded Cambodia to overthrow the KHMER ROUGE regime between 1975 and 1979, and then suffered heavily in a brief border war with China in 1979. The south of the country had been devastated by the war and many had become homeless. Floods and droughts disrupted agriculture and caused rice shortages. Attempts to restructure the south produced a flood of refugees, damaging Vietnam's international standing and increasing its economic dependence on the Soviet Union.

In 1989 Vietnamese troops withdrew from Cambodia. With the disintegration of the Soviet Union in 1991, Vietnam worked to improve its relations with China and the USA. A new constitution was adopted in 1992, incorporating major economic and political reforms. Economic links were forged with the USA, Britain and Japan, particularly to exploit Vietnam's oil and natural gas reserves. The Communist Party of Vietnam remains the country's sole political party.

vigilante Member of a self-appointed body for maintaining law and order in US frontier towns in the 18th and 19th centuries. With the slow development of official policing vigilance committees, organised by local citizens, frequently took the law into their own hands, meting out rough justice and sometimes resorting to lynching. Notable vigilante groups sprang up in the 1850s to bring order to the waterfront at San Francisco, known as the Barbary Coast and notorious for the brothels and gambling saloons spawned by the 1849 GOLD RUSH. Vigilante groups formed in modern times include a force active on the New York subway.

Vikings Scandinavian maritime people who were active from the 8th century to the 12th century. Vikings in the 8th century began one of the most remarkable periods of expansion in history. Sailing from Denmark, Norway and Sweden they voyaged westwards in their longships as far as VINLAND in eastern Canada. They invaded Britain and Ireland, ravaged the coast of continental Europe and struck far inland, sailing up rivers in search of plunder and land. Eastwards they expanded to Kiev in the Ukraine and Novgorod in Russia. The Vikings were also traders and farmers. They produced skilled work in wood and metal, and manufactured fine jewellery. They had a powerful oral poetic tradition, later recorded in

their prose histories, the Norse sagas. An adaptable people, the Vikings were able to absorb the culture and languages of the areas they settled. (See feature, page 685.)

Villa, Francisco (1877-1923) Mexican revolutionary leader, born Doroteo Arango and later nicknamed Pancho. He pursued an early career as a bandit and merchant before taking up the cause of Francisco Madero, a leading figure in the MEXICAN REVOLUTION of 1910. Villa and another northern rebel leader, Pascual Orozco, provided the military leadership that was responsible for Madero's defeat of the dictator Porfirio DIAZ, and his subsequent presidency. Villa was imprisoned by General Victoriano Huerta, the commandant of the government forces, in 1912, but escaped and fled to the USA. After Huerta's betrayal and assassination of Madero in 1913, Villa returned to Mexico and gathered together a fighting force, joining up with Venustiano Carranza to oust Huerta. The following year, Villa became governor of Chihuahua, and with his cavalry, *los dorados*, expropriated holdings of large landowners, using their revenues to equip the revolutionary army in Mexico.

By late 1915, rivalry with Carranza had begun to cause conflict with other revolutionary factions. Villa moved north with the guerrilla army leader Emiliano ZAPATA, and demonstrating his military power, ordered an attack in 1916 on the US town of Columbus, New Mexico, killing a group of Americans and provoking retaliation from a punitive expedition under General John Pershing. Villa continued his guerrilla activities until Carranza's government was overthrown in 1920, then received a pardon and lived in retirement until he was assassinated three years later.

An 11th-century Italian manuscript shows villeins tilling the soil and harvesting grapes for their overlord.

villein Medieval peasant subject to a lord or attached to a manor, a member of a class of SERFS. Villeins and serfs were subject to the MANORIAL SYSTEM which dominated Europe between the 9th and 14th centuries. The word villein comes from the Latin *villanus*, 'villager'; DOMESDAY BOOK records that more than 40 per cent of English households were *villani*. Villeins were the backbone of the rural economy. They provided labour services to their lord, gave him gifts of produce in return for their land, and were subject to the judicial system of the manor. Villeins in England later became bonded tenants, receiving cash for their labour and paying rent to their lord. By the 15th century social and economic changes following labour shortages as a result of the BLACK DEATH ended the manorial system and villeinage.

Vimy Ridge, Battle of (April 9, 1917) Allied attack on a German position near Arras, France, in the First World War. One of the key points on the WESTERN FRONT, Vimy Ridge had long resisted Allied attacks. Canadian troops led by Lieutenant-General Julian Byng and General Henry Horne launched the offensive. They had successfully located the majority of the German gun positions, and Allied gun positions were camouflaged so well that they were almost invisible. Despite heavy Allied casualties, most of Vimy Ridge was captured and 4000 prisoners were taken. The battle was a tactical success; it inflicted many casualties on the German line of defence and captured ground of considerable strategic importance.

Vinland Name given by the VIKINGS to part of eastern Canada, meaning 'Vine Land'; other parts were called Helluland ('Stone Land') and Markland ('Forest Land'). Norse sagas record the accidental landfall in North America by Bjarni Herjolfsson, blown off course while on his way to Viking settlements already on GREENLAND in about 985, and short-lived settlement in the late 10th and early 11th centuries by the Viking explorers Leif Ericsson, his brother Thorvald, and Thorfinn Karlsefni. Incontestable traces of a Norse presence are known only from remains of Viking buildings and other objects at Ellesmere Island, in the Arctic Ocean, and a site at L'Anse aux Meadows in Newfoundland, and from a coin found in Maine, just south of the Canadian-US border.

Raiders from the north

Manning the finest ships of their day, the Vikings were superb sailors who terrified the people of northern Europe with their lightning raids. But soon they were settling and pioneering trade routes throughout the known world.

The Vikings first erupted out of Scandinavia in the AD790s sailing forth to ransack monasteries on the islands of Lindisfarne and Iona in the British Isles, and Noirmoutier in the Loire estuary in France. This marked the start of an explosion of activity. Well into the 11th century, bands of Scandinavians left their farming and fishing communities in the north to travel. In their longships they voyaged in search of profit, power, land and adventure, raiding and trading in the wealthy Christian realms of Europe, and even farther afield.

The Vikings probably began their expansion partly because of increasing populations and shortage of land, and tension between Franks and Danes. But the main attraction was northern Europe's trade. There were rich pickings to be had, and the development of the longship in Scandinavia had given the Vikings the means to acquire unheard-of wealth. The shallow-draughted ships could navigate rivers and be beached almost anywhere giving the vital element of surprise.

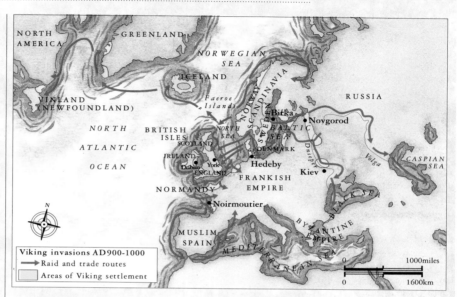

The early Viking raiders made only brief forays across the North Sea, but their descendants traded and settled as far as Newfoundland to the west and the Caspian Sea to the east.

The Oseberg ship emerges from the earth in 1903. Treasures inside it included this carved post.

Initially they plagued the coastlines of Britain and the Continent, and sailed up rivers to penetrate deep inland, seizing goods and slaves. During the 9th century, the weakness of the warring kingdoms of north-western Europe encouraged the Vikings to grow more daring. Instead of attacks on monasteries and villages, they conducted small campaigns against towns and whole districts. Some longships ranged as far south as the Mediterranean.

THE VIKINGS BECOME NORMANS

Sometimes Viking leaders were granted land in return for peace. Around 911 the French king Charles the Simple gave a chieftain called Rollo territory around the mouth of the Seine, which became known as Normandy, land of the 'Northmen'.

In England, Danish Viking armies conquered Northumbria, Mercia and East Anglia by the 870s. Only Alfred, king of Wessex, withstood them; his descendants eventually retook the 'Danelaw', the territory settled by the Scandinavians.

In the late 10th century the Vikings renewed their raids and again conquered the rich lands of England. From 1016 to 1042 the Danish king Canute ruled England, followed by his two sons. Norwegian Vikings settled the Scottish islands and founded and ruled the first towns in Ireland. Swedes navigated the hazardous waterways from the Baltic across Russia to the Black Sea and the Caspian, seeking silks and silver coins from the Arab merchants of the east. They established ruling dynasties over the principalities of Novgorod and Kiev, from where they threatened Byzantium, capital of the Eastern Roman Empire.

The Vikings were not only warlords. Their reputation as ferocious murderers is partly myth, created by monastic writers. The Vikings were no more bloodthirsty than many Christian contemporaries. Having seized territories they settled down to rule, trade and farm. They were single-minded people of enterprise, to whom trade was as important as conquest, and they plied the shipping routes from the Atlantic to the Caspian Sea. Many became explorers, and in the 9th and 10th centuries whole households braved the North Atlantic to settle in the Faroes, Iceland and Greenland. Pioneers sailing from Greenland around 1000 were the first Europeans to reach America.

Viollet-le-Duc, Eugène Emmanuel

(1814-79) French architect, engineer, writer and archaeologist, the dominant figure of the Gothic revival in France when the Gothic style of the Middle Ages was reintroduced. Viollet-le-Duc is known mainly for his restorations of medieval buildings. His opportunities in this field arose from his friendship with the writer and historian Prosper Mérimée, who was also Inspector of Ancient Monuments. His restorations, including work at Nôtre Dame in Paris and the walled town of Carcassonne, have been attacked as too sweeping, obscuring the original fabric with romantic reconstructions, but his efforts saved some buildings from total demolition or collapse. Viollet-le-Duc wrote a vast amount about architecture, promoting the Gothic style as a basis for a modern system of iron skeletal construction. His own buildings, built in a RENAISSANCE style, were not of the same standard as his restoration work.

Eugène Viollet-le-Duc (left) executed this scale drawing of the apse of St Saturnin church in Toulouse, which was one of his restoration projects.

Virgil

(70-19 BC) Roman poet born near Mantua. Virgil (also spelt Vergil) was educated in Cremona and later studied in Milan, Naples and Rome. He then worked for about ten years on his father's farm and wrote poetry. In 41 BC the farm was confiscated to provide land for soldiers and Virgil went to Rome, joining the literary circle there. His first poems, *Eclogues,* finished in 37 BC, idealise rural life. His following pastoral poems, the *Georgics* were, in contrast, realistic. His last and most famous work was the *Aeneid*, an epic poem in 12 books which relates the wanderings of the Trojan hero Aeneas after the fall of Troy. His wish that the poem, which was unfinished at his death, should be burnt was not respected. Virgil's works quickly established themselves as the greatest classics of Latin poetry and influenced poets, including Dante, Milton and Dryden, right up to the ROMANTIC period.

Virginia

Colony and state of the USA, which stretches from the Atlantic coast, including Chesapeake Bay, inland to the the eastern slopes of the Allegheny Mountains. JAMESTOWN, the first permanent British colony in America, was settled 15 miles (24 km) inland from Chesapeake Bay in 1607 by the Virginia Company of London, who inherited the name from Sir Walter RALEIGH's compliment to the 'virgin queen', Elizabeth I. Survival and later prosperity were based on tobacco, cultivated by White servants at first and by Black slaves after the 1690s, when a rural gentry of plantation owners, or planters, emerged. In the 18th century the land at the foot of the Allegheny Mountains, the Piedmont, was settled by Germans and Scots-Irish. Whatever their country of origin, Virginians were united in their mutual opposition to the British Government – from their early resistance to the colonial taxation of the STAMP ACT of 1765 to the DECLARATION OF INDEPENDENCE by Thomas JEFFERSON, state governor from 1779 to 1781 when the last major action of the War of Independence occurred at YORKTOWN, Chesapeake Bay.

Though deeply divided over the constitution because of controversy surrounding the rights of the different states, Virginia provided four of the first five presidents of the USA, including the first, George Washington and became the heartland of the Democratic Republican Party. In 1861, the state withdrew from the Union to become part of the Southern Confederacy, and the AMERICAN CIVIL WAR began when unionists in northwest Virginia tried to leave the Confederacy. The village of Appomattox in Virginia was the scene of the Confederates' surrender. The state adopted a new constitution in 1902, which was revised in 1971.

Virgin Islands

Group of around 100 islands and cays at the eastern extremity of the Greater Antilles in the Caribbean Sea. The westerly islands including St Thomas, St John and St Croix belong to the USA; Tortola, Virgin Gorda, Anegada and Jost Van Dyke are part of the British Virgin Islands, farther east. The islands were reached by Columbus in 1493 and claims for territory were later made by France and Spain, though effective settlement did not occur until the arrival of British and Danish planters in the 17th century. Denmark claimed St Thomas and St John, and later purchased St Croix from the French. In 1666 Britain took over Tortola from the Dutch pirates who had settled there. African slaves were then imported to work on the sugar plantations until slavery was abolished in the 19th century. Their descendants make up the majority of the population of the islands today. In 1917 Denmark sold its islands to the USA, and their people first elected a governor in 1970. More immigrants from mainland USA joined the settlers between 1960 and 1975.

From 1872 to 1956 the British Virgin Islands comprised part of the British colony of Leeward Islands, but since 1956, following defederation, they have been administered separately by British governors who have gradually extended self-government.

Visconti, Gian Galeazzo

(1351-1402) Italian statesman and patron of the arts who raised the Visconti dynasty of the 14th and 15th centuries to the height of its power. Gian Galeazzo was married in 1360 to Isabella of Valois, the daughter of John II of France, and in 1378 became ruler of Milan as successor to his father Galeazzo II. He ruled jointly with his brother, Bernabò, until 1385, when Bernabò's arrangement of marriage alliances between his family and French royalty led to a feud between them and the arrest of Bernabò, who died in prison.

Gian Galeazzo's expansionist policies united independent cities such as Pisa and Siena under Milanese rule, and made the Visconti dynasty the ruling force of northern Italy. He arranged marriage alliances with most of the western European powers in order to strengthen Italy's position. After Gian Galeazzo's death, the unity of his dominions was temporarily disrupted by the regency of his widow and the rule of his son, Giovanni Maria; during this period many of his conquests were lost. Unity was restored by Giovanni's brother, Filippo Maria, who ruled as duke from 1412 to 1447. On Filippo Maria's death Milan passed to the SFORZAS.

Visigoths see GOTHS

Vittoria, Battle of (June 21, 1813) Conflict fought between the French and a combined English, Spanish and Portuguese army near the Basque city of Vittoria in the PENINSULAR WAR, which followed Napoleon's invasion of Portugal in 1807. The combined forces led by Arthur Wellesley, who was created 1st Duke of Wellington the following year, decisively defeated the French under King Joseph Bonaparte, driving them back over the Pyrenees into France. News of this victory inspired Austria, Russia and Prussia to renew their plans to attack France, and they declared war on Napoleon on August 13.

vizier Leading court official of a traditional Islamic regime, from the Arabic *wazir*. Viziers were frequently the power behind nominal rulers. In some courts – such as those of the early ABBASSID dynasty of the 8th century – the office was hereditary: viziers of the Barmakid family, originally from Persia, served under the Abbassid caliphs, or heads of state. The OTTOMANS first conferred the title of vizier in the late 14th century, and until the conquest of Constantinople in 1453 viziers held the highest rank in the ruling administration. In the 15th century the Ottomans under Sultan Mehmed II assumed the old Islamic practice of giving the title to the office of the chief minister, who became the grand vizier, assisted by 'dome' viziers. The grand vizier represented the sultan, whose signet ring he kept as an insignia of office. In 1654 the grand vizier acquired an official residence which effectively replaced the palace as the centre of Ottoman government.

Mehmed Köprülü, a respected governor who had previously served as a vizier, became grand vizier in 1656, and brought control under one central authority by suppressing dissenters and rivals, reorganising the army and reforming the empire's finances. The position was inherited by the Köprülü family for nearly 80 years. In the 19th century the grand viziers presided over the council of ministers and after 1908 had power to appoint the Cabinet ministers. With the collapse of the Ottoman Empire after the First World War, the title of vizier disappeared.

Vladimir I, St (956-1015) Patron saint of Russia and Grand Duke of KIEV, the capital of the first Russian state, from *c.*980. Vladimir was an ardent pagan until his conversion to Christianity in about 987, and subsequent marriage to the sister of the Byzantine emperor Basil II. He initiated the Russian branch of the Eastern ORTHODOX CHURCH by inviting missionaries from Greece to his territories. Vladimir then devoted the remaining years of his life to building churches, including the magnificent Cathedral of the Tithes.

The powerful Ottoman grand vizier sits in audience with his master, Sultan Suleiman I, in the gardens of the Topkapi Palace in 1524.

Vogel, Sir Julius (1835-99) New Zealand statesman, born in London. Vogel founded and edited newspapers in Australia and in New Zealand, where he entered national politics in 1863. He was elected colonial treasurer from 1869, and as premier from 1873 to 1875 was responsible for a bold and successful policy of borrowing to promote immigration and enlarge the labour force, road and railway building, and land development. He was knighted in 1875, and returned briefly as premier in 1876. After four years in London as agent-general he returned to New Zealand and served as treasurer from 1884 to 1887. Unable to prevent the economic depression caused by growing public debt and high interest rates, he resigned in 1889.

Volta, Alessandro, Count (1745-1827) Italian physicist, inventor in 1800 of the electrochemical battery, or voltaic pile, the first device to produce a continuous electrical current. The impetus for this invention was the Italian physiologist Luigi Galvani's contention in 1791 that he had discovered a new kind of electricity, 'animal electricity', produced in animal tissue, when he connected two different metals to either end of a frog's leg and made it move. Volta ascribed the result to normal electricity, claiming that the contact of the two dissimilar metals would cause the current, with or without the frog's leg – which simply conducted the current – between them. His battery worked on this principle; after its demonstration to Napoleon in 1801, he was made a count. In 1815, he became director of the philosophical faculty at the University of Padua, where he had held the chair of physics for more than 35 years. Volta also invented a number of electrical instruments, including the electrophorus, which generated static electricity, and the condensing electroscope, used to detect an electric charge. The volt, a unit of electrical potential difference, is named in his honour.

Voltaire (1694-1778) Pseudonym of the French writer François-Marie Arouet, one of the dominating figures of the ENLIGHTENMENT, a movement which attacked the government, the Church and the judiciary system during the 18th century and laid the groundwork for the FRENCH REVOLUTION. Voltaire was educated by the Jesuits and went on to study law, but gave it up to become a writer. In 1723 he ridiculed the regency of Philip, Duke of Orleans, in his epic poem, *La Henriade*. For this and for his liberal religious opinions he was imprisoned in the fortress of the Bastille in Paris and then exiled to London in 1726. Voltaire returned to France two years later. In 1734 his *Lettres philosophiques sur les Anglais* (*Philosophical letters on the English*), expressing his admiration for English freedom and the English system of government, caused a scandal in Paris. Voltaire withdrew east of the city to Cirey with his mistress, Madame du Châtelet, where he studied religion, culture and science. FREDERICK the Great invited him to his court in 1750, but the two men quarrelled after two years and Voltaire finally settled in Switzerland. His satire *Candide* (1759) ridiculed the spirit of optimism found in some 18th-century philosophers and reflected his harsh sense of realism. Voltaire received a rapturous reception when he visited Paris in 1778, and died there later that year.

Voortrekkers see feature, page 270

Vortigern Legendary 5th-century Romano-British king, said by the early English scholar and historian BEDE in his *Historia Brittonum* (*History of Britain*) to have invited the first Anglo-Saxon leaders, HENGIST and HORSA, to Britain. Vortigern had requested their help as mercenaries to enable him to withstand raids by the PICTS and the Scots; however, the plan rebounded when Hengist and Horsa turned on the king in 455 and seized lands in Kent. In the 6th-century document *De excidio et conquestu Britanniae* (*The overthrow and conquest of Britain*), the British historian and monk Gildas blamed Vortigern for the loss of British lands to the ANGLO-SAXONS.

> **DID YOU KNOW?**
>
> Voltaire was a rationalist who abhorred conventional Christianity but professed an aggressive Deism. 'If God did not exist,' he wrote, 'it would be necessary to invent him.'

Wagner, Richard (1813-83) German opera composer, founder of the Bayreuth Festival Theatre. He had a profound influence on 19th-century music, particularly opera, and is notable for introducing the *leitmotiv*, a recurring theme that depicts characters and their emotions in rich orchestral passages. Wagner wrote his first opera, *The Marriage*, in 1832, but later destroyed it. In 1834 he completed the opera *The Fairies*. Work as a chorus master and conductor increased his understanding of operatic techniques and he enhanced his reputation with *The Flying Dutchman* (1841), *Tannhäuser* (1842-5) and *Lohengrin* (1846-8), before embarking on the four operas that were to make up his greatest achievement: *The Ring of the Nibelung* (1852-74), based on a Teutonic legend and consisting of *The Rhine Gold*, *The Valkyrie*, *Siegfried* and *The Twilight of the Gods*.

Wagner lived in considerable poverty, moving from Dresden to Weimar to Vienna and then to Stuttgart, where he came under the patronage of King Ludwig of Bavaria. Ludwig encouraged the successful production of *Tristan and Isolde* in 1865. Wagner settled in Switzerland with his second wife, Cosima von Bülow, the daughter of the composer Franz Liszt, and began to raise funds to fulfil his dream to build a theatre. The Bayreuth Festival Theatre opened in 1876 with an acclaimed full-length performance of the *Ring* cycle. Wagner completed the sacred festival drama *Parsifal* in 1882, the year before his death. Cosima and their son, Siegfried, carried on Wagner's work at Bayreuth.

Wagram, Battle of (July 5-6, 1809) Battle between the combined French and Italian forces led by Napoleon Bonaparte (see feature, page 437) and the Austrians under the Archduke Charles at the village of Wagram, near Vienna. Napoleon, determined to offset earlier setbacks, ordered a massive attack on the well-chosen Austrian position. The first day's fighting was inconclusive. The following day Napoleon renewed his assault and the Austrian army began to retreat. The French claimed the victory, but their losses outnumbered those of the Austrians. The battle was followed by the Treaty of Schönbrunn in which Austria lost territory and agreed to join the CONTINENTAL SYSTEM against Britain.

Waitangi, Treaty of (February 6, 1840) Pact between MAORI chiefs and the British Government over Maori land rights in New Zealand. Several hundred Maoris gathered at Waitangi to discuss Britain's annexation of New Zealand. One chief, Tamati Waka Nene, swayed opinion in favour of the treaty, which was signed by 50 chiefs and carried around the country for further signatures. However, many Maoris were opposed to the terms of the agreement, under which Maori sovereignty was ceded to Queen Victoria in return for protection of their land rights, and fighting broke out. Subsequent encroachment on Maori land by British settlers led to the ANGLO-MAORI WARS of 1860 to 1872, in which Maori claims to independence were defeated. Since its recognition by New Zealand statutes, the Treaty of Waitangi assumed new importance from 1975 as a basis of relations between Maori and non-Maori New Zealanders. The Waitangi Tribunal was reconvened in 1975 to consider Maori land claims and in 1985 was given authority to settle claims dating from 1840. In 1994 and 1995 the government agreed to pay compensation to certain Maori tribes whose land was seized illegally by settlers.

> **DID YOU KNOW?**
>
> The Maoris have their own queen. Dame Te Ata-I-Rangikaahu is the sixth sovereign of a royal line that dates from 1858 and which was inspired by the British monarchy.

Wakefield, Edward Gibbon (1796-1862) British colonial reformer and writer. After being sentenced to three years in London's Newgate prison in 1827 for abduction, he learned much about the consequences of the forcible removal of convicts to British overseas territories. In *A Letter from Sydney* (1829), Wakefield proposed the sale of small tracts of land to settlers at a 'sufficient price', rather than freely giving away large tracts. This, he suggested, would finance the regulated emigration of labourers of both sexes, and so create a more balanced colonial society. Wakefield's ideas, taken up and implemented from 1831, became law under the South Australia Act of 1834. At the peak of the system between 1831 and 1841, 51 200 migrants travelled to Australia. In 1837 Wakefield founded the NEW ZEALAND ASSOCIATION. He was largely responsible for British settlement in New Zealand.

Waldenses Christian sect of medieval origins founded by Peter Valdes, or Waldo, in France around 1170. Also known as the Vaudois and the 'Poor Men of Lyons', Valdes and his followers assumed a life of poverty and religious devotion. They lived mostly in southern France and in Piedmont in northern Italy. Persecuted in France as heretics and almost destroyed, the Waldenses formed an alliance with the Swiss Reformed Church in 1532. Today, Waldensian communities survive on the French-Italian border and in the USA around Valdense in North Carolina.

Wales Principality of the United Kingdom, known in Welsh as Cymru. The capital is Cardiff. Wales has retained a distinctive culture, and the Welsh language is spoken by nearly 20 per cent of the population. The original inhabitants were Celts, driven into Wales by Anglo-Saxon invaders of Britain who called them *Waelisc*, 'foreign'. They were relatively unaffected by the Romans, who penetrated as far as Anglesey between AD 50 and 60. By the 3rd century the country had become Christian, but politically the land remained disunited, with Gwynedd, Powys, Deheubarth and Dyfed the largest kingdoms. In the 8th century, King OFFA of Mercia, built a great earthwork running from the river Dee southwards to the Severn Estuary to mark

Maori chiefs sign the Treaty of Waitangi in 1840. The treaty was signed in two versions, one Maori, the other English. Waitangi Day, February 6, has since become New Zealand's national birthday.

Lech Walesa addresses a crowd during the Solidarity election of 1989, when the trade union was legalised and allowed to campaign as a political party.

the boundary between England and Wales. In the 10th century, Hywel the Good (904-50) introduced a code of laws.

From the 11th century the Normans colonised Wales and Romanised the Church. The Welsh revolted, but as each revolt was crushed the English kings tightened their grip on the country. LLYWELYN the Great (1194-1240) recovered a measure of independence, but the invasion of EDWARD I in 1277 ended hopes of a Welsh state. Edward's son, the future EDWARD II, was created the first Prince of Wales in 1301. The revolt of Owen GLYNDWR in the early 15th century revived Welsh aspirations, but they were dashed in 1536 when Henry VIII's Act of UNION formally united Wales with England.

As the gentry and Church became Anglicised, Wales developed into a centre of nonconformity, particularly for Baptists and Methodists. As a result, the position of the Anglican Church became a dominant question in Welsh politics, eventually leading to the disestablishment of the Church from

> ❝ There you saw the peculiar habits of the Welsh. In the very depth of winter they were running about bare-legged... I never saw them wear armour... They endamaged the Flemings very much. ❞
>
> *A Flemish observer studying the Welsh soldiers in Edward I's army in 1297*

1920. Social unrest in rural Wales, voiced in the REBECCA RIOTS of 1838-43, resulted in significant emigration. The INDUSTRIAL REVOLUTION brought prosperity to South Wales, and by the late 19th century the resulting boom in coal-mining had transformed Wales into the world's chief coal-exporting region.

By the 1980s many of Wales's coalfields had closed and industry had diversified. Welsh nationalism has been a powerful force, and in 1966 PLAID CYMRU returned its first member to Parliament. In a Welsh referendum in

1979, however, devolution from the United Kingdom was overwhelmingly opposed.

Walesa, Lech (1943-)

President of Poland from 1990 to 1995 and a leading figure in his country's democratisation in 1989. The son of a carpenter, Walesa worked as an electrician in the Gdánsk shipyard. In 1980 he founded SOLIDARITY, the first free – that is, not state-controlled – trade union in Eastern Europe. Walesa's dismissal as a union activist, together with food shortages and price rises, led to a series of strikes in 1980 and 1981 that attracted widespread public support for Solidarity and achieved a number of concessions from the government, including the right for workers to organise freely.

In late 1981 Solidarity was outlawed by the regime of General Wojciech Jaruzelski, and Walesa was imprisoned for nearly a year. In 1983 he was awarded the Nobel peace prize for his efforts to improve workers' rights. He played a major role in talks with the government in 1988 and 1989, which resulted in the legalisation of Solidarity and other trade unions and also paved the way for the introduction of a socialist democracy. In 1990 Walesa was elected president in a landslide victory. He faced the challenges of political instability and moving Poland towards a free-market economy. Defeated by Aleksander Kwasniewski in the presidential elections of 1995, Walesa nominally returned to his former job as a shipyard electrician in 1996.

Wallace, George Corley (1919-)

US politician, district judge and state governor of Alabama for four terms beginning in 1962, 1970, 1974 and 1982. Wallace ran for the presidency on three occasions. In 1968 he stood as leader of the newly established DIXIE-CRAT AMERICAN INDEPENDENT PARTY, polling more than 10 million votes, mainly in the South. In the 1972 presidential election Wallace sought the DEMOCRATIC PARTY's nomination, but his campaign was thwarted by an assassination attempt that left him paralysed. He was becoming reconciled to the issue of CIVIL RIGHTS when he made a final unsuccessful attempt to win the presidency in 1976. For the 1982 election as governor, Wallace publicly recanted his opposition to the desegregation of state schools and polled a substantial number of Black votes. He was re-elected and remained in office until 1987.

Wallace, Henry Agard (1888-1965)

US politician and agricultural reformer. As an agriculturist, Wallace developed successful varieties of corn. In 1932 he helped to swing the state of Iowa to the Democratic Party and the following year became Roosevelt's secretary of agriculture. He supported Roosevelt's NEW DEAL, and from 1940 to 1944 served as Roosevelt's vice-president. Wallace chaired the Board of Economic Warfare from 1941, but fell out with President Harry S Truman's Cold War policy and resigned in 1946. In 1948 he formed the Progressive Party and ran unsuccessfully against Truman for the presidency. Wallace then retired to continue his agricultural research.

Wallace, Sir William (c.1270-1305)

Scottish soldier who became a national hero for his resistance to English rule. After attacking the English garrison at Lanark, defeating Edward I's army at Stirling Bridge and banishing the English from Scotland in 1297, Wallace became guardian of Scotland. He then raided northern England and recaptured Berwick. In 1298 EDWARD I invaded Scotland with 88000 men and defeated Wallace at FALKIRK. Wallace fled, possibly to France, but was later captured, tried in London and hanged, drawn and quartered.

Wallenstein, Albrecht von (1583-1634)

Duke of Friedland from 1625, Duke of Mecklenburg from 1629, and general of the

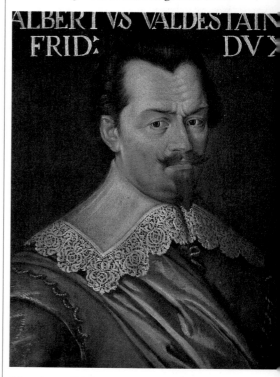

Albrecht von Wallenstein was assassinated in 1634 by an English captain who woke him up before striking him dead with his halberd.

Holy Roman imperial forces. Wallenstein remained loyal to the Holy Roman emperor Ferdinand on the outbreak of the THIRTY YEARS' WAR in 1618 and was appointed governor of Bohemia. He served as commander in chief of the emperor's forces from 1625 to 1630, drove the Danes out of northern Germany, overran Mecklenburg and tried to establish his own empire on the Baltic, but German princes forced his dismissal. In 1632 he was recalled as imperial general to halt a Swedish invasion. He connived to build up his power, secretly negotiating with Catholics and Protestants, but his plans were discovered and once again Ferdinand dismissed him. Soon afterwards Wallenstein was assassinated.

Walpole, Sir Robert, 1st Earl of Orford (1676-1745) Britain's first prime minister. Walpole led the government as chief minister from 1721 to 1742. Born in Norfolk, he entered the House of Commons in 1701 as a member of the WHIG party, rising to become first lord of the treasury and chancellor of the exchequer by 1715. He restored confidence after the stock market panic that followed the SOUTH SEA BUBBLE crisis in 1720 and came to power the following year.

GEORGE I's lack of interest in parliamentary procedures gave Walpole considerable freedom to govern. He strove for peace abroad, strengthened the economy at home, set up a fund to pay off the national debt and maintained political stability. He chaired meetings of a small group of ministers, later known as the CABINET. Walpole had to face increasing antagonism within his parliamentary party,

Robert Walpole, left, seen here in Parliament, is credited with establishing the office of prime minister, but never officially bore the title.

particularly over his opposition to foreign wars and his attempt to impose taxes on wine and tobacco in 1733. In 1739 Walpole was reluctantly drawn into conflict with Spain in the War of JENKINS' EAR. Three years later he resigned after the government was accused of rigging a by-election.

Walsingham, Sir Francis (c.1532-90) English politician and diplomat, and a principal secretary of state to ELIZABETH I. A zealous Protestant, Walsingham maintained an efficient network of spies that spanned Europe and enabled him to uncover such intrigues as the BABINGTON plot to put MARY, QUEEN OF SCOTS on the English throne in place of Elizabeth. In 1588 he obtained preparatory plans for the SPANISH ARMADA. Although he was valued by Elizabeth, Walsingham was not honoured for his work and died in poverty.

Walter, Hubert (d.1205) English churchman and statesman, ruler of England during the frequent absences abroad of RICHARD I. Walter accompanied Richard on the Third CRUSADE, and on his return in 1193 was appointed Archbishop of Canterbury and justiciar, or chief political and legal officer. His legal and administrative skills were recognised by Richard, for whose release from captivity by the German emperor Henry VI he raised a £100000 ransom, as well as by JOHN, whose accession he secured and who made him chancellor in 1199. Walter made extensive financial and judicial reforms, and also introduced the positions of justice of the peace and coroner.

Warbeck, Perkin (1474-99) PRETENDER to the throne of England, who led a rising against HENRY VII. Warbeck was in the service of a merchant who was friendly with EDWARD IV of England. From 1491 to 1497 he posed as Richard, Duke of York, the younger of Edward's sons who were supposed to have been murdered in the Tower. Warbeck was well received in Ireland, France and Flanders, but soon after he invaded England in 1497 he was captured, imprisoned in the Tower of London and executed.

Ward, Sir Joseph (1856-1930) Liberal prime minister of New Zealand from 1906 to 1912 and again from 1928 to 1930. Ward had a reputation as a financial 'wizard'. He was noted both for his successful loan raising and for the provision of low-interest credit to farmers, but he failed to solve the economic crises brought on by the Great DEPRESSION that began in 1929.

Wardrobe Department in the household of English royalty and nobility. The royal Wardrobe was first introduced in the 12th century to supply the king with cash while

travelling. In the 13th century HENRY III used it as a convenient alternative to the more bureaucratic and hidebound exchequer. His successor, EDWARD I, treated it as his war treasury to pay for military expenditure. The Wardrobe declined in importance in the 15th century and assumed its current role of responsibility for robes, clothing and jewels.

warlord Chinese regional military ruler in the early 20th century. Following the death in 1916 of Yuan Shikai, republican China's first president, local rulers, or warlords, established their own fiefdoms, which they controlled with private armies. The warlords were mostly former imperial and republican army soldiers, bandits and local officials. They waged civil war until 1928, when the government of CHIANG KAI-SHEK re-established

Chang Tso-lin was a warlord of Manchuria who in 1928 was assassinated by the Japanese after taking their money and then betraying them.

central authority. Some military rulers persisted in the west of China until the communists came to power in 1949.

War of 1812 (1812-15) War between the USA and Britain. The USA had become frustrated over trade and shipping restrictions imposed on it by Britain in the NAPOLEONIC WARS and that, combined with a desire to remove British and Canadian obstacles to US westward expansion, led Congress to declare war on Britain in June 1812. American forces attempted to invade Canada, but were driven back by the British. At sea, the USA won a

British troops burn public buildings in Washington, DC in the War of 1812. The burning, on August 24, 1814, was in retaliation for the destruction of York (present-day Toronto) the previous year.

number of victories, but the British naval blockade inflicted considerable harm on the US economy. In 1814 the British occupied Washington, burning the White House and other buildings. War-weariness brought the sides together, and in December the Treaty of GHENT restored all conquered territories to their original owners. The British shelling of Fort McHenry in the war inspired Francis Scott Key to write the 'The Star-spangled Banner', which became the national anthem.

Warsaw Pact Treaty of military alliance signed in Warsaw in 1955 by the Soviet Union and the Eastern Bloc countries it dominated, including Bulgaria, East Germany, Czechoslovakia, Hungary, Poland, Romania and Albania, which withdrew in 1968. Also known as the Eastern European Mutual Assistance Pact, it was drawn up in response to West Germany's membership of NATO, and provided for a unified military command, the maintenance of Soviet units in member states, and mutual assistance. This last provision was applied by the USSR in 1968 to launch an invasion of Czechoslovakia by member states against the liberal regime of Alexander DUBČEK. The Warsaw Pact was ended in Prague on July 1, 1991, following the collapse of the USSR. By then troops and equipment had been withdrawn from Hungary and Czechoslovakia. Withdrawal from Poland and Germany was completed in 1994.

Warsaw Rising (1944) Polish insurrection in Warsaw in the Second World War, in which Poles tried to expel the

During the Warsaw Rising the Polish underground army had to recruit soldiers of 16 to replace those who had fallen.

German forces before Soviet forces occupied the city. Polish resistance groups, supported by the exiled Polish government in London, rose up against German occupying forces to gain control of the city. Germany responded with a series of air raids lasting 63 days. Meanwhile, the advancing Red Army would not allow the Western Allies to use Soviet air bases to airlift food and equipment to the resistance forces. On October 2 supplies ran out and the Poles surrendered. The Germans then systematically deported Warsaw's population and destroyed the city, eliminating the main body of Poles who supported the government in exile. The Red Army continued its advance into Poland, and a communist provisional government was imposed in 1945.

Warwick, Richard Neville, Earl of (1428-71) English politician and soldier. Warwick earned the title of 'kingmaker' as a result of the influence he exerted during the Wars of the ROSES. Fighting first on the side of the Yorkists against the Lancastrians, he established EDWARD IV, son of Richard Plantagenet, Duke of York, on the throne in place of HENRY VI in 1461. Warwick then

fell out with Edward and fled to France. He invaded England in 1470, this time on the side of the Lancastrians, and reinstated Henry VI. Edward retaliated at the Battle of Barnet in 1471: the Lancastrians were defeated, Henry was captured and Warwick was killed.

Washington, Booker T(aliaferro) (1856-1915) US educationalist and the undeclared leader of Black people in their campaign for CIVIL RIGHTS. Washington was born in Virginia to a Black slave and a White father. He worked as a caretaker to help pay for his college education before becoming a teacher, writer and speaker on Black problems. From 1881 he was principal of Tuskegee Industrial Institute in Alabama, where he helped Black people to train in the trades and professions.

Washington emphasised the importance of economic independence in achieving social equality, a view he expounded in 1895 in a well-publicised speech known as the Atlanta Compromise. He also won the sponsorship of

> **❝ In all things that are purely social we can be separate as the fingers, yet one as the hand in all things essential to mutual progress. ❞**
>
> *Booker T. Washington, Atlanta, September 18, 1895*

White businessmen for his National Negro Business League of 1900 and advised two presidents – Theodore Roosevelt and William Taft – on racial issues.

Washington Conference (November 1921-February 1922) Conference held in Washington, USA, that placed restraints on the naval arms race and Japanese expansionism in the Far East. It was attended by Britain, Belgium, China, France, Holland, Portugal Italy, Japan and the USA. Several treaties were drawn up, including a nine-power agreement guaranteeing China's independence; a naval agreement limiting the sea power of Britain, the USA, Japan, France and Italy; and the Shantung Treaty, under which Japan had to return Shantung and Kiaochow to China and withdraw its troops from Siberia. The effect of the treaties was limited, however, and problems broke out afresh during the 1930s.

Washington, George (1732-99) First president of the USA from 1789 to 1797. Washington commanded the campaign that ended the American Revolution (see feature, page 31). Regarded as the father of his nation, Washington showed powers of leadership, stoicism and integrity that earned him widespread admiration. He was born into a wealthy Virginian family, started his career as a surveyor, and served in the last of the French and Indian Wars of 1755 to 1763. Politically, he supported American resistance to British colonial policy. He was also a member of the Virginia House of Burgesses from 1759 to 1774 and a delegate to the CONTINENTAL CONGRESSES of 1774 and 1775.

When the American Revolution broke out Washington was elected commander in chief of Continental forces. Taking command of 16000 volunteers, he drove the British from Boston in March 1776 and continued to fight with mixed success until the arrival of French troops as allies in 1780. In a final victorious campaign in 1781, Washington besieged YORKTOWN in Virginia and forced the British to surrender.

American independence was recognised by the Treaty of PARIS in 1783. Anxious about postwar political anarchy, Washington supported the Constitutional Convention in 1787 and the resulting CONSTITUTION OF THE USA. Washington was twice elected unanimously to the presidency. At first he was noted for his political neutrality, but ultimately he aligned himself with the FEDERAL-IST PARTY. His federalist policies, suppression of the WHISKEY REBELLION and approval of John JAY's treaty provoked attacks from Jeffersonian Republicans. In his farewell address Washington deplored factionalism and called for US neutrality in foreign affairs.

The Duke of Wellington rallies his troops at Waterloo. He later said of the battle: 'In all my life I have not experienced such anxiety, for I must confess that I have never been so close to defeat.'

watch and ward System developed in 13th-century England to preserve the peace. Guards were appointed and the duties of the constables at night (watch) and in daytime (ward) were defined. Town gates were closed from dusk to dawn, and strangers had to produce sureties. Modifications to the system were made during the 13th century and were eventually incorporated in the Statute of Winchester of 1285.

Watergate US political scandal that led to the resignation of President Richard NIXON. During the 1972 presidential election campaign, burglars with electronic surveillance equipment were caught breaking into the headquarters of the Democratic Party in the Watergate building, Washington, DC. It was soon discovered that their actions formed part of the Republican campaign to re-elect Nixon. At first the White House denied all knowledge of the incident, but after intensive investigations led by journalists on the *Washington Post* it became apparent that members of the president's staff had participated in illegal activities and had attempted to cover up the operation. Several White House officials were indicted and convicted on criminal charges

and Nixon himself was implicated. In August 1974 Nixon resigned in order to avoid impeachment. He was later pardoned for any federal offences he might have committed by his successor as president, Gerald FORD.

Waterloo, Battle of (June 18, 1815) Final action of the NAPOLEONIC WARS in which the British and Prussian armies defeated the French near the Belgian village of Waterloo, leading to the abdication of the French emperor Napoleon (see feature, page 437). In an attempt to regain power after escaping from Elba in February 1815, Napoleon had hastily recruited an army in the hope of defeating the Duke of WELLINGTON's allied forces of British, Dutch, Belgian and German soldiers, and General BLÜCHER's army of Prussians.

On June 16, Napoleon attacked and defeated the Prussians at Ligny; the British then repulsed the French at Quatre Bras before retreating towards Brussels. On June 18, Napoleon attacked with 72000 men to Wellington's 68000. The British stood firm until Blücher's 61000 Prussians arrived and attacked Napoleon in the flank. Wellington ordered a general advance and the French were routed. There were 30000 French casualties, and 13000 British and 7000 Prussian dead or wounded. On June 22 Napoleon signed his second and final abdication.

water supply In ancient times small communities depended on water from streams and springs to sustain life and irrigate the land for crops. They sank wells to draw water to the surface. Larger civilisations grew up along rivers such as the Nile, Tigris and Euphrates. Gradually populations outstripped local sources and water had to be brought in by canals and aqueducts and stored in reservoirs and cisterns. Around AD 100 the city of Rome was supplied by eight aqueducts delivering

Watergate investigations close in on John Ehrlichman, one of the president's chief aides, in May 1973 (below). A year later, Nixon resigned.

222 million gallons (1000 million litres) of water daily. This was distributed to public fountains and baths by means of lead pipes, gravity and pumps. The Romans built great stone aqueducts across Italy, France and Spain. In Britain their aqueducts were smaller, and earthenware pipes were used to channel water for short distances. From 1285 London had a system of conduits with water distributed along 3½ miles (6 km) of leather pipes.

It was not until the 17th and 18th centuries that a link was made between contaminated water and the spread of disease. Cities such as London and Paris began to install distribution networks using cast-iron pipes, aqueducts and pumps. In 1613 the 38 mile (61 km) New River was completed to feed a reservoir for London at Islington. Water was also pumped from the Thames by water wheels installed under London Bridge. In the 19th century reservoirs were constructed by flooding valleys, and treatment plants and pumping stations were built. Supplies are now augmented by purifying recycled water. In arid areas, such as the Gulf States, sea water is desalinated in special plants. In the 1990s the World Health Organisation estimates that while three-quarters of urban residents in developing countries have access to safe water (often from standpipes), only half of rural residents do.

Watling Street see ROAD

Watt, James (1736-1819) Scottish engineer and inventor who invented the modern steam condensing engine. His name was also given to the 'watt' unit of electrical power, and he devised the term 'horsepower'. Watt trained as a mathematical-instrument maker and worked as a canal surveyor before being asked to repair one of Thomas Newcomen's steam engines in 1764. To improve its efficiency, Watt introduced a separate condenser to cool the used steam and made further modifications. He then went into partnership with Matthew Boulton to manufacture the new engine, producing the first in 1774 at the Soho Engineering Works near Birmingham. Watt's other inventions include his design for a steam locomotive in 1784.

Wavell, Archibald, 1st Earl (1883-1950) British field-marshal. During the Second World War Wavell served as commander in chief of British forces in the Middle East from 1939 to 1941. In 1940-1 he won acclaim for his victories over the numerically greater Italian armies in North Africa, but was defeated by the Germans under General Erwin ROMMEL. Appointed supreme commander Far East just after the Japanese attack on Pearl Harbor in December 1941, Wavell lost Malaya, Burma and Singapore to the Japanese. In 1943 he was appointed viceroy of India, where he remained until he resigned from the post in 1947.

Webb, Sidney, Baron Passfield (1859-1947) English social reformer and founder of the London School of Economics in 1895 with his wife, Beatrice (1858-1943). Webb's writings, many of them joint studies with Beatrice on trade unionism and local government, had considerable influence on political theory and social reform. In 1884 the couple helped to found the FABIAN Society to promote the spread of democratic socialism. As a member of the Royal Commission on the Poor Law (1905-9), Beatrice produced a Minority Report outlining the idea of social insurance. Sidney Webb served as a Labour Member of Parliament from 1922 to 1929 and also held a number of government posts.

DID YOU KNOW?

Wavell, an officer untrammelled by convention, once declared that his ideal infantryman was a cross between a poacher, a gunman and a cat burglar.

Weber, Max (1864-1920) German sociologist, one of the founders of modern SOCIOLOGY. Weber's wide-ranging ideas on social stratification, large-scale institutions, power, law and religion continue to have an influence on sociological thinking. Weber argued that an individual's class could depend on the possession of skills as well as on property ownership and occupation. He believed that sociology should concern itself with the interpretation and explanation of social behaviour, not simply with its observation and description. He was concerned with the responsibilities of the social scientist and felt strongly that personal beliefs must not interfere with investigation and analysis. Weber's major work, *Economy and Society*, was published posthumously in 1922.

Webster, Daniel (1782-1852) US orator, lawyer and statesman. Webster served as a congressman (1813-17) and then as a senator (1827-41; 1845-50), securing his reputation through winning a series of cases before the Supreme Court. Among his many great orations, Webster delivered a staunch defence of the Union in 1830. During the 1830s and 1840s Webster was one of the leaders of the Whig Party. He failed to fulfil his presidential ambitions, but served as secretary of state under Benjamin Harrison and John Tyler between 1841 and 1843, during which time he negotiated the WEBSTER-ASHBURTON TREATY. He served again under President Millard Fillmore from 1850 to 1852.

Webster-Ashburton Treaty (1842) Agreement between Britain and the USA that settled the border between Maine and New Brunswick and established Anglo-US cooperation on the naval suppression of the slave trade off the African coast. The treaty, negotiated by the US secretary of state Daniel WEBSTER and the British minister Lord Ashburton, settled disputed boundaries in the north-east USA, including the Canadian-US boundary in the Great Lakes region. Maine won navigation rights on the St John River.

James Watt's rotative beam engine, patented in 1782, had an instant impact on industrial production as the first engine to provide rotary power.

Wedgwood, Josiah

Wedgwood, Josiah (1730-95) British potter and fellow of the Royal Society who was largely responsible for the great expansion of the Staffordshire pottery industry in the mid 18th century. Wedgwood was born into a family of potters and in 1759 he founded his own business at Burslem. There he produced Queens ware, a strong, cream-coloured earthenware that could be left plain or decorated in neoclassical style with the newly invented technique of transfer printing. Queens ware came to rival porcelain. In 1774 the Russian empress Catherine the Great ordered a service of 952 pieces.

In 1768 Wedgwood opened a new factory in the village he had built to house his workers, and called it Etruria. There he employed artists and the sculptor John Flaxman to make decorative pieces. In 1775 Wedgwood introduced jasper ware. This matt-finished, tinted – especially 'Wedgwood blue' – pottery decorated with contrasting white ornamentation became immensely popular and is still made today. His shrewd business sense also led him to pioneer sales catalogues for the public.

Josiah Wedgwood made 25 copies of the Portland Vase, a Roman burial urn, in black unglazed stoneware before the original was smashed by a vandal.

Weimar Republic

(1919-33) Republic of Germany formed after the end of the First World War, on the abdication of Emperor WILHELM II. The republic was proclaimed in Berlin on November 9, 1918. In January 1919 a democratic constitution was agreed in Weimar, and Friedrich EBERT, a Social Democrat, was elected first president. The new republic had to face the VERSAILLES PEACE SETTLEMENT, involving the loss of territory and overseas colonies, and a vast REPARATIONS debt. France occupied the Ruhr in 1923 in protest at

In Weimar Germany, bank customers used laundry baskets to collect their almost worthless banknotes.

Germany's failure to meet reparations payments. High inflation and mass unemployment fuelled the rise of right-wing extremists, who included Adolf HITLER. In 1925 Paul von HINDENBURG succeeded Ebert as president; adjustments were made to reparations payments in agreement with the USA; and France withdrew from the Ruhr. Germany began to recover economically, but the Great DEPRESSION of 1929 increased unemployment, and support for the Nazi and Communist parties gained ground. In 1933 Hindenburg was persuaded to accept Hitler as chancellor. Hitler exploited anticommunist fears and anti-Semitic prejudice to win a small majority for the nationalist parties in the elections of March 1933 that followed the REICHSTAG fire. On Hindenburg's death in 1934, Hitler made himself president and proclaimed the THIRD REICH.

Weizmann, Chaim (1874-1952) First president of Israel (1948-52), Zionist leader and scientist. Born in Russia, Weizmann became a British subject in 1910. As director of the Admiralty laboratories during the First World War, he developed a method for manufacturing the solvent acetone. His work brought him to the attention of the prime minister, Lloyd George. Weizmann exploited his contacts to help obtain the 1917 BALFOUR DECLARATION by which the Jews were promised a home in Palestine. He was also president of the World Zionist Organisation (1920-30; 1935-46), played a major role in shaping the PALESTINE mandate (1948), and became head of the Hebrew University in Jerusalem before taking up office as president of the new state of Israel.

Welensky, Sir Roy (1907-91) Prime minister of the Federation of Rhodesia and Nyasaland from 1956 to 1963. Welensky was born in Salisbury, Southern Rhodesia. He entered politics in 1938 and in 1953 founded the Federal Party, which was dedicated to racial partnership. He was chief architect and an enthusiastic supporter of the Central African Federation that brought together Northern Rhodesia (present-day Zambia), Southern Rhodesia (Zimbabwe) and Nyasaland (Malawi). However, when the federation was dissolved in 1963, Welensky lost

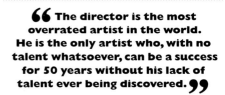

the support of the White Rhodesians, the majority of whom gave their allegiance to the Rhodesian Front of Ian Smith.

welfare state see feature, page 695

Welles, Orson (1915-85) US actor and film and theatre director. Born in Wisconsin, he became a radio producer in 1934 and in 1937 founded the Mercury Theater in New York. His first major work, a radio production of H.G. Wells's *The War of the Worlds* (1938), was so convincing that it caused panic among American listeners, who feared that a Martian

> **❝ The director is the most overrated artist in the world. He is the only artist who, with no talent whatsoever, can be a success for 50 years without his lack of talent ever being discovered. ❞**
>
> *Orson Welles in* Time *magazine, 1982*

invasion was taking place. Welles's first film, *Citizen Kane* (1941), the story of a press baron, which he wrote, produced, directed and acted in, was a landmark in the use of new cinema techniques. His other films include *The Magnificent Ambersons* (1942), *Macbeth* (1948), *Othello* (1951), Kafka's *The Trial* (1962), and *Chimes at Midnight* (1966). As an actor, Welles is particularly remembered for the role of Harry Lime in the film *The Third Man* (1949).

Wellington, Arthur Wellesley, 1st Duke of (1769-1852) British soldier and statesman, prime minister from 1828 to 1830. Known as the Iron Duke for his military achievements, Wellington is renowned for commanding the forces that defeated the French emperor Napoleon (see feature, page 437) at the Battle of WATERLOO in June 1815.

Wellington was born in Ireland and in 1787 joined the army. In 1796 he was posted to India, where he distinguished himself as both a soldier and an administrator. On his return

Welfare from the cradle to the grave

After the end of the Second World War Britain's Labour government set about creating a system to look after the basic needs of all its citizens, from health and education to housing and employment.

The origins of Britain's welfare state lie in the early 19th century, when legislators first acknowledged the despair of the poor. For, as the French historian Alexis de Tocqueville said after journeying through Britain in 1835, 'in every country it is unfortunate not to be rich; in England it is a horrible misfortune to be poor'. The result was piecemeal legislation, such as a grant of £20000 to help Church societies to educate the poor – though this was less than was spent annually on the royal stables.

When the Boer War broke out in 1899, the army discovered that many potential recruits were too unfit to serve. As a result, the Liberal government of 1906 introduced a number of reforms, among them Britain's first health and unemployment insurance, modelled on the pensions and sickness insurance introduced in Germany by Otto von Bismarck in the 1890s. The health package was promoted by the prime minister, David Lloyd George, with the slogan 'Ninepence for fourpence': employees contributed fourpence, employers threepence and the state twopence a week to provide the benefits.

The Great Depression and mass unemployment of the 1930s placed severe strains on this system, and it was realised that further reforms were needed. As a result, the economist William Beveridge was commissioned by Britain's wartime government to report on social security. His findings, published in 1942 as *Social Insurance and Allied Services*, recommended an entirely restructured welfare system providing universal pensions, social security, a National Health Service (NHS), child benefit and a commitment to full employment – a system that would meet the essential needs of all individuals 'from the cradle to the grave'.

THE LIMITS OF WELFARE

By the end of 1944 the wartime coalition had laid plans for the NHS and a modern social security system; it had also abolished fees in state-maintained schools. But it was under the postwar Labour government, from 1945 to 1951, that Beveridge's ambitious plans (with some modifications) were implemented, and the welfare state was launched.

The British welfare state provided inspiration for the creation of similar systems elsewhere, notably in New Zealand, the Netherlands and Scandinavia. The following 30 years saw the expansion of Britain's welfare system under both Labour and Conservative governments, despite repeated conflicts over where its boundaries should be drawn.

Rising oil prices in the 1970s and increasing unemployment in the 1980s slowed the development of the welfare state, as did Prime Minister Margaret Thatcher's adherence to the notion that individuals should take greater responsibility for themselves. As a result, the 1990s have seen the most intense debate about the future of the welfare state since the Second World War: whether it should continue to provide universal assistance; whether it should provide assistance directly, or by means of loans; and whether or not it should be reduced to a safety net for the most underprivileged members of society, with those who can afford to pay being encouraged, or compelled, to make private provision for themselves.

A cartoon from 1948 pokes gentle fun at the NHS (right), while a happy boy shows off his new spectacles (below).

Universal family allowance (also known as child benefit) was one of the first provisions of the British welfare state. It was widely advertised, as in this poster (above).

to Britain he was knighted. In 1808 he was sent to Portugal to lead an army against the French, then took up command of the British, Spanish and Portuguese forces in the PENINSULAR WAR, driving the French from Spain in 1813. The following year he was created Duke of Wellington.

Napoleon surrendered in 1814, but in 1815 he escaped from exile to lead the French army against Wellington's allied forces in Belgium. Supported by the Prussian army, Wellington defeated the French at Waterloo, breaking Napoleon's power and becoming a national hero. Afterwards, Wellington, in tears for the dead, said: 'I hope to God I have fought my last battle. It is a bad thing to be always fighting.'

Wellington never fought again. He had already embarked on a political career, and in 1806 had been elected to Parliament as a Tory. In 1819 he joined the Cabinet as master-general of the ordnance. After becoming prime minister in 1828, Wellington reluctantly agreed to CATHOLIC EMANCIPATION, but his opposition to parliamentary reform made him unpopular and he resigned. From 1834 to 1835 he served as foreign secretary under Sir Robert PEEL. In 1842 Wellington was made commander in chief of the army. Four years later he retired from public life.

Wells, Fargo and Company

US transport and banking organisation. The company was founded by Henry Wells and William G. Fargo in 1852 to handle the banking and transportation of gold bullion and other goods generated by the California GOLD RUSH. By 1866 Wells,

Fargo had established a monopoly of stagecoach lines west of the Mississippi, and for 20 years it dominated the postal service in the west. The stagecoach business declined with the introduction of railways. In 1905 the banking operation merged to form the Wells Fargo Nevada National Bank; in 1918 the transport side became the American Railway Express Company.

Wells, H(erbert) G(eorge) (1866-1946)

British novelist, historian and journalist. Wells is particularly known for his science fiction and satirical novels, including *The Time Machine* (1895), *The Invisible Man* (1897) and *The War of the Worlds* (1898). He was an advocate of socialism, women's rights and the advancement of science, as well as an active member of the FABIAN Society. Wells also produced works of scientific and political speculation, including *The Outline of History* (1920).

Welsh Nationalist Party see PLAID CYMRU

Wenceslas IV (1361-1419)

King of BOHEMIA from 1376 to 1402 and from 1404 until his death, also king of Germany and Holy Roman Emperor from 1378 to 1400. A weak king who allowed Germany to slip from his hands, he was overcome by the ambitions of the imperial princes and by his brother SIGISMUND. He was twice imprisoned by his nobles in Bohemia and briefly deposed. In Germany, the princes deposed him in 1400. The end of his reign was disturbed by the HUSSITE movement.

Henry Wells (left) and William Fargo (right) carried bullion from the American goldfields under armed guard. Stagecoach routes followed the wagons, and made Wells, Fargo an enduring legend of the West.

St Wenceslas became famous in England with the Victorian Christmas carol, which was not based on any known incident in the saint's life.

Wenceslas, St (c.907-29)

Prince and patron saint of BOHEMIA, immortalised as 'good King Wenceslas' in the popular carol. According to tradition, Wenceslas was raised as a Christian by his grandmother St Ludmilla, who was later murdered by his pagan mother, Drahomíra. Until he came of age, Drahomíra acted as regent. Wenceslas, who was noted for his piety, worked to promote Christianity. He incurred the wrath of the nobles, who disapproved of his subordination to Henry I, king of Germany. Wenceslas was murdered by his heathen brother, Boleslav, in the Church of St George in Prague.

Wentworth, Thomas see Thomas Wentworth, 1st Earl of STRAFFORD

Wesley, John (1703-91)

English clergyman, the founder of Methodism (see METHODISTS). Wesley was born in Lincolnshire, the son of an Anglican clergyman. At Oxford University he became the leader of a devout group whose members included his brother Charles, the hymn writer. After being ordained as a priest in the Church of England in 1728, Wesley went to Georgia in the USA to work as a missionary. On his return to England in 1738 he experienced a profound spiritual conversion and became a fervent evangelical.

Wesley began widespread preaching, but his zeal antagonised many Church of England clergy, who banned him from their pulpits. As a result, he took to preaching in the open air. In 1739 in Bristol he founded the first Methodist chapel, and from then on he set up Methodist societies wherever he preached. In 1744 he drew up his rule book for Methodist societies. Over 50 years, Wesley stimulated a religious revival in England, delivering 40 000 sermons and travelling some 250 000 miles (400 000 km), mainly on horseback.

Wessex Kingdom of the West Saxons, whose royal dynasty achieved the unification of England in the early 10th century. Wessex is said to have been founded in *c.*495 by two Saxon chieftains, Cerdic and Cynric, who landed near Southampton and advanced across Hampshire and the basin of the upper Thames. Under Cerdic's grandson, Ceawlin (560-*c.*91), expansion continued towards the lower Severn to encompass Gloucester, Bath and Cirencester. During the 7th century the growth of Wessex was challenged by the rise of its northern neighbour, MERCIA. Under Ine (688-726), Wessex incorporated Somerset.

Egbert (802-39) became overlord of all England, but his successors lost many of his gains fighting the invading Danes. In 926 Athelstan ousted the Danes to become ruler of all England. The writer Thomas Hardy (1840-1928) used the term Wessex in his novels to denote a fictional area of southern England centred on Dorset.

Western Australia Largest of Australia's states, bounded by the Timor Sea to the north, the Indian Ocean to the west, and the Southern Ocean and the Great Australian Bight to the south. Western Australia is separated from the Northern Territory and South Australia by desert, which was first crossed in 1873 by the English explorer Peter Warburton. The state's capital, Perth, was founded in 1829. The first European voyagers to Western Australia included the Dutchman Dirk Hartog in 1616, and the Englishman William Dampier in 1688.

Settlement did not begin until 1826, when the British sent soldiers and convicts to King George Sound on the south-east coast. In 1829 Britain founded Western Australia as its second Australian colony, and between 1850 and 1868 transported 10 000 convicts to boost its labour force and to accelerate its development. In 1890 a government was established under the leadership of Western Australia's first premier, John Forrest, a surveyor who in 1870 had found a route from Perth to South Australia along the south coast. In 1901 Western Australia became a state of the Commonwealth of Australia. In a 1933 referendum its citizens voted in favour of secession, but because of constitutional difficulties this was not implemented.

Western Front Battle zone during the FIRST WORLD WAR where German forces confronted French and British troops. Lines of trenches were constructed along the front, stretching from Nieuport on the Belgian coast to the Vosges mountains in north-east France. In the TRENCH WARFARE of 1915-18 battles

A tank, the Western Front's newest weapon of war, proved no match for the mud of Ypres. It adds its derelict hulk to the scene of desolation as in 1918 both sides staggered towards an armistice.

were numerous and casualties high. Poison gas was used for the first time in the second Battle of Ypres from April to May 1915.

In 1916 the German attack on Verdun nearly destroyed the French army, but failed to break through. To relieve the French, the British bore the brunt of the SOMME offensive, one of the bloodiest engagements in history. Early in 1917 the Germans withdrew to new trenches, the SIEGFRIED LINE. Some 300 000 men died later that year in a major British offensive, the third Battle of Ypres, known as the Battle of PASSCHENDAELE. In March 1918 German troops reached the Marne in France before they were halted by US troops at Château-Thierry. Allied forces then advanced along the front, gaining ground from the Germans until on November 11, 1918, an armistice was signed ending the war.

West Indies Archipelago of 1200 islands separating the Atlantic Ocean from the Gulf of Mexico and the Caribbean Sea. The islands are divided into three groups: the Bahamas, the Greater Antilles and the Lesser Antilles. Running south-west from Florida in the USA, the Bahamas comprise 700 islands, 22 of which are inhabited. The Greater Antilles

form a chain running east-west, consisting of CUBA, JAMAICA, Hispaniola (HAITI and the DOMINICAN REPUBLIC), and PUERTO RICO, the Caymans, Curacao and Aruba. The Lesser Antilles run north-south towards the coast of Venezuela. They are grouped into the Leeward Islands (the Virgin Islands, St Kitts-Nevis, Antigua and Barbuda, Anguilla, Montserrat and Guadaloupe); the Windward Islands (Dominica, Martinique, St Lucia, St Vincent, the Grenadines, Barbados and Grenada); and Trinidad and Tobago.

Christopher COLUMBUS landed on Cuba in 1492. Believing that he had found the western route to India, he named the islands the West Indies. Spanish settlers arrived soon afterwards, followed by the British, Dutch and French. By the 17th century the indigenous Carib and Arawak peoples had largely disappeared as a result of new diseases. They were replaced by African slaves who were imported by the Spanish to work on the newly established sugar plantations. Slavery was abolished between 1834 and 1863.

Within the British West Indian colonies during the 19th century, pressure grew for greater participation in government, but in 1865 a Black rising in Jamaica was ruthlessly suppressed. Following a Jamaican deputation to London in 1884, elected legislatures to advise governors were introduced.

In 1940 the British Government set up a Commission for Development and Welfare in the West Indies and financial aid was given to the region. The principle of self-government was also accepted. Believing that the islands could never be viable as independent states, however, Britain supported the formation of the Federation of the West Indies in 1958. When this failed in 1962, Jamaica, Trinidad and Tobago were granted full independence within the COMMONWEALTH OF NATIONS. Barbados followed in 1966, GRENADA in 1974, Dominica in 1978, St Vincent and St Lucia in 1979, Antigua-Barbuda in 1981 and St Kitts-Nevis in 1983. Anguilla became a self-governing dependency of the United Kingdom in 1969.

Economically, the islands declined with the fall in demand for West Indian sugar cane as the sugar-beet industry developed in Europe. But emigration, the growth of air transport and tourism, better education and attempts to diversify – in Trinidad, for example, with oil – all helped to improve prosperity. The Caribbean Community and Common Market was established in 1973 in order to coordinate economic and foreign policy in the region. However, the rise in oil prices, the fall in commodity prices and a world recession all created new debt problems during the 1980s and 1990s. Emigration to Europe fell, with many West Indians moving to the USA in search of work.

Westminster, Statute of (1931)

Legislation on the status of Britain's dominions that established the COMMONWEALTH OF NATIONS. At the Imperial Conferences held in 1926 and 1930, pressure was exerted by South Africa, Canada, Newfoundland, Australia, New Zealand and Eire for full autonomy within the British Commonwealth. The Statute of Westminster recognised the right of the dominions to control their own domestic and foreign affairs, to establish a diplomatic corps and to be represented at the League of Nations while maintaining their allegiance to the British Crown.

Westphalia, Treaty of (1648)

Treaty signed at Münster and Osnabrück in Westphalia that ended the THIRTY YEARS' WAR and which also marked the end of the supremacy of the HOLY ROMAN EMPIRE. By the terms of the treaty, France emerged as the dominant power, and gained Alsace as well as the bishoprics of Metz, Toul and Verdun. The peace acknowledged the independence of Switzerland, the Netherlands and the German states, while Sweden acquired West Pomerania. Equal rights were granted to Lutherans, Calvinists and Roman Catholics.

Whig leader Charles Fox gains another backer in Parliament, after a London by-election tainted by corruption. The figure of a fox raised high above crowds in Covent Garden salutes his triumph.

Weygand, Maxime (1867-1965)

French general. Weygand served as Marshal FOCH's chief of staff in the First World War, and in 1920 the French government sent him to help the Poles in their successful defence against the advancing Soviet Red Army. From 1931 to 1935 he was chief of staff of the French army. At the outbreak of the Second World War in 1939 Weygand was recalled from retirement, and in May 1940 he assumed command of the French forces attempting to stem German BLITZKRIEG attacks. Later he commanded the VICHY forces in North Africa, but tried to escape to Allied lines and was captured and imprisoned by the Germans. After the war Charles DE GAULLE's provisional government tried and acquitted Weygand on a charge of collaboration with the Germans.

Wheatstone, Sir Charles (1802-75)

English physicist and inventor noted for his experiments in sound. Originally a musical-instrument maker, Wheatstone invented both the concertina and the harmonica. With fellow inventor Sir William Cooke, he patented the electric telegraph in 1837. He also invented a device to magnify sound, calling it a 'microphone', and developed Samuel Christie's idea to produce the Wheatstone Bridge, a device to measure electrical resistance. Wheatstone was appointed professor of experimental psychology at King's College, London, in 1834.

Whig Party

British political party formed in 1679, the forerunner of the 19th-century Liberal Party. The Whigs emerged during the reign of CHARLES II, when they unsuccessfully attempted to force through a bill to prevent the succession of Charles's brother, James, Duke of York, on the grounds that he was a Catholic. They were named Whigs by their Tory opponents, probably after the Whiggamores, who were militant Scottish Presbyterians. In 1688 the Whigs joined the TORIES in inviting the Protestant William of Orange and his wife to take the English throne as WILLIAM III and MARY. After securing the trust of GEORGE I and the Hanoverian kings, the Whigs held office from 1714 to 1760.

The early Whigs represented the aristocracy. They sought to curb the power of the monarchy, tolerated religious dissenters and played an active role in Europe. In the 18th and 19th centuries the Whigs represented the rising industrial and commercial interests and became a party of reform. Notable Whig politicians included Robert WALPOLE, the Marquis of ROCKINGHAM, and Charles FOX, who served as leader of the Opposition to the government of William PITT THE YOUNGER.

The US Whig Party was formed in the mid 1830s in opposition to President Andrew JACKSON. William Harrison briefly served as a Whig president in 1841, and Zachary TAYLOR in 1848-50. Taylor was succeeded by his vice-president, Millard Fillmore. In the mid 19th century disunity on the issue of slavery split the party: the northern Whigs joined the Republican Party, while the southern Whigs merged with the Democrats.

Whiskey Rebellion (1794)

Uprising of farmers in western Pennsylvania, USA, in protest at a tax levied by secretary of the treasury Alexander HAMILTON in 1791. The farmers, who made quantities of whiskey from their crops of grain, considered the tax discriminatory. President George WASHINGTON called out 13000 troops to quell the rioting and thereby demonstrated the federal government's power to enforce the country's laws.

Whitbread, Samuel (1758-1815) British politician, son of Samuel Whitbread, the founder of the brewing business. Whitbread the younger entered Parliament in 1790 as a member of the WHIG PARTY, becoming a notable champion of reform and of the liberties of the individual. Allying himself with Charles James FOX, he became a dominant figure in the opposition to the government of William PITT THE YOUNGER.

Whitbread's Poor Law Bill of 1807, which included a proposal to offer free education to those unable to pay, was well received but not adopted. He was a fervent advocate of the abolition of slavery, and a vociferous debater on foreign affairs. It is said that from 1809 until his death he spoke more frequently than any other member of the House of Commons.

Whitby, Synod of (664) Church meeting in the Anglo-Saxon kingdom of NORTHUMBRIA that resolved to adopt Roman rather than Celtic Christianity, and which had a far-reaching effect on the development of the English Church. Differences between the Celtic and Roman forms of order were debated before King OSWY and included the method used for calculating the date of Easter, which had been under dispute since the arrival of St AUGUSTINE's mission from Rome in 596. The Celtic case was presented by Bishop Colman of Lindisfarne, while the Roman case was put by Queen Eanfled and Bishop Wilfrid of Ripon. The king's decision in favour of Rome was accepted throughout England and moved the Church closer to Europe.

White Australia policy Immigration policy pursued in Australia between 1901 and the late 1960s to exclude non-European migrants. In the 1850s and 1870s large numbers of gold seekers came from south China, and their presence led to anti-Chinese riots. Between 1864 and 1904 Kanakas (Pacific Islanders) were brought in to provide cheap labour, mainly on the Queensland cane fields. By the 1880s the trade unions were calling for a policy to protect the 'White working man' from the threat of Asian domination, and from the undermining of wage rates. Within the next ten years all states had legislated to ensure an exclusively White Australia. This policy was reinforced by the national Immigration Restriction Act of 1901, which from 1902 to 1958 aimed to exclude non-Europeans through the use of a dictation test in a 'prescribed' language specifically chosen to ensure failure.

Whitefield, George (1714-70) English evangelist. Together with John WESLEY, Whitefield was a founder member of the METHODISTS at Oxford in the early 1730s. In 1738 he followed the Wesleys to Georgia on the first of several visits to America. On his return in 1739 he became a priest, but finding the pulpits closed to his form of preaching he took to the open air. Followers of his Calvinist views built Whitefield a tabernacle in London in 1756. The Countess of Huntingdon, to whom he became chaplain, also built and endowed many chapels for him. Whitefield spent his life on preaching tours throughout Britain and America. In America he played an important role in the movement known as the Great Awakening, a period of intense religious revivalism that by 1742 threatened the existence of many established Churches.

Whitehead, Alfred (1861-1947) English mathematician and philosopher. Whitehead was a professor of mathematics at Imperial College, London, from 1914 to 1924, when he was appointed professor of philosophy at Harvard in the USA, a position he held until 1937. He collaborated with his former pupil Bertrand RUSSELL on *Principia Mathematica* (1910-13), which was regarded as a landmark in the study of logic. His philosophical works included *The Concept of Nature* (1920) and *Process and Reality* (1929), in which he explored metaphysics. He was also greatly admired, and young people would flock to hear him at his 'Sunday evening' gatherings. Among Whitehead's books for a popular audience is *Adventures of Ideas* (1933).

White Russians Those who opposed the Bolshevik revolution of 1917. The White Russians formed a counterrevolutionary army which was defeated by the Bolshevik RED ARMY in the RUSSIAN CIVIL WAR (1918-21). The name was taken from the royalist opponents of the French Revolution, who were known as Whites because they adopted the white flag of the Bourbon dynasty. The White Army, though smaller than the Red, was better equipped and had an abundance of ex-tsarist officers. Its two main bases were in the south and in Siberia, where Alexsandr KOLCHAK was head of a provisional government at Omsk. Internal quarrels, a refusal to grant land reforms in the areas under White Army domination, the Red Army's control of the railways and the withdrawal of British, American, French and Japanese military support led to its collapse.

DID YOU KNOW?

Anton Denikin, a serf's son who rose to command the White Russian army in the south, gave half his salary to army funds and owned a single, threadbare uniform.

Whitlam crisis (1975) Australian political and constitutional crisis caused when the opposition in the Senate refused to pass the Labor government's financial legislation unless a federal election was called. As the arguments raged, private banks would not release funds to allow the business of government to continue. As prime minister, Gough Whitlam did not agree to a dissolution, and Sir John Kerr, the governor-general, took the unprecedented step of dismissing him. Malcolm Fraser, leader of the Opposition, formed a caretaker government and won the subsequent election. Kerr's decision became the subject of debate and he resigned in 1977. The crisis led many to question the power of the governor-general as the Queen's representative in Australia.

Western backing for the anticommunist White Russians extended to a visit to army commander General Denikin (left) and his team by American Red Cross envoy Major George Ryden (right).

Whittle, Sir Frank (1907-96) British aeronautical engineer and inventor. Whittle designed the first British jet engine which was fitted to a specially built Gloster E 28/39 aircraft; its maiden flight took place on May 15, 1941. The success of this flight led to the introduction of jet engines in aircraft worldwide. Whittle joined the Royal Air Force in 1923 and began research into the problems of jet propulsion while a student at Cranwell and Cambridge. He became the government's technical adviser on engine design in 1946, and was knighted in 1948.

WHO see WORLD HEALTH ORGANISATION

Wiener, Norbert (1894-1964) American mathematician and founder of cybernetics. A child prodigy, Wiener went to university at the age of 11. He studied zoology and philosophy in the USA and Europe, and became professor of mathematics at Massachusetts Institute of Technology in 1932. During the Second World War, Wiener worked on guided missiles. In the course of his work he developed an interest in the mathematical analysis of the flow of information using electronic devices, for which he coined the term 'cybernetics'. His book, *Cybernetics, or control and communication in the animal and the machine*, was published in 1948.

Wilberforce, William (1759-1833) British philanthropist, and driving force behind the antislavery movement. He studied at Cambridge with William PITT the Younger and remained a staunch supporter and friend. Entering the House of Commons in 1780 as MP for Hull, Wilberforce lost no opportunity to denounce the horrors of the slave trade. In 1788 he began the movement which led to the abolition of slavery in the British West Indies in 1807. He then supported the campaign to outlaw slavery throughout the British Empire, which culminated in the passing of the Emancipation Act of 1833, a month after his death. His evangelical Christian beliefs also led Wilberforce to promote a number of schemes for the welfare of the community.

Wilde, Oscar (1854-1900) Irish playwright, novelist, and poet. Wilde was renowned for his wit and flamboyance. He studied at Trinity College, Dublin, and also at Magdalen College, Oxford, where he became a supporter of the Aesthetic 'art for art's sake' movement. In 1891 he achieved recognition with his novel, *The Picture of Dorian Gray*. Wilde's early works included *Poems* (1881), and *The Happy Prince and Other Tales* (1888), written for his sons. The most notable among his comic plays were *Lady Windermere's Fan* (1892) and *The Importance of Being Earnest* (1895), in which he exposed Victorian hypocrisies. His career was ruined, however, when in 1895 he was imprisoned for homosexual offences revealed during an abortive libel action against the Marquess of Queensberry, who disapproved of Wilde's friendship with his son, Lord Alfred Douglas. He wrote *The Ballad of Reading Gaol* (1898)

and *De Profundis* (1905) in prison. After his release in 1897 Wilde assumed the name Sebastian Melmoth and settled in France.

Wild West Name given to the western USA in the 19th century, during its period of settlement. North America had a succession of 'wests', as pioneers pressed on towards the Pacific coast; the Wild West of Texas and California was the last. It was a period epitomised by GOLD RUSHES, COWBOY cattle-drives, banditry and general lawlessness, which bred its own mythology. The era was romanticised by writers such as Edward Judson, who under the pseudonym Ned Buntline wrote penny (dime) novels about the

> **❝A land of scattered ranches, of herds of long-horned cattle, and of reckless riders who unmoved looked in the eyes of life or death.❞**
>
> *Theodore Roosevelt on the Wild West in his autobiography (1913)*

exploits of his friend William Cody as 'Buffalo Bill'. Out of these tales the Wild West shows developed from 1883; these included the appearance of the Indian Chief SITTING BULL. In the 20th century Western films became popular. The Wild West faded after 1890, with the end of American Indian hostilities, the decline of long-distance cattle drives, the building of railways and population growth.

Wilhelm I (1797-1888) King of Prussia from 1861, and first Emperor of Germany from 1871. Born in Berlin, Wilhelm was the son of Friedrich-Wilhelm III. He devoted himself to the Prussian army, and fought in the Napoleonic Wars (1814-15). Wilhelm's use of force against his people in the REVOLUTION OF 1848 earned him the nickname Prince of Grapeshot, and made him so unpopular that he fled to London for a year. Soon after succeeding to the throne of Prussia, Wilhelm invited Otto von BISMARCK to become his minister-president.

Thereafter his reign was dominated by Bismarck's ambitious policies. Wilhelm won victories over Denmark (1864), Austria (1866) and France (1871), after which he was proclaimed emperor of a unified GERMAN SECOND EMPIRE. He dealt harshly with the rising socialists, and survived two assassination attempts.

Wilhelm II (1859-1941) King of Prussia and Emperor of Germany from 1888 to 1918. Wilhelm was the grandson of Queen Victoria of Great Britain and William I of Prussia. In 1890 he forced the resignation of his chancellor, Otto von BISMARCK, and embarked on a period of personal rule. Wilhelm was regarded as a warmonger. He backed plans by his naval

Wilhelm II wearing the uniform of the Totenkopf Hussars, one of some 150 regimental uniforms to which he was entitled, tours with his wife, the Empress Augusta Victoria, in November 1907.

secretary, Alfred von TIRPITZ, to build a fleet to rival that of Britain. He made friendly overtures to the Boer leader, President Paul KRUGER, to whom he sent a congratulatory telegram on the failure of the JAMESON RAID in 1896 which offended Britain. Finally, Wilhelm's support of Austria-Hungary against SERBIA in 1914, after the assassination of Archduke Franz FERDINAND, contributed to the start of the First World War. Following Germany's defeat in 1918 Wilhelm abdicated, and retired to the Netherlands.

Wilhelmina (1880-1962), Queen of the Netherlands from 1890 to 1948. The daughter of William III, Wilhelmina upheld the principles of constitutional monarchy. She won the admiration of her people during the Second World War, following Germany's invasion of the Netherlands; through her frequent radio broadcasts from London, where she maintained a government-in-exile, she became a symbol of resistance to the Dutch people. Wilhelmina abdicated in 1948 in favour of her daughter Juliana.

Wilkes, John (1727-97) British journalist and politician. Wilkes was hailed as a champion of free speech. He was born in London, studied in Leyden, and entered Parliament as a Whig in 1757. In 1763, in his weekly journal *North Briton,* Wilkes attacked GEORGE III's ministers and by implication the king himself. He was imprisoned for libel, and released on the grounds of parliamentary privilege. The House of Commons then expelled him for obscenity, in particular for the publication of his *Essay on Woman.* Wilkes fled to France in 1764. He returned in 1768 to serve a 22 month sentence for his earlier obscenity

offences. Re-elected MP for Middlesex on four occasions, Parliament refused to let him take his seat until 1774, the year in which he became mayor of London. Wilkes enjoyed public support and could always summon a crowd to rally to his cause.

Wilkinson, James (1757-1825) US army general, adventurer and double agent. Wilkinson distinguished himself in the War of Independence (1775-83). He settled in Kentucky, where he worked both for Spain in

John Wilkes, whose tireless journalism brought him charges of libel and obscenity, wields his quill in defence of the freedom of the press.

conspiring to bring part of Kentucky under the control of Louisiana, and against Spain as a lieutenant-colonel in the US army. When the USA purchased Louisiana, Wilkinson was appointed governor (1805-6). During his term he became involved with the former vice-president Aaron BURR's conspiracy to set up a separate confederacy in the west, but betrayed him and acted as prosecution witness in Burr's trial for treason. The failure of Wilkinson's campaign to capture Montreal in the early stages of the War of 1812 led to his removal from command and to his retirement.

Willard, Emma (1787-1870) US pioneer of women's education. Concerned that girls were never taught subjects such as geometry and philosophy, Willard (née Hart) opened the Middlebury Female Seminary, Vermont, in 1814, to provide them with a wider range of studies. Her appeal to the New York legislature for finance, her *Plan for Improving Female Education* (1819), gained her the support of Governor De Witt Clinton. This led her to open the Troy Female Seminary (now the Emma Willard School) in New York State, which offered an intellectually demanding secondary education and became a model for similar establishments in Europe and the USA. In 1854, she and the educator Henry Barnard were the US representatives to the World's Educational Convention in London.

William I 'the Conqueror' (1028-87) First Norman king of England from 1066, on whose orders the DOMESDAY BOOK was compiled in 1086. The illegitimate son of Robert the Devil, Duke of Normandy, William succeeded to the dukedom in 1035. His early life was fraught with danger and twice he faced major rebellions. William's claim to the English throne was based on a promise allegedly given to him in 1051 by his cousin, EDWARD THE CONFESSOR. With papal backing he landed in England in 1066 and at the Battle of HASTINGS defeated and killed Edward's successor, HAROLD II.

William was crowned king on December 25 at Westminster Abbey. He swiftly quashed all pockets of resistance before any new leaders could emerge. The Norman Church flourished during his rule but was subordinate to him; he refused to tolerate interference from bishops, abbots or the papacy. He crushed a number of uprisings, including a rebellion under HEREWARD THE WAKE in 1070, and replaced Anglo-Saxon leaders with his own Norman, Breton and Fleming supporters. William spent much of his later life in Normandy fighting against the French king, PHILIP I. Shortly before his death he initiated the Domesday survey of English landowners and their properties. Injured during a campaign against Philip I, William died in Rouen and was buried at St Stephen's Church which

An illustration of William the Conqueror from a medieval manuscript depicts the Norman king of England at the head of his troops riding through London where he had been crowned in 1066.

he had founded in Caen. He left Normandy and Maine to his elder son Robert Curthose and England to his second son William Rufus.

William I 'the Lion' (1143-1214) King of Scotland from 1165. In 1174 William invaded Northumberland. He was captured at Alnwick, and at the subsequent Treaty of Falaise (1174) William was forced to recognise HENRY II of England as his feudal superior. The terms of the treaty were reversed and Scotland's independence restored in 1189, when William made a payment of 10 000 marks to RICHARD I. During his reign, William extended the frontiers of his kingdom to the north and consolidated his authority by developing an efficient central administrative bureaucracy. He helped to establish the independence of the Church of Scotland and in 1178 founded Arbroath Abbey, which at his death was among the wealthiest Scottish monasteries.

William I 'the Silent' (1533-84) Prince of ORANGE and Count of Nassau-Dillenburg. William is regarded as the founding father of the United Provinces of the Netherlands. He was opposed both to Spanish rule in the

Netherlands and to the tyrannical treatment of Dutch Protestants by the Catholic king of Spain, PHILIP II. Yet Philip trusted William and made him STADHOLDER (chief magistrate) of Holland, Zeeland and Utrecht in 1559. In 1567 William resigned and led his countrymen in the DUTCH REVOLTS against Spain. He joined the Calvinist Church in 1573. For a brief period in 1576 he succeeded in fulfilling his dream by uniting the Catholic south and Protestant north, before the south (now Belgium and Luxembourg) was repossessed by Spain.

In 1579 the northern provinces formed a federation, with William as its first stadholder, and declared its independence from Spain. William was assassinated by a Spanish agent in Delft in 1584.

William II 'Rufus' (c.1056-1100), King of England from 1087. William was the second son of WILLIAM I, the Conqueror, and Matilda. His succession was challenged by the Norman barons in England who rebelled in 1087 in favour of his elder brother Robert II, Duke of Normandy. William crushed this revolt, and another in 1095. His ruthless government, and the exploitation of Church properties and

revenues, brought him into conflict with the Church led by the Archbishop of Canterbury, Anselm. William fought Robert for possession of Normandy, which he finally secured for himself on Robert's departure for the First CRUSADE in 1096. Some have thought that William's death from an arrow while hunting in the New Forest was organised by his younger brother, who succeeded him as HENRY I, but it was probably an accident.

William III (1650-1702) King of Great Britain from 1689 with MARY, and STADHOLDER of the United Provinces of the Netherlands from 1672. His arrival in England in 1688 with his wife, the daughter of JAMES II of England, marked the start of the GLORIOUS REVOLUTION. William was the grandson of Charles I of England. In 1688 when a son was born to James, a Roman Catholic, English politicians asked William to intervene and save the country from a probable Catholic succession. William landed with his army at Torbay; James fled to France and in 1689 William and Mary jointly accepted the British crown.

William put an end to Jacobite resistance by suppressing a rebellion in Scotland (1689) and defeating James II in the Battle of the BOYNE in 1690. He was not popular, however, and his reputation suffered when he failed to honour his undertaking, made in the Treaty of Limerick (1691), to guarantee political and religious freedom to Irish Catholics. Leaving Mary as regent, he turned his attention to the war against France, which ended in 1697 with the PEACE OF RYSWICK. Financing of the war led to the founding of the Bank of England in 1694. William died after falling off his horse and was succeeded by Mary's sister, ANNE.

William III and Mary, the cousin he married in Holland in 1677, shared the throne of England for five years until Mary died in 1694.

William IV 'the Sailor King' (1765-1837)

King of Great Britain and Hanover from 1830. The third son of George III, William's reign marked a further decline in the political influence of the Crown. He joined the navy in 1778, subsequently becoming a close friend of Admiral Horatio NELSON, and an admiral himself in 1811. In 1790 he set up house with an Irish actress, Dorothea Jordan, by whom he had ten children. To secure the succession to the throne he married Adelaide of Saxe-Meiningen in 1818 and had two daughters, but both died in infancy. When he became king, William did much to obstruct the first REFORM ACT in 1832, but finally overcame his conservative sympathies and allowed its passage. His niece, VICTORIA, succeeded him.

William of Malmesbury (c.1090-c.1143)

English Benedictine monk and historian. William was librarian at Malmesbury Abbey, Wiltshire. He wrote a number of books chronicling the history of England, and the lives of St Dunstan and St Wulfstan. He is best known for *Gesta Regum Anglorum* (*Acts of the English Kings*), which covers the period from the arrival of the Saxons, and *Historia Novella* (*Modern History*) which continues the account to 1142. His *Gesta Pontificum Anglorum* is an ecclesiastical history to 1123. William's work is notable for its attempt to understand and interpret events rather than to simply record them in an uncritical fashion.

William of Ockham

(c.1285–c.1349) English theologian and philosopher. William was a Franciscan friar who developed an antipapal theory of the state – denying the pope secular authority – and defended evangelical poverty, for which he became known as the Invincible Doctor. He was imprisoned in Avignon in 1328 by Pope John XXII on charges of heresy, but escaped to Munich, and was excommunicated. William published works on logic and political theory. His form of nominalism, a doctrine that holds that abstract concepts exist only as names, saw God as beyond human powers of reasoning, and things as being capable of proof only by experience or by scriptural authority. His maxim that, when explaining something, all unnecessary factors should be excluded is known as 'Ockham's razor'.

William of Wykeham (1324-1404)

English politician, administrator and patron of education. William founded New College, Oxford, in 1379, and Winchester College in 1382, 'first for the glory of God and the promotion of divine service, and secondarily for scholarship'. Although he was allegedly the son of a serf, William became EDWARD III's

---

Harold Wilson speaks in 1974 when two general elections were called. Labour won a clear majority in the second.

most trusted minister. He was made Bishop of Winchester in 1367 and was twice appointed Chancellor of England, first under Edward and later under RICHARD II.

Williams, Eric (1911-81)

First prime minister of Trinidad and Tobago from 1961 to 1981. Williams was born in Trinidad, and educated at Oxford University and Howard University, USA. In 1955 he returned to Trinidad to found the People's National Movement (PNM), winning a landslide victory in the national elections of 1961. In 1962 he led his country to independence, becoming prime minister first of the colony and then of the republic (1976) of Trinidad and Tobago. He stressed the importance of social services, education and economic development. He attracted foreign capital through tax incentives, and helped to make Trinidad and Tobago the richest Commonwealth nation in the WEST INDIES. However, before his death, Williams faced militant opposition to his government.

> ### DID YOU KNOW?
> *When Harold Wilson succeeded Hugh Gaitskell in 1963 he became – at the age of 46 – the youngest leader in the history of the Labour Party.*

Wilson, Harold, Baron Wilson of Rievaulx (1916-1995)

British prime minister from 1964 to 1970, and from 1974 to 1976. Wilson was born in Huddersfield, West Yorkshire, and educated at Oxford University, where he became a lecturer in economics. He entered Parliament in 1945, and rose to succeed Hugh Gaitskell as leader of the Labour Party in 1963, winning the general election the following year.

Wilson's period in office was marked by the abolition of the death penalty (1965), the devaluation of the pound (1967), and the introduction of comprehensive education. He sent British troops into Northern Ireland in 1969 to control the outbreak of sectarian violence. In 1975 the first referendum was held in Britain, in which the majority voted in favour of joining the European Community, ending a period of division on the issue within Labour Party ranks. Overseas, Wilson attempted unsuccessfully to tackle the problem of the declaration of independence by Rhodesia's White government through negotiation and the imposition of economic sanctions. He lost the 1970 election, but returned as prime minister in 1974. In March 1976, Wilson

resigned unexpectedly. He was knighted the following month and became a life peer in 1983. He was succeeded by James Callaghan.

Wilson, (Thomas) Woodrow (1856-1924)

Twenty-eighth president of the USA from 1913 to 1921. Wilson was born in Staunton, Virginia, the son of a Presbyterian minister. He embarked on an academic career that led to him being appointed president of Princeton University in 1902. In 1910 he accepted the Democratic nomination and was elected governor of New Jersey. A skilled orator, with a magnetic personality, Wilson's success earned him the Democratic nomination for the presidency in 1912. Once in office, he proceeded to introduce his 'New Freedom' policy in a bid to stimulate competition, promote equal opportunity, and halt corruption. Amendments were made to the constitution on prohibition and women's suffrage.

Faced with the outbreak of the First World War in 1914, he concentrated on preserving US neutrality; however, the German policy of unrestricted submarine warfare led to the declaration of war in April 1917. From then on Wilson worked to realise his vision, proposed in the FOURTEEN POINTS, of a peaceful postwar world and the establishment of a LEAGUE OF NATIONS. After negotiating the VERSAILLES PEACE SETTLEMENT, his bid to enlist popular support for both the treaty and the League brought on a severe stroke. For his last year in office his wife Edith took responsibility for many of his presidential duties.

'wind of change'

Phrase contained in a speech by the British Conservative prime minister, Harold MACMILLAN, to the South African Parliament on February 3, 1960. He used it to draw attention to the growth of national consciousness and demands for independence which were then sweeping like a 'wind of change' across the African continent.

window tax English tax on any window or window-like opening, which was in force from 1696 to 1851. It was introduced to pay for the massive reform of English coinage in 1696 and finally applied to all houses with more than six windows. In older houses windows bricked up to avoid the tax are still seen.

wind power Wind has been harnessed as a source of energy since ancient times. In the 12th century windmills were introduced into Germany and the Netherlands to drive machinery to grind corn or pump water, and their use spread throughout Europe. More efficient, taller tower-mills were developed in the early 15th century. In 1745 Englishman Edmund Lee invented the fantail, which took over the manual task of turning the sails to the wind. By 1840 there were as many as 10 000 windmills in England and Wales and 8000 in Holland. The use of windmills declined in the later 19th century but in the American west the railroads still used them to raise underground water for their locomotives and settlers needed them for irrigation and water supply. In the 20th century, wind turbines, of which there are more than 20 000 worldwide, have been used for generating electricity.

Windsor Name of the British royal family since July 17, 1917. The designation House of Windsor was adopted by George V to replace the German title of Saxe-Coburg-Gotha, derived from the marriage of Queen Victoria to Prince Albert. 'Windsor' was chosen because Windsor Castle, Berkshire, has been a principal Royal residence since the 12th century. In 1960 Elizabeth II declared that those of her descendants who were not princes or princesses would take the surname Mountbatten-Windsor.

wine The vine that produces wine grapes, *Vitis vinifera*, is thought to be a native of Persia where wine was drunk as far back as 5000 BC. Its cultivation spread with the ancient Greeks who introduced wine to Italy, and the Romans who took it to Gaul (France). After the fall of the Roman Empire, wine-making skills were kept alive by the Church. Success and variety depended then, as now, on climatic and soil conditions. England produced wine on a large scale until the 12th century when Bordeaux wines became fashionable. From the end of the 17th century, the use of corks enabled wine to be aged in a bottle instead of being consumed young from a barrel. During the mid 1750s, Madeira shippers produced the first fortified wines by adding a proportion of brandy.

The early 19th century was known as the Golden Age of wine, until catastrophe struck in the 1860s when the beetle-like creature *Phylloxera vitifoliae*, which fed upon the roots of vines, devastated the vineyards of Europe. Wine-making was revived with the introduction of a North American vine resistant to the insect, on to which cuttings were grafted. Settlers had planted the first vines in the New World in the 17th century and today vineyards are found wherever conditions permit.

Wingate, Orde (1903-44) British general renowned for his guerrilla warfare tactics in Burma during the Second World War. In the 1930s Wingate helped to establish and train a Jewish defence force operating in Palestine. In Abyssinia in 1941 he took Addis Ababa from the Italians and successfully restored Emperor Haile Selassie to the throne. Two years later in Burma Wingate created and led the Chindits, a group of jungle fighters which operated behind Japanese lines to disrupt enemy communications. He died in a plane crash in Burma at the outset of a second and greatly enlarged Chindit offensive.

Winstanley, Gerrard (c.1609-c.60) English radical Puritan. Winstanley was the leader of the DIGGERS, a communist group who cultivated common land in Surrey between 1649 and 1650, when food prices were rising sharply. They were forced off the land by the authorities. Winstanley later became prominent as a pamphleteer. In 1652, he dedicated his most famous pamphlet on his ideas for a communist society, *The Law of Freedom in a Platform*, to Oliver Cromwell, in his belief that the ENGLISH CIVIL WAR had been fought against all who were enemies of the poor, including landlords and priests.

Winthrop, John (1606-76) American colonist, governor of Connecticut from 1657. Winthrop, son of John Winthrop, first governor of the Massachusetts Bay Colony, emigrated from England to Massachusetts in 1631. In 1635 he established the colony of Saybrook. Winthrop encouraged industrialisation, erecting two ironworks in Massachusetts in 1644. As governor of Connecticut, in 1662 he obtained a charter from Charles II uniting the colonies of Connecticut and New Haven. A notable physician and scientist, Winthrop became in 1663 the first fellow of the ROYAL SOCIETY in England to be resident in the USA.

Wishart, George (c.1513-46) Scottish Protestant preacher and martyr. A schoolmaster, Wishart fled to England and the Continent in 1538, having been charged with heresy for teaching the Greek New Testament. Returning to Scotland in 1543, he preached the doctrines of the Swiss reformers, incurring the anger of Cardinal BEATON, Archbishop of St Andrews. On his orders Wishart was charged with heresy and burnt at St Andrews. John KNOX, the Scottish Protestant reformer, was a disciple of Wishart.

witan (Old English *witenagemot*, meeting of the king's councillors) Council summoned by the Anglo-Saxon kings, a forerunner of the English Parliament. These formal gatherings of high-ranking nobles, great landowners, and bishops in the 10th and 11th centuries advised the king on such matters as royal grants of land, Church benefices, charters, taxation, and the prosecution of traitors. In most cases, the succession of a monarch had to be acknowledged by the witan.

witchcraft see feature, page 707

A witan, or council of wise men, elected and advised Saxon kings of England. Aelfric, an 11th-century monk, shows the witan hanging a criminal.

James Wolfe lies mortally wounded (right) at Quebec. His body was brought back to England wrapped in his dressing gown (below), now at Quebec House, Westerham in Kent.

Witt, Johan de (1625-72) Dutch political leader from 1653, republican opponent of the princes of Orange and mathematician. De Witt's eloquence, political skill and knowledge of foreign affairs led to his appointment as leader of the United Provinces during the minority of WILLIAM III, whom he refused to allow to be appointed STADHOLDER. He successfully ended the Dutch wars with England, and in 1668 signed the Triple Alliance with England and Sweden to thwart LOUIS XIV's designs on the Netherlands. However, when Louis invaded in 1672 the Dutch people demanded that William lead them. De Witt's power declined and he and his brother Cornelius, who was charged with conspiracy, were killed by a mob in The Hague. De Witt wrote one of the first books on analytical geometry, *Elementa curvarum linearum* (1659).

Witte, Sergei Yulyevich, Count (1849-1915) Russian statesman. As finance minister from 1892 to 1903, and prime minister from 1905 to 1906, Witte presided over the industrialisation of Russia, encouraging investment and foreign loans. New railways were built, steel production started and sufficient petroleum was produced to satisfy Russia's needs and for export. His ideal was economic modernisation combined with authoritarian rule. However, in the RUSSIAN REVOLUTION of 1905 Witte persuaded the tsar, NICHOLAS II, to issue the October Manifesto, which granted Russia a measure of representative government, and to establish the state DUMA. Tsar Nicholas, who feared and disliked his powerful minister, dismissed him in 1906.

Wittelsbach German ruling dynasty in Bavaria between 1180 and 1918. Otto, Count of Scheyern, moved to Wittelsbach castle in 1115, and adopted the name for his family. His son was invested Otto I, Duke of Bavaria, in 1180. From that time Wittelsbach dukes, Electors and kings ruled Bavaria. The Elector Charles Albert of Bavaria (1697-1745) became Holy Roman Emperor as Charles VII from 1742. The last king, Louis III, who abdicated in 1918, left a son, Prince Rupert who had a potential claim to the English throne through his female descent from the Stuarts. Rupert died in 1955.

Wittgenstein, Ludwig (1889-1951) Austrian philosopher. Wittgenstein became an influential figure among English-speaking philosophers. He trained as an engineer, but his interest in mathematical logic led him to study under Bertrand RUSSELL at Cambridge (1912-13). In his first book, *Tractatus Logico-Philosophicus* (1921), completed while a prisoner in Italy during the First World War, Wittgenstein attempted to construct a system of language which was as logical as mathematics. He gave away his inherited wealth to work in Austria as an elementary schoolmaster, a gardener's assistant and an amateur architect and builder. He returned to Cambridge in 1929 and in 1939 became professor of philosophy. His other important work, *Philosophical Investigations,* published posthumously in 1953, examined the philosophy of language.

Wolfe, James (1727-59) British general whose surprise attack on Quebec in 1759 and defeat of the French under General Montcalm on the Plains of Abraham, won Canada for Britain but cost him his life. Wolfe first won acclaim fighting the Jacobites at Falkirk and CULLODEN in the 1740s. After the outbreak of the SEVEN YEARS' WAR (1756-63) he was sent to Canada, and, as brigadier general and second-in-command to Jeffrey AMHERST, he forced the surrender of Louisburg, a fortress on Cape Breton Island in 1758. William Pitt the Elder chose him to lead the Quebec assault.

Wolseley, Garnet Joseph, 1st Viscount (1833-1913) British field-marshal, commander in chief of Britain's forces from 1895 to 1901. Wolseley was instrumental in modernising the army. A highly regarded officer, he served in Burma, the Crimea (where he lost an eye), the Indian Mutiny and the Second Opium War with China. At 25 he became the youngest lieutenant-colonel in the British army. In 1870 he put down the Red River rebellion in Canada. In 1873 he commanded the ASHANTI EXPEDITION in West Africa. Wolseley later served in South Africa, and in Egypt where he successfully crushed an uprising in 1882 and was rewarded with a barony. In 1885 he arrived too late to rescue his friend General Charles GORDON, besieged and killed at Khartoum in the Sudan, but was elevated to viscount for his brave attempt.

Gripped by the terror of witchcraft

For 300 years Europe and later North America was possessed by the idea that misfortune was caused by the evil intervention of witches. The result was the horrifying mass persecution of innocent people.

Fear stalked Europe during the witch hunts of the 15th to the 18th centuries. In the eyes of the Church, witches were heretics to be rooted out, tried and executed. Many thousands of people were put to death.

The practice of 'black' magic or sorcery was common in European pagan culture. Although it was condemned in the Bible, the early Church had a generally lenient attitude towards witchcraft, believing that its followers could be persuaded away from their delusions. Attitudes began to change from the 12th century. Even the scholastic philosophers speculated on the possible powers of magic used for evil purposes. Witches, who were believed to have been given malevolent powers by Satan and to be his agents on earth, became figures of hatred.

THE WITCH'S HAMMER

In 1484 two Dominican friars persuaded Pope Innocent VIII to authorise the suppression of witchcraft. Their book, *The Witch's Hammer*, became the handbook of demonology in Europe. It taught that the guilty were condemned but that their souls could be saved by confession, usually obtained by torture. Those who confessed quickly might be granted an 'easier' death such as hanging, rather than being burned alive.

The 'holy war' against witchcraft, begun before the Reformation, was carried on by both Catholics and Protestants. Old women were often accused, but anyone – priests, nuns, magistrates – could attract suspicion. Sickness, crop failure and other misfortunes were blamed on individuals accused of witchcraft.

Matthew Hopkins persecuted the women of eastern England before being hanged as a sorcerer in 1647.

A woodcut of about 1580 shows witches being burned to death in Guernsey's marketplace. They were believed to be able to escape their bodies and fly, like this French witch (top).

Allegations were sometimes made to gain revenge or the land or property of those condemned.

Witch hunts were not as widespread in England as in continental Europe, where witches were fanatically pursued. In Elizabeth I's reign witchcraft was punishable by death, but the accused were usually pilloried for the first offence and were put to death only if convicted of persisting in malevolent magic. They were not burnt at the stake but hanged, and confessions were not extracted from them by torture.

The prosecution of witches increased in 17th-century England, a time of war and religious division. Matthew Hopkins, self-styled 'Witchfinder-General' and author of a 1647 pamphlet, *The Discovery of Witches*, was among the most feared. Between 1645 and 1647 he was responsible for sending some 200 people to the gallows. Among the most notorious American witchcraft trials were those in Salem, Massachusetts, in 1692, in which village girls accused a group of respectable citizens of witchcraft. The girls' hallucinations and dreams were accepted as evidence, and 20 innocent people were put to death. When the injustice of the verdict became widely recognised, it led to the end of such trials in the American colonies and Britain. Despite the growth of a more rational society, the prioress of a German convent was burnt at the stake as late as 1749.

The wave of hysteria over witchcraft is linked to the destabilisation of society caused by plague, war and religious strife. The Black Death killed a quarter of Europe's population in the 14th century. Such disasters left people demoralised and puzzled about their causes. Witches were not alone in taking the blame: the persecution of Jews also increased. Witchcraft is still practised in nonliterate societies, where misfortunes are often attributed to malevolent spells.

Wolsey founded Cardinal's College (later Christ Church), Oxford, where his hat is now preserved.

Wolsey, Thomas (c.1475-1530) English cardinal and statesman, Lord Chancellor from 1515 to 1529. The son of a butcher, Wolsey was ordained in 1498 and rose to become the wealthiest and most powerful figure in the land, second only to HENRY VIII. He entered royal service as chaplain to Henry VII, then under Henry VIII acquired a string of rich benefices, culminating in the archbishopric of York (1514). Wolsey became a cardinal in 1515 and a papal legate in 1518. As Lord Chancellor, he ran the government, began the dissolution of the monasteries, and presided over the court of the STAR CHAMBER where his influence on legal reform was substantial.

In foreign affairs Wolsey was determined to make England a major European power. His unsuccessful interference in the war between France and Spain, and his attempts to raise taxes to meet the costs, increased his unpopularity at home. Wolsey's failure to persuade the pope to grant Henry an annulment of his marriage to Catherine of Aragon led to the cardinal's downfall. He was stripped of his offices and arrested on a charge of treason, but died before he could be brought to trial.

women in history see feature, page 708

women's movement Social movement that has campaigned since the 18th century for women to be granted equal rights to men. In 1792 the British feminist Mary Wollstonecraft, in her book *A Vindication of the Rights of Woman*, demanded equal opportunities. Other campaigners such as Elizabeth Cady STANTON who founded the National Woman Suffrage Association in the USA in 1869, and

Emmeline PANKHURST (1858-1928), the leading English SUFFRAGETTE, fought for women's rights to vote, to own property, and to receive higher education. The right to vote (WOMEN'S SUFFRAGE) was achieved for all women in Britain in 1928, and Cambridge University began awarding degrees to women in 1948. The movement gathered support after the Second World War with campaigners including Simone de Beauvoir in France, Betty Friedan in the USA, and Germaine Greer in Britain arguing the case for reform. In 1966 the National Organisation for Women (NOW) was formed in the USA, demanding the right to equal opportunities and equal pay. In Britain in 1971 the movement called for equal pay, equal opportunities for jobs and education, free contraception, abortion on demand and 24-hour nurseries. The Equal Pay Acts (1970 and 1975), the Sex Discrimination Act (1975) and the creation of the Equal Opportunities Commission (1975) have given legal effect to some demands.

women's suffrage The right of women to vote in national and local elections was first attained at national level in New Zealand in 1893, although the US state of Wyoming introduced women's suffrage in 1869. Women were not allowed to vote in ancient Greece and Rome, and it was not until Mary Wollstonecraft published *A Vindication of the Rights of Woman* in 1792 that women's suffrage

became an issue in Britain. Her cause was taken up by the social reformer John Stuart MILL who presented a petition to Parliament in 1867 which demanded for women the right to vote. In 1897 the National Union of Women's Suffrage Societies was formed to focus the campaign, but every suffrage bill brought before Parliament was defeated. Frustrated by this lack of progress a group of women known as SUFFRAGETTES, led by Emmeline PANKHURST, began taking militant action. The Suffragettes won considerable public support, and in 1918 Parliament passed the Representation of the People Act granting women over the age of 30 the right to vote. In 1928 this was extended to include women over 21 on the same terms as men.

In the USA a similar campaign was fought through the 19th and early 20th century. The antislavery campaigners Lucretia Mott and Elizabeth Cady STANTON called a convention on women's rights and suffrage at Seneca Falls in 1848. It was the first of many such events. The National Woman Suffrage Association was formed in 1869 to demand an amendment to the constitution, but it was not until 1920 that women's right to vote was granted under the 19th Amendment. During the 20th century women have achieved the right to vote in most countries, with the exception of certain Arab states on the Persian Gulf.

wool Fibre from the fleece of sheep, llamas, angora goats, vicunas and camels has long been prized for its warmth, elasticity and resilience. The raising of sheep to produce wool for clothing can be traced back 10 000 years to central Asia, but it was not until

Australian wool sorters grade fleeces. Merino flocks, descended from 13 sheep brought from Cape Town in 1797, were the mainstay of the nation's wealth for more than 140 years.

The secret history of women: a fight for independence

Although by virtue of their birth a few women have wielded power and made their mark on history, the silent majority have passed their years unrecorded. Only the reforms of the 20th century started to bring them equality with men.

Motherhood has been the main obstacle to women's independence. Until the 20th-century transformation of obstetrics and birth control, women spent much of their lives pregnant. Childbirth was dangerous and infant mortality high. Women's preoccupation with child-rearing largely accounts for their relatively minor role in history, yet they have also had to overcome deep-seated prejudice to gain equal rights.

The Greek philosopher Plato classed women with children and slaves as unreasoning beings: he believed that their nature was inferior to men's 'in capacity for virtue'. This attitude was commonplace in the ancient world and persisted for centuries in almost every society.

Most ancient societies were patriarchal. Women were homekeepers, with no say in the major issues of their lives. A woman was a mere chattel, as the poet Hesiod observed when issuing this advice to his fellow men: 'First of all get yourself a house and a woman and an ox to plough with.' Women were never free to choose a husband and could be passed on from one to another, as happened to the Athenian statesman Pericles's first wife. The Code of

Manu, a Sanskrit code of law, consigned Indian women to absolute control by men. A wife's duty was to worship her husband as a god, even if he was a tyrant.

Persian wives lived in strict seclusion within the harem, seeing no men except their husbands and sons, and the eunuchs who looked after them. When the beautiful queen Vashti of Persia rejected her husband's demand to parade herself in front of his drinking companions, the men feared that such rebellion could spread to their wives as well.

In the early Christian Church, women were almost as zealous as the Apostles in spreading the gospel. Some were ministers in the first churches, and took part in public worship. But in later books of the Bible's New Testament, such as St Paul's Epistles to Timothy, women are seen as unsuitable to teach or to have authority over men on the grounds that it was a woman, Eve, who introduced sin into the world. The Catholic Church later decreed that women should not receive Orders and banned them from ministering at the altar.

When the Church became politically influential, it ensured that women were not given civil rights which would be contrary to its doctrine. It was particularly opposed

to greater rights for married women and preferred the Roman law that kept women under the protection of their fathers and subsequently their husbands.

When the skills of reading and writing were developed in Sumer and Babylon in the second millennium BC, women were denied the chance to learn them. For thousands of years their descendants had little formal schooling: the purpose of education was seen as the preparation of

The lot of some 17th-century wives is illustrated by the number of children carved on their tombs.

American college girls take part in a physics lesson in 1900. University education had been open to privileged women for a generation, but job opportunities remained extremely limited.

Women such as Mary Magdalene had a central role in the Gospels and in the early Church.

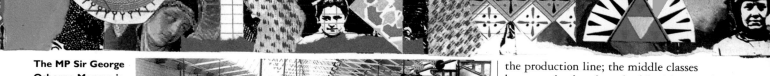

The MP Sir George Osborne Morgan is thanked for helping to pass the Married Women's Property Act.

Women prove capable of doing 'men's work' as they sort fuses for shells in a British munitions factory during the First World War.

men for leadership. But women were not entirely deprived of education. There were no girls' schools until the 16th century AD, but in earlier centuries wealthy families employed a tutor for their daughters or paid a dowry to have them educated in a convent. The Venetian-born Christine de Pisan (1363-1429), a prolific writer who championed the rights of women, and Elizabeth I of England were both well educated at home.

Nuns were trained to transcribe and illuminate manuscripts and made a major contribution to the spread of culture. In early convents there were many learned women, such as the visionary abbess Hildegard of Bingen (1098-1179), who founded several religious houses and wrote poetry and plays. But in Europe after the 13th century women's education declined into the study of the mystical. The rise of universities, which admitted only men, undermined convents as centres of learning.

THE FIRST GIRLS' SCHOOLS
The 16th-century Protestant reformer Martin Luther brought a new attitude to education. He favoured compulsory schooling for boys and girls and believed that able girls should be offered higher education, but it took 300 years for his ideas to be applied in Germany. The Scottish reformer John Knox (c.1514-72) created the foundations of universal education in Scotland, but only boys could go to university.

Girls' schools were set up in France, such as the Congrégation de Notre Dame founded by St Peter Fourier in Paris. In England there were no girls' schools until the 17th century, when private schools were established for the wealthy and the Red Maids' school was founded in Bristol to educate poor girls. Universal education in England arrived only with the Education Act of 1870, at about the time that university education was opened to women in Europe and the United States.

Married women in most of Europe through the centuries had no independent legal existence. Under English common law, for example, 'husband and wife are one person in law', the one person being the husband. A woman had no right to income from her property until the reforms of the Married Women's Property Act of 1870. Not until 1907 did French women win the right to keep their own earnings.

Ancient and medieval literature makes it clear that women were skilled in pharmacy. The Greek dramatist Euripides tells of females dealing with women's diseases. There were women doctors in the Greco-Roman period and female medical students during the Italian Renaissance, especially at the university of Bologna, which employed professors in the 18th century such as Anna Morandi-Manzolini in anatomy and Maria Dalle Donne in obstetrics.

Despite these examples, after the 15th century the role of women in medicine declined. With increasing scientific knowledge of disease, the prejudice about women's intellectual inferiority gained renewed force. In some countries it was joined by another: that a woman skilful in medicine might be a witch. Persecution of witches in the 16th and 17th centuries claimed thousands of lives. Only in the second half of the 19th century did higher education begin to break down the barriers.

The demands of industrial society in the late 19th century created a mass female work force, but women were still paid less than men and remained excluded from the professions. Working-class women joined the production line; the middle classes became schoolteachers, health visitors and junior civil servants. During the First World War, when millions of men went off to fight, women in Western societies were in demand for a wide range of traditional men's work and showed they could do it.

EQUAL PAY FOR EQUAL WORK
Women were slow to organise into trade unions, partly because many saw work as an interlude before having children. This made it difficult for working married women to demand more money to improve their families' standard of life. The International Labour Organisation, founded in 1919, laid down the principle that men and women should receive equal pay for work of equal value, but as late as the 1920s the need of women for protection from abuse was still seen as more important than equality.

Women played little part in politics until the 20th century. It was believed that they were guided more by emotion than by reason or conscience. There were exceptional periods. Women played a leading role at the start of the French Revolution: during the Insurrection of Women, led by Théroigne de Méricourt, a group of radical women of Paris marched to the palace of Versailles to escort Louis XVI back to imprisonment in the capital. But powerful women's clubs were suppressed by male revolutionary leaders, who argued that women did not possess the 'imperturbable equanimity' needed for politics.

Although some women had ruled as monarchs, until the end of the 19th century they could neither vote nor run for political office. New Zealand women were allowed to vote in 1893; the first European women to vote were the Finns in 1906. American women gained the vote in 1920, but in Britain it was not until 1928 that women could vote on equal terms with men. Women continued to move towards greater equality in the 1920s, particularly in Russia following the 1917 revolution.

After the Second World War the United Nations decreed that both sexes should have similar rights, but in countries such as Kuwait and Saudi Arabia women can neither vote nor stand in elections. Females remain under-represented in the parliaments of most countries, though Sirimavo Bandaranaike in Sri Lanka (the former Ceylon), Margaret Thatcher in Britain and Benazir Bhutto in Pakistan have succeeded in reaching the highest public office. There is still more illiteracy among women than men and there are fewer women in the work force – only 24 per cent in Latin America, for example. Of all the obstacles to the progress of women, the domestic burden remains the greatest.

the BRONZE AGE that people began to spin wool into yarn. Woollen materials have been found in the tombs of ancient Egypt and Babylon. Improved methods of sheep breeding by the Romans produced the ancestors of the Merino sheep, first bred in Spain. The Merino still produces the world's finest wool.

The first wool factory in England was set up by the Romans in Winchester in AD 50, and from the Middle Ages the wool industry flourished. In the 17th century the export of woollen textiles made up two-thirds of England's foreign trade, and today although wool production has declined, Britain remains an important producer.

The British Government failed in its attempts to discourage settlers from introducing the wool industry to the New World. The first sheep were imported into Australia at the end of the 18th century; now it has 150 million and is the largest producer of merino wool. New Zealand, the USA, South America and South Africa are also major wool producers. The quality of the fleeces varies among the breeds, the finest wool being used for dress fabrics and coarser wool for carpets. Synthetic fibres developed in the 20th century are often blended with wool.

wool staple Town in England, Wales, Ireland or continental Europe through which wool merchants traded. Staple towns were set up by Edward III of England in the 14th century as a means of controlling exports, so that he could be guaranteed the tax due on them at the customs point. The Ordinances of the Staple in 1353-4 established 15 staple towns in Britain. In 1363 Calais, on the northern French coast, became the wool staple through which all wool exports had to pass. A Continental staple existed until the export of wool was banned in 1617.

workhouse British public institution in which people unable to earn a living were housed, and forced to work if able-bodied. The 1601 POOR LAW Act made parishes responsible for their own workhouses. Parishes combined in the 18th century to build workhouses for the poor, elderly, disabled and orphans. By the 1723 Workhouse Test Act financial relief was denied to able-bodied paupers who refused to enter. Government policy to build more such institutions in the 19th century was widely criticised by refor-mers and humanitarians. Workhouses were often indistinguishable from 'houses of correction' set up to discipline vagrants, and remained a symbol of degradation until their abolition in the late 1920s.

Works Projects Administration (WPA) US federal agency established by President Franklin D. Roosevelt in 1935 to counteract severe unemployment during the

World fairs provided an international stage for nations to show off a great range of products – from pearls to preserved meats or steam engines. New York's first fair (above) was held in 1853.

Great DEPRESSION. The idea was that the payment of wages to those formerly on relief would increase their purchasing power and stimulate the economy. The WPA, led by Harry HOPKINS, created work for 8.5 million people in its lifetime, at a cost of $11 billion. Hospitals, schools, playgrounds, parks, roads and airports were constructed; art, theatre, writing and educational projects were set up. With the increase in employment in the private sector the WPA came to an end in 1943.

World Bank Financial agency of the UNITED NATIONS, also known as the International Bank for Reconstruction and Development, established in 1945 to make long-term loans available for economic development. The World Bank was first proposed at the BRETTON WOODS CONFERENCE in 1944. The World Bank has more than 177 members, and gets its income from interest and loan repayments, and from borrowing on the world money markets. Initially it gave loans for reconstruction in the aftermath of the Second World War, but by 1949 it was concentrating on loans for economic development, particularly in the Third World. Since 1970 it has concentrated on agricultural and rural development, education, health, and public hygiene, as well as helping to plan strategies for industrialisation. The bank is controlled by a board of representatives of member countries.

World Council of Churches Interdenominational organisation of Protestant and Orthodox Eastern churches, formed in Amsterdam in 1948 to further the unity of the Christian Church. Council members include more than 100 countries and 300 churches, and it maintains close links with the Roman Catholic Church which is not a member. Most of the work of the council is advisory. Its headquarters are in Geneva, and its ruling body, the assembly, meets about every seven years.

world fairs The first exhibitions highlighting the industrial, scientific and technological achievements of participating nations were held in Britain and France in the 18th century. They culminated in the GREAT EXHIBITION at the Crystal Palace in London's Hyde Park in 1851, and the Paris Exhibition of 1861. The Universal Exposition of 1889 in Paris, for which the Eiffel Tower was built, attracted 32 million visitors. In the USA the first New York Fair was held in 1853, and the Philadelphia Centennial Exhibition in 1876.

The most important world fairs of the 20th century include the British Empire Exhibition in London, from 1924 to 1925; Expo 67 in Montreal, Canada; Expo 70, Japan; and the Spanish Expo 92 in Seville.

World Health Organisation (WHO) Specialist agency of the UNITED NATIONS, founded in 1948 to promote international cooperation to achieve 'the highest possible level of health' of all people in all countries. The main concern of the WHO is the control of epidemic diseases, and it has had notable success in eradicating smallpox and reducing the incidence of cholera, polio, malaria,

---

DID YOU KNOW?

The World Bank estimates that the average income in the developing world has doubled since 1960. Yet a billion people still live on less than 70 pence a day.

---

tuberculosis and leprosy. The agency develops international vaccination programmes, lays down quarantine and sanitation rules, and funds international research programmes. Its headquarters are in Geneva.

World War I see FIRST WORLD WAR

World War II see SECOND WORLD WAR

Worms, Diet of (1521) Meeting of the Diet (assembly) of the Holy Roman Empire at Worms, Germany, before which the Protestant reformer Martin LUTHER appeared to defend his publications on religious matters. In 1521 Luther was excommunicated by Pope Leo X for criticising the papacy. He was summoned to appear before Emperor CHARLES V and the Diet. Luther refused to retract his views. The Diet condemned his teachings in the Edict of Worms, and demanded his capture as a heretic. The edict was never enforced, but it strengthened the resolve of his followers, and led ultimately to a split within the Roman Catholic Church in Germany.

Wounded Knee, Battle of (December 29, 1890) Last major battle between the US army and the Sioux Indians on the Pine Ridge reservation, South Dakota. In the 1880s the Sioux Indians were reduced to near-starvation after their reservation had been reduced in size. A Paiute prophet called Wovoka promised the return of their land from the White man if certain dances were performed. The resulting 'Ghost Dance' movement unsettled the White population. The federal army intervened, and in a conflict on December 15,

In 1675 Wren laid the foundation block of St Paul's Cathedral, his classical baroque masterpiece designed in the shape of a Greek cross. Thirty-five years later he put the final stone in place.

1890, Chief SITTING BULL was killed. A band of Sioux, led by Big Foot, escaped into the Badlands but was captured by the 7th Cavalry and taken to Wounded Knee Creek. Here, when a medicine man threw dust into the air, a warrior shot and wounded an officer. The US troops then opened fire on the Sioux, killing 200 men, women and children.

Wren, Sir Christopher (1632-1723) Influential English architect, noted for designing St Paul's Cathedral, London. Wren was also highly regarded as a scientist, and helped to found the ROYAL SOCIETY. Wren studied at Oxford University and in 1657 he became professor of astronomy at Gresham College in London. His first buildings were Pembroke College chapel, Cambridge (1663), and the Sheldonian Theatre, Oxford. After a visit to Paris in 1665, he returned to London inspired by French baroque architecture, many elements of which can be seen in his work. The Great FIRE OF LONDON in 1666 gave Wren the opportunity to show his architectural skills. He drew

Felled at Wounded Knee Creek, the frozen body of Chief Big Foot lies on the battlefield. He and the remnants of his tribe were defenceless against the guns of the 7th Cavalry.

up a plan for rebuilding the City based on wide avenues and squares, but his designs were not implemented on grounds of cost and vested interests. Instead he was commissioned to rebuild 51 City churches (1670-86) and the new St Paul's Cathedral (1675-1711). His

> **❝ Sir Christopher Wren said, I am going to dine with some men. If anybody calls, say I am designing St Paul's. ❞**
>
> *Edmund Clerihew Bentley (1875-1956)*

designs for public buildings included the Royal Hospital at Chelsea, Greenwich Hospital, and additions to Hampton Court Palace. He was buried in St Paul's where an inscription above his tomb reads: *Si monumentum requiris, circumspice* (if you seek his monument, look around you).

Wright, Frank Lloyd (1869-1959) US architect, renowned for the originality of his designs. Wright studied civil engineering at Wisconsin University. His first buildings were a series of low-built, prairie-style houses in Chicago, which established his reputation. Wright was an innovator in open-planning. He exploited modern technology, often producing controversial designs. He achieved worldwide recognition later in life, with buildings such as the Imperial Hotel, Tokyo (1915-22); the Johnson Wax factory, Wisconsin (1936-9), an office block with walls of brick and glass tubes; and the Guggenheim

Wright's 'Falling Water' weekend retreat, built in Pennsylvania in 1939, epitomises his masterful blend of architecture and nature.

Museum of Art, New York (1942-1959), in which the exhibits are viewed from a spiral ramp. Wright established the Taliesin architectural community, and built his own home and school, Taliesin West, in Arizona in 1938.

writing see feature, page 712

Wyatt's Rebellion (February 1554) Conspiracy in England against the proposed marriage of MARY I to the future PHILIP II of Spain. The rebellion was led by Sir Thomas Wyatt, a Kentish landowner. Convinced that the marriage would turn England into 'a cockleboat towed by a Spanish galleon', Wyatt led 3000 Kentishmen in a march on London. There he found most Londoners' loyalty to Mary stronger than their antipathy to Spain. He surrendered, was taken prisoner and executed.

Wycliffe, John (c.1330-84) English religious reformer, whose views inspired his followers to undertake a translation of the Bible into English. Wycliffe was born in Yorkshire and studied at Oxford, where he later taught and in 1360 became master of Balliol College. In 1361 he was made rector of the first of three parishes. Wycliffe attracted attention through his theological tracts, written mainly

How the world learned to make words immortal

Writing is among the greatest inventions in history – perhaps the greatest of all, since written records are the beginning of history and one of the foundations of civilisation.

Without writing, human society depended on memory; with writing, anything could be put on record. The transactions of the merchant, the command of the king or the priest, the calculations of the architect were made available far beyond the individual's sight and voice and lifetime. Writing enormously assisted the growth of nations larger than the old city-states. Yet no one knows how it was invented, or even where the first alphabet came from.

During the last ice age, some 20000 years ago, humans drew pictures of animals and people along with enigmatic graffiti on the walls of caves in southern France. One cave shows a horse surrounded by 80 'P' signs. But these signs are not writing: like modern mathematical symbols and musical notation, they convey information but are not flexible enough to express even simple thoughts or ideas.

THE FIRST WRITERS
The first people with a true writing system were the Sumerians, who lived in Mesopotamia (present-day Iraq) just before 3000 BC. Their writing appears to have grown out of a system of accountancy, driven by the compelling demands of a fast-expanding economy. The earliest known 'document' seems to have formed part of a tax account.

The Sumerians wrote chiefly on clay tablets by pressing the wedge-shaped end of a reed into moist clay, making marks which look something like bird tracks in mud. The symbols began as representations of specific objects, or 'pictographs', but later took on more abstract meanings. This writing is known as 'cuneiform', after the Latin word *cuneus*, meaning wedge. Cuneiform was later the writing system of the Babylonian, Assyrian and Persian empires; it was used in the Middle East for 3000 years.

At the same time, in ancient Egypt, the priests were developing hieroglyphs – that is, 'sacred carvings'. These beautiful symbols, unlike cuneiform, were often composed of recognisable images: an owl,

This colourful page from the ancient Egyptian *Book of the Dead* uses hieroglyphs to explain how the dead must behave in the underworld.

a serpent, a hand or even a human figure standing on its head. Ideas and sounds were both represented in the symbols. They were carved in stone, painted on objects or brushed onto papyrus, the Egyptian paper. The last known hieroglyphic inscription was carved in Egypt in AD 394.

Chinese script, composed of abstract 'characters', developed sometime in the second millennium BC. Some early characters are clearly stylised drawings of, say, the human figure, the moon, a horse, a tree, but most are not recognisable as the object they represent. They do, however, resemble the characters used in China today: the modern Chinese reader can understand the writings of his earliest literate ancestors. The Chinese script, with its thousands of symbols, is the world's oldest living writing system, and it has strongly influenced other Far Eastern scripts, especially that of Japan.

Most of the rest of the world writes using an alphabet – a system in which symbols represent sounds, and are combined to form words. The most important alphabets are Roman, used in modern forms by English and most other languages of Western Europe; Cyrillic, employed by the Russians and certain other Slavic peoples; Devanagari, the script of Sanskrit; as well as Greek, Arabic and Hebrew. Many languages use versions of these alphabets, adding letters for special sounds, or dropping them as necessary.

In spite of the differences in appearance between these alphabets, and their many offshoots, they are all related, since they have all evolved from a common ancestor.

GETTING DOWN THE MESSAGE

The first alphabet, which has been called North Semitic, seems to have been used in the 17th or 16th centuries BC in Palestine. No one knows precisely how it emerged, but perhaps it was invented by Phoenician merchants trading around the Mediterranean who required a quicker means of writing down transactions than cuneiform or hieroglyphs, and a system flexible enough to record the babel of languages spoken by their customers.

The alphabet consisted of 22 letters, and its usefulness was quickly established. Within a few centuries different versions of it had been adopted throughout the Middle East and had spread as far afield as Italy and India.

The letters of this Greek inscription remain perfectly legible after more than 2000 years.

Phoenician	⟨	9	ꙇ	△	ⱻ	Y	ꙅ	⯖	⟨
Early Greek	△	8	⌁	△	ⱻ	⅂	⟨	日	⏐
Classical Greek	A	B	Γ	△	E	Φ	Γ	H	⏐
Roman	A	B	C	D	E	F	G	H	I

Many letters in the modern Roman alphabet can be traced to ancient Phoenician originals (above); the letters G and J are omitted because they evolved from C and I respectively. The Phoenician text (left) dates from the 3rd century BC, while the Latin inscription (below) commemorates the building of the circus at Pompeii in 80 BC.

in English rather than Latin. He attacked the Church hierarchy, enforced confession, priestly powers and the doctrine stating that the Eucharist bread and wine was transformed

into the body and blood of Jesus Christ. In 1382 Wycliffe's views were condemned as heretical. He was forced to retire to his parish in Leicestershire, where he continued to write prolifically. His followers, who were known as LOLLARDS, formed the link between Wycliffe and the Protestant REFORMATION.

Xenophon (c.430–c.355 BC) Greek historian, philosopher and military commander. Xenophon was a pupil of SOCRATES before leaving Athens in 401 BC to join 10 000 Greek mercenaries hired by CYRUS THE YOUNGER to win the Persian throne from his elder brother Artaxerxes. After Cyrus's defeat at Cunaxa, the mercenaries chose Xenophon as their general and he led them back 900 miles (1500 km) across Asia Minor to the Black Sea. He later recorded his experiences in the *Anabasis*, (*Expedition*). Xenophon fought under the Spartan king Agesilaus in a campaign which led to victory over Athens and Thebes. The Athenians banished him, and the Spartans gave him an estate near Olympia. He later moved to Corinth, and in 365 back to Athens, where he spent the rest of his life.

Among Xenophon's other works was a history, the *Hellenica*, which continued the history of Greece from where THUCYDIDES ended in 411, and the *Memorabilia*, in which he recorded his memories of Socrates.

Xerxes I Ruler of the Achaemenid Persian empire from 486 to 465 BC; son of Darius I. Xerxes set out to avenge his father's defeat at Marathon in 490 by leading an expedition of 360 000 men against Greece. It took seven days for his army to cross two bridges of boats which spanned the Hellespont between Asia and Europe. After victory at the Battle of THERMOPYLAE, he pillaged Athens, but the defeat of his fleet at SALAMIS in 480 left him without means of supplying his army. He withdrew, leaving his cousin Mardonius in command of the Persian army, which was defeated at PLATAEA in 479. Subsequently, Xerxes gave up his ambitions to conquer Greece and extended his father's monumental building programme at the capital,

In a relief from Persepolis, Xerxes stands behind the throne as Darius gives audience to one of his priests.

Persepolis. He became increasingly caught up in harem intrigues, one of which led to his murder by the captain of his bodyguard.

Xhosa Wars (1779-1879) Frontier wars in South Africa between the Xhosa (NGUNI) people and European colonists in present-day Eastern Cape and Ciskei. From the late 1770s Boers and Xhosa were locked in intense competition for the rich grazing lands of the eastern Cape, and skirmishes gave way to wars. After the British occupied the Cape in 1806, British troops intervened to support the settlers, and from 1811 they began a policy of clearing the land of Xhosa people. Some 4000 British colonists were installed along the Great Fish River, following a year of fighting in 1818 and 1819. Xhosa cattle raids resulted in retaliation – the war of 1834-5 yielded 60 000 cattle to the colonists. From 1846 to 1853 the Xhosa adopted a scorched earth policy against the British, a policy which resulted in the starvation of many of their own people. The final Xhosa War, between 1877 and 1879, was a vain attempt by Xhosa returning from the diamond fields to regain their land. Subsequently, all Xhosa territory became European-owned farmland within Cape Colony (CAPE PROVINCE).

Yalta Conference (February 4-11, 1945) Meeting between the Allied leaders Joseph Stalin, Winston Churchill and Franklin D. Roosevelt at the Crimean city of Yalta. The leaders agreed that once victory had been won in the Second World War, Germany would be divided into four zones run by American, British, French and Soviet forces. The founding conference of the United Nations was set for two months later. Stalin gave a secret undertaking to enter the war against Japan, in return for the southern part of Sakhalin Island and the Kurile Islands, and for Soviet control of Outer Mongolia and Manchuria. He also made pledges concerning the independence of the countries of eastern Europe, pledges

which in the event he failed to honour. The leaders met again at the POTS-DAM CONFERENCE five months later.

Yeltsin, Boris (1931-) Russian president since 1991. From 1955 to 1968 Yeltsin was a construction worker in Sverdlovsk. He joined the Communist Party in 1961, and became first secretary of the Sverdlovsk region in 1976. In 1985, Mikhail GORBACHEV invited Yeltsin to reform the party organisation in the capital as mayor of Moscow. He lost his job in 1987 after criticising the slow pace of reform. In 1989 the people of Moscow elected him to the Congress of People's Deputies (the Soviet parliament), and a year later the Congress declared him leader of the Russian Republic.

Yeltsin became the first popularly elected leader in Russian history when he won the presidential elections in June 1991. In August he played a courageous role in defying an abortive military coup. Further confrontation with conservative hardliners in October 1993 led him to send in tanks to close the Russian parliament. In 1994 he sent Russian troops to the Caucasian republic of Chechnya which had declared its independence from Russia. This resulted in fierce fighting. He presided over the dissolution of the Soviet Union, and encouraged the Commonwealth of Independent States that replaced it, with Russia assuming the leading role. In July 1996 Yeltsin was re-elected president.

Yemen, Republic of Country incorporating the former Yemen Arab Republic (North Yemen) and People's Democratic Republic of Yemen (South Yemen) in the south-west of the Arabian peninsula. Between about 950

and 115 BC Yemen was known as Saba – part of the kingdom of the biblical Queen of Sheba. After around 100 BC it declined when the overland incense trade was largely superseded by sea routes. Yemen was converted to Islam in the 7th century AD and became a province of the Muslim CALIPHATE. The religious dynasty of the Zaidi sect ruled from the 9th century until 1972. Yemen was part of the OTTOMAN EMPIRE from 1517 until 1918, although Britain annexed ADEN in 1839.

In 1918, North Yemen was proclaimed a kingdom under Imam Yahya. He was assassinated in 1948, and his son Ahmad ruled until his death in 1962. An army coup led to the proclamation of a republic, and civil war followed until 1967 when a moderate government was formed. In 1972 war broke out with the neighbouring People's Democratic Republic of Yemen, formerly the British Protectorate of Aden. Intermittent talks to unite the two republics followed, and the unified Republic of Yemen was proclaimed in 1990. Under President Ali Abdullah Saleh, its political capital was San'aa and its commercial capital Aden.

After the Iraqi invasion of Kuwait in 1990, Yemen was the only member of the UN Security Council to oppose the Allied intervention which led to the GULF WAR. After a series of armed clashes the south seceded from the union in May 1994, but Aden soon fell to northern forces. In October Saleh formed a new united government of Yemen.

yeoman Member of the rural middle class in England. In the 13th and 14th centuries yeomen were landholding peasants, and as the medieval system of land tenure broke down their numbers increased. The name came to be used to describe certain high-ranking retainers in noble households, and from 1485 the bodyguards of the monarch were known as Yeomen of the Guard. In the 18th century cavalry units called yeomanry were formed.

Yom Kippur War Arab-Israeli war in October 1973, known in the Arab world as 'the October War'. On October 6, the Feast of Yom Kippur (the 'Day of Atonement' and the holiest day in the Jewish calendar) Egyptian forces crossed the Suez Canal into Israeli-held territory in the Sinai desert. Syria recovered the Golan Heights, occupied by Israel since the SIX DAY WAR. The war lasted three weeks, during which Israel pushed Syrian

Boris Yeltsin urges a crowd outside the Russian parliament to resist the organisers of a coup d'état in August 1991.

son won the battle of Towton in 1461 and became EDWARD IV, but his fourth son, RICHARD III, brought ruin on the YORKISTS.

Yorkists The descendants or supporters of Richard, 3rd Duke of YORK. Yorkists held the throne of England under Edward IV, Edward V and Richard III. Their emblem was a white rose. The Plantagenet royal Houses of York and Lancaster were both descended from Edward III and competed for the throne in the Wars of the ROSES of the 15th century. Despite Richard, Duke of York's death at the Battle of Wakefield in 1460, the Yorkists quickly regained the ascendancy over the LANCASTRIAN forces and Richard's son Edward became king in 1461 as EDWARD IV. On his death in 1483 he was succeeded by his 13-year-old elder son, EDWARD V, who was deposed three months later by his uncle RICHARD III. Richard's death at the Battle of BOSWORTH FIELD in 1485 opened the way for the last Lancastrian claimant Henry TUDOR to gain the throne. As HENRY VII he neutralised the Yorkist claim by marrying the heiress Elizabeth of York, Edward IV's eldest daughter, and beheading the last surviving male in the Yorkist line, Edward, Earl of Warwick, in 1499.

Yorktown Site of Britain's final defeat in the AMERICAN REVOLUTION. In August 1781, after suffering many casualties in an unsuccessful campaign in the Carolinas, the British general Charles CORNWALLIS seized and fortified the Yorktown peninsula in Chesapeake Bay and waited for the support of the British fleet. Cornwallis soon found he had led his army into a trap. In August a French fleet arrived and blockaded Chesapeake Bay, fighting off British naval forces. The French persuaded George WASHINGTON to hurry

Israeli defence minister Moshe Dayan confers with troops (left) during the Yom Kippur War, before the army moves through Sinai to the Suez Canal.

forces back into Syria and crossed the Canal, encircling part of the Egyptian army. Disengagement agreements were signed by Israel with Syria in 1974, and with Egypt in 1974 and 1975. The Israeli withdrawal from Sinai was completed in 1982, following a peace treaty, the CAMP DAVID ACCORD, in 1978.

York, Richard, 3rd Duke of (1411-60) Noble whose claim to the English throne started the Wars of the ROSES between his supporters, the YORKISTS, and the rival LANCASTRIAN forces.

Richard was descended from Edward III through both his father, Richard, Earl of Cambridge, and his mother, Anne Mortimer, and believed that he had a better claim to the English crown than HENRY VI, who ascended the throne in 1422. When the king's uncle Humphrey, Duke of Gloucester, died in 1447 York became next in line to the throne of England, and was sent in virtual banishment to Ireland as Lieutenant. He returned in 1450 to struggle against the growing power of the king's chief minister, Edmund Beaufort, Duke of Somerset, and of the queen, Margaret of Anjou. In 1453 Margaret gave birth to a son, Edward, who replaced York as Henry VI's heir. When the king suffered a period of insanity the following year Margaret, backed by Somerset, attempted to rule; but Parliament appointed York as Protector of the Realm in March 1454. York's forces killed Somerset at

the first Battle of ST ALBANS in 1455, but by 1456 the queen and her supporters had regained power.

It was not until 1460, when York's brother-in-law Richard Neville, Earl of Warwick, captured the king at Northampton, that a compromise was reached whereby Henry was to remain king for life and York was to succeed him. Margaret broke the agreement that disinherited her son, and in October her forces defeated the Yorkists at the Battle of Wakefield, in which Richard was killed. The Yorkist party survived him, and won the second battle of St Albans in 1460. His eldest

British redcoats serving in General Charles Cornwallis' army march in dignified procession out of Yorktown to surrender to George Washington's Franco-American forces on October 19, 1781.

These 19th-century Yoruba sculptures, or *ibejis*, representing twins were made when twins were born and were also used in funeral rites.

south from New York and lay siege to Yorktown. Surprised by Washington's advance, Cornwallis was cut off by land and sea, and surrendered on October 19, effectively ending the American War of Independence.

Yoruba People of NIGERIA whose Oyo empire was a loose confederation of kingdoms from the 17th to the 19th century, dominated by the northernmost kingdom, Oyo. The empire declined in the early 19th century with the end of the slave trade and the rise of the militant Muslim Fulani, who destroyed the city of Oyo and went on to create the emirate of Ilorin.

Alafin Atiba, the ruler of the empire from 1836 to 1859, allied Oyo with the city state of Ibadan; but on his death civil war broke out. In 1888 a treaty was made with the Alafin of Oyo, bringing all the Yoruba kingdoms under British protection. The Yoruba were under British control until 1960 when the federation of Nigeria became an independent state.

Young, Brigham (1801-77) US leader of the MORMONS. After Joseph SMITH's killing in Illinois in 1844, Young became the dominant figure of Mormonism. In 1847 he led the Mormon migration west to Salt Lake City, Utah, ruling over the new community with autocratic firmness, and turning a desert waste into a prosperous and flourishing city.

Young Plan Programme for the settlement of German REPARATIONS payments after the First World War. The plan was presented by a committee which met in Paris in 1929 under the chairmanship of a US financier, Owen D. Young, to revise the Dawes Plan (1924). The total sum due from Germany was reduced by 75 per cent to 121 billion Reichsmark, to be paid in 59 annual instalments. Foreign controls on Germany's economy were lifted. The first instalment was paid in 1930, but further payments lapsed until Adolf HITLER repudiated all reparations debts in 1933.

Young Turks European name applied to late 19th-century and early 20th-century reformers in the OTTOMAN EMPIRE who led a revolution in 1908. The main political party was the Committee of Union and Progress which seized power in 1913 and, under the triumvirate of Talat, Jamal and ENVER PASHA, ruled the Ottoman Empire until 1918, supporting Germany, Austria-Hungary and Bulgaria in the First World War.

Ypsilanti, Alexander (1792-1828) The Greek nationalist leader Ypsilanti served as a general in the Russian army and was elected leader of the Philike Hetairia, a secret organisation that sought Greek independence from the Ottoman Empire. In 1821 he raised a revolt in Moldavia, proclaiming the independence of Greece, but lacking the support of Russia or Romania he was defeated by the Turks and imprisoned in Austria. Together with the successful Greek rebellion in the Peloponnese, his uprising marked the beginning of the GREEK WAR OF INDEPENDENCE.

Yuan (1279-1368) MONGOL dynasty that ruled China following KUBLAI KHAN's defeat of the Song dynasty. Kublai Khan's reign and that of his grandson Temur (1294-1307) saw the re-establishment of trade links with the West along the Silk Road (see feature, page 595). MARCO POLO worked for the Yuan dynasty. After the death of Temur, the empire was unsettled by rebellion. From 1348 there was continuous conflict, with rebel Chinese armies fighting each other as well as the Mongols. In 1368 the last Yuan emperor fled to Mongolia when the rebel leader Zhu Yuanzhang captured Cambaluc (now Beijing) and founded the MING DYNASTY.

Yucatán State on a peninsula in the southeast of Mexico. Yucatán was the northern area of MAYA civilisation, and the region included some cities which were inhabited as early as 750 BC. Starting from about AD 800 many Maya migrated from the Southern Lowlands (present-day Guatemala) into the Northern Lowlands of the peninsula and founded new states at Chichén Itzá, Izamal, Mayapán and Uxmal, linked by political alliances and trade. At first Chichén Itzá was dominant, then Mayapán, until in the late 15th century 17 small principalities were formed. Fernández de Córdoba explored the coast in 1516-17, sighting several cities which were not fully subdued until the 1540s.

Yugoslavia Country in south-east Europe which, until 1991, comprised the states of BOSNIA-HERZEGOVINA, CROATIA, Macedonia, Montenegro, SERBIA and SLOVENIA, and two autonomous Serbian provinces, Kosovo and Vojvodina. The country came into being after the First World War as the Kingdom of the Serbs, Croats and Slovenes, made up of the

A painting from the Yuan dynasty illustrates the technology used by Chinese peasants more than 600 years ago to pump water from a river in order to irrigate their paddy fields.

A reclining god or chacmal (left), stands at the head of the steps at the Temple of the Warrior at Chichén Itzá, one of Yucatán's Maya cities.

south Slavic provinces of the former AUSTRO-HUNGARIAN EMPIRE. In 1921, King Peter I was succeeded by his son ALEXANDER I. The Serbian premier Nikola PASIC held the rival nations together, but after his death in 1926 political turmoil led the new king to establish a royal dictatorship, renaming the country Yugoslavia in 1929. Moves towards democracy ended with his assassination in 1934.

During the Second World War Yugoslavia was overrun by German forces, and the fascist puppet state of Croatia was established under Ante Pavelíc. A civil war began between supporters of Draza MIHAILOVIC and Marshal TITO's communist partisans, both of whom were fighting the Germans. In 1945 Tito, supported by the Soviet Union, proclaimed the Socialist Federal Republic of Yugoslavia. In 1948 the country was expelled by Joseph Stalin from the Soviet bloc for asserting its 'positive neutrality'. Improved relations with the West followed and, after Stalin's death, diplomatic ties with the Soviet Union were restored in 1955. Tito died in 1980, and in 1989 multiparty systems were introduced in Croatia and Slovenia. In 1990 a rebellion by Croatia's minority Serb population received support from Serbia, while in the same year Serbia suppressed a rebellion by its Albanian majority in the province of Kosovo. Full-scale civil war erupted in 1991. War continued in Bosnia – between Serbs, Muslims and Croats – until November 1995, when a peace accord was signed in Dayton, USA.

Yunnan Mountainous province in south-western China with a wide mixture of racial groups and a long history of Chinese encroachment. In the 8th century native Thais set up a kingdom called Nanchao. They managed to defy the Chinese but were conquered by KUBLAI KHAN's Mongols, accelerating Thai expansion towards the south. Islam was introduced by a Mongol general. Yunnan was integrated into China by the QING dynasty in the 17th century. It was a major centre of Chinese resistance in the Second World War.

Zaharoff, Sir Basil (1849-1936) International financier and arms manufacturer. Born Zacharias Basileios, from Anatolia (Turkey), he worked for a succession of Swedish, German and British armament firms in the Balkans, Eastern Europe and Russia before becoming director and chairman of the British Vickers-Armstrong arms firm. In 1913 Zaharoff became a French citizen, and during the First World War he served as an Allied secret agent. He was subsequently knighted by George V and awarded the Legion of Honour by the French government. He retired to Monte Carlo, where he controlled the casino.

Zaire Central African country. The original inhabitants were pygmies. During the first centuries AD Bantu-speakers migrated from north-west Africa, and from about 700 on they worked and traded the rich copper deposits of Katanga (present-day Shaba). The precolonial 19th-century history of Zaire was dominated by the Arab slave trade. David

LIVINGSTONE was the first European explorer of the country. In the 1870s Henry STANLEY's exploration of the river Zaire, then called the Congo, prompted LEOPOLD II of Belgium to found the Congo Free State. Maladministration obliged Leopold to hand over the state to the Belgian parliament in 1908.

Independence was granted in 1960. Within weeks, the regime of Patrice LUMUMBA was undermined by civil war and the secession under Moïse TSHOMBE of the province of Katanga. In 1965 General MOBUTU SESE SEKO seized power in a coup. He changed the country's name to Zaire, a local name for the river Congo, in 1971 and Zaire became a one-party state the following year. The sole candidate, Mobutu was elected president in 1970, 1977 and 1984. In 1991 multiparty elections were promised but opposition parties refused to support the prime minister nominated by the president. Riots followed until, in 1992, Mobutu accepted an opposition-led government, but the power struggle continued until April 1994, when a period of 15 months was set for a transition to democracy. This was extended in July 1995 for a further two years. In 1994 more than a million refugees from the civil war in RWANDA fled to Zaire; repatriation of these refugees began in September 1995.

Zambia Landlocked central African country, formerly called Northern Rhodesia (see ZIMBABWE). Most Zambian ethnic groups arrived from present-day ANGOLA and ZAIRE between the 16th and the 18th centuries. NGUNI people fleeing from Zululand settled in Zambia in 1835.

Granted responsibility for the area in its charter of 1889, Cecil RHODES' British South Africa Company worked the rich copper deposits from 1902. The country was named Northern Rhodesia in 1911, and the British Government administered it from 1924 until independence was granted in 1964. Kenneth

KAUNDA was elected president of the new republic of Zambia. International sanctions against its neighbour Rhodesia between 1965 and 1980 blocked the traditional route through Rhodesia for Zambian exports. From 1975 the problem was relieved by a new railway through Tanzania. The country had been a one-party state since 1972, but in 1990 Kaunda agreed to hold a referendum on the introduction of a multiparty system. In 1991

Traders offer their wares, in a 19th-century impression of Zanzibar's market. The slave fort looms in the background.

the Movement for Multiparty Democracy (MMD) was elected, with Frederick Chiluba as president. Kaunda returned to politics in 1995 as the leader of the United National Independence Party (UNIP).

Zanzibar Island off the East African coast. Around 1100 Zanzibar was importing pottery from the Persian Gulf and it soon became a base for Arab traders. The first European to visit the island was the Portuguese explorer Vasco da Gama in 1499, and the Portuguese went on to establish a trading post and a Catholic mission. In 1698 the sultanate of OMAN took Zanzibar, which became the commercial centre of the western Indian Ocean, selling slaves and ivory in the Arab world, India and across the Atlantic. In 1841 Said Ibn Sultan (1805-1856) moved his court from Oman to Zanzibar. In 1873 Sir John Kirk, British consul from 1866 to 1887, persuaded the sultan to end the slave trade. From 1890 to 1963 Zanzibar was a British protectorate.

Zanzibar became a republic in 1963, and united with Tanganyika in 1964 to form TANZANIA. In 1985 a new constitution was announced, and in 1990 Salmin Amour became president. He was re-elected in 1995.

Zapata, Emiliano (1879-1919) One of the leaders in the Mexican Revolution. A mixed-race, or *mestizo*, peasant, Zapata occupied land previously appropriated by the owners of large estates, or HACIENDAS, and distributed it to peasants. He joined the revolution in 1910 when the reformer Francisco Madero replaced the dictator Porfirio Díaz as president. Once in office, Madero failed to implement his promised programmes of agrarian reform, so Zapata opposed him. In 1911 his Plan of Ayala called for land to be returned to the Amerindians. For eight years he led guerrilla

armies against the owners of the haciendas, but was assassinated at Chinameca. Zapata's creed, *zapatismo*, came to be identified with *agrarianismo*, which called for the return of land to the Mexican Indians, and *indianismo*, the cultural and nationalist movement of the Mexican Indians. Zapata's influence still survives; insurgents in the Chiapas region of MEXICO in 1994 styled themselves the Zapatista National Liberation Army.

Zealots Militant Jewish sect in Roman Palestine, so called because of their intense religious observance and the fanaticism, or 'zeal', of their revolt against the Romans. They may have originated in the revolt of the Maccabees in the 2nd century BC. Zealots were fiercely opposed to the Romans, who worshipped many gods, and they attacked Jews who sought peace with Rome. An attempt in AD 6 by Quirinius, the Roman governor of Syria, to make a census of the Jews, caused the Zealots to revolt. Zealots have been identified with the 'Daggermen' (Sicarii) of the Jewish Revolt of 66-70 which ended in the Roman destruction of Jerusalem. The 900 occupants of the mountain fortress at MASADA (see feature, page 397) who committed suicide in 73 rather than surrender to the Romans are also said to have been Zealots.

Zen Buddhist sect in Japan (see BUDDHISM). Influenced by TAOISM, Zen originated in China and spread to Japan during the KAMAKURA period from 1192 to 1333. It seeks salvation through meditation and enlightenment – revelation of the Buddha-nature said to be in everyone. Training is transmitted personally from master to disciple.

In Japan, two sects developed: the Rinzai sect which uses *koans*, riddles that break down logical reasoning; and the Soto sect that stresses meditation and study. With its austere discipline and emphasis on fearlessness, Zen appealed to the SAMURAI warrior class. It flowered under the Ashikaga shogunate from 1339 to 1579, and declined in the 17th century. It was revived by Hakuin (1686-1769); present-day Rinzai masters trace their descent from him. Zen was introduced to the West by D. T. Suzuki (1870-1966), and interest in Zen meditation has subsequently expanded.

Zeng Guofan (1811-72) Chinese general and statesman of the Qing dynasty. A scholar, Zeng Guofan served for many years as an imperial official. In 1852 he raised the first of several regional armies, the Hunan Army, to crush the TAIPING REBELLION in south-east China. The rebellion lasted 14 years and cost 20 million lives before it ended in 1864 with the fall of the rebel capital Nanjing. Zeng Guofan later became governor-general of Jiangsu, Anhui and Jianxi provinces. In 1865 he sponsored the Jianyang Arsenal, which produced the first modern weapons and ships in China, and whose translation office introduced Western thought to the country. He supported the Self-Strengthening Movement, which in the 1860s and 1870s aimed to adapt Chinese institutions to Western innovation.

The emphasis Zen masters gave to harmony with nature had much influence on aesthetics, and an austere style of garden emerged which featured carefully placed rocks in raked gravel.

The cigar-shaped Graf Zeppelin airship, named after its inventor (left), first flew in 1928, made a round-the-world flight in 1929 and remained in trans-Atlantic service until 1937.

more than 100 'Zeppelins' were built, some of which made bombing raids over Britain. Zeppelin airships were later used for commercial flights, but when the world's largest airship, the *Hindenburg*, burst into flames in 1937 the accident signalled the end of the airship era.

Zeppelin, Ferdinand Count von (1838-1917) German pioneer of the rigid, metal-framed airship. An army officer, Zeppelin was impressed by the use of balloons while a military observer in the American Civil War in 1863, and again during the Prussian siege of Paris in 1870. In 1900 his first rigid airship, the LZ-1, made its maiden flight. It had an aluminium frame covered with cotton, 420 ft (128 m) long. Lift was provided by huge bags of hydrogen, which is lighter than air. Six years and several models later, he achieved a 24-hour flight. During the First World War

Zhao Mengfu (1254-1332) Chinese painter and calligrapher. Born a descendant of the imperial Sung dynasty, Zhao Mengfu was court painter to the Mongol emperor Kublai Khan and one of his finest calligraphers. His wife Kuan Tao-sheng and son Chao Yung were also notable painters.

Zheng He (d. c.1433) Chinese explorer. A Muslim court eunuch from YUNNAN province, Zheng He commanded seven voyages between 1405 and 1433. On his first voyage, from 1405 to 1407, he sailed with 62 ships,

Zhao Mengfu was particularly well known for his paintings of horses – here a horse is being tamed. Many of his pictures, which also covered other subjects such as landscapes, survive today.

calling at MALACCA and India. Later, Zheng He reached the Persian Gulf and, on his last voyage between 1431 and 1433, as far as East Africa. His journeys were made possible by Chinese advances in shipbuilding and by the use of the compass.

Zhou (11th century BC-256BC) Chinese dynasty founded by Wu the Martial; also called Chou. Wu overthrew the Shang emperor Zhou, and in 1027 BC established his capital at Hao near present-day Xi'an. From Hao the Western or Early Zhou emperors ruled over feudal vassal states until 771, when the capital was moved east to Luoyang. The anarchic era of the Warring States lasted from 403 until 221. In 256 the last Zhou sovereign was overthrown by Prince Zheng of the state of Qin.

In the later Zhou period there was a flowering of philosophy known as the 'hundred schools of thought', with exponents such as CONFUCIUS, MENCIUS and Chuang-tse. Trade also flourished with the demand for silk, faster transport by canals and increased use of coins.

Zhou En-lai (1898-1976) Chinese premier from 1949 to his death, also written Chou En-Lai, who helped to establish closer relations with Western nations. Born into a mandarin family, Zhou studied in Japan where he was imprisoned for his radical politics. From 1920 to 1922 he studied in France, where he became a communist. He returned to China in 1924 to become deputy political director of the GUOMINDANG Whampoa Military Academy commanded by CHIANG KAI-SHEK. In 1927 Zhou organised a general strike in Shanghai, opening the city to Chiang's forces. Chiang then turned against the communists and executed many of his former allies.

Escaping to Jiangxi, Zhou took part in the LONG MARCH and became MAO ZE-DONG's chief adviser. In December 1936 Chiang Kai-Shek was arrested by his own generals, who wanted to stop the civil war with the communists and unite with them against Japan, which had invaded Manchuria. Zhou was made chief communist liaison officer with the Guomindang, and remained in this position until the Japanese surrender in 1945.

When the People's Republic of China was established in 1949, he became prime minister and served as foreign minister until 1958. He played a major role at a conference in Geneva in 1954 which ended the INDO-CHINESE WAR, and at the 1955 Bandung Conference which set up a non-aligned group of Asian countries. In the 1970s Zhou worked to re-establish Chinese contacts with the West. He was an early supporter of the modernisations later encouraged by DENG XIAO-PING.

Zhukov, Georgi (1896-1974) Soviet commander in the Second World War. Zhukov fought in the Russian Revolution in 1917, and as a cavalry commander in the Russian Civil War from 1918 to 1921. In 1939 he led the defence against Japanese attacks in the Far East. Put in command on the south-western front, he defeated the Germans at STALINGRAD in 1943 and, with Marshal Voroshilov, raised the siege of Leningrad. Zhukov led the assault on Germany in 1945, captured Berlin and became commander of the Soviet zone in occupied Germany. In 1946 he became commander of all Soviet ground forces but was later demoted by Joseph Stalin. After Stalin's death he became defence minister. Zhukov supported Nikita KHRUSHCHEV against his political enemies in 1957, but was dismissed for insisting on reducing the role of the Communist Party in the army. He was reinstated after Khrushchev was deposed in 1964.

Zia ul-Haq, General Mohammed

(1924-88) Pakistani army officer and politician. In 1977 Zia ul-Haq, as army chief of staff, led a military coup against Zulfikar Ali BHUTTO. Zia then introduced a strict Islamic code of law. In 1978 he became president of Pakistan. His refusal to prevent Bhutto's execution in 1979 was internationally condemned. Martial law was lifted in 1986, but Zia remained in dispute with his provincial governments. He was killed in a plane crash, in which sabotage was suspected.

ziggurat Temple in the shape of a stepped pyramid found in ancient Babylonia and Assyria, where they were built from the 3rd millennium BC to the 6th century BC. Access to the shrine was by a ramp or stairway on one side, but nearly half the known ziggurats had no means of ascent. The Mayan people of Central America built similar structures.

Zimbabwe Country in south-east Africa, formerly the British colony of Southern Rhodesia. Between the 5th and 10th centuries AD

Bantu-speaking peoples (whose descendants are the Shona people) moved south of the Zambezi river. They displaced the indigenous Bushmen, established settlements and worked metal. By the 10th century gold and copper were being exported to Arabia from more than 1000 mines. For two centuries from about 1250, Great Zimbabwe was the capital of the Shona kingdom of the Mwene Mutapa, which extended from the river Zambezi to the river

Zimbabwe, an African word for 'stone houses', is named after the ruins of Great Zimbabwe, where this conical tower still stands within high walls.

Limpopo. The kingdom's wealth was founded on the Indian Ocean gold trade, and on tin, iron, copper, salt and grain.

The Portuguese began to make incursions in the 1530s. In the 17th century the fortunes of the Mwene Mutapa started to decline. In the 1690s the Portuguese were driven out by the Rozwi empire. Rozwi rule remained a major force in southern Africa in the 18th century but was ended in the 1830s by an invasion of the Ndebele from the south under their leader Mzilikazi. He created the kingdom of Matabeleland, and secured a peace treaty with the Boer Republic of the TRANSVAAL. In 1888 his son, Lobengula, granted mineral rights to agents of Cecil RHODES. Pioneers from South Africa arrived in 1890, and in 1896 Rhodesia was founded.

In 1923 Rhodesia became the self-governing British colony of Southern Rhodesia. After the victory of the right-wing Rhodesia Front in 1962, the colony refused British demands for Black political participation in government. In 1965 Prime Minister Ian Smith issued a Unilateral Declaration of Independence (UDI) for Rhodesia, and the guerrilla forces of the Zimbabwe African People's Union (ZAPU) and the Zimbabwe African National Union (ZANU) waged war in the country.

After the Lancaster House Conference in London in 1979, Robert MUGABE, the leader of ZANU, was elected prime minister, and the following year Rhodesia became the Republic of Zimbabwe. In 1987 a new constitution was introduced and ZAPU and ZANU were merged into one party. In 1995 Mugabe's government was re-elected for the fourth time. The leader of the only opposition party to win seats, Ndabaningi Sithole, was arrested later the same year on charges of conspiracy to assassinate Mugabe.

Zimmermann telegram (January 19, 1917) German secret telegram, the interception of which led to the USA entering the First World War. The telegram contained a coded message from the German foreign secretary Alfred Zimmermann to the German minister in Mexico City, instructing him to propose an alliance with Mexico against the USA, and offering territories which Mexico had lost to the United States in 1848: Texas, New Mexico and Arizona. The British intercepted the message and gave a copy to the US ambassador. The possibility of a German-backed attack through Mexico removed support in the USA for ISOLATIONISM, and on April 6, 1917, the USA declared war on Germany.

Zinoviev, Grigori (1883-1936) Soviet communist leader. Despite originally opposing the Russian Revolution, he became chairman from 1919 to 1926 of the COMINTERN, the world organisation of communist parties. In October 1924 a letter, apparently signed by him but almost certainly a forgery, was sent to the British Communist Party, urging revolution in Britain. Appearing in British newspapers four days before the general election, it swung votes away from Britain's first Labour government, which lost the election. On Vladimir Lenin's death in January 1924, Zinoviev formed a triumvirate with Joseph STALIN and Lev Kamenev, but he lost power and was executed after Stalin's first show trial.

Zionism Political movement advocating the return of Jews to Palestine. The founder of Zionism was Theodor HERZL, who in 1896

published his *Jewish State,* an outline scheme for a Jewish state under Ottoman rule. In 1897 he established the World Zionist Congress in Basel, Switzerland. In 1917 the British Government expressed support for a homeland for the Jews in the BALFOUR DECLARATION. To implement this, in 1920 Britain received a mandate from the League of Nations to govern Palestine, which lasted until 1948. During this period the World Zionist Organisation under Chaim WEIZMANN played a major part in the development of the Jewish community in Palestine, despite conflict with both Palestinian Arabs and the British. The massacres of the Nazi HOLOCAUST increased international support for the creation of a Jewish homeland, Israel, in 1948.

Zog (1895-1961) King of Albania. Born Ahmed Bey Zogu, he was prime minister of ALBANIA from 1922 to 1924, president from 1925 to 1928 and King Zog I from 1928 to 1939. A constitution gave Zog control of the country, and he championed its modernisation. He relied on Italy for financial help, and by 1939 the Italian dictator Benito Mussolini controlled both Albania's finances and its army. An Italian invasion in April ended Albania's independence, forcing Zog into exile. He died in France.

Zollverein German customs union established in 1834. In 1818 Prussia abolished all internal trade customs, and in 1828 the union was extended to the first of several neighbouring states. In 1834 18 German states joined the Zollverein – German for 'customs union' – to make a common market of 26 million people. Member states had the advantages of access to the sea, funding for building roads (and later railways), their own customs administrations and a veto over economic policy. Since receipts were divided by population and not by business transacted, smaller states received proportionally more income than Prussia, the state which dominated the union. Other than Bremen and Hamburg, all the German states had joined by 1867, the year a German parliament was established for economic matters.

The Zollverein led to increased industrial prosperity, and was a significant step in the unification of Germany, completed with the proclamation of the German Empire in 1871.

Zoroastrian Follower of the religious doctrines originally spread in Persia by Zarathustra – also known as Zoroaster – in the 6th century BC. Zoroastrians believe that the world is the site of a cosmic battle that is continually raging between good and evil, with man free to choose between the two.

Eventually the good god and creator Ahura Mazda, the Wise Lord, will defeat the power of evil personified by Ahriman. The Zoroastrian scriptures, the *Avesta,* contain the *Ahura Vairya,* their most sacred prayer, and relate the creation history of the world as a drama divided into four periods of 3000 years each.

Zoroastrianism was the state religion in Persia under the Sassanian dynasty (3rd-7th century AD), but an Islamic invasion in 642 resulted in the persecution and emigration of believers. Isolated groups survived there, but the focus of emigration was Gujarat, India, where the new cult flourished due to Hindu toleration. There Zoroastrians became known as Parsees (from the Persian *parsi,* 'Persian'). Characteristic religious practices include the preservation of the sacred fire, and disposal of the dead by exposure on 'towers of silence'.

Zulu War (1879) War fought between Britain and Zululand in eastern SOUTH AFRICA. By 1843 Britain had two colonies in South Africa: the Cape and Natal. The discovery of gold and diamonds in the 1860s made the Colonial Office under Lord Carnarvon consider forming all southern Africa into a British confederation, which would involve annexing fiercely independent local states such as the Transvaal and Zululand. In 1877 the Transvaal was duly annexed.

In 1878 a pretext for invading Zululand was discovered: the existence of a huge Zulu army of around 60000 men. The Zulu king Cetshwayo ignored an ultimatum to disband this force, and in January 1879 a British army entered Zululand. On January 22 the British suffered one of their worst defeats in any colonial war, when an ill-prepared column of some 1700 troops was almost entirely wiped out at Isandhlwana. Later the same day a garrison of about 120 British and Boer soldiers fended off an attack by several thousand Zulus at the mission station at Rorke's Drift with minimal loss of life. The heroic defence resulted in the award of 11 Victoria Crosses – a record for a single engagement. Pausing for reinforcements, the British invaded again in March, defeated the Zulus and burned their capital Ulundi. Cetshwayo was captured and taken to Cape Town, and then London. Zululand was annexed in 1887, and became part of Natal in 1897.

DID YOU KNOW?

The captured Zulu king, Cetshwayo, was taken to London to plead his cause. Installed in a house in Kensington, he was taken on tours of the capital and had lunch with the Queen.

Zwingli, Ulrich (1484-1531) Swiss Protestant reformer. A fine scholar who had taught himself Greek, Zwingli studied at the universities of Berne, Vienna and Basel before being ordained and becoming a pastor at Glarus in Switzerland in 1506. He fell deeply under the influence of the Dutch humanist Desiderius ERASMUS. As pastor at Einsiedeln from 1516

The British expected an easy victory in the Zulu War, and were astonished by the fierce and determined resistance of the Zulus.

to 1518, Zwingli began to formulate doctrines which led him to renounce the Roman Catholic Church. Like Martin LUTHER, but probably independently of him, he recognised the scriptures as the only spiritual authority. He believed that priests should have the right to marry, and sought to abolish monasteries and ban the sale of indulgences, which offered remission of the punishment for sins in return for payments of money to the Church.

After becoming preacher at the Great Minster in Zürich in 1518, he played a significant part in converting the city's authorities to Protestantism. At a public disputation with a papal representative in 1523 Zwingli presented his doctrines in 67 theses, and these were adopted by the general council of Zürich as the official Reformed creed to be followed by all priests within the canton. His secret and illegal marriage of two years standing was publicly celebrated in 1524.

Zwingli denied the bodily presence of Christ in the bread at Eucharist, and split with Luther over this question. The division was so deep that any union of the Protestant branches proved impossible.

Zwingli was killed at the Battle of Kappel in which Zürich was defending itself against the Roman Catholic cantons of Switzerland. John CALVIN succeeded Zwingli as the champion of the Reformation in Switzerland.

Timelines in history

The charts on the next 20 pages present an at-a-glance overview of world history from the earliest times to our own. They show which events, though often widely separated geographically, happened at the same time, and help to explain how political and cultural events may have influenced each other.

A shaman or sorcerer kills a bison, in a cave painting of around 10 000 BC at Lascaux, France.

EUROPE

c.10 000 Ice sheet recedes; hunter-gatherers colonise northern Europe
c.9000 First settlement of islands in the Mediterranean

Gold chest ornament, Bulgaria c.6000 BC.

c.6500 Agriculture spreads into south-east Europe
c.6000 First pottery produced
c.5200 Farming spreads widely into south-east Europe

c.5000 First ships appear in Mediterranean
c.5000 First metal objects, in gold and copper
c.5000 Pottery and carved figurines in Balkans
c.4500 Plough first used in south-east Europe
c.4500 Chamber tombs built in France
c.3500 Wheeled vehicles in central Europe

c.3000 Olives, vines, cereals in Aegean area
c.2300 Start of Bronze Age in Europe
c.2100 Stonehenge, England, in final form
c.1600 Mycenaeans dominant in Greece
c.1600 Linear A writing in Crete;
c.1450 Linear B
c.1250 Sack of Troy ends Trojan War
c.1200 Dark Age in Greece follows Mycenaean fall

c.1000 Greek settlers colonise Aegean coast
c.900 Etruscans in north Italy
c.800 First iron-using societies, Hallstatt, Austria
c.750 Greeks adopt Phoenician alphabet

ASIA

Clay mask of c.10 000 BC found in Amman, Jordan.

c.10 000 Food plants grown in Fertile Crescent, Middle East
c.10 000 First pottery made in Japan
c.9750 Peas, beans, water chestnuts grown in Thailand
c.9000 Jericho growing into a town of 2000 people
c.8500 Sheep domesticated in Fertile Crescent
c.8000 First farmers bring revolution in human culture

c.7000 Domestication of cattle and pigs
c.7000 Pottery, spinning, weaving, copper in western Asia
c.6500 Plaster human statues, Ain Ghazal, Jordan
c.6500 Çatal Hüyük, Anatolia growing into a town of 10 000 people
c.6000 First irrigation schemes, in Tigris and Euphrates valleys
c.6000 First farming in India
c.6000 Domesticated plants and animals in China
c.6000 Earliest pottery made in China

c.5000 Wet-field rice in China
c.4500 World's first temple at Eridu, Sumer
c.3500 Earliest cities develop in Mesopotamia
c.3000 First writing, cuneiform, at Uruk, Sumer
c.3000 Development of civilisation along Indus Valley

Pictograms, Uruk, Sumer, c.3000 BC.

c.2350 King Sargon of Akkad founds first great empire
c.1810-1750 First Assyrian Empire at its height
c.1595 Hittites sack Babylon
c.1500 Collapse of Indus Valley cities
c.1500 Aryan invasions into northern India
1450 Hittite Empire
1250 Israelites return to Canaan
c.1010 David unites Jews; capital at Jerusalem

Board game from Ur, Sumer, 3000 BC.

c.1000 Maps, dictionary in China
c.970 Solomon builds first temple in Jerusalem
c.922 Solomon dies: Judah and Israel split
911 New Assyrian Empire major power in Middle East

AMERICA

c.10 000 Hunter-gatherers in nomadic groups
c.9000 Hunters spread south through the Americas
c.8500 First experiments with farming in the Andes

c.7000 Squash, beans, chilli peppers grown in Mexico
c.7000 Potatoes and other root crops grown in Andes
c.7000 Manioc (cassava) grown in Amazon

c.5000 Maize grown in Tehuacán Valley, Mexico
c.4000 Amazon pottery, the earliest known in the Americas
c.3500 Farmers in Peru grow cotton; **c.3200** maize

c.3000 Pottery in Ecuador, Colombia; **c.2300** Mexico
c.1200 Agriculture spreads through North America
c.1150 Beginning of Olmec civilisation in Mexico

c.1000 Copper smelting in the Andes
c.900 La Venta becomes new Olmec centre
c.850 Chavín culture emerges in Peru

AFRICA

c.10 000 Hunter-gatherers in nomadic groups
c.9000 Stone used to rub husks off grain in Egypt
c.9000 Nile burials show evidence of wounds and war

c.7000 Pastoral farmers in Libya and Algeria
c.6000 Rock paintings in central Sahara

c.5000 Cattle herding in fertile Sahara
c.5000 Farming begins in Egypt
c.3100 King Menes unites Egypt; capital at Memphis
c.3100 Hieroglyphic writing in Egypt

c.2686-2181 Egypt: Old Kingdom; **c.2040-1782** Middle Kingdom; **c.1570-1070** New Kingdom
c.2650 Step Pyramid; **c.2584-2465** Pyramids, Sphinx at Giza

Chavín bottle with effigy, Peru, c.800 BC.

c.900 Kingdom of Napata, north-east Africa, founded
814 Phoenicians found Carthage

| 10 000 BC | 7000 BC | 5000 BC | 3000 BC | 1000 BC |

The Greek sphinx, as in this marble of around 570 BC, was unlike the Egyptian sphinx in its woman's head and bird's wings.

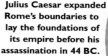

A head of Apollo in Syria (left) honoured King Antiochus I who claimed descent from the Greek god.

Julius Caesar expanded Rome's boundaries to lay the foundations of its empire before his assassination in 44 BC.

---

776 First Olympic Games
c.750 *Odyssey* and *Iliad* completed in modern form
c.753 Legendary founding of Rome by Romulus
c.683 Athens replaces kings with elected officials

A later minting of one of the first coins, Lydia c.800 BC.

c.800 Hinduism spreads south and east
722 Sargon II of Assyria conquers Babylon, Judah
700 First coins struck in Lydia
689 Babylon falls to Assyrians
660 Legend says Japan founded by Jimmu
650 Zoroaster in Persia
c.614 Medes and Babylonians destroy Assyria
c.600 Nebuchadnezzar II builds Hanging Gardens of Babylon

c.800 Monte Albán, Oaxaca, Mexico founded
c.700 Bering Straits peoples develop Arctic fishing life

750 Nubians conquer Egypt
c.700 Iron tools and weapons used in North Africa
671 Assyrians conquer Egypt
664-332 Princes of Sais reunite Egypt

---

510 Rome a republic: last Etruscan king expelled
480 Greek navy destroys Persians at Salamis
c.480 Classical age of Greek culture begins
478 Delian League formed, core of Athenian empire
431-404 Peloponnesian War, Sparta defeats Athens
c.430 Hippocrates revolutionises ideas on medicine

600 Taoism in China
587 Nebuchadnezzar II destroys Jerusalem
550 Persian empire founded by Cyrus II
539 Persians destroy Babylonian empire
c.500 Parts of Indian epic *Ramayana* written
c.500 Cast iron in China
473 Prince Vijaya founds new kingdom in Sri Lanka
460 Parchment replaces clay tablets in Persia

The 'Candelabra' is among the enigmatic patterns of c.200 BC in the Nazca Desert of Peru.

c.600 Adena culture in N. America builds earthworks
c.500 Early hieroglyphics at Monte Albán, Mexico
c.450-250 Peak of Chavín influence in Andes

510 First treaty between Rome and Carthage
c.500-AD 200 Nok civilisation in Nigeria
450 Iron-making in sub-Saharan Africa
404 Egyptian rebels revolt against Persian rule

---

390 Celts sack Rome
334-326 Alexander the Great's campaigns
c.280 Colossus of Rhodes built
264-241 First Punic War: Rome fights Carthage
218-201 Second Punic War: Carthage invades Italy
218 Hannibal of Carthage crosses Alps with elephants

331 Alexander routs Persians at Gaugamela
326 Alexander turns back from India
304-64 Seleucid empire in Persia
269-38 Asoka establishes Buddhist empire in India
221-210 First Emperor of China, Shih Huang-Di
210 Soldiers in terracotta guard Emperor Shih's tomb

c.5300-AD 300 Peak of Gallinazo culture, Peru
c.250 Emergence of lowland Maya centres, Guatemala

331 Alexander captures Egypt
323 Ptolemies rule Egypt from Alexandria
c.280 Pharos (lighthouse) of Alexandria built
202 Scipio defeats Hannibal of Carthage at Zama

---

c.200 Continental Celts push back Ancient Britons
c.200 Romans develop concrete as a building material
186 Bacchanalian orgies banned in Rome
c.160 Public libraries in Rome
149-146 Third Punic War: Rome defeats Carthage
c.140 Venus de Milo

c.202-AD 220 Han reunite China
c.200 Parts of Indian epic *Mahabharata* written
165-163 Maccabean revolt in Judah
142 Jews liberate Jerusalem and make it their capital
136 Confucianism becomes state religion of China
c.112 Silk Road opens between China and West

c.200 Nazca Lines, huge patterns in Peruvian desert
c.100-AD 750 Teotihuacán, Mexico, at its height

c.197 Rosetta Stone inscribed in Egypt
146 Carthage razed by Rome at end of Punic War
146 Rome founds province of Africa
c.100 Ptolemaic dynasty weakens hold on south Egypt

73-71 Spartacus leads Roman slave revolt
58-51 Caesar conquers Gaul
55 Caesar lands in Britain
49 Caesar crosses Rubicon, starts civil war
48 Caesar defeats Pompey, ends Republic
44 Caesar murdered on ides of March
31 Octavius wins Battle of Actium against Egypt
30 Octavius becomes Roman emperor Augustus

64 Pompey conquers Syria; end of Seleucid empire
63 Romans capture Jerusalem
53 Battle of Carrhae: Parthians defeat Romans
c.5 Strabo compiles Geography of known world
c.4 Jesus Christ born

Copper bird with pearl eye, Hopewell culture c.100 BC.

c.100 Hopewell phase succeeds Adena in Ohio valley
36 Earliest dated stele (gravestone), Chiapa de Corzo

51-30 Cleopatra VII, Queen of Egypt
47 Fire destroys great library of Alexandria
46 Numidia in North Africa under Roman control

---

800 BC   **600 BC**   **400 BC**   **200 BC**   **100 BC**

Roman engineers built the Pont du Gard aqueduct to bring water to Nîmes, France.

This portrait of a couple was buried in the ruins of Pompeii after Vesuvius erupted in 79.

Hadrian's Wall was the northernmost frontier of Rome.

EUROPE

c.5 Ovid: *Metamorphoses*
9 Romans beaten at Teutoburg Forest, Germany
c.10 Torches used to light main roads in Rome
14 Emperor Augustus succeeded by Tiberius
c.14 Pont du Gard, aqueduct, built at Nîmes
41-54 Claudius Emperor of Rome
43 Romans invade Britain; **c.43** found City of London
1st century: Latin writers Tacitus, Juvenal, Martial,

54-68 Nero, Emperor of Rome
c.58 St Paul: *Letters to the Corinthians*
61 Iceni under Boudicca revolt against Romans in Britain
64 Great Fire of Rome
64 First persecution of Christians
68-9 Vespasian Emperor of Rome
c.70-79 Pliny the Elder: *Natural History*
79 Vesuvius erupts, destroying Pompeii, Herculaneum
80 Colosseum opened in Rome
98-117 Trajan Emperor of Rome

106 Romans conquer Dacia
c.110 Aqueduct at Segovia, Spain
c.110 Trajan's Column erected in Rome
117 Roman Empire reaches greatest extent
117-38 Hadrian Emperor of Rome
118-30 Pantheon rebuilt; first large dome in Rome
122-26 Hadrian's Wall built across northern Britain; **c.142** Antonine Wall built farther north in Britain
138-61 Antoninus Pius Emperor of Rome
2nd century: Temple of Mithras built in London.

164-80 Roman Empire stricken by plague
174-80 Marcus Aurelius: *Meditations*
177 Christian uprising in Lyons
179 Romans defeat Marcomanni at Vindobona
180 Romans pushed back behind Hadrian's Wall
c.190 Galen extracts plant juices for medicinal purposes
192-97 Civil War in Roman Empire
193-211 Septimus Severus Emperor of Rome

c.200 Germanic tribes attack Roman frontiers
208 Britain divided into two Roman provinces
212 Roman citizenship given to all free people of empire
212-17 Baths of Caracalla built in Rome
220 Goths invade Balkans
c.225 *Origen Hexapla*, version of Old Testament
233-8 Franks make incursions into Roman Empire
c.250 Persecution of Christians increases

ASIA

6 Judaea becomes Roman province
9-25 China's 400-year Han dynasty briefly interrupted by Wang Mang's Xin dynasty
c.27 Jesus begins ministry in Galilee
c.33 Jesus crucified by the Romans
43-57 Missionary journeys of St Paul
c.50 Porcelain first made in China

c.60 Rise of Kushan Empire
66-70 Jews of Judaea revolt against Roman rule
70 Romans sack Jerusalem and destroy Temple
c.78-102 Kushan Empire gains control of northern India
91 Chinese defeat Huns (Hsiung-nu) in Mongolia
c.58 St Paul: *Epistle to the Romans*
Gospels: St Mark **c.70**; St Matthew **c.80**; St Luke **c.80**; St John **c.100**

c.100 First metal working on South-east Asian islands
c.105 Ts'ai Lun makes paper in China
c.106 Romans annex Arabia
114 Romans take Armenia
116 Romans complete conquest of Mesopotamia
132-5 Jews revolt against Romans in Judaea
132 Romans raze Jerusalem

150 Earliest surviving Sanskrit inscription
155 Parthians invade Armenia, defeated by Romans
162-6 Romans fight Parthian wars
165 Romans conquer northern Mesopotamia; **166** Ctesiphon and Seleucia burnt by Romans
184 'Yellow Turbans' rebel in Han China
c.190 Abacus in use in China

Scene from the life of Rama in the Indian epic *Ramayana*.

c.200 Indian Sanskrit epics *Ramayana, Mahabharata* take on their definitive form
200-540 White Huns invade Afghanistan
220 End of Han Dynasty: China splits into three

AMERICA

c.1 Complex cultures emerge on North Pacific coast
c.1-700 Moche dominate coast of northern Peru

c.50-600 Peak of Recuay culture, Santa Valley, Peru

c.100 Anasazi farmers in south-west North America
c.100 Moche Pyramids of Sun and Moon, Peru

c.150 Pyramids of Sun and Moon at Teotihuacán, Mexico

A Nok head.

c.200-700 Monte Albán, Mexico, at peak
c.250 Maya city of Tikal remodelled under new dynasty

AFRICA

44 Mauretania annexed by Romans
c.50 Kingdom of Axum (Ethiopia) expands

c.70 Christianity reaches Alexandria
c.80 Hero of Alexandria attempts steam propulsion

115-17 Jews riot against Romans in Cyrenaica
c.150 Berber, Mandingo tribes begin to dominate Sudan

c.150 Nok culture continues to flourish, Nigeria
c.150 Ptolemy: *Geographia*

c.200 Coptic Church founded
c.250 Diophantus of Alexandria: *Arithmetica*

AD 1　　**50**　　**100**　　**150**　　**200**

Pyramids in two continents: The Pyramid of the Sun and the Avenue of the Dead of 150 in Mexico (above), and pyramids of 300 in the Meroë region, Sudan (right).

Maya sun-god carved on an incense burner, Mexico.

251 Visigoths invade Roman provinces in Dacia
253 Franks and Alemanni invade Gaul
257 Franks invade Spain
268 Goths sack Athens, Sparta and Corinth
269 Romans defeat Goths at Doberus and Naissus
277 Romans recapture Gaul from Franks and Alemanni
285 Diocletian splits Roman empire into east and west
286 British rebels under Carausius drive out Romans
296 Romans recover Britain

Roman gold coin depicting Emperor Valerian.

260 Persians defeat Romans, capture Valerian
265-316 Succession of small states in China
268 Palmyrenes conquer Syria and Mesopotamia
273 Romans overthrow kingdom of Palmyra
297 Romans drive Persians from Armenia

c.290 Lord of Sipan buried with rich grave goods, Peru
c.300 Mexican city of Cuicuilco devastated by volcanic lava

269 Palmyrenes conquer parts of Egypt
c.300 Axum gains control of Red Sea trade

---

c.300 Large-scale iron production in northern Europe
312 Constantine wins Battle of Milvian Bridge
313 Edict of Milan grants tolerance of Christianity
324-30 Constantinople founded on site of Byzantium, and becomes capital of Roman Empire
325 Constantine forbids public gladiatorial combats.
4th century: plainsong develops.

300 Formation of Yamoto state, Japan
304 Hsiung-nu (Huns) invade China
310-79 Shapur II, ruler of Persia
316 China divided into northern and southern realms
320 Chandragupta I founds Gupta Empire, north India
c.350 Hun invasions of Persia and India

c.300 Hopewell Indian chiefdoms set up, North America
c.300-900 Maya civilisation in classic period

Vessel cover, Meroë, Sudan.

350 Axum destroys kingdom of Meroë (Kush)

---

357 Romans defeat Alemanni at Strasbourg
c.360 Scrolls begin to be replaced by books
360 Picts and Scots break through Hadrian's Wall; **370** driven back by Theodosius
362 First public hospital for the sick, Rome
c.370 Huns appear in Europe
c.375 Goths allowed to settle within Roman Empire
378 Visigoths defeat Romans at Adrianople
392 Pagan worship prohibited in the Roman Empire
393 Olympic Games banned
396 Visigoths invade Greece

359 Persians invade Syria
c.360 Chinese merchants reach Euphrates
365 Persia and Armenia unite; **386** Union ends: Romans and Persians divide Armenia
386 Northern Wei dynasty founded in China
c.399-420 Yazdegerd I, ruler of Persia

c.350-1200 Tiahuanaco culture dominates Andes
c.350-500 Peak of Nazca culture, Peru

395 (-430) St Augustine is Bishop of Hippo

---

402 Western Imperial Court moves from Milan to Ravenna
406 Vandals, Alans and Sueves invade Roman Empire
410 Visigoths under Alaric sack Rome
410 Roman legions withdraw from Britain to protect Italy
415 Visigoths establish kingdom at Toulouse
416 Visigoths conquer Vandal kingdom in Spain
435 St Patrick begins mission in Ireland
c.440 Theodosian Code summarises Roman law
c.450 Angles, Saxons, Jutes begin conquest of Britain

c.400 Writing begins in Japan with Chinese ideographs
405 Kingdom of Yamoto gains supremacy in Japan
420 Nanking becomes capital of northern China
428 Reunion of Persia and Armenia
430 Hephtalite Huns of central Asia invade Persia
434 (-453) Attila rules the Huns

c.400 Rise of Amazonian Marajoara culture
c.450 Teotihuacán influence found in Maya territory

c.400 First towns in sub-Saharan Africa
429 Vandal kingdom set up in North Africa

---

451 Battle of Catalaunian Fields: Huns leave Gaul
452 Huns invade Italy, but are persuaded by Pope Leo I to stop
452 Venice founded
455 Vandals sack Rome;
468 Vandals take Sicily
470 Huns withdraw from Europe
476 Romulus Augustulus abdicates; end of Roman Empire in West
486 Frankish Kingdom founded by Clovis
488 Ostrogoths invade Italy; **493** take Ravenna; Theodoric establishes kingdom of Italy

Palace of the Ostrogoth king Theodoric in Ravenna, Italy.

477 Buddhism becomes state religion in China
479-502 Ch'i dynasty established in southern China
c.480 White Huns destroy Gupta Empire in India
c.480 First Shinto shrines built in Japan

c.500 Huari peoples rising to power in Peru
c.500 Teotihuacán, Mexico, sixth largest city in the world

c.500 Bantu farmers and herdsmen reach South Africa

250　　　**300**　　　**350**　　　**400**　　　**450**

The flowering of Byzantine art produced mosaics such as this in Ravenna showing the Three Wise Men.

A miniature of St Mark adorns the Lindisfarne Gospels (right), produced on Holy Island in c.700.

Figures erected by the Toltec peoples in the 8th century stand guard on a pyramid in Tula, Mexico.

EUROPE

507 Franks under Clovis defeat Visigoths at Vouillé

507-11 Visigoth kingdom established in Spain

527-65 Justinian Emperor of Byzantium

533 Justinian restores Roman power in Italy

536 Byzantines take Naples and Rome from Ostrogoths

c.550 Bubonic plague ravages Europe

Alaric II of Visigoths submits to Clovis.

c.550 Church bells first used in France

c.550 Golden age of art in Byzantium

c.554 Justinian reconquers part of Spain

c.555 Franks take Bavaria

c.568 Lombards take over northern Italy

597 St Augustine begins mission to Britain

600 Arles Cathedral, France, begun

603 Lombards convert to Christianity

603 Slavs invade Balkan peninsula

610-41 Heraclius Emperor of Byzantium

c.625 Sutton Hoo ship burial in England

633 Byzantines driven out of Spain by Arabs

c.674-8 Arabs win extensive territory from Byzantium

c.680 Bulgars invade the Balkans

685 Picts fight off Northumbrian invasion of Scotland

687 Battle of Tertry: Pepin II sole ruler of Franks

698 Monastery of St Peter's, Salzburg

c.700 Lindisfarne Gospels: first Anglo-Saxon psalms

711-18 Muslim invasion of Spain

c.715 Anglo-Saxon epic *Beowulf* written down

716 Bulgar state recognised by Byzantine Empire

718 Arab siege of Constantinople fails

720 Arabs occupy Narbonne, France

722 St Boniface begins conversion of Germans

732 Franks under Charles Martel defeat Arabs at Poitiers

ASIA

c.500 Decimal system devised in India

503-5 War between Byzantium and Persia

c.531 Persian Sassanid empire at greatest extent

535 Northern Wei dynasty in China splits into two

540-62 Renewed war between Byzantium and Persia

Persian Sassanid coin depicting Shapur II.

c.550 Buddhism introduced to Japan from South Korea

562 Japanese driven from Korea

589 Sui dynasty reunites China

c.618-906 China united under Tang dynasty

622 Hijra: migration from Mecca and birth of Islam

630 Mecca submits to Muhammad

632 Death of Muhammad: Arab expansion begins

638 Jerusalem captured by Muslims

642-51 Arabs conquer Sassanid empire

c.645 Buddhism reaches Tibet

Great Mosque of Okba, Tunisia, 7th century.

661 Ummayad Caliphs: Islam rules a third of the Old World

665 Expansion of Tibet

668 Korea unified under Silla

676 Chinese withdraw from Korea

685 Buddhism becomes state religion of Japan

691 Dome of the Rock built in Jerusalem

c.700 Golden age of Chinese poetry

705 Great Mosque, Damascus

705 Arabs invade Turkistan and gradually win control

710-94 Nara period, Japan

714 Arabs conquer Sind and Samarkand

745 Beginning of Uighur empire in Mongolia

748 First printed newspaper, Beijing

AMERICA

c.500 Flutes, horns, tubas and drums used in Peru

562-94 Thirty-two-year drought in Mochica kingdom of Peru

c.600-900 Peak of Maya civilisation in Mexico

c.600 Peak of Peruvian empire based on Tiahuanaco

628 Copán, Honduras, becomes a major city of Maya civilisation

c.700 Hohokam, Mogollon, Anasazi cultures, N America

c.700 Mississippi temple-mounds: Cahokia first town in North America

c.700 Height of Tikal, Maya centre in Guatemala

c.700-900 Colombia society centred on Murillo

750 Rise of Toltecs in Mexico; Tollan (Tula) becomes capital

AFRICA

533-48 Byzantines conquer Vandal kingdom in North Africa

540 Nubians convert to Christianity

547 Byzantines crush rebellious Berber tribes

c.550 Draw looms used in Egypt to weave patterned silk

c.570 Sef ibn Dhi Yazan founds Kanem-Borno

615 Muslim refugees from Arabia given refuge in Axum

642 Arabs conquer Egypt

646 Governor of Carthage rebels against Byzantium

647 Arabs conquer Tripoli

651 Arabs invade Nubia; **694** take Maghreb; **697** overrun Carthage; Berber revolt against Arabs crushed

670 Kairouan founded in Tunisia; **c.690** State of Gao founded on Upper Niger

c.700 Rise of empire of Ghana

700 Arabs conquer Algiers; **720** Eritrea; **742** crush revolt of Berbers and Kharajites

745 Nubians invade Egypt

AD 500　　　**550**　　　**600**　　　**650**　　　**700**

Pepin III, King of the Franks from 751, was Charlemagne's father.

Moorish arches span Córdoba's 8th-century Great Mosque.

St Mark's, Venice (left), begun in 980, took 300 years to complete.

An effigy of the Maya god Chac at Chichén Itzá may have been used as an altar for sacrifices from 750.

751-68 Pepin III, first Carolingian king of France
751 Lombards take Ravenna, last Byzantine base in Italy
756-1031 Ummayad Caliphate in Córdoba, Spain
768-814 Charlemagne King of Franks
778 Charlemagne defeated at Roncesvalles
788 Great Mosque built at Córdoba, Spain
793-4 Vikings sack Lindisfarne

800 Charlemagne crowned Emperor of the Western Roman Empire
835 Danes begin raids on England, and establish Danelaw settlements
838 Vikings establish permanent base at Dublin
843 Treaty of Verdun: partition of Carolingian Empire

Votive crown of Leo VI, 9th century Byzantine emperor.

859-62 Vikings begin raids into Mediterranean
861 Vikings reach Iceland
863 Cyrillic alphabet created in eastern Europe
866 Conversion of Russia to Christianity begins
871 Alfred the Great halts Danish advance in England
885 Vikings besiege Paris
896 Magyars invade Hungary, set up state

900 Medical school founded in Salerno
c.900 First musical manuscripts, West Europe
911 Rollo the Viking given Dukedom of Normandy
c.930 Flowering of Arab learning in Córdoba, Spain

955 Battle of Lechfeld: Otto I defeats Magyars
962 Otto I of Germany Holy Roman Emperor
972 Beginning of Hungarian state under Duke Geisa
976-1025 Basil II extends frontiers of Byzantium
c.980 St Mark's Cathedral, Venice, begun
c.980-1015 Vladimir ruler of Kiev Russia; **987** adopts Byzantine Christianity
987 End of Carolingian dynasty, France

750 Abbassids overthrow Ummayad Caliphate
c.750-1258 Golden age of Islamic culture
751 Arabs defeat Chinese at Talas river
751 Paper making spreads from China to Muslim world
755-7 Rebellion of An Lu-han in China
760 Arabs develop own system of numerals
762 Abbassids found capital at Baghdad

c.800 First Muslim threat to north India
c.802 Angkorean kingdom founded (later Cambodia)
838 Arabs take city of Armorium, Asia Minor
840 Empire of Uighur Turks in central Asia collapses
c.840 Al Khwarizmi introduces algebra, Baghdad
842 Tibetan Empire disintegrates

850 Arab navigators Wahab and Abu Said reach China
c.850 Arabs perfect astrolabe
c.850 Arabs discover coffee
868 *Diamond Sutra,* first printed book, China
874-1005 Samanid dynasty established in Persia
879 Nepal gains independence from Tibet
c.890 Japanese renaissance: poetry, painting, novels

900 Cholas dominant power in southern India
c.900 *Sepher Yetzirah*, Jewish book of Creation
906 Tang dynasty collapses in China
916 Mongol Khitan empire founded
935 Text of Koran takes its definitive form
939 Vietnam independent of China
947 Khitans overrun N China, establish Liao dynasty

960 Sung dynasty founded in China
c.960 Samanids of Bukhara conquer Afghanistan
967 Fujiwara family establish power in Japan
977-84 Chinese compile 1000-volume encyclopedia
979-1279 Sung dynasty reunites China
986 Khitan Mongols defeat Sung Chinese
988 Central Asian Ghaznavids occupy Kabul
c.1000 Great age of Chinese painting and ceramics

China's Sung dynasty was noted for porcelain.

750 Ceremonies at Maya centre of Chichén Itzá feature ritual offerings
800 First use of bow and arrow in Mississippi valley

800 Beginning of Dorset culture in Greenland and N E Canada
c.800 Last traces of Peru's Mochica civilisation
c.800-1000 Uxmal, Yucatán, an important Maya city

c.900 Chimú city of Chan Chan founded in Peru
c.900 Decline of Nazca culture, Peru
c.900 Collapse of Classic phase of Maya culture

c.900 Chichén Itzá becomes centre of Maya culture
900 Hohokam make irrigation canals
c.900 Anasazi people build pueblos

c.990 Incas lay foundations of their empire in Peru
1000 Viking settlements Labrador, Newfoundland
c.1000 Huari, in the Andes, abandoned

761 Rustamid dynasty founded at Tahert, Algeria
788 Shiite kingdom established in Morocco
793 Fez founded in Morocco

800-1800 Kanem-Borno a great trading empire
828 Kingdom of Morocco divided on death of King Idris II

868-905 Tulunid dynasty established in Egypt and Syria
c.880 Falasha Jews settle in Ethiopia
800 Songhay kingdom of central Africa conquers Gao

900 Arab merchants settle East African coast
901-11 Berbers revolt against Aghlabid emir
909 Fatimid Caliph proclaimed at Mahdiya, Tunisia

957 Kilwa sultanate founded in southern Tanzania
969 Fatimids of Tunisia conquer Egypt, found Cairo
990 Kingdom of Ghana conquers Audaghost

750   **800**   **850**   **900**   **950**

The Normans sail, from the Bayeux tapestry of 1077.

Spanish 11th-century hero El Cid overcomes the Moors.

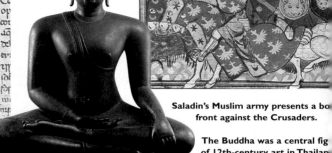

The Buddha was a central figure of 12th-century art in Thailand.

Saladin's Muslim army presents a bold front against the Crusaders.

	AD 1000	1040	1080	1120	1160
EUROPE	**1002** Danes under Sweyn I invade England; **1013** expel English king Ethelred II **1002-24** Henry II, Holy Roman Emperor **1016** Danish king Canute becomes ruler of England **1018** Council of Pavia enforces celibacy of clergy **1021** Epidemic of St Vitus' dance breaks out in Europe **1025** Byzantine Empire at its greatest extent **1031** Hisham III deposed; end of caliphate of Córdoba **1035** William I becomes Duke of Normandy	**1053** Normans conquer south Italy and found empire; **1061** invade Sicily **1054** Kievan Russia begins to decline **1054** Schism between Latin and Greek Churches **1057** Macbeth of Scotland defeated at Dunsinane **1066** English defeat Norwegians at Stamford Bridge **1066** Normans defeat English at Battle of Hastings **1067-77** Bayeux tapestry embroidered **1073** Gregory VII pope: Empire and Papacy in conflict	**1084** Normans sack Rome **1085** Castilians take Toledo from Muslims **1086** Domesday Book completed for William I **1094** El Cid captures Valencia, Spain, from Moors **1095** Pope Urban proclaims First Crusade; **1096** leaves Cologne for Jerusalem **c.1100** Leprosy reappears in Europe **1115** Florence becomes free republic	**1122** Concordat of Worms allows election of bishops **1125** Venetians pillage Rhodes, Chios and Lesbos **1125** Civil war over succession of emperor, Germany **1130** Normans establish kingdom of Sicily **1139** Civil war in England over succession to throne **1147-9** Second Crusade ends in failure **1150-1450** Gothic period in art and architecture **1154** Henry II: Angevin Empire in England and France **1155** Roman Republic crushed by Emperor Frederick I	**1162** Emperor Frederick I seizes and destroys Milan **c.1165** Lombard League founded by 16 north Italian cities **1170** Thomas Becket murdered at Canterbury **1176** Emperor Frederick I accepts papal authority **c.1180** Windmills with vertical sails appear in Europe **1189-92** Richard I of England, 'the Lionheart', leads Third Crusade **1192** Sicily united with Holy Roman Empire **1193** Richard I of England held to ransom in Austria
ASIA	**c.1000** Chinese use gunpowder for fireworks **c.1009** Muslims desecrate Holy Sepulchre, Jerusalem **1018** Mahmud of Ghazni breaks power of Hindu states **1018** Cholas conquer Ceylon; **1021** invade Bengal **1038-1194** Seljuks found Turkish Muslim dynasty	**1040** Seljuk Turks defeat Ghaznavids; **1055** sack Baghdad; **1063** conquer Georgia and Armenia; **1062-71** invade Syria and Asia Minor; take Jerusalem; **1071** defeat Byzantine emperor at Manzikert **1044** First Burmese national state at Pagan **c.1050** First printing from movable type, China **1068-85** She-tsung becomes emperor of China	**Coat-of-arms, Knights of St John, Turkey.** **1095** First Crusade: Franks invade Anatolia, Syria; **1097** Crusaders defeat Turks at Dorylaeum; **1098** take Antioch; **1099** Jerusalem **1113** Order of Knights Hospitallers of St John founded; **1119** Order of Knights Templars founded **1115** Chin Dynasty founded in North China	**1124** Crusaders capture Tyre **1126** Ch'in (Quin) dynasty overrun North China: Sung rule in south only **1144** Seljuk Turks capture kingdom of Edessa; **1148** Turks take Damascus **c.1150** Golden age of Buddhist art **1156-81** Civil war in Japan; **1159** Minamoto defeated by Taira clan in uprising	**1169-1250** Saladin founds Ayyubid dynasty; **1173** conquers Yemen; **1174** Syria; **1183** Aleppo; **1187** Jerusalem **1175** First Muslim empire in India **1176** Byzantines defeated by Seljuks at Myriokephalon **1177** Baldwin IV of Jerusalem beats Saladin at Ramlech **1191** Crusaders capture Acre; **1191** Richard I of England defeats Saladin
AMERICA	**c.1000** Cuzco, southern Peru, founded by Incas **c.1000-1530** Flourishing of Tairona culture, Colombia	**c.1040** Tiahuanaco style pottery in Ayacucho, Peru **c.1060** Decline of Coclé culture in Panama	**c.1100** Cliff homes at Mesa Verde, Colorado, built **1115** Chaco Canyon develops as a social and trade centre	**c.1120** Peak of Lamayeque culture, Peru **c.1150** End of Toltec dominance in central Mexico	**Chimú gold and turquoise ceremonial knife, Peru, c.1200.** **1168** Chichimecs take Toltec capital of Tula **c.1200** Chimú culture expands along coast of Peru
AFRICA	**c.1000** First Iron Age settlements at Zimbabwe **1034** Genoa and Pisa take Bône, Tunis	**1054-1147** Almoravids rule N Africa, Spain; **1062** capital at Marrakesh; **1076** destroy kingdom of Ghana	**c.1100-1250** Rise of Zimbabwe kingdom **c.1100-1600** Muslims convert Ghana	**1135-1269** Almohads rule kingdom in North Africa **1148** Normans subdue Tunis and Tripoli	**1171** Saladin becomes effective ruler of Egypt **1196-1465** Marinid dynasty founded at Fez, Morocco

Ceremonial soapstone pipe, from Oklahoma, USA, 13th century.

Palace of the Popes, Avignon, France.

Dogon horseman from 14th-century Mali.

John Ball, a leader of the 1381 Peasants' Revolt, addresses London crowds.

1202 Arab numerals adopted
1202-4 Fourth Crusade: Franks take Byzantium
1209 St Francis of Assisi sets out rules for his brotherhood
1209-29 Crusade against Albigensians in France
1215 King John of England sets his seal to Magna Carta
1215 Order of friars founded by St Dominic
1236 Ferdinand III captures Córdoba from Moors
1236 Mongols invade Russia, starting conquest

c.1240 Mongols take Russia: Khanate of the Golden Horde; **1241** invade Poland, Hungary, Bohemia
1241 Hanseatic League founded by German trading towns
1242 Alexander Nevsky defeats Teutonic Knights at Lake Peipus
1250 Collapse of imperial power in Germany and Italy
1252 First gold florins struck in Florence
1265 England's first Parliament at Westminster Hall
1276 Muscovite dynasty founded by Daniel, son of Alexander Nevsky

1282 Sicilian Vespers: massacre of French in Sicily
1291 Swiss Confederation established
1295 'Model Parliament' meets in England
c.1300 Gunpowder first manufactured in the West
1306 Philip IV expels Jews from France
1309 Papacy transfers to Avignon: 'Babylonian Captivity'
1313 Knights Templar dissolved by papal decree
1315-19 Widespread floods, famine. cattle plague

c.1320 Cultural revival in Italy
1328 Philip VI founds Valois dynasty in France
1328 Ivan I begins expansion of Moscow
1329 Scottish king Robert Bruce dies of leprosy
1330 Longbow achieves supremacy over crossbow
1338 France and England start 100 Years' War (-1453)
1343 Teutonic Knights buy Estonia from Denmark
1348 Black Death: about 25 million people die in Europe
c.1350 Muzzle-loading guns developed
1358 Revolt of the Jacquerie (peasants) in France

1360 First francs coined in France
1369 Bastille built, Paris
1372 Spanish fleets defeat English off La Rochelle
c.1375 John Wyclif tries to reform English Church
1378 Wyclif denounced by Pope Gregory XI
1378-1417 Great Schism in Papacy
1381 Venice defeats Genoa
1381 Wat Tyler and John Ball lead Peasants' Revolt in England
1387-1400 Geoffrey Chaucer: *Canterbury Tales*
1388 First urban Sanitary Act passed in England
1389 Battle of Kosovo: Ottomans capture Balkans

c.1205 Minamotos replaced by Hojo family, Japan
c.1200 Genghis Khan's Mongols begin conquest of Asia
1206-1526 Sultanate of Delhi
1227 Genghis Khan dies; empire divided between sons
1228-9 Sixth Crusade wins back Jerusalem
1234 Mongols destroy Chin Empire, China
c.1238 First Thai kingdoms emerge

1248-54 Seventh Crusade, led by Louis IX
1251 Kublai Khan, governor of China; **1279** establishes Yuan Dynasty in China
1258 Mongols sack Baghdad: end of Abbassid Caliphate
1270-2 Eighth Crusade
1275 Marco Polo arrives in Beijing

1291 Port of Acre falls to Mamelukes
1293 First Christian missionaries reach China
1294 Kublai Khan dies
1299 Ottoman Empire founded by Osman I, in succession to Seljuk empire
1303 Mongol invaders of Syria defeated at Damascus

1321 Sultanate of Delhi reaches greatest extent
1338 First of Ashikaga shoguns in Japan
c.1341 Black Death in Asia
1354 Ottoman Turks capture Gallipoli
c.1350 Cultural revival in Japan

1368 Ming dynasty succeeds Mongols in China

1369-1405 Tamerlane rules Mongols; **1383** begins conquest of central Asia; **1398** invades India and sacks Delhi
1394 Thais invade Cambodia

Mongols sack Isfahan, 1387.

c.1200 Aztecs occupy valley of Mexico
1225 Moundville settlement, Mississippi valley, North America

c.1250 Decline of Tajín, Veracruz culture, Mexico
c.1260 Chichimec tribes become powerful in Mexico

Pueblo Indian cliff dwellings at Mesa Verde, USA, date from the 11th to 14th centuries.

1283 Mayapán, Maya capital of Yucatán, at its peak
c.1300 Anasazi abandon Mesa Verde

1345 Tenochtitlán, Aztec capital, founded in Mexico
1350 Inca and Chimú states in conflict

c.1370 Chimú ruler Michancamon seized by Incas
c.1380 Expansion of Aztec state in Mexico

c.1200 Emergence of Hausa city states, Nigeria
1219 Fifth Crusade, against Egypt

1250-1517 Mameluke dynasty founded in Egypt
c.1250 Mali empire at its height, West Africa

c.1300 Emergence of empire of Benin, Nigeria

c.1321 Palace of Husuni Kubwa, Kilwa, East Africa
c.1340 Mali, great mosque of Djenné; **1352** Ibn Battuta crosses Sahara to Mali

c.1400 Great Zimbawe enclosures reach final form
c.1400 Bronze heads made in Benin, Nigeria

1200   **1240**   **1280**   **1320**   **1360**

Van Eyck made oil painting show new colours and light.

A bronze lion guards the Forbidden City.

Botticelli's famed *Primavera* ('Spring') is in Florence.

Vlad impaled his enemies on sharp stakes.

EUROPE

c.1400 Portuguese develop three-masted caravel
1400 Leprosy eradicated in Europe
1410 Poles defeat Teutonic Order at Tannenberg
1415 Jan Hus, Bohemian, burnt at stake for heresy
1415 English defeat French at Agincourt
1415 Jan and Hubert van Eyck introduce oil paints
1417 Martin V elected sole pope, ending Great Schism
1419 Hussite Wars break out in Bohemia

1420 Dome of Florence Cathedral begun
1421 Explosive shells, Corsica
1429 Joan of Arc enters Rheims; 1431 burnt at the stake at Rouen for heresy
c.1430 Chain mail succeeded by metal armour
1434-94 Medici ascendancy in Florence
1435 Treaty of Arras between Burgundy and France
1439 Greek and Roman churches unite under pope

c.1450 Dentures made from bone, Switzerland
1450 Florence, Naples and Milan ally to dominate Italy
1454 Peace of Lodi ends feuding among Italian states
c.1450 Gutenberg introduces printing press; c.1455 prints first book: Mazarin Bible
1453 England driven from Continent except Calais
1455 Wars of the Roses begin in England
1456-77 Vlad the Impaler (Dracula) king of Romania

1462-1505 Ivan III 'the Great' rules Moscow
1469-70 Malory: *Le Morte d'Arthur*
1471 Lancastrian forces crushed at Tewkesbury
1472 Printed music published in Bologna, Italy
1475 Peace of Picquigny: English withdraw from France
1476 Caxton establishes printing press at Westminster, London
1479 Aragon and Castile unite to form Spain
1479 Spanish Inquisition begins

1480 Ivan III frees Russia from Mongol rule
1480 Italian Renaissance paintings – Botticelli *Birth of Venus*; 1495-7 Da Vinci *Last Supper*
1483 Torquemada appointed Grand Inquisitor
1494 Spanish drive Moors from Granada, completing *Reconquista*
1494 Treaty of Tordesillas: New World split between Spain and Portugal

ASIA

White marble and glazed blue tiles adorn Beijing's Temple of Heaven.

1401-2 Mongols under Tamerlane defeat Ottomans
1405-33 Cheng Ho's voyages from China to Africa
1406 Temple of Heaven built, China

c.1420 Chinese emperor moves capital to Beijing
1420 Forbidden City begun in Beijing
1421-51 Murad II restores Ottoman power

1447 Tamerlane's empire disintegrates
1451-81 Mohammed II emir of Turks
1453 Ottoman Turks take Constantinople

The tomb of Tamerlane.

1467-77 Onin war causes break-up of Japan
1468 Ottoman Turks conquer Karaman; 1472 defeat Persians at Otlukbeli; 1475 conquer Crimea
1473 Venetians destroy Smyrna

1483 Yoshimasa builds the Silver Pavilion, Japan
1498 Da Gama reaches India round Cape of Good Hope
1498 First toothbrushes in use, in China

AMERICA

1400 Inca empire begins expansion under Viracocha
c.1420 Chimús conquer Lambayeque culture, north Peru

1428 Aztecs conquer rival city of Azcapotzalco
1434 Tenochtitlán, Tlacopán and Texcoco form alliance
1438 Incas defeat rival state of Chanca
1438-71 Pachacuti becomes Inca emperor

1440-69 Montezuma I becomes ruler of the Aztecs
1445 Inca explorers reach Pacific Ocean
c.1450 Middle Mississippi area of North America abandoned

1465 Incas conquer Chimú kingdom in northern Peru
1469-81 Axayácatl ruler of Aztec empire
1471-93 Topa Inca ruler of Inca empire
1476 Incas conquer south coast of Peru

Vespucci's book on America.

1486-1502 Ahuitzotl ruler of Aztec empire
1492 Columbus lands at San Salvador
1499 Amerigo Vespucci reaches South America

AFRICA

c.1400 Gold trade established in Zambezi valley
1402-5 Castilians explore Canary Islands
1415 Portuguese conquer Ceuta, Morocco

1432 Portuguese explorers reach Azores
1434 Portuguese round Cape Bojador, West Africa

1444-5 Portuguese sailors reach Senegal
c.1450 Songhay empire in western Africa at its height

1470 Portuguese reach Gold Coast
1479 Portugal gains trade monopoly of African west coast

1484-6 Diego Cão explores Congo and Zaire rivers
1488 Dias rounds Cape of Good Hope
c.1494 Pedro de Covilhão reaches Ethiopia

AD 1400   1420   1440   1460   1480

Giuliano de Medici, painted by Botticelli.

Babylon burns (above) in Luther's Bible.

Paré, a French surgeon, made this artificial hand.

Arctic Inuit fight Frobisher's crew, who voyaged north to seek gold.

Lord Howard led the English against the Spanish Armada.

c.1500 Peak of the Italian Renaissance – **1503** Da Vinci *Mona Lisa;* **1504** Michelangelo *David,* and **1505-12** Sistine ceiling; **1509** Erasmus *In Praise of Folly;* **1513** Machiavelli *The Prince*

1513 English defeat Scots at Flodden

1516 Coffee, from Arabia

1517 Luther's 95 Theses spark Reformation

1519 Charles V of Spain elected Holy Roman Emperor

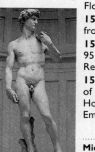

Michelangelo took four years to sculpt *David*.

1501 Shah Ismail founds Safavid dynasty, Persia

1504 Babur occupies Kabul

1511 Portuguese take Malacca

1517 Ottoman Turks capture Palestine

c.1519 Nanak founds Sikhism

1500 Portugal colonises Brazil

1500 Aztec empire at peak

c.1511 Spanish bring African slaves to Caribbean

1519 Magellan sails through straits later named after him

1504 Nubians destroy Christian kingdom of Meroë

1505 Portuguese sack Kilwa and settle in Mozambique

c.1517 Ottomans conquer Egypt

1521 Martin Luther excommunicated at Diet of Worms

1522 Portuguese complete world circumnavigation

1526 Ottoman Turks defeat Hungary at Battle of Mohacs

1527 Charles V, Holy Roman Emperor, sacks Rome

1530 Knights Hospitallers established in Malta

c.1530 Potato introduced from South America

1534 Ignatius Loyola founds Jesuit Order

1534 Henry VIII becomes head of English Church

1534 Luther: German Bible

1539 Ambroise Paré invents artificial hands and limbs

1520 Ferdinand Magellan, navigator, killed in Philippines

1520-66 Suleiman the Magnificent, Ottoman Sultan

1526 Babur defeats Sultan of Delhi at Panipat and begins Mughal dynasty

1521 Spanish conquistador Cortés captures Aztec city of Tenochtitlán

1531-3 Pizarro conquers Incas of Peru

1535 Lima founded

1520 Organised slavery from Africa to New World begins

1529 Ottomans complete conquest of Algeria

1535 Charles V, Holy Roman Emperor, takes Tunis

1541 Ottomans take Hungary

1541 John Calvin founds Reformed Church at Geneva

1543 Copernicus concludes that Earth orbits Sun

1545 Council of Trent: start of Counter-Reformation

1547 Ivan IV 'the Terrible' tsar of Russia

1549 Cranmer: *Book of Common Prayer*

1559 Tobacco from Central America

Copernicus's system (left) put the Sun at the centre, not the Earth.

1549 Christianity introduced to Japan

1552 Ivan IV conquers Tatars of Kazan

1556 Emperor Akbar defeats Hindus at Panipat

1557 Portuguese at Macao

The mountain at Potosi and its mines of silver.

1541 De Soto, Spaniard, reaches Mississippi

1542 Cabrillo, Spaniard, explores Californian coast

1545 Silver mining in Potosi, Bolivia

1544 Portuguese open trading posts in Mozambique

1546 Songhay destroys Mali empire

1554-6 Turks conquer coast of North Africa

1572 St Bartholomew's Day Massacre in French Wars of Religion

1562 English slave trading begins

1563 Seven Years' War between Sweden and Denmark

1564 Peace of Troyes ends Anglo-French War

1569 Mercator produces map of world

1571 Spanish-Venetian fleet beats Ottomans at Lepanto

1572-1648 Dutch revolt against Spain

1565 Mughals defeat Vijayanagara empire, India

1567 Nobunaga deposes Shogunate, Japan

1575 Akbar conquers Bengal

1565 Portuguese found Rio de Janeiro

1565 Spanish destroy Fort Caroline, Florida

1576 Martin Frobisher discovers Frobisher Bay

1576 Portuguese found Luanda

1578 Moroccans defeat Portuguese at Al-Kasr al-Kebir

1580 Spain annexes Portugal

1582 Gregorian calendar introduced

1588 English defeat Spanish Armada

c.1590 First microscope, by Hans and Zacharias Jansen

An Elizabethan playing card.

1592 William Shakespeare: *Richard III;* **1596** *Romeo and Juliet*

1595 Galileo makes first thermometer

1598-1648 Time of Troubles in Russia

1598 Edict of Nantes: religious toleration, France

1581 Yermak begins Russian conquest of Siberia

1590 Hideyoshi unifies Japan

1595 Dutch settlement at Java

1598-1868 Tokugawa restores Shogunate in Japan

1580 Juan de Garay, Spaniard, founds Buenos Aires

1583 English found colony at Newfoundland

1595 Raleigh explores Venezuela in search of El Dorado

1587 War breaks out among Chewa of south-east Africa

1591 Battle of Tondibi: Morocco destroys Songhay

1596 Portuguese build fort at Mombasa

1500   **1520**   **1540**   **1560**   **1580**

Portuguese traders do business after the English leave Japan.

The oak that sheltered the future Charles II is felled after the English Civil War.

EUROPE

1600 English East India Company founded
1602 Dutch East India Company founded
1603 Shakespeare *Hamlet*, *Macbeth*
1605 Gunpowder Plot, London
1608 Telescope invented by Hans Lippershey
1609 Spain expels Moriscos
1609 Dutch and Spanish sign truce in Netherlands

1610 Henry IV of France assassinated
1610 Galileo's discoveries challenge Church
1612 Last two people burnt for heresy in England
1614 French Estates General meets for last time (to 1789)
1618 Sir Walter Raleigh executed
1618 Thirty Years' War started by Defenestration of Prague (-1648)

A 'Coranto' carried foreign news in the 1620s.

1620 Battle of White Mountain: Bohemians defeated
1622 England's *Coranto* among earliest printed newspapers
1625 Denmark enters Thirty Years' War
1628 William Harvey publishes discovery of circulation of the blood
1630 Gustavus Adolphus of Sweden enters Thirty Years' War

1632 Battle of Lützen: Gustavus Adolphus killed
1632 William Oughtred invents slide rule
1635 Peace of Prague ends German part of Thirty Years' War
1635 France enters Thirty Years' War
1639 First milled-edged coins, in France

1640 Portugal regains independence from Spain
1642-5 English Civil War
1649 Execution of King Charles I of England
1649-53 Commonwealth rule in England
1643 Barometer invented by Evangelista Torricelli
1648 Treaty of Westphalia ends Thirty Years' War
1648 Fronde revolts against court in France

Medal marking the execution of Charles I.

ASIA

1603 Tokugawa (Edo) period begins in Japan
1605 Jahangir succeeds Akbar as Mughal emperor
1609 Illustrated encyclopedia in Chinese
1609-16 Blue Mosque built at Constantinople

Blue Mosque, Constantinople.

1613 Akbar's tomb, Sikandra
1614 First English trading post in India, at Surat
1616 Manchus invade China
1617 Jahangir bans smoking
1619 Dutch found Batavia

1623 English leave Japan
1624 Dutch establish trading posts in Taiwan
1627-57 Shah Jahan succeeds Jahangir
1629-42 Safi succeeds Shah Abbas as Safavid ruler

1632 Taj Mahal, India, begun
1635 Shah Jahan first sits on peacock throne
1637 Korea becomes Manchu vassal state
1637 Japan adopts isolationist policies
1638 Mughal court moves from Agra to Delhi

1641 Dutch capture Malacca from Portuguese
1644 Manchus found Ch'ing Dynasty
1645 Manchus make Chinese wear pigtails
1648 Red Fort built at Delhi
1649 Russians reach Pacific

AMERICA

1607 First permanent English settlement, at Jamestown, Virginia
1608 Jesuit state established in Paraguay
1608 Samuel de Champlain founds Quebec
1610 Hudson reaches southern end of Hudson Bay

1612 Tobacco cultivated in Virginia
1613 Champlain establishes fur trade route into interior
1619 First African slaves in North America
1619 First representative assembly, at Jamestown

Tobacco plant in a 1576 woodcut.

1620 Pilgrims cross Atlantic in *Mayflower*
1626 Founding of New Amsterdam
1626 Peter Minuit buys Manhattan for 24 dollars
1628 Nevis the first English settlement in Caribbean

1630-40 Waves of English settlers reach Massachusetts
1636 Harvard College founded
1639 First printing press, Cambridge, Massachusetts

1641 Dutch sugar plantations based on slavery, West Indies
1641 Law code established in Massachusetts
1642 Paul de Maisonneuve founds Montreal
1643 Colonies of New England form federation

AFRICA

1600 Oyo empire, Nigeria, at its height

1613 Paez reaches source of Blue Nile

1626 French settlement in Madagascar
1628 Empire of Mwenemutapa ended by Portuguese

1637 Dutch take El Mina, West Africa, from Portuguese

1642 Portuguese cede Gold Coast to Dutch
1645 Capuchin monks sail up river Congo

AD 1600   **1610**   **1620**   **1630**   **1640**

In 1666 the Great Fire devastated the City of London.

John Bunyan dreams of the sin-laden Christian, at the start of his *Pilgrim's Progress*.

The dodo, a flightless bird, was as big as a swan but unable to defend its eggs from pigs and monkeys.

1652 Russia bans drink shops
1652 End of the Fronde revolts in France
1652-3 First Anglo-Dutch War: Dutch decline begins
1653-8 Oliver Cromwell Lord Protector of England
1654 Russia gains Ukraine in war with Poland
1654 Blaise Pascal states theory of probability
1656 St Peter's, Rome, completed by Bernini
1659 Peace of Pyrenees marks Spanish decline

c.1660 Golden age of French culture at its peak
1660 Restoration of Charles II in Britain
1661 Louis XIV becomes absolute French monarch
1662 Boyle's Law stated
1664 Ottoman Turks occupy Hungary
1665-7 Second Anglo-Dutch War
c.1665 Great Plague in London: 70000 die
1666 Great Fire of London
1667 John Milton: *Paradise Lost*

1670 Jan Sobieski suppresses Ukrainian Cossacks
1670 Minute hand on pocket watches
1671 Spain and United Provinces ally against France
1671 Hungarian Revolt: Reign of Terror
1672-4 Third Anglo-Dutch War
1678 John Bunyan: *The Pilgrim's Progress*
1678 Chrysanthemums reach Holland from Japan

1682 Spain and Holy Roman Empire form league against France
1682 Edmond Halley observes 'Halley's Comet'
1683 Turks besiege Vienna
1685 Edict of Nantes revoked: Huguenots flee France
1686 League of Augsburg against Louis XIV
1687 Battle of Mohács: Holy Roman Empire defeats Turks 1687
1687 Venice captures Athens from Ottoman Turks
1688 'Glorious Revolution' in England

1690 John Locke: *Essay Concerning Human Understanding*
1690 Huygens develops wave theory of light
c.1690 Violins by Stradivari
1697 Treaty of Ryswick ends war of League of Augsburg
1698 Treaty of Partition, on Spanish succession problem
1698 Newton calculates speed of sound
1699 Habsburgs recover Hungary from Turks
1699 Holy League War

1650 First Roman Catholic church in Beijing
1652 Manchus control most of China
1655 Missionary in China invents steam-driven vehicle
1658-1707 Aurangzeb I, last great Mughal emperor

1660 Mughals ban cannabis
1661 England acquires Bombay from Portugal
1663 Japan bans fireworks
1669 Aurangzeb rejects freedom of worship in India

1674-81 Three Feudatories Rebellion, China
1674 Hindu Maratha Kingdom founded
1676 Intellectual history of Ming era published in China
1679 First English ship enters Ganges

1681 Dodo of Mauritius becomes extinct
1683 Chinese conquer Formosa (Taiwan)
1685 Chinese ports opened to foreign trade
1685 Aurangzeb's Mughals at war with East India Company
1689 Treaty of Nerchinsk between Russia and China

1690 Calcutta founded by English
1691 Mughal empire at greatest extent
1697 Chinese occupy Outer Mongolia
1699 Treaty of Karlowitz ends years of Muslim expansion

Aurangzeb I holds court in Mughal style

1654 Dutch sugar planters expelled from Brazil
1655 England takes Jamaica from Spain

1664 British take New Amsterdam, now New York
1669 Carolinas adopt the Constitutions of John Locke

1674 Plantations in Quebec become French royal colonies
1675 New England settlers defeat Native Americans
1676 Nathaniel Bacon leads Virginians' rebellion
1679 New Hampshire separates from Massachusetts

c.1680 French colonial empire established
1681 Royal Charter for Pennsylvania
1682 Explorer La Salle claims Louisiana for France
1683 Start of German immigration into Pennsylvania

1692 Salem witchcraft trials
1693 Gold discovered in Brazil
1699 Virginia becomes the most populous colony

1652 Dutch found Cape Town
1659 French found trading post on Senegal coast

1660 Rise of Bambara kingdoms of Upper Niger
1662 Battle of Ambuila: Portuguese end Kongo kingdom

1672 English Royal Africa Company founded
1674 French expelled from Madagascar

1682 Danes on Gold Coast
1684 Sultan of Morocco takes Tangier from British

c.1698 Waves of Omani Arabs settle on East coast

1650   **1660**   **1670**   **1680**   **1690**

In Peter the Great's new capital of St Petersburg, the Winter Palace flanks the River Neva on the right bank.

William Hogarth's Rake carouses at the Rose Tavern.

Gulliver captures Lilliput's fleet, in Swift's 1726 satire.

EUROPE

1700-21 Northern War between Sweden and Russia
1701 Holland, England and Austria form Grand Alliance; **1704** Allies defeat France at Blenheim
1701-14 War of Spanish Succession
1702 *The Daily Courant*, first daily newspaper in England
1703 St Petersburg founded by Peter the Great
1704 Isaac Newton: *Opticks* (principles of light)
1707 Act of Union unites England and Scotland
1709 Battle of Poltava: Russia defeats Sweden

1712 St Petersburg becomes capital of Russia
1712 Pope: *The Rape of the Lock*
1713-14 Peace of Utrecht ends War of Spanish Succession
1714 Gabriel Fahrenheit devises temperature scale
1715 (-74) Louis XV King of France
1715 Jacobite Rebellion in Scotland
1718 First banknotes used in England
1719 Daniel Defoe: *Robinson Crusoe*

1720 J.S. Bach: *Brandenburg Concertos*
1721 Treaty of Nystadt ends Northern War
1726 Jonathan Swift: *Gulliver's Travels*
1726 Stephen Hales measures blood pressure
1727-9 Spain and England at war over Gibraltar; **1729** Treaty of Seville: France, Britain, Holland, Spain
1739 John Wesley founds Methodism

1730-50 Height of rococo period in art and architecture
1733 Hogarth: *A Rake's Progress*
1733 John Kay invents flying shuttle loom, England
1734 Spain takes kingdom of Naples
1735 Treaty of Vienna ends War of Polish Succession
1736 Rubber introduced from Central America
1739 Anglo-Spanish war over trade in New World

1740-86 Prussia rises under Frederick the Great
1740-8 War of Austrian Succession
1742 Anders Celsius devises centigrade scale
1742 Handel: *Messiah*; **1749** *Music for Royal Fireworks*
1744-1815 War between France and Britain
1746 Battle of Culloden: English defeat Jacobites
1748 Steel pens introduced
1749 Henry Fielding: *Tom Jones*

The original 1742 score of Handel's *Messiah*.

ASIA

1707 Death of Aurangzeb: decline of Mughal power
1709 Afghan rising against Persians

1710-11 Turkey at war with Russia
1711 Turks defeat Russians at river Pruth

1720 Tibet becomes tributary to China
1722-30 Persia comes under Afghan rule
1728 Explorer Vitus Bering discovers Bering Strait between Russia and Alaska

1736 Safavid dynasty deposed by Nadir Shah
1737 Marathas extend power in northern India
1737-47 Persians occupy Afghanistan

1740-56 Alvardi Khan independent ruler of Bengal
1746-61 French take Madras: Anglo-French rivalry in India
1747 Kingdom of Afghanistan founded

AMERICA

1702-13 English at war with French over North American territories
1704 Colony of Delaware has own Assembly
1706 Juan de Uribarri claims Colorado for Spain

1713 French cede Newfoundland to Britain
1716 Frezier explores coast of Chile and Peru
1718 Jean Baptiste le Moyne founds New Orleans

1726 Montevideo founded
1727 Coffee first planted in Brazil

1732 Georgia, last of Thirteen Colonies, founded
1735 French found first permanent settlement in Indiana

Vitus Bering finds the Bering Strait.

1741 Bering reaches Alaska
1743 French explore Rocky Mountains
1745 British take French fort of Louisbourg, Canada

AFRICA

c.1700 Rise of Ashanti power on Gold Coast
c.1700 Rise of Bantu kingdom of Buganda, East Africa

1712 Kingdom of Segu founded in West Africa
1713 Smallpox epidemic devastates Khoisan of the Cape

1723 British Africa Company gains land in The Gambia

c.1730 Revival of ancient empire of Borno in Sudan
1737 Persians invade Oman;

c.1740 Lunda kingdom established in central Africa
1744-8 Yoruba conquer Dahomey, Benin

Ashanti bracelets and an elephant ring.

OCEANIA

1688 William Dampier reaches Australia; **1699** explores South Seas

1722 Dutch discover Samoa, Easter Island, Society Islands

AD 1700   **1710**   **1720**   **1730**   **1740**

Catherine II became Russia's empress after a coup ousted her husband.

Adventure Bay, Tasmania, painted soon after the discovery of the island.

The first manned flight was by the Montgolfier brothers in their own balloon.

1751-80 Denis Diderot: *Encyclopédie*
1754 Joseph Black discovers carbon dioxide
1755 Earthquake in Lisbon kills 60 000 people
1755 S. Johnson: *Dictionary*
1756 Mayonnaise invented in France
1756-63 Britain leading world power after winning Seven Years' War with France
1757 Frederick the Great beats Austria at Leuthen
1759 Voltaire: *Candide*

Hargreaves' spinning jenny.

1756 Deaths in Black Hole of Calcutta
1757 Clive of India defeats forces of Bengal at Plassey

1759 British defeat French at Quebec
1752 Benjamin Franklin invents lightning conductor

1758 British in conflict with French over Senegal

1762 Earl of Sandwich creates first sandwich
1762 J.J. Rousseau: *Social Contract*
1762 (-96) Catherine the Great Empress of Russia
1763 Treaty of Paris ends Seven Years' War
1767 James Hargreaves invents the spinning jenny
1769 Genoa cedes Corsica to France

1761 Muslim Afghans defeat Hindu Marathas at Battle of Panipat
1761 British defeat French in India at Pondicherry

1763 France cedes Canada to Britain
1765 Stamp Act causes unrest in British colonies

George Washington, first president of the USA.

1768 Ali becomes Mameluke dynasty Bey (Prince) of Egypt

1769 James Cook charts east coast of Australia
1769 James Cook reaches New Zealand

1771 Russia conquers Crimea, destroys Turkish fleet
1771 Richard Arkwright introduces water-powered spinning frame
1771 *Encyclopaedia Britannica* first published
1772 Partition of Poland: Russia, Prussia, Austria
1773-4 Peasant uprisings in Russia led by Pugachev
1774 James Watt makes first steam engine
1776 Adam Smith: *The Wealth of Nations*
1778 La Scala, Milan, built
1779 Velocipede, early bicycle, appears in Paris

1774 Warren Hastings appointed Governor of Bengal
1774 Russians defeat Turks near Shumla

1773 Boston Tea Party: protest at British taxes
1775-83 American War of Independence

1772 James Bruce rediscovers source of Blue Nile
1776 French make slave treaty with Sultan of Kilwa

1773 James Cook first to cross Antarctic Circle
1779 James Cook killed in Hawaii

1781 Joseph II frees serfs in Habsburg Empire
1783 First manned flight made in hot-air balloon
1788 Mozart: *Symphonies 39-41*
1789 French Revolution: Parisians storm the Bastille

The velocipede, an early French version of the bicycle.

1782 Rama I founds Chakkri dynasty in Siam
1784 India Act: British Government to control British India

1783 Treaty of Paris recognises American independence
1789-97 George Washington first president of the United States

c.**1780** Masai expand in eastern Africa

1788 'First Fleet' of convict ships arrives in Botany Bay;
1788 British colony of Australia founded
1789 *Bounty* mutineers settle on Pitcairn Island

1792 France proclaimed a republic
1792 Edmund Cartwright invents steam-powered loom
1793 Louis XVI of France guillotined
1793 Metric system introduced in France
1793-4 France suffers Reign of Terror
1794 Robespierre guillotined
1796 Edward Jenner gives first smallpox vaccination
1796-7 Napoleon conquers much of Italy; **1799** proclaims himself First Consul of France

1796 British conquer Ceylon
1799 French besiege Acre, Palestine
1799 British take control of southern India

1792 Dollar becomes currency of United States
1792-1809 White House, Washington, built
1800 Washington becomes home of US government

1796 Mungo Park reaches river Niger
1798 Nelson defeats French fleet at Battle of Nile

1797 First missionaries arrive in Tahiti
1798 Flinders and Bass confirm Tasmania an island

1750   **1760**   **1770**   **1780**   **1790**

Trevithick ran his locomotive at Euston in 1808.

The horrors of the Napoleonic wars inspired Goya to etchings such as *'What Courage!'*, showing a young woman left alone to fire the cannon.

Niépce took eight hours to expose the first photograph.

EUROPE

1800 French under Napoleon conquer Italy
1802 Napoleon becomes President of Italian republic; **1804** crowned Emperor of France; **1805** defeats Russians at Austerlitz
1803 Richard Trevithick produces first steam locomotive
1805 Nelson defeats French fleet at Trafalgar
1806 Holy Roman Empire dissolved
1807 Abolition of slave trade by Britain
1808-14 Peninsula War: Britain fights France in Spain
1808 Beethoven Symphony No. 6

1810-14 Goya: *Los Desastres de la Guerra* ('The Disasters of War')
1811 Luddites wreck machinery in N. England
1812 Brothers Grimm: *Fairy Tales*
1812 Napoleon invades Russia and captures Moscow; **1812-13** retreats from Russia; **1814** Paris surrenders to Allied forces; Napoleon exiled to Elba; **1814-15** Congress of Vienna meets on peace terms; **1815** Napoleon escapes from Elba but is defeated at Waterloo

c.1820 Romanticism in art and literature
1821 Michael Faraday's first electric motor
1821-9 Greek War of Independence from Turkey
1823 Beethoven: Symphony No. 9 (*Choral*)
1825 Decembrist Uprising in Russia crushed
1827 First known photograph taken by Joseph Niépce
1828-9 Russo-Turkish War

1830 Revolutionary movements formed in Germany, Italy, Poland and France
1830 Belgium independent from Holland
1831 Faraday discovers principle of electric dynamo

Brunel beside launch chains.

1832 First Parliamentary Reform Act in Britain
1838 Isambard Brunel's steam ship *Great Western* launched
1839 Dickens: *Oliver Twist*

1840 Penny Post introduced
1842 Tennyson: *Morte D'Arthur*
1845 Irish Potato Famine
1846 Corn Laws repealed in Britain
1846 Anaesthetics used in operating theatre
1848 Marx, Engels publish Communist Manifesto
1848 Revolutions in France, Italy, Hungary, Germany
1849 Giuseppe Mazzini proclaims Rome a republic

Faraday built the first dynamo (left) in 1831.

ASIA

c.1800 British export Indian opium to China

1818 British defeat Marathas
1819 British East India Company buys Singapore

1825-30 Indonesians revolt against Dutch
1826 British take Lower Burma and Assam

1830 British East India Company takes Mysore
1838-42 War between Afghanistan and Britain
1839 Britain takes Aden

1842 Opium War: Britain annexes Hong Kong
1843 British conquer Sind
1845-9 British conquer Punjab and Kashmir

AMERICA

1803 Louisiana Purchase nearly doubles size of USA
1804-6 Lewis and Clark open route to West Coast
1804 Haiti first independent Latin-American country

1812-15 War with Britain; White House burned
1813 Mexico independent
1819-26 Simon Bolívar liberates South America
1819 USA purchases Florida

1823 Monroe doctrine opposes European role in USA
1825 Bolivia and Uruguay become independent

1833 First mechanical reaper
1840 Colombia, Ecuador, Venezuela independent republics

1840 Upper and Lower Canada unite
1846 USA gains Oregon; **1848** takes New Mexico and California from Mexico; **1848-9** California Gold Rush

AFRICA

1806 British reoccupy Cape
1808 British take control in Sierra Leone

c.1815-30s Tribal wars in South Africa
1818 Shaka forms Zulu kingdom

1820 Egypt conquers Sudan
1821 Gold Coast and The Gambia British colonies
1822 Slaves freed in Liberia

1830 French conquer Algeria
1835-9 Boers' Great Trek;
1838 Battle of Blood River

1843 Britain annexes Natal, South Africa
1849 David Livingstone crosses Kalahari Desert.

OCEANIA

1801-4 Flinders circumnavigates Australia
1804 Hobart founded as penal colony

1814 First British missionaries arrive in New Zealand
1817 Australia gains its name

1824 Brisbane founded
1828-29 Sturt explores Murray-Darling river system

1835 Foundation of Melbourne; **1836** Adelaide
1838 Massacre of Aboriginals at Myall Creek

1840 Treaty of Waitangi: Britain annexes New Zealand
1840 Maori revolts against British, New Zealand

AD 1800   **1810**   **1820**   **1830**   **1840**

Bell, a teacher of the deaf, invented the telephone in 1876.

Eiffel was a bridge builder, and in 1889 his tower in Paris showed what he knew about strong light arches of iron.

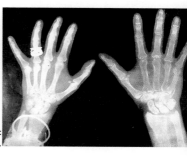

Hands of the Duke and Duchess of Kent were among the earliest X-rays in 1896.

1848 Wagner: *Lohengrin*
1852 Louis Napoleon becomes Emperor Napoleon III of France
1853 Verdi: *La Traviata*
1853-6 Crimean War: Britain, France and Turkey against Russia
1856 Louis Pasteur finds that bacteria spread disease
1857 Flaubert: *Madame Bovary*
1859 Darwin: *The Origin of Species*
1859 Battles of Solferino and Magenta; French and Piedmontese defeat Austria
1861 Emancipation of Russian serfs

1860 Giuseppe Garibaldi's 'Thousand' begin Italian unification
1862 Hugo: *Les Misérables*
1864 Prussia defeats Denmark, gaining Schleswig-Holstein
1864 Red Cross founded in Switzerland
1865-9 Joseph Lister pioneers antiseptic surgery
1866 Seven Weeks' War: Prussia defeats Austria
1866 Mendel publishes theories on genetics
1867-1918 Austro-Hungarian dual monarchy
1867-94 Marx: *Das Kapital*

1870-1 Franco-Prussian War; **1871** Prussians besiege Paris
1871-1940 Third French Republic
1871 Paris Commune suppressed
1874 Impressionists hold first exhibition, in Paris
1875 Bizet: *Carmen*
1875 Tchaikovsky: Piano Concerto No. 1
1877-8 Russo-Turkish War
1878 Berlin Treaty: Romania, Serbia, Montenegro, Bulgaria
1879 Dual Alliance: Germany and Austria-Hungary

1881 Tsar Alexander II of Russia assassinated
1884-5 Reform Acts: vote for all males over 21, Britain
1884 Charles Parsons develops steam turbine
1885 Brahms: Symphony No. 4
1885 Gilbert and Sullivan: *The Mikado*
1885 Gottlieb Daimler produces first motorcycle
1885 Karl Benz makes first practical petrol-burning car
1887-9 Eiffel Tower built
1888 Heinrich Hertz detects radio waves

1891-1904 Trans-Siberian railway constructed
1894 Alfred Dreyfus convicted of espionage, France
1895-9 Guglielmo Marconi uses radio waves for communication
1895 Wilhelm Röntgen discovers X-rays
1895 Lumière brothers' first film show, Paris
1895 Tchaikovsky: *Swan Lake*
1896 Theodor Herzl calls for Jewish National Home
1898 Start of German naval building programme
1898 Pierre and Marie Curie discover radium

1850-64 Taiping rebellion in China
1854 US forces Japan to open up to foreign traders
1857 Indian Mutiny: Siege of Lucknow

1862 French establish protectorate in Indo-China
1868-1912 Meiji Restoration: Japan modernises

1877-1901 Queen Victoria, Empress of India
1878-80 Second Anglo-Afghan war

1883 Krakatoa, Java, erupts
1885 Indian National Congress founded
1886 British annex Upper Burma

1890 Elected parliament in Japan
1893 French protectorate over Laos

Railroad poster.

1851-2 Beecher Stowe: *Uncle Tom's Cabin*
1853 Levi Strauss makes 'jeans' for miners

1861-5 American Civil War
1860s-70s Battles between settlers and Native Americans
1869 Coast-to-coast railway

1876 Sioux win Battle of Little Bighorn, kill Custer
1876 Bell invents the telephone

1886 Charles Tainter introduces wax discs for Edison's phonograph
1886 Statue of Liberty dedicated, New York

1892 Ellis Island opens
1898 Spanish-American War: Cuba gains independence

1854 Britain recognises independence of Transvaal and Orange Free State

1861 Lagos annexed as British colony
1869 Suez Canal opened

1871 Henry Stanley finds Livingstone at Ujiji
1875 Britain buys Suez shares

1880-1 Anglo-Boer War
1881 French occupy Tunisia
1882 British occupy Egypt
1885 Belgians acquire Congo

1896 Battle of Adowa: Ethiopians defeat Italians
1899-1902 Second Anglo-Boer War

1851 First Gold Rush
1851-9 Beginnings of self-government in Australia and New Zealand
1854 Eureka Stockade revolt

1860-70 Maoris and settlers at war in New Zealand
1862 Stuart crosses Australia from south to north

1870 Last British troops to serve in Australia withdraw
1874 Britain annexes Fiji Islands

1880 Australian bank robber Ned Kelly executed

1893 New Zealand is the first nation to give women the vote
1893 USA annexes Hawaii

1850 | **1860** | **1870** | **1880** | **1890**

Charlie Chaplin and child star Jackie Coogan in *The Kid*, 1921.

Bakst's design for Nijinsky's costume in *L'Après Midi d'un Faune*.

EUROPE

1900 Labour Party founded in Britain
1900 Chekhov: *Three Sisters*
1901 Marconi transmits wireless signal across Atlantic
1901 First Nobel prizes
1903 Tour de France bicycle race inaugurated
1904 J.M. Barrie: *Peter Pan*
1904 Puccini: *Madame Butterfly*

1905 Bloody Sunday massacre, during failed Russian Revolution
1905 Theory of relativity published by Albert Einstein
1907 Baden-Powell starts Boy Scout movement
1908 Austria-Hungary takes Bosnia and Herzegovina

1912-13 Balkan Wars
1912 Nijinsky dances *L'Après Midi d'un Faune*
1913 Stravinsky: *The Rite of Spring*
1913 Proust: *A la Recherche du Temps Perdu*
1914 Archduke Franz Ferdinand assassinated
1914 (-18) First World War

1916 Easter Rising in Dublin
1916 Battles of Somme and Verdun, France
1917 Bolsheviks storm Winter Palace, Russia
1919 Paris treaties redraw map of Europe
1919 Ernest Rutherford splits atom
1919 Bauhaus movement founded by Walter Gropius in Germany

1919 League of Nations
1922 Mussolini forms Fascist government in Italy
1921 Irish Free State (Eire) established
1922 Joyce: *Ulysses*
1923 Tuberculosis vaccine developed, France
1923 Unsuccessful Nazi rising, Germany

ASIA

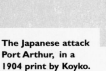

The Japanese attack Port Arthur, in a 1904 print by Koyko.

1900 Russia takes Manchuria
1900-1 Climax of Boxer Rising in China
1904-5 Russo-Japanese War

1905 Japanese destroy Russian fleet at Tsushima
1906 Revolution in Persia
1909 Young Turks topple Ottoman sultan

1911 Chinese revolution: Manchu dynasty overthrown
1912 Guomindang (Chinese National Party) founded
1916 Arab revolt against Ottomans begins

1917 Balfour Declaration supports Jewish homeland
1918 Guomindang create provisional government in China
1919 Massacre at Amritsar, India

1920 British and French mandates in Middle East
1920 Mohandas Gandhi begins resistance to British rule in India
1921 Communist Party founded in China

AMERICA

1900 First hamburger made in Connecticut
1903 Panama Canal Zone ceded to USA
1903 Wright brothers' first controlled powered flight

1906 Last British troops leave Canada
1906 San Francisco earthquake
1907 Bakelite, first plastic
1908 Model T car produced by Henry Ford

1910 (-40) Mexican Revolution
1911 Ziegfeld Follies established in New York
1912 Sinking of the *Titanic*
1913 (-24) Woodrow Wilson president of USA
1914 Panama Canal opened

1915 Film maker D.W. Griffith's *Birth of a Nation*
1917 First Pulitzer prizes
1917 USA declares war on Germany
1918 President Woodrow Wilson outlines 'Fourteen Points' world peace plan

c.1920 Start of the Jazz Age
1920 Prohibition in USA
1921 Chaplin in *The Kid*
1921 Valentino in *The Sheikh*
1922 Insulin therapy first used for diabetes

AFRICA

1900 British troops relieve Mafeking, in Boer War
1900 Britain annexes Orange River Colony and Transvaal
1901 Britain annexes state of Ashanti

1906 British quell revolt in Nigeria
1906 Zulu revolt crushed
1907 Transvaal regains autonomy
1908 Belgium takes over Congo

1910 Union of South Africa
1911 Italy conquers Libya
1912 African National Congress founded
1914 Egypt becomes a British protectorate

1915 South Africa defeats German South West Africa
1919 (-24) Jan Smuts prime minister of South Africa

1922 Egypt given nominal independence
1924 South Africa adopts Afrikaans as official language

OCEANIA

1901 Australia becomes Commonwealth
1902 Drought kills 50 per cent of Australian sheep

1906 Australia acquires Papua
1907 New Zealand adopts title of dominion

1914 Australia enters First World War
1914 New Zealand occupies Western Samoa

1916 First celebration of Anzac Day

1925 Ratana church founded in New Zealand

AD 1900   **1905**   **1910**   **1915**   **1920**

British soldiers man a barricade in Dublin during the Easter Rising, 1916.

Al Jolson and May McAvoy in *The Jazz Singer*, 1927.

An American supply plane lands at Tempelhof during the Berlin airlift.

Mohandas Gandhi, India's Nationalist leader.

1925 Adolf Hitler: *Mein Kampf* **1925** Franz Kafka: *The Trial* **1926** General Strike in Britain **1926** John Logie Baird demonstrates his television system **1928** Collectivisation of agriculture in USSR **1928** Alexander Fleming discovers penicillin **1929** Hergé: *Tintin*	**1930** Marlene Dietrich stars in *The Blue Angel* **1931** Spain declared republic **1932** Aldous Huxley: *Brave New World* **1932** Broadcasting House opens in Britain **1933** Reichstag fire **1933** Falange (Spanish Fascist Party) founded **1933** Hitler German Chancellor; **1934-45** Führer	**1936** Jesse Owens wins four gold medals at Berlin Olympics **1936-9** Spanish Civil War **1936** Rome and Berlin sign Axis Pact **1937** Guernica, Spain, destroyed by aerial bombing **1937** Jet engine tested, UK **1937** Picasso: *Guernica* **1939** Germany invades Poland, Second World War **1940** Germany overruns Belgium, Netherlands and France	**1940** Franco-German armistice signed **1940** Battle of Britain **1940-1** 'Blitz' on London **1941** Germany invades Soviet Union **1941** Whittle: jet engine **1942-3** Battle of Stalingrad **1943** Fall of Mussolini; Italy surrenders to Allies **1943** Barnes Wallis invents the 'bouncing bomb' **1944** 'D-Day': Allied Normandy landings	**1945** Germany surrenders to Allies **1945** Nuremberg trials of Nazi war criminals begin **1947** Marshall Plan for aid to Europe from USA **1948** Beginning of National Health Service in Britain **1948** Communist takeover in Hungary, Czechoslovakia **1948-9** Berlin airlift **1949** NATO formed
1925 Vietnamese Nationalist Party formed under Ho Chi Minh **1925** Chiang Kai-shek takes over Kuomintang in China	**1931** Japan occupies Manchuria **1934** Rearmament in Japan **1934-5** Long March by Chinese Communists **1935** Persia becomes Iran	**1935** Chinese Communists end Long March at Yan'an **1937** Full-scale war between China and Japan **1939** Siam renamed Praethet Thai, 'Land of the Free'	**1940-1** Japanese begin occupation of Indochina **1941** Britain and Soviet Union invade Iran **1943** Churchill, Roosevelt and Stalin meet in Teheran	**1945** USA drops atomic bomb on Hiroshima **1947** India, Pakistan states **1948** Mohandas Gandhi assassinated **1948** State of Israel **1949** Communist victory in China
1925 Fitzgerald: *The Great Gatsby* **1927** Jolson in *The Jazz Singer* **1928** Walt Disney creates Mickey Mouse **1929** Wall Street Crash begins the Great Depression	**1931** Empire State Building, New York, completed **1933** US President Roosevelt introduces New Deal	**1935** Land redistribution in Mexico **1936** Fascist regime established in Paraguay **1939** Selznick films *Gone with the Wind*	**1940** Hemingway: *For Whom the Bell Tolls* **1941** Orson Welles: *Citizen Kane* **1941** USA enters war against Germany and Japan **1942** Enrico Fermi builds nuclear reactor, USA **1943** Military dictatorship assumes power in Argentina	**1945** Constitution for United Nations established **1946** Churchill makes 'Iron Curtain' speech **1946** First electronic digital computer built, USA **1947** Williams: *A Streetcar Named Desire* **1947** CIA founded, USA

Empire State Building, on its completion in 1931 the tallest building in the world.

1925 Blacks banned from skilled jobs in South Africa **1926** Revolt of Abd-el Krim crushed, Morocco	**1930** Haile Selassie becomes emperor of Ethiopia; **1932** abolishes slavery in Ethiopia	**1935** Italy invades Ethiopia; **1936** annexes country **1936** Anglo-Egyptian alliance: British in Suez Canal Zone	**1940-1** Italians expelled from Eritrea, Somalia and Ethiopia **1942** Allies defeat Germans at El Alamein, Egypt **1943** Germans surrender in North Africa	**1947** Mau Mau secret society formed in Kenya **1948** Policy of apartheid introduced in South Africa
1927 Parliament House, Canberra, opened **1928** Trans-Pacific flight by *Southern Cross*	**1932** Sydney Harbour Bridge completed **1932-3** Australia v England 'bodyline' cricket series	**1939** Australia declares war on Germany **1939** New Zealand declares war on Germany	**1941** Pearl Harbor bombed **1942** Battle of Midway: USA halts Japanese in Pacific	**1946** USA carries out atomic bomb test on Bikini Atoll, Marshall Islands

1925 **1930** **1935** **1940** **1945**

In 1952 the USA explodes the first hydrogen bomb, on the Pacific atoll of Eniwatok.

Hitchcock's *Psycho*: Janet Leigh screams in the shower.

Buzz Aldrin walks on the Moon in 1969.

EUROPE

1953 Soviets crush East Berlin revolt
1953 Structure of DNA discovered
1954 England's Roger Bannister runs the mile in less than four minutes

1955 Warsaw Pact signed
1956 Hungarian uprising crushed by USSR
1957 Treaty of Rome: formation of the EEC
1957 USSR launches Sputnik 1 satellite
1957 USSR tests intercontinental ballistic missile

1961 Yuri Gagarin, Soviet Union, is first man in space
1961 Berlin Wall built
1963 Hotline telephone between USA and USSR
1963 Beatles' first album, *Please Please Me*
1963 Kodak markets instant picture cameras

1966 Buñuel: *Belle de Jour*
1967 King Constantine of Greece deposed
1968 Student unrest throughout Europe
1968 Revolution in Czechoslovakia crushed by USSR
1969 First human egg fertilised outside mother's body
1969 First flight by Concorde

1970 First heart pacemaker
1972 Terrorists kill Israeli Olympic athletes, Munich
1973 Military takeover in Greece
1974 End of dictatorship in Portugal
1974 Solzhenitsyn: *The Gulag Archipelago*
1974 Turks invade Cyprus

Russian novelist Solzhenitsyn.

ASIA

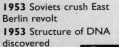

Sherpa Tensing on Everest.

1950 China invades Tibet
1950-3 Korean War
1953 Coup in Persia
1953 Hillary and Tensing first to climb Everest
1954 Kurosawa: *The Seven Samurai*

1955 Baghdad Pact
1956 Pakistan becomes first Islamic republic
1957 Malaya independent
1958-60 'Great Leap Forward' in China
1958 Military coup in Iraq
1959 Dalai Lama flees from Tibet after rebellion fails

1960 China-Soviet dispute
1961 Fugitive Nazi Adolf Eichmann on trial in Israel
1961 USA increases number of military advisers in South Vietnam
1964 Palestine Liberation Organisation created
1964 Mao Ze-dong: *Thoughts of Chairman Mao*

1965 Military takeover in Indonesia
1966 Cultural Revolution begins in China
1967 Israel and Arab states fight Six-Day War

1971 East Pakistan becomes Bangladesh
1973 Yom Kippur War between Israel and Arabs
1973 OPEC countries triple oil prices
1973 US forces withdraw from South Vietnam

AMERICA

1950 McCarthy witch hunt of communists begins
1951 Salinger: *Catcher in the Rye*
1952 Contraceptive pill, USA
1953 Miller: *The Crucible*
1954 Segregation in US schools ruled unconstitutional

1954 Bill Haley: *Rock Around the Clock*
1956 Lerner and Loewe: *My Fair Lady*
1956 Elvis Presley: *Hound Dog*
1958 NASA founded, USA
1959 Cuban Revolution: Fidel Castro takes power

1960 Hitchcock: *Psycho*
1960 Heller: *Catch 22*
1962 Cuban missile crisis
1963 President Kennedy assassinated
1963 Martin Luther King leads Civil Rights Campaign
1964 Beatles arrive in the USA

1965 Black activist Malcolm X assassinated
1968 Martin Luther King assassinated
1968 Kubrick: *2001: A Space Odyssey*
1969 Apollo 11's *Eagle* module lands on Moon
1969 Woodstock Music and Arts Festival

1972 USA begins policy of détente with China, USSR
1973 Military takeover in Chile
1973 Skylab space stations
1974 US President Nixon resigns over Watergate scandal
1975 US Apollo and Soviet Soyuz link up in space

AFRICA

1952 Revolution in Egypt: republic proclaimed
1952-6 Mau Mau uprising in Kenya
1954-62 Algerian guerrillas fight for independence

1956 French and Spanish Morocco unite
1956 Sudan independent
1956 Suez Canal crisis
1960 Civil war in former Belgian Congo

1960 Wind of Change: ten African states independent
1961 White South Africans vote to become republic
1965 Rhodesia declares independence

1967-70 Civil war in Nigeria, secession of Biafra
1967 Christian Barnard performs first human heart transplant, South Africa

1974 Ethiopian Emperor Haile Selassie deposed by Marxists

OCEANIA

1951 Australia, New Zealand, USA sign Anzus Pact

1955 Patrick White: *The Tree of Man*
1959 Antarctic Treaty signed

1963 Blood transfusion to unborn child, New Zealand
1963 First edition of *Oz* magazine, Australia

1967 Last execution in Australia
1968 Nauru independent

1970 Tonga and Fiji independent
1973 Aboriginals given vote in Australia

AD 1950   **1955**   **1960**   **1965**   **1970**

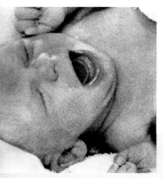

A yell from Louise Brown, the first 'test tube baby'.

Mandela's release after 28 years in prison spelt the end of apartheid.

1995: Russian troops patrol a devastated Chechnya.

1975 Death of Franco: Juan Carlos King of Spain
1977 First democratic elections held in Spain for 40 years
1978 First 'test tube baby' born, in Britain
1979 First direct elections to the European Parliament

1980 Solidarity trade union founded in Poland
1981 Martial law in Poland
1981 Francois Mitterrand becomes president of France
1981 Humber Bridge, UK

1986 Explosion at Chernobyl nuclear reactor in USSR
1988 Soviet cosmonauts spend 326 days on space station
1989 Fall of communist regimes in East Europe; Berlin Wall dismantled; Nationalist parties formed across USSR

1990 East and West Germany are reunified
1991 Croatia and Slovenia split from Yugoslavia
1991 Beginning of civil war in former Yugoslavia
1993 Czechoslovakia splits, Czech Republic and Slovakia
1994 Channel Tunnel linking France and England opens

1994-5 Turkey launches military attacks on Kurdish guerrillas
1995 Leaders of warring Balkan nations sign US-brokered peace accord
1995 'Reformed' communists win Polish election
1996 Yeltsin wins second Russian election
1996 Islamic Welfare Party forms government in Turkey

1975 Communists take Vietnam, Laos, Cambodia
1975 Civil war in Lebanon
1975 First video game, Japan
1979 Ayatollah Khomeini gains power in Iran
1979 Soviet Union invades Afghanistan

1980 Sony Walkman, Japan
1980-8 Iran-Iraq War
1982 Israel invades Lebanon
1984 Indira Gandhi, Indian prime minister, assassinated

Tiananmen just before the killing.

1988 Palestinians rise up in Israel
1988 Soviet Union withdraws from Afghanistan
1989 Chinese troops crush student protests in Tiananmen Square

1990 Iraq invades Kuwait;
1991 Gulf War: Allied forces defeat Iraqis back
1991 Ayodha Mosque, India, destroyed: 1000 die
1991 Russian government crushes communist coup bid
1993 Israel and PLO sign deal in Washington on Gaza and West Bank control

1995 Israeli Prime Minister Yitzhak Rabin assassinated over peace moves; **1996** Israel launches attacks on southern Lebanon 'terrorist camps'; Netanyahu elected prime minister
1995-6 Russian troops and Chechen rebels battle for Grozny

1976 Viking I probe lands on Mars
1977 Neutron bomb developed
1978 Mass suicide of Jim Jones's followers, Guyana
1977-9 Civil war in Nicaragua ends in victory for Sandinistas
1979-92 Civil war in El Salvador

1980s Computer revolution
1981 Scientists identify AIDS virus
1982 Britain and Argentina go to war over Falklands
1983 US troops invade Grenada

1986 'Baby Doc' Duvalier, Haitian president, overthrown
1987 Treaty USA/USSR to eliminate nuclear weapons
1987 World stock market prices crash
1989 US intervention in Panama; Noriega arrested

1991 Soviet Union withdraws troops from Cuba
1991 START I Treaty on nuclear disarmament USA/USSR
1993 Waco Cult siege, Texas: 87 die
1993 Five die in bombing of New York World Trade Center

Oklahoma bomb site.

1995 Bomb kills 166 in Oklahoma
1995 Million Man March in Washington
1996 230 die in TWA crash

1975 Angola and Mozambique independent
1976 Schoolchildren riot in Soweto, South Africa
1979 President Idi Amin expelled from Uganda

1980 Zimbabwe becomes a republic
1981 President Sadat of Egypt assassinated
1984-7 Famine in Ethiopia

1985 AIDS epidemic in East Africa
1986 USA bombs Libya for terrorist activities
1988 Sanctions introduced against South Africa

1990 South Africa frees Nelson Mandela; **1994** Mandela elected president in first all-race polls
1994 Rwandan civil war: thousands die

1995 Nigerian author Ken Saro-Wiwa executed
1996 Coup in Burundi

1975 Governor-General dismisses Gough Whitlam government, Australia
1975 Papua New Guinea becomes independent.

1983 Opposition leader Aquino killed, Philippines
1984 First frozen embryo baby born, Melbourne

1986 President Marcos flees Philippines

1991 Mount Pinatubo erupts in Philippines

1995 France holds nuclear tests in Polynesia; riots in Tahiti, and world protests

1975   **1980**   **1985**   **1990**   **1995**

ROMAN EMPERORS

THE JULIO-CLAUDIAN EMPERORS

27 BC-AD 14 Augustus
14-37 Tiberius
37-41 Caligula
41-54 Claudius
54-68 Nero
68-9 Galba
69 Otho
69 Vitellius

THE FLAVIAN EMPERORS

69-79 Vespasian
79-81 Titus
81-96 Domitian

THE ANTONINE EMPERORS

96-8 Nerva
98-117 Trajan
117-38 Hadrian
138-61 Antoninus Pius
161-9 Lucius Verus
161-80 Marcus Aurelius
180-92 Commodus
193 Pertinax
193 Didius Julianus

THE SEVERI

193-211 Septimius Severus
211 Geta

211-17 Caracalla
217-18 Macrinus
218 Diadumenian
218-22 Elagabalus
222-35 Alexander Severus

THE SOLDIER EMPERORS

235-8 Maximinus the Thracian
238 Gordian I/Gordian II
238 Balbinus/Pupienus Maximus
238-44 Gordian III
244-9 Philip I 'the Arabian'
247-9 Philip II
249-51 Decius
251 Herennius Etruscus
251 Hostilian
251-3 Trebonianus Gallus
251-3 Volusian
253 Aemilian
253-9 Valerian
259-68 Gallienus
260 Saloninus
268-70 Claudius II Gothicus
270 Quintillus
270-5 Aurelian
275-6 Tacitus
276 Florian
276-82 Probus
282-3 Carus

283-4 Numerian
283-5 Carinus

THE 'GALLIC EMPIRE'

260-9 Postumus
269 Laelian
269 Marius
269-71 Victorinus
271-4 Tetricus

DIOCLETIAN AND THE TETRARCHY

284-305 Diocletian (East)
286-305 Maximian (West)
305-6 Constantius I 'Chlorus' (West)
305-11 Galerius (East)
306-7 Severus (West)
307-12 Maxentius (West)

DYNASTY OF CONSTANTINE

308-13 Maximinus II
311-24 Licinius (East)
316-17 Valerius Valens
324 Martinian
324-37 Constantine I 'the Great'
337-40 Constantine II
337-50 Constans
337-61 Constantius II
350-3 Magnentius
360-3 Julian the Apostate
363-4 Jovian

DYNASTY OF VALENTINIAN

364-75 Valentinian I (West)
364-72 Valens (East)
375-83 Gratian (West)
383-92 Valentinian II (West)

DYNASTY OF THEODOSIUS

379-95 Theodosius I 'the Great'
383-7 Maximus
387-8 Victor
392-4 Eugenius

WESTERN ROMAN EMPERORS

395-423 Honorius
421 Constantius III
423-5 John
425-55 Valentinian III
455 Petronius Maximus
455-6 Avitus
457-61 Majorian
461-5 Libius Severus
467-72 Anthemius
472 Olybrius
473-4 Glycerius
474-80 Julius Nepos
475-6 Romulus Augustulus
476 Romulus Augustulus deposed; end of direct imperial rule in the West

HOLY ROMAN EMPERORS

CAROLINGIAN HOUSE

800-14 Charles I 'the Great' (Charlemagne)
814-40 Louis I 'the Pious'
840-55 Lothair I
855-75 Louis II
875-7 Charles II 'the Bald'
877-87 Charles III 'the Fat'
887-98 Arnulf of Carinthia
899-911 Louis III 'the Child'

HOUSE OF FRANCONIA

911-18 Conrad I

HOUSE OF SAXONY

919-36 Henry I 'the Fowler'
936-73 Otto I 'the Great'
973-83 Otto II
983-1002 Otto III
1002-24 St Henry II

SALIAN HOUSE

1024-39 Conrad II
1039-56 Henry III
1077-80 Rudolf of Swabia (rival)
1081-8 Herman of Salm (rival)
1056-1105 Henry IV
1087-98 Conrad
1105-25 Henry V

HOUSE OF SUPPLINBURG

1125-37 Lothair II of Saxony

HOUSE OF HOHENSTAUFEN

1138-52 Conrad III
1147-50 Henry

1155-90 Frederick I 'Barbarossa'
1190-7 Henry VI
1198-1208 Philip of Swabia

HOUSE OF WELF

1198-1218 Otto IV of Brunswick

HOUSE OF HOHENSTAUFEN

1220-50 Frederick II
1220-35 Henry
1246-7 Henry Raspe of Thuringia (rival)
1247-56 William of Holland (rival)
1250-4 Conrad IV
1257-72 Richard of Cornwall (rival)

HOUSE OF HABSBURG

1273-91 Rudolf I

HOUSE OF NASSAU

1292-8 Adolf

HOUSE OF HABSBURG

1298-1308 Albert I of Austria

HOUSE OF LUXEMBOURG

1308-13 Henry VII

HOUSE OF WITTELSBACH

1314-47 Louis IV of Bavaria
1314-30 Frederick of Austria (rival)

HOUSE OF LUXEMBOURG

1347-78 Charles IV
1349 Günther of Schwarzburg (rival)
1378-1400 Wenceslas

HOUSE OF WITTELSBACH

1400-10 Rupert of the Palatinate

HOUSE OF LUXEMBOURG

1410-37 Sigismund
1410-11 Jobst of Moravia (rival)

HOUSE OF HABSBURG

1438-9 Albert II of Austria
1440-93 Frederick III
1493-1519 Maximilian I
1519-58 Charles V
1558-64 Ferdinand I
1564-76 Maximilian II
1576-1612 Rudolf II
1612-19 Matthias
1619-37 Ferdinand II
1637-57 Ferdinand III
1658-1705 Leopold I
1705-11 Joseph I
1711-40 Charles VI

HOUSE OF WITTELSBACH

1742-5 Charles VII of Bavaria

HOUSE OF HABSBURG-LORRAINE

1745-65 Francis I of Lorraine
1765-90 Joseph II
1790-2 Leopold II
1792-1806 Francis II
Renunciation of the title of Holy Roman Emperor

ANCIENT EGYPT

DYNASTIC PERIOD	DYNASTY	DATES (BC)	IMPORTANT RULERS
Early Period	First Dynasty	c.3100-2905	Menes unites Upper and Lower Egypt
	Second Dynasty	c.2905-2700	Mastaba tombs
Old Kingdom	Third Dynasty	c.2700-2680	Zozer Step pyramid at Saqqara
	Fourth Dynasty	c.2680-2544	Cheops pyramid at Giza
	Fifth Dynasty	c.2544-2407	
	Sixth Dynasty	c.2407-2200	
First Intermediate Period	Seventh to Tenth Dynasties	c.2200-c.2100	Collapse of central rule from Memphis
Middle Kingdom	Eleventh Dynasty	c.2100-1991	Thebes emerges as capital under Mentuhotep II
	Twelfth Dynasty	c.1991-1786	Sesostis III conquers Nubia
Second Intermediate Period	Thirteenth to Seventeenth Dynasty	c.1786-1570	Hyksos kings rule
New Kingdom	Eighteenth Dynasty	c.1570-1293	Amenhotep III, Tuthmosis III, civilisation at height, Akhenaten heresy, Tutankhamun tomb
	Nineteenth Dynasty	c.1293-1185	Thebes at height of power under Rameses II
	Twentieth Dynasty	c.1185-1100	Sea People invade. Defeated by Rameses III
Third Intermediate Period	Twenty-first to Twenty-sixth Dynasties	c.1100-525	Nubians invade, followed by Assyrians who sack Thebes c.655 BC
Late Dynastic Period	Twenty-seventh to Thirty-first Dynasties	c.525-332	Persian domination, Alexander the Great arrives

JAPAN

ERAS

1600-1868 Tokugawa (or Edo)
1868-1912 Meiji
1912-26 Taishō
1926-89 Shōwa
1989- Heisei

SHOGUNS

1603-5 Tokugawa Ieyasu
1605-23 Hidetada
1623-51 Iemitsu
1651-80 Ietsuna
1680-1709 Tsunayoshi
1709-13 Ienobu
1713-16 Ietsugu
1716-45 Yoshimune
1745-61 Ieshige
1761-86 Ieharu
1787-1838 Ienari
1838-53 Ieyoshi
1853-8 Iesada

1858-66 Iemochi
1866-7 Yoshinobu

EMPERORS

1586-1611 Go-Yōzei
1611-29 Go-Mizunoo
1629-43 Meishō
1643-54 Go-Kōmyō
1655-63 Go-Sai
1663-87 Reigen
1687-1709 Higashiyama
1709-35 Nakamikado
1735-47 Sakuramachi
1747-62 Momozono
1762-71 Go-Sakuramachi
1771-9 Go-Momozono
1780-1817 Kōkaku
1817-46 Ninkō
1846-67 Kōmei
1868-1912 Mutsuhito
1912-26 Yoshihito
1926-89 Hirohito
1989- Akihito

DYNASTIES OF ISLAM

THE CALIPHATES

632-61 Orthodox Caliphate
661-750 Umayyad Dynasty
750-1258 Abbassid Dynasty

THE OTTOMANS

1280-1924 Osmanli Dynasty

THE INDIAN DYNASTIES

1526-40 Mughal Dynasty
1540-55 Suri Dynasty
1555-1857 Mughal Dynasty
(See also next column)

DYNASTIES OF INDIA

MUGHAL DYNASTY

1526-30 Babur
1530-40 Humayun

SURI DYNASTY

1540-5 Shir Shah Sur
1545-53 Islam Shah
1553-5 Muhammad Adil
1555 Ibrahim III
1555 Sikander III

MUGHAL DYNASTY

1555-6 Humayun
1556-1605 Akbar I 'the Great'
1605-27 Jahangir
1627-58 Shah Jahan I
1658-1707 Aurangzib Alamgir I
1707-12 Bahadur Shah I
1712-13 Jahandar Shah
1713-19 Farrukhsiyar
1719 Rafi al-Darajat
1719 Shah Jahan II
1719-48 Muhammad Shah
1748-54 Ahmad Shah
1754-9 Alamgir II
1759-1806 Shah Alam II
1806-37 Akbar II
1837-57 Bahadur Shah II

DYNASTIES OF CHINA

2250-2140 BC Five Emperors
2140-1711 BC Xia
1711-1066 BC Shang
1066-256 BC Zhou
(1066-771 BC Western Zhou)
(770-256 BC Eastern Zhou)
475-221 BC Warring States
221-206 BC Qin
206 BC-AD 220 Han
(206 BC-AD 25 Western Han)
(AD 25-220 Eastern Han)
220-280 Three Kingdoms
265-420 Jin
(265-317 Western Jin)
(317-420 Eastern Jin)
420-589 South and North Dynasties
581-618 Sui
618-906 Tang
906-60 Five Dynasties
960-1279 Sung
(960-1127 Northern Sung)
(1127-1279 Southern Sung)
1279-1368 Yuan
1368-1644 Ming
1644-1911 Qing
1911-49 Republic
1949- People's Republic

RULERS OF ENGLAND AND OF THE UNITED KINGDOM

SAXON LINE

955-9 Edwy
959-75 Edgar
975-8 Edward the Martyr
978-1016 Ethelred the Unready
1016 Edmund Ironside

DANISH LINE

1016-35 Canute (Cnut)
1035-40 Harold I
1040-2 Hardicanute (Harthacnut)

SAXON LINE

1042-66 Edward the Confessor
1066 Harold II

HOUSE OF NORMANDY

1066-87 William I 'the Conqueror'
1087-1100 William II
1100-35 Henry I
1135-54 Stephen

HOUSE OF PLANTAGENET

1154-89 Henry II
1189-99 Richard I
1199-1216 John
1216-72 Henry III
1272-1307 Edward I
1307-27 Edward II
1327-77 Edward III
1377-99 Richard II

HOUSE OF LANCASTER

1399-1413 Henry IV
1413-22 Henry V
1422-61;1470-1 Henry VI

HOUSE OF YORK

1461-70; 1471-83 Edward IV
1483 Edward V
1483-5 Richard III

HOUSE OF TUDOR

1485-1509 Henry VII
1509-47 Henry VIII
1547-53 Edward VI
1553-8 Mary I
1558-1603 Elizabeth I

HOUSE OF STUART

1603-25 James I of England and VI of Scotland
1625-49 Charles I

COMMONWEALTH (DECLARED 1649)

1653-8 Oliver Cromwell, Lord Protector
1658-9 Richard Cromwell

HOUSE OF STUART

1660-85 Charles II
1685-8 James II
1689-1702 William III and Mary II (Mary died 1694)
1702-14 Anne

HOUSE OF HANOVER

1714-27 George I
1727-60 George II
1760-1820 George III
1820-30 George IV
1830-37 William IV
1837-1901 Victoria

HOUSE OF SAXE-COBURG-GOTHA

1901-10 Edward VII

HOUSE OF WINDSOR

1910-36 George V
1936 Edward VIII
1936-52 George VI
1952- Elizabeth II

AUSTRIAN EMPERORS

HOUSE OF HABSBURG-LORRAINE

1804-35 Francis I
1835-48 Ferdinand I
1848-1916 Franz Joseph I
1916-18 Charles I
Proclamation of the republic

KINGS OF PRUSSIA

HOUSE OF HOHENZOLLERN

1701-13 Frederick I
1713-40 Frederick William I
1740-86 Frederick II 'the Great'
1786-97 Frederick Willliam II
1797-1840 Frederick William III
1840-61 Frederick William IV

RULERS OF SERBIA

1804-17 Karageorge (as ruler)
1817-39 Milos Obrenović (as Prince)
1839 Milan I Obrenović
1839-42 Michael III Obrenović
1842-58 Alexander Karageorgević
1858-60 Milos Obrenović
1860-8 Michael III Obrenović
1868-82 Milan II Obrenović (as Prince)
1882-9 Milan II Obrenović (as King)
1889-1903 Alexander Obrenović
1903-21 Peter I Karageorgević
1921-34 Alexander I Karageorgević
1934-45 Peter II Karageorgević

GERMAN EMPERORS

1871-88 Wilhelm I
1888 Frederick III
1888-1918 Wilhelm II
1918 Proclamation of the republic

RULERS OF SCOTLAND

1034-40 Duncan I
1040-57 Macbeth (usurper)
1057-93 Malcolm III
1093-4; 1094-7 Donalbane
1094 Duncan II
1097-1107 Edgar
1107-24 Alexander I
1124-53 David I
1153-65 Malcolm IV
1165-1214 William the Lion
1214-49 Alexander II
1249-86 Alexander III
1286-90 Margaret, Maid of Norway
1292-6 John Balliol
1306-29 Robert I
1329-71 David II

HOUSE OF STEWART

1371-90 Robert II
1390-1406 Robert III
1406-37 James I
1437-60 James II
1460-88 James III
1488-1513 James IV
1513-42 James V
1542-67 Mary Stuart
1567-1625 James VI (James I of England)
1685-8 James VII (James II of England)

RULERS OF SWEDEN

HOUSE OF VASA

1523-60 Gustavus I Vasa
1560-8 Eric XIV
1568-92 John III
1592-9 Sigismund
1599-11 Charles IX
1611-32 Gustavus II Adolphus
1632-54 Christina
1654-60 Charles X
1660-97 Charles XI
1697-1718 Charles XII
1718-20 Ulrica Eleanora (married Frederick
of Hesse-Cassell, King of Sweden)
1720-51 Frederick of Hesse-Cassell
1751-71 Adolphus Frederick
1771-92 Gustavus III
1792-1809 Gustavus IV Adolphus
1809-18 Charles XIII

HOUSE OF BERNADOTTE

1818-44 Charles XIV
1844-59 Oscar I
1859-72 Charles XV
1872-1907 Oscar II
1907-50 Gustavus V
1950-73 Gustavus VI Adolphus
1973- Charles XVI Gustavus

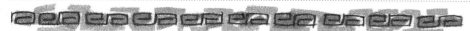

RULERS OF FRANCE

CAROLINGIAN HOUSE

751-68 Pepin the Short
768-71 Carloman
768-814 Charles 'the Great' (Charlemagne)
814-40 Louis I 'the Pious'
840-77 Charles I 'the Bald'
877-9 Louis II 'the Stammerer'
879-82 Louis III
882-4 Carloman
884-8 Charles II 'the Fat'

ROBERTIAN HOUSE

888-98 Eudes

CAROLINGIAN HOUSE

893-922 Charles III 'the Simple'

ROBERTIAN HOUSE

922-3 Robert I
923-36 Rudolf

CAROLINGIAN HOUSE

936-54 Louis IV of Outremer
954-86 Lothair
986-7 Louis V 'the Sluggard'

CAPETIAN HOUSE

987-96 Hugh 'Capet
996-1031 Robert II 'the Pious'
1017-25 Hugh
1031-60 Henry I
1060-1108 Philip I
1108-37 Louis VI 'the Fat'
1137-80 Louis VII 'the Younger'
1180-1223 Philip II, Augustus
1223-6 Louis VIII 'the Lion'
1226-70 St Louis IX
1270-85 Philip III 'the Bold'
1285-1314 Philip IV 'the Fair'
1314-16 Louis X 'the Stubborn'
1316 John I
1316-22 Philip V 'the Tall'
1322-8 Charles IV 'the Fair'

HOUSE OF VALOIS

1328-50 Philip VI
1350-64 John II 'the Good'

1364-80 Charles V 'the Wise'
1380-1422 Charles VI 'the Mad'
1422-61 Charles VII 'the Victorious'
1461-83 Louis XI
1483-98 Charles VIII

LINE OF ORLÉANS

1498-1515 Louis XII

LINE OF ANGOULÊME

1515-47 Francis I
1547-59 Henry II
1559-60 Francis II
1560-74 Charles IX
1574-89 Henry III

HOUSE OF BOURBON

1589-1610 Henry IV
1610-43 Louis XIII
1643-1715 Louis XIV
1715-74 Louis XV
1774-92 Louis XVI
1793-95 Louis XVII

FIRST REPUBLIC

1792-5 National Convention
1795-9 Directory
1799-1804 Consulate: Napoleon Bonaparte, First Consul

HOUSE OF BONAPARTE – FIRST EMPIRE

1804-14, 1815 Napoleon I
1815 Napoleon II (as Duke of Reichstadt)

HOUSE OF BOURBON

1795-1824 Louis XVIII
1824-30 Charles X

LINE OF ORLÉANS

1830-48 Louis Philippe I

SECOND REPUBLIC

1848-52 Louis Napoleon Bonaparte, President

HOUSE OF BONAPARTE – SECOND EMPIRE

1852-70 Napoleon III
Proclamation of the Third Republic

THE KINGDOM OF THE NETHERLANDS

HOUSE OF ORANGE-NASSU

1815-40 William I
1840-9 William II
1849-90 William III
1890-1948 Wilhelmina
1948-80 Juliana
1980- Beatrix

THE KINGDOM OF SPAIN

HOUSE OF HABSBURG

1516-56 Charles I
1556-98 Philip II
1598-1621 Philip III
1621-65 Philip IV
1665-1700 Charles II

HOUSE OF BOURBON

1700-24 Philip V
1724 Louis I
1724-46 Philip V
1746-59 Ferdinand VI
1759-88 Charles III
1788-1808 Charles IV

HOUSE OF BONAPARTE

1808-13 Joseph Napoleon

HOUSE OF BOURBON

1808-33 Ferdinand VII
1833-68 Isabella II
1868-70 Provisional Government

HOUSE OF SAVOY

1870-3 Amadeus I
1873-4 First Republic

HOUSE OF BOURBON

1874-85 Alfonso XII
1886-1931 Alfonso XIII

REPUBLIC AND STATE

1931-9 Second Republic
1939-75 Spanish State: Francisco Franco Bahamonde, chief of state

HOUSE OF BOURBON

1975- Juan Carlos I

TSARS OF RUSSIA

1547-84 Ivan IV 'the Terrible'
1584-98 Theodore I

HOUSE OF GODUNOV

1598-1605 Boris Godunov
1605 Theodore II
1605-6 Dimitri

HOUSE OF SHUISKII

1606-10 Basil IV Shuiskii

HOUSE OF ROMANOV

1613-45 Michael Romanov
1645-76 Alexis
1676-82 Theodore III
1682-96 Ivan V (co-tsar)
1682-1725 Peter I, 'the Great'

1725-7 Catherine I (Martha)
1727-30 Peter II
1730-40 Anne
1740-1 Ivan VI
1741-62 Elizabeth

HOUSE OF HOLSTEIN-GOTTORP-ROMANOV

1762 Peter III
1762-96 Catherine II 'the Great' (Sophia of Anhalt)
1796-1801 Paul I
1801-25 Alexander I
1825-55 Nicholas I
1855-81 Alexander II
1881-94 Alexander III
1894-1917 Nicholas II
Provisional government, Soviet rule, then republic

KINGS OF ITALY

HOUSE OF SAVOY

1849-78 Victor Emmanuel II
1878-1900 Umberto I
1900-46 Victor Emmanuel III
1946 Umberto II. Proclamation of the republic

PRIME MINISTERS OF GREAT BRITAIN AND OF THE UNITED KINGDOM

1721-42	Sir Robert Walpole	Whig
1742-3	Earl of Wilmington	Whig
1743-54	Henry Pelham	Whig
1754-6	Duke of Newcastle	Whig
1756-7	Duke of Devonshire	Whig
1757-62	Duke of Newcastle	Whig
1762-3	Earl of Bute	Tory
1763-5	George Grenville	Whig
1765-6	Marquis of Rockingham	Whig
1766-8	Earl of Chatham	Whig
1768-70	Duke of Grafton	Whig
1770-82	Lord North	Tory
1782	Marquis of Rockingham	Whig
1782-3	Earl of Shelburne	Whig
1783	Duke of Portland	coalition
1783-1801	William Pitt	Tory
1801-4	Henry Addington	Tory
1804-6	William Pitt	Tory
1806-7	Lord William Grenville	Whig
1807-9	Duke of Portland	Tory
1809-12	Spencer Perceval	Tory
1812-27	Earl of Liverpool	Tory
1827	George Canning	Tory
1827-8	Viscount Goderich	Tory

1828-30	Duke of Wellington	Tory
1830-4	Earl Grey	Whig
1834	Viscount Melbourne	Whig
1834	Duke of Wellington	Tory
1834-5	Sir Robert Peel	Conservative
1835-41	Viscount Melbourne	Whig
1841-6	Sir Robert Peel	Conservative
1846-52	Lord John Russell	Whig
1852	Earl of Derby	Conservative
1852-5	Earl of Aberdeen	coalition
1855-8	Viscount Palmerston	Liberal
1858-9	Earl of Derby	Conservative
1859-65	Viscount Palmerston	Liberal
1865-6	Earl Russell	Liberal
1866-8	Earl of Derby	Conservative
1868	Benjamin Disraeli	Conservative
1868-74	William Ewart Gladstone	Liberal
1874-80	Benjamin Disraeli	Conservative
1880-5	William Ewart Gladstone	Liberal
1885-6	Marquis of Salisbury	Conservative
1886	William Ewart Gladstone	Liberal
1886-92	Marquis of Salisbury	Conservative
1892-4	William Ewart Gladstone	Liberal
1894-5	Earl of Rosebery	Liberal

1895-1902	Marquis of Salisbury	Conservative
1902-5	Arthur James Balfour	Conservative
1905-8	Sir H. Campbell-Bannerman	Liberal
1908-16	Herbert Henry Asquith	Liberal
1916-22	David Lloyd George	coalition
1922-3	Andrew Bonar Law	Conservative
1923-4	Stanley Baldwin	Conservative
1924	James Ramsay MacDonald	Labour
1924-9	Stanley Baldwin	Conservative
1929-35	James Ramsay MacDonald	coalition
1935-7	Stanley Baldwin	coalition
1937-40	Neville Chamberlain	coalition
1940-5	Winston Spencer Churchill	coalition
1945-51	Clement Richard Attlee	Labour
1951-5	Sir Winston S. Churchill	Conservative
1955-7	Sir Anthony Eden	Conservative
1957-63	Harold Macmillan	Conservative
1963-4	Sir Alec Douglas-Home	Conservative
1964-70	Harold Wilson	Labour
1970-4	Edward Heath	Conservative
1974-6	Harold Wilson	Labour
1976-9	James Callaghan	Labour
1979-90	Margaret Thatcher	Conservative
1990-	John Major	Conservative

PRESIDENTS OF THE UNITED STATES OF AMERICA

1	1789-97	George Washington	Federalist
2	1797-1801	John Adams	Federalist
3	1801-9	Thomas Jefferson	Democratic-Republican
4	1809-17	James Madison	Democratic-Republican
5	1817-25	James Monroe	Democratic-Republican
6	1825-9	John Quincy Adams	Independent
7	1829-37	Andrew Jackson	Democrat
8	1837-41	Martin Van Buren	Democrat
9	1841	William H. Harrison	Whig
10	1841-5	John Tyler	Whig, then Democrat
11	1845-9	James K. Polk	Democrat
12	1849-50	Zachary Taylor	Whig
13	1850-3	Millard Fillmore	Whig
14	1853-7	Franklin Pierce	Democrat
15	1857-61	James Buchanan	Democrat
16	1861-5	Abraham Lincoln	Republican
17	1865-9	Andrew Johnson	Democrat
18	1869-77	Ulysses S. Grant	Republican
19	1877-81	Rutherford B. Hayes	Republican
20	1881	James A. Garfield	Republican
21	1881-5	Chester A. Arthur	Republican
22	1885-9	Grover Cleveland	Democrat
23	1889-93	Benjamin Harrison	Republican
24	1893-7	Grover Cleveland	Democrat
25	1897-1901	William McKinley	Republican
26	1901-9	Theodore Roosevelt	Republican
27	1909-13	William H. Taft	Republican
28	1913-21	Woodrow Wilson	Democrat
29	1921-3	Warren G. Harding	Republican
30	1923-9	Calvin Coolidge	Republican
31	1929-33	Herbert Hoover	Republican
32	1933-45	Franklin D. Roosevelt	Democrat
33	1945-53	Harry S Truman	Democrat
34	1953-61	Dwight D. Eisenhower	Republican
35	1961-3	John F. Kennedy	Democrat
36	1963-9	Lyndon B. Johnson	Democrat
37	1969-74	Richard M. Nixon	Republican
38	1974-7	Gerald R. Ford	Republican
39	1977-81	James Earl Carter	Democrat
40	1981-9	Ronald W. Reagan	Republican
41	1989-93	George H. W. Bush	Republican
42	1993-	William J. Clinton	Democrat

PRIME MINISTERS OF AUSTRALIA

1901-3	Edmund Barton
1903-4	Alfred Deakin
1904	John C. Watson
1904-5	George Houstoun Reid
1905-8	Alfred Deakin
1908-9	Andrew Fisher
1909-10	Alfred Deakin
1910-13	Andrew Fisher
1913-14	Joseph Cook
1914-15	Andrew Fisher
1915-23	William M. Hughes
1923-9	Stanley M. Bruce
1929-31	James H. Scullin
1932-9	Joseph A. Lyons
1939-41	Robert Gordon Menzies
1941	Arthur William Fadden
1941-5	John Curtin
1945-9	Joseph Benedict Chifley
1949-66	Robert Gordon Menzies
1966-7	Harold Edward Holt
1968-71	John Grey Gorton
1971-2	William McMahon
1972-5	Gough Whitlam
1975-83	J. Malcolm Fraser
1983-91	Robert J. L. Hawke
1991-6	Paul Keating
1996-	John Howard

PRIME MINISTERS OF CANADA

1867-73	John A. Macdonald	1926-30	W. L. Mackenzie King
1873-8	Alexander Mackenzie	1930-5	Richard B. Bennett
1878-91	John A. Macdonald	1935-48	W. L. Mackenzie King
1891-2	John J. C. Abbott	1948-57	Louis Stephen St Laurent
1892-4	John S. D. Thompson	1957-63	John George Diefenbaker
1894-6	Mackenzie Bowell	1963-8	Lester B. Pearson
1896	Charles Tupper	1968-79	Pierre Elliott Trudeau
1896-1911	Wilfrid Laurier	1979-80	Joseph Clark
1911-20	Robert L. Borden	1980-4	Pierre Elliott Trudeau
1920-1	Arthur Meighen	1984	John Turner
1921-6	W. L. Mackenzie King	1984-93	Brian Mulroney
1926	Arthur Meighen	1993-	Jean Chrétien

SECRETARIES GENERAL OF THE UNITED NATIONS

SECRETARY GENERAL	COUNTRY	DATES
Trygve Lie	Norway	1946-52
Dag Hammarskjöld	Sweden	1953-61
U Thant	Burma	1962-72
Kurt Waldheim	Austria	1972-81
Javier Pérez de Cuéllar	Peru	1982-91
Boutros Boutros-Ghali	Egypt	1992-

PRESIDENTS OF FRANCE

THIRD REPUBLIC

1899-1906 Emile Loubet
1906-13 Armand Fallières
1913-20 Raymond Poincaré
1920 Paul Deschanel
1920-4 Alexandre Millerand
1924-31 Gaston Doumergue
1931-2 Paul Doumer
1932-40 Albert Lebrun

FOURTH REPUBLIC

1947-54 Vincent Auriol
1954-8 René Coty

FIFTH REPUBLIC

1959-69 Charles de Gaulle
1969-74 Georges Pompidou
1974-81 Valéry Giscard d'Estaing
1981-95 François Mitterrand
1995- Jacques Chirac

PRIME MINISTERS OF NEW ZEALAND

1856 Henry Sewell
1856 William Fox
1856-61 Edward William Stafford
1861-2 William Fox
1862-3 Alfred Domett
1863-4 Frederick Whitaker
1864-5 Frederick Aloysius Weld
1865-9 Edward William Stafford
1869-72 William Fox
1872 Edward William Stafford
1872-3 George Marsden Waterhouse
1873 William Fox
1873-5 Julius Vogel
1875-6 Daniel Pollen
1876 Julius Vogel
1876-7 Harry Albert Atkinson
1877-9 George Grey
1879-82 John Hall
1882-3 Frederick Whitaker
1883-4 Harry Albert Atkinson
1884 Robert Stout
1884 Harry Albert Atkinson
1884-7 Robert Stout
1887-91 Harry Albert Atkinson
1891-3 John Ballance
1893-1906 Richard John Seddon
1906 William Hall Jones
1906-12 Joseph George Ward
1912 Thomas Mackenzie
1912-25 William Ferguson Massey
1925 Francis Henry Dillion Bell
1925-8 Joseph Gordon Coates
1928-30 Joseph George Ward
1930-5 George William Forbes
1935-40 Michael J. Savage
1940-9 Peter Fraser
1949-57 Sidney J. Holland
1957 Keith J. Holyoake
1957-60 Walter Nash
1960-72 Keith J. Holyoake
1972 John R. Marshall
1972-4 Norman Kirk
1974-5 Wallace Rowling
1975-84 Robert D. Muldoon
1984-9 David Lange
1989-90 Geoffrey Palmer
1990 Michael Moore
1990- James Bolger

GERMANY

WEIMAR REPUBLIC

1919-25	Friedrich Ebert	President
1925-34	Paul von Hindenburg	President

THIRD REICH

1934-45	Adolf Hitler	President and Führer

GERMAN DEMOCRATIC REPUBLIC

1949-60	Wilhelm Pieck	President
1949-64	Otto Grotewohl	Premier
1960-73	Walter Ernst Karl Ulbricht	Chairman of State Council
1964-73	Willi Stoph	Premier
1973-6	Willi Stoph	Chairman
1973-6	Horst Sindermann	Premier
1976-89	Erich Honecker	Chairman
1976-89	Willi Stoph	Premier
1989	Egon Krenz	Chairman
1989-	Gregor Gysi	Chairman
1989	Hans Modrow	Chairman
1989-90	Lothar de Maizière	Chairman of Council of Ministers

GERMAN FEDERAL REPUBLIC

1949-59	Theodor Heuss	President
1949-63	Konrad Adenauer	Chancellor
1959-69	Heinrich Lübke	President
1963-6	Ludwig Erhard	Chancellor
1966-9	Kurt Georg Keisinger	Chancellor
1969-74	Gustav Heinemann	President
1969-74	Willy Brandt	Chancellor
1974-9	Walter Scheel	President
1974-82	Helmut Schmidt	Chancellor
1979-84	Karl Carstens	President
1982-	Helmut Kohl	Chancellor
1984-94	Richard von Weizsäcker	President
1990-	(after unification with German Democratic Republic) Helmut Kohl	Chancellor
1994-	Roman Herzog	President

THE SOVIET UNION

PRESIDENTS

1917 Leo Borisovitch Kamenev
1917-19 Yakov Mikhailovitch Sverlov
1919-46 Mikhail Ivanovitch Kalinin
1946-53 Nikolai Shvernik
1953-60 Klimentiy Voroshilov
1960-4 Leonid Brezhnev
1964-5 Anastas Mikoyan
1965-77 Nikolai Podgorny
1977-82 Leonid Brezhnev
1982-3 Vasily Kuznetsov (Acting President)
1983-4 Yuri Andropov
1984 Vasily Kuznetsov (Acting President)
1984-5 Konstantin Chernenko
1985 Vasily Kuznetsov (Acting President)
1985-8 Andrei Gromyko
1988-90 Mikhail Gorbachev

EXECUTIVE PRESIDENT

1990-1 Mikhail Gorbachev

GENERAL SECRETARIES

1922-53 Joseph Stalin
1953 Georgiy Malenkov
1953-64 Nikita Khrushchev

1964-82 Leonid Brezhnev
1982-4 Yuri Andropov
1984-5 Konstantin Chernenko
1985-91 Mikhail Gorbachev

CHAIRMEN (PRIME MINISTERS) COUNCIL OF MINISTERS

1917 Georgy Evgenyevich Lvov
1917 Aleksandr Fyodorovich Kerensky

COUNCIL OF PEOPLE'S COMMISSARS

1917-24 Vladimir Ilyich Lenin
1924-30 Aleksei Ivanoch Rykov
1930-41 Vyacheslav Mikailovich Molotov
1941-53 Joseph Stalin

COUNCIL OF MINISTERS

1953-5 Georgiy Malenkov
1955-8 Nikolai Bulganin
1958-64 Nikita Khrushchev
1964-80 Alexei Kosygin
1980-5 Nikolai Tikhonov
1985-91 Nikolai Ryzhkov

THE RUSSIAN FEDERATION

PRESIDENT

1991- Boris Yeltsin

IRELAND

GOVERNORS GENERAL

1922-8 Timothy Michael Healy
1927-32 James McNeill
1932-6 Donald Buckley

PRESIDENTS

1938-45 Douglas Hyde
1945-59 Sean Thomas O'Kelly
1959-73 Eamon de Valera
1973-4 Erskine H. Childers
1974-6 Caroll Daly
1976-90 Patrick J. Hillery
1990- Mary Robinson

PRIME MINISTERS (TAOISEACH)

1919-21 Eamon de Valera

1922 Arthur Griffith
1922-32 William Cosgrave
1932-48 Eamon de Valera
1948-51 John Aloysius Costello
1951-4 Eamon de Valera
1954-7 John Aloysius Costello
1957-9 Eamon de Valera
1959-66 Sean Lemass
1966-73 John Lynch
1973-7 Liam Cosgrave
1977-9 John Lynch
1979-82 Charles Haughey
1982-7 Garret Fitzgerald
1987-92 Charles Haughey
1992-94 Albert Reynolds
1994- John Bruton

POPES AND ANTIPOPES

(antipopes shown in bold)

c.64 Peter	366-84 Damasus I	640 Severinus	855-8 Benedict III
c.67-76/79 Linus	**366-7 Ursinus**	640-2 John IV	**855 Anastasius (Anastasius the Librarian)**
76-88 or 79-91 Anacletus	384-99 Siricius	642-9 Theodore I	
88-97 or 92-101 Clement I	399-401 Anastasius I	649-55 Martin I	858-67 Nicholas I
c.97-c.107 Evaristus	401-17 Innocent I	654-7 Eugenius I	867-72 Adrian II
105-15 or 109-19 Alexander I	417-18 Zosimus	657-72 Vitalian	872-82 John VIII
c.115-c.25 Sixtus I	418-22 Boniface I	672-6 Adeodatus II	882-4 Marinus I
c.125-c.36 Telesphorus	**418-19 Eulalius**	676-8 Donus	884-5 Adrian III
c.136-c.40 Hyginus	422-32 Celestine I	678-81 Agatho	885-91 Stephen V (or VI)
c.140-55 Pius I	432-40 Sixtus III	682-3 Leo II	891-6 Formosus
c.155-c.66 Anicetus	440-61 Leo I	684-5 Benedict II	896 Boniface VI
c.166-c.75 Soter	461-8 Hilary	685-6 John V	896 Stephen VI (or VII)
c.175-89 Eleutherius	468-83 Simplicius	686-7 Conon	897 Romanus
c.189-99 Victor I	483-92 Felix III (or II)	687-701 Sergius I	897 Theodore II
c.199-217 Zephyrinus	492-6 Gelasius I	**687 Theodore**	898-900 John IX
217-22 Calixtus I (Callistus)	496-8 Anastasius II	**687 Paschal**	900-903 Benedict IV
222-30 Urban I	498-514 Symmachus	701-5 John VI	903 Leo V
230-5 Pontian	**498-c.505 Laurentius**	705-7 John VII	**903-4 Christopher**
235-6 Anterus	514-23 Hormisdas	708 Sisinnius	904-11 Sergius III
236-50 Fabian	523-6 John I	708-15 Constantine	911-13 Anastasius III
251-3 Cornelius	526-30 Felix IV (or III)	715-31 Gregory II	913-14 Lando
251 Novatian	**530 Dioscorus**	731-41 Gregory III	914-28 John X
253-4 Lucius I	530-2 Boniface II	741-52 Zacharias (Zachary)	928 Leo VI
254-7 Stephen I	533-5 John II	**752 Stephen (II)**	929-31 Stephen VII (or VIII)
257-8 Sixtus II	535-6 Agapetus I	752-7 Stephen II (or III)	931-5 John XI
259-68 Dionysius	536-7 Silverius	757-67 Paul I	936-9 Leo VII
269-74 Felix I	537-55 Vigilius	**767-8 Constantine (II)**	939-42 Stephen VIII (or IX)
275-83 Eutychian	556-61 Pelagius I	**768 Philip**	942-6 Marinus II
283-96 Gaius	561-74 John III	768-72 Stephen III (or IV)	946-55 Agapetus II
296-304 Marcellinus	575-9 Benedict I	772-95 Adrian I	955-64 John XII
308-9 Marcellus I	579-90 Pelagius II	795-816 Leo III	963-5 Leo VIII
309-c.310 Eusebius	590-604 Gregory I	816-17 Stephen IV (or V)	964-6 Benedict V
311-14 Miltiades (Melchiades)	604-6 Sabinian	817-24 Paschal I	965-72 John XIII
314-35 Sylvester I	607 Boniface III	824-7 Eugenius II	973-4 Benedict VI
336 Mark	608-15 Boniface IV	827 Valentine	**974 Boniface VII (1st time)**
337-52 Julius I	615-18 Deusdedit (also called Adeodatus I)	827-44 Gregory IV	974-83 Benedict VII
352-66 Liberius	619-25 Boniface V	844 John	983-4 John XIV
355-8 Felix (II)	625-38 Honorius I	844-7 Sergius II	**984-5 Boniface VII (2nd time)**
		847-55 Leo IV	985-96 John XV (or XVI)

CHRISTIAN SAINTS

NAME AND FEAST DAY	IDENTITY AND ASSOCIATIONS	NAME AND FEAST DAY	IDENTITY AND ASSOCIATIONS
Agnes, January 21	Virgin martyr; patron of betrothed couples maidens and gardeners.	Boniface, June 5	Archbishop and martyr, Apostle of Frisia and Germany, patron of brewers and tailors.
Ambrose, December 7	Opposer of heresy; associated with Ambrosian chant, patron of bee-keepers and domestic animals.	Bridget of Kildare (Brigid/Bride), February 1	Second patron of Ireland, venerated in Wales, Alsace, Flanders and Portugal. Patron of poets, blacksmiths, dairymaids or cattle, fugitives and healers.
Andrew, November 30	Patron of Scotland, Russia, fishermen and sailors. Apostle and martyr.		
Anselm, April 21	Archbishop, influential theologian, founder of scholasticism.	Cecilia (Cecily/Celia), November 22	Virgin martyr, patron of musicians.
Antony of Egypt, January 17	Abbot, patriarch and patron of monks, healer of men and animals.	Christopher, July 25 (Reduced to a local cult 1969)	Martyr, patron of sailors, travellers, motorists, invoked against water, tempest, plague and sudden death.
Augustine of Canterbury, May 26, May 27 and May 13 at Canterbury	Monk, prior and archbishop, evangeliser of the Anglo-Saxons.	Columba of Iona, June 9	Apostle of Scotland, abbot and missionary.
Augustine of Hippo, August 28	Author of Confessions On the Trinity and The City of God, patron of theologians.	Cornelius, September 16 or 26	Pope and martyr, associated with St Cyprian in Western Church.
Barnabas, June 11	Apostle (not one of the 12) and martyr accompanied St Paul on first missionary journey, legendary first bishop of Milan.	Cuthbert, March 20	Monk, prior and bishop; most popular saint of northern England; patron of shepherds and seafarers.
Bartholomew, August 24	Apostle and martyr, patron of tanners and all who work with skins.	David of Wales, March 1	Monk and bishop; patron saint of Wales and only canonised Welsh saint; nicknamed Aquaticus because he drank no wine or beer.
Benedict of Nursia, July 11	Founder of the Benedictine order, patriarch of Western monasticism. Patron of Europe, schoolboys and coppersmiths.	Dominic, August 8 or 4	Founder of the Order of Friars Preachers (Dominicans); sent to preach against the Albigensian heresy in Languedoc.
Bernard of Clairvaux, August 20	Founder of 163 Cistercian monasteries patron of bee-keepers.	Dorothy (Dorothea), February 6	Virgin, martyr, patron of brides.

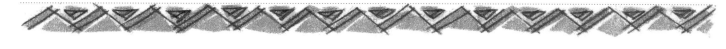

996-9 Gregory V
997-8 John XVI (or XVII)
999-1003 Sylvester II
1003 John XVII (or XVIII)
1004-9 John XVIII (or XIX)
1009-12 Sergius IV
1012 Gregory (VI)
1012-24 Benedict VIII
1024-32 John XIX (or XX)
1032-44 Benedict IX (1st time)
1045 Sylvester III
1045 Benedict IX (2nd time)
1045-6 Gregory VI
1046-7 Clement II
1047-8 Benedict IX (3rd time)
1048 Damasus II
1049-54 Leo IX
1055-7 Victor II
1057-8 Stephen IX (or X)
1058-9 Benedict X
1059-61 Nicholas II
1061-73 Alexander II
1061-72 Honorius (II)
1073-85 Gregory VII
1080-1100 Clement (III)
1086-7 Victor III
1088-99 Urban II
1099-1118 Paschal II
1100-2 Theodoric
1102 Albert (also called Aleric)
1105-11 Sylvester (IV)
1118-19 Gelasius II
1118-21 Gregory (VIII)
1119-24 Calixtus II (Callistus)
1124-30 Honorius II
1124 Celestine (II)
1130-43 Innocent II
1130-8 Anacletus (II)
1138 Victor (IV)

1143-4 Celestine II
1144-5 Lucius II
1145-53 Eugenius III
1153-4 Anastasius IV
1154-9 Adrian IV
1159-81 Alexander III
1159-64 Victor (IV)
1164-8 Paschal (III)
1168-78 Calixtus (III)
1179-80 Innocent (III)
1181-5 Lucius III
1185-7 Urban III
1187 Gregory VIII
1187-91 Clement III
1191-8 Celestine III
1198-1216 Innocent III
1216-27 Honorius III
1227-41 Gregory IX
1241 Celestine IV
1243-54 Innocent IV
1254-61 Alexander IV
1261-4 Urban IV
1265-8 Clement IV
1271-6 Gregory X
1276 Innocent V
1276 Adrian V
1276-7 John XXI
1277-80 Nicholas III
1281-5 Martin IV
1285-7 Honorius IV
1288-92 Nicholas IV
1294 Celestine V
1294-1303 Boniface VIII
1303-4 Benedict XI
1305-14 Clement V (at Avignon, from 1309)
1316-34 John XXII (at Avignon)
1328-30 Nicholas (V) (at Rome)
1334-42 Benedict XII (at Avignon)

1342-52 Clement VI (at Avignon)
1352-62 Innocent VI (at Avignon)
1362-70 Urban V (at Avignon)
1370-8 Gregory XI (at Avignon, then Rome from 1377)
1378-89 Urban VI
1378-94 Clement (VII) (at Avignon)
1389-1404 Boniface IX
1394-1423 Benedict (XIII) (at Avignon)
1404-6 Innocent VII
1406-15 Gregory XII
1409-10 Alexander (V) (at Bologna)
1410-15 John (XXIII) (at Bologna)
1417-31 Martin V
1431-47 Eugenius IV
1439-49 Felix (V) (also called Amadeus VIII of Savoy)
1447-55 Nicholas V
1455-8 Calixtus III (Callistus)
1458-64 Pius II
1464-71 Paul II
1471-84 Sixtus IV
1484-92 Innocent VIII
1492-1503 Alexander VI
1503 Pius III
1503-13 Julius II
1513-21 Leo X
1522-3 Adrian VI
1523-34 Clement VII
1534-49 Paul III
1550-5 Julius III
1555 Marcellus II
1555-9 Paul IV
1559-65 Pius IV
1566-72 Pius V
1572-85 Gregory XIII
1585-90 Sixtus V
1590 Urban VII

1590-1 Gregory XIV
1591 Innocent IX
1592-1605 Clement VIII
1605 Leo XI
1605-21 Paul V
1621-3 Gregory XV
1623-44 Urban VIII
1644-55 Innocent X
1655-67 Alexander VII
1667-9 Clement IX
1670-6 Clement X
1676-89 Innocent XI
1689-91 Alexander VIII
1691-1700 Innocent XII
1700-21 Clement XI
1721-4 Innocent XIII
1724-30 Benedict XIII
1730-40 Clement XII
1740-58 Benedict XIV
1758-69 Clement XIII
1769-74 Clement XIV
1775-99 Pius VI
1800-23 Pius VII
1823-9 Leo XII
1829-30 Pius VIII
1831-46 Gregory XVI
1846-78 Pius IX
1878-1903 Leo XIII
1903-14 Pius X
1914-22 Benedict XV
1922-39 Pius XI
1939-58 Pius XII
1958-63 John XXIII
1963-78 Paul VI
1978 John Paul I
1978- John Paul II

NAME AND FEAST DAY	IDENTITY AND ASSOCIATIONS	NAME AND FEAST DAY	IDENTITY AND ASSOCIATIONS
Dunstan, May 19	Benedictine monk, abbot and reformer; Archbishop of Canterbury; musician patron of goldsmiths, jewellers, locksmiths and armourers.	Joseph of Nazareth, March 19 (May 1, Joseph the Worker)	Foster-father of Jesus and husband of Virgin Mary, carpenter, patron of fathers of families, bursars, procurators, manual workers, engineers and all who desire a holy death.
Eligius (Loi, Eloi), December 1	Bishop, evangeliser of Flanders, goldsmith, patron of smiths and metal-workers.		
Francis of Assisi, October 4	Friar, founder of the Franciscan Order; preacher; lover of absolute poverty and nature, bearer of the stigmata, patron of ecologists and animals.	Luke, October 18	Evangelist, author of the Third Gospel and Acts, physician and possibly painter, disciple of St Paul, patron of artists, sculptors, doctors and surgeons.
Gabriel, September 29	One of seven archangels, patron of post office, telephone and telegraph workers.	Mark, April 25	Evangelist, author of the Second Gospel, patron of Venice, secretaries, notaries and glaziers.
George, April 23 (Reduced to a local cult 1969)	Martyr; soldier; patron saint of England, and of Venice, Genoa, Portugal, Catalonia; invoked against plague, leprosy, syphilis.	Mary Magdalene, July 22	Follower of Christ, the sinner who anointed Jesus's feet, present at the Crucifixion and first witness of his Resurrection, patron of repentant sinners and the contemplative life.
Gregory the Great, March 12 and September 3	Apostle of the English, writer and benefactor of the poor, patron of musicians, associated with Gregorian chant.		
John the Baptist, June 24	Hermit then preacher, son of the temple priest Zacharias and his wife Elizabeth, cousin of the Virgin Mary, the forerunner of Jesus Christ, patron of farriers and tailors.	Matthew, September 21	Apostle, evangelist and martyr, author of the First Gospel, publican (tax-collector), patron of bankers.
John the Evangelist, December 27	Apostle and evangelist, brother of St James the Great, author of the Fourth Gospel, entrusted with care of Mary, patron of theologians, booksellers.	Michael, September 29 (with All Angels)	Messenger of God, principal fighter against the devil or dragons, captain of the celestial armies, invoked for care of the sick, patron of radiologists, artists and soldiers.

Abbreviations: T = Top; B = Bottom; L = Left; C = Centre; R = Right

BAL = The Bridgeman Art Library, London
BLIB = Permission of the Board of the British Library
BM = Permission of the Trustees of the British Museum
BPK = Bildarchiv Preussischer Kulterbesitz, Berlin
ET = ET Archive, London
MEPL = Mary Evans Picture Library
RHPL = Robert Harding Picture Library

9 (T) Metropolitan Museum of Art/Gift of Mr and Mrs Carl Stoekel, 1897 (97.5). (B) Hulton Getty. 10 (T) Giraudon. (B) Giraudon/Musée des Arts Africains, Paris. 11 (TL) ET/National Library of Ireland. (B) Courtesy of the Massachusetts Historical Society. 12 (T) ET. (BR) AKG London. (B) Corbis-Bettmann. 13 (T) Science Photo Library/St Mary's Hospital Medical School. (BL) Sygma/Igor Kostin/Imago. (BR) AKG London. 16 Science Photo Library/John Reader. 17 (TL) Science Photo Library/John Reader. (TR) John Davies Fine Paintings, Stow-on-the-Wold. (footprint) Science Photo Library/John Reader. (skull) Science Photo Library/John Reader. (B) Science Photo Library/John Reader. 18 (TL) Scotland in Focus/J Weir. (BR) Giraudon/Musée du Louvre, Paris. 19 (T) BAL/Victoria and Albert Museum, London. (CR) Kunsthistorisches Museum, Vienna. (BR) BAL/Noortman (London) Ltd. 20 (C) Museum of London. (B) National Geographic Society. 20-21 Museum of London. 21 (T) AKG London/Musée Condé, Chantilly. (B) ET/Freer Gallery, Washington. 23 (T) The Brooklyn Museum (54.162)/Charles Edwin Wilbour Fund (B) C. M. Dixon/Arkeoloji Muzeleri, Istanbul. 24 (T) Novosti. (B) Ashmolean Museum, Oxford. 25 Magnum/Marc Ribaud. 26 BLIB/India Office. 27 (T) Hulton Getty. (B) MEPL. 28 (T) Metropolitan Museum of Art/Gift of Mrs Frank B. Porter, 1922/ (C) Corbis-Bettmann. (BR) Peter Newark's Pictures. 28-29 Paul Warchol/West Point Museum, US Military Academy, West Point, New York. 29 Private Collection/National Archives, Washington. 30 (CL) Aspect/Larry Burrows (BL). RHPL/Tim Hall. 31 (BL) Courtesy of the Director, National Army Museum, London. (BC) Paul Warchol/ West Point Museum, US Military Academy, West Point, New York. 32 (T) National Maritime Museum, London. (B) Rex Features Ltd/Alain Mingam/Sipa. 33 AKG London/Erich Lessing/ Musée du Louvre, Paris. 34 (B) Corbis-Bettmann. 35 (TL) Ikona, Rome/Bibliothèque Municipale, Avignon (Ms.136 C.241). (BR) ET/Bundesarchiv, Koblenz. 36 (T) US National Archives,Washington/Signal Corps. (B) Imperial War Museum. 37 (T) Werner Forman Archive. (B) Magnum/Ian Berry. 38 RHPL/US Army. 40 (L) BAL/private collection. (R) Science & Society Picture Library. 42 AKG London/ Bibliothèque Nationale, Paris. 43 AKG London/Erich Lessing/ British Museum, London. 44 (T) BPK/Musée Condé, Chantilly. (B) Ullstein. 45 BM. 46 Stadtisches Kunstsammlungen, Augsberg. 47 (TR) Giraudon. (C) Bibliothèque Nationale, Paris. (BL) Corbis-Bettmann. 48 (R) BM. (B) RHPL/John Ross/Vatican Museum. 49 Reproduced by courtesy of the Trustees of the Chester Beatty Library, Dublin. 50 (T) BAL. (B) Jean-Loup Charmet. 51 The Robert Hunt Library. 52 Popperfoto. (CR) Science Photo Library/David Parker/600 Group. (BR) Corbis-Bettmann. 54 (T) AKG London/Erich Lessing/Archaeological Museum, Istanbul. (B) AKG London. 55 (T) National Portrait Gallery, London (detail). (C) BLIB (8821 a21). (BR) Hulton Getty. 56 (TL) Science & Society Picture Library. (C) Peter Newark's Pictures. 58 Camera Press/Eastlight. 60 The Mansell Collection. 61 (T) Barnardos. (C) Sonia Halliday/Topkapi Palace Museum, Istanbul. (B) Sonia Halliday/Topkapi Palace Museum, Istanbul. 62 (TR) Bank of England. (C) ET. (BL) BAL/Seminario Patriacale, Venice. 64 (TL) Jean-Loup Charmet/Musée Carnavalet, Paris. (CR) Bauhaus-Archiv/ © Frite Bliefernichte. (BR) Bauhaus-Archiv/ © Dr F Karsten, London. 65 Redferns. 66 BAL/British Library. 67 (BL) Frank Spooner/Gamma. 68 (T) BPK/National Gallery, London. (B) ET. 69 (T) University College London. (B) AKG London. 70 (TR) The Field Museum, Chicago, IL. (Neg. A99505). (C) BPK/Volkerkunde-Museum, Vienna. (B) Werner Forman Archive. 71 Ullstein/Wolfgang Bera. 72 (C) Jean-Loup Charmet/Bibliothèque Nationale, Paris. (BL) Science & Society Picture Library. 73 Rex Features Ltd/Goksin Sipahioglu. 74 (T) BLIB (C351.13 (1) TP). (C) AKG London/British Library. (B) BAL/Kremlin Museums, Moscow. 75 (BC) Peter Newark's Pictures. (BR) Peter Newark's Pictures. 76 The Mansell Collection. 77 (T) Magnum/Raymond Depardone. (B) National Maritime Museum, London. 79 (T) Bibliothèque Royale Albert 1er, Brussels. (CL) Hubert Josse/Bibliothèque Nationale, Paris. (BL) (upper) Science & Society Picture Library. (BL) (lower) Science & Society Picture Library. (BC) The Wellcome Institute Library, London. 80 Bundesarchiv. 81 Hulton Getty. 82 (T) BM. (B) Dave King Collection. 83 (Bolivar) ET/(Boyaca) Alfredo Padron/Painting by Martin Tovar y Tovar, Presidential Palace, Caracas. 84 (TL) Corbis-Bettmann. (gun) Peter Newark's Pictures. (TC) Bibliothèque Nationale, Paris (Ms.Gr.1807 f69v). (TR) BLIB (G.6368 TP). (C) BLIB (Ms. Add. 14,448 f334). (CR) Private Collection. (B) Private Collection. 85 (TL) BLIB (12554.TT.20-T/P). (TR) 'One Day in the Life of Ivan Denisovich' Alexander Solzhenitsyn, translated by Ralph Parker published by Victor Gollancz. (C) BLIB (B7583.de/19/p/195) from 'Baby and Child Care' Dr Spock, Random House (UK) Ltd. (BL) The Penguin Group. (BR) Richard and Sally Greenhill. 86 (T) AKG London/Versailles. (B) BPK. 87 By permission of The Metropolitan Police. 88 BLIB (OR 5896 13). 89 (T) National Gallery of Ireland. (B) BPK/Hanns Hubmann. 90 BLIB (6 50.b.5.Pl.6). 91 BAL/Crawford Municipal Art Gallery, Cork. 92 BAL/Imperial War Museum London/Crown Copyright. 93 BLIB/India Office (Add. Or. 888 3). 94 (TR) Public Record Office/(Ryvita) Robert Opie. (brooch) ET. (B) BAL/Guildhall Art Gallery, Corporation of London. 95 BAL. 96 National Portrait Gallery, London. 97 Magnum/Abbas. 98 Private Collection. 99 (T) BPK/The Master, Fellows and Scholars of Corpus Christi College, Cambridge. (B) Corbis-Bettmann. 100 (C) Courtesy of the Trustees of the Victoria and Albert Museum, London. (B) BAL/Christie's Images. 101 BPK. 103 (R) Imperial War Museum. (B) Imperial War Museum. 104 Black Star, New York/Ken Love. 105 Scala. 106 (TL) Cadbury Limited. (TC) Cadbury Limited. (BR) Giraudon/Alinari Uffizi, Florence. 107 (T) AKG London. (B) Bibliothèque Publique et Universitaire, Geneva. 108 (R) Magnum/Chris Steele-Perkins. (B) Popperfoto. 109 (TC) Hulton Getty. (TR) Peter Newark's Pictures. 111 (BC) Camera Press. (BR) King Features. 113 (T) Andrew Carnegie Birthplace Museum, Dunfirmline. (B) BLIB (CUP.410.g.74). 114 (T) ET/Bardo Museum, Tunis. (B) Jean-Loup Charmet. 115 (TR) Hulton Getty. (C) ET/Ford Motor Company. (BL) Mercedes-Benz Classic Archiv, Stuttgart. 116 (T) AKG London. (B) MEPL. 118-19 Julian Cotton Picture Library/Jason Hawkes. 119 (CR) Aerofilms. (R) RHPL. 120 BAL/British Library, London. 121 (T) BAL/Hermitage, St Petersburg. (B) BAL/Broadlands Trust, Hants. 122 (TL) Hulton Getty. (TC) BLIB. 123 (T) Magnum. (B) ET/Trinity College, Dublin. 124 The Royal Collection © Her Majesty The Queen. 125 (T) The Ronald Grant Archive. (Chaplin) The Ronald Grant Archive. (BR) RHPL. 126 (BL) private collection. (B) The Fotomas Index. 127 AKG London/Aachen/Erich Lessing. 128 (TL) Scala/Palazzo Farnesse, Caprarola. (C) BAL Gruuthusemuseum, Bruges. 129 (TR) Michael Holford/ Hudson's Bay Company. (C) Guildhall Library, Corporation of London. (BL) Konstmuseum, Gothenburg/'The body of Charles XII being carried home from Norway' by Gustaf Cederstrom. 130 (T) Sygma/Igor Kostin/Imago. (B) RHPL/Courtesy of the Masters and Fellows of Corpus Christi College, Cambridge (Ms. 61 f1 verso). 131 Bazaar/Mats Ohman. 132 (T) Bibliothèque Nationale, Paris (Ms. Lat. 9333 f8). 132-3 Staatliche Museum, Kassel. 133 (T) Bibliothèque Nationale, Paris (Ms.Fr.134 f92v). (C) ET. (B) ET. 135 (TL) The Mansell Collection. (CL) Art Resource, NY/The Danny & Hettie Heineman Collection/ The Pierpont Morgan Library, New York. (CR) By Permission of the Christian Science Board of Directors. (BR) Brown Brothers. 136 (L) Schweizerisches Lanesmuseum, Zurich (LM-3405.178 Neg. CO-2543). (B) BAL/Bibliothèque Nationale, Paris. 136-7 (T) AKG London/ Universitatsbibliothek, Heidelberg. (B) Giraudon/ Bibliothèque de l'Arsenal, Paris. 137 (TL) ET/Universitatsbibliothek, Heidelberg. (CL) ET/ Universitatsbibliothek, Heidelberg. (BL) Giraudon/ Archive de France, Paris. 138 ET/Gripsholm Castle, Sweden. 139 (T) Jean-Loup Charmet. (B) National Maritime Museum, London. 140 (T) Pictorial Press. (B) Imperial War Museum. 141 (T) Giraudon/Bibliothèque Nationale, Paris. (B) ET 144 Roger-Viollet. 145 (C) BPK/ Antiken Museum, Berlin. (BR) Hubert Josse/Musée des Beaux-Arts, Lyon. 146 (T) Frank Spooner/Markel/Liaison/Gamma. (B) BLIB. 147 (TR)/The Medieval Academy of America. (C) Musée Ochier, Cluny. (BL) BAL/Bibliothèque Nationale, Paris. 148 ET/British Museum, London. 149 (T) Hulton Getty. (B) RHPL/Réunion de la Musées Nationaux/Musée de Versailles. 150 (L) Corbis-Bettmann. (C) CIRIP/Alain Gesgon. (B) BPK. 151 The Bodleian Library, Oxford (Ms. Maps Notts. 92 sheet1). 153 Dave King Collection. 154 Giraudon. 154-5 National Maritime Museum, London. 155 (T) BAL/Musée Bargoin, Clermont-Ferrand. (C) Giancarlo Costa. (B) BAL/Museo Civico, Turin. 156 (T) Science Photo Library/NASA. (B) Jean-Loup Charmet/Musée de la Poste, Paris. 156-7 Imperial War Museum. 158 (T) Dave King Collection. (TR) Dave King Collection. 159 (TL) Novosti. (CR) Magnum/Bruno Barbey. (B) Novosti. 160 (T) Giraudon/Musée du Louvre, Paris. (B) National Palace Museum, Taipei, Taiwan, Republic of China. 161 (T) Corbis-Bettmann. (B) The Bodleian Library, Oxford. 163 Roger-Viollet. 164 (T) ET/National Maritime Museum, London. (B) National Maritime Museum, London. 165 (T) BLIB (Ms. Or. 7028). 166 (T) The Mansell Collection. (B) G.Dagli Orti/Biblioteca Nacional, Madrid. 167 Scala/Russian State Museum, St Petersburg. 168 (T) MEPL. (B) Brown Brothers. 169 (T) Yale Collection of Western Americana/Beinecke Rare Books and Manuscripts Library. (B) BAL/Bibliothèque Nationale, Paris. 170 ET. 171 (TL) Peter Newark's Pictures. (CL) The Alamo, Daughters of the Republic of Texas. (B) National Portrait Gallery, London. 172 Bibliothèque Nationale, Paris (Ms Fr 5594 f213). 174 (T) The Fotomas Index. (B) Popperfoto. 175 (T) BLIB(10815. dd. TP). (B) Peter Newark's Pictures. 176 South America Pictures. 177 Société Francaise de Photographie, Paris. 178 (T) BPK. (B) BPK. 179 (T) ET/Pitti Palace, Florence. (B) Giraudon/Musée Carnavalet. 180 MEPL. 181 (T) Giraudon/Musée du Louvre, Paris/(Davy)Hulton Getty. (BR) Michael Holford/Royal Institution, London. 182 (TC) Giraudon/Palazzo Reale. (CL) ET/Czartrysky Museum, Cracow. (CR) Giraudon/Alinari. 183 (T) Frank Spooner/Burrows/Liaison USA. (C) Peter Newark's Pictures. (BR) The Fotomas Index. 184 (T) Statni Galerie, Zlin. (C) Woodfin Camp & Associates/Alexandra Avakian. (B) RHPL/National Achives, Washington. 185 Imperial War Museum. 186 (T) Giraudon/Musée du Louvre, Paris. (B) BLIB (Add. Or. 948). 187 (TL) ZEFA. (C) Scala/Delfi Museum. (BR) Sygma. 188 (T) BM. (B) American School of Classical Studies at Athens: Agora Excavations. 189 Culver Pictures, New York. 190 (T) Syndication International/National Gallery, London. (B) Magnum/B. Glinn. 191 (L) The Fotomas Index. (R) Hulton Getty. 192 (T) BAL/Giraudon/Musée de la Venerie, Senlis. 193 (T) Canadian War Museum/National Museums of Canada/Painting by Charles Comfort. (B) AKG London. 194 (T) Giraudon. (B) The Kobal Collection. 195 (T) Giraudon/Versailles. (C) BLIB (8005.aa.11). 196 (T) Punch. (B) BAL/Pushkin Museum, Moscow. 197 (T) BAL/Christies's, London. 198 (L) Trinity College Library, Cambridge (Ms.R.17.1.f284v/285r). (R) Werner Forman Archive/British Museum. (BR) Ancient Art and Achitecture Collection. 198-9 Werner Forman Archive/British Museum. 199 (TR) Arcaid/Richard Bryant. (CL) Edifice. (BL) BAL/Christie's, London. 200 MEPL. 201 (T) Jean-Loup Charmet. 202 (T) Frank Spooner/Gamma. (B) BAL/British Library. (B) The Fotomas Index. 203 (T) Hulton Getty. (B) MEPL. 204 (B) Sygma. 205 (TL) BAL/Guild Hall Library, London. (TR) ET/India Office Library, London. (BL) Tony Stone Photo Library, London/Tom Till. (BC) Photo: The Kon-Tiki Museum, Oslo, Norway. 206 (T) ET. (B). 207 (T) ET. (B) National Portrait Gallery, London. 209 Popperfoto. 210 (TR) Giraudon/Museum of Gold, Lima. (BL) Corbis-Bettmann/Penguin. (equation) The Hebrew University of Jerusalem/Albert Einstein Archives. 211 (T) Culver Pictures, New York. (B) Hulton Getty. 212 (C) Courtesy of the Trustees of the Victoria and Albert Museum, London. (B) The Fotomas Index. 213 (T) County Record Office, Bedford. (B) ET/Carl Marx Museum, Trier. 215 (T) BLIB (65.g.6 pl. 11). (C) BAL/Giraudon/Musée des Beax-Arts, Valenciennes. (B) Hubert Josse/Musée des Beaux-Arts, Rouen. 216 RHPL/Robert Freck/Odyssey. 217 ET/Palazzo Barberini, Rome. 218 (T) Michael Holford/British Library, London. (B) Scala/Museo Etrusco Guarnacci, Volterra. 219 (T) Popperfoto (BL) MEPL. (BR) ET. 221 Scala/Biblioteca Nazionale, Florence. 222 (T) Sonia Halliday/Biblioteca Nacional, Madrid. (C) ET/ Christchurch College, Oxford. (B) RHPL. 223 (T) Hulton Getty. (B) Scala/Galleria Sabauda, Turin. 224 Scala/Sala Regia, Vatican. (T) Popperfoto. 225 Museo del Prado Madrid. 226 (T) Weidenfeld and Nicolson. (CR) Moro Roma. (B) BLIB. (10231;29(1934)114). 227 (T) ET/Royal Chapel, Granada. (B) The Royal Collection © Her Majesty The Queen. 228 (T) Michael Holford/Musée de Bayeux. 228-9 (B) ET/Achives Nationales, Paris. 229 (T) BAL/National Maritime Museum, London. (BL) Giraudon/Musée Condé, Chantilly. 230 BAL/Guildhall Library, London. 231 (T) Science Photo Library/St Mary's Hospital Medical School. (B) Michael Holford. 232 (TR) John Frost Historical Newspaper Service. (B) Imperial War Museum. 232-3 BAL/Imperial War Museum, London. 233 (C) Imperial War Museum, London. (BL) Imperial War Museum, London. (BC) Imperial War Museum, London. (BR) Imperial War Museum, London. 234 (TL) Süddeutscher Verlag. (BR) Corbis-Bettmann. 235 Scala. 236 (T) Hulton Getty. (B) Popperfoto. 236-7 RAF Museum, Hendon. 237 (TL) Corbis-Bettmann. (CL) Corbis-Bettmann. (C) BPK/Kunst Bibliothek, Berlin/Artist Jupp Wiertz, photo D. Katz. (BL) Telegraph Colour Library. 238 BAL/Giraudon. 239 (T) BPK/Staatsbibliothek, Berlin. (R) Corbis-Bettmann. (BL) The Associated Press. 240 AKG London. 241 Philadelphia Museum of Art/The Mr & Mrs Wharton Sinkler Collection. 242 Marshall Cavendish Ltd/By permission of the United Grand Lodge, London. 243 MEPL. 244 (T) Scala/Versailles. (B) ET. 245 (TL) ET. (fan) Giraudon/Musée Carnavalet, Paris. (CL) Giraudon/Musée Carnavalet, Paris. (music) BAL/British Library. (B) BAL/Bibliothèque Nationale, Paris/Giraudon. 246 (T) MEPL/Sigmund Freud Copyrights. (B) ET/Bibliothèque Nationale, Paris. (Ms Harl 4379 f.112v). 247 (T) Hulton Getty. (B) AKG London. 248 (T) Giancarlo Costa. (B) Punch. 249 (TC) ET. (TR) Imperial War Museum. (B) Scala/Academia, Venice. 250 (BL) BAL/Biblioteca Marucelliana, Florence. (B) Hubert Josse/Louvre, Paris. 251 (TC) Rex Features Ltd/SIPA. (TR) Sygma/Chine Nouvelle. 252 (T) Hulton Getty. (B) Katz Pictures Limited/Margaret Bourke-White/LIFE Magazine © 1946 Time Inc. 253 (T) Scala/Museo del Risorgimento, Milan. (B) South America Pictures. 254 (T) RCS Libri & Grandi Opere, Milan/Société Archeologique et Historique de la Charente, Angoulême. (B) The Mansell Collection. 255 (T) National Portrait Gallery, London. (B) ET/Topkapi Museum, Istanbul. 256 (T) Sonia Halliday. (B) Rex Features Ltd. 259 Katz Pictures

Limited/LIFE Magazine © 1936 Time Inc. 260 (T) Wallace Collection, London. (B) Jean-Loup Charmet/Bibliothèque de la Ville de Paris. 261 (T) Hulton Getty. (B) © Glasgow Museum & Art Galleries. 262 Giraudon/Bibliothèque Nationale, Paris. 263 (T) Popperfoto. (B) Frank Spooner/V Shone/GAMMA. 264 (CL) Peter Newark's Pictures. (BL) Peter Newark's Pictures. 265 (TL) ET/Gordon Boy's School, Woking. (TR) Michael Holford/Statens Historiska Museum, Stockholm. (B) Novosti/N Petrov. 266 (T) BAL. (B) US Army Military History Institute, Carlisle, PA/Massachusetts Commandery. 267 (T) BAL/Stapleton Collection. (B) Magnum/Henri Cartier-Bresson. 268 (TR) Yale Center for British Art/Paul Mellon Collection (detail). (B) BLIB (Add Ms 36488 A ff 63v-64). 269 Colorific/Stan Grossfield/Black Star. 271 Rex Features Ltd/Action Press. 272 (TC) Werner Forman Archive. (tokens) Kostos Kontos, Athens. (mask) Museum of Fine Arts Boston/Gift of Dr Herbert A. Cahn. (BL) Ikona, Rome/Musei Vaticani, Rome. 273 (T) By courtesy of The Mercers' Company/Thomas Gresham, 1544, Flemish school, oil on panel. (B) BAL/National Gallery, London. 274 (T) BLIB. (Ms. Roy. 6 E IX f24). (B) Corbis-Bettmann. 275 (T) Giraudon/Lauros/Musée Carnavalet, Paris. (B) AKG London/Museo Correr, Venice. 276 (T) Michael Holford/Musée Guimet, Paris. (B) Rex Features Ltd. (T) Doccon-Gibod/SIPA. 277 (T) ET/(B) ET/Uffizi, Florence. 278 (T) National Portrait Gallery, London (detail). (B) Jean-Loup Charmet. 279 (T) Private Collection. (B) Imperial War Museum. 280 MEPL. 281 RCS Libri & Grandi Opere, Milan/Naturhistorisches Museum, Vienna. 282 (T) ET/Staatsarchiv, Hamburg. (BL) Private Collection. (BL) Private Collection. 283 (T) Michael Holford/Musée de Bayeux. (B) Private collection. 284. (T) ET. (B) Jürgen Liepe, Berlin. 285 (T) Rex Features Ltd/CIK/SIPA. (B) Deutsches Theatermuseum, Munich. 286 (TL) Colorific/Alon Reininger. (TC) Corbis-Bettmann. 286-7 The Mansell Collection. 287 (T) Scala/S. Groce, Florence. 288 BAL/Musée Crozatier, Le Puy en Velay. 289 Réunion des Musées Nationaux. 290 (T) BAL/Thyssen-Boremisza Collection, Lugano-Castgnola. (B) Bibliothèque Nationale, Paris (Ms. Fr. 2695 f11). 291 (T) BAL/Wadsworth Atheneum, Hartford, Conn. (B) ET/Museo Correr, Venice. 292 (T) Imperial War Museum. (B) RHPL. 293 By courtesy of The Mitchell Library, Glasgow City Libraries. 294 (T) BAL/British Library, London. (B) Popperfoto. 295 (TL) AKG London. (C) Imperial War Museum. (BR) Corbis-Bettmann. 296 (TR) National Portrait Gallery, London. (C) AKG London/Hubert Lanzinger. (BL) AKG London. 297 (BC) The Ronald Grant Archive. (BR) The Ronald Grant Archive. 298 (CR) Wiener Library/Zydowski Institute. (BL) Katz Pictures Limited/Margaret Bourke-White/LIFE Magazine © Time Warner Inc. 300 (T) Rex Features Ltd/Clevenger/SIPA. (R) Rex Features Ltd/Bill Gentile/SIPA. (B) MEPL. 301 National Archives, Washington. 302 Jean-Loup Charmet. 303 (TL) BLIB (1367 c2 Fr.). (C) BAL/Victoria and Albert Museum, London. (B) AKG London/Alte Nationalgalerie, Berlin. 305 Magnum/Erich Lessing. 306 (T) The Associated Press. (B) ET. 307 (T) Michael Holford/British Museum, London. (B) ZEFA. 308 (BL)/CNMHS/Philippe Berthe. © DACS 1996. (BC) BAL/Vatican Museums and Art Galleries, Rome. (BR) Scala/Prado, Madrid. 308-9 The Board of Trinity College, Dublin (Ms.58 f27v). 309 (TL) Colorific/Dr Abraham Zapruder. (TC) British Film Institute. (TR) Images Colour Library. (CL) BAL/Musées Royaux des Beax-Arts, Brussels. (BL) Kingston Corporation. (BR) BAL/Nasjonalgalleriet, Oslo/ © The Munch Museum/The Munch-Ellingsen Group/DACS 1996. 310 (T) Jean-Loup Charmet. (B) BAL/Musée Marmottan, Paris/ © ADAGP, Paris and DACS, London 1996. 311 Corbis-Bettmann. 312 (T) BLIB (Add. Ms. 27255 f22v). (B) BLIB (Add. Ms. 27255 f70v). 313 (TL) BLIB. (Add. Ms. 27255 f75v). (CL) BLIB (Add. Ms. 27255 f96v). (BR) ET/Prado, Madrid. 314 Courtesy of the Trustees of the Victoria and Albert Museum, London. 314-15 RHPL/FPG International. 315 (CL) Corbis-Bettmann. (BL) Rex Features Ltd/Patrick Lucero. (BR) Science Photo Library/Allen Green. 316 (T) Peter Newark's Pictures. (BC) Michael Holford/Andre Breton Collection, Paris. (BR) Bryan & Cherry Alexander. 317 (T) Hulton Getty. (B) Rex Features Ltd/Luc Delahaye. 318 (T) Scala. (B) Frank Spooner/Alain Mingam. 319 Slide File. 320 (fr) Réunion des Musées Nationaux/J. Schosmans/Musée des Antiquites Nationales, St-German-en-Laye./(sickle) private collection. (agriculture) AKG London/Erich Lessing. (writing) Giraudon/Iraq Museum, Baghdad. (counting) Département des Antiquites Orientales, Musée du Louvre, Paris. 320-2 (counting) Département des Antiquites Orientales, Musée du Louvre, Paris. 321 (counting) Département des Antiquites Orientales, Musée du Louvre, Paris. (counting) Département des Antiquites Orientales, Musée du Louvre, Paris. (counting) Département des Antiquites Orientales, Musée du Louvre, Paris. (printing) AKG London/Guttenberg Museum, Mainz/Erich Lessing. (steam) Science & Society Picture Library. (motor) The National Motor Museum, Beaulieu. (photography) Science & Society Picture Library. (radio) GEC-Marconi Ltd. (computer) Corbis-Bettmann. 322 (TL) Sonia Halliday. (TR) Jean-Loup Charmet. (B) Hulton Getty. 323 (T) Science & Society Picture Library. (C) RCS Libri & Grandi Opere, Milan/Musée Archaeologique, Épernay. (B) Kodak Museum. 324. (T) The Robert Hunt Library. 325 ET/Historical Museum, Moscow. 326 (C) ET. (BR) Lynn Abercrombie. 327 (CL) Sonia Halliday/Topkapi Museum, Istanbul. (BL) BAL/V&A Museum, London. 328 (T) BAL/Tate Gallery, London. (BL) Bulloz, Paris/Archives Nationales. (BR) Michael Holford/V&A Museum, London. 329 Bruce Coleman Ltd/Dr Stephen Coyne. 330 Independent Newspapers, Johannesburg. 331 BAL/British Library, London. 332 (T) Colorific/Michael Yamashita. (CL) The Associated Press/Kutsumi Kasahara. (B) RHPL. 333 (TL) Courtesy of Soni Music. (TC) AKG London. (B) Syndication International. 334 BAL/V & A Museum, London. 335 (T) RHPL/British Library (Ms Azz NS 2868). (B) Comstock Photofile Limited. 336 (TL) Popperfoto 337 (TL) BAL/Prado, Madrid. (TR) BAL/Museo S. Marco, Florence/Giraudon. (BL) BAL/Fitzwilliam Museum, Universitiy of Cambridge. (BR) Robert Opie. 338 (TR) (lower) BAL/Lauros-Giraudon/Musée du Louvre, Paris. (TR) ET. 339 Magnum/Scheiwzer Illustrierte/Dolf Preisig. 340 (T) Giraudon/Musée du Louvre, Paris. (B) private collection. 341 (T) Corbis-Bettmann. (B) BLIB (Ms Roy. 15 E. 11 f.265). 342 (T) Giraudon/Musée du Louvre, Paris. (B) Magnum/James Nachtwey. 343 (T) Michael Holford/Ministry of Defence. (B) AKG London. 344 (T) Tony Stone Photo Library, London/Richard Passmore. (B) Hulton Getty. 345 BPK/Hanns Hubmann. 346 AKG London. 347 Magnum/Ian Berry. 349 (T) Magnum/Dennis Stock. (B) Magnum/Abbas. 350 (TC) ET. (TR) National Portrait Gallery, London. (detail). 351 (T) AKG London/Erich Lessing. (B) ET/Imperial War Museum, London. 352 (TL) Michael Holford. (TC) Michael Holford. 353 (TC) AKG London. (TR) Jean-Loup Charmet. (B) AKG London/Bayerische Staatsbibliothek, Munich. 354 British Museum. 355 Frank Spooner/Fox-Liaison. 357 ET/Museum of Labour History. 358 (T) The Bodleian Library, Oxford (Ms Bodley 569 f1). (B) Tony Stone Photo Library, London/Gerard Pile. 359 (CR) A.D.L./M. Lariviere. (BR) National Geographic Society/Sisse Brimberg. 360 (T) Jean-Loup Charmet/Archive Nationale, Paris. (B) BAL/Tate Gallery, London/Permission of the Executors of Vivien White. 361 BAL/Penshurst Place, Kent. 362 AKG London. 363 (TL) BAL/Novosti. (TR) Michael Holford/National Maritime Museum, London. (B) Novosti. 364 (T) BAL/private collection/artist, Oscar Beringhaus. (L) Syndication International/Missouri Historical Society. 365 Corbis-Bettmann. 366 AKG London. 367 (T) The Wellcome Institute Library, London. (B) Corbis-Bettmann. 368 (T) BAL. (B) Hulton Getty. 369 Arcaid/Richard Bryant. 370 (TL) Permission of the National Museum of Labour History. (TC) Permission of the National Museum of Labour History. (B) Rex Features Ltd/Kazuyoshi Nomachi. 371 (BL) BAL/Bibliothèque Nationale, Paris. (BR) Scala. 372 BAL/Chateau de Versailles. 373 (T) Corbis-Bettmann. (B) Giraudon/National Portrait Gallery, London. 374 (T) MEPL. (B) MEPL. 375 (T) AKG London/artist Gerhard Kurt Muller. (B) AKG London. 376 (T) ET. (B) MEPL. 377 AKG London/Palazzo Vecchio, Florence. 378 Corbis-Bettmann. 380 (T) AKG London/der Stadt, Vienna/Photo Erich Lessing/artist Emil Orlik. (B) Magnum/George Rodger. 382 Magnum/Eve Arnold. 383 (T) BLIB (Ms Add 18866 f135). (B) Giraudon. 384 (T) Rex Features Ltd/Jacques Witt. (B) Bailey's African History Archives. 385 (T) BAL/Musées Royaux des Beax-Arts, Brussels. (B) BAL British Library. 386 (T) Camera Press/Interfoto. (C) ET. (B) Sovfoto, New York. 387 (T) Sygma/A Hernandez. (B) ET/Bibliothèque Nationale, Paris. 388 (T) BM. (B) BLIB. (Map C.1.d.2 world). 389 (T) AKG London/Akademie der Bildenden Kuenste, Vienna. (B) The Mansell Collection. 390 BAL/Blenheim Palace, Oxfordshire. 391 BPK/Alte Pinakothek, Munich/Photo Lutze Brown. 392 (BC) BPK/A Dagli Orti. (book) private collection. 393 (T) BAL/Trustees of the Bedford Estate. (BC) (C) The Trustees of the National Museums of Scotland. (BR) private collection. 394 ET/Museo Nazionale, Reggio Calabris. 394-5 AKG London. 395 (TL) Giraudon/Bibliothèque Municipale, Laon. (TR) ET/V&A Museum, London. (C) BAL/Tretjakoff Gallery, Moscow. (CR) Impact/Mohamed Ansar. 396 Camera Press. 397 (T) Colorific/Richard Nowitz/Black Star. (C) Private Collection. (B) AKG London/Erich Lessing. 398 The Illustrated London News Picture Library. 399 Hulton Getty. 400 (TR) Network/Dod Miller. (CR) Rex Features Ltd/Frank Griffin. (B) The Associated Press/Nguyen Kong/SIPA. 401 (TL) Dave King Collection. (TC) Corbis-Bettmann. (C) Rex Features Ltd. (BL) Photograph by Tim Graham. (BC) Photograph by Tim Graham. 402 (TR) AKG London/Erich Lessing. (CR) Corbis-Bettmann. (BL) BAL/Kunsthalle, Mannheim. 403 (L) Corbis-Bettmann. (B) Corbis-Bettmann. 404 (BL) BLIB. (LR 275.a.1 Pl.24). (BC) ET/Museum of Mankind, London. 405 private collection. (C) BAL/Museum of Mankind, London. (BC) South America Pictures. (BR) ET/Museo Arqueologico, Lima. 406 (T) Scala/Palazzo Medici Riccardi, Florence. (B) ET/V&A Museum, London. 407 (T) Camera Press/Penny Tweedie. (B) Tony Stone Photo Library, London/Hugh Sitton. 408 (TR) ET/Guildhall Library, London. (BL) The Image Bank/Cyril Isy-Schwart. (BR) ET. 409 (T) ET. (C) US Naval Academy Museum, Annapolis. (B) Sygma/Patrick Durand/Jacques Langevin. 410 AKG London/North Brabant Museum/Erich Lessing. 411 (T). (B) BPK. 412 (TC) Camera Press. (The Times). (TR) Camera Press/Peter Keen. (C) Camera Press. (CR) Corbis-Bettmann. 413 (CR) AKG London/Musée du Louvre/Erich Lessing. (B) AKG London/Musée du Louvre/Erich Lessing. 414 (BL) Scala. (BC) Scala Uffizi, Florence. 415 MEPL. 416 (T) Christie's Colour Library. (B) Scala/Archaeological Museum, Heraklion. 417 BAL/Christopher Wood Gallery, London. 418 (T) BAL/Musée des Beaux-Arts, Rouen/Giraudon. (BL) BPK/photo W. Schneider-Schultz/Museum fur Volkerkunde, Berlin. (BR) BPK/Antikensammlung, Berlin. 419 BPK. 421 (TL) Angelo Hornak. (TC) Royal Geographical Society. (B) BPK Orientabteilung, Berlin. 422 The Kobal Collection. 423 BPK/Palazzo Pitti, Florence/A Dagli Orti. 424 (T) Imperial War Museum. (B) Scala. 425 (TL) National Portrait Gallery, London (detail). (TR) Topham Picture Library. (B) ET/National Maritime Museum, London. 426 (T) National Portrait Gallery, London (detail). (C) National Portrait Gallery, London (detail). (B) Frank Spooner. 427 BAL/Musée Condé, Chantilly. 428 (T) Magnum/Henri Cartier-Bresson. (B) Michael Holford/British Museum. 429 Hulton Getty. 430 (TL) Neil Leifer. (TR) Magnum/Marilyn Silverstone. (B) BAL/Louvre, Paris. 431 (T) Peter Sanders. (C) Peter Sanders. (B) The Illustrated London News Picture Library. 432 Rijksmuseum, Amsterdam. 433 (TL) private collection. (C) MEPL. 434 (T) Giraudon/National Museum, Athens. (B) Courtesy of the Trustees of the Victoria and Albert Museum, London. 435 (C) Corbis-Bettmann (BL) Military Archive & Research Services/USAF. 436 (T) AKG London/Palais de Versaillles. 438 (TR) Giraudon/Chateau de Versailles. (B) ET/British Museum, London. 439 (T) Camera Press/Richard Ellis. (B) Peter Newark's Pictures. 440 (TR) AKG London. (B) AKG London/Erich Lessing/Historisches Museum, Vienna. 441 (TL) Jean-Loup Charmet. (TR) Magnum/Marc Ribaud (BL) AKG London/Erich Lessing/Musée du Petit Palais, Paris. (BC) ET/National Historical Museum, Bucharest. 442 BAL/Phillips. 443 ET. 444 (TR) (both) BM. (C) Trustees of the British Museum (Natural History). (CR) (upper) BM. (CR) (lower) BM. (BR) Science Photo Library/John Reader. 446 (TL) National Maritime Museum, London/(coat) National Maritime Museum, London. 447 (T) Östasiaska Museet, Stockholm/Erik Cornelius. (B) BPK/Prado, Madrid/A. Dagli Orti. 448 The Granger Collection. 450 (TR) The Mansell Collection. (CR) The Board of Trustees of the Royal Armouries. 451 (T) The Mansell Collection. (B) BAL National Library of Australia, Canberra. 452 (BL) Jeremy Whitaker/By permission of the Portsmouth Estate. (BC) BAL/Royal Society, London. 453 The Illustrated London News Picture Library. 454 Rex Features Ltd/SIPA/Bill Gentile. 455 (T) Popperfoto. (B) AKG London/Goethe Museum, Weimar. 456 (TR) The Robert Hunt Library. (C) Süddeutscher Verlag. 457 BAL/Leger Gallery, London. 458 (T) Scala/Iraq Museum, Baghdad. (B) Hulton Getty. 459 (T) Hulton Getty. (medal) Corbis-Bettmann. (BC) MEPL. 460 (T) BPK. (C) Museum fur Volkerkunde, Hamburg. (B) Giraudon/Musée d'Orsay, Paris. 461 Magnum/Robert Capa. 462 Impact/Jeremy Nicholl. 463 (T) BAL. (B) BAL/British Library. 464 ET/Versailles. 465 (T) BM (Copy by Nina Davies). (B) AKG London. 466 (TR) RHPL/USAF. (C) TRH Pictures/US Navy. (B) Rex Features Ltd/The Times. 467 (T) National Geographic Society/US Government photo. (CL) National Geographic Society/USAF. 468 (T) ET. (B) BAL. 470 Magnum/W. Eugene Smith/Black Star. 471 (T) Science Photo Library/Simon Fraser. (CR) Science Photo Library/Peter Menzel. (BC) Corbis-Bettmann. 472 (T) Sonia Halliday. (B) Hulton Getty. 473 (TR) BM (Owens) BPK. (C) BPK/K. Peterson. (B) BAL/British Museum. 474 (T) BAL/SPK, Berlin. (B) Corbis-Bettmann. 475 Peter Newark's Pictures. 476 (TL) Mick Sharp. (TC) Charles Tait. 477 Michael Holford/Countess Bobrinskoy Collection. 478 Popperfoto. 479 Sonia Halliday/Topkapi Palace. 480 Royal Geographical Society. 481 (TR) BAL/National; Portrait Gallery, Smithsonian Institution, Washington (medal) Michael Holford. (B) RHPL/Navy Dept. National Archives, Washington. 483 (T) Popperfoto/Ahmed Jadallah/Reuter. (B) Punch. 484 Magnum. 485 (CL) Impact/Colin Jones. (B) The Illustrated London News Picture Library. 486 Magnum/B. Glinn. 487 (T) Bulloz, Paris. (B) Giraudon/Musée du Louvre, Paris. 488 (T) MEPL. (B) National Portrait Gallery, London. 489 (T) Popperfoto. (B) Frank Spooner/Van Der Hilst. 490 (TC) Giraudon/Musée d'Orsay, Paris. (C) RHPL/Institute Pasteur, Paris. 491 (T) ET/Capidimonte, Naples. (B) ET/National Archives, Washington. 493 BAL/Friends' House, Euston. 494 (TL) National Portrait Gallery, London (detail). (diary) Master and Fellows Magdalene College Cambridge/Pepys Library. (BR) Corbis-Bettmann. 495 Sonia Halliday/T C Rising. 497 (T) ET. (B) Sonia Halliday/Jane Taylor. 498 (T) ZEFA. (C) State Hermitage Museum, St, Petersburg. (B) BAL/Fitzwilliam Museum, University of Cambridge. 499 BPK/Prado, Madrid/Joseph Martin. 500 AKG London/National Archaeological Museum, Beirut/Erich Lessing. 501 Science & Society Picture Library. 502 (T) AKG London. (B) BAL/Jamestown-Yorktown Educational trust, VA. 503 (TR) BAL/Geological Society, London/Arthur Claude Cooke. (CR) MEPL 504 (T) Museum of London. (C) Michael Holford/British Library. (B) Southampton City Council. 505 (T) MAS, Barcelona. (B) BAL/Bibliothèque Nationale, Paris. 506 (T)

ACKNOWLEDGMENTS

Hulton Getty. (B) Giancarlo Costa. 508 AKG London/Museo de America, Madrid. 509 (T) Popperfoto. (CL) ET. (BL) ET. 510 (T) BPK/A Dagli Orti. (BC)/Hereford Library (man trap) ET/Pitt Rivers Museum, Oxford. 511 (T) Hulton Getty. (B) BAL/Bibliothèque Nationale, Paris. 512 (T) Art Resource, NY/National Portrait Gallery, Smithsonian Institution Washington. (BL) Sygma/Christine Spengler. (BC) Popperfoto/Dudman. 513 MEPL. 514 (T) Corbis-Bettmann. (B) Dave King Collection. 515 (T) BAL/British Museum. (B) BAL/National Gallery of Scotland. 516 (TL) Camera Press/William MacQuitty. (TC) ET/Museo Archeologico, Naples. (B) Arcaid/Richard Einzig. 517 (T) MEPL. (B) BAL. 518 (T) Popperfoto. (B) BAL/Louvre, Paris. 519 MEPL. 520 (T) Pictorial Press/Keese. (B) ET/British Library. 521 Corbis-Bettmann. 522 (TR) BAL/Knebworth House, Herts. (C) Science & Society Picture Library. (B) private collection. 523 Corbis-Bettmann. 525 Aspect/J. Alex Langley. 526 Sygma/C. Spengler. 527 (T) ET/Bibliothèque Nationale, Paris. (R) RHPL. (B) RHPL. 528 (T) Hulton Getty/Peter Jones. (B) BAL/British Library. 529 AKG London. 530 (T) ET/Imperial War Museum, London. (BL) Corbis-Bettmann/Gary Hershorn/Reuter. (BC) Popperfoto/Jim Hollander courtesy Yedioth Ahronoth/Reuters. 532 (T) private collection. (L) RHPL/Union Pacific Railroad Collection. (B) RHPL/Science Museum, London. 533 (T) Hulton Getty. (B) BAL/Louvre, Paris. 534 BAL/National Galleries of Scotland, Edinburgh. 535 (TR) Dave King Collection (badge) Peter Newark's Pictures. (BL) Corbis-Bettmann. 536 (T) Popperfoto/Jack Dabaghian. (B) Roger-Viollet. 537 Christie's Colour Library. 538 (C) AKG London/Museum of Art, Toledo, Ohio. (B) Foto & Studio Heckel/Windsheim Town Hall. 539 (T) AKG London. (B) Peter Newark's Pictures. 540 RHPL/ACI. 541 (TL) AKG London/Herbert Kraft. (BL) AKG London/Naturhistorisches Museum, Vienna/Erich Lessing. (BC) ET. (BR) AKG London/Louvre/Erich Lessing. 542 (TR) Hulton Getty. (CR) AKG London/Imperial War Museum, London/Erich Lessing. 543 ET/Museo Correr, Venice. 544 (TR) Royal Institute of British Architects. (C) Ikona, Rome/Schioppetto, Florence. 544-5 Scala. 545 (TL) Scala/Musei Capitolini, Rome. (TC) Scala/Uffizi, Florence. (CL) Scala. 546 (T) Hulton Getty. (B) Corbis-Bettmann. 547 (T) Hulton Getty. (B) National Portrait Gallery, London. 548 (T) Giraudon/Musée Carnavalet, Paris. (B) Jean-Loup Charmet/Sorbonne, Paris. 549 (C) Scala/Museo del Risorgimento, Milan. (B) AKG London/Comune di Genova. 550 (TC) Giraudon/Musée Carnavalet, Paris. (TR) Jean-Loup Charmet/Bibliothèque Nationale, Paris. (B) Scotland in Focus. 551 (T) Peter Newark's Pictures. (B) ET/Imperial War Museum, London. 552 AKG London/Palazzo Madama, Rome. 553 (T) BAL/Walker Art Gallery, Liverpool. (B) Camera Press/Imperial War Museum, London. 554 (T) John Hillelson. (BL) John Hillelson/Brian Brake. (BR) private collection. 556 (T) Hulton Getty. (B) Universiteitsbibliotheek Gent (Ms. 236). 557 (T) Katz Pictures Limited/LIFE Magazine © Time Inc./George Skadding. (C) BAL/National Archives Trust, Pennsylvania. 558 (TL) The National Trust, Waddesdon Manor/M. Charles. (TC) BM. (B) ET. 559 (TL) Bulloz, Paris/Bibliothèque Nationale, Paris. (TC) BLIB. (10662. aaa22 3rd pr.p). 560 Popperfoto. 562 (T) BPK. (B) Dave King Collection. 563 Magnum/Luc Delahaye. 564 Corbis-Bettmann. 565 (T) AKG London/Musée Cantonal des Beax-Arts, Lausanne. (B) ET. 566 (T) Peabody Essex Museum Salem, Mass./Photo Mark Sexton. (B) The Salvation Army. 567 AKG London. 568 (T) Hulton Getty. (B) The Illustrated London News Picture Library. 569 Sonia Halliday. 570 Scala/Museo di S. Marco, Venice. 571 (T) AKG London/Niedersachsisches Landemuseum, Hanover. (B) Ullstein. 572 Ullstein. 574 (T) BAL/Pushkin Museum, Moscow. (B) Magnum/Anne Hamann/Fred Mayer. 575 (T) Corbis-Bettmann. (B) BAL/National Museum of India, New Delhi. 576 (T) BLIB (C. 54. K12). (B) AKG London/Collegium Maius Library, Cracow. 577 (L) BLIB (C.54.K12 TP). (C) Science Photo Library. (B) Ann Ronan at Image Select. 578 (T) Jean-Loup Charmet/Musée Carnavalet, Paris. (B) Sonia Halliday/Topkapi Palace Museum, Istanbul. 579 The Granger Collection. 580 (TR) RHPL/FPG. (B) Hulton Getty. 581 (T) ET. (C) RHPL. (B) Bundesarchiv, Koblenz. 582 ET/British Library. 583 (BL) BAL/Fratelli Fabri, Milan. (BR) BAL/SMPK, Berlin. 586 (T) Michael Holford/V&A Museum, London. (B) ET/Brera, Milan. 587 (T) Magnum/Ian Berry (B) Hulton Getty. 588 (T) Christie's Colour Library. (C) RHPL. 589 (T) MEPL. (BL) Japan Archive. (BC) Japan Archive. 590 (TL) Staatsarchiv Hamburg/Trummer-Sammlung (801VI7). (TR) BAL. (B) ET. 591 (BL) ET. (BC) Scala. 592 (T) Siemens. (B) Magnum/P. Zachmann. 593 (T) Rex Features Ltd. (B) Jean-Loup Charmet/A. Draeger 1940. 594 (T) The Image Bank/Steve Proehl. (B) RHPL/Imperial War Museum, London. 595 Museum of Fine Arts Boston/Chinese and Japanese Special Fund. 596 (T) Rex Features Ltd/George Sweeney. (B) Magnum/Bosshard. 597 (T) Giraudon/Louvre, Paris. (B) Magnum/C. Capa. 598 (TC) Chicago Historical Society (DIA 1920.1274). (CL) Chicago Historical Society (ICHi-22000). (C) Chicago Historical Society. (DIA 1920-732). (B) ET. 599 The Granger Collection. 600 (T) The Wellcome Institute Library, London. (B) Roger-Viollet. 601 AKG London/Historisches Museum, Vienna. 602 (L) Scottish National Portrait Gallery, Edinburgh. (C) private collection. 603 (T) Permission of the National Museum of Labour History. (B) Ullstein. 604 Rex Features Ltd/SIPA. 605 (TL) BM. (TR) BPK/Uffizi, Florence/A Dagli Orti. (B) Scala/Galleria Palatina, Florence. 606 (T) Still Pictures/Heldur Metocny. (B) The Robert Hunt Library/Imperial War Museum, London. 607 Brown Brothers. 608 (T) MEPL. (BC) Frank Spooner/Ken Oosterbroek/GAMMA. (BR) Frank Spooner/Ken Oosterbroek/GAMMA. 609 Jean-Loup Charmet. 610 (CL) Science Photo Library/NASA. (C) Novosti. (B) ET/NASA. 611 Oronoz, Madrid. 612 (TL) AKG London/Musée Vivenel, Compiegne. (TR) MEPL. (C) Scala/Museo di S. Marco, Florence. (B) AKG London/Staatsgallerie, Stuttgart. 613 (T) Hulton Getty. (C) Corbis-Bettmann. (B) Corbis-Bettmann. 614 (T) BPK. (B) Ullstein. 615 (TL) The Associated Press. (C) John Frost Historical Newspaper Service/Scottish Daily Express. 616 (CL) Reproduced by permission of Lipton and Van den Bergh Foods Ltd from an original in the Unilever Historical Archive. (BL) Reproduced by permission of Lipton and Van den Bergh Foods Ltd from an original in the Unilever Historical Archive/Liptons. 617 Hulton Getty. 618 MEPL. 619 US Dept. of the Interior, National Parks Service. 620 Hulton Getty. 621 Popperfoto. 622 English Heritage. 623 Hulton Getty. 624 (TR) Rex Features Ltd/Henri Bureau/GAMMA. (C) Jean-Loup Charmet. (B) Rex Features Ltd/Dagbladet/SIPA. 625 (T) Jean-Loup Charmet. (B) Corbis-Bettmann/UPI. 626 Hulton Getty. 627 (TL) Corbis-Bettmann. (C) The Fotomas Index. 628 (T) Sonia Halliday/Topkapi Palace Museum, Istanbul. (R) Giraudon/Musée Bonnat, Bayonne. 629 BAL/British Museum. 630 (TC) Jean-Loup Charmet. (TR) Giraudon. 631 (T) Michael Holford/British Museum. (C) BM. (B) BM. 632 Giraudon/Musée Guimet, Paris. 633 The Granger Collection. 634 ET. 635 (T) Giraudon/Musée Condé, Chantilly. (B) Images Colour Library. 636 (T) Corbis-Bettmann. (B) The Tank Museum. 637 (L) MEPL. (R) RHPL. (BR) BAL/Oriental Museum, Durham University. 638 BPK/Kunstbibliothek, Berlin. 639 (TR) Corbis-Bettmann. (BL) Michael Holford/British Museum. (BR) The Granger Collection. 640 (T) Corbis-Bettmann. (CR) R. Twining and Company Limited. 641 (T) Popperfoto. (B) The Image Bank. 642 Scala. 643 Popperfoto. 644 (T) BPK/Schloss Charlottenburg. (C) Scala/S. Pietro, Vatican. (BC) ET/Archaeological Museum, Lima. 645. (T) Magnum/Bruno Barbey. (B) Hulton Getty. 648 (T) Scala/Museo Nazionale, Naples. (B) Giraudon/Louvre, Paris. 649 AKG London. 650 (T) MEPL. (B) BPK/SBPK, Agytisches Museum, Berlin/Phot Jürgen Liepe 1991. 651 AKG London/Akademie der Bildenden Kuenste, Vienna/Erich Lessing. 652 Camera Press. 653 Girauden. 654 The Associated Press. 655 Novosti. 657 (T) Roger-Viollet. (B) Jean-Loup Charmet. 658 (T) AKG London. (C) AKG London. (B) The Illustrated London News Picture Library. 659 (T) AKG London/Musée de la Marine, Paris. (B) AKG London. 660 (T) Staadt Nuremberg. (L) National Archives of the Netherlands 9VOC 7474). (B) National Maritime Museum, London. 661 (T) AKG London. (B) Popperfoto. 662 (T) ET. (BL) Corbis-Bettmann. 663 Jean-Loup Charmet. 665 (T) Scala/Montecassino. (B) Corbis-Bettmann. 666 (T) Popperfoto. (B) Corbis-Bettmann. 667 (TL) The Bodleian Library, Oxford (Douce Bible Eng. 1583). (CL) ET/V&A, London. (B) Roger-Viollet. 668 Science Photo Library/Gianni Tortoli. 669 (T) Hulton Getty. (B) BPK/Egyptian Museum, Cairo/Margarete Euesing. 670 Roger-Viollet/Harlingue. 673 Giraudon. (T) Fitzwilliam Museum. (BL) Giraudon. 674 (T) Trustees of the British Museum (Natural History). (B) Scala. 675 MEPL. 676 (T) AKG London/Versailles. (B) Courtesy of The Valley Forge Historical Society. 677 (TR) Magnum/Raghu Rai. (B) Corbis-Bettmann. 678 Tony Stone Photo Library, London/Jean Pragen. 679 (T) BPK/Museo Correr. (B) BAL. 680 (BC) Corbis-Bettmann. (BR) Popperfoto. 681 (CL) BAL. (C) RHPL. (B) Giraudon. 682 AKG London/Herzog August Bibliothek, Wolfenbuettel. 683 Corbis-Bettmann. 684 Scala/Montecassino. 685 (CL) © University Museum of National Antiquities, Oslo, Norway/Eirik Irgens Johnsen. (BC) ©University Museum of National Antiquities, Oslo, Norway. 686 (TR) Jean-Loup Charmet. (C) MEPL. 687 Sonia Halliday/Topkapi Palace Museum, Istanbul. 688 BAL/New Zealand High Commission, London. 689 (T) Sygma/B. Bisson. (B) Scala/Uffizi, Florence. 690 (L) Corbis-Bettmann. (R) Roger-Viollet/Branger. 691 (T) The Granger Collection. (B) ET. 692 (T) Giraudon/Bridgeman. (B) John Frost Historical Newspaper Service. 693 (BL) Giraudon/National Portrait Gallery, London. (BC) Science & Society Picture Library. 694 (TR) Popperfoto. (CL) By Courtesy of the Wedgwood Museum Trustees, Barlaston, Stoke-on-Trent, Staffordshire. (vase) Josiah Wedgwood & Sons Ltd. 695 (C) BLIB. (R) Public Record Office. (BL) Hulton Getty. 696 (TR) ET. (CL) Corbis-Bettmann. (C) Corbis-Bettmann. (BL) Corbis-Bettmann. 697 Imperial War Museum. 698 Museum of London. 699 BPK. 700 (T) Hulton Getty. (B) Hulton Getty. 701 (T) AKG London. (B) Hulton Getty. 702 (TL) Giraudon. (B) Rijksmuseum, Amsterdam. 703 Magnum/P. Jones-Griffiths. 704 BLIB (Ms Claud. BIV f59). 705 (T) ET. (TR) BPK. 706 (T) Bibliothèque Nationale, Paris (Ms.Fr.12 476 f105v). (C) AKG London. (B) MEPL. 707 (TL) BPK. (C) Christchurch College, Oxford. (BR) ET. 708 (CR) private collection. (BL) Corbis-Bettmann. (BR) BAL/Museo di San Marco della Angelico, Florence. 709 (TL) RHPL/Imperial War Museum, London. (CL) Punch. 710 BPK. 711 (TC) Giraudon. (TR) BAL/Guildhall Library, Corporation of London. (B) Peter Newark's Pictures. 712 (TL) Arcaid/Scott Frances/Esto. 713 (L) BM. (TR) (BR). 714 (T) The Mansell Collection. (B) Features Ltd. 715 (T) Popperfoto. (CL) Magnum/Micha Bar-Am. (BR) Giraudon. 716 (T) BAL/Bonhams, London. (BR) ET. 717 (TL) Giraudon. (CL) South America Pictures. 718 (T) MEPL. (BR) Jerry Harpur. 719 (T) Royal Aeronautical Society. (C) The Fotomas Index. (B) National Palace Museum, Taipei, Taiwan, Republic of China. 720 Aspect/H. Gossler. 721 Jean-Loup Charmet. (TC) Giraudon. (TR) Scala/Museo Pio-Clementino, Vatican. (CL) Private Collection. (CR) Werner Forman Archive/Field Museum of Natural History, Chicago. (BR) RHPL. 722 (TL) Ancient Art and Achitecture Collection. (TC) Ancient Art and Achitecture Collection. (CL) Giraudon/Archaeological Museum, Amman. (CR) BAL/British Museum. (BC) Michael Holford/British Museum. (BR) ET/Museo Armano, Lima. 722-3 ET/Kerameikos Museum, Athens. 724 (TL) Michael Holford. (TC) BAL/Museo Archeolgico Nazionale, Naples. (TR) English Heritage. (CL) Giraudon/Anthropological Museum, Mexico City. (CR) Giraudon/National Museum, Dehli. (BC) Ancient Art and Achitecture Collection. 724-5 RHPL/Robert Frerck/Odyssey, Chicago. 725 (TC) ET. (TR) Werner Forman Archive/private collection, New York. (CL) private collection. (CR) Scala. (B) Werner Forman Archive/Sudan Archaeological Museum, Khartoum. 726 (TL) AKG London. (TC) BLIB. (Ms.Cott.Nero DIV f93). (TR) Michael Holford. (CL) Giraudon/Musée Condé, Chantilly. (B) private collection. 727 (TL) Giraudon. (left) John Hillelson/Roland Michaud (right) Michael Holford. (TR) RHPL/Chris Rennie. (C) BAL/San Marco, Venice. (BR) BAL/V&A Museum, London. 728 (TL) AKG London/Bayeux Museum/Erich Lessing. (El Cid) G.Dagli Orti/Academy of Science, Lisbon (Buddha) Giraudon. (TR) Giraudon/Bibliothèque Nationale, Paris. (C) Ancient Art and Achitecture Collection. (B) RHPL/Robert Frerck/Odyssey, Chicago. 729 (TL) Werner Forman Archive/Museum of the American Indian, Heye Foundation, New York. (Avignon) RHPL/David Hughes. (horseman) RHPL. (TR) BAL/British Library. (BL) Werner Forman Archive. (BR) BAL. 730 (TL) AKG London/Ca d'Oro, Venice (TC) (right) BAL/Kunsthistorisches Museum, Vienna (left) RHPL (TR) BAL/Uffizi, Florence. (CL) RHPL. (BC) Ancient Art and Achitecture Collection. (BR) BAL/British Library. 731 (TL) ET (bible) BAL. (TC) Jean-Loup Charmet/Musée d'Histoire de la Medecine, Paris/(Eskimos) The Granger Collection. (TR) BAL/V&A Museum, London. (CL) AKG London/Accademia, Florence/Erich Lessing. (C) Ann Ronan at Image Select/CR RHPL. (B) ET. 732 (TL) BAL/British Library. (TC) BLIB. (TR). (CL) John Hillelson/Roland and Sabrina Michaud. (CR) private collection. (B) The Granger Collection. 733 (TL) BAL/National Library of Australia, Canberra. (TC) Peter Newark's Pictures. (TR) ET/Museum of London. (Charles) BAL. (B) BAL/Chester Beatty Library, Dublin. 734 (TL) Michael Holford. (TC) Ann Ronan at Image Select. (TR) BAL/Sir John Soane Museum London. (C) BAL/Coram Foundation, London. (BL) Werner Forman Archive/Asantehene of Kumasi. (BC) Werner Forman Archive/Asantehene of Kumasi. 735 (TL) Michael Holford. (TC) MEPL. (TR) ET. (CL) Michael Holford/Science Museum, London. (R) Hulton Getty. (B) BAL/National Portrait Gallery, Smithsonian Institute, Washington/Art Resource. 736 MEPL. (TC). (TR) Hulton Getty. (CL) Michael Holford. (CR) BAL/Stapleton Collection. 737 (TL) BAL/National Portrait Gallery, Smithsonian Institution, Washington/Art Resource/(left) Jean-Loup Charmet/Collection Historique de France Telecom. (TC) (right) ET. (TR) Science & Society Picture Library. (B) Peter Newark's Pictures. 738 (TL) BAL/Bibliothèque Nationale, Paris. (TC) British Film Institute. (TR) Camera Press/ILN. (C) BAL/V&A Museum, London. 739 (TL) British Film Institute. (TC) AKG London. (TR) Popperfoto. (BL) Hulton Getty. 740 (TL) Science Photo Library/US Department of Energy. (TC) The Kobal Collection. (TR) Science Photo Library/NASA. (CL) Royal Geographical Society/Sir Edmund Hillary. (CR) Popperfoto. 740-1 Popperfoto. 741 (TL) Corbis-Bettmann/Reuter. (TC) Magnum/Steve McCurry. (TR) Network/Anthony Sau. (C) Frank Spooner/F. Anderson. (BR) Popperfoto/Mark Moore/Reuters.

With thanks to the Trireme Trust 664.

ORIGINATION Dot Gradations Ltd, Essex, England
PAPER Townsend Hook Ltd, Snodland, England
PRINTING Maury Imprimeur SA, Malesherbes, France
BINDING Reliures Brun SA, Malesherbes, France

40-575-1